# THE 21ST
# CENTURY
## CROSSWORD PUZZLE DICTIONARY

# THE 21ST CENTURY CROSSWORD PUZZLE DICTIONARY

### KEVIN McCANN & MARK DIEHL

PUZZLE WRIGHT PRESS

An imprint of Sterling
Publishing Co., Inc.

www.puzzlewright.com

Puzzlewright Press and the distinctive Puzzlewright Press logo are trademarks of
Sterling Publishing Co., Inc.

Library of Congress Cataloging-in-Publication Data Available

2   4   6   8   10   9   7   5   3   1

Published by Sterling Publishing Co., Inc.
387 Park Avenue South, New York, NY 10016
© 2009 by Kevin McCann & Mark Diehl
Distributed in Canada by Sterling Publishing
c/o Canadian Manda Group, 165 Dufferin Street
Toronto, Ontario, Canada M6K 3H6
Distributed in the United Kingdom by GMC Distribution Services
Castle Place, 166 High Street, Lewes, East Sussex, England BN7 1XU
Distributed in Australia by Capricorn Link (Australia) Pty. Ltd.
P.O. Box 704, Windsor, NSW 2756, Australia

Sterling ISBN 978-1-4027-2134-2

For information about custom editions, special sales, premium and
corporate purchases, please contact Sterling Special Sales
Department at 800-805-5489 or specialsales@sterlingpublishing.com.

# Contents

 **Introduction**

Crossword puzzles have been a part of American culture for nearly 100 years. The first crossword puzzle, then known as a "Word-Cross," was created by Arthur Wynne and appeared in the *New York World* on Dec. 21, 1913. In the 1920s, America experienced the "crossword craze," and since then crossword puzzles have been a regular feature in most daily newspapers. They can be found in magazine and book collections, topical publications, and now on the Internet.

But the puzzles we encounter today are not the same as those of the '20s, the '30s, or even the '80s. In days of yore, crossword puzzles were solely tests of vocabulary and facts, which did reward people who had broad knowledge of geography, mythology, history, and literature, but also tended to be dry and contained a great many entries that were highly obscure.

The 1990s brought in a new crossword era. Top puzzlemakers such as Merl Reagle and Stanley Newman sought to make the crossword puzzle less stodgy and more hip. And when Will Shortz took the helm as crossword editor of *The New York Times* in 1993, his goal was to make puzzles more appealing to a broader and younger audience by expanding the required knowledge, by including pop culture references, by using humorous wordplay, and by using unique and clever themes. In short, it was felt that crossword puzzles should be more fun. Nearly every syndicated publication has adopted this new style to some degree. Today's solver is the beneficiary of these changes.

Crossword puzzles are no longer just a test of one's vocabulary. They demand more from a solver and offer more in return. References to pop singers and television shows are commonplace. Tricky, punny, and sometimes diabolical clues are to be expected. But when solvers go to a typical crossword dictionary for assistance they find it to be of limited value. Most any dictionary will suffice if all the solver needs is a synonym for a straightforward clue. But most clues are not simple synonym clues. What about pop culture references, or clues that engage in wordplay? Today's crossword solver needs a better resource.

## The 21st Century Crossword Puzzle Dictionary

As creators of *The 21st Century Crossword Puzzle Dictionary*, we set out with one primary goal: to create a more useful resource for the modern crossword puzzle solver. We believe that goal has been reached.

How is *The 21st Century Crossword Puzzle Dictionary* more useful?

- It has real answers to real clues, taken from a database of thousands of crossword puzzles.
- It does not aim to be a thesaurus with synonyms that never show up in puzzles.
- It highlights very common clue/answer pairs.
- It has up-to-date pop culture references.
- It uses entire clues, broken up into main entries and subentries.
- Its appendix includes lists of the commonest crossword answers.
- Its appendix includes a description of the types of themes found in modern puzzles.

## Uses data from crossword database

*The 21st Century Crossword Puzzle Dictionary* creators are also the maintainers of the cruciverb.com crossword database. This database includes, among other things, clues and answers extracted from thousands of puzzles offered by mainstream crossword publishers, and is used by most of today's professional crossword constructors and editors. This very same database was used to create *The 21st Century Crossword Puzzle Dictionary*. What other dictionary can claim to derive its content from the same resource used by nearly every crossword professional?

## Not a thesaurus

Typical crossword dictionaries burden the solver with an abundance of synonyms, many of which have never appeared in crossword puzzles and likely never will. Such dictionaries are more like a thesaurus and tend to hide possible answers rather than highlight them. *The 21st Century Crossword Puzzle Dictionary* only includes clue/answer pairs that have appeared at least twice in puzzles published from 1997 to 2008. What this means is that you might see an entry like this:

**Bashful**
  companion: 3 DOC 5 DOPEY

Only Doc and Dopey are listed as answers because Grumpy, Happy, Sleepy, and Sneezy don't show up often enough to merit inclusion.

## Common clue/answer pairs are highlighted

If certain clue/answer pairs have appeared *many* times in previously published crosswords, *The 21st Century Crossword Puzzle Dictionary* will highlight the answer in color. While there is no guarantee that a highlighted answer will be the one that a solver is looking for, the high occurrence rate indicates that it is a very strong possibility. No other crossword dictionary offers this highlighting feature.

## Includes up-to-date pop culture references

Unlike crossword puzzles of yesteryear, today's puzzles contain a healthy amount of references to pop culture. *The 21st Century Crossword Puzzle Dictionary* includes clues and answers that refer to recent songs, movies, television programs, authors, politicians, etc. It also includes common slang and other "in the language" words and phrases that have found their way into mainstream crossword puzzles. Some dictionaries have no pop culture references at all.

## Uses the entire clue

*The 21st Century Crossword Puzzle Dictionary* is made up of main entries, often with many subentries underneath. For example, the clues "Extinct bird" (answer: DODO or MOA) and "Flightless bird" (answer: EMU, KIWI, or RHEA) would share the same main

entry of "Bird" and then have the rest of the clue in the subentries, like this:

**Bird**
  Extinct: 3 MOA 4 DODO
  Flightless: 3 EMU 4 KIWI RHEA

Other dictionaries may have one basic entry for "Bird," followed by the many possible answers:

**Bird** EMU MOA DODO KIWI RHEA

The first method is more helpful, since the solver has more specific information and can narrow down the possibilities.

## Dictionary Comparison

To further illustrate the difference between *The 21st Century Crossword Puzzle Dictionary* and other dictionaries, see the table on the next page.

The differences are significant.

Many of the answers offered by other dictionaries have likely *never* appeared in a mainstream crossword puzzle. In fact, this is the case for the large majority of the answers provided for the "Agent" entry at right. Including these obscurities as if they were legitimately possible answers does nothing more than throw the solver off.

Other dictionaries lump all their answers together, separating them only by length. Our dictionary includes subentries such as "action" under "Affirmative," which help direct the solver to a smaller set of possible answers (in this case, one answer: NOD).

Also, since other crossword dictionaries largely contain nothing but synonyms, they're no help with more complex clues. Since we use whole clues, we can include very common answers such as ANT for "Aardvark morsel" and AGER for "Maturing agent." Other dictionaries do not offer this level of detail. Nor do they contain any references to pop culture (such as "American Idol").

For all these reasons, we think you'll find that *The 21st Century Crossword Puzzle Dictionary* is clearly a more useful resource for today's crossword solver.

—Kevin McCann & Mark Diehl

| *The 21st Century* <br> *Crossword Puzzle Dictionary* | Other <br> Dictionary |
|---|---|
| **Aardvark:** 6 MAMMAL 7 ANTBEAR <br> 8 ANTEATER <br> feature: 5 SNOUT <br> land: 6 AFRICA <br> meal: 4 ANTS <br> morsel: 3 ANT | **Aardvark:** ANTEATER EARTHHOG <br> EDENTATE |
| **Affirmative:** 3 YES <br> action: 3 NOD <br> Emphatic: 6 YESSIR <br> French: 3 OUI <br> NASA: 3 AOK <br> Sailor: 3 AYE <br> Shipboard: 6 AYEAYE <br> Slangy: 4 YEAH <br> Spanish: 4 SISI <br> vote: 3 AYE YEA YES | **Affirmative:** AYE NOD YAH YEA YEP YES <br> AMEN ATEN YEAH PONENT <br> DOGMATIC POSITIVE |
| **Agent:** 3 FED REP SPY 7 VEHICLE <br> amount: 3 CUT FEE <br> Antiquing: 4 AGER <br> Bleaching: 3 LYE <br> Cleansing: 4 SOAP 5 BORAX <br> DEA: 4 NARC 5 NARCO <br> Diplomatic: 5 ENVOY <br> Double: 4 MOLE <br> Fed.: 4 GMAN TMAN <br> Kind of: 3 IRS <br> Leavening: 5 YEAST <br> Maturing: 4 AGER <br> of retribution: 7 NEMESIS <br> Sales: 3 REP <br> Secret: 3 SPY <br> take: 5 TENTH <br> Thickening: 4 AGAR <br> Undercover: 3 SPY 4 NARC <br> ~ 86: 5 SMART <br> ~ Ness: 5 ELIOT <br> ~ Scully: 4 DANA | **Agent:** SPY AMIN DOER ETCH GENE ACTOR <br> AMEEN BUYER CAUSE ENVOY MEANS <br> ORGAN PROXY REEVE RIDER VAKIL WALLA <br> ADUROL ASSIGN ATOPEN BROKER BURSAR <br> COMMIS DEALER DEPUTY ENINE FACTOR <br> FITTER KEYAHA LEDGER MEDIUM MINION <br> MUKTAR PESKAR SELLER SYNDIC VAKEEL <br> WALLAH BAILIFF BLISTER CHANNEL <br> COUCHER DRASTIC FACIENT FEDERAL <br> HUSBAND LEAGUER MOOKTAR MOUNTAR <br> MUKTEAR MUTAGEN OFFICER PESHKAR <br> PROCTOR SCALPER APPROVER ATTORNEY <br> AUMILDAR CATALYST EMISSARY EXECUTOR <br> GOMASHTA GOMASTAH IMPROVER <br> INCITANT INSTITOR MINISTER MITICIDE <br> MOOKHTAR OPERATOR PROMOTER <br> QUAESTOR RESIDENT SALESMAN VIRUCIDE <br> MIDDLEMAN OPERATIVE SATELLITE <br> SENESCHAL MAINSPRING PROCURATOR <br> PLENIPOTENTIARY |
| **"American Idol"** <br> winner Studdard: 5 RUBEN | No entry for **"American Idol"** |

# How to Use This Book

## Entry Parts

The user of this crossword dictionary needs to be familiar with the various entry parts. Here are some sample entries, followed by short descriptions of their different parts:

**Affirmative:** 3 YES
  action: 3 NOD
**Tail**
  **Info:** Suffix cue
**Tribute**
  Pay ~ to: 5 HONOR 6 SALUTE

**Main entries:** Affirmative, Tail, and Tribute
**Subentries:** "action" and "Pay ~ to"
**Answers:** YES, NOD, HONOR, and SALUTE (answers in red indicate very common clue/answer pairs)
**Info indicator:** provides further information
**The swung dash (~):** found in subentries and used to signify the part of the clue where the main entry would appear
**Numbers:** 3, 5, and 6 indicate the length of the answers

## Main entries

Main entries often consist of a single word, which may be the only word in a clue, or the most prominent one. Other main entries consist of more than one word: Full names, places, titles, common phrases, and fill-in-the-blank clues account for many of these. When a clue ends with "e.g." or "for example" or "for one" or anything similar, the ending is dropped from the clue and the answer is listed under what remains. For example, the answer PET is listed under "Cat," even though the clue for PET would be "Cat, e.g." or "Cat, for example." Certain punctuation marks have also been removed, including question marks (which indicate punny clues) and some possessive indicators.

## Subentries

Subentries are used in combination with main entries to provide a more detailed clue to an answer. Subentries that begin with a capital letter precede the main entry in their clues. Subentries that begin with a lowercase letter follow the main entry. A swung dash (~) is used as a placeholder when the main entry

falls within the subentry, when it leads or follows a number, or when there is an exception to the capital letter rule.

Observe the following examples:

**Thick:** 3 FAT 5 DENSE MIDST
  In the ~ of: 3 MID 4 AMID 5 AMONG 6 AMIDST
  Lay on: 7 SLATHER
  slice: 4 SLAB
**Woods**
  Actor: 5 JAMES
  Golfer: 5 TIGER
  Neck of the: 4 AREA
  prop: 3 TEE

Joining the subentries with their main entries, the full clues are:
  Thick; In the thick of; Lay on thick; Thick slice
  Actor Woods; Golfer Woods; Neck of the woods; Woods's prop

## Choose the Most Prominent Word(s)

When looking up a crossword entry, choose the most prominent word in the clue. If you have a clue such as "Aardvark feature" (answer: SNOUT), go to the "A" chapter and look up Aardvark, since "Aardvark" is more prominent than "feature."

Often two or more words in a clue will have equal prominence. In such cases, entries may be present for each word. For example, both "bleaching" and "agent" in the clue "Bleaching agent" are prominent. "Bleaching" may be somewhat stronger, but "agent" still has enough prominence to warrant inclusion.

For clues containing numbers, there will usually be an entry in the numbers chapter (the first chapter of the dictionary) in addition to any prominent word. For example, "36 inches" (answer: YARD) would have an entry under both "36" (in the numbers chapter) and "Inches" (in the I chapter).

## Plurals, Tenses, and Other Inflections

Inflected forms of a word usually won't have their own entries and will instead be found under the root word. This is especially true where both the clue and answer end in -S, -ES, -ED, and -ING. For example, if a clue is "Extinct birds," the main entry would be "Bird." There would be no separate entry for "Birds."

**Bird**
    Extinct: 3 MOA 4 DODO

But since the real clue has "birds" and not "bird," the solver must append an S to the possible answer that will be placed in the grid. In the above example, the possible answers would be MOAS and DODOS.

There are exceptions. If either the answer or the clue is a less common inflection, such as a Latin or French plural, there will be a separate entry. If a plural word is part of a clue that has a non-plural answer, it, too, will have a separate entry. Plurals have their own entries when the answers are 3-letter plurals of 2-letter words. For example:

**Addresses**
    Change: 4 MOVE
**Eggs:** 3 OVA ROE
**Vaccines:** 4 SERA
**VIPs**
    Baseball: 3 GMS
    Courtroom: 3 DAS
    Hospital: 3 DRS MDS RNS
    Magazine: 3 EDS
    Radio: 3 DJS

## People

These clues can include first names, middle names, last names, titles, and blanks. If a clue contains only a first name or last name, the main entry will be that single name. If a clue has both the first and last name, the main entry will be the last name followed by first name (e.g.: Nixon, Richard). Name titles such as Sir, Mr., and Mrs. will usually follow the last name (e.g.: O'Leary, Mrs.) unless the title and name is a film or book title (e.g., "Mrs. Miniver"). Name titles may also appear in the subentry instead of the main entry.

## Places

Countries, cities, towns, rivers, buildings, monuments, and so forth are found under their *full name*. For example: South America, Niagara Falls, Lake Victoria, Eiffel Tower.

## Titles of Works

Titles of books, film, plays, and the like are entered under the first letter of the first word unless the title begins with "The," "A," or "An." These entries will be found under the first letter of the next word. For example, if a clue contains "The Odd Couple," the solver should look for the entry "Odd Couple, The" in the O chapter.

## Phrases With Quote Marks

Phrases with quote marks are found in their entirety under the first letter of the first word.

## Phrases With Blanks

Phrases with blanks are found in their entirety under the first letter of the first word.

## Alphabetization

Entries are alphabetized strictly on a letter-by-letter basis, ignoring all punctuation and spaces. The ampersand symbol (&) is counted as the letters "and." If two answers use the same letters, the simpler version comes first, with "simpler" meaning lowercase and no punctuation. So "Al" comes before "A.L." and they both come before "Al ___." Names listed under the last name are an exception to the strict alphabetization rule. They are alphabetized under the last name, following any listings that have the same letters.

Another exception to the alphabetization rule is when a parenthetical part follows a fill-in-the-blank clue; such clues are alphabetized immediately following the same clue without parentheses (or the place where such a clue would be). Note the order of these two, even though "Willa" follows "days" alphabetically:

**"One of ___"** (Willa Cather novel): 4 OURS
**"One of ___ days ...":** 5 THESE

In subentries, the same alphabetization rules are followed. The only difference is the swung dash (~). If that's at the start of the subentry, it's listed at the end. If it's in the middle, then alphabetization stops at the swung dash.

If you can't find what you're looking for, look up and down a few inches and you might find it. Once you get used to the system, it will become easier.

## Examples

Observing the above rules, some main entry examples can be found below.

| | |
|---|---|
| Al | Stone |
| AL | ___ Stone |
| A.L. | Stone, Oliver |
| Al ___ | Stone Age |
| Al-___ | "Stoned Soul Picnic" |
| al-___, Bashar | Stone-faced |
| Ala. | Stonehenge |
| À la ___ | Stones |
| "Al Aaraaf" | Stoneworker |

## Other Information

In deciding which entries to include in this dictionary, the basic rule was that the clue/answer pairs had to have appeared in recent puzzles at least twice. Sometimes an answer that wouldn't have made the cut was added because we felt it was just a matter of time before that clue would appear in a crossword, but this was rare.

## Bonus Sections

In addition to the regular letter chapters that contain clues and answers, *The 21st Century Crossword Puzzle Dictionary* offers bonus sections that will no doubt aid the solver.

Some main entries will refer you to the **Useful Lists** section, starting on page 709; for instance, the entry for "Indianapolis 500," refers you to the list of winners on page 714.

An index on page 816 shows all the lists in the section.

The **Themes in Crosswords** section identifies and describes the various types of themes that are used in modern crossword puzzles. By understanding the different tricks and devices that crossword constructors use, the solver will have a better chance of solving crossword puzzles that contain themes.

The **Commonest Crossword Answers** section is a list of the top 3-, 4-, 5-, 6-, and 7-letter answers found in recent crossword puzzles. Solvers can use this section to become familiar with answers that often show up in puzzles due to their common letters and accommodating consonant/vowel patterns. Starting on page 755, you will find common clues to all the commonest answers.

| Main entry | Type | Chapter | Comment |
|---|---|---|---|
| 1998 | Number | #'s | Most numbers in a clue will have own entry |
| Aardvark | Single word | A | Normal lookup using first letter |
| West, Mae | Person | W | Last name, first name |
| Gellar, ___ Michelle | Person | G | Last name, other names |
| Atlas Mountains | Place | A | Full name |
| "Atlas Shrugged" | Title | A | First letter of title |
| "Simpsons, The" | Title | S | First letter of title, excluding "The," "An," or "A" |
| "Take it easy!" | Phrase | T | First letter of quote |
| "The doctor ___" | Phrase | T | First letter of quote, *including* "The," "An," or "A" |
| ___ no good | Phrase | N | First letter of phrase |

# #'s

**0:** 3 NIL 8 GOOSEEGG
   Letter above: 4 OPER
   on a phone: 4 OPER
   Put back to: 5 RESET
**0% ___:** 3 APR
**000**
   Put back to: 5 RESET
**007:** 3 SPY 4 BOND 5 AGENT
   alma mater: 4 ETON
   creator Fleming: 3 IAN
   First ~ film: 4 DRNO
   foe: 3 KGB 4 DRNO
      6 SMERSH
   How ~ likes his martinis:
      6 SHAKEN
   portrayer Roger: 5 MOORE
   portrayer Timothy: 6 DALTON
**¹/₆₄₀**
   of a square mile: 4 ACRE
**¹/₂₀**
   of a ream: 5 QUIRE
**¹/₈**
   cup: 5 OUNCE
   ounce: 4 DRAM
**¹/₆**
   fl. oz.: 3 TSP
   inch: 4 PICA
**1:** 3 ODD RTE 4 CUBE 5 DIGIT
**1-1**
   score: 3 TIE
**1/1**
   song ender: 4 SYNE
   word: 4 AULD LANG SYNE
**"1-2-3"**
   singer Barry: 3 LEN
**1.3**
   cubic yards: 5 STERE
**1.609**
   kilometers: 4 MILE
**1-800-COLLECT**
   pitchman: 3 MRT
**1-800-FLOWERS**
   rival: 3 FTD
**2**
   on a phone : 3 ABC
**2%**
   The ~ in milk: 3 FAT
**2.0**
   average: 3 CEE
   average components: 4 CEES
**2:1:** 5 RATIO
**2.2**
   pounds: 4 KILO
**2.54**
   centimeters: 4 INCH
**2 to 1:** 5 RATIO
**3**
   on a phone: 3 DEF

**3.0**
   ~, for example: 3 GPA
**3:00:** 4 EAST HOUR
**3:1:** 4 ODDS 5 RATIO
**3.26**
   light years: 6 PARSEC
**3.5**
   One of ~ billion: 5 ASIAN
   ~, for example: 3 GPA
**3/17**
   honoree: 5 STPAT
**3-in-One**
   product: 3 OIL
**3-pointers**
   in football: 3 FGS
   in Scrabble: 3 EMS
**4**
   He wore a: 3 ORR
   on a phone: 3 GHI
   ~ P.M.: 7 TEATIME
**4.0**
   ~, for example: 3 GPA
**4-0**
   The big ~, for one: 3 AGE
**4:00**
   social: 3 TEA
   ~ P.M.: 7 TEATIME
**4×4:** 3 UTE
**4-F**
   Like a: 5 UNFIT
**4-sided**
   fig.: 4 RECT
**5**
   on a phone: 3 JKL
**5½-point**
   type: 5 AGATE
**5.5**
   yards: 3 ROD
**5.5-point**
   type: 5 AGATE
**5.88**
   About ~ trillion mi.: 4 LTYR
**5K:** 4 RACE
**5th:** 3 AVE
**6**
   on a phone: 3 MNO
   They're worth ~ pts.: 3 TDS
   ___ 6: 5 MOTEL
**6/6/44:** 4 DDAY
**6:50:** 5 TENOF TENTO
**6-pointers:** 3 TDS
**6-pt.**
   plays: 3 TDS
**6th**
   sense: 3 ESP
**7:** 3 ODD 7 NATURAL
   on a phone: 3 PRS
**7-10:** 5 SPLIT

**7/10/62**
   launch: 7 TELSTAR
**7/28/1914**
   It started: 3 WWI
**"7 Faces of Dr. ___":** 3 LAO
**7th-century**
   date: 4 DCVI
   pope: 5 LEOII
   start: 3 DCI
**7-Up**
   rival: 6 FRESCA SPRITE
   ~, in old ads: 6 UNCOLA
**8**
   In base: 5 OCTAL
   on a phone: 3 TUV
   pts.: 3 GAL
**8×10**
   ~, often: 6 GLOSSY
**"8 Mile"**
   actress Basinger: 3 KIM
   star: 6 EMINEM
**9**
   on a phone: 3 WXY
   to 5: 5 RATIO SHIFT
**9-3**
   automaker: 4 SAAB
**9-5**
   automaker: 4 SAAB
**9/8/66**
   Noted debut of: 8 STARTREK
**9-iron**
   Use a: 4 LOFT
**9mm**
   weapon: 3 UZI
**10**
   No.: 4 NEON
   out of 10: 5 IDEAL
**"10"**
   actress Bo: 5 DEREK
   director Edwards: 5 BLAKE
   music: 6 BOLERO
**10%**
   Give: 5 TITHE
   taker: 5 AGENT
**10/7/82**
   Notable debut of: 4 CATS
**10/10/73**
   resignee: 5 AGNEW
**10/11/75**
   Show that debuted: 3 SNL
**10/30/74**
   Champ of: 3 ALI
**10K:** 4 RACE
   Compete in a: 3 RUN
**10-point**
   type: 5 ELITE
**10th anniversary**
   gift: 3 TIN

**10th-century**
  emperor: 5 OTTOI
  pope: 4 LEOV 5 LEOVI
**10th-grader:** 4 SOPH
**"10 Things ___ About You":**
    5 IHATE
**11:** 3 ACE 5 PRIME
  Like: 3 ODD
**11/11**
  honorees: 4 VETS
**12**
  Name of ~ popes: 4 PIUS
**12:00**
  flasher: 3 VCR
  Revert to: 5 RESET
**12/24:** 3 EVE
**12/31:** 3 EVE
**"12 Angry Men"**
  role: 5 JUROR
**12-point**
  type: 4 PICA
**12th-century**
  poet: 4 OMAR
  year: 3 MCL 4 MCII
**12-year-old:** 5 TWEEN
    7 PRETEEN
**13:** 5 PRIME
  Group of: 5 COVEN
**13th-century**
  invader: 5 TATAR
  writings: 4 EDDA
**14**
  pounds, in Britain: 5 STONE
**14-line**
  poem: 6 RONDEL SONNET
**14th-century**
  ruler: 5 IVANI
**15**
  Score before: 4 LOVE
**15.432**
  grains: 4 GRAM
**15th**
  of a month: 4 IDES
**15th-century**
  vessel: 4 NINA 5 PINTA
**16**
  drams: 5 OUNCE
  Name of ~ popes:
    7 GREGORY
**16.5**
  feet: 3 ROD
**16th**
  president: 3 ABE
**16th-century**
  circumnavigator: 5 DRAKE
  fleet: 6 ARMADA
  start: 3 MDI
**17**
  Poem with ~ syllables:
    5 HAIKU
**"___ 17" (1953 film):**
    6 STALAG
**17th-century**
  diarist: 5 PEPYS
  poet laureate: 6 DRYDEN
  start: 4 MDCI

**18**
  holes: 5 ROUND
  Not yet: 8 UNDERAGE
  Play: 4 GOLF
**"___ 18" (Uris novel):** 4 MILA
**18-wheeler:** 3 RIG 4 SEMI
**19th Amendment**
  beneficiaries: 5 WOMEN
**19th-century**
  literary inits.: 3 RLS
**20**
  providers: 4 ATMS
  quires: 4 REAM
**20%**
  It might be: 3 TIP
  of cuarenta: 4 OCHO
**20-20:** 3 TIE
  It may be: 9 HINDSIGHT
**"20/20"**
  former cohost Downs:
    4 HUGH
  former cohost Hugh:
    5 DOWNS
  network: 3 ABC
**20 Questions**
  category: 6 ANIMAL
    7 MINERAL
**20s**
  dispenser: 3 ATM
**20th-century**
  art movement: 4 DADA
  Name of three ~ popes: 4 PIUS
**20-vol.**
  reference: 3 OED
**21:** 3 AGE 5 LEGAL OFAGE
  Cube with ~ dots: 3 DIE
  Exceeds: 5 BUSTS
**21st-century**
  start: 3 MMI
**21-year-old:** 5 ADULT
**22**
  One of ~ cards: 5 TAROT
**22.5**
  degrees: 3 NNE
**22-mile-high**
  layer: 5 OZONE
**23**
  follower: 6 SKIDOO
**23rd**
  ~ Greek letter: 3 PSI
**24**
  cans: 4 CASE
  Every ~ hours: 4 ADAY
    5 DAILY
  horas: 3 DIA
  One of: 4 HOUR
  Poem of ~ books: 5 ILIAD
  sheets of paper: 5 QUIRE
**24/7:** 7 NONSTOP
  auction site: 4 EBAY
  bank device: 3 ATM
**24-hr.**
  bank feature: 3 ATM
  breakfast place: 4 IHOP
  convenience: 3 ATM
**24-karat:** 4 PURE

**26**
  fortnights: 4 YEAR
  Last of: 3 ZEE
**27**
  ~, to 3: 4 CUBE
**"28 Days"**
  subject: 5 REHAB
**30**
  ~, to a reporter: 3 END
**30%**
  of Africa: 6 SAHARA
  of the Earth's landmass: 4 ASIA
**30-day**
  mo.: 3 APR SEP
  month: 5 APRIL
**30th**
  Around the ~ (abbr.): 3 EOM
**30-ton**
  computer: 5 ENIAC
**32**
  Game sometimes using ~ cards:
    6 EUCHRE
  Game using ~ cards: 4 SKAT
**32-card**
  game: 4 SKAT
**"32 Flavors"**
  singer Davis: 5 ALANA
**33rd**
  pres.: 3 HST
**34th**
  pres.: 3 DDE IKE
**34th Street**
  happening: 7 MIRACLE
**35.3**
  cubic feet: 5 STERE
**35mm**
  camera type: 3 SLR
  Early ~ camera: 5 LEICA
  setting: 5 FSTOP
**36**
  inches: 4 YARD
**36-24-36**
  Part of: 4 HIPS 5 WAIST
**38th**
  parallel land: 5 KOREA
**39**
  About ~ inches: 5 METER
  ~, to Benny: 3 AGE
**39.37**
  inches: 5 METER
    8 ONEMETER
**39-line**
  poem: 7 SESTINA
**"39 Steps, The"**
  actress Taina: 3 ELG
  star: 5 DONAT
**40**
  winks: 3 NAP 6 CATNAP
**40-card**
  Game with a ~ deck: 5 MONTE
**40-day**
  period: 4 LENT
**41st**
  president: 4 BUSH
**42**
  gal.: 3 BBL

**"42nd Street"**
tune: 5 DAMES
**43rd**
pres.: 4 BUSH 5 DUBYA
**45:** 4 DISC
Half a: 5 BSIDE SIDEA
inches: 3 ELL
Old ~ player: 4 HIFI
player: 5 PHONO
**45th**
of 50: 4 UTAH
**47-stringed**
instrument: 4 HARP
**"48 ___":** 3 HRS
**"48HRS"**
actor Nick: 5 NOLTE
**49%**
About ~ of the world's
population: 3 MEN
**49th**
state: 6 ALASKA
**50%:** 4 HALF
**50–50:** 3 TIE 4 EVEN
chance: 6 TOSSUP
proposition: 7 EVENBET
**50-and-over**
org.: 4 AARP
**50 Cent:** 7 RAPSTAR
**50-oared**
ship: 4 ARGO
**52:** 3 LII
**54**
Element: 5 XENON
**55 minutes past the hour:**
6 FIVETO
**55th anniversary**
stone: 7 EMERALD
**56:** 3 LVI
**56-5**
His won-lost record was: 3 ALI
**60**
Every ~ minutes: 5 HORAL
grains: 4 DRAM
secs.: 3 MIN
**60%**
Like ~ of the world's
population: 5 ASIAN
**60-homer**
Three-time ~ man: 4 SOSA
**"60 Minutes"**
Alexander, formerly of:
5 SHANA
Andy of: 6 ROONEY
Lesley of: 5 STAHL
Morley of: 5 SAFER
network: 3 CBS
Original ~ correspondent:
8 REASONER
regular: 9 EDBRADLEY
Rooney of: 4 ANDY
**60th**
Capital near the ~ parallel:
4 OSLO
**61**
He hit ~ in '61: 5 MARIS
**66:** 3 RTE 5 ROUTE

**67.5**
deg.: 3 ENE
**70**
Did: 4 SPED
**70%**
of M: 3 DCC
**70-millimeter**
film format: 4 IMAX
**72**
~, often: 3 PAR
**75%:** 3 CEE
**76ers**
org.: 3 NBA
**"77 Sunset Strip"**
actor Byrnes: 3 EDD
character: 6 KOOKIE
costar of Edd: 5 EFREM
**78:** 4 DISC
**79**
for gold (abbr.): 4 ATNO
**"80's Ladies"**
singer: 5 OSLIN 7 KTOSLIN
**86:** 3 CAN NIX
Agent: 5 SMART
**87**
at the pump: 6 OCTANE
**88**
Piano's: 4 KEYS
~, briefly: 4 OLDS
**90**
degrees: 4 EAST
degrees from norte: 4 ESTE
Drove ~ mph: 4 SPED
Less than ~ degrees: 5 ACUTE
More than ~ degrees:
6 OBTUSE
**90-degree**
angle: 3 ELL
**90s**
It may be in the low:
6 OCTANE
**90th**
Hrs. on the ~ meridian: 3 CST
**92**
Pertaining to element:
6 URANIC
**95:** 3 RTE
**98**
~, briefly: 4 OLDS
**98.6**
Like a body temperature of:
6 NORMAL
**"99 Luftballons"**
pop group: 4 NENA
**100**
clams: 5 CNOTE
cts.: 3 DOL
Got ~ on: 4 ACED
It seats: 6 SENATE
lbs.: 3 CWT
Less than ~ shares: 6 ODDLOT
One of ~ (abbr.): 3 SEN
percent: 3 ALL
yrs.: 3 CEN
**100%:** 3 ALL 4 PURE 6 PURELY
8 ENTIRELY

**100-eyed**
giant: 5 ARGUS
**100-meter**
race: 4 DASH
**100-yard**
race: 4 DASH
**"101 Dalmatians"**
dog: 5 PONGO
**106:** 3 CVI
**108**
Game with ~ cards: 3 UNO
**114**
It has ~ suras: 5 KORAN
**128**
cubic feet: 4 CORD
**150**
One of ~ songs: 5 PSALM
**151:** 3 CLI
**160**
square rods: 4 ACRE
**180:** 3 UEY 5 UTURN
**___ 180:** 3 DOA
**180-degree**
maneuver: 5 UTURN
**180 degrees**
from NNW: 3 SSE
from WNW: 3 ESE
from WSW: 3 ENE
turn: 3 UEY
**200**
fins: 3 GEE
milligrams: 5 CARAT
**201:** 3 CCI
**202:** 4 CCII
**212:** 8 AREACODE
Bring to ~ degrees: 4 BOIL
**251:** 4 CCLI
**251.9**
calories: 3 BTU
**252**
wine gallons: 3 TUN
**300:** 3 CCC
**301:** 4 CCCI
**325i**
maker: 3 BMW
**347**
Football coach with ~ victories:
5 SHULA
**365**
days: 4 YEAR
dias: 3 ANO
**389**
Old car wih a ~ engine:
3 GTO
**400**
Society's: 5 ELITE
**401:** 3 CDI
**401(k):** 4 PLAN
alternative: 3 IRA
cousin: 3 IRA
**404:** 4 CDIV
**435**
One of: 3 REP
**440:** 4 RACE
**440–461**
pope: 4 LEOI

**440-yard-long**
  path: 4 OVAL
**450:** 3 CDL
**451:** 4 CDLI
**500**
  letters: 3 STP
  sheets: 4 REAM
  spot: 4 INDY
  ___ 500: 4 INDY
**500-mile**
  race: 4 INDY
**501**
  brand: 5 LEVIS
**502:** 3 DII
**503:** 4 DIII
**507:** 4 DVII
**511:** 3 DXI
  Hitter of ~ homers: 3 OTT
**516**
  sheets: 4 REAM
**525i**
  maker: 3 BMW
**551:** 3 DLI
**552:** 4 DLII
**601:** 3 DCI
**602:** 4 DCII
**640**
  acres (abbr.): 4 SQMI
**650:** 3 DCL
**660**
  Hitter of ~ home runs:
    4 MAYS
**700:** 3 DCC
**705:** 4 DCCV
**747:** 3 JET 5 PLANE
**755**
  Hitter with ~ homers:
    5 AARON
**800**
  preceder: 3 ONE
**801**
  Area code ~ locale: 4 UTAH
**900**
  automaker: 4 SAAB
**901:** 3 CMI
**905:** 3 CMV
**911**
  respondent: 3 EMT
  Subj. of a ~ call: 4 EMER
**950:** 3 CML
**1,000**
  G's: 3 MIL
  kilograms: 5 TONNE
  One in: 5 COMMA
**"1000 Oceans"**
  singer Tori: 4 AMOS
**"1,001 ___":** 4 USES
**1002:** 3 MII
**1040:** 4 FORM
  data: 6 INCOME
  info: 3 SSN
  issuer: 3 IRS
  reviewer: 3 CPA
**1040EZ**
  issuer: 3 IRS
**1052:** 4 MLII

**1,093**
  Holder of ~ patents:
    6 EDISON
**1102:** 4 MCII
**"___ 1138" (sci-fi film):** 3 THX
**1200**
  hours: 4 NOON
**1,281**
  Scorer of ~ goals: 4 PELE
**1300:** 4 MCCC 5 ONEPM
  hours: 3 ONE
**1302**
  Exile of: 5 DANTE
**1400:** 5 TWOPM
**1409**
  Council site of: 4 PISA
**1440**
  School since: 4 ETON
**1492**
  discovery: 5 HAITI
  Ship of: 4 NINA 5 PINTA
**1493**
  landing site: 7 ANTIGUA
**1500-meter**
  gold medalist: 3 COE
**1501:** 3 MDI
**1551:** 4 MDLI
**1600:** 3 MDC
**1605**
  Pope of: 5 LEOXI
**1614**
  Groom of: 5 ROLFE
**1692**
  trial site: 5 SALEM
**1701**
  Institution since: 4 YALE
**1711**
  Race site since: 5 ASCOT
**1719**
  Classic of: 6 CRUSOE
**1,760**
  A mi. has: 3 YDS
  yards: 4 MILE
**1773**
  Jetsam of: 3 TEA
**1776**
  battleground: 7 TRENTON
  pamphleteer: 5 PAINE
**"1776"**
  role: 5 ADAMS
**1777**
  battle site: 5 PAOLI
    8 SARATOGA
**1781**
  discovery: 6 URANUS
**1799**
  discovery:
    15 THEROSETTASTONE
**1801**
  Company since: 6 DUPONT
  discovery: 5 CERES
**1804**
  dueler: 4 BURR
  symphony: 6 EROICA
**1806**
  It ended in ~ (abbr.): 3 HRE

**1813**
  battle site: 4 ERIE
**1814**
  exile site: 4 ELBA
  treaty site: 5 GHENT
**1816**
  notable novel: 4 EMMA
**1825**
  Canal completed in: 4 ERIE
  It opened in: 9 ERIECANAL
**1829**
  Mount first climbed in:
    6 ARARAT
**1831**
  Noted poem of: 6 LENORE
**1836**
  battle site: 5 ALAMO
**1839–42**
  war cause: 5 OPIUM
**1846**
  discovery: 7 NEPTUNE
**1847**
  noted novel: 4 OMOO
**1850s**
  war site: 6 CRIMEA
**1852**
  erupter: 4 ETNA
**1,852**
  meters: 7 SEAMILE
**1,859**
  Mel who scored ~ runs: 3 OTT
**1860s**
  govt.: 3 CSA
  insignia: 3 CSA
  nickname: 3 ABE
**1862**
  battle site: 6 SHILOH
    8 ANTIETAM
**1864**
  battle site: 9 MOBILEBAY
**1867**
  purchase: 6 ALASKA
**1871**
  opera debut: 4 AIDA
**1876**
  victor, by one vote: 5 HAYES
**1880**
  novel: 4 NANA
**1883**
  erupter: 8 KRAKATOA
**1887**
  novel: 3 SHE
  opera debut: 6 OTELLO
**1890**
  Org. since: 3 DAR
  State since: 5 IDAHO
**1890s:** 11 MAUVEDECADE
  ideal female: 10 GIBSONGIRL
**1896**
  State since: 4 UTAH
**1898**
  annexation: 6 HAWAII
  Famed hill of: 7 SANJUAN
  She sank in: 8 THEMAINE
    USSMAINE
  Soft drink since: 5 PEPSI

**1899–1902**
war participant: 4 BOER
**1900**
opera debut: 5 TOSCA
**1903**
He debuted at the Met in:
6 CARUSO
**1909**
Pole seeker of: 5 PEARY
**1912**
Cookie since: 4 OREO
headline name: 7 TITANIC
**1914**
battle site: 4 YSER 5 MARNE
**"1914"**
poet: 6 BROOKE
**1915**
Service club since: 7 KIWANIS
**1917**
newsmaker: 5 LENIN
Ruler until: 4 TSAR
**1918**
hit song: 7 KKKKATY
**1919**
musical: 5 IRENE
**1920**
novel: 5 CHERI
Rights org. since: 4 ACLU
**1920s**
auto: 3 REO
designer: 4 ERTE
style: 7 ARTDECO
**1921**
sci-fi play: 3 RUR
**1922**
discovery, familiarly: 3 TUT
documentary: 6 NANOOK
**1923**
Capital since: 6 ANKARA
**1925**
defendant: 6 SCOPES
Girl in a ~ musical:
7 NANETTE
musical: 11 NONONANETTE
**1926**
Channel crosser of: 6 EDERLE
**1927**
Movie award since: 5 OSCAR
New auto of: 7 LASALLE
**1928**
musical, with "The":
15 THREEPENNYOPERA
New auto of: 6 DESOTO
MODELA
**1930**
discovery: 5 PLUTO
**1930s**
boxing champ: 4 BAER
From the: 6 PREWAR
migrant: 4 OKIE
movie dog: 4 ASTA
**1931**
convictee: 8 ALCAPONE
**1933**
film classic: 8 KINGKONG
Initials since: 3 TVA

**1935**
Country renamed in: 4 IRAN
musical: 7 ROBERTA
**1936**
best-selling novel:
15 GONEWITHTHEWIND
First name in ~ politics: 3 ALF
**1939**
epic film:
15 GONEWITHTHEWIND
film setting: 4 TARA
movie dog: 4 TOTO
**1940s**
agcy.: 3 OPA
computer: 5 ENIAC
first lady: 4 BESS
radio quiz show: 4 DRIQ
**1941**
attack site:
11 PEARLHARBOR
comics debut: 6 ARCHIE
musical:
13 MOONOVERMIAMI
**1942**
battle site: 8 CORALSEA
9 ELALAMEIN
**1944**
battle site: 4 STLO 5 LEYTE
initials: 3 ETO
invasion city: 4 STLO
June 6: 4 DDAY
Paper launched in:
7 LEMONDE
Town in a ~ novel: 5 ADANO
turning point: 4 DDAY
**1945**
Aug. 15: 5 VJDAY
battle site: 7 OKINAWA
conference site: 5 YALTA
7 POTSDAM
It started in: 9 ATOMICAGE
May 8: 5 VEDAY
summit site: 5 YALTA
**1946**
Airline founded in: 3 SAS
Computer unveiled in:
5 ENIAC
Govt. org. since: 3 SSA
**1947**
Mil. org. since: 4 USAF
**1948**
Airline since: 4 ELAL
Org. formed in: 3 OAS
political quote:
15 GIVEEMHELLHARRY
**1949**
Defense org. since: 4 NATO
Prize since: 4 EMMY
**1950**
film noir classic: 3 DOA
**1950s**
bomb: 5 EDSEL
campaign name: 3 IKE
experiment: 5 HTEST
First name in ~ TV: 4 DESI
political inits.: 3 AES

**1952**
Magazine since: 3 MAD
Weapon since: 5 HBOMB
**1953**
classic film: 5 SHANE
conquest: 7 EVEREST
western: 5 SHANE
**1954**
Alliance created in: 5 SEATO
**1954–77**
alliance: 5 SEATO
**1955**
animated film:
15 LADYANDTHETRAMP
hit song: 7 ONLYYOU
merger gp.: 3 AFL CIO
Name in ~ news:
9 ROSAPARKS
**1956**
Awards since: 5 OBIES
invasion site: 5 SINAI
sci-fi classic:
15 FORBIDDENPLANET
trouble spot: 4 SUEZ
**1957**
Car until: 4 NASH
hit song: 5 DIANA
River in a ~ film: 4 KWAI
**1958**
chiller, with "The": 4 BLOB
musical: 4 GIGI
News org. since: 3 UPI
Org. since: 4 NASA
~ #1 song: 6 VOLARE
**1958–61**
political org.: 3 UAR
**1959**
doo-wop classic:
15 ATEENAGERINLOVE
**1960**
Cartel since: 4 OPEC
Fuel org. since: 4 OPEC
hit song: 9 TEENANGEL
inauguration speaker: 5 FROST
U.N. member since: 4 TOGO
**1960s**
atty. gen.: 3 RFK
campus gp.: 3 SDS
civil rights org.: 4 SNCC
dance: 4 FRUG 5 TWIST
do: 4 AFRO
foursome: 7 BEATLES
It was dropped in the: 3 LSD
jacket style: 5 NEHRU
protest: 5 SITIN
radical gp.: 3 SDS
Sign of the: 5 PEACE
symbol: 5 PEACE
war zone: 3 NAM
~ TV boy: 4 OPIE
**1961**
space chimp: 4 ENOS
**1962**
Launch of: 7 TELSTAR
Retail chain since: 5 KMART
spy film: 4 DRNO

**1963–78**
pope: 6 PAULVI
**1964**
Car of a ~ song: 3 GTO
~ #1 hit: 5 RINGO
**1965**
march site: 5 SELMA
unrest site: 5 WATTS
**1966**
movie or song: 5 ALFIE
**1967**
seceder: 6 BIAFRA
war site: 5 SINAI
**1968**
folk album: 4 ARLO
groom, familiarly: 3 ARI
New flier of: 3 SST
**1969**
bride: 3 ONO
Clothing retailer since:
　6 THEGAP
jazz album: 4 ELLA
landing site: 4 MOON
miracle team: 4 METS
Team created in: 5 EXPOS
**1969–73**
lottery org.: 3 SSS
**1970**
Govt. agency since: 3 EPA
hurricane: 5 CELIA
~ #1 hit: 7 LETITBE
**1970s**
bombing target: 5 HANOI
compact: 5 LECAR
hairdo: 4 AFRO
hit show: 5 RHODA
radical gp.: 3 SLA
sitcom: 5 ARNIE
space station: 6 SKYLAB
spin-off: 5 RHODA
**1971**
courtroom drama: 5 THEDA
Govt. agency since: 4 OSHA
**1972**
hit song: 5 LAYLA
hurricane: 5 AGNES
treaty subj.: 3 ABM
**1973**
court alias: 3 ROE
resignee: 5 AGNEW
space station: 6 SKYLAB
**1974**
abductee: 6 HEARST
biopic: 5 LENNY
dog film: 5 BENJI
Radical gp. in ~ news: 3 SLA
**1975**
blockbuster film: 4 JAWS
Comedy show since: 3 SNL
**1976**
bestseller: 5 ROOTS
raid site: 7 ENTEBBE
uprising site: 6 SOWETO
**1977**
Org. abolished in: 5 SEATO
TV event of: 5 ROOTS

**1978**
cult film: 10 ERASERHEAD
Science magazine since:
　4 OMNI
thriller film: 4 COMA
**1979**
accident site: 3 TMI
disco hit: 4 YMCA
exile: 4 AMIN SHAH
　7 IDIAMIN
It left orbit in: 6 SKYLAB
revolution locale: 4 IRAN
sci-fi classic: 5 ALIEN
**1980**
erupter: 8 STHELENS
　10 MTSTHELENS
~ TV debut: 3 CNN
**1980s**
Dolls of the: 3 ETS
Half of a ~ TV duo: 4 KATE
　5 ALLIE
**1981**
bride: 5 DIANA 6 LADYDI
**1982**
media debut: 8 USATODAY
recall subject: 7 TYLENOL
sci-fi film: 4 TRON
**1983**
invasion site: 7 GRENADA
**1984:** 4 YEAR 8 LEAPYEAR
Eclectic magazine started in:
　4 UTNE
film catchphrase:
　9 ILLBEBACK
gas leak site: 6 BHOPAL
historical novel: 6 THEHAJ
sci-fi film: 7 STARMAN
**"1984"**
author: 6 ORWELL
setting: 7 OCEANIA
**1986**
It was launched in: 3 MIR
rock autobiography: 5 ITINA
sci-fi sequel: 6 ALIENS
self-titled album:
　6 ARETHA
**1988**
country album: 4 REBA
**1989**
auto debut: 3 GEO
**1990**
Nation since: 7 NAMIBIA
~ #1 rap hit:
　10 ICEICEBABY
**1990s**
music genre: 6 TECHNO
party: 4 RAVE
sitcom: 5 ELLEN
**1991**
Agcy. dismantled in: 3 KGB
Divorcée of: 5 IVANA
It dissolved in: 4 USSR
It regained independence in:
　7 ESTONIA
They broke up in ~ (abbr.):
　4 SSRS

**1992**
also-ran: 5 PEROT
erupter: 4 ETNA
presidential candidate:
　5 PEROT 7 TSONGAS
TV host since: 4 LENO
**1993**
accord site: 4 OSLO
Nation since: 7 ERITREA
treaty: 5 NAFTA
**1994**
campus comedy: 3 PCU
**1995**
court VIP: 3 ITO
earthquake site: 4 KOBE
hurricane: 4 OPAL
Name in ~ news: 3 ITO
pig movie: 4 BABE
**1996**
also-ran: 4 DOLE
candidate: 4 DOLE
golf movie: 6 TINCUP
horror flick: 6 SCREAM
presidential hopeful: 5 LAMAR
　PEROT
running mate: 4 KEMP
**1997**
basketball film: 6 AIRBUD
biopic: 6 SELENA
blockbuster film: 7 TITANIC
Carrier until: 5 USAIR
**1998**
animated film: 4 ANTZ
　5 MULAN
Car reintroduced in:
　6 BEETLE
Computer since: 4 IMAC
report author: 5 STARR
**1999**
hurricane: 5 IRENE
name in the news: 5 ELIAN
**2000:** 4 YEAR 8 LEAPYEAR
also-ran: 4 GORE 5 NADER
Flier grounded in: 3 SST
Name in ~ news: 5 ELIAN
sci-fi film: 4 XMEN
World leader since:
　5 PUTIN
**2,000**
pounds: 3 TON 6 ONETON
**2001:** 4 YEAR
biopic: 3 ALI
Carrier acquired in: 3 TWA
Co. in a ~ merger: 3 AOL
erupter: 4 ETNA
It came down in: 3 MIR
**"2001: A Space Odyssey"**
actor Dullea: 4 KEIR
computer: 3 HAL
extras: 4 APES
**2002**
erupter: 4 ETNA
scandal subject: 5 ENRON
**2003**
Its last trip was in: 3 SST
movie bomb: 5 GIGLI

**2004**
Auto discontinued in: 5 ALERO
biopic: 3 RAY
candidate: 5 NADER
hurricane: 4 IVAN
**2005**
hurricane: 4 RITA
**2006:** 4 YEAR
**2,213**
Ruth's: 4 RBIS
**2,297**
Aaron's: 4 RBIS
**4,047**
square meters: 4 ACRE

**4,840**
square yards: 4 ACRE
    7 ONEACRE
**5,000**
Game played to ~ points:
    7 CANASTA
**"5,000 Fingers of ___, The":**
    3 DRT
**5,280**
feet: 4 MILE
**5,714**
He fanned: 4 RYAN
**9000**
automaker: 4 SAAB

**11,000-foot**
peak: 4 ETNA
**24,902**
Line that extends for ~ miles:
    7 EQUATOR
**32,000**
ounces: 3 TON
**512,000**
drams: 3 TON
**6,272,640**
square inches: 4 ACRE
**1,000,000,000**
years: 3 EON

**A:** 3 ONE 4 MARK SIDE TYPE
5 GRADE 7 ARTICLE
Get all ~ grades: 5 EXCEL
Got an ~ on: 4 ACED
in communications: 4 ALFA
major: 3 KEY
opposite, in England: 3 ZED
Took the ~ train: 4 RODE
Vitamin: 7 RETINOL
~, abroad: 3 EIN UNA UNE
**A ___ (nonanalytic):** 6 PRIORI
**___ A:** 4 QAND
**A4**
maker: 4 AUDI
**A6**
maker: 4 AUDI
**A8**
maker: 4 AUDI
**AA:** 7 BATTERY
concern: 3 DTS
offshoot: 6 ALANON
**AAA**
AA and: 4 ORGS
baseball team of Buffalo:
6 BISONS
offering: 3 MAP TOW
opposite: 3 EEE
Part of: 4 AMER ASSN
suggestion: 3 RTE
**Aachen**
article: 3 DER EIN
**"Aah!"**
accompanier: 3 OOH
**A&E**
Part of: 4 ARTS
**A&M**
Texas ~ player: 5 AGGIE
**A&P**
Part of: 3 ATL
**A&W**
rival: 4 DADS 5 HIRES
**A ___ apple:** 4 ASIN
**Aar**
Capital on the: 4 BERN
City on the: 5 BERNE
**Aardvark:** 6 MAMMAL
7 ANTBEAR
8 ANTEATER
feature: 5 SNOUT
land: 6 AFRICA
meal: 4 ANTS
morsel: 3 ANT
**Aare**
Capital on the: 4 BERN
City on the: 5 BERNE
**Aaron**
Brother of: 5 MOSES
Daughter of: 4 TORI

had 2,297: 4 RBIS
or Raymond: 4 BURR
Son of: 7 ELEAZAR
**Aaron, Hank:** 8 ALABAMAN
**AARP**
members: 3 SRS
membership determinant:
3 AGE
Part of: 3 RET 4 AMER ASSN
**AAUW**
Part of: 4 UNIV
**Ab**
neighbor: 3 PEC
**Ab ___ (from the start):** 3 OVO
6 INITIO
**ABA**
member: 3 ATT 4 ATTY
members: 3 DAS
superstar: 3 DRJ
**___ Ababa:** 5 ADDIS
**Aback**
Take: 4 STUN
**Abacus**
piece: 4 BEAD
Use an: 3 ADD
user: 5 ADDER
**"Aba ___ Honeymoon, The":**
4 DABA
**Abalone**
eater: 5 OTTER
**Abandon:** 4 DROP SHED
5 DITCH LEAVE SCRAP
6 DESERT 7 FORSAKE
~, as a lover: 4 JILT
**Abase:** 6 DEMEAN
**Abate:** 3 EBB 4 EASE WANE
5 LETUP 6 EASEUP
LESSEN
**Abba**
1975 ~ hit: 3 SOS
1976 ~ hit:
15 IDOIDOIDOIDOIDO
Music of: 7 EUROPOP
of Israel: 4 EBAN
roots: 6 SWEDEN
**Abba, Mahmoud**
gp.: 3 PLO
**Abbe**
or Nathan: 4 LANE
**Abbé de l'___:** 4 EPEE
**Abbess**
Rank below: 8 PRIORESS
underling: 3 NUN
**Abbey:** 4 ROAD
and others: 3 RDS
biggie: 5 PRIOR
**Abbey Theatre**
name: 6 OCASEY

**Abbott**
~, to Costello: 6 COHORT
**Abbott & Costello:** 3 DUO
1942 ~ movie: 7 RIORITA
**Abbreviation**
An ~ of: 8 SHORTFOR
**Abby**
Twin of: 3 ANN
~, to Ann: 6 SISTER
**ABC:** 7 NETWORK TRIGRAM
Arledge of: 5 ROONE
Early ~ show: 3 GMA
Former ~ sitcom: 5 ELLEN
Roberts of: 5 COKIE
Sawyer of: 5 DIANE
**ABC's:** 6 BASICS
**Abdicator**
of 1917: 4 TSAR
**Abdomen:** 3 GUT
**Abduct:** 6 KIDNAP
**Abductee**
Paris: 5 HELEN
**Abduction**
1974 ~ gp.: 3 SLA
**Abductor**
craft: 3 UFO
Elephant: 3 ROC
Hearst: 3 SLA
Helen: 5 PARIS
**Abdul**
Singer: 5 PAULA
**Abdul-___, Kareem:**
6 JABBAR
**"Abdul Abulbul ___":** 4 AMIR
**___ Abdul-Jabbar:** 6 KAREEM
**Abe**
Like: 6 HONEST
Son of: 3 TAD
**Abecedarian**
phrase: 4 ASIN
**Abed**
Still: 5 NOTUP
**Abel**
Brother of: 4 CAIN SETH
Father of: 4 ADAM
Mother of: 3 EVE
Nephew of: 4 ENOS
Newsman: 4 ELIE
**Aberdeen**
denial: 3 NAE
miss: 4 LASS
native: 4 SCOT
river: 3 DEE
**Abet:** 3 AID 4 HELP 5 COACT
**Abeyance**
In: 5 ONICE
**Abhor:** 4 HATE 6 DETEST
LOATHE

**Abide**
Can't: 4 HATE 6 DETEST
    LOATHE
**Abie**
Girl of: 4 ROSE
**Ability:** 5 SKILL 6 TALENT
Creative: 3 ART
Instinctive: 4 FEEL
Musical: 3 EAR
Paranormal: 3 ESP PSI
to hit a target: 3 AIM
**"A bit of talcum/Is always**
    **walcum"**
poet: 4 NASH
**Abject:** 7 HANGDOG
**Able**
Art ~ to: 5 CANST
Is ~ to: 3 CAN
Isn't ~ to: 4 CANT
More than: 5 ADEPT
to feel: 7 SENSATE
to see through: 4 ONTO
**"Able was ___ ...":** 4 IERE
**"Able was I ___ ...":** 3 ERE
    4 EREI
**Ablutionary**
vessel: 4 EWER
**ABM**
Part of: 4 ANTI
**Abner**
artist: 4 CAPP
last name: 5 YOKUM
love: 8 DAISYMAE
radio partner: 3 LUM
**"___ Abner":** 3 LIL
**Abnormal**
sac: 4 CYST
Suffix for the: 3 OSE
**Abnormally:** 3 TOO
**Aboard:** 4 ONTO
Put: 4 LADE STOW
**Abode:** 4 HOME 5 HOUSE
Alpine: 6 CHALET
Animal: 4 LAIR
Bird: 4 NEST
Conical: 5 TEPEE
Heavenly: 4 EDEN
Lofty: 5 AERIE
**Abolish:** 3 END 5 ANNUL
**Abolished**
Defense gp. ~ in 1977:
    5 SEATO
**Abolitionist**
~ Harriet: 6 TUBMAN
**Abominable:** 6 HORRID
    7 OBSCENE
Find: 4 HATE 6 DETEST
    LOATHE
**Abominable Snowman:**
    4 YETI
**Abominate:** 4 HATE 6 DETEST
    LOATHE
**___ a bone:** 5 DRYAS
**Aborigine**
of Japan: 4 AINU
of New Zealand: 5 MAORI

**Aborted**
mission words: 4 NOGO
**"Abou Ben ___":** 5 ADHEM
**Abound:** 4 TEEM
**Abounding:** 4 RIFE
**About:** 4 ASTO INRE ORSO
    5 ANENT CIRCA
Be up and: 4 STIR
Just: 4 NEAR ORSO
    6 ALMOST NEARLY
to happen: 8 IMMINENT
**___ about:** 4 NOSE ONOR
**About-face:** 5 UTURN
**Above:** 4 ATOP OVER UPON
    5 SUPRA
As: 4 IDEM
From: 6 AERIAL
it all: 5 ALOOF
None of the: 5 OTHER
Word often seen from:
    7 WELCOME
~, in German: 4 UBER
~, poetically: 3 OER
**___ above:** 4 ACUT
**Aboveground**
trains: 3 ELS
**___ above the rest:** 4 ACUT
**Abracadabra**
alternative: 6 PRESTO
**Abrade:** 3 RUB 4 RASP
**Abraded:** 4 WORE
**Abraham**
Grandson of: 4 ESAU
    5 JACOB
Oscar role for: 7 SALIERI
Son of: 5 ISAAC
Wife of: 5 SARAH
**Abrasion:** 6 SCRAPE
**Abrasive**
cloth: 5 EMERY
particles: 4 GRIT
Use an: 5 SCOUR
**"Abra was ready ___ called her**
    **name": Prior:** 4 EREI
**Abreast**
of: 4 UPON
**Abridged**
Not: 5 UNCUT
**Abroad**
Go: 4 TOUR 6 TRAVEL
**Abrogate:** 6 REPEAL
**Abrupt:** 4 CURT
transition: 4 LEAP
**Abruptly:** 10 COLDTURKEY
fired: 4 AXED
Turn: 6 SWERVE
**Abruzzi**
bell town: 4 ATRI
**Abs**
exercise: 5 SITUP
They're above the: 4 PECS
**Abscam**
org.: 3 FBI
**Absence:** 4 LACK
Feel the ~ of: 4 MISS
**Absent:** 4 AWAY

**Absentee**
Roll call: 4 AWOL
**Absinthe**
flavor: 5 ANISE
**Absolut**
rival: 5 STOLI
**Absolute:** 5 FINAL SHEER
    TOTAL UTTER
Not: 8 RELATIVE
worst: 4 PITS
**"Absolutely!":** 3 YES 4 AMEN
    6 YOUBET
**"Absolutely Fabulous"**
Patsy's pal on: 5 EDINA
**Absorb:** 3 EAT SOP 5 LEARN
    SOPUP
**Absorbed:** 4 RAPT
as a cost: 3 ATE
Be ~ slowly: 6 OSMOSE
by: 4 INTO
the loss: 5 ATEIT
**Absorbent**
application: 4 TALC
cloth: 5 TERRY
Use ~ paper: 4 BLOT
**Absorption**
Gradual: 7 OSMOSIS
**Abstain**
from: 4 SHUN 5 AVOID
    6 ESCHEW RESIST
**Abstract**
artist Mark: 6 ROTHKO
composer Erik: 5 SATIE
sculpture: 7 STABILE
style: 5 OPART
Swiss ~ artist: 4 KLEE
**Abstraction:** 4 IDEA
**Abstractionist**
~ Paul: 4 KLEE
**Abstruse:** 4 DEEP 6 ARCANE
    8 ESOTERIC
stuff: 7 ESOTERY
**Absurd:** 4 ZANY 5 GOOFY
    INANE
**Absurdist**
movement: 4 DADA
**Abt.:** 3 CIR
**Abu ___:** 5 DHABI
**Abu Dhabi:** 7 EMIRATE
denizen: 4 ARAB
dignitary: 4 EMIR
fed.: 3 UAE
**Abuja**
Capital before: 5 LAGOS
country: 7 NIGERIA
**Abundance**
In: 6 GALORE
Rapunzel: 4 HAIR
**Abundant:** 4 LUSH MUCH RIFE
    5 AMPLE
Be: 4 TEEM
Far from: 6 SPARSE
**Abuse:** 8 MALTREAT
    MISTREAT
**Abut:** 6 BORDER
on: 6 ADJOIN

**Abutting:** 6 BESIDE NEXTTO
**Abuzz**
It's ~ with activity: 4 HIVE
**Abysmal:** 4 DEEP
**Abyss:** 4 GULF 5 CHASM
**Abyssinian:** 3 CAT
**Abzug**
Politico: 5 BELLA
**AC:** 4 ELEC
**A/C**
measure: 3 BTU
unit: 3 BTU
**Acad.:** 3 SCH 4 INST
goal: 3 PHD
**Academic**
achievement: 6 TENURE
enclave: 10 IVORYTOWER
figure: 4 DEAN
Meas. of ~ excellence: 3 GPA
Purely: 4 MOOT
term: 8 SEMESTER
type: 7 SCHOLAR
**Academy**
founder: 5 PLATO
freshman: 5 PLEBE
graduate: 6 ENSIGN
Its ~ is in Colo. Spr.: 4 USAF
student: 5 CADET
**Academy Award:** *see pages*
*718–721* 5 OSCAR
**Acadia National Park**
locale: 5 MAINE
**Acapulco**
**Info:** Spanish cue
appetizer: 5 NACHO
article: 3 LAS LOS UNA
assent: 4 SISI
aunt: 3 TIA
beach: 5 PLAYA
gold: 3 ORO
Other, in: 4 OTRO
sun: 3 SOL
**ACC**
member: 3 UVA
Part of: 3 ATL
**Accelerate:** 3 REV 6 STEPUP
~, with "up": 3 REV
**Accelerated:** 6 SPEDUP
**Acceleration**
unit: 4 ONEG
**Accelerator:** 3 GAS 5 PEDAL
7 SMASHER
particle: 3 ION 4 ATOM
suffix: 4 TRON
**Accent:** 6 STRESS
Brand name with an:
4 RAGU
Irish: 6 BROGUE
Scottish: 4 BURR
Speak with a Jersey: 3 MOO
**Accents**
Like some: 5 ACUTE GRAVE
**Accept:** 3 BUY 5 ADOPT
HONOR 7 AGREETO
eagerly: 5 LAPUP 6 LEAPAT
**Acceptable:** 4 OKAY

**Acceptance**
Gain ~ from: 7 GETINTO
on the street: 4 CRED
speech word: 5 THANK
**Acceptances:** 5 YESES
6 YESSES
**Accepted:** 3 OKD
customs: 5 MORES
eagerly: 7 LEAPTAT
practice: 5 USAGE
rule: 5 AXIOM
standard: 3 PAR 4 NORM
5 CANON
**Accepter**
Bet: 5 TAKER
**Accepting**
of: 6 OPENTO
**Access:** 5 ENTRY 6 ENTREE
7 TAPINTO
ATM: 3 PIN
Freeway: 4 RAMP 6 ONRAMP
Gain computer: 5 LOGIN
Means of: 4 DOOR 6 AVENUE
Mine: 4 ADIT
suffix: 3 ORY
the Web: 5 LOGON
~, with "into": 3 TAP
**"Access Hollywood"**
host Nancy: 5 ODELL
**Accessible**
Most: 7 NEAREST
**Accessory:** 5 ADDON EXTRA
**Accident:** 3 HAP 6 MISHAP
1979 Pa. ~ site: 3 TMI
Comment after an: 4 IMOK
OHNO OOPS UHOH
monitoring agcy.: 4 OSHA
Multicar: 6 PILEUP
scene fig.: 3 EMT
U.S. ~ investigator: 4 NTSB
**Accidental**
Certain: 4 FLAT
**Accidentally**
Bump: 4 STUB
reveal: 7 LETSLIP
**"Accidental Tourist, The"**
Oscar winner for:
10 GEENADAVIS
**Acclaim:** 4 LAUD 5 ECLAT
KUDOS
**Acclaimed**
Not: 6 UNSUNG
**Accolade:** 4 RAVE 5 AWARD
**Accolades:** 5 KUDOS
**Accommodate:** 3 FIT 4 SEAT
5 FITIN 6 OBLIGE
**Accommodating:** 4 EASY
6 PLIANT
person: 5 SPORT
place: 3 INN
**Accommodations**
Cheap: 8 STEERAGE
Deluxe: 5 SUITE
Liner: 6 CABINS
**Accompaniment**
Improvised: 4 VAMP

Without: 4 SOLO
**Accompany:** 6 ESCORT
to the airport: 6 SEEOFF
**Accompanying:** 4 WITH
"___ accompli": 4 FAIT
**Accomplice:** 6 COHORT
STOOGE
Con artist: 5 SHILL
Work without an:
8 ACTALONE
**Accomplish:** 6 ATTAIN
7 ACHIEVE
perfectly: 4 NAIL
**Accomplished:** 3 DID 4 ABLE
DONE FINE 7 PUTOVER
**Accomplishes:** 4 DOES
**Accomplishment:** 4 DEED FEAT
Cry of: 4 TADA 6 IDIDIT
**Accord:** 3 CAR 5 AMITY UNITY
6 TREATY UNISON
7 ENTENTE
1993 ~ site: 4 OSLO
Be in: 4 JIBE 5 ADDUP
AGREE
Bring into: 6 ATTUNE
In: 5 ASONE
International: 4 PACT
7 ENTENTE
maker: 5 HONDA
Perfect: 6 UNISON
Reach an: 5 AGREE
signed in 1992: 5 NAFTA
Were in: 5 JIBED
___ **Accord:** 3 WYE
**Accordance**
In ~ with: 3 PER 5 ASPER
**According**
to: 3 ALA PER 5 ASPER
**Accordingly:** 4 ERGO THEN
THUS
**According to ___:** 5 HOYLE
**"According to Jim"**
actor: 7 BELUSHI
**Accordion**
feature: 5 PLEAT
**Accost**
for money: 5 HITUP
**Account:** 3 LOG 4 SAKE TALE
amt.: 3 BAL
book: 6 LEDGER
Contribute to an: 5 PAYIN
exec: 3 REP
Firsthand: 6 MEMOIR
Gave an: 4 TOLD
It may be called on ~ of rain:
3 CAB
Kind of checking: 5 NOFEE
Long: 4 EPIC
Major: 4 SAGA
Rainy day: 7 NESTEGG
Settle an: 5 PAYUP
subtraction: 5 DEBIT
Third-party: 6 ESCROW
___ **account (never):** 4 ONNO
**Accountant:** 7 AUDITOR
8 PREPARER

closing time: 7 YEAREND
job: 5 AUDIT
**Accounting**
plus: 5 ASSET
principle: 4 LIFO
Young's ~ partner: 5 ERNST
**Accouter**
anew: 5 REFIT
**Accra**
land: 5 GHANA
**Accrual**
IRA: 3 INT
**Acct.**
addition: 3 INT
datum: 3 SSN
entry: 3 BAL DEP
figures: 4 AMTS
**Accumulate:** 5 AMASS RUNUP
STORE 6 ACCRUE
PILEUP SAVEUP
7 ACCRETE STOREUP
**Accumulated:** 5 RANUP
**Accumulation:** 4 MASS 5 STACK
STORE
Chimney: 4 SOOT
**Accuracy**
Check for: 3 VET
**Accurate:** 4 TRUE 5 RIGHT
6 DEADON SPOTON
**Accusation**
Caesar's: 4 ETTU
Unjust: 6 BADRAP
**Accuse:** 5 BLAME 7 IMPEACH
Formally: 6 INDICT
**Accused**
cry: 5 WHOME
excuse: 5 ALIBI
**Accustom:** 5 ADAPT ENURE
INURE 6 ORIENT
**AC/DC**
record label: 3 EMI
**Ace:** 3 PRO 4 CARD WHIZ
5 FLIER PILOT 6 TIPTOP
TOPGUN 7 AVIATOR
9 HOLEINONE
Act like an: 6 AVIATE
place: 4 HOLE 6 SLEEVE
**Acela:** 5 TRAIN
operator: 6 AMTRAK
**Acerbic:** 4 TART 5 HARSH
**Aces**
Game with ~ and chips:
4 GOLF
**Acetate**
Any: 5 ESTER
Word before: 5 ETHYL
**Acetyl**
suffix: 3 ENE
**Acetylacetone**
form: 4 ENOL
**Acetylene**
prefix: 3 OXY
**Ache:** 4 HURT 5 YEARN
(for): 4 LONG PINE
**Aches**
and pains: 4 ILLS

**Aches and ___:** 5 PAINS
**Acheson**
Reader's Digest cofounder:
4 LILA
**Achieve**
success: 6 ARRIVE
**Achievement:** 4 DEED FEAT
Base runner: 5 STEAL
Grand: 4 COUP
**Achille ___:** 5 LAURO
**Achilles:** 6 TENDON
He rescued the body of: 4 AJAX
Story of: 5 ILIAD
victim: 6 HECTOR
was dipped in it: 4 STYX
weak spot: 4 HEEL
**"Achtung Baby"**
producer Brian: 3 ENO
**Achy:** 4 SORE
Feels: 4 AILS
**Acid:** 3 LSD 4 TART
Antiseptic: 5 BORIC
Apple: 5 MALIC
Carbolic: 6 PHENOL
Draw with: 4 ETCH
Essential: 5 AMINO
Fatty: 5 OLEIC
head: 5 AMINO
in tea: 6 TANNIC
Kind of: 5 AMINO BORIC
MALIC OLEIC SALIC
6 ACETIC CITRIC NITRIC
TANNIC
letters: 3 LSD
neutralizer: 4 BASE 6 ALKALI
plus alcohol: 5 ESTER
Protein: 5 AMINO
Strong: 3 HCL 6 NITRIC
user: 6 ETCHER
**Acid ___:** 4 RAIN TEST
**___ acid:** 5 AMINO BORIC
FOLIC OLEIC 6 ACETIC
FORMIC NITRIC
**Acid-alcohol**
compound: 5 ESTER
**Acidic:** 4 TART
**Acidity**
nos.: 3 PHS
**Acknowledge:** 3 OWN 4 AVOW
5 ADMIT NODTO THANK
applause: 3 BOW
frankly: 4 AVOW
**Acknowledgment:** 6 CREDIT
Cockpit: 5 ROGER
Debt: 3 IOU
Frank: 6 AVOWAL
Performer's: 11 CURTAINCALL
**"A ___'clock scholar":** 4 TENO
**ACLU**
concerns: 3 RTS 6 RIGHTS
Part of: 4 AMER
**"A clue!":** 3 AHA
**Acme:** 4 APEX PEAK
At the ~ of: 4 ATOP
**Acne**
sufferer: 4 TEEN

**Aconcagua**
range: 5 ANDES
**Acorn:** 3 NUT 4 SEED
source: 3 OAK 7 OAKTREE
**A-courting**
Go: 3 SUE WOO
**Acoustic**
unit: 4 SONE
**"Acoustic Soul"**
singer: 9 INDIAARIE
**Acquaintance**
Make the ~ of: 4 MEET
**Acquainted**
Be ~ with: 4 KNOW
Was ~ with: 4 KNEW
**Acquiesce:** 5 AGREE 6 ACCEDE
ASSENT
**Acquire:** 3 GET NET WIN
4 GAIN REAP 5 GETIN
INCUR 6 OBTAIN
SECURE 8 COMEINTO
molars: 6 TEETHE
**Acquired:** 6 CAMEBY
deservedly: 6 EARNED
It may be: 5 TASTE
kin: 5 INLAW
**Acquisition**
American: 3 TWA
Aquarium: 5 TETRA
Beach: 3 TAN
Disney: 3 ABC
Marriage: 5 INLAW
Owner: 4 DEED
**Acquitted**
Is: 11 BEATOTHERAP
**Acre**
home: 6 ISRAEL
**Acreage:** 4 AREA LAND
**Acred**
homes: 7 ESTATES
**Acrimonious:** 6 BITTER
**Acrimony:** 3 IRE 5 SPITE
**Acrobat**
maker: 5 ADOBE
security: 3 NET
**Acrobatic:** 5 AGILE
performance: 5 STUNT
**Acrobatics**
performed to music:
10 BREAKDANCE
**Acronym**
Alliance: 4 NATO 5 SEATO
Anticrime: 4 RICO
Breakfast: 4 IHOP
Broadway: 4 ANTA
Cartel: 4 OPEC
Computer: 3 ROM 4 GIGO
5 ASCII MSDOS
Disney World: 5 EPCOT
Diving: 5 SCUBA
formed from Standard Oil:
4 ESSO
Great Lakes: 5 HOMES
Military: 3 SAC 5 AWACS
NORAD
Navigation: 5 LORAN

Oil: 4 OPEC
part: 4 INIT
Police jacket: 4 SWAT
Record: 5 ASCAP
Restaurant: 4 IHOP
Sleep: 3 REM
Sunscreen: 4 PABA
Wall St.: 4 AMEX

**Acrophobe**
dread: 6 HEIGHT

**Acropolis**
figure: 6 ATHENA
locale: 6 ATHENS

**Across:** 4 OVER
Came: 3 MET
Come: 4 FIND
Come ~ as: 4 SEEM
Directly ~ from (abbr.): 3 OPP
Go: 4 SPAN
Reach: 4 SPAN
the ocean: 7 OVERSEA
~, in verse: 3 OER

**Acrylic**
fiber: 5 ORLON

**Act:** 4 DEED 6 BEHAVE
7 STATUTE
as censor: 5 BLEEP
badly: 5 EMOTE
Catch in the: 3 NAB
Caught in the: 4 SEEN
Ceremonial: 4 RITE
crabby: 5 SIDLE
Failed to: 3 SAT
Formal: 7 STATUTE
human: 3 ERR
It's an: 4 SKIT
like: 3 APE 7 EMULATE
of faith: 4 LEAP
of war: 3 TUG
opener: 6 SCENEI
8 SCENEONE
Part of an: 5 SCENE
Prohibited: 4 NONO
properly: 6 BEHAVE
servile: 6 GROVEL
the ham: 5 RADIO
the snitch: 6 TATTLE
the snoop: 3 PRY
They: 5 DOERS
Time to: 5 DDAY
Trusting: 11 LEAPOFFAITH
Wrongful: 4 TORT

**Act.**
Not: 3 RET 4 RETD

**Acting**
ambassador: 5 AGENT
award: 4 OBIE
ensemble: 4 CAST
family: 5 ALDAS 6 FONDAS
like: 5 APING
Majors in: 3 LEE
part: 4 ROLE

**Action:** 4 DEED 5 STEPS
Affirmative: 3 NOD
Break in the: 4 LULL
centers: 6 ARENAS

figure: 5 GIJOE
film staple: 5 CHASE
First course of: 5 PLANA
Get ready for: 6 GEARUP
Inadvisable: 4 NONO
Incite to: 5 EGGON IMPEL
One who suspends an:
6 ABATOR
Out of: 5 IDLED ONICE
6 LAIDUP
People of: 5 DOERS
Piece of the: 3 CUT 5 SHARE
Prepare for: 4 GIRD 6 GEARUP
Put into: 3 USE 5 EXERT
6 DEPLOY
Rash: 5 HASTE
Refrain from taking: 6 SITPAT
spot: 5 ARENA
Stir to: 4 PROD URGE
6 AROUSE
Take ~ against: 3 SUE
Where the ~ is: 5 ARENA
word: 4 VERB

**Actionable**
words: 5 LIBEL

**Action-filled:** 8 SLAMBANG

**Actium**
Victor at: 7 AGRIPPA

**Activate:** 3 USE 5 SPARK START
6 ENABLE TURNON

**Active:** 4 SPRY 5 DOING
7 ONTHEGO
by day: 7 DIURNAL
Not: 4 IDLE 5 INERT
6 ONHOLD
Not ~ (abbr.): 3 RET 4 RETD
one: 4 DOER
volcano: 4 ETNA

**Activist:** 4 DOER
An ~ has one: 5 CAUSE
Old ~ org.: 3 SDS
~ Chavez: 5 CESAR
~ Davis: 6 ANGELA
~ Parks: 4 ROSA

**Activity**
Busy: 3 ADO
Center of: 3 HUB
Centers of: 4 LOCI
Dirty: 4 POOL
Flurry of: 3 ADO 5 SPASM
Productive: 4 WORK
Spurts of: 6 SPASMS

**"Act now!":** 4 DOIT

**Actor:** 7 ARTISTE
accessory: 4 PROP
aid: 3 CUE
award: 5 OSCAR
Biggest fan of a child:
8 STAGEMOM
Chain-wearing: 3 MRT
Crowd scene: 5 EXTRA
Lionized: 4 LAHR
milieu: 5 STAGE
minimum: 5 SCALE
Overacting: 3 HAM
part: 4 ROLE

Rapping: 4 ICET
rep: 5 AGENT
study: 5 LINES
Uncredited: 5 EXTRA
with no lines: 4 MIME

**Actors**
Change the: 6 RECAST
How ~ enter: 5 ONCUE
org.: 5 AFTRA

**Actual:** 4 REAL TRUE
7 DEFACTO
being: 4 ESSE

**Actually:** 6 INESSE INFACT
9 INREALITY
existing: 6 INESSE

**"Act your ___!":** 3 AGE

**Acuff**
Singer: 3 ROY

**Acuity**
Mental: 4 WITS
Musical: 3 EAR

**Acupressure:** 7 SHIATSU

**Acupuncturist**
life force: 3 CHI

**Acura**
model: 6 LEGEND 7 INTEGRA
___ a customer: 5 ONETO

**Acute:** 4 DIRE KEEN 5 SHARP
6 SEVERE 7 INTENSE

**Ad:** 4 SPOT 5 PROMO
abbr.: 3 APR
Attack: 5 SMEAR
award: 4 CLIO
catchphrase: 6 SLOGAN
follower: 3 HOC LIB

**A.D.**
It began in 800: 3 HRE
Part of: 4 ANNO 6 DOMINI

**Ad-___:** 3 HOC LIB 4 LIBS

**ADA**
member: 3 DDS

**Adage:** 3 SAW 5 AXIOM
MAXIM

**Adagio:** 4 SLOW
and allegro: 5 TEMPI
Slower than: 5 LENTO

**Adah**
Husband of: 4 ESAU

**Adam**
Actor: 5 ARKIN
and Eve locale: 4 EDEN
and Mae: 5 WESTS
First wife of ~, in Jewish lore:
6 LILITH
Grandson of: 4 ENOS SETH
madam: 3 EVE
Son of: 4 ABEL CAIN SETH

**"Adam ___": Eliot:** 4 BEDE

**"Adam Bede"**
author: 5 ELIOT

**Adams**
Actor: 3 DON
Actress: 4 EDIE MAUD
Mrs. John Quincy: 6 LOUISA
Photographer: 5 ANSEL
Singer: 4 EDIE 5 BRYAN

**Adams, John Quincy**
Mrs.: 6 LOUISA
**Adams, Scott**
character: 7 DILBERT
**Adam's ___ (water):** 3 ALE
**Adam's apple**
locale: 4 EDEN 6 LARYNX
provider: 3 EVE
**Adamson**
lioness: 4 ELSA
**Adaptable:** 6 PLIANT
7 ELASTIC
aircraft: 4 STOL
truck: 3 UTE
**Adapter**
letters: 4 ACDC
**Adar**
Month after: 5 NISAN
Month before: 6 SHEBAT
**"Ad astra per ___":** 6 ASPERA
**Ad-___ committee:** 3 HOC
**ADCs:** 5 ASSTS
**Add:** 5 MIXIN PUTIN TOTUP
6 APPEND TACKON
a lane to: 5 WIDEN
as a bonus: 7 THROWIN
booze to: 4 LACE
color to: 4 TINT
fizz to: 6 AERATE
fringe to: 4 EDGE
herbs to: 6 SEASON
on: 5 ANNEX 6 APPEND
ATTACH
sugar: 7 SWEETEN
to the payroll: 4 HIRE
turf to: 5 RESOD
up: 4 TOTE 5 TALLY TOTAL
6 ACCRUE
up (to): 6 AMOUNT
value to: 6 ENRICH
yeast to: 6 LEAVEN
**Addams**
Cartoonist: 4 CHAS
cousin: 3 ITT
Mrs. ~, to Gomez: 4 TISH
**Addams, Gomez**
portrayer: 5 ASTIN
**"Addams Family, The"**
actor: 5 ASTIN
actor Julia: 4 RAUL
butler: 5 LURCH
cousin: 3 ITT
**Added**
details: 4 ANDS
It's ~ to the bill: 5 RIDER
stipulations: 4 ANDS
topsoil to: 6 LOAMED
**Addenda**
Ltr.: 3 PSS
**Addendum**
Info: Suffix cue
**Adder:** 5 SNAKE
kin: 3 ASP
**Adderley**
instrument: 3 SAX
Jazzman: 3 NAT

**Adders:** 5 ABACI
**Addict:** 4 USER 6 ABUSER
helper: 7 ENABLER
program: 5 DETOX REHAB
**Adding**
Keep: 6 PILEON
**Addis ___:** 5 ABABA
**Addis Ababa**
land (abbr.): 3 ETH
**Addison**
colleague: 6 STEELE
**Addition:** 3 ELL 4 GAIN WING
Info: Suffix cue
Acct.: 3 INT
Building: 3 ELL 4 WING
5 ANNEX
column: 4 ONES TENS
In: 3 AND TOO YET 4 ALSO
ELSE PLUS 6 ATTHAT
TOBOOT
In ~ to: 8 ASWELLAS
problems: 4 SUMS
sign: 5 CARET
Slight: 5 TINGE
**Additional:** 4 ELSE MORE
5 EXTRA OTHER
7 ANOTHER
For an ~ cost: 5 EXTRA
Make ~ changes to: 6 REEDIT
ones: 6 OTHERS
~, in ads: 4 XTRA
**Additionally:** 3 AND TOO
4 ALSO ELSE PLUS
**Additive**
Café: 4 LAIT
Chinese food: 3 MSG
Copier: 5 TONER
Gas: 3 STP 5 ETHYL
Lotion: 4 ALOE
Tissue: 4 ALOE
**Addle:** 6 BEMUSE
add-on: 5 PATED
**Addlebrained:** 4 DAFT 5 DITSY
**Add-on:** 3 ELL 5 EXTRA
7 ADJUNCT
Info: Suffix cue
**Address:** 4 TALK 6 SPEECH
TALKTO 7 ORATION
SPEAKTO
abbr.: 3 RTE
Abbr. under an: 4 ATTN
a crowd: 5 ORATE
book no.: 3 TEL
Family: 3 SIS
GI: 3 APO
Give an: 5 ORATE
Hood: 3 BRO
Indian: 5 SAHIB
Kingly: 4 SIRE
Mil.: 3 APO
Net: 3 URL
One sans permanent:
5 NOMAD
One with an: 8 KEYNOTER
Palindromic: 4 MAAM
5 MADAM

Polite: 3 SIR 4 MAAM
5 MADAM
Rev.: 3 SER
Royal: 4 SIRE 6 MYLORD
WWW: 3 URL
**Addressee**
Apr.: 3 IRS
**Addresses**
Change: 4 MOVE
**Ade**
Astronaut's: 4 TANG
cooler: 3 ICE
flavor: 4 LIME
**"A debt ... we ___ Adam":**
Twain: 5 OWETO
**Adele**
Dancer: 7 ASTAIRE
**Aden**
land: 5 YEMEN
native: 6 YEMENI
**Adenauer**
epithet: 4 ALTE
German chancellor: 6 KONRAD
successor: 6 ERHARD
**Adept:** 3 ACE 4 DEFT
7 SKILLED
More: 5 ABLER
**Adequacy**
Phrase of: 6 ITLLDO
**Adequate:** 4 OKAY SOSO
6 DECENT ENOUGH
8 PASSABLE
Barely: 5 SCANT 6 SCANTY
7 MINIMAL
More than: 5 AMPLE EXTRA
~, old-style: 4 ENOW
~, slangily: 4 ENUF
**Adhere:** 3 HEW 4 BOND
5 CLING STICK
**Adherent**
in Iran: 5 BAHAI
suffix: 3 IST ITE
**Adhesive:** 3 GUM 4 GLUE
Kindergarten: 5 PASTE
Strong: 5 EPOXY
**Adidas**
rival: 4 AVIA FILA KEDS
NIKE PUMA
**Adieu**
Bid the bed: 5 ARISE
**Adipose:** 5 FATTY
**Adj.**
modifier: 3 ADV
**Adjacent**
Be ~ to: 4 ABUT
**Adjective**
suffix: 3 ENT IAL ILE INE
4 IBLE ICAL
**Adjoin:** 4 ABUT
**Adjudge:** 3 TRY 4 DEEM
**Adjunct:** 4 AIDE
**Adjust:** 4 GEAR TUNE 5 ALIGN
ALTER RESET
6 ATTUNE ORIENT
a brooch: 5 REPIN
a clock: 5 RESET

a hem: 5 RESEW
for: 6 GEARTO
one's sights: 5 REAIM
shoelaces: 5 RETIE
slightly: 5 TWEAK
to fit: 5 ADAPT
**Adjustable**
It has an ~ nose: 3 SST
loop: 5 NOOSE
**Adjuster**
concern: 5 CLAIM
Piano: 5 TUNER
**Adjustment**
Small: 5 TWEAK
Steering: 5 TOEIN
TV: 3 HOR
**Adjutant:** 4 AIDE
**Adlai**
running mate: 5 ESTES
**Adler**
of Holmes stories: 5 IRENE
**Ad-lib:** 4 SCAT 6 FAKEIT
        WINGIT 9 IMPROVISE
**Adm.**
org.: 3 USN
**Adman:** 9 SLOGANEER
award: 4 CLIO
~ Burnett: 3 LEO
**Admin.**
aide: 4 ASST
**Administer:** 4 DEAL
an oath to: 7 SWEARIN
EMTs ~ it: 3 CPR
medicine: 4 DOSE
the oath of office to:
        7 INSTATE
They may ~ IVs: 3 RNS
**Administration**
Current: 3 INS
ER: 3 CPR
Hosp.: 3 TLC
**Administrative**
center: 4 SEAT
**Administrator**
CPR: 3 EMT
Online: 5 SYSOP
SAT: 3 ETS
Superfund ~ (abbr.): 3 EPA
**Admiral**
force: 4 NAVY 5 FLEET
German: 4 SPEE
Kind of: 4 REAR
org.: 3 USN
position: 4 REAR
WWII: 6 HALSEY
~ Zumwalt: 4 ELMO
**Admiral Byrd**
book: 5 ALONE
**Admiration**
Induce: 4 AWE
Sound of: 3 OOH
**Admire**
a lot: 7 ADULATE
amorously: 4 OGLE
**Admired**
one: 4 HERO IDOL

**Admirer:** 3 FAN 4 BEAU
Beauty: 5 BEAST
Male: 5 SWAIN
of Narcissus: 4 ECHO
**Admiringly**
fearful: 5 INAWE
**Admission:** 6 ACCESS AVOWAL
exams: 4 SATS
Fibber's: 5 ILIED
Frank: 6 AVOWAL
of 1890: 5 IDAHO
of defeat: 5 ILOSE ILOST
**Admit:** 3 OWN 4 AVOW
        5 COPTO LETIN LETON
        OWNUP SEEIN
        7 CONCEDE OWNUPTO
a mistake: 7 EATCROW
openly: 4 AVOW
Refuse to: 4 DENY
to a poker game: 6 DEALIN
~, with "up": 3 OWN 4 FESS
**Admittedly:** 8 TOBESURE
**Admitting**
a draft: 4 AJAR
**Admonish:** 5 CHIDE 6 REBUKE
        7 REPROVE
**Admonishing**
sounds: 4 TSKS
**Admonition**
Archie's ~ to Edith: 6 STIFLE
Librarian's: 3 SHH
to a child: 4 NONO 6 BENICE
to Fido: 4 STAY
**Ado:** 4 FLAP FUSS STIR
        5 HOOHA 6 HOOPLA
**Adobe**
offering: 4 FONT
**Adolescent:** 4 TEEN 5 YOUTH
        6 TEENER 7 TEENAGE
        8 TEENAGER
**Adolph**
Brewer: 5 COORS
Publisher: 4 OCHS
**"Adonais"**
Shelley's: 5 ELEGY
**Adonis:** 4 HUNK STUD
killer: 4 BOAR
**Adopt:** 6 TAKEIN 7 EMBRACE
        ESPOUSE
**Adopt-a-Dog**
month: 3 OCT
**Adopted**
name of Makonnen: 5 HAILE
son of Claudius: 4 NERO
**Adoption**
agcy.: 4 SPCA 5 ASPCA
**Adorable:** 4 CUTE
one: 4 IDOL 5 CUTIE
**Adoration**
Object of: 4 IDOL
Shout of: 7 HOSANNA
**Adore:** 4 LOVE 6 DOTEON
        REVERE
~, informally: 3 LUV
**Adored**
one: 4 IDOL

**Adorée**
Actress: 5 RENEE
**Adoring**
trio: 4 MAGI
**Adorn:** 4 DECK 5 DRESS
        GRACE 6 BEDECK
Richly: 4 GILD
**Adorned**
Elaborately: 6 ORNATE
Less: 5 BARER
~, as an entrée: 5 GARNI
**Adornment:** 7 GARNISH
Bejeweled: 5 TIARA
Chin: 6 GOATEE
Letter: 5 SERIF
Model: 5 DECAL
Uniform: 7 EPAULET
**"Ad ___ per aspera":** 5 ASTRA
**Adrian**
Director: 4 LYNE
portrayer: 5 TALIA
**Adriatic**
Capital near the: 6 TIRANA
country: 7 CROATIA
feeder: 5 ADIGE
peninsula: 6 ISTRIA
port: 4 BARI 7 TRIESTE
resort: 4 LIDO
wind: 4 BORA
**Adrien**
of cosmetics: 5 ARPEL
**Adrienne**
Actress: 5 CORRI
**Adroit:** 4 ABLE DEFT 6 FACILE
        HABILE
prefix: 3 MAL
**Adroitness**
With: 4 ABLY
**Ads**
Additional, in: 4 XTRA
Dietary, in: 4 LITE
Evening, in: 4 NITE
Flat, in: 3 APT
Shine, in: 3 GLO
Skip the: 3 ZAP
Times to call, in: 4 EVES
Up to, in: 3 TIL
**Adult:** 5 GROWN OFAGE
        6 XRATED
acorn: 3 OAK
grig: 3 EEL
insect: 5 IMAGO
polliwog: 4 TOAD
**Adulterate:** 5 TAINT 6 DEBASE
**Adulterated**
Less: 5 PURER
**Adult-to-be:** 4 TEEN
**Advance:** 4 GAIN LEND LOAN
        SPOT STEP 6 MOVEUP
        STEPUP STRIDE
furtively: 5 SIDLE
Have ready in: 6 PRESET
in age: 5 GETON
In ~ of: 3 ERE 5 AFORE
Settled in: 7 PREPAID
Take care of in: 6 PREPAY

Take ~ orders for: **7** PRESELL
warning: **5** ALERT
**Advanced: 4** LENT
deg.: **3** MBA PHD
degree: **3** NTH
degs.: **3** MAS
More: **5** OLDER
study group: **7** SEMINAR
tests: **5** ORALS
**Advantage: 3** PRO **4** EDGE
**5** ASSET AVAIL LEGUP
STEAD
Competitive: **4** EDGE
Initial: **7** TOEHOLD
Slight: **4** EDGE
Take ~ of: **3** USE
Used one's standing to:
**10** PULLEDRANK
___ advantage: **4** ATAN
**Advantageous**
Be: **3** PAY
**Advent**
song: **4** NOEL
**Adventure: 4** GEST SAGA
African: **6** SAFARI
Carefree: **4** LARK
Computer ~ game: **4** MYST
hero Williams: **4** REMO
Seeking: **6** ERRANT
story: **4** GEST SAGA
**"Adventures of Robin Hood,
The"**
Little John portrayer in:
**8** ALANHALE
**Adventurous**
rover: **6** ERRANT
trip: **7** ODYSSEY
**Adverb**
ending: **3** IAL
Latin: **3** HIC HOC
Legalese: **7** THERETO
Nautical: **4** ALEE
Poetic: **3** EEN EER OFT
**4** ANON NEER
Salty: **4** THAR
**Adversary: 3** FOE **5** ENEMY
RIVAL
**Adverse**
fate: **4** DOOM
**Adversely**
Affect: **8** WHIPLASH
**Adversity**
Handle: **4** COPE
**Advertise: 4** PLUG **5** PITCH
**6** MARKET
**Advertiser: 7** SPONSOR
award: **4** CLIO
purchase: **7** AIRTIME
**Advertising**
award: **4** CLIO
photo label: **5** AFTER
section: **6** INSERT
sign: **4** NEON
suffix: **5** ORAMA
**Advice: 5** INPUT
Ambulance chaser's: **3** SUE

Bear: **4** SELL
First name in: **3** ANN
Follow, as: **5** ACTON
Give meddlesome: **6** KIBITZ
Kind of: **5** LEGAL
**8** PATERNAL
Medical: **4** REST
One sought for: **5** ELDER
Piece of: **3** TIP
Takes, as: **6** ACTSON
**Advil**
rival: **5** ALEVE
**Advise: 4** WARN
Strongly: **4** URGE
**Adviser**
Apr. 15: **3** CPA
Bush: **4** RICE ROVE
Delphic: **6** ORACLE
Reagan: **5** MEESE
Spiritual: **4** GURU
~ Landers: **3** ANN
**Advisory: 5** ALERT
Defense ~ org.: **3** NSC
group: **5** PANEL **7** CABINET
P.D.: **3** APB
**Advocacy**
Fem. ~ org.: **4** YWCA
Rights ~ org.: **4** ACLU
Sch. ~ org.: **3** PTA
**Advocate: 7** ESPOUSE
**8** PROMOTER
(abbr.): **4** ATTY
Consumer: **5** NADER
**Adz: 4** TOOL
**Aeaea**
Sorceress of: **5** CIRCE
**AEC**
logo: **4** ATOM
successor: **3** NRC
**Aegean: 3** SEA
island: **5** SAMOS
On the: **4** ASEA
region: **5** IONIA
vacation locale: **5** CRETE
**Aeneas**
Lover of: **4** DIDO
**"Aeneid": 4** EPIC
First word of: **4** ARMA
poet: **6** VIRGIL
**Aerial: 7** ANTENNA
defense acronym: **5** AWACS
maneuver: **4** LOOP ROLL SPIN
**Aerialist**
getup: **7** LEOTARD
insurance: **3** NET
**Aerie: 4** NEST
baby: **6** EAGLET
builder: **5** EAGLE
**Aero**
suffix: **3** SOL
**Aerobatics**
Do: **6** AVIATE
feat: **4** LOOP
**Aerobics**
action: **4** STEP
Kind of: **4** STEP

Rue the: **4** ACHE
**Aerodynamic: 5** SLEEK
force: **4** DRAG
**Aeronautics**
feat: **4** SOLO
**Aerosmith**
1993 ~ hit: **5** CRYIN
vocalist: **5** TYLER
**Aerosol**
output: **4** MIST **5** SPRAY
**Aerospatiale**
Onetime ~ product: **3** SST
**AES**
defeater: **3** DDE
**Aeschylus**
trilogy: **8** ORESTEIA
**Aesir**
bigwig: **4** ODIN
**Aesop**
also-ran: **4** HARE
conclusion: **5** MORAL
Like ~ grapes: **4** SOUR
tale: **5** FABLE
**Aesthetic**
Affectedly: **4** ARTY
**Aetna: 7** INSURER
offering: **3** HMO
**Afar**
Friend from: **6** PENPAL
Greet from: **6** WAVETO
Visitor from: **5** ALIEN
Visitors from: **3** ETS
**AFC**
1993 ~ Rookie of the Year:
**5** MIRER
**Affable**
Least: **6** ICIEST
**Affair: 5** EVENT FLING
**7** LIAISON
Afternoon: **3** TEA
Court: **5** TRIAL
Debutante: **4** BALL
Evening: **6** SOIREE
Festive: **4** GALA
Genteel: **3** TEA
Hatfield-McCoy: **4** FEUD
Illicit: **5** AMOUR
Love: **5** AMOUR
Men-only: **4** STAG
of honor: **4** DUEL
Tortoise-hare: **4** RACE
Vanity: **7** EGOTRIP
___ Affair (1797–98): **3** XYZ
**Affaire**
de coeur: **5** AMOUR
d'honneur: **4** DUEL
**Affairs: 3** DOS
**Affect: 4** DOTO MOVE **5** ACTON
FEIGN GETTO **6** IMPACT
drastically: **5** UPEND
strongly: **4** STIR
~, as opinion: **4** SWAY
**Affectation: 4** AIRS POSE
**Affected: 4** ARTY **5** ARTSY
GOTTO STAGY
**6** TOOTOO

Elegantly: 6 CHICHI
Excessively: 6 TOOTOO
look: 5 SMIRK
Tastelessly: 6 TOOTOO
**Affection:** 4 LOVE 8 FONDNESS
Lavish: 4 DOTE
Seek the ~ of: 3 WOO
Sign of: 4 KISS
Term of: 3 HON 5 CUTIE
6 DEARIE
**Affectionate:** 4 FOND
7 AMATIVE
10 LOVEYDOVEY
gesture: 3 PAT
touch: 6 CARESS
~, in slang: 5 KISSY
**Affiliation:** 3 TIE
**Affirm:** 4 AVER AVOW 5 STATE
SWEAR 7 PROFESS
SWEARTO
**Affirmation**
Altar: 3 IDO
Solemn: 4 OATH
**Affirmative:** 3 YES
action: 3 NOD
Emphatic: 6 YESSIR
French: 3 OUI
NASA: 3 AOK
Sailor: 3 AYE
Shipboard: 6 AYEAYE
Slangy: 4 YEAH
Spanish: 4 SISI
vote: 3 AYE YEA YES
**Affix:** 3 SET 4 GLUE 5 PASTE
7 STICKON
a brand to: 4 SEAR
a patch: 6 IRONON
**Affleck**
Actor: 3 BEN 5 CASEY
Oscar co-winner of: 5 DAMON
**Afflict:** 3 AIL 5 SMITE
**Afflicted:** 3 ILL 8 STRICKEN
Be ~ with: 4 HAVE
Is ~ with: 3 HAS
**Affliction:** 3 WOE 4 BANE
6 MALADY
Complexion: 4 ACNE
FDR: 5 POLIO
Skid row: 3 DTS
Teen: 4 ACNE
**"Affliction"**
actor Nick: 5 NOLTE
**Affluence:** 4 EASE 5 MEANS
**Affront:** 4 SLAP 6 OFFEND
7 OUTRAGE
Deliberate: 4 SNUB
**Afghan:** 5 ASIAN
capital: 5 KABUL
neighbor: 5 IRANI
**Afghanistan**
capital: 5 KABUL
city: 5 HERAT
neighbor: 4 IRAN
Pass to: 6 KHYBER
**Aficionado:** 3 FAN NUT
5 LOVER

cheer: 3 OLE
**"A fickle food upon a shifting
plate": Dickinson:** 4 FAME
___ a fiddle: 5 FITAS
**Afield**
Go far: 4 TREK
**Afire**
Set: 3 LIT 6 IGNITE
**AFL**
partner: 3 CIO
**AFL-___:** 3 CIO
**Aflame**
Set: 6 IGNITE
**AFL-CIO**
First president of the:
5 MEANY
head John: 7 SWEENEY
Part of: 4 AMER
**Afloat:** 6 NATANT
Kept: 6 BUOYED
**Afore:** 3 ERE
**Aforementioned:** 4 SAID SAME
**"A ___ formality":** 4 MERE
___ a fox: 5 SLYAS
**Afr.**
It's north of: 3 EUR
nation: 3 ALG ETH
**Afraid:** 6 SCARED TREPID
Be ~ to: 7 DARENOT
**A-frame**
feature: 5 EAVES
**Afresh:** 5 NEWLY
Lease: 5 RELET
**Africa**
Film set in: 6 HATARI
Fly from: 6 TSETSE
Horn of ~ native: 6 SOMALI
Lake of southeast: 5 NYASA
Largest city in: 5 CAIRO
Largest country in: 5 SUDAN
Longest river of: 4 NILE
Third-longest river of: 5 NIGER
**African**
adventure: 6 SAFARI
antelope: 3 GNU KOB 4 ORYX
5 ELAND NYALA ORIBI
6 IMPALA RHEBOK
bloodsucker: 6 TSETSE
capital: 5 ACCRA CAIRO
RABAT TUNIS 7 ALGIERS
NAIROBI
cattle pen: 5 KRAAL
charger: 5 RHINO
cobra: 3 ASP
danger: 9 TSETSEFLY
desert: 5 NAMIB 6 SAHARA
8 KALAHARI
fly: 6 TSETSE
Former ~ capital: 5 LAGOS
fox: 4 ASSE
grassland: 5 VELDT
grazer: 3 GNU
language: 5 BANTU
6 RUANDA
lily: 4 ALOE
master: 5 BWANA

menace: 3 ASP 6 TSETSE
nation: 4 CHAD MALI TOGO
5 BENIN GABON LIBYA
SUDAN 6 ANGOLA
UGANDA 7 ERITREA
LESOTHO SENEGAL
pullover: 7 DASHIKI
queen: 4 CLEO
river: 4 NILE 5 NIGER
6 UBANGI
snake: 3 ASP 5 MAMBA
streambed: 4 WADI
tree: 4 KOLA
virus: 5 EBOLA
Westernmost ~ city: 5 DAKAR
**African-American:** 5 BLACK
**"African Queen, The"**
author: 8 FORESTER
screenwriter: 4 AGEE
**Afrika Korps**
leader: 6 ROMMEL
**Afrikaner:** 4 BOER
**Afros:** 3 DOS
**Aft:** 5 ABACK 6 ASTERN
**AFT**
rival: 3 NEA
**After:** 3 ALA 4 PAST 6 BEHIND
a long wait: 6 ATLAST
a while: 4 ANON
Come: 5 ENSUE
curfew: 4 LATE
expenses: 3 NET
Go: 3 SUE 4 SEEK SHAG
5 CHASE SETAT 6 ASSAIL
ATTACK PURSUE
hours: 4 LATE
Immediately: 4 UPON
Look: 3 RUN 4 TEND 5 SEETO
6 TENDTO
Soon: 4 UPON
Take: 5 CHASE 7 EMULATE
Taking: 3 ALA
taxes: 3 NET
the bell: 4 LATE 5 TARDY
the hour: 4 PAST
Went: 8 ASSAILED
~, in French: 5 APRES
**"___ After" (1998 film):** 4 EVER
**After-bath**
powder: 4 TALC
wear: 4 ROBE
**After-Christmas**
event: 4 SALE
**After-class**
aide: 5 TUTOR
**After-dinner**
candy: 4 MINT
drink: 4 PORT 6 BRANDY
8 ANISETTE
offering: 3 TEA
wine: 4 PORT
**Aftereffect**
Lasting: 4 SCAR
Workout: 4 ACHE
**After-hours:** 4 LATE
depository: 3 ATM

**After-lunch**
sandwich: 4 OREO
**Aftermath:** 4 WAKE
Exercise: 4 ACHE
**Afternoon**
affair: 3 TEA
break: 3 NAP TEA
delight: 6 SIESTA
Early: 3 ONE TWO
Early ~ time: 6 ONETEN
fare: 4 SOAP
gathering: 3 TEA
Have an ~ break: 7 TAKETEA
Rest of the: 6 SIESTA
service: 6 TEASET
show: 7 MATINEE
social: 3 TEA
~, in Spanish: 5 TARDE
**After-school**
drink: 5 COCOA
gp.: 3 PTA
treat: 4 OREO
**Aftershock:** 6 TREMOR
**After-shower**
sprinkle: 4 TALC
**Aftertaste**
Compound with a nutty:
6 ACETAL
**After-tax**
amount: 3 NET
**"After the Bath"**
painter: 5 DEGAS
**Afterthought**
Architectural: 5 ANNEX
Legislative: 5 RIDER
Second: 3 PPS
**Afterward**
Come: 5 ENSUE
Right: 4 THEN
**A.G.**
Part of: 4 ATTY
**Again:** 4 ANEW OVER
6 AFRESH
and again: 5 OFTEN 6 THRICE
TRIPLY
Back: 3 FRO
Come up: 5 RECUR
Employ: 5 REUSE
Enlist: 4 REUP
Go over: 6 REHASH
7 ITERATE RETRACE
Happen: 5 RECUR
Here: 4 BACK
Over: 4 ANEW
Say: 4 ECHO 6 REPEAT
9 REITERATE
Showed: 5 RERAN
**Against:** 3 CON 4 ANTI INTO
6 VERSUS
Dead: 4 ANTI
Decide: 3 NIX
Fit up: 6 BUTTTO
Go up: 4 ABUT 6 OPPOSE
TAKEON
Lean: 6 RESTON
Not: 3 FOR

One: 4 ANTI
Rest: 6 LEANON
Stand: 6 OPPOSE
Took action: 4 SUED
Vote: 3 NAY
Votes: 3 NOS 4 NOES
**"... against ___ of troubles":**
4 ASEA
**Aga Khan**
Son of: 3 ALY
**Agamemnon**
Son of: 7 ORESTES
**Agassi:** 4 ACER
It means nothing to: 4 LOVE
of tennis: 5 ANDRE
**Agate**
variety: 4 ONYX
**Agatha**
contemporary: 4 ERLE
**Agave**
fiber: 5 ISTLE SISAL
root: 5 AMOLE
**Agcy.:** 3 ORG 4 DEPT
**Age:** 3 EON ERA 4 AEON
5 EPOCH RIPEN
7 SENESCE
A dog's: 4 EONS 5 YEARS
Advance in: 5 GETON
Come of: 5 RIPEN
Golden: 3 ERA 6 HEYDAY
Of: 5 ADULT
Of an: 4 ERAL
**Aged:** 3 OLD 6 GRAYED
beer: 5 LAGER
**Agee**
of baseball: 6 TOMMIE
**Ageless:** 7 ETERNAL
~, in poetry: 6 ETERNE
**Agency**
By the ~ of: 3 VIA
exec.: 3 DIR
Govt.: 3 EPA GAO GSA IRS
OMB SBA SSA
Old news: 4 TASS
Peace org.: 6 UNESCO
U.N.: 3 ILO
under FDR: 3 WPA
WWII: 3 OPA
**"Agency, The"**
actor Bellows: 3 GIL
**Agenda:** 4 LIST PLAN 5 SLATE
entry: 4 ITEM 7 ITEMONE
Hidden:
15 ULTERIORMOTIVES
Opening words on an: 4 TODO
~, for short: 4 SKED
**Agendum:** 4 ITEM
**Agent:** 3 FED REP SPY
7 VEHICLE
amount: 3 CUT FEE
Antiquing: 4 AGER
Bleaching: 3 LYE
Cleansing: 4 SOAP 5 BORAX
DEA: 4 NARC 5 NARCO
Diplomatic: 5 ENVOY
Double: 4 MOLE

Fed.: 4 GMAN TMAN
Kind of: 3 IRS
Leavening: 5 YEAST
Maturing: 4 AGER
of retribution: 7 NEMESIS
Sales: 3 REP
Secret: 3 SPY
take: 5 TENTH
Thickening: 4 AGAR
Undercover: 3 SPY 4 NARC
~ 86: 5 SMART
~ Ness: 5 ELIOT
~ Scully: 4 DANA
**"Age of Anxiety, The"**
author: 5 AUDEN
7 WHAUDEN
**Age of Aquarius:** 3 ERA
**"Age of Bronze, The"**
artist: 5 RODIN
**"Age of Reason, The"**
author: 5 PAINE
**Ages:** 3 EON
badly: 5 RUSTS
Wisdom of the: 4 LORE
**Aggravate:** 3 IRK 4 RILE ROIL
5 EATAT
**Aggravated:** 5 WORSE
**Aggregate:** 3 SUM 4 PILE
5 TOTAL 6 ENTIRE
8 SUMTOTAL
**Aggressive:** 4 GOGO 5 PUSHY
10 INYOURFACE
dog: 5 BITER
god: 4 ARES
one: 5 TYPEA
reformist: 9 YOUNGTURK
**Aggressively**
Greet: 6 ACCOST
Promote: 4 FLOG
Went after: 5 HADAT
**Agile:** 4 SPRY 6 NIMBLE
7 LISSOME
**Agin**
Not: 3 FER
One: 4 ANTI
**Agitate:** 4 RILE ROIL STIR
5 CHURN SHAKE
**Agitated:** 5 ABOIL 7 INASTEW
INASTIR 8 INASTATE
9 INALATHER
It may get: 4 WASH
state: 4 FLAP SNIT STEW
6 DITHER LATHER
~, with "up": 3 HET
**Agitation:** 6 UNREST
State of: 4 FLAP SNIT STEW
6 DITHER LATHER
**Aglet**
site: 4 LACE
**Agnes**
role: 6 ENDORA
~, to Cecil B.: 5 NIECE
**"Agnes Grey"**
author: 6 BRONTE
**Agnew**
Former veep: 5 SPIRO

plea: 4 NOLO
**"Agnus ___":** 3 DEI
**"___ agnus Dei":** 4 ECCE
**Ago:** 4 PAST
A while: 4 ONCE
Long: 4 ONCE YORE 5 OFOLD
Scottish: 4 SYNE
**Agog:** 7 BUGEYED
All: 5 EAGER
Stare: 4 GAPE
**Agonize:** 4 FRET STEW
**Agony:** 3 WOE 7 TORMENT
Sound of: 4 MOAN
**"A good walk spoiled": Twain:**
　4 GOLF
**Agorot**
100 ~: 6 SHEKEL
**Agouti**
cousin: 4 PACA
**Agra**
attire: 4 SARI
locale: 5 INDIA
**Agree:** 4 JIBE 5 MATCH
　6 ACCEDE ASSENT
　CONCUR SAYYES
　7 CONSENT
　11 SEEEYETOEYE
with: 4 ECHO
without a word: 3 NOD
**Agreeable:** 4 NICE 6 GENIAL
answer: 3 YES
odor: 5 AROMA
**"Agreed!":** 3 YES 4 DEAL
**Agreement:** 4 DEAL PACT
　5 TERMS UNITY
　6 ACCORD ASSENT
Altar: 3 IDO
at sea: 3 AYE
Emphatic: 4 AMEN 5 OHYES
　6 YESYES 8 YESSIREE
Flat: 5 LEASE
Formal: 4 PACT
In: 3 ONE 5 ASONE ATONE
Indicate: 3 NOD
International: 6 ACCORD
　7 DETENTE ENTENTE
Kind of: 4 ORAL 5 TOKEN
Nonverbal: 3 NOD
Nuptial: 3 IDO
Rental: 5 LEASE
Sign, as an: 9 ENTERINTO
Slangy: 3 YEP 4 YEAH
Word of: 3 AYE YES 4 AMEN
Words of: 4 ITOO 5 METOO
　SOAMI SODOI 6 IDOTOO
**Agricultural**
business: 4 FARM
**Agriculture**
Goddess of: 5 CERES
　7 DEMETER
**Agrippina**
Son of: 4 NERO
**Agronomist**
concern: 4 SOIL
**Agt.:** 3 REP
cut: 3 PCT

under Ness: 4 TMAN
**Agua**
~, in French: 3 EAU
**Aguilera**
Singer: 9 CHRISTINA
**Ah**
follower: 4 CHOO
**"Ah!":** 4 ISEE 6 IGETIT
**"Aha!":** 4 ISEE 5 GOTIT
　6 EUREKA GOTCHA
　IGETIT 7 THATSIT
**Ahab**
and crew: 7 WHALERS
Father of: 4 OMRI
obsession: 5 WHALE
~, in a song: 4 ARAB
**A hard row ___:** 5 TOHOE
**Ahead:** 5 ONTOP 6 ONWARD
　TOCOME 7 EARLIER
　LEADING 9 INTHELEAD
Look: 4 PLAN
Neither ~ nor behind: 4 TIED
of the game: 5 ONEUP
of the pack: 5 FIRST
of time: 5 EARLY
One looking: 4 SEER
Opposite of: 6 ASTERN
Slightly: 5 ONEUP
Spring: 5 RESET
Think: 4 PLAN
Time to look: 3 EVE
Was: 3 LED
**"A ___ help you are!":** 5 LOTTA
**Ahem**
Cousin of: 4 PSST
**Ahmad**
Sportscaster: 6 RASHAD
**"Ah, me!":** 3 WOE 4 ALAS
**"Ah'm ___ it!":** 4 AGIN
**"A house ___ a home":** 5 ISNOT
**"Ah, Wilderness!"**
character: 3 NAT
mother: 5 ESSIE
playwright: 6 ONEILL
**Aid:** 6 SUCCOR
Aiming: 5 SCOPE
Ask, as for: 6 TURNTO
Band: 3 AMP
Cleaning: 3 MOP
Driving: 3 TEE
Financial ~ criterion: 4 NEED
in crime: 4 ABET
Partner of: 4 ABET
Shopping: 4 CART LIST
Traction: 4 CLEAT
**Aida:** 5 SLAVE
Love of: 7 RADAMES
**"Aida":** 5 OPERA
backdrop: 4 NILE
composer: 5 VERDI
Where ~ premiered: 5 CAIRO
**Aid and ___:** 4 ABET
**Aide:** 6 HELPER
(abbr.): 4 ASST
Band: 6 ROADIE
DA: 4 ASST

Dictator: 5 STENO
Legal ~, briefly: 4 PARA
Mgr.: 4 ASST
Reagan: 5 MEESE
**Aide-___:** 7 MEMOIRE
**Aiea**
locale: 4 OAHU
**___ Aigner:** 7 ETIENNE
**Aikman**
alma mater: 4 UCLA
of football: 4 TROY
**Ailey**
Choreographer: 5 ALVIN
**Ailing:** 3 ILL 4 SICK 6 LAIDUP
**Ailment**
Common: 4 COLD
Eye: 4 STYE
Skid row: 3 DTS
Stomach: 5 ULCER
Throat: 5 STREP
Winter: 3 FLU
**Aim:** 3 END TRY 4 GOAL MEAN
　5 POINT 6 ASPIRE
　INTEND INTENT
　TARGET
Game: 3 WIN
improver: 5 SCOPE
Peddler: 4 SALE
Perfectionist: 5 IDEAL
Take careful ~ at:
　11 DRAWABEADON
**Aimée**
Actress: 5 ANOUK
title role: 4 LOLA
**Aiming**
aid: 5 SCOPE
**Aimless:** 6 ADRIFT ERRANT
**Aimlessly**
Move: 3 GAD 4 MILL
Wander: 4 ROAM ROVE
**Ain't**
right: 4 ISNT 5 ARENT
Say it ~ so: 4 DENY
**"___ ain't broke ...":** 4 IFIT
**"Ain't it the truth!":** 4 AMEN
　6 ILLSAY
**"Ain't She Sweet"**
composer: 4 AGER
**"___ ain't so!":** 5 SAYIT
**"Ain't That a Shame"**
singer: 8 PATBOONE
**Air:** 4 AURA MIEN SHOW
　SONG TUNE 6 MANNER
　8 TELEVISE
About one percent of: 5 ARGON
agcy.: 3 FAA
Alpine: 5 YODEL
alternative: 4 RAIL
apparent: 4 SMOG
Attack from the: 6 STRAFE
bag: 4 LUNG
Bear in the: 4 URSA
Chair in the: 5 SEDAN
Christmas: 4 NOEL
Dairy: 3 MOO
December: 4 NOEL

Distinctive: 4 AURA
Drops in the: 4 MIST
Eastern: 4 RAGA
Get some: 6 INHALE
    7 BREATHE RESPIRE
gun ammo: 3 BBS
hero: 3 ACE
Hot: 3 GAS
In the: 5 ALOFT
Light: 4 LILT
Like fall: 5 BRISK
Like ocean: 5 SALTY
Mountain: 5 YODEL
Move on a puff of: 4 WAFT
mover: 3 FAN
Operated by: 9 PNEUMATIC
out: 4 VENT 7 FRESHEN
passage: 4 DUCT 7 NOSTRIL
pollution: 4 SMOG 5 SMAZE
prefix: 4 ATMO
quality org.: 3 EPA
safety org.: 3 FAA
Struggle for: 4 GASP
Take to the: 3 FLY 4 SOAR
    6 AVIATE
Took to the: 4 FLEW
Up in the: 4 IFFY 5 ALOFT
Walking on: 6 ELATED
Winter: 4 NOEL 5 CAROL
**Airborne**
honkers: 5 GEESE
targets: 5 SKEET
**Airbrush:** 7 RETOUCH
**Air conditioner:** 4 UNIT
measure (abbr.): 3 BTU
**Aircraft:** 4 BIRD
Arctic: 8 SKIPLANE
**Aire**
City of the: 5 LEEDS
**Aired**
again: 5 RERAN
**Airedale:** 7 TERRIER
Like an ~ coat: 4 WIRY
**Airfone**
corporation: 3 GTE
**Air Force**
1950s–60s ~ Chief of Staff:
    5 LEMAY
gp.: 3 SAC
hero: 3 ACE
**Air Force One:** 3 JET 5 PLANE
passenger (abbr.): 3 CIC 4 PRES
**Air France**
destination: 4 ORLY
plane: 3 SST
**Air freshener**
option: 4 PINE 5 LILAC
target: 4 ODOR
**Airhead:** 4 DITZ DOLT
    5 SCHMO
**Airing:** 4 ONTV
Program: 8 TELECAST
**Air Jordans**
maker: 4 NIKE
**Airline**
Atlanta-based: 5 DELTA

Brazilian: 5 VARIG
Chilean: 3 LAN
Dutch: 3 KLM
European: 3 SAS
Israeli: 4 ELAL
Japanese: 3 ANA
patron: 5 FLIER
since 1948: 4 ELAL
**Airliner**
walkway: 5 AISLE
**"Air Music"**
composer: 5 ROREM
**Airplane**
boarding site: 4 GATE
Model ~ wood: 5 BALSA
roll control: 7 AILERON
seat feature: 7 ARMREST
seat option: 5 AISLE
server: 4 TRAY
shelter: 6 HANGAR
tracker: 5 RADAR
wing parts: 5 SLATS
**"Airplane!"**
actor Bridges: 5 LLOYD
actor Robert: 4 HAYS
heroine: 6 ELAINE
**Airport**
abbr.: 3 ARR ETA ETD
Accompany to the: 6 SEEOFF
area: 4 GATE
Bay area: 3 SFO
board word: 7 NONSTOP
Boston: 5 LOGAN
Calif.: 3 LAX
Chicago: 3 ORD 5 OHARE
conveyance: 4 TRAM
event: 7 ARRIVAL
French: 4 ORLY
info: 3 ARR ETA ETD
Israeli: 3 LOD
lineup: 4 CABS
Long Island: 5 ISLIP
Major: 3 HUB
National: 6 REAGAN
near Paris: 4 ORLY
near Tel Aviv: 3 LOD
NYC: 3 LGA
Paris: 4 ORLY
pickup: 4 LIMO 6 RENTAL
surface: 6 TARMAC
waiter: 3 CAB
Washington: 6 SEATAC
worry: 5 DELAY
**Air-quality**
org.: 3 EPA
**Air rifle:** 5 BBGUN
ammo: 3 BBS 6 BBSHOT
**Air-safety**
org.: 3 FAA
**Airtight**
It may be: 5 ALIBI
Make: 4 SEAL 6 SEALUP
**Air traffic**
control device: 5 RADAR
screen sight: 4 BLIP
**Airwaves:** 5 ETHER

Govt. ~ agency: 3 FCC
**Airy**
Light and: 8 ETHEREAL
melody: 4 LILT
**Aisle**
Choose the window over the:
    5 ELOPE
walker: 5 USHER
**Aisles**
Have rolling in the: 4 SLAY
Work the: 3 USH
**AJ**
of Indy: 4 FOYT
**Ajar:** 8 HALFOPEN
More than: 4 OPEN
Not: 4 SHUT
~, poetically: 3 OPE
**Ajax**
rival: 5 COMET
**"A jealous mistress": Emerson:**
    3 ART
**"A jug of wine ..."**
poet: 4 OMAR
**AKA**
Part of: 4 ALSO 5 KNOWN
**Akaka**
of Hawaii (abbr.): 3 SEN
**Akbar**
capital: 4 AGRA
**Akela**
org.: 3 BSA
**Aker**
Capital on the: 4 OSLO
**Akhmatova**
Poet: 4 ANNA
**Akihito:** 7 EMPEROR
(abbr.): 3 EMP
**___ a kind:** 5 ONEOF TWOOF
**Akins**
Playwright: 3 ZOE
**"Akira"**
genre: 5 ANIME
**Akita**
home: 5 JAPAN
**Akron**
baseball player: 4 AERO
home: 4 OHIO
product: 4 TIRE
Rock group from: 4 DEVO
**Al**
and Tipper: 5 GORES
Discus champ: 6 OERTER
of Indy: 5 UNSER
Scarface: 6 CAPONE
Trumpeter: 4 HIRT
Veep before: 3 DAN
Weatherman: 5 ROKER
who drew Abner: 4 CAPP
**AL**
and ME: 3 STS
**A.L.**
1953 ~ MVP: 5 ROSEN
1966 ~ Rookie of the Year:
    4 AGEE
1993 ~ batting champ:
    6 OLERUD

1996 ~ Rookie of the Year:
    5 JETER
2002 ~ MVP: 4 AROD
and N.L. city: 3 CHI
Seven-time ~ batting champ:
    5 CAREW
Some ~ batters: 3 DHS
Three-time ~ batting champ:
    5 BRETT OLIVA
Three-time ~ MVP: 5 BERRA
**Al ___**: 5 DENTE FATAH
**Al-___**: 4 ANON
**al-___, Bashar**: 5 ASSAD
**Ala.**
Neighbor of: 3 FLA
**À la ___**: 5 CARTE
**"Al Aaraaf"**
author: 3 POE
**Alabama**
city: 5 SELMA
footballers: 11 CRIMSONTIDE
native: 5 CREEK
One-named singer from:
    6 ODETTA
port: 6 MOBILE
**Alack**
partner: 4 ALAS
**Aladdin**: 4 ARAB
**"Aladdin"**
baddie: 5 JAFAR
find: 4 LAMP
monkey: 3 ABU
parrot: 4 IAGO
prince: 3 ALI
vehicle: 6 CARPET
wish-granter: 5 GENIE
**al-Ahmed al-Sabah**: 4 EMIR
___ **alai**: 3 JAI
**Alain**
Actor: 5 DELON
Novelist: 6 LESAGE
**Alamance County**
college: 4 ELON
___ **Alamitos**: 3 LOS
**Alamo**: 6 SHRINE
defender: 5 BOWIE 6 TRAVIS
Mexican leader at the:
    9 SANTAANNA
offering: 6 RENTAL
rival: 4 AVIS 5 HERTZ
**À la mode**: 4 CHIC
**Alamogordo**
county: 5 OTERO
event: 5 ATEST
___ **Alamos, New Mexico**:
    3 LOS
**Alan**
Actor: 4 ALDA LADD 5 ARKIN
    6 THICKE
Conservative: 5 KEYES
South African author: 5 PATON
**Alarm**: 4 FEAR 5 SCARE
    6 DISMAY
Anticipate with: 5 DREAD
bell: 6 TOCSIN
Car: 4 HORN

Cause for: 4 FIRE
False: 5 SCARE
Gives a false: 9 CRIESWOLF
Heed the: 4 RISE
Ignore the: 7 SLEEPIN
Nature's ~ clock: 7 ROOSTER
Sound the: 4 WARN
**Alarmed**
Easily: 5 TIMID
**Alas**
Partner of: 5 ALACK
**"Alas!"**: 4 AHME 5 SOSAD
    6 DEARME 7 WOEISME
~, in German: 3 ACH
**Alaska**: 5 STATE
buyer: 6 SEWARD
city: 4 NOME
First capital of: 5 SITKA
First governor of: 4 EGAN
National park in: 6 DENALI
native: 5 ALEUT INUIT
    6 ESKIMO
radar site: 4 ATTU
river: 5 YUKON
Sen. Stevens of: 3 TED
~, at one time (abbr.): 4 TERR
___ **Alaska**: 5 BAKED
**Alaskan**
bay: 7 PRUDHOE
Certain: 5 ALEUT INUIT
    6 ESKIMO
city: 4 NOME
island: 4 ATTU 6 KODIAK
islander: 5 ALEUT
native: 5 ALEUT INUIT
    6 ESKIMO
port: 4 NOME 5 SITKA
sled race: 8 IDITAROD
volcano: 6 KATMAI
**Alaskan Klee ___**: 3 KAI
**Al-Assad**
land: 5 SYRIA
**Alastair**
Actor: 3 SIM
___ **alba (gypsum)**: 5 TERRA
**Albacore**: 4 TUNA
**Alban**
Composer: 4 BERG
**Albania**
Capital of: 6 TIRANA
    TIRANE
**Albanian**
coin: 3 LEK
**Albany**
canal: 4 ERIE
City near: 4 TROY
College near: 5 SIENA
leader: 6 PATAKI
**Albatross**: 4 ONUS 7 SEABIRD
Black-footed: 6 GOONEY
**Albee**
Alice from: 4 TINY
Playwright: 6 EDWARD
**Albéniz**
Composer: 5 ISAAC
piano work: 6 IBERIA

**Albers**
Artist: 5 JOSEF
**Albert**
Actor: 5 EDDIE SALMI
Author: 5 CAMUS
of Minnesota: 3 LEA
Sportscaster: 4 MARV
~, to Victoria: 7 CONSORT
**Albert, Marv**
catchword: 3 YES
**Alberta**
park: 5 BANFF 6 JASPER
**Alberthal**
CEO: 3 LES
**Albert the Alligator**
Friend of: 4 POGO
**Albertville**
Skating medalist at: 3 ITO
**Albion**
neighbor: 4 ERIN
**Alborg**
native: 4 DANE
**Albrecht**
Artist: 5 DURER
**Albright**
headed it: 5 STATE
or Falana: 4 LOLA
**Album**
1968 folk ~: 4 ARLO
1969 jazz ~: 4 ELLA
1986 self-titled ~:
    6 ARETHA
1988 country ~: 4 REBA
2001 self-titled ~: 3 JLO
Country: 5 ATLAS
**Albums**
Mini record: 3 EPS
Old: 3 LPS
**Alcatraz**
(abbr.): 3 ISL
Birdman of: 5 LIFER
    6 STROUD
inmate: 7 BIRDMAN
**Alchemist**
concoction: 6 ELIXIR
**Alcindor**
of basketball: 3 LEW
**Alcoa**
purchase: 3 ORE
**Alcohol**
Allowing: 3 WET
An end to: 3 ISM
Grain: 7 ETHANOL
Kind of: 4 AMYL 5 ETHYL
Make ~ undrinkable:
    8 DENATURE
plus acid: 5 ESTER
Solid: 6 STEROL
___ **alcohol**: 5 BUTYL CETYL
    ETHYL
**Alcohol-based**
solvent: 6 ACETAL
**Alcoholic**
Excuse maker for an:
    7 ENABLER
Hot ~ drink: 5 TODDY

**Alcohol-laced**
dessert: 4 BABA
**Alcott**
book: 11 LITTLEWOMEN
Golfer: 3 AMY
**Alcove:** 3 BAY 4 NOOK 5 NICHE
6 RECESS
Church: 4 APSE
Eating: 7 DINETTE
Shady: 5 ARBOR
**Alda**
Actor: 4 ALAN
sitcom series: 4 MASH
**Aldebaran:** 4 STAR 5 KSTAR
**Al dente:** 4 FIRM
It might be cooked: 5 PASTA
**Alder:** 4 TREE
**Alderaan**
Princess from: 4 LEIA
**Aldo**
Italian politician: 4 MORO
**Aldrich**
Spy: 4 AMES
**Aldrin, Buzz**
birth name: 5 EDWIN
org.: 4 NASA
**Ale:** 4 BREW
alternative: 5 LAGER
cask: 3 TUN
fellow: 6 BREWER
Half ~, half stout:
11 BLACKANDTAN
holder: 3 MUG 5 STEIN
order: 4 PINT
quantity: 4 YARD
seller: 3 PUB
**Alec**
role: 6 OBIWAN
___ Alegre, Brazil: 5 PORTO
**Alehouse:** 3 PUB 6 TAVERN
**Aleichem**
Writer: 6 SHOLOM
**Alejandro**
Actor: 3 REY
of baseball: 4 PENA
**Alençon**
department: 4 ORNE
product: 4 LACE
**Aleppo**
land: 5 SYRIA
**Alero**
maker: 4 OLDS
**ALers**
Some: 3 DHS
**Alert:** 4 WARN 5 READY
6 TIPOFF
10 ONONESTOES
Coast Guard: 3 SOS
color: 3 RED
Golfer: 4 FORE
Kind of: 4 SMOG
Not: 7 NAPPING
Not be: 4 DOZE
P.D.: 3 APB
Studio: 5 ONAIR
Theater: 3 SRO

___ alert: 3 RED
**Alerting**
light: 5 FLARE
**Alessandro**
Physicist: 5 VOLTA
**Aleutian**
island: 4 ADAK ATKA ATTU
**Alewife**
relative: 4 SHAD
**Alex**
Author: 5 HALEY
Host: 6 TREBEK
**Alexander:** 4 TSAR
1996 candidate ~: 5 LAMAR
Aristotle, to: 5 TUTOR
Artist: 6 CALDER
Author: 5 SHANA
Former Sec. of State: 4 HAIG
Form of: 5 SASHA
He slew: 5 AARON
**Alexandra:** 7 TSARINA
husband: 4 TSAR
**Alexandre**
Author: 5 DUMAS
**Alexandria**
Capital near: 5 CAIRO
river: 4 NILE
**Alf**
and others: 3 ETS
home planet: 6 MELMAC
**Alfa ___:** 5 ROMEO
**Alfalfa:** 6 RASCAL
girlfriend: 5 DARLA
**Alfa Romeo**
rival: 4 FIAT
**Al Fatah**
Former ~ leader: 6 ARAFAT
gp.: 3 PLO
**"Alfie"**
lyricist David: 3 HAL
star: 5 CAINE
12 MICHAELCAINE
**Alfonso**
queen: 3 ENA
**Alfred**
GM president: 5 SLOAN
IQ tester: 5 BINET
of the theater: 4 LUNT
Poet: 5 NOYES
Psychologist: 5 ADLER
**"Alfred"**
composer: 4 ARNE
**Alfresco**
eatery: 4 CAFE
meal: 6 PICNIC
Not: 6 INDOOR INSIDE
**Alga**
Microscopic: 6 DIATOM
**Algae**
product: 4 AGAR
Red: 7 SEAMOSS
**Algebra:** 4 MATH
Early writer on: 4 OMAR
equation: 9 QUADRATIC
Kind of: 6 LINEAR
7 BOOLEAN

topic: 6 MATRIX
**Alger**
beginning: 4 RAGS
**Algeria**
neighbor: 4 MALI
**Algerian**
pop music: 3 RAI
port: 4 ORAN
**Algiers**
area: 6 CASBAH KASBAH
governors: 4 DEYS
**"Algiers"**
actor Charles: 5 BOYER
actress Hedy: 6 LAMARR
**Algonquian**
language: 4 CREE 7 ARAPAHO
tribe: 6 MIAMIS 7 OTTAWAS
~ Indian: 8 KICKAPOO
**Algonquin**
home: 6 WIGWAM
**Alhambra:** 6 PALACE
builder: 4 MOOR
Site of the: 7 GRANADA
**Ali**
Boxer: 5 LAILA
Muhammad: 5 PASHA
Sharp left from: 3 JAB
trainer Dundee: 6 ANGELO
Where ~ KO'd Foreman:
5 ZAIRE
**Ali ___:** 4 BABA
**"___ alia":** 5 INTER
**"Ali ___ and the 40 Thieves":**
4 BABA
**Alias:** 3 AKA
Common: 5 SMITH
Dickens: 3 BOZ
Essayist: 4 ELIA
Lamb: 4 ELIA
Patty Hearst: 5 TANIA
Superman: 4 KENT
**"Alias"**
actress Lena: 4 OLIN
network: 3 ABC
**Alibi:** 5 STORY 6 EXCUSE
guy: 3 IKE
Perfect, as an: 8 AIRTIGHT
IRONCLAD
**Alibi ___ (liars):** 4 IKES
**"___ Alibi":** 3 HER
**Alice**
boss: 3 MEL
cat: 5 DINAH
chronicler: 4 ARLO
Event for: 8 TEAPARTY
He sang about: 4 ARLO
Musical star: 4 FAYE
She played ~ on TV: 5 LINDA
**"Alice"**
actress Martha: 4 RAYE
Alice, in: 8 WAITRESS
diner: 4 MELS
spin-off: 3 FLO
star: 5 LAVIN
**"Alice in Wonderland"**
cat: 5 DINAH

**"Alice's Restaurant"**
  singer Guthrie: 4 ARLO
**Alicia**
  Actress: 3 ANA
  Ballerina: 6 ALONSO
**Alien:** 7 FOREIGN
  Furry TV: 3 ALF
  TV ~ home: 3 ORK
**"Alien"**
  actor Holm: 3 IAN
**Alienate:** 8 ESTRANGE
**"Alienist, The"**
  author: 4 CARR
  author Carr: 5 CALEB
**Aliens:** 3 ETS
  Course for U.S.: 3 ESL
**Align:** 4 TRUE
  the cross hairs: 3 AIM
**Alignment**
  Front wheel: 5 TOEIN
  In: 4 TRUE
**Alike**
  Think: 5 AGREE
  ~, in French: 4 EGAL
**"A likely story!":** 3 HAH 4 IBET
**Alimony**
  receiver: 6 EXMATE EXWIFE
  receivers: 4 EXES
**A-line**
  line: 3 HEM 4 SEAM
**Alison**
  Author: 5 LURIE
  A-list: 5 ELITE
**Alistair**
  Sam and: 6 COOKES
**Alitalia**
  stop: 4 ROMA
**"Alive"**
  Setting of ~: 5 ANDES
**"___ alive!":** 5 SAKES
**"___ Alive!" (1974 film):** 3 ITS
**Al-Jazeera**
  viewer: 4 ARAB
**Alkali:** 4 BASE
  neutralizer: 4 ACID
**Alkaline**
  solution: 3 LYE
**Alka-Seltzer**
  guy: 6 SPEEDY
  sound: 4 PLOP
**All**
  agog: 5 EAGER
  alternative: 3 ERA 4 NONE
    TIDE 5 CHEER
  At: 3 ANY 4 EVER
  At ~ times: 4 EVER
  done: 4 OVER
  ears: 4 RAPT
  excited: 4 AGOG 7 ATINGLE
  fired up: 4 AVID 5 EAGER
  First of: 4 ADAM
  For ~ time: 4 EVER
    9 AGELESSLY
  For ~ to hear: 5 ALOUD
  For ~ to see: 5 OVERT
    6 OPENLY

hands on deck: 4 CREW
Highest of: 7 TOPMOST
in: 4 BEAT 5 SPENT TIRED
  WEARY
Nearly: 4 MOST
Not: 4 SOME
Not at: 5 NOHOW 6 NOWISE
Not ~ there: 5 DOTTY
Opposite of: 4 NONE
  6 NOTONE
over: 4 ANEW 7 ATANEND
over again: 4 ANEW 6 AFRESH
possible: 5 EVERY
prefix: 4 OMNI
Second of: 3 EVE
set: 5 READY
smiles: 5 HAPPY
spruced up: 4 NEAT
Still and: 3 YET
there: 4 SANE 6 INTACT
the time: 4 ALOT 5 OFTEN
They're ~ in the family: 4 SIBS
tied up: 4 EVEN
together: 5 ASONE 6 INTOTO
  7 ENMASSE
tucked in: 4 ABED
tuckered out: 5 SPENT
With ~ one's might: 5 AMAIN
worked up: 4 AGOG 5 IRATE
you can carry: 7 ARMLOAD
you can eat: 7 EDIBLES
~, in music: 5 TUTTI
**All ___:** 3 WET 4 EARS
**"All ___!":** 4 RISE 6 ABOARD
**"All ___" (1967 hit):** 5 INEED
**"All ___" ('30s hit song):**
  4 OFME
**"All ___" (Martin/Tomlin film):**
  4 OFME
**All-4-One**
  ~ #1 hit: 6 ISWEAR
**Alla ___ (2/2 time):** 5 BREVE
**"All About ___" (1950 film):**
  3 EVE
**"All About Eve"**
  actress Bette: 5 DAVIS
  actress Holm: 7 CELESTE
  role: 5 MARGO
**Allah**
  Religion of: 5 ISLAM
**All-American**
  name: 5 KNUTE
**"All-American Girl"**
  star Margaret: 3 CHO
**"All ___ are off!":** 4 BETS
**Allay:** 4 EASE
**"All clear"**
  signal: 5 SIREN
**Allegation:** 5 CLAIM
**Allege:** 4 AVER
**Allegheny**
  City on the: 5 OLEAN
  Company once called: 5 USAIR
  The ~ flows into it: 4 OHIO
**Allegory:** 7 PARABLE
**Allegro:** 4 FAST 5 TEMPO

and others: 5 TEMPI
**Allegro ___:** 5 ASSAI
**Allen**
  Actor: 3 TIM
  Burns and ~ (abbr.): 4 SENS
  Burns, to: 7 PARTNER
  of the Green Mountain Boys:
    5 ETHAN
  or Martin: 5 STEVE
  Patriot: 5 ETHAN
  Sportscaster: 3 MEL
  successor: 4 PAAR
**Allen, Ira**
  Brother of: 5 ETHAN
**Allen, Jay Presson**
  play: 3 TRU
**Allen, Woody**
  1977 ~ film: 9 ANNIEHALL
  1978 ~ film: 9 INTERIORS
  1983 ~ film: 5 ZELIG
  1987 ~ film: 9 SEPTEMBER
  1998 film featuring the voice of:
    4 ANTZ
  Feeling for: 5 ANGST
**All-encompassing:** 5 BROAD
**Allen County, Kansas**
  Seat of: 4 IOLA
**Allende**
  Author: 6 ISABEL
**___ aller (last resort):** 3 PIS
**Allergen**
  Common: 4 DUST 6 DANDER
    POLLEN SPORES
    7 PETHAIR
**Allergic**
  reaction: 4 ITCH RASH
    5 ACHOO 6 ASTHMA
    SNEEZE
**Allergy**
  symptom: 4 RASH 5 HIVES
**Alleviate:** 4 EASE 6 SOOTHE
**Alleviator:** 5 EASER
**Alley**
  Bowling: 4 LANE
  button: 5 RESET
  cat: 5 STRAY
  Caveman: 3 OOP
  challenge: 5 SPLIT
  cry: 4 MEOW
  denizen: 3 RAT TOM 5 STRAY
  follower: 3 OOP
  game: 7 TENPINS
  Kind of: 5 BLIND
  Like an ~ cat: 5 FERAL
  org.: 3 PBA
  pickup: 5 SPARE
  Play in the: 4 BOWL
  prowler: 3 TOM 6 TOMCAT
  target, at times: 7 NINEPIN
  targets: 4 PINS
**"Alley ___":** 3 OOP
**Alley-___:** 3 OOP
**"___ all, folks!":** 5 THATS
**All Fools' Day**
  mo.: 3 APR
**"All gone!":** 4 PFFT

**Allgood**
  Actress: 4 SARA
**Alliance:** 4 BLOC PACT
    6 LEAGUE 7 ENTENTE
  acronym: 4 NATO 5 SEATO
  Defunct: 5 SEATO
  dissolved in 1977: 5 SEATO
  Onetime Egypt-Syr.: 3 UAR
  since 1948: 3 OAS
  since 1949: 4 NATO
**"All I ___ Do" (Sheryl Crow hit):**
  5 WANNA
**Allie**
  flat mate: 4 KATE
**Allied:** 5 SIDED
  1945 ~ conference site:
    5 YALTA 7 POTSDAM
  invasion site in WWII: 4 ORAN
  Menace to ~ ships: 5 UBOAT
  victory site: 4 STLO
**Allies**
  foe: 4 AXIS
**Alligator**
  kin: 6 CAIMAN
  pear: 7 AVOCADO
  Urban ~ home, they say:
    5 SEWER
**Alligator ___:** 4 PEAR
**"All I gotta do ___ naturally":**
  **Beatles:** 5 ISACT
**All-inclusive:** 4 ATOZ FULL
  6 ENTIRE
**All-in-one**
  meal: 4 STEW
**"All in the Family"**
  actress Stapleton: 4 JEAN
  daughter: 6 GLORIA
  producer Norman: 4 LEAR
  spin-off: 5 MAUDE
**All in ___ work:** 5 ADAYS
**Allison**
  Jazzman: 4 MOSE
**"All I Wanna Do"**
  singer: 10 SHERYLCROW
**"All kidding ___ ...":** 5 ASIDE
**All-knowing:** 4 WISE
**"___ All Laughed":** 4 THEY
**All-male:** 4 STAG
**Allman Brothers, The**
  One of: 5 DUANE GREGG
**"All My Children"**
  actress Susan: 5 LUCCI
  character: 5 ERICA
**"All My ___ Live in Texas":**
  3 EXS
**All-natural**
  food no-no: 3 BHT
**All-night**
  bash: 4 RAVE
**All-nighter**
  Pull an: 4 CRAM
**Allocate:** 4 METE 6 ASSIGN
  DEVOTE 7 DOLEOUT
**"All of Me"**
  director: 6 REINER
**Allot:** 4 METE

~, with "out": 4 METE
**Alloted**
  amount: 6 RATION
**Allotment:** 4 DOLE 5 PIECE
  QUOTA SHARE
  6 RATION
  words: 4 APOP
**All-out:** 5 TOTAL 7 DOORDIE
**Allow:** 3 LET OWN 5 ADMIT
  OPINE 6 ENABLE
  PERMIT
  in: 5 ADMIT
  to pass: 5 LETBY
  to use: 4 LEND
**Allowable:** 5 LICIT
**Allowance:** 7 STIPEND
  Waste: 4 TRET
  Weight: 4 TARE TRET
**Allowed:** 5 LICIT
  number: 5 QUOTA
**Allowing**
  a draft: 4 AJAR
  alcohol: 3 WET
**Alloy**
  component: 5 METAL
  Electrician: 6 SOLDER
  Gold-imitating: 6 ORMOLU
  Iron: 5 STEEL
  Magnet: 6 ALNICO
  Tin: 6 PEWTER
**All-points bulletin:** 5 ALERT
**All-purpose**
  truck: 3 UTE
**"All Quiet on the Western**
  **Front"**
  star: 5 AYRES
**"All right!":** 3 YES
  ~, slangily: 3 OKE
**All's**
  opposite: 5 NOONE 6 NOTONE
    7 NOTABIT
  partner: 5 WARTS
**All-star**
  game side: 4 EAST WEST
  Player in 24 ~ games: 4 MAYS
**Allstate**
  rival: 5 AETNA
**"All systems ___":** 5 AREGO
**"All systems go!":** 3 AOK
**"All That Jazz"**
  actress Reinking: 3 ANN
  director: 5 FOSSE
**All the ___:** 4 RAGE SAME
**"All the King's Men"**
  actress Joanne: 3 DRU
**"All the Things You ___":** 3 ARE
**"All the Way"**
  lyricist: 4 CAHN
**"All Things Considered"**
  network: 3 NPR
**___ all-time high:** 4 ATAN
**All together:** 5 ASONE INSUM
  6 INTOTO
**Allude:** 5 REFER
  to: 4 CITE 5 GETAT 6 HINTAT
**All ___ up:** 3 HET

**Allure:** 5 CHARM TEMPT
  Coffee: 5 AROMA
  competitor: 4 ELLE
**Alluring:** 4 FOXY SEXY
  6 EROTIC
  skirt feature: 4 SLIT
**Allusion**
  Make: 5 REFER
**Ally**
  Actress: 6 SHEEDY
  Gulf war: 4 OMAN
  Missouri: 4 OTOE
  of Captain Hook: 4 SMEE
  WWII: 4 USSR
**"___ All Ye Faithful":** 5 OCOME
**"Ally McBeal"**
  actress Lucy: 3 LIU
  lawyer: 4 LING NELL
    7 GEORGIA
  secretary: 6 ELAINE
**"All you had to do was ___":**
  3 ASK
**"All You Need Is ___" (Beatles**
  **song):** 4 LOVE
**Alma ___:** 5 MATER
**Almanac**
  datum: 4 STAT
  entry: 4 FACT
  tidbit: 5 ADAGE
  topic: 4 TIDE
**Almighty:** 3 GOD
  Muslim's: 5 ALLAH
  ~, in French: 4 DIEU
**Almodóvar**
  Director: 5 PEDRO
**Almond:** 3 TAN 4 ECRU
  confection: 6 NOUGAT
  flavored liqueur: 8 AMARETTO
  paste: 8 MARZIPAN
**Almost:** 4 NIGH 6 NEARLY
  NIGHON
  boil: 5 SCALD 6 SIMMER
  closed: 4 AJAR
  forever: 4 EON 4 EONS
  here: 4 NEAR
  never: 4 ONCE
**"Almost!":**
  15 CLOSEBUTNOCIGAR
**Alms**
  Ask for: 3 BEG
**Alnico:** 5 ALLOY
**"A loaf of bread ..."**
  poet: 4 OMAR
**Aloe ___:** 4 VERA
**Aloft**
  Glide: 4 SOAR
**Aloha**
  gift: 3 LEI
**Aloha State**
  bird: 4 NENE
  port: 4 HILO
**Alone:** 4 SOLO STAG
  Go it: 4 SOLO
  Leave: 5 LETBE
  Taken: 5 PERSE
  **___ alone (solo):** 4 GOIT

**Along**
 Get: 4 FARE
 Go: 5 AGREE 6 SAYYES
 the way: 7 ENROUTE
**Alongside**
 Lie: 4 ABUT
**Alonso**
 Ballerina: 6 ALICIA
**Aloof:** 4 COOL
 Beyond: 3 ICY
**Aloofness**
 With: 5 ICILY
**Alou**
 of baseball: 5 JESUS 6 FELIPE
**Aloud**
 Marvel: 3 OOH
 Weep: 3 SOB
**Alpaca**
 kin: 5 CAMEL LLAMA
 tender: 5 INCAN
**Alpes**
 peak: 4 MONT
**Alpha**
 follower: 4 BETA
 opposite: 5 OMEGA
**Alpha ___ :** 4 MALE
**Alphabet**
 book phrase: 4 ASIN
 ender: 3 ZEE
 finaliser: 3 ZED
 quartet: 4 ABCD BCDE CDEF
  *etc.*
 quintet: 5 AEIOU 6 VOWELS
 soup letter: 6 NOODLE
 trio: 3 ABC BCD CDE *etc.*
**Alphabetize:** 4 SORT 5 ORDER
**Alphonse**
 partner: 6 GASTON
**Alpine**
 abode: 6 CHALET
 air: 5 YODEL
 assent: 3 OUI
 call: 5 YODEL
 capital: 4 BERN 5 BERNE
 heroine: 5 HEIDI
 region: 5 TIROL TYROL
 river: 3 AAR 4 AARE 5 ISERE
 sight: 4 MONT
 song: 5 YODEL
 tool: 5 ICEAX
 transport: 4 TBAR TRAM
**Alpine Museum**
 site: 4 BERN
**Alps**
 lake: 4 COMO
 peak: 5 EIGER
 river: 5 ISERE
 Sing in the: 5 YODEL
**Already:** 5 BYNOW
 in use: 5 TAKEN
**"Already?":** 6 SOSOON
**Also:** 3 AND TOO 4 PLUS
  6 ASWELL
 known as: 5 ALIAS
**Also-ran:** 5 LOSER
 1992 ~: 5 PEROT

 1996 ~: 4 DOLE
 2000 ~: 4 GORE 5 NADER
  6 ALGORE
 Aesop: 4 HARE
 Fabled: 4 HARE
**Alt:** 3 KEY
 Opposite of: 3 NEU
**Alt.:** 4 ELEV
 spelling: 3 VAR
**Altair:** 5 ASTAR
 constellation: 6 AQUILA
**Altar**
 agreement: 3 IDO
 area: 4 APSE
 boy: 7 ACOLYTE
 Bypass the: 5 ELOPE
 constellation: 3 ARA
 ego: 3 MRS
 Leave at the: 4 JILT
 words: 3 IDO 4 IDOS
**Altared**
 Get: 3 WED
**Altdorf**
 is its capital: 3 URI
**"___ Alte" (Adenauer):** 3 DER
**Alter:** 3 HEM 4 EDIT SPAY
  5 EMEND RESEW
  6 MUTATE
**Alter ___ :** 3 EGO 4 IDEM
**Alterations**
 Make ~ to: 5 REFIT
**Altercation:** 3 ROW 5 MELEE
  RUNIN SETTO 6 AFFRAY
  7 RHUBARB
 Minor: 4 SPAT
**Alter ego**
 Dracula: 3 BAT
 Famous: 4 HYDE 6 MRHYDE
 Jekyll: 4 HYDE
 Superman: 4 KENT
**Alterer:** 6 TAILOR
**Alternate:** 5 OTHER 6 SEESAW
  7 STANDIN
  9 TAKETURNS
 handle: 5 ALIAS
 sp.: 3 VAR
**Alternative:** 5 OTHER
  6 BACKUP CHOICE
  OPTION
 fuel: 7 ETHANOL GASOHOL
 magazine: 4 UTNE
 word: 4 ELSE 6 RATHER
**Alternatively:** 4 ELSE 5 IFNOT
  7 INSTEAD
**Altima**
 maker: 6 NISSAN
**Altitude**
 Gain: 4 SOAR
**___ Alto, California:** 4 PALO
**Altogether**
 In the: 4 BARE NUDE
**Altoids**
 rival: 5 CERTS
**___ Altos, California:** 3 LOS
**Altruist**
 opposite: 6 EGOIST

**Alts.:** 3 HTS
**Alum:** 4 GRAD
 to be: 6 SENIOR
**Aluminum**
 It may be: 6 SIDING
 sheet: 4 FOIL
 source: 3 ORE 7 BAUXITE
**Alumna**
 word: 3 NEE
**Alumni**
 Baseball: 9 OLDTIMERS
**Alvar**
 Architect: 5 AALTO
**Alvarado**
 Actress: 5 TRINI
**Alveolus:** 3 SAC
**Alvin**
 Choreographer: 5 AILEY
**Alway:** 3 EER
 Opposite of: 4 NEER
**Always:** 4 EVER
  8 EVERMORE
 ~, in Italian: 6 SEMPRE
 ~, poetically: 3 ERE
**"___ always say ...":** 3 ASI
**Alzheimer, Dr.:** 5 ALOIS
**A.M.**
 Part of: 4 ANTE
 ~ TV show: 3 GMA
**AMA**
 members: 3 DRS GPS MDS
**"Amadeus"**
 director Forman: 5 MILOS
 star Tom: 5 HULCE
**Amado**
 Novelist: 5 JORGE
**Amahl**
 creator: 7 MENOTTI
**Amalgamate:** 3 WED 4 MELD
  5 MERGE
**Amanda**
 Actress: 4 PEET
**"___ a man who wasn't ...":**
  4 IMET
**Amaretto**
 flavor: 6 ALMOND
**___, amas, amat:** 3 AMO
**"___, amas, I love ...":** 3 AMO
**Amass:** 5 RUNUP 6 GARNER
  PILEUP RACKUP
  RAKEIN
**Amateur:** 3 LAY 4 TYRO
  6 NONPRO
 Leave the ~ ranks: 5 GOPRO
 No: 3 PRO
 sports org.: 4 NCAA
**Amateurish:** 4 BUSH
  10 BUSHLEAGUE
**Amateurishly**
 Paint: 4 DAUB
**Amati**
 Violinmaker: 6 NICOLO
**Amatol**
 ingredient: 3 TNT
**"___ Amatoria":** 3 ARS
**Amatory:** 6 EROTIC

**Amaze:** 3 AWE WOW 4 STUN
   13 SETONONESEARS
**Amazed:** 5 INAWE
  Obviously: 5 AGAPE
  outcries: 4 OOHS
**Amazement:** 3 AWE
  Sound of: 4 GASP
  Sounds of: 4 OOHS
**"Amazin'"**
  team: 4 METS
**Amazing**
  to behold: 10 EYEPOPPING
**"Amazing"**
  magician: 5 RANDI
**"Amazing!":** 3 OOH
**A-mazing**
  animal: 6 LABRAT
**Amazing ___, The:** 5 RANDI
**"Amazing Grace"**
  ending: 4 ISEE
**Amazon**
  burrower: 4 PACA
  How the ~ flows: 4 EAST
  River to the: 5 NEGRO
  sales: 5 ETAIL
  Source of the: 4 PERU
    5 ANDES
  squeezer: 3 BOA
  zapper: 3 EEL
**Ambassador**
  forte: 4 TACT
  Israel's first U.N.: 4 EBAN
  Jack's U.N.: 5 ADLAI
  JFK's U.N.: 3 AES
    15 ADLAIESTEVENSON
  of old cars: 4 NASH
  Papal: 6 NUNCIO
**"Am ___ believe ...?":** 3 ITO
**Amber:** 5 RESIN
  brew: 3 ALE
  colored wine: 7 MADEIRA
**Ambience:** 4 AURA
**Ambient**
  music pioneer: 3 ENO
**Ambiguous**
  patterned style: 5 OPART
**Ambition:** 3 AIM
**Ambitious**
  Be: 6 ASPIRE
**"Am ___ blame?":** 3 ITO
**Amble:** 4 LOPE ROVE 5 MOSEY
  7 SAUNTER
  along: 6 STROLL
**Ambler**
  Author: 4 ERIC
**Ambrose**
  Writer: 6 BIERCE
**Ambrosia**
  accompaniment: 6 NECTAR
**"Am ___ brother's keeper?":**
  3 IMY
**Ambulance**
  attachment: 5 SIREN
  attendant (abbr.): 3 EMT
  chaser advice: 3 SUE
  destinations (abbr.): 3 ERS

  initials: 3 EMS
  ~ VIP: 3 EMT
**Ambulatory**
  Area next to an: 4 APSE
**Ambush:** 4 TRAP 6 WAYLAY
  7 SANDBAG
  One who waits in: 4 LIER
  Prepare for an: 4 LURK
**AMC**
  Old ~ model: 5 PACER
**Amelia**
  Women's rights advocate:
    7 BLOOMER
**Ameliorate:** 4 EASE
**"Amen!":** 3 YES 5 RIGHT
    6 IAGREE ILLSAY ITISSO
    SOBEIT 9 YOUSAIDIT
**Amenable:** 4 OPEN
**Amend:** 4 EDIT 5 ALTER
  6 REVISE
**Amendment**
  18th ~ state: 3 DRY
  19th ~ beneficiaries:
    5 WOMEN
  First ~ defender: 4 ACLU
  Second ~ concern: 4 ARMS
  Second ~ supporter: 3 NRA
**Amends**
  Make: 5 ATONE
  One who makes: 6 ATONER
**Amenhotep**
  god: 4 ATEN ATON
**Amenity**
  Hotel: 3 ICE 4 POOL
  Suite: 6 WETBAR
**Amer.**
  counterpart: 4 NATL
**Amerada** 4 HESS
**America:** 9 THESTATES
**"America"**
  Third word in: 3 TIS
**___ America:** 4 MISS
**American**
  Airline bought by: 3 TWA
  An ~ in Paris, maybe: 5 EXPAT
  Ancient: 4 INCA
  anthropologist: 4 MEAD
  buffalo: 5 BISON
  charge: 7 AIRFARE
  craft: 3 JET 5 PLANE
  dogwood: 5 OSIER
  First ~ in orbit: 5 GLENN
  First ~ saint: 5 SETON
  Native ~ group: 5 TRIBE
  naturalist: 4 MUIR
  of Japanese descent: 5 NISEI
  operative: 6 CIASPY
  plan offering: 4 MEAL
  rival: 5 DELTA 6 UNITED
  symbol: 5 EAGLE
  Traditionally: 8 APPLEPIE
  Typical ~, they say:
    7 PEORIAN
  uncle: 3 SAM
  ~, to a Brit: 4 YANK
**American ___:** 3 ELM

**"American ___"**
  (Gere film): 6 GIGOLO
  (TV show): 4 IDOL
**___ American:** 6 NATIVE
**___-American:** 4 SINO
**American Airlines Arena**
  team: 9 MIAMIHEAT
**"American Appetites"**
  author: 5 OATES
**American Beauty:** 4 ROSE
  kin: 7 TEAROSE
**"American Beauty"**
  actor Bentley: 3 WES
  actress Suvari: 4 MENA
  director: 6 MENDES
**American-born**
  queen of Jordan: 4 NOOR
**"American Buffalo"**
  playwright: 5 MAMET
**"___ American Cousin":** 3 OUR
**American Dance Theater**
  founder: 5 AILEY
    10 ALVINAILEY
**"American Dream, The"**
  playwright: 5 ALBEE
**American Express**
  rival: 4 VISA
**American Fur Company**
  founder: 5 ASTOR
**"American Gigolo"**
  star: 4 GERE
**"American Gothic"**
  artist: 4 WOOD
**"American Graffiti"**
  actor Paul: 5 LEMAT
  director: 5 LUCAS
**American Greetings**
  logo: 4 ROSE
**"American Idol"**
  Compete on: 4 SING
  judge Abdul: 5 PAULA
  judge Cowell: 5 SIMON
  judge Paula: 5 ABDUL
  winner Studdard: 5 RUBEN
**"American in Paris, An"**
  actress: 8 NINAFOCH
  star: 5 CARON
**Americanism**
  Symbol of: 8 APPLEPIE
**American League**
  division: 4 EAST WEST
  team: 5 THEAS TWINS
    7 ORIOLES
**American Legion**
  member: 3 VET
**"American Pie"**
  actress Reid: 4 TARA
**American Revolution**
  general: 6 PUTNAM
**Americans**
  Faith of more than 5 million:
    5 ISLAM
  Like about 13% of: 6 LATINO
  Some: 6 LATINS
**American Samoa**
  capital: 8 PAGOPAGO

**American Shakers**
founder: 6 ANNLEE
**"American Tail, An"**
director: 5 BLUTH
**American Theater Wing**
award: 4 TONY
**"American Tragedy, An"**
writer: 7 DREISER
**America's Cup**
activity: 8 YACHTING
racer: 5 YACHT 7 YACHTER
winner, perhaps:
9 CATAMARAN
**"___ America Singing":**
Whitman: 5 IHEAR
**"America's Most Wanted"**
host John: 5 WALSH
letters: 3 AKA
**"America, the Beautiful"**
closer: 3 SEA
color: 5 AMBER
pronoun: 4 THEE
**"Amerika"**
author: 5 KAFKA
**Amerind**
Western: 3 UTE
**Amérique:** 9 ETATSUNIS
**"A merry heart ___ good like**
medicine": 5 DOETH
**Ames**
and others: 3 EDS
**AMEX**
counterpart: 4 NYSE
listings: 3 COS
unit: 3 SHR
**AM/FM**
device: 5 RADIO
**Amherst**
sch.: 5 UMASS
**Amicus ___:** 6 CURIAE
**Amiens**
Info: French cue
assent: 3 OUI
is its capital: 5 SOMME
Mine, in: 4 AMOI
**Amigo:** 3 PAL
**"___ amigos!":** 5 ADIOS
**Amin**
Dictator: 3 IDI
fate: 5 EXILE
land: 6 UGANDA
predecessor: 5 OBOTE
**Amino ___:** 4 ACID
**Amino acid:** 6 LYSINE
___ amis: 3 MES
**Amish:** 4 SECT
feature: 5 BEARD
pronoun: 4 THEE
**Amiss:** 3 OFF 5 WRONG
**"Amistad"**
character: 5 SLAVE
**"Amityville Horror, The"**
author Jay: 5 ANSON
**"Am ___ late?":** 4 ITOO
**Amman**
land: 6 JORDAN

**Ammo**
Air rifle: 3 BBS 6 BBSHOT
Blowgun: 3 PEA 4 DART
Put in more: 6 RELOAD
Put ~ into: 4 LOAD
Shooter: 3 PEA
Slapstick: 3 PIE
Sling: 5 STONE
Toy pistol: 4 CAPS
**Ammonia**
compound: 5 AMIDE AMINE
IMIDE IMINE
___ ammoniac: 3 SAL
**Ammunition**
Leading ~ maker: 4 OLIN
unit: 5 ROUND
**Amneris**
rival: 4 AIDA
**Amnesiac**
question: 6 WHOAMI
**Amniotic ___:** 3 SAC
**"Am not!"**
retort: 5 ARESO
**Amo:** 5 ILOVE
**Amo, amas, ___:** 4 AMAT
**Amo, ___, amat:** 4 AMAS
**Amoeba:** 4 BLOB
An ~ has one: 4 CELL
feature: 7 ONECELL
**Amok**
Run: 4 RIOT
**Among:** 4 WITH
others: 9 INTERALIA
**"Am ___ only one?":** 4 ITHE
**Amontillado**
holder: 4 CASK
**"___ Amore":** 5 THATS
**"Amores"**
poet: 4 OVID
**Amorous**
complication: 8 TRIANGLE
**Amorously**
Eye: 4 OGLE
Talk: 3 COO
**Amorphous**
critter: 5 AMEBA
hunk: 4 GLOB
**Amos**
and Spelling: 5 TORIS
Book before: 4 JOEL
Famous: 4 TORI
partner: 4 ANDY
Singer: 4 TORI
**Amos Alonso ___:** 5 STAGG
**"Amos 'n' Andy"**
Amos last name on: 5 JONES
**Amount:** 3 SUM 4 DOSE
A smaller: 4 LESS
Huge: 3 SEA TON 4 LOAD
PILE RAFT SCAD SLEW
5 OCEAN
Minimal: 5 LEAST
Minimum: 4 WAGE
Minute: 4 IOTA
9 SCINTILLA
Paltry: 3 SOU

Small: 3 BIT DAB FIG JOT
SOU TAD TOT 4 ATOM
DRAM DRIB GRAM IOTA
MITE WHIT 5 PINCH
TRACE 7 REDCENT
Vague: 4 SOME
**"A mouse!":** 3 EEK
**Amp**
attachment: 4 MIKE
toter: 6 ROADIE
**Ampersand**
follower, sometimes: 3 SON
**Amphibian**
Mil.: 3 LST
Small: 3 EFT 4 NEWT
Warty: 4 TOAD
**Amphibious**
carriers: 4 LSTS
**Amphilochus:** 4 SEER
**Amphitheater:** 5 ARENA
section: 4 TIER
shape: 4 OVAL
**Ample:** 4 WIDE
**Amplifier**
setting: 6 TREBLE
Voice: 4 MIKE 9 MEGAPHONE
**Ampule:** 4 VIAL
**"Amscray!":** 3 GIT 4 SCAT
SHOO 5 SCOOT
**Amsterdam**
Airline to: 3 KLM
Comic: 5 MOREY
**Amt.:** 3 QTY
**"Am ___ time?":** 3 IIN
**"Am too!"**
Reply to: 6 ARENOT
**Amtrak**
express train: 5 ACELA
stop (abbr.): 3 STA
track: 4 RAIL
**Amu Darya**
Sea the ~ flows into: 4 ARAL
**Amulet:** 5 CHARM 8 TALISMAN
Egyptian: 6 SCARAB
Polynesian: 4 TIKI
Voodoo: 4 MOJO
**Amundsen**
Explorer: 5 ROALD
**Amuse:** 6 DIVERT TICKLE
9 ENTERTAIN
immensely: 4 SLAY
**Amused**
Be ~ by: 6 GRINAT
**Amusement:** 5 MIRTH
park lure: 4 RIDE
Show: 4 GRIN 5 SMILE
**Amusing**
Bitterly: 3 WRY
Oddly: 5 DROLL
**Amy**
Author: 3 TAN
Sister of: 3 MEG 4 BETH
~, to Jo, Meg, or Beth: 3 SIS
**"Am ___ your way?":** 3 IIN
**An:** 7 ARTICLE
**Anabaptists:** 4 SECT

**Anaconda:** 3 BOA
**Anaheim**
  City north of: 4 BREA
  pro: 5 ANGEL
  team: 6 ANGELS
**Anaïs**
  Diarist: 3 NIN
**Anakin**
  Daughter of: 4 LEIA
  Son of: 4 LUKE
**Analgesic**
  target: 4 ACHE PAIN
**Analogous:** 4 AKIN LIKE
    5 ALIKE 7 SIMILAR
**Analogy**
  mark: 5 COLON
  words: 4 ISTO
**Analysis:** 5 ASSAY
**Analyst:** 7 ASSAYER
  concerns: 7 SYSTEMS
  need: 4 DATA
**Analytical Psychology**
  founder: 4 JUNG
**Analytic Geometry**
  giant: 5 EULER
**Analyze:** 4 TEST 5 ASSAY
  Figures to: 7 RAWDATA
  grammatically: 5 PARSE
  verse: 4 SCAN
**Analyzer**
  Echo: 5 SONAR
**"Analyze This"**
  actor: 6 DENIRO
**Ananias:** 4 LIAR
**"An apple ___ ...":** 4 ADAY
**Anarchist**
  1920s ~: 5 SACCO
**Anastasia**
  dad: 4 TSAR
**"Anastasia"**
  actor Brynner: 3 YUL
  Oscar winner: 7 BERGMAN
**Anat.:** 3 SCI
**Anatolia:** 9 ASIAMINOR
**Anatomical**
  canal: 4 ITER
  cavity: 5 FOSSA
  container: 3 SAC
  duct: 3 VAS
  foot: 3 PES
  interstice: 6 AREOLE
  knot: 4 NODE
  network: 4 RETE
  passage: 4 ITER
  pouch: 3 SAC
  ring: 6 AREOLA
  sac: 5 BURSA
**Anatomist**
  Second-century: 5 GALEN
**Anatomy**
  class model: 8 SKELETON
**Ancestral**
  group: 5 TRIBE
**Ancestry:** 4 LINE 5 ROOTS
    6 ORIGIN 7 LINEAGE
  One of mixed: 7 MULATTO

  record: 4 TREE
**Anchor:** 4 MOOR
  concern: 4 NEWS
  Drop: 4 MOOR
  Lift: 4 SAIL
  NBC: 6 BROKAW
  Pitch heavily at: 5 HAWSE
  Plant: 4 ROOT
  position: 4 DESK 5 APEAK
    ATRIP
  Raise an: 5 HEAVE WEIGH
  Small: 5 KEDGE 7 GRAPNEL
  Tooth: 4 ROOT
  ~ Paula: 4 ZAHN
  ~ Rather: 3 DAN
**Anchorman**
  WJM: 3 TED
  ~ Rather: 3 DAN
**"Anchors ___":** 6 AWEIGH
**"Anchors Aweigh"**
  gp.: 3 USN
**Anchovies**
  How ~ are packed: 5 INOIL
**Anchovy**
  container: 3 TIN
**Ancient:** 3 OLD 4 AGED
    5 HOARY OLDEN
    6 AGEOLD
  article: 5 RELIC
  ascetic: 6 ESSENE
  beauty: 5 HELEN
  character: 4 RUNE
  colonnade: 4 STOA
  consultant: 6 ORACLE
  epoch: 6 ICEAGE
  galley: 7 TRIREME
  greeting: 3 AVE
  kingdom: 4 MOAB
  laborer: 4 ESNE
  land: 5 IONIA 7 ALSATIA
  lawgiver: 5 SOLON
  letter: 4 RUNE
  mariner: 4 NOAH
  marketplace: 5 AGORA
  medium: 6 ORACLE
  meeting place: 4 STOA
    5 AGORA
  moralist: 5 AESOP
  portico: 4 STOA
  theaters: 4 ODEA
  times, old-style: 3 ELD
  ~ Andean: 4 INCA
  ~ Briton: 4 CELT PICT
  ~ Celt: 5 DRUID
  ~ Iranian: 4 MEDE
  ~ Italian: 6 SABINE
    8 ETRUSCAN
  ~ Mexican: 5 AZTEC OLMEC
    6 TOLTEC
  ~ Palestinian: 6 ESSENE
  ~ Persian: 4 MEDE
  ~ Peruvian: 4 INCA
**Ancient Greek**
  city-state: 5 POLIS 6 SPARTA
  coin: 4 OBOL 6 STATER
  colony: 5 IONIA

  dialect (var.): 5 EOLIC
  garment: 5 TUNIC
  lyric poet: 6 SAPPHO
    8 ANACREON
  marketplace: 5 AGORA
  physician: 5 GALEN
  portico: 4 STOA
  region: 5 IONIA
  state: 6 ATTICA
  theater: 5 ODEON
**Ancient Mariner**
  poem: 4 RIME
**Ancient Roman**
  historian: 4 LIVY
  magistrate: 5 EDILE
  road: 4 ITER
**And:** 4 ALSO PLUS
  more: 3 ETC
  not: 3 NOR
  others: 3 ETC 4 ETAL
    6 ETALIA ETALII
  so forth: 3 ETC 6 ETCETC
    8 ETCETERA
  the following: 5 ETSEQ
**___ and aah:** 3 OOH
**"... and ___ a good-night!":**
    5 TOALL
**___ and all:** 5 WARTS
**Andalusia**
  **Info:** Spanish cue
  Another, in: 4 OTRO
  home (abbr.): 3 ALA
**Andalusian**
  title: 5 SENOR 6 SENORA
  **___ and anon:** 4 EVER
**Andante**
  or allegro: 5 TEMPO
  Slower than: 6 ADAGIO
**"And a Voice to Sing With"**
  writer: 4 BAEZ
**"And away ___!":** 4 WEGO
**"___ and away!":** 4 UPUP
**"And ___ bed": Pepys:** 4 SOTO
**___ and blood:** 5 FLESH
**___ and crafts:** 4 ARTS
**___ and dined:** 5 WINED
**___ and don'ts:** 3 DOS
**Andean**
  Ancient: 4 INCA
  animal: 5 LLAMA 6 ALPACA
    VICUNA
  capital: 4 LIMA
  nation: 4 PERU
  shrub: 4 COCA
  tuber: 3 OCA
**Andersen**
  birthplace: 6 ODENSE
  countrymen: 5 DANES
  portrayer: 4 KAYE
**Anderson**
  Actress: 4 LONI 6 PAMELA
  Comedian: 5 LOUIE
  Composer: 5 LEROY
  Director: 3 WES
  Jazz singer: 4 IVIE
  Like ~ in 1980 (abbr.): 3 IND

**Anderson, Marian:** 4 ALTO
**Andes**
(abbr.): 3 MTS
animal: 5 LLAMA
capital: 4 LIMA
High in the: 4 ALTO
land: 4 PERU
tuber: 3 OCA
___ and far between: 3 FEW
___ and for all: 4 ONCE
"___ and gimble ...": 4 GYRE
"And giving ___, up the
    chimney ...": 4 ANOD
"And ___ grow on":
    5 ONETO
___ and hearty: 4 HALE
"And here it is!": 4 TADA
"___ and his money ...":
    5 AFOOL
"And how!": 3 DOI
"... ___ and hungry look":
    Shakespeare: 5 ALEAN
"And I Love ___": 3 HER
Andiron: 7 FIREDOG
"And ___ I wrote ...": 4 THEN
___ and kicking: 5 ALIVE
___ and kin: 4 KITH
"___ and Lovers": 4 SONS
"And ___ off!": 6 THEYRE
___ and outs: 3 INS
**Andover**
rival: 6 EXETER
"... and pretty maids all in ___":
    4 AROW
"___ and Punishment":
    5 CRIME
**Andre**
Ex of ~ and Frank: 3 MIA
Literature Nobelist: 4 GIDE
Pianist: 5 WATTS
**Andrea ___:** 5 DORIA
**Andrea del ___:** 5 SARTO
**Andrea ___ Sarto:** 3 DEL
___ Andreas fault: 3 SAN
**Andrés**
Guitarist: 7 SEGOVIA
**Andress**
Actress: 6 URSULA
film: 3 SHE
**Andretti**
Racer: 5 MARIO
**Andrew**
Actor: 4 SHUE
Brother of the Apostle:
    7 STPETER
Painter: 5 WYETH
Prince ~, to York: 4 DUKE
**Andrews**
Actor: 4 DANA
Cry at St.: 4 FORE
or Vandenberg (abbr.): 3 AFB
**Andrews Sisters, The:** 4 TRIO
One of: 6 MAXENE
    7 LAVERNE
**Andric**
Literature Nobelist: 3 IVO

**Androcles**
extraction: 5 THORN
Friend of: 4 LION
Where ~ was spared: 5 ARENA
**Android**
on the Enterprise: 4 DATA
"**Andromeda Strain, The**"
actor James: 5 OLSON
"___ **Andronicus**": 5 TITUS
**Androphobe**
fear: 3 MEN
**Andropov**
Former Soviet leader: 4 YURI
___ and sciences: 4 ARTS
"And so ___": Pepys: 5 TOBED
"**And So It Goes**"
author: 8 ELLERBEE
"___ and sometimes ...":
    5 AEIOU
___ and Span: 4 SPIC
"**And Still I Rise**"
poet: 7 ANGELOU
"___ & Stitch": 4 LILO
___ and terminer: 4 OYER
"... and that ___ hay!": 4 AINT
"___ and the Art of Motorcycle
    Maintenance": 3 ZEN
"___ and the King": 4 ANNA
"And then again ...": 5 ORNOT
"___ and the Night Visitors":
    5 AMAHL
"**And Then There Were ___**":
    4 NONE
"___ and the Pussycats":
    5 JOSIE
"And thereby hangs ___":
    Shakespeare: 5 ATALE
"And there you are!":
    5 VOILA
"And there you have it!":
    4 TADA 5 VOILA
"___ and the Swan": Yeats:
    4 LEDA
"And this is the thanks ___?":
    4 IGET
___ and tuck: 3 NIP
___ and void: 4 NULL
"___ and weep!": 6 READEM
"And what ___ rare as ...":
    4 ISSO
"And what's he then that says
    I play the villain?"
    speaker: 4 IAGO
**Andy**
Aunt of: 3 BEE
of the comics: 4 CAPP
or Ann: 7 RAGDOLL
partner: 4 AMOS
Son of: 4 OPIE
"**Andy Capp**"
beverage: 3 ALE
cartoonist Smythe: 3 REG
hangout: 3 PUB
wife: 3 FLO
"**Andy Griffith Show, The**"
son: 4 OPIE

"___ **Andy Warhol**" (1996 film):
    5 ISHOT
**Anecdotal**
collection: 3 ANA
knowledge: 4 LORE
**Anemic**
need: 4 IRON
**Anent:** 4 ASTO INRE
**Anesthetic**
gas: 6 ETHENE 8 ETHYLENE
Old: 5 ETHER
**Anesthetics**
Like some: 5 LOCAL
    7 TOPICAL
**Anesthetized:** 4 NUMB
    5 UNDER 7 SEDATED
**Anew:** 7 FRESHLY
**Ang**
Director: 3 LEE
**Angel:** 4 ALER 5 SAINT
    6 SERAPH
Charlie's: 4 OONA
child: 6 CHERUB
dust: 3 PCP
Fallen: 5 SATAN
favorite letters: 3 SRO
hair: 5 PASTA
High-ranking: 6 SERAPH
instrument: 4 HARP
Jockey: 7 CORDERO
Kind of: 4 TEEN
No: 4 BRAT
topper: 5 HALO
TV ~ portrayer: 4 ROMA
    5 REESE
"___ **Angel**" (Mae West film):
    4 IMNO
"**Angela's ___**": 5 ASHES
"**Angela's Ashes**"
sequel: 3 TIS
___ **Angeles:** 3 LOS
**Angelic**
aura: 4 HALO
**Angelica:** 4 HERB
**Angelico**
Painter: 3 FRA
**Angelina**
Actress: 5 JOLIE
role: 4 LARA
**Angelou**
Poet: 4 MAYA
**Angels**
High-ranking: 8 SERAPHIM
home: 6 HEAVEN 7 ANAHEIM
in many images: 8 HARPISTS
"**Angels in America**"
figure: 4 COHN
**Anger:** 3 IRE 4 RAGE RILE
    5 PIQUE STEAM UPSET
    WRATH 6 ENRAGE
    SPLEEN
Erupt in: 6 REARUP
Intense: 3 IRE 4 FURY RAGE
Internalize: 4 STEW
Shut in: 4 SLAM
With: 7 IRATELY

**"Angie"**
Stephen of: 3 REA
**"Angie Baby"**
singer: 5 REDDY
**Angkor ___** : 3 WAT
**___ anglais (English horn):**
3 COR
**Angle:** 4 FISH SKEW 5 SLANT
90-degree ~: 3 ELL
Cut at an: 5 BEVEL
iron: 4 LBAR
Leaf: 4 AXIL
prefix: 3 TRI
Right: 3 ELL
symbol: 5 THETA
**Angler**
aid: 4 LURE
basket: 5 CREEL
boot: 5 WADER
Certain: 5 EELER
gear: 6 TACKLE
hope: 4 BITE
need: 3 ROD 4 LURE REEL
spot: 4 PIER
**Angles**
At right ~ to the keel:
5 ABEAM
Like some: 5 ACUTE
They knew the: 6 SAXONS
**Anglican**
headgear: 5 MITRE
parish priest: 5 VICAR
**Angling**
area: 4 PIER
Go: 4 FISH
**Anglo-___** : 5 SAXON
**Anglo-Saxon**
laborer: 4 ESNE
lord: 5 THANE
**Angola**
capital: 6 LUANDA
**Angora**
fabric: 6 MOHAIR
output: 4 WOOL
**Angrily**
Speak: 5 SNARL
Stare: 5 GLARE
**Angry:** 3 HOT MAD 4 IRED
SORE 5 CROSS IRATE
IRKED RILED 6 IREFUL
dispute: 7 QUARREL
fits: 5 HUFFS
Get: 6 SEERED
Make: 3 IRE 4 RILE
6 ENRAGE
Plenty: 4 SORE
reaction: 4 RISE
stare: 5 GLARE
state: 4 SNIT
Very: 5 IRATE LIVID
with: 5 MADAT
young man: 5 REBEL
~, with "off": 4 TEED
~, with "up": 3 HET
**Angst**
Cause of Apr.: 3 IRS

**Anguish:** 3 WOE 4 PAIN
5 AGONY
Cause ~ to: 6 TEARAT
Extreme: 7 TORTURE
**Angular**
prefix: 3 TRI 4 EQUI RECT
shape: 3 ELL
**Angus**
refusal: 3 NAE
**Anima**
doctor: 4 JUNG
**Animal:** 5 BEAST
catcher: 4 TRAP 5 SNARE
den: 4 LAIR
doc: 3 VET
group suffix: 3 ZOA
gullet: 3 MAW
hide: 4 PELT
home: 4 LAIR
house: 3 ZOO 4 BARN CAGE
LAIR
in a roundup: 5 STEER
life: 5 FAUNA
park: 3 ZOO
pouch: 3 SAC
rights org.: 4 PETA SPCA
shelter: 3 ARK 4 LAIR
5 POUND
skin: 4 HIDE PELT
stomach: 4 CRAW
that bugles: 3 ELK
that sleeps upside-down:
5 SLOTH
track: 5 SPOOR
welfare org.: 4 SPCA
with a snout: 5 TAPIR
with striped legs: 5 OKAPI
**"Animal Farm"**
author: 6 ORWELL
form: 5 FABLE
**"Animal House"**
brother: 5 OTTER
group: 4 FRAT
house: 5 DELTA
party wear: 4 TOGA
**Animals:** 5 FAUNA
**Animate:** 5 ALIVE PEPUP
7 ENLIVEN
**Animated:** 5 ALIVE
1998 ~ film: 4 ANTZ
5 MULAN
character: 4 TOON
~ Chihuahua: 3 REN
~ Olive: 3 OYL
**Animation:** 3 PEP VIM 4 LIFE
ZING
First name in: 4 WALT
frame: 3 CEL
**Animator**
unit: 3 CEL
~ Tex: 5 AVERY
**Animosity:** 6 HATRED
**Anise-flavored**
liqueur: 4 OUZO 6 PERNOD
**Aniston**
ex: 4 PITT

**Anita**
Author: 4 LOOS
Jazz singer: 4 ODAY
**Anjou:** 4 PEAR
agreement: 3 OUI
alternative: 4 BOSC
**Anka, Paul**
1957 ~ hit: 5 DIANA
1962 ~ hit: 7 ESOBESO
**Ankara**
coin: 4 LIRA
resident: 4 TURK
title: 3 AGA
**Ankh**
feature: 4 LOOP
**Ankle**
bone: 5 TALUS
bones: 5 TARSI
Of the: 6 TARSAL
**Anklebone:** 5 TALUS
**Anklebones:** 4 TALI 5 TARSI
**Ankle-knee**
connector: 4 SHIN
**Ankle-length**
skirt: 4 MAXI
**Ankles**
Go in up to the: 4 WADE
**Anklets:** 5 SOCKS
**Ann**
and May: 5 CAPES
or Andy: 7 RAGDOLL
Shaker: 3 LEE
Sister of: 4 ABBY
**Anna**
Actress: 4 STEN
Author: 6 SEWELL
Diva: 5 MOFFO
Like students of: 7 SIAMESE
or Evangeline: 7 HEROINE
Where ~ taught: 4 SIAM
**"Anna Christie"**
playwright: 6 ONEILL
**"Anna Karenina"**
actress Garbo: 5 GRETA
author: 7 TOLSTOY
**Annan**
land: 5 GHANA
of the U.N.: 4 KOFI
**Annan, Kofi ___** : 4 ATTA
**Annapolis**
frosh: 5 PLEBE
grad.: 3 ENS
sch.: 4 USNA
**Anne**
Actress: 5 HECHE
Author: 4 RICE
Funny: 5 MEARA
Pulitzer novelist: 5 TYLER
**___ Anne de Beaupré:** 3 STE
**Annette**
Actress: 6 OTOOLE
**Annex:** 3 ADD ELL 4 WING
5 ADDON
**Info:** Suffix cue
**Annexation**
1898 ~: 6 HAWAII

**Annie:** 6 ORPHAN 7 ADOPTEE
  Actress: 5 POTTS
  Deadeye: 6 OAKLEY
  Dog of: 5 SANDY
  of the comics: 6 ORPHAN
  ~, to Warbucks: 4 WARD
**"Annie"**
  actress Quinn: 6 AILEEN
  song: 8 TOMORROW
**___ Annie ("Oklahoma!" role):**
    3 ADO
**"Annie Get Your Gun"**
  1999 ~ star: 6 PETERS
  subject: 6 OAKLEY
**"Annie Hall"**
  actress Keaton: 5 DIANE
  star: 6 KEATON
  Woody role in: 4 ALVY
**Anniversary:** see page 725
    4 DATE
  4th ~ gift: 5 LINEN
  10th ~ gift: 3 TIN
  20th ~ gift: 5 CHINA
  55th ~ gift: 7 EMERALD
  Golden ~ number: 5 FIFTY
  party: 7 JUBILEE
**Ann-Margret**
  ~, by birth: 5 SWEDE
**Ann ___, Michigan:** 5 ARBOR
**Anno ___:** 6 DOMINI
**Annotation**
  Proof: 4 STET
**Announce:** 6 HERALD
**Announcement**
  Circular: 4 SALE
  "Coming soon": 5 PROMO
  fanfare: 4 TADA
  JFK: 3 ETA ETD
  Marriage: 5 BANNS
  Merger: 3 IDO
  Proctor: 4 TIME
**Announcements**
  It's used for: 8 PASYSTEM
**Announcer**
  Baseball ~ phrase: 6 HESOUT
  "Heeere's Johnny!":
    7 MCMAHON
  Jay's former: 3 EDD
  Old: 5 CRIER
  Public: 5 CRIER
  Soccer ~ cry: 4 GOAL
  ~ Don: 5 PARDO
  ~ Hall: 3 EDD
  ~ Johnny: 5 OLSON
**Annoy:** 3 EAT IRK VEX 4 MIFF
    RILE 5 BESET EATAT
    GETTO GRATE PEEVE
    TEASE 6 BOTHER
    HASSLE MOLEST
    NETTLE PESTER
    RANKLE 7 AGITATE
**Annoyance:** 3 IRE 4 PEST
    5 PEEVE THORN
    6 HASSLE
  Dorm: 5 SNORE 6 SNORER
  Exclamation of: 4 DRAT

**Eye:** 4 STYE
  Online: 4 SPAM 7 POPUPAD
**Annoyed:** 4 SORE
  More than: 5 IRATE
**Annoyer:** 4 PEST PILL
**Annoying:** 5 PESKY
    7 IRKSOME
  child: 4 BRAT
  insect: 4 GNAT
  one: 4 PEST 5 VEXER
  spots: 4 ACNE
**Annuaire**
  listing: 3 NOM
**Annual**
  award giver: 3 MTV
  Bright: 6 ZINNIA
  exhibition: 4 FAIR
  foursome: 7 SEASONS
  parade honoree: 5 STPAT
  reference book: 7 ALMANAC
  sled race: 8 IDITAROD
**Annually:** 7 PERYEAR
    9 ONCEAYEAR
**Annul:** 4 UNDO VOID
    6 REPEAL REVOKE
    7 RESCIND
**Annum**
  Per: 5 AYEAR
  ___ annum: 3 PER
**"Annus Mirabilis"**
  poet: 6 DRYDEN
**Año**
  starter: 5 ENERO
**Anomalous:** 3 ODD
**Anon:** 4 SOON 5 LATER
    6 INABIT
  Partner of: 4 EVER
**Anonymity**
  Woman of: 7 JANEDOE
**Anonymous:** 6 NONAME
    7 UNNAMED
    8 NAMELESS
  ~ Jane: 3 DOE
  ~ John: 3 DOE
  ~ Richard: 3 ROE
**Another:** 7 ONEMORE
  At ~ time: 4 ANON
  Do ~ hitch: 4 REUP
  One thing after: 6 SERIES
  Put ~ way: 7 REWRITE
  Take ~ shot: 5 RETRY
  time: 4 ANEW 5 AGAIN
    7 LATERON
  ~, in Spanish: 4 OTRA OTRO
**"Another Green World"**
  composer: 3 ENO
**"Another interruption?":**
    7 WHATNOW
**"Another Pyramid"**
  musical: 4 AIDA
**"Another Time"**
  poet: 5 AUDEN
**"Another Woman"**
  actress Rowlands: 4 GENA
**Anouk**
  Actress: 5 AIMEE

**Ans.**
  Opposite of: 4 QUES
**Answer:** 4 RSVP 5 REACT
    REPLY
  a charge: 5 PLEAD
  Affirmative: 3 YES
  Altar: 3 IDO
  an invitation: 4 RSVP 5 REPLY
  back: 4 SASS
  (for): 5 ATONE
  incorrectly: 3 ERR
  man Trebek: 4 ALEX
  Noncommittal: 5 MAYBE
  Not ~ directly: 5 EVADE
  Quiz: 4 TRUE 5 FALSE
  to a charge: 4 PLEA
**Answered**
  a charge: 4 PLED
  a summons: 4 CAME
**Answering**
  Avoid: 5 EVADE
  machine button: 5 ERASE
**Answers**
  Like some: 3 PAT
  Man with all the: 6 TREBEK
  Seek: 3 ASK
**Ant:** 5 EMMET 7 PISMIRE
  group: 4 ARMY
  magnet: 6 PICNIC
  place: 6 COLONY
  Pop singer: 4 ADAM
**Ant.:** 3 OPP
  Opp. of: 3 SYN
**Antacid**
  choice: 6 BICARB
**Antagonist:** 3 FOE 5 ENEMY
    RIVAL
**Antagonistic:** 7 HOSTILE
**Antal**
  Conductor: 6 DORATI
**Antarctic**
  explorer Richard: 4 BYRD
  explorer Shackleton: 6 ERNEST
  explorer Sir James: 4 ROSS
  flier: 4 SKUA
  penguin: 6 ADELIE
  sight: 6 ICECAP
  volcano: 6 EREBUS
  waters: 7 ROSSSEA
**Antares:** 4 STAR 7 REDSTAR
**Ante**
  body: 3 POT
  matter: 3 BET
  Poker: 4 CHIP
  Raised the: 5 UPPED
  Up the: 5 RAISE
**Ante-:** 3 PRE
**Anteater**
  feature: 5 SNOUT
  Spiny: 7 ECHIDNA
**Antebellum:** 6 PREWAR
**Antelope**
  African: 3 GNU KOB 4 ORYX
    5 ELAND NYALA ORIBI
    6 IMPALA RHEBOK
  Bearded: 3 GNU

Female: 3 DOE
Small: 5 ORIBI
Where deer and ~ play:
    5 RANGE
with twisty horns: 4 KUDU
    5 ELAND
**Antenna:** 6 AERIAL
holder: 3 ANT
housing: 6 RADOME
Kind of: 4 DISH 6 DIPOLE
TV: 6 AERIAL
TV-top: 10 RABBITEARS
**Antepenultimate**
Greek letter: 3 CHI
**Anthem**
author: 3 KEY
contraction: 3 OER
opener: 4 OSAY
preposition: 3 OER
Show respect for the national:
    4 RISE 5 STAND
up north: 7 OCANADA
**Anther**
It's got the: 6 STAMEN
**Anthology:** 3 ANA 6 READER
    7 OMNIBUS
**Anthony**
Bowler: 4 EARL
British P.M.: 4 EDEN
Singer: 4 MARC 6 NEWLEY
~ Eden: 4 EARL
**Anthony, ___ B.:** 5 SUSAN
**Anthony, St.**
cross: 3 TAU
**Anthropologist**
~ Fossey: 4 DIAN
~ Margaret: 4 MEAD
**Anti:** 7 AGAINST
body: 3 CON
vote: 3 NAY
**Antiaircraft**
fire: 4 FLAK 6 ACKACK
**Anti-art**
art: 4 DADA
**Antibiotic**
target: 5 STREP
**Antibody**
sources: 4 SERA
**Anti-Brady**
org.: 3 NRA
**Antic:** 4 DIDO 5 CAPER
    6 MADCAP
**Anticipate:** 5 AWAIT 6 PLANON
    7 FORESEE
with alarm: 5 DREAD
**Anticipated:** 7 FORESAW
**Anticipation**
Time of: 3 EVE
**Anticipatory**
cry: 4 OHOH
times: 4 EVES
**Anticrime**
acronym: 4 RICO
**Antidiscrimination**
agcy.: 4 EEOC
**Antidote:** 4 CURE

**Antidrug**
cop: 4 NARC
honcho: 4 CZAR
mantra: 9 JUSTSAYNO
**Anti-DWI**
org.: 4 MADD
**Antietam**
fighter: 3 REB
general: 3 LEE
**Antifreeze**
additive: 8 METHANOL
**Antifur**
org.: 4 PETA
**Antigen**
attacker: 5 TCELL
**Antigone**
Father of: 7 OEDIPUS
Mother of: 7 JOCASTA
Uncle of: 5 CREON
**Anti-gun-control**
gp.: 3 NRA
**Anti-ICBM**
plan: 3 SDI
**Antiknock**
fluid: 5 ETHYL
**Antilles**
native: 5 CARIB
**Antinuclear**
treaty: 7 TESTBAN
**Antiparticle**
Certain: 8 POSITRON
**Antipasto**
ingredient: 5 OLIVE
    6 SALAMI
**Antipathetic:** 6 AVERSE
**Antipathy**
Feel ~ toward: 4 HATE
**Antipollution**
org.: 3 EPA
**Antiprohibitionist:** 3 WET
**___ Antiqua:** 3 ARS
**Antiquark**
A quark and an: 5 MESON
**Antiquated:** 3 OLD 5 FUSTY
    MOLDY MOSSY OLDEN
    PASSE
interjection: 4 EGAD
Somewhat: 6 OLDISH
**Antique:** 3 OLD
auto: 3 REO
dealer's deal: 6 RESALE
gun: 4 STEN
shop item: 5 CURIO
~, once: 4 OLDE
**"Antiques Roadshow"**
network: 3 PBS
**Antiquing**
agent: 4 AGER
**Antiquity:** 3 ELD
Antony of: 4 MARC
**Anti-Red**
gp.: 4 HUAC
**Antiroyalist:** 4 WHIG
**Antis:** 3 NOS
**Antiseptic**
acid: 5 BORIC

element: 6 IODINE
**Antislavery**
leader Tuner: 3 NAT
**Antismog**
org.: 3 EPA
**Antismoking**
org.: 3 AMA
**Antisocial**
sort: 5 LONER
**Antisubversive**
Old ~ gp.: 4 HUAC
**Antitank**
weapon: 7 BAZOOKA
**Antithesis:** 8 OPPOSITE
Farm ~, in song: 5 PAREE
Jock: 4 NERD
**Antitoxin:** 5 SERUM
**Antitoxins:** 4 SERA
**Antitrust**
org.: 3 FTC
suit defendant: 3 ITT
**Antivenins:** 4 SERA
**Antiviral**
drug: 3 AZT
**Antiwar**
gp.: 3 SDS
**Antler**
point: 4 TINE 5 PRONG
**Antlered**
animal: 3 ELK 4 DEER HART
    STAG 5 MOOSE
    7 ROEDEER
**Antoine**
~ Domino: 4 FATS
**Antoinette**
Tony award namesake:
    5 PERRY
**___ Antoinette:** 5 MARIE
**Antoinette, Marie:** 5 REINE
**Antonio**
Actor: 6 SABATO
role: 3 CHE 5 ZORRO
**___ Antonio:** 3 SAN
**Antony**
addressee: 5 ROMAN
Love of: 4 AMOR CLEO
    9 CLEOPATRA
of antiquity: 4 MARC
**"Antony and Cleopatra"**
servant: 4 EROS
**Antonym:** 3 OPP
opp.: 3 SYN
**Ants**
flick: 4 THEM
**Antsy:** 6 ONEDGE
    7 RESTIVE
**Anvil:** 7 EARBONE
location: 3 EAR
user: 5 SMITH
**Anwar**
of Egypt: 5 SADAT
successor: 5 HOSNI
**Anxiety:** 4 CARE 5 ANGST
    6 UNEASE 7 TENSION
High: 6 STRESS
Medication for: 6 VALIUM

**Anxious:** 4 EDGY 5 ANTSY
    EAGER ITCHY
    6 ONEDGE RARING
    UNEASY 7 ALARMED
  Be: 4 STEW
**Any:** 4 SOME
  At ~ time: 3 EER 4 EVER
  boat: 3 SHE
  day now: 4 ANON SOON
  doctrine: 3 ISM
  Hardly: 3 FEW ONE 4 ATAD
    5 SCANT
  In ~ case: 7 ATLEAST
  In ~ way: 4 EVER 5 ATALL
    NOHOW
  Not: 4 NARY NONE ZERO
  Not in ~ way: 5 NOHOW
    6 NOWISE
  Not just: 3 THE
**"Any ___?":** 5 IDEAS 6 TAKERS
**Anya**
  Author: 5 SETON
**Anybody:** 7 SOMEONE
**"... ___ any drop to drink":**
    3 NOR
**"Any Given Sunday"**
  star: 6 PACINO 8 ALPACINO
**"Anyone home?":** 6 YOOHOO
**Anything**
  He'll eat: 8 OMNIVORE
  Ready for: 5 ALERT
    7 ONALERT
  Without doing: 4 IDLY
**"Anything ___":** 4 GOES
**"Anything ___?":** 4 ELSE
**"___ Anything":** 4 IDDO
**"Anything for You"**
  singer: 7 ESTEFAN
**"Anything Goes"**
  songwriter Porter: 4 COLE
**"Anything you want!":**
    6 NAMEIT
**Anytown, USA**
  address: 6 MAINST
**Anywhere**
  Not going: 4 IDLE 7 STALLED
  on earth: 11 UNDERTHESUN
**Aoki**
  Golfer: 4 ISAO
**AOL:** 3 ISP
  delivery: 5 EMAIL
  exchanges: 3 IMS
  Part of: 6 ONLINE
  rival: 3 MSN
**A-one:** 5 SUPER
    8 TOPNOTCH
**___ a one:** 4 NARY
**Aotearoa**
  people: 5 MAORI
**Août**
  time: 3 ETE
**AP**
  Part of: 5 ASSOC
  rival: 3 UPI
**Aparicio**
  of baseball: 4 LUIS

**Apart**
  Come: 3 RIP 4 FRAY
    7 UNRAVEL
  Fall: 3 ROT 7 GOTOPOT
  from this: 4 ELSE
  Kept: 6 SPACED
  Pull: 4 TEAR 8 SEPARATE
  Rip: 4 REND
  Set: 5 ALLOT 7 ISOLATE
  Split: 4 REND
  Spread: 5 SPLAY
  Take: 4 UNDO
  Tear: 3 RIP 4 REND RIVE
**Apartment:** 3 PAD 4 FLAT UNIT
    6 RENTAL
  Certain: 4 COOP LOFT
    6 SUBLET
  dweller: 6 TENANT
  Owned: 5 CONDO
  sharer: 6 ROOMIE
  sign: 5 TOLET
  Small: 6 STUDIO
  Super's ~, often: 4 ONEA
  Take an: 4 RENT
**Apartments**
  Like some: 5 RELET
**Apathetic:** 5 BLASE
  Isn't: 5 CARES
**APB**
  Part of: 3 ALL
  sources: 3 PDS
**Ape:** 4 COPY 5 MIMIC
    6 SIMIAN 7 IMITATE
    PRIMATE
  Big: 4 LOUT 5 ORANG
    7 GORILLA PALOOKA
  Go: 4 FLIP RANT 6 LOSEIT
  Movie: 4 KONG
**Apennine**
  Ancient ~ dweller: 6 SABINE
  volcano: 4 ETNA
**Apéritif**
  Cassis-flavored: 3 KIR
  Italian: 7 CAMPARI
  White wine: 3 KIR
**Aperture:** 4 HOLE
  Narrow: 4 SLIT SLOT
  Tiny: 7 PINHOLE
**Apertures**
  Leaf: 7 STOMATA
**Apex:** 3 TOP 4 ACME PEAK
  At the ~ of: 4 ATOP
**Aphid:** 4 PEST
  milker: 3 ANT
**Aphorism:** 3 SAW 5 GNOME
    MAXIM
  Hindu: 5 SUTRA
**Aphrodite:** 5 VENUS
  Beloved of: 6 ADONIS
  domain: 4 LOVE
  Lover of: 4 ARES
  Son of: 4 EROS
**Apia**
  is its capital: 5 SAMOA
**Apiarist**
  hazard: 8 BEESTING

**Apiary:** 4 HIVE
  resident: 3 BEE
**Apiece:** 3 PER 4 EACH
  ~, in scores: 3 ALL
**A ___ pittance:** 4 MERE
**"A ___ plan, a canal ...":**
    4 MANA
**Aplenty:** 6 GALORE
  ~, old-style: 4 ENOW
**Aplomb:** 5 POISE
**Apocalypse:** 4 DOOM
**"Apocalypse Now"**
  setting: 3 NAM
**Apocrypha**
  archangel: 5 URIEL
  book: 5 TOBIT
  character: 3 BEL
**Apollo**
  approval: 3 AOK
  astronaut Slayton: 4 DEKE
  birthplace: 5 DELOS
  destination: 4 MOON
  instrument: 4 LYRE
  launcher: 4 NASA
  Mother of: 4 LETO
  Nymph loved by: 6 DAPHNE
  or Ares: 3 GOD 5 DEITY
  path: 5 ORBIT
  Sister of: 7 ARTEMIS
  Son of: 3 ION
  twin: 7 ARTEMIS
  vehicle: 3 LEM
**Apollo 11**
  destination: 4 MOON
  lunar module: 5 EAGLE
  name: 4 NEIL
**Apollo 13**
  astronaut: 6 LOVELL
**"Apollo 13"**
  actor Gary: 6 SINISE
  actor Joe: 5 SPANO
  director Howard: 3 RON
**Apollo 15**
  astronaut James: 5 IRWIN
**Apolo Anton ___**
  Speed skater: 4 OHNO
**Apology**
  Brief: 5 SORRY
  Cause for an: 4 BUMP
  preceder: 4 OOPS
  Start of an: 3 MEA
**Apostate:** 8 RENEGADE
**Apostle**
  Brother of ~ Andrew:
    7 STPETER
  Epistle: 4 PAUL
**Apostles**
  One of the: 4 LUKE PAUL
    5 JUDAS PETER
**"Apostles, The"**
  composer: 5 ELGAR
**Apostles' ___:** 5 CREED
**Apothecary**
  weight: 4 DRAM
**Apotheosis:** 5 IDEAL
    7 EPITOME

"... ___ a pound": 5 INFOR
"A pox upon thee!": 3 FIE
**App.**
  Job ~ no.: 3 SSN
**Appalachian Trail**
  Enjoy the: 4 HIKE
  terminus: 5 MAINE
**Appalled:** 6 AGHAST
**Appaloosa**
  Infant: 4 FOAL
**Apparatus:** 3 RIG 4 GEAR UNIT
    7 MACHINE
  Drilling: 6 OILRIG
  Gymnast's: 5 HORSE
  Lifting: 5 HOIST
  Playground: 5 SLIDE
    6 SEESAW
  Weaving: 4 LOOM
**Apparel:** 4 GARB 5 DRESS
    7 RAIMENT
  Like some holiday: 3 GAY
  Mass: 3 ALB
**Apparent:** 5 OVERT
  Air: 4 SMOG
  Become ~ to: 6 DAWNON
  With no hair: 4 BALD
**Apparently**
  are: 4 SEEM
"Apparently": 6 SOISEE
**Apparition:** 5 GHOST 6 SPIRIT
    WRAITH 7 SPECTER
    8 PHANTASM
**Appeal:** 3 ASK 4 PLEA
    5 CHARM
  Kind of: 3 SEX 4 SNOB
  Lose: 8 WEARTHIN
  Sex: 5 OOMPH
  strongly to: 5 TEMPT
  ___ appeal: 4 SNOB
**Appealing:** 4 CUTE SEXY
    5 SUING
**Appear:** 3 ACT 4 SEEM
    6 SHOWUP TURNUP
  dramatically: 4 LOOM
  gradually: 6 FADEIN
  suddenly: 5 ERUPT POPUP
**Appearance:** 3 AIR 4 LOOK
    MIEN 5 GUISE 6 ASPECT
    VISAGE
  Brief: 5 CAMEO
  First: 5 DEBUT ONSET
  Make an: 4 COME SHOW
    6 SHOWUP
  Plate: 5 ATBAT
  TV: 6 AIRING
**Appeared:** 4 CAME 5 AROSE
**Appearing**
  live: 8 INPERSON
**Appease:** 4 CALM 7 PLACATE
  fully: 4 SATE
**Appellation:** 4 NAME
**Append:** 3 ADD 5 ADDON
    AFFIX TAGON 6 TACKON
**Appendage**
  Grain: 6 ARISTA
  Grass: 3 AWN

  Neural: 4 AXON
**Appendages**
  Winglike: 4 ALAE
**Appendectomy**
  evidence: 4 SCAR
**Appendices:** 7 ADDENDA
"___ appétit!": 3 BON
**Appetite:** 3 YEN
  arouser: 5 AROMA
  Stimulate an: 4 WHET
**Appetizer**
  Chinese: 7 EGGROLL
  French: 4 PATE
  Italian ~ plates:
    9 ANTIPASTI
  Luau ~ array:
    11 PUPUPLATTER
  Mexican: 5 NACHO
  Spanish: 4 TAPA
**Appetizing:** 5 TASTY 6 SAVORY
**___ Appia:** 3 VIA
**Applaud:** 4 CLAP 6 PRAISE
    7 CLAPFOR
  (for): 4 ROOT
**Applause:** 4 HAND
  Acknowledge: 3 BOW
    8 TAKEABOW
  Round of: 4 HAND
**Apple:** 4 POME TREE
  acid: 5 MALIC
  alternative: 3 IBM
  Apple's: 4 LOGO
  application, once: 4 ALAR
  Autumn: 6 RUSSET
  Banned ~ spray: 4 ALAR
  center: 4 CORE
  coating: 7 CARAMEL
  cofounder: 4 JOBS
  Colorful: 4 IMAC
  computer: 4 IMAC
  drink: 5 CIDER
  eater: 3 EVE
  gadget: 5 CORER PARER
  Go after an: 3 BOB
  leftover: 4 CORE
  Love: 6 TOMATO
  MP3 player by: 4 IPOD
  offering: 3 MAC 4 IMAC
  pesticide: 4 ALAR
  picker: 3 EVE
  polisher: 5 TOADY
  Prepare an: 4 CORE
  product: 3 MAC 4 IMAC IPOD
    5 CIDER IBOOK
  Singer: 5 FIONA
  Skin an: 4 PARE
  spray: 4 ALAR
  Translucent: 4 IMAC
  variety: 3 MAC 4 IMAC ROME
    6 RUSSET 7 WINESAP
  Winter: 6 RUSSET
  ___ apple: 5 ADAMS
**Appleby, Inspector**
  creator: 5 INNES
**Applegate, Christina**
  sitcom: 5 JESSE

**Apple of Discord**
  thrower: 4 ERIS
**Apple pie**
  In ~ order: 4 NEAT TIDY
  Like: 8 AMERICAN
  order: 7 ALAMODE
  pro: 3 MOM
**Apples**
  Like some: 4 TART
**Applesauce**
  maker: 5 MOTTS
**Appleseed, Johnny**
  real surname: 7 CHAPMAN
**Appliance**
  designation: 4 ACDC
  Kitchen: 4 OVEN 5 RANGE
    STOVE 6 FRIDGE
  Laundry: 5 DRYER
  maker: 5 AMANA
  on a board: 4 IRON
  that sucks: 6 VACUUM
  ~, for short: 3 VAC
**Applicable:** 7 INFORCE
**Applicant**
  goal: 3 JOB
**Applicants**
  Coll.: 3 SRS
**Application:** 3 USE 5 USAGE
  Absorbent: 4 TALC
  After-bath: 4 TALC
    6 TALCUM
  Apple: 4 ALAR
  Bow: 5 ROSIN
  College ~ part: 5 ESSAY
  Cut: 6 IODINE
  datum: 3 AGE SEX SSN
    4 NAME
  Light: 3 DAB
  Lip: 4 BALM 5 GLOSS LINER
  Salon: 3 DYE GEL
  Soothing: 4 TALC
  Submit an: 6 SENDIN
**Applier**
  Pressure: 4 PEER
**Appliqué:** 5 SEWON
**Apply:** 3 USE 5 EXERT LAYON
    RUBON
  a basecoat to: 5 PRIME
  balm to: 6 SOOTHE
  crudely: 4 DAUB
  gently: 3 DAB
  haphazardly: 6 SLAPON
  macadam to: 4 PAVE
  oil to: 6 ANOINT
  spin to: 4 SKEW
  turf to: 3 SOD
**Appoint:** 4 NAME 6 ORDAIN
**Appointee**
  Pres.: 3 AMB 4 SECY
**Appointment:** 4 DATE POST
**Appointments:** 5 DECOR
**Appomattox**
  general: 3 LEE
**Apportion:** 4 METE 5 ALLOT
    7 PRORATE
  ~, with "out": 4 METE

**Appraisal**
Nasal: 5 AROMA
**Appraise:** 4 RATE 6 ASSESS
7 VALUATE
**Appraiser:** 6 VALUER
**Appreciate:** 3 GET 5 SAVOR
VALUE
**Appreciation**
Damsel's cry of: 6 MYHERO
Express ~ to: 5 THANK
Show: 4 CLAP
**Apprehend:** 3 BAG NAB 4 NAIL
6 COLLAR
**Apprehension:** 4 FEAR
5 ALARM ANGST DREAD
6 UNEASE
**Apprehensive:** 5 ANTSY LEERY
6 UNEASY
feeling: 5 ANGST
**Apprentice:** 3 CUB 4 TYRO
5 TUTEE 6 INTERN
7 LEARNER TRAINEE
**Apprised:** 5 AWARE
of: 4 INON
**Approach:** 4 COME NEAR
PATH 6 GOUPTO
7 CLOSEIN
for a loan: 5 HITUP
Means of: 6 ACCESS AVENUE
midnight: 5 LATEN
sneakily: 7 CREEPUP
Special: 5 ANGLE
the runway: 4 TAXI
~, with "for": 4 MAKE
**Approaching:** 4 NEAR NIGH
6 ALMOST NEARTO
the hour: 5 TENTO
**Appropriate:** 3 APT DUE FIT
4 GRAB TAKE 5 ALLOT
ANNEX COOPT RIGHT
SEIZE STEAL SWIPE
USURP 6 ASSUME
SEEMLY SUITED
Deem: 6 SEEFIT
Most: 6 NICEST
Not: 5 INAPT
What a family film is ~ for:
7 ALLAGES
**Appropriating:** 6 TAKING
**Approval:** 3 YES 5 SAYSO
6 ASSENT 7 GOAHEAD
Apollo: 3 AOK
Express: 4 CLAP
Final: 5 SAYSO
Give: 4 OKAY
Medicine ~ agcy.: 3 FDA
Quick ~ (abbr.): 4 INIT
Shout of: 3 OLE
Sign of: 3 NOD
Stamp of: 4 USDA
**Approvals:** 3 OKS 5 YESES
6 YESSES
**Approve:** 4 OKAY 6 RATIFY
**Approved:** 3 OKD 4 OKED
Generally: 8 ORTHODOX
**Approves:** 3 OKS

**Approving**
cry: 3 OLE
**Approx.:** 3 EST
**Approximately:** 3 SAY 4 ORSO
SOME 5 ABOUT CIRCA
**Approximation**
Sched.: 3 ETA ETD
suffix: 3 ISH
Words of: 4 ORSO
**Appt.**
book lines: 3 HRS
calendar item: 3 MTG
**APR**
Part of: 3 PCT 4 RATE
**Apr.**
addressee: 3 IRS
Busy one in: 3 CPA
**Après-ski**
drink: 5 COCOA
**April**
forecast: 4 RAIN
honoree: 4 FOOL
Many an ~ baby: 5 ARIES
payment: 3 TAX
~, May, and June, to Daisy:
6 NIECES
**April 1**
victim: 4 FOOL
**April 13:** 4 IDES
**April 15**
addressee: 3 IRS
**April 22**
saint: 6 ANSELM
**"April Love"**
composer Sammy: 4 FAIN
singer: 5 BOONE
**Apropos**
of: 4 ASTO INRE
___ apso (dog): 5 LHASA
**Apt:** 6 LIABLE LIKELY
name for a cook: 3 STU
to pry: 4 NOSY
**Apt.**
coolers: 3 ACS'
divisions: 3 RMS
feature: 3 EIK
features: 3 BRS
part: 4 BDRM
**Apteryx australis:** 4 KIWI
**Aptitude:** 4 BENT GIFT
5 KNACK SKILL
6 TALENT
Musical: 3 EAR
**Aptiva**
maker: 3 IBM
**Aqua**
Color close to: 4 TEAL
suffix: 4 NAUT
**Aqua ___:** 4 PURA 5 REGIA
VITAE
**Aqua-___:** 4 LUNG
**Aquamarine:** 7 SEABLUE
**Aquanaut**
base: 6 SEALAB
**Aquarium:** 4 TANK
attraction: 8 PORPOISE

bubbler: 7 AERATOR
buildup: 5 ALGAE
fish: 4 NEON 5 DANIO
GUPPY TETRA
6 WRASSE
9 NEONTETRA
performer: 4 SEAL
problem: 5 ALGAE
**Aquarius**
Words with: 5 AGEOF
**"Aquarius"**
musical: 4 HAIR
**Aquatic**
bird: 4 COOT GULL TERN
mammal: 4 SEAL 5 OTTER
nymph: 5 NAIAD
organisms: 5 ALGAE
plant: 4 ALGA
**Aquatint**
Make an: 4 ETCH
**Aqua Velva**
rival: 4 AFTA
**Aqueduct**
action: 3 BET
**Aqueduct of Sylvius:** 4 ITER
**Aqueduct Racetrack**
nickname: 4 BIGA
**Aquila**
Brightest star in: 6 ALTAIR
**Aquiline**
weapon: 5 TALON
**Aquitaine**
Home of ancient: 4 GAUL
queen: 7 ELEANOR
**Aquitania**
land: 4 GAUL
**Arab:** 5 HORSE 6 SEMITE
Certain: 6 YEMENI
ender: 5 ESQUE
land: 7 EMIRATE
leader: 4 EMIR 5 AMEER
EMEER SHEIK
lute: 3 OUD
name part: 3 IBN
Young: 4 FOAL
**"Arabesque"**
actress: 5 LOREN
___ Arabia: 5 SAUDI
**Arabian**
capital: 4 SANA
Certain: 5 OMANI SAUDI
cloak: 8 BURNOOSE
gulf: 4 ADEN
prince: 4 EMIR
sailing vessel: 4 DHOW
sultanate: 4 OMAN
**"Arabian Nights"**
bird: 3 ROC
group: 5 HAREM
hero: 7 ALIBABA
**Arabian Peninsula**
capital: 4 SANA
land: 4 OMAN
**Arabian Sea**
gulf: 4 ADEN
nation: 4 OMAN

**Arabic**
 Gum: 6 ACACIA
 letter: 4 ALIF
 "reading": 5 KORAN
 "son of": 3 IBN
**Arab League**
 member: 3 PLO 4 IRAQ OMAN
  5 QATAR SYRIA YEMEN
**Arachnid**
 Tiny: 4 MITE
**Arachnophobia:** 4 FEAR
**Arafat:** 4 ARAB
 birthplace: 5 CAIRO
 gp.: 3 PLO
 of the PLO: 5 YASIR 6 YASSER
**Arafat, Yasir**
 gp.: 3 PLO
**Aragón**
 **Info:** Spanish cue
 Are, in: 4 ESTA
 River of: 4 EBRO
**Aral:** 3 SEA
**Aramis**
 Athos, to: 3 AMI
 friend: 5 ATHOS
**Arapaho:** 5 TRIBE
 foe: 3 UTE
**Ararat**
 lander: 3 ARK 4 NOAH
**"A rat!":** 3 EEK
**Arbiter:** 3 REF UMP 6 UMPIRE
  7 REFEREE
**Arbitrarily**
 fine: 6 AMERCE
**Arbitrary**
 decree: 4 FIAT
**Arbor**
 abode: 4 NEST
**Arbor Day**
 honoree: 4 TREE
**Arboreal**
 abode: 4 NEST
 ape: 5 ORANG
 croaker: 8 TREETOAD
 lizard: 6 IGUANA
**Arboretum**
 item: 4 TREE
**Arborist**
 specimen: 4 TREE
**___ Arbor, Michigan:** 3 ANN
**Arbuckle**
 Like ~ films: 6 SILENT
**Arbuckle, Jon**
 dog: 4 ODIE
**Arbus**
 Photographer: 5 DIANE
**Arc**
 Hit in a high: 3 LOB
 lamp gas: 5 XENON
 on a score: 4 SLUR
**Arcade**
 attraction: 4 GAME 6 PACMAN
 coin: 5 TOKEN
 flub: 4 TILT
 name: 4 SEGA 5 ATARI
**Arcade game:** 6 TETRIS

 maker: 5 ATARI
 starter: 4 SKEE
**Arcane:** 8 ESOTERIC
**Arcangelo**
 Violinist: 7 CORELLI
**___ Arc, Arkansas:** 3 DES
**Arcaro**
 Jockey: 5 EDDIE
**Arc de Triomphe**
 site: 5 PARIS
**Arch:** 3 SLY 4 SPAN 6 IRONIC
 Kind of: 4 OGEE
 locale: 6 INSTEP
 Pointed: 4 OGEE 5 OGIVE
 type: 4 OGEE 6 GOTHIC
**Arch.**
 Kin of: 3 OBS
**Archaeological**
 find: 4 BONE TOMB 5 RELIC
  SHARD
 site: 3 DIG 4 RUIN
**Archaeologist**
 find: 4 BONE TOMB 5 RELIC
  SHARD
**Archaeology**
 site: 3 DIG
**Archaic**
 preposition: 3 ERE
 verb ending: 3 ETH
**Archangel**
 Apocryphal: 5 URIEL
**Archbishop**
 New York ~ before O'Connor:
  5 COOKE
 of New York: 4 EGAN
**"Archduke ___":** 4 TRIO
**Archenemy:** 7 NEMESIS
**Archer:** 5 AIMER
 Actress: 4 ANNE
 asset: 3 AIM
 bow wood: 3 YEW
 item: 3 BOW
 MacDonald's gumshoe: 3 LEW
 of myth: 4 AMOR EROS
 ~ William: 4 TELL
**Arches National Park**
 City near: 4 MOAB
 locale: 4 UTAH
**Archibald**
 of basketball: 4 NATE
 Watergate prosecutor: 3 COX
**Archie:** 4 TEEN
 admonition to Edith: 6 STIFLE
 Chum of: 5 MOOSE
 Mike, to: 5 INLAW
 Wife of: 5 EDITH
**Archies, The**
 1969 ~ hit: 10 SUGARSUGAR
**Archilochus**
 work: 5 EPODE
**Archimedean**
 tool: 5 LEVER
**Archimedes**
 cry: 6 EUREKA
**Archipelago**
 Pacific: 4 FIJI

 part: 4 ISLE 6 ISLAND
 unit (abbr.): 3 ISL
**Architect**
 addition: 3 ELL 5 ANNEX
 Kennedy Library: 5 IMPEI
 St. Louis bridge: 4 EADS
 St. Paul's: 4 WREN
 ~ Alvar: 5 AALTO
 ~ Christopher: 4 WREN
 ~ I.M.: 3 PEI
 ~ Jones: 5 INIGO
 ~ Lin: 4 MAYA
 ~ Maya: 3 LIN
 ~ Richard: 5 MEIER
 ~ Saarinen: 4 EERO 5 ELIEL
 ~ Sir Basil: 6 SPENCE
**Architectural**
 addition: 3 ELL 5 ANNEX
 curve: 4 OGEE
 detail: 4 SPEC
 drawing: 4 PLAN
 order: 5 DORIC IONIC
 Ornamental ~ style:
  6 ROCOCO
 pier: 4 ANTA
 sidepiece: 4 JAMB
 style: 5 DORIC IONIC TUDOR
  6 GOTHIC
 supporter: 6 LINTEL
 wing: 3 ELL
**Architecture**
 First name in: 4 EERO
  5 ELIEL
**Archives**
 Put in the: 4 FILE
**Archrival:** 7 NEMESIS
**Arcing**
 shot: 3 LOB
**Arco ___:** 5 ARENA
**Arctic:** 5 GELID OCEAN
  POLAR
 aircraft: 8 SKIPLANE
 assistant: 3 ELF
 barker: 4 SEAL
 bird: 3 AUK 4 SKUA TERN
 cover: 8 ICESHEET
 dweller: 4 LAPP 5 INUIT
 explorer John: 3 RAE
 explorer Robert: 5 PERRY
 floater: 4 BERG
 ice: 4 FLOE
 jacket: 5 PARKA 6 ANORAK
 plain: 6 TUNDRA
 sight: 4 FLOE
 transport: 4 SLED 6 SLEDGE
**Arctic Ocean**
 arm: 7 KARASEA
 hazard: 4 BERG
 sheet: 7 ICEFLOE
**Arcturus:** 4 STAR 5 KSTAR
**Arden**
 Actress: 3 EVE
 Fictional: 5 ENOCH
**"___ Arden":** 5 ENOCH
**Ardennes**
 river: 4 OISE

**Ardent:** 4 AVID 5 AFIRE EAGER
  7 AMATIVE DEVOTED
**Ardor:** 4 ELAN ZEAL
**Arduous**
  journey: 4 TREK
**Are:** 5 EXIST
  Apparently: 4 SEEM
  in the past: 4 WERE
  ~, in French: 4 ERES
  ~, in Spanish: 4 ESTA
**Area:** 4 ZONE 6 SECTOR
  SPHERE
  away from the battle: 4 REAR
  Dark: 5 UMBRA
  Depressed: 6 GHETTO
  Developing: 4 WOMB
    8 DARKROOM
  Grassy: 3 LEA
  Low-lying: 4 VALE 5 SWALE
  Marshy: 3 FEN
  meas.: 4 SQIN
  of land: 5 TRACT
  of London: 7 EASTEND
  of South Africa: 5 NATAL
  Outlying: 5 EXURB
  Recessed: 4 APSE 5 NICHE
  Run-down: 4 SLUM
  Swampy: 4 MIRE
**Area ___:** 3 RUG 4 CODE
**Area code**
  preceder: 3 ONE
**Areas**
  Fertile: 5 OASES
**Arena**
  Asian: 3 NAM
  DDE: 3 ETO
  Detroit: 4 COBO
  Former Atlanta: 4 OMNI
  Jousting: 4 LIST
  Kentucky: 4 RUPP
  level: 4 TIER
  NYC: 3 MSG
  Sacramento: 4 ARCO
  San Antonio:
    9 ALAMODOME
  shout: 3 OLE RAH
  WWII: 3 ETO
**Arenas:** 6 STADIA
**___ Arenas:** 5 PUNTA
**Arendt**
  Author: 6 HANNAH
**"Are not!"**
  retort: 4 AMSO 5 AMTOO
**Arens**
  of Israel: 5 MOSHE
**"Aren't ___ lucky one!":** 4 ITHE
**"Aren't ___ pair?":** 3 WEA
**Ares:** 3 GOD
  area: 3 WAR
  Mother of: 4 HERA
  Sister of: 4 ERIS
**Aretha**
  genre: 4 SOUL
**"Are we there ___?":** 3 YET
**"Are you a man ___ mouse?":**
  3 ORA

**"Are you calling me ___?":**
  5 ALIAR
**"Are you coming ___ not?":**
  4 INOR
**"Are you looking ___?":** 4 ATME
**"Are you ___ out?":** 4 INOR
**"Are you some kind of ___?":**
  4 ANUT
**Arg.**
  neighbor: 3 URU
**Argentina**
  Info: Spanish cue
  Are, in: 4 ESTA
  Big name in: 5 PERON
  Eva of: 5 PERON
  Hot time in: 5 ENERO
  Musical set in: 5 EVITA
  Perón of: 3 EVA
**Argentine**
  Info: Spanish cue
  article: 3 LAS
  aunt: 3 TIA
  dance: 5 TANGO
  plain: 5 PAMPA
**Argon:** 3 GAS 7 RAREGAS
  Like: 5 INERT
**"Argonautica"**
  character: 5 MEDEA
**Argonne Forest**
  river: 5 AISNE
**Arguable:** 4 MOOT
**Argue:** 5 PLEAD 6 DEBATE
  against: 7 CONTEST
  Point to: 3 NIT
**Argued:** 4 PLED
**Argues:** 7 HASAROW
  8 HASWORDS
**Arguing:** 4 ATIT
**Argument:** 3 ROW 4 FLAP
  5 RUNIN SETTO
  7 DISPUTE
  Brief: 5 SETTO
  Like a sound: 7 TENABLE
  Minor: 4 SPAT
  retort: 5 ISTOO
**Arguments**
  Like some: 4 ORAL
    6 HEATED
  Some: 3 PRO
**Argus**
  feature: 4 EYES
**Argus-eyed:** 5 ALERT
**Argyle:** 4 SOCK
**Argyles:** 4 HOSE
**Aria:** 4 SOLO
  area: 5 OPERA
  Perform an: 4 SING
  singer: 4 DIVA
  Verdi: 5 ERITU
**Arias:** 4 SOLI 5 SOLOS
**Arid:** 3 DRY 4 SERE 7 STERILE
  expanse: 6 SAHARA
  to the max: 7 SAHARAN
**Ariel**
  of Israel: 6 SHARON
  predecessor: 4 EHUD

**Aries:** 3 CAR RAM 4 AUTO
  6 THERAM
**Arise:** 4 DAWN STEM 5 OCCUR
  6 COMEUP CROPUP
  (from): 4 STEM
  without warning: 5 POPUP
**Arista**
  or Epic: 5 LABEL
**Aristocracy:** 5 ELITE 6 GENTRY
  7 PEERAGE
**Aristocrat:** 5 NOBLE
  9 BLUEBLOOD
  of old: 5 THANE
**Aristocratic:** 5 ELITE NOBLE
**Aristophanes**
  comedy, with "The": 5 WASPS
**Aristotle**
  subject: 5 LOGIC 6 ETHICS
  Teacher of: 5 PLATO
  walkway: 4 STOA
  ~, to Alexander the Great:
    5 TUTOR
**Arithmetic**
  Do basic: 3 ADD
  homework: 4 SUMS
  Make, in: 3 ARE
**Ariz.**
  clock setting: 3 MST
  neighbor: 3 NEV 4 NMEX
    5 CALIF
**Arizona**
  building block: 5 ADOBE
  city: 4 MESA YUMA 5 TEMPE
    7 NOGALES
  Former ~ congressman:
    5 UDALL
  Morris of: 5 UDALL
  necktie: 4 BOLO
  neighbor: 6 SONORA
  river: 4 GILA
  sight: 4 MESA
  symbol: 7 SAGUARO
  tourist locale: 6 SEDONA
  ~ Indian: 4 HOPI PIMA
    6 NAVAHO NAVAJO
**___ Arizona:** 3 USS
**Arizona State**
  home: 5 TEMPE
**Ark**
  berth: 6 ARARAT
  builder: 4 NOAH
  contents: 5 TORAH
    6 TORAHS
  Holy ~ home: 4 SHUL
  measure: 5 CUBIT
  units: 4 TWOS 5 PAIRS
**Ark.**
  neighbor: 4 OKLA
**___ Ark:** 5 NOAHS
**Arkansas**
  capital: 10 LITTLEROCK
  City on the: 5 TULSA
  footballer: 9 RAZORBACK
  Former ~ senator:
    11 DALEBUMPERS
  resort: 10 HOTSPRINGS

**Arkin**
1969 ~ film: 4 POPI
Actor: 4 ADAM ALAN
**Arledge**
Late TV exec: 5 ROONE
**Arlene**
Actress: 4 DAHL
**Arles**
Info: French cue
After, in: 5 APRES
agreement: 3 OUI
A, in: 3 UNE
Are, in: 4 ETES
article: 3 LES UNE
river: 5 RHONE
**Arlington**
landmark: 8 PENTAGON
melody: 4 TAPS
**Arlo**
Where ~ ate: 6 ALICES
**Arm:** 4 COVE LIMB 5 INLET
    6 WEAPON
art: 6 TATTOO
bone: 4 ULNA
bones: 5 RADII ULNAE
    ULNAS 6 HUMERI
Broken ~ holder: 5 SLING
Futuristic: 6 RAYGUN
holder: 6 SLEEVE
joint: 5 ELBOW
Mediterranean: 6 AEGEAN
muscle: 5 BICEP 6 BICEPS
Of an ~ bone: 5 ULNAR
of the sea: 5 INLET
Shot in the: 4 HYPO 5 BOOST
Tone ~ insert: 6 NEEDLE
U.N.: 3 ILO
--, in French: 4 BRAS
**Armada:** 5 FLEET
**Armageddon:** 3 END 4 DOOM
nation: 3 GOG 5 MAGOG
**"Armageddon"**
actress Tyler: 3 LIV
author: 4 URIS
**Armand**
Actor: 7 ASSANTE
**Armbone:** 4 ULNA
**Armchair**
quarterback channel: 4 ESPN
**Armed**
conflict: 3 WAR
**Armed Forces Day**
month: 3 MAY
**Armenia**
capital: 7 YEREVAN
capital, old-style: 6 ERIVAN
neighbor: 4 IRAN
peak: 6 ARARAT
~, formerly (abbr.): 3 SSR
**Armistice:** 5 TRUCE
**Armistice Day**
mo.: 3 NOV
**Armless**
couch: 5 DIVAN
**Armor**
Fish: 5 SCALE

Flexible: 9 CHAINMAIL
plate: 6 TUILLE
trouble: 5 CHINK
Type of: 4 MAIL
**Armor-busting**
weapon: 4 MACE
**Armored**
goddess: 6 ATHENA
vehicle: 4 TANK
**Armory**
supply: 4 AMMO
**Armour**
Parent company of: 4 DIAL
**Armpit:** 6 AXILLA
**Armrest:** 5 SLING
**Arms**
Commando: 4 UZIS
Comrade in: 4 ALLY
Doll with: 5 GIJOE
In the ~ of Morpheus:
    6 ASLEEP
Israeli: 4 UZIS
Like some: 6 AKIMBO
Org. with many: 3 NRA
Supply of: 7 ARSENAL
Up in: 5 IRATE
___ arms: 4 UPIN
**Armstrong**
Actress: 4 BESS
Astronaut: 4 NEIL
Cyclist: 5 LANCE
nickname: 7 SATCHMO
of football: 4 OTIS
**Arm-twisting:** 6 DURESS
Do some: 4 URGE 6 COERCE
**Army**
address: 3 SIR
attack helicopter: 5 COBRA
base: 4 FORT
bed: 3 COT
brass: 5 BUGLE
command: 6 ATEASE
cops: 3 MPS
corpsman: 5 MEDIC
Golfer with an: 5 ARNIE
group: 4 UNIT
Healthy, to the: 4 ONEA
helicopter: 4 HUEY 6 APACHE
Join the: 6 ENLIST
Kind of: 6 ONEMAN
leader: 5 ARNIE
meal: 4 MESS
member: 3 ANT
mule: 6 MASCOT
outfit: 4 UNIT
post: 4 BASE FORT
surgeon Walter: 4 REED
survey: 5 RECON
training center: 5 FTLEE
training loc.: 3 OCS
U.S. ~ medal: 3 DSC
vehicle: 4 JEEP TANK
~ E-3: 3 PFC
~ E-5: 3 NCO
~ NCO: 3 SGT 4 SSGT
~ VIP: 3 COL MAJ

___ **Army:** 6 ARNIES
**Army of the Potomac**
leader: 5 MEADE
**Army-style**
Polish: 9 SPITSHINE
**Arnaz**
and Ball studio: 6 DESILU
Entertainer: 4 DESI
**Arnhem**
City near: 3 EDE
**Arno**
Actor: 3 SIG
Ancient land between ~ and
    Tiber: 7 ETRURIA
Cartoonist: 5 PETER
City on the: 4 PISA
**Arnold**
Actor: 3 TOM
co-conspirator: 5 ANDRE
Comic: 5 STANG
Country singer: 4 EDDY
General: 3 HAP
Wife of: 5 MARIA
**" ___ a Rock":** 3 IAM
**A-Rod**
first name: 4 ALEX
**" ___ a roll!":** 4 IMON
**Aroma:** 4 NOSE ODOR
    5 SCENT SMELL
Travel, like an: 4 WAFT
~, to a Brit: 5 ODOUR
**Aromatic:** 8 REDOLENT
compound: 5 ESTER
herb: 5 ANISE BASIL CUMIN
ointment: 4 BALM NARD
wood: 5 CEDAR
**Arose:** 5 GOTUP STOOD
    6 CAMEUP
**Around:** 4 NEAR ORSO
    5 ABOUT CIRCA
Carry: 4 TOTE
Crowd: 3 MOB
Get: 4 ROVE 5 AVOID ELUDE
    EVADE SKIRT
Go: 4 SPIN 5 AVOID ORBIT
    SKIRT 6 BYPASS ROTATE
Going: 7 INORBIT
Hang: 4 LOLL STAY WAIT
    6 LINGER LOITER
It goes: 7 ORBITER
Kid: 4 JEST JOSH
Knock: 4 ROAM
Nosed: 5 PRIED
Once: 3 LAP 5 ORBIT
Poke: 4 NOSE 5 SNOOP
Spread: 5 STREW
Stick: 4 STAY
Swing: 4 SLUE
the 30th (abbr.): 3 EOM
Way: 5 ORBIT
**" ___ Around" (Beach Boys hit):**
    4 IGET
**Arouse:** 4 STIR 6 AWAKEN
    EXCITE FIREUP
    FOMENT
interest: 5 PIQUE

**Arousing:** 4 SEXY 6 EROTIC
**Arp:** 7 DADAIST
  art: 4 DADA
  contemporary: 5 ERNST
  Dadaist: 4 JEAN
**Arpel**
  of cosmetics: 6 ADRIEN
**Arraignment**
  offering: 4 PLEA
**Arrange:** 3 SET 4 SORT
    5 ORDER SETUP
    6 LAYOUT
  by class: 6 ASSORT
  hair: 4 DOUP
  in order: 7 SERIATE
  strategically: 6 DEPLOY
**Arrangement:** 4 PLAN 5 SETUP
  Driving: 7 CARPOOL
  Floral: 3 LEI 4 POSY 5 SPRAY
  Hair: 4 COIF
  Kind of: 6 FLORAL
  Orderly: 5 ARRAY
**Arrangements**
  Make table: 7 PRESEAT
**Array:** 4 ROBE 5 ORDER
    6 ATTIRE
**Arrears:** 4 DEBT
  Be in: 3 OWE
  In: 4 LATE
**Arrest:** 3 NAB 4 BUST STOP
    5 RUNIN 6 COLLAR
    HAULIN
**Arrested:** 5 RANIN
**Arrid**
  rival: 3 BAN 4 SURE
  target: 4 ODOR
**Arrival:** 6 ADVENT
  Early: 6 REDEYE 7 PREEMIE
  JFK: 3 SST
  New: 6 EMIGRE
  Recent: 6 NEWKID
    8 NEWCOMER
  Spring: 5 ARIES
  Stable: 4 FOAL
  Winter: 6 PISCES
**Arrive:** 4 COME LAND 5 GETIN
    6 PULLIN SHOWUP
  at: 5 GETTO REACH
    6 ATTAIN
  by air: 5 FLYIN
  Expected to: 3 DUE
  jauntily: 8 BREEZEIN
  rapidly: 6 POURIN
**Arrived:** 4 CAME 5 GOTIN
    6 MADEIT
  in time for: 4 MADE
**"Arrivederci, ___":** 4 ROMA
**Arrogance:** 6 HUBRIS
    7 HAUTEUR
**Arrogant**
  one: 4 SNOB
**Arrow**
  competitor: 4 IZOD
  poison: 4 INEE 6 CURARE
  shooter: 3 BOW 4 EROS
  stopper: 5 ARMOR

Words on an: 6 ONEWAY
**Arrow-shaped**
  Plant with ~ leaves: 5 CALLA
**Arrowsmith**
  Wife of: 5 LEORA
**Arroz con ___:** 5 POLLO
**Arroz ___ pollo:** 3 CON
**"Ars Amatoria"**
  About when ~ was written:
    5 ONEBC
  poet: 4 OVID
**Arsenal**
  contents: 4 AMMO
  Part of a nuclear: 4 ICBM
  Update the: 5 REARM
**Arsene**
  Gentleman burglar: 5 LUPIN
**Arsenic:** 6 POISON
  user, perhaps: 8 POISONER
**"Arsenic and Old Lace"**
  director: 5 CAPRA
**"Ars longa, ___ brevis":** 4 VITA
**Arson:** 6 FELONY
  evidence: 5 ASHES
**Arsonist:** 5 FELON TORCH
**"Ars Poetica"**
  poet: 6 HORACE
**"Ars ___, vita brevis":** 5 LONGA
**Art**
  able to: 5 CANST
  Body of: 5 TORSO
  Cartoon: 5 ANIME
  class: 5 GENRE
  collectible: 3 CEL
  colony of the Southwest:
    4 TAOS
  drawing: 5 SEPIA
  follower: 4 DECO
  gum: 6 ERASER
  Italian ~ patron: 4 ESTE
  Japanese: 7 ORIGAMI
  Joan of: 4 MIRO
  Kind of: 4 CAVE CLIP
  Love of fine: 5 VIRTU
  lover: 7 ESTHETE
  major subj.: 4 ANAT
  medium: 4 OILS 6 PASTEL
  Modern: 3 ARE
  Nihilistic: 4 DADA
  of jazz: 5 TATUM
  Paper: 7 ORIGAMI
  photo: 5 SEPIA
  print: 5 LITHO
  songs: 6 LIEDER
  stand: 5 EASEL
  subject: 4 NUDE VASE
    5 MODEL TORSO
  supporter: 5 EASEL
  TV doc: 5 ULENE
**Art ___:** 4 DECO
**"Artaxerxes"**
  composer: 4 ARNE
**Art Deco**
  designer: 4 ERTE
**Artemis**
  Mother of: 4 LETO

  slew him: 5 ORION
  twin: 6 APOLLO
  ~, to the Romans: 5 DIANA
**Arterial**
  trunk: 5 AORTA
**Artery:** 4 ROAD
  Kind of: 5 ILIAC RENAL
  Main: 5 AORTA
  Of a main: 6 AORTIC
**Artful:** 3 SLY 4 WILY 6 CLEVER
  dodge: 4 RUSE
  dodger: 6 EVADER
  tactic: 4 PLOY
**Artful Dodger:** 5 REESE
**Art gallery:** 5 SALON
  London: 4 TATE
  Manhattan ~ district: 4 SOHO
**Artgum:** 6 ERASER
**Arthr-**
  suffix: 4 ITIC
**Arthritis**
  prefix: 5 OSTEO
**Arthroscopy**
  site: 4 KNEE
**Arthur**
  Actress: 3 BEA
  Author: 6 CLARKE
  He beat ~ at the 1972 U.S.
    Open: 4 ILIE
  His real name was: 5 HARPO
  of tennis: 4 ASHE
**Arthur, Chester**
  middle name: 4 ALAN
**Arthur Conan ___:** 5 DOYLE
**Arthur Gordon ___:** 3 PYM
**Arthurian**
  isle: 6 AVALON
  lady: 4 ENID
  locale: 7 ASTOLAT
  magician: 6 MERLIN
  paradise: 6 AVALON
  times: 4 YORE
**Artichoke**
  center: 5 HEART
  Jerusalem: 5 TUBER
**Article:** 4 ITEM
  addendum: 7 ENDNOTE
  Common: 3 THE
  French: 3 LES UNE
  German: 3 DAS DER EIN
    4 EINE
  Italian: 3 GLI UNA
  lead-in: 8 DATELINE
  News: 4 ITEM
  of faith: 5 TENET
  Spanish: 3 LAS LOS UNA UNO
  supplement: 7 SIDEBAR
  Useful: 3 THE
**Articulate:** 3 SAY 5 UTTER
    6 FLUENT 7 ENOUNCE
**Articulated:** 4 SAID
**Artie**
  Clarinetist: 4 SHAW
  Ex of: 3 AVA 4 LANA
**Artifact**
  Ming: 4 VASE

Religious: 4 ICON
**Artifice:** 4 RUSE WILE
**Artificial:** 4 FAUX 6 ERSATZ
7 PLASTIC
bait: 4 LURE
leg: 5 STILT
sweetener: 5 EQUAL
tooth: 7 DENTURE
waterway: 5 CANAL 6 SLUICE
**Artillery**
burst: 5 SALVO
**Artist**
apartment: 4 LOFT
Art Deco: 4 ERTE
cap: 5 BERET
inspiration: 4 MUSE
medium: 4 OILS
One-named: 4 ERTE
paint holder: 5 PALETTE
pigment: 5 OCHER
plaster: 5 GESSO
prop: 5 EASEL
stand: 5 EASEL
studio: 7 ATELIER
~ Albrecht: 5 DURER
~ Guido: 4 RENI
~ Henri: 7 MATISSE
~ Jan: 5 STEEN
~ Joan: 4 MIRO
~ LeRoy: 6 NEIMAN
~ Mark: 6 ROTHKO
~ Max: 5 ERNST WEBER
~ Paul: 4 KLEE
~ Salvador: 4 DALI
**Artistes**
wear them: 7 CRAVATS
**Artistic**
category: 5 GENRE
dynasty: 4 MING
judgment: 5 TASTE
Make an ~ impression:
4 ETCH
**Artists**
Some: 7 ETCHERS
**Artless**
one: 4 NAIF
**Artlessness:** 7 NAIVETE
**"Art of Love, The"**
poet: 4 OVID
**"Art of Loving, The"**
author: 5 FROMM
**"Art of the Fugue"**
composer: 4 BACH
**Artoo ___:** 5 DETOO
**Art-rock**
British ~ combo: 3 XTC
**Art Ross Trophy**
org.: 3 NHL
Two-time ~ winner: 3 ORR
**Arts**
partner: 8 SCIENCES
**Artsy**
~ NYC area: 4 SOHO
**Artsy-___:** 7 CRAFTSY
**Artwork**
Religious: 5 PIETA

**Arty**
area: 7 BOHEMIA
~ NYC area: 4 SOHO
**Aruba:** 4 ISLE
**Arugula**
alternative: 8 ESCAROLE
**Arum**
family member: 4 TARO
lily: 5 CALLA
**As:** 3 QUA
a companion: 5 ALONG
a group: 7 ENMASSE
a joke: 5 INFUN
an alternative: 7 INSTEAD
a precaution: 6 INCASE
a result: 4 ERGO THUS
a rule: 9 INGENERAL
a substitute: 7 INSTEAD
a whole: 5 INALL 6 ENBLOC
expected: 4 DULY 5 ONCUE
far as: 4 UPTO
good as ever: 7 LIKENEW
it happens: 4 LIVE
located: 6 INSITU
many as: 4 UPTO
much: 6 NOLESS
much as you like: 5 AGOGO
of: 5 SINCE
of now: 6 TODATE
often as not: 9 ONAVERAGE
one: 6 UNITED
recently as: 4 ONLY
regards: 4 INRE
soon as: 4 ONCE
to: 4 INRE
well: 3 TOO 4 ALSO
6 TOBOOT
well as: 3 AND
we speak: 3 NOW
written: 3 SIC
yet: 5 SOFAR 6 ERENOW
you like it: 7 TOTASTE
**A's**
Former ~ player Sal: 5 BANDO
**As ___:** 5 ARULE
**"As ___ and breathe!":** 5 ILIVE
**ASAP:** 3 PDQ
in the ER: 4 STAT
Part of: 6 SOONAS
**"As brisk as ___ in
conversation":** 4 ABEE
**ASCAP**
Part of: 3 SOC 4 AMER
rival: 3 BMI
**Ascend:** 4 RISE 5 ARISE CLIMB
**Ascended:** 4 ROSE 5 AROSE
RISEN 6 ARISEN
UPROSE
**Ascent:** 4 RISE
**Ascetic**
Ancient: 6 ESSENE
Hindu: 5 FAKIR
**Ascot:** 3 TIE
**Ascribe:** 6 IMPUTE
blame for: 5 PINON
to: 6 CREDIT

**"... as devoid of rights as ___:**
5 ABALE
**"___ as directed":** 3 USE
**Asea**
Assents: 4 AYES
**Asgard**
leader: 4 ODIN
prankster: 4 LOKI
**"As Good As It Gets"**
actor: 7 KINNEAR
11 GREGKINNEAR
studio: 7 TRISTAR
**Ash:** 4 TREE
**Ashamed**
Make: 5 ABASH
**Ashcan School**
painter: 6 SLOANE
**Ashcroft**
predecessor: 4 RENO
**Ashe, Arthur**
alma mater: 4 UCLA
**Ashen:** 3 WAN 4 GRAY PALE
5 PASTY
Turn: 4 PALE
**Ashes**
Don sackcloth and: 6 REPENT
holder: 3 URN
**"___ Ashes":** 7 ANGELAS
**Ashe Stadium**
Ballpark near: 4 SHEA
do-over: 3 LET
event: 6 USOPEN
org.: 4 USTA
**"Ashes to Ashes"**
author Hoag: 4 TAMI
**Ashley**
Actress: 4 JUDD 5 OLSEN
Mom of: 5 NAOMI
rival: 5 RHETT
~, to Mary-Kate: 4 TWIN
**Ashore**
Go: 6 DEBARK
**Ashram**
figure: 4 GURU
visitor: 4 YOGI
**Ashtabula**
lake: 4 ERIE
**Ashtray**
item: 4 BUTT
**Ashuelot**
City on the: 5 KEENE
**Ash Wednesday**
start: 4 LENT
**"Ash Wednesday"**
poet: 5 ELIOT
**Ashworth**
Novelist: 5 ADELE
**Asia**
About 25,000 square miles of:
7 ARALSEA
Inland sea of: 4 ARAL
Turkey in: 8 ANATOLIA
Western boundary of:
5 URALS
**Asia Minor**
region: 5 IONIA 6 AEOLIA

**Asian**
arena: 3 NAM
border range: 4 URAL
capital: 3 YEN 5 AMMAN
　　DACCA HANOI KABUL
　　LHASA SEOUL 6 TAIPEI
　　TEHRAN 7 JAKARTA
carrier to Seoul: 3 KAL
Central: 5 TATAR
cuisine: 4 THAI
desert: 4 GOBI
destiny: 5 KARMA
festival: 3 TET
holiday: 3 TET
inland sea: 4 ARAL
language: 3 TAI 4 SHAN
nanny: 4 AMAH
nation: 4 LAOS 5 NEPAL
nursemaid: 4 AMAH
occasion: 3 TET
palm: 5 ARECA BETEL
peninsula: 5 KOREA MALAY
　　6 ARABIA MALAYA
place-name suffix: 4 STAN
prefix: 3 EUR
republic: 4 IRAN LAOS
royal: 4 RANI
sash: 3 OBI
sea: 4 ARAL
secret society: 4 TONG
shrub: 5 HENNA
Southeast: 3 LAO 4 THAI VIET
tents: 5 YURTS
title: 3 AGA SRI
tongue: 4 THAI URDU
weight: 4 TAEL
Wild ~ dog: 5 DHOLE
~ New Year: 3 TET

**Aside**
Brush: 5 SPURN
Money set: 6 ESCROW
Move: 5 SHUNT
Put: 5 ALLOT 6 SHELVE
Set: 4 SAVE 5 ALLOT
　　8 RESERVED
Sighed: 4 AHME
Temporarily put: 5 ONICE
Turn: 4 SNUB VEER 5 AVERT
　　PARRY SHUNT 6 DIVERT
　　7 DEFLECT
**"As if!":** 3 HAH NOT 4 IBET
　　5 PSHAW
**"As if ___!":** 5 ICARE
**"As if I care":** 6 SOWHAT
**"As I Lay Dying"**
father: 4 ANSE
**Asimov**
Author: 5 ISAAC
classic: 6 IROBOT
genre: 5 SCIFI
**Asinine:** 4 DUMB 5 INANE
**"As I ___ saying ...":** 3 WAS
**As it ___:** 4 WERE
**Ask:** 4 POSE 5 QUERY
　　7 INQUIRE REQUEST
for: 3 BEG 4 SEEK 7 SOLICIT

for a hand: 7 PROPOSE
for aid: 6 TURNTO
for an opinion: 4 POLL
for donations:
　　10 PASSTHEHAT
for ID: 4 CARD
for money: 5 HITUP
More than just: 6 DEMAND
___ A Sketch: 4 ETCH
**Asking**
For the: 4 FREE
**ASL**
Use: 4 SIGN
**Aslan:** 4 LION
**Asleep**
Be half: 6 DROWSE
Fall: 5 CRASH
Sound: 5 SNORE
**Asmara**
is its capital: 7 ERITREA
**Asner**
and others: 3 EDS
array: 5 EMMYS
title role: 8 LOUGRANT
**"As ___ on TV!":** 4 SEEN
___ a sour note: 5 ENDON
**Asparagus**
unit: 5 SPEAR
**ASPCA**
Part of: 3 SOC
**Aspect:** 4 AURA VIEW 5 ANGLE
　　FACET PHASE
　　6 REGARD
Harmful: 4 EVIL
Negative: 3 CON
Positive: 3 PRO 6 UPSIDE
**Aspen:** 4 TREE
abode: 6 CHALET
alternative: 4 VAIL 5 STOWE
attire: 7 SKISUIT
Do: 3 SKI
feature: 6 SKITOW
visitor: 5 SKIER
**Asperity:** 5 RIGOR
**Aspersion:** 4 SLUR
**Asphalt:** 4 PAVE
**Aspin**
Former defense secretary:
　　3 LES
**Aspiration:** 3 AIM 4 HOPE
　　5 DREAM
Common: 5 AITCH
**Aspirin**
allotment: 4 DOSE
maker: 5 BAYER
Need an: 4 ACHE
Open an ~ bottle: 5 UNCAP
target: 4 ACHE 8 HEADACHE
unit: 4 PILL
**Aspiring**
atty. exam: 4 LSAT
doc exam (abbr.): 4 MCAT
musician handout: 4 DEMO
one: 5 HOPER
**As ___ resort:** 5 ALAST
**Ass:** 4 DOPE

Act like an: 4 BRAY
Half: 4 MULE
Wild Asian: 6 ONAGER
**Assad:** 6 SYRIAN
**Assail:** 5 BESET SETAT
　　6 ATTACK
**Assailed:** 5 BESET HADAT
　　SETAT 6 CAMEAT
　　8 TOREINTO
**Assassin:** 6 SLAYER
Stealthy: 5 NINJA
**Assassinated:** 5 SLAIN
**Assassination**
Do some character: 5 ERASE
**Assault:** 5 ONSET 6 ATTACK
　　ONRUSH
Campaign: 5 SMEAR
from Moe: 4 POKE SLAP
or battery: 4 TORT
Verbal: 4 SLAP
**Assay:** 3 TRY 4 TEST
specimen: 3 ORE
**Assayer**
concern: 3 ORE
**"As ___ saying ...":** 4 IWAS
**Assemble:** 3 SIT 5 ERECT
　　RIGUP 6 GATHER
Parts to: 3 KIT
**Assembled:** 3 MET 4 MADE
again: 5 RESAT
**Assemblies**
General: 5 PLENA 6 ARMIES
**Assembly:** 4 DIET
Ancient ~ area: 5 AGORA
Church: 5 SYNOD
French: 5 SENAT
Full: 6 PLENUM
General: 4 ARMY 8 TOPBRASS
line worker: 5 ROBOT
**Assent:** 3 YEA YES 4 AMEN
　　6 SAYYES
French: 3 OUI
Indicate: 3 NOD
Informal: 3 YEH YEP 4 YEAH
Sailor's: 3 AYE 6 AYEAYE
Silent: 3 NOD
Slangy: 3 YEH YEP 4 YEAH
Spanish: 4 SISI
Sweetheart's: 7 YESDEAR
**Assert:** 4 AVER AVOW POSE
　　5 CLAIM POSIT STATE
　　6 ALLEGE
without proof: 6 ALLEGE
**Assertion:** 5 SAYSO
**Assertions**
Malicious: 3 MUD
**Assertive**
personality type: 5 ARIES
**Assess:** 4 RATE 5 GAUGE
　　VALUE 6 SIZEUP
**Assessment:** 4 LEVY
**Asset:** 4 PLUS
**Asseverate:** 4 AVOW
**"___ as she goes!":** 6 STEADY
**Assign:** 3 PUT 5 ALLOT
　　8 DELEGATE

blame to: 5 PINON
new actors: 6 RECAST
stars to: 4 RATE
workers to: 3 MAN
**Assignation:** 5 TRYST
**Assignment:** 4 POST TASK
Detective: 4 CASE
English: 5 ESSAY THEME
P.O.: 3 RTE
RN: 3 ICU
School: 5 ESSAY 6 REPORT
Swimmer: 4 LANE
Teaching: 5 CLASS
**Assignments**
Between: 4 IDLE
**Assimilate:** 5 COOPT
**Assimilation**
process: 7 OSMOSIS
**Assist:** 3 AID 4 HELP 5 SERVE
in crime: 4 ABET
**Assistance:** 3 AID 4 HELP
6 RELIEF SUCCOR
Passing: 3 YEA
Road ~ org.: 3 AAA
Without: 5 ALONE
7 UNAIDED
**Assistant:** 4 AIDE 6 HELPER
Arctic: 3 ELF
Fictional: 4 IGOR
mil. branch: 3 ADC
with a hunch: 4 IGOR
**Assn.:** 3 ORG SOC
Hemispheric: 3 OAS
**Associate:** 4 ALLY PEER
6 COHORT HOBNOB
7 CONSORT
Close: 3 PAL
Staff: 3 ROD
with: 5 TIETO
**Associated Press**
rival: 7 REUTERS
**Association:** 3 TIE 4 CLUB
**Assortment:** 4 OLIO 5 ARRAY
8 MIXEDBAG
___ asst.: 5 ADMIN
**Assuage:** 4 EASE 5 ALLAY
**Assume:** 5 ADOPT POSIT
USURP 6 TAKEON
blame: 10 TAKETHERAP
the role of: 5 ACTAS
**Assumed:** 5 GIVEN TACIT
It's: 5 ALIAS
truth: 5 AXIOM
**Assuming**
that: 4 IFSO
**Assumption**
Basic: 5 AXIOM
**Assurance:** 3 VOW 4 WORD
Say with: 4 AVER 5 CLAIM
Written: 9 GUARANTEE
**Assure:** 3 ICE
**Assyrian**
capital: 7 NINEVEH
king: 6 SARGON
**Asta:** 3 PET
owner: 4 NORA

**Astaire**
Dancer: 4 FRED 5 ADELE
headwear: 6 TOPHAT
partner: 6 ROGERS
12 GINGERROGERS
sister: 5 ADELE
**Astaire/Rogers**
destination: 3 RIO
film: 6 TOPHAT
**Asterisk:** 4 STAR
**Astern:** 3 AFT
**Asteroid**
discovered in 1898: 4 EROS
First known: 5 CERES
Largest: 5 CERES
maker: 5 ATARI
path: 5 ORBIT
Third-largest: 5 VESTA
Underwater: 7 SEASTAR
**As the ___ flies:** 4 CROW
**Asthmatic**
need: 7 INHALER
**"As Time Goes By"**
pianist: 3 SAM
requester: 4 ILSA
**Astin**
Actor: 4 SEAN
**Astolat**
Maid of: 6 ELAINE
**Astonish:** 3 AWE 4 STUN
5 AMAZE
**Astonished**
Sound: 4 GASP
Visibly: 5 AGAPE
**Astonishment:** 3 AWE
Show: 4 GASP 6 GOGGLE
**Astor**
Actress: 4 MARY
line: 3 FUR
**Astound:** 4 DAZE STUN
5 AMAZE FLOOR
**Astounded:** 4 AGOG 5 AGAPE
**Astral**
hunter: 5 ORION
**Astray:** 5 AMISS 6 ERRING
Go: 3 ERR SIN 6 DERAIL
**Astringent:** 4 ALUM 6 TANNIC
**Astro**
or Asta: 3 PET
**Astrodome**
Former ~ player: 5 OILER
**Astrologer**
~ Sydney: 5 OMARR
**Astrological**
border: 4 CUSP
lion: 3 LEO
ram: 5 ARIES
scales: 5 LIBRA
**Astronaut**
apparel: 5 GSUIT
drink: 4 TANG
Elton John song about an:
9 ROCKETMAN
excursion: 3 EVA
Friendship 7: 5 GLENN
milieu: 5 SPACE

org.: 4 NASA
"Thumbs up" to an: 3 AOK
~ Armstrong: 4 NEIL
~ Bean: 4 ALAN
~ Buzz: 6 ALDRIN
~ Collins: 6 EILEEN
~ Deke: 7 SLAYTON
~ Grissom: 3 GUS
~ James: 5 IRWIN
~ Jemison: 3 MAE
~ Judith: 6 RESNIK
~ Sally: 4 RIDE
~ Shepard: 4 ALAN
~ Slayton: 4 DEKE
~ Walter: 7 SCHIRRA
**Astronomer**
British: 6 HALLEY
favorite sky: 6 STARRY
Italian: 7 GALILEO
sighting: 4 NOVA STAR
6 NEBULA
~ Carl: 5 SAGAN
~ Hubble: 5 EDWIN
~ Sagan: 4 CARL
~ Tycho: 5 BRAHE
**Astronomical**
altar: 3 ARA
bear: 4 URSA
distance: 6 PARSEC
event: 7 ECLIPSE MOONSET
object: 6 PULSAR QUASAR
phenomena: 5 NOVAE
**Astronomy**
Major in: 4 URSA
Muse of: 6 URANIA
Star in: 5 SAGAN
**AstroTurf**
alternative: 3 SOD 5 GRASS
component: 5 VINYL
**Asturias**
Capital of: 6 OVIEDO
**Astute:** 3 SLY 4 WILY 5 CANNY
SHARP 6 SHREWD
**Astuteness:** 6 ACUMEN
**Asunder:** 5 RIVEN
Tear: 4 REND
**Aswan Dam**
builder: 6 NASSER
river: 4 NILE
**Asylum:** 5 HAVEN
Early: 3 ARK
seeker: 6 EMIGRE
7 REFUGEE
**"As you ___":** 4 WERE
**"As You Like It"**
forest: 5 ARDEN
woman: 5 CELIA
**"As you sew, so shall you**
**also ___":** 3 RIP
**"As you wish":** 6 SOBEIT
**At**
a distance: 3 FAR 4 AFAR
a good clip: 5 APACE
all: 3 ANY 4 EVER
all times: 4 EVER
any time: 4 EVER

a premium: 4 RARE
attention: 5 ERECT
birth: 3 NEE
fault: 6 GUILTY
first: 6 ONBASE
first (abbr.): 4 ORIG
full speed: 5 AMAIN
hand: 4 NEAR NIGH
　　6 NEARBY
large: 4 FREE 5 LOOSE
　　10 ONTHELOOSE
least one: 3 ANY
liberty: 4 FREE
lunch: 3 OUT
no cost: 4 FREE
no time: 4 NEER 5 NEVER
once: 3 NOW 4 STAT
one's post: 6 ONDUTY
peace: 5 SERENE
rest: 4 IDLE
right angles to: 5 ABEAM
risk: 8 INDANGER
that time: 4 THEN
the center of: 4 AMID
the home of: 4 CHEZ
the movies: 7 ONADATE
the peak of: 4 ATOP
the right time: 5 ONCUE
the summit of: 4 ATOP
the time of: 4 UPON
this point: 4 HERE
what time: 4 WHEN

**At ___**
(disagreeing): 4 ODDS
(free): 5 LARGE
(perplexed): 5 ALOSS
(with consequences): 5 ACOST

**Atahualpa**
land: 4 PERU
subject: 4 INCA 5 INCAN

**AT&SF**
and others: 3 RRS
stop: 3 STA

**AT&T**
acquisition: 3 NCR
Cable co. that merged with:
　　3 TCI
computer system: 4 UNIX
Former rival of: 3 GTE MCI
Part of: 3 TEL
wireless service: 5 MLIFE

**Atari**
founder Bushnell: 5 NOLAN

**Ataturk**
mausoleum city: 6 ANKARA

**At-bat**
Successful: 3 HIT

**Ate:** 3 HAD 5 DINED
into: 6 ERODED
like a bird: 6 PECKED

**"A-Team, The"**
member: 3 MRT

**Atelier**
item: 5 EASEL 7 PALETTE

**ATF**
agents: 4 FEDS

employee: 3 AGT

**At ___ for words:** 5 ALOSS

**Atheist**
~ Madalyn: 5 OHAIR

**Athena**
changed her into a spider:
　　7 ARACHNE
Epithet of: 4 ALEA
Roman counterpart of:
　　7 MINERVA
shield: 5 AEGIS
symbol: 3 OWL

**Athenian**
emblem: 3 OWL
lawgiver: 5 DRACO SOLON
marketplace: 5 AGORA
meeting place: 4 STOA
or Corinthian: 7 HELLENE
Shakespearean: 5 TIMON
vowel: 3 ETA
Wise: 5 PLATO

**Athens**
attractions: 5 RUINS
From: 5 GREEK
Letter from: 3 ETA
portico: 4 STOA
Region around: 6 ATTICA
rival: 6 SPARTA
University in: 4 OHIO

**Atherton, California**
college: 5 MENLO

**"A thing of beauty is a joy**
　　**forever"**
poet: 5 KEATS

**Athirst:** 5 EAGER

**Athlete**
Career: 3 PRO
Paid: 3 PRO
prefix: 3 TRI
trouble spot: 4 KNEE
~ Jim: 6 THORPE

**Athletic**
award: 5 MEDAL 6 LETTER
Onetime ~ org.: 4 NASL
shoe brand: 4 AVIA NIKE
supporter: 3 TEE
type: 5 ARIES
wear company: 6 SPEEDO

**Athos**
~, to Porthos: 3 AMI
___ a time: 5 ONEAT

**Atkins**
Actress: 6 EILEEN
diet concern: 4 CARB
Guitarist: 4 CHET
plan: 4 DIET

**Atkinson, Rowan**
role: 4 BEAN

**Atkov**
Salyut cosmonaut: 4 OLEG

**Atl.**
based cable network: 3 TNT
crosser: 3 SST
It's across the: 3 EUR

**Atlanta**
cable sta.: 3 TBS

Former ~ arena: 4 OMNI
player: 5 BRAVE
Turner of: 3 TED
university: 5 EMORY

**Atlanta-based**
airline: 5 DELTA
cable sta.: 3 TBS TNT
health agcy.: 3 CDC

**Atlantic:** 5 OCEAN
Arm of the: 8 IRISHSEA
crosser: 3 SST
food fish: 3 COD 4 SCUP
island group: 6 AZORES

**Atlantic City**
attraction: 4 KENO SLOT
casino, with "The": 3 TAJ
event: 7 PAGEANT

**"Atlantic City"**
director: 5 MALLE

**Atlantis**
docked with it: 3 MIR

**Atlas:** 4 ICBM 5 TITAN
abbr.: 3 ISL MTN STR TPK
　　4 ELEV USSR
contents: 4 MAPS
feature: 5 INSET
It's right in the: 4 EAST
Old ~ letters: 3 SSR 4 USSR
page: 3 MAP
rocket stage: 5 AGENA
section: 4 ASIA
stat: 4 AREA
Update an: 5 REMAP

**Atlas, Charles:** 5 HEMAN

**Atlas Mountains**
site: 7 ALGERIA

**"Atlas Shrugged"**
author Ayn: 4 RAND
author Rand: 3 AYN

**ATM**
input: 3 PIN
maker: 3 NCR
need: 3 PIN
part: 6 KEYPAD

**Atmosphere:** 3 AIR 4 AURA
　　8 AMBIENCE
About 1% of the: 5 ARGON
Bad: 6 MIASMA
Distinctive: 4 AURA
layer: 5 OZONE
prefix: 3 AER

**Atoll**
barrier: 4 REEF
Bikini ~ event: 5 ATEST
Bomb test: 8 ENIWETOK
feature: 6 LAGOON
material: 5 CORAL

**Atom**
Charged: 3 ION
Negatively charged:
　　5 ANION

**Atomic:** 3 WEE 4 TINY
　　6 MINUTE
cores: 6 NUCLEI
energy org.: 3 NRC
number 30: 4 ZINC

particle: 5 MESON 6 PROTON
   7 NEUTRON
**Atomizer**
  output: 4 MIST 5 SPRAY
**"At once!":** 4 STAT
**Atone:** 6 REPENT 7 EXPIATE
  Reason to: 3 SIN
**Atop:** 4 ONTO OVER UPON
  Lie: 6 RESTON
  Place: 5 SETON
  Rest: 5 LIEON
**"At Random"**
  autobiographer: 4 CERF
**At ___ rate:** 3 ANY
**Atrium**
  locale: 5 HEART
**Atropos:** 4 FATE
  ~ , Clotho, and Lachesis:
    5 FATES
**"At Seventeen"**
  singer: 3 IAN
**Atsuta Shrine**
  city: 6 NAGOYA
**Attach:** 5 ADDON AFFIX
    SCREW SEWON
    6 APPEND GLUEON
    SNAPON 7 PASTEON
  a brooch: 5 PINON
  a button: 5 SEWON
  a patch: 3 SEW 5 SEWON
  with a rope: 5 TIEON
**Attached**
  at the base: 7 SESSILE
  Be ~ (to): 6 ADHERE
  They come with strings:
    5 KITES 6 APRONS
**Attachment:** 3 TIE
  Info: Prefix or suffix cue
  adverb: 6 HERETO
**Attack:** 4 BOUT GOAT 5 BESET
    FLYAT ONSET RUNAT
    SETAT SETON SIEGE
    STORM 6 ASSAIL
    COMEAT HAVEAT
    JUMPON 7 SETUPON
    8 TEARINTO
  ad: 5 SMEAR
  a sub: 3 EAT
  by plane: 6 STRAFE
  Cause to: 5 SETAT SETON
  deterrent: 4 MACE MOAT
  Free to: 5 LETAT
  from above: 6 STRAFE
    7 AIRRAID
  from all sides: 5 BESET
  like an eagle: 5 SWOOP
  Main force of: 5 BRUNT
  Prolonged: 5 SIEGE
  Sneak: 4 RAID 6 AMBUSH
  Spirited: 5 SALVO
  Time to: 4 DDAY
  verbally: 8 TEARINTO
  vigorously: 6 ASSAIL
  word: 3 SIC
  ~, with "into": 3 LAY 4 LACE
**___ attack:** 4 SHAQ

**Attacked:** 5 HADAT RANAT
    SETAT 6 CAMEAT
    FELLON 7 LITINTO
    8 LAIDINTO
  violently: 6 TOREAT
**Attacker:** 3 FOE 9 ASSAILANT
  WWII: 5 UBOAT
**"Attack, Fido!":** 3 SIC
**Attacking:** 7 GOINGAT
**Attacks:** 5 HASAT 6 GOESAT
    8 LAYSINTO
**Attain**
  Endeavor to: 4 SEEK
  status: 4 RISE
**Attar**
  Major ~ source:
    10 DAMASKROSE
**"Atta Troll"**
  poet: 5 HEINE
**Attempt:** 3 TRY 4 SHOT STAB
    5 ASSAY ESSAY GOFOR
    6 EFFORT
  Failed: 4 NOGO
  Made an: 5 TRIED
  Make a new: 5 RETRY
  to get: 6 TRYFOR
  Wild: 4 STAB
**Attempts**
  ~, with "at": 6 HASAGO
**Attend:** 4 GOTO
  Fail to: 4 MISS SKIP
**Attendance**
  bk. entry: 3 ABS
  fig.: 3 EST
  In: 6 ONHAND
  taking: 8 ROLLCALL
  Was in: 4 CAME
**Attendance book**
  notation: 7 ABSENCE
**Attendant:** 5 VALET 6 ESCORT
**Attendants:** 7 RETINUE
**Attended:** 5 WASAT
**Attendee:** 4 GOER
**Attends:** 6 GOESTO
**Attention:** 3 EAR 4 CARE HEED
    MIND
  At: 5 ERECT
  Centers of: 4 FOCI
  getter: 3 HEY TAP 4 AHEM
    PSST 5 NUDGE
  Give careful ~ to: 4 HEED
  Hold, as: 5 RIVET
  Lavish ~ (on): 4 DOTE
  Media: 3 INK
  Pay: 4 HARK 6 LISTEN
    8 TAKENOTE
    9 LENDANEAR
  Paying: 5 ALERT AWARE
  Pay no ~ to: 6 IGNORE
    7 NEGLECT
  Pay ~ to: 4 HEED
  Sound for: 4 AHEM
  Special: 3 TLC
  Steal ~ from: 7 UPSTAGE
  Sympathetic: 3 EAR
**Attention ___:** 4 SPAN

**Attention-getter:** 3 HEY 4 AHEM
    PSST
  First-grader's: 4 MEME
  Half an: 3 YOO
**Attentive:** 7 ALLEARS
  Fully: 4 RAPT
**"At the ___" (1978 song**
    **phrase):** 4 COPA
**At the drop of ___:** 4 AHAT
**"___ at the office!":** 5 IGAVE
**Attic:** 6 GARRET
  In the: 6 STORED
  Like an ~, perhaps: 5 DUSTY
  sights: 4 WEBS
**Atila:** 3 HUN
  group: 4 HUNS
  Pope who persuaded ~ to spare
    Rome: 4 LEOI
  ~, to God: 7 SCOURGE
**Attila the ___:** 3 HUN
**Attire:** 4 GARB TOGS 5 DRESS
    HABIT 6 CLOTHE
    ENROBE 7 RAIMENT
  Casual: 5 DENIM JEANS
  Foreign: 4 SARI
  Formal: 3 TUX
  Senate: 4 TOGA
  Summer: 6 SHORTS
  Tattered: 4 RAGS
**Attired:** 4 CLAD
**Attitude:** 4 POSE 5 STAND
    6 STANCE
  Confident, as an: 5 CANDO
  Pretentious: 4 AIRS
**Attitudinize:** 4 POSE
**Attn.**
  Special: 3 TLC
**Attorney**
  Abbr. after an ~ name: 3 ESQ
  deg.: 3 LLB LLD
  field: 3 LAW
  follower: 5 ATLAW
  Future ~ exam: 4 LSAT
  org.: 3 ABA
  Scopes: 6 DARROW
  ~ Melvin: 5 BELLI
**Attorney-___:** 5 ATLAW
**Attorney General**
  1960s ~: 6 RAMSEY
  1970s ~: 6 ELLIOT
  1980s ~: 5 MEESE
    7 EDMEESE
  1990s ~: 4 RENO
  Clinton's: 4 RENO
  Reagan's: 5 MEESE
  ~ Janet: 4 RENO
**Attract:** 4 DRAW 6 DRAWIN
    ENTICE
**Attracted:** 4 DREW
**Attraction:** 4 DRAW LURE
    6 ALLURE
  Fair: 4 RIDE
  Main: 4 STAR
  near Orlando: 5 EPCOT
  Rush: 3 ORE
**"___ Attraction":** 5 FATAL

**Attractive:** 6 PRETTY
  It's: 3 ION 6 MAGNET
  legs: 4 GAMS
  Make more: 7 SWEETEN
  one: 5 CUTIE
  quality: 6 APPEAL
    15 ANIMALMAGNETISM
**Attribute:** 3 OWE 5 REFER
    TRAIT 6 IMPUTE
    7 ASCRIBE
  Golden: 7 SILENCE
  Psychic: 3 ESP
  Slot machine: 6 ONEARM
  Winemaking: 4 NOSE
**Attu**
  resident: 5 ALEUT
**Attucks**
  Patriot: 7 CRISPUS
**Attuned:** 5 KEYED
**Atty.**
  degree: 3 LLD
  Future ~ exam: 4 LSAT
  Kind of: 4 DIST
  org.: 3 ABA
  title: 3 ESQ
**Atty. Gen.**
  1960s ~: 3 RFK
**ATV**
  Part of: 3 ALL
**"At Wit's End"**
  author Bombeck: 4 ERMA
**Au**
  79, for ~ (abbr.): 4 ATNO
  courant: 5 AWARE
  fait: 4 ABLE
  naturel: 4 BARE NUDE
  revoir: 5 ADIEU
**Au ___:** 3 JUS
**Auberge:** 3 INN
**Auberjonois**
  Actor: 4 RENE
**Auburn**
  hair dye: 5 HENNA
**"Au contraire!":** 5 NOTSO
**Auction**
  action: 3 BID NOD 4 BIDS
  amount: 3 LOT
  caveat: 4 ASIS
  cry: 4 SOLD
  ending: 3 EER
  Exceed at an: 6 OUTBID
  Keep an ~ going: 5 REBID
  off: 4 SELL
  offering: 3 ART LOT
  Online ~ site: 4 EBAY
  Try for, at: 5 BIDON
  vehicle, often: 4 REPO
**Auctioneer**
  aid: 5 GAVEL
  cry: 4 GONE SOLD
**Audacity:** 5 NERVE 7 CHUTZPA
**Auden, ___ Hugh:** 6 WYSTAN
**Audi**
  rival: 3 BMW
**Audible**
  range: 7 EARSHOT

  relief: 4 SIGH
  warning: 3 GRR
**Audibly:** 5 ALOUD
  censor: 5 BLEEP
  Cry: 3 SOB
**Audience:** 3 EAR 9 LISTENERS
  Comment to the: 5 ASIDE
  member: 8 ATTENDEE
  shill: 5 PLANT
  Talk before an:
    15 PANELDISCUSSION
  USO: 3 GIS
**Audiences**
  For mature: 6 RATEDR
  Suitable for all: 6 RATEDG
**Audio**
  effect: 4 ECHO
  Match ~ and video: 4 SYNC
  system: 4 HIFI 6 STEREO
  systems, for short: 3 PAS
**Audiophile**
  collection: 3 CDS LPS
  purchase: 4 HIFI
  setup: 6 STEREO
**Audit:** 7 SITINON
  pro: 3 CPA
**Audited:** 7 SATINON
**Auditing**
  ace: 3 CPA
  Fed. ~ agency: 3 GAO
**Audition:** 4 TEST 6 TRYOUT
  (for): 4 READ
  Open: 10 CATTLECALL
  tape: 4 DEMO
**Auditioner**
  goal: 4 ROLE
**Auditor**
  Govt.: 3 GAO IRS
  initials: 3 CPA
**Auditorium:** 4 HALL
**Auditory:** 4 OTIC
  sensor: 3 EAR
**Audrey**
  1964 role for ~: 5 ELIZA
**Audubon**
  Of interest to: 5 AVIAN
**Auel**
  Author: 4 JEAN
  heroine: 4 AYLA
**Auerbach**
  Comic: 5 ARTIE
**Aug.**
  follower: 3 SEP 4 SEPT
  setting: 3 DST
**Auger**
  Use an: 4 BORE
**Augment:** 5 ADDTO
**Augsburg**
  **Info:** German cue
  Alas, in: 3 ACH
  article: 3 EIN
**Augur:** 4 OMEN SEER
    7 PORTEND
**Augury:** 4 OMEN 7 PORTENT
**August:** 5 NOBLE REGAL
    7 EMINENT

  birthstone: 7 PERIDOT
  hrs.: 3 DST
  Like Kansas in: 5 CORNY
  Most ~ babies: 4 LEOS
  person: 3 LEO
**August 13:** 4 IDES
**Augusta**
  11 through 13 at ~:
    10 AMENCORNER
  home: 5 MAINE
**Auguste**
  Painter: 6 RENOIR
  Sculpter: 5 RODIN
**Auld**
  lang syne: 4 YORE
**"Auld Lang ___":** 4 SYNE
**Auld Sod, The:** 4 EIRE ERIN
**Aulin**
  Actress: 3 EWA
**Aunt**
  Broadway: 4 MAME 5 ELLER
  Mayberry: 3 BEE
  ~, in French: 5 TANTE
  ~, in Spanish: 3 TIA
**Aunt Bee**
  charge: 4 OPIE
**"Aunt ___ Cope Book":**
    5 ERMAS
**"Auntie ___":** 4 MAME
**Aunt Jemima**
  rival: 4 EGGO
**Aunt Polly**
  nephew: 3 TOM
**"Au poivre"**
  serving: 5 STEAK
**Aura:** 3 AIR 5 VIBES 6 NIMBUS
    8 MYSTIQUE
  Angelic: 4 HALO
**Auréole**
  wearer: 4 ANGE
**"Au revoir!":** 4 TATA 5 ADIEU
**___ au rhum:** 4 BABA
**Auric**
  creator: 3 IAN
**Auricular:** 4 OTIC
**Auriga**
  Star in: 7 CAPELLA
**Aurora**
  counterpart: 3 EOS
  or Alero: 4 OLDS
**Aurora ___:** 8 BOREALIS
**Aus.**
  neighbor: 3 GER
**Auspices:** 4 EGIS 5 AEGIS
**Auspicious:** 4 RIPE
**Aussie**
  **Info:** Australian cue
  bear: 5 KOALA
  bird: 3 EMU
  bounder: 3 ROO
  buddy: 4 MATE
  Colleges, to an: 4 UNIS
  gems: 5 OPALS
  greeting: 4 GDAY
  Grounded: 3 EMU
  hopper: 3 ROO

lassie: 6 SHEILA
marsupial: 5 KOALA
  6 WOMBAT
outlaw Kelly: 3 NED
runner: 3 EMU
**Austen**
  Author: 4 JANE
  heroine: 4 EMMA
  novel: 4 EMMA
**Austen, Jane**
  novel: 4 EMMA
**Austere:** 5 HARSH STARK
  6 LENTEN 7 SPARTAN
**Austerlitz**
  Dancer born: 7 ASTAIRE
**Austin**
  Actress: 4 TERI
**Australia**
  Bird of: 3 EMU
  Gateway to: 6 SYDNEY
  Island off: 5 TIMOR
  Largest lake in: 4 EYRE
  Water off: 10 BASSSTRAIT
  Woman, in: 6 SHEILA
**Australian**
  bear: 5 KOALA
  bird: 3 EMU
  export: 4 OPAL
  Flightless: 3 EMU
  gem: 4 OPAL
  hard rock band: 4 ACDC
  marsupial: 5 KOALA
  outlaw Kelly: 3 NED
**Australian Open**
  1970 ~ champ: 4 ASHE
  1998 ~ champ: 5 KORDA
  2000 ~ champ: 6 AGASSI
  Four-time ~ champ: 5 SELES
**Austria**
  A as in: 3 EIN
  Alpine region of: 5 TIROL
    TYROL
  article: 3 EIN
  Capital of: 6 VIENNA
  capital, to locals: 4 WIEN
**Austrian**
  composer: 5 ALBAN
    6 MAHLER
  peak: 3 ALP
  psychologist: 5 ADLER
  region: 5 TIROL TYROL
  river: 4 ENNS
**Auteur**
  art: 6 CINEMA
**Auth.**
  unknown: 4 ANON
**Authentic:** 4 REAL TRUE
  5 LEGIT VALID
  7 GENUINE
**Author:** 3 PEN 6 PENNER
  of a 1998 report: 5 STARR
  offerings (abbr.): 3 MSS
  Rags-to-riches: 5 ALGER
  Uncredited: 5 GHOST
  unknown: 4 ANON
  Western: 4 GREY

~ Alexander: 5 SHANA
~ Ayn: 4 RAND
~ Bret: 5 HARTE
~ Eda: 6 LESHAN
~ Ennis: 4 REES
~ Frederik: 4 POHL
~ Hermann: 5 HESSE
~ James: 4 AGEE
~ John Dickson ___: 4 CARR
~ John Dos ___: 6 PASSOS
~ Josephine: 3 TEY
~ Joyce Carol: 5 OATES
~ Leonard: 6 ELMORE
~ Martin: 4 AMIS
~ Roald: 4 DAHL
~ Rona: 5 JAFFE
~ Scott: 5 ODELL
~ Umberto: 3 ECO
**"Author! Author!"**
  actress: 10 DYANCANNON
  star: 8 ALPACINO
**Authoritative**
  decree: 4 FIAT
  doctrine: 5 DOGMA
  order: 7 MANDATE
  source: 5 BIBLE
**Authority:** 5 POWER SAYSO
  6 PUNDIT
  Defy: 5 REBEL
  Final: 5 SAYSO
  Level of: 7 ECHELON
  Mil.: 3 CMD
  On the ~ of: 3 PER
  Position of: 5 CHAIR
  Quote an: 4 CITE
  Symbol of: 4 MACE ROBE
    5 BADGE 6 MANTLE
  Wield, as: 5 EXERT
**Authorize:** 3 LET 4 OKAY
  7 EMPOWER ENTITLE
**Authorizes:** 3 OKS
**"Author unknown":** 4 ANON
**Auto:** 3 CAR
  1950s ~: 5 EDSEL
  additive: 3 STP
  Antique: 3 REO
  Autobahn: 3 BMW 4 AUDI
    OPEL
  buyer's bargain: 4 DEMO
  Bygone ~ ornament: 3 FIN
  Classic: 3 REO
  club offering: 3 MAP TOW
  damage: 5 DENTS
  European: 4 OPEL YUGO
  Family: 5 SEDAN
  financing co.: 3 GMC
  Former ~ mfr.: 3 AMC
  frontpiece: 6 GRILLE
  fuel: 3 GAS
  German: 4 AUDI OPEL
  graph: 3 MAP
  Imported: 3 KIA 4 AUDI SAAB
  inflatable: 6 AIRBAG
  Italian: 4 ALFA FIAT
  Like ~ shop floors: 4 OILY
  loan letters: 3 APR

make: 4 MERC
making a comeback: 4 REPO
manufacturer woe: 6 RECALL
mechanic tool: 9 GREASEGUN
option: 3 AIR 5 ALARM
part: 3 CAM 4 CARB 6 GASCAP
parts brand: 4 NAPA
pioneer: 4 BENZ OLDS
race: 4 INDY 6 LEMANS
reversal: 3 UEY
Sad-sounding: 4 SAAB
safety device: 6 AIRBAG
  7 ROLLBAR
selection: 5 SEDAN
steering system link: 6 TIEROD
style: 5 SEDAN
suffix: 4 CRAT
Swedish: 4 SAAB
trim: 6 CHROME
Vintage: 3 REO 5 ESSEX
**Autobahn**
  auto: 3 BMW 4 AUDI OPEL
**Autobio**
  Turner: 5 ITINA
**Autobiographer**
  ~ Bobby: 5 SEALE
**Autobiography:** 6 MEMOIR
  7 MEMOIRS
  Moss Hart: 6 ACTONE
  Sammy Davis Jr.: 7 YESICAN
**Auto-correcting**
  device: 5 SERVO
**Autocrat:** 4 CZAR TSAR
  6 DESPOT
**Auto financing**
  abbr.: 3 APR
**Autograph:** 4 SIGN
**Auto grille**
  covering: 3 BRA
**Automaker**
  9000 ~: 4 SAAB
  Early: 4 OLDS 6 DURYEA
  German: 4 AUDI OPEL
  Japanese: 5 ACURA
  ~ Citroën: 5 ANDRE
  ~ Ferrari: 4 ENZO
  ~ Maserati: 7 ERNESTO
**Automat:** 6 EATERY
**Automatic:** 4 ROTE
  pistol: 7 BURPGUN
  prefix: 4 SEMI
**Automaton:** 5 GOLEM ROBOT
  7 ANDROID
  play: 3 RUR
  ~, briefly: 3 BOT 5 DROID
**Automne**
  preceder: 3 ETE
**Automobile**
  pioneer: 4 OLDS
  sticker fig.: 3 MPG
**Auto racer**
  ~ Al: 5 UNSER
  ~ Bobby: 5 UNSER
    7 ALLISON
  ~ Fabi: 3 TEO
  ~ Luyendyk: 4 ARIE

**Autostrada**
auto: 4 ALFA FIAT
**Autry**
pic: 5 OATER
**Autumn:** 4 FALL
apple: 6 RUSSET 7 WINESAP
birthstone: 4 OPAL
bloomer: 5 ASTER
color: 5 OCHER OCHRE
drink: 5 CIDER
mo.: 3 NOV OCT
pear: 4 BOSC
Sign of: 5 FROST
toiler: 5 RAKER
"___ Autumn": 3 TIS
**Autumnal equinox**
mo.: 3 SEP
**"Autumn Sonata"**
actress Ullmann: 3 LIV
___ au vin: 3 COQ
**Auxiliary:** 3 AID 4 AIDE
action: 7 SIDEBET
proposition: 5 LEMMA
track: 4 SPUR
verb: 3 ARE
WWII: 4 WACS
**Av**
Month after: 4 ELUL
**A/V**
Part of: 5 AUDIO
**Ava**
Ex of: 5 ARTIE
"___ a vacation!": 5 INEED
**Avail**
oneself of: 3 USE
To no: 6 FUTILE INVAIN
7 USELESS
___ avail: 4 TONO
**Available:** 3 OUT 4 OPEN
5 ONTAP 6 ATHAND
ONCALL ONHAND
UNUSED 7 FORHIRE
for rent: 5 TOLET 6 VACANT
for work: 6 ONCALL
from the publisher: 7 INPRINT
Make: 6 FREEUP
No longer: 4 SOLD 5 TAKEN
Not: 5 INUSE 6 TIEDUP
Readily: 5 ONTAP 6 ONCALL
ONHAND
**Avalanche:** 5 SPATE
**Avalon:** 4 ISLE
**Avalon, Frankie**
hit: 4 DEDE
**Avant-___:** 5 GARDE
**Avant-garde**
artist: 3 ARP
**Avarice:** 5 GREED
**"Avast!"**
responder: 4 SWAB
**Avatar**
of Vishnu: 4 RAMA
**Ave.**
crossers: 3 RDS STS
**"Ave Maria"**
Opera with: 6 OTELLO

**"Avengers, The"**
actor Patrick: 6 MACNEE
actress Diana: 4 RIGG
actress Rigg: 5 DIANA
actress Thurman: 3 UMA
character Emma: 4 PEEL
Emma player in: 3 UMA
guy: 5 STEED
Mrs. Peel of: 4 EMMA
**Avenging**
spirits: 6 FURIES
**Avenue**
crosser: 6 STREET
liners: 4 ELMS
Monopoly: 8 ORIENTAL
that changes into Amsterdam
Avenue: 5 TENTH
**Average:** 3 CEE PAR 4 MEAN
NORM SOSO
Better than: 8 ABOVEPAR
grade: 3 CEE
guy: 3 JOE 4 NORM
Just above: 5 CPLUS
name: 3 DOE DOW
producer: 8 DOWJONES
They ~ 100: 3 IQS
**Averred:** 4 SAID 6 STATED
**Averse:** 5 LOATH
to exertion: 4 LAZY
**Aversion:** 5 ODIUM
8 DISTASTE
Cry of: 3 UGH
**Avert**
~, with "off": 4 WARD
**Avery**
Animator: 3 TEX
**Aves.:** 3 STS
**Avg.:** 3 PCT REG STD
**Avian**
chatterbox: 5 MYNAH
food holder: 4 CRAW
home: 4 NEST
mimic: 4 MYNA
wader: 5 STILT
~ Australians: 4 EMUS
**Aviary:** 4 CAGE
abode: 4 NEST
sound: 3 CAW 5 CHEEP
TWEET
**Aviate:** 3 FLY
**Aviation**
First name in: 6 AMELIA
pioneer Clyde: 6 CESSNA
pioneer Post: 5 WILEY
pioneer Sikorsky: 4 IGOR
prefix: 3 AER 4 AERO
**Aviator:** 5 FLIER
Dance named for an: 5 LINDY
Famed: 8 REDBARON
~ Balbo: 5 ITALO
~ Earhart: 6 AMELIA
~ Post: 5 WILEY
**Aviators**
in tabloids: 3 ETS
**Aviatrix**
~ Earhart: 6 AMELIA

**Avid:** 4 KEEN 5 EAGER
6 GUNGHO RAHRAH
**Avignon**
**Info:** French cue
aunt: 5 TANTE
River of: 5 RHONE
**Avis**
adjective: 4 RARA
Eventual: 4 OVUM
pair: 4 ALAE
Rara: 4 ONER
rival: 5 ALAMO HERTZ
___ avis: 4 RARA
___ Aviv: 3 TEL
___ Avivian: 3 TEL
**Avocation:** 3 BAG
**Avoid:** 4 SHUN 5 ELUDE SKIRT
6 ESCHEW
a big wedding: 5 ELOPE
a trial: 6 SETTLE
Didn't: 5 FACED
doing: 5 EVADE
humiliation: 8 SAVEFACE
Publicly: 4 SHUN
responsibility:
11 PASSTHEBUCK
Something to: 4 NONO
5 TABOO
Try to ~ a tag: 5 SLIDE
Want to: 5 DREAD
**Avoirdupois**
alternative: 4 TROY
**Avon**
First Earl of: 4 EDEN
**Avowal**
Altar: 3 IDO
**Avril**
follower: 3 MAI
**"Aw, ___!":** 6 SHUCKS
**Await**
judgment: 4 PEND
**Awaiting:** 5 INFOR 7 INSTORE
service: 6 INLINE
**Awake**
Wide: 5 ALERT
**"Awake and Sing!"**
playwright: 5 ODETS
**Awaken:** 4 STIR 5 GETUP
ROUSE 6 AROUSE
COMETO
rudely: 5 ROUST
**Awakening:** 7 AROUSAL
Cause of a rude: 5 SNORE
**Awaker:** 5 ALARM
**"A waking dream": Aristotle:**
4 HOPE
**Award:** 5 PRIZE
Advertising: 4 CLIO
Athletic: 5 MEDAL 6 LETTER
bestowed by a queen: 3 OBE
Broadway: 4 TONY
Cable sports: 4 ESPY
Drama: 4 OBIE
Film: 5 OSCAR
French film: 5 CESAR
given by Chris Berman: 4 ESPY

given by The Village Voice:
4 OBIE
Mystery writer: 5 EDGAR
Off-Broadway: 4 OBIE
Olympic: 5 MEDAL
recipient: 7 HONOREE
Romance novelist: 4 RITA
Science fiction: 4 HUGO
since 1956: 4 OBIE
Sports: 4 ESPY
Television: 4 EMMY
Theater: 4 OBIE TONY
TV: 4 EMMY
U.K.: 3 OBE
**Aware**
Be ~ of: 4 KNOW
Become ~ of: 5 LEARN SENSE
Fully ~ of: 4 ONTO
Make: 5 CUEIN 6 CLUEIN
of: 4 INON ONTO UPON
5 HEPTO HIPTO
6 WISETO
Was ~ of: 4 KNEW
~, with "in": 5 CLUED
**Away:** 3 OFF OUT 5 ASIDE
NOTIN 6 ABSENT
7 NOTHOME ONLEAVE
A ways: 4 AFAR
Do ~ with: 3 OFF RID 4 OMIT
5 ERASE 7 ABOLISH
from land: 4 ASEA
from the bow: 3 AFT
6 ASTERN
from the mouth: 6 ABORAL
from the wind: 4 ALEE
Get: 3 LAM 4 EXIT SLIP
6 ESCAPE
Get ~ from: 5 ELUDE EVADE
6 ESCAPE
Go: 5 LEAVE 6 DEPART
VACATE
Not: 6 ATHOME
Partner of: 3 FAR
They got: 7 EVADERS
**Awe:** 3 WOW 5 AMAZE
In: 4 AGOG 5 AGAPE

Regard with: 8 VENERATE
Sound of: 3 OOH
**Aweather**
Opposite of: 4 ALEE
**"Awesome!":** 3 OOH RAD
**Awestruck:** 4 AGOG RAPT
5 AGAPE
one: 5 GAPER
**Awful:** 3 BAD 4 DIRE
7 THEPITS
Feel: 3 AIL
smell: 5 FETOR
tasting: 4 VILE
Was: 5 STANK
**"Aw, gee!":** 4 DARN
**Awkward:** 5 GOONY 6 GANGLY
It can put one in an ~ position:
4 YOGA
situation: 12 STICKYWICKET
**Awl:** 4 TOOL
**Awoke:** 5 GOTUP 6 CAMETO
**AWOL**
chasers: 3 MPS
Part of: 5 LEAVE 6 ABSENT
student: 6 TRUANT
**"Awright!":** 4 YEAH
**Awry:** 3 OFF 5 AMISS ASKEW
Go: 3 ERR
Seriously ~ scheme: 5 SNAFU
**Ax:** 3 CAN HEW 4 FIRE SACK
5 LETGO
Given the ~, with "off": 4 LAID
Give the: 3 CAN 4 FIRE SACK
5 LETGO
One with an ~ to grind:
5 HONER
relative: 3 ADZ
to grind: 6 AGENDA
wielder: 5 HEWER
**Axed:** 4 HEWN
**Axel:** 4 LEAP
Do an: 5 SKATE
**Axes**
Standard: 5 XANDY
**Axis**
foes: 6 ALLIES

leader: 4 TOJO
Turn on an: 4 SLUE 6 ROTATE
**Axis of ___:** 4 EVIL
**Axle:** 3 BAR
end: 3 HUB
holder: 5 UBOLT
**Axlike**
tool: 3 ADZ 4 ADZE
**Axton**
Country singer: 4 HOYT
**Ayatollah:** 4 IMAM
land: 4 IRAN
predecessor: 4 SHAH
**Ayckbourn**
Playwright: 4 ALAN
**Aye**
Apt anagram for: 3 YEA
opposite: 3 NAY
sayer: 3 PRO
**Ayes**
Spanish: 3 SIS 4 SISI
**Aykroyd**
Actor: 3 DAN
**Ayn**
Author: 4 RAND
**Ayres**
Actor: 3 LEW
**Azalea:** 5 HEATH
**Azer.**
~, once: 3 SSR
**Azerbaijan**
Capital of: 4 BAKU
~, once (abbr.): 3 SSR
**Azerbaijani**
neighbor: 5 IRANI
**Azores**
loc.: 3 ATL
**Azov**
On the: 4 ASEA
**AZT**
approver: 3 FDA
**Azure:** 4 BLUE 5 SKYEY
**Azzo, Alberto**
family name: 4 ESTE

# Bb

**B:** 3 KEY 4 TYPE 6 LETTER
  followers: 3 CDE
  in chemistry: 5 BORON
**B-2**
  letters: 4 USAF
**B-29**
  Name on a famous: 5 ENOLA
**B-52**
  home: 3 AFB
**B.A.**
  Part of: 4 ARTS
**Baa:** 5 BLEAT
  maid: 3 EWE
**Baal:** 4 IDOL
**Baba**
  Fabled woodcutter: 3 ALI
  ingredient: 3 RUM
**Baba ___ (Radner role):** 4 WAWA
  **___ Baba:** 3 ALI
**Babar**
  Wife of: 7 CELESTE
**Babble:** 5 PRATE RUNON
      7 PRATTLE
**Babe**
  Beasts like: 4 OXEN
  Family of: 5 RUTHS
  in the stable: 4 FOAL
  in the woods: 4 FAWN NAIF
**"Babe"**
  band: 4 STYX
  character Maa: 3 EWE
  Home for filmdom's: 3 STY
  in films: 3 PIG
**Babel:** 3 DIN
  building: 5 TOWER
**Babilonia**
  Skater: 3 TAI
**Babka**
  flavoring: 3 RUM
**Babushka:** 5 SCARF
**Baby:** 6 COSSET PAMPER
  bed: 4 CRIB
  bird: 5 OWLET STORK
      6 EAGLET
  bloomer: 3 BUD
  blues: 4 EYES 7 PEEPERS
  bouncer: 4 KNEE
  buggy: 4 PRAM
  carrier: 4 WOMB
  Cry like a: 4 MEWL
  food: 3 PAP
  goat: 3 KID
  grand: 5 PIANO
  in blue: 3 BOY
  powder: 4 TALC
  seal: 3 PUP
  seat: 3 LAP
  specialist: 7 DRSPOCK

  whale: 4 CALF
  word: 3 GOO 4 DADA MAMA
**"Baby Baby"**
  singer: 8 AMYGRANT
**Baby-faced:** 4 CUTE
**Babylonian**
  goddess: 6 ISHTAR
**Babysit:** 4 MIND TEND
**Babysitter:** 4 NANA
  bane: 3 IMP 4 BRAT
**Bacall**
  mate, familiarly: 5 BOGIE
**Baccarat**
  alternative: 4 FARO
  Best ~ hand: 4 NINE
  call: 5 BANCO
**Bacchanal:** 4 ORGY
**Bacchanalian**
  bash: 4 ORGY
**Bacchus**
  attendant: 5 SATYR
**Bach**
  contemporary: 6 HANDEL
  instrument: 5 ORGAN
  piece: 5 SUITE 7 CANTATA
      CHORALE TOCCATA
**Bacharach**
  Songwriter: 4 BURT
**Bachelor**
  home: 3 PAD
  Last words of a: 3 IDO
  pads, maybe: 5 STIES
  party: 4 STAG
  suffix: 4 ETTE
**"Bachelor Father"**
  actress Corcoran: 6 NOREEN
**Bachman**
  Singer: 3 TAL
**Bacillus**
  shape: 3 ROD
**Back:** 3 AGO FRO 4 HIND REAR
      5 STERN 7 ENDORSE
  Info: Suffix cue
  again: 3 FRO
  at sea: 3 AFT
  at the track: 5 BETON
  biter: 5 MOLAR
  bones: 5 SACRA
  Book: 5 SPINE
  Bounce: 4 ECHO
  Bring: 6 REVIVE 7 RESTORE
  Buy: 6 REDEEM
  Chair: 5 SPLAT
  Come: 4 ECHO 5 RECUR
  Come ~ again: 6 REECHO
  Cut: 4 PARE 5 PRUNE
  door: 7 POSTERN
  Draw: 6 RECEDE

  Drew: 5 SHIED
  Drive: 5 REPEL 7 REPULSE
  Drop: 3 LAG
  Fall: 3 EBB LAG 6 REVERT
      7 RELAPSE
  Far: 7 AGESAGO LONGAGO
  Flow: 3 EBB
  Force: 5 REPEL
  From way: 5 OFOLD
  Get: 6 RECOUP REGAIN
  Get ~ at: 5 SPITE
  Get ~ for: 6 AVENGE
  Give: 5 REPAY 7 RESTORE
  Go: 3 EBB 6 RETURN
      REVERT 7 REGRESS
  Go ~ over: 7 RETRACE
  Hang: 3 LAG 5 TARRY
  Hold: 4 STEM 6 IMPEDE
      RETARD
  in: 5 RETRO
  in time: 3 AGO
  Kick: 4 LOAF REST
  Let ~ in: 7 READMIT
  Lying on one's: 6 SUPINE
  muscle: 3 LAT
  of a boat: 5 STERN
  of the neck: 4 NAPE
  out: 6 RENEGE
  Pay: 3 OLA 6 AVENGE
  Put: 4 STET 5 RESET
      7 RESTORE
  Quarter: 5 EAGLE
  Send: 4 ECHO 6 REMAND
  Set: 7 SCENERY
  Slip: 7 RELAPSE
  Spring: 6 RECOIL
  street: 5 ALLEY
  Strike: 5 REACT
  Take: 4 UNDO 6 RECANT
  talk: 3 LIP 4 ECHO GUFF
      SASS 6 STATIC
  Talk ~ to: 4 SASS
  then: 4 ONCE
  tooth: 5 MOLAR
  Toward the: 5 AREAR
  Turn: 5 REPEL 6 REVERT
  Way ~ when: 4 ONCE
      7 AGESAGO LONGAGO
**Backbone:** 5 SPINE
  of a ship: 4 KEEL
**Backbreaker**
  Proverbial: 5 STRAW
**"Backdraft"**
  crime: 5 ARSON
**Backdrop:** 5 SCENE
  Theatrical: 5 SCRIM
**Backfire:** 9 BOOMERANG
  sound: 4 BANG

**Backgammom**
impossibility: 3 TIE
need: 4 DICE
piece: 5 STONE
**"Back in Black"**
band: 4 ACDC
**"Back in the ___": 4 USSR**
**Backless**
couch: 5 DIVAN
divan: 7 OTTOMAN
**Backpacker:** 5 HIKER
**Backrub:** 7 MASSAGE
response: 3 AAH
**Backs:** 5 DORSA
**Backside:** 4 DUFF REAR
**Backslide:** 7 REGRESS
RELAPSE
**Backstabber:** 3 RAT
Comment to a: 4 ETTU
**Backstreet Boys**
fan, usually: 4 TEEN
rivals: 5 NSYNC
**Backtalk:** 3 LIP 4 ECHO SASS
**Backup:** 4 COPY
procedure: 5 PLANB
**Backward:** 5 AREAR 6 ASTERN
**Backwash**
creator: 3 OAR
**Backwater**
Kind of: 5 BAYOU
**Backyard**
building: 4 SHED
8 TOOLSHED
**Baclanova**
Actress. 4 OLGA
**Bacon:** 6 AUTHOR
Actor: 5 KEVIN
bit: 5 ESSAY
Bring home the: 4 EARN
partner: 4 EGGS
piece: 5 ESSAY
portion: 4 SLAB 5 STRIP
serving: 6 RASHER
**Bacteria:** 5 GERMS
Dangerous: 5 ECOLI
prefix: 6 ENTERO
Spherical: 5 COCCI
**Bacterium:** 4 GERM
Dangerous: 5 ECOLI
Kind of: 6 AEROBE
**Bad:** 4 EVIL
atmosphere: 6 MIASMA
behavior: 3 SIN
blood: 6 ANIMUS
cut: 4 GASH
dog: 5 BITER
end: 4 DOOM
Feel: 3 AIL
Feel ~ about: 3 RUE
Go: 3 ROT 4 TURN 5 SPOIL
Gone: 6 SPOILT
habit: 4 VICE
impression: 4 DENT
In a ~ way: 4 ILLY 6 EVILLY
lighting: 5 ARSON
look: 4 LEER 5 SNEER

mark: 3 DEE ZIT 4 SCAR
6 STIGMA 7 DEMERIT
marks: 4 ACNE
mood: 4 SNIT
Not: 4 SOSO
points: 4 CONS
prefix: 3 DYS MAL 4 CACO
reception: 4 HISS
review: 3 PAN
Smell: 4 REEK
spell: 3 HEX
start: 3 DYS MAL
temper: 3 IRE
throw: 5 ERROR
Too: 4 ALAS
to the bone: 4 EVIL
treatment: 5 ABUSE
Very: 5 AWFUL 7 ABYSMAL
**"Bad, Bad Leroy Brown"**
singer: 5 CROCE
**"Bad Behavior"**
actor: 3 REA
**"Bad Boys"**
actor Morales: 4 ESAI
**Baddie**
Barrie: 4 SMEE
Bond: 4 DRNO
Fairy tale: 4 OGRE
Shakespeare: 4 IAGO
**Bad Ems:** 3 SPA
**Baden-Baden:** 3 SPA
**Badge**
holder: 4 SASH
Kind of: 5 MERIT
material: 3 TIN
Sheriff's: 4 STAR 7 TINSTAR
**Badger:** 3 NAG 6 HARASS
PESTER
group: 4 CETE
Honey: 5 RATEL
**Badges**
with names: 6 IDTAGS
**Badlands**
sights: 5 MESAS
state (abbr.): 4 SDAK
**Badminton**
need: 3 NET
11 SHUTTLECOCK
**Bad-mouth:** 3 DIS 6 MALIGN
REVILE
**Baer**
Boxer: 3 MAX
**Baez**
Folk singer: 4 JOAN
**Baffin Bay**
sight: 4 BERG FLOE
**Baffle:** 5 STUMP
**Baffled:** 5 ATSEA 7 ATALOSS
**Bag:** 3 NAB SAC 5 SNARE
6 VALISE
Freezer: 6 ZIPLOC
It's in the: 3 TEA
Kind of: 4 GRAB TOTE
Mixed: 4 OLIO
**Bagatelle:** 6 TRIFLE
___ **bagatelle:** 5 AMERE

**Bagel**
alternative: 4 ROLL
flavoring: 6 SESAME
9 POPPYSEED
topper: 3 LOX 4 NOVA
variety: 5 PLAIN 6 SESAME
**Baggage**
handler: 6 PORTER REDCAP
**Baggy:** 5 LOOSE
**Baghdad**
country: 4 IRAQ
native: 5 IRAQI
river: 6 TIGRIS
**Baglike**
structure: 3 SAC
**Bagnold**
Author: 4 ENID
**Bagpipe**
part: 5 DRONE
sound: 5 DRONE
**Bagpiper**
garment: 4 KILT
wear: 6 TARTAN
**Baguette:** 3 GEM 4 ROLL
**Bah:** 3 FIE
___ **Bah:** 4 POOH
**Baha'i**
birthplace: 4 IRAN
**Bahamas**
capital: 6 NASSAU
**Bahrain**
bigwig: 4 EMIR 5 AMEER
native: 4 ARAB
**Baht**
spender: 4 THAI
**Bailey**
bailiwick: 3 LAW
partner: 6 BARNUM
Singer: 5 PEARL
**Bailey, F. ___**
Attorney: 3 LEE
**Bailiff**
bellow: 4 OYEZ
command: 4 RISE 7 ALLRISE
execution: 4 WRIT
Reply to a: 3 IDO
**Bailiwick:** 4 AREA TURF
6 SPHERE
DDE: 3 ETO
Reporter's: 4 BEAT
**Bailout**
button: 5 EJECT
PC: 3 ESC
**Baird**
Attorney General nominee:
3 ZOE
Puppeteer: 3 BIL
**Bairn**
Like a: 3 SMA WEE
**Bait:** 4 LURE 5 TEASE
TEMPT
Artificial: 4 LURE
buyer: 6 ANGLER
Drop ~ lightly: 3 DAP
Fish: 4 CHUM WORM
Take the: 4 BITE

**Baiul**
Ice skater: 6 OKSANA
**Baja**
Info: Spanish cue
bear: 3 OSO
buck: 4 PESO
capital: 8 MEXICALI
cheer: 3 OLE
Opposite of: 4 ALTA
port: 8 ENSENADA
**Bake**
eggs: 5 SHIRR
sale org.: 3 PTA
**Baked**
alternative: 6 MASHED
dessert: 6 ALASKA
~, in Bologna: 5 COTTA
**Baked in ___:** 4 APIE
**Bake-off**
appliance: 4 OVEN
**Baker**
Brick: 4 KILN
Corporate: 7 SARALEE
dozen: 4 EGGS
implement: 4 PEEL
Jazz trumpeter: 4 CHET
need: 4 OVEN 5 YEAST
quantity: 5 BATCH
Singer: 5 ANITA
**___-Baker, Mark**
Actor: 4 LINN
**Bakersfield**
neighbor: 6 DELANO
**Bakery**
call: 4 NEXT
emanation: 5 AROMA
employee: 4 ICER
enticement: 5 AROMA
fixture: 4 OVEN
need: 5 YEAST
purchase: 4 LOAF
treat: 4 TART 5 SCONE
6 ECLAIR
worker: 4 ICER
**Baking**
chamber: 4 OVEN
follower: 4 SODA
ingredient: 5 YEAST
Lee of: 4 SARA
pan: 3 TIN
soda target: 4 ODOR
**Bakker, Jim**
former org.: 3 PTL
**Balaam**
beast: 3 ASS
**"Balalaika"**
actress Massey: 5 ILONA
**Balance:** 4 REST 6 SANITY
STASIS
Card: 4 DEBT
Fight for: 6 TEETER
Hanging in the: 7 ATSTAKE
Hang in the: 4 PEND
Have a: 3 OWE
Lose one's: 5 SPEND
part: 3 PAN

provider: 3 ATM
sheet item: 5 ASSET
sign: 5 LIBRA
**Balanced:** 4 EVEN SANE
**Balancing**
pro: 3 CPA
**Balbo**
Aviator: 5 ITALO
**Balboa**
Explorer: 5 VASCO
Mrs. Rocky: 6 ADRIAN
Where to spend a: 6 PANAMA
**Balbriggan**
Sight from: 8 IRISHSEA
**Balcony**
barrier: 7 PARAPET
Play to the: 5 EMOTE
7 OVERACT
section: 4 LOGE
**"Balcony, The"**
playwright Jean: 5 GENET
**Bald**
It's ~, possibly: 4 PATE
Loss at a ~ spot: 5 TREAD
spot cover: 3 SOD
**Balder**
Father of: 4 ODIN
**Balderdash:** 3 ROT 4 HOKE
5 HOKUM PSHAW
7 EYEWASH
8 NONSENSE
**Baldness:** 8 ALOPECIA
**Baldwin**
Actor: 4 ADAM ALEC
**Bale**
binder: 4 WIRE 5 TWINE
contents: 3 HAY
**Balearic Islands**
One of the: 5 IBIZA
7 MAJORCA MINORCA
**"Bali ___":** 3 HAI
**Balin**
Actress: 3 INA
**Balkan**
capital: 5 SOFIA 6 TIRANA
native: 4 SERB SLAV 5 CROAT
**Ball:** 3 ORB 4 GALA 6 SPHERE
Bobble the: 3 ERR
Cheese: 4 EDAM
costar: 5 VANCE
Drop the: 3 ERR
game: 5 BOCCE LOTTO
girl: 3 DEB 5 BELLE
Great ~ of fire: 3 SUN 4 STAR
Hand: 4 FIST
High: 3 LOB
holder: 3 TEE
"i" ~: 3 DOT
mate: 5 ARNAZ
of yarn: 4 CLEW
On the: 5 ALERT
Soft ~ material: 4 NERF
suffix: 3 OON
**Ball, Lucille:** 7 REDHEAD
**Ballad:** 3 LAY
suffix: 3 EER

**Ballade**
ending: 5 ENVOI
**Balladeer**
aid: 4 LUTE
**"Ballad of Jed Clampett, The"**
Oil, in: 8 TEXASTEA
**"Ballad of John and ___, The":**
4 YOKO
**"Ballad of Reading ___, The":**
4 GAOL
**Ballantine**
brew: 3 ALE
Publisher: 3 IAN
**Ballerina**
exercise: 4 PLIE
perch: 3 TOE
Prima: 6 ETOILE
skirt: 4 TUTU
support: 5 BARRE
Word before: 5 PRIMA
**Ballesteros**
Golfer: 4 SEVE
**Ballet:** 5 DANCE
bend: 4 PLIE
Copland: 5 RODEO
leap: 4 JETE
rail: 5 BARRE
Russian ~ company: 5 KIROV
skirt: 4 TUTU
slipper: 7 TOESHOE
step: 3 PAS
Stravinsky: 4 AGON
Stravinsky ~ character:
4 SWAN
**Ballet ___:** 5 RUSSE
**"Ballet Rehearsal"**
artist: 5 DEGAS
**Ballfield**
cover: 4 TARP
**Ballistic**
Go: 4 RAGE RAVE 6 LOSEIT
SEERED
**Ballmer, Steve:** 3 CEO
**Balloon:** 5 BLOAT SWELL
8 AEROSTAT
Bust, like a: 3 POP
filler: 3 AIR 5 WATER
6 HOTAIR
Trial: 6 FEELER
Water ~ sound: 5 SPLAT
**Ballot:** 4 VOTE
Cast a: 4 VOTE
Defeat by: 7 OUTVOTE
Marked, as a: 4 XED
marks: 3 XES 4 EXES
Paper ~ part: 4 CHAD
**Ballpark**
Big Apple: 4 SHEA
Bite at the: 5 FRANK
figure: 4 RBIS STAT
8 ESTIMATE
figure (abbr.): 3 EST
figure follower: 4 ORSO
instrument: 5 ORGAN
level: 4 TIER
official: 3 UMP

**Ballpoint:** 3 PEN
  brand: 3 BIC
**Ballroom**
  beat: 5 SAMBA
  Castle of the: 5 IRENE
  dance: 5 MAMBO TANGO
    6 CHACHA 7 ONESTEP
    TWOSTEP
  dance, when doubled: 3 CHA
  One of a ~ couple: 4 LEAD
**Ball-shaped:** 7 SPHERIC
  cheese: 4 EDAM
**Ballyhoo:** 4 HYPE 6 HOOPLA
    7 PROMOTE
**Balm:** 5 SALVE
  Apply ~ to: 6 SOOTHE
  Burn: 4 ALOE
  ingredient: 4 ALOE
  target: 3 LIP
**Balmoral:** 3 CAP
  relative: 3 TAM
**Balmoral Castle**
  river: 3 DEE
**Balmy:** 4 WARM
**Baloney:** 3 ROT 4 JIVE LIES
    5 TRIPE 7 EYEWASH
    HOGWASH 8 NONSENSE
  Bit of: 3 FIB
  Brit's: 4 TOSH
**Balsa:** 4 TREE
  vessel: 4 RAFT
**Balsam:** 3 FIR 4 TREE
**Baltic**
  capital: 4 RIGA
  native: 4 LETT
  One of the ~ States: 6 LATVIA
    7 ESTONIA
  On the: 4 ASEA
  republic: 7 ESTONIA
  River to the: 4 ODER
**Baltic Sea**
  feeder: 4 ODER
**Baltimore**
  athlete: 5 RAVEN 6 ORIOLE
  bird: 6 ORIOLE
  paper: 3 SUN
**"___ Baltimore, The":** 4 HOTL
**Balzac**
  character: 10 PEREGORIOT
  character Père: 6 GORIOT
**Bamako**
  is its capital: 4 MALI
**Bambi:** 4 DEER FAWN
  aunt: 3 ENA
  Father of: 4 STAG
  kin: 4 DEER
  Mother of: 3 DOE
**Bambino:** 3 TOT 4 TYKE
  of baseball: 4 RUTH
  watcher: 5 MAMMA
**Bamboo**
  eater: 5 PANDA
  swordplay: 5 KENDO
**Bamboozle:** 3 CON 4 FOOL
    SNOW 6 TAKEIN
**Ban:** 6 OUTLAW

  rival: 5 ARRID
  site: 6 ARMPIT
  target: 4 ODOR
**Banana**
  oil, for one: 5 ESTER
  relative: 8 PLANTAIN
  skin: 4 PEEL
  Top: 4 STAR
**Bananas:** 4 LOCO 5 CRAZY
  Go: 4 RAVE
  Go ~ over: 5 EATUP
**"Bananas"**
  director: 5 ALLEN
  star: 3 RAE
**Bancroft**
  Actress: 4 ANNE
**Band:** 4 GANG 5 COMBO
    STRAP 6 STRIPE
    8 ENSEMBLE
  aid: 3 AMP
  aide: 6 ROADIE
  Booking for a: 3 GIG
  Bride's: 4 RING
  command: 5 HITIT
  Decorative: 6 ARMLET
  Eight-man: 5 OCTET
  follower: 3 AID
  Heraldic: 4 ORLE
  instrument: 3 SAX 4 FIFE
    OBOE TUBA
  Kind of: 6 ONEMAN
  Palindromic: 4 ABBA
  Sheriff's: 5 POSSE
  Small: 4 TRIO 5 COMBO
  together: 5 UNITE
  TV: 3 UHF VHF
**Bandage:** 6 SWATHE
    7 SWADDLE
  brand: 3 ACE
**Band-aid**
  rival: 5 CURAD
  site: 3 CUT 4 GASH
**B&B:** 3 INN 5 BETAS
  Part of: 3 BED
**Banded**
  quartz: 4 ONYX
  rock: 6 GNEISS
  stone: 5 AGATE
**Banderas**
  Actor: 7 ANTONIO
  role: 5 ZORRO
**Banderillero**
  Cheer for a: 3 OLE
  target: 6 ELTORO
**Bandit**
  Hun-armed: 6 ATTILA
  One-armed: 4 SLOT
  Title ~ of opera: 6 ERNANI
**Bando**
  of baseball: 3 SAL
**B&O**
  Part of: 4 OHIO
  stop: 3 STA
  ~, et al.: 3 RRS
**"Band of Gold"**
  singer Payne: 5 FREDA

**Bandstand**
  box: 3 AMP
**Bandy:** 4 SWAP
  words: 4 SPAR 5 ARGUE
**Bang**
  Big ~ producer: 3 TNT
    5 NITRO
  shut: 4 SLAM
  up: 5 SMASH
**Banger:** 7 SAUSAGE
**Bangkok**
  bread: 4 BAHT
  money: 4 BAHT
  native: 4 THAI
**Bangladesh**
  capital: 5 DACCA
**Bangor**
  state: 5 MAINE
  Town near: 5 ORONO
**Banish:** 5 EXILE
**Banished:** 6 EXILED 7 INEXILE
  person: 5 EXILE 7 EVICTEE
**Banister:** 4 RAIL 7 RAILING
  post: 5 NEWEL
  Rode the: 4 SLID
**Banjo**
  perch: 4 KNEE
  Play a: 5 STRUM
  sound: 5 TWANG
**Banjoist**
  ~ Fleck: 4 BELA
  ~ Scruggs: 4 EARL
**Bank:** 4 RELY TIER 5 CAROM
    LEVEE 6 LIENOR
  acct. entry: 3 INT
  addition: 8 INTEREST
  claim: 4 LIEN
  customer: 5 SAVER
  deposit: 3 ORE 4 SILT SNOW
  device (abbr.): 3 ATM
  employee: 6 TELLER
  fixture: 4 SAFE
  holding: 4 LIEN
  holding (abbr.): 4 MTGE
  job: 5 HEIST
  offering: 3 IRA 4 LOAN
    7 CARLOAN
  of France: 4 RIVE
  (on): 4 RELY
  posting: 4 RATE
  Put in the: 4 SAVE 5 SAVED
  regulating gp.: 4 FDIC
  sign number: 6 CDRATE
  takeback: 4 REPO
**Bankbook**
  entry (abbr.): 3 DEP INT
**Bankhead**
  Actress: 8 TALLULAH
**Banking**
  British ~ name: 7 BARCLAY
  controller: 7 AILERON
  convenience: 3 ATM
  initials: 4 FDIC
**Bankroll:** 3 WAD 4 FUND
**Bankrupt:** 4 RUIN SUNK
**Bankruptcy:** 4 RUIN

Be near: 3 AIL
follow-up: 4 SALE
**Banks**
It's found in: 3 ORE
of baseball: 5 ERNIE
Supermodel: 4 TYRA
They may be found in: 4 OARS
___ Banks: 5 OUTER
**Banner:** 4 FLAG 6 ENSIGN
**Banners**
Internet: 3 ADS
**Bannister:** 5 MILER
Runner: 5 ROGER
**Banquet:** 3 SUP 4 DINE FETE
    MEAL 5 FEAST
    6 DINNER
host: 5 EMCEE
hosts (abbr.): 3 MCS
platform: 4 DAIS
with barbs: 5 ROAST
**Banquo:** 5 THANE
**Banshee**
Act the: 4 KEEN
Cry like a: 4 WAIL
land: 4 EIRE
Like a: 6 GAELIC
**Banter:** 4 JEST 8 REPARTEE
Engage in: 4 JOSH
Online: 4 CHAT
Talent for: 3 WIT
**Bantu**
language: 4 ZULU 6 RUANDA
tribe: 6 RUANDA
tribesman: 4 ZULU
**Banyan:** 4 TREE
**Bao** ___ : 3 DAI
**Baptism:** 4 RITE
One sponsored at a: 6 GODSON
**Baptist**
prefix: 3 ANA
**Bar:** 5 ESTOP INGOT
    7 MEASURE
at the bar: 5 ESTOP
    8 ESTOPPEL
Barbecue: 4 SPIT
Bathroom: 4 SOAP
bill: 3 TAB
Car: 4 AXLE
Car with a: 4 LIMO
chaser: 4 SHOT
employee: 7 BOUNCER
fare: 5 SALAD SUSHI
flier: 4 DART
Gold: 5 INGOT
High: 5 ROOST
ingredient: 7 GRANOLA
in the fridge: 4 OLEO
intro: 3 ISO
Kind of: 5 CANDY PIANO
    SPACE
Metal: 5 INGOT
One who can't pass the: 3 SOT
order: 3 ALE RUM RYE
    4 BEER NEAT 5 LAGER
    6 CHASER REFILL
    7 MARTINI

order, with "the": 4 SAME
    5 USUAL
Read a ~ code: 4 SCAN
regular: 6 PATRON
rocks: 3 ICE
Sand: 5 SHOAL
seat: 5 STOOL
Shot at the: 5 SNORT
sing-along: 7 KARAOKE
Snack: 7 GRANOLA
sound: 3 HIC
Straight, at the: 4 NEAT
Typing: 6 SPACER
**Bar** ___ : 4 NONE
**Bara**
Actress: 5 THEDA
**Baracus, B.A.**
portrayer: 3 MRT
**Barak:** 7 ISRAELI
country: 6 ISRAEL
of Israel: 4 EHUD
**Barb:** 3 DIG
**Barbara**
Actress: 4 BAIN EDEN HALE
nickname: 4 BABS
**"Barbara ___" (Beach Boys hit):**
    3 ANN
**"Barbarella"**
actor Milo: 5 OSHEA
**Barbarian:** 3 HUN 4 GOTH
    OGRE
___ the: 5 CONAN
**Barbaric:** 5 CRUEL 6 SAVAGE
**Barbarossa**
realm (abbr.): 3 HRE
**Barbary**
beast: 3 APE
**Barbary Coast**
city: 5 TUNIS
**Barbary State:** 7 TRIPOLI
Former: 5 TUNIS
    7 ALGIERS
**Barbecue:** 5 BROIL
bar: 4 SPIT
bit: 3 RIB
fare: 4 RIBS 9 SPARERIBS
fuel: 7 PROPANE
nugget: 4 COAL
offering: 5 KABOB KEBAB
receptacle: 6 ASHPIT
rod: 4 SPIT
site: 4 YARD 5 PATIO
**Barbed**
barricade: 6 ABATIS
comment: 3 JAB 4 GIBE
It may be: 4 WIRE
**Barbell**
abbr.: 3 LBS
metal: 4 IRON
**Barber**
call: 4 NEXT
chair attachment: 5 STROP
focus: 4 HAIR
job: 4 TRIM 5 SHAVE
motion: 4 SNIP
obstacle: 3 EAR

of music: 6 SAMUEL
of Seville: 6 FIGARO
powder: 4 TALC
sharpener: 5 STROP
shop sound: 4 SNIP
Sports broadcaster: 3 RED
**Barbera**
partner: 5 HANNA
**"Barber of Seville, The":**
    5 OPERA
composer: 7 ROSSINI
role: 6 FIGARO
**Barbershop**
band: 5 STROP
call: 4 NEXT
quartet member: 4 BASS
    5 TENOR
request: 4 TRIM
sound: 4 SNIP
symbol: 4 POLE
**Barbie:** 4 DOLL
beau: 3 KEN
boyfriend: 3 KEN
maker: 6 MATTEL
**Barbieri**
Jazzman: 4 GATO
**Barbizon School**
artist: 5 COROT DUPRE
**Barbuda**
Island near: 7 ANTIGUA
**Barcelona**
Info: Spanish cue
beach: 5 PLAYA
bear: 3 OSO
boy: 4 NINO
bravo: 3 OLE
buck: 6 PESETA
buddy: 5 AMIGO
bull: 4 TORO
**Bard:** 4 POET
Above, to a: 3 OER
Before, to a: 3 ERE
Below, to a: 5 NEATH
Between, to a: 5 TWIXT
Black, to a: 4 EBON
Inspiration, to a: 5 ERATO
Nightfall, to a: 3 EEN
of boxing: 3 ALI
River, to a: 4 AVON
Soon, to a: 4 ANON
Unclose, to a: 3 OPE
**Bard of** ___ : 4 AVON
**Bare:** 4 MERE 6 DENUDE
Lay: 6 DENUDE
Not: 4 CLAD
**Barefaced:** 4 BOLD 6 BRAZEN
    7 BLATANT
**Barefoot:** 6 UNSHOD
Not: 4 SHOD
**"Barefoot Contessa, The"**
actor Brazzi: 7 ROSSANO
actor O'Brien: 6 EDMOND
actress Gardner: 3 AVA
**Barents:** 3 SEA
**Barfly:** 3 SOT
perch: 5 STOOL

**Bargain:** 4 DEAL PACT PLEA
    5 STEAL 9 NEGOTIATE
  event: 4 SALE
  for leniency: 8 COPAPLEA
  Great: 5 STEAL
  hunter's stop: 7 TAGSALE
  site: 8 YARDSALE
**Bargain-basement:** 7 CUTRATE
**Barge:** 4 SCOW
**Barge ___:** 4 INON
**Barilla**
  rival: 4 RAGU
**Baritone**
  Voice above: 5 TENOR
**Bark:** 3 YAP 4 YELL
  beetle target: 3 ELM
  Comics: 3 ARF
  Little: 3 YIP
  Sharp: 3 YIP 4 YELP
**Barker**
  and others: 3 MAS
  Arctic: 4 SEAL
  Baum: 4 TOTO
  Circus: 4 SEAL
  Novelist: 5 CLIVE
**Barkin**
  Actress: 5 ELLEN
**Barkless**
  dog: 7 BASENJI
**Barkley**
  Boxer: 4 IRAN
  title, slangily: 4 VEEP
  Truman veep: 5 ALBEN
**Barley**
  beard: 3 AWN
  Germinated: 4 MALT
**Bar mitzvah:** 4 RITE
  boy: 4 TEEN
  dance: 4 HORA
  official: 5 RABBI
  reading: 5 TORAH
**Barn**
  area: 4 LOFT
  baby: 5 OWLET
  bedding: 5 STRAW
  bird: 3 OWL
  dance: 4 REEL 7 HOEDOWN
  neighbor: 4 SILO
  Pile in a: 6 HAYMOW
  topper: 4 VANE
**"Barnaby Jones"**
  actor Buddy: 5 EBSEN
**Barnard**
  graduate: 6 ALUMNA
**Barnes**
  Critic: 5 CLIVE
  of hockey: 3 STU
  partner: 5 NOBLE
**Barney**
  fan: 3 TOT
  Neighbor of: 4 FRED
**"Barney Miller"**
  actor Jack: 3 SOO
  actor Linden: 3 HAL
  actor Max: 4 GAIL
  actor Vigoda: 3 ABE

**Barnstorm:** 6 AVIATE
**Barnum, P.T.:** 6 HOAXER
  7 SHOWMAN
  Exit, to: 6 EGRESS
  Soprano who worked for:
    4 LIND
**Barnyard**
  baby: 3 KID
  beast: 4 GOAT
  bird: 4 FOWL
  bleat: 3 MAA
  cry: 5 BLEAT
  enclosure: 3 STY
  honker: 5 GOOSE
  layer: 3 HEN
  male: 3 TOM
  mom: 3 EWE
  perch: 5 ROOST
**Barometer**
  type: 7 ANEROID
**Baron**
  Scottish: 5 THANE
**Baronet**
  title: 3 SIR
**Baroque:** 5 STYLE 6 ORNATE
  composer: 4 BACH
  style: 6 ROCOCO
**Barr, William**
  successor: 4 RENO
**Barracks**
  bed: 3 COT
  boss: 5 SARGE
  ~ VIP: 3 NCO
**Barracuda**
  Baby: 4 SPET
**Barrage:** 4 PELT 5 BLITZ
  SALVO
**Barre**
  room bend: 4 PLIE
**Barrel:** 3 KEG 4 CASK
  Beer: 3 KEG
  Bottom of the: 4 LEES
  Kind of: 4 PORK
  Large: 4 DRUM
  Lock, stock, and: 3 ALL
  maker: 6 COOPER
  material: 3 ELM
  of laughs: 4 RIOT
  part: 5 STAVE
  Wine: 4 CASK
  ___ barrel: 5 OVERA
**Barreled**
  along: 4 TORE
**Barrelhead**
  bills: 4 CASH
**Barrel race**
  participant: 7 COWGIRL
  site: 5 RODEO
**Barren:** 4 ARID 6 DESERT
  7 STERILE
  8 DESOLATE
**Barrett**
  Gossip columnist: 4 RONA
  of Pink Floyd: 3 SYD
**Barricade:** 4 SHUT
  Barbed-wire: 6 ABATIS

**Barrie**
  baddie: 4 SMEE
  boy: 3 PAN
  dog: 4 NANA
**Barrier:** 4 WALL
  Atoll: 4 REEF
  Badminton: 3 NET
  breaker: 3 SST
  Cold War: 11 IRONCURTAIN
  Corporate: 12 GLASSCEILING
  Flood: 5 LEVEE
  Subway: 5 STILE
  Tennis: 3 NET
  Water: 4 DIKE MOAT
  Zoo: 4 MOAT
**Barrio**
  Calif. ~ city: 6 EASTLA
  grocery: 6 BODEGA
  outsider: 5 ANGLO
  resident: 6 LATINO
**Barris, Chuck**
  game show prop: 4 GONG
**Barrister**
  accessory: 3 WIG
**Barroom**
  brawl: 5 MELEE
**Barrow**
  native: 6 ESKIMO
**Barry**
  Humorist: 4 DAVE
  Singer: 3 LEN
**Barrymore**
  Actress: 4 DREW 5 ETHEL
**Bars**
  Behind: 5 CAGED
  It's sold in: 4 OLEO SOAP
  One behind: 3 CON
  Opening: 5 INTRO
**Bart**
  Father of: 5 HOMER
  Football legend: 5 STARR
  Grandpa of: 3 ABE
  Homer, to: 3 DAD
  Lisa, to: 3 SIS
  Mother of: 5 MARGE
  Sister of: 4 LISA
  ~, to Homer: 3 SON
**Bartender**
  A ~ may run one: 3 TAB
  need: 3 ICE
  requests: 3 IDS
  Rocks, to a: 3 ICE
**Barter:** 4 SWAP 5 TRADE
**"Bartered Bride, The":**
  5 OPERA
  composer: 7 SMETANA
  mezzo: 5 AGNES
**Barterer**
  Biblical: 4 ESAU
**Bartlett:** 4 PEAR
  Abbr. from: 4 ANON
  kin: 4 BOSC
  piece: 5 QUOTE
**Bartok**
  Actress: 3 EVA
  Composer: 4 BELA

**Bartoli**
piece: 4 ARIA
**Bartolomeu**
Explorer: 4 DIAS
**Barton**
Red Cross nurse: 5 CLARA
___ **Barton (Triple Crown winner):** 3 SIR
**Baryshnikov, Mikhail**
birthplace: 4 RIGA 6 LATVIA
early influence: 7 ASTAIRE
leap: 4 JETE
nickname: 5 MISHA
~, by birth: 4 LETT
**Basalt**
source: 4 LAVA
**Base:** 4 EVIL VILE 6 ALKALI SORDID TAWDRY 7 IGNOBLE IMMORAL NONACID 8 SINISTER
address: 3 SIR
Be off: 3 ERR
eatery: 7 CANTEEN 8 MESSHALL
figure (abbr.): 3 NCO
greeting: 6 SALUTE
horn: 5 BUGLE
Illegally off: 4 AWOL
information: 4 DATA
kid: 8 ARMYBRAT
Off: 4 AWOL 7 INERROR
Off ~ with permission: 7 ONLEAVE
runner's achievement: 5 STEAL
stealer Brock: 3 LOU
tune: 4 TAPS
~ 8: 5 OCTAL
**Baseball**
ancestor: 8 ROUNDERS
base: 3 BAG
bat wood: 3 ASH
blunder: 5 ERROR
club: 3 BAT
commissioner Bud: 5 SELIG
deal: 5 TRADE
diamond cover: 4 TARP
execs: 3 GMS
family name: 4 ALOU
feature: 4 SEAM
Former ~ commissioner Bowie: 4 KUHN
glove: 4 MITT
rarity: 3 TIE
stat: 3 ERA RBI 6 ATBATS ERRORS STEALS
team: 4 NINE 6 ENNEAD
**Baseballer**
Certain ~ (abbr.): 4 ALER NLER
Detroit: 5 TIGER
Houston: 5 ASTRO
Montreal: 4 EXPO
San Diego: 5 PADRE
**"Baseball Tonight"**
network: 4 ESPN

**Basecoat**
Apply a: 5 PRIME
Paint: 6 SEALER
**Baseless**
rumor: 6 CANARD
**Baseman**
blunder: 5 ERROR
First ~ in a comedy routine: 3 WHO
Second ~ in a comedy routine: 4 WHAT
**Basement**
Bargain ~ sign: 4 SAVE
feature: 7 RECROOM
fixture: 7 FURNACE
Like a finished: 7 PANELED
**Baserunner:** 7 STEALER
**Bash:** 4 FETE
All-night: 4 RAVE
Bacchanalian: 4 ORGY
Big: 4 FETE GALA 7 SHINDIG
Evening: 6 SOIREE
Maui: 4 LUAU
**Bashar**
of Syria: 5 ASSAD
**Bashful:** 3 SHY 5 DWARF 6 DEMURE
companion: 3 DOC 5 DOPEY
**Basic:** 4 BARE MERE 6 ALKALI 8 NOFRILLS 9 ELEMENTAL 11 FUNDAMENTAL
bit: 4 ATOM
command: 4 GOTO
element: 4 UNIT
stuff: 4 ABCS
**Basically:** 9 INESSENCE
**Basics:** 4 ABCS
**Basie, William "Count"**
instrument: 5 PIANO
**Basil:** 4 HERB
sauce: 5 PESTO
**Basil ___, Sir:** 6 SPENCE
**Basilica**
area: 4 APSE NAVE
bench: 3 PEW
center: 4 NAVE
section: 4 APSE
**Basin**
accessory: 4 EWER
Boat: 6 MARINA
Essen: 4 RUHR
German: 4 SAAR
Holy-water: 5 STOUP
type: 4 TIDAL
**Basinger**
Actress: 3 KIM
**Basis:** 4 ROOT SEED 6 REASON
**Bask:** 3 TAN
**Basket**
Angler's: 5 CREEL
Easy: 5 LAYUP TAPIN TIPIN
fiber: 5 ISTLE
Jai alai: 5 CESTA
Long ~, in hoops lingo: 4 TREY
material: 5 OSIER 6 RAFFIA

**Basketball**
brand: 4 VOIT
College ~ tourney: 3 NIT
defense: 4 ZONE
hoop: 3 RIM
player: 5 CAGER
rim: 4 HOOP
shot: 5 LAYUP TIPIN
stadium: 5 ARENA
stat: 6 ASSIST 7 REBOUND
tactic: 5 PRESS 9 FASTBREAK
target: 4 HOOP
Two-player ~ game: 8 ONEONONE
**Basketballer:** 5 CAGER
Beehive State: 3 UTE
Boston: 6 CELTIC
Indiana: 5 PACER
**Basketmaking**
branch: 5 OSIER
need: 5 ISTLE
Palm used in: 4 NIPA
**Baskin-Robbins**
purchase: 4 CONE
serving: 5 SCOOP
**Basque:** 7 IBERIAN
ancestor: 7 IBERIAN
kingdom: 7 NAVARRE
org.: 3 ETA
**Basra**
land: 4 IRAQ
resident: 5 IRAQI
**Bas-relief**
medium: 5 GESSO
**Bass:** 3 ALE LOW 4 CLEF DEEP FISH 5 VOICE
line player: 4 TUBA
player: 6 ANGLER
product: 3 ALE
suffix: 3 OON
**Bass ___:** 3 ALE
**Basset hound**
feature: 4 EARS
Like ~ ears: 6 DROOPY
**Bassett**
Actress: 6 ANGELA
**Basso**
~ Pinza: 4 EZIO
**Bassoon:** 4 REED
Like a: 5 REEDY
relative: 4 OBOE
**Bassoonist**
purchase: 4 REED
**Baste:** 3 SEW
**Bastille Day**
season: 3 ETE
**Basutoland**
~, today: 7 LESOTHO
**Bat**
again: 5 REHIT
home: 4 CAVE
navigation aid: 4 ECHO
Next to: 6 ONDECK
one's eyelashes: 5 FLIRT
Substance on a: 7 PINETAR
wood: 3 ASH

**Batch**
Auctioneer: 3 LOT
Dryer: 4 LOAD
Matched: 3 SET
of stew: 6 POTFUL
**Bates**
Actor: 4 ALAN
Actress: 5 KATHY
Author/poet: 4 ARLO
establishment: 5 MOTEL
**Bath:** 3 SPA
Info: British cue
county: 4 AVON
Enjoy a long: 4 SOAK
Finnish: 5 SAUNA
Need a ~ badly: 4 REEK
powder: 4 TALC
Relaxing: 4 SOAK
site (abbr.): 3 ENG
sponge: 6 LOOFAH
Steam: 5 SAUNA
suds: 3 ALE
Take a: 4 LAVE
water: 4 AVON
___ bath: 4 SITZ
**Bathday**
cake: 4 SOAP
**Bathe:** 4 LAVE 7 CLEANSE
**"Bathers, The"**
painter: 6 RENOIR
7 CEZANNE
**Bathhouse:** 6 CABANA
**Bathing**
suit top: 3 BRA
Type of ~ suit: 8 ONEPIECE
vessel: 3 TUB
**Bathroom**
bar: 4 SOAP
Bath: 3 LOO
flooring: 4 TILE
installation: 3 SPA
item: 3 MAT 5 SCALE
Like a ~ floor: 5 TILED
powder: 4 TALC
**Bathsheba**
husband: 5 URIAH
Son of: 7 SOLOMON
**Baths of Caracalla**
site: 4 ROME
**Bathtub**
booze: 3 GIN
Dirty ~ trait: 4 RING
feature: 5 DRAIN
murder victim: 5 MARAT
**Bathwater**
additive: 3 OIL
tester: 3 TOE
**Bathysphere**
designer: 5 BEEBE
**Batik**
artisan: 4 DYER
need: 3 DYE
**Batista**
successor: 6 CASTRO
**Batman**
and Robin: 3 DUO

and Robin, to villains:
7 NEMESES
butler: 6 ALFRED
costume part: 4 CAPE COWL
headquarters: 4 CAVE
Like: 5 CAPED
portrayer Adam: 4 WEST
portrayer Christian: 4 BALE
portrayer Kilmer: 3 VAL
sidekick: 5 ROBIN
~, to villains: 7 NEMESIS
**"Batman"**
actress Basinger: 3 KIM
sound effect: 3 BAM POW
**Bat Masterson**
trademark: 4 CANE 5 DERBY
**Baton:** 4 WAND 5 STICK
Handle a: 5 TWIRL
race: 5 RELAY
wielder: 7 MAESTRO
**Baton Rouge**
school (abbr.): 3 LSU
___ Bator: 4 ULAN
**Bats:** 4 LOCO 5 DAFFY LOONY
NUTTY
**Button**
down: 6 SECURE
**Batter**
Blend: 4 STIR
concern: 6 STANCE
position: 5 PLATE 6 STANCE
stat.: 3 RBI
success: 3 HIT 7 BASEHIT
**Batteries**
Small: 3 AAS 4 AAAS
Some: 3 AAS 4 AAAS
They may come in: 5 TESTS
Walkman: 3 AAS
**Battering**
device: 3 RAM
wind: 4 GALE
**Battery**
brand: 5 DELCO
component: 4 TEST
Electric ~ inventor: 5 VOLTA
fluid: 4 ACID
Of a ~ type: 6 ANODAL
part: 5 ANODE
size: 3 AAA
Small ~ size: 3 AAA
terminal: 5 ANODE
terminal (abbr.): 3 NEG POS
type: 5 NICAD SOLAR
7 DRYCELL
unit: 4 TEST VOLT
**Batting**
avg.: 3 PCT
stat.: 3 AVG RBI
**Batting champ**
1966 N.L. ~: 4 ALOU
Five-time: 5 BOGGS
Seven-time ~ Rod: 5 CAREW
Three-time ~ Tony: 5 OLIVA
**Battle**
Area away from the: 4 REAR
Court: 6 TENNIS

Engaged in: 5 ATWAR
Equip for: 3 ARM
field: 5 OPERA
memento: 4 SCAR
of behemoths: 4 SUMO
of wits: 5 CHESS
One-on-one: 4 DUEL
Ready for: 5 ARMED
song: 4 ARIA
Stage a ~, maybe: 7 REENACT
the clock: 4 RACE
**"Battle Cry"**
author Leon: 4 URIS
**Battlefield:** 5 ARENA
healer: 5 MEDIC
shout: 5 MEDIC
**Battleground:** 5 ARENA
**Battle of Britain**
gp.: 3 RAF
**Battle of the ___:** 5 BANDS
SEXES
**Battle of the Bulge**
locale: 8 ARDENNES
**Battlers**
Proverbial: 5 SEXES
**Battleship**
blast: 5 SALVO
color: 4 GRAY
letters: 3 USS
U.S. ~ destroyed in 1898:
5 MAINE
**Battle site**
1836 ~: 5 ALAMO
1862 ~: 6 SHILOH
8 ANTIETAM
1914 ~: 4 YSER 5 MARNE
1944 ~: 4 STLO 5 BULGE
LEYTE
490 B.C. ~: 8 MARATHON
Civil War: 6 SHILOH
Normandy: 4 STLO
Pacific: 7 OKINAWA
War of 1812: 4 ERIE
WWI: 4 YSER 5 MARNE
SOMME YPRES
WWII: 4 STLO 6 BATAAN
WWII ~, for short: 3 IWO
**"Battlestar Galactica"**
commander: 5 ADAMA
**Battling:** 5 ATWAR
**Batt. terminal:** 3 POS
**Batty:** 4 LOCO 5 NUTSO
**Bauble:** 3 TOY 6 DOODAD
GEEGAW GEWGAW
**"Baudolino"**
author Umberto: 3 ECO
**Bauhaus**
artist: 4 KLEE
**Baum**
canine: 4 TOTO
End of a ~ title: 4 OFOZ
princess: 4 OZMA
**Bausch**
partner: 4 LOMB
**Bauxite:** 3 ORE
component: 7 ALUMINA

**Bavaria**
river: 4 EGER ISAR
**Bawdy:** 4 LEWD
**Bawdyhouse**
manager: 5 MADAM
**Bawl:** 3 CRY SOB
Have a: 3 CRY SOB 4 WEEP
(out): 4 CHEW REAM
**Baxter**
Actress: 4 ANNE
Bandleader: 3 LES
Sitcom newsman: 3 TED
**Bay:** 4 COVE MARE 5 INLET
at the moon: 4 HOWL
Bring to: 4 TREE
Brought to: 5 TREED
city: 5 TAMPA
Maine: 5 CASCO
Scottish: 4 LOCH
Small: 5 INLET
Sound from a: 5 NEIGH
window: 5 ORIEL
**Bay ___ :** 4 AREA
**Bayer**
alternative: 6 ANACIN
brand: 5 ALEVE 7 ONEADAY
**Bayes**
Vaudevillian: 4 NORA
**Bayh**
Indiana senator: 4 EVAN
**Baylor**
Basketball player: 5 ELGIN
**Baylor University**
city: 4 WACO
**Bay of Bengal**
city: 6 MADRAS
**Bay of Biscay**
feeder: 5 LOIRE
**Bay of Fundy**
feature: 4 TIDE
**Bay of Naples**
isle: 5 CAPRI
**Bay of Pigs**
locale: 4 CUBA
**Bay of Whales**
sea: 4 ROSS
**Bayonet:** 4 STAB
**Bay State**
cape: 3 ANN
sch.: 5 UMASS
symbol: 7 ELMTREE
**Baywatch**
actress Anderson: 6 PAMELA
actress Bingham: 5 TRACI
actress Eleniak: 5 ERIKA
actress ___ Lee Nolin: 4 GENA
event: 6 RESCUE
**Bazaar**
merchant: 4 ARAB
**Bazin**
Author: 4 RENE
**Bazooka:** 4 TUBE
product: 3 GUM
**Bazooka Joe**
pal: 4 MORT
**BB:** 4 AMMO 6 PELLET

gun: 8 AIRRIFLE
**B-ball**
connection: 4 ASIN
Place to play: 4 YMCA
**BBC**
comedy: 5 ABFAB
rival: 3 ITN
Something to watch the ~ on:
5 TELLY
**"B ___ boy":** 4 ASIN
**BBS**
manager: 5 SYSOP
**B.C.**
cartoonist: 4 HART
neighbor: 4 ALTA
**BCE**
Part of: 3 ERA
**Be:** 5 EXIST
To ~, in French: 4 ETRE
To ~, in Latin: 4 ESSE
To ~, in Spanish: 3 SER
**"Be ___ !":** 4 APAL
**Bea**
Role for: 5 MAUDE
**Beach:** 5 SHORE 6 STRAND
acquisition: 3 TAN
Barcelona: 5 PLAYA
bird: 4 TERN
blanket: 4 SAND
color: 3 TAN
D-Day: 4 UTAH 5 OMAHA
feature: 4 DUNE
house: 6 CABANA
Like a: 5 SANDY
On the: 6 ASHORE
Reach the: 4 LAND
Rio: 7 IPANEMA
scavenger: 4 GULL
shade: 3 TAN
sidler: 4 CRAB
site: 4 ISLE
souvenir: 5 SHELL
They're caught at the:
4 RAYS
toy: 4 PAIL
**___ Beach:** 4 VERO 5 PISMO
6 LAGUNA MYRTLE
**Beach Boys**
Car in a ~ tune: 5 TBIRD
Girl in a ~ song: 6 RHONDA
hit song: 6 KOKOMO
15 CALIFORNIAGIRLS
**Beachgoer**
goal: 3 TAN
worry: 4 BURN
**Beachhead**
D-Day: 4 UTAH 5 OMAHA
of 1/22/44: 5 ANZIO
**Beachwear:** 5 THONG
6 BIKINI
**Beacon:** 4 LAMP 5 LIGHT
**Bead**
counters: 5 ABACI
Draw a: 3 AIM
Draw a ~ on: 5 AIMAT
material: 5 NACRE

Rosary ~ representation:
8 AVEMARIA
**Beads**
Item with: 6 ABACUS
on blades: 3 DEW
Prayer: 6 ROSARY
Produce: 8 PERSPIRE
**Beagle**
LBJ: 3 HER HIM
Writer aboard the: 6 DARWIN
**Beak:** 3 NEB NIB 4 NOSE
5 SNOOT 6 SCHNOZ
Use the ~ on: 5 PREEN
**"Be All That You Can Be"**
group: 4 ARMY 6 USARMY
**Beam:** 3 RAY 4 GRIN 5 SMILE
Building: 4 IBAR 5 JOIST
Construction: 4 IBAR
of light: 3 RAY 6 SUNRAY
splitter: 5 PRISM
Support: 4 IBAR 5 JOIST
TRUSS
Surgical: 5 LASER
Type of: 5 LASER
Use a surgical: 4 LASE
**Beame**
Mayor: 3 ABE
**Beaming:** 5 AGLOW 7 RADIANT
**"Beam ___ , Scotty!":** 4 MEUP
**Bean:** 3 NOB 4 CONK HEAD
6 NOGGIN NOODLE
Actor: 4 SEAN 5 ORSON
Astronaut: 4 ALAN
Broad: 4 FAVA
counter, for short: 3 CPA
cover: 3 HAT
curd: 4 TOFU
French: 4 TETE
holder: 3 POD
Judge: 3 ROY
Kind of: 4 FAVA NAVY SOYA
5 CACAO CAROB PINTO
6 KIDNEY
product: 4 IDEA
Protein: 4 SOYA
Succotash: 4 LIMA
town: 4 LIMA
**Beanery**
fare: 4 HASH
handout: 4 MENU
side: 4 SLAW
sign: 4 EATS
**Beanie:** 3 CAP HAT
**Beanie Babies:** 3 FAD 5 CRAZE
**Beans:** 8 SIDEDISH
Cook, as: 5 REFRY
It may be full of: 4 TACO
7 BURRITO
partner: 4 RICE
Spill the: 3 RAT 4 BLAB SING
TALK TELL 5 LETON
6 TATTLE
**Beantown**
team: 3 SOX
**Beany**
friend: 5 CECIL

**Bear:** 5 ABIDE STAND
    6 ENDURE MAMMAL
    8 TOLERATE
Act like a: 4 SELL
advice: 4 SELL
Barcelona: 3 OSA OSO
Bring to: 5 EXERT
Cartoon: 4 YOGI
Celestial: 4 URSA
claw: 6 PASTRY
Cuddly: 5 TEDDY
feet: 4 PAWS
hands: 4 PAWS
Heavenly: 4 URSA
home: 3 DEN
in the air: 4 URSA
in the sky: 4 URSA
lair: 3 DEN 4 CAVE
Load to: 4 ONUS
Milne: 4 POOH
of literature: 4 MAMA PAPA
of note: 6 SMOKEY
Sky: 4 URSA
suffix: 3 ISH
witness: 6 ATTEST
young, as sheep: 4 YEAN
**Bearable**
Make: 4 EASE
**Beard**
Barley: 3 AWN
Pointed: 6 GOATEE
**Bearded**
animal: 4 GOAT
antelope: 3 GNU
beast: 3 GNU
bloom: 4 IRIS
~, as barley: 5 AWNED
**Beardless:** 6 SHAVEN
**Bearer**
Acorn: 3 OAK
Biblical: 3 ASS
Bindle: 4 HOBO
Blame: 4 GOAT
Cone: 3 FIR
Flag: 4 MAST
Needle: 4 PINE
Ring: 4 WIFE 6 SATURN
Sheepskin: 4 GRAD
**Bearing:** 3 AIR 4 MIEN
    6 MANNER 8 CARRIAGE
    DEMEANOR PRESENCE
**Bearings**
Find one's: 6 ORIENT
**Bearish:** 6 URSINE
**Bearlike**
beast: 5 KOALA PANDA
**Béarnaise:** 5 SAUCE
ingredient: 8 TARRAGON
**Bears:** 4 TEAM
coach: 5 DITKA HALAS
What ~ do: 4 SELL
**Beast:** 4 OGRE 5 BRUTE
    6 ANIMAL
African: 5 RHINO
Andean: 5 LLAMA
Antlered: 3 ELK

Balaam: 3 ASS
Barbary: 3 APE
Bearded: 3 GNU
Borneo: 5 ORANG
Braying: 3 ASS
Burrowing: 4 MOLE
Caravan: 5 CAMEL
Grimm: 4 OGRE
Himalayan: 3 YAK
Horned: 5 RHINO
Long-snouted: 5 TAPIR
of Borden: 5 ELSIE
of burden: 3 ASS 5 LLAMA
Stubborn: 4 MULE
Tolkien: 3 ORC
Zodiac: 3 RAM
**Beasts**
Branded: 6 CATTLE
Yoked: 4 OXEN
**Beat:** 3 TOP 4 BEST 5 ALLIN
    OUTDO PULSE TEMPO
    THROB TIRED 6 BESTED
    PUMMEL 7 PULSATE
    8 DEFEATED
at the polls: 7 OUTVOTE
back: 7 REPULSE
badly: 4 ROUT 5 CREAM
    TROMP 7 SHELLAC
Barely: 3 NIP 4 EDGE
    5 EDGED 7 EDGEOUT
    NOSEOUT 8 EDGEDOUT
Brazilian: 5 SAMBA
ending: 3 NIK
it: 3 LAM 4 FLED FLEE
    5 BONGO SCRAM
Mailman's: 5 ROUTE
One with a: 3 COP
the draft: 6 ENLIST
the wheat: 6 THRESH
to a pulp: 4 MASH
to the tape: 6 OUTRAN
    OUTRUN
Usher's: 5 AISLE
Walk a: 6 PATROL
walker: 3 COP
with a stick: 4 FLOG
**Beaten**
It may be: 3 EGG RAP 4 PATH
It may be ~ at a party:
    6 PINATA
Was ~ by: 6 LOSTTO
**Beater**
Birdie: 5 EAGLE
Bogey: 3 PAR
Breast: 5 HEART
Deuce: 4 TREY
Egg: 5 WHISK
King: 3 ACE
Proverbial sword: 3 PEN
Rock: 5 PAPER
**Beating:** 4 LOSS 6 ATHROB
sound: 7 PITAPAT
**Beatle**
bride: 3 ONO
drummer: 5 RINGO STARR
Early ~ Sutcliffe: 3 STU

**Beatles**
adjective: 3 FAB
album: 4 HELP 9 ABBEYROAD
Best of the: 4 PETE
Country in a ~ song: 4 USSR
film: 4 HELP
Girl in a ~ song: 4 ANNA RITA
    5 RIGBY SADIE
hit song: 4 HELP 7 IMEMINE
    LETITBE 8 LOVEMEDO
    9 IFEELFINE
    15 HERECOMESTHESUN
    WHENIMSIXTYFOUR
    YELLOWSUBMARINE
Instrument on some ~ songs:
    5 SITAR
manager: 7 EPSTEIN
meter maid: 4 RITA
phenomenon: 5 MANIA
refrain: 4 YEAH
Start of a ~ title: 6 OBLADI
**Beatnik**
abode: 3 PAD
exclamation: 3 MAN 4 IDIG
    5 IMHIP
instrument: 5 BONGO
**Beatrice**
admirer: 5 DANTE
**"Beats me!":** 5 DUNNO
    6 IDUNNO NOIDEA
**Beattie**
Author: 3 ANN
**Beat ___ to one's door:**
    5 APATH
**Beatty**
Actor: 3 NED 6 WARREN
bomb: 6 ISHTAR
film: 4 REDS 5 BUGSY
    6 ISHTAR
flop: 6 ISHTAR
role: 5 BUGSY
**Beau:** 5 ROMEO SWAIN
    WOOER
Barbie's: 3 KEN
Bordeaux: 3 AMI
Doe's: 4 STAG
Ewe's: 3 RAM
Former: 8 OLDFLAME
Rose's: 4 ABIE
**Beau ___ (noble deed):**
    5 GESTE
**"Beau ___":** 5 GESTE
**Beau Brummel:** 3 FOP 5 DANDY
concern: 6 ATTIRE
school: 4 ETON
**___ beaucoup:** 5 MERCI
**Beaufort:** 5 SCALE
scale category: 4 GALE
    5 STORM
    11 FRESHBREEZE
**Beaujolais:** 4 WINE
**Beauregard**
boss: 3 LEE
**Beautician:** 4 DYER
    7 ADORNER
**Beauties:** 6 BELLES

Group of: 4 BEVY
"Beautiful Mind, A": 6 BIOPIC
   actor: 5 CROWE 8 EDHARRIS
   subject: 4 NASH
Beauty: 3 GEM
   admirer: 5 BEAST
   Ancient: 5 HELEN
   Hardly a: 3 HAG
      9 PLAINJANE
   Like a ~ queen: 7 TIARAED
   mark: 3 TEN
   pageant wear: 4 SASH
   parlor: 5 SALON
   preceder: 3 AGE
   queen's crown: 5 TIARA
   ___ Beauty (apple type):
      4 ROME
"Beauty and the Beast"
   character: 5 BELLE
Beauvais
   department: 4 OISE
Beaux-Arts
   ___ des ~: 5 ECOLE
Beaver: 6 RODENT
   brother: 5 WALLY
   Chew like a: 4 GNAW
   creation: 3 DAM
   Like a: 5 EAGER
Beaver State: 6 OREGON
   (abbr.): 3 ORE 4 OREG
   capital: 5 SALEM
"Be-Bop-___": 5 ALULA
Because: 3 FOR 5 SINCE
      6 INTHAT
   of: 5 DUETO
   of this: 6 HEREAT
"Because ___!": 6 ISAYSO
Becker
   of tennis: 5 BORIS
"Becker"
   actor Danson: 3 TED
"Becket"
   actor Peter: 6 OTOOLE
Beckett
   award: 4 OBIE
   no-show: 5 GODOT
   title character: 5 GODOT
Beckon: 6 CALLTO INVITE
Becloud: 5 MUDDY
      6 DARKEN
Become: 4 SUIT 8 TURNINTO
   ~, finally: 5 ENDUP
Bed
   Army: 3 COT
   Baby: 4 CRIB 6 CRADLE
   Barracks: 3 COT
   board: 4 SLAT
   ending: 5 STEAD
   Feather: 3 TAR
   Get out of: 4 RISE 5 ARISE
      ROUST
   Go to: 6 RETIRE
   Got out of: 5 AROSE
   Gotten out of: 6 ARISEN
   Kebab: 5 PILAF
   Make a: 3 HOE

Out of: 5 ASTIR RISEN
      6 ARISEN
   Portable: 3 COT
   Push out of: 5 ROUST
   size: 4 TWIN
   Still in: 5 NOTUP
   support: 4 SLAT
Bed-and-breakfast: 3 INN
Bedaub: 5 SMEAR
Bedazzle: 3 AWE
Bedazzled: 5 INAWE
Bedding: 5 LINEN
   Barn: 5 STRAW
   item: 4 SHAM
   material: 5 LINEN SATIN
   Whack: 9 RAPSHEETS
Beddy-bye
   outfit: 7 JAMMIES
Bedeck: 4 DOUP 5 ADORN
Bedevil: 3 VEX 5 NAGAT TEASE
Bedim: 5 BLEAR
"Bed-in for Peace"
   participant: 3 ONO
Bedlam: 3 DIN 5 CHAOS
Bedmate
   Bother a: 5 SNORE
   Bothersome: 6 SNORER
Bedouin: 4 ARAB 5 NOMAD
   bigwig: 4 EMIR
   home: 4 TENT
   transport: 5 CAMEL
"Bed Riddance"
   poet: 4 NASH
Bedridden
   Be: 3 AIL
Bedrock
   pet: 4 DINO
Bedroom
   furniture: 6 BUREAU
      7 ARMOIRE DRESSER
Beds
   Like some: 4 MADE
      6 UNMADE
Bedside
   awakener: 5 ALARM
   light: 4 LAMP
Bedtime
   Child's ~ request: 5 STORY
   Entertain at: 6 READTO
   Late: 5 ONEAM
   Nearing: 6 LATISH
   Put off: 6 STAYUP
   story: 5 DREAM
Bedwear
   ~, briefly: 3 PJS
Bee: 4 AUNT
   Be in a: 5 SPELL
   charge: 4 OPIE
   chaser: 3 CEE
   Competed in a: 5 SPELT
   flat: 4 HIVE
   formation: 5 SWARM
   He stung like a: 3 ALI
   house: 6 APIARY
   Male: 5 DRONE
   nephew: 4 ANDY OPIE

product: 5 QUILT
Bee ___: 4 GEES
Beech: 4 TREE
   family member: 3 OAK
Beef: 4 CARP MEAT 5 GRIPE
      7 REDMEAT
   Big piece of: 4 SIDE
   Corned ~ concoction: 4 HASH
   cut: 4 LOIN RUMP 5 TBONE
      9 CLUBSTEAK
   dish: 4 STEW 10 SWISSSTEAK
   How ~ may be served:
      5 AUJUS
   Improve, as: 3 AGE
   Like some: 6 CORNED
   One way to cook: 5 ROAST
   on the hoof: 5 STEER
   order: 4 RARE
   rating org.: 4 USDA
   Tenderized cut of:
      9 CUBESTEAK
Beefcake: 4 HUNK
Beef-rating
   agcy.: 4 USDA
Bee Gees, The: 4 TRIO 5 GIBBS
Beehive: 4 UPDO 5 STYLE
      6 HAIRDO
   and others: 3 DOS
   Build a: 5 TEASE
   protector: 7 HAIRNET
Beehive State: 4 UTAH
   athlete: 3 UTE
   native: 3 UTE
Beekeeper: 8 APIARIST
   in a 1997 film: 4 ULEE
Beelike: 5 APIAN
Beeline
   Make a: 6 HASTEN
Beelzebub: 5 DEVIL SATAN
   bailiwick: 4 EVIL
Been
   Had: 3 WAS
"___ been fun!": 3 ITS
"___ been had!": 3 IVE
"Been there, done that":
      7 TRIEDIT
Beep: 4 PAGE
Beeper: 4 HORN 5 PAGER
   Use a: 4 PAGE
Beer: 4 SUDS
   Aged: 5 LAGER
   barrel: 3 KEG
   belly: 3 POT
   Big name in: 5 PABST
      6 AMSTEL
   buy: 4 CASE
   cheer: 5 SKOAL
   Dark: 4 BOCK
   holder: 5 STEIN
   ingredient: 4 HOPS MALT
   Japanese ~ brand: 5 ASAHI
   keg outlet: 3 TAP
   Like some: 5 ONTAP
   Make: 4 BREW
   mug: 5 STEIN
   relative: 3 ALE

topper: 4 HEAD
variety: 4 LITE 5 LAGER
Word with: 4 NEAR
~, at times: 6 CHASER
"Beer Barrel ___": 5 POLKA
**Beersheba**
locale: 5 NEGEV
**Beery**
Actor: 4 NOAH
**Beery, Wallace**
film: 8 THECHAMP
**Bees**
Bunch of: 5 SWARM
home: 4 HIVE
Pertaining to: 5 APIAN
**Beet**
Comparable to a: 5 ASRED
extract: 5 SUGAR
variety: 5 CHARD
**Beethoven**
birthplace: 4 BONN
dedicatee: 5 ELISE
opera: 7 FIDELIO
Schiller work adapted by:
8 ODETOJOY
symphony: 6 EROICA
wrote one: 5 OPERA
"**Beethoven**"
actor Charles: 6 GRODIN
**Beetle:** 3 CAR 4 AUTO
cousin: 5 JETTA
Egyptian: 6 SCARAB
juice: 3 GAS
Kind of: 3 ELM 4 STAG
larvae: 5 GRUBS
Spotted: 7 LADYBUG
"**Beetle Bailey**"
boss: 5 SARGE
creator Walker: 4 MORT
dog: 4 OTTO
**Beeweed:** 5 ASTER
**Befit:** 4 SUIT
**Befitting:** 3 APT
**Before:** 3 ERE 5 UNTIL
7 AHEADOF PRIORTO
Come: 7 PRECEDE PREDATE
8 ANTEDATE
long: 4 ANON SOON
Night: 3 EVE
now: 3 AGO
prefix: 3 PRE
surgery: 5 PREOP
the deadline: 5 EARLY
6 INTIME
Time: 3 EVE
~, once: 3 ERE
~, poetically: 3 ERE
**Befoul:** 4 SOIL
**Befuddled:** 4 ASEA 5 ATSEA
**Beg:** 5 PLEAD 7 ENTREAT
One might ~ to do this:
6 DIFFER
**Began:** 5 AROSE 6 OPENED
**Begat:** 5 SIRED 7 SPAWNED
**Begawan, Bandar ___:** 4 SERI
**Beget:** 4 SIRE 5 SPAWN

**Beggar**
request: 4 ALMS
**Beggar's-___ (sticky seeds):**
4 LICE
**Begged:** 4 PLED 5 ASKED
8 IMPLORED
**Begin:** 5 SETTO START
7 ISRAELI STARTON
8 STARTOFF
again: 4 REDO
a journey: 6 SETOUT
co-Nobelist: 5 SADAT
of Israel: 7 MENACHEM
**Beginner:** 4 TYRO
8 NEOPHYTE
**Beginning:** 3 TOP 4 ASOF SEED
5 BIRTH ONSET START
6 ORIGIN OUTSET
7 INITIAL
From the: 4 ANEW 6 AFRESH
From the ~, in Latin: 5 ABOVO
The very: 6 DAYONE
7 YEARONE
~, slangily: 5 GETGO
"**Begin the Beguine**"
bandleader Artie: 4 SHAW
**Begley**
and others: 3 EDS
"**Begone!**": 4 SCAT SHOO
5 SCRAM 6 GETOUT
**Begot:** 5 SIRED
"**Beg pardon ...**": 4 AHEM
**Begrudge:** 4 ENVY 6 RESENT
**Beguile:** 5 AMUSE TEMPT
6 SEDUCE 8 ENTRANCE
**Beguiler:** 5 SIREN
**Beguiling**
trick: 4 WILE
**Behalf**
On ~ of: 3 FOR
**Behave:** 3 ACT
badly: 3 ERR
rudely: 5 ACTUP
**Behaving:** 6 ACTING
Men ~ badly: 4 CADS
**Behavior**
Bad: 4 SINS
pattern: 5 HABIT
**Behemoth:** 5 TITAN
Highway: 4 SEMI
Sport for a: 4 SUMO
**Behind:** 3 AFT 4 LATE REAR
9 INARREARS
bars: 5 CAGED
Be: 3 OWE 5 TRAIL
closed doors: 9 INPRIVATE
Come from: 5 RALLY
Fall: 3 LAG 8 LOSETIME
Following: 5 INTOW
Get: 7 ENDORSE 8 LOSETIME
Hit from: 7 REAREND
Is: 6 TRAILS
Not: 4 ANTI
One ~ bars: 3 CON
One ~ the other: 6 TANDEM
Pull from: 3 TOW

Running: 4 LATE
schedule: 4 LATE
Stay: 6 REMAIN
the eight ball: 7 INAHOLE
the scenes: 8 OFFSTAGE
Was ~ schedule: 7 RANLATE
Wet ~ the ears: 3 RAW
5 NAIVE
**Behold:** 3 SEE 8 LOOKUPON
Amazing to: 10 EYEPOPPING
"**Behold!**": 4 ECCE TADA
~, in Latin: 4 ECCE
"___ behold!": 5 LOAND
**Beholden**
Be ~ to: 3 OWE
**Beholder:** 4 EYER
**Beiderbecke**
Jazz musician: 3 BIX
**Beige:** 3 TAN 4 ECRU
**Being:** 4 ESSE 6 ENTITY
9 EXISTENCE
Came into: 5 AROSE
For the time: 6 PROTEM
Have: 5 EXIST
Supreme: 3 GOD
Time: 5 NONCE
~, in French: 4 ETRE
~, in Latin: 4 ESSE
**Beirut**
country (abbr.): 3 LEB
**Bejewel:** 5 ADORN
**Bejeweled**
headgear: 5 TIARA
**Bel ___:** 5 PAESE
**Bela**
Actor: 6 LUGOSI
Colleague of: 3 LON
Composer: 6 BARTOK
**Belafonte**
Actress: 5 SHARI
**Belafonte, Harry**
Daughter of: 5 SHARI
song: 4 DAYO
**Belarus**
capital: 5 MINSK
~, once (abbr.): 3 SSR
**Belbenoit**
Devil's Island escapee: 4 RENE
**Belch**
forth: 4 SPEW
Shakespeare character: 4 TOBY
**Belfast**
gp.: 3 IRA
Town near: 6 ANTRIM
**Belfry**
locale: 7 STEEPLE
resident: 3 BAT
**Belgian**
city: 5 YPRES
composer Jacques: 4 BREL
Former ~ airline: 6 SABENA
resort: 3 SPA
river: 4 YSER
**Belgium**
City in: 5 YPRES
River in: 4 YSER

**Belgrade**
country: 6 SERBIA
Former ~ bigwig: 4 TITO
resident: 4 SERB SLAV
**Belief:** 3 ISM 5 CREDO TENET
Established: 5 DOGMA
in God: 5 DEISM 6 THEISM
Mideast: 5 ISLAM
Statement of: 5 CREDO CREED
system: 3 ISM
**Beliefs**
of a group: 5 ETHOS
**Believable**
Not: 4 LAME
**Believe:** 4 DEEM FEEL
Hard to: 4 TALL
Make: 7 PLAYACT PRETEND
without question: 5 EATUP
~, as a story: 3 BUY
**"Believe"**
singer: 4 CHER
**Believed:** 4 FELT HELD
without question: 5 ATEUP
**"Believe it ___!":** 5 ORNOT
**"Believe ___ not!":** 4 ITOR
**Believer:** 3 IST 5 DEIST
6 THEIST
Suffix for a: 3 IST
**"___ Believer":** 3 IMA
**Belittle:** 3 DIS 5 ABASE
9 DISPARAGE
**Bell**
After the: 4 LATE
Alarm: 6 TOCSIN
and others: 3 MAS
Evening: 6 VESPER
Noted ~ ringer: 8 AVONLADY
Ring a: 4 PEAL TOLL
ringer: 6 SEXTON
site: 7 STEEPLE
sound: 4 BONG DONG PEAL
TING
the cat: 4 DARE
town: 4 ATRI 5 ADANO
**Bell ___:** 4 LABS
**___ Bell:** 4 TACO
**Bella**
Feminist politician: 5 ABZUG
**Bell-bottoms**
feature: 5 FLARE
Like: 5 RETRO
**Belle**
Bleating: 3 EWE
counterpart: 4 BETE
of the ball: 3 DEB
of the Old West: 5 STARR
**"Bellefleur"**
author: 5 OATES
**"Bell for ___, A":** 5 ADANO
**Bellhop:** 4 PAGE 5 TOTER
burden: 4 BAGS
employer: 5 HOTEL
**Belli**
Attorney: 6 MELVIN
**Bellicose**
god: 4 ARES

**Belligerent**
god: 4 ARES
**"Belling the Cat"**
author: 5 AESOP
**Bellini:** 7 ITALIAN
opera: 5 NORMA
**"Bell Jar, The"**
author: 5 PLATH
**Belloc**
Author: 7 HILAIRE
**Bellow:** 4 ROAR 5 SHOUT
Author: 4 SAUL
Bovine: 3 MOO
Bullring: 3 OLE
character March: 5 AUGIE
**Bellowing:** 5 AROAR
**Bellows**
Actor: 3 GIL
**"Bells, The"**
author: 3 POE
**Bell-shaped**
flower: 4 SEGO 5 TULIP
**"Bells ___ Mary's, The":** 4 OFST
**"Bells of St. ___, The":**
5 MARYS
**Bellum**
opposite: 3 PAX
**Belly:** 3 GUT 7 ABDOMEN
STOMACH
Beer: 3 POT
Go ~ up: 4 FAIL FOLD
laugh: 4 ROAR
muscles: 3 ABS
On one's: 5 PRONE
pain: 4 ACHE
**Bellyache:** 4 BEEF CRAB MOAN
5 GRIPE WHINE
**Bellyacher:** 4 CRAB 5 GRUMP
**Bellybutton**
type: 5 INNIE OUTIE
**Bellyful**
Give a: 4 SATE
Had a: 3 ATE
**Belmont**
bet: 6 EXACTA
event: 9 HORSERACE
**Belmonts**
lead singer: 4 DION
**Belong:** 3 FIT 5 FITIN
6 INHERE
**Belonging**
Cost of: 4 DUES
to moi: 3 MES
to us: 4 OURS
**Belongings:** 4 GEAR 6 ASSETS
ESTATE
**Beloved:** 4 DEAR
animal: 3 PET
folk: 5 DEARS
Make: 6 ENDEAR
Name meaning: 5 AIMEE
**"Beloved"**
author Morrison: 4 TONI
director: 5 DEMME
**Below:** 5 UNDER
low: 5 EMPTY

~, in poetry: 5 NEATH
**Belowdecks**
Put: 4 STOW
**Belt:** 4 AREA ZONE 5 PASTE
STRAP 6 REGION
WALLOP
Bar: 4 SHOT
clip-on: 5 PAGER
Imaginary: 6 ZODIAC
maker's tool: 3 AWL
Ornamental: 4 SASH
out: 4 SING
site: 5 WAIST
Tighten, as a: 4 GIRD
**___ Belt (constellation part):**
6 ORIONS
**Beluga**
delicacy: 3 ROE
**Belushi**
venue, briefly: 3 SNL
**Bemoan:** 3 RUE 4 WAIL
6 LAMENT REGRET
**"Be My Baby"**
group: 8 RONETTES
**Ben**
Golfer: 5 HOGAN
Screenwriter: 5 HECHT
**Ben-___:** 3 HUR
**Benaderet**
Actress: 3 BEA
**"___ Ben Adhem":** 4 ABOU
**Ben and Jerry's**
alternative: 4 EDYS
**Benatar**
Singer: 3 PAT
**___ Ben Canaan:** 3 ARI
**Bench:** 4 SEAT
Church: 3 PEW
Cry from the: 5 ORDER
Lance of the: 3 ITO
outfit: 4 ROBE
site: 5 PIANO
Warmed the: 3 SAT
**Bench, Johnny**
team: 4 REDS
**Bench-clearing**
incident: 5 MELEE SETTO
**Benchley, Peter**
novel: 4 JAWS 7 THEDEEP
**Benchmark:** 4 NORM
(abbr.): 3 STD
**Bench-press**
unit: 3 REP
**Benchwarmer:** 3 SUB 5 SCRUB
7 RESERVE
**Bend:** 3 ARC 4 FLEX
6 RELENT
Ballet: 4 PLIE
down: 5 STOOP
out of shape: 4 WARP
Pipe: 3 ELL
Right-angle: 3 ELL
Something to: 3 EAR
Something to ~ or lend:
5 ANEAR
under pressure: 3 SAG

**Bended**
Asked on ~ knee: 4 PLED
**Bender:** 3 JAG 4 TEAR TOOT
    5 BINGE SPREE
Eyeball: 5 OPART
Fender: 4 DENT 6 MISHAP
___ bender: 6 FENDER
**Bending**
muscle: 6 FLEXOR
readily: 5 LITHE
**Bendix**
role: 5 RILEY
___ bene: 4 NOTA
**Beneath:** 5 UNDER
**Benedict**
suffix: 3 INE
Traitor: 6 ARNOLD
___ Benedict: 4 EGGS
**Benedictine**
title: 3 DOM
**Benediction**
Give a ~ to: 5 BLESS
**Benefactor:** 5 ANGEL
    6 PATRON 7 DONATOR
PBS: 3 NEA
**Beneficial:** 5 OFUSE UTILE
    6 USEFUL
**Beneficiary:** 4 HEIR 5 DONEE
    7 LEGATEE
Primogeniture: 3 SON
**Benefit:** 3 AID 4 BOON PLUS
    SAKE 5 AVAIL
Employee: 4 PERK
event: 4 GALA
Fed. ~ source: 3 SSA
Fringe: 4 PERK
**Benevolence:** 5 MERCY
**Benevolent:** 4 KIND
order member: 3 ELK
**Bengali**
language group: 5 INDIC
**Ben-Gay**
target: 4 ACHE
**Ben-Gurion**
airline: 4 ELAL
**Ben-Hur:** 10 CHARIOTEER
**"Ben-Hur":** 4 EPIC
author Wallace: 3 LEW
studio: 3 MGM
**Benigni**
Actor/director: 7 ROBERTO
**Benin**
~, once: 7 DAHOMEY
**Bening**
Actress: 7 ANNETTE
**Benjamin:** 5 CNOTE
British Prime Minister:
    8 DISRAELI
Guitarist: 3 ORR
"___ Ben Jonson!": 5 ORARE
**Bennett**
Publisher: 4 CERF
Singer: 4 TONY
**Bennett, Tony**
birthplace: 7 ASTORIA
song title start: 5 ILEFT

**Benny, Jack**
39, to ~: 3 AGE
Like: 5 CHEAP
sponsor: 5 JELLO
**"Benny & Joon"**
actor Quinn: 5 AIDAN
**"Benson"**
actress Swenson: 4 INGA
**Bent:** 7 STOOPED
It may be ~ or lent: 3 EAR
out of shape: 5 IRATE
    6 WARPED
over: 6 ASTOOP
**Bentley**
Actor: 3 WES
**Bentley, E.C.**
detective: 5 TRENT
**Bentsen**
Former senator: 5 LLOYD
**Benz**
Auto pioneer: 4 KARL
end: 3 ENE
**Benzene**
prefix: 3 AZO
source: 3 TAR
**Benzi Box**
contents: 8 CARRADIO
**Benzoyl peroxide**
target: 4 ACNE
**Beowulf**
~, to Grendel: 6 SLAYER
**"Beowulf":** 4 EPIC EPOS SAGA
beast: 7 GRENDEL
beverage: 4 MEAD
**"Be patient":** 6 NOTYET
    8 SITTIGHT
**"Be Prepared"**
gp.: 3 BSA
**Bequeath:** 5 LEAVE
**"Be quiet!":** 4 HUSH
**Berate:** 5 SCOLD 6 RAILAT
    YELLAT
**Bereavement:** 5 GRIEF
**Bereft:** 4 LORN 6 DEVOID
**Berenstain**
Writer: 4 STAN
**Beret:** 3 CAP HAT
Leader in a: 3 CHE
Place for a: 4 TETE
Scottish: 3 TAM
**Berg**
Composer: 5 ALBAN
of baseball: 3 MOE
opera: 4 LULU
**Berganza**
Mezzo: 6 TERESA
**Bergen**
dummy Mortimer: 5 SNERD
Ventriloquist: 5 EDGAR
**Berger**
Actress: 5 SENTA
**Bergman:** 5 SWEDE
Actress: 6 INGRID
Director: 6 INGMAR
Last role for: 4 MEIR
Oscar role for: 9 ANASTASIA

**"Be right with you!":** 6 INASEC
    ONESEC
**Bering:** 3 SEA 4 DANE
    6 STRAIT
(abbr.): 3 STR
**Bering Sea**
bird: 3 AUK
island: 4 ATTU
native: 5 ALEUT
**Berkeley**
School with a ~ campus (abbr.):
    4 UCAL
**Berkow**
Sports columnist: 3 IRA
**Berkshire**
school: 4 ETON
**Berkshire Music Festival**
site: 5 LENOX
**Berle, Milton**
sidekick Arnold: 5 STANG
sponsor: 6 TEXACO
theme: 7 NEARYOU
**Berlin, Irving**
Original surname of:
    6 BALINE
output: 5 SONGS
song: 6 ALWAYS
    15 PUTTINONTHERITZ
**Berliner**
Inventor: 5 EMILE
**Berman**
Sportscaster: 3 LEN
**Berman, Chris**
award: 4 ESPY
**Bermuda:** 4 ISLE 5 ONION
vehicle: 5 MOPED
wear: 6 SHORTS
**Bern**
river: 3 AAR 4 AARE
**Bernadette**
(abbr.): 3 STE
Performer: 6 PETERS
**Bernard**
Author: 7 MALAMUD
News anchor: 4 SHAW
___ Bernardino: 3 SAN
**Berne**
river: 3 AAR 4 AARE
**Bernese Alps**
Peak in the: 5 EIGER
river: 3 AAR 4 AARE
**Bernhardt**
Actress: 5 SARAH
**Bernie**
Quarterback: 5 KOSAR
Songwriting partner of:
    5 ELTON
**Bernini**
Sculptor: 4 GIAN
**Bernstein**
Composer: 5 ELMER
Journalist: 4 CARL
musical: 7 CANDIDE
**Berra**
of baseball: 4 YOGI
teammate: 5 MARIS

*(handwritten marginal notes:)* VITUS EXPLORER

*(handwritten marginal note, left side:)* Del Toro Benicio - "TRAFFIC"

**Berry**
Actress: 5 HALLE
Fuzzy: 4 KIWI
Motown founder: 5 GORDY
of baseball: 3 KEN
prefix: 4 CRAN
___ Berry Farm: 6 KNOTTS
**Berserk:** 4 AMOK LOCO
Go: 4 RAGE SNAP
7 RUNAMOK
**Bert**
Actor: 4 LAHR
Buddy of: 5 ERNIE
Twin of: 3 NAN
**Berth:** 4 SLOT 5 SPACE
Ark: 6 ARARAT
Give a wide: 5 AVOID
place: 4 DOCK PIER SLIP
5 UPPER 6 MARINA
Prebirth: 4 WOMB
**Beryl**
variety: 7 EMERALD
**Beseech:** 3 BEG 4 PRAY
5 PLEAD 7 ENTREAT
IMPLORE 8 APPEALTO
**Beset:** 6 ASSAIL
**Beside:** 5 ALONG
oneself: 3 MAD 5 IRATE
**Besides:** 3 TOO 4 ALSO ELSE
6 ATTHAT
**Be silent**
~, in music: 5 TACET
**Besmirch:** 3 TAR 4 SOIL
5 DIRTY SULLY
8 DISCOLOR
**"___ Beso":** 3 ESO
**Bess**
follower: 5 MAMIE
Harry and: 7 TRUMANS
partner: 5 PORGY
predecessor: 7 ELEANOR
**Besson**
Director: 3 LUC
**Best:** 3 TOP 4 AONE BEAT
TOPS 5 ELITE IDEAL
OUTDO 6 FINEST
7 OPTIMAL OPTIMUM
Actress: 4 EDNA
conditions: 6 OPTIMA
In the ~ case: 7 IDEALLY
of the Beatles: 4 PETE
suited: 6 APTEST
The ~ of times:
9 GOLDENAGE
**Best Actor:** see pages 719–720
of 1958: 5 NIVEN
of 1961: 6 SCHELL
of 1967: 7 STEIGER
of 1971: 7 HACKMAN
of 1990: 5 IRONS
of 2000: 5 CROWE
**Best Actress:** see pages 720–721
of 1961: 5 LOREN
of 1963: 4 NEAL
of 1987: 4 CHER
of 1990: 5 BATES

of 1998: 4 HUNT
of 1999: 5 SWANK
**Best Director:** see pages 718–719
**Bested:** 6 OUTDID 7 OUTDONE
8 OVERCAME
Be: 4 LOSE
**Bestial**
hideaway: 4 LAIR
**"Best in Show"**
org.: 3 AKC
**Best Musical:** see pages 722–723
**Best of the best:** 8 CHOICEST
**Bestow:** 4 GIVE 5 AWARD
ENDUE GRANT
6 IMPART
**Best Picture:** see page 718
of 1955: 5 MARTY
of 1958: 4 GIGI
of 1968: 6 OLIVER
of 1977: 9 ANNIEHALL
of 1982: 6 GANDHI
of 1984: 7 AMADEUS
of 1986: 7 PLATOON
of 1997: 7 TITANIC
of 1998: 7 RAINMAN
**Best Play:** see page 722
**Best Supporting Actor:** see page
720
**Best Supporting Actress:** see
pages 720–721
**Best Western**
competitor: 6 RAMADA
**Bet:** 4 LAID 5 WAGER
7 WAGERED
Match a: 3 SEE
preceder: 4 ANTE
Track: 6 EXACTA
**Beta**
follower: 3 RAY 5 GAMMA
___ Beta Kappa: 3 PHI
**Betamax**
creator: 4 SONY
**Bête ___:** 5 NOIRE
**Betel**
palm: 5 ARECA
**Betelgeuse:** 4 STAR
constellation: 5 ORION
**Beth**
preceder: 5 ALEPH
**Bethlehem**
product: 5 STEEL
school: 6 LEHIGH
visitors: 4 MAGI
Woman from: 5 NAOMI
**Betray:** 5 RATON
7 TWOTIME
boredom: 4 YAWN
**Betrothal**
symbol: 4 RING
**Betrothed:** 7 ENGAGED
**Betsy**
Seamstress: 4 ROSS
**"Betsy's Wedding"**
actor Alan: 4 ALDA
**"Bette Davis Eyes"**
singer Carnes: 3 KIM

**Bettelheim**
Psychologist: 5 BRUNO
**Better:** 5 AMEND EMEND
6 ENRICH 7 ENHANCE
IMPROVE
10 AMELIORATE
copy: 4 EDIT
equipped: 5 ABLER
Get: 4 HEAL
Get the ~ of: 5 ONEUP
WORST
Go one: 3 TOP 5 OUTDO
half: 6 SPOUSE
informed: 5 WISER
Make: 4 CURE HEAL
5 AMEND
No ~ than: 4 MERE
than average: 8 ABOVEPAR
**"Better ___ than never":** 4 LATE
**Betting**
game: 5 BEANO
group: 4 POOL
info: 4 ODDS
odds: 4 LINE
setting: 4 RENO 5 VEGAS
6 CASINO
**Bettor**
aid: 6 SYSTEM
figures: 4 ODDS
**Betty**
of cartoons: 4 BOOP
Pinup girl: 6 GRABLE
**Between**
assignments: 4 IDLE
Few and far: 4 RARE 6 SPARSE
ports: 4 ASEA 5 ATSEA
~, in French: 5 ENTRE
~, poetically: 5 TWIXT
**Beulah**
Actress: 5 BONDI
**Bevan, Bev**
band: 3 ELO
**Beveled**
edges: 5 CANTS
**Beverage:** 5 DRINK
Ballpark: 4 BEER
Brewed: 3 ALE
Brown: 4 COLA
Brunch: 6 MIMOSA
Bubbly: 4 SODA
French: 3 THE
Honey: 4 MEAD
Japanese: 4 SAKE
Malt: 3 ALE
nut: 4 KOLA
Seasonal: 3 NOG
Social: 3 TEA
Wine and fruit: 7 SANGRIA
**"Beverly Hillbillies, The"**
actor Buddy: 5 EBSEN
actor Max: 4 BAER
actress Ryan: 5 IRENE
role: 3 JED 6 JETHRO
role ___ May: 4 ELLY
**"Beverly Hills Cop"**
character Foley: 4 AXEL

**Beverly Hills Drive:** 5 RODEO
**Bewail:** 5 MOURN 6 LAMENT
**Beware**
  Dog to: 5 BITER
  One who should: 5 BUYER
  Sign to: 4 OMEN
  Time to: 4 IDES
**"Beware ... of jealousy"**
  speaker: 4 IAGO
**Bewhiskered:** 5 HAIRY
    7 HIRSUTE
  animal: 4 SEAL 5 OTTER
    6 WALRUS
**Bewilder:** 4 DAZE 5 ADDLE
    AMAZE 6 PUZZLE
**Bewildered:** 4 ASEA LOST
    5 ATSEA 7 ATALOSS
    INADAZE
**Bewitch:** 3 HEX 6 ENAMOR
    7 ENCHANT
**"Bewitched"**
  actress Moorehead: 5 AGNES
  aunt: 5 CLARA
  character: 6 ENDORA
    7 TABITHA
**Beyond:** 4 PAST
  Go: 8 OVERSTEP
  partner: 5 ABOVE
**"Beyond Good and Evil"**
  author: 9 NIETZSCHE
**"Beyond the Sea"**
  singer: 5 DARIN
**B flat**
  equivalent: 6 ASHARP
**Bhutan**
  locale: 4 ASIA
  neighbor: 5 ASSAM
**Bi**
  halved: 3 UNI
  plus one: 3 TRI
**Bias:** 4 SKEW 5 SLANT
**Biased:** 7 COLORED SLANTED
    8 ONASLANT ONESIDED
    PARTISAN
  person: 5 BIGOT
**Biathlon**
  need: 4 SKIS 5 RIFLE
**Bib**
  Need a: 5 DROOL
**Bible**
  book: 4 ACTS AMOS 5 HOSEA
    MICAH 6 ESTHER
  book (abbr.): 3 NEH 4 ESTH
  division: 5 VERSE
  Hotel ~ provider: 6 GIDEON
  It has a part in the: 6 REDSEA
  Last word of the: 4 AMEN
  verb ending: 3 ETH
**Biblical**
  beast: 3 ASS
  Bit of ~ writing: 4 MENE
  boat: 3 ARK
  boat builder: 4 NOAH
  brother: 4 ABEL ESAU
    5 AARON
  bushel: 4 EPHA

footwear: 6 SANDAL
garden: 4 EDEN
gift: 5 MYRRH
judge: 3 ELI
king: 5 HEROD
kingdom: 4 EDOM ELAM
    MOAB
measure: 5 CUBIT
miracle site: 4 CANA
no-no: 3 SIN
patriarch: 5 ISAAC
peak: 5 HOREB SINAI
    6 ARARAT
poem: 5 PSALM
possessive: 5 THINE
preposition: 4 UNTO
priest: 3 ELI
pronoun: 3 THY 4 THEE
    THOU
prophet: 4 AMOS 5 HOSEA
queendom: 5 SHEBA
query: 5 ISITI
shepherd: 4 ABEL
sin city: 5 SODOM
song: 5 PSALM
spy: 5 CALEB
strongman: 6 SAMSON
suffix: 3 ETH
twin: 4 ESAU
verb: 4 DOTH HAST HATH
    5 HADST
verb ending: 3 ETH
vessel: 3 ARK
villain: 5 HEROD
weed: 4 TARE
**Bibliography**
  abbr.: 4 AUTH ETAL 5 OPCIT
  info: 5 TITLE
  phrase: 6 ETALII
  word: 4 IDEM
**Bibliophile**
  concern: 7 EDITION
  purchase: 4 TOME
  room: 3 DEN
  Suffix for a: 3 ANA 4 IANA
**Bic**
  buy: 3 PEN
  filler: 3 INK
**Biceps:** 6 FLEXOR MUSCLE
  builders: 7 CHINUPS
  Show one's: 4 FLEX
**Bicker:** 5 ARGUE
**Bickering:** 4 ATIT TIFF
**Bickle, Travis**
  drove one: 4 TAXI
**Bicolor**
  bite: 4 OREO
**Bicuspid:** 5 TOOTH
  base: 4 ROOT
  neighbor: 5 MOLAR
**Bicycle**
  built for two: 6 TANDEM
  part: 4 DECK SEAT
    10 BANANASEAT
  wheel part: 5 SPOKE
  with an engine: 5 MOPED

**"Bicycle Thief, The"**
  director: 6 DESICA
**Bid:** 5 OFFER
  Bridge: 5 ONENO
  Final: 4 PASS
  first: 4 OPEN 6 OPENED
  It may be: 5 ADIEU
  No: 5 IPASS
  the bed adieu: 5 ARISE
**Bidding:** 6 BEHEST
  Begin: 4 OPEN
  Do the ~ of: 4 OBEY
  Place to do one's: 4 EBAY
  site: 4 EBAY
**Biddy:** 3 HEN
**Bide**
  one's time: 4 WAIT 5 AWAIT
**Bide-___ :** 4 AWEE
**Bien**
  opposite: 3 MAL
**"___ bien!":** 4 TRES
**Biennial**
  vegetable: 4 BEET
**___ Bien Phu:** 4 DIEN
**Bierce**
  Author: 7 AMBROSE
  In bad company, according to:
    5 ALONE
**Big:** 4 HUGE 5 LARGE OBESE
  do: 4 AFRO GALA
  game: 4 DEER ELKS
  Make it: 6 ARRIVE
  prefix: 4 MAXI MEGA
  shot: 3 VIP 4 CZAR 5 CELEB
    6 FATCAT
  show: 4 EXPO
  wheel: 5 CHIEF NABOB
    7 MAGNATE
**Big ___ :** 3 BEN MAC SUR
    6 BERTHA
**"Big ___"**
  of the comic pages: 4 NATE
**Big Apple**
  award: 4 OBIE
  ballpark: 4 ASHE SHEA
  cardinal: 4 EGAN
  inits.: 3 NYC 4 NYNY
  neighborhood: 4 SOHO
  stadium: 4 ASHE SHEA
  subway stop (abbr.): 3 LEX
**"Big Bad John"**
  actor Jack: 4 ELAM
**Big Band:** 3 ERA
  brother: 6 DORSEY
  follower: 3 ERA
  member: 3 SAX
  music: 5 SWING
**Big bang**
  producer: 3 TNT 5 NITRO
**Big Bertha:** 3 GUN
  birthplace: 5 ESSEN
**Big-billed**
  bird: 6 TOUCAN 7 PELICAN
**"Big Blue":** 3 IBM
**Big Board**
  letters: 4 NYSE

**Big deal:** 3 ADO
**"Big deal!":** 6 SOWHAT
**Big East**
team: 4 PITT 5 HOYAS MIAMI
6 SAINTS
**Bigfoot**
cousin: 4 YETI
Like: 5 HAIRY
**Bigger**
Get: 4 GROW
than med.: 3 LGE
**Biggers**
detective: 4 CHAN
**Biggers, Earl ___**
Author: 4 DERR
**"___ bigger than a breadbox?":**
4 ISIT
**Biggie**
Business: 3 CEO 4 EXEC
5 TITAN
Media: 5 MOGUL
Valhalla: 4 ODIN
**Bight of Benin**
capital: 5 ACCRA
city: 5 LAGOS
**Big Mama:** 4 CASS
**Bigmouth:** 4 BASS
**Big-mouthed**
pitcher: 4 EWER
**Bigot:** 5 HATER 6 RACIST
on TV: 12 ARCHIEBUNKER
**Big ___ outdoors:** 5 ASALL
**Big Red:** 5 LENIN 6 STALIN
opponent: 3 ELI
**"Big Red, The":** 7 CORNELL
**Big-screen**
format: 4 IMAX
**Big Ten**
sch.: 3 OSU
school: 4 IOWA
team: 6 ILLINI
**Big Twelve**
athlete: 5 AGGIE
school: 6 KANSAS
**Bigwig:** 3 VIP 5 NABOB
Aesir: 4 ODIN
Business: 4 CZAR 5 MOGUL
Campus: 4 DEAN
Corp.: 3 CEO 4 EXEC
D.C.: 3 SEN
Kuwaiti: 4 EMIR
Mafia: 4 CAPO
Mideast: 4 EMIR 6 SULTAN
Mosque: 4 IMAM
Turkish: 3 AGA 5 PASHA
Valhalla: 4 ODIN
Venetian: 4 DOGE
**Bijou:** 3 GEM
Sign at the: 3 SRO
**Bike:** 5 CYCLE PEDAL
Go by: 5 PEDAL
type: 6 TANDEM 8 TENSPEED
with a small engine: 5 MOPED
**Biker**
A ~ might pop one:
7 WHEELIE

protection: 6 HELMET
wear: 7 LEATHER
**Bikini:** 5 ATOLL ISLET
alternative: 8 ONEPIECE
blast: 5 ATEST
experiment: 5 NTEST
part: 3 BRA
top: 3 BRA
~, once: 8 TESTSITE
**Bil**
Cartoonist: 5 KEANE
Puppeteer: 5 BAIRD
**Bilbo:** 5 SWORD
**Bile:** 3 IRE
**Bilko:** 5 ERNIE
actor: 7 SILVERS
nickname: 5 SARGE
rank (abbr.): 3 SGT 4 MSGT
**Bilko, Sgt.:** 5 ERNIE
**Bill:** 3 TAB 4 BEAK
(abbr.): 3 INV
add-on: 3 TAX 5 RIDER
8 SALESTAX
Bar: 3 TAB
Big: 5 CNOTE
Comedian ~, informally: 3 COS
Designer: 5 BLASS
Fill the: 3 EAT
Govt.: 5 TNOTE
Humorist: 3 NYE
in Washington: 5 GATES
killer: 4 VETO
Monthly: 5 CABLE
of fare: 4 MENU 5 CARTE
partner: 3 COO
Pass a: 5 ENACT
provider (abbr.): 3 ATM
Small: 3 ONE
Take care of, as a: 3 PAY
4 FOOT
They fill the: 5 CENTS
Till: 3 ONE
Utility ~ (abbr.): 4 ELEC
with a pyramid: 3 ONE
**"Bill & ___ Excellent Adventure":**
4 TEDS
**Billboard:** 4 SIGN
displays: 3 ADS
listings: 4 HITS
**Billet-___:** 4 DOUX
**Billet-doux**
beginner: 4 CHER DEAR
**Billfold:** 6 WALLET
contents: 4 ONES
**Billiards**
gadget: 4 RACK
need: 5 CHALK
shot: 5 CAROM MASSE
stick: 3 CUE
stroke: 5 MASSE
8 SIDESPIN
**Billing**
cycle: 5 MONTH
Get top: 4 STAR
One with equal: 6 COSTAR
unit: 4 HOUR

**Billion**
A ~ years: 3 EON 4 AEON
add-on: 4 AIRE
Faith of more than one:
5 ISLAM
Home to over one: 5 INDIA
Home to over three: 4 ASIA
**Billionaire**
Pockets of a: 4 DEEP
~ Bill: 5 GATES
**Billions:** 4 ALOT
Home to: 4 ASIA
**Billionth**
prefix: 4 NANO
**Bill of Rights**
defender (abbr.): 4 ACLU
**Bills:** 4 CASH 5 DEBTS
Big: 5 THOUS
Bologna: 4 LIRE
Bunch of: 3 WAD
Has: 4 OWES
Rare: 4 TWOS
Roll of: 3 WAD
Some: 4 TENS
**Bill the Cat**
statement: 3 ACK
**"Bill ___, the Science Guy":**
3 NYE
**Billy**
Actor: 4 ZANE
Evangelist: 6 GRAHAM
Melville's: 4 BUDD
Rocker: 4 IDOL
Singer: 4 JOEL 5 OCEAN
~, for one: 3 KID
**"Billy Budd":** 5 OPERA
captain: 4 VERE
**"Billy, Don't Be ___":**
5 AHERO
**"Billy, Don't ___ Hero":** 3 BEA
**"___ Billy Joe":** 5 ODETO
**Biloxi-to-Mobile**
dir.: 3 ENE
**Binary:** 4 DUAL
digit: 3 ONE
**Binchy**
Author: 5 MAEVE
**Bind:** 3 TIE 4 YOKE 5 UNITE
6 CEMENT ENLACE
OBLIGE
~, as fowl: 5 TRUSS
**Binding**
agreement: 3 IDO
material: 5 TWINE
Not: 4 VOID
order: 5 EDICT
**Bindle**
bearer: 4 HOBO
stiff: 4 HOBO
**Binet, Alfred**
creation: 6 IQTEST
data: 3 IQS
**Bing**
label: 5 DECCA
Milieu for ~ and Bob: 4 ROAD
Sing like: 5 CROON

**Binge:** 3 JAG 4 TOOT 5 SPREE
    10 GOONASPREE
**Bingham**
  Actress: 5 TRACI
**Binghamton**
  City near: 5 OWEGO
    6 ELMIRA 7 ONEONTA
**"___ Bingle":** 3 DER
**Bingo**
  call: 4 BTEN
  relative: 4 KENO 5 BEANO
**"Bingo!":** 3 AHA 5 RIGHT
**Binoculars**
  Use: 3 SPY 4 SCAN
**Bio:** 4 LIFE 7 PROFILE
  bit: 3 AGE
  Broadway: 3 TRU
  lab specimen: 6 AMOEBA
  Postmortem: 4 OBIT
  word: 3 NEE
**Biochemical**
  catalyst: 6 ENZYME
    7 OXIDASE
**Bioelectric**
  swimmer: 3 EEL
**Biography:** 4 LIFE
    9 LIFESTORY
**"Biography"**
  network: 5 AANDE
**Biol.:** 3 SCI
  branch: 4 ECOL
  course: 4 ANAT
**Biological**
  bristle: 4 SETA
  classification: 7 SPECIES
  classifications: 4 TAXA
    6 GENERA
  container: 3 SAC
  group: 5 GENUS
  ring of color: 6 AREOLA
  sci.: 4 ANAT
  walls: 5 SEPTA
**Biology**
  Attached, in: 6 ADNATE
  prefix: 3 EXO 4 AERO AGRO
    5 ETHNO PALEO
  subj.: 4 ANAT
  topic: 3 DNA RNA
**Bioluminescence**
  Marine: 7 SEAFIRE
**Biondi**
  Swimmer: 4 MATT
**"Bionic Woman, The"**
  role: 5 JAIME
**Biopic**
  2001 ~: 3 ALI
**Biotite:** 4 MICA
**Biplane**
  part: 5 STRUT
**Birch:** 4 TREE
  craft: 5 CANOE
  family member: 5 ALDER
  of Indiana: 4 BAYH
**Birchbark:** 5 CANOE
**Bird**
  abode: 4 NEST

beak: 3 NEB NIB
Big: 3 EMU
Diving: 3 AUK 4 LOON
  5 GREBE
Extinct: 3 MOA 4 DODO
Fabulous: 3 ROC
Flightless: 3 EMU 4 KIWI
  RHEA
Flightless (var.): 4 EMEU
Hawaiian: 4 NENE
home: 4 NEST
instrument: 3 SAX
  7 ALTOSAX
Marsh: 4 RAIL SORA 5 CRAKE
  EGRET HERON SNIPE
Mythical: 3 ROC
Night: 3 OWL
Nile: 4 IBIS
prefix: 3 AVI
raised on ranches: 3 EMU
Sea: 3 ERN 4 ERNE
Shore: 3 ERN 4 ERNE GULL
  TERN 5 HERON
Sinbad: 3 ROC
Small: 3 TIT 6 TOMTIT
sound: 5 TRILL
State: *see page 723*
Talking: 4 MYNA
Three-toed: 4 RHEA
Wading: 4 IBIS 5 CRANE
  EGRET STILT STORK
Water: 4 COOT
White-tailed: 3 ERN 4 ERNE
Whooping: 5 CRANE
Word from a: 5 TWEET
~, in Latin: 4 AVIS
**Birdbrain:** 3 ASS 4 DODO DOLT
  5 IDIOT 6 NITWIT
**Birdhouse**
  dweller: 4 WREN
**Birdie:** 8 UNDERPAR
  beater: 5 EAGLE
  Miss a: 7 MAKEPAR
  plus one: 3 PAR
**Birdlike:** 5 AVIAN
**Birdman of Alcatraz:** 5 LIFER
  6 STROUD
**"Bird on ___":** 5 AWIRE
**Bird-related:** 5 AVIAN
**Birds**
  For the: 5 AVIAN
  It's for the: 6 AVIARY
**"Birds, The"**
  actress Hedren: 5 TIPPI
  heroine: 7 MELANIE
  screenwriter Hunter: 4 EVAN
**Birds-feather**
  connection: 3 OFA
**Bird-to-be:** 3 EGG
**Birdy:** 5 AVIAN
**Bireme**
  feature: 3 OAR 4 TIER
**Birkerts**
  Author: 4 SVEN
**Birling**
  surface: 3 LOG

**Birney, Alfred ___**
  Poet: 5 EARLE
**Birth:** 5 ONSET
  Before: 7 INUTERO
  cert.: 5 IDENT
  control device (abbr.): 3 IUD
  Give ~ to: 4 HAVE 5 SPAWN
  Present from: 6 INNATE
  Regarding: 5 NATAL
**Birthday**
  attire: 4 SUIT
  dessert: 4 CAKE
  figure: 3 AGE
  In one's ~ suit: 4 BARE
    6 UNCLAD
  Like some ~ wishes:
    7 BELATED
  suit: 4 SKIN
**"Birth of a Nation, The"**
  gp.: 3 KKK
  group: 4 KLAN
**Birth-related:** 5 NATAL
**Birthright:** 8 HERITAGE
  Biblical ~ seller: 4 ESAU
**Birthstone:** *see page 725*
  Fall: 4 OPAL 5 TOPAZ
  February: 8 AMETHYST
  January: 6 GARNET
  July: 4 RUBY
  June: 5 PEARL
  May: 7 EMERALD
  November: 5 TOPAZ
  October: 4 OPAL
  September: 8 SAPPHIRE
**Biscayne Bay**
  city: 5 MIAMI
**Biscotti**
  flavoring: 5 ANISE
**Biscuit**
  English: 5 SCONE
  Teatime: 5 SCONE
**Bisect:** 5 HALVE
**Bisected:** 5 INTWO
**Bisector**
  Leaf: 6 MIDRIB
  Paris: 5 SEINE
**Bishop:** 7 PRELATE
  Comedian: 4 JOEY
  domain: 7 DIOCESE
  First ~ of Paris: 7 STDENIS
  First ~ of Rome: 7 STPETER
  headdress: 5 MITER
  headdress, in England:
    5 MITRE
  jurisdiction: 3 SEE
  of early TV: 4 JOEY
    5 SHEEN
  of Rome: 4 POPE
  South African: 4 TUTU
  subordinate: 6 PRIEST
**Bishopric:** 3 SEE
**Bismarck**
  state (abbr.): 4 NDAK
**Bison**
  Bunch of: 4 HERD
  feature: 4 MANE

**Bisque:** 4 SOUP
morsel: 4 CLAM
**Bissett**
Actress: 5 JOSIE
**Bistro:** 4 CAFE 6 EATERY
menu: 5 CARTE
sign word: 4 CHEZ
**Bit:** 3 DAB TAD 4 ATOM IOTA
SOME 5 SHRED
8 SOMEWHAT
attachment: 4 REIN
Basic: 4 ATOM
Even a: 5 ATALL
for a dog: 3 ORT
for a horse: 3 OAT
In a: 4 ANON SOON
Least: 4 IOTA WHIT
Little: 3 DAB JOT TAD
4 ATOM IOTA MITE
modifier: 3 WEE
Quite a: 4 LOTS 5 OFTEN
Tiny: 3 DAB 4 ATOM IOTA
MITE MOTE 5 TRACE
Wee: 3 TAD
___ bit: 3 INA 4 AWEE NOTA
**Bite:** 3 NIP 4 NOSH TANG
5 CHOMP NIPAT
Grab a: 3 EAT
Had a: 3 ATE
Have a: 3 EAT SUP 4 NOSH
5 TASTE
Least likely to: 6 TAMEST
like a beaver: 4 GNAW
Prepare to: 6 TEETHE
site: 4 CAFE
Small: 3 NIP
Sound: 5 QUOTE
Unlikely to: 4 TAME
**Biter**
Back: 5 MOLAR
Dog: 4 FLEA
Nile: 3 ASP
Small: 4 GNAT
**Biting:** 4 TART 5 ACERB ACRID
TANGY 6 ACIDIC
7 ACERBIC
remark: 4 BARB
wit: 4 ACID
___ bitten: 4 ONCE
**Bitter:** 5 ACERB ACRID
conflict: 6 STRIFE
drink: 3 ALE
end: 4 NESS
It may be: 3 ALE END
salad item: 9 DANDELION
**Bitter-___:** 5 ENDER
**Bittern:** 5 HERON
relative: 5 EGRET
**Bitterness:** 8 ACRIDITY
ACRIMONY
**Bivouac:** 6 ENCAMP
bed: 3 COT
facility: 7 LATRINE
shelter: 4 TENT
**Biz**
biggie: 3 CEO 4 EXEC

**Bizarre:** 3 ODD 5 EERIE
OUTRE WEIRD
**Bizet**
opera: 6 CARMEN
priestess: 5 LEILA
work: 4 ARIA 5 OPERA
6 CARMEN
**Bjorn**
of tennis: 4 BORG
rival: 4 ILIE
**Blab:** 3 YAK 4 SING TELL
7 TELLALL
**Blabbed:** 4 SUNG TOLD
15 SPILLEDTHEBEANS
**Blabbermouth:** 5 YENTA
Hardly a: 4 CLAM
**Black:** 3 SEA 4 EBON INKY
5 EBONY SABLE
Actress: 5 KAREN
bird: 3 ANI DAW 5 RAVEN
cat: 4 OMEN
cuckoo: 3 ANI
Deep: 3 JET 4 EBON INKY
5 RAVEN SABLE
eye: 6 SHINER
fly: 4 GNAT
gold: 3 OIL
gunk: 3 TAR
ink item: 5 ASSET
In the: 4 ASEA
Jet: 4 ONYX 5 SABLE
Justice: 4 HUGO
key: 5 AFLAT EFLAT
6 ASHARP
Lustrous: 5 RAVEN
mark: 6 STIGMA
One in a ~ suit: 5 SPADE
shade: 3 INK 4 COAL
Singer: 5 CLINT
tea: 5 PEKOE
Wear: 5 MOURN
wood: 5 EBONY
~, in French: 4 NOIR
~, to a bard: 4 EBON
~, to Blake: 4 EBON
"___ Black" (sci-fi film):
5 MENIN
**Black and ___** (dog breed):
3 TAN
**Black-and-orange**
bird: 6 ORIOLE
**Black-and-white**
bamboo eater: 5 PANDA
cookie: 4 OREO
diver: 3 AUK
driver: 3 COP
killer: 4 ORCA
treat: 4 OREO
**Blackball:** 4 SHUN
9 OSTRACIZE
**Black Bears**
home: 5 ORONO
**"Black Beauty"**
actress Freeman: 4 MONA
author Anna: 6 SEWELL
**Blackbird:** 3 ANI 4 MERL

Where to find a baked:
6 INAPIE
**Blackboard:** 5 SLATE
Clear the: 5 ERASE
**"Blackboard Jungle, The"**
author Hunter: 4 EVAN
**Black-bordered**
bio: 4 OBIT
**"Black Camel, The"**
detective: 4 CHAN
**Black ___ cattle:** 5 ANGUS
**Blacken:** 3 TAR 4 CHAR SEAR
**Black-eyed**
legume: 3 PEA 6 COWPEA
**Black-eyed ___:** 3 PEA 5 SUSAN
**Black-footed**
animal: 6 FERRET
**Blackguard:** 3 CAD CUR RAT
4 HEEL
**Blackjack:** 4 COSH
card: 3 ACE TEN
dealer's tip: 4 TOKE
Good score in: 8 NINETEEN
option: 4 STAY
request: 5 HITME
**Blackmore**
heroine: 5 DOONE
10 LORNADOONE
heroine Doone: 5 LORNA
**"Black Narcissus"**
actress Deborah: 4 KERR
**"Black Orpheus"**
setting: 3 RIO
**Blackout:** 3 BAN
**Black Panthers**
founder Bobby: 5 SEALE
**"Black Pearl, The":** 4 PELE
**Blacks**
out: 6 SWOONS
**Black Sea**
country: 7 ROMANIA
port: 6 ODESSA
**Blacksmith:** 5 SHOER
attire: 5 APRON
block: 5 ANVIL
metal: 4 IRON
tool: 4 RASP
**"Black Stallion, The"**
boy: 4 ALEC
horse: 7 ARABIAN
**"Black Star, Bright Dawn"**
author Scott: 5 ODELL
**Blackthorn:** 4 SLOE
fruit: 4 SLOE
**Blade:** 3 OAR
Blunted: 4 EPEE
brand: 4 ATRA
Bygone: 4 SNEE
Chopper: 5 ROTOR
Fencing: 4 EPEE
Fictional: 5 ATHOS
Gangster: 4 SHIV
handle: 4 HILT
metal: 5 STEEL
Precision: 5 XACTO
Shoulder: 7 SCAPULA

site: 5 SKATE
Sporting: 4 EPEE
Windmill: 4 VANE
**Blades**
Singer: 5 RUBEN
Use ~ on: 3 MOW
**Blah:** 5 HOHUM 7 PROSAIC
**"Blah, blah, blah":** 6 ETCETC
**Blahs:** 5 ENNUI
Have the: 3 AIL
**Blair**
Actress: 5 LINDA
and others (abbr.): 3 PMS
of Britain: 4 TONY
**Blair, Tony**
Party of: 6 LABOUR
**Blaise**
Mathematician: 6 PASCAL
**Blake**
Actress: 6 AMANDA
Jazz musician: 5 EUBIE
**Blake, Robert**
series: 7 BARETTA
**Blakey**
Jazz musician: 3 ART
**Blakley**
Actress: 5 RONEE
**Blame:** 3 RAP 4 ONUS 5 FAULT
6 ACCUSE
Accept: 7 EATDIRT
Assign, as: 5 PINON
bearer: 4 GOAT
Unfair: 6 BADRAP
Who might be to: 5 NOONE
**"Blame It on ___":** 3 RIO
**"Blame it on the ___ Nova":**
5 BOSSA
**Blanc:** 3 MEL
of Bugs Bunny: 3 MEL
**___ Blanc:** 4 MONT 6 CHENIN
**Blanche**
Carte: 8 FREEREIN
Fictional: 6 DUBOIS
Sister of: 6 STELLA
**___ blanche:** 5 CARTE
**Blanched:** 3 WAN 4 PALE
5 ASHEN
**Blanchett**
Actress: 4 CATE
**Blandness:** 7 NOTASTE
**Blank**
Draw a: 6 FORGET
It may be: 5 STARE
look: 5 STARE
Make: 5 ERASE
Word after: 5 VERSE
**Blanket:** 7 OVERLIE
Beach: 4 SAND
Boy with a: 5 LINUS
Knitted: 6 AFGHAN
Wet: 7 KILLJOY
11 PARTYPOOPER
Winter: 4 SNOW
**___ blanket:** 3 WET
**Blanks, Billy**
workout program: 5 TAEBO

**Blare**
Trumpet: 7 TANTARA
**Blaring:** 4 LOUD 6 BRASSY
**Blarney Stone**
home: 4 EIRE ERIN
**"___ Blas" (LeSage novel):** 3 GIL
**Blasé:** 5 BORED JADED
**Blass**
competitor: 5 BEENE
**Blast:** 3 GAS 5 SALVO
Clarion: 7 TANTARA
from the past: 5 ATEST NTEST
OLDIE
furnace input: 3 ORE
7 IRONORE
It's a: 3 TNT
maker: 3 TNT
of wind: 4 GUST
Short: 4 TOOT
Trumpet: 7 TANTARA
**"Blast!":** 4 DANG DARN
**Blaster**
need: 3 TNT
Rock: 3 AMP
**___ blaster:** 6 GHETTO
**Blastoff**
preceder: 3 ONE
**Blatant:** 5 OVERT
deception: 7 CHARADE
**Blather:** 3 GAS 5 PRATE
RUNON 6 HOTAIR
**Blaze**
Big: 7 BONFIRE
~, in French: 3 FEU
**Blazer:** 3 SUV
cleaner: 7 CARWASH
part: 5 LAPEL
Slit in a: 4 VENT
**Blazes**
It may go to: 4 HOSE
Went like the: 4 TORE
**Blazing:** 3 LIT 5 AFIRE
6 AFLAME AFLARE
AGLARE
**"Blazing Saddles"**
actress Madeline: 4 KAHN
director Brooks: 3 MEL
**Bldg.**
Municipal: 3 CTR
unit: 3 APT
**Bleach:** 6 WHITEN 8 ETIOLATE
**Bleacher**
creature: 3 FAN
feature: 4 TIER
suffix: 3 ITE
**Bleachers**
Sell in the: 4 VEND
sound: 3 BOO RAH
**Bleaching**
agent: 3 LYE
**Bleak:** 4 GRIM 6 DISMAL
~, in verse: 5 DREAR
**Bleat:** 3 BAA MAA
**Bleater:** 3 EWE 4 LAMB
Baby: 3 KID
**"Blecch!":** 3 UGH

**Bled:** 3 RAN
**Bleed:** 3 RUN
**Bleep:** 7 EDITOUT
out: 5 ERASE 6 CENSOR
**Bleeped**
It may be: 4 OATH
**Blemish:** 3 MAR 4 FLAW MOLE
SCAR SPOT 5 STAIN
Fender: 4 DENT
Shoe: 5 SCUFF
Skin: 4 MOLE WART
**Blend:** 3 MIX 4 MELD STIR
5 ADMIX IMMIX
with traffic: 5 MERGE
**Blender**
brand: 5 OSTER
setting: 3 MIX 5 PUREE
sound: 4 WHIR
**Blessed**
bread holder: 5 PATEN
event: 6 SNEEZE
It may be: 5 EVENT
**Blessing:** 4 BOON 7 GODSEND
Cause for a: 5 ACHOO
6 SNEEZE
preceder: 5 ACHOO 6 SNEEZE
**"___ bleu!":** 5 SACRE
**Blight:** 7 EYESORE
Tomato: 5 EDEMA
Urban: 4 SLUM SMOG
victim: 3 ELM
**Blimpie**
rival: 7 QUIZNOS
**Blind**
It may be: 5 ALLEY
part: 4 SLAT
spot location: 6 RETINA
**Blind as ___:** 4 ABAT
**Blindly**
Search: 5 GROPE
**Blini:** 6 CREPES
**Blink:** 3 BAT
of an eye: 3 SEC
**Blinker:** 3 EYE 6 EYELID
10 TURNSIGNAL
Broadway: 4 NEON
Screen: 6 CURSOR
**Blip**
producer: 5 RADAR SONAR
**Bliss:** 6 HEAVEN 7 ECSTASY
8 EUPHORIA PARADISE
Place of: 4 EDEN
**Blissful:** 6 EDENIC ELATED
7 ELYSIAN
state: 4 EDEN
**Blithe:** 8 CAREFREE
spirit: 4 ELAN
**Blithering**
person: 5 IDIOT
**"Blithe Spirit"**
playwright: 10 NOELCOWARD
**Blitz:** 6 REDDOG
Kind of: 5 MEDIA
**Blitzer**
employer: 3 CNN
Journalist: 4 WOLF

**Blixen**
 pseudonym: 7 DINESEN
**Bloated:** 5 GASSY
**Blob**
 Move like the: 4 OOZE
**Bloc:** 5 UNION
 Big voting: 5 LABOR
 Doc: 3 AMA
**Block:** 3 BAN BAR 5 DAMUP
  DETER 6 IMPEDE
 Building: 4 UNIT 5 ADOBE
  BRICK
 Building ~ brand: 4 LEGO
 buster: 6 ICEMAN
 end: 3 ADE
 house: 5 IGLOO
 Illegal: 4 CLIP
 legally: 5 ESTOP
 Recent ~ arrival: 6 NEWKID
 suffix: 3 ADE
 Sun: 5 CLOUD 7 ECLIPSE
 Tiny building: 4 ATOM
 Toy ~ company: 4 LEGO
 up: 3 DAM
**Blockade:** 5 SIEGE
**Blockage:** 4 CLOG CLOT
  6 LOGJAM
 Blood: 4 CLOT
**Blockbuster**
 of 1975: 4 JAWS
 rental: 3 DVD 5 VIDEO
 transaction: 6 RENTAL
**Blocker:** 3 DAM
 Actor: 3 DAN
 Kind of: 4 BETA
 Sun: 5 CLOUD
 Ultraviolet: 5 OZONE
 X-ray: 4 LEAD
 ___ blocker: 4 BETA
**Blocker, Dan**
 role: 4 HOSS
**Blockhead:** 3 ASS LUG OAF
  SAP 4 CLOD DODO DOLT
  FOOL
**Bloke:** 3 EGG 4 CHAP GENT
  MATE
**Blonde**
 Go ~, maybe: 3 DYE
 Like some ~ hair: 4 DYED
 shade: 3 ASH 5 SANDY
**Blondie:** 7 CATERER
 Husband of: 7 DAGWOOD
**"Blondie":** 5 STRIP
 boy: 4 ELMO
 creator Young: 4 CHIC
 Mrs. Dithers of: 4 CORA
**Blood:** 3 KIN
 Bad: 6 ANIMUS ENMITY
  RANCOR
 bank supply: 6 PLASMA
 blockage: 4 CLOT
 carrier: 5 AORTA
 classification: 5 TYPEA TYPEB
 classification system: 3 ABO
 component: 5 SERUM
  6 PLASMA

 components: 4 SERA
 Flesh and: 3 KIN
 giver: 5 DONOR
 Hot: 3 IRE 5 ARDOR
 line: 4 VEIN 5 AORTA
  6 ARTERY
 measure: 4 UNIT
 Of the: 5 HEMAL
 of the gods: 5 ICHOR
 pigment: 4 HEME
 prefix: 4 HEMA HEMO
 Rare: 6 TYPEAB
 Related by: 4 AKIN
 type, briefly: 4 APOS ONEG
 vessel: 5 AORTA
**Bloodhound:** 7 TRACKER
 asset: 4 NOSE
 clue: 4 ODOR 5 SCENT
 trail: 5 SCENT
**Bloodmobile**
 Visit a: 6 DONATE
**Bloodshot:** 3 RED
**Bloodsucker:** 5 LEECH
 African: 6 TSETSE
**Blood-typing**
 letters: 3 ABO
 system: 3 ABO
**Bloom**
 Actress: 6 CLAIRE
 Daisylike: 5 ASTER
 Purple: 5 LILAC
 September: 5 ASTER
 Spring: 4 IRIS 5 PEONY
 Thorny: 4 ROSE
**"Bloom County"**
 penguin: 4 OPUS
**Bloomer**
 Autumn: 5 ASTER
 Fall: 5 ASTER
 Late: 5 ASTER
 Spring: 5 LILAC 6 AZALEA
 Suffragist: 6 AMELIA
 Whitman: 5 LILAC
**Blooming:** 8 INFLOWER
 business: 3 FTD
 month: 5 APRIL
 neckwear: 3 LEI
**Bloomingdale's**
 competitor: 4 SAKS
**Blooper:** 4 SLIP 5 ERROR
  GAFFE
 Made a: 5 ERRED
**Blossom:** 5 BLOOM
 holder: 4 STEM
**Blossom-to-be:** 3 BUD
**Blot:** 6 STIGMA 7 EYESORE
 out: 5 ERASE
**Blotch:** 4 SPOT 5 STAIN
 Driveway: 3 OIL
**Blotter**
 info: 5 ALIAS
 letters: 3 AKA
**Blotto:** 3 LIT 5 FRIED OILED
  STIFF 6 LOOPED
  SOUSED STEWED
  STONED TANKED

**Blount**
 of football: 3 MEL
**Blouse:** 3 TOP 5 SHIRT
 Kind of: 7 PEASANT
**Bloviate:** 5 ORATE
**Blow:** 5 ERUPT
 a gasket: 5 GOAPE
 away: 3 AWE 5 AMAZE
 Big: 4 GALE
 gently: 4 WAFT
 it: 3 ERR
 Karate: 4 CHOP
 off steam: 4 HISS VENT
 one's horn: 4 TOOT
 one's top: 5 ERUPT
 out: 6 EXHALE
 Powerful: 4 SWAT
 React to a: 8 SEESTARS
 Severe: 4 GALE
 Sharp: 4 SLAP
 Sudden: 4 GUST
 the whistle: 3 RAT
 up: 4 RAGE 5 ERUPT
  6 GETMAD 7 ENLARGE
  GETSORE
 up (abbr.): 3 ENL
 ~, as a game: 4 LOSE
**Blower**
 Sicilian: 4 ETNA
 Whistle: 3 REF 6 TOOTER
**Blowfish:** 6 PUFFER
 ___ & the: 6 HOOTIE
**Blowgun**
 ammo: 3 PEA 4 DART
**Blowhard**
 Act the: 4 BRAG
 offering: 5 BOAST
 trait: 3 EGO
**Blowhole:** 4 VENT
**"Blowin' in the Wind"**
 singer/composer: 5 DYLAN
**Blown**
 away: 4 AWED 5 INAWE
  6 AMAZED 7 STUNNED
 It may be: 4 FUSE 6 GASKET
**Blowout:** 4 BASH GALA
**Blows**
 Come to: 4 SPAR
 It ~ off steam: 6 GEYSER
 Where she: 4 THAR
**Blowtorch**
 Use a: 4 WELD
**Blowup**
 (abbr.): 3 ENL
 Atlas: 5 INSET
 Cause of a: 3 TNT
**BLT**
 part: 5 BACON 6 TOMATO
 spread: 4 MAYO
**Blubber:** 3 CRY FAT SOB
  4 BAWL WEEP
  6 BOOHOO
 Strip ~ from: 6 FLENSE
**Bludgeon:** 4 COSH
**"___ Blu Dipinto di Blu":** 3 NEL
**Blue:** 3 LOW SAD 6 EROTIC

bird: 3 JAY
blood, briefly: 6 ARISTO
bloods: 5 ELITE
Bluer than: 7 OBSCENE
books: 4 PORN SMUT
   7 EROTICA
cartoon character: 5 SMURF
chip: 4 ANTE
Dark: 4 NAVY
Deep: 4 ANIL
dye: 4 ANIL 6 INDIGO
eyes: 5 TRAIT
Feeling: 3 SAD
flag: 4 IRIS
follower: 4 NILE
Get a ~ ribbon: 3 WIN
Greenish: 4 AQUA CYAN
   TEAL
Heraldic: 5 AZURE
hue: 4 AQUA CYAN NAVY
   TEAL 5 AZURE
In a ~ funk: 3 SAD
jeans: 5 LEVIS
Like a ~ moon: 4 RARE
of baseball: 4 VIDA
ox: 4 BABE
prints: 7 EROTICA
shade: 3 SKY 4 ANIL AQUA
   NAVY NILE TEAL 5 ROYAL
   6 COBALT
Sky: 5 AZURE
Somewhat: 4 RACY
Talk a ~ streak: 3 GAB YAK
   4 CUSS 5 RUNON SWEAR
toon: 5 SMURF
True: 5 LOYAL
Turn: 3 DYE 6 SADDEN
Wild ~ yonder: 3 SKY
   5 ETHER
"___ Blue": 4 NYPD
"___ Blue?": 3 AMI
**Bluebeard**
Last wife of: 6 FATIMA
**"Blueberry Hill"**
singer Domino: 4 FATS
**Blue Bonnet**
product: 4 OLEO
**Blue-book**
filler: 5 ESSAY
**"Blue Chips"**
actor Nick: 5 NOLTE
**BlueChoice:** 3 HMO
**Blue Cross**
alternative: 5 AETNA
**"Blue Dahlia, The"**
actor: 4 LADD
actress: 12 VERONICALAKE
**Blue Devils**
home: 4 DUKE
**Blue Eagle**
org.: 3 NRA
**Bluefin:** 4 TUNA
**Bluegill**
relative: 5 BREAM
**Bluegrass**
instrument: 5 BANJO

musician Bill: 6 MONROE
musician Lester: 5 FLATT
**Blue-green:** 4 AQUA CYAN
   TEAL
**Blue Grotto**
locale: 5 CAPRI
**"Blue Hawaii"**
star: 5 ELVIS
**Bluejacket:** 3 TAR
**Blue Jays**
home: 7 TORONTO
player: 4 ALER
song: 7 OCANADA
**Blue-law**
subject: 6 SUNDAY
**"Blue Moon"**
of baseball: 4 ODOM
**Blueness:** 6 SORROW
**Bluenose:** 4 PRIG 5 PRISS
   PRUDE 7 PURITAN
   9 NICENELLY
**Blue-pencil:** 4 EDIT 5 EMEND
user: 6 EDITOR
**Bluepoint:** 6 OYSTER
**Blueprint:** 4 PLAN
detail: 4 SPEC
**Blue-ribbon:** 5 FIRST
**Blue Ribbon**
maker: 5 PABST
**Blues:** 5 MUSIC
Baby: 4 EYES
singer Bonnie: 5 RAITT
singer James: 4 ETTA
singer Ma: 6 RAINEY
singer Simone: 4 NINA
singer Smith: 6 BESSIE
singer Washington: 5 DINAH
Singing the: 3 SAD
Sing the: 4 WAIL
street: 5 BEALE
**"Blues Brothers, The"**
director: 6 LANDIS
venue: 3 SNL
**"Blue ___ Shoes":** 5 SUEDE
**"Blues in the Night"**
composer Harold: 5 ARLEN
**"Blue Sky"**
actress Jessica: 5 LANGE
**Bluesman**
~ Mahal: 3 TAJ
~ Mo': 3 KEB
~ Spann: 4 OTIS
**Blue ___ special:** 5 PLATE
**"Blue Suede Shoes"**
singer: 5 ELVIS
songwriter Perkins: 4 CARL
**Blue Triangle**
gp.: 4 YWCA
**"Blue Velvet"**
actress Laura: 4 DERN
**Bluffer**
game: 5 POKER
ploy: 5 RAISE
**Bluish**
duck: 4 TEAL
gray: 5 SLATY

green: 4 TEAL
purple: 5 MAUVE
**Blunder:** 3 ERR 4 FLUB GOOF
   5 ERROR GAFFE
   7 MISSTEP
Baseball: 5 ERROR
Bridge: 6 RENEGE
Make a: 3 ERR
Social: 5 GAFFE
**Blunderer:** 7 SADSACK
**Blunt:** 6 OBTUSE
blade: 4 EPEE
sword: 4 EPEE
**Blunted**
blade: 4 EPEE
sword: 4 EPEE
**Blurbs:** 3 ADS 4 BIOS
**Blurt**
Bleeped: 4 OATH
Pert: 4 SASS
**Blush:** 5 ROUGE 6 REDDEN
**Blushing:** 3 RED
**Bluster:** 4 BRAG RANT
**Blustery:** 3 RAW
**Bluto:** 6 SAILOR
dream girl: 5 OLIVE
rival: 6 POPEYE
**Blvd.:** 3 AVE
crossers: 3 RDS STS
**Blyleven**
of baseball: 4 BERT
**Blynken**
Partner of Wynken and: 3 NOD
**Blyth**
Actress: 3 ANN
**Blyton**
Author: 4 ENID
**BMI**
rival: 5 ASCAP
**B-movie**
bad guy: 4 YEGG
**BMW:** 6 IMPORT
rival: 4 AUDI
**Bo**
Actress: 5 DEREK
**B.O.**
sign: 3 SRO
___ Bo: 3 TAE
**Boa:** 5 SCARF SNAKE
   6 PYTHON 7 FEATHER
**Boar**
abode: 6 PIGSTY
mate: 3 SOW
**Board:** 5 GETON HOPON
   MEALS 7 CLIMBIN
   ENPLANE
and lodging: 4 KEEP
Back on: 3 AFT
Bed: 4 SLAT
Bring on: 4 HIRE
Clear the: 5 ERASE
game: 5 CHESS
Manicurist's: 5 EMERY
material: 5 EMERY
member: 4 EXEC 7 TRUSTEE
member (abbr.): 3 DIR

Mystical: 5 OUIJA
partner: 4 ROOM
Put on: 4 LADE STOW
Ship: 5 PLANK
Thin: 4 SLAT
**Boarded:** 5 GOTON
**Boarding**
area: 4 GATE
place: 4 STOP
place (abbr.): 3 STA
sch.: 4 ACAD
**Boardroom**
bigwig: 3 CEO
visual aid: 5 GRAPH
**Boards**
Clear the: 5 ERASE
treader: 5 ACTOR
Treading the: 7 ONSTAGE
Tread the: 3 ACT
**Boardwalk**
diversion: 6 STROLL
refreshments: 4 ICES
**Boars:** 3 HES 5 MALES
Place for: 3 STY
**Boast:** 4 BRAG CROW
7 POSSESS
End of Jack's: 3 AMI
Part of a famous: 4 ISAW VENI
VICI VIDI 5 ICAME
**Boaster:** 6 GASBAG
**Boastful:** 5 GASSY
**Boat:** 3 HER SHE
Back of a: 3 AFT 5 STERN
basin: 6 MARINA
Biblical: 3 ARK
Biblical ~ builder: 4 NOAH
bottom: 4 KEEL
Coal: 4 SCOW
contents: 5 GRAVY
Dispatch: 5 AVISO
Eskimo: 5 UMIAK
Flat-bottomed: 4 DORY SCOW
Garbage: 4 SCOW
Genesis: 3 ARK
Lake: 5 CANOE
Malayan: 4 PROA
Miss the: 7 LOSEOUT
Off the: 6 ASHORE
One-person: 5 SKIFF
Propel a: 3 ROW
propeller: 3 OAR
race: 7 REGATTA
Racing: 5 SCULL
trailer: 4 WAKE
Twin-hulled: 9 CATAMARAN
**Boater:** 3 HAT 8 STRAWHAT
**Boathouse**
inventory: 4 OARS
**Bob:** 6 HAIRDO
Choreographer: 5 FOSSE
Comedian: 5 SAGET
companion: 5 WEAVE
cousin: 4 LUGE
Former Ontario Premier: 3 RAE
Handyman: 4 VILA
of football: 6 GRIESE

of the Bob and Ray comedy
team: 6 ELLIOT
Rock singer: 5 SEGER
who lost to Bill: 4 DOLE
**Bobbettes**
hit song: 5 MRLEE
**Bobbin:** 5 SPOOL
**Bobble:** 3 ERR 4 MUFF
5 ERROR
**Bobbsey**
One of the ~ twins: 3 NAN
4 BERT 7 FLOSSIE
FREDDIE
**Bobby**
1960s radical ~: 5 SEALE
Auto racer: 5 RAHAL UNSER
Child star: 5 BREEN
of football: 5 LAYNE
of hockey: 3 ORR
of tennis: 5 RIGGS
of the Black Panthers: 5 SEALE
Singer: 3 VEE 5 DARIN
**Bobby-___:** 6 SOXERS
**"___ Bobby McGee":** 5 MEAND
**Bobbysoxer:** 4 GIRL
event: 3 HOP
**Boca ___:** 5 RATON
**Bocelli, Andrea:** 5 TENOR
performance: 4 ARIA
**Bochco**
Producer: 6 STEVEN
**Bochco, Steven**
series: 5 LALAW
**Bock**
holder: 5 STEIN
**Bodega**
owner: 6 GROCER
patron: 6 LATINO
setting: 6 BARRIO
**Bodhidharma**
philosophy: 3 ZEN
**Bodine, Jethro**
portrayer Max: 4 BAER
**___ bodkins:** 3 ODS
**Body:** 5 TORSO 6 CORPSE
7 CADAVER
Ante: 3 POT
Anti: 3 CON
build: 5 FRAME
fluids: 4 SERA
French: 5 SENAT
Heavenly: 3 ORB 5 ANGEL
of art: 5 TORSO
of knowledge: 4 LORE
of speech: 4 TEXT
of values: 5 ETHIC
of water: 3 SEA 4 POND
5 OCEAN
of work: 6 OEUVRE
passage: 4 ITER
Sci. of the: 4 ANAT
Study of the ~ (abbr.): 4 ANAT
Upper: 5 TORSO
Without: 4 LIMP
work: 6 TATTOO
wrap: 4 SKIN

**Bodybuilder:** 5 HEMAN
bane: 4 FLAB
pride: 3 ABS 4 LATS PECS
6 BICEPS
unit: 3 REP
~ Charles: 5 ATLAS
~ Reeves: 5 STEVE
**"Body Count"**
rapper: 4 ICET
**Bodyguards:** 6 MUSCLE
**Body shop:** 3 SPA
challenge: 4 DENT
fig.: 3 EST
offering: 6 LOANER
**Bodywork**
In need of: 6 DENTED
**Boeing:** 3 JET 8 JETLINER
rival: 6 AIRBUS
Scrapped ~ project: 3 SST
**Boer**
migration: 4 TREK
**Boesky**
of Wall Street: 4 IVAN
**Boff**
suffix: 3 OLA
**Boffo**
letters: 3 SRO
review: 4 RAVE
show: 5 SMASH
**Bog:** 3 FEN 4 MIRE
down: 4 MIRE
fuel: 4 PEAT
Like a: 4 MIRY 5 PEATY
**Bogarde**
Actor: 4 DIRK
**Bogart, Humphrey**
costar: 6 BACALL
9 IDALUPINO
film: 6 SAHARA 8 KEYLARGO
role: 5 EARLE QUEEG SPADE
Spade, to: 4 ROLE
title role: 3 MRX
topper: 6 FEDORA
**Bogey:** 7 ONEOVER
8 ABOVEPAR
beater: 3 PAR
**Bogeyman:** 4 OGRE 6 SCARER
**Bogged**
down: 5 MIRED 6 INARUT
**Boggs**
of baseball: 4 WADE
**Boggy:** 4 MIRY
area: 3 FEN 4 MIRE 5 SWAMP
**Bogosian**
Actor: 4 ERIC
**Bogotá**
babies: 5 NENES
City southwest of: 4 CALI
Gp. founded in: 3 OAS
**Bogus:** 4 FAKE SHAM 5 FALSE
PHONY 6 ERSATZ
butter: 4 OLEO
Not: 4 REAL
**Bohemian:** 4 ARTY 5 ARTSY
CZECH
dance: 5 POLKA

More: 6 ARTIER
**Bohr:** 4 DANE
  Physicist: 5 NIELS
  study: 4 ATOM
**Boiardo**
  patron: 4 ESTE
**Boil:** 6 SEETHE
  Almost: 5 SCALD
  Bring to a: 5 ANGER
    6 ENRAGE
  down: 6 DECOCT
  in oil: 3 FRY
**Boilermaker**
  Beer, in a: 6 CHASER
  part: 4 BEER
**"Boiler Room"**
  actress Long: 3 NIA
**Boiling:** 3 HOT MAD 5 IRATE
    7 INARAGE
  Extract by: 6 DECOCT
  Heat without: 5 SCALD
  ___ **Boingo (rock band):**
    5 OINGO
**Boise**
  county: 3 ADA
  state: 5 IDAHO
  state (abbr.): 3 IDA
**Boisterous:** 4 LOUD 5 AROAR
  Be: 7 ROLLICK
  festivity: 5 REVEL
**Boitano**
  Skater: 5 BRIAN
**Bojangles**
  Emulate: 3 TAP 8 TAPDANCE
**Bok** ___: 4 CHOY
**Bold:** 5 BRAVE GUTSY
  Be: 4 DARE
  Not: 3 SHY 4 MEEK 5 TIMID
  one: 5 DARER
**Bolero**
  composer: 5 RAVEL
**Boleyn:** 4 ANNE
**Bolger**
  costar: 4 LAHR
**Bolívar, Simón**
  birthplace: 7 CARACAS
**Bolivia**
  Bear, in: 3 OSO
  capital: 5 LAPAZ SUCRE
  export: 3 TIN
  neighbor: 4 PERU
**Bollix:** 4 FLUB 5 SNAFU
**Bollixed**
  All ~ up: 7 INAMESS
**Bolo:** 3 TIE
**Bologna:** 8 DELIMEAT
  alternative: 6 SALAMI
  bills: 4 LIRE
  bread: 4 LIRA
  neighbor: 6 MODENA
  unit: 5 SLICE
**Bolshevik:** 3 RED
  leader: 5 LENIN 7 TROTSKY
  target: 4 TSAR
**Bolshevism**
  founder: 5 LENIN

**Bolshoi**
  rival: 5 KIROV
**Bolt:** 3 LAM RUN 4 FLEE
  down: 3 EAT
  fastener: 3 NUT
  holder: 4 TNUT
  to bond: 5 ELOPE
**Bomb:** 4 FLOP 6 TURKEY
    7 FAILURE 8 LAYANEGG
  Car: 5 EDSEL LEMON
  Kind of: 7 AEROSOL
  squad member: 5 ROBOT
  trial: 5 ATEST
**Bombard:** 4 PELT 5 SHELL
  suffix: 3 IER
**Bombast:** 3 GAS 8 RHETORIC
**Bombastic:** 5 GASSY TUMID
**Bombay**
  City ESE of: 5 POONA
  country: 5 INDIA
  garb: 4 SARI
  royal: 4 RANI
**Bombeck**
  Humorist: 4 ERMA
**Bomber**
  letters: 4 USAF
  Name on a: 5 ENOLA
  Noted: 8 ENOLAGAY
**Bombs**
  Like some: 5 SMART
**"... bombs bursting ___ ...":**
    5 INAIR
**Bombshell:** 6 SEXPOT
  actress Diana: 4 DORS
  actress Jean: 6 HARLOW
**Bon** ___: 3 MOT 4 SOIR
  of rock: 4 JOVI
**"Bon** ___!":** 7 APPETIT
**"___ bon!":** 4 CEST
**Bona** ___: 4 FIDE 5 FIDES
**Bona fide:** 4 REAL 6 ACTUAL
**Bon Ami**
  competitor: 4 AJAX
**Bonanza:** 4 LODE
  find: 3 ORE
  Miner's: 4 LODE
**"Bonanza"**
  actor Blocker: 3 DAN
  actor Greene: 5 LORNE
  brother: 4 ADAM HOSS
**Bonbon:** 5 SWEET TREAT
**Bond:** 3 SPY 4 GLUE 5 AGENT
    UNITE 6 SURETY
  alma mater: 4 ETON
  creator Fleming: 3 IAN
  foe: 4 DRNO 6 SMERSH
  Govt.: 5 TNOTE
  on the run: 5 ELOPE
  order: 7 MARTINI
    10 DRYMARTINI
  portrayer: 5 MOORE
    6 DALTON
  prefix: 4 EURO
  rating: 3 AAA BBB CCC
  recipient: 7 OBLIGEE
  Tax-free: 4 MUNI

Type of: 5 EPOXY
**Bond, James:** 3 SPY
  (abbr.): 3 AGT
  alma mater: 4 ETON
  cocktail: 7 MARTINI
    10 DRYMARTINI
  creator Fleming: 3 IAN
  film: 4 DRNO 9 MOONRAKER
    10 GOLDFINGER
  foe: 4 DRNO 6 SMERSH
  portrayer: 5 MOORE
    6 DALTON
**Bonds**
  How some ~ are sold: 5 ATPAR
  Like some: 5 RATED
    6 RATEDA 7 TAXFREE
**Bonds, Barry**
  stat: 3 HRS RBI
**Bondsman:** 4 SERF
  payment: 4 BAIL
**Bone:** 5 FILET
  Arm: 4 ULNA
  Bad to the: 4 EVIL
  connector: 5 SINEW
  Dry as a: 4 ARID
  Ear: 5 INCUS 6 STAPES
  First ~ donor: 4 ADAM
  Forearm: 4 ULNA
  Largest human: 5 FEMUR
  Leg: 4 SHIN 5 FEMUR TIBIA
  Mouth: 3 JAW
  Of an arm: 5 ULNAR
  Pelvic: 5 ILIUM
  prefix: 3 OST 4 OSSE OSTE
    5 OSSEO OSTEO
  Small: 7 OSSICLE
  Smallest human: 6 STAPES
  to pick: 4 BEEF 5 GRIPE
  Work on a: 4 GNAW
  ~, in Latin: 4 OSSO
**Bone-dry:** 4 ARID SERE
**Bonehead:** 3 ASS OAF SAP
    4 DOLT 5 IDIOT
**Boneless**
  entrée: 5 FILET
**Boner:** 5 ERROR
  Pull a: 3 ERR 4 GOOF
**Bones:** 4 DICE OSSA
  Ankle: 5 TARSI
  Arm: 5 RADII ULNAE ULNAS
    6 HUMERI
  Back: 5 SACRA
  Foot: 5 TARSI
  Forearm: 5 RADII ULNAE
    ULNAS
  Hip: 4 ILIA
  Pelvic: 4 ILIA 5 SACRA
  Wrist: 5 CARPI
  ___ **Bones (Ichabod's foe):**
    4 BROM
**"Bonesetter's Daughter, The"**
  author: 3 TAN 6 AMYTAN
**Bonet**
  Actress: 4 LISA
**Bonfire**
  remnant: 3 ASH

**Bongo:** 4 DRUM
**Bonheur**
  Painter: 4 ROSA
**Bon Jovi**
  Singer: 3 JON
**Bonkers:** 3 MAD 4 AMOK DAFT
    GAGA LOCO NUTS
    5 NUTSO 6 INSANE
  Go: 4 RAVE SNAP
  Not: 4 SANE
**Bon mot:** 4 QUIP 7 EPIGRAM
**Bonn**
  **Info:** German cue
  City near: 5 ESSEN
  mister: 4 HERR
  One in: 4 EINE
  river: 5 RHINE
**Bonner**
  Russian activist: 5 ELENA
**Bonnet:** 3 HAT
  bug: 3 BEE
  in Britain: 4 HOOD
**Bonneville Flats**
  locale: 4 UTAH
**Bonnie**
  Actress: 7 BEDELIA
  partner: 5 CLYDE
  portrayer: 4 FAYE
  Singer: 5 RAITT
**Bonnie Blue**
  Father of: 5 RHETT
**Bonny**
  miss: 4 LASS
**Bono**
  Pro: 6 UNPAID
**Bonus:** 3 TIP 5 EXTRA
  Concert: 6 ENCORE
**Bony:** 6 OSTEAL 7 OSSEOUS
  prefix: 5 OSTEO
**Boo:** 4 JEER
  follower: 3 HOO
  relative: 4 HISS
**Boob:** 3 ASS OAF
**Boob ___:** 4 TUBE
**Boo-boo:** 4 SLIP 5 BONER
    ERROR 7 MISTAKE
  Book ~ (plural): 6 ERRATA
  remover: 6 ERASER
**Boo Boo:** 4 BEAR
  buddy: 4 YOGI
**Boob tube:** 5 TVSET
  (plural): 3 TVS
  ~, in Britain: 5 TELLY
**Booby**
  Get the ~ prize: 4 LOSE
  Taking the ~ prize: 4 LAST
  trap: 4 MINE 5 SNARE
**Book**
  after Daniel: 5 HOSEA
  after Ezra: 8 NEHEMIAH
  after Ezra (abbr.): 3 NEH
  after Galatians (abbr.): 3 EPH
  after II Chronicles: 4 EZRA
  after Joel: 4 AMOS
  after John: 4 ACTS
  after Jonah: 5 MICAH

  after Nehemiah: 6 ESTHER
  after Proverbs (abbr.): 4 ECCL
  back: 5 SPINE
  backbone: 5 SPINE
  before Amos: 4 JOEL
  before Daniel (abbr.): 4 EZEK
  before Deut.: 3 NUM
  before Esther (abbr.): 3 NEH
  before Jeremiah: 6 ISAIAH
  before Job (abbr.): 4 ESTH
  before Joel: 5 HOSEA
  before Micah: 5 JONAH
  before Nahum: 5 MICAH
  before Nehemiah: 4 EZRA
  before Obadiah: 4 AMOS
  before Romans: 4 ACTS
  Big: 4 TOME 5 FOLIO
  Cook: 4 COMA
  end: 5 INDEX
  Enjoy a: 4 READ
  Enjoy a ~ again: 6 REREAD
  Holy: 5 BIBLE KORAN
  jacket item: 3 BIO 5 BLURB
  leaf: 4 PAGE
  of Changes: 6 ICHING
  of hymns: 7 PSALTER
  of legends: 5 ATLAS
  of maps: 5 ATLAS
  of memories: 5 ALBUM
  of prophecies: 4 AMOS
    5 HOSEA
  OT: 3 LEV NEH 4 EZEK OBAD
  page: 4 LEAF
  Photo: 5 ALBUM
  Prayer: 6 MISSAL
  Ref.: 4 DICT
  School: 4 TEXT 6 PRIMER
    7 SPELLER
  size: 6 OCTAVO
  supplements: 7 ADDENDA
  World: 5 ATLAS
  ~ ID: 4 ISBN
  ~, in Spanish: 5 LIBRO
**Bookbag**
  item: 4 TEXT
**Bookbinding**
  leather: 4 ROAN
**"Book 'em, ___!":** 4 DANO
**Booker T.**
  backup band: 3 MGS
**Bookie**
  concern: 4 ODDS
  records: 4 BETS
**Booking**
  for a band: 3 GIG
  Take in for: 6 ARREST
**Bookish:** 8 STUDIOUS
  type: 4 NERD
**Book jacket**
  hype: 5 BLURB
**Bookkeeper**
  ~, at times: 5 ADDER
**Bookkeeping**
  entry: 5 DEBIT
**Booklet**
  Mass: 4 ORDO

**Bookmark:** 6 DOGEAR
  Browser: 3 URL
**"Book of Days"**
  singer: 4 ENYA
**Books**
  Blue: 4 PORN SMUT
  Check: 5 AUDIT
  Crack the: 4 READ
  He's found in: 5 WALDO
  Put on the: 5 ENACT
  Reviewer of ~, for short: 3 CPA
**Bookseller**
  Online: 6 AMAZON
**Bookstore**
  Campus ~ purchase: 4 TEXT
  Enjoy a: 6 BROWSE
  feature: 4 CAFE
  section: 5 HOWTO HUMOR
    SCIFI
  section (abbr.): 4 BIOG
**Bookworm:** 4 NERD 6 READER
**"Boola Boola"**
  singer: 3 ELI
**Boom:** 4 SPAR 5 NOISE
  Kind of: 5 SONIC
  producer: 3 SST
  support: 4 MAST
  times: 3 UPS
  ___ boom: 5 SONIC
**Boom-bah**
  preceder: 3 SIS
**Boom box:** 5 RADIO
  button: 3 REC
  letters: 4 AMFM
  platters: 3 CDS
**Boomer**
  followers: 4 GENX
  of football: 7 ESIASON
**Boomerang:** 8 BACKFIRE
**Booms:** 9 GOODTIMES
  Like some: 5 SONIC
**Boone**
  of baseball: 4 BRET
  Singer: 3 PAT 5 DEBBY
  ~, to friends: 4 DANL
**Boone, Daniel**
  portrayer Parker: 4 FESS
**Boop**
  Miss: 5 BETTY
**Boor:** 3 CAD OAF 4 CLOD
    LOUT 5 CHURL YAHOO
**Boorish:** 4 RUDE 5 CRASS
  sort: 3 CAD OAF 4 CLOD
    LOUT 5 CHURL YAHOO
**Boosler**
  Comic: 6 ELAYNE
**Boost:** 3 AID 4 PUSH 5 LEGUP
    RAISE 7 ELEVATE
  It may need a: 3 EGO
    6 MORALE
  Salary: 5 RAISE
**Booster:** 5 AGENA
  GI morale: 3 USO
  Paycheck: 8 OVERTIME
  Sound: 3 AMP
**Boot:** 4 OUST 6 UNSEAT

attachment: 4 SPUR
bottom: 4 SOLE
Give the: 3 AXE CAN 4 OUST
out: 5 EXPEL
part: 3 TOE 6 TOECAP
To: 3 TOO 4 ALSO 6 NOLESS
"___ Boot": 3 DAS
**Bootblack**
offering: 5 SHINE
**Boot camp**
boss: 5 SARGE
reply: 6 YESSIR
**Booted:** 4 SHOD
**Bootees**
Make: 4 KNIT
**Booth**
Actor: 5 EDWIN
Mall: 5 KIOSK
Merchandise: 5 STALL
Person in a: 5 VOTER
___ **Boothe Luce:** 5 CLARE
**Bootlicker:** 6 YESMAN
**Bootlicking:** 4 OILY
**Boot-shaped**
country: 5 ITALY
**Booty:** 4 LOOT SWAG 6 SPOILS
**Booze:** 5 HOOCH SAUCE
6 HOOTCH
Add ~ to: 4 LACE
Avoid: 8 TEETOTAL
Shot of: 5 SNORT
**Boozehound:** 3 SOT 4 LUSH
WINO 5 DIPSO TOPER
**Boozer:** 3 SOT 4 LUSH WINO
5 DIPSO TOPER
**Bop:** 4 CONK
"___ Bop" (Lauper hit): 3 SHE
**Bo-Peep**
Call to: 3 BAA
charges: 5 SHEEP
Like ~ charges: 5 OVINE
___ **Bora:** 4 TORA
**Bora Bora**
neighbor: 6 TAHITI
___ **Borch, Gerard**
Painter: 3 TER
**Bordeaux:** 3 VIN 4 WINE
**Info:** French cue
bean: 4 TETE
beau: 3 AMI
Born, in: 3 NEE
But, in: 4 MAIS
To be, in: 4 ETRE
wine: 5 MEDOC 6 CLARET
**Bordelaise:** 5 SAUCE
ingredient: 7 SHALLOT
**Borden**
Beast of: 5 ELSIE
brand: 6 ELMERS
cow: 5 ELSIE
weapon: 3 AXE
**Border:** 4 ABUT EDGE SIDE
marker: 5 FENCE
on: 4 ABUT
patrol concern: 6 ALIENS
Put a ~ on: 5 EDGED

Shield: 4 ORLE
Stitched: 3 HEM
**Bore:** 4 DRAG DRIP TIRE
6 NUDNIK
Crashing: 4 DRIP
It's a: 6 YAWNER
Respond to a: 4 YAWN
Utter: 4 DRAG
Word before: 5 TIDAL
___ **borealis:** 6 AURORA
**Bored**
Become: 4 TIRE
**Boredom:** 5 ENNUI
Indicate: 4 SIGH YAWN
**Borg:** 5 SWEDE
contemporary: 4 ASHE
homeland: 6 SWEDEN
of tennis: 5 BJORN
**Borge, Victor:** 4 DANE
7 PIANIST
instrument: 5 PIANO
**Borges, Jorge ___**
Author: 4 LUIS
**Borgia**
Cardinal: 6 CESARE
in-law: 4 ESTE
**Borgnine**
Actor: 6 ERNEST
Oscar-winning title role for:
5 MARTY
**Boric acid**
target: 4 ANTS
**Boring:** 4 BLAH DULL
5 HOHUM
Become: 4 CLOY
Do ~ work: 4 REAM
Got: 4 WORE
It may be: 3 BIT 5 DRILL
person: 4 DRIP
routine: 3 RUT
tool: 5 AUGER 6 REAMER
TREPAN
voice: 8 MONOTONE
**Boris**
contemporary: 3 LON 4 BELA
partner: 7 NATASHA
refusal: 4 NYET
rival: 4 IVAN
**Born:** 3 NEE
earlier: 5 ELDER OLDER
First: 4 CAIN 6 ELDEST
OLDEST
in: 4 FROM
yesterday: 5 NAIVE
~, in French: 3 NEE
**Born and ___:** 4 BRED
**Borneo**
beast: 5 ORANG
Island south of: 4 BALI
ruler: 5 RAJAH
Sultanate on: 6 BRUNEI
___ **Bornes (card game):**
5 MILLE
**"Born Free"**
lioness: 4 ELSA
**"Born in the ___":** 3 USA

**Borodin**
prince: 4 IGOR
**Borodina**
Mezzo: 4 OLGA
**Borrowed:** 6 ONLOAN
**Borscht:** 4 SOUP
belt bit: 3 GAG
ingredient: 4 BEET 5 BEETS
**"Borstal Boy"**
author Brendan: 5 BEHAN
**Bosc:** 4 PEAR
**Bosley**
Actor: 3 TOM
**Bosnia**
peacekeeping org.: 4 NATO
**Bosnian:** 4 SERB
**Bosom**
buddy: 3 PAL 4 CHUM
**"Bosom Buddies"**
musical: 4 MAME
**Bosox**
outfielder: 3 YAZ
**Bosporus:** 6 STRAIT
(abbr.): 3 STR
**Boss:** 4 HEAD 6 HONCHO
8 OVERSEER
(abbr.): 3 MGR
Barracks: 5 SARGE
Bus.: 3 CEO
Mafia: 3 DON 4 CAPO
Pfc.: 3 CPL
Pvt.: 3 SGT
request: 5 SEEME
Safari: 5 BWANA
Street: 5 MASON
**Bossa nova**
relative: 5 SAMBA
**Boss Tweed**
cartoonist: 4 NAST
**Bossy:** 3 COW
baby: 4 CALF
boss: 6 TYRANT
chew: 3 CUD
remark: 3 MOO
**Boston**
airport: 5 LOGAN
cager: 4 CELT
newspaper: 5 GLOBE
orchestra: 4 POPS
suburb: 4 LYNN
~ NHLer: 5 BRUIN
**Boston Bruins**
legend: 3 ORR
**"Bostonians, The"**
actor: 5 REEVE
**Boston Marathon**
month: 5 APRIL
**"Boston Public"**
actor McBride: 3 CHI
extra: 4 TEEN
**Boston Red ___:** 3 SOX
**Boston Symphony**
Former ~ conductor: 5 OZAWA
**Bot.:** 3 SCI
**Botanical**
beard: 3 AWN

opening: 5 STOMA
support: 4 STEM
**Botanist**
  expertise: 5 FLORA
  Flower named for a: 6 DAHLIA
  ~ Gray: 3 ASA
  ~ Mendel: 6 GREGOR
**Botch:** 3 ERR 4 BLOW FLUB
    MUFF RUIN 5 MISDO
    6 FOULUP MANGLE
**"Botch-___" (Clooney tune):**
    3 AME
**Both**
  prefix: 4 AMBI
**Bother:** 3 ADO AIL IRE IRK
    VEX 4 FUSS PEST TODO
    5 ANNOY EATAT UPSET
    6 HARASS HASSLE
    PESTER
  Don't: 8 LETALONE
    10 LEAVEALONE
  persistently: 5 EATAT NAGAT
    6 HARASS
**Botheration:** 3 ADO
**Bothered:** 5 ATEAT GOTAT
**Botswana**
  blight: 6 TSETSE
**Botticelli**
  Painter: 6 SANDRO
**Bottle**
  Baby: 6 NURSER
  Dressing: 5 CRUET
  Hit the: 4 TOPE 5 BOOZE
  Large: 6 MAGNUM
  Medicine: 4 VIAL
  Message in a: 3 SOS
  Model in a: 4 SHIP
  Open, as a: 5 UNCAP
  part: 4 NECK
  Perfume: 4 VIAL
  size: 5 LITER
  size (British): 5 LITRE
  stopper: 4 CORK
  Tiny: 4 VIAL
  top: 3 CAP 6 NIPPLE
    8 SCREWCAP
  Wicker-covered:
    8 DEMIJOHN
**Bottled**
  Not: 5 ONTAP
  spirit: 4 DJIN 5 GENIE
  (up): 4 PENT
  water brand: 5 EVIAN
**Bottleneck:** 3 JAM 5 SNARL
**Bottom:** 4 FOOT 5 FANNY
    NADIR
  Boat: 4 KEEL
  Boot: 4 SOLE
  Clear of the: 6 AWEIGH
  Go to the: 4 SINK
  Hit: 5 SPANK
  It's on the: 6 DIAPER
  line: 3 HEM NET SUM
    5 TOTAL YIELD
    6 AMOUNT
    10 NETRESULTS

of the barrel: 4 LEES 5 DREGS
    WORST
  Rock: 5 NADIR
  Shoe: 4 SOLE
**Bottomless:** 4 DEEP
  It may be: 3 PIT
  pit: 5 ABYSM ABYSS
**Bottom-of-the-barrel:** 5 WORST
  stuff: 4 LEES 5 DREGS
**"Bottoms up!":** 5 SKOAL
**Botulin:** 5 TOXIN
**Botvinnik**
  Defeater of ~ in chess: 3 TAL
**Bough:** 4 LIMB
  Take a: 3 LOP
**Bought:** 7 PAIDFOR
  and sold: 5 DEALT
  back: 8 REDEEMED
  It's ~ by the bar: 4 SOAP
**Bouillabaisse:** 4 STEW
**Boulanger**
  Composer: 5 NADIA
**Boulder:** 3 DAM 4 ROCK
    5 STONE
  hrs.: 3 MST
**Boulevard:** 4 ROAD
    6 AVENUE
  Hollywood: 6 SUNSET
  liners: 5 TREES
**Boult**
  Conductor: 6 ADRIAN
**Bounce:** 3 BOB 4 BOOT ECHO
    LILT OUST 5 EJECT
    EVICT
  back: 4 ECHO
  Billiards: 5 CAROM
  setting: 5 DRYER
  Sonic: 4 ECHO
**Bounced**
  check letters: 3 NSF
**Bouncer:** 4 BALL
  Baby: 4 KNEE
  requests: 3 IDS 7 IDCARDS
**Bouncing**
  off the walls: 5 HYPER
**Bouncy:** 4 PERT 7 UPTEMPO
  step: 4 LILT
**Bound:** 4 LEAP LOPE TIED
    6 LASHED
  bundle: 5 SHEAF
**Boundary:** 3 END 4 EDGE
    5 AMBIT LIMIT
  Plateau: 7 RIMROCK
  Property: 5 FENCE
  Racetrack: 4 RAIL
  Sector: 3 ARC
  Statistical: 8 QUARTILE
  Strike zone: 5 KNEES
**"Bound East for Cardiff"**
  Like O'Neill's: 5 ONEACT
**Bounder:** 3 CAD 4 ROUE
  Aussie: 3 ROO
**Bounding main:** 3 SEA
    5 OCEAN
  On the: 4 ASEA 5 ATSEA
**Boundless:** 4 VAST

**Bountiful**
  locale: 4 UTAH
**Bounty:** 5 PRICE 6 REWARD
  competitor: 4 VIVA
  destination: 6 TAHITI
**Bouquet:** 4 NOSE ODOR POSY
    5 AROMA SCENT
    7 NOSEGAY
  Fall: 6 ASTERS
  garni element: 5 THYME
  holder: 4 VASE
  item: 4 ROSE
  Small: 4 POSY
  Wine: 4 NOSE
**Bouquet ___:** 5 GARNI
**Bouquets**
  Big name in: 3 FTD
**Bourbon**
  and others (abbr.): 3 STS
  Like good: 4 AGED
**"Bourne Identity, The"**
  actor: 5 DAMON
    9 MATTDAMON
  Bourne, in: 5 JASON
    8 AMNESIAC
  Bourne's problem, in:
    7 AMNESIA
**Bout**
  ender: 3 TKO
  Ends a ~ early: 3 KOS
  locale: 5 ARENA
  Prepare for a: 4 SPAR 5 TRAIN
**Boutique:** 4 SHOP 5 STORE
**Boutonniere**
  site: 5 LAPEL
**Boutros-___, Boutros**
  Diplomat: 5 GHALI
**Boutros-Ghali, Boutros**
  successor: 4 KOFI 5 ANNAN
  ~, by birth: 7 CAIRENE
**Bovary**
  Madame: 4 EMMA
**Bovine**
  baby: 4 CALF
  beasts: 4 OXEN
  Borden: 5 ELSIE
  bunch: 4 HERD
  cry: 3 MOO
  Hairy: 3 YAK 5 BISON
  Humped: 4 ZEBU
**Bow:** 3 ARC
  Actress: 5 CLARA
  and scrape: 4 FAWN
  application: 5 ROSIN
  Away from the: 3 AFT
    6 ASTERN
  Boy with a: 4 AMOR EROS
  God with a: 4 AMOR EROS
  Low: 6 SALAAM
  Make a: 3 TIE
  Ma with a: 4 YOYO
  of silents: 5 CLARA
  Part of a: 4 LOOP 5 HAWSE
  Polite: 6 CURTSY
  Stern with a: 5 ISAAC
  (to): 6 KOWTOW

With the ~, in music: 4 ARCO
wood: 3 YEW
**Bowdlerize:** 4 EDIT
**Bower:** 5 ARBOR
**Bowery**
  bum: 4 WINO
  __ **Bowes (postage company):**
    6 PITNEY
**Bowie:** 3 JIM
  Former baseball commissioner:
    4 KUHN
  last stand: 5 ALAMO
  weapon: 5 KNIFE
**Bowie, David**
  #1 hit of: 9 LETSDANCE
  collaborator Brian: 3 ENO
  Wife of: 4 IMAN
**Bowl:** 5 ARENA
  org.: 4 NCAA
  over: 3 AWE WOW 4 STUN
    5 AMAZE
  yell: 3 RAH
**Bowler:** 3 HAT 5 DERBY
  button: 5 RESET
  challenge: 5 SPLIT
  edge: 4 BRIM
  hangout: 5 ALLEY
  pickup: 5 SPARE
  target: 3 PIN 6 TENPIN
**Bowlful**
  Bowser's: 4 ALPO
  Breakfast: 6 CEREAL
    FARINA
  Party: 8 ONIONDIP
**Bowling**
  ball material: 7 EBONITE
  British ~ pin: 7 SKITTLE
  green: 4 LAWN
  lane: 5 ALLEY
  Lawn: 5 BOCCE BOCCI
  pin wood: 5 MAPLE
  site: 4 LANE LAWN
  target: 3 PIN 6 TENPIN
  unit: 5 FRAME
**Bowling alley:** 4 LANE
  button: 5 RESET
  letters: 3 AMF
**"Bowling for Columbine"**
  Org. targeted in: 3 NRA
**Bowser:** 5 POOCH
  alternative: 3 REX
  bowlful: 4 ALPO
  Brand for: 4 ALPO
  Leftover for: 5 TBONE
**Bowwow:** 5 POOCH
  Nickelodeon: 3 REN
**Box:** 4 LOGE SPAR 5 CRATE
    6 ENCASE
  Balcony: 4 LOGE
  Band: 3 AMP
  Idiot: 5 TVSET 6 TEEVEE
  In the: 5 ATBAT
  Jewel: 6 CDCASE
  Kind of: 5 IDIOT MITER
    PRESS 6 LITTER
  top: 3 LID

**Boxcar**
  rider: 4 HOBO
**Boxcars:** 5 SIXES 6 TWELVE
**Boxer:** 3 DOG PUG
  Baby: 3 PUP
  bane: 5 FLEAS
  blow: 3 JAB
  Breathe like a: 4 PANT
  Certain ~, informally:
    6 WELTER
  combination: 6 ONETWO
  comment: 3 ARF GRR
  doctor: 3 VET
  fare: 4 ALPO
  group: 6 SENATE
  Instruction to a: 4 STAY
  Rope-a-dope: 3 ALI
  stat: 5 REACH
  target: 3 JAW
  vulnerability: 8 GLASSJAW
  wear: 4 ROBE
**Boxers**
  alternative: 6 BRIEFS
**Boxing**
  Bard of: 3 ALI
  boundary: 4 ROPE
  decision: 3 TKO
  great: 3 ALI
  locale: 5 ARENA
  match: 4 BOUT
  official: 3 REF
  Practice: 4 SPAR
  prize: 4 BELT
  punch: 3 JAB
  signal: 4 BELL
  stats: 3 KOS 4 TKOS
  trainer Dundee: 6 ANGELO
  venue: 5 ARENA
  victory: 3 TKO 4 KAYO
**Box office:** 4 GATE
  failure: 4 BOMB
  sales, slangily: 3 TIX
  sign: 3 SRO
**Box score**
  blemish: 5 ERROR
  numbers: 5 STATS
  stats: 3 RBI
**Boy:** 3 LAD TAD
  king: 3 TUT
  lead-in: 4 ATTA
  Mama's: 3 SON
  Mammy's: 5 ABNER
  of TV: 4 BART OPIE
  Poster: 4 IDOL 6 ADONIS
  Sonny: 3 LAD
  suffix: 3 ISH
  toy: 3 KEN
  Whipping: 4 GOAT
  with a blanket: 5 LINUS
  with a bow: 4 AMOR EROS
  ~, in Spanish: 4 NINO
  __ boy: 5 MAMAS
  "__ boy!": 4 ATTA ITSA
**"Boy, am __ trouble!":** 3 IIN
**Boyer**
  of baseball: 5 CLETE

**Boyer, Charles**
  costar in "Algiers":
    6 LAMARR
  film: 7 ALGIERS
**Boyfriend:** 4 BEAU
**Boyle**
  Cookbook author: 4 TISH
**Boyle, __ Flynn**
  Actress: 4 LARA
**"Boy Named Sue, A"**
  singer: 4 CASH
    10 JOHNNYCASH
**Boys**
  Big: 3 MEN
  club: 4 FRAT
  in the hood: 4 BROS
  Some ~ of summer: 4 LEOS
  "__ Boys" (Alcott novel): 3 JOS
**Boy Scout**
  action: 4 DEED
  novice: 10 TENDERFOOT
  outing: 4 HIKE
  unit: 5 TROOP
**"Boys Don't Cry"**
  actor Brandon: 5 TEENA
  actress Swank: 6 HILARY
**"Boys From Brazil, The"**
  author Levin: 3 IRA
**"Boys Town"**
  neighbor: 5 OMAHA
**Bozo:** 3 ASS OAF 4 DOLT DOPE
    TWIT 5 CLOWN MORON
**BP**
  It merged with: 5 AMOCO
  purchase: 5 LITRE
**BPOE**
  Part of: 4 ELKS
**Bra**
  part: 5 STRAP
**Brace:** 3 DUO TWO 4 PAIR
    PROP 5 STEEL
    7 SHOREUP
  (oneself): 4 GIRD 5 STEEL
**Bracelet**
  attachment: 5 CHARM
  Rigid: 6 BANGLE
  site: 5 ANKLE
**Bracer:** 5 TONIC
**Brachial:** 7 ARMLIKE
**Bracket**
  Candle: 6 SCONCE
  Shelf: 3 ELL
**Brackets**
  Word in: 3 SIC
**Brad:** 4 NAIL
  Actor: 4 PITT 6 RENFRO
**Bradbury**
  Sci-fi writer: 3 RAY
**Braddock**
  Loser to: 4 BAER
**Bradley**
  and others: 3 EDS
  colleague: 5 STAHL
  General: 4 OMAR
**Bradley University**
  site: 6 PEORIA

**Bradshaw**
of football: 5 TERRY
**Bradstreet, Anne:** 4 POET
**Brady Bill**
opposers: 3 NRA
**"Brady Bunch, The"**
actor Robert: 4 REED
actress: 11 SHELLEYLONG
actress Plumb: 3 EVE
daughter: 3 JAN 5 CINDY
6 MARCIA
Greg, Peter, or Bobby, to Carol
in: 7 STEPSON
housekeeper: 5 ALICE
son: 4 GREG 5 BOBBY
PETER
**Brag:** 4 CROW 5 BOAST GLOAT
VAUNT
**Braga**
Actress: 5 SONIA
**Bragg:** 4 FORT
**Braggart:** 6 CROWER
A ~ has a big one: 3 EGO
Fabled: 4 HARE
Suffix for a: 3 EST
"___ bragh!": 6 ERINGO
**Brahe:** 4 DANE
**Brahma**
sounds: 3 OMS
**Brahman:** 5 CASTE
**Brahms**
Key of ~ Symphony No. 4:
6 EMINOR
Like ~ Symphony No. 3: 3 INF
**Braid:** 5 PLAIT TRESS
7 PIGTAIL
Gold: 5 ORRIS
Narrow hair: 7 CORNROW
**Braille**
Bit of: 3 DOT
**Brain**
area: 4 LOBE
cell: 6 NEURON
passage: 4 ITER
PC's: 3 CPU
protector: 5 SKULL
Relating to the: 6 NEURAL
scan (abbr.): 3 EEG
Small ~ size: 3 PEA
wave: 4 IDEA
**Brainard**
Absent-minded professor:
3 NED
**Braincases:** 6 CRANIA
**Brainchild:** 4 IDEA
**Brainiac:** 4 WHIZ 6 GENIUS
7 EGGHEAD
8 EINSTEIN
**Brainpower:** 3 WIT 5 SENSE
measurer: 6 IQTEST
**Brains:** 5 SENSE
Collection of: 5 MENSA
Like: 5 LOBED
They have: 6 CRANIA
**Brainstorm:** 4 IDEA 6 IDEATE
announcement: 3 AHA

product: 4 IDEA
**Brainteaser:** 5 POSER
6 ENIGMA
**Brainy:** 5 SMART 6 BRIGHT
bunch: 5 MENSA
Not too: 3 DIM 5 DENSE
**Brake:** 5 PEDAL
Do a ~ job: 6 RELINE
Horse: 4 REIN
part: 4 DISC SHOE
**Brakes**
Apply quickly, as: 6 SLAMON
Fix, as: 6 RELINE
Hit the: 4 SLOW
Type of: 4 DISC
**Bran**
accompanier: 6 RAISIN
source: 3 OAT
substance: 5 FIBER
**Branagh, Kenneth**
role of 1995: 4 IAGO
**Branch:** 3 ARM 4 LIMB
headquarters: 4 NEST
location: 4 TREE
offshoot: 4 TWIG
Peace: 5 OLIVE
point: 4 NODE
Religious: 4 SECT
Small: 4 TWIG 5 SPRIG
Union: 5 LOCAL
**Branches:** 4 RAMI
Cut off, as: 3 LOP
Remove: 5 PRUNE
Tree with rooting: 6 BANYAN
~, in botany: 4 RAMI
**Brand:** 4 SEAR
Name: 5 LABEL
**Brandenburg**
river: 4 ODER
**Brandenburg Concertos**
composer: 4 BACH
**Branding**
Mark with a ~ iron: 4 SEAR
tool: 4 IRON
**Brandish:** 5 WIELD
**Brandless:** 6 NONAME
**Brand-new:** 6 UNUSED
**Brando, Marlon**
birthplace: 5 OMAHA
by birth: 6 OMAHAN
film: 8 SAYONARA
role: 6 ZAPATA
**Brandy:** 6 COGNAC
base: 4 PLUM
cocktail: 7 SIDECAR
STINGER
flavor: 4 PEAR 7 APRICOT
French: 6 COGNAC
8 ARMAGNAC
glass: 7 SNIFTER
Grape: 4 MARC
Italian: 6 GRAPPA
letters: 3 VSO 4 VSOP
Sitcom starring singer:
6 MOESHA
**Braque:** 6 CUBIST

**Brasi**
"The Godfather" villain:
4 LUCA
**Brass:** 4 GALL 5 ALLOY CHEEK
NERVE 8 GENERALS
OFFICERS
Big: 4 TUBA 5 TUBAS
component: 4 ZINC
instrument: 4 TUBA
10 FRENCHHORN
Invigorate the: 7 REPLATE
Military: 5 BUGLE
**Brasserie**
order: 8 OMELETTE
**Brat:** 3 IMP 4 PEST 6 TERROR
look: 5 SMIRK
More than a: 5 DEMON
**Brat Pack**
member: 4 LOWE 6 SHEEDY
**Brauhaus**
brew: 4 BIER
**Braun**
Hitler consort: 3 EVA
**Braun, ___ Jackson:** 6 LILIAN
**___ Braun, Wernher:** 3 VON
**___ Brava:** 5 COSTA
**Brave:** 4 DARE NLER 5 GUTSY
6 HEROIC
Home of the: 5 TEPEE
legend: 5 AARON
**"Braveheart"**
actor Gibson: 3 MEL
group: 4 CLAN
**"Brave New World"**
drug: 4 SOMA
**Bravery:** 5 VALOR
Commend, as for: 4 CITE
**Braves**
home: 7 ATLANTA
home (abbr.): 3 ATL
network (abbr.): 3 TBS
player: 5 AARON
**Braving**
the waves: 4 ASEA
**Bravo:** 3 RIO
Bullring: 3 OLE
competitor: 3 AMC
preceder: 4 ALFA
**"Bravo!":** 3 OLE 8 WELLDONE
**___ Bravo:** 3 RIO
**Bravura:** 5 ECLAT
**Brawl:** 4 FRAY RIOT 5 MELEE
SETTO 6 AFFRAY
FRACAS
Barroom: 5 MELEE
Brief: 5 SETTO
site: 6 SALOON
souvenir: 6 SHINER
**Brawny:** 8 MUSCULAR
guys: 5 HEMEN
**Braxton**
Singer: 4 TONI
**Bray:** 6 HEEHAW
beginning: 3 HEE
ending: 3 HAW
They: 5 ASSES

**Brayer:** 3 ASS 6 DONKEY
**Braz.**
neighbor: 3 ARG BOL URU
**Brazen:** 5 SAUCY
9 SHAMELESS
type: 5 HUSSY
**Brazil**
neighbor: 4 PERU
port: 5 BELEM NATAL
**"Brazil"**
bandleader: 5 CUGAT
**Brazilian**
airline: 5 VARIG
dance: 5 SAMBA
metropolis: 8 SAOPAULO
port: 5 BELEM NATAL
resort: 3 RIO
soccer star: 4 PELE
state: 5 BAHIA
**Brazos River**
city: 4 WACO
**Brazzi**
Actor: 7 ROSSANO
**Breach:** 3 GAP
of security: 4 LEAK
**Bread:** 3 SOP 5 MOOLA
6 STAPLE
11 STAFFOFLIFE
Bit of: 5 CRUMB
Break: 3 EAT 4 DINE
Breakfast: 5 BAGEL TOAST
13 ENGLISHMUFFIN
Broke: 3 ATE
Brown: 5 TOAST
browner: 7 TOASTER
chamber: 4 OVEN
Corn: 4 PONE
10 JOHNNYCAKE
Deli: 3 RYE
Kind of: 3 RYE 6 RAISIN
Like old: 5 STALE
Like some: 5 OATEN
6 CRUSTY
maker: 4 OVEN 5 BAKER
of India: 3 NAN
Pocket: 4 PITA
Quick: 5 SCONE
Ritual: 5 WAFER
spread: 3 JAM 4 MAYO OLEO
unit: 4 LOAF
___ bread: 4 PITA
**Breadbasket:** 5 BELLY TUMMY
Square in a: 3 PAT
**Breadth:** 4 SPAN 5 RANGE
SCOPE
**Breadwinner:** 6 EARNER
**Break:** 3 GAP NAP 4 REST RIFT
TAME 6 HIATUS RECESS
7 TAKETEN
10 RESTPERIOD
a fast: 3 EAT
Afternoon: 3 NAP TEA
an oath: 3 LIE
away: 6 SECEDE
bread: 3 EAT
British: 7 TEATIME

Day: 3 NAP
down: 3 SOB 4 WEEP 5 PARSE
7 ANALYZE
follower: 4 ALEG
ground: 3 HOE
in relations: 4 RIFT
in the action: 4 LULL
into bits: 5 SMASH
7 SHATTER
It's a good thing to: 5 HABIT
off: 3 END 4 WEAN 5 CEASE
SEVER
out: 5 ERUPT 6 ESCAPE
point: 5 ADOUT
sharply: 4 SNAP
Something hard to: 5 HABIT
Take a: 4 REST
time: 5 TENAM
up: 5 ENDIT
Without a: 5 ONEND
6 ONEACT
**"Break ___!":** 4 ALEG
**Breakaway**
Glacier: 4 BERG
group: 4 SECT
**Breakdown:** 8 COLLAPSE
Diplomacy: 4 RIFT
It causes a: 6 ENZYME
Request after a: 3 TOW
Societal: 6 ANOMIE
**Breaker**
Barrier: 3 SST
Code: 3 KEY
Ground: 3 HOE 4 HOER
Ice: 4 PICK
Mach 1: 3 SST
on the road: 4 CBER
Tend to a: 5 RESET
Word before: 3 JAW
**Breakfast:** 4 MEAL
acronym: 4 IHOP
area: 4 NOOK
beverage: 5 JUICE
brand: 4 EGGO
bread: 5 BAGEL TOAST
13 ENGLISHMUFFIN
chain: 4 IHOP
choice: 4 EGGS
companion: 3 BED
dish: 6 OMELET
drinks: 3 OJS
food: 7 GRANOLA
for Brutus: 3 OVA
fruit: 5 MELON
Had: 3 ATE
Hot: 7 OATMEAL
meat: 3 HAM 5 BACON
13 CANADIANBACON
nook: 6 ALCOVE
pastry: 6 DANISH
sizzler: 5 BACON
staple: 4 EGGS
**"Breakfast at Tiffany's"**
author: 6 CAPOTE
**Break-in**
for snooping: 6 BAGJOB

Sound of a: 4 AHEM
**"Breaking Away"**
director Peter: 5 YATES
**"Breaking Up Is Hard to Do"**
singer Neil: 6 SEDAKA
**Breakout:** 6 ESCAPE
High school: 4 ACNE
**Breakup**
comment: 7 ITSOVER
**"___ Breaky Heart":** 4 ACHY
**Breastbone:** 7 STERNUM
Of the: 7 STERNAL
**Breastbones:** 6 STERNA
**Breath**
candy: 6 TICTAC
Catch one's: 4 REST
Dog: 4 PANT
Kind of: 5 BATED
mint: 5 CERTS 6 TICTAC
Struggle for: 4 GASP
Take a: 6 INHALE
Take a deep: 4 SIGH
**Breathe:** 7 RESPIRE
heavily: 4 PANT
life into: 7 ANIMATE
Live and: 3 ARE 5 EXIST
out: 6 EXHALE
**Breather:** 4 LUNG REST
Skin: 4 PORE
Take a: 4 REST 5 PAUSE
**Breathing:** 5 ALIVE
fire: 5 IRATE
organ: 4 GILL LUNG
problem: 5 APNEA
room: 5 SPACE
sound: 4 RALE
spell: 4 REST
**Breathless:** 5 EAGER
condition: 5 APNEA
Leave: 3 AWE
**"Breathless"**
actress Jean: 6 SEBERG
**Breathtaking**
beast: 3 BOA
**Brecht**
collaborator: 5 WEILL
**Breck**
competitor: 5 PRELL
**"___ Breckinridge":** 4 MYRA
**Breed:** 3 ILK 4 REAR SIRE
SORT TYPE
Mixed: 4 MUTT
**Breeze:** 4 EASY SNAP
5 CINCH
Float on the: 4 WAFT
Gentle: 6 ZEPHYR
Like a certain: 7 ONSHORE
producer: 3 FAN
Shoot the: 3 FAN GAB JAW
YAK 4 CHAT
through: 3 ACE
(through): 4 SAIL
**Breezy:** 4 AIRY
In a ~ way: 6 AIRILY
**"Breezy"**
actress Kay: 4 LENZ

**Brenda**
  of the comics: 5 STARR
  Singer: 3 LEE
**Brendan**
  Playwright: 5 BEHAN
**Brennan**
  Actress: 6 EILEEN
  Justice who replaced:
    6 SOUTER
**Brenneman**
  Actress: 3 AMY
**Breslau**
  river: 4 ODER
**Brest**
  **Info:** French cue
  bridge: 4 PONT
  friend: 3 AMI 4 AMIE
  milk: 4 LAIT
  To be, in: 4 ETRE
**Bret**
  Author: 5 HARTE
**Bret Easton ___**
  Author: 5 ELLIS
**Breton: 4 CELT**
**___ breve: 4 ALLA**
**Brew: 3 ALE TEA 4 BEER**
    5 STEEP
  Chinese: 3 CHA
  hue: 5 AMBER
  Japanese: 5 KIRIN
  Malt: 5 STOUT
  Pub: 3 ALE
  Weak: 8 NEARBEER
  Witch: 6 POTION
  ~, in German: 4 BIER
**Brewed**
  beverage: 3 ALE
  drink: 7 ICEDTEA
  Not: 7 INSTANT
**Brewer**
  Canadian: 6 LABATT
  Coffee: 3 URN
  need: 4 HOPS MALT 5 YEAST
  oven: 4 OAST
  Singer: 6 TERESA
**Brewery**
  container: 3 VAT
  fixture: 4 OAST
  need: 4 HOPS MALT 5 YEAST
**Brewpub**
  offering: 3 ALE
**Brewski: 4 BEER SUDS**
    7 COLDONE
  location: 6 COOLER
  topper: 4 HEAD
**Breyers**
  rival: 4 EDYS
**Brezhnev**
  Soviet leader: 6 LEONID
**Brian**
  Actor: 6 AHERNE
  Beatles manager: 7 EPSTEIN
  Figure skater: 5 ORSER
  of Roxy Music: 3 ENO
  Rock producer: 3 ENO
**Bribe: 3 OIL SOP 6 GREASE**

Open to a: 5 VENAL
  9 ONTHETAKE
  to a DJ: 6 PAYOLA
**Bric-a-___ : 4 BRAC**
**Bric-a-brac**
  event: 7 TAGSALE
  stand: 7 ETAGERE WHATNOT
**Brice, Fanny**
  theme song: 5 MYMAN
**Brick**
  bond: 6 MORTAR
  carrier: 3 HOD
  Hacienda: 5 ADOBE
  oven: 4 KILN
  Sun-dried: 5 ADOBE
  Toy ~ brand: 4 LEGO
  worker: 5 MASON
**Brickell**
  Singer: 4 EDIE
**Bricklayer: 5 MASON**
  burden: 3 HOD
**Bricks**
  measure: 3 TON
**Bridal**
  bio word: 3 NEE
  covering: 4 VEIL
  Part of a ~ dress: 5 TRAIN
  party: 4 WIFE
  path: 5 AISLE
  shower: 4 RICE
  wreath: 6 SPIREA
**Bride**
  band: 4 RING
  destination: 5 ALTAR
  headgear: 4 VEIL
  ride: 4 LIMO
  title: 3 MRS
  words: 3 IDO
**"Bride of Frankenstein, The"**
  actress Lanchester: 4 ELSA
**Bridesmaid**
  Many a: 6 SISTER
**Bridge: 4 SPAN**
  action: 3 BID 5 REBID
  ancestor: 5 WHIST
  beam: 4 IBAR
  bid, briefly: 5 ONENO
  blunder: 6 RENEGE
  call: 4 AHOY 5 IPASS
  coup: 4 SLAM
  declaration: 3 BID 5 IPASS
  Defeats in: 4 SETS
  Electrical: 3 ARC
  expert Charles: 5 GOREN
  expert Culbertson: 3 ELY
  expert Sharif: 4 OMAR
  feat: 4 SLAM
  fee: 4 TOLL
  First name in: 4 OMAR
  guard of folklore: 5 TROLL
  holding: 4 HAND 6 TENACE
  ploy: 7 FINESSE
  position: 4 EAST WEST
    5 NORTH SOUTH
  section: 4 SPAN
  site: 4 NOSE

support: 4 IBAR 5 TRUSS
  6 GIRDER 7 TRESTLE
  tower: 5 PYLON
  ~, in French: 4 PONT
  ~, in Italian: 5 PONTE
**"Bridge of San Luis ___, The":**
  3 REY
**"Bridge on the River ___, The":**
  4 KWAI
**Bridges**
  Actor: 4 BEAU JEFF 5 LLOYD
  Like some rural: 7 ONELANE
**Bridges, Jeff**
  brother: 4 BEAU
  film: 4 TRON 7 STARMAN
**Bridget**
  She played ~ in 2001:
    5 RENEE
  ~, to Jane: 5 NIECE
**"Bridget Jones's Diary"**
  actress Zellweger: 5 RENEE
**"Bridge Too Far, A"**
  author Cornelius: 4 RYAN
**Bridle**
  part: 3 BIT 4 REIN
  strap: 4 REIN
**Brie**
  carrier: 7 SALTINE
  covering: 4 RIND
  Mature, as: 3 AGE
  Mold, in: 7 RIPENER
**Brief: 4 MINI 6 LITTLE**
    7 CURSORY
  appearance: 5 CAMEO
  brawl: 5 SETTO
  message: 4 NOTE
  story: 3 BIO
  summary: 5 RECAP
  time: 6 MOMENT
  upturn: 4 BLIP
**Briefly: 7 INAWORD INSHORT**
  Visit: 6 STOPIN
**Briefs**
  alternative: 6 BOXERS
    11 BOXERSHORTS
  brand: 5 HANES
  ~, briefly: 4 BVDS
**Brig**
  British: 4 GAOL
  pair: 5 MASTS
**Brigadier**
  Like a ~ general: 7 ONESTAR
**"Brigadoon"**
  composer: 5 LOEWE
  lyricist: 6 LERNER
**Brigantine**
  gear: 4 SAIL
**Brigham Young University**
  city: 5 PROVO
**Bright: 3 LIT 5 SMART SUNNY**
    6 BRAINY
  annual: 6 ZINNIA
  bunch: 5 MENSA
  Extremely: 4 NEON
  It may be: 4 IDEA
  lights: 5 NEONS

**Not too:** 4 PALE 5 DENSE
**star:** 4 NOVA
**thought:** 4 IDEA
**Brighten:** 6 PERKUP
**Brightest**
  star in a constellation:
    5 ALPHA
**Brightly**
  Burn: 5 BLAZE
  colored: 4 LOUD
  colored bird: 6 ORIOLE
  colored fish: 4 OPAH
  Shine: 7 RADIATE
  Shining: 6 AGLARE
**Brightness**
  Measurer of: 5 MENSA
  unit: 7 LAMBERT
**Brighton**
  Info: Spanish cue
  buggy: 4 PRAM
  bye-bye: 4 TATA
**Brigitte**
  Actress: 6 BARDOT
**Brilliance:** 5 ECLAT 6 LUSTER
  Flash of: 4 IDEA
  Lose: 4 FADE
**Brilliant:** 6 SUPERB 7 STELLAR
  display: 4 RIOT
  stroke: 4 COUP
  success: 5 ECLAT
  suffix: 3 INE
**"___ brillig ...":** 4 TWAS
**Brillo**
  rival: 3 SOS
**Brim:** 4 EDGE TEEM
  Fill to the: 4 SATE
  Snap: 6 FEDORA
**Brimless**
  cap: 5 BERET
  hat: 3 FEZ 5 BERET TOQUE
  topper: 10 PILLBOXHAT
**Brimstone:** 6 SULFUR
  Spew fire and: 4 RANT
**Brine-cured**
  cheese: 4 FETA
  salmon: 3 LOX
**Bring**
  about: 5 BEGET CAUSE
    6 INDUCE 8 ENGENDER
  action: 3 SUE
  back: 6 REVIVE 7 RESTORE
  bad luck to: 4 JINX
  dishonor: 5 SHAME
  down: 4 RUIN UNDO 5 ABASE
  down the house: 4 RAZE
  forth: 6 ELICIT
  home: 3 NET 4 EARN
  home the bacon: 4 EARN
    11 MAKEALIVING
  in: 3 NET 4 EARN REAP
    6 IMPORT
  in the harvest: 4 REAP
  into accord: 6 ATTUNE
  into being: 6 CREATE
  into harmony: 6 ATTUNE
  into play: 3 USE 6 ENTAIL

**joy to:** 5 ELATE
  on: 4 HIRE
  out: 5 EDUCE 6 ELICIT
  (out): 4 TROT
  the food: 5 CATER
  to a boil: 6 ENRAGE
  to a near boil: 5 SCALD
  to bay: 4 TREE
  to bear: 5 EXERT
  together: 5 UNITE
  to life: 7 ANIMATE
  to light: 6 EXHUME
    EXPOSE
  to mind: 5 EVOKE
  to naught: 4 UNDO
  to ruin: 4 UNDO
  to the surface: 6 ELICIT
  under control: 4 TAME
  up: 4 REAR 5 RAISE
    7 MENTION
  upon oneself: 5 INCUR
  up the rear: 3 LAG 4 MOON
    5 TRAIL
**"Bring ___!":** 4 ITON
**Brink:** 3 EVE RIM 4 EDGE
    5 VERGE
  Be on the: 6 TEETER
**Brinker**
  Skater: 4 HANS
**Briny:** 3 SEA 5 OCEAN
  Back on the: 3 AFT 5 STERN
  On the: 4 ASEA 5 ATSEA
  septet: 4 SEAS
**Brio:** 4 ELAN 6 SPIRIT
**Brioche**
  ingredient: 3 EGG
**Bris:** 4 RITE
**Brisk:** 4 SPRY 5 NIPPY PERKY
    7 ALLEGRO
**Bristle:** 3 AWN 4 SETA
  at: 6 RESENT
  Barley: 3 AWN
  Biological: 4 SETA
  Grain: 6 ARISTA
**Bristles:** 5 SETAE 7 SEESRED
  Grain: 7 ARISTAE ARISTAS
**Bristly:** 6 SETOSE
**Bristol**
  baby carriage: 4 PRAM
  cable channel: 4 ESPN
  county: 4 AVON
**Brit**
  Conservative: 4 TORY
  Early: 4 PICT
  Noble ~, briefly: 6 ARISTO
**Brit.**
  fliers: 3 RAF
  honor: 3 OBE
  legislators: 3 MPS
  lexicon: 3 OED
  military decoration: 3 DSO
  money: 4 STER
  recording label: 3 EMI
  sports cars: 3 MGS
**Britannicus**
  Poisoner of: 4 NERO

**___ B'rith:** 4 BNAI
**British**
  architect: 4 WREN 6 SPENCE
  biscuit: 5 SCONE
  blackbird: 4 MERL
  bowling pin: 7 SKITTLE
  break: 3 TEA
  brew: 3 ALE
  buddy: 5 MATEY
  buggy: 4 PRAM
  carbine: 4 STEN
  coins: 5 PENCE
  colony: 4 ADEN
  composer: 4 ARNE
  conservative: 4 TORY
  ending: 3 ZED
  exam: 6 ALEVEL OLEVEL
  exclamation: 4 ISAY
  flag: 9 UNIONJACK
  flashlight: 5 TORCH
  fliers (abbr.): 3 RAF
  gun: 4 STEN
  john: 3 LOO
  music co.: 3 EMI
  noble: 4 DAME DUKE EARL
    5 BARON
  novelist: 5 READE
  peer: 4 EARL 5 BARON
  prep school: 4 ETON
  prime minister: 4 EDEN
    5 BLAIR HEATH 6 ATTLEE
    8 DISRAELI
  quart: 5 LITRE
  racecourse: 5 ASCOT
  raincoat: 3 MAC
  record label: 3 EMI
  ref. work: 3 OED
  royal: 4 ANNE
  rule in India: 3 RAJ
  runner: 3 COE 5 OVETT
  school: 4 ETON
  servicewoman: 4 WREN
  sports cars: 3 MGS
  streetcar: 4 TRAM
  submachine gun: 4 STEN
  tar: 5 LIMEY
  tax: 4 CESS
  title: 4 DAME EARL
  verb ending: 3 ISE
  weapon: 4 STEN
  weight: 5 STONE
**British ___:** 5 ISLES
**British Honduras**
  ~, today: 6 BELIZE
**British Open:** see page 714
  winner: 3 ELS 4 DALY LEMA
    6 OMEARA WATSON
**British Petroleum**
  acquisition: 5 AMOCO
**Briton**
  Ancient: 4 CELT PICT
**Brittany**
  Info: French cue
  Being, in: 4 ETRE
  port: 5 BREST
**Brittle:** 5 CRISP

cookie: 4 SNAP
  10 GINGERSNAP
  pastry: 7 OATCAKE
**Brno**
  locale: 7 MORAVIA
**Bro:** 3 REL SIB 4 DUDE
  counterpart: 3 SIS
  of Dad or Mom: 3 UNC
  sib: 3 SIS
**Broad:** 4 DAME VAST WIDE
  bean: 4 FAVA
  necktie: 5 ASCOT
  sash: 3 OBI
  shoe size: 3 EEE
  tie: 5 ASCOT
  valley: 4 DALE
**Broadbent, Jim**
  film: 4 IRIS
**Broadcast:** 3 AIR 4 EMIT ONTV
  SHOW 5 AIRED
  6 STREWN
  Being: 4 ONTV 5 ONAIR
  6 AIRING
  component: 5 AUDIO
  inits.: 3 APB
  Not: 7 UNAIRED
  sign: 5 ONAIR
  slot: 7 AIRTIME
**Broadcaster:** 5 AIRER
  Cold war ~ (abbr.): 3 VOA
  Senate: 5 CSPAN
**Broadcasting:** 5 ONAIR
  8 ONTHEAIR
  watchdog (abbr.): 3 FCC
**Broaden:** 5 WIDEN
  7 ENLARGE
**Broadside**
  Hit: 3 RAM
  Not: 5 ENDON
**Broad-topped**
  hill: 4 LOMA
**Broadway**
  1973 ~ revival: 5 IRENE
  1978 ~ musical: 5 EUBIE
  1990 one-man ~ show: 3 TRU
  1990s ~ smash: 4 RENT
  acronym: 4 ANTA
  aunt: 4 MAME 5 ELLER
  Auntie of: 4 MAME
  award: 4 TONY
  backer: 5 ANGEL
  Began on: 6 OPENED
  bio: 3 TRU
  brightener: 4 NEON
  hit: 4 CATS RENT
  hit letters: 3 SRO
  opening: 4 ACTI 6 ACTONE
  production: 4 PLAY SHOW
  role: 4 AIDA 5 ANNIE
**Broadway Joe:** 6 NAMATH
**Brobdingnagian:** 4 HUGE
  5 GIANT
**Brocaded**
  fabric: 4 LAME
**Broccoli**
  bit: 5 SPEAR 6 FLORET

**Broccoli ___:** 4 RABE
**___ broche:** 3 ALA
**Brock**
  of baseball: 3 LOU
**"___ Brockovich":** 4 ERIN
**Brogan:** 4 SHOE
  bottom: 4 SOLE
**Brogna**
  of baseball: 4 RICO
**Broil:** 4 COOK
  Place to: 4 OVEN
**Brokaw:** 6 ANCHOR
  network: 3 NBC
  Newsman: 3 TOM
**Broke:** 8 STRAPPED
**Broken:** 4 TAME 5 KAPUT
  arm holder: 5 SLING
  It's ~ at parties: 6 PINATA
  THEICE
  Like a ~ horse: 4 TAME
  mirror: 4 OMEN
  piece: 5 SHARD
  They're ~ up: 4 EXES
  They run when: 4 EGGS
**Broker:** 5 AGENT
  charge: 3 FEE
  Information: 7 TIPSTER
  offering: 3 IRA TIP
  order: 4 SELL
  stat: 5 QUOTE
  suggestion: 3 BUY
**Brokerage**
  Online: 6 ETRADE
  phrase: 5 ATPAR
**Brolly**
  go-withs: 4 MACS
**Bromide:** 3 SAW 6 CLICHE
  OLDSAW
**Bronco**
  Break a: 4 TAME
  buster: 5 TAMER
  catcher: 5 LASSO
**Broncos**
  quarterback John: 5 ELWAY
**Brontë**
  Author: 4 ANNE 5 EMILY
  heroine Jane: 4 EYRE
  novel: 8 JANEEYRE
**Bronx**
  attraction: 3 ZOO
  cheer: 4 JEER RAZZ
  Give a ~ cheer: 4 JEER RAZZ
  Rhymer of ~ and thonx:
  4 NASH
**Bronx Bomber:** 6 YANKEE
**Bronx Zoo**
  beasts: 4 APES
**"Bronx Zoo, The"**
  actor Ed: 5 ASNER
**Bronze:** 3 AGE 5 ALLOY
  coating: 6 PATINA
  component: 3 TIN
  Go for the: 3 TAN
**Bronze ___:** 3 AGE
**Brooch:** 3 PIN 5 CLASP
  Adjust, as a: 5 REPIN

Attach, as a: 5 PINON
  fastener: 5 CLASP
**Brood:** 3 SIT 4 CLAN MOPE
  POUT STEW SULK
  creator: 3 HEN
  Place to: 4 NEST
**Brooder:** 3 HEN
  place: 4 NEST
**Brooding**
  author: 3 POE
  place: 4 NEST
  type: 3 HEN
**Brook:** 4 RILL
  catch: 5 TROUT
  Small: 4 RILL
**Brooke**
  Ex-husband of: 5 ANDRE
**Brooklet:** 4 RILL
**Brooklyn**
  institute: 5 PRATT
  island: 5 CONEY
  pronoun: 3 DEM
  school (abbr.): 3 LIU
  suffix: 3 ESE ITE
  West of: 3 MAE
**Brooklyn Dodgers**
  Duke of the: 6 SNIDER
  great: 5 REESE
  ~, affectionately: 4 BUMS
**Brookner**
  Author: 5 ANITA
**Brooks**
  Actor: 5 AVERY 6 ALBERT
  Country singer: 5 GARTH
  Director: 3 MEL
**Brooks, Foster**
  persona: 3 SOT
**Brooks, Garth**
  birthplace: 5 TULSA
**Brookville**
  campus: 6 CWPOST
**Broom**
  Curling: 5 BESOM
  rider: 3 HAG
  Twig: 5 BESOM
  Use a: 5 SWEEP
  Used a: 5 SWEPT
**"Broom ___":** 5 HILDA
**"Broom Hilda"**
  cartoonist: 5 MYERS
**Brosnan, Pierce**
  role: 4 BOND 6 STEELE
**Broten**
  of hockey: 4 NEAL
**Brother:** 3 FRA SIB 4 MONK
  address: 3 FRA
  Biblical: 4 ABEL ESAU
  5 AARON
  Daughter of a: 5 NIECE
  Kid ~, maybe: 4 PEST
  Lodge: 3 ELK
**Brought**
  about: 5 LEDTO
  forth: 5 BEGAT
  to life: 4 BORN
  up: 4 BRED

**Brouhaha:** 3 ADO 4 FLAP STIR
  TODO 5 SCENE
  6 UPROAR
**Browbeat:** 7 HENPECK
**Brown:** 3 IVY 5 SAUTE
  and others: 5 IVIES
  bagger: 4 WINO
  Bandleader: 3 LES
  beverage: 3 ALE
  bread: 5 TOAST
  building: 4 DORM
  Dark: 5 SEPIA
  Editor: 4 TINA
  ermine: 5 STOAT
  Grayish: 3 DUN
  hue: 4 ECRU 5 SEPIA
  Light: 3 TAN 4 ECRU 5 BEIGE
  pigment: 5 SEPIA
  Question for a ~ cow:
    6 HOWNOW
  quickly: 4 SEAR
  rival: 4 PENN YALE
  seaweed: 4 KELP
  shade: 3 TAN 4 ECRU RUST
    5 BEIGE SEPIA TAUPE
    UMBER
**Brown, Buster**
  dog: 4 TIGE
**Brown, Charlie**
  exclamation: 4 RATS
**Brown, ___ Mae**
  Novelist: 4 RITA
**Brown, Molly**
  portrayer: 6 GRIMES
**Brown, Murphy**
  program: 3 FYI
  Son of: 5 AVERY
**Brown, Rita ___**
  Author: 3 MAE
**Brown Bomber, The:**
  8 JOELOUIS
**Browne**
  Cartoonist: 3 DIK
**Browner, Carol**
  org.: 3 EPA
**Brownie:** 3 ELF 6 SPRITE
  9 GIRLSCOUT
  bunch: 5 TROOP
  org.: 3 GSA
  topper: 6 BEANIE
**Brownie ___:** 6 POINTS
**Browning:** 4 POET
  character: 5 PIPPA
  Director: 3 TOD
  output: 4 POEM
**Brownish:** 5 UMBER
  gray: 5 TAUPE
  purple: 4 PUCE
  yellow: 5 TAWNY
**Brownstone**
  feature: 5 STOOP
**Brown-tinted**
  photo: 5 SEPIA
**Browse**
  from outside:
    10 WINDOWSHOP

(through): 4 LEAF
  ~, in a way: 4 SURF
**Browser**
  bookmark: 3 URL
  target: 3 WEB
**Broz, Josip:** 4 TITO
**"Brrr!":** 6 IMCOLD
**Brubeck**
  Jazz pianist: 4 DAVE
  music: 4 JAZZ
**Bruce**
  Actor: 4 DERN 5 NIGEL
  Comedian: 5 LENNY
  Ex of: 4 DEMI
**Bruckner**
  Composer: 5 ANTON
  Like Symphony No. 7 by:
    3 INE
**Bruhn**
  of ballet: 4 ERIK
**Bruins:** 4 TEAM
  home: 4 UCLA
  legend: 3 ORR
  player Phil, familiarly:
    4 ESPO
  sch.: 4 UCLA
**Bruised:** 6 PURPLE
  It may be easily: 3 EGO
**Bruiser:** 5 HEMAN PASTE
  opposite: 5 SISSY
**___ brûlée:** 5 CREME
**Brummell, Beau:** 3 FOP
  5 DANDY
  school: 4 ETON
**Brunch:** 4 MEAL
  beverage: 6 MIMOSA
  entrée: 6 OMELET
  fish: 3 LOX
  Have: 3 EAT
  selection: 5 BAGEL CREPE
    6 OMELET QUICHE
    7 SAUSAGE
  time: 5 TENAM
**Brundage**
  Former Olympics head:
    5 AVERY
**Brunei:** 9 SULTANATE
  locale: 4 ASIA 6 BORNEO
**Brunette**
  Become a: 3 DYE
  Go back to being a: 5 REDYE
**Brunswick**
  competitor: 3 AMF
**Brunswick stew**
  need: 5 ONION
**Brush**
  off: 4 SNUB 5 SPURN
  Ranch: 4 SAGE
  (up): 4 BONE
  up on: 7 RELEARN
**Brusque:** 4 CURT RUDE
  5 GRUFF SHORT TERSE
  6 ABRUPT
**Brussels**
  Alliance based in: 4 NATO
**Brutal:** 5 CRUEL 6 SAVAGE

**Brute:** 3 APE 4 LOUT OGRE
  5 BEAST 6 ANIMAL
  7 RUFFIAN
  leader: 4 ETTU
**___ Brute:** 4 ETTU
**Brutus**
  Info: Latin cue
  Bear, to: 4 URSA
  Behold, to: 4 ECCE
  Being, to: 4 ESSE
  Bird, to: 4 AVIS
  Breakfast for: 3 OVA
  Burdens, to: 5 ONERA
  But, to: 3 SED
  co-conspirator: 5 CASCA
  Rebuke to: 4 ETTU
**Bryan:** 6 ORATOR
  defeater, in 1908: 4 TAFT
**Bryan, William Jennings**
  birthplace: 5 SALEM
  Emulate: 5 ORATE
**Bryant:** 5 LAKER
  of basketball: 4 KOBE
  Singer: 5 ANITA
**Bryant, Paul**
  Movie about: 7 THEBEAR
  team, for short: 4 BAMA
**Bryce Canyon**
  locale: 4 UTAH
**Brylcreem**
  amount: 3 DAB
**Bryn ___:** 4 MAWR
**Brynhild**
  brother: 4 ATLI
**Bryn Mawr**
  grad: 6 ALUMNA
**Brynner**
  Actor: 3 YUL
**Bryologist**
  What a ~ studies: 4 MOSS
**Bryson**
  Singer: 5 PEABO
**B's**
  One of the three: 4 BACH
**B.S.:** 3 DEG
**BSA**
  part: 4 AMER
**BTU**
  Part of: 4 UNIT
  relative: 3 CAL
**Bub:** 3 MAC
**Bubble:** 4 BOIL 6 AERATE
  Enjoy ~ gum: 4 CHEW
  source: 3 GUM 4 SOAP
**Bubble ___:** 4 WRAP
**"Bubble, bubble, ___ and**
  **trouble":** 4 TOIL
**Bubblehead:** 3 ASS 4 DOLT
**Bubbler:** 7 AERATOR
**"Bubbles in the Wine"**
  was his theme song: 4 WELK
**Bubbletop:** 4 DOME
**Bubbling:** 5 ABOIL
**Bubbly**
  beverage: 4 COLA SODA
  7 SELTZER

Make: 6 AERATE
name: 4 MOET
prefix: 3 AER
source: 4 ASTI
**Bubkes:** 3 NIL 4 NADA ZERO
**Buccaneers**
home: 5 TAMPA
**Buchanan**
Mystery writer: 4 EDNA
Politico: 3 PAT
**Buchholz**
Actor: 5 HORST
**Buchwald**
Columnist: 3 ART
**Buck:** 4 CLAM DEER DEFY
MALE STAG 6 DOLLAR
RESIST 7 ONESPOT
8 SIMOLEON
add-on: 4 AROO
Author: 5 PEARL
Bird on a: 5 EAGLE
Country singer: 5 OWENS
ender: 4 AROO
feature: 6 ANTLER
7 ANTLERS
heroine: 4 OLAN
mate: 3 DOE
of baseball: 5 ONEIL
**Buck, Pearl S.**
book: 12 THEGOODEARTH
heroine: 4 OLAN
**Bucked**
It may be: 6 SYSTEM
**Bucker:** 5 BRONC
**Bucket:** 4 PAIL SEAT
Champagne: 4 ICER
contents: 4 DROP
Item in a: 3 MOP
Like the ~ of song: 5 OAKEN
locale: 4 WELL
material: 3 OAK
of bolts: 4 HEAP 5 CRATE
LEMON 6 JALOPY
**Buckets:** 4 ALOT
Come down in: 4 POUR
**Buckeye:** 6 OHIOAN
sch.: 3 OSU
**Buckeye State:** 4 OHIO
**Buckingham:** 6 PALACE
**Buckingham Palace**
letters: 3 HRH
**Buckinghamshire**
school: 4 ETON
**Buckle:** 4 CAVE GIVE WARP
6 FASTEN
opener: 5 SWASH
site: 4 BELT
up: 7 STRAPIN
**Buckley**
Actress: 5 BETTY
**Bucko:** 3 LAD
**Bucks:** 3 HES 4 CASH DEER
KALE 5 DOUGH MONEY
MOOLA
prefix: 4 MEGA
**Buckwheat:** 6 RASCAL

dish: 5 KASHA
pancakes: 5 BLINI
**Bucky Beaver**
brand: 5 IPANA
**Buco**
Osso ~ meat: 4 VEAL
___ buco: 4 OSSO
**Bucolic:** 5 RURAL
byway: 4 LANE
**Bucs**
home: 5 TAMPA
**Bud:** 3 BRO MAC PAL 4 BEER
CHUM PARD 5 CRONY
6 FRIEND
Baseball commissioner:
5 SELIG
holder: 3 KEG 4 VASE
partner: 3 LOU
Pickled: 5 CAPER
~, to a botanist: 5 GEMMA
**Budd**
Olympic runner: 4 ZOLA
**"Buddenbrooks"**
novelist Thomas: 4 MANN
**Buddha**
birthplace: 5 NEPAL
sermon: 5 SUTRA
shade-giver: 6 BOTREE
**Buddhist**
discipline: 3 ZEN
Dome-shaped ~ shrine:
5 STUPA
language: 4 PALI
monk: 4 LAMA
sect: 3 ZEN
who has attained Nirvana:
5 ARHAT
**Buddy:** 3 BRO BUB MAC PAL
4 CHUM MATE PARD
5 AMIGO CRONY KIDDO
Actor: 5 EBSEN
British: 5 MATEY
Good: 3 PAL 4 CBER
Kind of: 5 BOSOM
of Bert: 5 ERNIE
of Bud: 3 LOU
of Ollie: 4 STAN
~, in French: 3 AMI
~, in Spanish: 5 AMIGO
**Buddy-buddy:** 5 CLOSE
**"Buddy Holly Story, The"**
actor Gary: 5 BUSEY
**Budge:** 4 MOVE STIR
Doesn't: 8 STAYSPUT
One who won't: 4 MULE
**Budget**
Monthly ~ item: 4 RENT
offering: 6 RENTAL
rival: 4 AVIS 5 ALAMO
**Budgetary:** 6 FISCAL
excess: 3 FAT
**Budging**
Not: 7 ADAMANT
**Budweiser**
rival: 5 COORS PABST
6 STROHS

___ Buena Island: 5 YERBA
**Buenos ___:** 5 AIRES
**"Buenos ___":** 4 DIAS
**Buenos Aires**
musical: 5 EVITA
**Buff:** 3 FAN NUT RUB TAN
5 LOVER MAVEN SHINE
7 BURNISH
10 AFICIONADO
In the: 4 BARE NUDE
5 NAKED
**Buffalo:** 5 BISON STUMP
AAA baseball team: 6 BISONS
bunch: 4 HERD
canal: 4 ERIE
City near: 5 OLEAN
county: 4 ERIE
hockey player: 5 SABRE
hunter: 4 CREE
lake: 4 ERIE
**Buffalo Bill:** 4 CODY 5 IOWAN
colleague: 5 ANNIE
**Buffalo Bob Smith**
puppet: 10 HOWDYDOODY
**Buffet:** 4 MEAL PELT 6 REPAST
Enjoy a: 3 EAT 7 OVEREAT
patron: 5 EATER
table item: 3 URN
warmer: 6 STERNO
**Buffoon:** 3 ASS OAF 4 DOLT
**Buffoonery:** 5 ANTIC 6 ANTICS
8 ZANINESS
**Buffy:** 6 SLAYER
portrayer: 5 SARAH
weapon: 5 STAKE
**"Buffy the Vampire Slayer"**
actor Green: 4 SETH
actress ___ Michelle Gellar:
5 SARAH
**Bug:** 3 FLU IRK TAP VEX
4 GERM RILE 5 ANNOY
PEEVE TEASE VIRUS
6 HASSLE INSECT
NEEDLE NETTLE
PESTER 7 WIRETAP
Baby: 5 LARVA
Busy: 3 BEE
Computer: 6 GLITCH
ending: 4 ABOO
Fire: 3 ANT
Have a: 3 AIL
June ~, for one: 6 BEETLE
killer: 3 DDT
Like a ~ in a rug: 4 SNUG
no end: 5 EATAT
out: 5 LEAVE
Pesky: 4 GNAT
Tiny: 4 MITE
with bounce: 4 FLEA
**Bugaboo:** 4 BANE FEAR
**Bugbear:** 4 OGRE 8 PETPEEVE
9 BETENOIRE
**Bug-eyed:** 4 AGOG GAGA
monsters: 3 ETS
**Buggy**
Baby: 4 PRAM

British: 4 PRAM
Moon ~ (abbr.): 3 LEM
Off-road ~ (abbr.): 3 ATV
place: 4 DUNE
power: 5 HORSE
**Bugler**
call: 7 RETREAT
evening call: 4 TAPS
of the wild: 3 ELK
**Bugling**
beast: 3 ELK
**Bugs:** 3 VWS 6 RABBIT
chaser: 4 FUDD 5 ELMER
    9 ELMERFUDD
co-creator Chuck: 5 JONES
Columnist: 4 BAER
Elmer, to: 3 DOC
Gangster: 5 MORAN
treat: 6 CARROT
Voice of: 3 MEL 5 BLANC
**"Bug's Life, A"**
character: 3 ANT
princess: 4 ATTA
**Build:** 5 ERECT
a fire under: 6 AROUSE
on: 5 ADDTO
(on): 3 ADD
Place to: 4 SITE
up: 5 AMASS 6 ACCRUE
**Builder:** 7 ERECTOR
Ark: 4 NOAH
Chair: 5 CANER
Delta: 4 SILT
Empire: 4 INCA
guide: 5 SPECS
Hill: 3 ANT
Lodge: 6 BEAVER
Molecule: 4 ATOM
Navy: 6 SEABEE
Nest: 3 ANT 4 BIRD
Pot: 4 ANTE
**Builders**
Pyramid: 5 MAYAS 6 MAYANS
**Building**
addition: 3 ELL 4 WING
    5 ANNEX
annex: 3 ELL 4 WING
Babel: 5 TOWER
Backyard: 4 SHED
beam: 4 IBAR 5 JOIST
block: 4 UNIT 5 ADOBE
    BRICK
block brand: 4 LEGO
brick: 5 ADOBE
Brown: 4 DORM
Campus: 4 DORM HALL
courtyards: 5 ATRIA
Diplomat's: 7 EMBASSY
Domed: 7 ROTUNDA
Farm: 4 BARN SILO
front: 6 FACADE
location: 4 SITE
material: 5 ADOBE STONE
near a silo: 4 BARN
Quad: 4 DORM HALL
site: 3 LOT

support: 4 IBAR
wing: 3 ELL
**Buildup:** 4 HYPE 6 HOOPLA
Aquarium: 5 ALGAE
Dryer: 4 LINT
Flue: 4 SOOT
Musical: 9 CRESCENDO
Navel: 4 LINT
Polar: 6 ICECAP
Pond: 5 ALGAE
**Built:** 4 MADE
for speed: 5 SLEEK
**Built-up:** 5 URBAN
**Bulb:** 5 CLOVE
Cartoon: 4 IDEA
Garden: 5 TULIP
holder: 6 SOCKET
Pungent: 5 ONION
unit: 4 WATT
___ **Bulba:** 5 TARAS
**Bulfinch**
subject: 4 MYTH
**Bulgar:** 4 SLAV
**Bulgaria**
capital: 5 SOFIA
money: 3 LEV
**Bulgy**
Battle of the: 4 SUMO
**Bulk:** 4 HEFT MASS
**Bull:** 4 MALE 5 EDICT
    NBAER
and others: 3 HES
artist: 4 LIAR
Barcelona: 4 TORO
Borden: 5 ELMER
Bullfight: 4 TORO
issuer: 4 POPE
It's no: 3 COW
markets: 3 UPS
prefix: 4 TAUR 5 TAURO
Rodeo: 6 BRAHMA
run: 3 LEA
sound: 5 SNORT
suffix: 3 ISH
target: 4 CAPE
Type of: 5 PAPAL
**Bulldog:** 3 ELI 5 YALIE
    7 EDITION
of the comics: 4 OTTO
**Bulldoze:** 4 RAZE
**Bullet:** 4 SLUG
in a deck: 3 ACE
point: 4 ITEM
**Bulletin:** 5 ALERT
News: 6 UPDATE
**Bulletin board**
fastener: 4 TACK 7 PUSHPIN
notice: 4 MEMO 7 POSTING
overseer: 5 SYSOP
Put on a: 4 POST
**Bullets:** 4 AMMO
Fill with: 4 LOAD
**Bullfight:** 7 CORRIDA
bull: 4 TORO
cheer: 3 OLE
figure: 6 TORERO

**Bullfighter:** 6 TORERO
    8 TOREADOR
cloak: 4 CAPA
**Bullish:** 7 TAURINE
**"Bullitt"**
director Peter: 5 YATES
**Bullock**
Actress: 6 SANDRA
film: 6 THENET
**Bullpen**
ace: 6 CLOSER
sound: 5 SNORT
stat: 3 ERA
**Bullring**
beast: 4 TORO
cheer: 3 OLE
Injured in the: 5 GORED
**Bull Run**
general: 5 MEADE 6 STUART
~, to the Rebs: 8 MANASSAS
**Bulls:** 4 TEAM
Like some: 5 PAPAL
org.: 3 NBA
**Bull's-eye**
(abbr.): 3 CTR
Eye the: 3 AIM
hitter: 4 DART
Like a: 8 ONTARGET
**Bullwinkle:** 5 MOOSE
foe: 5 BORIS 7 NATASHA
**Bully:** 3 COW 6 ABASER
    ABUSER MEANIE
    10 BROWBEATER
target: 4 NERD
**Bullying:** 6 DURESS
Engage in: 8 BROWBEAT
**Bulova**
rival: 5 ROLEX SEIKO TIMEX
**Bulrush:** 4 TULE 5 SEDGE
**Bulwer-___**
English author: 6 LYTTON
**"Bulworth"**
actress Berry: 5 HALLE
**Bum:** 4 HOBO REAR
Bowery: 4 WINO
off of: 5 CADGE
Word with: 3 SKI
**Bum ___:** 3 RAP 5 STEER
**Bumble Bee**
product: 4 TUNA
**Bumbler:** 3 OAF 7 SADSACK
cry: 4 OOPS
**Bumbling:** 5 INEPT
**Bummed:** 3 SAD
out: 3 SAD 4 BLUE
    6 MOROSE
**"Bummer!":** 4 ALAS DRAG
**Bump:** 3 JAR 4 OUST STUB
    7 PREEMPT
in the road: 4 SNAG
into: 4 MEET
Like a ~ on a log: 5 INERT
off: 3 ICE 4 DOIN SLAY
    5 ERASE WASTE
on a log: 4 KNUR NODE
Place for a: 3 LOG

**Bumper**
  bruise: 4 DENT
  coating: 6 CHROME
  sticker word: 4 HONK
**Bumpkin:** 4 HICK RUBE
       5 YAHOO YOKEL
**Bumpy:** 6 UNEVEN
  Not: 4 EVEN
**Bumstead**
  boss: 7 DITHERS
  Dithers, to: 4 BOSS
**Bun:** 4 ROLL 6 HAIRDO
  Buttery: 7 BRIOCHE
  seed: 6 SESAME
**Bunch:** 4 HERD SLEW
       6 PASSEL
  A whole: 4 LOTS TONS
  Brainy: 5 MENSA
  Bright: 5 MENSA
  Crude: 4 OPEC
  Honey: 4 BEES
  of bees: 5 SWARM
  of bills: 3 WAD
  of brownies: 5 TROOP
**"___ Bunch, The":** 5 BRADY
**Bunche**
  Peace Nobelist: 5 RALPH
**Bunco:** 4 SCAM
**Bundle:** 5 SHEAF 6 PACKET
  Make a: 4 BALE
  of bills: 3 WAD
  of cotton: 4 BALE
  of energy: 6 DYNAMO
  of hay: 4 BALE
  of papers: 5 SHEAF
**Bundy**
  and others: 3 ALS
  Mrs.: 3 PEG
**Bungle:** 3 ERR 4 FLUB MUFF
       5 BOTCH GUMUP MISDO
       7 LOUSEUP SCREWUP
       8 BOLLIXUP
**Bungling:** 5 INEPT
**Bunion**
  locale: 3 TOE
**Bunk:** 3 COT ROT 4 GUFF
       5 HOKUM HOOEY
  Army: 3 COT
**Bunker:** 4 HILL
  Mr.: 6 ARCHIE
  Mrs.: 5 EDITH
  portrayer: 7 OCONNOR
**Bunker, Archie:** 5 BIGOT
  command: 6 STIFLE
  furniture: 8 ARMCHAIR
  humor: 6 ETHNIC
  portrayer: 7 OCONNOR
  Wife of: 5 EDITH
**Bunny**
  boss, briefly: 3 HEF
  bounce: 3 HOP
  Dumb: 5 STUPE
  makeup: 4 DUST
  Move like a: 3 HOP
  tail: 4 SCUT
**Buns:** 3 DOS

Pat on the: 4 OLEO
**Bunsen**
  burner relative: 4 ETNA
  creation: 6 BURNER
**Bunt**
  situation: 5 ONEON
  ~, on a scorecard: 3 SAC
**Bunting:** 5 FINCH
  place: 4 NEST
**Buntline**
  Novelist: 3 NED
**Buñuel**
  collaborator: 4 DALI
  Director: 4 LUIS
**Bunyan, Paul**
  ox: 4 BABE
  tool: 3 AXE
**"Buona ___":** 4 SERA
**Buoy:** 5 ELATE
  Red: 3 NUN
  Where ~ meets gull: 3 SEA
       5 OCEAN
**Buoyancy:** 10 RESILIENCE
**Buoyant:** 5 PERKY 6 FLOATY
       7 SPRINGY
  tune: 4 LILT
**Burden:** 3 TAX 4 LOAD ONUS
       6 SADDLE
  bearer: 5 BEAST
  Beast of: 3 ASS YAK 5 CAMEL
       LLAMA
  Financial: 4 DEBT
  of proof: 4 ONUS
**Burdened:** 5 LADEN
  No longer ~ by: 5 RIDOF
**Burdensome:** 7 ONEROUS
**Burdette**
  of '50s–'60s baseball: 3 LEW
**Burdon**
  Singer: 4 ERIC
**Bureau:** 5 CHEST 6 AGENCY
       7 DRESSER
  ender: 4 CRAT
**Bureaucratic**
  bigwig: 6 POOBAH
  tangle: 7 REDTAPE
**Burg:** 4 TOWN
  Cheese: 4 EDAM
  Icy: 4 NOME
**Burger**
  bread: 3 BUN
  side: 4 SLAW
  topping: 5 ONION
**Burglar:** 4 YEGG 5 FELON
       THIEF
  alarm feature: 6 SENSOR
  deterrent: 4 BARK 5 ALARM
  Kind of: 3 CAT
  Like a cat: 8 STEALTHY
  take: 4 LOOT
**Burgle:** 3 ROB 5 STEAL
**Burgoo:** 4 STEW
**Burgundy:** 3 VIN 4 WINE
  being: 4 ETRE
  buddy: 3 AMI
  by another name: 5 ARLES

grape: 5 PINOT
**Burial**
  vault: 4 TOMB 5 CRYPT
**"Burial of the Count Orgaz"**
  painter: 7 ELGRECO
**"Burke's Law"**
  Burke of: 4 AMOS
**Burkina ___:** 4 FASO
**Burkina Faso**
  neighbor: 4 MALI
**Burl**
  Folk singer: 4 IVES
**Burlap**
  bag: 4 SACK
  material: 4 HEMP JUTE
**Burlesque:** 3 APE
  bit: 4 SKIT
  prop: 3 BOA
**Burmese**
  prime minister: 3 UNU
**Burn:** 4 CHAR SEAR 5 SCALD
       6 SCORCH
  balm: 4 ALOE 8 ALOEVERA
  brightly: 5 BLAZE
  Do a slow: 4 STEW 6 SEETHE
       7 SMOLDER
  Kind of: 4 SLOW
  like a candle: 7 FLICKER
  rubber: 5 SPEED
  slightly: 5 SINGE
  soother: 4 ALOE
       8 ALOEVERA
  up: 3 IRE
  without a flame: 7 SMOLDER
  with water: 5 SCALD
**Burner**
  Ceremonial: 6 CENSER
  inventor: 6 BUNSEN
  Lab: 4 ETNA
  Oil: 4 LAMP
**Burnett**
  Actress: 5 CAROL
  Adman: 3 LEO
**Burning:** 3 LIT 5 AFIRE
       AGLOW 6 AFLAME
       ONFIRE
  desire: 5 ARSON
  It's often: 6 DESIRE
  Like ~ plastic: 5 ACRID
  remnant: 3 ASH
  the midnight oil: 6 UPLATE
  with desire: 6 ARDENT
**Burnish:** 3 RUB
**Burnoose**
  wearer: 4 ARAB
**Burnout**
  cause: 6 STRESS
  treatment: 8 RESTCURE
**Burns:** 4 POET SCOT
  **Info:** Scottish cue
  and Allen (abbr.): 4 SENS
  Before, to: 3 ERE
  Bestow, to: 3 GIE
  birthplace: 3 AYR
  Documentarian: 3 KEN
  Hillside, to: 4 BRAE

land: 6 SCOTIA
Not large, to: 3 SMA WEE
Not, to: 3 NAE
partner: 5 ALLEN
Possess, to: 3 HAE
Pretty, to: 5 BONNY
"sweet" stream: 5 AFTON
title starter: 4 AULD
~, to Allen: 7 PARTNER
**Burns, George**
　film: 5 OHGOD
　partner ___ Allen: 6 GRACIE
　role: 3 GOD
　trademark: 5 CIGAR
**Burnt**
　color: 6 SIENNA
　residue: 3 ASH
**Burnt ___ crisp: 3 TOA**
**Burpee**
　unit: 4 SEED
**Burr**
　Duel participant: 5 AARON
　Event for ~ and Hamilton:
　　4 DUEL
**Burr, Raymond**
　role: 5 MASON 8 IRONSIDE
**Burrito**
　alternative: 4 TACO
　filler: 4 BEEF
　kin: 6 TAMALE
　topping: 5 SALSA
　wrapper: 8 TORTILLA
**Burro: 3 ASS 10 PACKANIMAL**
　bellow: 4 BRAY
**Burrow: 3 DEN 4 HOLE LAIR**
**Burrower**
　Lawn: 4 MOLE
**Burrowing**
　animal: 4 MOLE 6 GERBIL
　　WOMBAT
**Burrows**
　Playwright: 3 ABE
**Bursa: 3 SAC**
**Burst: 3 POP 5 ERUPT**
　Artillery: 5 SALVO
　of activity: 5 SPURT
　of energy: 5 SPASM
　of laughter: 4 PEAL
　of speed: 6 SPRINT
　of wind: 4 GUST
　Ready to: 5 SATED
　with pride: 5 KVELL
**Bursting**
　star: 4 NOVA
**Burstyn**
　Actress: 5 ELLEN
**Burt**
　and Loni: 4 EXES
　Ex of: 4 LONI
**Burton**
　Actor: 5 LEVAR
　Director: 3 TIM
　Miniseries role for: 5 KINTE
**Burton, Richard**
　film: 5 EQUUS 7 THEROBE
　Like: 5 WELSH

**Burundi**
　neighbor: 6 RWANDA
**Bury: 5 INTER INURN
　　6 ENTOMB INHUME**
**Bus**
　alternative: 4 RAIL
　Board a: 5 GETON
　front: 4 OMNI
　Parks on a: 4 ROSA
　passenger request:
　　8 TRANSFER
　route: 4 LINE
　starter: 4 MINI OMNI
　station: 5 DEPOT
　station info: 3 ETA
　terminal (abbr.): 3 STN
**Bus.**
　abbr.: 3 INC
　bigwig: 3 CEO
　card info: 3 TEL
　heads: 4 MGMT
　helper: 4 ASST
　leader: 3 MGR
　letter abbr.: 3 ENC 4 ATTN
　school course: 4 ECON
**Busboy**
　load: 4 TRAY
**Busby: 3 HAT**
**Buscaglia**
　Author: 3 LEO
**Busch Gardens**
　locale: 5 TAMPA
**Busch Stadium: 5 ARENA**
　team (abbr.): 3 STL
**Bush: 5 SHRUB**
　league: 3 GOP
　outing: 6 SAFARI
　Singer: 4 KATE
**Bush, George H.W.: 3 ELI
　　5 TEXAN YALIE**
　adviser Scowcroft: 5 BRENT
　campaign adviser:
　　7 ATWATER
　chief of staff: 6 SUNUNU
　former org.: 3 CIA
**Bush, George W.: 3 ELI
　　5 TEXAN YALIE**
　adviser Karl: 4 ROVE
　alma mater: 4 YALE
　degree (abbr.): 3 MBA
　nickname: 5 DUBYA
　opponent: 4 GORE
　party: 3 GOP
　spokesman Fleischer: 3 ARI
　Wife of: 5 LAURA
**Bush, Gov.**
　of Florida: 3 JEB
　state (abbr.): 3 FLA
**Bushed: 5 ALLIN TIRED
　　WEARY**
　Become: 4 TIRE
**Bushel**
　Biblical: 4 EPHA
　fraction: 4 PECK
**Bushel ___ peck: 4 ANDA**
**Bushels: 4 ALOT GOBS**

**Bushes**
　are in it: 3 GOP
　One of the: 3 JEB
**Bushmiller**
　Cartoonist: 5 ERNIE
**Bushnell, Nolan**
　company: 5 ATARI
**Bushwhacked: 7 WAYLAID**
**Bushy**
　hairdo: 4 AFRO
**Bushy-tailed**
　beast: 7 RACCOON
　rodent: 6 MARMOT
**Busiest: 4 PEAK**
**Busily**
　Employ: 3 PLY
　working: 4 ATIT
**Business: 4 SHOP 5 TRADE**
　abbr.: 3 INC 4 CORP
　attire: 4 SUIT 7 NECKTIE
　banter: 8 SHOPTALK
　bigwig: 4 CZAR EXEC
　　5 BARON MOGUL TITAN
　Brand-new: 7 STARTUP
　card abbr.: 3 EXT TEL
　Do: 4 DEAL 8 TRANSACT
　Do ~ with: 6 SELLTO
　Doing: 4 OPEN
　Funny: 5 ANTIC 6 ANTICS
　Get down to: 10 TALKTURKEY
　Go back into: 6 REOPEN
　Head for: 4 BOSS
　Its ~ is folding: 7 ORIGAMI
　Its ~ was booming: 3 SST
　letter abbr.: 3 ENC 4 ATTN
　　ENCL
　letters: 3 INC
　lunch locale: 5 HOTEL
　mag: 3 INC
　marriage: 6 MERGER
　Monkey: 5 APERY
　news: 6 MERGER
　Online: 5 ETAIL
　Order of: 6 AGENDA
　Out of: 4 SHUT 6 CLOSED
　　7 BELLYUP
　partner, often: 3 SON
　Place of: 4 SHOP
　Port: 6 WINERY
　prefix: 4 AGRI AGRO
　Ready for: 4 OPEN
　school subj.: 4 ECON
　sign abbr.: 4 ESTD 5 ESTAB
　solicitor: 3 REP
　transaction: 4 DEAL
　You might give him the: 3 SON
　~ VIP: 3 CEO
　~, facetiously: 7 BEESWAX
**Businessman**
　offering: 4 CARD
**Businessmen: 5 SUITS**
**"Bus Stop"**
　playwright: 4 INGE
**Bust: 3 NAB 4 RAID 5 RUNIN
　　6 ARREST
　　10 POLICERAID**

It may be a: **6** STATUE
Make a: **4** RAID **6** SCULPT
maker: **4** NARC
makers (abbr.): **3** DEA
opposite: **4** BOOM
**Bust ___:** **4** AGUT
**Buster:** **4** NARC
Drought: **4** RAIN
Drug: **4** NARC
of Flash Gordon fame:
 **6** CRABBE
of silent comedies: **6** KEATON
~, old-style: **6** SIRRAH
**Bustle:** **3** ADO HUM **4** STIR
 TODO
**Busy:** **4** ATIT **5** INUSE
 **6** ORNATE TIEDUP
 **7** ONTHEGO
activity: **3** ADO
as a bee: **8** HARDATIT
bug: **3** BEE
Keep: **5** AMUSE
Not: **4** FREE IDLE SLOW
one: **3** BEE **4** DOER
one in Apr.: **3** CPA
place: **4** HIVE
time for the IRS: **3** APR
**Busy as ___:** **4** ABEE
**Busybody:** **5** SNOOP YENTA
 **7** MEDDLER
 **10** NOSYPARKER
Be a: **3** PRY **4** NOSE **5** SNOOP
Like a: **4** NOSY
**But**
end: **3** ANE
~, for short: **3** THO
~, in French: **4** MAIS
~, in German: **4** ABER
~, in Latin: **3** SED
**"But ___ art?":** **4** ISIT
**Butcher**
cut: **4** LOIN **5** TBONE
device: **5** SCALE
offering: **4** BEEF MEAT
 **5** STEAK TBONE
 **10** SHELLSTEAK
**Butches:** **3** DOS
**Butler:** **4** HELP
Comic: **5** BRETT
Do the job of a: **5** ASKIN
 SEEIN
final word: **4** DAMN
love: **5** OHARA
of Batman: **6** ALFRED
of fiction: **5** RHETT
portrayer: **5** GABLE
request: **5** ENTER
~, to Gable: **4** ROLE
**Butler, Robert ___**
Author: **4** OLEN
**"But ___ me, give me**
 **liberty ...":** **5** ASFOR
**"But of course!":** **3** AHA
 **5** OHYES
**Butt:** **3** END
Info: Suffix cue

bit: **3** ASH
Cigar: **4** ETTE
into: **3** RAM
place: **7** ASHTRAY
**Butte**
Big: **4** MESA
kin: **4** MESA
locale: **6** MONTANA
**Butter:** **3** RAM
alternative: **4** OLEO
Bit of: **3** PAT
Clarified: **4** GHEE
holder: **3** TUB
Indian: **4** GHEE
knife: **8** SPREADER
Make: **5** CHURN
maker: **5** CHURN
serving: **3** PAT
substitute: **4** OLEO
up: **5** BASTE
**Buttercup**
relative: **7** ANEMONE
 **8** LARKSPUR
**"BUtterfield 8"**
author John: **5** OHARA
**Butterfingers:** **3** OAF **5** KLUTZ
cry: **4** OOPS
**Butterflies:** **5** ANGST **6** NERVES
 **7** ANXIETY
**"Butterflies ___ Free":** **3** ARE
**Butterfly:** **6** MADAME
Brightly colored: **7** MONARCH
 **10** REDADMIRAL
catcher: **3** NET
Did the: **4** SWAM
Float like a: **4** FLIT
relative: **4** MOTH
**"Butterfly"**
actress Zadora: **3** PIA
**"___ Butterfly":** **6** MADAMA
**"___ Buttermilk Sky":** **3** OLE
**Butterworth:** **3** MRS
**"___ but the Brave":** **4** NONE
**"___ but the wind":** **4** TWAS
**Butting**
heads: **6** ATODDS
**Buttinsky:** **4** PEST **5** PRIER
 YENTA YENTE
Barbecue: **3** ANT
Like a: **4** NOSY
**Button**
Alley: **5** RESET
Attach, as a: **5** SEWON
Blender: **5** PUREE
Boom box: **3** REC
Bowling alley: **5** RESET
Calculator: **5** CLEAR
Campaign ~ word: **5** ELECT
Car radio: **6** PRESET
Cash register: **6** NOSALE
Cell phone: **4** SEND
Clock radio: **5** SNOOZE
Cockpit: **5** EJECT
Cute as a: **8** ADORABLE
Email: **4** SEND
Fax: **4** SEND

Furnace: **5** RESET
Kind of: **5** PANIC
Like a: **4** CUTE
material: **5** NACRE
On the: **5** EXACT
PC panic: **3** ESC
Phone: **4** OPER STAR
 **6** REDIAL
Phone ~ trio: **3** ABC DEF
 GHI JKL MNO PRS TUV
 WXY
Skater: **4** DICK
up: **6** FASTEN
~, to Frosty: **4** NOSE
**Buttoned:** **4** SHUT
Not: **4** OPEN
**Buttonhole:** **3** SEW **4** SLIT
 **6** ACCOST
locale: **5** LAPEL
**Buttonless**
shirt: **3** TEE
**Buttonlike:** **4** CUTE
**Buttons**
Comedian: **3** RED
**Buttonwood:** **8** SYCAMORE
**Butyl**
suffix: **3** ENE
**Buy**
alternative: **5** LEASE
and sell: **5** TRADE **6** DEALIN
back: **6** REDEEM
Great: **5** STEAL
in a hurry: **6** SNAPUP
One way to: **8** ONCREDIT
stocks: **6** INVEST
stuff: **4** SHOP
**Buyer:** **6** VENDEE
Car ~ protection:
 **8** LEMONLAW
caution: **4** ASIS
concern: **4** COST
incentive: **6** REBATE
~, in Latin: **6** EMPTOR
**Buyoff:** **5** BRIBE
**Buzz:** **3** HUM **4** NEWS **5** DRONE
 RUMOR
Astronaut: **6** ALDRIN
Gave a: **4** RANG
in space: **6** ALDRIN
Moonmate of: **4** NEIL
producer: **5** KAZOO
**Buzzard**
relative: **7** VULTURE
**Buzzards Bay:** **5** INLET
**Buzzer:** **3** BEE
Bothersome: **4** GNAT
 **8** HOUSEFLY
Tiny: **4** GNAT
**Buzzi**
Comedian: **4** RUTH
**Buzzing:** **4** AHUM **5** ASTIR
about: **3** ADO
cloud: **5** SWARM
location: **6** APIARY
pest: **4** GNAT
with excitement: **5** ABOIL

**"Buzz off!":** 4 SHOO 5 SCRAM
**B'way**
  hit sign: 3 SRO
**By:** 3 VIA
  and by: 4 ANON SOON
      7 ERELONG
  and large: 7 ASARULE
      9 INTHEMAIN
  any chance: 4 EVER
  birth: 3 NEE
  far: 6 EASILY
  itself: 5 PERSE
  means of: 3 PER VIA
  way of: 3 VIA
  way of, briefly: 4 THRU
**"By ___!":** 3 GAR 4 JOVE
      6 JIMINY
**"Bye!":** 4 CIAO TATA 5 ADIEU
      SEEYA 6 SEEYOU
**"Bye-bye!":** 4 CIAO TATA
      5 ADIEU SEEYA
      6 SEEYOU
**"Bye Bye Birdie"**
  song: 4 KIDS 5 ROSIE
      15 PUTONAHAPPYFACE

  star: 10 JANETLEIGH
**"Bye Bye Bye"**
  pop group: 5 NSYNC
**"By gar!":** 4 EGAD
**Bygone:** 3 OLD 4 PAST
      5 OLDEN 7 OLDTIME
  days: 4 PAST YORE
**"By Jove!":** 4 EGAD ISAY
      5 EGADS
**"___ by land ...":** 5 ONEIF
**Bylaw**
  ~, briefly: 3 REG
**Byline**
  Essay: 4 ELIA
**"By me":** 5 IPASS
**BYOB**
  Part of: 3 OWN 4 YOUR
      5 BOOZE BRING
  provision: 5 SETUP
**Bypass:** 4 OMIT SKIP 5 SKIRT
  the altar: 5 ELOPE
**Byrd, Admiral**
  book: 5 ALONE
**Byrnes**
  Actor: 3 EDD

**Byron:** 4 POET
  daughter: 3 ADA
  piece written to Napoleon:
      3 ODE
  poem: 4 LARA
**"___ by Starlight":**
      6 STELLA
**Byte**
  parts: 4 BITS
  prefix: 4 GIGA KILO MEGA
      TERA
**"___ by the bell!":** 5 SAVED
**"By the way ...":** 3 SAY
**Bytown**
  was its first name:
      6 OTTAWA
**Byway:** 4 LANE ROAD
      6 AVENUE
      8 SIDEROAD
  Country: 4 LANE
**Byways**
  (abbr.): 3 RDS
**Byword:** 5 ADAGE MAXIM
**"By yesterday!":** 4 ASAP

**C:** 4 FAIR 5 GRADE 7 AVERAGE
D and ~, in D.C.: 3 STS
follower: 4 SPAN
G in the key of: 3 SOL
in a C scale: 5 TONIC
in shop class: 5 CLAMP
in UPC: 4 CODE
Mark added to a: 7 CEDILLA
minor: 3 KEY
natural: 6 BSHARP
Note above: 5 DFLAT
sharp: 5 DFLAT
The ~ of C.S. Lewis: 5 CLIVE
to C: 6 OCTAVE
Vehicle for the high: 4 ARIA
What a ~ might be: 4 SOFT
Work in: 4 CODE
Worth a: 4 FAIR SOSO
**C-___:** 4 SPAN 5 CLAMP
**$C_2H_6$:** 6 ETHANE
**C-3PO:** 5 DROID ROBOT
**$C_4H_8$:** 6 BUTENE
**$C_4H_8O_2$:** 5 ESTER
**$C_{14}H_9Cl_5$:** 3 DDT
**$Ca^{++}$:** 3 ION
**CAA**
   employee: 3 AGT
**Cab:** 4 HACK TAXI
   caller: 6 HAILER
   counter: 5 METER
   Early: 6 HANSOM
   Flag a: 4 HAIL
   prefix: 4 PEDI
   Take a: 4 RIDE
**Cabal:** 4 PLOT RING
      5 JUNTA
   member: 7 PLOTTER
**"Cabaret"**
   actor Grey: 4 JOEL
   actor Joel: 4 GREY
   actress Minnelli: 4 LIZA
   basis: 10 IAMACAMERA
   director Bob: 5 FOSSE
   lyricist: 3 EBB
   ~ Klub: 6 KITKAT
**Cabbage:** 4 GELT KALE LOOT
      5 MOOLA 6 DINERO
      MOOLAH
   **Info:** Money cue
   dish: 4 SLAW
   kin: 4 KALE
   Kobe: 3 YEN
   salad: 4 SLAW
   Spanish: 6 PESETA
**Cabby:** 4 HACK
   Call to a: 4 HAIL
   client: 4 FARE
   query: 7 WHERETO

**Caber**
   tosser: 4 SCOT
**Cabernet:** 3 RED 4 WINE
**Cabeza**
   across the Pyrenees: 4 TETE
**Cabin**
   bed: 3 COT
   component: 3 LOG
   Place for a: 4 LAKE
**Cabinet**
   Cleaning ~ supplies: 4 LYES
   department: 5 LABOR STATE
      7 DEFENSE 8 INTERIOR
   dept.: 3 AGR DOD HUD INT
      4 EDUC ENER USDA
   div.: 4 DEPT
   Kitchen: 8 CUPBOARD
   Medicine ~ item: 4 QTIP
      6 IODINE
   off.: 4 SECY
   TV: 7 CONSOLE
   wood: 5 ALDER CEDAR
**Cabinet member**
   Clinton: 4 PENA RENO
      5 COHEN 7 SHALALA
   Nixon: 6 ELLIOT
   Reagan: 4 HAIG 5 MEESE
**Cable:** 4 WIRE 5 PAYTV
   Atlanta-based ~ sta.: 3 TBS
      TNT
   Basic ~ channel: 3 TNN
   car: 4 TRAM
   chan. for old films: 3 AMC
      TCM
   channel: 3 AMC HBO SHO TBS
      TNN TNT USA
   connection: 5 TVSET
   co. that merged with AT&T:
      3 TCI
   kingpin Turner: 3 TED
   modem alternative: 3 DSL
   network: 3 AMC HBO SHO
      TBS TNN TNT USA
   Provide with a new: 6 REWIRE
   sports award: 4 ESPY
   sports channel: 4 ESPN
   superstation: 3 TBS
   syst.: 4 CATV
   worker: 5 WIRER
**Caboodle**
   companion: 3 KIT
   Kit and: 3 ALL LOT
**Caboose:** 4 REAR
   place: 4 REAR
**Cabral**
   Explorer: 5 PEDRO
**Cabriolet**
   maker: 4 AUDI

**Cache:** 5 HOARD STORE
      TROVE 7 SECRETE
   Cash: 3 ATM 4 TILL
**Cachet:** 4 SEAL
**Cackleberry:** 3 EGG
   producer: 3 HEN
**Cackler:** 3 HEN
**Cacophony:** 3 DIN 5 BLARE
      NOISE
**Cacti**
   Flowering: 8 SAGUAROS
**Cactus**
   Hallucinogenic: 6 MESCAL
      PEYOTE
   Large: 7 SAGUARO
   Like: 5 SPINY
   ring: 6 AREOLE
**Cad:** 4 HEEL LOUT RAKE
      ROUE 5 BEAST CREEP
      LOUSE 6 ROTTER
      7 BOUNDER
   comeuppance: 4 SLAP
**Cadbury**
   confection: 3 EGG
**Caddie:** 5 TOTER
   suggestion: 4 IRON
   supplies: 4 TEES
**Caddies**
   Events with: 4 TEAS
**Caddy**
   contents: 3 TEA
   shack: 6 GARAGE
   Word with: 3 TEA
**Cadence**
   Rhythmic: 4 LILT
   sound: 3 HUP
**Cadenza**
   It might have a: 4 ARIA
   Perform a: 4 SOLO
   player: 7 SOLOIST
**Cadet**
   First-year: 4 PLEB 5 PLEBE
   org.: 4 ROTC
   sch.: 4 USMA
   Space ~ place:
      8 LALALAND
**Cadge:** 3 BUM
**Cadillac**
   model: 6 CATERA 7 SEVILLE
      8 ELDORADO
**Cádiz**
   **Info:** Spanish cue
   Cold, in: 4 FRIO
   crafts: 5 ARTES
**Cadmus**
   Daughter of: 3 INO
**Caduceus**
   Org. with a ~ logo: 3 AMA

**Caen**
Info: French cue
In conclusion, in: 5 ENFIN
river: 4 ORNE
Town near: 4 STLO
**Caesar:** 3 SID 5 ROMAN SALAD
Info: Latin cue
accusation: 4 ETTU
cohort: 4 COCA
Comic: 3 SID
Cry of: 4 ETTU
Dying words from: 4 ETTU
End of a ~ boast: 4 VICI
existence: 4 ESSE
farewell: 4 VALE
Fateful day for: 4 IDES
Hail, to: 3 AVE
hello: 3 AVE
Mo. named for a: 3 AUG
Opponent of: 4 CATO
Part of a ~ boast: 4 ISAW
      5 ICAME
port: 5 OSTIA
Rebuke from: 4 ETTU
robe: 4 TOGA
salad ingredient: 3 OVA
server: 9 SALADBOWL
suffix: 3 EAN
That is, to: 5 IDEST
To be, to: 4 ESSE
tongue: 5 LATIN
topper: 7 CROUTON
Words from: 4 ETTU
      5 ICAME
___ Caesar: 5 GAIUS
**Caesarean**
conquest: 4 GAUL
phrase: 4 ETTU
**Caesura:** 4 REST 5 PAUSE
**Café:** 6 BISTRO EATERY
additive: 4 LAIT
alternative: 3 THE
clientele: 6 EATERS
cup: 5 TASSE
feature: 6 AWNING
**Café ___:** 4 NOIR 6 AULAIT
**Café au ___:** 4 LAIT
**Café con ___:** 5 LECHE
**Cafeteria**
carrier: 4 TRAY
customer: 5 EATER
of yore: 7 AUTOMAT
Unappetizing ~ serving:
      4 GLOP
wear: 7 HAIRNET
**Caffè ___:** 5 LATTE
**Caffeinated**
drink: 4 COLA
**Caffeine**
source: 3 TEA 4 COLA KOLA
**Caftan:** 4 ROBE
**Cage**
Actor ~, to friends: 3 NIC
part: 3 RIB
Talker in a: 4 MYNA
Worker in a: 6 TELLER

**Cage, Nicolas**
1997 ~ film: 6 CONAIR
**Cager**
Boston: 4 CELT
Cleveland: 3 CAV
Dallas: 3 MAV
favorite sound: 5 SWISH
Los Angeles: 5 LAKER
New Jersey: 3 NET
offense: 4 FOUL
org.: 3 NBA
San Antonio: 4 SPUR
target: 4 HOOP
~ Archibald: 4 NATE
~ Gilmore: 5 ARTIS
~ Mashburn: 5 JAMAL
~ O'Neal: 4 SHAQ
~ Shaq: 5 ONEAL
**Cagers**
Like most: 4 TALL
**Cagey:** 3 SLY
**Cagney**
1935 ~ film: 4 GMEN
1949 ~ film: 9 WHITEHEAT
portrayer: 5 GLESS
role: 5 COHAN
TV partner of: 5 LACEY
**"Cagney & Lacey"**
costar: 4 TYNE 5 GLESS
**Cahoots**
In: 6 ALLIED
**Cain**
Brother of: 4 ABEL SETH
Father of: 4 ADAM
Land where ~ dwelt: 3 NOD
Nephew of: 4 ENOS
Raise: 4 RAGE
raiser: 3 EVE 4 ADAM
Son of: 5 ENOCH
**Caine**
1966 ~ role: 5 ALFIE
title: 3 SIR
**"Caine Mutiny, The"**
author: 4 WOUK
captain: 5 QUEEG
**Cairn**
composition: 6 STONES
**Cairngorms**
River in the: 3 DEE
**Cairo**
debut of 1871: 4 AIDA
river: 4 NILE OHIO
suburb: 4 GIZA
**Cajole:** 4 COAX URGE
**Cajun**
"Dirty" ~ dish: 4 RICE
staple: 4 OKRA
waterway: 5 BAYOU
**Cake**
Bathday: 4 SOAP
Corn: 4 PONE
decoration: 5 ICING
decorator: 4 ICER
feature: 4 TIER 5 LAYER
finisher: 4 ICER
Finish the: 3 ICE

ingredient: 5 SUGAR
It's a piece of: 5 SLICE
It takes the: 4 OVEN
Kind of: 3 OAT 5 BUNDT
      LAYER 6 SPONGE
layer: 4 TIER
Like a wedding: 6 TIERED
Like fresh: 5 MOIST
Make a: 4 BAKE
Message on a: 5 EATME
name: 7 SARALEE
Nut: 5 TORTE
Piece of: 4 EASY SNAP TIER
      5 CINCH LAYER WEDGE
      6 BREEZE PICNIC
Popular snack: 5 SUZYQ
Rich: 5 TORTE 6 GATEAU
Rum: 4 BABA
Small sponge:
      10 LADYFINGER
Spongy: 5 BABKA
Take the: 3 EAT WIN
Tea: 5 SCONE
topper: 4 ICER 5 ICING
Wedding ~ feature: 4 TIER
**Cake pan**
type: 5 BUNDT
**Cakes**
partner: 3 ALE
Rich: 7 GATEAUX
**Cakewalk:** 4 ROMP SNAP
      6 PICNIC
**Cal**
Twin of: 4 ARON
**Cal.**
Boxer from: 3 SEN
column: 3 FRI MON SAT SUN
      THU TUE WED 4 THUR
      TUES
entry: 4 APPT
neighbor: 3 NEV ORE
opener: 3 JAN
page: 3 APR AUG FEB DEC
      JAN JUL JUN MAR NOV
      OCT SEP 4 SEPT
pages: 3 MOS
periods: 3 YRS
**Cal ___:** 4 TECH
**Calabash:** 3 MRS
**Calaboose:** 4 STIR
**Calais**
Info: French cue
Cup, in: 5 TASSE
___ Calais: 5 PASDE
**Calamari:** 5 SQUID
**Calamine**
ingredient: 4 ZINC
target: 4 BITE ITCH
**Calamitous:** 4 DIRE 5 FATAL
      6 TRAGIC
**Calamity:** 3 ILL WOE
      7 TROUBLE
**Calc**
cousin: 4 TRIG
prerequisite: 3 ALG
readout: 3 LCD

**Calcium-rich**
green: 4 KALE
**Calculate**
astrologically: 4 CAST
**Calculated**
It may be: 4 RISK
**Calculating**
sort: 3 CPA
subject: 4 MATH
**Calculation**
Carpet: 4 AREA
Cash register: 3 TAX
Gambling: 4 ODDS
Geometry: 4 AREA
Graph: 5 SLOPE
Physics: 4 MASS
Statistics: 4 MEAN MODE
5 RANGE
Trig: 5 SLOPE
**Calculator:** 5 ADDER
Basic (plural): 5 ABACI
button: 5 CLEAR
display: 3 LED
Early: 6 ABACUS
9 SLIDERULE
element: 5 DIODE
figure: 6 ADDEND
key: 3 COS 5 ENTER
MPG: 3 EPA
Use a: 3 ADD
**Calculus:** 6 TARTAR
calculation: 4 AREA 5 LIMIT
SLOPE
pioneer: 5 EULER
___ calculus: 5 RENAL
**Calcutta**
coin: 5 RUPEE
costume: 4 SARI
home: 5 INDIA
Mother of: 6 TERESA
**Calder, Alexander**
creation: 6 MOBILE
7 STABILE
**Caldwell**
Actress: 3 ZOE
Author: 7 ERSKINE
Conductor: 5 SARAH
**Caleb**
Author: 4 CARR
**Caledonian:** 4 SCOT
**Calendar**
abbr.: 3 APR AUG DEC FEB
FRI JAN JUL JUN MAR
MON NOV OCT SAT SEP
SUN THU TUE WED
4 SEPT THUR TUES
Appt. ~ item: 3 MTG
Church: 4 ORDO
divs: 3 WKS
End of the Jewish: 4 ELUL
Kind of: 5 MAYAN PINUP
6 JEWISH 7 ISLAMIC
length: 4 YEAR
Like the Muslim: 5 LUNAR
line: 4 WEEK
Lunar ~ event: 3 TET

period: 4 WEEK YEAR
pgs.: 3 MOS
square: 3 DAY
**"Calendar Girl"**
singer: 6 SEDAKA
**Calendario**
opener: 5 ENERO
**Calf**
catcher: 5 LASSO RIATA
cry: 3 MAA 5 BLEAT
Golden: 4 IDOL
It covers half a: 4 MIDI
meat: 4 VEAL
Motherless: 5 DOGIE
roping site: 5 RODEO
Stray: 4 WAIF 5 DOGIE
**Calf-length**
skirt: 4 MIDI
**Calfless**
cow: 6 HEIFER
**Calgary**
native: 8 ALBERTAN
prov.: 4 ALTA
province: 7 ALBERTA
**Calgary Stampede:** 5 RODEO
**Calhoun**
Actor: 4 RORY
**Calibrate:** 3 SET
**Calico**
comment: 4 MEOW
**Calif.**
airport: 3 LAX
barrio city: 6 EASTLA
neighbor: 3 NEV 4 ARIZ OREG
Old ~ fort: 3 ORD
zone: 3 PST
**California**
A ~ Santa: 3 ANA 5 CLARA
Big in: 3 SUR
border lake: 5 TAHOE
city: 4 OJAI 6 ELTORO IRVINE
college: 6 POMONA
county: 4 NAPA 5 MARIN
6 FRESNO ORANGE
POMONA SHASTA
first lady: 3 MARIA
flag symbol: 4 BEAR
Former ~ fort: 3 ORD
giant: 7 REDWOOD
gold rush name: 6 SUTTER
golf locale: 11 PEBBLEBEACH
hrs.: 3 PDT
Island off: 8 CATALINA
missionary: 5 SERRA
National forest in: 6 SHASTA
oak: 5 ROBLE
Onetime ~ capital:
8 MONTEREY
peak: 6 LASSEN SHASTA
peninsula: 4 BAJA
raisin center: 6 FRESNO
resort: 11 PALMSPRINGS
senator: 12 BARBARABOXER
Start of many ~ city names:
3 SAN
valley: 4 NAPA SIMI

wind: 8 SANTAANA
wine region: 4 NAPA
6 SONOMA
___ California: 4 BAJA
**Californie:** 4 ETAT
**Caligula**
Nephew of: 4 NERO
**"Caligula"**
author: 5 CAMUS
**Caliph**
Early Muslim: 3 ALI 4 OMAR
faith: 5 ISLAM
**Calista**
role: 4 ALLY
**Call:** 3 REF SEE UMP 4 DIAL
NAME TERM 5 PHONE
RADIO VISIT
a game: 3 REF
a halt to: 3 END
at first: 4 SAFE
at home: 4 SAFE
before court: 7 ARRAIGN
Close: 5 SCARE
8 NEARMISS
counterpart: 3 PUT
for: 4 NEED PAGE 5 MERIT
6 ENTAIL INVOKE
(for): 3 ASK
for attention: 4 PSST
for help: 3 SOS 6 MAYDAY
forth: 5 EVOKE
for the salt: 4 AHOY
into question: 6 OPPUGN
it a day: 4 QUIT STOP
6 RETIRE
Kind of: 4 MAIL TOLL
5 CLOSE 6 MATING
WAKEUP 7 COLLECT
Like a 911: 4 EMER
Make a: 3 OPT 4 RULE
5 PHONE
off: 3 END 5 ABORT
6 CANCEL
of the wild: 4 ROAR
on: 3 SEE TAP USE 5 VISIT
out: 3 CRY
partner: 4 BECK
Part of an 800 collect ~
number: 3 ATT
Place to ~ home: 5 ABODE
the shots: 4 LEAD 6 DIRECT
Times to ~, in ads: 4 EVES
to a mate: 4 AHOY
to attention: 4 PSST
to Bo Peep: 3 BAA
to court: 4 CITE
to Fido: 4 HERE
to mind: 5 EVOKE
to the USCG: 3 SOS
up: 4 DIAL RING 5 EVOKE
PHONE
upon: 3 ASK 4 CITE 5 VISIT
6 INVOKE
___ call: 4 TOLL
**Calla lily**
family: 4 ARUM

**Callao**
Capital near: 4 LIMA
country: 4 PERU
**Callas:** 4 DIVA
courter Onassis: 3 ARI
Soprano: 5 MARIA
**"Call ___ cab!":** 3 MEA
**Call___ day:** 3 ITA
**Called**
First to be: 4 ONEA
Formerly: 3 NEE
It may be ~ on account of rain:
3 CAB
Once: 3 NEE
Originally: 3 NEE
**Caller**
Cab: 6 HAILER
Frequent: 4 AVON
8 AVONLADY
Strike: 3 UMP 5 UNION
6 UMPIRE
Tech support: 4 USER
TKO: 3 REF
**Calligrapher:** 6 PENMAN
liquid: 3 INK
**Calligraphy**
need: 3 INK
stroke: 5 SERIF
**Calling:** 4 URGE 5 TRADE
6 CAREER
company: 4 AVON
Old ~ fee: 7 ONEDIME
**"___ calling!":** 4 AVON
**Calliope:** 4 MUSE
Sister of: 5 ERATO
**Callisto**
~, to Jupiter: 4 MOON
**"Call Me ___":** 5 MADAM
**"Call Me Irresponsible"**
songwriter Sammy: 4 CAHN
**Callow**
Less: 5 OLDER
**Calloway, Cab**
catchphrase: 6 HIDEHO
forte: 4 SCAT
**"___ Calloways":** 5 THOSE
**"___ calls?":** 3 ANY
**"___ call us ...":** 4 DONT
**Calm:** 4 COOL 5 ALLAY STILL
6 REPOSE SEDATE
SERENE 7 APPEASE
ATPEACE HALCYON
SILENCE
8 COMPOSED
Completely: 6 SERENE
down: 4 LULL 6 COOLIT
PACIFY SEDATE
On the ~ side: 4 ALEE
side: 3 LEE
**"... calm, ___ bright":** 5 ALLIS
**"Calm down!":** 4 EASY
6 NOWNOW
**Calmer:** 6 OPIATE
**Calmness:** 4 EASE 6 REPOSE
**Caloric:** 4 RICH
**Calorie-laden:** 4 RICH

**Calories**
Approx. 252: 3 BTU
Count: 4 DIET
**Caltech**
grad: 4 ENGR
Some ~ grads: 3 EES
**Calumet:** 9 PEACEPIPE
**Calvary**
letters: 4 INRI
**Calverton**
TV series set in: 6 LASSIE
**Calvin**
Columnist: 7 TRILLIN
Golfer: 5 PEETE
**"Calvin and Hobbes"**
bully: 3 MOE
girl: 5 SUSIE
**Calvino**
Author: 5 ITALO
**Calypso**
kin: 3 SKA
**Calyx**
component: 5 SEPAL
**Cam**
Bruin great: 5 NEELY
**Camaro**
model: 4 IROC
Onetime ~ rival: 3 GTO
**Camay**
alternative: 4 DOVE
**Cambodia**
continent: 4 ASIA
Lon of: 3 NOL
neighbor: 4 LAOS
**Cambodian**
currency: 4 RIEL
Former ~ leader: 3 NOL
6 LONNOL
neighbor: 3 LAO 4 THAI
**Cambria:** 5 WALES
**Cambridge**
bigwig: 3 DON
old coin: 5 PENCE
sch.: 3 MIT
**Cambridgeshire**
town: 3 ELY
**Camcorder**
abbr.: 3 REC
**Camden Yards**
player: 6 ORIOLE
**Came**
across: 3 MET SAW
after: 6 ENSUED
clean: 4 TOLD 8 FESSEDUP
down: 4 ALIT 6 RAINED
down to earth: 4 ALIT
down with: 3 GOT HAD
from behind: 7 RALLIED
home: 4 SLID
in: 7 ENTERED
in first: 3 WON
into being: 5 AROSE
on stage: 7 ENTERED
out: 7 EMERGED
out on top: 3 WON
out with: 4 SAID

to: 4 WOKE 5 AWOKE
7 EQUALED
to a fast stop: 3 ATE
to a halt: 5 ENDED 6 CEASED
to a point: 7 TAPERED
to earth: 4 ALIT
together: 3 MET WED
6 GELLED JELLED
MASSED
to rest: 4 ALIT
to visit: 8 CALLEDON
up: 5 AROSE
upon: 3 MET
**"___ Came Jones":** 5 ALONG
**Camel:** 9 CIGARETTE
dropping: 3 ASH
feature: 4 HUMP
kin: 5 LLAMA 6 ALPACA
7 GUANACO
lot: 5 OASIS
performer: 6 SKATER
pitstops: 5 OASES
resting place: 7 ASHTRAY
**"Camel News Caravan"**
anchor: 6 SWAYZE
**Camelot**
lady: 4 ENID
weapon: 5 LANCE
~, to Arthur: 5 REALM
7 KINGDOM
**"Camelot"**
actor Franco: 4 NERO
composer: 5 LOEWE
**Camembert**
alternative: 4 BRIE
**Cameo:** 4 ROLE 7 BITPART
carving: 6 RELIEF
role of an actress, perhaps:
7 HERSELF
shape: 4 OVAL
stone: 4 ONYX
**Camera**
attachment: 4 LENS
8 ZOOMLENS
Canon: 3 EOS
Clown for the: 3 MUG
diaphragm: 4 IRIS
feature: 4 ZOOM
Follow with the: 3 PAN
inits.: 3 SLR
maker: 4 FUJI 5 CANON
KODAK LEICA NIKON
7 MINOLTA
man: 4 FUNT
Mug for the: 4 POSE
part: 4 IRIS LENS 7 SHUTTER
Popular: 5 NIKON
Prepare a: 4 LOAD
protection: 7 LENSCAP
setting: 4 AUTO 5 FOCUS
FSTOP
shop display: 4 SLRS
stand: 6 TRIPOD UNIPOD
type: 3 SLR
Words mouthed to a: 5 HIMOM
Word with: 4 DISC

Caméra ___ (Cannes prize):
   3 DOR
"___ Camera": 4 IAMA
Cameraman
   org.: 3 ASC
Cameron
   Actor: 4 KIRK
   Actress: 4 DIAZ
Cameron, James
   1989 ~ film: 8 THEABYSS
Cameroon
   neighbor: 4 CHAD 5 GABON
      7 NIGERIA
Camille
   portrayer: 5 GRETA
Caminiti
   of baseball: 3 KEN
Camouflage: 4 HIDE 5 BELIE
      7 BLENDIN
Camp
   bed: 3 COT
   Captives: 6 STALAG
   craft: 5 CANOE
   facility: 7 LATRINE
   German prison: 6 STALAG
   Military: 5 ETAPE
   shelter: 4 TENT
   Soviet labor: 5 GULAG
   Word with: 3 DAY
   WWII: 6 STALAG
Campaign: 3 RUN 4 RACE
      7 CRUSADE
   1950s ~ nickname: 3 IKE
   1996 ~ name: 4 DOLE
   assault: 5 SMEAR
   asset: 8 MOMENTUM
   button word: 5 ELECT
   concern: 5 IMAGE
   contributor: 3 PAC
   creator: 5 ADMAN
   Dirty ~ stuff: 3 MUD
   event: 6 DEBATE
   (for): 3 RUN
   funder: 3 PAC 6 FATCAT
   Intense: 5 BLITZ
   Long: 5 SIEGE
   Perennial ~ issue: 4 JOBS
   poster word: 7 REELECT
   promise: 6 TAXCUT
   strategy: 6 ATTACK
   tactic: 5 SMEAR
   Type of: 5 SMEAR
   vet: 3 POL
   worker: 4 AIDE
Campaigner: 3 POL
   Dirty: 10 MUDSLINGER
Campanella
   of baseball: 3 ROY
Campanile
   Site of a famous: 4 PISA
   sound: 4 PEAL
Campbell
   Actress: 4 NEVE 5 TISHA
   Country singer: 4 GLEN
   creation: 4 SOUP
   Supermodel: 5 NAOMI

Camp David Accords
   participant: 5 BEGIN SADAT
Camped
   out: 6 TENTED
Camper: 3 VAN 7 TRAILER
   cover: 4 TENT
   gear: 7 MESSKIT
Campers: 3 RVS
Campfire
   remains: 3 ASH 5 ASHES
      EMBER
   They're passed around a:
      5 TALES
   treat: 5 SMORE
Campground
   letters: 3 KOA
Camphor: 6 KETONE
Camping
   gear: 4 TENT
Campion
   Director: 4 JANE
Camp Lejeune
   letters: 5 USMC
Camp-out
   treat: 5 SMORE
Camp Pendleton
   City near: 9 OCEANSIDE
Campsite
   Infantry: 5 ETAPE
   sight: 4 TENT
Camp Swampy
   dog: 4 OTTO
"Camptown Races"
   syllable: 3 DAH
   word: 6 DOODAH
Campus
   1960s ~ gp.: 3 SDS
   1994 ~ comedy: 3 PCU
   Amherst: 5 UMASS
   area: 4 QUAD
   Baton Rouge: 3 LSU
   Big man on: 4 DEAN
   bigwig: 4 DEAN PROF
   Brooklyn: 3 LIU
   Bruin: 4 UCLA
   building: 4 DORM HALL
   buys: 5 TEXTS
   Cambridge: 3 MIT
   Cedar Rapids: 3 COE
   climber: 3 IVY
   Connecticut: 4 YALE
   digs: 4 DORM
   E. Lansing: 3 MSU
   figure: 4 COED
   gp.: 4 ROTC
   hangout: 4 QUAD
   Jewish ~ organization:
      6 HILLEL
   L.A.: 3 USC
   letter: 3 ETA RHO 4 BETA
      5 SIGMA THETA
   Lewiston: 5 BATES
   Maine ~ site: 5 ORONO
   marchers: 4 ROTC
   Militant ~ org.: 3 SDS
   military org.: 4 ROTC

New Haven: 4 YALE
   official: 4 DEAN
   quarters: 4 DORM 5 DORMS
   Sch. with a Berkeley: 4 UCAL
   Sch. with a Providence: 3 URI
   sports org.: 4 NCAA
   tie-ups: 6 SITINS
   West Coast: 4 UCLA
Camry
   maker: 6 TOYOTA
Camus
   birthplace: 7 ALGERIA
   Plague, to: 5 PESTE
Can: 3 AXE MAY TIN 4 FIRE
      JAIL JOHN SACK
      5 LETGO 6 LAYOFF
   Kind of: 7 AEROSOL
   material: 3 TIN
   Meat in a: 4 SPAM
   opener: 3 CEE TAB
      7 PULLTAB
      9 CHURCHKEY
   Spray: 7 AEROSOL
   Word on a drink: 4 LITE
Can.
   heads: 3 PMS
   neighbor: 3 USA
   province: 3 ONT PEI QUE
      4 ALTA NFLD SASK
"Can ___?": 4 ITBE
"___ Can" (Sammy Davis Jr.
      book): 4 YESI
Canaan
   spy: 5 CALEB
   suffix: 3 ITE
Canaanite
   deity: 4 BAAL
Canada
   capital: 6 OTTAWA
   Exxon, in: 4 ESSO
   lake: 4 ERIE
   province: 7 ONTARIO
Canada Day
   month: 4 JULY
Canadian
   Abbr. in many ~ city names:
      3 STE
   capital: 3 CEE 6 OTTAWA
   coin: 4 CENT
   coin bird: 4 LOON
   comedian Mort: 4 SAHL
   cop: 7 MOUNTIE
   distance measures (abbr.):
      3 KMS
   Eastern ~ Indian: 6 MICMAC
   flag symbol: 4 LEAF
   gas name: 4 ESSO
   mayor: 5 REEVE
   Native: 4 CREE
   peninsula: 5 GASPE
   prov.: 3 ONT PEI QUE 4 ALTA
      NFLD SASK
   province: 7 ONTARIO
   territory: 5 YUKON
   tribe: 4 CREE
   verb ending: 3 ISE

~ Arctic explorer: 3 RAE
~ Conservative: 4 TORY
~ Indian: 4 CREE
**"Canadian Bacon"**
president portrayer: 4 ALDA
**Canadiens:** 4 TEAM
org.: 3 NHL
**Canal:** 4 DUCT 7 SHIPWAY
Albany: 4 ERIE
Anatomical: 4 ITER
buildup: 6 EARWAX
completed in 1825: 4 ERIE
craft: 5 BARGE
Egyptian: 4 SUEZ
examiner aid: 8 OTOSCOPE
feature: 4 LOCK
of Sal: 4 ERIE
of song: 4 ERIE
opened in 1869: 4 SUEZ
problem: 7 EARACHE
River connected by ~ to the
    Tiber: 4 ARNO
site: 3 EAR 6 PANAMA
to Buffalo: 4 ERIE
to the Baltic: 4 KIEL
to the Hudson: 4 ERIE
to the Mediterranean: 4 SUEZ
Word before: 4 ROOT
zone: 3 EAR
___ **Canals:** 3 SOO
**Canapé**
and so on: 10 FINGERFOOD
topper: 4 PATE
**Canary:** 3 PET 6 YELLOW
kin: 5 SERIN
Largest: 8 TENERIFE
nose: 4 CERE
sound: 5 TWEET
**Canary Islands**
One of the: 7 LAPALMA
**Canasta**
combo: 4 MELD
**Canaveral**
org.: 4 NASA
stop: 5 ABORT
**Canberra**
comrade: 4 MATE
**Cancel:** 3 AXE NIX 4 NULL
    UNDO XOUT 5 ABORT
    ANNUL ERASE SCRAP
    SCRUB 6 NEGATE
    REPEAL REVOKE
    7 CALLOFF REDLINE
    VOIDOUT
a dele: 4 STET
out: 6 NEGATE
**Canceled:** 4 NOGO VOID
    6 XEDOUT
**Canceler**
Nay: 3 YEA
**Cancer**
follower: 3 LEO
"___ **Can Cook":** 3 YAN
**Cancún**
**Info:** Spanish cue
coin: 4 PESO

kin: 3 TIO
**Candelabrum**
Religious: 7 MENORAH
**Candice**
Father of: 5 EDGAR
**Candid:** 4 OPEN 5 FRANK
    6 HONEST
Be: 5 LEVEL
**"Candida"**
playwright: 4 SHAW
**Candidate**
1936 ~ Landon: 3 ALF
1950s ~ Stevenson: 5 ADLAI
1992 ~: 5 PEROT
1996 ~: 4 DOLE 5 LAMAR
    NADER PEROT
2000 ~: 5 NADER 6 ALGORE
2004 ~: 4 DEAN 5 NADER
concern: 4 POLL 5 IMAGE
Day care: 3 TOT
Florida governor: 4 RENO
goal: 4 SEAT
Green Party: 5 NADER
list: 5 SLATE
Losing: 7 ALSORAN
Perennial ~ of old: 7 STASSEN
Reform Party: 5 PEROT
Tony: 4 PLAY
Unlikely ~ for prom king:
    4 NERD
**Candidates**
discussion: 6 DEBATE
Like some ~ (abbr.): 3 IND
**"Candid Camera"**
cohost Durward: 5 KIRBY
host Allen: 4 FUNT
**"Candide"**
author: 8 VOLTAIRE
**Candied:** 5 GLACE SWEET
dish: 4 YAMS
**Candies**
Cinnamon: 7 REDHOTS
Spicy: 7 REDHOTS
**Candle**
Add a ~ to the cake: 3 AGE
bracket: 6 SCONCE
Burn like a: 7 FLICKER
center: 4 WICK
count: 3 AGE
dripping: 3 WAX
holder: 4 CAKE 6 SCONCE
Kind of: 5 ROMAN
Like a: 5 WAXEN
material: 3 WAX 4 SUET
    6 TALLOW
Slender: 5 TAPER
**Candlelight**
Song sung by: 4 NOEL
**Candler**
Coca-Cola founder: 3 ASA
**Candles**
Like prank: 5 RELIT
Like some: 7 SCENTED
What ~ may reveal: 3 AGE
**C&O**
and others: 3 RRS

**C&W**
Chet of: 6 ATKINS
Former ~ channel: 3 TNN
K.T. of: 5 OSLIN
Leann of: 5 RIMES
McEntire of: 4 REBA
Tritt of: 6 TRAVIS
**Candy:** 6 SWEETS
After-dinner: 4 MINT
Big name in: 4 MARS
brand: 3 PEZ 4 ROLO
    6 KITKAT REESES
    RIESEN
Caramel: 4 ROLO
Chewy: 5 TAFFY 6 NOUGAT
    TOFFEE 7 CARAMEL
Coated: 5 MANDM
Craving for: 10 SWEETTOOTH
Dispenser: 3 PEZ
Hard: 10 JAWBREAKER
Hard ~, in Britain: 5 LOLLY
Hershey: 4 HUGS ROLO
    6 KITKAT
in a dispenser: 3 PEZ
Ingredient in some ~ bars:
    6 ALMOND
Lemon: 4 DROP
Like cotton: 4 SPUN
Like taking ~ from a baby:
    4 EASY
shape: 3 BAR 4 CANE
striper: 4 AIDE
**Candy, John**
Old show featuring: 4 SCTV
**Cane:** 4 FLOG 5 STICK
    6 RATTAN
cutter: 7 MACHETE
extract: 5 SUGAR
Sugar ~ menace: 6 AGOUTI
~, to Charlie Chaplin: 4 PROP
**Canea**
Where ~ is capital: 5 CRETE
**Canetti**
Literature Nobelist: 5 ELIAS
**Canful**
Cook's: 4 LARD
**Canin**
Novelist: 5 ETHAN
**Canine:** 5 TOOTH
    8 EYETOOTH
Camp Swampy: 4 OTTO
Cartoon: 3 REN 4 ODIE
checker (abbr.): 3 DDS
coat: 6 ENAMEL
Comics: 4 ODIE OTTO
    5 SNERT
command: 3 BEG SIT 4 HEEL
    STAY
comment: 3 ARF 4 WOOF
cry: 3 ARF 4 HOWL YELP
from Kansas: 4 TOTO
Hollywood: 4 ASTA
Kiddie lit: 4 SPOT
neighbor: 8 PREMOLAR
Oz: 4 TOTO
warning: 3 GRR

Welsh: 5 CORGI
**Canines:** 5 TEETH
    8 EYETEETH
Cut: 6 TEETHE
Raise: 6 TEETHE
**Caning**
material: 6 RATTAN
**Canis Major**
Constellation south of:
    4 ARGO
**Canned**
heat: 6 STERNO
meat: 4 SPAM
**Canner**
job: 5 AXING
supply: 4 LIDS
**Cannery**
row: 4 JARS TINS
**Cannes**
**Info:** French cue
cap: 5 BERET
cash: 5 FRANC
co.: 3 CIE
concept: 4 IDEE
confidant: 3 AMI
cup: 5 TASSE
showing: 4 CINE
Water in: 3 EAU
**Cannibal**
Tolkien: 3 ORC
**Cannon**
Actress: 4 DYAN
Kind of: 5 LOOSE
Loose: 6 MENACE
suffix: 3 ADE EER
Water ~ target: 6 RIOTER
"___ Cannonball": 6 WABASH
**Cannonballs:** 4 AMMO
**Cannoneer**
command: 4 FIRE
"Can ___ now?": 3 IGO
**Canny:** 3 SLY 5 SMART
    6 SHREWD
**Canoe**
challenge: 6 RAPIDS
Enclosed: 5 KAYAK
paddle: 3 OAR
___ can of worms: 5 OPENA
**Canon**
camera: 3 EOS
competitor: 4 MITA 5 KODAK
    LEICA NIKON RICOH
    6 KONICA 7 MINOLTA
**Canonical**
hour: 4 NONE 5 MATIN
    NONES
**Canonized**
mlle.: 3 STE
pope known as "the Great":
    5 STLEO
**Canopy:** 6 TESTER
support: 7 BEDPOST
**Cans**
24 ~: 4 CASE
**Canseco**
of baseball: 4 JOSE

**Cant:** 4 LEAN 5 ARGOT
    6 JARGON
**Can't**
abide: 6 DETEST
bear: 4 HATE
do without: 4 NEED 5 NEEDS
help but: 4 MUST 5 HASTO
stand: 4 HATE 5 ABHOR
    HATES 6 DETEST
    LOATHE 7 DETESTS
stomach: 4 HATE 5 ABHOR
wait for: 8 NEEDASAP
**Cantab**
rival: 3 ELI
**Cantabrian Mountains**
river: 4 EBRO
**Cantaloupe:** 5 MELON
cover: 4 RIND
kin: 6 CASABA 8 HONEYDEW
**Cantankerous:** 5 TESTY
    6 ORNERY
~ Ryan: 5 IRENE
**Cantata**
composer: 4 BACH
melody: 4 ARIA
singers: 5 CHOIR
"... can't believe ___ the whole
    thing": 4 IATE
**Canter:** 4 GAIT LOPE
**Canterbury**
can: 3 LOO TIN 4 GAOL
county: 4 KENT
John of: 3 LOO
saint: 6 ANSELM
"Canterbury"
episode: 4 TALE
"Canterbury Tales, The"
author: 7 CHAUCER
pilgrim: 5 REEVE
"Can't Fight the Moonlight"
singer: 5 RIMES
"Can't Get It Out of My Head"
rock gp.: 3 ELO
"Can't Get Used to Losing You"
singer Williams: 4 ANDY
"Can't Help Lovin' ___ Man":
    3 DAT
**Canticle:** 3 ODE
Perform a: 6 INTONE
**Cantilevered**
window: 5 ORIEL
**Cantina**
cooker: 4 OLLA
offering: 4 TACO 6 TAMALE
tidbit: 4 TAPA
___ canto: 3 BEL
**Canton**
designer: 3 PEI
locale: 4 OHIO
neighbor: 5 AKRON
suffix: 3 ESE
Swiss: 3 URI 6 GENEVA
William Tell: 3 URI
**Cantor**
Mrs.: 3 IDA
"Cantos de ___": 6 ESPANA

**Cantrell**
Singer: 4 LANA
"Can ___ true?": 4 ITBE
"Can't Take My Eyes Off You"
singer Frankie: 5 VALLI
**Canucks:** 4 TEAM
**Canute**
foe: 4 OLAF
**Canvas**
bag: 4 TOTE
cover: 4 TARP 8 OILPAINT
holder: 5 EASEL
Knock on the: 4 DECK
Practice on: 4 SPAR
Send to the: 4 KAYO
shelter: 4 TENT
sunscreen: 6 AWNING
support: 5 EASEL
Waterproof: 4 TARP
**Canvasback**
cousin: 4 TEAL
"Can we talk?"
comic: 6 RIVERS
    10 JOANRIVERS
**Canyon:** 5 GORGE
comeback: 4 ECHO
edge: 3 RIM
of comics: 5 STEVE
phenomenon: 4 ECHO
sound: 4 ECHO
Utah: 4 SEGO 5 BRYCE
**Canyonlands**
locale: 4 UTAH
___ Canyon National Park:
    5 BRYCE
**Cap:** 3 LID TAM 4 ACME COIF
    5 LIMIT
Artist: 5 BERET
attachment: 5 PLUME
    6 EARLAP
Bird on a: 6 ORIOLE
Brimless: 5 BERET 6 BEANIE
Capitol: 4 DOME
Cardinal ~ letters: 3 STL
Clergy: 7 BIRETTA
Dunce: 4 CONE
feature: 5 VISOR
flap: 6 EARLAP
Foreign Legion: 4 KEPI
Freshman's: 6 BEANIE
Joint with a: 4 KNEE
Like a dunce: 5 CONIC
locale: 4 KNEE
material: 3 ICE
Military force: 4 KEPI
Mushroom ~ part: 4 GILL
Nut with a: 5 ACORN
on a leg: 7 PATELLA
Put a ~ on: 5 LIMIT
Put on one's thinking:
    6 IDEATE
Red: 3 FEZ
Scottish: 3 TAM
setting: 4 KNEE
Shriner's: 3 FEZ
Skye: 3 TAM

source: 4 COON
Special Forces: 5 BERET
Tasseled: 3 FEZ
Tip a: 4 DOFF
Visored: 4 KEPI
**Cap.**
Abu Dhabi is its: 3 UAE
Dover is its: 3 DEL
Vilnius is its: 4 LITH
**Cap-___ (head-to-toe):**
4 APIE
**Capability**
Military: 9 FIREPOWER
**Capable**
More than: 5 ADEPT
of: 4 UPTO
**Capacious: 5 AMPLE ROOMY**
**Capacitance**
Unit of: 5 FARAD
**Capacitor**
Primitive: 9 LEYDENJAR
**Capacity: 4 ROLE ROOM**
AC ~ measure: 3 BTU
Calendar: 4 YEAR
Computer ~ unit: 4 BYTE
descriptor: 3 SRO
Diary: 4 YEAR
Garage: 6 ONECAR
Hospital: 4 BEDS
In the ~ of: 3 QUA
Serve in the ~ of: 5 ACTAS
**Cape: 4 NESS 5 CLOAK**
Bay State: 3 ANN
Massachusetts: 3 ANN COD
North Carolina: 4 FEAR
8 HATTERAS
of Portugal: 4 ROCA
Pope: 5 ORALE
**Cape ___: 3 ANN COD 4 ROCA**
5 VERDE
**"Cape ___" (De Niro film):**
4 FEAR
**Cape Canaveral**
org.: 4 NASA
**Cape Cod**
catch: 4 TUNA
town: 5 TRURO
**"Cape Fear"**
actor: 5 NOLTE
**Capek**
play: 3 RUR
Playwright: 5 KAREL
**Cape of Good Hope**
country (abbr.): 3 RSA
discoverer: 4 DIAS
**Caper: 4 DIDO LARK 5 ANTIC**
PRANK
Bank: 5 HEIST
**Cape Town**
cash: 4 RAND
Diplomat born in: 4 EBAN
home (abbr.): 3 RSA
**Cape Tres Puntas**
locale (abbr.): 3 ARG
**Capework**
reaction: 3 OLE

**Capita**
Per: 4 EACH
___ capita: 3 PER
**Capital: 4 AONE**
Info: Money cue
Info: See specific country, state,
etc.
African: 5 ACCRA CAIRO
RABAT TUNIS
Alpine: 4 BERN
Andean: 4 LIMA
Arabian: 4 SANA
Asian: 5 AMMAN DACCA
HANOI KABUL LHASA
SEOUL 6 TAIPEI TEHRAN
7 JAKARTA
Assyrian: 7 NINEVEH
at the center of Czechoslovakia:
4 OSLO
Balkan: 5 SOFIA 6 TIRANA
Baltic: 4 RIGA
before Brasilia: 3 RIO
Chinese: 6 TAIPEI
Cold: 4 OSLO 8 HELSINKI
Continental: 4 EURO
European: 4 BERN KIEV OSLO
RIGA 6 TIRANA ZAGREB
First U.S.: 3 NYC
Former European: 4 BONN
Former Japanese: 4 NARA
5 KYOTO
Former Polish: 6 KRAKOW
Former Serbian: 3 NIS
Mediterranean: 5 TUNIS
7 NICOSIA
Mideast: 4 SANA 5 AMMAN
6 TEHRAN 7 TEHERAN
Mogul: 4 AGRA
near the 60th parallel: 4 OSLO
North African: 5 RABAT
TUNIS
Northern: 4 OSLO
of Österreich: 4 WIEN
on a fjord: 4 OSLO
Pacific: 4 APIA
South American: 4 LIMA
5 LAPAZ QUITO SUCRE
transit: 5 METRO
Western: 5 BOISE SALEM
6 HELENA
Westernmost African:
5 DAKAR
Working: 3 PAY
**Capitale**
European: 4 ROMA
**Capitalist**
Fur: 5 ASTOR
**Capitalize**
on: 3 USE
**Capitol: 10 STATEHOUSE**
feature: 4 DOME 7 ROTUNDA
fig.: 3 POL SEN
Like the: 5 DOMED
Record label with: 3 EMI
topper: 4 DOME
worker: 4 AIDE

~ VIPs: 4 SENS
**Capitol ___, The: 5 STEPS**
**Capitol Hill**
fig.: 3 SEN
figure: 3 POL
first name: 4 NEWT
prize: 4 SEAT
~ VIP: 3 SEN
**Capitulate: 6 CAVEIN**
**Caplet**
count: 4 DOSE
**Cap'n**
mate: 4 BOSN
Say "~": 5 ELIDE
**Capo**
crew: 5 MAFIA
**Capone**
and others: 3 ALS
associate: 5 NITTI
captor: 4 NESS
facial feature: 4 SCAR
nemeses: 4 TMEN
nemesis: 4 NESS
rival: 5 MORAN
**Capote**
nickname: 3 TRU
Play about: 3 TRU
**Capp**
and others: 3 ALS
contraction: 3 LIL
creation: 5 ABNER
hyena: 4 LENA
of comics: 4 ANDY
**Capp, Andy**
hangout: 3 PUB
quaff: 3 ALE
Wife of: 3 FLO
wife, often: 3 NAG
**Capped**
joint: 4 KNEE
They're: 5 KNEES
**Capping: 4 ATOP**
**Cappuccino**
cousin: 5 LATTE
Prepare milk for: 5 STEAM
topper: 4 FOAM 5 FROTH
**Capri: 4 ISLE 5 ISOLA**
attraction: 6 GROTTO
cash: 4 LIRA
suffix: 3 OTE
**Caprice: 4 WHIM**
**Capricious: 9 WHIMSICAL**
notion: 4 WHIM
**Capriciously: 7 ONAWHIM**
**Capricorn: 4 GOAT**
**Capris: 5 PANTS**
**Caps**
Like some: 6 WOOLEN
**Capsize: 5 UPEND UPSET**
**Caps Lock**
neighbor: 3 TAB
**Capstone: 4 ACME**
**Capsule**
contents: 4 DOSE
Cotton: 4 BOLL
Time ~ event: 6 BURIAL

**Capsule-mate**
  of Buzz: 4 NEIL
**Capt.**
  aide: 3 ENS
  heading: 3 ESE SSE
  prediction: 3 ETA
  Rank below: 5 LIEUT
  saluters: 3 LTS
  superior: 3 MAJ
**Captain:** 4 RANK
  command: 5 AVAST TOSEA
  diary: 3 LOG
  Enterprise: 4 KIRK
  Fictional: 4 AHAB NEMO
  Golden Hind: 5 DRAKE
  Melville: 4 AHAB
  offering: 4 MENU
  of Ishmael: 4 AHAB
  of Queequeg: 4 AHAB
  of Starbuck: 4 AHAB
  One-handed: 4 HOOK
  position: 4 HELM
  Reply to the: 3 AYE 6 AYEAYE
  staff: 4 CREW
  superior: 5 MAJOR
  Verne: 4 NEMO
  Wouk: 5 QUEEG
**"Captain Blood"**
  actor Flynn: 5 ERROL
  costar of Basil: 5 ERROL
**Captain Davies**
  portrayer: 7 EDASNER
**Captain Hook**
  sidekick: 4 SMEE
**Captain Kangaroo**
  portrayer: 7 KEESHAN
**Captain Kirk**
  helmsman: 4 SULU
**Captain Lou Albano:**
    7 RASSLER
**Captain Marvel**
  magic word: 6 SHAZAM
**Captain Nemo**
  creator: 5 VERNE
**Captain Picard**
  counselor: 4 TROI
**Capt. Davies**
  portrayer: 5 ASNER
**Capt. Hook**
  biter: 4 CROC
**Caption**
  Diet-ad photo: 5 AFTER
    6 BEFORE
**Captivate:** 6 ENAMOR ENGAGE
    RAVISH 8 ENTHRALL
  a crowd, perhaps: 5 ORATE
**Captivated**
  by: 4 INTO
**Captive**
  MP's: 4 AWOL
  of Hercules: 4 IOLE
  of Paris: 5 HELEN
**Captor**
  Capone: 4 NESS
**Captors**
  Patty Hearst: 3 SLA

**Capture:** 3 BAG GET NAB NET
    WIN 4 CAGE GRAB LAND
    TAKE 5 LASSO SEIZE
    SNARE 6 CORRAL
    7 ENSNARE
  electronically: 4 SCAN
  the bronze: 3 TAN
**Captured:** 3 WON 4 TOOK
  again: 5 REWON
**Car:** 4 AUTO
  1960s muscle ~: 3 GTO
  accessory: 3 MAG
  ad abbr.: 3 APR MPG
  alarm: 4 HORN
  Antique: 3 REO
  Balloon: 7 NACELLE
  bar: 4 AXLE 5 STRUT
  bomb: 5 EDSEL LEMON
  buyer protection:
    8 LEMONLAW
  Cable: 4 TRAM
  Classic: 3 GTO REO 5 TBIRD
    6 MODELA 7 BEARCAT
  club: 3 AAA
  co. bought by Chrysler: 3 AMC
  Collectible: 5 EDSEL
  Company: 4 PERK
  contract: 5 LEASE
  dealer offering: 5 LEASE
  Drive the getaway: 4 ABET
  Early touring: 3 REO
  Enter a: 5 GETIN
  European: 4 OPEL
  Family: 5 SEDAN
  Fancy: 5 ROLLS
  for hire: 3 CAB
  Four-door: 5 SEDAN
  "Fun, Fun, Fun": 5 TBIRD
  German: 4 AUDI OPEL
  Gun in a: 3 REV
  Italian: 4 FIAT
  Italian ~, for short: 4 ALFA
  Junky: 4 HEAP
  Kind of: 4 SLOT TOWN USED
    5 SQUAD 6 KIDDIE
    MUSCLE PATROL
  Korean: 3 KIA
  Last: 6 HEARSE 7 CABOOSE
  lifter: 4 JACK
  Light: 4 NEON
  "Little" ~ of song: 3 GTO
  loan fig.: 3 APR
  Long: 4 LIMO
  Lousy: 5 LEMON
  Mine: 4 TRAM
  Monogrammatic: 3 REO
  nut: 3 LUG
  Olds: 3 REO
  owner proof: 5 TITLE
  parker: 5 VALET
  part: 4 AXLE FUSE TIRE
  payment: 4 TOLL
  Police ~ device: 5 SIREN
  prefix: 4 SIDE
  protector: 3 BRA 5 ALARM
  Race ~ sponsor: 3 STP

  rack item: 3 SKI
  radio button: 6 PRESET
  Railroad: 5 DINER
  Retro: 6 BEETLE
  roof feature: 4 TTOP
  safety feature: 6 AIRBAG
    7 ROLLBAR
  scar: 4 DENT DING
  Seized: 4 REPO
  shopper option: 5 LEASE
  show car: 9 STREETROD
  Showroom: 4 DEMO
  since 1949: 4 SAAB
  Sleek, in ~ lingo: 4 AERO
  sound: 7 SCREECH
  Souped-up: 6 HOTROD
  Sports ~, for short: 3 JAG
    4 ALFA
  Squad: 7 CRUISER
  starter: 5 CRANK
  starter (abbr.): 3 IGN
  Subway ~ part: 5 STRAP
  Swedish: 4 SAAB
  Taken-back: 4 REPO
  Test-driven: 4 DEMO
  top: 4 ROOF
  Touring: 5 SEDAN
  Two-door: 5 COUPE
  until 1957: 4 NASH
  Used ~ deal: 6 RESALE
  Vintage: 3 REO
  Wait in the: 4 IDLE
  wash option: 3 WAX
  window sticker: 5 DECAL
  with a bar: 4 LIMO
  with four linked rings:
    4 AUDI
**Cara**
  Singer/actress: 5 IRENE
**Caracas**
  lass (abbr.): 4 SRTA
**Carafe**
  kin: 4 EWER
  size: 5 LITER
**Caramel**
  candy brand: 4 ROLO
  Crème: 4 FLAN
  Like: 5 CHEWY
  topped dessert: 4 FLAN
**Carangi**
  Supermodel: 3 GIA
**Carapace:** 5 SHELL
**Caravan**
  beast: 5 CAMEL
  maker: 5 DODGE
  stop: 5 OASIS
  stops: 5 OASES
**Caravel**
  Historic: 4 NINA 5 PINTA
**Caraway:** 4 HERB SEED
**Carbine**
  British: 4 STEN
**Carbohydrate**
  ending: 3 OSE
**Carbolic**
  acid: 6 PHENOL

**Carbo-loader**
fare: 5 PASTA
**Carbon**
compound: 4 ENOL 5 ESTER
  6 KETONE
compound suffix: 3 ENE
monoxide lack: 4 ODOR
Test for ~ 14: 4 DATE
~ 13: 7 ISOTOPE
**Carbon ___:** 7 DIOXIDE
**Carbonated**
drink: 4 COLA SODA
**Carbon dioxide**
Treat with: 6 AERATE
**Carbonium:** 3 ION
**Carbs**
Cut: 4 DIET
**Carburetor**
regulator: 5 CHOKE
**Card:** 3 WIT 4 NLER RIOT
  5 CUTUP
balance: 4 DEBT
Birthday ~ subject: 3 AGE
Blackjack: 3 ACE TEN
Bus. ~ info: 3 TEL
combination: 4 MELD
Conceal a: 4 PALM
Diner's: 4 MENU
Drawing: 4 LURE
Green ~ holder: 5 ALIEN
Greeting ~ item: 4 POEM
He's a real: 4 JACK
High: 3 ACE
"in the hole": 3 ACE
Kind of: 3 ATM 5 HONOR
  INDEX 6 CREDIT
Low: 3 TWO 4 TREY
  5 DEUCE
Low ~ in a royal flush: 3 TEN
Low ~ in euchre: 5 SEVEN
Low ~ in pinochle: 4 NINE
Monopoly: 4 DEED
Picture: 5 TAROT
Plays the wrong: 7 RENEGES
Poker: 3 ACE 4 TREY
  5 DEUCE
Punch ~ remnant: 4 CHAD
Read a credit: 5 SWIPE
Restaurant: 4 MENU
Sci-fi writer: 5 ORSON
Seer's: 5 TAROT
spot: 3 PIP
Take a: 4 DRAW
Tarot ~ user: 4 SEER
Took a: 4 DREW
Top: 3 ACE
Used a credit: 4 OWED
Wild: 5 JOKER
with one pip: 3 ACE
X, on a greeting: 4 KISS
**Card-carrying:** 4 REAL
**Card catalogue**
abbr.: 4 ETAL
entry: 5 TITLE
**Carder**
requests: 3 IDS

**Card game:** 3 GIN LOO UNO
  WAR 4 SKAT STUD
  6 ECARTE GOFISH
  7 CANASTA
also called sevens: 6 FANTAN
authority Edmond: 5 HOYLE
Children's: 3 UNO WAR
  6 GOFISH 7 OLDMAID
  11 CRAZYEIGHTS
cry: 3 GIN 6 GOFISH
Easy: 3 WAR
Family: 3 UNO
Fast-paced: 4 SPIT
for three: 4 SKAT 5 OMBRE
Fortuneteller: 5 TAROT
for two: 3 WAR 6 ECARTE
Lively: 3 UNO
Old: 3 LOO 4 SKAT 5 OMBER
  OMBRE
Popular: 3 UNO
stake: 4 ANTE
start: 4 DEAL
Trick-taking: 6 EUCHRE
with a "good ten": 6 CASINO
with forfeits: 3 LOO
**Cardiff**
country: 5 WALES
natives: 5 WELSH
**Cardigan:** 4 KNIT
Make a: 4 KNIT
**Cardin**
rival: 6 ARMANI
**Cardinal:** 4 MAIN 7 DEEPRED
  REDBIRD
Big Apple: 4 EGAN
insignia: 3 STL
letters: 3 STL
point: 4 NEST
The first: 3 ONE
topper: 6 REDHAT
~ O'Connor successor: 4 EGAN
~ Slaughter: 4 ENOS
**Cardinale**
Actress: 7 CLAUDIA
**Cardinals**
great Brock: 3 LOU
great Musial: 4 STAN
home (abbr.): 3 STL
manager: 4 POPE
Marrero of the: 3 ELI
**Cardiologist**
concern: 5 AORTA
**Cards**
Big name in sports: 5 FLEER
  TOPPS
Cost of: 4 ANTE
Distributed the: 5 DEALT
Extra hand of: 5 WIDOW
Hard-to-find: 5 RARES
In the: 5 FATED
Like some: 5 SMART
Place for: 5 TABLE
**Care**
Day ~ attendee: 3 TOT
Dress with: 5 PREEN PRIMP
Enter with: 6 EASEIN

for: 4 LIKE MIND REAR
  TEND 5 NURSE SEETO
  VALUE 6 TENDTO
Great: 5 PAINS
Handle without: 3 PAW
Managed ~ gp.: 3 HMO
Med. ~ option: 3 HMO
packages: 3 AID
prefix: 4 MEDI
Taken ~ of: 6 SEENTO
Take ~ of: 4 TEND 5 SEETO
  TREAT 6 HANDLE
  TENDTO 8 SEEAFTER
Take ~ of business: 7 SEETOIT
Taking ~ of business: 4 ONIT
Took ~ of: 3 DID 4 KEPT
  5 SAWTO
Tooth ~ org.: 3 ADA
Word with: 3 DAY
"___ care!": 5 IDONT
**Career:** 4 TEAR
athlete: 3 PRO
Calls it a: 7 RETIRES
Certain ~ path:
  10 MOMMYTRACK
soldier: 5 LIFER
**Carefree:** 3 GAY 4 EASY
  6 BLITHE 7 CONTENT
adventure: 4 LARK
**Careful**
about spending: 6 FRUGAL
Give ~ attention to: 4 HEED
"___ careful!": 4 DOBE
**Carefully**
Enter: 6 EASEIN EDGEIN
Examine: 4 SIFT
Move: 4 EASE
Not ~ considered: 4 RASH
Read: 6 PERUSE
Study ~, with "over": 4 PORE
Watch: 3 EYE
**Caregivers**
Hosp.: 3 RNS
**___ care in the world:** 4 NOTA
**Careless:** 3 LAX 6 REMISS
  8 SLAPDASH SLIPSHOD
**"Careless Hands"**
singer: 5 TORME
**Carelessly**
Let fall: 5 DRAPE
**Caress:** 3 PET 5 TOUCH
**Caretaker:** 6 SITTER
Baby: 4 NANA
**Carey**
Comic: 4 DREW
Singer: 6 MARIAH
**Carey, Mariah**
Former label of: 3 EMI
**Cargo:** 4 LOAD
carrier: 4 SEMI
Clipper ship: 3 TEA
Fill with: 4 LADE
hauler: 3 VAN
Load: 4 STOW
measure: 3 TON
Put on: 4 LADE

Schooner: 3 ALE
Stow: 4 LADE
Tram: 3 ORE
**Carhop**
load: 4 TRAY
**Caribbean:** 3 SEA
and others: 4 SEAS
getaway: 5 ARUBA
group: 7 CAYMANS
  8 ANTILLES
music: 3 SKA
republic: 5 HAITI
resort island: 5 ARUBA
**Caribou**
kin: 3 ELK 4 DEER
**Caricaturist**
Tweed: 4 NAST
~ Daumier: 6 HONORE
~ Thomas: 4 NAST
**Caring:** 6 HUMANE
**Carioca**
city: 3 RIO
country: 6 BRASIL
**Cariou**
Actor: 3 LEN
**Carl**
Astronomer: 5 SAGAN
Composer: 4 ORFF
Corporate raider: 5 ICAHN
Ex-Viking: 5 ELLER
or Rob: 6 REINER
Rob, to: 3 SON
**Carle**
Author: 4 ERIC
**Carle, Frankie**
theme song:
  15 SUNRISESERENADE
**Carlisle, Belinda**
was one: 4 GOGO
**Carlo**
Author: 4 LEVI
Sophia's: 5 PONTI
___ Carlo: 5 MONTE
**Carlos**
Spanish king before Juan:
  7 ALFONSO
**Carlos, Juan:** 3 REY
Daughter of: 5 ELENA
**Carlos III**
Museum founded by:
  5 PRADO
**Carlsbad**
river: 5 PECOS
**Carlson**
Former governor: 4 ARNE
**Carly**
Singer: 5 SIMON
**Carmaker**
9-5 ~: 4 SAAB
French: 7 PEUGEOT
Korean: 3 KIA
woe: 6 RECALL
~ Maserati: 7 ERNESTO
~ Ransom Eli: 4 OLDS
**Carmela**
player: 4 EDIE

**Carmen**
Jazz singer: 5 MCRAE
Pop singer: 4 ERIC
Spanish actress: 5 MAURA
**"Carmen":** 5 OPERA
composer: 5 BIZET
highlight: 4 ARIA
  8 HABANERA
**Carmichael**
Composer: 5 HOAGY
**Carmichael, Hoagy**
classic: 8 STARDUST
**"Carmina Burana"**
composer: 4 ORFF
**Carmine:** 3 RED
**Carnaby Street**
setting: 4 SOHO
**Carnac:** 4 SEER
**Carnation:** 4 PINK
container: 4 VASE
emanation: 5 AROMA
site: 5 LAPEL
**Carnegie:** 4 SCOT
Author: 4 DALE
foundation: 5 STEEL
or Mellon: 6 ANDREW
**Carnegie ___:** 4 DELI HALL
**Carnegie Hall**
event: 7 RECITAL
**Carnera**
Champ after: 4 BAER
**Carnes**
Singer: 3 KIM
**Carney**
Actor: 3 ART
role: 6 NORTON
**Carney, Art**
role: 8 EDNORTON
**Carnival**
area: 6 MIDWAY
attraction: 4 RIDE
city: 3 RIO
doll: 6 KEWPIE
follower: 4 LENT
locale: 3 RIO
oddball: 4 GEEK
prize: 5 PANDA
show: 5 RAREE
sight: 4 TENT
stock-in-trade: 3 FUN
treat: 7 SNOCONE
**"Carnivàle"**
network: 3 HBO
**Carnivore:** 9 MEATEATER
Catlike: 5 CIVET
diet: 4 MEAT
Doglike: 5 HYENA
Jurassic: 8 ALLOSAUR
Mountain: 4 PUMA
**Carol:** 4 NOEL SING SONG
contraction: 3 TIS
Cover girl: 3 ALT
Greg Brady, to: 7 STEPSON
Model: 3 ALT
starter: 5 OCOME 6 ADESTE
syllables: 3 LAS

time: 4 YULE
**Carole Bayer ___**
Songwriter: 5 SAGER
**Caroled:** 4 SANG
**Caroler**
song: 4 NOEL
syllable: 3 TRA
**Carolina**
college: 4 ELON
First name in ~ politics:
  5 STROM
rail: 4 SORA
river: 6 PEEDEE
**Caroline**
group: 5 PALAU
of TV: 4 RHEA
Uncle of: 3 TED
**"Caroline in the City"**
Thompson of: 3 LEA
**Carolyn**
Nancy Drew creator: 5 KEENE
**Caron**
1953 ~ film: 4 LILI
Actress: 6 LESLIE
role: 4 GIGI LILI
**"Caro nome":** 4 ARIA
___ carotene: 4 BETA
**Carouse:** 5 REVEL
**"Carousel"**
choreographer: 7 DEMILLE
**"___ Carousel" (Hollies hit):**
  3 ONA
**Carousing:** 7 ONATEAR
  8 ONASPREE
**Carp:** 5 CAVIL
at: 3 NAG
Japanese: 3 KOI
Tiny: 3 NIT
**Carpe ___:** 4 DIEM
**"Carpe diem!":**
  11 SEIZETHEDAY
**Carpenter:** 5 KAREN
clamp: 4 VISE
cutter: 3 SAW
fastener: 4 TNUT
groove: 4 DADO
machine: 5 LATHE 6 PLANER
  SANDER
mouthful: 5 NAILS
Singer: 5 KAREN
tool: 3 ADZ AWL SAW 4 ADZE
  RASP VISE 5 DRILL
  LATHE LEVEL PLANE
  6 NAILER RIPSAW
  ROUTER SANDER
wear: 5 APRON
~, at times: 6 NAILER
  PLANER SANDER
  7 STAINER TENONER
**Carpenter, John**
movie: 6 THEFOG
**Carpenters**
Some: 4 ANTS
**Carpentry:** 5 TRADE
fastener: 4 NAIL 5 SCREW
groove: 4 DADO

joint: 5 MITER
tool: 3 ADZ AWL SAW 4 ADZE
    RASP VISE 5 DRILL
    LATHE LEVEL PLANE
    6 NAILER RIPSAW
    ROUTER SANDER
**Carper:** 3 NAG
**Carpet:** 3 RUG
  calculation: 4 AREA
  cleaner: 3 VAC
  color: 3 RED
  fastener: 4 TACK
  feature: 3 NAP 4 PILE
  fiber: 5 ISTLE
  Install: 3 LAY
  Kind of: 4 SHAG
  leftover: 7 REMNANT
  Like a: 5 PILED
  meas.: 4 SQYD
  measure: 4 AREA
  quality: 4 PILE
  store purchase: 7 AREARUG
  Thick: 4 SHAG
  Wear out the: 4 PACE
**Carpooling**
  Lane for ~ (abbr.): 3 HOV
  path: 7 HOVLANE
**Carr**
  Author: 5 CALEB
  Singer: 5 VIKKI
**Carreras:** 5 TENOR
  piece: 4 ARIA
  Tenor: 4 JOSE
**Carreras, Jose:** 5 TENOR
**Carrere**
  Actress: 3 TIA
**Carrey**
  Comical: 3 JIM
  role: 7 VENTURA
**Carrey, Jim**
  1994 ~ movie: 7 THEMASK
  1997 ~ movie: 8 LIARLIAR
  role: 6 GRINCH
    10 ACEVENTURA
**Carriage:** 4 MIEN 5 COACH
  Brit's baby: 4 PRAM
  Four-wheel: 6 LANDAU
  Fringed: 6 SURREY
  Light: 8 STANHOPE
  One-horse: 3 GIG 4 SHAY
  Open: 4 SHAY
  Russian: 6 TROIKA
  Three-horse: 6 TROIKA
  Traveling: 4 SHAY
**Carrie**
  Actress: 3 NYE
  Role for: 4 LEIA
  Suffragist: 4 CATT
**"Carrie"**
  star: 6 SPACEK
**Carried:** 5 BORNE
  chair: 5 SEDAN
  Get ~ away: 4 RIDE
  on: 5 PLIED WAGED
  out: 3 DID
**Carrier:** 4 CASE 5 TOTER

Common: 3 BUS
European: 3 SAS 8 ALITALIA
Former U.K.: 4 BOAC
name until 1997: 5 USAIR
since 1948: 4 ELAL
to Ben-Gurion: 4 ELAL
to Copenhagen: 3 SAS
to Karachi: 3 PIA
to Kyoto: 3 JAL
to Stockholm: 3 SAS
to Tel Aviv: 4 ELAL
**Carrion**
  feeder: 5 HYENA
**Carroll**
  Actor: 4 LEOG
  cake phrase: 5 EATME
  creature: 5 SNARK
  heroine: 4 ALICE
  slithy thing: 4 TOVE
**Carroll, Lewis:** 7 PENNAME
  critter: 5 SNARK
  heroine: 5 ALICE
**Carrot:** 4 ROOT 6 VEGGIE
    7 TAPROOT
  cutter: 5 DICER
  Dangle a.: 5 TEMPT 6 ENTICE
  on a snowman: 4 NOSE
**Carrot-top:** 7 REDHEAD
**Carry:** 4 BEAR HAUL TOTE
    6 SCHLEP
  All you can: 7 ARMLOAD
  along: 4 TOTE
  A movie star may – one:
    4 AURA
  away: 5 ELATE
  It's hard for some to: 4 TUNE
  off: 6 ABDUCT
  on: 3 PLY 4 RAGE RANT
    RAVE WAGE 8 TRANSACT
  out: 4 OBEY 5 ACTON STAGE
    7 ENFORCE EXECUTE
  Partner of: 4 CASH
  Runners ~ it: 4 SLED
  the day: 3 WIN
  They ~ a charge: 4 IONS
  They ~ on: 7 RANTERS
  to excess: 6 OVERDO
  with effort: 3 LUG
**Carry-___:** 3 ONS
**Carryall:** 4 CASE TOTE
  Western: 9 SADDLEBAG
**Carrying**
  a grudge: 4 SORE
  current: 4 LIVE
  no guarantees: 4 ASIS
**Carry-on:** 4 TOTE 7 TOTEBAG
**Cars**
  British sports: 3 MGS
  Some sports: 3 GTS
  Used: 4 RODE
**Cars, The**
  Ocasek of: 3 RIC
**Carson**
  Author: 6 RACHEL
  character: 6 CARNAC
  Frontiersman: 3 KIT

predecessor: 4 PAAR
successor: 4 LENO
target: 3 DDT
**Carson, Johnny:** 5 IOWAN
  announcer: 7 MCMAHON
**Carson, Kit**
  home: 4 TAOS
**Carson City**
  City north of: 4 RENO
  Lake near: 5 TAHOE
  state: 6 NEVADA
  state (abbr.): 3 NEV
**Cart:** 4 HAUL
  before the ores: 4 TRAM
  Bring by ~, maybe:
    7 WHEELIN
  Farm: 4 WAIN
  Kind of: 4 GOLF
  Shopping ~ path: 5 AISLE
  Sturdy: 4 DRAY
**___ Carta:** 5 MAGNA
**"Car Talk"**
  network: 3 NPR
**Carte**
  du jour: 4 MENU
  start: 3 ALA
**___ carte:** 3 ALA
**Carte blanche:** 8 FREEREIN
  offer: 6 NAMEIT
**Cartel:** 4 BLOC
  acronym: 4 OPEC
  city: 4 CALI
  Oil: 4 OPEC
**Carter**
  Actress: 4 NELL 5 LYNDA
  and Grant: 4 AMYS
  and Gwyn: 5 NELLS
  Country singer: 5 DEANA
  First daughter: 3 AMY
  had one: 4 TERM
  sch.: 4 USNA
  Secretary of State under:
    5 VANCE
  Singer: 4 NELL
  successor: 6 REAGAN
**Carter, Howard**
  discovery: 3 TUT
**Carter, James ___:** 4 EARL
**Carter, Jimmy**
  coll.: 4 USNA
  Daughter of: 3 AMY
  Where ~ taught: 5 EMORY
**Carter Center**
  university: 5 EMORY
**Cartesian**
  conclusion: 3 IAM
  conjunction: 4 ERGO
  line: 4 AXIS
**Carthage**
  founder: 4 DIDO
  hater: 4 CATO
  language: 5 PUNIC
  neighbor: 5 TUNIS UTICA
**"Carthage must be destroyed"**
  speaker: 4 CATO
**Carthaginian:** 5 PUNIC

**Cartier-Bresson**
  Photographer: 5 HENRI
**Cartland**
  title: 4 DAME
**Cartographer**
  creation: 3 MAP
  do over: 5 REMAP
**Cartographic**
  collection: 5 ATLAS
  extra: 5 INSET
**Carton**
  contents: 4 EGGS
  count: 5 DOZEN
  Egg ~ abbr.: 3 DOZ 4 USDA
  sealer: 4 TAPE
**Cartoon**
  art: 3 CEL 5 ANIME
  bear: 4 YOGI
  Bilingual ~ character:
      4 DORA
  bird: 10 ROADRUNNER
  Blue ~ character: 5 SMURF
  canine: 3 REN 4 ODIE
      5 ASTRO GOOFY PLUTO
      SNERT 9 SCOOBYDOO
  cat: 3 TOM 6 STIMPY
  catalog company: 4 ACME
  caveman: 3 OOP
  chihuahua: 3 REN
  chipmunk: 4 DALE 5 ALVIN
      SIMON
  clown: 4 KOKO
  collectible: 3 CEL
  cry: 3 EEK
  First Mickey Mouse:
      15 STEAMBOATWILLIE
  flapper: 4 BOOP
  frame: 3 CEL
  George Herriman:
      8 KRAZYKAT
  Half a ~ duo: 3 REN 4 LOIS
  Japanese ~ art: 5 ANIME
  light bulb: 4 IDEA
  mirage: 5 OASIS
  Nearsighted ~ character:
      5 MAGOO
  part: 5 PANEL
  partner of Barbera: 5 HANNA
  shriek: 4 YEOW
  sidekick: 5 BORIS
  skunk: 4 PEPE 5 LEPEW
  squeal: 3 EEK
  therapist Dr. ___: 4 KATZ
  voiceman Mel: 5 BLANC
**Cartoonist**
  Cat: 6 KLIBAN
  Dogpatch: 4 CAPP
  Harper's Weekly: 4 NAST
  ~ Addams: 4 CHAS
  ~ Browne: 3 DIK
  ~ Chast: 3 ROZ
  ~ Drake: 4 STAN
  ~ Drucker: 4 MORT
  ~ Edward: 5 SOREL
  ~ Gardner: 3 REA
  ~ Goldberg: 4 RUBE

  ~ Groening: 4 MATT
  ~ Guisewite: 5 CATHY
  ~ Hoff: 3 SYD
  ~ Johnny: 4 HART
  ~ Keane: 3 BIL
  ~ Kelly: 4 WALT
  ~ Key: 3 TED
  ~ Larson: 4 GARY
  ~ Lazarus: 4 MELL
  ~ Peter: 4 ARNO
  ~ Rall: 3 TED
  ~ Silverstein: 4 SHEL
  ~ Soglow: 4 OTTO
  ~ Tex: 5 AVERY
  ~ Thomas: 4 NAST
  ~ Trudeau: 5 GARRY
  ~ Walker: 4 MORT
  ~ Wilson: 5 GAHAN
**Cartridge**
  contents: 3 INK 4 AMMO
      5 TONER
  holder: 3 PEN
**Cartridges:** 4 AMMO
**Cartwheel**
  spinner: 4 AXLE
**Cartwright, Ben**
  ~, for one: 7 NEVADAN
**Cartwright, Hoss**
  real name: 4 ERIC
**Cartwright, Nancy**
  supplies his voice: 4 BART
**Cartwrights**
  One of the: 3 BEN 4 ADAM
      HOSS
**Caruso:** 5 TENOR
  portrayer: 5 LANZA
  Singer: 6 ENRICO
**Carve:** 6 INCISE
  with acid: 4 ETCH
**Carved**
  gem: 4 JADE 5 CAMEO
  Island with ~ heads: 6 EASTER
  Letters ~ in stone: 3 RIP
  out: 4 HEWN
  pillar: 5 STELA
  pole: 5 TOTEM
**Carver**
  Kachina: 4 HOPI
**Carver, G.W.**
  concern: 6 PEANUT
**Carvey**
  Comedian: 4 DANA
**Carving**
  Cameo: 6 RELIEF
  Green: 4 JADE
  Polynesian: 4 TIKI
**Cary**
  Actor: 5 ELWES
  Ex of: 4 DYAN
**Casa**
  cookware: 4 OLLA
  division: 4 SALA
  Lady of la: 6 SENORA
  material: 5 ADOBE
  title: 5 SENOR
**Casa ___:** 4 LOMA

**Casaba:** 5 MELON
**Casablanca**
  Capital near: 5 RABAT
  City near: 3 FEZ
**"Casablanca"**
  actor: 5 LORRE RAINS
  actor Wilson: 6 DOOLEY
  Bergman role in: 4 LUND
  café: 5 RICKS
  café owner: 4 RICK
  heroine: 4 ILSA
  Ingrid role in: 4 ILSA
  Lorre role in: 6 UGARTE
  pianist: 3 SAM
  producer Hal: 6 WALLIS
  Rick's love in: 4 ILSA
**Casals:** 5 PABLO
  instrument: 5 CELLO
**Casanova:** 4 RAKE ROUE
      9 LADIESMAN
**Casbah**
  headgear: 3 FEZ
**Cascade Range**
  peak: 6 SHASTA
**Cascades**
  mount: 4 HOOD
  peak: 6 MTHOOD SHASTA
      7 RAINIER
**Case:** 6 SHEATH 8 INSTANCE
  Dairy ~ item: 4 OLEO
  Decorative: 4 ETUI
  for a lawyer: 7 ATTACHE
  Hopeless: 5 GONER
  In: 4 LEST
  In any: 4 EVER 7 ATLEAST
  In that: 4 IFSO THEN
  Just in: 4 LEST
  Kind of: 4 TEST 6 CLOSET
      DATIVE 7 ATTACHE
  Knickknack: 7 ETAGERE
  Latin: 6 DATIVE
  Make a: 5 ARGUE PLEAD
  maker: 4 SUER
  Name in a famous: 3 ROE
      4 DRED
  Needle: 4 ETUI
  Nut: 3 BUR 5 CRANK
  Seed: 4 ARIL
  Sewing: 4 ETUI
  Should the be: 4 IFSO
  Small: 4 ETUI
  Stated one's: 4 PLED
  State one's: 5 OPINE
  Try a: 4 HEAR
  Vanity: 7 EGOTRIP
  worker: 5 JUROR 6 LAWYER
  worker org.: 3 ABA
  workers (abbr.): 3 DAS
      5 ATTYS
**___ case-by-case basis:** 3 ONA
**Casement:** 4 SASH
**Cases**
  Head: 6 CRANIA
  Some ER: 3 ODS
  Spore: 4 ASCI
  Vanity: 4 EGOS

**Casey**
Deejay: 5 KASEM
Storied: 5 JONES
**Cash: 5 ASSET MOOLA**
24-hr. ~ source: 3 ATM
Boy in a ~ tune: 3 SUE
cache: 3 ATM 4 TILL
closing: 3 IER
dispenser, for short: 3 ATM
drawer: 4 TILL
in: 6 REDEEM
Large amount of: 3 WAD
    4 PILE
of the courts: 3 PAT
on hand: 4 ANTE
Prison in a ~ tune: 6 FOLSOM
source: 3 ATM
Strapped for: 5 SHORT
substitute: 3 IOU
suffix: 3 IER
**Casher**
Check: 5 PAYEE
**Cashew:** 3 NUT 4 TREE
kin: 5 SUMAC
**Cashier:** 4 FIRE
stack: 4 ONES
**Cashless**
deal: 4 SWAP 5 TRADE
trade: 6 BARTER
**Cash lost in 'em:**
    12 SLOTMACHINES
**Cashmere:** 4 WOOL
brand: 3 TSE
**Cash register:** 4 TILL
calculation: 3 TAX
key: 6 NOSALE
output: 4 TAPE
stack: 4 ONES TENS
**Casing:** 4 SKIN
Prickly: 3 BUR
**Casino**
action: 4 BETS
area: 3 PIT
Atlantic City ~, with "The":
    3 TAJ
city: 4 RENO
cube: 3 DIE
cubes: 4 DICE
Does ~ work: 5 DEALS
employee: 6 DEALER
figures: 4 ODDS
game: 4 FARO KENO 5 CRAPS
    POKER
gear: 5 RAKES
gratuity: 4 TOKE
lure: 5 SLOTS
machine: 4 SLOT
opening: 4 SLOT
request: 5 HITME
supervisor: 7 PITBOSS
three: 4 TREY
Throw in a: 4 ROLL
Vegas ~, with "The":
    5 DUNES
**"Casino"**
costar: 5 PESCI

**Cask**
contents: 3 ALE
dregs: 4 LEES
Large: 3 TUN VAT
Put another hole in a: 5 RETAP
Unfilled part of a: 6 ULLAGE
Wine: 3 TUN
wood: 3 OAK
**"Cask of Amontillado, The"**
author: 3 POE
**Casks**
Like some: 5 OAKEN
**Caspary**
Author: 4 VERA
novel: 5 LAURA
**Casper:** 5 GHOST
**Caspian:** 3 SEA
Capital on the: 4 BAKU
Country on the: 4 IRAN
feeder: 4 URAL
neighbor: 4 ARAL
River to the: 4 URAL
Sea east of the: 4 ARAL
**Cass:** 4 MAMA
Mama: 6 ELLIOT
**Cassandra:** 4 SEER 6 ORACLE
alter ego: 6 ELVIRA
Brother of: 7 TROILUS
Father of: 5 PRIAM
**Cassatt**
Painter: 4 MARY
**Cassava**
product: 7 TAPIOCA
**Casserole**
Kind of: 5 DIVAN
staple: 4 TUNA
**Cassette:** 4 TAPE
contents: 5 VIDEO
half: 5 SIDEA SIDEB
Make a new: 6 RETAPE
**Cassidy, Hopalong**
portrayer: 4 BOYD
**Cassin**
Peace Nobelist: 4 RENE
**Cassini**
Designer: 4 OLEG
**Cassino**
cash: 4 LIRA LIRE
**Cassio**
rival: 4 IAGO
**Cassis**
aperitif: 3 KIR
**Cassiterite:** 6 TINORE
**Cassius**
Loser to: 5 SONNY
**Cassowary**
kin: 3 EMU 4 RHEA
**Cast:** 3 HUE 4 HURL MIEN
    SENT SHED TOSS
    5 FLING FLUNG HEAVE
    SLING SLUNG THREW
    TINGE 6 ACTORS
    HURLED THROWN
a ballot: 4 VOTE
aspersions on: 4 SLUR
Be a ~ member of: 5 ACTIN

Be in a: 3 ACT
forth: 4 EMIT 6 SPEWED
Head the ~ of: 6 STARIN
iron: 5 ALLOY
It may be: 3 DIE 4 IRON ROLE
    5 SPELL
Join the ~ of: 5 ACTIN
leader: 4 TELE
member: 5 ACTOR 6 PLAYER
off: 4 SHED
off from the body: 5 EGEST
of mind: 4 BENT
One in a: 5 ACTOR
out: 4 SPEW 5 EGEST EXILE
    6 BANISH 7 EGESTED
Something to: 6 BALLOT
supporter: 5 SLING
They're: 6 ACTORS
wearer problem: 4 ITCH
**Castaway**
call: 3 SOS
creation: 4 RAFT
home: 4 ISLE 5 ISLET
Literary: 6 CRUSOE
**"Cast Away"**
setting: 4 ISLE
**Caste**
member: 3 ANT 5 HINDU
**Castel Gandolfo**
resident: 4 POPE
**Castel Nuovo**
site: 6 NAPLES
**Caster**
Ballot: 5 VOTER
**Castile**
Hero of: 5 ELCID
**Castilian**
hero: 5 ELCID
kinsmen: 4 TIOS
**Casting**
assignment: 4 ROLE
Do some: 4 FISH
requirement: 3 ROD 4 REEL
**Castle:** 4 ROOK
Cuban: 5 MORRO
defense: 4 MOAT
feature: 4 KEEP 5 TOWER
    6 TURRET
material: 4 SAND
mistress: 10 CHATELAINE
Movable: 4 ROOK
of dance: 5 IRENE
or Cara: 5 IRENE
protector: 4 MOAT
Queenside ~, in notation:
    3 OOO
with lots of steps: 5 IRENE
___ Castle: 5 MORRO
**"Castle, The"**
author: 5 KAFKA
**Cast-of-thousands**
film: 4 EPIC
**Castor**
Mother of: 4 LEDA
or Olive: 3 OYL
or Pollux: 4 STAR TWIN

**Castro**
country: 4 CUBA
Cuba, to: 4 ISLA
of Cuba: 5 FIDEL
predecessor: 7 BATISTA
**Casual**
attire: 5 DENIM JEANS
day (abbr.): 3 FRI
eatery: 6 BISTRO
fabric: 5 DENIM
pants: 5 JEANS
shirt: 3 TEE 4 POLO
talk: 4 CHAT
top: 3 TEE 6 TSHIRT
wear: 5 JEANS LEVIS
    6 CHINOS DENIMS
**Casually**
Turns ~, with "through":
    5 LEAFS
**Casualty**
Euro: 5 FRANC
Hamelin: 3 RAT
Titanic: 5 ASTOR
**Cat:** 3 PET
Alice's: 5 DINAH
Alley ~, perhaps: 5 STRAY
Bell the: 4 DARE
Big: 4 LION LYNX PUMA
Black: 7 PANTHER
Black ~, maybe: 4 OMEN
breed: 7 SIAMESE
call: 3 MEW 4 MEOW
Cartoon: 3 TOM
cartoonist: 6 KLIBAN
catcher: 4 CLAW
Colorful: 6 CALICO
Cool: 6 DADDYO
Curly-haired: 3 REX
Dogs on a: 4 PAWS
Drink like a: 3 LAP 5 LAPUP
Endangered: 4 PUMA
    6 OCELOT
Fast: 7 CHEETAH
Fat: 5 MOGUL NABOB
    9 MONEYBAGS
feet: 4 PAWS
food flavoring: 4 TUNA
hangout: 5 ALLEY
Kind of: 3 HEP 4 MANX
    5 ALLEY 7 SIAMESE
Leopardlike: 6 OCELOT
Let the ~ out of the bag:
    4 BLAB TOLD
Like a ~ burglar: 8 STEALTHY
Like an alley: 5 FERAL
Long-haired: 6 ANGORA
Made ~ calls: 5 MEWED
Male: 3 GIB TOM
Mountain ~ perch: 5 ARETE
of ads: 6 MORRIS
pajamas: 3 FUR
preceder: 3 SNO 4 ONEO
prey: 3 RAT
scanner: 3 VET
Spotted: 5 CIVET 6 CALICO
    OCELOT

Tailless: 4 MANX
that earns its keep: 6 MOUSER
weapon: 4 CLAW
Wild: 4 PUMA
with ear tufts: 4 LYNX
~, in Spanish: 4 GATO
**CAT**
scan kin: 3 MRI
**CAT ___:** 4 SCAN
**Catalan**
artist: 4 MIRO
**Catalina:** 4 ISLE 6 ISLAND
    (abbr.): 3 ISL
**Catalog:** 4 LIST 6 ASSORT
abbr.: 4 ETAL
Card ~ entry: 5 TITLE
Kind of: 9 MAILORDER
Old ~ maker: 5 SEARS
**Catalogs**
Big name in: 5 JCREW
    6 LLBEAN 7 SPIEGEL
**Catalonia**
cat: 4 GATO
**Catalyst**
Biochemical: 6 ENZYME
**Catamaran**
mover: 4 SAIL
**Catamount:** 4 PUMA
**"Cat and the Curmudgeon,
    The"**
author: 5 AMORY
**Catania**
View from: 4 ETNA
**Catapult:** 4 HURL
Medieval: 6 ONAGER
**Catastrophe**
prefix: 3 ECO
Word before: 4 NEAR
**"Cat Ballou"**
actor Marvin: 3 LEE
**Catbird**
seat: 4 NEST TREE 5 PERCH
    ROOST
**Catboat**
has one: 4 MAST
**Catcall:** 3 BOO 4 HISS HOOT
    JEER
**Catch:** 3 BAG GET NAB NET
    RUB SEE 4 HEAR HOOK
    LAND NAIL ROPE SNAG
    5 CLASP LASSO SNARE
    6 ENMESH REELIN
    7 ENSNARE
a break: 5 SLEEP
a glimpse of: 4 ESPY SPOT
Atlantic: 3 COD
Brook: 5 TROUT
but good: 4 NAIL
Cape Cod: 4 TUNA
Coastal: 4 SOLE
Cop's: 4 PERP
forty winks: 3 NAP
Hard to: 4 EELY
in a net: 6 ENMESH
in a sting: 6 ENTRAP
in the act: 3 NAB

Marine: 7 SEABASS
New England: 3 COD 5 SCROD
on: 3 SEE 5 LEARN SEEIT
one's breath: 4 REST
on to: 3 GET 5 GRASP
phrase: 6 IGOTIT SLOGAN
red-handed: 3 NAB 4 NAIL
sight of: 4 ESPY SPOT
    6 DESCRY
some extra Z's: 7 SLEEPIN
some rays: 3 SUN TAN 4 BASK
    6 SUNTAN
some z's: 3 NAP 4 DOZE
    5 SLEEP 6 SNOOZE
up with: 8 OVERTAKE
What nodders: 4 ZEES
**"Catch!":** 4 HERE
**Catch ___:** 4 ONTO
**Catch-22:** 4 SNAG 7 DILEMMA
**"Catch-22"**
actor: 5 ARKIN
Minderbinder of: 4 MILO
pilot: 3 ORR
**"Catch a Falling Star"**
singer: 4 COMO
**Catchall**
abbr.: 3 ETC 4 ETAL MISC
category: 5 OTHER 6 OTHERS
    7 POTLUCK
**Catcher:** 3 NET 5 SNARE
Animal: 4 TRAP
Catcher's: 4 MITT
Circus: 3 NET
communication: 4 SIGN
Cow: 5 LASSO REATA RIATA
    6 LARIAT
Drip: 3 BIB
Fly: 3 WEB 4 MITT
in the Rhine: 5 SEINE
in the wry: 5 BERRA
locale: 3 RYE
Mouse: 3 OWL 4 TRAP
Pass: 3 END
position: 5 SQUAT 6 CROUCH
Quotable: 5 BERRA
Read the sign of a: 6 PEERIN
Splash: 5 APRON
Wave: 7 ANTENNA
~ Berra: 4 YOGI
~ Tony: 4 PENA
**"Catcher in the ___, The":**
    3 RYE
**"Catcher in the Rye, The"**
author: 8 SALINGER
**Catching**
It may be: 4 TRAP
**Catchphrase:** 6 SLOGAN
Austin Powers: 8 OHBEHAVE
Chef: 3 ALA
Skelton: 7 IDOODIT
**Catchword:** 6 SLOGAN
1960s ~: 5 PEACE
Belafonte: 4 DAYO
Dieter's: 4 LITE 5 LOFAT
    6 LOWFAT NONFAT
Emeril: 3 BAM

Jack Benny: 4 WELL
Marv Albert: 3 YES
Procrastinator's: 6 MANANA
"Catch you later!": 3 BYE
"Categorical imperative"
  philosopher: 4 KANT
**Categorically**
  State: 4 AVER 6 ASSERT
**Categorize:** 4 SORT 5 LABEL
    6 ASSORT
**Category:** 4 TYPE 5 CLASS
    GENRE
  Artistic: 5 GENRE
  Blood: 4 TYPE
  Book: 5 HOWTO
  Catchall: 5 OTHER 6 OTHERS
    7 POTLUCK
  Clothing: 4 MENS
  Fencing: 4 EPEE
  Figure skating: 5 PAIRS
  Grammy: 3 POP RAP 4 FOLK
    ROCK 5 LATIN RANDB
    6 GOSPEL
  Literary: 5 GENRE
  Music: 4 SOUL
  Nobel: 4 ECON 5 PEACE
  Poll: 9 UNDECIDED
  Pulitzer: 5 DRAMA
  Skating: 5 PAIRS
  Skiing: 6 ALPINE
  SSS: 4 ONEA
  Ticket: 5 ADULT
  Trivia: 6 SPORTS
  Twenty Questions: 6 ANIMAL
    7 MINERAL
**Cater**
  basely: 6 PANDER
**Catered**
  event: 6 AFFAIR
**Caterer**
  carrier: 4 TRAY
  coffeepot: 3 URN
  heater: 6 STERNO
  job: 5 EVENT
**Caterpillar:** 5 LARVA
  case: 6 COCOON
  construction: 4 TENT
  hairs: 5 SETAE
  product: 7 TRACTOR
  rival: 5 DEERE
  Tent: 5 EGGER
  Vehicle with ~ treads:
    6 SNOCAT
**Caterwaul:** 4 HOOT HOWL
    YOWL
**Cathartic**
  herb: 5 SENNA
**Cathay**
  visitor: 4 POLO
**Cathedral**
  area: 4 APSE
  center: 4 NAVE
  English ~ city: 3 ELY
    6 EXETER
  French ~ city: 5 REIMS
    6 AMIENS

topper: 5 SPIRE
Tuscany ~ city: 5 SIENA
**Cather**
  Author: 5 WILLA
  title heroine: 7 ANTONIA
**Catherine**
  Henry VIII's: 4 PARR
  Home of: 6 ARAGON
  Husband of: 5 HENRY
**Catherine of ___:** 6 ARAGON
**Catherine the Great:**
    7 EMPRESS TSARINA
**Cathode**
  counterpoint: 5 ANODE
**Catholic**
  devotion: 6 NOVENA
  Eastern: 5 UNIAT
  prayer: 8 AVEMARIA
  ~ Bible version: 5 DOUAY
**"Cat ___ Hot Tin Roof":** 3 ONA
**Catkin**
  producer: 5 ALDER
**Catlike:** 5 AGILE 6 FELINE
  carnivore: 5 CIVET
**Cat-mouse**
  connector: 3 AND
**Catnap:** 4 DOZE
**Cat Nation**
  members: 5 ERIES
**Cato:** 5 ROMAN
  **Info:** Latin cue
  To be, to: 4 ESSE
**"Cat on a Hot Tin Roof"**
  actor Burl: 4 IVES
**Cat-o'-nine-tails**
  blow: 4 LASH
  Use a: 4 FLOG
**"Cat on ___ Tin Roof":** 4 AHOT
**Cats**
  Copy: 3 MEW 4 MEOW PURR
  Like some: 3 HEP
  Rain ~ and dogs: 4 POUR
  Striped: 7 TABBIES
**"Cats"**
  director Trevor: 4 NUNN
  monogram: 3 TSE
  poet: 5 ELIOT
**Cat's ___:** 7 PAJAMAS
**Catskills**
  resort area: 11 BORSCHTBELT
**Cat's-paw:** 3 SAP 4 DUPE
    TOOL 6 STOOGE
**Catsup**
  catcher: 3 TIE
**Cattail:** 4 REED
  setting: 5 MARSH
**Cattails**
  Full of: 5 REEDY
**Cat-tails**
  connector: 5 ONINE
**Cattle:** 4 KINE 5 STEER
  African ~ pen: 5 KRAAL
  Black ~ breed: 5 ANGUS
  call: 3 LOW MOO
  catcher: 5 LASSO REATA
    RIATA

catching weapon: 4 BOLA
encourager: 4 PROD
English ~ breed: 5 DEVON
genus: 3 BOS
group: 4 HERD
identifier: 5 BRAND
Raised: 4 BRED
Scottish ~ breed: 5 ANGUS
Steal: 6 RUSTLE
unit: 4 HEAD
Work with: 6 DEHORN
**Cattleman**
  concern: 4 BEEF
**Catty**
  remark: 3 MEW 4 MEOW
**Catullus**
  composition: 3 ODE
**Catwoman**
  portrayer Kitt: 6 EARTHA
  ~, to Batman: 3 FOE
**Caucasus**
  native: 5 OSSET
**Caucus**
  selection: 8 DELEGATE
  state: 4 IOWA
**Caught:** 3 GOT 4 SEEN
    5 ROPED 6 NAILED
    NETTED SNARED
    7 INATRAP SNAGGED
    8 ENSNARED
a calf: 5 ROPED
a few winks: 5 SLEPT
Fish ~ in a pot: 3 EEL
Fish ~ in winter: 4 SHAD
He ~ a perfect game:
    9 YOGIBERRA
He ~ his adversary's ear:
    5 TYSON
in a trap: 6 SNARED
in the act: 4 SEEN
One ~ off base: 4 AWOL
on video: 5 TAPED
on, with "up": 5 WISED
sight of: 5 SPIED 6 ESPIED
some rays: 6 SUNNED
    TANNED
some Z's: 5 SLEPT
They're ~ at the beach:
    4 RAYS
up in a cliffhanger: 6 ONEDGE
Where some fish are:
    6 EELERY
**Caught in ___:** 4 ALIE
**"Caught you!":** 3 AHA
**Cauldron**
  1996 Olympic ~ lighter: 3 ALI
  stirrer: 3 HAG
**Caulfield**
  creator: 8 SALINGER
**Cauliflower**
  cousin: 8 BROCCOLI
**Caulk:** 4 SEAL 7 SEALANT
**Caulking**
  material: 5 OAKUM PUTTY
**Cause:** 4 SAKE 7 CRUSADE
  '70s–'80s ~: 3 ERA

a major disturbance in:
   7 UPHEAVE
anguish to: 6 TEARAT
Bygone polit.: 3 ERA
damage to: 3 MAR
for a blessing: 5 ACHOO
   6 SNEEZE
for alarm: 4 FIRE
for an apology: 4 BUMP
for a pause: 5 COMMA
for cramming: 4 EXAM
for overtime: 3 TIE
Interruption: 5 PAGER
It can ~ a blowup: 3 TNT
Losing: 4 DIET
Lost: 5 GONER
NOW: 3 ERA
of burnout: 6 STRESS
of inflation: 3 AIR
of ruin: 4 BANE
Overtime: 3 TIE
They ~ breakdowns:
   7 ENZYMES
to attack: 5 SETAT SETON
to err: 6 TRIPUP
to expand: 6 DILATE
to laugh: 5 AMUSE
to see red: 6 ENRAGE
to swell: 5 BLOAT
to vanish: 6 DISPEL
to yawn: 4 BORE
trouble:
   15 CREATEANUISANCE
Underlying: 4 ROOT
**Cause ___:** 7 CELEBRE
**Caused:** 5 LEDTO 7 LEDUPTO
by: 5 DUETO
to go: 6 BETOOK
**Causing**
goose bumps: 5 EERIE
   6 CREEPY
laughter: 7 COMICAL
**Caustic:** 4 TART 5 ACRID
   7 EROSIVE
chemical: 3 LYE
Comparatively: 6 TARTER
stuff: 3 LYE
wit: 7 SARCASM
**Cauterize:** 4 SEAR
**Cauthen**
Jockey: 5 STEVE
**Caution:** 4 WARN
Road: 3 SLO 4 SLOW
Sale: 4 ASIS
**Cautionary**
word: 4 DONT
**Cautious:** 4 WARY
**Cautiously**
Enter: 6 EASEIN EDGEIN
Move: 6 TIPTOE
**___ cava:** 4 VENA
**Cavaliers**
NCAA: 3 UVA
**Cavalry**
British ~ sword: 5 SABRE
command: 6 CHARGE

member: 6 LANCER
unit: 5 TROOP
weapon: 5 LANCE SABER
**Cavalryman**
European ~ sight: 6 HUSSAR
in an oater: 5 EXTRA
**Cavaradossi**
Lover of: 5 TOSCA
**Cave:** 3 DEN 4 LAIR 5 ANTRE
   6 GROTTO RELENT
Alley in a: 3 OOP
art: 5 MURAL
dweller: 3 BAT 5 TROLL
effect: 4 ECHO
Explore a: 7 SPELUNK
Small: 6 GROTTO
**Caveat**
Issue a ~ to: 4 WARN
Sale: 4 ASIS
**Caveat ___:** 6 EMPTOR
**Caveman:** 9 SPELUNKER
Comics: 3 OOP 8 ALLEYOOP
discovery: 4 FIRE
weapon: 4 CLUB
~ Alley: 3 OOP
**Cavern:** 6 GROTTO
comeback: 4 ECHO
~, in poetry: 4 GROT 5 ANTRE
**Caviar:** 3 ROE 4 EGGS
Roman: 3 OVA
source: 6 BELUGA
   8 STURGEON
They may be served with:
   5 BLINI
variety: 7 SHADROE
**Caving**
Go: 7 SPELUNK
**Cavities:** 6 FOSSAE
Bone: 5 ANTRA
**Cavity:** 4 HOLE
Deep: 5 ABYSM
filler: 5 GROUT
filler (abbr.): 3 DDS
Kind of: 5 NASAL
Skull: 5 SINUS
**Cavort:** 4 ROMP 6 PRANCE
**Cavs**
org.: 3 NBA
**Cavy**
Spotted: 4 PACA
**Cay:** 4 ISLE 5 ISLET
**___ Cayes, Haiti:** 3 LES
**Cayuga**
relative: 6 SENECA
**Cayuga Lake**
City on: 6 ITHACA
**Cayuse**
controller: 4 REIN
**CB:** 5 RADIO
Emergency ~ channel: 4 NINE
**CBC**
Onetime ~ newsman:
   6 TREBEK
**CBer**
relative: 3 HAM
sign-off: 4 OVER

**CBS**
anchor Dan: 6 RATHER
eye: 4 LOGO
forensic drama: 3 CSI
Former ~ anchor: 4 MUDD
   6 RATHER
Former ~ chairman Laurence:
   5 TISCH
founder: 5 PALEY
hit series: 3 CSI
logo: 3 EYE
Part of: 3 SYS 4 SYST
Rather of: 3 DAN
**CD:** 4 ACCT
acronym: 5 ASCAP
earnings: 3 INT
follower: 3 ROM
Make a: 4 BURN
Part of: 4 DISC
Pitch a: 4 TOUR
player part: 5 LASER
players: 3 DJS
predecessors: 3 LPS
Promo: 4 DEMO
selection: 4 SONG 5 TRACK
source: 5 SANDL
**CD-___:** 3 ROM
**Cease:** 3 END 4 HALT STOP
   6 DESIST
**"Cease!"**
at sea: 5 AVAST
**Cease-fire:** 5 TRUCE
**Ceaselessly:** 5 NOEND ONEND
   7 ONANDON
**Cecil**
Cartoon pal of: 5 BEANY
**Cecil B.**
Agnes, to: 5 NIECE
**Cedar Rapids**
college: 3 COE
**Ceded:** 6 GAVEUP
**Ceiling:** 3 CAP LID 5 LIMIT
fixture: 3 FAN
Sistine ~ figure: 4 ADAM
support: 5 JOIST
**Cel**
character: 4 TOON
mates: 5 TOONS
**Celeb:** 4 NAME STAR
life story: 3 BIO
Soccer: 4 PELE
**Celebrant**
June: 4 GRAD
**Celebrate:** 5 REVEL
   15 PAINTTHETOWNRED
Time to: 3 EVE
**Celebrated:** 4 STAR 5 FAMED
   FETED 7 EMINENT
   STORIED
**Celebration:** 4 FEST FETE
   GALA 5 PARTY REVEL
   6 FIESTA
Asian: 3 TET
Day of: 4 FETE
Environmentalist:
   8 EARTHDAY

Passover: 5 SEDER
Sunday: 4 MASS
Thanksgiving: 5 FEAST
times: 4 EVES
**Celebratory**
dance: 4 HORA
poem: 3 ODE
___ célèbre: 5 CAUSE
**Celebrex**
maker: 6 SEARLE
**Celebrity:** 4 FAME LION NAME
    5 ECLAT 6 RENOWN
    7 STARDOM
    9 SUPERSTAR
A ~ may have one: 4 AURA
concern: 5 IMAGE
Treat as a: 7 LIONIZE
**Celerity:** 5 HASTE SPEED
With: 5 APACE
**Celery**
piece: 5 STALK
**Celeste**
Husband of: 5 BABAR
Oscar winner: 4 HOLM
**Celestial**
altar: 3 ARA
array: 4 ORBS
bear: 4 URSA
being: 6 SERAPH
hunter: 5 ORION
ice ball: 5 COMET
It lies on the ~ equator:
    5 ORION
messenger: 5 ANGEL
radio source: 6 PULSAR
ram: 5 ARIES
sphere: 3 ORB
**Celestial Seasonings**
product: 3 TEA
**Celine**
Singer: 4 DION
**Cell**
Brain: 6 NEURON
centers: 6 NUCLEI
component: 3 DNA RNA
division: 7 MITOSIS
Egg: 4 OVUM
Germ: 5 SPORE
Immature egg: 6 OOCYTE
Kind of: 4 GERM STEM
    5 SOLAR
messenger: 3 RNA
Nerve: 6 NEURON
Nerve ~ part: 4 AXON
Reproductive: 5 OVULE
    6 GAMETE
Retina: 3 ROD
Sea: 4 BRIG
Stuff in a: 3 RNA
terminal: 5 ANODE
**Cellar**
door device: 4 HASP
dweller's place: 4 LAST
It's in the: 9 TABLESALT
Like many a: 4 DAMP DANK
Sit in the: 3 AGE

stock: 4 WINE
Word before: 5 STORM
**Cellist**
direction: 4 ARCO
French-born: 6 YOYOMA
purchase: 5 ROSIN
~ Casals: 5 PABLO
~ Ma: 4 YOYO
~ Starker: 5 JANOS
**Cello**
feature: 5 FHOLE
kin: 4 VIOL 5 VIOLA
Ma with a: 4 YOYO
**Cellophane:** 4 WRAP
**Cell phone**
button: 4 SEND
kin: 5 PAGER
lack: 4 CORD
maker: 5 NOKIA
Pioneer ~ co.: 3 GTE
**Cells**
Dissolve: 4 LYSE
Egg: 3 OVA
Element in photoelectric:
    6 CESIUM
Reproductive: 3 OVA
**Cellular**
prefix: 3 UNI 5 MULTI
stuff: 3 RNA
**Cellular ___:** 3 ONE 5 PHONE
**Celluloid**
canine: 4 ASTA
**Cellulose**
fiber brand: 5 ARNEL
**Celsius:** 5 SWEDE
freezing point: 4 ZERO
Thermometer developer:
    6 ANDERS
**Celt:** 4 GAEL
Ancient: 5 DRUID
**Celtic**
group: 4 CLAN
language: 4 ERSE 5 IRISH
    6 GAELIC
priest of old: 5 DRUID
sea god: 3 LER
tongue: 4 ERSE
~ Bird: 5 LARRY
**Celtics**
coach, 1995–97: 6 MLCARR
Hall of Famer: 7 KCJONES
M.L. of the: 4 CARR
star White: 4 JOJO
**"Celts, The"**
singer: 4 ENYA
**Cement:** 4 GLUE 5 PASTE
Like the "c" in: 4 SOFT
Like wet: 5 UNSET
**Cemetery**
sights: 4 URNS
**Cen.**
parts: 3 YRS
**Cenozoic:** 3 ERA
**Censor:** 5 BLEEP
concern: 4 OATH SMUT
Roman: 4 CATO

**"Censor, The":** 4 CATO
**Censoring**
device: 5 VCHIP
**Censorship**
fighting gp.: 4 ACLU
**Censure:** 4 DAMN 7 DEPLORE
    REPROVE
**Census**
data: 4 AGES
info: 3 AGE SEX 4 RACE
**Cent:** 5 PENNY
Word on a: 4 UNUM
**Cent.**
parts: 3 YRS
**Centaur**
~, in part: 5 HORSE
**Centaurs**
Home of the: 6 PELION
**Centavos**
100 ~: 4 PESO
**Centennial**
prefix: 3 TER
**Center:** 3 HUB 4 CORE SNAP
    5 FOCUS HEART MIDST
At the ~ of: 4 AMID
Bagel: 4 HOLE
Basilica: 4 NAVE
Church: 4 NAVE
Combat: 4 ARENA
County: 4 SEAT
Cyclone: 3 EYE
Dead: 4 TOMB
Diamond: 5 MOUND
Fitness: 3 SPA
Florida citrus: 5 OCALA
Football: 3 AIR
front: 3 EPI
Fruit: 3 PIT 4 CORE
Game: 3 TAC
Health: 3 SPA
Heat ~, once: 5 ONEAL
Hurricane: 3 EYE
In the ~ of: 4 AMID
It may be left of: 3 EPI
Kind of: 3 REC 4 ARTS
    5 REHAB 6 CRISIS
    TRAUMA
Lincoln: 3 CEE
Lines from the: 5 RADII
Military: 4 BASE
Nearest the: 7 MIDMOST
Near the: 3 MID
Nut: 4 MEAT
of a ball: 3 DEB 5 BELLE
of activity: 3 HUB 4 HIVE
    5 LOCUS
of a roast: 7 HONOREE
of Florida: 5 EPCOT
of government: 4 SEAT
of Miami, once: 4 SHAQ
    5 ONEAL
of power: 5 LOCUS
of rotation: 4 AXIS
opening: 3 EPI
or end: 7 ATHLETE
prefix: 3 EPI

Raisin: 6 FRESNO
Remove the ~ of: 4 CORE
Self: 3 EGO
Shopping: 4 MALL MART
　5 PLAZA
Simile: 3 ASA 4 ASAN
Sports: 5 ARENA
starter: 3 EPI
Storm: 3 EYE
Taste: 6 PALATE
Third from: 3 END
Trade: 4 MART
Wheel: 3 HUB
X or O: 3 TAC
___ center: 3 REC
___ Center: 5 EPCOT
**Centerpiece**
Still-life: 4 VASE
Wedding reception: 4 CAKE
**Centers**
Cell: 6 NUCLEI
of activity: 4 LOCI
of attention: 4 FOCI
of power: 4 LOCI
Trauma: 3 ERS
**Centesimi**
100 ~: 4 LIRA 7 ONELIRA
**Centesimos**
100 ~: 4 PESO
**Centimes**
Five or ten ~, once: 3 SOU
**Centimeter-gram-second**
unit: 3 ERG 4 DYNE
**Centimeters**
2.54 ~: 4 INCH
**Centimos**
100 ~: 6 PESETA
**Centipede**
maker: 5 ATARI
**Central:** 3 MID 4 MAIN
　5 FOCAL INNER NODAL
church area: 4 NAVE
computer: 4 HOST 6 SERVER
courtyards: 5 ATRIA
feature: 4 CRUX
leaf vein: 6 MIDRIB
line: 4 AXIS
part: 4 CORE PITH YOLK
　5 MIDST
parts: 6 NUCLEI
point: 4 CRUX GIST NODE
　5 HEART MIDST NAVEL
　NEXUS 6 THESIS
points: 4 FOCI
spots: 4 LOCI
street: 4 MAIN
truth: 3 TAO
**Central American**
~ Indian: 4 MAYA
**Central Florida**
city: 5 OCALA
**Central New York**
city: 5 UTICA
**Central Pennsylvania**
city: 7 ALTOONA
___ **Centre:** 5 EATON

**Centric**
prefix: 4 AFRO ENDO EURO
　5 ETHNO HELIO
**Centrifuge**
stresses: 7 GFORCES
**Centripetally:** 7 INWARDS
**Centrum**
rival: 7 ONEADAY
**Cents**
100 ~: 4 EURO RAND
　5 RUPEE
Make: 4 MINT
Put in one's two: 4 ANTE
　5 OPINE
**Centuries**
and centuries: 3 EON
**Century**
1st ~ emperor: 4 NERO
4th ~ invader: 4 GOTH
5th ~ pope: 5 STLEO
10th ~ emperor: 5 OTTOI
11th ~ hero: 5 ELCID
13th ~ invader: 5 TATAR
16th ~ council site: 5 TRENT
16th ~ painter: 5 PAOLO
16th ~ poet: 5 TASSO
divs.: 3 YRS
Like some 20th ~ music:
　6 ATONAL
One of a 15th ~ trio: 4 NINA
plant: 4 ALOE 5 AGAVE
**Century 21**
rival: 3 ERA
**CEO:** 3 VIP 4 PRES
aide: 4 ASST
degree: 3 MBA
Former Disney: 6 EISNER
Part of: 4 EXEC
perk: 3 JET
"stat!": 4 ASAP
**Ceramic**
square: 4 TILE
**Ceramics:** 5 CRAFT
oven: 4 KILN
**Cereal:** 5 GRAIN
brand: 3 KIX 4 CHEX 5 TOTAL
　10 FROOTLOOPS
choice: 4 BRAN 6 FLAKES
Cooked: 6 FARINA
fruit: 6 BANANA RAISIN
fungus: 5 ERGOT
grain: 3 OAT RYE 4 RICE
　6 BARLEY
grass: 3 RYE
ingredient: 4 BRAN
Kids': 4 TRIX
　10 CAPNCRUNCH
killer: 5 ERGOT
Like some: 4 OATY 5 OATEN
Quaker: 3 OHS
serving: 4 BOWL
sound: 4 SNAP
utensil: 5 SPOON
**Cereal box**
stat.: 3 RDA 5 NETWT
tiger: 4 TONY

**Cerebellum**
section: 4 LOBE
**Cerebral**
output: 4 IDEA
**Cerebral ___:** 6 CORTEX
**Ceremonial**
act: 4 RITE
dinner: 5 SEDER
gown: 4 TOGA
procession: 6 PARADE
splendor: 4 POMP
staff: 4 MACE
**Ceremony:** 4 POMP RITE
　6 RITUAL
Skip the: 5 ELOPE
Solemn: 4 RITE
___ ceremony: 7 STOODON
**Ceres:** 8 ASTEROID
　9 PLANETOID
birthplace: 4 ENNA
**Cereus**
and others: 5 CACTI
**Cerf**
Publisher: 7 BENNETT
specialty: 3 PUN
**Cerium:** 9 RAREEARTH
**Cert.**
Birth: 5 IDENT
**Certain:** 4 SURE
Far from: 4 IFFY
Made: 7 SAWTOIT
Make: 6 ASSURE ENSURE
　INSURE
That ~ something: 4 AURA
　6 ALLURE
To a ~ extent: 6 INPART
Was ~ of: 4 KNEW
**"Certainly!":** 3 YES 4 SURE
　5 NATCH
**Certainty:** 5 CINCH
State with: 4 AVER
**Certifiable:** 3 MAD 6 INSANE
**Certificate:** 5 SCRIP
Ownership: 4 DEED 5 TITLE
Village Voice: 4 OBIE
**Certified**
It may be: 4 MAIL
**Certify:** 6 ATTEST 8 ACCREDIT
　ATTESTTO
~, in a way: 8 NOTARIZE
**Certs**
rival: 6 TICTAC 7 TICTACS
**Cerulean:** 5 AZURE
**Cervantes**
title: 5 SENOR
**Cerveza**
Snack with: 4 TAPA
**Cesar**
Actor: 6 ROMERO
**Cessation:** 3 END 4 HALT
　REST
**Cesspool:** 3 STY 4 SUMP
**"C'est ___":** 5 LAVIE
**"C'est magnifique!":** 6 OOLALA
　7 OOHLALA
**"___ c'est moi":** 5 LETAT

**Cetus**
Star in: 4 MIRA
**C. Everett ___:** 4 KOOP
**Ceylon**
~, today: 8 SRILANKA
**Cézanne**
Artist: 4 PAUL
summer: 3 ETE
**CFO:** 4 EXEC
**CGS**
unit: 3 ERG
**Chablis:** 4 WINE
**Cha-cha**
cousin: 5 MAMBO
**Cha cha cha:** 5 STEPS
**Chachi**
portrayer: 4 BAIO
**Chacon**
of baseball: 4 ELIO
**"Chacun ___ goût":** 4 ASON
**Chad**
Cont. of: 3 AFR
neighbor: 5 LIBYA NIGER
8 CAMEROON
**Chadwick, Sir James**
discovery: 7 NEUTRON
**Chafe:** 3 IRK RUB 6 ABRADE
**Chaff**
Free grain from: 6 WINNOW
**Chaffee**
Skier: 4 SUZY
**Chagall**
Artist: 4 MARC
**Chai:** 9 SPICEDTEA
**Chain**
Breakfast restaurant:
4 IHOP
Cinema: 5 LOEWS
component: 4 LINK 5 DAISY
concern: 8 WEAKLINK
Early discount gas: 4 HESS
European: 4 ALPS
Fast-food: 3 KFC 4 ROYS
5 ARBYS 7 HARDEES
Flowery: 3 LEI
found in cells: 3 RNA
Home furnishings: 4 IKEA
hotel, for short: 4 HOJO
Island: 3 LEI
letters: 3 DNA RNA
Mountain: 5 RANGE RIDGE
6 SIERRA 7 SIERRAS
of hills: 5 RIDGE 6 SIERRA
Sawlike: 6 SIERRA
Supermarket: 5 AANDP
Swedish: 4 IKEA
units (abbr.): 3 MTS
Watch: 3 FOB
wearer: 3 MRT
with links: 4 IHOP
**"Chain Gang"**
singer: 5 COOKE
**"Chain Reaction"**
actor Reeves: 5 KEANU
**Chains**
Actor in: 3 MRT

**Chair:** 4 SEAT
back: 5 SPLAT
Barber ~ attachment: 5 STROP
builder: 5 CANER
Carried: 5 SEDAN
designer: 5 EAMES
Easy ~ site: 3 DEN
Fall into a: 4 PLOP
Kind of: 5 EAMES
Left the: 5 AROSE
man: 5 EAMES
part: 3 ARM LEG 4 SLAT
person: 5 TAMER
piece: 4 SLAT
Pull up a: 3 SIT
raising experience: 4 HORA
supporter: 3 LEG
Take a: 3 SIT
Took a: 3 SAT
Use an easy: 7 RECLINE
Working on a ~, perhaps:
6 CANING
**Chaired:** 3 LED
**Chairlift**
alternative: 4 TBAR
**Chairmaker:** 5 CANER
**Chairman**
Chinese: 3 MAO
Former CBS: 5 TISCH
need: 5 GAVEL 6 AGENDA
Nixon impeachment:
6 RODINO
of note: 3 MAO
~ Arafat: 5 YASIR
~ Greenspan: 4 ALAN
**Chairperson:** 5 CANER
list: 6 AGENDA
**Chairs**
Like some: 5 CANED
**Chairwoman:** 5 MADAM
**Chaka**
Singer: 4 KHAN
**Chakra**
releasing discipline: 4 YOGA
**Chalcedony:** 4 SARD 5 AGATE
**Chalet**
backdrop: 3 ALP
environs: 7 SKIAREA
Like a: 5 EAVED
shape: 6 AFRAME
Strand at the: 5 ICEIN
**Chaliapin:** 5 BASSO
and others: 5 BASSI
**Chalice:** 5 GRAIL
partner: 5 PATEN
**Chalk**
French: 4 TALC
remover: 6 ERASER
user: 6 TAILOR
**Chalkboard**
Clear the: 5 ERASE
**Chalky-cheeked:** 5 ASHEN
**Challenge:** 4 DARE DEFY
Alley: 5 SPLIT
Barber's: 3 MOP
Climber's: 3 ALP 4 CRAG

for a nonnative speaker:
5 IDIOM
Golfer's: 6 DOGLEG
Lab rat: 4 MAZE
Laundry: 5 STAIN 6 GREASE
Mover's: 5 PIANO
Oater's: 4 DRAW
Parenting: 4 TEEN
Poker: 5 ICALL
Presents a:
15 TESTSONESMETTLE
Ready for any: 5 CANDO
Schoolyard: 4 DARE
6 MAKEME
~, metaphorically: 4 HILL
**Challenged**
Socially ~ person: 4 NERD
When: 7 ONADARE
**Challenger:** 5 RIVAL
astronaut Judith: 6 RESNIK
Clinton's: 4 DOLE
Dwight's: 5 ADLAI
letters: 4 NASA
quest: 5 TITLE
Stalin's: 4 TITO
**Chalmers**
business partner: 5 ALLIS
**Châlons**
Loser at: 6 ATTILA
**Chalupa**
kin: 4 TACO
**Chamber:** 4 ROOM
Baking: 4 OVEN
Casa: 4 SALA
Cloud ~ particle: 3 ION
composition: 5 NONET
Firing: 4 KILN
group: 4 TRIO 5 NONET
OCTET 6 SEPTET
Harem: 3 ODA
Kind of: 3 ION 4 ECHO
opening: 4 ANTE
piece: 7 ARMOIRE
Schubert ~ work:
12 TROUTQUINTET
Underground: 4 CAVE
5 CRYPT
worker (abbr.): 3 SEN
**Chambered**
mollusks: 7 NAUTILI
**Chamberlain**
of basketball: 4 WILT
TV role for: 7 KILDARE
**Chamberlain, Neville**
reputation: 8 APPEASER
**Chambers**
Heart: 5 ATRIA
**Chamomile:** 3 TEA
**Chamonix**
nix: 3 NON
View from: 3 ALP 4 ALPE
ALPS 5 ALPES
**Champ**
Batting: 4 ALOU 5 BRETT
CAREW OLIVA
Boxing: 3 ALI 4 BAER ZALE

Chess: 3 TAL
Golf: 3 ELS 4 LEMA 5 SNEAD
  15 SEVEBALLESTEROS
holding: 5 TITLE
Home run: 3 OTT 5 KINER
  MARIS
Indy: 4 ARIE
Ski: 5 MAHRE
Tennis: 4 ASHE BORG GRAF
  5 EVERT LAVER LENDL
  SELES 6 AGASSI
**Champagne**
bucket: 4 ICER
city: 5 REIMS
cocktail: 6 MIMOSA
designation: 3 SEC 4 BRUT
does this: 7 SPARKLE
Dry: 4 BRUT
glass: 5 FLUTE
glass part: 4 STEM
name: 4 MOET MUMM
**"Champagne music"**
player: 4 WELK
**Champagne Tony**
of golf: 4 LEMA
**Champaign**
st.: 3 ILL
**Champigny-___-Marne:** 3 SUR
**Champing**
at the bit: 5 ANTSY EAGER
  READY
**Champion:** 3 ACE
boast: 4 IWON
claim: 5 TITLE
Its ~ is called "yokozuna":
  4 SUMO
rider: 5 AUTRY
**Championship:** 5 TITLE
**Champs ___:** 6 ELYSEE
**Champs Élysées**
feature: 4 CAFE
**Chan**
phrase: 4 AHSO
player of TV: 5 NAISH
portrayer: 5 OLAND TOLER
**Chan, Charlie**
creator Earl ___ Biggers:
  4 DERR
**Chance:** 3 BET HAP LOT
  4 RISK 5 BETON
50–50 ~: 6 TOSSUP
By any: 4 EVER
Discover by: 5 HITON
Discovered by: 5 LITON
Even: 6 TOSSUP
for a hit: 5 ATBAT
Game of: 4 KENO 5 BEANO
  LOTTO
Meet by: 8 BUMPINTO
Second:
  15 ANEWLEASEONLIFE
Student's second: 6 RETEST
Take a: 3 BET 4 DARE
  5 WAGER 6 GAMBLE
Take a ~ on: 4 RISK
Take the: 6 RISKIT

to play: 4 TURN
to speak: 3 SAY
upon: 4 MEET
With zero: 5 NOHOW
**"___ chance!":** 3 FAT 4 NOTA
**Chanced**
upon: 3 MET
**Chancel**
cross: 4 ROOD
**Chancellor**
First ~ of reunified Germany:
  4 KOHL
~ Adenauer: 6 KONRAD
~ Bismarck: 4 OTTO
~ Willy: 6 BRANDT
**Chancellorsville**
fighter: 3 REB
**Chances:** 4 ODDS
Like some: 4 SLIM
~, briefly: 3 OPS
**"Chances ___":** 3 ARE
**"Chances Are"**
singer: 6 MATHIS
**Chandler**
Actress: 5 ESTEE
Buddy of: 4 ROSS
Publisher: 4 OTIS
**___ & Chandon:** 4 MOET
**Chanel**
Designer: 4 COCO
**Chaney**
Actor: 3 LON
**Chang:** 4 TWIN
homeland: 4 SIAM
Twin of: 3 ENG
**Change:** 4 REDO VARY
  5 ALTER AMEND
  EMEND 6 AFFECT
  MUTATE REVISE
  SWITCH
a bill: 5 AMEND
addresses: 4 MOVE
Bit of: 4 CENT DIME
chemically: 5 REACT
color: 3 DYE
color again: 5 REDYE
Continuous: 4 FLUX
course: 3 ZIG 4 TURN VEER
Editor's ~ of heart: 4 STET
Element of: 4 CENT COIN
  DIME
for a five: 4 ONES
for a twenty: 4 TENS
form: 5 MORPH
for the better: 4 EDIT
  5 AMEND
in Chile: 4 PESO
Kind of: 5 LOOSE
machine input: 4 ONES
Minimal: 4 CENT
on the beach: 3 TAN
over time: 6 EVOLVE
places: 4 MOVE 7 MIGRATE
Resist: 8 STANDPAT
Resistance to: 7 INERTIA
Seek: 3 BEG

Sharp ~ in direction: 3 ZIG
Short: 3 CTS
Small: 5 CENTS DIMES
  PENNY
Spare: 4 TIRE
states: 4 MELT
the borders of: 5 REMAP
  6 REZONE
the décor: 4 REDO
the focus of: 8 REDIRECT
the look of: 7 RESTYLE
the price on: 5 RETAG
to suit: 5 ADAPT
Without: 4 ASIS
**"___ changed man!":** 3 IMA
**Changer**
Lane ~ concern: 9 BLINDSPOT
Money: 6 EDITOR
**Changes**
Book of: 6 ICHING
If nothing: 6 ASITIS
Scene of many: 6 CABANA
**Changing**
place: 6 CABANA
Without money ~ hands:
  7 INTRADE
**Channel:** 3 RUT WAY 4 DUCT
  LANE 5 STEER
  6 GROOVE STRAIT
  STREAM TRENCH
Artificial water: 6 SLUICE
Cable: 3 AMC HBO TNT USA
  4 ESPN 5 AANDE
Chimney: 4 FLUE
choker: 4 SILT
Emergency CB: 4 NINE
English: 3 BBC
Former cable: 3 TNN
marker: 4 BUOY
Political: 5 CSPAN
Premium: 3 HBO
Shopping: 3 QVC
surfer locale: 8 RECLINER
swimmer Gertrude: 6 EDERLE
Water: 6 SLUICE
**___ Channel:** 5 SCIFI
**Channeling**
state: 6 TRANCE
**Channel Islands**
One of the: 4 SARK 6 JERSEY
**Channels**
Turner of: 3 TED
TV ~ 2–13: 3 VHF
TV ~ 14 and up: 3 UHF
Went through: 6 SURFED
**Channing**
of Broadway: 5 CAROL
**Chanson de ___:** 5 GESTE
**Chant:** 6 INTONE
Olympics: 3 USA 6 USAUSA
Start of a pirate: 4 YOHO
with the cheerleaders: 4 ROOT
**Chanted**
word: 6 MANTRA
**Chanteuse**
~ Adams: 4 EDIE

~ Edith: 4 PIAF
~ Horne: 4 LENA
**Chantey**
locale: 3 SEA
singer: 6 SAILOR
**Chantilly:** 4 LACE
department: 4 OISE
product: 4 LACE
river: 4 OISE
**Chaos:** 4 MESS RIOT
6 MAYHEM 7 ANARCHY
Daughter of: 4 GAEA GAIA
It's: 3 ZOO
Son of: 4 EROS
Tendency toward: 7 ENTROPY
Utter: 6 BEDLAM
**Chaotic:** 5 MESSY SNAFU
6 HECTIC
Cause of ~ weather: 6 ELNINO
scene: 3 ZOO
situation: 5 SNAFU
**Chap:** 3 GUY JOE LAD MAN
4 DUDE GENT 5 BLOKE
BUCKO FELLA
Chelsea: 4 BRIT
Words to an old: 4 ISAY
**Chapeau:** 3 HAT 5 BERET
holder: 4 TETE
**Chapel**
fixture: 3 PEW
part: 4 APSE
Run off to the: 5 ELOPE
Sound from a ~ tower: 4 PEAL
top: 5 SPIRE
vow: 3 IDO
___ **Chapel:** 7 SISTINE
**Chapel Hill**
sch.: 3 UNC
student: 7 TARHEEL
**Chaperone:** 6 ESCORT
**Chaplain**
Military: 5 PADRE
**Chaplin**
brother: 3 SYD
employer: 7 SENNETT
Mrs.: 4 OONA
persona: 5 TRAMP
prop: 4 CANE
title: 3 SIR
**"Chaplin"**
actress Kelly: 5 MOIRA
**Chaplin, Geraldine**
Mother of: 4 OONA
**Chapped:** 3 RED
**Chaps:** 3 MEN
**Chapter:** 4 PART
Chaucer: 4 TALE
in history: 3 ERA
partner: 5 VERSE
Serial: 7 EPISODE
Textbook: 4 UNIT
**Chapter 11**
cause: 4 DEBT
**Chapter and ___:** 5 VERSE
**"Chapter on Ears, A"**
writer: 4 ELIA

**Chapters**
They have: 6 UNIONS
**Char:** 4 SEAR 5 SINGE
**Character:** 4 ROLE TONE
5 AROMA ETHOS TENOR
6 ASPECT NATURE
Ancient: 4 RUNE
Animated: 4 TOON
Blue: 5 SMURF
builder: 4 GENE
Community: 5 ETHOS
Crowd-scene: 5 EXTRA
Do some ~ assassination:
5 ERASE
Homeric: 3 ETA
Mysterious: 4 RUNE
Opposite in: 5 POLAR
part: 4 GENE 5 TRAIT
PC ~ set: 5 ASCII
Step into: 3 ACT
Uncool: 4 NERD
**Characteristic:** 5 TRAIT
carrier: 4 GENE
**Characterize:** 6 DEPICT
**Charade:** 3 ACT 4 MIME
**Charades:** 4 GAME
Play: 4 MIME 6 ACTOUT
~, basically: 6 MIMING
8 GESTURES
**Charcoal**
wood: 5 ALDER
**Chardonnay:** 4 WINE
**Charen**
Author: 4 MONA
**Charge:** 3 FEE 4 BILL CARE
COST FARE GOAT TASK
WARD 5 DEBIT PRICE
RUNAT STORM
6 ACCUSE ALLEGE
INDICT IONIZE ONRUSH
RUSHAT TILTAT
Answer a: 5 PLEAD
Answered a: 4 PLED
Answer to a: 4 PLEA
At no: 4 FREE
Atom with a: 3 ION
Bee's: 4 OPIE
Be in: 4 RULE 5 REIGN
Be in ~ of: 4 HEAD
carrier: 3 ION
Club: 4 FEES
Criminal: 3 RAP
Daily: 4 RATE
Depth: 6 ASHCAN
Eunuch's: 3 ODA 5 HAREM
Extra: 5 ADDON
Fixed: 6 SETFEE
In: 15 WEARINGTHEPANTS
In ~ of: 4 OVER
It has a negative: 5 ANION
It's not free of: 3 ION
Membership: 3 FEE
per unit: 4 RATE
Professional: 3 FEE
Service: 3 FEE 4 TOLL
Sitter: 3 TOT

the passer: 5 BLITZ
Took: 3 LED
Took ~ of: 3 RAN
Unfair: 6 BADRAP BUMRAP
**Charged:** 5 HADAT IONIC
RANAT 6 WENTAT
Create ~ particles: 6 IONIZE
Negatively: 7 ANIONIC
particle: 3 ION 5 ANION
Weight not ~ for: 4 TARE
**Charger:** 5 STEED
8 WARHORSE
African: 5 RHINO
array: 5 DEBTS
Corrida: 4 TORO 6 ELTORO
**Chargers:** 4 TEAM
home: 8 SANDIEGO
**Charges**
Facing: 7 ONTRIAL
Teacher's: 5 CLASS
**Charging**
need: 6 CREDIT
**Chariot**
rider of myth: 3 EOS 4 THOR
suffix: 3 EER
**"Chariots of Fire"**
actor Charleson: 3 IAN
**Charismatic**
trait: 4 AURA
**Charisse**
Dancer: 3 CYD
**Charitable**
Be: 6 DONATE
donation: 4 ALMS
offering: 4 ALMS
**Charitably**
hand out: 4 DOLE
**Charity:** 4 ALMS DOLE
5 DONEE
event: 5 BAZAAR
Give to: 6 DONATE
Hope and ~ partner: 5 FAITH
Popular: 9 UNITEDWAY
recipient: 5 DONEE
**Charlatan:** 5 FAKER FRAUD
**Charlemagne**
capital: 6 AACHEN
domain:
15 HOLYROMANEMPIRE
domain (abbr.): 3 HRE
**Charles:** 3 ROI 4 HEIR
and others: 4 RAYS 5 NORAS
Author: 5 READE
barker: 4 ASTA
Bodybuilder: 5 ATLAS
Bridge expert: 5 GOREN
Chair designer: 5 EAMES
Composer: 4 IVES
Former senator: 4 ROBB
Mrs.: 4 NORA
Newsman: 6 OSGOOD
Newsreel pioneer: 5 PATHE
or Louis: 3 ROI
pastime: 4 POLO
Poet: 5 OLSON
Sch. on the: 3 MIT

Singer: 3 RAY
**Charles, Ray**
hit: 5 NOONE
    15 GEORGIAONMYMIND
**Charles ___, Sir**
Geologist: 5 LYELL
**Charles II**
mistress: 4 NELL
painter: 4 LELY
**"Charles in Charge"**
actor Willie: 5 AAMES
star: 4 BAIO
**Charleston**
fort: 6 SUMTER
st.: 3 WVA
**Charley**
horse: 4 ACHE 5 CRAMP
    SPASM
**Charlie:** 4 TUNA
Actor: 5 SHEEN
Detective: 4 CHAN
of PBS: 4 ROSE
of the Honolulu P.D.: 4 CHAN
Wife of: 4 OONA
**"Charlie and the Chocolate
    Factory"**
author: 4 DAHL
**"Charlie Hustle":** 4 ROSE
    8 PETEROSE
**"Charlie's Angels"**
actress Lucy: 3 LIU
actress Roberts: 5 TANYA
actress Smith: 6 JACLYN
angel: 4 KRIS
**Charlize**
Actress: 6 THERON
**Charlotte**
Actress: 3 RAE
Comic: 3 RAE
creation: 3 WEB
**Charlotte ___:** 5 RUSSE
    6 AMALIE
**Charlottesville**
sch.: 3 UVA
**"Charlotte's Web"**
author: 7 EBWHITE
boy: 5 AVERY
monogram: 3 EBW
**Charlottetown**
prov.: 3 PEI
**Charlton**
Actor: 6 HESTON
role: 5 MOSES
**"Charly"**
actress Bloom: 6 CLAIRE
**Charm:** 3 HEX 4 MOJO
    5 AMUSE 6 ALLURE
    AMULET DISARM
    ENAMOR ENDEAR
    FETISH 7 ENCHANT
    8 TALISMAN
Magic: 4 MOJO 6 AMULET
Radiate: 4 OOZE 5 EXUDE
Voodoo: 4 MOJO 5 OBEAH
**Charmed**
one: 5 COBRA

particle: 5 QUARK
**Charmee**
Snake: 3 EVE
**Charmer**
Snake for a: 5 COBRA
**Charming:** 6 QUAINT
    8 ENGAGING
**Charon**
is its moon: 5 PLUTO
river: 4 STYX
**Charred:** 5 BURNT
**Chart:** 3 MAP 5 GRAPH TABLE
anew: 5 REMAP
Genealogy: 4 TREE
Heart: 3 EKG
holder: 5 EASEL
Kind of: 3 PIE 4 FLIP 5 NATAL
shape: 3 PIE
topper: 3 HIT
**Charter:** 3 LET 4 HIRE RENT
    5 LEASE
again: 5 RELET
**Chas.**
Mother of: 4 ELIZ
**Chase:** 4 SHAG SHOO
    7 GOAFTER
Actress: 4 ILKA
off: 4 SHOO
**Chaser**
Info: Suffix cue
Bar: 4 SHOT
Bugs: 5 ELMER
Magnum: 4 OPUS
Mob: 4 STER
Narc: 4 OTIC
Nymph: 5 SATYR
Pusher: 4 NARC
Status: 3 QUO
Whiskey: 5 AGOGO
**Chasers:** 5 POSSE
AWOL: 3 MPS
**Chasing:** 5 AFTER
**Chasm:** 4 GULF 5 ABYSS
    GORGE
Deep: 5 ABYSS 6 CANYON
**Chast**
Cartoonist: 3 ROZ
**Chaste:** 4 PURE
**Chastity**
Mom of: 4 CHER
Sonny or: 4 BONO
**Chat:** 3 JAW 4 TALK
    9 TETEATETE
    14 SHOOTTHEBREEZE
Cat: 4 MEOW
Have a ~ with: 6 TALKTO
Informal: 10 RAPSESSION
Private: 9 TETEATETE
sites: 9 FIRESIDES
You may ~ on it: 3 AOL
___ chat: 5 PASDE
**Chateaubriand:** 5 STEAK
**Chateau-Thierry**
river: 5 MARNE
**Chatelaine**
rival: 4 ELLE

**Chat room**
chuckle: 3 LOL
initials: 4 IMHO
nonparticipant: 6 LURKER
provider: 3 AOL
**Chats**
online: 3 IMS
**Chatter:** 3 GAB JAW YAK YAP
    4 BLAB 5 PRATE RUNON
Idle: 10 YACKETYYAK
Like some: 4 IDLE
on the road: 4 CBER
**Chatterbox:** 6 MAGPIE TALKER
    YABBER
**Chatty**
bird: 4 MYNA 5 MYNAH
**Chaucer**
offering: 4 TALE
pilgrim: 5 REEVE
Wife's place in a ~ tale:
    4 BATH
**Chaud**
time: 3 ETE
**Chauffeur:** 6 DRIVER
Order to a: 4 HOME
vehicle: 4 LIMO
Word to the: 5 DRIVE
**Chauncey**
Orator: 5 DEPEW
**Chauvinistic**
type: 6 SEXIST
**Chavez**
Labor leader: 5 CESAR
**Che**
compadre: 5 FIDEL
Revolutionary: 7 GUEVARA
~, formally: 7 ERNESTO
**Cheap:** 5 TATTY 6 TRASHY
    7 CHINTZY
accommodations:
    8 STEERAGE
bar: 7 GINMILL
cigar: 6 STOGIE
jewelry: 5 PASTE
Like ~ pianos: 5 TINNY
liquor: 6 ROTGUT
mags: 5 PULPS
Not: 4 DEAR
so-and-so: 5 PIKER
tire: 7 RETREAD
way to live: 8 RENTFREE
**"Cheap Detective, The"**
star: 4 FALK
**Cheapen:** 6 DEBASE
    7 DEVALUE
**Cheaper:** 6 ONSALE
**Cheaply:** 8 FORASONG
**Cheapskate:** 5 MISER PIKER
    7 SCROOGE STINTER
**Cheat:** 3 GYP 4 BILK GULL
    HOSE REAM ROOK
    SCAM 5 COZEN 6 CHISEL
    CONMAN
on: 7 TWOTIME
sheet: 4 TROT
~, in a way: 4 COPY PEEK

**Cheater**
aid: 4 CRIB
**Check:** 3 TAB 4 BILL CURB
HALT REIN STEM STOP
TEST 5 BLOCK DETER
6 ARREST REININ
REREAD STANCH
Alimony ~ cashers: 4 EXES
Bad ~ letters: 3 NSF
books: 5 AUDIT
Bouncers ~ them: 3 IDS
casher: 5 PAYEE
copy: 4 EDIT
endorser: 5 PAYEE
entry: 4 DATE 6 AMOUNT
falsifier: 5 KITER
fig.: 3 AMT
for accuracy: 3 VET
for Checkers: 5 LEASH
for fit: 5 TRYON
for prints: 4 DUST
Grab the: 5 TREAT
In: 5 ATBAY
letters: 3 NSF
Make a ~ for later:
8 POSTDATE
mark: 4 TICK
mate: 4 STUB
out: 3 EYE VET 4 OGLE SCAN
TEST 5 AUDIT TALLY
7 EXAMINE 8 LOOKINTO
(out): 5 SCOPE
out before a heist: 4 CASE
out the sites: 4 SURF
payee: 6 BEARER
Pick up the: 5 TREAT
point: 4 BANK
Rain ~, often: 4 STUB
recipient: 5 PAYEE
Sign the back of a: 7 ENDORSE
Something to: 3 BAG HAT IDS
4 COAT
the check: 3 ADD 5 READD
Traveler's: 3 MAP
Word on a sample: 4 VOID
words: 5 PAYTO
writer: 5 PAYER
**Checkbook**
item: 4 STUB
**Check-cashing**
needs: 3 IDS
**Checked**
for fit: 7 TRIEDON
**Checker:** 4 DISC TAXI
Double: 4 KING
Spot: 3 VET 4 SPCA 5 LEASH
**Checker, Chubby**
dance: 5 TWIST
**Checkerboard**
rows, e.g.: 6 OCTETS
**Checkered:** 5 PLAID
It has a ~ past: 4 TAXI
It may be: 4 PAST
**Checkers:** 3 MEN 4 GAME
Check for: 5 LEASH
color: 3 RED

Half the: 4 REDS
**Checking**
Kind of ~ account: 5 NOFEE
out: 5 EYING 6 EYEING
**"check is in the mail, The":**
3 LIE
**"Check it out!":** 4 LOOK
5 GOSEE
**Checklist**
part: 4 ITEM
**Checkout**
bars (abbr.): 3 UPC
count: 5 ITEMS
item: 7 SCANNER
task: 4 SCAN
Work at a ~ counter: 3 BAG
**Checkpoint**
requests: 3 IDS
**Checkroom**
item: 3 HAT 4 COAT
**Checks**
Like some ~ (abbr.): 4 CERT
**"Check this out!":** 4 PSST
**Checkup:** 4 EXAM TEST
request: 5 SAYAH
sounds: 3 AHS
**Cheddar**
Like some: 4 AGED MILD
5 SHARP
**Cheech**
Actor: 5 MARIN
Ex-partner of: 5 CHONG
**Cheek:** 4 JOWL SASS 5 NERVE
coloring: 5 ROUGE
dampener: 4 TEAR
Of the: 5 MALAR
**Cheekiness:** 4 SASS
**Cheeks**
Like some: 4 ROSY
**"Cheek to Cheek"**
musical: 6 TOPHAT
**Cheeky:** 4 PERT WISE
5 SASSY
**Cheep**
place: 4 NEST
**Cheer:** 3 RAH 4 ROOT YELL
5 ELATE 7 GLADDEN
HEARTEN
Beer: 5 SKOAL
Bronx: 4 GIBE HOOT JEER
RAZZ
Bullring: 3 OLE
competitor: 3 ERA
(for): 4 ROOT
Full of: 5 MERRY
Half a: 5 BOOLA
Object of an old French:
5 LEROI
Olympics: 3 USA
Palindromic: 3 YAY
School: 4 YELL 6 GOTEAM
Spanish: 3 OLE
Stadium: 3 RAH
starter: 3 HIP SIS 4 VIVA
Word of: 3 RAH YEA
Yale: 5 BOOLA

**Cheerful:** 3 GAY 4 GLAD ROSY
5 RIANT SUNNY
6 BLITHE UPBEAT
8 SANGUINE
tune: 4 LILT
**Cheering:** 5 AROAR
sound: 3 RAH
**"Cheerio!":** 4 TATA 5 SEEYA
**Cheerios**
grain: 3 OAT
Like: 4 OATY 5 OATEN
**Cheerleader**
cheer: 4 YELL
cry: 3 RAH 6 GOTEAM
feat: 6 SPLITS
skirt: 4 MINI
**Cheerleaders**
Chant with the: 4 ROOT
Group of: 5 SQUAD
Most: 4 SHES
**Cheerless:** 4 DRAB GRIM
5 BLEAK DREAR STARK
6 DISMAL
**"Cheers"**
actor Danson: 3 TED
actor George: 5 WENDT
actor Roger: 4 REES
actress Neuwirth: 4 BEBE
actress Perlman: 4 RHEA
barfly: 4 NORM
barmaid: 5 CARLA
bartender: 3 SAM 6 MALONE
Bebe on: 6 LILITH
Carla on: 4 RHEA
Diane's successor on:
7 REBECCA
fixture: 8 BARSTOOL
Norm's wife on: 4 VERA
perch: 5 STOOL
regular: 4 NORM
Rhea on: 5 CARLA
role: 3 SAM 5 CARLA DIANE
setting: 3 BAR
star: 6 DANSON
waitress: 5 CARLA DIANE
**"Cheers!":** 5 SKOAL
9 BOTTOMSUP
**Cheery:** 3 GAY 4 GLAD ROSY
5 RIANT SUNNY
6 BLITHE UPBEAT
8 SANGUINE
tune: 4 LILT
**Cheese**
Ball-shaped: 4 EDAM
Big: 4 BOSS EXEC 5 NABOB
6 TOPDOG
Big name in: 5 KRAFT
Brine-cured: 4 FETA
burg: 4 EDAM
choice: 4 BRIE 5 SWISS
coating: 4 RIND
Creamy: 4 BRIE
Crumbly: 4 FETA
dish: 7 RAREBIT
Dutch: 4 EDAM 5 GOUDA
etc.: 5 DAIRY

for crackers: 4 BRIE
French: 4 BRIE
Goat: 4 FETA
Greek: 4 FETA
Hunk of: 4 SLAB
Italian: 6 ROMANO
  8 PARMESAN
Kind of: 5 NACHO
  7 PIMENTO
Like some: 4 AGED 5 SHARP
Like Swiss: 5 HOLEY
made from ewe's milk:
  6 ROMANO
Mild: 4 EDAM 5 GOUDA
Mold-ripened: 4 BRIE
nibblers: 4 MICE
Party: 4 BRIE EDAM
Pickled: 4 FETA
Red-wrapped: 4 EDAM
  5 GOUDA
region: 4 BRIE
Romano ~ source: 3 EWE
Round: 4 EDAM
Salad: 4 FETA
Sharp: 6 ROMANO
Soft: 4 BRIE
Spreadable: 4 BRIE
Wax-coated: 4 EDAM
White: 4 BRIE
with holes: 7 HAVARTI
**"Cheese"**
action: 5 SMILE
___ cheese: 4 BLEU
**Cheeseboard**
ball: 4 EDAM
**Cheesecake**
Bit of: 3 GAM
**Cheesehead**
st.: 4 WISC
**Cheesemaking**
leftover: 4 WHEY
**Cheesy**
dish: 7 RAREBIT
morsel: 5 NACHO
sandwich: 4 MELT
**Cheetah**
Like a: 4 FAST
**Chef**
catchphrase: 3 ALA
collection: 7 RECIPES
d'état: 3 ROI
direction: 4 STIR
flavoring: 4 HERB
French ~ cry: 7 ETVOILA
gadget: 5 DICER RICER
Good name for a: 3 STU
herb: 4 SAGE
mixture: 4 ROUX
phrase: 3 ALA
protector: 5 APRON
protectors: 5 MITTS
seasoning: 4 HERB
~, at times: 4 ICER 5 DICER
  6 SPICER
~ Graham: 4 KERR
~ Julia: 5 CHILD

~ Lagasse: 6 EMERIL
~ Martin: 3 YAN
**"Che gelida manina"**: 4 ARIA
**Chekhov**
First play of: 6 IVANOV
Playwright: 5 ANTON
Sister in a ~ play: 4 OLGA
  5 IRINA MASHA
Uncle in a ~ play: 5 VANYA
**Chekov**
neighbor: 4 SULU
**Chelsea**
Info: British cue
chap: 4 BRIT
**Chem.:** 3 SCI
class: 3 LAB
class data: 5 ATNOS
lab array: 5 ACIDS
neurotransmitter: 3 ATP
pollutant: 3 PCB
unit: 3 MOL
**Chemical**
analysis: 5 ASSAY
Aromatic: 5 ESTER
Caustic: 3 LYE
compound: 4 ENOL 5 ESTER
  6 ISOMER
Copier: 5 TONER
Corrosive: 4 ACID
ending: 3 ANE ENE IDE INE
  ITE
extract: 5 EDUCT
Fertilizer: 4 UREA
prefix: 5 PETRO
salt: 6 IODIDE
suffix: 3 ANE ENE IDE INE
  ITE
Type of ~ bond: 5 IONIC
**Chemical-free:** 7 NATURAL
**Chemically**
Change: 5 REACT
nonreactive: 5 INERT
**Chemicals**
Big name in: 3 DOW 4 OLIN
  6 DUPONT
**Chemin de ___:** 3 FER
**Chemist**
condiment: 4 NACL
workplace: 3 LAB
**Chemistry**
B in: 5 BORON
class cost: 6 LABFEE
Kind of: 7 ORGANIC
Nobelist in: 4 HAHN UREY
  5 CURIE
Twin, in: 6 ISOMER
~ Nobelist: *see pages 730–731*
**Cheney:** 4 VEEP
predecessor: 4 GORE
  6 ALGORE
**Cheng-chou**
province: 5 HONAN
**Chenin ___:** 5 BLANC
**Cher**
Ex of: 4 BONO 5 SONNY
film: 4 MASK

**Cherbourg**
Info: French cue
**"Cherchez la ___":** 5 FEMME
**Cheri**
Actress: 5 OTERI
**Cherish:** 4 LOVE 5 ADORE
  PRIZE 6 ESTEEM
**Cherished**
relation: 8 LOVEDONE
**Chero-Cola**
Company formerly known as:
  4 NEHI
**Cherokee:** 4 JEEP
**Cherokee Strip**
city: 4 ENID
**Cheroot:** 5 CIGAR 6 STOGIE
**Cherry:** 3 RED 4 TREE
and others: 4 REDS
brandy: 6 KIRSCH
holder: 4 STEM
picker: 5 CRANE
Pie: 7 MORELLO
pit: 5 STONE
red: 6 CERISE
Singer: 5 NENEH
stone: 3 PIT
Sweet: 4 BING
variety: 4 BING
**Cherry ___:** 4 COLA
**Cherub:** 5 ANGEL
archer: 4 AMOR
superior: 6 SERAPH
**Chervil:** 4 HERB
**Cheryl**
Actress: 4 LADD
and Alan: 5 LADDS
Supermodel: 5 TIEGS
**Chesapeake**
catch: 4 CRAB
**Cheshire Cat**
look: 4 GRIN
**Chess:** 4 GAME
1960 ~ champ: 3 TAL
action: 4 MOVE
castle: 4 ROOK
champion Mikhail: 3 TAL
Computer ~ machine:
  8 DEEPBLUE
ending: 4 MATE
Japanese: 5 SHOGI
Least valuable ~ piece: 4 PAWN
opening: 3 CEE 6 GAMBIT
piece: 3 MAN 4 KING PAWN
  ROOK
pieces (abbr.): 3 KTS
Queenside castle, in ~ notation:
  3 OOO
rival of Bobby: 5 BORIS
sequence: 7 ENDGAME
Won at: 5 MATED
World ~ org.: 4 FIDE
**Chessboard**
row: 4 RANK
**Chest:** 5 TORSO 6 THORAX
beater: 3 APE 5 HEART
display: 5 MEDAL

filler: 4 LUNG
Kind of: 3 ICE TOY WAR
   5 CEDAR
material: 5 CEDAR
Medieval: 4 ARCA
muscle: 3 PEC
of drawers: 6 BUREAU
   7 DRESSER
part: 6 DRAWER
protector: 3 BIB RIB 4 VEST
Sacred: 3 ARC
Trunk with a: 5 TORSO
wood: 5 CEDAR
**Chesterfield:** 4 COAT SOFA
   8 OVERCOAT
**Chester White**
home: 3 STY
**Chestnut:** 4 TREE 5 HORSE
coating: 3 BUR
horse: 4 ROAN
**Chestnut-colored:** 4 ROAN
ruminant: 7 REDDEER
**Chestnuts**
Cook: 5 ROAST
**Chest-thumping:** 5 MACHO
**Chet**
Guitarist: 6 ATKINS
**Chevalier**
film: 4 GIGI
song: 4 MIMI
trademark: 8 STRAWHAT
**Chevrolet**
introduced in 1966: 6 CAMARO
**Chevron**
Chevron's: 4 LOGO
rival: 4 ARCO ESSO
wearer (abbr.): 3 NCO
**Chevy**
Classic: 6 IMPALA
cohort: 5 GILDA
minivan: 5 ASTRO
model: 4 AVEO 6 CAMARO
   LUMINA MALIBU
   7 CORSICA
Old: 4 NOVA VEGA
   6 IMPALA
Sporty: 5 VETTE 6 CAMARO
truck: 5 TAHOE
vehicle of the 1970s: 3 SNL
~ SUV: 5 TAHOE 6 BLAZER
**Chew:** 4 GNAW
Cow: 3 CUD
(on): 4 GNAW 5 MUNCH
out: 5 SCOLD 7 TELLOFF
Something to: 3 CUD GUM
   6 THEFAT
the fat: 3 GAB JAW YAK
   4 CHAT 8 SCHMOOZE
the rag: 3 YAK
the scenery: 5 EMOTE
   7 HAMITUP OVERACT
**Chewable**
nut: 5 BETEL
**Chewer**
Bamboo: 5 PANDA
Scenery: 3 HAM 6 EMOTER

**Chewing gum:** 6 CHICLE
**Chewy**
candy: 5 TAFFY 6 NOUGAT
   TOFFEE 7 CARAMEL
**Cheyenne**
ally: 7 ARAPAHO
county: 7 LARAMIE
shelter: 5 TEPEE
**Chg.**
Type of: 3 NEG
**Chi**
follower: 3 PSI 4 MINH
hrs.: 3 CDT CST
paper: 4 TRIB
preceder: 3 TAI
**Chi.**
setting: 3 CDT CST
___ chi: 3 TAI
**Chiang**
opponent: 3 MAO
**Chiang Kai-shek**
capital: 6 TAIPEI
**Chiang** ___-shek: 3 KAI
**Chianti:** 4 VINO WINE
color: 3 RED
Like: 3 DRY SEC
**Chic:** 5 STYLE 6 CLASSY
   SWANKY TRENDY
   7 ALAMODE ELEGANT
   INSTYLE STYLISH
getaways: 4 SPAS
More: 6 TONIER
Revivalist: 5 RETRO
___ chic: 4 TRES
**Chicago**
1974 ~ hit: 8 CALLONME
airport: 5 OHARE
airport code: 3 ORD
area: 4 LOOP
Banks of: 5 ERNIE
Big name in: 5 DALEY
Boston or: 4 BAND
critic: 5 EBERT
Downtown: 7 THELOOP
exchange: 4 MERC
footballer: 4 BEAR
hrs.: 3 CST
hub: 5 OHARE
Like: 5 WINDY
maestro: 5 SOLTI
mayor: 5 DALEY
Mrs. of: 6 OLEARY
paper, briefly: 4 TRIB
state (abbr.): 3 ILL
suburb: 5 ELGIN NILES
   6 CICERO SKOKIE
   7 OAKLAWN
team: 3 SOX 4 CUBS
terminal: 5 OHARE
trains: 3 ELS
university: 6 DEPAUL
   LOYOLA
**"Chicago"**
actor: 4 GERE
actress Lucy: 3 LIU
actress Neuwirth: 4 BEBE

actress Zellweger: 5 RENEE
lyricist: 3 EBB
role: 5 VELMA
**Chicagoan**
Legendary: 9 MRSOLEARY
**Chicago Cubs**
Sammy of the: 4 SOSA
spring training site: 4 MESA
**"Chicago Hope"**
actor Adam: 5 ARKIN
actor Arkin: 4 ADAM
actress: 5 LAHTI
**Chichén** ___: 4 ITZA
**Chichén Itzá**
attraction: 5 RUINS
resident: 4 MAYA
**Chichester**
chap: 3 SOD 5 BLOKE
**Chichi:** 4 ARTY TONY 5 ARTSY
   SWANK 7 ALAMODE
___ chi ch'uan: 3 TAI
**Chick**
Jazz pianist: 5 COREA
mate: 4 DUDE
sound: 4 PEEP
suffix: 4 ADEE
**Chick-**___**-A:** 3 FIL
**Chickadee:** 8 TITMOUSE
**Chickadees:** 7 TITMICE
**Chickasaw:** 5 TRIBE
**Chicken:** 4 WIMP 5 SISSY
   6 COWARD SCARED
   TREPID
Big name in: 5 TYSON
   7 SANDERS
choice: 3 LEG 4 WING
   5 FRYER THIGH 6 BREAST
   7 ROASTER
dinner: 4 FEED
dish: 8 YAKITORI
Fixed: 5 CAPON
General ___ ~: 4 TSOS
house: 4 COOP 5 ROOST
in some dish names: 3 COQ
Little: 6 BANTAM
organ: 6 GIBLET
part: 4 NECK
preceder: 3 EGG
style: 4 KIEV 7 ALAKING
~, in Spanish: 5 POLLO
**Chicken** ___: 3 POX 4 KIEV
   6 LITTLE
**Chicken cordon** ___: 4 BLEU
**Chicken-king**
link: 3 ALA
**Chicken** ___ **king:** 3 ALA
**Chicken Little:** 8 ALARMIST
   9 PESSIMIST
**"Chicken Run"**
characters: 4 HENS
**Chickens**
and others: 4 FOWL
**Chico:** 4 MARX
**Chide:** 3 NAG 5 SCOLD
**Chiding**
sound: 3 TSK

**Chief:** 3 KEY TOP 4 ARCH
BOSS HEAD MAIN
5 MAJOR 6 LEADER
7 HEADMAN
Arab: 4 EMIR 5 EMEER
Clan: 5 THANE
Corp.: 4 EXEC
exec: 4 PRES PREZ
Former ~ Palestinian:
6 ARAFAT
Indian: 5 RAJAH
Magazine: 6 EDITOR
Muslim: 4 IMAM
point: 9 ESSENTIAL
steward: 9 MAJORDOMO
Tribal: 4 KHAN 6 SACHEM
Turkish: 3 AGA
~ Big Bear: 4 CREE
~ Greek god: 4 ZEUS
~ Norse god: 4 ODIN
~ Pontiac: 6 OTTAWA
~ Whitehorse: 4 OTOE
**Chief Justice**
1836–64 ~: 5 TANEY
1920s ~: 4 TAFT
1953–69 ~: 10 EARLWARREN
Dred Scott: 5 TANEY
First: 7 JOHNJAY
~ Warren: 4 EARL
**Chief of Staff**
Bush: 6 SUNUNU
Nixon: 4 HAIG
Reagan: 5 REGAN
**Chieftain**
Arab: 4 EMIR 5 EMEER
Mafia: 4 CAPO
Norse: 5 ROLLO
**Chiffon**
Like: 5 SHEER
Sturdy: 5 NINON
**Chiffons**
hit: 10 ONEFINEDAY
**Chigger:** 5 LARVA
**Chignon**
setting: 4 NAPE
**Chihuahua:** 5 STATE
**Info:** Spanish cue
Bark like a: 4 YELP
Cartoon: 3 REN
cash: 4 PESO
celebration: 6 FIESTA
cheer: 3 OLE
chicken: 5 POLLO
child: 4 NINO
home: 4 CASA
neighbor (abbr.): 4 NMEX
TV: 3 REN
wrap: 6 SERAPE
**Child:** 3 KID SON 4 BABE TYKE
Admonition to a: 4 NONO
6 BENICE
Annoying: 4 BRAT
appliance: 4 OVEN
Chihuahua: 4 NINO
direction: 4 STIR
Flower: 4 SEED 6 HIPPIE

god: 4 AMOR
Homeless: 4 WAIF
hood: 3 IMP
Kind of: 4 ONLY 5 INNER
Love: 4 EROS
Mexican: 4 NINA
of fortune: 4 HEIR
play: 3 TAG
seat: 3 LAP
Small: 3 TAD TOT
Spoiled: 4 BRAT
support: 4 KNEE
Wee: 5 BAIRN
welfare gps.: 4 PTAS
~, for one: 4 CHEF
~, in Spanish: 4 NINO
**Child-care**
writer LeShan: 3 EDA
**Childhood**
They're often removed in:
8 ADENOIDS
**Childish:** 7 PUERILE
**Children**
Bring up: 4 REAR
Card game for: 3 WAR
7 OLDMAID
doctor: 5 SEUSS
Game for: 3 TAG
Like proper: 4 SEEN
Nursery rhyme home of many:
4 SHOE
rhyme start: 4 EENY
song refrain: 5 EIEIO
**"Children of a ___ God":**
6 LESSER
**"Children of a Lesser God"**
director Haines: 5 RANDA
**"Children of the Albatross"**
author: 3 NIN
**"Children of the Poor"**
author: 4 RIIS
**Children's author**
~ Blyton: 4 ENID
~ Eleanor: 5 ESTES
~ Ennis: 4 REES
~ Scott: 5 ODELL
**Chile**
Much of: 5 ANDES
neighbor: 4 PERU
Range in: 5 ANDES
When it's warm in: 5 ENERO
**Chilean**
1970s ~ leader: 7 ALLENDE
airline: 3 LAN
change: 4 PESO
pianist: 5 ARRAU
poet Pablo: 6 NERUDA
range: 5 ANDES
**Chili**
companion: 5 CARNE
hotness unit: 5 ALARM
ingredient: 10 PINTOBEANS
powder ingredient: 5 CUMIN
verde: 4 STEW
**Chiliads**
Many: 3 EON

**Chili ___ carne:** 3 CON
**Chili con ___:** 5 CARNE
**Chill:** 3 NIP 4 REST 5 RELAX
Causing ~ bumps: 5 EERIE
Feverish: 4 AGUE
out: 5 RELAX
Take a ~ pill: 6 COOLIT
**"Chill!":** 5 RELAX
**Chilled:** 4 COLD ICED 5 ONICE
garnish: 5 ASPIC
soup: 5 SCHAV
**Chiller:** 3 ICE
1958 ~, with "The": 4 BLOB
**Chill-inducing:** 5 EERIE
**Chilling:** 3 ICY 5 EERIE ONICE
out: 6 ATEASE ATREST
~ Chaney: 3 LON
**Chills:** 4 AGUE
and fever: 4 AGUE
**Chilly**
and damp: 3 RAW
and wet: 4 DANK
powder: 4 SNOW
Really: 6 ARCTIC
**Chime:** 4 RING
ominously: 5 KNELL
time: 4 NOON
**Chimed:** 4 RANG
**Chimers:** 5 BELLS
**Chimney**
channel: 4 FLUE
Like a: 5 SOOTY
nester: 5 STORK
residue: 4 SOOT
Vulcan's: 4 ETNA
**Chimp:** 3 APE
in space: 4 ENOS
relative: 5 ORANG
**Chimpanzee:** 3 APE 5 JOCKO
**Chin**
adornment: 6 GOATEE
end: 3 ESE
indentation: 5 CLEFT
stroker's words: 4 ISEE
Take it on the: 4 LOSE
**Ch'in**
Dynasty after: 3 HAN
**China**
and others: 7 FAREAST
border river: 4 YALU
city: 8 SHANGHAI
Fine: 5 SPODE
Former leader of: 3 MAO
group: 6 TEASET
name: 5 SPODE
neighbor: 4 LAOS
piece: 4 DISH 5 PLATE
6 TEACUP
prefix: 4 INDO
problem: 4 CHIP
province: 5 HONAN HUNAN
purchase: 6 TEASET
river: 7 YANGTZE
setting: 4 ASIA 7 FAREAST
shop problem: 4 BULL
prefix: 4 SINO

Use: 5 EATON
Used: 5 ATEIN
Zhou of: 5 ENLAI
China ___: 5 ASTER
**"China Beach"**
  setting: 3 NAM
  star Dana: 6 DELANY
**Chinatown**
  Street in New York's: 4 MOTT
**"Chinatown"**
  screenwriter Robert: 5 TOWNE
**Chinchilla:** 3 FUR 6 RODENT
**Chinese:** 5 ASIAN
  4th to 6th century ~ dynasty:
    3 WEI
  1960s ~ leader: 3 MAO
  appetizer: 7 EGGROLL
  Artistic ~ dynasty: 4 MING
  association: 4 TONG
  Big name in ~ history:
    5 ENLAI
  boat: 4 JUNK
  brew: 3 CHA
  calendar animal: 3 RAT
  capital: 6 TAIPEI
  coin: 4 YUAN
  cuisine: 5 HUNAN
  Dark ~ principle: 3 YIN
  discipline: 3 ZEN 6 TAICHI
  dollar: 4 YUAN
  drink: 3 TEA 8 GREENTEA
  dumpling: 6 WONTON
  dynasty: 3 HAN 4 CHOU HSIA
    MING TONG 5 LIANG
    SHANG
  dynasty overthrown by the
    Mongols: 4 SUNG
  food additive: 3 MSG
  Former ~ leader: 3 MAO
    4 DENG
  gang: 4 TONG
  gelatin: 4 AGAR
  general: 3 TSO
  gooseberry: 4 KIWI
  ideal: 3 TAO
  idol: 4 JOSS
  island: 6 TAIWAN
  leader: 4 INDO SINO
  Like some ~ dishes:
    9 STIRFRIED
  martial art: 6 KUNGFU
  menu general: 3 TSO
  menu phrase: 5 NOMSG
  money: 4 YUAN
  nurse: 4 AMAH
  nut: 6 LITCHI
  Old ~ money: 4 TAEL
  opening: 4 SINO
  percussion: 4 GONG
  philosopher: 5 LAOTSE
  philosophy: 3 TAO
  poet: 4 LIPO
  port: 4 AMOY
  potable: 8 GREENTEA
  prefix: 4 INDO SINO
  principle: 3 TAO

  secret society: 4 TONG
  Start of a ~ game: 3 MAH
  takeout freebie: 4 RICE
  tea: 3 CHA
  temple: 6 PAGODA
  toy: 4 PEKE
  way: 3 TAO
  ~ Chairman: 3 MAO
**"Chinese Parrot, The"**
  hero: 4 CHAN
**Chinese restaurant**
  drink: 6 HOTTEA
  flower: 7 TEAROSE
  freebie: 3 TEA
  offering: 8 GREENTEA
**Chinese restaurant syndrome**
  cause: 3 MSG
**___ Chinmoy:** 3 SRI
**Chinny**
  chatter: 4 LENO
**Chinook:** 6 SALMON
**Chinua**
  Novelist: 6 ACHEBE
**Chinwag:** 3 GAB
**Chip**
  accompanier: 8 ONIONDIP
  away at: 5 ERODE
  Blue or white: 4 ANTE
  Cheesy ~ flavor: 5 NACHO
  dip: 5 SALSA
  feature: 5 RIDGE
  flavoring: 4 SALT
  giant: 5 INTEL
  in: 4 ANTE
  Initial: 4 ANTE
  Kick in a: 4 ANTE
  Kind of: 5 NACHO
  Main ~, for short: 3 CPU
  maker: 3 AXE 4 WISE 5 INTEL
    7 ICEPICK
  making supply: 4 LARD
  off the old block: 3 LAD SON
    5 IMAGE 6 SLIVER
  on the table: 4 ANTE
  or drive: 6 STROKE
  Partner of: 4 DALE
  Popular: 5 FRITO
  Snack: 5 NACHO
  Snack for ~ or Dale: 5 ACORN
  topper: 3 DIP
  tossing comment: 4 IMIN
  ~, to a Brit: 5 CRISP
**Chipmunk:** 6 RODENT
  Cartoon: 4 DALE 5 ALVIN
**Chippendale**
  feature: 4 OGEE
  Like ~ furniture: 6 ROCOCO
**Chipper:** 3 GAY 4 PERT
    5 PERKY
  Nipper and ~ co.: 3 RCA
**Chips**
  and such: 4 NOSH
    8 JUNKFOOD
    9 SNACKFOOD
  Apples with: 4 MACS
  Bag of: 4 NOSH

  Big name in: 4 LAYS WISE
    5 INTEL 6 FRITOS
  Element in: 7 SILICON
  Game with aces and: 4 GOLF
  Have some: 4 NOSH
  In the: 4 RICH
  Like some: 5 SALTY
    6 RIDGED
**"CHiPs"**
  actor Erik: 7 ESTRADA
  actor Estrada: 4 ERIK
  actress Oakes: 5 RANDI
**Chips, Mr.**
  portrayer: 5 DONAT
    6 OTOOLE
  subject: 5 LATIN
**"Chiquitita"**
  quartet: 4 ABBA
**Chirac**
  palace: 6 ELYSEE
  state: 4 ETAT
**Chiromancer**
  study: 5 PALMS
**Chiropractor**
  concern: 5 SPINE
**Chirp:** 4 PEEP 5 TWEET
**Chirper**
  Little: 4 WREN
  Tiny: 7 KATYDID
**Chisel:** 4 TOOL 5 GOUGE
  feature: 4 EDGE
  relative: 3 ADZ
**Chisholm Trail**
  city: 4 ENID WACO
  group: 4 HERD
  terminus: 7 ABILENE
**Chit:** 3 IOU
  Has a ~ out: 4 OWES
**Chitchat:** 3 GAB YAK 4 TALK
    7 PALAVER
**Chi-town**
  paper: 4 TRIB
**"Chitty Chitty Bang Bang"**
  actor Frobe: 4 GERT
  screenwriter: 4 DAHL
  ~, literarily:
    12 ONOMATOPOEIA
**Chivalrous:** 5 NOBLE
    7 GALLANT
  Hardly: 4 RUDE
**Chive:** 4 HERB
**Chloe**
  Love of: 7 DAPHNIS
**Chlor-**
  suffix: 3 IDE
**Chloride**
  prefix: 3 TRI
  Sodium: 4 SALT
**Chlorine**
  compound: 6 HALIDE
**Chloroform**
  kin: 5 ETHER
**Chlorophyll**
  maker: 4 ALGA 5 PLANT
**Chmn.**
  cousin: 4 PRES

**Choate**
  Attend: 4 PREP
**Chocoholic**
  bane: 5 CAROB
**"Chocolat"**
  actress Lena: 4 OLIN
**Chocolate**
  bar nut: 6 ALMOND
  bean: 5 CACAO
  Big name in: 6 NESTLE
  candy brand: 6 RIESEN
  dessert: 6 MOUSSE MUDPIE
  Ersatz: 5 CAROB
  flavoring: 5 MOCHA
  Half a ~ drink: 3 YOO
  marshmallow snack: 5 SMORE
  sauce: 4 MOLE
  shape: 3 BAR 4 KISS
  snacks: 5 ROLOS
  source: 5 CACAO
  substitute: 5 CAROB
  syrup brand: 5 BOSCO
  treat: 3 BAR 4 KISS OREO
    5 FUDGE 6 MOUSSE
    7 MARSBAR
**Chocolate Creme**
  cookie: 4 OREO
**Chocolatier**
  Fictional: 5 WONKA
**Choctaw:** 5 TRIBE
**Choice:** 4 PICK PLUM RARE
    5 ELECT ELITE PRIME
    6 OPTION
  cut: 4 LOIN 5 FILET
  location: 4 FORK MENU
  marble: 3 TAW
  morsel: 6 TIDBIT
  word: 3 ANY 4 EENY ELSE
    5 OTHER 6 EITHER
  words: 3 ORS 4 IFSO 5 ANDOR
    6 ORELSE
**"___ Choice":** 7 SOPHIES
**Choir**
  attire: 4 ROBE
  member: 4 ALTO 5 TENOR
  neighbor: 4 APSE
  section: 5 ALTOS
  Some ~ members: 4 ALTI
    5 ALTOS 6 BASSES
  stands: 6 RISERS
  voice: 4 ALTO
**Choke:** 3 GAG JAM
    8 OVERGROW
**Choker:** 5 NOOSE
  Channel: 4 SILT
  site: 4 NECK
**Choler:** 3 IRE 5 ANGER
    WRATH
**Cholesterol**
  Bad ~ letters: 3 LDL
  Good ~ letters: 3 HDL
**Chollas:** 5 CACTI
**Chomolungma**
  alias: 7 EVEREST
**Chomsky**
  Linguist: 4 NOAM

**Chong, ___ Dawn:** 3 RAE
**Choo-choo**
  part: 6 ENGINE
  sound: 4 TOOT
**Choose:** 3 OPT TAP 4 PICK
    5 ELECT 6 DECIDE
    OPTFOR SELECT
  not to choose: 7 ABSTAIN
  the window instead of the aisle:
    5 ELOPE
**Chooser**
  word: 4 EENY
**Choosing**
  Having a hard time: 4 TORN
**Chop:** 3 HEW 5 MINCE
  down: 3 AXE HEW 4 FELL
  finely: 4 HASH 5 MINCE
  In a ~ shop: 6 STOLEN
  into cubes: 4 DICE
  Kind of: 4 JUDO LOIN PORK
    6 KARATE
  off: 3 LOP
  up: 4 HASH 5 MINCE
**Chop ___:** 4 SUEY
**Chop-chop:** 4 ASAP 5 APACE
    6 PRESTO
  Go: 3 HEW
**Chophouse**
  choice: 5 STEAK TBONE
  request: 4 RARE
**Chopin**
  piece: 5 ETUDE WALTZ
    7 MAZURKA 9 POLONAISE
  Sand, to: 4 AMIE
  work: 8 NOCTURNE
**Chopped**
  side dish: 4 SLAW
**Chopper:** 3 AXE
  blade: 5 ROTOR
  Clod: 3 HOE
**Choppers:** 5 TEETH
  Grow: 6 TEETHE
**Chopping**
  tool: 3 AXE 4 ADZE
**Chops:** 4 MEAT
**Chop suey**
  additive: 3 MSG
**Choral**
  part: 4 ALTO
  piece: 5 MOTET 7 CANTATA
  section: 5 ALTOS
  syllable: 3 TRA
**"Choral"**
  Beethoven's ~ Symphony:
    5 NINTH
**Chord**
  Common: 5 TRIAD
**Chore:** 4 TASK 6 ERRAND
  list header: 4 TODO
  shortcut: 9 TIMESAVER
**Choreographer**
  ~ Agnes de ___: 5 MILLE
  ~ Ailey: 5 ALVIN
  ~ Alvin: 5 AILEY
  ~ Bob: 5 FOSSE
  ~ Cunningham: 5 MERCE

  ~ de Mille: 5 AGNES
  ~ Lubovitch: 3 LAR
  ~ Sir Frederick: 6 ASHTON
  ~ Tharp: 5 TWYLA
  ~ Twyla: 5 THARP
**Choreography**
  bit: 4 STEP
**Choristers**
  Some: 4 ALTI 5 ALTOS
**Chorus:** 7 REFRAIN
  A ~ line: 4 ALTO 5 TRALA
  Church: 5 AMENS
  girl: 4 ALTO
  member: 4 ALTO BASS
    5 TENOR
  syllable: 3 TRA
  voice: 4 ALTO
**"Chorus Line, A"**
  producer: 4 PAPP
  song: 3 ONE
**Chose:** 5 OPTED
**Chosen:** 5 ALIST ELECT
  few: 5 ELITE
  number: 3 FEW
  one: 8 SELECTEE
  ones: 5 ELECT
**Chou ___:** 5 ENLAI
**Chou En-___:** 3 LAI
**Chow:** 4 EATS FEED FOOD
    GRUB 5 SPITZ
  chow: 4 ALPO
  down: 3 EAT
  holder: 5 LEASH
  Luau: 3 POI
  mein additive: 3 MSG
  Sow: 4 SLOP
**Chow ___:** 4 MEIN
**Chowder**
  ingredient: 4 CLAM
  Manhattan clam ~ seasoning:
    5 THYME
**Chowderhead:** 3 ASS LUG SAP
    4 DOLT DOPE SIMP
    5 IDIOT STUPE
**___ choy:** 3 BOK
**Chris**
  NHL goalie: 6 OSGOOD
  of tennis: 5 EVERT
  Singer: 3 REA 5 ISAAK
**Christ**
  Follower of: 3 IAN
  Sect member during time of:
    6 ESSENE
  Vicar of: 4 POPE
**Christen:** 4 NAME
**Christian:** 3 ERA
  Egyptian: 4 COPT
  of fashion: 4 DIOR
  symbol: 5 CROSS
**Christian ___:** 3 ERA
**Christiania**
  Capital formerly called: 4 OSLO
**Christianity**
  (abbr.): 3 REL
  Creed of: 6 NICENE
  Early center of: 6 EDESSA

**Christians**
Like some: 6 REBORN
  9 BORNAGAIN
**Christian Science**
founder: 4 EDDY
**"___ Christian Soldiers":**
  6 ONWARD
**Christie's**
and Karenina: 5 ANNAS
contemporary: 3 TEY
detective: 6 MARPLE POIROT
of mystery: 6 AGATHA
Singer: 3 LOU
**"___ Christie":** 4 ANNA
**Christie, Agatha**
River in an ~ title: 4 NILE
title: 4 DAME
**Christie's**
Compete at: 3 BID
**Christina**
Actress: 5 RICCI
Father of: 3 ARI
Singer: 8 AGUILERA
**"Christina's World"**
painter: 5 WYETH
**Christine**
Actress: 5 LAHTI
TV actress: 5 ELISE
**Christmas:** 4 NOEL YULE
(abbr.): 3 ISL
air: 4 NOEL
buy: 3 FIR TOY 4 TREE
carol: 4 NOEL
Classic ~ present: 4 SLED
decoration: 4 TREE 5 HOLLY
  SANTA 6 WREATH
display: 6 CRECHE
eave decoration: 6 ICICLE
poem opener: 4 TWAS
quaff: 3 NOG 6 EGGNOG
season: 4 NOEL YULE
song: 4 NOEL 5 CAROL
sounds: 3 HOS
stamp subject: 7 MADONNA
Start of a ~ carol: 5 OCOME
  6 ADESTE
Start of a ~ poem: 4 TWAS
time (abbr.): 3 DEC
~, in Italian: 6 NATALE
**Christmas ___:** 3 EVE 4 SEAL
  5 CAROL SEALS
**"Christmas Carol, A"**
character: 3 TIM
exclamation: 3 BAH
**"Christmas Song, The"**
co-composer: 5 TORME
**Christmas tree:** 3 FIR
glitter: 6 TINSEL
topper: 4 STAR 5 ANGEL
**"Christ of St. John of the Cross"**
artist: 4 DALI
**Christogram**
letter: 3 RHO
**Christopher**
Actor: 5 LLOYD REEVE
Architect: 4 WREN

Connecticut senator: 4 DODD
**"Christ's Entry Into Brussels"**
painter James: 5 ENSOR
**"Christ Stopped at ___":**
  5 EBOLI
**"Christ Stopped at Eboli"**
author: 4 LEVI
**Chromosome**
component: 3 DNA 4 GENE
map: 6 GENOME
molecule: 3 RNA
Y ~ carrier: 4 MALE
**Chronic**
critic: 3 NAG
nag: 5 SHREW
Not: 5 ACUTE
**Chronicler**
1666 London fire ~: 5 PEPYS
Alice's: 4 ARLO 5 LEWIS
Narnia: 7 CSLEWIS
Poker Flat: 5 HARTE
**Chronicles:** 6 ANNALS
**"Chronicles of ___":** 6 NARNIA
**Chronological**
brinks: 4 EVES
**Chronology**
component: 3 ERA
**Chrysalis:** 4 PUPA
**Chrysler:** 4 AUTO
1980s ~ model: 4 KCAR
Car co. bought by: 3 AMC
Former head of: 7 IACOCCA
Old ~ model: 6 DESOTO
**Chrysler Building**
architect William Van ___:
  4 ALEN
style: 4 DECO
**"Chuang Tzu"**
principle: 3 TAO
**Chubby:** 3 FAT 5 PLUMP
**Chuck:** 3 PEG 4 HURL TOSS
  5 FLING 7 DEEPSIX
A ~ holds it: 3 BIT
alternative: 4 CHAS
Former Steelers coach: 4 NOLL
of Watergate: 6 COLSON
Test pilot: 6 YEAGER
wagon honcho: 4 COOK
**Chuckle**
Bit of a: 3 HEH
Cause to: 5 AMUSE
Chat room: 3 LOL
More than: 4 ROAR
**Chucklehead:** 3 ASS SAP
  4 BOOB DOPE 5 DUNCE
  SCHMO
**Chug-___:** 4 ALUG
**Chukkers**
Game of: 4 POLO
**Chum:** 3 BRO BUB BUD PAL
  5 AMIGO CRONY
Longtime: 6 OLDPAL
~, to a Brit: 4 MATE
**Chump:** 3 SAP 5 SCHMO
**Chung, Connie**
employer: 3 CNN

**Chunk:** 3 GOB 4 SLAB
Big ~ of earth: 4 ASIA
in the Arctic Ocean: 4 BERG
of fairway: 5 DIVOT
of history: 3 ERA
**Chunky**
More than: 5 OBESE
**Church**
agreement: 4 AMEN
area: 4 APSE NAVE 5 ALTAR
  6 VESTRY
assembly: 5 SYNOD
bench: 3 PEW
calendar: 4 ORDO
center: 4 NAVE
chorus: 5 AMENS
council: 5 SYNOD
dignitary: 7 PRELATE
donation: 5 TITHE
ending: 4 GOER
feature: 5 SPIRE
gallery: 4 LOFT
holding: 5 DOGMA TENET
instrument: 5 ORGAN
key: 6 OPENER
lady: 3 NUN
law: 5 CANON
leader: 5 ELDER
Letters in some ~ names:
  3 AME
Like a ~ mouse: 4 POOR
Like some ~ matters: 4 LAIC
Millennial ~ member:
  6 SHAKER
music: 5 MOTET
niche: 4 APSE
offering: 5 TITHE
official: 5 ABBOT ELDER
  VICAR 6 DEACON
  PASTOR SEXTON
  7 PRELATE
recess: 4 APSE
seating: 3 PEW
service: 4 MASS
singers: 5 CHOIR
song: 4 HYMN 5 MOTET
Split for: 5 TITHE
support: 5 TITHE
Title acquired in: 3 MRS
topper: 5 SPIRE 7 STEEPLE
Unification ~ member:
  6 MOONIE
Vaulted ~ area: 4 APSE
vestment: 3 ALB
**Churchgoers**
Many ~ (abbr.): 5 CATHS
**Churchill:** 4 TORY
Barrier named by:
  11 IRONCURTAIN
gesture: 3 VEE 5 VSIGN
"So few," to: 3 RAF
successor: 4 EDEN 6 ATTLEE
The RAF, to: 5 SOFEW
**Churchill Downs**
drink: 5 JULEP
event: 5 DERBY

**Church Lady**
sound: 3 TSK
**Churchyard**
tree: 3 YEW
**Churl:** 3 CAD OAF 4 BOOR
LOUT
Like a: 4 RUDE
**Churn**
up: 4 RILE ROIL
**Chute**
Deliver by: 4 DROP
fabric: 5 NYLON
opener: 4 PARA
**Chutist**
~, briefly: 4 PARA
**Chutney**
fruit: 5 MANGO
ingredient: 8 TAMARIND
**Chutzpah:** 4 GALL 5 BRASS
CRUST MOXIE NERVE
6 HUBRIS
Full of: 5 BRASH NERVY
**CIA**
1980s ~ director: 5 CASEY
agent: 3 SPY
director under Bush and
Clinton: 5 TENET
film spoof: 4 SPYS
Former ~ opponent: 3 KGB
operative: 3 AGT
Part of: 6 AGENCY
predecessor: 3 OSS
problem: 4 MOLE
relative: 3 NSA
**"Ciao!":** 3 BYE 4 TATA 5 LATER
SEEYA
~, in Spanish: 5 ADIOS
**Cicatrix:** 4 SCAR
**Cicely**
Emmy winner: 5 TYSON
**Cicero**
Emulate: 5 ORATE
**Cider**
girl: 3 IDA
Like some: 4 HARD
**"Cider House Rules, The"**
Oscar winner: 5 CAINE
12 MICHAELCAINE
**Cigar**
butt: 4 ETTE
Cheap: 6 STOGIE
Cherished: 6 HAVANA
choice: 6 CORONA
holder: 7 HUMIDOR
Kind of: 5 CUBAN
Long: 9 PANATELLA
Mild: 5 CLARO
residue: 3 ASH
suffix: 4 ETTE
tip: 3 ASH 4 ETTE
**Cigarette:** 4 WEED
Illicit: 6 REEFER
ingredient: 3 TAR
pkg.: 3 CTN
residue: 3 ASH
stuff: 3 TAR

**Cigs:** 5 WEEDS
**Cilium:** 4 LASH
**"Cimarron"**
actress Dunne: 5 IRENE
**C in C:** 4 PRES 5 POTUS
Part of: 3 CDR
**Cinch:** 3 ICE 4 SNAP 6 ENSURE
in Japan: 3 OBI
**Cincinnati**
state: 4 OHIO
team: 4 REDS 7 BENGALS
**Cinco**
follower: 4 SEIS
y dos: 5 SIETE
y tres: 4 OCHO
**Cinco de Mayo:** 3 DIA
event: 6 FIESTA
**Cincy**
player: 3 RED
**Cinderella**
event: 4 BALL
horses: 4 MICE
Like stepsisters of: 4 UGLY
loss: 7 SLIPPER
**"Cinderella Liberty"**
Wallach of: 3 ELI
**Cinders**
of comics: 4 ELLA
Turn to: 4 CHAR
**"___ Cinders" (old comic):**
4 ELLA
**Cine**
suffix: 4 RAMA
**Cinema**
canine: 4 ASTA
chain: 5 LOEWS
Delon of: 5 ALAIN
Hall of: 5 ANNIE
name: 5 ODEON
snippet: 4 CLIP
Sommer of: 4 ELKE
statuette: 5 OSCAR
supplies: 5 REELS
trigram: 3 MGM
West of: 3 MAE
**Cinemas**
Local: 5 NABES
**Cinematographer**
org.: 3 ASC
~ Nykvist: 4 SVEN
**Cinemax**
sister: 3 HBO
**Cineplex ___:** 5 ODEON
**Cinerary**
vessel: 3 URN
**Cinergy Field**
team: 4 REDS
**Cinnabar:** 3 ORE
**Cinnamon:** 5 SPICE
candy: 6 REDHOT
Chinese: 6 CASSIA
**Cinque**
follower: 3 SEI
minus due: 3 TRE
**CIO**
partner: 3 AFL

**Cio-Cio-___:** 3 SAN
**Cipher:** 4 CODE NULL ZERO
Put in: 6 ENCODE
**Circa:** 4 NEAR 5 ABOUT
6 AROUND
**Circle:** 3 SET 4 AREA LOOP
RING 5 ORBIT
7 COTERIE
bit: 3 ARC
Colorful: 6 AREOLA
constants: 3 PIS
dance: 4 HORA
Flattened: 4 OVAL
Floral: 3 LEI
Form a: 4 LOOP
Full: 3 LAP
Inner: 4 LOOP 5 CADRE
Kind of: 5 INNER
line: 6 RADIUS
Line connecting points on a:
5 CHORD
lines: 5 RADII
Line through a: 6 SECANT
meas.: 4 DIAM
of light: 4 HALO
overhead: 4 HALO
preceder: 5 INNER
section: 3 ARC
stat: 8 DIAMETER
Tiny: 3 DOT
Traffic: 6 ROTARY
Word with: 5 INNER
**"Circle of Friends"**
author Binchy: 5 MAEVE
**Circles**
Colorful: 7 AREOLAE
Go around in: 4 EDDY ROLL
SPIN 5 ORBIT
Going in: 4 LOST
**Circlet**
Angelic: 4 HALO
**Circling:** 7 INORBIT
**Circuit:** 4 LOOP
breaker word: 3 AMP
Full: 3 LAP
part: 4 FUSE
Racing: 3 LAP
**Circuitous**
path: 3 ARC
**Circular:** 5 FLIER 6 MAILER
announcement: 4 SALE
course: 4 GYRE
current: 4 EDDY
file: 7 ROLODEX
gasket: 5 ORING
waffle: 4 EGGO
**"Circular file":** 8 TRASHCAN
**Circulation**
Took out of: 8 CALLEDIN
~, in a way: 7 READERS
**Circulatory**
blockage: 4 CLOT
**Circumference:** 5 AMBIT GIRTH
part: 3 ARC
**Circumflex**
lookalike: 5 CARET

**Circumnavigator**
16th-century ~: 5 DRAKE
Fictional: 4 FOGG
**Circumspect:** 5 CHARY
**Circumstance**
Partner of: 4 POMP
**Circumstances**
Under any: 5 ATALL
Under the most favorable:
6 ATBEST
**Circumvent:** 5 AVOID ELUDE
EVADE 6 BYPASS
OUTWIT
**Circus**
act: 4 FEAT
barker: 4 SEAL
catcher: 3 NET
clapper: 4 SEAL
clown Kelly: 6 EMMETT
cries: 3 OHS 4 OOHS
employee: 5 TAMER
housing: 4 TENT
Kind of: 4 FLEA 5 MEDIA
Like ~ lions: 5 TAMED
lineup: 4 ACTS
performer: 4 FLEA SEAL
5 CLOWN TAMER
7 ACROBAT 9 AERIALIST
LIONTAMER
prop: 5 STILT
safeguard: 3 NET
setups: 5 TENTS
sight: 4 TENT 5 STILT
site: 5 ARENA
Work with ~ cats: 4 TAME
___ Circus: 5 NEROS
**Circus Hall of Fame**
site: 8 SARASOTA
**Cirque du ___:** 6 SOLEIL
**Cirrus:** 5 CLOUD
cloud formation: 4 WISP
**CIS**
members, once: 4 SSRS
predecessor: 4 USSR
**Cisco Kid**
horse: 6 DIABLO
player: 6 ROMERO
~, to Pancho: 5 AMIGO
**Cistern:** 3 VAT
___ cit.: 3 LOC
**Citadel**
Like The ~, now: 4 COED
student: 5 CADET
The ~ rival, briefly: 3 VMI
**Citation**
and Corsair: 6 EDSELS
Court ~ abbr.: 5 ETSEQ
Earned a: 4 SPED
jockey: 6 ARCARO
Reason for a ~ (abbr.):
3 DWI
___ citato: 5 OPERE
**Cite:** 5 QUOTE 6 ADDUCE
7 REFERTO
**"Cities of the Interior"**
author: 3 NIN 8 ANAISNIN

**Cities Service**
competitor: 4 ESSO
**Citified:** 5 URBAN
**Citium**
Stoic from: 4 ZENO
**Citizen:** 7 FREEMAN
Muscat: 5 OMANI
New: 6 EMIGRE
Noted: 4 KANE
rights org.: 4 ACLU
Riyadh: 4 ARAB
Saudi: 4 ARAB
Seoul: 6 KOREAN
Sultanate: 5 OMANI
U.S. ~ to be: 9 DECLARANT
**"Citizen ___":** 4 KANE
**"Citizen Kane"**
actor Everett: 6 SLOANE
actor Joseph: 6 COTTEN
Last word of: 7 ROSEBUD
portrayer: 6 WELLES
prop: 4 SLED
sled: 7 ROSEBUD
studio: 3 RKO
**Citizenship**
Good ~ org.: 3 GSA
**"Citizen X"**
actor: 3 REA
**Citric ___:** 4 ACID
**Citrine**
cooler: 3 ADE
**Citroën**
Automaker: 5 ANDRE
**Citron**
suffix: 4 ELLA
**Citrus**
Big ~ fruit: 6 POMELO
city: 5 OCALA
cooler: 3 ADE
drink: 3 ADE 7 LIMEADE
fruit: 4 LIME UGLI 5 LEMON
6 ORANGE
hybrid: 4 UGLI 5 LIMON
7 TANGELO
Jamaican: 4 UGLI
juice cocktail: 7 SIDECAR
peel: 4 ZEST 5 TWIST
source: 8 LIMETREE
Wrinkly: 4 UGLI
**Città**
capitale: 4 ROMA
**Città ___ Vaticano:** 3 DEL
**City:** 4 BURG 5 URBAN
Ancient: 5 TANIS UTICA
6 EDESSA SPARTA
7 BABYLON
area: 3 URB
Bay: 5 TAMPA
Biblical: 5 SODOM
Big ~ woe: 4 SMOG
bond, for short: 4 MUNI
"by the sea, oh": 3 RIO
council rep.: 3 ALD
"Gay": 5 PAREE
Half a: 4 PAGO 5 WALLA
Holy: 5 MECCA 6 TOLEDO

Inner ~ area: 6 BARRIO
GHETTO
It's far from the big city:
5 EXURB
leader: 5 MAYOR
map: 4 PLAT
NFL: 5 TAMPA
NHL: 6 OTTAWA
N.L.: 3 ATL STL
Sin: 5 SODOM
Southernmost U.S.: 4 HILO
Strange-sounding: 4 ERIE
Word with: 5 INNER
___ City
(easy street): 3 FAT
(PC game): 3 SIM
**City-state**
Greek: 5 POLIS 6 SPARTA
7 CORINTH
**"City Without Clocks, The":**
5 VEGAS
**"City Without Walls"**
poet: 5 AUDEN
**Ciudad Juárez**
neighbor: 6 ELPASO
**Civic:** 5 HONDA
group: 4 ELKS 5 LIONS
**Civil:** 6 POLITE
action cause: 4 TORT
disorder: 4 RIOT
It may be: 3 WAR
punishment: 4 FINE
suffix: 3 ITY
They may be ~ (abbr.): 3 RTS
wrong: 4 TORT
**"Civil Disobedience"**
author: 7 THOREAU
**Civilian**
clothes: 5 MUFTI
**Civil rights**
1960s ~ gp.: 4 SNCC
city: 5 SELMA
figure Parks: 4 ROSA
lawyer Morris: 4 DEES
leader Medgar: 5 EVERS
org.: 5 NAACP
**Civil Rights Memorial**
designer: 3 LIN
**Civil War**
authority Shelby: 5 FOOTE
battle site: 6 SHILOH
biography: 5 RELEE
fort: 6 SUMTER
general: 3 LEE 4 RENO
5 GRANT MEADE
7 SHERMAN
gp.: 3 CSA
guerrilla: 6 REDLEG
nickname: 3 ABE
photographer: 5 BRADY
side: 4 REBS 5 NORTH
SOUTH UNION
soldier: 3 REB 4 GRAY
song:
15 TRAMPTRAMPTRAMP
veterans gp.: 3 GAR

Civvies: 5 MUFTI
Cl⁻: 3 ION 5 ANION
Clack: 5 NOISE
Clad: 7 ATTIRED
Was ~ in: 4 WORE
Claiborne
  Designer: 3 LIZ
  Food writer: 5 CRAIG
Claim: 4 AVER AVOW DIBS
    6 ALLEGE ASSERT
    7 PROFESS PURPORT
  Champion's: 5 TITLE
  Clairvoyant's: 3 ESP
  Ex: 7 ALIMONY
  First: 4 DIBS
  Legal: 4 LIEN
  Property: 4 LIEN
  Psychic's: 3 ESP
  Vain: 5 BOAST
Claimant: 6 LIENOR
  cry: 4 DIBS
Claimed
  the title: 3 WON
Claiming
  Quit: 5 CEDED
Clair
  Director: 4 RENE
"Clair de ___": 4 LUNE
Claire
  Actress: 3 INA
  ___ Claire
    (Quebec): 6 POINTE
    (Wisconsin): 3 EAU
Clairol
  choice: 4 TINT 8 BRUNETTE
  user: 4 DYER
Clairvoyance: 3 ESP PSI
Clairvoyant: 4 SEER 5 SIBYL
  cards: 5 TAROT
  claim: 3 ESP
  gift: 3 ESP
  opener: 4 ISEE
Clam
  digs: 5 SHORE
  Edible: 6 QUAHOG
  home: 5 SHELL
  Soft-shell: 7 STEAMER
Clambake
  item: 7 STEAMER
Clammy: 4 DAMP DANK
    5 MOIST
Clamor: 3 ADO CRY DIN HUE
    5 HOOHA NOISE
    6 RACKET
Clamorous: 4 LOUD 5 AROAR
    NOISY VOCAL
  criticism: 4 FLAK
Clamp: 4 VISE
  shape: 3 CEE
Clampett
  patriarch: 3 JED
Clampett, Jed: 9 HILLBILLY
  portrayer: 5 EBSEN
Clampett, ___ May: 4 ELLY
Clams
  100 ~: 5 CNOTE CSPOT

Cook: 5 STEAM
  or lettuce: 5 BREAD
Clan
  chief: 5 THANE
  clash: 4 FEUD
  emblem: 5 TOTEM
  pattern: 6 TARTAN
  unit: 4 SEPT
Clancy
  Author: 3 TOM
Clancy, Tom
  hero: 4 RYAN
  org.: 3 CIA
  subj.: 3 CIA
Clandestine: 3 SLY 6 SECRET
  maritime org.: 3 ONI
  meeting: 5 TRYST
Clangor: 3 DIN 5 NOISE
"Clan of the Cave Bear, The"
  author: 4 AUEL
  heroine: 4 AYLA
Clansman
  cap: 3 TAM
Clanton
  foe: 4 EARP
  gang leader: 3 IKE
Clap: 4 PEAL
Clapper
  Circus: 4 SEAL
Clapton
  Guitarist: 4 ERIC
  tune: 5 LAYLA
  ___ Clara, California: 5 SANTA
Clare
  and Henry: 5 LUCES
Clarence
  accuser: 5 ANITA
  Saxophonist: 7 CLEMONS
Claret: 4 WINE
  and chianti: 4 REDS
  color: 3 RED
  relative, for short: 3 ZIN
Clarification
  preceder: 5 IDEST
  starter: 5 IMEAN
  Words of: 4 ASIN 5 IDEST
    TOWIT
Clarified
  butter: 4 GHEE
Clarifier
  Latin: 5 IDEST
  words: 5 IMEAN
Clarinet: 4 REED
  cousin: 4 OBOE
  part: 4 REED
Clarinetist
  Dixieland: 12 PETEFOUNTAIN
  need: 4 REED
  ~ Artie: 4 SHAW
  ~ Shaw: 5 ARTIE
Clarion
  blast: 7 TANTARA
Clark
  Country singer: 3 ROY 5 TERRI
  of The Daily Planet: 4 KENT
  partner: 4 LOIS 5 LEWIS

Role for: 5 RHETT
  Singer: 6 PETULA
Clark, Gen. Wesley
  Like: 3 RET
Clarke
  Actress: 3 MAE
  computer: 3 HAL
Claro: 5 CIGAR
Clash
  of clans: 4 FEUD
  of heavyweights: 4 SUMO
  Petty: 4 SPAT
  They may: 4 EGOS
"Clash by Night"
  playwright: 5 ODETS
Clasp
  Men's: 6 TIEBAR
  Resting spot for a: 4 NAPE
  Tie with a: 4 BOLO
Class: 3 ILK 4 SORT TIER
    5 CASTE GENRE GRADE
    STYLE
  action gp.: 3 PTA
  Airline: 7 ECONOMY
  Anatomy ~ model:
    8 SKELETON
  Arrange by: 6 ASSORT
  Art: 5 GENRE
  Audited a: 5 SATIN
  Beginning drawing: 4 ARTI
  Biology ~ subject: 6 AMOEBA
  Chem: 3 LAB
  Cushy: 5 EASYA
  cutter: 6 TRUANT
  ender: 4 BELL
  for new arrivals (abbr.): 3 ESL
  Grad.: 3 SRS
  High school: 3 GYM 4 MATH
    SHOP
  H.S.: 3 ALG ENG SCI 4 ECON
    GEOG GEOM TRIG
    5 SEXED
  Law school: 5 TORTS
  leader: 4 PROF
  Math ~ abbr.: 3 QED 4 CALC
  Med. school: 4 ANAT
  of racing car: 6 MIDGET
  of submarines: 4 ALFA
  Physics ~ topic: 3 ERG
  pres.: 4 BMOC
  Privileged: 5 ELITE
  reunion attendee: 4 ALUM
  Science: 3 LAB
  Ship: 8 STEERAGE
  Social: 5 CASTE
  struggle: 4 EXAM TEST
  Unlikely ~ president:
    4 NERD
  With: 6 FINELY
  work: 6 LESSON
  Yoga ~ need: 3 MAT
Class-conscious
  gp.: 3 PTA
Classic
  art subject: 4 NUDE
  beginning: 3 NEO

board game: 4 LIFE RISK
  5 SORRY
car: 3 GTO REO 5 TBIRD
  VETTE 6 MODELA
card game: 3 UNO
clown: 4 BOZO
computer game: 4 MYST
film noir: 3 DOA
gas brand: 4 ESSO
opener: 3 NEO
sneakers: 4 KEDS
soft drink: 4 NEHI
sports cars: 3 MGS
theater: 4 ROXY 5 ODEON
western: 5 SHANE

**Classical**
beginning: 3 NEO
finale: 5 OMEGA
Light ~ music orchestra:
  4 POPS
lyric poet: 6 SAPPHO
meeting place: 4 STOA
prefix: 3 NEO
style: 5 DORIC IONIC

**Classification: 4 TYPE 5 GENRE**
Biological: 6 FAMILY
Blood ~ system: 3 ABO
Draft: 4 ONEA
Kennel club: 5 BREED
Racehorse: 3 AGE

**Classifications**
Biological: 6 GENERA

**Classified: 6 SECRET SORTED**
  WANTAD
ad abbr.: 3 EEO EOE
ad no.: 3 TEL
Highly: 9 TOPSECRET
info: 3 ADS
It's: 6 WANTAD
offers: 4 JOBS

**Classifieds: 3 ADS**
Times in: 4 EVES

**Classifier: 8 ASSORTER**

**Classify: 3 PEG 4 SORT**
  5 LABEL 6 ASSORT

**Classmates**
See old: 5 REUNE

**"Class Reunion"**
author Jaffe: 4 RONA

**Classroom**
aid: 5 GLOBE
book: 4 TEXT
drudgery: 4 ROTE
favorite: 3 PET
furniture: 5 DESKS
helper: 4 AIDE
need: 7 ERASERS
supply: 5 CHALK

**Classy: 4 POSH 7 ELEGANT**
entrance: 4 ARCH

**Clatter: 3 DIN 5 NOISE**

**Clattery**
trains: 3 ELS

**Claude**
Actor: 5 AKINS RAINS
Author: 5 MCKAY

**Claudio**
Pianist: 5 ARRAU

**Claudius**
Info: Latin cue
I, to: 3 EGO
Successor to: 4 NERO
To be, to: 4 ESSE

**Claus**
Subordinate: 3 ELF

**Clause**
connector: 3 AND
Contract ~ (abbr.): 4 COLA
Escape: 3 OUT
negator: 3 NOR

**Claustrophobic**
patient's dread: 3 MRI

**Clavell, James**
novel: 6 SHOGUN TAIPAN
  7 KINGRAT

**"C'___ la vie!": 3 EST**

**Claw: 5 TALON 6 TEARAT**
Bear: 6 PASTRY
Lobster: 6 PINCER

**Clay**
brick: 5 ADOBE
clump: 4 CLOD
Desert: 5 ADOBE
Lump of: 4 GLOB
Made of: 7 EARTHEN
Nee: 3 ALI
Remodeled: 3 ALI
today: 3 ALI
Work: 5 KNEAD

**Clay, Henry: 6 ORATOR**

**Clayey**
deposit: 4 MARL

**Clay pigeon: 5 SKEET**
  6 TARGET
tosser: 4 TRAP

**Clean: 5 MOPUP**
air org.: 3 EPA
Came: 4 TOLD
Come: 5 ADMIT BATHE
  6 FESSUP
Hard to: 5 GRIMY
It's not: 4 SMUT
kind of energy: 5 SOLAR
Make: 5 REHAB
off: 5 ERASE
Squeaky: 6 CHASTE
tables: 3 BUS
the deck: 4 SWAB
the furniture: 4 DUST
the slate: 5 ERASE
They ~ locks: 8 SHAMPOOS
up: 4 LAVE WASH 5 BATHE
up copy: 4 EDIT
Wipe: 5 ERASE
with effort: 5 SCOUR SCRUB

**Clean Air Act**
concern: 4 SMOG
org.: 3 EPA

**Cleaned**
one's plate: 3 ATE

**Cleaner**
Blazer: 7 CARWASH

Caustic: 3 LYE
Clorox: 7 PINESOL
Cotton-tipped: 4 SWAB
Dry ~ challenge: 4 SPOT
Ear: 4 QTIP SWAB
Flat: 4 CHAR
Pipe: 5 DRANO 6 REAMER
Plate: 3 UMP 7 DISHRAG
Rug: 3 VAC
Strong: 3 LYE

**Cleaners**
One may be taken to the:
  5 STAIN
Take to the: 4 BILK SOAK
  6 FLEECE 7 SWINDLE

**Cleaning**
agent: 3 LYE
aid: 3 MOP 5 BROOM
  6 SPONGE 7 DUSTMOP
cloth: 3 RAG 4 WIPE
Do a ~ chore: 4 DUST
Spring ~ event: 7 TAGSALE

**Cleanliness: 7 HYGIENE**

**Cleanse: 3 RID 4 LAVE**
  5 BATHE PURGE
  7 DETERGE

**Cleanser**
brand: 4 AJAX 5 COMET
  LYSOL 6 BONAMI
scent: 4 PINE
Strong: 3 LYE

**Cleansing**
agent: 4 SOAP 5 BORAX

**Cleanup**
Fall ~ aid: 4 RAKE
org.: 3 EPA

**Clear: 3 NET RID 4 EARN**
  5 DEFOG ERASE LUCID
  PLAIN 6 DELETE
  LIMPID PATENT
  UNCLOG UNSTOP
  7 EVIDENT
  9 EXONERATE
a hurdle: 4 LEAP
Became: 6 SANKIN
for takeoff: 5 DEICE
Just ~ of the bottom:
  5 ATRIP
(of): 3 RID
off: 4 WIPE 5 ERASE
of the bottom: 6 AWEIGH
of vermin: 5 DERAT
Partner of: 4 LOUD
Perfectly: 5 LUCID
sky: 5 ETHER
sky color: 5 AZURE
soup: 8 CONSOMME
Steer ~ of: 4 DUCK SHUN
  5 AVOID ELUDE EVADE
tables: 3 BUS
the board: 5 ERASE
the leaves: 4 RAKE
the tape: 5 ERASE
the windshield: 5 DEFOG
up: 5 SOLVE
Words before: 5 INTHE

**Clearance**
  condition: 4 ASIS
  event: 4 SALE
  sign: 6 ONSALE
**Clear as ___:** 5 ABELL
**Clearasil**
  target: 3 ZIT 4 ACNE
**Clear-cut**
  They're often: 5 TREES
**"___ Clear Day ...":** 3 ONA
**Clearheaded:** 4 SANE 5 LUCID
    SOBER
**Clearing**
  Forest: 5 GLADE
  Throat: 4 AHEM
**Clearly**
  Hears: 4 GETS
  Outline: 4 ETCH
  Show: 6 EVINCE
**Cleary, Beverly**
  character: 6 RAMONA
**Cleats**
  What ~ increase: 4 GRIP
**Cleave:** 4 REND TEAR 5 SEVER
    6 ADHERE
**Cleaver**
  Mrs.: 4 JUNE
**Cleaver, Theodore**
  ~, to Wally: 4 BEAV
**Cleaver, Wally**
  pal: 5 EDDIE
  portrayer: 3 DOW 7 TONYDOW
**Cleaving**
  tool: 3 AXE 4 FROE
**Cleek:** 7 ONEIRON
**Cleese**
  cohort: 4 IDLE 5 PALIN
  Fish in a ~ film: 5 WANDA
**Clef**
  Kind of: 4 ALTO BASS
    6 TREBLE
  Violinist: 4 ALTO
**Clematis:** 4 VINE
**Clemens**
  pen name: 5 TWAIN
  Pitcher: 5 ROGER
  stat: 3 ERA
  ~, as of 2004: 5 ASTRO
**Clement**
  Director: 4 RENE
  Poet: 5 MOORE
**___ Clemente:** 3 SAN
**Clementine**
  Father of: 5 MINER
**Clemson**
  athlete: 5 TIGER
**Cleo**
  of jazz: 5 LAINE
  river: 4 NILE
  undoing: 3 ASP
  wooer: 4 MARC
**Cleopatra**
  charm: 6 SCARAB
  He defeated Antony and:
    7 AGRIPPA
  killer: 3 ASP

  love: 4 MARC 6 ANTONY
  portrayer in 1917: 4 BARA
  river: 4 NILE
**"Cleopatra"**
  backdrop: 4 NILE 5 EGYPT
  portrayer:
    15 ELIZABETHTAYLOR
**Cleopatra's Needle:** 7 OBELISK
**Clergy**
  Not of the: 4 LAIC
  Some French: 5 ABBES
**Clergyman:** 5 VICAR
    7 PRELATE
  cap: 7 BIRETTA
  Catholic: 6 PRIEST
  French: 4 ABBE
  Noted: 5 PEALE
  quarters: 5 MANSE
**Cleric:** 5 VICAR 6 DEACON
    PRIEST
  council: 5 SYNOD
  famous for bloopers:
    7 SPOONER
  French: 4 ABBE
**Clerical**
  abode: 5 MANSE
  garb: 3 ALB
  Not: 4 LAIC
  One doing ~ work: 6 PRIEST
  vestment: 4 ROBE 5 AMICE
**Clerk:** 6 SELLER
  Dickens: 4 HEEP 5 URIAH
    8 CRATCHIT
  Do a ~ job: 4 SELL
  File: 12 PENCILPUSHER
  Kwik-E-Mart: 3 APU
  "M*A*S*H": 5 RADAR
**Clermont**
  designer: 6 FULTON
  power: 5 STEAM
**Cleveland:** 4 CITY 6 GROVER
  Abbr. after: 3 HTS
  Author: 5 AMORY
  cager: 3 CAV
  City near: 5 AKRON 6 ELYRIA
  lake: 4 ERIE
  ~ Indian: 4 ERIE
**Cleveland Indians**
  mascot: 5 WAHOO
**Clever:** 3 APT 4 CAGY DEFT
    WILY 5 CANNY QUICK
    SHARP SLICK SMART
  comment: 3 MOT 4 QUIP
  maneuver: 4 PLOY
  one: 3 WIT
  opening: 3 CEE
  ploy: 4 RUSE
**Cleverly**
  effective: 4 NEAT
  skillful: 6 ADROIT
**Cliburn:** 7 PIANIST
**Clichéd:** 5 BANAL TRITE
  movie ending: 6 SUNSET
**Click:** 8 HITITOFF
  beetle: 6 ELATER
  It's sent with a: 5 EMAIL

  Morse: 3 DIT
  Request before a: 5 SMILE
  site: 4 ICON
  They: 8 TAPSHOES
**Clickable**
  image: 4 ICON
**Clicked**
  image: 4 ICON
  "send": 7 EMAILED
**Clicker:** 6 REMOTE
    8 CASTANET
**Clickers:** 4 MICE
**Client:** 4 USER
  of Darrow: 4 LOEB
**"Client, The"**
  actor Brad: 6 RENFRO
**Clientele**
  Café: 6 EATERS
**Cliff:** 5 SCARP 6 ESCARP
  dwelling: 5 AERIE
  hanger: 5 AERIE
  line: 5 SCARP
  Rocky: 4 SCAR
  Rough: 4 CRAG
**Clifford**
  Playwright: 5 ODETS
**Cliffside**
  dwelling: 5 AERIE
**Climactic**
  opening: 4 ANTI
  time in a Cooper film: 4 NOON
**Climatologist**
  concern: 6 ELNINO
**Climax:** 3 CAP 4 ACME PEAK
  Musical: 4 CODA
  Oater: 8 SHOOTOUT
  Race: 7 LASTLAP
**Climb:** 4 GOUP RISE SHIN
    5 SCALE 6 ASCEND
    ASCENT SHINNY
  They ~ walls: 5 IVIES VINES
  Tough to: 5 STEEP
  up: 5 MOUNT 6 ASCEND
**Climber:** 4 SNOB VINE
  Campus: 3 IVY
  challenge: 3 ALP 4 CRAG
  descent: 6 RAPPEL
  Hill: 3 ANT
  Mountain: 4 TBAR
  need: 7 TOEHOLD
  Showy: 8 CLEMATIS
  Social ~ goal: 6 STATUS
  spike: 5 PITON
  stop: 5 LEDGE
  tool: 5 ICEAX
**Climbing**
  plant: 3 IVY 4 VINE 5 LIANA
    8 SWEETPEA
  spike: 5 PITON
  vine: 5 LIANA
**Clinch:** 3 ICE 4 NAIL SEAL
    5 SEWUP
**Cline**
  Country singer: 5 PATSY
  record label: 5 DECCA
**Cling:** 6 ADHERE COHERE

Word before: 6 STATIC
**Clinger**
  Sock: 3 BUR
**Clinic**
  name: 4 MAYO
  Recovery: 5 REHAB
  ___ Clinic: 4 MAYO
**Clink:** 3 CAN 4 JAIL STIR
  glasses: 5 TOAST
  Klink: 6 STALAG
  Ship: 4 BRIG
**Clinker:** 3 DUD 4 GOOF
    5 ERROR
  Drink: 3 ICE
**Clinky:** 8 METALLIC
**Clint**
  "costar": 5 ORANG
**Clinton:** 8 ARKANSAN
  (abbr.): 3 DEM SEN
  aide Leon: 7 PANETTA
  aide Myers: 6 DEEDEE
  alma mater: 4 YALE
  and Bush: 4 ELIS
  attorney general: 4 RENO
  birthplace: 4 HOPE
  blew it: 3 SAX
  cabinet member: 4 PENA
    RENO 7 SHALALA
  canal: 4 ERIE
  cat: 5 SOCKS
  CIA director under: 5 TENET
  defense secretary: 5 COHEN
  inaugural poet: 7 ANGELOU
  investigator: 5 STARR
  opponent: 4 DOLE
  or Kennedy: 7 SENATOR
  treaty: 5 NAFTA
  veep: 4 GORE 6 ALGORE
  was one: 5 YALIE
  Where Bill and Hillary ~ met:
    4 YALE
  ~ FBI director: 5 FREEH
  ~, to Yale: 4 ALUM
**"Clinton's Ditch":** 9 ERIECANAL
**Clio:** 4 MUSE 5 AWARD
  Sister of: 5 ERATO 6 THALIA
    URANIA
  winner: 5 ADMAN
  winners: 3 ADS 5 ADMEN
**Clip:** 4 CHOP GAIT PACE RATE
    5 SHEAR 6 ATTACH
    7 SCISSOR
  alternative: 6 STAPLE
  At a good: 5 APACE
  News: 5 VIDEO 7 FOOTAGE
  out: 7 SCISSOR
  wool: 5 SHEAR
**Clip-fed**
  machine gun: 4 BREN
**Clip-on**
  Belt: 5 PAGER
**Clipped:** 5 SHORN TERSE
  Musically: 8 STACCATO
**Clipper:** 4 SHIP
  feature: 4 MAST SAIL
  name: 5 PANAM

target: 4 NAIL 7 TOENAIL
**Clippers:** 6 SHEARS
  org.: 3 NBA
  Using: 4 ASEA
**Clipper-ship**
  cargo: 3 TEA
**Clipping:** 4 ITEM
  holder: 9 SCRAPBOOK
  Item for: 7 TOENAIL
  Shopper's: 6 COUPON
**Clique:** 3 SET 4 GANG
    7 COTERIE FACTION
    INCROWD INGROUP
  member: 7 INSIDER
**Cloak:** 4 CAPE 6 MANTLE
  Arabian: 8 BURNOOSE
  Bullfighter: 4 CAPA
  partner: 6 DAGGER
  Roman: 4 TOGA
  Sleeveless: 6 MANTLE
**Cloak-and-dagger**
  org.: 3 CIA
  type: 3 SPY
**Clobber:** 3 BOP LAM 4 BASH
    DECK DRUB ROUT
    5 PASTE SMITE TROMP
    6 THRASH 7 SHELLAC
  with snowballs: 4 PELT
**Clobbered**
  Is: 9 SEESSTARS
**Clock**
  Adjust a: 3 SET 5 RESET
  face: 4 DIAL
  function: 5 ALARM
  Kind of: 4 SHOT 6 ANALOG
    ATOMIC 7 DIGITAL
  Midnight on a grandfather:
    3 XII
  numeral: 3 III VII XII 4 IIII
    VIII
  part: 4 DIAL FACE GEAR
  radio button: 6 SNOOZE
  sound: 4 TICK TOCK
  std.: 3 GMT GST
**"Clockers"**
  director Spike: 3 LEE
**Clockmaker**
  ~ Terry: 3 ELI
  ~ Thomas: 4 SETH
**Clock setting**
  Ala.: 3 CST
  Ariz.: 3 MST
  at LAX: 3 PST
  Cal.: 3 PST
  Chi.: 3 CDT CST
  Colo.: 3 MST
  D.C.: 3 EDT EST
  Halifax ~ (abbr.): 3 AST
  L.A.: 3 PST
  N.S.: 3 AST
  NYC: 3 EDT EST
  Okla.: 3 CST
  Penna.: 3 EST
  Phila.: 3 EST
  Seattle ~ (abbr.): 3 PST
  S.F.: 3 PST

Summer ~ (abbr.): 3 DST EDT
**"Clockwork Orange, A"**
  hooligan: 4 ALEX
**Clod:** 3 ASS OAF 4 BOOR
  Big: 3 APE
  chopper: 3 HOE
**Clodhopper:** 3 OAF 4 BOOR
    LOUT
**Clog:** 4 SHOE 5 DAMUP JAMUP
    6 STOPUP
  bottom: 4 SOLE
  clearer: 5 DRANO
  kin: 5 SABOT
**Cloisonné:** 6 ENAMEL
**"Cloister and the Hearth, The"**
  author: 5 READE
**Cloistresse:** 3 NUN
**Clone:** 4 COPY 7 REPLICA
  Famous: 5 DOLLY
**Cloned**
  They may be: 3 PCS
**Cloning**
  basic: 3 DNA
**Clop**
  Foot that goes: 4 HOOF
**Clorox**
  cleaner: 7 LESTOIL PINESOL
**Close:** 3 END 4 NEAR SHUT
    5 LATCH TIGHT ZIPUP
    6 ENDING NEARBY
    NEARTO
  Actress: 5 GLENN
  again: 6 RESEAL
  associate: 3 PAL
  at hand: 4 NEAR NIGH
    6 NEARBY
  Brings to a: 4 ENDS
  by: 4 NEAR NIGH 6 ATHAND
    NEARTO
  by, once: 5 ANEAR
  call: 5 SCARE 8 NEARMISS
  Came to a: 5 ENDED
  companion: 8 SOULMATE
  Cut: 4 CROP MOWN 5 SHAVE
  Doesn't just: 5 SLAMS
  down: 3 END
  Draw to a: 3 END 4 WANE
  enough: 7 INRANGE
  friend: 3 PAL 8 SIDEKICK
  Get: 6 NESTLE
  Get ~ to: 4 NEAR
  Getting: 4 WARM
  Hardly a ~ win: 4 ROMP
  (in): 3 HEM
  in films: 5 GLENN
  in on: 4 NEAR
  It may be: 5 SHAVE
  Like a ~ neighbor:
    8 NEXTDOOR
  loudly: 4 SLAM
  Not: 4 AFAR 5 APART
  Not even: 3 FAR
  one: 3 PAL
  Reason to ~ up shop: 6 SIESTA
  shave: 5 SCARE
  tightly: 4 SEAL 6 SEALUP

to: 4 NEAR WARM 5 ABOUT
to closed: 4 AJAR
up: 4 SEAL
**Closed**
Almost: 4 AJAR
Behind ~ doors: 9 INPRIVATE
Not quite: 4 AJAR
Sing with a ~ mouth: 3 HUM
**Close-fitting:** 4 SNUG
hat: 5 TOQUE
**Closely**
confined, with "up": 4 PENT
connected: 7 SIAMESE
Examine: 4 SIFT
Follow: 3 APE DOG 4 HEEL
TAIL 5 STALK 6 SHADOW
Following: 6 ATHEEL
Look: 4 PEER 5 DELVE
Read: 6 PERUSE
resemble: 5 MIMIC
Watch: 3 EYE
15 KEEPASHARPEYEON
**Closemouthed:** 3 MUM
**Closeout**
caveat: 4 ASIS
**Closer**
Clothes: 4 SNAP
Fairy tale: 5 AFTER
Gate: 5 LATCH
Get ~ to: 6 GAINON
Kimono: 3 OBI 4 SASH
Letter: 5 YOURS
Newscast: 5 RECAP
Prayer: 4 AMEN
stat: 3 ERA
**Closest:** 8 NEARMOST
**Closet**
contents: 5 LINEN
Forced from the: 5 OUTED
invader: 4 MOTH
item: 5 BROOM 6 HANGER
items: 6 SHEETS
Kind of: 5 CEDAR LINEN
pest: 4 MOTH
___ close to schedule: 4 ONOR
**Close-up**
map: 5 INSET
**Closing**
**Info:** Suffix cue
Auctioneer's ~ word: 4 SOLD
document: 4 DEED
notes: 4 CODA
passage: 4 CODA
remarks: 4 OBIT
Road: 4 STER
**Cloth**
Abrasive: 5 EMERY
Absorbent: 5 TERRY
Cleaning: 3 RAG
Coarse: 5 TWEED
Cover with: 5 DRAPE
Cut from the same: 4 AKIN
finish: 3 IER
joint: 4 SEAM
Kind of: 4 LOIN
Not of the: 3 LAY 4 LAIC

sample: 6 SWATCH
Scrap of: 3 RAG
suffix: 3 IER
unit: 4 BOLT
Woolen: 7 WORSTED
Worsted: 6 TRICOT
**Clothed:** 6 DECENT
**Clothes:** 4 DUDS GARB TOGS
6 ATTIRE 7 THREADS
alterer: 6 TAILOR
Civilian: 5 MUFTI
closer: 4 SNAP
Iron: 5 ARMOR PRESS
Knight: 4 MAIL 5 ARMOR
line: 3 HEM 4 SEAM
6 CREASE INSEAM
Nice, as: 6 DRESSY
presser: 4 IRON
Put some ~ on: 6 ENROBE
with slogans: 7 TSHIRTS
**Clothes-drying**
frame: 5 AIRER
**Clothesline**
alternative: 5 DRYER
**Clothespin:** 3 PEG
Reason for a comic strip:
4 ODOR
**Clothier**
concern: 3 FIT
~ Strauss: 4 LEVI
**Clothing:** 3 TOG 4 DUDS GARB
GEAR TOGS 5 DRESS
6 ATTIRE 7 RAIMENT
Calcutta: 4 SARI
category: 4 MENS SIZE
6 MISSES
chain, with "The": 3 GAP
Food, ~, or shelter: 4 NEED
Knight: 5 ARMOR
label word: 4 MADE
line: 3 HEM 4 SEAM
6 CREASE INSEAM
size: 6 PETITE
Without: 5 NAKED
**Clothing store:** 6 THEGAP
department: 4 MENS
designations: 9 MENSSIZES
**Clotho:** 4 FATE
**Cloud:** 4 BLUR
Bit of a: 4 WISP
chamber particle: 3 ION
Interstellar: 6 NEBULA
layers: 6 STRATA
locale: 3 SKY
Low-altitude: 7 STRATUS
Mushroom ~ maker: 5 ABOMB
HBOMB
number: 4 NINE
On ~ nine: 6 ELATED
Put on ~ nine: 5 ELATE
Space: 6 NEBULA
Start of some ~ names: 4 ALTO
___ cloud: 4 OORT
**Cloudiness:** 5 BLEAR
**Cloudless:** 5 CLEAR
sky hue: 5 AZURE

**Cloud-nine**
feeling: 7 ELATION
**Clouds**
Dark: 4 OMEN
Dense: 6 CUMULI
in space: 7 NEBULAE
Move quickly, as: 4 SCUD
Rain: 5 NIMBI
Wispy: 5 CIRRI
**Clouseau**
portrayer: 7 SELLERS
valet: 4 KATO
~, briefly: 4 INSP
**Clove hitch:** 4 KNOT
**Clover**
Kind of: 8 FOURLEAF
**Cloverleaf**
feature: 4 LOOP RAMP
6 ONRAMP
parts: 5 EXITS LOOPS ROADS
**Clown:** 4 BOZO
Cartoon: 4 KOKO
Court: 6 JESTER
first name: 6 RONALD
of renown: 4 BOZO KOKO
"Pagliacci": 5 TONIO
pole: 5 STILT
prop: 3 PIE WIG 5 STILT
Sidewalk: 4 MIME
suffix: 3 ISH
TV: 4 BOZO
~ Kelly: 6 EMMETT
"___ Clown": 3 BEA
**Clownish:** 4 ZANY
**Cloying**
stuff: 7 TREACLE
**Club:** 6 CUDGEL
alternative: 3 BLT
at a club: 4 IRON 5 WEDGE
Baseball: 3 BAT
Big: 3 ACE
Car: 3 AAA
charge: 4 DUES
Cricket: 3 BAT
Cub with a: 4 SOSA
date: 3 GIG
Diamond: 3 BAT
dressing: 4 MAYO
for swingers: 3 BAT
Golf: 4 IRON WOOD 5 WEDGE
6 PUTTER
Health: 3 SPA
High-IQ: 5 MENSA
Join, as a: 5 ENTER
Kind of: 3 FAN 4 GLEE GOLF
6 KENNEL
Knight: 4 MACE
of song: 4 COPA
Private: 3 USO
soda: 7 SELTZER
Some ~ members: 4 ELKS
Spiked: 4 MACE
steak: 9 DELMONICO
U.S. motor: 3 AAA
Word after: 4 SODA
**Club ___:** 3 MED 4 SODA

___ **Club:** 4 SAMS 6 SIERRA
"___ **Club, The":** 3 PTL
**Club Med**
locale: 4 ISLE
**Clubroot**
cause: 9 SLIMEMOLD
**Clubs**
Big name in book: 5 OPRAH
or spades: 4 SUIT
Woods with: 5 TIGER
**Cluck:** 3 OAF
Condescending: 3 TSK
Dumb: 4 DODO 5 IDIOT
**Clucker:** 3 HEN
**Clucking**
sounds: 4 TSKS
**Clue:** 4 HINT IDEA
Bloodhound: 4 ODOR 5 SCENT
character: 11 MISSSCARLET
Give a: 4 HINT
hunter: 3 TEC
Misleading: 10 REDHERRING
room: 4 HALL 5 STUDY
Small: 4 HINT
weapon: 4 ROPE 8 LEADPIPE
**Clued**
in: 5 AWARE
in about: 4 ONTO
**Clueless:** 4 LOST 5 ATSEA
BLANK INEPT NAIVE
7 ATALOSS
**"Clueless"**
actress Dash: 6 STACEY
catchphrase: 4 ASIF
Cher in: 6 ALICIA
Inspiration for: 4 EMMA
lead role: 4 CHER
**Clues**
Some crossword: 4 PUNS
~, to a cop: 5 LEADS
**Clump:** 4 GLOB
Clay: 4 CLOD
of grass: 4 TUFT
of hair: 4 TUFT
Small: 4 TUFT
**Clumsily**
Handle: 3 PAW 5 PAWAT
Move: 6 LUMBER
Spill: 5 SLOSH
**Clumsy:** 5 INEPT 6 OAFISH
9 ALLTHUMBS
craft: 3 ARK
dancer's problems: 4 TOES
one: 3 OAF 4 LOUT
5 KLUTZ
one's cry: 4 OOPS
ship: 3 TUB
**Clunker:** 3 DUD 4 BOMB HEAP
5 LEMON 6 JALOPY
**Clunky**
shoe: 5 SABOT
**Cluster:** 4 CLOT KNOT TUFT
5 BUNCH GROUP
**Clutch:** 4 GRAB GRIP 5 CLASP
GRASP PEDAL
neighbor: 5 BRAKE

producer: 3 HEN
**Clutched:** 4 HELD
**Clutcher:** 4 CLAW 5 TALON
**Clutches**
Escape the ~ of: 5 ELUDE
**Clutter:** 4 MESS
E-mail: 4 SPAM
Sink: 6 DISHES
Web site: 3 ADS
**Cluttered:** 5 MESSY
Less: 5 BARER 6 NEATER
**Clutter-free:** 4 NEAT
**Clyde**
Aviation pioneer: 6 CESSNA
Cap on the: 3 TAM
City on the: 7 GLASGOW
Partner of: 6 BONNIE
**Clytemnestra**
Mother of: 4 LEDA
Slayer of: 7 ORESTES
**"C'mon in!":** 5 ENTER
**CNBC**
analyst Ron: 6 INSANA
**CNN**
anchor Paula: 4 ZAHN
founder: 6 TURNER
home (abbr.): 3 ATL
interviewer: 9 LARRYKING
offering (abbr.): 4 REPT
Part of: 4 NEWS 5 CABLE
reporter David: 5 ENSOR
**C-note**
Change for a: 4 TENS
**C-notes**
Ten: 3 GEE 4 ONEG THOU
**CN Tower**
city: 7 TORONTO
**CO**
setting: 3 MST
**Co.**
auditors: 4 CPAS
bigwig: 3 CEO 4 PRES
designation: 3 INC
Electric: 4 UTIL
French: 3 CIE
unit: 4 DEPT
**Coach:** 3 BUS 5 CLASS TRAIN
TUTOR 6 ADVISE
MENTOR 7 TRAINER
~ Chuck: 4 NOLL
~ Dan: 5 ISSEL
~ Don: 5 SHULA
~ Ewbank: 4 WEEB
~ George: 5 HALAS
~ Greasy: 5 NEALE
~ Hank: 5 STRAM
~ Jackson: 4 PHIL
~ Joe: 7 PATERNO
~ Karolyi: 4 BELA
~ Mike: 5 DITKA
~ Parseghian: 3 ARA
~ Pat: 5 RILEY
~ Rockne: 5 KNUTE
**"Coach"**
actress Georgia: 5 ENGEL
**Coagulate:** 3 SET 4 CLOT

**Coal**
boat: 4 SCOW
carrier: 3 HOD 4 TRAM
container: 3 BIN
Covers with ~ dust: 5 SOOTS
deposit: 4 SEAM
German ~ region: 4 RUHR
SAAR
hole: 4 MINE
Hot: 5 EMBER
layer: 4 VEIN
product: 4 COKE
scuttle: 3 HOD
stratum: 4 SEAM
unit: 3 TON 4 LUMP
**Coalfield**
city: 5 ESSEN
**Coalition:** 4 BLOC 5 UNION
Form a: 5 UNITE
**"Coal Miner's Daughter"**
subject: 4 LYNN
**Coals**
Rake over the: 5 CHIDE
ROAST SCOLD
**Coarse:** 4 LEWD 5 BAWDY
ROUGH 6 EARTHY
fabric: 5 TWEED
file: 4 RASP
flour: 4 MEAL
Opposite of: 4 FINE
person: 5 BEAST
**Coarsely**
irreverent: 6 RIBALD
**Coast:** 5 GLIDE SHORE
7 SEASIDE
On the: 6 INLAND
___ **Coast, Antarctica:** 6 ADELIE
**Coastal**
catch: 4 SOLE
city: 4 PORT
feature: 5 INLET
flier: 3 ERN 4 ERNE
prefix: 5 INTRA
region: 8 SEABOARD
resorts: 8 RIVIERAS
**Coasted:** 4 SLID
**Coaster:** 4 LUGE SLED
cry: 4 WHEE
Roller: 4 RIDE
**Coast Guard**
alert: 3 SOS
rank (abbr.): 3 ADM CPO ENS
___ **Coast, Hawaii:** 4 KONA
**Coastline**
feature: 3 RIA 5 INLET
**Coat:** 5 LAYER
Apply a new: 7 REPAINT
Canine: 6 ENAMEL
Expensive: 3 FUR
feature: 5 LAPEL
Fir: 4 BARK
First: 6 PRIMER
Fix a: 6 RELINE
Grass: 3 DEW
Heavy: 6 ULSTER
holder: 3 PEG

House: 5 PAINT
It has a red: 4 EDAM
Kind of: 3 LAB PEA 4 BASE
Like an Airedale: 4 WIRY
Mink: 3 FUR
of paint: 5 LAYER
on Santa's coat: 4 SOOT
Orange: 4 RIND SKIN
part: 3 ARM 4 HOOD
Put a ~ on: 4 GILD 5 PAINT
Red: 4 RUST
Seaman's: 9 PEAJACKET
Seed: 4 ARIL 5 TESTA
Short: 5 TUNIC 6 REEFER
   TABARD
Sugar: 5 ICING
Take a ~ off: 4 PARE
White: 4 RIME
Winter: 3 ICE 4 RIME SNOW
   6 ANORAK ULSTER
with a coat of arms: 6 TABARD
with gold: 4 GILD 5 PLATE
**Coated**
candy: 5 MANDM
**Coating:** 4 FILM RIND 5 LAYER
Bronze: 6 PATINA
Bumper: 6 CHROME
Canine: 6 ENAMEL
Ember: 3 ASH
Floss: 3 WAX
Icy: 4 HOAR RIME
Nonstick: 6 TEFLON
Sandpaper: 4 GRIT
**Coat-of-arms**
border: 4 ORLE
**Coatrack**
item: 3 PEG
**Coax:** 4 URGE
**Cob:** 3 PEN
**Cobalt**
~ 60: 7 ISOTOPE
**Cobb**
Actor: 4 LEEJ
and others: 3 TYS
salad ingredient: 5 BACON
**"Cobb"**
Ty Cobb portrayer, in:
   13 TOMMYLEEJONES
**Cobbled**
together: 4 MADE
~, in a way: 5 SOLED
**Cobbler:** 3 PIE
container: 6 PIEPAN PIETIN
Do a ~ job: 6 REHEEL
   RESOLE
form: 4 LAST
output: 5 SHOES
stock: 5 HEELS SOLES
tool: 3 AWL
~, at times: 5 SOLER
**Cobblestone**
sound: 4 CLOP
___ Cob, Connecticut: 3 COS
**Cobra:** 5 SNAKE
Egyptian: 3 ASP
killer: 8 MONGOOSE

kin: 3 ASP 5 MAMBA
**Coburn, D.L.**
~ Pulitzer play, with "The":
   7 GINGAME
**Cobweb**
Filmy: 8 GOSSAMER
site: 5 ATTIC
**Coca**
Comic: 7 IMOGENE
**Coca-Cola**
brand: 3 TAB 6 FRESCA
   MRPIBB
**Cochise:** 6 APACHE
player Michael: 6 ANSARA
**Cochran**
Mississippi senator: 4 THAD
**Cock**
and bull: 3 HES 5 MALES
**Cock-a-doodle-doo:** 4 CROW
**Cockamamie:** 5 INANE
   7 ASININE
**Cockatoo**
kin: 5 MACAW
**Cocked:** 5 ATILT
It may be: 3 HAT
**Cockeyed:** 4 ALOP LOCO
   5 AMISS ASKEW INANE
   6 ABSURD ALLWET
   ASLANT
**Cockney:** 4 BRIT
**Info:** British cue
coins: 5 PENCE
greeting: 4 ELLO
residence: 3 OME
**Cockpit**
abbr.: 3 ALT
acknowledgment: 5 ROGER
button: 5 EJECT
calculation: 3 ETA
figure: 5 PILOT 7 COPILOT
**Cockroach**
Fictional keyboarding:
   5 ARCHY
**Cocktail**
Brandy: 7 SIDECAR
   STINGER
Brunch: 6 MIMOSA
Champagne: 6 MIMOSA
Fruit ~ fruit: 4 PEAR
Fruity: 6 MAITAI
Gin and lime: 6 GIMLET
Half a: 3 MAI TAI
made with grenadine:
   7 BACARDI
Molotov ~ fuse: 3 RAG
nibble: 6 CANAPE
party spread: 4 PATE
Popular: 7 MARTINI
Rum: 6 MAITAI
Vodka: 12 WHITERUSSIAN
**Coco**
of fashion: 6 CHANEL
**Coconut**
cookie: 8 MACAROON
Dried: 5 COPRA
fiber: 4 COIR

Oranges and shredded:
   8 AMBROSIA
source: 4 PALM
**Cocoon**
dwellers: 5 PUPAE
Exit one's: 6 EMERGE
fiber: 4 SILK
resident: 4 PUPA
**"Cocoon"**
actor: 6 AMECHE
actor Cronyn: 4 HUME
director Howard: 3 RON
**Cod:** 4 CAPE
kin: 4 HAKE
piece: 3 FIN
___ Cod: 4 CAPE LING
**Coda**
kin: 6 EPILOG 8 EPILOGUE
place: 3 END
**Coddle:** 4 BABY 6 PAMPER
**Coddled**
It may be: 3 EGG
**Code**
ATM: 3 PIN
Bar: 3 LAW
Bar ~ reader: 7 SCANNER
breaker: 3 KEY
carrier: 3 DNA 4 GENE
component: 3 LAW
Computer: 5 ASCII
cracker comment: 3 AHA
creator: 5 MORSE
Gangster: 6 OMERTA
Genetic: 3 DNA
Govt. ~ breakers: 3 NSA
It has a: 4 AREA GENE
Kind of: 3 ZIP 4 AREA
   5 DRESS MORSE PENAL
Long, in: 3 DAH 4 DASH
Moral: 5 ETHIC
name: 5 MORSE
of conduct: 5 ETHIC
of silence: 6 OMERTA
Org. with a: 3 IRS
subject: 4 AREA 5 DRESS
syllable: 3 DAH 4 DASH
Web prog.: 4 HTML
word: 3 DAH DIT 4 ALFA
   6 SIERRA
___ code: 3 ZIP 4 AREA
   5 MORSE PENAL
**Code-cracking**
org.: 3 NSA
**Coded**
message: 6 CIPHER
**Codeine:** 6 OPIATE
source: 5 OPIUM
**Codfish**
Young: 5 SCROD
**Codger:** 4 COOT CUSS
   6 GEEZER
replies: 3 EHS
**Coed**
It may be: 4 DORM
**Coeducation**
pioneering college: 7 OBERLIN

**Coen**
brothers film: 5 FARGO
Filmmaker: 4 JOEL 5 ETHAN
**Coerce:** 5 FORCE
**Coercion:** 6 DURESS
___ **Coeur:** 5 SACRE
**Coeur d'___, Idaho:** 5 ALENE
**Coffee:** 3 JOE 4 JAVA
add-in: 5 CREAM
allure: 5 AROMA
alternative: 3 TEA
brewer: 3 URN
choice: 7 INSTANT
container: 3 URN
flavor: 5 MOCHA
gathering: 6 KLATCH
7 KLATSCH
harvest: 5 BEANS
Hawaiian: 4 KONA
holder: 3 CUP MUG POT URN
Hot ~ hazard: 5 SCALD
How ~ may be served:
6 AULAIT
Just sit, like: 7 GETCOLD
Kind of: 4 DRIP ICED
5 DECAF IRISH
lightener: 5 CREAM
Like some: 4 ICED
liqueur: 6 KAHLUA
8 TIAMARIA
Made: 6 PERKED
maker: 3 URN
order: 5 BLACK DECAF
LATTE LIGHT MOCHA
SANKA 6 GRANDE
7 REGULAR
order (abbr.): 3 REG
Place for: 5 TABLE
Quick: 7 INSTANT
server: 3 URN
size: 4 TALL
source: 4 BEAN
Strong black ~ after dinner:
9 DEMITASSE
table item: 7 ARTBOOK
variety: 5 MOCHA
~, in slang: 3 JOE MUD
4 JAVA
**Coffee ___:** 3 URN
**"Coffee ___?":** 5 ORTEA
___ **coffee:** 5 IRISH
**" ___ coffee?":** 5 TEAOR
**Coffee break**
hr.: 5 TENAM
snack: 5 DONUT
time: 3 TEN
When some take a: 5 ATTEN
**Coffeehouse**
choice: 5 MOCHA
container: 3 URN
draw: 5 AROMA
order: 5 LATTE
8 ESPRESSO
**"Coffee, ___ Me?":** 5 TEAOR
**Coffeepot:** 3 URN
**"Coffee, Tea ___?":** 4 ORME

**Coffee-to-go**
need: 3 LID
**Coffin**
stand: 4 BIER
**Cog**
Slip a: 3 ERR
**Coghlan, Eamonn:** 5 MILER
**Cogitate:** 5 THINK
**Cogitating**
Result of: 4 IDEA
**"Cogito ___ sum":** 4 ERGO
**Cognac**
Big name in: 4 REMY
**Cognate:** 4 AKIN
**Cognizant:** 5 AWARE
of: 4 INON ONTO 5 HIPTO
**Cohabitant:** 6 POSSLQ ROOMIE
**Cohen**
Skater: 5 SASHA
**Coherent**
Emit ~ light: 4 LASE
**Cohesive**
group: 4 UNIT
**Cohn**
Grammy winner: 4 MARC
**Coho:** 6 SALMON
**Cohort:** 3 PAL 4 ALLY CHUM
5 CRONY
**Coif**
Frizzy: 4 AFRO
High: 4 UPDO
**Coiffure:** 6 HAIRDO
**Coiffures:** 3 DOS
**Coil:** 5 HELIX SKEIN TWINE
6 SPIRAL
Inventor of a: 5 TESLA
of hair: 4 HANK
___ **coil:** 5 TESLA
**Coiled:** 5 WOUND
**Coin:** 4 MINT 6 INVENT
SPECIE
$10 ~: 5 EAGLE
collection: 4 ROLL
collector: 4 SOFA
factory: 4 MINT
Fake: 4 SLUG
flip: 4 TOSS
flipper phrase: 6 CALLIT
hole: 4 SLOT
New: 4 EURO
Old gold: 5 DUCAT
reverse: 5 TAILS
side: 7 OBVERSE
Small: 3 SOU 4 CENT
Thin: 4 DIME
toss call: 5 HEADS TAILS
word: 3 GOD 4 UNUM
5 TRUST
Worthless: 3 SOU
**Coincide:** 5 AGREE
with: 7 OVERLAP
**Coined**
money: 6 SPECIE
word: 4 UNUM
**Coin-edge**
ridge: 5 KNURL

**Coins:** 6 SPECIE
and bills: 4 CASH
Roll of: 7 ROULEAU
Some: 6 TOKENS
**Coke:** 4 COLA
alternative: 5 PEPSI
and Pepsi: 5 COLAS
partner: 3 RUM
vs. Pepsi event: 9 TASTETEST
**Col.**
boss: 3 GEN
**Cola**
choice: 5 PEPSI
container: 3 CAN
cooler: 3 ICE
Part of: 4 COST
**Colada**
liquor: 3 RUM
___ **colada:** 4 PINA
**Colander:** 8 STRAINER
kin: 5 SIEVE
**Colbert**
role: 9 CLEOPATRA
**Colchester**
county: 5 ESSEX
**Colchis**
Ship to: 4 ARGO
**Cold:** 4 ICED 5 ALGID HARSH
RHEUM 6 WINTRY
8 UNHEATED
and clammy: 4 DANK
and damp: 6 CLAMMY
and wet: 3 RAW
Bitterly: 3 RAW 7 GLACIAL
call: 3 BRR
capital: 4 BERN OSLO
8 HELSINKI
Crack from the: 4 CHAP
cube: 3 ICE
cuts: 4 MEAT
desserts: 4 ICES
development: 7 REDNOSE
draft: 4 BEER
drops: 5 SLEET
era: 6 ICEAGE
feet: 4 FEAR
front: 3 CEE
Give the ~ shoulder: 4 SHUN
SNUB 5 SPURN
Go ~ turkey: 4 QUIT
Had down: 4 KNEW
Like a ~ shower: 6 SLEETY
Like many ~ meds: 3 OTC
mold: 5 ASPIC
one: 4 BEER BREW
or hot drink: 5 CIDER
reaction: 3 BRR
Really: 3 ICY 6 FROSTY
response: 5 ACHOO
shoulder: 4 SNUB
shower: 4 HAIL 5 SLEET
Soup served: 5 SCHAV
spell: 6 ICEAGE
symptom: 7 SNIFFLE
temperatures: 5 TEENS
Very: 3 ICY 5 GELID 6 ARCTIC

weather protector: 5 PARKA
7 EARFLAP
~, in Spanish: 4 FRIA FRIO

**Cold-blooded**
killer: 3 ASP 4 TREX

**Cold-caller**
goal: 4 SALE

**"Cold Case Files"**
carrier: 5 AANDE

**Cold-cock:** 4 STUN

**"Cold Mountain"**
role for Nicole: 3 ADA

**"Cold one":** 4 BEER

**Cold-shoulder:** 4 SHUN SNUB
5 SPURN

**Cold War**
abbr.: 3 SSR
capital: 4 BONN
concern: 5 HBOMB
country: 4 USSR
defense gp.: 4 NATO
foe: 4 REDS USSR
initials: 3 SDI 4 USSR
news name: 4 TASS
org.: 3 KGB
power: 4 USSR
threat: 5 HBOMB
winner: 4 NATO

**Cold-weather**
cap part: 6 EARLAP
coat: 5 PARKA

**Cole**
of song: 3 NAT 7 NATALIE
or Abdul: 5 PAULA

**Cole ___:** 4 SLAW

**Coleman**
Songwriter ~ et al.: 3 CYS

**Coleridge**
character: 7 MARINER
sacred river: 4 ALPH
work: 3 ODE 4 RIME

**Coles**
Dancer: 4 HONI

**Colette**
1920 ~ novel: 5 CHERI
pal: 4 AMIE
work: 4 GIGI

**Colgate**
rival: 3 AIM 5 CREST GLEEM

**Coliseum:** 5 ARENA

**Coll.:** 3 SCH
admissions concerns: 4 SATS
aides: 3 TAS
course: 3 SOC 4 ECON
degrees: 3 BAS
dorm figures: 3 RAS
figure: 4 PROF
hoops competition: 3 NIT
hopefuls: 3 SRS
hotshot: 4 BMOC
major: 3 BIO ENG SOC
4 ECON
marchers: 4 ROTC
record no.: 3 GPA
senior's test: 3 GRE
Some ~ exams: 5 LSATS

Some ~ students: 3 SRS
sports group: 4 NCAA

**Collaborative**
number: 4 DUET

**"Collages"**
author: 3 NIN

**Collagist**
French: 3 ARP
need: 4 GLUE

**Collapse:** 4 GIVE 6 CAVEIN
FALLIN

**Collapsed:** 4 FELL GAVE
WENT

**Collapsible**
bed: 3 COT
lid: 8 OPERAHAT

**Collar:** 3 NAB 4 NAIL 5 PINCH
RUNIN SEIZE 6 ARREST
attachment: 5 IDTAG LEASH
extension: 5 LAPEL
Hot under the: 4 SORE
5 ANGRY IRATE RILED
Inquisition: 7 GAROTTE
insert: 4 STAY
Kind of: 4 ETON FLEA
Make a: 3 NAB 4 BUST
6 ARREST
on a pipe: 6 FLANGE
Put the ~ on: 3 NAB 5 RANIN
6 ARREST
Ring around the: 3 LEI TIE
stiffener: 4 STAY
victim: 4 PERP
White ~ worker: 6 CLERIC

**Collared:** 5 RANIN

**Collate:** 4 SORT

**Colleague:** 4 PEER

**Collect:** 4 REAP SAVE 5 AMASS
RAISE 6 GATHER
Part of a ~ call number: 3 ATT
slowly: 5 GLEAN

**Collected:** 3 MET 4 CALM COOL
6 SEDATE SERENE
dust: 3 SAT
sayings: 3 ANA

**Collectible:** 5 CURIO
candy dispenser: 3 PEZ
cap: 3 POG
car: 5 EDSEL
Cartoon: 3 CEL
illustrator: 4 ERTE
~ Ming: 4 VASE

**Collectibles**
Music: 3 LPS

**Collecting**
a pension (abbr.): 3 RET

**Collection:** 3 ANA SET 5 ARRAY
BATCH TROVE
8 ENSEMBLE
agcy.: 3 IRS
Complete: 3 SET
Literary: 3 ANA
Map: 5 ATLAS
Monopoly: 4 RENT
of anecdotes: 3 ANA
of brains: 5 MENSA

of Hindu truths: 5 SUTRA
of online discussion groups:
6 USENET
of poetry: 4 EDDA EPOS
Record: 7 DATASET
8 DATABASE
Smithsonian: 9 AMERICANA
Stock: 4 HERD
Valuable: 5 TROVE
Vinyl: 3 LPS

**Collectively:** 5 ASONE INALL

**Collector**
Coin: 4 SOFA
Garbage: 6 ASHMAN
goal: 3 SET
Lint: 4 TRAP 5 INNIE
Nectar: 3 BEE
quests: 4 SETS
Specimen: 4 SWAP
Trash: 3 BIN

**"Collector, The"**
actress Samantha: 5 EGGAR

**Colleen:** 4 LASS
country: 4 EIRE

**College**
administrator: 4 DEAN
application part: 5 ESSAY
area: 4 QUAD
bigwig: 4 DEAN 7 PROVOST
book: 4 TEXT
bulldogs: 4 ELIS
California: 6 POMONA
Carolina: 4 ELON
Cedar Rapids: 3 COE
Certify, as a: 8 ACCREDIT
cheer: 3 RAH
course, briefly: 3 LIT 5 PSYCH
entrance exam: 3 SAT
exam: 4 ORAL
First coed ~ in U.S.:
7 OBERLIN
grad: 4 ALUM
head: 5 PREXY
Hold aside as a ~ athlete:
8 REDSHIRT
housing: 4 DORM
Iowa: 3 COE
Kentucky: 5 BEREA
lecturer: 4 PROF
life: 7 ACADEME
Like some ~ curricula: 4 CORE
Like some ~ walls: 5 IVIED
maj.: 5 PSYCH
major: 3 ART 4 MATH
5 DRAMA
member: 7 ELECTOR
Michigan: 4 ALMA
military gp.: 4 ROTC
New Rochelle: 4 IONA
North Carolina: 4 ELON
NY: 3 RPI
official: 4 DEAN 6 BURSAR
7 PROVOST
Ohio: 4 KENT 5 HIRAM
7 OBERLIN
Portland: 4 REED

Poughkeepsie: 6 MARIST
   VASSAR
quarters: 5 DORMS
Some ~ students: 5 COEDS
sports org.: 4 NCAA
sr.'s exam: 4 GMAT LSAT
sr.'s test: 3 GRE
unit: 6 CREDIT
web address suffix: 3 EDU
Wisconsin: 5 RIPON 6 BELOIT
Word in many ~ names:
   4 TECH
~ QB, often: 4 BMOC
~, to Aussies: 3 UNI
~ VIP: 4 BMOC DEAN
**College Park**
   athlete: 4 TERP
**College World Series**
   site: 5 OMAHA
**Collegian**
   Connecticut: 3 ELI
   declaration: 5 MAJOR
   Florida: 5 GATOR
   Maryland: 4 TERP
   New Haven: 3 ELI 5 YALIE
   quest: 6 DEGREE
**Collette**
   Actress: 4 TONI
**Collide**
   with: 7 REAREND
**Collie**
   of film: 6 LASSIE
**Colliery**
   carrier: 4 TRAM
**Collin**
   Country singer: 4 RAYE
**Collins**
   Astronaut: 6 EILEEN
   Pop singer: 4 PHIL
**Collins, Michael**
   land: 4 EIRE
   Org. founded by: 3 IRA
**Collision:** 5 CRASH 6 IMPACT
   Kind of: 6 MIDAIR
   result: 4 DENT
   Serious: 7 SMASHUP
   sound: 3 BAM 4 BANG
**Colloquialism:** 5 IDIOM SLANG
**Collusion:** 7 CAHOOTS
**Colmes**
   of Hannity & Colmes: 4 ALAN
**Colo.**
   clock setting: 3 MST
   neighbor: 3 KAN NEB WYO
   4 NEBR
**Cologne**
   Info: German cue
   Article of: 3 EIN
   City near: 5 ESSEN
   conjunction: 3 UND
   cooler: 3 EIS
   cry: 3 ACH
   German name for: 4 KOLN
   "Oh!" de: 3 ACH
   Popular: 4 TABU
   river: 5 RHINE

scent: 4 MUSK
trio: 4 DREI
water: 3 EAU
___ **Cologne:** 5 EAUDE
**Colombian**
   border river: 7 ORINOCO
   capital: 6 BOGOTA
   city: 4 CALI
   coin: 4 PESO
   kin: 4 TIOS
   Onetime ~ drug kingpin:
   7 ESCOBAR
**Colon**
   Abbr. that may precede a:
   4 ATTN
   translation: 4 ISTO
**Colonel:** 4 RANK
   Comics: 5 BLIMP
   insignia: 5 EAGLE
   TV: 5 HOGAN
**Colonel Klink**
   Foil for: 5 HOGAN
**Colonel Mustard**
   game: 4 CLUE
**Colonel Sanders**
   feature: 6 GOATEE
**Colonel Tibbets**
   Mother of: 5 ENOLA
**Colonial**
   descendants gp.: 3 DAR
   diplomat Silas: 5 DEANE
   estate owner: 5 SAHIB
   insect: 3 ANT
   leader: 3 NEO
   newsman: 5 CRIER
   or Cape Cod: 5 HOUSE
   prefix: 3 NEO
   ~ British rule in India: 3 RAJ
   ~ Virginia: 4 DARE
**Colonies**
   Like some: 5 APIAN
   One of the 13 orig.: 3 DEL
   4 CONN PENN
**Colonist**
   Molokai: 5 LEPER
   Small: 3 ANT
   Virginia: 5 ROLFE
**Colonizer**
   of Greenland: 4 ERIC
**Colonnade**
   Ancient: 4 STOA
   tree: 3 ELM
**Colony**
   Ancient Greek: 5 IONIA
   Art ~ of New Mexico: 4 TAOS
   Former British: 4 ADEN
   Former Portuguese: 3 GOA
   5 MACAO
   Insect: 4 HIVE
   Kind of: 5 PENAL 6 NUDIST
   member: 3 ANT BEE 4 WASP
   5 LEPER
   Southwestern art: 4 TAOS
**Color:** 3 DYE HUE 5 TINCT
   Add ~ to: 4 TINT
   anew: 5 REDYE

Burnt: 6 SIENNA
Change: 3 DYE
changer: 4 DYER
Drained of: 3 WAN 4 PALE
   5 ASHEN
fabric: 6 TIEDYE
Get some: 3 TAN
Intense, as: 5 VIVID
Lacking: 4 PALE
Lack of: 6 PALLOR
lightly: 4 TINT
Lose: 4 FADE PALE
Lost: 5 FADED PALED
Neutral: 3 TAN 4 ECRU
   5 FLESH
of honey: 4 GOLD 5 AMBER
of money: 5 GREEN
of raw silk: 4 ECRU
of sand: 3 TAN
of water: 4 AQUA
on the Irish flag: 6 ORANGE
prefix: 3 TRI UNI
Primary: 3 RED
quality: 4 TONE
Ring of: 6 AREOLA
separator: 5 PRISM
Subdued: 6 PASTEL
Touch of: 5 TINCT TINGE
Turn: 5 RIPEN
variation: 5 SHADE
wheel display: 5 TONES
**Coloradan**
   Early: 3 UTE
**Colorado**
   city: 5 ASPEN 7 DURANGO
   creek: 3 RIA
   Former ~ governor Roy:
   5 ROMER
   hrs.: 3 MST
   native: 3 UTE
   neighbor: 4 UTAH
   resort: 4 VAIL 5 ASPEN
   Western ~ sight: 4 MESA
   ~ NHL team: 3 AVS
   ~ Park: 5 ESTES
**Colorado River**
   city: 4 YUMA
   feeder: 4 GILA
**"Colorado Serenade":** 5 OATER
**Colorado Springs**
   initials: 4 USAF
**Colorado State**
   player: 3 RAM
**Colorant:** 3 DYE
**Coloration:** 5 TINCT
   Slight: 4 TINT 5 TINGE
**Coloratura**
   piece: 4 ARIA
**Colored**
   Brightly: 4 LOUD NEON
   Brightly ~ bird: 6 ORIOLE
   Brightly ~ fish: 4 OPAH
   eye part: 4 IRIS
   glasses color: 4 ROSE
**Colorfast**
   Wasn't: 3 RAN 4 BLED

**Colorful**
amphibian: 4 NEWT
arc: 7 RAINBOW
bands: 7 SPECTRA
card game: 3 UNO
cat: 6 CALICO
circle: 6 AREOLA
computer: 4 IMAC
diaphragm: 4 IRIS
fish: 4 OPAH 5 TETRA
   6 TETRAS
Hardly: 4 DRAB 5 ASHEN
horse: 4 ROAN
insects: 7 REDANTS
Least: 6 PALEST
parrot: 5 MACAW
seashell: 6 TRITON
songbird: 6 ORIOLE
talk: 5 SLANG
Used ~ language: 5 SWORE
wrap: 6 SERAPE
writing: 7 IMAGERY
~ Apple: 4 IMAC
**Coloring:** 4 TINT 5 TINCT
Cheek: 5 ROUGE
expert: 4 DYER
Hair: 3 DYE
Horse: 4 ROAN
Salon: 5 HENNA
**Colorist:** 4 DYER
**Colorless:** 3 WAN 4 DRAB PALE
ketone: 6 ACETOL
liqueur: 4 OUZO
liquor: 7 TEQUILA
solvent: 7 ACETONE
**"Color Purple, The"**
author Walker: 5 ALICE
role: 5 CELIE
Sofia in: 5 OPRAH
Whoopi in: 5 CELIE
**Colors**
Having a range of: 7 OPALINE
Like some: 4 NEON
Pass with flying: 3 ACE
**"Colors"**
actor Sean: 4 PENN
actress Maria Conchita:
   6 ALONSO
**Color TV**
knob: 4 TINT
pioneer: 3 RCA
**Colo. Spr.**
Initials at: 4 USAF
**Colossal:** 4 EPIC HUGE
   7 TITANIC
**Colosseum**
sights: 5 LIONS
wear: 4 TOGA
**Colossus:** 5 TITAN
locale: 6 RHODES
**"Colossus, The"**
poet: 5 PLATH
**Colour**
Autumn: 5 OCHRE
**Colt**
coddler: 4 MARE

mother: 4 MARE
of fame: 6 UNITAS
**Colt 45**
maker: 5 PABST
**Colt .45s**
~, today: 6 ASTROS
**Columba**
island: 4 IONA
**Columbia**
athlete: 4 LION
City on the: 7 ASTORIA
launcher: 4 NASA
**Columbian**
prefix: 3 PRE
vessel: 5 PINTA
**Columbia Pictures**
cofounder: 4 COHN
**Columbo:** 3 TEC
and others (abbr.): 3 LTS
Bandleader: 4 RUSS
employer: 4 LAPD
portrayer: 4 FALK
**Columbus**
birthplace: 5 GENOA
death year: 5 MDVI
discovery: 5 HAITI 7 ANTIGUA
   JAMAICA
Home to: 4 OHIO
in NYC: 3 AVE
Native encountered by:
   5 CARIB
port: 5 PALOS
sch.: 3 OSU
Second voyage start for:
   5 CADIZ
ship: 4 NINA 5 PINTA
**Columbus Day**
event: 4 SALE 6 PARADE
mo.: 3 OCT
**Column:** 6 PILLAR
Addition: 4 ONES TENS
Cal.: 3 FRI MON SAT SUN
   THU TUE WED 4 THUR
   TUES
crossers: 4 ROWS
Grooved, as a: 6 FLUTED
Kind of: 4 LOSS ONES OPED
   5 IONIC 6 SPINAL
Ledger: 6 ASSETS
Memorial: 4 OBIT
P&L ~ heading: 3 YTD
piece: 4 ITEM
Rightmost: 4 ONES
Society ~ word: 3 NEE
Sports: 4 WINS 6 LOSSES
style: 5 DORIC IONIC
worker: 5 ADDER
~ A or B selection:
   6 ENTREE
**Columnist**
Advice: 3 ANN 4 ABBY
page: 4 OPED
~ Barrett: 4 RONA
~ Bombeck: 4 ERMA
~ Buchwald: 3 ART
~ Coulter: 3 ANN

~ Goodman: 5 ELLEN
~ Herb: 4 CAEN
~ Hopper: 5 HEDDA
~ Joseph: 5 ALSOP
~ Landers: 3 ANN
~ LeShan: 3 EDA
~ Marilyn ___ Savant: 3 VOS
~ Maureen: 4 DOWD
~ Mike: 5 ROYKO
~ Rowland: 5 EVANS
~ Smith: 3 LIZ
**Com**
preceder: 3 DOT
prefix: 4 TELE
relative: 3 EDU GOV ORG
**Comanche**
enemy: 3 UTE
**Comaneci**
Gymnast: 5 NADIA
**Comb**
again and again: 5 PREEN
backwards: 5 TEASE
Divide with a: 4 PART
Kind of: 7 RATTAIL
maker: 3 BEE
Place for a: 4 HIVE MANE
   5 TRESS
projections: 5 TEETH
**Combat:** 3 WAR 4 DUEL
   6 OPPOSE
area: 7 WARZONE
gear: 5 ARMOR
zone: 5 ARENA 6 SECTOR
**Combatant:** 3 FOE 4 VIER
   5 ENEMY
1999 ~: 4 SERB
Civil War: 3 REB
Corrida: 6 TORERO
**Combative**
Small ~ ones: 7 BANTAMS
**Combination:** 7 AMALGAM
Boxing: 6 ONETWO
Card: 4 MELD
**Combinations**
Info: Prefix cue
**Combine:** 3 ADD MIX WED
   4 MELD POOL 5 UNITE
with: 5 ADDTO
~, as resources: 4 POOL
**Combined:** 5 INONE
   8 ALLINONE
**Combing**
attractions: 6 SHELLS
**Combo:** 4 BAND
Card: 4 MELD
Largish: 5 NONET OCTET
Musical: 5 CHORD
offering: 3 SET
Ring: 6 ONETWO
Small: 4 TRIO
**Combs**
of baseball: 5 EARLE
Ones with: 4 BEES
Rapper: 4 SEAN
**Combs, ___ "Puffy":** 4 SEAN
**Combust:** 4 BURN

**Combustible**
heap: 4 PYRE
**Come:** 6 ARRIVE
about: 4 TURN 5 ARISE
    OCCUR PIVOT
across: 4 FIND
across as: 4 SEEM
after: 5 ENSUE
again: 5 RECUR
and go: 5 RECUR
apart: 3 RIP 7 UNRAVEL
apart at the seams: 4 FRAY
back: 4 ECHO 5 RECUR
    6 ANSWER
back again: 6 REECHO
before: 6 LEADTO 7 PRECEDE
    PREDATE 8 ANTECEDE
    ANTEDATE
by: 3 GET 5 VISIT 6 ATTAIN
clean: 4 TELL 5 ADMIT
    BATHE LEVEL 6 FESSUP
clean, with "up": 4 FESS
closer to: 4 NEAR
down: 3 SET 4 LAND RAIN
    TEEM
down hard: 4 POUR TEEM
down to earth: 4 LAND
down with: 3 GET 5 CATCH
forth: 6 EMERGE
from behind: 5 RALLY
Hard to ~ by: 4 RARE
in: 5 ENTER 6 ARRIVE
in second: 4 LOSE 5 PLACE
in third: 4 SHOW
into one's own: 7 BLOSSOM
into view: 4 LOOM 6 APPEAR
    EMERGE
It may ~ after you: 3 ARE
It may ~ before long: 3 ERE
next: 5 ENSUE 6 FOLLOW
out: 5 DEBUT 6 EMERGE
    7 EMANATE
out on top: 3 WIN
Really ~ down: 4 POUR
Sign of things to: 4 OMEN
to: 5 REACH TOTAL WAKEN
    6 ATTEND AWAKEN
    8 ARRIVEAT
to a halt: 3 END 4 STOP
    5 CEASE
to a point: 5 TAPER
together: 3 GEL 4 JELL KNIT
    MASS MESH 5 AMASS
    MERGE REUNE UNITE
    8 COALESCE
to light: 5 ARISE 6 EMERGE
to mind: 5 ARISE OCCUR
too: 8 TAGALONG
to pass: 5 ENSUE OCCUR
    6 BETIDE HAPPEN
to terms: 5 AGREE
to the plate: 3 BAT
to the rescue of: 3 AID
up: 5 ARISE
up again: 5 RECUR
up against: 4 ABUT

up short: 3 OWE 4 FAIL FALL
    LOSE
up with: 6 CREATE
**Come-___:** 3 ONS 6 HITHER
**"Come again?":** 3 HUH
    4 WHAT
**Comeback:** 4 ECHO 5 REPLY
    6 ANSWER RETORT
    7 RIPOSTE 8 RESPONSE
Playground: 5 AMNOT ARESO
    ISNOT ISTOO 6 CANTOO
Snappy: 6 RETORT
**"Come Back, Little ___":**
    5 SHEBA
**"Come Back, Little Sheba"**
playwright: 4 INGE
wife: 4 LOLA
**Comedian:** 6 AMUSER
stock: 4 GAGS
Violin-playing: 5 BENNY
~ Bill, briefly: 3 COS
~ Bruce: 5 LENNY
~ Charlotte: 3 RAE
~ George: 5 GOBEL
~ Louis: 3 NYE
~ Margaret: 3 CHO
~ Martha: 4 RAYE
~ Richard: 5 PRYOR
**Comedians**
-- Bob and Chris: 8 ELLIOTTS
**Comedy**
Anne of: 5 MEARA
Caesar of: 3 SID
club sound: 4 HAHA ROAR
Costello of: 3 LOU
Fields of: 5 TOTIE
First name in: 3 EMO
Half a ~ duo: 5 MEARA OLLIE
Idle in: 4 ERIC
Inits. in: 3 SNL
King of: 4 ALAN
Muse of: 6 THALIA
props: 4 PIES
Rivers of: 4 JOAN
Rock of: 5 CHRIS
**Comedy Central**
game show host: 5 STEIN
**Come from ___:** 4 AFAR
**"Come here ___?":** 5 OFTEN
**"Come in!":** 5 ENTER
**Come-on:** 4 LINE LURE
    5 OFFER 6 TEASER
Commercial: 6 TRYONE
Credit card: 5 NOFEE
**Comet:** 8 REINDEER
competitor: 4 AJAX 6 BONAMI
head: 4 COMA
leader: 5 SANTA
Moves like a: 4 ARCS
**Cometh**
He: 6 ICEMAN
**"___ Cometh, The":** 6 ICEMAN
**Comets**
Leader of the: 5 HALEY
**Comeuppance**
Cad's: 4 SLAP

Defaulter's: 4 REPO
Mugger's: 4 MACE
**Comfort:** 4 EASE 5 SALVE
    6 RELIEF SOLACE
    SOOTHE 7 CONSOLE
Give ~ to: 6 SOOTHE
    8 REASSURE
Words of: 5 ITSOK
**Comfortable:** 5 HOMEY
    6 ATEASE ATIIOME
room: 3 DEN
with: 6 USEDTO
**Comfortable ___ old shoe:**
    4 ASAN
**Comforter:** 5 DUVET
filling: 5 EIDER
**Comforting**
words: 5 ICARE
**Comforts**
Forgo: 7 ROUGHIT
**Comfy:** 4 SNUG 5 HOMEY
    6 ATEASE
Get: 6 NESTLE
room: 3 DEN
shirt: 3 TEE
shoe: 3 MOC
spot: 4 SOFA
Warm and: 6 TOASTY
**Comic:** 3 WIT
actor Jack: 5 OAKIE
actress Tessie: 5 OSHEA
bit: 3 GAG
intro: 5 SERIO
pianist Victor: 5 BORGE
prefix: 5 SERIO
reward: 4 HAHA
~ Charlotte: 3 RAE
~ Cheech: 5 MARIN
~ Howie: 6 MANDEL
~ Judy: 6 TENUTA
~ Lillie: 3 BEA
~ Louie: 3 NYE
~ Margaret: 3 CHO
~ Martha: 4 RAYE
~ Mort: 4 SAHL
~ Soupy: 5 SALES
**Comic book**
cry: 3 EEK
punch sound: 3 POW
**Comics**
Andy of: 4 CAPP
bark: 3 ARF
Brenda of: 5 STARR
canine: 4 ODIE OTTO
    5 SNERT
Canyon of: 5 STEVE
Capp of: 4 ANDY
caveman: 3 OOP 8 ALLEYOOP
Cinders of: 4 ELLA
colonel: 5 BLIMP
cry: 3 EEK
diminutive: 3 LIL
Etta of: 4 KETT
exclamation: 3 ACK
ghost: 6 CASPER
heroes: 4 XMEN

Kett of: 4 ETTA
Krazy ___ of: 3 KAT
Light bulb, in: 4 IDEA
Magician of: 8 MANDRAKE
Miss in the: 5 PEACH
Morgan of: 3 REX
Mrs. Dithers of: 4 CORA
Olive in: 3 OYL
orphan: 5 ANNIE
possum: 4 POGO
Rich kid in: 5 ROLLO
Snores, in: 4 ZEES
sound: 5 SPLAT
Spitting sound, in: 4 PTUI
Trueheart of: 4 TESS
Wavy lines, in: 4 ODOR

**Comic strip**
canine: 4 ODIE 5 SNERT
Greg Evans: 5 LUANN
Jeff MacNelly: 4 SHOE
Jerry Marcus: 5 TRUDY
Mell Lazarus: 5 MOMMA
pair: 11 MUTTANDJEFF
segment: 5 PANEL
viking: 5 HAGAR

**"Comin' ___!": 4 ATYA**

**Coming:** 3 DUE 6 ADVENT
   7 ENROUTE ONORDER
before (abbr.): 4 PREC
Have: 4 EARN 5 MERIT
   7 DESERVE
into existence: 7 NASCENT
Keep it: 5 RENEW
One who has it: 4 HEIR
or going: 7 ENROUTE
out even: 5 TYING
Second: 6 ENCORE
Short: 3 ARR
up: 5 AHEAD ONTAP
   7 INSTORE
Young lady ~ out: 3 DEB

**"___ Coming": 4 ELIS**

**"Coming Home"**
actor: 4 DERN 6 VOIGHT
subject: 3 NAM

**Coming-out:** 5 DEBUT
party: 3 DEB

**Comings**
Word used for ~ and goings:
   5 ALOHA

**"Comin' ___ the Rye": 4 THRO**

**Comma**
Abbr. after a: 3 ETC
connotation: 5 PAUSE

**Command:** 4 FIAT LEAD
   5 ORDER PILOT
   6 BEHEST ORDAIN
for DDE: 3 ETO
for Queeg: 5 CAINE
level (abbr.): 3 ECH
posts (abbr.): 3 HQS
to a dog: 3 BEG SIT 4 HEEL
   STAY 5 FETCH SICEM
   SPEAK
to a horse: 3 GEE 4 WHOA
to a sailor: 5 AVAST

to Macduff: 5 LAYON
to the band: 5 HITIT
Took: 3 LED

**Commanded:** 3 LED RAN
   4 BADE

**Commander**
Arabic: 4 EMIR
British: 4 HOWE
ETO: 3 DDE
Revolutionary War: 4 ASHE
Waterloo: 3 NEY

**Commanding**
phrase: 4 DOIT

**Commandment:** 7 PRECEPT
Break a: 3 SIN 5 COVET
count: 3 TEN
Final: 5 TENTH
pronoun: 3 THY
verb: 5 SHALT
word: 3 NOT THY 5 COVET
   SHALT

**Commando:** 6 RAIDER
action: 4 RAID
Navy: 4 SEAL
weapon: 3 UZI

**"Comme ci, comme ça":**
   4 SOSO 8 NOTSOHOT

**Commedia dell'___: 4 ARTE**

**Commemoration**
Exodus: 5 SEDER

**Commemorative**
marker: 5 STELE
writing: 3 ODE

**Commence:** 5 ARISE ENTER
   START 7 STARTIN

**Commenced:** 5 BEGAN
   BEGUN

**Commencement:** 5 ONSET
   START
composer: 5 ELGAR

**Commencement Bay**
city: 6 TACOMA

**Commencing:** 4 ASOF

**Commend:** 4 CITE 6 SALUTE

**Commendation:** 4 STAR
   6 PRAISE
School: 8 GOLDSTAR

**Comment**
after an accident: 4 IMOK
after the fog clears: 4 ISEE
Barbed: 3 JAB
Clever: 3 MOT 4 QUIP
Cutting: 4 BARB
Disparaging: 4 SLUR
Klutz's: 4 OOPS
Quitter's: 5 ICANT
Skeptic's: 4 IBET
suffix: 4 ATOR
to the audience: 5 ASIDE
Winter: 3 BRR 4 BRRR

**Commentator**
page: 4 OPED
~ Rooney: 4 ANDY

**Comments**
Make nasty: 5 SNIPE
Puzzled: 3 EHS

**Commerce**
agcy.: 3 FTC
Online: 5 ETAIL 6 ETRADE
org.: 4 GATT
pact: 5 NAFTA
restriction: 7 EMBARGO

**Commerce Secretary**
~ Maurice: 5 STANS

**Commercial**
bovine: 5 ELSIE
Designate as: 6 REZONE
designer: 5 ADMAN
makers: 5 ADMEN
prefix for winter items: 3 SNO
prefix with foam: 5 STYRO
producer: 7 SPONSOR
shine: 3 GLO
silencer: 4 MUTE
suffix with Motor: 3 OLA
TV: 4 SPOT

**Commercially**
Become ~ successful:
   6 GETHOT

**Commercials:** 3 ADS
Cow of: 5 ELSIE
Skip the: 3 ZAP

**Commies:** 4 REDS

**Commiserate**
with: 4 PITY

**Commiserative**
comment: 4 ALAS

**"Commish, The"**
actress McGraw: 7 MELINDA

**Commission**
Out of: 5 KAPUT 6 LAIDUP
Put out of: 7 DISABLE

**Commissioned**
Lowest ~ USN officer: 3 ENS

**Commit**
a court infraction: 6 TRAVEL
a deadly sin: 4 LUST
a faux pas: 3 ERR
perjury: 3 LIE
to memory: 5 LEARN
unalterably: 6 LOCKIN

**Commitment**
Avoid: 5 HEDGE
Words of: 3 IDO

**Committee:** 5 PANEL
head: 5 CHAIR
Judiciary ~ head: 5 BIDEN
Kind of: 5 ADHOC
sess.: 3 MTG

**Committer**
Crime: 4 PERP

**Commodious:** 5 ROOMY

**Commodity**
OPEC: 3 OIL

**Commodore**
Old ~ computer: 5 AMIGA

**Commodore Perry**
headquarters: 4 ERIE

**Common:** 4 MERE 6 COARSE
   NORMAL VULGAR
It may be: 5 SENSE
Least: 6 ODDEST RAREST

Not so: 7 SCARCER
sense: 5 SIGHT SMELL TASTE
   6 SMARTS
**Commoner:** 4 PLEB
**Common-interest**
   group: 4 BLOC
**Commonly:** 4 ALOT 5 OFTEN
**Common Market**
   initials: 3 EEC
   money: 3 ECU 4 EURO
**Common Mkt.:** 3 EEC
**Commonplace:** 5 BANAL TRITE
   USUAL 6 OLDHAT
**"Common Sense":** 5 TRACT
   author: 5 PAINE
**Commonsensical:** 4 SANE
**Commotion:** 3 ADO 4 FUSS
   STIR TODO 5 HOOHA
   6 CLAMOR HOOPLA
   TUMULT UPROAR
   7 TEMPEST
   Public: 5 SCENE
**Commune**
   Dutch: 3 EDE
   Iowa: 5 AMANA
   Italian: 4 ESTE
**Communicate**
   manually: 4 SIGN
   online: 5 EMAIL
**Communication**
   Catcher's: 4 SIGN
   Mass: 5 LATIN
   Office: 3 FAX
   Old style of: 5 TELEX
   syst.: 3 ASL
**Communications**
   A, in: 4 ALFA
   co.: 3 GTE ITT
   satellite: 5 RELAY 7 TELSTAR
**Communion:** 4 RITE
   cup: 7 CHALICE
   plates: 7 PLATENS
   site: 5 ALTAR
**Communiqué**
   Interoffice: 4 MEMO
   segue: 4 ASTO
**Communism**
   First name in: 4 KARL
**Communist**
   Old ~ letters: 3 SSR
**Communist-hunting**
   gp.: 4 HUAC
**"Communist Manifesto"**
   coauthor: 6 ENGELS
**Communities**
   Like some: 5 GATED
**Community**
   bldg.: 3 CTR
   characteristic: 5 ETHOS
   Complex: 5 BIOME
   contest: 3 BEE
   Jewish: 6 SHTETL
   org.: 4 YMCA
   outside the city: 5 EXURB
   program: 8 OUTREACH
   spirit: 5 ETHOS

**Commute:** 4 RIDE
   prefix: 4 TELE
**Commuter**
   cost: 4 TOLL
   hassle: 5 TIEUP
   home: 5 BURBS EXURB
   6 SUBURB
   line: 4 RAIL
   NYC ~ line: 4 LIRR
   obstacle: 5 SNARL
   prefix: 4 TELE
   Some ~ trains: 3 ELS
**"Cómo ___?":** 4 ESTA
**Como, Perry**
   1956 ~ hit: 4 MORE
**"Cómo ___ usted?":** 4 ESTA
**"___ Como Va":** 3 OYE
**Comp.**
   course: 3 ENG
   key: 3 ESC
**Compact:** 5 DENSE TERSE
   6 TREATY 7 ENTENTE
   Dodge: 4 NEON
   item: 4 DISC 5 ROUGE
   name: 5 ESTEE
   Saturn: 3 ION
   weapon: 3 UZI
**Compact ___:** 4 DISC
**Compacted**
   coal: 6 CANNEL
**Compadre:** 3 PAL 5 AMIGO
   of Che: 5 FIDEL
   of Fidel: 3 CHE
**Companies**
   Combine: 5 MERGE
**Companion:** 3 PAL 6 COHORT
   As a: 5 ALONG
   Close: 8 SOULMATE
**Companionless:** 5 ALONE
**Company:** 4 FIRM 5 TROOP
   avoider: 5 LONER
   Calling: 4 AVON
   car: 4 PERK
   dishes: 5 CHINA
   emblem: 4 LOGO
   In need of: 8 LONESOME
   in the news: 5 ENRON
   In the ~ of: 4 WITH 5 AMONG
   Keep ~ with: 3 SEE
   lover: 6 MISERY
   name tag: 3 INC
   that has its ups and downs:
   4 OTIS
   Theater: 3 REP
   Without: 4 LONE
   8 ALLALONE
   LONESOME
   Word after some ~ names:
   3 SON
   ~, in French: 3 CIE
   ~, proverbially: 3 TWO
   ~ VIP: 3 CEO 4 EXEC PRES
**"___ company, ...":** 4 TWOS
**"Company, The":** 3 CIA
**"company for women, The":**
   4 AVON

**Compaq**
   acquisition: 3 DEC
   competitor: 3 IBM 4 DELL
   products: 3 PCS
**Comparable:** 4 AKIN 5 ALIKE
   EQUAL
   to a beet: 5 ASRED
   to a pancake: 6 ASFLAT
   to a pig: 5 ASFAT
   to a pin: 6 ASNEAT
**Comparably:** 5 ALIKE
**Comparative**
   phrase: 4 ASAN ISTO
   suffix: 3 IER
   word: 4 THAN
**Compare:** 5 LIKEN
**Compared**
   to: 4 THAN 7 AGAINST
**Comparison:** 6 SIMILE
   center: 3 ASA
   figure: 4 NORM
   Numeric: 5 RATIO
   word: 4 THAN
   words: 3 ASA
**Compartment:** 5 STALL
   Elevator: 3 CAB CAR
   Glove ~ item: 3 MAP
   Protective: 3 POD
   Put in the overhead: 4 STOW
   Till: 4 ONES TENS
   Truck: 3 CAB
**Compass:** 4 AREA 6 EXTENT
   Any point of the: 5 RHUMB
   creation: 3 ARC
   • dir.: 3 ENE ESE NNE NNW
   SSE SSW WNW WSW
   line: 3 ARC
   Spanish ~ point: 4 ESTE
   Use a: 6 ORIENT
**Compassion:** 4 PITY 5 HEART
   MERCY 6 PATHOS
   Feel: 4 ACHE
   Lacking: 8 INHUMANE
   Letters of: 3 TLC
**Compassionate:** 4 KIND
   6 CARING HUMANE
   letters: 3 TLC
**Compel:** 4 HALE 5 EXACT
   FORCE 6 COERCE
**Compelled**
   Was: 5 HADTO
**Compensate:** 3 PAY 5 ATONE
   REPAY
   for: 6 OFFSET
**Compensation:** 3 PAY 4 WAGE
   6 OFFSET SALARY
   7 PAYMENT
**"___ Compères":** 3 LES
**Compete:** 3 VIE 4 RACE
   6 STRIVE
   in logrolling: 4 BIRL
   with: 5 RIVAL
**Competence**
   With: 4 ABLY
**Competent:** 4 ABLE
   ~, slangily: 3 EPT

**Competing**
team: 4 SIDE

**Competition:** 3 BEE 4 MEET
Crush, in: 4 ROUT
In: 5 VYING
Lumberjack: 5 ROLEO
Pub: 5 DARTS
site: 5 ARENA
Spelling: 3 BEE
Trucker: 6 ROADEO

**Competitive:** 9 RIVALROUS
advantage: 4 EDGE
personality: 5 TYPEA
Ruthlessly: 9 DOGEATDOG

**Competitor:** 3 FOE 5 RIVAL
7 ENTRANT

**Complacent:** 4 SMUG

**Complain:** 4 CARP CRAB FUSS
MOAN 5 GRIPE GROAN
6 GROUSE REPINE
YAMMER
bitterly: 4 RAIL
in a murmur: 6 MUTTER
loudly: 12 RAISETHEROOF
too often: 3 NAG

**Complainer:** 4 CRAB 5 GRUMP
6 MOANER WHINER

**Complaining:** 5 GRIPY WHINY

**Complaint:** 4 BEEF MOAN
5 GRIPE PEEVE WHINE
6 MALADY 7 AILMENT
Grounds for: 5 ACHES
9 GRIEVANCE
Long: 4 RANT

**"Compleat Angler, The"**
author Walton: 5 IZAAK

**Complement**
Baseball: 4 NINE
Football: 6 ELEVEN
Lacrosse: 3 TEN

**Complete:** 4 ATOZ OVER REAL
5 TOTAL UTTER WHOLE
6 ENTIRE
a sentence: 6 DOTIME
9 SERVETIME
a street: 3 TAR
collection: 3 SET
failure: 6 FIASCO
prefix: 3 HOL
range: 4 ATOZ
reversal: 5 UTURN
~, informally: 5 THORO

**Completed:** 3 DID 4 DONE
OVER

**Completely:** 3 ALL 4 ATOZ
5 FULLY INALL QUITE
6 INFULL INTOTO
8 FROMATOZ
9 EVERYINCH
botch: 4 RUIN
confused: 7 CHAOTIC
consumed: 5 ATEUP
7 ALLGONE
convinced: 4 SOLD SURE
cooked: 4 DONE
demolish: 4 RAZE

full: 5 SATED
infatuated: 4 GAGA
mistaken: 6 ALLWET
new: 6 REMADE
surrounding: 7 AMBIENT

**Completeness**
Sense of: 7 CLOSURE

**Complex**
division: 4 UNIT
Like a certain: 7 OEDIPAL
Sports: 5 ARENA

**Complexion**
affliction: 4 ACNE
tone: 5 OLIVE

**Compliant**
Be: 4 OBEY
one: 6 OBEYER

**Complicated**
Less: 6 EASIER

**Complication:** 3 ADO RUB
4 SNAG 5 SNARL

**Compliment**
Give, as a: 3 PAY
Response to a: 4 ITRY
to the cook: 3 YUM

**Complimentary:** 4 FREE

**Compliments:** 5 KUDOS

**Comply:** 4 OBEY
with: 4 MEET OBEY
8 ADHERETO

**Component:** 6 FACTOR
MODULE 7 ELEMENT

**Comportment:** 4 MIEN

**Compose:** 3 PEN 4 CALM
7 TYPESET
prose: 5 WRITE

**Composed:** 4 EVEN 5 STAID
WROTE 6 SEDATE
SERENE

**Composer**
base: 5 THEME
British: 4 ARNE
French: 5 SATIE
Hungarian: 5 LISZT 6 BARTOK
Knighted: 5 ELGAR
New Age: 4 TESH
Norwegian: 5 GRIEG
org.: 5 ASCAP
Rock: 3 ENO
work: 4 OPUS
~ Alban: 4 BERG
~ ___ Carlo Menotti: 4 GIAN
~ Charles: 4 IVES
~ Erik: 5 SATIE
~ Gustav: 6 MAHLER
~ Harold: 5 ARLEN
~ Jacques: 4 BREL 5 IBERT
~ Jerome: 4 KERN
~ Ned: 5 ROREM
~ Thomas: 4 ARNE

**Composite**
Bilingual: 6 PIDGIN
kin: 5 DORIC

**Composition:** 4 OPUS 5 ESSAY
Musical: 4 OPUS 5 ETUDE
6 ARIOSO SONATA

Short: 8 SONATINA

**Compos mentis:** 4 SANE
___ compos mentis: 3 NON

**Compost**
Become: 3 ROT

**Composure:** 4 COOL WITS
5 POISE 6 APLOMB

**Compote**
fruit: 4 PEAR 5 PEARS

**Compound**
Aromatic: 5 ESTER
Carbon: 4 ENOL
Chemical: 4 ENOL 5 ESTER
6 ISOMER
Fatty: 5 LIPID
Fragrant: 5 ESTER
Hydroxyl: 4 ENOL
Nitrogen: 5 AMIDE AMINE
AZIDE
Organic: 4 ENOL 5 AMIDE
ESTER
with two double bonds:
5 DIENE

**Comprehend:** 3 GET SEE
4 KNOW 5 GRASP
6 FATHOM
Hard to: 4 DEEP

**Comprehension:** 3 KEN
5 GRASP 6 UPTAKE
Words of: 4 ISEE

**Comprehensive:** 5 BROAD
6 GLOBAL 7 OVERALL

**Compress**
a file: 3 ZIP
~, informally: 5 SMUSH

**Compression**
It operates by: 6 AIRGUN

**Compromise:** 5 BUDGE
8 TRADEOFF

**Compromised**
Financially: 7 INAHOLE

**"Compromising Positions"**
author Susan: 6 ISAACS

**Compulsion:** 4 NEED URGE

**Compulsive**
thief: 6 KLEPTO

**Compunction:** 7 REMORSE

**Computation**
Carpet: 4 AREA

**Computer**
1940s ~: 5 ENIAC
accessory: 5 MODEM MOUSE
7 PRINTER
acronym: 4 GIGO 5 ASCII
add-on: 3 ESE
Apple: 4 IMAC
bug: 6 GLITCH
bulletin board manager:
5 SYSOP
capacity: 5 BYTES
6 MEMORY
Central: 6 SERVER
chip maker: 5 INTEL
choice: 3 MAC
clickers: 4 MICE
Colorful: 4 IMAC

command: 4 GOTO OPEN
    SAVE UNDO 5 ENTER
    ERASE PRINT
    7 RESTART
core (abbr.): 3 CPU
data unit: 4 BYTE
device: 5 MODEM MOUSE
document: 4 FILE
Dot on a: 5 PIXEL
Early: 5 ENIAC 6 UNIVAC
expert: 6 TECHIE
fodder: 4 DATA 5 INPUT
game: 4 MYST 6 TETRIS
game maker: 5 ATARI
geek: 4 NERD
giant: 3 NEC 4 DELL 5 APPLE
graphic: 4 ICON
image: 4 ICON
image file format: 4 JPEG
input: 4 DATA 7 DATASET
introduced in 1985: 5 AMIGA
Japanese ~ giant: 3 NEC
Jobs in the ~ biz: 5 STEVE
key: 3 ALT ESC TAB 5 ARROW
    ENTER 6 DELETE
Kind of ~ drive: 5 CDROM
language: 4 JAVA 5 ALGOL
    BASIC COBOL 6 PASCAL
    7 FORTRAN
letters: 5 EMAIL
Like a certain ~ system:
    5 OCTAL
list: 4 MENU
memory unit: 3 MEG 4 BYTE
message: 5 EMAIL
monitor, for short: 3 CRT
Most ~ buyers: 8 ENDUSERS
network: 6 SYSTEM
networking device:
    6 ROUTER
Old: 5 AMIGA
Old ~ tube: 6 TRIODE
operating system: 4 UNIX
    5 MSDOS
operator: 4 USER
owner: 4 USER
peripheral: 7 SCANNER
picture: 4 SCAN
Pioneer: 5 ENIAC
Portable: 6 LAPTOP
printer maker: 5 EPSON
problem: 5 CRASH VIRUS
program feature: 4 LOOP
program, for short: 3 APP
record: 7 DATASET
reseller (abbr.): 3 OEM
screen, for short: 3 CRT
Shared ~ sys.: 3 LAN
shortcut: 5 MACRO
Start up a: 4 BOOT
suffix: 3 ESE IZE
symbol: 4 ICON
text: 5 ASCII
TRS-80 ~ maker: 5 TANDY
unit: 3 MEG 4 BYTE
whiz: 6 TECHIE

Computerphile: 4 USER
Computes
    net weight: 5 TARES
Comrade: 3 PAL 4 ALLY
    British: 4 MATE
    French: 3 AMI
    Russian: 8 TOVARICH
Comstock
    load: 3 ORE
Comtes
    etc.: 8 NOBLESSE
"Comus"
    composer: 4 ARNE
Con: 4 ANTI DUPE RUSE
    SCAM SNOW 6 INMATE
    counter: 3 PRO
    cover: 5 ALIAS
    decoy: 5 SHILL
    game: 4 SCAM 5 BUNCO
       BUNKO STING
    Help with a: 4 ABET
    man: 4 ANTI
    men: 5 ANTIS
    Pro or: 4 SIDE
    Three-card: 5 MONTE
    vote: 3 NAY
Con ___ : 4 BRIO 5 AMORE
ConAgra
    Home of: 5 OMAHA
"Con Air"
    actor Nicolas: 4 CAGE
Conan
    former sidekick: 4 ANDY
    Host: 6 OBRIEN
Con artist: 5 DUPER
    7 FLEECER
    aide: 5 SHILL
    art: 4 SCAM
Concave
    lint trap: 5 INNIE
Conceal: 4 BURY HIDE MASK
    PALM VEIL 6 HUSHUP
    SCREEN SHIELD
    7 SECRETE
Concealed: 3 HID 5 PERDU
    6 HIDDEN UNSEEN
    Not: 5 OVERT
Concealer
    Floorboard: 7 AREARUG
Concealment
    Hunter: 5 BLIND
Concede: 4 GIVE 5 ADMIT
    ALLOW YIELD
Conceit: 3 EGO 4 IDEA
    7 EGOTISM
Conceited: 4 VAIN
Conceive: 6 IDEATE
Concentrate: 5 FOCUS
    7 DISTILL
Concentration
    Points of: 4 FOCI
"Concentration"
    puzzle: 5 REBUS
Concept: 4 IDEA
    Cannes: 4 IDEE
    Confucian: 3 TAO

Flawless: 5 IDEAL
Freudian: 3 EGO 6 LIBIDO
Newtonian: 7 INERTIA
Physics: 4 MASS
Conception: 4 IDEA 5 IMAGE
Conceptualize: 6 IDEATE
Concern: 4 CARE FIRM NEED
    5 ALARM WORRY
    6 MATTER 8 INTEREST
Concerned
    with: 4 INTO
Concerning: 4 ASTO INRE
    5 ABOUT ANENT ASFOR
    this: 6 HEREOF
    ~, in legalese: 4 INRE
Concert: 5 EVENT
    bonus: 6 ENCORE
    ending: 3 INA
    equipment: 4 AMPS
    hall: 5 ODEUM
    halls: 4 ODEA
    In: 5 ASONE
    pianist Claudio: 5 ARRAU
    setting: 5 ARENA
    souvenir: 3 TEE 6 TSHIRT
    take: 4 GATE
    venue: 5 ARENA
Concertina: 10 SQUEEZEBOX
Concerto
    climax: 7 CADENZA
    finale: 4 CODA
    highlight: 4 SOLO
    instrument: 4 OBOE 5 PIANO
    movement: 5 RONDO
Concession
    Concise: 5 ILOSE
    Make a: 4 BEND
    suffix: 4 AIRE
Conch
    cousin: 6 LIMPET
Conciliatory: 6 IRENIC
    gift: 3 SOP
Concise: 4 CURT 5 PITHY
    SHORT TERSE
    summary: 5 RECAP 6 PRECIS
Concisely
    Describe: 5 SUMUP
Conclude: 3 END 4 WRAP
    5 ENDUP INFER
    by: 5 ENDAT
Concluded: 4 DONE OVER
    6 SEWNUP
Concluding
    passage: 4 CODA
Conclusion: 3 END 4 CODA
    5 FINIS 6 ENDING
    EPILOG FINALE
Info: Suffix cue
    Cartesian: 3 IAM
    Congregational: 4 AMEN
    Draw a: 5 INFER
    Horner: 3 AMI
    In: 6 LASTLY
    In ~, in French: 5 ENFIN
    lead-in: 4 ERGO IFSO
    5 HENCE

Legal: 3 ESE
Major: 4 ETTE
Musical: 4 CODA
Start of a legal: 5 IREST
**Conclusive:** 4 LAST
trial: 8 ACIDTEST
**Concoct:** 4 BREW 5 HATCH
6 DEVISE 7 DREAMUP
**Concoction**
Bean: 4 IDEA
Café: 5 MOCHA
Corn: 4 PONE
Corned beef: 4 HASH
Crockpot: 4 STEW
Custard: 4 FLAN
Noodle: 4 IDEA
Scotch: 6 ROBROY
Witches': 4 BREW
**Concord:** 5 AMITY PEACE
UNITY 6 UNISON
**Concorde:** 3 SST
maker: 8 CHRYSLER
Take a: 3 JET
**"Concord Sonata"**
composer: 4 IVES
**Concrete:** 4 REAL 6 ACTUAL
Cover with: 4 PAVE
kin: 6 CEMENT
Like fresh: 5 UNSET
reinforcer: 5 REBAR
section: 4 SLAB
**Concubine**
room: 3 ODA
**Concur:** 5 AGREE 6 ACCEDE
ASSENT 7 GOALONG
11 SEEEYETOEYE
**Condé ___:** 4 NAST
**Condemn:** 4 DOOM
openly: 5 DECRY
**Condé Nast**
magazine: 4 SELF
**Condensation**
Morning: 3 DEW
**Condense:** 7 ABRIDGE
on a surface: 6 ADSORB
**Condensed**
In ~ form: 8 CAPSULAR
**Condescend:** 5 DEIGN
STOOP
**Condescending**
cluck: 3 TSK
one: 4 SNOB 5 SNOOT
**Condiment**
Breakfast: 5 SYRUP
Cannes: 3 SEL
Chemist: 4 NACL
Chili: 8 HOTSAUCE
Japanese: 8 SOYSAUCE
9 SOYASAUCE
Ocean: 7 SEASALT
source: 8 SALTMINE
Sushi: 6 WASABI
TexMex: 5 SALSA
**Condition:** 4 MODE 5 INURE
SHAPE STATE 6 FETTLE
7 PROVISO

In perfect: 4 MINT
Muscle: 4 TONE
Physical: 5 SHAPE
Pique: 3 IRE
Sale: 4 ASIS
Undesirable: 6 MALADY
Untidy: 4 MESS
**Conditional**
release: 6 PAROLE
**Conditionally**
out: 8 ONPAROLE
**Conditioned**
reflex researcher: 6 PAVLOV
**Conditioner**
Kind of: 3 AIR
**Conditions:** 3 IFS
Best: 6 OPTIMA
Contract: 5 TERMS
Harsh: 6 RIGORS
Prevailing: 7 CLIMATE
**Condo:** 4 UNIT
alternative: 4 COOP
division: 4 UNIT
**Condor**
claw: 5 TALON
condo: 4 NEST 5 AERIE
Kind of: 6 ANDEAN
Like a ~ in the wild: 4 RARE
**Conduct:** 3 RUN 4 LEAD
Code of: 5 ETHIC
(oneself): 6 DEPORT
**Conductance**
unit: 3 MHO
**Conducted:** 3 LED
**Conducting**
First name in: 6 ARTURO
rod: 5 BATON
**Conductor:** 7 MAESTRO
Bombay-born: 5 MEHTA
concern: 5 TEMPO
Former Boston Symphony:
5 OZAWA
Hungarian-born: 5 SOLTI
intro: 4 SEMI
Longtime NBC Symphony:
9 TOSCANINI
platforms: 5 PODIA
reference: 5 SCORE
Semi: 4 CBER
Slowly, to a: 6 ADAGIO
stick: 5 BATON
~ Antal: 6 DORATI
~ Georg: 5 SOLTI
~ Kurt: 5 MASUR
~ Lucas: 4 FOSS
~ Riccardo: 4 MUTI
~ Seiji: 5 OZAWA
~ Sir Georg: 5 SOLTI
~ Walter: 5 BRUNO
~ Zubin: 5 MEHTA
**Conduit:** 4 DUCT 8 PIPELINE
bend: 3 ELL
Engine: 4 HOSE
in an ICU: 6 IVTUBE
Poison: 4 FANG
Underground: 5 SEWER

Vital engine: 7 OILLINE
Water: 4 MAIN
**Cone**
bearer: 3 FIR 4 PINE
It may be found in a: 4 LAVA
prefix: 3 SNO
Traffic: 5 PYLON
**Cone-bearing**
tree: 3 FIR 7 CYPRESS
**Cones**
It contains rods and: 6 RETINA
Partners of: 4 RODS
**Cone-shaped**
heater: 4 ETNA
**Conestoga:** 5 WAGON
**Confection**
Cadbury: 3 EGG
Cold: 3 ICE 5 BOMBE
French: 7 PRALINE
Frozen: 4 ICEE
Nutty: 6 NOUGAT 7 PRALINE
**Confectionary**
worker: 4 ICER
**Confederacy**
foe: 5 UNION
**"Confederacy of Dunces, A"**
author: 5 TOOLE
**Confederate:** 4 ALLY
general: 3 LEE 6 STUART
Quebec: 3 AMI
soldier: 3 REB
**Confer:** 6 BESTOW
**Conference:** 6 POWWOW
7 PALAVER SEMINAR
1945 ~ site: 5 YALTA
Court: 7 SIDEBAR
Football: 6 HUDDLE
prefix: 4 TELE
Press ~ activity: 5 QANDA
WWII ~ site: 5 CAIRO YALTA
**Conferral**
A-student: 5 HONOR
College: 6 DEGREE
**Confess:** 3 OWN 4 AVOW TALK
TELL 5 ADMIT OWNTO
OWNUP
~, with "up": 3 OWN
**Confession**
collection: 4 SINS
starter: 3 MEA
**Confessions**
Like some: 4 ORAL
**"Confessions of ___ Turner,
The":** 3 NAT
**Confetti:** 6 SHREDS
Make: 5 SHRED
Turn into: 5 RIPUP
**Confidante:** 4 AMIE
**Confidence:** 5 FAITH TRUST
6 SECRET SURETY
Declare with: 4 AVER
6 ASSERT
game: 4 SCAM 5 BUNKO
STING
Give ~ to: 6 ASSURE
Have: 4 RELY

Have ~ in: 5 TRUST
Restore ~ to: 8 REASSURE
Vote of: 3 AYE
Words of: 4 ICAN
**Confident:** 4 SURE
solver's tool: 3 PEN
way to solve: 5 ININK
**Confidential**
matter: 6 SECRET
**Confidently**
State: 4 AVER 6 ASSERT
   ASSURE
**Confine:** 4 SHUT 5 BOXIN
   HEMIN LIMIT PENIN
   6 COOPUP ENCAGE
   INTERN
~, with "in": 3 HEM
**Confined:** 4 PENT
**Confines:** 3 RIM 4 AREA
   7 PURLIEU SHUTSIN
Swine: 5 STIES
**Confirmation:** 4 RITE
Used as: 5 CITED
**Confiscate:** 5 SEIZE
~, in law: 7 ESCHEAT
**Conflagration:** 5 BLAZE
**Conflict:** 3 WAR 4 SPAT
   5 CLASH 6 STRIFE
   7 COLLIDE
1960s ~ site: 3 NAM
Armed: 3 WAR
Confused: 5 MELEE
Field of: 5 ARENA
In: 4 TORN 5 ATWAR
   6 ATODDS
In ~ with, with "of": 5 AFOUL
Literary: 4 AGON
**Conflicted:** 4 TORN
**Conform:** 4 JIBE 5 ADAPT
   FITIN 6 ADHERE
(to): 3 HEW
**Conforming:** 6 INSTEP
**Confound:** 5 ADDLE 6 BEMUSE
**Confounded:** 5 ATSEA
**"Confound it!":** 4 DANG DRAT
**Confront:** 4 FACE MEET
   6 ACCOST
**Confrontation:** 5 RUNIN
   8 ONEONONE
   SHOWDOWN
In direct: 8 TOETOTOE
Rink: 7 FACEOFF
**Confronted**
with: 9 UPAGAINST
**Confucian**
path: 3 TAO
**Confucius**
Dynasty of: 4 CHOU
**Confuse:** 3 VEX 5 ADDLE
   BEFOG MUDDY RAVEL
   6 BAFFLE TANGLE
**Confused:** 4 LOST 5 ATSEA
   MUDDY 6 INAFOG
   7 OUTOFIT
Completely: 7 CHAOTIC
fight: 5 MELEE

Make: 5 ADDLE
state: 3 FOG 4 HAZE
**Confusing**
pathway: 4 MAZE
**Confusion:** 4 HAZE MESS MOIL
   8 DISARRAY
Total: 5 CHAOS
**Cong.**
meeting: 4 SESS
member: 3 SEN
___ **Cong:** 4 VIET
**Conga:** 4 DRUM
**"Conga"**
singer: 7 ESTEFAN
**Congeal:** 3 GEL SET 4 CLOT
   CURD JELL
**Congenial:** 4 NICE
Less: 5 ICIER
Like Miss: 6 NICEST
**Congenital:** 6 INNATE
**Conger:** 3 EEL 6 SEAEEL
catcher: 5 EELER
Caught a: 5 EELED
**Congested**
area: 5 SINUS
**Conglomerate:** 5 AMASS
   UNITE
Corp.: 3 ITT
**Conglomeration:** 4 OLIO
   6 RAGBAG
**Congo**
animal: 5 HIPPO OKAPI
   RHINO
First ~ P.M. Lumumba:
   7 PATRICE
neighbor: 6 ANGOLA RWANDA
river: 4 UELE 5 EBOLA
   6 URANGI
suffix: 4 LESE
~, formerly: 5 ZAIRE
**"Congratulations!":** 5 KUDOS
   8 MAZELTOV
in action: 3 PAT
**Congregate:** 4 MEET
**Congregation**
area: 4 NAVE
divider: 5 AISLE
leader: 5 RABBI 6 PASTOR
members: 5 LAITY
shout: 4 AMEN
**Congress**
creation: 3 ACT
Mem. of: 3 REP
Part of: 6 SENATE
Send to: 5 ELECT
Vote in: 3 YEA
Where to see: 5 CSPAN
**Congressional**
approval: 3 YEA
committee: 6 ETHICS
gofer: 4 PAGE
mtg.: 4 SESS
output: 3 ACT 4 ACTS BILL
   LAWS
period: 7 SESSION
~ VIP: 4 WHIP

**Conical**
dryer: 4 OAST
home: 5 TEPEE
**Coniferous**
tree: 3 YEW 4 PINE 5 CEDAR
   LARCH
**Conjecture:** 5 GUESS
   7 GUESSAT SURMISE
**Conjugation**
Latin I: 3 AMO 4 AMAS AMAT
**Conjunction**
Cartesian: 4 ERGO
Common: 3 AND NOR
couplet: 5 ANDOR
German: 3 UND
Latin: 4 ERGO
Negative: 3 NOR
Poetic: 3 ERE
**Conjure**
up: 5 EVOKE
**Conjurer**
prop: 4 WAND
**Conk:** 3 BOP 4 BEAN 5 BRAIN
   CROWN
out: 3 DIE 4 FAIL QUIT
   5 STALL
**Conker**
Curly: 3 MOE
**Conn**
Actress: 4 DIDI
Take the: 5 STEER
**Conn.**
school: 5 YALEU
**Connect:** 3 TIE 4 JOIN LINK
   5 TIEIN UNITE
   6 FASTEN PLUGIN
to an outlet: 6 PLUGIN
via phone: 6 DIALIN
with: 5 TIETO 7 TIEINTO
**Connected**
Closely: 7 SIAMESE
Is: 6 TIESIN
to the Internet: 6 ONLINE
**Connecticut**
campus: 4 YALE
city: 7 BRISTOL
collegian: 3 ELI 5 YALIE
Former ~ governor: 6 GRASSO
motto word: 3 QUI
senator: 4 DODD
**Connecting**
flight: 9 STAIRCASE
point: 4 NODE
strips of land: 6 ISTHMI
wd.: 4 CONJ
word: 3 AND
**Connection:** 3 TIE 4 BOND
   LINK 5 NEXUS TIEIN
   6 HOOKUP 7 LIAISON
Have a: 6 RELATE
Inner: 5 SINEW
**Connections:** 3 INS
French: 3 ETS
**Connective tissue:** 6 TENDON
**Connect the ___:** 4 DOTS
**Conned:** 3 GOT HAD 5 TAKEN

**Connell**
Author: 4 EVAN
**Connelly**
Playwright: 4 MARC
**Connery**
Actor: 4 SEAN
role: 4 BOND
successor: 5 MOORE
~, by birth: 4 SCOT
**Connick Jr., Harry**
1994 ~ album: 3 SHE
Sing like: 5 CROON
**Connie**
Newswoman: 5 CHUNG
of baseball: 4 MACK
portrayer: 5 TALIA
**Conniption:** 6 CATFIT
**Connivance:** 6 SCHEME
**Connive:** 4 PLAN 6 SCHEME
with: 4 ABET
**Conniving:** 3 SLY
sort: 7 SCHEMER
**Connoisseur:** 5 MAVEN
Food: 7 EPICURE GOURMET
Wine ~ concern: 4 YEAR
**Connors**
adversary: 4 ASHE BORG
**Conoco**
rival: 4 ESSO
___ con pollo: 5 ARROZ
**Conquer:** 4 BEAT BEST TAME
**Conqueror**
11th century ~: 6 NORMAN
of Mexico: 6 CORTEZ
of Valencia: 5 ELCID
Sword: 3 PEN
**Conquest**
for Caesar: 4 GAUL
Hillary: 7 EVEREST
of 1953: 7 EVEREST
Salk's: 5 POLIO
**Conquistador**
fighter: 4 INCA
quest: 3 ORO
**Conrad**
Actor: 4 BAIN
novel: 7 LORDJIM
of old films: 5 NAGEL
**Conrad, Robert**
series: 5 THEDA
**Conried**
Actor: 4 HANS
**Cons**
Discuss pros and: 6 DEBATE
do it: 4 TIME
**Conscience:** 8 SUPEREGO
burden: 5 GUILT
**Conscious:** 5 ALERT AWARE
8 SENTIENT
prefix: 3 ECO
**Consciousness**
Lose: 5 SWOON
Regained: 6 CAMETO
**Conscriptable:** 4 ONEA
**Conscription**
org.: 3 SSS

**Conseco Fieldhouse**
player: 5 PACER
**Consecrate:** 5 BLESS 6 ANOINT
HALLOW ORDAIN
**Consecrated:** 4 HOLY 5 BLEST
6 SACRED
**Consecutively:** 6 INAROW
**Consensus**
Come to a: 5 AGREE
**Consent:** 9 ACQUIESCE
Give: 5 AGREE 6 ACCEDE
**Consequence:** 6 IMPORT
RESULT
Workout: 4 ACHE
___ consequence: 4 OFNO
**Consequently:** 4 ERGO THEN
THUS 5 HENCE
**Conservationist**
~ John: 4 MUIR
**Conservative:** 4 TORY 5 STAID
prefix: 3 NEO 5 ULTRA
~ Alan: 5 KEYES
**Conservatives:** 5 RIGHT
**Conservatory**
Ohio: 7 OBERLIN
subj.: 3 MUS
**Consider:** 4 DEEM HEED
5 WEIGH 6 DEBATE
HEAROF LOOKAT
again: 6 REHEAR
officially: 4 HEAR
~, with "over": 4 CHEW MULL
**Considerable:** 4 TIDY 5 AMPLE
BROAD LARGE
amount: 3 TON
sum: 11 PRETTYPENNY
**Considerably:** 3 FAR 4 ALOT
MUCH 5 QUITE
**Considerate:** 4 KIND NICE
**Consideration:** 4 HEED SAKE
**Considered**
Everything: 8 ALLINALL
Not carefully: 4 RASH
**"Consider it done":** 6 IMONIT
**Consign:** 6 DEVOTE
8 RELEGATE
to oblivion: 4 DOOM
**Consist**
suffix: 3 ENT 4 ENCY
**Consistency**
It's used for the sake of:
7 THINNER
**Consolidate:** 4 MELD POOL
5 MERGE UNITE
**Consonant:** 6 INSYNC
Greek: 3 CHI PSI RHO TAU
4 BETA ZETA 5 SIGMA
**Consonants**
Greek: 3 MUS NUS 6 THETAS
Some: 6 NASALS
**Consort**
of Aphrodite: 4 ARES
of Zeus: 4 HERA
**Conspicuous:** 5 OVERT
7 EMINENT SALIENT
success: 5 ECLAT

**Conspiracy:** 4 PLOT
5 CABAL
**"Conspiracy Against Childhood,
The"**
author LeShan: 3 EDA
**"Conspiracy Zone, The"**
network: 3 TNN
**Conspirator**
Shakespearean: 4 IAGO
~ Guy: 6 FAWKES
**Conspiratorial**
group: 5 CABAL
**Conspire:** 4 PLOT 6 SCHEME
7 COLLUDE
with: 4 ABET
**Constable**
Where to see a: 4 TATE
**"Constant Craving"**
singer: 4 LANG 6 KDLANG
**Constantine**
Mother of: 6 HELENA
**Constantly:** 4 EVER 5 NOEND
find fault with: 3 NAG
~, to Keats: 3 EER
**Constants**
Circle: 3 PIS
**Constellation**
Altar: 3 ARA
animal: 4 URSA
Belted: 5 ORION
brightest star: 5 ALPHA
component: 4 STAR
Northern: 5 DRACO
Peacock: 4 PAVO
Southern: 3 ARA 4 ARGO
Vega: 4 LYRA
**Consternate:** 6 APPALL
**Consternation:** 5 ALARM
6 DISMAY
**Constituent:** 4 PART 6 MEMBER
7 ELEMENT
Cell: 3 RNA
Convoy: 4 SEMI
**Constitution**
Change the: 5 AMEND
clause: 7 ARTICLE
drafter: 6 FRAMER
lead-in: 3 USS
States' rights amendment to
the: 5 TENTH
___ Constitution: 3 USS
**Constitutional:** 4 WALK
6 STROLL
Failed ~ amendment: 3 ERA
**Constriction**
of the pupils: 6 MIOSIS
**Constrictor:** 3 BOA
___ constrictor: 3 BOA
**Construct:** 4 MAKE 5 BUILD
ERECT
**Constructed:** 4 MADE
**Construction**
beam: 4 IBAR
Big name in: 4 LEGO
Caterpillar: 4 TENT
co. project: 4 BLDG

Coral: 4 REEF
crew: 8 HARDHATS
Fed. ~ overseer: 3 GSA
girder: 5 IBEAM
Naval ~ crew: 7 SEABEES
piece: 4 IBAR ZBAR 5 IBEAM
setting: 4 SITE
site sight: 4 CONE 5 CRANE
   7 HARDHAT
Stage: 3 SET
support: 4 IBAR
worker: 7 ERECTER
   HARDHAT
**Constructive**
Be: 6 CREATE
**Constructor**
Crossword ~, seemingly:
   6 SADIST
**Consult:** 3 SEE 6 LOOKTO
**Consultant**
Ancient: 6 ORACLE
Manual: 4 USER
**Consultation**
Send for: 5 REFER
**Consume:** 3 EAT USE 5 EATUP
Safe to: 6 EDIBLE
**Consumed:** 3 ATE HAD
   4 GONE 5 EATEN
   6 USEDUP
Completely: 7 ALLGONE
quickly: 5 ATEUP
**Consumer:** 4 USER 5 BUYER
   EATER 7 ENDUSER
advocate Ralph: 5 NADER
concern: 4 COST
protection org.: 3 BBB
reading: 5 LABEL
**Consumerist**
~ Ralph: 5 NADER
**Consumer Reports**
employee: 5 RATER 6 TESTER
"___ consummation
   devoutly ...": Hamlet:
   4 TISA
**Consumption:** 3 USE
Fit for: 6 EDIBLE
**Cont.**
Second-largest: 3 AFR
**Contact:** 4 LENS 5 EMAIL
   RADIO
contact: 6 CORNEA
Don't make ~ with: 4 MISS
Make: 6 LIAISE
Reporter: 6 SOURCE
site: 3 EYE
**"Contact"**
author: 5 SAGAN
They make contact in: 3 ETS
**Contact ___:** 4 LENS
**Container:** 3 BIN CAN JAR TUB
Big: 3 VAT
cover: 3 LID
Small: 4 VIAL
weight: 4 TARE
**Containing**
nothing: 5 EMPTY

**Contains:** 3 HAS
**Contaminant**
Chem.: 3 PCB
free: 4 PURE
Water: 5 ECOLI
**Contaminate:** 5 TAINT
   6 DEFILE INFECT
   POISON 7 POLLUTE
**Contemplate:** 4 MUSE
   6 PONDER
Subject to: 5 NAVEL
**Contemporary:** 6 COEVAL
   MODERN
**Contempt:** 5 ODIUM SCORN
Beneath: 4 VILE
Cry of: 3 BAH 4 PISH POOH
   TUSH
Show: 4 JEER 5 SCOFF
   SNEER
Treat with: 4 SNUB 5 SCORN
   SPURN 6 DERIDE
Uttered with: 4 SPAT
**Contemptible:** 4 BASE MEAN
   VILE 5 MANGY
one: 3 CAD CUR 4 CRUD
   HEEL TOAD WORM
   5 LOUSE SWINE TWERP
   7 DASTARD
**Contemptuous**
look: 5 SNEER
noise: 5 SNORT
**Contend:** 3 VIE 6 STRIVE
colloquially: 6 RASSLE
**Contender:** 4 VIER
___ contendere: 4 NOLO
**Content:** 7 ATPEACE
prefix: 3 MAL
**Contented**
sound: 3 AAH 4 PURR
**Contention**
Drop out of: 4 FADE
Matter of: 4 BONE
Still in: 5 ALIVE
**Contentment:** 4 EASE
Sound of: 3 AAH 4 PURR
Sounds of: 3 AHS
**Contest:** 3 BEE VIE 4 BOUT
   MEET 5 ARGUE
Cowboy: 5 RODEO
form: 5 ENTRY
for two: 4 DUEL
Greek: 4 AGON
hopeful: 7 ENTRANT
Kind of: 3 BEE
Logger: 5 ROLEO
Medieval: 4 TILT
No: 4 ROMP
Oldest hoops: 3 NIT
Ring: 4 SUMO
Speed: 4 RACE
Spelling: 3 BEE
submission: 5 ENTRY
venue: 5 ARENA
**Contestant:** 4 VIER 5 ENTRY
Become a: 5 ENTER
rank: 4 SEED

Regatta: 3 OAR
Slalom: 5 SKIER
**Continent**
Currency on the: 4 EURO
Largest: 4 ASIA
Second-largest: 6 AFRICA
separator: 5 OCEAN
south of Eur.: 3 AFR
The: 6 EUROPE
**"Continent, The":** 6 EUROPE
**Continental**
border: 5 URALS
competitor: 5 DELTA
currency: 4 EURO 5 EUROS
divide: 5 OCEAN
prefix: 4 AFRO EURO
trade gp.: 3 EEC
**Continental Airlines Arena**
team: 4 NETS
**Continental Congress**
Silas of the: 5 DEANE
**Contingencies:** 3 IFS
**Contingency**
Event: 8 RAINDATE
**Continually:** 4 EVER
Bother: 5 EATAT NAGAT
   6 HARASS
**Continue:** 3 ADD 4 GOON
   MOVE 6 KEEPON
   MOVEON ROLLON
a subscription: 5 RENEW
**Continued:** 6 KEPTON
   WENTON
drama: 6 SERIAL
~, with "on": 4 KEPT
**Continuing**
story: 6 SERIAL
**Continuous**
change: 4 FLUX
**Continuously:** 4 EVER
   5 ONEND
**Contort:** 4 BEND CURL WARP
   5 GNARL 6 DEFORM
**Contoured**
Finely: 5 SLEEK
**Contra-**
relative: 4 ANTI
**Contract:** 3 GET 4 HIRE PACT
   WANE
add-on: 5 RIDER
Certain: 5 LEASE
conditions: 5 TERMS
Defeat a ~ in bridge: 3 SET
escalator: 4 COLA
Extend a: 5 RENEW
Kind of: 10 SWEETHEART
Lucrative, as a: 3 FAT
negotiator: 5 AGENT
negotiator (abbr.): 3 AGT
provision: 6 CLAUSE
Rental: 5 LEASE
seeker: 9 FREEAGENT
Sign a: 3 INK
Unbreakable, as a:
   8 IRONCLAD
Without a: 6 ONSPEC

worker: 6 HITMAN
**"Contract Bridge Complete"**
author: 5 GOREN
**Contracted:** 3 GOT
8 SHRUNKEN
cost: 7 SETRATE
**Contraction:** 5 SPASM
Anthem: 3 OER
Carol: 3 TIS
Muscle: 5 SPASM
Poetic: 3 EEN EER OER TIS
4 NEER
Quaint: 5 SHANT TWERE
**Contractor**
detail: 4 SPEC
fig.: 3 EST
Sub: 4 DELI
Top: 6 ROOFER
**Contracts**
Like some: 4 ORAL
**Contradict:** 4 DENY 5 BELIE
REBUT
**Contradicted**
Apt to be: 8 DENIABLE
**Contrapuntal**
composition: 5 CANON
**Contrary**
girl: 4 MARY
to expectation: 5 ODDLY
votes: 4 NAYS
**Contrasts**
Like some: 5 STARK
Opposite of: 6 LIKENS
**Contretemps:** 6 MISHAP
**Contribute:** 3 ADD 5 ADDIN
PAYIN PUTIN 6 CHIPIN
DONATE IMPART
KICKIN
**Contributing**
element: 6 FACTOR
**Contribution**
Church: 5 TITHE
Insured's: 5 COPAY
Kind of: 3 IRA
of ideas: 5 INPUT
Pot: 4 ANTE
**Contributor**
Campaign: 3 PAC
Wealthy: 6 FATCAT
**Contrite:** 5 SORRY
Feel: 6 REPENT
one: 4 RUER
**Contrition:** 6 REGRET
7 REMORSE
Show: 3 RUE
**Contrive:** 4 BREW MAKE PLAN
5 HATCH STAGE
6 DEVISE
**Contrived:** 5 HOKEY
7 TREACLE
**Control:** 3 OWN 4 REIN
5 REINS 7 HARNESS
Bring under: 4 TAME
6 REININ
Crew's: 3 OAR
Dashboard: 5 DEFOG

Electronic ~ system:
5 SERVO
Emissions ~ gp.: 3 EPA
Flood ~ device: 4 DIKE
Have ~ of: 3 OWN
Lose: 4 FLIP RAGE SKID
SNAP
Means of: 4 REIN
Mission ~, for short: 3 OPS
Organ: 4 STOP
Out of: 4 AMOK WILD
5 ARIOT 7 ONATEAR
Pest ~ brand: 4 DCON
Pollution ~ org.: 3 EPA
post: 4 HELM
Steer out of: 8 STAMPEDE
tower image: 4 BLIP
TV: 3 VOL 4 DIAL TINT
5 TUNER
Under: 4 TAME 5 TAMED
6 INHAND INLINE
**Controller**
Horse: 4 REIN
Pupil: 4 IRIS
Traffic: 5 LIGHT
**Controls**
Like some: 4 DUAL
**Controversial:** 7 ERISTIC
1990s ~ sitcom: 5 ELLEN
blowup: 5 ATEST
chemical: 3 PCB
spray: 4 ALAR
talk: 7 EBONICS
Very: 6 REDHOT
war zone: 3 NAM
**Controvert:** 4 DENY 5 BELIE
REBUT
**Contumely:** 5 SCORN
**Conundrum:** 5 POSER
6 ENIGMA RIDDLE
**Convection:** 4 OVEN
**Convene:** 3 SIT 4 MEET
**Convened:** 3 MET SAT
again: 5 REMET
**Convenience:** 4 EASE
24-hr. ~: 3 ATM
Airline: 7 ETICKET
Bank: 3 ATM
Hotel: 4 SAFE
Shopping: 4 TOTE
store convenience: 3 ATM
**Convenient:** 5 HANDY
enc.: 3 SAE
**Convent**
dweller: 3 NUN
leader: 6 ABBESS
**Convention:** 4 MORE NORM
5 USAGE
address: 7 KEYNOTE
center event: 4 EXPO
group: 4 BLOC
handout: 5 IDTAG
7 NAMETAG
site: 4 HALL
~ VIP: 7 NOMINEE
8 KEYNOTER

**Conventional**
Make: 7 STYLIZE
**Convergence**
points: 4 FOCI
**Conversant**
with: 4 UPON
**Conversation:** 6 DIALOG
filler: 4 ISEE
Friendly: 4 CHAT
Have a: 4 TALK
piece: 5 PHONE
starter: 5 HELLO 6 LISTEN
**Conversational**
filler: 5 IMEAN
fillers: 3 ERS
**Conversationalist:** 6 TALKER
**Converse:** 3 RAP 4 CHAT TALK
5 SPEAK
competitor: 4 AVIA KEDS
To's: 3 FRO
**Convert:** 5 ADAPT
~, with "over": 3 WIN
**Converted:** 6 REBORN
**Convertible:** 6 RAGTOP
7 SOFABED
alternative: 5 SEDAN
couch: 6 DAYBED 7 SOFABED
cover: 7 SOFTTOP
It may be: 4 SOFA
Mazda: 5 MIATA
**Convertiplane:** 4 STOL
**Convex**
molding: 5 OVOLO
**Conveyance**
Airport: 4 TRAM
Skier's: 4 TBAR
Whitewater: 4 RAFT
Winter: 4 SLED
**Conveyed:** 6 DEEDED
**Conveyor**
Tear: 4 DUCT
**Conviction:** 5 FAITH TENET
6 BELIEF
One with a: 5 FELON
State with: 4 AVER
6 ASSERT
Unfair: 3 RAP
**Convince:** 4 SELL SWAY
**Convinced:** 4 SOLD SURE
**Convincing**
one: 6 SWAYER
**Convocation**
Quilting: 3 BEE
**Convoy**
component: 3 RIG 4 SEMI
**Convulsive**
sound: 3 SOB
**Convy:** 4 BERT
**Conway**
Comic: 3 TIM
**Cooer:** 4 DOVE
**Cook:** 4 CHEF 7 PREPARE
abbr.: 3 TSP
Apt name for a: 3 STU
book: 4 COMA
canful: 4 LARD

clams: 5 STEAM
cookies: 4 BAKE
cover-up: 5 APRON
exhortation: 5 DIGIN
Gourmet: 4 CHEF
in a microwave: 3 ZAP
    4 NUKE
in a wok: 5 SAUTE
in the oven: 5 ROAST
meas.: 3 TSP
one's goose: 5 ROAST
One way to: 3 FRY 4 BOIL
    STEW 5 BROIL ROAST
    6 BRAISE
too long: 6 OVERDO
up: 4 BREW 5 HATCH
    6 INVENT
wear: 5 APRON
**Cook, Robin**
book: 4 COMA
**Cookbook**
abbr.: 3 TBS TSP 4 TBSP
    TSPS
author Boyle: 4 TISH
author Rombauer: 4 IRMA
direction: 4 SIFT STIR
    5 PUREE
phrase: 3 ALA 5 ADDIN
**Cooke**
Singer: 3 SAM
TV host: 8 ALISTAIR
**Cooked:** 4 DONE MADE
    5 READY 6 STEWED
cereal: 6 FARINA
It's ~ up: 3 LIE
Less: 5 RARER RAWER
Not: 3 RAW
~ Indian-style: 8 TANDOORI
**Cooker:** 4 OVEN 5 STOVE
    7 ROASTER
Asian: 3 WOK
Cantina: 4 OLLA
Old-fashioned: 8 OILSTOVE
Stew: 3 POT
**Cookie**
Black-and-white: 4 OREO
Brittle: 4 SNAP
    10 GINGERSNAP
Computer: 4 DATA
cooker: 4 OVEN
Creme-filled: 4 OREO
"Famous" ~ maker: 4 AMOS
filling: 5 CREME
flavorer: 5 ANISE
Ginger: 4 SNAP
holder: 3 JAR TIN
Keebler ~ maker: 3 ELF
Kind of: 5 SMART 7 OATMEAL
litter: 6 CRUMBS
maker Wally: 4 AMOS
Nabisco: 4 OREO
Pepperidge Farm: 6 MILANO
sandwich: 4 OREO
since 1912: 4 OREO
**Cookies**
Cook: 4 BAKE

quantity: 5 BATCH
**"Cookie's Fortune"**
actress Patricia: 4 NEAL
director: 6 ALTMAN
**Cooking**
direction: 4 HEAT
Enjoyed home: 5 ATEIN
fat: 4 LARD SUET
First name in: 6 EMERIL
Leaves for: 4 SAGE
meas.: 3 TSP
output: 5 AROMA
pot: 4 OLLA
Prepares for: 7 DRESSES
spray brand: 3 PAM
style: 4 THAI 6 CREOLE
Sunken ~ site: 7 FIREPIT
up: 6 MAKING
**Cook Inlet**
city: 9 ANCHORAGE
**Cook-off**
dish: 5 CHILI
**Cookout:** 3 BBQ
fare: 4 RIBS 5 STEAK
Hawaiian: 4 LUAU
intruder: 3 ANT
leftover: 3 ASH 5 EMBER
locale: 5 PATIO
throwaway: 3 COB
**Cookware**
Big name in nonstick: 4 TFAL
Glass: 5 PYREX
item: 3 POT WOK
**Cool:** 3 FAN HEP HIP RAD
    4 CALM NEAT 5 ALOOF
    NEATO NIFTY POISE
    6 APLOMB SEDATE
    SERENE
    10 NONCHALANT
drink: 3 ADE
dude: 3 CAT 6 HEPCAT
Heat and then: 6 ANNEAL
in manner: 5 ALOOF
it: 4 STOP 5 CEASE 6 DESIST
    8 CHILLOUT
Lose one's: 4 SNAP 5 PANIC
Not: 5 UNHIP
rap artist: 4 ICET
red giants: 6 SSTARS
treat: 6 SUNDAE 7 SHERBET
    SNOCONE
Way: 3 RAD 5 GELID
~, updated: 3 DEF 4 PHAT
**"Cool!":** 3 RAD 4 NEAT
    5 NEATO
"___ cool!": 3 WAY
**Cool, Joe**
Hardly: 4 NERD
**Coolant**
Nature's: 5 SWEAT
**Cool ___ Bell (of baseball):**
    4 PAPA
**Cool cat:** 6 DADDYO
Like a: 3 HEP
quality: 7 HIPNESS
**Cool ___ cucumber:** 3 ASA

**"Cool, dude!":** 3 RAD
**Cooled:** 4 ICED
**Cooler:** 3 FAN PEN 4 JAIL STIR
    6 ICEBOX
Citrus: 3 ADE
Drink: 3 ICE
in a cooler: 3 ADE
In the: 5 ONICE
Sailor's: 4 BRIG
Stay in the: 6 DOTIME
Summer: 3 ADE FAN 4 POOL
    6 ICETEA
than cool: 3 RAD
Water: 3 ICE
**Coolers**
Apt.: 3 ACS
**Coolidge:** 3 DAM
President: 3 CAL
Singer: 4 RITA
veep: 5 DAWES
**Coolidge Dam**
river: 4 GILA
**Cooling-off**
period: 6 ICEAGE
place: 4 SILL
**Coolio**
genre: 3 RAP
**"Cool it!":** 4 STOP 5 CHILL
**Coolpix**
maker: 5 NIKON
**Coon**
kin: 5 COATI
**Coop:** 3 PEN 5 HUTCH
clutch: 4 EGGS
flier: 7 ESCAPEE
group: 4 HENS
Pigeon: 4 COTE
**Co-op**
Soviet: 5 ARTEL
unit (abbr.): 3 APT
**Cooped**
(up): 4 PENT
**Cooper**
1936 ~ role: 5 DEEDS
    7 MRDEEDS
Actress: 6 GLADYS
classic: 9 BEAUGESTE
hero: 5 UNCAS
piece: 5 STAVE
Time in a ~ film: 4 NOON
tool: 4 ADZE
**Cooperate**
Won't: 7 RESISTS
**Cooperative**
action: 7 SYNERGY
    8 TEAMWORK
Iowa: 5 AMANA
Russian: 5 ARTEL
**Cooperstown**
Info: Baseball cue
Banks in: 5 ERNIE
bldg.: 3 HOF
first elected member:
    6 TYCOBB
Mel in: 3 OTT
Monte of: 5 IRVIN

nickname: 4 TRIS YOGI
Slaughter in: 4 ENOS
Speaker in: 4 TRIS
Warren of: 5 SPAHN
**Coordinate:** 4 MESH
  system base: 5 XAXIS
**Coordinated:** 5 AGILE
**Coordination:** 4 SYNC
  Loss of: 6 ATAXIA
**Coordinators**
  Flight ~ (abbr.): 3 ATC
**Coors**
  brand: 4 ZIMA
  Brewer: 6 ADOLPH
  rival: 5 PABST 6 STROHS
**Coos Bay**
  state: 6 OREGON
**Coot:** 6 GEEZER
**Cooties:** 4 LICE
**Cop**
  Antidrug: 4 NARC
  calls (abbr.): 4 APBS
  catch: 4 PERP
  French: 8 GENDARME
  milieu: 4 BEAT
  Offender, to a: 4 PERP
  out: 6 RENEGE
  Traffic ~, at times: 5 CITER
  Unarmed, to a: 5 CLEAN
  ~ ID: 5 BADGE
**Cop ___:** 5 APLEA
**Cop a ___:** 4 PLEA
**Copacabana**
  site: 3 RIO
**"Copacabana"**
  showgirl: 4 LOLA
**Copacetic:** 3 AOK 4 JAKE OKAY
**Copal:** 5 RESIN
**Copays**
  Gp. requiring: 3 HMO
**Cope:** 4 DEAL 6 HACKIT
    MAKEDO MANAGE
  with: 5 STAND 6 HANDLE
**"Cope Book"**
  aunt: 4 ERMA
**Coped:** 5 DEALT 6 MADEDO
**Copenhagen**
  carrier: 3 SAS
  currency: 5 KRONE
  park: 6 TIVOLI
  resident: 4 DANE
**Copernicus:** 6 CRATER
  sci.: 4 ASTR
**Copied:** 4 APED 7 XEROXED
  Something ~ (abbr.): 4 ORIG
**Copier:** 3 APE 4 APER 5 MIMIC
    6 SCRIBE
  additive: 5 TONER
  company: 4 MITA 5 CANON
    RICOH
  function: 4 SORT
  Large: 3 APE
  Old-style: 5 MIMEO
  setting: 5 LEGAL
**Copilot**
  Fly without a: 4 SOLO

**Copious:** 5 AMPLE
**"Cop Killer"**
  rapper: 4 ICET
**Copland**
  ballet: 5 RODEO
  composer: 5 AARON
**Copley**
  Actress: 4 TERI
**Copped**
  Something: 4 PLEA
**"Coppélia"**
  costume: 4 TUTU
**Copper:** 4 CENT 5 PENNY
  Big ~ exporter: 4 PERU
  coverings: 7 PATINAE
  head: 3 ABE
**Copperfield**
  field: 5 MAGIC
  Mrs.: 4 DORA
  villain: 4 HEEP
**Copperhead:** 5 SNAKE
**Coppers**
  English: 5 PENCE
**Coppertone**
  no.: 3 SPF
**Coppola**
  Director: 5 SOFIA
**Coppola, Francis**
  Sister of: 5 TALIA
**Cops:** 6 POLICE
  Army: 3 MPS
  Like some undercover:
    5 WIRED
  Pressure from the: 4 HEAT
  Watch for the: 4 ABET
**Copter**
  Early: 4 GIRO
  part: 5 ROTOR
**Coptic**
  title: 4 ABBA
**Copy:** 3 APE 4 DUPE TEXT
    5 CLONE MIMEO MIMIC
    REPRO XEROX
    6 PARROT 7 EMULATE
    IMITATE REPLICA
  Better: 4 EDIT
  cats: 3 MEW 4 MEOW PURR
  Check: 4 EDIT
  Exact: 4 TWIN 5 CLONE
  Hard: 8 PRINTOUT
  machine need: 5 TONER
  Magazine: 5 ISSUE
  Not a ~ (abbr.): 4 ORIG
  Old: 5 MIMEO
  Remove from: 4 DELE
  to a floppy: 4 SAVE
**Copycat:** 3 APE 4 APER
    5 MIMIC 7 METOOER
  cry: 5 METOO
**Copying:** 3 ALA
  Worth: 8 IMITABLE
**Copyist:** 4 APER 6 SCRIBE
    9 SCRIVENER
**Copyright**
  letter: 3 CEE
  page abbr.: 4 ISBN

**"Copy that":** 5 ROGER
**Coq au ___:** 3 VIN
**Coquette:** 4 MINX VAMP
    5 FLIRT TEASE
  Like a: 3 COY
**Coquettish:** 3 COY
**Coral:** 3 SEA 4 PINK
  formation: 4 REEF 5 ATOLL
  island: 3 CAY
  producer: 5 POLYP
**Coral ___:** 3 SEA
**Corbeled-out**
  window: 5 ORIEL
**Corby**
  Actress: 5 ELLEN
**Corcoran**
  Actress: 6 NOREEN
**Cord:** 5 TWINE
  About ¼: 5 STERE
  components: 4 LOGS
  Jumper's: 6 BUNGEE
  Kind of: 3 RIP 6 SPINAL
  Sailor: 7 LANYARD
  Strong: 4 ROPE
  Tie with a: 4 BOLO
**___ corda:** 3 UNA
**Cordage**
  fiber: 5 ISTLE SISAL
**Corday**
  victim: 5 MARAT
**Cordelia**
  Father of: 4 LEAR
  Sister of: 5 REGAN
**Cordial:** 4 WARM
    8 ANISETTE
  flavoring: 5 ANISE
  French ~ flavoring: 4 ANIS
  Less: 5 ICIER
**Cordiant**
  ad agency: 5 BATES
**Cordillera Real**
  home: 5 ANDES
**Córdoba**
  Info: Spanish cue
  cheer: 3 OLE
  kinswoman: 3 TIA
**Cordon ___:** 4 BLEU
**Cords:** 5 PANTS
  Cut: 3 HEW
**Corduroy**
  feature: 3 RIB 4 WALE
    5 RIDGE
  Like: 5 WALED 6 RIBBED
    RIDGED
**Cordwood**
  measure: 5 STERE
**Core:** 3 HUB NUB NUT 4 GIST
    PITH 5 HEART MIDST
    7 ESSENCE
  Corn: 3 COB
  group: 5 CADRE
  PC: 3 CPU
  Peach: 3 PIT
**CORE**
  Roy of: 5 INNIS
**Cores:** 6 NUCLEI

**Corey**
Actor: 4 HAIM
Professor: 5 IRWIN
**Corfu**
Letter from: 3 ETA
**Corgi**
or collie: 5 BREED
**Coriander**
cousin: 5 ANISE
or basil: 4 HERB
**Corinth**
Play set in: 5 MEDEA
**Corinthian:** 7 HELLENE
alternative: 5 DORIC
**"Coriolanus"**
setting: 4 ROME
**Cork:** 7 STOPPER
dance: 3 JIG
locale: 4 EIRE 7 IRELAND
shooter: 6 POPGUN
source: 3 OAK 4 BARK
**Corker:** 3 PIP 4 LULU
**Corkers:** 5 IRISH
**Corkscrew:** 4 COIL 6 SPIRAL
pasta: 6 ROTINI
**Corkwood:** 5 BALSA
**Corleone:** 5 FREDO SONNY
creator: 4 PUZO
Head: 4 VITO
title: 3 DON
**Corleone, Sonny**
portrayer: 4 CAAN
**Corn:** 4 CROP 5 MAIZE
Bit of: 6 KERNEL
bread: 4 PONE
    10 JOHNNYCAKE
concoction: 4 PONE
core: 3 COB
country: 4 IOWA
covering: 4 HUSK
flower: 6 TASSEL
Golden-___: 5 EARED
grower: 3 TOE
holder: 3 CAN COB 4 CRIB
How ~ is planted:
    6 INROWS
Indian: 5 MAIZE
Order of: 3 EAR
prefix: 3 TRI UNI
product: 4 OLEO
serving: 3 EAR
site: 3 TOE
spikes: 4 EARS
Store, as: 6 ENSILE
syrup brand: 4 KARO
unit: 3 COB EAR
**Corn ___:** 4 BELT CHEX PONE
    5 SYRUP
**Cornball:** 5 HOKEY TRITE
**Corn Belt**
state: 4 IOWA
**Cornbread**
cake: 4 PONE
**Cornea**
companion: 6 SCLERA
repository: 7 EYEBANK

**Corned beef**
concoction: 4 HASH 6 REUBEN
sandwich bread: 3 RYE
**Corneille**
play: 5 ELCID
**Cornell**
city: 6 ITHACA
rival: 4 PENN YALE
**Cornell University**
founder: 4 EZRA
**Corner:** 4 NOOK TREE
    5 ANGLE HEMIN NICHE
Cozy: 4 NOOK
Diamond: 3 BAG 4 BASE
    6 SECOND
From ~ to ~ (abbr.): 4 DIAG
In a: 5 TREED
Just around the: 4 SOON
key: 3 ESC
map: 5 INSET
Monopoly: 4 JAIL
One in your: 4 ALLY
piece: 3 ELL 4 ROOK
Secluded: 4 NOOK
**Cornerback**
~ Sanders: 5 DEION
**Cornered:** 5 ATBAY TREED
    7 UPATREE
**Cornerstone**
abbr.: 3 EST 4 ESTD 5 ESTAB
features: 5 DATES
word: 4 ANNO
**Cornetist**
~ Adderley: 3 NAT
~ Beiderbecke: 3 BIX
**Cornfield**
bird: 4 CROW
cry: 3 CAW
measure: 4 ACRE
**"Cornflake Girl"**
singer Tori: 4 AMOS
**"... corn ___ high ...":** 4 ISAS
**Cornhusker**
city: 5 OMAHA
rival: 6 SOONER
st.: 3 NEB 4 NEBR
___ Corning: 5 OWENS
**Cornishman:** 4 CELT
**Cornmeal**
bread: 4 PONE
mush: 7 POLENTA
treat: 7 HOECAKE
**Corn-oil**
spread: 4 OLEO
**Cornrow:** 5 PLAIT
**Cornrows**
Like: 7 PLAITED
**Cornstalks**
Like: 5 EARED
**Cornstarch**
brand: 4 ARGO
**Cornwall:** 5 SHIRE
**Cornwallis**
surrender site: 8 YORKTOWN
**Corny**
bit: 6 KERNEL

item: 3 EAR 4 PONE
**"___ corny as Kansas ...":**
    4 IMAS
**Corolla**
part: 5 PETAL
**Corona:** 5 CIGAR 7 AUREOLE
**Coronado**
quest: 3 ORO
**Coronet:** 5 TIARA
**Corot**
Painter: 4 JEAN
**Corp.**
bigwig: 3 CEO 4 EXEC PRES
exec degree: 3 MBA
money handler: 3 CFO
takeover: 3 LBO
**Corporal**
punishment unit: 4 LASH
**Corporally**
punish: 5 SPANK
**Corporate**
alias (abbr.): 3 DBA
baker: 7 SARALEE
budget part: 5 RANDD
cow: 5 ELSIE
department: 5 LEGAL SALES
exec.: 3 CEO CFO
flunky: 5 DRONE
image: 4 LOGO
mouthpiece: 9 SPOKESMAN
raider Carl: 5 ICAHN
rule: 5 BYLAW
symbol: 4 LOGO
~ VIP: 3 CEO 4 EXEC
**Corporation**
called "Big Blue": 3 IBM
Giant chemicals: 4 OLIN
that gave a bad account of
    itself: 5 ENRON
**Corporeal**
quintet: 6 SENSES
**Corps**
member: 6 MARINE
**Corpsman:** 5 MEDIC
**Corpulent:** 3 FAT 5 OBESE
    STOUT
**Corpus**
follower: 7 DELICTI
Habeas: 4 WRIT
___ corpus: 6 HABEAS
**Corral:** 3 PEN 5 PENIN
    6 ROPEIN 7 ENCLOSE
**Correct:** 4 MEND TRUE
    5 AMEND EMEND
    RIGHT 6 PROPER
    REMEDY 7 REDRESS
Ain't: 4 ISNT 5 ARENT
copy: 4 EDIT 5 EMEND
**Correction:** 7 ERASURE
list: 6 ERRATA
Make a ~ to: 5 EMEND
Need: 3 ERR
**Correctly:** 6 ARIGHT
**Correlative**
Common: 3 NOR
**Correo ___ (airmail):** 5 AEREO

**Correspond:** 5 AGREE TALLY
**Corresponded:** 5 WROTE
**Correspondence:** 4 MAIL
  6 PARITY 7 LETTERS
  High-tech: 5 EMAIL
  Kind of: 8 ONETOONE
  Office: 4 MEMO
**Correspondent**
  Foreign: 6 PENPAL
  WWII ~ Pyle: 5 ERNIE
**Corresponding:** 4 SAME
**Corrida**
  beast: 4 TORO 6 ELTORO
  cheer: 3 OLE
  combatant: 6 TORERO
  Enthusiastic ~ cry: 6 OLEOLE
  Hurt in the: 5 GORED
**Corridor:** 4 HALL 5 AISLE
  bullet train: 5 ACELA
**Corrode:** 3 EAT 4 RUST
  7 EATINTO
**Corroded:** 3 ATE 5 ATEAT
  EATEN 7 ATEINTO
**Corrosive**
  chemical: 4 ACID
**Corrupt:** 3 BAD ROT 4 HOSE
  5 TAINT VENAL
  6 DEBASE POISON
  7 DEPRAVE SUBVERT
**Corruptible:** 5 VENAL
**Corsage**
  Attach, as a: 5 PINON
  flower: 6 ORCHID
**Corsair:** 5 EDSEL
**Corset**
  part: 4 STAY
  tightener: 5 LACER
**Corsica:** 3 CAR
  Isle near: 4 ELBA
**Corsican**
  hero: 5 PAOLI
**Cortés**
  quest: 3 ORO
  victim: 5 AZTEC
**Cortex**
  prefix: 3 NEO
  product: 4 IDEA
**Cortisone:** 7 STEROID
**Corundum:** 4 RUBY
**Corvair**
  critic: 5 NADER
**Corvine**
  cry: 3 CAW
**Cosa ___:** 6 NOSTRA
  **___ cosa:** 4 OTRA
**Cosby**
  1960s ~ show: 4 ISPY
  costar: 4 CULP 6 RASHAD
  heavy creation: 6 ALBERT
  specialty: 8 ANECDOTE
**"Cosby Show, The"**
  actress Lisa: 5 BONET
  actress Phylicia: 6 RASHAD
  kid: 4 THEO
**Cosecant**
  reciprocal: 4 SINE

**Cosell**
  Longtime ~ foil: 3 ALI
**Cosgrave**
  Former Irish P.M.: 4 LIAM
**Cosine:** 5 RATIO
**Cosmetic**
  additive: 4 ALOE
  Cheek: 5 ROUGE
  goo: 5 GELEE
  Lash: 7 MASCARA
  Liquid: 6 LOTION
**Cosmetician**
  ~ Lauder: 5 ESTEE
**Cosmetics**
  Adrien of: 5 ARPEL
  Arpel of: 6 ADRIEN
  company: 4 AVON
  Curtis of: 6 HELENE
  dye: 5 EOSIN
  First name in: 5 ESTEE
  MERLE
  Mary ___ of: 3 KAY
  name: 4 COTY 5 ESTEE
  overseeing agcy.: 3 FDA
**"Cosmicomics"**
  author Calvino: 5 ITALO
**Cosmo:** 3 MAG
  feature: 7 SEXQUIZ
  rival: 4 ELLE
**Cosmonaut:** 7 RUSSIAN
  home: 3 MIR
  insignia, once: 4 CCCP
  ~ Atkov: 4 OLEG
  ~ Gagarin: 4 YURI
**Cosmopolitan**
  rival: 4 ELLE
**Cosmos**
  star: 4 PELE
**"Cosmos"**
  creator: 5 SAGAN
**Cost:** 5 PRICE RANTO RUNTO
  6 OUTLAY 7 EXPENSE
  Absorb, as: 3 EAT
  At no: 4 FREE
  Contracted: 7 SETRATE
  Determine: 5 PRICE
  For an additional: 5 EXTRA
  Housing: 4 RENT
  Maintenance: 6 UPKEEP
  of belonging: 4 DUES
  of leaving: 4 BAIL
  of living: 4 RENT
  Pump: 6 GASTAX
  to cross: 4 TOLL
  ~, in slang: 6 DAMAGE
  ___ cost: 4 ATNO
**Costa ___:** 4 MESA RICA
**Costa del ___:** 3 SOL
**Costa del Sol**
  feature: 5 PLAYA
**Costanza**
  Mother of George: 7 ESTELLE
**Costa ___ Sol:** 3 DEL
**Costello**
  Abbott and: 3 DUO
  Abbott, to: 6 COHORT

  Comedian: 3 LOU
  Partner of: 6 ABBOTT
**Costly:** 4 DEAR
**Costner**
  1987 ~ role: 4 NESS
  1988 ~ film:
  10 BULLDURHAM
  1994 ~ role: 4 EARP
  1996 ~ film: 6 TINCUP
  Actor: 5 KEVIN
**Cost-of-living**
  stat: 3 CPI
**Costs**
  (abbr.): 3 EXP
  Cover: 9 BREAKEVEN
  ~, with "to": 5 COMES
  "___ cost to you!": 4 ATNO
**Costume:** 5 GETUP GUISE
  6 ATTIRE
  Ballet: 4 TUTU
  Calcutta: 4 SARI
  Halloween: 5 GHOST SHEET
  part: 4 CAPE MASK
**"___ cost you!":** 4 ITLL
**Cote**
  call: 3 BAA COO
  girls: 4 EWES
  It's off la: 3 MER
**Côte ___:** 3 DOR
**Côte d'___:** 4 AZUR
**Cotillion:** 4 BALL
  honoree: 3 DEB
  **___ cotta:** 5 TERRA
**Cottage**
  and condo: 6 REALTY
  site: 4 LAKE
  Ski: 5 LODGE 6 CHALET
  Summer: 5 DACHA LODGE
  Summer ~, often: 6 RENTAL
**Cotton:** 7 TEXTILE
  bundle: 4 BALE
  bundler: 5 BALER
  candy: 5 SUGAR
  fabric: 4 PIMA 5 CHINO
  RAMIE 6 DAMASK
  SATEEN 7 GINGHAM
  Fine: 4 PIMA 5 LISLE
  fuzz: 4 LINT
  gin inventor Whitney: 3 ELI
  Lightweight: 7 ETAMINE
  Like ~ candy: 4 SPUN
  pest: 6 WEEVIL
  pod: 4 BOLL
  Process: 3 GIN
  Sheer: 5 TOILE
  Strong: 4 PIMA
  stuffing: 4 BATT
  thread: 5 LISLE
  unit: 4 BALE
**Cotton Bowl**
  city: 6 DALLAS
  Three-time ~ champs: 3 SMU
**"Cotton Candy"**
  trumpeter: 4 HIRT 6 ALHIRT
**Cotton Club**
  site: 6 HARLEM

**"Cotton Club, The"**
　setting: 6 HARLEM
　star: 4 GERE
**Cotton State (abbr.):** 3 ALA
**Cottontail:** 6 RABBIT
　tail: 4 SCUT
**Cotton-tipped**
　cleaner: 4 SWAB
**Cottonwood:** 5 ALAMO
　　6 POPLAR
　　10 POPLARTREE
**Coty**
　of France: 4 RENE
**Couch:** 4 SOFA 6 PHRASE
　　SETTEE
　Backless: 5 DIVAN
　Convertible: 6 DAYBED
**Couch potato:** 5 IDLER
　Be a: 4 LAZE LOLL
　device: 6 REMOTE
　　13 REMOTECONTROL
　Like a: 4 IDLE 5 INERT
　No: 4 DOER
　perch: 4 SOFA
**Cougar:** 3 CAR CAT 4 AUTO
　　PUMA
　maker: 4 MERC
　quarters: 4 LAIR
**Cough**
　drop flavor: 5 ANISE
　　7 MENTHOL
　Polite: 4 AHEM
　quieter: 7 CODEINE
　syrup amt.: 3 TSP
　up: 4 ANTE
**Could**
　It ~ be a lot: 4 ACRE
　tell: 6 SENSED
**"... could ___ fat":** 5 EATNO
**Couldn't**
　abide: 5 HATED
　help but: 5 HADTO
　remember: 6 FORGOT
　stand: 5 HATED
　　8 DETESTED
**"Couldn't help it!":** 5 HADTO
**Coulomb**
　per sec: 3 AMP 6 AMPERE
**Coulter**
　Author: 3 ANN
**Council**
　1409 ~ site: 4 PISA
　1545 ~ site: 5 TRENT
　Church: 5 SYNOD
　City ~ rep.: 3 ALD
　member: 5 ELDER
**___ Council:** 6 NICENE
**Council Bluffs**
　neighbor: 5 OMAHA
**Counsel:** 4 WARN 6 ADVISE
　Hire, as ~: 6 RETAIN
**Counseling:** 4 HELP
**Counselor**
　at Troy: 6 NESTOR
　org.: 3 ABA
　Personal: 6 MENTOR

**Count:** 3 ADD 4 RELY
　　6 MATTER
　Attendance: 5 NOSES
　calories: 4 DIET
　Candle: 3 AGE
　Checkout: 5 ITEMS
　Commandments: 3 TEN
　Down for the: 3 KOD
　Drop for the: 4 KAYO
　ending: 3 ESS
　equivalent: 4 EARL
　Hospital: 4 BEDS
　It may: 8 NEATNESS
　of jazz: 5 BASIE
　(on): 4 RELY
　player: 6 LUGOSI
　Ring: 3 TEN
　Start for a Spanish: 3 UNO
　Start of a: 4 EENY 5 BALLS
　suffix: 3 ESS
　Supreme Court: 4 NINE
　Swimmer's: 4 LAPS
　Workout: 3 REP
　You can ~ on it: 6 ABACUS
**"Count ___":** 4 MEIN
**Countdown**
　deejay Casey: 5 KASEM
　start: 3 TEN
**Counted**
　Fully: 5 INALL
　They're: 5 NOSES
**Countenance:** 4 MIEN
　　6 VISAGE
**Counter:** 5 REBUT 6 OPPOSE
　　7 RESPOND
　Cab: 5 METER
　call: 4 NEXT
　Kind of: 5 LUNCH 6 GEIGER
　　7 CALORIE
　Kitchen: 5 TIMER
　KO: 3 REF
　man: 6 GEIGER
　Mileage: 8 ODOMETER
　offer: 3 BLT 4 SODA
　opener: 4 EENY
**Counteract:** 6 NEGATE OFFSET
**Counterargue:** 5 REBUT
**Counterbalance:** 6 OFFSET
　　SETOFF
**Counterculture**
　guru: 5 LEARY
**Countercurrent:** 4 EDDY
**Counterfeit:** 3 BAD 4 FAKE
　　SHAM 5 BOGUS
　catcher: 4 TMAN
　coin: 4 SLUG
**Countermand:** 3 NIX 6 CANCEL
　　NEGATE
**Countermeasures**
　Take: 5 REACT
**Counterpart:** 4 MATE
　　8 OPPOSITE
**Counters:** 5 ABACI
　11 to 20, for some ~: 4 TOES
　What ~ count: 5 NOSES
**Counterstroke:** 6 RIPOST

**Countertenor:** 4 ALTO
**Countess**
　spouse: 4 EARL
**Counting**
　everything: 5 INALL
　　6 INTOTO
　method: 4 TENS
　(on): 7 RELIANT
　rhyme start: 4 EENY
　Stop ~ sheep: 5 SLEEP
**Counting-out**
　word: 4 EENY
**Countless:** 4 MANY
　　6 UNTOLD
　years: 3 EON 4 AGES
**"Count me in!":** 6 IMGAME
　　7 IMFORIT
**"Count of ___ Cristo, The":**
　　5 MONTE
**"Count of Monte ___, The":**
　　6 CRISTO
**"Count of Monte Cristo, The"**
　setting: 7 DUNGEON
**Countrified:** 5 RURAL
**Country:** 4 LAND 5 RURAL
　　6 NATION
　1988 ~ album: 4 REBA
　African: 4 MALI 5 SUDAN
　album: 5 ATLAS
　Andean: 4 PERU
　Arabian: 4 OMAN
　Biblical: 4 EDOM
　Black of: 5 CLINT
　Boot-shaped: 5 ITALY
　bumpkin: 4 CLOD JAKE RUBE
　　5 YAHOO YOKEL
　Bush: 5 USOFA
　byway: 4 LANE
　cousin: 4 RUBE
　crossing: 5 STILE
　Divided: 5 KOREA
　estate: 5 MANOR VILLA
　First name in: 4 REBA
　founded by freed slaves:
　　7 LIBERIA
　Hill of: 5 FAITH
　in a Beatles song: 4 USSR
　It's a free: 3 USA
　Leave the: 6 SECEDE
　lodging: 3 INN
　mail rte.: 3 RFD
　Medit.: 3 ISR
　Mideast: 5 YEMEN
　name: 4 REBA
　Of ~ life: 5 RURAL
　on the Caspian: 4 IRAN
　Out of the: 6 ABROAD
　quartet: 7 ALABAMA
　rtes.: 3 RDS
　SA: 3 ARG
　Scand.: 4 NORW
　Split: 5 KOREA
　U.K.: 3 ENG
　with a blue, black, and white
　　flag: 7 ESTONIA
**"___ Country":** 4 AFAR

**Country club**
(abbr.): 5 THEUN
figure: 3 PRO
rental: 4 CART
**Country dance:** 4 REEL
spot: 4 BARN
**"Country Doctor, A"**
author Sarah ___ Jewett:
4 ORNE
**"Country Gentleman"**
Atkins: 4 CHET
**"Country Girl, The"**
playwright: 5 ODETS
Tony winner: 8 UTAHAGEN
**Countryman**
Neither a friend nor a:
5 ROMAN
**Country music:** 6 ANTHEM
network, once: 3 TNN
**Country road:** 4 LANE
feature: 3 ESS RUT
Unlike a: 5 PAVED
**Country singer**
~ Black: 5 CLINT
~ Bonnie: 5 RAITT
~ Brenda: 3 LEE
~ Brooks: 5 GARTH
~ Carter: 5 DEANA
~ Clark: 3 ROY 5 TERRI
~ Collin: 4 RAYE
~ Crystal: 5 GAYLE
~ David Allan ___: 3 COE
~ Davis: 3 MAC 7 SKEETER
~ Evans: 4 SARA
~ George: 6 STRAIT
~ Gibbs: 5 TERRI
~ Haggard: 5 MERLE
~ Jackson: 4 ALAN
~ Kathy: 6 MATTEA
~ Ketchum: 3 HAL
~ K.T.: 5 OSLIN
~ LeAnn: 5 RIMES
~ Lynn: 7 LORETTA
~ McCann: 4 LILA
~ McCoy: 4 NEAL
~ McDaniel: 3 MEL
~ McEntire: 4 REBA
~ McGraw: 3 TIM
~ Morgan: 6 LORRIE
~ Murray: 4 ANNE
~ Randy: 6 TRAVIS
~ Reeves: 3 DEL
~ Rimes: 5 LEANN
~ Tillis: 3 MEL PAM
~ Travis: 5 TRITT
~ Tubb: 6 ERNEST
~ Tucker: 5 TANYA
~ Yearwood: 6 TRISHA
**County**
center: 4 SEAT
English: 4 AVON KENT
5 ESSEX SHIRE
6 DORSET
festival: 4 FAIR
Scottish: 5 CLARE KERRY
SLIGO 6 ARGYLL

**County Clare**
capital: 5 ENNIS
**County Kerry**
seat: 6 TRALEE
**Coup**
Bridge: 4 SLAM
Court: 3 ACE
follower: 5 DETAT
Golf: 3 ACE 5 EAGLE
group: 5 CABAL JUNTA
Narc's: 4 BUST
**Coup ___:** 5 DETAT
**Coup d'___:** 4 ETAT
**Coupe:** 3 CAR 4 AUTO
alternative: 5 SEDAN
**Couple:** 3 DUO TWO WED
4 DUAD DYAD ITEM
PAIR 5 UNITE
7 TWOSOME
Divorced: 4 EXES
in the news: 4 ITEM
Odd: 4 DEES
of cups: 3 BRA
pronoun: 3 OUR 4 OURS
**Coupler:** 4 YOKE
**Couples**
carrier: 3 ARK
Golfer: 4 FRED
may swing here: 3 TEE
**Coupling**
device: 4 YOKE
**Coupon**
clipper: 8 REDEEMER
for the needy: 9 FOODSTAMP
Removes, as a: 5 CLIPS
8 TEARSOUT
**Courage:** 4 GUTS 5 HEART
NERVE PLUCK SPINE
Deprive of: 5 UNMAN
Have the: 4 DARE
**Courageous:** 5 BRAVE
6 GRITTY
Be: 4 DARE
**Couric**
Former ~ cohost: 5 LAUER
Former ~ show: 5 TODAY
Newscaster: 5 KATIE
**Courier:** 4 FONT
**Course:** 4 DISH FLOW PATH
ROAD 5 ROUTE TREND
6 STREAM
Change: 3 ZIG 4 TURN VEER
Circular: 4 GYRE
climax: 4 TEST
Coll.: 3 SOC 4 ECON
Cushy: 5 EASYA
deviation: 3 YAW
Dinner: 4 SOUP 5 SALAD
6 ENTREE 7 DESSERT
dir.: 3 ENE ESE NNE SSE
Downhill: 6 SKIRUN
Early: 5 SALAD
First: 4 SOUP 5 PLANA
for U.S. aliens: 3 ESL
Freshman language: 6 LATINI
Go off: 3 ERR YAW 4 VEER

guide: 3 PAR
Gut: 5 EASYA
hazard: 4 TRAP
Horse: 4 OATS OVAL
H.S.: 3 ENG 4 TRIG
list abbr.: 3 TBA
listing: 4 MENU
Main: 6 ENTREE
Math: 4 CALC TRIG
Med.: 4 ANAT
of events: 4 TIDE
Off: 4 AWRY 6 ASTRAY
ERRANT
requirement: 3 TEE
Second: 5 PLANB
section: 4 UNIT
start: 3 TEE
Took a: 3 ATE
with greens: 5 SALAD
Zigzag: 6 SLALOM
**Courses**
Like some golf: 8 NINEHOLE
Slalom: 5 ESSES
Takes: 4 SUPS
**Court:** 3 WOO
1973 ~ name: 3 ROE
1995 ~ VIP: 3 ITO
action: 4 PLEA
activity: 5 TRIAL
arbiter: 3 REF
Argued in: 4 PLED
battle: 6 TENNIS
Bring to: 3 SUE
calendar: 6 DOCKET
call: 3 LET 4 ADIN 5 ORDER
Call before a: 7 ARRAIGN
Call to: 4 CITE
clown: 6 JESTER
conference: 7 SIDEBAR
coup: 3 ACE
covering: 4 ROBE
cry: 4 OYEZ 6 HEARYE
decision: 3 LET
defense: 4 ZONE
divider: 3 NET
Dressed for: 5 ROBED
event: 5 TRIAL
fig.: 3 ATT 4 ATTY
figs.: 3 DAS
figure: 4 EARL SUER 5 JUROR
NOBLE STENO
game: 8 ONEONONE
Gentleman of the: 4 ASHE
hearing: 4 OYER
Hoop at a: 3 RIM
huddle: 7 SIDEBAR
legend: 3 DRJ 4 ASHE
Like ~ testimony: 5 SWORN
matter: 3 RES
Open: 6 ATRIUM
order: 4 RISE WRIT
7 ALLRISE
org.: 3 ABA 4 USTA
Papal: 5 CURIA
plea, briefly: 4 NOLO
procedure: 4 OATH

records: 4 ACTA
reporter: 5 STENO
response: 4 PLEA
ruling: 3 LET
score: 4 ADIN
Send back to a lower:
    6 REMAND
site, with "The": 5 HAGUE
statistic: 4 PLEA
story: 5 ALIBI
summons: 8 SUBPOENA
Take to: 3 SUE
They come to: 5 BEAUS
They're taken in: 5 OATHS
Zero, on a: 4 LOVE
~ VIPs: 3 DAS
**Courteney**
Actress: 3 COX
**Courteous:** 4 NICE 5 CIVIL
    6 POLITE 7 GENTEEL
**Courtesan**
Zola: 4 NANA
**Courtesy**
Reply ~, briefly: 4 SASE
**"Court Jester, The"**
star: 9 DANNYKAYE
**Courtroom**
1970s ~ drama: 5 THEDA
attire: 4 ROBE
entry: 4 PLEA
fig.: 3 ATT
First name in ~ fiction: 4 ERLE
pledge: 4 OATH
statement: 4 PLEA
~ VIPs: 3 DAS
**Courts:** 5 ATRIA
**Court TV**
fare: 5 TRIAL
topic: 3 LAW
**Courtyard:** 6 ATRIUM
**Courtyards:** 5 ATRIA
**Cous.:** 3 REL
**Cousins:** 3 KIN
mothers: 5 AUNTS
**Cousteau**
milieu: 3 MER 5 OCEAN
**Cousy, Bob**
team: 7 CELTICS
**Couth**
Lacking: 4 RUDE 5 CRASS
___ couture: 5 HAUTE
**Couturier**
initials: 3 YSL
~ Cassini: 4 OLEG
~ Christian: 4 DIOR
**Cove:** 3 BAY RIA 5 INLET
___ Cove: 5 CABOT
**Covenant:** 4 PACT
holder: 3 ARK
**Covent Garden**
architect Jones: 5 INIGO
landmark: 10 OPERAHOUSE
offering: 5 OPERA
solo: 4 ARIA
**Coventry**
Info: British cue

cleaner: 4 CHAR
coins: 5 PENCE
**Cover:** 3 LID 4 COAT VEIL
    5 ALIAS ALIBI 6 CLOTHE
    ENCASE INSURE
    7 OVERLAY OVERLIE
After-bath: 4 ROBE
anew: 5 RESOD
Arctic: 8 ICESHEET
Camper: 4 TENT
Canvas: 4 TARP
Catch-basin: 5 GRATE
Crown: 6 ENAMEL
Diamond: 4 TARP
Engine: 4 HOOD
Front end: 3 BRA
Ground: 3 SOD 7 MACADAM
Head: 3 HAT
Infield: 4 TARP
Lamp: 5 SHADE
Lens: 6 EYELID
letter letters: 3 SAE
Orange: 4 PEEL RIND
over: 6 REWRAP 7 REPAPER
Pillow: 4 CASE SHAM
Pot: 3 LID
Road: 3 TAR
Seed: 4 ARIL
Slip: 5 DRESS
Stadium: 4 DOME
story: 5 ALIBI
Take: 4 HIDE
Teapot: 4 COZY
Took: 3 HID
Under: 4 ABED 5 INBED
up: 4 HIDE VEIL 6 ENROBE
Waterproof: 4 TARP
Wheel: 6 HUBCAP
Window: 5 BLIND DRAPE
with crumbs: 5 BREAD
with dirt: 4 BURY
with goo: 5 SLIME
with graffiti: 6 DEFACE
with turf: 3 SOD
Wound: 4 SCAB
**Coverage**
letters: 3 HMO
Press: 3 INK
Rug: 4 AREA
**Covered:** 4 CLAD
(in): 5 AWASH
It's got you: 4 SKIN
passageway: 6 ARCADE
with dirt: 5 GRIMY
with vines: 5 IVIED
**Cover girl**
~ Banks: 4 TYRA
~ Carol: 3 ALT
**Covering:** 4 ATOP
Head: 3 CAP 4 HAIR
Outer: 4 PEEL RIND SKIN
Polar: 6 ICECAP
Pond: 5 ALGAE
Protective: 4 TARP
Seed: 4 ARIL HULL 5 TESTA
up: 6 HIDING

**Coverlet:** 5 QUILT 6 AFGHAN
**Covert**
org.: 3 CIA
~ WWII org.: 3 OSS
**Cover-up:** 4 ROBE TARP TOGA
    5 APRON 6 CAFTAN
Calcutta: 4 SARI
**Covet:** 4 ENVY WANT
    6 DESIRE
**Coveted**
statue: 5 OSCAR
**Covetous**
feeling: 4 ENVY
**Covetousness:** 4 ENVY
    5 GREED
**Cow:** 3 AWE 5 BULLY DAUNT
catcher: 5 LASSO REATA
    RIATA 6 LARIAT
chew: 3 CUD
comment: 3 MOO
Corporate: 5 ELSIE
Dairy: 8 HOLSTEIN
hand: 4 HOOF
Have a: 5 CALVE
Having a: 5 UPSET
Her symbol was a: 4 ISIS
hurdle, in rhyme: 4 MOON
kid: 4 CALF
name: 5 BOSSY
or sow: 3 SHE 6 FEMALE
owner: 6 OLEARY
Query to a: 6 HOWNOW
Sea: 7 MANATEE
**Coward:** 10 WEAKSISTER
    11 YELLOWBELLY
lack: 5 HEART SPINE
Playwright: 4 NOEL
**Cowardly Lion**
alter ego: 4 ZEKE
portrayer: 4 LAHR
**"Coward of the County"**
actress Alicia: 3 ANA
**Cowboy:** 5 ROPER 6 HERDER
boot attachment: 4 SPUR
contest: 5 RODEO
date: 3 GAL
gear: 5 RIATA 6 LARIAT
Legendary: 9 PECOSBILL
Mexican: 6 CHARRO
nickname: 5 SLIM
pal: 4 PARD
rope: 5 LASSO REATA RIATA
Singing: 5 AUTRY
stray: 5 DOGIE
~ Ritter: 3 TEX
~ Rogers: 3 ROY
**Cowboys**
gp.: 3 NFL
home: 6 DALLAS
or Indians: 4 TEAM
**"Cowboys"**
Like Shepard's: 6 ONEACT
**Cowcatcher:** 6 GRILLE
**"Cow Cow Boogie"**
singer Morse: 7 ELLAMAE
**Cower:** 5 QUAIL

**Cowgirl**
~ Dale: 5 EVANS
**Cowhand**
moniker: 3 TEX
**Cow-horned**
goddess: 4 ISIS
**Cowley**
composition: 3 ODE
**Cowpoke**
contest: 5 RODEO
pal: 4 PARD
Pampas: 6 GAUCHO
rope: 5 RIATA 6 LARIAT
**Cows:** 4 KINE
Like some: 6 SACRED
**Cox**
TV role for: 7 PEEPERS
**Coxcomb:** 3 FOP
**Coxswain**
charges: 4 OARS
Obey the: 3 ROW
**Coyote**
Cartoon: 5 WILEE
clamor: 4 HOWL
supplier: 4 ACME
___ **Coyote:** 5 WILEE
**Coyote, ___ E.:** 4 WILE
**Cozumel**
Info: Spanish cue
cash: 4 PESO
**Cozy:** 4 SNUG 5 COMFY
HOMEY
contents: 6 TEAPOT
corner: 4 NOOK
Get: 6 NESTLE
Kind of: 3 TEA
retreat: 3 DEN 4 NEST
up: 6 NESTLE
**CPA**
busy mo.: 3 APR
concern: 6 TAXLAW
employer: 3 IRS
expertise: 3 NOS
Part of: 3 ACC 4 ACCT CERT
suggestion: 3 IRA
**Cpl.:** 3 NCO
NCO two levels above: 4 SSGT
Rank above: 3 SGT
Rank below: 3 PFC PVT
**CPO**
org.: 3 USN
**CPR**
expert: 3 EMT
**CPU**
attachment: 3 CRT
Part of: 4 UNIT
**CQD**
successor: 3 SOS
**Crab:** 3 NAG 5 GRIPE
Move like a: 5 SIDLE
weapon: 4 CLAW
**Crab ___:** 6 NEBULA
**Crabby**
Act: 5 SIDLE
**Crab Key**
resident: 4 DRNO

**Crack:** 3 ACE TRY 4 CHAP
JOKE OPEN QUIP SLIT
STAB 5 ADEPT SOLVE
7 ATTEMPT FISSURE
8 APERTURE
a book: 4 READ
and redden: 4 CHAP
At the ~ of dawn: 5 EARLY
cop: 4 NARC
Creep through the: 4 SEEP
Enter via a: 6 SEEPIN
fighter pilot: 3 ACE
in the cold: 4 CHAP
Likely to: 7 BRITTLE
Open a: 4 AJAR
Org. with a ~ staff: 3 DEA
result: 4 HAHA
Something to: 4 CODE
squad: 5 ATEAM
Take a ~ at: 3 TRY
Tough nut to: 5 POSER
6 ENIGMA
**Cracked:** 3 MAD 4 AJAR BATS
DAFT LOCO NUTS
5 BATTY LOONY NUTTY
6 INSANE
It might be: 4 SAFE
open: 4 AJAR
**Cracker**
box: 4 SAFE
brand: 4 HIHO RITZ
flavoring: 6 SESAME
Kind of: 6 GRAHAM
Seder: 5 MATZO
shape: 6 ANIMAL
Soup: 7 SALTINE
spread: 3 ROE 4 PATE
topper: 4 BRIE
Vault: 4 YEGG
**Crackerjack:** 3 ACE PRO
5 ADEPT
**Cracker Jack**
surprise: 3 TOY
**Crackers:** 3 MAD 4 BATS DAFT
LOCO NUTS 5 BATTY
LOONY NUTTY
6 INSANE
**Cracking**
Get: 5 START
**Crackle**
colleague: 4 SNAP
**Crackler**
Year-end: 7 YULELOG
**Crackpot:** 3 NUT 6 MANIAC
**Cradle**
Odd place for a: 7 TREETOP
part: 6 ROCKER
**"Cradle of Love"**
singer Billy: 4 IDOL
**Craft:** 3 ART 4 BOAT MAKE
SHIP 5 GUILE SKILL
6 VESSEL
Camp: 5 CANOE
Canal: 5 BARGE
Clumsy: 3 ARK
Eskimo: 5 KAYAK UMIAK

E.T.: 3 UFO
Harbor: 3 TUG
Indian: 5 CANOE
Lunar: 3 LEM 6 LANDER
Paper: 7 ORIGAMI
Simple: 4 DORY
Small-runway: 4 STOL
WWII: 3 LST 5 EBOAT
**Crafted:** 4 MADE
on a loom: 5 WOVEN
**Craftiness:** 5 GUILE
**Crafts**
Cádiz: 5 ARTES
partner: 4 ARTS
**Craftsperson:** 7 ARTISAN
**Crafty:** 3 SLY 4 ARCH WILY
5 SLICK 6 ASTUTE
More: 5 SLIER SLYER
move: 4 RUSE
one: 5 SNEAK 7 ARTISAN
**Crag:** 3 TOR
**Craggy**
hill: 3 TOR
ridge: 5 ARETE
**Craig, Jenny**
client: 6 DIETER
**Cram:** 4 SATE 5 STUFF
6 BONEUP PACKIN
Reason to: 4 EXAM TEST
**Crammed:** 5 DENSE
**Cramp:** 5 SPASM
**Cranberry:** 3 RED
locale: 3 BOG
product: 5 SAUCE
**Crane:** 5 DAVIT HOIST WADER
cousin: 5 HERON
Irving's: 7 ICHABOD
Poet: 4 HART
**Crane, Frasier**
Brother of: 5 NILES
**Crane, Martin**
dog: 5 EDDIE
**Crane, Niles**
Wife of: 6 DAPHNE
**Crank**
up: 3 REV
**Crankcase**
base: 6 OILPAN
fluid: 3 OIL
**Crankshaft**
attachment: 7 FANBELT
**Cranky**
one: 5 GRUMP
**Cranny**
partner: 4 NOOK
**Cranston**
of old radio: 6 LAMONT
**Craps**
action: 3 BET
Losing come-out roll in: 3 TWO
5 THREE
natural: 5 SEVEN 6 ELEVEN
need: 4 DICE
turn: 4 ROLL
**Crapshoot:** 4 RISK
**Crash:** 4 REST

cause: 5 PANIC
course: 4 ECON
into: 3 RAM
Prepares for a: 6 BRACES
Roswell ~ victim, supposedly:
    5 ALIEN
site: 3 PAD 4 SOFA 5 PARTY
**Crashed**
It ~ in 2001: 3 MIR
**Crasher**
Garden: 4 WEED
Picnic: 3 ANT
**Crashing**
bore: 4 DRIP
Bring ~ down: 4 RUIN
sound: 3 BAM
**Crass**
one: 3 OAF
**Cratchit:** 5 CLERK
Cry to: 3 BAH
Son of: 7 TINYTIM
Tiny Tim, to: 3 SON
**Crate:** 3 BOX 4 HEAP
    6 ENCASE
component: 4 SLAT
marking: 7 STENCIL
Upturned, as a: 5 ONEND
**Crater:** 4 LAKE
feature: 3 RIM
Volcanic: 7 CALDERA
**Crater Lake**
Like: 4 DEEP
state: 6 OREGON
___ Crater, Maui: 3 EKE
**Craters of the Moon**
locale: 5 IDAHO
**Cravat:** 3 TIE
cousin: 5 ASCOT
**Crave:** 4 WANT 6 BEGFOR
    DESIRE
**Craved:** 8 THIRSTED
**Craven**
Director: 3 WES
**Craving:** 3 YEN 4 ITCH LUST
    NEED URGE 6 DESIRE
    THIRST
**Crawford**
Model: 5 CINDY
**Crawford, Christina**
book: 13 MOMMIEDEAREST
**Crawford, Cindy**
Ex of: 4 GERE
**Crawl:** 4 WORM 6 GROVEL
    10 SNAILSPACE
Did the: 4 SWAM
Do the: 4 SWIM
(with): 4 TEEM
**Crawler:** 3 TOT
Dangerous: 3 ASP
Hairy: 9 TARANTULA
Night ~, perhaps: 4 BAIT
stop: 3 PUB
Tiny: 3 ANT
**Crawling:** 6 ASWARM
**Cray**
ending: 3 OLA

**Crayola**
choice: 5 COLOR
color until 1990:
    9 ORANGERED
shade: 6 SIENNA
**Crayon**
Burnt ~ color: 6 SIENNA
Like a: 4 WAXY
Use a: 5 COLOR
**Craze:** 3 FAD 5 FEVER MANIA
    TREND
Latest: 4 RAGE
**Crazed:** 5 MANIC
**Crazily:** 4 AMOK
busy: 6 HECTIC
**Craziness**
Symbol of: 4 LOON
**Crazy:** 4 BATS GAGA LOCO
    NUTS 5 GONZO LOONY
    NUTSO WACKO
    6 ABSURD INSANE
Be ~ about: 5 ADORE
Like: 4 ALOT
Not: 4 SANE
quilt: 4 OLIO
Talk like: 4 RANT
**"Crazy"**
singer: 5 CLINE
**Crazy ___:** 6 EIGHTS
**Crazy as ___:** 5 ALOON
**Crazy as a ___:** 4 LOON
**Crazy Eights**
Game similar to: 3 UNO
**"Crazy for You"**
singer: 7 MADONNA
**Crazy Horse:** 5 CHIEF
    6 LAKOTA OGLALA
**Crazy Horse Memorial**
loc.: 4 SDAK
**Cream:** 4 TRIO 5 ELITE
Bit of: 3 DAB
cooler: 4 SODA
Depilatory: 4 NAIR
ingredient: 4 ALOE
of the crop: 4 BEST 5 ATEAM
    ELITE
puff: 4 WIMP 6 ECLAIR
quantity: 4 PINT
Whipped ~ amount: 4 GLOB
    6 DOLLOP
**Cream ___:** 3 ALE 4 SODA
**Creamer**
etc.: 6 TEASET
**Cream-filled**
cookie: 4 OREO
pastry: 6 ECLAIR
**Cream-of-the-crop:** 4 AONE
**Creamy**
cheese: 4 BRIE
dessert: 6 MOUSSE
white: 5 IVORY
**Crease**
It has a ~ on top: 6 FEDORA
player: 6 GOALIE
**Creasing**
Skill in: 7 ORIGAMI

**Create:** 4 FORM MAKE
    5 CRAFT
batik: 3 DYE
friction: 5 CLASH
~, as a word: 4 COIN
**Created:** 4 MADE
a basket: 4 WOVE
a web site: 4 SPUN
**Creation**
at the Creation: 3 MAN
**"Creation, The"**
composer: 5 HAYDN
**Creative:** 4 ARTY
ability: 3 ART
person: 7 IDEAMAN
spark: 4 IDEA
story: 3 LIE
types: 7 IDEAMEN
work: 4 OPUS
**Creator:** 3 GOD 5 MAKER
**Creature:** 5 BEING 6 ANIMAL
Bearded: 3 GNU
Carroll: 5 SNARK
Elusive: 4 YETI
Folklore: 3 ROC 5 GNOME
home, in film: 6 LAGOON
Microscopic: 5 AMEBA
    6 AMOEBA
of habit: 3 NUN
Sea: 7 ANEMONE
Seuss: 5 LORAX
Shy: 4 DEER
Thick-skinned: 5 RHINO
Tolkien: 3 ENT ORC 6 HOBBIT
Two footed: 5 BIPED
Zodiac: 3 RAM
**Crèche**
trio: 4 MAGI
**Credibility**
problem: 3 GAP
**Credit:** 7 ASCRIBE
    12 BROWNIEPOINT
agcy.: 3 TRW
counterpart: 5 DEBIT
Extend: 4 LEND
Letters of: 3 IOU
Take: 3 OWE
union offering: 4 LOAN
Used: 4 OWED
Write without: 5 GHOST
**Credit card**
ad abbr.: 3 APR
alternative: 4 CASH
Bank name on a: 6 ISSUER
come-on: 5 NOFEE
feature: 6 STRIPE
kind: 4 VISA
Read, as a: 5 SWIPE
**Credit-checking**
corp.: 3 TRW
**Creditor**
claim: 4 LIEN
**Credits**
listing: 4 ROLE
Part of the: 4 CAST
**Credo:** 3 ISM 5 ETHIC TENET

**Creed**
  Kind of: 6 NICENE
  Postal ~ word: 3 NOR
  ___ Creed: 6 NICENE
**Creedence Clearwater Revival**
  1968 ~ hit: 6 SUZIEQ
**Creek:** 3 RIA 6 STREAM
  barrier: 4 WEIR
  Up the: 6 INAJAM 7 INASPOT
     9 INTROUBLE
  ___ creek: 5 UPTHE
**Creep:** 4 BOZO DRIP INCH
     POKE 5 STEAL
     6 GOSLOW
  Look like a: 4 LEER
  through the cracks: 4 SEEP
**Creeper:** 3 IVY TOT 4 VINE
     5 SNAIL
  keeper: 7 TRELLIS
**"Creepshow"**
  director: 6 ROMERO
**Creepy:** 5 EERIE SCARY
     WEIRD
  feeling: 6 UNEASE
  one: 5 SNAIL
  thing: 4 VINE
**Creepy-crawlies:** 6 LARVAE
**Creepy-crawly:** 6 SPIDER
**Creighton**
  Vietnam War general:
     6 ABRAMS
**Creighton University**
  site: 5 OMAHA
**Crème**
  caramel: 4 FLAN
  cookie: 4 OREO
  flavorer: 6 MENTHE
**Crème ___ crème:** 4 DELA
**Crème de ___:** 5 CACAO
     6 MENTHE
**Crème de la crème:** 4 BEST
     5 ELITE
**Creme-filled**
  cookie: 4 OREO
**Cremona**
  artisan: 5 AMATI
  crowd: 3 TRE
  Former coin of: 4 LIRA
  product: 5 STRAD
**Crenshaw:** 5 MELON
  Golfer: 3 BEN
  Relative of: 6 CASABA
**Creole**
  veggie: 4 OKRA
**Creosote**
  source: 3 TAR
**Crepe**
  de Chine: 4 SILK
**Crêpe ___:** 7 SUZETTE
**Crescent:** 4 LUNE
  Its emblem is the: 5 ISLAM
  point: 4 CUSP
  shape: 3 ARC
**Crescent-shaped:** 6 LUNATE
**Cressida**
  Love of: 7 TROILUS

**Crest:** 4 ACME APEX 5 RIDGE
     6 SUMMIT
  competitor: 3 AIM
  Mountain: 5 ARETE
  On the ~ of: 4 ATOP
**Crested**
  bird: 3 JAY 7 BLUEJAY
     8 COCKATOO
**Crestfallen:** 3 SAD
**Cretan**
  king: 5 MINOS
  peak: 3 IDA
**Crete**
  Capital of: 5 CANEA
  Highest peak in: 5 MTIDA
**Crew:** 4 GANG 5 HANDS
  Ahab and: 7 WHALERS
  Construction: 8 HARDHATS
  equipment: 4 OARS
  Film ~ member: 4 GRIP
  Hotel: 5 MAIDS
  leader: 3 COX
  member: 3 OAR 5 ROWER
     7 OARSMAN
  Naval construction:
     7 SEABEES
  need: 3 OAR
  Participate in: 3 ROW
  Road ~ supply: 3 TAR
  UFO: 3 ETS 6 ALIENS
**Crewman:** 4 HAND
  Dhow: 4 ARAB
  under Kirk: 4 SULU
**Crib:** 3 BIN PEN 4 TAKE
     5 FILCH STEAL
  cry: 4 MAMA
  kid: 3 TOT
  part: 4 SLAT
  toy: 6 RATTLE
  Use ~ notes: 5 CHEAT
**Cribbage**
  knave: 3 NOB
  piece: 3 PEG
**Crichton**
  critter: 8 DINOSAUR
**Crick**
  site: 4 NECK
  spirals: 3 DNA
**Cricket:** 4 FAIR
  club: 3 BAT
  player: 7 BATSMAN
  position: 4 SLIP
  sides: 3 ONS
  sound: 5 CHIRP
  team: 6 ELEVEN
  wicket: 3 END
**Crickets, The**
  1957 hit for ~: 5 OHBOY
**Cried:** 4 WEPT 6 SOBBED
**"___ Cried" (1962 hit):** 3 SHE
**Crier**
  Kind of: 4 TOWN
**"Crikey!":** 4 EGAD
**Crime**
  Aid in: 4 ABET
  boss: 4 CAPO

  committer: 4 PERP
  fiction name: 4 ERLE
  Fiery: 5 ARSON
  job: 5 CAPER
  Lure into: 6 ENTRAP
  scene find: 5 PRINT
  Torch: 5 ARSON
  White collar: 5 FRAUD
**"___ crime?":** 5 ISITA
**Crimean**
  conference site: 5 YALTA
  native: 5 TATAR
  resort: 5 YALTA
**"Crime and Punishment"**
  heroine: 5 SONYA
**Crime-fighter**
  ~ Eliot: 4 NESS
**Crime lab**
  job: 7 DNATEST
  study: 3 DNA
**"Crimes & Misdemeanors"**
  actor: 4 ALDA
**"Crimes of Love, The"**
  author: 6 DESADE
**Crime-solving**
  game: 4 CLUE
**Criminal:** 4 PERP THUG
     5 FELON 7 ILLEGAL
  A ~ may have one: 5 ALIAS
  charge: 3 RAP
  haul: 4 LOOT
  patterns: 3 MOS
  Serious: 5 FELON
  They are broken by a: 4 LAWS
**Criminalize:** 3 BAN
**Crimp:** 4 KINK
**Crimson:** 3 RED 7 DARKRED
     8 BLOODRED
     9 CHERRYRED
  rival: 3 ELI
**Crimson Glory:** 4 ROSE
**Crimson Tide:** 4 BAMA
**Cringe:** 5 COWER
**Crinkled**
  fabric: 5 CREPE
**Cripple:** 4 MAIM
**Crisis**
  period: 8 REDALERT
  point: 4 HEAD
**Crisp**
  biscuit: 4 RUSK
  Burn to a: 4 CHAR
  cookie: 4 SNAP
  fabric: 7 TAFFETA
  veggie: 8 SNAPBEAN
**Crisper:** 3 BIN
**Crispy**
  sandwich: 3 BLT
**Crisscross**
  pattern: 4 GRID 7 LATTICE
  ___ Cristo: 5 MONTE
**Criteria**
  (abbr.): 4 STDS
  Coll. entrance: 4 SATS
**Criterion**
  (abbr.): 3 STD

Scholarship: 4 NEED
**Critic:** 5 RATER
1987 Pulitzer ~: 4 EDER
Be a: 4 RATE
Canadian literary: 4 FRYE
Chicago film: 5 EBERT
Film: 7 REXREED
pick: 3 NIT
Thumb-turning: 5 EBERT
~ Barnes: 5 CLIVE
~ James: 4 AGEE
~ Janet: 6 MASLIN
~ Pauline: 4 KAEL
~ Rex: 4 REED
~ Roger: 5 EBERT
~ Sheraton: 4 MIMI
~ Walter: 4 KERR
**Critical:** 3 KEY 5 ACUTE
      GRAVE VITAL
care ctrs.: 3 ERS
evaluation: 4 TEST
      8 ACIDTEST
inning: 5 NINTH
It may be: 4 MASS
point: 4 CRUX 5 BRINK
**Criticism:** 3 DIG 4 FLAK GAFF
      6 STATIC
Defend against: 6 UPHOLD
Harsh: 5 LUMPS
Random: 7 POTSHOT
Strong: 4 FLAK
Tiny: 3 NIT
**Criticize:** 3 DIS PAN RAP RIP
      4 CARP FLAY REAM
      SLAM 5 CAVIL FAULT
      KNOCK SNIPE TRASH
      6 ATTACK IMPUGN
      LEANON RAILAT
      RAILON SCATHE
      YELLAT
**"Critique of Pure Reason"**
writer: 4 KANT
**Croak:** 4 RASP
**Croaker:** 4 FROG TOAD
**Croat:** 4 SLAV
**Croatian**
born inventor: 5 TESLA
capital: 6 ZAGREB
prefix: 5 SERBO
**Croc**
cousin: 5 GATOR
**Crock:** 3 JAR POT 4 OLLA
suffix: 3 ERY
**Crockett**
cohort: 5 BOWIE
Frontiersman: 4 DAVY
hat critter: 4 COON
last stand: 5 ALAMO
portrayer Parker: 4 FESS
rifle: 5 BETSY
**Crockpot**
concoction: 4 STEW
**Crocodile**
shirt maker: 4 IZOD
**Crocodile Dundee**
greeting: 4 GDAY

**"Crocodile Rock"**
rocker John: 5 ELTON
**Crocus:** 4 IRID
bulb: 4 CORM
cousin: 4 IRIS
**Croesus**
Conquest of: 5 IONIA
kingdom: 5 LYDIA
**"___ Croft: Tomb Raider":**
      4 LARA
**Croissant:** 4 ROLL
**Crone:** 3 HAG
Like a: 5 ANILE
**Cronus:** 5 TITAN
Daughter of: 4 HERA
Son of: 4 ZEUS
**Crony:** 3 PAL
**Cronyn**
Actor: 4 HUME
**Crook:** 4 BEND CANE 5 THIEF
      8 CHISELER
      9 CHISELLER
Help a: 4 ABET
**Crooked:** 4 ALOP AWRY BENT
      5 ASKEW 6 ASLANT
lass of rhyme: 6 BOPEEP
**"Crooklyn"**
director: 3 LEE
**Crooned:** 4 SANG
**Crooner**
Hawaiian: 5 DONHO
~ Cole: 3 NAT
~ Columbo: 4 RUSS
~ Jerry: 4 VALE
~ Paul: 4 ANKA
~ Perry: 4 COMO
**Crooning**
First name in: 4 BING
**Crop:** 3 MAW 4 CRAW TRIM
Bring in the: 4 REAP
Cream of the: 4 BEST
      5 ATEAM ELITE
Many a ~ duster: 7 BIPLANE
pest: 5 APHID
Raise a: 4 FARM
up: 5 ARISE 6 EMERGE
**Cropped**
up: 5 AROSE
**Cropper**
Come a: 4 FAIL
**___ cropper:** 5 CAMEA
      COMEA
**Croquet**
area: 4 LAWN
need: 6 MALLET
**Crosby**
Bandmate of ~ and Stills:
      4 NASH
Love interest of ~ and Hope:
      6 LAMOUR
partner: 4 HOPE
Sing like: 5 CROON
~, Stills, and Nash: 4 TRIO
**Crosby, Bing**
1944 ~ hit: 4 AMOR
Emulate: 5 CROON

record label: 5 DECCA
**Cross:** 4 FORD ROOD SPAN
      5 MEDAL TESTY
      6 GOOVER 8 TRAVERSE
Align the ~ hairs: 3 AIM
Ancient: 3 TAU
a shallow creek: 4 WADE
Cost to: 4 TOLL
Egyptian: 4 ANKH
Greek: 3 TAU
It may have a ~ to bear:
      5 ALTAR
Kind of: 3 TAU 5 PAPAL
Large: 4 ROOD
letters: 4 INRI
over: 4 SPAN
product: 3 PEN
shape: 3 TAU
Sportscaster: 3 IRV
St. Anthony's: 3 TAU
the goal line: 5 SCORE
the threshold: 4 GOIN
      5 ENTER 6 STEPIN
to bear: 4 ONUS
word: 3 BAH
words: 4 SPAT
**___ cross:** 3 TAU
**Crossbones**
partner: 5 SKULL
Word seen on a skull and:
      6 POISON
**Crossbow**
Medieval: 8 ARBALEST
**Crossbreed:** 3 MIX
**Cross-country**
gear: 4 SKIS
Go: 3 SKI
**Crosscut:** 3 SAW
**Crossed:** 3 MET
one's fingers: 5 HOPED
out: 3 XED 4 EXED
They can be: 4 EYES
They're ~ in competition:
      5 EPEES
**Crosser**
Atl.: 3 SST
Avenue: 6 STREET
Column: 3 ROW
Gorge: 7 TRESTLE
Hollywood: 4 VINE
Line: 4 SCAB
Long.: 3 LAT
Ocean: 5 LINER
Rubicon: 6 CAESAR
St.: 3 AVE
Street: 6 AVENUE
**Crossing**
cost: 4 TOLL
Country: 5 STILE
Exodus: 6 REDSEA
Kind of: 5 ZEBRA
Making a: 4 ASEA
sign silhouette: 4 DEER
swords: 5 ATWAR
**Crosspiece:** 4 RUNG
**___ crossroads:** 3 ATA

**Crosswise:** 5 ABEAM
  7 ATHWART
**Crossword**
  Complete a: 5 SOLVE
  hint: 4 CLUE
  maker, at times: 5 CLUER
  pattern: 4 GRID
  Potential ~ clue: 7 SYNONYM
  solving tool: 3 PEN
  Some ~ clues: 4 PUNS
  wipeout: 7 ERASURE
  worker: 4 ESNE
**Crotchety**
  sort: 4 COOT
**Crothers**
  Actor: 7 SCATMAN
**Crouch**
  down: 5 SQUAT
**"Crouching Tiger, Hidden**
    **Dragon"**
  director: 3 LEE 6 ANGLEE
**Croupier:** 5 RAKER
  accessory: 8 EYESHADE
  tool: 4 RAKE
**Croutons**
  Place for: 5 SALAD
**Crow:** 4 BRAG 5 BOAST EXULT
    7 AMERIND
  cousin: 3 DAW
  cry: 3 CAW
  home: 4 NEST 5 TEPEE
    6 TEEPEE
  Time to: 4 DAWN 5 SUNUP
**Crowbar:** 3 PRY 5 LEVER
  Use a ~ on: 5 FORCE
    7 PRYOPEN
**Crowd:** 3 MOB 4 CRAM HERD
    HOST SLEW 5 HORDE
    THREE 6 THRONG
  Address a: 5 ORATE
  Cremona: 3 TRE
  Feed a: 5 CATER
  German: 4 DREI
  In: 5 ELITE
  Like a loud: 5 AROAR
  noise: 3 BOO RAH 4 ROAR
    8 APPLAUSE
  One in a: 5 EXTRA
  scene actor: 5 EXTRA
  Sign near a: 3 SRO
  Spanish: 4 TRES
  to capacity: 7 JAMPACK
**Crowd-___:** 7 PLEASER
**Crowded:** 5 DENSE
**Crowd-pleasing**
  hit: 7 HOMERUN
**Crowds**
  Like some: 4 UGLY 5 AROAR
**Crowe**
  2001 ~ role: 4 NASH
**Crower:** 7 ROOSTER
**___ crow flies:** 5 ASTHE
**Crown:** 3 TOP 4 APEX PATE
    5 TIARA 6 DIADEM
    7 CORONET
  and scepter: 7 REGALIA

  covering: 6 ENAMEL
  Jeweled: 5 TIARA
  sparkler: 5 JEWEL
**Crowned**
  It may be: 5 MOLAR
**Crowning:** 4 ATOP
  event: 8 CAPSTONE
  glory: 4 MANE
  point: 4 ACME APEX
**Crown jewels**
  quality: 6 LUSTRE
**Crows**
  Collection of: 6 MURDER
**Crow's-feet:** 5 LINES
**Crow's-nest**
  cry: 4 AHOY LAND 5 AVAST
    6 LANDHO
  locale: 4 MAST
**CRT**
  Part of: 3 RAY
**Cru**
  product: 3 VIN
  ___ Cruces, New Mexico: 3 LAS
**Crucial:** 3 KEY
**"Crucible, The"**
  actress: 5 RYDER
  setting: 5 SALEM
**Crucifix:** 4 ROOD
  inscription: 4 INRI
**Crucifixion**
  site: 8 GOLGOTHA
**Crude:** 3 RAW
  bunch: 4 OPEC
  carrier: 5 OILER
  dude: 3 CAD 4 BOOR
  dwelling: 3 HUT 5 SHACK
  gp.: 4 OPEC
  metal: 3 ORE
  stuff: 3 OIL
**Crudely**
  Apply: 4 DAUB
**Cruel:** 6 UNKIND
    8 INHUMANE
  fellow: 4 OGRE
  one: 6 SADIST
**"Cruel Intentions"**
  costar Phillippe: 4 RYAN
**Cruellest**
  month: 5 APRIL
**Cruelty:** 6 SADISM
**Cruet**
  contents: 3 OIL
**Cruise**
  destination: 3 RIO 6 NASSAU
  in style: 5 YACHT
  On a: 4 ASEA
  or Mix: 3 TOM
  quarters: 5 CABIN
    9 STATEROOM
  ship: 5 LINER
  ship deck: 4 LIDO
  stop: 4 ISLE PORT 5 ISLET
**Cruiser**
  Highway: 7 TROOPER
  Retired: 3 SST
**Cruising:** 4 ASEA 5 ATSEA

**Cruller**
  cousin: 5 DONUT
**Crumb:** 3 ORT 6 MORSEL
  Tiniest: 4 IOTA
**Crumble:** 3 ROT 5 ERODE
    6 MOLDER 7 GOTOPOT
**Crumbly:** 7 FRIABLE
  and dry: 5 MEALY
  cheese: 4 FETA
**Crumbs**
  Cover with: 5 BREAD
**Crumhorn**
  cousin: 4 OBOE
**Crummy**
  Feel: 3 AIL
**Crumpets**
  partner: 3 TEA
**Crumple**
  into a ball: 5 WADUP
**Crumpled:** 4 GAVE
**Crunch**
  creator: 6 NESTLE
  Lunch with a: 4 TACO
  Numbers to: 4 DATA
  targets: 3 ABS
  ___ Crunch: 4 CAPN
**Cruncher**
  No.: 3 CPA
**Crunchy:** 5 CRISP
  Like ~ vegetables: 3 RAW
  munchie: 4 TACO
  salad toppers: 5 BACOS
  sandwich: 3 BLT 4 TACO
  vegetable: 6 CELERY
**Crusade:** 5 JIHAD
    7 HOLYWAR
**"Crusade in Europe"**
  auth.: 3 DDE
**Crusader**
  foes: 8 SARACENS
  ~ Ralph: 5 NADER
**Crusader Rabbit**
  weapon: 5 LANCE
**Crush:** 4 MASH RUIN
    7 SODAPOP TRAMPLE
  Have a ~ on: 5 ADORE
  in a Cuisinart: 5 PUREE
  with one's foot: 6 STEPON
    7 STAMPON
**Crushed:** 4 TROD
**Crusher:** 6 PESTLE
**Crusoe**
  creator: 5 DEFOE
  Strand like: 6 ENISLE
**Crust**
  Dessert with a: 3 PIE
  Form a: 4 CAKE
  layer of Earth: 4 SIMA
  Like a pie: 5 FLAKY
  Pie ~ ingredient: 4 LARD
  Upper: 5 ELITE
  Word before: 5 UPPER
**Crustacean:** 4 CRAB 6 ISOPOD
**Crusted:** 5 CAKED
**Cruster**
  Upper: 7 ELITIST

**Crusty**
Get: 4 CAKE
one: 3 PIE
**Crux**: 4 ESSE GIST MEAT
7 ESSENCE
**Cruz**
Salsa singer: 5 CELIA
**Cry**: 3 SOB 4 WEEP YELL YELP
6 HOLLER
a river: 4 BAWL
at home: 4 SAFE
before a fall: 6 TIMBER
before disaster: 4 OHNO
companion: 3 HUE
for help: 3 SOS
from above: 6 UPHERE
from the bench: 5 ORDER
like a baby: 4 BAWL MEWL
PULE
loudly: 3 SOB 4 BAWL
out: 4 WAIL YELL YELP
out for: 4 NEED
over: 6 BEMOAN
___ cry: 4 AFAR
**Crybaby**: 6 WEEPER
Be a: 4 PULE
**Crying**: 7 INTEARS
shame: 4 PITY
**"Crying"**
singer Orbison: 3 ROY
**"Crying Game, The"**
star: 3 REA
**Cryogenic**
refrigerant: 4 NEON
**Cryptic**
character: 4 RUNE
Make: 6 ENCODE
**Cryptogram**: 4 CODE
Solve a: 6 DECODE
**Cryptographer**
aid: 3 KEY
**Cryptologic**
gp.: 3 NSA
**Cryptozoology**
subject: 6 NESSIE
**"Cry ___ River"**: 3 MEA
**Crystal**
Country singer: 5 GAYLE
**Crystal ball**: 3 ORB 5 GEODE
gazer: 4 SEER
Look into a: 4 GAZE
**Crystalline**
rock: 6 SCHIST
**Crystal-lined**
rock: 5 GEODE
**Crystallize**: 3 GEL
**Crystals**
1960s ~ hit: 9 HESAREBEL
11 DADOORONRON
Icy: 4 HOAR RIME
**"Cry, the Beloved Country"**
author: 5 PATON
**CSA**
general: 5 RELEE
monogram: 3 REL
Part of a ~ signature: 4 ELEE

soldier: 3 REB
state: 3 ALA
**"CSI"**: 5 DRAMA
actress Helgenberger: 4 MARG
evidence: 3 DNA
network: 3 CBS
**"CSI: Miami"**
network: 3 CBS
**CST**
Part of: 3 STD
**Ctrl**
cousin: 3 ALT
**Cuatro**
halved: 3 DOS
Twice: 4 OCHO
**Cub**: 4 NLER
Former ~ Sandberg: 4 RYNE
house: 3 DEN 4 LAIR
Joy's: 4 ELSA
slugger: 4 SOSA
**Cuba**: 4 ISLA ISLE
(abbr.): 3 ISL
Coin of: 4 PESO
Dance from: 5 MAMBO
RUMBA 6 RHUMBA
Gp. of which ~ is a member:
3 OAS
is in it: 8 ANTILLES
leader: 5 FIDEL 6 CASTRO
U.S. base in: 5 GITMO
**Cuba ___**: 5 LIBRE
**Cuban**
boy: 4 NINO 5 ELIAN
currency: 4 PESO 5 PESOS
dance: 5 MAMBO RUMBA
6 RHUMBA
drum: 5 CONGA
leader: 5 FIDEL 6 CASTRO
line dance: 5 CONGA
patriot: 5 MARTI
**Cuban Revolution**
figure: 3 CHE 7 GUEVARA
**Cubby**
hole: 3 DEN
**Cubbyhole**: 4 CELL NOOK
5 NICHE
**Cube**: 4 DICE
A ~ has twelve: 5 EDGES
Casino: 3 DIE
Gaming: 3 DIE
grippers: 5 TONGS
inventor Rubik: 4 ERNO
Like a: 5 SOLID
Sugar: 4 LUMP
with 21 dots: 3 DIE
**Cubed**
Dos: 4 OCHO
Zwei: 4 ACHT
**Cubemaker**
~ Rubik: 4 ERNO
**Cubes**: 4 DICE 5 DICES
Cut into: 5 DICED
Grab, as ice: 4 TONG
Some: 5 SUGAR
**Cubic**
128 ~ feet: 4 CORD

decimeter: 5 LITER
meter: 5 STERE
~ Rubik: 4 ERNO
**Cubicle**
fixture: 4 DESK
**Cubist**
~ Fernand: 5 LEGER
~ Juan: 4 GRIS
~ Rubik: 4 ERNO
**Cubits**
Vessel measured in: 3 ARK
**Cubs**: 4 TEAM
Banks of the: 5 ERNIE
Home of the: 3 DEN
Org. with ~ and Eagles:
3 BSA
Sammy of the: 4 SOSA
~, on scoreboards: 3 CHI
**Cub Scout**: 3 LAD
group: 3 DEN
leader: 5 AKELA
**Cuckoo**: 3 ANI MAD 4 NUTS
5 CRAZY INANE NUTSY
NUTTY 6 INSANE
Black: 3 ANI
**Cucumber**
Like a: 4 COOL
**Cuddle**: 5 SPOON 6 NESTLE
**Cuddly**
carnival prize: 5 PANDA
pet: 6 LAPDOG
**Cuddly-looking**
critter: 5 KOALA
**Cue**: 6 PROMPT
application: 5 CHALK
Fix a: 5 RETIP
Jazzman's: 5 HITIT
Queue: 4 NEXT
**Cuff**
Speak off the: 5 ADLIB
**Cuffs**
Put on ~, perhaps: 5 ALTER
Slap ~ on: 3 NAB 6 ARREST
**Cugat, Xavier**
Half a ~ hit: 4 TICO
Lane who sang with: 4 ABBE
**Cuisinart**
Crush in a: 5 PUREE
**Cuisine**
Asian: 4 THAI
Chinese: 5 HUNAN
Curried: 6 INDIAN
Hardly haute: 4 GLOP SLOP
Kind of: 5 HAUTE 6 ETHNIC
8 NOUVELLE
Lover of lean: 5 SPRAT
New Orleans: 5 CAJUN
Spicy: 4 THAI 6 CREOLE
TEXMEX
___ cuisine: 5 HAUTE
**Cul-___**: 5 DESAC
**Culbertson**
Bridge expert: 3 ELY
**Cul-de-___**: 3 SAC
**Culinary**
artiste: 4 CHEF

cover-up: 5 APRON
directive: 4 STIR
herb: 5 THYME
**Culkin**
Actor: 4 RORY
**Cull**: 6 SCREEN SELECT
7 WEEDOUT
**Culmination**: 4 ACME
6 APOGEE
**Culp**
and Cosby TV series: 4 ISPY
___ culpa: 3 MEA
**Culpable**: 7 ATFAULT
___ Culp Hobby: 5 OVETA
**Cultist**
Jamaican: 5 RASTA
**Cultivate**: 3 HOE 4 FARM GROW
PLOW TEND TILL WEED
5 BREED
**Cultivation**
Fit for: 6 ARABLE
**Cultivator**: 3 HOE
**Cultural**: 6 ETHNIC
character: 5 ETHOS
funding org.: 3 NEA
Govt. ~ org.: 4 USIA
interests: 4 ARTS
Intl. ~ org.: 6 UNESCO
NYC ~ center: 4 MOMA
prefix: 4 AGRI 5 MULTI
values: 5 ETHOS
**Culturally**
showy: 4 ARTY
**Cultural Revolution**
figure: 3 MAO
**Culture**
base: 4 AGAR
character: 5 ETHOS
dish: 5 PETRI
Kind of: 3 POP
medium: 4 AGAR
prefix: 3 AVI 4 AGRI
**Cultured**
gem: 5 PEARL
With ~ airs: 4 ARTY
**Cum ___** : 5 LAUDE
**Cumberland ___** : 3 GAP
**Cumberland Gap**
explorer: 5 BOONE
___ cum laude: 5 MAGNA
SUMMA
**Cummerbund**: 4 SASH
feature: 5 PLEAT
kin: 3 OBI
**Cumming**
Tony winner: 4 ALAN
**Cumulus**
prefix: 4 ALTO
**Cuneiform**
discovery site: 6 AMARNA
**Cunning**: 3 ART SLY 4 ARCH
CAGY FOXY WILE WILY
5 GUILE 7 SLYNESS
More: 5 CUTER SLIER SLYER
6 WILIER
With: 5 SLYLY

**Cunningham**
Choreographer: 5 MERCE
**Cuomo**
Former governor: 5 MARIO
successor: 6 PATAKI
**Cup**: 5 CALIX 6 TROPHY
1/16 of a ~ (abbr.): 4 TBSP
Café: 5 TASSE
Court: 5 DAVIS
Golf: 5 RYDER
handle: 3 EAR
holder: 6 SAUCER
part: 3 RIM 4 BRIM 5 OUNCE
Place to buy a: 4 CAFE
Put in the: 5 HOLED
___ Cup: 5 DAVIS 8 AMERICAS
**Cup-and-saucer**
heaters: 5 ETNAS
**Cupboard**
Like Hubbard's: 4 BARE
Tall: 7 ARMOIRE
**Cupcake**
topper: 4 ICER 5 ICING
**Cupful**
Diner: 3 JOE 4 JAVA
**Cupid**: 4 AMOR EROS
8 AMORETTO
REINDEER
projectile: 5 ARROW
Struck by: 6 INLOVE
7 SMITTEN
~, to Greeks: 4 EROS
**Cupidity**: 5 GREED 7 AVARICE
**Cupids**
Little: 8 AMORETTI
**"Cup of Tea, The"**
painter: 7 CASSATT
**Cupola**: 4 DOME
**Cuppa**
contents: 3 TEA
**Cuprite**: 3 ORE
**Cups**
A couple of: 3 BRA
deck: 5 TAROT
etc.: 6 TEASET
**Cur**
curb: 5 LEASH
**Curaçao**
has one: 7 CEDILLA
neighbor: 5 ARUBA
**Curative**
locale: 3 SPA
**Curator**
deg.: 3 MFA
**Curb**: 4 REIN 6 REININ
STIFLE
Get to the other: 5 CROSS
Run at the: 4 IDLE
**Curbside**
call: 4 TAXI
fixture: 5 METER
**Curd**
Bean: 4 TOFU
**Curdle**: 5 GOBAD
**Curdler**
Milk: 6 RENNET

**Cure**: 4 HEAL 6 REMEDY
hides: 3 TAN
Place to take a: 3 SPA
prefix: 3 EPI 4 PEDI
**Cure-all**: 6 ELIXIR 7 PANACEA
**Cured**
cheese: 4 FETA
Something to be: 3 HAM
**Curfew**
After: 4 LATE
___ curiae: 5 AMICI
**Curie**
Daughter of: 5 IRENE
Madame: 5 MARIE
title: 6 MADAME
title (abbr.): 3 MME
**Curio**: 9 OBJETDART
shelf: 7 WHATNOT
**Curiosity**
Raise: 5 PIQUE
Show: 3 ASK
**Curious**: 3 ODD 4 NOSY
5 NOSEY 7 STRANGE
**"Curious George"**
author: 3 REY
**Curl**: 7 RINGLET
Kind of: 4 SPIT
One ~, say: 3 REP
one's lip: 5 SNEER
Place to ~ up and dye:
5 SALON
**Curled**
Dog with a ~ tail: 3 PUG
lip look: 5 SNEER
Tightly: 5 KINKY
**Curler**: 7 ATHLETE
place: 4 RINK
**Curlew**
cousin: 5 SNIPE
**Curlicue**: 4 COIL LOOP
**Curling**
lines: 4 ARCS
Mark aimed at in: 3 TEE
place: 4 RINK
surface: 3 ICE
**Curly**: 6 STOOGE
associate: 3 MOE
bopper: 3 MOE
cabbage: 4 KALE
coif: 4 AFRO
diacritic: 5 TILDE
do: 4 AFRO
lock: 5 TRESS
of the Globetrotters: 4 NEAL
replacement: 5 SHEMP
strand: 7 TENDRIL
syllable: 3 WOO
**Curly-haired**
cat: 3 REX
**Curly-leafed**
cabbage: 4 KALE
**Curly-tailed**
dog: 5 AKITA
**Curmudgeon**: 4 COOT CRAB
6 GROUCH
TV: 6 ROONEY

**Currant**
Black ~ liqueur: 6 CASSIS
**Currency**
U.S.: *see page 724*
**Current:** 3 HIP NEW 4 FLOW
    TIDE 5 TREND 6 LATEST
    7 PRESENT
    8 UPTODATE
    10 PRESENTDAY
administration: 3 INS
amount: 6 AMPERE
Carrying: 4 LIVE
choice: 4 ACDC
Circular: 4 EDDY
Dangerous: 3 RIP 7 RIPTIDE
entry points: 6 ANODES
event: 4 TIDE 6 ELNINO
fashion: 4 MODE RAGE
    5 TREND
gadget: 7 AMMETER
letters: 4 ACDC
location: 5 OCEAN
measure: 4 VOLT WATT
    6 AMPERE
strength: 8 AMPERAGE
unit: 3 AMP 6 AMPERE
Weather-affecting: 6 ELNINO
with the wind: 7 LEETIDE
**Currently**
employed: 5 INUSE
popular: 3 HOT
serving status: 4 ONEC
**Curricula vitae:** 4 BIOS
**Curriculum**
division: 4 UNIT 6 MODULE
Gp. concerned with: 3 PTA
range, briefly: 4 ELHI
**Curriculum ___:** 5 VITAE
**Curried**
cuisine: 6 INDIAN
**Currier**
Lithographer: 3 NAT
    9 NATHANIEL
Partner of: 4 IVES
**Curry**
herb: 5 CUMIN
or Rice: 3 TIM
powder ingredient:
    8 TURMERIC
**Curse:** 3 HEX POX 4 BANE
    DAMN DOOM OATH
    5 SWEAR 6 REVILE
**"___ Curse, The":** 4 DAIN
**Cursed:** 5 SWORE 7 SWOREAT
team, some say: 3 SOX
**"Curse of the Starving Class"**
Award for: 4 OBIE
**"Curses!":** 3 BAH 4 DRAT
    OHNO
**Cursive**
opposite: 5 PRINT
**Cursor**
mover: 5 MOUSE
target: 4 ICON
**Curt:** 5 SHORT TERSE
    6 ABRUPT SNIPPY

Sportscaster: 5 GOWDY
**Curtail:** 4 CLIP PARE TRIM
    5 ELIDE 8 CUTSHORT
**Curtain:** 5 DRAPE
call: 6 ENCORE
call call: 5 BRAVO
Drop the ~ on: 3 END
fabric: 4 LACE 5 NINON
    SCRIM VOILE
folds: 6 PLEATS
holder: 3 ROD
raiser: 4 ACTI
shade: 4 ECRU
**___ Curtain:** 4 IRON
**Curtin**
Comical: 4 JANE
**Curtin, Jane**
role: 5 ALLIE
**Curtis**
Actor: 4 TONY
of cosmetics: 6 HELENE
**Curtsy**
Ballet: 4 PLIE
**Curvaceous**
character: 3 ESS
**Curve:** 3 ARC 4 ARCH BEND
Architectural: 4 OGEE
Double: 3 ESS 4 OGEE
Geometric: 3 ARC 7 ELLIPSE
    8 PARABOLA
Kind of: 4 BELL SINE
shape: 3 ESS
Slalom: 3 ESS
**Curved:** 4 BENT
arch: 4 OGEE
basket: 5 CESTA
entranceway: 4 ARCH
letter: 3 ESS
molding: 4 OGEE
shape: 3 ESS
sword: 5 SABER 8 SCIMITAR
**Curvy**
letter: 3 ESS
**Cushiness:** 4 EASE
**Cushion:** 3 PAD
Billiard: 4 BANK RAIL
Hit the: 5 CAROM
It gives players a:
    9 POOLTABLE
Pin: 3 MAT
**Cushy:** 4 EASY SOFT 5 DOWNY
course: 5 EASYA
**Cusp:** 4 EDGE
Holiday: 3 EVE
**Cuspid:** 5 TOOTH
**Cuspidor**
Used the: 4 SPAT
**Cuss:** 5 SWEAR
**Cussed:** 5 SWORE
**Cussler**
Author: 5 CLIVE
**Custard**
apple relative: 5 PAPAW
base: 3 EGG
dessert: 4 FLAN
Like: 4 EGGY

**Custer**
colleague: 4 RENO
**Custodian:** 5 SUPER
collection: 4 KEYS
**Custody:** 7 KEEPING
Hold in: 6 DETAIN
In: 4 HELD 8 ARRESTED
Take into: 3 NAB 6 ARREST
**Custom:** 3 TAX 4 WONT
    5 HABIT USAGE
    6 MANNER
**Customarily:** 7 ASARULE
**Customary:** 5 USUAL
practice: 4 RITE 5 USAGE
**Customer:** 4 USER 6 CLIENT
    PATRON
Cafeteria: 5 EATER
file entry: 8 AREACODE
Hack: 4 FARE
Have as a: 6 SELLTO
S&L: 4 ACCT
Utility: 4 USER
**Customers**
Ready for: 4 OPEN
**Customs:** 5 MORES
duty: 6 IMPOST
**Cut:** 3 AXE HEW LOP MOW
    SAW 4 AXED DELE ETCH
    HEWN MOWN OMIT
    SAWN SLIT SNIP
    5 HEWED SAWED SEVER
    SHARE SHEAR SHORN
    6 DELETE DILUTE
    FELLED 7 ABRIDGE
    SHEARED 8 DECREASE
abruptly: 3 AXE
and paste: 4 EDIT
application: 6 IODINE
a rug: 5 DANCE
at an angle: 5 BEVEL
back: 4 PARE 5 PARED
    PRUNE
Bad: 4 GASH
Beef: 4 LOIN RUMP 5 TBONE
    9 CLUBSTEAK
Boneless: 5 FILET
canines: 6 TEETHE
close: 4 CROP MOWN
    5 SHAVE
corners: 5 SKIMP 6 SCRIMP
Deep: 4 GASH
down: 3 HEW 4 AXED FELL
    5 HEWED
down on: 6 LESSEN
drastically: 5 SLASH
Dress: 4 BIAS 5 ALINE
flower: 4 STEM
from the same cloth: 4 AKIN
glass: 4 ETCH
into: 5 ERODE 6 INCISE
into cubes: 5 DICE 5 DICED
into pieces: 4 CHOP
It may be ~ and dried: 3 HAY
line: 4 SCAR
Narrow: 4 SLIT
Neckline: 3 VEE

off: 3 END LOP 4 CROP STEM
   5 ALONE APART SEVER
   7 ABSCISE ISOLATE
of marble: 4 SLAB
One getting a: 5 AGENT
out: 3 END 4 BAIL CLIP OMIT
   STOP 5 CEASE
partner: 5 DRIED PASTE
Quick: 4 SNIP
short: 3 END 4 CLIP CROP
   SNIP 5 ABORT ELIDE
   7 CURTAIL
taker: 5 AGENT
the grass: 3 MOW
through: 9 PENETRATE
time: 9 ALLABREVE
Took a: 5 SWUNG
up: 4 DICE 5 SHRED
V-shaped: 5 NOTCH
with a knife, old-style: 4 SNEE
with small strokes: 4 SNIP
wood: 5 SAWED
~, old-style: 4 SNEE
**Cut ___:** 4 ARUG 5 INTWO
**Cute**
as a button: 8 ADORABLE
**Cutesy-___:** 3 POO
**Cutie:** 4 DOLL
**Cutie ___:** 3 PIE
**"Cut it out!":** 4 DONT STOP
   5 CEASE 6 DESIST
**Cutlass**
Former ~ model: 5 CIERA
maker: 4 OLDS
**Cutlery:** 6 KNIVES
**Cutlet:** 4 NICK SNIP
meat: 4 VEAL
**Cutoff**
point: 3 END
**Cutter:** 3 AXE SAW 4 EDGE
   SHIP 5 PARER
Cane: 7 MACHETE
Carrot: 5 DICER
Class: 6 TRUANT
kin: 5 SLOOP
part: 4 MAST
Portable: 8 SABERSAW
Record: 6 STYLUS
Wood: 3 AXE SAW 4 ADZE
**"Cut that out!":** 4 STOP
   6 STOPIT
**Cutting:** 4 KEEN TART
   5 SNIDE
edge: 5 BLADE
It lacks a ~ edge: 4 EPEE
It may be: 4 EDGE
Make ~ remarks: 5 SNIPE
remark: 3 DIG 4 BARB
the mustard: 4 ABLE
tool: 3 ADZ AXE BUR 4 ADZE
   5 KNIFE
Work in the ~ room: 4 EDIT
**Cuttlefish**
ejection: 3 INK

ink: 5 SEPIA
**"Cutty ___":** 4 SARK
**Cutup:** 4 CARD
Act the: 7 OPERATE
**Cuyahoga**
outlet: 4 ERIE
**Cuzco**
From: 5 INCAN
land: 4 PERU
native: 4 INCA
**C-worthy:** 4 FAIR SOSO
**Cyber**
chuckle: 3 LOL
junk: 4 SPAM
**Cyberauction**
site: 4 EBAY
**Cybercafe**
patron: 4 USER
**Cyberflick**
1982 ~: 4 TRON
**Cyberheads**
Where ~ surf: 3 NET
**Cybermessage:** 5 EMAIL
**Cybername:** 6 USERID
**Cyberspace**
bidding site: 4 EBAY
initials: 3 AOL
letters: 5 EMAIL
nuisance: 6 HACKER
traveler: 4 USER
**"Cybill"**
actress Witt: 6 ALICIA
**Cyborg**
enforcer: 7 ROBOCOP
movie prefix: 4 ROBO
**Cyclades**
island: 3 IOS
sea: 6 AEGEAN
**Cycle**
Economic:
   11 BOOMANDBUST
Gentle ~ items: 5 KNITS
Kind of: 5 LUNAR SLEEP
   SOLAR
part: 5 PHASE
prefix: 3 EPI TRI UNI
Wash: 4 SPIN 5 RINSE
**Cyclist**
choice: 4 GEAR
protection: 6 HELMET
stunt: 7 WHEELIE
~ Armstrong: 5 LANCE
~ LeMond: 4 GREG
**Cyclo-**
suffix: 4 TRON
**Cyclone**
center: 3 EYE
**Cyclones**
Home of the: 4 AMES
   9 IOWASTATE
**Cyclopes**
workplace: 4 ETNA
**Cyclops**
and others: 4 XMEN

Site of the smithy of: 4 ETNA
**Cyclotron**
bit: 3 ION 4 ATOM
**Cygnet**
Former: 4 SWAN
mother: 3 PEN
**Cygnus**
Bright star in: 5 DENEB
**Cylinder**
filler: 6 PISTON
Storage: 4 SILO
**Cylindrical:** 6 TERETE
structure: 4 SILO
**Cymbal**
relative: 4 GONG
sound: 5 CLASH
**"Cymbeline"**
heroine: 6 IMOGEN
**Cyndi**
Singer: 6 LAUPER
**Cynic**
look: 5 SNEER
retort: 4 IBET
**Cynical**
Cause to be: 4 JADE
**Cynthia**
Author: 5 OZICK
**___ Cynwyd, Pennsylvania:**
   4 BALA
**Cypress**
feature: 4 KNEE
**Cyprus**
capital: 7 NICOSIA
Opera set in: 6 OTELLO
**Cyrano**
Love of: 6 ROXANE
portrayer: 6 GERARD
**Cyrus**
Book that tells of: 4 EZRA
realm: 6 PERSIA
**Cyst:** 3 WEN
**Cytoplasm**
material: 3 RNA
**Cy Young Award:** *see page 711*
**Czar:** 5 RULER
edict: 5 UKASE
Terrible: 4 IVAN
The Great: 6 PETERI
**Czarist**
edict: 5 UKASE
parliament: 4 DUMA
**Czech:** 4 SLAV
chief Vaclav: 5 HAVEL
composer Janacek: 4 LEOS
dialect: 8 MORAVIAN
mark: 5 HACEK
river: 4 ODER OHRE
runner Zatopek: 4 EMIL
tennis star Ivan: 5 LENDL
**Czechoslovakia**
Capital in the middle of:
   4 OSLO
**Czechs**
neighbors: 7 SLOVAKS

**D:** 4 POOR
  Half of: 3 CCL
  neighbor: 5 EFLAT
  Worth a: 4 POOR
  ___ d': 6 MAITRE
**Da**
  opposite: 4 NYET
**Da ___ (from the beginning):**
  4 CAPO
**D.A.**
  Kind of: 4 ASST
  Part of: 3 ATT
**da ___, Leonardo:** 5 VINCI
**da ___, Vasco**
  Explorer: 4 GAMA
**"___ Daba Honeymoon, The":**
  3 ABA
**Dabble**
  in: 6 PLAYAT 7 SMATTER
**Dabbler:** 4 TEAL
**Dabbling**
  duck: 4 TEAL
**Dachshund**
  doc: 3 VET
  features: 4 EARS
**Dacia**
  Year ~ was captured by Trajan:
    3 CVI
**Dacron:** 8 MATERIAL
**Dactyl:** 3 TOE
  opening: 5 PTERO
**Dad:** 3 POP 4 PAPA 6 OLDMAN
  Bro of: 3 UNC
  Mate of: 3 MOM
  Mom and: 7 PARENTS
  Sister of: 4 AUNT
  ~, to Grandpa: 3 SON
**Dada**
  artist: 3 ARP
  daddy: 3 ARP
  pioneer: 3 ARP
**Dadaism**
  founder: 3 ARP
**Dadaist**
  Early: 7 JEANARP
  German: 5 ERNST
  ~ Jean: 3 ARP
  ~ Max: 5 ERNST
**Dad-blasted:** 8 DOGGONED
**Daddy:** 4 PAPA 5 POPPA
**Daddy-longlegs:**
  8 ARACHNID
**Daddy-o:** 4 POPS
**Daddy Warbucks**
  kid: 5 ANNIE
**Daedalus**
  creation: 4 MAZE
  Son of: 6 ICARUS

**Daffy Duck:** 4 TOON
  impediment: 4 LISP
  Speak like: 4 LISP
  Voice of: 3 MEL
**da Gama**
  destination: 5 INDIA
  Explorer: 5 VASCO
**Dagger**
  handle: 4 HAFT HILT
  Highlands: 4 DIRK
  of yore: 4 SNEE
  Old: 4 SNEE
  partner: 5 CLOAK
  Slender: 6 STYLET
    8 STILETTO
  Small: 7 PONIARD
    8 STILETTO
**Daggers**
  Look: 5 GLARE 6 GLOWER
**"Dagnabbit!":** 5 NERTS
**Dagwood:** 8 BUMSTEAD
  Herb, to: 8 NEIGHBOR
  Neighbor of: 4 HERB
  Wife of: 7 BLONDIE
  Young neighbor of: 4 ELMO
**Dah**
  partner: 3 DIT
**Dahl**
  Actress: 6 ARLENE
  Author: 5 ROALD
  ex: 5 LAMAS
**Dahl, Roald**
  book: 7 MATILDA
**Dahomey**
  ~, today: 5 BENIN
**Dail**
  land: 4 EIRE
**Daily**
  delivery: 4 MAIL 6 USMAIL
  drama: 4 SOAP
  event: 7 SUNRISE
  grind: 3 RUT 7 RATRACE
  One of a ~ trio: 4 MEAL
  record: 3 LOG
**Daily Bruin**
  sch.: 4 UCLA
**Daily Planet**
  Clark of the: 4 KENT
  Lois of the: 4 LANE
  name: 4 LOIS
  reporter: 5 OLSEN
    8 LOISLANE
**Daintily**
  Drink: 3 SIP
  Walk: 5 MINCE
**Dainty:** 4 TWEE 8 DELICATE
**Daiquiri**
  ingredient: 3 RUM

**Dairy**
  animal: 3 COW
  case purchase: 4 OLEO
  cow: 8 HOLSTEIN
  Cultured ~ product:
    6 YOGURT
  dozen: 4 EGGS
  herd: 4 COWS
  implement: 5 CHURN
  purchase: 5 CREAM
  section selection: 5 OLEOS
  staple: 4 MILK
**Dairy Queen**
  order: 4 CONE 6 SUNDAE
**Daisy**
  Michaelmas: 5 ASTER
  relative: 5 ASTER
  variety: 5 OXEYE 6 SHASTA
  White: 5 OXEYE
**Daisy ___:** 3 MAE
**Daisylike**
  flower: 5 ASTER
**Daisy Mae**
  creator: 4 CAPP
  Husband of: 5 ABNER
**Daisy ___ Yokum:** 3 MAE
**Dakar**
  land: 7 SENEGAL
**Dakota**
  home: 5 TEPEE
  ~ Indian: 3 REE 6 OGLALA
  ~, once (abbr.): 4 TERR
**Dalai ___:** 4 LAMA
**Dalai Lama**
  land: 5 TIBET
**Dale**
  Cowgirl: 5 EVANS
  Husband of: 3 ROY
  Snack for: 5 ACORN
**Dalgliesh, Adam**
  creator: 7 PDJAMES
**Dali**
  contemporary: 4 MIRO
  Like a ~ watch: 4 LIMP
**Dallas**
  cager: 3 MAV
  campus (abbr.): 3 SMU
  City north of: 5 PLANO
  City SSW of: 4 WACO
  hoopster: 3 MAV
  sch.: 3 SMU
  suburb: 5 PLANO
**"Dallas"**
  actor Larry: 6 HAGMAN
  family name: 5 EWING
  Jock's wife, in: 5 ELLIE
  matriarch: 5 ELLIE
  Miss on: 5 ELLIE

One of the Ewings on: 3 PAM
setting: 5 RANCH
**Dallas Cowboys**
emblem: 4 STAR
**Dallas-to-Houston**
dir.: 3 SSE
**"___ Dalloway":** 3 MRS
**Dalmatia**
native: 5 CROAT
**Dalmatian:** 5 CROAT
detail: 4 SPOT
Good name for a: 4 SPOT
marking: 4 SPOT
**Daly**
Actress: 4 TYNE
costar: 5 GLESS
**Daly, Tyne**
role: 5 LACEY
**Dam:** 3 SHE 4 WEIR
Egyptian: 5 ASWAN
mate: 4 SIRE
on the Nile: 5 ASWAN
org.: 3 TVA
Ram's: 3 EWE
River: 4 WEIR
Small: 4 WEIR
**Damage:** 3 MAR 4 COST HARM
6 IMPAIR
Auto: 5 DENTS
Cause ~ to: 3 MAR
Do ~ to: 4 HARM
done: 4 TOLL
Sign of: 4 SCAR
Widespread: 5 HAVOC
**"Damage"**
director: 5 MALLE
**Damages**
Seek: 3 SUE
**Damascus**
land: 5 SYRIA
native: 6 SYRIAN
**D'Amato**
and others: 3 ALS
**Dam-building**
org.: 3 TVA
**Dame:** 5 TITLE
intro: 5 NOTRE
of the piano: 4 HESS
**___ Dame:** 5 NOTRE
**Daminozide**
brand: 4 ALAR
**"Damn Yankees"**
composer Richard: 5 ADLER
Lola portrayer in: 4 GWEN
role: 4 LOLA
vamp: 4 LOLA
**Damocles**
Sword of: 5 PERIL
**Damon**
Actor: 4 MATT
Writer: 6 RUNYON
**Damone**
Singer: 3 VIC
**___ d'amore:** 4 OBOE
**Damp:** 4 DANK DEWY 5 MOIST
SOGGY

More than: 3 WET
**Dampen:** 3 WET
**Damper**
Put a ~ on: 5 DETER
**Damsel:** 4 GIRL LASS MAID
cry: 4 HELP 6 MYHERO
deliverer: 4 HERO
Yonder: 3 HER
**___ Dan (rock group):** 6 STEELY
**Dana**
Actor: 5 ELCAR
Actress: 6 DELANY
perfume brand: 4 TABU
**Dance:** 3 ART HOP
1860s ~ tune:
15 BLUEDANUBEWALTZ
1930s ~: 5 LINDY
1940s ~:
15 BEERBARRELPOLKA
1960s ~: 4 FRUG 6 WATUSI
1960s ~ tune:
15 PEPPERMINTTWIST
1970s ~ music: 5 DISCO
1990s ~ craze: 8 MACARENA
All-night ~ party: 4 RAVE
Ballroom: 5 TANGO
7 ONESTEP TWOSTEP
Barn: 4 REEL 7 HOEDOWN
bit: 4 STEP
Brazilian: 5 SAMBA
Circle: 4 HORA
Cork: 3 JIG
Country: 4 REEL
Cuban: 5 CONGA MAMBO
RUMBA 6 RHUMBA
Dramatic: 5 TANGO
energetically: 6 BOOGIE
First name in: 5 TWYLA
7 ISADORA
Formal: 4 BALL
for two: 5 TANGO
Gliding ~ step: 6 CHASSE
Half a: 3 CAN CHA
Hawaiian: 4 HULA
Hip: 4 HULA
in duple (2/4) time: 5 POLKA
in quadruple (4/4) time:
7 GAVOTTE
instruction: 4 STEP
Interrupt on the ~ floor:
5 CUTIN
Island: 4 HULA
Israeli: 4 HORA
Jazz: 5 STOMP
Jewish: 4 HORA
Latin: 5 MAMBO SAMBA
TANGO
Latin ~ music: 5 SALSA
lesson: 4 STEP
Line: 5 CONGA
Lively: 4 HORA REEL
5 GALOP GIGUE
Maui: 4 HULA
move: 3 DIP 4 STEP
Old French: 7 GAVOTTE
partner: 4 SONG

pattern: 4 STEP
Ragtime: 7 ONESTEP
Ring: 4 HORA
Round: 4 HORA
Sailor's: 8 HORNPIPE
School: 3 HOP
Sensuous: 5 TANGO
Song and: 4 ARTS
Spring: 7 MAYPOLE
Stately: 6 MINUET PAVANE
step: 3 CHA PAS
under the bar: 5 LIMBO
unit: 4 STEP
U.S. ~ gp.: 3 ABT
Vigorous: 8 FLAMENCO
Virginia: 4 REEL
Wedding: 4 HORA
When repeated, a: 3 CHA
with a kick: 5 CONGA
~, in French: 3 BAL
**"Dance On Little Girl"**
singer: 4 ANKA
**Dancer**
1968 ~ biopic: 7 ISADORA
garment: 4 TUTU 7 LEOTARD
handrail: 5 BARRE
Kind of: 4 GOGO
**Dancers**
Like some: 6 EXOTIC
Snake: 4 HOPI
**"___ Dances" (Dvořák work):**
8 SLAVONIC
**"Dancing Queen"**
group: 4 ABBA
**Dandelion:** 4 WEED
**Dander:** 3 IRE 5 IRISH
Get one's ~ up: 3 IRE 4 RILE
**Dandling**
spot: 4 KNEE
**Dandy:** 3 FOP 4 FINE
beginning: 3 JIM
dresser: 3 FOP
Fine and: 3 AOK
neckwear: 5 ASCOT
**Danes**
Actress: 6 CLAIRE
**Danger:** 4 RISK 5 PERIL
In: 6 ATRISK
Inviting:
15 PLAYINGWITHFIRE
Out of: 4 SAFE
sign: 7 REDFLAG
signal: 5 ALERT 7 REDFLAG
**Dangerfield**
Comedian: 6 RODNEY
**Dangerous:** 5 RISKY 6 UNSAFE
Least: 6 SAFEST
partner: 5 ARMED
**"Dangerous When Wet"**
star: 5 LAMAS
**Dangle:** 4 HANG
a carrot in front of: 5 TEMPT
Decorative: 6 TASSEL
**Dangler:** 6 TASSEL
Deli: 6 SALAMI
Palate: 5 UVULA

Throat: 5 UVULA
**Daniel**
Book after: 5 HOSEA
Follower of: 5 HOSEA
Hawaiian senator: 6 INOUYE
of Nicaragua: 6 ORTEGA
Trailblazer: 5 BOONE
**"Daniel Boone"**
actor: 4 AMES 6 EDAMES
actor Parker: 4 FESS
**"Daniel Deronda"**
author: 5 ELIOT
**Danielle**
Novelist: 5 STEEL
**Danilova**
dip: 4 PLIE
**Danish**
city: 6 ODENSE
coin: 5 KRONE
filler: 5 PRUNE
Kind of: 5 PRUNE
money: 5 KRONE
seaport: 6 ODENSE
show brand: 4 ECCO
toy company: 4 LEGO
**Danish-born**
journalist: 4 RIIS
reformer: 4 RIIS
**Danny**
Actor: 6 AIELLO DEVITO
Comedic actor: 4 KAYE
Daughter of: 5 MARLO
of basketball: 5 AINGE
**"Danny Boy"**
actor: 3 REA
**Danson**
Actor: 3 TED
**Dante**
locale: 7 INFERNO
translator John: 6 CIARDI
**Dantès**
Dumas character:
6 EDMOND
**Danube**
City on the: 3 ULM 4 LINZ
**Danza**
Actor: 4 TONY
**Daphnis**
God offended by: 4 EROS
Lover of: 5 CHLOE
**"Daphnis et ___" (Ravel work):**
5 CHLOE
**Dapper:** 5 NATTY SMART
6 SPORTY
fellow: 3 DAN
**Dapper ___:** 3 DAN
**Dappled:** 4 PIED
horse: 4 ROAN
**d'Arc, Jeanne:** 6 SAINTE
(abbr.): 3 STE
**Dare**
alternative: 5 TRUTH
Defiant: 6 MAKEME
**Daredevil:** 6 RISKER
name: 4 EVEL
Robbie's ~ dad: 4 EVEL

**Daredeviltry**
First name in: 4 EVEL
**Daring:** 4 BOLD
deed: 4 GEST
exploit: 4 GEST
feat: 5 STUNT
Hardly a ~ do: 3 BUN
**Darius I**
land: 6 PERSIA
**Darjeeling:** 3 TEA
duds: 4 SARI
**Dark:** 5 UNLIT 6 GLOOMY
and dreary: 5 DINGY
area: 5 UMBRA
Grow: 5 LATEN
In the: 7 UNAWARE
Not in the ~ about: 5 HEPTO
suit: 6 SPADES
The ~ force: 4 EVIL
The ~ side: 3 YIN
times, in verse: 4 EENS
Very: 4 INKY
~, in poetry: 4 EBON
**"Dark Angel"**
actress Jessica: 4 ALBA
**"Dark at the Top of the Stairs, The"**
playwright: 4 INGE
**Dark-complexioned:**
7 SWARTHY
**Darken:** 3 DIM TAN 5 BEDIM
**Darkening:** 7 ECLIPSE
**"Dark Lady"**
singer: 4 CHER
**Darkness:** 4 MURK
Force of: 4 EVIL
personified: 6 EREBUS
**Darkroom**
abbr.: 3 ENL NEG
**Darlin':** 3 HON
**"___ Darlin":** 3 LIL
**Darling:** 3 PET 4 DEAR IDOL
7 SWEETIE
dog: 4 NANA
of baseball: 3 RON
~, in French: 5 CHERI
6 CHERIE
**Darn:** 3 SEW 4 MEND
Give a: 3 SEW 4 CARE MIND
**"Darn!":** 4 DRAT NUTS RATS
5 SHOOT
**"Darn ___!":** 5 ITALL
**Darned:** 4 SEWN VERY
spot: 3 TOE 4 TEAR
**"Darn it!":** 4 DRAT HECK
NUTS RATS
**"Da ___ Ron Ron":** 3 DOO
**Darrow**
Actress: 3 ANN
client: 4 LOEB 6 SCOPES
**Dart:** 3 ZIP 4 FLIT 5 SCOOT
about: 4 FLIT
Make a: 3 SEW
**___ d'art:** 5 OBJET
**D'Artagnan**
creator: 5 DUMAS

Friend of: 5 ATHOS 6 ARAMIS
**Dartboard:** 6 TARGET
Drink by a: 3 ALE
**Darth Vader**
Daughter of: 4 LEIA
Like: 4 EVIL
Son of: 4 LUKE
**Dartmoor**
crag: 3 TOR
**Darts**
quaff: 3 ALE
venue: 3 PUB
**"Das Boot"**
setting: 5 UBOAT
**Dash:** 3 PEP RUN VIM 4 ELAN
RACE 5 VERVE 6 SPRINT
7 PANACHE
counter: 8 ODOMETER
gauge: 4 TACH
lengths: 3 EMS ENS
off: 5 WRITE
**Dashboard**
abbr.: 3 MPH RPM
control: 5 DEFOG
device: 4 DIAL
dial: 4 TACH
gauge: 4 TACH 8 ODOMETER
**Dashed:** 3 RAN 4 TORE
**Dashes:** 3 EMS ENS
**Dashiell**
contemporary: 4 ERLE
detective: 4 NORA
dog: 4 ASTA
**Dashing:** 5 SHARP
sort: 5 RACER
style: 4 ELAN
**___ dash of ...:** 4 ADDA
**"Das Kapital"**
author: 4 MARX
**"Das Lied von der Erde"**
composer: 6 MAHLER
**"Das Rheingold"**
goddess: 4 ERDA
**Dastardly:** 4 EVIL
**Data:** 4 INFO 5 STATS
holder: 4 DISK
Like some: 3 RAW
storage medium: 5 CDROM
to enter: 5 INPUT
transfer rate unit: 4 BAUD
transmission path: 6 UPLINK
**Database**
operation: 4 SORT
**Data-sharing**
system (abbr.): 3 LAN
**Date:** 3 SEE
Get ready for a: 5 PRIMP
Guy's: 3 GAL
Have a: 3 EAT
Invite on a: 6 ASKOUT
Kind of: 3 DUE
On a: 3 OUT
producer: 4 PALM
Prom: 6 ESCORT
To: 3 YET 5 ASYET SOFAR
Where to get a: 5 OASIS

with a Dr.: 4 APPT
Without a: 4 STAG
___ date (makes wedding
     plans): 5 SETSA
"___ date!": 4 ITSA
**Datebook**
abbr.: 3 APR AUG DEC FEB
     FRI JAN JUL JUN MAR
     MON NOV OCT SAT SEP
     SUN THU TUE WED
     4 APPT THUR TUES
**Dated:** 3 OLD SAW 4 SEEN
     5 PASSE 6 OLDHAT
**Dateless:** 4 STAG 5 ALONE
**Dates**
Like some: 6 PITTED
Where to find: 5 OASES OASIS
**Dating**
couple: 4 ITEM
from: 4 ASOF
letters: 3 BCE
Word used in: 4 ANNO
**Datum:** 4 FACT STAT
**Daughter**
Brother's: 5 NIECE
Mom's: 3 SIS
Sister's: 5 NIECE
~, for example: 3 SHE
**Daumier**
Artist: 6 HONORE
**Daunt:** 4 FAZE 5 SCARE
     6 DISMAY
**Dauntless:** 5 STOUT 6 HEROIC
**Dave**
Computer nemesis of: 3 HAL
Humorist: 5 BARRY
of baseball: 5 STIEB
of the PGA: 4 MARR
**"Dave"**
star: 5 KLINE
**Davenport:** 4 SOFA
resident: 5 IOWAN
site: 4 IOWA
**David:** 4 CAMP 6 STATUE
Actor: 5 NIVEN 6 CARUSO
Coanchor of: 4 CHET
Golfer: 5 DUVAL
Impressionist: 4 FRYE
Journalist: 5 ENSOR
Lyricist: 3 HAL
Philosopher: 4 HUME
Playwright: 5 MAMET
Song of: 5 PSALM
Weapon used by: 5 SLING
___ David (Jewish star):
     5 MOGEN
**Davidic**
song: 5 PSALM
**Davies**
Golfer: 5 LAURA
**Davies, Capt.**
portrayer: 7 EDASNER
___-Davies, John: 4 RHYS
**Da ___, Vietnam:** 4 NANG
**Davis**
Activist: 6 ANGELA

Actor: 5 OSSIE
Actress: 5 BETTE GEENA
Nutritionist: 6 ADELLE
Singer: 3 MAC 7 SKEETER
**Davis, Jefferson**
org.: 3 CSA
supporter: 3 REB
**Davis, Jim**
dog: 4 ODIE
**Davis Cup**
Former ~ captain: 4 ASHE
**Davis Jr., Sammy**
book: 7 YESICAN
**Davit:** 5 CRANE HOIST
**Daw, Marjorie**
vehicle: 6 SEESAW
**Dawber**
Actress: 3 PAM
**Dawdle:** 3 LAG 5 TARRY
     6 LOITER 8 LOSETIME
**Dawdling:** 4 POKY
**Dawn:** 4 MORN 5 ARISE
     ONSET SUNUP
     6 AURORA
deity: 3 EOS
droplets: 3 DEW
goddess: 3 EOS 6 AURORA
Greet the: 5 ARISE
riser: 3 SUN
to dusk: 3 DAY
Toward the: 4 EAST
**Dawnlike:** 7 AURORAL
**Dawson**
of football: 3 LEN
**"Dawson's Creek"**
actress Holmes: 5 KATIE
extra: 4 TEEN
**Day**
Actress: 5 DORIS
Any ~ now: 4 SOON
at the movies: 5 DORIS
break: 3 NAP 6 RECESS
     SIESTA
Break of: 4 DAWN MORN
     5 SUNUP 6 SIESTA
Call it a: 4 QUIT
care attendee: 3 TOT
divs.: 3 HRS
Face the: 5 ARISE
Fateful: 4 IDES
fraction: 4 HOUR
Greet the: 4 RISE 5 ARISE
Hebrew: 3 YOM
It's another: 8 TOMORROW
laborer: 4 PEON
march: 5 ETAPE
of celebration: 4 FETE
of rest: 7 SABBATH
of the wk.: 3 FRI MON SAT
     SUN THU TUE WED
Plain as: 8 CLEARCUT
preceding: 3 EVE
prefix: 3 MID 6 YESTER
saver: 4 HERO
To this: 3 YET
~, in Spanish: 3 DIA

**Day-___:** 3 GLO
___ day (dosage): 4 ONEA
___ Day (November 2):
     8 ALLSOULS
**Day, Doris**
film: 10 PILLOWTALK
Word repeated in a ~ song:
     4 SERA
**Dayan**
contemporary: 4 MEIR
of Israel: 5 MOSHE
**Daybed:** 6 CHAISE
**Daybreak:** 4 DAWN 5 SUNUP
**Daydream:** 4 MOON 7 REVERIE
     10 WOOLGATHER
"___ day now ...": 3 ANY
**Days**
Bygone: 4 PAST YORE
In the old: 4 ONCE
In those: 4 THEN
In ~ past: 3 AGO
Like ~ of yore: 5 OLDEN
of old: 4 YORE
of yore: 3 ELD 4 PAST
**Days ___:** 3 INN 5 OFOLD
"___ Days" (Woody Allen film):
     5 RADIO
"___ Day's Night": 5 AHARD
**Days of ___:** 4 YORE
**"Days of ___ Lives":** 3 OUR
**Daytime**
drama: 4 SOAP 6 SERIAL
First name in ~ TV: 5 OPRAH
show: 7 MATINEE
**Dayton**
City near: 5 XENIA
**Daytona 500:** 4 RACE
entrant: 7 RACECAR
org.: 6 NASCAR
**Daytona Beach**
City west of: 5 OCALA
"___ Day Will Come": 3 OUR
**"Day Without Rain, A"**
singer: 4 ENYA
**Daze:** 3 FOG 4 STUN 6 STUPOR
**Dazed:** 4 ASEA 6 INAFOG
and confused: 5 ATSEA
     6 INAFOG 7 OUTOFIT
condition: 6 STUPOR
___ d'Azur: 4 COTE
**Dazzle:** 3 AWE 4 STUN
     5 AMAZE ECLAT
**Dazzled:** 5 INAWE
**Dazzling**
display: 5 ECLAT
effect: 5 ECLAT
light: 5 GLARE
performance:
     11 SHOWSTOPPER
success: 5 ECLAT
**D'back:** 4 NLER
**D.C.**
bigwig: 3 SEN
donor: 3 PAC
figure: 3 POL SEN
fund-raiser: 3 PAC

insider: 3 POL
lobby: 3 NRA 4 AARP
lobbying gp.: 3 PAC
One of a ~ 100: 3 SEN
pol: 3 SEN
setting: 3 EDT EST
stadium: 3 RFK
TV from: 5 CSPAN
type: 3 POL
~ VIP: 3 SEN

**D-Day**
beach: 4 UTAH 5 OMAHA
craft: 3 LST 4 LSTS
invasion town: 4 STLO
link: 4 ASIN
transport: 3 LST
vessel: 3 LST

**DDE**
command: 3 ETO
foe: 3 AES
follower: 3 JFK
Loser to: 3 AES
nickname: 3 IKE
party: 3 GOP
predecessor: 3 HST

**DDT**
Org. that banned: 3 EPA

**De ___**
(actual): 5 FACTO
(again): 4 NOVO
(excessive): 4 TROP

**De ___, Brian**
Director: 5 PALMA

**de ___, Cabeza**
Explorer: 4 VACA

**de ___, Charles:** 6 GAULLE
**de ___, Cyrano:** 8 BERGERAC

**de ___, Hernando**
Explorer: 4 SOTO

**de ___, Honoré**
Novelist: 6 BALZAC

**De ___, Robert**
Actor: 4 NIRO

**De ___, Vittorio**
Director: 4 SICA

**DEA**
agent: 4 NARC

**Dead:** 3 SEA
against: 4 ANTI
center: 4 TOMB
duck: 5 GONER
end: 3 DEE
    10 BLINDALLEY
follower: 3 END
giveaway: 6 ESTATE
heat: 3 TIE
In a ~ heat: 4 EVEN
It may be: 3 END
letters: 3 RIP
to the world: 5 INERT
    6 ASLEEP
~, as an engine: 5 KAPUT

**"Dead ___"**
Francis book: 4 CERT

**Deaden:** 4 DAMP MUTE NUMB
    6 BENUMB

**Dead-end**
job: 3 RUT
street: 8 CULDESAC

**Deadeye**
of legend: 6 OAKLEY

**Deadline**
Add just before the: 6 EDGEIN
After the: 4 LATE
Before the: 5 EARLY 6 INTIME
Past the: 4 LAST

**Deadlock:** 3 TIE 4 DRAW
    7 IMPASSE

**Deadlocked:** 4 EVEN TIED

**Deadly:** 5 FATAL 6 LETHAL
defoliant: 11 AGENTORANGE
poison: 4 BANE
sin: 4 ENVY LUST 5 ANGER
    GREED PRIDE SLOTH
    8 GLUTTONY
sin count: 5 SEVEN
snake: 3 ASP 5 KRAIT MAMBA
virus: 5 EBOLA

**Dead Sea**
document: 6 SCROLL
kingdom: 4 MOAB
region: 4 EDOM
scribe: 6 ESSENE

**Dead Sea Scrolls**
language: 7 ARAMAIC
Presumed authors of:
    7 ESSENES

**"Dead Souls"**
novelist: 5 GOGOL

**Deaf**
Communication for the ~
    (abbr.): 3 ASL
Falling on ~ ears: 7 UNHEARD

**Deaf as ___:** 5 APOST
**___ deaf ear to:** 5 TURNA

**Deafening:** 4 LOUD 5 AROAR

**Deal:** 4 PACT
Bank: 4 LOAN
Big: 3 ADO
Cashless: 4 SWAP 5 TRADE
Conclude, as a: 5 CLOSE
Get in on a: 4 ANTE
Good: 3 BUY LOT 4 LOTS
Great: 3 LOT TON 4 SLEW
    5 NOEND
in: 4 SELL
Kind of: 10 SWEETHEART
maker: 5 AGENT
preceder: 4 ANTE
Secondhand: 6 RESALE
Secure, as a: 3 ICE
Sports: 4 SWAP 5 TRADE
with: 5 TREAT 7 ADDRESS
(with): 4 COPE

**"___ deal!":** 4 ITSA

**Dealer**
buster: 4 NARC
in cloth: 6 DRAPER
in stolen goods: 5 FENCE
Kind of: 4 ARMS
nemesis: 4 NARC
Order to a: 5 HITME

request: 4 ANTE
Tip for a: 4 TOKE

**Dealt**
(with): 5 COPED

**Dean**
concern: 8 ACADEMIA
list fig.: 3 GPA
of diplomacy: 7 ACHESON
of Jan & Dean: 8 TORRENCE
Partner of: 3 JAN

**Dean, James:** 4 ICON
film: 5 GIANT
persona: 5 REBEL

**Deane**
Diplomat: 5 SILAS

**Deanna**
Enterprise counselor: 4 TROI

**Dear:** 6 VALUED 7 BELOVED
companion: 4 NEAR
Hold: 4 LOVE 5 ADORE
    7 CHERISH
~, in French: 5 CHERE CHERI
~, in Italian: 4 CARA CARO
~, in Spanish: 4 CARA CARO

**"Dear"**
advice-giver: 4 ABBY
one: 3 SIR 4 ABBY

**Dear Abby**
Sister of: 3 ANN

**"___ Dearest":** 6 MOMMIE
**Dearie:** 3 HON PET
**"Dear me!":** 4 ALAS

**"Dear old"**
family member: 3 DAD

**Dearth:** 4 LACK

**Death**
Done to: 3 OLD
Love to: 5 ADORE
Thrill to: 5 ELATE

**"___ Death" (Grieg work):**
    4 ASES

**"Death Be Not Proud"**
author: 5 DONNE

**"Death in the Family, A"**
author: 4 AGEE

**"Death in Venice"**
author: 4 MANN

**"Death of a Naturalist"**
poet: 6 HEANEY

**"Death of a Salesman"**
name: 5 LOMAN

**"Death on the ___":** 4 NILE

**Death Valley**
Like: 4 ARID

**Debacle:** 6 FIASCO

**___ de Balzac**
Novelist: 6 HONORE

**Debatable:** 4 MOOT

**Debate:** 5 ARGUE
focus: 5 TOPIC
side: 3 CON PRO 4 ANTI
subject: 5 ISSUE TOPIC
topic: 5 ISSUE
Under: 7 ATISSUE

**Debating**
Not worth: 4 MOOT

**Debauchee:** 4 ROUE 5 SATYR
**Debbie**
  Actress: 8 REYNOLDS
  Swimmer: 5 MEYER
**Debby**
  Singer: 5 BOONE
**de Beauvoir**
  Writer: 6 SIMONE
**Debilitated:** 6 FEEBLE
**Debonair:** 5 SUAVE 6 URBANE
**Deborah**
  Actress: 4 KERR 5 ADAIR
  ___ de Boulogne (Paris park):
      4 BOIS
**Debra**
  Actress: 5 PAGET
**Debra Jo**
  Actress: 4 RUPP
**Debris**
  Ocean: 6 JETSAM 7 FLOTSAM
  Rocky: 5 SCREE
**Debt**
  acknowledgment: 3 IOU
  Be in: 3 OWE
  Clear a: 5 REPAY
  Govt.: 5 TNOTE
  Letters of: 3 IOU
  memo: 3 IOU
  National ~ word: 8 TRILLION
  Satisfy, as a: 5 REPAY
  security: 4 LIEN
  Settle a: 5 REPAY 6 PONYUP
  Unpaid: 6 ARREAR
**Debtor**
  claim: 4 LIEN
  letters: 3 IOU
  note: 3 IOU
  woe: 4 REPO
**Debt-ridden:** 8 INTHERED
**Debts:** 6 REDINK
  Acquire, as: 5 INCUR RUNUP
  Have: 3 OWE
**Debussy**
  Composer: 6 CLAUDE
  contemporary: 5 SATIE
  subject: 3 MER
  work: 5 LAMER
**Debut:** 5 ENTRY 7 PREMIER
      ROLLOUT
  NASDAQ: 3 IPO
  NYSE: 3 IPO
  of Oct. 7, 1982: 4 CATS
  of Oct. 11, 1975: 3 SNL
  Wall St.: 3 IPO
**Débutante**
  affair: 3 BAL 4 BALL
**Dec.**
  holiday: 4 XMAS
**Decade**
  divs.: 3 YRS
**Decadent:** 6 EFFETE
**Decaf**
  brand: 5 SANKA
**Decalogue**
  deliverer: 5 MOSES
  word: 5 SHALT

**Decant:** 4 POUR
**Decapitate:** 6 BEHEAD
**DeCarlo**
  Actress: 6 YVONNE
**Decathlon**
  component: 5 EVENT
  event: 7 JAVELIN
      SHOTPUT
**Decay:** 3 ROT
  Sign of: 4 RUST
**Deceit:** 4 RUSE 5 GUILE
**Deceitful**
  Be: 3 LIE 8 TELLALIE
  one: 4 LIAR
**Deceive:** 4 DUPE SNOW
      5 COZEN LIETO
      6 LEADON
**Deceived:** 5 LEDON 6 LIEDTO
      MISLED
  Not ~ by: 4 ONTO
**Deceiving:** 7 LYINGTO
**Decelerate:** 4 SLOW
**December**
  24th or 31st: 3 EVE
  air: 4 NOEL
  decoration: 8 ORNAMENT
  song: 4 NOEL 5 CAROL
  temp: 5 SANTA
  The first of: 3 DEE
**Decennial**
  event: 6 CENSUS
**Decent:** 4 CLAD
  chap: 4 GENT
  Not: 4 LEWD
  sort: 6 MENSCH
**Deception:** 3 LIE 4 HOAX RUSE
      SHAM
  Blatant: 7 CHARADE
  on the ice: 4 DEKE
**Deceptive:** 6 TRICKY
  move: 5 FEINT
  plan: 4 RUSE
**Decide:** 3 OPT
  against: 3 NIX
  on: 5 ELECT
  to withdraw: 6 OPTOUT
  Unable to: 4 TORN
**Decide at the flip of ___:**
      5 ACOIN
**Deciding**
  Have trouble: 6 SEESAW
**Decimal**
  base: 3 TEN
  follower: 5 CENTS
  fraction: 5 TENTH
  No. after the: 3 CTS
  point: 3 DOT
  unit: 3 TEN
  ___ decimal system: 5 DEWEY
**Decimeter**
  Cubic: 5 LITER
**Decision:** 4 CALL
  Await a: 4 PEND
  Bout: 3 TKO
  Court: 3 LET
  Judicial: 5 AWARD

  Make a: 3 OPT 4 RULE
      5 ELECT
  point: 4 FORK
  Ref's: 3 TKO
  Right of: 5 SAYSO
  Ring: 3 TKO
  Split: 7 DIVORCE
  Time of: 4 DDAY
**Decisive**
  Be: 3 OPT
  defeat: 8 WATERLOO
  time: 4 DDAY
**Deck:** 4 KAYO
  22-card ~: 5 TAROT
  assent: 6 AYEAYE
  Clean the: 4 SWAB
  Diviner's: 5 TAROT
  expert: 9 CARDSHARK
  Fortuneteller's: 5 TAROT
  Gave from a: 5 DEALT
  hands: 4 CREW
  Lowest: 5 ORLOP
  Mystical: 5 TAROT
  No longer on: 5 ATBAT
  Not on: 5 BELOW
  On: 4 NEXT 7 TOPSIDE
  On a ~, perhaps: 4 ASEA
  out: 5 ADORN ARRAY
      6 CLOTHE 7 FESTOON
  Playing with a full: 4 SANE
      8 ALLTHERE
  salt: 3 TAR
  Seer's: 5 TAROT
  Ship: 5 ORLOP
  wood: 4 TEAK
**Decked:** 3 KOD 4 CLAD
  Get ~ out: 5 DRESS
  out: 4 CLAD 7 ADORNED
      ARRAYED
**Decks:** 3 KOS
**"Deck the Halls":** 5 CAROL
  contraction: 3 TIS
  sequence: 6 LALALA
  syllables: 3 LAS
**Declaim:** 5 ORATE SPOUT
**Declaration**
  Altar: 3 IDO
  Bridge: 5 IPASS
  Formal: 6 DICTUM
  Make a: 4 AVER
  Pinochle: 4 MELD
  Poker: 4 IMIN 5 ICALL
      6 IRAISE
  Senate: 3 YEA
  Solemn: 4 OATH
  Wedding: 3 IDO
**Declare:** 3 SAY 4 AVER AVOW
      5 STATE 6 ASSERT
  false: 4 DENY
  openly: 4 AVOW
  positively: 4 AVER
  untrue: 4 DENY
**Decline:** 3 EBB SAG 4 DROP
      FALL PASS WANE
      5 SAYNO SLIDE
      6 REFUSE WORSEN

in value: 3 SAG
On the: 6 ASLOPE WANING
Period of: 3 EBB 7 EBBTIDE
to bid: 4 PASS
to vote: 7 ABSTAIN
___ Deco: 3 ART
___ de coeur: 3 CRI
___ de Cologne: 3 EAU
___ de combat: 4 HORS
**Decompose:** 3 ROT
**Décor**
Change the: 4 REDO
Wall: 5 MURAL
**Decorate:** 5 ADORN
7 GARNISH
anew: 4 REDO
**Decorated**
Richly: 6 ORNATE
**Decoration:** 5 AWARD
9 ADORNMENT
Cake: 5 ICING
Christmas: 4 TREE 5 HOLLY
6 TINSEL
Garden: 3 URN 5 GNOME
Gift: 3 BOW
Hat: 5 PLUME
Mil.: 3 DSC DSM
Object of: 4 HERO
Party: 8 STREAMER
Shoe: 6 TASSEL
Uniform: 7 EPAULET
**Decorative**
band: 6 ARMLET FRIEZE
case: 4 ETUI
jug: 4 EWER
metalwork: 6 NIELLO
noose: 3 TIE
Not just: 5 UTILE
pitcher: 4 EWER
trim: 4 LACE
vase: 3 URN
**Decorator**
Cake: 4 ICER
Hire a: 4 REDO
shade: 4 ECRU
suggestion: 3 HUE
**Decorous:** 4 PRIM 6 SEEMLY
___ de corps: 6 ESPRIT
**Decoy:** 4 LURE
Con's: 5 SHILL
**Decrease:** 3 EBB 4 WANE
5 ABATE LOWER
**De-crease:** 4 IRON 5 PRESS
**Decree:** 4 FIAT RULE
5 EDICT UKASE
6 ORDAIN
Imperial: 5 UKASE
Islamic: 5 FATWA
Not final, as a: 4 NISI
Official: 5 EDICT
**Decrepit:** 6 CREAKY
horse: 3 NAG
___ de deux: 3 PAS
**Dedicated:** 4 AVID 5 LOYAL
6 ARDENT
poem: 3 ODE

**Dedicatory**
verse: 3 ODE
words: 3 TOA
**Deduce:** 5 GLEAN INFER
6 GATHER
**Deduction**
Scale: 4 TARE
**Deductions**
After: 3 NET
**Deductive:** 7 APRIORI
**Dee**
Actress: 6 SANDRA
predecessor: 3 CEE
Singer: 4 KIKI
**Dee, Ruby**
Husband of: 5 OSSIE
**Deed:** 3 ACT
Daring: 4 GEST
Have the ~ to: 3 OWN
Heroic: 4 FEAT 7 EXPLOIT
holder: 5 OWNER
No good: 3 SIN
**"Deed I Do"**
singer: 5 HORNE
**Deejay:** 7 SPINNER
worry: 4 SKIP
**Deem**
appropriate: 6 SEEFIT
**Deep:** 4 RICH 7 INTENSE
black: 3 JET 4 EBON INKY
blue: 4 ANIL
cavity: 5 ABYSM
chasm: 5 ABYSS 6 CANYON
cut: 4 GASH
dish: 6 TUREEN
down: 7 ATHEART
8 INWARDLY
draft: 4 SWIG
Go off the ~ end: 4 DIVE SNAP
green: 7 EMERALD
pink: 4 ROSE 5 MELON
pit: 5 ABYSS
red: 4 RUBY 6 CERISE
secrets: 6 ARCANA
sleep: 4 COMA 5 SOPOR
voice: 4 BASS
**Deep Blue**
game: 5 CHESS
maker: 3 IBM
**Deep-dish**
meal: 6 POTPIE
**Deepen**
~, as a canal: 6 DREDGE
**Deep-frying**
need: 3 OIL 6 HOTOIL
**"Deep Impact"**
star: 5 LEONI
**Deep-seated:** 6 INBRED
INNATE
**Deep-six:** 3 CAN 4 TOSS
5 DITCH SCRAP TRASH
**Deep-space**
energy source: 6 QUASAR
mission: 5 PROBE
**"Deep Space Nine"**
character: 3 ODO

**Deep Throat:** 6 SOURCE
**Deep-voiced**
singer: 5 BASSO
**Deer:** 3 DOE ROE
Baby: 4 FAWN
cousin: 3 ELK
dad: 4 STAG
Female: 3 DOE 4 HIND
herder: 4 LAPP
Male: 4 HART STAG
mom: 3 DOE
sir: 4 STAG
Young: 4 FAWN
**Deere**
headquarters: 6 MOLINE
product: 4 PLOW
___ Dee River: 3 PEE
**Deerstalker:** 3 HAT
**Deface:** 3 MAR
**De facto:** 6 ACTUAL
**Defamation**
Written: 5 LIBEL
**Defame:** 5 ABASE LIBEL
in print: 5 LIBEL
**Defat**
~, as a whale: 6 FLENSE
**Defaulter**
loss: 4 REPO
**Defeat:** 3 TOP 4 BEST LICK
LOSS 5 WORST
Admission of: 5 ILOSE ILOST
Barely: 4 EDGE
Cry of: 5 UNCLE
decisively: 4 DRUB ROUT
5 STOMP 6 THRASH
15 MOPTHEFLOORWITH
Narrowly: 3 NIP 4 EDGE
Overwhelmingly: 4 ROUT
**Defeated:** 5 DIDIN 6 BEATEN
**Defeatist**
word: 4 CANT 6 CANNOT
**Defect:** 4 FLAW 5 FAULT
**Defective:** 3 BAD
Slightly ~ (abbr.): 3 IRR
**Defector:** 6 EMIGRE
**Defendant**
answer: 4 PLEA
excuse: 5 ALIBI
of 1925: 6 SCOPES
**Defendants**
~, in old law: 3 REI
**Defender**
Bridge: 4 EAST
Perennial: 4 EAST
**Defense**
acronym: 4 NATO
advisory org.: 3 NSC
Castle: 4 MOAT
Court: 4 ZONE
Former ~ gp.: 5 SEATO
gp.: 4 NATO
Medieval: 4 MOAT
org.: 4 NATO
Polecat's: 4 ODOR
Skunk's: 4 ODOR
type: 4 ZONE

Weaponless ~ system: 4 JUDO
**Defenseless:** 5 NAKED
  Render: 5 UNARM
**Defenseman**
  Legendary: 3 ORR
**Defensive**
  ditch: 4 MOAT
  effort: 5 STAND
  spray: 4 MACE
  wall: 7 PARAPET
**Defer**
  Suffix with: 4 ENCE
  (to): 6 KOWTOW
  ___ deferens: 3 VAS
**Defiant**
  act: 4 DARE
  remark: 7 SOTHERE
  reply: 5 NEVER
  words: 6 MAKEME
**Defibrillator**
  yell: 5 CLEAR
**Deficiency:** 3 GAP 5 MINUS
    8 SHORTAGE
  Result of iron: 6 ANEMIA
  Result of thiamine:
    8 BERIBERI
**Deficient**
  Be ~ in: 4 LACK
**Deficit**
  indicator: 6 REDINK
**Definitive**
  statement: 8 LASTWORD
**Deflated**
  It can be: 3 EGO
**Deflation**
  victim: 3 EGO
**Deflect:** 5 AVERT
**Defoe**
  Author: 6 DANIEL
  character: 6 CRUSOE
    12 MOLLFLANDERS
  character Flanders: 4 MOLL
**Defoliant**
  Deadly: 11 AGENTORANGE
  ___ de France: 3 ILE
**Defraud:** 4 BILK SCAM
    5 CHEAT COZEN
    6 FLEECE
**Defrost:** 4 MELT THAW
**Deft:** 5 AGILE HANDY SLICK
    6 ADROIT
**Deftness:** 4 EASE 5 SKILL
**Defunct**
  alliance: 5 SEATO
  humor magazine: 3 SPY
  sports org.: 3 ABA
**Defy:** 4 DARE
**Degas**
  Artist: 5 EDGAR
  Item in a ~ painting: 4 TUTU
  Many a: 6 PASTEL
  subject: 7 DANCERS
**De Gaulle**
  alternative: 4 ORLY 5 LILLE
  birthplace: 5 LILLE
**Degauss:** 5 ERASE

**DeGeneres**
  Comic: 5 ELLEN
**Degrade:** 5 ABASE
**Degree:** 4 STEP 6 EXTENT
  Advanced: 3 NTH PHD
  Atty.'s: 3 LLD
  CEO's: 3 MBA
  div.: 3 MIN
  High: 3 NTH PHD 7 MASTERS
  Highest: 3 NTH
  In the slightest: 5 ATALL
  Math: 3 NTH
  Nth: 3 MAX
  Prof.'s: 3 PHD
  Second: 3 MBA
  Third: 3 PHD
  To a: 4 SOME 5 QUITE
  To any: 5 ATALL
  Ultimate: 3 NTH
  Utmost: 3 NTH
  ___ degree: 3 NTH TOA
**Degrees**
  22.5 ~: 3 NNE
  90 ~: 4 EAST
  ___ de guerre: 3 NOM
**Dehydrated:** 4 SERE
**Dehydration**
  remedy: 7 LIQUIDS
**"___ Dei":** 5 AGNUS
**Deicer**
  Road: 4 SALT
**Deighton**
  Author: 3 LEN
**Deimos:** 4 MOON
  Father of: 4 ARES
**Deity**
  Bellicose: 4 ARES
  Dawn: 3 EOS
  Discord: 4 ERIS
  dismisser: 7 ATHEIST
  doubter: 8 AGNOSTIC
  Hindu: 4 RAMA 5 SHIVA
    6 VISHNU
  Islamic: 5 ALLAH
  Lascivious: 5 SATYR
  Lustful: 5 SATYR
  Semitic: 4 BAAL
  Shi'ite: 5 ALLAH
  Subordinate: 6 DAEMON
  Supreme Greek: 4 ZEUS
  Supreme Norse: 4 ODIN
  Supreme Theban: 6 AMENRA
  Viking: 4 ODIN
  War: 4 ARES
  Woodland: 4 FAUN 5 SATYR
  ___ de Janeiro: 3 RIO
**Déjà vu**
  Have: 6 RELIVE
**Dejected:** 3 SAD 4 BLUE DOWN
    GLUM 5 MOPEY
**Deke:** 5 FEINT
  Astronaut: 7 SLAYTON
**de la ___, Oscar**
  Boxer: 4 HOYA
  Designer: 5 RENTA
  ___ de la Cité: 3 ILE

**Delaney**
  Actress: 3 KIM
**Delany**
  Actress: 4 DANA
**de la Renta**
  Designer: 5 OSCAR
**De Laurentiis**
  Producer: 4 DINO
**Delaware**
  Capital on the: 7 TRENTON
  City on the: 6 CAMDEN
  senator: 4 ROTH 5 BIDEN
  ~ Indian: 6 LENAPE
**"Delaware Water Gap"**
  painter George: 6 INNESS
**Delay:** 5 SITON TARRY
    6 PUTOFF 7 TIMELAG
  After much: 6 ATLAST
  progress: 6 RETARD
  Time: 3 LAG
  Without: 3 NOW 5 APACE
    6 ATONCE
    15 ATTHEDROPOFAHAT
  Without ~, in a memo: 4 ASAP
**Delayed:** 4 LATE 6 HELDUP
**Dele**
  Cancel a: 4 STET
  undoer: 4 STET
**Delectable:** 5 TASTY YUMMY
**Delegate:** 5 ENVOY 8 EMISSARY
  U.N.: 3 AMB
**___ de Leon**
  Explorer: 5 PONCE
**Delete:** 3 ZAP 4 XOUT 5 ERASE
**Deleted:** 3 XED 6 XEDOUT
**___ del Fuego:** 6 TIERRA
**Delhi**
  **Info:** Indian cue
  address: 3 SRI
  bread: 5 RUPEE
  dough: 5 RUPEE
  dress: 4 SARI
  dweller: 5 HINDU
  language: 5 HINDI
  princess: 4 RANI
  wrap: 4 SARI
**Deli**
  bread: 3 RYE
  dangler: 6 SALAMI
  display: 5 MEATS
  donut: 5 BAGEL
  fixture: 6 SLICER
  jarful: 4 MAYO
  loaf: 3 RYE
  loaves: 4 RYES
  meat: 3 HAM 6 SALAMI
    7 BOLOGNA
  need: 6 SLICER
  order: 3 BLT 5 SWISS
    6 REUBEN 8 HAMONRYE
    PASTRAMI
  request: 3 BLT 5 ONRYE
    6 NOMAYO
  sandwich: 3 BLT 4 HERO
    6 REUBEN
  sausage: 6 SALAMI

side: 4 SLAW
spread: 4 MAYO
Word on a ~ scale: 4 TARE
**Deliberate:** 4 MUSE SLOW
loss: 4 DIVE
**Delibes**
Composer: 3 LEO
**Delicacy:** 4 TACT 7 FINESSE
Fish: 3 EEL 7 SHADROE
Jellied: 3 EEL
Pickled: 3 EEL
Seafood: 3 ROE
Shad: 3 ROE
Stuffed: 5 DERMA
Sturgeon: 3 ROE
**Delicate:** 4 FINE LACY SOFT
5 FRAIL 6 TENDER
8 ETHEREAL
fabric: 4 LACE
**"Delicate Balance, A"**
playwright: 5 ALBEE
**Delicious:** 5 TASTY
discard: 4 CORE
leftover: 4 CORE
thing: 5 APPLE
**"Delicious!":** 3 MMM YUM
4 MMMM 5 TASTY
**Delight:** 3 JOY 4 GLEE 5 ELATE
6 PLEASE REGALE
TICKLE
in: 5 ENJOY
Insurer's: 7 LOWRISK
Sound of: 3 AAH OOH
Sounds of: 3 AHS
___ delight: 6 IDIOTS
**Delighted:** 4 GLAD SENT
6 ENRAPT
exclamation: 3 AAH OOH
"___ delighted!": 4 IDBE
**Delightful:** 4 NICE 8 PLEASING
place: 4 EDEN
**Delilah**
portrayer: 6 LAMARR
wooer: 6 SAMSON
**DeLillo**
Writer: 3 DON
**Delineate:** 4 ETCH LIMN
**Delirious:** 4 AGOG 5 GIDDY
6 RAVING
person: 5 RAVER
**Deliver:** 6 RESCUE
a diatribe: 4 RANT
an address: 5 ORATE
a speech: 5 ORATE
a tirade: 4 RANT
by parachute: 4 DROP
7 AIRDROP
It may ~ the goods: 4 SEMI
Suffix with: 4 ANCE
**Deliverance:** 6 RESCUE
7 RELEASE
**"Deliverance"**
actor Beatty: 3 NED
**Delivered:** 4 BORN 5 DEALT
6 SENTIN
Had food: 5 ATEIN

Have food: 5 EATIN
7 ORDERIN
**Deliverer**
Baby: 5 STORK
Damsel's: 4 HERO
of old: 6 ICEMAN
Pkg.: 3 UPS
Serum: 7 SYRINGE
**Delivery**
AOL: 5 EMAIL
co.: 3 UPS
Daily: 4 MAIL 6 USMAIL
Diva's: 4 ARIA
docs: 3 OBS
Early: 7 PREEMIE
entrance: 8 SIDEDOOR
Fast: 5 SPIEL
Male: 3 SON
Postal: 4 MAIL
Sun.: 3 SER
Sunday: 6 SERMON
truck: 3 VAN
UPS: 3 PKG
USPS: 3 LTR
**Dell:** 4 VALE
competitor: 3 IBM 4 ACER
products: 3 PCS
**Della**
Actress: 5 REESE
creator: 4 ERLE
of mystery: 6 STREET
Singer: 5 REESE
**Delmonico**
alternative: 5 TBONE
order: 4 RARE
**Delon**
Actor: 5 ALAIN
**"___ De-Lovely":** 3 ITS
**Delphi**
figure: 6 ORACLE
prophet: 6 ORACLE
temple god: 6 APOLLO
**Delphic:** 8 ORACULAR
medium: 6 ORACLE
shrine: 6 ORACLE
**Del Rio**
Actress: 7 DOLORES
**___ del Sol:** 5 COSTA
**Delt**
neighbor: 3 LAT PEC
**Delta:** 7 AIRLINE
Actress: 5 BURKE
builder: 4 SILT
deposit: 4 SILT
Former ~ competitor: 3 TWA
**"Delta Dawn"**
singer Tucker: 5 TANYA
**"Delta of Venus"**
author Anais: 3 NIN
**Delude:** 6 LEADON
**Deluge:** 6 ENGULF
7 TORRENT
**DeLuise**
Comic: 3 DOM
**DeLuise, Dom**
film: 5 FATSO

**"___ de Lune":** 5 CLAIR
**Deluxe:** 4 POSH
accommodations: 5 SUITE
seat: 3 BOX
sheet fabric: 5 SATIN
**Dem.**
foe: 3 REP
Neither ~ nor Rep.: 3 IND
**Demagnetize:** 5 ERASE
**Demand:** 5 EXACT
Court: 5 ORDER
In: 3 HOT 7 DESIRED
Kidnapper's: 6 RANSOM
payment: 3 DUN
Striker's: 5 RAISE
Union: 5 RAISE
**Demanding:** 5 STERN
7 EXIGENT
Less: 6 EASIER
star: 4 DIVA
**Demarcate:** 6 DEFINE
**Demarcation**
Mountain: 8 TREELINE
Pool: 4 LANE
**___ de Mayo:** 5 CINCO
**Demean:** 5 ABASE
**Demeanor:** 3 AIR 4 MIEN
MOOD
**de' Medici, Catherine:** 5 REINE
**___ de menthe:** 5 CREME
**Dementieva**
of tennis: 5 ELENA
**"___ de mer":** 3 MAL
**Demeter**
counterpart: 5 CERES
**Demi**
Actress: 5 MOORE
and Bruce: 4 EXES
**"Demian"**
author: 5 HESSE
**de Mille**
Choreographer: 5 AGNES
Dancer: 5 AGNES
**DeMille**
Director: 5 CECIL
film: 4 EPIC
specialty: 4 EPIC
**Demise:** 3 END
**Demme**
Director: 3 TED
**Demo**
ender: 4 CRAT
**Democratic**
donkey creator: 4 NAST
**Democratic Party**
symbol: 6 DONKEY
**Demoiselle:** 3 GAL 4 GIRL
**Demolish:** 4 RAZE RUIN
5 LEVEL TOTAL WRECK
**Demolition**
compound: 3 TNT
letters: 3 TNT
**Demolitionist**
supply: 3 TNT
**Demon:** 3 IMP
Female: 5 LAMIA

Little: 3 IMP
Speed: 5 RACER
Demon ___: 3 RUM
Demond
TV costar: 4 REDD
Demonic: 4 EVIL
Demonstrate: 4 SHOW 5 PROVE
Demonstration
End of a: 3 QED
Nonviolent: 5 SITIN
Demosthenes: 6 ORATOR
Emulate: 5 ORATE
Demure: 3 COY
Den: 4 LAIR NEST
denizen: 4 BEAR 7 BEARCUB
din: 4 ROAR
Kind of: 5 OPIUM
Lion's: 4 LAIR
mother: 7 LIONESS
outburst: 4 ROAR
sets: 3 TVS
system: 6 STEREO
Den ___ (Dutch city): 4 HAAG
Dench
Actress: 4 JUDI
film: 4 IRIS
title: 4 DAME
Dendrologist
study: 5 TREES
Deng
land: 5 CHINA
Denial: 4 VETO 7 REFUSAL
Dundee: 3 NAE
Military: 5 NOSIR
Slangy: 3 NAH 4 NOPE
Spouse's: 6 NODEAR
Terse: 5 NOTME
Words of: 4 NOTI 5 NOTME
6 IDONOT
Denials: 3 NOS 4 NOES
Denier
words: 4 NOTI 5 NOTME
Denim: 8 MATERIAL
fabric: 8 DUNGAREE
First name in: 4 LEVI
De Niro, Robert
film: 5 RONIN 6 CASINO
8 CAPEFEAR
10 GOODFELLAS
role: 6 CAPONE
Denison
denizen: 5 TEXAN
Denizen
Alley: 3 TOM
Coop: 3 HEN
Den: 4 BEAR 7 BEARCUB
Desert: 5 CAMEL
Dorm: 4 COED
Down under: 3 EMU 6 AUSSIE
Forest: 4 DEER
Hill: 3 ANT
Marsh: 4 RAIL 5 HERON
Pen: 3 CON
Pond: 4 NEWT TOAD
Dennis: 6 MENACE
Actor: 3 DAY

of basketball: 6 RODMAN
Dennis the Menace: 4 BRAT
dog: 4 RUFF
girl: 4 GINA
Like: 5 PESKY
Mother of: 5 ALICE
Denomination: 4 SECT
5 ORDER
Denouement: 3 END 6 ENDING
FINALE
Denounce: 4 DAMN 6 RAILAT
7 CONDEMN
De novo: 4 ANEW
Dense: 6 OBTUSE
fog: 7 PEASOUP
Not: 4 RARE 6 SPARSE
Density
symbol: 3 RHO
Dent: 3 MAR 4 DING
prefix: 3 TRI
Dental
cleaner: 5 FLOSS
exam: 4 ORAL
filling: 5 INLAY
records: 5 XRAYS
Dentist
deg.: 3 DDS
directive: 4 BITE OPEN
5 RINSE WIDER
8 OPENWIDE
handiwork: 5 INLAY
org.: 3 ADA
request: 4 BITE OPEN
5 RINSE WIDER
8 OPENWIDE
tool: 5 DRILL
Denver
dish: 6 OMELET
elevation: 4 MILE
hrs.: 3 MST
summer hrs.: 3 MDT
university: 5 REGIS
Denver-to-Chicago
dir.: 3 ENE
Deny: 6 NAYSAY NEGATE
Deodorant
type: 5 SPRAY 6 ROLLON
7 AEROSOL
"De oratore"
author: 6 CICERO
Dep.
opposite: 3 ARR
De Palma
Director: 5 BRIAN
Depardieu
Actor: 6 GERARD
Depart: 5 LEAVE 6 SETOFF
9 TAKELEAVE
Departed: 4 GONE LEFT
WENT
Department: 4 AREA
Cabinet: 5 LABOR STATE
7 DEFENSE 8 INTERIOR
Corporate: 5 LEGAL SALES
French: 3 AIN 4 OISE ORNE
5 AISNE

Department of Labor
agcy.: 4 OSHA
Department store
section: 4 MENS 6 LINENS
MISSES 8 MENSWEAR
~ Santa: 4 TEMP
Departs: 4 GOES
Departure: 4 EXIT 5 DEATH
Mass: 6 EXODUS
notice: 4 OBIT
Depend: 4 RELY 5 HINGE
(on): 4 RELY 5 HINGE
suffix: 4 ENCE
Dependable: 4 SAFE 5 SOLID
6 TRUSTY
Dependent
Be: 4 RELY
Depict: 4 LIMN
unfairly: 4 SKEW
Depilatory
brand: 4 NAIR NEET
Deplaned: 4 ALIT
Deplete: 3 SAP 5 DRAIN EATUP
USEUP 7 EATINTO
Depleting: 7 USINGUP
___ de plume: 3 NOM
Deportment: 4 MIEN
Depose: 4 OUST
Deposed
leader: 4 SHAH 5 EXILE
Deposit: 3 BED LAY PUT
5 PLACE
Bank: 3 ORE 4 SILT SNOW
Big: 4 LODE
Clayey: 4 MARL
Coal: 4 SEAM
Delta: 4 SILT 8 SEDIMENT
Earthy: 4 MARL
Glacial: 7 MORAINE
Gold: 4 LODE
in a tray: 3 ASH
Loamy: 5 LOESS
Metal: 4 LODE
Mineral: 4 VEIN
Rich: 4 LODE
River: 4 SILT
Silt: 5 LOESS
Depot: 4 STOP 7 STATION
(abbr.): 3 STA
letters (abbr.): 3 ARR
posting, for short: 4 SKED
RR: 3 STA STN
Depp, Johnny
role: 6 BRASCO EDWOOD
Depraved: 4 EVIL
Depreciation
cause: 11 WEARANDTEAR
Depressed: 3 LOW SAD 4 BLUE
DOWN 7 INAFUNK
area: 6 GHETTO
Depressing: 3 SAD 6 DREARY
GLOOMY
situation: 6 DOWNER
Depression: 3 ERA 4 DALE
DENT FUNK HOLE
agcy.: 3 NRA TVA

Big: 6 CRATER
Geological: 5 BASIN
Great: 5 ABYSS
migrant: 4 OKIE
**Deprive**
of courage: 5 UNMAN
of food: 6 STARVE
of heat: 5 UNARM 6 DISARM
of weapons: 5 UNARM
**Deprived:** 6 BEREFT
**Dept.**
head: 3 MGR
store stock: 4 MDSE
**Depth:** 5 ABYSS NADIR
checker: 5 PLUMB
Lacking: 4 TWOD
Lacking ~ and width: 4 ONED
Like a ~ finder: 5 SONIC
**Depth charge:** 6 ASHCAN
target: 5 UBOAT
**Dept. of Justice**
employee: 4 ATTY
**Dept. of Labor**
agency: 4 OSHA
division: 4 OSHA
**Deputized**
group: 5 POSSE
**Deputy:** 4 AIDE
(abbr.): 4 ASST
**Deputy ___ (cartoon character):**
4 DAWG
**Der ___ (Adenauer):** 4 ALTE
**Deranged:** 3 MAD 6 INSANE
**Derby:** 3 HAT 4 RACE
distance: 4 MILE 5 METRE
feature: 4 BRIM
material: 4 FELT
prize: 5 PURSE ROSES
prospect: 4 COLT
site: 5 EPSOM
town: 5 EPSOM
**Derek**
and others: 3 BOS
of baseball: 5 JETER
**Derek, Bo**
film: 3 TEN 4 ORCA
**Derek and the Dominos**
hit song: 5 LAYLA
**Derelict:** 3 BUM 4 HOBO
6 REMISS TRUANT
**Deride:** 4 GIBE JEER
7 SCOFFAT SNEERAT
**Derision:** 5 SCORN
Express: 4 JEER 5 SNEER
Sound of: 5 SNORT
**Derisive:** 5 SNIDE
cry: 3 YAH
laugh: 3 HAH 4 HAHA
look: 5 SNEER
sound: 5 SNORT
**Derive:** 5 INFER
**Derm**
prefix: 4 ECTO ENDO ENTO
**Dermal**
dilemma: 4 ACNE
opening: 3 EPI 4 PORE

prefix: 3 EPI 4 ENTO
**Dermatologist**
concern: 4 ACNE CYST ITCH
MOLE
**Dermis**
prefix: 3 EPI
**Dern**
Actor: 5 BRUCE
Actress: 5 LAURA
**Dernier ___ :** 3 CRI
**Derogatory:** 5 SNIDE
**Derrière:** 4 REAR TUSH
**Derring-do**
Bit of: 4 FEAT
First name in: 4 EVEL
Tale of: 5 GESTE
**Derringer:** 3 GUN 8 SMALLARM
**"___ Derringer" (TV oldie):**
5 YANCY
**"Der Ring ___ Nibelungen":**
3 DES
**Dershowitz**
field: 3 LAW
Lawyer: 4 ALAN
**Der Spiegel**
Article in: 3 EIN 4 EINE
**Dervish:** 5 FAKIR
faith: 5 ISLAM
**Des ___ :** 6 MOINES
**___ de sac:** 3 CUL
**Desai**
Author: 5 ANITA
**___ des Beaux-Arts:** 5 ECOLE
**Descartes**
concept: 4 IDEE
conclusion: 3 IAM
Philosopher: 4 RENE
quote word: 4 ERGO
Therefore, to: 4 ERGO
**Descend:** 4 SINK
**Descendant:** 5 SCION
**Descent:** 4 DROP
Climber's: 6 RAPPEL
Hawk's: 5 SWOOP
**Describe:** 4 LIMN 6 RELATE
**Descriptive**
wd.: 3 ADJ
**Desdemona**
Husband of: 7 OTHELLO
opera: 6 OTELLO
**Desecrate:** 6 DEFILE
**Desert**
African: 6 SAHARA
8 KALAHARI
Asian: 4 GOBI
bloomers: 5 CACTI
clay: 5 ADOBE
denizen: 5 CAMEL
Dry as a: 4 ARID 7 SAHARAN
flora: 5 CACTI
group: 7 CARAVAN
havens: 5 OASES
home: 5 ADOBE
Israeli: 5 NEGEV
Like ~ vegetation: 6 SPARSE
Mideast: 5 NEGEV

Mongolian: 4 GOBI
near Sinai: 5 NEGEV
plant: 5 AGAVE
plants: 5 CACTI
rest stop: 5 OASIS
rest stops: 5 OASES
sight: 4 DUNE 6 MIRAGE
stopover: 5 OASIS
stream: 4 WADI
wanderer: 5 NOMAD
Western: 6 MOHAVE MOJAVE
World's largest: 6 SAHARA
**Deserted:** 5 ALONE 6 LONELY
**Deserter:** 3 RAT 7 RUNAWAY
8 RENEGADE
**Desert Fox, The:** 6 ROMMEL
**Desertlike:** 4 ARID SERE
7 SAHARAN
**___ Desert of the Southwest:**
7 SONORAN
**Desert Storm**
missile: 4 SCUD
reporter Peter: 6 ARNETT
site: 4 IRAQ
**Deserve:** 4 EARN RATE
5 MERIT
a hand: 4 ANTE
**Deserved:** 3 DUE
**Desi**
Bandleader: 5 ARNAZ
Daughter of: 5 LUCIE
Wife of: 4 LUCY
**Desideratum:** 4 NEED
**Design:** 3 AIM 4 PLAN
detail: 4 SPEC
Inlaid: 6 MOSAIC
Interior: 5 DECOR
Stick-on: 5 DECAL
with acid: 4 ETCH
**Designate:** 3 TAP 4 NAME
TERM 5 ALLOT ELECT
6 ANOINT DENOTE
a new use for: 6 REZONE
**Designation:** 4 NAME 5 TITLE
**Designer**
concern: 5 DECOR
One-named: 4 ERTE
studio: 7 ATELIER
tool: 7 STENCIL
**"Designing Women"**
actress: 10 DELTABURKE
actress Annie: 5 POTTS
actress Delta: 5 BURKE
**Desilu**
partner: 5 ARNAZ
**Desirable**
guests: 5 ALIST
Most: 7 OPTIMAL
position: 4 PLUM
quality: 5 ASSET
**Desire:** 3 YEN 4 EROS ITCH
URGE WANT 5 COVET
CRAVE 6 THIRST
7 HOPEFOR
9 STREETCAR
Burning: 5 ARSON

Passionate: 4 LUST
Persistent: 7 CRAVING
Restless: 4 ITCH
Strong: 3 YEN 4 URGE
   6 THIRST
**Desist:** 4 STOP 5 CEASE
partner: 5 CEASE
**Desk**
item: 6 ERASER 7 STAPLER
type: 7 ROLLTOP
wood: 3 OAK
words: 5 INOUT
**Desktop**
item: 4 ICON
products: 3 PCS
symbol: 4 ICON
**Des Moines**
hrs.: 3 CST
resident: 5 IOWAN
state: 4 IOWA
university: 5 DRAKE
**Desmond**
of South Africa: 4 TUTU
___ de soie: 4 PEAU
**Desolate:** 4 LORN 5 STARK
region: 5 WILDS
**Despair**
Cry of: 4 OHNO
**Desperate:** 4 DIRE 7 DOORDIE
measure: 10 LASTRESORT
**"Desperate Housewives"**
actress Hatcher: 4 TERI
Longoria of: 3 EVA
network: 3 ABC
role: 4 EDIE BREE
**Desperation**
Act of:
   15 LASTDITCHEFFORT
tactic: 8 LASTGASP
**Despicable:** 3 LOW 4 VILE
More: 5 BASER
sort: 3 CUR 4 TOAD WORM
**Despise:** 4 HATE 5 ABHOR
   6 LOATHE
**Despoil:** 3 ROB 5 TAINT
**Despondent:** 3 SAD
cry: 4 OHME
**Despot:** 4 TSAR 6 TYRANT
1970s ~: 7 IDIAMIN
Bygone: 4 TSAR
Persian: 6 SATRAP
Roman: 4 NERO
Ugandan: 4 AMIN 7 IDIAMIN
**Despotism:** 7 TYRANNY
First name in: 3 IDI
**Dessert**
choice: 3 PIE 4 CAKE
Cold: 3 ICE 6 GELATO
   SORBET 7 SHERBET
Creamy: 6 MOUSSE
Crusty: 3 PIE
Custard: 4 FLAN
Dense: 6 GELATO
Dixie: 8 PECANPIE
Double: 10 PIEALAMODE
Eggy: 4 FLAN

Frozen: 6 SORBET
   7 SHERBET
Fruity: 3 PIE 4 TART
Green: 7 LIMEPIE
Rich: 4 CAKE 5 TORTE
   8 TIRAMISU
   9 CREAMCAKE
   10 CHEESECAKE
sandwich: 4 OREO
Southern: 8 PECANPIE
   10 SHOOFLYPIE
Spanish: 4 FLAN
style: 7 ALAMODE
vehicle: 4 CART
Wedding: 4 CAKE
wine: 4 PORT 6 MALAGA
   8 SAUTERNE
**Dessert ___:** 4 MENU
**Dest.**
Mail: 5 POBOX
**Destiny:** 3 LOT 4 FATE
   5 KARMA 6 KISMET
Asian: 5 KARMA
Dire: 4 DOOM
**Destiny's Child:** 4 TRIO
**Destitute:** 4 POOR 5 NEEDY
**Destroy:** 4 RUIN UNDO
   5 ERASE TOTAL TRASH
by degrees: 5 ERODE
gradually: 5 ERODE
~, as documents: 5 SHRED
**Destroyed:** 7 INRUINS
   8 TOREDOWN
Not: 6 EXTANT
**Destroyer**
detector: 5 SONAR
Hindu: 4 SIVA 5 SHIVA
letters: 3 USS
~, slangily: 6 TINCAN
**Destroyer, The:** 4 SIVA
   5 SHIVA
**Destruction:** 4 BANE LOSS
   RUIN 5 HAVOC
**Destructive**
compound: 3 TNT
episode: 7 RAMPAGE
insect: 5 BORER
**Detach:** 5 UNFIX UNPIN
   6 UNCLIP UNHOOK
   7 TEAROFF
gradually: 4 WEAN
**Detached:** 5 ALOOF APART
   8 STACCATO
~, in mus.: 4 STAC
**Detail:** 4 ITEM 7 ITEMIZE
Job: 4 SPEC
Map: 5 INSET
Small: 4 SPEC
Type: 5 SERIF
**Details**
Contract: 10 SMALLPRINT
Like some: 4 GORY
Missing: 7 SKETCHY
**Detained:** 4 HELD
**Detainee:** 6 INTERN
privilege: 7 ONECALL

**Detect:** 4 SPOT 5 SENSE
**Detected:** 4 SEEN
**Detection**
device: 5 RADAR SONAR
Escape: 5 ELUDE
Means of: 5 SCENT
**Detective:** 4 TAIL 6 SLEUTH
   TRACER 7 GUMSHOE
1950s ~: 4 GUNN
1970s TV ~: 4 TOMA
1990s TV ~ drama:
   15 DIAGNOSISMURDER
assignment: 4 CASE
dilemmas: 8 DEADENDS
discovery: 4 CLUE
dog: 4 ASTA
Fictional ~ name: 4 CHAN
   ERLE NERO
need: 4 LEAD
**Detectives:** 3 PIS
**Detective story:** 7 MYSTERY
discovery: 4 BODY
pioneer: 3 POE
writer ___ Stanley Gardner:
   4 ERLE
**Detector**
Destroyer: 5 SONAR
Motion: 6 SENSOR
Smoke: 4 NOSE
Sub: 5 SONAR
Submarine: 5 SONAR
Type of: 3 LIE 5 METAL
**Détente:** 4 THAW
Abandon: 5 REARM
**Detergent:** 4 SOAP
brand: 3 ERA 4 TIDE 5 CHEER
   PUREX
ingredient: 5 BORAX
Old ~ brand: 3 DUZ
target: 4 DIRT
**Deteriorate:** 3 ROT 4 RUST
   6 WORSEN 7 GOTOPOT
   8 GOTOSEED
Gradually: 5 ERODE
**Deterioration:** 4 WEAR
**Determinant**
Gender: 11 XCHROMOSOME
Trait: 4 GENE
**Determination:** 7 RESOLVE
   8 SELFWILL
**Determined:** 3 SET
   8 RESOLUTE
to follow: 5 SETON
**Deterrent**
Attack: 4 MACE MOAT
Burglar: 4 BARK 5 ALARM
Teamwork: 3 EGO
**Detest:** 4 HATE 5 ABHOR
   6 LOATHE
**Detestation:** 5 ODIUM
**Dethrone:** 4 OUST
**de Tirtoff, Romain**
pseudonym: 4 ERTE
___ de toilette: 3 EAU
**Detonate:** 6 SETOFF
   7 EXPLODE

It doesn't: 3 DUD
**Detonating**
device: 3 CAP 6 PETARD
___ **Detoo:** 5 ARTOO
**de Torquemada, ___:** 5 TOMAS
**Detour:** 5 AVERT 6 BYPASS
    DIVERT
Send on a: 7 REROUTE
**Detox**
center: 5 REHAB
**Detractor:** 4 ANTI
**Detrained:** 4 ALIT
___ **d'etre:** 6 RAISON
**Detriment:** 4 HARM
___ **de Triomphe:** 3 ARC
**Detritus:** 7 REMAINS
Cigarette: 3 ASH
Dryer: 4 LINT
Volcano: 3 ASH
___ **de trois:** 3 PAS
**Detroit**
baseballer: 5 TIGER
brewery name: 5 STROH
dud: 5 EDSEL
footballer: 4 LION
founder: 8 CADILLAC
labor gp.: 3 UAW
org.: 3 UAW
product: 3 CAR 4 AUTO
**Deuce:** 3 TWO 4 CARD
beater: 4 TREY
follower: 4 ADIN
pair: 4 PIPS
Score after: 4 ADIN 5 ADOUT
topper: 4 TREY
~, in tennis: 3 TIE
**Deucey**
lead-in: 4 ACEY
**Deut.**
Book before: 3 NUM
**Deuterium**
discoverer: 4 UREY
**Deutsch:** 6 GERMAN
**"Deutschland ___ Alles":**
    4 UBER
**"Deutschland uber ___":**
    5 ALLES
**Deux**
follower: 5 TROIS
Pas de ~ section: 6 ADAGIO
plus trois: 4 CINQ
preceder: 3 UNE
___ **deux:** 5 PASDE
**De Valera**
land: 4 EIRE
of Ireland: 5 EAMON
**Devalue:** 7 CHEAPEN
**Devastate:** 4 RUIN 6 RAVAGE
**Devastation:** 4 RUIN 5 HAVOC
**Develop:** 4 GROW 5 ARISE
    6 EMERGE EVOLVE
    UNFOLD
Begin to: 4 DAWN
into: 6 BECOME
slowly: 6 EVOLVE 7 GESTATE
Starting to: 7 NASCENT

**Developed:** 6 MATURE
Fully: 4 RIPE
**Developer**
map: 4 PLAT
site: 3 LOT
**Developing:** 7 NASCENT
    9 INCIPIENT
area: 4 WOMB 8 DARKROOM
**Development**
Land: 6 CAMERA
phase: 5 STAGE
Place for: 7 SEEDBED
site: 8 PHOTOLAB
Stage of: 5 PHASE
unit: 4 ACRE HOME
**Devereux, Robert**
earldom: 5 ESSEX
**Devers**
Runner: 4 GAIL
**Deviate:** 3 YAW 4 SKEW VARY
    VEER
**Deviation:** 3 YAW 7 ANOMALY
    9 ABERRANCE
Course: 3 YAW
Standard ~ symbol: 5 SIGMA
**Device:** 4 RUSE 6 GADGET
**"___ de vie" (brandy):** 3 EAU
**Devil:** 5 DEMON SATAN
dog: 6 MARINE
doing: 4 EVIL
Little: 3 IMP
**"Devil and Daniel Webster,**
    **The"**
author: 5 BENET
**Deviled**
item: 3 EGG
**Devilfish:** 5 MANTA
**Devilish:** 7 SATANIC
look: 4 GRIN
sort: 3 IMP
**Devilkin:** 3 IMP
**DeVille:** 3 CAR 4 AUTO
**Devil-may-care:** 4 RASH
**Devil Rays**
home: 5 TAMPA
**Devil's Island**
escapee Belbenoit: 4 RENE
**Devious:** 3 SLY
More: 5 SLYER
move: 4 PLOY
plan: 5 ANGLE 6 SCHEME
**Devise:** 6 CREATE
~, as a plot: 5 HATCH
**Devitalize:** 3 SAP
**DeVito**
Actor: 5 DANNY
sitcom: 4 TAXI
___ **de vivre:** 4 JOIE
**Devoid:** 6 BEREFT
**Devon**
capital: 6 EXETER
river: 3 EXE
**Devonshire**
city: 6 EXETER
dad: 5 PATER
river: 3 EXE

seat: 6 EXETER
**Devoted:** 5 LOYAL 6 ARDENT
**Devotee:** 3 FAN NUT
    7 ACOLYTE
    8 IDOLATER
**Devotion:** 6 NOVENA
Blind: 8 IDOLATRY
Intense: 5 ARDOR
Object of: 4 IDOL
**Devour:** 3 EAT 5 EATUP
**Devoured:** 3 ATE 5 EATEN
**Devout:** 5 GODLY PIOUS
petition: 6 ORISON
**Devoutness:** 5 PIETY
**Dew**
Bit of: 4 DROP
Frozen: 4 HOAR
**de Waart**
Conductor: 3 EDO
**Dewey**
Donald, to: 4 UNCA
~, for one (abbr.): 3 ADM
~, to Donald Duck:
    6 NEPHEW
**Dewey, Thomas**
hometown: 6 OWOSSO
**Dewlap:** 4 JOWL
**de Wolfe**
Decorator: 5 ELSIE
**De-wrinkle:** 4 IRON
**Dewy:** 3 WET 4 DAMP
**Dewy-eyed:** 5 NAIVE
Get: 4 TEAR
**Dexterity:** 3 ART 4 EASE
    5 CRAFT SKILL
prefix: 4 AMBI
**Dexterous:** 4 DEFT 5 AGILE
    6 ADROIT
**Dextrous**
prefix: 4 AMBI
**Dey, Susan**
TV series: 5 LALAW
**D flat**
equivalent: 6 CSHARP
**DH:** 4 ALER
stat: 3 RBI
___ **Dhabi:** 3 ABU
**Dharma**
Husband of: 4 GREG
She played: 5 JENNA
**"Dharma & Greg"**
actress Elfman: 5 JENNA
actress Jenna: 6 ELFMAN
**d'honneur**
Affaire: 4 DUEL
___ **d'hôtel:** 6 MAITRE
**Dhow:** 4 BOAT
crewman: 4 ARAB
**Di-**
doubled: 5 TETRA
**Diablo**
He rode: 5 CISCO
**Diabolical:** 4 EVIL 5 CRUEL
**Diacritical**
mark: 5 HACEK TILDE
    6 UMLAUT

**Diagnostic**
scanner (abbr.): 3 MRI
test: 4 SCAN
tool: 6 CTSCAN 7 TESTKIT
tool (abbr.): 3 EEG MRI
**Diagonal:** 4 BIAS
**Diagonally:** 6 ASLOPE
     11 KITTYCORNER
**Diagram:** 4 GRID 6 SCHEMA
Family: 4 TREE
Genealogy: 4 TREE
grammatically: 5 PARSE
Guitar: 5 CHORD
**Dial:** 4 KNOB
0 on a ~: 4 OPER
2 on a ~: 3 ABC
3 on a ~: 3 DEF
4 on a ~: 3 GHI
5 on a ~: 3 JKL
6 on a ~: 3 MNO
7 on a ~: 3 PRS
8 on a ~: 3 TUV
9 on a ~: 3 WXY
Dashboard: 4 TACH
Find on the: 6 TUNETO
on a dash: 4 TACH
Radio: 4 KNOB
sound: 4 TONE
Top of a: 3 XII
**Dialect:** 5 ARGOT IDIOM
     LINGO 6 PATOIS
**Dialogue**
writer: 5 PLATO
**Dial-up**
device: 5 MODEM
**Diameter**
halves: 5 RADII
Inside: 4 BORE
Wire ~ measure: 3 MIL
~, in ballistics: 7 CALIBER
**Diametrically**
opposed: 5 POLAR
**Diamond:** 4 CARD 5 SHAPE
Info: Baseball cue
arbiter: 3 UMP
authority: 3 UMP
bag: 4 BASE
call: 3 OUT 4 SAFE
center: 5 MOUND
club: 3 BAT
corner: 3 BAG 4 BASE
cover: 4 TARP
data: 4 OUTS 5 STATS
datum: 5 STEAL
execs: 3 GMS
family name: 4 ALOU
flaw: 5 ERROR
girl: 3 LIL
group: 4 NINE
makeup: 6 CARBON
number: 4 NINE
of note: 4 NEIL
pattern: 6 ARGYLE
plate: 4 HOME
protection: 4 TARP
side: 5 FACET

Singer: 4 NEIL
situation: 5 ONEON
stat: 3 ERA RBI 5 ATBAT
sultanate: 4 SWAT
surface: 5 FACET
Up on the: 5 ATBAT
weight: 5 CARAT
**Diamond ___:** 3 LIL
**Diamondback:** 8 TERRAPIN
**Diamondbacks, The**
~, on scoreboards: 3 ARI
**Diamond Head**
locale: 4 OAHU
**Diamonds:** 3 ICE 4 SUIT
Big name in: 7 DEBEERS
**"Diamonds and Rust"**
singer Joan: 4 BAEZ
**"Diamonds ___ Forever":** 3 ARE
**Diamond-shaped**
pattern: 6 ARGYLE
**Diana**
Actress: 4 DORS RIGG
Singer: 4 ROSS
Swimmer: 4 NYAD
**"Diana"**
singer: 4 ANKA
**Diane**
Actress: 4 LADD 6 KEATON
**"Dianetics"**
author Hubbard: 4 LRON
**Dianne**
Actress: 5 WIEST
**Diaper**
~, in Britain: 5 NAPPY
**Diaphanous:** 4 THIN 5 SHEER
**Diaphragm**
Camera: 4 IRIS
Colorful: 4 IRIS
spasm noise: 3 HIC
**Diarist**
French: 3 NIN
of note: 3 NIN 5 PEPYS
Palindromic: 3 NIN
**Diary:** 3 LOG 6 MEMOIR
     7 JOURNAL
capacity: 4 YEAR
item: 5 ENTRY
name: 4 ANNE
opener: 4 DEAR
passage: 5 ENTRY
**"Diary of ___ Housewife":**
     4 AMAD
**Dias**
365 ~: 3 ANO
**Diatribe:** 4 RANT 6 SCREED
     TIRADE
**Diaz de Vivar, Rodrigo:** 5 ELCID
**DiCaprio**
role: 5 ROMEO
~, to friends: 3 LEO
**Dice:** 5 BONES CUBES
Loser at the ~ table:
     9 SNAKEEYES
roll: 5 THROW
Throw, as: 4 CAST TOSS
Throw the ~ again: 6 REROLL

**Diciembre**
follower: 5 ENERO
**Dick**
1956 counterpart of ~:
     5 ESTES
Detective: 5 TRACY
Ex of: 3 LIZ
Sportscaster: 6 ENBERG
Tom, ~, or Harry: 4 MALE
     NAME
**"___ Dick":** 4 MOBY
**Dick and Jane**
dog: 4 SPOT
**Dickens**
alias: 3 BOZ
boy: 3 TIM 7 TINYTIM
character: 5 DROOD RUDGE
     URIAH 7 TINYTIM
character Drood: 5 EDWIN
character Heep: 5 URIAH
character Pecksniff: 4 SETH
character Uriah: 4 HEEP
clerk: 4 HEEP
girl: 4 NELL
pen name: 3 BOZ
title starter: 5 ATALE
villain: 5 FAGIN
Went like the: 4 FLEW SPED
     TORE
**Dickensian**
clerk: 5 URIAH
cry: 3 BAH
lad: 3 TIM
outburst: 3 BAH
**Dicker:** 6 HAGGLE
**Dickerson**
of football: 4 ERIC
**Dickinson:** 4 POET
Actress: 5 ANGIE
Poet: 5 EMILY
**Dickinson, Emily:** 4 POET
     7 POETESS
home: 7 AMHERST
**Dict.**
entries: 3 WDS
entry: 3 DEF SYN
label: 3 ADJ OBS
listing: 3 SYN
offering: 3 DEF SYN 4 ETYM
**Dictation**
taker: 5 STENO
**Dictator:** 8 AUTOCRAT
aide: 5 STENO
problem: 8 EGOMANIA
**Dictatorship:** 10 ONEMANRULE
**Dictionary**
abbr.: 3 OBS VAR
entry: 4 WORD
Hi-tech ~ medium: 5 CDROM
info: 5 USAGE
listing: 5 ENTRY
word: 5 ENTRY
**___ dictum:** 6 OBITER
**Did**
in: 4 SLEW
nothing: 3 SAT 5 SATBY

**Diddley**
and others: 3 BOS
**Diddley, Bo**
hit song: 6 IMAMAN
**Diddly:** 3 NIL
**Diddly-squat:** 3 NIL
**Diddy, P.**
First name of: 4 SEAN
**Didion**
Novelist: 4 JOAN
**"Didn't I tell you?":** 3 SEE
**Dido**
Lover of: 6 AENEAS
Work in which ~ died:
6 AENEID
**Didrikson**
Sportswoman: 4 BABE
**"Did you ___?":** 4 EVER
**"Did You Ever ___ Lassie?":**
4 SEEA
**"Did you forget about me?":**
4 AHEM
**Die:** 4 CUBE 6 EXPIRE
down: 3 EBB 4 WANE
5 ABATE
(out): 5 PETER
**Dieciseis**
Half of: 4 OCHO
**"Die Fledermaus":** 5 OPERA
composer: 7 STRAUSS
maid: 5 ADELE
**___ Diego:** 3 SAN
**Diehard**
Like ~ fans: 4 AVID
**"Die Lorelei"**
poet: 5 HEINE
**___ diem:** 3 PER 5 CARPE
**"Die Meistersinger"**
soprano: 3 EVA
**"___ Dien" (Prince of Wales**
motto): 3 ICH
**"Dies ___":** 4 IRAE
**Diesel**
Actor: 3 VIN
**Diet:** 4 FARE 5 LOFAT NOCAL
6 LOWCAL
doctor: 6 ATKINS
Kind of: 6 NOSALT
9 SCARSDALE
Like many ~ foods: 6 NONFAT
Overdo a: 6 STARVE
Soft: 3 PAP
Stable: 4 OATS
successfully: 4 LOSE
Word on a ~ product: 4 LITE
**___ diet:** 3 ONA
**Dietary**
abbr.: 3 RDA
concern: 3 FAT
label: 5 LOFAT
need: 4 IRON
~, in ads: 4 LITE
**Diet Coke**
forerunner: 3 TAB
**Dieter**
concern: 3 FAT 9 WAISTLINE

**dish:** 5 SALAD
**dread:** 4 GAIN
no-no: 3 FAT 6 SWEETS
of rhyme: 5 SPRAT
temptation: 5 AROMA
unit: 7 CALORIE
word: 4 LITE
**Dietetic:** 5 LOFAT NOFAT
**"___ dieu!":** 3 MON
**Differ**
suffix: 3 ENT 4 ENCE
**Difference**
Make a: 5 ALTER 6 MATTER
14 CHANGETHEWORLD
Subtle: 6 NUANCE
Time: 3 LAG
**"___ difference!":** 4 SAME
**Different:** 4 ELSE 5 OTHER
In a ~ form: 4 ANEW
In a ~ manner: 4 ELSE
**Differently:** 4 ELSE
**"Different Read on Life, A"**
magazine: 4 UTNE
**Difficult:** 4 HARD 6 ORNERY
TAXING TRYING
7 LABORED
duty: 4 ONUS
journey: 4 TREK
Make less: 4 EASE
Not: 4 EASY
spot: 7 HOTSEAT
test: 6 ORDEAL
**Difficulty:** 3 ADO RUB 4 SNAG
Got with: 3 EKE
Manage with: 4 COPE
**Diffident:** 3 SHY
**"Diff'rent Strokes"**
actress Charlotte: 3 RAE
actress Plato: 4 DANA
**Diffuse:** 6 OSMOSE
**DiFranco**
Singer: 3 ANI
**Dig:** 5 DELVE 6 TUNNEL
a lot: 5 ADORE
deeply: 5 ADORE
find: 5 RELIC
for: 4 SEEK
fragment: 5 SHARD
in: 3 EAT
into: 3 EAT
(into): 5 DELVE
it: 3 ORE 4 HOLE
like a pig: 4 ROOT
this: 3 ORE
(up): 6 DREDGE
You can ~ it: 3 ORE 4 HOLE
6 TRENCH
**"Dig?":** 5 GETIT
**Digestive:** 6 PEPTIC
aid: 4 BILE 6 SALIVA
**Digger:** 5 SPADE 6 TROWEL
Gold: 5 MINER
**Digging:** 4 INTO
tool: 5 SPADE 6 SHOVEL
**Diggs**
Actor: 4 TAYE

**"Dig in!":** 3 EAT 7 LETSEAT
**Digit**
Binary: 3 ONE
Hitchhiker's: 5 THUMB
Largest: 4 NINE
Low: 3 TOE
Pedal: 3 TOE
**Digital**
communication (abbr.): 3 ASL
First ~ computer: 5 ENIAC
Not: 6 ANALOG
readout: 3 LCD
**Digitize:** 4 SCAN
**Digits**
ID: 3 SSN
Number with 101: 6 GOOGOL
**Dignified:** 5 STAID
Stiffly: 7 STILTED
woman: 6 MATRON
**Dignify:** 7 ENNOBLE
**Dignitary:** 3 VIP
Church: 7 PRELATE
Foreign: 4 EMIR
Indian: 5 RANEE
**Dignity**
Amount of: 5 SHRED
Retain some: 8 SAVEFACE
With: 5 NOBLY
**Digress:** 5 STRAY
15 GOOFFONATANGENT
**Digression:** 5 ASIDE
7 TANGENT
**Digs:** 5 ABODE
Campus: 4 DORM
Dirty: 3 STY
Dog's: 6 KENNEL
of twigs: 4 NEST
Pig's: 3 PEN STY
Squalid: 4 SLUM
**DIII**
doubled: 3 MVI
**Dik-dik:** 8 ANTELOPE
**Dike:** 5 LEVEE
problem: 4 LEAK
~, Eunomia, and Irene:
5 HORAE
**Dilapidated:** 5 RATTY
6 SHABBY 8 DECREPIT
dwelling: 5 SHACK
7 RATTRAP
**Dilbert**
creator: 5 ADAMS
Like: 5 NERDY
Note for: 4 MEMO
**"Dilbert"**
cartoonist: 5 ADAMS
10 SCOTTADAMS
intern: 4 ASOK
**Dilemma:** 4 BIND
Dermal: 4 ACNE
**Dilettante:** 7 AMATEUR
Be a: 6 DABBLE
dabblings: 4 ARTS
**Dilettantish:** 4 ARTY 5 ARTSY
**Diligent**
worker: 5 PLIER

**Diligently**
  Work: 3 PLY
**Dillinger**
  Org. that stopped: 3 FBI
**Dillon**
  Actor: 4 MATT
  Actress: 7 MELINDA
**Dillon, Marshal**
  portrayer: 6 ARNESS
**Dilly:** 4 LULU ONER 5 BEAUT
    PEACH
**Dillydally:** 3 LAG 4 IDLE
    6 DAWDLE LOITER
**Dilute:** 4 THIN
**Diluted:** 4 WEAK 6 WATERY
  Not: 4 PURE
**Dim:** 4 FADE 5 BLEAR UNLIT
    6 DARKEN
  Become: 4 FADE
**DiMaggio**
  nickname:
    13 YANKEECLIPPER
  of baseball: 3 DOM JOE
**Dime:** 4 COIN
  A ~ a dozen: 4 RATE
  Item shown on a: 5 TORCH
  Like a: 4 THIN
  Word on a: 3 ONE
    7 LIBERTY
  Words before: 3 ONA
**Dimension:** 5 DEPTH WIDTH
  The fourth: 4 TIME
**Dimensions:** 4 SIZE
**Dimethyl**
  sulfate: 5 ESTER
**Dimin.**
  Opposite of: 5 CRESC
**Diminish:** 3 EBB 4 BATE FADE
    WANE 5 ABATE
    6 LESSEN RECEDE
**Diminished**
  by: 4 LESS 5 MINUS
**Diminutive:** 3 WEE 5 SMALL
    TEENY 6 PETITE
    TEENSY
  Comics: 3 LIL
  Dogpatch: 3 LIL
  suffix: 3 CLE INO ULA ULE
    4 ETTA ETTE LING
**Dimmer:** 8 RHEOSTAT
**Dimwit:** 4 BOZO DOLT SIMP
    5 IDIOT STUPE
    6 STOOGE
**Din:** 4 ROAR 5 NOISE
    7 CLATTER
  Den: 4 ROAR
**"___ Din":** 5 GUNGA
**Dinah**
  Singer: 5 SHORE
**"___ Dinah"** (Frankie Avalon
    hit): 4 DEDE
**Dinars**
  100 ~: 4 RIAL
  spender: 5 IRANI IRAQI
**Dine:** 3 EAT SUP
  at home: 5 EATIN

Wine and: 3 WOO 4 FETE
    6 REGALE
**Dined:** 3 ATE 5 ATEIN
**Diner:** 3 CAR 5 EATER
    6 EATERY
  card: 4 MENU
  cupful: 3 JOE
  dish: 4 HASH
  display: 4 PIES
  Down, at a: 7 ONTOAST
  employee: 7 FRYCOOK
  handout: 4 MENU
  hodgepodge: 4 HASH
  On toast, at a: 4 DOWN
  order: 3 BLT 6 OMELET
  sandwich: 3 BLT
  side dish: 4 SLAW
  sign: 4 EATS 7 EATHERE
  Sitcom: 4 MELS
  Sitcom ~ owner: 3 MEL
  TV: 4 MELS
  TV ~ owner: 3 MEL
**Dinero:** 4 GELT 5 MOOLA
    PESOS 6 MOOLAH
  Bit of: 4 PESO
**Dines**
  at home: 6 EATSIN
**Dinesen**
  Author: 4 ISAK
  Real name of: 6 BLIXEN
**Dinette**
  spot: 4 NOOK
**Ding:** 4 DENT
**Ding-a-___:** 4 LING
**Dingbat:** 5 IDIOT NINNY
**Dinghy:** 4 BOAT
  need: 3 OAR
  propeller: 3 OAR
**___ Dinh Diem:** 3 NGO
**Dining**
  Like patio: 8 ALFRESCO
  option: 8 ALACARTE
**"___ Dinka Doo":** 4 INKA
**Dinner:** 4 MEAL
  and a movie: 4 DATE
  Ceremonial: 5 SEDER
  course: 4 SOUP 5 SALAD
    6 ENTREE 7 DESSERT
  Had: 3 ATE
  Had ~ at home: 5 ATEIN
  Have: 3 EAT SUP
  Have ~ at home: 5 EATIN
  jacket: 6 TUXEDO
  Offers for: 8 SERVESUP
  Pay for: 5 TREAT
  Point at the ~ table: 4 TINE
  Private: 4 MESS
  Rude ~ guest: 7 REACHER
  Served ~ to: 3 FED
**Dinnerware:** 5 CHINA
    6 PLATES
  Piece of: 5 PLATE
**Dinning, Mark**
  hit song: 9 TEENANGEL
**Dino**
  Master of: 4 FRED

tail: 4 SAUR
  ~, to Fred: 3 PET
**Dinosaur:** 5 RELIC
    7 HASBEEN
  Frightening: 4 TREX
  Tall: 4 TREX
**Dinsdale, Shirley**
  award: 4 EMMY
**Dinsmore**
  of children's literature:
    5 ELSIE
**Dinty Moore**
  product: 4 STEW
**Diocese**
  head: 6 BISHOP
**Diogenes:** 5 CYNIC 6 SEEKER
**Dion**
  Singer: 6 CELINE
**Dion and the Belmonts**
  hit song: 10 NOONEKNOWS
    15 ATEENAGERINLOVE
**Dionne**
  kid: 5 QUINT
  Where the ~ quints were born:
    7 ONTARIO
**Dionysus**
  attendant: 5 SATYR
  Bride of: 7 ARIADNE
  Mother of: 6 SEMELE
  Priestess of: 6 MAENAD
**Dior**
  creation: 5 ALINE
**Dip:** 3 SAG
  Chip: 5 SALSA
  Go for a: 4 SWIM
  into coffee: 4 DUNK
  Zesty: 5 SALSA
**Diphthong:** 7 PHONEME
**Diploma**
  (abbr.): 4 CERT
  holder: 4 GRAD
  word: 3 CUM 5 LAUDE
    MAGNA SUMMA
**Diplomacy:** 4 TACT
  breakdown: 4 RIFT
  Root of: 5 ELIHU
**Diplomatic**
  agent: 5 ENVOY
  etiquette: 8 PROTOCOL
  goal: 7 ENTENTE
  representative: 5 ENVOY
  trait: 4 TACT
  woe: 4 RIFT
**Dipper**
  Big: 5 LADLE
  Skinny: 3 EEL
  unit: 4 STAR
**Dipsomaniac:** 3 SOT
**Dipstick:** 3 ROD
  word: 3 ADD
**Dir.:** 3 ENE ESE NNE NNW SSE
    SSW WNW WSW
**Dire**
  fate: 4 DOOM
  In ~ straits: 5 NEEDY
**___ dire:** 4 VOIR

**Direct:** 5 ORDER REFER
STEER 6 HEADON
7 OVERSEE
15 STRAIGHTFORWARD
elsewhere: 5 REFER
ending: 3 IVE
route: 7 BEELINE
**Directed:** 3 LED RAN 4 BADE
against a thing: 5 INREM
at: 6 SENTTO
Do as: 4 OBEY
skyward: 6 UPCAST
**"___ directed":** 5 USEAS
**Direction:** 4 PATH 5 ROUTE
(abbr.): 3 ENE ESE NNE NNW
SSE SSW WNW WSW
Change: 4 VEER
Chef's: 4 STIR
Cookbook: 4 HEAT STIR
5 PUREE
Dawn's: 4 EAST
General: 5 TREND
German: 3 OST
In the ~ of: 6 TOWARD
Nautical: 3 AFT 4 ALEE
5 ABEAM APORT
Paint can: 4 STIR
Point in the right: 6 ORIENT
Recipe: 4 STIR 6 STIRIN
Sailor's: 4 ALEE
Script: 5 ENTER
Stage: 4 EXIT 5 ENTER
Sunrise: 4 EAST
Sunset: 4 WEST
Sunup: 4 EAST
Whaler's: 4 THAR
**Directional**
prefix: 3 UNI
suffix: 3 ERN
**Directions**
In need of: 4 LOST
It follows: 3 ERN
**Directive:** 5 ORDER 6 BEHEST
7 PRECEPT
Culinary: 4 STIR
Drill: 6 ATEASE
Memo: 4 ASAP
Recipe: 4 STIR
**Directly:** 3 DUE 4 ANON
8 ONEONONE
Go: 7 BEELINE
opposed: 8 TOETOTOE
**Direct-mail**
sticker: 3 YES
**Director:** 4 BOSS
bane: 3 HAM
cry: 3 CUT 6 ACTION
Personnel: 5 HIRER
prerogative: 5 RECUT
6 RETAKE
Traffic: 4 CONE 5 ARROW
**Directory:** 4 LIST
contents: 5 NAMES
**Dirigible:** 5 BLIMP
8 AEROSTAT
Like a: 5 RIGID

parts: 5 KEELS
**Dirk:** 6 DAGGER
Use a: 4 STAB
**Dirksen**
Senator: 7 EVERETT
**Dirndl:** 5 SKIRT
**Dirt:** 4 INFO SMUT 5 FILTH
GRIME PORNO
bike cousin: 3 ATV
Dish the: 6 GOSSIP
Flue: 4 SOOT
Lump of: 4 CLOD
Pay: 3 ORE
road feature: 3 RUT
Stubborn: 5 GRIME
Treat like: 5 ABUSE
**Dirtbag:** 3 CAD
**Dirty:** 4 LEWD SOIL 6 SOILED
7 POLLUTE UNCLEAN
air: 4 SMOG
dealing: 8 FOULPLAY
digs: 3 STY
dog: 3 CAD CUR RAT
Get: 4 SOIL
look: 4 LEER 5 GLARE
Make: 4 SOIL
money: 4 PELF
rat: 5 LOUSE 7 SOANDSO
**"Dirty"**
activity: 4 POOL
dish: 4 RICE
**"Dirty Dancing"**
star: 6 SWAYZE
**Dirty Harry**
employer (abbr.): 4 SFPD
portrayer: 5 CLINT
**Dis:** 4 SASS SLAM 6 INSULT
Not: 3 DAT
**Disable:** 4 MAIM
**Disabled**
On the ~ list: 4 HURT
___ disadvantage: 3 ATA
**Disadvantaged:** 5 NEEDY
**Disagree:** 5 CLASH 6 DIFFER
**Disagreeable:** 4 SOUR UGLY
5 TESTY
burden: 4 ONUS
people: 5 PILLS
**Disagreeing:** 6 ATODDS
**Disagreement:** 3 ROW 4 SPAT
In: 6 ATODDS
**Disallow:** 3 BAN 4 DENY
**Disappear:** 6 PERISH VANISH
gradually: 4 FADE
into thin air: 9 EVAPORATE
Some things ~ into it:
7 THINAIR
**Disappearance**
Sound of: 4 POOF
**Disappearing**
sea: 4 ARAL
transports: 3 ELS
**Disappoint:** 7 LETDOWN
**Disappointment:** 7 LETDOWN
Sound of: 3 TSK
Sounds of: 3 AWS

**Disapproval**
Look of: 5 FROWN
One showing: 6 CHIDER
Shout of: 3 BOO
Sound of: 3 TSK TUT
6 TUTTUT 9 RASPBERRY
Voice ~ of: 6 HISSAT
**Disapproving**
sound: 3 TSK TUT
**Disarrange:** 4 MUSS
7 UNSTACK
**Disarray:** 4 MESS
In: 5 MESSY 7 CHAOTIC
**Disassemble:** 5 UNRIG
**Disaster:** 6 FIASCO 7 DEBACLE
8 CALAMITY
Environmental: 7 ECOCIDE
relief org.: 4 FEMA
Small: 6 MISHAP
**Disastrous:** 4 DIRE 5 FATAL
**Disavow:** 4 DENY
**Disburden:** 4 EASE
**Disburse:** 5 SPEND
**Discard:** 5 SCRAP
Corn eater's: 3 COB
Delicious: 4 CORE
**Discarded:** 7 OFFCAST
9 TOSSEDOUT
**Discern:** 3 SEE 4 ESPY TELL
**Discerning:** 4 SAGE 7 SAPIENT
**Discernment:** 3 EYE 5 TASTE
Musical: 3 EAR
**Discharge:** 4 EMIT FIRE SPEW
5 EGEST LETGO
7 RELEASE 8 EMISSION
Brit's: 5 DEMOB
letters: 3 TNT
**Disciple:** 7 APOSTLE
query: 5 ISITI
**Disciplinarian**
Like a: 5 STERN
reading: 7 RIOTACT
**Discipline:** 5 RIGOR
Dojo: 6 KARATE
Eastern: 3 ZEN 4 YOGA
Exercise: 4 YOGA
Hindu: 4 YOGA
Meditative: 3 ZEN
Tranquil: 4 YOGA
**Disclaimer:** 8 NEGATION
Tag: 4 ASIS
**Disclose:** 6 IMPART REVEAL
7 CONFIDE
**Disco**
dancer type: 4 GOGO
fixture: 6 STROBE
hit song: 4 YMCA
light: 6 STROBE
musical style: 6 TECHNO
Phrase in ~ names: 5 AGOGO
Rick of: 4 DEES
**Disco ___ (character on "The
Simpsons"):** 3 STU
**Discolor:** 5 STAIN
**Discombobulate:** 5 ADDLE
UPSET

Discombobulated: 5 ATSEA
Discomfit: 4 FAZE 5 ABASH
UPSET
Discomfort: 4 ACHE 6 UNEASE
7 MALAISE
Discompose: 5 ABASH
7 PERTURB
Disconcert: 4 FAZE 5 ABASH
Disconnect: 6 UNPLUG
Discontinue: 4 DROP QUIT
STOP 5 CEASE SEVER
8 SURCEASE
Discord: 6 STRIFE
Goddess of: 4 ERIS
Norse god of: 4 LOKI
Discordant: 4 AJAR
Discordia
counterpart: 4 ERIS
Discotheque
effect: 6 STROBE
phrase: 5 AGOGO
Discount: 6 IGNORE REBATE
label abbr.: 3 IRR
rack abbr.: 3 IRR 5 IRREG
With a ~ of: 4 LESS
Words before: 3 ATA
Discounted: 4 LESS 6 ONSALE
by: 4 LESS
Some ~ items: 5 DEMOS
Discourage: 5 DETER
Discouraging
word: 3 BAH TUT
words: 3 NOS 4 NOES
Discourse
Lengthy: 6 SCREED
Discourteous: 4 RUDE
Discover: 5 LEARN 6 DETECT
7 FINDOUT UNEARTH
by chance: 5 HITON
~, as an idea: 5 HITON
Discovered: 5 FOUND 6 LEARNT
Discoverer
cry: 3 AHA OHO
Discovery: 4 FIND
Cry of: 3 AHA OHO 6 EUREKA
Dawn: 3 DEW
Detective's: 4 CLUE
Dig: 5 RELIC
gp.: 4 NASA
Pollster's: 5 TREND
Valuable: 5 TROVE
Discovery Channel
subj.: 3 SCI
Discredit: 5 DECRY TAINT
6 DEFAME 8 TEARDOWN
Discreet: 7 POLITIC
Discrete: 5 APART
part: 4 UNIT
unit: 6 ENTITY
Discretion: 4 TACT 5 SAYSO
Discriminating
person: 6 AGEIST
Discrimination: 5 TASTE
basis: 4 RACE
Type of: 6 AGEISM SEXISM
watchdog (abbr.): 4 EEOC

Discriminator: 6 AGEIST
SEXIST
Discs: 3 LPS
Discus
champ Al: 6 OERTER
Discuss: 6 GOINTO 7 GETINTO
again: 6 REHASH
in detail: 7 HASHOUT
pros and cons: 6 DEBATE
~, with "out": 4 HASH
Discussion: 7 PALAVER
group: 5 PANEL
Informal: 10 RAPSESSION
11 BULLSESSION
Online: 4 CHAT
panel: 5 FORUM
Under: 7 ATISSUE
venue: 5 FORUM
Disdain: 5 SCORN
8 CONTEMPT
Feigned: 10 SOURGRAPES
Look of: 5 SNEER
Reject with: 5 SPURN
Show: 5 SCORN SNEER
Word of: 4 POOH
Disease
Grass: 5 ERGOT
Teen: 4 MONO
Disenchanted
Become: 4 SOUR
Disencumber: 3 RID
Disentangle: 5 RAVEL
6 UNKNOT 7 UNSNARL
Disfigure: 3 MAR 4 MAIM
Disgorge: 4 SPEW
Disgrace: 5 ODIUM SHAME
Disgruntled: 4 SORE
sound: 3 UGH
Disguise: 4 MASK 5 CLOAK
Disguised: 9 INCOGNITO
~, for short: 5 INCOG
Disgust: 6 NAUSEA OFFEND
SICKEN
Cry of: 3 BAH FIE PAH UGH
Sound of: 3 UGH
Disgusted: 5 FEDUP
Disgusting: 4 ICKY 5 GROSS
Dish: 5 CUTEY CUTIE PLATE
alternative: 5 CABLE
7 ANTENNA
Beef: 4 STEW
Brunch: 6 OMELET
Cabbage: 4 SLAW
Cheese: 7 RAREBIT
Deep: 6 TUREEN
Diner: 4 HASH
Dixie: 5 GRITS
Dover: 4 SOLE
Egg: 6 OMELET
Fish: 3 COD 4 HAKE SOLE
5 SCROD
Folded: 6 OMELET
for culture: 5 PETRI
Garlicky: 6 SCAMPI
Hawaiian: 3 POI
Islands: 3 POI

Japanese: 5 SUSHI
Jellied: 5 ASPIC
Kind of: 5 PETRI
Leftovers: 4 HASH
Luau: 3 POI
Main: 6 ENTREE
manufacturer: 3 RCA
Meat: 4 STEW 7 ROULADE
name: 5 PETRI
Picnic: 4 SLAW
Rice: 5 PILAF 6 PAELLA
Russian: 5 BLINI
Scottish: 6 HAGGIS
Shrimp: 6 SCAMPI
Side: 4 DISH
Slung: 4 HASH
Southern: 5 GRITS
Spanish: 6 PAELLA
Taro: 3 POI
Tasty: 5 VIAND
___ dish: 5 PETRI
Dishearten: 5 DAUNT
6 DEJECT 7 DEPRESS
Dishes
Company: 5 CHINA
Help with the: 3 DRY 4 WIPE
List of: 4 MENU
Dishevel: 6 TOUSLE
Disheveled: 5 MESSY
6 RAGTAG 7 UNKEMPT
Dishonest
Be ~ with: 5 LIETO
sort: 5 SNEAK
Was ~ with: 6 LIEDTO
Dishonesty
Suspect: 9 SMELLARAT
Dishonor: 5 ABASE SHAME
STAIN TAINT
Trace of: 5 TAINT
Dishwasher
cycle: 5 RINSE
Dishwater
Dull as: 4 BLAH DRAB
Like: 4 DULL 5 SUDSY
Disinclined: 5 LOATH
6 AVERSE
Disinfectant: 5 LYSOL
Disinfest: 5 DERAT
Disk
Clear, as a: 5 ERASE
contents: 4 DATA
function: 7 STORAGE
On: 6 STORED
Prepare a ~ for writing:
6 FORMAT
suffix: 4 ETTE
Thrown: 7 FRISBEE
Dislike
Intense: 5 ODIUM 6 HATRED
More than: 4 HATE 5 ABHOR
6 DETEST LOATHE
Disloyal: 5 FALSE 6 UNTRUE
Dismal: 4 GRIM 5 AWFUL
SORRY 6 DREARY
Dismay: 4 FAZE 5 ALARM
APPAL 6 APPALL

Cries of: 3 OYS
Cry of: 4 ALAS OHNO
Words of: 4 OHNO 5 OYVEY
**Dismiss:** 3 AXE 4 SACK
    5 LETGO
derisively: 7 SNEERAT
lightly: 8 POOHPOOH
unceremoniously: 4 BOOT
**Dismounted:** 4 ALIT
**Disney**
1940 ~ film: 8 FANTASIA
1955 ~ film:
    15 LADYANDTHETRAMP
1957 ~ film: 9 OLDYELLER
1982 ~ film: 4 TRON
1998 ~ film: 5 MULAN
acquisition: 3 ABC
Animator: 4 WALT
collectible: 3 CEL
deer: 3 ENA 5 BAMBI
dog: 4 LADY 5 PLUTO SCAMP
duck: 6 DONALD
dwarf: 3 DOC
dwarfs: 6 SEPTET
fish: 4 NEMO
Former ~ head: 6 EISNER
frame: 3 CEL
leader: 4 EURO
lioness: 4 NALA
mermaid: 5 ARIEL
middle name: 5 ELIAS
musical: 4 AIDA
parrot: 4 IAGO
prefix: 4 EURO
sci-fi film: 4 TRON
**Disney, Walt**
Middle name of: 5 ELIAS
**Disneyland**
attraction: 4 RIDE
locale: 7 ANAHEIM
transport: 8 MONORAIL
**Disney World**
anagram: 5 EPCOT
attraction: 4 RIDE 5 EPCOT
city: 7 ORLANDO
transport: 4 TRAM
**Disobedience:**
    15 INSUBORDINATION
**Disorder:** 4 MESS 5 CHAOS
    HAVOC 6 MAYHEM
Civil: 4 RIOT
Sleep: 5 APNEA
Utter: 5 CHAOS
**Disordered:** 5 MESSY 6 UNTIDY
**Disorderly:** 6 UNRULY UNTIDY
    7 INAMESS
crowd: 3 MOB
disturbance: 6 FRACAS
do: 3 MOP
group: 3 MOB
**Disoriented:** 4 LOST
**Disown:** 8 RENOUNCE
**Disparage:** 4 SLUR 5 DECRY
    8 BADMOUTH
**Disparaging:** 5 SNIDE
comment: 4 SLUR

**Disparity:** 3 GAP
**Dispatch:** 4 SEND SHIP
    5 HASTE
boat: 5 AVISO
identifier: 8 DATELINE
~, as a dragon: 4 SLAY
**Dispatched:** 4 SENT
    7 SENTOUT
**Dispensable**
candy: 3 PEZ
**Dispense:** 5 ALLOT
    7 DOLEOUT METEOUT
~, with "out": 4 METE
**Dispenser**
candy: 3 PEZ
Cash: 3 ATM
Coffee: 3 URN
Dough: 3 ATM
**Disperse:** 5 STREW 6 FANOUT
    7 SCATTER
**Disperser**
Light: 5 PRISM
**Dispirit:** 5 UNMAN
**Displace:** 4 BUMP 6 UPROOT
**Displaced**
person: 5 EXILE 6 EMIGRE
**Display:** 3 AIR 4 SHOW
    5 SPORT 6 EVINCE
Calc.: 3 LCD
case: 7 ETAGERE
Dazzling: 5 ECLAT
Deli: 5 MEATS
Dizzying: 5 OPART
Elaborate: 5 ECLAT
Embarrassing: 5 SCENE
Gallery: 3 ART
Historical: 7 DIORAMA
Met: 3 ART
Museum: 3 ART
Ostentatious: 4 POMP RITZ
Showy: 5 ECLAT
Wide-ranging: 7 PANOPLY
Wild: 4 RIOT
**Displeased**
look: 5 FROWN
with: 5 MADAT
**Displeasure:** 7 UMBRAGE
Look of: 5 SCOWL
Show: 3 BOO 4 HISS SULK
**Disposable**
Some are: 7 INCOMES
**Disposal**
button: 5 RESET
item: 3 ORT
**Disposed:** 3 APT 5 GIVEN
    PRONE
**Disposition:** 4 BENT MOOD
    6 NATURE
    8 ATTITUDE
**Dispossess:** 4 OUST 5 EVICT
**Disprove:** 5 REBUT
**Dispute:** 3 ROW 4 DENY SPAR
    SPAT 5 ARGUE
    7 QUARREL
handler: 8 MEDIATOR
Matter of: 5 ISSUE

**Disqualify:** 6 RECUSE
**Disquiet:** 4 ROIL 6 UNEASE
    UNREST
**Disraeli:** 4 EARL TORY
**"Disraeli"**
actor George: 6 ARLISS
**Disregard:** 4 OMIT SKIP
    6 IGNORE 8 SHRUGOFF
**Disreputable:** 5 SEAMY SEEDY
    SHADY SLIMY
group: 8 RIFFRAFF
newspaper: 3 RAG
**Disrepute:** 5 ODIUM
**Disrespect:** 4 SASS 7 IMPIETY
    9 INSOLENCE
Show ~ to: 4 SASS
**Disrobe:** 4 PEEL 7 UNDRESS
**Dissect:** 5 PARSE
**Disseminate:** 3 SOW 5 STREW
    6 EFFUSE
**Dissent**
Vote of: 3 NAY
Without: 5 ASONE
**Dissenter:** 4 ANTI
Religious: 7 HERETIC
word: 3 NAY
**Dissenting**
vote: 3 NAY
votes: 3 NOS
**Dissertation:** 6 THESIS
    8 TREATISE
**Dissertations:** 6 THESES
**Disservice:** 4 HARM
**Dissimilar:** 6 UNLIKE
**Dissolute**
man: 4 ROUE
**Dissolve:** 4 MELT 5 SEVER
~, as cells: 4 LYSE
**Dissonant**
Not: 5 TONAL
**Dissuade:** 5 DETER
**Distance**
Astronomical: 6 PARSEC
At a: 3 FAR 4 AFAR
Derby: 5 METRE
Dueler's: 4 PACE
From a: 4 AFAR
Go the: 4 LAST
In the: 3 YON 4 AFAR
Long ~ letters: 3 ATT MCI
Off in the: 4 AFAR
Pool: 3 LAP
Race: 4 MILE
runner: 5 MILER
Short: 4 STEP
    11 STONESTHROW
**Distant:** 3 FAR ICY 4 AFAR
    5 ALOOF 6 REMOTE
beginning: 4 EQUI
friends: 7 PENPALS
prefix: 4 TELE
Prefix with ~: 4 EQUI
**Distaste:** 8 AVERSION
Cry of: 3 FIE UGH
**Distasteful:** 4 ICKY
    8 UNSAVORY

**Distillery**
ingredient: 4 MALT
tank: 3 VAT
**Distinct:** 8 SEPARATE
period: 3 ERA
style: 5 IDIOM
**Distinction:** 4 NOTE
Subtle: 6 NUANCE
Woman of: 4 DAME
**Distinctive**
air: 4 AURA
atmosphere: 4 AURA
doctrine: 3 ISM
flavor: 4 TANG
manner: 5 STYLE
period: 3 ERA 5 EPOCH
quality: 4 AURA
style: 4 ELAN
time: 3 ERA
**Distinguish:** 8 SETAPART
**Distinguished:** 5 GREAT
6 OFNOTE 7 EMINENT
NOTABLE 8 SETAPART
**Distort:** 4 BEND SKEW WARP
5 COLOR GNARL
**Distress:** 3 AIL WOE 4 PAIN
5 ANGST 6 UNEASE
call: 3 SOS
Cry of: 4 YOWL
In: 6 PAINED
Muscular: 4 ACHE
Sighs of: 3 OHS
signal: 3 SOS 4 ACHE
5 FLARE
Sound of: 5 GRUNT
Woman in: 6 DAMSEL
**Distribute:** 4 DOLE METE
5 ALLOT 7 DOLEOUT
HANDOUT
anew: 6 REDEAL
cards: 4 DEAL
~, with "out": 4 METE
**Distributed:** 5 DEALT
**District:** 4 AREA ZONE
Theater: 6 RIALTO
Voting: 5 WARDS
**Distrustful:** 5 LEERY
**Disturb:** 4 RILE ROIL
Do not: 5 LETBE
**Disturbance:** 5 MELEE SCENE
6 POTHER
Civil: 4 RIOT
Disorderly: 6 FRACAS
**Disturbed:** 5 UPSET
6 AWOKEN
state: 4 SNIT
**Disuse**
Fall into: 5 LAPSE
Sign of: 4 RUST
**Dit**
partner: 3 DAH
**Ditch:** 4 LOSE 6 TRENCH
digger: 5 SPADE
that divides: 9 SUNKFENCE
Watery: 4 MOAT
**Dither:** 4 STEW

**Dithers**
Mrs.: 4 CORA
~, to Bumstead: 4 BOSS
**"Ditto":** 4 SAME 5 METOO
SODOI 8 SAMEHERE
**Ditty:** 4 LILT TUNE
December: 4 NOEL 5 CAROL
**Ditz:** 7 AIRHEAD
**Diurnal:** 5 DAILY
**Diva**
delivery: 4 ARIA
problem: 3 EGO
solo: 4 ARIA
song: 4 ARIA
**Divan:** 4 SOFA
Backless: 7 OTTOMAN
**Dive:** 6 PLUNGE
Hollywood: 5 STUNT
Splashy: 9 BELLYFLOP
Takes a: 5 SCUBA
Type of: 4 SWAN
**Diver**
acronym: 5 SCUBA
Black-and-white: 3 AUK
concern: 5 BENDS
device: 5 SCUBA
Flying: 3 AUK
Kind of: 7 DEEPSEA
Navy: 4 SEAL
Ocean: 3 ERN
Skilled: 4 LOON
wear: 7 WETSUIT
**Divergence:** 3 GAP
**Diverse:** 6 MOTLEY VARIED
**Diversify:** 4 VARY 9 VARIEGATE
**Diversion:** 3 TOY 4 RUSE
5 SPORT 7 PASTIME
9 AMUSEMENT
**Divert:** 5 AMUSE SHUNT
**Divest:** 3 RID
**Divide:** 4 REND
equally: 5 HALVE
in threes: 7 TRISECT
up: 5 ALLOT
**Divided:** 4 TORN 5 CLEFT
INTWO
country: 5 KOREA
~, as a highway: 5 LANED
**Dividend:** 6 PAYOUT
**Divider**
Continent: 5 OCEAN
Court: 3 NET
Highway: 6 MEDIAN
Notebook: 3 TAB
Room: 4 WALL
Tennis: 3 NET
Theater: 5 AISLE
word: 4 INTO
**Dividers**
Nasal: 5 SEPTA
**Dividing**
It multiplies by: 6 AMOEBA
membranes: 5 SEPTA
walls: 5 SEPTA
word: 4 INTO
**Divination:** 4 OMEN 6 AUGURY

Book of: 6 ICHING
deck: 5 TAROT
practitioner: 4 SEER
**Divine**
entertainer: 5 MISSM
food: 5 MANNA
hunter: 5 DIANA
revelation: 6 ORACLE
**"Divine Comedy, The"**
opening: 7 INFERNO
poet: 5 DANTE
**"Divine Miss M, The":** 5 BETTE
**Diviner**
deck: 5 TAROT
**Diving**
acronym: 5 SCUBA
bird: 3 AUK 4 LOON
5 GREBE
duck: 4 SMEW 6 SCOTER
position: 4 PIKE TUCK
seabird: 3 AUK 6 PETREL
**Divining**
one: 6 DOWSER
tool: 3 ROD
Use a ~ rod: 5 DOWSE
**Divisible**
by two: 4 EVEN
**Division:** 6 SCHISM SECTOR
7 SEGMENT
Cell: 7 MITOSIS
Condo: 4 UNIT
Corporate: 5 SALES
Farm: 4 ACRE
Game: 4 HALF
Hair: 4 PART
Like some: 4 LONG
Match: 3 SET
Opera: 3 ACT
Play: 3 ACT
Poem: 5 CANTO
Pool: 4 LANE
preposition: 4 INTO
result: 8 QUOTIENT
School: 5 GRADE
Social: 5 CASTE
Timeline: 3 ERA
word: 4 INTO
**Divorce**
mecca: 4 RENO
**Divorced**
couple: 4 EXES
**"___ Divorcee, The":** 3 GAY
**Divorcees:** 4 EXES
**Divorces**
Like some: 5 MESSY
7 NOFAULT
**Divulge:** 4 TELL 5 LETON
SPILL 6 EXPOSE
LETOUT REVEAL
**Divulged:** 4 TOLD
**Divvy**
up: 5 ALLOT SHARE
6 RATION
**Dix**
follower: 4 ONZE
Painter: 4 OTTO

**Dixie: 9** DEEPSOUTH
bread: **4** PONE
dessert: **8** PECANPIE
dish: **5** GRITS
drink: **5** JULEP
letters: **3** CSA
pronoun: **4** YALL
soldier: **3** REB
suffix: **4** CRAT
talk: **5** DRAWL
**"Dixie"**
composer: **6** EMMETT
**Dixie Chicks, The: 4** TRIO
**Dixieland**
clarinetist:
   **12** PETEFOUNTAIN
favorite: **8** TIGERRAG
trumpeter Al: **4** HIRT
___ dixit: **4** IPSE
**Dixon, Jeane**
supposed gift: **3** ESP
**Dizzy: 5** AREEL
Feel: **8** SEESTARS
of baseball: **4** DEAN
**Dizzying**
designs: **5** OPART
display: **5** OPART
pictures: **5** OPART
**DJ**
assortment: **3** CDS LPS
gear: **3** AMP
**DJIA**
Part of: **3** DOW
**Djibouti**
language: **6** SOMALI
neighbor: **7** ERITREA
**DKNY**
Part of: **5** DONNA
**Dmitri**
denial: **4** NYET
**DMV**
datum: **3** DOB
document: **3** LIC
offering: **7** EYETEST
**DMZ**
Part of: **4** ZONE
**DNA**
component: **7** ADENINE
holder: **4** GENE
source: **8** GENEPOOL
structure: **4** GENE **5** HELIX
**Dnieper**
Capital on the: **4** KIEV
**Do: 4** COIF NOTE PERM
   **5** PARTY **6** SOIREE
   **7** HAIRCUT
1960s ~: **4** AFRO
as told: **4** OBEY
away with: **5** ERASE
   **7** ABOLISH
Big: **4** AFRO BASH FETE
   GALA
Bushy: **4** AFRO
Can't ~ without: **4** NEED
   **5** NEEDS
doer: **7** STYLIST

followers: **4** REMI
in: **4** KILL SLAY
nothing: **4** IDLE LAZE LOAF
over: **7** ITERATE
poorly: **3** AIL
well: **7** PROSPER
without: **5** FORGO
**"Do ___!": 4** TELL
**Do-___: 4** REMI **5** ORDIE
**Dobbin**
command: **4** WHOA
home: **6** STABLE
morsel: **3** OAT
pulls one: **4** SHAY
tow: **4** SHAY
**Dobbs**
of CNN: **3** LOU
**Doberman**
boss: **5** BILKO
doc: **3** VET
___ doble: **4** PASO
**Doc: 5** MEDIC **6** MEDICO
bloc: **3** AMA
Dog: **3** VET
Friend of: **5** WYATT
Future ~ exam: **4** MCAT
**Docile: 4** MEEK TAME
**Dock: 4** PIER QUAY **5** WHARF
Tie up at the: **4** MOOR
Work on the: **4** LADE
**Docked**
Not: **4** ASEA
**Dockers**
org.: **3** ILA
**Dockworkers**
org.: **3** ILA
**Docs: 3** GPS MDS
Delivery: **3** OBS
org.: **3** AMA
**Doctor: 5** ALTER CURER
   MEDIC TREAT
   **6** HEALER
aid: **5** PAGER
Available, as a: **6** ONCALL
charge: **3** FEE
directive: **5** SAYAH
interruption: **4** PAGE
Kind of: **4** SPIN
New: **6** INTERN
Nonresident: **6** EXTERN
order: **4** REST TEST **5** REHAB
   SAYAH
prescription: **4** DOSE
Sci-fi: **3** WHO
Spin: **5** PRMAN
TV: **4** PHIL
Word to a: **3** AAH
**Doctorate**
dissertations: **6** THESES
hurdle: **5** ORALS
   **8** ORALEXAM
**Doctorow**
novel: **7** RAGTIME
**Doctors**
make them: **6** ROUNDS
org.: **3** AMA

Spin: **5** PRMEN
**"Doctor Zhivago"**
heroine: **4** LARA
**Doctrine: 3** ISM **5** CREDO
   CREED DOGMA TENET
doubter: **7** HERETIC
Prescribed: **5** DOGMA
Religious: **5** TENET
Secret: **6** CABALA
**Document**
Computer: **4** FILE
end: **3** ARY
Legal: **4** DEED WRIT
Owner's: **4** DEED **5** TITLE
subsection: **7** ARTICLE
Title: **4** DEED
**Documentation: 6** PAPERS
**Doddering: 5** ANILE **6** SENILE
**Dodecanese Islands**
Largest of the: **6** RHODES
**Dodge: 4** RUSE **5** AVOID
   ELUDE EVADE SHIRK
compact: **4** NEON
model: **4** DART OMNI **5** ARIES
Old: **4** DART OMNI **5** ARIES
truck: **3** RAM
**Dodge City**
lawman: **4** EARP
**Dodger**
Artful: **5** REESE **6** EVADER
Like a certain: **6** ARTFUL
**"Do ___ Diddy Diddy": 3** WAH
**Dodo: 4** BIRD
Like the: **7** EXTINCT
**Doe: 3** SHE **4** DEER
beau: **4** STAG
follower in song: **5** ADEER
mate: **4** STAG
**"Doe, ___ ...": 5** ADEER
**Doer**
of dos: **7** STYLIST
suffix: **3** IST
~, in crime-speak: **4** PERP
**Does: 4** DEER
___ d'oeuvres: **4** HORS
**Dog: 3** PET **5** POOCH
   **6** HARASS PURSUE
Bad: **5** BITER
bane: **4** FLEA LICE **5** FLEAS
bark: **3** YIP
biter: **4** FLEA
Cartoon: **3** REN **4** ODIE
collar attachment: **5** IDTAG
Comics: **4** ODIE **5** SNERT
command: **3** SIC SIT **4** COME
   STAY **5** SICEM
days mo.: **3** AUG
Devil: **6** MARINE
Dirty: **3** CUR
doc: **3** VET
Drink like a: **3** LAP **5** LAPUP
English: **6** SETTER
Film: **4** ASTA TOTO
food brand: **4** ALPO
hand: **3** PAW
Have ~ breath: **4** PANT

Herding: 6 COLLIE
holder: 3 BUN
Hot: 6 WEENIE WIENER
Hunting: 6 SETTER
in Oz: 4 TOTO
Irish: 6 SETTER
Is a good: 5 OBEYS
Japanese: 5 AKITA
Junkyard: 3 CUR
Kind of: 4 SLED
Lap ~, for short: 3 POM
    4 PEKE
Latin: 5 CANIS
Movie: 4 ASTA TOTO
Outback: 5 DINGO
pest: 4 FLEA
Put on the: 3 SIC
Sea: 3 GOB TAR 4 SALT
Snarly: 3 CUR
Snub-nosed: 3 PUG
star: 4 ASTA 5 BENJI
    6 LASSIE
Start of a ~ name: 3 RIN
tag datum: 5 OWNER
Top: 5 CHAMP
    9 NUMEROUNO
treat: 4 BONE
TV: 3 REN 5 ASTRO
warning: 3 GRR
Welsh: 5 CORGI
Wild: 5 DINGO
Wiry-coated: 8 AIREDALE
with a blue-black tongue:
    4 CHOW
with a curled tail: 3 PUG
    5 AKITA
Word before: 3 RED SEA
Work like a: 4 TOIL 5 SLAVE
    SWEAT
Wrinkled: 3 PUG
**Dog-___:** 5 EARED
**Dogbane**
shrub: 8 OLEANDER
**Dogcatcher**
quarry: 5 STRAY
**Dog-eared:** 4 WORN
**Dogfaces:** 3 GIS
**Dogfight**
participant: 3 ACE
**Doggie bag**
morsel: 3 ORT
**Doggone:** 7 DRATTED
**"Doggone it!":** 4 DRAT RATS
**Doggy:** 5 POOCH
**Dogie:** 4 CALF 6 ORPHAN
catcher: 5 LASSO RIATA
**Doglike**
scavenger: 5 HYENA
**Dogma:** 5 TENET 6 BELIEF
disputer: 7 HERETIC
**"Dog of Flanders, A"**
author: 5 OUIDA
**Dog-paddle:** 4 SWIM
**Dog-paddled:** 4 SWAM SWUM
**Dogpatch**
adjective: 3 LIL

cartoonist: 4 CAPP
creator: 4 CAPP 6 ALCAPP
denizen: 5 ABNER SADIE
    8 LILABNER
    10 MAMMYYOKUM
diminutive: 3 LIL
Hawkins of: 5 SADIE
Opposed to, in: 4 AGIN
possessive: 4 HISN
resident: 5 ABNER
**Dog-tired:** 5 ALLIN 6 POOPED
**Dogwood**
variety: 5 OSIER
**Doha**
land: 5 QATAR
**Doherty**
Actress: 7 SHANNEN
of the Mamas & the Papas:
    5 DENNY
**Dohnányi**
Composer: 4 ERNO
**"Do I dare to ___ peach?":**
    4 EATA
**Doilies**
Make: 3 TAT
**Doily**
Like a: 4 LACY
Make a: 3 TAT
material: 4 LACE
**Doing:** 4 DEED UPTO
Not ~ much: 4 IDLE
nothing: 4 IDLE
Without ~ much: 4 IDLY
**Do-it-yourselfer**
purchase: 3 KIT
words: 5 HOWTO
**Dojo**
teaching: 6 KARATE
**Dol.**
parts: 3 CTS
**Doldrums:** 5 BLAHS
In the: 3 SAD
**Dole:** 4 METE
out: 5 ALLOT
(out): 4 METE
running mate: 4 KEMP
**Dolin**
Dancer: 5 ANTON
**Doll:** 3 HON TOY 5 CUTIE
    SUGAR
Carnival: 6 KEWPIE
cry: 4 DADA MAMA
Fad: 5 TROLL
for boys: 5 GIJOE
He's a: 3 KEN 4 ELMO
Kachina ~ maker: 4 HOPI
Kind of: 6 VOODOO
Living: 5 CUTIE
Mattel: 3 KEN
Raggedy: 3 ANN 4 ANDY
She's a: 3 ANN
Ticklish: 4 ELMO
**Dollar**
bill: 3 ONE
competitor: 4 AVIS 5 ALAMO
divs.: 3 CTS

Kind of: 4 SAND
Latin word on a: 4 ORDO
Like a new ~ bill: 5 CRISP
Parts of a: 5 CENTS
prefix: 4 EURO
rival: 4 AVIS EURO 5 ALAMO
**Dollop:** 3 DAB GOB 4 GLOB
**Dolls**
companions: 4 GUYS
Like some Russian: 6 NESTED
of the 1980s: 3 ETS
**"Doll's House, A"**
author: 5 IBSEN
heroine: 4 NORA
**Dolly:** 3 EWE 5 CLONE SHEEP
Singer: 6 PARTON
the clone: 3 EWE
**Dolores**
Actress: 6 DELRIO
**Dolphin**
habitat: 5 MIAMI OCEAN
Largest: 4 ORCA
relative: 4 ORCA
**Dolphins**
coach: 5 SHULA
Dan of the: 6 MARINO
home: 5 MIAMI
**Dolt:** 3 ASS OAF 4 BOOB CLOD
    LOUT 5 IDIOT MORON
    SCHMO 6 NITWIT
    11 KNUCKLEHEAD
**Domain:** 4 AREA LAND
    5 REALM
Royal: 5 REALM
**"Domani"**
singer: 6 LAROSA
**Dome:** 6 CUPOLA
home: 5 IGLOO
openings: 5 OCULI
player: 5 ASTRO
**Domed**
building: 7 ROTUNDA
home: 5 IGLOO
recess: 4 APSE
**Domenica**
Day before: 6 SABATO
**Domenici**
Senator: 4 PETE
**Dome-shaped**
building: 7 ROTUNDA
home: 5 IGLOO
~ Buddhist memorial: 5 STUPA
**Domestic:** 4 MAID 6 AUPAIR
    8 HOMEMADE
Some are: 4 ARTS
**Domesticate:** 4 TAME
**Domesticated:** 4 TAME
insect: 3 BEE
Not: 4 WILD 5 FERAL
**Domicile:** 5 ABODE
**Dominant:** 5 ONTOP
It may be: 4 GENE
Socially: 5 ALPHA
**Domineering:** 5 BOSSY
**Domingo:** 3 DIA 5 TENOR
domain: 5 OPERA

solo: 4 ARIA
___ Domingo: 5 SANTO
___ Domini: 4 ANNO
**Dominican**
dollar: 4 PESO
slugger: 4 SOSA
**Dominican Republic**
neighbor: 5 HAITI
**Dominik**
NHL goalie: 5 HASEK
**Dominion:** 5 REALM
**Domino:** 4 MASK
dot: 3 PIP
Middle: 4 TREY
Singer: 4 FATS
**Don:** 4 WEAR 8 SLIPINTO
Announcer: 5 PARDO
Deejay: 4 IMUS
of football: 5 SHULA
of game shows: 5 PARDO
of talk radio: 4 IMUS
**Doña ___ (Las Cruces's county):**
3 ANA
**Donahue**
Actor: 4 TROY
Actress: 6 ELINOR
TV host: 4 PHIL
**Donald**
and Ivana: 4 EXES
Ex of: 5 IVANA MARLA
First ex of: 5 IVANA
**Donald Duck:** 4 TOON
nephew: 4 HUEY 5 DEWEY
LOUIE
~, to his nephews: 4 UNCA
**Donaldson**
TV newsman: 3 SAM
**Donate:** 4 GIVE
**Donation**
Charitable: 4 ALMS
Church: 5 TITHE
Eye bank: 6 CORNEA
Generous: 5 ORGAN
Parish: 5 TITHE
**Donations:** 4 ALMS
Ask for: 10 PASSTHEHAT
**Don ___ de la Vega:** 5 DIEGO
**Done:** 4 OVER 5 ENDED
7 THROUGH
for: 4 DEAD SUNK 5 KAPUT
SPENT
in: 5 SLAIN
It's: 4 DEED
Just not: 5 TABOO
Less: 5 RARER
to death: 3 OLD
with: 4 OVER
with a wink: 3 SLY
~, in French: 4 FINI
~, to Donne: 3 OER
"___ done!": 6 NICELY
**Donegal**
From: 5 IRISH
Island of: 4 ARAN
**Donegal Bay**
River to: 4 ERNE

"___ Done Him Wrong": 3 SHE
**Done to ___:** 5 ATURN
**Done ___ turn:** 3 TOA
**"Don Giovanni":** 5 OPERA
composer: 6 MOZART
**"Don Juan"**
poet: 5 BYRON
**"Don Juan DeMarco"**
actor: 4 DEPP
**Donkey:** 3 ASS
remark: 6 HEEHAW
sound: 4 BRAY
uncle: 3 ASS
~, in German: 4 ESEL
**Donna**
Designer: 5 KARAN
___ donna: 5 PRIMA
**Donne:** 4 POET
**Info:** Poetic cue
Dawn, to: 4 MORN
Done, to: 3 OER
Dusk, to: 3 EEN
**Donner Pass**
City near: 4 RENO
**Donny**
Marie, to: 3 SIS
Singer: 6 OSMOND
Sister of: 5 MARIE
**Donnybrook:** 3 ROW 4 FRAY
RIOT 5 MELEE SETTO
6 FRACAS
**Donohoe**
Actress: 6 AMANDA
**Donor**
Become a: 4 GIVE
Big: 3 PAC
D.C.: 3 PAC
Noted bone: 4 ADAM
Universal: 5 TYPEO
**"Do not give up !":** 3 TRY
**Do-nothing:** 5 IDLER
**Donovan**
crew: 3 OSS
Daughter of: 4 IONE
**"Don't ___ !":** 3 ASK
**"Don't bet ___ !":** 4 ONIT
**"Don't bother":** 6 NONEED
**"Don't Bring Me Down"**
gp.: 3 ELO
**"Don't count ___ !":** 4 ONIT
**"Don't Cry for Me, Argentina"**
musical: 5 EVITA
**"Don't dawdle!":** 4 ASAP
**"Don't ___, don't tell":** 3 ASK
**"Don't Drop Bombs"**
singer Minnelli: 4 LIZA
**"Don't evade the question!":**
7 YESORNO
**"Don't even bother":** 5 NOUSE
**"Don't even go ___ !":** 5 THERE
**"Don't get any funny ___ !":**
5 IDEAS
**"Don't give up!":** 3 TRY
**"Don't go":** 4 STAY
**"Don't have ___, man!":**
4 ACOW

**"Don't look ___ !":** 4 ATME
**"Don't look at me!":** 4 NOTI
**"Don't make ___ !":** 5 AMESS
AMOVE
**"Don't mind ___ !":** 5 IFIDO
**"Don't mind ___ do":** 3 IFI
**"Don't move!":** 4 STAY
7 STAYPUT
**"Don't ___ surprised":** 5 ACTSO
**"Don't tell ___ !":** 5 ASOUL
**"Don't tell me!":** 4 OHNO
**"Don't throw bouquets ___":**
4 ATME
**"Don't You Know"**
singer: 5 REESE
**Donut**
Dip, as a: 3 SOP
feature: 4 HOLE
quantity: 5 DOZEN
shape: 5 TORUS 6 TOROID
**Donut-and-dance**
org.: 3 USO
**Doo-___:** 3 WOP
**Doodlebug**
Adult: 7 ANTLION
prey: 3 ANT
**Doodler**
aid: 10 SCRATCHPAD
**Doofus:** 3 ASS OAF 4 BOOB
BOZO CLOD DODO DOLT
TWIT 5 IDIOT SCHMO
6 NITWIT
10 STUMBLEDUM
**Doohickey:** 5 GIZMO 6 GADGET
**Doolittle**
Ms.: 5 ELIZA
Poet: 5 HILDA
**Doolittle, Eliza**
Inspiration for: 7 GALATEA
**Doom:** 3 END 4 FATE
partner: 5 GLOOM
**Doomsayer:** 9 PESSIMIST
sign: 6 REPENT
**Doone**
of fiction: 5 LORNA
"___ Doone": 5 LORNA
**"Doonesbury"**
cartoonist: 7 TRUDEAU
character: 4 DUKE
**Door:** 5 ENTRY 8 ENTRANCE
fastener: 4 HASP
feature: 4 KNOB
frame: 4 JAMB
frame part: 6 LINTEL
handle: 4 KNOB
opener: 3 KEY 4 KNOB
Open the ~ to: 5 LETIN
part: 4 JAMB 5 HINGE
sign: 3 MEN 4 EXIT PULL
PUSH 5 ENTER
sound: 4 SLAM
Sound at the: 3 RAP
word: 3 MEN 4 PULL PUSH
**Doorbell**
Eschew the: 5 KNOCK
Used a: 4 RANG

**Doorframe**
part: 4 JAMB
**Doorkeeper**
Masonic: 5 TILER
**Doors**
Like French: 5 PANED
Like many: 4 AJAR
Opener of many: 7 PASSKEY
**Doorway:** 5 ENTRY 6 PORTAL
8 ENTRANCE
part: 4 JAMB
**"Do ___ others ...":** 4 UNTO
**Do-over**
Tennis: 3 LET
**Doo-wop**
instrument: 3 SAX
member: 4 ALTO
song: 5 OLDIE
syllable: 3 SHA
**Doozy:** 3 PIP 4 LULU ONER
**Dope:** 3 SAP 4 INFO POOP
7 SCHNOOK
**Dopey:** 5 DWARF INANE
picture: 3 CEL
**Doppelgänger:** 4 TWIN
5 CLONE
**___ d'Or (award at Cannes):**
5 PALME
**Dorati**
Conductor: 5 ANTAL
**Do-re-mi:** 4 GELT KALE LOOT
5 MOOLA 6 DINERO
**"___ Doria":** 6 ANDREA
**Do-Right, Dudley**
beloved: 4 NELL
org.: 4 RCMP
**Doris**
Actress and singer: 3 DAY
**Dork:** 4 NERD 5 DWEEB
SCHMO 6 DOOFUS
**___ d'Orléans:** 3 ILE
**Dorm**
alternative: 4 FRAT
annoyance: 5 SNORE
dweller: 4 COED
sharer: 6 ROOMIE
unit: 4 ROOM
~ VIPs: 3 RAS
**Dormant:** 6 ASLEEP LATENT
7 RESTING
**Dormitory:** 4 HALL
annoyance: 6 SNORER
**Dorothea**
Reformer: 3 DIX
**Dorothy**
dog: 4 TOTO
Em, to: 4 AUNT
home: 6 KANSAS
Mystery writer: 6 SAYERS
Skater: 6 HAMILL
~, to Em: 5 NIECE
**Dors**
Actress: 5 DIANA
**___ d'Orsay:** 4 QUAI
**Dorsey, Jimmy**
hit: 6 SORARE

**Dorsey, Tommy**
hit: 7 OPUSONE
**Dortmund-___Canal:** 3 EMS
**Dory:** 4 BOAT
propeller: 3 OAR
**Dos:** 6 NUMERO
cubed: 4 OCHO
follower: 4 TRES
halved: 3 UNO
Notes after: 3 RES
preceder: 3 UNO
Uno plus: 4 TRES
Where ~ are done: 5 SALON
**Dos ___, John**
Author: 6 PASSOS
**Dosage**
amt.: 3 TSP
Radiation: 3 REM
unit: 3 RAD 4 PILL
units: 3 CCS
**Do-say**
link: 3 ASI
**"Do ___ say":** 3 ASI
**Dose**
amt.: 3 TSP
Medicinal: 4 PILL
prefix: 4 MEGA
Prevention: 5 OUNCE
**Do-___ situation:** 5 ORDIE
**Dos Passos, John**
trilogy: 3 USA
**Dossier:** 4 FILE
letters: 3 AKA
**Dostoevsky**
Author: 6 FYODOR
novel: 8 THEIDIOT
title character: 5 IDIOT
**Dot**
follower: 3 COM ORG
Map: 4 ISLE TOWN 5 ISLET
of land: 5 ISLET
on a domino: 3 PIP
on a monitor: 5 PIXEL
On the: 5 SHARP
Small: 6 TITTLE
Video: 5 PIXEL
**Dot-___:** 3 COM
**Dotage**
In one's: 6 SENILE
**Dot-com:** 7 STARTUP
address: 3 URL
giant: 6 AMAZON
**Dote**
on: 5 ADORE
**Doth**
speak: 5 SAITH
**"Do the ___!":** 4 MATH
**"Do the Right Thing"**
pizzeria: 4 SALS
star: 6 AIELLO
**Doting:** 4 FOND
**Dotty:** 4 DAFT GAGA
6 SENILE
Not as: 5 SANER
**Douay**
prophet: 4 OSEE

**Double:** 3 HIT 4 TWIN
7 STANDIN TWOFOLD
agent: 4 MOLE
curve: 3 ESS 4 OGEE
dessert: 10 PIEALAMODE
duty: 5 STUNT
Exact: 5 CLONE
fold: 5 PLEAT
header: 3 DUO
job: 5 STUNT
negative: 4 NONO
On the: 4 ASAP 5 APACE
6 ATONCE PRONTO
reed: 4 OBOE
standard: 3 TWO
Stunt: 7 STANDIN
twist: 3 ESS
whole note: 5 BREVE
**Double ___:** 4 DARE
8 ENTENDRE
**Double-___:** 5 EDGED
6 TALKER 7 CROSSER
**Double-check:** 6 REREAD
RETEST
a sum: 5 READD
**Double-clicked**
item: 4 ICON
**Double-crosser:** 5 SNAKE
8 TWOTIMER
**Doubleday**
of baseball: 5 ABNER
**Double-decker:** 3 BUS
part: 4 TIER
**Double Delight**
snack: 4 OREO
**Double-edged:** 6 IRONIC
**"Double Fantasy"**
singer: 3 ONO 7 YOKOONO
**Doubleheader**
First game of a: 6 OPENER
**Double-helix**
stuff: 3 DNA
**"Double Indemnity"**
novelist: 4 CAIN
**Doublemint:** 3 GUM
figures: 5 TWINS
**Double-reed**
instrument: 4 OBOE
player: 6 OBOIST
**Double Stuf**
cookie: 4 OREO
**___ double take:** 3 DOA
**Doubly:** 5 TWICE
**Doubt:** 8 MISTRUST
QUESTION
Free from: 6 ASSURE
Free of: 4 SURE
Had no: 4 KNEW
Sounds of: 3 EHS
Without a: 4 SURE
**Doubter:** 7 SKEPTIC
Deity: 8 AGNOSTIC
Response to a: 6 ICANSO
words: 4 IBET
**"___ Doubtfire":** 3 MRS
**Doubtful:** 4 IFFY

**Doubting Thomas:** 5 CYNIC
**Doubtless:** 4 SURE
**Dough:** 4 KALE 5 BREAD
  MONEY MOOLA
  6 MOOLAH
Delhi: 5 RUPEE
dispenser: 3 ATM
Like: 6 YEASTY
Like some: 4 SOUR
Pisa: 4 LIRA
raiser: 5 YEAST
Rolling in: 4 RICH
Turkish: 4 LIRA
Work: 5 KNEAD
**Doughnut**
  center: 4 HOLE
  Dip, as a: 4 DUNK
  Finish a: 5 GLAZE
  shape: 5 TORUS
  shapes: 4 TORI
**Doughnut-shaped:** 5 TORIC
**Douglas:** 3 FIR 7 DEBATER
**Douglas ___:** 3 FIR
**Douglas, Michael**
  film: 4 COMA
  ~, to Kirk: 3 SON
**Douglas-Home**
  British P.M.: 4 ALEC
**Dour:** 4 GLUM 5 MOODY
  6 SULLEN
**Dove:** 4 SOAP 5 COOER
  8 PACIFIST
call: 3 COO
goal: 5 PEACE
into second: 4 SLID
Like a: 7 ANTIWAR
Poet: 4 RITA
shelter: 4 COTE
sound: 3 COO
**Dover**
  dish: 4 SOLE
  state (abbr.): 3 DEL
**Dovetail:** 4 MESII
  part: 5 TENON
**Dow:** 5 INDEX
  figures: 5 HIGHS
  rise: 4 GAIN
**Do-well**
  starter: 4 NEER
**Down:** 3 EAT SAD 4 BLUE
  GLUM 6 MOROSE
at the heels: 5 SEEDY
at the pond: 5 EIDER
for the count: 3 KOD
Go: 3 SET 4 DROP LOSE SINK
  WANE 5 ABATE 6 SHRINK
Got: 3 ATE 4 ALIT
Had ~ pat: 4 KNEW
in the dumps: 3 SAD 4 BLUE
  GLUM 6 MOROSE
in the mouth: 3 SAD 4 BLUE
  GLUM 6 MOROSE
Is ~ with: 3 HAS
It may be laid: 6 THELAW
Marked: 6 ONSALE
opposite: 6 ACROSS

Put: 3 DIS LAY SET 4 LAID
  5 ABASE QUELL
  6 BERATE DEMEAN
  DERIDE DISSED STIFLE
Set: 3 LAY PUT 4 ALIT LAID
  5 WROTE
source: 5 EIDER
the road: 5 AHEAD 6 INTIME
too much: 7 OVEREAT
Went: 4 FELL SANK SLID
Where to get: 5 EIDER
with, in French: 4 ABAS
with the flu: 3 ILL
~, at a diner: 7 ONTOAST
**Down ___ (Maine):** 4 EAST
**Down-and-out:** 5 NEEDY
**Downcast:** 3 SAD 4 BLUE
  GLUM 6 MOROSE
**Down East:** 5 MAINE
**Downed:** 3 ATE 5 EATEN
**Downer:** 4 DRAG
It's a real: 6 OPIATE
Scud: 3 ABM
**Downey**
  Actress: 4 ROMA
  costar: 5 REESE
  TV angel: 4 ROMA
**Downfall:** 4 BANE RUIN
  6 DEMISE
**Downhearted:** 3 SAD 4 BLUE
  GLUM 6 MOROSE
**Downhill**
  course: 6 SKIRUN SLALOM
  Go: 4 SLED 6 WORSEN
  8 GETWORSE
  Go ~ fast: 3 SKI 4 LUGE SLED
  6 SCHUSS
  racer: 4 LUGE SLED
  runner: 3 SKI
**Downpour:** 4 RAIN
**Downright:** 5 PLUMB SHEER
  6 ARRANT 7 UTTERLY
**Downs**
  It has its ups and: 4 YOYO
  6 SEESAW
  town: 5 EPSOM
  TV host: 4 HUGH
  ___ Downs: 5 EPSOM
**Downsize:** 4 PARE 7 RESCALE
**Downspout**
  site: 4 EAVE
**Downstairs**
  ~, at sea: 5 BELOW
**Downtime:** 4 LULL REST
  5 RANDR
  Toddler's: 3 NAP
**Down-to-earth:** 4 REAL
  folks: 3 ETS
**"Downtown"**
  singer Clark: 6 PETULA
**Downturn:** 3 DIP
**Down Under**
  Info: Australian cue
  bird: 3 EMU
  critter: 5 KOALA
  denizen: 6 AUSSIE

dog: 5 DINGO
girl: 6 SHEILA
hopper: 3 ROO
soldier: 5 ANZAC
**Downward**
  bend: 3 SAG
**Downwind:** 4 ALEE
**Downy:** 4 SOFT
  duck: 5 EIDER
  surface: 3 NAP
**Dowsing**
  tool: 3 ROD
**Dowson**
  English poet: 6 ERNEST
**"Do Ya"**
  rock gp.: 3 ELO
**Doyle, Popeye**
  prototype Eddie: 4 EGAN
**Doyle, Sir Arthur ___:** 5 CONAN
**"Do you come here often?":**
  4 LINE
**"Do you get it?":** 3 SEE
**Doz.**
  Twelve: 3 GRO
**Doze:** 3 NAP NOD 6 NODOFF
  (off): 3 NOD
**Dozed:** 5 SLEPT
**Dozen**
  A dime a: 4 RATE
  Baker's: 4 EGGS 8 THIRTEEN
  Dairy: 4 EGGS
  Half a: 3 SIX
  Item sold by the: 5 DONUT
  Price of a: 4 DIME
**DPL**
  One with ~ plates: 3 AMB EMB
**Dr.**
  group: 3 AMA HMO
  magazine: 4 JAMA
  of literature: 5 SEUSS
  of rap: 3 DRE
  order: 3 MRI
  orders: 3 RXS
  org.: 3 AMA
  TV: 4 PHIL
**Dr. ___**
  Rapper: 3 DRE
**Drab:** 4 BLAH PALE
  color: 5 OLIVE
**Drachma**
  replacer: 4 EURO
**Draconian:** 5 HARSH 6 SEVERE
**Dracula:** 5 COUNT 7 VAMPIRE
  creator: 6 STOKER
  Inspiration for: 4 VLAD
  Mother-in-law of: 6 OLDBAT
  portrayer: 6 LUGOSI
  portrayer Lugosi: 4 BELA
  ~, at times: 3 BAT
**"Dracula"**
  author: 6 STOKER
  author Stoker: 4 BRAM
  director Browning: 3 TOD
**Draft:** 4 BEER
  Admitting a: 4 AJAR
  animals: 4 OXEN

Beat the: 6 ENLIST
Bit of a: 3 SIP
choice: 3 ALE
classification: 4 ONEA
device: 3 TAP 4 YOKE
drink: 3 ALE
Hearty: 5 QUAFF
holder: 8 SCHOONER
letters: 3 SSS
org.: 3 NBA NFL SSS
pick: 3 ALE
rating: 4 ONEA
source: 7 BEERKEG
status: 4 ONEA 5 ONTAP
**Draftable:** 4 ONEA 5 ONTAP
**"Draft Dodger Rag"**
singer Phil: 4 OCHS
**Drafting**
Fit for: 4 ONEA
**Drag:** 4 BORE HAUL TOKE
It's a: 3 TOW
It's off the main:
    10 SIDESTREET
Kind of a: 4 MAIN
one's feet: 5 STALL
Prepare to: 3 REV
race participant: 6 HOTROD
through the mud: 5 SMEAR
**Dragnet:** 5 TRAWL
**"Dragnet"**
background for credits:
    5 BADGE
org.: 4 LAPD
role: 9 JOEFRIDAY
star: 4 WEBB
**Dragon:** 6 TATTOO
Did in, as a: 4 SLEW
Do in, as a: 4 SLAY
land: 7 HONALEE
puppet: 5 OLLIE
___ dragon: 6 KOMODO
**"Dragons of ___, The" (Carl**
   **Sagan novel):** 4 EDEN
**"Dragons of Eden, The"**
author: 5 SAGAN
**"Dragonwyck"**
author Anya: 5 SETON
author Seton: 4 ANYA
**Drag queen**
topper: 3 WIG
wrap: 3 BOA
**Drain:** 3 SAP 4 TIRE 5 EMPTY
    SEWER
bane: 4 CLOG
cleaner: 3 LYE
of color: 8 ETIOLATE
problem: 4 CLOG
sight: 4 EDDY
**Drained:** 5 SPENT
of color: 5 ASHEN
**Drainer**
Pasta: 5 SIEVE
**Drainpipe**
section: 4 TRAP
**Drake:** 4 MALE
Cartoonist: 4 STAN

Fake: 5 DECOY
**"Drake"**
poet: 5 NOYES
**Drake, Francis**
title: 3 SIR
**Dram:** 3 TOT
**Drama**
award: 4 OBIE
Daytime: 4 SOAP 6 SERIAL
Forensic: 3 CSI
Japanese: 3 NOH 6 KABUKI
Musical: 5 OPERA
opening: 4 ACTI
prefix: 4 MELO
Robot: 3 RUR
Short: 7 PLAYLET
TV ~ settings: 3 ERS
**Dramatic**
beginning: 4 ACTI
dance: 5 TANGO
opening: 4 ACTI MELO
Overly: 5 HAMMY
segment: 3 ACT 5 SCENE
wail: 4 ALAS
**Dramatist**
French: 6 SARTRE
Irish: 5 SYNGE
**Drambuie**
Scotch and ~ drink:
    9 RUSTYNAIL
**Drams**
16 ~: 5 OUNCE
512,000 ~: 3 TON
**Drang**
partner: 5 STURM
**Drano**
ingredient: 3 LYE
target: 4 CLOG
**Drape**
edge: 3 HEM
**Draped**
garment: 4 SARI TOGA
**Draperies**
Decorative: 5 SWAGS
**"Drat!":** 4 DANG OATH
    5 NERTS
**Draught:** 3 ALE 4 SWIG
**Dravidian**
language: 5 TAMIL
**Draw:** 3 TIE 4 PULL 6 ALLURE
    7 ATTRACT TIEGAME
a bead: 3 AIM
a bead on: 5 AIMAT
a blank: 6 FORGET
a conclusion: 5 INFER
forth: 5 EDUCE EVOKE
    6 ELICIT
in: 6 ENTICE
on a board: 9 STALEMATE
on glass: 4 ETCH
out: 5 EDUCE 6 ELICIT
Ready to: 5 ONTAP
Something to: 4 BATH
to a close: 3 END 4 WANE
upon: 3 USE 7 TAPINTO
with acid: 4 ETCH

**Drawbridge**
Water under the: 4 MOAT
**Drawer**
Big: 5 MECCA
Cash: 4 TILL
part: 4 KNOB
Produce: 7 CRISPER
Top: 4 AONE
**Drawers**
Chest of: 6 BUREAU
    7 DRESSER
**Drawing:** 6 SKETCH
card: 4 LURE
place: 4 WELL
Ready for: 5 ONTAP
Represent in: 4 LIMN
room: 5 SALON
support: 5 EASEL
**Drawing board**
staple: 7 TSQUARE
**Drawings**
Like some: 6 RANDOM
**Drawn**
Ready to be: 5 ONTAP
They're: 4 LOTS
**Dre, Dr.**
genre: 3 RAP
**Dread:** 4 FEAR 5 ANGST
Cry of: 4 OHNO
Feeling of: 5 ANGST
**Dreadful:** 3 BAD 4 DIRE
    6 HORRID 9 ATROCIOUS
**Dreadlocks**
wearer: 5 RASTA
**Dream:** 6 ASPIRE
Kind of: 4 PIPE
location: 3 BED
state: 3 REM
up: 6 DEVISE 7 CONCOCT
~, in French: 4 REVE
**"Dream a Little Dream of Me"**
singer: 8 MAMACASS
    14 MAMACASSELLIOT
**Dreamcast**
maker: 4 SEGA
**Dreamer:** 8 IDEALIST
    10 LOTUSEATER
 Fictional: 5 ALICE
opposite: 7 REALIST
**Dreaming**
phenomenon: 3 REM
**"___ dreaming?":** 3 AMI
**Dreamland:** 5 SLEEP 6 UTOPIA
Out of: 5 AWAKE
**"Dreamlover"**
singer Carey: 6 MARIAH
**Dreamscape**
artist: 4 DALI
**Dreary:** 4 DRAB GREY 5 BLEAK
    7 HUMDRUM
**Dregs:** 4 LEES
**Drench:** 3 SOP 4 SOAK
    5 DOUSE
**Drenched:** 3 WET 5 SOGGY
**Drescher**
Actress: 4 FRAN

**Drescher, Fran**
  Like the voice of: 5 NASAL
  role: 5 NANNY
**Dresden**
  Info: German cue
  denial: 4 NEIN
  native: 5 SAXON
  river: 4 ELBE
**Dress:** 4 GARB 6 ATTIRE
  Ballet: 4 TUTU
  cut: 5 ALINE
  Delhi: 5 SARI
  down: 5 BASTE 6 BERATE
  Elegant: 5 SATIN
  Formal: 4 GOWN
  Indian: 4 SARI
  line: 4 SEAM
  Longish: 4 MIDI
  Loose-fitting: 4 TENT
  Mend a: 5 REHEM
  Peasant: 6 DIRNDL
  Prom: 4 GOWN
  Prom ~ material: 5 TULLE
  Roomy: 5 ALINE
  size: 6 PETITE
  smartly: 5 PREEN
  style: 4 MAXI 5 ALINE
  up: 5 ADORN PREEN
    6 TOGOUT
  (up): 3 TOG
  up, with "out": 3 TOG
  with a flare: 5 ALINE
**Dressed:** 4 CLAD 6 GARBED
  Get: 5 TOGUP
  It's often: 5 SALAD
  like a judge: 5 ROBED
  Sharply: 5 NATTY
  to the nines: 7 DUDEDUP
**Dressed to the ___:** 5 NINES
**Dresser**
  Dandy: 3 FOP
  Messy: 4 SLOB
  Smart: 3 FOP
**Dressing**
  bottle: 5 CRUET
  choice: 5 RANCH 7 ITALIAN
    RUSSIAN
  Course with: 5 SALAD
  holder: 5 CRUET
  ingredient: 3 OIL 7 VINEGAR
  Surgical: 5 GAUZE
  tool: 3 ADZ
  Window: 5 DRAPE 6 FACADE
**Dressmaker**
  cut: 4 BIAS
  dummy: 4 FORM
**Dress to the ___:** 5 NINES
**Dressy**
  accessory: 3 TIE
  event: 4 GALA
**Drew**
  a blank: 6 FORGOT
  Actor: 5 CAREY
  back: 5 SHIED
  in: 5 LURED
  in novels: 5 NANCY

  on: 4 USED
**Drew, Nancy**
  beau: 3 NED
  boyfriend: 3 NED
  creator Carolyn: 5 KEENE
**"Drew Carey Show, The"**
  character: 4 MIMI
  setting: 4 OHIO
**Drexler**
  of basketball: 5 CLYDE
**Dreyer**
  partner in ice cream: 3 EDY
**Dreyfus**
  Defender of: 4 ZOLA
    9 EMILEZOLA
  trial city: 6 RENNES
**Dribble:** 4 SEEP
**Dried**
  fruit: 5 PRUNE
  It may be cut and: 3 HAY
  out: 4 SERE 5 SOBER
  up: 4 SERE
**Drier:** 5 TOWEL
  Hops: 4 OAST
**Drift:** 4 ROAM ROVE 5 STRAY
    TENOR
  Get the: 3 SEE
  off: 4 DOZE
**Drifter:** 4 HOBO
**Drifters**
  hit song: 11 UPONTHEROOF
    15 THISMAGICMOMENT
  Plains: 5 BISON
**Driftwood**
  Groucho's: 4 OTIS
  Where ~ drifts: 6 ASHORE
**Drill:** 4 BORE 5 BORER
  command: 6 ATEASE
  License to: 3 DDS
  through: 6 PIERCE
**Driller:** 3 SGT
  deg.: 3 DDS
  org.: 3 ADA
**Drilling**
  gp.: 4 ROTC
  machine: 6 OILRIG
  Ready for: 4 NUMB
  tool: 8 BRACEBIT
**Drill sergeant**
  call: 3 HEP HUP
  command: 6 ATEASE FALLIN
  Obey the:
    15 SNAPTOATTENTION
**Drink:** 3 SEA 5 OCEAN
    6 IMBIBE
  After-dinner: 4 PORT
    8 ANISETTE
  a little: 3 SIP
  Apple: 5 CIDER
  Autumn: 5 CIDER
  Big: 4 SWIG
  Brewed: 7 ICEDTEA
  Brunch: 6 MIMOSA
  Carbonated: 4 SODA
  Chinese: 6 HOTTEA
    8 GREENTEA

  Citrus: 3 ADE 7 LIMEADE
  cooler: 3 ICE
  Dad's: 8 ROOTBEER
  daintily: 3 SIP
  Dixie: 5 JULEP
  Draft: 3 ALE
  Eggy: 3 NOG
  Fizzy: 4 COLA SODA
  from a bag: 3 TEA
  from a dish: 3 LAP
  Fruit: 3 ADE
  Fruity: 3 ADE 7 SANGRIA
  garnish: 4 LIME PEEL
    5 TWIST
  Green: 3 TEA
  Half a: 3 MAI TAI
  Herbal: 3 TEA
  Holiday: 3 NOG
  Honey: 4 MEAD
  Hot: 3 TEA 5 COCOA TODDY
  impolitely: 5 SLURP
  in a can: 4 COLA
  in a mug: 3 ALE
  Japanese: 4 SAKE
  Juice: 3 ADE
  like a cat: 3 LAP 5 LAPUP
  like a dog: 3 LAP 5 LAPUP
  like a fish: 4 TOPE
  Lime: 3 ADE
  Malt: 3 ALE
  mixer: 4 SODA
  No-cal: 5 WATER
  noisily: 5 SLURP
  of the gods: 6 NECTAR
  on board: 4 GROG
  on draft: 3 ALE
  Orange: 3 ADE
  Pirate's: 3 RUM
  Pub: 3 ALE
  Quick: 3 NIP 5 SNORT
  Rum: 4 GROG 6 COLADA
    MAITAI
  Sailor's: 4 GROG
  slowly: 3 SIP
  Small: 3 NIP SIP
  Soft: 4 COLA SODA
    7 SODAPOP
  Stiff: 6 BRACER
  suffix: 3 ADE
  Summer: 3 ADE
  too much: 4 TOPE
  with a straw: 4 SODA 5 FLOAT
  Yule: 3 NOG
**Drinker**
  debt: 6 BARTAB
  Heavy: 3 SOT
**Drinking**
  Marked by: 3 WET
  party: 7 WASSAIL
  spree: 6 BENDER
**Drinks**
  Like some: 4 NEAT
    10 ONTHEHOUSE
**"Drinks are ___!":** 4 ONME
**Drip:** 4 BORE
  catcher: 3 BIB

drops: 4 OOZE
site: 4 EAVE
**Dripping:** 3 WET
Candle: 3 WAX
Plant: 5 RESIN
sound: 4 PLOP
**Drive:** 4 URGE 5 IMPEL
   MOTOR 6 COMPEL
   STROKE
away: 4 SHOO 5 REPEL
   6 BANISH 8 ALIENATE
back: 5 REPEL 7 REPULSE
bananas: 5 ANNOY
   7 DERANGE
Finish a: 4 PAVE
forward: 5 IMPEL 6 PROPEL
Get ready to: 5 TEEUP
Got ready to: 4 TEED
Inner: 4 URGE
Kind of: 5 CDROM
off: 4 SHOO 5 REPEL
Prepare to: 3 TEE 5 TEEUP
Quick: 4 SPIN
the getaway car: 4 ABET
**Drive-___:** 4 THRU
**Drive-in**
employee: 6 CARHOP
**Drivel:** 3 PAP ROT 5 BILGE
   DROOL TRIPE 6 SALIVA
   SLAVER
**Driven**
group: 4 HERD
Like the ~ snow: 4 PURE
They're: 4 CARS
**Driver:** 4 WOOD
aid: 3 TEE
Back seat: 3 NAG
caution: 3 SLO
choice: 4 GEAR 5 SEDAN
device: 3 TEE
Dory: 3 OAR
Elephant: 6 MAHOUT
Gondola: 5 POLER
invitation: 5 HOPIN
lic. *(plural)*: 3 IDS
license datum: 3 AGE DOB
   SEX
licenses: 3 IDS
lic. info: 3 DOB HGT 5 IDENT
need: 3 GAS
need (abbr.): 3 LIC
New: 4 TEEN
one-eighty: 5 UTURN
org.: 3 AAA PGA
shield: 5 VISOR
Stake: 4 MAUL
warning: 4 FORE
**Drive-thru**
dispenser: 3 ATM
request: 5 ORDER
**Driveway**
blotch: 3 OIL
surface: 3 TAR 6 GRAVEL
**Driving**
aid: 3 TEE
choice: 7 ONEIRON

danger: 3 FOG ICE 4 SNOW
   5 GLARE SLEET
hazard: 3 FOG ICE 4 SNOW
   5 GLARE SLEET
need: 3 GAS TEE 7 EYETEST
place: 3 TEE 4 LANE
Rare ~ result: 3 ACE
**Drizzle:** 4 MIST RAIN
**"Dr. Kildare"**
actor Raymond: 6 MASSEY
**"Dr. No"**
actor Connery: 4 SEAN
Sean's costar in: 6 URSULA
**Droid**
of movies: 5 ARTOO
**Droll:** 3 WRY 7 AMUSING
folks: 4 WAGS
**Drome**
prefix: 4 AERO
**Drone:** 3 BEE 4 MALE
home: 4 HIVE
**Drones:** 4 HUMS
Like some: 5 APIAN
**Droning**
reed: 7 BAGPIPE
sound: 3 HUM
**Drood**
Dickens character: 5 EDWIN
**Drool:** 6 SLAVER 7 SLOBBER
**Drooling**
dog of comics: 4 ODIE
**Droop:** 3 LOP SAG 4 WILT
**Drooping:** 5 SAGGY
**Droopy-eared**
dog: 7 SPANIEL
hound: 6 BASSET
**Drop:** 3 EBB 4 LOSE OMIT
   6 PLUNGE 7 DESCEND
a line: 4 FISH
back: 3 LAG
by: 5 POPIN 6 STOPIN
down: 4 MOLT
Eye: 4 TEAR
for the count: 4 KAYO
from the eye: 4 TEAR
Get the ~ on: 3 NAB
in: 5 VISIT
in on: 3 SEE
in the ocean: 3 EBB
off: 3 NAP NOD 4 DOZE
   WANE 5 ABATE SLEEP
one's jaw: 4 GAPE
out: 6 SECEDE
Ready to: 5 ALLIN SPENT
Salty: 4 TEAR
shot: 4 DINK
Sweat: 4 BEAD
Theater: 5 SCRIM
the ball: 3 ERR
**Drop ___ (write):** 5 ALINE
**Drop-down**
list: 4 MENU
**Droplets**
Adorn with: 5 BEDEW
Form: 4 BEAD
Morning: 3 DEW

**___ drop of a hat:** 5 ATTHE
**Drop-off**
point: 4 EDGE
**Dropout**
doc.: 3 GED
**Dropped**
a line: 5 WROTE
It was ~ in the 1960s: 3 LSD
   4 ACID
off: 8 TOOKANAP
   10 FELLASLEEP
**Dropper**
Acorn: 3 OAK
Eaves: 6 ICICLE
Needle: 4 PINE
**Drought**
buster: 4 RAIN
ender: 4 RAIN
**Drought-damaged:** 4 SERE
**Drove:** 4 HERD
(around): 6 TOOLED
too fast: 4 SPED
**Drowned**
valley: 3 RIA
**"Drowning ___" (2000 film):**
   4 MONA
**Drowse**
Begin to: 3 NOD
**Droxie**
rival: 4 OREO
**"Dr. Strangelove"**
actor Wynn: 6 KEENAN
**Drub:** 4 LICK 5 PASTE
**Drubbing:** 4 ROUT
**Drucker**
Mad cartoonist: 4 MORT
**Drudge:** 4 MOIL PEON SERF
   5 SLAVE
Feudal: 4 SERF
Internet columnist: 4 MATT
work: 4 TOIL
**Drudgery:** 4 TOIL 5 LABOR
Classroom: 4 ROTE
Do: 4 MOIL
**Drug:** 6 OPIATE SEDATE
agent: 4 NARC 5 NARCO
buster: 4 NARC 5 NARCO
cop: 4 NARC 5 NARCO
Hallucinogenic: 3 LSD
Psychedelic: 3 LSD
source: 4 IPECAC
unit: 4 KILO
**Druggie:** 4 USER
**Druggist**
Thrice, to a: 3 TER
~, to a Brit: 7 CHEMIST
**Druid:** 4 CELT 6 PRIEST
**Drum**
accompanier: 4 FIFE
attachment: 5 SNARE
Beatnik's: 5 BONGO
Fifer's: 5 TABOR
Hand: 6 TOMTOM
Indian: 5 TABLA
major's hat: 5 SHAKO
material: 5 STEEL

out: 4 OUST
part: 5 SNARE
played with the hands:
    5 BONGO
site: 3 EAR
Small: 5 TABLA TABOR
sound: 4 ROLL
string: 5 SNARE
**Drummer:** 8 SALESMAN
**"Drums Along the Mohawk"**
    hero: 3 GIL
**Drumstick:** 3 LEG
    source: 4 FOWL
**Drunk:** 3 SOT 5 SOUSE
    7 PIEEYED
    Get: 5 BESOT
    suffix: 3 ARD
**Drunkard:** 3 SOT 4 LUSH
    5 SOUSE
**Drunken:** 5 BEERY
    6 SOTTED
    daze: 6 STUPOR
**Drury**
    Novelist: 5 ALLEN
**Drury Lane**
    composer: 4 ARNE
**Dry:** 3 SEC ARID SERE
    7 SAHARAN
    and crumbly: 5 MEALY
    as a bone: 4 ARID
    as a desert: 7 SAHARAN
    as dust: 4 ARID SERE
    Extra: 4 ARID
    In a ~ manner: 6 ARIDLY
    Make: 5 PARCH
    Not quite: 4 DAMP
    (off): 5 TOWEL
    On ~ land: 6 ASHORE
    out: 5 DETOX PARCH
    Place to ~ out: 5 REHAB
    run: 4 TEST
    Stay: 8 TEETOTAL
    Very: 4 ARID BRUT SERE
    ~, as Champagne: 4 BRUT
    ~, as wine: 3 SEC
    ~, in a way: 5 WRING
**Dry ___:** 3 MOP ROT
**Dry as ___:** 5 ABONE
**Dryden, John**
    year of death: 4 MDCC
**Dryer**
    batch: 4 LOAD
    buildup: 4 LINT
    Hops: 4 OAST
    Like a ~ trap: 5 LINTY
    outlet: 4 VENT
    residue: 4 LINT
**Drying**
    cloth: 5 TOWEL
    Keep from ~ out: 5 REWET
    oven: 4 OAST
**Drying-out**
    facility: 5 REHAB
    stint: 5 REHAB
**Drysdale**
    of baseball: 3 DON

**"Dr. Zhivago"**
    actor Rod: 7 STEIGER
    heroine: 4 LARA
**D sharp**
    equivalent: 5 EFLAT
**DST**
    When ~ begins: 3 APR
    When ~ ends: 3 OCT
**Duane**
    Guitarist: 4 EDDY
**Duarte, Maria Eva**
    after marriage:
      10 EVITAPERON
    He married: 5 PERON
**Dub:** 4 NAME
**Dubai:** 7 EMIRATE
    dignitary: 4 EMIR
**Dubbed:** 5 NAMED 6 TITLED
    one: 3 SIR
    Prepared to be: 5 KNELT
**Dubious:** 4 IFFY
    gift: 3 ESP
**Dublin**
    dance: 3 JIG
    denizens: 5 IRISH
    land: 4 EIRE ERIN
    theater: 5 ABBEY
**Dublin-born:** 5 IRISH
    poet: 5 YEATS
**Dubuque**
    native: 5 IOWAN
    state: 4 IOWA
**Dubya**
    and classmates: 4 ELIS
    deg.: 3 MBA
    Wife of: 5 LAURA
    ~, as a collegian: 3 ELI
**Ducat**
    word: 5 ADMIT
**Duchamp**
    art movement: 4 DADA
    contemporary: 3 ARP
**Duchess:** 5 TITLE
    Goya's: 4 ALBA
**Duchess of ___:** 4 YORK
**"Duchess of ___" (Goya work):**
    4 ALBA
**"Duchess of Alba"**
    painter: 4 GOYA
**Duchess of York:** 5 SARAH
**Duchin**
    Bandleader: 5 PETER
**Duchovny, David**
    Wife of: 3 TEA 8 TEALEONI
**Duchy**
    Old German: 4 SAXE
**Duck:** 5 AVERT AVOID DODGE
      ELUDE EVADE
      8 SIDESTEP
    Dabbling: 4 TEAL
    Dead: 5 GONER
    Diving: 4 SMEW 6 SCOTER
    down: 4 HIDE 5 EIDER
    Downy: 5 EIDER
    Eurasian: 4 SMEW
    Freshwater: 4 TEAL

    home: 4 POND
    Male: 5 DRAKE
    Pintail: 4 SMEE
    Pond: 4 TEAL
    Sea: 5 EIDER
    Small: 4 TEAL
    suffix: 4 LING
    Walk like a: 6 WADDLE
**"Duck ___":** 4 SOUP
**Duck, Daffy:** 4 TOON
**"___ Duckling, The":** 4 UGLY
**"Duck soup!":** 4 EASY
**"Duck Soup"**
    name: 4 MARX
**Ducky**
    color: 4 TEAL
    Just: 3 AOK
**Ducommun**
    Nobelist: 4 ELIE
**Duct:** 4 MAIN 5 CANAL
    Anatomical: 3 VAS
    Chimney: 4 FLUE
    follower: 4 TAPE
    prefix: 3 OVI
    suffix: 3 ILE
**Ductile**
    element: 3 TIN
**Dud:** 4 FLOP 5 LEMON
    Detroit: 5 EDSEL
    Social: 6 MISFIT
**Dude:** 3 BRO BUB CAT 5 FELLA
    Cool: 3 CAT
    Crude: 3 CAD 4 BOOR
    Macho: 5 HEMAN
    Mean: 4 OGRE
    Rich: 6 FATCAT
    Rude: 3 CAD 4 BOOR
    Stewed: 3 SOT
**Dudgeon:** 3 IRE 5 ANGER
    High: 3 IRE
**___ du Diable:** 3 ILE
**Dudley**
    Actor: 5 MOORE
    Beloved of: 4 NELL
**Duds:** 4 GARB 5 GETUP
    6 ATTIRE 7 THREADS
**Due:** 4 OWED
    Amount past: 3 TRE
    Before the ~ date: 5 EARLY
    follower: 3 TRE
    In ~ time: 4 ANON
    It may be: 4 EAST RENT
      WEST 5 NORTH SOUTH
    It's past: 3 TRE
    Landlord's: 4 RENT
    Past: 4 LATE
    Uno plus: 3 TRE
**Duel**
    invitation: 4 SLAP
    personality: 4 BURR
    6 SECOND
    prelude: 4 SLAP
    souvenir: 4 SCAR
    tool: 4 EPEE 5 SABER
**Dueler**
    distance: 4 PACE

**Dueling**
souvenir: 4 SCAR
sword: 4 EPEE
weapon: 4 EPEE
**Dues**
payer: 6 MEMBER
payer (abbr.): 3 MEM
receiver: 4 CLUB
**Duet:** 4 PAIR
plus one: 4 TRIO
**Duff:** 4 REAR RUMP
**Duffel:** 4 GEAR
filler: 4 GEAR
**Duffer**
cry: 4 FORE
dream: 3 ACE 5 EAGLE
goal: 3 PAR
headache: 4 TRAP
problem: 5 SLICE
**Dufy**
Artist: 5 RAOUL
**Dug:** 3 GOT
in: 3 ATE 10 ENTRENCHED
Really: 5 ATEUP
up: 5 MINED
~, in a way: 6 SPADED
**Dugong:** 6 SEACOW
**Dugout:** 4 BOAT 5 CANOE
fig.: 3 MGR
gear: 5 MITTS
shelter: 4 ABRI
vessel: 5 CANOE
~ VIP: 3 MGR
**Duisburg**
river: 4 RUHR
___ du jour: 4 PLAT
**Duke:** 4 FIST PEER 5 NOBLE
TITLE
(abbr.): 4 UNIV
His wife was a: 5 ASTIN
home: 4 DORM
of baseball: 6 SNIDER
She performed with: 4 ELLA
st.: 4 NCAR
**Duke, The:** 5 WAYNE
**"Duke Bluebeard's Castle"**
composer: 6 BARTOK
**Dukedom**
Notable: 4 YORK
**"Duke of ___" (1962 hit):**
4 EARL
**Duke of York:** 6 ANDREW
**"___ Dukes, The" (Ted Nugent's
old band):** 5 AMBOY
**"Dukes of Hazzard, The"**
Boss of: 4 HOGG
deputy: 4 ENOS
spin-off: 4 ENOS
**Duke University**
locale: 6 DURHAM
**"___ du lieber!":** 3 ACH
**Dull:** 4 BLAH DRAB 5 HOHUM
6 BORING
finish: 3 ARD 5 MATTE
pain: 4 ACHE
routine: 3 RUT 4 ROTE

sound: 4 THUD
suffix: 3 ARD
~, as text: 5 PROSY
**Dullard:** 4 BORE CLOD SIMP
**Dull-colored:** 4 DRAB
**Dullea**
Actor: 4 KEIR
**Dulles, Allen**
org.: 3 CIA
**Dulles Airport**
designer: 12 EEROSAARINEN
**Dullsville:** 4 BLAH 5 NOFUN
**Dull-witted**
person: 4 DODO
**Duma**
denial: 4 NYET
**Dumas**
character: 5 ATHOS 6 ARAMIS
7 PORTHOS
9 MUSKETEER
motto word: 3 ALL
**Dumb:** 5 INANE 7 ASININE
bunny: 5 STUPE
cluck: 4 DODO 5 IDIOT
**"Dumb"**
girl of comics: 4 DORA
**"Dumb & Dumber"**
actress: 4 GARR
**Dumbarton**
denial: 3 NAE
denizen: 4 SCOT
**Dumbarton ___:** 4 OAKS
**Dumbbell:** 4 DODO DOLT
5 IDIOT SCHMO STUPE
material: 4 IRON
**Dumbfound:** 3 AWE WOW
4 DAZE 5 AMAZE
7 STUPEFY
**Dumbo**
wing: 3 EAR
**Dumbstruck:** 4 AWED 5 AGAPE
INAWE
Leave: 3 AWE
**Dumfries**
denial: 3 NAE
denizen: 4 SCOT
**Dummkopf:** 3 ASS 4 CLOD
DODO 5 IDIOT
**Dummy:** 3 ASS 4 BOZO DODO
DOLT 6 NITWIT
STOOGE
name: 5 SNERD
perch: 4 KNEE
~, at times: 4 EAST WEST
5 NORTH SOUTH
**Dump:** 3 CAN STY 4 JILT
5 SCRAP 6 UNLOAD
7 EYESORE
emanation: 4 ODOR
output: 4 ODOR
**Dumpling**
Chinese: 6 WONTON
Potato: 7 GNOCCHI
**Dumps:** 5 STIES
Down in the: 3 SAD 4 BLUE
GLUM 6 MOROSE

**Dumpster**
contents: 5 TRASH
emanation: 4 ODOR
**Dunaway**
Actress: 4 FAYE
**Dunaway, Faye**
film: 13 MOMMIEDEAREST
15 EYESOFLAURAMARS
**Duncan**
Dancer: 7 ISADORA
of basketball: 3 TIM
product: 4 YOYO
When Macbeth slays: 5 ACTII
**Dunce:** 3 OAF 4 SIMP
7 AIRHEAD PINHEAD
**Dunce cap:** 4 CONE
shape: 5 CONIC
wearer: 4 DOLT DOPE
**"Dunciad, The"**
poet: 4 ROPE
**Dundee**
Info: Scottish cue
Boxing trainer: 6 ANGELO
denial: 3 NAE
denizen: 4 SCOT
portrayer: 5 HOGAN
Wee, in: 3 SMA
**Dunderhead:** 3 ASS OAF SAP
4 BOZO DOLT DOPE
5 IDIOT MORON
**"Dune"**
composer Brian: 3 ENO
**Dungeon**
Like a: 4 DANK
restraints: 5 IRONS
**Dungeons & Dragons**
co.: 3 TSR
fan: 5 GAMER
monster: 3 ORC
spellcaster: 4 MAGE
**Dunk:** 7 IMMERSE
___ dunk: 4 SLAM
**Dunkable**
cookie: 4 OREO
treat: 4 OREO 5 DONUT
**Dunked**
It may be: 4 OREO 5 DONUT
**Dunkers:** 4 SECT
**Dunn**
Comic: 4 NORA
**Dunne**
Actress: 5 IRENE
**Dunne, Irene**
film: 13 IREMEMBERMAMA
**Duo:** 3 TWO
times four: 5 OCTET
**Dup.**
Not a: 4 ORIG
___ du pays: 3 MAL
**Dupe:** 3 SAP 5 REPRO
6 DELUDE 7 CATSPAW
**Duped:** 3 HAD 7 TAKENIN
Easily: 5 NAIVE
Not ~ by: 4 ONTO
**Dupin**
creator: 3 POE

**Duple**
Dance in ~ time: 5 POLKA
**Duplicate:** 4 TWIN 5 CLONE
    DITTO REPRO
Sent a: 4 CCED
**Duplicitous:** 6 SNEAKY
    7 CROOKED
**Duplicity:** 5 GUILE 6 DECEIT
**DuPont**
introduced it: 5 ORLON
invention: 6 LUCITE
**Durability:** 4 WEAR
**Durable**
fabric: 5 CHINO SERGE
wood: 3 OAK 4 TEAK 5 LARCH
**Duracell**
competitor: 7 RAYOVAC
**Durango**
**Info:** Mexican cue
day: 3 DIA
dough: 5 PESOS
dwelling: 4 CASA
**Durant**
Historian: 5 ARIEL
**Durante**
Prominent ~ feature: 4 NOSE
song starter: 4 INKA
**Duration:** 4 TERM 6 LENGTH
    7 STRETCH
**D'Urbervilles**
lass: 4 TESS
**Durbeyfield**
girl: 4 TESS
**Durbin**
Actress: 6 DEANNA
**Dürer**
Emulate: 4 ETCH
**Durham**
sch.: 3 UNH
**During:** 4 AMID 6 AMIDST
the time that: 5 WHILE
**Durkheim**
Sociologist: 5 EMILE
**"___ durn tootin'!":** 3 YER
**___ Duro Canyon:** 4 PALO
**Durocher**
Baseball manager: 3 LEO
shortstop: 5 REESE
**Dusk**
Like: 6 TWILIT
Poet's: 3 EEN
~, to Donne: 3 EEN
**Düsseldorf**
**Info:** German cue
denial: 4 NEIN
direction: 3 OST
donkey: 4 ESEL
**Dust**
Bit of: 4 MOTE
Chimney: 4 SOOT
Collected: 3 SAT
Dry as: 4 ARID SERE
jacket feature: 3 BIO
Kind of: 6 COSMIC
Leave in the: 4 LOSE
Like a ~ bowl: 4 ARID

speck: 4 MOTE
Volcanic: 3 ASH
Word after: 3 BIN 5 CLOTH
**___ dust:** 5 DRYAS
**Dust Bowl**
migrant: 4 OKIE
refugee: 4 OKIE
**Dustcloth:** 3 RAG
**Duster:** 3 RAG 4 MAID
**Dustin**
Role for: 5 RATSO
**Dusting:** 5 CHORE
cloth: 3 RAG
target: 4 CROP
**"Dust in the Wind"**
group: 6 KANSAS
**Dustup:** 3 ROW 4 SPAT STIR
    5 SETTO
**Dutch**
airline: 3 KLM
bloom: 5 TULIP
carrier: 3 KLM
cheese: 4 EDAM 5 GOUDA
city: 3 EDE
commune: 3 EDE
explorer: 6 TASMAN
export: 4 EDAM 5 TULIP
humanist: 7 ERASMUS
It may be ~: 4 DOOR OVEN
It may be ~ or French: 4 DOOR
master: 5 STEEN
painter: 4 HALS 5 STEEN
sights: 5 DIKES
town: 4 EDAM
treat: 4 EDAM 5 GOUDA
**Dutch ___:** 4 OVEN
**Dutch Guiana**
~, today: 7 SURINAM
    8 SURINAME
**Dutch South African:** 4 BOER
**Dutra**
Golfer: 4 OLIN
**Duty:** 3 TAX 4 ONUS TASK
    6 IMPOST TARIFF
Customs: 6 IMPOST
Import: 6 TARIFF
Kind of: 5 CIVIC
Period of: 4 TOUR
Tour of: 5 STINT
**Duun**
Novelist: 4 OLAV
**Duvalier, Papa Doc:** 6 DESPOT
domain, once: 5 HAITI
**Duvall, Robert**
title role: 7 SANTINI
**Duvall, Shelley**
role: 8 OLIVEOYL
**___ du Vent:** 4 ILES
**DVD**
maker: 3 RCA
part: 5 VIDEO
**DVD player**
alternative: 3 VCR
maker: 3 RCA
necessities: 3 TVS
**Dvorak:** 5 CZECH

**Dwarf:** 4 STAR
Bespectacled: 3 DOC
complement: 5 SEVEN
Folklore: 5 GNOME
Silent: 5 DOPEY
Subterranean: 5 GNOME
tree: 6 BONSAI
**Dwarfs**
Disney's: 6 SEPTET
**Dweeb:** 4 GEEK NERD TWIT
    5 LOSER
**Dweebish:** 5 NERDY
**Dweezil**
Musician: 5 ZAPPA
**Dwell:** 4 BIDE 5 ABIDE
    6 RESIDE
on: 6 PONDER 7 BELABOR
(on): 4 HARP
permanently: 6 RESIDE
**Dweller**
Apartment: 6 TENANT
Arctic: 4 LAPP 5 INUIT
Attu: 5 ALEUT
Brook: 5 TROUT
Cave: 3 BAT
Convent: 3 NUN
Coop: 3 HEN
Cuzco: 4 INCA
Delhi: 5 HINDU
Dorm: 4 COED
Flat: 6 LESSEE
Forest: 3 DOE
Hill: 3 ANT
Igloo: 6 ESKIMO
Lamp: 5 GENIE
Mesa: 4 HOPI
Palace: 5 ROYAL
Pueblo: 4 HOPI
Reef: 3 EEL
Sty: 3 HOG SOW
**Dwelling:** 5 ABODE
Cliffside: 5 AERIE
Conical: 5 TEPEE
Crude: 3 HUT 5 SHACK
Durango: 4 CASA
Indian: 5 TEPEE
Lofty: 5 AERIE
Makeshift: 3 HUT
Miserable: 5 HOVEL
Navajo: 5 HOGAN
**Dwelt:** 5 LIVED 7 RESIDED
**Dwight**
General under: 4 OMAR
Loser to: 5 ADLAI
Opponent of: 5 ADLAI
**Dwindle:** 3 EBB 4 WANE
~, with "out": 5 PETER
**Dye:** 5 TINCT
at the salon: 5 HENNA
Blue: 4 ANIL 6 INDIGO
Hair: 5 HENNA
Indigo: 4 ANIL
Nitrogen-based: 3 AZO
Place to curl up and: 5 SALON
plant: 4 ANIL
Red: 5 EOSIN HENNA

worker: 7 STAINER
**Dyeing**
  art: 5 BATIK
**Dyemaking**
  chemical: 7 ANILINE
**Dyer**
  container: 3 VAT
**Dye-yielding**
  plant: 4 ANIL
**Dying**
  words: 4 ETTU
**Dykstra**
  of baseball: 3 LEN
**Dylan**
  Singer: 3 BOB

**Dynamic**
  Leader: 4 AERO
  opening: 4 AERO
  Prefix for: 4 AERO
  start: 4 AERO
**Dynamite:** 3 FAB 4 AONE
  Form of: 7 GELATIN
  ingredient, for short:
    5 NITRO
  inventor: 5 NOBEL
**Dynamo:** 8 FIREBALL
    LIVEWIRE
  part: 6 STATOR
**Dynasty**
  after the Ch'in: 3 HAN

  Chinese: 3 HAN WEI 4 CHOU
    MING
  Early Chinese: 4 HSIA
  of Confucius: 4 CHOU
**"Dynasty"**
  actress Emma: 5 SAMMS
  actress Linda: 5 EVANS
  conniver: 6 ALEXIS
  role for Joan: 6 ALEXIS
**Dyne**
  Prefix with: 4 AERO
**Dyne-centimeter:** 3 ERG
**Dzhugashvili**
  Leader originally surnamed:
    6 STALIN

# Ee

**E:** 3 DIR KEY 4 NOTE
  Morse: 3 DIT DOT
  Three before: 3 BCD
**E-3:** 3 PFC
**E-4**
  to E-7: 3 NCO
**Each:** 3 PER 4 APOP 5 AHEAD
    EVERY 6 APIECE
    ATHROW
  and every: 3 ALL
  For: 3 PER 6 APIECE
  in scores: 3 ALL
  Partner of: 5 EVERY
**"Each Dawn ___":** 4 IDIE
**"___ each life ...":** 4 INTO
**Eager:** 4 AGOG AVID KEEN
    5 DYING 6 ARDENT
    7 ATHIRST
  eater: 9 CHOWHOUND
  Far from: 5 LOATH
  Like an ~ guest: 5 EARLY
  to try: 6 KEENON
**Eagerly**
  Accept: 5 LAPUP 6 LEAPAT
  excited: 4 AGOG
  expectant: 4 ATIP
**Eagerness:** 4 ZEAL 5 ARDOR
**Eagle:** 6 SOARER
  Attack like an: 5 SWOOP
  claw: 5 TALON
  Fish-eating: 4 ERNE
  Fly like an: 4 SOAR
  Like an: 7 TALONED
  Muppet: 3 SAM
  nest: 5 AERIE
  org.: 3 BSA
  Sea: 3 ERN 4 ERNE
  Silver ~ wearer: 7 COLONEL
  The ~ that landed: 3 LEM
**Eagles:** 4 TEAM
**Eagles, The**
  Glenn of: 4 FREY
**Eaglet**
  nursery: 5 AERIE
**Ear:** 5 ORGAN
  bone: 5 INCUS 6 STAPES
  cleaner: 4 QTIP SWAB
  coverings: 5 MUFFS
  Inner: 3 COB
  Lend an: 4 HEED 6 LISTEN
  Like a turned: 4 DEAF
  Of the: 4 OTIC 5 AURAL
  part: 4 DRUM LOBE 5 CANAL
  prefix: 3 OTO
  problem: 6 OTITIS
  Stick it in your: 4 QTIP
  Word before: 3 TIN 5 INNER
**Earache:** 7 OTALGIA

**"___ ear and out ...":** 5 INONE
**Eared**
  pitcher: 4 EWER
  seal: 5 OTARY
**Earhart:** 8 AVIATRIX
  Aviator: 6 AMELIA
  Emulate: 6 AVIATE
  plane: 7 ELECTRA
**Earl:** 4 PEER 5 NOBLE TITLE
  Banjo player: 7 SCRUGGS
  French: 5 COMTE
  Jockey: 5 SANDE
  of Avon: 4 EDEN
  of jazz: 5 HINES
  Tea: 4 GREY
**Earldom**
  Anthony Eden: 4 AVON
  Devereux: 5 ESSEX
**Earl Grey:** 3 TEA
**Earlier:** 3 AGO ERE 5 OLDER
    PRIOR 6 BEFORE
  At an ~ time: 4 ONCE
  Born: 5 OLDER
  Of an ~ style: 5 RETRO
  Throwback to an ~ time:
    7 ATAVIST
**Early:** 3 WEE
  afternoon: 3 ONE TWO
    5 ONEPM
  afternoon time: 6 ONETEN
  arrival: 6 PREMIE
  bird: 3 EGG
  cab: 6 HANSOM
  car: 3 REO
  course: 4 SOUP 5 SALAD
  End: 5 ABORT
  evening: 5 SEVEN
  evictee: 3 EVE
  game score: 6 ONEONE
  hour: 5 ONEAM
  hrs.: 3 AMS
  in the morning: 6 ATDAWN
  man prefix: 3 CRO
  pulpit: 4 AMBO
  Put an ~ end to:
    11 NIPINTHEBUD
  release: 6 PAROLE
  round: 6 PRELIM
  stage: 5 ONSET
  times: 3 AMS 5 MORNS
  Very: 3 WEE
  word: 4 MAMA
  years: 5 YOUTH
  ~ P.M.: 3 AFT
**"Early Edition"**
  network: 3 CNN
**Earmark:** 5 ALLOT 7 DESTINE
    8 SETAPART

**Earn:** 4 MAKE 5 CLEAR GROSS
    MERIT 6 PULLIN
    TAKEIN 7 BRINGIN
    REALIZE
  after taxes: 3 NET
  and then some: 6 RAKEIN
**Earned:** 3 WON 4 MADE
  a citation: 4 SPED
**Earnest:** 7 INTENSE SINCERE
  request: 4 PLEA
**Earnestly**
  hope: 4 PRAY
**Earnhardt**
  Racer: 4 DALE
**Earnings:** 5 WAGES 6 SALARY
  Acct.: 3 INT
**Earp**
  Lawman: 5 WYATT
**Ear-piercing**
  It can be: 4 STUD
**Earring**
  site: 4 LOBE
  Small: 4 STUD
  style: 4 HOOP
**Ears**
  All: 4 RAPT
  Falling on deaf: 7 UNHEARD
  It's all: 4 CORN 5 MAIZE
  Like basset: 6 DROOPY
  Like some: 3 TIN
  Rabbit: 6 DIPOLE
    7 ANTENNA
  Up to one's: 5 AWASH
  Wet behind the: 3 RAW
    5 NAIVE
**Earshot**
  Within: 4 NEAR
**Earsplitting:** 4 LOUD
**Earth:** 3 SOD 4 DIRT LOAM
    SOIL 5 TERRA 6 SPHERE
  Anywhere on:
    11 UNDERTHESUN
  Came down to: 4 ALIT
  Clump of: 4 CLOD
  Come down to: 4 LAND
  crust layer: 4 SIMA
  Ends of the: 5 POLES
  force: 4 ONEG
  goddess: 4 GAEA GAIA
  Good: 4 LOAM
  Heaven on: 4 EDEN 6 UTOPIA
  hue: 5 OCHER OCHRE
  inheritors: 4 MEEK
  Most of ~ surface: 5 OCEAN
  Not from: 5 ALIEN
  On: 4 HERE
  Orbital point farthest from:
    6 APOGEE

orbiter: 3 MIR
pigment: 5 OCHER OCHRE
   6 SIENNA
remover: 6 DREDGE
sci.: 4 ECOL GEOG
tone: 4 ECRU 5 BEIGE OCHER
   OCHRE UMBER
Wet: 3 MUD 4 CLAY MIRE
Word after: 4 TONE
~, in German: 4 ERDE
~, in sci-fi: 5 TERRA
**Eartha**
Singer: 4 KITT
**Earthbound**
bird: 3 EMU
**Earth Day**
mo.: 3 APR
month: 5 APRIL
subj.: 4 ECOL
**Earthen**
pot: 4 OLLA
**Earthenware**
pot: 4 OLLA 5 CROCK
source: 4 CLAY
**Earth First**
prefix: 3 ECO
**Earth-friendly**
prefix: 3 ECO
sci.: 4 ECOL
**"Earth in the Balance"**
author: 4 GORE 6 ALGORE
**Earthling:** 5 HUMAN
~, in sci-fi: 6 TERRAN
**Earthlings**
Most: 6 ASIANS
**EarthLink:** 3 ISP
competitor: 3 AOL
**Earthmover:** 5 DOZER
maker, for short: 3 CAT
**Earthquake:** 5 SEISM
   7 TEMBLOR
1995 ~ site: 4 KOBE
origins: 4 FOCI
**Earthquake-related:** 7 SEISMAL
   SEISMIC
**Earthshaking:** 7 SEISMIC
It's: 6 TREMOR
**Earth-sky**
boundary (abbr.): 3 HOR
**Earth Summit**
site: 3 RIO
**Earthy**
deposit: 4 MARL
desire: 4 LUST
pigment: 5 OCHER OCHRE
   UMBER
**Ear-to-ear**
smile: 4 GRIN
**Ease:** 5 ABATE LETUP
   6 LESSEN
Less at: 6 EDGIER
up: 5 ABATE 6 LOOSEN
___ ease: 5 ILLAT
**Easel:** 5 STAND
**"Ease on Down the Road"**
musical: 6 THEWIZ

**Easier**
Make ~ to take: 9 SUGARCOAT
version, in music: 5 OSSIA
**"Easier said ___ done":** 4 THAN
**Easiness**
Epitome of: 3 ABC PIE
**Easing**
of tension: 4 THAW
**East:** 6 ORIENT
end: 3 ERN
ender: 3 ERN
From the: 5 ASIAN
of the Urals: 4 ASIA
Priest of the: 4 LAMA
suffix: 3 ERN
The: 4 ASIA 6 ORIENT
Way of the: 3 TAO
wind: 5 EURUS
~, in German: 3 OST
~, in Spanish: 7 ORIENTE
**East China Sea**
island: 5 MATSU
**East Coast**
rte.: 5 USONE
**Easter**
egg coloring: 3 DYE
entrée: 3 HAM 4 LAMB
event: 6 PARADE
flower: 4 LILY
follower: 4 SEAL
headgear: 6 BONNET
lead-in: 3 NOR
Like ~ eggs: 4 DYED
or Christmas (abbr.): 3 ISL
preceder: 3 NOR 4 LENT
   10 PALMSUNDAY
**Easter Island**
owner: 5 CHILE
statues: 7 COLOSSI
**Eastern:** 5 ASIAN
air: 4 RAGA
cuisine: 4 THAI
discipline: 3 ZEN 4 YOGA
holiday: 3 TET
ideal: 3 TAO
leader: 3 AGA
music: 4 RAGA
nanny: 4 AMAH
nursemaid: 4 AMAH
philosophy: 3 TAO
royal: 4 RANI
sash: 3 OBI
tie: 3 OBI
title: 3 AGA SRI
way: 3 TAO
wrap: 4 SARI
~ Canadian indian: 6 MICMAC
~ Christian: 6 UNIATE
~ European: 4 SERB SLAV
~ Indian: 4 ERIE
**East German**
secret police: 5 STASI
**East Indian**
sailor: 6 LASCAR
**East Lansing**
sch.: 3 MSU

**"East of ___":** 4 EDEN
**"East of Eden"**
brother: 3 CAL 4 ARON
character Cathy: 4 AMES
director Kazan: 4 ELIA
family name: 5 TRASK
girl: 4 ABRA
**Easton**
Singer: 6 SHEENA
**Easton ___, Bret**
Author: 5 ELLIS
**Eastwood**
1980 ~ film:
   11 BRONCOBILLY
Actor: 5 CLINT
series: 7 RAWHIDE
TV role for: 5 YATES
**Easy:** 7 LENIENT
basket: 5 LAYUP
dupe: 3 SAP
gait: 4 LOPE TROT 5 AMBLE
gallop: 6 CANTER
job: 4 SNAP
mark: 3 SAP 4 DUPE PREY
   SIMP 5 CHUMP PATSY
   6 PIGEON 7 LIVEONE
Not ~ to find: 4 RARE
on the eyes: 6 PRETTY
out: 5 POPUP
pace: 4 LOPE TROT 5 AMBLE
Proverbial ~ life leader:
   5 RILEY
Take it: 4 LAZE LOAF LOLL
   REST 5 COAST RELAX
target: 3 SAP
   11 SITTINGDUCK
task: 4 SNAP
The ~ life: 10 BEDOFROSES
threesome: 3 ABC
throw: 3 LOB 4 TOSS
to fool: 5 NAIVE
to manage: 4 TAME
to understand: 5 CLEAR
two-pointer: 4 DUNK
victory: 4 ROMP ROUT
   7 RUNAWAY
way out: 4 DOOR
**"Easy!":** 5 ASNAP
**Easy ___:** 5 ASABC ASPIE
   6 STREET
**"___ Easy" (1977 hit):** 5 ITSSO
**Easy as ___:** 3 ABC
**Easy as falling off ___:** 4 ALOG
**Easy chair**
site: 3 DEN
Use an: 7 RECLINE
**Easygoing**
Not: 5 TESTY
**Easy-listening:** 4 LITE
**Easy Street**
On: 4 RICH
Was on: 9 HADITMADE
Where ~ is: 7 FATCITY
**"Easy to Be Hard"**
musical: 4 HAIR
**Easy-to-prepare:** 6 NOBAKE

**Eat:** 3 SUP 4 DINE HAVE
    6 FEEDON INGEST
All you can: 7 EDIBLES
away: 4 GNAW 5 ERODE
    7 CORRODE
away at: 5 ERODE
between meals: 4 NOSH
    5 SNACK
He'll ~ anything:
    8 OMNIVORE
in style: 4 DINE
into: 5 ERODE
like a bird: 4 PECK
Ready to: 4 DONE RIPE
sumptuously: 5 FEAST
Unable to ~ another bite:
    7 STUFFED
voraciously: 5 SCARF
well: 4 DINE
What you: 4 DIET
**"Eat Drink Man Woman"**
director Lee: 3 ANG
**"Eat ___ eaten!":** 4 ORBE
**Eaten**
up: 4 GONE
**Eater**
Abalone: 5 OTTER
Apple: 3 EVE
Bamboo: 5 PANDA
Eucalyptus: 5 KOALA
Lean: 5 SPRAT
Pumpkin: 5 PETER
Seaweed: 7 ABALONE
Slop: 5 SWINE
Sweater: 4 MOTH
**Eatery:** 4 CAFE 5 DINER
Casual: 6 BISTRO
Famed New York: 7 ELAINES
Outmoded: 7 AUTOMAT
Puck's: 5 SPAGO
Small: 7 TEAROOM
**"Eat hearty!":** 5 DIGIN
**Eating**
alcove: 7 DINETTE
plan: 4 DIET
Start: 5 DIGIN
**"Eating ___" (1982 film):**
    5 RAOUL
**Eat like ___:** 4 APIG 5 ABIRD
    6 AHORSE
**Eats:** 3 HAS 4 CHOW GRUB
**Eau ___, Wisconsin:** 6 CLAIRE
**Eaves**
dropper: 6 ICICLE
**Eavesdrop:** 3 TAP 4 HEAR
**Eavesdropper:** 5 SNOOP
**Eban**
of Israel: 4 ABBA
**eBay**
action: 3 BID
Beat on: 6 OUTBID
user: 6 SELLER
**Ebb:** 4 WANE WILT
    6 RECEDE
and neap: 5 TIDES
Of ~ and neap: 5 TIDAL

**Ebbets Field**
great: 5 REESE
**Ebenezer**
exclamation: 3 BAH
Partner of: 5 JACOB
**Eberhard ___:** 5 FABER
**Ebert**
Emulate: 4 RATE
Former partner of: 6 SISKEL
**Ebony**
counterpart of song: 5 IVORY
**Ebro:** 3 RIO
City on the: 9 SARAGOSSA
**Ebullience:** 3 VIM
**Ecbatana**
resident: 4 MEDE
**Eccentric:** 3 NUT ODD 4 KOOK
    5 BATTY DOTTY KOOKY
    LOOPY NUTTY OUTRE
    WACKO 6 SCREWY
    7 ODDBALL
people: 9 HEADCASES
type: 5 FLAKE
wheel: 3 CAM
**Eccentricity:** 3 TIC 7 ODDNESS
**Ecclesiastes**
Phrase repeated in: 5 ATIME
**Ecclesiastical**
council: 5 SYNOD
office: 3 SEE
**Echelon:** 4 RANK TIER
Top: 5 ELITE
**Echidna**
morsel: 3 ANT
**Echo:** 4 RING 5 NYMPH OREAD
    6 ANSWER REPEAT
    7 ITERATE RESOUND
    8 RESONATE
effect: 6 REVERB
Emulate: 4 PINE
finder: 5 SONAR
spot: 6 CANYON
**Echolocation**
device: 5 SONAR
**"Echo Park"**
actress: 3 DEY
**Eclectic**
magazine: 4 UTNE
mix: 4 OLIO
**Eclipse:** 4 OMEN
Kind of: 5 LUNAR SOLAR
shadow: 5 UMBRA
sight: 4 RING 6 CORONA
**Eco-friendly**
org.: 3 EPA
**Ecol.**
watchdog: 3 EPA
**Ecological**
adjective: 5 SERAL
community: 5 BIOME
**Econ.**
measure: 3 GNP
**Economic**
cycle: 11 BOOMANDBUST
extremes: 10 BOOMORBUST
fig.: 3 GNP

prefix: 5 SOCIO
stat.: 3 CPI
warfare tactic: 7 EMBARGO
What ~ sanctions can lead to:
    8 TRADEWAR
**Economical:** 4 LEAN
**Economics**
prefix: 5 MACRO MICRO
~ Nobelist: *see page 736*
**Economize:** 4 SAVE 6 SCRIMP
    10 CUTCORNERS
**Economy:** 4 SIZE 6 THRIFT
Failed ~ car: 4 YUGO
Lack of: 5 WASTE
**Economy-size:** 5 GIANT JUMBO
**Ecru:** 5 BEIGE
**Ecstasy:** 5 BLISS
Go into: 5 SWOON
In: 4 SENT
**"Ecstasy"**
actress Hedy: 6 LAMARR
**Ecstatic**
Make: 5 ELATE
**Ecto-**
Opposite of: 4 ENDO ENTO
**Ecuador**
Capital of: 5 QUITO
East, in: 7 ORIENTE
Ending for: 3 EAN
**Ecuadoran**
cash: 6 SUCRES
**Ed**
Actor: 5 ASNER
and Mel of baseball: 4 OTTS
Comedian: 4 WYNN
Former NYC mayor: 4 KOCH
Former SAG president:
    5 ASNER
Mingo portrayer: 4 AMES
of the Reagan cabinet:
    5 MEESE
Singer: 4 AMES
Wife of: 6 TRIXIE
**"Ed"**
network: 3 NBC
**Ed.**
Enclosure to an: 4 SASE
First: 4 ORIG
Fixed by an: 4 CORR
group: 3 PTA
provider: 3 SCH
Submissions to an: 3 MSS
___ Ed.: 4 PHYS
**Eda**
Author: 6 LESHAN
**Edam:** 6 CHEESE
relative: 5 GOUDA
**Edberg**
of tennis: 6 STEFAN
or Borg: 5 SWEDE
**Eddas**
Language of the: 8 OLDNORSE
**Eddie**
and Edward: 7 ALBERTS
Ex of: 3 LIZ
Famous cop: 4 EGAN

of baseball: 4 YOST 5 LOPAT
Rocker: 8 VANHALEN
Vaudevillian: 3 FOY
**Eddy:** 5 SWIRL
Guitarist: 5 DUANE
**Eddying:** 6 ASWIRL
**Edelweiss**
source: 4 ALPS
**Eden**
event: 4 FALL
evictee: 3 EVE 4 ADAM
Like Nod, to: 4 EAST
**Eden, Anthony:** 4 EARL
earldom: 4 AVON
**Eden, Barbara**
role: 5 GENIE
**"___ ed Euridice":** 5 ORFEO
**Edgar:** 5 AWARD
Painter: 5 DEGAS
Psychic: 5 CAYCE
**Edgar Allan ___:** 3 POE
**Edgard**
Composer: 6 VARESE
**Edge:** 3 HEM LIP RIM 4 TRIM
6 BORDER
along: 5 SIDLE
Beveled: 4 CANT
Bowler: 4 BRIM
Canyon: 3 RIM
Cutting: 3 LIP 5 BLADE
Drape: 3 HEM
Extreme: 5 BRINK
Give an ~ to: 4 HONE WHET
Golf-hole: 3 LIP
Had an: 3 LED
Hat: 4 BRIM
Have an ~ against: 4 ABUT
It lacks a cutting: 4 EPEE
On: 5 JUMPY TENSE TESTY
6 UNEASY
Outer: 3 RIM 6 FRINGE
Put an ~ on: 4 HONE WHET
Racer's: 9 HEADSTART
Rock on the: 6 TEETER
Roof: 4 EAVE
Server: 4 ADIN
Skirt: 3 HEM
Tennis: 4 ADIN
The ~ of night: 4 DUSK
Water's: 5 SHORE
Wear at the: 4 FRAY
**Edger**
Lid: 8 EYELINER
**Edgy:** 5 TENSE WIRED
**Edible**
Become: 5 RIPEN
clam: 6 QUAHOG
mollusk: 6 OYSTER
7 ABALONE
mushroom: 5 MOREL
No longer: 3 BAD
pocket: 4 PITA
pod: 4 OKRA 5 CAROB
root: 3 YAM 4 TARO
snail: 8 ESCARGOT
spikes: 4 EARS

tuber: 3 OCA YAM 4 TARO
6 POTATO
**Edict:** 4 FIAT 6 DECREE
7 MANDATE
1598 ~ site: 6 NANTES
Czar: 5 UKASE
**Edinburgh**
native: 4 SCOT
**Edison**
contemporary: 5 TESLA
grant: 6 PATENT
middle name: 4 ALVA
product: 4 IDEA
**Edison, Thomas ___:** 4 ALVA
**Edit:** 5 AMEND EMEND
6 REDACT REVISE
anew: 5 RECUT
film: 6 SPLICE
menu choice: 4 UNDO
out: 4 DELE 5 BLEEP
6 DELETE
**Edited**
Not: 5 UNCUT
**Edith**
Archie's admonition to:
6 STIFLE
Chanteuse: 4 PIAF
Mike, to: 5 INLAW
portrayer: 4 JEAN
~, to Archie: 7 DINGBAT
**Edith ___**
Tomlin character: 3 ANN
**Editing**
Do some film: 6 SPLICE
Do some tape: 3 DUB
Film ~ technique: 4 WIPE
Work at film: 5 RECUT
**Edition**
Later: 7 REPRINT
Mag.: 3 ISS
Magazine: 5 ISSUE
Most-used ~ (abbr.): 3 STD
Special: 5 EXTRA
**Editor**
Encl. to an: 3 SAE 4 SASE
Film: 7 SPLICER
find: 4 TYPO
Leave in, to an: 4 STET
mark: 4 DELE STET
Material for an: 4 COPY
of the New Yorker: 4 ROSS
Remove, to an: 4 DELE
~ Brown: 4 TINA
**Editorial**
submissions (abbr.): 3 MSS
**Editorialize:** 5 OPINE
**"Editorially speaking"**
~, in chat rooms: 3 IMO
**Edmond**
Card game authority: 5 HOYLE
**Edmonton**
hockey player: 5 OILER
province: 7 ALBERTA
**Edmund**
Actor: 5 GWENN
Shakespearean actor: 4 KEAN

**"Ed, ___ n' Eddy":** 3 EDD
**Edom**
Ancient kingdom near: 4 MOAB
**Edomite**
city: 5 PETRA
**Edouard**
Composer: 4 LALO
**Eds.**
Submissions to: 3 MSS
**Edson**
Athlete born: 4 PELE
**"EDtv"**
director Howard: 3 RON
**Edu**
alternative: 3 ORG
**Educ.**
group: 3 PTA
institution: 3 SCH
**Educate:** 5 TEACH 6 SCHOOL
**Educated**
It may be: 5 GUESS
**Education**
Basics of: 3 RRR
Early: 4 ABCS
gp.: 3 PTA
grant name: 4 PELL
K-12, in: 4 ELHI
station: 4 DESK
Uncreative: 4 ROTE
**Educational**
items used to illustrate
everyday life: 6 REALIA
**Educator**
org.: 3 NEA
Royal: 4 ETON
**Edward**
and Eddie: 7 ALBERTS
Archbishop: 4 EGAN
New Yorker cartoonist:
5 SOREL
Playwright: 5 ALBEE
Poet: 4 LEAR
**Edward G.**
role: 4 RICO
**Edward James ___**
Actor: 5 OLMOS
**Edwards**
(abbr.): 3 AFB
Director: 5 BLAKE
**Edwin**
Former Attorney General:
5 MEESE
**"Ed Wood"**
director Burton: 3 TIM
star: 4 DEPP
~ Oscar winner: 6 LANDAU
**EEC**
Part of: 3 EUR
**Eel:** 6 CONGER
Feared: 5 MORAY
Glass: 5 ELVER
lookalike: 7 LAMPREY
Where to find: 8 SUSHIBAR
Young: 5 ELVER
**E'en**
if: 3 THO

Not ~ once: 4 NEER
**Eerie:** 6 SPOOKY 7 STRANGE
feeling: 6 DEJAVU
sighting: 3 UFO
**E'erlasting:** 6 ETERNE
**Eero**
Dad of: 5 ELIEL
**Eeyore**
Creator of: 5 MILNE
7 AAMILNE
**Effect**
Audio: 4 ECHO
Canyon: 4 ECHO
Dazzling: 5 ECLAT
Discotheque: 6 STROBE
Echo: 6 REVERB
Guitar: 4 WAWA
Have an: 4 TELL WORK
Having: 7 INURING
Ice cream: 5 SWIRL
Jacuzzi: 4 EDDY
Lasting: 4 SCAR
Lunar: 4 TIDE
Magic sound: 4 POOF
Meteorological: 4 HALO
Muted: 4 WAWA
Organ: 7 TREMOLO
Partner of: 5 CAUSE
Put into: 5 ENACT
Replay: 5 SLOMO
Singing: 7 TREMOLO
Sound: 4 ECHO
Take: 5 INURE SETIN
Vibrating: 7 TREMOLO
**Effective:** 7 INFORCE
OPERANT
Cleverly: 4 NEAT
power: 5 TEETH
**Effectively**
Use: 5 WIELD
**Effectiveness**
Range of: 5 SCOPE
**Effects**
Reverse the ~ of: 4 UNDO
**Effervescent**
Make: 6 AERATE
**Efficiency**
experts:
15 SYSTEMSANALYSTS
Fuel ~ abbr.: 3 MPG
symbol: 3 ETA
**Efficient:** 4 ABLE
**Effigy:** 5 IMAGE
**Effluvia**
Noxious: 6 MIASMA
**Effluvium**
Emit: 4 REEK
**Effort:** 4 DINT STAB
Carry with: 3 LUG 4 HAUL
Clean with: 5 SCRUB
Contest: 5 ENTRY
Exert no: 5 COAST
Gather with: 7 SCAREUP
High mark with low: 5 EASYA
Kind of: 9 LASTDITCH
Last-ditch: 5 STAND

Lift with: 4 HEFT 5 HEAVE
Make an: 3 TRY 6 STRIVE
Put forth: 5 EXERT
Throw with: 5 HEAVE
Vigorous: 11 ELBOWGREASE
Walk with: 4 PLOD SLOG
6 TRUDGE
Waste: 14 SPINONESWHEELS
With little: 6 EASILY
___ effort: 4 AFOR EFOR
**Effortless:** 4 EASY
pace: 4 ROMP
**Effortlessly**
Move: 5 GLIDE
**Effortlessness:** 4 EASE
**Effrontery:** 4 GALL 5 BRASS
CHEEK
**Effusive**
Be: 4 GUSH
**E-file**
org.: 3 IRS
**E flat**
equivalent: 6 DSHARP
**Eft:** 4 NEWT
**Eg.**
and Syr., once: 3 UAR
**E.g.**
relative: 3 VIZ
**"Egad!":** 4 OATH OHMY YIPE
**Egg:** 4 OVUM URGE 6 GAMETE
beater: 5 WHISK
carton abbr.: 3 DOZ 4 USDA
cell: 4 OVUM
cells: 3 OVA
container: 4 NEST 6 OVISAC
cream ingredient: 4 SODA
5 SYRUP
dish: 6 OMELET
drink: 3 NOG
Goose: 3 NIL ZIP 4 NADA
ZERO 6 NAUGHT
holder: 3 SAC 4 NEST
Immature ~ cell: 6 OOCYTE
Kind of nest: 7 ROTHIRA
Lay an: 4 BOMB FLOP
layers: 4 HENS
Like a good: 6 GRADEA
Louse: 3 NIT
Nest: 3 IRA 7 ROTHIRA
on: 4 COAX DARE GOAD
PROD SPUR URGE
6 INCITE
One with a nest: 3 HEN
order: 4 OVER
11 SUNNYSIDEUP
Paint with ~ in it: 7 TEMPERA
part: 4 YOLK
prefix: 3 OVI OVO
Prepare an: 5 POACH
producer: 3 HEN
purchase: 5 DOZEN
qty.: 3 DOZ
shape: 4 OVAL
size: 5 JUMBO LARGE
Small: 5 OVULE
warmer: 3 HEN

white: 7 ALBUMIN
Word following: 4 ROLL
**"Egg ___, The":** 4 ANDI
**Egg foo ___:** 4 YUNG
**Egghead:** 4 NERD 5 BRAIN
6 SAVANT
**Egg-laying**
animal: 7 ECHIDNA
**Egglike:** 6 OVULAR
**Eggnog**
spice: 6 NUTMEG
Time for: 4 NOEL YULE
**Eggplant**
dish: 8 MOUSSAKA
**Egg roll**
place: 4 LAWN
time: 6 EASTER
**Eggs:** 3 OVA ROE
Bake: 5 SHIRR
partner: 3 HAM
**Egg-shaped:** 4 OVAL 5 OVATE
OVOID
instrument: 7 OCARINA
**Eggshell:** 4 ECRU
**Eggy**
cake: 5 TORTE
dessert: 4 FLAN
drink: 3 NOG
entrée: 6 OMELET
**Egg ___ yung:** 3 FOO
**Ego:** 4 SELF
Altar: 3 MRS 5 GROOM
of Freud: 3 ICH
**Egotist**
interest: 4 SELF
**Egoyan**
Director: 4 ATOM
**Egret:** 5 WADER
relative: 4 IBIS 5 HERON
**Egypt**
Anwar of: 5 SADAT
Capital of: 5 CAIRO
Gulf between Saudi Arabia and:
5 AQABA
Lake of: 6 NASSER
Mubarak of: 5 HOSNI
Nasser of: 5 GAMAL
neighbor (abbr.): 3 ISR
Opera set in: 4 AIDA
Port of: 4 SAID
President of: 7 MUBARAK
River of: 4 NILE
Sacred bird of: 4 IBIS
Sadat of: 5 ANWAR
Symbol of ancient: 3 ASP
~, in the 1960s: 3 UAR
**Egyptian**
beetle: 6 SCARAB
bird: 4 IBIS
boy king: 3 TUT
canal: 4 SUEZ
cobra: 3 ASP
cross: 4 ANKH
dam: 5 ASWAN
deity: 6 AMENRA
Former ~ leader: 5 SADAT

god: 4 PTAH
goddess of fertility: 4 ISIS
god of the underworld:
   6 OSIRIS
money: 7 PIASTER
peninsula: 5 SINAI
pharoah: 7 RAMESES
port: 4 SUEZ
pyramid: 4 TOMB
queen: 4 CLEO
snake: 3 ASP
sun deity: 4 ATEN
symbol of life: 4 ANKH
symbol of resurrection:
   6 SCARAB
viper: 3 ASP
~ Christian: 4 COPT
**"Eh":** 4 SOSO
**Ehud**
of Israel: 5 BARAK
successor: 5 ARIEL
**E-I**
connection: 3 FGH
**Eiffel ___:** 5 TOWER
**Eiffel Tower**
home: 5 PARIS
**Eiger:** 3 ALP
**Eight**
Based on: 5 OCTAL
Behind the ~ ball: 6 INAJAM
   7 INAHOLE
bits: 4 BYTE
furlongs: 4 MILE
Group of: 5 OCTAD OCTET
Half a figure: 3 ESS
Name of ~ popes: 5 URBAN
One of ~ Eng. kings: 3 EDW
prefix: 4 OCTA OCTO
pts.: 3 GAL
quarts: 4 PECK
Word in ~ Commandments:
   3 NOT
~, in German: 4 ACHT
~, in Spanish: 4 OCHO
**Eight-armed**
creature: 7 OCTOPUS
creatures: 6 OCTOPI
**Eightball**
choice: 6 SOLIDS
shot: 5 MASSE
**Eight-based:** 5 OCTAL
**Eight-day**
observance: 8 CHANUKAH
**"Eight Days ___":** 5 AWEEK
**Eighteenth Amendment**
state: 3 DRY
**Eighteen-wheeler:** 3 RIG
   4 SEMI
**Eighth**
Greek letter: 5 THETA
**"Eight Is Enough"**
actor Willie: 5 AAMES
**Eight-legged**
Deity with an ~ horse: 4 ODIN
**Eight-line**
verse: 7 TRIOLET

**Eight-member**
ensemble: 5 OCTET
**Eightsome:** 5 OCTAD OCTET
**Eighty Eight:** 4 OLDS
**Eighty-eight:** 5 PIANO
**Eighty-six:** 3 NIX 4 TOSS
   5 DITCH
**EIK**
Part of: 5 EATIN
site: 3 APT
**Eins**
und zwei: 4 DREI
**Einstein:** 5 BRAIN
birthplace: 3 ULM
Everything, to: 5 ALLES
factor: 4 MASS
~, for one: 6 EMIGRE
**Eisaku**
1974 Peace Nobelist: 4 SATO
**Eisenhower**
and others: 4 IKES
Mrs.: 5 MAMIE
nickname: 3 IKE
Secretary of State under:
   6 DULLES
WWII command: 3 ETO
**Eisenhower Center**
city: 7 ABILENE
**Eisenstein**
Director: 6 SERGEI
**"Either he goes, ___ do!":** 3 ORI
**Eithne Ní Bhraonáin**
Singer born: 4 ENYA
**Eject:** 4 BOOT OUST SPEW
   6 CASTUP
lava: 5 ERUPT
**E-junk:** 4 SPAM
**Ekberg**
Actress: 5 ANITA
**Eke**
out a living: 6 MAKEDO
**EKG**
Part of: 4 GRAM
**Ekland**
Actress: 5 BRITT
**El ___**
(Spanish hero): 3 CID
(Spanish painter): 5 GRECO
(Texas city): 4 PASO
(treasure city): 6 DORADO
(weather phenomenon):
   4 NINO
(western peak): 7 CAPITAN
(WWII battle site): 7 ALAMEIN
**"El ___" (Marty Robbins hit):**
   4 PASO
**Elaborate:** 6 ORNATE
display: 5 ECLAT
party: 4 FETE GALA
tapestry: 5 ARRAS
**Elaine**
Friend of Jerry and: 5 COSMO
Home of: 7 ASTOLAT
**El Al**
destination: 3 LOD 7 TELAVIV
**___ el Amarna, Egypt:** 3 TEL

**Elan:** 4 DASH
**Elapse:** 4 GOBY
**Elastic:** 7 RUBBERY
wood: 3 ASH YEW
**Elasticity:** 4 GIVE
**Elate:** 4 SEND 7 OVERJOY
**Elated:** 4 GLAD SENT 5 HAPPY
   11 ONCLOUDNINE
Be visibly: 4 GLOW
Where the ~ walk: 5 ONAIR
**Elath**
neighbor: 5 AQABA
**Elation:** 3 JOY 4 GLEE
**Elba**
Send to: 5 EXILE
**Elbe**
tributary: 4 EGER
**Elbow:** 3 JAB 4 POKE PROD
   5 JOINT NUDGE SHOVE
   6 JOSTLE
Bend one's: 4 TOPE 6 IMBIBE
Bone below the: 4 ULNA
Gently: 5 NUDGE
site: 3 ARM
Use ~ grease: 4 TOIL 5 SCOUR
   SCRUB
**Elbow-bender:** 3 SOT 4 LUSH
   5 SOUSE
**Elbow room:** 5 SPACE
**Elbows:** 5 PASTA
on the table: 5 PASTA
   8 MACARONI
Pipe: 4 ELLS
**Elbow-wrist**
connection: 4 ULNA
**El Capitan**
Like the face of: 5 STEEP
**El Cid:** 4 HERO
foe: 4 MOOR
**Elder:** 4 TREE
elver: 3 EEL
of Isaac: 4 ESAU
~ Judd: 5 NAOMI
~ Saarinen: 5 ELIEL
**"Elder"**
Roman: 4 CATO
**Elderly:** 3 OLD 4 AGED
**Eldest**
of Cain: 5 ENOCH
of Eve: 4 CAIN
of Isaac: 4 ESAU
of Noah: 4 SHEM
**El Dorado**
treasure: 3 ORO
**"Eldorado"**
rock gp.: 3 ELO
**"___ e Leandro":** 3 ERO
**Eleanor**
Children's author: 5 ESTES
Feminist: 5 SMEAL
First Lady before: 3 LOU
in a Beatles hit: 5 RIGBY
successor: 4 BESS
~, to Teddy: 5 NIECE
**Eleanora**
Actress: 4 DUSE

**Eleazar:** 8 AARONITE
**Elec.**
  company: 4 UTIL
  designation: 4 ACDC
  system component: 3 IGN
**Elect:** 3 OPT 6 CHOOSE
    CHOSEN VOTEIN
**Elected**
  officials: 3 INS
  Try to get: 3 RUN
**Electees:** 3 INS
**Election**
  data: 7 RETURNS
  day (abbr.): 4 TUES
  Fix an: 3 RIG
  hanger-on: 4 CHAD
  loser: 3 OUT 7 ALSORAN
  mo.: 3 NOV
  news: 5 UPSET
  winners: 3 INS
**Elective**
  High school: 3 ART
**Electoral**
  Winner by one ~ vote:
    5 HAYES
**Electorate:** 6 VOTERS
**Electra**
  Brother of: 4 ORIN 7 ORESTES
**Electric**
  co.: 4 UTIL
  coil inventor: 5 TESLA
  current blocker: 8 RESISTOR
  eye: 6 SENSOR
  fish: 3 EEL
  flux symbol: 3 PSI
  measure: 3 AMP
  One with ~ organs: 3 EEL
  partner: 3 GAS
  swimmer: 3 EEL
  unit: 4 VOLT
**Electric ___:** 3 ARC EEL EYE
**Electrical**
  bridge: 3 ARC
  device: 7 ADAPTER ADAPTOR
  Do ~ work: 4 WIRE
  gauge: 7 AMMETER
  inventor Nikola: 5 TESLA
  letters: 4 ACDC
  Make ~ improvements:
    6 REWIRE
  network: 4 GRID
  pioneer: 5 TESLA
  problem: 9 SHORTFUSE
  resistance: 6 OHMAGE
  resistance unit: 3 OHM
  safeguard: 4 FUSE
  unit: 3 AMP MHO OHM REL
    4 VOLT WATT 5 FARAD
    6 AMPERE
**Electrically**
  flexible: 4 ACDC
**Electric guitar**
  effect: 4 WAWA
  hookup: 3 AMP
**Electrician:** 5 WIRER
  alloy: 6 SOLDER

  need: 6 PLIERS
**Electricity:** 5 JUICE POWER
  Jolt with: 3 ZAP
  Kind of: 6 STATIC
  pioneer: 5 TESLA VOLTA
**Electrified**
  fish: 3 EEL
  particle: 3 ION
**Electrify:** 3 AWE WOW 4 WIRE
    6 AROUSE THRILL
**Electrode**
  Certain: 7 EMITTER
  flow: 3 ARC
**Electrolux:** 3 VAC
**Electrolysis**
  particle: 3 ION 5 ANION
**Electrolytic**
  cell part: 5 ANODE
**Electromagnetic**
  wave amplifier: 5 MASER
**Electron**
  home: 4 ATOM
  loser or gainer: 3 ION
  stream: 7 BETARAY
  tube: 5 DIODE
**Electronic**
  control system: 5 SERVO
  drug in Shatner novels: 3 TEK
  First ~ computer: 5 ENIAC
  game pioneer: 5 ATARI
  info source: 5 CDROM
  music pioneer: 4 MOOG
    6 VARESE
**Electronically**
  Capture: 4 SCAN
**Electronic Data Systems**
  founder: 5 PEROT
**Electronics**
  Big name in: 3 IBM RCA
    4 SONY 5 CASIO SANYO
    7 TOSHIBA 8 MOTOROLA
  co.: 3 ITT RCA
  device: 5 DIODE
  expert: 4 TECH 6 TECHIE
**Electrophorus**
  member: 3 EEL
**Elegance:** 4 LUXE TONE
    5 CLASS GRACE STYLE
    6 POLISH
**Elegant:** 4 FINE POSH 5 SLEEK
    SWANK 6 CLASSY
    SWANKY 7 REFINED
  Has an ~ supper: 5 DINES
**Elegantly**
  lean: 6 SVELTE
  stylish: 6 CLASSY
**"___ eleison":** 5 KYRIE
**"Elektra"**
  composer: 7 STRAUSS
**Elem.**
  school aux.: 3 PTA
**Element:** 4 UNIT
  Antiseptic: 6 IODINE
  Blind: 4 SLAT
  Brake: 4 SHOE
  Brass: 4 ZINC

  Containing ~ 76: 5 OSMIC
  Contributing: 6 FACTOR
  element: 4 ATOM
  Forest: 4 TREE
  Graphite: 6 CARBON
  Jigsaw: 5 PIECE
  Moral: 5 ETHOS
  of change: 4 CENT COIN DIME
  Ointment: 4 ZINC
  Photoelectric cell: 6 CESIUM
  Psyche: 3 EGO
  Revue: 4 SKIT
  Solder: 3 TIN
  The fifth: 5 BORON
  ~ 5: 5 BORON
  ~ 5 compound: 6 BORATE
  ~ 10: 4 NEON
  ~ 34: 8 SELENIUM
  ~ 39: 7 YTTRIUM
  ~ 50: 3 TIN
  ~ 53 salt: 6 IODATE
  ~ 54: 5 XENON
  ~ 76: 6 OSMIUM
  ~ 77: 7 IRIDIUM
  ~ 86: 5 RADON
**Elemental**
  ending: 3 IUM
  unit: 4 ATOM
  variant: 7 ISOTOPE
**Elementary:** 4 EASY 5 BASIC
  education: 4 ABCS
  particle: 3 ION 4 ATOM MUON
    5 MESON QUARK
    8 NEUTRINO
  school trio: 3 RRR
**Elements**
  One of the four: 3 AIR
  Protected from the: 6 INDOOR
    INSIDE
**"Elements"**
  author: 6 EUCLID
**___ elements:** 9 RAREEARTH
**"Elements of Style, The"**
  coauthor: 6 STRUNK
**"Eleni"**
  author Nicholas: 4 GAGE
  director Peter: 5 YATES
  star: 8 NELLIGAN
**Eleniak**
  Actress: 5 ERIKA
**Elephant**
  abductor: 3 ROC
  ancestor: 8 MASTODON
  Big ~ features: 4 EARS
  driver: 6 MAHOUT
  group: 3 GOP
  Kid-lit: 5 BABAR
  Republican ~ creator: 4 NAST
  seat: 6 HOWDAH
  suffix: 3 INE
  tooth: 4 TUSK
  Vicious: 5 ROGUE
  White: 6 ALBINO
**"Elephant Boy"**
  boy: 4 SABU
**Elephantine:** 4 HUGE 5 GIANT

**Elephants**
Opera with: 4 AIDA
Some: 4 COWS
**Elev.:** 3 ALT HGT
**Elevate:** 4 LIFT REAR
5 EXALT RAISE
6 UPLIFT 7 ENHANCE
RAISEUP
Lines that: 3 ODE
**Elevated**
dwelling: 5 AERIE
**Elevation:** 4 HILL
Western: 4 MESA
**Elevator**
alternative: 6 STAIRS
8 STAIRWAY
compartment: 3 CAR
inventor: 4 OTIS
Links: 3 TEE
man: 4 OTIS
part: 3 CAR
pioneer Otis: 6 ELISHA
Some ~ buttons: 3 UPS
**Élève**
place: 5 ECOLE
**Eleven**
through thirteen at Augusta:
10 AMENCORNER
Two of these make: 4 ONES
~, in French: 4 ONZE
**Eleventh ___:** 4 HOUR
**Eleventh-hour:** 4 LATE
**Elevs.:** 3 HTS
**Elf:** 3 HOB 6 SPRITE
**"Elf"**
Ed who played Santa in:
5 ASNER
**Elfin:** 3 WEE 6 LITTLE
**Elfman**
Actress: 5 JENNA
**Elfman, Danny**
band: 11 OINGOBOINGO
**Elfman, Jenna**
role: 6 DHARMA
**Elgar**
King in an ~ work: 4 OLAF
**Elgart**
Bandleader: 3 LES
**El Greco:** 6 CRETAN
homeland: 5 CRETE
subject: 6 TOLEDO
**Elhi**
org.: 3 PTA
**Eli**
school: 4 YALE
word: 5 BOOLA
**Eli, Ransom**
Carmaker: 4 OLDS
**Elia:** 7 PENNAME
output: 5 ESSAY
**Elias**
Inventor: 4 HOWE
**Elicit:** 5 EDUCE EVOKE
**Elicitor**
Groan: 3 PUN
**Elide:** 4 OMIT

**Eliel**
Son of: 4 EERO
**Eligibility**
Org. with ~ rules: 4 NCAA
**Eligible**
for Mensa: 5 SMART
for service: 4 ONEA
Most: 4 ONEA
**Elijah**
role: 5 FRODO
**Elimelech**
Wife of: 5 NAOMI
**Eliminate:** 3 BAR END RID
5 ERASE 6 REMOVE
**Elimination**
game: 9 ODDMANOUT
**Elinor**
Poet: 5 WYLIE
Writer: 4 GLYN
**Eliot:** 4 POET
character: 4 ADAM BEDE
5 SILAS 6 MARNER
Untouchable: 4 NESS
**Eliot, George**
Real last name of: 5 EVANS
**Eliphaz**
Father of: 4 ESAU
**Elisabeth**
Actress: 4 SHUE
**Elisha**
Inventor: 4 OTIS
**Elite:** 3 TOP 5 ALIST CREAM
6 CHOSEN 7 ALLSTAR
alternative: 4 PICA
athlete: 11 ALLAMERICAN
group: 5 ALIST ATEAM
Navy: 4 SEAL 5 SEALS
seats: 4 LOGE
Sports: 6 ALLPRO
**Elitist:** 4 SNOB 5 SNOOT
**Elixir:** 5 TONIC
**Eliz., Queen**
Honor from: 3 OBE
**Eliza**
Inspiration for: 7 GALATEA
Mentor of: 4 ENRY
**Elizabeth**
Actress: 4 PENA
Bob or: 4 DOLE
Initials for: 3 HRH
Makeup mogul: 5 ARDEN
player: 4 CATE
TV newswoman: 6 VARGAS
**"Elizabeth"**
actress Blanchett: 4 CATE
**Elizabethan ___:** 3 ERA
**Elizabeth I**
Elizabeth II, to:
8 NAMESAKE
favorite: 5 ESSEX
Mother of: 4 ANNE
Sister of: 4 MARY
**Elk:** 7 WAPITIS
feature: 6 ANTLER
**Elke**
Actress: 6 SOMMER

**Elks**
Group of: 5 LODGE
**Ella**
Actress: 6 RAINES
Emulate: 4 SCAT
Former Conn. governor:
6 GRASSO
**Elle**
rival: 5 VOGUE
**"Ellen":** 6 SITCOM
**Ellerbee**
Newscaster: 5 LINDA
**Ellington**
Bandleader: 4 DUKE
classic: 9 SATINDOLL
13 TAKETHEATRAIN
colleague: 5 BASIE
inits.: 3 EKE
mood: 6 INDIGO
vehicle: 6 ATRAIN
**Elliot, ___ Cass:** 4 MAMA
**Elliot, Mama ___:** 4 CASS
**Ellipse:** 4 OVAL
points: 4 LOCI
**Ellipsis:** 4 DOTS
part: 3 DOT
**Ellipsoid:** 4 OVAL
**Elliptical:** 4 OVAL 5 OVATE
OVOID TERSE
**Ellis**
(abbr.): 3 ISL
Novelist: 4 BRET
**Ellison**
Sci-fi writer: 6 HARLAN
**Ellison, Larry**
company: 6 ORACLE
**Elly May**
Pa of: 3 JED
**Elm:** 4 TREE 9 SHADETREE
and others (abbr.): 3 STS
offering: 5 SHADE
**Elm City**
student: 3 ELI
**Elmer**
Partner of: 5 ELSIE
Voice of: 3 MEL
who bugs Bugs: 4 FUDD
~, to Bugs: 3 DOC
**Elmer's:** 4 GLUE
**El Misti**
locale: 4 PERU
range: 5 ANDES
**Elmore**
of basketball: 3 LEN
**Elm Street**
terrorizer: 6 FREDDY
**Elocution**
Practice: 5 ORATE
**Eloise**
creator Thompson: 3 KAY
The likes of: 4 IMPS
**Elongated**
fish: 3 EEL
pastry: 6 ECLAIR
**Eloquent:** 10 ORATORICAL
equine: 4 MRED

speaker: 6 ORATOR
Wax: 5 ORATE
**El Prado**
city: 6 MADRID
**Elroy**
Dog belonging to: 5 ASTRO
**Els**
followers: 3 EMS
Golfer: 5 ERNIE
org.: 3 PGA
**Elsa:** 7 LIONESS
chronicler: 7 ADAMSON
**Else**
Everything: 4 REST
**Elsewhere:** 4 AWAY
7 NOTHERE
Direct: 5 REFER
Here: 3 ICI
Usher: 6 RESEAT
**Elsie**
chew: 3 CUD
Emulate: 3 MOO
**Elton**
john: 3 LOO
Partner of: 6 BERNIE
Title for: 3 SIR
**Elude:** 4 LOSE 5 AVOID DODGE
the seeker: 4 HIDE
**Elusive:** 4 EELY 6 SCARCE
creature: 4 YETI
one: 3 EEL
**Elver:** 3 EEL
**Elvin**
of basketball: 5 HAYES
**Elvis:** 4 IDOL
1956 ~ song: 6 LOVEME
15 HEARTBREAKHOTEL
1958 ~ song: 4 DONT
15 HARDHEADEDWOMAN
1961 ~ song: 10 BLUEHAWAII
1964 ~ song: 5 ASKME
1969 ~ movie: 6 CHARRO
birthplace: 6 TUPELO
Emulate: 6 GYRATE
first label: 3 SUN
hit: 13 JAILHOUSEROCK
middle name: 4 ARON
record label: 3 RCA
Rocker: 8 COSTELLO
swiveled his: 4 HIPS
**Elwes**
Actor: 4 CARY
**Elwood P. ___:** 4 DOWD
**Ely**
Actor: 3 RON
**Elysium:** 4 EDEN
**Elzie**
Popeye creator: 5 SEGAR
**Em:** 6 AUNTIE
and Bee: 5 AUNTS
Dorothy, to: 5 NIECE
~, to Dorothy: 4 AUNT
**E-mail:** 4 MEMO SEND
7 MESSAGE WRITETO
8 MESSAGES
(abbr.): 3 MSG

address ending: 3 COM EDU
GOV ORG
address part: 3 AOL DOT
again: 6 REPOST RESEND
alternative: 3 FAX 6 LETTER
button: 4 SEND
command: 4 SEND
forerunner: 5 TELEX
guffaw: 3 LOL
header: 4 FROM
Junk: 4 SPAM
nuisance: 4 SPAM
option: 5 REPLY
symbol: 8 EMOTICON
Unwanted: 4 SPAM
**E-mailed:** 4 SENT 5 WROTE
**Emanate:** 4 EMIT 5 ARISE
**Emanation:** 4 AURA
Bakery: 5 AROMA
Kitchen: 4 ODOR 5 AROMA
Radiator: 4 HEAT
Sachet: 5 AROMA SCENT
Sun: 3 RAY
**Emancipate:** 4 FREE
7 MANUMIT SETFREE
**Emasculate:** 4 GELD
5 UNMAN
**Embankment:** 5 LEVEE
Build an: 5 REVET
Protective: 6 ESCARP
Soil: 4 BERM
**Embargo:** 3 BAN
**Embargoed**
land: 4 CUBA
**Embarrass:** 5 ABASH SHAME
**Embarrassed:** 3 RED
Visibly: 7 BEETRED
10 REDASABEET
**Embarrassing**
display: 5 SCENE
situation: 7 HOTSEAT
**Embarrassment:** 5 SHAME
Show: 5 BLUSH
**Embassy**
fig.: 3 AMB
**Embattle:** 5 BESET
**Embellish:** 5 ADORN 6 BEDECK
7 DRESSUP
richly: 4 GILD
**Embellished:** 6 ORNATE
**Embellishment**
Entrée: 5 GARNI
Letter: 5 SERIF
Musical: 5 TRILL 7 ROULADE
9 GRACENOTE
**Ember**
coating: 3 ASH
**Embezzler**
fear: 5 AUDIT
**Emblem:** 4 ICON
Clan: 5 TOTEM
Company: 4 LOGO
Its ~ is the crescent:
5 ISLAM
Official: 4 SEAL
of power: 3 ORB

of victory: 6 LAUREL
**Embodiment:** 6 AVATAR
7 EPITOME
**Embrace:** 3 HUG 5 ADOPT
7 ESPOUSE
Strong: 7 BEARHUG
**Embroider:** 3 SEW
**Embroidered**
mat: 5 DOILY
**Embroidery**
aid: 4 HOOP
Bit of ~ (abbr.): 4 INIT
loop: 5 PICOT
style: 11 CROSSSTITCH
Towel: 3 HIS
yarn: 6 CREWEL
**Embroiled**
Seriously: 8 KNEEDEEP
**Embryo**
Of the ~ sac: 8 AMNIOTIC
**Embryonic**
Beyond: 5 FETAL
plant: 5 OVULE
sac: 6 AMNION
**Emcee:** 4 HOST
need: 4 MIKE
task: 5 INTRO
**Emerald:** 3 GEM 5 BERYL
**Emerald ___:** 4 ISLE
**Emerald City**
creator: 4 BAUM
princess: 4 OZMA
**Emerald Isle:** 4 EIRE ERIN
From the: 5 IRISH
**Emerge:** 4 DAWN 5 ARISE
6 APPEAR
from being out: 6 COMETO
**Emerged:** 5 AROSE
7 CAMEOUT
**Emergencies:** 6 CRISES
**Emergency:** 4 NEED 6 CRISIS
exit: 10 FIREESCAPE
fund: 8 MADMONEY
job: 3 TOW
light: 5 FLARE
link: 7 HOTLINE
safeguard: 8 FIREDOOR
signal: 5 FLARE SIREN
supply: 5 SERUM 6 PLASMA
treatment: 8 FIRSTAID
~ CB channel: 4 NINE
~ PC key: 3 ESC
**Emerging:** 7 NASCENT
**Emeril:** 4 CHEF
exclamation: 3 BAM
need: 4 OVEN
**Emeritus**
(abbr.): 3 RET 4 RETD
**Emerson**
contemporary: 4 ASHE
middle name: 5 WALDO
of tennis: 3 ROY
piece: 5 ESSAY
**Emerson, Ralph ___:** 5 WALDO
**Emery**
Use ~ on: 6 ABRADE

**Emetic**
plant: 6 IPECAC
**Emigration**
Loss through: 10 BRAINDRAIN
Mass: 6 EXODUS
**Emil**
Expressionist: 5 NOLDE
of track: 7 ZATOPEK
**Emile**
Author: 4 ZOLA
portrayer: 4 EZIO
**Emilia**
Husband of: 4 IAGO
**Emiliano**
Mexican revolutionary:
6 ZAPATA
**Emilio**
Actor: 7 ESTEVEZ
Designer: 5 PUCCI
~, to Martin: 3 SON
**Emily**
Sister of: 4 ANNE
**Eminem:** 7 RAPSTAR
genre: 3 RAP
Mentor of: 3 DRE 5 DRDRE
**Eminent:** 4 HIGH 5 NOTED
6 OFNOTE
**Emirate**
Mideast: 4 OMAN 5 DUBAI
QATAR 8 ABUDHABI
**Emissary:** 6 LEGATE
**Emission**
control gp.: 3 EPA
Volcanic: 3 ASH 4 LAVA
**Emit:** 4 SHED 7 GIVEOFF
SENDOUT
coherent light: 4 LASE
**EMK:** 3 SEN
**Emma**
Actress: 5 SAMMS
Avenger: 4 PEEL
**"Emma"**
author Austen: 4 JANE
**Emmenthaler:** 5 SWISS
6 CHEESE
**Emmet**
Muppet: 5 OTTER
**Emmy:** 5 AWARD
1977 ~ winner: 5 ROOTS
1986–87 ~ winner: 5 GLESS
Daytime ~ candidate: 4 SOAP
Four-time ~ winner: 5 LALAW
Sally Field ~ role: 5 SYBIL
Seven-time ~ winner: 5 ASNER
7 EDASNER
Susan Lucci ~ role: 5 ERICA
winner Arthur: 3 BEA
winner Christine: 5 LAHTI
winner Cicely: 5 TYSON
winner Falco: 4 EDIE
winner Lewis: 5 SHARI
winner Loretta: 4 SWIT
winner Lucci: 5 SUSAN
winner Susan: 5 LUCCI
winner Thompson: 4 SADA
winner Ward: 4 SELA

**Emollient:** 4 BALM 6 LOTION
Natural: 4 ALOE
**Emolument:** 3 FEE
**Emote**
Hardly: 8 UNDERACT
**Emotion**
A verse to: 3 ODE
Overwhelming: 3 AWE
**Emotional:** 5 TEARY 6 MOVING
8 CHOKEDUP
feeling: 4 VIBE
flower: 4 TEAR
Less: 5 ICIER
Not: 5 STOIC
pang: 6 TWINGE
poem: 3 ODE
situation: 5 DRAMA
**Emotionally**
Affect: 4 MOVE STIR 5 GETTO
TOUCH
**Emotions**
Has: 5 FEELS
Like some: 6 PENTUP
**Empathetic**
words: 5 ICARE
**Empathize:** 6 RELATE
**Empathy**
One showing: 7 SOLACER
Words of: 10 ICANRELATE
**"Empedocles on ___":** 4 ETNA
**Emperor**
10th-century ~: 5 OTTOI
after Galba: 4 OTHO
after Nero: 5 GALBA
Cruel: 4 NERO
Fiddling: 4 NERO
Holy Roman: 4 OTTO
6 TRAJAN 7 LOTHAIR
Japanese: 7 AKIHITO
Mo. named for an: 3 AUG
**"Emperor Jones, The"**
playwright: 6 ONEILL
star: 7 ROBESON
**Emphasis:** 6 STRESS
Phrase tacked on for: 6 NOLESS
**Emphasize:** 6 ACCENT STRESS
**Emphatic**
agreement: 4 AMEN 6 IDOIDO
YESYES 8 YESSIREE
Be: 6 INSIST
denial: 5 NOSIR 6 NONONO
7 NOSIREE
ending: 5 SIREE
refusal: 5 NEVER NOHOW
6 NOMAAM
type (abbr.): 4 ITAL
**Empire:** 5 REALM
Bygone: 4 INCA
Former: 4 USSR
Like a bygone: 5 INCAN
**Empire State**
canal: 4 ERIE
leader: 6 PATAKI
**Empire State Building**
climber: 4 KONG
site: 3 NYC

style: 7 ARTDECO
**Employ:** 3 USE 4 HIRE 5 APPLY
6 HIREON
again: 5 REUSE
They: 5 USERS
vigorously: 5 EXERT
**Employed**
as: 7 USEDFOR
Currently: 5 INUSE
**Employee:** 6 EARNER
benefit: 4 PERK 7 DAYCARE
request: 5 RAISE
reward: 5 BONUS
Transferred ~ concern:
4 RELO
~ ID: 3 SSN
**Employees:** 4 HELP 5 STAFF
**Employer:** 4 USER 5 HIRER
**Employment:** 3 USE
agency listing: 3 JOB
extra: 4 PERK
**Emporium:** 4 MART
event: 4 SALE
**Empower:** 3 LET 6 ENABLE
**Empowered:** 4 ABLE
**Empress**
Former Iranian: 5 FARAH
Russian: 7 TSARINA
**Emptiness:** 4 VOID
**Empty:** 4 BARE IDLE NULL
VOID 5 DRAIN INANE
6 HOLLOW VACANT
VACATE 7 DEPLETE
hand, literally: 6 KARATE
house feature: 4 ECHO
(of): 3 RID
out: 6 UNPACK
space: 4 VOID
stomach sound: 5 GROWL
talk: 3 GAS 4 CANT WIND
5 HOKUM 6 HOTAIR
~, as an apartment: 5 UNLET
**Empty ___:** 4 NEST 6 NESTER
**Empty-headed:** 5 INANE
**___ empty stomach:** 4 ONAN
**Empty-vehicle**
weight: 4 TARE
**Ems:** 3 SPA
followers: 3 ENS
**EMT**
destinations: 3 ERS
Part of: 4 EMER
skill: 3 CPR
**Emu**
kin: 4 RHEA
or ostrich: 6 RATITE
**Emulate:** 3 APE
**Emulsion**
Photo lab ~ compound:
6 HALIDE
**En ___:** 5 MASSE
**"En ___!":** 5 GARDE
**Enact**
anew: 8 REORDAIN
**Enameled**
metalware: 4 TOLE

**Enamored**
of: 4 INTO 6 KEENON
**Enc.**
to an editor: 3 SAE 4 SASE
**Encase:** 7 SHEATHE
**Enceladus**
burial place: 4 ETNA
**Enchanted:** 3 FEY 4 RAPT
"___ Enchanted": 4 ELLA
**"Enchanted April"**
setting: 5 ITALY
**Enchanting:** 7 MAGICAL
**Enchantress:** 5 SIREN
Mythical: 5 CIRCE
**Enchilada**
alternative: 6 TAMALE
The whole: 3 ALL 4 ATOZ
5 TOTAL
**Encircle:** 4 GIRD RING
5 HEMIN 7 CLOSEIN
**Encircled:** 4 GIRT
**Encirclements:** 5 SIEGE
**Encl.**
to an editor: 3 SAE 4 SASE
**Enclave**
Academic: 10 IVORYTOWER
**Enclose:** 7 ROPEOFF
**Enclosed**
canoe: 5 KAYAK
car: 5 SEDAN
**Enclosure**
Baby: 7 PLAYPEN
Farm: 3 PEN STY
Jamboree: 4 TENT
Ms.: 3 SAE 4 SASE
Ranch: 6 CORRAL
Software: 5 CDROM
Yard: 5 HEDGE
Zoo: 4 CAGE
**"Encomium Moriae"**
author: 7 ERASMUS
**Encompassing:** 7 AMBIENT
**Encore**
performance: 5 RERUN
**"Encore!":** 4 MORE 5 AGAIN
**Encounter:** 4 MEET 5 RUNIN
7 MEETING RUNINTO
8 MEETWITH
**Encountered:** 3 MET
7 RANINTO
**Encourage:** 4 COAX URGE
5 EGGON 6 EXHORT
FOSTER SPURON
URGEON 7 HEARTEN
NURTURE
a crook: 4 ABET
**Encouragement**
at the bullring: 3 OLE
Shout of: 5 CHEER
Word of: 3 OLE RAH TRY YES
4 AMEN CMON
**Encourager**
Cattle: 4 PROD
**Encouraging**
sound: 3 RAH
touch: 3 PAT

word: 3 OLE RAH TRY YES
4 AMEN CMON
**Encroach:** 7 IMPINGE
on: 6 INVADE
**Encroachment:** 6 INROAD
**Encrusted:** 4 CAKY 5 CAKED
**Encrypted:** 5 CODED
**Encumbered**
Be: 3 OWE
**Encumbrance:** 4 LIEN ONUS
**Encyclopedia**
medium: 5 CDROM
unit (abbr.): 3 VOL
volume: 5 ATLAS INDEX
Walking: 7 EGGHEAD
**End:** 3 TIP 4 GOAL HALT REAR
STOP 5 CEASE DEATH
FINIS OMEGA 6 RESULT
WRAPUP
Info: Suffix cue
a fast: 3 EAT
Ages on: 4 EONS
at: 4 ABUT
Bad: 4 DOOM
Book: 5 INDEX
Dead: 3 DEE 10 BLINDALLEY
early: 5 ABORT
Go off the deep: 4 DIVE SNAP
Hammer: 4 CLAW PEEN
Land's: 5 SCAPE
Match: 3 TKO
notes: 4 CODA
of a #2: 6 ERASER
of a 1/1 song: 4 SYNE
of a bridal path: 5 ALTAR
of a demonstration: 3 QED
of a list abbr.: 4 ETAL
of a race: 8 ELECTION
of a series: 3 ZEE 5 OMEGA
of a shooting: 4 WRAP
of a threat: 4 ELSE 6 ORELSE
of grace: 4 AMEN
piece: 4 CODA
product: 6 RESULT
Put an early ~ to:
11 NIPINTHEBUD
Put an ~ to: 3 CAN 4 DOIN
STOP 5 CEASE
result: 6 UPSHOT
River: 7 ESTUARY
Shoelace: 5 AGLET
Short: 4 STUB
Short ~ of the stick:
7 BUMDEAL RAWDEAL
Striking: 4 PEEN
Tail: 4 REAR
The: 3 ZEE 5 FINIS OMEGA
Time on: 3 EON
to sex: 3 ISM
Untimely: 6 DEMISE
up with: 3 NET
What some games ~ in:
4 ATIE
Where breeches: 4 KNEE
**End ___:** 4 USER
**___ end:** 4 ATAN

**Endangered:** 4 RARE
antelope: 4 ORYX
cat: 4 PUMA 6 OCELOT
goose: 4 NENE
layer: 5 OZONE
sea cow: 7 MANATEE
state bird: 4 NENE
**Endearment**
Italian term of: 7 CARAMIA
Term of: 3 HON PET 4 BABE
5 HONEY TOOTS
7 TOOTSIE
10 HONEYBUNCH
**Endeavor:** 3 AIM TRY
7 VENTURE
to attain: 4 SEEK
**Endeavored:** 6 STROVE
**Endeavour**
org.: 4 NASA
Travel like: 5 ORBIT
**Ended:** 4 OVER
~, as a subscription: 6 LAPSED
**Ender**
Info: Suffix cue
**Endgame**
ender: 4 MATE
**End in ___:** 4 ATIE
**Ending**
Info: Suffix cue
**Endless**
~, in poetry: 6 ETERNE
**Endnote**
abbr.: 4 ETAL IBID
**Endo-**
Opposite of: 3 EXO 4 ECTO
**End of ___:** 5 ANERA
**End-of-class**
signal: 4 BELL
**End-of-proof**
letters: 3 QED
**End-of-week**
cry: 4 TGIF
**Endora**
portrayer: 5 AGNES
**Endorse:** 4 OKAY SIGN
**Endorsed:** 3 OKD 4 OKED
**Endorsement**
Passport: 4 VISA
**Endorser:** 6 SIGNEE
Check: 5 PAYEE
Toothpaste ~ (abbr.): 3 ADA
**Endorses:** 3 OKS
**Endow:** 4 FUND VEST 5 BLESS
GRANT 6 PAYFOR
**Endower**
College: 4 ALUM
Cornell: 4 EZRA
**Endowment:** 4 GIFT 5 GRANT
**Ends**
Book: 7 ADDENDA
It ~ in a point: 5 FABLE
It ~ in Oct.: 3 DST
Leave no loose: 3 TIE
of letters: 3 PSS
of the earth: 5 POLES
**Endurance:** 4 LEGS 7 STAMINA

**Endure:** 4 BEAR COPE LAST
  5 ABIDE 7 PERSIST
    WEATHER
  successfully: 7 RIDEOUT
**Endured:** 5 STOOD 7 RODEOUT
**Enduring:** 7 ETERNAL
**"Endymion"**
  poet: 5 KEATS
**ENE**
  Opposite of: 3 WSW
**Enemy:** 3 FOE
  Allies: 4 AXIS
  C.O.N.T.R.O.L.: 4 KAOS
  Iroquois: 4 ERIE
  Kind of: 6 MORTAL
  leader: 4 ARCH
  Minuteman: 7 REDCOAT
  Superman: 6 LUTHOR
  The: 4 THEM
**Energetic:** 4 GOGO SPRY
  5 BRISK
**Energetically**
  Begin: 5 WADEIN
    8 WADEINTO
  Dance: 6 BOOGIE
**Energize:** 4 STIR 5 LIVEN
    REVUP 7 ANIMATE
**Energy:** 3 GAS PEP VIM ZIP
  4 ZEST 5 DRIVE POWER
    STEAM
  bit: 3 ERG
  Bundle of: 6 DYNAMO
  Burst of: 5 SPASM
  choice: 5 SOLAR
  Clean kind of: 5 SOLAR
  Former ~ giant: 5 ENRON
  Full of: 4 GOGO 5 ALIVE
    PEPPY VITAL ZIPPY
    6 BOUNCY
  Full of nervous: 5 ANTSY
  Kind of: 5 SOLAR
  Lack of: 6 ANEMIA
  Lose: 3 SAG 4 TIRE 5 DROOP
  source: 3 SUN 4 ATOM COAL
    FUEL
  unit: 3 ERG 5 JOULE
**Enero:** 3 MES
  to enero: 3 ANO
**Enervate:** 3 SAP 4 TIRE
    6 WEAKEN
**Enfants**
  Place for les: 5 ECOLE
  Song pour les: 8 ALOUETTE
**Enfield:** 5 RIFLE
**Enforcement**
  Big Apple ~ gp.: 4 NYPD
  orgs.: 3 PDS
  Ottawa-based ~ gp.: 4 RCMP
  power: 5 TEETH
**Enforcer:** 7 EXACTER
  Law ~ since 1873: 7 MOUNTIE
  Yukon law: 4 RCMP
**"Enforcer, The"**
  Frank: 5 NITTI
**Eng**
  homeland: 4 SIAM

  Twin of: 5 CHANG
**Eng.**
  award: 3 OBE
  channel: 3 BBC
  course: 3 LIT
**Engage:** 4 HIRE MESH
  in logrolling: 4 BIRL
**Engaged:** 4 ATIT
  in: 4 UPTO
  in battle: 5 ATWAR
  Not: 4 IDLE 5 ALOOF
**Engagement:** 6 BATTLE
  Arranged: 9 BLINDDATE
  Evening: 6 SOIREE
  gift: 4 RING
  Ring: 4 BOUT
**Engagements**
  Series of: 4 TOUR
**Engager**
  Ratchet: 4 PAWL
**Engaging:** 7 WINSOME
  one: 5 HIRER
**Engels**
  collaborator: 4 MARX
**Engender:** 4 SIRE 5 BEGET
    10 GIVERISETO
**Engendered:** 4 BRED 5 BEGOT
**Engine:** 5 MOTOR
  additive: 3 OIL STP
  Aircraft: 6 RAMJET
  Air to a jet: 6 INTAKE
  attachment: 4 HOSE
  Bike with an: 5 MOPED
  booster: 5 TURBO
  cover: 4 HOOD
  Gun the: 3 REV
  housing: 9 CRANKCASE
  knock: 4 PING
  need: 3 OIL
  part: 3 CAM ROD 4 GEAR
    5 ROTOR 7 STARTER
  part, briefly: 4 CARB
  Powerful: 4 VTEN 5 TURBO
  Rev an: 3 GUN
  Rotating ~ part: 3 CAM
  sound: 4 PING PURR ROAR
    WHIR 5 COUGH KNOCK
    8 PUTTPUTT
  stat: 3 RPM
  type: 4 HEMI VSIX 5 TURBO
    6 DIESEL
  Vital ~ conduit: 7 OILLINE
**Engineer**
  French: 6 EIFFEL
  Kind of: 5 CIVIL
  place: 3 CAB
**Engineering**
  NY ~ sch.: 3 RPI
  project: 4 DIKE 7 TRESTLE
  sch.: 4 TECH
**England**
  County of: 5 ESSEX
  French port nearest: 6 CALAIS
  Head of: 3 LOO
  John of: 3 LOO 5 ELTON
  River in: 4 OUSE

**English:** 4 SPIN 7 BRITONS
  Any of three ~ rivers: 4 OUSE
  article: 3 THE
  assignment: 5 ESSAY THEME
  cathedral city: 3 ELY
    6 EXETER
  cattle breed: 5 DEVON
  channel: 3 BBC
  channel, with "the": 4 BEEB
  china: 5 SPODE
  composer: 4 ARNE
  coppers: 5 PENCE
  county: 4 AVON KENT
    5 ESSEX SHIRE
  earldom: 5 ESSEX
  earth tone: 5 OCHRE
  equivalent of a count: 4 EARL
  governor: 4 EARL
  homework: 5 ESSAY
  paper: 5 ESSAY
  Pigeon: 3 COO
  poet: 5 KEATS
  prep school: 4 ETON
  race place: 5 ASCOT EPSOM
  river: 3 EXE 4 AVON OUSE
    TYNE 5 TRENT
  royal house: 4 YORK 5 TUDOR
  spa: 4 BATH
  sports car: 3 JAG
  university city: 5 LEEDS
  variety: 5 SCOTS
**English ___ :** 3 LIT
**English Channel**
  1926 ~ swimmer: 6 EDERLE
  county: 6 DORSET
  feeder: 3 EXE 4 AVON ORNE
    5 SEINE SOMME
  isle: 5 WIGHT
  seaport: 7 LEHAVRE
**English horn**
  cousin: 4 OBOE
  need: 4 REED
**"English Patient, The"**
  setting: 6 SAHARA
**Engorge**
  oneself: 6 PIGOUT
**Engr.**
  Kind of: 4 ELEC MECH
**Engrave:** 4 ETCH 6 INCISE
  with acid: 4 ETCH
**Engraver:** 6 ETCHER
**Engraving:** 7 LINECUT
  tools: 5 STYLI
**Engrossed:** 4 RAPT
  by: 4 INTO
**Engulf:** 5 DROWN WHELM
**Enhance:** 5 ADDTO
**Enhancer**
  Café: 4 LAIT
  Flavor: 3 MSG 4 SALT
    5 SPICE
  Grade: 4 PLUS
**Enid**
  Knight who wed: 7 GERAINT
**Enigma:** 5 POSER 6 RIDDLE
  Extraterrestrial: 3 UFO

**"Enigma Variations"**
composer: 5 ELGAR
**Enjoined:** 4 BADE
**Enjoy:** 4 LIKE 5 EATUP SAVOR
6 RELISH
a favorite book: 6 REREAD
a long bath: 4 SOAK
a novel: 4 READ
a snowy slope: 3 SKI 4 SLED
bubble gum: 4 CHEW
fine whiskey: 3 SIP
the sun: 4 BASK
**Enjoyed**
home cooking: 5 ATEIN
immensely: 5 ATEUP
oneself: 7 ATEITUP
9 HADABLAST
**Enjoying:** 4 INTO
**Enjoyment:** 3 FUN 5 KICKS
8 PLEASURE
___ **En-lai:** 4 CHOU
**Enlarge:** 4 GROW 6 DILATE
a hole: 4 REAM
a house: 7 ADDONTO
a photo: 6 BLOWUP
**Enlargement**
Atlas: 5 INSET
**Enlighten:** 5 EDIFY TEACH
**Enlightenment**
Cry of: 3 AHA
Means of: 3 ZEN
Mock words of: 4 AHSO
Zen: 6 SATORI
**Enlist**
again: 4 REUP
in: 4 JOIN
**Enlisted**
men: 3 GIS
~ VIPs: 4 NCOS
**Enlistee**
WWII: 3 WAC 5 GIJOE
**Enlistees**
Some: 4 PFCS
**Enliven:** 5 PEPUP
~, with "up": 3 PEP 4 PERK
5 SPICE
**En masse**
Enter: 6 PILEIN
Exist: 3 ARE
**Enmity:** 4 HATE 6 ANIMUS
**Ennead:** 5 NONET
Feline: 5 LIVES
**Ennis**
Author: 4 REES
**Ennoble:** 5 EXALT 7 ELEVATE
**Ennui:** 5 BLAHS 6 TEDIUM
7 BOREDOM
8 THEBLAHS
Exhibit: 4 YAWN
**Enoch**
Tennyson's: 5 ARDEN
**Enola Gay**
payload: 5 ABOMB
**Enormous:** 4 HUGE VAST
6 COSMIC
bird of myth: 3 ROC

**Enormously:** 4 ALOT
**Enos**
Father of: 4 SETH
**Enough:** 5 AMPLE
Close: 7 INRANGE
Hardly: 5 SCANT 6 SCANTY
It may be: 4 ONCE
Just firm: 7 ALDENTE
Just ~ to wet the lips: 3 SIP
More than: 4 MANY 5 AMPLE
6 OODLES PLENTY
Not good ~ for: 7 BENEATH
Old: 5 OFAGE
Old ~ to know better:
5 ADULT
Quite: 5 AMPLE
Seen: 5 HADIT
~, for some: 4 ONCE
~, in Italian: 5 BASTA
**"Enough!":** 4 STOP 5 CANIT
IGIVE UNCLE 6 DROPIT
NOMORE QUITIT
STOPIT 7 SPAREME
**"Enough already!":** 5 CANIT
UNCLE 6 QUITIT
STOPIT 8 IVEHADIT
**En passant**
capture: 4 PAWN
**"___ en paz, fierro en guerra":**
3 ORO
**Enrage:** 3 IRE 4 GALL
**Enrapture:** 4 SEND 5 RIVET
**Enraptured:** 4 GAGA SENT
**Enrich:** 4 LARD
**Enrico**
Physicist: 5 FERMI
Tenor: 6 CARUSO
**Enríquez**
Actor: 4 RENE
**En route:** 4 SENT
by ship: 4 ASEA
**Ens.**
producer: 4 USNA
**"___ en scene":** 4 MISE
**Ensemble:** 4 CAST 6 OUTFIT
Acting: 4 CAST
Certain string: 5 NONET
Furniture: 5 SUITE
Jazz: 4 TRIO 5 COMBO
Midsized: 5 OCTET
**Ensign**
Shakespearean: 4 IAGO
**Ensler**
Playwright: 3 EVE
**Ensnare:** 4 TRAP
**Ensuing:** 4 NEXT
**Ensure**
failure: 4 DOOM
~, with "up": 3 SEW
**Entail:** 7 INVOLVE
**Entangle:** 4 MIRE 5 SNARE
SNARL
**Entangled:** 5 AFOUL
**Entanglement:** 3 WEB 4 KNOT
MESH SNAG 5 SKEIN
SNARL TIEUP

**Enter:** 3 LOG 4 GOIN 5 INPUT
KEYIN 6 GOINTO
READIN STEPIN TYPEIN
7 GETINTO
again: 5 REKEY
cautiously: 6 EASEIN EDGEIN
forcefully: 6 BUSTIN INVADE
gradually: 6 EASEIN
Invite to: 5 ASKIN
One way to: 5 ONCUE
secretly: 7 SNEAKIN
Signal to: 3 CUE
the picture: 6 APPEAR
uninvited: 7 BARGEIN
via cracks: 6 SEEPIN
with care: 6 EASEIN
**Entered:** 6 CAMEIN GONEIN
WENTIN 7 KEYEDIN
en masse: 9 PILEDINTO
in the record: 6 LOGGED
the race: 3 RAN
**Enterprise:** 8 STARSHIP
captain: 4 KIRK
communications officer:
5 UHURA
counselor: 4 TROI
helmsman: 4 SULU
initials: 3 USS
Klingon on the: 4 WORF
Letters on the: 3 NCC
navigator: 4 SULU
off.: 3 ENS
rival: 4 AVIS 5 ALAMO
voyage: 4 TREK
**"___ Enterprise":** 3 USS
**Enterprising**
one: 8 GOGETTER
**Entertain:** 4 DINE FETE HOST
WINE 5 AMUSE
6 DIVERT REGALE
at bedtime: 6 READTO
lavishly: 6 REGALE
**Entertainer:** 4 HOST 7 ARTISTE
Island: 5 DONHO
Japanese: 6 GEISHA
Late, great: 7 BOBHOPE
trademark: 7 TAGLINE
**Entertainers**
GI: 3 USO
**"Entertaining Mr. ___":**
6 SLOANE
**Entertainment**
Cowboy: 5 RODEO
GI: 7 USOSHOW
gp.: 3 USO
Home ~ option: 5 WEBTV
Luau: 4 HULA
**"___ Entertainment!":** 5 THATS
**"Entertainment Tonight"**
Former host of: 4 TESH
Gibbons of: 5 LEEZA
topic: 4 ITEM
**"___ Entertain You":** 5 LETME
**Enthrall:** 4 SEND 6 RAVISH
**Enthralled:** 4 AGOG RAPT
**Enthuse:** 4 RAVE

**Enthusiasm:** 4 ELAN FIRE ZEAL ZEST 5 ARDOR DRIVE GUSTO 6 SPIRIT
Excessive: 5 MANIA
Infuse with: 6 PUMPUP
With: 6 AVIDLY
**Enthusiast:** 3 NUT 4 BUFF 5 LOVER
Extreme: 4 NERD
**Enthusiastic:** 4 AVID GOGO KEEN WILD 5 CANDO EAGER HETUP 6 ONFIRE RAHRAH STOKED
about: 4 INTO 5 UPFOR 6 HIGHON KEENON
approval: 6 YESYES
Became ~ about: 7 GOTINTO
Extremely: 5 RABID
Hardly: 5 TEPID
Like ~ fans: 5 AROAR
overseas assent: 4 SISI
verse: 3 ODE
Wildly: 4 GAGA
words: 5 YESES
~, with "up": 3 HET
**Enthusiastically**
Receive: 5 LAPUP
**Entice:** 4 BAIT COAX LURE 5 TEMPT 6 BECKON LEADON LUREIN ROPEIN
**Enticement:** 4 BAIT HOOK WILE 6 ALLURE COMEON
Bakery: 4 ODOR 5 AROMA
Fish: 4 LURE
**Entire**
range: 5 GAMUT
**Entirely:** 3 ALL 5 FULLY INALL 6 INTOTO
sensible: 4 SANE
**Entity:** 4 UNIT
Single: 5 MONAD
**Entomb:** 5 INTER
**Entomologist**
subject: 6 INSECT 7 INSECTS
**Entourage:** 7 RETINUE
**Entr'___:** 4 ACTE
**Entrance:** 4 ADIT DOOR 5 INLET WAYIN 6 PORTAL 7 BEWITCH GATEWAY
Classy: 4 ARCH
College ~ exam: 3 SAT
Curved: 4 ARCH
Delivery: 8 SIDEDOOR
Freeway: 4 RAMP 6 ONRAMP
Metro: 5 STILE
Mine: 4 ADIT
**Entranced:** 4 RAPT
**Entrant**
Derby: 5 HORSE
Iditarod: 4 SLED 5 RACER
Indy: 5 RACER
Regatta: 5 YACHT

**Entrap:** 5 SNARE
~, with "up": 3 SET
**Entre ___:** 4 NOUS
**Entreat:** 3 ASK BEG 4 PRAY URGE
**Entreated:** 4 PLED
**Entreaty:** 4 PLEA
**Entrée:** 5 WAYIN 6 ACCESS 8 MAINDISH
Barbecue: 4 RIBS
Brunch: 6 OMELET
Crusty: 6 POTPIE
Easter: 3 HAM 4 LAMB
Eggy: 6 OMELET
fowl: 5 CAPON
Greek: 4 GYRO
Hearty: 5 STEAK TBONE
item: 4 MEAT
Layered: 7 LASAGNA
Mexican: 4 TACO 7 TOSTADA
Pounded: 10 SWISSSTEAK
preceder: 5 SALAD
Salsa-topped: 4 TACO
School-lunch: 11 MYSTERYMEAT
Seafood: 4 SOLE 5 FILET SCROD 11 FILETOFSOLE
Shrimp: 6 SCAMPI
Sunday: 5 ROAST 8 POTROAST
**Entrench:** 5 DIGIN
**Entrepreneur**
deg.: 3 MBA
mag.: 3 INC
**Entrepreneur-aiding**
org.: 3 SBA
**Entry:** 4 DOOR 6 ACCESS 7 LISTING
Agenda: 4 ITEM 7 ITEMONE
Almanac: 4 FACT
Bank acct.: 3 DEP INT
Black ink: 5 ASSET
Bookkeeping: 5 DEBIT
Cal.: 4 APPT
Card catalogue: 5 TITLE
Check: 4 DATE 6 AMOUNT
Courtroom: 4 PLEA
Customer file: 8 AREACODE
Dict.: 3 DEF SYN
Dictionary: 4 WORD
Gain: 5 GETIN
Glossary: 4 TERM
Grant ~ to: 5 ADMIT LETIN
Illegal: 6 BAGJOB
Indy: 7 RACECAR
Ledger: 4 ITEM 5 ASSET DEBIT 6 CREDIT
List: 4 ITEM
PDA: 4 APPT
permit: 4 VISA
Poker ~ fee: 4 ANTE
Rap sheet: 5 PRIOR
Red ink: 4 DEBT 5 DEBIT
requirement: 5 IDTAG
Savings acct.: 3 INT
Sched.: 3 ETD 4 APPT

Thesaurus ~ (abbr.): 3 SYN
To-do list: 4 TASK
Web browser: 3 URL
**"Entry of Christ Into Brussels"**
artist: 5 ENSOR
**Entryway:** 4 DOOR 6 PORTAL
**Enumerate:** 4 LIST 6 DETAIL RECITE 7 ITEMIZE
**Enumeration**
abbr.: 3 ETC
**Env.**
contents: 3 LTR 4 ENCS
extra: 3 ENC
info: 4 ADDR
In this: 4 ENCL
notation: 4 ATTN
stuffer: 3 ENC
**Envelope**
abbr.: 4 ATTN
closer: 4 FLAP SEAL 5 CLASP
encl.: 4 SASE
feature: 5 CLASP
Kind of: 6 MANILA
Letters on a love letter: 4 SWAK
Open an: 4 SLIT 6 UNSEAL
part: 4 FLAP GLUE
sticker: 5 STAMP
**Enveloping**
glow: 4 AURA
**Environment:** 6 MILIEU
Stable: 5 STALL
**Environmental**
disaster: 7 ECOCIDE
prefix: 3 ECO
sci.: 4 ECOL
subgroup: 7 ECOTYPE
subj.: 4 ECOL
toxin: 3 PCB
**Environmentalist**
celebration: 8 EARTHDAY
concern: 4 SMOG
Dr. Seuss's: 5 LORAX
magazine: 6 SIERRA
maj.: 4 ECOL
**Environs:** 4 AREA 6 CLIMES MILIEU
Chalet: 7 SKIAREA
**Envision:** 3 SEE
**Envy:** 3 SIN
**Enya**
Musical style of: 6 NEWAGE
**Enzyme**
ending: 3 ASE
Kidney: 5 RENIN
suffix: 3 ASE
**Eocene:** 5 EPOCH
**Eon:** 3 AGE
subdivision: 3 ERA
**Eos**
Lover of: 5 ORION
**EPA**
banned it: 3 DDT
concern: 4 ECOL SMOG
determination: 3 MPG

**Epcot**
home: 3 FLA

**Épée**
Wield an: 5 FENCE

**Ephesus**
Home of: 5 IONIA

**Ephron**
Author: 4 NORA 5 DELIA
Director: 4 NORA
Screenwriter: 4 NORA
5 DELIA

**Epic**
Homeric: 5 ILIAD
Icelandic: 4 EDDA
poem: 5 ILIAD
tale: 4 SAGA
Trojan War: 5 ILIAD
Virgil: 6 AENEID
___ epic scale: 4 ONAN

**Epicure**
asset: 6 PALATE

**Epidermal**
eruption: 4 RASH

**Epilogue:** 3 END
Musical: 4 CODA

**Epinephrine**
prefix: 3 NOR
producer: 7 ADRENAL

**Epinicion:** 3 ODE

**Epiphany**
figures: 4 MAGI
sound: 3 AHA

**Episcopal**
cleric: 6 RECTOR

**Episode:** 5 EVENT 8 INCIDENT
Old TV show: 5 RERUN

**Epistle**
apostle: 4 PAUL
writer: 4 PAUL

**Epistolary**
friend: 6 PENPAL

**Epitaph**
opener: 4 HERE

**Epithet:** 4 NAME SLUR 5 LABEL
Dickensian: 3 BAH
Homer: 3 DOH
Mild: 4 EGAD
of Athena: 4 ALEA

**Epitome:** 5 IDEAL 8 PARADIGM
of easiness: 3 ABC PIE
of hardness: 5 NAILS
of neatness: 3 PIN
of redness: 4 BEET
of simplicity: 3 ABC
of slowness: 5 SNAIL
8 MOLASSES
of thinness: 4 RAIL REED
5 RAZOR

**"E pluribus ___":** 4 UNUM
**"E pluribus unum":** 5 MOTTO

**Epoch:** 3 AGE ERA
Ancient: 6 ICEAGE
from 10 to 2 million years ago:
8 PLIOCENE
Glacial: 6 ICEAGE
Pleistocene: 6 ICEAGE

when mammals arose:
6 EOCENE

**Eponym**
for failure: 5 EDSEL
of a lemon: 9 EDSELFORD

**Eponymous**
general: 3 TSO

**Epoxy:** 4 GLUE 5 RESIN

**Epps**
Actor: 4 OMAR

**Epsilon**
follower: 4 ZETA

**Epsilon ___:** 3 ERI

**Equal:** 3 ARE 4 PEER SAME
Miss: 4 MILE
prefix: 3 ISO 4 PARI
Sharing ~ value: 6 ONAPAR
Social: 4 PEER
to the task: 4 ABLE
Try to: 7 EMULATE
Without: 5 ALONE

**Equally:** 5 ALIKE
Divide: 5 HALVE
divided: 4 EVEN
matched: 4 EVEN

**Equanimity:** 6 APLOMB

**Equation**
Kind of: 6 LINEAR

**Equator**
Constellation above the:
5 ORION
Fly over the: 6 TSETSE
Island crossed by the:
7 SUMATRA

**Equatorial**
Opposite of: 5 AXIAL

**Equestrian:** 5 RIDER
attire: 5 HABIT
brake: 4 REIN
equipment: 10 RIDINGCROP
event: 8 DRESSAGE

**Equi-:** 3 ISO

**Equiangular:** 8 ISOGONAL
figure: 6 ISOGON

**Equilibrium:** 6 STASIS

**Equine:** 5 HORSY
Eloquent: 4 MRED
Energetic: 5 STEED
Striped: 5 ZEBRA
Stubborn: 3 ASS 4 MULE

**Equinox**
mo.: 3 SEP 4 SEPT

**Equip:** 3 RIG 6 TOOLUP
anew: 5 REFIT RERIG
for battle: 4 ARM

**Equipment:** 4 GEAR
Backgammon: 4 DICE
Bowling ~ mfr.: 3 AMF
Brewery: 4 OAST
Coffeehouse: 3 URN
Concert: 3 AMP
Crew: 4 OARS
ER: 3 IVS
Farm ~ name: 5 DEERE
Fire truck: 6 LADDER
Fronton: 5 CESTA

Lab: 4 ETNA
Olympics: 4 EPEE
Playground: 5 SWING
6 SEESAW SLIDES
SWINGS
Trawling: 3 NET

**Equipped:** 4 ABLE

**Equitable:** 4 EVEN FAIR JUST
5 RIGHT

**Equitably**
Assessed: 7 PRORATA

**Equivalent**
Aurora: 3 EOS
C: 6 BSHARP
Count: 4 EARL
C sharp: 5 DFLAT
D flat: 6 CSHARP
D sharp: 5 EFLAT
E flat: 6 DSHARP
F: 6 ESHARP
French ~ of the Oscar:
5 CESAR
F sharp: 5 GFLAT
G sharp: 5 AFLAT
Helios: 3 SOL

**Equivocator**
spot: 5 FENCE

**Equivoque:** 3 PUN

**ER**
cry: 4 STAT
equipment: 3 IVS
figure: 3 DOC
hookups: 3 IVS
locale: 4 HOSP
Part of: 4 EMER
pronouncement: 3 DOA
readout: 3 EEG
skill: 3 CPR
Some ~ cases: 3 ODS
units: 3 CCS
workers: 3 DRS MDS RNS

**"ER"**
actor Epps: 4 OMAR
actor La Salle: 4 ERIQ
actor Noah: 4 WYLE
actress Laura: 5 INNES
and others: 6 DRAMAS
doctor: 4 ROSS
extra: 5 NURSE
extras: 3 RNS
network: 3 NBC
order: 4 STAT
roles: 3 MDS
setting: 3 ICU

**"Er ...":** 5 IMEAN

**Era:** 3 AGE 4 TIME 5 EPOCH
TIMES
From a prior: 3 OLD
Suffix on ~ names: 4 ZOIC

**ERA:** 4 STAT
Part of: 5 EQUAL 6 EARNED

**Eras**
Two or more: 3 EON 4 AEON

**Erase:** 4 UNDO WIPE
6 DELETE
a magnetic tape: 7 DEGAUSS

**Eraser**
Kind of: 6 ARTGUM
leaving: 6 SMUDGE
**"Eraser"**
star: 4 CAAN
**"Eraserhead"**
actor Jack: 5 NANCE
**Erasers**
Clean: 4 CLAP
**Erato:** 4 MUSE
instrument: 4 LYRE
is their Muse: 5 POETS
**Ere:** 5 AFORE
**Erect**
Not quite: 5 ATILT
Wasn't: 5 LEANT
___ erectus: 4 HOMO
**Erelong:** 4 ANON SOON
**Eremite:** 5 LONER
Like an: 4 LONE 5 ALONE
**Erenow:** 3 AGO
**Ergo:** 4 THEN THUS 5 HENCE
**Ergs**
100 ~ per gram: 3 RAD
Ten million: 5 JOULE
**Erhard, Werner**
system: 3 EST
**Eric**
Actor: 4 IDLE 5 BLORE
6 STOLTZ
Author: 6 AMBLER
Magazine founder: 4 UTNE
Son of: 4 LEIF
**Erica**
Author: 4 JONG
**Erich**
Author: 5 SEGAL
**Ericson**
Mariner: 4 LEIF
tongue: 5 NORSE
**Eric the Red:** 5 NORSE
Son of: 4 LEIF
**Erie:** 4 LAKE 5 CANAL
hockey player: 5 OTTER
**Erie Canal**
city: 5 UTICA
mule: 3 SAL
**Erik**
Actor: 7 ESTRADA
Composer: 5 SATIE
**Erin**
Actress: 5 MORAN
**"Erin go ___!":** 5 BRAGH
**Eritrea**
border: 6 REDSEA
Capital of: 6 ASMARA
**"Eri tu":** 4 ARIA
**Erle**
Contemporary of: 6 AGATHA
**Ermine:** 6 WEASEL
Brown: 5 STOAT
Summer: 5 STOAT
**Erne:** 7 SEABIRD 8 SEAEAGLE
**Ernest**
Offscreen pal of: 4 VERN
of honky-tonk: 4 TUBB

Winemaker: 5 GALLO
**Ernestine**
~, for one: 8 OPERATOR
**Ernesto**
nickname: 3 CHE
**Ernie**
Golfer: 3 ELS
Home of: 12 SESAMESTREET
Journalist: 4 PYLE
Keebler's: 3 ELF
Pal of: 4 BERT
**Ernst**
colleague: 3 ARP
style: 4 DADA
**Ernst & Young**
staff: 4 CPAS
**Erode:** 3 EAT 4 GNAW WEAR
5 DECAY EATAT
7 EATAWAY EATINTO
**Eroded:** 3 ATE 4 WORE WORN
5 ATEAT EATEN
7 ATEINTO
8 WOREDOWN
valley: 6 RAVINE
**"Eroica"**
Key of: 5 EFLAT
**Eros**
Love of: 6 PSYCHE
Roman: 4 AMOR
**Erosion**
cause: 4 TIDE
loss: 4 SOIL
Product of: 6 RAVINE
**Erotic:** 4 SEXY 6 STEAMY
**Erotica**
First name in: 5 ANAIS
**Err:** 4 GOOF SLIP
Cause to: 4 TRIP
**Errand:** 3 JOB 4 TASK
runner: 4 PAGE 5 GOFER
**Erratic**
move: 3 ZAG ZIG 4 FLIT
**Erratum:** 4 SLIP
**Errol**
Emulate: 11 SWASHBUCKLE
**Erroneous**
conviction: 6 BUMRAP
**Error:** 6 MISCUE 7 MISSTEP
indicator: 3 SIC
Key: 4 TYPO
message: 4 OOPS
Minor: 5 LAPSE
Partner of: 5 TRIAL
Pitching: 4 BALK
Remove an: 5 DEBUG
Sign of an: 7 ERASURE
**Errors:** 4 STAT
**Ersatz:** 4 FAKE SHAM
(abbr.): 4 IMIT
butter: 4 OLEO
chocolate: 5 CAROB
fat: 5 OLEAN
gold: 6 ORMOLU
**Erstwhile:** 3 OLD 4 ONCE
**Erté**
forte: 4 DECO 7 ARTDECO

**Erudite:** 4 WISE 7 LEARNED
**Erudition:** 4 LORE
**Erupt:** 4 SPEW 7 FLAREUP
suddenly: 5 FLARE
**Erupter**
1786 ~: 8 MTSHASTA
European: 4 ETNA
Sicilian: 4 ETNA
**Eruption**
Epidermal: 4 RASH
**Erving**
nickname: 3 DRJ
**Erwin**
Actor: 3 STU
**Erykah**
Singer: 4 BADU
**Esai**
Actor: 7 MORALES
**Esau**
Descendant of: 7 EDOMITE
Father of: 5 ISAAC
home: 4 EDOM
Jacob, to: 4 TWIN
Twin of: 5 JACOB
Wife of: 4 ADAH
**ESC:** 3 KEY
**Escalator**
clause: 4 COLA
feature: 5 TREAD
part: 4 STEP
**"Escales"**
composer: 5 IBERT
**Escamillo**
Cheer for: 3 OLE
**Escapade:** 4 LARK 5 CAPER
**Escape:** 3 FLY LAM 4 BOLT
FLEE 5 ELUDE
6 GETOUT 7 RUNAWAY
10 FLYTHECOOP
artist: 6 ELUDER
clause: 3 OUT
Close, as an: 6 NARROW
from: 5 EVADE
Hasty: 3 LAM
mechanism: 4 VENT
slowly: 4 SEEP
Unable to: 5 TREED
vehicle: 3 POD
**Escapee:** 6 ELUDER
Pandora: 4 EVIL
Political: 6 EMIGRE
Sodom: 3 LOT
**Escaping**
Keep from: 6 SEALIN
**Escargot:** 5 SNAIL
**Escher**
genre: 5 OPART
**Eschew:** 4 SHUN 5 AVOID
the doorbell: 5 KNOCK
the leftovers: 6 EATOUT
**Eschewed**
fast food: 5 ATEIN
**Escort:** 3 SEE 6 GIGOLO
SQUIRE 7 TAKEOUT
Lady's: 4 GENT
offering: 3 ARM

to the door: 6 SEEOUT
**Escorted:** 3 LED 5 LEDIN
  by: 4 WITH
**Escorts**
  to the penthouse: 6 SEESUP
**ESE**
  Opposite of: 3 WNW
  ___ e sempre: 3 ORA
**Eshkol**
  of Israel: 4 LEVI
  successor: 4 MEIR
**Eskimo:** 5 INUIT
  craft: 5 KAYAK UMIAK
  home: 5 IGLOO 6 ALASKA
  knife: 3 ULU
  relative: 5 ALEUT
  transport: 4 SLED
**ESL**
  student challenge: 5 IDIOM
**Esne:** 4 SERF
**Eso**
  Not esto or: 4 OTRO
**"Eso ___" (Anka hit):** 4 BESO
**Esophagus:** 6 GULLET
**Esoteric:** 4 DEEP 6 ARCANE
    OCCULT
**ESP:** 4 GIFT
  and such: 3 PSI
**España**
  Info: Spanish cue
**"___ espanol?":** 5 HABLA
**Espied:** 3 SAW 4 SEEN
**Espionage**
  1960 ~ show: 4 ISPY
  First name in: 4 MATA
  insider: 4 MOLE
  org.: 3 CIA
**ESPN**
  figure: 4 STAT
  subject: 4 NCAA
**"Espolio"**
  artist: 7 ELGRECO
**Esposito**
  of hockey: 4 PHIL
  teammate: 3 ORR
**Espouse:** 5 ADOPT
**Espresso**
  drink: 5 LATTE
  Spot for: 4 CAFE
**Esprit de corps:** 6 MORALE
**Espy:** 3 SEE 4 SPOT 6 DETECT
    NOTICE
**Esq.**
  user: 4 ATTY
**Esquivel**
  1980 Peace Nobelist:
    6 ADOLFO
  ___ es Salaam: 3 DAR
**Essay:** 3 TRY 5 PROSE
    7 ATTEMPT
  An ~ may be part of it: 4 EXAM
  byline: 4 ELIA
  page: 4 OPED
**"Essay ___, An":** 5 ONMAN
**Essayist**
  alias: 4 ELIA

Newspaper ~ page: 4 OPED
**"Essay on Criticism, An"**
  writer: 4 POPE
**"Essay on Man"**
  author: 4 POPE
**"Essays of ___":** 4 LAMB
**Essen**
  Info: German cue
  exclamation: 3 ACH
  river: 4 RUHR
**Essence:** 3 NUB 4 CORE CRUX
    GIST MEAT ODOR PITH
    SOUL 6 FLAVOR KERNEL
    THRUST 8 SUMTOTAL
  Rose: 5 ATTAR
  Spiritual: 4 SOUL
**Essential:** 3 KEY 4 NEED
    5 VITAL 6 NEEDED
  acid: 5 AMINO
  Be an ~ part of: 6 INHERE
  It may be: 3 OIL
  part: 4 GIST PITH ROOT
**Essentially:** 7 ATHEART
**Essentials:** 4 ABCS
    10 BRASSTACKS
**Esses**
  Have trouble with: 4 LISP
**Essex:** 3 CAR
  contemporary: 3 REO
**Est**
  founder: 6 ERHARD
**EST**
  Part of: 3 STD
**Est.:** 3 SSR
**Esta**
  Not ~ or esa: 4 OTRA
**Establish:** 3 SET 5 ERECT
    SETUP
  as fact: 5 PROVE
  as law: 5 ENACT
**Established**
  Become: 5 SETIN
  fact: 5 GIVEN
  Long: 7 OLDTIME
  rule: 5 AXIOM
**Establishment**
  Quaint: 6 SHOPPE
**Estate:** 5 MANOR
  Country: 5 MANOR VILLA
  division: 4 ACRE
  Feudal: 4 FIEF
  Fourth: 5 PRESS
  home: 5 MANOR
  Kane: 6 XANADU
  Lord's: 7 DEMESNE
  Luxurious: 5 VILLA
  Rancher's: 8 HACIENDA
  recipient: 4 HEIR
  Scarlett's: 4 TARA
**Estates**
  Like some: 5 GATED
**"¿___ está usted?":** 4 COMO
**Estee**
  Cosmetician: 6 LAUDER
**Esteem:** 5 VALUE 6 ADMIRE
    REGARD REPUTE

Lower in: 5 ABASE
  Object of: 4 ICON
  to the extreme: 5 ADORE
**Esteemed**
  one: 3 GEM
  title: 3 SIR
**Estefan**
  Singer: 6 GLORIA
**Estelle**
  Actress: 5 GETTY
  Costar of: 3 BEA
**Ester**
  Soap: 6 OLEATE
**Estevez**
  Actor: 6 EMILIO
  Dad of: 5 SHEEN
**Esth.**
  Book before: 3 NEH
**Esther**
  Actress: 5 ROLLE
  festival: 5 PURIM
**Estimate:** 4 STAB 5 ASSAY
    GAUGE
  follower: 4 ORSO
  formally: 6 ASSESS
**Estimator**
  words: 4 ORSO
**Esto**
  Not ~ or eso: 4 OTRO
**Estonia**
  ~, once (abbr.): 3 SSR
**"___ est percipi":** 4 ESSE
**Estrada**
  Actor: 4 ERIK
**Estragon**
  expected him: 5 GODOT
**Estrange:** 8 ALIENATE
**Estrangement:** 4 RIFT
**Estuary:** 3 RIA 5 DELTA
    INLET
**ET**
  craft: 3 UFO
  on TV: 3 ALF
**"E.T."**
  Wallace of: 3 DEE
**Et ___:** 3 SEQ 4 ALIA ALII
    6 CETERA
**Eta**
  Letter after: 5 THETA
**ETA**
  Part of: 3 ARR
**Et al.**
  and others: 5 ABBRS
**Etats-___:** 4 UNIS
**Etc.**
  kin: 4 ETAL
**Etch:** 4 DRAW LIMN
**___ et Chandon:** 4 MOET
**Etch-a-Sketch**
  feature: 4 KNOB
  Shake an: 5 ERASE
**Etcher**
  need: 4 ACID
**Etching**
  fluid: 4 ACID
**Etchings:** 3 ART

**Eternal:** 7 AGELESS AGELONG
  UNAGING UNDYING
  It springs: 4 HOPE
**Eternal City:** 4 ROME
**Eternally:** 4 EVER
  ~, in poetry: 3 EER
**Eternity:** 3 EON 4 AEON
**Ethan**
  Actor: 5 HAWKE
  Filmmaker: 4 COEN
  "Ethan ___": 5 FROME
**Ethel**
  or Fred: 5 MERTZ
**Ethelbert**
  Composer: 5 NEVIN
**Ethelred**
  Descriptor for: 7 UNREADY
**Ethereal:** 4 AERY AIRY
  prefix: 4 AERI
**Etheridge**
  Singer: 7 MELISSA
**Ethical:** 5 MORAL
  standards: 5 MORES
**Ethically**
  neutral: 6 AMORAL
**Ethiopian**
  emperor Selassie: 5 HAILE
  map word: 5 ABABA
  neighbor: 6 SOMALI
  of opera: 4 AIDA
  title: 3 RAS
**Ethnic:** 6 RACIAL
  cuisine: 4 THAI
  suffix: 3 ESE
**Ethyl**
  acetate: 5 ESTER
  ending: 3 ENE
**Ethylene:** 4 AGER 7 RIPENER
**Etiquette**
  Diplomatic: 8 PROTOCOL
  expert: 4 POST
    11 MISSMANNERS
  Post of: 5 EMILY
  subjects: 5 NONOS
  "___ et labora": 3 ORA
  "___ et mon droit": 4 DIEU
**Etna**
  Emulate: 5 ERUPT
  Gush like: 4 SPEW
  output: 3 ASH 4 LAVA
**ETO**
  commander: 3 DDE
  name: 3 IKE
**Etonian**
  dad: 5 PATER
**ETS**
  exam: 3 SAT
  offering: 4 PSAT
**Etta**
  Jazz singer: 5 JAMES
  of old comics: 4 KETT
  "Et voilà!": 4 TADA
**EU**
  language: 3 ENG GER
  member: 3 GER
  Part of: 3 EUR

**Eubanks**
  is on his show: 4 LENO
**Eucalyptivore:** 5 KOALA
**Eucalyptus**
  eater: 5 KOALA
**Eucharist**
  bread: 5 WAFER
  plate: 5 PATEN
  vessel: 3 PYX
**Euchre**
  kin: 6 ECARTE
  low card: 5 SEVEN
**Euclid**
  lake: 4 ERIE
  subj.: 4 GEOM
  suffix: 3 EAN
**Eugene**
  Belgian composer: 5 YSAYE
  Daughter of: 4 OONA
  home: 6 OREGON
  Playwright: 6 ONEILL
    7 IONESCO
  Socialist: 4 DEBS
**"Eugene Onegin"**
  mezzo: 4 OLGA
**Eulogist**
  B.C.: 6 ANTONY
**Eulogize:** 4 LAUD 5 EXTOL
**Eunomia**
  ~, Dike, and Irene: 5 HORAE
**Eunuch**
  Area guarded by a: 5 HAREM
**Euphoric:** 5 GIDDY
  states: 5 HIGHS
  Where the ~ walk: 5 ONAIR
**Euphrates**
  land: 4 IRAQ 5 SYRIA
**Eur.**
  Bygone ~ realm: 3 HRE
  carrier: 3 SAS
  Former ~ carrier: 4 BOAC
  It's south of: 3 AFR
  nation: 3 GER IRE
**Eurasian**
  divide: 5 URALS
  duck: 4 SMEW
  wild goat: 4 IBEX
**Eure-et-Loir**
  neighbor: 4 ORNE
**"Eureka!":** 3 AHA OHO
    5 MOTTO 7 THATSIT
  cause: 8 SOLUTION
**Euripides**
  play: 3 ION 5 HELEN MEDEA
    7 ELECTRA ORESTES
**Euro**
  exchange (abbr.): 3 DOL
  fraction: 4 CENT
  predecessor: 3 ECU 4 LIRA
    5 FRANC 6 PESETA
**Europe**
  "boot": 5 ITALY
  East end of: 5 URALS
  highest volcano: 4 ETNA
  In: 6 ABROAD
  Longest river of: 5 VOLGA

  ~, to the U.S.: 8 OLDWORLD
**European**
  airline: 3 SAS
  auto: 4 AUDI OPEL SAAB
    YUGO
  blackbird: 4 MERL
  capital: 4 BERN KIEV OSLO
    RIGA 5 BERNE MINSK
    6 TIRANA VIENNA
    ZAGREB 7 TALLINN
  chain: 4 ALPS
  Eastern: 4 SERB SLAV
  erupter: 4 ETNA
  fashion center: 5 MILAN
  finch: 5 SERIN 6 LINNET
  Former ~ capital: 4 BONN
  high points: 4 ALPS
  hot spot: 4 ETNA
  language: 4 ERSE
  peak: 3 ALP
  peninsula: 6 IBERIA
  prefix: 4 INDO
  river: 4 ARNO ELBE
  rocket: 6 ARIANE
  stock exchange: 6 BOURSE
  tree: 4 SORB
  viper: 3 ASP 5 ADDER
**European-made**
  jet: 6 AIRBUS
**Europe-Asia**
  divider: 5 URALS
**Eurydice**
  Lover of: 7 ORPHEUS
**Euterpe:** 4 MUSE
  Sister of: 4 CLIO 5 ERATO
**Eva**
  half-sister: 3 ZSA
  of Argentina: 5 PERON
  or Zsa Zsa: 5 GABOR
  Sister of: 5 MAGDA 6 ZSAZSA
**Evade:** 5 DODGE SHIRK SKIRT
  ~, with "out of": 6 WEASEL
**Evader**
  Famed tax: 6 CAPONE
  Tax ~ nightmare: 5 AUDIT
**Evaluate:** 4 RATE 5 ASSAY
    WEIGH 6 ASSESS
    SIZEUP 8 APPRAISE
**Evaluation:** 4 TEST
  Critical: 8 ACIDTEST
**Evan**
  Senator: 4 BAYH
  suffix: 4 ESCE
**Evanesce:** 4 FADE WANE
    8 FADEAWAY
**Evangeline:** 7 ACADIAN
**"Evangeline"**
  setting: 6 ACADIA
**Evangelist**
  cry: 6 REPENT
  Early: 11 BILLYSUNDAY
  Eminent: 11 BILLYGRAHAM
  prefix: 3 TEL
**Evans**
  Actress: 5 LINDA
  Country singer: 4 SARA

Cowgirl: 4 DALE
Jazz arranger: 3 GIL
partner in journalism:
    5 NOVAK
**Evans, Greg**
comic strip: 5 LUANN
**Evans, Janet**
Emulated: 4 SWAM
**Evaporation**
product: 7 SEASALT
**Evasive:** 3 COY 4 EELY 5 CAGEY
maneuver: 4 SLASH STALL
    6 ENDRUN
**Eve**
Actress: 5 ARDEN
counterpart: 4 MORN
Early: 3 RIB
Eldest of: 4 CAIN
Grandson of: 4 ENOS
Home of: 4 EDEN
Mate of: 4 ADAM
Second son of: 4 ABEL
Son of: 4 ABEL CAIN SETH
Tempter of: 7 SERPENT
Youngest of: 4 SETH
Yves's: 4 SOIR
**Evel**
deed: 5 STUNT
**Evelyn**
Actress: 5 KEYES
Writing brother of: 4 ALEC
**Even:** 3 TIE YET 4 TIED
    5 ALIGN FLUSH
    6 INATIE ONAPAR
    SEDATE TIEDUP
a little: 3 ANY 5 ATALL
chance: 6 TOSSUP
Get ~ for: 6 AVENGE
if: 3 THO 5 ALTHO 6 ALBEIT
Make: 4 TRUE
Not: 3 ODD 5 ASKEW
    6 ASLOPE UNTRUE
one: 3 ANY
prime: 3 TWO
score: 3 TIE
so: 3 YET 5 STILL
start: 4 EQUI
though: 6 ALBEIT
~, once: 4 EVER
~, with "in": 4 ATIE
**Evenhanded:** 4 FAIR
**Evening**
affair: 6 SOIREE
bell: 6 VESPER
do: 6 SOIREE
Early: 5 SEVEN
Eat in the: 3 SUP 4 DINE
event: 6 SOIREE SUNSET
hour: 3 TEN 4 NINE
Informal: 4 NITE
Like a romantic: 7 MOONLIT
Like some ~ gowns:
    9 STRAPLESS
party: 6 SOIREE
Suitable for ~ wear: 6 DRESSY
~, in French: 4 SOIR

~, in Italian: 4 SERA
___ even keel: 4 ONAN
**Evenly**
matched: 8 ONETOONE
Split: 6 BISECT
**"Even ___ speak ...":** 4 ASWE
**Even-steven:** 4 TIED
**Event**
1944 ~: 4 DDAY
1977 ~: 5 ROOTS
1998 ~: 5 NTEST
After-Christmas: 4 SALE
Airport: 7 ARRIVAL
Annual sports: 6 USOPEN
Annual TV: 6 OSCARS
Bargain: 4 SALE
Blessed: 6 SNEEZE
Campaign: 6 DEBATE
Catered: 6 AFFAIR
Community: 4 SING
Court: 5 TRIAL
Current: 4 EDDY TIDE
    6 ELNINO
Dressy: 4 GALA
Easter: 6 PARADE
Eden: 4 FALL
Emotional: 5 DRAMA
Equestrian: 8 DRESSAGE
Festive: 4 GALA
Field: 7 SHOTPUT
for Alice: 8 TEAPARTY
Friars: 5 ROAST
Fundraising: 8 BAKESALE
Gallery: 7 ARTSALE
Garage: 4 SALE
Hoops: 3 NIT
Ice skating: 5 PAIRS
Inauguration: 4 OATH
Lunar: 7 ECLIPSE
Mall: 4 SALE
May: 4 INDY
Meet: 4 DASH RACE
Musical: 7 RECITAL
Olympic: 4 EPEE LUGE
Pentathlon: 4 EPEE
Pointless: 4 EPEE
Prefight: 7 WEIGHIN
Quadrennial:
    11 SUMMERGAMES
Quantum: 4 LEAP
Red-tag: 4 SALE
Significant: 9 MILESTONE
Speakeasy: 4 RAID
Sports: 4 MEET
Spring: 4 THAW
Stock mkt.: 3 IPO
Tent: 4 SALE
Thanksgiving Day: 6 PARADE
Track: 3 BET 4 DASH MEET
    RACE TROT 5 RELAY
    6 SPRINT 7 JAVELIN
with caddies: 3 TEA
WWII: 4 DDAY
Yachting: 7 SEARACE
Yard: 4 SALE
**Events:** 6 DOINGS

Course of: 4 TIDE
**Eventual**
avis: 4 OVUM
**Eventually:** 3 YET 6 INTIME
    ONEDAY 7 SOMEDAY
    13 SOONERORLATER
become: 5 ENDUP
**Ever**
As good as: 7 LIKENEW
Hardly: 6 RARELY
Partner of: 4 ANON
so slight: 3 WEE
**Everage**
Dame: 4 EDNA
Title: 4 DAME
**Ever and ___:** 4 ANON
**Everest:** 5 MOUNT
and others: 3 MTS
guide: 6 SHERPA
locale: 5 NEPAL
**Everett**
Actor: 4 CHAD 6 SLOANE
**Everglades**
bird: 5 EGRET
deposit: 4 PEAT
terrain: 5 SWAMP
wader: 4 IBIS 5 EGRET HERON
**Everglades Parkway**
City west of: 6 NAPLES
**Evergreen:** 3 FIR YEW 4 PINE
    6 SPRUCE 7 CONIFER
hedge: 6 PRIVET
Northern ~ forest: 5 TAIGA
Poisonous: 8 OLEANDER
scented: 4 PINY
Tropical: 5 CACAO
West Coast: 6 TANOAK
**Everhart**
Model: 5 ANGIE
**Everlasting:** 7 AGELESS
    ETERNAL 8 CONSTANT
~, old-style: 6 ETERNE
**Everly Brothers:** 3 DUO 4 DUET
1957 ~ hit: 10 BYEBYELOVE
1960 ~ hit: 5 SOSAD
    9 LETITBEME
One of the: 4 PHIL
Sleeping girl in an ~ hit:
    5 SUSIE
**"___ Ever Need Is You":** 4 ALLI
**"___ ever so humble ...":**
    4 BEIT
**Evert**
of tennis: 5 CHRIS
**Every:** 3 ALL 4 EACH
bit: 3 ALL
Each and: 3 ALL
For: 3 PER
last one: 3 ALL
~ 24 hours: 4 ADAY 5 DAILY
~, on an Rx: 3 OMN
**Everybody:** 3 ALL
Opposite of: 5 NOONE
**"Everybody Loves Raymond":**
    6 SITCOM
actor Peter: 5 BOYLE

actor Ray: 6 ROMANO
network: 3 CBS
**"Everybody's Talkin'"**
singer: 7 NILSSON
**Everyday:** 5 PLAIN USUAL
   6 NORMAL 7 PROSAIC
   ROUTINE
vocabulary: 10 VERNACULAR
**Everydog:** 4 FIDO
**Everyone:** 3 ALL
Buy ~ beers: 9 GETAROUND
For: 4 COED 6 RATEDG
For ~ to hear: 5 ALOUD
~, on boxes: 7 ALLAGES
**Everything:** 3 ALL 6 THELOT
considered: 8 ALLINALL
Counting: 5 INALL 6 INTOTO
   7 ALLTOLD INTOTAL
   OVERALL
else: 4 REST
It means: 4 OMNI
Lose: 6 GOBUST
They fix: 8 PANACEAS
~, in German: 5 ALLES
**Everytown, USA:** 6 PEORIA
**Everywhere:** 7 ALLOVER
   10 HIGHANDLOW
**"Every ___ winner!":** 4 ONEA
**Evian**
and others: 4 SPAS
output: 3 EAU
**Evict:** 4 OUST SHOO
**Evictee**
Early: 3 EVE 4 ADAM
**Eviction:** 6 OUSTER
site: 4 EDEN
**Evidence**
Appendectomy: 4 SCAR
Burning: 5 SMOKE
Carpet: 6 FIBERS
Conclude from the: 5 INFER
Examine: 4 SIFT
Hide: 15 COVERONESTRACKS
in court: 7 EXHIBIT
Indisputable: 5 PROOF
Minimal: 5 SHRED
Modern-day: 3 DNA
of change: 7 ERASURE
of rot: 4 ODOR
of sloppiness: 5 TYPOS
Paternity suit: 3 DNA
Piece of: 4 TAPE
Stop introducing: 4 REST
Type of: 3 DNA
Watergate: 4 TAPE
**Evil:** 3 BAD ILL 4 BASE
   6 UNHOLY 7 SATANIC
Believer in good and:
   7 DUALIST
deed: 3 SIN
emperor: 4 NERO
It may be: 3 EYE
Like a certain: 6 LESSER
look: 4 LEER
one: 3 ORC 4 OGRE 5 DEMON
   FIEND SATAN

repeller: 6 AMULET
spell: 3 HEX
spirit: 5 DEMON
spirits: 6 INCUBI
~, in French: 3 MAL
~ Norse god: 4 LOKI
**"___ evil ...":** 5 SEENO
**"Evil That ___, The":** 5 MENDO
**"Evil Ways"**
band: 7 SANTANA
**"Evil Woman"**
band: 3 ELO
**Evinced:** 5 SHOWN
**Eviscerate:** 3 GUT
**"Evita"**
Antonio in: 3 CHE
Madonna costar in:
   7 ANTONIO
role: 3 CHE 5 PERON
**Evoke:** 6 ELICIT
love: 6 ENDEAR
**Evoker**
Blessing: 5 ACHOO 6 AHCHOO
**Evoking**
the past: 5 RETRO
**Evolution**
Steps in human: 4 APES
**Evolutionary**
link: 6 APEMAN
**Evolutionist**
interest: 7 ORIGINS
**"___ Ev'ry Mountain":** 5 CLIMB
**Ewbank**
Coach: 4 WEEB
**Ewe**
Cheese from ~ milk:
   6 ROMANO
He loves: 3 RAM
It comes from: 4 WOOL
kids: 5 LAMBS
Like a: 5 OVINE
milieu: 3 LEA
said it: 3 BAA MAA
**Ewing**
A ~ on TV: 3 PAM
mother: 5 ELLIE
**Ewing, J.R.:** 6 OILMAN
Mother of: 5 ELLIE
show: 6 DALLAS
**Ewing, Patrick:** 6 CENTER
**Ewok**
home: 5 ENDOR
**"Ew-w-w!":** 3 ICK 5 GROSS
**Ex**
claim: 7 ALIMONY
of André: 3 MIA
of Artie: 3 AVA 4 LANA
of Barbie: 3 KEN
of Brooke: 5 ANDRE
of Bruce: 4 DEMI
of Burt: 4 LONI
of Cher: 4 BONO 5 SONNY
of Crawford: 4 GERE
of Dahl: 5 LAMAS
of Dick: 3 LIZ
of Donald: 5 IVANA 6 MAPLES

of Duke: 5 ASTIN
of Frank: 3 AVA MIA
of Frasier: 6 LILITH
of George Hamilton: 5 ALANA
of Ike: 4 TINA
of Julia: 4 LYLE
of Loni: 4 BURT
of Madonna: 4 SEAN
of Mick: 6 BIANCA
of Mickey: 3 AVA
of Puffy: 3 JLO
of Richard Gere: 5 CINDY
of Rita: 3 ALY
of Rod Stewart: 5 ALANA
of Sonny: 4 CHER
of Tina: 3 IKE
of Turner: 5 FONDA
of Woody: 3 MIA
of Xavier: 4 ABBE 5 CHARO
~ GI: 3 VET
**Exact:** 4 EVEN VERY 6 STRICT
   7 LITERAL PRECISE
copy: 4 TWIN 5 CLONE
   7 REPLICA
Not an ~ fig.: 3 EST
satisfaction for: 6 AVENGE
**Exacta:** 3 BET
**"Exactamundo!":** 5 RIGHT
**Exacting:** 5 HARSH RIGID
   STERN 6 SEVERE
   STRICT
**Exactitude:** 5 RIGOR
**Exactly:** 3 PAT 4 TOAT
   6 NOLESS TOATEE
   8 ONTHEDOT
   SMACKDAB VERBATIM
   9 ONTHENOSE
like this: 6 JUSTSO
right: 6 DEADON SPOTON
**"Exactly!":** 5 RIGHT
**Exaggerate:** 6 OVERDO
   7 INFLATE
**Exaggerated:** 4 TALL
melodrama:
   15 BLOODANDTHUNDER
publicity: 4 HYPE
sense of power: 8 MACHISMO
**Exaggerator**
ending: 3 EST
**Exalt:** 4 LAUD 6 LIFTUP
   7 ENNOBLE LIONIZE
**Exam:** 4 TEST
3-D ~: 3 MRI
Atty.-to-be: 4 LSAT
Breeze through an: 3 ACE
British: 6 ALEVEL OLEVEL
College: 4 ORAL
Coll. senior's: 3 GRE 4 GMAT
Cram for an: 6 BONEUP
Dental: 4 ORAL XRAY
Doc-to-be: 4 MCAT
English: 5 ESSAY
Face-to-face: 4 ORAL
for jrs.: 4 PSAT
H.S.: 3 SAT 4 PSAT
Jr.: 4 PSAT

Kind of: 4 ORAL 5 FINAL
   8 OPENBOOK
Makeup: 6 RETEST
no-no: 4 CRIB
part: 5 ESSAY
Sr.: 3 SAT
taker: 6 TESTEE
Tough: 4 BEAR ORAL
**Examination:** 4 TEST 5 ASSAY
Stiff: 7 AUTOPSY
**Examine:** 3 EYE 4 QUIZ TEST
   5 ASSAY STUDY
   6 GOINTO GOOVER
   LOOKAT PERUSE
again: 5 RESEE
closely: 4 SIFT
hastily: 4 SCAN
in detail: 4 SCAN 5 PROBE
~, with "out": 5 SCOPE
**Examiner:** 6 TESTER
Ear: 8 OTOSCOPE
Future: 4 SEER
Ticket: 5 VOTER
X-file: 4 GMAN
**Example:** 4 TYPE 5 MODEL
   6 LESSON
   8 SPECIMEN
Fine: 5 PEARL
One with an: 5 CITER
___ example: 4 ASAN
**Exasperate:** 3 IRE IRK VEX
   4 GALL RILE
**Exasperation:** 3 IRE
**Excalibur:** 5 SWORD
**Excavate:** 3 DIG 6 DEEPEN
**Excavated**
again: 5 REDUG
**Excavation**
find: 3 ORE 5 RELIC
**Excedrin**
rival: 5 ALEVE BAYER
   6 ANACIN
**Exceed:** 3 TOP 5 OUTDO
   6 GOOVER 7 OUTSTEP
   RUNOVER
   8 OVERSTEP
the limit: 5 SPEED
**Exceeding:** 4 OVER 5 ABOVE
**Exceedingly:** 4 VERY 5 NOEND
   6 EVERSO
**Excel:** 4 STAR 5 SHINE
   7 ACHIEVE
**Excelled:** 5 SHONE
**Excellence:** 5 MERIT
Mark of: 3 TEN 5 APLUS
Meas. of academic: 3 GPA
Model of: 7 PARAGON
Standard of: 5 IDEAL
**Excellent:** 4 AONE 5 AOKAY
   SUPER 6 BANGUP
   SUPERB TIPTOP
   8 SPLENDID
mark: 5 APLUS
rating: 4 AONE
service: 3 ACE
Unusually: 4 RARE

~, slangily: 3 DEF RAD
   4 PHAT 5 PRIMO
**"Excellent!":** 5 GREAT
   SWELL
**Except:** 3 BAR BUT 4 OMIT
   SAVE 5 DEBAR
   6 ALLBUT 7 BESIDES
if: 6 UNLESS
**Exception:** 7 ANOMALY
Take: 5 DEMUR 6 OBJECT
   RESENT
Without: 3 ALL 6 ALWAYS
   TOAMAN 7 BARNONE
**Exceptional:** 4 RARE
   8 ABERRANT
**Excerpt:** 5 QUOTE
Film: 4 CLIP
Opera: 4 ARIA
**Excess:** 3 FAT
Carry to: 6 OVERDO
Drink to: 4 TOPE
Fill to: 4 SATE 7 SATIATE
In ~ of: 4 OVER
   8 MORETHAN
Love to: 4 DOTE
Spell of: 5 SPREE
Use to: 6 OVERDO
Weary by: 4 CLOY
**Excessive:** 5 ULTRA UNDUE
   6 DETROP 8 ALLFIRED
   10 INORDINATE
excitement: 5 MANIA
fondness: 6 DOTAGE
interest: 5 USURY
pride: 6 HUBRIS
sentimentality:
   8 SCHMALTZ
sweetness: 7 TREACLE
**Excessively:** 3 TOO 4 OHSO
affected: 6 TOOTOO
excited: 5 MANIC
glib: 3 PAT
Talk: 5 PRATE
**Exchange:** 4 MART SWAP
   5 BANDY TRADE
   6 SWITCH 7 TRADEIN
allowance: 4 AGIO
Chicago: 4 MERC
Church: 4 IDOS
Currency ~ board (abbr.):
   3 USD
European stock: 6 BOURSE
Foreign: 4 EURO
membership: 4 SEAT
premium: 4 AGIO
Tech-heavy: 6 NASDAQ
verbal blows: 4 SPAR
vows: 3 WED
Wedding: 4 IDOS
**Exchanged**
items: 4 IONS
Where vows are: 5 ALTAR
words: 3 IDO 4 IDOS
**Exchanges**
AOL: 3 IMS
**Excise:** 3 TAX 4 DELE

**Excite:** 3 WOW 4 SEND
   5 KEYUP REVUP
   6 AROUSE THRILL
   TICKLE TURNON
   7 ENTHUSE
~, as interest: 5 PIQUE
**Excited:** 4 AGOG SENT
   5 HETUP 6 INHEAT
   ONFIRE PUMPED
   7 ATINGLE KEYEDUP
about: 4 INTO 5 UPFOR
Got: 5 RAVED
sensation: 6 TINGLE
"___ Excited": 4 IMSO
**Excitedly:** 4 AGOG
**Excitement:** 3 ADO 5 DRAMA
   6 HOOPLA 7 AROUSAL
Buzzing with: 5 ABOIL
Cry of: 4 OHOH
Excessive: 5 MANIA
Full of: 4 AGOG
**Exciting**
Far from: 4 BLAH TAME
**Exclaim**
over: 3 OOH
**Exclamation**
Beatnik: 3 MAN
Brit: 4 ISAY
Comics: 3 ACK
Ebenezer: 3 BAH
Emeril: 3 BAM
French: 5 VOILA 7 OOHLALA
German: 3 ACH
Magician: 6 PRESTO
of annoyance: 4 DRAT
of discovery: 3 AHA
of disdain: 4 POOH
of disgust: 3 UGH
of relief: 4 PHEW
of surprise: 3 OHO 4 LORD
   YIPE 5 WOWIE
Old-time: 3 FIE 4 EGAD
Part of a WWII: 4 TORA
Taunting: 3 OHO
Triumphant: 3 AHA
Weary worker: 4 TGIF
**Exclamations**
Surprised: 3 OHS
**Exclude:** 3 BAN BAR 4 OMIT
   5 DEBAR
**Excluding:** 3 NOT 7 SHORTOF
**Exclusive:** 4 SOLE 5 ELITE
   SCOOP 6 SNOOTY
group: 4 CULT 5 CASTE
   ELITE 6 CHOSEN
   7 COTERIE INCROWD
**Exclusively:** 3 ALL 4 ONLY
   5 ALONE
**Excommunication**
Reason for: 6 HERESY
**Excoriate:** 4 FLAY PARE SKIN
   6 REVILE SAVAGE
   SCATHE 7 CHEWOUT
**Excursion:** 4 RAID TRIP
   5 FORAY JAUNT
NASA: 3 EVA

**Excursions**
Like some: 5 LUNAR
**Excuse:** 3 OUT 5 ALIBI
6 LETOFF PARDON
7 CONDONE FORGIVE
Kind of: 4 LAME
Lame: 6 COPOUT 7 IFORGET
Legal: 5 ALIBI
Like a poor: 4 LAME
Many an: 3 LIE
**"Excuse me ...":** 4 AHEM
**Exec:** 4 SUIT
Agency: 3 DIR
Chief: 4 PRES PREZ
College: 5 PREXY
Corp.: 4 PRES 5 TREAS
degree: 3 MBA
Ex-Disney: 6 EISNER
extra: 4 PERK
Fiscal: 3 CFO
note: 4 MEMO
request: 4 ASAP
Right away, to an: 4 ASAP
TV ~ work: 4 SKED
**Execrate:** 5 ABHOR 6 DETEST
LOATHE
**Execs**
Account: 4 REPS
Baseball: 3 GMS
Magazine: 3 EDS
Mag for: 3 INC
Some: 3 VPS
**Execute**
perfectly: 4 NAIL
**Executed:** 3 DID
**Executes:** 4 DOES
**Executive:** 4 SUIT
7 MANAGER
(abbr.): 4 PRES
extra: 4 PERK
11 STOCKOPTION
staff: 5 AIDES
~ Roone: 7 ARLEDGE
**Executor**
concern: 6 ESTATE
**Exemplar:** 5 IDEAL
of easiness: 3 PIE
of grace: 4 SWAN
of greed: 5 MIDAS
of might: 3 OAK
of twinship: 4 PEAS
**Exempt:** 4 FREE 6 IMMUNE
**Exemption**
Tournament: 3 BYE
**Exercise:** 3 PLY USE 5 EXERT
WIELD
aftermath: 4 ACHE
Ballerina: 4 PLIE
Bar: 6 CHINUP
based on karate: 5 TAEBO
discipline: 4 YOGA
Dumbbell: 4 CURL
for the abs: 5 SITUP
Kind of: 7 AEROBIC
Swimming: 4 LAPS
target: 3 ABS 4 DELT FLAB

unit: 3 SET 5 SITUP
6 PULLUP
Weightlifting: 4 CURL
**Exerciser**
target: 3 ABS 4 FLAB
wear: 7 SPANDEX
**Exert**
One may ~ pressure: 4 PEER
**Exertion:** 4 DINT TOIL
5 SWEAT 6 EFFORT
STRAIN
Averse to: 4 LAZY
Aversion to: 5 SLOTH
**Exhalation**
Wistful: 4 SIGH
**Exhaust:** 3 SAP 4 POOP TIRE
5 DRAIN SPEND USEUP
7 DEPLETE TIREOUT
WEAROUT
tube: 8 TAILPIPE
**Exhausted:** 4 BEAT DEAD
SHOT 5 ALLIN SPENT
WEARY 6 DONEIN
USEDUP 9 WASHEDOUT
~, slangily: 5 FRIED
**Exhausts**
Like some: 4 DUAL
**Exhibit:** 4 SHOW
scorn: 5 SNEER
subject: 3 ART
**Exhibition:** 4 FAIR SHOW
**Exhibitionist:** 8 SHOWBOAT
**Exhibits:** 8 EVIDENCE
**Exhilarate:** 5 ELATE
**Exhort:** 4 URGE
**Exhortation**
Cook's: 5 DIGIN
Demonstration: 5 UNITE
November: 4 VOTE
**Exigency:** 4 NEED
**Exile**
1979 ~: 4 AMIN SHAH
7 IDIAMIN
Early: 3 EVE 4 ADAM
isle: 4 ELBA 8 STHELENA
of 1302: 5 DANTE
Political: 5 EXPAT
Renowned: 9 DALAILAMA
**Exiled**
Leader ~ to Hawaii: 4 RHEE
Where Napoleon was: 4 ELBA
~ Amin: 3 IDI
~ Cambodian leader:
6 LONNOL
~ Irani: 4 SHAH
~ Roman poet: 4 OVID
~ Ugandan: 4 AMIN
**Exist:** 3 ARE 4 LIVE
Did not: 6 WERENT
Does not: 4 ISNT
Do not: 5 ARENT
suffix: 3 ENT 4 ENCE
**Existed:** 3 WAS 4 BEEN WERE
Never: 5 WASNT
**Existence:** 4 LIFE 5 BEING
Coming into: 7 NASCENT

Have: 3 ARE
Hectic: 7 RATRACE
Latin: 4 ESSE
**Existential**
woe: 5 ANGST
**Existing:** 5 ALIVE
**Exit:** 4 DOOR 5 LEAVE
6 BOWOUT DEPART
EGRESS WAYOUT
7 STEPOUT
Discreet: 8 SIDEDOOR
Emergency: 10 FIREESCAPE
Freeway: 4 RAMP
Head for the: 5 LEAVE
location: 4 REAR
one's cocoon: 6 EMERGE
Secret: 8 TRAPDOOR
___ ex machina: 4 DEUS
**Exmoor**
Doone of: 5 LORNA
**Exo-**
Opposite of: 4 ENDO ENTO
**Exodus**
Bk. after: 3 LEV
commemoration: 5 SEDER
crossing: 6 REDSEA
figure: 5 MOSES 7 PHARAOH
food: 5 MANNA
High priest in: 5 AARON
miracle: 5 MANNA
mount: 5 SINAI
pharoah: 6 RAMSES
vllain: 7 PHARAOH
**"Exodus"**
actor: 5 MINEO
actor John: 5 DEREK
actor Mineo: 3 SAL
author: 4 URIS
author Uris: 4 LEON
director Preminger: 4 OTTO
hero: 3 ARI
role for Paul Newman: 3 ARI
**Exonerate:** 5 CLEAR
**Exorbitant:** 4 HIGH 5 STEEP
interest: 5 USURY
**"Exorcist, The"**
actress Blair: 5 LINDA
Board used in: 5 OUIJA
quarry: 5 DEMON
**Exotic:** 5 ALIEN 7 STRANGE
fruit: 5 MANGO
meat: 3 EMU
stamp receiver: 6 PENPAL
**Expand:** 4 GROW 5 ADDON
SPLAY WIDEN 6 DILATE
7 ADDONTO BROADEN
ENLARGE
Cause to: 6 DILATE
**Expanded:** 4 GREW
**Expanding**
gp.: 4 NATO
**Expanse:** 3 SEA 4 AREA
6 SPREAD
African: 6 SAHARA
Argentine: 5 PAMPA
Arid: 6 SAHARA

Green: 3 LEA 4 ACRE LAWN
Iranian:
   15 GREATSALTDESERT
Mongolian: 4 GOBI
of land: 5 TRACT
Pastoral: 3 LEA
Sandy: 6 DESERT
Treeless: 5 PAMPA
Vast: 3 SEA 5 OCEAN
**Expansion**
Room for: 5 ANNEX
team of 1962: 4 METS
**Expansive:** 4 VAST 5 BROAD
   7 OCEANIC
**Expatriate:** 8 EMIGRANT
**Expect:** 4 HOPE 5 AWAIT
   6 PLANON 7 WAITFOR
**Expectant**
Act the ~ father: 4 PACE
Eagerly: 4 ATIP
father: 5 PACER
parent: 5 NAMER
**Expectations**
Grate: 3 ASH 5 ASHES
Like some: 5 UNMET
Meet, as: 6 RISETO
Met: 5 ARIAS 6 OPERAS
**Expected:** 3 DUE 5 USUAL
   6 NORMAL
As: 4 DULY 5 ONCUE
   7 UPTOPAR
Exactly what's:
   15 PARFORTHECOURSE
Is ~ (to): 5 OUGHT
It's: 3 PAR
result: 3 PAR 4 NORM
soon: 4 NIGH
to arrive: 3 DUE
What's: 4 NORM
When: 5 ONCUE
**Expecting:** 8 PREGNANT
Eagerly: 4 ATIP
the worse: 7 BEARISH
**Expectorate:** 4 SPIT
**Expedition:** 4 TREK 5 HASTE
   SPEED
African: 6 SAFARI
**Expeditious:** 6 PROMPT
   SPEEDY
**Expel:** 4 OUST SPEW
   5 EJECT EVICT
   6 DEPORT
from law practice: 6 DISBAR
**Expend:** 3 USE 5 USEUP
**Expenditure:** 4 COST 5 OUTGO
   6 OUTLAY
**Expense:** 4 COST 6 OUTLAY
Monthly: 4 RENT
Nightclub:
   11 COVERCHARGE
Trucker: 4 TOLL
**Expenses**
After: 3 NET
Reduce: 4 PARE
**Expensive:** 4 DEAR HIGH
   , 5 STEEP 6 COSTLY

**Experience:** 4 FEEL HAVE
   7 UNDERGO
again: 6 RELIVE
Bound to: 5 INFOR
Chair-raising: 4 HORA
Exciting: 4 TRIP
Pique: 3 IRE 4 SNIT
Trying: 6 ORDEAL
**Experienced:** 3 PRO 4 FELT
   KNEW 7 VETERAN
Least: 6 RAWEST
~, old-style: 5 VERST
**Experiences:** 3 HAS
**Experiment:** 4 TEST 5 TRIAL
Alamogordo: 5 ATEST
Bikini: 5 NTEST
site: 3 LAB
subject: 6 LABRAT
Subject of a psych.: 3 ESP
Underwater ~ site: 6 SEALAB
**Expert:** 3 ACE PRO WIZ
   4 GURU WHIZ 5 ADEPT
   MAVEN SHARP
   7 MAESTRO OLDHAND
Bridge: 5 GOREN
Card game: 5 HOYLE
Coloring: 4 DYER
CPR.: 3 EMT
ending: 3 ISE
Gregg: 5 STENO
group: 5 PANEL
in futures: 4 SEER
Law: 6 JURIST
Martial arts: 5 NINJA
Mideast: 7 ARABIST
PC: 4 TECH
Policy: 4 WONK
Service: 4 ACER
suffix: 3 ISE
Talmud: 5 RABBI
Tax prep.: 3 CPA
with a deck: 9 CARDSHARK
"___ expert, but ...": 4 IMNO
**Expertise:** 3 ART 5 SKILL
   7 KNOWHOW
Field of: 4 AREA
Level of karate: 3 DAN
PT: 5 REHAB
Sailor: 5 KNOTS
**Expiate:** 5 ATONE
**Expire:** 3 DIE END 5 LAPSE
   6 RUNOUT
**Explain**
away, with "over": 5 GLOSS
Hard to: 5 EERIE
"___ Explains It All":
   8 CLARISSA
**Explanation:** 3 WHY
Phrase of: 5 IDEST
Propose as an: 5 POSIT
**Expletive**
Charlie Brown: 4 RATS
Dated: 4 EGAD
Ebenezer: 3 BAH
Fields: 4 DRAT
Mild: 4 EGAD

**Explicable**
Least: 6 ODDEST
**Explicit**
Not: 5 VAGUE
**Explode:** 5 BURST ERUPT
   6 BLOWUP GOBOOM
Ready to: 5 IRATE
**Exploded:** 4 BLEW 7 WENTOFF
**Exploding**
gag item: 5 CIGAR
star: 4 NOVA
stars: 5 NOVAE
Still capable of: 4 LIVE
**Exploit:** 3 ACT USE 4 DEED
   FEAT GEST MILK
   5 GESTE 7 TRADEON
   UTILIZE
**Exploitive**
boss: 7 PADRONE
one: 4 USER
**Exploration**
org.: 4 NASA
**Exploratory**
expedition: 5 PROBE
**Explore:** 5 DELVE PROBE
   6 GOINTO
caves: 7 SPELUNK
**Explorer**
Antarctic: 4 BYRD ROSS
   6 ERNEST
Arctic: 3 RAE 5 PEARY
called "the Red": 4 ERIC
Cumberland Gap: 5 BOONE
Down Under: 6 TASMAN
Early: 4 ERIC
Ford: 3 SUV
Internet: 4 USER
maker: 4 FORD
Mississippi River: 6 DESOTO
   7 LASALLE
NASA: 5 ROBOT
need: 3 MAP
Norse: 4 ERIC
of Florida: 6 DESOTO
org.: 3 BSA
Scottish: 3 RAE
Space: 5 PROBE
Victoria Island: 3 RAE
who named Louisiana:
   7 LASALLE
~ La ___: 5 SALLE
~ Polo: 5 MARCO
**Explosion:** 5 BLAST
**Explosive:** 3 TNT 5 NITRO
compound: 6 AMATOL
letters: 3 TNT
liquid: 5 NITRO
sound: 4 BANG BLAM WHAM
   6 KABOOM
trial: 5 NTEST
**Expo**
1970 ~ site: 5 OSAKA
**Exponential**
inverse: 7 ANTILOG
**Export**
Australian: 4 OPAL

Bolivian: 3 TIN
Dutch: 4 EDAM 5 TULIP
Holland: 5 TULIP
Jamaican: 3 RUM
Malaysian: 3 TIN
Mideast: 3 OIL
North Pole: 3 TOY
Sri Lanka: 3 TEA 5 PEKOE
   8 PEKOETEA
Swedish: 4 SAAB
Venezuelan: 3 OIL

**Expos**
Former ~ manager: 4 ALOU
**Expose:** 4 BARE 6 DEBUNK
   UNMASK 7 LAYBARE
   LAYOPEN
~, in verse: 3 OPE
**Exposed:** 4 OPEN SEEN
   5 NAKED 8 LAIDBARE
**Exposition:** 4 FAIR
**Exposure:** 4 RISK
**Express:** 3 AIR SAY 4 AVER
   VENT 5 OPINE STATE
   UTTER VOICE 6 PHRASE
alternative: 5 LOCAL
appreciation to: 5 THANK
approval: 4 CLAP
checkout word: 4 ITEM
   5 ITEMS
disapproval: 4 HISS
discontent: 6 REPINE
disdain: 3 TUT
gratitude to: 5 THANK
grief: 5 MOURN
letters: 4 ASAP
Not: 5 LOCAL TACIT
regret: 4 MOAN SIGH
shock: 4 GASP
**Expressed:** 3 PUT 4 SAID
delight: 5 AAHED OOHED
disapproval: 5 TSKED
joy: 4 WEPT
Vocally: 4 ORAL
~, as a farewell: 4 BADE
**Expression:** 4 LOOK TERM
   5 IDIOM VOICE
All-inclusive: 4 ATOZ
following an accident: 4 UHOH
of contempt: 5 SNEER
of discovery: 3 AHA
of pride: 4 ROAR
of sorrow: 4 ALAS 6 LAMENT
of surprise: 3 OHO
Unhappy: 5 SCOWL
Without: 5 STONY 7 STONILY
**Expressionist**
~ Nolde: 4 EMIL
~ Schiele: 4 EGON
**Expressionless:** 5 BLANK
   STONY 6 GLASSY
**Expressions**
of surprise: 3 OHS
Pained: 3 OWS
**Expressway**
access: 4 RAMP
___ **Expressway:** 5 EDENS

**Expunge:** 4 DELE 5 ERASE
   6 EFFACE
**Exquisite:** 6 DAINTY
trinket: 5 BIJOU
**Extend:** 3 ADD JUT RUN
   5 RANGE RENEW SPLAY
   6 OUTLIE 7 ADDONTO
across: 4 SPAN
a subscription: 5 RENEW
credit: 4 LEND
**Extended:** 4 LONG
family: 4 CLAN 5 TRIBE
period: 3 EON ERA 4 AEON
**Extender**
  **Info:** Suffix cue
  List: 4 ETAL
  Pay: 3 OLA
  Sail: 5 SPRIT
**Extension:** 3 ARM 4 LIMB
   5 ADDON
  **Info:** Suffix cue
  Building: 3 ELL 4 WING
   5 ANNEX
  Computer filename: 3 EXE
  East: 3 ERN
  Florida: 4 KEYS
  Home: 5 STEAD
  Keel: 4 SKEG
  Kitchen: 4 ETTE
  Manila folder: 3 TAB
  Program file: 3 EXE
  Right-angled: 3 ELL
  Shoulder: 6 SLEEVE
  Stage: 5 APRON
  Switch: 4 EROO
  Table: 4 LEAF
**Extensive:** 4 VAST WIDE
   5 MAJOR
**Extensively:** 4 ALOT
   8 ATLENGTH
**Extent:** 4 AREA SIZE SPAN
   5 GAMUT REACH SCOPE
   6 DEGREE
Full: 4 SPAN
Fullest: 4 HILT
To a certain: 6 INPART
To a greater: 6 MORESO
To any: 5 ATALL
To a smaller: 4 LESS
To some: 3 ANY 4 ATAD
To such an: 7 INSOFAR
To the ~ that: 7 ASFARAS
Two-dimensional: 4 AREA
Utmost: 9 NTHDEGREE
**Extents**
Vast: 5 DEEPS
**Exterior:** 5 OUTER
finish: 6 STUCCO
Tough: 4 HIDE
**Exterminator**
target: 4 PEST
**External:** 5 OUTER
Not: 5 INNER
**Extinct**
Become: 3 DIE 6 DIEOUT
bird: 3 MOA 4 DODO

**Extinction**
Facing: 4 RARE
**Extinguish:** 4 DAMP KILL
   5 DOUSE SNUFF
   6 PUTOUT
**Extol:** 4 LAUD TOUT 6 PRAISE
**Extort:** 5 BLEED WREST
   WRING
**Extorted:** 4 BLED
**Extra:** 4 MORE 5 ADDED
   ADDON SPARE
   7 ADDEDON SURPLUS
   TOSPARE
(abbr.): 4 ADDL
Bus. letter: 3 ENC
charge: 5 ADDON
dry: 4 ARID
Env.: 3 ENC
Exec: 4 PERK
inning: 5 TENTH
innings cause: 3 TIE
It's a lot of ~ work:
   11 ELBOWGREASE
Ltr.: 3 ENC
Movie ~, for short: 4 SUPE
number: 6 ENCORE
periods: 3 OTS
perk: 5 FRILL
Something: 3 TIP 4 PLUS
   5 BONUS
stipulations: 4 ANDS
tire: 5 SPARE
wager: 7 SIDEBET
___ **extra cost:** 4 ATNO
**Extract:** 5 WREST 6 ELICIT
Beet: 5 SUGAR 7 SUCROSE
Rose: 5 ATTAR
Seaweed: 4 AGAR 6 POTASH
Shale: 3 OIL
Soybean: 4 TOFU
**Extraction:** 7 LINEAGE
Androcles: 5 THORN
Mine: 3 ORE
**Extracts**
Make: 6 DECOCT
**Extra-large:** 4 SIZE
**Extra-long:** 4 MAXI
**Extraordinary:** 4 EPIC
Be: 11 TAKETHECAKE
Most: 6 RAREST
server: 4 ACER
talent: 6 PHENOM
**Extras**
These have many: 5 EPICS
**Extraterrestrial:** 5 ALIEN
TV: 3 ALF
**Extravagant:** 6 LAVISH
party: 4 GALA
**Extravagantly**
theatrical: 4 CAMP
**Extra-wide:** 3 EEE 4 EEEE
**Extreme:** 3 END FAR NTH
   5 ACUTE OUTER ULTRA
   UNDUE 6 ARRANT
   SEVERE 7 INTENSE
   RADICAL

anguish: 7 TORTURE
cruelty: 6 SADISM
degree: 3 NTH
dislike: 6 HATRED
edge: 5 BRINK
fear: 5 DREAD 6 TERROR
Global: 4 POLE
Orbital: 6 APOGEE
suffix: 3 EST
~, as a fan: 5 RABID
**Extremely:** 3 TOO 4 VERY
    5 AWFUL NOEND QUITE
    SUPER 6 DAMNED
    EVERSO SORELY
**Extremes**
Go to: 6 OVERDO
**Extremist:** 5 ULTRA 6 ZEALOT
    7 RADICAL
group: 4 CULT
**Extremity:** 3 END TOE
**Extrinsic:** 5 ALIEN
**Exuberance:** 3 PEP VIM 4 ELAN
    GLEE
**Exuberant:** 6 ELATED HEARTY
    YEASTY 7 RIOTOUS
    ZESTFUL
cry: 5 WAHOO
**Exudate**
Tree: 3 SAP
**Exudation**
Pine: 5 RESIN
**Exude:** 4 EMIT OOZE SEEP
    5 REEKOF 7 SECRETE
**Exult:** 4 CROW 7 REJOICE
**Exultant**
joy: 4 GLEE
**Exultation:** 4 GLEE
**Exxon**
It merged with: 5 MOBIL
rival: 4 ARCO HESS 5 AMOCO
    SHELL
tiger: 4 TONY
~, formerly: 4 ESSO
**Exxon Valdez:** 5 OILER
mishap: 5 SPILL 8 OILSPILL
**Eye:** 3 TEC 4 HOLE LENS
    OGLE 5 ORGAN
    6 PEEPER 7 STAREAT
amorously: 4 OGLE
annoyance: 4 STYE
bank donation: 6 CORNEA
Black: 5 MOUSE 6 SHINER
    STIGMA
Blink of an: 3 SEC
Camera: 4 LENS
closer: 3 LID
color: 5 HAZEL
Colored ~ part: 4 IRIS

covering: 3 LID 6 SCLERA
drop: 4 TEAR
Electric: 6 SENSOR
Flower of one's: 4 IRIS
Give the: 4 OGLE 6 LEERAT
irritation: 4 STYE
It brings a tear to the: 4 DUCT
It keeps an ~ on TV: 3 CBS
It may have a black: 3 PEA
Keep an ~ on: 4 TEND
lasciviously: 6 LEERAT
layer: 4 UVEA 6 RETINA
liner: 3 LID
Of the: 5 OPTIC
opener: 5 ALARM
opening: 4 SLIT
part: 4 IRIS UVEA
parts (var.): 6 IRIDES
Perform ~ surgery: 4 LASE
piece: 4 LENS
Poetic: 3 ORB
prefix: 5 OCULO
Private: 3 TEC 5 SNOOP
    6 SHAMUS
problem: 4 STYE 6 IRITIS
protector: 4 LASH
rakishly: 4 OGLE
shade: 5 HAZEL
shape: 6 ALMOND
signal: 4 WINK
site: 5 STORM 6 POTATO
slyly: 4 OGLE
Snake: 7 ONESPOT
sore: 4 STYE
surgery procedure: 5 LASIK
the bull's-eye: 3 AIM
up and down: 4 OGLE
Use the mind's: 7 IMAGINE
White of the: 6 SCLERA
woe: 4 STYE 6 IRITIS
~, in Spanish: 3 OJO
**Eyeball:** 3 ORB 4 LEER OGLE
    6 GAPEAT SIZEUP
benders: 5 OPART
part: 6 RETINA
**Eyebrow**
Pluck ~ hairs: 6 TWEEZE
shape: 4 ARCH
**Eyeful**
Get an: 4 GAPE GAWK LEER
    OGLE
**Eyeglass**
frames: 4 RIMS
part: 4 LENS
parts: 7 TEMPLES
**Eyeglasses:** 5 SPECS
**Eyelash**
cosmetic: 7 MASCARA

**Eyelashes:** 5 CILIA
Bat one's: 5 FLIRT
**Eyelet**
maker: 8 STILETTO
**Eyelid**
attachment: 4 LASH
problem: 4 STYE
**Eye of ___ :** 4 NEWT
**Eye-opener:** 5 LATTE
**Eyepiece:** 6 OCULAR
**Eye-related:** 5 OPTIC
**Eyes:** 5 OCULI
Blue ~, for one: 5 TRAIT
Cry one's ~ out: 4 BAWL
Easy on the: 6 PRETTY
Frosty's: 4 COAL
Hard on the: 4 UGLY
It brings tears to one's:
    4 DUCT
Kind of: 6 GOOGOO
Lay ~ on: 3 SEE 4 ESPY SPOT
Like some: 5 BEADY
    7 DEEPSET
Make ~ at: 4 OGLE
Open your: 5 AWAKE
Snake: 3 TWO 4 ACES ONES
Some have black: 4 PEAS
The ~ have them: 4 LIDS
They may make your ~ roll:
    4 PUNS
Turn away, as one's: 5 AVERT
What some ~ do: 4 DART
**"___ Eyes" (Eagles hit):** 4 LYIN
**Eyesore:** 3 STY 4 DUMP
Garden: 4 WEED
Urban: 4 SLUM
**"Eyes Wide ___" (Cruise film):**
    4 SHUT
**Eye to eye**
Not seeing: 6 ATODDS
    10 ATVARIANCE
See: 4 JIBE 5 AGREE
    6 CONCUR
**Eyetooth:** 6 CANINE
**Eyewear:** 5 SPECS 6 SHADES
**Eyewitness**
phrase: 4 ISAW
**Eyre, Jane:** 7 HEROINE
pupil: 5 ADELE
**Ezekiel**
Book after: 6 DANIEL
Prince in: 3 GOG
**Ezio:** 4 BASS 5 BASSO
and others: 5 BASSI
Basso: 5 PINZA
**Ezra**
Bk. after: 3 NEH
Book after: 8 NEHEMIAH

# Ff

**F**
Avoid an: 4 PASS
equivalent: 6 ESHARP
Letters before: 3 CDE TGI
major or minor: 3 KEY
M or: 3 SEX
on a test: 5 FALSE
sharp equivalent: 5 GFLAT
T or: 3 ANS

**F-14**
fighter: 6 TOMCAT
home: 3 AFB

**Fa**
follower: 3 SOL
followers: 4 LALA
lead-in: 4 REMI

**Fab:** 5 BOFFO SUPER
intro: 3 PRE
rival: 3 ERA

**Fabergé**
creation: 3 EGG

**Fab Four:** 7 BEATLES
film: 4 HELP
member: 4 PAUL 5 RINGO
STARR 6 GEORGE
LENNON

**Fabi**
Auto racer: 3 TEO

**Fabian**
~, once: 4 IDOL

**Fable**
creator: 4 LIAR 5 AESOP

**Fabled**
also-ran: 4 HARE
bird: 3 ROC
cow owner: 6 OLEARY
ending: 5 MORAL
Like the ~ piper: 4 PIED
monster: 4 OGRE
racer: 4 HARE 8 TORTOISE
warrior: 6 AMAZON
"___ Fables": 6 AESOPS

**"Fables in Slang"**
author: 3 ADE

**Fabray**
Emmy winner: 7 NANETTE

**Fabric:** 4 WEFT 5 CLOTH
Angora: 6 MOHAIR
Brocaded: 4 LAME
Casual: 5 DENIM
Colorful: 6 TIEDYE
Cotton: 6 SATEEN
Crinkled: 5 CREPE
Crisp: 7 TAFFETA
Curtain: 4 LACE 5 NINON
SCRIM
Decorative strip of: 6 RIBAND
Delicate: 4 LACE

Durable: 5 SERGE
Fancy: 6 SATEEN
Feltlike: 5 BAIZE
Filmy: 5 GAUZE
Fine: 5 SATIN
Flaxen: 5 LINEN
fold: 5 PLEAT
fuzz: 4 LINT
Glazed: 6 CHINTZ
Glossy: 5 SATIN 6 SATEEN
Gown: 5 TULLE
Hat: 4 FELT
Jeans: 5 DENIM
Lightweight: 5 VOILE
Linen: 5 TOILE
Lustrous: 5 SATIN 6 SATEEN
7 TAFFETA
meas.: 3 YDS
Metallic: 4 LAME
Open: 4 MESH
Pants: 5 CHINO
Patterned: 5 TOILE 6 DAMASK
MADRAS
Puckered: 6 PLISSE
Reversible: 6 DAMASK
rib: 4 WANE
Ribbed: 5 TWILL 6 FAILLE
Robe: 5 TERRY
Roll of: 4 BOLT
Sheer: 5 NINON
Sheet: 7 PERCALE
Shiny: 4 LAME
Soft: 5 TERRY
suffix: 3 EEN 4 ATOR
Suit: 4 WOOL 5 SERGE
TWEED
Synthetic: 5 ORLON
Tie: 3 REP
Twilled: 5 SERGE
Upholstery: 5 TOILE
6 VELOUR
Veil: 5 TULLE
with metallic threads: 4 LAME
Wrinkle-resistant: 5 ORLON

**Fabricate:** 4 FAKE MAKE SPIN
6 MAKEUP

**Fabrication:** 3 LIE 4 TALE
YARN 5 STORY

**Fabricator:** 4 LIAR

**Fabrics**
for sale: 8 DRYGOODS

**Fabulist**
Greek: 5 AESOP

**Fabulous:** 5 SUPER
bird: 3 ROC
fellow: 5 AESOP

**"Fabulous Baker Boys, The"**
star: 7 BRIDGES

**Façade:** 4 POSE 5 FRONT
6 VENEER
part: 7 CEDILLA

**Face:** 4 MEET PUSS 6 VISAGE
Certain watch: 3 LCD
Clock: 4 DIAL
cover: 4 VEIL
defacer: 4 ACNE
down: 5 BEARD PRONE
Fly in the ~ of: 4 DEFY
Happy: 4 BEAM GRIN
5 SMILE
Have a long: 4 MOPE
In the ~ of: 7 DESPITE
It makes your ~ red: 5 ROUGE
Make a: 4 GRIN 5 SCOWL
SNEER
Make a funny: 3 MUG
mask wearer: 6 GOALIE
New: 8 STRANGER
on a five: 3 ABE
Pouty: 4 MOUE
prefix: 5 INTER
shape: 4 OVAL
Smack in the: 4 KISS
Stuff one's: 6 PIGOUT
that launched a thousand ships:
5 HELEN
the day: 5 ARISE
the pitcher: 3 BAT
Watch: 4 DIAL
Wear a long: 4 MOPE POUT
Without ~ value: 5 NOPAR
~, in French: 3 VIS

**Face-off:** 4 DUEL
preceder, often: 7 OCANADA

**"Face/Off"**
director John: 3 WOO

**Facet:** 6 ASPECT

**"Face the Nation"**
network: 3 CBS

**Facetious:** 5 DROLL 7 JOCULAR
five: 5 AEIOU

**Face-to-face**
exam: 4 ORAL

**Face-up:** 6 SUPINE

**Face-valued:** 5 ATPAR

**Facial**
feature: 4 JOWL MOLE NOSE
firmer-upper: 5 TONER
hair: 4 LASH 7 EYELASH
movement: 3 TIC
spot: 3 SPA
tissue additive: 4 ALOE

**Facil.**
Research: 4 INST

**Facile**
Unconvincingly: 3 PAT

**Facilitate:** 4 EASE 6 ENABLE
  a felony: 4 ABET
**Facilitator**
  Breakfast-in-bed: 4 TRAY
  Rush-hour traffic: 7 HOVLANE
**Facilities:** 4 JOHN 7 LATRINE
  Sports: 6 STADIA
**Facility:** 4 EASE
  Health: 3 SPA 6 CLINIC
  London: 3 LOO
  Medical: 6 CLINIC
  Mil. ed.: 3 OCS
  Research ~ (abbr.): 4 INST
  Sports: 5 ARENA
  Underground: 4 SILO
**Facing:** 6 TOWARD
  charges: 7 ONTRIAL
  extinction: 4 RARE
  Not ~ the truth: 8 INDENIAL
  the pitcher: 5 ATBAT
**Facsimile:** 4 COPY
**Fact:** 5 GIVEN
  Allege as: 4 AVER
  Assume as: 5 POSIT
  Declare as: 5 STATE
  Despite the ~ that, for short:
    3 THO
  Establish as: 5 PROVE
  filled volume: 7 ALMANAC
  fudger: 4 LIAR
  It's a: 5 DATUM
  Perceive as: 4 KNOW
  State as: 5 SAYSO
  suffix: 3 OID
**Faction:** 4 BLOC CAMP SECT
    SIDE
  Political: 4 BLOC
  Religious: 4 SECT
  ___ facto: 4 IPSO
**Factoid:** 4 STAT 5 DATUM
**Factor:** 5 PIECE
  in: 8 ALLOWFOR
  Inheritance: 4 GENE
  Weigh station: 4 TARE
**Factory:** 4 SHOP 5 PLANT
  Flour: 4 MILL
  Honey: 4 HIVE
  item: 4 TOOL
  Modern ~ worker: 5 ROBOT
  Right from the: 3 NEW
  second (abbr.): 3 IRR
  Update a: 6 RETOOL
**Factotum:** 5 DOALL
  Frankenstein: 4 IGOR
**Facts:** 4 DATA INFO 6 SKINNY
  Had the: 4 KNEW
  The ~ of life: 3 BIO
**"Facts of Life, The"**
  actress Charlotte: 3 RAE
  actress Mindy: 4 COHN
  Mrs. Garrett of: 4 EDNA
**Factual:** 4 TRUE
**Faculties:** 6 SENSES
  They keep control of their:
    5 DEANS
**Faculty:** 5 KNACK SKILL STAFF

  head: 4 DEAN
**Fad:** 4 RAGE 5 CRAZE MANIA
    TREND
  1950s ~: 8 HULAHOOP
  1961 ~: 4 YOYO
  1970s ~: 7 PETROCK
  1970s ~ participant:
    8 STREAKER
  1990s ~: 7 CHIAPET
  doll: 5 TROLL
  Therapy: 3 EST
**Faddish**
  pet: 4 CHIA
**Fade**
  away: 3 DIE EBB 6 DIEOUT
    8 EVANESCE
  out: 3 DIE DIM
**Faded**
  star: 7 HASBEEN
**"Faerie Queene, The"**
  division: 5 CANTO
  victim: 5 IRENA
**Fahd:** 4 ARAB 5 SAUDI
  subject: 4 ARAB 5 SAUDI
**Fail:** 4 BOMB TANK 5 FLUNK
    7 LOSEOUT
  Does not: 6 PASSES
  suffix: 3 URE
  to attend: 4 MISS SKIP
  to impress: 8 CUTNOICE
  to include: 4 OMIT
  to make: 4 MISS
  to medal: 4 LOSE
  to mention: 4 OMIT
  to pronounce: 5 ELIDE
  to see: 4 MISS
**___ Fail (Irish coronation stone):**
    3 LIA
**Failed**
  amendment: 3 ERA
  attempt: 4 NOGO
  to: 5 DIDNT
  to act: 3 SAT
**Fails**
  If all else: 7 ATWORST
  to: 6 DOESNT
**Failure:** 3 DUD 4 FLOP MISS
    5 LAPSE
  Ensure the ~ of: 4 DOOM
  Memory: 5 LAPSE
  Power: 6 OUTAGE
  Show-biz: 4 BOMB
  Total: 6 FIASCO
**Faint:** 3 WAN 4 PALE 5 SWOON
    WISPY 7 PASSOUT
  from excitement: 5 PLOTZ
  Grow: 3 DIM 4 WANE
  ~, with "over": 4 KEEL
**"Faint heart ___ won ...":**
    4 NEER
**Fainthearted:** 5 TIMID
**Fair:** 4 EVEN EXPO JUST
    SOSO 5 BLOND CLEAR
    6 HONEST 7 AVERAGE
    CRICKET 8 UNBIASED
  attraction: 4 RIDE

  Big: 4 EXPO
  features: 5 TENTS
  grade: 3 CEE
  hiring abbr.: 3 EOE
  It may be: 4 DEAL
  Kind of ~ (abbr.): 3 SCI
  Like a ~ playing field: 5 LEVEL
  mark: 3 CEE
  Not: 5 RAINY
  share: 4 HALF
  sight: 4 TENT
  to middling: 4 SOSO
**"___ Fair" (Cornell song):**
    6 ITISNT
**Fair, A.A.**
  monogram: 3 ESG
  real first name: 4 ERLE
**Fairbanks**
  Highway to: 5 ALCAN
**Fair Deal**
  pres.: 3 HST
  president: 6 TRUMAN
**Fairground**
  attraction: 4 RIDE
**Fair-haired:** 5 BLOND
**Fair-hiring**
  letters: 3 EEO 4 EEOC
**Fairies**
  King of the: 6 OBERON
  Queen of the: 3 MAB
**"___ fair in love ...":** 4 ALLS
**Fairly**
  modern: 6 NEWISH
**Fair-minded:** 4 JUST
**Fairness:** 6 EQUITY
  in hiring (abbr.): 3 EEO
**Fair-sized**
  musical group: 5 NONET
**Fairway**
  border: 5 ROUGH
  choice: 4 IRON
  chunk: 5 DIVOT
  Fix the: 5 RESOD
  position: 3 LIE
  vehicle: 4 CART
  warning: 4 FORE
**Fairy**
  Kind of: 5 TOOTH
  king: 6 OBERON
  Persian: 4 PERI
  queen: 3 MAB
  story: 4 TALE
**Fairy tale**
  baddie: 4 OGRE
  beginning: 4 ONCE
  closer: 5 AFTER
  figure: 3 HAG 5 GNOME
  heroine: 6 GRETEL
  last word: 5 AFTER
  meanie: 4 OGRE
    10 STEPSISTER
  opener: 4 ONCE
  penultimate word: 4 EVER
  second word: 4 UPON
  start: 4 ONCE
**Faisal II:** 5 IRAQI

**Faith:** 5 CREED TRUST
  Act of: 4 LEAP
  Article of: 5 TENET
  Fight to keep the: 7 HOLYWAR
  Forsaker of the: 8 APOSTATE
  Have: 4 RELY 5 TRUST
  healer command: 4 RISE
  of over one billion: 5 ISLAM
  prefix: 5 INTER
  that arose in Persia: 5 BAHAI
**Faith-based**
  system (abbr.): 3 REL
**Faithful:** 4 TRUE 5 LOYAL
  Is: 7 ADHERES
**Fajita**
  cuisine: 6 TEXMEX
  flavorer: 5 SALSA
**Fake:** 4 COPY MOCK SHAM
     5 BOGUS FEIGN PHONY
     6 ERSATZ RINGER
     7 NOTREAL 8 IMPOSTER
  coin: 4 SLUG
  drake: 5 DECOY
  fanfare: 4 TADA
  fat: 5 OLEAN
  handle: 5 ALIAS
  it: 3 ACT 7 PRETEND
  jewelry: 5 PASTE
  Not: 4 REAL
  on the ice: 4 DEKE
  Teens may have ~ ones: 3 IDS
**Fala:** 7 SCOTTIE
**Falafel**
  holder: 4 PITA
  sauce: 6 TAHINI
**Falana**
  Entertainer: 4 LOLA
**Falco**
  Emmy winner: 4 EDIE
**Falcon**
  Fictional ~ home: 5 MALTA
  Small: 7 KESTREL
**"___ Falcon, The":** 7 MALTESE
**"Falcon Crest"**
  actress Alicia: 3 ANA
**Falcon-headed**
  god: 5 HORUS
**Falcons:** 4 TEAM
  home (abbr.): 3 ATL
**Faline**
  Mother of: 3 ENA
**Falkland Islands**
  city: 7 STANLEY
**Falklands War**
  participant: 4 BRIT
**Fall:** 3 ERR 4 DROP 6 AUTUMN
     7 DESCEND
  apart: 3 ROT 7 GOTOPOT
  away: 3 EBB
  back: 3 EBB LAG 4 REEL
     5 RESET 6 REVERT
     7 RELAPSE
  behind: 3 LAG OWE 5 TRAIL
     8 LOSETIME
  birthstone: 4 OPAL 5 TOPAZ
  bloomer: 5 ASTER

  color: 4 RUST 5 OCHRE
     6 ORANGE
  Cry before a: 6 TIMBER
  Do a ~ chore: 4 RAKE
  drink: 5 CIDER
  faller: 4 LEAF
  flower: 5 ASTER
  for: 4 BITE
  from grace: 3 ERR SIN
  guy: 3 SAP 4 ADAM GOAT
     5 CHUMP PATSY RAKER
     6 STOOGE 9 SCAPEGOAT
  heavily: 4 PLOP THUD
  Kind of: 4 PRAT
  lead-in: 4 PRAT
  Let: 4 DROP
  Like ~ weather: 5 BRISK
  locale: 4 EDEN
  mo.: 3 NOV OCT SEP 4 SEPT
  off: 3 DIP EBB 4 WANE
     5 ABATE ERODE
  Opposite of: 4 RISE
  (over): 4 KEEL
  over in a faint: 5 PLOTZ
  place: 4 EDEN
  planting: 4 BULB
  preceder: 4 PRAT TRIP
     5 PRIDE 6 TIMBER
  setting: 4 EDEN
  shade: 4 RUST
  short: 4 FAIL
  sign: 5 LIBRA 7 SCORPIO
  site: 4 EDEN
  sound: 4 PLOP THUD
  Start to: 3 TIP
  Threaten to: 6 TEETER
  times (abbr.): 4 OCTS
  tool: 4 RAKE
  Winter: 4 SNOW 5 SLEET
  worker: 5 RAKER
**Fallaci**
  Auhor: 6 ORIANA
**Fallback**
  option: 5 PLANB
**Fallen**
  angel: 5 SATAN
  space station: 3 MIR
**"___ fallen ...":** 3 IVE
**Fallibility**
  Show: 5 ERASE
**Falling**
  flakes: 4 SNOW
  Like ~ off a log: 4 EASY
  out: 4 RIFT
  pellets: 4 HAIL
  star: 6 METEOR
**Falling-out:** 4 SPAT TIFF
**"Fall of the House of Usher, The"**
  author: 3 POE
**Fallopian tube**
  travelers: 3 OVA
**Fallout**
  Volcanic: 3 ASH
**Fall River**
  tool: 3 AXE

**Falls**
  for lovers: 7 NIAGARA
  on the border: 7 NIAGARA
  on, as responsibility:
     8 LIESWITH
**___ Falls (Venezuela):** 5 ANGEL
**"Fall, The"**
  author: 5 CAMUS
**False:** 5 NOTSO 6 PSEUDO
     UNTRUE
  alarm: 5 SCARE
  coin: 5 SLUG
  Declare: 4 DENY
  Expose as: 6 DEBUNK
  friend: 4 IAGO
  front: 3 ACT 4 POSE 5 GUISE
     PSEUD 6 FACADE
  Gives a ~ alarm:
     9 CRIESWOLF
  god: 4 BAAL IDOL
  It may be: 5 ALARM
  locks: 4 WIGS
  move: 5 FEINT
  Not: 4 TRUE
  prefix: 6 PSEUDO
  Prove: 5 BELIE
  Reject as: 4 DENY
  rumor: 6 CANARD
  Some are: 5 HOPES
  start: 6 PSEUDO
  Was: 4 LIED
  witness: 4 LIAR
**"False!":** 5 NOTSO
**Falsehood:** 3 FIB LIE
**Falsetto**
  1960s ~ singer: 7 TINYTIM
**Falsified:** 6 COOKED
**Falsifier**
  Check: 5 KITER
**Falstaff**
  Like: 3 FAT
**"Falstaff":** 5 OPERA
  composer: 5 VERDI
  prince: 3 HAL
**Fam.**
  doctors: 3 GPS
  member: 3 BRO REL SIS
  tree member: 4 DESC
**Fame:** 5 ECLAT 6 RENOWN
     REPUTE
**"Fame"**
  actress Irene: 4 CARA
  actress Peeples: 3 NIA
  singer: 9 IRENECARA
  singer Irene: 4 CARA
**Familia**
  member: 3 TIA TIO
  New ~ member: 4 BEBE
**Familial**
  address: 3 SIS
**Familiar**
  Become ~ with: 8 EASEINTO
     9 GETTOKNOW
  Comfortably: 5 HOMEY
  saying: 6 OLDSAW
  Sound: 9 RINGABELL

Was ~ with: 4 KNEW
with: 4 INTO UPON
  6 USEDTO
~, as friends: 3 OLD
**Familiarize:** 6 ORIENT
  8 ACQUAINT
**Famille**
  member: 4 MERE PERE
    5 FRERE
**Family:** 3 ILK KIN 4 CLAN
  5 GROUP
  1950s TV ~: 7 NELSONS
  Acting: 6 FONDAS
  auto: 5 SEDAN
  Big: 5 TRIBE
  Blended ~ member:
    7 STEPSON
  card game: 3 UNO
  diagram: 4 TREE
  docs: 3 GPS
  dog: 3 LAB
  emblem: 5 TOTEM
  Extended: 4 CLAN 5 TRIBE
  follower: 4 TREE
  girl: 3 SIS 5 NIECE
  group: 4 CLAN
  guy: 3 BRO DAD
  head: 3 DON 4 CAPO
  life, figuratively: 6 HEARTH
  Like ~ films: 6 RATEDG
  man: 3 DAD
  map: 4 TREE
  mem.: 3 REL
  member: 3 DAD SIR SIS SON
    4 AUNT 5 NIECE UNCLE
    6 SISTER
  men: 3 PAS
  nickname: 3 SIS UNC 4 NANA
    6 GRAMPA
  problem: 4 FEUD
  subdivision: 5 GENUS
  subdivisions: 6 GENERA
  They're all in the: 4 SIBS
  They're new to the:
    9 SONSINLAW
  tree word: 3 NEE
  Word after: 4 TREE
    8 ORIENTED
**"Family Circus, The"**
  cartoonist Bil: 5 KEANE
  cartoonist Keane: 3 BIL
**Family-friendly**
  ~, in films: 6 RATEDG
**"Family Matters"**
  nerd: 5 URKEL
**"Family Plot"**
  actor Bruce: 4 DERN
**Family reunion**
  attendee: 5 NIECE
**Family room:** 3 DEN
  piece: 6 SETTEE
**"Family Ties"**
  mother: 5 ELYSE
  son: 4 ALEX
**Famished**
  Far from: 5 SATED

**Famous:** 3 BIG 5 KNOWN
  NOTED 7 EMINENT
  NOTABLE
  cow owner: 6 OLEARY
  fed: 4 NESS
  fiddle: 5 STRAD
  fiddler: 4 NERO
  flop: 5 EDSEL
  fountain piazza: 5 TREVI
  jour.: 3 AMA
  last word: 4 AMEN
  last words: 3 IDO 4 ETTU
    5 ELEGY 6 THEEND
  lioness: 4 ELSA
  loch: 4 NESS
  palindrome middle: 5 IEREI
  redhead: 4 ERIC
  Site of some ~ hangings:
    5 PRADO
  twin: 3 ENG
  ~ B-29: 5 ENOLA
**"Famous"**
  cookie maker: 4 AMOS
**Famous ___:** 4 AMOS
**"Famous Potatoes"**
  Its license plates say:
    5 IDAHO
**Fan:** 3 BUG 4 COOL 5 LOVER
  6 ADORER ROOTER
  7 DEVOTEE
  8 ADULATOR
  A ~ of: 4 INTO
  club focus: 4 IDOL
  Extreme, as a: 5 RABID
  fave: 4 IDOL
  Jazz: 3 CAT 6 UTAHAN
  mag: 4 ZINE
  noise: 3 RAH
  setting: 3 LOW 5 ARENA
  sound: 3 RAH 4 CLAP WHIR
  Unhappy: 5 BOOER
  Unhappy ~ noise: 4 HISS
**Fanatic:** 3 NUT 5 ULTRA
  6 MANIAC ZEALOT
**Fanatical:** 5 RABID 7 EXTREME
  8 OBSESSED
  devotion: 8 ZEALOTRY
**Fanciful:** 4 TALL
  story: 8 TALLTALE
**Fancily**
  Dress ~, with "out": 3 TOG
  Walk: 6 SASHAY
**Fancy:** 4 IDEA WHIM 5 ADORE
  COVET DREAM HAUTE
  6 DESIRE ORNATE
  PREFER 7 IMAGINE
  case: 4 ETUI
  cover: 4 SHAM
  desk: 7 ROLLTOP
  dinnerware: 5 CHINA
  fabric: 4 LAME
  Made: 5 DIDUP
  Not ~ at all: 6 LOATHE
  Passing: 3 FAD
  Really: 5 ADORE
  Sudden: 4 WHIM

  Tickle the: 5 AMUSE
**"Fancy"**
  singer McEntire: 4 REBA
**Fancy-schmancy:** 4 POSH
  5 RITZY 7 ELEGANT
**"Fancy that!":** 3 GEE 4 GOSH
  MYMY
**Fanfare:** 5 ECLAT 6 HOOPLA
  7 TANTARA
  Mock: 4 TADA
**Fangs:** 7 CANINES
**Fannie**
  Author: 5 FLAGG HURST
  Funny: 5 FLAGG
**Fannie ___:** 3 MAE
**Fanny:** 4 DUFF REAR TUSH
**"Fanny"**
  author Jong: 5 ERICA
**Fans**
  Like: 4 AVID 7 ADORING
  Like enthusiastic: 5 AROAR
  Where ~ may be found:
    6 STANDS
**Fantail:** 4 DEER
**Fan-tan:** 6 SEVENS
**Fantasia**
  alternative: 7 TOCCATA
**"Fantasia"**
  dancer: 5 HIPPO
  frame: 3 CEL
**Fantasize:** 5 DREAM
**Fantastic:** 5 GREAT SUPER
  6 UNREAL 7 SURREAL
**"Fantastic Mr. Fox"**
  author Roald: 4 DAHL
**"Fantasy Island"**
  prop: 3 LEI
**"___ fan tutte":** 4 COSI
**Fanzine:** 3 MAG
  focus: 4 IDOL 5 CELEB
  Streisand, in a: 4 BABS
**FAO Schwarz**
  offering: 3 TOY
**Far**
  As ~ as: 4 UPTO
  back: 7 AGESAGO
  By: 6 EASILY
  Few and ~ between: 4 RARE
    6 SPARSE
  Not: 4 NEAR
  So: 3 YET 5 ASYET 6 TODATE
    7 UPTONOW
  Take too: 6 OVERDO
  Thus: 3 YET 5 ASYET
    6 TODATE
**Far ___:** 4 EAST
**Faraway**
  place: 8 TIMBUKTU
**Fare:** 4 DIET FOOD 5 GETON
  Had: 3 ATE
  question: 7 WHERETO
  reduction: 4 DIET
  Trendy: 5 SUSHI
  Unappetizing: 4 GLOP MUSH
    SLOP
  War: 4 SPAM

**Far East**
cuisine: 4 THAI
From the: 5 ASIAN
nurse: 4 AMAH
**Farewell:** 5 ADIEU
Expressed a: 4 BADE
Forum: 3 AVE 4 VALE
French: 5 ADIEU
Informal: 5 LATER
Italian: 4 CIAO
party: 7 SENDOFF
Spanish: 5 ADIOS
**"Farewell!":** 4 TATA 5 ADIEU
ADIOS
**Farewells**
Like some: 4 FOND
**"Farewell to ___, A":** 4 ARMS
**"Farewell to Thee"**
translated: 7 ALOHAOE
**"___ far, far better thing ...":**
5 ITISA
**Farfetched:** 4 TALL
**Far-flung:** 4 VAST
**Far-flying**
seabird: 6 PETREL
**Fargo**
Partner of: 5 WELLS
state (abbr.): 4 NDAK
**"Fargo"**
director: 4 COEN
**Faris**
Actress: 4 ANNA
**Farlow**
Jazz guitarist: 3 TAL
**Farm**
animal: 3 ANT ASS EWE
4 GOAT
antithesis, in song: 5 PAREE
building: 4 BARN
bundle: 4 BALE
butter: 3 RAM
call: 3 BAA 5 SOOEY
cart: 4 WAIN
crawler: 3 ANT
cry: 4 OINK
division: 4 ACRE
dweller: 3 ANT
enclosure: 3 PEN STY
equipment name: 5 DEERE
fare: 4 SLOP
Fat: 3 SPA
father: 4 SIRE
feature: 4 SILO
female: 3 DAM EWE HEN
SOW 4 MARE
gathering: 3 HAY
hauler: 4 DRAY
Health: 3 SPA
It's left on the: 3 HAW
It's pulled on a: 5 UDDER
It's raised on a: 4 SILO
layer: 3 HEN
letters: 5 EIEIO
machine: 5 BALER 6 REAPER
SEEDER TILLER
7 COMBINE

measure: 4 ACRE
Milk: 5 DAIRY
prefix: 4 AGRI AGRO
soil: 4 LOAM
sound: 3 BAA CAW MOO
4 BRAY OINK 5 BLEAT
Store on a: 6 ENSILE
structure: 4 BARN SILO
team: 4 OXEN SPAN
team unifier: 4 YOKE
tool: 6 SCYTHE
tower: 4 SILO
unit: 4 ACRE
vehicle: 7 TRACTOR
worker: 3 ANT 9 PLOWHORSE
yield: 4 CROP
**Farmed**
Fit to be: 6 ARABLE
**Farmer:** 4 HOER 6 PLOWER
SEEDER TILLER
Feudal: 4 SERF
field: 3 LEA
field (abbr.): 3 AGR
in the spring: 5 SOWER
place: 4 DELL 7 THEDELL
purchase: 4 SEED
Transvaal: 4 BOER
victims of the ~'s wife: 4 MICE
**"Farmer in the Dell, The"**
syllables: 4 HIHO
**"Farmer's Daughter, The"**
actress Stevens: 5 INGER
**Farming**
abbr.: 3 AGR
Fit for: 6 ARABLE
Kind of: 7 ONECROP
prefix: 4 AGRI AGRO
Refrain from: 5 EIEIO
**Farmland:** 5 ACRES
unit: 4 ACRE
**Far-out:** 5 OUTRE WACKO
Org. with ~ goals: 4 NASA
**"Far out!":** 3 RAD 5 NEATO
6 UNREAL 7 AWESOME
**Farr**
Actor: 5 JAMIE
**Farragut**
word: 4 DAMN
**Far-reaching**
view: 5 VISTA
**Farrell**
costar: 4 ALDA
Soprano: 6 EILEEN
**Farrier**
tool: 4 RASP
**Farrow**
Actress: 3 MIA
**Farsi**
speaker: 5 IRANI 7 IRANIAN
Where ~ is spoken: 4 IRAN
**"Far Side, The"**
cartoonist Gary: 6 LARSON
**Farsighted**
one: 4 SEER
**Farther**
Extend ~ down: 6 DEEPEN

**Farthest:** 6 UTMOST
7 ENDMOST
from the hole: 4 AWAY
orbital point: 6 APOGEE
**Fascinated**
by: 4 INTO
**Fascination:** 6 ALLURE
**Fashion:** 3 TON WAY 4 FORM
MAKE MODE 5 CRAFT
SHAPE STYLE TREND
VOGUE 6 CREATE
1970s ~ fad: 8 HOTPANTS
Big name in: 4 DIOR IZOD
5 BLASS KLEIN PRADA
6 ARMANI
center: 5 MILAN
Current: 4 MODE RAGE
5 TREND
First name in: 3 LIZ 4 COCO
OLEG YVES
Fleeting: 3 FAD
High: 3 TON
illustrator: 4 ERTE
In: 3 HIP HOT 4 CHIC
industry: 8 RAGTRADE
initials: 3 YSL 4 DKNY
issue: 4 ELLE
It's long in: 4 MAXI
letters: 3 YSL
line: 3 HEM
magazine: 4 ELLE
model: 4 IMAN
monogram: 3 YSL
Nostalgic: 5 RETRO
Out of: 5 PASSE
**Fashionable:** 3 MOD 4 CHIC
LATE 6 MODISH
TRENDY 7 INSTYLE
cashmere company: 3 TSE
monogram: 3 YSL
necktie: 5 ASCOT
resort: 3 SPA
~ Christian: 4 DIOR
~ Geoffrey: 5 BEENE
~ Simpson: 5 ADELE
**Fashion designer**
monogram: 3 YSL
~ Geoffrey: 5 BEENE
~ Giorgio: 6 ARMANI
~ Ralph: 6 LAUREN
~ Vera: 4 WANG
**Fashioned:** 4 MADE
**"Fashion Emergency"**
host: 4 EMME
**Fast:** 5 APACE BRISK QUICK
RAPID
Break a: 3 EAT
Came to a ~ stop: 3 ATE
feline: 4 PUMA
finish: 4 MEAL
flier: 3 JET SST
food order: 6 BURGER
gait: 6 GALLOP
Hold: 6 ADHERE COHERE
horse: 4 ARAB
Make: 3 TIE

movement: 7 ALLEGRO
Not very: 7 ANDANTE
pace: 4 CLIP
Pull a ~ one: 4 YANK
Ran ~, to a Brit: 5 HARED
runner: 4 HARE
start: 5 STEAD
time: 4 LENT 7 RAMADAN
Went: 4 SPED TORE
"___ fast!": 5 NOTSO
**Fastball:** 4 HEAT 6 HEATER
Famous ~ thrower: 4 RYAN
   5 NOLAN
**Fasten:** 3 TIE 4 BIND DOUP
   SHUT 5 LATCH SCREW
   6 ATTACH
again: 5 RETIE
anew: 5 REPIN
at sea: 5 BELAY
with a pop: 6 SNAPON
with rope: 4 LASH
**Fastened:** 5 DIDUP 6 HASPED
**Fastener:** 4 BOND SNAP STUD
   5 CLASP LATCH
Bolt: 3 NUT 4 TNUT
Door: 4 HASP
for Rosie: 5 RIVET
Gate: 4 HASP 5 LATCH
Letter-shaped: 4 TNUT
   5 UBOLT
Metal: 4 BOLT HASP NAIL
   5 RIVET SCREW
Necklace: 5 CLASP
Office: 9 PAPERCLIP
Paper: 6 STAPLE
Small: 4 BRAD TACK
Threaded: 4 TNUT 5 SCREW
**Fastening**
device: 4 HASP TNUT
pin: 5 RIVET
**Faster**
No: 5 EATER
**Fastest**
runner: 7 CHEETAH
**Fast-food**
chain: 4 ROYS 5 ARBYS
   7 HARDEES
drink: 4 COLA SODA
inits.: 3 KFC
option: 4 TOGO
**Fast ___ get-out:** 5 ASALL
**Fastidious:** 4 NEAT TIDY
   5 FUSSY
**Fast-moving**
object: 4 BLUR
**Fast-shrinking**
sea: 4 ARAL
**Fast-talking:** 4 GLIB
**Fat:** 4 LARD 5 LIPID 6 TALLOW
Big ~ mouth: 3 YAP
Big ~ zero: 3 NIL
cat: 5 NABOB 9 MONEYBAGS
Chew the: 3 GAB JAW YAK
   4 CHAT 8 SCHMOOZE
Cooking: 4 LARD SUET
Cut the: 4 TRIM

Fake: 5 OLEAN 7 OLESTRA
farm: 3 SPA
foot spec: 3 EEE
in a can: 4 LARD
letters: 3 EMS
Liquid: 5 OLEIN
Low in: 4 LEAN
More than: 5 OBESE
Pat of: 4 OLEO
substitute: 5 OLEAN
   7 OLESTRA
unit: 4 GRAM
Wool: 7 LANOLIN
~, in French: 4 GRAS
**"Fatal Attraction"**
director Adrian: 4 LYNE
___ fatale: 5 FEMME
**Fatality**
Genesis: 4 ABEL
**Fata morgana:** 6 MIRAGE
**"Fat chance!":** 3 HAH 4 NOPE
   5 NEVER 6 NOSOAP
**Fate:** 3 LOT 4 DOOM 5 KARMA
   6 KISMET
Adverse: 4 DOOM
of Wednesday's child: 3 WOE
Tempt: 4 DARE
**Fateful**
date: 4 IDES
**Fates, The:** 4 TRIO
One of: 6 CLOTHO
   7 ATROPOS
**Fat-free:** 4 SLIM
**"Fatha"**
Jazzman: 5 HINES
~ Hines: 4 EARL
**Father:** 3 DAD 4 PAPA SIRE
   5 BEGET
Act the expectant: 4 PACE
Become a: 4 SIRE
Expectant: 5 PACER
First: 4 ADAM
in the army: 5 PADRE
in the Bible: 4 ABBA
Make a: 6 ORDAIN
Related on the ~ side:
   5 AGATE
talk (abbr.): 3 SER
wear: 3 ALB
word form: 5 PATRI
~, in French: 4 PERE
**Father ___:** 6 DAMIEN
**Father-and-son**
actors: 5 ALDAS
physicists: 5 BOHRS
**Fathered:** 5 BEGAT BEGOT
**Father-in-law**
of Jacob: 5 LABAN
of Meathead: 6 ARCHIE
**"Father Knows Best"**
family name: 8 ANDERSON
**"Father Murphy"**
actor Merlin: 5 OLSEN
extra: 6 ORPHAN
**"Father of the Bride"**
actor Martin: 5 SHORT STEVE

**Fathers**
and sons: 3 HES MEN
Unwed: 7 PRIESTS
**"Fathers and Sons"**
novelist Turgenev: 4 IVAN
**Father's Day**
gift: 3 TIE 4 BELT 5 RAZOR
   6 TIEPIN TIETAC WALLET
month: 4 JUNE
**Fathom:** 3 GET 5 GRASP
Hard to: 4 DEEP 6 ARCANE
**Fatigue:** 4 TIRE
Showing: 3 WAN
**Fatima**
faith: 5 ISLAM
Husband of: 3 ALI
**Fat lady**
What the ~ sings: 4 ARIA
Where the ~ sings: 5 OPERA
**Fatman, The**
Partner of: 4 JAKE
**Fat-removing**
surgery: 4 LIPO
**Fat Tuesday**
Fat, in: 4 GRAS
**Fatty:** 7 ADIPOSE
acid: 5 OLEIC
compound: 5 LIPID
It may be: 4 ACID
Not: 4 LEAN
oil: 6 CANOLA
tissue: 4 SUET
**Fatuous:** 5 INANE SILLY
   7 ASININE
___ fatuus (delusion): 5 IGNIS
**Faucet:** 3 TAP 6 SPIGOT
attachment: 7 AERATOR
brand: 4 MOEN
fault: 4 DRIP LEAK
problem: 4 DRIP LEAK
**Faulkner**
character Varner: 4 EULA
title start: 3 ASI
**Fault:** 3 SIN 4 FLAW 5 ERROR
At: 6 GUILTY
Find: 4 CARP CRAB 5 BLAME
   CAVIL
Find ~ with: 5 NAGAT
**Faults**
It has its: 6 TENNIS
**Faulty:** 5 AMISS
Most: 5 WORST
**Faun**
half: 4 GOAT
**Fauna**
collection: 3 ZOO
Flora and: 4 LIFE 5 BIOTA
Partner of: 5 FLORA
prefix: 3 AVI
**Fauntleroy**
title: 4 LORD
**"Faust":** 5 OPERA
author: 6 GOETHE
**Fauvism**
founder: 7 MATISSE
**Faux:** 4 FAKE MOCK SHAM

(abbr.): 4 IMIT
**Faux ___ (social misstep):** 3 PAS
**Faux pas:** 4 NONO SLIP
    5 ERROR GAFFE
    6 BOOBOO 7 MISSTEP
Commit a: 3 ERR
**Fava:** 4 BEAN
**Fave**
Teacher: 3 PET
Teen: 4 IDOL
**Favor:** 4 BOON 5 BLESS
    6 ESTEEM PREFER
Do a ~ for: 6 OBLIGE
In ~ of: 3 FOR PRO
Not in ~ of: 4 ANTI
one side: 4 LIMP
Out of: 5 INBAD
Return the: 5 REPAY
Seek ~ with: 3 WOO
Votes in: 4 YEAS 5 YESES
___ favor: 3 POR
**Favorable:** 6 BENIGN
factor: 4 PLUS
Less: 5 WORSE
opinion: 6 ESTEEM
Under the most ~ conditions:
    6 ATBEST
**Favored**
few: 5 ELITE
Highly: 6 ODDSON
**Favoring:** 3 PRO
**Favorite:** 3 PET 4 IDOL SEED
    5 TOAST 7 TOPSEED
Crowd: 7 PLEASER
Enjoy a ~ book: 6 REREAD
hangout: 5 HAUNT
Hardly a: 8 LONGSHOT
one: 3 SON
son, maybe: 6 ELDEST
Tournament: 4 SEED
**Favoritism:** 4 BIAS
**Favre**
Quarterback: 5 BRETT
target: 3 END
___ Fawkes Day: 3 GUY
**"Fawlty Towers"**
airer: 3 BBC
star John: 6 CLEESE
**Fawn:** 5 TOADY
Mature: 4 DEER
mom: 3 DOE
(on): 4 DOTE
over: 7 ADULATE
**Fawning:** 7 SERVILE
one: 3 DOE
**Fax:** 4 SEND
button: 4 SEND
cover-page word: 4 FROM
forerunner: 5 TELEX
user: 6 SENDER
**Faxed:** 4 SENT
**Fayed**
"Hook" producer: 4 DODI
**Faze:** 5 DAUNT 6 RATTLE
**FBI**
agent: 4 GMAN

datum: 5 CRIME
director after Sessions:
    5 FREEH
employee: 3 AGT 4 GMAN
    5 AGENT
info: 4 FILE
Part of: 7 FEDERAL
sting of the late 1970s:
    6 ABSCAM
**FCC**
concerns (abbr.): 4 STDS
**FDR:** 3 DEM 4 PRES
coin: 4 DIME
Mother of: 4 SARA
opponent Landon: 3 ALF
Part of: 4 INIT 6 DELANO
program: 3 CCC NRA TVA
    WPA
project: 3 TVA
quote word: 6 INFAMY
successor: 3 HST
~ Interior Secretary: 5 ICKES
~ Scottie: 4 FALA
~ Secretary of State: 4 HULL
**Fe:** 4 IRON
**Fear:** 4 CAPE 6 PHOBIA
and wonder: 3 AWE
For ~ that: 4 LEST
Great: 5 DREAD
Instill ~ in: 5 SCARE
Intense: 5 PANIC 6 TERROR
Reduce a: 5 ALLAY
Show: 4 PALE 5 COWER
    QUAKE 7 TREMBLE
Shrink in: 6 CRINGE
**Feared**
fly: 6 TSETSE
mosquito: 5 AEDES
**Fearful:** 5 MOUSY 6 AFRAID
    TREPID
Be ~ of: 5 DREAD
fate: 4 DOOM
**Fearless:** 4 BOLD
flyer: 3 ACE
**Fearless Fosdick**
creator: 6 ALCAPP
**"Fear of Fifty"**
author: 9 ERICAJONG
author Erica: 4 JONG
author Jong: 5 ERICA
**Fearsome**
dinosaur: 4 TREX
fellow: 4 OGRE
fly: 6 TSETSE
**Fearsome Foursome**
member: 5 GRIER
**Feast:** 4 DINE 6 REPAST
finale: 7 DESSERT
Island: 4 LUAU
Passover: 5 SEDER
Put on a: 6 REGALE
Spring: 5 SEDER
**Feast of Lots**
book: 6 ESTHER
**Feat:** 3 ACT 4 DEED
Brilliant: 4 COUP

Daring: 5 STUNT
on ice: 4 AXEL
**Feather:** 5 PENNA PINNA
    PLUME
bed: 3 TAR
Light as a: 4 AIRY
partner: 3 TAR
scarf: 3 BOA
**Feathered**
bigfoot: 3 EMU
fisher: 6 OSPREY
stole: 3 BOA
**Feathers**
Duck: 5 EIDER
Fix: 5 PREEN
Fuss and: 3 ADO
Lose: 4 MOLT
Ruffle: 3 IRE IRK VEX
    4 RILE
**Feathery:** 4 SOFT
wrap: 3 BOA
**Feature:** 5 MOVIE TRAIT
    6 ASPECT
**Feb.**
Month after: 3 MAR
**Febrero**
preceder: 5 ENERO
**Febreze**
target: 4 ODOR
**February**
birthstone: 8 AMETHYST
forecast: 5 SLEET
**February 14**
figure: 4 EROS
word: 4 LOVE
**February 29:** 7 LEAPDAY
**Fed:** 4 GMAN TMAN
after a dealer: 4 NARC
Famous: 4 NESS
first name: 4 ALAN
Got ~ up: 3 ATE
on: 3 ATE
the kitty: 5 ANTED
They're ~ at curbside:
    6 METERS
**Fed.**
Abu Dhabi: 3 UAE
agent: 4 GMAN TMAN
auditors: 3 GAO
benefit source: 3 SSA
emissions watchdog: 3 EPA
fiscal agency: 3 OMB
funder: 3 NEA
hush-hush group: 3 NSA
loan agency: 3 SBA
med. research agency: 3 NIH
monetary-aid program: 3 SSI
money overseer: 3 OMB
pollution monitor: 3 EPA
property overseer: 3 GSA
retirement org.: 3 SSI
support benefit: 3 SSI
watchdog: 3 EPA
workplace watchdog: 4 OSHA
**Federal**
agcy.: 3 AEC

agt.: 4 GMAN TMAN
Like ~ tax laws: 6 ARCANE
purchasing org.: 3 GSA
**"Federalist, The"**
   pieces: 6 ESSAYS
**Federation**
   Mideast ~ (abbr.): 3 UAE
**Federico**
   Clinton Cabinet member:
      4 PENA
**Federico Garcia ___**
   Poet: 5 LORCA
**FedEx:** 4 SEND SHIP
   arrival: 6 PARCEL
   rival: 3 UPS
**Fedora:** 3 HAT
   feature: 4 BRIM 6 CREASE
**Feds:** 4 GMEN TMEN
**Fee:** 6 CHARGE
   Bridge: 4 TOLL
   Currency exchange: 4 AGIO
   Docking: 7 MOORAGE
   Flat: 4 RENT
   Hourly: 4 RATE
   Import: 6 TARIFF
   Lawyer: 8 RETAINER
   Mutual fund: 4 LOAD
   Old calling: 7 ONEDIME
   Poker: 4 ANTE
   Stud: 4 ANTE
**Feeble:** 6 ANEMIC
**Feeble-minded:** 4 DOTY
**Feebly**
   Walk: 6 TOTTER
**Feed:** 4 SLOP 6 REPAST
      7 NOURISH
   a crowd: 5 CATER
   Don't: 6 FAMISH
   fuel to: 5 STOKE
   Livestock: 4 MASH SLOP
      7 SOILAGE
   Off one's: 3 ILL
   Part of a TV: 5 AUDIO
   seed: 3 OAT
   the kitty: 4 ANTE
   the pigs: 4 SLOP
**Feedback:** 5 INPUT
   Positive: 5 YESES
**Feed bag**
   Attach, as a: 5 TIEON
   Don the: 3 EAT
   feed: 4 OATS
   item: 3 OAT
**Feeder**
   filler: 4 SEED SUET
   Horse: 7 NOSEBAG
   Line: 4 CUER
   Pig: 6 TROUGH
**"Fee, fi, fo, fum"**
   caller: 4 OGRE 5 GIANT
**Feel:** 4 AURA 5 GROPE SENSE
      7 BELIEVE
   Able to: 7 SENSATE
   bad: 3 AIL
   bad about: 3 RUE
   contrite: 6 REPENT

excitement: 6 TINGLE
indignant toward: 6 RESENT
in one's bones: 4 KNOW
   5 SENSE
longing for: 4 MISS
Nice way to: 6 NEEDED
off: 3 AIL
one's way: 5 GROPE
poorly: 3 AIL
remorse: 3 RUE
sore: 4 ACHE
sorry about: 3 RUE 6 LAMENT
sorry for: 4 PITY
the same: 5 AGREE
**Feeler:** 4 PALP TEST
      7 ANTENNA
**Feelers:** 8 ANTENNAE
**Feeling:** 4 AURA VIBE
      5 CHORD SENSE
      7 SENSATE TACTILE
   Apprehensive: 5 ANGST
   blue: 3 SAD 4 DOUR GLUM
   Cloud-nine: 7 ELATION
   Covetous: 4 ENVY
   Creepy: 6 UNEASE
   Distressed: 4 PANG
   Emotional: 4 VIBE
   faint: 5 WOOZY
   Fluish: 4 AGUE
   Full of: 5 LYRIC
   Gung-ho: 4 ZEAL
   Have a: 5 SENSE
   Kind of: 3 GUT
   no pain: 4 NUMB
   off: 3 ILL
   of hunger: 4 PANG
   of pity: 6 PATHOS
   Parched: 6 THIRST
   poorly: 3 ILL
   Queasy: 6 NAUSEA
   sore: 4 ACHY
   Tickled-pink: 4 GLEE
   Uneasy: 5 ANGST QUALM
   Vengeful: 5 SPITE
**Feelings:** 3 EGO
   Feign: 5 EMOTE
   Have good ~ about: 4 LIKE
   Ill: 10 NOLOVELOST
**Feet:** 4 DOGS
   128 cubic ~: 4 CORD
   43,560 square ~: 4 ACRE
   5,280 ~: 4 MILE
   Cold: 4 FEAR
   Drag one's: 5 STALL
   Feline: 4 PAWS
   Get one's ~ wet: 4 WADE
   Got to one's: 5 STOOD
   Hard on the: 6 PEBBLY
   Having ~ pointing inward:
      10 PIGEONTOED
   in meter: 5 IAMBS
   Light on one's: 4 SPRY
      5 AGILE
   One who works with: 4 POET
   Poetic: 5 IAMBS
   Work with: 4 POEM

**Feign:** 3 ACT 6 AFFECT
      7 PRETEND 8 SIMULATE
   feelings: 5 EMOTE
**___ Fein:** 4 SINN
**Feinstein**
   (abbr.): 3 DEM SEN
   Senator: 6 DIANNE
**Feint:** 4 PLOY RUSE
   Fencing: 5 APPEL
   Football: 4 JUKE
   Hockey: 4 DEKE
**Feldman**
   Actor: 5 COREY
   Comical: 5 MARTY
**Feldman, Marty**
   role: 4 IGOR
**Felicia**
   Actress: 4 FARR
**Feliciano**
   Singer: 4 JOSE
**"Felicity"**
   star Russell: 4 KERI
**Feline:** 5 CATTY
   defense: 5 CLAWS
   ennead: 5 LIVES
   fancy: 6 CATNIP
   Fast: 4 PUMA 7 CHEETAH
   feet: 4 PAWS
   female: 7 TIGRESS
   Film: 4 ELSA
   film heroine: 4 ELSA
   hybrid: 5 LIGER
   line: 4 MEOW
   Male: 6 TOMCAT
   sign: 3 LEO
   Spotted: 6 OCELOT
   ~, in Spanish: 4 GATO
   ~, to Tweety: 3 TAT
**Felipe**
   farewell: 5 ADIOS
   of baseball: 4 ALOU
**Felis**
   member: 4 PUMA
**Felix:** 3 CAT
   Like: 4 NEAT TIDY
   roommate: 5 OSCAR
**"Feliz ___ Nuevo!":** 3 ANO
**Fell:** 3 HEW 4 SLAY
   It ~ in 1836: 5 ALAMO
   It ~ in 2001: 3 MIR
   off: 5 EBBED WANED
   with a blade: 3 MOW
**Fell, Gideon**
   creator: 4 CARR
**Fella:** 3 BUD GUY MAC 4 CHAP
      GENT 5 KIDDO
**Feller:** 3 AXE MAN
   targets: 5 TREES
   What a ~ needs: 3 AXE SAW
      8 CHAINSAW
**Fellini:** 7 ITALIAN
   film: 8 LASTRADA
   Musical based on a ~ film:
      4 NINE
**Fellow:** 3 BUB GUY LAD MAN
      4 CHAP GENT

Ale: 6 BREWER
Clumsy: 3 OAF
Contemptible: 3 CAD
Cruel: 4 OGRE
Dapper: 3 DAN
Deer: 4 STAG
Fabulous: 5 AESOP
Fiery: 7 HOTHEAD
Foolish: 4 TWIT
Fraternal: 3 ELK
Fun-loving:
    15 GOODTIMECHARLIE
Furtive: 5 SNEAK
Hilarious: 3 WAG 4 RIOT
Ode: 4 POET
Philandering: 4 ROUE
Singular: 4 ONER
Smart: 5 ALECK
Young: 3 LAD SON
**Fellows:** 3 HES MEN
For ~ only: 4 STAG
**Fellowship**
Fund a: 5 ENDOW
**Felon**
Aid a: 4 ABET
**Felony**
Fiery: 5 ARSON
**Felt:** 6 SENSED
hat: 6 FEDORA
**Feltlike**
fabric: 5 BAIZE
**Fem.**
leadership gp.: 4 YWCA
Neither ~ nor masc.: 4 NEUT
Not: 4 MASC
**Female:** 3 SEX
antelope: 3 DOE
cells: 3 OVA
Common ~ middle name:
    3 MAE
deer: 3 DOE 4 HIND
demon: 5 LAMIA
domestic: 4 MAID
donkey: 5 JENNY
Farm: 3 DAM EWE HEN SOW
    4 MARE
Feline ~ of film: 4 ELSA
Fleecy: 3 EWE
Forest: 3 DOE
fowl: 3 HEN 6 PEAHEN
fox: 5 VIXEN
friend, in French: 4 AMIE
gamete: 4 OVUM
hare: 3 DOE
horse: 4 MARE
kangaroo: 3 DOE
lobster: 3 HEN
Low ~ voice: 4 ALTO
Male and: 5 SEXES
octopus: 3 HEN
pheasant: 6 PEAHEN
pig: 3 SOW
principle: 3 YIN
pronoun: 3 SHE
prophet: 5 SIBYL
rabbit: 3 DOE

red deer: 4 HIND
sheep: 3 EWE
suffix: 3 INE 4 ENNE
swan: 3 PEN
swimmer: 5 NAIAD
vampire: 5 LAMIA
whale: 3 COW
WWII gp.: 4 WAAC WACS
~ bear, in Spanish: 3 OSA
**"Female Eunuch, The"**
author: 5 GREER
**Feminine:** 7 WOMANLY
Hardly: 7 MANNISH
principle: 3 YIN
suffix: 3 ESS INA 4 ENNE
    ETTA ETTE TRIX
**Feminist**
~ Abzug: 5 BELLA
~ Bella: 5 ABZUG
~ Eleanor: 5 SMEAL
~ Germaine: 5 GREER
~ Lucretia: 4 MOTT
**Femme**
Canonized ~ (abbr.): 3 STE
fatale: 5 SIREN 7 MANTRAP
    8 MANEATER
That: 4 ELLE
**Femme ___:** 6 FATALE
**Fen-___ (diet drug combo):**
    4 PHEN
**Fence**
alternative: 5 HEDGE
Be a ~ for: 4 ABET
feature: 4 GATE POST RAIL
    5 STILE
Get off the: 3 ACT OPT
    6 CHOOSE DECIDE
Like ~ wares: 6 STOLEN
On the: 4 TORN
opening: 4 GATE 5 STILE
Racetrack: 4 RAIL
stake: 4 PALE
Steps over a: 5 STILE
supplier: 5 THIEF
**Fencer**
blade: 4 EPEE
cry: 7 ENGARDE
defense: 5 PARRY
feint: 5 APPEL
move: 5 LUNGE
**Fence-sitter**
sounds: 3 ERS
**Fencing**
blade: 4 EPEE
event: 4 EPEE 5 SABER
Japanese: 5 KENDO
move: 5 LUNGE PARRY
    6 THRUST
piece: 4 RAIL
sword: 4 EPEE 5 SABER
**Fender**
bender: 4 DENT 6 MISHAP
flaw: 4 DENT DING
**Fenway**
Imposing ~ sight:
    15 THEGREENMONSTER

team: 5 BOSOX
**Feodor:** 4 TSAR
**Fer**
Not: 4 AGIN
**Feral:** 6 UNTAME
Least: 6 TAMEST
**Ferber**
Author: 4 EDNA
novel: 5 GIANT SOBIG
    8 CIMARRON
    9 ICEPALACE
**Ferde**
Composer: 5 GROFE
**Ferdinand**
First lady of: 6 IMELDA
kingdom: 6 ARAGON
of WWI: 4 FOCH
queen: 8 ISABELLA
**Ferdinand III**
Daughter of: 7 ELEANOR
**Fergie**
~, formally: 5 SARAH
**Ferment:** 6 SIMMER
**Fermentation**
ingredient: 5 YEAST
**Fermented:** 7 YEASTED
drink: 3 ALE
honey drink: 4 MEAD
milk drink: 5 KEFIR
rice drink: 4 SAKE SAKI
**Fermenter:** 5 YEAST
**Fermi**
Physicist: 6 ENRICO
study: 4 ATOM
**Fern**
Future: 5 SPORE
leaf: 5 FROND
seed: 5 SPORE
**Fernand**
Cubist: 5 LEGER
**Fernandez**
Pitcher: 3 SID
**Fernando**
Info: Spanish cue
Actor: 3 REY 5 LAMAS
**"Fernando"**
group: 4 ABBA
**Ferocious:** 6 SAVAGE
fish: 7 PIRANHA
**Ferrara**
Director: 4 ABEL
family name: 4 ESTE
**Ferrari**
Automaker: 4 ENZO
**Ferraro**
Ms. ~, to friends: 4 GERI
**Ferrell**
film: 3 ELF
**Ferrer**
Actor: 3 MEL 4 JOSE
**Ferret**
foot: 3 PAW
kin: 5 OTTER
out: 4 FIND SEEK 5 DIGUP
**Ferrigno**
Actor: 3 LOU

**Ferris wheel:** 4 RIDE
**Ferry**
  destination: 4 ISLE
  How a ~ goes: 8 TOANDFRO
  river of myth: 4 STYX
**Ferryman**
  Styx: 6 CHARON
**Fertile**
  area: 5 OASIS
  areas: 5 OASES
  soil: 4 LOAM 5 LOESS
**Fertile Crescent**
  land: 4 ASIA 5 SYRIA
  river: 6 TIGRIS
**Fertility**
  god: 6 OSIRIS
  goddess: 4 ISIS 7 ASTARTE
**Fertilization**
  Kind of: 7 INVITRO
  site: 5 OVULE
  targets: 3 OVA
**Fertilizer**
  brand: 5 ORTHO
  chemical: 4 UREA 7 NITRATE
  ingredient: 4 PEAT 5 NITER
    6 MANURE POTASH
  Loamy: 4 MARL
  Organic: 5 GUANO
  source: 7 PEATBOG
**Fervency:** 4 ZEAL
**Fervent:** 4 AVID 5 EAGER RAPID
**Fervid:** 6 ARDENT
**Fervor:** 4 ZEAL 5 ARDOR
  Full of: 6 ONFIRE
  With: 5 HOTLY
**Fess**
  up: 4 AVOW 5 ADMIT
  (up): 3 OWN
**Fest**
  month: 7 OKTOBER
**Fester**
  Morticia, to: 5 NIECE
**Festival**
  Asian: 3 TET
  Colorado ~ site: 5 ASPEN
  County: 4 FAIR
  Jewish: 5 PURIM
  opener: 3 EVE
  Redford: 8 SUNDANCE
  Spring: 6 EASTER
  Vietnamese: 3 TET
**Festival d' ___ :** 3 ETE
**Festive:** 3 GAY 4 GALA
  event: 4 FETE GALA
  night: 3 EVE
  time: 4 YULE
**Festoon:** 4 SWAG 5 ADORN
    DRAPE
**Fetch:** 3 GET 4 SHAG 5 BRING
    GOFOR GOGET
  Thing to: 5 STICK
  with force: 3 LUG
**Fetching:** 4 CUTE
  ones: 6 GOFERS
**Fete:** 4 GALA 5 HONOR
    6 REGALE

**Friars:** 5 ROAST
**Feted**
  with alcohol: 5 WINED
**Fetes**
  Fancy: 3 DOS
**Fettle**
  In fine: 3 AOK FIT 4 HALE
    WELL
**Fettuccine:** 5 PASTA
**Fettuccine ___ :** 7 ALFREDO
**Feud**
  Bitter: 8 VENDETTA
  family: 6 MCCOYS
**Feudal**
  estate: 4 FIEF
  Like ~ times: 8 MEDIEVAL
  lord: 5 LIEGE
  worker: 4 ESNE SERF
    6 VASSAL
**Feudin'**
  with: 4 AGIN
**Feuding:** 4 ATIT 5 ATWAR
**Fever**
  cause: 3 FLU
  Chills and: 4 AGUE
  Have, as a: 3 RUN
  Malarial: 4 AGUE
  symptom: 5 CHILL
**"Fever"**
  singer Peggy: 3 LEE
**___ fever:** 4 RANA
**Feverish:** 3 ILL 4 WARM
    6 HECTIC
  chill: 4 AGUE
  Feel: 3 AIL
**Few**
  A: 4 SOME
  A ~ bucks: 4 DEER
  A ~ chips: 4 ANTE
  A ~ last words: 4 OBIT
  A ~ laughs: 4 HAHA
  and far between: 4 RARE
    6 SPARSE
  Favored: 5 ELITE
  Known by: 6 ARCANE
  Like very ~ games:
    5 NOHIT
  Of ~ words: 5 TERSE
  Select: 5 ELITE
  Understood by: 8 ESOTERIC
**Fewer:** 4 LESS
  No ~ than: 7 ATLEAST
**"Few Good ___ , A":** 3 MEN
**"Few Good Men, A"**
  actress: 5 MOORE
  director: 6 REINER
    9 ROBREINER
**___ few rounds:** 3 GOA
**Fey**
  Comedienne: 4 TINA
**Fez:** 3 HAT
  feature: 6 TASSEL
**F.G.s**
  They're worth two: 3 TDS
**Fi**
  lead-in: 3 SCI

**Fiasco:** 4 BOMB 7 DEBACLE
    8 DISASTER
  Ford: 5 EDSEL
**Fiat:** 5 EDICT
  homeland: 5 ITALY
**Fib:** 3 LIE 8 TELLALIE
**Fibber:** 4 LIAR
  admission: 5 ILIED
  and Molly: 6 MCGEES
  of old radio: 5 MCGEE
**Fiber**
  Acrylic: 5 ORLON
  Agave: 5 SISAL
  Basket: 5 ISTLE
  Burlap: 4 JUTE
  Carpet: 5 ISTLE
  Caulking: 5 OAKUM
  Cellulose: 5 ARNEL RAYON
  Cereal: 4 BRAN
  Coconut: 4 COIR
  Cocoon: 4 SILK
  Cordage: 5 SISAL
  Dupont: 5 ORLON
  Flaxlike: 5 RAMIE
  Hemp: 5 SISAL
  Rope: 4 BAST COIR HEMP
    JUTE 5 SISAL 6 STRAND
  source: 4 BEAN BRAN HEMP
    5 AGAVE
  Strong: 5 RAMIE
  Synthetic: 5 ARNEL NYLON
    ORLON RAYON
    7 ACETATE
  Twine: 5 SISAL
**Fiber-yielding**
  plant: 4 ALOE
**Fibster:** 4 LIAR
**Fibula:** 4 BONE
  neighbor: 5 TIBIA
**FICA**
  funds it: 3 SSA
**Fiction:** 5 GENRE 6 NOVELS
  expert: 4 LIAR
  Opposite of: 4 FACT
  Work of: 5 NOVEL
**Fictional**
  alter ego: 4 HYDE
  bell town: 5 ADANO
  blade: 5 ATHOS
  captain: 4 AHAB NEMO
  circumnavigator: 4 FOGG
  dreamer: 5 ALICE
  elephant: 5 BABAR
  governess: 4 ANNA EYRE
  hunchback: 4 IGOR
  lab assistant: 4 IGOR
  pirate: 4 SMEE
  planet: 3 ORK
  plantation: 4 TARA
  salesman: 5 LOMAN
  surname of 1847: 4 EYRE
  terrier: 4 ASTA
  weaver: 6 MARNER
  wirehair: 4 ASTA
  ~ Butler: 5 RHETT
  ~ Doone: 5 LORNA

~ Frome: 5 ETHAN
~ Gantry: 5 ELMER
~ Georgia home: 4 TARA
~ Heep: 5 URIAH
~ Helm: 4 MATT
~ Honolulu detective: 4 CHAN
~ Italian town: 5 ADANO
~ Jane: 4 EYRE
~ Lorna: 5 DOONE
~ Marner: 5 SILAS
~ Plaza Hotel brat: 6 ELOISE
~ Swiss miss: 5 HEIDI
~ Uncle: 5 REMUS
~ Uriah: 4 HEEP
~ Wolfe: 4 NERO

**Fictitious**
~ Richard: 3 ROE

**Fiddle**
Early: 4 VIOL
Emperor with a: 4 NERO
finale: 5 DEDEE 6 DEEDEE
Fine: 5 AMATI STRAD
Fit as a: 4 HALE
Kind of: 4 BASS
Like a: 3 FIT
Renaissance: 5 REBEC
stick: 3 BOW
(with): 6 TAMPER
with a fiddle: 4 TUNE
**Fiddled:** 5 TOYED
**Fiddle-de-___:** 3 DEE
**Fiddlehead:** 4 FERN
**Fiddlemaker**
Famed: 5 AMATI
**Fiddler**
Famous: 4 NERO
of kids' rhyme: 3 CAT
on the reef: 4 CRAB
**"Fiddler on the Roof"**
concern: 6 POGROM
matchmaker: 5 YENTE
role: 5 TEVYE
setting: 6 SHTETL
star: 5 TOPOL
**"Fiddlesticks!":** 4 BOSH DRAT
POSH RATS 5 PSHAW
SHOOT
**___ fide:** 4 BONA
**Fidel**
Friend of: 3 CHE
Philippine president: 5 RAMOS
**"___ Fideles":** 6 ADESTE
**"Fidelio":** 5 OPERA
jailer: 5 ROCCO
**Fidelity:** 5 TROTH
High: 5 TROTH
**Fidget**
Inclined to: 5 ANTSY
**Fidgety:** 5 ANTSY 8 RESTLESS
**Fido**
Bit for: 3 ORT 5 SCRAP
Call to: 4 HERE
Command to: 3 BEG SIT
4 HEEL STAY 5 FETCH
SICEM SPEAK 6 DROPIT
doc: 3 VET

Food for: 4 ALPO
foot: 3 PAW
Friend of: 3 REX 5 ROVER
warning: 5 SNARL
**Fiduciary**
entity: 5 TRUST
**Field:** 4 AREA 5 ARENA
6 DOMAIN MEADOW
METIER SPHERE
Attorney: 3 LAW
Battle: 5 OPERA
call: 3 CAW
Clear the: 4 REAP
cover: 4 TARP
event: 7 SHOTPUT
Farmer ~ (abbr.): 3 AGR
furrower: 4 PLOW
Grassy: 3 LEA
house: 5 TEPEE
Level the playing: 3 MOW
Like a fair playing: 5 LEVEL
marshal: 3 REF
measure: 4 ACRE
mouse: 4 VOLE
of expertise: 4 AREA
official: 3 REF UMP
of honor event: 4 DUEL
of play: 5 ARENA
of study: 4 AREA
of work: 4 LINE
Partner of: 5 TRACK
Plow the: 4 TILL
prefix: 4 AGRO
protector: 4 TARP
Rice: 5 PADDY
Rock ~ (abbr.): 4 GEOL
Small: 4 ACRE
trip: 5 ERROR
unit: 4 ACRE
Word before: 3 AIR
yield: 4 CROP
**Field ___:** 4 GOAL
**Field, Sally**
Emmy-winning role: 5 SYBIL
Oscar film: 8 NORMARAE
TV role: 3 NUN
**Fielding**
goof: 5 ERROR
novel: 6 AMELIA
**"Field of Dreams"**
setting: 4 IOWA
**Fields**
Bandleader: 4 SHEP
Comedienne: 5 TOTIE
oath: 4 DRAT
persona: 3 SOT
School with historic playing:
4 ETON
**___ Fields (mythical paradise):**
7 ELYSIAN
**Fields, W.C.**
expletive: 4 DRAT
persona: 3 SOT 4 LUSH
5 SOUSE
**Fiend:** 3 NUT 4 OGRE
5 DEMON

**Fiendish:** 4 EVIL VILE
7 SATANIC
**Fiennes**
1998 ~ role: 5 STEED
**Fierce**
fighter: 7 BEARCAT
one: 5 TIGER
Smell something: 4 REEK
**"Fierce Creatures"**
star John: 6 CLEESE
**Fierceness:** 4 FURY
**Fierstein, Harvey**
Talk like: 4 RASP
**Fiery**
crime: 5 ARSON
fellow: 7 HOTHEAD
gemstone: 4 OPAL
heap: 5 PYRE
saint: 4 ELMO
**"Fiesque"**
composer: 4 LALO
**Fiesta:** 4 GALA
fare: 5 TACOS
prop: 6 PINATA
**Fiesta Bowl**
site: 5 TEMPE
**Fife**
accompaniment: 5 TABOR
companion: 4 DRUM
player: 6 KNOTTS
**Fifth**
element: 5 BORON
note: 3 SOL
of NYC: 3 AVE
qtrs.: 3 OTS
wheel: 5 SPARE
zodiac sign: 3 LEO
**Fifth Avenue**
store: 4 SAKS
**"Fifth Beatle"**
~ Sutcliffe: 3 STU
**Fifth-century**
pope: 4 LEOI 5 STLEO
scourge: 6 ATTILA
start: 3 CDI
warrior: 3 HUN
**Fifty**
Change for a: 4 TENS
minutes past: 5 TENTO
One of: 5 STATE
percent: 4 HALF
Two of: 4 EFFS
**Fifty-fifty:** 4 EVEN
**"Fifty-four-forty or Fight"**
territory: 6 OREGON
**Fig**
Give a: 4 CARE
pollinator: 4 WASP
**Fig.**
Attendance: 3 EST
Ballpark: 3 AVG EST
Capitol: 3 SEN
Check: 3 AMT
Court: 3 ATT 4 ATTY
Dugout: 3 MGR
Financial: 3 APR

**Geometric:** 3 CIR 4 RECT
**Global positioning:** 3 LAT
**Invoice:** 3 AMT
**Nutritional:** 3 CAL RDA
**Pilot:** 3 ALT
**Transcript:** 3 GPA
**Yield:** 3 ROI
**Fight:** 3 ROW 4 BOUT 5 MELEE
    SETTO 6 OPPOSE
    SCRAPE TUSSLE
  back: 6 RESIST
  Brief: 5 SETTO
  Confused: 5 MELEE
  down and dirty: 6 RASSLE
  ender: 3 TKO
  enders: 3 KOS
  Fix a: 3 RIG
  for balance: 6 TEETER
  Give up the: 4 CAVE
  grime: 5 CLEAN
  like a knight: 4 TILT
  Noisy: 5 BRAWL
  off: 5 REPEL
  Prepare to: 4 SPAR
    9 SQUAREOFF
  Put up a: 6 RESIST
  Rural: 6 RASSLE
  site: 4 RING 5 ARENA
  Slight: 4 SPAT
  to keep the faith: 7 HOLYWAR
  Two-person: 4 DUEL
  Valiant: 5 STAND
  with fists: 3 BOX
**Fighter**
  Crack ~ pilot: 3 ACE
  Fierce: 7 BEARCAT
  Fire: 4 HOSE
  Flu: 5 SERUM
  Good: 4 EVIL
  Infection: 5 SULFA
  Inflation:
    15 PRICEREGULATION
  in grey: 3 REB
  Korean War: 3 MIG
  Polio: 5 SABIN
  Russian: 3 MIG
**Fighters**
  Flu: 4 SERA
  ___ Fighters: 3 FOO
**Fighting:** 4 ATIT 5 ATWAR
    7 HOSTILE WARFARE
  fleet: 6 ARMADA
  In ~ shape: 4 TRIM
  Scene of WWI: 4 YSER
  Them's ~ words: 7 ENGARDE
**"Fighting"**
  ~ Big Ten team: 6 ILLINI
**Fighting ___:** 5 IRISH
**Fighting Irish**
  Rockne of the: 5 KNUTE
**Fighting Tigers**
  sch.: 3 LSU
**"___ fightin' words!":**
    5 THEMS
**Figs.:** 3 NOS
  Court: 3 DAS

**Figure:** 3 BOD 4 STAT 5 ADDUP
    TOTUP 6 DECIDE
    PERSON RECKON
    7 NUMERAL
  Adored: 4 IDOL
  Do ~ eights: 5 SKATE
  Go: 3 ADD
  Half a ~ eight: 3 ESS
  in geometry: 4 AREA
  of speech: 5 IDIOM TROPE
    6 LECTOR ORATOR
    SIMILE
  on a fin: 3 ABE
  out: 3 GET SEE 5 INFER
    SOLVE 6 DECODE
    DEDUCE REASON
    7 REALIZE
  (out): 4 DOPE SUSS
**Figured**
  out: 3 GOT
**Figurehead**
  place: 4 PROW
**Figures:** 4 DATA
  to analyze: 7 RAWDATA
  Watch the: 4 OGLE
**Figure skater**
  category: 5 PAIRS
  figure: 5 EIGHT
  jump: 4 AXEL
  ~ Babilonia: 3 TAI
  ~ Baiul: 6 OKSANA
  ~ Cohen: 5 SASHA
  ~ Katarina: 4 WITT
  ~ Lipinski: 4 TARA
  ~ Paulsen: 4 AXEL
  ~ Rodnina: 5 IRINA
  ~ Sasha: 5 COHEN
  ~ Sonja: 5 HENIE
  ~ Thomas: 4 DEBI
**Figurine**
  mineral: 4 ONYX
  Polynesian: 4 TIKI
**Fiji**
  Neighbor of: 5 SAMOA TONGA
  One of three in: 3 DOT
**Filament:** 6 THREAD
  element: 8 TUNGSTEN
**Filbert:** 3 NUT
**Filch:** 3 COP ROB 5 STEAL
    SWIPE 6 THIEVE
**File:** 4 RASP SORT 5 EMERY
    QUEUE
  box filler: 6 RECIPE
  Brokerage ~ (abbr.): 4 ACCT
  Change a ~ listing: 6 RENAME
  Circular: 7 ROLODEX
    8 TRASHCAN
  Coarse: 4 RASP
  Common text ~ name:
    6 README
  Compress a data: 3 ZIP
  Computer ~ format: 4 JPEG
  Customer ~ entry:
    8 AREACODE
  Delete a: 5 ERASE
  Expand a: 5 UNZIP

**folder feature:** 3 TAB
  holder: 4 DISC 6 FOLDER
  material: 5 EMERY
  Program ~ extension: 3 EXE
**"___ File, The":** 6 ODESSA
**Filed**
  item: 4 NAIL
**Filer:** 4 RASP 5 EMERY
  Form: 3 CPA
  worry: 5 AUDIT
**Filet**
  fish: 4 SOLE
**Filet ___:** 6 MIGNON
**Filet mignon**
  source: 4 LOIN
**Filigreed:** 4 LACY
**Filing**
  aid: 3 TAB 5 EMERY
  Court: 10 LEGALBRIEF
  Miner: 5 CLAIM
  mo.: 3 APR
**Filippo Lippi:** 3 FRA
**Fill:** 4 SATE 7 SATIATE
  a hold: 4 LADE
  Get one's: 6 LOADUP
  in: 4 TELL TEMP 5 BRIEF
  Something to ~ out: 4 FORM
  space: 3 ARE
  the bill: 3 EAT
  the lungs: 6 INHALE
  the tank: 5 GASUP
  They ~ the bill: 5 CENTS
  Till: 4 CASH ONES
  up: 4 SATE 7 SATIATE
  with cargo: 4 LADE
  with fizz: 6 AERATE
  with joy: 5 ELATE
  with love: 6 ENAMOR
  with resolution: 5 STEEL
  with wonder: 3 AWE
**Filled**
  pastry: 6 ECLAIR
  They may be ~ with jets:
    4 SPAS
  to overflowing: 5 ABRIM
  tortilla: 4 TACO
  up: 3 ATE
  with wonder: 5 INAWE
**Filler**
  Balloon: 3 AIR
  Boat: 5 GRAVY
  Conversation: 4 ISEE 5 IMEAN
  Duffel: 4 GEAR
  Feeder: 4 SEED SUET
  Flagon: 3 ALE
  Flask: 5 BOOZE
  Floppy: 4 DATA
  Football: 3 AIR
  Hourglass: 4 SAND
  Pen: 3 INK
  Pillow: 4 FOAM 5 EIDER
  Reservoir: 4 RAIN
  Sandwich: 4 TUNA
    8 TUNAFISH
  Scuttle: 4 COAL
  Sleeve: 3 ARM

Slot: 3 TAB
Tank: 3 GAS
Tankard: 3 ALE
Tire: 3 AIR
Tram: 3 ORE
**Fillet:** 4 BONE 6 DEBONE
Like a: 8 BONELESS
**Filleted**
  fish: 3 COD 4 SHAD SOLE
**Fill-in:** 3 SUB 4 TEMP
**Filling**
  Bagel: 3 LOX
  Burrito: 4 BEEF
  Cookie: 5 CREME
  Dental: 5 INLAY
  It's removed before ~ up:
    6 GASCAP
  material: 7 AMALGAM
  Pie: 3 MUD
  Pillow: 5 EIDER
  station letters: 3 DDS
**Fillmore:** 4 WHIG
**Filly:** 4 LASS
  brother: 4 COLT
  father: 4 SIRE
  filler: 4 OATS
  footfall: 4 CLOP
  Former: 4 MARE
**Film:** 4 CINE 5 MOVIE
  6 PATINA
  1944 ~: 5 LAURA
  1950 ~: 3 DOA
  1953 ~: 4 LILI
  1958 ~: 4 GIGI
  1962 ~: 4 DRNO
  1965 ~: 4 HELP
  1971 ~: 5 KLUTE
  1974 ~: 5 BENJI
  1975 ~:
    15 DOGDAYAFTERNOON
  1977 ~: 4 ORCA
  1978 ~: 4 COMA
    10 ERASERHEAD
  1979 ~: 5 ALIEN
  1982 ~: 4 TRON
  1985 ~: 5 ELENI
  1996 ~: 5 FARGO
  1997 ~: 7 TITANIC
  1998 ~: 4 ANTZ
  1999 ~: 4 EDTV
    13 THESIXTHSENSE
  2001 ~: 3 ALI 6 AMELIE
  Action ~ highlight: 5 CHASE
  award: 5 OSCAR
  Big name in: 5 KODAK
  box letters: 3 ASA
  buff network: 3 AMC
  Cast-of-thousands: 4 EPIC
  changes: 5 EDITS
  composer Morricone: 5 ENNIO
  composer Nino: 4 ROTA
  composer Rota: 4 NINO
  composer Schifrin: 4 LALO
  crew member: 4 GRIP
  critic James: 4 AGEE
  critic Pauline: 4 KAEL

critic Reed: 3 REX
critic Rex: 4 REED
critic Roger: 5 EBERT
Do ~ work: 3 ACT
dog: 4 ASTA
Do some ~ editing: 6 SPLICE
editing effect: 4 WIPE
editor: 7 SPLICER
ending: 4 GOER
excerpt: 4 CLIP
feline: 4 ELSA
festival site: 6 CANNES
fish: 4 NEMO 5 WANDA
format: 4 IMAX
fragment: 4 CLIP
frame: 3 CEL
French ~ award: 5 CESAR
genre: 4 NOIR 6 ACTION
  HORROR 7 ROMANCE
holder: 4 REEL
Home ~ player: 3 VCR
Kind of: 4 CULT
material: 7 ACETATE
Non-studio: 5 INDIE
ogre: 5 SHREK
part: 4 ROLE
plantation: 4 TARA
Pond: 4 SCUM
princess: 4 LEIA
Private ~ producer: 5 INDIE
Put in more: 6 RELOAD
Put ~ into: 4 LOAD
rat: 3 BEN
rating org.: 4 MPAA
river: 4 KWAI
Sci-fi ~ extra: 5 ALIEN
segment: 4 CLIP
Some ~ ratings: 3 PGS
spool: 4 REEL
studio: 3 LOT
technique: 5 SLOMO
terrier: 4 ASTA
unit: 4 REEL
Western: 5 OATER
What a family ~ is appropriate
  for: 7 ALLAGES
winds up on it: 4 REEL
Word with: 3 ART
~, in French: 4 CINE
**Film ___:** 4 NOIR
**Film director**
  cry: 3 CUT
  unit: 4 TAKE
  ~ Kazan: 4 ELIA
  ~ Lee: 3 ANG
  ~ Nicolas: 4 ROEG
  ~ Petri: 4 ELIO
  ~ Resnais: 5 ALAIN
**Filmed:** 4 SHOT
  again: 6 RESHOT
**Filming**
  Bit of: 4 TAKE
  locale: 3 SET
**Filmmaker**
  with creative control:
    6 AUTEUR

~ Craven: 3 WES
~ Lee: 3 ANG
~ Riefenstahl: 4 LENI
~ Spike: 3 LEE
~ Wertmuller: 4 LINA
**Film noir:** 5 GENRE
  classic: 3 DOA
**Films**
  Its ~ begin with a roar: 3 MGM
  Like horror: 6 RATEDR
    RRATED
  Like many independent:
    4 ARTY
  Like some R-rated: 4 GORY
    6 EROTIC
**Filmy:** 8 GOSSAMER
  fabric: 5 GAUZE
**Fils**
  father: 4 PERE
**Filter:** 4 SEEP 6 SCREEN
  Flounder: 4 GILL
**Filthy**
  lucre: 4 PELF
  money: 5 LUCRE
  place: 3 STY
**Fin:** 5 FIVER
  Change for a: 4 ONES
  Figure on a: 3 ABE
**Finagle:** 3 RIG 6 WANGLE
**Final:** 3 NET 4 EXAM LAST
    TEST
  **Info:** Suffix cue
  (abbr.): 3 ULT
  authority: 5 SAYSO
  bio: 4 OBIT
  exams: 5 ORALS
  inning, usually: 5 NINTH
  Let have the ~ word:
    7 DEFERTO
  notice: 4 OBIT
  Not yet: 4 NISI
  preceder: 4 SEMI
  Prepare for a: 4 CRAM
  stage: 7 ENDGAME
  stanza: 5 ENVOI
  story: 4 OBIT
  taker: 6 TESTEE
  transport: 6 HEARSE
  word: 4 AMEN 5 ADIEU
    SAYSO
  ~ Commandment: 5 TENTH
**"Final answer?"**
  asker: 5 REGIS
**"Final Days, The"**
  author: 5 OLSON
**Finale:** 3 END 4 CODA
    5 OMEGA 6 ENDING
  **Info:** Suffix cue
  Brit: 3 ZED
  Classical: 5 OMEGA
  English-exam: 5 ESSAY
  Fable: 5 MORAL
  Feast: 7 DESSERT
  Gerund: 3 ING
  Grand: 3 DEE 4 PRIX
  Major: 4 ETTE

Musical: 4 CODA
Proof: 3 QED
Series: 3 ETC 4 ETAL
Social: 3 ITE
Threat: 6 ORELSE
Waltz: 3 ZEE
**Final Four**
1998 ~ team: 4 UTES
game: 4 SEMI
org.: 4 NCAA
**"Final frontier"**: 5 SPACE
**Finalize**: 8 NAILDOWN
~, as a deal: 3 INK
~, with "up": 3 SEW
**Finally:** 6 ATLAST
Become,: 5 ENDUP
~, in French: 5 ENFIN
**"Finally!":** 3 AHA 6 ATLAST
**Finance**
co. takeback: 4 REPO
deg.: 3 MBA
Fannie of: 3 MAE
**Financial:** 6 FISCAL
8 ECONOMIC
aid criterion: 4 NEED
backer: 5 ANGEL
Bit of ~ planning: 3 IRA
burden: 4 DEBT
claim: 4 LIEN
Federal ~ planning gp.: 3 OMB
fig.: 3 APR
independence:
10 EASYSTREET
It may be: 3 AID
obligation: 4 DEBT
page letters: 4 NYSE
Party to a ~ exchange:
6 DRAWEE
standing: 5 WORTH
transaction: 4 LOAN
wherewithal: 5 MEANS
windfall: 5 MELON
**Financial ___ :** 3 AID
**Financially**
compromised: 7 INAHOLE
Set up: 5 ENDOW
solvent: 6 AFLOAT
**Financier**
Fugitive ~ Robert: 5 VESCO
Powerful: 5 BARON
with his own law: 7 GRESHAM
~ Cornell: 4 EZRA
**Financing**
abbr.: 3 APR
Auto ~ co.: 4 GMAC
___ financing: 3 APR
**Finch**
European: 6 LINNET
home: 4 NEST
Long-tailed: 6 TOWHEE
Small: 5 SERIN
**Finch, Atticus**
creator: 3 LEE
**Find:** 4 SPOT 5 DIGUP
6 DETECT LOCATE
7 UNEARTH

Hard to: 4 RARE 5 SCANT
6 SCARCE
Hard to ~, in Latin: 4 RARA
Manage to: 7 SCAREUP
out: 3 SEE 4 HEAR 5 LEARN
7 UNCOVER
out about: 6 HEAROF
the origin of: 5 TRACE
Try to: 4 SEEK
Try to ~ out: 3 ASK
**Fin de ___ :** 6 SIECLE
**Finder**
cry: 3 AHA
Fish: 5 SONAR
Like a depth: 5 SONIC
Scent: 4 NOSE
Stash: 4 NARC
View: 3 EYE
**Finder's ___ :** 3 FEE
**Find ___ for:** 5 AMATE
**"Finding ___ ":** 4 NEMO
**Findlay, Mrs. Walter:** 5 MAUDE
**Fine:** 3 AOK 4 GOOD NICE
OKAY 6 AMERCE
CHOICE 7 PENALTY
and dandy: 3 AOK
china: 5 SPODE
cotton: 4 PIMA
cotton thread: 5 LISLE
dinnerware: 5 CHINA
Enjoy ~ food: 4 DINE
fabric: 5 SATIN
fur: 5 SABLE 6 ERMINE
Impose a: 6 AMERCE
In ~ fettle: 3 AOK FIT 4 HALE
WELL
Just: 3 AOK
Like ~ wine: 4 AGED
Love of ~ art: 5 VIRTU
netting: 5 TULLE
or Howard: 6 STOOGE
point: 6 DETAIL NICETY
Punish by: 6 AMERCE
rain: 4 MIST
Risk a: 5 SPEED
silver: 8 STERLING
Some are: 4 ARTS
spray: 4 MIST
suit material: 5 TWILL
They may be: 4 ARTS
things: 4 ARTS
wool: 6 MERINO
work: 3 ART
**"Fine!:** 3 AOK
**" ___ Fine":** 5 HESSO
**" ___ Fine Day":** 3 ONE
**Fine-grained**
wood: 3 YEW
**Finely**
Chop: 4 DICE HASH 5 MINCE
contoured: 5 SLEEK
sharpened: 4 KEEN
**Fineness**
unit: 5 KARAT
**Finer**
Made: 6 SIFTED

**Finesse:** 4 TACT
With: 4 ABLY
**Finest:** 4 BEST
One of the: 3 COP
**" ___ Finest Hour":** 5 THEIR
**Fine-tune:** 4 HONE 5 TWEAK
6 ADJUST
**Fine-tuned**
engine sound: 4 PURR
**Finger:** 4 FEEL NAME 5 DIGIT
RATON
Do ~ painting: 5 SMEAR
feature: 4 NAIL
Jab with a: 4 POKE
Largest ~ Lake: 6 SENECA
Little: 5 PINKY
Luau ~ food: 3 POI
Point a ~ at: 5 BLAME RATON
6 ACCUSE
pointer: 6 BLAMER
7 ACCUSER
Put one's ~ on: 7 PINDOWN
Use the ~ bowl: 5 RINSE
**Fingerboard**
ridge: 4 FRET
**Finger-choosing**
call: 5 EVENS
**Fingered:** 4 IDED
**Finger-paint:** 4 DAUB 5 SMEAR
**Fingerprint:** 4 CLUE
feature: 5 WHORL
Kind of: 3 DNA
**Fingerprints**
Check for: 4 DUST
Like some: 6 LATENT
**Fingers:** 3 IDS
count: 3 TEN
Cross one's: 4 HOPE
Work your ~ to the bone:
5 SLAVE
**Fingertip:** 4 NAIL
**Finger-wagging:** 5 STERN
**Finis:** 3 END 4 OVER 5 DEATH
**Finish:** 3 END 5 ENDUP
MOPUP SEWUP USEUP
6 VENEER WRAPUP
9 POLISHOFF
Info: Suffix cue
a basement: 5 PANEL
a drive: 4 PAVE
a highway: 3 TAR
Big: 6 FINALE
by: 5 ENDAT
Dull: 3 ARD 5 MATTE
Exterior: 6 STUCCO
first: 3 WIN
line: 4 TAPE WIRE
Lineup: 4 ETAL
Lusterless: 5 MATTE
off: 3 EAT 4 DOIN 5 USEUP
6 DEVOUR
option: 5 GLOSS MATTE
Photo: 5 GENIC MATTE
Pottery: 5 GLAZE
protector: 7 COASTER
second: 5 PLACE

Stay to the: 4 LAST
the cake: 3 ICE
third: 4 SHOW
(up): 3 MOP SEW 4 WRAP
with: 5 ENDAT ENDON
Wood: 5 STAIN
**Finished:** 3 DID 4 DONE OVER
  THRU 5 ENDED KAPUT
  6 CAMEIN 7 ALLDONE
  ALLOVER ATANEND
  ENDEDUP
Expensively: 4 GILT
first: 3 WON
with: 5 RIDOF
**"Finished!":** 5 THERE
**Finisher**
  Cake: 4 ICER
  Furniture: 7 STAINER
  Late: 7 ALSORAN
**Finito:** 4 DONE OVER 5 ENDED
  KAPUT
**Fink:** 3 RAT 4 SCAB SING TELL
  6 TELLON 7 STOOLIE
  TATTLER
**Finless**
  fish: 3 EEL
**Finn**
  carrier: 4 RAFT
  chronicler: 5 TWAIN
  Fictional: 4 HUCK
**"Finnegans Wake"**
  author James: 5 JOYCE
  wife: 4 ANNA
**Finnish**
  architect Alvar: 5 AALTO
  bath: 5 SAUNA
**Fins**
  200 ~: 3 GEE
  Twenty: 5 CNOTE
  Two: 6 TENNER
    7 TENSPOT
**Fiord**
  city: 4 OSLO
**Fir**
  coat: 4 BARK
  fluid: 3 SAP
  Kind of: 6 BALSAM
**Fire:** 3 AXE CAN 4 SACK ZEAL
  5 ARDOR BLAZE LETGO
  6 EXCITE
  Antiaircraft: 4 FLAK
  Baptism of: 6 ORDEAL
  Breathing: 5 IRATE
  bug: 3 ANT
  Build a ~ under: 6 AROUSE
  Dying ~ feature: 5 EMBER
  engine warning: 5 SIREN
  Feed a: 5 STOKE
  fiddler: 4 NERO
  fighters: 5 HOSES
  from a plane: 6 STRAFE
  Great ball of: 3 SUN 4 STAR
  Hang: 4 PEND
  Kind of: 5 ENEMY
  man: 4 ELMO
  On: 3 LIT 6 ABLAZE AFLAME

On ~, in a restaurant:
  6 FLAMBE
  opal: 7 GIRASOL
  Partner of: 9 BRIMSTONE
  preceder: 3 AIM
  Prepare to: 3 AIM
  proof: 3 ASH
  Ready to: 5 ARMED 6 COCKED
  remnant: 3 ASH 5 EMBER
  saint: 4 ELMO
  Set on: 3 LIT 6 IGNITE
  Set ~ to: 5 TORCH
  sign: 3 LEO 5 EMBER SMOKE
  Spew ~ and brimstone: 4 RANT
  Started a ~ again: 5 RELIT
  starter: 5 SPARK 6 TINDER
  Trial by: 6 ORDEAL
  truck item: 3 AXE 4 HOSE
    6 LADDER
  up: 6 AROUSE ENRAGE
    FOMENT 7 INSPIRE
  Went out, as a: 4 DIED
  work: 5 ARSON
  ~, in French: 3 FEU
  ~, in Spanish: 5 FUEGO
**"Fire!"**
  preceder: 3 AIM
**Fire ___:** 3 ANT 4 OPAL
**"___ Fire" (Springsteen hit):**
  4 IMON
**Firearm:** 6 WEAPON
  filler: 4 AMMO
**Fireballer**
  ~ Nolan: 4 RYAN
  ~ Ryan: 5 NOLAN
**Firebird:** 6 ORIOLE
**Firebox**
  feature: 5 ALARM
**Fire-breathing**
  beast: 6 DRAGON 7 CHIMERA
**Firebug**
  crime: 5 ARSON
**Firecracker**
  Fizzled: 3 DUD
  Kind of: 6 PETARD
    10 CHERRYBOMB
**Fired**
  on: 6 SHOTAT
  Singer ~ on live TV: 6 LAROSA
  up: 4 AVID 5 EAGER
    6 AFLAME
**"___ fired!":** 5 YOURE
**Firedog:** 7 ANDIRON
**Firedome:** 6 DESOTO
**Firefighter:** 5 HOSER
    7 RESCUER
  fixture: 7 HYDRANT
  need: 4 HOSE
  protection: 7 GASMASK
  tool: 3 AXE 7 BROADAX
  ~ Red: 5 ADAIR
**Firehouse**
  Used a ~ pole: 4 SLID
**Firenze**
  **Info:** Italian cue
  farewell: 4 CIAO

friends: 5 AMICI
  land: 6 ITALIA
**Fireplace:** 5 INGLE
  accessory: 7 ANDIRON
  adjunct: 6 MANTEL
  fill: 4 LOGS
  floor: 6 HEARTH
  frame: 5 GRATE 6 MANTEL
  glower: 5 EMBER
  Like a: 4 ASHY
  projection: 3 HOB
  receptacle: 6 ASHPIT
  residue: 3 ASH 5 ASHES
  shelf: 3 HOB 6 MANTEL
  tool: 5 POKER
**Firepower**
  Exceed in: 6 OUTGUN
**Fireproof**
  material: 8 ASBESTOS
**Fireside:** 6 HEARTH
  chat medium: 5 RADIO
**Firewood**
  measure: 4 CORD 5 STERE
**Firework**
  Revolving: 8 PINWHEEL
**Fireworks**
  Big name in: 6 GRUCCI
  cries: 3 AHS 4 OOHS
**Firing**
  It does a lot of: 6 NEURON
  place: 4 KILN 5 RANGE
  squad (abbr.): 3 NRA
  Unlawful: 5 ARSON
**Firm:** 3 SET 5 SOLID
    7 ALDENTE STAUNCH
  and fresh: 5 CRISP
  Be: 6 INSIST
  head: 4 EXEC PRES
  Just ~ enough: 7 ALDENTE
  Law ~ employee: 4 PARA
  Stand: 6 INSIST RESIST
  Stood: 4 HELD
  up: 3 GEL
**___ firma:** 5 TERRA
**Firmament:** 3 SKY
**Firmer-upper**
  Facial: 5 TONER
**Firm-fleshed**
  pear: 5 ANJOU
**Firmly**
  Declare: 4 AVER
  Fix: 4 MOOR 5 EMBED IMBED
    RIVET 8 ENSCONCE
  Hold: 4 GRIP
  Imprint: 4 ETCH
  Plant: 5 EMBED
  State: 4 AVER
  Stick: 6 ADHERE
**Firms**
  (abbr.): 3 COS
**First:** 4 BASE GEAR 6 PRIMAL
    7 INITIAL ORDINAL
  and second: 8 ORDINALS
  appearance: 5 DEBUT ONSET
  At: 6 ONBASE
  At ~ (abbr.): 4 ORIG

born: 4 CAIN 6 ELDEST
  OLDEST
cardinal: 3 ONE
claim: 4 DIBS
coat: 6 PRIMER
Come in: 3 WIN
course: 4 SOUP 5 PLANA
  SALAD
Finish: 3 WIN
follower: 3 AID
game: 6 OPENER
garden: 4 EDEN
Go: 5 START
home: 4 EDEN
in a series: 5 ALPHA
In ~ place: 5 AHEAD
  ONTOP
It's a: 8 PREMIERE
light: 4 DAWN
Make the ~ bid: 4 OPEN
man: 4 ADAM
man, to Polynesians: 4 TIKI
mate: 3 EVE 4 ADAM
miracle site: 4 CANA
of all: 4 ADAM
of December: 3 DEE
of September: 3 ESS
person, in German: 3 ICH
place: 4 EDEN
Play: 4 LEAD
Played: 3 LED
Ran: 3 LED
Show for the ~ time:
  6 UNVEIL
sign: 5 ARIES
state (abbr.): 3 DEL
strategy: 5 PLANA
to be called: 4 ONEA
to be counted: 4 EENY
Took: 3 WON
to putt: 4 AWAY
victim: 4 ABEL
video game: 4 PONG
Went: 3 LED 6 LEDOFF
X: 3 TIC
~, in German: 4 ERST
First ___: 3 AID 4 BASE GEAR
"First ___, The": 4 NOEL
First-aid
  item: 6 IODINE
  provider: 5 MEDIC
First Amendment
  defenders: 4 ACLU
"First Blood"
  director Kotcheff: 3 TED
  hero: 5 RAMBO
Firstborn: 6 ELDEST OLDEST
  Genesis: 4 CAIN
  Ingrid's: 3 PIA
  Isaac's: 4 ESAU
First-century
  emperor: 4 NERO
First-class: 3 ACE 4 AONE
  5 ELITE PRIMO
  6 GRADEA
  Not: 5 COACH

First Daughter
  1970s ~: 3 AMY
  1990s ~: 7 CHELSEA
First Dog
  ~, once: 4 FALA
First-draft: 8 UNEDITED
First-grade
  attention-getter: 4 MEME
First Lady: 3 EVE
  1940s ~: 4 BESS 7 ELEANOR
  1950s ~: 5 MAMIE
  after Hillary: 5 LAURA
  before Eleanor: 3 LOU
  before Mamie: 4 BESS
  First: 6 MARTHA
  in 1900: 3 IDA
  of Harry: 4 BESS
  of jazz: 4 ELLA
  Second: 7 ABIGAIL
"First Lady of Song": 4 ELLA
First name
  at Gettysburg: 3 ABE
  at the Fed: 4 ALAN
  at Woodstock: 4 ARLO JIMI
  Dickensian: 5 URIAH
  Dog star's: 3 RIN
  in 1950s TV: 4 DESI
  in 1970s tennis: 4 ILIE
  in 1970s TV comedy: 4 REDD
  in 2000 news: 5 ELIAN
  in advice: 3 ANN
  in animation: 4 WALT
  in architecture: 4 EERO
  5 ELIEL
  in aviation: 6 AMELIA
  in bridge: 4 OMAR
  in clowns: 6 RONALD
  in coaching: 3 ARA
  in comedy: 3 EMO
  in Communism: 4 KARL
  in conducting: 6 ARTURO
  in cooking: 6 EMERIL
  in cosmetics: 5 ESTEE MERLE
  in country: 4 REBA
  in courtroom fiction: 4 ERLE
  in crooning: 4 BING
  in dance: 7 ISADORA
  in daredeviltry: 4 EVEL
  in daytime TV: 5 OPRAH
  in despotism: 3 IDI
  in diaries: 5 ANAIS
  in espionage: 4 MATA
  in exiles: 3 IDI
  in exploration: 7 AMERIGO
  in fashion: 3 LIZ 4 COCO
  OLEG YVES
  in game shows: 4 ALEX MERV
  5 REGIS
  in gins: 3 ELI
  in gospel: 7 MAHALIA
  in gossip: 4 RONA
  in gymnastics: 4 OLGA
  5 NADIA
  in horror: 3 LON WES 4 BELA
  BRAM 6 FREDDY
  in humor: 4 ERMA

in jazz: 4 ELLA
in jeans: 4 LEVI
in late-night TV: 5 CONAN
in lexicography: 4 NOAH
in linguistics: 4 NOAM
in modern dance: 5 TWYLA
in mysteries: 4 ERLE
  6 AGATHA
in one-liners: 5 HENNY
in photography: 5 ANSEL
in puppetry: 5 SHARI
in rock: 5 ELTON
in scat: 4 ELLA
in shoes: 6 IMELDA
in Solidarity: 4 LECH
in soul: 6 ARETHA
in spydom: 4 MATA
in stunts: 4 EVEL
in swashbuckling: 5 ERROL
in swing: 5 ARTIE
in talk: 5 CONAN ELLEN
  OPRAH REGIS ROSIE
  6 MONTEL
in tyranny: 3 IDI
in westerns: 5 CLINT
in whodunits: 4 ERLE
of Fergie: 5 SARAH
Whale: 4 MOBY
___ first-name basis: 3 ONA
First-place: 4 BEST GOLD
First-rate: 3 ACE DEF TIP TOP
  4 ACES AONE BEST
  NEAT TOPS 5 PRIME
  PRIMO 6 CHOICE
  CLASSA TIPTOP
  7 STELLAR
First-stringer: 7 STARTER
First-stringers: 5 ATEAM
"First Time Ever ___ Your Face,
  The": 4 ISAW
"First Wives' Club, The"
  actress: 4 HAWN
  members: 4 EXES
First word
  Baby's: 4 DADA
  Giant's: 3 FEE
  in a fairy tale: 4 ONCE
  in Massachusetts' motto:
  4 ENSE
First-year
  cadet: 5 PLEBE
  law student: 4 ONEL
  student: 5 FROSH
"___ first you don't ...": 4 IFAT
Firth of Clyde
  island: 5 ARRAN
  port: 3 AYR
Firth of Tay
  port: 6 DUNDEE
Fiscal
  exec: 3 CFO
  Fed. ~ agency: 3 OMB
  period: 4 YEAR
Fischer
  forte: 5 CHESS
  opponent: 7 SPASSKY

Hissy: 4 SNIT
in: 6 BELONG
It's ~ for a queen: 5 TIARA
It's ~ to be tied: 8 SNEAKERS
Kind of: 5 HISSY
Make: 5 ADAPT ALTER
   6 TAILOR
Not: 5 UNAPT
of agitation: 4 SNIT
of fever: 4 AGUE
of pique: 4 SNIT
of wrath: 4 RAGE
one inside another: 4 NEST
out: 3 RIG 5 EQUIP
Shivering: 4 AGUE
Snit: 5 ANGER
Test for: 5 TRYON
Think: 5 DEIGN
Throw a: 4 RAGE
to be tied: 3 MAD 5 IRATE
   LIVID RILED 7 INARAGE
   STEAMED
to be tried: 4 SANE
together: 4 MESH NEST
Trim to: 4 EDIT
up against: 6 BUTTTO
well: 4 MESH
within: 6 NESTED
___ fit: 4 HADA
Fit ___ fiddle: 3 ASA
Fitness: 6 HEALTH
  center: 3 SPA
  Muscular: 4 TONE
Fitting: 3 APT DUE 4 MEET
   5 RIGHT TRYON
   7 APROPOS
As is: 4 DULY
End of a ~ phrase: 4 ATEE
In a ~ manner: 5 APTLY
Not: 5 INAPT UNAPT
Fit to ___: 4 ATEE
Fitzgerald
  Singer: 4 ELLA
  specialty: 4 SCAT
Fitzgerald, F. Scott
  Wife of: 5 ZELDA
Five
  centimes: 3 SOU
  cents a minute, say: 4 RATE
  Change for a: 4 ONES
  Cleveland: 4 CAVS
  Group of: 6 PENTAD
  Having ~ sharps: 3 INB
  High: 4 SLAP
  hundred sheets: 4 REAM
  in front: 5 PENTA
  iron: 6 MASHIE
  It follows four but not: 4 TEEN
  New Jersey: 4 NETS
  One of: 5 QUINT SENSE
  prefix: 5 PENTA
  Take: 4 REST 5 RELAX
  word form: 5 PENTA
  ~, in French: 4 CINQ
Five-alarm
  item: 5 CHILI

Five-alarmer: 5 BLAZE
Five-dollar
  bill: 3 FIN
"Five Guys Named ___": 3 MOE
Five-line
  verse: 8 LIMERICK
Five Nations
  tribe: 6 ONEIDA SENECA
Five o'clock shadow:
   7 STUBBLE
  remover: 5 RAZOR
Fiver: 3 FIN
  Face on a: 3 ABE
Fivescore
  yrs.: 3 CEN
Five-spot: 3 FIN
Five-star
  name: 4 OMAR
Five-time
  Derby winner: 6 ARCARO
   7 HARTACK
  Wimbledon champ: 4 BORG
Five W's
  One of the: 3 WHO WHY
   4 WHAT WHEN 5 WHERE
Fix: 3 JAM PUT RIG SET
   4 CURE DARN MEND
   MESS REDO SPAY
   5 ALTER AMEND DEBUG
   EMBED EMEND
   6 DEFINE REMEDY
   REPAIR SCRAPE
  a loose lace: 5 RETIE
  a road: 5 RETAR
  a seam: 3 SEW
  a squeak: 3 OIL
  deeply: 5 EMBED 7 INGRAIN
  feathers: 5 PREEN
  firmly: 4 MOOR 5 EMBED
   RIVET 8 ENSCONCE
  illegally: 3 RIG
  program problems: 5 DEBUG
  Start to: 3 PRE
  Temporary: 7 STOPGAP
  text: 4 EDIT
  the fairway: 5 RESOD
  the soundtrack: 5 REDUB
  They ~ locks: 6 SALONS
  up: 4 MEND REDO 5 REHAB
  ~, as a fight: 3 RIG
Fixate: 6 OBSESS
___ fixe: 4 IDEE PRIX
Fixed: 3 SET 5 RIGID 6 INTENT
   REDONE
  by an ed.: 4 CORR
  charge: 3 FEE 4 RATE
  chicken: 5 CAPON
  look: 4 GAZE 5 STARE
  Not: 7 MOVABLE
   8 MOVEABLE
  quantity: 4 UNIT
  They may be: 6 ASSETS
  up: 6 REDONE
Fixer
  Boxer: 3 VET
  Flat: 5 SUPER

Piano: 5 TUNER
Fixer-upper: 8 REPAIRER
Fizz
  Add ~ to: 6 AERATE
  ingredient: 7 SLOEGIN
  producer: 4 SODA
Fizzle
  out: 3 DIE
  sound: 3 SSS
Fizzler: 3 DUD
Fizzless: 4 FLAT
Fizzling-out
  sound: 4 PFFT
Fizzy
  drink: 4 COLA SODA
  Make: 6 AERATE
  No longer: 4 FLAT
  prefix: 3 AER
Fjord: 5 INLET
  Capital on a: 4 OSLO
  kin: 3 RIA
  land (abbr.): 4 ICEL
Fla.
  It borders: 3 ALA ATL
  Living in ~, maybe: 4 RETD
Flabbergast: 3 AWE 4 DAZE
  STUN 5 AMAZE FLOOR
  SHOCK 7 ASTOUND
Flabby
  Not: 5 TONED
Flaccid: 4 LIMP
  flesh: 4 FLAB
Flack
  forte: 4 SPIN
Flag: 3 SAG 4 FADE IRIS TIRE
  WANE 6 COLORS
  British: 9 UNIONJACK
  Common ~ feature: 4 STAR
  Country with a blue, black, and
   white: 7 ESTONIA
  down: 4 HAIL
  holder: 4 POLE
  Open a: 6 UNFURL
  Red: 5 ALERT
  Roll up a: 4 FURL
  tosser: 3 REF
  Verbal white: 5 UNCLE
  waver: 4 WIND
  White ~ message: 5 TRUCE
Flagmaker
  Betsy: 4 ROSS
Flagon
  filler: 3 ALE
Flagrant: 5 GROSS
Flagstaff
  sch.: 3 NAU
  setting: 7 ARIZONA
Flagston, Mrs.
  of the comics: 4 LOIS
Flaherty
  man: 4 ARAN
Flair: 4 BENT ELAN 5 ECLAT
  KNACK STYLE 6 PIZAZZ
  TALENT
  Musical: 3 EAR
  of wrestling: 3 RIC

**Flake:** 4 CHIP KOOK PEEL
   5 WACKO 6 WEIRDO
   10 SPACECADET
Feedbag: 3 OAT
  material: 4 BRAN
**Flakes**
Falling: 4 SNOW
Fireplace: 5 ASHES
**Flaky**
dessert: 3 PIE
mineral: 4 MICA
pastry: 4 FILO
**Flamboyance:** 4 ELAN
   7 PANACHE
**Flamboyant**
pianist: 8 LIBERACE
~ Flynn: 5 ERROL
**Flame**
Burn without: 7 SMOLDER
follower: 4 MOTH
Rick's: 4 ILSA
**Flamenco**
cheer: 3 OLE
clicker: 8 CASTANET
**Flames**
In: 5 AFIRE 6 ABLAZE
Old: 4 EXES
Stand in the: 4 PYRE
**Flamethrower**
fuel: 6 NAPALM
**Flaming:** 5 AFIRE
felony: 5 ARSON
**Flamingo**
color: 4 PINK
**Flammable**
garment: 3 BRA
gas: 6 ETHANE ETHENE
jelly: 6 STERNO
**Flanders**
fields flower: 5 POPPY
of fiction: 4 MOLL
river: 4 YSER
"___ Flanders": 4 MOLL
**Flanders, Rod**
Dad of: 3 NED
**Flange:** 3 RIM
**Flanged**
girder: 5 IBEAM
**Flank**
alternative: 5 TBONE
**Flannel**
makeup: 4 WOOL
**Flap:** 3 ADO TAB 4 BEAT SNIT
   SPAT STIR TODO
Cap: 6 EARLAP
Home with a ~ door: 5 TEPEE
Jacket: 5 LAPEL
Public: 5 SCENE
**Flapjack:** 7 PANCAKE
Fancy: 5 CREPE
flipper: 7 SPATULA
franchise: 4 IHOP
**Flapper**
Cartoon: 4 BOOP
hairdo: 3 BOB
wrapper: 3 BOA

**Flare:** 5 FUSEE
Dress with a: 5 ALINE
Kind of: 5 SOLAR
**Flareup**
of crime: 5 ARSON
**Flash:** 3 SEC 4 IDEA JIFF
   7 INSTANT
in the can: 6 GORDON
light: 6 STROBE
Mental: 4 IDEA
of brilliance: 4 IDEA
of light: 5 GLEAM GLINT
point: 6 CAMERA
Radar screen: 4 BLIP
___ flash: 3 INA
**Flashback**
causer: 3 LSD
**"Flashdance"**
singer Irene: 4 CARA
song: 6 MANIAC
star Jennifer: 5 BEALS
**Flashed**
sign: 3 VEE
**Flasher**
Disco: 6 STROBE
on the Strip: 4 NEON
**Flashing**
lights: 6 ALERTS 7 STROBES
**Flashlight**
British: 5 TORCH
carrier: 5 USHER
**Flashy:** 5 GAUDY 6 SPORTY
car accessories: 4 MAGS
display: 10 RAZZMATAZZ
flower: 5 PEONY
outfit: 8 ZOOTSUIT
**Flask**
Drink from a: 4 SWIG
filler: 5 BOOZE
Vacuum ~ inventor: 5 DEWAR
___ flask: 5 DEWAR
**Flat:** 4 EVEN TWOD 5 LEVEL
   PRONE 6 PLANAR
   7 INSIPID
agreement: 5 LEASE
B ~: 6 ASHARP
Bee: 4 HIVE
cleaner: 4 CHAR
D ~: 6 CSHARP
dweller: 6 LESSEE
fee: 4 RENT
fish: 3 RAY 4 SOLE
fixer: 5 PATCH SUPER
floater: 4 RAFT
Go: 3 LIE
hat: 3 TAM 5 BERET
Having one: 3 INF
High ~ area: 4 MESA
in ads: 3 APT
key material: 5 EBONY
Knock: 4 DECK
land: 7 PRAIRIE
Leave: 6 DESERT
Lying: 5 PRONE
Neither sharp nor: 5 ONKEY
on one's back: 6 SUPINE

payment: 4 RENT
rate: 4 RENT
replacement: 5 SPARE
sharer: 6 ROOMIE
sign: 5 TOLET
sound: 3 SSS 4 SSSS
spot: 4 MESA
surface: 5 PLANE
They pay a ~ rate: 6 RENTER
Where the world is: 3 MAP
Word after: 4 RATE
**Flatboat:** 4 SCOW
Old: 3 ARK
**Flat-bottomed**
boat: 4 DORY SCOW 5 BARGE
**Flatbush**
Duke of: 6 SNIDER
**Flatfish:** 4 SOLE 6 PLAICE
**Flat-fixing**
tool: 8 TIREIRON
**Flatfoot:** 3 COP
lack: 4 ARCH
**Flatow**
Host: 3 IRA
**Flat ___ pancake:** 3 ASA
**Flats**
Key with no ~ or sharps:
   6 AMINOR
Level: 4 RASE
**Flatt**
Bluegrass musician: 6 LESTER
**Flat-tasting:** 5 BLAND
**Flatten:** 4 DECK IRON KAYO
   MASH RAZE 5 PRESS
   6 LAYLOW
~, in Britain: 4 RASE
**Flattened:** 6 OBLATE
circle: 4 OVAL
**Flattener**
Fly: 7 SWATTER
**Flattens:** 3 KOS
**Flatter:** 7 IMITATE
servilely: 7 ADULATE
**Flattering:** 6 SMARMY
deception: 7 SNOWJOB
**Flattery**
False: 5 SMARM
**Flattop:** 7 CARRIER
letters: 3 USS
**Flat-topped**
hill: 4 MESA 5 BUTTE
**Flaubert**
birthplace: 5 ROUEN
character: 6 BOVARY
heroine: 4 EMMA
**Flaunt:** 6 PARADE
**Flavius**
Foot, to: 3 PES
**Flavor:** 5 SAPOR TASTE
Absinthe: 5 ANISE
Amaretto: 6 ALMOND
Brandy: 4 PEAR 7 APRICOT
Coffee: 5 MOCHA
Distinctive: 4 TANG
Dressing: 5 RANCH
enhancer: 3 MSG 4 SALT

Fudge: 5 MAPLE
Gin: 4 SLOE
Half a: 5 TUTTI
Ice cream: 4 OREO 5 PECAN
Jelly: 5 GUAVA
Jelly bean: 8 LICORICE
Nectar: 4 PEAR
Nehi: 5 GRAPE
Pernod: 5 ANISE
Pop: 4 COLA
Popsicle: 6 ORANGE
Potato chip: 3 BBQ
Sharp: 3 NIP 4 TANG
Soda: 4 COLA 5 GRAPE
Syrup: 5 MAPLE
Tangy pie: 5 LEMON
Tropical: 5 MANGO
**Flavorer**
Amaretto: 6 ALMOND
Crème: 6 MENTHE
Liqueur: 5 ANISE 7 ANISEED
**Flavorful:** 5 SAPID TANGY
     TASTY
**Flavoring**
Bagel: 6 SESAME
Biscotto: 5 ANISE
Brandy: 7 APRICOT
Cat food: 4 TUNA
Chef's: 4 HERB
Coffee: 5 MOCHA
Cordial: 5 ANISE
Cream soda: 7 VANILLA
French cordial: 4 ANIS
Gimlet: 4 LIME
Gin: 4 SLOE
Julep: 4 MINT
Licorice: 5 ANISE
Ouzo: 5 ANISE 7 ANISEED
Soup: 4 DILL MISO
**Flaw:** 4 WART 6 DEFECT
Diamond: 5 ERROR
Face: 3 ZIT
Fairway: 5 DIVOT
Faucet: 4 DRIP LEAK
Fender: 4 DENT
Fruit: 6 BRUISE
Logical: 4 HOLE
LP: 4 SKIP
Surfboard: 4 DING
Upholstery: 3 RIP
Without a: 5 IDEAL
**Flawed**
~, as mdse.: 3 IRR
**Flaws**
Like some: 6 TRAGIC
**Flax**
fabric: 5 LINEN
Soak: 3 RET
**Flaxlike**
fiber: 5 RAMIE
**Flea:** 4 PEST
**Fleabag**
Like a: 5 SEEDY
**Flea market**
find: 5 CURIO
warning: 4 ASIS

**Fleck:** 4 SPOT
Banjoist: 4 BELA
**Fled:** 3 RAN
**Fledgling:** 4 TYRO
Barn: 5 OWLET
pigeon: 5 SQUAB
**Flee:** 3 LAM
to wed: 5 ELOPE
Unable to: 5 ATBAY
**Fleece:** 3 CON ROB 4 BILK
        CLIP MILK ROOK SCAM
        SKIN 5 SHEAR
Fine: 5 LLAMA
Made from: 6 WOOLEN
ship: 4 ARGO
**Fleeced:** 5 SHORN
They get: 4 EWES
**Fleecy**
babe: 4 LAMB
female: 3 EWE
**Fleeing:** 8 ONTHELAM
**Fleet:** 4 FAST NAVY 5 RAPID
        6 ARMADA SPEEDY
Far from: 4 POKY
fleet: 4 SSTS
letters: 3 USS
member: 4 TAXI
One of a 15th-century: 4 NINA
Street: 4 CABS
WWII: 3 RAF
~ VIP: 3 ADM
**FleetCenter**
player: 4 CELT
**Fleeting**
fashion: 3 FAD
trace: 4 WISP
**Fleetwood ___:** 3 MAC
**Fleetwoods, The:** 4 TRIO
1959 #1 hit for ~: 6 MRBLUE
**Flegenheimer, Arthur**
Gangster: 12 DUTCHSCHULTZ
**Fleischer**
Boxing historian: 3 NAT
Bush spokesman: 3 ARI
**Fleming**
Actress: 6 RHONDA
Author: 3 IAN
Soprano: 5 RENEE
villain: 4 DRNO
**Flesh**
and blood: 3 KIN
Flaccid: 4 FLAB
In the: 4 LIVE
Pound of: 4 DEBT
**Fleshy**
fruit: 4 PEAR POME 5 PAPAW
mushroom: 3 CEP
part: 4 JOWL
**Fleshy-leafed**
plant: 4 ALOE
**Fleshy-snouted**
beast: 5 TAPIR
**Fletcher**
product: 5 ARROW
**Fleur-___:** 5 DELYS
**Fleur-de-___:** 3 LIS LYS

**Flew:** 4 SPED TORE 7 AVIATED
alone: 6 SOLOED
**Flex:** 4 BEND
suffix: 4 IBLE
**Flexed**
It may be: 6 BICEPS
**Flexibility:** 4 GIVE PLAY
Show: 4 BEND 5 ADAPT
**Flexible:** 5 AGILE LITHE
        6 LIMBER PLIANT
        7 ELASTIC
armor: 9 CHAINMAIL
Electrically: 4 ACDC
fish: 3 EEL
mineral: 4 MICA
Most: 7 LOOSEST
response: 6 EITHER
schedule part: 8 OPENDATE
wood: 3 YEW
**Flexible Flyer:** 4 SLED
**Flick:** 3 PIC 5 MOVIE
Hot: 3 ASH
Local ~ shower: 4 NABE
Mix: 5 OATER
**Flicks:** 3 PIX
Like horror: 4 GORY
**"___ fliegende Holländer":**
        3 DER
**Flier**
Andean: 6 CONDOR
Bar: 4 DART
Coastal: 3 ERN 4 ERNE
Coop: 7 ESCAPEE
Fabled: 3 ROC
Fast: 3 JET SST
Fork-tailed: 4 TERN
Frequent: 4 BIRD
Grounded: 3 SST
Hawaiian: 4 NENE
Ill-fated: 6 ICARUS
Israeli: 4 ELAL
Mythical: 3 ROC
Night: 3 OWL 4 MOTH
Pesky: 4 GNAT
seat choice: 5 AISLE
Swedish: 3 SAS
Tabloid: 3 UFO
Tailed: 4 KITE
**Fliers**
Brit.: 3 RAF
Formation: 5 GEESE
Mil.: 4 USAF
WWII: 3 RAF
**Flies:** 5 PESTS
Chase: 4 SHAG
Dangerous: 7 TSETSES
in the face of: 6 DEFIES
Small: 5 GNATS
without a motor: 6 GLIDES
**"Flies, The"**
playwright: 6 SARTRE
**Flight:** 3 LAM 4 WING
board abbr.: 3 ARR ETA
component: 5 STAIR
Connecting: 9 STAIRCASE
coordinators (abbr.): 3 ATC

data: 4 ETAS
Designed for: 4 AERO
Expensive: 3 SST
formation: 3 VEE
from justice: 3 LAM
Hasty: 3 LAM
Incoming ~ info: 3 ETA
Night: 6 REDEYE
part: 4 STEP 5 RISER STAIR
Post in a: 5 NEWEL
Short: 3 HOP
stat.: 3 ALT
student's test: 4 SOLO
Take: 4 SOAR
Take ~ to unite: 5 ELOPE
**Flight-board**
abbr.: 3 ARR
**Flightless**
bird: 3 EMU 4 KIWI RHEA
bird (var.): 4 EMEU
Extinct ~ bird: 3 MOA
**Flights**
First name in: 6 AMELIA
Like many JFK: 4 INTL
Like some: 6 SPIRAL
7 NONSTOP
**Flighty**
Far from: 5 STAID
**Flimflam**: 3 CON GYP 4 FOOL
SCAM 5 BUNCO
6 CONJOB EUCHRE
FAKERY
**"Flim ___ Man, The": 4 FLAM**
**Flimsy**
~, as an excuse: 4 LAME
**Flinch**: 5 REACT START
WINCE
**Fling**: 4 CAST HURL TOSS
5 SPREE
with effort: 5 HEAVE
**Flintstone**
Mr.: 4 FRED
Mrs.: 5 WILMA
yell part: 5 DABBA YABBA
**"Flintstones, The"**
boss: 5 SLATE
pet: 4 DINO
setting: 8 STONEAGE
wife: 5 WILMA
**Flip**: 4 PERT TOSS 5 EVERT
GOAPE SASSY UPEND
6 INVERT LOSEIT
RESELL 7 REVERSE
and bob: 3 DOS
Coin: 4 TOSS
out: 4 SNAP 5 GOAPE
6 LOSEIT 8 HAVEACOW
over: 5 ADORE UPEND
6 INVERT
response: 5 HEADS TAILS
7 SOSUEME
Something to: 3 LID
through: 4 SCAN
**Flip ___ : 5 ACOIN**
**Flip-chart**
stand: 5 EASEL

**Flip-flop**: 5 THONG UTURN
6 SANDAL
Wearing a: 4 SHOD
**Flippant**: 4 PERT 5 SASSY
SAUCY
**Flipped**: 7 WENTAPE
Heads: 5 TAILS
It may be: 3 LID
**Flipper**: 3 FIN 7 ACROBAT
SPATULA 8 FORELIMB
**Flippered**
animal: 4 SEAL 7 SEALION
**Flirt**: 5 TEASE
badly: 4 OGLE
signal: 4 WINK
**Flirtatious**
overture: 4 PASS
signal: 4 WINK
sort: 4 MINX
stare: 4 OGLE
**Flit**: 3 GAD
**___ Flite (bicycle brand):**
4 AERO
**Flo**
TV boss of: 3 MEL
**Float**: 3 BOB 4 BUOY RAFT
WAFT
base: 4 COLA
ingredient: 8 ICECREAM
ROOTBEER
material: 5 BALSA
**Float ___ (finance): 5 ALOAN**
**Floater**
Arctic: 4 BERG
Flat: 4 RAFT
Genesis: 3 ARK
Pond: 4 ALGA
**Floating**: 4 ASEA 6 NATANT
Go for ~ apples: 3 BOB
zoo: 3 ARK
**"Float like a butterfly"**
boxer: 3 ALI
**Flock**: 4 BEVY 5 COVEY
DROVE
female: 3 EWE
Flightless: 4 EMUS
head (abbr.): 3 REV
holder: 3 PEW
leader: 3 RAM 6 PASTOR
PRIEST
Leave the: 5 STRAY
member: 3 EWE RAM
Of the: 4 LAIC
place: 3 LEA
Sea: 5 ERNES
sound: 3 BAA
**Flockhart**
Actress: 7 CALISTA
role: 6 MCBEAL
**Flog**: 4 CANE LASH WHIP
6 THRASH
**Flo-Jo**
alma mater: 4 UCLA
**Flood**: 5 SPATE 6 DELUGE
7 TORRENT
8 ACTOFGOD INUNDATE

barrier: 5 LEVEE
prevention: 3 DAM 4 DIKE
refuge: 3 ARK
survivor: 4 NOAH
**Flooded: 5 AWASH**
**Floodgate**: 3 DAM 6 SLUICE
**Flooding**
factor: 4 TIDE
**Flooey**
lead-in: 3 KER
**Floor**: 4 STUN 5 AMAZE
NADIR STORY
7 ASTOUND
8 ASTONISH
Clean a tile: 7 DAMPMOP
cleaner: 7 DUSTMOP
covering: 3 MAT RUG 4 LINO
7 AREARUG
10 SHAGCARPET
Fireplace: 6 HEARTH
Food on the: 4 ALPO
Hold the: 5 ORATE
Interrupt on the dance:
5 CUTIN
it: 4 TEAR 5 SPEED
Japanese ~ covering:
6 TATAMI
layer: 5 TILER
model: 4 DEMO
Ocean: 6 SEABED
piece: 4 TILE
Some ~ votes: 4 NAYS
square: 4 TILE
Top: 5 ATTIC
worker: 5 TILER WAXER
6 TRADER
Work on the: 6 RETILE
~, in French: 5 ETAGE
**Floorboard**
concealer: 7 AREARUG
sound: 5 CREAK
**Floored: 5 INAWE**
it: 4 SPED TORE
**Flooring**
calculation: 4 AREA
material: 3 OAK 4 TEAK
5 VINYL
Short: 4 LINO
square: 4 TILE
**Floors: 3 KOS**
Like some: 4 WAXY 5 TILED
**Floozy: 4 TART**
**Flop**: 3 DUD 4 BOMB BUST
Famed film: 6 ISHTAR
Ford: 5 EDSEL
Opposite of: 5 SMASH
prefix: 3 KER
**Floppy: 4 DISK**
Copy to a: 4 SAVE
filler: 4 DATA
**Flora**
and fauna: 4 LIFE 5 BIOTA
Desert: 5 CACTI
partner: 5 FAUNA
Unwanted: 5 WEEDS
Wrigley Field: 3 IVY

**Floral**
arrangement: 4 POSY 5 SPRAY
    7 COROLLA
fragrance: 5 ATTAR
leaf: 5 SEPAL
loop: 3 LEI
**Florence**
City near: 5 SIENA
flooder: 4 ARNO
river: 4 ARNO
ruling family: 6 MEDICI
**Florentine**
artist: 6 GIOTTO
attraction: 5 DAVID
family: 6 MEDICI
flower: 4 ARNO
poet: 5 DANTE
river: 4 ARNO
**Florid:** 3 RED 6 ORNATE
    ROCOCO
Far from: 5 ASHEN
**Florida:** 9 PENINSULA
Bush of: 3 JEB
Center of: 5 EPCOT
city: 5 OCALA TAMPA
city, for short: 4 BOCA
collegian: 5 GATOR
county: 4 DADE
explorer: 6 DESOTO
extension: 4 KEYS
footballer: 5 GATOR
football stadium:
    10 ORANGEBOWL
fruit: 6 ORANGE
island: 7 SANIBEL
islands: 4 KEYS
keys: 5 ISLES
port: 5 TAMPA
port, for short: 3 JAX
sea creature: 7 MANATEE
swinger: 4 CHAD
vacation area: 4 KEYS
~ ZIP code starter: 5 THREE
**Florida State**
player: 8 SEMINOLE
rival: 5 MIAMI
**Florist**
piece: 4 VASE
unit: 4 STEM
**Floss**
coating: 3 WAX
Kind of: 6 DENTAL
**Flossing**
advocacy gp.: 3 ADA
**Flotilla:** 6 ARMADA
**Flounder**
Future: 3 ROE
through water: 5 SLOSH
**Flour**
factory: 4 MILL
Future: 5 GRIST
Kind of: 3 RYE SOY 6 FARINA
or sugar: 6 STAPLE
Prepare: 4 SIFT
**Flourish:** 5 BLOOM 6 THRIVE
    7 BLOSSOM

Letter: 5 SERIF
Signer: 8 CURLICUE
**Flourless**
cake: 5 TORTE
**Flout:** 4 DEFY 6 DERIDE
**Flouter**
Union: 4 SCAB
**Flow:** 6 STREAM
back: 3 EBB
Forceful: 5 SPATE
Go with the: 5 ADAPT
It goes with the: 4 LAVA
out: 6 EFFUSE 7 EMANATE
Outward: 3 EBB
Partner of: 3 EBB
Rhythmic: 7 CADENCE
slowly: 4 OOZE SEEP
    7 TRICKLE
Steady: 6 STREAM
stoppage: 4 CLOT 6 STASIS
stopper: 4 CLOG
Volcanic: 4 LAVA
**Flower:** 4 POSY 5 BLOOM
    RIPEN 6 MATURE
    7 BLOSSOM
base: 5 BRACT
Bell-shaped: 4 SEGO 5 TULIP
child: 4 SEED 6 HIPPIE
Corsage: 6 ORCHID
Daisylike: 5 ASTER
Dutch: 5 TULIP
Easter: 4 LILY
Fall: 5 ASTER
feature: 5 PETAL
Flashy: 5 PEONY
Fragrant: 7 TEAROSE
    8 GARDENIA
Fresh: 5 DAISY
Friend of: 5 BAMBI
Funnel-shaped: 7 PETUNIA
Garden: 4 IRIS 5 PANSY
    TULIP 10 SNAPDRAGON
girl, perhaps: 5 NIECE
holder: 3 POT URN 4 STEM
    VASE 5 LAPEL
Imaginary eternal:
    8 AMARANTH
In full: 4 OPEN 6 ABLOOM
of one's eye: 4 IRIS
Ornamental: 6 DAHLIA
part: 4 STEM 5 CALYX OVARY
    PETAL SEPAL 6 ANTHER
    PISTIL RACEME STAMEN
    7 COROLLA
Purple: 5 LILAC
Red: 4 ROSE
shop letters: 3 FTD
Showy: 4 IRIS LILY ROSE
    5 ASTER CALLA CANNA
    PEONY PHLOX POPPY
    6 AZALEA DAHLIA
    7 ANEMONE 8 HIBISCUS
Showy ~, for short: 4 GLAD
site: 3 BED
Spring: 4 IRIS
stalk: 4 STEM

State: *see page 724*
visitor: 3 BEE
**"Flower Drum Song"**
actor: 3 SOO
**Flowering:** 6 ABLOOM
    7 INBLOOM
shrub: 6 AZALEA SPIREA
**"Flowering Peach, The"**
playwright: 5 ODETS
**Flowerless**
plant: 4 FERN
**Flowerlike**
polyp: 7 ANEMONE
**"Flower of my heart":**
    7 ADELINE
**Flowerpot**
spot: 4 SILL 5 LEDGE
**Flowers**
Like: 7 PETALED
Oil from: 5 ATTAR
**"... flowers that bloom in the
    spring, ___":** 5 TRALA
**Flowery:** 6 ORNATE
greeting: 3 LEI
verse: 3 ODE
**"Flow gently, sweet ___":** Burns:
    5 AFTON
**Flowing**
Musically: 6 LEGATO
tresses: 5 MANES
**___ Flow, Scotland:** 5 SCAPA
**Fl. oz.**
1/6 ~: 3 TSP
Half a: 4 TBSP
**Flu**
Down with the: 3 ILL
fighter: 4 SHOT 5 SERUM
    6 HOTTEA
fighters: 4 SERA
Kind of: 5 ASIAN
Like the: 5 VIRAL
symptom: 4 ACHE AGUE
    5 FEVER
**___ flu:** 5 ASIAN
**Flub:** 3 ERR 5 ERROR MISDO
Arcade: 4 TILT
**Fluctuate:** 4 VARY YOYO
**Flue**
residue: 4 SOOT
**Fluent:** 4 GLIB
**Fluff:** 4 LINT
up: 5 TEASE WHISK
**Fluffy**
scarf: 3 BOA
trio: 4 EFFS
**Fluid**
1/8 of a ~ ounce: 4 DRAM
Antiknock: 5 ETHYL
Battery: 4 ACID
Blood: 5 SERUM
container: 3 SAC
rock: 4 LAVA
Tree: 3 SAP
**Fluidity**
unit: 3 RHE
**Fluids:** 4 SERA

**Fluke:** 8 ACCIDENT
**Flummox:** 4 FOOL 5 ADDLE
**Flummoxed:** 5 ATSEA
    7 ATALOSS
**Flung:** 5 THREW
**Flunk:** 4 FAIL
**Flunking**
  letters: 3 EFS
**Flunky:** 4 AIDE 6 STOOGE
    YESMAN
  Corporate: 5 DRONE
  Frankenstein: 4 IGOR
  reply: 3 YES
**Fluor-**
  suffix: 3 IDE 4 ESCE
**Fluorescent**
  lamp filler: 5 ARGON
  paint: 6 DAYGLO
**Fluoride**
  prefix: 5 TETRA
**Flurry:** 3 ADO
**Flush:** 4 EVEN 5 COLOR
    LEVEL 6 LOADED
    7 REDNESS TURNRED
    8 ROSINESS
**Flushed:** 3 RED 4 ROSY
  Hardly: 4 PALE
**Flushes**
  Like some: 5 ROYAL
    7 ACEHIGH
**Flushing**
  stadium: 4 ASHE
**Fluster:** 4 FAZE
**Flute**
  innovator Theobald: 5 BOEHM
  Kind of: 4 ALTO
  Small: 4 FIFE
  sound: 6 TOOTLE
**Flutie**
  Quarterback: 4 DOUG
**Flutist**
  ~ Herbie: 4 MANN
**Fluttering**
  tree: 5 ASPEN
**Flux**
  Symbol of electric: 3 PSI
  Unit of magnetic: 5 WEBER
  Unit of magnetic ~ density:
    5 TESLA
**Fly:** 4 LURE PEST SOAR TEAR
    6 AVIATE
  African: 6 TSETSE
  alone: 4 SOLO
  Attack a: 4 SWAT
  ball path: 3 ARC
  Biting: 4 GNAT
  catcher: 3 WEB 4 MITT
  Dangerous: 6 TSETSE
  flattener: 7 SWATTER
  Flew like a: 5 ARCED
  Half a: 3 TSE
  Harvest: 6 CICADA
  high: 4 SOAR
  in the face of: 4 DEFY
  in the ointment: 3 RUB 4 SNAG
  It'll never: 3 EMU

  like a butterfly: 4 FLIT
  like an eagle: 4 SOAR
    5 SWOOP
  off the handle: 4 RAGE RANT
    RAVE
  Prepare to: 4 TAXI
  Run after a: 5 TAGUP
  Sacrifice ~ stat: 3 RBI
  Small: 4 GNAT
  They ~ by night: 4 OWLS
  trap: 3 WEB
  Try for a: 4 SWAT 6 SWATAT
  Word to a: 4 SHOO
  ___ fly: 3 SAC 6 TSETSE
**"Fly away home"**
  nursery rhyme critter:
    7 LADYBUG
**Flybelt**
  pest: 6 TSETSE
**Flyboy**
  place: 7 AIRBASE
**Fly-by-night:** 6 REDEYE
  sort: 3 OWL
**Flycatcher:** 4 MITT 5 PEWEE
**Flyer**
  Coastal: 4 ERNE
  Fast: 3 SST
  Fearless: 3 ACE
  Flexible: 4 SLED
  Night: 3 OWL
  Transatlantic: 3 SST
**Flyers**
  org.: 3 NHL
  WWII Brit.: 3 RAF
**Flying:** 5 ALOFT
  fish eater: 3 ERN 4 ERNE
  formation: 3 VEE
  Go like a ~ squirrel: 5 GLIDE
  honkers: 5 GEESE
  jib: 4 SAIL
  mammal: 3 BAT
  monster: 5 RODAN
  Pass with ~ colors: 3 ACE
  pest: 4 GNAT
  prefix: 4 AERO
  solo: 5 ALONE
  start: 4 AERO
  stinger: 4 WASP
  watchdog (abbr.): 3 FAA
  ~ Pan: 5 PETER
**Flying "A"**
  rival: 4 ESSO
**Flying Cloud**
  automaker: 3 REO
**"Flying Down to ___":** 3 RIO
**"Flying Dutchman, The"**
  heroine: 5 SENTA
  huntsman: 4 ERIK
**Flying Dutchman's**
  choice: 3 KLM
**Flying Finn:** 5 PAAVO
**Flying saucer:** 3 UFO
  pilots: 3 ETS
**Flynn**
  Actor: 5 ERROL
**"___ Fly Now":** 5 GONNA

**Flyspeck:** 3 DOT 4 MOTE SPOT
**Flytrap, Venus**
  radio station: 4 WKRP
**Fo**
  Playwright: 5 DARIO
**Foal**
  father: 4 SIRE
  mother: 4 MARE
**Foam:** 4 SUDS 5 FROTH
    SPUME
  at the mouth: 4 RAGE
    6 SEETHE
  ingredient: 8 URETHANE
  prefix: 5 STYRO
**Foaming**
  at the mouth: 5 IRATE RABID
**"Foaming cleanser":** 4 AJAX
**Foamy**
  brew: 3 ALE
**Fob:** 10 WATCHCHAIN
  locale: 4 VEST
**Focal**
  point: 3 HUB 4 NODE
    9 EPICENTER
  points: 4 LOCI
  prefix: 3 TRI
**Foch**
  Actress: 4 NINA
**Focus:** 3 AIM HUB 5 RIVET
    6 ZEROIN
  again: 5 REAIM
  Debate: 5 TOPIC
  I ~: 3 EGO
  Lose: 4 BLUR
**Focused:** 6 INTENT
**Focusing**
  agent: 4 LENS
**Fodder:** 3 HAY 6 SILAGE
  grain: 3 OAT
  holder: 4 SILO
  Store: 6 ENSILE
**Foe:** 4 ANTI 5 ENEMY RIVAL
**Fog:** 4 HAZE 7 STEAMUP
  Comment after the ~ clears:
    4 ISEE
  Dense: 7 PEASOUP
    9 PEASOUPER
  In a: 5 ATSEA DAZED
  Light: 4 MIST
  Mental: 4 DAZE
  Not in a: 5 AWARE
**Fogelberg**
  Singer: 3 DAN
**Fogg, Phileas**
  creator: 5 VERNE
  portrayer: 5 NIVEN
**"Fog of War, The"**
  director Morris: 5 ERROL
**Fogy:** 4 DODO
**Foible:** 3 TIC
**Foie ___:** 4 GRAS
**Foie gras**
  source: 5 GOOSE
**Foil:** 4 EPEE 6 STOOGE
    STYMIE THWART
    TRIPUP

alternative: 4 EPEE 5 SABER
   SARAN
Big name in: 5 ALCOA
for Bugs: 5 ELMER
for Colonel Klink: 5 HOGAN
for Garfield: 4 ODIE
kin: 4 EPEE
material: 3 TIN
prefix: 4 AERO
Tin: 4 WRAP
**Foist:** 6 IMPOSE
**Fold:** 3 PEN 4 BEND TUCK
   5 PLAIT PLEAT
   6 CREASE
Don't: 4 STAY 6 STAYIN
female: 3 EWE
Press, ~, and stretch:
   5 KNEAD
sound: 3 BAA
~, spindle, or mutilate: 3 MAR
**Folded**
food: 4 TACO 5 CREPE TACOS
   6 OMELET 7 OMELETS
   8 OMELETTE
**Folder**
feature: 3 TAB
What a ~ wouldn't say: 4 IMIN
Words from a: 5 IMOUT
work: 7 ORIGAMI
**Fold-in**
Magazine with a ~ cover:
   3 MAD
**Folding**
Its business is: 7 ORIGAMI
**Folds**
Arrange in: 5 DRAPE
**Fold-up**
bed: 3 COT
mattress: 5 FUTON
**Folgers**
rival: 5 SANKA 7 NESCAFE
**Foliage**
Bit of: 4 LEAF
**Folies-Bergère**
designer: 4 ERTE
**Foliovore:** 5 KOALA
**Folk**
1968 ~ album: 4 ARLO
Beloved: 5 DEARS
First name in: 4 ARLO JONI
history: 4 LORE
music instrument: 5 BANJO
Simple: 5 AMISH
story: 4 TALE
wisdom: 4 LORE
**Folklore**
being: 3 ORC 4 OGRE
   5 GNOME TROLL
Bridge protector of: 5 TROLL
Door opener of: 7 ALIBABA
Dream producer of: 3 MAB
fiend: 4 OGRE
Wailer of: 7 BANSHEE
**Folks:** 3 KIN 7 PARENTS
Droll: 4 WAGS
Food for regular: 4 BRAN

Funny: 5 RIOTS
**Folk singer**
Irish: 4 ENYA
One-named: 6 ODETTA
~ Burl: 4 IVES
~ DiFranco: 3 ANI
~ Guthrie: 4 ARLO
~ Joan: 4 BAEZ
~ Mitchell: 4 JONI
~ Pete: 6 SEEGER
~ Phil: 4 OCHS
~ Seeger: 4 PETE
**Folk-song**
mule: 3 SAL
**Folktales:** 4 LORE
**Folkways:** 5 MORES
**Follett**
Author: 3 KEN
**Follow:** 3 DOG GET 4 HEED
   OBEY TAIL 5 ACTON
   ENSUE TRACE TRAIL
   6 GONEXT 7 ABIDEBY
   ACTUPON EMULATE
   IMITATE SUCCEED
   8 ADHERETO
   9 COMELATER
a pattern: 3 SEW
a trail: 4 HIKE
closely: 3 APE DOG 4 HEEL
   TAIL 5 STALK 6 SHADOW
Fail to ~ suit: 6 RENEGE
   REVOKE
It may ~ a dot: 3 COM
It may ~ directions: 3 ERN
It may ~ something: 4 ELSE
It may ~ you: 3 ARE
orders: 4 OBEY
Something to: 4 SUIT
   5 ARROW
the rainbow: 3 ARC
too closely: 8 TAILGATE
**Follow ___:** 5 ALEAD
**Follower:** 3 FAN IST 4 TAIL
   8 ADHERENT
**Info:** Suffix cue
follower: 3 IST
suffix: 3 IST ITE
**Followers:** 5 SHEEP
**Following:** 3 ALA 4 NEXT SECT
   THEN 5 AFTER INTOW
   7 RETINUE
And the ~ (abbr.): 5 ETSEQ
behind: 5 INTOW
closely: 6 ATHEEL
Loyally: 6 TRUETO
orders: 8 OBEDIENT
**"Follow me!":** 4 CMON COME
**Follows**
He ~ Jay: 5 CONAN
He ~ the news: 4 LENO
It often ~ you: 3 ARE
It ~ that: 4 ERGO
**Follow-up**
(abbr.): 3 SEQ
**Folly:** 7 MADNESS
Ford: 5 EDSEL

**"___ Folly" (Alaska):**
   7 SEWARDS
**"___ folly to be wise": Gray:**
   3 TIS
**Foment:** 3 SOW
**Fond**
Become ~ of: 6 TAKETO
Be too: 4 DOTE
of: 4 INTO 5 BIGON
   6 KEENON
**Fonda**
1940 ~ role: 4 JOAD
1981 ~ film:
   12 ONGOLDENPOND
1997 ~ role: 4 ULEE
Actor: 5 PETER
Actress: 4 JANE 7 BRIDGET
**Fonda, Jane**
role: 9 CATBALLOU
~ Oscar movie: 5 KLUTE
**Fonda, Peter**
title role: 4 ULEE
**Fond du ___:** 3 LAC
**Fondle:** 3 PET
**Fondness:** 8 APPETITE
Excessive: 6 DOTAGE
Show much: 4 DOTE
**Fondue:** 3 DIP
**Fong**
Senator: 5 HIRAM
**Font**
flourish: 5 SERIF
**Fontana di ___:** 5 TREVI
**Fontanne**
of Broadway: 4 LYNN
Partner of: 4 LUNT
**Fonteyn**
garb: 4 TUTU
title: 4 DAME
**Fonz**
Richie's father, to the: 3 MRC
Richie's mother, to the: 4 MRSC
sitcom: 9 HAPPYDAYS
**Food:** 4 CHOW EATS FARE
   7 ALIMENT EDIBLES
   VICTUAL
additive: 3 DYE MSG
All-natural ~ no-no: 3 BHT
and drink: 6 REPAST
and shelter: 5 NEEDS
Baby: 3 PAP 5 PUREE
bar: 4 OLEO 5 SALAD
Bird: 4 SEED SUET
Breakfast: 6 CEREAL
Bring the: 5 CATER
Deprive of: 6 STARVE
Divine: 5 MANNA
Dog: 4 ALPO
fish: 3 COD 4 BASS CARP
   LING PIKE SHAD SOLE
   5 SMELT 7 HALIBUT
   SEABASS SNAPPER
Folded: 4 TACO 5 CREPE
   TACOS 6 OMELET
   7 OMELETS 8 OMELETTE
from heaven: 5 MANNA

Frozen ~ brand: 6 OREIDA
8 BIRDSEYE
Furnish: 5 CATER
Half a ~ fish: 4 MAHI
Health ~ flavor: 5 CAROB
High-fiber: 4 BRAN
Hog: 4 SLOP
holder: 3 TIN
in a red coat: 4 EDAM
in a shell: 4 TACO
Infant: 3 PAP
Italian: 5 PIZZA
label abbr.: 3 RDA 4 NTWT
Luau: 3 POI
Mexican: 4 TACO
morsel: 3 ORT
Mushy: 3 PAP
of the gods: 8 AMBROSIA
on the floor, maybe: 4 ALPO
Orange: 3 YAM
order: 4 TOGO
Pig: 4 SLOP
plan: 4 DIET
poisoning: 8 PTOMAINE
preparer: 4 COOK
Provide: 5 CATER
Put through a ~ press: 4 RICE
pyramid org.: 4 USDA
scrap: 3 ORT
Search for: 6 FORAGE
seeker: 7 FORAGER
Shell: 4 TACO
shop: 4 DELI
Soft: 3 PAP
Squirrel: 3 NUT 5 ACORN
stabilizer: 4 AGAR
stamp: 4 USDA
stat.: 3 RDA
sticker: 4 TINE
storage material: 5 SARAN
supply: 6 LARDER
Supply the: 5 CATER
thickener: 4 AGAR
Twice-chewed: 3 CUD
Word with: 6 ETHNIC
**"Food Glorious Food"**
musical: 6 OLIVER
**Foodie:** 5 EATER
**Food Network**
chef: 6 EMERIL
**Foofaraw:** 3 ADO 4 TODO
5 HOOHA
**Fool:** 3 ASS CON KID SAP
4 BOOB BOZO DOPE
DUPE SIMP 5 BOOBY
CLOWN GOOSE IDIOT
MORON NINNY
6 DELUDE
(around): 5 HORSE
follower: 3 ISH
Old: 4 COOT
Pompous: 3 ASS
**"___ Fool Believes" (1979 hit):**
5 WHATA
**Fooled:** 3 GOT HAD
Not ~ by: 4 ONTO 6 WISETO

on the ice: 5 DEKED
**Fooler**
Fish: 4 BAIT
**Foolhardy:** 4 RASH 5 BRASH
HASTY 6 UNWISE
**Foolish:** 4 DAFT GAGA
5 GOOSY INANE LOONY
SAPPY 6 UNWISE
7 WITLESS
behavior: 6 IDIOCY
fellow: 4 COOT SIMP TWIT
It might be: 4 GRIN
month: 5 APRIL
**"___ Foolish Things":** 5 THESE
**"Fool Such ___, A":** 3 ASI
**"___ Fool to Care":** 5 IWASA
**"___ Fool to Want You":** 3 IMA
**Foot:** 4 IAMB
Anatomical: 3 PES
Big: 3 EEE
bones: 5 TARSI
Crush with the: 7 STAMPON
fault: 4 CORN
Feline: 3 PAW
fraction: 4 INCH
Furry: 3 PAW
Hand or: 4 UNIT
It's about a: 4 SHOE
It's just over a: 5 ANKLE
It's under: 4 SOLE
Latin: 3 PES
Left ~ of Orion: 5 RIGEL
Measured on: 5 PACED
Metric: 4 IAMB
Move a: 4 STEP
part: 3 TOE 4 ARCH BALL
HEEL INCH SOLE
6 INSTEP
Poetic: 4 IAMB
prefix: 4 PEDI
Put one's ~ down: 4 STEP
TROD 5 STOMP TREAD
Wait on hand and: 7 CATERTO
Wide ~ spec: 3 EEE
word form: 4 PEDE PEDI
PEDO
**Footage**
Square: 4 AREA
**Football**
blitz: 6 REDDOG
center: 3 AIR
conference: 6 HUDDLE
feint: 4 JUKE
filler: 3 AIR
formation: 7 SHOTGUN
gains: 5 YARDS
gains (abbr.): 3 YDS
gear: 4 PADS
holder: 3 TEE
Kind of: 5 ARENA
Kind of ~ kick: 6 ONSIDE
lineman: 3 END
official: 3 REF
part: 4 LACE
play: 4 PASS TRAP
7 LATERAL REVERSE

position: 3 END 7 LINEMAN
positions (abbr.): 3 RTS
scores (abbr.): 3 TDS
shorthand: 7 XSANDOS
shutout line score: 4 OOOO
squad: 6 ELEVEN
stat.: 3 INT YDS
supporter: 3 TEE
team: 6 ELEVEN
**___ football:** 5 ARENA
**Football-shaped:** 4 OVAL
5 OVATE OVOID
**Footboard-headboard**
connector: 7 BEDRAIL
**Footed**
vase: 3 URN
**Footfall:** 4 STEP
Horse: 4 CLOP
**Footing**
Lose one's: 4 SLIP
**Footless**
animal: 4 APOD
**Footlike**
part: 3 PES
**"Footloose"**
singer: 7 LOGGINS
Singer of: 4 LORI
**Footnote**
abbr.: 3 VID 4 ETAL IBID
IDEM 5 ETSEQ OPCIT
datum: 4 PAGE
word: 4 IDEM 6 IBIDEM
**Footprint:** 4 CLUE STEP
5 TRACK
maker: 4 SOLE
**Footrest:** 7 OTTOMAN
Pole with: 5 STILT
**Footstool:** 7 OTTOMAN
**Footwear:** 5 PUMPS
Quaint: 5 SPATS
Summer: 7 SANDALS
Winter: 5 BOOTS
Wooden: 5 SABOT
**Fop:** 5 DANDY
prop: 4 CANE
**For:** 3 PRO
each: 3 PER 6 APIECE
every: 3 PER
everyone: 6 RATEDG
example: 3 SAY 6 SUCHAS
fear that: 4 LEST
fun: 7 ONALARK
instance: 3 SAY
now: 6 PROTEM
one: 3 PER 4 APOP EACH
6 APIECE
real: 5 LEGIT
rent: 5 TOLET
the most part: 6 MAINLY
Those: 4 AYES YEAS
**For ___**
(cheap): 5 ASONG
(suitable for everyone):
7 ALLAGES
**Forage**
holder: 4 SILO

**Forager**
Forest: 4 DEER
Tiny: 3 ANT
**"For ___ a jolly ...":** 3 HES
**"___ for All Seasons":** 4 AMAN
**Foray:** 4 RAID 6 SORTIE
**Forbear:** 7 ABSTAIN
**"For better or for ___":**
    5 WORSE
**Forbid:** 3 BAN
**Forbidden:** 5 TABOO
  fruit site: 4 EDEN
  They're: 5 NONOS
  thing: 4 NONO
  (var.): 4 TABU
**"Forbidden City, The":** 5 LHASA
**Forbidding:** 3 ICY 4 DOUR
    GRIM 5 STERN
    6 SEVERE
**Force:** 4 DINT 5 IMPEL MIGHT
    6 COERCE COMPEL
    OBLIGE
  along: 4 URGE
  (apart): 3 PRY
  back: 5 REPEL
  Bit of: 4 DYNE
  Cold war: 4 NATO
  Dark: 4 EVIL
  down: 4 TAMP
  Driving: 5 MOTOR
  Earth: 4 ONEG
  Fetch with: 3 LUG
  Fighting: 6 ARMADA
  Fling with: 4 HURL
  French: 5 ARMEE
  Full: 5 BRUNT
  Gaza: 3 PLO
  Having no: 4 NULL
  In: 5 VALID
  Kind of: 4 GALE 5 BRUTE
  Life: 3 CHI
  Main: 5 BRUNT
  Naval: 5 FLEET
  One on a: 3 REP 8 SALESREP
  One with the: 4 JEDI
  open: 5 JIMMY
  Opposing: 5 ENEMY
  out: 4 OUST 5 EVICT EXILE
    ROUST 6 DEPOSE
  Rotational: 6 TORQUE
  Sales: 4 REPS
  Take by: 4 REFT 5 SEIZE
    USURP WREST
  Throw with: 5 HEAVE
  to leave: 5 EXILE 6 UPROOT
  unit: 4 DYNE
  Wield: 5 EXERT
  With full: 5 AMAIN
  ~, in Latin: 3 VIS
**Forced**
Was: 5 HADTO
**Forceful:** 6 COGENT
    7 DYNAMIC
  flow: 5 SPATE
**Forcefully**
Eject: 4 SPEW

Fling: 4 HURL
Say: 4 AVER
Take: 5 WREST
**Forces**
Join: 4 ALLY 5 MERGE UNITE
    6 TEAMUP
**Forcibly**
Put down: 5 QUELL
Take: 5 USURP WREST
**Ford**
1950s ~: 5 EDSEL
Actor: 5 GLENN
A Tennessee: 5 ERNIE
Classic: 3 LTD 5 TBIRD
    WOODY 6 MODELA
    MODELT 7 MUSTANG
contemporary: 4 OLDS
flop: 5 EDSEL
model: 5 PINTO 6 ESCORT
    FIESTA TAURUS
of fashion: 6 EILEEN
of football: 4 LEN
Old: 3 LTD 5 EDSEL PINTO
or Lincoln: 3 CAR 4 AUTO
predecessor: 5 AGNEW
press secretary: 6 NESSEN
product, briefly: 4 MERC
role: 4 SOLO
son: 5 EDSEL
~ Explorer: 3 SUV
**Ford, President:** 6 GERALD
**Fore**
for four: 5 TETRA
Opposite of: 3 AFT
site: 3 TEE
**Fore-and-after:** 4 YAWL 5 SLOOP
**Forearm**
bone: 4 ULNA
bones: 5 ULNAE
**Forebear:** 8 ANCESTOR
**Foreboding:** 4 OMEN
Feeling of: 5 DREAD
**Forecast**
April: 4 RAIN
Icy: 5 SLEET
Part of a summer: 4 HAZE
Welcome: 5 CLEAR
Wet: 4 RAIN
Winter: 4 SNOW 5 SLEET
    TEENS
**Forecaster**
~ Al: 5 ROKER
**Forecasting**
aid: 5 RADAR
**Forehead:** 4 BROW
cover: 5 BANGS
**Foreign:** 5 ALIEN
assembly: 5 SENAT
correspondent: 6 PENPAL
dignitary: 3 AGA 4 EMIR
follower: 3 AID
Like some ~ films:
    7 UNRATED
money: 4 LIRE
prefix: 4 XENO
settler: 6 EMIGRE

**"Foreign Affairs"**
author Alison: 5 LURIE
~ Pulitzer-winner Lurie:
    6 ALISON
**Foreigner:** 5 ALIEN
prefix: 4 XENO
**Forelimb**
bone: 4 ULNA
**Foreman**
Deck: 4 BOSN
KO'er of: 3 ALI
place: 4 RING
Where Ali kayoed: 5 ZAIRE
**Foremast**
attachment: 8 HEADSAIL
**Forensic**
CBS ~ show: 3 CSI
tool: 3 DNA
workplace: 8 CRIMELAB
**Forensics**
expert: 7 DEBATER
**Foresail:** 3 JIB
**Foreshadow:** 4 BODE OMEN
    5 AUGUR
**Forest**
clearing: 5 GLADE
denizen: 3 ELK 4 DEER
element: 4 TREE
feller: 3 AXE
female: 3 DOE
growth: 4 MOSS
Like a rain: 4 LUSH 5 DENSE
plant: 4 FERN
quaker: 5 ASPEN
ranger: 3 ELK
runner: 3 SAP
Shakespearean: 5 ARDEN
Subarctic: 5 TAIGA
unit: 4 TREE
vine: 5 LIANA
**Forestall:** 5 AVERT
**Forest floor**
sight: 8 PINECONE
**Forest Service**
dept.: 4 USDA
**Foretopman**
Melville: 4 BUDD
**Forever:** 4 AGES 6 ALWAYS
    9 INDELIBLY
Almost: 3 EON 4 EONS
Lasting: 7 ETERNAL
Partner of: 4 ADAY
Seemingly: 3 EON 4 AEON
    AGES EONS
young: 7 AGELESS
~, poetically: 6 ETERNE
**"Forever, ___" (1996 humor**
    **book):** 4 ERMA
**Forever and ___:** 4 ADAY
**Forever ___ day:** 4 ANDA
**"Forever Your Girl"**
singer: 5 ABDUL
**"___ for Evidence" (Grafton**
    **novel):** 3 EIS
**Forewarned:** 8 ONNOTICE
**Foreword:** 5 INTRO

(abbr.): 4 INTR
**Forfeit:** 4 CEDE LOSE 5 WAIVE
**Forfeits**
  Card game with: 3 LOO
**Forge**
  worker: 5 SMITH
**Forgery:** 4 FAKE
**Forget:** 4 OMIT
**Forget-___:** 5 MENOT
**"___ Forget":** 5 TRYTO
**Forgetfulness**
  Drink of: 8 NEPENTHE
  River of: 5 LETHE
**"Forget it!":** 3 NAH NOT
    4 NOPE UHUH 5 IWONT
    IXNAY NOHOW NOWAY
    6 ISAYNO NODEAL
    NODICE NOSOAP
**Forging**
  When ~ began: 7 IRONAGE
**"___ forgiven":** 5 ALLIS
**Forgiveness**
  Start of a saying on: 5 TOERR
**"... ___ forgive those ...":**
    4 ASWE
**Forgiving:** 8 PLACABLE
  Less: 7 STERNER
**Forgo**
  Cannot: 5 NEEDS
**"For goodness ___!":** 4 SAKE
    5 SAKES
**"Forgot About ___" (rap song):**
    3 DRE
**"___ for Innocent" (Grafton**
    **novel):** 3 IIS
**"For ___ jolly ...":** 4 HESA
**Fork:** 7 DIVERGE UTENSIL
  feature: 4 TINE 5 PRONG
  in the road: 3 WYE
  Kind of: 5 SALAD 6 OYSTER
  Like a: 5 TINED
  One with a: 5 TUNER
  over: 3 PAY 5 REMIT SPEND
  over, with "up": 4 ANTE
  part: 4 TINE
  site: 4 ROAD
  Stick a ~ in: 4 STAB
**Forked**
  Not yet ~ over: 4 OWED
  Speak with ~ tongue: 3 LIE
**"For ___ know ...":** 4 ALLI
**Fork-tailed**
  flier: 4 TERN 6 MARTIN
**Form:** 4 MODE 7 FASHION
  a coalition: 5 UNITE
  a jury: 7 EMPANEL
  an opinion: 4 DEEM
  follower: 3 ULA
  Foundary: 4 MOLD
  Good: 7 DECORUM
  heading: 3 UNI
  In a different: 4 ANEW
  letters: 3 IRS
  of ID: 3 LIC
  Poetic: 3 ODE
  prefix: 3 UNI

Relating to: 5 MODAL
Sculpted: 5 TORSO
Shoemaking: 4 LAST
Short: 4 ABBR
suffix: 3 ULA
Tax: 6 RETURN
Tiny life: 5 AMEBA
Vb.: 3 INF
**Form 1040**
  completer: 3 CPA
  deduction: 3 IRA
  issuer: 3 IRS
  ~ ID: 3 SSN
**Formal:** 4 PRIM 6 DRESSY
  accessory: 4 STUD
  act: 7 STATUTE
  agreement: 4 PACT
  attire: 3 TUX
  avenue: 5 ALLEE
  ceremony: 4 RITE
  dance: 4 BALL
  declaration: 6 DICTUM
  decree: 5 EDICT
  dress: 4 GOWN
  Go: 5 DRESS 7 DRESSUP
  headgear: 6 TOPHAT
  introduction: 4 SEMI
  need: 3 TIE
  order: 4 WRIT 6 DECREE
  pronoun: 7 ROYALWE
  rulings: 5 DICTA
  speech: 7 ORATION
  Spring: 4 PROM
  Stiffly: 7 STILTED
  wear: 3 TUX 5 TAILS
**"___ for Malice" (Grafton**
    **novel):** 3 MIS
**Forman**
  Director: 5 MILOS
**Format**
  Big-screen: 4 IMAX
  Computer data: 5 ASCII
  Early VCR: 4 BETA
  Home movie: 3 DVD
  Image file: 4 JPEG
  Interview: 5 QANDA
  Radio: 4 TALK 6 OLDIES
  Videotape: 3 VHS 4 BETA
**Formation**
  Coral: 4 REEF 5 ATOLL
  fliers: 5 GEESE
  Flight: 3 VEE
  Glacial: 5 ARETE
  In: 7 ARRAYED
  Orderly: 5 ARRAY
  River mouth: 5 DELTA
  Sand: 4 DUNE
  Southwestern land: 4 MESA
  Triangular: 5 DELTA
**Formative:** 7 SEMINAL
**Formatting**
  key: 6 TABSET
**"For Me and My ___":** 3 GAL
**Former:** 3 OLD 4 ONCE PAST
    5 PRIOR 6 BYGONE
    7 CREATOR ONETIME

**Formerly:** 3 AGO NEE 4 ERST
    ONCE 9 ATONETIME
**Formic acid**
  source: 3 ANT
**Formicary:** 4 NEST
  resident: 3 ANT
**Formidable**
  foe: 7 NEMESIS
**Formosa:** 6 TAIWAN
**Formula:** 6 RECIPE
  of belief: 5 CREDO
  Part of a circle: 3 PIR
  Salt: 4 NACL
**Formula ___:** 3 ONE
**Formulary**
  entry: 4 DRUG
**Formulate:** 4 DRAW 5 FRAME
    SHAPE
**"___ for Murder":** 5 DIALM
**"___ for Noose" (Grafton**
    **novel):** 3 NIS
**___ for oneself:** 4 FEND
**"Forrest Gump"**
  actor Gary: 6 SINISE
  Oscar actor for: 8 TOMHANKS
**Forsake:** 6 DESERT
**"For ___ sake!":** 5 PETES
**Forsaken:** 4 LORN 5 ALONE
  child: 4 WAIF
**Forsaker**
  of the faith: 8 APOSTATE
**"For shame!":** 3 FIE TSK TUT
    6 TSKTSK TUTTUT
**Forster**
  novel: 15 APASSAGETOINDIA
  novel setting: 5 INDIA
  title with a view: 5 AROOM
**Forsyth**
  title city: 6 ODESSA
**Fort:** 7 BASTION 8 GARRISON
  attacked by Goldfinger:
    4 KNOX
  California: 3 ORD
  Civil War: 6 SUMTER
  Kentucky: 4 KNOX
  near McGuire Air Force Base:
    3 DIX
  North Carolina: 5 BRAGG
**Fort ___**
  (California): 3 ORD
  (Florida): 5 MYERS
  (gold site): 4 KNOX
  (North Carolina): 5 BRAGG
  (New Jersey): 3 DIX
  (Ontario): 4 ERIE
  (South Carolina): 6 SUMTER
**Fortas**
  Justice: 3 ABE
**___ for tat:** 3 TIT
**Fort Baxter**
  sergeant: 5 BILKO
**Fort Bliss**
  city: 6 ELPASO
**Fort Courage**
  company: 6 FTROOP
  group: 6 FTROOP

**Forte:** 4 LOUD 5 SKILL
   6 METIER
**Fort Erie**
  home (abbr.): 3 ONT
**Forth**
  And so: 3 ETC 8 ETCETERA
  Belch: 4 SPEW
  Bring: 5 EDUCE SPAWN
   6 ELICIT
  Call: 5 EVOKE
  Cast: 4 EMIT 6 SPEWED
  Come: 6 EMERGE
  Draw: 5 EDUCE EVOKE
   6 ELICIT
  Flow: 7 EMANATE
  Give: 4 EMIT 5 EXUDE
  Gush: 4 SPEW
  Hold: 5 OPINE ORATE
  Issue: 4 EMIT
  Put: 3 ASK 5 EXERT POSIT
  Send: 4 EMIT
  Spew: 5 ERUPT
  They go back and: 4 SAWS
  Walk back and: 4 PACE
  Words before: 5 ANDSO
**Forthcoming**
  Not: 3 SHY 5 CAGEY
**"For ___ the Bell Tolls":**
  4 WHOM
**"For the Boys"**
  gp.: 3 USO
**"For the life ___, ...":** 4 OFME
**"___ for the Misbegotten":**
  5 AMOON
**___ for the money:** 4 INIT
**"___ for the poor!":** 4 ALMS
**Forthright:** 4 BOLD OPEN
  6 CANDID 7 SINCERE
**Fortification:** 7 RAMPART
  V-shaped: 5 REDAN
**Fortify:** 3 ARM MAN 4 GIRD
  5 STEEL 7 BOLSTER
**Fortitude:** 4 GRIT GUTS
  6 METTLE
**Fort Knox**
  bar: 5 INGOT
**Fort Lauderdale**
  City near: 5 MIAMI
**Fortnight**
  fourteen: 4 DAYS
  Half a: 4 WEEK
**Fortnights**
  26 ~: 4 YEAR
**Fort Peck:** 3 DAM
**Fortress:** 7 CITADEL
  Dead Sea: 6 MASADA
  Medieval Italian: 4 ESTE
  Mountaintop: 5 AERIE
**Fortunate:** 5 LUCKY 6 INLUCK
**Fortune:** 3 HAP LOT 4 FATE
  PILE 6 KISMET RICHES
  WEALTH
  Good ~ source: 6 AMULET
  partner: 4 FAME
  Soldier of: 4 MERC
  Wheels of: 4 LIMO

**Fortune 500**
  abbr.: 3 INC 4 CORP
  inits.: 3 ITT
  listings (abbr.): 3 COS
**Fortuneteller:** 4 SEER
  6 ORACLE
  deck: 5 TAROT
  phrase: 4 ISEE
  sign: 4 OMEN
**Fort Wayne**
  river: 7 STMARYS
  state (abbr.): 3 IND
**Fort Worth**
  sch.: 3 TCU
**Forty**
  One of the back: 4 ACRE
  winks: 3 NAP 4 DOZE
  6 CATNAP SNOOZE
  7 SHUTEYE
**Forty-___:** 5 NINER
**Forty-niner:** 5 MINER
  filing: 5 CLAIM
  find: 3 ORE
**Forum**
  **Info:** Latin cue
  farewell: 3 AVE
  garb: 4 TOGA
  greeting: 3 AVE
  language: 5 LATIN
  matter: 3 RES
  player: 5 LAKER
  site: 4 ROME
  wear: 4 TOGA 5 TOGAE
  TOGAS
**"For ___ us a child ...":** 4 UNTO
**"For want of ___ ...":** 5 ANAIL
**Forward:** 4 BOLD PERT
  5 AHEAD BRASH FRESH
  REMIT 6 BRASSY
  RESEND SENDON
  Come: 6 EMERGE
  Drive: 5 IMPEL 6 PROPEL
  Look ~ to: 5 AWAIT
  Move: 6 PROPEL
  Nudge: 4 PROD
  pass: 6 AERIAL
  Put: 4 POSE 5 OFFER POSED
  POSIT 6 ASSERT
  sail: 3 JIB
  Urge: 5 IMPEL
**Forwarded:** 4 SENT 6 SENTON
**Forward-looking**
  group: 5 SEERS
**"For Your Eyes Only"**
  singer Sheena: 6 EASTON
**Fosse**
  film: 11 ALLTHATJAZZ
  musical: 6 DANCIN
  7 CABARET CHICAGO
**Fossey**
  Anthropologist: 4 DIAN
  subject: 3 APE 6 SIMIAN
**Fossil**
  Famed ~ site: 4 JAVA
  fuel blocks: 5 PEATS
  holder: 5 SHALE

  preserver: 6 TARPIT
  resin: 5 AMBER
**Fossil fuel:** 3 GAS OIL 4 COAL
**Foster:** 4 ABET REAR 5 BREED
  RAISE 7 NURTURE
  Actress: 5 JODIE
  home crowd: 5 FOLKS
  uncle: 3 NED
**Foster, Jodie**
  1999 ~ role: 4 ANNA
  alma mater: 4 YALE
  movie: 4 NELL
  role: 4 ANNA NELL
  title role: 4 NELL
**"Foucault's Pendulum"**
  author: 3 ECO
**Foul:** 4 VILE 5 NASTY
  6 PUTRID SORDID
  7 NOTFAIR
  caller: 3 REF UMP
  mood: 4 SNIT
  odor: 6 STENCH
  Pinball: 4 TILT
  up: 3 ERR 5 BOTCH MISDO
  (up): 6 BOLLIX
**Foul-mouth:** 6 CURSER
**Foul-smelling:** 4 OLID RIPE
  5 FETID FUNKY
  6 PUTRID RANCID
**Foul-tempered**
  fellow: 4 OGRE
**Foul-up:** 4 GOOF 5 BONER
  ERROR SNAFU
  6 BOOBOO
**Found:** 5 BEGIN 6 CREATE
  7 LOCATED
  As originally: 6 INSITU
  out: 6 LEARNT 7 LEARNED
  Partner of: 4 LOST
**Foundation:** 3 BED 4 BASE
  5 BASIS 7 ENDOWER
  Carnegie: 5 STEEL
  figure: 7 TRUSTEE
  garment: 6 CORSET
  Oxford: 4 SOLE
  plant: 5 SHRUB
  Plaster: 4 LATH
  Stone: 6 RIPRAP
**"Foundation"**
  author: 6 ASIMOV
**Founded:** 5 BASED
  (abbr.): 3 EST 4 ESTD 5 ESTAB
**"Found it!":** 3 AHA
**Foundry**
  form: 4 MOLD
  need: 3 ORE
  refuse: 4 SLAG
**Fountain**
  drink: 4 COKE COLA MALT
  SODA 5 SHAKE 6 MALTED
  Famous: 5 TREVI
  freebie: 5 STRAW
  of jazz: 4 PETE
  Roman: 5 TREVI
  treat: 4 MALT 6 MALTED
  11 BANANASPLIT

**Fountain, Pete**
collaborator: 6 ALHIRT
**"Fountainhead, The"**
author Rand: 3 AYN
character: 5 ROARK
**Four**
A quarter of: 3 ONE
duos: 5 OCTET
gills: 4 PINT
Give ~ stars: 4 RATE
Having ~ sharps: 3 INE
inferior: 4 TREY
It follows ~ but not five:
   4 TEEN
Key with ~ sharps: 6 EMAJOR
Lake in ~ states: 4 ERIE
of a kind: 6 TETRAD
One of the ~ elements: 3 AIR
prefix: 5 TETRA
quarters: 3 ONE 4 YEAR
Round of: 5 SEMIS
seasons in Spain: 3 ANO
Three or: 4 AFEW
times a day, on an Rx: 3 QID
Top: 4 ACES
**Four-___: 7 ALARMER**
**___ four: 5 PETIT**
**___ Four, The: 3 FAB**
**Fourbagger: 5 HOMER**
**Fourbaggers**
in MLB: 3 HRS
**Four Corners**
state: 4 UTAH
**Four-door: 5 SEDAN**
**"Four Essays on Liberty"**
author Berlin: 6 ISAIAH
**Four-footed**
friend: 3 PET
**Four Forest Cantons**
lake: 7 LUCERNE
**Four Freedoms**
subject: 4 FEAR
**Four-hand**
piano piece: 4 DUET
**Four Horsemen**
One of the: 3 WAR
**Four-in-hand: 3 TIE**
**Four-letter**
Use a ~ word: 4 CUSS
word: 4 OATH 5 SWEAR
**Four o'clock**
fare: 8 TEACAKES
Leaves at: 3 TEA
service: 6 TEASET
**Four-page**
sheet: 5 FOLIO
**Four-person**
event: 5 RELAY
**Fourposter: 3 BED**
**"Four Quartets"**
poet: 5 ELIOT 7 TSELIOT
**Fours: 5 CAKES**
**___ fours (crawling): 5 ONALL**
**Fourscore: 6 EIGHTY**
**Four Seasons, The**
Frankie of: 5 VALLI

song: 6 SHERRY
**"Four Seasons, The"**
director: 4 ALDA
**Four-sided**
fig.: 4 RECT
**Foursome: 6 TETRAD**
Annual: 7 SEASONS
Grand slam: 4 RBIS
Half a 1960s: 5 MAMAS PAPAS
Monopoly ~ (abbr.): 3 RRS
**Four-star: 4 AONE RAVE**
   5 GREAT
Hardly ~ fare: 4 SLOP
review: 4 RAVE
**Four-stringed**
instrument: 3 UKE
**Four-term**
pres.: 3 FDR
**Fourth**
anniversary gift: 5 LINEN
dimension: 4 TIME
in a series: 3 DEE
little piggy's share: 4 NONE
man: 4 SETH
person: 4 ABEL
planet: 4 MARS
**Fourth-down**
option: 4 PUNT
**Fourth Estate: 5 PRESS**
**Fourth-largest**
lake: 7 ARALSEA
**Fourths**
of gals.: 3 QTS
**Four-time**
~ Australian Open champ:
   5 SELES
~ Emmy-winning drama:
   5 LALAW
~ Indy 500 winner: 4 FOYT
   5 UNSER 7 ALUNSER
~ Japanese P.M.: 3 ITO
~ Super Bowl champs:
   8 STEELERS
~ Wimbledon champ: 5 LAVER
**Four-to-midnight**
group: 10 SWINGSHIFT
**Four-wheeler: 5 WAGON**
   6 LANDAU
Recreational: 3 ATV
**Four-year**
degs.: 3 BAS BSS
**Fowl**
Entrée: 5 CAPON
Female: 3 HEN 6 PEAHEN
Flightless: 3 EMU
pole: 5 ROOST
product: 3 EGG
territory: 4 COOP
Young: 5 POULT
**Fox: 7 REYNARD**
African: 4 ASSE
comedy series: 5 MADTV
Female: 5 VIXEN
follower: 4 TROT
Former ~ sitcom: 3 ROC
   6 MARTIN

Fox Mulder program on:
   9 THEXFILES
honorific: 4 BRER
hunt cry: 5 HALLO 6 YOICKS
   7 TALLYHO
kin: 3 SAC
Like a: 3 SLY
Partner of: 4 DANA
prey: 4 HARE
relative: 7 ARAPAHO
show: 4 COPS
Young: 3 KIT
~, in Spanish: 5 ZORRO
**___ Fox: 4 BRER**
**"Fox and the Grapes, The"**
storyteller: 5 AESOP
**Foxhole**
Fix a: 5 REDIG
**Foxlike: 3 SLY**
**Foxx**
Actor: 5 JAMIE
Comedian: 4 REDD
Singer: 4 INEZ
**Foxy: 3 SLY**
lady: 5 VIXEN
**Foy**
Vaudevillian: 5 EDDIE
**Foyer: 4 HALL**
**Foyt**
et al.: 3 AJS
**Fr.**
company: 3 CIE
father: 4 PERE
holy woman: 3 STE
holy women: 4 STES
miss: 4 MLLE
title: 3 MME 4 MLLE
**Fra**
Painting: 5 LIPPI
**Fracas: 4 TODO 5 MELEE**
   SCRAP SETTO
**Fraction**
Bushel: 4 PECK
Day: 4 HOUR
Farm: 4 ACRE
Foot: 4 INCH
Inch: 3 MIL
Joule: 3 ERG
Min.: 4 NSEC
Newton: 4 DYNE
Ounce: 4 DRAM
Peso: 7 CENTAVO
Sawbuck: 3 ONE
Sen: 3 RIN
Square-mile: 4 ACRE
**Fractional**
prefix: 4 DEMI HEMI NANO
**Fractions**
Make: 6 DIVIDE
Ton ~ (abbr.): 3 LBS
**Fragile**
It may be: 3 EGO
layer: 5 OZONE
**Fragment: 5 PIECE SCRAP**
   SHARD 7 ATOMIZE
   SNIPPET

Pottery: 5 SHARD
**Fragrance: 4 ODOR** 5 AROMA
    SCENT
Floral: 5 ATTAR
Gucci: 4 ENVY
Popular: 4 COCO TABU
    6 ARAMIS
YSL: 5 OPIUM
**Fragrant: 8 REDOLENT**
compound: 5 ESTER
fir: 6 BALSAM
flower: 5 LILAC 7 TEAROSE
    8 GARDENIA
oil: 5 ATTAR
resin: 5 ELEMI
ring: 3 LEI
root: 5 ORRIS
shrub: 5 LILAC 6 AZALEA
tree: 3 FIR 4 PINE
wood: 5 CEDAR 8 REDCEDAR
___ fraîche: 5 CREME
**Fraidy-cat: 5 SISSY**
**Frame: 5 SETUP**
Animation: 3 CEL
a photo again: 5 REMAT
Clothes-drying: 5 AIRER
Door ~ part: 4 JAMB
    6 LINTEL
Fireplace: 5 GRATE
insert: 4 LENS
of mind: 4 MOOD 5 HUMOR
    6 MORALE
Pane: 4 SASH
shape: 4 OVAL
Ship: 4 HULL
Time: 3 ERA
Window: 4 SASH
**Framed: 5 SETUP**
It may be: 3 ART CEL
**Framer**
need: 3 MAT
**Framework: 7 LATTICE**
Bridge: 7 TRESTLE
Rigid: 5 TRUSS
Window: 4 SASH
**Fran**
Friend of: 5 KUKLA OLLIE
**Franc**
Former ~ fraction: 3 SOU
successor: 4 EURO
**Française**
feature: 7 CEDILLA
___ française: 3 ALA
**France**
Ancient region of: 7 ALSATIA
Author: 7 ANATOLE
Bank of: 4 RIVE
Born in: 3 NEE
City of: 4 CAEN 5 LILLE
Department of: 3 AIN
France of: 7 ANATOLE
Friend in: 3 AMI 4 AMIE
Head of: 4 TETE
King of: 3 ROI
Longest river in: 5 LOIRE
Neighbor of: 7 ANDORRA

One in: 3 UNE
Patron saint of: 5 DENIS
President of: 4 COTY
Queen of: 5 REINE
Region of: 4 BRIE
River of: 4 OISE YSER 5 ISERE
    RHONE
Saint of: 6 TROPEZ
State of: 4 ETAT
Story of: 5 ETAGE
Summer in: 3 ETE
The king of: 5 LEROI
The south of: 4 MIDI
~, formerly: 4 GAUL
___ France: 5 ILEDE
**Franchise: 4 VOTE**
Flapjack: 4 IHOP
**Francis: 5 SAINT**
Actress: 6 ARLENE
of 1950s films: 4 MULE
or Frank: 4 ANNE
**Francis ___, Sir**
Explorer: 5 DRAKE
**Francis, St.**
birthplace: 6 ASSISI
**Franciscan: 5 FRIAR**
___ Francisco: 3 SAN
**Franck**
Composer: 5 CESAR
**Franco**
Actor: 4 NERO
friend: 5 AMIGO
**François**
**Info:** French cue
Farewell from: 5 ADIEU
Friend of: 3 AMI 4 AMIE
**Frank: 3 DOG** 4 OPEN
    6 CANDID DIRECT
    HONEST REDHOT
    WIENER
admission: 6 AVOWAL
comic colleague: 6 ERNEST
Diarist: 4 ANNE
Director: 5 CAPRA
Ex of: 3 AVA MIA
Gangster: 5 NITTI
of rock: 5 ZAPPA
Songwriter: 7 LOESSER
topper: 5 KRAUT 6 RELISH
work: 5 DIARY
**Frank, Anne**
account: 5 DIARY
**Franken**
and others: 3 ALS
**Frankenstein**
assistant: 4 IGOR
feature: 4 SCAR
workplace: 3 LAB
**"Frankenstein"**
Like: 6 GOTHIC
**Frankfurt**
**Info:** German cue
First in: 4 ERST
river: 4 ODER
**Frankfurter**
Justice: 5 FELIX

link: 3 UND
**Frankie**
Singer: 5 LAINE VALLI
**Franklin**
flier: 4 KITE
forte: 4 SOUL
invention: 5 STOVE
invention (abbr.): 3 DST
is on it: 5 CNOTE
Loser to ~ in 1936: 3 ALF
Mother of: 4 SARA
of soul: 6 ARETHA
or Jefferson: 5 DEIST
successor: 5 HARRY
Wife of: 7 ELEANOR
**Franks**
Of: 5 SALIC
**Franny**
Father of: 3 LES
**Frans**
Painter: 4 HALS
**Frantic**
Get: 13 CLIMBTHEWALLS
**Franz**
Author: 5 KAFKA
Composer: 5 LEHAR LISZT
Hypnotist: 6 MESMER
**Fraser**
of tennis: 5 NEALE
**"Frasier"**
actress Gilpin: 4 PERI
actress Peri: 6 GILPIN
brother: 5 NILES
character: 3 ROZ 5 NILES
    6 DAPHNE
dog: 5 EDDIE
Ex-wife on: 5 MARIS
Peri on: 3 ROZ
portrayer: 6 KELSEY
Surname on: 5 CRANE
**Frat**
house wear: 4 TOGA
letter: 3 CHI ETA PHI PSI
    RHO TAU 4 BETA ZETA
    5 KAPPA SIGMA THETA
party staple: 3 KEG
recruits: 5 FROSH
**Fraternal**
group: 4 BPOE ELKS
    6 MASONS
member: 3 ELK
twin, in chemistry: 6 ISOMER
**Fraternity**
hopeful: 6 RUSHEE
letter: 3 CHI ETA PHI PSI
    RHO TAU 4 BETA ZETA
    5 KAPPA SIGMA THETA
letters: 3 NUS XIS
member: 5 GREEK
members: 3 MEN
party wear: 4 TOGA
travail: 8 HELLWEEK
**Fratricide**
victim: 4 ABEL
**Frau**
abode: 4 HAUS

mate: 4 HERR
**Fraud:** 4 HOAX SCAM SHAM
    6 POSEUR
  finder (abbr.): 3 BBB
  monitoring agcy.: 3 FTC
**Fray:** 4 WEAR 5 RAVEL SETTO
**Frayed:** 4 WORN
**Frazier**
  foe: 3 ALI
**Freak**
  out: 5 GOAPE 6 LOSEIT
**Freaked**
  out: 6 LOSTIT 7 GONEAPE
    HADACOW
**"Freaks"**
  director Browning: 3 TOD
  Hyams of: 5 LEILA
**Freberg**
  Satirist: 4 STAN
**Fred**
  1966 U.S. Open champ ~:
    6 STOLLE
  Dancer: 7 ASTAIRE
  Lyricist: 3 EBB
  Partner of: 5 ADELE
  Ricky vis-à-vis: 6 TENANT
  Sister of: 5 ADELE
  Wife of: 5 WILMA
  ~, to Pebbles: 3 DAD
**Freda**
  Singer: 5 PAYNE
**"Fred Basset"**
  cartoonist Graham: 4 ALEX
**Freddie**
  Comic: 6 PRINZE
**Freddie the Freeloader:** 4 HOBO
    5 TRAMP
  portrayer: 10 REDSKELTON
**Freddy**
  street: 3 ELM
**Frederic**
  Photoengraving innovator:
    4 IVES
**Frederick**
  Composer: 5 LOEWE
**Frederick ___, Sir**
  Choreographer: 6 ASHTON
**Fredericksburg**
  Victor at: 3 LEE
**Frederik**
  Sci-fi author: 4 POHL
**Free:** 3 RID 4 ONME 5 LETGO
    LOOSE UNTIE 6 GRATIS
    LETOUT 7 ATLARGE
    MANUMIT PROBONO
    RELEASE UNLOOSE
    8 ATNOCOST LIBERATE
    SETLOOSE
  Add for: 7 THROWIN
  from: 5 RIDOF
  from contaminants: 4 PURE
  from strife: 7 ATPEACE
  gift, sometimes: 7 TOTEBAG
  It may be: 4 RIDE 5 TRIAL
    VERSE
  It's a ~ country: 3 USA

It's not ~ of charge: 3 ION
Let: 5 UNTIE
Not: 5 CAGED INUSE
    6 EARNED
  (of): 3 RID
  of charge: 6 GRATIS
  of frost: 5 DEICE
  Set: 5 UNTIE 6 UNCAGE
    7 UNLOOSE
  speech obstacle: 3 GAG
  suffix: 3 DOM
  throw score: 3 ONE
  ticket: 4 COMP PASS
  tix: 5 COMPS
  to attack: 5 LETAT
  ~, in French: 5 LIBRE
  ~ TV ad: 3 PSA
**Free as ___:** 5 ABIRD
**Freebie:** 4 COMP PASS
  Chinese restaurant: 3 TEA
  Chinese takeout: 4 RICE
  Diner: 5 MINTS
  Gas station: 3 AIR
  Hotel: 3 ICE 4 SOAP
  Motel: 3 ICE 4 SOAP
  Restaurant: 4 ROLL 5 WATER
    8 ICEWATER
  Soda shop: 5 STRAW
**Freebooter:** 6 PIRATE
**Freed**
  Rock pioneer: 4 ALAN
**Freedom**
  from worry: 4 EASE
  Put a price on: 7 SETBAIL
  Swahili for: 5 UHURU
  ~, briefly: 3 LIB
**Free-for-all:** 4 RIOT 5 BRAWL
    MELEE 6 FRACAS
**Freeh**
  org.: 3 FBI
**Freelancer**
  encl.: 4 SASE
**Freeload:** 5 MOOCH
**Freeloader:** 5 LEECH
    6 SPONGE 7 SPONGER
**Freely:** 6 ATWILL
**Freeman**
  Actress: 4 MONA
**Freemen**
  Anglo-Saxon: 6 CEORLS
**Freesia**
  family: 4 IRIS
**Freestone**
  fruit: 5 PEACH
**Freethinker:** 7 HERETIC
**Free-throw**
  area: 4 LANE
**Freetown**
  currency: 5 LEONE
**Freeway**
  access: 4 RAMP
  caution: 7 NOUTURN
  Enter the: 5 MERGE
  feature: 6 ONRAMP
**Freeze:** 5 ICEUP
  over: 5 ICEUP

  prefix: 4 ANTI
  Word with: 4 DEEP
**Freezer**
  bag name: 6 ZIPLOC
  brand: 5 AMANA
  stuff: 3 ICE
  Take out of the: 4 THAW
**Freezing:** 4 COLD 7 ICECOLD
  point: 4 ZERO
  temperatures: 5 TEENS
**Freight:** 5 CARGO
  carrier: 6 BOXCAR 7 FLATCAR
  Filled with: 5 LADEN
  hauler: 4 SEMI
  unit: 6 ONETON
  weight: 3 TON
**Freighter**
  filler: 5 CARGO
**"___ Freischütz" (Weber opera):**
    3 DER
**Freleng**
  Animator: 7 ISADORE
**Fremont**
  guide: 9 KITCARSON
**French:** 6 GALLIC
    15 ROMANCELANGUAGE
  1950s ~ president: 4 COTY
  2001 ~ film: 6 AMELIE
  actor Delon: 5 ALAIN
  actress Anouk: 5 AIMEE
  affirmative: 3 OUI
  airport: 4 ORLY
  article: 3 LES UNE
  assembly: 5 SENAT
  avant-garde artist: 3 ARP
  bank: 4 RIVE
  bean: 4 TETE
  bench: 4 BANC
  beverage: 3 THE
  brandy: 6 COGNAC
    8 ARMAGNAC
  bread: 5 FRANC
  brother: 5 FRERE
  cathedral city: 5 REIMS
  chalk: 4 TALC
  cheer ending: 5 LEROI
  cheese: 4 BRIE 7 FROMAGE
  city: 4 CAEN LYON METZ
    NICE 5 ARLES 6 CALAIS
  cleric: 4 ABBE
  collagist: 3 ARP
  composer Edouard: 4 LALO
  composer Erik: 5 SATIE
  connections: 3 ETS
  cop: 8 GENDARME
  cordial flavoring: 4 ANIS
  corp.: 3 CIE
  cubist Fernand: 5 LEGER
  cup: 5 TASSE
  curve creation: 3 ARC
  dear: 5 CHERI
  department: 4 OISE ORNE
    5 AISNE
  diarist: 3 NIN
  director Clair: 4 RENE
  door part: 4 PANE

evening: 4 SOIR
existentialist: 6 SARTRE
explorer: 7 LASALLE
farewell: 5 ADIEU
fashion designer: 6 CHANEL
    10 COCOCHANEL
fashion magazine: 4 ELLE
father: 4 PERE
females: 5 ELLES
film: 4 CINE
film award: 5 CESAR
force: 5 ARMEE
Former ~ coin: 3 SOU
friar: 4 ABBE
friend: 3 AMI 4 AMIE
friends: 4 AMIS
funnyman Jacques: 4 TATI
girlfriend: 4 AMIE
handle: 3 NOM
hat: 5 BERET
head: 4 TETE
holy woman (abbr.): 3 STE
honey: 5 CHERI
illustrator Gustave: 4 DORE
impressionist: 5 DEGAS
    MANET MONET
income: 5 RENTE
infinitive: 4 ETRE
inn: 7 AUBERGE
islands: 4 ILES
jeweler Lalique: 4 RENE
key: 3 CLE
king: 3 ROI
king Hugh: 5 CAPET
landscapist: 5 COROT
leave: 5 ADIEU
legislature: 5 SENAT
Like some ~ accents: 5 ACUTE
Like some ~ sounds: 5 NASAL
Like ~ doors: 5 PANED
Like ~ toast: 4 EGGY
love: 5 AMOUR
map word: 3 ILE
mark below C: 7 CEDILLA
mathematician: 6 PASCAL
military cap: 4 KEPI
mother: 4 MERE
movie: 4 CINE
mushroom: 4 CEPE
naval base: 5 BREST
negative: 3 NON
nobleman: 3 DUC 5 COMTE
noodle: 4 TETE
novelist: 4 GIDE LOTI ZOLA
    6 BALZAC
Old ~ coin: 3 ECU SOU
Old ~ dance: 7 GAVOTTE
one: 3 UNE
painter: 5 COROT LEGER
    MANET MONET 6 RENOIR
    7 UTRILLO
peak: 4 ALPE
physicist: 6 AMPERE
pianist: 5 SATIE
play part: 4 ACTE
pointillist: 6 SEURAT

port: 5 BREST ROUEN
    6 CALAIS 7 LEHAVRE
possessive: 3 MES SES TES
    4 AMOI ATOI
preposition: 3 DES 4 AVEC
    SANS 5 APRES ENTRE
president Jacques: 6 CHIRAC
president residence: 6 ELYSEE
pronoun: 3 CES ILS LUI MOI
    MON SES TES TOI UNE
    4 AMOI ELLE
protest phrase: 4 ABAS
pupil: 5 ELEVE
queen: 5 REINE
restaurant name part: 4 CHEZ
revolutionary: 5 MARAT
river: 4 EURE OISE ORNE
    5 ISERE LOIRE MARNE
    RHONE SAONE SARRE
    SELLE SOMME
roast: 4 ROTI
rocket: 6 ARIANE
romance: 5 AMOUR
room: 5 SALLE
satellite launcher: 6 ARIANE
school: 5 ECOLE LYCEE
sculptor: 5 RODIN
sea: 3 MER
seaport: 5 BREST
season: 3 ETE
seasoning: 3 SEL
silk: 4 SOIE
silk center: 4 LYON
soldier: 5 POILU
Some ~ sounds: 6 NASALS
soul: 3 AME
spa: 5 EVIAN
spot of land: 3 ILE
star: 6 ETOILE
states: 5 ETATS
story: 5 ETAGE
street: 3 RUE
student: 5 ELEVE
summer: 3 ETE
surname start: 3 DES
teacher: 6 MAITRE
textile city: 5 LILLE
tire: 4 PNEU
toast: 5 SALUT
toast portion: 5 SANTE
verb: 4 ETRE
vineyard: 3 CRU
water: 3 EAU 5 EVIAN
wave: 4 ONDE
way: 3 RUE
weapon: 4 ARME
When the ~ fry: 3 ETE
wine: 3 VIN 5 MEDOC
wine region: 6 ALSACE
wine valley: 5 LOIRE
~ Mrs.: 3 MME
~ Nobelist André: 4 GIDE
~ Oscar: 5 CESAR
French Chantilly: 4 LACE
"French Connection, The"
    Hackman role in ~: 5 DOYLE

French Foreign ___: 6 LEGION
"French Kiss"
    actress Meg: 4 RYAN
    costar: 5 KLINE
Frenchman: 4 GAUL
French Open
    1973 ~ champ Nastase: 4 ILIE
    1983 ~ champ: 4 NOAH
    1989 ~ champ: 5 CHANG
    1990–92 ~ champ: 5 SELES
    1999 ~ champ: 6 AGASSI
    Three-time ~ champ: 5 SELES
French Polynesia
    capital: 7 PAPEETE
French Riviera
    city: 4 NICE
French Sudan
    ~, today: 4 MALI
Frenzied: 4 AGOG AMOK WILD
    5 MANIC 6 HECTIC
    RAVING 7 BERSERK
    In a ~ way: 4 AMOK
    routine: 7 RATRACE
    (var.): 5 AMUCK
Frenzy: 4 RAGE 5 FUROR
    MANIA
    In a: 4 AMOK
Freon: 3 GAS
Frequency
    unit: 5 HERTZ
Frequent: 5 HAUNT
    author: 4 ANON
    caller: 4 AVON
    Far from: 4 RARE
    flier: 4 BIRD 5 PILOT
    fliers: 6 JETSET
    hangout: 5 HAUNT
    song subject: 4 LOVE
    ~ 007 foe: 3 KGB
Frequently: 3 OFT 4 ALOT
    5 OFTEN 8 OFTTIMES
    It's ~ 72: 3 PAR
    ~, in poetry: 3 OFT
Frère
    sibling: 5 SOEUR
Fresh: 3 NEW 4 AIRY ANEW
    PERT 5 NOVEL SASSY
    6 RECENT RESTED
    UNUSED
    and firm: 5 CRISP
    Far from: 5 BANAL TRITE
    from the laundry: 5 CLEAN
    Get ~ with: 4 SASS
    information: 4 NEWS
    kid: 4 BRAT
    Least: 7 STALEST TRITEST
    Like ~ cake: 5 MOIST
    More: 5 NEWER
    No longer: 5 STALE
    Not: 5 STALE TRITE
    start: 3 NEO 7 RENEWAL
    Stay: 4 KEEP
    Still: 7 UNJADED
    talk: 4 SASS
"Fresh Air"
    airer: 3 NPR

**Fresh as a ___:** 5 DAISY
**Freshen:** 5 RENEW 6 AERATE
   AIROUT
**Freshener:** 6 SACHET
  Breath: 6 TICTAC
  scent: 4 PINE
  target: 4 ODOR
**Freshly:** 4 ANEW
  made: 3 NEW
  painted: 3 WET
**"Freshmaker, The":** 6 MENTOS
**Freshman:** 4 TEEN
  Academy: 5 PLEBE
  cap: 6 BEANIE
  language course: 6 LATINI
**Fresh-mouthed:** 4 PERT 5 SASSY
**Freshness:** 3 LIP 4 SASS
  Lose: 4 WILT 5 STALE
  Protect: 6 SEALIN
  Sign of: 4 SLAP
  Symbol of: 5 DAISY
**"Fresh Prince of Bel Air"**
  actress Tatyana: 3 ALI
**Freshwater**
  crustacean: 6 ISOPOD
  duck: 4 TEAL
  fish: 4 CHUB DACE PIKE
    RUDD 5 BREAM 6 DARTER
  minnow: 6 REDFIN
**Fresno**
  paper: 3 BEE
**Fret:** 4 STEW 5 WORRY
**Fretful:** 7 INASTEW
**Freud**
  Article written by: 3 DER
  contemporary: 4 JUNG
    5 ADLER
  ego: 3 ICH
  First stage of: 4 ORAL
  focus: 3 EGO
  focus (abbr.): 4 ANAL
  Psychoanalyst: 4 ANNA
  Surrealist influenced by:
    4 DALI
**Freudian**
  concept: 3 EGO 6 LIBIDO
  error: 4 SLIP
  subject: 5 DREAM
  subjects: 3 IDS
**Fri.**
  Gal: 4 ASST
  preceder: 3 THU
**___ Fria National Monument:**
  4 AGUA
**Friar:** 5 ABBOT
  French: 4 ABBE
  Sherwood: 4 TUCK
**Friars Club**
  event: 5 ROAST
  official: 5 ABBOT
**Frick**
  collection: 3 ART
**Friction:** 6 STRIFE
  easer: 3 OIL
**"Frida"**
  actress Hayek: 5 SALMA

**Friday:** 3 COP
  Abbr. before: 3 SGT
  and Bilko: 4 SGTS
  Casual ~ castoff: 3 TIE
  catchphrase ender: 4 MAAM
  creator: 5 DEFOE
  Friend of: 6 CRUSOE
  Man: 4 AIDE
  org.: 4 LAPD
  player: 4 WEBB
  preceder: 3 GAL
  program: 7 DRAGNET
  rank (abbr.): 3 SGT
  Sergeant: 3 JOE
  What ~ wanted: 5 FACTS
**___ Friday:** 3 GAL SGT
**Friday, Joe:** 3 COP
**Friday, Sgt.**
  employer: 4 LAPD
**___ Friday's (restaurant):** 3 TGI
**Fridge**
  accessory: 6 MAGNET
  foray: 4 RAID
  name: 5 AMANA
  Old: 6 ICEBOX
  Raid the: 4 NOSH
  Stick in the: 4 OLEO
**Fried**
  lightly: 7 SAUTEED
  Pan for ~ rice: 3 WOK
**"Fried Green Tomatoes"**
  actress Cicely: 5 TYSON
  author Fannie: 5 FLAGG
**Friedman**
  subj.: 4 ECON
**Friedrich**
  German mineralogist: 4 MOHS
**Friend:** 3 PAL 4 ALLY 5 AMIGO
  address: 4 THEE
  As a ~, in French: 5 ENAMI
  Close: 3 PAL
  False: 4 IAGO USER 5 JUDAS
  Formal: 4 ALLY
  Four-footed: 3 PET
  French: 3 AMI 4 AMIE
  from afar: 6 PENPAL
  Good: 6 BONAMI
  in the 'hood: 3 BRO
  in war: 4 ALLY
  Like a best: 6 TRUEST
  opposite: 3 FOE
  Spanish: 5 AMIGO
  Western: 4 PARD
**"Friend ___?":** 5 ORFOE
**Friendlier**
  Become: 4 THAW
**Friendliness:** 5 AMITY
    8 BONHOMIE
**Friendly:** 4 WARM 6 GENIAL
    7 AMIABLE CORDIAL
  Become: 4 WARM
  Break in ~ relations: 4 RIFT
  conversation: 4 CHAT
  dog offering: 3 PAW
  femme: 4 AMIE
  intro: 3 ECO 4 USER

  Kind of: 4 USER
  Less: 5 ICIER
  nation: 4 ALLY
  prefix: 3 ECO
  term of address: 5 KIDDO
  Very: 5 CLOSE
    10 BUDDYBUDDY
**Friendly Islands:** 5 TONGA
**Friends**
  and family: 4 KITH
  Familiar, as: 3 OLD
  in France: 5 AMIES
  in Italy: 5 AMICI
  pronoun: 4 THEE THOU
**"Friends":** 6 SITCOM
  actor Matt: 7 LEBLANC
  actor Matthew: 5 PERRY
  baby: 4 EMMA
  costar: 3 COX 6 KUDROW
    7 ANISTON
  friend: 4 JOEY ROSS
    6 MONICA PHOEBE
  network: 3 NBC
  Phoebe's sister on: 6 URSULA
**___ friends:** 5 AMONG
**Friendship:** 5 AMITY
**Friendship 7**
  astronaut: 5 GLENN
**Fries:** 6 TATERS
  condiment: 4 SALT
  Future: 4 SPUD
  go-with: 6 CATSUP
  Kind of: 4 HOME
  order: 5 LARGE
  or slaw: 4 SIDE 8 SIDEDISH
**Frigate**
  front: 4 PROW
**Frigg**
  Husband of: 4 ODIN
**Fright:** 5 SCARE 6 TERROR
  Pale with: 5 ASHEN
  site: 5 STAGE
  Sound of: 3 EEK 4 GASP
  Sudden: 5 PANIC START
**Frighten:** 5 ALARM DAUNT
    SCARE UNMAN
    7 STARTLE
  off: 5 DETER
**Frightened**
  horse: 6 REARER
  Visibly: 5 ASHEN
**Frightening:** 5 EERIE
    8 FEARSOME
  shout: 3 BOO
**Frigid:** 3 ICY 4 ICED 5 POLAR
    6 ARCTIC
  finish: 4 AIRE
  time: 6 ICEAGE
**Frigidaire**
  rival: 5 AMANA
**Frilly:** 4 LACY
**Fringe:** 4 EDGE
  benefit: 4 PERK
  Beyond the: 5 OUTRE
  material: 7 TASSELS
**Frisbee:** 4 DISC DISK

inspiration: **6** PIETIN
maker: **5** WHAMO
**Frisco**
footballer: **5** NINER
**Frisk**
~, with "down": **3** PAT
**Friskies**
Ask for: **3** MEW
eater: **3** CAT
**Frisky**
mammal: **5** OTTER
pet: **6** KITTEN
**Frist**
predecessor: **4** LOTT
**Frito-Lay**
product: **9** CORNCHIPS
**Frittata: 6** OMELET
needs: **4** EGGS
**Fritter**
away: **5** WASTE
**Fritz**
Director: **4** LANG
Go on the: **4** FAIL **5** ACTUP
On the: **5** KAPUT
**Frivolous**
gal of song: **3** SAL
**Frizzy**
coif: **4** AFRO
**Fro**
Flowed to and: **5** TIDED
Go to and: **4** SWAY
___ fro: **5** TOAND
**Frobe**
Actor: **4** GERT
**Frock: 5** DRESS
Forum: **4** TOGA
German: **6** DIRNDL
wearer: **5** FRIAR
**Frodo**
Friend of: **3** ENT SAM
portrayer: **10** ELIJAHWOOD
**Frog: 6** LEAPER **7** CROAKER
Future: **7** TADPOLE
genus: **4** RANA
kin: **4** TOAD
Made like a: **5** LEAPT
seat: **7** LILYPAD
sound: **5** CROAK
spit: **4** ALGA
Twain's: **4** DANL
**Froggy**
Talk like: **4** RASP
**Frogman**
gear: **5** SCUBA
**Frogner Park**
city: **4** OSLO
**Frolic: 4** LARK PLAY ROMP
**5** SPORT **6** CAVORT
PRANCE
**Frolicking**
animal: **5** OTTER
**From: 4** ASOF **5** SINCE
above: **6** AERIAL
birth: **6** INNATE
l. to r.: **3** ACR
now: **5** HENCE

scratch: **4** ANEW **6** AFRESH
square one: **4** ANEW **5** AGAIN
**6** AFRESH
that place: **6** THENCE
the beginning: **4** ANEW
**5** ABOVO **6** AFRESH
DENOVO
the beginning, in music:
**6** DACAPO
the heart: **6** AORTAL
**7** EARNEST
then on: **5** SINCE
the top: **4** ANEW **5** AGAIN
the U.S.: **4** AMER
the year one: **3** OLD
way back: **5** OFOLD
what source: **6** WHENCE
**From ___**
(completely): **4** ATOZ
(opening bit): **4** ATOB
**From A ___: 3** TOZ
**Frome**
Fictional: **5** ETHAN
"___ Frome": **5** ETHAN
**From head ___: 5** TOTOE
**"From Here to Eternity"**
actor Montgomery: **5** CLIFT
actress: **4** KERR
wife: **5** KAREN
**Fromm**
Psychoanalyst: **5** ERICH
**"___ From Muskogee": 4** OKIE
**From the ___: 5** GETGO
**"From the Earth to the Moon"**
writer: **5** VERNE
**"From the Terrace"**
author: **5** OHARA
**"From ___ to Eternity": 4** HERE
**"From ___ to Mozart": 3** MAO
**"From where ___ ...": 4** ISIT
**"From ___ With Love":**
**6** RUSSIA
**From ___ Z: 3** ATO
**Fronds**
Plant with: **4** FERN
With ~ aplenty: **5** FERNY
**Front: 3** ACT **4** FORE
**6** VENEER
**Info:** Prefix cue
At the ~ of the line: **4** NEXT
Back at the: **5** RETRO
end: **3** IER
False: **3** ACT **4** POSE **5** GUISE
PSEUD **6** FACADE
In: **5** AHEAD
line: **6** ISOBAR
money: **4** ANTE
Out in: **5** AHEAD
part: **11** BUSINESSEND
porch: **5** STOOP
Ship: **4** PROW
Sock: **3** TOE
Stage: **5** APRON
Was in: **3** LED
wheel alignment: **5** TOEIN
**Fronted: 3** LED

**Frontier**
Final: **5** SPACE
nickname: **4** DANL
settlement: **7** OUTPOST
trophy: **5** SCALP
**Frontiersman**
~ Carson: **3** KIT
~ Crockett: **4** DAVY
**Frontman**
U2: **4** BONO
**Fronton**
gear: **6** CESTAS
**Front-page**
stuff: **4** NEWS
**"Front Page, The"**
coauthor: **5** HECHT
**Front-runner: 6** LEADER
**Frosh**
Academy: **5** PLEBE
Former: **4** SOPH
topper: **6** BEANIE
**Frost: 3** ICE **4** HOAR POET
RIME
bite: **3** NIP
Bit of: **4** POEM
lines: **4** POEM **5** VERSE
Melt the ~ from: **5** DEICE
over: **5** ICEUP
prefix: **5** PERMA
remover: **6** DEICER
Touch of: **3** NIP
**Frost, Jack**
touch: **3** NIP
**Frost, Robert**
farm site: **5** DERRY
piece: **4** POEM
**Frost-covered: 4** RIMY **5** RIMED
**Frosted: 4** ICED RIMY
Get: **5** ICEUP
**Frostflower: 5** ASTER
**Frostiness: 3** NIP
**Frosting**
pro: **4** ICER
Put ~ on: **3** ICE
**Frosty: 3** ICY **5** CRISP
**7** SNOWMAN
Button, to: **4** NOSE
covering: **4** HOAR RIME
eyes: **4** COAL
**Froth: 4** FOAM
**Frothy: 5** BARMY FOAMY
LIGHT
Get: **4** FOAM
quaff: **3** ALE
**Frowned-on**
thing: **4** NONO
thing (var.): **4** TABU
**Frowning: 3** SAD
**Frozen**
confection brand: **4** ICEE
dessert: **3** ICE **6** GELATO
SORBET **7** SHERBET
dessert chain: **4** TCBY
dew: **4** HOAR
food brand: **4** EGGO **6** OREIDA
**8** BIRDSEYE

quarters: 6 IGLOOS
rain: 4 HAIL 5 SLEET
They can be: 6 ASSETS
treats: 4 ICES
waffle brand: 4 EGGO
~ Wasser: 3 EIS

**Frug**
Dance like the:
10 HULLYGULLY

**Frugal**
Be: 5 STINT 6 SCRIMP
fellow: 5 SAVER

**Fruit**
Aptly named: 4 UGLI
Big citrus: 6 POMELO
Big name in: 4 DOLE
Big name in ~ drinks:
5 MOTTS
Blackthorn: 4 SLOE
Breakfast: 5 MELON
center: 3 PIT 4 CORE
Cereal: 6 RAISIN
Chinese: 6 LITCHI
Chutney: 5 MANGO
Citrus: 4 LIME UGLI
5 LEMON 6 ORANGE
cocktail fruit: 4 PEAR
Compote: 4 PEAR
covering: 4 RIND
Dried: 5 PRUNE
Early winter: 9 SNOWAPPLE
flaw: 6 BRUISE
Fleshy: 4 PEAR POME
5 PAPAW
for a twist: 4 LIME
Forbidden ~ site: 4 EDEN
Fuzzy: 4 KIWI 5 PEACH
Green: 4 KIWI LIME 5 OLIVE
Hybrid: 4 UGLI 7 TANGELO
Jamaican: 4 UGLI
Jelly: 5 GRAPE GUAVA
Juicy: 4 PEAR 5 MELON
PEACH 6 ORANGE
Margarita: 4 LIME
Mediterranean: 3 FIG 4 DATE
Melonlike: 5 PAPAW 6 PAPAYA
Newton: 3 FIG
Not a pretty: 4 UGLI
Oak: 5 ACORN
Oblong: 5 PAPAW
Orchard: 4 PEAR
Palm: 4 DATE
pastry: 7 STRUDEL
peel: 4 RIND SKIN
Pie: 5 APPLE
Plumlike: 4 SLOE
Purple: 4 SLOE
Sour: 4 SLOE 5 LEMON
spray: 4 ALAR
Tart: 4 SLOE
Trademarked: 4 UGLI
tree: 4 PEAR
Trifling: 3 FIG
Tropical: 4 DATE 5 DATES
GUAVA MANGO 6 PAPAYA
Turkish: 3 FIG

Wintergreen: 8 TEABERRY
Wrinkly: 4 UGLI 5 PRUNE
**Fruitcake:** 3 NUT 4 LOON
Nutty as a: 5 LOOPY
**Fruit drink:** 3 ADE 5 CIDER
brand: 3 HIC
suffix: 3 ADE
**Fruit-filled**
dessert: 3 PIE
pastry: 7 STRUDEL
**Fruitless:** 4 ARID VAIN
**Fruit of the Loom**
rival: 5 HANES
**Fruits de ___ :** 3 MER
**Fruity**
cocktail: 6 MAITAI
cooler: 3 ADE
dessert: 3 PIE 4 TART
drink: 3 ADE 7 SANGRIA
liqueur: 7 SLOEGIN
pastry: 4 TART
quaff: 3 ADE
spread: 3 JAM
**Fruity-smelling**
compound: 5 ESTER
**Frustrate:** 4 FOIL 6 STYMIE
THWART
**Frustration**
Cry of: 5 AARGH
___-frutti: 5 TUTTI
**Fry:** 5 SAUTE
Fish ~ sound: 3 SSS
Small: 3 TOT 4 TOTS TYKE
6 NIPPER
When the French: 3 ETE
Word before: 4 DEEP STIR
5 SMALL
**Frying**
medium: 4 LARD 7 DEEPFAT
pan: 7 SKILLET
Prepare for: 5 FLOUR
Source of rings for: 5 ONION
**Frypan**
Chinese: 3 WOK
**"F Troop"**
corporal: 5 AGARN
sergeant: 7 OROURKE
**Ft. Worth**
school: 3 TCU
**"___ Fu" (1970s western):**
4 KUNG
**Fudd**
Elmer: 4 TOON
of cartoons: 5 ELMER
**Fuddy-duddy:** 4 DODO FOGY
6 GEEZER STODGY
13 STICKINTHEMUD
**Fudge:** 5 CHEAT
flavor: 5 MAPLE MOCHA
~, to a dieter: 4 NONO
**"Fudge!":** 4 DARN RATS
**Fudger**
Fact: 4 LIAR
**Fuel**
Add ~ to: 5 STOKE
additive: 3 STP

Alternative: 7 GASOHOL
Auto: 3 GAS
Barbecue: 7 PROPANE
Blast-furnace: 4 COKE
Bog: 4 PEAT
carrier: 5 OILER 6 TANKER
cartel: 4 OPEC
Chafing dish: 6 STERNO
Commercial: 7 COALGAS
efficiency abbr.: 3 MPG
Flamethrower: 6 NAPALM
Fossil: 3 GAS OIL 4 COAL
Funny-car: 5 NITRO
Furnace: 4 COKE
gas: 6 ETHANE
Hybrid: 7 GASOHOL
Lighter: 6 BUTANE
org.: 4 OPEC
Organic: 4 PEAT
prefix: 3 SYN
Vegetable: 4 PEAT
**Fugard**
Playwright: 5 ATHOL
title word: 5 ALOES
**Fugitive:** 7 ESCAPEE
financier: 5 VESCO
Help a: 4 ABET
**"Fugitive, The"**
actor Barry: 5 MORSE
actress Ward: 4 SELA
pursuer: 6 GERARD
**Fugue**
master: 4 BACH
**Fuji**
competitor: 4 AGFA 5 KODAK
outflow: 4 LAVA
**Fujimori**
land: 4 PERU
of Peru: 7 ALBERTO
**Fulcrum**
locale: 6 SEESAW
Oar: 5 THOLE
**Fulda**
feeder: 4 EDER
**Fulfill**
Fully: 4 SATE
**Fulfilled:** 3 MET
Not: 5 UNMET
**Full:** 5 LADEN SATED
6 ENTIRE
assemblies: 5 PLENA
At ~ gallop: 5 APACE
At ~ speed: 5 AMAIN
circle: 3 LAP
Completely: 5 SATED
Do a ~ monty: 5 STRIP
extent: 4 SPAN
Fill beyond: 4 SATE 7 SATIATE
force: 5 BRUNT
For the ~ orchestra: 5 TUTTI
Going ~ tilt: 4 ATIT
Hardly the ~ gamut: 4 ATOB
house: 4 HAND
house sign: 3 SRO
In ~ flower: 4 OPEN
6 ABLOOM

moon: 5 PHASE
name part: 3 III
Not at ~ power: 5 ONLOW
of (suffix): 3 OSE
of back talk: 5 SASSY
of chutzpah: 5 NERVY
of energy: 4 GOGO 5 ALIVE
   PEPPY VITAL ZIPPY
of excitement: 4 AGOG
of feeling: 5 LYRIC
of fervor: 6 ONFIRE
of good cheer: 5 MERRY
of gossip: 5 DISHY
of guile: 3 SLY 4 WILY
of meaning: 4 DEEP
of merriment: 6 JOCOSE
of nervous energy: 5 ANTSY
of oneself: 4 SMUG VAIN
of pep: 4 PERT SPRY 5 ALIVE
of school spirit: 6 RAHRAH
of streaks: 4 LINY
of substance: 5 MEATY
of vice: 4 EVIL
of vinegar: 5 PEPPY
   6 ACETIC
of wonder: 5 INAWE
of zip: 4 PERT
Playing with a ~ deck: 4 SANE
   8 ALLTHERE
range: 5 GAMUT
skirt: 6 DIRNDL
With ~ force: 5 AMAIN
**Full-bodied:** 4 RICH
   6 ROBUST
**Fuller**
figure: 4 DOME
**Fullest**
Enjoy to the: 5 SAVOR
extent: 4 HILT
**Full-house**
notice: 3 SRO
**"Full House"**
actor Bob: 5 SAGET
**Full-length:** 5 UNCUT
**"Full Metal Jacket"**
setting: 3 NAM
**Fullness:** 7 SATIETY
**Full-price**
payer: 5 ADULT
**Full-scale:** 6 ALLOUT
**Fully:** 3 ALL 5 INALL
fulfill: 4 SATE
grown: 5 ADULT
Not ~ closed: 4 AJAR
**Fulminate:** 4 RAGE RAIL
**Fulton**
power: 5 STEAM
**Fumble:** 3 ERR
for words: 3 HAW
**Fume:** 4 BOIL STEW 5 STEAM
   6 SEERED SEETHE
More than: 4 RAGE
**Fuming:** 5 IRATE 7 ENRAGED
**Fun:** 4 JEST
For: 7 ONALARK
Have: 4 PLAY 5 ENJOY

Make ~ of: 3 RAG RIB 4 JAPE
   MOCK RAZZ 5 RAGON
   TEASE 6 DERIDE
   HOOTAT JEERAT PARODY
   7 SNEERAT
Partner of: 5 GAMES
Poke ~ at: 3 KID RIB 4 MOCK
   TWIT 5 TEASE 6 NEEDLE
time: 3 GAS
~, for short: 3 REC
**Function:** 3 ACT JOB USE
   4 ROLE TASK WORK
Kind of: 4 TRIG
prefix: 3 DYS MAL
suffix: 3 ARY
Trig: 4 SINE 5 COSEC COTAN
   6 COSINE SECANT
   7 ARCSINE
**Functional:** 5 UTILE 6 USABLE
prefix: 3 DYS
**Fund:** 5 ENDOW
for the future: 7 NESTEGG
Kind of: 5 SLUSH TRUST
   6 NOLOAD
org.: 3 SSA
Svgs.: 3 IRA
**Fundamental:** 3 KEY 4 CORE
   5 BASAL BASIC
position: 5 TENET
**Fundamentals:** 4 ABCS
**Funder**
Campaign: 3 PAC
PBS: 3 NEA
**Fund-raiser:** 7 BENEFIT
   8 TELETHON
D.C.: 3 PAC
Government: 5 LOTTO
Popular: 6 RAFFLE
   8 BAKESALE
**Fund-raisers**
pass it: 3 HAT
Some: 7 DINNERS
**Fund-raising**
gp.: 3 PAC PTA
letter: 6 APPEAL
suffix: 4 THON
**Funeral**
bell: 5 KNELL
fire: 4 PYRE
march symphony: 6 EROICA
stand: 4 BIER
**"Funeral in Berlin"**
author Deighton: 3 LEN
**Funereal**
fires: 5 PYRES
**Funfair**
feature: 4 RIDE
**"Fun, Fun, Fun"**
car: 5 TBIRD
**Fungi**
Fermenting: 6 YEASTS
partner to form lichens:
   5 ALGAE
Tasty: 6 MORELS
**Fungus**
Cereal: 5 ERGOT

Grain: 4 SMUT
growth: 4 MOLD 6 MILDEW
**Funhouse**
sounds: 4 EEKS
**Funk**
In a: 3 SAD
of Funk & Wagnalls: 5 ISAAC
Puts in a: 7 BUMSOUT
**"Funky Cold Medina"**
rapper: 7 TONELOC
**Fun-loving**
fellow:
   15 GOODTIMECHARLIE
**Funnel**
shape: 4 CONE
**Funnel-shaped:** 5 CONED
   CONIC
flower: 7 PETUNIA
**Funnies:** 6 COMICS
**Funny:** 3 ODD 4 JOKE 5 ANTIC
   COMIC 7 COMEDIC
   RISIBLE STRANGE
brothers: 6 MARXES
business: 5 ANTIC 6 ANTICS
guy: 3 WAG
Have a ~ feeling: 5 SENSE
Ironically: 3 WRY
joke: 6 GASSER
one: 4 RIOT 5 COMIC
person: 4 CARD 5 CUTUP
sketch: 4 SKIT
**"Funny!":** 4 HAHA
**Funny-car**
fuel: 5 NITRO
**"Funny Girl"**
actor Omar: 6 SHARIF
composer Jule: 5 STYNE
**Funnyman:** 3 WIT
~ Jacques: 4 TATI
~ Jay: 4 LENO
~ Mort: 4 SAHL
**Funt**
gear: 6 CAMERA
TV host: 5 ALLEN
Word from: 5 SMILE
**Fur:** 4 COAT HIDE 6 PELAGE
Brown: 5 OTTER STOAT
   6 NUTRIA
Expensive: 4 MINK 5 SABLE
   6 ERMINE
Like the ~ seal: 5 EARED
Lose: 4 SHED
Make the ~ fly: 4 SHED
piece: 4 WRAP 5 STOLE
Rabbit: 4 CONY 5 CONEY
   LAPIN
Royal: 6 ERMINE
tycoon: 5 ASTOR
**"Für ___":** 5 ELISE
**Furbys**
and others: 4 FADS
**Furies**
Avenging: 9 EUMENIDES
One of the: 6 ALECTO
**Furious:** 5 ANGRY IRATE
with: 5 MADAT

**"Fur Is Dead"**
org.: 4 PETA
**Furlongs**
Eight: 4 MILE
**Furlough:** 5 LEAVE
**Furloughed:** 7 ONLEAVE
**Furnace:** 4 KILN
Blast ~ input: 3 ORE
   7 IRONORE
button: 5 RESET
fodder: 4 COAL
fuel: 3 OIL 4 COKE
output: 4 HEAT
Put through a: 5 SMELT
tender: 6 STOKER
**Furnish:** 4 LEND 5 ENDOW
   EQUIP YIELD 6 RENDER
   7 ENTITLE
food: 5 CATER
with gear: 5 EQUIP
**Furnished**
Less: 5 BARER
**Furnishing**
Cubicle: 4 DESK
style: 5 DECOR
**Furnishings:** 5 DECOR
Big name in: 4 IKEA
**Furniture**
Bar: 5 STOOL 6 STOOLS
Classroom: 5 DESKS
Clean the: 4 DUST
designer Charles: 5 EAMES
ensemble: 5 SUITE
finisher: 7 STAINER
Fix some: 6 RECANE
giant: 4 IKEA
Hawaiian ~ wood: 3 KOA
Like Chippendale: 6 ROCOCO
Like some: 5 OAKEN 6 INLAID
Living room: 4 SOFA 5 DIVAN
   8 ARMCHAIR
mover: 3 VAN
Nursery: 4 CRIB
Office: 4 DESK 5 DESKS
Parlor: 10 POOLTABLES
polish scent: 5 LEMON
store section: 5 SOFAS
Versatile: 6 DAYBED
   7 SOFABED
wheel: 6 CASTER
wood: 3 ASH OAK 4 TEAK
   5 CEDAR
worker: 7 STAINER
**Furor:** 3 ADO 4 RAGE 5 MANIA
**Furrier**
Famed: 5 ASTOR
offering: 4 PELT 6 ERMINE
**Furrow:** 3 RUT 4 KNIT LINE
   SEAM

fillers: 5 SEEDS
former: 3 HOE 4 PLOW
Narrow: 5 STRIA
**Furrowed:** 4 KNIT 7 STRIATE
It may be: 4 BROW
**Furry:** 6 PILOSE
feet: 4 PAWS
frolicker: 5 OTTER
neckwear: 3 BOA
sci-fi critter: 4 EWOK
sitcom E.T.: 3 ALF
swimmer: 5 OTTER
~ Australian: 5 KOALA
**Furry-tailed**
rodent: 8 DORMOUSE
**Furtado**
Singer: 5 NELLY
**Further:** 3 AND TOO 4 ALSO
   ELSE MORE
Go no: 3 END 4 STOP
Refrain from taking ~ action:
   6 SITPAT
Say: 3 ADD
shorten: 5 RESAW
Without ~ delay: 3 NOW
**Furthermore:** 3 AND TOO
   4 ALSO PLUS
**Furtive:** 3 SLY 6 SNEAKY
In a ~ manner: 5 SLYLY
look: 4 PEEK
one: 5 SNEAK
whisper: 4 PSST
**Furtively:** 8 ONTHESLY
Follow: 4 TAIL
Move: 5 SIDLE SLINK SNEAK
   6 TIPTOE
**Fury:** 3 IRE 4 RAGE 5 ANGER
   WRATH
**Fusco, Paul**
TV puppet voiced by: 3 ALF
**Fuse:** 3 WED 4 MELD WELD
   5 SMELT UNITE
   6 CEMENT SOLDER
metal: 4 WELD
Molotov cocktail: 3 RAG
unit: 3 AMP 6 AMPERE
Word on a: 4 AMPS
**Fuselage**
fastener: 5 RIVET
**Fusilli:** 5 PASTA
**Fusion:** 5 ALLOY
**Fuss:** 3 ADO 4 FRET STEW
   STIR TODO 5 HOOHA
   STINK 6 HASSLE
   HOOPLA
over oneself: 5 PREEN
over, with "on": 4 DOTE
Put up a: 4 BALK 6 BEEFED
   7 PROTEST

**Fussbudget:** 4 PRIG 5 BIDDY
**Futhark**
symbol: 4 RUNE
**Futile:** 4 VAIN 5 NOUSE
   6 OTIOSE 7 USELESS
**Future**
atty.'s exam: 4 LSAT
DA's course: 6 PRELAW
Deck of the: 5 TAROT
doc's exam: 4 MCAT
examiner: 4 SEER 6 ORACLE
   7 SEERESS
fern: 5 SPORE
fish: 3 ROE
flour: 5 GRIST
flower: 4 SEED
frog: 7 TADPOLE
fry: 3 ROE
Funds for the: 8 NESTEGGS
indicator: 4 OMEN
In the: 5 AHEAD HENCE
   LATER
In the near: 4 ANON SOON
Know the: 7 SEEINTO
Near: 6 OFFING
Now or in the: 4 EVER
oak: 5 ACORN
One with a promising:
   7 STARLET
Past, present, or: 5 TENSE
plant: 4 SEED
queen: 4 PAWN
school: 3 ROE
Sign of the: 4 OMEN
tulip: 4 BULB
**"Future Shock"**
writer Toffler: 5 ALVIN
**Futurist:** 4 SEER
**Futuristic**
play: 3 RUR
servant: 5 ROBOT
**Fuzz:** 3 NAP 4 COPS HEAT
   LINT
**Fuzzbuster**
finding: 5 RADAR
**Fuzzy:** 5 VAGUE 7 UNCLEAR
Become: 4 BLUR
fruit: 4 KIWI 5 PEACH
hang-ups: 4 DICE
image: 4 BLUR
**Fuzzy Wuzzy**
lack: 4 HAIR
**"Fuzzy Wuzzy ___ fuzzy":**
   5 WASNT
**FX**
subjects: 3 ETS
**FYI**
Part of: 3 FOR
**___ Fyne, Scotland:** 4 LOCH

# Gg

**G:** 3 KEY 4 CLEF NOTE THOU
  Black key above: 5 AFLAT
  follower: 4 SUIT
  neighbor: 5 AFLAT
  The ~ in GTO: 4 GRAN
**G, Kenny**
  buy: 4 REED
  instrument: 3 SAX
  record label: 6 ARISTA
**G4**
  computer: 3 MAC
**G-8**
  member: 3 USA
**Ga.**
  city: 3 ATL
  neighbor: 3 ALA FLA 4 TENN
  setting: 3 EST
**Gab:** 3 JAW YAK 4 CHAT CHIN
     TALK 6 NATTER
     7 PRATTLE
  suffix: 4 FEST
**Gab and gab:** 5 RUNON
     8 NATTERON
**Gable**
  Butler, for: 4 ROLE
  part: 4 EAVE
  place: 4 ROOF
**Gabler**
  creator: 5 IBSEN
  Ibsen's: 5 HEDDA
**"___ Gabler":** 5 HEDDA
**___ Gables, Florida:** 5 CORAL
**Gabor**
  and Perón: 4 EVAS
  sister: 3 EVA 5 MAGDA
     6 ZSAZSA
**Gabor, Zsa Zsa**
  1966 ~ comedy:
     15 ARRIVEDERCIBABY
**Gabriel:** 3 SAN
  companion: 5 URIEL
  ___ Gabriel: 3 SAN
**Gabrielle**
  Model: 5 REECE
**Gad**
  about: 4 ROAM ROVE
     6 RAMBLE 7 TRAIPSE
**Gadabout:** 4 GOER 5 ROVER
     6 ROAMER
**Gadget:** 5 GIZMO 6 DOODAD
  Kitchen: 5 CORER DICER
     PARER RICER TIMER
     6 BASTER BEATER
     GRATER OPENER
     PEELER REAMER
  Sharp: 3 AWL
**Gadsden Purchase**
  city: 6 TUCSON

**"Gadzooks!":** 4 EGAD OATH
**Gaea**
  Child of: 5 TITAN
**Gael:** 4 CELT SCOT
  college: 4 IONA
  tongue: 4 ERSE
**Gaelic:** 4 ERSE
  name for Ireland: 4 EIRE
  poet: 6 OSSIAN
  pop star: 4 ENYA
  Scots: 4 ERSE
  tongue: 4 ERSE
**Gaetano**
  Librettist: 5 ROSSI
**Gaff:** 4 SPAR
**Gaffe:** 5 ERROR
  Half a: 3 BOO
**Gaffer**
  aide: 7 BESTBOY
**Gag:** 4 JAPE JEST JOKE
  reflex: 4 HAHA
  response, informally: 4 LAFF
**Gaga**
  Be ~ over: 4 RAVE 5 ADORE
  Went ~ over: 5 LOVED
**Gagarin**
  Cosmonaut: 4 YURI
**Gage, Nicholas**
  book: 5 ELENI
**Gaggle**
  formation: 3 VEE
  greeting: 4 HONK
  member: 5 GOOSE
  members: 5 GEESE
**Gagné**
  of baseball: 4 ERIC
**Gailey**
  Actor: 4 FRED
**Gain**
  access: 5 ENTER LOGIN
  altitude: 4 SOAR
  entry: 5 GETIN
  Grid: 5 YARDS
  in the polls: 5 SURGE
  Monetary: 5 LUCRE
  Small football: 4 YARD
  Unrealized: 11 PAPERPROFIT
**Gained**
  a lap: 3 SAT
**Gainesville**
  athlete: 5 GATOR
  City near: 5 OCALA
**Gains**
  Ill-gotten: 4 LOOT PELF
     SWAG 5 BOOTY LUCRE
     11 FILTHYLUCRE
  NFL: 3 YDS
**Gainsay:** 4 DENY 5 BELIE

**Gait:** 4 PACE STEP
  Easy: 4 LOPE TROT 5 AMBLE
  Fast: 6 GALLOP
  Hobbling: 4 GIMP
**Gaius**
  garb: 4 TOGA
  greeting: 3 AVE
**Gal**
  counterpart: 3 GUY
  of song: 3 SAL
  Society: 3 DEB
  ~ Fri.: 4 ASST
**Gal.**
  Book before: 3 EPH
  parts: 3 QTS
**Gala:** 4 BASH FETE 5 EVENT
     6 SOIREE
**Galahad**
  Like: 4 PURE
  Mother of: 6 ELAINE
  title: 3 SIR
**Galápagos**
  creature: 6 IGUANA
  owner: 7 ECUADOR
**Galatea**
  Love of: 4 ACIS
**Galatians**
  Book before ~ (abbr.): 3 EPH
**Galba**
  Emperor after: 4 OTHO
  greeting: 3 AVE
  predecessor: 4 NERO
**Gale:** 5 STORM
  family pet: 4 TOTO
  Novelist: 4 ZONA
  Sail in a: 4 SCUD
**Galena:** 3 ORE 7 LEADORE
**Galería de ___:** 4 ARTE
**Galilee:** 3 SEA
  town: 4 CANA
**Galileo:** 5 PISAN
  birthplace: 4 PISA
**Gall:** 5 CRUST NERVE
**Gallagher**
  Actress: 5 MEGAN
  of Oasis: 4 NOEL
**Gallantry**
  RAF award for: 3 DSO
**Gallery**
  Art: 5 SALON
  display: 3 ART
  district of NYC: 4 SOHO
  Do a ~ job: 4 HANG
     6 REHANG
  Flashy ~ display: 5 OPART
  Fruit in a: 9 STILLLIFE
  London: 4 TATE
  NYC: 4 MOMA

Washington: 5 FREER
**Galley**
Ancient: 7 TRIREME
Do ~ work: 4 EDIT
　7 TYPESET
gear: 4 OARS
goofs: 5 TYPOS 6 ERRATA
Like a: 5 OARED
marking: 4 STET 5 CARET
need: 3 OAR
Remove from the: 4 DELE
tool: 3 OAR
Two-tiered: 6 BIREME
**Gallic**
girlfriend: 4 AMIE
goodbye: 5 ADIEU
**Gallico, Paul**
title character: 5 ARRIS
**Gallic Wars**
hero: 6 CAESAR
**Gallimaufry:** 4 OLIO
　7 MELANGE
**Gallivant:** 3 GAD 4 ROAM ROVE
　7 TRAIPSE
**Gallo**
brother: 5 JULIO 6 ERNEST
**Gallon**
fraction: 4 PINT 5 QUART
**Gallons**
252 wine ~: 3 TUN
**Gallop:** 3 HIE 4 GAIT LOPE
　RACE
At full: 5 APACE
Easy: 6 CANTER
**Galloper**
Graceful: 4 ARAB
**Galloping:** 5 RAPID SWIFT
**"Galloping Ghost"**
of football: 9 REDGRANGE
**"Galloping Gourmet, The"**
Graham: 4 KERR
**Galloway**
gal: 4 LASS
**Gallows**
loop: 5 NOOSE
reprieve: 4 STAY
**Gallup**
concern: 5 TREND
work: 4 POLL
**Galoot:** 3 APE LUG MUG OAF
　6 BIGAPE
**Galore:** 7 APLENTY
**Gals.**
Fourths of: 3 QTS
**Galvanization**
metal: 4 ZINC
**Galway, James**
hometown: 7 BELFAST
instrument: 5 FLUTE
**Galway Bay**
island group: 4 ARAN
**Gambia**
neighbor: 7 SENEGAL
**Gambit:** 4 RUSE 6 TACTIC
**Gamble:** 3 BET 4 DARE
　RISK

**Gambler**
asset: 4 LUCK
loss: 5 SHIRT
marker: 3 IOU 4 CHIT
mecca: 4 RENO 6 CASINO
method: 6 SYSTEM
money: 5 STAKE
woe: 4 LOSS
**Gambling:** 4 VICE
city: 4 RENO
game: 3 LOO 4 FARO KENO
　5 BEANO LOTTO MONTE
mecca: 4 RENO
site (abbr.): 3 OTB
**Gambol:** 4 PLAY ROMP SKIP
Place to: 3 LEA
**Game**
32-card ~: 4 SKAT
48-card ~: 8 PINOCHLE
accessory: 8 EGGTIMER
Ahead of the: 5 ONEUP
aim: 3 WIN
Alley: 7 TENPINS
Ball: 5 BOCCE
Be in the: 4 PLAY
Big: 3 ELK 4 DEER
Big ~ venue: 5 ARENA
bird: 8 PHEASANT
Board: 5 CHESS PENTE
　SORRY
Call a: 3 REF UMP
Card: 3 GIN LOO UNO WAR
　4 SKAT STUD 6 CASINO
　ECARTE FANTAN GOFISH
　7 OLDMAID
Casino: 4 FARO KENO
　5 CRAPS
catcher: 5 SNARE
center: 3 TAC
Close, in a: 4 WARM
Computer: 4 DOOM MYST
Con: 4 SCAM 5 BUNKO
　STING 8 FLIMFLAM
division: 4 HALF
ender: 4 HORN MATE
ending: 4 ALAI
Final Four: 4 SEMI
First: 6 OPENER
fish: 4 BASS TUNA 5 TROUT
　6 MARLIN TARPON
Gets: 6 SNARES
Go for: 4 HUNT
Half court: 4 ALAI
High-risk:
　15 RUSSIANROULETTE
"It": 3 TAG
keeper: 5 SNARE 6 ARCADE
Kids': 3 TAG 8 PATACAKE
　REDROVER 9 HOPSCOTCH
　SIMONSAYS
　11 HIDEANDSEEK
Lawn: 5 BOCCI
Like a perfect: 5 NOHIT
maker: 5 ATARI
Match: 3 NIM 7 OLDMAID
Mating: 5 CHESS

Middle of a: 3 TAC
named for a king: 4 FARO
needs: 5 RULES
Numbers: 4 KENO 5 BEANO
　BINGO LOTTO
of chance: 4 KENO 5 BEANO
　LOTTO
of chukkers: 4 POLO
one: 6 OPENER
on horseback: 4 POLO
opener: 3 TIC
piece: 3 DIE MAN PEG 4 TILE
plan: 4 IDEA 8 SCENARIO
　STRATEGY
played with dollar bills:
　10 LIARSPOKER
point: 4 ADIN
Pub: 5 DARTS 7 SNOOKER
ragout: 5 SALMI
room: 3 DEN 6 ARCADE
Running: 3 TAG
segment: 4 HALF
Shell: 4 SCAM
Simple: 4 PONG
Small: 4 PREY 5 HARES
Spelling: 5 GHOST
stick: 6 CROSSE
stickers: 6 SPEARS
Still in the: 5 ALIVE
Three-card: 5 MONTE
Three-player: 4 SKAT
winner: 3 OOO
with aces and chips: 4 GOLF
with car tokens: 4 LIFE
with mallets: 4 POLO
with matchsticks: 3 NIM
with pitching: 4 GOLF
with Skip cards: 3 UNO
with trump cards: 4 SKAT
with two bases: 7 ONEACAT
Won every: 5 SWEPT
Word: 5 GHOST
**"___ Game, The":** 6 PAJAMA
**"Game, ___, and match":** 3 SET
**Game-ending**
cry: 3 GIN 4 IWIN MATE
**Games**
Big name in: 4 SEGA 5 ATARI
　HOYLE
Fun and: 3 REC
gp.: 3 IOC
Like some: 5 NOHIT
Site of ancient: 5 NEMEA
Some big: 5 BOWLS
What some ~ end in: 4 ATIE
**Game show**
announcer Don: 5 PARDO
announcer Johnny: 5 OLSON
Comedy Central ~ host:
　5 STEIN
first name: 4 ALEX MERV
　5 REGIS
host: 5 EMCEE
host Pat: 5 SAJAK
host Trebek: 4 ALEX
offer: 5 PRIZE

panelist Peggy: 4 CASS
prize: 3 CAR 4 TRIP 6 NEWCAR
request: 3 ANA ANE ANI ANO
**Gamesmanship**
Turn on the: 5 PSYCH
**"Games People Play"**
author: 5 BERNE
**Gamete**
Female: 4 OVUM
**Gametes:** 3 OVA
**Gaming**
cube: 3 DIE
device: 10 PUNCHBOARD
**Gamma**
preceder: 4 BETA
**Gamma ___:** 8 GLOBULIN
**Gamut:** 4 ATOZ 5 RANGE
Hardly the full: 4 ATOB
**Gamy:** 3 OFF
**Gance**
Director: 4 ABEL
**Gandalf**
Letter for: 4 RUNE
portrayer McKellen: 3 IAN
**Gander:** 4 MALE 5 GOOSE
Take a ~ at: 3 EYE SEE
**Ganders:** 5 GEESE
**Gandhi:** 5 HINDU RAJIV
6 INDIRA
associate: 5 NEHRU
Father of: 5 NEHRU
land: 5 INDIA
Mrs. ~: 6 INDIRA
Rule opposed by: 3 RAJ
Title for: 7 MAHATMA
**Gandolfini**
costar: 5 FALCO
role: 7 SOPRANO
**G&S**
title character: 3 IDA
**Gang:** 3 MOB 5 POSSE
6 CIRCLE
addition: 4 STER
Chinese: 4 TONG
L.A. ~ member: 4 CRIP
land: 4 TURF
leader: 4 KOOL
Like the ~, in song:
7 ALLHERE
See the old: 5 REUNE
Some ~ members: 6 BIKERS
suffix: 4 STER
territory: 4 TURF
weapon: 4 SHIV
**"___ Gang":** 3 OUR
**Gangbuster**
~ Ness: 5 ELIOT
**Ganges**
city: 5 PATNA
garb: 4 SARI 5 SARIS
Where the ~ flows: 5 INDIA
**Gangling:** 5 LANKY
**Gangplank:** 4 RAMP
Down the: 6 ASHORE
**Gangsta**
recitals: 4 RAPS

**"Gangsta's Paradise"**
rapper: 6 COOLIO
**Gangster:** 4 HOOD THUG
blade: 4 SHIV
chaser: 4 GMAN
gal: 4 MOLL
gun: 3 GAT 6 ROSCOE
known as Scarface:
6 CAPONE
nickname: 5 BUGSY
toppers: 7 FEDORAS
~ Frank: 5 NITTI
~ Lansky: 5 MEYER
**Gangway:** 5 AISLE
**Gannet:** 5 SOLAN
**Gannon University**
locale: 4 ERIE
**"___ Gantry":** 5 ELMER
**Ganymede:** 4 MOON
**Gap:** 4 VOID 5 CHASM SPACE
6 HIATUS LACUNA
Neuron: 7 SYNAPSE
**Gape:** 4 GAWK OGLE YAWN
**Gaping**
hole: 3 MAW 5 CHASM
pit: 5 ABYSS
**Garage**
band tape: 4 DEMO
capacity: 6 ONECAR
contents: 3 CAR 4 AUTO
event: 4 SALE
figs.: 4 ESTS
Gun in the: 3 REV
job: 4 LUBE
Kind of: 6 ONECAR TWOCAR
Large: 4 BARN
Like most ~ sale goods:
4 USED
occupant: 4 AUTO
sale caveat: 4 ASIS
Sitcom in a: 4 TAXI
stain: 3 OIL
**Garam ___ (spice mix):**
6 MASALA
**Garb:** 4 TOGS 5 DRESS
6 ATTIRE ENROBE
**Garbage:** 5 TRASH
barge: 4 SCOW
can, on a PC: 4 ICON
collector: 6 ASHMAN
hauler: 4 SCOW
receptacle: 3 BIN 6 ASHCAN
Taking out the: 5 CHORE
**Garbed:** 4 CLAD 5 ROBED
**Garbo:** 5 SWEDE 7 SWEDISH
1932 ~ role: 8 MATAHARI
1936 ~ role: 7 CAMILLE
Actress: 5 GRETA
homeland: 6 SWEDEN
line ender: 5 ALONE
**Garcia**
Actor: 4 ANDY
**Garcia ___, Frederico**
Poet: 5 LORCA
**Garciaparra**
of baseball: 5 NOMAR

**Garçon:** 6 WAITER
has one: 7 CEDILLA
list: 5 CARTE
**Garden**
area: 3 BED 4 PLOT
Biblical: 4 EDEN
bulb: 5 TULIP
decoration: 3 URN 5 GNOME
Do ~ work: 3 HOE 4 WEED
entrance: 4 GATE
fertilizer: 4 PEAT
fertilizer brand: 5 ORTHO
figure: 4 ADAM 5 GNOME
First: 4 EDEN
flower: 4 IRIS 5 PANSY
7 BEGONIA TEAROSE
10 SNAPDRAGON
Genesis: 4 EDEN
Hose not for the: 6 NYLONS
hose problem: 4 KINK
intruder: 4 WEED
Kind of: 4 BEER
Make a row in the: 3 HOE
party: 3 EVE 4 ADAM
pest: 4 SLUG 5 APHID
products name: 5 ORTHO
product word: 3 GRO
Rock ~ herb: 5 SEDUM
shelter: 5 ARBOR 6 GAZEBO
shrub: 6 AZALEA
spot: 4 EDEN
spot of London: 3 KEW
star: 5 ASTER
starter: 4 SEED
statue: 5 GNOME
tool: 3 HOE 4 RAKE 5 EDGER
SPADE
variety: 4 SOSO
worker: 4 HOER
**Garden City**
~ University: 7 ADELPHI
**Gardener**
bane: 5 WEEDS
in action: 4 HOER
need: 4 HOSE
of rhyme: 4 MARY
Original: 4 ADAM
purchase: 4 BULB LIME
SEED
soil: 4 LOAM 5 LOESS
tool: 3 HOE 4 RAKE 5 EDGER
SPADE 6 TROWEL
~, at times: 4 HOER 5 HOSER
RAKER 6 PRUNER
SPADER WEEDER
**Gardening**
Do some: 4 WEED
tool: 3 HOE 5 EDGER SPADE
6 WEEDER
**"Garden of ___, The" (Wilde):**
4 EROS
**"Garden of Earthly Delights"**
author: 5 OATES
painter: 5 BOSCH
**___ Gardens:** 3 KEW
5 BUSCH

**Garden-variety:** 5 PLAIN
    USUAL 6 NORMAL
    7 AVERAGE
**Gardner**
    1948 ~ film:
        15 ONETOUCHOFVENUS
    Actress: 3 AVA
    Author: 4 ERLE
    creation: 5 MASON
    pen name: 6 AAFAIR
**Garfield:** 3 CAT 6 PETCAT
    TOMCAT
    middle name: 5 ABRAM
    predecessor: 5 HAYES
    successor: 6 ARTHUR
**"Garfield"**
    dog: 4 ODIE
    foil: 4 ODIE
    girlfriend: 6 ARLENE
    guy: 3 JON
    waitress: 4 IRMA
**Garfield, James ___:** 5 ABRAM
**Garfield County, Oklahoma**
    Seat of: 4 ENID
**Garfunkel**
    Ex-partner of: 5 SIMON
    Singer: 3 ART
**"Gargantua and Pantagruel"**
    author: 8 RABELAIS
**Gargantuan:** 4 HUGE
**Gargle:** 5 RINSE
**Gargoyle**
    Like a: 4 UGLY
**Garibaldi**
    Gen.: 8 GIUSEPPE
**Garish:** 4 LOUD 5 GAUDY
    6 ROCOCO
    light: 4 NEON
**Garland**
    Hawaiian: 3 LEI
    ~, originally: 4 GUMM
**Garlic**
    Dish made with ~ and butter:
        6 SCAMPI
    mayonnaise: 5 AIOLI
    portion: 5 CLOVE
    trait: 4 ODOR
**Garment**
    border: 3 HEM
    Draped: 4 SARI TOGA
    Foundation: 6 CORSET
    Hooded: 4 COWL 5 PARKA
    Loose: 4 ROBE SARI TOGA
        5 TUNIC
    Protective: 5 SMOCK
    Sleeveless: 4 CAPE VEST
**Garner:** 3 NET 4 EARN
    5 AMASS 6 TAKEIN
    of jazz: 6 ERROLL
**Garner, Jennifer**
    series: 5 ALIAS
**Garner, John ___:** 5 NANCE
**Garnet:** 3 RED 7 DEEPRED
**Garnish**
    Bar: 5 OLIVE
    Burger: 5 ONION

Drink: 4 LIME RIND 5 OLIVE
Gelatin: 5 ASPIC
Gibson: 5 ONION
Gimlet: 4 LIME
Green: 5 CRESS
Martini: 5 OLIVE
Meat: 5 ASPIC
Salad: 5 CRESS
**Garr**
    Actress: 4 TERI
    role: 4 INGA
**Garret:** 4 LOFT
**Garrick**
    Newsman: 5 UTLEY
**Garrison:** 8 PRESIDIO
    pl. (abbr.): 3 FTS
**Garroway**
    TV host: 4 DAVE
**Garson**
    Actress: 5 GREER
**Garson, Greer**
    role: 5 CURIE 7 MINIVER
**Gary**
    Actor: 5 BUSEY 6 OLDMAN
        SINISE
    Cartoonist: 6 LARSON
    Former senator: 4 HART
    Golfer: 6 PLAYER
    Pundit: 5 BAUER
    state (abbr.): 3 IND
**Gas:** 4 FUEL
    additive: 3 STP 5 ETHYL
    Anesthetic: 6 ETHENE
    Bottled: 7 PROPANE
    brand in Canada: 4 ESSO
    choice: 8 UNLEADED
    co.: 4 UTIL
    Dangerous: 5 RADON
    Early discount ~ chain: 4 HESS
    E, on a ~ gauge: 5 EMPTY
    Flammable: 6 ETHANE
    from the past: 4 ESSO
    Fuel: 6 ETHANE
    gauge reading: 4 FULL
    gauge warning: 5 EMPTY
    Give the: 3 REV
    guzzler: 6 ENGINE
    Inert: 4 NEON 5 ARGON
        XENON
    in glass: 4 NEON
    It's a: 4 NEON
    Laughing: 5 OXIDE
    Light: 4 NEON
    Like some: 6 LEADED
    Marsh: 7 METHANE
    Natural ~ component:
        6 ETHANE
    Nerve: 5 SARIN
    Noble: 4 NEON 5 XENON
    Odorless: 5 ARGON
        6 ETHANE
    Old ~ brand: 4 ESSO
    or clutch: 5 PEDAL
    Out of: 5 TIRED
    Past: 4 ESSO
    prefix: 3 AER

provider: 4 PUMP
pump choice (abbr.): 3 REG
Radioactive: 5 RADON
rating: 6 OCTANE
Refrigerant: 5 FREON
Run out of: 4 TIRE
Sign: 4 NEON
thief device: 6 SIPHON
Treat with: 6 AERATE
~, to a Brit: 6 PETROL
**Gasconade:** 4 BRAG
**Gases**
    Heaviest of the noble:
        5 RADON
    Like some: 5 INERT
**Gasket:** 5 ORING
    Blow a: 4 RAGE 5 GOAPE
**Gaslight ___:** 3 ERA
**Gasohol:** 4 FUEL
**Gasoline:** 4 FUEL
    rating: 6 OCTANE
    type: 6 HITEST
**Gasp:** 4 PANT
    Famous last ~ start: 4 ETTU
    in delight: 3 OOH
**"Gaspard de la ___":** 4 NUIT
**Gasser:** 4 RIOT
**Gasset, ___ y**
    Philosopher: 6 ORTEGA
**Gas station**
    freebie: 3 AIR
    store: 8 MINIMART
**Gasteyer**
    Comic: 3 ANA
**Gaston**
    of baseball: 4 CITO
**Gastric**
    Like ~ juice: 4 ACID
**Gastroenteritis**
    cause: 5 ECOLI
**Gastronome:** 7 EPICURE
**Gat:** 3 ROD 6 HEATER
**Gate:** 4 TAKE
    fastener: 4 HASP 5 LATCH
    Get out of the: 5 START
    Give the: 4 OUST
    Open, as a: 5 UNBAR
    part: 5 HINGE
    Starting: 4 POST
    Water: 3 DAM
**Gate-crash:** 6 IMPOSE
    7 INTRUDE
**Gatekeeper:** 5 GUARD
    7 STPETER
**Gates**
    and others: 4 CEOS
    Like heaven's: 6 PEARLY
    Race with: 6 SLALOM
**Gateway**
    Like a: 6 ARCHED
    products: 3 PCS
    rival: 4 DELL
    Shinto temple: 5 TORII
    to Australia: 6 SYDNEY
**Gateway Arch**
    designer Saarinen: 4 EERO

**Gather:** 4 CULL REAP
　　　5 AMASS GLEAN INFER
　　　6 RAKEIN
　gradually: 5 GLEAN
　grain: 4 REAP
　in bundles: 6 SHEAVE
　intelligence: 3 SPY
　leaves: 4 RAKE
　on a surface: 4 SORB
　　　6 ADSORB
　one's strength: 6 RESTUP
　together: 5 AMASS
　with difficulty: 8 SCRAPEUP
　with effort: 7 SCAREUP
**Gatherer**
　Clue ~ (abbr.): 3 DET
　Pollen: 3 BEE
**Gathering:** 3 BEE 4 BEVY
　　　5 GROUP
　Afternoon: 3 TEA
　Ancient ~ place: 4 STOA
　　　5 AGORA
　clouds: 4 OMEN
　Farm: 3 HAY
　Hippie: 4 BEIN
　Social: 3 BEE 5 EVENT
　　　6 AFFAIR
　tool: 4 RAKE
**Gator:** 7 REPTILE
　kin: 4 CROC
　tail: 3 ADE
**___ Gatos, California:** 3 LOS
**Gatsby**
　portrayer of 1949: 4 LADD
**"Gattaca"**
　actor Hawke: 5 ETHAN
　actress Thurman: 3 UMA
**Gauche:** 6 COARSE
**"___ gauche":** 4 RIVE
**Gaucho**
　area: 6 PAMPAS
　gear: 5 REATA RIATA
　gold: 3 ORO
　plain: 5 LLANO
　rope: 5 REATA RIATA
　weapon: 4 BOLA
**Gaudy:** 4 LOUD 6 ORNATE
　sign: 4 NEON
**Gauge:** 4 DIAL 5 METER
　　　6 ASSESS
　Dash: 4 TACH
　Electrical: 7 AMMETER
**Gauguin**
　Artist: 4 PAUL
　island home: 6 TAHITI
**Gaul**
　girlfriend: 4 AMIE
　invader: 6 ATTILA
**Gaunt:** 4 BONY LANK
　　　8 RAWBONED
**Gauntlet:** 5 GLOVE
　Throw down the: 4 DARE
**Gauze**
　fabric: 5 LISSE
**Gave**
　in: 5 CAVED

　it a go: 5 TRIED
　off: 7 EMITTED
　out: 8 ASSIGNED
　up: 5 CEDED 6 WAIVED
　what for: 7 TOLDOFF
**Gavel**
　pounder's word: 4 SOLD
　　　5 ORDER
　word: 4 GONE
**Gawk:** 4 GAPE 5 STARE
　at: 3 EYE 4 OGLE
**Gawking**
　sort: 6 STARER
**Gay**
　Author: 6 TALESE
　leader: 5 ENOLA
**"Gay ___":** 5 PAREE
**___ Gay:** 5 ENOLA
**Gaye, Marvin**
　genre: 4 SOUL
**Gay Nineties:** 3 ERA 6 DECADE
**Gaynor**
　Actress: 5 MITZI
**Gaza**
　gp.: 3 PLO
**Gaze:** 5 STARE
　at: 3 EYE 6 BEHOLD
**Gazelle**
　hound: 6 SALUKI
　~, at times: 5 LOPER
**Gazer**
　Crystal: 4 SEER
**Gazetteer**
　datum: 4 AREA
**Gazillions:** 4 ALOT ATON
　　　5 SCADS
**Gazpacho**
　ingredient: 5 ONION
　　　6 TOMATO
　Like: 4 COLD
**Gazzara**
　Actor: 3 BEN
**Gdansk**
　resident: 4 POLE
**"G'day"**
　recipient: 4 MATE
**Gds.:** 4 MDSE
**GE**
　competitor: 5 AMANA
　Part of: 4 ELEC
　product: 5 TVSET
　purchase of 1986: 3 RCA
　subsidiary: 3 NBC
**Gear:** 9 EQUIPMENT
　Run out of: 4 IDLE
　tooth: 3 COG
**Gearshift**
　sequence: 5 PRNDL
**Gecko:** 6 LIZARD
**___ Geddes, Barbara**
　Actress: 3 BEL
**Gee:** 4 THOU
　follower: 5 AITCH
　preceder: 3 EFF
　preceders: 3 EFS
**"Gee!":** 4 GOSH

　Scottish: 3 OCH
**Geek:** 4 NERD
**Geeky:** 5 UNHIP
　sort: 4 NERD
**Geena**
　Actress: 5 DAVIS
　Role for: 6 THELMA
**Geese**
　formation: 3 VEE
　Why ~ migrate: 8 INSTINCT
**"Gee whillikers!":** 4 GOSH
**"Gee whiz!":** 3 BOY MAN
　　　4 GOSH
**Geezer:** 4 COOT
　queries: 3 EHS
**Gefilte-fish**
　fish: 4 CARP
**Gehrig**
　of baseball: 3 LOU
　on the diamond: 4 FOUR
**"___ geht's?":** 3 WIE
**Geiger**
　Element in a ~ counter:
　　　4 NEON
　Mr.: 4 HANS
**Geisel**
　pen name: 5 SEUSS
**Geisha**
　garb: 6 KIMONO
　sash: 3 OBI
**Gel:** 3 SET
　additive: 4 ALOE
　amount: 3 DAB
　effect: 7 WETLOOK
　Lab: 4 AGAR
**Gelatin**
　Culture: 4 AGAR
　garnish: 5 ASPIC
　shaper: 4 MOLD
**Gelcap**
　alternative: 6 TABLET
**Gellar**
　role: 5 BUFFY
**Gellar, ___ Michelle:** 5 SARAH
**Geller**
　Mentalist: 3 URI
**Gem**
　Australian: 4 OPAL
　Cameo: 4 ONYX
　Carvable: 4 JADE
　Fiery: 4 OPAL
　Green: 4 JADE 5 BERYL
　　　7 EMERALD PERIDOT
　Iridescent: 4 OPAL 5 PEARL
　Milky: 4 OPAL
　mineral: 5 BERYL
　Necklace: 5 PEARL
　Pendant ~ shape:
　　　8 TEARDROP
　Red: 4 RUBY 6 SPINEL
　Reddish-brown: 4 SARD
　shape: 6 SCARAB
　Silicon: 4 OPAL
　surface: 5 FACET
　Verbal: 3 MOT
　weight: 5 CARAT

**Gemini:**
15 CASTORANDPOLLUX
figure: 6 CASTOR
month: 4 JUNE
rocket: 5 AGENA
**Gemologist**
concern: 6 CARATS
**Gems**
Like some: 7 OPALINE
**Gemsbok:** 4 ORYX
**Gem State:** 5 IDAHO
capital: 5 BOISE
product: 5 TATER
**Gemstone:** 4 JADE OPAL
5 LAPIS 7 CATSEYE
**Gen.**
CSA: 5 RELEE
follower: 4 EXOD
WWII: 3 DDE
**Gen-___ :** 3 XER
**Gender:** 3 SEX
(abbr.): 3 FEM 4 MASC
**Gender-neutral**
Make: 5 DESEX
**Gene**
Actress: 7 TIERNEY
Critic: 6 SHALIT
Drummer: 5 KRUPA
Film cowboy: 5 AUTRY
form: 6 ALLELE
Golfer: 7 SARAZEN
material: 3 DNA RNA
**Genealogical**
record: 4 TREE
**Genealogy:** 5 ROOTS
7 LINEAGE
chart: 4 TREE
10 FAMILYTREE
gp.: 3 DAR
word: 3 NEE
**General**
address: 3 SIR
assemblies: 5 PLENA
6 ARMIES
assembly: 4 ARMY
8 TOPBRASS
command: 6 ATEASE
direction: 5 TREND
drift: 5 TENOR
Gettysburg: 5 MEADE
Greet a: 6 SALUTE
helper: 4 AIDE
In: 7 ASARULE OVERALL
in gray: 3 LEE
insignia: 4 STAR
Japanese: 4 TOJO
Kind of: 7 ONESTAR
meaning: 4 GIST
on Chinese menus: 3 TSO
pardon: 7 AMNESTY
plan: 7 ROADMAP
Revolutionary War: 4 GAGE
Turkish: 3 AGA 4 AGHA
under Dwight: 4 OMAR
vicinity: 4 AREA
**General ___ chicken:** 4 TSOS

**"General Hospital":** 4 SOAP
extra: 5 NURSE
**Generally:** 7 ASARULE
8 ALLINALL
approved: 8 ORTHODOX
**General Mills**
brand: 3 KIX 4 CHEX TRIX
5 TOTAL
**General Motors**
division: 3 GEO 4 SAAB
6 SATURN
**Generals:** 5 BRASS
Like some: 7 TWOSTAR
**Generate:** 5 SPAWN
It can ~ some interest: 4 LOAN
**Generation:** 3 AGE ERA
**Generation ___ :** 3 XER
**Generational**
misunderstanding: 3 GAP
**Generations**
Story of: 4 SAGA
**"Generations of healthy, happy
pets"**
brand: 4 ALPO
**Generator**
part: 5 ROTOR
Random number: 3 DIE
Rumor: 4 MILL
**Generic:** 6 NONAME
dog: 4 FIDO
**___ generis:** 3 SUI
**Generous:** 5 AMPLE
6 GIVING
Be: 4 GIVE 5 TREAT
6 DONATE
donation: 5 ORGAN
gifts: 8 LARGESSE
sort: 5 DONOR 6 SHARER
7 DONATOR
**Generously**
Gave: 8 LAVISHED
**Genesis:** 4 SEED 5 ONSET
START 6 ORIGIN
SOURCE
boat: 3 ARK
brother: 4 ABEL CAIN ESAU
SETH
builder: 4 NOAH
City destroyed in: 5 SODOM
figure: 3 EVE 4 ADAM
garden: 4 EDEN
grandchild: 4 ENOS
setting: 4 EDEN
son: 4 ABEL CAIN ENOS
SETH
twin: 4 ESAU
victim: 4 ABEL
**Genetic**
attribute: 5 TRAIT
carrier: 3 DNA RNA
double: 5 CLONE
letters: 3 DNA RNA
material: 3 DNA RNA
**Genetically**
Copy: 5 CLONE
related organisms: 7 BIOTYPE

**Geneticist**
creation: 5 CLONE
Pioneering: 6 MENDEL
study: 3 RNA
**Geneva**
native: 5 SWISS
**Genève**
nation: 6 SUISSE
**Genevieve:** 3 STE
**Genghis ___ :** 4 KHAN
**Genghis Khan:** 6 MONGOL
follower: 5 TATAR
**Genie**
home: 4 LAMP
offering: 4 WISH
on TV: 4 EDEN
summoner: 7 ALADDIN
**Genius:** 5 BRAIN 8 EINSTEIN
Not exactly a: 5 DENSE
**Genoa**
Region NW of: 4 ASTI
**Genome**
stuff: 3 DNA
**Genre**
1960s ~: 5 OPART
1970s ~: 5 DISCO
Comedy: 7 STANDUP
Film: 4 NOIR 5 ANIME SCIFI
6 ACTION HORROR
8 WHODUNIT
Jazz: 3 BOP 4 JIVE 5 BEBOP
Music: 3 POP RAP 4 FOLK
ROCK 5 METAL RANDB
Novel: 7 ROMANCE
Practical literary: 5 HOWTO
**Gent:** 4 CHAP
German: 4 HERR
Spanish: 5 SENOR
**Genteel:** 4 NICE
affair: 3 TEA
Hardly: 4 RUDE 5 CRASS
**Gentile:** 6 NONJEW
**Gentle:** 4 KIND MILD SOFT
TAME
breeze: 6 ZEPHYR
cycle items: 5 KNITS
handling: 3 TLC
In a ~ way: 6 TAMELY
Isn't ~ with: 4 PAWS
one: 4 LAMB
pace: 7 DOGTROT
prod: 5 NUDGE
rhythm: 4 LILT
slope: 4 RISE 6 GLACIS
touch: 3 PAT 6 CARESS
TV bear: 3 BEN
**Gentle as ___ :** 5 ALAMB
**Gentleman**
Gentleman's: 5 VALET
Hindu: 5 BABU
No: 3 CAD 4 BOOR 5 BRUTE
of the court: 4 ASHE
**"Gentleman Jim"**
Jim in: 5 ERROL
**"Gentleman's Agreement"**
director Kazan: 4 ELIA

~ Oscar winner Celeste:
  4 HOLM
**Gentlemen:** 4 SIRS
**"Gentlemen Prefer Blondes"**
  author: 4 LOOS 9 ANITALOOS
**Gentlewoman:** 4 DAME
  5 MADAM
**Gently**
  Apply: 3 DAB
  Blow: 4 WAFT
  Hold: 6 CRADLE
  Pat: 3 DAB 5 DABAT
  persuade: 4 COAX
  Prod: 5 NUDGE
  Stroke: 3 PAT PET
**Gentry:** 5 ELITE
**Genuflected:** 5 KNELT
**Genuflection**
  point: 4 KNEE
**Genuine:** 4 REAL TRUE
  6 KOSHER 8 BONAFIDE
  article: 3 THE
  Not ~ (abbr.): 4 IMIT
**Genuine Risk:** 4 MARE
**Genus**
  Cattle: 3 BOS
  Dog: 5 CANIS
  Goose: 5 ANSER
  Holly: 4 ILEX
  Maple: 4 ACER
  of garden pests: 5 APHIS
  Olive: 4 OLEA
  Our: 4 HOMO
**Gen Xer**
  predecessor: 6 BOOMER
**Geo:** 3 CAR
  model: 5 METRO PRIZM
  STORM
**Geodesic**
  item: 4 DOME
**Geoffrey**
  Designer: 5 BEENE
**Geog.**
  Old ~ initials: 3 SSR
**Geographic**
  area: 7 TERRAIN
**Géographie**
  feature: 3 ILE
**Geol.:** 3 SCI
**Geological**
  layers: 6 STRATA
  period: 3 AGE EON ERA
  5 EPOCH
  ridge: 5 ARETE ESKER
**Geom.**
  figure: 3 CIR 4 RECT
  Kin of: 3 ALG
  point: 3 CTR
  solid: 3 SPH
**Geometer**
  product: 4 AREA
**Geometric**
  calculation: 4 AREA
  curve: 3 ARC
  fig.: 3 CIR 4 RECT
  figure: 5 PRISM

locus: 7 EVOLUTE
reference line: 4 AXIS
solid: 5 TORUS
solids: 4 TORI
suffix: 3 GON
Works with ~ patterns:
  5 OPART
**Geometry**
  adjective: 7 SCALENE
  Big name in: 5 EULER
  calculation: 4 AREA
  curve: 8 PARABOLA
  Kind of: 5 PLANE SOLID
  line: 4 AXIS
  ratios: 3 PIS
**Geopolitical**
  Former ~ initials: 3 SSR
  4 USSR
**Georg**
  Physicist: 3 OHM
**Georg ___, Sir**
  Conductor: 5 SOLTI
**George**
  Actor: 5 SEGAL TAKEI
  WENDT 6 ARLISS
  7 PEPPARD
  and George W.: 4 ELIS
  Author: 5 ELIOT
  bill: 3 ONE
  Brother of: 3 IRA JEB
  Colleague of ~, Hap, and Ike:
  4 OMAR
  Comedian: 5 GOBEL 6 CARLIN
  Country singer: 6 STRAIT
  Director: 5 LUCAS
  English dramatist: 5 PEELE
  He ran against ~ and Bill:
  4 ROSS
  Humorist: 3 ADE
  John, Paul, and ~ (abbr.):
  3 STS
  Logician: 5 BOOLE
  NFL pioneer: 5 HALAS
  of baseball: 5 BRETT
  of jazz: 6 BENSON
  or Victoria: 4 LAKE
  Partner of: 6 GRACIE
  Partner of John, Paul, and:
  5 RINGO
  spokesman: 3 ARI
  TV friend of Jerry and:
  6 ELAINE
  Veep after: 3 DAN
  Wife of: 6 MARTHA
**George ___:** 3 III
**George M. ___:** 5 COHAN
**"George of the Jungle"**
  elephant: 4 SHEP
  obstacle: 4 TREE
**Georges**
  Composer: 6 ENESCO
  French writer: 5 PEREC
  Pointillism founder: 6 SEURAT
**Georgetown**
  athlete: 4 HOYA
**Georgia:** 3 SSR 5 STATE

Actress: 5 ENGEL
capital: 7 ATLANTA
city: 5 MACON 6 ATHENS
  8 MARIETTA SAVANNAH
Ex-Senator from: 4 NUNN
Fictional ~ home: 4 TARA
It's south of: 4 IRAN
Leader born in: 6 STALIN
neighbor: 7 ARMENIA
product: 7 PEACHES
Rock group from: 3 REM
state tree: 7 LIVEOAK
Where ~ is: 4 ASIA
~, et al.: 4 SSRS
**Georgia ___:** 4 TECH
**Georgian**
  neighbor: 8 ARMENIAN
**"Georgia Peach":** 4 COBB
**Georgia Tech**
  grad: 4 ENGR
**Géorgie**
  ~, for one: 4 ETAT
**"Georgy Girl"**
  star: 8 REDGRAVE
**Geppetto**
  goldfish: 4 CLEO
**Geraint**
  Love of: 4 ENID
**Geraint, Sir**
  Wife of: 4 ENID
**Gerald**
  Veep before: 5 SPIRO
**Geraldo**
  News reporter: 6 RIVERA
**Gerard**
  Actor: 3 GIL
**Gerbil:** 3 PET
**Gere**
  title role: 3 DRT
**Geriatrics**
  subject: 6 OLDAGE
**Geritol**
  ingredient: 4 IRON
**Germ:** 4 SEED 5 SPORE
  It has a: 4 IDEA
  Rod-shaped: 5 ECOLI
  Some ~ cells: 3 OVA
**Germaine**
  Feminist: 5 GREER
**German:** 6 TEUTON
  8 TEUTONIC
  admiral: 4 SPEE
  article: 3 DAS DER EIN
  4 EINE
  art songs: 6 LIEDER
  auto: 4 AUDI OPEL
  auto pioneer: 4 BENZ
  border river: 4 ODER
  capital: 4 BONN
  city: 5 BADEN ESSEN STADT
  6 BREMEN
  city with a canal: 4 KIEL
  coal region: 4 RUHR SAAR
  crowd: 4 DREI
  cry: 3 ACH
  dadaist: 5 ERNST

direction: 3 OST
donkey: 4 ESEL
Early: 6 TEUTON
First president of the ~
　republic: 5 EBERT
Former ~ chancellor: 4 KOHL
　6 BRANDT
Former ~ state: 5 BADEN
　LIPPE
gent: 4 HERR
gun: 5 LUGER 6 MAUSER
historian: 5 WEBER
industrial city: 5 ESSEN
industrial family: 6 KRUPPS
industrial region: 4 RUHR
king: 4 OTTO
mark: 6 UMLAUT
mister: 4 HERR
name part: 3 VON
one: 3 EIN 4 EINS
philosopher: 4 KANT
physicist: 3 OHM
port: 4 KIEL 5 EMDEN ESSEN
　6 BREMEN
Pre-euro ~ money: 5 MARKS
prison camp: 6 STALAG
pronoun: 3 ICH SIE 4 EINE
resort: 3 EMS
river: 3 EMS 4 EDER ELBE
　ODER RUHR SAAR
　5 FULDA RHINE WESER
ruler: 6 KAISER
series start: 4 EINS
spa: 3 EMS 5 BADEN
　10 BADENBADEN
steel city: 5 ESSEN
sub: 5 UBOAT
surrealist: 5 ERNST
thoroughfare: 7 STRASSE
title: 4 HERR
town: 5 STADT
valley: 4 RUHR SAAR
wine valley: 5 MOSEL RHINE
　~ 101 word: 3 ICH
Germane: 3 APT 8 RELEVANT
Germanic
　invader: 4 GOTH
　tribesman: 6 TEUTON
Germ-free: 7 ASEPTIC
　STERILE
"Germinal"
　author Émile: 4 ZOLA
Germinated
　barley: 4 MALT
Germs
　may grow in it: 4 AGAR
Gernreich
　Designer: 4 RUDI
Geronimo: 6 APACHE
"Gerontion"
　monogram: 3 TSE
　poet: 5 ELIOT
Gerontologist
　study: 6 OLDAGE
Gershon
　Actress: 4 GINA

Gershwin
　biographer David: 4 EWEN
　first hit: 6 SWANEE
　hero: 5 PORGY
　heroine: 4 BESS
　Lyricist: 3 IRA
　tune: 4 LIZA
Gershwin, Ira
　creation: 5 LYRIC
Gerstner
　of IBM: 3 LOU
Gertrude
　and Hamlet: 5 DANES
　Channel swimmer: 6 EDERLE
　Writer: 5 STEIN
Gerund: 4 NOUN
　maker: 3 ING
　___ gestae: 3 RES
Gesturer: 4 MIME
"Gesundheit!"
　preceder: 5 ACHOO
　6 AHCHOO
　Reason to say: 6 SNEEZE
Get: 3 NAB 4 EARN REAP
　5 GRASP 6 ATTAIN
　OBTAIN 7 RECEIVE
　by: 4 COPE PASS 5 ELUDE
　EXIST 6 MAKEDO
　MANAGE
　in: 6 ARRIVE
　it: 3 SEE
　off: 6 DEBARK
　on: 3 AGE 4 RIDE 5 BOARD
　TEASE
　to: 3 IRK 4 RILE 5 ANNOY
　REACH 6 ATTAIN
　RANKLE
　up: 4 RISE 5 ARISE AWAKE
　ROUST STAND
　~, as a job: 4 LAND
"Get ___!": 4 REAL 5 AGRIP
　ALIFE AROOM
　(hit song): 4 AJOB
Get ___ a good thing: 4 INON
Get an ___ effort: 4 AFOR
　EFOR
Getaway
　Chic: 3 SPA
　Drive a ~ car: 4 ABET
　Healthful: 3 SPA
　spot: 4 ISLE 6 RESORT
　Summer: 4 CAMP
　time: 7 WEEKEND
　Weekend: 3 INN 5 BANDB
"Get away!": 4 SCAT SHOO
"Get clean"
　program: 5 REHAB
Get ___ for effort: 3 ANA ANE
Get ___ for one's money:
　4 ARUN
Get-go: 5 ONSET
Get ___ goat: 4 ONES
"Get going!": 3 NOW 4 MOVE
　6 MOVEIT
"Get it?": 3 SEE
"___ get it": 5 IDONT

"Get lost!": 4 SCAT SHOO
　5 SCRAM 6 BEATIT
　BEGONE GOHOME
"Get my drift?": 3 SEE
Get ___ of: 3 RID 5 AHOLD
"Get ___ of yourself!": 5 AHOLD
Get ___ on the back: 4 APAT
Get ___ on the wrist: 5 ASLAP
"Get out!": 4 SCAT 5 LEAVE
　SCRAM
Get-out-of-jail
　money: 4 BAIL
"Get outta here!": 4 SCAT
　SHOO 5 SCRAM
"Get real!": 4 ASIF 6 COMEON
Get-rich-quick
　scheme: 5 HEIST
Get ___ shape: 4 INTO
"Get Shorty"
　author: 6 ELMORE
"Get Smart"
　evil gp.: 4 KAOS
Getter
　Attention: 3 HEY TAP 4 AHEM
　PSST 5 NUDGE
Get ___ the ground floor:
　4 INON
"Get the picture?": 3 SEE
Getting
　on: 3 OLD 5 AGING 6 AGEING
Getting ___ years: 4 ONIN
Get-together
　Coffee: 6 KLATCH
　Evening: 6 SOIREE
　Gala: 4 FETE
　Island: 4 LUAU
　Rural: 3 BEE
Getty
　Actress: 7 ESTELLE
Getty Center
　architect: 5 MEIER
Gettysburg
　First name at: 3 ABE
　general: 5 MEADE
　loser: 3 LEE
　victor: 5 MEADE
Gettysburg Address
　adjective: 3 AGO
Getup: 4 TOGS 5 DRESS
　6 ATTIRE
Get-up-and-go: 3 PEP VIM ZIP
　4 BRIO PUSH ZEAL ZEST
　5 DRIVE MOXIE OOMPH
　6 ENERGY
Get-well
　program: 5 REHAB
Get ___ writing: 4 ITIN
Getz
　instrument: 3 SAX
　8 TENORSAX
　of jazz: 4 STAN
Geyser
　output: 5 STEAM
Ghana
　capital: 5 ACCRA
　neighbor: 4 TOGO

people: 7 ASHANTI
river: 5 VOLTA
___ ghanouj: 4 BABA
**Ghastly:** 7 MACABRE
**Ghent**
river: 3 LYS
**Ghost**
Comics: 6 CASPER
cry: 3 BOO
Give up the: 3 DIE
Like ~ stories: 5 EERIE
Pale as a: 4 ASHY
When Hamlet sees the:
  4 ACTI
White as a: 3 WAN 4 ASHY
  PALE 5 ASHEN
Word following: 4 TOWN
**"Ghost"**
costar: 4 DEMI
role: 3 ODA
**"... ___ ghost!":** 5 SEENA
**"Ghost and Mrs. ___, The":**
  4 MUIR
**"Ghost and ___ Muir, The":**
  3 MRS
**"Ghostbusters"**
actor Harold: 5 RAMIS
character: 4 EGON
goo: 5 SLIME
**Ghostlike:** 5 ASHEN
**Ghostly:** 4 PALE 5 ASHEN
  EERIE
greeting: 3 BOO
**"Ghosts"**
playwright: 5 IBSEN
**GI**
address: 3 APO
ally of the 1950s: 3 ROK
chow: 3 MRE
duties: 3 KPS
entertainers: 3 USO
entertainment: 7 USOSHOW
gear: 7 MESSKIT
Like a ~ series: 5 BARIC
mail drop: 3 APO
meal: 7 CRATION
Missing: 4 AWOL
neckwear: 5 IDTAG
offense: 4 AWOL
squads: 3 KPS
uniforms: 3 ODS
**Gia**
Actress: 5 SCALA
**Giant:** 4 NLER 5 LARGE
  TITAN
100-eyed ~: 5 ARGUS
Global: 4 ASIA
Himalayan: 4 YETI
Rabelaisian: 9 GARGANTUA
Red: 4 MIRA 5 SSTAR
  7 ANTARES
screen format: 4 IMAX
syllable: 3 FEE FIE FUM
Tolkien: 3 ENT
Took ~ steps: 6 STRODE
Wrestling: 5 ANDRE

**"Giant"**
author Ferber: 4 EDNA
ranch: 5 REATA
**Giants**
Former ~ manager Felipe:
  4 ALOU
Hollywood: 4 EGOS
Mel of the: 3 OTT
Some: 5 OGRES
**Gibb**
Singer: 4 ANDY
**Gibbon:** 3 APE
**Gibbons**
Oscar designer: 6 CEDRIC
TV host: 5 LEEZA
**Gibbs**
Actress: 5 MARLA
Country singer: 5 TERRI
**Giblets**
part: 5 LIVER
**Gibraltar**
City near: 5 CADIZ
Port near: 7 TANGIER
~, for one (abbr.): 3 STR
**Gibran**
birthplace: 7 LEBANON
**Gibson**
1981 ~ film, with "The":
  11 ROADWARRIOR
1996 ~ film: 6 RANSOM
Actor: 3 MEL
garnish: 5 ONION
of tennis: 6 ALTHEA
role: 5 RIGGS 6 MADMAX
**Giddy**
Make: 5 ELATE
**Gide**
Author: 5 ANDRE
God, to: 4 DIEU
**"Gidget"**
actress Sandra: 3 DEE
**Gift:** 7 PRESENT
10th anniversary ~: 3 TIN
20th anniversary ~: 5 CHINA
55th anniversary ~:
  7 EMERALD
bearers: 4 MAGI
Biblical: 5 MYRRH
Clairvoyant: 3 ESP
Conciliatory: 3 SOP
decoration: 3 BOW
Diplomat: 4 TACT
Dubious: 3 ESP GAB
Engagement: 4 RING
for Dad: 3 TIE 5 RAZOR
  6 TIEPIN
for an exec: 7 DESKSET
Fourth anniversary: 5 LINEN
Give as a: 6 BESTOW
Hanukkah: 4 GELT
Hawaiian: 3 LEI
Heavenly: 5 MANNA
holder: 3 BOX
It's a: 3 GAB
Musical: 3 EAR
Pledge drive: 4 TOTE

recipient: 5 DONEE
tag word: 4 FROM
Temporary: 4 LOAN
**Gift ___:** 5 OFGAB
**Gifted**
person: 5 DONEE
**Gift-giver**
urging: 6 OPENIT
**"Gift of the ___, The":** 4 MAGI
**"Gift of the Magi, The"**
author: 6 OHENRY
gift: 3 FOB 5 COMBS
Like: 6 IRONIC
**Gifts:** 7 TALENTS
Generous: 8 LARGESSE
**Gift-wrapping**
time: 3 EVE
**Gig**
Acting: 4 ROLE
after gig: 4 TOUR
gear: 3 AMP
Part of a: 3 SET
**Gigantic:** 4 HUGE
**Giggle:** 5 LAUGH TEHEE
  6 TEEHEE TITTER
Part of a: 3 HEE
Start of a: 3 TEE
**Giggling**
muppet: 4 ELMO
sound: 5 TEHEE 6 TEEHEE
**"Gigi"**
actress Leslie: 5 CARON
**___ Gigio (TV mouse):** 4 TOPO
**"___ Gigolo" (Cole Porter):**
  3 IMA
**Gigs**
Between: 4 IDLE
**"G.I. Jane"**
actress Demi: 5 MOORE
actress Moore: 4 DEMI
**"Gil ___":** 4 BLAS
**Gila monster**
home: 6 DESERT
**Gilbert**
Actress: 4 SARA 7 MELISSA
**Gilbert & Sullivan**
fairy queen: 8 IOLANTHE
princess: 3 IDA
production: 8 OPERETTA
work, with "The": 6 MIKADO
**Gilberto**
Singer: 6 ASTRUD
**"Gil Blas"**
novelist Alain: 6 LESAGE
novelist Lesage: 5 ALAIN
**Gilda**
character Baba: 4 WAWA
Comic: 6 RADNER
**"Gilda"**
star Hayworth: 4 RITA
**Gilded:** 7 AUREATE
**Gilels**
Pianist: 4 EMIL
**"Gilgamesh":** 4 EPIC
**Gill**
of country music: 5 VINCE

opening: 4 SLIT
**Gillespie**
genre: 3 BOP 5 BEBOP
~, to fans: 3 DIZ
**Gillette**
brand: 4 ATRA
product: 5 FOAMY RAZOR
razor brand: 4 ATRA
6 SENSOR
**Gilliam**
Comic: 3 STU
**Gillian**
role: 4 DANA
**Gilligan**
boat: 6 MINNOW
was stranded on one: 4 ISLE
**"Gilligan's Island"**
actor Hale: 4 ALAN
actress Louise: 4 TINA
Ginger portrayer on: 4 TINA
Skipper portrayer on:
8 ALANHALE
**Gillis**
buddy: 5 KREBS
of TV: 5 DOBIE
**Gills**
Fill to the: 4 SATE
Four: 4 PINT
Green around the: 3 ILL
4 SICK
**Gilmore**
of basketball: 5 ARTIS
**Gilpin**
Actress: 4 PERI
**Gimel**
Letter before: 4 BETH
**Gimlet:** 4 TOOL
garnish: 4 LIME
ingredient: 9 LIMEJUICE
liquor: 3 GIN
**Gimme**
Like a: 4 EASY
on the green: 5 TAPIN
**"Gimme ___!":** 3 ANA ANE
**"Gimme a Break"**
star Carter: 4 NELL
**"Gimme a break!":** 4 CMON
**"Gimme a ...!" etc.:** 4 YELL
**Gimmick:** 4 PLOY 6 SHTICK
Marketing: 5 TIEIN
**Gin**
accompanier: 5 TONIC
drink: 4 FIZZ
flavoring: 4 SLOE
game: 5 RUMMY
Kind of: 4 SLOE
___ gin fizz: 4 SLOE
**Ginger:** 3 PEP
cookie: 4 SNAP
**Ginger ale**
Like: 7 PALEDRY
**Gingerbread**
house visitor: 6 HANSEL
**Gingerly**
Drink: 3 SIP
Go: 4 EASE

**Gingersnap:** 6 COOKIE
**Gingivitis**
What ~ affects: 4 GUMS
**Gingrich**
Former Speaker: 4 NEWT
Speaker before: 5 FOLEY
**Ginnie ___:** 3 MAE
**Ginsberg, Allen:** 8 BEATPOET
and others: 5 BEATS
poem: 4 HOWL
**Ginsburg**
Garbed like: 5 ROBED
**Ginsburg, Ruth ___**
Justice: 5 BADER
**Ginza**
cash: 3 YEN
girdle: 3 OBI
light: 4 NEON
locale: 5 TOKYO
**Giorgio**
Fashion designer: 6 ARMANI
**"___ giorno!":** 4 BUON
**Giotto**
fresco town: 6 ASSISI
work: 5 MURAL
**"Giovanna d'___":** 4 ARCO
**Gipper**
grippers: 6 CLEATS
**Gipper, The:** 6 REAGAN
**Giraffe**
feature: 4 NECK
kin: 5 OKAPI
**Girasol:** 4 OPAL
**Gird:** 5 STEEL
**Girded**
They may be: 5 LOINS
**Girder:** 4 IBAR 5 IBEAM
Letter-shaped: 5 HBEAM
IBEAM
material: 5 STEEL
**Girdle:** 6 CORSET
**Girl:** 4 LASS 5 MISSY 6 LASSIE
Ball: 3 DEB 5 BELLE
Chorus: 4 ALTO
Diamond: 3 LIL
Dickens: 4 NELL
Down Under: 6 SHEILA
Family: 3 SIS 5 NIECE
Graceful: 5 SYLPH
Hardy: 4 TESS
Impudent: 5 HUSSY
Mischievous: 6 GAMINE
Nice: 5 NELLY
or boy of song: 3 SUE
preceder: 4 ATTA
Salinger: 4 ESME
Slave ~ of opera: 4 AIDA
Society: 3 DEB
Stowe: 3 EVA
That: 3 HER SHE
Valley: 4 LILY
Young: 5 MISSY
**"___ girl!":** 4 ATTA
**"___ Girl Friday":** 3 HIS
**Girlfriend**
French: 4 AMIE

of Peter Gunn: 4 EDIE
of Sundance: 4 ETTA
of Superboy: 4 LANA LANG
**"Girl Like I, A"**
author: 4 LOOS 9 ANITALOOS
**"___ Girl Like You Loved a Boy
Like Me":** 3 IFA
**"___ Girls":** 3 LES
**Girl Scout**
emblem: 7 TREFOIL
group: 5 TROOP
**"___ Girls Go":** 5 ASTHE
**Girl-watch:** 4 OGLE
**Girth**
They practice ~ control:
7 DIETERS
**Gish, Lillian**
film, with "The":
14 BIRTHOFANATION
**Gist:** 3 NUB 4 CRUX IDEA
MEAT 5 HEART POINT
6 UPSHOT 7 ESSENCE
8 MAINIDEA
**"Git!":** 4 SCAT SHOO
5 SCRAM
**"Git ___ Little Dogies":**
5 ALONG
**Giuliani**
Former mayor: 4 RUDY
**Give:** 4 PLAY 5 ENDOW GRANT
6 DONATE
away: 4 CEDE 6 REVEAL
in: 4 CAVE 5 YIELD 6 ACCEDE
RELENT
off: 4 EMIT OMIT 5 EGEST
EXUDE 7 RADIATE
or take: 5 ABOUT
out: 3 DIE 4 CEDE EMIT FAIL
5 ALLOT ISSUE 6 ASSIGN
(out): 4 METE
up: 3 DIE 4 CEDE EMIT QUIT
5 FORGO WAIVE YIELD
6 VACATE
**Giveaway**
Gambler: 4 TELL
**"Give ___ break!":** 3 MEA
**Give ___ for one's money:**
4 ARUN
**Give-go**
link: 3 ITA
**Give ___ go:** 3 ITA
**Give-hand**
connection: 3 MEA
**"Give it ___!":** 3 AGO 4 ATRY
5 AREST
**Given**
away: 6 UNKEPT
**Give ___ of one's own
medicine:** 5 ADOSE
**Give ___ on the back:** 4 APAT
**Giver**
Blood: 5 DONOR
CPR: 3 EMT
Party: 4 HOST
Shade: 3 ELM 4 TREE
**"Give ___ rest!":** 3 ITA

**Giverny**
Artist at: 5 MONET
**Givers**
Hug: 4 ARMS
TLC: 3 RNS
**Give ___ to Cerberus:** 4 ASOP
**"Give ___ whirl!":** 3 ITA
**Giza**
neighbor: 5 CAIRO
**Gizmo:** 6 DOODAD GADGET
Kitchen: 5 CORER DICER
PARER
Office: 7 LABELER
Post office: 5 DATER
Tackle box: 6 SCALER
**Glace**
Melted: 3 EAU
**Glacial**
deposit: 7 MORAINE
epoch: 6 ICEAGE
matter: 7 ICEFALL
pinnacle: 5 SERAC
ridge: 5 ARETE ESKER
**Gladden:** 4 BUOY 5 ELATE
**Glade**
rival: 5 LYSOL
target: 4 ODOR
**Gladiator**
domain: 5 ARENA
weapon: 7 TRIDENT
**"Gladiator"**
actor Russell: 5 CROWE
garment: 4 TOGA
setting: 4 ROME 5 ARENA
**Gladly:** 4 FAIN LIEF
**Gladstone**
P.M. before: 8 DISRAELI
**"Glad that's over!":** 4 WHEW
**Gladys**
guys: 4 PIPS
**Glamour**
rival: 4 ELLE
**Glance:** 5 CAROM
8 ONCEOVER
at: 3 EYE
Impolite: 4 LEER
over: 4 READ SCAN SKIM
Quick: 4 PEEK
___ glance: 3 ATA
**Glances**
Like some: 8 SIDELONG
**Gland**
Kind of: 6 PINEAL
7 ADRENAL
prefix: 5 ADENO
Reproductive: 5 OVARY
**Glare**
Villainous: 5 SNEER
**Glaringly**
vivid: 5 LURID
**Glasgow**
gal: 4 LASS
negative: 3 NAE
Novelist: 5 ELLEN
resident: 4 SCOT
river: 5 CLYDE

**Glass**
Actor: 3 RON
Brandy: 7 SNIFTER
component: 6 SILICA
Cut: 4 ETCH
eels: 6 ELVERS
finish: 3 INE
Gas in: 4 NEON
Heat-resistant: 5 PYREX
SILEX
Jeweler: 5 LOUPE
Like some: 6 LEADED
7 STAINED
Makeshift drinking:
8 JELLYJAR
marble: 5 AGATE
of public radio: 3 IRA
part: 4 STEM
Raise a ~ to: 5 TOAST
sheet: 4 PANE
Small liqueur: 4 PONY
Small ~ container: 4 VIAL
5 PHIAL
suffix: 3 INE
Toughen, as: 6 ANNEAL
Type of: 4 SHOT
Window: 4 PANE
Word with: 3 ART
**Glass-enclosed**
porches: 7 SOLARIA
**Glasses:** 5 SPECS
Champagne: 6 FLUTES
Clink: 5 TOAST
Colored ~ color: 4 ROSE
Kind of: 5 OPERA
Like some: 6 TINTED
Opera: 9 LORGNETTE
option: 4 TINT
parts: 4 RIMS
piece: 4 LENS
**Glassful**
Toddler's: 4 WAWA
**Glassmaker**
~ Lalique: 4 RENE
**Glass-polishing**
compound: 5 CERIA
**Glassware**
material: 5 PYREX
oven: 4 LEHR
**Glassworker:** 8 ANNEALER
**Glassy**
look: 5 STARE
**Glaswegian:** 4 SCOT
negative: 3 NAE
**Glaze**
Pottery: 6 ENAMEL
**Glazed**
fabric: 6 CHINTZ TAMMIE
square: 4 TILE
**Glazier**
need: 5 PUTTY
unit: 4 PANE
**Gleam:** 5 SHINE
**Gleamed:** 5 SHONE
**Gleason**
Early ~ role: 5 RILEY

**Glee:** 5 MIRTH
club member: 4 ALTO
**"Glengarry Glen Ross"**
actor Baldwin: 4 ALEC
playwright: 5 MAMET
**Glenn**
Actress: 5 CLOSE
of the Eagles: 4 FREY
represented it: 4 OHIO
Rocker: 4 FREY
**Glenn, John**
portrayer: 8 EDHARRIS
state: 4 OHIO
**Glib**
Excessively: 3 PAT
Gift of the: 3 GAB
quality: 7 PATNESS
responses: 10 PATANSWERS
**Glide:** 5 COAST SKATE
6 SASHAY 8 ICESKATE
high: 4 SOAR
on snow: 3 SKI
**Glided:** 4 SLID
**Glider:** 5 SKATE
On a: 5 ALOFT
Snow: 4 SLED
wood: 5 BALSA
**Gliding**
Go: 4 SOAR
step: 6 CHASSE 8 GLISSADE
**Glimmering:** 4 IDEA
**Glimpse:** 3 SEE 4 ESPY LOOK
PEEK 5 SIGHT 6 PEEKAT
**Glimpsed:** 4 SEEN
**Glisten:** 5 SHINE
**Glistened:** 5 SHONE
**Glistener**
Cheek: 4 TEAR
Morning: 3 DEW
**Glistens**
It: 3 DEW 5 ASPIC
**Glitch:** 3 BUG 4 SNAG
**Glitter:** 6 TINSEL
Bit of: 7 SPANGLE
**Glitterati:** 5 ELITE 6 JETSET
8 SMARTSET
**Glittery**
material: 4 LAME
stone: 5 GEODE
topper: 5 TIARA
**Gloaming:** 3 EVE 4 DUSK
**Gloater**
cry: 3 HAH SEE
**Glob**
suffix: 3 ULE
**Global**
currency org.: 3 IMF
extreme: 4 POLE
giant: 4 ASIA
positioning fig.: 3 LAT
septet: 4 SEAS
warming treaty city: 5 KYOTO
**Globe:** 3 ORB 6 SPHERE
7 THEATRE
Company with a blue ~ logo:
5 PANAM

It circles the: 6 TROPIC
plotter: 4 IAGO
**Globin**
  prefix: 4 HEMO
**Globular:** 5 ORBED
**Globule:** 4 BEAD DROP
**Gloom:** 4 MURK 7 SADNESS
  Mood of: 4 PALL
  Partner of: 4 DOOM
**"___ gloom of night ...":** 3 NOR
**Gloomy:** 3 DUN 4 DARK DOUR
  DRAB GRAY GRIM
  6 MOROSE SOLEMN
  Act: 4 MOPE
  guy: 3 GUS
  More: 5 BLUER
  ~, in poetry: 5 DREAR
**Gloomy Gus:** 4 MOPE
**Glop:** 3 GOO
**Gloria**
  Pop singer: 7 ESTEFAN
  Writer: 7 STEINEM
**"Gloria"**
  actress Rowlands: 4 GENA
**Gloria ___ :** 5 PATRI
**"Gloria in excelsis ___":** 3 DEO
**Glorified**
  gofer: 4 AIDE
**Glorify:** 4 LAUD 5 ADORE
  BLESS EXALT EXTOL
**Glory:** 4 KUDO 5 ECLAT EXALT
  Crowning: 4 MANE
  Vein: 3 ORE 4 LODE
**Gloss:** 5 SHEEN
  target: 3 LIP 4 LIPS
**Glossary**
  entry: 4 TERM
**Glossed**
  It might be ~ over: 3 LIP
**Glossina**
  Fly of the genus: 6 TSETSE
**Glossiness:** 5 SHEEN
**Glossy:** 5 SLEEK
  brown fur: 5 OTTER
  coating: 6 ENAMEL
  fabric: 5 SATIN 6 SATEEN
  Not: 5 MATTE
  paint: 6 ENAMEL
**Glottis**
  prefix: 3 EPI
**Gloucester**
  cape: 3 ANN
**Glove**
  Baseball: 4 MITT
  compartment item: 3 MAP
  material: 5 LATEX LISLE
  SUEDE
  Oven: 4 MITT
**Gloves**
  Place to wear: 4 OVEN
  Train with: 4 SPAR
**Glow:** 4 AURA 5 ARDOR
  SHINE 8 RADIANCE
  Saintly: 4 AURA HALO
  Vegas: 4 NEON
**Glower:** 4 NEON

Fireplace: 5 EMBER
**Glowing:** 3 LIT 6 ASHINE
  7 RADIANT
  personality: 4 AURA
  remnant: 5 EMBER
  review: 4 RAVE
**Gluck**
  hero: 5 ORFEO
  Soprano: 4 ALMA
**Glue:** 4 BIND TACK 5 EPOXY
  PASTE 6 CEMENT
  Bull on ~ bottles: 5 ELMER
  name: 5 ELMER
  Stick like: 6 ADHERE
  Strong: 5 EPOXY
**Glued**
  Stay ~ to: 7 STAREAT
**Glum:** 3 SAD 4 DOUR
  6 MOROSE
  drop: 4 TEAR
**Glut:** 4 SATE 7 ENGORGE
  SATIATE
**Glutton:** 3 HOG PIG
**Gluttony:** 3 SIN
**Glyceride:** 5 ESTER
**Glycerin**
  opener: 5 NITRO
**Glyn**
  Author: 6 ELINOR
**Glyph**
  prefix: 3 TRI 5 HIERO
**GM**
  line: 4 OLDS
  Negotiator with: 3 UAW
  subsidiary: 4 OPEL
**G-man:** 3 FED 4 NARC
  8 FBIAGENT
  (abbr.): 3 AGT
  org.: 3 FBI
**GMC**
  truck: 6 SIERRA
**GMT**
  Part of: 4 MEAN
**Gnat:** 4 PEST
  Go after a: 4 SWAT
  Like a: 5 PESKY
**Gnatlike**
  insect: 5 MIDGE
**Gnaw**
  on: 5 EATAT
**Gnawed**
  away: 5 EROSE
**Gnocchi**
  ingredient: 6 POTATO
**Gnome**
  kin: 5 TROLL
**GNP:** 4 STAT
**Gnu**
  kin: 5 ELAND
**Go:** 3 TRY 4 EXIT PART
  5 LEAVE 6 ELAPSE
  across: 4 SPAN
  after: 3 SUE 4 SEEK SHAG
  5 CHASE SETAT 6 ASSAIL
  ATTACK PURSUE
  along: 5 AGREE 6 SAYYES

along (with): 5 AGREE
along with: 6 ESCORT
  7 AGREETO
around: 4 SPIN 5 AVOID
  ORBIT SKIRT 6 BYPASS
at it: 5 ARGUE 6 TUSSLE
away: 5 LEAVE
by: 4 PASS 6 ELAPSE
Caused to: 6 BETOOK
Cause to: 4 SEND
Come and: 5 RECUR
Doesn't: 5 STAYS
for: 4 COST LIKE
(for): 3 OPT TRY VIE
Get up and: 4 MOVE
Give it a: 3 TRY
Have a ~ at: 3 TRY
in: 5 ENTER
It must ~ on: 7 THESHOW
Let: 3 AXE CAN CUT 4 AXED
  CEDE DROP FIRE FREE
  SACK 5 FIRED FREED
  RELAX WAIVE 6 LAYOFF
  UNHAND 7 RELEASE
  UNLOOSE
  15 RELEASEONESHOLD
off: 3 ERR 5 ERUPT LEAVE
on: 4 LAST RANT 6 NATTER
One way to: 3 APE
On the: 6 ACTIVE
out: 3 DIE EBB 4 EXIT
  5 LEAVE SLEEP 6 EGRESS
over: 3 TOP 4 READ SPAN
  5 CROSS ELIDE RECAP
  7 RUNLATE
(over): 4 PORE
Partner of: 5 GETUP
through: 5 SPEND
(through): 4 SIFT
to: 3 SEE 6 ATTEND
to the dogs: 4 MUSH
under: 4 FAIL FOLD SINK
  5 DROWN
up: 4 RISE SOAR 5 CLIMB
  SCALE 6 ASCEND
Way to ~ (abbr.): 3 RTE
with: 3 SEE 4 DATE 6 ESCORT
without: 4 FAST
**Go ___ :** 3 APE 4 ATIT 5 ALONG
  6 TOSEED
**Go-___ :** 4 KART 6 GETTER
**"___ go!":** 4 LETS 5 GOTTA
**Goad:** 4 PROD SPUR URGE
  5 EGGON
**Go-ahead:** 3 NOD 4 OKAY
  5 SAYSO 6 ASSENT
  Gave the: 3 OKD 4 OKED
  6 OKAYED
  Gives the: 3 OKS 5 OKAYS
**"Go ahead!":** 4 DOIT 5 SHOOT
**Goal:** 3 AIM END
  Set a high: 6 ASPIRE
**Goalie**
  area: 6 CREASE
  Beat the: 5 SCORE
  feat: 4 SAVE

protection: 4 MASK PADS
**Goalpost**
part: 8 CROSSBAR
**Goals**
(abbr.): 3 PTS
or assists: 4 STAT
**Goat**
Baby: 3 KID
cheese: 4 FETA
coat: 6 MOHAIR
Get one's: 3 IRK 4 RILE
Half: 5 SATYR
Mountain: 4 IBEX
Navy ~, e.g.: 6 MASCOT
or rabbit: 6 ANGORA
sound: 3 MAA
Wild: 4 IBEX
~, ox, or sheep: 5 BOVID
**"Goat, The"**
playwright: 5 ALBEE
**"___ Goat-Boy":** 5 GILES
**Goat-drawn**
chariot rider: 4 THOR
**Goatee:** 5 BEARD
site: 4 CHIN
**Goat-footed**
one: 5 SATYR
**Goatish**
glance: 4 LEER
**Goat-man:** 4 FAUN 5 SATYR
**"Go away!":** 4 SCAT
**Gob:** 3 TAR WAD 4 SALT
6 SEAMAN
greeting: 4 AHOY
**"Go back!"**
in word processing: 4 UNDO
on a PC: 3 ESC
**Gobble:** 3 EAT
up: 3 EAT 5 SCARF 6 DEVOUR
**Gobbled**
up: 3 ATE 5 EATEN
**Gobbler:** 3 TOM
**Go-between:** 5 AGENT
7 LIAISON 8 EMISSARY
MEDIATOR
Man-mouse: 3 ORA
Pi-sigma: 3 RHO
**Gobi:** 6 DESERT
continent: 4 ASIA
Like the: 4 ARID SERE
refuge: 5 OASIS
**Goblet:** 7 CHALICE
part: 4 STEM
**Goblin**
prefix: 3 HOB
word: 3 BOO
**"___ go bragh!":** 4 ERIN
**Gobs:** 4 ALOT ATON 5 SLEWS
6 SEAMEN
**Go-cart:** 5 RACER
**God:** 4 LORD 5 DEITY
Aggressive: 4 ARES
attended by Valkyries: 4 ODIN
Belief in: 6 THEISM
Celtic sea: 3 LER
Chariot-riding: 4 THOR

Chief Greek: 4 ZEUS
Chief Norse: 4 ODIN
Child: 4 AMOR
Egyptian: 4 ATEN PTAH
6 AMENRA OSIRIS
Falcon-headed: 5 HORUS
False: 4 BAAL IDOL
Greek love: 4 EROS
Greek war: 4 ARES
Greek wind: 6 AEOLUS
Handsome: 6 APOLLO
Hebrew title for: 6 ADONAI
He played: 5 BURNS
Hindu: 4 DEVA SIVA 5 SHIVA
Love: 4 AMOR EROS
Mischievous: 4 LOKI
Norse: 4 ODIN
Norse peace: 4 FREY
Norse war: 3 TYR 4 ODIN
Norse ~ of discord: 4 LOKI
of Islam: 5 ALLAH
of love: 4 AMOR EROS
of the Koran: 5 ALLAH
of thunder: 4 THOR
of war: 4 ARES MARS ODIN
One-handed: 3 TYR
prefix: 4 DEMI
Red-bearded: 4 THOR
Roman household: 3 LAR
Roman love: 4 AMOR
Roman sun: 3 SOL
Scandinavian: 4 ODIN
Sea: 7 NEPTUNE
Theban: 4 AMON
The Lion of: 3 ALI
Thunder: 4 THOR
War: 4 ARES MARS
Winged: 4 EROS
with a bow: 4 AMOR EROS
5 CUPID
with a hammer: 4 THOR
with an eight-legged horse:
4 ODIN
You may thank ~ for it (abbr.):
3 FRI
~, in French: 4 DIEU
~, in Italian: 3 DIO
~, in Spanish: 4 DIOS
~, with "the": 7 CREATOR
ETERNAL
**Godard**
Actress: 8 PAULETTE
style: 7 NEWWAVE
**Godard, Jean-___:** 3 LUC
**God-awful:** 5 LOUSY
**Goddess**
Agriculture: 5 CERES
Armored: 6 ATHENA
Babylonian: 6 ISHTAR
Cow-horned: 4 ISIS
Dawn: 3 EOS 6 AURORA
Earth: 4 GAEA GAIA
Egyptian: 4 ISIS
Fertility: 4 ISIS 7 ASTARTE
Greek war: 4 ENYO
Harvest: 3 OPS

Hearth: 5 VESTA 6 HESTIA
Moon: 4 LUNA 6 SELENA
SELENE
Nature: 4 ISIS
Norse: 3 HEL 4 NORN
5 FREYA
of discord: 4 ERIS
of plenty: 3 OPS
of recklessness: 3 ATE
of sorcery: 6 HECATE
of the hunt: 5 DIANA
7 ARTEMIS
of wisdom: 6 ATHENA
Parthenon: 6 ATHENA
Peace: 5 IRENE
Rainbow: 4 IRIS
Victory: 4 NIKE
Vindictive: 4 HERA
Winged: 4 NIKE
**Goddesses**
of the seasons: 5 HORAE
Trio of: 5 FATES
**"Godfather, The"**
actor: 4 CAAN
actress Shire: 5 TALIA
author: 4 PUZO
character: 5 SONNY
composer Nino: 4 ROTA
Henchman Luca of: 5 BRASI
John Cazale in: 5 FREDO
Marlon's role in: 4 VITO
Portrayer of Connie in: 5 TALIA
star: 6 BRANDO
Word not used in: 5 MAFIA
**Godfrey**
instrument: 3 UKE
Singer fired by: 6 LAROSA
**Godhead**
Like the: 6 TRIUNE
**"God in Ruins, A"**
author: 4 URIS
**Godiva:** 4 LADY
Emulate: 4 RIDE
Unlike: 4 CLAD
**Godlike:** 6 DIVINE
**Godliness:** 5 PIETY
**Gods**
Blood of the: 5 ICHOR
Drink of the: 6 NECTAR
Food of the: 5 MANNA
8 AMBROSIA
Home of the Norse: 6 ASGARD
Household: 5 LARES
Queen of the: 4 HERA
Race of Norse: 5 AESIR
Way of the: 6 SHINTO
**Godsend:** 4 BOON
**"God's Little ___":** 4 ACRE
**Godunov, Boris:** 4 TSAR
singer: 5 BASSO
**"God willing!":** 7 IHOPESO
**Godzilla**
creator: 6 TANAKA
target: 5 TOKYO
**"Go Eat Worms!"**
author: 7 RLSTINE

"___ goes": 4 SOIT
"___ goes nothing!": 4 HERE
**Goethe**
  classic: 5 FAUST
  Playwright: 6 JOHANN
**Gofer:** 4 AIDE
  (abbr.): 4 ASST
  job: 6 ERRAND
  Senate: 4 PAGE
**"Go fly ___!":** 5 AKITE
**Go ___ for:** 5 TOBAT
**Go-getter:** 4 DOER 5 TIGER
  6 DYNAMO
**Goggle:** 4 GAPE GAWK GAZE
  5 STARE
  at: 4 LEER OGLE
**Go-go**
  Like ~ boots, nowadays:
    5 RETRO
**Going**
  Coming or: 7 ENROUTE
  Get: 4 MOVE ROLL 5 HOPTO
    START 6 BOOGIE
    8 COMMENCE
  It'll keep you: 7 INERTIA
  Keep: 4 LAST 5 RUNON
    7 PERSIST
  on and on: 7 ETERNAL
  out: 6 DATING
**Going ___:** 4 ATIT
**Goings-on:** 3 ADO 6 EVENTS
**Goiter**
  treatment: 6 IODINE
**Gold:** 5 METAL 7 ELEMENT
  $10 ~ piece: 5 EAGLE
  79, for ~ (abbr.): 4 ATNO
  Band of: 3 ORE
  bar: 5 INGOT
  Black: 3 OIL 8 TEXASTEA
  braid: 5 ORRIS
  brick: 5 INGOT
  Coat with: 4 GILD
  compound: 6 AURATE
  Containing: 5 AURIC
  deposit: 4 LODE
  digger: 5 MINER
  Ersatz: 6 ORMOLU
  fabric: 4 LAME
  Fort of: 4 KNOX
  Go for the: 3 DIG PAN VIE
    4 MINE 7 COMPETE
  Got the: 3 WON
  Legendary city of:
    8 ELDORADO
  Look for: 3 PAN
  measure: 5 KARAT
  measures (abbr.): 3 KTS
  mine: 9 MONEYTREE
  mold: 5 INGOT
  Old ~ coin: 5 DUCAT
  prefix: 3 AUR
  standard: 5 KARAT
  statuette: 5 OSCAR
  Take the: 3 WIN
  They go for the: 6 MINERS
  unit: 3 BAR 5 KARAT OUNCE

  watch recipient: 7 RETIREE
  ~, in Spanish: 3 ORO
**Gold ___:** 4 LAME
**"___ Gold" (1997 film):**
    5 ULEES
**Golda**
  of Israel: 4 MEIR
**Goldberg**
  Cartoonist: 4 RUBE
  Oscar emcee: 6 WHOOPI
**"Goldberg Variations"**
  composer: 4 BACH
**Goldbrick:** 4 LOAF 5 DOGIT
    IDLER SHIRK
    7 SHIRKER SLACKER
**"Gold Bug, The"**
  author: 3 POE
  author monogram: 3 EAP
**Gold Coast**
  locale: 5 GHANA
**Golden:** 5 AURIC 7 AUREATE
  age: 6 HEYDAY
  ager: 7 OLDSTER
  anniversary number: 5 FIFTY
  attribute: 7 SILENCE
  boy of film: 5 OSCAR
  finish: 4 AGER
  It may be: 5 OLDIE
  King with a ~ touch: 5 MIDAS
  rule word: 4 UNTO
  song: 5 OLDIE
  years: 6 OLDAGE
  ~, in French: 3 DOR
**Golden ___:** 4 AGER GATE
    RULE 5 OLDIE
**Golden-___:** 4 AGER
  corn: 5 EARED
**Golden ___, The:** 4 HIND
**Golden Arches**
  offering: 6 BIGMAC
**Golden Bears**
  (abbr.): 4 UCAL
**"Golden Boy"**
  playwright: 5 ODETS
**Golden-brown**
  quartz: 8 TIGEREYE
**Golden Calf:** 4 IDOL
  builder: 5 AARON
**Golden-coated**
  horse: 8 PALOMINO
**Golden-egg**
  layer: 5 GOOSE
**Golden Fleece**
  hunter: 5 JASON
  princess: 5 MEDEA
  ship: 4 ARGO
**"Goldengirl"**
  actress Susan: 5 ANTON
**"Golden Girls, The"**
  actress Arthur: 3 BEA
  actress Getty: 7 ESTELLE
  actress McClanahan: 3 RUE
  Blanche portrayer on: 3 RUE
  character: 4 ROSE
**Golden Hind**
  skipper: 5 DRAKE

**Golden Horde**
  member: 5 TATAR 6 MONGOL
**Golden Pong**
  bird: 4 LOON
**"Golden rule"**
  last word: 3 YOU
  preposition: 4 UNTO
**Golden Spike**
  locale: 4 UTAH
**Golden State**
  sch.: 3 USC 4 UCLA
**Golden Triangle**
  country: 4 LAOS
  native: 4 THAI
**Goldfinger**
  assistant: 6 ODDJOB
  first name: 5 AURIC
  Fort attacked by: 4 KNOX
  portrayer Frobe: 4 GERT
**Goldie**
  Actress: 4 HAWN
  Costar of ~ and Ruth: 4 ARTE
**Goldilocks**
  adversary: 8 PAPABEAR
  Like some porridge, to:
    6 TOOHOT
**Goldin**
  Photographer: 3 NAN
**Goldman**
  Anarchist: 4 EMMA
  broker partner: 5 SACHS
**Gold Rush**
  mecca: 4 NOME
  name: 6 SUTTER
  territory: 5 YUKON
**Goldsmith:** 7 ARTISAN
**Goldwyn:** 6 SAMUEL
  star Anna: 4 STEN
**Golf**
  1996 ~ movie: 6 TINCUP
  bag item: 3 TEE 4 IRON
  Best, in a ~ score: 6 FEWEST
  California ~ locale:
    11 PEBBLEBEACH
  coup: 3 ACE 5 EAGLE
  Easy ~ shot: 5 TAPIN
  Farthest from the hole, in:
    4 AWAY
  gadget: 3 TEE
  goal: 3 PAR
  goof: 4 HOOK
  great: 5 SNEAD
  Half a ~ course: 4 NINE
  hazard: 4 TRAP
  instructor: 3 PRO
  lesson topic: 6 STANCE
  Like some ~ balls: 4 TEED
  Like some ~ courses:
    8 NINEHOLE
  Like some ~ tourneys:
    5 PROAM
  Major ~ event: 6 USOPEN
  Miami ~ resort: 5 DORAL
  peg: 3 TEE
  position: 3 LIE
  Rare ~ shot: 3 ACE

shoe feature: 5 CLEAT
stroke: 4 CHIP PUTT SHOT
Word after: 5 WIDOW
**Golf ball**
material: 6 BALATA
position: 3 LIE
support: 3 TEE
**"Golf Begins at Forty"**
author: 5 SNEAD
**Golf club:** 4 IRON WOOD
6 DRIVER
part: 3 TOE 4 GRIP 5 SHAFT
socket: 5 HOSEL
**Golf course**
area: 3 TEE
feature: 6 DOGLEG
**Golfer**
accessory: 5 VISOR
aide: 5 CADDY
bagful: 4 TEES
challenge: 6 DOGLEG
choice: 4 IRON NINE
5 WEDGE
concern: 3 LIE 4 GRIP
5 SWING 6 STANCE
coup: 3 ACE
cry: 4 FORE
gadget: 3 TEE
goal: 3 PAR 4 HOLE
headache: 6 BADLIE
purchase: 5 BALLS IRONS
target: 4 HOLE
transport: 4 CART
with an army: 5 ARNIE
~ Aoki: 4 ISAO
~, at times: 4 TEER
~ Ballesteros: 4 SEVE
~ Calvin: 5 PEETE
~ Dutra: 4 OLIN
~ Hale: 5 IRWIN
~ Isao: 4 AOKI
~ Mattiace: 3 LEN
~ Mediate: 5 ROCCO
~ Norman: 4 GREG
~ Palmer: 5 ARNIE
~ Trevino: 3 LEE
~ Wadkins: 5 LANNY
**Golf hole**
edge: 3 LIP
start: 3 TEE
**Golfing**
group: 8 FOURSOME
**Golgi**
Physician: 7 CAMILLO
**Goliath:** 5 GIANT
**Golightly**
creator: 6 CAPOTE
**"Golly!":** 3 GEE
**Gomer**
and Goober: 5 PYLES
**"Gomer ___, U.S.M.C.":** 4 PYLE
**Gomez**
Cousin of: 3 ITT
Mrs. Addams, to: 4 TISH
**Gomorrah**
Sister city of: 5 SODOM

**Gompers, Samuel**
org.: 3 AFL
org., informally: 5 AFOFL
**Gondola**
driver: 5 POLER
locale: 5 CANAL
propeller: 4 POLE
Some ~ users: 6 SKIERS
**Gondolier:** 5 POLER
need: 4 POLE
**"Gondoliers, The"**
girl: 5 TESSA
**Gone:** 4 AWAY DEAD 5 EATEN
6 USEDUP 7 EXTINCT
bad: 6 SPOILT
by: 3 AGO 4 PAST 5 OFOLD
out with: 4 SEEN
wrong: 4 AWOL
**"___ Gone":** 4 SHES
**Goner:** 5 TOAST 8 DEADDUCK
**Goneril**
Father of: 4 LEAR
Sister of: 5 REGAN
**"Gone ___ the Wind":** 4 WITH
**"Gone With the Wind"**
actor Howard: 6 LESLIE
actress Barbara: 5 ONEIL
actress McDaniel: 6 HATTIE
actress Vivien: 5 LEIGH
plantation: 4 TARA
star: 5 GABLE
**Gong:** 6 TAMTAM
**"___ Gonna Take It":**
7 WERENOT
**Gonzales**
of tennis: 6 PANCHO
**González**
in 2000 news: 5 ELIAN
**Goo:** 4 GLOP MIRE 5 SLIME
7 TREACLE
Cosmetic: 5 GELEE
Do: 3 GEL
Greasy: 4 GUNK
Hair: 3 GEL
La Brea: 3 TAR
Lip: 4 BALM
Road: 3 TAR
Styling: 3 GEL
**Goober**
of Mayberry: 4 PYLE
**Good**
A ~ deal: 4 TONS
As ~ as ever: 7 LIKENEW
Believer in ~ and evil:
7 DUELIST
Body of ~ conduct: 5 ETHIC
buddy: 3 BRO PAL 4 CBER
CHUM 6 FRIEND
buy: 4 DEAL
cheer: 3 OLE
deal: 3 BUY LOT TON
earth: 4 LOAM
feller: 3 AXE
form: 7 DECORUM
Full of ~ cheer: 5 MERRY
grade: 5 BPLUS

guy: 6 MENSCH
In ~ health: 4 HALE WELL
In ~ order: 4 NEAT TIDY
In ~ shape: 3 FIT 4 HALE
TRIM
It doesn't look: 7 EYESORE
It's not: 4 EVIL
judgment: 5 SENSE
10 HORSESENSE
looker: 3 EYE
Make: 5 ATONE REPAY
7 RESTORE
name: 3 REP 6 REPUTE
Not as: 5 WORSE
Not ~ enough for: 7 BENEATH
ol' boy: 5 BUBBA
Partner of: 4 EVIL
point: 5 ASSET
relations: 5 AMITY
run: 6 STREAK
shot: 4 GOAL 6 RINGER
Show a really ~ time:
6 REGALE
sign: 4 HALO
Tell a ~ one: 3 LIE
The ~ life: 4 EASE
thing: 4 PLUS 5 ASSET
times: 3 UPS
witch: 6 GLINDA
~, in French: 4 BIEN
~, in slang: 3 BAD DEF
~, in Spanish: 5 BUENO
**Good ___:** 5 ASNEW
**"Good ___!":** 5 GRIEF
**Good Book:** 5 BIBLE
**"Good buddy":** 4 CBER
**Goodbye:** 4 CIAO TATA
5 ADIEU
Hello or: 5 ALOHA 6 SHALOM
**"Goodbye Columbus"**
author: 4 ROTH
**"Goodbye Girl, The"**
Mason of: 6 MARSHA
**"___ good cheer!":** 4 BEOF
**___ good deed:** 3 DOA
**"Good Earth, The"**
author: 9 PEARLBUCK
heroine: 4 OLAN
**___ good example:** 4 SETA
**___ Good Feeling:** 5 ERAOF
**"GoodFellas"**
costar: 6 LIOTTA
9 RAYLIOTTA
Oscar winner: 5 PESCI
star: 6 DENIRO
**Goodfellow**
(abbr.): 3 AFB
**Goodfellow, Robin:** 3 IMP
6 SPRITE
**Good-for-nothing:** 3 BUM
5 IDLER ROGUE
6 BADEGG 7 NOCOUNT
USELESS
**Good-gets**
connector: 4 ASIT
**"Good going!":** 4 NICE

**"Good grief!":** 4 EGAD
    5 EGADS
**Good Housekeeping**
  award: 4 SEAL
**Good-humored:** 7 AMIABLE
**Goodie:** 5 TREAT
  Bakery: 5 SCONE
  from Linz: 5 TORTE
  Fruity: 4 TART
  Gumbo: 4 OKRA
**Gooding Jr., ___**
  Actor: 4 CUBA
**Good-looking**
  guy: 10 STUDMUFFIN
**"Good Luck, Miss Wyckoff"**
  novelist: 4 INGE
**Goodly**
  A ~ number: 4 MANY
**Goodman**
  Columnist: 5 ELLEN
  drummer: 5 KRUPA
**Goodman, Benny**
  genre: 5 SWING
**"___ Good Men":** 4 AFEW
**Good-natured:** 4 NICE
  banter: 4 JOSH
**Goodness:** 5 WORTH 6 VIRTUE
  Symbol of: 4 HALO
**"Goodness!":** 4 MYMY OHMY
  6 DEARME
**"Goodness gracious!":** 4 EGAD
  MYMY OHMY
  6 DEARME
**Goodnight**
  girl: 5 IRENE
**"Goodnight ___":** 5 IRENE
**"Good one!":** 4 NICE
**___ good race:** 4 RANA
**"Good riddance":** 6 NOLOSS
**Goods:** 5 WARES
  It may deliver the: 4 SEMI
  Piece: 5 CLOTH
  Stolen: 4 LOOT
  Store ~ (abbr.): 4 MDSE
**Good Samaritan:** 5 AIDER
**"Good shot!":** 4 NICE
  7 NICEONE
**Good-sized**
  combo: 5 NONET OCTET
**Goodson**
  TV partner of: 6 TODMAN
**"Good Times"**
  actress Esther: 5 ROLLE
**___ good turn:** 3 DOA
**Goodwill:** 5 ASSET
**"... good will ___":** 5 TOMEN
**Goodwill Ambassadors**
  org.: 6 UNESCO
**"Good Will Hunting"**
  actor: 5 DAMON
  actress: 12 MINNIEDRIVER
  campus: 3 MIT
**"Good work!":** 4 NICE
**"Goody!":** 5 OHBOY
**Goody, Sam**
  purchases: 3 CDS

**Goodyear**
  home: 5 AKRON
  product: 4 TIRE
**Goody-goody:** 5 PRUDE
**"Goody Two Shoes"**
  singer Adam: 3 ANT
**Gooey**
  dessert: 5 SMORE
  stuff: 3 GEL 4 GLOP MIRE
  OOZE 5 SLIME
**Goof:** 3 ERR 4 SLIP 5 ERROR
  6 BOOBOO MISCUE
  off: 4 LAZE LOAF
  Printing: 4 TYPO
  up: 3 ERR 4 FLUB
**Goofball:** 4 BOZO NERD YOYO
  5 FLAKE
**Goof-off:** 5 IDLER
**Goofs:** 6 ERRATA
**Goofy:** 3 ODD 4 DAFT LOCO
  TOON 5 INANE SAPPY
**Google**
  rival: 5 YAHOO
**Goo-goo**
  Make ~ eyes at: 4 OGLE
**Goo Goo Dolls**
  1998 ~ hit: 4 IRIS
**Goolagong**
  of tennis: 6 EVONNE
  rival: 5 EVERT
**Goombah:** 3 PAL
**Goon:** 3 APE 4 HOOD THUG
  6 GALOOT
**"Go on!":** 6 DOTELL
**"Go on ...":** 3 AND
**"___ go on?":** 6 SHALLI
**Goop**
  Hair: 3 GEL
**Goose**
  Black-necked: 5 BRANT
  Causing ~ bumps: 5 EERIE
  Cook one's: 5 ROAST
  egg: 3 NIL ZIP 4 NADA ZERO
  6 NAUGHT
  genus: 5 ANSER
  Hawaiian: 4 NENE
  Like a: 8 ANSERINE
  Silly: 3 ASS 5 NINNY
  sound: 4 HONK
**Gooseberry**
  Chinese: 4 KIWI
**Goosebumps**
  Causing: 5 EERIE 6 CREEPY
**"Goosebumps"**
  author: 5 STINE 7 RLSTINE
**Goosefoot**
  plant: 4 BEET
**Gooselike:** 8 ANSERINE
**Gooseneck:** 4 LAMP
**Goosey:** 5 INANE
**GOP**
  elephant drawer: 4 NAST
  foe: 3 DEM
  hq.: 3 RNC
  member: 3 REP
  Part of: 3 OLD

**Gopher wood**
  vessel: 3 ARK
**Gorbachev**
  Its last pres. was: 4 USSR
  Mrs.: 5 RAISA
  policy: 8 GLASNOST
**Gorcey**
  Actor: 3 LEO
**Gordie**
  of hockey: 4 HOWE
**Gordimer**
  Novelist: 6 NADINE
**Gordius**
  tied one: 4 KNOT
**Gordon**
  Auto racer: 4 JEFF
**Gordon, Flash**
  foe: 4 MING
  portrayer Buster: 6 CRABBE
**Gordon, Jeff**
  org.: 6 NASCAR
**Gore**
  and others: 3 ALS
  gp.: 4 DEMS
  home st.: 4 TENN
  ~, formerly: 4 VEEP
**Gorge:** 4 SATE 5 CHASM
  FEAST 6 RAVINE
  7 SATIATE
  crosser: 7 TRESTLE
**Gorged:** 7 ATEALOT
**Gorgon:** 3 HAG 6 MEDUSA
  Like a: 4 UGLY
**Gorilla:** 3 APE 4 HOOD THUG
  leader: 10 SILVERBACK
  researcher Fossey: 4 DIAN
  Sign language: 4 KOKO
  Toon: 7 MAGILLA
**"Gorillas in the Mist"**
  author Dian: 6 FOSSEY
  author Fossey: 4 DIAN
**Gorky Park**
  setting: 6 MOSCOW
**Gormé**
  Singer: 5 EYDIE
**Gorton**
  Senator: 5 SLADE
**"Gosh!":** 3 GEE OOH 4 ISAY
**Gospel**
  First name in: 7 MAHALIA
  singer Winans: 4 CECE
  writer: 4 JOHN LUKE MARK
**Gospels**
  follower: 4 ACTS
  One of the: 4 JOHN LUKE
  MARK
**Gossamer:** 4 AIRY LACY
  5 LIGHT WISPY
  7 SPIDERY 8 ETHEREAL
**Gossip:** 3 GAB JAW YAK 4 BLAB
  CHIN DIRT DISH POOP
  TALK 5 YENTA 6 TATTLE
  Bit of: 4 ITEM 5 ONDIT
  columnist Barrett: 4 RONA
  columnist Smith: 3 LIZ
  Full of: 5 DISHY

Juicy: 4 DIRT 6 EARFUL
Piece of: 4 ITEM 5 ONDIT
tidbit, with "the": 6 LATEST
**Gossipy:** 5 NEWSY
**Got**
along: 5 FARED 6 MADEDO
by: 6 MADEDO
down: 3 ATE 4 ALIT
off: 4 ALIT
on: 5 FARED
up: 4 ROSE WOKE 5 AROSE
    AWOKE STOOD
**"Got ___?":** 4 MILK
**"___ Got a Crush on You":**
    3 IVE
**"___ Got a Secret":** 3 IVE
**"Gotcha!":** 3 AHA OHO 4 IDIG
    ISEE
**"Go team!":** 3 RAH
**Gotham City**
protector: 6 BATMAN
**Gothic**
adornment: 5 GABLE
governess: 4 EYRE
**"Got it!":** 3 AHA 4 IDIG ISEE
**"___ got it!":** 3 IVE
**"Got me!":** 5 DUNNO
**"Got milk?"**
cry: 4 MEOW
**"___ Got Sixpence":** 3 IVE
**"___ gotta be kidding!":** 3 YOU
**"___ Gotta Be Me":** 3 IVE
**"___ Gotta Crow":** 3 IVE
**"Gotta have it"**
sloganeer: 5 PEPSI
**"___ Gotta Have It":** 4 SHES
**"Gotti"**
actor Armand: 7 ASSANTE
**"___ Got You Under My Skin":**
    3 IVE
**Gouda**
alternative: 4 EDAM
**Gouge:** 4 TOOL
**Goulash:** 4 STEW
seasoning: 7 PAPRIKA
**Gould**
Novelist: 4 LOIS
railroad: 4 ERIE
**Gould, Jay**
railroad: 4 ERIE
**Gould/Sutherland**
film: 4 SPYS
**Gounod**
composition: 8 AVEMARIA
opera: 5 FAUST
**Gourd**
fruit: 4 PEPO
instrument: 6 MARACA
Out of one's: 4 LOCO
**Gourde**
Its currency is the: 5 HAITI
**Gourmand:** 5 EATER
    6 GORGER
**Gourmet**
cook: 4 CHEF
mushroom: 5 MOREL

sense: 6 PALATE
**Govern:** 4 RULE
**Governess**
Fictional: 4 ANNA EYRE
**Governessy:** 4 PRIM
**Governing**
body: 6 SENATE
**Government**
agent: 3 FED 4 TMAN
Center of: 4 SEAT
in power: 6 REGIME
issue: 5 TNOTE
security: 5 TNOTE
worker: 10 BUREAUCRAT
**Governor**
domain: 5 STATE
First ~ of Alaska: 4 EGAN
Former Connecticut: 6 GRASSO
Former NJ: 6 FLORIO
Former NY: 5 CUOMO
    6 PATAKI
option: 4 VETO
**Govt.**
1860s ~: 3 CSA
agent: 4 TMAN
airwaves board: 3 FCC
auditor: 3 IRS
banking org.: 4 FDIC
certified: 4 REGD
code breakers: 3 NSA
home loan gp.: 3 FHA
hush-hush gp.: 3 NSA
investigation: 3 INQ
lawyers: 3 DAS
lender: 3 SBA
medical agcy.: 3 NIH
mortgage gp.: 3 FHA
narcotics watchdog: 3 DEA
obligation: 5 TBILL TNOTE
old-age insurer: 3 SSA
product-testing org.: 3 FDA
property overseer: 3 GSA
security: 5 TNOTE
watchdog: 3 EPA 4 OSHA
**Go-with**
Brolly: 3 MAC
Early PC: 5 MSDOS
Gin: 5 TONIC
Muumuu: 3 LEI
Oil change: 4 LUBE
Soup: 7 SALTINE
Tonic: 3 GIN
**Gown:** 5 DRESS
accessory: 5 STOLE
fabric: 5 SATIN TULLE
Kind of: 6 BRIDAL
Priest: 3 ALB
renters (abbr.): 3 SRS
**Gowns**
Like some: 9 STRAPLESS
partners: 4 CAPS
Pricey: 5 DIORS
**Goya**
homeland: 5 SPAIN
museum: 5 PRADO
    7 ELPRADO

patron: 4 ALBA
subject: 4 MAJA
**Gp.:** 3 ORG 4 ASSN
**G.P.**
gp.: 3 AMA
**G.P.'s:** 3 MDS
**GQ:** 3 MAG
**Grab:** 5 SEIZE 6 SNAPUP
    SNATCH
a bite: 3 EAT
bag: 4 OLIO
by the collar: 6 ACCOST
(onto): 4 GLOM
some z's: 5 SLEEP
the check: 5 TREAT
tightly: 6 CLENCH
~, in a way: 4 TONG
**Grab ___:** 5 ABITE
**"Grab ___!":** 5 AHOLD
**Grabber:** 4 CLAW 5 TALON
Tab ~ words: 4 ONME
**Grabbers:** 5 TONGS
**Grable, Betty**
asset: 4 LEGS
**Grabs**
Up for: 4 FREE OPEN
___ grabs: 5 UPFOR
**Grace:** 6 PRAYER
End of: 4 AMEN
Fall from: 3 SIN
land: 6 MONACO
period: 4 AMEN
Say: 4 PRAY
Symbol of: 4 SWAN
under pressure: 5 POISE
word: 5 BLESS
**Grace, Bud**
strip: 5 ERNIE
**Graceful**
bend: 4 PLIE
bird: 4 SWAN
girl: 5 SYLPH
horse: 4 ARAB
plunge: 8 SWANDIVE
runner: 7 ARABIAN
seabird: 4 TERN
Trim and: 5 SLEEK
**Graceland:** 6 ESTATE
home (abbr.): 4 TENN
icon: 5 ELVIS
**"... grace of God ___":** 3 GOI
**"Gracias"**
reply: 6 DENADA
**Gracile:** 4 SLIM
**Grad:** 4 ALUM
class: 3 SRS
Gregg: 5 STENO
MIT: 4 ENGR
USNA: 3 ENS
Yale: 3 ELI
**Grade:** 4 HILL RATE 5 SLOPE
    7 INCLINE
Average: 3 CEE
Barely passing: 3 DEE
    5 DPLUS
enhancer: 4 PLUS

Good: 5 BPLUS
Great: 5 APLUS
of tea: 5 PEKOE
point avg.: 4 CUME
Poor: 3 DEE
prefix: 5 CENTI
school class (abbr.): 3 SCI
They make the: 5 TESTS

**Grader**
Govt. beef: 4 USDA
Seventh: 7 PRETEEN

**Grades**
~ 1–12: 4 ELHI
~ K–6 (abbr.): 4 ELEM

**Grads**
Many college: 3 BAS
Many MIT: 3 EES
OCS: 3 LTS

**Grads-to-be**
(abbr.): 3 SRS

**Grad student**
hurdle: 4 ORAL
work: 6 THESIS

**Grad-to-be:** 6 SENIOR

**Gradually:** 8 BITBYBIT
OVERTIME
10 STEPBYSTEP

**Graduate:** 6 ALUMNA
Academy: 6 ENSIGN
deg.: 3 PHD
garb: 4 GOWN
Seminary: 5 RABBI
USNA: 3 ENS

**"Graduate, The"**
actress Katharine: 4 ROSS
hero: 3 BEN
heroine: 6 ELAINE

**Graduated:** 6 SCALAR

**Graduates:** 6 ALUMNI
7 ALUMNAE

**Graduating**
class (abbr.): 3 SRS

**Graduation**
composer: 5 ELGAR
dangler: 6 TASSEL
month: 4 JUNE

**Graf**
Husband of: 6 AGASSI
of tennis: 6 STEFFI
rival: 5 SELES

**Graf ___:** 4 SPEE

**Graff**
Actress: 5 ILENE

**Graffiti**
artist: 6 VANDAL
Biblical ~ start: 4 MENE
Cover with: 6 DEFACE
Like most ~ (abbr.): 4 ANON
~, to some: 3 ART

**Graft:** 6 BOODLE

**Grafting**
shoot: 5 SCION

**Grafton**
Author: 3 SUE

**Graham**
Author: 6 GREENE

Cartoonist: 4 ALEX
of football: 4 OTTO
of rock: 4 NASH

**Grain**
alcohol: 7 ETHANOL
beard: 3 AWN
Brewer: 4 MALT
bristle: 6 ARISTA
bristles: 7 ARISTAE
Cereal: 3 OAT RYE
for grinding: 5 GRIST
Free ~ from chaff: 6 WINNOW
fungus: 4 SMUT
Gather: 4 REAP
Granola: 3 OAT
grinder: 4 MILL
Ground: 4 MEAL 5 GRIST
holder: 3 BIN 4 SILO
husk: 4 BRAN
Made of a certain: 5 OATEN
Saw with the: 3 RIP
Skeptic's: 4 SALT
Store: 6 ENSILE
thresher: 5 FLAIL

**Grains**
60 ~: 4 DRAM
About 3 ~: 5 CARAT
About 15 ~: 4 GRAM
Buckwheat: 6 KASHAS
Gritty: 4 SAND

**Grain-sized**
Made: 5 RICED

**Grainy:** 5 OATEN

**Gram:** 4 NANA
prefix: 3 ANA EPI 4 IDEO

**Gramercy Five**
leader Shaw: 5 ARTIE

**Gramm:** 7 SENATOR
Senator: 4 PHIL

**Grammar**
Analyze: 5 PARSE
class subject: 5 NOUNS TENSE
no-no: 4 AINT
school trio: 3 RRR
Subj. including: 3 ENG

**Grammarian**
concern: 5 USAGE

**Grammy**
1988 ~ winner: 5 OSLIN
1989 ~ winner: 5 RAITT
1991 ~ winner: 6 ARETHA
1992 ~ winner: 4 ENYA
6 KDLANG
2003 ~ winner Jones:
5 NORAH
category: 3 RAP 4 FOLK JAZZ
5 RANDB 6 GOSPEL
winner Bonnie: 5 RAITT
winner Cohn: 4 MARC

**Gramps**
Wife of: 4 NANA

**Grams**
1000 ~: 4 KILO
Like: 6 METRIC

**Granada**
Info: Spanish cue

God, in: 4 DIOS
gold: 3 ORO
Good, in: 5 BUENO
greeting: 4 HOLA

**Gran Canaria:** 4 ISLA

**Grand:** 3 GEE 4 EPIC POSH
THOU 6 SUPERB
8 THOUSAND
Baby: 5 PIANO
duke's father: 4 CZAR
finale: 4 PRIX
It may be: 4 TOUR
7 LARCENY
It's less than: 6 SPINET
On a ~ scale: 4 EPIC
slam foursome: 4 RBIS
theft: 6 FELONY
Word after: 5 OPERA

**"Grand"**
hotel: 5 HYATT
ice cream: 4 EDYS
island: 6 BAHAMA
thing: 5 PIANO

**Grand ___:** 3 CRU PRE 4 PRIX

**Grand Canal**
bridge: 6 RIALTO

**Grand Canyon**
beast: 5 BURRO
feature: 3 RIM
sight: 4 MESA
st.: 4 ARIZ
transport: 5 BURRO
view: 8 PANORAMA

**"Grand Canyon Suite"**
composer Ferde: 5 GROFE
composer Grofé: 5 FERDE

**Grand Central**
(abbr.): 3 STA

**Grandchild**
Genesis: 4 ENOS

**Grandchildren**
Watch the: 3 SIT

**Grand Coulee:** 3 DAM

**Granddaddy**
of computers: 5 ENIAC

**Grand ___ Dam:** 6 COULEE

**Grande:** 3 RIO

**___ Grande:** 3 RIO 4 CASA

**Grandee**
inferior: 7 HIDALGO

**Grandfather**
Hour not on a ~ clock: 4 XIII
of Bart: 3 ABE

**"Grand Illusion"**
director: 6 RENOIR

**Grandiloquize:** 5 ORATE

**Grand ___ island:** 6 BAHAMA

**Grandma:** 4 NANA
impersonator: 4 WOLF
in galleries: 5 MOSES

**Grand Marquis**
~, for short: 4 MERC

**Grandmother:** 4 NANA

**Grand ___ National Park:**
5 TETON

**Grand Ole ___:** 4 OPRY

**"Grand Ole Opry"**
network: 3 TNN
**Grand ___ Opry:** 3 OLE
**Grandparent**
~, often: 5 DOTER
**Grand Prix**
feature: 3 ESS
site: 6 LEMANS
**Grand Slam**
winner: 4 GRAF 5 LAVER
**Grandson**
add-on: 3 III
of Abraham: 4 ESAU
of Adam: 4 ENOS
**Grandstand**
shout: 3 RAH
**Grand Teton**
grazer: 3 ELK
**Granny:** 4 KNOT NANA
portrayer: 5 IRENE
**Granola**
grain: 3 OAT
ingredient: 6 RAISIN
Like: 5 OATEN
**___ grano salis:** 3 CUM
**Grant:** 4 CEDE GIVE 5 AWARD
ENDOW 6 BESTOW
7 STIPEND
(abbr.): 3 GEN
Actor: 4 CARY HUGH
basis: 4 NEED
bill: 5 FIFTY
entry to: 5 LETIN
foe: 3 LEE
General: 7 ULYSSES
Genie: 4 WISH
money: 5 ENDOW
portrayer: 5 ASNER
7 EDASNER
Singer: 3 AMY 4 GOGI
source (abbr.): 3 NEA
successor: 5 HAYES
Tey investigator: 4 ALAN
**Grant-___:** 5 INAID
**Grant, Inspector**
creator: 3 TEY
**Grant, Lou**
paper: 4 TRIB
portrayer: 5 ASNER
7 EDASNER
**Grant, U.S.**
birthplace: 4 OHIO
**Granted:** 4 GAVE
Be: 7 RECEIVE
Take for: 6 ASSUME
**Granter**
Wish: 5 GENIE
**Granters**
Wish: 5 GENII
**Granting**
gp.: 3 NEA
that, briefly: 3 THO
**Grantorto**
victim: 5 IRENA
**Granular**
coating: 4 RIME

**Grape**
Burgundy: 5 PINOT
Dried: 6 RAISIN
holder: 4 VINE
Red wine: 6 MERLOT
soda: 4 NEHI
suffix: 3 ADE
Wine: 5 PINOT
**Grapefruit**
kin: 6 POMELO
**Grapefruit League**
state (abbr.): 3 FLA
**Grapes**
Like some: 4 SOUR
8 SEEDLESS
Like sour: 4 TART 6 ACIDIC
**"Grapes of Wrath"**
character: 4 OKIE
family name: 4 JOAD
star: 5 FONDA
**Grapevine**
Get from the: 4 HEAR
item: 5 RUMOR
**Graph:** 5 CHART
(0,0) on a: 6 ORIGIN
3-D ~ line: 5 ZAXIS
calculation: 5 SLOPE
horizontal line: 5 XAXIS
line: 4 AXIS
lines: 4 AXES
Make a: 4 PLOT
pattern: 4 GRID
point: 4 PEAK
points: 4 LOCI
prefix: 3 EPI 4 IDEO PARA
TELE
vertical line: 5 YAXIS
X or Y, on a: 4 AXIS
**Graphic**
Computer: 4 ICON
descriptions: 6 IMAGES
prefix: 3 GEO 4 IDEO
symbol: 4 ICON
**Graphic ___:** 4 ARTS
**Graphics**
machine: 6 IMAGER
**Graphite**
element: 6 CARBON
remover: 6 ERASER
**Grapple:** 6 RASSLE
**Grappler**
surface: 3 MAT
**___ Gras:** 5 MARDI
**Grasp:** 3 GET KEN SEE
4 HOLD KNOW 5 SEIZE
6 ATTAIN FATHOM
Hard to: 4 DEEP EELY
Mental: 6 UPTAKE
**Grasped:** 4 HELD
**Graspers:** 5 TONGS
**Grass:** 4 LAWN
appendage: 3 AWN
Cereal: 3 OAT
Clump of: 4 TUFT
coat: 3 DEW
Cut the: 3 MOW

Drops on the: 3 DEW
Kind of: 3 OAT
Like early morning: 4 DEWY
Marsh: 4 REED 5 SEDGE
Put in new: 5 RESOD
Rye ~ disease: 5 ERGOT
section: 3 SOD
unit: 5 BLADE
Word with: 5 WIDOW
**___ grass:** 3 OAT
**Grasshopper**
associate: 3 ANT
kin: 7 KATYDID
sound: 5 CHIRR
**Grassland:** 3 LEA
African: 5 VELDT
Russian: 6 STEPPE
**Grasso**
Former governor: 4 ELLA
**Grassy**
area: 3 LEA
expanse: 5 LLANO
field: 3 LEA
plain: 5 LLANO 7 SAVANNA
surface: 5 SWARD
**Grate:** 4 RASP
expectations: 3 ASH 5 ASHES
on: 3 IRK
stuff: 3 ASH 5 ASHES
**G-rated:** 5 CLEAN
What ~ is for: 7 ALLAGES
**Grateful:** 5 ASHES
**Grater**
input: 6 ROMANO
**___ gratia:** 3 DEI
**"___ gratia artis":** 3 ARS
**___ gratias:** 3 DEO
**Gratify:** 4 FEED SATE
6 PLEASE
**Grating:** 4 GRID 5 HARSH
RASPY 6 HOARSE
8 STRIDENT
sound: 4 RASP
Window: 6 GRILLE
**Gratis:** 4 COMP FREE
7 FORFREE
**Gratitude**
Express ~ to: 5 THANK
**Gratuity:** 3 TIP
Casino: 4 TOKE
**Grave:** 4 TOMB 5 ACUTE
SOBER STAID STERN
6 SEVERE SOLEMN
SOMBER 7 SERIOUS
marker: 5 STELA STONE
risk: 5 PERIL
robber: 5 GHOUL
**Gravel ___ (Dick Tracy**
**character):** 6 GERTIE
**Gravelly**
ridge: 5 ESKER
utterance: 4 RASP
**Graven**
image: 4 IDOL
**Graves**
Actress: 6 TERESA

**Gravitate:** 4 TEND
(toward): 4 LEAN
**Gravity**
Give in to: 3 SAG 5 DROOP
**Gravity-powered**
vehicle: 4 SLED
**Gravy**
Absorb, as: 5 SOPUP
absorber: 3 SOP
flaw: 4 LUMP
holder: 4 BOAT
Like bad: 5 LUMPY
morsel: 6 GIBLET
Red-eye ~ base: 3 HAM
**Gravy Train**
rival: 4 ALPO
**Gray:** 3 AGE CSA REB 4 ASHY
DRAB REBS 5 ASHEN
7 ELEGIST
Actress: 4 ERIN
area (abbr.): 4 ANAT
Botanist: 3 ASA
Brownish: 5 TAUPE
Fighter in: 3 REB
General in: 3 LEE
Go: 3 AGE
Like the ~ mare: 3 OLD
matter output: 4 IDEA
piece: 3 ODE 5 ELEGY
remover: 4 DYER
shade: 5 TAUPE
Silvery: 3 ASH
Soldier in: 3 REB 5 REBEL
subj.: 4 ANAT
wolf: 4 LOBO
**Gray ___ :** 4 AREA
**Gray, Dorian**
creator: 5 WILDE
What ~ didn't do: 3 AGE
**Gray, Thomas**
ode subject: 4 ETON
work: 3 ODE 5 ELEGY
**Grayback:** 3 REB
**Graycoat:** 3 REB
**Grayish:** 4 ASHY DRAB
5 ASHEN
brown: 3 DUN
yellow: 4 ECRU
**Gray Panthers**
(abbr.): 3 SRS
**Graze:** 3 EAT 4 FEED
Place to: 3 LEA
**Grazed:** 3 ATE
**Grazer**
African: 3 GNU
Bearded: 3 GNU
Female: 3 EWE
Grand Teton: 3 ELK
Roadside: 4 DEER
Serengeti: 3 GNU 5 ELAND
6 IMPALA
**Grazie**
Response to: 5 PREGO
**Grazing**
ground: 3 LEA 6 MEADOW
7 PASTURE

**GRE**
takers: 3 SRS
**Grease:** 4 LARD LUBE
Clean with elbow: 5 SCOUR
SCRUB
job: 4 LUBE
target: 4 AXLE
**"Grease"**
actress: 8 EVEARDEN
actress Conn: 4 DIDI
actress Eve: 5 ARDEN
Costar of John in: 6 OLIVIA
girl: 5 SANDY
group: 7 SHANANA
singer: 5 VALLI
**Greasy:** 4 OILY
goo: 4 GUNK
of football: 5 NEALE
**Greasy spoon:** 5 DINER
sign: 4 EATS
**Great:** 3 RAD 4 AONE EPIC
5 NOTED SWELL
ball of fire: 4 STAR
bargain: 5 STEAL
care: 5 PAINS
deal: 3 LOT TON 4 HEAP
SCAD SLEW
In ~ shape: 3 FIT
move: 4 COUP
Neither ~ nor terrible: 4 SOSO
No ~ shakes: 4 SOSO
number: 3 TON 4 HEAP RAFT
SCAD
review: 4 RAVE
score: 3 TEN
service: 3 ACE
time: 3 ERA GAS 4 BALL
5 BLAST
unwashed: 5 PLEBS
work: 4 OPUS
**"Great"**
czar: 6 PETERI
detective of kid lit: 4 NATE
pope: 5 STLEO
**"Great!":** 5 NEATO SUPER
SWELL
**Great ___ :** 4 DANE 6 DIVIDE
**"Great, The"**
Pope known as: 4 LEOI
**"Great ___, The":** 7 SANTINI
**Great Britain**
emblem: 4 LION
**"Great Dictator, The"**
costar Jack: 5 OAKIE
**Greater:** 4 MORE
To a ~ extent: 6 MORESO
**Greatest:** 6 UTMOST
degree: 3 MAX
part: 4 MOST
**"Greatest, The":** 3 ALI
**"Great Expectations"**
girl: 7 ESTELLA
hero: 3 PIP
Magwitch of: 4 ABEL
**"Great Forest, The"**
painter: 6 ERNEST

**Great Lake:** 4 ERIE
Second largest: 5 HURON
Shallowest: 4 ERIE
Smallest: 7 ONTARIO
Southernmost: 4 ERIE
**Great Lakes**
acronym: 5 HOMES
fish: 4 CHUB 5 CISCO SMELT
port: 4 ERIE
salmon: 4 COHO
whitefish: 5 CISCO
~ Indians: 5 ERIES
**Great Leap Forward**
leader: 3 MAO
**Great Mosque**
site: 6 ALEPPO
**Great ___ Mountains:** 5 SMOKY
**"Great ___ Pepper, The":**
5 WALDO
**Great Salt Lake**
site: 4 UTAH
**Great Society**
pres.: 3 LBJ
**Great Trek**
participant: 4 BOER
**Great white ___ :** 5 HERON
**Great White North, The:**
6 CANADA
**Grecian**
urn work: 3 ODE
**Grecian Formula**
target: 8 GRAYHAIR
**Greece**
Dawn of: 3 EOS
Divine agency of: 6 ORACLE
Letter from: 3 ETA RHO TAU
Peak in NE: 6 MTOSSA
Region of ancient: 5 IONIA
~, to the Greeks: 5 ELLAS
**Greed:** 3 SIN 7 AVARICE
Exemplar of: 5 MIDAS
**Greedy**
Be: 3 HOG
cry: 4 MINE 5 METOO
one: 3 HOG PIG 5 TAKER
**Greek:** 7 HELLENE
1st ~ letter: 5 ALPHA
3rd ~ letter: 5 GAMMA
6th ~ letter: 4 ZETA
7th ~ letter: 3 ETA
8th ~ letter: 5 THETA
19th ~ letter: 3 TAU
Ancient ~ coin: 4 OBOL
6 STATER
Ancient ~ colony: 5 IONIA
Ancient ~ dialect: 5 EOLIC
Ancient ~ lyric poet:
6 SAPPHO 8 ANACREON
Ancient ~ physician: 5 GALEN
Ancient ~ region: 5 IONIA
Ancient ~ state: 6 ATTICA
bread: 4 PITA
cheese: 4 FETA
Chief ~ god: 4 ZEUS
city-state: 5 POLIS 6 SPARTA
7 CORINTH

colonnade: 4 STOA
column style: 5 IONIC
consonant: 3 CHI RHO TAU
   4 BETA ZETA 5 SIGMA
consonants: 3 MUS NUS
cross: 3 TAU
ending: 5 OMEGA
epic: 5 ILIAD
fabulist: 5 AESOP
for "many": 6 POLLOI
garment: 5 TUNIC
god of love: 4 EROS
god of war: 4 ARES
group: 4 FRAT
harp: 4 LYRE
island: 5 CRETE SAMOS
legislature: 5 BOULE
letter: 3 CHI ETA PHI PSI
   RHO TAU 4 BETA IOTA
   ZETA 5 ALPHA GAMMA
   KAPPA OMEGA SIGMA
   THETA
letters: 3 MUS NUS PIS XIS
liqueur: 4 OUZO
marketplace: 5 AGORA
mountain: 4 OSSA
Paradoxical. 4 ZENO
peak: 4 OSSA
philosopher: 4 ZENO
   5 PLATO
portico: 4 STOA
sandwich: 4 GYRO
sea: 6 AEGEAN
temple: 4 NAOS
theater: 5 ODEON
theaters: 4 ODEA
Triangular ~ letter: 5 DELTA
underworld: 5 HADES
vowel: 3 ETA 4 IOTA
   7 OMICRON UPSILON
wine: 7 RETSINA
~ H: 3 ETA
~ I: 4 IOTA
~ P: 3 RHO
~ T: 3 TAU
~ X: 3 CHI
**Greek salad**
cheese: 4 FETA
**Greeley**
direction: 4 WEST
Newsman: 6 HORACE
**Green:** 3 ECO NEW RAW
   4 CASH 5 MOOLA NAIVE
   6 MOOLA UNRIPE
   8 IMMATURE
Actor: 4 SETH
and others: 3 ALS
around the gills: 3 ILL
   4 SICK
beans: 5 LIMAS
beginner: 4 EVER
Bluish: 4 AQUA TEAL
Bowling: 4 LAWN
carvings: 4 JADE
course: 5 SALAD
Deep: 7 EMERALD

dessert: 7 LIMEPIE
drink: 3 TEA 7 LIMEADE
eggs and ham promoter:
   6 SAMIAM
feeling: 4 ENVY
film: 6 PATINA
fruit: 4 KIWI LIME 5 OLIVE
garnish: 5 CRESS
gem: 4 JADE 5 BERYL
   7 EMERALD PERIDOT
Gimme on the: 5 TAPIN
Gives the ~ light: 3 OKS
growth: 4 ALGA MOSS
guarder: 4 TRAP
hole: 3 CUP
hue: 4 JADE
land: 4 EIRE ERIN
light: 4 OKAY 6 ASSENT
lights: 3 OKS 5 YESES
liqueur: 8 ABSINTHE
Little ~ man: 5 ALIEN
Little ~ men: 3 ETS
Long: 4 CASH KALE 5 BREAD
   DOUGH MONEY MOOLA
   6 MOOLAH
moth: 4 LUNA
perimeters: 6 APRONS
pet: 4 CHIA
prefix: 3 ECO
Pungent: 5 CRESS
Salad: 3 COS 5 CRESS
   6 CELERY ENDIVE
   8 ESCAROLE
sauce: 5 PESTO
sci.: 4 ECOL
shade: 3 PEA SEA 4 JADE
   LEEK LIME MOSS NILE
   5 BERYL KELLY OLIVE
   7 AVOCADO
shot: 4 PUTT
spot: 5 OASIS
stuff: 4 CASH 5 MOOLA
   6 DOREMI
suffix: 3 ERY
target: 3 CUP PIN 4 HOLE
Turn: 3 DYE 4 ENVY
Word seen in: 4 WALK
**"Green ___":** 5 ACRES
**"Green ___, The":** 4 MILE
**"Green Acres"**
costar: 5 GABOR 6 ALBERT
Gabor of: 3 EVA
pig: 6 ARNOLD
**Green Bay**
gridder: 6 PACKER
**"Green Berets, The"**
actor Ray: 4 ALDO
**Green card**
holder: 5 ALIEN
org.: 3 INS
~, informally: 4 AMEX
**Greene**
Actor: 5 LORNE
Critic: 4 GAEL
**Greene, Mean Joe:**
   7 STEELER

**Greene County, Ohio**
seat: 5 XENIA
**Greenery**
Pond: 5 ALGAE
Yuletide: 5 HOLLY
**Green-eyed**
monster: 4 ENVY
**Greenfield**
Columnist: 3 MEG
**Green Gables**
girl: 4 ANNE
**Greenhorn:** 4 COLT NAIF TIRO
   TYRO 6 ROOKIE
Like a: 3 NEW
**Green Hornet**
real first name: 5 BRITT
real last name: 4 REID
sidekick: 4 KATO
**Greenhouse**
area: 6 HOTBED
Do a ~ job: 5 REPOT
gadget: 6 MISTER
**Greenish:** 5 OLIVE
blue: 4 AQUA CYAN NILE
   TEAL
yellow pear: 4 BOSC
**Greenland**
air base site: 5 THULE
explorer: 4 ERIC
feature: 6 ICECAP
**Green Mountain Boys**
leader Allen: 5 ETHAN
**Green Party**
candidate: 5 NADER
**Greens:** 5 SALAD
___ greens: 4 BEET
**Greenside**
hazard: 4 TRAP
**Greenskeeper**
supply: 3 SOD
**Greenspan**
Economist: 4 ALAN
group: 3 FED 6 THEFED
subj.: 4 ECON
**Green Wave**
school: 6 TULANE
**Greenwich**
Songwriter: 5 ELLIE
**Greenwich Village**
Area below: 4 SOHO
Like: 4 ARTY
**Greet:** 4 HAIL 7 SAYHITO
and seat: 5 SEEIN
from afar: 6 WAVETO
the day: 4 RISE 5 ARISE
the judge: 4 RISE
the villain: 3 BOO 4 HISS
with laughter: 6 ROARAT
**Greeting:** 5 HELLO
at sea: 4 AHOY
Aussie: 4 GDAY
Bygone: 3 AVE
Cockney: 4 ELLO
Cowboy: 5 HOWDY
Flowery: 3 LEI
Forum: 3 AVE

Informal: 3 HEY 4 HIHO HIYA
  5 HOWDY HULLO
  6 YOOHOO 7 HITHERE
Island: 5 ALOHA
On-field: 5 HIMOM
Ritual: 6 SALAAM
Silent: 4 WAVE
Spanish: 4 HOLA
Tail: 3 WAG
**"Greetings": 5 HELLO**
  org.: 3 SSS
**Greg**
  Actor: 6 EVIGAN 7 KINNEAR
  TV wife of: 6 DHARMA
**Gregarious: 6 SOCIAL**
  Not: 7 ASOCIAL
  Not the ~ type: 5 LONER
**Gregg**
  expert: 5 STENO
  Rocker: 6 ALLMAN
**Gregor**
  Kafka hero: 5 SAMSA
**Gregory**
  Dancer: 5 HINES
  of reggae: 6 ISAACS
**Gregory I**
  papacy year: 3 DCI
**Gremlin**
  maker: 3 AMC
**Gremlins: 4 AMCS**
**Grenada: 4 ISLE**
  **Info:** Spanish cue
  gold: 3 ORO
**Grenade**
  throw: 3 LOB
**Grenadine**
  Cocktail made with: 7 BACARDI
**Grenoble**
  **Info:** French cue
  girlfriend: 4 AMIE
  Goodbye, in: 5 ADIEU
  Good, in: 4 BIEN
  river: 5 ISERE
**Greta**
  Actress: 5 GARBO
  role: 4 MATA
**Gretel**
  Brother of: 6 HANSEL
**Gretna Green**
  Visit: 5 ELOPE
**Gretzky**
  of hockey: 5 WAYNE
  score: 4 GOAL
  was one: 5 OILER
**Grew**
  fond of: 6 TOOKTO
  like ivy: 5 VINED
**Grey**
  Actor: 4 JOEL
  Actress: 3 NAN
  Author: 4 ZANE
  ___ Grey: 4 EARL
**Grey Cup**
  org.: 3 CFL
**Greyhound: 3 BUS**
  stop (abbr.): 3 STN

**Grid**
  figure, slangily: 5 ZEBRA
  infraction: 4 CLIP
  stat: 4 GAIN
  TV screen: 6 RASTER
**Gridder**
  Frisco: 5 NINER
  Green Bay: 6 PACKER
  St. Louis: 3 RAM
  Tennessee: 5 TITAN
**Griddle**
  sound: 3 SSS
**Gridiron**
  complement: 6 ELEVEN
  divs.: 3 YDS
  figure: 3 REF
  gains: 5 YARDS
  kick: 4 PUNT
  official: 3 REF
  org.: 3 NFL
  pass: 7 LATERAL
  play: 5 SNEAK 6 ENDRUN
  prop: 3 TEE
  stat: 3 YDS 5 SACKS
  team: 6 ELEVEN
  unit: 4 YARD
  "zebra": 3 REF
**Gridlock: 3 JAM**
  component: 3 CAR 4 AUTO
**Grief: 3 WOE 4 PAIN 5 DOLOR**
  6 SORROW
  Express: 5 MOURN
**Grief-stricken**
  cry: 4 ALAS
**Grieg**
  Composer: 6 EDVARD
  dancer: 6 ANITRA
  homeland: 6 NORWAY
  Peer of: 4 GYNT
  ~ Piano Concerto key:
    6 AMINOR
**Grier**
  Actress: 3 PAM
  of football: 5 ROSEY
**Grievance: 4 BEEF**
**Grieve: 5 MOURN**
  (for): 4 WEEP
**Griever**
  word: 4 ALAS
**Grievously: 6 SORELY**
  Injure: 4 MAIM
**Griffey**
  of baseball: 3 KEN
  stat: 3 RBI
**Griffin**
  Game show creator:
    4 MERV
  Half of a: 4 LION 5 EAGLE
**Griffith**
  Actor: 4 ANDY
  Actress: 7 MELANIE
  Boxer: 5 EMILE
  Folk singer: 5 NANCI
  role: 7 MATLOCK
**Grifter**
  speciality: 4 SCAM

**Grig**
  Adult: 3 EEL
**Grill: 3 ASK 5 BROIL**
  Blacken on a: 4 SEAR
  partner: 3 BAR
  Patio: 7 HIBACHI
**Grille**
  cover: 3 BRA
  Horse-collar ~ car: 5 EDSEL
**Grilled**
  sandwich: 4 MELT 6 PANINI
**Grim**
  figure: 6 REAPER
**Grimace: 4 MOUE 5 WINCE**
  Uttered: 3 UGH
**Grimaldis**
  ruling site: 6 MONACO
**Grime: 4 DIRT SOIL**
  Fight: 5 CLEAN
**Grimm**
  beast: 4 OGRE
  Elder ~ brother: 5 JACOB
  girl: 6 GRETEL
  lad: 6 HANSEL
  offering: 4 TALE
**Grim Reaper**
  prop: 6 SCYTHE
**Grin: 5 SMILE**
  Begin to: 11 CRACKASMILE
  Big ~ terminus: 3 EAR
  from ear to ear: 4 BEAM
  Twisted, as a: 3 WRY
**Grinch**
  creator: 5 SEUSS
  dog: 3 MAX
  smile: 5 SNEER
  victim: 3 WHO
**Grind: 3 RUT 5 GNASH**
  6 ABRADE CRUNCH
  7 RATRACE
  Axe to: 6 AGENDA
  Daily: 3 RUT 7 RATRACE
  One with an axe to: 5 HONER
**Grinder: 3 SUB 4 HERO MILL**
  5 HOAGY MOLAR
  6 HOAGIE
  Grain: 4 MILL
  Pepper: 4 MILL
**Grinding**
  Grain for: 5 GRIST
  material: 5 EMERY
  tool: 6 PESTLE
  tooth: 5 MOLAR
**Grinned: 5 LITUP**
**Grins**
  Like some: 3 SLY 6 TOOTHY
    8 SHEEPISH
**Grip: 5 CLASP**
  Get a ~ on: 4 HOLD 5 GRASP
  It helps you get a: 4 VISE
    7 PINETAR
  workplace: 3 SET
**Gripe: 4 BEEF MOAN**
  5 PEEVE 6 KVETCH
  PLAINT
**Grippe: 3 FLU**

**Gripper:** 5 TALON
  for the Gipper: 5 CLEAT
  Workbench: 4 VISE 5 CLAMP
    6 CCLAMP
**Gris-gris:** 6 AMULET
**Grisham**
  title bird: 7 PELICAN
**Grissom**
  Astronaut: 3 GUS
  TV show featuring: 3 CSI
**Grist**
  for processors: 4 DATA
  place: 4 MILL
**Grit:** 4 GUTS SAND 5 GNASH
    SPUNK 6 METTLE
**Gritty**
  intro: 5 NITTY
**Grizabella:** 3 CAT
**Grizzlies**
  org.: 3 NBA
**Grizzly:** 3 OLD 4 BEAR
  home: 4 LAIR
  Young: 3 CUB
**Groan**
  causer: 3 PUN 4 CORN
**Groaner:** 3 PUN
**Groats**
  Buckwheat: 5 KASHA
**Groceries**
  holder: 3 BAG
  Pack the ~ again: 5 REBAG
**Grocery**
  carrier: 4 CART
  containers: 5 SACKS
  holder: 3 BAG
  part: 5 AISLE
  Spanish: 6 BODEGA
  stick: 4 OLEO
**Groening**
  Cartoonist: 4 MATT
**Grofé**
  Composer: 5 FERDE
**Grog**
  house: 3 INN
  ingredient: 3 RUM
**Groggery:** 3 BAR
**Grok:** 3 GET
**Grommet:** 6 EYELET
**Gromyko**
  Diplomat: 6 ANDREI
**Groom:** 5 PRIMP
  attendant: 5 USHER
  carefully: 5 PREEN
  garb: 3 TUX
  Greek ~ of 1968: 3 ARI
  of 1614: 5 ROLFE
  vow: 3 IDO
**Groomer**
  Jungle: 3 APE
**Grooming**
  process: 6 TOILET
**Groove:** 3 RUT 4 SLOT_
  Carpentry: 4 DADO
    6 RABBET
  It's in the: 6 NEEDLE
  Narrow: 5 STRIA

**Groove-billed**
  bird: 3 ANI
**Grooved**
  Toy on a ~ track: 7 SLOTCAR
  ~, as a column: 6 FLUTED
**Grooving**
  on: 4 INTO
**Groovy**
  music: 3 LPS
  track: 3 RUT
**"Groovy!":** 3 FAB RAD 4 COOL
    NEAT 5 NEATO
**Grope:** 3 PAW
  for words: 3 HEM
**Grosbard**
  Director: 3 ULU
**Gross:** 4 ICKY
  minus net: 4 TARE
  minus taxes: 3 NET
  out: 5 REPEL
**"Gross!":** 3 ICK UGH 4 YUCK
    5 YECCH
**Grosse ___, Michigan:**
    6 POINTE
**Grotesque**
  figure: 8 GARGOYLE
  imitation: 8 TRAVESTY
**Grotto:** 4 CAVE 6 CAVERN
**Grouch:** 4 CRAB 5 CRANK
    8 SOURPUSS
**Groucho**
  Glance from: 4 LEER
  of comedy: 4 MARX
  prop: 5 CIGAR
  remark: 4 QUIP
  role: 4 OTIS 5 RUFUS
  Tattooed lady of: 5 LYDIA
**Grouchy:** 4 SOUR
  person: 4 CRAB 5 CRANK
  ~ Muppet: 5 OSCAR
**Ground:** 4 SOIL 5 EARTH
  Break: 3 HOE
  breaker: 3 HOE 4 HOER
  cover: 3 SOD 4 TARP 5 GRASS
    MULCH 7 MACADAM
  Drops on the: 3 DEW
  Gooey: 4 MIRE
  grain: 4 MEAL 5 GRIST
  Grazing: 3 LEA
  High: 6 UPLAND
  Hit the: 4 ALIT
  Hold one's: 8 STANDPAT
  It's found in the: 3 ORE
  Lose: 5 ERODE
  Marshy: 6 MORASS
  On solid: 6 ASHORE
  Play: 5 ARENA
  Soggy: 4 MIRE
  Solid: 10 TERRAFIRMA
  Swampy: 3 BOG 4 MIRE
  They never get off the:
    4 EMUS
  Touched: 4 ALIT
**Groundbreaker:** 3 HOE
**Groundbreaking**
  discovery: 3 ORE

**Grounded**
  bird: 3 EMU
  flier: 3 SST
**Grounder**
  Kicks a: 4 ERRS
  Like an easy: 6 ONEHOP
**Ground-floor**
  apartment, perhaps: 4 ONEB
**Groundhog**
  Noted: 4 PHIL
**"Groundhog Day"**
  actress MacDowell: 5 ANDIE
**Groundless:** 4 IDLE
**Grounds:** 5 BASIS DREGS
  for complaint: 9 GRIEVANCE
  for excommunication:
    6 HERESY
  Grand: 6 ESTATE
**Groundskeeper**
  purchase: 3 SOD
  ~, at times: 5 RAKER
**Ground-up**
  bait: 4 CHUM
**Groundwork:** 5 BASIS
**Group:** 3 LOT SET 4 BLOC
    6 ASSORT
  belief: 5 TENET
  character: 5 ETHOS
  "In": 5 ELITE
  In a ~ of: 4 AMID
  Kind of: 3 AGE 4 PEER
  Large: 4 BEVY 5 ARRAY
  of 13: 5 COVEN
  of associates: 6 COHORT
  of beauties: 4 BEVY
  of bees: 5 SWARM
  of cattle: 4 HERD
  of eight: 5 OCTAD OCTET
  of experts: 5 PANEL
  of fish: 6 SCHOOL
  of five: 6 PENTAD
  of horses: 4 TEAM
  of lions: 5 PRIDE
  of nine: 5 NONET
    6 ENNEAD
  of officers: 5 CADRE
  of periods: 3 ERA
  of planes: 5 FLEET
  of seven: 6 HEPTAD
  of ships: 5 FLEET
  of students: 5 CLASS
  of three: 5 TRIAD TRINE
    6 TROIKA
  of two: 4 DUAD DYAD
  of whales: 3 POD
  of witches: 5 COVEN
  principle: 5 TENET
  spirit: 6 MORALE
  values: 5 ETHOS
  voters: 4 BLOC
**Grouper**
  group: 6 SCHOOL
**Groupie:** 3 FAN
**Grouping:** 5 ARRAY
**Group Theatre**
  playwright: 5 ODETS

**Grouse:** 4 BEEF CRAB KICK
RAIL
**Grove**
fruit: 6 ORANGE
growth: 10 ORANGETREE
**Grovel:** 7 EATDIRT
**Grover**
Second veep of: 5 ADLAI
___ **Grove Village, Illinois:**
3 ELK
**Grow**
dark: 5 LATEN
dim: 4 FADE
faint: 4 WANE
It'll ~ on you: 4 HAIR
old: 3 AGE 7 SENESCE
One to ~ on: 4 ACRE
together: 7 ACCRETE
up: 3 AGE
wearisome: 4 PALL
weary: 4 TIRE
**Grower:** 6 FARMER
concern: 6 WEEVIL
Vegetable:
11 TRUCKFARMER
**Growing**
area: 4 FARM
10 GREENHOUSE
Good for: 6 ARABLE
out: 5 ENATE
room: 4 ACRE
**"Growing Pains"**
actor Alan: 6 THICKE
**"Growing Up in ___":**
9 NEWGUINEA
**"Growing Up in New Guinea"**
author: 4 MEAD
**Growl:** 4 GNAR
**Grown:** 5 ADULT
**Grownup:** 5 ADULT
**Grown-up:** 5 ADULT
acorn: 3 OAK
kid: 4 GOAT
**"___ Grows in Brooklyn":**
5 ATREE
**Growth**
Forest: 4 MOSS
Marsh: 4 REED
Pond: 4 ALGA
Rock: 4 MOSS
Sea: 5 ALGAE
~, briefly: 4 INCR
**Groza**
of football: 3 LOU
**Grp.:** 3 ORG 4 ASSN
**Grub:** 4 CHOW EATS FOOD
5 LARVA
Give ~ to: 4 FEED
**Grubstake:** 4 LOAN
**Grudge**
Carrying a: 4 SORE
**Grueling**
test: 4 ORAL
**Gruesome:** 5 LURID
6 MORBID
**Gruff:** 6 HOARSE

**Grumble:** 4 CARP CRAB
5 GRIPE 6 GROUSE
MUTTER
**Grump:** 4 CRAB
**"Grumpier Old Men"**
actress Sophia: 5 LOREN
**Grumpy:** 4 SOUR
companion: 3 DOC
glare: 5 SCOWL
mood: 4 SNIT
**"Grumpy ___" (1993 film):**
6 OLDMEN
**"Grumpy Old Men"**
actor Davis: 5 OSSIE
**Grunt**
Disgusted: 3 UGH
of surprise: 3 HUH
**Grunts:** 3 GIS
**GTO**
The "G" in: 4 GRAN
**Guacamole:** 3 DIP
ingredient: 7 AVOCADO
**Guadalajara**
**Info:** Spanish cue
gold: 3 ORO
goodbye: 5 ADIOS
Good, in: 5 BUENO
guy: 5 SENOR
**Guadalquivir**
and others: 4 RIOS
**Guadeloupe**
and others: 4 ILES
**Guam**
(abbr.): 3 TER 4 TERR
capital: 5 AGANA
Point between ~ and Hawaii:
10 WAKEISLAND
**Guanabara Bay**
city: 3 RIO
**Guanaco**
kin: 5 LLAMA
**Guantánamo**
locale: 4 CUBA
**Guarantee:** 4 AVOW SEAL
6 ASSURE AVOUCH
ENSURE INSURE
**Guaranteed:** 4 ICED MADE
6 NOLOSE 8 FAILSAFE
(abbr.): 4 CERT
to work: 8 SUREFIRE
**Guarantees**
Carrying no: 4 ASIS
**Guarantor**
Acct.: 4 FDIC
**Guard:** 4 TEND 6 PATROL
SENTRY SHIELD
7 GATEMAN PROTECT
8 SENTINEL
dog warning: 5 SNARL
Harem: 6 EUNUCH
Like a good: 5 ALERT
On: 4 WARY 5 ALERT
Place for a: 4 SHIN
Prison: 5 SCREW
shout: 4 HALT
Some ~ dogs: 5 SHEPS

**Guarded:** 4 SAFE 5 LEERY
Sword with a ~ tip: 4 EPEE
**Guarder**
Green: 4 TRAP
**Guardian**
charge: 4 WARD
spirits: 5 GENII LARES
Treasures: 5 GNOME
**Guardian Angels**
wear: 5 BERET
**"Guarding ___" (1994 film):**
4 TESS
**Guards:** 7 LINEMEN
**Guatemala**
**Info:** Spanish cue
gold: 3 ORO
native: 4 MAYA
**Guayaquil**
locale: 7 ECUADOR
**Gucci**
Designer: 4 ALDO
fragrance: 4 ENVY
rival: 5 FENDI
**Guernsey:** 3 COW 4 ISLE
greeting: 3 MOO
___ **guerre:** 5 NOMDE
**Guerrero**
of baseball: 5 PEDRO
**Guerrilla**
1970s ~ org.: 3 SLA
action: 4 RAID
**Guess:** 4 IDEA STAB 5 OPINE
6 RECKON
(abbr.): 3 EST
Didn't: 4 KNEW
Hazard a: 5 OPINE
Sked: 3 ETA ETD
Wild: 4 STAB
Winetaster: 4 YEAR
**Guessing**
Close to: 4 WARM
**Guesstimate**
phrase: 4 ORSO
**Guest**
Homecoming: 4 ALUM
Honored ~ spot: 4 DAIS
Like an eager: 5 EARLY
of note: 5 EDGAR
Uninvited:
11 GATECRASHER
Unwelcome: 4 BOOR PEST
work: 5 VERSE
**Guesthouse:** 3 INN
**Guests**
Desirable: 5 ALIST
**Guevara**
Revolutionary: 3 CHE
**Guevara, Che**
real first name: 7 ERNESTO
**Guff:** 3 GAS LIP 4 SASS
**Guffaw:** 3 YUK 4 ROAR
E-mail: 3 LOL
Hardly a: 5 TEHEE
React to with a: 6 ROARAT
syllable: 3 HAR
~, à la Variety: 4 LAFF

**Guggenheim**
(abbr.): 3 MUS
display: 3 ART
**"Guh-ross!":** 5 YECCH
**Guidance**
Seek divine: 4 PRAY
**Guide:** 4 LEAD 5 PILOT STEER
    8 LODESTAR
Himalayan: 6 SHERPA
Magi: 4 STAR
Museum: 6 DOCENT
posts: 5 TOURS
Road: 3 MAP
Saw: 3 JIG
Spiritual: 4 GURU
Theater: 5 USHER
the ride: 5 STEER
Tour: 3 MAP
Travel ~ name: 5 FODOR
**Guidebook**
for travelers: 8 BAEDEKER
**Guided:** 3 LED
It might be: 7 MISSILE
trip: 4 TOUR
**Guideline**
FDA: 3 RDA
**Guiding**
beliefs: 5 ETHOS
light: 6 BEACON
    7 POLARIS 8 LODESTAR
    POLESTAR
principle: 5 CREDO CREED
    ETHIC TENET
tower: 5 PYLON
**Guido**
high note: 3 ELA
Italian artist: 4 RENI
**Guidry**
Pitcher: 3 RON
**Guild**
Medieval: 5 HANSA HANSE
**Guildenstern**
or Rosencrantz: 4 DANE
    8 COURTIER
**Guile**
Full of: 3 SLY 4 WILY
**Guileful:** 3 SLY 4 WILY
**Guilt:** 7 REMORSE
Sign of: 3 TIC
**Guilty:** 4 PLEA
Find not: 6 ACQUIT
**Guinea**
pig: 3 PET 4 CAVY
**"Guinevere"**
actor Stephen: 3 REA
**Guinier**
Legal scholar: 4 LANI
**Guinness**
Actor: 4 ALEC
adjective: 5 FIRST
category: 7 LARGEST
order: 4 PINT
suffix: 3 EST
**Guinness, Alec**
film, with "The":
    15 LAVENDERHILLMOB

**Guisado**
cooker: 4 OLLA
**Guisewite**
Cartoonist: 5 CATHY
**Guitar**
Adjust a: 4 TUNE
attachment: 5 STRAP
bar: 4 FRET
book diagrams: 6 CHORDS
Country music: 5 DOBRO
cousin: 3 UKE 4 LUTE
    5 BANJO SITAR
device: 4 CAPO
Electric ~ effect: 4 WAWA
forerunner: 4 LUTE
innovator Paul: 3 LES
One of two on a: 7 ESTRING
part: 4 FRET NECK
picker Chet: 6 ATKINS
Play the: 5 STRUM THRUM
sound: 5 TWANG
suffix: 3 IST
Twang, as a: 5 PLUNK
~, slangily: 3 AXE
**Guitarist**
Classical: 7 SEGOVIA
**"Guitar Town"**
singer Steve: 5 EARLE
**Gulager**
Actor: 3 CLU
**Gulch:** 6 ARROYO RAVINE
biter: 4 TOTO
**Gules**
~, in heraldry: 3 RED
**Gulf:** 3 GAP 5 ABYSS BIGHT
    CHASM
Arabian: 4 ADEN
Bottomless: 5 ABYSS
competitor: 4 ESSO 5 AMOCO
    SHELL
emirate: 5 QATAR
    8 ABUDHABI
leader: 4 EMIR
Libyan: 5 SIDRA
Mideast: 4 ADEN OMAN
    5 AQABA
north of Somalia: 4 ADEN
port: 4 ADEN
Red Sea: 5 AQABA
relatives: 4 BAYS
ship: 5 OILER
st.: 3 ALA
sultanate: 4 OMAN
**Gulf of ___**
(Algeria): 4 ORAN
(Arabia): 4 ADEN
(Baltic): 4 RIGA
(Caribbean): 7 SANBLAS
(China): 6 TONKIN
(Mideast): 4 ADEN OMAN
    5 AQABA
(New Guinea): 5 PAPUA
(Spain): 5 CADIZ
(Yemen): 4 ADEN
**Gulf of Aden**
country: 5 YEMEN

**Gulf of Aqaba**
city: 5 EILAT
**Gulf of Bothnia**
country: 6 SWEDEN
**Gulf of California**
peninsula: 4 BAJA
**Gulf of Finland**
capital: 8 HELSINKI
feeder: 4 NEVA
Land on the: 7 ESTONIA
**Gulf of Guinea**
capital: 5 ACCRA
river: 5 NIGER
**Gulf of Mexico**
sight: 6 OILRIG
**Gulf State:** 4 OMAN
    7 ALABAMA
**Gulf War**
ally: 4 OMAN
foe: 4 IRAQ
gulf: 4 ADEN
missile: 4 SCUD
planes: 5 AWACS
**Gulfweed:** 8 SARGASSO
**Gull:** 4 DUPE 6 VICTIM
relative: 4 SKUA TERN
Where buoy meets: 5 OCEAN
**Gullet:** 3 MAW 4 CRAW
**Gullible:** 5 NAIVE
one: 3 SAP 4 DUPE FOOL
    5 PATSY
**"Gulliver's Travels"**
author:
    13 JONATHANSWIFT
brute: 5 YAHOO
Like: 7 SATIRIC
**Gully:** 6 RAVINE
**Gulp**
Big: 4 SWIG
down: 4 CHUG
**Gulped**
down: 3 ATE
**Gum:** 4 TREE 5 RESIN
arabic tree: 6 ACACIA
Art: 6 ERASER
Chewing ~ base: 6 CHICLE
Enjoy some: 4 CHEW
gob: 3 WAD
source: 6 CHICLE
tree dweller: 5 KOALA
Use art: 5 ERASE
___ gum: 4 GUAR
**Gumball**
machine feature: 4 SLOT
**Gumbo**
ingredient: 4 OKRA
**Gummo**
Last name of: 4 MARX
**Gump**
of the comics: 4 ANDY
**Gumption:** 4 GRIT GUTS
    5 MOXIE NERVE SPINE
    SPUNK 6 METTLE
Have the: 4 DARE
**Gums**
Beat one's: 3 YAP

**Gumshoe:** 3 TEC 4 DICK
  6 SHAMUS SLEUTH
job: 4 CASE
**Gun:** 3 REV 6 HEATER
Air ~ ammo: 3 BBS
Big: 6 BERTHA CANNON
  MORTAR
British: 4 STEN
cleaner: 4 SWAB
Clip-fed machine: 4 BREN
Gangster: 3 GAT
German: 5 LUGER
gp.: 3 NRA
Hit with a ray: 3 ZAP
Hood: 3 GAT
Israeli: 3 UZI
Kind of: 3 CAP RAY 5 RADAR
  SPRAY
Machine ~ sound:
  7 RATATAT
Machine ~ syllable: 3 TAT
maker: 7 ARMORER
offspring: 3 SON
Radar ~ wielder: 3 COP
recoil: 4 KICK
stat: 4 BORE
Stun: 5 TASER
Submachine: 3 UZI 4 BREN
  STEN
the engine: 3 REV
Top: 3 ACE
Toy ~ ammo: 3 CAP
WWII: 4 STEN
**"___ Gun, The":** 5 NAKED
**Gund Arena**
player: 3 CAV
**Gunfight**
command: 4 DRAW
**"Gunfight at the O.K. Corral"**
role: 4 EARP
**Gunfighter**
cry: 4 DRAW
**"___ Gun for Hire":** 4 THIS
**"Gunga Din"**
setting: 5 INDIA
**Gung-ho:** 4 AVID 5 CANDO
  EAGER 6 ARDENT
  RAHRAH
about: 4 INTO
feeling: 4 ZEAL
sort: 6 ZEALOT
**Gunk:** 4 CRUD GLOP GOOP
  MUCK OOZE 5 SLIME
  6 SLUDGE
Roofer: 3 TAR
**Gunn, Peter**
girlfriend: 4 EDIE
**Gunners**
org.: 3 NRA
**Gunning**
for: 5 AFTER
**Gunpowder:** 3 TEA
ingredient: 5 NITER
**Guns**
Filler for some: 4 GLUE
Give ~ to: 3 ARM

**Gunslinger**
cry: 4 DRAW
**"Gunsmoke"**
actor James: 6 ARNESS
actress Blake: 6 AMANDA
bartender: 3 SAM
deputy: 7 CHESTER
role: 3 DOC
**Guns N' Roses**
singer Rose: 3 AXL
**Gunther, John**
book: 10 INSIDEASIA
**Gunwale**
pin: 5 THOLE
**Gurkha:** 6 NEPALI
home: 5 NEPAL
**Gurley**
mag: 5 COSMO
**Gurney**
Poet: 4 IVOR
**Guru:** 4 SAGE 5 TUTOR
  6 MASTER
1960s ~: 5 LEARY
Counterculture: 5 LEARY
Home repair: 4 VILA
Policy: 4 WONK
**Gus**
Gloomy: 4 MOPE
Lyricist: 4 KAHN
**Gush:** 4 RAVE SPEW 5 EMOTE
  SPOUT SPURT
**Gussy**
up: 5 ADORN PREEN
  PRIMP
**Gustatory**
organ: 8 TASTEBUD
**Gustav**
Composer: 5 HOLST
  6 MAHLER
**Gustave**
Artist: 4 DORE
**Gustavus**
subject: 5 SWEDE
**Gusto:** 3 PEP 4 BRIO ELAN
  ZEAL ZEST
**Gut**
course: 5 EASYA
feeling: 4 PANG
Get a ~ feeling: 5 SENSE
Listen to one's: 3 EAT
reaction: 3 OOF
**"___ gut!":** 4 SEHR
**Guthrie**
Folk singer: 4 ARLO
restaurant owner: 5 ALICE
**Guts:** 4 GRIT 5 MOXIE VALOR
  7 INSIDES
Have the: 4 DARE
Scarecrow: 5 STRAW
**Guttenberg**
Actor: 5 STEVE
**Gutter**
site: 4 EAVE
**Guy:** 3 MAC MAN 4 CHAP
  DUDE GENT MALE
  5 FELLA

Average: 3 JOE 4 NORM
Belonging to that: 3 HIS
Big ~ nickname: 4 TINY
Fall: 3 SAP 4 ADAM GOAT
  5 CHUMP PATSY
  6 STOOGE
  9 SCAPEGOAT
Funny: 3 WAG
Gloomy: 3 GUS
Good: 6 MENSCH
Great: 5 SCOTT
Grim: 6 REAPER
Handsome: 6 ADONIS
Little: 3 LAD
Macho: 5 HEMAN
Partner of: 3 GAL
Regular: 4 BEAU
Sly: 5 RAMBO
Smart: 4 ALEC 5 ALECK
  BRAIN
Sneaky: 4 PETE
Stand-up kind of: 5 COMIC
Sty: 4 BOAR
That: 3 HIM
Tough: 7 IRONMAN
  8 HARDNOSE
Wise: 3 OWL 4 GURU
  SAGE 5 SWAMI
  6 SAVANT SMARTY
  11 SMARTYPANTS
**Guy Fawkes Day**
mo.: 3 NOV
sight: 7 BONFIRE
**Guys**
only: 4 STAG
partners: 4 GALS
  5 DOLLS
The bad: 4 THEM
Wise: 4 MAGI
**"Guys and Dolls"**
actor Robert: 4 ALDA
composer: 7 LOESSER
guy: 7 DETROIT
  13 NATHANDETROIT
song: 5 SUEME
  15 ADELAIDESLAMENT
writer: 6 RUNYON
**Guzzle:** 4 CHUG
Not: 3 SIP
What cars: 3 GAS
**Guzzled:** 5 DRANK
**Guzzler:** 3 SOT
Gas: 6 ENGINE
**Gwen**
Role for: 4 LOLA
**Gwyn**
Actress: 4 NELL
**Gwyneth**
1996 role for: 4 EMMA
**Gym**
accessory: 3 MAT
ball: 4 PROM
exercise: 4 CHIN
garb: 6 SWEATS
It's pumped at a: 4 IRON
pad: 3 MAT

set: 4 REPS
site: 4 YMCA
stretcher: 7 SPANDEX
**Gym-goer**
concern: 3 BOD
**Gymnast**
assistant: 7 SPOTTER
dream: 3 TEN
goal: 3 TEN
Like a: 5 AGILE LITHE
Olympic ~, often: 4 TEEN
perch: 4 BEAM
**Gymnastic**
event: 5 HORSE RINGS
feat: 6 SPLITS

finale: 8 DISMOUNT
**Gymnastics**
coach Karolyi: 4 BELA
competition: 4 MEET
device: 3 BAR
First name in: 4 OLGA
5 NADIA
move: 4 FLIP
Rare ~ score: 3 TEN
**"Gymnopédies"**
composer Erik: 5 SATIE
**Gynt, Peer**
composer: 5 GRIEG
creator: 5 IBSEN
Mother of: 3 ASE

**Gypsum**
painting surface: 5 GESSO
variety: 8 SELENITE
**Gypsy:** 6 ROMANY
deck: 5 TAROT
**"Gypsy"**
composer Jule: 5 STYNE
**Gyrate:** 4 SPIN 5 WHIRL
**Gyrene**
org.: 4 USMC
**Gyro**
bread: 4 PITA
meat: 4 LAMB
**Gyrocompass**
part: 5 ROTOR

# Hh

**H**
Greek: 3 ETA
Hellenic: 3 ETA
lookalike: 3 ETA
**Häagen-___:** 4 DAZS
**Häagen-Dazs**
alternative: 4 EDYS
**Haakon**
successor: 4 OLAV
**Habaneros**
Like: 3 HOT
**Habeas corpus:** 4 WRIT
**Haberdashery**
item: 3 TIE 6 TIEBAR TIEPIN
7 TIETACK
**Habiliments:** 4 GARB
6 ATTIRE
**Habit:** 4 GARB WONT 5 USAGE
6 ATTIRE
Bad: 4 VICE
Creature of: 3 NUN
In the ~ of: 6 USEDTO
Woman of: 3 NUN
**Habitation:** 5 ABODE
**Habitually:** 5 OFTEN
Take: 3 USE
**Habituate:** 5 ENURE INURE
**Habitué:** 7 REGULAR
**Hacienda:** 5 RANCH
brick: 5 ADOBE
hand: 4 PEON
room: 4 SALA
**Hack:** 3 CAB HEW 4 CHOP
TAXI 6 CABBIE
7 TAXICAB
auto: 3 CAB
charge: 7 CABFARE
customer: 4 FARE
it: 4 COPE
off: 3 LOP
question: 7 WHERETO
**Hackberry**
cousin: 3 ELM
**Hackensack**
City near: 4 LODI
**Hacker:** 3 AXE
Cry from a: 4 IMIN
**Hacking**
fee: 4 FARE
knife: 4 BOLO
**Hackles**
Raise one's: 3 IRK 4 RILE
**Hackman**
Actor: 4 GENE
role: 5 DOYLE
**Hackneyed:** 5 BANAL STALE
TIRED TRITE
**Had:** 3 ATE 5 OWNED

been: 3 WAS
on: 4 WORE
**"___ Had a Hammer":** 3 IFI
**Haddock**
Young: 5 SCROD
**"Had enough?":** 4 GIVE
**Hades**
entryway: 6 EREBUS
Mother of: 4 RHEA
river: 4 STYX 5 LETHE
Traveler to: 7 ORPHEUS
**"___ had it!":** 3 IVE
**Hadn't**
Wish one: 3 RUE
**Hadrian:** 7 EMPEROR
Info: Latin cue
**Hafez al-___:** 5 ASSAD
**Hafiz**
object of study: 5 KORAN
**Hag:** 5 CRONE
**Hägar the Horrible**
creator Browne: 3 DIK
Daughter of: 4 HONI
dog: 5 SNERT
Wife of: 5 HELGA
**Hagen**
Actress: 3 UTA
Tony winner: 3 UTA
**Hagfish**
relative: 3 EEL
**Haggadah**
Meal at which the ~ is read:
5 SEDER
**Haggard:** 4 WORN 5 DRAWN
GAUNT
Country singer: 5 MERLE
heroine: 3 SHE
**Haggard, H. Rider**
book: 3 SHE
**Haggis**
ingredient: 4 SUET
**Hagia ___:** 6 SOPHIA
**Hagiologist**
subject: 5 SAINT
**Hagman**
costar: 4 EDEN
role: 5 EWING
**"Ha-ha"**
Mini: 5 TEHEE
Online: 3 LOL
**Hahn**
Nobelist: 4 OTTO
**"___ Ha'i":** 4 BALI
**Haifa**
airline: 4 ELAL
country: 6 ISRAEL
country (abbr.): 3 ISR
greeting: 6 SHALOM

**Haig**
and others: 3 ALS
**Haiku:** 4 POEM 5 VERSE
**Hail:** 5 EXTOL GREET
Sailor's: 4 AHOY
sound: 7 PITAPAT
~, in Latin: 3 AVE
**Hail ___:** 4 ACAB
**Haile ___:** 8 SELASSIE
**Hailed**
vehicle: 3 CAB 4 TAXI
**Hailey, Arthur**
novel: 5 HOTEL
**Hailing**
Sailing: 4 AHOY
**Hail Mary:** 4 PASS
**"Hail the Conquering Hero"**
actress Raines: 4 ELLA
**Haiphong**
Capital west of: 5 HANOI
holiday: 3 TET
**Hair**
Angel: 5 PASTA
application: 3 GEL
Bit of: 4 HANK
braid: 5 PLAIT
cluster: 4 TUFT
color: 3 ASH
colorer: 3 DYE
conditioner: 5 RINSE
dressing: 6 POMADE
dryer brand: 6 CONAIR
feature: 5 BRAID
goo: 3 GEL
goop: 3 GEL
He had a bad ~ day:
6 SAMSON
High ~ style: 4 UPDO
highlights: 7 STREAKS
holder: 3 GEL
Horse: 4 MANE
Lid: 4 LASH
Like permed: 4 WAVY
line: 4 PART
Lock of: 5 TRESS
Long: 4 MANE
Lose: 4 SHED
Make big, as: 5 TEASE
Mass of: 4 SHAG
Muss one's: 6 TOUSLE
net: 5 SNOOD
ointment: 6 POMADE
piece: 4 CURL 5 TRESS
6 STRAND
removal brand: 4 NAIR NEET
rinse: 5 HENNA
Stiff: 4 SETA
style: 3 BUN 4 AFRO COIF

Thick: 3 MOP 4 MANE
treatment: 6 POMADE
Unruly head of: 3 MOP
untangler: 4 COMB
**"Hair"**
cowriter James: 4 RADO
producer: 4 PAPP
**Haircut**
Layered: 4 SHAG
Quick: 4 TRIM
Short: 3 BOB
Very short: 4 BURR
**Hairdo:** 4 COIF
Bushy: 4 AFRO
Short: 3 BOB
Spheroid: 4 AFRO
Uneven: 4 SHAG
**Hairless:** 4 BALD
**Hairnet:** 5 SNOOD
**Hairpiece:** 3 RUG WIG
**Hair-raiser:** 7 ROGAINE
**Hair-raising:** 5 EERIE SCARY
place: 5 SALON
**Hairs**
Split: 7 NITPICK
Stiff: 5 SETAE
**Hairsplitter:** 6 PEDANT
**"Hairspray"**
actress Zadora: 3 PIA
award: 4 TONY
**Hairstyle:** 4 COIF
Bushy: 4 AFRO
High: 4 UPDO
**Hairstyles:** 3 DOS
**Hairstyling**
goo: 3 GEL
**Hairy:** 6 PILOSE 7 HIRSUTE
bovine: 3 YAK
crawler: 9 TARANTULA
~ Himalayan: 4 YETI
~ TV cousin: 3 ITT
**Hairy-chested:** 5 MANLY
6 VIRILE
**Haiti**
**Info:** French cue
Head of: 4 TETE
Here in: 3 ICI
season: 3 ETE
**Haitian**
dictator: 7 PAPADOC
leader: 8 ARISTIDE
monetary unit: 6 GOURDE
season: 3 ETE
**"Haj, The"**
author Leon: 4 URIS
**Hajj**
destination: 5 MECCA
**Hajji**
belief: 5 ISLAM
destination: 5 MECCA
**Hal**
Actor: 6 LINDEN
**Hale:** 3 FIT 5 SOUND
Actor: 4 ALAN
alma mater: 4 YALE
Golfer: 5 IRWIN

Not: 3 ILL
Patriot: 6 NATHAN
**Hale-___ (comet):** 4 BOPP
**Hale, Edward Everett**
character: 5 NOLAN
**Haleakala National Park**
locale: 4 MAUI
**Hale-Bopp:** 5 COMET
**Haley**
Author: 4 ALEX
costar: 4 LAHR
**Haley, Alex**
saga: 5 ROOTS
**Haley, Bill**
group: 6 COMETS
**Half:** 6 MOIETY
Better: 6 SPOUSE
More than: 4 MOST
prefix: 4 DEMI HEMI SEMI
**Half-___**
(flag position): 4 MAST
(ill-considered): 5 BAKED
**Half and half:** 3 ONE
**Half-and-half**
half: 3 ALE 5 CREAM
**Half-asleep:** 4 DOZY 6 DROWSY
**Half-baked:** 4 DONE
Not even: 3 RAW
**Half-brother**
of Ishmael: 5 ISAAC
of Tom Sawyer: 3 SID
**Half-dozen**
~, in Spanish: 4 SEIS
**Halfhearted:** 5 TEPID
**Half-inch**
stripe wearer (abbr.): 3 ENS
**"Half ___ is better than none":**
5 ALOAF
**Half-moon**
shape: 4 LUNE
tide: 4 NEAP
**Half-pint:** 6 PEEWEE
**Half-sister**
Eva's: 3 ZSA
**Halftime**
lead: 4 EDGE
marchers: 4 BAND
**Halfway**
house: 3 INN
**Half-witted:** 4 DUMB
**Halifax**
clock setting (abbr.): 3 AST
**Hall**
Comedian: 7 ARSENIO
Concert: 5 ODEUM
Former late show announcer:
3 EDD
Kind of: 4 BEER
Large: 4 SALA
Music: 5 ODEUM
partner: 5 OATES
watcher: 7 MONITOR
Word with: 4 CITY
___ hall: 3 REC
___ Hall: 5 SETON
**Hall & Oates:** 3 DUO

**Halle**
Actress: 5 BERRY
**"Hallelujah, ___ Bum":** 3 IMA
**Halley**
observation: 5 COMET
**Halliday, Brett**
detective: 6 SHAYNE
**Halliwell**
Former Spice Girl: 4 GERI
**Hallmark**
card feature: 4 POEM
product: 4 CARD
**Hall of Famer:** 5 GREAT
6 LEGEND
Giant: 3 OTT 6 MELOTT
pitcher Warren: 5 SPAHN
Polo Grounds: 3 OTT
with exactly 3,000 hits:
8 CLEMENTE
~ Aparicio: 4 LUIS
~ Bobby: 3 ORR
~ Combs: 5 EARLE
~ Hank: 5 AARON
~ Hubbard: 3 CAL
~ Koufax: 5 SANDY
~ Mel: 3 OTT
~ QB Bob: 6 GRIESE
~ QB Johnny: 6 UNITAS
~ QB Y.A.: 6 TITTLE
~ Ralph: 5 KINER
~ Ryan: 5 NOLAN
~ Slaughter: 4 ENOS
~ Tony: 5 PEREZ
~ Williams: 3 TED
~ Yogi: 5 BERRA
**Hall of Famer, Aviation**
member: 6 CESSNA
**Hall of Famer, Baseball**
First: 4 COBB
~ Al: 6 KALINE
~ Combs: 5 EARLE
~ Duke: 6 SNIDER
~ Mel: 3 OTT
~ Rod: 5 CAREW
~ Roush: 3 EDD
~ Slaughter: 4 ENOS
~ Speaker: 4 TRIS
~ Waite: 4 HOYT
~ Warren: 5 SPAHN
**Hall of Famer, Basketball**
nickname: 3 DRJ
~ Archibald: 4 NATE
~ Dan: 5 ISSEL 6 LANIER
~ Harshman: 4 MARV
~ Holman: 3 NAT
~ Monroe: 4 EARL
~ Thurmond: 4 NATE
~ Unseld: 3 WES
**Hall of Famer, Football**
coach Greasy: 5 NEALE
~ Blount: 3 MEL
~ Dawson: 3 LEN
~ Ewbank: 4 WEEB
~ Ford: 3 LEN
~ George: 5 HALAS
~ Graham: 4 OTTO

~ Hirsch: 5 ELROY
~ Luckman: 3 SID
~ Lynn: 5 SWANN
~ Marchetti: 4 GINO
~ Merlin: 5 OLSEN
~ Ronnie: 4 LOTT
~ Sayers: 4 GALE
~ Wellington: 4 MARA
**Hall of Famer, Golf**
  ~ Sam: 5 SNEAD
**Hall of Famer, Hockey**
  ~ Bobby: 3 ORR
  ~ Phil, familiarly: 4 ESPO
**Hall of Famer, Horse racing**
  ~ Earl: 5 SANDE
**Hall of Famer, Rock and Roll**
  ~ James: 4 ETTA
  ~ Shannon: 3 DEL
**Hallow:** 5 BLESS
  ending: 3 EEN
**Hallowed:** 6 SACRED
  site: 6 SHRINE
  ~, old-style: 5 BLEST
**Halloween**
  Basic ~ costume: 5 GHOST
    SHEET
  choice: 5 TREAT
  color: 6 ORANGE
  costume part: 4 MASK
  decoration: 3 BAT
    8 SKELETON
  greeting: 3 BOO
  hue: 6 ORANGE
  mo.: 3 OCT
  option: 5 TREAT
**Halls**
  Concert: 4 ODEA
  Music: 4 ODEA
**Hallucinogen:** 3 LSD
**Hallucinogenic**
  cactus: 6 MESCAL PEYOTE
  drug: 3 LSD
**Halo:** 4 AURA 6 NIMBUS
    7 AUREOLE
  wearer: 5 ANGEL
**Halogen**
  salt: 6 IODATE
  suffix: 3 INE
**Halsey, William:** 3 ADM
**Halt:** 3 END 4 STEM STOP
    5 ABORT CEASE
  Call a ~ to: 3 END
  Come to a: 5 CEASE
**"Halt!"**
  ~, to a salt: 5 AVAST
**Halter:** 3 TOP 6 SENTRY
  Horse: 4 REIN WHOA
  Traffic: 8 STOPSIGN
**"Halt, salt!":** 5 AVAST
**Halvah**
  ingredient: 6 SESAME
**Halved:** 5 INTWO
  Bi-: 3 UNI
  Dos: 3 UNO
  Sei: 3 TRE
**Halves:** 8 MOIETIES

Course: 5 NINES
Diameter: 5 RADII
Sawbuck: 4 FINS
Sextet: 5 TRIOS
**Ham:** 4 MEAT 6 EMOTER
    8 BADACTOR
  Brother of: 4 SHEM
  Father of: 4 NOAH
  holder: 3 RYE
  How ~ may be ordered:
    5 ONRYE
  it up: 5 EMOTE
  need: 5 RADIO 7 ANTENNA
  Place for a: 4 DELI
  raiser: 4 NOAH
  spice: 5 CLOVE
  ~, to Noah: 3 SON
**Ham ___ (overact):** 4 ITUP
**Hambletonian**
  Compete in the: 4 TROT
  pace: 4 TROT
**Hamburg**
  river: 4 ELBE
**Hamburger:** 5 PATTY
  grade: 4 LEAN
  holder: 3 BUN
  topping: 5 ONION
  unit: 5 PATTY
**Hamelin**
  casualty: 3 RAT
  hero: 5 PIPER
  Like the ~ piper: 4 PIED
**Ham-handed:** 5 INEPT
**Hamill**
  Actor: 4 MARK
  Journalist: 4 PETE
**Hamilton:** 10 FEDERALIST
  Actress: 5 LINDA
  bill: 3 TEN
  dueling opponent: 4 BURR
  place: 3 TEN
  prov.: 3 ONT
  Skater: 5 SCOTT
  undoing: 4 DUEL
**Hamilton, George**
  Ex of: 5 ALANA
**Hamilton, Scott:** 6 SKATER
  gear: 9 ICESKATES
**Hamilton-Burr**
  event: 4 DUEL
**Hamlet:** 4 BURG DANE ROLE
  choice: 4 TOBE
  cousin: 4 TOWN
  expression: 4 ALAS
  Father of ~, for one: 5 GHOST
  friend: 6 YORICK 7 HORATIO
  home: 8 ELSINORE
  Mother of: 8 GERTRUDE
  realm: 7 DENMARK
  slayer: 7 LAERTES
  What ~ smelled: 4 ARAT
  When ~ dies: 4 ACTV
  When ~ goes mad: 5 ACTII
  When ~ see his father's ghost:
    4 ACTI
**"Hamlet":** 5 DRAMA

actor Hawke: 5 ETHAN
courtier: 5 OSRIC
has five: 4 ACTS
hiding place: 5 ARRAS
maiden: 7 OPHELIA
setting: 8 ELSINORE
soliloquy starter: 4 TOBE
**Hamlin, Harry**
  onetime costar: 3 DEY
  series: 5 LALAW
**Hamm**
  of soccer: 3 MIA
  score: 4 GOAL
**Hammarskjöld**
  Nobelist: 3 DAG
  successor: 6 UTHANT
  U.N. Secretary: 3 DAG
**Hammer:** 4 TOOL
  Businessman: 6 ARMAND
  end: 4 PEEN
  God with a: 4 THOR
  Heavy: 4 MAUL 6 SLEDGE
  in oil: 6 ARMAND
  on a slant: 3 TOE
  part: 4 CLAW PEEN
  Shape with a: 4 PEEN
  site: 3 EAR
  sound: 3 BAM
  target: 4 NAIL
  Tool used with a: 7 NAILSET
  user: 6 NAILER
  wielder: 4 THOR
**Hammer, Mike**
  actor Keach: 5 STACY
  creator Mickey: 8 SPILLANE
**Hammering**
  block: 5 ANVIL
**Hammerin' Hank:** 5 AARON
**Hammers**
  Instrument with: 5 PIANO
**Hammerstein**
  creation: 5 LYRIC
**Hammer-wielding**
  god: 4 THOR
**Hammett**
  detective: 5 SPADE
  heroine: 4 NORA
  hound: 4 ASTA
  sleuth: 5 SPADE
**Hammock**
  holder: 4 TREE
  Use a: 4 LAZE LOLL REST
**Hammond**
  product: 5 ATLAS ORGAN
**Hamper:** 5 CRIMP
  filler: 4 WASH 7 LAUNDRY
**Hamperer**
  Picnic: 4 ANTS RAIN
  Tamperer: 4 SEAL
**Hampton**
  instrument: 5 VIBES
  of jazz: 6 LIONEL
**Hampton Court**
  feature: 4 MAZE
**Hamster:** 3 PET
  home: 4 CAGE

**Hamsun**
  Author: 4 KNUT
**Han**
  beloved: 4 LEIA
  Furry ally of: 4 EWOK
  of sci-fi: 4 SOLO
**Hancock, John:** 6 SIGNEE
      SIGNER
  (abbr.): 3 SIG
  Add your: 3 INK
  Put your ~ on: 4 SIGN
  site: 10 DOTTEDLINE
**Hand:** 4 UNIT
  Ask for a: 7 PROPOSE
  At: 4 NEAR NIGH 6 NEARBY
  At ~, old style: 5 ANEAR
  ball: 4 FIST
  Band: 6 ROADIE
  Bridge: 4 EAST
  Cash on: 4 ANTE
  Close at: 4 NEAR NIGH
      6 NEARBY
  Cow: 4 HOOF
  cream ingredient: 4 ALOE
  Gave a: 5 DEALT
  Give a: 3 AID 4 CLAP DEAL
  Helping: 3 AID
  holder: 3 ARM 4 MITT
      5 GLOVE
  Hook: 4 SMEE
  Lend a: 3 AID 4 ABET HELP
      6 ASSIST
  lotion ingredient: 4 ALOE
  Old: 3 PRO
  One in a: 3 ACE
  On the other: 3 BUT YET
      5 AGAIN
  out: 3 PAY 4 DEAL 5 ALLOT
  (out): 4 METE
  over: 4 CEDE 5 REFER
  Part of a: 4 CARD
  Pay for a: 4 ANTE
  Ranch: 7 COWPOKE
  Right: 4 AIDE
  Seek the ~ of: 3 WOO
  Start a: 4 ANTE DEAL
  suffix: 3 FUL
  Turn one's ~ down: 4 FOLD
  Upper: 4 EDGE
  Wait on ~ and foot:
      7 CATERTO
  warmer: 4 MITT 5 GLOVE
      6 MITTEN
  Word before: 3 OLD 5 UPPER
  You may have a ~ in it:
      5 GLOVE 6 MITTEN
  ~ down, as a verdict:
      6 RENDER
  ~, in Spanish: 4 MANO
  ~, slangily: 3 PAW
**"___ hand?":** 5 NEEDA
**___ hand (help):** 5 LENDA
**Handbag:** 5 PURSE
  handle: 5 STRAP
  Large: 4 TOTE
  material: 5 SUEDE

  Open: 4 TOTE
**Handball**
  relative: 7 JAIALAI
**Handbill:** 5 FLIER FLYER
**Handbook:** 5 GUIDE
**Hand-color:** 6 TIEDYE
**Handcuff:** 7 MANACLE
**Hand-dyed**
  fabric: 5 BATIK
  technique: 5 BATIK
**Handed**
  down: 6 RETOLD
  out: 5 DEALT
**Handed-down**
  history: 4 LORE
**Handel**
  bars: 6 SONATA 8 ORATORIO
  contemporary: 4 ARNE
  oratorio: 4 SAUL
**Handford, Martin**
  character: 5 WALDO
**Handful:** 3 FEW
  A ~ of: 4 SOME
**Handheld**
  computer (abbr.): 3 PDA
  harp: 4 LYRE
  lunch: 4 WRAP
**Handhold**
  Subway: 5 STRAP
**Handicapper**
  hangout, for short: 3 OTB
**"Hand it over!":** 4 GIVE
**Handle:** 3 USE 4 NAME
      5 SEETO WIELD
  adversity: 4 COPE
  Alternate: 5 ALIAS
  clumsily: 3 PAW 5 PAWAT
  Cup: 3 EAR
  Dagger: 4 HAFT
  Door: 4 KNOB
  Fake: 5 ALIAS
  Fly off the: 4 RAGE RANT
      RAVE
  holder: 4 CBER
  Hook on a: 4 GAFF
  Jug: 3 EAR
  Knife: 4 HAFT HILT
  Looped: 4 ANSA
  One with a: 4 CBER
  Razor: 4 ATRA
  roughly: 4 MAUL
  Scythe: 5 SNATH
  Sword: 4 HAFT HILT
  Teacup: 3 EAR
  the helm: 5 STEER
  Tractor: 5 DEERE
  Vase: 4 ANSA
  Word above a: 4 PULL
**Handled:** 3 RAN 5 SAWTO
      6 SEENTO
  Easily ~, as a ship: 4 YARE
**Handler**
  Baggage: 6 REDCAP
  Honey: 3 BEE
  Horse: 5 GROOM
  Money: 6 TELLER

  Pan: 4 CHEF
**Handling**
  Gentle ~, initially: 3 TLC
**Handout:** 4 ALMS DOLE
  Beanery: 4 MENU
  Diner: 4 MENU
  New father's: 5 CIGAR
  Party: 5 FAVOR
  Revival: 5 TRACT
  Spa: 5 TOWEL
  Waiter's: 4 MENU
**Handrail**
  Ballet: 5 BARRE
**H&R Block**
  employee: 3 CPA
**Hands**
  Deck: 4 CREW
  Gave new: 7 REDEALT
  Join: 4 CLAP
  One's ~ and knees:
      8 ALLFOURS
  Put your ~ together: 4 CLAP
  Shake ~ with: 4 MEET
      5 GREET
  Show of: 4 VOTE
  Sitting on one's: 4 IDLE
  Talk with one's: 4 SIGN
  Time when both ~ are up:
      4 NOON
  With ~ on hips: 6 AKIMBO
  Work with the: 5 KNEAD
**Handshake**
  Reason for a: 4 DEAL
  Result of a: 4 PACT
  words: 8 ITSADEAL
**Handsome**
  god: 6 APOLLO
  guy: 6 ADONIS
  Hardly: 4 UGLY
**"Handsome ___ handsome**
      **does":** 4 ISAS
**Hands-up**
  time: 4 NOON
**Handwriting**
  feature: 5 SLANT
  on the wall: 4 OMEN
**Handy:** 4 DEFT 5 OFUSE
      UTILE 6 NEARBY
  bag: 4 TOTE
  reference: 7 ALMANAC
**"Handy"**
  man: 4 ANDY
**Handyman:** 5 DOALL FIXER
  need: 4 TOOL
  TV ~ Bob: 4 VILA
**Hanes**
  competitor: 3 BVD 5 LEGGS
**Hanff**
  Author: 6 HELENE
**Hang:** 4 PEND 5 DRAPE
      HOVER 7 SUSPEND
  around: 4 LOLL STAY WAIT
      6 LINGER LOITER
  around for: 5 AWAIT
  back: 3 LAG 5 TARRY
  Hard to ~ on to: 4 EELY

in the air: 5 HOVER
in the balance: 4 PEND
in there: 4 LAST 6 ENDURE
It may ~ by the neck: 4 JOWL
loose: 4 LOLL 5 CHILL RELAX
loosely: 3 LOP 5 DRAPE
   6 DANGLE
One to ~ with: 3 PAL
on the line: 6 AIRDRY
on to: 4 KEEP 6 RETAIN
out: 4 LOLL 6 AIRDRY
   LOITER
out (with): 6 HOBNOB
over one's head: 4 LOOM
ten: 4 SURF
**Hangar**
Cliff: 5 AERIE
**Hanged Man, The:** 5 TAROT
**Hanger**
Cliff: 5 AERIE
Deli: 6 SALAMI
Frozen: 6 ICICLE
Hat: 3 PEG
Throat: 5 UVULA
**Hanger-on:** 5 LEECH
Boat: 8 BARNACLE
Election: 4 CHAD
**Hang-glide:** 4 SOAR
**Hang ___ Index:** 4 SENG
**Hanging**
around: 4 IDLE
Deli: 6 SALAMI
Elegant: 5 ARRAS
in the balance: 7 ATSTAKE
It's often left: 3 ART
Kind of: 3 OIL
Locker: 5 PINUP
loose: 6 ATEASE
need: 5 NOOSE
Public: 3 ART
tapestry: 5 ARRAS
Wall: 5 ARRAS
**Hangings**
Public: 7 ARTSHOW
Site of some: 5 PRADO
**"Hanging Up"**
novelist Ephron: 5 DELIA
**Hangman**
knot: 5 NOOSE
line: 3 ARM
request: 3 ANI
**Hangout:** 3 DEN 4 LAIR
   5 HAUNT 7 PURLIEU
Bowler's: 5 ALLEY
Campus: 4 QUAD
Cat's: 5 ALLEY
GI: 3 USO
Handicapper: 3 OTB
Herd: 3 LEA
High king: 4 TARA
Hippie: 3 PAD
Jersey: 3 LEA
Oater's: 6 SALOON
Owl's: 4 BARN
Regular: 5 HAUNT 7 PURLIEU
Sloth's: 4 TREE

Teal: 4 POND
Teen: 4 MALL
Thieves': 3 DEN
Tout: 3 OTB
**Hangover:** 4 EAVE
**Hang-up:** 4 SNAG
**Hang-ups**
Serious: 3 ART
**Hank**
Football coach: 5 STRAM
of baseball: 5 AARON BAUER
Slugger: 5 AARON
**Hanker:** 5 YEARN
(for): 5 YEARN
**Hankering:** 3 YEN 4 ITCH
   URGE
Have a: 5 YEARN
**Hanks**
Actor: 3 TOM
**Hanks, Tom**
awards: 6 OSCARS
film: 3 BIG 11 THEMONEYPIT
film, with "The": 5 BURBS
Wife of: 4 RITA
**Hanky**
Use a: 4 WIPE
**Hanna**
animation partner: 7 BARBERA
**Hannah**
Actress: 5 DARYL
**Hannah, Daryl**
film: 6 SPLASH
**"Hannah and Her Sisters"**
actress Farrow: 3 MIA
**Hannibal**
hurdle: 4 ALPS
Mountains crossed by: 4 ALPS
opponent: 6 SCIPIO
**Hannity**
Talk show host: 4 SEAN
**Hanoi**
holiday: 3 TET
**Hans**
Dadaist: 3 ARP
~, in Ireland: 4 SEAN
**"Hansel and Gretel"**
prop: 4 OVEN
**Hansen**
NPR host: 5 LIANE
**Hanson:** 4 TRIO
hit song: 6 MMMBOP
**Hanukkah**
centerpiece: 7 MENORAH
gift: 4 GELT
treat: 5 LATKE
**Haole**
gift: 3 LEI
**Haphazard:** 6 RANDOM
   8 SLAPDASH
**Haphazardly:** 6 ANYHOW
   8 ATRANDOM
Apply: 6 SLAPON
**Happen:** 4 PASS 5 ARISE
   OCCUR
About to: 8 IMMINENT
again: 5 RECUR

Be about to: 6 IMPEND
They may not: 3 IFS
to: 6 BEFALL BETIDE
**Happening:** 5 AFOOT EVENT
   7 EPISODE
Hippie: 4 BEIN 6 LOVEIN
Keep: 5 RECUR
Keep from: 5 AVERT
place: 5 ARENA SCENE
Spring: 4 THAW
Track: 4 MEET
What's: 4 NEWS 5 EVENT
   TREND 6 DOINGS
**Happens**
As it: 4 LIVE
It: 5 EVENT
"___ happens ...": 4 ASIT
"... happily ___ after": 4 EVER
**Happiness:** 4 GLEE
Bird symbolizing: 4 LARK
Symbol of: 4 CLAM LARK
**Happy:** 4 GLAD 6 ELATED
   7 CONTENT
colleague: 6 SLEEPY SNEEZY
ending: 4 HOUR
follower: 4 MEAL
loser: 6 DIETER
Make: 5 ELATE
Not: 5 UPSET
Not a ~ fate: 4 DOOM
Put on a ~ face: 4 BEAM
   5 SMILE
song: 4 LILT
sounds: 3 AHS
Very: 6 ELATED
Visibly: 5 AGLOW
**Happy ___:** 4 HOUR
**"Happy Anniversary"**
writer: 4 ICER
**Happy as ___:** 5 ACLAM
**"Happy Birthday"**
writer: 4 ICER
**"Happy Birthday ___":** 5 TOYOU
**"Happy Days"**
actor Howard: 3 RON
actor Scott: 4 BAIO
actor Williams: 5 ANSON
actress: 9 ERINMORAN
actress Erin: 5 MORAN
actress Moran: 4 ERIN
character: 4 FONZ 6 CHACHI
malt shop owner: 6 ARNOLD
role: 6 RICHIE
surname: 5 MALPH
**"Happy Days Are Here Again"**
composer Milton: 4 AGER
**Happy-go-lucky:** 8 CAREFREE
syllables: 7 TRALALA
**"Happy Motoring"**
company: 4 ESSO
**Harald**
Capital city founded by:
   4 OSLO
Father of: 4 OLAV
**Harangue:** 4 RANT 5 ORATE
   6 BERATE TIRADE

**Harass:** 4 RIDE 5 ANNOY
    BESET NAGAT TEASE
    6 BADGER MOLEST
  ~, in a way: 4 HAZE
**Harassed:** 4 RODE
**Harbach**
  Lyricist: 4 OTTO
**Harbinger:** 4 OMEN 6 HERALD
  Spring: 5 ROBIN
**Harbor:** 4 HIDE PORT
  alert: 4 TOOT
  craft: 3 TUG
  hauler: 4 SCOW
  Leave the: 4 SAIL
  marker: 4 BUOY
  pronoun: 3 SHE
  protection: 5 JETTY
  pusher: 3 TUG
  Safe: 4 COVE
  sight: 3 TUG 4 SHIP
  structure: 5 WHARF
  Tie up in the: 4 MOOR
  workhorse: 3 TUG
**___ Harbour, Florida:** 3 BAL
**Harburg**
  Lyricist: 3 YIP
**Hard:** 6 STEELY
  candy: 10 JAWBREAKER
  Come down: 4 POUR TEEM
  copy: 8 PRINTOUT
  ending: 4 WARE
  finish: 6 ENAMEL
  Get: 3 SET
  Give a ~ time to: 6 HARASS
    HASSLE
  Hit: 3 RAM 5 SMITE WHACK
  It's ~ to believe: 4 TALE
  It's ~ to tell: 4 SAGA
  knocks: 4 BOPS
  Not as: 6 EASIER
  on the eyes: 4 UGLY
  on the feet: 6 PEBBLY
  Playing ~ to get: 3 COY
  rain: 4 HAIL
  rubber: 7 EBONITE
  shot: 5 SMASH
  stuff: 5 BOOZE SAUCE
  suffix: 4 WARE
  throw: 3 PEG
  to believe: 4 TALL
  to catch: 4 EELY
  to clean: 5 GRIMY
  to come by: 4 RARE
  to comprehend: 4 DEEP
  to fathom: 4 DEEP
  to find: 4 RARE 6 SCARCE
  to get: 4 RARE 7 ELUSIVE
  to grasp: 4 EELY
  to hold: 4 EELY
  to lift: 6 LEADEN
  to make out: 5 FAINT
  to penetrate: 5 DENSE
  to please: 5 PICKY
  to resolve: 5 MESSY
  to understand: 6 OPAQUE
  Tried: 6 STROVE

  Try: 6 STRIVE
  up: 4 POOR 5 NEEDY
  water: 3 ICE 4 HAIL
  wear: 5 ARMOR
  wood: 3 ASH OAK
  work: 4 TOIL 5 SWEAT
  worker: 6 TOILER
**Hard ___ (slaving away):** 4 ATIT
**"Hard ___!" (ship command):**
  4 ALEE
**"Hardball"**
  broadcaster: 5 MSNBC
**"Hard Cash"**
  author Charles: 5 READE
**"Hard Day's Night, A"**
  director Richard: 6 LESTER
**Harden:** 3 SET 5 ENURE
  INURE
  in the heat: 4 BAKE
**Hardhearted:** 5 STONY
**"Hard Hearted Hannah"**
  composer: 4 AGER
**Hardin**
  Actor ~ and others: 3 TYS
**Harding**
  Actress: 3 ANN
  opponent: 3 COX
  Skater: 5 TONYA
  successor: 8 COOLIDGE
**Hardliner:** 4 HAWK
**Hardly**
  any: 3 FEW 4 ATAD 5 SCANT
  enough: 5 SCANT
  ever: 6 RARELY SELDOM
  seen: 4 RARE
**"Hardly!":** 3 NOT
**"___ hardly wait!":** 4 ICAN
**Hardness**
  Epitome of: 5 NAILS
**Hard-nosed:** 5 STERN
  Hardly: 3 LAX
**"Hard Road to Glory, A"**
  author: 4 ASHE
**Hard-rock**
  connection: 3 ASA
**Hardship:** 5 RIGOR
  Accustom to: 5 INURE
**Hardware**
  item: 4 BOLT BRAD TNUT
  5 UBOLT
**Hardwood**
  Made of a: 5 OAKEN
  source: 6 REDOAK
  7 OAKTREE
  tree: 3 ASH OAK 5 MAPLE
**Hardy:** 4 HALE
  follower: 3 HAR
  heroine: 4 TESS
  lass: 4 TESS
  partner: 6 LAUREL
  soul: 4 TESS
  ~, to Laurel: 5 OLLIE
  ~, vis-à-vis Laurel: 6 LARGER
**Hardy, Joe**
  tempter: 4 LOLA
**Hare:** 6 MAMMAL

  constellation: 5 LEPUS
  Female: 3 DOE
  opponent: 8 TORTOISE
  tail: 4 SCUT
  Young: 7 LEVERET
**Harebrained:** 5 INANE
  6 ABSURD
**Harem:** 8 SERAGLIO
  chamber: 3 ODA
  guard: 6 EUNUCH
  room: 3 ODA
**___ Hari:** 4 MATA
**Hari, Mata:** 3 SPY
**Haricot:** 4 STEW
**Harkin, Tom**
  state: 4 IOWA
**Harlem**
  suffix: 3 ITE
  theater: 6 APOLLO
**Harlem Globetrotters**
  promoter Saperstein: 3 ABE
  star:
    15 MEADOWLARKLEMON
**Harley:** 3 HOG
**Harlin**
  Director: 5 RENNY
**Harlow:**
    14 PLATINUMBLONDE
  Actress: 4 JEAN
**Harm:** 3 ILL 4 MAIM
  6 DAMAGE INJURE
**Harmless:** 6 BENIGN
  Render: 5 UNARM 6 DEFANG
  DEFUSE DISARM
**Harmon**
  Actor: 4 MARK
  Actress: 5 ANGIE
**Harmonia**
  Father of: 4 ARES
**Harmonica**
  part: 4 REED
**Harmonious**
  Make: 6 ATTUNE
**Harmonize:** 5 AGREE
  6 ATTUNE 7 BLENDIN
**Harmony:** 4 SYNC 5 AMITY
  ORDER 6 ACCORD
  Be in: 4 JIBE 5 AGREE
  Bring into: 4 SYNC
  6 ATTUNE
  Having: 5 TONAL
  In: 5 ASONE
**Harness**
  Oxen: 4 YOKE
  part: 4 HAME REIN
  race: 4 TROT
  race pace: 4 TROT
  racer: 5 PACER
  ring: 6 TERRET
  strap: 4 REIN
**Harold**   LLOYD - Silent MOVIE
  Chemistry Nobelist: 4 UREY
  Composer: 5 ARLEN
  Editor: 5 EVANS
  Presidential candidate:
    7 STASSEN

**Haroseth**
When ~ is eaten: 5 SEDER
**Harp**
cousin: 4 LYRE
ending: 3 IST
on: 7 BELABOR
output: 3 ALE
**Harped:** 5 DWELT
**Harper**
Actress: 4 TESS
Author: 3 LEE
**Harper, Valerie**
role: 5 RHODA
**Harper's Bazaar**
illustrator: 4 ERTE
**Harper's Weekly**
artist: 4 NAST
Piece in: 5 ESSAY
**Harper Valley**
gp.: 3 PTA
**"Harper Valley ___":** 3 PTA
**Harpist**
Heavenly: 5 ANGEL
**Harpo**
of comedy: 4 MARX
**Harpoon:** 5 SPEAR
**Harpoonist**
Nemo's: 3 NED
**Harpo Productions**
Head of: 5 OPRAH
**Harp seal**
lack: 4 EARS
**Harpsichord:** 7 CLAVIER
Small: 6 SPINET
**Harrah's**
locale: 4 RENO
**Harridan:** 3 NAG
**Harriet**
hubby: 5 OZZIE
**Harriman**
Diplomat: 6 PAMELA
**Harris**
Actress: 3 MEL
and others: 3 EDS
Country singer: 7 EMMYLOU
**Harris, Joel Chandler**
creation: 10 UNCLEREMUS
title: 4 BRER
Uncle: 5 REMUS
**Harrisburg**
suburb: 5 ENOLA
**Harrison**
Actor: 3 REX
associate: 5 STARR
role: 3 HAN
**Harrison, George:** 6 BEATLE
Instrument played by: 5 SITAR
**Harrow**
blade: 4 DISK
rival: 4 ETON
**"Harrumph":** 3 BAH
**Harry:** 4 MALE NAME
6 MOLEST
Candy maker: 5 REESE
Mother of: 5 DIANA
successor: 3 IKE

**U.S. President:** 6 TRUMAN
veep: 5 ALBEN
Wife of: 4 BESS 5 LEONA
**Harsh:** 5 STERN 6 COARSE
SEVERE
conditions: 6 RIGORS
cry: 3 CAW
light: 5 GLARE
Not: 3 LAX
review: 3 PAN
sound: 4 RASP
treatment: 4 GAFF
**Harshman**
of basketball: 4 MARV
**Hart, Moss**
autobiography: 6 ACTONE
memoir: 6 ACTONE
**Harte**
Author: 4 BRET
**Harte, Bret**
play: 5 AHSIN
**Hartebeest**
cousin: 3 GNU
**Hartford**
home (abbr.): 4 CONN
symbol: 3 ELK
**Hartman**
Comedian: 4 PHIL
portrayer: 6 LASSER
**Hart Trophy**
winner: 3 ORR
**Harvard**
and others: 5 IVIES
First-year ~ law student:
4 ONEL
hater: 3 ELI
Like ~ walls: 5 IVIED
rival: 4 YALE
Sch. near: 3 MIT
Some ~ grads: 3 DRS
student: 6 CANTAB
**Harvest:** 4 REAP
Bring in the: 4 REAP
fly: 6 CICADA
goddess: 3 OPS
Ready for: 4 RIPE
wool: 5 SHEAR
**Harvester:** 3 ANT
Anglo-Saxon: 4 ESNE
haul: 4 CROP
**Harvey**
Actor: 6 KEITEL
**"Harvey"**
hero: 4 DOWD
**Harvey ___ College:** 4 MUDD
**Has:** 4 OWNS
been: 3 WAS
on: 5 WEARS
to: 4 MUST
to have: 5 NEEDS
too much: 3 ODS
**Has ___ (is connected):** 4 ANIN
**Has-been**
Track: 3 NAG
**Hasbro**
division: 9 PLAYSKOOL

line of trucks: 5 TONKA
**Hasbrouck ___, N.J.:** 3 HTS
**Hasenpfeffer:** 4 STEW
**Has ___ for (is skilled at):**
5 ABENT
**___ Hashanah:** 4 ROSH
**___ ha-Shanah:** 4 ROSH
**Hash house:** 5 DINER
7 BEANERY
handout: 4 MENU
**Hasidic**
leaders: 6 REBBES
**Hasidism:** 4 SECT
**Hassle:** 4 FUSS 5 ANNOY
6 PESTER
**Hasso**
Actress: 5 SIGNE
**Hassock**
Use a: 5 KNEEL
**"Hasta ___!":** 5 LUEGO
**"Hasta la ___!":** 5 VISTA
**Haste:** 5 SPEED
Go in: 3 HIE
Make: 3 HIE
Marry in: 5 ELOPE
**"Haste makes waste":** 5 ADAGE
**Hasten:** 3 HIE
**Hasty:** 4 RASH
**___ hasty retreat:** 5 BEATA
**Hat:** 3 LID
Brimless: 3 FEZ 5 BERET
TOQUE
Canterbury: 5 MITRE
Close-fitting: 5 TOQUE
edge: 4 BRIM
fabric: 4 FELT
Felt: 6 FEDORA
Flat: 3 TAM 5 BERET
French: 5 BERET
High: 5 MITER
9 STOVEPIPE
Highland: 3 TAM
Jipijapa: 6 PANAMA
material: 4 FELT 5 STRAW
Military: 5 SHAKO
Old: 5 DATED PASSE STALE
TRITE
Part of a ~ trick: 4 GOAL
Place to hang your: 3 PEG
Remove, as a: 4 DOFF
Shriner's: 3 FEZ
stand: 4 HEAD
Straw: 6 BOATER
Summer: 6 PANAMA
Tasseled: 3 FEZ
Tip, as a: 4 DOFF
White ~ wearer: 4 CHEF
with a pompon: 3 TAM
Word before: 3 OLD
**Hatch:** 6 DEVISE
Senator: 5 ORRIN
state: 4 UTAH
**Hatcher**
Actress: 4 TERI
**Hatcher, Teri**
role: 8 LOISLANE

**Hatchery**
sound: 4 PEEP
supply: 3 ROE
**Hatchet:** 3 AXE
handle: 4 HAFT
Native: 8 TOMAHAWK
Shaped with a: 4 HEWN
**Hatching**
place: 4 NEST
**Hatchling**
Aerie: 6 EAGLET
group: 5 BROOD
home: 4 NEST
Nocturnal: 5 OWLET
noise: 4 PEEP
**Hate:** 5 ABHOR VENOM
6 DETEST LOATHE
group: 4 KLAN
State of: 5 ODIUM
the thought of: 5 DREAD
**Hatfield**
foe: 5 MCCOY
~, to a McCoy: 3 FOE
5 ENEMY
**Hatfield-McCoy**
affair: 4 FEUD
**Hatfields:** 4 CLAN
**Hathaway**
Shakespeare's: 4 ANNE
**"Hath ___ sister?":**
**Shakespeare:** 3 HEA
**Hatred:** 5 ODIUM 6 ANIMUS
ENMITY
**Hatter**
Like the: 3 MAD
**Hat-tipper**
word: 4 MAAM
**Haughtiness:** 4 AIRS
**Haughty:** 5 PROUD
one: 4 SNOB
response: 5 SNIFF
**Haul:** 3 LUG TOW 4 DRAG
TOTE 5 CARRY
6 SCHLEP
Heist: 4 LOOT
into court: 3 SUE
Long: 4 TREK
to jail: 5 RUNIN
**Hauled**
Being: 5 INTOW
**Hauler**
Cargo: 3 VAN
Farm: 4 DRAY
Freight: 4 SEMI
Garbage: 4 SCOW
Highway: 3 RIG 4 SEMI
Long: 4 SEMI
**Haunt:** 6 OBSESS
**Haunted house**
Like a: 5 EERIE
reaction: 6 SCREAM
sound: 4 MOAN 5 CREAK
**Haunting:** 5 EERIE
**Haus**
Man of the: 4 HERR
wife: 4 FRAU

Woman of the: 4 FRAU
**Hautboy:** 4 OBOE
**Haute**
Hardly ~ cuisine: 4 GLOP
SLOP
___ Haute, Indiana: 5 TERRE
**Hauteur:** 4 AIRS
**Havana**
castle: 5 MORRO
country: 4 CUBA
home: 4 CASA
honcho: 6 CASTRO
residue: 3 ASH
**"Havana"**
actress Lena: 4 OLIN
actress Olin: 4 LENA
**Have:** 3 OWN 7 POSSESS
a go at: 3 TRY
Had to: 6 NEEDED
Has to: 5 NEEDS
Long to: 5 COVET
Must: 4 NEED
no use for: 4 HATE 6 DETEST
on: 4 WEAR
one's say: 5 OPINE
something: 3 AIL EAT
What we: 4 OURS
What we ~ here: 4 THIS
**Have ___**
(be connected): 4 ANIN
(freak out): 4 ACOW
**"Have a bite":** 5 TRYIT
**"Have a good time!":** 5 ENJOY
**"Have a piece!":** 6 TRYONE
**Have ___ at:** 3 AGO
**"Have ___ day":** 5 ANICE
**Have ___ for:** 4 ITIN 5 ANEED
**Have ___ for news:** 5 ANOSE
**Have ___ good authority:**
4 ITON
**Have ___ in one's bonnet:**
4 ABEE
**Havelock**
Author: 5 ELLIS
**Haven:** 5 OASIS
Gambling: 4 RENO
Health: 3 SPA
Hog: 3 STY
Safe: 4 NEST
**Havens:** 5 ASYLA OASES
**"Haven't a clue":** 6 NOIDEA
**"Haven't ___ you somewhere**
**before?":** 4 IMET
**"Have one":** 5 TRYIT
**Have ___ on one's shoulder:**
5 ACHIP
**Haves**
One of the: 5 NABOB
The ~ have it: 6 WEALTH
**"Have some":** 3 EAT
**Have ___ to grind:** 4 ANAX
5 ANAXE
**Have to have:** 4 NEED
**Have ___ to pick:** 4 ANIT
5 ABONE
**Have ___ to play:** 5 AROLE

**Have ___ with**
(know well): 4 ANIN
(speak to): 5 ACHAT
**"Have you ___ wool?":** 3 ANY
**Having "it":** 4 SEXY
**Havoc:** 4 RUIN
Cause: 5 WREAK
**Havoline**
competitor: 3 STP
**Haw**
Hem and: 7 STAMMER
partner: 3 HEM
preceder: 3 HEE
**"___ Haw":** 3 HEE
**Hawaii:** 5 STATE
10 ALOHASTATE
coastal region: 4 KONA
hi: 5 ALOHA
Ho of: 3 DON
It gets picked in: 3 UKE
Outsider, in: 5 HAOLE
porch: 5 LANAI
senator Hiram: 4 FONG
state bird: 4 NENE
**Hawaiian**
bird: 4 NENE
carving: 4 TIKI
city: 4 HILO
coffee: 4 KONA
crooner: 5 DONHO
dance: 4 HULA
dish: 3 POI
feast: 4 LUAU
garland: 3 LEI
goose: 4 NENE
hello: 5 ALOHA
honker: 4 NENE
instrument: 3 UKE
island: 4 MAUI OAHU
5 LANAI 7 MOLOKAI
Like ~ shirts: 4 LOUD
music maker: 3 UKE
necklace: 3 LEI
porch: 5 LANAI
port: 4 HILO
souvenir: 3 LEI
state bird: 4 NENE
tree: 3 KOA
tuber: 4 TARO
tuna: 3 AHI
veranda: 5 LANAI
wind: 4 KONA
**Hawaii County**
seat: 4 HILO
**"Hawaii Five-O"**
locale: 4 OAHU
network: 3 CBS
nickname: 4 DANO 5 DANNO
star: 4 LORD
**Hawk:** 4 SELL VEND 5 NBAER
6 PEDDLE
descent: 5 SWOOP
Fish: 6 OSPREY
gripper: 5 TALON
home: 4 NEST 5 AERIE
Like a: 7 TALONED

Mythical: 4 ARES
opposite: 4 DOVE
weapon: 5 TALON
**Hawke**
Actor: 5 ETHAN
**Hawkeye:** 5 IOWAN
home: 4 IOWA
portrayer: 4 ALDA
show: 4 MASH
Where ~ served: 5 KOREA
**Hawkeye State:** 4 IOWA
**Hawkins**
creator: 4 CAPP
of Dogpatch: 5 SADIE
___ Hawkins Day: 5 SADIE
**Hawkish:** 6 PROWAR
deity: 4 ARES
**Hawks**
former home: 4 OMNI
**Hawley**
cosponsor: 5 SMOOT
**Hawley-___ Tariff Act:** 5 SMOOT
**Haws**
Hems and: 3 ERS
**Hawthorne**
birthplace: 5 SALEM
English actor: 5 NIGEL
**Hay**
bundle: 4 BALE
Hit the: 5 CRASH SLEEP
home: 4 BARN
Ready to hit the: 4 BEAT
Spread, as: 3 TED
storage area: 4 LOFT
Store, as: 6 ENSILE
unit: 4 BALE
**Haydn:** 4 PAPA
piece: 6 SONATA 8 ORATORIO
sobriquet: 4 PAPA
**Hayek**
Actress: 5 SALMA
**Hayes**
Actress: 5 HELEN
of basketball: 5 ELVIN
Singer: 5 ISAAC
**Hayloft**
bundle: 4 BALE
site: 4 BARN
**Haymaker**
Nails with a: 3 KOS
React to a: 4 REEL
    8 SEESTARS
**Haymarket Square**
event: 4 RIOT
**Hayseed:** 4 HICK RUBE
    5 YOKEL
**Haystack**
hider: 6 NEEDLE
**"Haystacks"**
painter: 5 MONET
**Hayworth**
Actress: 4 RITA
husband Khan: 3 ALY
**Hazard:** 4 RISK 5 PERIL
a guess: 5 OPINE
Arctic: 4 BERG

Boating: 4 EDDY
Course: 4 TRAP
Driving: 3 FOG ICE 4 SNOW
    5 GLARE SLEET
Golf: 4 TRAP 8 SANDTRAP
Home: 5 RADON
Links: 4 TRAP
Navigational: 4 BERG REEF
prefix: 3 BIO ECO HAP
River: 5 SHOAL
Road: 3 ICE
Sailing: 5 SHOAL
Shipping: 4 FLOE 7 ICEBERG
Underwater: 4 REEF
Urban: 4 SMOG
Water: 4 REEF
Winter: 3 ICE 5 SLEET
**Hazardous:** 5 RISKY
for driving: 6 SLEETY
gas: 5 RADON
Less: 5 SAFER
**Haze**
London: 3 FOG
Morning: 4 MIST
Urban: 4 SMOG
**Hazel**
cousin: 5 BIRCH
occupation: 4 MAID
**"Hazel"**
cartoonist Key: 3 TED
**Hazy:** 6 UNSURE
Become: 4 BLUR
**Hazzard County**
boss: 4 HOGG
deputy: 4 ENOS
**HBO**
alternative: 3 AMC SHO TMC
    TNT
Part of: 4 HOME
sports agent: 6 ARLISS
**HCl:** 4 ACID
**Head:** 3 NOB 4 BEAN BOSS
    DOME FOAM PATE
    5 FROTH 6 NOODLE
A: 4 EACH
Big: 3 EGO
cases: 6 CRANIA
Cone: 3 SNO
Corp.: 3 CEO
cover: 3 HAT 5 SCALP
covering: 3 CAP 4 HAIR
    5 SCALP
Dept.: 3 MGR
Egg: 3 OVI OVO
follower: 4 ACHE
for: 4 GOTO
for the hills: 4 BOLT FLEE
Hit on the: 3 BOP 4 CONK
Hole in the: 4 PORE 5 SINUS
honcho: 4 BOSS 5 MRBIG
    6 TOPDOG
hunters: 4 LICE
It comes to a: 4 BEER
It gets hit on the: 4 NAIL
It has a ~ and hops: 4 BEER
It may have a big: 4 BEER

It's over your: 3 SKY 4 ROOF
light: 4 HALO IDEA
lines: 3 EEG
lock: 4 HAIR 5 TRESS
of the class: 4 PROF
off: 5 AVERT
out: 5 LEAVE
over heels: 4 GAGA
Red: 5 LENIN
set: 4 EARS EYES
start: 4 EDGE
Swelled: 3 EGO
Top of the: 4 PATE
toward: 7 MAKEFOR
up: 5 CLIMB
wreath: 6 ANADEM
~, in French: 4 TETE
**Head-___ (thorough):** 5 TOTOE
**Headache:** 6 HASSLE
augmenter: 5 NOISE
helper: 7 ASPIRIN
Highway: 5 TIEUP
**Headband:** 4 HALO
Jeweled: 5 TIARA
Royal: 6 DIADEM
Sidekick with a: 5 TONTO
**Headdress**
Bishop's: 5 MITER
British bishop's: 5 MITRE
Egyptian ~ symbol: 3 ASP
Jeweled: 5 TIARA
Wound: 6 TURBAN
**Headed:** 3 LED RAN
(for): 5 BOUND
**Header**
Double: 3 DUO
Take a: 4 FALL TRIP
**Headey**
Actress: 4 LENA
**Headgear**
Angel's: 4 HALO
Bride's: 4 VEIL
Formal: 6 TOPHAT
Hardy: 5 DERBY
Highland: 3 TAM
Pageant: 5 TIARA
Royal: 5 CROWN TIARA
Soldier's: 6 TINHAT
**Heading:** 3 ENE ESE NNE
    NNW SSE SSW WNW
    WSW 6 COURSE
Invitation: 5 WHERE
List: 4 TODO
Memo: 4 INRE
Menu: 7 ENTREES
Pioneer: 4 WEST
Poster: 6 WANTED
**Headland:** 3 RAS 4 CAPE NESS
**Headley, Heather**
role: 4 AIDA
**Headlight:** 4 HALO
component: 4 LENS
lamp type: 7 HALOGEN
setting: 3 DIM
**Headline:** 4 STAR 6 BANNER
Sensational: 8 SCREAMER

**Headliner:** 4 STAR
**"Headlines"**
host: 4 LENO
**Headlong:** 4 RASH
Rush: 4 TEAR 8 STAMPEDE
Rushed: 4 TORE
Send: 4 TRIP
**Headly**
Actress: 6 GLENNE
**Head-on**
Hit: 3 RAM
Meet: 4 FACE
**Head-over-heels:** 4 GAGA
**Headphones:** 4 EARS
**Headpiece:** 5 TIARA
**Headquartered:** 5 BASED
**Headquarters:** 4 BASE HOME
SEAT
Branch: 4 NEST TREE
**"___ Headroom":** 3 MAX
**"Heads ___ ...":** 4 IWIN
**Headstone**
letters: 3 RIP
**Heads-up:** 5 ALERT
**"Heads up!":** 4 FORE 5 ALERT
**Headwaiter:** 7 MAITRED
**Headware**
Angel's: 4 HALO
Heavenly: 4 HALO
Regal: 5 TIARA
**Headway:** 4 DENT
**Heady**
posture: 3 EGO
stuff: 3 ALE 4 BEER
**Heal:** 4 KNIT MEND
~, as bones: 4 KNIT
**Healer**
Animal: 3 VET
Battlefield: 5 MEDIC
Tribal: 6 SHAMAN
Ward: 5 NURSE
**Healing**
attn.: 3 TLC
ointment: 4 BALM
plant: 4 ALOE
sign: 4 SCAB
**Health**
Atlanta-based ~ agcy.: 3 CDC
club: 3 SPA
Drink to one's: 7 WASSAIL
facility: 3 SPA
food flavor: 5 CAROB
Home ~ hazard: 5 RADON
In good: 4 HALE WELL
org.: 3 AMA
Picture of: 4 XRAY
resort: 3 SPA 6 CLINIC
Restore to: 4 CURE
Run for: 3 JOG
Urban ~ hazard: 4 SMOG
~, in French: 5 SANTE
**Health and Human Services**
division (abbr.): 3 FDA
**Healthful:** 8 SALUTARY
getaway: 3 SPA
resort: 3 SPA

routine: 7 REGIMEN
**Healthy:** 4 HALE WELL
5 SOUND
look: 4 GLOW
Not: 3 ILL
Perfectly ~, to the Army:
4 ONEA
**Heaney**
Poet: 6 SEAMUS
**Heap:** 3 TON 4 PILE
A: 5 LOADS SCADS
Combustible: 4 PYRE
Fiery: 4 PYRE
Hearth: 5 ASHES
Top of the: 4 ACME
Whole: 4 SLEW
**Heaps:** 4 ALOT ATON 5 APILE
**Hear:** 3 TRY
For all to: 5 ALOUD
So all can: 5 ALOUD
**"___ Hear a Waltz?":** 3 DOI
**Heard:** 5 AURAL
**Hearing:** 5 SENSE
aid: 3 AMP EAR 5 STENO
Court: 4 OYER
Of: 5 AURAL
Open: 4 OYER
things: 4 EARS
**Hearing-related:** 4 OTIC
5 AURAL 8 AUDITORY
**Hearst**
book division: 4 AVON
**Hearst, Patty:** 7 HEIRESS
alias: 5 TANIA
kidnap gp.: 3 SLA
**Heart:** 3 NUB 4 CORE CRUX
ESSE GIST PITH
5 ORGAN 6 TICKER
7 ESSENCE
Big: 3 ACE
chambers: 5 ATRIA
chart (abbr.): 3 ECG EKG
Eat one's ~ out: 5 YEARN
From the: 6 AORTAL
7 EARNEST
It comes from the: 5 AORTA
PULSE
It gets to your: 8 VENACAVA
It's from the: 5 AORTA
line: 5 AORTA
of a PC: 3 CPU
Of a ~ part: 6 ATRIAL
of the matter: 3 NUB 4 CRUX
MEAT PITH
outlet: 5 AORTA
Say by: 6 RECITE
starter: 3 CPR
Take to: 4 HEED
Take to one's: 6 ENDEAR
test (abbr.): 3 EKG
The way to a man's: 4 VEIN
ward (abbr.): 3 CCU
Where the ~ is: 4 HOME
5 CHEST
Win the ~ of: 6 ENAMOR
Word after: 4 ACHE

~, in French: 5 COEUR
**Heartache:** 3 WOE 5 GRIEF
**"___ Heartache" (Bonnie Tyler**
hit): 4 ITSA
**Heartbeat:** 5 PULSE
**___ heartbeat:** 3 INA
**"___ Heartbeat" (Amy Grant**
hit): 5 EVERY
**Heartbreaker:** 3 CAD
type: 8 CASANOVA
**"Heartbreak House"**
author: 4 SHAW
**Heartburn:** 5 AGITA
remedy: 7 ANTACID
**Heartfelt:** 4 DEEP REAL
7 EARNEST SINCERE
**Hearth:** 5 INGLE 8 FIRESIDE
goddess: 6 HESTIA
heap: 5 ASHES
residue: 3 ASH 5 ASHES
Roman ~ goddess: 5 VESTA
**Heartless:** 4 COLD 5 CRUEL
fellow: 6 TINMAN
**Heart of Dixie (abbr.):** 3 ALA
**Hearts**
How two ~ may beat: 5 ASONE
Parts of: 5 ATRIA
Two: 3 BID
What lurks in the ~ of men:
4 EVIL
**Heart-shaped**
Tree with ~ leaves: 6 LINDEN
**Heartthrob:** 4 IDOL
Small-screen: 6 TVIDOL
**Hearty**
brew: 3 ALE
cheer: 3 OLE
companion: 4 HALE
draft: 5 QUAFF
entrée: 5 STEAK TBONE
hello: 4 HAIL
partner: 4 HALE
Party: 5 REVEL 8 LIVEITUP
pint: 5 STOUT
**Heat:** 4 COPS TEAM
and then cool: 6 ANNEAL
Beat the: 7 AIRCOOL
Canned: 6 STERNO
center, once: 5 ONEAL
Cook with high: 4 SEAR
Dead: 3 TIE
Deprive of: 6 DISARM
Feel the: 4 BAKE
home: 5 MIAMI
In a dead: 4 EVEN
meas.: 3 BTU
Packing: 5 ARMED
shield location: 8 NOSECONE
source: 3 GAS SUN 5 STEAM
6 BOILER
Source of: 3 IRE
unit: 5 THERM
up: 4 WARM
without boiling: 5 SCALD
**"Heat"**
actor: 8 ALPACINO

**"Heat ___, The":** 4 ISON
**Heated:** 4 WARM 5 ANGRY
  argument: 5 SETTO
**Heater:** 3 GAT ROD
  Caterer's: 6 STERNO
  feature: 4 COIL
  Lab: 4 ETNA
  Space: 3 SOL
**Heath**
  family shrub: 5 ERICA
    6 AZALEA
  ___ **Heath ("The Return of the**
    **Native" setting):**
    5 EGDON
**Heathcliff:** 3 CAT
**Heathen:** 5 PAGAN
**Heather:** 5 ERICA
  lands: 5 MOORS
**Heathrow**
  Former ~ arrival: 3 SST
**Heating**
  device: 4 ETNA
  fuel: 3 GAS OIL 7 COALGAS
  Strengthen by: 6 ANNEAL
**Heat-resistant**
  glass: 5 PYREX
**Heaved**
  It may be: 4 SIGH
**Heave-ho:** 4 BOOT
  6 OUSTER
  Give the: 3 CAN 4 OUST TOSS
    5 EJECT
**Heaven:** 3 SKY 5 BLISS
  Food from: 5 MANNA
  Hog: 3 STY
  In: 5 ABOVE 6 ONHIGH
  In seventh: 6 ELATED
  on earth: 4 EDEN 6 UTOPIA
  Queen of: 4 HERA
  Seventh: 5 BLISS 7 ECSTASY
    8 EUPHORIA
    9 CLOUDNINE
  Smell to high: 4 REEK
**"Heaven forbid!":** 4 OHNO
**Heavenly:** 6 DIVINE
    9 CELESTIAL
  altar: 3 ARA
  bear: 4 URSA
  body: 3 ORB 5 ANGEL
  circle: 4 HALO
  food: 5 MANNA
  gift: 5 MANNA
  glow: 4 AURA
  headwear: 4 HALO
  hunter: 5 ORION
  instrument: 4 HARP
  opener: 5 URANO
  ring: 4 HALO
  streaker: 6 METEOR
**Heavenly ___ (ice cream flavor):**
  4 HASH
**Heavens:** 3 SKY 5 ETHER
  Head for the: 4 SOAR
  Hunter in the: 5 ORION
  In the: 6 ONHIGH
  prefix: 5 URANO

**"Heavens!":** 4 EGAD
  6 DEARME
**Heaven-sent**
  food: 5 MANNA
**"Heavens to Betsy!":** 4 EGAD
**Heavenward:** 5 ABOVE
**Heavily**
  Breathe: 4 PANT
  Drop: 4 PLOP THUD
  favored: 6 ODDSON
  Sit: 4 PLOP
  Stepped: 4 TROD
  Walk: 4 PLOD SLOG 5 STOMP
    TROMP
  Walked: 4 TROD
  Weigh: 8 MILITATE
**Heavy:** 6 LEADEN 7 VILLAIN
  book: 4 TOME
  burden: 4 LOAD
  cart: 4 DRAY
  Fairy-tale: 4 OGRE
  hammer: 4 MAUL 6 SLEDGE
  knock: 5 THUMP
  metal: 4 LEAD
  More than: 5 OBESE
  overcoat: 6 ULSTER
  reading: 4 TOME
  weight: 3 TON
  wts.: 3 TNS
**Heavy ___ music:** 5 METAL
**Heavyweight**
  Japanese: 4 SUMO
  Light: 6 EDISON
  Zoo: 5 HIPPO RHINO
**Heavyweight champ**
  1930s ~: 4 BAER
  1940s ~: 8 JOELOUIS
  Three-time: 3 ALI
  ~ Holyfield: 7 EVANDER
  ~ Johansson: 7 INGEMAR
  ~ Max: 4 BAER
  ~ Willard: 4 JESS
**Heb.**
  judge: 4 SAML
**Hebrew:** 6 SEMITE
  beginning: 4 ROSH
  day: 3 YOM
  First ~ letter: 4 ALEF
    5 ALEPH
  judge: 3 ELI
  letter: 3 MEM TAV YOD
    4 ALEF TETH YODH
    5 ALEPH
  month: 4 ADAR ELUL
  opener: 5 ALEPH
  prophet: 4 AMOS 5 HOSEA
    6 ELIJAH ISAIAH
  Sons of, in: 4 BNAI
  title of respect for God:
    6 ADONAI
**Hebrews**
  Bk. after: 3 JAS
**Hebrides**
  hill: 4 BRAE
  island: 4 IONA SKYE
  language: 4 ERSE

**Heche**
  Actress: 4 ANNE
**Heckart**
  Actress: 6 EILEEN
**Heckelphone**
  cousin: 4 OBOE
**Heckerling**
  Director: 3 AMY
**Heckle:** 3 BOO 4 BAIT HISS
  RAZZ RIDE 6 HARASS
  NEEDLE
**Heckler**
  holler: 3 BOO
  missile: 3 EGG
**Hector:** 6 TROJAN
  died in it: 5 ILIAD
  Father of: 5 PRIAM
**"Hedda Gabler"**
  playwright Henrik: 5 IBSEN
**Hedgehog**
  of video games: 5 SONIC
**Hedin**
  Explorer: 4 SVEN
**Hedonistic:**
    15 PLEASURESEEKING
**Hedren**
  Actress: 5 TIPPI
**"___ he drove out of sight ...":**
  3 ERE
**Hedwig**
  Harry Potter's: 3 OWL
**Hedy**
  Actress: 6 LAMARR
**Hee**
  follower: 3 HAW
**"Hee ___":** 3 HAW
**Heed:** 4 OBEY 8 LISTENTO
  Give: 6 HARKEN
  Pay: 4 OBEY
  Pay no ~ to: 6 IGNORE
  Sign to: 4 OMEN
  the alarm: 4 RISE
**Heedless:** 4 DEAF
**"Hee Haw"**
  character: 4 RUBE
  cohost: 5 OWENS
  performer Pickens: 4 SLIM
**Heel:** 3 CAD CUR 5 LOUSE
  Kind of: 8 STILETTO
**Heeler**
  Ward: 3 POL
**Heelless**
  shoe: 4 FLAT
**Heels**
  Bite, as the: 5 NIPAT
  Cool one's: 4 WAIT
  Down at the: 5 SEEDY
  Head over: 4 GAGA
  Kick up one's: 6 GAMBOL
  Took to one's: 3 RAN
**Heep:** 5 CLERK
  Dickens's: 5 URIAH
  of fiction: 5 URIAH
**Hefty**
  competitor: 4 GLAD
  sandwich: 4 HERO

volume: 4 TOME
**Hegelian**
  article: 3 EIN
**"___ he grown!": 5 HASNT**
**Heidelberg**
  trio: 4 DREI
**Heiden**
  Skater: 4 ERIC
**Heidi:** 5 SWISS
  height: 3 ALP
  Hollywood madam: 6 FLEISS
  home: 4 ALPS 6 CHALET
**"Heidi"**
  author: 5 SPYRI
**Heifer:** 3 SHE
  housing: 4 BARN
**Heifetz**
  teacher: 4 AUER
  Violinist: 6 JASCHA
**Height:** 4 ACME APEX
    7 STATURE
  (abbr.): 3 ALT 4 ELEV
  Having ~, width, and depth:
    6 THREED
  Lacking ~ or depth: 4 ONED
  prefix: 3 ACR 4 ACRO ALTI
**Heighten:** 5 RAISE 7 ENHANCE
**Heights**
  Mideast: 5 GOLAN
**___ Heights:** 5 GOLAN
**Hein**
  Mathematician: 4 PIET
**Heineken**
  brand: 6 AMSTEL
  symbol: 4 STAR
**Heinie:** 4 TUSH
**Heinous:** 4 EVIL
**Heinrich**
  Poet: 5 HEINE
**Heinz, H.J.**
  Company owned by: 6 OREIDA
**"Heinz 57"**
  dog: 4 MUTT
**Heinz Field**
  player: 7 STEELER
**Heir:** 7 LEGATEE
  concern: 6 ESTATE
  lines: 4 WILL
  ~, in law: 7 ALIENEE
  ~, often: 3 SON 6 ELDEST
**Heiress**
  ~, perhaps: 5 NIECE
**Heirloom**
  locale: 5 ATTIC
**Heirs**
  Biblical: 4 MEEK
**Heisman Trophy**
  winner Doug: 6 FLUTIE
**Heist:** 5 CAPER
  haul: 4 LOOT
  Help in a: 4 ABET
**Held:** 3 HAD 4 KEPT
    6 DEEMED
  off: 5 ATBAY
  on to: 4 KEPT
  up: 4 LATE 5 BORNE

**"___ Heldenleben" (Strauss
    opus):** 3 EIN
**Helen**
  Actress: 5 HAYES
  of radio soaps: 5 TRENT
  Paris dumped her for:
    6 OENONE
  Singer: 5 REDDY
  Where Paris took: 4 TROY
**Helena**
  rival: 5 ESTEE
**Helen of ___:** 4 TROY
**Helen of Troy**
  abductor: 5 PARIS
  Mother of: 4 LEDA
**Helga**
  Husband of: 5 HAGAR
**Helgenberger**
  Actress: 4 MARG
  hit on CBS: 3 CSI
**Helicopter**
  Army: 5 COBRA 6 APACHE
  blade: 5 ROTOR
  inventor Igor: 8 SIKORSKY
  part: 5 ROTOR
  pioneer Sikorsky: 4 IGOR
**Helios:** 6 SUNGOD
  Mother of: 4 THEA
  Roman counterpart of: 3 SOL
**Helium:** 3 GAS 8 INERTGAS
  Like: 5 INERT
  One of a ~ pair: 6 PROTON
**Helix:** 4 COIL 6 SPIRAL
  Heredity: 3 DNA
**Hell**
  He went to ~, so to speak:
    5 DANTE
  Like: 6 ABLAZE
  of a place: 5 HADES
**Hellenic**
  hangouts: 6 AGORAE
  ~ H: 3 ETA
**Hellish:** 7 AVERNAL
    8 INFERNAL
**"Hell ___ no fury ...":** 4 HATH
**Hello**
  Caesar's: 3 AVE
  Hawaiian: 5 ALOHA
  Hilo: 5 ALOHA
  Sailor's: 4 AHOY
**"Hello":** 7 HITHERE
  follower, often: 9 HOWAREYOU
  It may say: 7 NAMETAG
**"Hello, Dolly!"**
  character Dolly: 4 LEVI
**Hells Canyon**
  state: 5 IDAHO
**"Hellzapoppin"**
  actress Martha: 4 RAYE
  star Ole: 5 OLSEN
**Helm**
  Fictional spy: 4 MATT
  Handle the: 5 STEER
  Have the: 5 STEER
  heading: 3 ENE ESE NNE
    NNW SSE SSW WNW WSW

position: 4 ALEE
  Quick to the: 3 YAR 4 YARE
  Take the: 5 STEER
**Helmet:** 7 HARDHAT
  accessory: 5 PLUME
  feature: 5 STRAP
  Pith: 5 TOPEE
  plume: 5 CREST
  Soldier's: 6 TINHAT
  Visored: 5 ARMET
**___ helmet (safari wear):**
    4 PITH
**Helmets:** 8 HEADGEAR
**Helmsley**
  Hotelier: 5 LEONA
**Helmsman:** 7 STEERER
  Enterprise: 4 SULU
**Helmut**
  German statesman: 4 KOHL
**Heloise**
  Info: French cue
  love: 7 ABELARD
  offering: 4 HINT
**Help:** 3 AID 4 ABET 5 AVAIL
  a hood: 4 ABET
  a hooligan: 4 ABET
  Bit of: 4 HINT
  Call for: 3 SOS 6 MAYDAY
  Can't ~ but: 5 HASTO
  Couldn't ~ but: 5 HADTO
  for the stumped: 4 HINT
  Holiday: 3 ELF
  in a heist: 4 ABET
  It'll ~ you up: 4 TBAR
  on the way up: 4 STEP
  out: 6 ASSIST
  Requiring: 6 INNEED
  Seek ~ from: 6 PRAYTO
    TURNTO
  settle: 7 MEDIATE
  with homework: 5 TUTOR
  Without: 4 SOLO 5 ALONE
    7 UNAIDED
  with the dishes: 3 DRY 4 WIPE
**"Help!":** 3 SOS 6 SAVEME
**Helper:** 4 AIDE
  (abbr.): 4 ASST
  Dictator's: 5 STENO
  Driver's: 3 TEE
  Holiday: 3 ELF
  Hook's: 4 SMEE
  Little: 3 ELF 4 ASST
  Mgr.'s: 4 ASST
  Mother's: 9 NURSEMAID
  Off.: 4 ASST
  Reception: 6 AERIAL
    7 ANTENNA
  Santa's: 3 ELF
  Wedding: 5 USHER
**Helpers**
  Hwy.: 3 AAA
  Prof's: 3 TAS
**Helpful:** 5 OFUSE UTILE
  contacts: 3 INS
  hint: 3 TIP
  sort: 5 AIDER

**Helpless:** 4 SOLO 5 ALONE
    6 UNABLE
**Helpmate:** 6 SPOUSE
**"Help ___ the way!":** 4 ISON
**Help wanted**
    abbr.: 3 EEO EOE
**"___ help you?":** 4 CANI MAYI
**Helsinki**
    native: 4 FINN
    Year ~ was founded: 3 MDL
**Helter-skelter:** 8 PELLMELL
**Helvetica:** 4 FONT
**Hem**
    again: 5 RESEW
    and haw: 7 STAMMER
    Fix, as a: 5 RESEW
    in: 5 BESET
    line: 4 KNEE
    partner: 3 HAW
    Prepare to: 5 PINUP
    Raise the: 5 ALTER
**He-man**
    Hardly a: 5 SISSY
    Like a: 5 MACHO
**Hematite:** 3 ORE 7 IRONORE
**Hemingway**
    Actress: 6 MARIEL
    Author: 6 ERNEST
    End of a ~ title: 6 THESEA
    nickname: 4 PAPA
    novel:
        15 AFAREWELLTOARMS
    Pronoun in a ~ title: 4 WHOM
    sobriquet: 4 PAPA
    title character: 6 OLDMAN
    Writer: 6 ERNEST
**Hemispherical**
    home: 5 IGLOO
    roof: 4 DOME
**Hemmed:** 4 SEWN
**Hemming**
    and hawing: 3 ERS
**Hemoglobin**
    component: 4 IRON
**Hemp:** 5 BHANG
    fiber: 5 SISAL
**Hems**
    and haws: 3 ERS
**Hen:** 5 LAYER 6 FEMALE
    home: 4 COOP
    pen: 4 COOP
    Type of: 7 CORNISH
**Hence:** 4 ERGO THUS
**Henchman**
    Hook's: 4 SMEE
**Henderson, Rickey**
    Emulate: 5 STEAL
**Hendricks**
    of football: 3 TED
**Hendrix**
    genre: 8 ACIDROCK
    Guitarist: 4 JIMI
    hairdo: 4 AFRO
**Hendryx**
    Singer: 4 NONA
**Henhouse:** 4 COOP 5 ROOST

unit: 3 EGG
**Henie**
    Skater: 5 SONJA
**Henie, Sonja**
    birthplace: 4 OSLO
**Henley**
    crew: 4 OARS
    event: 7 REGATTA
    Playwright: 4 BETH
    propeller: 3 OAR
**Henley-on-Thames**
    Annual ~ event: 7 REGATTA
**Henley Regatta**
    site: 6 THAMES
**Henna:** 3 DYE
    user: 4 DYER
**Henner**
    Actress: 6 MARILU
**Henning**
    Magician: 4 DOUG
**Henpeck:** 3 NAG
**Henri:** 3 NOM
    **Info:** French clue
    Painter: 7 MATISSE
**Henrik**
    Playwright: 5 IBSEN
**Henry**
    Actor: 5 FONDA
    Publisher: 4 LUCE
    Sculptor: 5 MOORE
    Son of: 5 EDSEL
    tutee: 5 ELIZA
**Henry ___:** 4 VIII
**Henry, O.**
    device: 5 IRONY
    Like a story by: 6 IRONIC
**Henry ___, Sir**
    gallery: 4 TATE
**"Henry & June"**
    character: 3 NIN 5 ANAIS
    She was June in: 3 UMA
**Henry II**
    He played ~ twice: 6 OTOOLE
    Queen of: 7 ELEANOR
**Henry VI**
    School founded by: 4 ETON
**Henry VIII**
    family: 5 TUDOR
    house: 5 TUDOR
    Last wife of: 4 PARR
    Like: 5 OBESE
    Second wife of: 4 ANNE
    sextet: 5 WIVES
    Sixth wife of: 4 PARR
    wife Boleyn: 4 ANNE
    wife Catherine: 4 PARR
**Henson**
    of Muppets fame: 3 JIM
**Hentoff**
    Writer: 3 NAT
**Heparin**
    target: 4 CLOT
**Hepburn**
    film: 8 ADAMSRIB
        12 MORNINGGLORY
        15 THELIONINWINTER

quartet: 6 OSCARS
    role: 7 SABRINA
**Hepcat**
    jargon: 4 JIVE
**Hephaestus**
    workshop: 4 ETNA 6 MTETNA
**Hepta-**
    plus one: 4 OCTA
**Her**
    His and: 5 THEIR
    partner: 3 HIS
    ~, in French: 3 SES
**"Her ___" ("Miss Saigon" song):**
    4 ORME
**Hera**
    counterpart: 4 JUNO
    Husband of: 4 ZEUS
    Mother of: 4 RHEA
    Son of: 4 ARES
**Herald:** 7 USHERIN
    Home of the: 5 MIAMI
**Heraldic**
    band: 4 ORLE
    blue: 5 AZURE
    border: 4 ORLE
**Herb**
    Aromatic: 5 ANISE
    Cathartic: 5 SENNA
    Chef's: 4 SAGE
    Columnist: 4 CAEN
    Culinary: 5 THYME
        8 MARJORAM
    Curry: 5 CUMIN
    Medicinal: 5 SENNA
    of regret: 3 RUE
    of the parsley family:
        8 ANGELICA
    Pesto: 5 BASIL
    Pickling: 4 DILL
    Pizza: 7 OREGANO
    Stuffing: 4 SAGE
    "Sweet": 5 BASIL
    Trumpeter: 6 ALPERT
**Herbal**
    drink: 3 TEA
    quaff: 3 TEA
**Herber**
    of football: 5 ARNIE
**Herbert**
    Actor: 3 LOM
    Pulitzer winner: 4 AGAR
**Herbert, Frank**
    classic novel: 4 DUNE
**Herbicide**
    target: 4 WEED
**Herbie**
    Jazz flutist: 4 MANN
    ~, in Disney films: 5 VWBUG
**Herbivore**
    Horned: 5 RHINO
    Hulking: 5 HIPPO
**Hercule**
    creator: 6 AGATHA
**Herculean**
    dozen: 5 TASKS
    Hardly: 4 PUNY

labor site: 5 NEMEA
**Hercules:** 5 HEMAN
  captive: 4 IOLE
  challenges: 6 LABORS
  victim: 5 HYDRA
  Where ~ slew a lion: 5 NEMEA
**"Hercules"**
  spin-off: 4 XENA
**Herd:** 5 DROVE
  bird: 3 EMU
  Dairy: 4 COWS
  hangout: 3 LEA
  in Africa: 5 ELAND
  It's heard in a: 3 BAA MOO
  Name for a ~ dog: 4 SHEP
  noise: 3 MOO
  of seals: 3 POD
  orphan: 5 DOGIE
  word: 3 MOO
**Herder**
  Reindeer: 4 LAPP
**Herding**
  dog: 6 COLLIE
  dog name: 4 SHEP
**Here**
  again: 4 BACK
  Almost: 4 NEAR
  and there: 5 ABOUT APART
    6 PASSIM
  Go ~ and there: 4 ROAM
    ROVE
  It's neither ~ nor there:
    5 LIMBO
  No longer: 4 GONE
  Not for: 4 TOGO
  The one: 4 THIS
  The ones: 5 THESE
  What's: 5 THESE
  You are: 5 EARTH
  ~, in French: 3 ICI
  ~, in Spanish: 3 ACA 4 AQUI
**"Here ___ Again":** 3 IGO
**"Here comes trouble!":** 4 OHOH
  UHOH
**Hereditary:** 6 INBORN INBRED
  INNATE LINEAL
  8 FAMILIAL
  helix: 3 DNA
  ruler: 6 DYNAST
  unit: 4 GENE
**Heredity:** 5 GENES
  carrier: 4 GENE
  helix: 3 DNA
**"Here Is Your War"**
  author Ernie: 4 PYLE
**"Here it is!":** 4 TADA
**"Here's to you!":** 5 SKOAL
  TOAST
  The "you" of: 7 TOASTEE
**Here today, gone tomorrow:**
  9 EPHEMERAL
**Heretofore:** 5 ASYET SOFAR
  6 ERENOW
**"Here we ___!":** 3 ARE
**"___ Her Go"** (Frankie Laine
  song): 4 ILET

**Herman, Jerry**
  musical: 4 MAME
**Hermann**
  Author: 5 HESSE
  Gold medalist skier: 5 MAIER
**Herman's Hermits**
  singer Peter: 5 NOONE
**Hermes**
  Half brother of: 4 ARES
  Mother of: 4 MAIA
**Hermit:** 5 LONER 7 RECLUSE
  It may be a ~ or fiddler:
    4 CRAB
  Like a: 5 ALONE
**Hermitic:** 4 LONE
**Hernando**
  Info: Spanish cue
**Hernando de ___**
  Explorer: 4 SOTO
**"Hernando's Hideaway":**
  5 TANGO
**Hero:** 3 SUB 4 IDOL
  Air: 3 ACE
  ending: 3 INE
  love: 7 LEANDER
  maker: 4 DELI
  Place for a: 4 DELI
  reward: 5 MEDAL
  suffix: 3 INE ISM
  worshiper: 7 LEANDER
**"Hero"**
  singer Mariah: 5 CAREY
**Heroes**
  Like some: 6 UNSUNG
  Where ~ are made: 4 DELI
**Heroic:** 5 BRAVE
  act: 6 RESCUE
  action: 9 DERRINGDO
  deed: 4 FEAT
  narrative: 4 SAGA
  story: 4 EPIC
  tale: 4 EPIC SAGA
**Heroics:** 9 DERRINGDO
**Heron:** 5 WADER
  home: 4 NEST
  Plumed: 5 EGRET
  relative: 4 IBIS
  Small: 7 BITTERN
  White: 5 EGRET
**Herr**
  home: 4 HAUS
  mate: 4 FRAU
**Herriman, George**
  cartoon: 8 KRAZYKAT
  "Krazy" creation of: 3 KAT
**Herring**
  cousin: 4 SHAD
  Red: 4 PLOY
  Type of: 4 SHAD 5 SPRAT
**Herringlike**
  fish: 4 SHAD
**Hersey**
  bell town: 5 ADANO
**Hershey**
  brand: 4 ROLO 6 REESES
  candy bar: 6 KITKAT

  product: 4 KISS
**Hershiser**
  of baseball: 4 OREL
**Hertz**
  prefix: 4 TERA
  rival: 4 AVIS
**Herzegovina**
  partner: 6 BOSNIA
**Herzigova**
  Model: 3 EVA
**"He's Got the Whole World ___**
  **Hands":** 5 INHIS
**Hesitant:** 6 UNSURE
  9 TENTATIVE
  sounds: 3 ERS UHS UMS
**Hesitate:** 3 HAW HEM 5 HEDGE
  WAVER
  It may make you: 5 COMMA
**Hesitation:** 3 HAW HEM
  Show: 6 FALTER
  Sounds of: 3 ERS UHS UMS
  Without: 6 FLATLY
**"He's ___ nowhere man"**
  **(Beatles lyric):** 5 AREAL
**Hess**
  Pianist: 4 MYRA
**Hesse**
  Novelist: 7 HERMANN
  River of: 4 EDER
  Sculptor: 3 EVA
**Hessian**
  pronoun: 3 ICH
  river: 4 EDER
**Hester**
  portrayer: 4 DEMI
**Heston, Charlton**
  film: 5 ELCID 6 BENHUR
  org.: 3 NRA
  role: 5 ELCID MOSES
    6 BENHUR
**Het**
  up: 5 IRATE
**Hew:** 3 AXE LOP 4 CHOP
**Hewing**
  tool: 3 AXE
**Hex:** 4 JINX 5 SPELL
  ending: 3 ANE
  halved: 3 TRI
  sign site: 4 BARN
**"Hey!":** 4 PSST
**Heyerdahl**
  Author: 4 THOR
  craft: 3 RAI
  Explorer: 4 THOR
  raft: 7 KONTIKI
**"Hey, over here!":** 4 PSST
**"Hey, sailor!":** 4 AHOY
**"Hey there!":** 4 PSST
**"Hey, wait ___!":** 4 ASEC
**"Hey, what's the big ___?":**
  4 IDEA
**"Hey you!":** 4 PSST
**Hgt.:** 3 ALT 4 ELEV
**HHH:** 4 ETAS
**HHS**
  division: 3 SSA

**Hi**
from Ho: 5 ALOHA
HI: 5 ALOHA
Wife of: 4 LOIS
**"Hi"**
Hawaiian: 5 ALOHA
Ho: 5 ALOHA
**Hi-___:** 3 FIS RES
graphics: 3 RES
monitor: 3 RES
**"Hi and Lois"**
pet: 4 DAWG
**Hiatus:** 3 GAP 5 LAPSE PAUSE
**Hiawatha**
craft: 5 CANOE
**Hibachi**
residue: 5 ASHES
site: 5 PATIO
**Hibernate**
Place to: 4 LAIR
**Hibernation:** 5 SLEEP
location: 3 DEN 4 LAIR
**Hibernia:** 4 EIRE ERIN
**Hibiscus:** 6 MALLOW
**Hiccup**
cause: 5 SPASM
cure: 5 SCARE
**Hic, ___, hoc:** 4 HAEC
**Hick:** 4 RUBE 5 YAHOO YOKEL
**Hickey**
beginning: 3 DOO
**Hickory:** 3 NUT
**Hid:** 7 HOLEDUP STASHED
**Hidalgo**
**Info:** Spanish cue
Here, in: 3 ACA
home: 4 CASA
hooray: 3 OLE
**Hidden:** 5 INNER PERDU
6 CACHED COVERT
LATENT UNSEEN
VEILED
advantage:
12 ACEINTHEHOLE
agenda:
15 ULTERIORMOTIVES
Hardly: 5 OVERT
It may be: 6 AGENDA
loot: 5 STASH
Not: 5 OVERT
obstacle: 4 SNAG
problem: 5 CATCH
supply: 5 CACHE STASH
treasure: 5 TROVE
valley: 4 GLEN
**Hide:** 4 MASK PELT SKIN
VEIL 5 CLOAK STASH
6 SCREEN 7 SECRETE
away: 5 STASH
from view: 6 SHROUD
out: 6 LIELOW
partner: 4 SEEK
Prepare: 3 TAN
Untanned: 4 PELT
well: 4 BURY
worker: 6 TANNER

**Hide-and-seek**
Cheat at: 4 PEEK
**Hideaway:** 3 DEN 4 CAVE LAIR
High: 5 AERIE
**"Hideaway"**
actress Christine: 5 LAHTI
**Hide-hair**
connector: 3 NOR
**Hideki**
Pitcher: 5 IRABU
**Hideo**
Pitcher: 4 NOMO
**Hideous:** 4 UGLY
fellow: 4 OGRE
**Hideout:** 3 DEN 4 LAIR
**Hider**
Haystack: 6 NEEDLE
**Hiding**
out: 8 ONTHELAM
place: 3 DEN 4 LAIR NOOK
5 CACHE
**Hierarchy:** 6 LADDER
9 TOTEMPOLE
level: 4 RUNG
Top, in a: 5 ALPHA
**Hieroglyphics**
bird: 4 IBIS
snake: 3 ASP
stone: 7 ROSETTA
**Hieronymus**
Painter: 5 BOSCH
**Hi-fi:** 6 STEREO
component: 3 AMP
discs: 3 LPS
pioneer Fisher: 5 AVERY
**Higgins, Henry**
creator: 4 SHAW
**High:** 4 TALL 5 LOFTY TIPSY
6 STONED WASTED
ball: 3 LOB
bar: 5 ROOST
card: 3 ACE
degree: 3 NTH PHD
dudgeon: 3 IRE
fashion: 3 TON
flier: 4 KITE
Fly: 4 SOAR
Get really: 4 SOAR
grade: 5 APLUS
ground: 6 UPLAND
guy: 4 ALTO
hat: 5 MITER 9 STOVEPIPE
Hold: 6 ESTEEM
home: 5 AERIE
Home on: 4 NEST 5 AERIE
It may be: 4 NOON
It may get ~ marks: 5 LEVEE
jinks: 6 ANTICS
land: 5 NEPAL
Leave ~ and dry: 6 STRAND
light: 4 HALO
lines: 3 ELS
mark with low effort: 5 EASYA
mountain: 3 ALP
note of old: 3 ELA
On: 5 ALOFT

On a: 6 ELATED
opening: 4 ALTI
peak: 3 ALP TOR
pitch: 3 LOB
point: 4 ACME APEX PEAK
6 APOGEE 7 EVEREST
8 PINNACLE
prefix: 4 ALTI
pt.: 3 MTN
regard: 6 ESTEEM
return: 3 LOB
rollers: 3 ELS
roller's roll: 3 WAD
schooler: 4 TEEN 6 TEENER
society: 5 ELITE
spirits: 4 GLEE 7 ELATION
spot: 3 ALP 4 APEX
standard: 5 IDEAL
station: 3 MIR
style: 4 UPDO
time: 4 BOOM NOON
times: 3 UPS
wind: 4 GALE OBOE 5 FLUTE
~, in music: 3 ALT
**High ___:** 3 TEA
**"High ___"**
(Anderson play): 3 TOR
(Bogart film): 6 SIERRA
**High-___:** 3 RES 4 TECH
**Highball**
ingredient: 3 RYE
**Highborn:** 5 NOBLE
**Highbrow:** 4 SNOB 5 SNOOT
**Highbrows:** 8 LITERATI
**Highchair**
feature: 4 TRAY
Like a baby in a: 6 BIBBED
wear: 3 BIB
**High-class:** 5 ELITE
tie: 5 ASCOT
**___ High Dam:** 5 ASWAN
**High-energy**
snack: 4 GORP
**Higher**
ground: 6 UPLAND
than: 4 OVER 5 ABOVE
**"Higher Learning"**
actor Epps: 4 OMAR
**Higher-ranking:** 6 SENIOR
**Higher-ups:** 8 TOPBRASS
**Highest:** 3 NTH
degree: 3 NTH PHD
honor: 3 ACE
of all: 7 TOPMOST
Of the ~ quality: 4 BEST
point: 4 ACME APEX 5 CREST
6 APOGEE ZENITH
power: 3 NTH
**Highfalutin:** 5 ARTSY LOFTY
6 SNOOTY
**High-fashion**
mag: 4 ELLE
**High-fiber**
food: 4 BRAN
**High-five:** 4 SLAP
sound: 4 SLAP

**Highflier**
home: 5 AERIE
**High-flying**
clique: 6 JETSET
toy: 4 KITE
**High-grade:** 6 RATEDA
**High-hat:** 4 SNOB 5 SNOOT
6 SNOOTY
**High-hatter:** 4 SNOB 5 SNOOT
**"High Hopes"**
insect: 3 ANT
lyricist Sammy: 4 CAHN
**High-IQ**
group: 5 MENSA
**High-jump**
hurdle: 3 BAR
**Highland**
girl: 4 LASS
hat: 3 TAM
headgear: 3 TAM
hillside: 4 BRAE
horde: 4 CLAN
pattern: 6 TARTAN
refusal: 3 NAE
tongue: 4 ERSE
topper: 3 TAM
valley: 4 CLAN
wear: 6 TARTAN
**Highlander:** 4 GAEL SCOT
8 CLANSMAN
hat: 3 TAM
**Highlight**
Opera: 4 ARIA
**Highlights**
ESPN: 3 TDS
Hair: 7 STREAKS
Musical: 4 SOLI
**Highminded:** 5 NOBLE
**High-minded:** 5 MORAL NOBLE
**High-muck-a-muck:** 5 MOGUL
NABOB
**"High Noon"**
heroine: 3 AMY
lawman: 4 KANE
**High-pH**
substance: 3 LYE 6 ALKALI
**High-pitched:** 5 SHARP
6 TREBLE
cry: 4 YELP
**High-priced**
spread: 6 ESTATE
ticket area: 4 LOGE
**High-profile**
hairdo: 4 AFRO
**High-protein**
food: 4 TOFU
**High-ranking**
angel: 6 SERAPH
clergyman: 7 PRELATE
NCO: 4 MSGT
**High-rise**
feature: 7 TERRACE
locales: 4 URBS
support: 4 IBAR
**High school**
book: 4 TEXT

breakout: 4 ACNE
class: 3 ART GYM 4 SHOP
dance: 4 PROM
exam: 4 PSAT
misfit: 4 NERD
subj.: 3 ALG ENG SCI 4 BIOL
HIST
**"High Sierra"**
actress: 9 IDALUPINO
actress Lupino: 3 IDA
director: 5 WALSH
role: 5 EARLE
**High-spirited:** 6 ELATED
horse: 5 STEED 7 ARABIAN
**High-strung:** 4 EDGY TAUT
5 HYPER TENSE
**Hightail**
it: 3 LAM 4 FLEE SCAT
TEAR
**Hightailed**
it: 3 RAN 4 SPED
**High-tech**
identifier: 3 DNA
memo: 5 EMAIL
recordings: 3 CDS
Suffix used in: 4 TRON
**Highway:** 4 ROAD 6 ARTERY
(abbr.): 3 RTE
access: 4 RAMP
behemoth: 4 SEMI
curve: 3 ESS
divider: 6 MEDIAN
division: 4 LANE
entrance: 4 RAMP
exit: 4 RAMP
fee: 4 TOLL
hauler: 3 RIG 4 SEMI
hazard: 5 SLEET
headache: 5 TIEUP
Like a main: 8 ARTERIAL
Main: 6 ARTERY
no-no: 5 UTURN
Northern: 5 ALCAN
Old ~ name: 5 ALCAN
owner: 7 ROADHOG
patroller: 7 TROOPER
rig: 4 SEMI
sign: 5 MERGE
warning: 3 SLO 5 FLARE
**Highwayman:** 6 BANDIT
**"Highwayman, The"**
poet Alfred: 5 NOYES
**"Hi-___, Hi-Lo":** 4 LILI
**Hike:** 4 SNAP TREK 5 BOOST
RAISE TROOP
Long: 4 TREK
Take a: 4 WALK
Words before a: 6 HUTONE
**Hiked:** 5 UPPED
**Hiker**
burden: 8 KNAPSACK
path: 5 TRAIL
route: 4 PATH 5 TRAIL
snack: 4 GORP
woe: 4 CORN
**Hikes:** 3 UPS 7 JACKSUP

**Hiking**
path: 5 TRAIL
trail: 4 PATH
**Hilarious**
joke: 11 KNEESLAPPER
person: 4 RIOT
**Hilarity:** 4 GLEE 5 MIRTH
**Hildegarde**
Actress: 4 NEFF
**Hill**
builder: 3 ANT 4 MOLE
climber: 3 ANT
companion: 4 DALE
Craggy: 3 TOR
dweller: 3 ANT
Flat-topped: 4 MESA 5 BUTTE
Highland: 4 BRAE
in 1991 news: 5 ANITA
Isolated: 5 BUTTE
resident: 3 ANT
Rocky: 3 TOR
Sand: 4 DUNE
Send to the: 5 ELECT
Small: 5 KNOLL
Way up a: 4 TBAR
worker: 3 ANT
**___ Hill**
of San Francisco: 3 NOB
R&B band: 3 DRU
**Hill, Faith**
hit song: 8 THISKISS
**Hillary**
challenge: 7 EVEREST
conquest: 7 EVEREST
successor: 5 LAURA
supporters: 7 SHERPAS
Where Bill met: 4 YALE
~, at birth: 6 RODHAM
**Hillenbrand**
of baseball: 4 SHEA
**Hillock:** 4 RISE 5 KNOLL
MOUND
**Hills**
Chain of: 5 RANGE
City of seven: 4 ROME
Head for the: 4 BOLT FLEE
Home in the: 3 DEN
Like the: 3 OLD
**Hillside:** 5 SLOPE
Highland: 4 BRAE
Scottish: 4 BRAE
shelter: 4 ABRI
**"Hill Street Blues"**
actor Joe: 5 SPANO
actress Veronica: 5 HAMEL
**Hilltop:** 3 TOR 4 RISE
**Hilo**
feast: 4 LUAU
garland: 3 LEI
hello: 5 ALOHA
strings: 4 UKES
**Hilton**
rival: 5 HYATT
**"___ Hilton, The":** 5 HANOI
**Him**
~, in French: 3 LUI

**Himalayan**
beast: 3 YAK
continent: 4 ASIA
country: 5 NEPAL
danger: 9 AVALANCHE
guide: 6 SHERPA
Hairy: 4 YETI
humanoid: 4 YETI
kingdom: 5 NEPAL 6 BHUTAN
legend: 4 YETI
sighting: 4 YETI
summit: 7 EVEREST

**Himalayas**
Area south of the: 5 ASSAM
continent: 4 ASIA

**"___ Him on a Sunday"**: 4 IMET

**Hind**: 3 DOE 4 DEER
mate: 4 STAG

**Hindenburg**
predecessor: 5 EBERT

**Hinder**: 5 DETER EMBAR
6 IMPEDE
legally: 5 ESTOP
Opposite of: 4 ABET

**Hindi**
language group: 5 INDIC
master: 5 SAHIB

**Hindquarters**: 4 RUMP

**Hindrance**: 5 CRIMP

**Hindu**
aphorism: 5 SUTRA
ascetic: 5 FAKIR
deity: 4 RAMA 5 SHIVA
6 VISHNU
destroyer: 4 SIVA
discipline: 4 YOGA
doctrine: 6 TANTRA
garment: 4 SARI
gentleman: 4 BABU
god: 4 DEVA SIVA
hero: 4 RAMA
honorific: 3 SRI 5 RAJAH
SWAMI
incarnation: 6 AVATAR
loincloth: 5 DHOTI
master: 5 SWAMI
melody: 4 RAGA
Member of a ~ trio: 5 SHIVA
monk: 5 SADHU
music: 4 RAGA
Of ~ scriptures: 5 VEDIC
prince: 5 RAJAH
princess: 4 RANI 5 RANEE
queen: 4 RANI 5 RANEE
religious teacher: 5 SWAMI
retreat: 6 ASHRAM
sacred writing: 4 VEDA
sage: 5 RISHI SWAMI
self: 5 ATMAN
social division: 5 CASTE
teacher: 4 GURU 5 SWAMI
title: 3 SRI
wrap: 4 SARI 5 SAREE

**Hinduism**
The Creator, in: 6 BRAHMA
The Destroyer, in: 4 SIVA

The Preserver, in: 6 VISHNU

**Hines**
Dance like: 3 TAP
Jazzman "Fatha": 4 EARL

**Hines, Earl**
nickname: 5 FATHA

**Hines, Gregory**
forte: 3 TAP

**Hinge**
Silence a: 3 OIL

**Hinged**
cover: 3 LID
fastener: 4 HASP

**Hingis**
of tennis: 7 MARTINA
rival: 4 GRAF 5 SELES

**Hinkle**
Golfer: 3 LON

**"Hinky Dinky Parlay ___"**:
3 VOO

**Hinny**
kin: 4 MULE

**Hint**: 3 TIP 4 CLUE 5 TINGE
TRACE
at: 7 SUGGEST
at, with "to": 6 ALLUDE
of color: 5 TINGE
of light: 5 GLEAM
Words before: 5 DROPA

**Hints**
Needing many: 4 SLOW
Woman with: 7 HELOISE

**Hip**: 3 MOD 4 COOL 5 AWARE
6 TRENDY WITHIT
bones: 4 ILIA
dance: 4 HULA
ending: 4 STER
Got: 5 WISED
joint: 4 COXA
Part of the: 6 HAUNCH
suffix: 4 STER

**Hipbone**: 5 ILIUM
Of the: 5 ILIAC
Of the ~ (prefix): 4 ILIO

**Hipbones**: 4 ILIA

**"Hip hip ___!"**: 6 HOORAH

**Hip-hop**: 3 RAP
Dr. of: 3 DRE
fan: 4 BBOY

**Hippie**: 11 FLOWERCHILD
attire: 5 BEADS
Color, as ~ clothing: 6 TIEDYE
greeting: 5 PEACE
happening: 4 BEIN 6 LOVEIN
home: 3 PAD
purchase: 4 WEED
Understand, like a: 3 DIG

**Hippo**
add-on: 5 DROME
relative: 5 TAPIR
tail: 5 DROME

**Hippodrome**: 5 ARENA
shape: 4 OVAL

**Hippomenes**
Loser to ~ in a footrace:
8 ATALANTA

**Hippy**
dance: 4 HULA

**Hips**
With hands on: 6 AKIMBO

**Hipster**: 3 CAT 7 COOLCAT
exclamation: 3 MAN
Not a: 4 NERD

**Hiram**
of Hawaii: 4 FONG

**Hire**: 6 ENGAGE TAKEON
Car for: 3 CAB
New: 7 TRAINEE
new staff: 5 REMAN
Summer: 4 TEMP
~, as a lawyer: 6 RETAIN

**Hired**
Just: 3 NEW

**Hiree**
Annual: 3 CPA
Holiday: 5 SANTA
Vacationer's: 6 SITTER

**Hires**: 7 TAKESON
8 ROOTBEER
competition: 4 DADS
New corp.: 4 MBAS

**Hirohito**: 7 EMPEROR

**"Hiroshima"**
writer: 6 HERSEY

**Hirsch**
of football: 5 ELROY

**Hirsch, Judd**
sitcom: 4 TAXI

**Hirschfeld**
and others: 3 ALS
daughter: 4 NINA

**Hirt**
and others: 3 ALS

**His**
and her: 5 THEIR
partner: 4 HERS
~, in French: 3 SES

**His ___ (big shot)**: 4 NIBS

**"His Master's Voice"**
org.: 3 RCA

**Hispanic**: 6 LATINO

**Hispaniola**: 4 ISLA 5 HAITI

**Hiss**: 8 SIBILATE
Gp. that accused: 4 HUAC
of history: 5 ALGER
relative: 3 BOO

**Hisser**
Household: 9 STEAMIRON

**Hissy fit**: 4 SNIT

**Historian**
German: 5 WEBER
interest: 4 PAST
Roman: 4 LIVY
subject: 3 ERA
unit: 3 ERA
Venerable: 4 BEDE
~ Muse: 4 CLIO

**Historic**
age: 3 ERA
beginning: 3 PRE
leader: 3 PRE
period: 3 ERA

start: 3 PRE
time: 3 ERA
**Historical**
display: 7 DIORAMA
memento: 5 RELIC
period: 3 AGE ERA
   5 EPOCH
records: 6 ANNALS
**History: 4 PAST**
Chapter in: 3 ERA
Folk: 4 LORE
Handed-down: 4 LORE
homework: 5 ESSAY
Hunk of: 3 ERA
Kind of: 4 ORAL
Muse of: 4 CLIO
Piece of: 3 ERA 5 RELIC
Time in: 3 ERA
___ history: 4 ORAL
**Hit: 3 BOP RAM 4 BEAT BELT**
   SLAP SWAT 5 SMACK
alternative: 4 MISS
Big: 5 HOMER SMASH
   6 TRIPLE 7 HOMERUN
bottom: 5 SPANK
broadside: 3 RAM
hard: 3 RAM 4 BELT SLAM
   5 SMACK SMITE SMOTE
letters: 3 SRO
lightly: 3 TAP
maker: 3 BAT
man: 4 ICER 8 ASSASSIN
music: 3 RAP
one's toe: 4 STUB
on the green: 4 PUTT
on the head: 3 BOP 4 CONK
openhanded: 4 SLAP
show sign: 3 SRO
sign: 3 SRO
Surprise: 7 SLEEPER
the beach: 4 LAND
the big time: 6 ARRIVE
   MAKEIT
the books: 5 STUDY
the bottle: 4 TOPE 5 BOOZE
the deck: 5 ARISE
the ground: 4 ALIT
the hay: 5 CRASH SLEEP
the jackpot:
   12 STRIKEITRICH
the mall: 4 SHOP
the road: 4 LEFT TOUR WENT
   5 LEAVE SCRAM
the roof: 6 SEERED
the slopes: 3 SKI
the spot: 7 SATISFY
the tarmac: 4 LAND
Try to ~, as a fly: 6 SWATAT
with a laser: 3 ZAP
~, old-style: 5 SMITE SMOTE
**Hitch: 4 KNOT SNAG YOKE**
Clove: 4 KNOT
Do another: 4 REUP
Half: 4 KNOT
on the run: 5 ELOPE
Start another: 4 REUP

**Hitchcock, Alfred**
film: 4 ROPE 5 TOPAZ
   6 FRENZY MARNIE
   PSYCHO 7 REBECCA
   VERTIGO
film appearance: 5 CAMEO
film title start: 5 DIALM
genre: 8 SUSPENSE
menaces: 5 BIRDS
Wife of: 4 ALMA
**Hitchcockian: 5 EERIE**
**Hitched: 3 WED**
Get: 3 WED
Get ~ quick: 5 ELOPE
It may be: 4 RIDE
Not: 5 UNWED
**Hitchhike: 4 RIDE**
**Hitchhiker: 5 RIDER**
digit: 5 THUMB
quest: 4 LIFT RIDE
Words to a: 5 GETIN HOPIN
**"Hitchin' ___" (1970 hit):**
   5 ARIDE
**Hitching**
place: 4 POST RENO
post: 5 ALTAR
**Hite**
Author: 5 SHERE
Sex researcher: 5 SHERE
**Hi-tech**
address: 3 URL
dictionary medium:
   5 CDROM
message: 5 EMAIL
**Hither**
partner: 3 YON
**Hither and ___: 3 YON**
**Hitherto: 5 ASYET SOFAR**
**Hit-or-miss: 6 RANDOM**
   8 SLAPDASH
**Hits**
Big ~ (abbr.): 3 HRS
the roof: 7 SEESRED
They're rarely: 6 BSIDES
**"Hits the spot"**
sloganeer: 5 PEPSI
**Hitter**
Heavy: 6 SLEDGE
of 660 home runs: 4 MAYS
of 755 home runs: 5 AARON
ploy: 4 BUNT
stat: 3 RBI
**Hitting: 5 ATBAT**
opportunity: 5 ATBAT
**Hittites**
home: 9 ASIAMINOR
**Hive**
dweller: 3 BEE 5 DRONE
house: 6 APIARY
**Hiver**
opposite: 3 ETE
**Hives**
Like: 5 APIAN
Person with: 8 APIARIST
problem: 4 ITCH
**Hizzoner: 5 MAYOR**

**H-L**
connectors: 3 IJK
**"Hmmm ...": 4 ISEE**
   7 LETSSEE
   8 LETMESEE
**HMO**
listing: 3 GPS
members: 3 MDS 4 DOCS
Part of: 6 HEALTH
**HMS**
Part of: 3 HER HIS
**Ho**
Hello from: 5 ALOHA
of Hawaii: 3 DON
**"___ ho!": 5 HEAVE**
**Ho, Don**
hit: 11 TINYBUBBLES
neckwear: 3 LEI
**Hoad**
of tennis: 3 LEW
**Hoag**
Author: 4 TAMI
**Hoagie**
Had a: 3 ATE
**Hoard: 5 CACHE STASH**
   TROVE
**Hoarfrost: 4 RIME**
**Hoarse: 5 RASPY**
sound: 4 RASP
**Hoarsely**
Speak: 4 RASP
**Hoary: 3 OLD 4 AGED**
**Hoax: 4 SHAM 6 CANARD**
**"Hobbit, The"**
character: 5 BILBO FRODO
home: 5 SHIRE
**Hobble: 4 LIMP**
**Hobbling: 4 GIMP LAME**
**Hobby: 7 PASTIME**
Making a ~ of: 4 INTO
shop purchase: 3 KIT
suffix: 3 IST
**Hobbyist**
purchase: 3 KIT
Radio: 3 HAM
**Hobnob: 9 ASSOCIATE**
**Hobo: 5 TRAMP 7 VAGRANT**
   8 VAGABOND
fare: 4 STEW
**Ho Chi ___: 4 MINH**
**Ho Chi Minh City**
former name: 6 SAIGON
**Hock: 4 PAWN**
Be in: 3 OWE
In: 6 PAWNED
**Hockey**
fake out: 4 DEKE
great Bobby: 3 ORR
great Gordie: 4 HOWE
infraction: 5 ICING
legend: 3 ORR
objective: 4 GOAL
official: 3 REF
position: 4 WING
score: 4 GOAL
shot: 4 SLAP

Song played at some ~ games:
   7 OCANADA
stat: 7 ASSISTS
stick wood: 3 ASH
surface: 3 ICE
team: 6 SEXTET
venue: 4 RINK
**"Hocus Pocus"**
actor Katz: 4 OMRI
**Hod**
worker: 5 MASON
**Hodgepodge:** 4 HASH MESS
   OLIO STEW 5 SALAD
   7 FARRAGO MELANGE
   8 PASTICHE
   10 CRAZYQUILT
**Hodges**
of baseball: 3 GIL
teammate: 5 REESE
**Hoe:** 4 TILL
home: 4 SHED
target: 4 WEED
**Hoedown**
move: 6 DOSIDO
participant: 3 GAL
seat: 4 BALE
setting: 4 BARN
**Hoff**
Cartoonist: 3 SYD
**"Hoffa"**
screenwriter: 5 MAMET
**Hoffer**
Author: 4 ERIC
**Hoffman**
Actor: 6 DUSTIN
Author: 5 ABBIE
offerings: 5 TALES
Radical: 5 ABBIE
**Hoffman, Dustin**
film: 5 LENNY 7 RAINMAN
   TOOTSIE
role: 5 LENNY RATSO
**Hog**
cheek: 4 JOWL
fat: 4 LARD
food: 4 SLOP
heaven: 3 STY
home: 3 STY
opposite: 6 SHARER
sound: 5 GRUNT
Stage: 3 HAM
Wild: 4 BOAR
**Hogan**
contemporary: 5 SNEAD
dweller: 6 NAVAHO NAVAJO
Golfer: 3 BEN
in a sitcom: 7 COLONEL
Wrestler: 4 HULK
**Hogan, Paul**
film: 15 CROCODILEDUNDEE
**"Hogan's Heroes"**
keeper: 12 COLONELKLINK
sergeant: 7 SCHULTZ
setting: 6 STALAG
**Hoggett, Farmer**
prize pig: 4 BABE

Wife of: 4 ESME
**Hoglike**
beast: 5 TAPIR
**Hogs**
Feed the: 4 SLOP
**Hogwarts**
accessory: 4 WAND
attendee: 11 HARRYPOTTER
mail carrier: 3 OWL
Malfoy at: 5 DRACO
**Hogwash:** 3 PAP ROT 4 BOSH
   BULL BUNK LIES SLOP
   5 BILGE HOOEY PSHAW
   TRIPE 6 HOTAIR
   7 BALONEY
**"Ho, ho, ho!"**
speaker:
   15 JOLLYGREENGIANT
**Ho-hum:** 4 BLAH DRAB DULL
   SOSO 5 BLASE
feeling: 5 ENNUI
grade: 3 CEE
~ TV fare: 5 RERUN
**"Ho-hum":** 7 IMBORED
**Hoi ___:** 6 POLLOI
**Hoi polloi:** 6 MASSES RABBLE
character: 7 OMICRON
disdainer: 4 SNOB 7 ELITIST
**Hoist:** 5 CRANE RAISE
   7 ELEVATE UPRAISE
Lifeboat: 5 DAVIT
**Hoisted**
~, nautically: 4 HOVE
**Hoister:** 6 PETARD
**Hoity-___:** 5 TOITY
**Hoity-toity**
type: 4 SNOB
**Hokey:** 5 CORNY
**Hokkaido**
city: 5 OTARU
native: 4 AINU
people: 4 AINU
port: 5 OTARU
**Hokum:** 3 ROT
**Holbein**
Painter: 4 HANS
**"Holberg Suite"**
composer: 5 GRIEG
**Holbrook**
Actor: 3 HAL
**Hold:** 3 OWN 4 DEEM GRIP
   5 GRASP 6 ASSERT
   DETAIN RETAIN
   7 POSSESS 8 MAINTAIN
back: 4 REIN STEM 6 IMPEDE
dear: 5 ADORE 7 CHERISH
Didn't: 3 RAN
Doesn't ~ up well: 4 SAGS
Don't ~ back: 4 TELL
fast: 6 ADHERE COHERE
Fill the: 4 LADE
firmly: 4 GRIP
forth: 5 ORATE
gently: 6 CRADLE
Hard to: 4 EELY
in high regard: 6 ADMIRE

In the: 4 ALOW 5 BELOW
off: 4 WAIT 5 DEFER
on: 4 WAIT
one's ground: 8 STANDPAT
one's horses: 4 WAIT
Put in the: 4 LADE STOW
Put on: 6 SHELVE
responsible: 5 BLAME
stuff: 5 CARGO
sway: 4 RULE 5 REIGN
Take: 5 SETIN
the deed to: 3 OWN
the floor: 5 ORATE
Tight: 4 GRIP
title to: 3 OWN
together: 6 COHERE
up: 3 ROB 4 LAST
Wrestling: 6 NELSON
~, as attention: 5 RIVET
**"___ Holden" (Bacheller novel):**
   4 EBEN
**Holding:** 5 ASSET TENET
gadget: 4 VISE
Third-party: 6 ESCROW
**Holdings:** 6 ESTATE
**"Hold it!":** 4 WHOA
**"Hold it right there!":**
   6 FREEZE
**"Hold Me"**
Grammy winner for: 5 OSLIN
**"Hold on!":** 4 WAIT 6 NOTYET
   ONESEC 8 WAITASEC
**"Hold on ___!":** 4 ASEC
**"Hold on a ___!":** 3 SEC
**"Hold on there!":** 4 WHOA
**"Hold On Tight"**
band: 3 ELO
**Holdover:** 5 RELIC
**Holds:** 3 HAS
**Holdup:** 4 SNAG 5 DELAY
   HEIST 7 BANKJOB
Help in a: 4 ABET
**"Hold your horses!":** 4 WAIT
   WHOA 6 NOTYET
**Hole**
Be in the: 3 OWE
enlarger: 6 REAMER
fixer: 6 DARNER
for a lace: 6 EYELET
Gaping: 5 CHASM
Get a ~ in one: 3 ACE
goal: 3 PAR
Green: 3 CUP
in one: 3 ACE
in the head: 5 SINUS
in the wall: 4 VENT
Is in the: 4 OWES
Make a new: 5 REDIG
maker: 3 AWL
Needle: 3 EYE
number: 3 PAR
Place to start a: 3 TEE
puncher: 3 AWL
Roll with a: 5 BAGEL
Shoe: 6 EYELET
Start a: 5 TEEUP

**Holy Roman**
emperor: 4 OTTO 5 OTTOI
7 LOTHAIR
**"Holy smokes!":** 3 GEE 4 EGAD
JEEZ YIPE 5 EGADS
GOLLY YIKES
**"Holy Sonnets"**
poet: 5 DONNE
**"Holy Toledo!":** 3 GEE 4 EGAD
JEEZ YIPE 5 EGADS
GOLLY YIKES
**Homage:** 6 SALUTE
Poetic: 3 ODE
**"Homage to Clio"**
poet: 5 AUDEN
**Hombre**
home: 4 CASA
title: 5 SENOR
**Home:** 4 BASE DIGS NEST
5 ABODE 6 HEARTH
7 HABITAT
9 RESIDENCE
Almost make it: 6 TRIPLE
At the ~ of: 4 CHEZ
Bring: 3 NET 4 EARN
5 CLEAR
Call at: 4 SAFE
Clay: 5 ADOBE
Conical: 5 TEPEE
Desert: 5 ADOBE
Dome: 5 IGLOO
ending: 5 STEAD
Estate: 5 MANOR
extension: 3 ELL 5 STEAD
Farm: 3 STY
First: 4 EDEN
fries: 6 TATERS
Get ~ safely: 5 SCORE
High: 5 AERIE
in a 1936 novel: 4 TARA
in a tree: 4 NEST
Leaves: 4 TREE
Log: 5 CABIN
Make a: 4 NEST
maker: 6 NESTER
Mobile: 4 TENT 5 TEPEE
7 ALABAMA
Not: 3 OUT 4 AWAY
Not at: 3 OUT 4 AWAY
of the brave: 5 TEPEE
One who works at: 3 UMP
on high: 5 AERIE
on the range: 5 TEPEE
6 TEEPEE
planet: 5 EARTH
products seller: 5 AMWAY
Remain at: 6 STAYIN
Returns: 3 IRS
room: 3 DEN
Rose: 3 BED
Royal: 6 CASTLE
site: 3 LOT
Stately: 5 MANOR
Stuck at ~, in a way:
9 SNOWBOUND
Take: 3 NET 4 EARN

territory: 4 TURF
to billions: 4 ASIA
to most: 4 ASIA
with a flap door: 5 TEPEE
with a view: 5 AERIE
wrecker: 7 TERMITE
**Home ___:** 4 INON 5 PLATE
**"Home ___":** 5 ALONE
**___ home (out):** 5 NOTAT
**"Home Alone"**
actor: 5 PESCI
**Homeboy:** 3 PAL
turf: 4 HOOD
**Homebuilders**
Storied:
15 THREELITTLEPIGS
**Homebuyer**
need: 4 LOAN
**Homecoming**
guest: 4 ALUM
guests: 6 ALUMNI
queen headwear: 5 TIARA
**"Homecoming, The"**
playwright: 6 PINTER
**Home-cooked**
Have a ~ meal: 5 EATIN
**Home Depot**
competitor: 5 LOWES
**Home ec**
alternative: 4 SHOP
**Homegrown:** 5 LOCAL
**"Home Improvement"**
actor Allen: 3 TIM
prop: 4 TOOL
star: 5 ALLEN
**Homeless**
animal: 5 STRAY
child: 4 WAIF
**Homemade**
hooch: 10 BATHTUBGIN
SNEAKYPETE
**Homeowner**
paper: 4 DEED
pride: 4 LAWN
pymt.: 4 MTGE
**Homer:** 3 HIT 4 POET
8 EPICPOET
Bart, to: 3 SON
Cry from: 3 DOH
Daughter of: 4 LISA
epic: 5 ILIAD
Father of: 3 ABE
leader: 5 AARON
neighbor: 3 NED
outburst: 3 DOH
Son of: 4 BART
Two-run ~ prerequisite:
5 ONEON
work: 4 EPIC EPOS
~, to Bart: 3 DAD
**Homeric:** 4 EPIC
epic: 5 ILIAD 7 ODYSSEY
work: 5 ILIAD
**Home run**
great: 5 MARIS
king: 5 AARON

pace: 4 TROT
~, slangily: 5 TATER
**HOMES**
member: 4 ERIE
Part of: 4 ERIE
**Homesite:** 3 LOT
**"Home to Harlem"**
novelist: 5 MCKAY
**Homework**
Arithmetic: 4 SUMS
English: 5 ESSAY
Give, as: 6 ASSIGN
Help with: 5 TUTOR
History: 5 ESSAY
**Homey:** 4 COZY
in the 'hood: 3 BRO
**Homicide**
First ~ victim: 4 ABEL
**Homily:** 6 SERMON
**Ho ___ Minh:** 3 CHI
**Hominoid**
family member: 3 APE
**Hominy**
kin: 4 SAMP
**Homme ___ (statesman):**
5 DETAT
**Homme d'___ (statesman):**
4 ETAT
**"___ homo!":** 4 ECCE
**Homo sapiens:** 7 SPECIES
Like: 5 ERECT
The "Homo" in: 5 GENUS
**Hon:** 3 PET 4 BABY DEAR
DOLL LOVE 5 DEARY
SUGAR TOOTS 6 DEARIE
7 DEAREST SWEETIE
10 SWEETIEPIE
**Honcho:** 4 BOSS 5 MRBIG
NABOB 8 BIGWHEEL
Corp.: 3 CEO 4 EXEC
Head: 4 BOSS 5 MRBIG
6 TOPDOG
Monastery: 5 ABBOT
**Honda:** 3 CAR 4 AUTO
competitor: 6 YAMAHA
division: 5 ACURA
model: 5 CIVIC 6 ACCORD
**Hone:** 7 SHARPEN
**Honed:** 4 KEEN
**Honest:** 4 REAL
Be ~ (with): 5 LEVEL
**"Honest"**
one: 3 ABE
president: 3 ABE
**"Honest!":** 5 NOLIE 6 ISWEAR
7 FORREAL TRUSTME
**Honest ___:** 3 ABE
**Honest-to-goodness:** 4 REAL
TRUE 6 ACTUAL
**Honey:** 3 PET 4 BABY DEAR
DOLL LOVE 5 DEARY
SUGAR TOOTS 6 DEARIE
7 DEAREST SWEETIE
10 SWEETIEPIE
badger: 5 RATEL
bunch: 4 BEES

drink: 4 MEAD
factory: 4 HIVE
Fermented: 4 MEAD
French: 5 CHERI
handler: 3 BEE
holder: 3 JAR
maker: 3 BEE
Take the ~ and run: 5 ELOPE
The color of: 4 GOLD 5 AMBER
Word after: 3 PIE
"Honey, ___!": 6 IMHOME
Honeybun: 3 PET 4 BABY
    DEAR DOLL LOVE
    5 DEARY SUGAR TOOTS
    6 DEARIE 7 DEAREST
    SWEETIE
    10 SWEETIEPIE
Honeybunch: 3 PET 4 BABY
    DEAR DOLL LOVE
    5 DEARY SUGAR TOOTS
    6 DEARIE 7 DEAREST
    SWEETIE
    10 SWEETIEPIE
Honeycomb
    maker: 3 BEE
    shape: 7 HEXAGON
    unit: 4 CELL
Honeycreeper
    cousin: 7 TANAGER
Honeydew: 5 MELON
    eater: 3 ANT
    relative: 6 CASABA
Honeyed
    beverage: 4 MEAD
Honeymoon
    choice: 5 SUITE
    haven: 7 NIAGARA
"Honeymooners, The"
    actor Carney: 3 ART
    actress Jane: 4 KEAN
    role: 5 ALICE 6 NORTON
    TRIXIE
Hong Kong
    harbor craft: 6 SAMPAN
    neighbor: 5 MACAO
Honk: 4 BEEP TOOT
    provoker: 7 ROADHOG
Honker: 4 BEAK HORN NOSE
    5 GOOSE
    Barnyard: 5 GOOSE
    Hawaiian: 4 NENE
Honkers: 5 GEESE
Honking
    birds: 5 GEESE
Honky-___: 4 TONK
Honky-tonk: 6 SALOON
    7 RAGTIME
    musician Ernest: 4 TUBB
    player: 5 PIANO
Honolulu
    fictional detective: 4 CHAN
    hello: 5 ALOHA
    home: 4 OAHU
    island: 4 OAHU
Honor: 4 LAUD 5 ADORE
    AWARD 6 ESTEEM

Brit.: 3 DSO
Highest: 3 ACE
In ~ of: 3 FOR
It's an: 3 TEN
Pay ~ to: 4 FETE
Place of: 4 DAIS
society letter: 3 PHI
Title of: 3 SIR
with a party: 4 FETE
with humor: 5 ROAST
Word of: 4 OATH
Honoraria: 4 FEES
Honorarium: 3 FEE
Honorary
    Brit. ~ title: 3 OBE
    deg.: 3 LLD
    title: 7 EMERITA
Honored
    lady: 4 DAME
Honoré de ___ (French novelist):
    6 BALZAC
Honoree
    April: 4 FOOL
    Cotillion: 3 DEB
    Jan.: 3 MLK
    June: 3 DAD
    Mar.: 5 STPAT
    March: 9 STPATRICK
    March ~, for short: 5 STPAT
    May: 3 MOM 6 MOTHER
    Nov.: 3 VET
    Parade: 4 HERO
    Parade ~, for short: 5 STPAT
    place: 4 DAIS
    Purim: 6 ESTHER
    Wartime: 4 HERO
Honorific: 5 TITLE
    Asian: 3 SRI
    Hindu: 3 SRI 5 SWAMI
    Honshu: 3 SAN
    Indian: 3 SRI 5 SAHIB
    Japanese: 3 SAN
    Royal: 4 SIRE
    Turkish: 3 AGA 4 AGHA
Honor ___ thieves: 5 AMONG
"Honor Thy Father"
    author: 6 TALESE
"Honour is ___ scutcheon":
    Shakespeare: 5 AMERE
Honshu
    city: 5 OSAKA
    honorific: 3 SAN
    peak: 4 FUJI
    port: 4 KOBE 5 OSAKA
Hoo
    preceder: 3 YOO
Hooch: 5 BOOZE
    holder: 5 FLASK
    Homemade: 10 BATHTUBGIN
    SNEAKYPETE
Hood: 4 COWL THUG
    Child actress: 5 DARLA
    gun: 3 GAT
    Help a: 4 ABET
    Job for a: 5 HEIST
    knife: 4 SHIV

Monk's: 4 COWL
weapon: 3 GAT
Young: 4 PUNK
~, to a Brit: 6 BONNET
Hood, Robin: 6 ARCHER
    OUTLAW
    gang: 8 MERRYMEN
    portrayer Flynn: 5 ERROL
    weapon: 5 ARROW
    7 LONGBOW
Hooded
    garment: 4 COWL 5 PARKA
    jacket: 6 ANORAK
    snake: 3 ASP 5 COBRA
Hoodlum: 4 GOON THUG
    Help a: 4 ABET
Hoodwink: 3 CON GYP 4 DUPE
    FOOL SCAM 5 LIETO
    9 BAMBOOZLE
Hooey: 3 ROT 4 BOSH
    5 PSHAW
Hoof
    Beef on the: 5 STEER
    it: 4 WALK
    protector: 4 SHOE
    sound: 4 CLOP
Hoofbeat: 4 CLOP
    sound: 4 CLOP
Hoo-ha: 3 ADO 4 FLAP STIR
    TODO
Hook: 6 PIRATE
    Fishing: 4 GAFF
    hand: 4 SMEE
    Hawk's: 5 TALON
    henchman: 4 SMEE
    It's on the: 4 BAIT
    Let off the: 6 EXEMPT
    mate: 4 SMEE
    nemesis: 4 CROC
    Off the: 4 FREE
    Prepare a: 4 BAIT
    projection: 4 BARB
    shape: 3 CEE ESS
    target: 3 JAW
"Hook"
    producer Fayed: 4 DODI
    role: 4 SMEE
Hook, Captain
    cohort: 4 SMEE
    nemesis: 4 CROC
Hookah
    part: 3 URN
Hooked
    It often gets: 4 BAIT
    on: 4 INTO
"___ hooks": 5 USENO
Hook-shaped
    peninsula: 7 CAPECOD
Hookup: 4 LINK
    Hydrant: 4 HOSE
    PC: 3 CRT LAN
    R-V: 3 STU
    TV: 3 VCR
Hookups
    ER: 3 IVS
    ICU: 3 IVS

**Hooky**
Playing: 4 AWOL 6 ABSENT
**Hooligan:** 4 GOON THUG
5 ROWDY
British: 3 YOB
Help a: 4 ABET
**Hoop**
edge: 3 RIM
gp.: 3 NBA
hanger: 3 NET
Hula: 3 LEI
Kind of: 4 HULA
site: 3 EAR
**Hoopla:** 3 ADO 4 HYPE TODO
**Hoople, Major**
outburst: 4 EGAD
**Hoops:** 5 BBALL
**Info:** Basketball cue
Coll. ~ competition: 3 NIT
gp.: 3 NBA
nickname: 4 SHAQ
org.: 3 NBA
pos.: 3 CTR
target: 3 RIM
tournament org.: 4 NCAA
**Hoopster:** 5 CAGER
**Info:** Basketball player cue
Boston ~, briefly: 4 CELT
Cleveland ~, briefly: 3 CAV
Dallas ~, briefly: 3 MAV
gp.: 3 NBA
Hoosier: 5 PACER
L.A.: 5 LAKER
New Jersey: 3 NET
New York: 5 KNICK
org.: 3 NBA
Salt Lake City: 3 UTE
Seattle: 5 SONIC
target: 3 RIM
**"Hooray!":** 3 OLE
~, to José: 3 OLE
**"Hooray for me!":** 4 TADA
**Hoosegow:** 3 CAN 4 STIR
5 POKEY
Naval: 4 BRIG
**Hoosier**
hoopster: 5 PACER
hub: 4 GARY
humorist: 3 ADE
state: 7 INDIANA
**"Hoosier Poet, The":** 5 RILEY
**Hoot**
Give a: 4 CARE HONK JEER
YELL
It gives a: 3 OWL
**Hootenanny:** 4 SING
**Hooter:** 3 OWL
Baby: 5 OWLET
Little: 5 OWLET
**Hoover:** 3 DAM
birthplace: 4 IOWA
org.: 3 FBI
rival: 5 ORECK 6 EUREKA
vice president: 6 CURTIS
~, briefly: 3 VAC
**Hoover ___ :** 3 DAM

**Hoover, Herbert:** 5 IOWAN
It was named for ~ in 1947:
10 BOULDERDAM
**Hoover, J. ___ :** 5 EDGAR
**Hoover, J. Edgar**
gp.: 3 FBI
**Hoover Dam**
lake: 4 MEAD
**Hooves**
Split like: 6 CLOVEN
**Hop**
Giant: 4 LEAP
Sock: 5 DANCE
~, skip, or jump: 4 VERB
**"Hop ___ !":** 4 TOIT
**Hopalong Cassidy**
portrayer William: 4 BOYD
**Hope:** 6 ASPIRE
Actress: 5 LANGE
and charity partner: 5 FAITH
Bit of: 3 RAY
Comic: 3 BOB
Give up: 7 DESPAIR
Gp. that brought ~ to the
troops: 3 USO
Lose: 7 DESPAIR
Losing: 4 DIET
Not much: 3 RAY
One beyond: 5 GONER
sponsor: 3 USO
**"___ Hope" (former soap):**
5 RYANS
**Hope/Crosby**
costar Dorothy: 6 LAMOUR
destination: 3 RIO 4 BALI
**Hoped-for**
reply: 3 YES
**"Hope Floats"**
actress Rowlands: 4 GENA
**Hopeful**
Contest: 7 ENTRANT
Fraternity: 6 RUSHEE
Hollywood: 7 STARLET
Military: 5 CADET
**Hopeless:** 5 NOWIN 6 ABJECT
case: 5 GONER
situation: 9 LOSTCAUSE
**Hopes**
Have high: 6 ASPIRE
**Hopi**
doll: 7 KACHINA
reservation site: 4 MESA
ritual: 9 RAINDANCE
**Hopkins, Anthony:** 5 WELSH
role: 5 NIXON 6 LECTER
title: 3 SIR
**___ Hopkins University:**
5 JOHNS
**Hopper:** 3 BIN ROO 4 FLEA
HARE TOAD
Aussie: 3 ROO
Columnist: 5 HEDDA
Gossipy: 5 HEDDA
load: 3 ORE
Long-eared: 4 HARE
Outback: 3 ROO

Warty: 4 TOAD
**Hopping**
Be ~ mad: 4 BOIL
mad: 5 IRATE LIVID
**Hoppy**
brew: 3 ALE
quaff: 3 ALE
**Hops**
dryer: 4 KILN OAST
It has a head and: 3 ALE
4 BEER
kiln: 4 OAST
product: 4 BEER
**"Hop to it!":** 4 MOVE
**Hor.**
Opposite of: 4 VERT
**Hora:** 5 DANCE
**Horace:** 5 ODIST
collection: 4 ODES
Educator: 4 MANN
work: 3 ODE
**Horae**
One of the: 5 IRENE
**Horas**
24 ~: 3 DIA
**Horatian**
creation: 3 ODE 5 EPODE
**Horatio**
Author: 5 ALGER
**Horde:** 4 SLEW 5 DROVE
6 THRONG
Highland: 4 CLAN
Member of a: 3 HUN
**Horizon**
Go below the: 3 SET
On the: 4 NIGH 5 AHEAD
Rise on the: 4 LOOM
**Horizontal**
handrail: 5 BARRE
line on a graph: 5 XAXIS
Make: 5 LEVEL
**Hormel**
product: 4 SPAM
**Hormone**
drug: 7 STEROID
Female: 8 ESTROGEN
Pituitary: 4 ACTH
**Horn:** 6 ANTLER
Big: 4 TUBA
blower: 6 TOOTER
Blow one's: 4 CROW TOOT
Get on the: 5 PHONE
Hit the: 4 HONK
Honk the: 4 TOOT
sound: 4 BEEP TOOT
Toot one's own: 4 BRAG
5 BOAST
**Horne:** 4 DIVA
Singer: 4 LENA
solo: 4 ARIA
**Horned**
beast: 5 RHINO
flyer: 3 OWL
goddess: 4 ISIS
lizard: 6 IGUANA
viper: 3 ASP

**Horned Frogs**
sch.: 3 TCU
**Horner, Little Jack**
dessert: 3 PIE
find: 4 PLUM
last words: 3 AMI
**Hornet**
home: 4 NEST
nest: 3 ADO
relative: 4 WASP
**Horn of Africa**
native: 6 SOMALI
**Horns**
Animal with curved: 4 IBEX
Animal with twisted: 5 ELAND
It may have: 7 DILEMMA
**Hornswoggle:** 3 CON 4 DUPE
HOAX HOSE ROOK
5 CHEAT
**Hornswoggled:** 3 HAD
**Horny**
bill: 4 BEAK
**Horoscope**
columnist Sydney: 5 OMARR
datum: 4 SIGN
**Horrible:** 5 AWFUL
8 GRUESOME
**"Horrible"**
comics character: 5 HAGAR
**Horrified:** 6 AGHAST
sound: 4 GASP
**Horrify:** 5 APPAL 6 APPALL
**Horripilation:** 10 GOOSEFLESH
Causing: 5 EERIE
**Horror**
Cry of: 4 OHNO
Cry of mock: 4 EGAD
First name in: 3 LON WES
4 BELA 5 BORIS 6 FREDDY
**Horror film**
actor Chaney: 3 LON
director Craven: 3 WES
Like a: 4 GORY 5 EERIE
11 HAIRRAISING
of 1954: 4 THEM
of 1996: 6 SCREAM
reaction: 4 GASP
sound: 6 SHRIEK
staple: 4 GORE
street: 3 ELM
Word in a ~ title:
8 CREATURE
**"Horrors!":** 3 EEK 4 EGAD
OHMY OHNO
**Hors d'oeuvre:** 6 CANAPE
Fancy: 6 CAVIAR
Spanish: 4 TAPA
spread: 4 PATE
**Horse:** 5 STEED 6 EQUINE
bit: 3 OAT
Came down off a: 4 ALIT
Charley: 4 ACHE
color: 4 ROAN
Colorful: 4 ROAN
controller: 4 REIN
course: 4 OATS OVAL

Dark: 4 ROAN
Fast: 4 ARAB
father: 4 SIRE
Female: 4 MARE
Fine: 4 ARAB 5 STEED
gait: 4 TROT
Graceful: 4 ARAB 7 ARABIAN
hair: 4 MANE
halter: 4 REIN WHOA
handler: 5 GROOM
High-spirited: 5 STEED
hoof sound: 4 CLOP
house: 4 BARN 6 STABLE
hue: 4 ROAN
Jousting: 5 STEED
lead: 6 HALTER
Like a: 5 MANED
Like a broken: 4 TAME
mackerel: 4 TUNA
morsel: 3 OAT
Mottled: 4 ROAN
of a different color: 4 ROAN
Old: 3 NAG
opera: 5 OATER
pace: 4 GAIT
play: 4 POLO 5 EQUUS
Reddish: 4 ROAN
Reddish-brown: 3 BAY
6 SORREL
River: 5 HIPPO
Show: 4 ARAB MRED
Small: 4 PONY
Spirited: 4 ARAB 5 STEED
Spot on a: 6 DAPPLE
Stereotypical: 6 DOBBIN
Swift: 4 ARAB
Talking ~ of TV: 4 MRED
TV: 4 MRED
Unbroken: 5 BRONC
War: 5 STEED
Winged ~ of myth: 7 PEGASUS
Word after: 5 SENSE
Young: 4 COLT
**"___ horse!":** 4 GETA
**Horse-and-buggy:** 3 ERA
travelers: 5 AMISH
**Horseback**
Game on: 4 POLO
Go on: 4 RIDE
**Horse-drawn**
vehicle: 6 HANSOM
**"Horsefeathers!":** 3 BAH ROT
5 PSHAW
**Horsehide:** 4 BALL
Pitch a: 4 HURL
**"Horsepower"**
coiner James: 4 WATT
**Horses**
Hold one's: 4 WAIT
Like show: 4 SHOD
**Horseshoe**
site: 4 HOOF
**Horseshoe Curve**
City near: 7 ALTOONA
**Horseshoes**
player: 6 TOSSER

scorer: 6 LEANER
**Horseshoe-shaped**
fastener: 5 UBOLT
symbol: 5 OMEGA
**"___ horse to water ...":**
5 LEADA
**Horticulturist**
of note: 13 LUTHERBURBANK
topic: 6 BOTANY
**Horton**
creator: 5 SEUSS
heard one: 3 WHO
Seuss's: 8 ELEPHANT
**"Horton Hears ___":** 4 AWHO
**"Horton Hears a ___":** 3 WHO
**Horus**
Father of: 6 OSIRIS
Mother of: 4 ISIS
**Hose:** 3 WET 5 SPRAY
6 NYLONS
color: 4 ECRU NUDE
Garden ~ problem: 4 KINK
hue: 4 ECRU 5 BEIGE TAUPE
ladder: 3 RUN
material: 5 NYLON
part: 3 TOE 6 NOZZLE
problem: 4 SNAG
shade: 4 ECRU 5 BEIGE
TAUPE
woe: 3 RUN 4 SNAG
Word before: 5 PANTY
**Hosea**
Book after: 4 JOEL
**Hosiery:** 6 NYLONS
choice: 5 LEGGS
hue: 4 ECRU 5 BEIGE TAUPE
item: 6 ANKLET
material: 5 LISLE NYLON
problem: 4 SNAG
shade: 4 ECRU NUDE
5 TAUPE
thread: 5 LISLE
woe: 4 SNAG
**Hoskins, Bob**
role: 4 SMEE
**Hosni**
predecessor: 5 ANWAR
**Hosp.**
aide: 3 LPN
area: 3 ICU
areas: 3 ERS ORS
diagnostic: 3 MRI
employees: 3 DRS RNS
hookups: 3 IVS
machine: 3 MRI
picture: 3 MRI
readout: 3 EEG EKG
section: 3 ICU
sections: 3 ERS
Some ~ cases: 3 ODS
specialty: 3 TLC
staffer: 3 LPN
staffers: 3 RNS
test: 3 EKG
units: 3 ERS
ward: 3 ICU

worker: 3 LPN
workers: 3 MDS RNS
**Hospice**
Eastern: 6 IMARET
**Hospitable: 8 PLEASANT**
Less: 5 ICIER
**Hospital**
area: 5 PREOP
capacity: 4 BEDS
depts.: 3 ERS
figure: 5 NURSE
fluids: 4 SERA
helper: 4 AIDE
item: 6 BEDPAN
Like some ~ care:
  8 NEONATAL
solution: 6 SALINE
staffer: 4 AIDE 6 INTERN
supplies: 4 SERA
unit: 3 BED
worker: 6 INTERN 7 ORDERLY
**Hospitality**
area: 5 SUITE
**Hoss**
brother: 4 ADAM
dad: 3 BEN
**Host: 4 ARMY SLEW 5 EMCEE**
Answer to the: 4 RSVP
handout: 4 MENU
Late-night: 4 LENO
Roast: 5 EMCEE
Show: 5 EMCEE
**Hostage**
1979–81 ~ site: 4 IRAN
crisis group: 4 SWAT
Former ~ Terry: 5 WAITE
**Hostel: 3 INN**
Ute: 5 TEPEE
**Hostelry: 3 INN**
**Hostess**
Famous: 5 MESTA
snack cakes: 5 HOHOS
**Hostile: 4 UGLY 5 ENEMY**
  **6 BITTER 7 ADVERSE**
party: 5 ENEMY
reaction: 4 FLAK
to: 4 ANTI
**Hostilities**
Break in: 5 TRUCE
ender: 4 PACT 6 TREATY
Ongoing: 4 FEUD
**Hosts: 3 MCS**
MTV: 3 VJS
Roast: 3 MCS
**Hot: 4 FOXY IRED RACY SEXY**
  **5 AFIRE IRATE RILED**
  **SPICY 6 EROTIC**
  **STOLEN TRENDY**
  **7 ONAROLL PICANTE**
  **STEAMED**
  **9 ONASTREAK**
  **10 ALLTHERAGE**
air: 3 GAS
and dry: 7 SAHARAN
blood: 3 IRE 5 ARDOR
coal: 5 EMBER

drink: 3 TEA 4 GROG
  5 TODDY
flick: 3 ASH
Get ~ and bothered:
  7 STEAMUP
Get really: 6 SEERED
issue: 4 LAVA
It gets in ~ water: 6 TEABAG
It makes one: 3 IRE
Leaves in ~ water: 3 TEA
No longer: 3 OUT
Not: 4 COLD MILD
Not so: 4 WARM 5 TEPID
Not too: 4 SOSO
Not very: 5 TEPID
off the press: 3 NEW
pepper: 7 CAYENNE
pot: 4 STEW
rock: 4 LAVA
sandwich: 4 MELT
sauce: 5 SALSA 7 TABASCO
shot: 3 ACE
Some like it: 3 TEA 5 TODDY
  6 CEREAL TAMALE
spot: 3 SPA 4 HELL OVEN
  5 HADES SAUNA STOVE
  7 INFERNO
spring: 3 SPA
stuff: 4 LAVA LOOT 5 ANGER
  CHILI SALSA 7 CAYENNE
  TABASCO
temper: 3 IRE 5 ANGER
time: 4 JULY
time (abbr.): 3 AUG
time, in French: 3 ETE 4 AOUT
to trot: 4 AGOG AVID KEEN
  5 EAGER
tub: 3 SPA
tub part: 3 JET
under the collar: 4 SORE
  5 ANGRY IRATE RILED
**Hot ___ (rock band): 4 TUNA**
**Hotbed: 4 NEST**
**Hotcakes**
Go like: 4 SELL
**"Hot Diggity"**
singer: 4 COMO
**Hot dog: 6 WEENIE WIENER**
  **WIENIE**
picker-upper: 5 TONGS
topping: 5 CHILI 6 RELISH
~, once: 6 LASSIE
**Hotel**
convenience: 4 SAFE
employee: 4 MAID 5 VALET
  11 BELLCAPTAIN
freebie: 3 ICE 4 SOAP
Luxury ~, familiarly:
  7 THERITZ
name: 4 RITZ 5 HYATT
  LEONA 6 HILTON
offering: 5 SUITE
posting: 5 RATES
Resort: 3 SPA
Rural: 3 INN
sign: 3 ICE

suffix: 3 IER
upgrade: 5 SUITE
~ Bible name: 6 GIDEON
**Hotfoot: 5 PRANK**
it: 3 HIE 5 SCOOT SPEED
**Hothead**
Italian: 4 ETNA
**Hotpoint**
competitor: 5 AMANA
**Hot rod**
propellant: 5 NITRO
rod: 4 AXLE
sound: 5 VROOM
**Hots: 4 LUST**
**Hotshot: 3 ACE**
Coll.: 4 BMOC
Company: 4 EXEC
pilot: 3 ACE
Univ.: 4 BMOC
**Hotsy-___: 5 TOTSY**
**"Hot Zone, The"**
topic: 5 EBOLA
**Houdini: 8 ESCAPIST**
  **MAGICIAN**
feat: 6 ESCAPE
**Houlihan**
portrayer: 4 SWIT
rank: 5 MAJOR
**Hound: 3 DOG NAG PET**
  **6 BASSET HARASS**
Gazelle: 6 SALUKI
hint: 5 SCENT
holder: 5 LEASH
hounder: 4 FLEA
Long-eared: 6 BASSET
Low-slung: 6 BASSET
prey: 4 HARE
**Hour**
After the: 4 PAST
Evening: 4 NINE 5 SEVEN
Lunch: 3 ONE
Man of the: 4 HERO
Nearing the: 5 TENOF TENTO
  6 FIVETO
News: 6 ELEVEN
Prime-time: 3 TEN 4 NINE
Wee: 3 ONE TWO 5 ONEAM
  THREE TWOAM
  6 FOURAM
Whistle: 4 NOON
**Hourglass: 5 TIMER**
filler: 4 SAND
**Hourly**
charge: 4 RATE
pay: 4 WAGE
wage: 4 RATE
**Hours**
1200 ~: 4 NOON
1300 ~: 3 ONE
After: 4 LATE
Every 24: 4 ADAY 5 DAILY
Keep late: 6 STAYUP
L.A.: 3 PST
Like early: 3 WEE
Many: 4 DAYS
Mass. summer: 3 EDT

NYC: 3 EST
Tenn.: 3 CST
**House:** 4 STOW 6 ENCASE
addition: 3 ELL
adjunct: 4 YARD
and grounds: 6 ESTATE
Animal: 3 ZOO 4 BARN CAGE
   LAIR
Bee: 6 APIARY
Big: 5 MANOR 7 MANSION
Bird: 4 CAGE NEST
Bring down the: 4 RAZE
call: 3 NAY YEA 4 VOTE
coat: 5 PAINT
Country: 5 DACHA
cover: 4 ROOF
extension: 3 ELL
Feature of an empty:
   4 ECHO
Field: 5 TEPEE
Full: 4 HAND
Hash: 5 DINER
Horse: 4 BARN 6 STABLE
Ice: 5 IGLOO
It may be on the: 4 LIEN
Lady of the: 5 MADAM
Lord's: 5 MANOR
mem.: 3 REP
member: 4 LORD
of the lord: 5 MANOR
of worship: 6 TEMPLE
On the: 4 FREE
pet: 3 CAT
Place for a small: 4 TREE
Public: 3 INN
Religious: 6 PRIORY
Rough: 6 LEANTO
School: 4 FRAT
shower: 5 CSPAN
Sign of a full: 3 SRO
style: 5 TUDOR 7 CAPECOD
   8 COLONIAL
The big: 4 STIR
top: 5 ATTIC
Tree: 4 NEST
Upper: 6 SENATE
vote: 3 NAY YEA
wing: 3 ELL
work: 3 ACT
wrecker: 7 TERMITE
~, in Spanish: 4 CASA
**"House"**
actor Epps: 4 OMAR
**Housecat:** 3 PET
perch: 4 SILL
**Housecleaning**
Do some: 4 DUST
**Housecoat:** 6 DUSTER
**Household:** 6 MENAGE
animal: 3 PET
helper: 7 HELOISE
pest: 3 ANT 5 ROACH
   6 REDANT
spirit: 3 LAR
spray target: 4 ODOR
task: 5 CHORE

**"House Is Not ___, A":**
   5 AHOME
**Housekeeping**
Do some light: 4 DUST
**"House of Blue Leaves, The"**
playwright: 5 GUARE
**House of Lords**
member: 4 PEER
**"House of the Seven Gables,
   The"**
locale: 5 SALEM
**House of York**
symbol: 4 ROSE
**Houseplant**
Popular: 4 ALOE
   8 ALOEVERA
   9 AMARYLLIS
Spiny: 4 ALOE
**Housework**
Do some: 4 DUST
**Housing**
College: 4 DORM
cost: 4 RENT
Engine: 9 CRANKCASE
Fodder: 4 SILO
Hen: 4 COOP
Missile: 4 SILO
unit: 5 CONDO
**Houston**
baseballer: 5 ASTRO
footballer: 5 OILER
hockey player: 4 AERO
of Texas: 3 SAM
player: 5 ASTRO
Private eye: 4 MATT
pro: 5 ASTRO
team: 6 ASTROS
university: 4 RICE
**Houston, Whitney**
recording label: 6 ARISTA
**Houstonian:** 5 TEXAN
**HOV**
lane users: 8 CARPOOLS
**Hovel:** 5 SHACK 6 SHANTY
**Hover:** 4 HANG
**Hoverer**
Sci-fi: 3 UFO
Stadium: 5 BLIMP
**How**
Show: 5 TEACH
**"How ___!":** 4 RUDE TRUE
**How-___ (instruction books):**
   3 TOS
**"How about that!":** 3 GEE
**Howard**
Actor: 4 DUFF
and others: 4 RONS
Director: 3 RON
of baseball: 6 ELSTON
Shock jock: 5 STERN
Sportscaster: 6 COSELL
**Howard, Ron**
film: 4 EDTV 6 RANSOM
role: 4 OPIE
**"How awful!":** 3 ICK 4 OHNO
**"How can ___?":** 5 ILOSE

**"How Can ___ Sure" (1967 hit):**
   3 IBE
**"How Can We Be Lovers"**
singer Michael: 6 BOLTON
**"How cute!"**
exclamations: 3 AWS
**"How disgusting!":** 3 ICK UGH
**"How Do I Live"**
singer LeAnn: 5 RIMES
**How-do-you-dos:** 3 HIS
**"How do you like ___ apples?":**
   4 THEM
**"How dry ___":** 3 IAM
**Howdy**
Hawaiian: 5 ALOHA
**"Howdy":** 4 HIYA
**Howdy Doody**
network: 3 NBC
original name: 5 ELMER
spot: 7 FRECKLE
**"___ Howdy Doody time!":**
   3 ITS
**Howe**
Inventor: 5 ELIAS
of hockey: 6 GORDIE
Playwright: 4 TINA
**Howe'er:** 3 THO
**However:** 3 BUT YET
~, briefly: 3 THO
**Howie**
Comic: 6 MANDEL
**Howl:** 3 BAY 7 ULULATE
**Howland Island**
She never made it to:
   7 EARHART
**Howler:** 4 RIOT WOLF
   6 COYOTE
**"How nice!":** 3 AAH
**"How obvious!":** 3 DUH
**"How revolting!":** 3 UGH
**"How sexy!":** 7 OOHLALA
**"How stupid of me!":** 3 DOH
**"How sweet ___!":** 4 ITIS
**"How the Grinch Stole
   Christmas"**
director Howard: 3 RON
**"How the Other Half Lives"**
author Jacob: 4 RIIS
**How-to**
help: 8 TUTORIAL
listing: 4 STEP
**"How to Handle a Woman"**
lyricist: 6 LERNER
**"How to Make an American
   Quilt"**
author Whitney: 4 OTTO
**"How to Murder Your Wife"**
actress Virna: 4 LISI
**"How've you ___?":** 4 BEEN
**"How was ___ know?":** 3 ITO
**___ Hoya, Oscar**
Boxer: 4 DELA
**Hoyle**
topic: 5 RULES
**Hr.**
Lunch: 5 ONEPM

part: 3 MIN
Wee: 5 ONEAM
**HRH**
Part of: 3 HER HIS
**Hrs.**
Early: 3 AMS
**H.S.**
class: 3 ALG ENG SCI 4 GEOG
    HIST TRIG
exam: 3 SAT 4 PSAT
math: 3 ALG 4 TRIG
proficiency test: 3 GED
promoter: 3 PTA
requirement: 3 ENG
subject: 3 ALG ENG SCI
    4 GEOG HIST TRIG
**Hsing-Hsing:** 5 PANDA
**___ Hsin-liang**
Taiwanese dissident: 3 HSU
**HST**
predecessor: 3 FDR
successor: 3 DDE
**Ht.:** 3 ALT 4 ELEV
**http**
Address that begins with:
    3 URL
**HUAC**
Part of: 4 COMM
**Huáscar**
subject: 4 INCA
**Hub:** 5 MECCA
In the ~ of: 4 AMID
Wheel: 4 NAVE
**"Hubba hubba!":** 6 OOLALA
    7 OOHLALA
Person who might say:
    5 OGLER
**Hubbard**
Author: 4 LRON
Hall of Famer: 3 CAL
Scientology founder: 4 LRON
**Hubbell**
of baseball: 4 CARL
teammate: 3 OTT
**Hubble**
Astronomer: 5 EDWIN
**Hubbub:** 3 ADO 4 STIR TODO
    5 NOISE 6 CLAMOR
    8 BROUHAHA
**Huber**
of tennis: 4 ANKE
**Hubert**
successor: 5 SPIRO
Veep after: 5 SPIRO
**Hubris**
source: 3 EGO
**Huck**
conveyance: 4 RAFT
follower: 4 STER
of fiction: 4 FINN
transport: 4 RAFT
**"Huckleberry Finn"**
character: 3 JIM
**HUD**
Former ~ head Jack: 4 KEMP
Part of: 5 URBAN

~, for one: 4 DEPT
**"Hud"**
actress Patricia: 4 NEAL
director Martin: 4 RITT
Oscar winner: 4 NEAL
**Huddle:** 6 POWWOW
Court: 7 SIDEBAR
**Hudson:** 3 CAR
Actress: 4 KATE
Canal to the: 4 ERIE
City on the: 4 TROY 6 ALBANY
N.J. city on the: 5 FTLEE
**Hudson, Henry**
ship: 8 HALFMOON
**Hudson Bay**
prov.: 3 ONT
tribe: 4 CREE
**Hudson/Day**
film: 10 PILLOWTALK
**Hue:** 4 TINT TONE 5 COLOR
    SHADE
and cry: 5 FUROR 6 CLAMOR
Blue: 4 AQUA NAVY TEAL
    5 AZURE
Earth: 5 OCHER OCHRE
Green: 4 JADE
Horse: 4 ROAN
Hose: 4 ECRU 5 BEIGE
    TAUPE
Linen: 4 ECRU
Neutral: 4 ECRU
partner: 3 CRY
Pastel: 4 AQUA
Purple: 5 LILAC MAUVE
Shoe: 3 TAN
**Huey**
of politics: 4 LONG
~, Dewey, and Louie: 4 TRIO
~, Dewey, or Louie:
    6 NEPHEW
**Huff:** 4 SNIT
and puff: 4 BLOW GASP PANT
Be in a: 4 STEW
Horsy: 5 SNORT
In a: 5 IRATE 7 STEAMED
Leave in a: 5 STORM
**Huffington**
Columnist: 7 ARIANNA
**Huffy:** 4 SORE
state: 4 SNIT
**Hug:** 5 CLASP 7 ENCLASP
givers: 4 ARMS
**Huge:** 4 EPIC VAST 5 GIANT
    7 IMMENSE MASSIVE
amount: 3 SEA TON 5 OCEAN
~, in French: 6 ENORME
~, poetically: 5 ENORM
**Hugh**
French king: 5 CAPET
Magazine publisher:
    6 HEFNER
nickname: 3 HEF
TV host: 5 DOWNS
**Hughes**
Poet: 3 TED
Skater: 5 SARAH

**Hughes, Howard**
aircraft: 11 SPRUCEGOOSE
Company once owned by:
    3 TWA
Studio once owned by: 3 RKO
**Hughes, Langston**
poem: 4 ITOO
**Hughes, Sarah**
Emulate: 5 SKATE
leap: 4 AXEL LUTZ
**Hugo:** 5 AWARD
fugitive: 7 VALJEAN
**Hugs**
~, in letters: 3 OOO
~, symbolically: 3 OOO
**"Huh?":** 3 WHA
    10 IDONTGETIT
**Huitzilopochtli:** 6 WARGOD
worshiper: 5 AZTEC
**Hula:** 5 DANCE
follower: 5 SKIRT
hoop: 3 FAD LEI
skirt material: 5 GRASS
**Hulk**
of wrestling: 5 HOGAN
**"Hulk, The"**
actor Bana: 4 ERIC
director Lee: 3 ANG
**Hull**
Captain: 5 ISAAC
marking: 8 LOADLINE
packing: 5 OAKUM
part: 4 KEEL 5 BILGE
**Hullabaloo:** 3 ADO DIN 4 STIR
    5 HOOHA 6 RUMPUS
**Hull House**
founder: 6 ADDAMS
**Hum:** 4 WHIR 5 DRONE
**Human:** 5 BIPED 6 MORTAL
    PERSON 7 ADAMITE
Act: 3 ERR
Be: 3 ERR
being: 5 BIPED 6 MORTAL
    PERSON 7 ADAMITE
It's: 5 TOERR
Largest ~ organ: 4 SKIN
Period in ~ development:
    7 IRONAGE
rights gp.: 3 ILO 4 ACLU
suffix: 3 OID
The ~ senses: 6 PENTAD
trunk: 5 TORSO
Was: 5 ERRED
**"Human Concretion"**
sculptor: 3 ARP
**"Human Condition, The"**
author Arendt: 6 HANNAH
**Humane**
org.: 4 SPCA 5 ASPCA
**Human Genome Project**
topic: 3 DNA
**Humanist**
Dutch: 7 ERASMUS
**Humanities:** 4 ARTS
degs.: 3 BAS MAS
subj.: 3 ENG

**Humanoid**
Hairy: 4 YETI 7 BIGFOOT
Himalayan: 4 YETI
**Humans:** 4 RACE 6 PEOPLE
**Humbert, Humbert**
obsession: 6 LOLITA
**Humble:** 5 ABASE LOWLY
6 DEMEAN
home: 3 HUT 5 ABODE
oneself: 7 EATDIRT
reply: 4 ITRY
Word after: 3 PIE
**Humbled**
Was: 7 ATECROW ATEDIRT
**Humble Oil**
Company that bought: 4 ESSO
**Humboldt**
City on the: 4 ELKO
**Humbug**
preceder: 3 BAH
**Humdinger:** 4 LULU ONER
5 BEAUT DILLY DOOZY
**Humdrum:** 4 BLAH
8 TIRESOME
**Humerus**
locale: 3 ARM
neighbor: 4 ULNA
**Humid:** 3 WET 4 DAMP
5 MOIST
**Humidifier**
output: 5 VAPOR
**Humidity**
React to: 4 WILT
**Humidor**
item: 5 CIGAR CLARO
6 HAVANA
**Humiliate:** 5 ABASE SHAME
6 DEMEAN 7 DEGRADE
**Humiliated**
person: 7 DOORMAT
Was: 7 ATECROW ATEDIRT
**Humiliation:** 5 SHAME
Avoid: 8 SAVEFACE
Suffer: 7 EATCROW
EATDIRT
**Hummable:** 6 CATCHY
**Humming:** 5 ABUZZ
**Hummingbird**
Hang like a: 5 HOVER
**Hummus**
holder: 4 PITA
ingredient: 6 SESAME
TAHINI
**Humongous:** 5 GIANT LARGE
**Humor:** 7 CATERTO
First name in: 4 ERMA
Good ~ man: 3 WIT
Ill: 4 BILE 6 SPLEEN
Like some: 3 DRY WRY
6 ETHNIC
magazine: 3 MAD
Often-missed: 5 IRONY
Old-fashioned: 4 CORN
Overwhelm with: 4 SLAY
Sense of: 3 WIT
with a twist: 5 IRONY

**Humorous**
Dryly: 3 WRY
fellow: 3 WAG
Whimsically: 5 DROLL
**Humpback:** 5 WHALE
herd: 3 POD
**Humpbacked**
helper: 4 IGOR
**Humped**
bovine: 4 ZEBU
**Humperdinck**
hero: 6 HANSEL
heroine: 6 GRETEL
**Humperdinck, Engelbert**
hit song: 9 RELEASEME
**Humphrey**
1960s veep ~: 6 HUBERT
costar: 3 IDA
nickname: 5 BOGIE
role: 3 SAM
successor: 5 AGNEW
**Humphries, Barry**
character: 8 DAMEEDNA
**Hump-shouldered**
animal: 3 GNU
**Humpty Dumpty:** 3 EGG
Like: 5 OBESE OVATE OVOID
**Humvee**
forerunner: 4 JEEP
**Hun**
Head: 6 ATTILA
king: 4 ATLI 6 ATTILA
**Hunch**
Assistant with a: 4 IGOR
Have a: 4 FEEL 5 SENSE
**Hunchback**
Fictional: 4 IGOR
**"Hunchback of Notre Dame,
The"**
woman: 9 ESMERALDA
**Hundred**
A ~ sawbucks: 4 ONEG
dollar bill: 5 CSPOT
Five ~ sheets: 4 REAM
One of a D.C.: 3 SEN
smackers: 5 CSPOT
**Hundred Acre Wood**
denizen: 3 ROO 4 POOH
**Hundredweight**
20 ~: 3 TON
**Hung.**
neighbor: 3 AUS
**Hungarian:** 6 MAGYAR
composer: 5 LISZT 6 BARTOK
conductor: 5 SOLTI
leader Kádár: 5 JANOS
premier Imre: 4 NAGY
premier Nagy: 4 IMRE
sheepdog: 4 PULI
spa town: 4 EGER
stew: 7 GOULASH
wine: 5 TOKAY
**"Hungarian Dances"**
composer: 6 BRAHMS
**"Hungarian Rhapsodies"**
composer: 5 LISZT

**Hungary**
Nagy of: 4 IMRE
**Hunger:** 3 YEN
Feeling of: 4 PANG
for: 5 CRAVE
(for): 4 LUST 5 YEARN
Halt a ~ strike: 3 EAT
It's from: 4 PANG
**Hung-jury**
result: 7 RETRIAL
**Hungry:** 5 UNFED
feeling: 4 PANG
Still: 7 UNSATED
**Hunk:** 3 GOB 4 SLAB 6 ADONIS
APOLLO
of cheese: 4 SLAB
of history: 3 ERA
of meat: 4 SLAB
pride: 3 BOD
**Hunker**
down: 5 SQUAT
**Hunky-dory:** 3 AOK 4 FINE
JAKE OKAY 5 DANDY
SWELL
**"Hunny"**
bear: 4 POOH
**Huns**
King of the: 4 ATLI
6 ATTILA
**Hunt:** 8 SCAVENGE
Actress: 5 HELEN LINDA
for: 4 SEEK
illegally: 5 POACH
partner: 4 PECK
**Hunted:** 4 PREY
animal: 4 PREY
spheroid: 3 EGG
**Hunter**
Actor: 3 IAN
Actress: 3 KIM
Author: 4 EVAN
Bugs: 4 FUDD 5 ELMER
Celestial: 5 ORION
dog: 6 SETTER
Heavenly: 5 ORION
in the night sky: 5 ORION
Moray: 5 EELER
Nocturnal: 3 OWL
Novelist: 4 EVAN
quarry: 3 ELK 4 PREY
target: 4 PREY
trail: 5 SPOOR
Writer: 4 EVAN
**Hunter, Kim**
role: 6 STELLA
**"___ Hunter, The":** 4 DEER
**Hunting**
dog: 5 HOUND 6 SETTER
expedition: 6 SAFARI
Legal ~ period:
10 OPENSEASON
**Huntley**
Newsman: 4 CHET
**Huntress**
Mythical: 5 DIANA
8 ATALANTA

**Hupmobile**
 contemporary: 3 REO
**Hurdle**
 Aspiring atty.'s: 4 LSAT
 Classroom: 4 EXAM TEST
 Clear a: 4 LEAP
 Cow's ~, in rhyme: 4 MOON
 Doctorate: 5 ORALS
 Hannibal: 4 ALPS
 Legal: 3 BAR
**Hurdy-gurdy:** 5 ORGAN
**Hurl:** 4 SPEW 5 THROW
**Hurler**
 asset: 3 ARM
 stat: 3 ERA
**Hurley**
 Actress: 3 LIZ
**Hurling:** 5 SPORT
 stat: 3 ERA
**"Hurlyburly"**
 actor Sean: 4 PENN
 playwright: 4 RABE
 ~ Tony winner Judith: 4 IVEY
**Hurly-burly:** 3 ADO
**Hurok**
 Impresario: 3 SOL
**Huron:** 4 LAKE
 neighbor: 4 ERIE
**"Hurrah!":** 3 YAY
 for José: 3 OLE
**"Hurray for me!":** 6 IDIDIT
**Hurricane:** 5 STORM
 center: 3 EYE
 heading (abbr.): 3 ENE ESE
  NNE NNW SSE SSW WNW
  WSW
 home: 5 MIAMI
 of 1964: 4 DORA
 of 1970: 5 CELIA
 of 1972: 5 AGNES
 of 1975: 6 ELOISE
 of 1995: 4 OPAL
 of 1999: 5 IRENE
 of 2004: 4 IVAN
**Hurriedly:** 5 APACE 7 INHASTE
**Hurry:** 3 HIE 4 RUSH 5 SPEED
 up: 4 RUSH
**"Hurry!":** 4 ASAP
**Hurry-scurry:** 3 ADO
**"Hurry up!":** 4 CMON
  6 COMEON 7 HOPTOIT
  8 STEPONIT
**Hurston, ___ Neale**
 Writer: 4 ZORA
**Hurston, Zora ___**
 Author: 5 NEALE
**Hurt:** 3 AIL MAR 4 ACHE HARM
  PAIN 5 ACHED AILED
  SMART 6 HARMED
  OFFEND 7 SMARTED
 badly: 4 MAIM
**Hurting:** 4 ACHY SORE
**Husband:** 4 MATE 5 STORE
  6 OLDMAN SAVEUP
  SPOUSE
 ~, in French: 4 MARI

**Hush-hush:** 6 SECRET
  9 TOPSECRET
 Govt. ~ group: 3 CIA NSA
 org.: 3 CIA NSA
 WWII ~ group: 3 OSS
**Hush puppy**
 material: 8 CORNMEAL
**Husk:** 8 SEEDCASE
 Prickly: 3 BUR
 site: 3 OAT
 Wheat: 4 BRAN
**Huskies**
 of the NCAA: 5 UCONN
**Husk-wrapped**
 dish: 6 TAMALE
**Husky:** 6 HOARSE
 burden: 4 SLED
 cry: 3 ARF
 trailer: 4 SLED
**Husky-voiced:** 6 HOARSE
**Hussein, King**
 Widow of: 4 NOOR
**Hussy:** 4 MINX 7 JEZEBEL
**Hustle:** 3 HIE 4 RACE
  5 DANCE SCOOT
  SPEED
 and bustle: 3 ADO
 music: 5 DISCO
**"Hustler, The"**
 actress Piper: 6 LAURIE
 game: 4 POOL
 locale: 8 POOLHALL
  POOLROOM
 prop: 3 CUE
 role: 5 EDDIE
**Hut:** 5 HOVEL
 material: 5 ADOBE
**Hutchinson**
 Congressman: 3 ASA
**Hutchison**
 Senator: 3 KAY
**Hutu**
 country: 6 RWANDA
**Huxley**
 Author: 6 ALDOUS
 work: 13 BRAVENEWWORLD
**Huxtable**
 mom: 5 CLAIR
 son: 4 THEO
**Huxtable, ___ Louise**
 Critic: 3 ADA
**"Huzzah!":** 3 YAY
 ~, in Spanish: 3 OLE
**HVAC**
 measure: 3 BTU
**Hwy.:** 3 RTE
 Coast: 4 RTEI
 helpers: 3 AAA
 Numbered: 3 RTE
 with tolls: 3 TPK
**Hwys.:** 3 RDS
**Hyacinth**
 holder: 4 VASE
**Hyalite:** 4 OPAL
**Hyams**
 Actress: 5 LEILA

**Hyannis**
 entrée: 5 SCROD
**Hybrid**
 animal yielding low-fat meat:
  7 BEEFALO
 cat: 5 LIGER TIGON
 fruit: 4 UGLI 7 TANGELO
 fuel: 7 GASOHOL
**Hyde:** 5 FIEND
 alterego: 6 JEKYLL
 ~, to Jekyll: 8 ALTEREGO
**Hyde Park**
 buggy: 4 PRAM
**Hydra:** 5 POLYP
**Hydrant**
 hookup: 4 HOSE
**___ hydrate (sedative):**
  7 CHLORAL
**Hydrocarbon**
 ending: 3 ANE ENE
 Simple: 6 ETHANE
 suffix: 3 ANE ENE
 Type of: 6 OLEFIN
 used as a solvent: 6 HEXANE
 with a double bond:
  6 ALKENE
**Hydroelectric**
 agcy.: 3 TVA
 project: 3 DAM
**Hydrogen:** 3 GAS
 atomic number: 3 ONE
 Heavy: 7 ISOTOPE
**Hydrolysis**
 atom: 3 ION
 product: 5 ANION
**Hydromassage**
 facility: 3 SPA
**Hydrophane:** 4 OPAL
**Hydrotherapy**
 place: 3 SPA
**Hydrox**
 rival: 4 OREO
**Hydroxide**
 Potassium: 3 LYE 6 ALKALI
 Sodium: 3 LYE
 Sodium ~, to a chemist:
  4 NAOH
**Hydroxyl**
 compound: 4 ENOL
**Hygiene**
 Kind of: 4 ORAL
**Hygienist**
 Dental ~ request: 5 RINSE
**Hymn:** 5 PSALM
  8 DOXOLOGY
 book: 7 PSALTER
 Joyous: 5 PAEAN
 Kind of: 7 CHORALE
 of praise: 5 PAEAN
 opener: 6 ADESTE
 part: 4 ALTO
 Sacred: 5 PSALM
 Start of a: 4 OGOD
 word: 4 AMEN
**Hymnal**
 holder: 3 PEW

**Hype:** 4 PLUG 6 HOOPLA
    7 PROMOTE 8 BALLYHOO
**Hyperion:** 5 TITAN
  Daughter of: 3 EON
**"Hyperion"**
  poet: 5 KEATS
**Hyphen:** 4 DASH
**Hyphenated**
  ~ ID: 3 SSN
**Hypnotic**
  name: 6 MESMER
  state: 6 TRANCE
**Hypnotist**
  command: 5 SLEEP

Evil ~ of fiction:
  8 SVENGALI
Pioneering ~ Franz:
  6 MESMER
**Hypnotized:** 5 UNDER
**Hypo**
  units: 3 CCS
**Hypothesis**
  Start of a: 4 IFSO
  ___ hypothesis: 4 GAIA
**Hypothesize:** 5 POSIT
**Hypothetical:** 4 MOOT
  6 WHATIF
  particle: 5 AXION

  primate: 6 APEMAN
  question: 6 WHATIF
**Hypotheticals:** 3 IFS
**Hyson:** 3 TEA
**Hysteria:** 5 PANIC
  area: 7 DEEPEND
**Hysterical:** 5 MANIC
  person: 4 RIOT
**Hyundai:** 3 CAR 4 AUTO
  competitor: 3 KIA
  model: 6 SONATA
    7 ELANTRA

**I:** 3 EGO ONE 4 ELEM
    5 VOWEL
  focus: 3 EGO
  It may start with: 3 RTE
  Latin: 3 EGO
  problem: 3 EGO 7 EGOTISM
    8 EGOMANIA
  The ~ of I.M. Pei: 4 IEOH
  The ~ of IV: 5 INTRA
  The ~ of TGIF: 3 ITS
  topper: 3 DOT
  ~, in German: 3 ICH
  ~, in Greek: 4 IOTA
**"¡"**
  ball: 3 DOT
**I-5:** 3 RTE
**I-79**
  terminus: 4 ERIE
**I-80:** 3 RTE
  Nevada city on: 4 ELKO
**I-95:** 3 RTE
**Iacocca**
  Businessman: 3 LEE
**IAD**
  posting: 3 ARR ETA ETD
**Iago:** 4 LIAR
  Superior of: 7 OTHELLO
  Wife of: 6 EMILIA
**"I agree!":** 4 AMEN
**"I Ain't Marching Anymore"**
  singer: 4 OCHS
**Iambs:** 4 FEET
**"I am ___ crook!": Nixon:**
    4 NOTA
**Iams**
  competitor: 4 ALPO
**"I Am Woman"**
  singer: 5 REDDY
**Ian**
  Actor: 4 HOLM
**"___ I a stinker?":** 4 AINT
**"___ I a woman?": Sojourner**
    Truth: 5 ARENT
**"I before E except after C":**
    4 RULE
**"I Believe"**
  singer Frankie: 5 LAINE
**Iberia**
  Part of: 5 SPAIN
  River that gives ~ its name:
    4 EBRO
**Ibid.**
  relative: 5 OPCIT
**IBM:** 4 CORP
  compatibles: 3 PCS
  competitor: 3 NEC
  Gerstner of: 3 LOU
  Part of: 4 INTL

  products: 3 PCS
**Ibn ___:** 4 SAUD
**iBook:** 3 MAC
**Ibsen**
  character: 3 ASE 4 GYNT
    6 GABLER
  city: 4 OSLO
  dancer: 6 ANITRA
  heroine: 4 NORA 5 HEDDA
  play: 6 GHOSTS 8 PEERGYNT
  Playwright: 6 HENRIK
**Ibuprofen**
  brand: 5 ADVIL
  target: 4 ACHE
**"I burn"**
  Mount whose name means:
    4 ETNA
**"I called it!":** 4 DIBS
**"I ___ Camera":** 3 AMA
**"___ I can help it!":** 5 NOTIF
**"I cannot ___ lie":** 5 TELLA
**"I cannot tell ___":** 4 ALIE
**"I can take ___!":** 5 AHINT
**"I can't believe ___ ...":** 4 IATE
**"I can't ___ satisfaction":**
    5 GETNO
**"I can't ___ thing!":** 4 EATA
**"___ I care!":** 4 ASIF
**Icarus**
  Father of: 8 DAEDALUS
**"Icarus Agenda, The"**
  author: 6 LUDLUM
**ICBM**
  First U.S.: 5 ATLAS
  Part of: 5 INTER
**Ice:** 3 OFF 6 ENSURE
  alternative: 7 SNOCONE
  Arctic: 4 FLOE
  Bobby on the: 3 ORR
  breaker: 4 PICK
  Celestial ~ ball: 5 COMET
  device: 5 TONGS
  Fake on the: 4 DEKE
  Glide on: 5 SKATE
  hockey team: 6 SEXTET
  house: 4 IGLU 5 IGLOO
  Jump on the: 4 AXEL
  legend: 3 ORR
  Lose control on: 5 SLIDE
  mass: 4 BERG
  melter: 3 SUN 4 SALT
  pick: 3 AWL
  pinnacle: 5 SERAC
  Put on: 4 COOL 5 CHILL
    TABLE
  Sans: 4 NEAT
  sheet: 4 FLOE
  They're kept on: 5 PUCKS

  unit: 4 CUBE
  Without: 4 NEAT
  ~, in German: 3 EIS
**Ice ___:** 3 AGE 4 FLOE
**Ice Age**
  elephant: 8 MASTODON
**Iceberg**
  alternative: 7 ROMAINE
**Ice cream**
  brand: 4 EDYS
  drink: 4 MALT SODA 5 FLOAT
  effect: 5 SWIRL
  flavor: 4 OREO 5 MOCHA
    PECAN 6 COFFEE
    7 VANILLA 9 ROCKYROAD
    11 COOKIEDOUGH
  Half an ~ flavor: 5 TUTTI
  holder: 4 CONE
  ingredient: 4 AGAR
  maker Joseph: 3 EDY
  One of an ~ duo: 3 BEN
  parlor order: 6 FRAPPE
    SUNDAE
  pattern: 5 SWIRL
  purchase: 4 PINT
  serving: 3 DIP 5 SCOOP
  thickener: 4 AGAR
  With: 7 ALAMODE
**Ice Cube:** 6 RAPPER
  Real first name of: 5 OSHEA
**Iced:** 5 DIDIN
  tea garnish: 5 LEMON
  ~, with "in": 3 DID
  ~, with "up": 4 SEWN
**Iceland**
  feature: 5 FJORD
  money: 5 KRONA
  ocean (abbr.): 3 ATL
**"Iceland"**
  star: 5 HENIE
**"Iceland Fisherman, An"**
  author Pierre: 4 LOTI
**Icelandic**
  epic: 4 EDDA
  singer: 5 BJORK
**Iceless:** 4 NEAT
**Iceman**
  Legendary: 3 ORR
**"Iceman ___, The":**
    6 COMETH
**"Iceman Cometh, The"**
  playwright: 6 ONEILL
**Ice skater**
  event: 5 PAIRS
  figures: 6 EIGHTS
  leap: 4 AXEL
**"Ice Storm, The"**
  director Lee: 3 ANG

**Ice-T**
genre: 3 RAP
**"Ich bin ___ Berliner":** 3 EIN
**"Ich ___ dich":** 5 LIEBE
**"I Ching"**
reader: 6 TAOIST
**Icicle**
former: 4 DRIP
site: 4 EAVE
**"Ici on ___ français":** 5 PARLE
**"Ick!":** 5 GROSS
**Icky**
stuff: 3 GOO 4 CRUD GLOP
GOOK GUNK OOZE
5 SLIME 6 SLUDGE
**"I, Claudius"**
role: 4 NERO
star: 6 JACOBI
**Icon:** 5 IMAGE
Place for an: 4 APSE
unit: 5 PIXEL
**"I could ___ horse!":** 4 EATA
**"I couldn't care less"**
attitude: 6 APATHY
**"I could write ___":** 5 ABOOK
**ICU**
conduit: 6 IVTUBE
hookups: 3 IVS
Quickly, in the: 4 STAT
staff: 3 RNS
The U in: 4 UNIT
**Icy:** 4 COLD 5 ALOOF GELID
burg: 4 NOME
coating: 4 HOAR RIME
forecast: 5 SLEET
It can be: 5 STARE
mass: 4 BERG
rain: 4 HAIL 5 SLEET
remark: 3 BRR
Tended to ~ roads: 6 SANDED
threat: 4 BERG
treat: 7 SNOCONE
**ID**
Ask for: 4 CARD
Book: 4 ISBN
Common: 3 SSN
Cop: 5 BADGE
Driver's: 3 LIC
High-tech: 3 DNA
IRS: 3 SSN
Library: 4 ISBN
Merchandise: 3 UPC
Nine-digit: 3 SSN
**"Id ___":** 3 EST
**Ida.**
neighbor: 3 NEV ORE WYO
4 MONT
**Idaho:** 4 SPUD 5 TATER
capital: 5 BOISE
motto word: 4 ESTO
nickname: 8 GEMSTATE
product: 4 SPUD 6 POTATO
**"I dare you!":** 4 DOIT 5 TRYME
**Idea:** 4 CLUE 6 NOTION
7 CONCEPT
Central ~, in music: 4 TEMA

**Discover, as an:** 5 HITON
7 HITUPON
Main: 4 GIST 5 THEME
Novel: 4 PLOT 5 STORY
Start of an: 4 GERM SEED
Took hold, as an: 6 SANKIN
Unifying: 5 THEME
**Ideal:** 5 DREAM 6 EDENIC
7 PARAGON
Eastern: 3 TAO
place: 4 EDEN 6 UTOPIA
___ ideal: 3 EGO
**Idealist:** 7 UTOPIAN
**Idealistic**
one: 7 QUIXOTE
**Ideally:** 6 ATBEST
15 INAPERFECTWORLD
**"___ Ideas" (1951 song):**
4 IGET
**Idée ___:** 4 FIXE
**Identical:** 4 SAME TWIN
5 ALIKE EQUAL
6 CLONED 8 SELFSAME
Regard as: 6 EQUATE
to: 6 SAMEAS
**Identification**
Formal phrase of: 5 ITISI
Miss: 3 SHE
Old station: 4 ESSO
**Identifier**
Corporate: 4 LOGO
High tech: 3 DNA
Wildlife: 6 EARTAG
**Identify:** 3 PEG 4 NAME
5 LABEL
**Identifying**
mark: 4 SCAR
**Identity:** 3 EGO 7 ONENESS
Assumed: 5 ALIAS
Give new ~ to: 6 RENAME
Question of: 3 WHO
Secret ~ preserver: 4 MASK
**"___ Identity, The":** 6 BOURNE
**Ideology:** 3 ISM
**Ides**
Ninth day before the: 5 NONES
rebuke: 4 ETTU
**"I'd hate to break up ___":**
4 ASET
**Idi**
Notorious: 4 AMIN
**"I did it!":** 4 TADA
**"I didn't know that!":** 3 GEE
**Idiom**
Specialized: 5 ARGOT
**Idiosyncrasy:** 3 TIC 5 QUIRK
**Idiosyncratic:** 3 ODD
**Idiot:** 4 BOZO DODO DOLT
5 MORON
box: 4 TVSET 6 TEEVEE
boxes: 3 TVS
light word: 3 OIL
**Idiotic:** 4 DUMB 5 INANE
7 ASININE
**Iditarod**
command: 4 MUSH

destination: 4 NOME
racer: 4 SLED
setting: 6 ALASKA
terminus: 4 NOME
vehicle: 4 SLED
**Idle:** 4 LOAF 5 NOTON
6 OTIOSE
Comic: 4 ERIC
Stays: 4 SITS
Was: 3 SAT
**Idler:** 9 DONOTHING
opposite: 4 DOER
**"I'd like to buy ___":** 3 ANA
ANE ANI ANO
**Idly**
Chatter: 5 PRATE
Pass time: 4 LAZE
Scribble: 6 DOODLE
**"I do":** 3 VOW
**"I do!":** 3 YES
**"I Do I Do I Do I Do I Do"**
group: 4 ABBA
**Idol**
Biblical: 4 BAAL
Chinese: 4 JOSS
Kind of: 4 TEEN 7 MATINEE
Like an: 6 ADORED
Polynesian: 4 TIKI
worshipper: 3 FAN
**Idolize:** 5 ADORE 6 DOTEON
**Idolizer:** 6 ADORER
**"I don't buy it!":** 5 PSHAW
**"I Don't Buy Kisses Anymore"**
costar Peoples: 3 NIA
**"I don't give ___!":** 4 ARAP
5 AHOOT
**"I don't think so!":** 3 NAH
4 NOPE UHUH
**"I don't want to hear it!":**
5 SHUSH 7 SPAREME
**"I'd rather not":** 3 NAH
**"I Dream of Jeannie"**
star Barbara: 4 EDEN
**"I dropped it!":** 4 OOPS
**IDs**
Corp.: 3 TMS
**"I'd walk ___ for ...":** 5 AMILE
**Idyllic**
place: 4 EDEN
setting: 3 LEA
**Idylls:** 5 POEMS
**"Idylls of the King"**
lady: 4 ENID
**i.e.:** 5 IDEST 6 THATIS
Part of: 3 EST
Relative of: 3 VIZ
**If:** 6 INCASE
all else fails: 7 ATWORST
all goes well: 6 ATBEST
E'en: 3 THO
Even: 3 THO 5 ALTHO
6 ALBEIT
Except: 6 UNLESS
need be: 8 INAPINCH
not: 4 ELSE
nothing changes: 6 ASITIS

"If all ___ fails ...": 4 ELSE
"I Fall to Pieces"
  singer Patsy: 5 CLINE
"If ___ a nickel ...": 4 IHAD
"If ___ Answers": 4 AMAN
"If ___ be so bold ...": 4 IMAY
"If He Walked Into My Life"
  musical: 4 MAME
"If I Could Turn Back Time"
  singer: 4 CHER
"If I Had a Hammer"
  singer: 10 PETESEEGER
"If I ___ Hammer": 4 HADA
Ifill
  Newswoman: 4 GWEN
"If I Only Had the Nerve"
  singer: 4 LAHR
"If I ___ Rich Man": 5 WEREA
"If I Ruled the World"
  rapper: 3 NAS
"If it ___ broke ...": 4 AINT
"If I Were a Rich Man"
  singer: 5 TEVYE
"If I Were King of the Forest"
  singer: 4 LAHR
"If I Were ___ Man": 5 ARICH
"If ___ nickel ...": 5 IHADA
"If only!": 5 IWISH
"If only that were true!":
  5 IWISH
"I forbid": 4 VETO
"I forgot the words"
  syllables: 4 LALA
"I found it!": 3 AHA
"If they could ___ now ...":
  5 SEEME
"If ___ Would Leave You":
  5 EVERI
"If ___ you ...": 5 IWERE
"If You Knew ___": 5 SUSIE
"I get it!": 3 AHA
"I give!": 5 UNCLE
"I give up!": 5 UNCLE
  8 ITSNOUSE
Iglesias
  tune: 4 AMOR
Igloo
  dweller: 5 INUIT 6 ESKIMO
  dwellers (abbr.): 4 ESKS
Ignatius
  of Loyola: 6 JESUIT
Igneous
  rock: 6 BASALT 7 DIORITE
    8 FELDSPAR
  rock source: 5 MAGMA
Ignite: 5 LIGHT 6 KINDLE
Ignited: 3 LIT
  again: 5 RELIT
Igniter
  Lighter: 5 FLINT
Ignominy: 5 ODIUM SHAME
Ignorance
  ~, in an adage: 5 BLISS
"Ignorance ___ excuse!":
  4 ISNO
Ignorant: 7 UNAWARE

of right and wrong: 6 AMORAL
Ignore: 4 OMIT SKIP 5 ELIDE
  7 TUNEOUT
  15 CLOSEONESEYESTO
Doesn't: 5 HEEDS OBEYS
intentionally: 4 SNUB
the alarm clock: 7 SLEEPIN
the limit: 5 SPEED
the script: 5 ADLIB
~, with "out": 4 TUNE
"I Got ___" (1973 song):
  5 ANAME
"I ___ Grow Up": 4 WONT
Iguana
  relative: 5 ANOLE
"I had no ___!": 4 IDEA
"I Hated, Hated, Hated This
  Movie"
  author: 5 EBERT
"I hate to break up ___":
  4 ASET
"I have found it!": 6 EUREKA
"I have ___ good authority":
  4 ITON
IHOP
  order: 5 STACK 7 LARGEOJ
    SMALLOJ
  Part of: 4 INTL
  ___ II (Gillette razor brand):
    4 TRAC
II Chronicles
  Book after: 4 EZRA
  ___ II Men: 4 BOYZ
"I ___ it!": Red Skelton: 4 DOOD
Ijsselmeer
  City on the: 4 EDAM
"I Just Wanna Stop"
  singer Vannelli: 4 GINO
Ike
  Colleague of: 4 OMAR
  command in WWII: 3 ETO
  Ex-wife of: 4 TINA
  hometown: 7 ABILENE
  initials: 3 DDE
  Opponent of: 5 ADLAI
  She didn't like: 4 TINA
  Wife of: 5 MAMIE
"___ Ike" ('50s slogan): 5 ILIKE
Ikhnaton
  successor: 3 TUT
"I ___ kick ...": 5 GETNO
"I Kid You Not"
  autobiographer: 4 PAAR
"I kiss'd thee ___ I kill'd thee":
  Othello: 3 ERE
"___ I Kissed You" (Everly
  Brothers hit): 3 TIL
"I knew it!": 3 AHA
"I know what you're up to!":
  3 OHO
Il ___ (Mussolini): 4 DUCE
Ile ___-Hélène: 3 STE
Iliac
  prefix: 5 SACRO
"Iliad": 4 EPIC EPOS
  bickerer: 4 HERA

king: 5 PRIAM
Like the: 4 EPIC
sage: 6 NESTOR
setting: 4 TROY
warrior: 4 AJAX ARES
Ilie
  of tennis: 7 NASTASE
Iliescu
  Former Romanian president:
    3 ION
"I Like ___" ('50s slogan): 3 IKE
Ilium: 4 TROY 7 HIPBONE
Ilk: 4 KIND SORT TYPE
Ill
  Be: 3 AIL
  feelings: 10 NOLOVELOST
  humor: 4 BILE 6 SPLEEN
  It may be: 6 REPUTE
  temper: 3 IRE 4 BILE
  treatment: 5 ABUSE
  Was ~ with: 3 HAD
  will: 3 IRE 4 HATE 5 SPITE
    6 ANIMUS ENMITY
    MALICE RANCOR
Ill.
  neighbor: 3 IND WIS
Ill at ___: 4 EASE
Ill-behaved: 3 BAD
"I'll be ___ of a gun!": 4 ASON
"I'll be right there!": 6 ONESEC
Ill-considered: 4 RASH 5 HASTY
    6 UNWISE 7 ASININE
"I'll do it!": 5 LETME
"I'll drink to that!": 4 AMEN
Illegal
  block: 4 CLIP
  entry: 6 BAGJOB
  firing: 5 ARSON
  interest: 5 USURY
  liquor: 9 MOONSHINE
  Make: 3 BAN
  parker's foe: 5 TOWER
Illegally
  Fix: 3 RIG
  Hunt: 5 POACH
  off base: 4 AWOL
  resell: 5 SCALP
  seize: 5 USURP
  Take: 3 ROB 4 SKIM
Illegible
  signature: 6 SCRAWL
Ill-fated: 5 HEXED 6 DAMNED
    DOOMED TRAGIC
  auto: 5 EDSEL
  flier: 6 ICARUS
  mission of 1967: 7 APOLLOI
  sub of 2000: 5 KURSK
"I'll get right ___!": 4 ONIT
"I'll go along with that":
  4 OKAY
Ill-gotten
  gains: 4 LOOT PELF SWAG
    5 BOOTY GRIFT
    11 FILTHYLUCRE
Ill-humored: 4 DOUR 5 CROSS
    SURLY

**Illicit**
cigarette: 6 REEFER
drug inits.: 3 PCP
**Illinois**
city: 5 ALTON CAIRO ELGIN
  SALEM 6 MOLINE PEORIA
  URBANA
City on the: 6 PEORIA
neighbor: 4 IOWA
port: 5 CAIRO 6 PEORIA
**Illiterate**
Signed like an: 3 XED
**Ill-mannered:** 4 RUDE
sort: 4 BOOR LOUT
**"Illmatic"**
rapper: 3 NAS
**Illness**
End of an: 4 ITIS
Infant: 5 COLIC
Severe: 7 BADCASE
**"I'll say!":** 4 AMEN
**"I'll speak a prophecy ___ go":**
  Shakespeare: 4 EREI
**Ill-suited:** 5 INAPT UNFIT
**"I'll take that as ___":** 3 ANO
**Ill-tempered:** 4 MEAN 5 NASTY
  SURLY TESTY 6 ORNERY
**Illuminated:** 5 LITUP
sign: 4 EXIT
**Illuminating**
gas: 4 NEON
**Illumination**
Evening: 10 NIGHTLIGHT
Vegas: 4 NEON
**Illusion:** 6 MIRAGE
**Illusionist**
feat: 15 DISAPPEARINGACT
**Illusory**
paintings: 5 OPART
promise: 11 PIEINTHESKY
**Illustrator**
One-named: 4 ERTE
**Illustrious:** 5 FAMED NOBLE
  NOTED 6 FAMOUS
  7 EMINENT
**"Ill wind that no one blows**
  **good":** 4 OBOE
**"Il mio tesoro":** 4 ARIA
**"Il Nome Della Rosa"**
author: 3 ECO
**"I Lost It at the Movies"**
author: 4 KAEL
**I love**
~, in French: 5 JAIME
~, in Latin: 3 AMO
**"I Love a Parade"**
composer: 5 ARLEN
**"I Love Lucy"**
network: 3 CBS
**"I Love Rock 'n Roll"**
singer Joan: 4 JETT
**"I Loves You, Porgy"**
singer: 4 BESS
singer Nina: 6 SIMONE
**Ilsa**
Love of: 4 RICK

maiden name: 4 LUND
Where ~ met Rick: 5 PARIS
~, to Rick: 3 KID
**"Il Trovatore":** 5 OPERA
soprano: 4 INEZ
**___ Ilyich**
Tolstoy's: 4 IVAN
**IM**
carrier: 3 AOL
**I.M.**
Architect: 3 PEI
**"I'm ___!":** 4 ONIT
**iMac**
maker: 5 APPLE
rivals: 3 PCS
**"___, I'm Adam":** 5 MADAM
**Image:** 4 ICON 7 PERSONA
  8 LIKENESS
Computer: 4 ICON
Computer ~ format: 3 GIF
  4 JPEG
Corporate: 4 LOGO
Graven: 4 IDOL
maker: 5 PRMAN
Medical: 4 SCAN
Photog: 3 NEG
Public: 3 REP 7 PERSONA
Radar: 4 BLIP
receiver: 6 RETINA
**Imaginary:** 6 UNREAL
belt: 6 ZODIAC
eternal flower:
  8 AMARANTH
line: 4 AXIS
Not: 4 REAL
**Imaginative:** 5 NOVEL
Was: 8 HADIDEAS
**Imagine:** 5 OPINE 6 IDEATE
  7 PICTURE
**"Imagine ___!":** 4 THAT
**Imagined:** 6 DREAMT
Not: 4 REAL
**Imago**
Future: 4 PUPA
**"I'm all ___":** 4 EARS
**"I'm all ears!":** 5 TRYME
  6 DOTELL
**Imam**
book: 5 KORAN
**Iman**
Model ~, for one: 6 SOMALI
**Imbalance**
Economic: 8 TRADEGAP
**Imbibe:** 5 DRINK
to excess: 4 TOPE
**Imbibed**
some: 7 HADANIP
**Imbroglio:** 4 MESS SPAT
**Imbue:** 5 STEEP 6 INFUSE
**"I mean ...":** 6 THATIS
**Imelda**
collection: 5 SHOES
**"___, I'm Falling in Love**
  **Again":** 4 OHOH
**"I'm freezing!":** 3 BRR
**"I'm game!":** 4 LETS

**"I'm ___ here!":** 4 OUTA
  5 OUTTA
**"I'm impressed!":** 3 GEE OOH
  WOW 4 NICE 5 NEATO
**I-minded**
individual: 6 EGOIST
**"I'm innocent!":** 5 NOTME
**Imitate:** 3 APE 4 COPY 5 MIMIC
  6 MIRROR PARROT
  7 ACTLIKE
**Imitating:** 5 APING
**Imitation:** 4 FAUX MOCK SHAM
  5 APERY 6 ERSATZ
Grotesque: 8 TRAVESTY
In ~ of: 5 AFTER
Prone to: 5 APISH
**Imitative:** 5 APISH 6 ECHOIC
  7 COPYCAT
sort: 4 APER
**Imitator:** 4 APER
Life: 3 ART
**"I'm kidding!":** 3 NOT
**"I'm listening":** 4 GOON
**Immaculate:** 4 PURE 5 CLEAN
**Immanuel**
Philosopher: 4 KANT
**Immature:** 5 YOUNG 6 UNRIPE
  7 PUERILE
egg cell: 5 OVULE 6 OOCYTE
newt: 3 EFT
**Immeasurable**
chasm: 5 ABYSS
time: 3 EON 4 AEON
**Immediate:** 4 NEAR
**Immediately:** 3 NOW 4 STAT
  6 ATONCE PRESTO
after: 4 UPON
if not sooner: 3 PDQ
~, in the ER: 4 STAT
**"Immediately!":** 4 ASAP STAT
**Immense:** 3 BIG 4 HUGE VAST
**Immensely:** 4 ALOT ATON
  5 NOEND
Enjoyed: 5 ATEUP
**Immerse:** 3 DIP 4 SOAK
  5 BATHE SOUSE STEEP
  6 PLUNGE
**Immigrant**
course (abbr.): 3 ESL
island: 5 ELLIS
Japanese: 5 ISSEI
Japanese ~ descendant:
  6 SANSEI
subj.: 3 ESL
**Immigration**
island: 5 ELLIS
**Imminent:** 4 NEAR
Be: 4 LOOM
**Imminently:** 4 SOON
**Immobilize:** 6 HOGTIE
  SPLINT
**Immobilized:** 7 INACAST
**Immoderate**
revelry: 4 ORGY
**"Immoralist, The"**
author: 4 GIDE

**Immortal**
  coaching name: 5 KNUTE
  Soccer: 4 PELE
  ~ Giant: 3 OTT
**Immovable**
  blockage: 6 LOGJAM
**Immune**
  response stimulus: 7 ANTIGEN
  system agent: 5 TCELL
**Immunity**
  One with: 8 DIPLOMAT
**Immunization:** 4 SHOT
  letters: 3 DPT
**Immunologist**
  study: 7 ANTIGEN
**"I'm not ___ complain ...":**
      5 ONETO
**Imogene**
  Comedienne: 4 COCA
  Partner of: 3 SID
**"I'm OK, You're OK"**
  author: 6 HARRIS
**"I'm outta here!":** 4 CIAO
      5 ADIOS LATER SEEYA
**Imp:** 4 BRAT PEST 5 DEMON
      DEVIL 6 RASCAL
      URCHIN 8 DEVILKIN
**Impact**
  Main: 5 BRUNT
  sound: 3 BAM 4 BANG THUD
      WHAM 5 SPLAT
**Impair:** 3 MAR 4 HARM HURT
      MAIM
**Impala**
  kin: 5 ELAND
**Impale:** 5 SPEAR
**Impaler, The**
  Ruler known as: 4 VLAD
**Impart:** 4 LEND LOAN
      7 INSTILL
**Impartial:** 4 FAIR JUST
  ___ impasse (stuck): 4 ATAN
**Impassioned:** 6 ARDENT
**Impassive:** 5 STOIC STONY
      6 STOLID WOODEN
      7 STOICAL
**Impatience:**
      15 ANTSINONESPANTS
  Sign of: 4 HONK
**Impatient:** 5 ANTSY HASTY
  acknowledgment: 6 YESYES
  cry: 3 NOW YAH
**Impeach:** 6 ACCUSE
**Impeachment**
  juror: 7 SENATOR
  Nixon ~ chairman: 6 RODINO
**Impecunious:** 4 POOR 5 NEEDY
**Impedance**
  unit: 3 OHM
**Impede:** 5 DETER 6 HINDER
      HOBBLE RETARD
  legally: 5 ESTOP
**Impeder**
  Progress: 4 SNAG
**Impediment:** 4 SNAG
  Speech: 4 LISP

**Impel:** 4 GOAD URGE 5 DRIVE
**Impend:** 4 LOOM
**Impending:** 4 NEAR
**Impenetrable:** 5 DENSE
**Imperative:** 4 MOOD 5 AMUST
  Sentry: 4 HALT
**Imperfect:** 6 MARRED
  Be: 3 ERR
  Make: 3 MAR
**Imperfection:** 4 FLAW WART
      5 STAIN 6 DEFECT
  Hose: 4 SNAG
  Mug: 3 ZIT
  Road: 4 BUMP
  Sign of: 7 ERASURE
**Imperial**
  autocrat: 4 TSAR
  decree: 5 UKASE
  product: 4 OLEO
**Imperil:** 8 ENDANGER
**Impersonate:** 3 APE 6 POSEAS
**Impersonator:** 4 APER
**Impertinence:** 3 LIP 4 SASS
      5 CHEEK
**Impertinent:** 4 FLIP RUDE
      5 SASSY SAUCY
  one: 4 SNIP
  stare: 4 OGLE
**Imperturbable:** 5 STOIC
      6 SERENE
**Impetuous:** 4 RASH 5 BRASH
      6 MADCAP
  ardor: 4 ELAN
  motion: 6 PLUNGE
**Impetuously:** 7 ONADARE
  Begin: 8 PLUNGEIN
**Impetus:** 4 FUEL 5 DRIVE
      FORCE
**Impiety:** 3 SIN
**Impish:** 6 ELFISH
  smile: 4 GRIN
  sort: 5 PIXIE
**Implant:** 3 SOW 5 EMBED
      6 ENROOT
**"I'm pleased!":** 4 GOOD
**Implement:** 4 TOOL
**Implied:** 5 GOTAT MEANT
      TACIT
**Implore:** 3 BEG 4 PRAY URGE
      5 PLEAD 7 ENTREAT
**Imply:** 4 MEAN 5 AIMAT
      GETAT 6 HINTAT
      7 CONNOTE
**Impolite:** 4 RUDE
  look: 4 LEER OGLE 5 STARE
  sound: 5 SLURP
**Import:** 5 SENSE TENOR
      6 WEIGHT
  duty: 6 TARIFF
**Importance**
  Of no: 5 PETTY
  ___ importance: 4 OFNO
**Important:** 3 BIG KEY
      6 OFNOTE
      9 REDLETTER
  exam: 5 FINAL

  grain: 4 OATS
  Is: 7 MATTERS
  Most: 4 MAIN
  Not as: 6 LESSER
  numero: 3 UNO
  period: 3 ERA
  sort: 7 SOMEONE
  time: 3 ERA
**Imported**
  auto: 4 AUDI
  cheese: 4 EDAM
**Imports**
  Pricey: 4 BMWS
**Importune:** 3 BEG 4 URGE
      7 ENTREAT
**Impose:** 3 PUT 4 LEVY 5 FOIST
  a fine: 6 AMERCE
  a second levy on: 5 RETAX
**Impose ___ on:** 4 ABAN
**Imposing**
  entrance: 6 PORTAL
  structure: 7 EDIFICE
**"Impossible!":** 6 CANTBE
      7 NOCANDO
**"___ impossible!":** 3 ITS
**Impostor:** 4 FAKE SHAM
**Impoverished:** 4 POOR
      5 NEEDY 6 INNEED
**Impractical:** 8 QUIXOTIC
  idealist: 9 STARGAZER
  one: 7 DREAMER
**Imprecise**
  ordinal: 3 NTH
**Impresario**
  production: 5 OPERA
**Impress:** 3 WOW 4 DENT
      5 PRINT
  deeply: 3 AWE 4 ETCH
  It may be added to: 3 IVE
  More than: 3 AWE
**Impressed**
  Not: 6 UNAWED
**Impression:** 4 DENT IDEA
      5 SENSE
  Do an ~ of: 3 APE
  Lasting: 4 SCAR
  Make an: 4 DENT ETCH
**Impressionist:** 4 APER
**Impressive**
  grouping: 5 ARRAY
  Long and: 4 EPIC
**Imprint:** 5 STAMP
  firmly: 4 ETCH
**Imprison:** 5 EMBAR
**Impromptu**
  bookmark: 6 DOGEAR
  percussion: 6 SPOONS
  playing: 10 JAMSESSION
**Improper:** 5 AMISS UNDUE
**Improprieties:** 5 NONOS
**Improv**
  style: 4 SCAT
**Improve:** 4 HONE MEND
      5 AMEND 6 ENRICH
      7 ENHANCE
  ~, as beef: 3 AGE

~, as text: 5 EMEND
**Improvement:** 7 UPGRADE
**Improvisational**
  composition: 7 TOCCATA
  style: 4 SCAT
**Improvise:** 4 VAMP 5 ADLIB
    6 FAKEIT NOODLE
    WINGIT
  vocally: 4 SCAT
**Improvised:** 5 ADHOC ADLIB
    7 STOPGAP
  accompaniment: 4 VAMP
**Impudence:** 3 LIP 4 GALL SASS
    5 BRASS CHEEK SAUCE
**Impudent:** 4 PERT 5 BRASH
    7 SASSY
  girl: 4 MINX 5 HUSSY
  talk: 3 LIP
  youth: 5 WHELP
**Impulse:** URGE WHIM
  carrier: 4 AXON
  conductor: 4 AXON 6 NEURON
  Nerve ~ region: 7 SYNAPSE
  transmitter: 4 AXON
**Impulsive:** 4 RASH
**Impurities**
  Free from: 6 REFINE
**Impute:** 7 ASCRIBE
**Imre**
  Former Hungarian premier:
    4 NAGY
**"I'm Real"**
  singer, familiarly: 3 JLO
**"I'm ___ Sexy":** 3 TOO
**"I'm so glad!":** 3 YAY
**"I'm Sorry"**
  singer Brenda: 3 LEE
**"I'm thinking ...":** 3 HMM
**"___ I'm told":** 4 ORSO
**"I'm too ___ for my shirt":**
    4 SEXY
**"I'm ___ you!":** 4 ONTO
**"I ___ my wit's end":** 4 AMAT
**In:** 3 HOT MOD 4 AMID CHIC
    6 AMIDST ATHOME
    TRENDY 7 ELECTED
    ELECTEE
  Not: 4 AWAY 5 PASSE UNHIP
  on: 5 HEPTO 6 WISETO
    7 PRIVYTO
**In ___**
  (actually): 4 ESSE
  (as found): 4 SITU
  (bored): 4 ARUT
  (calmly): 6 STRIDE
  (entirely): 4 TOTO
  (even): 4 ATIE
  (existing): 4 ESSE
  (harmonious): 4 SYNC
  (intrinsically): 6 ITSELF
  (lined up): 4 AROW
  (not yet born): 5 UTERO
  (soon): 4 ABIT
  (stuck): 4 AJAM ARUT
    5 ABIND
  (together): 4 SYNC 6 UNISON

  (unborn): 5 UTERO
  (undisturbed): 4 SITU
  (untidy): 5 AMESS
**___ in (cozy in bed):** 6 TUCKED
**"___ In" (1976 Wings hit):**
    5 LETEM
**Ina**
  Actress: 5 BALIN
**Inability**
  Musical: 6 TINEAR
**___ in a blue moon:** 4 ONCE
**Inaccurate:** 3 OFF 5 NOTSO
    6 UNTRUE
  Be: 3 ERR
**Inactive:** 4 IDLE 6 ATREST
    7 DORMANT
**Inactivity:** 6 STASIS 7 INERTIA
**Inadequate:** 3 BAD LOW
    4 LAME POOR 5 SCANT
    6 SCARCE
**Inadvertently**
  Say: 7 LETSLIP
**Inadvisable**
  action: 4 NONO
**"I ___ Name":** 4 GOTA
**___ in a million:** 3 ONE
**Inamorata**
  of Valentino: 5 NEGRI
**Inamorato:** 4 BEAU 5 LOVER
**Inane:** 5 DOPEY LOONY
    9 SENSELESS
**___ in apple:** 3 AAS
**"In apprehension how like
    ___": Hamlet:** 4 AGOD
**Inasmuch**
  as: 5 SINCE
  (as): 6 SEEING
**Inaugural**
  ball: 4 GALA
**Inauguration**
  1960 ~ speaker: 5 FROST
  highlight: 4 OATH
**In-basket**
  item: 4 MEMO
  stamp (abbr.): 4 RECD
**"___ in Boots":** 4 PUSS
**In-box**
  clutter: 4 SPAM
  Ed.'s ~ filler: 3 MSS
  filler: 5 MEMOS
  input: 5 EMAIL
**Inc.**
  alternative: 3 LTD
  workers: 3 EDS
  ~, abroad: 3 CIE LTD
**Inca**
  land: 4 PERU
**Incalculable:** 6 UNTOLD
**"___ in Calico":** 4 AGAL
**Incan**
  capital: 5 CUZCO
**Incandescence:** 4 GLOW
**Incandescent:** 5 AGLOW
  lamp gas: 5 ARGON
**Incantation:** 5 SPELL
  opener: 4 ABRA

**Incarcerate:** 4 JAIL
**Incarnation**
  Hindu: 6 AVATAR
  of Vishnu: 4 RAMA
**Incendiary:** 8 ARSONIST
  stuff: 6 NAPALM
**Incense:** 3 IRE 5 ANGER
    6 ENRAGE 7 MAKEMAD
  resin: 5 MYRRH
  stick: 4 JOSS
**Incensed:** 5 ANGRY IRATE
**Incentive**
  Sales: 6 REBATE
  Worker's: 5 BONUS
**Inception:** 4 DAWN 5 ONSET
    6 ORIGIN
**Incessantly:** 4 EVER 5 NOEND
    7 NONSTOP ONANDON
  Bother: 5 EATAT
**Inch:** 4 UNIT 5 SIDLE
  .001 ~: 3 MIL
  Part of an: 4 PICA
**___ in Charlie:** 3 CAS
**Inched:** 5 CREPT
**Inches**
  36 ~: 4 YARD
  45 ~: 3 ELL
  6,272,640 square ~: 4 ACRE
  About 39 ~: 5 METER
    METRE
  Nine: 4 SPAN
**Inchon**
  City near: 5 SEOUL
**Incident:** 5 EVENT 7 EPISODE
  Bench-clearing: 5 SETTO
**"___ Incident, The":** 5 OXBOW
**Incidentally**
  ~, in e-mail shorthand: 3 BTW
**Incidentals**
  cash: 8 PINMONEY
**Incision:** 4 SLIT 5 NOTCH
**Incisor:** 5 TOOTH
  neighbor: 6 CANINE
**Incite:** 4 GOAD PROD URGE
    5 EGGON ROUSE
    6 SPURON 7 PROVOKE
  to action: 5 EGGON IMPEL
**Inclement:** 5 NASTY RAINY
**Inclination:** 4 BENT BIAS
    5 BEVEL SLANT SLOPE
    7 MINDSET
    8 TENDENCY
**Incline:** 3 TIP 4 LEAN RAMP
    TEND TILT 5 GRADE
    SLANT SLOPE
    7 DISPOSE
**Inclined:** 3 APT 5 ATILT LEANT
    PRONE 6 ASLOPE
    7 OFAMIND
  Be: 4 TEND
  Not: 6 AVERSE
  Very: 5 STEEP
**Include:** 3 ADD 4 HAVE
    5 ADDIN
  Fail to: 4 OMIT
**Includes:** 3 HAS

**Including:** 4 WITH 6 SUCHAS
    8 ASWELLAS
**Inclusion**
  MS.: 4 SASE
  Phrase of: 6 ETALII
**Inclusive**
  abbr.: 3 ETC 4 ETAL
  ___ incognita: 5 TERRA
**Income:** 4 FEES 7 REVENUE
  component: 8 NETSALES
  French: 5 RENTE
  Landlord: 4 RENT
  Like some: 8 UNEARNED
  Madison Ave.: 6 ADFEES
  Magazine: 3 ADS
  Some ~ (abbr.): 3 INT
**Incoming**
  flight (abbr.): 3 ARR
  flight info: 3 ETA
**Incomparable:** 6 UNIQUE
  ending: 3 EST
**Incompatible**
  Be: 5 CLASH
**Incompetent:** 6 UNABLE
  sort: 3 OAF
**Incomplete:** 7 PARTIAL
**"Incompleteness theorem"**
  formulator: 5 GODEL
**Incongruity**
  Literary: 5 IRONY
**Inconsiderate:** 4 RUDE
**Inconsistent:** 6 SPOTTY
    UNEVEN 7 ERRATIC
  Be: 4 VARY
**Inconvenience:** 6 HASSLE
**Incorporate**
  new territory: 5 ANNEX
**Increase:** 4 BUMP GOUP
    GROW HIKE RISE
    5 ADDTO BOOST REVUP
    RUNUP 6 STEPUP
    7 ENHANCE
  by 200%: 6 TREBLE
  gradually: 6 ACCRUE
  Sudden: 5 SURGE
  ~, with "up": 3 REV
**Increaser**
  IRA: 3 INT
  Price: 3 TAX
  Signal: 3 AMP
**Incredible**
  bargain: 5 STEAL
  story: 4 YARN
**Incredulous**
  Visibly: 5 AGAPE
**Incriminate:** 5 RATON
**Incriminating**
  info: 4 DIRT
**Incubation**
  station: 4 NEST
**Incubator**
  occupant: 7 NEONATE
  spot (abbr.): 3 ICU
**Incur:** 5 RUNUP
**Incurred:** 5 RANUP
**Incursion:** 4 RAID 5 FORAY

**Ind.**
  neighbor: 3 ILL
**Indebted:** 7 OBLIGED
  Be ~ to: 3 OWE
**Indecisive**
  Be: 3 HEM 5 WAVER
    6 WAFFLE
**Indeed:** 3 YEA 6 REALLY
**"Indeed!":** 3 YES 5 OHYES
**Indelicate:** 4 RACY
**Indemnify:** 5 REPAY
**Indentation:** 5 CLEFT NOTCH
    6 RECESS
**Independence**
  Financial: 10 EASYSTREET
  It gained ~ in 1991:
    7 ESTONIA
**"Independence Day"**
  actor: 5 QUAID
  invaders: 3 ETS
**Independent**
  emirate since 1971: 5 QATAR
  land since 1991: 8 SLOVENIA
  Like many ~ films: 4 ARTY
  Make: 4 WEAN
**Independently:** 5 APART
**Index**
  Market: 3 DOW
  UV ~ monitor: 3 EPA
  Wall St.: 4 NYSE
**India**
  1998 headline event in ~:
    5 NTEST
  Ancient invader of: 5 ARYAN
  British rule in: 3 RAJ
  City of: 4 AGRA 5 DELHI
    6 MADRAS MYSORE
  Coin of: 5 RUPEE
  Conductor born in: 5 MEHTA
  First P.M. of: 5 NEHRU
  Language of: 5 HINDI TAMIL
  Like ~ paper: 4 THIN
  neighbor: 5 NEPAL
  Nursemaid of: 4 AMAH
  Prince of: 4 RAJA
  Princess of: 4 RANI 5 RANEE
  Sir, in: 5 SAHIB
  Song of: 4 RAGA
  State of: 5 ASSAM
  tourist mecca: 4 AGRA
  Where ~ is: 4 ASIA
  ~ Inc.: 3 LTD
**India.___**
  Singer: 4 ARIE
**Indian:** 5 ASIAN OCEAN
  address: 5 SAHIB
  Alabama: 4 CREE
  Andean: 4 INCA
  Arizona: 4 HOPI PIMA
    6 NAVAHO NAVAJO
  attire: 4 SARI
  Big: 4 RAJA
  bread: 3 NAN
  butter: 4 GHEE
  Canadian: 4 CREE
  chief: 4 RAJA 5 RAJAH

  city: 5 DELHI
  coin: 5 RUPEE
  Colorado: 3 UTE
  corn: 5 MAIZE
  craft: 5 CANOE
  Dakota: 3 REE
  Delaware: 6 LENAPE
  dress: 4 SARI
  drum: 5 TABLA 6 TOMTOM
  dwelling: 5 HOGAN TEPEE
  elephant driver: 6 MAHOUT
  garment: 4 SARI
  head: 4 CENT
  home: 4 ASIA
  honorific: 3 SRI 5 SAHIB
  instrument: 5 SITAR
  king: 4 RAJA
  Lake: 4 ERIE
  language: 5 HINDI
  lentil dish: 3 DAL
  Longfellow: 8 HIAWATHA
  Manitoba: 4 CREE
  Midwest: 3 SAC 4 OTOE
  movie area: 9 BOLLYWOOD
  music: 4 RAGA
  music first name: 4 RAVI
  Nebraska: 3 OTO 4 OTOE
    5 OMAHA 6 PAWNEE
  New Mexico: 4 ZUNI
  nursemaid: 4 AMAH
  Oklahoma: 3 OTO SAC
    4 OTOE 5 OSAGE
    6 PAWNEE
  Peruvian: 4 INCA
  Plains: 3 OTO 4 CREE OTOE
    5 KIOWA OSAGE
    6 PAWNEE 7 ARAPAHO
  poet: 6 TAGORE
  pole: 5 TOTEM
  Pre-Aztec: 6 TOLTEC
  prince: 4 RAJA 5 RAJAH
  princess: 4 RANI 5 RANEE
  Pueblo: 4 HOPI TIWA ZUNI
  silk center: 5 ASSAM
  Southwestern: 3 UTE 4 HOPI
  state: 5 ASSAM
  title: 3 SRI 5 SAHIB
  tourist city: 4 AGRA
  Western: 3 OTO UTE 4 HOPI
    OTOE
**Indian ___:** 5 OCEAN
**Indiana**
  basketballer: 5 PACER
  city: 4 GARY PERU
    7 ELKHART
  county: 7 LAPORTE
  Former ~ governor Bayh:
    4 EVAN
  Former ~ senator Birch:
    4 BAYH
  river: 6 WABASH
  senator: 5 LUGAR
  state flower: 5 PEONY
**Indiana Jones:** 4 HERO
  quest: 3 ARK
  trademark: 6 FEDORA

**Indianapolis**
team: 5 COLTS
university: 6 PURDUE
**Indianapolis 500:** *see pages*
714–715
**Indiana University**
locale: 6 KOKOMO
**Indian Ocean**
vessel: 4 DHOW
**Indians:** 4 TEAM 6 ASIANS
on scoreboards: 3 CLE
**Indic**
language: 4 URDU
**Indicate:** 6 DENOTE SIGNAL
7 BESPEAK POINTAT
POINTTO
assent: 3 NOD
**Indicated:** 7 BESPOKE
**Indication:** 4 HINT OMEN SIGN
Little-hand: 4 HOUR
Tree-ring: 3 AGE
**Indicator**
Econ.: 3 GNP
Future: 4 OMEN
Insertion: 5 CARET
Maiden-name: 3 NEE
Market: 3 DOW
Pause: 5 COMMA
Pitch: 4 CLEF NOTE
Price: 3 TAG
RPM: 4 TACH
Sale: 6 REDTAG
Second-sequel: 3 III
Sellout: 3 SRO
Tie: 3 ALL
Wind: 4 SOCK VANE
**Indifference:** 6 APATHY
**Indifferent:** 4 SOSO 5 ALOOF
JADED
Ethically: 6 AMORAL
**Indigence:** 4 NEED
**Indigenous:** 6 ETHNIC NATIVE
**Indigent:** 5 NEEDY
**Indigestion**
cause: 4 ACID
**Indignant:** 5 HETUP
Feel ~ about: 6 RESENT
reaction: 4 SLAP
~, with "up": 3 HET
**Indignation:** 3 IRE 7 OUTRAGE
**Indigo:** 3 DYE 4 ANIL
source: 4 ANIL
**Indira**
Father of: 5 NEHRU
Son of: 5 RAJIV
**Indirect:** 3 WRY
10 ROUNDABOUT
Make ~ reference: 6 ALLUDE
**Indiscretion:** 4 SLIP
**Indispensable:** 5 VITAL
**Indisposed:** 3 ILL 6 AVERSE
UNWELL
15 UNDERTHEWEATHER
**Indistinct:** 3 DIM 4 HAZY
5 BLEAR FAINT MISTY
Become: 4 BLUR FADE

**Indistinctly**
Speak: 4 SLUR 6 MUTTER
**Indistinguishable:** 4 SAME
**Individual:** 3 ONE 4 LONE SELF
6 ENTITY PERSON
effort: 4 SOLO
performances: 4 SOLI
share: 4 ANTE
**Individualist:** 5 LONER
**Individuality:** 4 SELF 5 STYLE
**Individually:** 4 APOP EACH
6 APIECE
**Indivisible:** 3 ONE
**Indochinese**
language: 3 LAO
**Indo-European:** 5 ARYAN
**Indolence:** 5 SLOTH
**Indolent:** 4 LAZY 6 OTIOSE
**Indomitable**
spirit: 4 GRIT
**Indonesia**
is in it: 4 OPEC
Part of: 4 BALI
**Indonesian**
ape: 5 ORANG
Certain: 8 SUMATRAN
island: 4 BALI JAVA 5 CERAM
TIMOR 6 BORNEO
7 SUMATRA
islands: 3 ARU
ox: 4 ANOA
**Indoor**
ball: 4 NERF
**"In Dreams"**
actor: 3 REA
**"Indubitably":** 3 YES
**Induce**
to a crime: 6 SUBORN
**Inducement**
Illegal: 5 BRIBE
**Inducer**
Admiration: 3 AWE
Sleep: 6 OPIATE 7 SANDMAN
Yawn: 4 BORE
**Induction**
motor inventor: 5 TESLA
unit: 5 GAUSS TESLA
**Indulge:** 5 HUMOR
7 CATERTO
in daydreaming:
10 WOOLGATHER
oneself: 7 SPLURGE
to excess: 6 OVERDO
**Indulged**
in vanity: 6 PRIDED
**Indulgence**
Bout of: 5 SPREE
Period of: 4 ORGY
**Indus**
Where the ~ flows: 4 ASIA
**Industrial**
container: 3 VAT
German ~ city: 5 ESSEN
German ~ region: 4 RUHR
giant: 4 CZAR
Japanese ~ center: 5 OSAKA

**Industrious**
group: 5 DOERS
insect: 3 ANT
**Industriousness**
Symbol of: 3 ANT
**Industry**
big shot: 4 CZAR 5 BARON
Captain of: 7 MAGNATE
Cloning: 7 BIOTECH
Fashion: 8 RAGTRADE
prefix: 4 AGRO
Symbol of: 3 ANT 4 LOGO
**"Industry"**
Its motto is: 4 UTAH
**Indy**
Al of: 5 UNSER
Big initials at: 3 STP
Compete at: 4 RACE
entrant: 5 RACER 7 RACECAR
Family name at: 5 UNSER
leader: 7 PACECAR
letters: 3 STP
mishap: 7 SPINOUT
path: 4 OVAL
service area: 3 PIT
sponsor: 3 STP
stop: 3 PIT
The Unsers of: 3 ALS
**Indy 500:** *see pages* 714–715
1983 ~ winner: 5 SNEVA
1986 ~ winner: 5 RAHAL
and others: 5 RACES
area: 3 PIT
entrant: 3 CAR 5 RACER
Four-time ~ winner: 4 FOYT
5 UNSER
letters: 3 STP
sponsor: 3 STP
winner Luyendyk: 4 ARIE
**Inebriate:** 3 SOT
**Inebriated:** 3 LIT
**Inedible**
Become: 3 ROT
mushroom: 9 TOADSTOOL
orange: 5 OSAGE
**"I Need to Know"**
singer Anthony: 4 MARC
**Ineffective:** 4 VOID WEAK
6 OTIOSE
Make: 6 NEGATE
**Ineffectual:** 6 NOHELP
**Inefficiency**
Eliminate: 10 CLEANHOUSE
**Inept:** 4 POOR 6 GAUCHE
Less: 5 ABLER
Socially: 5 NERDY
soldier: 7 SADSACK
**Ineptitude**
Musical: 6 TINEAR
**Inert**
gas: 4 NEON 5 ARGON
RADON XENON
Some are: 5 GASES
**Ines, ___ Juana (Mexican poet):**
3 SOR
**"I never ___ man ...":** 4 META

**Inevitable: 4** SURE **5** FATED
  **8** FOREGONE
**Inexact**
  words: **4** ORSO
**Inexperienced: 3** NEW RAW
  **5** GREEN **6** CALLOW
**Infamy**
  Symbol of: **6** STIGMA
**Infant: 4** BABY
  Appaloosa: **4** FOAL
  food: **3** PAP
  illness: **5** COLIC
  word: **4** DADA
**Infantile**
  outburst: **3** WAH
**Infantry**
  campsite: **5** ETAPE
  group: **11** SHOCKTROOPS
**Infatuate: 5** BESOT
**Infatuated: 4** GAGA **7** SMITTEN
  with: **6** SOFTON
**Infatuation: 5** CRUSH
**Infected: 5** GERMY **6** SEPTIC
**Infection**
  fighter: **5** SULFA
  Kind of: **5** STAPH VIRAL
  site: **4** STYE
  suppressants: **4** SERA
**Infer: 5** EDUCE **6** DERIVE
  GATHER
**Inferior: 4** POOR **5** WORSE
  **6** CHEAPO CHEESY
  LESSER SHABBY
  in quality: **6** TRASHY
  liquor: **6** ROTGUT
**"Inferiority complex"**
  coiner Alfred: **5** ADLER
**Infernal: 6** NETHER
**"Inferno, The"**
  author: **5** DANTE
  First word of: **3** NEL
**Infest: 7** OVERRUN
**Infidel**
  in Islam: **5** KAFIR
**Infield**
  cover: **4** TARP
  Hit beyond the: **5** BLOOP
**Infielder**
  stat.: **3** DPS
**Infiltrator: 4** MOLE **5** PLANT
**In fine ___: 6** FETTLE
**Infinitesimal: 4** TINY
  amount: **4** IOTA
**Infinitive**
  French 101: **4** ETRE
  Latin I: **4** ESSE
**Inflame: 5** ANGER
**Inflamed: 3** LIT RED **5** ANGRY
  suffix: **4** ITIC
**Inflammation**
  Eyelid: **4** STYE
  Joint: **4** GOUT
**Inflammatory**
  suffix: **4** ITIS
**Inflatable**
  item: **3** EGO **4** RAFT

**Inflate: 3** PAD
**Inflated**
  It may be: **3** EGO
  Sell at an ~ price: **5** SCALP
**Inflation**
  Cause of: **3** AIR
  fighter:
    **15** PRICEREGULATION
  fighting WWII org.: **3** OPA
  meas.: **3** CPI PSI
  victim: **3** EGO
**Inflationary**
  path: **6** SPIRAL
**Inflection: 4** TONE
**Inflexibility: 5** RIGOR
**Inflexible: 4** IRON **5** RIGID
  **7** ADAMANT **8** CASTIRON
  OBDURATE
**Inflict: 5** WREAK
  upon: **4** DOTO
**In-flight**
  info: **3** ETA **4** ETAS
**Influence: 4** BIAS HEFT PULL
  SWAY **5** CLOUT COLOR
  JUICE **6** AFFECT
  Area of: **6** SPHERE
  Sphere of: **5** ORBIT REALM
  **6** DOMAIN
  Wield: **5** EXERT
**Influential**
  group: **5** ELITE
  Highly ~ and original:
    **7** SEMINAL
  individual: **5** NABOB
  member: **5** ELDER
  Org. with an ~ journal: **3** AMA
**Info: 4** DATA DOPE NEWS
  POOP STAT
  gathering: **5** RECON
  Inside: **3** TIP **4** DOPE POOP
**Infomercial**
  directive: **5** TRYIT **6** ACTNOW
  muscles: **3** ABS
**Infomercials: 3** ADS
  Big name in: **5** RONCO
  Popeil of: **3** RON
**Inform: 7** APPRISE
  (on): **3** RAT
**Informal**
  affirmative: **3** YEP YUP
  **4** YEAH
  bid: **5** ONENO
  chat: **10** RAPSESSION
  evening: **4** NITE
  goodbyes: **5** CIAOS
  greeting: **3** HEY **4** HIHO HIYA
  **5** HOWDY HULLO
  refusal: **4** NOPE
  shirt: **3** TEE
  sign-off: **3** LUV **5** LATER
  speech: **5** SLANG
  talk: **4** CHAT
**Information: 4** DATA DOPE
  bank: **8** DATABASE
  Bit of: **4** FACT **5** DATUM
  broker: **7** TIPSTER

  Fresh: **4** NEWS
  Kind of: **6** INSIDE
  medium: **5** CDROM
  One way to get: **5** DIALO
  Seek: **3** ASK
  unit: **4** BYTE
**Informative: 5** NEWSY
**Informed: 5** AWARE CLUED
  about: **4** UPON
  Better: **5** WISER
  of: **4** ONTO
**Informer: 3** RAT **6** CANARY
  **7** STOOLIE
  **11** STOOLPIGEON
**Infraction**
  Grid: **4** CLIP
  Hockey: **5** ICING
  Pinball: **4** TILT
**Infrequent: 4** RARE
**Infrequently: 6** SELDOM
**Infuriate: 3** IRE **4** RILE
  **5** ANGER **6** ENRAGE
  MADDEN
**Infuse: 5** STEEP
  with oxygen: **6** AERATE
**Inge**
  dog: **5** SHEBA
**Ingenious: 6** CLEVER
**Ingenuous: 5** NAIVE
  Least: **6** SLYEST
**Ingest: 3** EAT
**Ingle**
  glowers: **5** COALS
**Ingot: 3** BAR
**Ingrain: 4** ETCH
**Ingratiate: 6** ENDEAR
**Ingredient: 6** FACTOR
**Ingrid**
  Daughter of: **3** PIA
  role: **4** ILSA
**Inhabitant**
  suffix: **3** ITE
**Inhalation**
  Noisy: **5** SNORT
  of fright: **4** GASP
**Inhaler**
  target: **6** ASTHMA
**Inherent**
  quality: **6** NATURE
**Inherently: 5** PERSE
**Inheritance**
  factor: **4** GENE
  Genetic: **5** TRAIT
**Inherited: 3** GOT **8** CAMEINTO
  They're: **5** GENES
  wealth: **8** OLDMONEY
**Inheritors**
  Earth: **4** MEEK
**"Inherit the Wind"**
  star: **5** TRACY
**Inhibit: 5** CRIMP DETER
**Inhibited**
  Less: **5** FREER
**Iniquity: 3** SIN **4** EVIL VICE
  site: **3** DEN
**Initial: 4** OKAY

advantage: **7** TOEHOLD
chip: **4** ANTE
instruction: **7** STEPONE
stake: **4** ANTE
**Initialed: 3** OKD
**Initiated: 5** BEGAN
**Initiation: 5** ONSET
practice: **4** RITE
**Initiative**
Took the: **3** LED
**Injecting**
device: **4** HYPO
**Injection: 4** SHOT
fluids: **4** SERA
selection: **7** SYRINGE
**Injure: 3** MAR **4** HARM HURT
MAIM **5** WOUND
a knee: **4** SKIN
**Injured: 4** HURT
sneakily: **5** KNEED
Support for an ~ arm: **5** SLING
~, literally: **4** LESE
**Injuries**
Like some: **6** SPINAL
**Injury: 4** HARM
Muscle: **6** STRAIN
Psychological: **6** TRAUMA
sign: **4** SCAR
**Injustice: 5** WRONG
**Ink: 4** SIGN
Black ~ entry: **5** ASSET
Cuttlefish: **5** SEPIA
Kind of: **3** SOY **5** INDIA
Like a debtor's: **3** RED
Like some: **8** ERASABLE
Like wet: **6** SMEARY
Red: **4** DEBT
Red ~ amount: **4** LOSS
smear: **4** BLOT
sources: **6** OCTOPI
stain: **4** BLOT
~, in French: **5** ENCRE
**Ink-jet**
alternative: **5** LASER
**Inkless**
pen: **3** STY
**Inkling: 4** CLUE HINT IDEA
**5** GLINT
Have an: **5** SENSE
**Inks**
Chemical salt in some:
**7** TANNATE
**Inky**
mess: **4** BLOT
**Inlaid**
design: **6** MOSAIC
**Inland**
sea: **4** ARAL
**In ___ land: 4** LALA
**In-law: 6** AFFINE
Borgia: **4** ESTE
LBJ: **4** ROBB
Lennon: **3** ONO
Lincoln: **4** TODD
**Inlay**
material: **5** NACRE **6** NIELLO

**Inlet: 3** ARM RIA **4** COVE
**7** ESTUARY
Marshy: **5** BAYOU
Narrow: **3** RIA **5** FJORD
River: **3** RIA
Scottish: **5** FIRTH
Sheltered: **4** COVE
**In-line**
item: **5** SKATE
**Inmate: 3** CON
hope: **6** PAROLE
Long-term: **5** LIFER
**In medias ___: 3** RES
**"In memoriam"**
item: **4** OBIT
**Inn: 5** HOTEL **8** HOSTELRY
Arabian: **5** SERAI
French: **7** AUBERGE
Inexpensive: **6** HOSTEL
inventory: **4** ALES BEDS
Kind of: **5** BANDB
name: **6** RAMADA
Spanish: **6** POSADA
Turkish: **5** SERAI **6** IMARET
**Innards**
Virus: **3** RNA
Watch: **5** WORKS
**Inner**
circle: **4** LOOP **5** CADRE
city area: **6** BARRIO GHETTO
connection: **5** SINEW
drive: **4** URGE
ear: **3** COB
prefix: **3** ESO **4** ENDO ENTO
self: **5** ANIMA
tubes: **4** TORI
tube surrounder: **4** TIRE
turmoil: **5** ANGST
vision: **4** XRAY
**Inner Hebrides**
island: **4** IONA SKYE
**Innermost: 4** CORE
**Innie: 5** NAVEL
**Inning**
enders: **4** OUTS
Extra: **5** TENTH
half: **6** BOTTOM
Last ~, usually: **5** NINTH
Like a good ~ for a pitcher:
**5** NOHIT
trio: **3** ENS
**Innings**
Cause for extra: **3** TIE
Pitches between: **3** ADS
**Innisfree**
He celebrated: **5** YEATS
**Innkeeper: 8** HOSTELER
Italian: **4** OSTE **7** PADRONE
**Innocence**
Affected: **7** COYNESS
Epitome of: **4** LAMB
**Innocent: 4** BABE LAMB NAIF
**5** NAIVE **6** CHASTE
CHERUB
and others: **5** POPES
one: **4** BABE LAMB

Plead: **4** DENY
remark: **5** NOTME
**Innovative: 3** NEW
**Innsbruck**
is its capital: **5** TYROL
province: **5** TIROL
**Innuendo: 4** SLUR
**Inoculation**
fluids: **4** SERA
**In ___ of: 4** LIEU
**___ in on (near): 4** HOME
**Inoperative: 4** NOGO
**Inopportune: 8** ILLTIMED
**"In other words ...": 5** IMEAN
**In ___ parentis (legal doctrine):**
**4** LOCO
**"In principio ___ verbum":**
**4** ERAT
**Input: 5** ENTER
anew: **6** RETYPE
**7** REENTER
**Inquest: 6** ASSIZE
**Inquire: 3** ASK
**Inquiries**
Make: **9** ASKAROUND
**Inquiry: 5** PROBE
Judicial: **6** ASSIZE
Shipping: **6** TRACER
**Inquisition**
choker: **7** GARROTE
**Inquisitive: 4** NOSY
Be: **3** PRY
**Ins.**
choice: **3** HMO
**Insane: 3** MAD **8** DERANGED
**Inscribe: 4** ETCH
**Inscribed**
pillar: **5** STELA STELE
**Inscription**
Ancient: **4** RUNE
Calvary: **4** INRI
Crucifix: **4** INRI
Part of a cornerstone:
**4** ANNO
Statue: **8** EPIGRAPH
Tombstone: **3** RIP
Towel: **3** HIS **4** HERS
**Insect**
Adult: **5** IMAGO
Annoying: **4** GNAT
Colorful hill: **6** REDANT
Destructive: **5** BORER
**6** LOCUST
Domesticated: **3** BEE
egg: **3** NIT
feelers: **5** PALPS
Flying: **4** MOTH
form: **4** PUPA
Gnatlike: **5** MIDGE
Industrious: **3** ANT
midsection: **6** THORAX
nest: **4** NIDI
Nocturnal: **6** EARWIG
Noisy: **6** CICADA
Pesky: **4** GNAT
Praying: **6** MANTIS

repellent: 4 DEET
Sap-sucking: 5 APHID
Showy: 6 IOMOTH
Shrill: 6 CICADA
Slender-waisted: 4 WASP
Social: 3 ANT
stage: 4 PUPA 5 IMAGO
  LARVA
Stinging: 4 WASP 6 HORNET
Strong: 3 ANT
study (abbr.): 5 ENTOM
wings: 4 ALAE
with pincers: 6 EARWIG
**Insecticide**
  Banned: 3 DDT
  ingredient: 7 ARSENIC
**Insectivorous**
  insect: 6 MANTIS
**Insensitive**
  Isn't: 5 FEELS
  sort: 4 BOOR
**Inseparable:** 3 ONE
  He and his brother were:
    3 ENG
**Insert:** 3 ADD 5 PANEL
  mark: 5 CARET
**Insertion**
  mark: 5 CARET
**Inset:** 3 MAP
  site: 5 ATLAS
**Inside**
  diameter: 4 BORE
  Fit one ~ another: 4 NEST
  Go: 5 ENTER
  info: 3 TIP 4 DOPE POOP
  look: 4 XRAY 7 CATSCAN
  prefix: 4 ENDO
  scoop: 4 DIRT
  shot: 4 XRAY
  Turn ~ out: 5 EVERT
**"Inside Politics"**
  broadcaster: 3 CNN
**Insider**
  D.C.: 3 POL
  Espionage: 4 MOLE
  vocabulary: 5 ARGOT
**"Inside the Actors Studio"**
  network: 5 BRAVO
**"Inside the NFL"**
  network: 3 HBO
**"Inside the Third Reich"**
  author: 5 SPEER
**Insidious:** 3 SLY 4 EVIL
  sort: 5 SNAKE
**Insight:** 5 SENSE 6 ACUMEN
  Cry of: 3 AHA
  Mock phrase of: 4 AHSO
**Insightful:** 4 DEEP KEEN
    6 ASTUTE
**Insignia:** 6 EMBLEM
  1860 ~: 3 CSA
  Cardinal: 3 STL
  Colonel: 5 EAGLE
  Old cosmonaut: 4 CCCP
  site: 3 CAP
  Superman: 3 ESS

**Insignificant:** 4 MERE PUNY
    SLIM 5 DINKY MINOR
    SMALL 6 MEASLY
    TWOBIT 8 ONEHORSE
    13 SMALLPOTATOES
  amount: 3 SOU TAD 4 IOTA
    5 MINIM
  one: 4 SNIP TWIT 5 TWERP
**Insincere:** 4 OILY 5 PHONY
  talk: 4 CANT 10 LIPSERVICE
  Verbally: 4 GLIB
**Insinuate:** 5 GETAT
**Insinuating:** 5 SNIDE
**Insinuation:** 8 OVERTONE
**Insinuative**
  remark: 5 SNEER
**Insipid:** 4 BLAH 5 BLAND
    6 JEJUNE
**Insist**
  on: 6 DEMAND
  suffix: 3 ENT
**Insolence:** 3 LIP
**Insolent:** 5 SASSY SAUCY
**Insomnia**
  Evidence of: 7 REDEYES
  Royal ~ cause: 3 PEA
**"Insomnia"**
  star: 6 PACINO
**Insomniac**
  lack: 5 SLEEP
**Inspect**
  the figures: 4 OGLE
**Inspection:** 7 LOOKSEE
  Food ~ inits.: 4 USDA
  Kind of: 6 ONSITE
**Inspector:** 4 EYER
  employer (abbr.): 4 USDA
  Nectar: 3 BEE
**Inspiration:** 4 IDEA
  Have a sudden: 4 GASP
  Poet: 5 ERATO
  Source of: 4 MUSE
**Inspirational**
  phrase: 5 MOTTO
  talk (abbr.): 3 SER
**Inspire:** 4 FIRE 5 ELATE
    IMBUE 6 AROUSE
    PROMPT
  reverence: 3 AWE
**Inspired**
  It's: 3 AIR AWE
  poem: 3 ODE
  with love, old-style: 4 SMIT
**Inst.:** 4 ACAD
**Instability**
  Show: 4 YOYO
  Social: 6 ANOMIE
**Install**
  a door: 4 HANG
  a sidewalk: 4 PAVE
  carpeting: 3 LAY
  to new specs: 5 REFIT
  turf: 3 SOD
**Installation**
  Bath: 3 SPA
  Glazier: 4 PANE

**Installed:** 4 LAID
**Installer**
  Floor: 5 TILER
**Installment:** 7 EPISODE
**Instamatic**
  maker: 5 KODAK
**Instance:** 4 CASE
  For: 3 SAY
**Instant:** 3 SEC 5 FLASH JIFFY
    TRICE 6 MOMENT
  brand: 7 NESCAFE
  lawn: 3 SOD
  message sender: 5 AOLER
  replay format: 5 SLOMO
  This: 3 NOW
  ___ instant (quickly): 4 INAN
**Instant Message**
  sender: 5 AOLER
**Instead:**
    15 ASANALTERNATIVE
  of: 3 FOR 4 THAN
**Instinctive:** 3 GUT
  ability: 4 FEEL
**Instinctual**
  energy: 6 LIBIDO
**Institute**
  Brooklyn: 5 PRATT
  Educ.: 3 SCH
  MD: 4 USNA
**Institutes**
  Prestigious: 5 IVIES
**In ___ straits:** 4 DIRE
**Instruct:** 5 EDIFY TEACH
**Instruction**
  Cookbook: 4 STIR
  Dance: 4 STEP
  Dotted-line: 4 TEAR
  Initial: 7 STEPONE
  Rx: 3 TID
  to a boxer: 4 STAY
  Yoga: 6 EXHALE
**Instructions**
  Set of: 6 RECIPE
**Instructor**
  Dance ~ call: 4 STEP
  Drill ~ directive: 6 ATEASE
  Golf: 3 PRO
  Private: 5 TUTOR
**Instrument:** 5 AGENT
    7 UTENSIL
  Kind of: 4 REED
  Long-necked: 4 LUTE 5 SITAR
**Insulated**
  Poorly: 6 DRAFTY
**Insulating**
  tubing: 9 SPAGHETTI
**Insulation**
  material: 4 MICA
**Insulin:** 7 HORMONE
**Insult:** 4 BARB SLAM SLAP
    SLUR
  response: 6 INEVER
  Response to an: 4 SLAP
  ~, slangily: 3 DIS RIP 4 ZING
**Insulting:** 5 SNIDE
  look: 5 SNEER

remark: 4 SLUR
**Insurable**
  item: 4 AUTO
  It's: 4 LIFE
**Insurance**
  Aerialist's: 3 NET
  Big name in: 5 AETNA GEICO
    6 LLOYDS
  Case for an ~ detective:
    5 ARSON
  city: 8 HARTFORD
  company with a duck: 5 AFLAC
  concern: 7 METLIFE
  Flood: 3 ARK
  Kind of: 4 TERM 7 NOFAULT
  Med. ~ group: 3 HMO
  seller: 5 AGENT
  spokeslizard: 5 GECKO
  subject: 4 LOSS
  worker: 5 AGENT
**Insured**
  contribution: 5 COPAY
  report: 4 LOSS
**Insurer**
  calculation: 4 RISK
  delight: 7 LOWRISK
  Mortgage: 3 FHA
**Insurgent**: 5 REBEL
**Insurrectionist**: 5 REBEL
**Int.**
  disclosure: 3 APR
  They earn: 3 ODS
**Intaglio**
  opposite: 5 CAMEO
  stone: 4 ONYX
**Intake**
  Limited food: 4 DIET
  Quick: 4 GASP
  Small: 3 SIP
**Intangible**
  quality: 4 AURA
**Integer**
  Smallest positive: 3 ONE
**Integers**
  Half of the: 4 ODDS 5 EVENS
**Integra**
  maker: 5 ACURA
**Integrated**
  circuit: 9 MICROCHIP
  It may be: 7 CIRCUIT
**Intel**
  Grove of: 4 ANDY
**Intellect**: 4 MIND
**Intellectuals**: 8 LITERATI
**Intelligence**: 4 NEWS 5 SENSE
  Former ~ org.: 3 OSS
  Gather: 3 SPY
  Lively: 6 ESPRIT
  org.: 3 NSA
  test developer: 5 BINET
**Intelligent**: 5 SMART
  Unusually: 3 APT
**Intelligently**
  planned progress: 7 TELESIS
**Intelligentsia**: 8 LITERATI
**Intend**: 3 AIM 4 MEAN

**Intended**: 5 MEANT 6 FIANCE
    TARGET 7 FIANCEE
**Intense**: 4 AVID DEEP EDGY
    5 ACUTE 6 FIERCE
    RAGING
  Become more: 6 DEEPEN
  desire: 4 ITCH
  devotion: 5 ARDOR
  dislike: 5 ODIUM
  fear: 6 TERROR
  Make less: 4 BATE
  More: 7 FIERCER
  pain: 5 AGONY
  ~, as color: 5 VIVID
**Intensifier**
  Slangy: 3 OLA
**Intensify**: 6 DEEPEN HEATUP
    STEPUP 7 ENHANCE
**Intensity**: 4 ZEAL ZEST
    5 ARDOR 6 FERVOR
  Diminish in: 5 ABATE
  With: 5 HOTLY
**Intent**: 3 AIM 4 RAPT
  look: 4 GAZE 5 STARE
**Intention**: 3 AIM END 4 IDEA
    PLAN 6 DESIGN
**Intentional**
  grounding: 3 SOD
**Intentionally**
  lose: 5 THROW
**Intentions**
  Have good: 8 MEANWELL
**Intently**
  Look: 4 GAZE PEER
  Staring: 5 AGAZE
**Inter ___ (among others):**
    4 ALIA
**Intercom**
  speaker: 9 SQUAWKBOX
**Interdiction**: 3 BAN
**Interest**: 4 GRAB 5 STAKE
    8 APPEALTO
  Accumulate: 6 ACCRUE
  Arouse: 5 PIQUE
  Excessive: 5 USURY
  Field of: 4 AREA
  figure: 4 RATE
  Garner: 4 EARN
  group: 4 BLOC
  Item of: 4 LOAN
  Lose: 4 TIRE
  Lose ~ in: 6 TIREOF
  One of great: 6 USURER
    9 LOANSHARK
  Place of: 4 BANK
  Show ~ in: 8 ASKABOUT
  Showed: 5 SATUP
**Interested**
  Overly: 4 NOSY
**Interfere**: 6 MEDDLE
    TAMPER
  (with): 4 MESS
**Interference**: 6 STATIC
  TV: 4 SNOW
**Interim**
  ruling group: 5 JUNTA

**Interior**
  design: 5 DECOR
**Interior Secretary**
  1960s ~: 5 UDALL
  FDR: 5 ICKES
  Reagan: 4 WATT
**Interject**: 3 ADD
**Interjection**
  Brit: 4 ISAY
  German: 3 ACH
  Klutz: 4 OOPS
  of disapproval: 3 TUT
  Old-style: 3 FIE
  Psalms: 5 SELAH
  Triumphant: 4 TADA
**Interjections**
  Pirate: 3 ARS
  Questioning: 3 EHS
**Interlace**: 4 KNIT
**Interlaced**: 5 WOVEN
    6 TWINED
**Interlaken**
  river: 4 AARE
**Interlock**: 4 MESH
**Interlude**
  Romantic: 4 IDYL 5 IDYLL
**Intermediary**: 9 GOBETWEEN
**Interminable**: 7 ENDLESS
  time: 3 EON
**Interminably**: 5 NOEND
    ONEND
**Intermission**: 4 LULL
    8 ENTRACTE
  follower: 5 ACTII 6 ACTTWO
  preceder: 4 ACTI
**Intermissionless**: 6 ONEACT
**Intermittently**: 8 ONANDOFF
**Intern**: 4 AIDE
**Internalize**
  anger: 4 STEW
**International**
  accord: 7 ENTENTE
  agcy.: 6 UNESCO
  agreement: 6 ACCORD
    7 ENTENTE
  court site, with "The":
    5 HAGUE
  money: 4 EURO
  thaw: 7 DETENTE
  trade spot: 8 OPENPORT
  waters: 7 OPENSEA
**Internet**
  abbr.: 3 WWW
  auction site: 4 EBAY
  Big name on the: 3 AOL
  Browse the: 4 SURF
  Connected to the: 6 ONLINE
  connection need: 5 MODEM
  Drudge of the: 4 MATT
  explorer: 4 USER
  High-speed ~ inits.: 3 DSL
  initials: 4 HTTP
  letters: 3 AOL WWW
  marketing: 5 ETAIL
  messages: 5 EMAIL
  novice: 6 NEWBIE

Popular ~ company: 5 YAHOO
popups: 3 ADS
Profitable ~ business: 4 PORN
program language: 4 JAVA
Short ~ message: 5 ENOTE
**Internet address:** 3 URL
component: 3 DOT
ending: 3 COM EDU ORG
starter: 4 HTTP
**Internist**
org.: 3 AMA
**Interoffice**
note: 4 MEMO
**Interpret:** 4 READ 8 CONSTRUE
incorrectly: 7 MISREAD
**Interpretation:** 4 SPIN
Kind of: 5 LOOSE
**Interpreter**
Omen: 4 SEER
**Interrogate:** 3 ASK 4 PUMP
QUIZ 5 GRILL
after a mission: 7 DEBRIEF
**Interrogation**
Intense: 11 THIRDDEGREE
room excuse: 5 ALIBI
**Interrogative**
interjections: 3 EHS
**Interrupt:** 5 CUTIN
**Interrupter**
word: 4 AHEM
**Interruption:** 3 GAP 4 AHEM
5 BREAK LAPSE
6 HIATUS
cause: 5 PAGER
Doctor's: 4 PAGE
Follow without: 5 SEGUE
TV show: 9 NEWSFLASH
Without: 5 ONEND
**Interruptions**
TV show: 3 ADS
**Intersect:** 4 MEET 5 CROSS
**Intersection:** 4 NODE
sign: 4 STOP
Three-way: 3 TEE
**Interstate**
entrance: 4 RAMP
sight: 4 SEMI
sign: 3 GAS 4 EXIT
stop: 8 RESTAREA
**Interstate H1**
Where ~ is: 4 OAHU
**Interstellar**
cloud: 6 NEBULA
dist.: 4 LTYR
**Interstice:** 3 GAP 6 AREOLA
Anatomical: 6 AREOLE
**Intertwine:** 4 LACE MESH
5 WEAVE 6 ENLACE
**Interval:** 3 GAP LAG 4 SPAN
between cause and effect:
7 TIMELAG
Musical: 4 REST 5 NINTH
6 OCTAVE 7 TRITONE
**Intervene:** 6 STEPIN
**Intervening**
stretch: 8 MEANTIME

**Interview:** 3 ASK
format: 5 QANDA
wear: 4 SUIT
**Interviewer**
CNN: 9 LARRYKING
Emmy-winning: 5 FROST
**"Interview With the Vampire"**
author Rice: 4 ANNE
vampire: 6 LESTAT
**Interweave:** 4 KNIT MESH
5 BRAID 7 ENTWINE
**Intestinal**
bacteria: 5 ECOLI
parts: 4 ILEA
prefix: 6 ENTERO
**Intestine**
Of the small: 5 ILEAC
**"In that case ...":** 4 IFSO
THEN
**"___ in the bag":** 3 ITS
**"In the Bedroom"**
actress: 5 TOMEI
In the blink ___ eye: 4 OFAN
In the blink of ___ : 5 ANEYE
___ in the bucket: 5 ADROP
**"___ in the Dark":** 5 ASHOT
**"___ in the Family":** 3 ALL
**"In the Good Old Summertime"**
lyricist Shields: 3 REN
**"In the headlights"**
animal: 4 DEER
**"In the Heat of the Night"**
setting: 6 SPARTA
**"In the Land of Israel"**
author: 6 AMOSOZ
**"___! In the Name of Love":**
4 STOP
**Intimate:** 3 PAL 4 CHUM HINT
NEAR 5 BOSOM CLOSE
CRONY GETAT 6 HINTAT
**"Intimate ___, The":** 4 ELLA
**"Intimations of Immortality":**
3 ODE
**Intimidate:** 3 COW 5 DAUNT
DETER PSYCH
7 OVERAWE
**Intimidating:** 6 FEARED
**Into**
Is: 4 DIGS
___ into (attack): 3 LAY
**Intolerance**
Source of: 7 LACTOSE
**Intolerant**
one: 5 BIGOT
**Intone:** 5 CHANT
**Intoxicate:** 5 BESOT ELATE
**Intoxicating:** 5 HEADY
drink: 4 KAVA
**"___ in Toyland":** 5 BABES
**Intraoffice**
linkup (abbr.): 3 LAN
**Intrepid:** 4 BOLD 5 BRAVE
8 FEARLESS
**Intricate**
Cleverly: 6 DAEDAL
pattern: 3 WEB

**Intrigue:** 4 PLOT 5 CABAL
League of: 5 CABAL
**Intrigued**
by: 4 INTO
**Intrinsically:** 5 PERSE
**Intro:** 5 PROEM 6 LEADIN
OPENER PROLOG
Info: Prefix cue
maker: 5 EMCEE
NYSE: 3 IPO
**Introduce**
slowly: 7 PHASEIN
to the mix: 5 ADDIN
**Introduction:** 5 DEBUT PROEM
6 LEADIN
Info: Prefix cue
**Introductory**
material: 4 ABCS
**Introvert:** 5 LONER
**Intrude:** 6 HORNIN
upon: 6 INVADE
~, with "in": 4 BUTT
5 BARGE
**Intruder**
Garden: 4 WEED
Kitchen: 3 ANT
**Intrusive:** 4 NOSY
**Intrusively**
Greet: 6 ACCOST
**Intuit:** 5 SENSE
**Intuition:** 5 HUNCH SENSE
More than: 3 ESP
**Intuitive**
ability: 4 FEEL
**Intuitively**
Feel: 5 SENSE
**Inuit:** 6 ESKIMO
craft: 5 KAYAK UMIAK
kin: 5 ALEUT
transport: 4 SLED
**Inundate:** 5 DROWN SWAMP
6 DELUGE ENGULF
**Inundated:** 5 AWASH
**Inundation:** 5 SPATE
**Invader**
5th-century ~: 6 ATTILA
13th-century ~: 5 TATAR
Ancient: 4 GOTH
Mongol: 5 TATAR
of Gaul: 6 ATTILA
of Rome: 4 GOTH
Picnic: 3 ANT
Sci-fi: 7 MARTIAN
**Invalid:** 4 NULL
Make: 4 VOID 6 NEGATE
**Invalidate:** 5 ANNUL
**Invasion**
Roman ~ resister: 5 DRUID
site of 1944: 4 STLO
site of 1956: 5 SINAI
site of 1983: 7 GRENADA
**"Invasion of the Body**
**Snatchers"**
prop: 3 POD
**Inveigh**
against: 6 RAILAT

**Inveigle:** 4 COAX LURE
6 ENTICE
**Inveigled:** 5 LEDON
**Invent:** 4 COIN 6 CREATE
DEVISE 7 DREAMUP
**Invented**
word: 7 COINAGE
**Invention**
beginning: 4 IDEA
Bell: 5 PHONE
Franklin: 5 STOVE
Whitney: 9 COTTONGIN
**Inventions:** 4 FIBS LIES
Second name in: 4 ALVA
**Inventor**
cry: 3 AHA
document: 6 PATENT
goal: 15 BETTERMOUSETRAP
monogram: 3 TAE
start: 4 IDEA
**Inventory:** 5 STOCK 6 STORES
(abbr.): 4 MDSE
Bit of: 4 ITEM
syst.: 4 FIFO LIFO
**"In ___ veritas":** 4 VINO
**Inverness**
inhabitant: 4 SCOT
instrument: 7 BAGPIPE
Lake near: 4 NESS
**Invert:** 5 UPEND
a pencil: 5 ERASE
**Inverted**
e: 5 SCHWA
**Invest:** 5 ENDUE
**Investigate:** 5 DELVE PLUMB
PROBE 7 DIGINTO
8 LOOKINTO
again: 6 REOPEN
**Investigation:** 5 PROBE
Govt.: 3 INQ
**Investigative**
gp.: 4 HUAC
tool: 13 FINETOOTHCOMB
**Investigator:** 6 PROBER
Crack: 4 NARC
P.D.: 3 DET
question: 3 WHY
U.S. accident: 4 NTSB
~, briefly: 3 TEC
**Investing**
Online ~ service: 6 ETRADE
options: 3 CDS
**Investment:** 5 STAKE
Certain: 4 BOND 5 TNOTE
Govt.: 5 TBILL
option: 3 IRA
options: 3 CDS
Sound: 3 AMP 6 STEREO
**Investor**
goal: 6 RETURN
hope: 4 GAIN
mail-in: 5 PROXY
Online ~ company: 6 ETRADE
Org. that protects an: 3 SEC
**Invigorate**
the brass: 7 REPLATE

**Invigorating:** 5 BRISK CRISP
drink: 5 TONIC
place: 3 SPA
**Invincible**
Not: 8 BEATABLE
**Inviolate:** 6 SACRED
**Invisible:** 6 UNSEEN
emanation: 4 AURA
follower: 3 INK
It may be: 3 INK
troublemaker: 7 GREMLIN
**"Invisible Man"**
author: 7 ELLISON
**"Invisible Man, The"**
author: 5 WELLS
**Invitation**
Answer an: 4 RSVP 5 REPLY
Driver's: 5 HOPIN
Duel: 4 SLAP
heading: 5 WHERE
letters: 4 BYOB RSVP
Positive reply to an: 4 LETS
turndown: 7 REGRETS
**Invite:** 3 ASK
on a date: 6 ASKOUT
to a penthouse: 5 ASKUP
to enter: 5 ASKIN
to one's house: 7 ASKOVER
**Invited**
Not: 7 UNASKED
**Invitee:** 5 GUEST
**Invitees**
Most-wanted: 5 ALIST
**Inviting**
smell: 5 AROMA
**Invoice**
abbr.: 3 AMT
amount: 3 FEE
fig.: 3 AMT
phrase: 6 SHIPTO
stamp: 4 PAID
word: 3 DUE NET 5 REMIT
**Invoke**
Bad thing to: 3 IRE
**Involuntary**
contraction: 5 SPASM
muscle movement: 3 TIC
**Involve:** 6 ENTAIL 7 EMBROIL
**Involved:** 9 ELABORATE
Get: 6 STEPIN
with: 4 INON INTO
6 SEEING
**In ___ way:** 4 ABAD 5 HARMS
**"In what way?":** 5 HOWSO
**"In your dreams!":** 4 ASIF
5 NOWAY
10 NOTACHANCE
**Io:** 4 MOTH
Protector of: 5 ARGUS
**Iodine**
creator: 5 HATLO
source: 4 KELP 7 SEAWEED
**Iolani Palace**
locale: 4 OAHU
**Ion**
suffix: 3 IZE

**Iona College**
athlete: 4 GAEL
**Ione**
Actress: 4 SKYE
**Ionian Sea**
island: 5 CORFU
Sight from the: 4 ETNA
**Ionic**
alternative: 5 DORIC
**Ionized**
gas: 6 PLASMA
**Iota:** 3 TAD 4 WHIT 5 SPECK
TRACE
follower: 5 KAPPA
preceder: 5 THETA
**IOU:** 4 CHIT DEBT NOTE
6 MARKER
Part of: 3 OWE
**Iowa**
city: 4 AMES
college: 3 COE
college town: 4 AMES
commune: 5 AMANA
state tree: 3 OAK
**Iowa State**
location: 4 AMES
**Ipanema**
locale: 3 RIO
**"I pass":** 5 NOBET
**"Ipcress File, The"**
author Deighton: 3 LEN
**Ipecac:** 6 EMETIC
**iPod**
maker: 5 APPLE
**Ipse ___:** 5 DIXIT
**Ipso**
Meaning of: 6 ITSELF
**Ipso ___:** 5 FACTO
**IQ**
test name: 5 BINET
**Ira**
Author: 5 LEVIN
**IRA:** 7 NESTEGG
holder: 5 SAVER
increaser: 3 INT
legislation: 5 ERISA
Part of: 3 RET 4 ACCT 5 IRISH
renewal: 8 ROLLOVER
Tapping an: 3 RET
type: 3 SEP 4 ROTH
**Iran**
Adherent in: 5 BAHAI
capital: 6 TEHRAN
Coin of: 4 RIAL
Former name of: 6 PERSIA
Former ruler of: 4 SHAH
**Iran-Contra**
name: 5 NORTH
North of: 5 OLLIE
org.: 3 CIA NSC
**Iranian:** 5 ASIAN
Ancient: 4 MEDE
city: 3 QOM
coin: 4 RIAL
expanse:
15 GREATSALTDESERT

Former ~ leader: 4 SHAH
island: 6 ABADAN
language: 5 FARSI
money: 4 RIAL
mountain dweller: 4 KURD
**Iraq**
money: 5 DINAR
neighbor: 4 IRAN
port: 5 BASRA
resource: 3 OIL
**Iraqi:** 4 ARAB
Northern: 4 KURD
**Irascible:** 4 EDGY 5 TESTY
7 BRISTLY
**Irate:** 3 MAD 4 SORE 5 ABOIL
6 FUMING 7 TEEDOFF
**Ire:** 5 ANGER 6 SPLEEN
**Ireland:** 4 EIRE ERIN
11 EMERALDISLE
County of: 4 CORK 5 CLARE
DERRY
De Valera of: 5 EAMON
Island off: 4 ARAN
John, in: 4 SEAN
poetic name: 5 IRENA
Singer from: 4 ENYA
**"I Remember Mama"**
son: 4 NELS
**Irene**
Actress: 4 RYAN 5 DUNNE
PAPAS
Dike, Eunomia, and: 5 HORAE
She played: 5 RENEE
Singer: 4 CARA
**"I ___ return":** 5 SHALL
**Iridescent:** 7 OPALINE
gem: 4 OPAL
**Iris**
center: 5 PUPIL
covering: 6 CORNEA
locale: 3 EYE 4 UVEA
Part of the: 6 AREOLA
**Irises:** 8 GLADIOLI
**Irish**
accent: 6 BROGUE
Ancient ~ capital: 4 TARA
county: 5 CLARE KERRY
SLIGO 6 GALWAY
7 DONEGAL
dance: 3 JIG
dramatist: 5 SYNGE
flag color: 6 ORANGE
folk singer: 4 ENYA
Former ~ P.M. Cosgrove:
4 LIAM
hero: 5 STPAT
homeland: 4 EIRE
instrument: 4 HARP
Ireland, to the: 4 EIRE
islands: 4 ARAN
lass: 7 COLLEEN
lass name: 4 ERIN
lullaby start: 5 TOORA
moonshine: 6 POTEEN
nationalist Robert: 5 EMMET
native: 4 CELT

offshoot: 4 ERSE
Old ~ alphabet: 5 OGHAM
poet: 5 YEATS
port: 4 COBH CORK 5 DERRY
SLIGO 6 GALWAY TRALEE
republic: 4 EIRE
singer: 4 ENYA
tongue: 4 ERSE
wailing spirit: 7 BANSHEE
word on coins: 4 EIRE
~ Gaelic: 4 ERSE
**Irish ___:** 6 SETTER
**Irishman:** 4 CELT
**Irish Rose**
lover: 4 ABIE
**"___ Irish Rose":** 5 ABIES
**Irk:** 3 VEX 4 RILE 5 ANNOY
GETAT GETTO PEEVE
6 NEEDLE NETTLE
PESTER
More than: 4 GALL
**Irked:** 4 SORE
**"I, Robot"**
author: 6 ASIMOV
author Asimov: 5 ISAAC
**"I ___ Rock" (Simon and**
Garfunkel song): 3 AMA
**Iron:** 5 PRESS
alloy: 5 STEEL
and Ice: 4 AGES
Angle: 4 LBAR
clothes: 5 ARMOR
fishhook: 4 GAFF
Five: 6 MASHIE
In need of: 6 ANEMIC
Kind of: 3 PIG 4 NINE
Mark with a branding: 4 SEAR
One with ~ hands: 6 DESPOT
output: 5 STEAM
pigment: 5 OCHER
prefix: 5 FERRI FERRO
product: 6 WAFFLE
Refined: 5 STEEL
setting: 5 STEAM
Shooting: 6 SIXGUN
source: 3 ORE 5 LIVER
target: 6 ANEMIA CREASE
Use an: 5 PRESS
**Ironed:** 9 DECREASED
**Ironfisted:** 5 STERN
**Ironic:** 3 WRY
**"Ironic"**
singer Morissette: 6 ALANIS
**"Iron Mike":** 5 DITKA TYSON
**Iron-on:** 5 DECAL
**Iron-pumper**
muscles: 4 LATS PECS
5 DELTS
unit: 3 REP
**Irons:** 5 ACTOR
Actor: 6 JEREMY
**Irony:** 5 TROPE
**Iroquoian**
Indian: 4 ERIE 6 SENECA
language: 4 ERIE 6 ONEIDA
8 CHEROKEE

tribe: 6 ONEIDA
**Iroquois**
foe: 4 ERIE
tribe: 5 HURON 6 ONEIDA
SENECA
**Irrational:** 3 MAD 6 INSANE
fear: 6 PHOBIA
numbers: 5 SURDS
**Irreconcilables:** 8 DIEHARDS
**Irrefutable:** 4 SURE TRUE
**Irregular:** 5 EROSE
**Irregularly**
notched: 5 EROSE
**Irrelevant:** 4 MOOT
**Irreligious**
one: 5 PAGAN
**Irresistible**
It may be: 4 URGE
**Irreverence:** 7 IMPIETY
**Irreverent:** 4 FLIP
Coarsely: 6 RIBALD
**Irrigation**
aid: 5 CANAL
Needing: 4 ARID
**Irritable:** 4 EDGY 5 TESTY
6 TETCHY 7 PECKISH
**Irritably**
Speak ~ to: 6 SNAPAT
**Irritant**
Dog's: 4 FLEA
Major: 5 THORN
Royal: 3 PEA
**Irritate:** 3 IRK NAG VEX 4 GALL
MIFF RASP RILE ROIL
5 CHAFE EATAT GRATE
PIQUE 6 BOTHER
NETTLE PESTER
RANKLE TEEOFF
**Irritated**
state: 4 SNIT
**Irritation:** 5 PEEVE
Eye: 4 STYE
State of: 4 SNIT
**IRS**
check: 5 AUDIT
employee: 3 AGT CPA 4 TMAN
mo.: 3 APR
Percentage for the: 7 TAXRATE
review (abbr.): 3 AUD
~ ID: 3 SSN
**IRT**
and BMT partner: 3 IND
**Irvin**
Illustrator: 3 REA
**Irving**
Actress: 3 AMY
hero: 3 RIP 4 GARP 6 TSGARP
Talent agent: 5 LAZAR
**Irving, John**
character: 4 GARP 6 TSGARP
**Irwin**
Actor: 3 STU
Golfer: 4 HALE
**Is:** 6 EXISTS
for two: 3 ARE
in the past: 3 WAS

no longer: 3 WAS
without: 6 HASNOT
~, in Spanish: 4 ESTA
"Is ___?": Matt. 26:22: 3 ITI
**Isaac**
Eldest son of: 4 ESAU
Mother of: 5 SARAH
Sci-fi writer: 6 ASIMOV
Singer/actor: 5 HAYES
Violinist: 5 STERN
**Isabel II:** 5 REINA
**Isabella:** 5 REINA
**Isabella d'___:** 4 ESTE
**Isaiah:** 7 PROPHET
**Isak**
Real first name of: 5 KAREN
**I Samuel**
priest: 3 ELI
"___ is an island": 5 NOMAN
**Isao**
Golfer: 4 AOKI
"___ is as good as a wink":
4 ANOD
"___ is a terrible thing ...":
5 AMIND
"... ___ I saw Elba": 3 ERE
"I saw ___ sawing wood ...":
4 ESAU
"I say!"
sayer: 4 BRIT CHAP
"___ I say!": 4 DOAS
"___ I say more?": 4 NEED
**ISBN**
Part of: 4 INTL
"___ Is Born": 5 ASTAR
"I see!": 3 AHA OHO
~, facetiously: 4 AHSO
"I see it now!": 3 AHA
"... is fear ___": FDR:
6 ITSELF
**Isherwood**
collaborator: 5 AUDEN
7 WHAUDEN
**Ishmael**
Captain of: 4 AHAB
One of ~'s people: 4 ARAB
"I Shot Andy Warhol"
star Taylor: 4 LILI
"Ishtar"
director: 9 ELAINEMAY
extras: 6 CAMELS
"___ is human ...": 5 TOERR
**Isidor**
Physics Nobelist: 4 RABI
**Isinglass:** 4 MICA
**Isis**
Brother of: 6 OSIRIS
"Is it soup ___?": 3 YET
**Islam**
(abbr.): 3 REL
follower: 3 ITE 5 SUNNI
God of: 5 ALLAH
holy city: 5 MECCA
One of the Pillars of: 4 HADJ
**Islamabad**
country: 8 PAKISTAN

**Islamic**
chief: 4 EMIR
crusade: 5 JIHAD
decree: 5 FATWA
deity: 5 ALLAH
holy war: 5 JIHAD
leader: 4 EMIR IMAM
5 AMEER
republic: 4 IRAN
spirit: 5 DJINN
text: 5 KORAN
title: 4 EMIR
**Island**
accompaniment: 3 UKE
Adriatic: 4 LIDO
Aegean: 5 SAMOS
Alaskan: 4 ATTU 6 KODIAK
Aleutian: 4 ADAK ATKA ATTU
Atlantic ~ group: 6 AZORES
attire: 6 SARONG
Bering Sea: 4 ATTU
Big ~ port: 4 HILO
Caribbean: 5 ARUBA
chain: 3 LEI
Chinese: 6 TAIWAN
Coral: 5 ATOLL
dance: 4 HULA
dish: 3 POI
East China Sea: 5 MATSU
east of Java: 4 BALI
Exile: 4 ELBA
feast: 4 LUAU
Firth of Clyde: 5 ARRAN
Florida: 7 SANIBEL
Greek: 5 CRETE SAMOS
6 LESBOS
greeting: 5 ALOHA
group near Fiji: 5 SAMOA
Hawaiian: 4 MAUI OAHU
5 LANAI 7 MOLOKAI
Hebrides: 4 IONA SKYE
Immigration: 5 ELLIS
in a computer game: 4 MYST
Indonesian: 4 BALI JAVA
5 CERAM TIMOR
6 BORNEO
Italian: 4 LIDO
Japanese: 6 HONSHU
7 OKINAWA
Largest Mediterranean:
6 SICILY
Low: 3 CAY
Mediterranean: 5 MALTA
More: 6 UTOPIA
New York: 5 CONEY ELLIS
6 STATEN
of Brooklyn: 5 CONEY
Philippine: 4 CEBU 5 LEYTE
LUZON PANAY SAMAR
ring: 3 LEI
River: 3 AIT
South Pacific: 5 SAMOA
6 EASTER TAHITI
8 BORABORA
strings: 3 UKE
U.S. Pacific: 4 GUAM

welcome: 3 LEI
West Indies: 5 ARUBA
WWII: 5 LEYTE
~, in French: 3 ILE
___ Island: 5 ELLIS RHODE
6 STATEN
~, Florida: 5 MARCO
**Islander**
Alaskan: 5 ALEUT
Pacific: 6 SAMOAN
**Islanders**
org.: 3 NHL
"Island of the Blue Dolphins"
author: 5 ODELL
"Island of the Day Before, The"
author Umberto: 3 ECO
___ Island Red: 5 RHODE
___ Islands: 6 BAHAMA BIMINI
"___ Island With You": 4 ONAN
**Isle of ___:** 5 WIGHT
**Isle of Man**
man: 4 GAEL
**Islet:** 3 AIT CAY
**Ism:** 5 DOGMA TENET
"___ is me!": 3 WOE
"I smell ___!": 4 ARAT
"Isn't ___ bit like you and me?":
3 HEA
**Iso-**
Relative of: 4 EQUI
**Isolate:** 5 ICEIN 6 ENISLE
8 SETAPART
**Isolated:** 4 LONE 5 ALONE
APART STRAY
8 ALLALONE
district: 7 ENCLAVE
hill: 5 BUTTE
**Isolde**
Love of: 7 TRISTAN
"I ___ Song Go Out of My
Heart": 4 LETA
**Isotope**
Radioactive: 6 IONIUM
**ISP**
Popular: 3 AOL
"I Spy"
costar Bill: 5 COSBY
costar Robert: 4 CULP
**Isr.**
neighbor: 3 LEB SYR
**Israel**
Abba of: 4 EBAN
Airline to: 4 ELAL
American Revolutionary
general: 6 PUTNAM
Ariel of: 6 SHARON
Bank ___ of: 5 LEUMI
Barak of: 4 EHUD
carrier to Seoul: 4 ELAL
Dayan of: 5 MOSHE
Eban of: 4 ABBA
First king of: 4 SAUL
Follower of: 3 ITE
Golda of: 4 MEIR
Gun designed in: 3 UZI
legislature: 7 KNESSET

Meir of: 5 GOLDA
Moshe of: 5 ARENS
neighbor: 5 SYRIA
Port of: 4 ACRE ELAT 5 EILAT
  HAIFA
Sharon of: 5 ARIEL
Shimon of: 5 PERES
suffix: 3 ITE
Tribe of: 3 DAN 5 ASHER
Weizman of: 4 EZER
**Israeli: 5 SABRA 6 SEMITE**
airline: 4 ELAL
airport: 3 LOD
author Oz: 4 AMOS
carrier: 4 ELAL
city: 5 HAIFA
dance: 4 HORA
desert: 5 NEGEV
Former ~ P.M.: 4 MEIR
  5 PERES RABIN
gun: 3 UZI
money: 6 SHEKEL
native: 5 SABRA
political party: 5 LIKUD
port: 4 ACRE ELAT 5 EILAT
  HAIFA
resort: 4 ELAT 5 EILAT
statesman Abba: 4 EBAN
statesman Dayan: 5 MOSHE
statesman Weizman: 4 EZER
weapon: 3 UZI
**"Is so!"**
rebuttal: 4 AINT
**Issue: 4 EMIT 5 SCION TOPIC**
  **6 EMERGE 7 EMANATE**
  **RELEASE**
a summons to: 4 CITE
Became an: 5 AROSE
Burning: 3 ASH
Business: 3 INC
Campaign: 4 JOBS
Fashion: 4 ELLE
forth: 4 EMIT
For the ~ price: 5 ATPAR
Government: 5 TNOTE
Hot: 4 LAVA
Labor: 5 CHILD
New: 3 IPO
Newspaper: 7 EDITION
One side of an: 3 CON
Royal: 6 PRINCE
**Issues**
Agree to more: 5 RENEW
How some ~ are debated:
  5 HOTLY
**Istanbul**
inn: 6 IMARET
native: 4 TURK
region: 6 THRACE
title: 3 AGA
**"Is that ___?": 3 ANO 5 AFACT**
**"Is that a fact!": 6 DOTELL**
**"Is That All There Is"**
singer: 8 PEGGYLEE
**"Is that so?": 3 GEE 6 DOTELL**
  **REALLY**

**"Is this a dagger which ___ ...":**
  **Macbeth: 4 ISEE**
**Isthmus**
Malay: 3 KRA
splitter: 5 CANAL
**"I Still See ___" ("Paint Your**
  **Wagon" tune): 5 ELISA**
**Isuzu**
model: 5 RODEO
**"I swear!": 5 NOLIE 6 HONEST**
**"Is Your Mama a ___?" (kids'**
  **book): 5 LLAMA**
**It**
game: 3 TAG
Like: 6 NEUTER
They may have: 4 AYES
~, in Italian: 4 ESSA ESSO
**It.**
is there: 3 EUR
It borders: 3 AUS
peak: 6 MTETNA
**"It ___": 3 ISI**
**"___ it!" ("Amen!"): 4 SOBE**
**"It ain't over till it's over"**
speaker: 5 BERRA
**Italia**
Capital of: 4 ROMA
city: 6 TORINO
seaport: 6 NAPOLI
**Italian: 6 ETHNIC**
alternative: 5 RANCH
Ancient: 6 SABINE
  8 ETRUSCAN
aperitif: 7 CAMPARI
article: 3 UNA
artist: 4 RENI
art patron: 4 ESTE
author: 3 ECO
auto: 4 ALFA FIAT
beach resort: 4 LIDO
brandy: 6 GRAPPA
bread: 4 LIRA LIRE
bridge: 5 PONTE
bubbly source: 4 ASTI
cheese: 6 ROMANO
  7 RICOTTA 8 PARMESAN
city: 4 ESTE PISA 5 CUNEO
  MILAN TURIN UDINE
  7 TARANTO
dessert: 3 ICE
dish: 5 PASTA
Fictional ~ town: 5 ADANO
Former ~ money: 4 LIRA LIRE
Former ~ P.M.: 4 MORO
holiday: 5 FESTA
hot spot: 4 ETNA
ice alternative: 7 SNOCONE
ice cream: 6 GELATI GELATO
innkeeper: 4 OSTE
  7 PADRONE
island resort: 4 LIDO
isle: 5 CAPRI
lady: 5 DONNA
lawn game: 5 BOCCI
love: 5 AMORE
loved one: 4 CARA

money: 4 LIRA LIRE
monk: 3 FRA
noble family: 4 ESTE
number: 3 TRE UNO
peak: 4 ETNA
poet: 5 TASSO
port: 4 BARI 5 GENOA
  6 NAPLES 7 SALERNO
  TRIESTE
possessive: 3 MIO
prime minister Aldo: 4 MORO
pronoun: 3 MIA
province: 4 ASTI 5 SIENA
  UDINE 7 SALERNO
resort: 4 LIDO
resort lake: 4 COMO
rice dish: 7 RISOTTO
river: 4 ARNO
sauce: 5 PESTO
sculptor: 6 PISANO
smoker: 4 ETNA
sonnet end: 6 SESTET
soup ingredient: 4 ORZO
staple: 5 PASTA
Stuffed ~ pockets: 7 RAVIOLI
term of endearment:
  7 CARAMIA
town: 6 ASSISI
treat: 3 ICE
trio: 3 TRE
volcano: 4 ETNA
white: 5 SOAVE
wine: 4 VINO 5 SOAVE
  7 MARSALA
wine region: 4 ASTI
**Italics**
Like: 6 ASLANT
What ~ do: 5 SLANT
**"It ___ All Velvet": 5 WASNT**
**Italy**
Alpine region of: 5 TIROL
Former denomination in:
  7 ONELIRA
Largest lake of: 5 GARDA
Moro of: 4 ALDO
Part of: 3 TOE
shape: 4 BOOT
Wine region of: 4 ASTI
**"___ It a Pity?": 4 ISNT**
**Itar-___: 4 TASS**
**"___ it a shame!": 4 ISNT**
**"I tawt I taw a puddy ___!":**
  3 TAT
**"It ___ Be You": 5 HADTO**
**"It can't be!": 4 OHNO**
**Itch: 3 YEN 4 URGE**
**Itchy: 5 EAGER 8 PRURIENT**
**Item: 7 ARTICLE**
of interest: 4 LOAN
of value: 5 ASSET
The ~ here: 4 THIS
**Itemize: 4 LIST**
**Iterate: 5 RESAY 6 RETELL**
**"___ It Goes": 5 ANDSO**
**"It Had to ___": 5 BEYOU**
**"It Had to Be ___": 3 YOU**

"It Had to Be You"
  composer Jones: 5 ISHAM
  lyricist Gus: 4 KAHN
"It Happened One Night"
  director: 5 CAPRA
  producer: 4 COHN
"I thought we ___ deal!":
    4 HADA
"I thought we had ___!":
    5 ADEAL
Itinerant: 5 NOMAD
  Be: 4 ROVE
Itinerary: 5 ROUTE
  abbr.: 3 ARR RTE
  Concert: 4 TOUR
  info: 4 ETAS
  word: 3 VIA
"It is rumored ...": 7 SOMESAY
"It is ___ told by an idiot ...":
    5 ATALE
"It Must Be ___": 3 HIM
"It must be him, ___ shall die":
    3 ORI
"It Must Be Him" singer:
    4 CARR
"It must have been
    something ___!": 4 IATE
"It must have been
    something I ___!": 3 ATE
"___ it my best": 5 IGAVE
"It ___ Necessarily So": 4 AINT
"I told you so!": 3 IIAH SEE
    5 THERE
  Word before: 3 SEE
"___ it or lose it": 3 USE
  ___ it over (dominated):
    6 LORDED
"___ It Romantic?": 4 ISNT
Its
  ~, in French: 3 SES
"It's ___!": 4 ABOY 5 ADATE
    ADEAL AGIRL ASNAP
"It's ___ ...": 4 AGAS
"It's about time!": 6 ATLAST
"It's a deal!": 4 DONE OKAY
"It's all ___": 5 ANACT
"It's all clear now": 4 ISEE
"It's Alright" singer: 3 ONO
"It's a ___ situation!": 5 NOWIN
"It's ___ a while": 4 BEEN
"It's a Wonderful Life"
  angel: 8 CLARENCE
  cabdriver: 5 ERNIE
  director Frank: 5 CAPRA
"It's been ___ pleasure":
    5 AREAL
"It's ___ big mistake!": 4 ALLA
"It's c-c-c-cold!": 3 BRR
"It's ___ country!": 5 AFREE
Itself
  By: 5 PERSE
  In: 5 PERSE 6 ASSUCH
  ~, in Latin: 4 IPSA

"It's ___ ever wanted": 4 ALLI
"It's ___ in the right direction":
    5 ASTEP
"It slices, it ___ ...": 5 DICES
"It's ___ Love": 4 YOUI
"It's My Party"
  singer: 4 GORE
"It's no ___!": 3 USE
"It's not gonna happen":
    4 NOPE
"It's only ___!": 5 AGAME
"It's on me!": 7 MYTREAT
"It's ___ real!": 4 BEEN
"It's rumored ...": 7 SOMESAY
"It's the end of ___": 5 ANERA
"It's the truth!": 5 NOLIE
"It's Too Late Now"
  autobiographer: 7 AAMILNE
"It's ___ to tell ...": 4 ASIN
"It's true!": 5 NOLIE
"It's ___ vu all over again!":
    4 DEJA
"It's ___-win situation": 3 ANO
"It's ___ world": 5 AMANS
"It's worth ___": 4 ATRY
    5 ASHOT
Itsy-___: 5 BITSY
Itsy-bitsy: 3 WEE 4 TINY
    5 TEENY 6 TEENSY
  biter: 4 GNAT MITE
  bits: 4 ATOMS
ITT
  Part of: 3 TEL
"It takes two"
  dance: 5 TANGO
"___ it the truth!": 4 AINT
Itty-___: 5 BITTY
Itty-bitty: 3 WEE 4 TINY
    5 TEENY 6 TEENSY
  bit: 4 IOTA
  bug: 4 MITE
"It Walks by Night" author:
    4 CARR
"It was ___ and ...": 5 ADARK
"It was ___ mistake!": 4 ALLA
"It was the ___ I could do":
    5 LEAST
"I understand": 4 AHSO
    5 GOTIT ROGER
IV
  givers: 3 RNS
  measurements: 3 CCS
  part: 5 INTRA
  place: 3 ICU
  sites: 3 ORS
"I ___ vacation!": 5 NEEDA
Ivan: 4 TSAR
  of tennis: 5 LENDL
Ivana
  and Donald: 4 EXES
"Ivanhoe"
  author: 5 SCOTT
  love: 6 ROWENA

  weapon: 5 LANCE
Ivan the Terrible: 4 TSAR
"I vant to be alone"
  actress: 5 GARBO
"I've been ___!": 3 HAD
"I've been framed!": 7 ITSALIE
"I've Got ___ in Kalamazoo":
    4 AGAL
"I've got it!": 3 AHA
"I've got my ___ you!":
    5 EYEON
"I've Gotta ___": 4 BEME
"I've ___ had!": 4 BEEN
Ives
  Oscar-winner: 4 BURL
  Singer: 4 BURL
"I've ___ up to here!": 5 HADIT
Ivey, Artis
  Rapper born: 6 COOLIO
Ivied
  alcove: 5 ARBOR
  Student inside ~ walls: 3 ELI
Ivies
  One of the: 4 PENN YALE
Ivins, Molly
  Presidential bio by: 5 SHRUB
Ivories: 4 KEYS
  place: 5 PIANO
  Tickle the: 4 PLAY
Ivory
  product: 4 SOAP
  rival: 4 DIAL 5 CAMAY
  source: 4 TUSK
  tower setting. 8 ACADEMIA
Ivory Coast
  neighbor: 4 MALI
Ivy
  feature: 4 VINE 7 TENDRIL
Ivy League
  city: 6 ITHACA
  school: 4 PENN YALE
    5 BROWN
  team: 4 ELIS PENN
Ivy Leaguer: 3 ELI 5 YALIE
I.W.
  Labor leader: 4 ABEL
"I ___ Walrus": 5 AMTHE
"I wanna!": 5 LEMME
"I want it!": 5 GIMME
"I was elsewhere"
  excuse: 5 ALIBI
"___ I Went Mad": 3 ERE
"I will sing ___ the Lord ...":
    Exodus: 4 UNTO
"I Will Survive"
  singer Gloria: 6 GAYNOR
Iwo ___: 4 JIMA
"I wouldn't send ___ out ...":
    4 ADOG
"I would rather not": 3 NAH
"Ixnay!": 6 NODICE
Izmir
  native: 4 TURK

# J

**J**
topper: 3 DOT
**Ja**
Opposite of: 4 NEIN
~, across the Rhine: 3 OUI
**Jab:** 4 POKE PROD
Many a: 4 LEFT
**Jabba**
prisoner: 4 LEIA
___-Jabbar, Kareem: 5 ABDUL
**Jabba the ___:** 4 HUTT
**Jabber:** 3 GAS JAW YAK YAP
5 PRATE
**"Jabberwocky"**
opener: 4 TWAS
Slithy ~ thing: 4 TOVE
**Jabs**
Trade: 4 SPAR
**"J'accuse"**
author: 4 ZOLA
author Zola: 5 EMILE
___ Jacinto: 3 SAN
**Jack:** 4 CARD 5 KNAVE
6 MOOLAH SEAMAN
Actor: 3 SOO 4 ELAM WEBB
5 BENNY OAKIE
6 LEMMON 7 PALANCE
9 ALBERTSON
NICHOLSON
and the missus: 6 SPRATS
Author: 7 KEROUAC
Boxer: 7 DEMPSEY
Clancy hero: 4 RYAN
Golfer: 8 NICKLAUS
inferior: 3 TEN
Like: 6 NIMBLE
of nursery rhyme: 5 SPRAT
of politics and football:
4 KEMP
partner: 4 JILL
predecessor: 3 IKE
TV host: 4 PAAR
___ Jack: 5 UNION
**Jackal:** 5 CANID
**Jack and Jill**
vessel: 4 PAIL
**Jacket:** 4 COAT 5 PARKA
6 BLAZER
1960s-style ~: 5 NEHRU
Arctic: 6 ANORAK
buildup: 4 LINT
fabric: 5 SUEDE TWEED
feature: 3 ARM 4 SNAP VENT
5 LAPEL 6 SLEEVE
8 COATTAIL
Kind of: 3 MAO 4 ETON FLAK
5 NEHRU
partner: 3 TIE

Police ~ letters: 4 SWAT
Short: 6 BOLERO
**Jackie**
Actor: 4 CHAN 7 GLEASON
Designer for: 4 OLEG
predecessor: 5 MAMIE
Sister of: 3 LEE
**"Jackie Brown"**
star: 5 GRIER
**"Jackie Gleason Show, The"**
network: 3 CBS
**Jackie O**
Husband of: 3 ARI
**"Jackie Robinson Story, The"**
actress: 7 RUBYDEE
**Jack-in-the-pulpit:** 4 ARUM
**Jackknife:** 4 DIVE
It may: 4 SEMI
**Jack-o'-lantern**
feature: 4 GRIN
**Jackpot**
game: 5 LOTTO
Hit the: 12 STRIKEITRICH
**Jacks:** 7 OPENERS
**Jackson**
Actress: 4 KATE 6 GLENDA
Country singer: 4 ALAN
Gospel singer: 7 MAHALIA
Jazzman: 4 MILT
NBA coach: 4 PHIL
Reverend: 5 JESSE
Singer: 5 JANET 6 BROWNE
LATOYA 7 MICHAEL
**Jackson, Jesse**
intro: 3 REV
**Jackson 5**
hairdo: 4 AFRO
hit song: 3 ABC
member: 4 TITO
**Jackson County, Texas**
seat: 4 EDNA
**Jackson Hole**
backdrop: 6 TETONS
beast: 3 ELK
**Jack-tar:** 3 GOB 6 SAILOR
SEAMAN
**Jaclyn**
TV angel: 5 SMITH
**Jacob**
Author: 4 RIIS
Father of: 5 ISAAC
Furrier: 5 ASTOR
Magnate: 5 ASTOR
Reformer: 4 RIIS
Son of: 4 LEVI 5 ASHER
Twin brother of: 4 ESAU
Wife of: 4 LEAH 6 RACHEL
~, to Esau: 4 TWIN

**Jacobi**
Actor: 5 DEREK
**Jacobin**
leader: 5 MARAT
**Jacob ___ Park:** 4 RIIS
**Jacqueline**
Actress: 6 BISSET
Author: 6 SUSANN
**Jacques:** 3 NOM
Actor: 4 TATI
Composer: 4 BREL 5 IBERT
Director: 4 TATI
French president: 6 CHIRAC
___ Jacques: 5 FRERE
**Jacuzzi:** 3 SPA
effect: 4 EDDY
feature: 3 JET
product: 6 HOTTUB
**Jaffe**
Author: 4 RONA
**Jag:** 5 SPREE
Classic: 3 XKE
rival: 3 BMW
**"JAG"**
network: 3 CBS
**Jagged:** 5 EROSE
6 UNEVEN
**Jagger**
and mates: 6 STONES
Ex of: 6 BIANCA
Rock star: 4 MICK
**Jaguar:** 3 CAR 4 AUTO
6 FELINE
Classic: 3 XKE
**Jahan:** 4 SHAH
city: 5 DELHI
tomb site: 4 AGRA
**Jai ___:** 4 ALAI
**Jai alai**
ball: 6 PELOTA
basket: 5 CESTA
locale: 7 FRONTON
**Jail:** 3 CAN 6 PRISON
feature: 7 IRONBAR
key: 9 CANOPENER
Navy: 4 BRIG
Out of: 4 FREE
Take to: 5 RUNIN
___ jail: 4 GOTO
**Jailbird:** 3 CON 6 INMATE
**Jailbreak:** 6 ESCAPE
participant: 7 ESCAPEE
**Jaipur**
City east of: 4 AGRA
**Jakarta**
island: 4 JAVA
**Jake:** 3 AOK
TV partner of: 6 FATMAN

**"Jake's Thing"**
  author: 4 AMIS
**Jalapeno:** 6 PEPPER
  Like a: 3 HOT
**Jalopy:** 4 HEAP 5 CRATE
    WRECK
**Jalousie**
  part: 4 SLAT
**Jam:** 3 FIX 4 CRAM MESS
    5 SNARL TIEUP
    6 SCRAPE
  ingredient: 3 CAR 4 AUTO
  Popular ~ band: 5 PHISH
  up: 4 CLOG
  Word with: 3 LOG
**Jamaica**
  gent: 3 MON
**"Jamaica ___":** 3 INN
**Jamaican**
  Certain: 5 RASTA
  export: 3 RUM
  fruit: 4 UGLI
  music: 3 SKA 6 REGGAE
**Jamb**
  insert: 4 DOOR
**Jambalaya**
  ingredient: 4 RICE
  Like: 6 CREOLE
**Jamboree**
  gp.: 3 BSA
  sight: 4 TENT
**James**
  Actor: 4 CAAN COCO
    5 WOODS 6 ARNESS
    SPADER
  Astronaut: 5 IRWIN
  Author: 4 AGEE 5 JOYCE
  Bk. before: 3 HEB
  Lyricist: 4 RADO
  Magician: 5 RANDI
  of the Met: 6 LEVINE
  Outlaw: 5 JESSE
  Revolutionary orator: 4 OTIS
  Singer: 4 ETTA
  Spy: 4 BOND
**"James and the Giant Peach"**
  author: 4 DAHL
**James II**
  Daughter of: 4 ANNE
**"James Joyce"**
  Author Leon: 4 EDEL
**Jamestown**
  John of: 5 ROLFE
**James Whitcomb ___**
  Poet: 5 RILEY
**Jamie**
  Actor: 4 FARR
**Jammies:** 3 PJS
**Jam-pack:** 4 CRAM
**Jan**
  Painter: 5 STEEN
**Jan.**
  honoree: 3 MLK
  preceder: 3 DEC
**Jan. 1**
  to now: 3 YTD

**Jan. 1, 1994**
  Act of: 5 NAFTA
**Janacek**
  Composer: 4 LEOS
**Jane**
  Actress: 5 FONDA
  Brother of: 5 PETER
  Dog of: 4 SPOT
  Fictional: 4 EYRE
  Lady: 4 GREY
**Jane ___:** 3 DOE
**"Jane ___":** 4 EYRE
**"Jane Eyre":** 7 HEROINE
  pupil: 5 ADELE
**Janeiro**
  starts it: 3 ANO
**___ Janeiro:** 5 RIODE
**Janet**
  Actress: 5 LEIGH
  Attorney General: 4 RENO
  Film critic: 6 MASLIN
  Olympic swimmer:
    5 EVANS
  ~, to Michael: 3 SIB SIS
**Janeway**
  Economist: 5 ELIOT
**Jangler:** 5 ALARM
**Janis**
  Actress: 5 PAIGE
  Comic strip mate of: 4 ARLO
  Old comic actress: 5 ELSIE
  Singer: 3 IAN
**Janitor**
  tool: 3 MOP
**Jann**
  Rolling Stone founder:
    6 WENNER
**Jannings**
  Actor: 4 EMIL
**Janowitz**
  Author: 4 TAMA
**January**
  Big game in: 8 ROSEBOWL
  birthstone: 6 GARNET
  popper: 4 CORK
  song word: 4 AULD SYNE
  warm spell: 4 THAW
  ~, in Spanish: 5 ENERO
**January 13th:** 4 IDES
**Japan:** 7 FAREAST
  capital: 5 TOKYO
  city: 5 OSAKA OTARU
  ending: 3 ESE
  Former capital of: 3 EDO
    4 NARA 5 KYOTO
  Highest peak of: 4 FUJI
  island: 6 HONSHU
    7 OKINAWA
  legislature: 4 DIET
**Japanese:** 5 ASIAN
    9 EASTASIAN
  airline: 3 ANA
  art form: 7 ORIGAMI
  assassin: 5 NINJA
  band: 3 OBI
  Beatle: 3 ONO

  beer: 5 ASAHI KIRIN
    7 SAPPORO
  capital: 3 YEN
  car: 5 MIATA
  carp: 3 KOI
  cartoon art: 5 ANIME
  Certain: 6 OSAKAN
  chess: 5 SHOGI
  computer giant: 3 NEC
  dish: 5 SUSHI 7 TEMPURA
    8 SUKIYAKI
  dog: 5 AKITA
  drama: 3 NOH 6 KABUKI
  entertainer: 6 GEISHA
  fencing: 5 KENDO
  gateway: 5 TORII
  honorific: 3 SAN
  immigrant: 5 ISSEI
  leader of old: 6 SHOGUN
  martial art: 6 AIKIDO
  mat: 6 TATAMI
  miniature tree: 6 BONSAI
  money: 3 YEN
  noodles: 5 RAMEN
  novelist Kobo: 3 ABE
  parliament: 4 DIET
  porcelain: 5 IMARI
  port: 4 KOBE 5 OSAKA
    OTARU 6 SASEBO
    9 HIROSHIMA
  prime minister: 4 SATO
  rice drink: 4 SAKE
  sandal: 4 ZORI
  sash: 3 OBI
  soup: 4 MISO
  statesman: 3 ITO
  stringed instrument: 4 KOTO
  temple: 6 PAGODA
  vegetable: 3 UDO
  verse: 5 HAIKU
  warrior: 7 SAMURAI
**Japanese-American:** 5 ISSEI
    NISEI 6 SANSEI
**Japheth**
  Brother of: 4 SHEM
  Father of: 4 NOAH
**Jar:** 4 STUN
  Kind of: 5 MASON 6 LEYDEN
  part: 3 LID
**Jardin zoologique**
  inhabitant: 4 BETE
**Jared**
  Actor: 4 LETO
**Jargon:** 4 CANT JIVE 5 ARGOT
    LINGO
  suffix: 3 ESE
**Jarreau**
  and others: 3 ALS
**Jarrett**
  Jazzman: 5 KEITH
  NASCAR racer: 3 NED
**Jasmine:** 4 VINE
**Jason**
  Field goal kicker: 4 ELAM
  Ship of: 4 ARGO
  Wife of: 5 MEDEA

**Jasper**
  Painter: 5 JOHNS
**Jaundiced:** 6 SALLOW
**Jaunt:** 4 RIDE TRIP 8 SIDETRIP
**Jauntily**
  Wear: 5 SPORT
**Jaunty:** 4 AIRY PERT 6 RAKISH
  greeting: 4 HIHO
  hat: 5 BERET
  rhythm: 4 LILT
**Java:** 3 JOE
  holder: 3 CUP MUG URN
  Island near: 4 BALI
  selection: 5 DECAF
**"Java"**
  trumpeter: 4 HIRT 6 ALHIRT
**Javelin:** 5 SPEAR
**Javits Center**
  architect: 3 PEI
**Jaw:** 3 GAB YAP
  Drop your: 4 GAPE
  Make the ~ drop: 3 AWE
  With dropped: 5 AGAPE
**Jawaharlal**
  Daughter of: 6 INDIRA
**Jawbone:** 8 MANDIBLE
  Biblical ~ source: 3 ASS
**Jaworski**
  of Watergate: 4 LEON
**"Jaws"**
  boat: 4 ORCA
  omen: 3 FIN
**Jay**
  Actor: 4 MOHR
  Author: 5 ANSON
  follower: 3 KAY
  Former announcer for: 3 EDD
  home: 4 NEST
  Host: 4 LENO
  Host after: 5 CONAN
  preceder: 3 DEE
  Rival of: 4 DAVE
**Jayvee**
  athlete, perhaps: 4 SOPH
**Jaywalking:** 4 NONO
**"Jaywalking"**
  comedian: 4 LENO
**Jay-Z:** 7 RAPSTAR
  genre: 3 RAP
**Jazz:** 4 TEAM
  accompaniment: 4 VAMP
  album: 4 ELLA
  bandleader: 5 SUNRA
  band member: 7 SIDEMAN
  bit: 4 RIFF
  club unit: 3 SET
  combo: 4 TRIO 5 OCTET
  dance: 5 STOMP
  drummer: 8 MAXROACH
  fan: 3 CAT 6 HEPCAT
  form: 5 BLUES
  genre: 4 JIVE
  gp.: 3 NBA
  group: 5 COMBO
  instrument: 3 SAX 7 ALTOSAX
    8 TENORSAX

**job:** 3 GIG
**lick:** 4 RIFF
**Like some:** 4 COOL
**nickname:** 5 SATCH
  7 SATCHMO
**performance:** 3 JAM
  10 JAMSESSION
**phrase:** 4 LICK RIFF
**pianist:** 5 TATUM
  8 ARTTATUM
  10 COUNTBASIE
  15 JELLYROLLMORTON
**saxophonist:** 8 COLTRANE
  STANGETZ
**score:** 4 HOOP
**setting:** 4 UTAH
**singing:** 4 SCAT
**style:** 3 BOP 5 BEBOP
**trumpeter:** 6 ALHIRT
**Type of:** 4 ACID
**up:** 7 ENLIVEN
**(up):** 4 HOKE 5 SPICE
**Jazzman:** 3 CAT
  cue: 5 HITIT
  instrument: 3 AXE
**"Jazz Singer, The":** 6 TALKIE
**J. Carroll ___ :** 5 NAISH
**JCPenney**
  rival: 5 SEARS
**Jct.**
  component: 3 HWY RTE
**J.D.**
  holder: 3 ATT
  hurdle: 4 LSAT
**Jean:** 3 NOM
  Actress: 6 HARLOW
  SEBERG
  Author: 4 AUEL
  Dadaist: 3 ARP
  Playwright: 5 GENET
  Psychologist: 6 PIAGET
**Jeanmaire**
  Dancer: 5 RENEE
**Jeanne:** 3 STE
**Jeanne ___ :** 4 DARC
**Jeannette**
  First Congresswoman:
  6 RANKIN
**Jean-Paul**
  French revolutionary:
  5 MARAT
**Jeans:** 5 LEVIS PANTS
  brand: 3 LEE
  fabric: 5 DENIM
  feature: 5 RIVET
  Like old: 5 FADED
**Jeb**
  of Bull Run: 6 STUART
**J.E.B. ___ :** 6 STUART
**Jedi**
  master: 4 YODA
**Jeep**
  maker, once: 3 AMC
**"Jeepers!":** 4 EGAD GOSH
**Jeer:** 4 GIBE HOOT 5 SCOFF
  TAUNT 7 CATCALL

**Jeff**
  Pal of: 4 MUTT
  Racer: 6 GORDON
**Jefferson:** 5 DEIST
  bill: 3 TWO
  portrayer: 5 NOLTE
  Pres.: 4 THOS
  Sch. founded by: 3 UVA
  veep: 4 BURR
**"Jefferson in Paris"**
  actor: 5 NOLTE 9 NICKNOLTE
**"Jeffersons, The"**
  Sanford of: 6 ISABEL
  star: 7 HEMSLEY
**Jehoshaphat**
  Father of: 3 ASA
**Jehovah's Witnesses:** 4 SECT
**Jejune:** 4 ARID 5 STALE
**Jekyll, Dr.**
  Alter ego of: 4 HYDE
  6 MRHYDE
  creator's initials: 3 RLS
  ~, to Mr. Hyde: 8 ALTEREGO
**"Jekyll & Hyde"**
  Linda of: 4 EDER
**Jellied**
  delicacy: 3 EEL
  garnish: 5 ASPIC
**Jelling**
  agent: 4 AGAR
**Jell-O**
  Like ~, often: 6 MOLDED
  Move like: 6 WIGGLE
**Jelly:** 6 SPREAD
  bean flavor: 8 LICORICE
  container: 3 JAR
  Flammable: 6 STERNO
  flavor: 4 MINT 5 GRAPE
  GUAVA
  Inedible: 8 VASELINE
  ingredient: 6 PECTIN
  Royal ~ maker: 3 BEE
  Savory: 5 ASPIC
  Word following: 4 ROLL
**Jellyfish:** 6 MEDUSA
  appendage: 8 TENTACLE
**Jelly Roll**
  of jazz: 6 MORTON
**"Jelly's Last Jam"**
  dancer: 5 HINES
**Jellystone Park**
  bear: 4 YOGI 6 BOOBOO
**Jemima:** 4 AUNT
**Jemison**
  Astronaut: 3 MAE
**Je ne ___ quoi:** 4 SAIS
**Jenna**
  Actress: 6 ELFMAN
**Jennifer**
  Actress: 5 BEALS LOPEZ
  Former husband of: 4 BRAD
**"Jennifer 8"**
  actress Thurman: 3 UMA
**Jennings:** 6 ANCHOR
  Newscaster: 5 PETER
**Jenny:** 3 ASS

Diet guru: 5 CRAIG
Little ~, in nursery rhyme:
   4 WREN
Soprano: 4 LIND
**Jeopardy:** 4 RISK 5 PERIL
In: 6 ATRISK
Out of: 8 HOMEFREE
**"Jeopardy!"**
ans.: 4 QUES
clue: 6 ANSWER
column: 8 CATEGORY
contestant: 5 ASKER
host Alex: 6 TREBEK
host Trebek: 4 ALEX
millionaire Jennings: 3 KEN
Respond on: 3 ASK
staple: 6 TRIVIA
**Jer.**
Book before: 3 ISA
**Jeremiah**
Book before: 6 ISAIAH
**"Jeremiah Johnson"**
actor Will: 4 GEER
**Jeremy**
Actor: 5 IRONS
Singing partner of: 4 CHAD
**Jerk:** 3 ASS BOB TIC TUG
   4 BOZO TWIT YANK
   5 IDIOT MORON REACT
   SCHMO SPASM
Kind of: 4 KNEE SODA
**Jerky**
Made: 5 DRIED
Make: 4 CURE
**Jermaine**
Brother of: 4 TITO
**Jerome**
Composer: 4 KERN
novel:
   15 THREEMENINABOAT
**Jerry**
Cartoonist: 6 SIEGEL
Comedian: 5 LEWIS
of basketball: 4 WEST
of the Grateful Dead:
   6 GARCIA
Partner of: 3 BEN 4 DEAN
Singer: 4 VALE
**Jerry-built:** 6 SHODDY
**Jerry Lee ___:** 5 LEWIS
**"Jerry Maguire"**
actress Zellweger: 5 RENEE
Oscar winner:
   13 CUBAGOODINGJR
**Jersey:** 3 COW 4 KNIT
chew: 3 CUD
hangout: 3 LEA
remark: 3 MOO
**"Jersey Lily, The":**
   7 LANGTRY
**Jerusalem**
airline: 4 ELAL
Capital east of: 5 AMMAN
country: 6 ISRAEL
day: 3 YOM
temple hill: 4 ZION

**Jesse**
Olympian: 5 OWENS
Outlaw: 5 JAMES
**Jessica**
Actress: 4 ALBA 5 LANGE
   TANDY
portrayer on TV: 6 ANGELA
**Jest:** 4 JAPE 5 PUTON
**Jester:** 4 FOOL
**Jesus**
Language of: 7 ARAMAIC
letters: 4 INRI
miracle site: 4 CANA
of baseball: 4 ALOU
story: 7 PARABLE
**"Jesus ___" (shortest Bible
   verse):** 4 WEPT
**Jet:** 4 EBON
Air, to a ~ engine: 6 INTAKE
black: 4 INKY ONYX 5 EBONY
   SABLE
follower: 3 LAG
giant: 4 LEAR
Mil. ~ letters: 4 USAF
Mil. ~ locale: 3 AFB
prefix: 5 TURBO
Russian: 3 MIG
speed unit: 4 MACH
stream heading: 4 EAST
**Jeté:** 4 LEAP
**Jeter**
of baseball: 5 DEREK
**Jethro**
Agriculturalist: 4 TULL
**Jethro ___ (rock band):**
   4 TULL
**Jet Propulsion Lab**
org.: 4 NASA
site: 7 CALTECH
**Jets:** 4 GANG TEAM
Joe of the: 6 NAMATH
Like the: 5 ANGLO
one-time org.: 3 AFL
**Jetsam**
of 1773: 3 TEA
**Jet-set**
destination: 7 RIVIERA
**Jetson**
dog: 5 ASTRO
maid: 5 ROSIE
mom: 4 JANE
son: 5 ELROY
**Jetson, Judy**
Brother of: 5 ELROY
**Jettison:** 4 DUMP TOSS
   5 SCRAP
**Jetty:** 4 PIER QUAY
**___ Jeunesse:** 3 UNE
**Jewel:** 3 GEM 5 BIJOU STONE
box: 6 CDCASE
**Jeweled**
crown: 5 TIARA
**Jeweler**
item: 3 GEM
magnifier: 5 LOUPE
unit: 5 CARAT KARAT

**Jewelry**
Big name in: 5 ZALES
Carved: 5 CAMEO
Fake: 5 PASTE
item: 3 PIN 4 RING 6 BROOCH
   CHOKER 7 PENDANT
   8 BRACELET
Showy ~, in slang:
   10 BLINGBLING
**"Jewel Song":** 4 ARIA
**Jewett, Sarah ___:** 4 ORNE
**Jewish**
campus organization:
   6 HILLEL
community: 6 SHTETL
dance: 4 HORA
feast: 5 SEDER
festival: 5 PURIM
Like much ~ food: 6 KOSHER
month: 4 ADAR ELUL
   6 TISHRI
mystical doctrine: 6 CABALA
Old ~ scholar: 4 ABBA
robot: 5 GOLEM
scripture: 5 TORAH
teacher: 5 RABBI REBBE
**Jew's-harp**
sound: 5 TWANG
**Jezebel:** 5 HUSSY
Husband of: 4 AHAB
idol: 4 BAAL
portrayer: 5 BETTE
**JFK:** 3 DEM 4 PRES 7 AIRPORT
arrival: 3 SST
carrier: 3 KLM 4 ELAL
info: 3 ARR ETA ETD
Like: 4 INTL
opponent: 3 RMN
part: 4 INIT
predecessor: 3 DDE
quote start: 3 ASK 6 ASKNOT
regulator: 3 FAA
successor: 3 LBJ
terminal: 3 TWA
was in it: 3 USN
~ U.N. ambassador: 3 AES
   15 ADLAIESTEVENSON
**"JFK"**
actor Joe: 5 PESCI
director Oliver: 5 STONE
**JFK Library**
designer: 3 PEI 5 IMPEI
**J. Geils Band**
song: 10 LOVESTINKS
**Jib:** 4 SAIL
Racing: 5 GENOA
**Jibe:** 4 MESH 5 AGREE
**Jidda**
locale: 6 REDSEA
**Jiff:** 3 SEC
**Jiffy:** 3 SEC 5 TRICE
   6 MOMENT
**Jiggermast**
Like a: 3 AFT
**Jigsaw**
part: 5 PIECE

**Jillian**
Actress: 3 ANN
**Jillions:** 4 ALOT LOTS
6 OODLES
**Jim**
Athlete: 6 THORPE
Newsman: 6 LEHRER
Olympics sportscaster:
5 MCKAY
Singer: 5 CROCE
___ **Jima:** 3 IWO
**Jim and Tammy**
org.: 3 PTL
**Jim-dandy:** 4 AONE NEAT
NICE 5 SWELL
**Jimenez, Jose**
portrayer: 4 DANA
8 BILLDANA
**Jimjams:** 3 DTS
**Jimmie**
Mouseketeer: 4 DODD
**Jimmy:** 3 PRY 5 LEVER
Actor: 5 SMITS
Labor leader: 5 HOFFA
Predecessor of: 6 GERALD
Rival of: 4 ILIE
Successor of: 6 RONALD
**Jingle**
writer: 5 ADMAN
**"Jingle Bells"**
contraction: 3 OER
**Jinx:** 3 HEX
**Jipijapa**
hat: 6 PANAMA
**Jitterbug**
relative: 5 LINDY
**Jitteriness:** 6 NERVES
**Jitters:** 6 UNEASE
Worse than: 5 ANGST
**Jittery:** 4 EDGY 5 ANTSY
TENSE 6 ONEDGE
**Jo**
Sister of: 4 BETH
**Joad, Tom:** 4 OKIE
**Joan:** 3 STE
Folk singer: 4 BAEZ
Rock singer: 4 JETT
Surrealist painter: 4 MIRO
**"Joanie Loves Chachi"**
costar Moran: 4 ERIN
**Joanna**
Actress: 5 KERNS
**Joanne**
Actress: 3 DRU
**Joan of ___:** 3 ARC
**Joan of Arc:** 6 MARTYR
City saved by: 7 ORLEANS
death site: 5 ROUEN
**"Joan of Arc"**
actress Sobieski: 6 LEELEE
___ **João:** 3 SAO
**Job:** 3 GIG 4 POST TASK
5 CHORE HEIST
ad letters: 3 EOE
Barber: 4 TRIM
Bk. before: 4 ESTH

**Con:** 4 SCAM
**Crime:** 5 CAPER
**Dead-end:** 3 RUT
**detail, briefly:** 4 SPEC
**Detective:** 4 CASE
**Did a smithy:** 4 SHOD
5 SHOED
**Double:** 5 STUNT
**Emcee:** 5 INTRO
**extra:** 4 PERK
**follower:** 6 PSALMS
**Friend of:** 5 ELIHU
**Grease:** 4 LUBE
**Kind of:** 4 RUSH SNOW
**Off the:** 4 IDLE
**On the:** 4 ATIT 6 ATWORK
**opening:** 4 SLOT
**preceder:** 6 ESTHER
**safety org.:** 4 OSHA
**Salon:** 3 SET 4 PERM TINT
5 RINSE
**Scout:** 5 RECON
**security:** 6 TENURE
**Time on the:** 5 STINT
**Torch:** 5 ARSON
**Tow:** 4 REPO
**Up to the:** 4 ABLE
**Wrecker:** 3 TOW
**"___ Job":** 4 GETA
**Jobs**
Like some: 3 ODD 5 CUSHY
6 INSIDE
of computers: 5 STEVE
offering: 4 IMAC
~, so to speak: 4 HATS
**Jock:** 7 ATHLETE
antithesis: 4 NERD
Wife of: 5 ELLIE
**Jockey:** 5 RIDER
1930 Triple-Crown ~: 5 SANDE
attire: 5 SILKS
Kind of: 4 DISC
need: 4 CROP
strap: 4 REIN
Two-time Triple-Crown:
6 ARCARO
~ Angel: 7 CORDERO
~ Arcaro: 5 EDDIE
**Jocular**
nickname: 5 KIDDO
**Joe:** 4 JAVA 6 COFFEE
Actor: 5 PESCI SPANO
and Jane: 3 GIS
Baseball manager: 5 TORRE
holder: 3 CUP URN
Joltless: 6 DECAF SANKA
Playwright: 5 ORTON
~, in French: 4 CAFE
___ **Joe:** 5 INJUN
**Joel**
Actor: 4 GREY 6 MCCREA
Book after: 4 AMOS
Book before: 5 HOSEA
Director: 4 COEN
**Joel, Billy**
instrument: 5 PIANO

**Joey**
mom: 8 KANGAROO
of twister fame: 3 DEE
Punk rocker: 6 RAMONE
**Joffrey**
of ballet: 6 ROBERT
**Jog:** 3 RUN 4 TROT
**Jogger**
purchase: 5 NIKES
**Johann**
Author: 4 WYSS
**Johannes**
Astronomer: 6 KEPLER
**Johann Sebastian ___:** 4 BACH
**Johansson**
Boxer: 7 INGEMAR
**John:** 3 LAV 4 POPE 6 TOILET
Actor: 5 ASTIN 6 CLEESE
AFL-CIO: 7 SWEENEY
Anonymous: 3 DOE
Arctic explorer: 3 RAE
Author: 5 OHARA 6 UPDIKE
7 GRISHAM
Batting champ: 6 OLERUD
Book after: 4 ACTS
Book before: 4 LUKE
Brewer: 6 LABATT
British: 3 LOO
Broncos QB: 5 ELWAY
Cards expert: 6 SCARNE
Comedian: 5 BYNER
Dante translator: 6 CIARDI
Director: 3 WOO
Explorer: 5 CABOT
Farm equipment maker:
5 DEERE
Former TV host: 4 TESH
Furrier ~ Jacob: 5 ASTOR
Justice: 3 JAY
Naturalist: 4 MUIR
New Age musician: 4 TESH
or Jane: 3 DOE
or Paul: 6 BEATLE
Painter: 4 OPIE
Philosopher: 5 LOCKE
Pilgrim: 5 ALDEN
Playwright: 7 OSBORNE
Poet: 5 DONNE KEATS
Politician: 6 SUNUNU
Russian: 4 IVAN
Scottish: 3 IAN
Singer: 5 ELTON RAITT
TV pioneer: 5 BAIRD
Welsh: 4 EVAN
Widow of: 4 YOKO
Wife of: 4 YOKO
with a wild wardrobe: 5 ELTON
~, Paul, and George (abbr.):
3 STS
**John ___:** 3 DOE
___ **John:** 4 DEAR
**John, Elton**
title: 3 SIR
**John Boy**
Sister of: 4 ERIN
**John Boyd ___:** 3 ORR

**"John Brown's Body"**
 poet: 5 BENET
**John Dickson ___**: 4 CARR
**"___ John, M.D."**: 7 TRAPPER
**Johnny**
 Actor: 4 DEPP
 Announcer: 5 OLSON
 of baseball: 4 MIZE
 Quarterback: 6 UNITAS
 Singer: 6 MATHIS
**Johnny ___**: 3 REB
**"___ Johnny!"**: 5 HERES
**Johnny Appleseed**
 last name: 7 CHAPMAN
**"Johnny B. ___"**: 5 GOODE
**Johnnycake**: 4 PONE
**"Johnny Mnemonic"**
 actor/rapper: 4 ICET
**Johnny Reb**
 gp.: 3 CSA
**John Paul II**: 4 POLE POPE
 Given name of: 5 KAROL
 Like: 5 PAPAL
**John Philip ___**: 5 SOUSA
**John/Rice**
 musical: 4 AIDA
**Johns, Jasper**
 genre: 6 POPART
**Johnson**
 Comic: 4 ARTE
 Decathlete: 5 RAFER
 dog: 3 HER HIM
 in-law: 4 ROBB
**Johnson, Claudia ___ Taylor:**
 4 ALTA
**Johnson, Dame ___**: 5 CELIA
**Johnson & Johnson**
 item: 4 QTIP
**Johnstown**
 disaster: 5 FLOOD
**John Wooden Center**
 site: 4 UCLA
**Joie de vivre**: 4 ELAN
**Join**: 3 WED 4 BAND KNIT
  LINK WELD 5 ENROL
  ENTER UNITE 6 ENLIST
 forces: 4 ALLY 5 MERGE
  UNITE 6 TEAMUP
 metal items: 6 SOLDER
 securely: 5 TENON
  7 MORTISE
 temporarily: 5 SITIN
 the team: 4 YOKE
 together: 4 TEAM 6 SPLICE
 up: 6 SIGNON
**Joiner**
 Common: 3 AND
 Woodworking: 5 DOWEL
**Joining**
 words: 3 IDO
**Joint**: 6 MUTUAL REEFER
 ailment: 4 GOUT
 Arm: 5 ELBOW
 Fix, as a pipe: 6 REWELD
 Jacuzzi: 3 SPA
 Kind of: 5 HINGE MITER

Leg: 4 KNEE 5 ANKLE
 Oink: 3 STY
 part: 5 TENON 7 MORTISE
 Pipe: 3 ELL TEE
 point: 4 NODE
 problem: 4 ACHE
 protection: 7 KNEEPAD
 Quirky: 9 TRICKKNEE
 Seedy: 4 DIVE
 Swivel: 3 HIP
 Tailor: 4 SEAM
 tenant: 3 CON 5 FELON
 Three-way: 3 TEE
**Jointly**
 Held: 6 POOLED
**Joke**: 3 GAG KID 4 JAPE JEST
 around with: 3 KID
 As a: 5 INFUN
 Butt of a: 4 GOAT
  6 STOOGE
 Cohort of priest and minister in
  a: 5 RABBI
 Funny: 4 RIOT 6 GASSER
 Get the: 5 LAUGH
 Kind of: 10 KNOCKKNOCK
 Knock-knock: 3 PUN
 Like an old: 5 CORNY STALE
 Old: 6 WHEEZE
 Online ~ response: 3 LOL
 Practical: 3 GAG 4 JAPE
  5 PRANK 7 LEGPULL
 React to a bad: 5 WINCE
 response: 4 HAHA 6 IGETIT
 setting: 3 BAR
 Short: 8 ONELINER
 target: 4 BUTT
 Way to pass on a: 5 EMAIL
**Joker**: 3 WAG 4 CARD
  5 CUTUP
 portrayer Cesar: 6 ROMERO
 Practical: 9 LEGPULLER
**Jokers**
 Game with four: 7 CANASTA
**Jokester**: 3 WAG
**Jokingly**: 5 INFUN 6 INJEST
**Jolie**
 Actress: 8 ANGELINA
**Jollies**: 3 FUN
**Jolliet**
 1669 ~ discovery: 4 ERIE
**Jollity**: 3 FUN 4 GLEE
  5 MIRTH
**Jolly**
 Season to be: 4 NOEL YULE
**Jolly ___**: 5 ROGER
**Jolly Roger**
 feature: 4 BONE 5 BONES
  SKULL
 mate: 4 SMEE
**"___ jolly swagman"**: 5 ONCEA
**Jolson**
 and others: 3 ALS
 portrayer Parks: 5 LARRY
 real first name: 3 ASA
 song: 6 SWANEE
  15 TOOTTOOTTOOTSIE

**Jolt**: 3 JAR ZAP 4 BUMP
  5 SHOCK
**"Joltin' Joe"**: 5 DIMAG
  6 YANKEE
**Joltless**
 joe: 5 DECAF SANKA
**Jon**
 Director: 5 AMIEL
 Dog of: 4 ODIE
 Illustrator: 4 AGEE
 Rock singer: 7 BONJOVI
**Jonah**
 Book after: 5 MICAH
 swallower: 5 WHALE
**Jonas**
 Vaccine developer: 4 SALK
**Jonathan**: 5 APPLE
 Director: 5 DEMME
**Jones**: 7 SURNAME
 Architect: 5 INIGO
 Bandleader: 5 SPIKE
 Casey: 8 ENGINEER
  TRAINMAN
 Composer: 5 ISHAM
 Grammy winner: 5 NORAH
 Jazz singer: 4 ETTA
 Jazz trumpeter: 4 THAD
 of the Miracle Mets: 5 CLEON
 Playwright: 5 LEROI
 Poet: 5 LEROI
**___ Jones**: 3 DOW
**Jones, Davy**
 domain: 3 SEA
**Jones, Dr.**
 nickname: 4 INDY
**Jones, Indiana**
 quest: 3 ARK
 trademark: 6 FEDORA
**Jones, Marion**
 Where ~ won: 6 SYDNEY
**Jones, Tommy Lee**
 movie: 4 COBB
**___ Jones's locker**: 4 DAVY
**Jong**
 Author: 5 ERICA
**Jonson**: 4 POET
 work: 3 ODE
**Joplin**
 genre: 7 RAGTIME
 Singer: 5 JANIS
**Joplin, Scott**
 piece: 3 RAG
**Jordan**
 capital: 5 AMMAN
 Director: 4 NEIL
 Former queen of: 4 NOOR
 neighbor: 5 SYRIA
 neighbor (abbr.): 3 SYR
 Seaport city of: 5 AQABA
**Jordan, Michael**
 alma mater (abbr.): 3 UNC
 epithet: 3 AIR
 former team: 5 BULLS
 org.: 3 NBA
 underwear: 5 HANES
**Jordanian**: 4 ARAB

**Jorge**
  Author: 5 AMADO
  Pianist: 5 BOLET
**"Jo's Boys"**
  author: 6 ALCOTT
**José**
  Flamenco dancer: 5 GRECO
  Pet name for: 4 PEPE
  Pianist: 6 ITURBI
  preceder: 3 SAN
  Uncle: 3 TIO
  World Series MVP: 4 RIJO
  ___ Jose: 3 SAN
**José Marie ___**
  Muralist: 4 SERT
**Joseph**
  Columnist: 5 ALSOP
  Journalist: 5 ALSOP
  Theater producer: 4 PAPP
**Josephine**
  Mystery author: 3 TEY
**Josh:** 3 KID RIB 5 TEASE
**Joss:** 4 IDOL
**Jostle:** 3 JAR 5 ELBOW
    SHOVE
**Jot:** 3 TAD 4 ATOM IOTA WHIT
    5 SPECK 6 TITTLE
  down: 4 NOTE
**Jottings:** 5 NOTES
**Joule**
  fraction: 3 ERG
  per second: 4 WATT
**"Jour de Fete"**
  star: 4 TATI
**Journal:** 3 LOG
  British medical: 6 LANCET
  ending: 3 ESE
  Nautical: 3 LOG
  Org. with a: 3 AMA
**Journalist:** 6 SCRIBE
  idea: 5 ANGLE
  WWII: 4 PYLE
**Journey:** 4 TREK TRIP
    7 ODYSSEY
  Begin a: 6 SETOUT
  Muslim: 4 HADJ HAJJ
  part: 3 LEG
  Self-directed: 7 EGOTRIP
  Tough: 4 TREK
**"Journey Into Fear"**
  author Ambler: 4 ERIC
  author Eric: 6 AMBLER
**"Journey of Natty ___, The":**
    4 GANN
**Joust:** 4 TILT
  verbally: 4 SPAR
**Jousting:** 5 ATILT
  arena: 5 LISTS
  Defeat at: 7 UNHORSE
  weapon: 5 LANCE
**Jovi, Jon ___:** 3 BON
**Joy:** 4 GLEE 7 ELATION
  Author: 7 ADAMSON
  Bring ~ to: 5 ELATE
  Express: 3 OOH 4 WEEP
  Exude: 4 BEAM

  Jump for: 5 EXULT
  Partner of: 5 PRIDE
  With: 5 GAILY
**"___ Joy":** 5 ODETO
**Joyce**
  epic: 7 ULYSSES
  Nation of: 4 EIRE
**Joyce Carol ___**
  Author: 5 OATES
**Joyful**
  dance: 4 HORA
  Make: 5 ELATE
**"___ joy keep you": Sandberg:**
    4 LETA
**"Joy Luck Club, The"**
  author: 3 TAN 6 AMYTAN
  game: 8 MAHJONGG
**"Joy of Cooking, The"**
  author: 8 ROMBAUER
  author Rombauer: 4 IRMA
**"___, Joy of Man's Desiring":**
    4 JESU
**"Joy of Sex, The"**
  Author Comfort: 4 ALEX
**Joyous:** 3 GAY 5 MERRY
  affair: 4 GALA
  hymn: 5 PAEAN
**Joyride:** 4 SPIN
**Joystick:** 5 LEVER
  Use a: 6 AVIATE
**J.P.**
  Flee to a: 5 ELOPE
  visitor: 6 ELOPER
**J. Paul**
  Oil magnate: 5 GETTY
**Jr.**
  exam: 4 PSAT
  Son of ~, maybe: 3 III
  Yr. before: 4 SOPH
**Jr. high**
  Sch. before: 4 ELEM
**Jrs.**
  Former: 3 SRS
**Juan**
  Cubist: 4 GRIS
  or Eva: 5 PERON
  preceder: 3 SAN
  Wife of: 3 EVA
**Juan, Don:** 4 ROUE
    9 LADIESMAN
  Mother of: 4 INEZ
**___ Juana Ines:** 3 SOR
**Juan Carlos:** 3 REY
  Daughter of: 5 ELENA
**Juárez**
  of Mexico: 6 BENITO
**Jubilance:** 7 ELATION
**Jubilant:** 6 ELATED
  Be: 5 EXULT
**Judah**
  Mother of: 4 LEAH
  Son of: 4 ONAN
**Judd**
  Actor: 6 HIRSCH
  Mother: 5 NAOMI
  Singer: 5 NAOMI

**Jude**
  Actor: 3 LAW
**Judean**
  king: 5 HEROD
**Judge:** 4 DEEM RATE 5 TRIER
    6 ASSESS CRITIC
    7 ARBITER
  Biblical: 3 ELI
  Consider, as a: 4 HEAR
  cry: 5 ORDER
  demand: 5 ORDER
  Dressed like a: 5 ROBED
  Former TV: 4 KOCH
    6 EDKOCH WAPNER
  garb: 4 ROBE
  in Judges: 6 GIDEON
  Like a: 5 SOBER
  need: 5 GAVEL
  O.J. Simpson: 3 ITO
    8 LANCEITO
  seat in court: 4 BANC
  TV: 4 JUDY
  ~ Fortas: 3 ABE
**Judges:** 4 REFS
  Book after: 4 RUTH
  Group of: 5 PANEL
  Judge in: 6 GIDEON
**"Judging Amy"**
  actress Daly: 4 TYNE
  actress Tyne: 4 DALY
**Judgment**
  Artistic: 5 TASTE
  Await: 4 PEND
  Good: 5 SENSE
    10 HORSESENSE
  Kind of: 4 SNAP
  Unjust: 6 BADRAP
**"Judgment at Nuremberg"**
  director: 6 KRAMER
**___ judicata:** 3 RES
**Judicial**
  comments: 5 DICTA
  delay: 4 STAY
  inquiry: 6 ASSIZE
  order: 4 WRIT
**Judicious:** 4 SAGE WISE
    5 SOBER
**Judith**
  Actress: 4 IVEY
  Astronaut: 6 RESNIK
**"Judith"**
  composer: 4 ARNE
**Judo**
  level: 3 DAN
  master: 6 SENSEI
**Judy**
  Comic: 5 CARNE 6 TENUTA
  Daughter of: 4 LIZA
**Jug:** 4 EWER
  band instrument: 5 KAZOO
  beverage: 5 CIDER
  handle: 3 EAR
  Wide-mouthed: 4 EWER OLLA
**Juggler**
  fruits: 7 ORANGES
**Jughead:** 4 TEEN 8 TEENAGER

Friend of: 6 ARCHIE
**Juice**
Beetle: 3 GAS
Bug: 3 GAS
drink: 3 ADE
Extract ~ from: 4 REAM
Kind of: 3 MOO
Medicinal: 4 ALOE
Pickle: 5 BRINE
Pour ~ over: 5 BASTE
Provide ~ for: 6 PLUGIN
source: 6 OUTLET
Tree: 3 SAP
with punch: 9 HARDCIDER
**Juicer:** 3 SOT
refuse: 4 PULP
**Juices:** 6 SALIVA
Big name in: 5 MOTTS
**Juicy:** 5 MOIST
fruit: 4 PEAR
gossip: 4 DIRT
morsel: 6 TIDBIT
**Juillet**
season: 3 ETE
**Juilliard**
deg.: 3 MFA
subj.: 3 MUS
**Juin**
preceder: 3 MAI
season: 3 ETE
**Juju:** 6 AMULET
**Jukebox**
part: 4 SLOT
verb: 6 SELECT
**Jule**
Composer: 5 STYNE
**Julep**
enhancer: 4 MINT
**Jules**
Author: 5 VERNE
Composer: 8 MASSENET
Painter: 5 DUPRE
school: 5 ECOLE
**Juli**
Golfer: 7 INKSTER
**Julia**
2000 role for ~: 4 ERIN
Actor: 4 RAUL
Ex of: 4 LYLE
TV chef: 5 CHILD
**Julian**
of rock music: 6 LENNON
**Julia Ward ___**
Reformer: 4 HOWE
**Juliet**
Beloved of: 5 ROMEO
Dancer: 6 PROWSE
Emulate: 5 ELOPE
Home of: 6 VERONA
Last name of: 7 CAPULET
Romeo, to: 5 LOVER
~, to Romeo: 3 SUN
**Julio:** 3 MES
Vintner: 5 GALLO
**Julius**
avenger: 4 MARC

Crooner: 6 LAROSA
Villain named: 4 DRNO
**"Julius Caesar"**
costume: 4 TOGA
role: 5 CASCA
setting: 4 ROME 6 SENATE
**Julius III**
Start of ~ papacy: 3 MDL
**July**
birthstone: 4 RUBY
Late ~ birth: 3 LEO
noisemaker: 11 FIRECRACKER
**July 4, 1776**
~, for one: 4 DATE
**July 15:** 4 IDES
**Jumble:** 4 HASH MESS OLIO
    5 CHAOS MIXUP
    8 MISHMASH
**Jumbo:** 5 LARGE
**Jumna**
City on the: 4 AGRA
**Jump:** 3 HOP 4 LEAP VERB
Ballet: 4 JETE 9 PASDECHAT
electrodes: 3 ARC
for joy: 5 EXULT
Make: 5 SCARE
of surprise: 5 START
on the ice: 4 AXEL LUTZ
    7 SALCHOW
over: 4 LEAP OMIT
Triple ~ feature: 3 HOP
What to ~ for: 3 JOY
**Jumped:** 5 LEAPT 6 SPRANG
It may be: 4 BAIL
to one's feet: 5 AROSE
**Jumper**
Aussie: 3 ROO
cable connection: 5 ANODE
Cord for a: 6 BUNGEE
High: 4 FLEA
**Jumping**
Big name in: 4 EVEL
Twain's ~ frog: 4 DANL
**Jumping-off**
point: 4 EDGE
**"Jumpin' Jack Flash, it's ___ ...":**
    4 AGAS
**Jump-starting**
org.: 3 AAA
**Jumpy:** 5 TENSE 6 ONEDGE
**Junction**
Petticoat: 4 SEAM
point: 4 NODE
**"___ Junction":** 9 PETTICOAT
**June:** 4 NAME
Actress: 5 HAVER HAVOC
bug: 6 BEETLE
celebrant: 4 GRAD
honoree: 3 DAD 4 GRAD
    8 OLDGLORY
Early ~ birth: 6 GEMINI
**June 6, 1944:** 4 DDAY
**June 14:** 7 FLAGDAY
**Jung**
Inner soul, to: 5 ANIMA
Psychiatrist: 4 CARL

**Jungfrau:** 3 ALP
**Jungian**
principle: 5 ANIMA
topic: 3 EGO
**Jungle**
crusher: 3 BOA 8 ANACONDA
groomer: 3 APE
growth: 4 VINE
King of the: 4 LION
sound: 4 ROAR
swinger: 3 APE
vine: 5 LIANA
woman: 4 JANE
**"Jungle, The"**
novelist: 8 SINCLAIR
novelist Sinclair: 5 UPTON
**"Jungle Book, The"**
bear: 5 BALOO
boy: 6 MOWGLI
setting: 5 INDIA
snake: 3 KAA
star: 4 SABU
tiger: 9 SHEREKHAN
**Junho to Junho:** 3 ANO
**Junior:** 3 SON 4 YEAR
Dolphins linebacker: 4 SEAU
Future: 4 SOPH
H.S. ~ test: 4 PSAT
of a junior: 3 III
Watch: 3 SIT
watcher: 6 SITTER
Whopper: 3 FIB
~, to Senior: 8 NAMESAKE
**Juniper**
drink: 3 GIN
**Junipero**
Missionary: 5 SERRA
**Junk:** 4 SHIP 5 SCRAP TRASH
e-mail: 4 SPAM
Some of it is: 4 MAIL
**Junket:** 4 TRIP 5 SPREE
**Junkie:** 4 USER
**Junk mail:** 3 ADS
Like much: 6 UNREAD
**Junky**
car: 4 HEAP
**Junkyard**
dog: 3 CUR
**Juno**
Greek counterpart of: 4 HERA
**"Juno and the Paycock"**
playwright: 6 OCASEY
**Junta:** 5 CABAL
**Jupiter:** 3 GOD 4 DEUS JOVE
    5 DEITY
Greek counterpart of: 4 ZEUS
Moon of: 3 OPS 4 LEDA
    6 EUROPA
probe: 7 GALILEO
Wife of: 4 JUNO
**Jurado**
Actress: 4 KATY
**Jurassic**
carnivore: 8 ALLOSAUR
**"Jurassic Park"**
actor Sam: 5 NEILL

actress Laura: 4 DERN
actress Richards: 6 ARIANA
mathematician ___ Malcolm:
   3 IAN
menace: 4 TREX 6 RAPTOR
role for Laura: 5 ELLIE
sequel: 12 THELOSTWORLD
**"Jurassic Park III"**
  star Téa: 5 LEONI
**___ jure: 4 IPSO**
**Jurgensen**
  Sportscaster: 5 SONNY
**Juries**
  Like some: 4 HUNG
  ___ juris: 3 SUI
**Jurisdiction**
  of a bishop: 7 DIOCESE
**Jurisprudence: 3 LAW**
**Juror: 4 PEER**
**Jury: 5 PANEL**
  member: 4 PEER
  Seat a: 7 EMPANEL IMPANEL
  Serve on a: 3 SIT
  size: 6 TWELVE
**Jury-___: 3 RIG**
  ___ jury: 5 PETIT
**"___ Jury": 4 ITHE**
**Just: 4 FAIR MERE ONLY**
     6 BARELY MERELY
  a bit: 3 TAD
  about: 6 ALMOST NEARLY
  above average: 5 CPLUS
  beat: 4 EDGE
  fine: 3 AOK
  for fun: 7 ONALARK

for kicks: 5 INFUN
get by: 6 EDGEIN
hired: 3 NEW
in case: 4 LEST
know: 5 SENSE 6 INTUIT
make, with "out": 3 EKE
not done: 5 TABOO
Not ~ any: 3 THE
Not ~ one: 4 BOTH
okay: 4 SOSO
one of those things: 4 THAT
open: 4 AJAR
out: 6 NEWEST 8 BRANDNEW
peachy: 3 AOK 5 SWELL
right: 4 TOAT 5 IDEAL
    6 TOATEE
slightly: 4 ATAD
They may be: 7 DESERTS
**Just ___: 4 ABIT ATAD**
**"Just ___": 4 ASEC DOIT**
    6 INCASE
**"Just a ___!": 3 SEC**
**"Just as I thought!": 3 AHA**
    OHO
**Just for Men**
  product: 3 DYE
**"Just for the heck ___": 4 OFIT**
**Justice**
  attire: 4 ROBE
  Flight from: 3 LAM
  Janet of: 4 RENO
  Kind of: 6 POETIC
  Wild West: 5 NOOSE
**Justice Dept.**
  division: 3 ATF DEA FBI

employee: 3 ATT
**Justification: 6 REASON**
**Justifiers**
  Means: 4 ENDS
**"Justine"**
  author: 4 SADE 6 DESADE
  star: 5 AIMEE
**Just ___ in the bucket:**
    5 ADROP
**"Just kidding!": 3 NOT**
**"___ just kidding!": 4 IWAS**
**Just-passing**
  grade: 3 DEE
**"Just say ___ drugs": 4 NOTO**
**"Just Shoot Me"**
  actor George: 5 SEGAL
  actress Malick: 6 WENDIE
**Just the ___: 4 SAME**
**"Just the facts, ___": 4 MAAM**
**"Just this ___": 4 ONCE**
**"Just ___ thought!": 3 ASI**
**"Just you wait, ___ 'iggins!":**
    4 ENRY
**Jute**
  Language that gives us:
    7 BENGALI
**Jutland**
  native: 4 DANE
  Old ~ resident: 6 TEUTON
**Jutlander: 4 DANE**
**___ Juvante (motto of Monaco):**
    3 DEO
**Juxtapose: 4 ABUT**
**JVC**
  competitor: 3 RCA

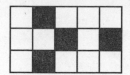

# Kk

**K**
follower: 4 MART
followers: 3 LMN 4 LMNO
through 12: 4 ELHI
**K-___:** 3 TEL
**K2**
continent: 4 ASIA
**K–5:** 4 ELEM
**Kabibble**
Comic: 3 ISH
**Kabob**
holder: 6 SKEWER
skewer: 4 SPIT
**Kabuki**
kin: 3 NOH
sash: 3 OBI
**Kachina:** 4 DOLL
carver: 4 HOPI
**Kadar**
Hungarian leader: 5 JANOS
**Kadett**
maker: 4 OPEL
**Kadiddlehopper**
Skelton character: 4 CLEM
**Kael**
Critic: 7 PAULINE
**Kaelin**
Simpson trial figure: 4 KATO
**Kaffiyeh**
wearer: 4 ARAB
**Kafka**
hero: 5 SAMSA
novel: 7 AMERIKA
Writer: 5 FRANZ
**Kaftan**
Kyoto: 6 KIMONO
**Kahanamoku, Duke**
Emulate: 4 SURF
**Kahlil**
Author: 6 GIBRAN
**Kahn**
Art patron: 4 OTTO
Banker: 4 OTTO
Composer: 3 GUS
**Kai-___, Chiang:** 4 SHEK
**Kaiser:** 4 ROLL 5 RULER
**Kai-shek, Chiang**
capital: 6 TAIPEI
**Ka Ka ___:** 3 LAE
**Kal-___:** 3 KAN
**Kalahari:** 6 DESERT
layover: 5 OASIS
layovers: 5 OASES
Like the: 4 ARID
**Kalamazoo**
lass: 3 GAL
**Kale**
Variety of: 7 COLLARD

**Kal-Kan**
rival: 4 ALPO
**Kama ___:** 5 SUTRA
**Kamali**
Designer: 5 NORMA
**Kamehameha**
Island conquered by:
4 OAHU
**Kaminska**
Actress: 3 IDA
**Kamoze**
Singer: 3 INI
**Kampala**
country: 6 UGANDA
native: 7 UGANDAN
**"___ Kampf":** 4 MEIN
**Kan.**
neighbor: 3 NEB 4 OKLA
**Kander**
Broadway partner of: 3 EBB
**Kandinsky**
contemporary: 3 ARP 4 KLEE
**Kane**
of "All My Children": 5 ERICA
portrayer on TV: 5 LUCCI
Rosebud, to: 4 SLED
**Kane, Marshall**
deadline: 4 NOON
Wife of: 3 AMY
**Kanga**
creator: 5 MILNE
Kid of: 3 ROO
**Kangaroo:** 6 HOPPER
Female: 3 DOE
Young: 4 JOEY
**___ Kangaroo:** 4 CAPT
**"___ Kangaroo Down, Sport":**
5 TIEME
**Kans.**
neighbor: 4 OKLA
**Kansai International Airport**
site: 5 OSAKA
**Kansas**
canine: 4 TOTO
capital: 6 TOPEKA
city: 4 IOLA
Dorothy of: 4 GALE
end of the Chisholm Trail:
7 ABILENE
Landon from: 3 ALF
Like ~ in August: 5 CORNY
motto word: 5 ASTRA
playwright: 4 INGE
She never left: 6 AUNTEM
8 AUNTIEEM
**Kansas City**
athlete: 5 CHIEF ROYAL
team: 6 CHIEFS ROYALS

**"___ Kapital":** 3 DAS
**Kaplan**
Comic: 4 GABE
**Kappa**
follower: 6 LAMBDA
preceder: 4 IOTA
**Kaput:** 4 DONE GONE OVER
SHOT 6 RUINED
Go: 3 DIE 4 FAIL
**Karachi**
airline: 3 PIA
**Karamazov**
brother: 4 IVAN 6 DMITRI
**Karan**
Designer: 5 DONNA
**Karaoke**
need: 4 MIKE
**Kara Sea**
border: 4 ASIA
**Karate**
award: 4 BELT
blow: 4 CHOP
Exercise based on: 5 TAEBO
instructor: 6 SENSEI
kin: 4 JUDO
level: 3 DAN
school: 4 DOJO
**"Karate Kid, The"**
costar Pat: 6 MORITA
hero: 6 DANIEL
**Kareem**
Alma mater of: 4 UCLA
~, as a kid: 3 LEW
**Karel**
Playwright: 5 CAPEK
**Karen**
Actress: 7 GRASSLE
**Karen ___ (Isak Dinesen):**
6 BLIXEN
**Karenina**
portrayer: 5 GARBO
**"___ Karenina":** 4 ANNA
**Karl**
Actor: 6 MALDEN
Auto pioneer: 4 BENZ
Bush adviser: 4 ROVE
of the NBA: 6 MALONE
**Karloff**
Actor: 5 BORIS
film: 6 THEAPE
Real last name of: 5 PRATT
role: 5 MUMMY
**Karma:** 5 VIBES
**Karmann ___:** 4 GHIA
**Karnak**
ruler: 6 RAMSES
**Karolyi**
Coach: 4 BELA

**Karras**
of football: 4 ALEX
**Karrie**
Golfer: 4 WEBB
**Karsavina**
Ballerina: 6 TAMARA
**Kasbah**
native: 4 ARAB
**Kasparov**
game: 5 CHESS
Queens, to: 3 MEN
sixteen: 3 MEN
win: 4 MATE
Youngest chess champion
before: 3 TAL
**Kassel**
river: 4 EDER
**Katarina**
Skater: 4 WITT
**Kate**
Model: 4 MOSS
TV mate of: 5 ALLIE
**Katey**
Actress: 5 SAGAL
**Katharina:** 5 SHREW
**Kathie Lee**
Former cohost of: 5 REGIS
~, formerly: 6 COHOST
**Kathmandu**
land: 5 NEPAL
native: 6 NEPALI
**Kathryn**
Actress: 4 ERBE
**Kathy**
Country singer: 6 MATTEA
**Katmandu**
land: 5 NEPAL
native: 6 NEPALI
**Katz**
Actor: 4 OMRI
**Katzenjammer**
kid: 4 HANS
**Kauai**
flier: 4 NENE
Island near: 4 OAHU
keepsake: 3 LEI
**Kaufman**
Comedian: 4 ANDY
role: 5 LATKA
TV show: 4 TAXI
**Kay**
Actress: 4 LENZ
Bandleader: 5 KYSER
follower: 3 ELL
Singer: 5 STARR
**Kayak**
kin: 5 CANOE UMIAK
propeller: 3 OAR
**Kaye**
Actor: 5 DANNY
Bandleader: 5 SAMMY
**Kayo**
count: 3 TEN
**Kayoed:** 3 OUT
**Kazakh**
river: 4 URAL

**Kazakhstan**
capital: 6 ASTANA
former capital: 6 ALMATY
7 ALMAATA
lake: 7 ARALSEA
river: 4 URAL
sea: 4 ARAL
~, formerly (abbr.): 3 SSR
**Kazakh-Uzbek**
sea: 4 ARAL
**Kazan**
Actress: 6 LAINIE
Director: 4 ELIA
native: 5 TATAR
**Kazoo**
Play a: 3 HUM
**k.d.**
Singer: 4 LANG
___ Kea: 5 MAUNA
**Keach**
Actor: 5 STACY
**Keane**
Cartoonist: 3 BIL
**Keanu**
Actor: 6 REEVES
**Keaton**
Actress: 5 DIANE
**Keaton, Buster**
Like: 7 DEADPAN
**Keaton, Michael**
film: 5 MRMOM 6 BATMAN
title role: 5 MRMOM
6 BATMAN
**Keats:** 4 POET 5 ODIST
Always, to: 3 EER
creation: 3 ODE
Frequently, to: 3 OFT
Shelley elegy to: 7 ADONAIS
subject: 3 URN
title starter: 5 ODEON
**Kebab**
bed: 5 PILAF
holder: 4 SPIT
Like: 8 SKEWERED
___ kebab: 5 SHISH
**Kedrova**
Actress: 4 LILA
**Keds**
competitor: 4 AVIA
**Keebler**
baker: 3 ELF
cracker: 4 HIHO
crew: 5 ELVES
spokes-elf: 5 ERNIE
**Keebler, Ernie**
Like: 5 ELFIN
**Keel**
Across the: 5 ABEAM
connector: 4 SKEG
**Keen:** 4 AVID NEAT WAIL
5 ACUTE NEATO
6 ASTUTE
about: 4 INTO
of sight: 9 EAGLEEYED
**Keenan**
Actor: 4 WYNN

**Keep:** 4 HAVE HOLD LAST
SAVE STOW 6 RETAIN
7 LEAVEIN
8 HANGONTO
adding: 6 PILEON
afloat: 4 BUOY
an eye on: 4 TEND
apart: 5 SPACE
at it: 4 GOON 8 PLUGAWAY
away: 5 REPEL
away from: 4 SHUN 5 AVOID
EVADE
company with: 3 SEE
Fail to: 3 ROT
Fail to ~ up: 3 LAG
for later: 5 STORE
from: 5 DETER
from happening: 5 AVERT
from leaving: 6 DETAIN
getting: 5 RENEW
going: 4 LAST 5 RUNON
7 PERSIST
happening: 5 RECUR
in: 4 STET
in a barrel: 3 AGE
in mind: 8 REMEMBER
It'll ~ you going: 7 INERTIA
It won't ~ you up: 5 DECAF
SANKA
out: 3 BAN BAR 5 DEBAR
possession of: 6 RETAIN
secret: 4 HIDE
time: 3 TAP
to oneself: 3 HOG
up: 7 SUSTAIN
8 MAINTAIN
**Keep ___:** 4 ATIT
**Keep an ___:** 5 EYEON
**Keep an ___ the ground:**
5 EARTO
**Keeper:** 6 WARDEN
A ~ may keep it: 3 INN
Creeper: 7 TRELLIS
Game: 5 SNARE 6 ARCADE
Key: 4 RING
Rhythm: 3 TOE
Sheep: 8 HERDSMAN
~, so it's said: 6 FINDER
**Keeping:** 7 CUSTODY
**Keep ___ on:** 5 ANEYE
**Keep ___ profile:** 4 ALOW
**Keepsake:** 5 RELIC TOKEN
7 MEMENTO
Concert: 4 STUB
holder: 6 LOCKET
Kauai: 3 LEI
Personal: 5 TRESS
Wedding: 5 ALBUM
**Kefauver**
Politician: 5 ESTES
**Keg**
contents: 4 BEER
From the: 5 ONTAP
outlet: 3 TAP
stopper: 4 BUNG
**Kegger:** 5 PARTY

**Kegler**
org.: 3 PBA
place: 5 ALLEY
target: 3 PIN 4 PINS
**Keillor, Garrison**
Where ~ began (abbr.): 3 NPR
**Keir**
Actor: 6 DULLEA
**Keister:** 4 REAR RUMP
**Keller, Helen**
birthplace: 7 ALABAMA
Org. cofounded by: 4 ACLU
**Kellogg**
brand: 4 EGGO
selection: 4 POPS
**Kelly**
Actor: 4 GENE
Actress: 5 GRACE MOIRA
Cartoonist: 4 WALT
Clown: 6 EMMETT
Cohost: 4 RIPA
Cohost of: 5 REGIS
Outlaw: 3 NED
**Kelly, Gene**
classic: 15 SINGININTHERAIN
**Kelly, Walt**
comic strip: 4 POGO
**Kelp:** 4 ALGA 5 ALGAE
7 SEAWEED
**Kelsey**
Costar of: 4 PERI RHEA
She played the ex of: 4 BEBE
**Kemal**
Turkish leader: 7 ATATURK
**Kemelman**
character: 5 RABBI
**Kemo ___:** 4 SABE
**Kemo Sabe**
sidekick: 5 TONTO
**Ken:** 4 DOLL
Actor: 4 OLIN
Author: 5 KESEY
Boxer: 6 NORTON
Friend of: 6 BARBIE
Golfer: 7 VENTURI
**Kenan**
Partner of: 3 KEL
**Ken-L Ration**
competitor: 4 ALPO
**Kenmore**
competitor: 5 AMANA
seller: 5 SEARS
**Kennedy:** 3 TED 4 ROSE
5 ETHEL JOHNF
6 EUNICE 7 SENATOR
8 CAROLINE
(abbr.): 3 SEN
coin: 4 HALF
colleague: 6 SCALIA
matriarch: 4 ROSE
Mrs.: 5 ETHEL
Start of a ~ quote: 6 ASKNOT
**Kennedy Center**
architect: 3 PEI 5 IMPEI
**Kennedy Library**
architect: 3 PEI 5 IMPEI

**Kennel**
club info: 5 BREED
command: 3 SIT
cry: 3 ARF YAP YIP
4 WOOF YELP YOWL
6 ARFARF
**Kenneth**
Critic: 5 TYNAN
Judge: 5 STARR
Prosecutor: 5 STARR
**Kenny**
Rocker: 7 LOGGINS
**Kenny G**
accessory: 4 REED
instrument: 3 SAX
label: 6 ARISTA
**Keno**
kin: 5 LOTTO
**Kenobi**
trainee: 5 VADER
**Kenobi, ___-Wan:** 3 OBI
**Kent**
associate: 4 LANE 5 OLSEN
**Kenton**
Director: 4 ERLE
Jazzman: 4 STAN
**Kent State**
state: 4 OHIO
**Kentucky**
college: 5 BEREA
fort: 4 KNOX
landmark:
11 MAMMOTHCAVE
**Kentucky Derby:** *see page 715*
1984 ~ winner: 5 SWALE
drink: 5 JULEP
Five-time ~ winner: 6 ARCARO
7 HARTACK
prize: 5 ROSES
time: 3 MAY
**Kenya**
capital: 7 NAIROBI
caravan: 6 SAFARI
neighbor: 6 SOMALI
president: 3 MOI
revolutionary: 6 MAUMAU
tribesman: 5 MASAI
**Kenyatta University**
city: 7 NAIROBI
**Keogh**
relative: 3 IRA
**Keokuk**
state: 4 IOWA
**Kepler**
Teacher of: 5 BRAHE
**Kerensky**
successor: 5 LENIN
**Kerfuffle:** 3 ADO 4 TODO
**Kern**
Composer: 6 JEROME
creation: 4 SONG
**Kernel:** 3 NUB 4 GIST
site: 3 COB EAR
**Kerns**
Actress: 6 JOANNA
**Kerouac:** 4 BEAT 7 BEATNIK

**Kerr**
Actress: 7 DEBORAH
**Kerri**
Gymnast: 5 STRUG
**Kerrigan**
Skater: 5 NANCY
**Kertesz**
Nobelist: 4 IMRE
**Kesey**
Author: 3 KEN
**Kesselring**
Killer in a ~ play: 7 ARSENIC
**Ketch:** 4 BOAT 5 YACHT
cousin: 4 YAWL
pair: 5 MASTS
**Ketcham**
Country singer: 3 HAL
menace: 6 DENNIS
**Ketone**
Colorless: 6 ACETOL
**Kett**
of comics: 4 ETTA
**Kettle**
and others: 3 MAS
Large: 8 CAULDRON
of fish: 4 MESS
**Kettles:** 7 MAANDPA
8 IRONWARE
**Kevin**
Actor: 5 KLINE 6 SPACEY
"SNL" alum: 6 NEALON
**Kewpie:** 4 DOLL
**Key:** 4 ISLE 5 ISLET 6 OPENER
7 CENTRAL
(abbr.): 3 ALT ESC MAJ MIN
Black: 5 AFLAT BFLAT DFLAT
EFLAT GFLAT 6 ASHARP
Calculator: 5 ENTER
Cartoonist: 3 TED
Cash register: 6 NOSALE
Church: 6 OPENER
color: 5 EBONY
Computer: 3 ALT DEL ESC
TAB 5 ENTER 6 DELETE
SPACER
contraction: 3 OER
food: 4 LIME
French: 3 CLE
Having a: 5 TONAL
Hit the plus: 3 ADD
Important piano: 7 MIDDLEC
in: 4 TYPE 5 ENTER
in again: 6 RETYPE
7 REENTER
Indent: 3 TAB
Jail: 9 CANOPENER
Lacking a: 6 ATONAL
letter: 3 PHI 4 BETA 5 KAPPA
locale: 5 PIANO
material: 5 CORAL EBONY
IVORY
Musical: 5 AFLAT BFLAT
CFLAT DFLAT EFLAT
FFLAT GFLAT 6 EMAJOR
PC: 3 ALT END ESC 5 ENTER
6 DELETE

player: 7 PIANIST
preposition: 3 OER
state (abbr.): 3 FLA
Type of: 5 MINOR
Wide: 5 ENTER
with four sharps: 6 EMAJOR
with no black keys: 6 CMAJOR
with no sharps or flats:
  6 AMINOR
with three sharps (abbr.):
  4 AMAJ
**Key ___:** 4 LIME 5 LARGO
**Key Arena**
team: 6 SONICS
  11 SUPERSONICS
**Keyboard**
bar: 6 SPACER
Count with a: 5 BASIE
expert: 6 TYPIST
instrument: 5 PIANO
  6 SPINET 7 CELESTA
key: 3 ALT DEL ESC TAB
  5 ENTER 6 DELETE
  SPACER
Largest ~ key: 8 SPACEBAR
symbol: 8 ASTERISK
Use a: 4 TYPE
**Keyed up:** 5 HYPER TENSE
**Keyes**
Commentator: 4 ALAN
**Keyhole**
Look through a: 3 SPY 4 PEEK
  6 PEERIN
**Keyless:** 6 ATONAL
**Keynes**
alma mater: 4 ETON
subj.: 4 ECON
**Keynote**
Giva a: 5 ORATE
**Keypad**
key: 5 ENTER
**Keystone**
officer: 3 KOP
place: 4 ARCH
**Keystone Kops:** 7 CHASERS
creator Mack: 7 SENNETT
Like the: 4 ZANY
**Keystone State**
city: 7 ALTOONA
founder: 4 PENN
port: 4 ERIE
**KFC**
piece: 3 LEG 4 WING 6 BREAST
side order: 4 SLAW
**KGB**
employee: 3 AGT
rival: 3 CIA
**Kgs.:** 3 WTS
**Khachaturian**
Composer: 4 ARAM
composition: 10 SABERDANCE
**Khakis:** 4 TANS
Like: 4 DRAB
**Khan**
foe: 4 KIRK
title: 3 AGA

**___ Khan:** 3 AGA ALY 4 AGHA
  BATU 5 SHERE
  7 GENGHIS
**Khan, Genghis**
follower: 5 TATAR 6 MONGOL
  TARTAR
**___ Khan, Yasmin:** 3 AGA
**Khartoum**
country: 5 SUDAN
river: 4 NILE
**Khayyam**
Poet: 4 OMAR
**Khomeini:** 5 IRANI 6 SHIITE
country: 4 IRAN
title: 4 IMAM
**Khrushchev**
country (abbr.): 4 USSR
Premier: 6 NIKITA
**Khyber Pass**
city: 5 KABUL
**Ki ___ (founder of Korea):** 3 TSE
**Kibbutz**
dance: 4 HORA
**Kibosh**
Put the ~ on: 3 END NIX
  4 KILL STOP VETO
  5 CEASE ENDED NIXED
**Kick:** 3 VIM 4 BOOT PUNT
  ZEST 5 GRIPE 6 GROUSE
  RECOIL
Add a ~ to: 4 LACE
a grounder: 3 ERR
back: 4 LOAF REST 5 RELAX
Cake with a: 4 BABA
Dance with a: 5 CONGA
in: 4 ANTE
Kind of: 6 ONSIDE 7 SCISSOR
Little: 4 TANG
off: 4 OPEN 5 BEGIN START
  8 INITIATE
out: 3 BAN 4 OUST 5 EJECT
  EVICT EXILE EXPEL
  6 BANISH DEPORT
  10 DISPOSSESS
Place to ~ something:
  5 REHAB
Stick with a: 3 TNT
target: 4 SHIN
Thing to: 5 HABIT
Top: 6 NONCOM
up your heels: 6 GAMBOL
**Kickback:** 6 RECOIL
**Kicker**
aid: 3 TEE
Famous: 4 PELE
target: 4 SHIN 8 CROSSBAR
  GOALPOST
**Kicking:** 5 ALIVE
partner: 5 ALIVE
**Kickoff:** 5 ONSET START
  6 OPENER OUTSET
aid: 3 TEE
NFL: 4 NATL
**"___ Kick Out of You":** 5 IGETA
**Kicks**
They get their: 5 TIRES

**Kid:** 3 RIB TOT 4 JEST JIVE
  JOKE JOSH TYKE
  5 TEASE
Annoying: 4 BRAT
Base: 8 ARMYBRAT
Composer: 3 ORY
Cow: 4 CALF
cry: 3 BAA MAA 5 MOMMY
Ewe: 4 LAMB
Grownup: 4 GOAT
Jazzman: 3 ORY
king: 3 TUT
name: 5 CISCO
plea: 4 CANI
retort: 5 CANSO DIDSO
Well-behaved: 4 DOLL
wheels: 4 BIKE 5 WAGON
  7 SCOOTER
  10 SKATEBOARD
**Kid-___:** 3 VID
**"___ Kid, The":** 5 CISCO
**Kidd**
Captain: 6 PIRATE
stuff: 5 BOOTY 6 PIRACY
**Kidd, Jason**
team: 4 NETS
**Kidder**
Actress: 6 MARGOT
**Kiddie**
Play in a ~ pool: 4 WADE
racer: 6 GOCART GOKART
transport: 7 SCOOTER
**Kiddie ___:** 3 LIT
**Kiddie lit**
brat: 6 ELOISE
dog: 4 SPOT
elephant: 5 BABAR
giant: 5 SEUSS
trio: 5 BEARS
**Kidding**
Just: 3 NOT
No: 3 GEE 4 GOSH 5 TRULY
  6 DOTELL HONEST
  7 IMEANIT ITSTRUE
  8 ITSAFACT
**Kiddy**
litter: 4 TOYS
**Kidman**
Actress: 6 NICOLE
**Kidnap:** 6 SNATCH
Hearst ~ gp.: 3 SLA
**Kidnapper**
demand: 6 RANSOM
**Kidney**
enzyme: 5 RENIN
related: 5 RENAL
**Kids**
card game: 3 UNO WAR
  6 GOFISH
cereal: 4 TRIX
  10 CAPNCRUNCH
game: 3 TAG 7 STATUES
  8 PATACAKE REDROVER
  9 HOPSCOTCH
  SIMONSAYS
  11 HIDEANDSEEK

Not for: 5 ADULT
question: 3 WHY
Raise: 4 REAR
Watch the: 3 SIT
wheels: 6 TRIKES
**Kierkegaard:** 4 DANE
Philosopher: 5 SOREN
**Kiev**
land: 7 UKRAINE
**Kigali**
land: 6 RWANDA
resident: 7 RWANDAN
**Kiki**
Singer: 3 DEE
**Kilauea**
flow: 4 LAVA
**Kilborn**
TV host: 5 CRAIG
**Kildare**
and others: 3 DRS
**Kilimanjaro**
covering: 4 SNOW
**Kill:** 3 NIX OFF 4 SLAY VETO
7 BUMPOFF
10 STRIKEDOWN
time: 4 IDLE LAZE LOAF
with a click: 3 ZAP
**Killarney**
From: 5 IRISH
Land of: 4 ERIN
**Killebrew**
of baseball: 6 HARMON
**Killed:** 4 SLEW 5 SLAIN
**Killer**
Banned: 3 DDT
Bill: 4 VETO
Bug: 3 DDT 4 DCON
Cereal: 5 ERGOT
Cobra: 8 MONGOOSE
Cold-blooded: 3 ASP 4 TREX
of Scarpia: 5 TOSCA
Sci-fi: 3 RAY
Weed: 3 HOE
whale: 3 ORC 4 ORCA
**Killer ___:** 3 APP
**"Killers, The"**
Gardner of: 3 AVA
**Killjoy:** 11 PARTYPOOPER
**Kill ___ killed:** 4 ORBE
**Kilmer**
Actor: 3 VAL
concern: 4 TREE
creation: 4 POEM
poem: 5 TREES
Poet: 5 JOYCE
**Kiln:** 4 OAST OVEN
Put in a: 3 DRY 4 FIRE
**Kilograms**
1,000 ~: 5 TONNE
**Kilometers**
1.6 ~: 4 MILE
**Kilowatt-hour**
fraction: 3 ERG
**Kilt**
accessory: 3 TAM
feature: 5 PLEAT

pattern: 5 PLAID 6 TARTAN
Pouch worn with a:
7 SPORRAN
wearer: 4 SCOT
**Kilter**
Out of: 4 AWRY 5 AMISS
ASKEW
**Kiltie**
dance: 5 FLING
Young: 3 LAD
**Kim**
Actress: 5 NOVAK
Ex-husband of: 4 ALEC
Singer: 6 CARNES
**___ Kim of hip-hop:** 3 LIL
**Kimberly**
Actress: 5 ELISE
**Kimono**
accessory: 3 OBI 4 SASH
kin: 4 ROBE 6 CAFTAN
**Kin:** 9 RELATIONS
(abbr.): 3 FAM REL
Acquired: 5 INLAW
Certain: 3 MAS
group: 4 CLAN
Kissin': 6 COUSIN
of a spouse: 5 INLAW
Partner of: 4 KITH
**Kind:** 3 ILK 4 NICE SORT TYPE
5 BREED 6 HUMANE
of: 5 QUASI SORTA
8 INASENSE
Of that: 4 SUCH
One of a: 4 UNIT
words: 6 PRAISE
**Kindergarten**
basics: 4 ABCS
break: 3 NAP
disrupter: 4 BRAT
period: 8 PLAYTIME
song start: 3 ABC 4 ABCD
5 ABCDE
**Kindergartner:** 3 TOT 4 TYKE
**Kindled:** 3 LIT
again: 5 RELIT
**Kindling**
Bit of: 4 TWIG
**"... kindness begets kindness
___":** 8 EVERMORE
**Kine:** 6 CATTLE
**Kinetoscope**
inventor: 6 EDISON
**Kinfolk:** 4 CLAN
(abbr.): 4 RELS
**King:** 4 CARD SIRE 5 PIECE
RULER TITLE
7 CHECKER ROYALTY
8 FACECARD
1965 ~ arrest site: 5 SELMA
Actor: 4 ALAN
address: 4 SIRE
À la: 5 EERIE REGAL
SCARY
beater: 3 ACE
Biblical: 4 JEHU OMRI SAUL
5 HEROD 7 SOLOMON

Boy: 3 TUT
Comic: 4 ALAN
Cretan: 5 MINOS
domain: 3 CNN 5 REALM
Egyptian: 3 TUT 6 RAMSES
7 RAMESES
Elgar: 4 OLAF
Eng.: 3 EDW
English: 5 HENRY 6 GEORGE
7 RICHARD
Fairy: 6 OBERON
First ~ of Israel: 4 SAUL
Fit for a: 5 NOBLE REGAL
ROYAL
Golden touch: 5 MIDAS
High ~ hangout: 4 TARA
Home run: 5 AARON
Indian: 4 RAJA 5 RAJAH
lead-in: 3 ALA
Merry old: 4 COLE
Norwegian: 4 OLAF OLAV
of beasts: 4 LION
of Judea: 5 HEROD
of Phrygia: 5 MIDAS
of Siam phrase: 8 ETCETERA
of the Huns: 4 ATLI 6 ATTILA
of the jungle: 4 LION
of the road: 4 HOBO
of tragedy: 4 LEAR
of Troy: 5 PRIAM
of TV talk: 5 LARRY
Persian: 4 SHAH
Place for a: 4 DECK PROM
Pop songwriter: 6 CAROLE
Portuguese: 3 REI
proclamation: 5 EDICT
protector: 4 PAWN ROOK
Ring: 3 ALI
ring thing: 4 SEAL
Saudi: 4 FAHD
seat: 6 THRONE
Shakespearean: 4 LEAR
6 OBERON
Strikeout: 4 RYAN
title (abbr.): 3 REV
topper: 3 ACE
~, in French: 3 ROI 5 LEROI
~, in Latin: 3 REX
~, in Spanish: 3 REY
**King ___:** 4 KONG 5 COBRA
**___ king:** 3 ALA
**King, Larry**
employer: 3 CNN
has a few: 4 EXES
**King, Stephen**
format: 5 EBOOK
home: 5 MAINE
novel: 4 CUJO 6 CARRIE
MISERY 8 THESTAND
9 SALEMSLOT
10 ROSEMADDER
11 FIRESTARTER
novel setting: 5 SALEM
9 SHAWSHANK
10 CASTLEROCK
11 BANGORMAINE

short story collection:
   12 SKELETONCREW
**King, The:** 5 ELVIS
   Middle name of: 4 ARON
**"King ___, The":** 4 ANDI
**"___ King, The":** 4 LION
   6 FISHER
**"___-King, The":** 3 ERL
**"King and I, The"**
   actor Brynner: 3 YUL
   actress: 4 KERR
   character: 4 ANNA
   country: 4 SIAM
   role: 4 ANNA
**King Arthur**
   Father of: 5 UTHER
   Foster brother of: 3 KAY
   6 SIRKAY
   home: 7 CAMELOT
   Nephew of: 6 GARETH
   paradise: 6 AVALON
   Sister of: 4 ANNE
   slayer: 7 MORDRED
**King Atahualpa:** 4 INCA
   5 INCAN
**King Cole**
   fiddlers: 4 TRIO 5 THREE
   request: 4 PIPE
**___ King Cole:** 3 NAT
**King David:** 8 PSALMIST
   creation: 5 PSALM
   Father of: 5 JESSE
   instrument: 4 HARP
   predecessor: 4 SAUL
   Son of: 7 ABSALOM
**Kingdom:** 5 REALM
   Ancient: 4 MOAB 5 NUBIA
   SHEBA
   Biblical: 4 EDOM ELAM
   MOAB
   Himalayan: 5 NEPAL
   6 BHUTAN
   of Croesus: 5 LYDIA
   of Henry IV: 7 NAVARRE
   Old Spanish: 4 LEON
   South Pacific: 5 TONGA
**King Faud:** 5 SAUDI
**King Features**
   competitor: 3 NEA
**King Harald**
   Father of: 4 OLAV
**King Hussein:** 4 ARAB
   Queen of: 4 NOOR
   Widow of: 4 NOOR
**King-jack**
   card combination: 6 TENACE
**King James**
   (abbr.): 3 VER
**"King Kong":** 3 APE
   costar: 4 WRAY
   studio: 3 RKO
**King Lear**
   Daughter of: 5 REGAN
**Kingly:** 5 REGAL ROYAL
   6 REGNAL
   address: 4 SIRE

**King Mark**
   Nephew of: 7 TRISTAN
   Wife of: 6 ISOLDE
**King Minos**
   Daughter of: 7 ARIADNE
   Mother of: 6 EUROPA
   realm: 5 CRETE
**King Mongkut**
   realm: 4 SIAM
   visitor: 4 ANNA
**"King of Comedy, The"**
   star: 6 DENIRO
**King of Torts, The:** 5 BELLI
**Kingpin:** 4 CZAR EXEC
   Kuwaiti: 4 EMIR
**King ___ Saud:** 3 IBN
**King Sisters, The**
   One of: 5 ALYCE
**Kingsley**
   Actor: 3 BEN
   Author: 4 AMIS
**Kings Peak**
   range: 5 UINTA
   state: 4 UTAH
**Kingston**
   group: 4 TRIO
   sch.: 3 URI
**Kingston Trio, The**
   hit song: 3 MTA
   9 TOMDOOLEY
**Kinison**
   Comic: 3 SAM
**Kinks, The**
   hit song: 4 LOLA
   Ray of: 6 DAVIES
**Kinky**
   do: 4 AFRO
**Kinnear**
   Actor: 4 GREG
**Kinshasa**
   country, once: 5 ZAIRE
   river: 5 CONGO
**Kinship:** 3 TIE
   emblem: 5 TOTEM
**Kinski**
   role: 4 TESS
**Kinsman:** 3 SIB
   (abbr.): 3 REL
   ~, in Spanish: 3 TIO
**___ Kinte:** 5 KUNTA
**Kip**
   spender: 7 LAOTIAN
   Where ~ are spent: 4 LAOS
**Kipling**
   lad: 3 KIM
   novel: 3 KIM
   poem: 8 GUNGADIN
   10 FUZZYWUZZY
   python: 3 KAA
   story setting: 5 INDIA
   wolf: 5 AKELA
**___ Kippur:** 3 YOM
**Kirby**
   Actor: 5 BRUNO
**Kirghizia**
   city: 3 OSH

**Kirk**
   (abbr.): 4 CAPT
   diary: 3 LOG
   Journey for: 4 TREK
   Officer under: 4 SULU
   5 UHURA
   portrayer: 7 SHATNER
**Kirkland**
   Labor-leader: 4 LANE
**Kirkuk**
   country: 4 IRAQ
   native: 4 KURD
**Kirlian**
   photography image: 4 AURA
**Kirsten**
   Actress: 5 DUNST
**Kishke:** 5 DERMA
**Kismet:** 4 FATE 5 KARMA
   7 DESTINY
**Kiss:** 4 BUSS 5 SMACK
   6 SMOOCH 8 OSCULATE
   partner: 4 TELL
   Prelude to a: 3 IDO
   Prepare to: 6 PUCKER
   Quick: 4 PECK
   sound: 5 SMACK
   ~, in Spanish: 4 BESO
**"Kiss, The"**
   sculptor: 5 RODIN
**Kisser:** 3 LIP MUG YAP 4 PUSS
   TRAP
   Baby: 3 POL
   Nickname for a good:
   7 HOTLIPS
**Kisses**
   Like some: 6 STOLEN
   partner: 4 HUGS
**Kit**
   and caboodle: 3 ALL 4 ALOT
   call: 4 MEOW
   First aid ~ item: 4 TAPE
   6 IPECAC
   item: 4 TOOL
   Like ~ pieces: 6 PRECUT
   Makeup ~ item: 5 LINER
   7 MASCARA
   partner: 8 CABOODLE
   Scout: 6 CARSON
   Sewing ~ item: 5 SPOOL
   6 NEEDLE
**Kitchen:** 4 ROOM
   add-on: 4 ETTE
   appliance: 4 OVEN 5 RANGE
   STOVE 6 FRIDGE
   7 TOASTER 8 DISPOSAL
   9 CANOPENER
   appliance brand: 5 AMANA
   bar: 4 OLEO SOAP
   basin: 4 SINK
   cleaner: 3 MOP 5 COMET
   cloth: 7 DISHRAG
   counter: 5 TIMER
   coverup: 5 APRON
   filter: 5 SIEVE
   fixture: 4 SINK 5 RANGE
   7 CABINET

foil: 5 ALCOA
gadget: 5 CORER DICER
   LADLE PARER RICER
   SIEVE TIMER TONGS
   6 BASTER BEATER
   GRATER OPENER
   PEELER SLICER
   7 SPATULA UTENSIL
   8 STRAINER
   9 CANOPENER
gadget maker: 3 OXO
glove: 4 MITT
hanger: 7 POTHOOK
intruder: 3 ANT
item: 6 SPONGE
   7 UTENSIL
It runs in the: 3 TAP
Kind of: 5 EATIN
light: 5 PILOT
pest: 3 ANT
spray: 3 PAM
spread: 4 OLEO
tear-jerker: 5 ONION
utensil maker: 3 OXO
vessel: 3 PAN POT
whistler: 6 TEAPOT
worker: 4 CHEF COOK
wrap: 5 SARAN
"Kitchen God's Wife, The"
   Author: 3 TAN
Kite: 4 BIRD
   Golfer: 3 TOM
   home: 4 NEST
   Kind of: 3 BOX
   part: 4 BEAK TAIL
Kith
   partner: 3 KIN
Kitsch
   opposite: 5 TASTE
Kitschy: 9 TASTELESS
   film monster: 5 RODAN
   lawn figure: 8 FLAMINGO
Kitt
   Singer/actress: 6 EARTHA
Kitt, Eartha
   hit: 9 CESTSIBON
Kitten
   cry: 3 MEW
   plaything: 4 YARN
   quality: 8 CUTENESS
Kitty: 3 POT 4 PUSS
   Comment to: 4 SCAT
   Contented ~ sound: 4 PURR
   cry: 3 MEW 4 MEOW
   Feed the: 4 ANTE
Kitty ___: 5 OSHEA 6 LITTER
Kiva
   builder: 4 HOPI
Kiwi: 6 RATITE
   Native: 5 MAORI
   relative: 3 EMU MOA
Klaxon: 5 ALARM
   cause: 5 ALERT
Klee: 5 SWISS
   Artist: 4 PAUL
   contemporary: 3 ARP

Klein
   Designer: 4 ANNE
"___ kleine Nachtmusik":
   4 EINE
Klemperer
   Actor: 6 WERNER
   Conductor: 4 OTTO
Klensch
   CNN style maven: 4 ELSA
Klimt
   birthplace: 6 VIENNA
   Painter: 6 GUSTAV
Kline
   Actor: 5 KEVIN
   movie: 4 DAVE
Kline, Kevin
   Wife of: 5 CATES
Klinger
   hometown: 6 TOLEDO
   portrayer: 4 FARR
   rank (abbr.): 3 CPL
Klingon: 5 ALIEN
   and others: 3 ETS
   Enterprise: 4 WORF
Klink
   clink: 6 STALAG
   Prisoner of: 5 HOGAN
   Secretary to: 5 HELGA
Klink, Colonel
   portrayer:
     15 WERNERKLEMPERER
KLM
   rival: 3 SAS
Klondike
   find: 3 ORE 4 GOLD
   territory: 5 YUKON
Kluszewski
   of baseball: 3 TED
Klutz: 3 OAF 4 CLOD
   6 GALOOT
   cry: 4 OHNO OOPS
Klutzy: 5 INEPT
   one: 3 OAF
Knack: 3 ART WAY 5 FLAIR
   6 TALENT
   Lacking the: 5 INEPT
Knapsack: 6 KITBAG
Knave: 3 CAD 5 ROGUE
   6 RASCAL
   loot: 4 TART
Knead: 7 MASSAGE
Kneading
   Needing: 4 ACHY SORE
   5 TENSE
Kneads
   Person who: 5 BAKER
   7 MASSEUR
   8 MASSEUSE
Knee: 5 HINGE JOINT
   Ask on bended: 5 PLEAD
   bend: 4 PLIE
   Injure a: 4 SKIN 6 SCRAPE
   It goes below the: 4 MIDI
   Jerk your: 5 REACT
   neighbor: 4 SHIN
   protector: 3 PAD

Knee-ankle
   connection: 5 TIBIA 6 FIBULA
Kneecap: 7 PATELLA
Knee-high
   to a grasshopper: 4 TINY
Knee-slapper: 4 HOOT JOKE
   RIOT 6 GASSER
   HOTONE
Knell: 4 PEAL
Knickers: 5 PANTS
Knickknack: 4 ITEM 5 CURIO
   6 DOODAD NOTION
   7 MEMENTO TRINKET
   holder: 5 SHELF 7 ETAGERE
Knicks
   coach: 5 RILEY
   coach Riley: 3 PAT
   org.: 3 NBA
   venue: 3 MSG
Knievel
   Daredevil: 4 EVEL
   specialty: 5 STUNT 6 STUNTS
Knife: 4 SHIV STAB 6 WEAPON
   Butter: 8 SPREADER
   Eskimo: 3 ULU
   Hacking: 4 BOLO 7 MACHETE
   handle: 4 HAFT HILT
   holder: 6 SHEATH
   Kind of: 5 BOWIE XACTO
   Large ~ of yore: 4 SNEE
   Like a good: 5 SHARP
   maker: 6 CUTLER
   on TV: 5 GINSU
   sharp part: 4 EDGE
   Use a: 4 PARE SLIT STAB
Knight: 3 SIR 5 TITLE
   Actor: 3 TED
   address: 3 SIR
   aide: 4 PAGE
   apprentice: 6 SQUIRE
   award (abbr.): 3 OBE
   cap: 6 HELMET
   clothes: 4 MAIL 5 ARMOR
   9 CHAINMAIL
   club: 4 MACE
   duel: 5 JOUST
   fight: 4 TILT
   game: 5 JOUST
   job: 5 QUEST
   lady: 4 DAME
   Like a: 6 TITLED
   Make a: 3 DUB
   mare: 5 STEED
   mount: 5 STEED
   neighbor: 4 ROOK 6 BISHOP
   noise: 5 CLANK
   of note: 6 GLADYS
   of the Round Table: 3 KAY
   4 BORS 6 GARETH
   GAWAIN 7 GALAHAD
   MORDRED TRISTAN
   8 LANCELOT
   Roving, as a: 6 ERRANT
   spot: 5 MALTA
   Star Wars: 4 JEDI
   superior: 7 BARONET

time: 4 YORE
title: 3 SIR
tunic: 6 TABARD
weapon: 5 LANCE
work: 5 QUEST
**Knight ___:** 7 TEMPLAR
**Knighted**
actor Guinness: 4 ALEC
actor McKellen: 3 IAN
architect: 4 WREN
composer: 5 ELGAR
conductor: 5 SOLTI 6 PREVIN
Prepare to be: 5 KNEEL
**Knightwear:** 5 ARMOR
**Knish**
ingredient: 6 POTATO
noshery: 4 DELI
**Knit:** 4 HEAL MEND
alternative: 4 PURL
shirt: 4 POLO
**Knitted**
blanket: 6 AFGHAN
shoe: 6 BOOTEE
wrap: 5 SHAWL
**Knitting**
item: 5 SKEIN
need: 4 YARN
project: 6 AFGHAN
stitch: 4 PURL
tool: 6 NEEDLE
**Knob:** 4 NODE
Control: 4 DIAL
Organ: 4 STOP
Radio: 5 TUNER
TV: 4 TINT VERT
**Knobby:** 5 NODAL
**Knock:** 3 DIS RAP
about: 4 ROAM
down: 4 DECK FELL RAZE
    TAMP 5 UPSET 6 DEBASE
    DEFAME DEMOTE
    LAYLOW
down a peg: 5 ABASE
Engine: 4 PING
follower: 5 KNEED
for a loop: 4 DAZE STUN
Hard: 3 BOP RAP 5 THUMP
It'll ~ you out: 5 ETHER
off: 4 DOIN SLAY STOP
    5 CEASE
on the noggin: 4 CONK
out: 3 AWE 6 SEDATE
    7 FLATTEN
over: 3 AWE ROB 6 TOPPLE
prefix: 4 ANTI
response: 5 ENTER
    6 COMEIN
senseless: 4 DAZE STUN
the socks off: 3 WOW 5 AMAZE
    6 DAZZLE
**Knock-___:** 5 KNEED
**Knocked**
for a loop: 5 AREEL
over: 5 SPILT
**Knocker:** 6 CRITIC
place: 4 DOOR

reply: 5 ITSME
**Knock for ___:** 5 ALOOP
**Knocking**
sound: 4 PING 7 RATATAT
    10 RATATATTAT
Source of: 3 GIN
**Knock-knock**
joke: 3 PUN
**Knockoff:** 5 CLONE
**Knockout:** 4 LULU
It's a: 5 ETHER
**Knoll:** 5 MOUND
**Knossos**
King of: 5 MINOS
locale: 5 CRETE
**Knot:** 3 TIE 4 NODE 5 SKEIN
    TIEUP UNITE
again: 5 RETIE
In a: 5 TENSE
Loosen a: 4 UNDO 5 UNTIE
Tie the: 3 WED
type: 7 BOWLINE
Wild West: 5 NOOSE
work: 7 MACRAME
**Knotted**
neckwear: 3 TIE 5 ASCOT
up: 5 TENSE
**Knotty**
craft: 7 MACRAME
wood: 4 PINE
**Knot-tying**
phrase: 3 IDO
place: 5 ALTAR 6 CHAPEL
**Know**
A way to: 3 ESP
Before you ~ it: 4 SOON
In the: 3 HEP HIP 5 AWARE
In the ~ about: 4 ONTO
    5 HEPTO
Just: 5 SENSE 6 INTUIT
Old enough to ~ better:
    5 ADULT
Wanted to: 5 ASKED
**___ Know:** 4 ALLI
**Know-how:** 3 ART
**Knowing**
about: 4 ONTO
**Know-it-all:** 8 WISEACRE
**Knowledge:** 3 KEN 4 LORE
    7 SCIENCE
Body of: 4 LORE
Field of: 6 SPHERE
Gain: 5 LEARN
Impart: 5 TEACH
Range of: 3 KEN
Traditional: 4 LORE
**"___ Knowledge":** 6 CARNAL
**Knowledgeable:** 4 WISE
    5 AWARE
about: 4 INON
**Known**
Least: 6 RAREST
Make: 3 AIR 4 TELL
Once ~ as: 3 NEE
Well: 8 ONTHEMAP
**___ known:** 4 HADI

**Knows**
about: 6 ISONTO
What the nose: 4 ODOR
    5 AROMA SMELL
**"___ Knows" (Dion & the
    Belmonts hit):** 5 NOONE
**"___ know you?":** 3 DOI
**Knox:** 4 FORT
and others (abbr.): 3 FTS
**Knoxville**
athlete: 3 VOL
org.: 3 TVA
sch.: 5 UTENN
**Knuckle:** 5 JOINT
dragger: 3 APE
**Knucklehead:** 4 BOZO DODO
    DOPE TWIT 5 IDIOT
    MORON
**KO**
counter: 3 REF
**K-O**
filler: 3 LMN
**Koala**
home: 4 TREE
**Koan**
teaching: 3 ZEN
**Kobe:** 5 LAKER
City near: 5 OSAKA
cummerbund: 3 OBI
currency: 3 YEN
**Koblenz**
cry: 3 ACH
**Koch**
and others: 3 EDS
Mayor before: 5 BEAME
memoir: 5 MAYOR
**Kodak**
competitor: 4 FUJI 8 FUJIFILM
film brand: 4 TMAX
moments: 3 ADS
**Kodaly**
Composer: 6 ZOLTAN
**Kofi**
country: 5 GHANA
of the U.N.: 5 ANNAN
predecessor: 3 DAG
**Koh-i-___:** 4 NOOR
**Kohoutek:** 5 COMET
**Kojak**
Detective: 4 THEO
Lt.: 4 THEO
portrayer: 7 SAVALAS
**Kol ___ (Hebrew prayer):**
    5 NIDRE
**Köln:** 5 STADT
crowd: 4 DREI
**Kong:** 3 APE
costar: 4 WRAY
**___ Kong:** 4 HONG
**Konica**
competitor: 4 AGFA
    5 CANON
**Königsberg**
philosopher: 4 KANT
**Kon-Tiki:** 4 RAFT
wood: 5 BALSA

**Kon-Tiki Museum**
site: 4 OSLO
**Kook:** 3 NUT
**Kooky:** 3 ODD 4 LOCO NUTS
    ZANY
**Koontz**
Author: 4 DEAN
**Koop**
and others: 3 SGS
**Kopecks**
100 ~: 5 RUBLE
**Koppel**
News host: 3 TED
**Koran**
deity: 5 ALLAH
language: 6 ARABIC
Like the: 7 ISLAMIC
religion: 5 ISLAM
**Korbut**
Gymnast: 4 OLGA
**Korda**
of tennis: 4 PETR
**Korea**
and others: 7 FAREAST
    8 EASTASIA
continent: 4 ASIA
Sitcom set in: 4 MASH
Syngman of: 4 RHEE
**Korea Bay**
feeder: 4 YALU
**Korean:** 5 ASIAN 9 EASTASIAN
carmaker: 3 KIA
money: 3 WON
river: 4 YALU
soldier: 3 ROK
statesman: 4 RHEE
**Korean War**
fighter: 3 MIG
**Korngold**
Composer: 5 ERICH
**Kosher:** 5 LEGIT LICIT
Airline that serves only ~ food:
    4 ELAL
It may be: 4 DELI
Not: 4 TREF
One who keeps things: 5 RABBI
**Kosovo**
ally: 7 ALBANIA
citizen: 4 SERB
defense gp.: 4 NATO
**Koss, Johann ___**
Speed skater: 4 OLAV
**Kostelanetz**
Conductor: 5 ANDRE
**Kosygin**
Soviet leader: 6 ALEXEI
**Kotcheff**
Director: 3 TED
**Kotter**
portrayer: 6 KAPLAN
portrayer Kaplan: 4 GABE
student: 8 SWEATHOG
**Kotter, Mrs.**
portrayer: 9 STRASSMAN
**Koufax**
Pitcher: 5 SANDY

stat.: 3 ERA
**Kournikova**
of tennis: 4 ANNA
**Koussevitzky**
Conductor: 5 SERGE
**Kovacs**
Comic: 5 ERNIE
**Kovacs, Mrs.:** 4 EDIE
**Kovic**
War memoirist: 3 RON
**Kowalski**
portrayer: 6 BRANDO
shout: 6 STELLA
**K.P.**
Do ~ work: 4 PEEL
tool: 5 PARER 6 PEELER
**K-P**
filler: 4 LMNO
**Kraft Foods**
brand: 4 OREO 5 SANKA
**Krait**
kin: 3 ASP
**Kramden**
laugh: 3 HAR
Mr.: 5 RALPH
Mrs.: 5 ALICE
Norton, to: 3 PAL
Pal of: 6 NORTON
    8 EDNORTON
portrayer: 7 GLEASON
vehicle: 3 BUS
**Kramer**
Quarterback: 4 ERIK
**"Kramer vs. Kramer"**
director: 6 BENTON
**Krantz, Judith**
novel: 8 SCRUPLES
**Krasner**
Artist: 3 LEE
**Krauss**
Pop singer: 6 ALISON
**Kravitz**
Pop singer: 5 LENNY
**Krazy**
of comics: 3 KAT
**Krazy ___:** 3 KAT
**Kresge, S.S.**
~, now: 5 KMART
**Kreskin**
forte: 3 ESP
**Kringle**
Mr.: 4 KRIS 5 KRISS
**Krishna**
chant: 6 MANTRA
preceder: 4 HARE
**Krispy ___:** 5 KREME
**Kristin**
Swimmer: 4 OTTO
**Kristofferson**
Actor/singer: 4 KRIS
**Kroc**
of McDonald's: 3 RAY
**"___ Kröger"** (Thomas Mann
    novella): 5 TONIO
**Krona**
part: 3 ORE

**Krone**
part: 3 ORE
**Kroon**
country: 7 ESTONIA
**___ Kross (rap duo):** 4 KRIS
**Krueger**
of Elm Street: 6 FREDDY
street: 3 ELM
**Kruger**
Actor: 4 OTTO
NBA coach: 3 LON
**Kruger, ___ Paul:** 3 OOM
**Krupa**
Drummer: 4 GENE
instrument: 4 DRUM
portrayer: 8 SALMINEO
**Krupp**
of hockey: 3 UWE
works city: 5 ESSEN
**Krusty:** 5 CLOWN
**Krypton:** 3 GAS 6 PLANET
    7 RAREGAS
Like: 5 INERT
**K.T.**
Singer: 5 OSLIN
**Kuala Lumpur**
country: 8 MALAYSIA
language: 5 MALAY
native: 5 MALAY
**Kublai ___:** 4 KHAN
**Kubrick**
computer: 3 HAL
Director: 7 STANLEY
**Kudos:** 5 HONOR 6 PRAISE
**Kudrow**
Actress: 4 LISA
**Kudu:** 8 ANTELOPE
**Kudzu:** 4 VINE
**Kukla**
friend: 4 FRAN 5 OLLIE
**Kukoc**
of basketball: 4 TONI
**Kulik**
Figure skater: 4 ILIA
**Kumar**
Actor: 4 HARI
**Kumquat**
shape: 4 OVAL
**Kung ___:** 3 PAO
**Kunta ___:** 5 KINTE
**Kunta Kinte**
slave name: 4 TOBY
**Kupcinet**
Journalist: 3 IRV
**Kurdistan**
Bit of: 4 IRAN
peak: 6 ARARAT
**Kurds**
Home to some: 4 IRAN IRAQ
**Kurosawa**
Director: 5 AKIRA
film: 3 RAN 8 RASHOMON
**Kurt**
Conductor: 5 ADLER MASUR
denial: 4 NEIN
Quarterback: 6 WARNER

Wife of: 5 LOTTE
**Kurtz**
  Actress: 7 SWOOSIE
  Conductor: 5 EFREM
**Kuwait:** 7 EMIRATE
  peninsula: 6 ARABIA
**Kuwaiti:** 4 ARAB
  money: 5 DINAR
  ruler: 4 EMIR 5 EMEER
**Kvass**
  ingredient: 3 RYE
**Kvetch:** 4 CARP CRAB MOAN
         5 GRIPE WHINE
         6 GROUSE MOANER
  cry: 5 OYVEY

**Kwai**
  River ~ locale: 4 SIAM
**Kwan:** 6 SKATER
  Actress: 5 NANCY
  move: 4 AXEL
**Kwanzaa**
  principle: 5 FAITH UNITY
**KwaZulu-___:** 5 NATAL
**Kwik-E-Mart**
  clerk: 3 APU
  ___ kwon do: 3 TAE
**Ky.**
  neighbor: 4 TENN
**Kyle**
  Brother of: 3 IKE

  of football: 4 ROTE
**Kyoto**
  carrier: 3 JAL
  cash: 3 YEN
  cummerbund: 3 OBI
  garment: 6 KIMONO
  killer: 5 NINJA
**Kyrgyz**
  city: 3 OSH
  range: 4 ALAI
**Kyrgyzstan**
  city: 3 OSH
  range: 4 ALAI
**Kyser**
  Bandleader: 3 KAY

# L1

**L:** 5 FIFTY LARGE
**La**
  lead-in: 3 SOL TRA
**La ___**
  (Milan opera house): 5 SCALA
  (San Diego resort): 5 JOLLA
**"La ___"**
  (Debussy work): 3 MER
  (Fellini film): 6 STRADA
  (Puccini work): 6 BOHEME
  (Ravel work): 5 VALSE
  (Ritchie Valens hit): 5 BAMBA
**Lab**
  animal: 3 RAT
  burner: 4 ETNA
  container: 4 VIAL
  cry: 3 AHA
  dish: 5 PETRI
  eggs: 3 OVA
  employee: 6 TESTER
  Fictional ~ assistant: 4 IGOR
  fluids: 4 SERA
  gel: 4 AGAR
  heater: 4 ETNA
  procedure: 4 TEST
  rat's course: 4 MAZE
  runner: 3 RAT
  slide objects: 6 AMEBAE
  subj.: 3 SCI
  swimmer: 5 AMEBA
  Take back to the: 6 RETEST
  tube: 7 BURETTE PIPETTE
  unit: 4 GRAM
  work: 5 TESTS
**"La Bamba"**
  actor Morales: 4 ESAI
  actress Elizabeth: 4 PENA
**Label:** 3 TAG 4 NAME 5 IDTAG
    7 NAMETAG
  anew: 5 RETAG
  info: 4 SIZE
  Lapel: 5 IDTAG
  Loo: 5 GENTS
  Put a new ~ on: 5 RETAG
    6 RENAME
  Record: 3 EMI MCA RCA SUN
    4 KTEL 5 ASCAP DECCA
    6 ARISTA
**LaBelle**
  Singer: 5 PATTI
  song: 13 LADYMARMALADE
**"La Belle et la ___":** 4 BETE
**Labine**
  Pitcher: 4 CLEM
**"La Bohème":** 5 OPERA
  heroine: 4 MIMI
  highlight: 4 ARIA
  Updated version of: 4 RENT

**La ___, Bolivia:** 3 PAZ
**"La ___ Bonita":** 4 ISLA
**Labor:** 4 TOIL WORK 6 STRIVE
  camp: 5 GULAG
  group: 5 UNION
  issue: 5 CHILD
  output: 4 BABY
  partner: 5 PARTS
**Labor Day**
  mo.: 3 SEP 4 SEPT
**Laborer**
  Anglo-Saxon: 4 ESNE
  Lowly: 4 PEON
  Medieval: 4 ESNE SERF
  Menial: 4 PEON
  Migrant: 7 BRACERO
**Laborious:** 6 UPHILL
    8 TOILSOME
  routine: 5 GRIND
**Labrador:** 3 DOG
  retriever: 4 SPCA
**La Brea**
  attraction: 6 TARPIT
  goo: 3 TAR
**Labyrinth:** 4 MAZE
  King who had the ~ built:
    5 MINOS
  suffix: 3 INE
**Lac**
  contents: 3 EAU
**"La Campanella":** 5 ETUDE
**Lace:** 3 TIE 7 TATTING
  again: 5 RETIE
  color: 4 ECRU
  Hole for a: 6 EYELET
  Loosen a: 5 UNTIE
  Made: 6 TATTED
  Make: 3 TAT
  place: 4 SHOE 6 EYELET
  tip: 5 AGLET
**Lacework**
  Do: 3 TAT
**Lachesis**
  Clotho, ~, and Atropos:
    5 FATES
**Lachrymal**
  secretion: 4 TEAR
**Lachrymose:** 5 TEARY
**Lack:** 4 NEED 6 DEARTH
    7 ABSENCE
**Lackadaisical:** 4 SLOW
  response: 6 MANANA
**Lackawanna**
  lake: 4 ERIE
**___ Lackawanna Railroad:**
    4 ERIE
**Lacking:** 3 SHY 4 LESS SANS
    5 NEEDY OUTOF SHORT

  a key: 6 ATONAL
  color: 4 PALE
  compassion: 8 INHUMANE
  couth: 4 RUDE
  in variety: 7 ONENOTE
  locks: 4 BALD
  moisture: 3 DRY 4 ARID
  muscle: 4 WEAK
  play: 4 TAUT
  principles: 6 AMORAL
  siblings: 4 ONLY
  skill: 5 INEPT
  slack: 4 TAUT
  substance: 4 AIRY 5 INANE
  value: 3 NIL
  vitality: 6 ANEMIC
**Lackluster:** 4 DRAB DULL
**Lacks:** 5 HASNT
**"L.A. Confidential"**
  actress Basinger: 3 KIM
**Laconic:** 5 TERSE
**Lacoste**
  of fashion: 4 IZOD
  of tennis: 4 RENE
**Lacquer:** 5 JAPAN
  ingredient: 5 ELEMI RESIN
**Lacquered**
  metalware: 4 TOLE
**Lacrosse**
  team: 3 TEN
**Lact-**
  suffix: 3 OSE
**Lacto-___ vegetarian:** 3 OVO
**Lacuna:** 3 GAP
**Lacy**
  item: 5 DOILY
  loop: 5 PICOT
**Lad:** 3 BOY
  love: 4 LASS
**Ladd**
  Actor: 4 ALAN
  Actress: 5 DIANE
    6 CHERYL
**Ladd, Alan**
  film: 3 OSS 5 SHANE
  role: 5 SHANE
**Ladder**
  Climb the: 4 RISE
  He dreamt about a: 5 JACOB
  Hose: 3 RUN
  Item with a: 5 SLIDE
  Lover with a: 6 ELOPER
  part: 4 RUNG STEP
  step: 4 RUNG
  Top of the corporate: 3 CEO
  ~, in Italian: 5 SCALA
**"Ladders to Fire"**
  novelist: 3 NIN

**Laddie:** 4 BOYO
  love: 4 LASS
**La-di-da:** 6 TOOTOO
**Ladies**
  man: 4 GENT 5 ROMEO
    8 CASANOVA
  room: 5 HAREM
**Ladle:** 5 SPOON 6 DIPPER
**"La Dolce ___":** 4 VITA
**"La Dolce Vita"**
  director: 7 FELLINI
  setting: 4 ROME
  star Anouk: 5 AIMEE
**"___ la Douce":** 4 IRMA
**Lady:** 7 PEERESS
  Church: 3 NUN
  escort: 4 GENT
  First: 3 EVE
  Foxy: 5 VIXEN
  Lea: 3 EWE
  Little: 4 GIRL
  Loved: 4 LUCY
  of the house: 5 MADAM
  of the knight: 4 DAME
  Scat: 4 ELLA
  That: 3 HER SHE
  title: 3 MRS 5 MADAM
  What the fat ~ sings: 4 ARIA
    5 OPERA
  Young: 4 GIRL LASS MISS
  ~, in Italian: 5 DONNA
  ~, in Spanish: 3 SRA 4 DONA
    6 SENORA
**"___ Lady":** 5 SHESA
**"Lady ___, The":** 3 EVE
  5 INRED
**"Lady and the Tramp"**
  breed: 7 SIAMESE
**Ladybug**
  feature: 5 SPOTS
  prey: 5 APHID
**"Lady Jane Grey"**
  dramatist: 4 ROWE
**Lady-killer:** 5 ROMEO
  8 LOTHARIO
**"Lady Lindy":** 7 EARHART
**"Lady Love"**
  singer: 5 RAWLS
**Lady Macbeth:** 4 ROLE
**___ Lady of Fatima:** 3 OUR
**"Lady of the Lake, The"**
  author: 5 SCOTT
**"Lady Sings the Blues"**
  star: 4 ROSS
**Lady's man:** 3 SIR 4 BEAU
  EARL GENT LORD
  5 ROMEO
**Lady's-slipper:** 6 ORCHID
**"Lady ___ Tramp, The":** 3 ISA
**Laertes**
  sister: 7 OPHELIA
**Lafayette**
  recruiter Silas: 5 DEANE
**Lafayette College**
  home: 6 EASTON
**Lag:** 5 TRAIL

**Lagasse**
  Chef: 6 EMERIL
**L'Age ___:** 3 DOR
**Lager**
  holder: 5 STEIN
  kin: 3 ALE
  Light: 7 PILSNER
**Lagerlöf**
  Novelist: 5 SELMA
**Laggard:** 4 POKE 6 SLOUCH
**Lago**
  contents: 4 AGUA
**Lagomorphic**
  leaper: 4 HARE
**Lagoon**
  surrounder: 5 ATOLL
**LaGuardia Airport**
  Stadium near: 4 ASHE SHEA
**"___ la guerre!":** 4 CEST
**"Lah-di-___!":** 3 DAH
**Lahore**
  garb: 4 SARI
  language: 4 URDU
**Lahr**
  Actor: 4 BERT
  role: 4 LION
**"La ___ Humaine" (Jean Renoir**
  **film):** 4 BETE
**Laid**
  Be ~ up: 3 AIL
  It's often ~ down: 6 THELAW
  low: 3 HID
  off: 5 IDLED
  up: 3 ILL 4 ABED 5 INBED
**Laid-back:** 5 STAID TYPEB
  6 ATEASE
  Hardly: 5 TYPEA
  In a ~ fashion: 4 IDLY
  quality: 4 EASE
  sort: 5 TYPEB
**Laila**
  Boxer: 3 ALI
**Laine**
  Jazz singer: 4 CLEO
**Laine, Frankie**
  hit song: 8 IBELIEVE
**Lair:** 3 DEN 7 HIDEOUT
  Bear: 3 DEN
  Lofty: 5 AERIE
**Laissez-___:** 5 FAIRE
**Lake**
  boat: 5 CANOE
  craft: 5 CANOE
  dweller: 5 TROUT
  Fictional: 7 WOBEGON
  lander: 8 SEAPLANE
  Land in a: 5 ISLET
  maker: 3 DAM
  rental: 5 CANOE
  Resort: 5 TAHOE
  tribe: 4 ERIE
  Western: 5 TAHOE
**Lake ___**
  (Blue Nile source): 4 TANA
  (Mississippi river source):
    6 ITASCA

**Lake Assad**
  setting: 5 SYRIA
**Lake Geneva**
  spa: 5 EVIAN
**Lake Mead**
  Like: 7 MANMADE
**Lake Michigan**
  city: 4 GARY 6 RACINE
**Lake Nasser**
  City near: 5 ASWAN
**"Lake ___ of Innisfree, The":**
  4 ISLE
**Lake Okeechobee**
  state: 3 FLA
**Lake Ontario**
  River to: 7 GENESEE
**Laker**
  Great: 4 SHAQ 5 ONEAL
  org.: 3 NBA
**Lake Tahoe**
  City near: 4 RENO
**Lake Titicaca**
  is partly here: 4 PERU
  locale: 5 ANDES
**Lake Volta**
  locale: 5 GHANA
**"Lakmé"**
  soprano: 5 ELLEN
**La-la**
  lead-in: 3 OOH TRA
**___ la la:** 3 TRA
**"___ La La" (Manfred Mann hit):**
  3 SHA
**"L.A. Law"**
  actor Richard: 6 DYSART
  actress Susan: 3 DEY
  lawyer: 5 ARNIE
**Lalique**
  Glassmaker and jeweler:
    4 RENE
**Lallygag:** 4 LOAF
**"La Loge"**
  painter: 6 RENOIR
**Lam**
  Go on the: 4 FLEE
  One on the: 5 FLEER
    7 ESCAPEE
  On the: 5 LOOSE
  Went on the: 6 LITOUT
**Lama**
  land: 5 TIBET
  Like Nash's: 4 ONEL
**___ Lama:** 5 DALAI
**"___ Lama Ding Dong":**
  4 RAMA
**La Mancha**
  Lady of: 6 SENORA
  Man of: 5 SENOR
**Lamarr**
  Actress: 4 HEDY
**"La Marseillaise":**
  6 ANTHEM
**Lamb:** 4 MEAT 8 ESSAYIST
  alias: 4 ELIA
  A little: 4 CHOP
  Had a little: 3 ATE

Like a: 4 MEEK
mother: 3 EWE
noise: 3 BAA
of literature: 4 ELIA
pen name: 4 ELIA
product: 5 ESSAY
sandwich: 4 GYRO
serving: 4 CHOP RACK
sound: 5 BLEAT
Tender: 3 EWE
**Lamb, Charles:** 8 ESSAYIST
pen name: 4 ELIA
**Lambaste:** 4 SLAM 5 CREAM
    SCOLD 6 RAILAT
**Lamb Chop**
puppeteer Lewis: 5 SHARI
**Lambert Airport**
code: 3 STL
**Lamborghini**
owner: 4 AUDI
**Lambs**
Like: 5 OVINE
~, in Latin: 4 AGNI
**Lame:** 6 FEEBLE FLIMSY
excuse: 7 IFORGOT
**Lament:** 3 RUE 4 MOAN
    5 MOURN 6 BEMOAN
    GRIEVE 7 DEPLORE
loudly: 4 KEEN WAIL
Poem of: 5 ELEGY
**Lamentation:** 4 MOAN
    6 PLAINT
in verse: 5 ELEGY
**Laminated**
rock: 5 SHALE
**Lammermoor**
bride: 5 LUCIA
**Lamont ___ ("The Shadow"):**
    8 CRANSTON
**LaMotta**
Boxer: 4 JAKE
**Lamour**
garment: 6 SARONG
**L'Amour, Louis**
novel: 5 HONDO
**Lamp**
cover: 5 SHADE
dweller: 5 GENIE
dwellers: 5 GENII
filler: 4 NEON 5 ARGON
    XENON
fuel: 8 KEROSENE
insert: 4 BULB
Kind of: 4 LAVA 7 HALOGEN
    8 INFRARED
locale: 8 ENDTABLE
On, as a: 3 LIT
part: 4 HARP
___ lamp: 3 ARC
**Lampblack:** 4 SOOT
**Lamplighter:** 8 KEROSENE
**Lampoon:** 5 SPOOF 6 SATIRE
    SENDUP
**Lamprey:** 3 EEL
hunter: 5 EELER
**Lamprey-like:** 4 EELY

**LAN**
Part of: 4 AREA
**Lana**
Ex of: 5 ARTIE
**Lanai**
event: 4 LUAU
neighbor: 4 MAUI OAHU
**Lancaster**
group: 5 AMISH
symbol: 4 ROSE 7 REDROSE
**Lancaster, Burt**
role: 4 EARP
thriller:
    14 SEVENDAYSINMAY
**Lancastrian**
symbol: 4 ROSE 7 REDROSE
**Lance:** 4 STAB 5 SPEAR
cpl. inferior: 3 PFC
Judge: 3 ITO
of the bench: 3 ITO
With ~ in hand: 5 ATILT
**Lancelot**
lover: 6 ELAINE
portrayer: 4 GERE
Son of: 7 GALAHAD
title: 3 SIR
**Lanchester**
Actress: 4 ELSA
**Land:** 5 TERRA 6 ALIGHT
    ARRIVE NATION
    REALTY 7 ACREAGE
Area of: 5 TRACT
development: 6 CAMERA
Divided: 5 KOREA
Dot of: 4 ISLE
down under: 5 HADES
Expanse of: 5 TRACT
Far from: 4 ASEA
Feudal: 4 FIEF
Flat: 4 MESA 7 PRAIRIE
French spot of: 3 ILE
Gang: 4 TURF
Grazing: 3 LEA
Green: 4 EIRE ERIN
Having: 5 ACRED
High: 5 NEPAL
hopper: 4 TOAD
in la mer: 3 ILE
in the lake: 5 ISLET
in the ocean: 5 ISLET
in the sea: 4 ISLE 5 ISLET
in the water: 4 ISLE 5 ISLET
Kind of: 4 LALA
Large ~ mass: 4 ASIA
    7 EURASIA
Lots of: 5 ACRES
Low bit of: 5 SWALE
map: 4 PLAT
measure: 4 ACRE
Narrow strip of: 7 ISTHMUS
Not on: 4 ASEA
of a billion: 5 INDIA
of literature: 4 ERIN
of poetry: 4 ERIN
On: 6 ASHORE
On dry: 6 ASHORE

Our ~, informally: 5 USOFA
parcel: 3 LOT 4 ACRE
Plot of: 4 ACRE 5 TRACT
Promised: 6 CANAAN UTOPIA
Speck of: 5 ISLET
Spot of: 4 ISLE
Stretch of: 5 TRACT
suffix: 5 SCAPE
unit: 4 ACRE
Work the: 4 FARM TILL
~, as a fish: 6 REELIN
~, in French: 5 TERRE
~, in Latin: 5 TERRA
**"Land ___!":** 5 SAKES
___ land: 4 LALA
**Landed:** 4 ALIT 5 ACRED
estate: 5 MANOR
property: 5 MANOR
**Landers**
Advice columnist: 3 ANN
**Landfall**
Biblical: 6 ARARAT
**Landfill:** 4 DUMP
emanation: 4 ODOR
**Landing:** 4 QUAY
area: 5 STRIP WHARF
field: 9 AERODROME
info: 3 ETA
pier: 4 DOCK
place: 4 PIER 8 AIRSTRIP
**Landlady**
Lucy's: 5 ETHEL
**Landlocked**
land: 4 MALI 6 UGANDA
    7 BOLIVIA
sea: 4 ARAL
**Landlord:** 5 OWNER 6 LESSOR
due: 4 RENT
income: 4 RENT
need: 6 TENANT
sign: 5 TOLET
    10 ROOMSTOLET
Sitcom: 5 MERTZ
**"Land of Smiles, The"**
composer Franz: 5 LEHAR
**Land of the Rising Sun:**
    5 JAPAN
**Landon**
1936 candidate ~: 3 ALF
**Landon, Michael**
role:
    15 TEENAGEWEREWOLF
**Landowner**
Like a: 5 ACRED
Scottish: 5 LAIRD
**Landscaper**
need: 3 SOD
tool: 5 EDGER
**Landscaping**
tool: 5 EDGER
**Landscapist**
French: 5 COROT
**Landvetter**
airline: 3 SAS
**Lane**
Add a ~ to: 5 WIDEN

Bowling: 5 ALLEY
changer's concern:
    9 BLINDSPOT
colleague: 4 KENT
for carpoolers: 3 HOV
Lovers': 5 AISLE
Singer: 4 ABBE
with lines: 6 NATHAN
**Lane, Rocky**
spoke for him: 4 MRED
**Lanes**
Join: 5 MERGE
org.: 3 PBA
**Lang**
of Smallville: 4 LANA
Superboy's girlfriend: 4 LANA
**Langdon, Sue ___**
Actress: 3 ANE
**Langer**
Philosopher: 7 SUSANNE
**Langerhans**
___ of ~ (pancreatic parts):
    6 ISLETS
**Langley**
org.: 3 CIA
**"___ Lang Syne": 4 AULD**
**Langtry**
Actress: 6 LILLIE
**Language**
columnist William: 6 SAFIRE
Computer: 4 JAVA 5 ALGOL
    BASIC COBOL
    7 FORTRAN
ending: 3 ESE
Forum: 5 LATIN
Highland: 4 ERSE
Kids': 8 PIGLATIN
Limerick: 4 ERSE
Mass: 5 LATIN
peculiarity: 5 IDIOM
Secret: 4 CODE
Sine: 4 TRIG
suffix: 3 ESE ISH
**Languish:** 3 ROT SAG 4 PINE
    5 DROOP
**Languor:** 5 ENNUI
**Lanin**
Bandleader: 6 LESTER
**Lanka**
lead-in: 3 SRI
___ Lanka: 3 SRI
**Lanky:** 4 LEAN SLIM THIN
    6 GANGLY
**L'année**
Part of: 3 ETE
**Lansbury**
Actress: 6 ANGELA
role: 4 MAME
**Lansing**
E. ~ school: 3 MSU
**Lansky**
Mobster: 5 MEYER
**Lantern-jawed**
celebrity: 4 LENO
**L.A.-N.Y.**
flight path: 3 ENE

**Lanza**
role: 6 CARUSO
Singer: 5 MARIO
**Lanzoni**
Male model: 5 FABIO
**Lao**
follower: 3 TSE
**Lao-___ :** 3 TSE TZU
**La ___ of Milan:** 5 SCALA
**Laos**
locale: 4 ASIA
**Laotian:** 5 ASIAN
money: 3 KIP
neighbor: 4 THAI
**Lao-tzu**
follower: 6 TAOIST
system: 6 TAOISM
way: 3 TAO
**Lap**
Create a: 3 SIT
dog, for short: 3 POM 4 PEKE
Gained a: 3 SAT
Lose a: 5 STAND
Made a: 3 SAT
**"___ Lap" (1983 film):** 4 PHAR
**La Paz**
country (abbr.): 3 BOL
**LAPD**
alert: 3 APB
rank: 3 DET
**Lapel**
device: 4 MIKE
jewelry: 3 PIN
label: 5 IDTAG
**Lapidarist**
item: 3 GEM
unit: 5 CARAT
**Lapin**
Lady: 3 DOE
**Laps**
Did: 4 SWAM
Do: 4 SWIM
Done: 4 SWUM
**Lapse:** 3 SIN 4 SLIP 5 ERROR
**Lapsed:** 6 RANOUT
**Lapses:** 6 ERRATA
**Laptev Sea**
River to the: 4 LENA
**Laptop**
Apple: 5 IBOOK
IBM: 8 THINKPAD
item: 6 NAPKIN
**Lara**
Tomb raider: 5 CROFT
**Laraine**
cohort: 5 GILDA
**Larcenous:** 7 PIRATIC
**Larceny:** 5 THEFT
Type of: 5 PETIT
**Larch:** 4 TREE 8 TAMARACK
___ Laredo, Mexico: 5 NUEVO
**Large:** 3 BIG 4 SIZE
amount: 3 SEA TON 4 SCAD
    5 OCEAN
At: 4 FREE 5 LOOSE
    10 ONTHELOOSE

group: 4 BEVY 5 ARRAY
More than: 4 HUGE 5 OBESE
number: 4 HERD HOST SLEW
quantity: 4 SCAD SLEW
    6 OODLES
Too: 5 OBESE
**Large-eyed**
lemur: 5 LORIS
primate: 5 LEMUR
**Larger ___ life:** 4 THAN
**Larger-than-life:** 4 EPIC
**Large-scale:** 4 EPIC MASS
**Large-screen**
film format: 4 IMAX
**Largo:** 5 TEMPO
and others: 5 TEMPI
Faster than: 6 ADAGIO
**Lariat:** 4 ROPE 5 LASSO REATA
    RIATA
loop: 5 NOOSE
**Lark:** 5 ANTIC SPREE
    8 ESCAPADE
Words before: 3 ONA
___ lark: 3 ONA
**"L'Arlésienne"**
composer: 5 BIZET
**Larrup:** 3 TAN
**Larry:** 6 STOOGE
Cohort of: 3 MOE
**"Larry King Live"**
broadcaster: 3 CNN
**Larsen**
of baseball: 3 DON
**Larson**
Cartoonist: 4 GARY
**Larson, Jonathan**
musical: 4 RENT
**Larvae**
Beetle: 5 GRUBS
Fly: 7 MAGGOTS
**Laryngology**
prefix: 3 OTO
**Lasagna**
ingredient: 7 RICOTTA
**La Salle**
Actor: 4 ERIQ
**La Scala**
1887 ~ debut: 6 OTELLO
highlight: 4 ARIA
home: 5 MILAN
offering: 5 OPERA
solo: 4 ARIA
star: 4 DIVA
**"La Scala di ___" (Rossini**
    **opera):** 4 SETA
**Las ___, Canary Islands:**
    6 PALMAS
**Lascivious:** 4 LEWD
deity: 5 SATYR
look: 4 LEER
**Lasciviously**
Look: 4 LEER OGLE
    6 LEERAT
**Laser**
Hit with a: 3 ZAP
light: 4 BEAM

output: 3 RAY 4 BEAM
**Lash:** 3 TAN TIE 4 CANE WHIP
cosmetic: 7 MASCARA
Cowboy star: 5 LARUE
of westerns: 5 LARUE
out at: 6 ASSAIL
**Lash ___:** 5 OUTAT
**"Lasher"**
novelist Anne: 4 RICE
**Lashes:** 5 CILIA
Site for: 6 EYELID
**Lashing**
reminder: 4 WELT
**Lass:** 3 GAL 4 GIRL 5 BELLE
    6 DAMSEL
partner: 3 LAD
**Lassie:** 6 COLLIE
Aussie: 6 SHEILA
mate: 3 LAD
**Lassitude:** 5 ENNUI
**Lasso:** 4 ROPE 5 REATA RIATA
    6 LARIAT
loop: 5 NOOSE
wielder: 5 ROPER
**Last:** 5 FINAL 6 ENDURE
(abbr.): 3 ULT
call: 4 TAPS
Come in: 4 LOSE
in a series. 3 NTH ZEE
    5 OMEGA
mo.: 3 DEC
part: 3 END
place: 6 CELLAR
shot: 4 PUTT
word: 3 END
**"Last Days of Pompeii, The"**
heroine: 4 IONE
**Last-ditch**
effort: 5 STAND
**"Last Don, The"**
author: 4 PUZO
**"Last Emperor, The"**
star: 4 LONE
**"Last Essays of ___," 1833:**
    4 ELIA
**Lasting:** 7 DURABLE
do: 4 PERM
forever: 7 ETERNAL
impression: 4 SCAR
start: 4 EVER
**"Last of the Mohicans, The"**
heroine: 4 CORA
**"Last one ___ a rotten egg!":**
    4 INIS
**Last Supper**
cup: 5 GRAIL
guest: 7 APOSTLE
query: 5 ISITI
**"Last Supper, The":** 5 MURAL
city: 5 MILAN
painter: 7 DAVINCI
**"Last Temptation of Christ, The"**
actor: 5 DAFOE
**Last word:** 3 END 4 AMEN
in a threat: 4 ELSE
in prayer: 4 AMEN

**Last words:** 4 OBIT 7 EPITAPH
Famous: 3 IDO 4 ETTU
    5 AMENS 6 THEEND
**Las Vegas**
area: 5 STRIP
gas: 4 NEON
illumination: 4 NEON
TV drama set in: 3 CSI
**"Las Vegas"**
actor James: 4 CAAN
**Laszlo**
of cosmetics: 4 ERNO
**Laszlo, Victor**
Wife of: 4 ILSA
**La ___ Tar Pits:** 4 BREA
**Latch:** 4 GLOM GRAB
Door: 4 HASP
Word after: 4 ONTO
**Latch ___:** 4 ONTO
**Latched**
Not: 4 AJAR
**Late:** 5 TARDY 6 RECENT
    7 OVERDUE
    8 DECEASED
news: 4 OBIT
Not: 5 ONCUE 6 ONTIME
Of: 5 NEWLY
Running: 5 TARDY
**Lateef**
Composer: 5 YUSEF
**Lateen-rigged**
vessel: 4 DHOW
**Late-night**
flight: 6 REDEYE
host: 4 LENO PAAR 5 CONAN
**Later:** 4 ANON 5 NEWER
    6 NOTNOW NOTYET
No ~ than: 3 TIL 5 UNTIL
**"Later!":** 3 BYE 4 TATA 5 ADIOS
    SEEYA 6 MANANA
    NOTNOW
**Lateral**
prefix: 3 TRI UNI 4 EQUI
remark: 5 ASIDE
**Laterally**
Move: 5 SIDLE
**Late-show**
watcher: 8 NIGHTOWL
**Latest**
info: 4 DOPE
The: 4 NEWS
thing: 4 RAGE
word: 4 NEWS 6 UPDATE
**Lather:** 4 FOAM SNIT STEW
In a: 3 MAD 4 AGOG 5 HETUP
    SOAPY
Producing: 5 SUDSY
**Lathered:** 6 SOAPED
**Latin**
abbr.: 3 ETC 4 ETAL
adverb: 3 HIC HOC
bear: 4 URSA
being: 4 ESSE
carol word: 6 ADESTE
case: 6 DATIVE
clarifier: 5 IDEST

dance: 5 SAMBA TANGO
dance music: 5 SALSA
dog: 5 CANIS
egg: 4 OVUM
eggs: 3 OVA
existence: 4 ESSE
First of a ~ trio: 3 AMO
foot: 3 PES
king: 3 REX
land: 5 TERRA
law: 3 LEX
Like ~, today: 4 DEAD
list ender: 6 ETALII
love: 4 AMOR
lover's word: 3 AMO 4 AMAT
music: 5 SALSA
others: 4 ALII
passage: 4 ITER
Pertinent, in: 5 ADREM
poet: 4 OVID
preposition: 4 ANTE
pronoun: 3 MEA 4 ILLE
salutation: 3 AVE
That is, in: 5 IDEST
thing: 3 RES
trio member: 3 AMO 4 AMAS
    AMAT
word on a coin: 4 UNUM
word on a dollar bill: 4 ORDO
year: 4 ANNO
**Latin 101**
word: 3 AMO EGO 4 AMAS
    AMAT ERAT ESSE
**Latino**
cry: 7 CARAMBA
**Latish**
bedtime: 5 ONEAM
lunch hr.: 5 ONEPM
lunchtime: 3 ONE
**Latitude:** 4 PLAY ROOM
    6 LEEWAY
Pole: 6 NINETY
**Latke**
ingredient: 6 POTATO
**"La Traviata"**
composer: 5 VERDI
mezzo: 5 FLORA
**Lats**
neighbors: 3 ABS
**___ latte:** 5 CAFFE
**Latter-day Saint:** 6 MORMON
**Lattice**
for plant growers: 7 TRELLIS
**Latticework**
strip: 4 LATH
**Lattisaw**
Singer: 5 STACY
**Latvia**
capital: 4 RIGA
Like: 6 BALTIC
~, once (abbr.): 3 SSR
**Latvian:** 4 BALT LETT
capital: 4 RIGA
**Laud:** 5 EXTOL 6 PRAISE
**Laudatory**
lines: 3 ODE

**Lauder**
  of cosmetics: 5 ESTEE
**Lauderdale**
  neighbor: 4 BOCA
**Lauer**
  Host: 4 MATT
  show: 5 TODAY
**Laugh**
  Belly: 4 ROAR
  Big: 6 HAHAHA
  Cause to: 5 AMUSE
  Derisive: 3 HAH 6 HAWHAW
  Half a: 3 HEE HEH
  Have a good: 4 HOOT ROAR
  Little: 5 TEHEE 6 GIGGLE
    TEEHEE
  Loud: 3 YUK 4 ROAR
  loudly: 4 ROAR
  Make: 5 AMUSE
  riot: 6 SCREAM
  syllable: 3 HAR HEE
  unit: 4 PEAL
  Witch's: 6 CACKLE
  ~, in French: 4 RIRE
**Laughable:** 5 COMIC INANE
    7 ASININE
**"Laughable Lyrics"**
  writer: 4 LEAR
**Laugh-a-minute:** 4 HOOT RIOT
  type: 4 RIOT
**Laughfest:** 4 HOOT RIOT
**"Laugh-In"**
  actress Goldie: 4 HAWN
  actress Judy: 5 CARNE
  cohost Dan: 5 ROWAN
  comedian Johnson: 4 ARTE
  comedienne Lily: 6 TOMLIN
  comedienne Ruth: 5 BUZZI
  line: 10 SOCKITTOME
  segment: 4 SKIT
**Laughing:** 5 RIANT
  animal: 5 HYENA
  gas: 5 OXIDE
  It may be: 3 GAS
  matter: 3 GAS
  scavenger: 5 HYENA
**"Laughing Cavalier, The"**
  painter: 4 HALS
**Laughs:** 4 HAHA
  Barrel of: 4 RIOT
**Laughter**
  Burst of: 4 GALE PEAL
  Cause of: 7 COMICAL
  Loud: 4 ROAR
  Sound of: 4 HAHA PEAL
    6 TEEHEE
**"Laughter in the Rain"**
  singer/songwriter: 6 SEDAKA
**Launch:** 4 BOAT 6 PROPEL
    8 INITIATE
  agcy.: 4 NASA
  Cancel a: 5 ABORT
  cancellation: 4 NOGO
  of 1962: 7 TELSTAR
  of 1986: 3 MIR
  Scrub, as a: 5 ABORT

  site: 3 PAD
**Launcher**
  French satellite: 6 ARIANE
  org.: 4 NASA
  Rocket: 4 NASA
**Launder:** 4 WASH 5 CLEAN
**Laundering**
  In need of: 6 SOILED
**Laundromat**
  appliance: 5 DRYER
  Like a ~ machine: 6 COINOP
**Laundry:** 4 WASH
  Do a ~ task: 4 SORT
  Early ~ brand: 5 RINSO
  load: 4 WASH
  mysteries: 8 ODDSOCKS
  Prepare: 4 SORT
  supply: 6 STARCH
  unit: 4 LOAD
  woe: 5 STAIN
  worker: 6 IRONER
**Lauper**
  Singer: 5 CYNDI
**Laura**
  Actress: 4 DERN 5 INNES
  Fashion designer: 6 ASHLEY
  Songwriter: 4 NYRO
**"Laura"**
  actress Gene: 7 TIERNEY
  author Caspary: 4 VERA
  director Preminger: 4 OTTO
**Laurel**
  Comedian: 4 STAN
  Hardy, to: 5 OLLIE
  Hardy, vis-à-vis: 6 LARGER
  topper: 5 DERBY
**Lauren**
  Actress: 5 TEWES
  Designer: 5 RALPH
**Lauren, Ralph**
  brand: 4 POLO
  line: 5 CHAPS
**Laurence**
  Former CBS chairman:
    5 TISCH
**Laurentiis, De**
  Film producer: 4 DINO
**Lav**
  of London: 3 LOO
**Lava**
  Eject: 4 SPEW 5 ERUPT
  Like: 6 MOLTEN
  rock: 6 BASALT
  Spew: 5 ERUPT
**Lavatory**
  London: 3 LOO
  sign: 5 INUSE
**Laver**
  of tennis: 3 ROD
**"___ la vie":** 4 CEST
**"La Vie en Rose"**
  singer Edith: 4 PIAF
**Lavigne**
  Singer: 5 AVRIL
**Lavin**
  Actress: 5 LINDA

**Lavish:** 7 OPULENT
  affection: 4 DOTE
  party: 4 FETE GALA
**"___ la vista":** 5 HASTA
**"La ___ Vita":** 5 DOLCE
**"La vita nuova"**
  poet: 5 DANTE
**Law:** 7 STATUTE
    9 ORDINANCE
  It's the: 5 EDICT
  Lay down the: 4 RULE
  Make into: 5 ENACT
  Man with a: 3 OHM
  partner: 5 ORDER
  Pass into: 5 ENACT
  Religious: 5 CANON
  school class: 5 TORTS
  suffix: 3 YER
  Thing, in: 3 RES
  ~, in French: 3 LOI
  ~, in Latin: 3 LEX
**___ law**
  (old German code): 5 SALIC
  (physics topic): 4 OHMS
**"Law & ___":** 5 ORDER
**"Law & Order: SVU"**
  actor: 4 ICET
**Lawful:** 5 LEGIT LICIT
**Lawgiver**
  Ancient: 5 SOLON
  Athenian: 5 DRACO SOLON
  Harsh: 5 DRACO
  Wise: 5 SOLON
**La ___, Wisconsin:** 6 CROSSE
**Lawless:** 8 ANARCHIC
  character: 4 XENA
**Lawman**
  Comical: 3 KOP
  Legendary: 4 EARP
  Tombstone: 4 EARP
**Lawn:** 5 GRASS
  additive: 4 LIME
  bowling: 5 BOCCE BOCCI
  burrower: 4 MOLE
  decoration: 5 GNOME
    8 FLAMINGO
  Do ~ work: 3 SOD 5 RESOD
    6 RESEED
  Instant: 3 SOD
  Lay down the: 3 SOD
  layer: 3 SOD
  Name in ~ care: 4 TORO
    5 ORTHO 6 SCOTTS
  Neaten the: 4 EDGE
  pest: 4 MOLE
  Start a: 4 SEED
  tool: 5 EDGER MOWER
    6 SEEDER
**Lawn mower**
  brand: 4 TORO 5 DEERE
  path: 5 SWATH
  site: 4 SHED
**"Lawnmower Man"**
  actor Jeff: 5 FAHEY
**Lawrence**
  land: 6 ARABIA

**Leading:** 3 TOP 5 AHEAD
    FIRST ONTOP
    7 AHEADOF INFRONT
**"Leading With My Chin"**
  author: 4 LENO 7 JAYLENO
**Leadoff**
  Result of a ~ walk: 5 ONEON
**Leaf:** 4 PAGE 5 FOLIO
  bisector: 6 MIDRIB
  Book: 4 PAGE
  Fern: 5 FROND
  Floral: 5 SEPAL
  gatherer: 4 RAKE
  Half a: 4 PAGE
  holder: 4 STEM
  line: 4 VEIN
  opening: 4 PORE 5 STOMA
  Palm: 5 FROND
  part: 6 MIDRIB
  pore: 5 STOMA
  Salad: 6 ENDIVE
  Uneven like a: 5 EROSE
  unit: 4 PAGE
  vein: 3 RIB
**Leafed:** 5 PAGED
  through: 4 READ
**Leaflike**
  appendage: 5 BRACT
**Leaf-loving**
  ~ Aussie: 5 KOALA
**Leafstalk:** 7 PETIOLE
**Leafy**
  climber: 3 IVY
  recess: 5 ARBOR BOWER
  shelter: 5 BOWER
  vegetable: 4 KALE
**League**
  Certain ~ (abbr.): 4 AMER
    NATL
  leader: 3 IVY
  member: 4 ARAB TEAM
  of intrigue: 5 CABAL
  ___ League: 3 IVY 4 ARAB
    6 LITTLE
**League of Nations**
  home: 6 GENEVA
**"League of ___ Own, A":**
  5 THEIR
**"League of Their ___, A":**
  3 OWN
**League of Women Voters**
  founder: 4 CATT
**Leah**
  Son of: 4 LEVI
**Leak:** 4 SEEP 6 GETOUT
  slowly: 4 OOZE SEEP
  sound: 3 SSS 4 SSSS
**Leakey, Richard:** 6 KENYAN
  home: 5 KENYA
**Leaking:** 4 OOZY 5 ADRIP
**Lean:** 4 LANK LIST THIN TILT
    TRIM WIRY 5 SPARE
    6 MEAGER
  against: 6 RESTON
  and lovely: 6 SVELTE
  and muscular: 4 WIRY

eater of rhyme: 5 SPRAT
Long and: 4 LANK
Make: 5 DEFAT
(on): 4 RELY
to one side: 4 LIST
toward: 5 FAVOR 6 PREFER
**Lean-___ (sheds):** 3 TOS
**Leander**
  love: 4 HERO
**Leaning:** 4 BENT BIAS 5 ATILT
    6 ASLANT
  against: 4 ANTI
  to the right: 6 ITALIC
**Leaning Tower**
  town: 4 PISA
**LeAnn**
  Country singer: 5 RIMES
**Lean-to:** 4 SHED
**Leap**
  at the rink: 4 AXEL
  Ballet: 4 JETE
  Skater's: 4 AXEL LUTZ
**"___ Leap":** 7 QUANTUM
**Leaper**
  Aussie: 3 ROO
  Long-eared: 4 HARE
  Savanna: 6 IMPALA
**Leapfrog:** 3 HOP
**Leaping:** 7 SALTANT
  game fish: 5 WAHOO
**"Leap of Faith"**
  Queen who wrote: 4 NOOR
**Leapt:** 6 SPRANG
**Lear:** 4 KING
  Daughter of: 5 REGAN
**Learn:** 4 HEAR
  about: 6 HEAROF
  gradually: 5 GLEAN
  One way to: 4 ROTE
    6 BYROTE
  Quick to: 3 APT
**Learned:** 4 SAGE 5 HEARD
    7 ERUDITE
    8 LITERATE
  Not: 6 INNATE
  one: 4 SAGE 6 SAVANT
**Learning:** 4 LORE
  inst.: 4 ACAD
  Mechanical: 4 ROTE
  method: 4 ROTE
  One ~ on the job: 7 TRAINEE
**Leary, Denis**
  1994 ~ film: 6 THEREF
**Leary, Timothy**
  drug: 3 LSD
**Lease:** 3 LET 4 RENT
  anew: 5 RELET
  length: 4 YEAR
**Leash:** 5 CHAIN 6 TETHER
  Off the: 5 LOOSE
**Least:** 6 FEWEST MEREST
    7 MINIMUM
  At ~ one: 3 ANY
  bit: 3 FIG 4 IOTA WHIT
  In the: 3 ANY 5 ATALL AWHIT
    6 ONEBIT

The ~ bit: 5 ATALL
  7 ONEIOTA
**Leather**
  Bookbinding: 4 ROAN
  ending: 4 ETTE
  Napped: 5 SUEDE
  piercer: 3 AWL
  Pliable: 3 ELK
  Prepare: 3 TAN
  Soft: 3 ELK 5 SUEDE
  sticker: 3 AWL
  strap: 4 REIN
  tool: 3 AWL
  Unpolished: 6 RUSSET
  worker: 6 TANNER
**Leatherneck:** 6 MARINE
  lunch: 4 MESS
  org.: 4 USMC
**Leatherworker**
  tool: 3 AWL
**L'eau**
  land: 3 ILE
**Leave:** 4 EXIT QUIT 5 SPLIT
    6 DEPART SECEDE
    7 HEADOUT PULLOUT
    TAKEOFF
  alone: 5 LETBE
  at the altar: 4 JILT
  be: 4 STET
  Force to: 5 EXILE 6 UPROOT
  in: 4 STET
  in a hurry: 4 BOLT
  in the dust: 4 LOSE
  Not: 4 STAY
  off: 4 OMIT 5 CEASE
  one's mark: 4 ETCH
    7 IMPRESS
  out: 4 OMIT SKIP 5 ELIDE
  port: 4 SAIL 7 SETSAIL
  the country: 6 SECEDE
  the flock: 5 STRAY
  the stage: 4 EXIT
  the union: 6 SECEDE
  unsaid: 4 OMIT
**Leave ___:** 4 ATIP
**"Leave ___ Beaver":** 4 ITTO
**"Leave it":** 4 STET
**"Leave It to Beaver"**
  role: 5 EDDIE
**Leaven:** 5 YEAST
**Leavening**
  agent: 5 YEAST
**Leavenworth:** 6 PRISON
**Leaves:** 4 GOES 7 FOLIAGE
  Clear the: 4 RAKE
  for lunch: 5 SALAD
  Gather: 4 RAKE
  home: 4 NEST TREE
    6 TEABAG
  in a bag: 3 TEA
  in hot water: 3 TEA
  Like some: 5 EROSE OVATE
    6 LOBATE 7 TERNATE
  Uneven, as: 5 EROSE
**Leaving:** 3 ORT
  Cost of: 4 BAIL 7 ALIMONY

Keep from: 6 DETAIN
"___ Leaving Home" (Beatles
    tune): 4 SHES
"Leaving Las Vegas"
    actress Elisabeth: 4 SHUE
Leb.
    neighbor: 3 ISR SYR
Lebanese: 4 ARAB
Lebanon
    capital: 6 BEIRUT
    tree: 5 CEDAR
Leblanc
    detective Lupin: 6 ARSENE
LeBlanc
    Actor: 4 MATT
Lebowitz
    Humorist: 4 FRAN
Le Carré
    character: 3 SPY 6 SMILEY
Lech
    of Poland: 6 WALESA
Lecher: 4 ROUE 5 SATYR
    look: 4 LEER OGLE
Lecherous: 5 RANDY
            7 GOATISH
    look: 4 LEER
    sort: 4 ROUE 5 SATYR
"Le Coq ___": 3 DOR
Lectern
    locale: 4 DAIS
Lecterns: 5 PODIA 6 ROSTRA
Lecture
    Give a: 5 ORATE
    hall: 6 LYCEUM
    jottings: 5 NOTES
    locale: 4 HALL
Lecturer: 4 PROF
    platform: 4 DAIS
    spots: 5 PODIA
Led: 3 RAN 5 PACED RULED
            7 USHERED
    on: 7 ENTICED
    to a seat: 7 USHERED
LED
    Part of: 5 DIODE
"Le ___ d'Arthur": 5 MORTE
Lederer
    known as Ann Landers:
            5 EPPIE
Ledge: 5 SHELF
    Window: 4 SILL
Ledger
    column: 6 ASSETS
    entry: 5 DEBIT
    item: 5 ENTRY
"Le ___ d'Or" (Rimsky-Korsakov
            title): 3 COQ
Le Duc Tho
    capital: 5 HANOI
"Le ___ du printemps":
            5 SACRE
Lee
    Actress: 4 RUTA
    Cake lady: 4 SARA
    Director: 3 ANG

foe: 5 MEADE
gp.: 3 CSA
of comics: 4 STAN
side: 3 CSA 4 GRAY
soldier: 3 REB
___ Lee: 4 SARA 6 KATHIE
" ___ Lee"
    (folk song): 4 AURA
    Poe work: 7 ANNABEL
Lee, Ann: 6 SHAKER
Lee, Brenda
    hit song: 7 IMSORRY
Lee, Peggy
    song: 5 FEVER
Lee, Robert E.: 3 GEN 4 GENL
    org.: 3 CSA
    soldier: 3 REB
    waiting area: 5 LEVEE
Lee, Spike
    film: 15 DOTHERIGHTTHING
Lee, Tsung-___
    Nobelist: 3 DAO
Leeds
    lockup: 4 GAOL
    river: 4 AIRE
Leek
    relative: 5 CHIVE ONION
Leer
    at: 4 OGLE
Lees: 5 DREGS
Leeward Island: 7 STKITTS
Leeway: 4 ROOM 7 LICENSE
            8 LATITUDE
"___ le feste": 5 TUTTE
Le ___, France: 5 HAVRE
Left: 4 GONE WENT
            7 VACATED 8 DEPARTED
    Are: 6 REMAIN
    at sea: 5 APORT
    end: 3 IST
    Go: 3 HAW 4 TURN
    in a hurry: 4 HIED
    in the dust: 6 OUTRAN
    Not ~ over: 5 EATEN
    on a map: 4 WEST
    one's seat: 5 AROSE
    out: 7 OMITTED
    over: 7 UNEATEN
    They're ~ behind: 7 ESTATES
    To the ~, at sea: 5 APORT
    What's: 3 NET 4 REST
            6 ESTATE
Left Bank
    city: 5 PARIS
    river: 5 SEINE
Left Coast
    airport, for short: 3 LAX
Left-hand
    entry: 5 DEBIT
    page: 5 VERSO
Left-handed
    Game that can't be played:
            4 POLO
Leftover: 3 ORT 5 CRUMB
            SCRAP 6 EXCESS
    Apple: 4 CORE

morsel: 3 ORT
Leftovers: 4 REST
    dish: 4 HASH
    Have: 5 EATIN
    Like: 7 UNEATEN
    Prepare: 6 REHEAT
Left-winger: 5 PINKO
            7 LIBERAL
Lefty: 8 SOUTHPAW
    of baseball: 5 ODOUL
Leg: 3 GAM 4 LIMB
    bone: 4 SHIN 5 FEMUR TIBIA
    Give a ~ up: 5 BOOST
    joint: 4 KNEE 5 ANKLE
    muscle: 4 QUAD
    part: 4 CALF SHIN 5 SHANK
    Shake a: 3 HIE 6 HASTEN
    up: 4 EDGE 5 BOOST
Legacy: 8 HERITAGE
    recipient: 4 HEIR
Legal: 5 LICIT OFAGE
    action: 4 SUIT 6 APPEAL
    add-on: 3 ESE
    aide: 4 PARA 5 CLERK
    claim: 4 LIEN
    conclusion: 3 ESE
    cover-up: 4 ROBE
    deg.: 3 LLB
    document: 4 DEED WRIT
    excuse: 5 ALIBI
    gp.: 3 ABA
    It may be: 6 TENDER
    Like some ~ proceedings:
            5 INREM
    matter: 3 RES
    memo opener: 4 INRE
    order: 4 WRIT
    org.: 3 ABA
    plea: 4 NOLO
    postponement: 4 STAY
    rep.: 4 ATTY
    rights org.: 4 ACLU
    scholar: 6 JURIST
    Some ~ tender: 6 TNOTES
    Start of a ~ conclusion:
            5 IREST
    suffix: 3 ESE
    thing: 3 RES
    wrong: 4 TORT
Legalese
    adverb: 6 HEREBY HEREIN
            HERETO 7 THEREIN
            THERETO
    Bit of: 4 INRE
Legalistic
    phrase: 4 INRE
Legally
    bar: 5 ESTOP
    prevent: 5 ESTOP
    responsible: 6 LIABLE
"Legally Blonde"
    actress Witherspoon: 5 REESE
    role: 4 ELLE
Legate: 8 EMISSARY
Legatee: 4 HEIR
Legend: 4 MYTH

maker: 5 ACURA
**Legends**
Book with: 5 ATLAS
The stuff of: 4 LORE
**"Leggo my ___!": 4 EGGO**
**L'eggs**
rival: 5 HANES
**Leghorn**
locale: 5 ITALY
**Legion: 4 ARMY**
**Legislate: 5 ENACT**
**Legislation: 3 LAW 4 ACTS**
Pass: 5 ENACT
Pension ~ letters: 5 ERISA
**Legislative**
add-on: 5 RIDER
assemblies: 5 PLENA
house: 6 SENATE
**Legislator: 3 SEN 7 ENACTOR**
Municipal ~ (abbr.): 3 ALD
Wise: 5 SOLON
**Legislature**
French: 5 SENAT
Greek: 5 BOULE
Japanese: 4 DIET
Russian: 4 DUMA
**Legit: 5 LICIT VALID 6 KOSHER**
**Legitimate: 5 LICIT VALID**
6 KOSHER
**Legman**
list: 7 ERRANDS
**Leg-puller: 5 JOKER 6 KIDDER**
**Legrand**
Composer: 6 MICHEL
**Legree, Simon: 6 TYRANT**
8 OVERSEER
creator: 5 STOWE
look: 5 SNEER
**Legume: 3 PEA**
Black-eyed: 6 COWPEA
Medicinal: 5 SENNA
Soup: 3 PEA 6 LENTIL
Southern: 6 COWPEA
Tiny: 3 PEA
**Le Havre**
**Info:** French cue
City near: 4 CAEN
**Lehman**
Conductor: 5 ENGEL
**Lehmann**
Soprano: 5 LOTTE
**Leia**
cohort: 3 HAN
Furry friend of: 4 EWOK
portrayer: 6 CARRIE
Princess ~ ___: 6 ORGANA
**Leibovitz**
Photographer: 5 ANNIE
**Leif**
Father of: 4 ERIC
language: 5 NORSE
**Leigh**
Actress: 5 JANET 6 VIVIEN
role: 5 OHARA
**Leinsdorf**
Conductor: 5 ERICH

**Leisure: 4 EASE 8 FREETIME**
Like a ~ suit: 5 RETRO
**Leisurely: 4 SLOW**
stroll: 5 PASEO
Walk: 5 AMBLE 6 STROLL
**LEM**
Part of: 5 LUNAR
___ Leman: 3 LAC
**LeMans: 3 GTO**
**Le Mans**
event: 4 RACE
**Lemieux**
milieu: 3 ICE 4 RINK
**"Lemme ___!": 4 ATEM**
**Lemmon, Jack**
comedy: 6 AVANTI
**"___ Le Moko": 4 PEPE**
**Lemon: 3 DUD**
candy: 4 DROP
drink: 3 ADE
Like a: 4 SOUR
Noted: 5 EDSEL
peel: 5 RIND ZEST
rind: 4 PEEL ZEST
suffix: 3 ADE
zest: 4 PEEL RIND
**LeMond**
Cyclist: 4 GREG
**Le Monde**
article: 3 UNE
**Lemons**
locale: 5 GROVE
Where to find: 6 CARLOT
**"Lemon Tree"**
singer Lopez: 5 TRINI
**Lemony: 4 SOUR TART**
**Lemur**
Large-eyed: 5 LORIS
**Len**
of football: 6 DAWSON
**Lena**
Actress: 4 OLIN
Singer: 5 HORNE
**Lend: 6 IMPART**
a hand: 3 AID 4 HELP
6 ASSIST
an ear: 6 LISTEN
Something to: 3 EAR 5 ANEAR
**Lend ___: 5 ANEAR**
**Lender**
claim: 4 LIEN
Govt.: 3 SBA
offering: 5 BAGEL
**Lending**
figures: 5 RATES
**Lendl**
of tennis: 4 IVAN
**Length**
Biblical: 5 CUBIT
Lease: 4 YEAR
of time: 5 SPELL
of yarn: 4 HANK 5 SKEIN
Ruler: 4 FOOT
Skirt: 4 MAXI MIDI MINI
times width: 4 AREA
**Lengthen: 3 EKE 6 EXTEND**

**Lengths**
Dash: 3 EMS ENS
**Lenient: 3 LAX 4 EASY SOFT**
Less: 7 STERNER
with: 6 SOFTON
**Lenin**
foe: 7 TSARIST
Leader before: 4 TSAR
middle name: 5 ILICH
**Lennon**
lady: 3 ONO
love: 3 ONO
Singer: 4 SEAN
widow: 3 ONO
**Lennon, John**
hit: 5 WOMAN 7 IMAGINE
middle name: 3 ONO
Wife of: 7 YOKOONO
**Lennon, Sean**
Mother of: 3 ONO 7 YOKOONO
**Lennox**
Singer: 5 ANNIE
**Lenny**
Comic: 5 BRUCE
**Leno**
Former ~ announcer Hall:
3 EDD
Host: 3 JAY
Notable ~ feature: 4 CHIN
predecessor: 6 CARSON
welcome: 5 INTRO
**"Lenore"**
poet: 3 POE
**Lens**
cover: 6 EYELID
holders: 4 RIMS
Instrument: 5 OPTIC
Powerful: 5 MACRO
setting: 5 FSTOP
type: 4 ZOOM 7 BIFOCAL
CONCAVE
**Lenska**
Actress: 4 RULA
**Lent: 4 GAVE**
a hand: 5 AIDED
ender: 6 EASTER
First day of:
12 ASHWEDNESDAY
It may be: 3 EAR
**Lenten**
symbol: 3 ASH
treat: 11 HOTCROSSBUN
**Lentil: 6 LEGUME**
Indian ~ dish: 3 DAL
**Lento: 4 SLOW 5 TEMPO**
**Lenya**
Actress: 5 LOTTE
**Leo: 4 SIGN**
follower: 5 VIRGO
home: 3 DEN 4 LAIR
Singer: 5 SAYER
sound: 4 ROAR
**Leon**
Actor: 4 AMES
Author: 4 URIS
Biographer: 4 EDEL

Clinton aide: 7 PANETTA
Singer: 7 REDBONE
**Leonard**
   Author: 6 ELMORE
   foe: 5 DURAN
   Songwriter: 5 COHEN
**Leonard ___ (Roy Rogers):**
   4 SLYE
**Leonardo da ___: 5 VINCI**
**Leoncavallo**
   opera: 9 PAGLIACCI
**Leone**
   Director: 6 SERGIO
   ___ Leone: 6 SIERRA
**Leonhard**
   Mathematician: 5 EULER
**Leoni**
   Actress: 3 TEA
**Leonine**
   locks: 4 MANE
   sound: 4 ROAR
**Leontyne**
   piece: 4 ARIA
**Leopard**
   Leap like a: 6 POUNCE
   markings: 5 SPOTS
   relative: 6 OCELOT
   spot: 7 ROSETTE
**Leopardlike**
   cat: 6 OCELOT
**Leopold**
   partner in crime: 4 LOEB
   Violinist: 4 AUER
**Le Pew**
   Cartoon skunk: 4 PEPE
**Lepidopterist**
   gear: 3 NET
**Leporine**
   creature: 4 HARE
   ___ Leppard: 3 DEF
**Leprechaun: 3 ELF**
   land: 4 EIRE ERIN
   Like a: 5 ELFIN
**Lepton**
   Kind of: 3 TAU
   locale: 4 ATOM
   Unstable: 4 MUON
**Lepus: 4 HARE**
**Lerner**
   partner: 5 LOEWE
**Lerner, ___ Jay: 4 ALAN**
**"___ le roi!": 4 ABAS VIVE**
**"Le roi d'Ys"**
   composer: 4 LALO
**LeRoy**
   Sports artist: 6 NEIMAN
**Les**
   WKRP news director:
     7 NESSMAN
**"Les ___" (Broadway show, for**
   **short): 3 MIZ**
**Lesage**
   Author: 5 ALAIN
   hero: 4 BLAS
**Lesbos**
   poet: 6 SAPPHO

**Les États-___: 4 UNIS**
**"Les Girls"**
   actress Taina: 3 ELG
**LeShan**
   Author: 3 EDA
**Lesley**
   Newscaster: 5 STAHL
**Leslie**
   Actress: 5 CARON
**"Les Misérables"**
   author: 4 HUGO
**Lesotho**
   capital: 6 MASERU
**Less: 5 MINUS NOTAS**
   Get for: 6 SAVEON
   More or: 5 ABOUT
   Much: 8 LETALONE
   No ~ than: 7 ATLEAST
   than: 5 UNDER
**Lessee: 6 TENANT**
**Lessen: 4 BATE EASE 5 ABATE**
   **8 DECREASE DIMINISH**
**Lesser of two ___: 5 EVILS**
**Lesser Sunda**
   island: 4 BALI 5 TIMOR
**Lessing**
   Author: 5 DORIS
**Lesson**
   Dance: 4 STEP
   Early: 4 ABCS
   Kindergarten: 4 ABCS
   Piano: 5 ETUDE
**"Lesson From ___, A" (Fugard**
   **play): 5 ALOES**
**"Less Than Zero"**
   author Bret Easton ___:
     5 ELLIS
**Lest: 6 INCASE**
**Lestat**
   creator Anne: 4 RICE
**Lester**
   Bluegrass guitarist: 5 FLATT
   Sci-fi writer: 6 DELREY
**"Lest we lose our ___":**
   5 EDENS
**Les ___-Unis: 5 ETATS**
**Let: 4 RENT 5 ALLOW LEASE**
   **6 RENTED**
   back in: 7 READMIT
   down: 5 ALTER
   fall: 4 DROP
   free: 5 UNTIE
   go: 3 AXE CAN 4 AXED FIRE
     FREE 5 FIRED FREED
     7 RELEASE UNLEASH
     UNLOOSE
     15 RELEASEONESHOLD
   go of: 4 DROP
   in: 5 ADMIT 8 ADMITTED
   loose: 5 FREED UNPEN
     UNTIE
   off: 4 VENT 6 ACQUIT
   out: 4 EMIT RENT 5 ALTER
     UNPEN WIDEN 6 LOOSEN
     PAROLE
   slip: 4 TELL TOLD

stand: 4 STET
up: 4 EASE 5 ABATE EASED
   6 ABATED LESSEN
   RELENT
~, in tennis: 6 DOOVER
**"Let ___" (Beatles song): 4 ITBE**
**Let ___ a secret: 4 INON**
**"Let ___ cake": 5 EMEAT**
**Letch: 5 SATYR**
**"Let 'er ___!": 3 RIP**
**"Lethal Weapon"**
   costar of Danny: 3 MEL
   director Richard: 6 DONNER
   role: 5 RIGGS
**"Let ___ hang out": 5 ITALL**
**Lethargic: 4 LOGY 5 INERT**
   **6 DROWSY SUPINE**
**Lethargy: 5 SOPOR 6 STUPOR**
   **TORPOR 7 MALAISE**
**"Let It ___ " (Everly Brothers**
   **hit): 4 BEME**
**"Let it stand": 4 STET**
**"Let me repeat ...": 5 ISAID**
   **7 ASISAID**
**"Let's ___": 4 ROLL**
**"Let's Dance"**
   singer David: 5 BOWIE
**"Let's Eat Right to Keep Fit"**
   author Davis: 6 ADELLE
**"Let's Fall in Love"**
   composer: 5 ARLEN
**"Let's get going!": 4 CMON**
**"Let's Get It On"**
   singer: 4 GAYE
**"Let's go!": 4 CMON**
**"Let's just leave ___ that":**
   4 ITAT
**"Let's Make ___": 5 ADEAL**
**"Let's Make a Deal"**
   option: 4 DOOR
**Letter: 7 EPISTLE**
   abbr.: 3 ENC PPS 4 ATTN
     ENCL
   additions (abbr.): 3 PSS
   adornment: 5 SERIF
   after chi: 3 PSI
   after epsilon: 4 ZETA
   after eta: 5 THETA
   after pi: 3 RHO
   after theta: 4 IOTA
   after zeta: 3 ETA
   Ancient: 4 RUNE
   before beth: 5 ALEPH
   before gimel: 4 BETH
   before iota: 5 THETA
   before omega: 3 PSI
   before sigma: 3 RHO
   before upsilon: 3 TAU
   Campus: 3 ETA RHO 5 THETA
   Curvy: 3 ESS
   embellishment: 5 SERIF
   enc.: 3 SAE 4 SASE
   flourish: 5 SERIF
   Frat: 3 CHI ETA PHI PSI
     RHO TAU 5 SIGMA
     THETA

Greek: 3 CHI ETA PHI PSI
 RHO TAU 4 IOTA ZETA
 5 ALPHA KAPPA OMEGA
 SIGMA THETA
Hebrew: 3 MEM TAV YOD
 4 ALEF KOPH TETH
 5 ALEPH
Key: 3 PHI 4 BETA 5 KAPPA
Kind of: 4 FORM 5 CHAIN
Last: 3 ZEE
Last ~ in London: 3 ZED
Old English: 3 EDH
Online: 5 EMAIL
opener: 3 SIR 4 DEAR SIRS
 5 STEAM 7 DEARSIR
Penultimate: 3 WYE
Pluralizing: 3 ESS
Scarlet: 6 STIGMA
signoff: 6 ASEVER
Sorority: 3 CHI ETA RHO
starter: 4 DEAR
Sweater: 3 RHO VEE 4 ZETA
 5 THETA
to Santa: 8 WISHLIST
Triangular: 5 DELTA
Trident-shaped: 3 PSI
Undeliverable: 5 NIXIE
Use a ~ opener: 4 SLIT
**Letterhead**
 abbr.: 3 INC TEL
 symbol: 4 LOGO
**Lettering**
 device: 7 STENCIL
**Letterless**
 phone button: 3 ONE
**Letterman**
 rival: 4 LENO
 ~, to pals: 4 DAVE
**Letterman, David**
 dental feature: 3 GAP
 list: 6 TOPTEN
 network: 3 CBS
 rival: 7 JAYLENO
**Lettermen, The:** 4 TRIO
**Letters:** 4 MAIL
 Alias: 3 AKA
 at sea: 3 HMS USS
 Chain: 3 DNA
 Cross: 4 INRI
 Dead: 3 RIP
 Draft: 3 SSS
 Explosive: 3 TNT
 Fashion: 3 YSL
 Fleet: 3 USS
 Form: 3 IRS
 Full house: 3 SRO
 Genetic: 3 DNA RNA
 Greek: 3 MUS NUS PIS XIS
 Hit: 3 SRO
 Invitation: 4 RSVP
 Key: 3 ESC
 Links: 3 PGA
 Lodge: 4 BPOE
 Lotion: 3 SPF
 Love: 4 SWAK
 Marker: 3 IOU

Memo: 3 FYI
News: 3 UPI
of concern: 3 TLC
of credit: 3 IOU
of success: 3 SRO
of urgency: 4 ASAP
Online: 5 EMAIL
Package: 3 COD
partner: 4 ARTS
Proof: 3 QED
Red: 4 USSR
Regal: 3 HRH
Rush: 4 ASAP
Shingle: 3 DDS
Tach: 3 RPM
Tanning: 3 SPF
Trading: 4 NYSE
Urgent: 4 ASAP
Wanted: 3 AKA
with no stamps: 5 EMAIL
Woman of: 5 VANNA
**Letter-shaped**
 beam: 4 IBAR
 fastener: 4 TNUT 5 UBOLT
 girder: 5 HBEAM
 opening: 5 TSLOT
 support: 5 IBEAM
**Letter-writing**
 device: 7 STENCIL
**Letts**
 live here: 4 RIGA
**Lettuce:** 5 BREAD MOOLA
 6 DOREMI
 Big piece of: 5 CNOTE
 Like: 5 LEAFY
 unit: 4 HEAD
 variety: 3 COS 4 BIBB
**Letup**
 Without: 5 NOEND ONEND
**"Let Us Now Praise Famous
 Men"**
 writer James: 4 AGEE
**Levant**
 Pianist: 5 OSCAR
**Levee:** 4 DIKE
**Level:** 4 EVEN RAZE TIER
 TOOL TRUE 5 PLANE
 7 ECHELON STRATUM
 Ballpark: 4 TIER
 connector: 4 RAMP
 Hierarchy: 4 RUNG
 Highest: 4 ACME
 Not: 5 ATILT 6 ASLOPE
 Not on the: 6 ASLANT
 SLOPED
 of authority: 7 ECHELON
 Stadium: 4 TIER
 Theater: 4 LOGE
 ~, in London: 4 RASE
**Levelheaded:** 4 SANE
**Leveling**
 device: 4 SHIM
**Levels:** 6 STRATA
 of society: 6 STRATA
**Lever:** 3 PRY
 Foot: 5 PEDAL

Kind of: 7 CROWBAR
**Leveret:** 4 HARE
**Levertov**
 Poet: 6 DENISE
**Lévesque**
 Former Quebec premier:
 4 RENE
**Levi**
 Former Israeli prime minister:
 6 ESHKOL
 Mother of: 4 LEAH
**Levi, Carlo**
 novel town: 5 EBOLI
**Leviathan:** 4 HULK
 8 BEHEMOTH
**Levin**
 Author: 3 IRA
**Levinson, Barry**
 film: 5 DINER 6 TINMEN
**Levi's**
 line: 4 SEAM
 material: 5 DENIM
 rival: 3 LEE
**Levitate:** 4 RISE 5 FLOAT
**Levy:** 3 TAX 6 IMPOSE
 collector: 3 IRS
**Lew**
 Actor: 5 AYRES
 Wimbledon champion: 4 HOAD
**Lewd:** 6 SMUTTY 7 OBSCENE
 look: 4 LEER
**Lewis**
 Bandleader: 3 TED
 Jazz pianist: 6 RAMSEY
 puppet: 8 LAMBCHOP
 Puppeteer: 5 SHARI
 Ventriloquist: 5 SHARI
 with Lamb Chop: 5 SHARI
**Lewis, C.S.**
 fictional land: 6 NARNIA
 The "C" of: 5 CLIVE
**Lewis, Huey (and the News)**
 hit song: 13 HIPTOBESQUARE
**Lewis, John L.**
 org.: 3 UMW
**Lewiston, Maine**
 campus: 5 BATES
**Lex**
 Superman foe: 6 LUTHOR
**Lexicographer**
 concern: 5 USAGE
**Lexicography**
 First name in: 4 NOAH
**Lexicon**
 Brit.: 3 OED
 U.K.: 3 OED
**Lexington:** 3 AVE
 sch.: 3 VMI
**Lhasa**
 land: 5 TIBET
 priest: 4 LAMA
**Lhasa ___:** 4 APSO
**Liability:** 4 DEBT
 Musical: 6 TINEAR
 opposite: 5 ASSET
**Liable:** 3 APT

Become: 5 INCUR
**Liam**
  Actor: 6 NEESON
**Liar**
  Biblical: 7 ANANIAS
**"Liar Liar"**
  actress Cheri: 5 OTERI
  star: 9 JIMCARREY
**Libation:** 8 BEVERAGE
  Postprandial: 4 PORT
  Yuletide: 3 NOG
**Libel:** 4 TORT
**Liberace:** 7 PIANIST
  Like a ~ outfit: 6 ORNATE
**Liberal**
  follower: 4 ARTS
  Former: 6 NEOCON
  leader: 3 NEO
  pursuits: 4 ARTS
**Liberal ___:** 4 ARTS
**Liberate:** 4 FREE
  ~, so to speak: 5 SWIPE
**Liberator**
  Simón: 7 BOLIVAR
**Liberia**
  capital: 8 MONROVIA
**Libertine:** 4 RAKE ROUE
  6 LECHER
  opposite: 4 PRIG
**Liberty:** 4 EASE 5 LEAVE
  6 STATUE 7 FREEDOM
  At: 4 FREE
  On: 6 ASHORE
  Taking: 6 ASHORE
**Libido:** 4 EROS
**Libra:** 4 SIGN
  Gem for a ~, maybe: 4 OPAL
**Librarian**
  admonition: 3 SHH
  gadget: 5 DATER
  motto: 15 SILENCEISGOLDEN
**Library**
  Bellow in the: 4 SAUL
  command: 3 SHH
  device: 5 DATER
  innovator: 5 DEWEY
  item: 4 BOOK
  microfilm: 5 FICHE
  no-no: 5 NOISE
  patron: 4 USER
  ref.: 3 OED
  study area: 6 CARREL
  unit: 5 SHELF
  Use a: 4 READ
  ~ ID: 4 ISBN
**Libreville**
  country: 5 GABON
**Libya**
  capital: 7 TRIPOLI
  Much of: 6 SAHARA
  Neighbor of: 4 CHAD
**Lice:** 4 NITS 6 VERMIN
**License:** 6 PERMIT 7 ENTITLE
  Driver's ~ datum: 3 DOB SEX
  4 NAME
  issuer (abbr.): 3 FCC

Kind of: 6 POETIC
  plate: 3 TAG
  to drill: 3 DDS
**Licenses:** 3 IDS
**Licentious:** 7 IMMORAL
  man: 4 ROUE
**Lichen**
  component: 4 ALGA 5 ALGAE
  Velvety: 4 MOSS
**Lichtenstein**
  Artist: 3 ROY
  output: 6 POPART
**Lick**
  Musical: 4 RIFF
  Not a: 4 NONE
**Lickable**
  cookie: 4 OREO
**Licked:** 6 BEATEN
  Get: 4 LOSE
**Lickety-split:** 3 PDQ 5 APACE
  8 INNOTIME
  Go: 4 TEAR
  Went: 4 SPED TORE
**Licking**
  It may get a ~ after dinner:
  4 OREO
**Lick ___ promise:** 4 ANDA
**Licorice**
  flavoring: 5 ANISE
  liqueur: 5 ANISE 8 ANISETTE
  plant: 5 ANISE
**Lid:** 3 CAP
  attachment: 4 LASH
  edger: 8 EYELINER
  problem: 4 STYE
  Take the ~ off: 5 UNCAP
**Liddy**
  of politics: 4 DOLE
**Lie:** 4 REST 7 UNTRUTH
  at rest: 6 REPOSE
  in store for: 5 AWAIT
  in the sun: 4 BASK
  in wait: 4 LURK
  Little: 3 FIB
  low: 4 HIDE
  next to: 4 ABUT
  One way to: 5 PRONE
  on the beach: 4 BAKE
  White: 3 FIB
**Liechtenstein**
  capital: 5 VADUZ
**Lied**
  article: 4 EINE
**"___ lied!":** 3 SOI
**Lieder:** 5 SONGS
  Follow the: 4 SING
**Life:** 3 PEP 6 CEREAL
  8 SENTENCE
  Animal: 5 FAUNA
  Bring to: 7 ANIMATE
  Brought to: 4 BORN
  College: 7 ACADEME
  Come back to: 7 REAWAKE
  follower: 4 SPAN
  form: 5 BEING
  Had a: 3 WAS

Have a: 3 ARE 5 EXIST
  jacket: 4 VEST 7 MAEWEST
  lines: 3 BIO 4 OBIT
  Local: 5 BIOTA
  Lot in: 4 FATE
  Low: 5 AMEBA
  Mark for: 4 SCAR
  Nice: 3 VIE
  partner: 4 LIMB MATE
  Pertaining to: 6 BIOTIC
  Plant: 5 FLORA
  Pool: 4 ALGA
  prefix: 3 MID
  preserver: 4 OBIT
  Regional: 5 BIOTA
  saver: 4 HERO
  Short: 3 BIO
  Show signs of: 4 STIR
  Sign of: 5 PULSE
  sources: 3 OVA
  story: 3 BIO
  Succeed in: 5 GOFAR
  support: 3 AIR
  Symbol of: 4 ANKH
  The easy: 10 BEDOFROSES
  The facts of: 3 BIO
  The good: 4 EASE
  This is your: 3 BIO
  time: 3 AGE
  Time of one's: 3 AGE
  Tiny ~ form: 5 AMEBA
  work: 6 CAREER
**"___ life!":** 4 GETA
**"Life ___ a dream":** 5 ISBUT
**Lifeboat**
  item: 3 OAR
  lowerer: 5 DAVIT
**"Lifeboat"**
  actress Bankhead:
  8 TALLULAH
**"Life ___ cabaret":** 3 ISA
**"Life in London"**
  author Pierce: 4 EGAN
**Lifeless:** 4 ARID DEAD 5 INERT
  ~, old-style: 5 AMORT
**Lifelike:** 4 REAL
**Lifeline**
  site: 4 PALM
**Lifelines**
  OR: 3 IVS
**Life of ___ (ease):** 5 RILEY
**"Life of Brian"**
  star: 8 ERICIDLE
**Life of Riley:** 4 EASE
**"Life of Riley, The"**
  character Digger: 5 ODELL
**Lifesaver:** 3 EMT NET 4 HERO
  6 AIRBAG
  Biblical: 3 ARK
**Lifesaving**
  skill: 3 CPR
**"Life ___ short ...":** 5 ISTOO
**"Lifestyles of the Rich and
  Famous"**
  host Robin: 5 LEACH
**Lifetime:** 3 AGE 4 DAYS

**Lifework:** 5 TRADE 6 CAREER
**Liffey**
  locale: 4 EIRE
**LIFO**
  Part of: 6 LASTIN
**Lift:** 3 COP 4 HIKE RIDE
      5 HOIST RAISE STEAL
      6 REPEAL THIEVE
      7 ELEVATE RESCIND
      UPRAISE 8 ELEVATOR
  anchor: 4 SAIL
  Hard to: 6 LEADEN
  He gave us a: 4 OTIS
  It might give you a: 4 TBAR
  Need a: 3 SAG
  Shoe: 7 HEELTAP
  Ski: 4 TBAR
  the spirits of: 5 ELATE
  They may need a: 6 SKIERS
  up: 5 ELATE EXALT HOIST
      RAISE 7 ELEVATE
  up a mountain: 4 TBAR
  with effort: 5 HEAVE
**"___ lift?":** 5 NEEDA
**Lifted:** 5 STOLE
  with effort: 4 HOVE
**Lifter**
  Car: 4 JACK
  Mythical: 5 ATLAS
  Weight: 5 CRANE
**Lifting**
  apparatus: 5 HOIST
  Job involving: 5 HEIST
  unit: 3 REP
**Light:** 4 AIRY LAMP PALE
      6 IGNITE
  air: 4 LILT
  Alerting: 5 FLARE
  and airy: 8 ETHEREAL
  as a feather: 4 AIRY
  Beam of: 3 RAY
  Blinding: 5 GLARE
  Bring to: 6 EXHUME EXPOSE
  Circle of: 4 HALO
  Come to: 5 ARISE 6 EMERGE
  Disco: 6 STROBE
  Emit coherent: 4 LASE
  Emitted: 5 SHONE
  First: 4 DAWN
  Flash of: 5 GLEAM GLINT
  Gas: 4 NEON
  Green: 4 OKAY 6 ASSENT
  Guiding: 6 BEACON
      7 POLARIS 8 POLESTAR
  Head: 4 HALO IDEA
  High: 4 HALO
  Hint of: 5 GLEAM
  into: 3 RIP 6 ASSAIL
  Kitchen: 5 PILOT
  Laser: 4 BEAM
  Make ~ of: 8 POOHPOOH
  Night: 4 NEON STAR
  on one's feet: 4 SPRY 5 AGILE
  opening: 3 TWI
  prefix: 3 TWI 4 PHOS
  Ray of: 4 BEAM

  Science of: 6 OPTICS
  show: 6 AURORA
  Sky: 3 UFO 4 STAR
  source: 3 SUN 4 LAMP
  splitter: 5 PRISM
  starter: 3 TWI
  Stove: 5 PILOT
  stuff: 4 NEON
  Theater: 4 SPOT
  unit: 5 LUMEN
**Light ___ :** 5 ASAIR
**Lighten:** 4 EASE
  up: 4 EASE PALE
**"Lighten up!":**
      10 TONEITDOWN
**Lighter:** 5 BARGE
  feature: 4 WICK
  fuel: 6 BUTANE
  Get: 4 FADE
  igniter: 5 FLINT
  Made: 5 EASED
  maker: 3 BIC
**Light-footed:** 5 AGILE
      6 NIMBLE
**Lightheaded:** 5 GIDDY WOOZY
**Light-Horse Harry:** 3 LEE
**Lighthouse**
  locale: 4 ISLE
  of note: 6 PHAROS
**Lighting**
  Bad: 5 ARSON
  Overhead: 4 HALO
**"Light My Fire"**
  band: 8 THEDOORS
**Lightning:** 4 TEAM
  drawer: 3 ROD
  home: 5 TAMPA
  sound: 3 ZAP
**"___ Light Up My Life":** 3 YOU
**Lightyear, Buzz**
  movie: 8 TOYSTORY
**Light-years**
  3.26 ~: 6 PARSEC
**Lignite:** 4 COAL
**Ligurian Sea**
  feeder: 4 ARNO
**Likable:** 4 NICE
**Like:** 3 ALA DIG 4 ASIF
      5 GOFOR 6 AKINTO
      SUCHAS 7 SIMILAR
  so: 4 THUS
  suffix: 3 ISH OID
**Like ___ (quickly):** 5 ASHOT
**Likeable**
  leader: 3 IKE
**Like a ___ bricks:** 5 TONOF
**"Like a Rock"**
  singer Bob: 5 SEGER
**"Like a Rolling Stone"**
  singer Bob: 5 DYLAN
**Liked:** 3 DUG
**Like ___ from the blue:**
      5 ABOLT
**"___ Like It Hot":** 4 SOME
**Likelihood:** 4 ODDS
**Likely:** 3 APT 6 LIABLE

  Not: 5 UNAPT
  (to): 5 PRONE
**Like-minded:** 9 SIMPATICO
  voters: 4 BLOC
**Likeness:** 5 IMAGE
  prefix: 5 ICONO
**"Like ___ not":** 4 ITOR
**"Like, no way!":** 4 ASIF
**Like ___ of bricks:** 4 ATON
**Like ___ of sunshine:** 4 ARAY
**Like ___ out of hell:** 4 ABAT
**"... like ___ planted by the**
      **rivers":** 5 ATREE
**Likewise:** 3 TOO 4 ALSO SAME
  not: 3 NOR
**"Likewise":** 5 DITTO
**Likhovtseva**
  of tennis: 5 ELENA
**Liking:** 3 YEN 4 INTO 5 FANCY
      TOOTH 7 SWEETON
  Start: 6 TAKETO
**Likud**
  leader: 6 SHAMIR
**"Li'l Abner"**
  cartoonist: 4 CAPP 6 ALCAPP
  Mother of: 10 PANSYYOKUM
  Opposed to, in: 4 AGIN
  Say: 5 ELIDE
**Lilac:** 4 ODOR 5 SHRUB
**"Lilies of the Field"**
  role: 3 NUN
**Lille**
  **Info:** French cue
  Laugh, in: 4 RIRE
  Lily, in: 3 LIS LYS
  Little, in: 3 PEU
  Love, in: 5 AMOUR
**Lillehammer**
  City near: 4 OSLO
  country: 6 NORWAY
**Lillian**
  Actress: 4 GISH
**Lillie**
  Comic: 3 BEA
**Lilliputian:** 3 WEE 4 TINY
**Lilly**
  of pharmaceuticals: 3 ELI
**___ Lilly & Co.:** 3 ELI
**Lilongwe**
  country: 6 MALAWI
**Lilting**
  refrain: 3 TRA 5 TRALA
**Lily**
  African: 4 ALOE
  Arum: 5 CALLA
  Medicinal: 4 ALOE
  plant: 4 ALOE
  Plantain: 5 HOSTA
  Showy: 4 SEGO
  Soprano: 5 PONS
  Type of: 5 CALLA
  Utah: 4 SEGO
  Western: 4 SEGO
**Lily-livered:** 6 CRAVEN
**Lily-white:** 4 PURE
**Lima:** 4 BEAN

land: 4 PERU
state: 4 OHIO
**Limb:** 3 ARM
grabber: 5 TALON
holder: 5 TORSO
It may be out on a: 4 NEST
Out on a: 5 TREED
**Limber:** 5 AGILE LITHE
**Limbo**
requirement: 3 BAR
resident: 4 SOUL
USPS: 3 DLO
**Limburger**
feature: 4 ODOR
relative: 6 TILSIT
**Lime:** 5 OXIDE
drink: 3 ADE
**Limelites**
leader: 4 SHEP
**Limerick:** 4 POEM
County north of: 5 CLARE
land: 4 EIRE ERIN
language: 4 ERSE
maker: 4 LEAR
Second word of a ~, often:
4 ONCE
Third word of a ~, often:
3 WAS
**Limit:** 3 CAP
Go over the: 5 SPEED
Kind of: 3 AGE
Outer: 3 RIM 4 EDGE
Salary: 3 CAP
Speed ~ letters: 3 MPH
Spending: 3 CAP
Upper: 3 CAP MAX
Went over the: 4 SPED
**Limited:** 5 SCANT 6 FINITE
NARROW
It may be: 7 EDITION
number: 3 FEW
support: 5 RAILS
**Limitless:** 4 VAST
quantity: 3 SEA 5 OCEAN
**Limo**
destination: 4 PROM
passenger: 3 VIP
**Limp**
Go: 4 WILT
watch painter: 4 DALI
**Limp as ___:** 4 ARAG
**Limping:** 4 LAME 5 LAMED
**Lin**
Architect: 4 MAYA
**Linchpin:** 8 KEYSTONE
site: 4 AXLE
**Lincoln:** 3 CAR 4 AUTO
7 CAPITAL
Actor: 4 ELMO
birthplace: 8 LOGCABIN
center: 3 CEE
feature: 5 BEARD
First VP of: 6 HAMLIN
in-law: 4 TODD
nickname: 3 ABE
portrait site: 4 CENT

President: 3 ABE
Son of: 3 TAD
**Lind, Jenny:** 5 SWEDE
**Linda**
Actress: 4 DANO HUNT
5 EVANS LAVIN
of the soaps: 4 DANO
Singer: 4 EDER
**___ Linda, California:** 4 LOMA
**Lindbergh**
feat: 10 SOLOFLIGHT
Like the ~ flight: 4 SOLO
Writer: 4 ANNE
**Lindbergh, Anne ___:**
6 MORROW
**Lindbergh, ___ Morrow:**
4 ANNE
**Linden:** 4 TREE
Actor: 3 HAL
**Lindgren**
character Longstocking:
5 PIPPI
Novelist: 6 ASTRID
**Lindley**
Actress: 5 AUDRA
of golf: 4 LETA
**Lindros**
of hockey: 4 ERIC
**Lindsay**
Poet: 6 VACHEL
**Lindstrom**
Newswoman: 3 PIA
**Lindy**
Fly like: 4 SOLO
**Line:** 5 QUEUE
Bottom: 3 HEM NET SUM
5 TOTAL 10 NETRESULTS
Central: 4 AXIS
crosser: 4 SCAB
Curved: 3 ARC
Cut: 4 SCAR
dance: 5 CONGA
Drop a: 4 FISH 5 WRITE
feeder: 6 STOOGE
Hang on the: 6 AIRDRY
It holds the: 4 REEL
Kind of: 3 AIR DEW 5 CONGA
WAIST
Like a ~, briefly: 4 ONED
Main: 5 AORTA 6 ARTERY
On the: 6 ATRISK
7 ATSTAKE
Out of: 5 ASKEW
Put on the: 4 RISK
Stand in: 4 WAIT
Stop on a: 5 DEPOT
Toe the: 4 OBEY
**Lineage:** 5 BREED 7 DESCENT
8 ANCESTRY
**Linear:** 4 ONED
prefix: 5 RECTI
**Lined**
up: 4 AROW 6 INAROW
**Lineman:** 3 END
**Linemen:** 3 LGS LTS RGS RTS
TES 4 ENDS

**Linen:** 5 CLOTH
color: 4 ECRU
fabric: 5 TOILE 6 DAMASK
items: 6 SHEETS
Sheer: 5 TOILE
source: 4 FLAX
Table: 6 NAPERY
tape: 5 INKLE
Transparent: 5 TOILE
vestment: 3 ALB
**Liner:** 4 SHIP
Eye: 3 LID
Kind of: 5 OCEAN
letters: 3 USS
On a: 4 ASEA
Place for a: 5 OCEAN
Shoe: 6 INSOLE
**Lines**
Circle: 5 RADII
Dedicated: 3 ODE
Graph: 4 AXES
Head: 3 EEG
Heir: 4 WILL
High: 3 ELS
Like some: 6 DOTTED
Lyrical: 3 ODE
Map – (abbr.): 3 RDS STS
of music: 5 STAFF
on a musical staff: 5 EGBDF
**Lineup:** 5 ARRAY
Circus: 4 ACTS
finish: 4 ETAL
Kind of: 7 ALLSTAR
Picked out of a: 4 IDED
Picks out of a: 3 IDS
Rest stop: 5 SEMIS
Wasn't in the: 6 SATOUT
**"Lineup, The"**
enforcement gp.: 4 SFPD
**___ Ling (Chinese mountain**
**range):** 3 NAN
**Linger:** 4 STAY WAIT
5 TARRY
**Lingerie**
item: 3 BRA 5 TEDDY
7 NIGHTIE
**Lingering**
effect: 4 ECHO
sensation: 10 AFTERTASTE
sign: 4 SCAR
**Ling-Ling:** 5 PANDA
**Lingo:** 5 ARGOT SLANG
6 PATOIS
**Lingua ___:** 6 FRANCA
**Lingual**
prefix: 3 TRI
**Linguine:** 5 PASTA
topper: 5 PESTO
**Linguistics**
First name in: 4 NOAM
gp.: 3 MLA
Suffix used in: 3 ESE
**___ Lingus:** 3 AER
**Liniment**
Need: 4 ACHE
Needing: 4 ACHY SORE

target: 4 ACHE
**Lining**
  Hat: 4 CAUL
  Warm: 3 FUR
**Link:** 3 TIE 4 BOND 5 NEXUS
    TIEIN UNITE
  with: 5 TIETO
**Linking**
  toy: 4 LEGO
  verb: 6 COPULA
**Linkletter**
  Emcee: 3 ART
**Links**
  **Info:** Golf cue
  carrier: 4 CART
  cry: 4 FORE
  figure: 3 PRO
  gadget: 3 TEE
  gp.: 3 PGA
  hazard: 4 TRAP
  letters: 3 PGA
  Missing: 6 APEMEN
  nickname: 5 ARNIE
  norm: 3 PAR
  org.: 3 PGA
  peg: 3 TEE
  position: 3 LIE
  rarity: 3 ACE 5 EAGLE
  rental: 4 CART
  Take to the: 4 GOLF
  target: 4 HOLE
**Linkup**
  PC: 3 LAN
**Linoleum**
  alternative: 4 TILE
  protector: 3 WAX
**Linseed oil**
  source: 4 FLAX
**Lint:** 5 FLUFF
  collector: 4 TRAP
  trap: 5 INNIE
**Lintel**
  locale: 9 DOORFRAME
**Linz**
  Goodie from: 5 TORTE
  locale (abbr.): 3 AUS
**Linzer**
  follower: 5 TORTE
**Lion:** 3 CAT
  den: 4 LAIR
  home: 3 DEN
  Like a: 5 MANED
  Like a sea: 5 EARED
  Mountain: 4 PUMA
  of Narnia: 5 ASLAN
  portrayer: 4 LAHR
  pride: 4 MANE
  share: 4 MOST
  sound: 4 ROAR
  suffix: 3 ESS IZE
  Young: 5 WHELP
  Zodiac: 3 LEO
**Lion-colored:** 5 TAWNY
**Lionel**
  product: 8 TRAINSET
  Sister of: 5 ETHEL

**Lioness**
  lack: 4 MANE
  Lionized: 4 ELSA
  Literary: 4 ELSA
  Movie: 4 ELSA
**"Lion in Winter, The"**
  queen: 7 ELEANOR
  star: 6 OTOOLE
**Lionized**
  actor: 4 LAHR
  lioness: 4 ELSA
**"Lion King, The"**
  hero: 5 SIMBA
  lion: 4 NALA 5 SIMBA
  villain: 4 SCAR
**Lions:** 4 TEAM
  Group of: 5 PRIDE
  Like circus: 5 TAMED
  org.: 3 NFC
**Lip:** 3 RIM 4 BRIM EDGE SASS
  application: 5 GLOSS LINER
  attachment: 4 SYNC
  Curl one's: 5 SNEER
  Give ~ to: 4 SASS
  goo: 4 BALM
  service: 4 KISS
**Lip-___:** 4 SYNC
**Lipinski**
  leap: 4 AXEL
  milieu: 3 ICE
  Skater: 4 TARA
**Lippi, Filippo:** 3 FRA
**Lipstick**
  container: 5 PURSE
  Like: 4 WAXY
  mishap: 5 SMEAR
**Lipton**
  offering: 3 TEA
  rival: 6 NESTEA SALADA
    TETLEY
**Liq.**
  measures: 3 PTS QTS
**Liquefy:** 4 MELT THAW
    5 PUREE
**Liqueur**
  Almond-flavored:
    8 AMARETTO
  Anise-flavored: 4 OUZO
    6 PERNOD
  Black currant: 6 CASSIS
  Coffee-flavored: 8 TIAMARIA
  flavoring: 5 ANISE 7 ANISEED
    APRICOT
  Greek: 4 OUZO
  Green: 8 ABSINTHE
  Small ~ glass: 4 PONY
  Spanish: 4 ANIS
  Sweet: 8 ANISETTE
  Thick: 5 CREME
**Liquid:** 5 FLUID
  asset: 4 CASH
  Burn with hot: 5 SCALD
  Corrosive: 4 ACID
  cosmetic: 6 LOTION
  Explosive: 5 NITRO
  fat: 5 OLEIN

  Make: 4 CASH
  Pickling: 5 BRINE
  suffix: 4 ATOR
  Volatile: 5 NITRO
**Liquidate:** 4 SELL 7 SELLOUT
**Liquid-Plumr**
  alternative: 5 DRANO
**Liquor**
  Colada: 3 RUM
  Gimlet: 3 GIN
  Jamaican: 3 RUM
  Kind of: 4 MALT
  lover: 3 SOT
  Martini: 3 GIN
  Selling: 3 WET
  Small drink of: 3 NIP
**Lira**
  replacement: 4 EURO
**Lire**
  Where ~ are spent: 5 ITALY
**Lisa**
  Actress: 5 BONET
  of basketball: 6 LESLIE
  Singer: 4 LOEB
  ~, to Bart: 3 SIS
**"___ Lisa":** 4 MONA
**Lisbon**
  **Info:** Portuguese cue
  City north of: 6 OPORTO
  Lady, in: 4 DONA 7 SENHORA
  Man, in: 6 SENHOR
  native: 7 IBERIAN
**Lisi**
  Actress: 5 VIRNA
**Lisper**
  Problematic letter for a: 3 ESS
**Lissome:** 5 AGILE
**List:** 4 MENU 6 ROSTER
  abbr.: 3 ETC 4 ETAL
  component: 4 ITEM
  divider: 5 COMMA
  ender: 3 ETC 4 ETAL
    6 ETALIA 8 ETCETERA
  entry: 4 ITEM
  Get on the: 5 ENROL
  heading: 4 TODO
  of candidates: 5 SLATE
  of choices: 4 MENU
  of dishes: 4 MENU
  Official with a: 4 DEAN
  of lapses: 6 ERRATA
  of options: 4 MENU
  of priors: 8 RAPSHEET
  of topics: 6 AGENDA
  One with a: 4 DEAN
  On the A: 5 ELITE
  On the disabled: 4 HURT
  Part of a: 4 ITEM
  preceder: 5 COLON
  price: 6 RETAIL
  recipient: 5 SANTA
  shortener: 3 ETC 4 ETAL
  Type of: 4 TODO
  ___ list: 4 TODO 5 DEANS
**Listed:** 5 LEANT
  Not ~ above: 5 OTHER

**Listen: 4** HARK **6** ATTEND
  here: **3** EAR
  in on: **7** WIRETAP
  Refusing to: **4** DEAF
  to: **4** HEAR HEED OBEY
**"Listen!": 4** HARK
**List-ending**
  abbr.: **3** ETC **4** ETAL
**Listener: 3** EAR
**Listening: 7** ALLEARS
    TUNEDIN
  device: **3** EAR
  to music, maybe: **6** ONHOLD
**"Listen up!": 3** HEY
    **8** TAKEHEED
**Listerine**
  target: **4** GERM
**Listlessness: 5** ENNUI
    **6** TORPOR **7** MALAISE
    **8** LETHARGY
**Liston**
  Boxer: **5** SONNY
  defeater: **3** ALI
**List-shortening**
  abbr.: **3** ETC **4** ETAL
**Liszt**
  Composer: **5** FRANZ
  Lively, to: **7** ANIMATO
  piece: **5** ETUDE
  symphonic poem: **5** TASSO
**Lit: 4** HIGH **5** AFIRE AGLOW
    OILED **6** LOOPED
    STONED **7** IGNITED
    SMASHED
  Barely: **3** DIM
  into: **5** HADAT
  No longer: **5** SOBER
  Poorly: **3** DIM
  up: **5** AGLOW
**Lit ___ (college course):**
    **4** CRIT
**Lite: 5** LOFAT NOCAL
**Literacy**
  Prove one's: **4** READ
**Literary**
  adverb: **3** OFT **4** NEER
  alias: **4** ELIA
  assortment: **3** ANA
  captain: **4** AHAB NEMO
  category: **5** GENRE
  collection: **3** ANA
  conflict: **4** AGON
  device: **5** IRONY **6** SIMILE
  figure: **4** LION
  inits.: **3** EAP GBS RLS RWE
    TSE
  lioness: **4** ELSA
  monogram: **3** EAP GBS RLS
    RWE TSE
  olio: **3** ANA
  pen name: **4** ELIA
  postscript: **6** EPILOG
  pseudonym: **4** ELIA
**Literature: 7** LETTERS
  Lewd: **4** PORN
  ~ Nobelist: *see pages 733–734*

**Liters**
  Like: **6** METRIC
**Lith.**
  ~, once: **3** SSR
**Lithe: 4** SLIM **6** SUPPLE
    SVELTE
**Lithographer**
  Highly collectible: **4** ERTE
  Noted: **4** IVES
**Litigant: 4** SUER
  Unnamed: **3** ROE
**Litigate: 3** SUE
**Litigator**
  org.: **3** ABA
**Litigious**
  Be: **3** SUE
  type: **4** SUER
**Litmus: 3** DYE
  It turns ~ blue: **6** ALKALI
  It turns ~ red: **4** ACID
  reddener: **4** ACID
**Litter: 5** BROOD
  critter: **3** PUP
  cry: **3** MEW
  Littlest of a: **4** RUNT
  member: **3** PUP **4** RUNT
  Theater: **5** STUBS
**Litterae: 3** ARS
**Litterbug: 4** SLOB
**Little: 3** WEE **5** SMALL
  A: **4** SOME
  bit: **3** DAB TAD **4** ATOM DRIB
    IOTA **5** SKOSH
  Even a: **3** ANY **5** ATALL
  Give a: **4** BEND
  more than: **4** MERE
  one: **3** ELF TAD TOT **4** RUNT
    TYKE
  'un: **3** TAD TOT
**"Little"**
  car of song: **3** GTO
  comics fellow: **4** NEMO
**Little ___**
  (nickname of a state): **5** RHODY
  (tots): **3** UNS
**"Little ___": 4** NEMO **5** WOMEN
**Little ___ (60's singer): 3** EVA
**Little, Rich: 4** APER
**"Little ___ Annie": 6** ORPHAN
**Little Anthony and the Imperials**
  hit song:
    **15** TEARSONMYPILLOW
**"Little Bitty Tear, A"**
  singer: **4** IVES
**"Little Caesar"**
  role: **4** RICO
**"Little Darlings"**
  actress: **5** ONEAL
**"Little Flower of Jesus":**
    **7** THERESA
**"Little Girls"**
  musical: **5** ANNIE
**Little-hand**
  indication: **4** HOUR
**"Little House on the Prairie"**
  actor Nels: **6** OLESON

**"___ Little Indians" (Christie**
    **mystery): 3** TEN
**Little Joe**
  Brother of: **4** ADAM
**Little League**
  coach, often: **3** DAD
  membership restriction:
    **8** AGELIMIT
  precursor: **5** TBALL
**Little Leaguer: 7** PRETEEN
**"Little Mermaid, The"**
  mermaid: **5** ARIEL
  prince: **4** ERIC
**Little Oil Drop**
  was its mascot: **4** ESSO
**Little pig**
  count: **5** THREE
**Little piggy: 3** TOE
  cry: **3** WEE
  What the fourth ~ had:
    **4** NONE
**"Little Plastic Castle"**
  singer DiFranco: **3** ANI
**"___ Little Prayer": 5** ISAYA
**"Little Red Book"**
  adherents: **7** MAOISTS
  author: **3** MAO
**"Little Red Hen, The"**
  reply: **4** NOTI
**"Little Shop of Horrors"**
  demand: **6** FEEDME
**Littlest**
  of a litter: **4** RUNT
**"___ little teapot ...": 3** IMA
**"___ Little Tenderness": 4** TRYA
**"Little Women"**
  author: **6** ALCOTT
  costar: **5** RYDER
  woman: **3** AMY **4** BETH
**Liturgy: 4** RITE
**Litvak**
  Director: **7** ANATOLE
**Liu**
  Actress: **4** LUCY
**Live: 3** ARE **5** EXIST **6** RESIDE
    **7** UNTAPED
  and breathe: **3** ARE **5** EXIST
  Appearing: **8** INPERSON
  Can't ~ without: **5** NEEDS
  in fear of: **5** DREAD
  it up: **5** REVEL
  Not: **5** TAPED **6** ONTAPE
  partner: **5** LEARN
  Place to: **5** ABODE
  (up): **3** PEP
  Where you: **5** ABODE
  wire: **4** DOER
**Live Aid: 7** BENEFIT
  founder Bob: **6** GELDOF
**"___ live and breathe!": 3** ASI
**Lived: 3** WAS **4** WERE **5** DWELT
    **7** RESIDED
  it up: **9** HADABLAST
**"Live Free or Die"**
  ~, to New Hampshire:
    **5** MOTTO

**Liveliness:** 4 BRIO ELAN
  5 VERVE 6 ENERGY
  ESPRIT
**Lively:** 4 PERT SPRY 5 AGILE
  BRISK 6 ACTIVE
  7 ANIMATO
  dance: 3 JIG 4 HORA REEL
    5 GALOP GIGUE
  Less: 8 SLEEPIER
  one: 4 GRIG
  outing: 5 SPREE
  party: 4 BASH
  wit: 6 ESPRIT
  ~, in music: 7 ANIMATO
  ~, in music (abbr.): 4 ANIM
**Liven:** 4 ZEST
**Liver:** 5 GLAND
  accompaniment: 6 ONIONS
  Chopped: 4 PATE
  product: 4 BILE
  ~, in French: 4 FOIE
**Liverpool**
  river: 6 MERSEY
**Liverpudlian:** 4 BRIT
**Livery**
  Did ~ work: 5 SHOED
**Livestock**
  farm: 5 RANCH
  feed: 4 MASH 7 SOILAGE
**Livid:** 5 ANGRY ASHEN IRATE
**Living:** 5 TRADE
  Barely make, as a: 6 EKEOUT
  Cost of: 4 RENT
  doll: 5 CUTIE
  Eke out a: 6 MAKEDO
  end, once: 9 BEESKNEES
  follower: 3 END
  quarters: 5 ABODE
  thing: 5 BEING
**Living room**
  furniture: 4 SOFA 5 COUCH
    6 SETTEE
**"Livin' La Vida ___" (Ricky
  Martin hit):** 4 LOCA
**Livorno**
  Info: Italian cue
  Love, in: 5 AMORE
**Livy**
  Info: Latin cue
  Land, to: 5 TERRA
  language: 5 LATIN
  Like: 5 ROMAN
  Love, to: 4 AMOR
**Lixivium:** 3 LYE
**Liz**
  Role for: 4 CLEO
**Liza**
  sister Lorna: 4 LUFT
**Lizard**
  Brightly-colored: 5 AGAMA
  Large: 6 IGUANA
  Like a: 5 SCALY 6 SCALED
  Small: 5 GECKO SKINK
  Tropical: 5 GECKO 6 IGUANA
  Type of: 6 LOUNGE
  ~, old-style: 3 EFT

**Lizardlike:** 5 SCALY
  7 SAURIAN
**Lizzie**
  Tin: 6 MODELT
  ___ Lizzie: 3 TIN
**Llama**
  country: 4 PERU
  cousin: 6 ALPACA VICUNA
    7 GUANACO
  feature: 7 SILENTL
  habitat: 5 ANDES
  land: 4 PERU
  Like the: 6 ANDEAN
**Llano**
  rarity: 4 TREE
**LLD**
  holder: 3 ATT 4 ATTY
**Lloyd**
  Actor: 5 NOLAN
**Lloyd Webber, Andrew:**
  6 KNIGHT
  musical: 4 CATS 5 EVITA
  title: 3 SIR
**"Lo!"**
  ~, in Latin: 4 ECCE
**Lo ___ (noodle dish):** 4 MEIN
**Lo-___:** 3 CAL RES
  ___ Loa: 5 MAUNA
**Load:** 4 ONUS SLEW STOW
  6 BURDEN
  Got a ~ of: 3 SAW 4 EYED
  hauler: 4 DRAY
  Heavy: 4 ONUS
  in a basket: 4 WASH
  Lode: 3 ORE
  on a ship: 5 CARGO
  Take a ~ off: 3 SIT 4 REST
    5 RELAX
  Tram: 3 ORE
**Loaded:** 4 RICH RIFE 6 STINKO
  7 WEALTHY
  It may be: 3 DIE
  They may be: 4 DICE 5 BASES
  They're: 7 FATCATS
**Loader**
  Musket: 6 RAMROD
  Muzzle: 6 RAMROD
**Loading**
  area: 4 DOCK
  site: 4 PIER
**Loads:** 4 ALOT ATON GOBS
  LOTS MANY TONS
  5 HEAPS SCADS
  6 OCEANS OODLES
  SCORES
**Loaf:** 4 LAZE
  about: 4 LOLL
  Deli: 3 RYE
  end: 4 HEEL
  on the job: 5 DOGIT
  part: 3 END
**Loafer:** 4 SHOE 5 IDLER
  6 SLIPON
  attachment: 6 TASSEL
  lack: 5 LACES
  sin: 5 SLOTH

**Loafers**
  Wearing: 4 SHOD
  Where to find: 8 SHOETREE
**Loafing:** 4 IDLE
**"___ loaf is better ...":** 5 HALFA
**Loam:** 4 SOIL
  component: 4 SILT
  Rich: 5 LOESS
**Loamy**
  deposit: 5 LOESS
  soil: 5 LOESS
**Loan**
  Ask for a: 5 HITUP
  figure (abbr.): 3 APR PCT
  Have a ~ from: 5 OWETO
  payment (abbr.): 3 INT
  Settle a: 5 REPAY
  source: 8 PAWNSHOP
**"Lo and behold!":** 3 OHO
**Loaned:** 4 LENT
**Loaner**
  Like a: 4 USED
**Loan shark:** 6 USURER
  offense: 5 USURY
**Loath:** 6 AVERSE
**Loathe:** 4 HATE 5 ABHOR
  6 DETEST 7 DESPISE
**Loathing:** 4 HATE 5 ODIUM
  6 HATRED
  Object of: 8 ANATHEMA
**Loathsome:** 4 VILE
  person: 4 TOAD
**Lob:** 4 TOSS
  path: 3 ARC
**Lobbed:** 5 THREW
**Lobby:** 4 URGE
  Big D.C.: 3 NRA
  Gun ~ org.: 3 NRA
  suffix: 3 IST
**Lobbying**
  org.: 3 PAC
**Lobe**
  locale: 3 EAR
**Loblolly:** 4 PINE
**"___ Lobo" (John Wayne film):**
  3 RIO
**___ Lobos:** 3 LOS
**Lobster**
  catcher: 4 TRAP
  eater's need: 3 BIB
  eggs: 3 ROE
  Female: 3 HEN
  Like a boiled: 3 RED
  locale: 5 MAINE
  pincer: 4 CLAW
  relative: 7 CRAWDAD
  serving: 4 TAIL
**Lobster ___ Diavolo:** 3 FRA
**"L'Oca ___ Cairo" (Mozart
  opera):** 3 DEL
**Local:** 4 NEAR 6 NATIVE
  cinema: 4 NABE
  group: 5 UNION
  life: 5 BIOTA
  self-government:
    8 HOMERULE

theater: 4 NABE
**Lo-cal:** 4 LITE
**Locale:** 4 AREA SITE ZONE
    5 PLACE SCENE
**Locality:** 4 AREA SITE
**Locate:** 4 FIND SITE
**Located:** 5 SITED
    As: 6 INSITU
**Location:** 4 AREA SITE SPOT
    5 PLACE
**Loch**
    Legendary: 4 NESS
    Monster's: 4 NESS
    monster's nickname:
      6 NESSIE
    Scottish: 4 NESS
**Loch ___:** 4 NESS
**Lock:** 5 TRESS 6 SHOOIN
    fastener: 4 HASP
    Head: 5 TRESS
    It fits in a: 3 OAR
    Long: 5 TRESS
    maker: 4 YALE
    of hair: 5 TRESS
    opener: 3 KEY
    prefix: 4 ANTI 5 INTER
    site: 5 CANAL
    Thin: 4 WISP
    (up): 3 SEW
    ~, stock, and barrel: 3 ALL
**Locked**
    in: 8 ICEBOUND
    They may be: 5 HORNS
    up: 5 CAGED 6 INJAIL JAILED
    (up): 4 PENT
**Locker**
    hanging: 5 PINUP
    photo: 5 PINUP
**Locker room**
    emanation: 4 ODOR
    item: 5 TOWEL
    powder: 4 TALC
    shower: 4 ESPN
**Locket**
    shape: 4 OVAL
**"Lockhorns, The"**
    husband: 5 LEROY
**Locks:** 4 HAIR
    Change: 3 DYE
    False: 3 WIG 6 TOUPEE
    Head: 4 HAIR
    in a barn: 4 MANE
    Lacking: 4 BALD
    Leonine: 4 MANE
    They can fix: 6 SALONS
    Unruly: 3 MOP
**Lockup:** 4 CELL JAIL
    London: 4 GAOL
    Navy: 4 BRIG
**Loco:** 4 BATS
    Less: 5 SANER
**"Loco-Motion, The"**
    singer: 9 LITTLEEVA
**Locomotive:** 6 ENGINE
    9 IRONHORSE
    fuel: 4 COAL

    power: 5 STEAM
    sound: 4 CHUG
**Locum ___ (temporary**
    **substitute):** 6 TENENS
**Locus**
    Geometrical: 7 EVOLUTE
**Locust:** 3 BUG 4 TREE
    tree: 6 ACACIA
**Lod**
    land (abbr.): 3 ISR
    lander: 4 ELAL
**Lod Airport**
    carrier: 4 ELAL
**Lode**
    Get a ~ of this: 3 ORE
    load: 3 ORE
    locale: 4 VEIN
**Lodge:** 3 INN 4 ROOM STOW
    6 HOSTEL RESIDE
    brother: 3 ELK
    builder: 6 BEAVER
    letters: 4 BPOE
    member: 3 ELK 5 MOOSE
    Motor: 3 INN
    opening: 5 ECONO
    resident: 5 SKIER
**___ Lodge (motel chain):**
    5 ECONO
**Lodging**
    Country: 3 INN
    Inexpensive: 6 HOSTEL
    Military: 6 BILLET
    Quaint: 3 INN
    Roadside: 5 MOTEL
**Loeb**
    Singer: 4 LISA
**___ l'oeil:** 6 TROMPE
**Loewe**
    Partner of: 6 LERNER
**Loewenstein, Laszlo**
    Actor born: 5 LORRE
**Lo-fat:** 4 LITE
**Lofgren**
    Guitarist: 4 NILS
**Loft:** 5 ATTIC
    contents: 3 HAY
    group: 5 CHOIR
    locale: 4 BARN
    Voice in a: 4 ALTO BASS
**Lofts**
    Author: 5 NORAH
**Lofty:** 4 HIGH TALL
    5 NOBLE 6 AERIAL
    8 RAREFIED
    abode: 5 AERIE
    lyric: 3 ODE
    nest: 5 AERIE
    poem: 3 ODE
    Set a ~ goal: 6 ASPIRE
**Log:** 5 ENTER
    Bump on a: 4 KNAR NODE
    cutter: 6 PITSAW
    home: 5 CABIN
    item: 5 ENTRY
    Kind of: 4 YULE
    prefix: 3 ANA EPI

**Logan**
    and others (abbr.): 3 MTS
    home: 4 UTAH
**Logarithms**
    inventor: 6 NAPIER
**Logged**
    One ~ on: 4 USER
**Loggers**
    contest: 5 ROLEO
**Loggins**
    partner: 7 MESSINA
    Singer: 5 KENNY
**Logic:** 5 SENSE 6 REASON
    Hence, in: 4 ERGO
    negation mark: 5 TILDE
    Use: 6 REASON
**Logical**
    Be: 6 REASON
    conclusion: 3 QED
    flaw: 4 HOLE
    prefix: 3 ECO GEO 4 IDEO
    THEO 5 PATHO
    6 CHRONO
**Logically**
    Think: 6 REASON
**Logician:** 8 REASONER
    letters: 3 QED
    phrase: 7 APRIORI
    word: 4 ERGO
**Logo:** 6 EMBLEM
**Log-on**
    need: 6 USERID
**Logos**
    (abbr.): 3 TMS
**Logrolling**
    Compete in: 4 BIRL
**Logs**
    Cut, as: 4 SAWN
    Like: 4 SAWN
    One who ~ on: 4 USER
    Saw: 5 SNORE
    Sawing: 6 ASLEEP
**Lohengrin**
    love: 4 ELSA
**"Lohengrin":** 5 OPERA
    role: 4 ELSA
**Loin**
    steak: 5 TBONE
**Loincloth**
    Hindu: 5 DHOTI
**Loire**
    City on the: 5 TOURS
    6 NANTES
**Lois**
    love: 5 CLARK
    portrayer: 4 TERI
**"Lois & Clark"**
    actor Dean: 4 CAIN
    actress Hatcher: 4 TERI
**Loiter:** 5 DALLY TARRY
**Loki**
    Daughter of: 3 HEL
**"LOL"**
    vocalized: 4 HAHA
**"Lola"**
    actress Anouk: 5 AIMEE

band: 8 THEKINKS
"Lolita"
  actress Lyon: 3 SUE
  actress Sue: 4 LYON
Loll: 4 LAZE
Lollapalooza: 3 PIP 4 LULU
    ONER 5 BEAUT
Lolling: 6 ATEASE
Lollobrigida
  Actress: 4 GINA
Lollygag: 4 IDLE LAZE LOAF
___ Loma, California:
    4 ALTA
Loman, Willy: 8 SALESMAN
  field: 5 SALES
  Son of: 4 BIFF
Lombard
  Actress: 6 CAROLE
Lombardi
  Coach: 5 VINCE
Lombardy
  Info: Italian cue
  attraction: 8 LAKECOMO
  city: 5 MILAN
  lake: 4 COMO
  Love, in: 5 AMORE
Lo mein
  morsel: 6 NOODLE
Lomond: 4 LOCH
Lon
  contemporary: 4 BELA
  of Cambodia: 3 NOL
London
  airport: 8 HEATHROW
  area: 4 SOHO 7 EASTEND
  district: 4 SOHO
  facility: 3 LOO
  gallery: 4 TATE
  Garden spot of: 3 KEW
  Inc., in: 3 LTD
  land (abbr.): 3 ENG
  landmark: 6 BIGBEN
    15 ROYALALBERTHALL
  Last letter in: 3 ZED
  lavatory: 3 LOO
  length: 5 METRE
  Level, in: 4 RASE
  locale: 7 ONTARIO
  lockup: 4 GAOL
  neighborhood: 4 SOHO
  Notorious ~ prison:
    7 NEWGATE
  park name: 4 HYDE
  Place to go in: 3 LOO
  river: 6 THAMES
  section: 7 EASTEND
  stroller: 4 PRAM
  subway: 4 TUBE
  theater: 6 OLDVIC
  ~ TV inits.: 3 BBC
London ___: 5 BROIL
Londoner: 4 BRIT 6 BRITON
  Wealthy: 3 NOB
London Magazine
  essayist: 4 ELIA
Lone: 4 SOLE

"Lonely Boy"
  singer Paul: 4 ANKA
"Lonely Rage, A"
  author Bobby: 5 SEALE
Loner: 6 HERMIT MISFIT
Lone Ranger
  sidekick: 5 TONTO
"Lonesome Dove"
  author: 13 LARRYMCMURTRY
Lonesome George
  of early TV: 5 GOBEL
Lone Star State: 5 TEXAS
  sch.: 4 UTEP
Long: 4 ACHE PINE 5 YEARN
    6 HANKER
  A ~ way off: 3 FAR 4 AFAR
  Actress: 3 NIA
  After a ~ wait: 6 ATLAST
  ago: 4 ONCE YORE
  and lean: 4 LANK
  Before: 4 ANON SOON
  Certain ~ shot: 8 ONEINTEN
  Football commentator:
    5 HOWIE
  for: 5 CRAVE 6 DESIRE
  Go: 5 RUNON
  intro: 3 ERE
  It comes before: 3 ERE
  It may be: 3 TON
  Politician: 4 HUEY
  Went: 7 RANOVER
Long.
  crosser: 3 LAT
Long ___: 3 AGO TON 5 JOHNS
"Long ___ and Far Away":
    3 AGO
Long-armed
  ape: 5 ORANG
  entity: 3 LAW
"___ longa, vita brevis": 3 ARS
Long-billed
  bird: 4 IBIS 5 HERON SNIPE
  wader: 4 IBIS 5 HERON
Longbow
  wood: 3 YEW
Long-distance
  letters: 3 ATT MCI
  Start of a ~ call: 3 ONE
Long-eared
  animal: 3 ASS 4 HARE
  hound: 6 BASSET
Longer: 4 MORE
  Is no: 3 WAS
  No: 4 ONCE
  No ~ here: 4 GONE
  No ~ hot: 3 OUT
  No ~ in: 5 DATED PASSE
  No ~ in bed: 5 ASTIR
  No ~ in use: 7 DEFUNCT
  No ~ lit: 5 SOBER
  No ~ mint: 4 USED
  No ~ on deck: 5 ATBAT
"Longest Day, The"
  city: 4 CAEN
Longevity: 4 LEGS
Long-faced: 3 SAD 6 SULLEN

Longfellow
  bell town: 4 ATRI
  ~ Indian: 8 HIAWATHA
Long-gone
  bird: 4 DODO
Longhair: 6 HIPPIE
Long-haired
  cat: 6 ANGORA
Longhorn: 5 STEER
  rival: 5 AGGIE
Longing: 3 YEN 4 ACHE ITCH
    6 DESIRE
  Feel ~ for: 4 MISS
Longish
  skirt: 4 MIDI
Long Island
  airport: 5 ISLIP
  town: 5 ISLIP
  university: 7 ADELPHI
Long-jawed
  fish: 3 GAR
Long John Silver
  feature: 6 PEGLEG
Long-lasting
  wave: 4 PERM
Long-legged
  bird: 4 IBIS 5 HERON STILT
    STORK 6 AVOCET
Longley
  of basketball: 3 LUC
Long-limbed: 5 LEGGY RANGY
"Long Long Time"
  singer Linda: 8 RONSTADT
Long March
  leader: 3 MAO
Long-necked
  bird: 4 SWAN 5 HERON
  instrument: 4 LUTE 5 SITAR
  lute: 5 SITAR
Long-nosed
  fish: 3 GAR 4 PIKE
Long-plumed
  bird: 5 EGRET
Long-range
  weapon: 4 ICBM
Longship
  mover: 3 OAR
Longshoreman: 5 LADER
    9 STEVEDORE
Long-snouted
  beast: 5 TAPIR
  fish: 3 GAR
Longstocking
  creator Lindgren: 6 ASTRID
  of children's books: 5 PIPPI
Long-tailed
  finch: 6 TOWHEE
  parrot: 5 MACAW
"Long time ___": 5 NOSEE
"Long Time No See"
  novelist Susan: 6 ISAACS
___ longue: 6 CHAISE
___ long way (last): 3 GOA
Long-winded: 5 GASSY
    6 PROLIX
  Less: 6 TERSER

type: 6 GASBAG
**Loni**
and Burt: 4 EXES
Ex of: 4 BURT
**Loo**
sign: 5 GENTS INUSE
**Looie**
subordinate: 5 SARGE
**Look:** 4 PEER SEEM
  6 APPEAR
Affected: 5 SMIRK
after: 4 TEND 5 SEETO
  6 TENDTO
at: 3 EYE SEE 4 VIEW
  6 REGARD
at the stars: 4 GAZE
Blank: 5 STARE
closely: 4 PEER 5 DELVE
Contemptuous: 5 SNEER
daggers: 5 GLARE
Derisive: 5 SNEER
Dirty: 4 LEER 5 GLARE
Displeased: 5 FROWN
Evil: 4 LEER
Fixed: 4 GAZE 5 STARE
for: 4 SEEK 5 AWAIT
forward to: 5 AWAIT
Give a new ~ to: 4 REDO
good on: 6 BECOME
Have a: 3 SEE
Healthy: 4 GLOW
Impolite: 4 LEER 5 STARE
Intent: 4 GAZE
It doesn't ~ good: 7 EYESORE
Lascivious: 4 LEER
Lecherous: 4 LEER
Lecher's: 4 LEER OGLE
like: 8 RESEMBLE
like a wolf: 4 LEER OGLE
Long: 4 GAZE 5 STARE
Lustful: 4 LEER
lustfully: 4 OGLE
of contempt: 5 SNEER
of disdain: 5 SNEER
over: 3 EYE 4 SCAN
Pouty: 4 MOUE
Quick: 4 PEER 6 GLANCE
  7 GLIMPSE
Salacious: 4 LEER
Scornful: 5 SNEER
Sheepish: 4 GRIN
Sinister: 4 LEER
Sly: 4 LEER
Sneak a: 4 PEEK
Suggestive: 4 LEER
sullen: 4 POUT
through a keyhole: 6 PEERIN
to be: 4 SEEM
up and down: 4 OGLE
upon: 6 REGARD
up to: 6 ADMIRE ESTEEM
  REVERE
Villainous: 4 LEER 5 SNEER
Wanton: 4 LEER
Wolfish: 4 LEER
~, slangily: 6 GANDER

**Look ___**
(explore): 4 INTO
(visit): 4 INON
**"Look ___ ..."** ("Misty" starter):
  4 ATME
**Lookalike:** 4 TWIN 6 RINGER
  10 CARBONCOPY
  DEADRINGER
  13 SPITTINGIMAGE
H ~: 3 ETA
Hydrox: 4 OREO
**"Look at Me, I'm Sandra ___":**
  3 DEE
**"Look Back in Anger"**
playwright John: 7 OSBORNE
**Looker:** 3 EYE
Good: 3 EYE 4 EYER
Lewd: 5 OGLER
**"Look ___ hands!":** 4 MANO
**"Look here!":** 3 OHO
**Looking**
down from: 4 ATOP
One ~ ahead: 4 SEER
over: 6 EYEING
up: 4 ROSY
**Lookout:** 8 SENTINEL
Act as: 4 ABET
Be a ~ for: 4 ABET
On the: 5 ALERT
point: 5 AERIE
**"Look out!":** 7 HEADSUP
**Look-see:** 4 PEEK PEEP
**"Looks ___ everything":** 5 ARENT
**"Looks like trouble!":** 4 UHOH
**"Look what I did!":** 4 TADA
**"Looky here!":** 3 OHO
**Loom**
Crafted on a: 5 WOVEN
Use a: 5 WEAVE
Used a: 4 WOVE
**Loon:** 8 CRACKPOT
  9 SCREWBALL
relative: 5 GREBE
**Looney Tunes**
devil, for short: 3 TAZ
prey: 6 TWEETY
**Loony:** 4 BATS DAFT NUTS
  5 NUTSO 6 INSANE
Less: 5 SANER
**Loop:** 4 COIL RING
Embroidery: 5 PICOT
Floral: 3 LEI
Gallows: 5 NOOSE
Knock for a: 4 DAZE JOLT
  STUN
Lariat: 5 NOOSE
Lasso: 5 NOOSE
loopers: 3 ELS
Throw for a: 4 FAZE STUN
**Looped**
fabric: 5 FRISE
handle: 4 ANSA
rope: 5 NOOSE
**Loophole:** 3 OUT
Use a: 5 EVADE
**Loopy:** 4 DAFT 6 SPACED

**Loos:** 3 WCS
Author: 5 ANITA
woman: 7 LORELEI
**Loose:** 3 LAX 4 FREE 5 FREED
  6 ATEASE 7 ATLARGE
  SETFREE
cannon: 6 MENACE
garment: 4 TOGA
Hang: 3 SAG 4 LOLL 5 CHILL
  RELAX
Hanging: 6 ATEASE
Let: 4 FREE 5 FREED UNPEN
  UNTIE 7 UNLEASH
Not: 6 CHASTE
On the: 7 ATLARGE
overcoat: 6 RAGLAN ULSTER
Set: 5 UNTIE
snow: 6 POWDER
Some are: 4 ENDS
talk: 5 SLANG
Turn: 7 UNLEASH
~, as shoelaces: 6 UNTIED
**Loose-fitting:** 5 BAGGY
dress: 4 TENT
**Loose-limbed:** 5 AGILE LITHE
**Loosen:** 4 THAW UNDO
  5 UNTIE 6 UNKNOT
  UNLACE
**Looseness:** 4 GIVE 5 SLACK
**Loosestrife**
dye: 5 HENNA
**Loot:** 3 ROB 4 SWAG
  7 RANSACK
Hidden: 5 STASH
Lot of: 4 PILE
Stolen: 4 HAUL
**"Loot"**
playwright Joe: 5 ORTON
**Lop**
off: 5 SEVER
the crop: 4 REAP
**Lopez**
Singer: 5 TRINI
**___ Lopez** (chess opening):
  3 RUY
**Lopez, Jennifer**
film: 6 SELENA 7 THECELL
role: 6 SELENA
**Lopez, Vincent**
theme song: 4 NOLA
**Lopsided:** 5 ASKEW ATILT
win: 4 ROUT
**Loquacious:** 5 TALKY
horse: 4 MRED
**"Lorax, The"**
author: 5 SEUSS
**Lord:** 4 PEER 5 LIEGE NOBLE
  TITLE
Feudal: 5 LIEGE
home: 5 MANOR
House of the: 5 MANOR
laborer: 4 SERF
land: 4 FIEF
mate: 4 LADY
of La Mancha: 5 SENOR
of poetry: 5 BYRON

Turkish: 3 AGA
worker: 4 SERF 5 THANE
**"Lord ___" (Conrad work):**
    3 JIM
**"Lord, ___?":** 5 ISITI
**"Lord, is ___?":** 3 ITI
**"Lord Jim"**
    actor: 6 OTOOLE
**"Lord of the Rings, The"**
    actor McKellen: 3 IAN
    actor Sean: 5 ASTIN
    actress Tyler: 3 LIV
    beast: 3 ORC 4 OGRE
    hero: 5 FRODO
    tree creature: 3 ENT
**Lords**
    Actress: 5 TRACI
**Lord's Prayer:** 5 PATER
    pronoun: 3 THY
    start: 3 OUR
**Lorelei:** 5 SIREN
    river: 5 RHINE
**Loren**
    Actress: 6 SOPHIA
    Husband of: 5 PONTI
**Lorenz**
    Lyricist: 4 HART
**Lorenzo**
    Actor: 5 LAMAS
**"Lorenzo's Oil"**
    actor Nick: 5 NOLTE
**Loretta**
    Actress: 4 SWIT
    portrayer: 5 SISSY
    Singer: 4 LYNN
**Lorgnette**
    part: 4 LENS
**Lorillard**
    brand: 4 KENT
**Lorna**
    Actress: 4 LUFT
    of literature: 5 DOONE
**"Lorna ___":** 5 DOONE
**Lorne**
    Actor: 6 GREENE
**Lorraine**
    neighbor: 6 ALSACE
**Lorre, Peter**
    role: 4 MOTO 6 MRMOTO
        UGARTE
**Los Alamos**
    scientist: 4 BOHR
**Los Angeles**
    Beach near: 6 MALIBU
    cager: 5 LAKER
    Center of ~, once: 5 ONEAL
    City near: 6 POMONA
    suburb: 6 ENCINO RESEDA
**Los ___, California:** 5 ALTOS
        GATOS
**Lose:** 4 SHED 6 MISLAY
    a lap: 5 STAND
    color: 4 FADE
    control: 4 SKID
    energy: 4 TIRE
    everything: 6 GOBUST

ground: 5 ERODE
hair: 4 SHED
Having a lot to: 5 OBESE
Intentionally: 5 THROW
it: 4 SNAP 5 GOAPE GOMAD
one's cool: 5 PANIC
one's footing: 4 SLIP
one's mind: 5 GOMAD
one's nerve: 10 CHICKENOUT
steam: 4 TIRE
strength: 4 FADE FLAG TIRE
traction: 4 SKID SLIP
Try to: 4 DIET
weight: 4 SLIM
You stand to ~ it: 3 LAP
**Loser:** 5 DWEEB 7 ALSORAN
    Election: 7 ALSORAN
    Fabled: 4 HARE
    Happy: 6 DIETER
    of 1588: 6 ARMADA
    of 1996: 4 DOLE
    to DDE: 3 AES
**Losers**
    Election: 4 OUTS
    Like some: 4 SORE
    Place for: 3 SPA
**Losing:** 7 ONADIET
    cause: 4 DIET
    money: 8 INTHERED
    proposition: 4 DIET
**"Losing My Religion"**
    band: 3 REM
**Los ___, New Mexico:**
        6 ALAMOS
**Loss**
    Deliberate: 4 DIVE
    leader: 3 ATA
    of coordination: 6 ATAXIA
    of courage: 8 COLDFEET
    of memory: 7 AMNESIA
    Suffer a: 5 EATIT
    ___ loss: 3 ATA
**Losses**
    How ~ are shown: 5 INRED
    ~, in accounting: 6 REDINK
    ___ loss for words: 3 ATA
**"Loss of Roses, A"**
    playwright: 4 INGE
**Lost:** 4 ASEA ATSEA
    a lap: 5 AROSE STOOD
    in thought: 7 PENSIVE
    on purpose: 5 THREW
    traction: 4 SLID
**"Lost Boys, The"**
    actor: 4 HAIM
**"Lost Horizon"**
    director: 5 CAPRA
**"Lost in Space"**
    character: 5 ROBOT
**"Lost World, The"**
    menace: 4 TREX
**Lot:** 3 TON 4 FATE GOBS HEAP
        MUCH SCAD SLEW
        TONS 5 BATCH LOADS
        OFTEN RAFTS
        8 GOODDEAL

A whole: 4 TONS 6 OCEANS
Bit of a: 4 ACRE
choice: 5 SEDAN
in life: 4 FATE
It could be a: 4 ACRE
Not a: 3 FEW
They make a: 5 ACRES
Use a: 4 PARK
Whole: 3 TON 4 SLEW
**Lothario:** 4 RAKE
    look: 4 OGLE
**Lotion**
    additive: 4 ALOE
    Apply, as: 5 RUBON
    ingredient: 4 ALOE
        8 ALOEVERA
    letters: 3 SPF
**Lots:** 4 AGOB ATON GOBS
        MUCH MANY TONS
        5 AHEAP LOADS OFTEN
        RAFTS REAMS SCADS
        6 OCEANS OODLES
        PLENTY
**Lott**
    of football: 6 RONNIE
    Senator: 5 TRENT
**Lotte**
    Actress: 5 LENYA
**Lottery**
    cry: 4 IWON
    Onetime ~ org.: 3 SSS
**Lotto**
    cousin: 4 KENO 5 BEANO
    variant: 4 KENO
**Lotto-like**
    game: 4 KENO
**Lotus**
    owner: 3 IBM
    position activity: 4 YOGA
**Lotus-___:** 5 EATER
**Lou**
    Singer: 5 RAWLS
**Loud:** 5 AROAR GAUDY NOISY
        6 BRASSY GARISH
    and clear: 7 CLARION
    laugh: 3 YUK 4 ROAR
    speaker: 7 STENTOR
    thud: 3 BAM
    Very ~, in music: 3 FFF
    ~, as a crowd: 5 AROAR
**Loudness**
    increaser: 3 AMP
    unit: 3 BEL 4 PHON SONE
**"Lou Dobbs Moneyline"**
    carrier: 3 CNN
**Louganis**
    Diver: 4 GREG
**Louganis, Greg:** 5 DIVER
**Loughlin**
    Actress: 4 LORI
**"Lou Grant"**
    reporter: 5 ROSSI
    star: 5 ASNER 7 EDASNER
**Louie**
    ~, to Donald Duck:
        6 NEPHEW

**Louis**
Comedian: 3 NYE
FBI director: 5 FREEH
**Louise**
Actress: 4 TINA 6 LASSER
cohort, in film: 6 THELMA
**"Louise"**
soprano: 4 IRMA
**Louisiana**
Capital of: 3 ELL
county: 6 PARISH
feature: 5 BAYOU
lingo: 6 CREOLE
marsh: 5 BAYOU
namer: 7 LASALLE
symbol: 7 PELICAN
~, in Orléans: 4 ETAT
**Louisville**
river: 4 OHIO
slugger: 3 ALI
**"Louisville Lip, The":** 3 ALI
**Louisville Slugger:** 3 BAT
wood: 3 ASH
**Louis XIV:** 3 ROI
~, to himself: 5 LETAT
**Lounge:** 3 LIE 4 IDLE LAZE
LOAF LOLL SOFA
6 REPOSE
group: 4 TRIO
**Lounging:** 6 ATEASE
robe: 6 CAFTAN
slipper: 4 MULE
**Louse:** 3 CAD
egg: 3 NIT
Plant: 5 APHID
up: 4 RUIN
Wood: 6 ISOPOD
**Lousy:** 3 BAD
car: 5 LEMON
egg: 3 NIT
Feel: 3 AIL
pick: 3 NIT
**Lout:** 3 APE OAF 4 BOOR CLOD
5 YAHOO
**Louver:** 4 SLAT
part: 4 SLAT
**Louvre:** 5 MUSEE
collection: 6 MANETS
7 RENOIRS
display: 3 ART
highlight: 8 MONALISA
sculpture: 11 VENUSDEMILO
Works at the: 4 OILS
**Louvre Pyramid**
architect: 3 PEI 5 IMPEI
**Lovable**
Make: 6 ENDEAR
**Love:** 5 ADORE
affair: 5 AMOUR
apple: 6 TOMATO
god: 4 AMOR EROS
Greek god of: 4 EROS
In: 7 SMITTEN
In ~ with oneself: 4 VAIN
Inspire ~ in: 6 ENAMOR
Latin: 4 AMOR

letters: 4 SWAK 6 XOXOXO
lots: 5 ADORE
Madly in: 4 GAGA
of fine art: 5 VIRTU
opposite: 4 HATE
personified: 4 AMOR EROS
Roman god of: 4 AMOR
song: 6 BALLAD
symbol: 4 EROS 7 REDROSE
To ~, in Italian: 5 AMARE
to death: 5 ADORE
to pieces: 5 ADORE
You ~, in Latin: 4 AMAS
~, in Italian: 5 AMORE
~, in Spanish: 4 AMOR
**Love ___:** 4 NEST
**"Love ___"** (Beatles hit):
4 MEDO
**"___ Love"** (Pat Boone hit):
5 APRIL
**"___ Love, The"**
(Gershwin tune): 4 MANI
(R.E.M. tune): 4 ONEI
**Love, Courtney**
band: 4 HOLE
**"___ Love Again"** (Porter song):
4 IMIN
**"Love and Basketball"**
actor Omar: 4 EPPS
**"Love Boat, The"**
actress Lauren: 5 TEWES
**Lovecraft, H.P.**
Like ~ stories: 5 EERIE
**Loved**
by: 6 DEARTO
Just: 5 ATEUP
one: 4 DEAR IDOL
**"Love Hangover"**
singer Ross: 5 DIANA
**"___ Love Her"** (Beatles hit):
4 ANDI
**"Love Is a Hurtin' Thing"**
singer: 5 RAWLS
**Lovelace**
Mathematician: 3 ADA
**"Love Letters in the Sand"**
singer: 8 PATBOONE
**"Lovely ___"** (Beatles tune):
4 RITA
**"Love ___ Madly"** (Doors hit):
3 HER
**"Love Me, I'm a Liberal"**
singer Phil: 4 OCHS
**"Love Me Tender"**
~, originally: 7 AURALEE
**"Love ___ neighbor ...":** 3 THY
**Lover:** 5 ROMEO
boy: 4 EROS
**Loverboy:** 4 BEAU 5 ROMEO
8 LOTHARIO
**"Lovergirl"**
singer Marie: 5 TEENA
singer Teena: 5 MARIE
**Lovers**
meeting: 5 TRYST
place: 4 LANE

**Loves**
He ~, in Latin: 4 AMAT
too much: 7 DOTESON
**"Love ___ Simple Thing":** 3 ISA
**"Love Sneakin' Up on You"**
singer: 5 RAITT
**"Love Story"**
author Erich: 5 SEGAL
author Segal: 5 ERICH
composer Francis: 3 LAI
**"Love the skin you're in"**
company: 4 OLAY
**Lovett**
label: 3 MCA
Singer: 4 LYLE
**Lovey:** 3 PET 4 DEAR
**Lovey-dovey:** 7 AMOROUS
Act: 3 COO
**"___ Love You"** (Beatles hit):
3 PSI
**"Love ___ you need"** (Beatles
lyric): 5 ISALL
**Loving**
Act: 4 DOTE
murmur: 3 COO
touch: 6 CARESS
Word before: 4 EVER
**Lovingly**
Talk: 3 COO
Touch: 6 FONDLE
**Low:** 3 MOO SAD 4 BASE
As ~ as it gets:
10 ROCKBOTTOM
Below: 5 EMPTY
bow: 6 SALAAM
card: 4 TREY
digit: 3 TOE
grade: 3 DEE
in fat: 4 LEAN
joint: 5 ANKLE
Laid: 3 HID
Lay: 3 HID 4 HIDE
7 HIDEOUT
Lie: 4 HIDE
life: 5 AMEBA
man: 5 BASSO
mark: 3 DEE
men: 5 BASSI 6 BASSOS
point: 5 NADIR
sock: 6 ANKLET
spot: 4 DELL
They get: 5 BASSI
tract: 4 VALE
voice: 4 BASS
woman: 4 ALTO
**Low-___:** 3 CAL
**Low-budget**
prefix: 5 ECONO
**Low-cal:** 4 DIET LITE
**Low-cholesterol**
spread: 4 OLEO
**Low-class**
~, in London: 4 NONU
**Low-___ diet:** 4 CARB
**Lowdown:** 4 DIRT DOPE INFO
POOP 5 SCOOP

**Low-down**
joint: 5 ANKLE
**Lowe**
Actor: 3 ROB 4 CHAD
**Lowell**
Poet: 3 AMY
**Lower:** 3 DIM 4 BATE LESS
5 ABASE SCOWL
6 NETHER 7 DEPRESS
oneself: 5 DEIGN STOOP
~, as lights: 3 DIM
~, south of the border: 4 BAJA
**Lowest**
deck: 5 ORLOP
lake: 7 DEADSEA
point: 5 NADIR
tide: 4 NEAP
**Lowey**
Congresswoman: 4 NITA
**Low-fat:** 4 LEAN
meat: 3 EMU 7 BEEFALO
**Low-grade**
wool: 5 MUNGO
**Low-heeled**
shoe: 6 BROGUE
**Lowland:** 4 DALE VALE
Boggy: 3 FEN
Wet: 5 SWALE
**Lowlife:** 3 CAD 4 SCUM
5 SLIME SNAKE SWINE
6 SLEAZE
**Lowly:** 4 BASE 6 MENIAL
worker: 3 ANT 4 PEON SERF
**Low-lying**
area: 4 VALE 5 SWALE
**Low-paying**
position: 5 MCJOB
**Low-pH**
substance: 4 ACID
**Low-pressure**
pitch: 8 SOFTSELL
**Low-quality:** 4 POOR
7 ONESTAR
**Lowry**
Newbery-winning author:
4 LOIS
**Low-slung**
hound: 6 BASSET
**Low-tech**
calculators: 5 ABACI
missile: 3 PEA
propeller: 3 OAR
**Low-voiced**
lady: 4 ALTO
man: 5 BASSO
**Lox**
Kind of: 4 NOVA
partner: 5 BAGEL
**Loy**
Actress: 5 MYRNA
**Loyal:** 4 TRUE 8 TRUEBLUE
lodger: 5 MOOSE
subject: 5 LIEGE
**Loyalist:** 4 TORY
**Loyally**
following: 6 TRUETO

**Lozenge:** 4 DROP PILL
6 TROCHE
**LP**
contents: 3 MNO
cover: 6 SLEEVE
flaw: 4 SKIP
measure: 3 RPM
player: 4 HIFI 5 PHONO
successors: 3 CDS
Word on an: 6 STEREO
**L-P**
filler: 3 MNO
**L-Q**
filler: 4 MNOP
**LSAT:** 4 EXAM
**LSD:** 4 ACID
**Lt.**
Rank below: 3 ENS
saluter: 3 NCO
superior: 4 CAPT
trainer: 3 OCS
**Ltd.**
~, in France: 3 CIE
~, in the U.S.: 3 INC
**Ltr.**
addenda: 3 PSS
addendum: 3 PPS
enclosure: 4 SASE
extra: 3 ENC
holder: 3 ENV
opener: 4 INIT
**Luanda**
land: 6 ANGOLA
**Luau**
chow: 3 POI
dance: 4 HULA
dish: 3 POI
fare: 3 POI
greeting: 5 ALOHA
instrument: 3 UKE
7 UKELELE UKULELE
memento: 3 LEI
souvenir: 3 LEI
staple: 3 POI
strings: 3 UKE
**Lubber:** 3 OAF
**Lubbock**
home: 5 TEXAS
**Lubitsch**
Director: 5 ERNST
**Lubovitch**
Choreographer: 3 LAR
**Lubricate:** 3 OIL 6 GREASE
**Lubrication**
opening: 7 OILHOLE
**Lucas, George**
critter: 4 EWOK
letters: 3 THX
**Lucci**
Actress: 5 SUSAN
**Lucci, Susan**
Award that ~ finally won:
4 EMMY
role: 5 ERICA
**Luce**
Playwright: 6 CLAIRE

**Lucerne**
view: 4 ALPS
**Lucid:** 4 SANE 5 CLEAR
**Lucie**
Brother of: 4 DESI
Father of: 4 DESI
**Lucifer:** 5 SATAN
Like: 4 EVIL
**Luck**
Bad: 6 HOODOO
Bring bad ~ to: 4 JINX
Down on one's: 5 NEEDY
personification: 4 LADY
Stroke of: 5 BREAK FLUKE
"___ luck!": 5 LOTSA
"___ luck?": 3 ANY
**Luckman**
of football: 3 SID
**Lucky**
charm: 6 AMULET
number: 5 SEVEN
strike: 3 OIL ORE 5 TROVE
tip: 3 ASH
**"Lucky Jim"**
author: 4 AMIS
**Lucrative:** 3 FAT
**Lucre**
Filthy: 4 PELF
**Lucretia**
Feminist: 4 MOTT
**Lucy**
Actress: 3 LIU 7 LAWLESS
He loved: 4 DESI
landlady: 5 ETHEL
neighbor: 5 ETHEL
partner: 4 DESI
Where ~ was found:
8 ETHIOPIA
**Ludicrous:** 5 ANTIC INANE
**Ludwig**
Biographer: 4 EMIL
dedicatee: 5 ELISE
lament: 3 ACH
"___ luego!": 5 HASTA
**Luening**
Composer: 4 OTTO
**Luft**
Actress: 5 LORNA
**Luftwaffe**
battler: 3 RAF
**Lug:** 3 APE 4 LOUT TOTE
5 SHLEP 6 SCHLEP
7 SCHLEPP
Big: 3 OAF
nut cover: 6 HUBCAP
**Luge:** 4 SLED
**Luggage:** 4 BAGS
attachment: 3 TAG 5 IDTAG
7 NAMETAG
**Lugosi**
Actor: 4 BELA
**Luigi**
**Info:** Italian cue
___ Luis, Brazil: 3 SAO
**Luise**
Actress: 6 RAINER

___ Luis Obispo: 3 SAN
"Luka"
  singer Suzanne: 4 VEGA
Lukas
  Actor: 4 HAAS
  Conductor: 4 FOSS
Luke
  Mentor of: 6 OBIWAN
  Sister of: 4 LEIA
  Teacher to: 4 YODA
Lukewarm: 5 TEPID
Lull: 4 REST 5 LETUP
Lullaby
  Irish ~ start: 5 TOORA
  Soldier's: 4 TAPS
Lulu: 3 PIP 4 ONER 5 BEAUT
    DOOZY 6 CORKER
"Lulu": 5 OPERA
  Composer Alban: 4 BERG
  Composer Berg: 5 ALBAN
Lum
  partner: 5 ABNER
Lumbago: 4 ACHE
Lumber: 4 WOOD
  mill fixture: 3 SAW
  processor: 7 SAWMILL
Lumberjack: 5 AXMAN HEWER
    6 AXEMAN LOGGER
  competition: 5 ROLEO
  shout: 6 TIMBER
  tool: 3 AXE
Luminary: 4 STAR
Luminous: 5 AGLOW
  radiation: 4 AURA
  ring: 4 HALO
  sign: 4 NEON
Lummox: 3 APE OAF 4 CLOD
    LOUT
Lump: 3 NUB 4 GLOB
  Large: 3 GOB
  of clay: 4 GLOB
  of dirt: 4 CLOD
___ Lumpur: 5 KUALA
Lumumba
  Congo P.M.: 7 PATRICE
Luna: 4 MOTH
Lunar
  calendar holiday: 3 TET
  craft: 6 LANDER
  descent: 7 MOONSET
  feature: 5 RILLE 6 CRATER
  new year: 3 TET
  plain: 4 MARE
  trench: 5 RILLE
  valley: 5 RILLE
___ Lunas, New Mexico: 3 LOS
Lunatic: 5 RAVER 6 MADMAN
Lunch: 4 MEAL
  At: 3 OUT
  Brief: 3 BLT
  Did: 3 ATE
  Dieter's: 5 SALAD
  Do: 5 CATER
  Had: 3 ATE
  Have: 3 EAT
  holder: 3 BAG

hour: 3 ONE
Light: 5 SALAD
Long: 4 HERO
meat: 3 HAM
order: 3 BLT
Out to: 6 EATING
time: 3 ONE 4 NOON
    5 ONEPM
Words before: 5 OUTTO
___ lunch: 5 OUTTO
Lunchbox
  fruit: 5 APPLE
  treat: 4 OREO
Luncheon
  ending: 4 ETTE
Luncheonette
  list: 4 MENU
"Luncheon on the Grass"
  painter: 5 MANET
Lunchtime: 3 ONE 4 NOON
    7 NOONDAY
  Latish: 3 ONE
___ Lund (of "Casablanca"):
    4 ILSA
Lundgren
  Actor: 5 DOLPH
Lundi
  Day after: 5 MARDI
Lunes: 3 DIA
Lung
  Of ~ membranes: 7 PLEURAL
  section: 4 LOBE
  starter: 4 AQUA
Lung, Wang
  Wife of: 4 OLAN
Lungful: 3 AIR
  Get a: 6 INHALE
Lungs
  Fill the: 6 INHALE
  Pertaining to the: 5 LOBAR
Lunkhead: 3 ASS SAP 4 CLOD
    DOLT
Lupin
  Fictional detective: 6 ARSENE
  Leblanc's: 6 ARSENE
Lupino
  Actress: 3 IDA
LuPone
  Actress: 5 PATTI
  role: 5 EVITA PERON
Lurch: 4 REEL 6 CAREEN
Lure: 4 BAIT 5 DECOY TEMPT
    6 COMEON ENTICE
    ENTRAP ROPEIN
  into crime: 6 ENTRAP
  with music: 7 TWEEDLE
Lurie
  Novelist: 6 ALISON
Lush: 3 SOT 4 WINO 5 SOUSE
    TOPER 7 TIPPLER
  locale: 3 BAR
  sound: 3 HIC
  with vegetation: 7 VERDANT
Lusitania: 5 LINER
  sinker: 5 UBOAT
Lust: 3 SIN

Look of: 4 LEER
Luster: 5 SHEEN
  Lacking: 5 MATTE
  Legendary: 5 SATYR
  Lose: 4 FADE
Lusterless: 4 DRAB
  finish: 5 MATTE
Lustful: 5 RANDY
  deity: 5 SATYR
  god: 4 EROS
  look: 4 LEER OGLE
Lustrous: 5 SILKY SLEEK
    6 GLOSSY PEARLY
    SHEENY
  black: 5 RAVEN
  fabric: 5 SATIN 6 SATEEN
  gem: 4 OPAL
Lusty
  deity: 5 SATYR
Lute
  Arab: 3 OUD
  Long-necked: 5 SITAR
  part: 4 FRET
  shape: 4 PEAR
Lutefisk
  fish: 3 COD
Lutetia
  Modern: 5 PARIS
Luth.: 3 REL
Luther, Martin
  article: 3 DER
  had 95: 6 THESES
  lang.: 3 GER
  opposer: 3 ECK
Luthor
  Superman foe: 3 LEX
Lutz: 4 LEAP
Lux.
  locale: 3 EUR
  neighbor: 3 GER 4 BELG
Luxemburg
  Revolutionary: 4 ROSA
Luxor
  river: 4 NILE
Luxuriant: 4 LUSH
Luxuriate: 4 BASK 5 REVEL
    6 WALLOW
Luxurious: 4 LUSH POSH TONY
    5 PLUSH 7 OPULENT
    UPSCALE
  fur: 5 SABLE
  life: 4 EASE
  material: 5 SATIN
  place: 3 LAP
  resort: 3 SPA
  retreat: 5 VILLA
Luxury: 4 EASE
  Big name in: 4 RITZ
  resort: 3 SPA
  resort feature: 5 SAUNA
  Seat of: 3 LAP
  ___ luxury: 5 LAPOF
Luyendyk
  Racer: 4 ARIE
Luzinski
  of baseball: 4 GREG

**Lycée:** 5 ECOLE
**Lydia**
 Foe of ancient: 5 IONIA
**Lying:** 4 ABED
 around: 4 IDLE
 facedown: 5 PRONE
 flat: 5 PRONE
 on: 4 ATOP
 on one's back: 6 SUPINE
 Stopped: 5 AROSE
**Lymph ___:** 4 NODE
**Lymphatic**
 mass: 4 NODE
**Lymphocyte**
 Immune system: 5 TCELL
**Lynch, David**
 film: 10 ERASERHEAD

**Lyne**
 Director: 6 ADRIAN
**Lynn**
 of country: 7 LORETTA
 of football: 5 SWANN
 sister: 7 VANESSA
**Lynne, Jeff**
 rock gp.: 3 ELO
**Lyon**
 **Info:** Also spelled Lyons
 Actress: 3 SUE
 Organization based in:
  8 INTERPOL
 river: 5 RHONE SAONE
**Lyonnaise**
 Ingredient in ~ cuisine:
  5 ONION

**Lyra**
 Star in: 4 VEGA
**Lyre**
 cousin: 4 HARP
 Muse with a: 5 ERATO
**Lyric**
 Lofty: 3 ODE
 poem: 3 ODE 5 EPODE
 poet: 4 BARD 5 ODIST
**Lyrical:** 4 ODIC 6 POETIC
 lines: 3 ODE
 work: 5 EPODE
**Lysol**
 target: 4 GERM ODOR

# Mm

**M:** 4 SIZE
  Quarter of: 3 CCL
  Two signal an: 4 DAHS
  What an ~ may indicate: 3 SEX
**"M"**
  director Fritz: 4 LANG
  star: 5 LORRE
**M.**
  mate: 3 MME
**M-1:** 5 RIFLE
  inventor: 6 GARAND
**M-16:** 5 RIFLE
  Equip with an: 3 ARM
**Ma**
  Cellist: 4 YOYO
  instrument: 5 CELLO
  or Pa: 6 KETTLE
  Sister of: 4 AUNT
**MA**
  and PA: 3 STS
**M.A.**
  entry test: 3 GRE
**Ma, Yo-Yo**
  instrument: 5 CELLO
**___ Maar (Picasso subject):**
    4 DORA
**___ Mable (WWI humor book):**
    4 DERE
**Mabley**
  Comic: 4 MOMS
**Mac:** 3 BUB 5 KIDDO
  alternatives: 3 PCS
  insert: 5 CDROM
  maker: 5 APPLE
**Macabre:** 5 EERIE
  In a ~ way: 6 EERILY
**___ Macabre:** 5 DANSE
**Macadam**
  Apply ~ to: 4 PAVE
**Macao**
  money: 3 AVO
**Macarena:** 3 FAD 5 DANCE
**Macaroni:** 5 PASTA
  shape: 5 ELBOW
**MacArthur**
  dismisser: 3 HST
  quote ender: 6 RETURN
  victory site: 5 LEYTE
**MacArthur Airport**
  site: 5 ISLIP
**Macaw:** 6 PARROT
**Macbeth**
  burial place: 4 IONA
  title: 5 THANE
  weapon: 6 DAGGER
  When ~ dies: 4 ACTV
  When ~ slays Duncan: 5 ACTII
**"Macbeth":** 5 DRAMA

opener: 4 ACTI
quintet: 4 ACTS
trio: 4 HAGS
witch: 6 HECATE
**MacDonald**
  Like: 3 OLD
  Partner of: 4 EDDY
  sleuth: 6 ARCHER
  spread: 4 FARM
**MacDowell**
  Actress: 5 ANDIE
**MacDuff:** 5 THANE
  Command to: 5 LAYON
**Mace**
  source: 6 NUTMEG
**Macedonia**
  Early capital of: 6 EDESSA
**Macedonian**
  neighbor: 4 SERB
**MacGraw**
  Actress: 3 ALI
**Mach**
  Physicist: 5 ERNST
**Mach 1**
  breaker: 3 SST
**Mach 2**
  plane: 3 SST
**Mach 3**
  alternative: 4 ATRA
**Machete:** 4 BOLO
**Machiavellian:** 3 SLY
**Machinating:** 4 UPTO
**Machine**
  Assembly line: 5 ROBOT
  Bread: 3 ATM
  Deli: 6 SLICER
  Farm: 5 BALER 6 REAPER
    SEEDER 7 COMBINE
  Graphics: 6 IMAGER
  Office: 5 ADDER
    8 SHREDDER
  part: 3 CAM COG 4 GEAR
    5 ROTOR
  Sowing: 6 SEEDER
  tooth: 3 COG
  Vegas: 4 SLOT
  Voting ~ part: 5 LEVER
  Weaving: 4 LOOM
  Woodworking: 5 LATHE
  Word with: 4 SLOT
**___ machine:** 4 SLOT
**Machine gun**
  sound: 7 RATATAT
  syllable: 3 TAT
**Machinery**
  Big name in farm: 5 DEERE
  Run, as: 7 OPERATE
  Update the: 6 RETOOL

**Macho:** 5 MANLY
  Hardly: 3 FEY 5 MOUSY SISSY
    6 GIRLIE
  type: 4 STUD 5 HEMAN
    RAMBO
  types: 5 HEMEN
**Machu Picchu**
  resident: 4 INCA 5 INCAN
  site: 4 PERU
**Macintosh**
  maker: 5 APPLE
**Mack**
  of early TV: 3 TED
  predecessor: 5 BOWES
  Producer: 7 SENNETT
**MacKenzie**
  Actor: 5 ASTIN
  Singer: 6 GISELE
**Mackerel**
  Horse: 4 TUNA
  kin: 6 BONITO
  Large: 5 WAHOO
  shark: 4 MAKO
**Mackinac Island**
  lake: 5 HURON
**"Mack the Knife"**
  singer: 5 DARIN
**MacLachlan**
  Actor: 4 KYLE
**MacLaine, Shirley**
  1963 ~ role: 4 IRMA
  1969 ~ musical:
    12 SWEETCHARITY
  1994 ~ role: 4 TESS
**MacLeod**
  Actor: 5 GAVIN
**Macmillan**
  predecessor: 4 EDEN
**MacMurray, Fred**
  sitcom: 11 MYTHREESONS
**MacNeil**
  Partner of: 6 LEHRER
**MacNelly, Jeff**
  comic strip: 4 SHOE
**Macon**
  breakfast: 5 GRITS
**Macpherson**
  Model: 4 ELLE
**Macramé:** 5 CRAFT
  unit: 4 KNOT
**Macro**
  suffix: 4 COSM
**Macroeconomic**
  stat: 3 GNP
**Macy's:** 5 STORE
  alternative: 5 SEARS
  event: 4 SALE
  section: 4 MENS

**Mad:** 4 LOCO 5 ANGRY FEDUP
   IRATE LIVID 7 STEAMED
  (at): 4 SORE
  Be ~ about: 5 ADORE
  Be hopping: 4 BOIL 6 SEETHE
  Get: 5 STEAM 6 SEERED
  one of fiction: 6 HATTER
  Plenty: 4 IRED
**Mad. ___:** 3 AVE
**"Mad About You"**
  actress Helen: 4 HUNT
  cousin: 3 IRA
**Madagascar:** 6 ISLAND
  primate: 5 LEMUR
**Madalyn**
  Atheist: 5 OHAIR
**Madam:** 4 BAWD 5 TITLE
  Mate of: 3 SIR
**"Madama Butterfly"**
  Pinkerton, in: 5 TENOR
**Madame**
  Reply to a: 6 OUIOUI
**Madame Bovary:** 4 EMMA
**Madame Butterfly**
  Sash for: 3 OBI
**Madame de ___:** 5 STAEL
**Madame Karenina:** 4 ANNA
**Madame Tussaud**
  medium: 3 WAX
**"Madame X"**
  painter: 7 SARGENT
**"Madamina":** 4 ARIA
**Madcap:** 4 ZANY 5 ANTIC
  comedy: 4 ROMP
**MADD**
  concern: 3 DUI
  Part of: 7 AGAINST
**Madden:** 3 IRE 4 RILE
  6 ENRAGE 7 DERANGE
**Maddox**
  Former Georgia governor:
  6 LESTER
**Maddux**
  of baseball: 4 GREG
**Made:** 6 EARNED
  Barely ~ it: 4 EKED
  certain: 7 SAWTOIT
  Freshly: 3 NEW
  like: 4 APED
  out: 5 FARED 6 NECKED
  over: 5 REDID 6 REDONE
  possible: 7 ENABLED
  up (for): 6 ATONED
  use of: 6 DREWON
**Made in the ___:** 3 USA
**Madeleine**
  Actress: 5 STOWE
**Madeline**
  Actress: 4 KAHN
**"___ Made to Love Her":**
  4 IWAS
**Mad Hatter**
  drink: 3 TEA
**Madhouse:** 3 ZOO
**Madigan**
  Actress: 3 AMY

**"___ Madigan":** 6 ELVIRA
**Madison:** 6 AVENUE
  (abbr.): 3 AVE JAS
  Friend of: 5 UNGER
  Mrs.: 6 DOLLEY
  Sch. in ~, N.J.: 5 DREWU
  state (abbr.): 3 WIS
  successor: 6 MONROE
  veep: 5 GERRY
**Madison, Oscar:** 4 SLOB
  Like: 5 MESSY
  secretary: 5 MYRNA
**Madison Ave.**
  address: 4 NYNY
  guys: 5 ADMEN
  income: 6 ADFEES
  output: 3 ADS
**Madison Avenue**
  award: 4 CLIO
  reading: 6 ADWEEK
  type: 5 ADMAN
  types: 5 ADMEN
  7 IDEAMEN
**Madison Square Garden:**
  5 ARENA
**Madlyn**
  Actress: 4 RHUE
**Mad magazine**
  cartoonist Drucker: 4 MORT
  Get ~ again: 5 RENEW
  piece: 6 SATIRE
  publisher: 6 GAINES
**Mad Max**
  portrayer: 3 MEL
**"Mad Max"**
  Max in: 3 MEL
  villain: 5 BIKER
**"___ Madness":** 6 REEFER
**Madonna**
  1996 ~ film: 5 EVITA
  Ex of: 4 SEAN
  portrayal: 5 PIETA
  role: 5 EVITA PERON
  8 EVAPERON
  stagewear: 3 BRA
**"___ Madonna"**
  (Beatles tune): 4 LADY
  (Raphael): 7 SISTINE
**Madras**
  **Info:** India cue
  dress: 4 SARI
  master: 5 SAHIB
  money: 5 RUPEE
  music: 4 RAGA
  ~ Mr.: 3 SRI
**Madre**
  Brother of: 3 TIO
  Child of: 4 NENE NINO
  title (abbr.): 3 SRA
**___ Madres:** 6 SIERRA
**Madrid**
  **Info:** Spanish cue
  airline: 6 IBERIA
  City NW of: 4 LEON
  mister: 5 SENOR
  money: 6 PESETA

  month: 5 ENERO
  museum: 5 PRADO
  Walled city near: 5 AVILA
  ~ Mrs.: 3 SRA 6 SENORA
  ~ Ms.: 4 SRTA
**Madrileña**
  Married: 6 SENORA
**Madrileño:** 5 SENOR
**"Mad TV"**
  rival: 3 SNL
**Mae**
  Actress: 4 WEST
  role: 3 LIL
**___ Mae (Oscar role for**
  **Whoopi):** 3 ODA
**Maelstrom:** 4 EDDY
**Maestro**
  Bombay-born: 5 MEHTA
  wand: 5 BATON
  ~ Georg: 5 SOLTI
**Mafia**
  boss: 3 DON 4 CAPO
  Chinese: 4 TONG
  code of silence: 6 OMERTA
**Mag**
  edition: 3 ISS
  Fan: 4 ZINE
  Fan ~ subject: 4 IDOL
  features: 3 ADS
  for execs: 3 INC
  magnate: 3 HEF
  Web: 5 EZINE
  workers: 3 EDS
**Magazine:** 7 ARSENAL
  about celebs: 6 PEOPLE
  Arm with a: 3 UZI
  Business: 3 INC
  contents: 4 AMMO
  copy: 5 ISSUE
  Do ~ work: 4 EDIT
  Dr.'s: 4 JAMA
  Eclectic: 4 UTNE
  execs.: 3 EDS
  extra: 6 INSERT
  Fashion: 4 ELLE
  fillers: 3 ADS
  for men: 7 DETAILS
  Former humor: 3 SPY
  Former science: 4 OMNI
  Former women's: 5 ROSIE
  for women: 4 SELF
  genre: 4 MENS
  magnate, for short: 3 HEF
  Noted online: 5 SLATE
  Satire: 3 MAD
  Women's ~, for short:
  5 COSMO
  Word in some ~ titles:
  6 DIGEST
  ~ VIPs: 3 EDS
**Magaziner:** 3 IRA
**Magazines**
  and papers: 10 PRINTMEDIA
**Magda**
  Sister of: 3 EVA 6 ZSAZSA
**Magellan:** 6 STRAIT

org.: 4 NASA
**Maggie**
Husband of: 5 JIGGS
**Maggot:** 5 LARVA
**Magi:** 4 TRIO
Any of the: 6 ADORER
gift: 5 MYRRH
guide: 4 STAR
Home of the: 6 ORIENT
Like the: 4 WISE
One of the: 6 CASPAR
origin: 4 EAST
**Magic**
charm: 4 MOJO 6 AMULET
org.: 3 NBA
stick: 4 WAND
The ~ word: 6 PLEASE
town: 7 ORLANDO
West Indies: 5 OBEAH
word: 6 PRESTO
words: 10 HOCUSPOCUS
~, formerly: 5 LAKER
7 LALAKER
*"___ magic!":* 3 ITS
___ magica: 3 ARS
**Magical**
character: 4 RUNE
Cult using ~ rites: 6 VOODOO
drink: 6 POTION
object: 6 FETISH
opening: 4 ABRA 5 HOCUS
sound: 4 POOF
wish granter: 5 GENIE
**"Magic Flute, The":** 5 OPERA
**Magician**
Amazing: 5 RANDI
cry: 5 VOILA 6 PRESTO
Famous: 7 HOUDINI
hiding place: 6 SLEEVE
hiding spot: 4 PALM
name suffix: 3 INI
prop: 3 HAT 4 WAND
secret exit: 8 TRAPDOOR
source: 7 THINAIR
Tribal: 6 SHAMAN
**Magistrate**
Muslim: 4 CADI
Roman: 5 EDILE
Venetian: 4 DOGE
**Maglie**
of baseball: 3 SAL
**Magma**
on the go: 4 LAVA
**Magna ___:** 5 CARTA
**Magna cum ___:** 5 LAUDE
**Magna ___ laude:** 3 CUM
**Magnani**
Actress: 4 ANNA
**Magnate:** 4 CZAR 5 BARON
TITAN
Fur: 5 ASTOR
nickname: 3 ARI HEF
**Magnavox**
rival: 3 RCA 4 SONY
**Magnet**
alloy: 6 ALNICO

end: 4 POLE
holder: 6 FRIDGE
Kitchen: 5 AROMA
metal: 4 IRON
Tourist: 5 MECCA
**"Magnet and Steel"**
singer Walter: 4 EGAN
**Magnetic**
flux unit: 5 WEBER
induction unit: 5 GAUSS
TESLA
prefix: 4 AERO
ribbon: 4 TAPE
**Magnetism:** 6 ALLURE
8 CHARISMA
**Magnetite:** 3 ORE 7 IRONORE
**Magnificence:** 4 POMP
8 SPLENDOR
**Magnificent:** 5 REGAL
**"Magnificent Seven, The"**
Chris in: 3 YUL
*"___ magnifique!":* 4 CEST
**Magnify:** 7 ENHANCE
**Magnifying**
device: 5 LOUPE
**Magniloquize:** 5 ORATE
**Magnitude:** 4 SIZE 6 EXTENT
Having ~, but no direction:
6 SCALAR
___ Magnon: 3 CRO
**Magnum**
and others (abbr.): 3 PIS
follower: 4 OPUS
**Magnus**
Newswoman: 4 EDIE
**Magoo:** 5 MYOPE
Nephew of: 5 WALDO
vision: 4 BLUR
voice: 6 BACKUS
**Magritte**
Painter: 4 RENE
___ Mahal: 3 TAJ
**Mahalia**
music: 6 GOSPEL
**Maharani**
garb: 4 SARI
**Mahayana**
master: 4 LAMA
movement: 3 ZEN
**"Ma, He's Making Eyes ___":**
4 ATME
**Mah-jongg**
piece: 4 TILE
**Mahler**
Composer: 6 GUSTAV
Earth, to: 4 ERDE
**Mahler, Gustav**
Wife of: 4 ALMA
**Mahogany:** 4 TREE
**Mahre**
Emulate: 3 SKI
**Mai ___ (cocktail):** 3 TAI
___ mai (dim sum dish): 3 SHU
**Maid**
Baa: 3 EWE
cloth: 3 RAG

Comics: 5 HAZEL
need: 7 PASSKEY
of Astolat: 6 ELAINE
**Maiden:** 4 LASS
name preceder: 3 NEE
Poe: 6 LENORE
voyage preceder:
15 SHAKEDOWNCRUISE
**Maidenform**
product: 3 BRA
**Maidenhair:** 4 FERN
**"Maid of Athens, ___ part":**
Byron: 5 EREWE
**"Maids, The"**
playwright: 5 GENET
*"... maids all in ___":* 4 AROW
**Maidstone**
county: 4 KENT
**Mail:** 4 POST SEND
7 SENDOUT
again: 6 RESEND
carrier beat: 5 ROUTE
carrier beat (abbr.): 3 RTE
Country ~ rte.: 3 RFD
French: 5 POSTE
GI ~ drop: 3 APO
In the: 4 SENT
Junk ~, often: 3 ADS
6 UNREAD
Kind of: 4 BULK HATE
5 SNAIL 7 METERED
Main ~ ctr.: 3 GPO
motto word: 3 NOR
opening: 4 SLOT
org.: 4 USPS
Piece of ~ (abbr.): 3 LTR
Put in the: 4 SEND SENT
Snail ~ attachment: 5 STAMP
The check is in the ~, often:
3 LIE
Unwelcome: 4 BILL
You've got ~ co.: 3 AOL
**Mailbox**
attachment: 4 FLAG
**Mail Boxes ___:** 3 ETC
**Mailed:** 6 SENTIN
**Mailer, Norman:** 6 AUTHOR
novel: 12 HARLOTSGHOST
**Mailing**
courtesy (abbr.): 4 SASE
list items: 5 NAMES
Ready for: 7 STAMPED
Software: 5 CDROM
supply: 6 LABELS
**Mailman**
beat: 5 ROUTE
"Cheers": 5 CLIFF
**Mail order**
giant: 6 LLBEAN
record co.: 4 KTEL
**Main:** 3 SEA 5 CHIEF OCEAN
and others (abbr.): 3 STS
artery: 5 AORTA
attraction: 4 STAR
course: 6 ENTREE
idea: 4 CRUX GIST

impact: 5 BRUNT
In the: 7 ASARULE
Like a ~ highway: 8 ARTERIAL
line: 5 AORTA 6 ARTERY
men: 4 TARS
Of a ~ line: 6 AORTIC
On the: 4 ASEA 5 ATSEA
pronoun: 3 HER
role: 4 LEAD
route: 7 SEALANE
squeeze: 6 STEADY
theme: 5 MOTIF
**Maine:** 5 STATE
Bay in: 5 CASCO
college town: 5 ORONO
national park: 6 ACADIA
resort: 9 BARHARBOR
symbol: 8 PINETREE
tree: 4 PINE
**Maine ___ cat:** 4 COON
**Mainframe**
2001 ~: 3 HAL
Send to a: 6 UPLOAD
**Maintain:** 4 AVER HOLD
5 CLAIM 6 ALLEGE
ASSERT HOLDTO
**Maintenance:** 6 UPKEEP
Like some computer: 6 ONSITE
worker: 7 JANITOR
**Mainz**
mister: 4 HERR
**"Mais ___!":** 3 OUI
**Mai tai**
ingredient: 3 RUM
**Maj.**
College: 3 BIO ENG SOC
4 ECOL ECON 5 PSYCH
Rank above: 3 COL 5 LTCOL
**Maja**
painter: 4 GOYA
**"Maja Nude"**
painter: 4 GOYA
**___ majesté:** 4 LESE
**Majestic:** 4 EPIC 5 GRAND
REGAL 7 STATELY
poem: 4 EPIC
**"___ Majesty's Secret Service":**
5 ONHER
**Major**
A: 3 KEY
account: 4 SAGA
addition: 4 ETTE
airport: 3 HUB
animal: 4 URSA
artery: 5 AORTA
Coll.: 3 BIO ENG SOC 4 ECOL
ECON 5 PSYCH
College: 3 ART 4 MATH
5 DRAMA
conflict: 3 WAR
in the sky: 4 URSA
leaguer: 5 FEAST
meal: 5 FEAST
mix-up: 5 SNAFU
successor: 5 BLAIR
Uncommon: 5 CFLAT

util.: 4 ELEC
work: 4 OPUS
**Major ___:** 4 DOMO
**___ Major:** 4 URSA 5 CANIS
**"Major Barbara"**
playwright: 4 SHAW
**Majorca:** 4 ISLA
capital: 5 PALMA
**Majorette**
motion: 5 TWIRL
need: 5 BATON
**Major Hoople**
holler: 4 EGAD
**Majority:** 4 MOST
**Major leagues**
One of the ~ (abbr.): 4 NATL
~, in slang: 4 BIGS
**Major Major**
portrayer: 7 NEWHART
**Majors**
Actor: 3 LEE
**Makarova**
Ballerina: 7 NATALIA
of tennis: 5 ELENA
**Make:** 4 EARN
amends: 5 ATONE
Barely: 6 EKEOUT
Barely ~ it: 5 GETBY
8 SQUEAKBY
better: 4 HEAL 5 AMEND
certain: 6 ASSURE ENSURE
INSURE
do: 4 COPE
Hard to ~ out: 5 FAINT
it: 3 TAG 4 COME 5 GOFAR
6 ARRIVE
like: 3 APE
one: 3 WED 5 UNITE
one's own: 5 ADOPT
(one's way): 4 WEND
out: 3 SEE 4 ESPY FARE
NECK READ 6 DETECT
7 DISCERN
(out): 3 EKE
over: 5 ALTER 7 RESTYLE
8 RECREATE
up: 5 ATONE ELATE
up for: 5 ATONE 6 RECOUP
use of: 3 TAP
**"Make ___!" (captain's order):**
4 ITSO
**Make ___ (get rich):** 5 AMINT
**Make ___ at:** 5 APASS
**Makeba**
Singer: 6 MIRIAM
**Make-believe:** 4 SHAM
8 PRETENSE
**Make ___ buck:** 5 AFAST
**Make ___ dash for:** 4 AMAD
**"Make ___ double":** 3 ITA
**Make ___ for:** 5 ACASE
**Make ___ for it:** 4 ARUN
**Make ___ for oneself:** 5 ANAME
**"Make it snappy!":** 4 ASAP
**"Make love, not war":**
6 SLOGAN

**Make ___ meet:** 4 ENDS
**Make ___ of:** 5 ANOTE
**Make ___ of things:** 5 AMESS
**Makeover:** 4 REDO
**Makes**
What one: 6 INCOME
**Makeshift:** 7 STOPGAP
drinking glass: 8 JELLYJAR
dwelling: 3 HUT
money: 5 SCRIP
swing: 4 TIRE
**Make the ___:** 6 MOSTOF
**Makeup:** 4 EXAM TEST
6 RETEST
artist: 4 LIAR
Cube: 3 ICE
Do a ~ job: 5 ATONE
Jury: 5 PEERS
Model: 5 BALSA
name: 5 ESTEE
Rio: 4 AGUA
**Make ___ with:** 4 AHIT
**Making**
a crossing: 4 ASEA
all stops: 5 LOCAL
no progress: 6 INARUT
no sense: 5 INANE
**"Makin' Whoopee"**
lyricist Gus: 4 KAHN
**Mal-**
relative: 3 MIS
**Mal ___:** 5 DEMER
**Malady:** 7 AILMENT DISEASE
**Malaga**
mister: 5 SENOR
Mmes. in: 4 SRAS
Mrs. in: 3 SRA
**Malaise:** 8 THEBLAHS
~, with "the": 5 BLAHS
**Malamud, Bernard**
novel: 10 THENATURAL
**Malamute**
tow: 4 SLED
**Malaprop:** 3 MRS
**Malaria**
symptom: 4 AGUE
**Malarkey:** 3 ROT
**Malay**
boat: 4 PROA
Export of: 3 TIN
isthmus: 3 KRA
monarch: 5 RAJAH
**Malay Archipelago**
island: 6 BORNEO
**Malcolm**
role: 4 THEO
TV dad of: 3 HAL
**Malcolm-___ Warner:** 5 JAMAL
**Malcolm X**
biographer: 9 ALEXHALEY
**"Malcolm X"**
director: 3 LEE 8 SPIKELEE
**Malcontent:** 5 REBEL
**Mal de ___:** 3 MER
**Malden**
Actor: 4 KARL

**Male**
admirer: 5 SWAIN
bee: 5 DRONE
cat: 3 TOM
deer: 4 HART STAG
duck: 5 DRAKE
heirs: 4 SONS
Kind of: 5 ALPHA
pig: 4 BOAR
sheep: 3 RAM
sibs: 4 BROS
swan: 3 COB
turkey: 3 TOM
___ male: 5 ALPHA
**Maleficent:** 4 EVIL
**Males:** 3 HES
**Malevolence:** 4 EVIL HATE
5 SPITE
**Malevolent:** 4 EVIL
**Malfoy**
of Hogwarts: 5 DRACO
**Malfunction:** 5 ACTUP
**Mali**
neighbor: 5 NIGER
river: 5 NIGER
**Malibu:** 4 AUTO 5 SEDAN
**Malice:** 5 SPITE
**"Malice"**
Baldwin of: 4 ALEC
**Malicious:** 4 EVIL MEAN
5 CATTY NASTY
SNIDE
gossip: 4 DIRT
look: 4 LEER
ones: 7 MEANIES
**Maliciously**
Treat: 5 SPITE
**Malick**
Actress: 6 WENDIE
**Malign:** 5 ABUSE 7 ASPERSE
TRADUCE
in print: 5 LIBEL
**Malihini**
Gift for a: 3 LEI
**Malkovich, John**
1985 ~ film: 5 ELENI
**Mall**
Ancient: 5 AGORA
areas: 5 ATRIA
bag: 4 TOTE
binge: 5 SPREE
chain, with "The": 3 GAP
event: 4 SALE
feature: 6 ARCADE CINEMA
Greek: 5 AGORA
Kind of: 5 STRIP
rat: 4 TEEN
Shopping: 8 GALLERIA
stand: 5 KIOSK
tenant: 10 CHAINSTORE
unit: 4 SHOP 5 STORE
**Mallard**
Male: 5 DRAKE
relative: 4 TEAL
**Mallet:** 5 GAVEL
game: 4 POLO

**Mallorca:** 4 ISLA
Info: Spanish cue
Mlle. in: 4 SRTA
Mrs. in: 3 SRA
**Mallow**
shrub: 4 OKRA
**Malmo**
citizen: 5 SWEDE
setting: 6 SWEDEN
**Malodorous:** 5 FETID
7 REEKING
animal: 7 POLECAT
**Malone**
Actress: 4 JENA
of basketball: 4 KARL
**Malraux**
Novelist: 5 ANDRE
**Malt**
alternative: 4 SODA
beverage: 3 ALE 4 BEER
5 STOUT
dryer: 4 OAST
kiln: 4 OAST
liquor yeast: 4 BARM
**Malta**
capital: 8 VALLETTA
money: 4 LIRA
**Maltese**
cry: 4 MEOW
**"Maltese Falcon, The"**
actor Peter: 5 LORRE
actress Mary: 5 ASTOR
role: 3 SAM 5 SPADE
**Maltreat:** 5 ABUSE 6 ILLUSE
___ **Malvinas (the Falklands):**
5 ISLAS
**Mama**
Big: 4 CASS
boy: 3 SON
Lamb: 3 EWE
of papa: 4 NANA
Partner of: 4 PAPA
~ bear, in Spanish: 3 OSA
**Mama Cass ___:** 6 ELLIOT
**"Mamas & the Papas, The"**
singer Doherty: 5 DENNY
singer Elliot: 4 CASS
**Mambo**
king Puente: 4 TITO
**"Mambo Kings, The"**
star: 7 ASSANTE
8 BANDERAS
**Mame:** 6 AUNTIE
**Mamet, David**
1992 ~ play: 7 OLEANNA
award: 4 OBIE
**Mamie**
Husband of: 3 IKE
predecessor: 4 BESS
**"Mamma ___!":** 3 MIA
**Mammal**
Aquatic: 4 SEAL 5 OTTER
Burrowing: 4 MOLE
Flying: 3 BAT
Long-eared: 4 HARE
Mammoth: 5 WHALE

**Marine:** 6 WALRUS
7 SEALION
of Madagascar: 5 LEMUR
Piglike: 5 TAPIR
Slow-moving: 5 SLOTH
Thick-skinned: 5 HIPPO
RHINO
Tropical: 5 TAPIR
**"Mamma Mia!"**
group: 4 ABBA
**Mammoth**
era: 6 ICEAGE
part: 4 TUSK
**Mammy Yokum**
creator: 6 ALCAPP
Son of: 5 ABNER
**Man:** 3 BRO 4 GENT ISLE
5 VALET 7 PRIMATE
(abbr.): 3 ISL
at the wheel: 5 SAJAK
Chair: 5 EAMES
Con: 4 ANTI
Dadaist: 3 RAY
Dirty old: 6 LECHER
Elevator: 4 OTIS
Family: 3 DAD
First: 4 ADAM
Fourth: 4 SETH
High: 4 ALTO
Hit: 4 ICER
in a suit: 5 SANTA
Iron: 5 ROBOT
Jazz: 3 CAT
Little green: 5 ALIEN
Low: 5 BASSO
Macho: 4 STUD
March: 5 SOUSA
of La Mancha: 5 SENOR
of many words: 5 ROGET
of morals: 5 AESOP
of mystery: 3 MRX
of parts: 5 ACTOR
of photos: 3 RAY
of Principle: 5 PETER
of the haus: 4 HERR
of the hour: 4 HERO
of the Year: see pages 725–726
Old: 3 DAD POP 5 POPPA
Right-hand: 4 AIDE
Straight: 4 FOIL 6 STOOGE
Third: 4 ABEL
Third ~ in the ring: 3 REF
Time magazine's ~ of the Year:
see pages 725–726
Top: 5 MRBIG
Tractor: 5 DEERE
Unmannered: 3 CAD
who would be queen: 4 PAWN
with a law: 3 OHM
with a mission: 5 PADRE
SERRA
Young: 3 LAD
~ Fri.: 4 ASST
~ Friday: 4 AIDE
~, in Italian: 4 UOMO
~, in Latin: 3 VIR

"Man!": 5 OHWOW
Man ___ (racehorse): 4 OWAR
___ man: 3 TOA
"___ Man"
  (1984 film): 4 REPO
  (1992 film): 6 ENCINO
  (Village People hit): 5 MACHO
"___ Man, The" (Heston film):
  5 OMEGA
Manacle: 8 HANDCUFF
Manage: 4 COPE FEND
  5 GETBY SEETO
  6 EKEOUT MAKEDO
  7 OPERATE OVERSEE
  SWINGIT
  Barely ~, with "out": 3 EKE
  Easy to: 4 TAME
  moguls: 3 SKI
  to find: 7 SCAREUP
Managed: 3 RAN 5 SAWTO
  care org.: 3 HMO
Management
  Fed. ~ gp.: 3 GSA
  Middle: 4 DIET
  prefix: 5 MICRO
Manager
  Cardinal: 4 POPE
  Corp. money: 3 CFO
  deg.: 3 MBA
  Fed. property: 3 GSA
  Money: 6 EDITOR
Manager of the Year
  1994 N.L.: 4 ALOU
  1998 A.L.: 5 TORRE
Mañana
  Opposite of: 4 AYER
  ___ mañana!: 5 HASTA
"Man and a Woman, A"
  actress: 5 AIMEE
"Man and Superman"
  playwright: 4 SHAW
"___ Man Answers" (1962 film):
  3 IFA
Manatee: 6 SEACOW
  home: 3 SEA
Manche
  capital: 4 STLO
Manchester
  man: 5 BLOKE
  Singer: 7 MELISSA
Manchurian
  border river: 4 YALU
Manco Capac: 4 INCA
Mandamus: 4 WRIT
Mandarin: 6 ORANGE
Mandate: 5 ORDER
Mandel
  Comic: 5 HOWIE
Mandela: 6 NELSON
  org.: 3 ANC
Mandible
  part: 4 JOWL
Mandlikova
  of tennis: 4 HANA
Mandolin
  feature: 4 FRET

kin: 4 LUTE
Mandrake
  assistant: 6 LOTHAR
  field: 5 MAGIC
"Mandy"
  singer: 7 MANILOW
Mane
  Antelope with a: 3 GNU
  area: 4 NAPE
  Thick: 3 MOP
  thing: 4 HAIR
Man-eating
  monster: 4 OGRE
Manet: 6 ARTIST
Maneuver
  180-degree ~: 5 UTURN
  carefully: 4 EASE
  Clever: 4 PLOY
  Dance: 3 DIP
  Evasive: 6 ENDRUN
  Sailing: 4 TACK
  Skating: 4 AXEL LOOP
  Skiing: 8 SIDESLIP
  Wall St.: 3 LBO
Maneuverable: 4 YARE
Manfred
  Detective story writer: 3 LEE
  Pop singer: 4 MANN
Mangel-wurzel: 4 BEET
Manger
  bedding: 3 HAY
  visitors: 4 MAGI
"Mangia!": 3 EAT
Mangle: 4 MAIM
  Use a: 4 IRON
Man-goat: 5 SATYR
Manhandle: 3 PAW 4 MAUL
  5 PAWAT
Manhattan: 5 DRINK 6 ISLAND
  (abbr.): 3 ISL
  Arty ~ district: 4 SOHO
  eatery: 7 ELAINES
  ingredient: 3 RYE
  Island near: 5 ELLIS
  landmark: 11 CENTRALPARK
  letters: 4 NYNY
  locale (abbr.): 4 KANS
  neighborhood: 4 SOHO
  7 TRIBECA
  sch.: 3 NYU 4 CCNY
  section: 8 EASTSIDE
  site: 3 BAR
  Suffix with: 3 ITE
  ~, for short: 4 BORO
"Manhattan Murder Mystery"
  star: 4 ALDA
Manhattan Project
  Agcy. created after the: 3 AEC
  It followed the: 9 ATOMICAGE
  result: 5 ABOMB
  scientist: 5 FERMI
Manhunt
  letters: 3 APB
  target: 7 ESCAPEE
Mania: 3 FAD 4 RAGE 5 CRAZE
  source of the 1630s: 5 TULIP

Maniac: 5 FIEND 6 MADMAN
  Kind of: 3 EGO
Manicured
  expanse: 4 LAWN
Manicurist
  board: 5 EMERY
  concern: 4 NAIL 7 CUTICLE
  tool: 4 FILE
Manifest: 5 OVERT 6 EVINCE
  7 EVIDENT
Manifesto
  writer: 4 MARX 6 ENGELS
Manila
  envelope fastener: 5 CLASP
  folder extension: 3 TAB
  island: 5 LUZON
  Territory east of: 4 GUAM
Manilow, Barry
  1975 ~ hit: 5 MANDY
  song setting: 4 COPA
"Man in Full, A"
  author: 5 WOLFE
Manipulate: 3 USE 5 WIELD
  dishonestly: 4 COOK
Manipulative
  one: 4 USER
Manipulator: 4 USER
Manitoba
  native: 4 CREE
Manjula
  Husband of: 3 APU
Manliness: 8 MACHISMO
Manly: 5 MACHO 6 VIRILE
Man-made
  Not: 7 NATURAL
"Man ___ Mancha": 4 OFLA
Man-mission
  link: 3 ONA
Man-mouse
  link: 3 ORA
"... man ___ mouse?": 3 ORA
Mann
  of education: 6 HORACE
  Singer: 5 AIMEE
Mann, Manfred
  1964 ~ hit: 7 SHALALA
Manner: 4 MIEN
  Cool in: 5 ALOOF
  Distinctive: 5 STYLE
  In the ~ of: 3 ALA
  In this: 6 LIKESO
  Kind of: 7 BEDSIDE
  of action: 4 MODE
  of speaking: 5 IDIOM
  suffix: 3 ISM
Mannerism: 5 TRAIT
  Odd: 3 TIC
Mannerly
  guy: 4 GENT
  ___ manner of speaking: 3 INA
Manners: 5 MODES
  7 PSANDQS
  of moving: 5 GAITS
  Post of: 5 EMILY
Mannheim
  Mr.: 4 HERR

**Manning**
of football: 3 ELI
**Manny**
of baseball: 4 MOTA
**Mano a mano:** 4 DUEL
8 ONEONONE
**"Man of ___":** 4 ARAN
**"Man of a Thousand Faces"**
actor Chaney: 3 LON
**Man of Steel**
portrayer: 5 REEVE
**Man of the Year:** *see pages*
*725–726*
1971 ~: 5 NIXON
1977 ~: 5 SADAT
**Manolete**
Cheer for: 3 OLE
nemesis: 6 ELTORO
**Manor:** 6 ESTATE
master: 4 LORD
Mitchell: 4 TARA
**... ___ man put asunder:**
5 LETNO
**Mansard:** 4 ROOF
overhang: 4 EAVE
**Manse**
dweller: 6 PARSON
**Man-shaped**
mug: 4 TOBY
**Mansion**
and grounds: 6 ESTATE
Man with a: 6 HEFNER
Mitchell: 4 TARA
**Mantel**
piece: 3 URN 4 VASE
**Mantilla:** 5 SCARF
**Mantle**
number: 5 SEVEN
teammate: 5 MARIS
**Mantra**
Antidrug: 9 JUSTSAYNO
sounds: 3 OMS
**Manual**
Kind of: 5 USERS
Not: 5 STICK
reader: 4 USER
transmission: 5 STICK
**Manufacture:** 4 MAKE
**Manufacturer:** 5 MAKER
bane: 6 RECALL
Dish: 3 RCA
Egg: 3 HEN
offer: 6 REBATE
**Manuscript**
book: 5 CODEX
copyist: 6 SCRIBE
Correct a: 4 EDIT
encl.: 4 SASE
Fix, as a: 6 RETYPE
marking: 4 STET
Pertaining to a:
7 TEXTUAL
Remove from a: 4 DELE
sheet: 5 FOLIO
**Manuscripts**
Unsolicited: 5 SLUSH

**Manute**
of basketball: 3 BOL
**"Man Who Fell to Earth, The"**
director: 4 ROEG
**"Man Who Knew Too Much,**
**The"**
actress: 8 EDNABEST
**... ___ man who wasn't there:**
5 IMETA
**"Man Who Wasn't There, The"**
director: 4 COEN
**"Man Without ___, The" (1993**
**film):** 5 AFACE
**"Man Without a Country, The":**
5 NOLAN
**... ___ man with seven wives:**
5 IMETA
**Manx:** 3 CAT
feature: 6 NOTAIL
lack: 4 TAIL
of the house: 3 PET
relative: 4 ERSE
thanks: 4 PURR
**Many:** 4 ALOT 6 ALOTOF
LOTSOF
As ~ as: 4 UPTO
(Greek): 6 POLLOI
Is for: 3 ARE
Not: 3 FEW 4 AFEW
Not as: 5 FEWER
**Many-___:** 4 HUED
**"___ many and many a**
**year ...": Poe:** 5 ITWAS
**___ many cooks ...:** 3 TOO
**Many-headed**
monster: 5 HYDRA
**Many moons ___:** 3 AGO
**___ many words:** 4 INSO
**Mao**
colleague: 4 CHOU
follower: 3 TSE
Like the Book of: 3 RED
opponent: 6 CHIANG
successor: 4 DENG
**Map**
abbr.: 3 AVE ISL LAT RTE
abbrs.: 3 STS
collection: 5 ATLAS
Corner: 5 INSET
dot: 4 ISLE TOWN 5 ISLET
Family: 4 TREE
feature: 5 INSET SCALE
Former ~ abbr: 4 USSR
In need of a: 4 LOST
It's right on the: 4 EAST
Land: 4 PLAT
line: 4 ROAD
lines (abbr.): 3 RDS STS
Modern ~ subject: 6 GENOME
out: 4 PLAN
overlay: 4 GRID
Surveyor: 4 PLAT
Treasure ~ distance: 4 PACE
Up, on a: 5 NORTH
Weather ~ line: 6 ISOBAR
within a map: 5 INSET

**WWII ~ (abbr.):** 3 ETO
**Maple**
fluid: 3 SAP
genus: 4 ACER
Like a ~ leaf: 5 EROSE
product: 5 SYRUP
**Maple Leaf**
org.: 3 NHL
**"Maple Leaf ___":** 3 RAG
**Maples**
Actress: 5 MARLA
**MapQuest**
request (abbr.): 3 RTE
**Maps**
Big name in: 4 RAND
Book of: 5 ATLAS
Org. with: 3 AAA
**Mar:** 4 DENT
Site in el: 4 ISLA
**Mar.**
follower: 3 APR
honoree: 5 STPAT
**Maracaibo:** 4 LAGO
**Maradona**
of soccer: 5 DIEGO
**Marais ___ Cygnes:** 3 DES
**Marañón**
Where the ~ flows: 4 PERU
**Marathon:** 4 RACE 5 EVENT
data: 5 TIMES
Do a: 3 RUN
mementos: 7 TSHIRTS
Prep for a ~, with "up":
4 CARB
unit: 4 MILE
**Marathoner**
gorge: 5 CARBS
need: 7 STAMINA
woe: 4 ACHE
**"Marat/Sade"**
Patrick of: 5 MAGEE
playwright Peter: 5 WEISS
**Maravich**
nickname: 10 PISTOLPETE
**Marble**
Cut of: 4 SLAB
Glass: 5 AGATE
Italian ~ city: 5 MASSA
Like: 6 VEINED
Metal: 7 STEELIE
Noted Italian: 5 PIETA
Playing: 3 TAW 5 AGATE
AGGIE IMMIE 7 CATSEYE
STEELIE
Shooting: 3 TAW 5 AGATE
**Marbled**
bread: 3 RYE
Fully: 4 SANE
stone: 5 AGATE
**Marbles**
game: 4 MIBS
Having all one's: 4 SANE
~, so to speak: 6 SANITY
**___ Marbles:** 5 ELGIN
**Marc**
Love of: 4 CLEO

of distinction: 6 ANTONY
Painter: 7 CHAGALL
**Marc Antony**
love: 4 AMOR
request: 4 EARS
Wife of: 7 OCTAVIA
9 CLEOPATRA
**Marceau**
character: 3 BIP
Emulate: 4 MIME
Mime: 6 MARCEL
**Marcel**
Mime: 7 MARCEAU
Mother, to: 4 MERE
Novelist: 6 PROUST
**Marcellus II**
Pope after: 6 PAULIV
**March:** 5 TROOP
1965 ~ city: 5 SELMA
event: 6 EASTER PARADE
follower: 4 HARE 5 APRIL
gp., once: 3 SDS
honoree: 5 STPAT
9 STPATRICK
Host: 3 HAL
It came down in ~ 2001: 3 MIR
lead-in (abbr.): 3 FEB
marchers: 5 IRISH
Military day's: 5 ETAPE
name: 5 SOUSA
sound: 3 HUP
**March 15:** 4 IDES
**March 17**
dance: 3 JIG
honoree, briefly: 5 STPAT
slogan word: 4 ERIN
**March 21**
occurrence: 7 EQUINOX
**"March comes in like ___ ...":**
5 ALION
**Marchers**
Coll.: 4 ROTC
March: 5 IRISH
November: 4 VETS
Sugar bowl: 4 ANTS
**Marchetti**
of football: 4 GINO
**Marching**
band instrument: 4 FIFE TUBA
5 FLUTE
order: 4 HALT
practice: 5 DRILL
together: 6 INSTEP
words: 4 HEPS
**"Marching Along"**
autobiographer: 5 SOUSA
**"March King, The":** 5 SOUSA
**"March Madness"**
org.: 4 NCAA
**March of ___:** 5 DIMES
**Marciano**
birth name: 5 ROCCO
**Marcie**
Peppermint Patty, to: 3 SIR
**Marco**
Traveler: 4 POLO

**Marcos**
Mrs.: 6 IMELDA
successor: 6 AQUINO
**Marcus**
MGM founder: 4 LOEW
Partner of: 6 NEIMAN
**Marcus, Jerry**
comic strip: 5 TRUDY
**"Marcus Welby, M.D."**
actress Verdugo: 5 ELENA
network: 3 ABC
**Mardi ___:** 4 GRAS
**Mardi Gras**
accessory: 4 MASK
follower: 4 LENT
~ VIP: 3 REX
**Mare**
Knight: 5 STEED
Like the gray: 3 OLD
meal: 4 OATS
Mottled: 5 PINTO
offspring: 4 FOAL
on the moon: 3 SEA
**Mare, Walter ___**
Poet: 4 DELA
**Mare's-nest:** 4 MESS
**Margaret**
Anthropologist: 4 MEAD
Comic: 3 CHO
Comics tormentor of:
6 DENNIS
hero: 5 RHETT
nickname: 3 PEG
**Margaret Higgins ___:**
6 SANGER
**Margarine:** 4 OLEO
**Margarita:** 4 ISLA
fruit: 4 LIME
need: 4 SALT
**Margery**
of rhyme: 3 DAW
**Margin:** 3 RIM 4 EDGE
Large: 4 MILE
mark: 4 STET
Narrow: 4 HAIR INCH
NOSE 7 EYELASH
WHISKER
Suffix with: 4 ALIA
Victory: 6 LENGTH
**Marginal:** 10 BORDERLINE
jotting: 8 NOTATION
mark: 4 STET
**Marginalia**
Bit of: 4 STET
**Margins**
Like some: 4 SLIM
**Margot**
role: 4 LOIS
**Margrethe**
Queen ~ subjects: 5 DANES
**Maria**
Soprano: 6 CALLAS
**"Maria ___" (old song):**
5 ELENA
**___ Maria (liqueur):** 3 TIA
**"___ Maria":** 3 AVE

**Mariachi**
wrap: 6 SERAPE
**Mariah**
Former label of: 3 EMI
Singer: 5 CAREY
**Marian:** 4 MAID
**Marianas**
Largest of the: 4 GUAM
One of the: 6 SAIPAN
**Marianne**
Poet: 5 MOORE
**Marie**
(abbr.): 3 STE
Donny or: 6 OSMOND
~, to Donny: 3 SIS
**___ Marie**
Singer: 5 TEENA
**Marie Claire**
rival: 4 ELLE
**Marienbad:** 3 SPA
**Marigold:** 6 ANNUAL
**Marijuana**
source: 4 HEMP
**Marilu**
Actress: 6 HENNER
role: 6 ELAINE
**Marilyn**
birth name: 5 NORMA
Like: 4 SEXY
Mezzo-soprano: 5 HORNE
**Marin**
Comic: 6 CHEECH
**Marin, Cheech**
film setting: 6 EASTLA
**Marina**
feature: 4 PIER
sight: 5 BOATS YACHT
**Marina del ___:** 3 REY
**Marinara:** 5 SAUCE
alternative: 5 PESTO
ingredient: 6 TOMATO
**Marinate:** 4 SOAK
**Marine:** 3 SEA 8 DEVILDOG
bioluminescence:
7 SEAFIRE
eagle: 3 ERN 4 ERNE
food fish: 7 SEABASS
mammal: 7 SEALION
meal: 4 MESS
menace: 4 ORCA
plant: 4 ALGA
rock-clinger: 7 ABALONE
shade: 4 AQUA
snail: 5 WHELK
TV ~ Gomer: 4 PYLE
**Marine ___:** 5 CORPS
**Mariner:** 3 TAR 6 SEAMAN
Ancient: 4 NOAH
call: 4 AHOY
Genesis: 4 NOAH
"Mayday!": 3 SOS
measure: 7 SEAMILE
menace: 3 FOG
patron: 6 STELMO
~ Ericson: 4 LEIF
~ Melville: 4 AHAB

**"Marines' Hymn, The"**
port: 7 TRIPOLI
**Marino**
Quarterback: 3 DAN
___ Marino: 3 SAN
**Mario**
Author: 4 PUZO
Former NY governor:
5 CUOMO
Linguist: 3 PEI
of basketball: 4 ELIE
Tenor: 5 LANZA
**Mario Brothers**
One of the: 5 LUIGI
**Marion County, Florida**
Seat of: 5 OCALA
**Marionette**
maker Tony: 4 SARG
surname: 5 DOODY
**Mariposa**
relative: 4 SEGO
**Maris**
~, to pals: 3 ROG
**Marisa**
Actress: 5 TOMEI
**Marital**
skirmish: 4 SPAT
**Maritime**
Clandestine ~ org.: 3 ONI
One of the ~ Provinces (abbr.):
3 PEI
trio member: 4 NINA
**Marjoram:** 4 HERB
Wild: 7 OREGANO
**Marjorie**
of rhyme: 3 DAW
**Mark:** 5 GRADE 6 DENOTE
7 APOSTLE
alternative: 4 EURO
Bad: 7 DEMERIT
Beauty: 3 TEN
below C in French: 7 CEDILLA
Black: 6 STIGMA
Check: 4 TICK
Czech: 5 HACEK
down, perhaps: 5 RETAG
Easy: 3 SAP 5 CHUMP PATSY
6 PIGEON 7 LIVEONE
Editor: 4 DELE STET
Excellent: 5 APLUS
for life: 4 SCAR
German: 6 UMLAUT
Golfer: 6 OMEARA
High ~ with low effort:
5 EASYA
Insertion: 5 CARET
Kind of: 4 SKID
King ~ queen: 6 ISOLDE
Leave a ~ on: 4 SCAR
Leave one's: 7 IMPRESS
Low: 3 DEE
Made one's: 3 XED
Make one's: 4 SIGN
Mediocre: 3 CEE
Miss the: 3 ERR
Musical: 4 REST

Official: 5 STAMP
Off the: 4 WIDE 6 AFIELD
ERRANT
On the: 3 APT 4 TRUE
or Dorothy: 6 HAMILL
permanently: 4 ETCH
Proofreader: 4 DELE STET
Punctuation: 5 COMMA
Spanish: 5 TILDE
Squiggly: 5 TILDE
Swimmer: 5 SPITZ
Tally: 5 NOTCH
the beginning of: 7 USHERIN
the boundaries of: 7 DELIMIT
Wide of the: 3 OFF 6 ERRANT
with blotches: 6 MOTTLE
**Markdown:** 4 SALE
**Marked**
a ballot: 3 XED
down: 6 ONSALE
Not ~ up: 6 ATCOST
**Marker:** 3 IOU 4 CHIT DEBT
5 STELE
Air-race: 5 PYLON
Channel: 4 BUOY
Commemorative: 5 STELE
Cribbage: 3 PEG
Desktop: 4 ICON
Gambling: 4 CHIT
Grave: 5 STONE
Highway: 8 MILEPOST
Traffic: 4 CONE
**Markers**
Has ~ out: 4 OWES
Spot.: 4 EXES
**Market:** 4 SELL
activity: 7 TRADING
aid: 4 CART
Ancient Greek: 5 AGORA
Ending for: 3 EER
figure: 6 SELLER
Fish ~ feature: 4 ODOR
Flea ~ find: 5 CURIO
indicator: 3 DOW
Kind of: 4 BULL FLEA
7 OPENAIR
opportunist, briefly: 3 ARB
oversupply: 4 GLUT
price: 5 VALUE
Put on the: 4 SELL
section: 4 DELI
town: 5 BOURG
unit: 5 SHARE
**Marketing**
Internet: 5 ETAIL
Intro to: 4 TELE
lures: 7 REBATES
ploy: 4 TEST 5 TIEIN
**Marketplace:** 6 BAZAAR
RIALTO
Ancient Greek: 5 AGORA
Online: 4 EBAY
**Markets**
Bull: 3 UPS
**Markey**
Silents actress: 4 ENID

**Marking**
Crate ~, often: 7 STENCIL
Manuscript: 4 STET
Martian: 5 CANAL
Maze: 5 ENTER
Meat: 4 USDA
Music: 4 SLUR
Shoebox: 3 EEE
**Markova**
Ballerina: 6 ALICIA
**Marks**
Bad: 4 ACNE
They take ~ off: 7 ERASERS
**Marksman:** 5 AIMER
7 DEADEYE
org.: 3 NRA
weapon: 5 RIFLE
**Marla**
predecessor: 5 IVANA
**Marlee**
Actress: 6 MATLIN
"___ Marlene": 4 LILI
**Marley, Bob:** 5 RASTA
genre: 6 REGGAE
**Marlin:** 4 NLER
**Marlon**
costar: 3 EVA
He directed: 4 ELIA
role: 4 VITO
**Marmalade**
ingredient: 4 RIND
**Marner:** 5 MISER
Fictional: 5 SILAS
"___ Marner": 5 SILAS
**Maroon:** 6 ENISLE STRAND
home: 4 ISLE
**"Mârouf"**
baritone: 3 ALI
**Marquand**
sleuth: 4 MOTO 6 MRMOTO
**Marquee**
filler: 4 NEON
name: 4 STAR
time: 4 NITE
word: 4 NITE 6 TONITE
**Marquette**
Title for: 4 PERE
**Marquis**
Rank above: 4 DUKE
Rank below: 4 EARL
**Marquis ___:** 6 DESADE
**Marquis de ___:** 4 SADE
**Marrero**
of baseball: 3 ELI
**Marriage:** 4 RITE 5 UNION
acquisition: 5 INLAW
Invalidate, as a: 5 ANNUL
Ready for: 6 NUBILE
requirement: 3 TWO
Unite in: 3 WED
vows: 4 IDOS
**Marriageable:** 6 NUBILE
**"Marriage of ___, The":**
6 FIGARO
**Married:** 3 ONE
mujer: 6 SENORA

"___ Married an Axe
    Murderer": 3 SOI
"Married ... With Children"
    actor Ed: 6 ONEILL
    actress Katey: 5 SAGAL
Marriott
    rival: 5 HYATT 6 RAMADA
Marrow, Tracy
    Rapper: 4 ICET
Marry: 3 WED
    in haste: 5 ELOPE
Marryin' Sam
    creator: 4 CAPP 6 ALCAPP
Mars: 3 GOD ORB 4 DEUS
        5 DEITY 6 WARGOD
        9 REDPLANET
    Counterpart of: 4 ARES
    Man from: 5 ALIEN
    Moon of: 6 DEIMOS
    Phobos, to: 4 MOON
    prefix: 4 AREO
Marsalis
    Jazz pianist: 5 ELLIS
Marseille
    Info: French cue
    Mail, in: 5 POSTE
    Mine, in: 4 AMOI
    Mrs., in: 3 MME
    They, in: 3 ILS
    View from: 3 MER
Marsh: 3 FEN
    Author: 5 NGAIO
    bird: 4 RAIL SORA 5 CRAKE
        EGRET HERON SNIPE
    critter: 4 CROC
    duck: 4 TEAL
    gas: 7 METHANE
    Like ~ plants: 5 REEDY
    Louisiana: 5 BAYOU
    material: 4 PEAT
    plant: 4 REED 5 SEDGE
        7 CATTAIL
    wader: 5 EGRET HERON
Marshal: 5 ARRAY
    at Waterloo: 3 NEY
    Field: 3 REF
    of Yugoslavia: 4 TITO
Marshaled: 3 LED
Marshall
    Director: 5 PENNY
Marshall ___: 4 PLAN
Marshall Islands: 6 ATOLLS
Marshland: 3 FEN
Marshmallow
    Chocolate ~ snack: 5 SMORE
    Drink with a: 5 COCOA
    sandwich: 7 MOONPIE
Marshy
    area: 3 FEN
    ground: 6 MORASS
    inlet: 5 BAYOU
Marsupial
    American: 7 OPOSSUM
    Australian: 5 KOALA
        6 WOMBAT
    Comics: 4 POGO

Milne: 3 ROO
Mart
    start: 4 EURO
Martes: 3 DIA
Martha
    Comedienne: 4 RAYE
    successor: 7 ABIGAIL
Martial ___: 4 ARTS
Martial art: 4 JUDO 6 KARATE
        TAICHI
    Japanese: 6 AIKIDO
Martial arts
    degree: 3 DAN
    expert: 5 NINJA
    master: 6 SENSEI
    school: 4 DOJO
"Martial Law"
    actor Hall: 7 ARSENIO
Martian: 5 ALIEN
    feature: 6 ICECAP
    marking: 5 CANAL
    rover: 3 UFO
Martians: 3 ETS
Martin
    Author: 4 AMIS
    Comic: 5 STEVE
    Director: 4 RITT
    of Broadway: 4 MARY
    Partner of: 5 ROWAN
    TV chef: 3 YAN
"Martin"
    actress Campbell: 5 TISHA
"Martin ___": 4 EDEN
___ Martin
    (auto): 5 ASTON
    (cognac): 4 REMY
Martin, Dean
    Home of: 4 OHIO
    subject: 5 AMORE
Martin, Mary
    1966 ~ musical: 6 IDOIDO
Martin, Ricky: 4 IDOL
    Like ~ "vida": 4 LOCA
Martin, Steve
    movie: 7 ALLOFME
    song: 7 KINGTUT
    ~, at the 2001 Oscars:
        5 EMCEE
Martin, ___ Sue
    Actress: 6 PAMELA
Martina
    of tennis: 6 HINGIS
    rival: 4 HANA 6 STEFFI
Martinelli
    Actress: 4 ELSA
Martinez
    of baseball: 4 TINO
    Pitcher: 5 PEDRO
Martinez, Pedro: 3 MET
    stat: 3 ERA
Martini
    garnish: 5 OLIVE
    ingredient: 3 GIN
    Like a James Bond: 6 SHAKEN
    Partner of: 5 ROSSI
    Ruin a James Bond: 4 STIR

Martinique: 3 ILE
    mountain: 5 PELEE
Martinis
    Like some: 3 DRY
Marty
    role: 4 IGOR
"Marty"
    Marty's friend in: 5 ANGIE
Marvel Comics
    founder Lee: 4 STAN
    superhero: 4 THOR
    superheroes: 4 XMEN
Marveled
    aloud: 5 OOHED
Marvin
    Actor: 3 LEE
    Journalist: 4 KALB
    Singer: 4 GAYE
Marvy: 3 FAB
Marx
    A ~ brother: 5 CHICO
        GUMMO HARPO ZEPPO
        7 GROUCHO
    article: 3 DAS 4 EINE
    collaborator: 6 ENGELS
    forte: 3 WIT 8 ONELINER
    Silent: 5 HARPO
    Socialist: 4 KARL
    with a horn: 5 HARPO
Marx, Groucho
    Prop for: 5 CIGAR
Marx Brothers
    Like the: 4 ZANY 5 ANTIC
        6 MADCAP
    mom: 6 MINNIE
Mary
    Actress: 3 URE 5 ASTOR
    and John Jacob: 6 ASTORS
    Fashion designer: 5 QUANT
    Follower of: 4 LAMB
    had a little one: 4 LAMB
    of Peter, Paul, and Mary:
        7 TRAVERS
    Painter: 7 CASSATT
    TV boss of: 3 LOU
Mary ___ (cosmetics): 3 KAY
Mary-Kate: 4 TWIN
    Actress: 5 OLSEN
Mary Kay
    rival: 4 AVON 5 ESTEE
Maryland
    athlete: 4 TERP 8 TERRAPIN
    battle site: 8 ANTIETAM
    pro: 6 ORIOLE
    state bird: 6 ORIOLE
"Mary ___ Little Lamb":
        4 HADA
Mary Lou
    Gymnast: 6 RETTON
"Mary, Mary, Quite Contrary"
    prop: 11 SILVERBELLS
Mary McLeod ___
    Educator: 7 BETHUNE
"Mary Poppins"
    chimney sweep: 4 BERT
Mary Tyler ___: 5 MOORE

**"Mary Tyler Moore Show, The"**
costar: 7 EDASNER
spin-off: 5 RHODA
unseen character: 4 LARS
**Mas**
mates: 3 PAS
**Masc.**
Neither ~ nor fem.: 4 NEUT
Not: 3 FEM
**Mascara**
First name in: 5 ESTEE
target: 4 LASH 7 EYELASH
**Mascot**
MGM: 4 LION
Navy: 4 GOAT
Qantas: 5 KOALA
**Masculine**
side: 4 YANG
**Maserati**
Carmaker: 7 ERNESTO
**"M*A*S*H"**
actor Jamie: 4 FARR
actress Loretta: 4 SWIT
cops: 3 MPS
extra: 5 MEDIC NURSE
Pierce portrayer on: 4 ALDA
procedure: 6 TRIAGE
role: 5 RADAR
    13 HAWKEYEPIERCE
    15 CORPORALKLINGER
setting: 5 KOREA
soda: 4 NEHI
staffers: 3 DRS 4 DOCS
Star of: 8 ASTERISK
vehicle: 4 JEEP
Winchester rank on: 3 MAJ
**Mashburn**
of basketball: 5 JAMAL
**Mashed**
dish: 4 YAMS
**Masher**
Response to a: 4 SLAP
**Mashie:** 4 IRON
**Mask**
feature: 7 EYEHOLE
Kind of: 3 SKI
wearer: 3 UMP 6 GOALIE
**"Mask"**
actor Eric: 6 STOLTZ
actor Stoltz: 4 ERIC
star: 4 CHER
**Masked**
critter: 4 COON
swordsman: 5 ZORRO
**Masks**
Play with: 3 NOH
Sport with: 4 EPEE
**Masochistic**
beginning: 4 SADO
**Mason**
(abbr.): 4 ATTY
Actress: 6 MARSHA
assistant: 6 STREET
burden: 3 HOD
field: 3 LAW
job: 4 CASE

portrayer: 4 BURR
tool: 6 TROWEL
wedge: 4 SHIM
**Mason, James**
1954 ~ role: 4 NEMO
**Masonic**
doorkeeper: 5 TILER
**Masqat**
land: 4 OMAN
___ masque: 3 BAL
**Masquerade:** 3 ACT
item: 6 DOMINO
**Mass:** 3 GOB 4 RITE 5 HORDE
    7 REQUIEM
apparel: 4 ALBS
booklet: 4 ORDO
confusion: 5 CHAOS
declaration: 4 AMEN
departure: 6 EXODUS
figure: 6 PRIEST
Icy: 4 BERG
Knotlike tissue: 4 NODE
language: 5 LATIN
Large land: 4 ASIA 7 EURASIA
music: 4 HYMN
name: 4 JESU
of hair: 3 MOP 4 SHAG
seating: 4 PEWS
segment: 5 CREDO
transit carrier: 3 BUS
unit: 4 GRAM KILO
**Mass.**
neighbor: 4 CONN
Sen. from: 3 EMK
setting: 3 EST
summer hours: 3 EDT
**Massachusetts**
cape: 3 ANN COD
motto opener: 4 ENSE
nickname: 8 BAYSTATE
senator John: 5 KERRY
state tree: 3 ELM
Tip of: 6 ONEILL
university: 5 TUFTS
**Massage:** 3 RUB 5 KNEAD
deeply: 4 ROLF
locale: 3 SPA
Need a: 4 ACHE
Needing a: 4 ACHY 5 TENSE
reaction: 3 AAH
reactions: 3 AHS
target: 5 SCALP 7 TENSION
**Massaged**
It may be: 3 EGO
**Massenet**
Composer: 5 JULES
opera: 5 LECID THAIS
**Masseur/Masseuse**
application: 6 HOTOIL
concern: 9 TENSENESS
employer: 3 SPA
In need of a: 4 SORE
supply: 3 OIL 4 OILS
target: 4 ACHE KNOT
**Massey**
Actress: 5 ILONA

**"Mass in B Minor"**
composer: 4 BACH
**Massive:** 4 HUGE 5 GREAT
**"Mass ___ Minor":** 3 INB
**Mast:** 4 SPAR
pole: 5 SPRIT
support: 4 STAY
Turn, as a: 4 SLUE
**Master:** 3 ACE PRO 4 GURU
    5 SAHIB
anew: 7 RELEARN
Fugue: 4 BACH
Hindu: 5 SWAMI
Judo: 6 SENSEI
Kind of: 3 ZEN
Madras: 5 SAHIB
Mahayana: 4 LAMA
Ring: 3 ALI 7 JEWELER
Scout: 5 TONTO
Web: 6 SPIDER
~, in Hindi: 5 SAHIB
~, in Swahili: 5 BWANA
**"Master Builder, The"**
playwright: 5 IBSEN
**MasterCard**
alternative: 4 VISA
**Masterful:** 5 ADEPT
**"Master Melvin"**
of baseball: 3 OTT
**Masterpiece:** 3 GEM
**"Masterpiece Theatre"**
airer: 3 PBS
**Masters**
1996 ~ winner: 5 FALDO
1997 ~ winner: 5 WOODS
    10 TIGERWOODS
1998 ~ winner: 6 OMEARA
and Jonson: 5 POETS
city: 7 AUGUSTA
holder (abbr.): 3 PGA
Old: 4 OILS
Three-time ~ winner: 5 FALDO
    SNEAD
Two-time ~ winner: 4 SEVE
    15 SEVEBALLESTEROS
**Master's**
follower: 3 PHD
ordeal: 5 ORALS
requirement: 6 THESIS
**Masterson**
Friend of: 4 EARP
weapon: 4 CANE
**Masterstroke:** 4 COUP
**"___ Master's Voice":** 3 HIS
**Masterwork:** 4 OPUS
**Masthead**
title: 6 EDITOR
~ VIPs: 3 EDS
**Mastic:** 5 RESIN
**Masticate:** 4 CHEW
**Mat**
Embroidered: 5 DOILY
Go to the ~, slangily:
    6 RASSLE
Japanese: 6 TATAMI
Lace: 5 DOILY

material: 5 SISAL
Sent to the: 3 KOD
Mata ___: 4 HARI
Matador: 6 TORERO
  Cheer for a: 3 OLE
  foe: 4 TORO 6 ELTORO
  move: 4 PASE
  trophy: 3 EAR
Mata Hari: 3 SPY
Matalin
  Martin and: 5 MARYS
Matamoros
  mister: 5 SENOR
  Mrs., in: 3 SRA
Match: 3 SEE 4 BOUT PAIR
    SYNC TWIN 5 AGREE
    EQUAL
  Don't: 5 CLASH
  ender: 3 TKO
  game: 7 OLDMAID
  Missing a: 3 ODD
  part: 3 SET
  play: 5 ARSON
  Put a ~ to: 3 LIT 6 IGNITE
  Shoving: 4 SUMO
  site: 5 ARENA
  Start a tennis: 5 SERVE
  Tournament: 4 SEMI
Matchbox
  item: 6 TOYCAR
Matched
  Equally: 4 EVEN
  Evenly: 8 ONETOONE
  Half a ~ set: 4 HERS
Matches
  Play with: 6 TENNIS
Matching: 4 SAME TWIN
Matchless: 3 ODD
Matchmaker: 5 CUPID
  Musical: 5 YENTE
  of myth: 4 EROS
  Play ~ for: 5 FIXUP
  Play ~ to: 5 SETUP
Matchstick
  game: 3 NIM
Match-up: 7 PAIRING
Mate: 3 PAL
  assent: 6 AYESIR
  First: 3 EVE 4 ADAM
  greeting: 4 AHOY GDAY
  Madam: 3 SIR
  preceder: 4 SOUL
  Quest for a: 5 CHESS
  Soul: 4 BODY
___ maté (tealike drink):
    5 YERBA
___ Mateo, California: 3 SAN
___ mater: 3 PIA 4 ALMA DURA
"___ Mater": 6 STABAT
Material
  Genetic: 3 DNA RNA
  Net: 4 MESH
  Pat: 4 OLEO
  Raw: 3 ORE
  Soft ball: 4 NERF
  Star: 3 TIN

Sturdy: 5 DENIM
Materialize: 6 APPEAR
Materiel
  Brief: 4 AMMO
Maternally
  related: 5 ENATE
Math
  abbr.: 3 QED
  amts.: 4 LCMS
  calculation: 4 AREA 5 SLOPE
  degree: 3 NTH
  Do the: 3 ADD
  Empty, in: 4 NULL
  groups: 4 SETS
  makes up half of it (abbr.):
    4 PSAT
  Old ~ tool: 9 SLIDERULE
  Ordered group in: 6 NTUPLE
  ratio: 4 SINE
  rings: 4 TORI
  Squiggly ~ symbol: 5 TILDE
  subj.: 3 ALG 4 CALC GEOM
    TRIG
Mathematical
  grouping: 5 COSET
  points: 4 LOCI
  proof letters: 3 QED
  proportion: 5 RATIO
  symbol: 7 NUMERAL
Mathematician
  Blind: 5 EULER
  ~ Blaise: 6 PASCAL
  ~ Charles: 7 BABBAGE
  ~ George: 5 BOOLE
  ~ Leonhard: 5 EULER
  ~ Lovelace: 3 ADA
  ~ Paul: 5 ERDOS
Mathers, Jerry
  role: 6 BEAVER
Mathew
  Photographer: 5 BRADY
Mathis, Johnny
  1959 ~ hit: 5 MISTY
  1962 ~ hit: 4 GINA
"Matilda"
  Wilson of: 4 MARA
Matinee
  hero: 4 IDOL
Matinee ___: 4 IDOL
Mating
  game: 5 CHESS
Matisse
  Painter: 5 HENRI
  pieces: 3 ART
Matriculate: 5 ENROL
    6 ENROLL
Matrimony
  Enter into: 3 WED
"Matrix, The"
  Keanu in: 3 NEO
  Neo in: 5 KEANU
Matson
  of football: 5 OLLIE
Matt
  Actor: 7 LEBLANC
  Former cohost with: 5 KATIE

Internet reporter: 6 DRUDGE
Olympic swimmer: 6 BIONDI
TV host: 5 LAUER
Mattel
  doll: 3 KEN
  game: 3 UNO
Matter: 4 CASE 5 COUNT
  Bit of: 4 ATOM
  Confidential: 6 SECRET
  Court: 3 RES
  Heart of the: 3 NUB 4 CRUX
    MEAT PITH
  In the ~ of: 4 ASTO
  Legal: 3 RES
  Mined-over: 3 ORE
  No ~ what:
    15 COMERAINORSHINE
  of contention: 4 BONE
  Subject: 5 TOPIC
  Will: 6 ESTATE
Matterhorn: 3 ALP
  (abbr.): 3 MTN
"Matter of Fact"
  columnist: 5 ALSOP
Matters: 6 COUNTS
  in dispute: 6 ISSUES
  Mysterious: 6 ARCANA
  PBS: 4 ARTS
Matthau
  Actor: 6 WALTER
Matthew: 7 APOSTLE
  Actor: 5 PERRY 6 MODINE
  Question in: 5 ISITI
  Trio in: 4 MAGI
Mattiace
  Golfer: 3 LEN
Mattingly
  of baseball: 3 DON
Mattress
  Fold-up: 5 FUTON
  maker: 5 SEALY SERTA
  part: 4 COIL
  problem: 3 SAG 4 LUMP
  support: 4 SLAT
  Thin: 5 FUTON
  type: 4 TWIN
Matty
  of baseball: 4 ALOU
Mature: 3 AGE 4 RIPE
    5 ADULT RIPEN
    7 GROWNUP
    9 COMEOFAGE
  For ~ audiences: 6 RATEDR
Matured: 4 GREW 6 GREWUP
Maturing
  agent: 4 AGER
Maturity
  Attain: 5 RIPEN
Matzo
  lack: 5 YEAST
  meal: 5 SEDER
Maude
  portrayer Arthur: 3 BEA
"Maude"
  Maude on: 3 BEA
Maudlin: 5 SAPPY

**Maugham, Somerset**
  heroine: **5** SADIE
  novel: **13** THERAZORSEDGE
  satire: **11** CAKESANDALE
**Maugham, W. ___:**
    **8** SOMERSET
**Maui**
  dance: **4** HULA
  dish: **3** POI
  flier: **4** NENE
  greeting: **5** ALOHA
  music-maker: **3** UKE
  necklace: **3** LEI
  neighbor: **5** LANAI
**Mauna ___: 3** KEA LOA
**Mauna Loa**
  City near: **4** HILO
  flow: **4** LAVA
**Maupin**
  effort: **4** TALE
**Maureen**
  Actress: **5** OHARA
  Columnist: **4** DOWD
**Maurice**
  Actor: **5** EVANS
  Author: **6** SENDAK
  Barry, Robin, and: **5** GIBBS
  Composer: **5** JARRE
  Illustrator: **6** SENDAK
  Nixon Commerce Secretary:
    **5** STANS
  Painter: **7** UTRILLO
**Mauritania**
  Most of: **6** SAHARA
  Neighbor of: **4** MALI
    **7** SENEGAL
**Mauritius**
  Extinct bird of: **4** DODO
**Mausoleum: 4** TOMB
  Ataturk ~ city: **6** ANKARA
**Maven: 3** PRO **4** GURU
  Media:
    **15** MARSHALLMCLUHAN
**Maverick**
  One of the ~ brothers: **4** BART
    BRET
  type: **5** LONER
**"Maverick"**
  Maverick of: **4** BRET
**Mavs**
  The ~ play in it: **3** NBA
**Mawkish: 5** SAPPY SOPPY
  material: **4** CORN
  ___ Mawr: **4** BRYN
**Max**
  Artist: **5** WEBER
  Author: **5** WEBER
  Boxer: **4** BAER
  Buddy, Bugs, or: **4** BAER
  Dadaist: **5** ERNST
  Movie scorer: **7** STEINER
  Surrealist: **5** ERNST
**Max.**
  Opposite of: **3** MIN
**Maxi**
  Opposite of: **4** MINI

**Maxim: 3** SAW **5** ADAGE
    MOTTO TENET
  Russian writer: **5** GORKI
**Maxima**
  maker: **6** NISSAN
  Maximally: **6** ATMOST
**Maximilian**
  Actor: **6** SCHELL
**Maximilian I**
  Realm of ~ (abbr.): **3** HRE
**Maxims**
  Religious: **5** LOGIA
**Maximum: 3** NTH **6** UTMOST
  Reach a: **4** PEAK
**"Maximus Poems, The"**
  author: **5** OLSON
**Maxwell**
  Hostess: **4** ELSA
  Socialite: **4** ELSA
**Maxwell House**
  brand: **5** SANKA
**May**
  April, ~, and June, to Daisy
    Duck: **6** NIECES
  Be that as it: **6** EVENSO
    **9** ATANYRATE
  birthstone: **7** EMERALD
  Director: **6** ELAINE
  event, for short: **4** INDY
  honoree: **3** MOM **6** MOTHER
  in New Jersey: **4** CAPE
  Psychologist: **5** ROLLO
**May 8, 1945: 5** VEDAY
**May 15: 4** IDES
**Maya**
  Architect: **3** LIN
**"Maybe": 6** ILLSEE
**"Maybellene"**
  singer: **5** BERRY
    **10** CHUCKBERRY
**Mayberry**
  aunt: **3** BEE
  Goober or Gomer of: **4** PYLE
  kid: **4** OPIE
  Like: **5** RURAL
  Pyle of: **5** GOMER
  sheriff: **4** ANDY
  tippler: **4** OTIS
**"Mayberry ___": 3** RFD
**Mayday: 3** SOS
**"Mayday!": 3** SOS
**Mayer, Louis B.**
  birthplace: **5** MINSK
**Mayfair**
  It borders: **4** SOHO
  moms: **6** MATERS
**Mayflower**
  employee: **5** MOVER
  pilgrim John: **5** ALDEN
**Mayhem: 5** HAVOC
**"May I have your attention?":**
    **4** AHEM
**"May I help you?": 3** YES
**"May I speak?": 4** AHEM
**Maynard G. ___: 5** KREBS
**"May ___ now?": 3** IGO

**Mayo: 3** MES
  Garlicky: **5** AIOLI
  holder: **3** JAR
  Sandwich with: **3** BLT
  serving: **4** GLOB
**"May ___ of service?": 3** IBE
**Mayonnaise**
  Garlic: **5** AIOLI
**Mayor**
  Canadian: **5** REEVE
  Chicago: **5** DALEY
  Former Cincinnati:
    **13** JERRYSPRINGER
  Former L.A. ~ Sam: **5** YORTY
  Former N.Y.: **6** EDKOCH
    **8** ABEBEAME
  Former N.Y. ~ Abe: **5** BEAME
  Former N.Y. ~ Beame: **3** ABE
  Former N.Y. ~ Ed: **4** KOCH
  Former N.Y. ~ Giuliani:
    **4** RUDY
  Former Philly ~ Wilson:
    **5** GOODE
  L.A. ~ Jim: **4** HAHN
**"Mayor"**
  author: **6** EDKOCH
  author Ed: **4** KOCH
**Mayo to Mayo: 3** ANO
**Maytag**
  rival: **5** AMANA
**Mazar**
  Actress: **4** DEBI
**Mazda**
  model: **5** MIATA
**Maze**
  runner: **3** RAT **6** LABRAT
  solution: **4** PATH
  word: **5** ENTER
**"Mazel ___!": 3** TOV
**"Mazes and Monsters"**
  author Jaffe: **4** RONA
**Mazuma**
  Monterrey: **4** PESO
**MB**
  It is measured in: **3** RAM ROM
**MBA: 3** DEG
  subj.: **4** ECON
**McAn**
  Shoemaker: **4** THOM
**McAn, Thom**
  spec: **3** EEE
**McArdle**
  of Broadway: **6** ANDREA
  role: **5** ANNIE
**McBain, Ed**
  Author Hunter who used the
    pen name: **4** EVAN
**McBeal: 6** LAWYER
  on TV: **4** ALLY
**McCaffrey**
  Sci-fi author: **4** ANNE
**McCain**
  State of ~ (abbr.): **4** ARIZ
  ~, once: **3** POW
**McCann**
  Country singer: **4** LILA

**McCarey**
Director: 3 LEO
**McCarthy**
aide Roy: 4 COHN
quarry: 3 RED 4 REDS
trunkmate: 5 SNERD
**McCarthy, Charlie**
Like: 6 WOODEN
**McCarthy, Joe**
attorney Roy: 4 COHN
**McCarthy-era**
hearings gp.: 4 HUAC
**McCartney, Paul:** 4 BRIT
1982 ~ hit with Stevie Wonder:
13 EBONYANDIVORY
1984 ~ hit: 5 SOBAD
instrument: 4 BASS
title: 3 SIR
**McCarver**
Sportscaster: 3 TIM
**McClanahan**
Actress: 3 RUE
**McClellan**
victory site: 8 ANTIETAM
**McClure**
Actor: 4 DOUG
**McClurg**
Actress: 4 EDIE
**McConaughey, Matthew**
1999 ~ film: 4 EDTV
**McCormack**
Actor: 4 ERIC
**McCormick**
Inventor: 5 CYRUS
**McCorvey, Norma**
alias in a famous court case:
3 ROE
**McCourt, Frank**
book: 3 TIS
Mother of: 6 ANGELA
**McCowen**
Actor: 4 ALEC
**McCoy**
Country singer: 4 NEAL
Hatfield, to a: 3 FOE
5 ENEMY
Jazz pianist: 5 TYNER
**McCoy, Dr.**
nickname: 5 BONES
spray: 4 HYPO
___ McCoy, The: 4 REAL
**McCoys:** 4 CLAN
**McCrea**
Actor: 4 JOEL
**McCullough**
Novelist: 7 COLLEEN
**McDaniel**
Actress: 6 HATTIE
Country singer: 3 MEL
**McDonald's**
arches: 4 LOGO
clown: 6 RONALD
equipment: 6 FRYERS
founder: 7 RAYKROC
founder Kroc: 3 RAY
founder Ray: 4 KROC

freebie: 6 CATSUP
order: 4 TOGO
symbol: 6 ARCHES
**McDonough**
Actor: 4 NEAL
**McDowall**
Actor: 5 RODDY
**McEnroe**
foe: 4 BORG 5 LENDL
**McEntire**
Country singer: 4 REBA
**McEwan**
Author: 3 IAN
**McFuzz, Gertrude**
creator: 5 SEUSS
**McGee**
Principal ~ portrayer:
8 EVEARDEN
**McGraw**
Actress: 7 MELINDA
Country singer: 3 TIM
of baseball: 3 TUG
**McGregor**
Actor: 4 EWAN
**McGrew**
Service's: 3 DAN
**McGuire Air Force Base**
Fort near: 3 DIX
**McGwire, Mark**
cap monogram: 3 STL
home run rival: 4 SOSA
speciality: 5 HOMER
stat (abbr.): 3 HRS
stats: 4 RBIS
**McHenry:** 4 FORT
and others (abbr.): 3 FTS
**McIntosh:** 5 APPLE
alternative: 7 WINESAP
**McKellen**
Actor: 3 IAN
**McKenna**
Folk singer: 4 LORI
**McKenzie**
Series set at ~, Brackman, et
al.: 5 LALAW
**McKinley**
and others (abbr.): 3 MTS
Mount: 6 DENALI
Mrs.: 3 IDA
Ohio birthplace of: 5 NILES
**McKinney**
Olympic skier: 6 TAMARA
**McKuen**
Poet: 3 ROD
**McLachlan**
Pop singer: 5 SARAH
**McLachlan, Sarah**
hit: 4 ADIA
**McLain**
of baseball: 5 DENNY
**McLean**
Singer: 3 DON
"___ McLean" (Owen Wister
novel): 3 LIN
**McLean, Don**
song: 11 AMERICANPIE

**McLean, VA**
Group based in: 3 CIA
**McLuhan**
study: 5 MEDIA
**McMahon**
and others: 3 EDS
**McMillan**
of basketball: 4 NATE
Writer: 5 TERRY
**McMuffin**
ingredient: 3 EGG
**McMurtry**
Film based on a ~ novel:
3 HUD
**McNally**
Partner of: 4 RAND
**McPherson**
Evangelist: 5 AIMEE
**"McQ"**
first name: 3 LON
**McQueen**
Actor: 4 CHAD 5 STEVE
**McQueen, Steve**
First movie starring:
7 THEBLOB
**McShane**
Actor: 3 IAN
**"McSorley's Bar"**
painter: 5 SLOAN
**M.D.:** 4 PHYS
ASAP, to an: 4 STAT
Date with an: 4 APPT
Family ~ (plural): 3 GPS
measures: 3 CCS
order: 3 MRI 6 CTSCAN
org.: 3 AMA
speciality: 3 ENT
wall hanging: 3 DEG
workplaces: 3 ERS ORS
**Md.**
neighbor: 3 DEL
**Mdse.:** 3 GDS
Flawed, as: 3 IRR
**Me**
It's all about: 6 EGOISM
7 EGOTISM
To ~, in French: 4 AMOI
~, in French: 3 MOI
~, myself, and I: 3 EGO
"___ me!": 5 WOEIS
"___ me?": 4 ISIT
**Mea ___:** 5 CULPA
**Mead**
base: 5 HONEY
research site: 5 SAMOA
subject: 5 SAMOA
**Mead, Margaret**
Island studied by: 5 SAMOA
subject: 6 SAMOAN
**Meadow:** 3 LEA
Like a: 6 GRASSY
mother: 3 EWE
mouse: 4 VOLE
sound: 3 BAA MAA
**Meadowlands**
pace: 4 TROT

**team:** 4 NETS
**Meadowlark**
  kin: 6 ORIOLE
**Meadowsweet:** 6 SPIREA
**Meager:** 4 SLIM 5 SCANT
    6 SCANTY SPARSE
  Not: 5 AMPLE
**Meagerly**
  maintain, with "out": 3 EKE
**Meal:** 6 REPAST
  Army: 4 MESS
  Carbo-loading: 5 PASTA
  Crusty: 6 POTPIE
  Exodus: 5 SEDER
  Gave a ~ to: 3 FED
  GI: 7 CRATION
  Had a home-cooked: 5 ATEIN
  Have a: 3 EAT SUP 4 DINE
  in a pot: 4 STEW
  in a shell: 4 TACO
  Kind of: 3 OAT
  Light: 5 SALAD
  Major: 5 FEAST
  Military: 4 MESS
  on a stick: 5 KABOB
  One-dish: 4 STEW
  Passover: 5 SEDER
  starter: 3 OAT 5 SALAD
  When repeated, a kid's: 3 DIN
**Meals**
  Eat between: 4 NOSH
    5 SNACK
**Mean:** 3 LOW 5 CRUEL NASTY
    6 DENOTE INTEND
    ORNERY STINGY
  Didn't ~ to tell: 7 LETSLIP
  dude: 4 OGRE
  It makes men: 3 ANA
  mien: 5 SNEER
  mood: 4 SNIT
  mutt: 3 CUR
  What little things: 4 ALOT
**"Me and Bobby ___":** 5 MCGEE
**Meander:** 3 GAD 4 ROAM ROVE
    WIND 5 AMBLE STRAY
    6 RAMBLE
**Meandering**
  curve: 3 ESS
**Meanie:** 4 OGRE
  face: 5 SCOWL
  Fairy tale: 4 OGRE
    10 STEPSISTER
**Meaning:** 5 SENSE 6 INTENT
  Full of: 4 DEEP
  General: 4 GIST
  Give the ~ of: 6 DEFINE
  Shade of: 6 NUANCE
**Meaningless**
  talk: 4 JIVE
**Meanness**
  Symbol of: 11 JUNKYARDDOG
**Means:** 4 MODE 6 AVENUE
  By ~ of: 3 PER VIA
  justifiers: 4 ENDS
  of access: 6 AVENUE
  of approach: 6 ACCESS

of control: 4 REIN
of enlightenment: 3 ZEN
of support: 3 BRA
Partner of: 4 WAYS
Without ~ of support:
    7 BRALESS
**Mean-spirited:** 5 NASTY SNIDE
    6 ORNERY
**Meantime:** 7 INTERIM
**Meany**
  Fairy tale: 4 OGRE
  Irving's: 4 OWEN
**Meara**
  Comic: 4 ANNE
  Partner of: 7 STILLER
**Measles**
  Like: 5 VIRAL
**Measly:** 4 MERE
  amount: 3 SOU
**Measure:** 3 ACT 4 METE STEP
    5 GAUGE 6 AMOUNT
  AC: 3 BTU
  Biblical: 5 CUBIT
  Blood: 4 UNIT
  Cordwood: 5 STERE
  Current: 6 AMPERE
  Econ.: 3 GNP
  Electrical: 3 AMP OHM 4 VOLT
  Energy: 3 ERG
  Gold: 5 KARAT
  Heavy: 3 TON
  Jeweler: 5 KARAT
  Land: 4 ACRE
  LP: 3 RPM
  Mariner's: 7 SEAMILE
  Memory: 4 BYTE
  metal: 5 ASSAY
  Metric: 3 ARE 4 KILO 5 LITER
  Musical: 3 BAR
  of conductance: 3 MHO
  of purity: 5 KARAT
  on foot: 4 PACE
  (out): 4 METE
  Paper: 4 REAM
  Petrol: 5 LITRE
  Prevention: 5 OUNCE
  Wire: 3 MIL
**"Measure for Measure"**
  heroine: 8 ISABELLA
  villain: 6 ANGELO
**Measurement**
  Middle: 5 WAIST
  of work: 3 ERG
  Pants: 6 INSEAM
  Wing: 4 SPAN
**Measurements**
  IV: 3 CCS
  Recipe ~ (abbr.): 4 TSPS
**Measurer**
  Brainpower: 6 IQTEST
  Current: 7 AMMETER
  RPM: 4 TACH
  Thickness: 7 CALIPER
**Measures**
  Liq.: 3 PTS QTS
  Mensa: 3 IQS

Printer's: 3 EMS ENS
Take: 3 ACT
**"Measure twice, cut ___":**
    4 ONCE
**Measuring**
  device: 4 TAPE 5 GAUGE
    SIZER
  instrument: 5 METER
**Meat:** 4 GIST
  and potatoes: 4 FOOD
  avoider: 5 VEGAN
  Breakfast: 3 HAM 5 BACON
  Calf: 4 VEAL
  Canned: 4 SPAM
  Cutlet: 4 VEAL
  Cut of: 4 LOIN 5 ROAST
    SHANK
  Deli: 3 HAM 6 SALAMI
  dish: 7 ROULADE
  filled treat: 4 TACO
  garnish: 5 ASPIC
  Gyro: 4 LAMB
  Hunk of: 4 SLAB
  inspection inits.: 4 USDA
  It does ~ to a turn:
    10 ROTISSERIE
  Like some: 4 LEAN
  locker, for example: 4 AGER
  Low-fat: 3 EMU 7 BEEFALO
  Lunch: 3 HAM
  marking: 4 USDA
  pie: 5 PASTY
  substitute: 5 TOFU
  The other white: 4 PORK
  Treat: 4 CORN CURE
**Meat-and-potatoes:** 5 BASIC
**Meathead:** 3 OAF
  Father-in-law of: 6 ARCHIE
  Mother-in-law of: 5 EDITH
  player: 6 REINER
**Meat-rating**
  org.: 4 USDA
**Mecca**
  Gambler's: 4 RENO 6 CASINO
  Indian: 4 AGRA
  Journey to: 4 HADJ HAJJ
  native: 4 ARAB 5 SAUDI
  Pilgrimage to: 4 HADJ HAJJ
  Pilgrim to: 5 HAJJI 6 MOSLEM
    MUSLIM
  Shopping: 4 MALL
  Ski: 4 ALPS 5 ASPEN
  Surfing: 4 OAHU 7 WAIKIKI
**Mechanic**
  Part of a ~ bill: 5 LABOR
  prefix: 4 AERO
  service: 4 LUBE
  tool: 9 GREASEGUN
**Mechanical**
  learning: 4 ROTE
  man: 5 ROBOT
  method: 4 ROTE
  Slangy prefix meaning: 4 ROBO
**Mechanism**
  Control: 5 SERVO
  Defense: 6 DENIAL

Watch: 6 DETENT

**Med**
school subj.: 4 ANAT

**Med.**
Bigger than: 3 LRG
care option: 3 HMO
country: 3 ISR LEB SYR
course: 4 ANAT
diagnostic tool: 3 EEG
drama sets: 3 ERS
people: 3 DRS RNS
plan: 3 HMO
readout: 3 EKG
research funder: 3 NIH
specialty: 3 ENT GYN
test: 3 MRI

**Medal:** 5 HONOR
Fail to: 4 LOSE
giver: 7 HONORER
Mil.: 3 DSC DSO
recipient: 4 HERO
U.K.: 3 OBE
U.S. Army: 3 DSC
Winning: 4 GOLD
worthy behavior: 5 VALOR

**Medalist**
1984 and 1988 skating ~:
4 WITT
1984 skiing ~: 5 MAHRE
1988 swimming ~ Kristin:
4 OTTO
Four-time Olympic discus:
6 OERTER
Gold ~ Lipinski: 4 TARA
Gold ~ skater Michelle:
4 KWAN
Gold ~ skier Hermann:
5 MAIER
Gold ~ skier Phil: 5 MAHRE
Gold ~ skier Tommy: 3 MOE
Three-time skating: 5 HENIE
Two-time 1500-meter gold:
3 COE

**Medallion**
site: 3 CAB 4 TAXI

**"Medallion, The"**
star: 4 CHAN

**Meddle:** 3 PRY 5 SNOOP
(with): 4 MESS

**Meddler:** 5 SNOOP YENTA

**Meddlesome:** 4 NOSY 5 NOSEY
sort: 5 YENTA

**Medea**
rode on it: 4 ARGO

**Medevac**
destinations: 3 ERS

**Medgar**
Civil rights leader: 5 EVERS

**Media**
Alternative ~ magazine:
4 UTNE
attention: 3 INK
exec Roger: 5 AILES
gadfly Huffington: 7 ARIANNA
Govt. ~ watchdog: 3 FCC
law topic: 5 LIBEL

maven:
15 MARSHALLMCLUHAN
Modern music: 3 CDS
mogul Turner: 3 TED
Noted ~ merger:
10 TIMEWARNER
Print: 5 PRESS
Toronto ~ inits.: 3 CBS
workers' union: 5 AFTRA

**Media ___:** 5 EVENT

**Mediate**
Golfer: 5 ROCCO

**Mediator**
Freudian: 3 EGO
skill: 4 TACT

**Medic:** 3 DOC
prefix: 4 PARA
treatment: 8 FIRSTAID

**Medical**
advice, often: 4 REST
amount: 4 DOSE
beam: 5 LASER
breakthrough: 4 CURE
British ~ journal: 6 LANCET
care gp.: 3 HMO
disappointment: 7 RELAPSE
facility: 6 CLINIC
Govt. ~ agency: 3 NIH
image: 4 SCAN
picture: 4 XRAY
plan, briefly: 3 HMO
prefix: 5 OSTEO
procedure: 4 TEST
research agcy.: 3 NIH
resident: 6 INTERN
staffer: 6 INTERN
suffix: 3 ESE OMA 4 ITIS OSIS
supply: 5 SERUM
test: 4 SCAN
wiper: 4 SWAB

**"Medical Center"**
star: 7 EVERETT
11 CHADEVERETT

**Medicare**
org.: 3 SSA

**Medicate:** 4 DOSE

**Medication**
for anxiety: 6 VALIUM
How most ~ is taken:
6 ORALLY
Sleep: 6 OPIATE

**Medicinal**
amount: 4 DOSE 6 DOSAGE
amt.: 3 TSP
fluids: 4 SERA
form: 4 PILL
herb: 5 SENNA
juice: 4 ALOE
plant: 4 ALOE HERB
5 SENNA
shrub: 5 SENNA 6 CASSIA
syrup: 6 IPECAC

**Medicine**
Amount of: 4 DOSE
bottle: 4 VIAL
cabinet item: 4 QTIP

holder: 7 CAPSULE
Like some: 4 ORAL
man: 6 HEALER SHAMAN
show product: 6 ELIXIR
Soothing: 7 NERVINE
yielding legume: 5 SENNA

**Medicine Nobelist:** *see pages*
*732–733*
~ Metchnikoff: 4 ELIE

**Medico:** 3 DOC

**Medieval**
catapult: 6 ONAGER
chest: 4 ARCA
contest: 4 TILT
defense: 4 MOAT
guild: 5 HANSA HANSE
helmet: 5 ARMET
Hero of ~ romances:
6 ROLAND
laborer: 4 ESNE SERF
weapon: 6 POLEAX
7 POLEAXE 8 CROSSBOW

**Medina**
resident: 4 ARAB

**Mediocre:** 4 BLAH SOSO
mark: 3 CEE
writer: 4 HACK

**Medit.**
country: 3 ISR

**Meditate:** 4 MUSE

**Meditation**
sounds: 3 OMS
system: 3 ZEN 4 YOGA

**Meditative**
discipline: 3 ZEN
sect: 3 ZEN
sounds: 3 OMS

**Meditator:** 4 YOGI

**Mediterranean**
Arm of the: 6 AEGEAN
8 ADRIATIC
Canal to the: 4 SUEZ
capital: 5 TUNIS 7 NICOSIA
feeder: 4 NILE 5 RHONE
fruit: 3 FIG
island: 5 MALTA 7 MINORCA
Largest ~ island: 6 SICILY
port: 4 GAZA ORAN
resort: 7 RIVIERA
Spanish river to the: 4 EBRO
tourist destination: 5 IBIZA

**Méditerranée:** 3 MER

**Medium:** 4 SEER SIZE SOSO
7 PSYCHIC
board: 5 OUIJA
distance run: 4 TENK
grade: 3 CEE
meeting: 6 SEANCE
range missile: 4 THOR
setting: 6 ORACLE
sized sofa: 6 SETTEE
skill: 3 ESP

**Medley:** 4 OLIO

**Médoc:** 3 RED 4 WINE

**"___ me down to rest me" (old**
**prayer start):** 4 ILAY

**Medulla**
place: 9 BRAINSTEM
**Medusa**
Snake, to: 5 TRESS
transformer: 6 ATHENA
**Meek**
Comics partner of: 3 EEK
one: 4 LAMB
**Meeny**
preceder: 4 EENY
**Meerschaum:** 4 PIPE
part: 4 STEM
**Meese**
and others: 3 EDS
**Meet:** 3 APT FIT SIT
6 RISETO
component: 4 RACE 5 EVENT
head-on: 4 FACE
in Las Vegas: 3 SEE
in poker: 3 SEE
Kind of: 4 SWAP
One you might not want to:
5 MAKER
people: 6 RACERS
They ~ at a center: 5 RADII
Tries not to: 6 AVOIDS
Where roads ~ (abbr.): 3 JCT
with: 3 SEE
~, as expectations: 6 RISETO
**Meeting:** 7 SESSION
1945 ~ site: 5 YALTA
Ancient ~ place: 4 STOA
5 AGORA
Big ~ (abbr.): 4 CONF
Cong.: 4 SESS
Hold a: 3 SIT
Kind of: 3 PTA 6 SUMMIT
leader: 5 CHAIR
Lovers': 5 TRYST
Medium: 6 SEANCE
minimum: 6 QUORUM
of the minds: 3 ESP
outline: 6 AGENDA
plan: 6 AGENDA
Propose at a: 4 MOVE
Public: 5 FORUM
Secret: 5 TRYST
Short: 4 SESS
Speak at a:
12 TAKETHEFLOOR
**Meetings**
Formal: 8 SYMPOSIA
Pregame: 10 PEPRALLIES
Town: 4 FORA
**"Meet Joe Black"**
actor: 4 PITT
**"Meet John Doe"**
director: 5 CAPRA
**"Meet Me ___ Louis":** 4 INST
**"Meet the Parents"**
actress Polo: 4 TERI
**"Meet the Press"**
host Russert: 3 TIM
**"Mefistofele":** 5 BASSO
composer: 5 BOITO
role: 5 ELENA

**Meg**
Actress: 4 RYAN 5 TILLY
Sibling of: 3 AMY 4 BETH
**Mega**
follower: 4 BYTE
**Megacorporation:** 5 GIANT
**Megalomaniac:** 6 MADMAN
**Megaphone**
Crooner with a: 6 VALLEE
Shaped like a: 5 CONIC
**Mehitabel**
Pal of: 5 ARCHY
**Mehta**
Conductor: 5 ZUBIN
**Meir:** 7 ISRAELI
Foreign minister under:
4 EBAN
of Israel: 5 GOLDA
successor: 5 RABIN
**Mei Xiang:** 5 PANDA
**Mekong**
nation: 4 LAOS
native: 3 LAO 7 LAOTIAN
**Mel**
Giant: 3 OTT
of baseball: 3 OTT
of many voices: 5 BLANC
Singer: 5 TORME
**Melancholy:** 3 SAD 6 SOMBER
poem: 5 ELEGY
**"___ Melancholy" (Keats work):**
5 ODEON
**Mélange:** 4 OLIO 8 MIXEDBAG
**Melba**
of peaches and toast: 6 NELLIE
**___ Melba:** 5 PEACH
**Melba, Nellie**
title: 4 DAME
**Meld**
40-point ~: 8 PINOCHLE
**Melee**
memento: 4 SCAR
**Mello ___ (Coca-Cola brand):**
5 YELLO
**Mellon:** 6 ANDREW
**Mellow:** 3 AGE
More: 5 RIPER
**Mellower**
Got: 4 AGED
**Melmac**
alien: 3 ALF
**Melodic:** 5 TONAL 6 ARIOSE
ARIOSO
passage: 6 ARIOSO
pieces: 6 ARIOSI
syllable: 3 TRA
~ Mel: 5 TORME
**___ Melodies (old cartoons):**
6 MERRIE
**Melodious:** 6 ARIOSE ARIOSO
singer: 4 WREN
~ Horne: 4 LENA
**Melodrama**
Exaggerated:
15 BLOODANDTHUNDER
Musical: 5 OPERA

**Melodramatic:** 5 SOAPY
SUDSY
cry: 4 ALAS
Get: 5 EMOTE
**Melody:** 3 AIR 4 TUNE
Airy: 4 LILT
Diva's: 4 ARIA
Hindu: 4 RAGA
Light: 4 LILT 6 ARIOSO
Little: 7 ARIETTA
Recurring: 5 MOTIF THEMA
**Melon**
Kind of: 6 CASABA
8 HONEYDEW
Winter: 6 CASABA
**Melonlike**
fruit: 5 PAPAW 6 PAPAYA
**Melpomene**
Sister of: 5 ERATO
**"Melrose Place"**
actor Andrew: 4 SHUE
actor Rob: 5 ESTES
role: 6 AMANDA
**Mel's:** 5 DINER
**Mel's Diner**
Waitress at: 3 FLO 4 VERA
5 ALICE
**Melt:** 4 THAW 5 DEICE
down: 6 RENDER
ingredient: 4 TUNA
It can ~ in your mouth:
4 OLEO
together: 4 FUSE
**Meltdown**
site: 4 CORE
victim of myth: 6 ICARUS
**Melted**
glace: 3 EAU
**Melter**
Ice: 4 SALT
**Mel-Tones**
leader: 5 TORME
**Melville**
Author: 6 HERMAN
captain: 4 AHAB
hero: 4 BUDD 9 BILLYBUDD
novel: 4 OMOO 5 TYPEE
**Melvin**
Attorney: 5 BELLI
**Mem.**
Bar: 3 ATT
Family: 3 REL
House: 3 REP
**Member**
Become a: 4 JOIN 5 ENROL
Influential: 5 ELDER
**Membership**
charge: 3 FEE
Exchange: 4 SEAT
fees: 4 DUES
Take out: 5 ENROL
**Membrane**
Eye: 6 SCLERA
Pass through a: 6 OSMOSE
**Membranes**
Of lung: 7 PLEURAL

**Memento:** 5 RELIC TOKEN
    8 KEEPSAKE
  Battle: 4 SCAR
  Historical: 5 RELIC
  Scuffle: 6 FATLIP
**Memnon**
  Mother of: 3 EOS
**Memo:** 4 NOTE
  abbr.: 4 ATTN
  Debt: 3 IOU
  directive: 4 ASAP
  heading: 4 ATTN
  opener: 4 INRE 5 ASPER
  phrase: 4 ASTO INRE
**Memorable:** 6 OFNOTE
    9 REDLETTER
  time: 3 ERA 5 EPOCH
**Memorial**
  column: 4 OBIT
  marker: 5 STELE
  Stone: 5 CAIRN
**Memorial Day**
  event: 4 INDY
  setting: 3 MAY
  solo: 4 TAPS
**Memories**
  Place for: 4 LANE
**"Memories Are Made of ___":**
  4 THIS
**Memorization:** 4 ROTE
**Memorize:** 5 LEARN
**Memorized**
  Have: 4 KNOW
**Memory:** 6 RECALL
  failure: 5 LAPSE
  Having a good:
    9 RETENTIVE
  Loss of: 7 AMNESIA
  Nudge the: 3 JOG
  Remove from: 5 ERASE
  Speak from: 6 RECITE
  trace: 6 ENGRAM
  unit: 3 MEG 4 BYTE
**"Memory"**
  musical: 4 CATS
**Memphis**
  home (abbr.): 4 TENN
  locale: 5 EGYPT
  middle name: 4 ARON
  Opera that opens in: 4 AIDA
  Sight in: 4 NILE
  street: 5 BEALE
**Memsahib**
  nurse: 4 AMAH
**"Me, myself ___":** 4 ANDI
**"Me, Myself & ___"** (Jim Carrey
  flick): 5 IRENE
**Men:** 3 HES 4 SIRS 5 MALES
  behaving badly: 4 CADS
  Con: 5 ANTIS
  Family: 3 PAS 4 DADS
  For ~ only: 4 STAG
  Holy ~ (abbr.): 3 STS
  It makes ~ mean: 3 ANA
  Little green: 3 ETS 6 ALIENS
  Main: 4 TARS

of La Mancha: 6 SENORS
Org. for young: 3 BSA
or women: 6 PLURAL
She turned ~ into swine:
  5 CIRCE
Wise: 4 MAGI 5 SAGES
Young: 4 LADS
**___ Men ("Who Let the Dogs**
  **Out" band):** 4 BAHA
**"___ Men" ("Kiss Me, Kate"**
  **tune):** 5 IHATE
**Menace:** 6 THREAT
  African: 3 ASP 6 TSETSE
  Marine: 4 ORCA
  Mariner: 3 FOG
  Meteorological: 6 ELNINO
  Toothy: 4 CROC
  WWII: 5 UBOAT
**Menachem**
  co-Nobelist of: 5 ANWAR
**Menacing:** 7 OMINOUS
  look: 5 GLARE
**Menagerie:** 3 ZOO
**Mend:** 3 FIX 4 DARN HEAL
    TAPE
  a dress: 5 REHEM
  again: 5 RESEW 6 REHEAL
  Be on the: 4 HEAL
**Mendel**
  Botanist: 6 GREGOR
  subject: 3 PEA
**Mendelssohn**
  Key of ~ Symphony No. 3:
    6 AMINOR
  oratorio: 6 ELIJAH
**Mendes**
  Actress: 3 EVA
  of the bossa nova: 6 SERGIO
**Mendicant**
  Money for: 4 ALMS
  moniker: 3 FRA
**"Me neither":** 4 NORI
**Menelaus**
  Realm of: 6 SPARTA
  Wife of: 5 HELEN
**"Mene, mene, ___, upharsin":**
  5 TEKEL
**"Men ___ From Mars, ...":**
  3 ARE
**Menial:** 4 PEON 6 FLUNKY
**"... men in ___":** 4 ATUB
**Menjou**
  Actor: 7 ADOLPHE
**Menken**
  1860s actress ~: 4 ADAH
**Menlo Park**
  middle name: 4 ALVA
  monogram: 3 TAE
  name: 6 EDISON
**Mennonite**
  group: 5 AMISH
**Meno ___ (less rapid):** 5 MOSSO
**Men-only:** 4 STAG
**Menotti**
  Composer: 4 GIAN
  title character: 5 AMAHL

**Mens ___ (criminal intent):**
  3 REA
**Mensa**
  data: 3 IQS
  Eligible for: 5 SMART
  Hardly ~ material: 5 DENSE
  hurdle: 6 IQTEST
**Menswear**
  brand: 4 IZOD
**Mental**
  acuity: 4 WITS
  flash: 4 IDEA
  fog: 4 DAZE
  grasp: 6 UPTAKE
  picture: 4 IDEA 5 IMAGE
  pictures: 7 IMAGERY
  quickness: 3 WIT
**Mentalist**
  claim: 3 ESP
  ~ Geller: 3 URI
**Mentality**
  Kind of: 5 SIEGE
**Mentally**
  quick: 5 AGILE
  twisted: 4 SICK
**Menth-**
  suffix: 3 ENE
**Mention:** 4 CITE 7 REFERTO
  Fail to: 4 OMIT
  Make ~ of: 4 NOTE
  Not to: 3 AND 4 ALSO PLUS
    8 LETALONE
  Passing: 4 OBIT
**Mentioned:** 4 SAID
  prefix: 5 AFORE
**Mentioning**
  Worth: 6 OFNOTE
**Mentor:** 4 GURU
  One under a: 7 PROTEGE
**Menu:** 5 CARTE
  Bistro: 5 CARTE
  Chinese ~ general: 3 TSO
  Chinese ~ letters: 3 MSG
  Chinese ~ phrase: 5 NOMSG
  heading: 7 ENTREES
    8 ALACARTE
  Japanese ~ item: 7 SASHIMI
    8 TERIYAKI
  option: 4 SAVE UNDO
  Phone ~ imperative: 5 PRESS
  phrase: 3 ALA 8 ALACARTE
  pick: 6 ENTREE
  Pick from the: 5 ORDER
**Menuhin**
  Violinist: 6 YEHUDI
**Méphistophélès**
  player: 5 BASSO
**Mer**
  contents: 3 EAU
  sight: 3 ILE
**Mercator**
  creation: 3 MAP
**Mercedes**
  rival: 3 BMW 4 AUDI
**Mercedes-___:** 4 BENZ
**Mercenary:** 5 VENAL

Japanese: 5 NINJA
Revolutionary: 7 HESSIAN
**Mercer**
Singer: 5 MABEL
**Merchandise:** 5 GOODS WARES
booth: 5 STALL
Stocking: 4 TOYS
~ ID: 3 UPC
**Merchant:** 6 SELLER
8 RETAILER
Food: 6 GROCER
Large ~ ship: 6 ARGOSY
Mail order: 6 LLBEAN
NYC ~ Horace: 4 SAKS
of music: 7 NATALIE
Online: 7 ETAILER
vessel officer: 5 BOSUN
vessel officer, briefly: 4 BOSN
**"Merchant of Venice, The"**
heroine: 6 PORTIA
title character: 7 ANTONIO
**Merci**
relative: 5 DANKE
**Merciless:** 5 CRUEL
one: 4 MING
**Mercilessly**
Tease: 4 RIDE
**Mercredi**
Day after: 5 JEUDI
**"Mercure"**
composer: 5 SATIE
**Mercury:** 5 METAL
model: 5 SABLE
org.: 4 NASA
or Saturn: 3 CAR GOD 4 AUTO
5 DEITY
**Mercutio**
Friend of: 5 ROMEO
Queen described by: 3 MAB
**Mercy**
Have ~ on: 5 SPARE
Mother of: 6 TERESA
Show: 5 SPARE
**Mercyhurst College**
site: 4 ERIE
**"... mercy on such ___": Kipling:**
4 ASWE
**Mere:** 4 POND 5 SCANT
No ~ spectator: 4 DOER
taste: 3 SIP
**Mère**
sibling: 5 ONCLE
**Merely:** 4 ONLY
**Merganser:** 4 SMEW
**Merge:** 5 UNITE
**Merged**
It ~ into Verizon: 3 GTE
It ~ with BP: 5 AMOCO
It ~ with Exxon: 5 MOBIL
It ~ with GE: 3 RCA
It ~ with Mobil: 5 EXXON
It ~ with Time Warner: 3 AOL
news agency: 4 TASS
**Merger:** 5 UNION
1955 ~: 3 AFL CIO
1998 ~: 5 AMOCO

2001 ~: 3 AOL
agreement: 3 IDO
Form a secret: 5 ELOPE
Have a: 3 WED
Media: 10 TIMEWARNER
**Mérida**
Mrs., in: 3 SRA
**Meridian:** 4 ACME
Hrs. on the 90th: 3 CST
___ meridiem: 4 ANTE
**Meringue**
ingredient: 8 EGGWHITE
**Merino**
coat: 4 WOOL
mama: 3 EWE
**Merit:** 4 EARN RATE
7 DESERVE
**Merit badge**
holder: 4 SASH
org.: 3 BSA
**Merkel**
Actress: 3 UNA
**Merle**
Actress: 6 OBERON
**Merlin:** 4 MAGE SEER
Actor: 5 OLSEN
of football: 5 OLSEN
Sportscaster: 5 OLSEN
**Merlot:** 3 RED 7 REDWINE
**Mermaid**
Disney: 5 ARIEL
feature: 4 TAIL
habitat: 3 SEA
movie: 6 SPLASH
**Merman**
Singer: 5 ETHEL
**Merrick**
Half a ~ musical: 3 IDO
**Merrie**
follower: 4 OLDE
**Merrill**
Actress: 4 DINA
**Merrily**
Play: 6 CAVORT
**"Merrily, we roll ___": 5 ALONG**
**Merrimack**
City on the: 6 NASHUA
**Merriment:** 4 GLEE
Full of: 6 JOCOSE
**Merry:** 3 GAY 4 GLAD
Make: 5 ELATE REVEL
month: 3 MAY
prank: 4 JEST
~, in Basque: 4 ALAI
**"Merry Company"**
artist: 5 STEEN
**"Merry Drinker, The"**
painter: 4 HALS
**Merry-go-round**
figure, to a kid: 5 HORSY
music: 4 LILT
**"Merry Widow, The"**
composer: 5 LEHAR
role: 5 SONIA
**Mertz**
Ethel: 8 LANDLADY

Mrs.: 5 ETHEL
Ricardo, to: 6 TENANT
**Meryl**
1982 ~ role: 6 SOPHIE
Actress: 6 STREEP
**Mes**
Primero: 5 ENERO
**Mesa**
dweller: 4 HOPI
Small: 5 BUTTE
**Mesa ___:** 5 VERDE
**Mesabi Range**
find: 3 ORE 7 IRONORE
___ Mesa, California: 5 COSTA
**Mescal**
source: 5 AGAVE
**Mescaline**
source: 6 PEYOTE
**Meses**
12 ~: 3 ANO
**Mesh:** 5 AGREE FITIN
It's a: 3 NET WEB
Like: 5 NETTY
Resembling: 7 NETLIKE
~, as gears: 6 ENGAGE
**Meshed**
land: 4 IRAN
resident: 5 IRANI
**Meshuga:** 6 INSANE
**Mesmerized:** 4 RAPT 6 ENRAPT
9 INATRANCE
**Mesopotamia**
today: 4 IRAQ
**Mesopotamian**
city: 6 EDESSA
ruler: 6 SARGON
**Mesozoic:** 3 ERA
**Mess**
Big: 5 SNAFU
hall mess: 4 SLOP
It's a: 3 STY
Make a ~ of: 4 RUIN
6 FOULUP
maker: 5 SLOB
One in a: 5 EATER
place: 4 HALL
Stuck in a: 4 ONKP
up: 3 ERR 4 FLUB 5 BOTCH
MISDO SPOIL 6 BLOWIT
Went to: 3 ATE
**Mess ___:** 3 KIT
**Message**
board: 5 OUIJA
Brief: 4 NOTE
Coded: 6 CIPHER
Computer: 5 EMAIL
Error: 4 OOPS
Get the: 3 SEE
Got the: 5 HEARD
in a bottle: 3 SOS
Kind of: 5 ERROR
Newsgroup: 4 POST
Office: 4 MEMO
Short Internet: 5 ENOTE
starter: 4 INRE
White flag: 5 TRUCE

**___ message:** 5 SENDA
**Messages**
Pitched: 3 ADS
**Messenger**
Genetic: 3 RNA
Official: 6 HERALD
**Messenger ___:** 3 RNA
**Messiah**
Muslim: 5 MAHDI
**"Messiah":** 8 ORATORIO
composer: 6 HANDEL
**Messina**
Sight from: 4 ETNA
**Messing**
Actress: 5 DEBRA
**Messy**
dresser: 4 SLOB
Less: 6 NEATER
mass: 4 GLOB
place: 3 STY
situation: 5 SNAFU
**Mesta**
Hostess: 5 PERLE
Perle: 7 HOSTESS
**Met:** 3 SAT 4 NLER 7 RANINTO
8 CONVENED
display: 3 ART
expectations: 5 ARIAS
6 OPERAS
He debuted at the ~ in 1903:
6 CARUSO
James of the: 6 LEVINE
offering: 4 ARIA 5 OPERA
solo: 4 ARIA
Some ~ stars: 6 TENORS
squarely: 5 FACED
star: 4 DIVA
**Metabolism**
Kind of: 5 BASAL
**Metal**
bar: 5 INGOT
Can: 3 TIN
container: 3 ORE
Crude: 3 ORE
Cut into: 4 ETCH
deposit: 4 LODE
Enameled: 4 TOLE
fastener: 4 BOLT HASP
5 RIVET SCREW UBOLT
Fuse: 4 WELD
Galvanizing: 4 ZINC
Heavy: 4 LEAD
in brass: 4 ZINC
in steel: 4 IRON
Join: 4 WELD 6 SOLDER
marble: 7 STEELIE
Measure: 5 ASSAY
mix: 5 ALLOY
mold: 3 PIG
Pewter: 3 TIN
Precious: 4 GOLD
Put the pedal to the: 4 SPED
Refine: 5 SMELT
refuse: 4 SLAG
rim: 6 FLANGE
shaping aid: 5 ANVIL

Soft: 3 TIN
source: 3 ORE
strand: 4 WIRE
Temper: 6 ANNEAL
Threaded ~ fastener: 4 TNUT
Unrefined: 3 ORE
waste: 5 DROSS
**Metal-bearing**
mineral: 3 ORE
**Metallic**
fabric: 4 LAME
marble: 7 STEELIE
mixture: 5 ALLOY
rock: 3 ORE
sound: 5 CLANG
waste: 4 SLAG
**Metallica**
drummer Ulrich: 4 LARS
**Metallurgist**
sample: 3 ORE
**Metals**
Big name in: 5 ALCOA
**Metalworker:** 5 SMITH
**Metamorphic**
rock: 5 SLATE
**"Metamorphoses"**
poet: 4 OVID
**Metamorphosis**
stage: 4 PUPA 5 LARVA
**"Metamorphosis, The"**
author: 5 KAFKA
Hero of: 5 SAMSA
**___ me tangere:** 4 NOLI
**Metaphor:** 5 TROPE
Economic: 3 PIE
Fog: 7 PEASOUP
Scolding: 7 RIOTACT
**Metaphorically**
Challenge, ~: 4 HILL
Punishment, ~: 3 ROD
**Metaphysical**
poet: 5 DONNE
**Metaphysics**
Giant of: 4 KANT
**Metcalf**
Actress: 6 LAURIE
**Metchnikoff**
Nobelist: 4 ELIE
**Mete**
out: 4 DOLE 5 ALLOT
**Meteor**
path: 3 ARC
tail: 3 ITE
**"Meteorologica"**
writer: 9 ARISTOTLE
**Meteorological**
concern: 7 AIRMASS
effect: 4 HALO 6 AURORA
line: 6 ISOBAR
menace: 6 ELNINO
**Meteorologist**
comfort meas.: 3 THI
device: 9 BAROMETER
study: 5 SKIES
**Meter**
Cubic: 5 STERE

feed: 5 DIMES
Feet in: 5 IAMBS
maid of song: 4 RITA
man: 4 POET
Millionth of a: 6 MICRON
Millionths of a: 5 MICRA
opening: 4 ALTI
prefix: 3 ODO 4 PERI
5 ANEMO
reader: 6 GASMAN
reading: 4 FARE 5 USAGE
site: 4 TAXI
**Metered**
vehicle: 3 CAB 4 TAXI
**Meters**
100 square ~: 3 ARE
1,852 ~: 7 SEAMILE
4,047 square ~: 4 ACRE
**Meth**
suffix: 3 ANE
**Meth.:** 3 REL SYS 4 PROT
**Methane**
lack: 4 ODOR
**Method:** 3 WAY 4 MODE
5 STYLE 6 SYSTEM
TACTIC
(abbr.): 3 SYS 4 SYST
A question of: 3 HOW
Counting: 4 TENS
Gambler's: 6 SYSTEM
Learning: 4 ROTE
7 OSMOSIS
of meditation: 3 ZEN 4 YOGA
of reasoning: 5 LOGIC
**Methuselah:** 7 OLDSTER
claim to fame: 6 OLDAGE
Father of: 5 ENOCH
Like: 3 OLD
**Methyl**
ending: 3 ENE
**Methyl acetate:** 5 ESTER
**Meticulousness:** 4 CARE
**Metier:** 5 TRADE
**MetLife:** 7 INSURER
competitor: 5 AETNA
**"Me too":** 5 ASAMI SODOI
**Metric**
distances (abbr.): 3 KMS
foot: 4 IAMB
heavyweight: 5 TONNE
mass unit: 4 GRAM
measure: 3 ARE 4 KILO
5 LITER STERE
prefix: 3 ISO 4 DECA DECI
5 CENTI MILLI
quart: 5 LITER
weight: 4 GRAM KILO
**Metro**
area: 3 URB
entrance: 5 STILE
maker: 3 GEO
**Metrodome**
lack: 4 TARP
player: 4 TWIN
**Metroliner**
company: 6 AMTRAK

**Metronome**
setting: 5 TEMPO
settings: 5 TEMPI
**Metropolis:** 4 CITY
Indian: 5 DELHI
Japanese: 5 OSAKA
Norwegian: 4 OSLO
Pakistani: 6 LAHORE
**Metropolitan:** 5 URBAN
**Mets:** 4 TEAM
1969 ~ victims: 7 ORIOLES
div.: 6 NLEAST
First ~ manager:
    7 STENGEL
Former ~ outfielder: 4 AGEE
Jones of the: 5 CLEON
stadium: 4 SHEA
Tommie in ~ history: 4 AGEE
**Mettle:** 4 GUTS 5 SPUNK
    VALOR
**Metz**
Mine, in: 4 AMOI
~ Mrs.: 3 MME
**Mex.:** 4 ABBR
miss: 4 SRTA
Neighbor of: 3 USA 4 ARIZ
~ Mrs.: 3 SRA
**Mexicali**
mister: 5 SENOR
peninsula: 4 BAJA
    15 LOWERCALIFORNIA
**Mexican**
Ancient: 5 AZTEC OLMEC
beans: 5 PESOS
blanket: 6 SERAPE
bread: 4 PESO
cactus: 6 PEYOTE
child: 4 NINA
coin: 4 PESO
cowboy: 6 CHARRO
food: 4 TACO 6 TAMALE
    7 TOSTADA
general: 9 SANTAANNA
mister: 5 SENOR
money: 4 PESO
month: 3 MES
munchie: 4 TACO
muralist: 6 RIVERA
peninsula: 4 BAJA
Prepare ~ beans: 5 REFRY
revolutionary: 5 VILLA
    6 ZAPATA
saloon: 7 CANTINA
sandal: 8 HUARACHE
sandwich: 4 TACO
shawl: 6 SERAPE
silverwork center: 5 TAXCO
snack: 4 TACO 5 NACHO
state: 7 TABASCO
The U.S., to a: 7 ELNORTE
treat holder: 6 PINATA
water: 4 AGUA
wrap: 6 SERAPE
~ Mrs.: 3 SRA
**Mexican War**
president: 4 POLK

**Mexico**
Conqueror of: 6 CORTES
It is in: 4 ESTA
Mme., in: 3 SRA
More, in: 3 MAS
State of: 6 OAXACA
This, in: 4 ESTO
Up from: 5 NORTE
**Meyer**
Crime boss: 6 LANSKY
Director: 4 RUSS
**Meyers**
Actress: 3 ARI
of basketball: 3 ANN
**Mezzo**
offering: 4 ARIA
~ Berganza: 6 TERESA
~ Borodina: 4 OLGA
**Mezzo-soprano**
~ Marilyn: 5 HORNE
**MFA**
Part of: 4 ARTS
"___ M for Murder": 4 DIAL
**Mfr.**
detail: 4 SPEC
**Mfume, Kweisi**
org.: 5 NAACP
**Mg.**
and others: 3 WTS
**MGM:** 6 STUDIO
Cofounder of: 4 LOEW
Former ~ rival: 3 RKO
lion: 3 LEO
motto word: 3 ARS 5 ARTIS
movie sound: 4 ROAR
Part of: 5 MAYER METRO
**Mgmt.:** 5 ADMIN
**Mgr.**
degree: 3 MBA
helper: 4 ASST
**Mgrs.**
Online: 6 SYSOPS
**MHz**
Part of: 4 MEGA
**Mi**
followers: 3 FAS
**Mi.**
A ~ has 1,760: 3 YDS
About ⅝: 3 KIL
About 5.88 trillion: 4 LTYR
**Mia**
An ex of: 5 ANDRE
of soccer: 4 HAMM
Role for: 6 HANNAH
"___ mia!": 5 MAMMA
"___ Mia" (1965 hit): 4 CARA
**Miami**
basketball team: 4 HEAT
City near: 11 CORALGABLES
county: 4 DADE
golf resort: 5 DORAL
newspaper: 6 HERALD
Tree in: 4 PALM
Where ~ is: 4 OHIO
**Miamian**
Certain: 5 ANGLO

**Miami Sound Machine**
singer: 7 ESTEFAN
**"Miami Vice"**
actor Edward James: 5 OLMOS
star: 10 DONJOHNSON
**Miata**
maker: 5 MAZDA
**Mica:** 8 SILICATE
**Micah**
Book before: 5 JONAH
**Mice**
catchers: 4 OWLS
Field: 4 VOLE
Reactions to: 4 EEKS
Sites for: 4 PADS
~, to cats: 4 PREY
**Mich.**
neighbor: 3 IND ONT 4 WISC
**Michael**
Actor: 5 NOURI
and others: 5 TSARS
Batman after: 3 VAL
Brother of: 4 TITO
Cochise portrayer: 6 ANSARA
Former Disney exec: 6 EISNER
Janet, to: 3 SIS
of tennis: 5 CHANG STICH
Sister of: 5 JANET 6 LATOYA
Sleuth: 6 SHAYNE
~, to Kirk: 3 SON
**"Michael"**
actress Garr: 4 TERI
actress MacDowell: 5 ANDIE
**"Michael Collins"**
star: 3 REA
**Michaelmas**
daisy: 5 ASTER
**Michaels**
TV producer: 5 LORNE
**Michel**
Napoleonic marshal: 3 NEY
**Michelangelo**
masterpiece: 5 DAVID PIETA
works: 4 ARTE 7 FRESCOS
**Michelin**
product: 4 TIRE 6 RADIAL
rival: 6 DUNLOP
**Michelle**
and Cass: 5 MAMAS
of soccer: 5 AKERS
Rival of: 4 TARA
Skater: 4 KWAN
**Michener**
epic: 5 SPACE TEXAS
    6 ALASKA HAWAII IBERIA
work: 4 EPIC SAGA
**"Mi chiamano Mimi":** 4 ARIA
**Michigan:** 4 LAKE 6 AVENUE
city: 6 OWOSSO 7 PONTIAC
    SAGINAW
college: 4 ALMA
**Mick**
Bandmates of: 6 STONES
Ex of: 6 BIANCA
**Mickey**
Actor: 6 ROONEY

and Minnie: 4 MICE
Ex of: 3 AVA
of baseball: 6 MANTLE
**Mickey ___ (loaded drink):**
   4 FINN
**Mickey Mouse**
   courses: 6 EASYAS
   creator: 4 WALT 6 DISNEY
   dog: 5 PLUTO
   First ~ cartoon:
      15 STEAMBOATWILLIE
   Girlfriend of: 6 MINNIE
   Like: 8 ANIMATED
**Microbe:** 4 GERM
**Microbiologist**
   gel: 4 AGAR
**Microbrewery**
   offering: 3 ALE 4 BEER
**Microfilm**
   sheet: 5 FICHE
**Micromanager**
   concern: 6 DETAIL
**Micronesia**
   Group that includes:
      7 OCEANIA
**Microphone**
   He patented the: 6 EDISON
   inventor Berliner: 5 EMILE
**Microscope**
   item: 5 SLIDE
   Kind of: 8 ELECTRON
   part: 4 LENS 5 OPTIC
   sample: 5 SMEAR
**Microscopic:** 3 WEE 4 TINY
   critter: 5 AMEBA 6 AMOEBA
   critters: 6 AMEBAE
   sea life: 4 ALGA
**Microscopy**
   supply: 5 STAIN
**Microsoft**
   boss: 5 GATES
   employee: 5 CODER
   game system: 4 XBOX
   product: 4 WORD
   reference: 7 ENCARTA
**Microwave:** 3 ZAP 4 NUKE
      OVEN
   brand: 5 AMANA
   option: 4 THAW
**Midafternoon:** 5 THREE
   on a sundial: 3 III
**Mid-American Conference**
   team: 6 TOLEDO
**Midas**
   undoing: 5 GREED
**Midday:** 4 NOON
   errand: 6 NOONER
   nap: 6 SIESTA
**Middies**
   sch.: 4 USNA
**Middle**
   (abbr.): 3 CTR
   ear bone: 5 INCUS
      6 STAPES
   Give in the: 3 SAG
   grade: 3 CEE

In the ~ of: 5 AMONG
   7 AMONGST
management: 4 DIET
measurement: 5 WAIST
middle: 4 DEES
Minuet: 4 TRIO
Most red in the: 6 RAREST
of a game: 3 TAC
of an insect: 6 THORAX
of March: 4 IDES
of some plays: 5 ACTII
of summer: 3 EMS
prefix: 4 MESO
QED: 4 ERAT
Simile: 3 ASA
Split down the: 6 BISECT
weight: 9 SPARETIRE
~ X or O: 3 TAC
**Middlecoff**
   Golfer: 4 CARY
**Middle East**
   bread: 4 PITA
   denizen: 4 ARAB
   faith: 5 ISLAM
   gp.: 3 PLO
   leader: 4 EMIR 5 EMEER
   port: 4 ADEN
   strip: 4 GAZA
   sultanate: 4 OMAN
**Middle Easterner:** 4 ARAB
      5 SAUDI 7 IRANIAN
**"Middlemarch"**
   author: 5 ELIOT
**Middle name**
   Common girl's: 3 ANN MAE
   Disney's: 5 ELIAS
   Edison's: 4 ALVA
   Elvis's: 4 ARON
   Emerson's: 5 WALDO
   Garfield's: 5 ABRAM
   Lenin's: 5 ILICH
   Lennon's: 3 ONO
   Mystery: 5 CONAN
   Poe's: 5 ALLAN
   Polk's: 4 KNOX
   Presidential: 4 ALAN 5 ABRAM
      6 DELANO
**Middlesex**
   Middle of: 6 CENTRE
**Middleweight**
   1940s ~ champ Tony: 4 ZALE
**Middling:** 4 FAIR SOSO
      7 AVERAGE
   grade: 3 CEE
**Mideast**
   airline: 4 ELAL
   belief: 5 ISLAM
   canal: 4 SUEZ
   capital: 4 SANA 5 AMMAN
      7 TEHERAN
   carrier: 4 ELAL
   chief: 4 EMIR
   chief (var.): 4 AMIR
   desert: 5 NEGEV
   emirate: 4 OMAN 5 DUBAI
   expert: 7 ARABIST

export: 3 OIL
federation (abbr.): 3 UAE
Former ~ first name: 5 YASIR
Former ~ gp.: 3 UAR
Former ~ leader: 4 SHAH
gp.: 3 PLO 5 HAMAS
gulf: 4 ADEN
heights: 5 GOLAN
land: 4 OMAN
land (abbr.): 3 ISR
leader: 5 ASSAD
Like some ~ politics:
   7 PANARAB
missile: 4 SCUD
money: 4 RIAL 5 DINAR
nation: 5 QATAR
peninsula: 5 SINAI 6 ARABIA
port: 4 ADEN
prince: 4 EMIR
region: 4 GAZA
royal name: 4 SAUD
ruler: 4 AMIR EMIR SHAH
      5 AMEER EMEER
sultanate: 4 OMAN
**Midge:** 4 GNAT
   Singer: 3 URE
**Midland**
   City near: 6 ODESSA
**Midleg:** 4 KNEE
**Midler:** 4 DIVA
   1979 ~ film: 7 THEROSE
   Singer: 5 BETTE
**Mid-level**
   army rank: 10 FIELDGRADE
**Mid-month**
   day: 4 IDES
**Midmorning:** 3 TEN 5 TENAM
**Midnight:** 3 XII
   Approach: 5 LATEN
   Burning the ~ oil: 6 UPLATE
   Burn the ~ oil: 6 STAYUP
   fridge visit: 4 RAID
   Hour after: 5 ONEAM
   Hour before: 6 ELEVEN
   rider: 6 REVERE
   Word heard around: 4 AULD
**"Midnight Cowboy"**
   role: 5 RATSO
**Midori**
   Skater: 3 ITO
**Midpoint**
   (abbr.): 3 CTR
**Midriff**
   revealing top: 6 HALTER
**Midsection:** 3 GUT 5 BELLY
      TORSO WAIST
**Midshipman**
   rival: 5 CADET
   sch.: 4 USNA
**Midshipmen, The:** 4 NAVY
**Mid-sized**
   ensemble: 5 OCTET
**Midst**
   In the ~ of: 5 AMONG
**Midsummer**
   sign: 3 LEO

**"Midsummer Night's Dream, A"**
King of: 6 OBERON
Queen of: 7 TITANIA
trickster: 4 PUCK
**Midterm:** 4 EXAM TEST
**Midvoyage:** 4 ASEA
**Midway**
alternative: 5 OHARE
attraction: 4 RIDE
**Midwest**
Big ~ sch.: 3 OSU
city: 5 OMAHA
city, familiarly: 3 CHI
hub: 5 OHARE
Indian: 3 SAC 4 OTOE
5 OMAHA
university town: 4 AMES
**Midwife**
instruction: 4 PUSH
**Midwives**
Some ~ (abbr.): 3 RNS
**Mien:** 3 AIR
Mean: 5 SNEER
**"Mi ___ es su ...":** 4 CASA
**Mies van der ___**
Architect Ludwig: 4 ROHE
**Mies van der Rohe**
More, to: 4 LESS
motto: 10 LESSISMORE
**Miff:** 3 IRE 4 RILE SNIT
5 STEAM
**Miffed:** 4 SORE
More than: 5 IRATE
state: 4 SNIT
~, with "off": 4 TEED
**Might:** 3 MAY 4 DINT 5 FORCE
POWER
Symbol of: 3 OAK
**Mighty**
long time: 3 EON
tree: 3 OAK
**"Mighty Aphrodite"**
Sorvino of: 4 MIRA
**"Mighty ___ a Rose":** 3 LAK
**Mighty Ducks**
Home of the: 7 ANAHEIM
org.: 3 NHL
**"Mighty Ducks, The"**
star: 7 ESTEVEZ
**Mighty Joe Young:** 3 APE
**"Mighty Lak' a Rose"**
composer: 5 NEVIN
**___ mignon:** 5 FILET
**Migraine**
omen: 4 AURA
omens: 5 AURAE
**Migrant:** 5 NOMAD
Depression era: 4 OKIE
**Migrate**
Why geese: 8 INSTINCT
**Migration:** 4 TREK
**Migratory**
fish: 3 EEL 4 SHAD
goose: 5 BRANT
**___ Miguel:** 3 SAO
**"Mikado, The":** 8 OPERETTA

attire: 3 OBI
role: 4 KOKO
weapon: 4 SNEE
**Mike**
Archie or Edith, to: 5 INLAW
Boxer: 5 TYSON
Columnist: 5 ROYKO
Hidden: 4 WIRE
holder: 4 BOOM 5 EMCEE
LAPEL STAND
Iron: 5 TYSON
of football: 5 DITKA
Producer ~ and others:
5 TODDS
**Mikhail**
of chess: 3 TAL
Wife of: 5 RAISA
**Mikita**
of hockey: 4 STAN
**"Mikrokosmos"**
composer: 6 BARTOK
**Mil.**
address: 3 APO
advisory gp.: 3 NSC
alliance: 4 NATO
assistant: 3 ADC
authority: 3 CMD
award: 3 DSC DSM DSO
bigwig: 3 GEN
branch: 4 USAF USAR USMC
drop site: 3 APO
entertainers: 3 USO
group on campus: 4 ROTC
jet locale: 3 AFB
mail drop: 3 APO
No longer in the: 3 RET
officers: 3 LTS
rank: 3 COL GEN MAJ PFC
PVT SGT 5 LTCOL
registration group: 3 SSS
school: 4 ACAD
stores: 3 PXS
student body: 4 ROTC
training academy: 3 OCS
transport: 3 LST
truant: 4 AWOL
unit: 4 REGT
**"Mila 18"**
author: 4 URIS
**Milan**
attraction: 7 LASCALA
money: 4 LIRA
Seaport south of: 5 GENOA
**Milano**
Actress: 6 ALYSSA
moola: 4 LIRA LIRE
**Mild:** 4 TAME 5 TEPID
cheese: 4 EDAM 5 GOUDA
cigar: 5 CLARO
oath: 4 DRAT EGAD GOSH
HECK 5 EGADS NERTS
~, as weather: 5 BALMY
**Mildew**
and mold: 5 FUNGI
**Mildly**
Scold: 5 CHIDE

**Mile**
1/640 of a square ~: 4 ACRE
A ~ a minute: 5 SIXTY
fraction: 4 YARD
**Mileage**
counter: 8 ODOMETER
Get more ~ out of: 5 REUSE
rating gp.: 3 EPA
Square: 4 AREA
**Mile High Center**
architect: 3 PEI
**Miler**
~ Sebastian: 3 COE
**Miles**
About 25,000 square ~ of Asia:
7 ARALSEA
Actress: 4 VERA 5 SARAH
and miles: 3 FAR
Many ~ off: 4 AFAR
of jazz: 5 DAVIS
per hour: 4 RATE
**Milestone**
Baby: 9 FIRSTSTEP
**Milieu:** 4 AREA 7 ELEMENT
**Militant**
campus gp.: 3 SDS
~ Muslim group: 5 HAMAS
**Military**
1980s ~ inits.: 3 SDI
academy frosh: 4 PLEB
address: 3 SIR
address (abbr.): 3 APO
adversary: 5 ENEMY
Arm of the British: 4 STEN
assault: 5 SIEGE
award: 5 MEDAL
band: 6 ARMLET
band instrument: 7 HELICON
bigwigs: 5 BRASS
Brit. ~ decoration: 3 DSO
camp: 5 ETAPE
Campus ~ org.: 4 ROTC
cap: 4 KEPI 5 SHAKO
capability: 9 FIREPOWER
chaplain: 5 PADRE
classification: 4 ONEA
command: 6 ATEASE
"Currently serving" ~ status:
4 ONEC
day's march: 5 ETAPE
defense parts: 4 SAMS
denial: 5 NOSIR
Discharge from the ~,
informally: 3 RIF
Elite ~ unit: 5 ATEAM
French ~ cap: 4 KEPI
group: 4 ARMY UNIT
helicopter: 4 HUEY 6 APACHE
hopeful: 5 CADET
inits.: 3 SDI
Join the: 6 ENLIST
meal: 4 MESS
mess: 5 SNAFU
mission: 5 RECON
pilots: 6 AIRMEN
Pres., to the: 3 CIC 4 CINC

response: 5 NOSIR 6 YESSIR
sch.: 4 ACAD
school: 7 ACADEMY
squad: 4 UNIT
station: 4 POST
stronghold: 4 FORT
student: 5 CADET
subdivision: 4 UNIT
tactic: 4 RAID
tenure: 4 TOUR
trainee: 5 CADET
training group: 5 CADRE
training site: 8 BOOTCAMP
U.K. ~ fliers: 3 RAF
unit: 5 SQUAD TROOP
vehicle: 4 JEEP

**Milk**
amts.: 3 QTS
Brest: 4 LAIT
choice: 4 SKIM
component: 4 WHEY
container: 6 CARTON
Cry over spilled: 3 RUE 4 OOPS
    5 WHINE
curdler: 6 RENNET
delivery cry: 3 MOO
Drink with: 5 LATTE
etc.: 5 DAIRY
farm: 5 DAIRY
Like skim: 6 NONFAT
Nonfat: 4 SKIM
pitcher: 5 ELSIE
prefix: 4 LACT 5 LACTI
    LACTO
Prepare cappuccino: 5 STEAM
Produce skim: 5 DEFAT
purchase: 5 QUART
related: 6 LACTIC
Remove from a mother's:
    4 WEAN
Request for: 3 MEW
snake: 5 ADDER
source: 3 COW EWE 4 GOAT
    5 UDDER
sugar: 7 LACTOSE
train: 5 LOCAL
Treat with: 4 OREO
Turn bad, as: 4 SOUR
Word before: 4 SOYA
~, in a way: 3 USE
~, in French: 4 LAIT
~, in prescriptions: 3 LAC
~, in Spanish: 5 LECHE
**Milk-Bone:** 5 TREAT
**Milker**
Aphid: 3 ANT
need: 4 PAIL 5 STOOL
**Milking**
machine attachment: 5 UDDER
the cows: 5 CHORE
**Milk of ___:** 8 MAGNESIA
**Milkshake**
in New England: 6 FRAPPE
insert: 5 STRAW
**Milksop:** 4 WIMP
lack: 5 SPINE

**Milky**
gemstone: 4 OPAL
**Milky Way:** 3 BAR
component: 6 NOUGAT
maker: 4 MARS
part: 4 STAR
**Mill:** 5 GRIND
fodder: 5 GRIST
input: 3 ORE 5 GRIST
Kind of: 3 GIN 5 GRIST STEEL
material: 4 IRON
output: 5 PAPER STEEL
site: 6 STREAM
Steel ~ refuse: 4 SLAG
**Millais**
Site of some ~ works: 4 TATE
**Millay**
muse: 5 ERATO
Poet: 4 EDNA
**Milldam:** 4 WEIR
**Millennia**
Many: 3 EON 4 AEON EONS
    5 AEONS
**Millennial Church**
member: 6 SHAKER
**Millennium**
start: 3 MMI
unit: 4 YEAR
**Millennium Falcon**
pilot: 7 HANSOLO
pilot Solo: 3 HAN
**Miller:** 4 BEER
Bandleader: 5 GLENN
    MITCH
beer: 4 LITE
character: 5 LOMAN
Comic ranter: 6 DENNIS
Dancer: 3 ANN
Designer: 6 NICOLE
mistress: 3 NIN
need: 5 GRIST
offering: 4 BEER LITE
salesman: 5 LOMAN
**Miller ___:** 4 LITE
**"___ Miller":** 5 LUISA
**Miller, Arthur**
character: 5 LOMAN
**Miller, Dennis**
monologue: 4 RANT
**Miller, Glenn**
protégé Ray: 6 EBERLE
**Miller, Henry**
Friend of: 8 ANAISNIN
genre: 7 EROTICA
title start: 6 TROPIC
**Miller, Mitch:** 6 OBOIST
instrument: 4 OBOE
**Miller, Roger**
hit: 6 DANGME
    13 KINGOFTHEROAD
**Miller, William E.**
was his running mate:
    14 BARRYGOLDWATER
**Miller Lite**
alternative: 6 AMSTEL
**Milli ___:** 7 VANILLI

**Milligrams**
200 ~: 5 CARAT
It may be measured in:
    4 DOSE
**Milliner:** 6 HATTER
stock: 4 HATS
**Millinery**
accessory: 6 HATPIN
**Million**
Capital of 2.6: 6 TAIPEI
Ending for: 4 AIRE
Most of a: 5 ZEROS
One in a: 4 RARE
suffix: 4 AIRE
**Millionaire**
maker: 5 LOTTO 7 LOTTERY
on the Titanic: 5 ASTOR
prefix: 5 MULTI
transport: 5 YACHT
**"Millionairess, The"**
star: 5 LOREN
**Million Moms March**
target: 3 NRA
**Millions**
of years: 4 EONS
**"___ Millions" (O'Neill play):**
    5 MARCO
**Millionth**
of a meter: 6 MICRON
**Millionths**
of a meter: 5 MICRA
**"Mill on the Floss, The"**
author: 5 ELIOT
**Mills**
or Sills: 4 DIVA
**Millstone:** 4 ONUS
**Milne**
baby: 3 ROO
bear: 4 POOH
marsupial: 3 ROO 5 KANGA
**Milo**
Actor: 5 OSHEA
Partner of ~ in film: 4 OTIS
**Milosevic:** 4 SERB
**Milquetoast:** 4 WIMP
Like a: 4 MEEK
**Milsap**
Singer: 6 RONNIE
**Miltie**
Memorable: 5 BERLE
**Milton:** 5 ODIST
Funnyman: 5 BERLE
muse: 5 ERATO
overthrower: 3 IDI
pearl: 3 ODE 5 ELEGY
**Mime:** 4 APER
Muse of: 5 ERATO
~ Marceau: 6 MARCEL
**Mimeo:** 4 COPY
**Mimic:** 3 APE 4 APER COPY
    ECHO MYNA 6 PARROT
    7 COPYCAT
ability: 5 APING
skill: 5 APERY
**Mimieux**
Actress: 6 YVETTE

**Miming**
dance: 4 HULA
**Mimosa**
family tree: 6 ACACIA
**Min.**
15 ~ of football: 3 QTR
Fraction of a: 4 NSEC
part: 3 SEC
Three ~ in the ring: 3 RND
**"Min and Bill"**
Oscar winner: 8 DRESSLER
**Mince:** 4 HASH
**Minced**
It may be: 4 OATH
**Mincemeat**
dessert: 3 PIE
ingredient: 4 SUET
**Mind:** 4 HEED OBEY TEND
5 SEETO 6 LISTEN
RESENT
Be of one: 5 AGREE
Bring to: 5 EVOKE
Call to: 5 EVOKE
Cast of: 4 BENT
Come to: 5 ARISE OCCUR
Frame of: 4 MOOD
Had in: 5 MEANT
Have in: 4 MEAN PLAN
6 INTEND
It comes to: 4 IDEA
Keep in: 8 REMEMBER
Kind of: 8 ONETRACK
Lose one's: 5 GOMAD
Of sound: 4 SANE
Peace of: 4 EASE REST
6 REPOSE
Prey on the: 5 EATAT
set: 5 IDEAS 6 IMAGES
Soundness of: 6 SANITY
Speak one's: 5 OPINE
State of: 4 MOOD
the kids: 3 SIT
Things to: 7 PSANDQS
What comes to: 4 IDEA
Words before: 5 OUTOF
**"___ mind?":** 5 DOYOU
**Mind-boggler:** 6 ENIGMA
**Mind-boggling**
span: 3 EON
**Minded**
junior: 3 SAT
**Minderbinder**
of fiction: 4 MILO
**Mindful:** 5 AWARE
**Mindless:** 5 INANE
card game: 3 WAR
process: 4 ROTE
**Mind reader**
(abbr.): 3 EEG
knack: 3 ESP
**Mind-reading:** 3 ESP
**Minds**
Meeting of the: 3 ESP
**Mind's**
eye view: 5 IMAGE
Use the ~ eye: 7 IMAGINE

**Mindspring**
(abbr.): 3 ISP
**Mindy**
portrayer: 3 PAM
Where ~ honeymooned:
3 ORK
**Mine**
access: 4 ADIT
A load off one's: 3 ORE
and yours: 4 OURS
A relative of: 4 OURS
car: 4 TRAM
entrance: 4 ADIT
find: 3 ORE
line: 4 SEAM
passage: 5 SHAFT
prefix: 5 UNDER
Stuff of: 3 ORE
yield: 3 ORE
~, in French: 4 AMOI
**"___ Mine"**
(Beatles song): 3 IME
(Platters song): 3 HES
**Mined**
find: 3 ORE 7 IRONORE
over matter: 3 ORE
**"Mine eyes have seen the
___ ...":** 5 GLORY
**Mineo**
Actor: 3 SAL
**Miner**
bonanza: 4 LODE
concern: 3 ORE
hat feature: 8 HEADLAMP
**Mineral**
Bone: 7 APATITE
Chalky: 4 TALC
deposit: 4 LODE VEIN
Figurine: 4 ONYX
Flaky: 4 MICA
Gem: 5 BERYL
Green: 4 JADE
hardness scale: 4 MOHS
in pesticide: 4 TALC
Iridescent: 4 OPAL
Layered: 4 MICA
Metal-bearing: 3 ORE
Monterrey: 3 ORO
Nail file: 5 EMERY
Nutritive: 4 IRON
Outback: 4 OPAL
Shiny: 4 MICA
Silica: 4 OPAL
Soft: 4 TALC
spring: 3 SPA
suffix: 3 ITE
Supplement: 4 ZINC
Translucent: 4 MICA
**___ minérale:** 3 EAU
**Minero**
find: 3 ORO
**Miners**
sch.: 4 UTEP
**Minerva**
Greek: 6 ATHENA
Symbol of: 3 OWL

**Minesweeper**
Fictional: 5 CAINE
**Miney**
follower: 3 MOE
**Ming:** 7 DYNASTY
artifact: 4 VASE
of basketball: 3 YAO
thing: 4 VASE
**Mingle**
at a banquet: 8 TABLEHOP
**Mingled**
with: 5 AMONG
**Mingo**
portrayer: 4 AMES 6 EDAMES
**___ Minh:** 4 VIET
**___ Minh City, Vietnam:**
5 HOCHI
**Mini**
albums, for short: 3 EPS
Change a: 5 REHEM
feature: 3 HEM
ha-ha: 5 TEHEE
map: 5 INSET
pictures: 5 ICONS
whirlpool: 4 EDDY
**Miniature:** 3 TOY 5 PYGMY
golf club: 6 PUTTER
map: 5 INSET
racer: 4 KART 6 GOCART
7 SLOTCAR
sci-fi vehicles: 4 PODS
**Minibar**
site: 4 LIMO
**Minibike**
kin: 5 MOPED
**Minicam**
abbr.: 3 REC
**Minima:** 6 LEASTS
**Minimal:** 5 LEAST 6 BAREST
amount: 4 IOTA 5 LEAST
change: 4 CENT 5 PENNY
evidence: 5 SHRED
money: 4 CENT
moola: 7 REDCENT
Most: 6 BAREST
swimwear: 5 THONG
**Minimalist**
More to a: 4 LESS
**Minimally:** 4 ATAD 7 ATLEAST
**Minimize**
Designed to ~ drag: 4 AERO
**Minimovies:** 6 SHORTS
**Minimum:** 5 LEAST 6 BAREST
amount: 4 WAGE
Meeting: 6 QUORUM
Morse: 3 DIT
Sales: 5 QUOTA
wage: 5 SCALE
**Minimum ___:** 4 WAGE
**Mining**
Montana ~ town: 5 BUTTE
nail: 4 SPAD
**Minirecord**
albums: 3 EPS
**Miniseries**
1981 ~: 6 MASADA

Haley: 5 ROOTS
role of 1977: 5 KINTE
**Minister: 6 PARSON**
(abbr.): 3 REV
assistant: 6 DEACON
cohort: 5 RABBI
home: 5 MANSE
nickname: 3 REV
request: 8 BESEATED
school: 8 SEMINARY
to: 4 TEND 5 CATER
**Ministry**
TV: 3 PTL
**Minivan**
alternative: 3 SUV
Chevy: 5 ASTRO
model: 8 AEROSTAR
**Miniver**
Mr.: 4 CLEM
"___ Miniver": 3 MRS
**Mink: 3 FUR**
kin: 5 OTTER STOAT
wrap: 5 STOLE
**Minn.**
neighbor: 3 ONT WIS 4 NDAK
SDAK WISC
**Minneapolis**
Magazine based in: 4 UTNE
suburb: 5 EDINA
**Minnelli**
Singer: 4 LIZA
**Minnelli, Liza**
1977 ~ musical: 6 THEACT
**Minnesota**
10,000 of ~: 5 LAKES
ballplayer: 4 TWIN
Former ~ governor Ventura:
5 JESSE
governor Carlson: 4 ARNE
lake: 6 ITASCA
range: 6 MESABI
state bird: 4 LOON
twin: 6 STPAUL
twins: 3 ENS
**Minnesota ___: 4 FATS**
**Minnesota Fats**
rival, in film: 9 FASTEDDIE
stick: 3 CUE
**Minnesotan: 6 GOPHER**
**Minnie**
Memorable: 5 PEARL
Mickey and: 4 MICE
**"Minnie the Moocher"**
singer: 11 CABCALLOWAY
**Minnow**
Freshwater: 6 REDFIN
variety: 4 DACE
**Minnows: 4 BAIT**
**Minoan**
domain: 5 CRETE
**Minolta**
rival: 5 RICOH
**Minolta Maxxum: 3 SLR**
**Minor: 4 TEEN 5 PETTY**
6 LESSER
A: 3 KEY

argument: 4 SPAT
dent: 4 DING
falling-out: 4 TIFF
First ~ prophet: 5 HOSEA
No longer a: 5 OFAGE
obsession:
15 BEEINONESBONNET
player: 3 COG
prophet: 5 JONAH
quarrel: 4 SPAT
setback: 4 SNAG 6 HICCUP
~, in law: 5 PETIT
___ Minor: 4 ASIA URSA
**Minorca**
Capital of: 5 MAHON
**Minority**
Mideastern: 4 KURD
Writer in the: 5 LEFTY
**Minors**
Not for: 5 ADULT
**Minos: 6 CRETAN**
Daughter of: 7 ARIADNE
King ~ capital: 7 KNOSSOS
Kingdom of: 5 CRETE
Mother of: 6 EUROPA
**Minotaur**
Half sister of: 7 ARIADNE
home: 5 CRETE
**Mins.**
Extra game: 3 OTS
Many: 3 HRS
Parts of: 4 SECS
**Minsk**
money: 5 RUBLE
**Minstrel**
instrument: 4 LUTE LYRE
song: 3 LAY
**Minstrel show**
figure: 6 ENDMAN
**Mint: 3 NEW 4 COIN HERB**
7 POTHERB
family member: 4 CHIA SAGE
5 BASIL THYME
7 OREGANO
No longer: 4 USED
output: 4 CENT COIN
Popular breath: 6 TICTAC
They make a: 5 CERTS
Weed of the ~ family:
6 HENBIT
**Mint-condition: 3 NEW**
**Minted**
Coin no longer: 4 LIRA
7 ONELIRA
**Mints**
Brand of: 5 CERTS
**Minty**
drink: 5 JULEP
**Minuet**
middle: 4 TRIO
**"Minuet ___": 3 ING**
**Minus: 4 LESS SANS**
**Minuscule: 3 WEE 4 ITSY TINY**
5 TEENY
amount: 3 TAD 4 IOTA
margin: 4 HAIR

part of a min.: 4 NSEC
**Minuses**
It has pluses and: 4 MATH
They have their pluses and:
4 IONS
**Minute: 3 WEE 4 TINY 5 MICRO**
TEENY 6 ATOMIC
TEENSY
A mile a: 5 SIXTY
amount: 4 IOTA 9 SCINTILLA
Any: 4 ANON SOON
bit: 4 ATOM
In a: 4 SOON
In a New York: 6 ATONCE
More: 7 TEENIER
opening: 4 PORE
piece: 6 SECOND
Right this: 3 NOW
Study at the last: 4 CRAM
This: 3 NOW 6 ATONCE
**Minute ___: 5 STEAK**
**Minute Maid**
product: 3 HIC
**Minute Maid Park**
player: 5 ASTRO
**Minuteman**
enemy: 7 REDCOAT
home: 4 SILO
**Minutemen**
of college sports: 5 UMASS
**Minutes**
30 ~ in football: 4 HALF
50 ~ spent with a shrink:
7 SESSION
55 ~ past the hour:
6 FIVETO
Fifty ~ past: 5 TENTO
Of sixty: 5 HORAL
taker: 5 STENO
**Minuti**
60 ~: 3 ORA
**Minx: 4 VAMP 5 HUSSY**
Like a: 4 PERT
"___ Mio": 5 OSOLE
**Miquelon: 3 ILE**
**Mir**
Travel à la: 5 ORBIT
**Mira**
Paul Sorvino, to: 3 DAD
**Miracle**
Biblical ~ site: 4 CANA
drink: 6 ELIXIR
Exodus: 5 MANNA
response: 3 AWE
team of 1969: 4 METS
**Miracle-___: 3 GRO**
**"Miracle Mets"**
manager: 6 HODGES
pitcher: 6 SEAVER
**"Miracle on 34th Street"**
actor Gailey: 4 FRED
actor John: 5 PAYNE
Oscar winner: 5 GWENN
store: 5 MACYS
**"Miracle Worker, The"**
actress Swenson: 4 INGA

**Mirage**
sight: 5 OASIS
**"___ Mir Bist Du Schön":**
3 BEI
**Mire**
Move in: 4 SLOG
**Mired:** 8 KNEEDEEP
**"Miró, Miró on the wall"**
Like: 5 PUNNY
**Mirror:** 3 APE 5 IMAGE
Broken ~, say: 4 OMEN
Fuss at the: 5 PREEN
marrer: 5 SMEAR
material: 5 GLASS
reflection: 5 IMAGE
**Mirrors**
Like some: 4 OVAL
10 FULLLENGTH
Partner of: 5 SMOKE
**Mirth:** 4 GLEE
**Mirthful:** 5 RIANT
sounds: 4 HAHA
**Mis**
followers: 3 FAS
preceders: 3 RES
**Misanthrope:** 5 HATER
**Misbehave:** 5 ACTUP
7 CARRYON
**Misbehaving:** 3 BAD
**Miscalculate:** 3 ERR
**Miscellaneous**
collection: 3 ANA
mixture: 4 OLIO
**Miscellany:** 3 ANA 4 OLIO
8 CATCHALL
**Mischa**
Actor: 4 AUER
Violinist: 5 ELMAN
**Mischief:** 4 HARM
night activity: 5 PRANK
**Mischief-maker:** 3 IMP 5 PIXIE
6 RASCAL
Norse: 4 LOKI
**Mischievous:** 3 BAD 4 ARCH
5 ELFIN 6 ELFISH
IMPISH
bird: 6 MAGPIE
one: 3 ELF IMP 5 DEVIL
PIXIE ROGUE 6 RASCAL
Small and: 5 ELFIN
sprite: 5 PIXIE
**Misconduct**
Mark for: 7 DEMERIT
**Miscue:** 4 SLIP 5 ERROR
**Misdeed:** 3 SIN
**Miser**
Fictional ~ Marner: 5 SILAS
fixation: 5 MONEY
word: 4 MINE
**Miserable**
dwelling: 5 HOVEL
**"___ Misérables":** 3 LES
**Miserably**
Fail: 4 BOMB
**Miserere:** 5 PSALM
**Misery:** 3 WOE

**"Misery"**
costar: 4 CAAN
director: 6 REINER
star: 5 BATES
~ Oscar winner Bates:
5 KATHY
**Misfire**
QB: 3 INT
**Misfit**
Social: 4 DORK GEEK NERD
5 DWEEB
**Misfortune:** 3 WOE
**Misfortunes:** 4 ILLS
**Misgivings:** 6 QUALMS
Have ~ about: 3 RUE
**Mishandle:** 4 MUFF 5 ABUSE
**Mishap**
One-in-a-million:
13 FREAKACCIDENT
Shaving: 4 NICK
**Mishmash:** 4 OLIO
**Misinform:** 5 LIETO
**Misjudge:** 3 ERR
**Mislay:** 4 LOSE
**Mislead:** 5 LIETO
**Misleading:** 8 ILLUSIVE
clue: 10 REDHERRING
**Misogynist:** 5 HATER
**Mispickel:** 3 ORE
**Misplace:** 4 LOSE
**Misplay:** 5 ERROR
**Misprints:** 6 ERRATA
**"Misreadings"**
author: 3 ECO
**Misrepresent:** 4 SKEW 5 BELIE
7 DISTORT
**Miss:** 3 GAL SHE 4 GIRL LASS
OMIT
a cue: 3 ERR
after marriage: 3 MRS
a step: 6 FALTER
Bonny: 4 LASS
counterpart: 3 HIT
equal: 4 MILE
Fictional Swiss: 5 HEIDI
identification: 3 SHE
in a 1934 song: 4 OTIS
Kind of: 4 NEAR
Mex.: 4 SRTA
Mexican: 8 SENORITA
of comics: 5 PEACH
out: 3 DEB
Oxford: 3 OLE
Porter's: 4 OTIS
the mark: 3 ERR
TV psychic: 4 CLEO
~, in French: 4 MLLE
~, in Spanish: 4 SRTA
**Miss.**
neighbor: 3 ALA 4 TENN
**___ miss:** 5 HITOR
**___ Miss:** 3 OLE
**Miss America**
Accessory for: 4 SASH 5 TIARA
Former ~ host Parks: 4 BERT
Former ~ host Ron: 3 ELY

to some: 5 IDEAL
**Miss Brooks**
Eve who played: 5 ARDEN
**"___ Miss Brooks":** 3 OUR
**Miss by ___:** 5 AMILE
**Miss Cinders**
of old comics: 4 ELLA
**Miss Clairol**
user: 4 DYER
**Miss Congeniality**
Like: 6 NICEST
**Miss Daisy**
Driver of: 4 HOKE
**Missed:** 5 UNHIT
It may be: 3 CUE
List of what was: 6 ERRATA
**Missile**
American: 5 TITAN
Blowgun: 4 DART
Deadly: 4 NUKE
Gulf War: 4 SCUD
Heckler: 3 EGG
housing: 4 SILO
Kind of: 6 CRUISE
8 AIRTOAIR
Low-tech: 3 PEA
Medium-range: 4 THOR
Mideast: 4 SCUD
path: 3 ARC
Pub: 4 DART
Slapstick: 3 PIE
Two-stage: 5 TITAN
Underwater: 7 POLARIS
**"Missile Crisis, The"**
author Abel: 4 ELIE
**Missing:** 4 GONE LOST
5 OUTOF 6 ABSENT
a deadline: 4 LATE
a match: 3 ODD
details: 7 SKETCHY
links: 6 APEMEN
nothing: 6 ENTIRE
~ GI: 4 AWOL
**Mission:** 4 TASK 5 QUEST
Aborted ~ words: 4 NOGO
Bomber: 6 SORTIE
control, for short: 3 OPS
Historic: 5 ALAMO
Ill-fated ~ of 1967: 7 APOLLOI
Info-gathering: 5 RECON
Interrogate after a:
7 DEBRIEF
Man with a: 5 PADRE SERRA
Memorable: 5 ALAMO
Person on a: 6 LEGATE
Scout: 5 RECON
Scrubbed: 4 NOGO
**___ mission:** 3 ONA
**Missionary**
Molokai: 6 DAMIEN
target: 5 PAGAN
~ Junipero: 5 SERRA
**Mission ___, California:** 5 VIEJO
**Mission Control**
gp.: 4 NASA'
order: 5 ABORT

**"Mission: Impossible"**
  actor Greg: 6 MORRIS
  actress Barbara: 4 BAIN
  Mr. on: 6 PHELPS
  theme composer Schifrin:
    4 LALO
**"Mission: Impossible II"**
  director: 3 WOO
**Mississippi**
  city: 6 BILOXI TUPELO
  City on the: 7 MEMPHIS
  explorer: 6 DESOTO
  feeder: 3 RED 4 OHIO
    5 YAZOO
  inlet: 5 BAYOU
  Lake source of the: 6 ITASCA
  Lott of: 5 TRENT
  Mouth of the: 5 DELTA
  Much of: 5 ESSES
  senator: 9 TRENTLOTT
  senator Cochran: 4 THAD
  senator Trent: 4 LOTT
  state tree: 8 MAGNOLIA
  Ward of: 4 SELA
**"Mississippi ___": 6 MASALA**
**Mississippi River**
  explorer: 6 DESOTO
  source: 6 ITASCA
  transport: 5 BARGE
**Missive: 6 LETTER**
  (abbr.): 3 LTR
  Modern: 5 EMAIL
  Unsigned:
    15 ANONYMOUSLETTER
**Miss Manners**
  Like: 6 POLITE
  Unlike: 4 RUDE
**Miss Marple**
  discovery: 4 CLEW
  of mystery: 4 JANE
**Miss Muffet**
  bugaboo: 6 SPIDER
  fare: 4 WHEY
  Like: 9 SCAREDOFF
  morsel: 4 CURD
**Miss-named: 3 NEE**
**Missouri: 5 RIVER**
  Capital on the: 6 PIERRE
  City on the: 5 OMAHA
  feeder: 5 OSAGE 6 PLATTE
  motto end: 4 ESTO
  mountains: 5 OZARK
  river: 5 OSAGE
  town where Truman was born:
    5 LAMAR
  tribe: 4 OTOE
**___ Missouri: 3 USS**
**"Miss Peaches"**
  James nicknamed: 4 ETTA
**Miss Piggy: 3 SOW**
  query: 3 MOI
**"Miss Pym Disposes"**
  author Josephine: 3 TEY
**"Miss ___ Regrets": 4 OTIS**
**"Miss Saigon"**
  homeland: 7 VIETNAM

  Salonga of: 3 LEA
  setting: 3 NAM
**Misstep: 4 TRIP 5 ERROR**
    GAFFE
  Make a: 3 ERR
**Missus**
  Jack and the: 6 SPRATS
**Miss Woodhouse**
  of fiction: 4 EMMA
**Mist: 4 HAZE 5 VAPOR**
  Get the ~ off: 5 DEFOG
**Mistake: 5 ERROR LAPSE**
    7 ERRATUM
  Big: 5 BONER
  By: 7 INERROR
  Like many a: 4 RUED
  Make a: 3 ERR
  Minor: 4 SLIP
  Printed: 4 TYPO
  QB: 3 INT
  remover: 6 ERASER
  Sign of a: 7 ERASURE
**Mistaken: 7 INERROR**
  Be: 3 ERR
**Mistakenly: 7 INERROR**
**Mistakes: 6 ERRATA**
**Mister: 3 SIR**
  Madras: 3 SRI
  ~, in German: 4 HERR
  ~, in Spanish: 5 SENOR
**"Mister Ed"**
  actor Leon: 4 AMES
  morsel: 3 OAT
**Mister Roberts**
  portrayer: 5 FONDA
**Mister Rogers: 4 FRED**
**Mistletoe**
  mo.: 3 DEC
**Mistreat: 5 ABUSE 6 ILLUSE**
**Mistreatment: 5 ABUSE**
**Mistress**
  Like ~ Mary's maids:
    6 INAROW
**"Mistress of the Dark":**
    6 ELVIRA
**"Misty"**
  composer Garner: 6 ERROLL
  Where to look, in: 4 ATME
**Misunderstanding: 4 TIFF**
  Generational: 3 GAP
**MIT: 3 SCH**
  grad: 4 ENGR
  Many ~ grads: 3 EES
  Part of: 4 INST TECH
**Mitchell**
  Actor: 5 SASHA
  Dennis: 4 BRAT
  Diva: 5 LEONA
  heroine: 5 OHARA
  mansion: 4 TARA
  Singer: 4 JONI
  Songwriter: 4 JONI
**Mite: 4 ATOM 6 ACARID**
**Mitigate: 4 EASE**
**"Mitla Pass"**
  author: 4 URIS

**Mitochondrion**
  material: 3 RNA
**Mitt: 5 GLOVE**
  Kind of: 4 OVEN
  Kit: 3 PAW
**Mittens**
  Make: 4 KNIT
**Mitterrand**
  successor: 6 CHIRAC
**Mittimus**
  or mandamus: 4 WRIT
**Mitty**
  portrayer: 4 KAYE
**Mitzi**
  Actress: 6 GAYNOR
**Mix: 4 STIR 5 BLEND**
  Actor: 3 TOM
  anew: 6 RETOSS
  Contribute to the: 5 ADDIN
  flick: 5 OATER
  it up: 6 RASSLE
  Metal: 5 ALLOY
  Moonshine: 4 MASH
  more thoroughly: 6 RESTIR
  movie: 5 OATER
  of football: 3 RON
  Snack: 4 GORP
  together: 5 STIR 5 BLEND
  Trail: 4 GORP
  Trail ~ fruit: 6 RAISIN
  up: 4 STIR 5 ADDLE
**Mix-a-Lot**
  title: 3 SIR
**Mixed**
  bag: 4 OLIO
  One of ~ ancestry:
    7 MULATTO
**Mixer: 5 TONIC 6 SOCIAL**
  Bar: 4 SODA 5 TONIC
    8 CLUBSODA
  Rum: 4 COLA
  Sans: 4 NEAT
**Mixologist**
  measure: 4 SHOT
  spot: 6 WETBAR
  workplace: 3 BAR
**Mixture: 4 MELD OLIO**
    7 AMALGAM
  Chef's: 4 ROUX
  Metal: 5 ALLOY
**Mix-up: 5 SNAFU**
**Miyoshi**
  Oscar winner: 5 UMEKI
**"___ Miz": 3 LES**
**Mizrahi**
  Designer: 5 ISAAC
**Mizzen: 4 SAIL**
**Mjolnir**
  His hammer was named:
    4 THOR
**Mkt.**
  Common: 3 EEC
  Like a school supplies: 4 ELHI
  Stock ~ event: 3 IPO
**ml.**
  About five: 3 TSP

**MLB**
stat: 3 ERA HRS
**MLK**
Part of: 6 MARTIN
title: 3 REV
**Mlle.**
Canonized: 3 STE
cousin: 4 SRTA
**Mme.**
of Madrid: 3 SRA
**"Mm-hmm!":** 4 ISEE
**"MMMBop"**
Group with 1997 hit:
6 HANSON
**"Mmm, mmm!":** 5 TASTY
**M ___ mnemonic:** 4 ASIN
**Mnemonic**
Lakes: 5 HOMES
**Mnemosyne**
Daughter of: 5 ERATO
**Mo**
preceder: 3 SLO
**MO**
city: 3 STL
**Mo.**
Autumn: 3 NOV OCT
Back-to-school: 4 SEPT
Dog days: 3 AUG
Equinox: 3 SEP 4 SEPT
Fall: 3 NOV OCT SEP
4 SEPT
Last: 3 DEC
named for a Caesar: 3 AUG
Presents: 3 DEC
Schoolmaster: 3 OCT
Showery: 3 APR
Spring: 3 APR
Summer: 3 AUG
town: 3 STL
Winter: 3 DEC FEB JAN
without a holiday: 3 AUG
**Moab**
Ancient region near: 4 EDOM
**Moat**
critter: 4 CROC
**Mob:** 4 BAND 5 HORDE
6 RABBLE THRONG
action: 4 RIOT
boss: 4 CAPO
follower: 4 STER
hitman weapon: 7 GARROTE
scene: 4 RIOT
thug: 4 GOON
tough: 8 ENFORCER
**"Mo' Better Blues"**
director Spike: 3 LEE
**Mobil**
Company that merged with:
5 EXXON
logo: 7 PEGASUS
rival: 5 AMOCO
**Mobile**
home: 4 TENT 5 TEPEE
6 TEEPEE 7 ALABAMA
home (abbr.): 3 ALA
person: 8 ALABAMAN

**Mobiles:** 3 ART
Big name in: 6 CALDER
**Mobuto**
land: 5 ZAIRE
**Mobuto Sese ___:** 4 SEKO
**Moby Dick:** 5 WHALE
**"Moby Dick"**
captain: 4 AHAB 5 PELEG
**Moccasin:** 4 SHOE
Move like a: 7 SLITHER
Water: 11 COTTONMOUTH
**Mocedades**
1974 ~ hit: 6 ERESTU
**Mocha**
setting: 5 YEMEN
**Mock:** 4 GIBE JAPE JEER
5 SCOFF SCORN TAUNT
TEASE 6 DERIDE
JEERAT
fanfare: 4 TADA
laugh syllable: 3 HAR
suffix: 3 ERY
words of understanding:
4 AHSO
~, in a way: 3 APE
**"Mocker Mocked, The"**
artist: 4 KLEE
**Mockery:** 5 FARCE
Make a ~ of: 7 SNEERAT
**"Mockingbird"**
singer Foxx: 4 INEZ
**Mockingly**
Laugh: 5 FLEER
**"Mod ___, The":** 5 SQUAD
**Mode:** 5 STYLE
lead-in: 3 ALA
**___ mode:** 3 ALA
**Model:** 4 POSE 5 IDEAL
adornment: 5 DECAL
airplane wood: 5 BALSA
asset: 4 FACE 5 POISE
Big name in ~ trains:
4 TYCO
Floor: 4 DEMO
from Somalia: 4 IMAN
in a bottle: 4 SHIP
Kind of: 4 ROLE 5 SCALE
maker's purchase: 3 KIT
material: 5 BALSA
of excellence: 7 PARAGON
of perfection: 5 IDEAL
One-named: 4 EMME IMAN
5 FABIO
partner: 4 MAKE
Perfect game: 5 IDEAL
Plus-size: 4 EMME
Role: 4 HERO IDOL 5 IDEAL
Rolled: 5 PINUP
Runway: 5 PLANE
session: 5 SHOOT
Showroom: 4 DEMO
stance: 4 POSE
train layout: 4 OVAL
wood: 5 BALSA
~ Carol: 3 ALT
~ Gabrielle: 5 REECE

~ Macpherson: 4 ELLE
**Modeler**
purchase: 3 KIT
wood: 5 BALSA
**Modeling**
material: 4 CLAY
wood: 5 BALSA
**Models**
Like many: 6 SVELTE
Like Playboy: 4 SEXY
Very thin: 5 WAIFS
**Model T:** 4 AUTO
contemporary: 3 REO
**Modem**
Cable ~ alternative (abbr.):
3 DSL
Kind of: 5 CABLE
message: 3 FAX
Message via: 5 EMAIL
speed unit: 4 BAUD
termini: 3 EMS
**Moderate:** 4 EASE 5 ABATE
TEPID 8 CENTRIST
Politically:
15 MIDDLEOFTHEROAD
**Moderately**
slow: 7 ANDANTE
**Moderator:** 4 HOST
~ Jim: 6 LEHRER
**Modern:** 3 NEW 8 UPTODATE
address: 3 URL
art: 3 ARE
evidence: 3 DNA
Fairly: 6 NEWISH
First name in ~ dance:
5 TWYLA
letters: 5 EMAIL
Like some ~ music:
6 ATONAL
map subject: 6 GENOME
music media: 3 CDS
music style: 3 RAP
office staples: 3 PCS
pentathlon weapon: 4 EPEE
phone feature: 6 REDIAL
prefix: 3 NEO
recorder: 4 TIVO
rock genre: 3 EMO
sci. course: 4 ECOL
surgical tool: 5 LASER
viewer's choice: 4 HDTV
workout system: 5 TAEBO
~, in German: 3 NEU
**Modernist:** 3 NEO
**"Modern Maturity"**
org.: 4 AARP
**Modest:** 6 DEMURE
response to praise: 4 ITRY
Skirt for the: 4 MAXI
**Modesto**
winery name: 5 GALLO
**"Modest Proposal, A"**
author: 5 SWIFT
**Modicum:** 3 TAD
**Modifier**
abbr.: 3 ADJ

**Modify: 4** EDIT **5** ADAPT
  ALTER AMEND
  **6** RECAST
  text: **4** EDIT
**Modifying**
  wd.: **3** ADJ
**Modigliani**
  Painter: **6** AMEDEO
**Modish: 4** CHIC
**"Mod Squad, The"**
  actor Andrews: **4** TIGE
  actor Epps: **4** OMAR
  costar: **4** EPPS
  role: **4** LINC PETE
**Modular**
  home: **6** PREFAB
**Module: 4** UNIT
  Apollo 11: **5** EAGLE
**Modus ___ : 8** OPERANDI
**Modus operandi: 3** HOW WAY
  **6** METHOD SYSTEM
**Moe: 6** STOOGE
  Assault from: **4** POKE SLAP
  Missile for: **3** PIE
**Moe, Tommy**
  Emulate: **3** SKI
**Moffo**
  Diva: **4** ANNA
  Soprano: **4** ANNA
**Mogadishu**
  country: **7** SOMALIA
  resident: **6** SOMALI
**"Mogambo"**
  costar: **3** AVA
**Mogul: 5** NABOB
  **6** TYCOON
  Early movie: **4** LOEW
  Industry: **4** CZAR
  Movie ~ Laemmle: **4** LOEW
**Mogul Empire**
  capital: **4** AGRA **5** DELHI
**Moguls**
  One among the: **5** SKIER
  Tackle: **3** SKI
**Mohair**
  source: **6** ANGORA
**Mohammed**
  Descendant of:
    **7** AGAKHAN
**Mohawk**
  Actor with a: **3** MRT
  City on the: **5** UTICA
  Literary: **5** UNCAS
**Mohs scale**
  1 on the ~: **4** TALC
  8 on the ~: **5** TOPAZ
  Higher on the: **6** HARDER
  top: **3** TEN
**Moi**
  Belonging to: **3** MES
  **___ Moines: 3** DES
**Moises**
  of baseball: **4** ALOU
**Moist: 3** WET **4** DAMP DEWY
  and musty: **4** DANK
  application: **3** DAB

In a ~ way: **5** WETLY
  Keep: **5** BASTE
  Less: **5** DRIER
  suffix: **3** URE
**Moisten: 5** BEDEW
  the turkey: **5** BASTE
**Moistener**
  Muffin: **4** OLEO
**Moisture: 7** WETNESS
  Lacking: **3** DRY **4** ARID
  Morning: **3** DEW
  remover: **5** DRIER
**Moistureless: 4** ARID
**Moisturizer**
  ingredient: **4** ALOE
**Mojave: 6** DESERT
  Like the: **4** ARID
  plant: **5** AGAVE
  state (abbr.): **5** CALIF
**Mojo: 6** AMULET
**Molar: 5** TOOTH
  Acquire a: **6** TEETHE
**Molars: 5** TEETH
**Molasses**
  Dessert made from:
    **10** SHOOFLYPIE
  Like: **4** SLOW
  Move like: **4** OOZE
  Slow as: **4** POKY
**Molasses-based**
  liquor: **3** RUM
**Mold: 5** SHAPE
  anew: **7** RESHAPE
  Cold: **5** ASPIC
  Gold: **5** INGOT
  Metal: **3** PIG
  React to: **5** RIPEN
  ripened cheese: **4** BRIE
  source: **5** SPORE
**Moldavia**
  ~, once (abbr.): **3** SSR
**Molded**
  dessert: **5** BOMBE
  dish: **5** ASPIC
  Easily: **4** SOFT
**Molder: 3** ROT
**Molding**
  Convex: **5** OVOLO
  Curved: **4** OGEE
  Horizontal: **7** CORNICE
  S-shaped: **4** OGEE
  Window: **5** LEDGE
**Moldings**
  Semicircular: **4** TORI
**Molds: 5** FUNGI
**Mole: 3** SPY **5** AGENT
  kin: **5** SHREW
  passageway: **6** TUNNEL
**Molecular**
  biology topic: **3** RNA
  bit: **4** ATOM
**Molecule**
  Genetic: **3** RNA
  part: **4** ATOM
  Part of a complex: **6** LIGAND
  Single-strand: **3** RNA

**Molehill**
  It can make a ~ out of a
    mountain: **3** TNT
**Molière**
  metier: **6** SATIRE
  play part: **4** ACTE
**Moline**
  Company based in: **5** DEERE
**"Moll Flanders"**
  author: **5** DEFOE
**Mollify: 4** CALM **5** ALLAY
  **6** SOFTEN SOOTHE
  **7** ASSUAGE PLACATE
**Mollusk**
  Bivalve: **4** CLAM
  Edible: **6** OYSTER **7** ABALONE
  Spiral-shelled: **5** SNAIL
    WHELK
  Tentacled: **5** SQUID
    **7** OCTOPOD
**Mollusks**
  Tentacled: **6** OCTOPI
**Molly**
  Fibber and: **6** MCGEES
**Mollycoddle: 4** BABY **6** PAMPER
**Molokai**
  meal: **4** LUAU
  neighbor: **4** MAUI OAHU
**Molotov cocktail**
  fuse: **3** RAG
**Molson**
  product: **4** BEER
**Molson Centre**
  music: **7** OCANADA
**Molt: 4** SHED
**Molten**
  rock: **4** LAVA **5** MAGMA
**Mom: 6** PARENT
  1950s sitcom ~: **4** REED
  Bro of: **3** UNC
  Coop: **3** HEN
  Cousin's: **4** AUNT
  Mate of: **3** DAD
  Meadow: **3** EWE
  Mom's: **4** GRAN NANA
  Question to ~ or dad: **4** CANI
  Related to: **5** ENATE
  Sister of: **4** AUNT
  specialty: **3** TLC
  Stable: **4** MARE
**MoMA**
  artist: **4** DALI KLEE MIRO
  Part of: **3** ART **6** MODERN
  Part of ~ address: **4** NYNY
**Mom-and-pop**
  lender (abbr.): **3** SBA
  org.: **3** PTA
**Mombasa**
  home: **5** KENYA
**Moment**
  Brief: **3** SEC
  Met: **4** ARIA
  Quiet: **4** LULL
  Senior: **4** PROM
  **___ moment: 3** INA
**Momentarily: 4** SOON **6** INASEC

**Momentary**
flash: 5 GLINT
"___ momento!": 3 UNO
**Momentous:** 8 EVENTFUL
15 EARTHSHATTERING
"___ Mommy Kissing Santa
Claus": 4 ISAW
**"Momo"**
author Michael: 4 ENDE
**Mon.**
follower: 3 TUE 4 TUES
**"Mon ___!":** 4 DIEU
**"Mona ___":** 4 LISA
**Monaco**
resort: 10 MONTECARLO
**Monarch:** 5 RULER
Be a: 4 RULE
Bygone: 4 TSAR
catcher: 3 NET
domain: 5 REALM
Future: 4 HEIR
Old: 4 SHAH
**Monarchy**
Himalayan: 5 NEPAL
near Fiji: 5 TONGA
**Monastery:** 5 ABBEY
address: 3 DOM
head: 5 ABBOT
music: 5 CHANT
resident: 4 MONK 6 OBLATE
**Monastic**
jurisdiction: 6 ABBACY
title: 3 FRA
**Mondale**
running mate: 7 FERRARO
**Mondavi**
rival: 5 GALLO
**"Monday, Monday"**
Half the ~ group: 5 MAMAS
PAPAS
**"Monday Night Football"**
Former ~ commentator:
7 ESIASON
network: 3 ABC
**___ monde (high society):**
4 HAUT
**Mondesi**
of baseball: 4 RAUL
**Mondrian**
Painter: 4 PIET
**Monet:** 6 ARTIST
medium: 4 OILS
**Monetary**
gain: 5 LUCRE
**Money:** 4 CASH KALE
5 MOOLA 6 TENDER
Advance: 4 LEND
back: 6 REBATE REFUND
Big: 9 MEGABUCKS
Box office: 4 GATE
Bribe: 4 SOAP
Bygone: 6 PESETA
changer: 6 EDITOR
Coined: 6 SPECIE
Color of: 5 GREEN
Continental: 4 EURO

Corp. ~ man: 3 CFO
Dirty: 4 PELF
dispenser: 3 ATM
drawer: 4 TILL
Extort ~ from: 5 BLEED
Fed. ~ overseer: 3 OMB
for old age (abbr.): 3 IRA
for the poor: 4 ALMS
Front: 4 ANTE
Get-out-of-jail: 4 BAIL
Grant: 5 ENDOW
guarantor, for short: 4 FDIC
handler: 6 TELLER
International: 4 EURO
In the: 4 RICH
in the bank: 5 ASSET
Kind of: 3 MAD 4 HUSH SEED
Lay ~ on: 3 BET
Losing: 8 INTHERED
machine: 3 ATM
Make: 4 COIN EARN MINT
maker: 4 MINT
Makeshift: 5 SCRIP
manager: 6 EDITOR
Minimal: 4 CENT
New: EURO 5 EUROS
Old: 4 LIRE 5 SCRIP
overseas: 5 EUROS
owed: 4 DEBT
Paper: 5 NOTES
player: 3 PRO
Prize: 5 PURSE
Provide ~ for: 5 ENDOW
Put ~ in the bank: 4 SAVE
Put up, as: 4 LEND
roll: 3 WAD
Run for the: 4 RACE
Send: 5 REMIT
set aside: 6 ESCROW
Slangy: 4 KALE
Slightest bit of: 3 SOU
Solicit ~ from: 5 HITUP
spent: 5 OUTGO
substitute: 5 SCRIP
Take the ~ and run: 3 ROB
7 ABSCOND
The color of no: 3 RED
Upfront: 4 ANTE
Use: 5 SPEND
Without ~ changing hands:
7 INTRADE
Words before: 7 ALACKOF
**"Money"**
novelist Martin: 4 AMIS
**Moneybags:** 5 NABOB
6 FATCAT
**Moneyed**
one: 4 HAVE
**"Money ___ everything!":**
4 ISNT
**Money-losing**
proposition: 4 SCAM
**Moneymaker:** 4 MINT
Sure: 7 CASHCOW
**Moneymakers**
Magazine: 3 ADS

**Money-making:** 3 PRO
device: 3 DIE
**Money-managing**
exec.: 3 CFO
**"Money ___ object!":** 4 ISNO
**Money-related**
(abbr.): 4 FISC
**Money-saving**
~, in product names: 5 ECONO
**Mongibello**
Mount known locally as:
4 ETNA
**Mongkut, King**
realm: 4 SIAM
visitor: 4 ANNA
**Mongol**
invader: 5 TATAR
ruler: 4 KHAN
tent: 4 YURT
**Mongolia**
Like: 4 ARID
Much of: 4 GOBI
**___ Mongolia:** 5 OUTER
**Mongolian:** 5 ASIAN
desert: 4 GOBI
expanse: 10 GOBIDESERT
It means "ocean" in: 5 DALAI
It means "red" in: 4 ULAN
monk: 4 LAMA
mountain range: 5 ALTAI
tent: 4 YURT
**Mongoose**
prey: 5 COBRA
**Mongrel:** 3 CUR 4 MUTT
**Monica**
of tennis: 5 SELES
**___ Monica, California:**
5 SANTA
**Monicagate**
prosecutor: 5 STARR
**Moniker:** 3 TAG 4 NAME
6 HANDLE
Cowboy: 3 TEX
Monk: 4 FRA
Monster: 6 NESSIE
Satanic: 7 EVILONE
**Monitor**
Airport ~ (abbr.): 3 ARR ETA
beat: 4 HALL
Dot on a: 5 PIXEL
image: 4 ICON
Kind of PC: 3 LCD
PC: 3 CRT
Place for a ~ (abbr.): 3 ICU
TV: 3 FCC 5 VCHIP
**Monk**
Buddhist: 4 LAMA
home: 5 ABBEY 6 PRIORY
hood: 4 COWL
Like a: 6 HOODED
Main: 5 ABBOT
music: 3 BOP
quarters: 4 CELL
title: 3 DOM FRA
**"Monkees"**
1967 ~ song: 3 SHE

Peter of the: 4 TORK
**Monkey**
African: 6 BABOON
Aladdin: 3 ABU
business: 5 APERY
Grease ~ job: 4 LUBE
Kind of: 6 RHESUS
Mini: 4 TITI
South American: 4 TITI
suit: 3 TUX
wrench: 4 SNAG
**Monkey's**
uncle: 3 APE
**Monkeyshine:** 5 ANTIC
**Monkey Trial**
defendant: 6 SCOPES
lawyer: 6 DARROW
**Mono**
Not: 6 STEREO
relative: 3 UNI
**Monocle**
part: 4 LENS
**Monogram**
1950s ~: 3 AES DDE
CSA: 3 REL
Fashion: 3 YSL
Inventor: 3 TAE
Jan.: 3 MLK
letter: 7 INITIAL
Literary: 3 EAP GBS RLS RWE
TSE
ltr.: 4 INIT
N.L.: 3 STL
Poet: 3 TSE
Presidential: 3 DDE FDR HST
pt.: 4 INIT
**Monogrammatic**
car: 3 REO
**Monokini**
lack: 3 BRA
**Monologist**
Late-night: 4 LENO
need: 5 STOOL
~ Mort: 4 SAHL
**Monologue**
Miller: 4 RANT
**"Mon Oncle"**
actor: 4 TATI
Tati's ~ Monsieur: 5 HULOT
**Monopolize:** 3 HOG
~, with "up": 3 SEW
**Monopoly:** 4 GAME
asset: 5 HOTEL
avenue: 8 ORIENTAL
card: 4 DEED
Cheap ~ purchase: 6 BALTIC
Corner square in: 4 JAIL
fee: 4 RENT
maker: 6 HASBRO
need: 4 DICE
payment: 4 RENT
props.: 3 RRS 4 AVES
purchase: 5 HOTEL HOUSE
purchase (abbr.): 4 UTIL
token: 3 HAT 4 IRON SHOE
7 SCOTTIE

White ~ bill: 3 ONE
**Monorail**
unit: 4 TRAM
**Monotone**
Speak in a: 5 DRONE
**Monotonous:** 7 ONENOTE
8 SINGSONG
**Monotonously**
Talked: 8 DRONEDON
**Monotony:** 6 TEDIUM
8 SAMENESS
**Monounsaturated**
Oil high in ~ fatty acids:
6 CANOLA
**Monroe:** 6 BLONDE
movie: 7 BUSSTOP
or Madison (abbr.): 3 JAS
policy: 8 DOCTRINE
successor: 5 ADAMS
**Monroe, Marilyn:** 4 ICON
6 BLONDE
birth name: 5 NORMA
feature: 4 MOLE
**Monsoon**
Like ~ season: 5 RAINY
**Monster:** 4 HUGE OGRE
Fairy tale: 4 OGRE
Flying ~ of sci-fi: 5 RODAN
Green-eyed: 4 ENVY
Kind of: 4 GILA
lizard: 4 GILA
loch: 4 NESS
Many-headed: 5 HYDRA
Mythical: 3 ORC 5 HARPY
7 GRIFFIN
nickname: 6 NESSIE
Sea: 3 ORC 6 SCYLLA
Southwestern: 4 GILA
___ monster: 4 GILA
**"Monsters, ___":** 3 INC
**"Monster's Ball"**
actress Berry: 5 HALLE
**Mont.**
neighbor: 3 IDA 4 ALTA NDAK
SASK SDAK
**Montague**
foe: 7 CAPULET
Young: 5 ROMEO
**Montaigne**
output: 5 ESSAI ESSAY
**Montana:** 3 JOE 5 STATE
capital: 6 HELENA
city: 5 BUTTE
motto starter: 3 ORO
native: 4 CREE
neighbor: 7 ALBERTA
tribe: 4 CROW
~, once: 5 NINER
**Montand**
Actor: 4 YVES
**Mont Blanc:** 3 ALP PEN
range: 4 ALPS
~, in French: 4 ALPE
**Monte**
Three-card: 4 SCAM
**Monte ___:** 5 CARLO 6 CRISTO

(peak): 4 ROSA
___ Monte: 3 DEL
**Monte Carlo:** 4 AUTO
**Montecristo**
Island north of: 4 ELBA
**Montel**
rival, once: 5 OPRAH
**Montenegro**
native: 4 SLAV
**Monterey**
Fort near: 3 ORD
**Monte Rosa:** 3 ALP
**Monterrey**
jack: 4 PESO
mineral: 3 ORO
~ Mrs.: 3 SRA
**Monteverdi**
opera: 5 ORFEO 7 ARIANNA
**Montevideo**
land (abbr.): 3 URU
**Montez**
Dancer: 4 LOLA
**Montezuma:** 5 AZTEC
**Montgomery**
Actor: 5 CLIFT
City SSE of: 5 OZARK
City west of: 5 SELMA
Jazz guitarist: 3 WES
**Month**
A ~ of Sundays: 4 AGES
Day of the: 4 IDES
First Spanish: 5 ENERO
Hebrew: 4 ADAR ELUL
5 NISAN
In the previous: 6 ULTIMO
"Merry": 3 MAY
~, in Spanish: 3 MES
**Monthly:** 6 MENSAL
bill: 4 RENT 5 CABLE
bill (abbr.): 3 TEL 4 ELEC
**Months**
Like non-oyster: 5 RLESS
**Monticello:** 6 ESTATE
**Montmartre**
menu: 5 CARTE
**Montreal:** 6 ISLAND
1967 ~ event: 4 EXPO
player: 4 EXPO
prov.: 3 QUE
season: 3 ETE
~ Mrs.: 3 MME
**Monty**
Do a full: 5 STRIP
**"Monty Python"**
actor Idle: 4 ERIC
actor John: 6 CLEESE
actor Michael: 5 PALIN
airer: 3 BBC
offering: 4 SKIT
**Monument:** 5 STELE
designer Maya: 3 LIN
rock: 7 GRANITE
Stone: 5 CAIRN STELE
Year, on a: 4 ANNO
**Monumental:** 4 EPIC
year: 4 ANNO

**Monument Valley**
feature: 4 MESA
state: 4 UTAH
**Moo:** 3 LOW
Alley from: 3 OOP
**Mooch:** 3 BUM 5 CADGE
6 SPONGE
**Mood:** 4 TONE
Foul: 4 SNIT
In a peeved: 5 TESTY
In the: 7 AMOROUS
ring, once: 3 FAD
**"Mood ___":** 6 INDIGO
**Moody:** 4 DOUR 6 MOROSE
Actor: 3 RON
**Moody Blues**
hit: 5 GONOW
**"Moody River"**
singer: 8 PATBOONE
**Moo ___ gai pan:** 3 GOO
**Moo goo gai pan**
pan: 3 WOK
**Moo goo ___ pan:** 3 GAI
**Mooing**
Still ~, so to speak: 4 RARE
**Moolah:** 4 CASH GELT JACK
KALE 5 BREAD DOUGH
LUCRE 6 DINERO
DOREMI
**Moon:** 3 ORB
Bay at the: 4 HOWL
Blue: 6 RARITY
craft: 3 LEM
First name on the: 4 NEIL
Full: 5 PHASE
goddess: 4 LUNA 6 SELENE
Howl at the: 3 BAY
lander: 3 LEM
Like a blue: 4 RARE
Many a: 4 AGES
material: 11 GREENCHEESE
mission name: 6 APOLLO
New: 5 PHASE
of Jupiter: 4 LEDA 6 EUROPA
of Mars: 6 DEIMOS PHOBOS
of Neptune: 6 NEREID
TRITON
of Saturn: 4 RHEA 5 DIONE
TITAN 6 TETHYS
Of the: 5 LUNAR
of Uranus: 5 ARIEL 6 OBERON
7 MIRANDA TITANIA
Once in a blue: 6 RARELY
ring: 4 HALO
Second man on the: 6 ALDRIN
shape: 8 CRESCENT
Shoot for the: 6 ASPIRE
stage: 5 PHASE
suffix: 5 SCAPE
Unseen part of the:
7 FARSIDE
valley: 4 RILL 5 RILLE
vehicle: 3 LEM
**Moonfish:** 4 OPAH
**"Moonlight ___":** 6 SONATA
8 SERENADE

**Moon of Endor**
critter: 4 EWOK
**"Moon Over Parador"**
actress: 5 BRAGA
**"Moonraker"**
actor Richard: 4 KIEL
**"Moon River"**
composer: 7 MANCINI
lyricist: 6 MERCER
**Moonroof**
alternative: 4 TTOP
**Moons**
Many: 3 EON 4 AGES
**Moonscape**
Like a: 5 STARK
**Moonshine:** 5 HOOCH
11 MOUNTAINDEW
Irish: 6 POTEEN
maker: 5 STILL
mix: 4 MASH
Mouthful of: 4 SWIG
**Moonstone:** 4 OPAL
**Moonstruck:** 4 DAFT GAGA
6 INLOVE
**"Moonstruck"**
Oscar winner: 4 CHER
**Moo ___ pork:** 3 SHU
**Moor:** 5 HEATH TIEUP
betrayer: 4 IAGO
Place to: 4 COVE 5 INLET
Shakespearean: 7 OTHELLO
**Moore**
Actress: 4 DEMI
costar: 5 ASNER
Filmmaker: 7 MICHAEL
poem opener: 4 TWAS
Singer: 5 MELBA
**___ Moore (stew):** 5 DINTY
**Moore, Demi**
1990 ~ film: 5 GHOST
1997 ~ film: 6 GIJANE
**Moore, Dudley**
film: 6 ARTHUR
**Moore, Mary ___:** 5 TYLER
**Moore, Thomas**
land: 4 ERIN
**Moorehead**
Actress: 5 AGNES
**Mooring**
rope: 6 HAWSER
**Moorish**
palace: 7 ALCAZAR
**Moose**
kin: 3 ELK 4 DEER
**Mop**
mate: 4 PAIL
up: 4 SWAB
**Mop & ___:** 3 GLO
**Mope:** 4 POUT SULK 5 BROOD
**Mopped**
It may be: 4 BROW
**Moppet:** 3 TOT 4 TYKE
Mayberry: 4 OPIE
**Moral**
author: 5 AESOP
element: 5 ETHOS

principle: 5 ETHIC
Story with a: 5 FABLE
7 PARABLE
values: 6 ETHICS
**Morale:** 6 ESPRIT
GI ~ booster: 3 USO
**Morales**
Actor: 4 ESAI
**Moralist**
Noted: 5 AESOP
Roman: 6 SENECA
**Morality:** 5 ETHIC
**Morally**
reprehensible: 6 SORDID
strict: 7 PURITAN
**Morals**
Man of: 5 AESOP
**Moran**
Actress: 4 ERIN
rival: 6 CAPONE
**Moranis**
Actor: 4 RICK
**Morante**
Novelist: 4 ELSA
**Moravia**
Capital of: 4 BRNO
**Moravian:** 4 SLAV
**Moray:** 3 EEL
home: 6 EELERY
hunter: 5 EELER
**Mordant:** 5 ACERB
-- Mort: 4 SAIL
**More:** 4 ELSE 5 EXTRA
And: 3 ETC 4 ETAL
Does ~ than see: 6 RAISES
Get ~ out of: 5 REUSE
Is for ~ than one: 3 ARE
Little ~ than: 4 MERE
No ~ than: 4 MERE ONLY
UPTO 6 ATMOST
of the same: 7 WHATNOT
Once: 4 ANEW 5 AGAIN
6 AFRESH
One: 7 ANOTHER
One or: 3 ANY 4 SOME
or less: 5 ABOUT SORTA
6 KINDOF
Say: 3 ADD
What's: 3 AND 4 ALSO
work: 6 UTOPIA
~, in Spanish: 3 MAS
~, musically: 3 PIU
~, proverbially: 4 LESS
**"More!":** 6 ENCORE
**Morel**
morsel: 4 STEM
**Morelos, José**
Place to see: 4 PESO
**Moreno**
Actress: 4 RITA
**More or ___:** 4 LESS
**Moreover:** 3 AND TOO 4 ALSO
**"More's the pity":** 4 ALAS
**Morgan**
Country singer: 6 LORRIE
of the comics: 3 REX

Senior golfer: 3 GIL
**Morgan, J.P.:** 6 BANKER
___ morgana (mirage): 4 FATA
**Morgenstern**
of TV: 5 RHODA
**Morgiana**
Master of: 7 ALIBABA
**Morgue:** 3 RUE
**"Moriae encomium"**
author: 7 ERASMUS
**Morissette**
hit: 6 IRONIC
singer: 6 ALANIS
**Morita**
Sony cofounder: 4 AKIO
**Mork:** 5 ALIEN
and others: 3 ETS
home planet: 3 ORK
Like: 5 ORKAN
sign-off: 8 NANUNANU
spaceship: 3 EGG
supervisor: 5 ORSON
word: 4 NANU
**"Mork & Mindy"**
actress Dawber: 3 PAM
leader: 5 ORSON
planet: 3 ORK
**Morley**
Reporter: 5 SAFER
**Morlocks**
victims: 4 ELOI
**Mormon**
gp.: 3 LDS
Many a: 6 UTAHAN
stronghold: 4 UTAH
**Mormon Church**
founder: 5 SMITH
**Morn**
Moist in the: 4 DEWY
opposite: 3 EVE
**Mornay:** 5 SAUCE
**Morning**
bowlful: 6 CEREAL
condensation: 3 DEW
Early ~ arrivals: 7 REDEYES
Early in the: 6 ATDAWN
eyeopener: 4 JAVA 5 LATTE
6 COFFEE
haze: 4 MIST
hrs.: 3 AMS
It breaks every: 3 DAY
Like ~ grass: 4 DEWY
NBC ~ show: 5 TODAY
noisemaker: 5 ALARM
radio host: 4 IMUS
Red sky at: 4 OMEN
talk show cohost: 4 RIPA
~, in French: 5 MATIN
**Morning ___:** 5 GLORY
**"Morning ___ Broken":** 3 HAS
**"Morning Edition"**
network: 3 NPR
**Mornings**
~, for short: 3 AMS
**"Morning Watch, The"**
writer: 4 AGEE

**Morns:** 3 AMS
opposites: 4 EENS
**Moro**
of Italy: 4 ALDO
**Moroccan**
city: 3 FES FEZ
**Morocco**
Capital of: 5 RABAT
Former Spanish enclave in:
4 IFNI
**Morocco-like**
leather: 4 ROAN
**Moron:** 3 ASS
**Moronic:** 3 DIM 5 INANE
intro: 3 OXY
**Morose:** 6 SULLEN
**Morph**
prefix: 4 ECTO ENDO
suffix: 3 EME
**Morpheus**
In the arms of: 6 ASLEEP
Realm of: 6 DREAMS
**Morphine:** 6 OPIATE
**Morricone**
Composer: 5 ENNIO
**Morris**
Civil rights lawyer: 4 DEES
Director: 5 ERROL
Politico: 5 UDALL
**Morrison**
Author: 4 TONI
Singer: 3 VAN
**Morrison, Jim**
group, with "The": 5 DOORS
portrayer Kilmer: 3 VAL
**Morrison, Toni**
novel: 4 SULA 7 BELOVED
TARBABY
**Morrow**
Actor: 3 VIC
**Morrow, Tracy**
Rapper born: 4 ICET
**Morse:** 4 CODE
bit: 3 DAH DIT DOT 4 DASH
"E": 3 DIT DOT
message: 3 SOS
Singer: 7 ELLAMAE
"T": 3 DAH
Three dots, in: 3 ESS
**Morse, Robert**
Tony role for: 3 TRU
**Morsel:** 3 ORT 4 BITE 6 TIDBIT
**Mort**
Comedian: 4 SAHL
Satirist: 4 SAHL
___ mort (melancholy): 3 ALA
**Mortal**
wrong: 3 SIN
___ mortals: 4 MERE
**Mortar**
partner: 6 PESTLE
tool: 6 TROWEL
tray: 3 HOD
**Mortarboard:** 3 CAP
attachment: 6 TASSEL
Like a: 8 TASSELED

wearer: 4 GRAD
**Mortgage:** 4 DEBT LIEN
figure: 4 RATE
Govt. ~ org.: 3 FHA
Have a: 3 OWE
Satisfy a: 5 REPAY
Take out a: 6 BORROW
**Morticia:** 6 ADDAMS
Cousin of: 3 ITT
creator, briefly: 4 CHAS
Husband of: 5 GOMEZ
**Mortification:** 5 SHAME
7 CHAGRIN
**Mortify:** 5 ABASE ABASH
APPAL 6 DEMEAN
**Mortimer**
Dummy: 5 SNERD
Philosopher: 5 ADLER
**Mortise**
mate: 5 TENON
**Morton**
product: 4 SALT
**Morton, ___ P.:** 4 LEVI
**Mos.**
Fall: 4 OCTS
Many: 3 YRS
School: 5 SEPTS
**Mosaic:** 5 INLAY
Like ~ stones: 6 INLAID
piece: 4 TILE 7 TESSERA
pieces: 8 TESSERAE
technique: 5 INLAY
**Mosconi**
game: 4 POOL
maneuver: 5 MASSE
**Moscow**
City near: 4 OREL
money: 5 RUBLE
**Mose**
Jazzman: 7 ALLISON
**Moselle**
City on the: 4 METZ
tributary: 4 SAAR
**Moses**
Brother of: 5 AARON
Grandma: 4 ANNA
mount: 4 NEBO
Mount climbed by: 5 SINAI
Obstacle for: 6 REDSEA
of basketball: 6 MALONE
of track: 5 EDWIN
portrayer: 6 HESTON
Successor of: 6 JOSHUA
Where ~ was buried: 4 MOAB
**"Moses"**
novelist: 4 ASCH
**Moses, Grandma**
first name: 4 ANNA
**"Moses und ___":** 4 ARON
**Mosey:** 5 AMBLE
**Mosh:** 9 SLAMDANCE
**Moshe**
Israeli general: 5 DAYAN
of Israel: 5 ARENS
**Moslem**
leader: 4 EMIR IMAM

**Mosque**
Great ~ site: 6 ALEPPO
leader: 4 IMAM
tower: 7 MINARET
**Mosque of ___:** 4 OMAR
**Mosquito:** 4 PEST 5 BITER
Dangerous: 5 AEDES
lookalike: 5 MIDGE
protection: 3 NET
~, to a dragonfly: 4 PREY
**Moss**
Kind of: 4 PEAT
maker: 5 SPORE
Model: 4 KATE
Sea: 4 ALGA
Sphagnum: 4 PEAT
___ moss: 4 PEAT
**Mossback:** 4 FOGY
**Most**
At: 4 TOPS
For the ~ part: 6 MAINLY
7 ASARULE
Home to: 4 ASIA
Like ~ of us: 5 ASIAN
likely: 6 APTEST
More than: 3 ALL
**Mostel**
Actor: 4 ZERO
role: 5 TEVYE
**"Most likely ...":** 7 ODDSARE
**"___ Most Unusual Day":**
4 ITSA
**Most-wanted**
group: 5 ALIST
**Mosul**
native: 5 IRAQI
**Mot**
Bon: 4 JEST QUIP 7 EPIGRAM
**Mote:** 5 SPECK
**Motel:** 3 INN
employee: 4 MAID
freebie: 3 ICE 4 SOAP
Kind of: 5 ROACH
meeting: 5 TRYST
posting: 5 RATES
rater: 3 AAA
They're non grata at a: 4 PETS
unit: 4 ROOM
___ motel (tryst site): 6 NOTELL
**Motet**
group: 5 CHOIR
**Moth**
Draw for a: 5 FLAME
Kind of: 4 LUNA
meal: 4 WOOL
repellent: 5 CEDAR
**Moth-___:** 5 EATEN
**Moth-eaten:** 3 OLD 5 RATTY
STALE TATTY
More: 6 HOLIER
**Mother**
Act the ~ hen: 4 FUSS
Brooding: 3 HEN
Farm: 3 EWE HEN SOW
group: 3 DEN
helper: 9 NURSEMAID

of renown: 6 TERESA
relative: 5 ENATE
superior: 6 ABBESS
~, in Spanish: 5 MADRE
**Mother ___:** 4 LODE 6 TERESA
**"Mother Goose Suite"**
composer: 5 RAVEL
**Mother Hubbard**
Like: 3 OLD
**Mothering**
sort: 5 DOTER
type: 3 HEN
**Mother-in-law**
of Dracula: 6 OLDBAT
of Meathead: 5 EDITH
of Ruth: 5 NAOMI
**Motherless**
calf: 5 DOGIE
**"Mother Night"**
star: 5 NOLTE
**Mother-of-pearl:** 5 NACRE
source: 7 ABALONE
**Mother's Day**
baby: 6 TAURUS
Busy co. on: 3 FTD
**Mothers of Invention**
rocker Frank: 5 ZAPPA
**Mother Teresa:** 3 NUN
**Moths**
Showy: 3 IOS
**Motif:** 5 THEME
Jazz: 4 RIFF
**Motion**
detector: 6 SENSOR
First law of ~ subject:
7 INERTIA
Manner of: 4 GAIT
Ocean: 4 TIDE
Pertaining to: 7 KINETIC
picture: 4 CINE
Put into: 7 ACTUATE
Put off, as a: 5 TABLE
Support a: 6 SECOND
**Motionless:** 5 INERT STILL
6 ATREST
**Motion picture**
spool: 4 REEL
**Motivate:** 4 STIR 5 IMPEL
7 INSPIRE
**Motivator**
Certain: 7 PEPTALK
**Motive:** 6 REASON
A question of: 3 WHY
Crime: 7 REVENGE
Secret: 5 ANGLE
**Motley:** 4 PIED 6 RAGTAG
**Mötley ___:** 4 CRUE
**Motor**
Adjust a: 4 TUNE
attachment: 4 CADE
club: 3 AAA
Fly without a: 5 GLIDE
Gun the: 3 REV
Induction ~ inventor: 5 TESLA
lodge: 3 INN
oil additive: 3 STP

oil amount: 5 QUART
suffix: 3 OLA 4 CADE
trailer: 4 CADE
vehicle: 3 CAR
**Motorboat**
tow: 9 AQUAPLANE
**Motor City**
gp.: 3 UAW
**Motorcycle**
attachment: 7 SIDECAR
Big: 3 HOG
daredevil: 7 KNIEVEL
First name in ~ stunts: 4 EVEL
maker: 6 YAMAHA
**Motorcyclist**
~ Knievel: 4 EVEL
**Motorist**
choices: 4 RTES
offense: 3 DWI
org.: 3 AAA
Red, to a: 4 STOP
Stranded ~ need: 3 TOW
Stranded ~ signal: 5 FLARE
**Motown:** 5 LABEL 7 DETROIT
Franklin of: 6 ARETHA
genre: 4 SOUL
Marvin of: 4 GAYE
**Motown Records**
founder Berry: 5 GORDY
**Motrin**
rival: 5 ADVIL ALEVE
6 ANACIN
**Mott**
Reformer: 8 LUCRETIA
**Mottled:** 4 PIED 5 PINTO
horse: 4 ROAN 5 PINTO
6 DAPPLE
**Motto**
U.S. ~ word: 4 UNUM
**"Moulin Rouge"**
actor McGregor: 4 EWAN
dance: 6 CANCAN
**Mound:** 4 DUNE HEAP HILL
PILE 5 KNOLL
builder: 3 ANT
Insect: 7 ANTHILL
stat: 3 ERA
Stone: 5 CAIRN
Take the: 4 HURL
**Mount:** 5 GETON HORSE
STEED
climbed by Moses: 5 SINAI
Colorful: 4 ROAN
for Noah: 6 ARARAT
in Crete: 3 IDA
near Catania: 4 ETNA
They may: 8 TENSIONS
whose name means "I burn":
4 ETNA
**Mount ___:** 5 SINAI 6 VERNON
**Mountain**
air: 5 YODEL
ashes: 6 ROWANS
Biblical: 5 HOREB
cat: 4 PUMA
chain: 5 RANGE 7 SIERRAS

climber equipment: 5 ICEAX
    PITON
crest: 5 ARETE RIDGE
curve: 3 ESS
debris: 5 SCREE
demarcation: 8 TREELINE
Genesis: 6 ARARAT
goat: 4 IBEX
Greek: 4 OSSA
High: 3 ALP
home: 5 AERIE 6 CHALET
lake: 4 TARN
Lift up a: 4 TBAR
lion: 4 PUMA
man pursuit: 4 PELT
man trap: 5 SNARE
Martinique: 5 PELEE
Mongolian ~ range: 5 ALTAI
nymph: 5 OREAD
pass: 3 COL GAP
pool: 4 TARN
ridge: 5 ARETE
road feature: 3 ESS
road sign: 10 STEEPGRADE
sighting: 4 YETI
sign (abbr.): 4 ELEV
suffix: 3 EER
top: 4 PEAK
topper: 4 SNOW
tree: 3 ASH
Trip up a: 6 ASCENT
Way up a: 4 TBAR
World's highest: 7 EVEREST
~, to some: 8 MOLEHILL
Mountain ___: 3 DEW
Mountaineer: 6 SCALER
    7 CLIMBER
challenge: 4 CRAG
descent: 6 RAPPEL
rest stop: 5 LEDGE
tool: 5 ICEAX
"Mountain Music"
    group: 7 ALABAMA
___ Mountains: 4 URAL
    5 OZARK UINTA
Mountaintop: 4 APEX PEAK
home: 5 AERIE
Mountbatten
    Lady: 6 EDWINA
Mount Carmel
    locale: 6 ISRAEL
Mount Desert Island
    park: 6 ACADIA
Mountebank: 4 FAKE 5 ROGUE
Mounted: 4 ROSE
on: 4 ATOP
Mount Fuji
    setting: 6 HONSHU
Mount Hood
    locale: 6 OREGON
Mount Katahdin
    locale: 5 MAINE
Mount McKinley: 6 DENALI
Mount Olympus
    chief: 4 ZEUS
    dwellers: 4 GODS

queen: 4 HERA
Mount Rainier
    range: 8 CASCADES
    View from: 6 TACOMA
Mount Rushmore
    pres.: 3 ABE
    state (abbr.): 4 SDAK
Mount Saint ___: 6 HELENS
Mount Saint Helens
    fallout: 3 ASH
Mount Vernon: 6 ESTATE
Mourn: 6 BEWAIL GRIEVE
Mournful: 7 ELEGIAC
    cry: 4 YOWL
    melody: 5 DIRGE
    peal: 5 KNELL
    poem: 5 ELEGY
Mourning
    of basketball: 6 ALONZO
"Mourning Becomes Electra"
    brother: 4 ORIN
    playwright: 6 ONEILL
Mouse: 6 RODENT
    catcher: 3 CAT OWL 4 TRAP
    Eat like a: 4 GNAW
    hater cry: 3 EEK
    home: 3 PAD
    Like a: 3 WEE
    Like a church: 4 POOR
    manipulator: 4 USER
    Move like a: 4 DRAG
    pad: 3 MAT
    Reaction to a: 3 EEK
    sound: 5 CLICK
    target: 4 ICON
    Word with: 3 PAD
    ~, to some: 4 PREY
Mouseketeer
    An original: 6 DOREEN
        7 ANNETTE
    ~ Jimmy: 4 DODD
Mouselike
    animal: 4 VOLE
Mousquetaires
    Number of: 5 TROIS
Moussaka
    meat: 4 LAMB
Mousse
    alternative: 3 GEL
Mousy: 3 SHY 4 MEEK 5 TIMID
Mouth
    area: 5 DELTA
    Away from the: 6 ABORAL
    Big: 3 MAW YAP 4 TRAP
    bone: 3 JAW
    By: 6 ORALLY
    Down in the: 3 SAD
    Foam at the: 4 RAGE
    Foaming at the: 5 RABID
    It has a big: 4 EWER
    off: 4 RANT SASS
    off to: 6 SNAPAT
    Of the: 4 ORAL
    part: 4 ROOF
    piece: 3 LIP
    prefix: 3 ORI

River: 5 DELTA
Roof of the: 6 PALATE
Run at the: 5 DROOL
Sing with closed: 3 HUM
Taken by: 4 ORAL
They exist from hand to:
    5 REINS
Toward the: 4 ORAD
Word of: 5 PAROL
~, in slang: 3 YAP 4 TRAP
Mouthed
    Words ~ to a camera:
        5 HIMOM
Mouthful: 3 WAD 4 CHAW
    Carpenter: 5 NAILS
    Cows': 3 CUD
    of a sort: 4 SWIG
Mouthing
    off: 8 INSOLENT
Mouthless
    comic strip character:
        7 DILBERT
Mouthpiece
    piece: 4 REED
Mouths: 3 ORA
Mouth-shaped
    flower: 10 SNAPDRAGON
Mouthwash
    Like a: 5 MINTY
    Use: 6 GARGLE
Mouth-watering: 5 TASTY
Mouthy: 4 ORAL
Movable
    castle: 4 ROOK
Movado
    rival: 5 ROLEX
Move: 4 STIR 8 RELOCATE
    RESETTLE
    a bit: 5 BUDGE
    aimlessly: 3 GAD 4 MILL ROVE
    a muscle: 4 STIR
    a picture: 6 REHANG
    a plant: 5 REPOT
    aside: 5 SHUNT
    away: 6 RECEDE
    Ballet: 4 PLIE
    carefully: 4 EASE
    cautiously: 6 TIPTOE
    Crafty: 4 RUSE
    Dance: 3 DIP 4 STEP
    Don't: 4 STAY STOP
    effortlessly: 5 GLIDE
    Erratic: 3 ZAG ZIG
    False: 5 FEINT
    Fencing: 5 LUNGE PARRY
    forward: 5 IMPEL 6 PROPEL
    furtively: 5 SIDLE SLINK
        SNEAK
    Get a ~ on: 3 HIE
    gradually: 4 OOZE
    Gymnastics: 4 FLIP
    Hard to: 6 LEADEN
    How groups: 7 ENMASSE
    it: 3 HIE
    It can ~ a star: 4 LIMO
    It may ~ you: 3 VAN

Karate: 4 CHOP
laterally: 5 SIDLE
like a bunny: 3 HOP
like a butterfly: 4 FLIT
like a cat: 5 PROWL
like a crab: 5 SIDLE
like a snake: 7 SLITHER
like Jell-o: 6 WIGGLE
like molasses: 4 OOZE
Make a: 3 ACT 4 STEP
    5 REACT
obliquely: 5 SIDLE
on all fours: 5 CRAWL
on a puff of air: 4 WAFT
One on the: 4 GOER
one's tail: 3 WAG
On the: 5 ASTIR GOING
    6 ACTIVE
out: 6 VACATE
Powerless to: 5 INERT
Priced to: 6 ONSALE
quickly: 3 HIE ZIP 4 DART
    RUSH SCUD
Really: 4 ZOOM
sideways: 4 CRAB
Skittish: 5 START
slowly: 4 INCH OOZE PLOD
    SLOG 5 MOSEY
stealthily: 5 SKULK SLINK
    SNEAK
to the side: 5 SHUNT
unsteadily: 6 TEETER
upward: 5 ARISE
with a hum: 4 WHIR
Wrong: 5 ERROR
~, in Realtor-speak: 4 RELO
"___ move": 4 YOUR
**Moved**
Barely: 5 CREPT
furtively: 5 SLUNK
**"Move it, already!":** 6 LETSGO
**Movement**
Art: 4 DADA
Ballet: 4 PLIE
Concerto: 5 RONDO
Dance: 4 STEP
Fast: 7 ALLEGRO
Hippy: 4 HULA
Muscle: 3 TIC
Slow: 4 OOZE 5 LARGO
    6 ADAGIO 7 ANDANTE
Sonata: 5 RONDO
Start of many ~ names: 3 NEO
Upward: 6 ASCENT
word: 3 LIB
**"Move on":** 7 LETITGO
**Mover:** 3 VAN
Air: 3 FAN
and shaker: 4 DOER 5 NABOB
Boat: 3 OAR
challenge: 5 PIANO
Cursor: 5 MOUSE
How a ~ moves a sofa:
    7 ENDWISE
need: 3 VAN
rental: 5 UHAUL

Slow: 5 SNAIL
**Movie:** 4 CINE FILM SHOW
    5 FLICK
1958 ~, with "The": 4 BLOB
1966 ~: 5 ALFIE
1969 ~: 3 CHE
1977 ~: 4 ORCA
1982 ~: 4 TRON
1987 ~: 6 ISHTAR
1997 ~: 7 AMISTAD
1998 ~: 4 ANTZ
2003 ~: 5 GIGLI
award: 5 OSCAR
backdrop: 3 SET
Beatles: 4 HELP
buy: 3 DVD
channel letters: 3 HBO
Chase: 10 CADDYSHACK
color: 4 BLUE
critic Roger: 5 EBERT
Dinner and a: 4 DATE
dog: 4 ASTA TOTO
Early ~ mogul: 4 LOEW
ending: 4 GOER
ending cliché: 6 SUNSET
extra, for short: 4 SUPE
French: 4 CINE
genre: 6 HORROR
    8 WHODUNIT
Hot: 14 CHARIOTSOFFIRE
    ISPARISBURNING
    15 TOWERINGINFERNO
house: 6 CINEMA
Jungle ~ omen: 5 DRUMS
lioness: 4 ELSA
location: 3 LOT SET
maven: 5 EBERT
monster: 4 BLOB
Part of a ~ collection:
    7 VCRTAPE
pooch: 4 ASTA
Poor ~ rating: 7 ONESTAR
preview: 7 TRAILER
previewer: 5 RATER
princess: 4 LEIA
promo: 7 TRAILER
ratings: 3 PGS
shot: 4 TAKE 5 STILL
spool: 4 REEL
that rates 0 stars: 4 BOMB
    7 STINKER
theater: 4 CINE 6 CINEMA
trailer: 4 GOER
Western: 5 OATER
Whale of a: 4 ORCA
**Movies:** 3 PIX 4 FLIX
At the ~, maybe: 7 ONADATE
Day at the: 5 DORIS
In the: 8 ONSCREEN
Like many ~ nowadays:
    5 ONDVD
Like most: 5 RATED
Power of the: 6 TYRONE
The last word in: 3 END
**Moving:** 5 ASTIR
aid: 3 VAN 6 CASTER

Not: 5 INERT 6 ATREST
part: 5 ROTOR
Run without: 4 IDLE
vehicle: 3 VAN
**Moviola**
Work at the: 4 EDIT
**Mowed**
row: 5 SWATH
**Mower**
maker: 4 TORO 5 DEERE
path: 5 SWATH
storage: 4 SHED
**Mowgli**
portrayer: 4 SABU
**Mowing:** 5 CHORE
**Moxie:** 3 PEP 4 GRIT 5 NERVE
Alternative to: 4 NEHI
Have the: 4 DARE
**Mozambique**
neighbor: 6 MALAWI
**Mozart**
article: 4 EINE
birthplace: 7 AUSTRIA
movement: 5 RONDO
opera title starter: 4 COSI
portrayer Tom: 5 HULCE
rival: 7 SALIERI
**MP**
quarry: 4 AWOL
**MP3**
player: 4 IPOD
**mpg**
Part of: 3 PER
rater: 3 EPA
**mph**
Part of: 3 PER
**Mr.**
and Mr.: 6 MESSRS
Cartoon: 5 MAGOO
German: 4 HERR
Hindu: 4 BABU
Myopic: 5 MAGOO
~, abroad: 3 SRI
**Mr. ___**
(baseball mascot): 3 MET
(old whodunit game): 3 REE
(soft drink): 4 PIBB
**"Mr. Apollinax"**
poet: 5 ELIOT
**"Mr. Belvedere"**
actress Graff: 5 ILENE
**Mr. Big:** 5 NABOB
**Mr. Bill**
shriek: 4 OHNO
**Mr. Boddy**
game: 4 CLUE
**Mr. Chips**
class: 5 LATIN
portrayer: 5 DONAT
    6 OTOOLE
**Mr. Cool**
Hardly: 4 NERD
**"Mr. Deeds Goes to Town"**
director: 5 CAPRA
**Mr. Green**
game: 4 CLUE

Mr. Heep: 5 URIAH
"Mr. Holland's ___": 4 OPUS
"Mr. Hulot's Holiday"
  star/director: 4 TATI
Mr. Hyde: 5 FIEND
  8 ALTEREGO
MRI: 4 SCAN
Mr. 'iggins: 4 ENRY
Mr. Kramden: 5 RALPH
Mr. Kringle: 4 KRIS 5 KRISS
Mr. Magoo: 5 MYOPE
  malady: 6 MYOPIA
  nephew: 5 WALDO
  portrayer: 7 NIELSEN
"Mr. Mom"
  actress: 8 TERIGARR
  actress Garr: 4 TERI
  Costar of Keaton in: 4 GARR
  Costar of Michael in: 4 TERI
Mr. Moneybags: 5 NABOB
Mr. Moto: 6 SLEUTH
  portrayer: 5 LORRE
  remark: 4 AHSO
Mr. Nahasapeemapetilon:
  3 APU
"___ Mr. Nice Guy!":
  6 NOMORE
"Mr. ___ Passes By": 3 PIM
Mr. Peanut
  attire: 5 SPATS
Mr. Pecksniff: 4 SETH
"Mr. Peepers"
  actor Wally: 3 COX
Mr. Potato Head: 3 TOY
  part: 3 EAR EYE 4 NOSE
Mr. Pulver
  rank: 3 ENS
Mr. Right
  Hardly: 5 CREEP
Mrs.
  and Mrs.: 4 MMES
  Chicago: 6 OLEARY
  German: 4 FRAU
  Spanish: 6 SENORA
  ~, in French: 3 MME
  ~, in Spanish: 3 SRA
Mrs. Addams
  ~, to Gomez: 4 TISH
Mrs. Andy Capp: 3 FLO
"Mrs. Bridge"
  author Connell: 4 EVAN
Mrs. Cleaver: 4 JUNE
Mrs. Copperfield: 4 DORA
Mrs. Dithers: 4 CORA
Mrs. Kramden: 5 ALICE
"Mrs. Miniver"
  Mr. Miniver in: 4 CLEM
  ~ Oscar winner: 6 GARSON
Mrs. Munster: 4 LILY
Mrs. Peel: 4 EMMA
  partner: 5 STEED
  portrayer: 4 RIGG
Mr. Spock
  forte: 5 LOGIC
  Like: 7 LOGICAL
  Mother of: 6 AMANDA

  portrayer: 5 NIMOY
Mrs. Smith
  product: 3 PIE
Mrs. Sprat
  no-no: 4 LEAN
Mrs. Zeus: 4 HERA
Mr. T
  group: 5 ATEAM
  movie: 5 DCCAB
"Mr. Tambourine Man"
  group, with "The": 5 BYRDS
Mr. Television: 5 BERLE
Mr. Turkey: 3 TOM
Mr. Unexciting: 4 DRIP
Mr. Universe
  pride: 3 ABS
"Mr. Wrong"
  actress: 9 DEGENERES
MS.
  enclosure: 4 SASE
  founder: 7 STEINEM
  markers: 3 EDS
  ~, in Spanish: 4 SRTA
MS-___ : 3 DOS
"MS. Found in a Bottle"
  author: 3 POE
MSG
  decisions: 4 TKOS
  Part of: 4 MONO
  tourney: 3 NIT
Msg.
  Sabbath: 3 SER
MSgt: 3 NCO
MSN: 3 ISP
  rival: 3 AOL
MSNBC
  entertainer: 4 IMUS
  7 DONIMUS
  rival: 3 CNN
Ms. Pac-Man
  ghost: 3 SUE
Mtg.: 4 SESS
Mtge.
  units: 3 PTS
MTM
  Part of: 5 TYLER
Mtn.
  stat: 3 ALT 4 ELEV
MTV
  cartoon girl: 5 DARIA
  fans: 5 TEENS
  fare: 6 VIDEOS
  figure: 6 VEEJAY
  hosts: 3 VJS
  prize: 3 AVA
Mubarak
  of Egypt: 5 HOSNI
  predecessor: 5 SADAT
Much: 3 FAR 4 ALOT 6 ALOTOF
  As: 6 NOLESS
  As ~ as you like: 5 AGOGO
  Be too: 4 CLOY
  Had too: 4 ODED
  Has too: 3 ODS
  It doesn't take: 4 TREY
  less: 8 LETALONE

Not: 4 ABIT ATAD
Not as: 4 LESS
Not so: 4 LESS
Not up to: 4 IDLE
So ~, musically: 5 TANTO
the same: 5 ALIKE
Too ~, musically: 6 TROPPO
Took too ~ of: 6 ODEDON
Very: 4 ALOT ATON TONS
  5 BYFAR NOEND
  6 SORELY
~, musically: 5 MOLTO
"___ Much" (Presley hit): 3 TOO
"Much ___ About Nothing":
  3 ADO
"Much Ado About Nothing"
  friar: 7 FRANCIS
Mucho: 4 ALOT LOTS 5 LOTSA
"Much obliged!": 6 THANKS
Much-quoted
  Org. with a ~ journal: 3 AMA
Much-used
  key: 5 ENTER
Mucilage: 4 GLUE 5 PASTE
Muck: 3 GOO 4 CRUD MIRE
  OOZE
Muck-a-muck
  High: 3 VIP 4 EXEC
  7 BIGSHOT
  Mideast: 4 AMIR
Muckraker
  ~ Sinclair: 5 UPTON
  ~ Tarbell: 3 IDA
Mud: 3 JOE 4 GOOP JAVA
  bath place: 3 SPA
  Drag through the: 5 SMEAR
  hole: 3 STY
  Like: 4 OOZY
  Like thick, dry: 5 CAKED
  Move through: 4 SLOG
  5 SLOSH
  Sling ~ at: 4 SLUR 5 SMEAR
  7 ASPERSE
  Stick in the: 4 MIRE 5 EMBED
"Mud": 3 JOE
Mud ___ : 3 EEL PIE
Mudder
  fodder: 3 HAY 4 OATS
Muddle: 4 HASH MESS
  5 BEDIM BEFOG SNAFU
  In a: 4 ASEA
Muddleheaded: 6 ADDLED
Muddy: 4 ROIL 6 OPAQUE
  up: 4 ROIL
Mudhole: 3 STY
"___ mud in your eye!":
  5 HERES
Mud-sliding
  mammal: 5 OTTER
Mudville
  complement: 4 NINE
  slugger: 5 CASEY
Mueller, Robert
  org.: 3 FBI
Muesli
  morsel: 3 OAT

**Muezzin**
call to prayer: 4 AZAN
perch: 7 MINARET
**Muff:** 3 ERR
site: 3 EAR
**Muffet**
bugaboo: 6 SPIDER
fare: 4 CURD WHEY 5 CURDS
**Muffet-to-tuffet**
words: 6 SATONA
**Muffin**
choice: 3 OAT 4 BRAN CORN
ingredient: 3 OAT 4 BRAN
Make a: 4 BAKE
topper: 4 OLEO
**Muffin Man**
lane: 5 DRURY
**Muffle:** 6 DEADEN
**Muffler:** 5 SCARF
Trumpet: 4 MUTE
**Mug:** 3 ROB 4 FACE PUSS
6 KISSER
Big: 5 STEIN
Drink in a: 3 ALE
filler: 3 ALE 4 BEER
for the camera: 4 POSE
imperfections: 4 ZITS
Man-shaped: 4 TOBY
**Mugger:** 3 HAM
repellent: 4 MACE
**Muggy:** 5 HUMID
**Muhammad**
birthplace: 5 MECCA
Boxer: 3 ALI
Descendant of: 4 EMIR
faith: 5 ISLAM
**Muhammad ___:** 3 ALI
**Muhammad Ali**
was one: 5 PASHA
**Muir**
milieu: 7 SIERRAS
Poet: 5 EDWIN
**Mujer**
Married: 6 SENORA
Married ~ (abbr.): 3 SRA
**___ Mujeres, Mexico:** 4 ISLA
**Mukluk**
material: 8 SEALSKIN
wearer: 5 INUIT
**Mulberry**
fruit: 3 FIG
relative: 5 OSAGE
**Mulder**
and Scully org.: 3 FBI
folder: 5 XFILE
or Scully: 5 AGENT
or Scully (abbr.): 3 AGT
**"Mulder, ___" (Gillian Anderson**
**biography):** 5 ITSME
**Mule:** 4 SHOE
Army: 6 MASCOT
Canal with a: 4 ERIE
Erie Canal: 3 SAL
father: 3 ASS
Like a: 7 STERILE
mother: 4 MARE

of song: 3 SAL
team: 4 ARMY
**"Mule Train"**
singer: 5 LAINE
**Mulgrew**
Actress: 4 KATE
**Mull**
Island near: 4 IONA
over: 6 PONDER
**Mullah**
home: 4 IRAN
Taliban: 4 OMAR
**Mullally**
Actress: 5 MEGAN
**Mullens, Miss**
Caller on: 5 ALDEN
**Mulligan:** 4 STEW
**Mulligatawny:** 4 SOUP
**Multi**
suffix: 4 PLEX
**Multichannel:** 6 STEREO
**Multicolored:** 4 PIED
**Multi-day**
prayer: 6 NOVENA
**Multilingual:** 8 POLYGLOT
**Multinational**
currency: 4 EURO
**Multiple**
Abbr. before ~ surnames:
6 MESSRS
**Multiple-choice**
choice: 5 OTHER
**"Multiplicity"**
director: 5 RAMIS
**Multiplies**
It ~ by dividing: 6 AMOEBA
**Multipurpose**
truck: 3 UTE
**Multiroofed**
structure: 6 PAGODA
**Multitude:** 3 SEA 4 ARMY BEVY
HEAP HOST SLEW
5 HORDE 6 LEGION
**Multivitamin**
brand: 7 GERITOL
supplement: 4 IRON
**Multivolume**
ref.: 3 OED
**Mum:** 5 MATER 6 SILENT
**Mummy**
Celebrated: 3 TUT
God in ~ wrappings:
6 OSIRIS
home: 4 TOMB
Make a: 6 EMBALM
**Mun.**
official: 3 ALD
**Munch:** 3 EAT 5 CHOMP
**Munch, Edvard**
subject: 6 SCREAM
**Munched**
on: 3 ATE
**München**
mister: 4 HERR
**Munches**
on: 5 CHEWS

**Münchhausen**
Baron: 4 KARL
**Munchie**
Crunchy: 4 TACO
Mexican: 4 TACO 7 TOSTADA
**Munchies:** 4 URGE
Party: 7 CANAPES
Satisfy the: 4 NOSH
**Munchkin:** 3 ELF
**Munch Museum**
site: 4 OSLO
**___ mundi:** 4 ANNO
**Mungojerrie**
musical: 4 CATS
**Muni**
role: 4 ZOLA
**Munic.**
legislator: 3 ALD
**Munich**
Info: German cue
river: 4 ISAR
**Munich ___ of 1938:** 4 PACT
**Municipal:** 5 CIVIC
offering: 4 BOND
**Municipality:** 4 TOWN
Suffix in some ~ names:
4 BORO
**Munro, H.H.**
pen name: 4 SAKI
**Munson**
Actress: 3 ONA
**Munster**
Mr.: 6 HERMAN
Mrs.: 4 LILY
pet bat: 4 IGOR
pet dinosaur: 4 SPOT
son: 5 EDDIE
**Münster**
mister: 4 HERR
**"Munsters, The"**
DeCarlo of: 6 YVONNE
**Muppet:** 4 ELMO 5 ERNIE
eagle: 3 SAM
Ernie's ~ pal: 4 BERT
Giggly: 4 ELMO
Grouchy: 5 OSCAR
Red: 4 ELMO
Spanish-speaking: 6 ROSITA
Ticklish: 4 ELMO
with a unibrow: 4 BERT
~ Emmet: 5 OTTER
**Muppets**
creator: 6 HENSON
creator Henson: 3 JIM
**Mural**
prefix: 5 INTRA
site: 4 WALL
**Muralist**
Mexican: 6 RIVERA
Spanish: 4 SERT
~ José María: 4 SERT
~ Rivera: 5 DIEGO
**Murals**
and such: 3 ART
**Murder**
Christie ~ setting: 4 NILE

First ~ victim: 4 ABEL
mystery plot device: 5 TWIST
Some ~ mystery suspects:
  5 HEIRS
~, in slang: 3 OFF
**"Murder, ___":** 3 INC
**"Murder in the Cathedral"**
  playwright: 5 ELIOT
**"Murder in the First"**
  Christian of: 6 SLATER
**"Murder Must Advertise"**
  writer: 6 SAYERS
**"Murder on the ___ Express":**
  6 ORIENT
**"Murders in the ___ Morgue,**
  **The":** 3 RUE
**"Murders in the Rue Morgue,**
  **The"**
  beast: 3 APE
**"Murder, ___ Wrote":** 3 SHE
**Murdoch**
  Author: 4 IRIS
**Murmur:** 3 COO
**Murphy:** 3 BED
  Actor: 5 EDDIE
  Actress: 4 ERIN
  bed place: 6 CLOSET
  Decorated: 5 AUDIE
  War hero: 5 AUDIE
**Murphy, Eddie**
  1996 ~ film: 5 METRO
  2002 ~ film: 4 ISPY
  old show, for short: 3 SNL
**"Murphy Brown"**
  bar owner: 4 PHIL
  show: 3 FYI
  son: 5 AVERY
  star: 6 BERGEN
**Murphy's ___:** 3 LAW
**Murray**
  Actor: 4 BILL
  Actress: 3 MAE
  ref. work: 3 OED
  Singer: 4 ANNE
**Murray, Arthur**
  lessons: 5 STEPS
**Murrow**
  and others: 3 EDS
  network: 3 CBS
**Mus.**
  Get slower, in: 3 RIT
  Lively, in: 4 ANIM
  major degrees: 3 BAS
  version: 3 ARR
**Musante, Tony**
  series: 4 TOMA
**Musberger**
  Sportscaster: 5 BRENT
**Muscat**
  land: 4 OMAN
  money: 5 RIALS
  resident: 5 OMANI
**Muscateer:** 5 OMANI
**Muscatel:** 4 WINE
**Muscle:** 5 SINEW
  Arm: 5 BICEP 6 BICEPS

Back: 3 LAT
Bending: 6 FLEXOR
car: 3 GTO
Certain: 6 TENSOR
Chest: 3 PEC
condition: 4 TONE
connector: 6 TENDON
contraction: 5 SPASM
fiber ridge: 5 STRIA
injury: 4 TEAR
Involuntary ~ movement:
  3 TIC 5 SPASM
Lacking: 4 WEAK
Leg: 4 QUAD
Move a: 4 STIR
pain: 4 ACHE
power: 5 SINEW
problem: 3 TIC 5 CRAMP
  SPASM 6 STRAIN
protein: 5 ACTIN
Shoulder: 4 DELT 7 DELTOID
  ROTATOR
Show: 4 FLEX
spasm: 4 KINK
Stretching: 6 TENSOR
Thoracic: 3 PEC
**Muscle Beach**
  sight: 3 BOD
**Musclebound**
  guy: 5 HEMAN
**Muscleman**
  Mohawked: 3 MRT
  ~ Reeves: 5 STEVE
  ~ Steve: 6 REEVES
**Muscles:** 5 BRAWN
  Belly: 3 ABS
  Like overused: 4 ACHY
  Mold: 6 TONEUP
  Sitting: 6 GLUTEI GLUTES
  Tummy: 3 ABS
**Muscular:** 4 ROPY 5 BEEFY
  BUILT 6 SINEWY
  condition: 4 TONE
  dog: 5 AKITA
  Lean and: 4 WIRY
  power: 5 SINEW
**Muse**
  Astronomy: 6 URANIA
  Comedy: 6 THALIA
  count: 4 NINE
  History: 4 CLIO
  instrument: 4 LYRE
  Music: 7 EUTERPE
  Poetry: 5 ERATO
  Tenth: 6 SAPPHO
**Museo**
  in Madrid: 5 PRADO
  works: 4 ARTE
**Muses, The:** 4 NINE 5 NONET
  6 ENNEAD
**Museum**
  area: 8 GIFTSHOP
  artifact: 5 RELIC
  display: 3 ART
  Do ~ work: 7 RESTORE
  guide: 6 DOCENT

Like some ~ exhibits:
  6 ONLOAN
Natural history ~ display:
  4 TREX
piece: 5 RELIC TORSO
worker deg.: 3 MFA
**Museum ___:** 5 OFART
**Museum Folkwang**
  setting: 5 ESSEN
**Mush**
  Cornmeal: 7 POLENTA
  Reduce to: 5 PUREE
**Musher**
  vehicle: 4 SLED
**Mushroom**
  cap part: 4 GILL
  cloud maker: 5 ABOMB
  Edible: 5 MOREL
  Fleshy: 3 CEP
  French chef's: 4 CEPE
  Gourmet: 5 MOREL
  Inedible: 9 TOADSTOOL
  Japanese: 5 ENOKI
  part: 3 CAP 4 STEM
  seed: 5 SPORE
  stem: 5 STIPE
**Mushy**
  food: 3 PAP
  Get all: 4 MELT
**Musial**
  of baseball: 4 STAN
**Musial, Stan**
  nickname: 6 THEMAN
**Music**
  "10" ~: 6 BOLERO
  1950s ~ store purchase: 4 HIFI
  African ~ genre: 3 BIS
  A little night: 4 TAPS 5 SNORE
  Ambient ~ composer: 3 ENO
  Be silent, in: 5 TACET
  Big Band: 5 SWING
  box: 6 CDCASE
  British ~ co.: 3 EMI
  Caribbean: 3 SKA
  carrier: 4 IPOD
  category: 4 SOUL
  Church: 5 MOTET
  collectibles: 3 LPS
  compilation name: 4 KTEL
  Count in: 5 BASIE
  Country: 6 ANTHEM
  creators' org.: 5 ASCAP
  Easier version, in: 5 OSSIA
  Eastern: 4 RAGA
  for two: 4 DUET
  genre: 3 POP RAP 4 FOLK
    ROCK SOUL 5 BLUES
  group: 4 BAND
  hall: 5 ODEON ODEUM
  halls: 4 ODEA
  Hit: 3 RAP
  Holiday: 5 BLUES
  Home ~ system: 6 STEREO
  Kind of: 5 SHEET
  Knack for: 3 EAR
  Latin: 5 SALSA

Like some: 6 ATONAL
Lines of: 5 STAFF
Lure with: 7 TWEEDLE
marking: 4 SLUR
Merchant of: 7 NATALIE
Mexican: 8 MARIACHI
Modern ~ media: 3 CDS
Modern ~ style: 3 RAP
Muse of: 7 EUTERPE
Music box: 4 LILT
Night: 4 TAPS
Page of: 5 PATTI
Piece of: 5 SHEET
player: 4 JUKE 6 STEREO
preceder: 4 SOUL
rights org.: 5 ASCAP
sampler: 4 DEMO
sheet abbr.: 3 ARR
Sound of: 4 TONE
Summer: 5 DISCO
Summer ~ festival site:
    5 ASPEN
Swing: 4 JIVE
TV ~ vendor: 4 KTEL
With the bow, in: 4 ARCO
~, to a matador: 3 OLE
~, to a musician: 5 FORTE
**Musical**
1925 ~: 11 NONONANETTE
1943 ~:
    15 ONETOUCHOFVENUS
1948 ~: 6 CASBAH
1953 ~: 4 LILI
1958 ~: 4 GIGI
1960s rock ~: 4 HAIR
1966 ~: 6 IDOIDO
1969 ~: 12 SWEETCHARITY
1973 ~: 6 PIPPIN
1978 ~: 5 EUBIE
1996 ~: 4 RENT 5 EVITA
ability: 3 EAR
based on a Fellini film: 4 NINE
based on a strip: 5 ANNIE
beat: 5 TEMPO
break: 4 REST
buildup: 9 CRESCENDO
chairs goal: 4 SEAT
chord: 5 TRIAD
climax: 4 CODA
combo: 5 CHORD
composition: 4 OPUS
    5 ETUDE
conclusion: 4 CODA
dir.: 3 RIT
direction: 5 LENTO
discernment: 3 EAR
drama: 5 OPERA
embellishment: 7 ROULADE
    9 GRACENOTE
ending: 4 CODA
event: 7 RECITAL
exercise: 5 ETUDE
Fair-sized ~ group: 5 NONET
gift: 3 EAR
gourd: 6 MARACA
ineptitude: 6 TINEAR

interval: 5 NINTH 6 OCTAVE
    7 TRITONE
key: 5 AFLAT BFLAT CFLAT
    DFLAT EFLAT FFLAT
    GFLAT 6 AMINOR
    BMINOR CMINOR
    DMINOR EMINOR
    FMINOR GMINOR
leads: 5 SOLOS
Light ~ work: 8 OPERETTA
mark: 4 NOTE REST SLUR
measure: 3 BAR
melodrama: 5 OPERA
miscellany: 4 OLIO
motif: 5 THEME
notes: 3 FAS LAS MIS RES TIS
number: 5 PIECE
Of ~ quality: 5 TONAL
Part of a ~ gig: 3 SET
pause: 4 REST
phrase: 5 TRALA
pitch: 4 TONE
postscript: 4 CODA
potpourri: 6 MEDLEY
quality: 4 TONE
refrain: 5 TRALA
sense: 3 EAR
Short ~ composition:
    8 SONATINA
sign: 4 CLEF
silence: 4 REST
speed: 5 TEMPO
staff lines: 5 EGBDF
study: 5 ETUDE
syllable: 3 TRA
symbol: 4 CLEF NOTE REST
talent: 3 EAR
theme: 5 MOTIF
toy: 5 KAZOO
vamp: 5 INTRO
work: 4 OPUS
**Musically**
A little, ~: 4 POCO
flowing: 6 LEGATO
From the top, ~: 6 DACAPO
keyless: 6 ATONAL
More, ~: 3 PIU
Slow, ~: 5 LARGO
Smooth, ~: 6 LEGATO
So much, ~: 5 TANTO
Together, ~: 4 ADUE
Twice, ~: 3 BIS
Very, ~: 5 ASSAI
Wing it, ~: 3 JAM
**"Music for Airports"**
composer: 3 ENO
**Musician**
asset: 3 EAR
booking: 3 GIG
gift: 3 EAR
inspiration: 5 ERATO
job: 3 GIG
of old: 6 LUTIST
One-named: 4 MOBY 5 YANNI
org.: 5 ASCAP
Rolling: 5 STONE

~ Brian: 3 ENO
~ John: 4 TESH
~ Yoko: 3 ONO
**Music-licensing**
org.: 5 ASCAP
**"Music Man, The"**
setting: 4 IOWA
**Music store**
frequenters: 5 TEENS
**Musing**
Meadow: 3 MOO
**Musk:** 4 ODOR 5 SCENT
secreter: 5 OTTER
**Musket**
ammo: 4 BALL
attachment: 3 EER
    7 BAYONET
loader: 6 RAMROD
suffix: 3 EER
**Musketeers:** 4 TRIO
One of the: 5 ATHOS
    6 ARAMIS
Three: 3 BAR
**Muskie**
successor: 4 HAIG
**Muskogee**
native: 4 OKIE
**Muslim:** 7 ISLAMIC
Certain: 5 SUNNI 6 SHIITE
chief: 4 IMAM
crusade: 5 JIHAD
destination: 5 MECCA
general: 4 AGHA
judge: 5 HAKIM
leader: 4 EMIR IMAM
Like the ~ calendar:
    5 LUNAR
magistrate: 4 CADI
messiah: 5 MAHDI
palace area: 5 HAREM
Philippine: 4 MORO
pilgrim: 4 HAJI
pilgrimage: 3 HAJ 4 HADJ
    HAJJ
sect: 5 SUNNI
title: 3 AGA 5 HAFIZ
~ Almighty: 5 ALLAH
**Muss:** 6 RUMPLE TOUSLE
**Mussel**
home: 6 SEABED
**Mussolini**
moniker: 4 DUCE 6 ILDUCE
**Mussorgsky**
bass: 5 BORIS
**Must:** 5 HASTO 6 HAVETO
    NEEDTO 7 NEEDSTO
have: 4 NEED
It ~ go on: 7 THESHOW
pay: 3 OWE
You ~ remember this:
    5 ALAMO
~, informally: 5 GOTTA
**"Musta been something ___":**
    4 IATE
**Mustache**
style: 9 HANDLEBAR

**Mustachioed**
artist: 4 DALI
Last ~ president: 4 TAFT
~ Surrealist: 4 DALI
**Mustang:** 3 CAR 4 AUTO
home: 6 GARAGE
**Mustangs**
Home of the: 3 SMU
**Mustard:** 7 COLONEL
Cut the: 4 REAP
Cutting the: 4 ABLE
family member: 4 KALE
6 RADISH WASABI
rank (abbr.): 3 COL
town: 5 DIJON
**Mustard, Colonel**
game: 4 CLUE
**"Must be something ___":**
4 IATE
**Must-have:** 4 NEED
**"Must've been something ___":**
4 IATE
**Musty:** 4 DANK
**Mutated**
gene: 6 ALLELE
**Mute**
Some are: 5 SWANS
~ Marx: 5 HARPO
**Muted**
effect: 4 WAWA
~, with "down": 5 TONED
**Mutilate:** 3 MAR 4 MAIM
**Mutineer:** 5 REBEL
**Mutinied**
ship: 7 AMISTAD
**Mutiny**
Potemkin ~ city: 6 ODESSA
site: 5 CAINE
**"___ Mutiny, The":** 5 CAINE
**Mutt:** 3 CUR 7 MONGREL
Pal of: 4 JEFF
**Mutton**
fat: 4 SUET
serving: 3 LEG
**"___ Mutual Friend":** 3 OUR
**Mutual fund**
fee: 4 LOAD
holdings: 7 NESTEGG
Kind of: 4 REIT 6 NOLOAD
Some ~ accts.: 4 IRAS
**Mutuel**
lead-in: 4 PARI
**Muumuu**
accessory: 3 LEI
Where to wear a: 4 LUAU
**Muzak**
locale: 8 ELEVATOR
**Muzzle:** 5 SNOUT
Gun with a flared:
11 BLUNDERBUSS
loader: 6 RAMROD
**MVP**
1953 A.L. ~: 5 ROSEN
1998 N.L. ~: 4 SOSA
2000 World Series ~: 5 JETER
10 DEREKJETER

First Super Bowl: 5 STARR
NBA: *see page 710*
Super Bowl: *see page 709*
Super Bowl III: 6 NAMATH
Super Bowl XXXIII: 5 ELWAY
Three-time NHL: 3 ORR
Three-time Super Bowl:
10 JOEMONTANA
World Series: *see page 710*
**My**
Your and: 3 OUR
~, in French: 3 MES
**"My ___!":** 4 HERO
**Myanmar**
locale: 4 ASIA
neighbor: 4 LAOS
~, formerly: 5 BURMA
**"My bad!":** 4 OOPS
**"My Big Fat Greek Wedding"**
Vardalos of: 3 NIA
**"My boy":** 3 SON
**"___ my brother's keeper?":**
3 AMI
**"___ my case":** 5 IREST
**"My Cherie ___":** 5 AMOUR
**"My Children! My ___!":**
6 AFRICA
**"My Country"**
author: 4 EBAN
**"My country, ___ of thee ...":**
3 TIS
**"My country, 'tis of thee"**
song: 7 AMERICA
**"My Cousin Vinny"**
actress Marisa: 5 TOMEI
Oscar winner: 5 TOMEI
star: 5 PESCI 8 JOEPESCI
**"My Cup Runneth Over"**
musical: 6 IDOIDO
singer: 6 EDAMES
**"My Darling Clementine"**
role: 4 EARP
**"My dear man":** 3 SIR
**"My Dinner With Andre"**
actor: 5 SHAWN
director: 5 MALLE
**"My dog ___ fleas":** 3 HAS
**Myers**
Former press secretary:
6 DEEDEE
Political analyst: 6 DEEDEE
**"___ Myers":** 3 NED
**Myerson**
Miss America: 4 BESS
**"My Fair Lady"**
composer: 5 LOEWE
director: 5 CUKOR
lady: 5 ELIZA
race place: 5 ASCOT
**"My fault!":** 5 SORRY
**"My Favorite Martian"**
headgear: 8 ANTENNAS
**"My Favorite Year"**
star: 6 OTOOLE
**"My Friend ___":** 4 IRMA
**"My Friend Flicka"**

author: 5 OHARA
**"My gal":** 3 SAL
**"___ my God, thou art very
great":** 5 OLORD
**"___, My God, to Thee":**
6 NEARER
**"My goodness!":** 5 EGADS
**"___ My Heart":** 4 PEGO
**"___ My Heart in San
Francisco":** 5 ILEFT
**"My Heart Will Go On"**
singer: 4 DION
**"My karma ran over my ___":**
5 DOGMA
**"My kingdom for ___":**
6 AHORSE
**"My Life as ___":** 4 ADOG
**"My life ___ open book":**
4 ISAN
**"___ my lips!":** 4 READ
**"My Little Chickadee"**
actress West: 3 MAE
costar: 7 MAEWEST
**"My mama done ___ me ...":**
3 TOL
**"My man!":** 3 BRO
**"My Michael"**
author Oz: 4 AMOS
**"My mistake!":** 4 OOPS
**"My Name Is ___":** 4 ARAM
**"My Name Is Asher ___":**
3 LEV
**"My Name Is ___ Lev":**
5 ASHER
**MYOB**
Part of: 3 OWN 4 YOUR
**Myopic**
Mr.: 5 MAGOO
**"___ My Party":** 3 ITS
**"My People"**
author: 4 EBAN
**Myra**
Dame: 4 HESS
Pianist: 4 HESS
**"Myra Breckinridge"**
author: 5 VIDAL
**"___ my reasons ...":** 5 IHAVE
**Myriad:** 4 MANY
**Myrmecologist**
study: 4 ANTS
**Myrna**
Actress: 3 LOY
Role for: 4 NORA
**Myron**
Humorist: 5 COHEN
**Myrrh:** 5 RESIN
**Myshkin:** 5 IDIOT
**"My So-Called Life"**
actor Jared: 4 LETO
actress Danes: 6 CLAIRE
**Mysore**
master: 5 SAHIB
mister: 3 SRI
**Myst:** 4 GAME
**"My stars!":** 4 EGAD 5 EGADS
**Mysteries:** 6 ARCANA

**Mysterious:** 5 EERIE QUEER
  6 ARCANE
  character: 4 RUNE
  matters: 6 ARCANA
  (var.): 4 EERY
**Mystery:** 5 GENRE 6 ENIGMA
  First name in: 4 ERLE
    5 EDGAR 6 AGATHA
  Man of: 3 MRX
  middle name: 5 CONAN
  Street of: 5 DELLA
**"Mystery!"**
  host Diana: 4 RIGG
  station: 3 PBS
**"Mystery of ___ Vep, The":**
    4 IRMA
**Mystery writer**
  award: 5 EDGAR RAVEN
  ~ Josephine: 3 TEY
**Mystic:** 4 YOGI 5 SWAMI
  letter: 4 RUNE
**Mystical:** 5 RUNIC
  character: 4 RUNE

  deck: 5 TAROT
  emanation: 4 AURA
  poem: 4 RUNE
**"Mystic Pizza"**
  actress Taylor: 4 LILI
**Mystique:** 4 AURA
**"___: My Story":** 3 AVA
    4 REBA
**Myth:** 4 TALE
  Peak of: 4 OSSA
  River of: 4 STYX
  Ship of: 4 ARGO
  Twin of: 5 REMUS
**Mythical**
  archer: 4 EROS
  beast: 3 ORC
  bird: 3 ROC
  goat-man: 4 FAUN
  hammer wielder: 4 THOR
  hunter: 5 ORION
  huntress: 5 DIANA
  man-goat: 3 PAN 5 SATYR
  meanie: 4 OGRE

  monster: 3 ORC 7 GRIFFIN
  river: 4 STYX
  sorceress: 5 CIRCE MEDEA
  strongman: 5 ATLAS
  trio: 5 FATES
  weaver: 7 ARACHNE
  weeper: 5 NIOBE
**Mythology**
  anthology: 4 EDDA
**Mythomaniac:** 4 LIAR
**"My Three ___":** 4 SONS
**"My Three Sons"**
  son: 5 ERNIE
**"My treat":** 4 ONME
**My ___, Vietnam:** 3 LAI
**"My Way"**
  songwriter: 4 ANKA
**"___ my way":** 4 IMON
**"My Wicked, Wicked Ways"**
  author: 5 ERROL
**"___ my wit's end!":** 4 IMAT
**"My word!":** 4 EGAD ISAY
**"___ my word!":** 4 UPON

# Nn

**N:** 3 DIR
  followers: 4 OPQR
**N/A**
  Part of: 4 APPL
**NAACP**
  Part of: 4 ASSN NATL
    5 ASSOC
**Nab:** 3 BAG 4 NAIL 5 CATCH
    6 ARREST COLLAR
**Nabber**
  Cry of a: 6 GOTCHA
**Nabisco**
  cookie: 4 OREO
  cracker: 4 RITZ
  steak sauce: 4 AONE
  wafer: 5 NILLA
**Nabokov, Vladimir**
  novel: 3 ADA 4 PNIN
    6 LOLITA
**Nabors, Jim**
  role: 4 PYLE
**Nachos**
  topping: 5 SALSA
**"___ Nacht" (German carol):**
    6 STILLE
**NaCl:** 4 SALT
  Containing: 6 SALINE
**Nada:** 3 NIL ZIP 4 NONE
    ZERO 5 ZILCH ZIPPO
  ~, in French: 4 RIEN
**Nadelman**
  Sculptor: 4 ELIE
**Nader:** 7 ALSORAN
  Activist: 5 RALPH
**Nadir:** 6 BOTTOM
  opposite: 6 ZENITH
**Nae**
  sayer: 4 SCOT
**NAFTA**
  Part of: 5 TRADE
  predecessor: 4 GATT
  signer: 3 USA
**Nag:** 4 CARP 5 SHREW
    6 BADGER 7 HENPECK
  nibble: 3 OAT
  pad: 6 STABLE
**Nagana**
  carrier: 6 TSETSE
**Nagano**
  noodles: 5 RAMEN
**Nagger:** 5 SHREW
**"___ Nagila":** 4 HAVA
**Nagy**
  Hungarian leader: 4 IMRE
**"Nah!":** 4 UHUH
**Nahuatl:** 5 AZTEC
**Nahum**
  Book before: 5 MICAH

British poet laureate: 4 TATE
**Naif:** 4 BABE
**Nail**
  cousin: 5 SCREW
  file: 5 EMERY
  holder: 3 TOE
  Mining: 4 SPAD
  polish: 6 ENAMEL
  puller: 4 CLAW
  site: 3 TOE
  Small: 4 BRAD
  Thin: 4 BRAD
**Nail-biters**
  (abbr.): 3 OTS
**Nails**
  100 pounds of ~: 3 KEG
  Target for: 4 ITCH
  Work on: 4 FILE
**Nair**
  rival: 4 NEET
**Nairn**
  negative: 3 NAE
**Nairobi**
  nation: 5 KENYA
  native: 6 KENYAN
**Naish, J. ___:** 7 CARROLL
**Naive:** 7 ARTLESS
  crusader: 8 DOGOODER
  Not so: 5 SLYER
**Naked:** 4 BARE 6 UNCLAD
  Make: 6 DENUDE
  Not: 4 CLAD
**"Naked ___" (Goya work):**
    4 MAJA
**___ naked:** 5 STARK
**"Naked Jungle, The"**
  menace: 4 ANTS
**"Naked Maja"**
  painter: 4 GOYA
**Nala:** 4 LION
**Naldi**
  Actress: 4 NITA
**Namath, Joe:** 3 JET
  Last team of: 4 RAMS
  Super Bowl with: 3 III
**Name:** 3 DUB 4 CITE 5 TITLE
    7 APPOINT
  Assumed: 5 ALIAS
  Average: 3 DOW
  Big: 4 STAR
  Fail to: 4 OMIT
  Give a ~ to: 3 DUB 7 ENTITLE
  Give a new ~ to: 7 RETITLE
  Given a: 6 TERMED
  Good: 6 REPUTE
  Good ~, briefly: 3 REP
  part (abbr.): 4 INIT
**Named:** 4 IDED

  names: 4 SANG
  Once: 3 NEE
  Originally: 3 NEE
**Name-dropper:** 4 SNOB
  word: 3 NEE
**"___ Named Sue":** 4 ABOY
**Namely:** 5 IDEST TOWIT
    (abbr.): 3 VIZ
**"Name of the Rose, The"**
  author: 3 ECO
**Namesake**
  of Jr.: 3 III
  (plural): 3 JRS SRS
**Nametag**
  Like many a: 7 STICKON
  word: 5 HELLO
**"Name That Tune"**
  clue: 4 NOTE
**Namibia**
  neighbor: 6 ANGOLA
    8 BOTSWANA
  ~, until 1990 (abbr.): 3 SWA
**"Nana"**
  actress Anna: 4 STEN
  author Émile: 4 ZOLA
  author Zola: 5 EMILE
**___ Na Na:** 3 SHA
**Nanakuli**
  necklace: 3 LEI
**Nancy**
  Actress: 5 OLSON
  City near: 4 METZ
  Friend of: 6 SLUGGO
  Golfer: 5 LOPEZ
  Rival of: 5 TONYA
  When ~ bakes: 3 ETE
**"Nancy"**
  rich kid: 5 ROLLO
**Nanette**
  Words to: 4 NONO
**"___ Nanette":** 4 NONO
**Nanjing**
  nanny: 4 AMAH
**Nanki-___:** 3 POO
**Nanking**
  nanny: 4 AMAH
**Nanny:** 4 GOAT 9 NURSEMAID
  Eastern: 4 AMAH
  trio: 3 ENS
**"Nanny, The"**
  actress Taylor: 5 RENEE
  butler: 5 NILES
  portrayer Drescher: 4 FRAN
**Nanook**
  nook: 5 IGLOO
**Nantes**
  Info: French cue
  noggin: 4 TETE

Nothing, in: 4 RIEN
notion: 4 IDEE
river: 5 LOIRE
**Nantucket:** 6 ISLAND
**Nap:** 4 DOZE 5 SLEEP
        6 SIESTA SNOOZE
        10 FORTYWINKS
It has a: 5 SUEDE
Long: 4 SHAG
Noontime: 6 SIESTA
Place for a: 3 COT
sack: 3 BED
Take a: 4 REST
**Napa**
business: 6 WINERY
County east of: 6 SOLANO
growth: 4 VINE
nabob: 5 GALLO
Prefix used in: 4 OENO
**Naphthalene**
target: 4 MOTH
**Napkin**
for a slob: 6 SLEEVE
holder: 3 LAP
material: 5 LINEN
**Naples**
City near: 7 SALERNO
**Napoleon:** 5 EXILE 7 DESSERT
(abbr.): 3 EMP
birthplace: 7 CORSICA
Exile site for: 4 ELBA
Fate of: 5 EXILE
Marshal under: 3 NEY
**Napoleon III**
Wife of: 7 EUGENIE
**Napoli**
City NW of: 4 ROMA
locale: 6 ITALIA
Nothing, in: 6 NIENTE
Three, in: 3 TRE
**Napping:** 5 ADOZE 6 ASLEEP
        ATREST
~, so to speak: 7 UNAWARE
**Narc**
activity: 4 BUST RAID
chaser: 4 OSIS OTIC
find: 3 PCP 4 KILO 5 STASH
org.: 3 DEA
**Narcissist**
love: 4 SELF
problem: 3 EGO
vacation: 7 EGOTRIP
**Narcissus**
Like: 4 VAIN
Lover of: 4 ECHO
**Narcotic:** 4 DRUG 6 OPIATE
Govt. ~ watchdog: 3 DEA
Poppy: 5 OPIUM
**Narnia**
chronicler: 7 CSLEWIS
lion: 5 ASLAN
**Narrate:** 4 TELL
anew: 6 RETELL
**Narration:** 4 TALE
**Narrative:** 4 TALE 5 STORY
Heroic: 4 SAGA

Lengthy: 4 EPIC
**Narrator**
Literary: 7 PERSONA
Notable: 7 ISHMAEL
**Narrow:** 5 TAPER
access: 5 ALLEY
Become: 5 TAPER
cut: 4 SLIT
groove: 5 STRIA
inlet: 3 RIA
margin: 4 HAIR NOSE
        7 EYELASH
opening: 5 SLIT
passage: 4 LANE 5 INLET
peninsula: 4 SPIT
piece: 5 STRIP
ridge: 5 STRIA
street: 4 LANE
strip: 4 SLAT
valley: 4 GLEN
waterway (abbr.): 3 STR
zone: 4 BELT
~, as a bridge or road:
        7 ONELANE
**Narrow-bodied**
fish: 3 GAR
**Narrowly:** 7 BYAHAIR
defeat: 3 NIP 4 EDGE
**Narrow-waisted**
insect: 4 WASP
**Narthex**
neighbor: 4 NAVE
**Nary**
a soul: 5 NOONE 6 NOTONE
**NASA**
affirmative: 3 AOK
cancellation: 4 NOGO
Cancel, to: 5 ABORT
chimp: 4 ENOS
concern: 3 UFO
Creator of: 3 DDE
gasket: 5 ORING
moon craft: 3 LEM
outfit: 5 GSUIT
Part of: 4 NATL 5 SPACE
Perfect, at: 3 AOK
rocket stage: 5 AGENA
spacewalk: 3 EVA
**Nasal**
appraisal: 4 ODOR 5 AROMA
cavity: 5 SINUS
partitions: 5 SEPTA
passage: 4 NARE
tone: 5 TWANG
**NASCAR**
qualifier: 9 TIMETRIAL
sponsor: 3 STP
**NASDAQ**
cousin: 3 ASE
debut: 3 IPO
Like ~ trades: 3 OTC
listings (abbr.): 3 COS
New ~ listing: 3 IPO
offering: 5 STOCK
Part of ~ (abbr.): 4 ASSN
        5 ASSOC

rival: 4 NYSE
**Nash**
Crosby, Stills, and: 4 TRIO
Like a ~ lama has: 4 ONEL
Poet: 5 OGDEN
portrayer: 5 CROWE
priest: 4 LAMA 8 ONELLAMA
specialty: 3 PUN
**Nashville**
attraction: 4 OPRY
school (abbr.): 3 TSU
venue: 4 OPRY
**"Nashville"**
actress: 10 KARENBLACK
actress Blakley: 5 RONEE
song: 6 IMEASY
**Nassau**
country: 7 BAHAMAS
**Nasser**
Egyptian leader: 5 GAMAL
org.: 3 UAR
successor: 5 SADAT
**Nast**
of publishing: 5 CONDE
target: 9 BOSSTWEED
___ Nast: 5 CONDE
**Nastase**
Netman: 4 ILIE
of tennis: 4 ILIE
**Nastassja**
Actress: 6 KINSKI
Father of: 5 KLAUS
Role for: 4 TESS
**Nasty:** 4 ACID BASE MEAN
        UGLY VILE 5 SNIDE
Not so: 5 NICER
sort: 4 OGRE 6 MEANIE
**Nasty-smelling:** 5 FETID
**Nat**
Singer: 4 COLE
**Natal**
native: 4 ZULU
starter: 3 NEO PRE
**Natalie**
Singer: 4 COLE
**Natasha**
No, to: 4 NYET
Partner of: 5 BORIS
**Nathan**
Actor: 4 LANE
Patriot: 4 HALE
**Nathanael**
Author: 4 WEST
**National**
competitor: 4 AVIS 5 ALAMO
prefix: 5 INTER
service: 8 RENTACAR
song: 6 ANTHEM
symbol: 5 EAGLE
___ National Forest, Florida:
        5 OCALA
**National Gallery**
architect: 3 PEI
center: 6 ARMORY
**National Institutes of Health**
city: 8 BETHESDA

**Nationalists**
city: 6 TAIPEI
**Nationality**
suffix: 3 ESE
**National League**
division: 4 EAST
stadium: 4 SHEA
team: 4 METS REDS
6 ASTROS
**National Park**
of Alaska: 6 DENALI
of California: 7 REDWOOD
of Canada: 5 BANFF
of Maine: 6 ACADIA
of Utah: 4 ZION
**"National Velvet"**
author Bagnold: 4 ENID
**National Zoo**
animal: 5 PANDA
**Native:** 6 INBRED 7 ENDEMIC
8 INHERENT
10 ABORIGINAL
suffix: 3 ITE OTE
**Nativity**
scene: 6 CRECHE
**Natl. Courtesy Mo.:** 4 SEPT
**NATO**
founder: 3 HST
member: 3 GER USA
member since '99: 3 POL
Part of ~ (abbr.): 3 ATL ORG
**Natter:** 3 GAB 4 CHAT
**Natterjack:** 4 TOAD
**Natty:** 4 NEAT
**Natural:** 4 BORN 6 INBORN
INNATE UNDYED
do: 4 AFRO
emollient: 4 ALOE
habitat: 7 ELEMENT
Isn't a: 4 DYES
It may be: 3 GAS
necklace: 3 LEI
Not: 4 DYED 7 MANMADE
resource: 3 ORE
talent: 4 GIFT 5 FLAIR
~, in craps: 5 SEVEN
**"Natural, The"**
role: 5 HOBBS
**Natural gas:** 4 FUEL
component: 6 ETHANE
**"Natural History"**
author: 5 PLINY
**Naturalist**
Roman: 5 PLINY
**"Natural Man, A"**
singer: 5 RAWLS
**Naturalness:** 4 EASE
**Nature:** 3 ILK 4 SORT
7 ASPECTS
By its very: 9 IPSOFACTO
goddess: 4 ISIS
prefix: 3 ECO
Similar in: 4 AKIN
**"Nature"**
author: 7 EMERSON
**Naught:** 3 NIL

Bring to: 4 UNDO
**Naughty:** 3 BAD
Not: 4 NICE
**"Naughty, naughty!":** 3 TSK
**"Naughty you!":** 5 SHAME
**"Nausea"**
novelist: 6 SARTRE
**Nautical**
adverb: 4 ALEE
assent: 3 AYE
cry: 4 AHOY 5 AVAST
danger: 4 REEF
direction: 4 ALEE 5 APORT
journal: 3 LOG
pole: 4 SPAR 5 SPRIT
prefix: 4 AERO
speed unit: 4 KNOT
**Nautilus:** 3 SUB
attacker: 5 SQUID
captain: 4 NEMO
**Nav.**
officer: 3 ADM ENS
rank: 3 CPO ENS
school: 4 ACAD
**Navajo:** 5 TRIBE
dwelling: 5 HOGAN
foes: 4 UTES
neighbor: 4 HOPI
**Naval**
agreement: 3 AYE
base: 4 KEEL
builder: 6 SEABEE
force: 5 FLEET 8 SEAPOWER
hoosegow: 4 BRIG
initials: 3 HMS USS
noncom: 3 CPO
officer (abbr.): 3 ADM ENS
petty officer: 6 YEOMAN
pronoun: 3 SHE
rank (abbr.): 3 CDR CPO ENS
standard: 6 ENSIGN
~ VIP: 3 ADM
**Naval Academy**
freshman: 4 PLEB 5 PLEBE
**Nave**
bench: 3 PEW
neighbor: 4 APSE
**Navel:** 6 ORANGE
buildup: 4 LINT
Type of: 5 INNIE OUTIE
**Navigate:** 5 PILOT STEER
**Navigation**
acronym: 5 LORAN
aid: 5 SONAR
Bat's ~ aid: 4 ECHO
need: 3 MAP
Old ~ instrument:
9 ASTROLABE
route: 7 SEALANE
tool: 7 SEXTANT
unit: 7 SEAMILE
**Navigator**
heading (abbr.): 3 ENE ESE
NNE NNW SSE SSW WNW
WSW
instrument: 6 OCTANT

need: 3 MAP
**Navigator Islands**
~, today: 5 SAMOA
**Navratilova**
It means nothing to: 4 LOVE
rival: 5 EVERT
**Navy:** 4 BEAN
builder: 6 SEABEE
commando: 4 SEAL
Elite ~ group: 5 SEALS
mascot: 4 GOAT
noncom: 3 CPO
officer: 6 ENSIGN
sport rival: 4 ARMY
**Nay**
canceler: 3 YEA
opposite: 3 YEA
sayer: 4 ANTI
**Naysay:** 4 DENY
**Naysayer:** 4 ANTI
**"Nazarene, The"**
novelist: 4 ASCH
**Nazarenes:** 4 SECT
**Nazareth**
native: 7 ISRAELI
**N.B.**
Part of: 4 BENE NOTA
Prov. east of: 3 PEI
**NBA**
Like many ~ players: 4 TALL
nickname: 4 SHAQ
Part of: 4 ASSN
stats: 3 PTS
team: 4 HEAT NETS 5 SPURS
6 LAKERS PACERS
~ MVP: *see page 710*
**NBC**
comedy show since '75: 3 SNL
founder: 3 RCA
host: 4 LENO
morning show: 5 TODAY
news show: 8 DATELINE
Part of: 4 NATL
Peacock, to: 4 LOGO
**N.C.**
city: 3 RAL
**NC-17:** 5 ADULT
assigning gp.: 4 MPAA
Reason for an ~ rating:
4 GORE
**NCAA**
1995 ~ champs: 4 UCLA
Part of: 3 ATH 4 ASSN
8 ATHLETIC
rival: 3 NIT
**NCO:** 3 CPL SGT 4 MSGT SSGT
Certain ~, familiarly: 5 SARGE
Navy: 3 CPO
Part of: 3 NON
USAF: 4 TSGT
**NEA**
member: 4 TCHR
Part of: 4 ARTS ASSN EDUC
**Neal, Patricia**
film: 3 HUD
**Neanderthal:** 7 CAVEMAN

wear: 4 PELT
**Neap:** 4 TIDE
  Pertaining to: 5 TIDAL
**Near:** 4 NIGH 5 ABOUT
  6 ATHAND BESIDE
  7 CLOSEBY CLOSETO
  Draw: 7 CLOSEIN
  future: 6 OFFING
  Not: 3 FAR
**Near ___:** 4 EAST
**Nearby:** 5 CLOSE LOCAL
  6 AROUND ATHAND
  Not: 4 AFAR
  things: 5 THESE
**Near East**
  inn: 5 SERAI
**Near Eastern**
  honorific: 3 AGA
  hotel: 5 SERAI
**Neared:** 10 CLOSEDINON
**Nearest:** 8 PROXIMAL
  the center: 7 MIDMOST
**Near-eternity:** 3 EON 4 AEON
**Nearing**
  bedtime: 6 LATISH
  the hour: 5 TENTO
**Nearly:** 4 NIGH 5 ABOUT
  6 ALMOST 7 CLOSETO
  all: 4 MOST
  Very: 6 ALLBUT
**Near-perfect**
  grade: 6 AMINUS
  rating: 4 NINE
**Neat:** 4 TIDY 5 KEMPT NIFTY
  7 INORDER
  Make: 5 GROOM
  Not: 5 MESSY ONICE
  7 OVERICE
  Stiffly: 4 PRIM
  suffix: 3 NIK
**Neat as ___:** 4 APIN
**Neaten:** 4 TIDY 6 TIDYUP
  8 SPRUCEUP
  ~, as a lawn: 4 EDGE
**Neath**
  Not: 3 OER
**Neatnik**
  opposite: 4 SLOB
**"Neato!":** 4 COOL KEEN
  5 SWELL
**Neb.**
  neighbor: 3 KAN WYO 4 SDAK
**Nebraska**
  city: 5 OMAHA
  county: 4 OTOE
  First capital of: 5 OMAHA
  native: 3 OTO 4 OTOE
  6 PAWNEE
  neighbor: 4 IOWA
  river: 6 PLATTE
**Nebuchadnezzar**
  realm: 7 BABYLON
**Nebula**
  composition: 10 COSMICDUST
**Necessary**
  (abbr.): 4 REQD

  Deem: 6 SEEFIT
**Necessitate:** 6 ENTAIL
**Necessity:** 4 MUST NEED
**Neck**
  and neck: 4 EVEN TIED
  6 INATIE
  Back of the: 4 NAPE
  It may hang by the: 4 JOWL
  of the woods: 4 AREA
  Pain in the: 4 KINK PEST
  5 CRICK 6 HASSLE
  part: 4 NAPE
  region: 6 SCRUFF
  shape: 3 VEE
  wrap: 3 BOA 5 ASCOT SCARF
  ~, slangily: 5 SCRAG
**Necklace**
  component: 4 BEAD
  fastener: 5 CLASP
  Floral: 3 LEI
  gem: 5 PEARL
  item: 6 AMULET
  Kind of: 6 CHOKER
  Natural: 3 LEI
**Neckline**
  shape: 3 VEE
  type: 3 VEE
**Neckpiece**
  Feathered: 3 BOA
**Necktie:** 6 CRAVAT
  Arizona: 4 BOLO
  Broad: 5 ASCOT
  Fancy: 5 ASCOT
  Western: 4 BOLO 5 NOOSE
**Neckwear:** 3 TIE
  Floral: 3 LEI
  Furry: 3 BOA
  Knotted: 5 ASCOT
  Oxen: 4 YOKE
  Winter: 5 SCARF
**Nectar**
  collector: 3 BEE
  inspector: 3 BEE
  source: 4 PEAR
**Ned**
  Composer: 5 ROREM
**Need**
  Has ~ of: 5 LACKS
  If ~ be: 8 INAPINCH
  It's all you: 4 LOVE
**Needle:** 4 RIDE TWIT 5 NAGAT
  TAUNT TEASE
  bearer: 4 PINE
  case: 4 ETUI
  holder: 3 FIR 4 ETUI
  7 TONEARM
  hole: 3 EYE
  part: 3 EYE
  Ply a: 3 SEW
  point: 3 ENE ESE NNE NNW
  SSE SSW WNW WSW
  4 EAST WEST 5 NORTH
  SOUTH
  source: 3 FIR
  Use a: 3 SEW
  With a ~ (prefix): 3 ACU

**Needlefish:** 3 GAR 4 GARS
**Needle-nosed**
  fish: 3 GAR
**Needles**
  On pins and: 4 EDGY 5 ANTSY
  TENSE
  Phonograph: 5 STYLI
  Work with: 4 KNIT
**Needle-shaped:** 7 ACEROSE
**Needlework**
  Do: 3 SEW
**Needs:** 5 HASNT
**Needy:** 4 POOR
  Is: 5 WANTS
**Ne'er-do-well:** 3 BUM 5 IDLER
  ROGUE 7 LOWLIFE
**Neeson**
  Actor: 4 LIAM
**Neet**
  rival: 4 NAIR
**Nefarious:** 4 EVIL
  plan: 6 SCHEME
**Neg.**
  blowup: 3 ENL
  opposite: 3 POS
**Negate:** 4 UNDO
**Negation**
  symbol, in logic: 5 TILDE
**Negative**
  conjunction: 3 NOR
  Double: 4 NONO
  link: 3 NOR
  particle: 5 ANION
  Poetic: 4 NEER
  Russian: 4 NYET
  Scottish: 3 NAE
  Slangy: 3 NAH
  vote: 3 NAY
  votes: 3 NOS 4 NOES
  ~, in German: 4 NEIN
**Negev**
  Like the: 4 ARID
**Neglect:** 4 OMIT 6 DISUSE
  May ~ to: 6 NEEDNT
  Sign of: 4 RUST
**Neglected**
  area: 4 SLUM
  ~, as a lawn: 5 WEEDY
**Neglectful:** 6 REMISS
**Negligent:** 3 LAX 6 REMISS
**Negligible:** 4 SLIM
**Negotiating**
  goal: 4 DEAL
**Negotiation**
  result: 4 DEAL
**Negotiations:** 5 TALKS
  hang-up: 4 SNAG
**Negotiator:** 5 AGENT
  asset: 4 TACT
**Negri**
  Silent film actress: 4 POLA
**Neh.**
  Book after: 4 ESTH
  Book before: 3 EZR
**Nehemiah**
  Book after: 6 ESTHER

**Book before:** 4 EZRA
**Nehi**
  drinker on TV: 5 RADAR
  flavor: 5 GRAPE
**Nehru**
  Daughter of: 6 INDIRA
**Neigh**
  sayer: 5 HORSE
**Neighbor:** 4 ABUT
  A: 5 BFLAT
  on: 4 ABUT
**Neighborhood:** 4 AREA
    5 LOCAL
  event: 10 GARAGESALE
  In the: 4 NEAR 5 ABOUT
    LOCAL 6 NEARBY
  Needy: 6 GHETTO
  store: 4 DELI
**Neigh-sayer:** 5 HORSE
  on TV: 4 MRED
**Neil**
  Playwright: 5 SIMON
  Singer: 6 SEDAKA
**Neill**
  Actor: 3 SAM
**Neiman**
  Artist: 5 LEROY
**Neisse**
  partner: 4 ODER
**Neither**
  partner: 3 NOR
**Neither fish ___ fowl:** 3 NOR
**Neither here nor there:**
    7 ENROUTE INLIMBO
**Neither here ___ there:** 3 NOR
**"Nel ___, dipinto ...":** 3 BLU
**Nell**
  British actress: 4 GWYN
**"Nell"**
  actor Neeson: 4 LIAM
  actress Foster: 5 JODIE
**Nellie**
  Journalist: 3 BLY
  Soprano: 5 MELBA
**Nelligan, Kate**
  film: 5 ELENI
**Nelly**
  Poet: 5 SACHS
**Nels**
  Actor: 6 OLESON
**Nelson**
  Nobelist: 7 MANDELA
  Singer: 4 EDDY
**Nelson, Willie**
  Like the voice of: 5 NASAL
  movie:
    15 HONEYSUCKLEROSE
**Nemesis:** 3 FOE 4 BANE
    5 ENEMY
**Nemo**
  creator: 5 VERNE
  harpoonist: 3 NED
**Nen**
  of baseball: 4 ROBB
**Neo**
  portrayer: 5 KEANU

**Neo-**
  opposite: 5 PALEO
**Neolith:** 4 TOOL
**Neologism:** 7 COINAGE
  Create, as a: 4 COIN
**Neon:** 3 GAS 7 RAREGAS
    8 INERTGAS
  Like: 5 INERT
**Neon ___:** 5 TETRA
**Neophyte:** 4 TYRO
    10 FIRSTTIMER
**Nepal**
  capital: 8 KATMANDU
  legend: 4 YETI
  locale: 4 ASIA
**Nephrite:** 4 JADE
**Nephritic:** 5 RENAL
**Ne plus ultra:** 4 ACME
**Nepotism**
  beneficiary (abbr.): 3 REL
**Neptune:** 3 GOD 6 SEAGOD
  Celtic: 3 LER
  moon: 6 NEREID TRITON
  neighbor: 6 URANUS
  realm: 3 SEA 5 OCEAN
  spear: 7 TRIDENT
**Nerd:** 4 GEEK 5 DWEEB
    TWERP
**Nerdy:** 5 UNHIP 6 UNCOOL
  Not: 3 HEP 4 COOL
**Nero**
  (abbr.): 3 EMP
  instrument: 5 PIANO
  successor: 5 GALBA
  Tutor of: 6 SENECA
  Wife of: 7 OCTAVIA
  Year during reign of: 3 LIV LIX
    LVI LXI
**"Nerts!":** 4 DRAT
**Neruda**
  Nobelist poet: 5 PABLO
  specialty: 4 ODES
**Nerve:** 5 CRUST MOXIE
  cell: 6 NEURON
  cell part: 4 AXON
  Deadly ~ gas: 5 SARIN
  Have the: 4 DARE
  impulse region: 7 SYNAPSE
  Kind of: 5 OPTIC
  Lose one's: 10 CHICKENOUT
  network: 4 RETE
  opening: 4 NEUR
  Some: 5 OPTIC
**___ nerve:** 5 OPTIC
**"___ nerve!":** 4 SOME
**Nerves**
  More than just: 4 FEAR
  Sign of: 3 TIC
**Nervous:** 4 EDGY 5 ANTSY
    TENSE 6 ONEDGE
    UNEASY 9 ILLATEASE
  girl: 6 NELLIE
  laugh: 6 TITTER
  spasm: 3 TIC
  twitch: 3 TIC
  ~, with "up": 5 KEYED

**Nervous ___:** 6 NELLIE
**Nervousness:** 6 UNEASE
**Nervy:** 4 BOLD 5 BRASH
**Ness:** 3 FED 4 LOCH TMAN
  Agent: 5 ELIOT
  nemesis: 5 NITTI
  Untouchable: 5 ELIOT
**Nessen**
  Press secretary: 3 RON
**Nessie**
  Home of: 4 LOCH
**Nessman**
  WKRP newsman: 3 LES
  ___ Ness monster: 4 LOCH
**Nest:** 5 NIDUS
  builder: 3 ANT 4 BIRD
  Eagle's: 5 AERIE
  Lofty: 5 AERIE
  Lofty ~ (var.): 5 EYRIE
  material: 5 TWIGS
  noise: 4 PEEP 5 CHEEP
    CHIRP TWEET
  part: 4 TWIG
**Nest egg:** 3 IRA
  choice: 7 ROTHIRA
**Nester:** 3 HEN
  Chimney: 5 STORK
**Nesting**
  spot: 4 EAVE
**Nestlé**
  pet food brand: 4 ALPO
**Nestling**
  noise: 4 PEEP 5 CHEEP
**Nestor:** 4 SAGE
**Nests**
  Insect: 4 NIDI
  Like some: 5 EMPTY
**Net:** 5 SNARE 7 REALIZE
    8 AFTERTAX
    TAKEHOME
  address: 3 URL
  Catch in a: 6 ENMESH
  domain part: 3 COM EDU ORG
  Fishing: 5 SEINE TRAWL
  giant: 3 AOL
  Hair: 5 SNOOD
  letters: 3 WWW
  material: 4 MESH
  Surfing the: 6 ONLINE
  Where the ~ hangs: 3 RIM
**Netanyahu**
  predecessor: 5 PERES
  ~, familiarly: 4 BIBI
**Neth.**
  neighbor: 3 GER
**Netherlands**
  cheese: 4 EDAM
  city: 3 EDE
**Netherlands Antilles**
  island: 5 ARUBA
**Netherworld:** 5 HADES
  river: 4 STYX
**Netizen:** 4 USER
**Netscape**
  purchaser: 3 AOL
**Netting:** 4 MESH

**Nettle:** 3 IRK 4 RILE ROIL
**Network:** 3 WEB 4 GRID
　　5 AIRER 6 SYSTEM
　(abbr.): 4 SYST
　Cable: 3 AMC HBO TNT USA
　Kind of: 6 NEURAL
　logo: 3 EYE
　Major TV: 3 ABC CBS NBC
　Nerve: 4 RETE
　Overseas: 3 BBC
　*(plural)*: 5 RETIA
　point: 4 NODE
　signal: 4 FEED
　Telly: 3 BBC
　terminal: 4 NODE
　U.K.: 3 BBC
**"Network"**
　actor: 10 PETERFINCH
　director: 5 LUMET
**"___ Network 90" (1980s**
　　comedy): 4 SCTV
**Neuman, Alfred E.**
　feature: 4 GRIN
　magazine: 3 MAD
**Neur-**
　Suffix: 4 OTIC
**Neural**
　transmitter: 4 AXON
**Neurologist**
　request: 3 EEG
**Neuron**
　gap: 7 SYNAPSE
　Part of a: 4 AXON
**Neurotransmission**
　site: 4 AXON
**Neuss**
　Never, in: 3 NIE
**Neut.**
　Not ~ or fem.: 4 MASC
**Neuter:** 4 GELD SPAY 5 DESEX
　　7 SEXLESS
**Neutral:** 4 GEAR
　color: 3 TAN 4 ECRU
　　5 BEIGE
　Ethically: 6 AMORAL
　Run in: 4 IDLE
**Neutrality**
　Eschew: 9 TAKESIDES
**Neutralize:** 5 ANNUL
**Neutralizer**
　Acid: 4 BASE 6 ALKALI
　Alkali: 4 ACID
**Neutrinos**
　Symbols for: 3 NUS
**Neuwirth**
　Actress: 4 BEBE
**Nev.**
　neighbor: 3 IDA ORE 4 ARIZ
　　5 CALIF
**Nevada**
　city: 4 ELKO RENO
　lake: 5 TAHOE
　Novelist: 4 BARR
　senator Harry: 4 REID
　town: 3 ELY 4 ELKO
**___ Nevada:** 6 SIERRA

**Never:** 4 NARY 5 NOHOW
　　7 NOTONCE
　　8 ATNOTIME
　Almost: 4 ONCE
　Better than: 4 LATE
　say this: 3 DIE
　~, in German: 3 NIE
**Never-ending:** 7 ETERNAL
　story: 9 SOAPOPERA
　~, in poetry: 6 ETERNE
**"Neverending Story, The"**
　author: 4 ENDE
**"___ never fly!":** 4 ITLL
**"___ never happen!":** 4 ITLL
**"Never mind!":** 6 SKIPIT
　　8 NOMATTER
　~, to an editor: 4 STET
**"Nevermore!"**
　speaker: 5 RAVEN
**Nevertheless:** 3 BUT THO YET
　　6 EVENSO 8 AFTERALL
**"___ never too late!":** 3 ITS
**"Never Wave at a ___" (1952**
　　fiilm): 3 WAC
**"___ never work!":** 4 ITLL
**Nevil**
　Novelist: 5 SHUTE
**Neville**
　Singer: 5 AARON
**Nevins**
　Biographer: 5 ALLAN
**Nevis**
　partner: 7 STKITTS
**New**
　follower: 4 AGER
　moon: 5 PHASE
　Not: 4 USED
　Not as: 5 OLDER
　prefix: 3 NEO
　~, in Spanish: 5 NUEVA
　　NUEVO
**New-___:** 4 AGER
**New Age**
　musician: 5 YANNI
　musician John: 4 TESH
　singer: 4 ENYA
**Newark**
　County of: 5 ESSEX
　neighbor: 10 EASTORANGE
**New Balance**
　competitor: 4 AVIA NIKE
**Newbery Medal**
　winner Lowry: 4 LOIS
　winner Scott: 5 ODELL
**Newbie:** 4 TYRO
　Military: 5 PLEBE
　Society: 3 DEB
**Newborn:** 4 BABE BABY
　　7 NEONATE
　outfit: 7 LAYETTE
　place: 4 CRIB
　Stable: 4 FOAL
**Newcastle**
　product: 4 COAL
　river: 4 TYNE
**Newcomer:** 3 NEO 6 ROOKIE

　Academy: 4 PLEB 5 PLEBE
　Law school: 4 ONEL
　Society: 3 DEB
　Stable: 4 FOAL
**New Deal**
　agcy.: 3 CCC NRA REA TVA
　　WPA
　monogram: 3 FDR
　org.: 3 CCC NRA REA TVA
　　WPA
　pres.: 3 FDR
　prog.: 3 CCC NRA REA TVA
　　WPA
**New Delhi**
　garment: 4 SARI
**New England**
　cape: 3 ANN
　catch: 3 COD 5 SCROD
　college town: 7 AMHERST
　collegian: 3 ELI
　player: 7 PATRIOT
　sch.: 3 UNH URI
　soda fountain: 3 SPA
**New Englander:** 6 YANKEE
**Newer:** 8 UPGRADED
　version: 6 REMAKE
**New Guinea**
　port: 3 LAE
**___ New Guinea:** 5 PAPUA
**New Hampshire**
　city: 5 KEENE 6 NASHUA
　college town: 5 KEENE
　prep school: 6 EXETER
　state flower: 5 LILAC
**Newhart**
　Comedian: 3 BOB
**"Newhart"**
　actor Tom: 6 POSTON
　setting: 3 INN
**New Haven**
　campus: 4 YALE
　collegian: 3 ELI
　founder Theophilus:
　　5 EATON
　nickname: 7 ELMCITY
　school: 4 YALE
　student: 3 ELI 5 YALIE
**Newhouser**
　of baseball: 3 HAL
**New ___, India:** 5 DELHI
**"New Jack City"**
　costar: 4 ICET
**New Jersey**
　county: 5 ESSEX
　five: 4 NETS
　hoopsters: 4 NETS
　resort: 7 CAPEMAY
　seaport: 10 PERTHAMBOY
　skater: 5 DEVIL
　state tree: 6 REDOAK
　team: 4 NETS
　town: 4 LODI 6 LEONIA
**"New Life, A"**
　actor and director: 4 ALDA
**New Look**
　designer: 4 DIOR

**Newly**
formed: 8 EMERGENT
made: 5 FRESH
**Newlyweds**
trip: 9 HONEYMOON
**Newman**
Newsman: 5 EDWIN
**Newman, Paul**
film: 3 HUD 10 THEHUSTLER
  12 COOLHANDLUKE
  15 THECOLOROFMONEY
role: 3 ARI HUD
  12 BUTCHCASSIDY
**Newman, Randy**
song: 7 ILOVELA
**New Mexico**
art colony: 4 TAOS
mountains: 6 SANDIA
native: 4 ZUNI
resort: 4 TAOS
state flower: 5 YUCCA
town: 4 TAOS
**New Orleans**
cuisine: 6 CREOLE
sandwich: 5 POBOY
  7 POORBOY
university: 6 TULANE
**Newport Folk Festival**
performer: 4 BAEZ
**New Rochelle**
college: 4 IONA
**News**
agcy.: 3 UPI
bit: 4 ITEM
bulletin: 4 UPDATE
Business: 6 MERGER
clip: 5 VIDEO
Election: 5 UPSET
feature: 5 STORY
hour: 6 ELEVEN
Late: 4 OBIT
Latest: 6 UPDATE
letters: 3 UPI
Like old: 5 PASSE
Old ~ source: 5 CRIER
org.: 3 UPI
Reaction to bad: 5 GROAN
segment: 5 RECAP
Short ~ bit: 5 SQUIB
source: 4 LEAK
Sports: 5 TRADE
subject: 5 EVENT
summary: 5 RECAP
TV ~ source: 3 CNN
When some ~ airs: 5 ATSIX
  ATTEN
**Newsboy**
cry: 5 EXTRA
**Newscast**
ender: 5 RECAP
feature: 6 SPORTS
**Newsgroup**
message: 4 POST
system: 6 USENET
**Newshawk**
asset: 4 NOSE

query: 3 HOW WHO WHY
  4 WHAT WHEN 4 WHERE
source: 4 LEAK
**"NewsHour"**
airer: 3 PBS
**Newsletter**
Corporate: 5 ORGAN
  10 HOUSEORGAN
**Newsman**
of yore: 5 CRIER
**New South Wales**
capital: 6 SYDNEY
**Newspaper**
advertising piece: 6 INSERT
Do ~ work: 4 EDIT
employee: 8 PRESSMAN
executive: 6 EDITOR
inserts: 3 ADS
issue: 7 EDITION
notice: 4 OBIT
Old ~ section: 4 ROTO
opinion piece: 9 EDITORIAL
page: 4 OPED
piece: 4 ITEM
section: 6 COMICS SPORTS
**Newspapers:** 5 PRESS
Like most: 5 DAILY
~, television, etc.: 5 MEDIA
**Newsreel**
inventor: 5 PATHE
segment: 5 EVENT
**Newsroom**
fixture: 4 DESK
Old ~ machine (abbr.): 3 TTY
unit: 4 PICA
**Newsstand:** 5 KIOSK
purchase: 5 DAILY
**Newsweek**
rival: 4 TIME
**Newswire**
initials: 3 UPI
**Newt:** 3 EFT
Young: 3 EFT
___ newt: 5 EYEOF
**New Testament**
book: 4 ACTS LUKE
king: 5 HEROD
letter: 7 EPISTLE
**Newton:** 4 UNIT
fraction: 4 DYNE
fruit: 3 FIG
Scientist: 5 ISAAC
**Newtonian**
concept: 7 INERTIA
**Newton-John**
Singer: 6 OLIVIA
**New World**
(abbr.): 4 AMER
gp.: 3 OAS
**New Year**
Vietnamese: 3 TET
**New Year's ___:** 3 EVE
**New Year's Day**
event: 4 BOWL
**New Year's Eve**
word: 4 AULD LANG SYNE

**New York:** 5 STATE 6 COLONY
  7 SEAPORT
archbishop: 4 EGAN
bridge, formerly: 7 TRIBORO
canal: 4 ERIE
city: 5 OLEAN UTICA
  6 ELMIRA
college: 4 IONA
county: 4 ERIE
gallery district: 4 SOHO
island: 5 CONEY ELLIS
  6 STATEN
lake: 6 ONEIDA
mayor Giuliani: 4 RUDY
mountains: 6 RAMAPO
Place name in: 5 ASTOR
port: 6 OSWEGO
restaurateur: 5 SARDI
river: 4 EAST 7 AUSABLE
  GENESEE
stadium: 4 ASHE
team: 4 METS
tribe: 7 ONEIDAS
university: 7 CORNELL
**New York City**
archbishop: 4 EGAN
former mayor: 8 ABEBEAME
**New Yorker, The**
cartoonist Edward: 5 SOREL
cartoonist Peter: 4 ARNO
___ New York minute: 3 INA
**New York Times**
publisher Adolph: 4 OCHS
**New York World**
journalist: 3 BLY
**New Zealand**
bird: 4 KIWI
native: 5 MAORI
parrot: 3 KEA
tongue: 5 MAORI
**New Zealander:** 4 KIWI
  5 MAORI
**Next:** 4 THEN 6 ONDECK
Be ~ to: 4 ABUT 6 ADJOIN
Come: 5 ENSUE
in line: 4 HEIR
Lie ~ to: 4 ABUT
Put ~ to: 6 APPOSE
to: 6 BESIDE
to bat: 6 ONDECK
Up: 6 ONDECK
"___ next?": 4 WHOS
**Next-to-last**
syllable: 6 PENULT
**Nez ___:** 5 PERCE
**Nez Perce**
leader: 6 JOSEPH
mount: 9 APPALOOSA
**NFL**
city: 5 TAMPA
coach Dan: 5 SHULA
gains: 3 YDS
linemen: 3 RTS TES
official: 3 REF
scores: 3 TDS
stat: 3 YDS

tiebreakers: 3 OTS
  ~ 3-pointers: 3 FGS
  ~ 6-pointers: 3 TDS
**NFLer:** 3 BUC PRO 7 STEELER
  Former: 5 LARAM
  Top: 6 ALLPRO
**Ngaio**
  Contemporary of: 4 ERLE
**Ngo Dinh ___ (Vietnamese**
  **dictator):** 4 DIEM
**NHL**
  city: 6 OTTAWA
  Extra ~ periods: 3 OTS
  legend: 3 ORR 4 HOWE
  player: 5 BRUIN OILER
    SABRE
  Play in the: 5 SKATE
**Niagara Falls**
  feeder: 4 ERIE
  Like: 5 MISTY
  prov.: 3 ONT
  sound: 4 ROAR
  veil: 4 MIST
**Niamey**
  Its capital is: 5 NIGER
**Nibble:** 4 GNAW NOSH
  Nag: 3 OAT
  on: 3 EAT 5 TASTE
  Take a: 5 TASTE
**Nibblers**
  Cheese: 4 MICE
**Niblick:** 4 IRON
**Nicaragua**
  city: 4 LEON
  Daniel of: 6 ORTEGA
  Nothing, in: 4 NADA
**Nice:** 4 KIND
  girl: 5 NELLY
  life: 3 VIE
  notion: 4 IDEE
  Not so: 7 NASTIER
  response: 3 OUI
  summer: 3 ETE
  touch: 6 CARESS
  view: 3 MER
  water: 3 EAU
**"Nice!":** 3 AAH OOH
  7 GOODONE
**Nice ___:** 5 NELLY
**"___ nice day!":** 5 HAVEA
**Niche:** 4 NOOK 6 RECESS
  Church: 4 APSE
**Nichelle**
  role: 5 UHURA
**Nicholas:** 4 TSAR 5 SAINT
  Poet: 4 ROWE
**"Nicholas Nickleby"**
  actor Roger: 4 REES
**Nichols**
  partner: 3 MAY
**Nichols, Anne**
  hero: 4 ABIE
**Nicholson, Jack**
  film: 14 FIVEEASYPIECES
  role: 5 HOFFA
**Nick:** 4 DENT DING 5 GRAZE

Actor: 5 NOLTE
  Golfer: 5 FALDO
  name: 5 SANTA
  Old: 5 SATAN 9 BEELZEBUB
  Wife of: 4 NORA
**Nick and Nora**
  dog: 4 ASTA
**Nick at ___:** 4 NITE
**Nickel:** 4 COIN 7 ELEMENT
  animal: 5 BISON
  Word on a: 5 CENTS
**Nickel-and-___:** 4 DIME
**Nickelodeon:** 7 JUKEBOX
  Kenan's pal on: 3 KEL
  pooch: 3 REN
**Nickels:** 6 CHANGE
**Nicklaus, Jack**
  Norm for: 3 PAR
  org.: 3 PGA
**Nickname:** 3 DUB TAG
  7 AGNOMEN EPITHET
**"Nick of Time"**
  singer: 5 RAITT
**Nicks**
  Singer: 6 STEVIE
**Nicolas**
  Actor: 4 CAGE
  Film director: 4 ROEG
**Nicolò**
  Violin maker: 5 AMATI
**Nicotine**
  partner: 3 TAR
  source: 5 PATCH
**___ Nidre (Hebrew prayer):**
  3 KOL
**Niels**
  Physicist: 4 BOHR
**Nielsen**
  Actor: 6 LESLIE
  Actress: 8 BRIGITTE
  output: 7 RATINGS
**Nieuwpoort**
  river: 4 YSER
**Nifty:** 4 NEAT 5 NEATO
**Niger**
  Much of: 6 SAHARA
  neighbor: 4 CHAD MALI
  5 BENIN
**Nigeria**
  city: 5 LAGOS
  Gp. that includes: 4 OPEC
  language: 3 EDO
  neighbor: 4 CHAD 5 BENIN
  8 CAMEROON
  Pop singer from: 4 SADE
  tribesman: 3 IBO
**Nigh:** 6 NEARBY
  Draw: 4 NEAR
  Draw ~ to: 5 ANEAR
  Not: 4 AFAR
**Night**
  before: 3 EVE
  bird: 3 OWL
  flier: 3 OWL 4 MOTH
  flight: 6 REDEYE
  In for the: 4 ABED

light: 4 NEON STAR
  8 MOONBEAM
  Like a clear: 6 STARRY
  7 STARLIT
  noise: 4 HOOT 5 SNORE
  Out for the: 4 ABED 6 ASLEEP
  Poetic: 3 EEN
  prefix: 3 MID TWI 5 NOCTI
  school subj.: 3 ESL
  sight: 4 STAR
  sound: 5 SNORE
  Spend the: 4 STAY
  spot: 3 BED
  star: 4 LENO
  stick: 5 ROOST
  The ~ before: 3 EVE
  vision: 5 DREAM
  watch: 5 VIGIL
**"Night"**
  author Wiesel: 4 ELIE
**"Night at the Opera, A"**
  song: 5 ALONE
**Nightclub:** 5 BOITE DISCO
  6 BISTRO 7 CABARET
  HOTSPOT
  employee: 5 BGIRL
  expense: 11 COVERCHARGE
  offering: 9 FLOORSHOW
  of song: 4 COPA
  performer: 5 COMIC
**Nightfall**
  Bard's: 3 EEN
**Nightgown**
  wearer of rhyme:
    15 WEEWILLIEWINKIE
**Nightingale:** 5 NURSE
**"Nightingale, The"**
  author: 8 ANDERSEN
**"Nightline"**
  host Koppel: 3 TED
  host Ted: 6 KOPPEL
  network: 3 ABC
**Nightly**
  comic: 4 LENO
**Nightmare:** 5 DREAM
  cause: 7 BUGABOO
  street: 3 ELM
**"Nightmare on ___ Street, A":**
  3 ELM
**Nightmarish**
  street: 3 ELM
**"Night Music"**
  playwright: 5 ODETS
**"Night of the Hunter, The"**
  screenwriter: 4 AGEE
**Nightshade**
  Plant of the ~ family:
    7 HENBANE
**"Nights in White ___":**
  5 SATIN
**Nightspot:** 4 CAFE 7 CABARET
**Nightstand:** 8 BEDTABLE
  item: 4 EWER LAMP
**"Night They Invented**
    **Champagne, The"**
  musical: 4 GIGI

**Nighttime**
disorder: 5 APNEA
noise: 5 SNORE
Poetic: 3 EEN
**"Night Watch, The"**
painter: 9 REMBRANDT
**Nightwear:** 3 PJS
**Nihilistic**
art: 4 DADA
**Nike:** 5 DEITY
home: 6 OREGON
logo: 6 SWOOSH
rival: 4 AVIA 6 ADIDAS
REEBOK
swoosh: 4 LOGO
**Nikita**
"No," to: 4 NYET
successor: 6 ALEXEI
**Nikkei**
unit: 3 YEN
**Nikola**
Inventor: 5 TESLA
**Nikolai**
Author: 5 GOGOL
**Nikon**
rival: 5 LEICA
**Nil:** 4 NADA ZERO
**Nile**
bird: 4 IBIS
biter: 3 ASP
city: 5 ASWAN CAIRO
delta town: 7 ROSETTA
Opera set on the: 4 AIDA
queen: 4 CLEO
reptile: 3 ASP
slitherer: 3 ASP
wader: 4 IBIS
**Nimbi:** 5 AURAS
**Nimble:** 4 DEFT SPRY 5 AGILE
LITHE 6 ADROIT
**Nimbus:** 4 AURA HALO
**NIMBY**
Part of: 3 NOT
**Nimitz**
title (abbr.): 3 ADM
**Nin**
Diarist: 5 ANAIS
**Nin, Anais**
output: 7 EROTICA
**Nina**
Actress: 4 FOCH
Designer: 5 RICCI
**Nincompoop:** 3 ASS SAP
4 BOZO SIMP TWIT
5 IDIOT
**Nine**
Group of: 6 ENNEAD
Half of: 3 ENS
inches: 4 SPAN
On cloud: 6 ELATED
One of: 6 INNING
Piece for: 5 NONET
Put on cloud: 5 ELATE
The whole ~ yards: 3 ALL
4 ATOZ
Third of ~, once: 5 EARTH

Two of: 3 ENS
**Nine-___ (short golf course):**
5 HOLER
**Nine-day**
ritual: 6 NOVENA
**Nine-digit**
no. issuer: 3 SSA
sequence: 3 ZIP
~ ID: 3 SSN
**Nine-headed**
serpent: 5 HYDRA
**Nine-millimetre**
gun: 4 STEN
**Nines**
Dressed to the: 7 DUDEDUP
9 GUSSIEDUP
Pair of: 3 ENS
**Nine-sided**
shape: 7 NONAGON
**Ninesome:** 6 ENNEAD
**Nine-to-fiver**
cry: 4 TGIF
**Nineveh**
Book about: 5 NAHUM
locale: 7 ASSYRIA
locale (abbr.): 5 ASSYR
Modern site of: 4 IRAQ
river: 6 TIGRIS
**Ninny:** 3 ASS SAP 4 BOOB
DODO DOLT DOPE SIMP
TWIT 5 GOOSE
**Nino**
Film composer: 4 ROTA
**"Ninotchka"**
actress: 9 INACLAIRE
director Lubitsch: 5 ERNST
portrayer: 5 GRETA
**Nino Tempo**
Singer with:
12 APRILSTEVENS
**Nintendo**
character: 5 MARIO
forerunner: 5 ATARI
rival: 4 SEGA
**Ninth**
day before the ides:
5 NONES
month (abbr.): 4 SEPT
**Niobe:** 6 WEEPER
**Nip:** 4 BITE
partner: 4 TUCK
**Nipper:** 3 DOG
co.: 3 RCA
company: 9 RCAVICTOR
Nile: 3 ASP
Nose: 9 JACKFROST
**Nirvana**
attainer: 5 ARHAT
seeker: 5 HINDU
**Nisan**
Month after: 4 IYAR
Month before: 4 ADAR
**Nissan**
model: 6 ALTIMA MAXIMA
SENTRA
~, once: 6 DATSUN

**Nita**
of silents: 5 NALDI
**Nitpick:** 5 CAVIL
10 SPLITHAIRS
**Nitpicker:** 6 PEDANT
**___ nitrate:** 4 AMYL
**___ nitrite:** 4 AMYL
**Nitrogen:** 3 GAS
compound: 5 AMIDE AMINE
AZINE
lack: 4 ODOR
**Nitrogen-based**
dye: 3 AZO
**Nitrous ___ (laughing gas):**
5 OXIDE
**Nits**
Adult: 4 LICE
**Nittany Lions**
school (abbr.): 3 PSU
**Nitti**
nemesis: 4 NESS
**Nitty-gritty:** 3 NUB 4 MEAT
PITH 6 BASICS
**Nitwit:** 3 ASS 4 BOOB DODO
DOLT FOOL
**Niven**
role: 4 FOGG
**Nix:** 4 VETO 6 SCOTCH
**Nixon**
aide: 5 STANS
chief of staff: 4 HAIG
Commerce Secretary of:
5 STANS
Defense Secretary of: 5 LAIRD
impeachment chairman:
6 RODINO
nemesis Sam: 5 ERVIN
policy: 7 DETENTE
target: 4 HISS
undoing: 5 TAPES
Vice President of: 5 AGNEW
**"Nixon in China":** 5 OPERA
role: 3 MAO
**"Nixon's the One":** 6 SLOGAN
**N.J.**
and others: 3 STS
base: 5 FTDIX
city: 5 FTLEE
neighbor: 3 DEL
summer hrs.: 3 EDT
**N.L.**
city: 3 ATL CHI STL
**N.L. Central**
team: 3 CHI MIL STL
**NNE**
opposite: 3 SSW
U-turn from: 3 SSW
**NNW**
opposite: 3 SSE
U-turn from: 3 SSE
**No**
and others: 3 DRS
follower: 3 SIR 5 SIREE
Russian: 4 NYET
vote: 3 NAY
voter: 4 ANTI

~, in German: 4 NEIN
**No.**
　after a no.: 3 EXT
**No-**
　follower: 3 CAL
**"No ___!":** 4 PROB
**No-___ (gnat):** 5 SEEUM
**"No ___" (menu phrase):** 3 MSG
**No. 2:** 4 ASST
**No. 5**
　maker: 6 CHANEL
**No. 10:** 4 NEON
**"No. 10"**
　painter: 6 ROTHKO
**Noah**
　Actor: 4 WYLE 5 BEERY
　boat: 3 ARK
　challenge: 5 FLOOD
　landfall: 6 ARARAT
　mount: 6 ARARAT
　number: 3 TWO
　Son of: 3 HAM 4 SHEM
**"___ No Angels":** 4 WERE
**Nob:** 4 HILL
**Nobel:** 5 SWEDE
　category: 5 PEACE
　category (abbr.): 4 CHEM
　　ECON
　Inventor: 6 ALFRED
　suffix: 3 IST
　~ Prize: *see pages 728–736*
**Nobel Institute**
　city: 4 OSLO
**Nobelist:** 8 LAUREATE
**Nobelist, Chemistry:** *see pages*
　　*730–731*
　1911 ~ Marie: 5 CURIE
　1913 ~ Alfred: 6 WERNER
　1918 ~ Fritz: 5 HABER
　1928 ~ Windhaus: 5 ADOLF
　1934 ~ Harold: 4 UREY
　1936 ~ Peter: 5 DEBYE
　1937 ~ Norman: 7 HAWORTH
　1944 ~ Hahn: 4 OTTO
　1944 ~ Otto: 4 HAHN
　1967 ~ Manfred: 5 EIGEN
　1968 ~ Onsager: 4 LARS
**Nobelist, Economics:** *see page*
　　*736*
　1974 ~ Myrdal: 6 GUNNAR
　1980 ~ Lawrence: 5 KLEIN
　1990 ~ William: 6 SHARPE
　1997 ~ Scholes: 5 MYRON
　2001 ~ Michael: 6 SPENCE
**Nobelist, Literature:** *see pages*
　　*733–734*
　1909 ~ Lagerlöf: 5 SELMA
　1913 ~ Rabindranath:
　　6 TAGORE
　1921 ~ France: 7 ANATOLE
　1923 ~ William Butler:
　　5 YEATS
　1927 ~ Henri: 7 BERGSON
　1929 ~ Thomas: 4 MANN
　1930 ~ Sinclair: 5 LEWIS
　1933 ~ Ivan: 5 BUNIN

　1936 ~ Eugene: 6 ONEILL
　1946 ~ Hermann: 5 HESSE
　1947 ~ André: 4 GIDE
　1948 ~: 5 ELIOT 7 TSELIOT
　1954 ~:
　　15 ERNESTHEMINGWAY
　1957 ~ Albert: 5 CAMUS
　1961 ~ Andric: 3 IVO
　1966 ~ Nelly: 5 SACHS
　1966 ~ Sachs: 5 NELLY
　1971 ~ Neruda: 5 PABLO
　1971 ~ Pablo: 6 NERUDA
　1976 ~ Bellow: 4 SAUL
　1981 ~ Canetti: 5 ELIAS
　1984 ~ Simon: 6 CLAUDE
　1989 ~ Camilo José: 4 CELA
　1990 ~ Octavio: 3 PAZ
　1990 ~ Paz: 7 OCTAVIO
　1991 ~ Gordimer: 6 NADINE
　1992 ~ Walcott: 5 DEREK
　1993 ~: 4 TONI
　　12 TONIMORRISON
　1995 ~ Seamus: 6 HEANEY
　1997 ~ Fo: 5 DARIO
　2002 ~ Kertesz: 4 IMRE
**Nobelist, Medicine:** *see pages*
　　*732–733*
　1904 ~ Pavlov: 4 IVAN
　1908 ~ Metchnikoff: 4 ELIE
　1919 ~ Jules: 6 BORDET
　1936 ~ Otto: 5 LOEWI
　1949 ~ Walter: 4 HESS
　1950 ~ Philip: 5 HENCH
　1970 ~ Bernard: 4 KATZ
　1970 ~ von Euler: 3 ULF
　1974 ~ George: 6 PALADE
　1975 ~ Dulbecco: 6 RENATO
　1977 ~ Rosalyn: 5 YALOW
　1977 ~ Yalow: 7 ROSALYN
**Nobelist, Peace:** *see pages*
　　*734–735*
　1907 ~ Ernesto: 6 MONETA
　1912 ~ Root: 5 ELIHU
　1925 ~ Charles: 5 DAWES
　1927 ~ Ludwig: 6 QUIDDE
　1946 ~ John: 4 MOTT
　1949 ~ John Boyd ___: 3 ORR
　1949 ~ John ___ Orr: 4 BOYD
　1950 ~: 6 BUNCHE
　　11 RALPHBUNCHE
　1958 ~ Georges: 4 PIRE
　1961 ~ Hammarskjöld: 3 DAG
　1963 ~: 7 PAULING
　　12 LINUSPAULING
　1968 ~ Cassin: 4 RENE
　1969 ~: 3 ILO
　1971 ~ Willy: 6 BRANDT
　1974 ~ Eisaku: 4 SATO
　1975 ~ Sakharov: 6 ANDREI
　1978 ~ Anwar: 5 SADAT
　1978 ~ Sadat: 5 ANWAR
　1980 ~ ___ Pérez Esquivel:
　　6 ADOLFO
　1983 ~ Lech: 6 WALESA
　1983 ~ Walesa: 4 LECH
　1984 ~ Desmond: 4 TUTU

　1986 ~ Elie: 6 WIESEL
　1986 ~ Wiesel: 4 ELIE
　1987 ~ Oscar ___ Sánchez:
　　5 ARIAS
　1989 ~: 9 DALAILAMA
　1989 ~ the ___ Lama: 5 DALAI
　1993 ~ Nelson: 7 MANDELA
　1994 ~ Shimon: 5 PERES
　1994 ~ Yasser: 6 ARAFAT
　1994 ~ Yitzhak: 5 RABIN
　2001 ~ Kofi: 5 ANNAN
**Nobelist, Physics:** *see pages*
　　*728–730*
　1902 ~ Pieter: 6 ZEEMAN
　1903 ~ Pierre and Marie:
　　5 CURIE
　1909 ~ Guglielmo: 7 MARCONI
　1918 ~ Max: 6 PLANCK
　1918 ~ Planck: 3 MAX
　1922 ~ Bohr: 5 NIELS
　1922 ~ Niels: 4 BOHR
　1930 ~ Venkata: 5 RAMAN
　1933 ~ Paul: 5 DIRAC
　1938 ~ Enrico: 5 FERMI
　1938 ~ Fermi: 6 ENRICO
　1944 ~ Isidor: 4 RABI
　1944 ~ Rabi: 6 ISIDOR
　1945 ~ Wolfgang: 5 PAULI
　1955 ~ Polykarp: 5 KUSCH
　1957 ~ Tsung-___ Lee: 3 DAO
　1958 ~ Tamm: 4 IGOR
　1959 ~ Segrè: 6 EMILIO
　1962 ~ Landau: 3 LEV
　1967 ~ Hans: 5 BETHE
　1973 ~ Giaever: 4 IVAR
　1978 ~ Penzias: 4 ARNO
**Nobel Prize:** *see pages 728–736*
**"No bid":** 5 IPASS
**Nobility:** 5 PEERS
　Indian: 5 RAJAS RANIS
　Some: 4 SIRS
**Noble**
　British: 4 EARL 5 BARON
　　7 BARONET
　British ~ (briefly): 6 ARISTO
　French: 5 COMTE
　gas: 4 NEON 5 XENON
　Heaviest ~ gas: 5 RADON
　Hindu: 4 RANI
　Italian ~ family: 4 ESTE
　It may be: 3 GAS
　mount: 5 STEED
　objective: 5 IDEAL
　Of a certain: 5 DUCAL
　partner: 6 BARNES
　state: 7 EARLDOM
**Nobleman:** 4 EARL LORD
　　5 BARON
　French: 3 DUC 5 COMTE
　Spanish: 7 GRANDEE
　　HIDALGO
**Noblewoman:** 7 PEERESS
　　8 BARONESS
**"No ___, Bob!":** 6 SIRREE
**Nobody**
　in particular: 6 ANYONE

**"Nobody doesn't like ___ Lee":**
4 SARA
**No-brainer:** 5 MORON
7 EASYONE
15 OPENANDSHUTCASE
Like a: 4 EASY
**No-cal**
drink: 5 WATER
**Noche**
opposite: 3 DIA
___ noche (tonight, in Spanish):
4 ESTA
**No-cholesterol**
spread: 4 OLEO
**Nocturnal**
bird: 3 OWL
flier: 4 MOTH
hunter: 5 ORION
insect: 6 EARWIG
lizard: 5 GECKO
primate: 5 LEMUR
**Nod:** 3 CUE 4 DOZE 5 SLEEP
6 ASSENT SIGNAL
ending: 3 ULE
Gives the: 3 OKS
Give the: 4 OKAY 5 AGREE
6 ASSENT
Land west of: 4 EDEN
off: 3 NAP 4 DOZE
6 DROWSE
to: 5 GREET
Visit the land of: 5 SLEEP
Words with a: 4 ISEE
**Nodding:** 6 ASLEEP SLEEPY
**"No dice":** 3 NAH 4 UHUH
**Nods:** 3 OKS 5 YESES
**Nodule:** 5 POLYP
Crystal-lined: 5 GEODE
**Noel:** 4 YULE 5 CAROL
___ Noël: 4 PERE
**"No Exit"**
playwright: 6 SARTRE
**No-frills:** 5 BASIC PLAIN
7 GENERIC SPARTAN
bed: 3 COT
**Nofziger**
Reagan aide: 3 LYN
**Nog**
ingredient: 3 EGG
**Nogales**
Info: Spanish cue
Nap, in: 6 SIESTA
Nothing, in: 4 NADA
Now, in: 5 AHORA
**Noggin:** 4 BEAN DOME HEAD
PATE 5 GOURD
6 NOODLE
Knock on the: 4 BONK CONK
~, in French: 4 TETE
**No-good:** 6 ROTTEN
___ no good: 4 UPTO
**No-goodnik:** 3 CAD RAT
4 HEEL 5 LOUSE
6 BADDIE BADEGG
MEANIE 7 SOANDSO
STINKER

**No-holds-barred:** 6 ALLOUT
7 EXTREME
___ No Hooks: 3 USE
"___ no idea!": 4 IHAD
**"No ifs, ands, or ___":** 4 BUTS
**"No ifs, ___, or buts!":** 4 ANDS
___ noir: 4 CAFE 5 PINOT
___ noire: 4 BETE
**Noise**
Crowd: 3 RAH 8 APPLAUSE
Fan: 3 RAH 4 WHIR
Herd: 3 MOO
Lot of: 3 DIN
Nest: 4 PEEP 5 CHEEP
Night: 5 SNORE
of the lambs: 3 BAA
Radio: 6 STATIC
Trumpet: 5 BLARE
**Noisemaker**
Celebration: 11 FIRECRACKER
Flying: 6 CICADA
Nighttime: 6 SNORER
Nursery: 6 RATTLE
**Noisily**
Drink: 5 SLURP
Proclaim: 5 BLARE
Revel: 7 ROISTER
Walk: 5 CLOMP
**Noisy:** 4 LOUD 5 AROAR
bird: 3 JAY
fight: 5 BRAWL
flier: 3 SST
insect: 6 CICADA
napper: 6 SNORER
quarrel: 3 ROW
sleeper: 6 SNORER
toy: 6 POPGUN
trains: 3 ELS
**"No kidding!":** 3 GEE 4 GOSH
6 DOTELL 7 IMEANIT
ITSTRUE 8 ITSAFACT
**Nol**
of Cambodia: 3 LON
**Nolan**
of baseball: 4 RYAN
**Nolan, Philip:** 5 EXILE
**No later than:** 3 TIL 5 UNTIL
**Nolde**
Expressionist painter: 4 EMIL
**No less than:** 7 ATLEAST
**Nolin, ___ Lee**
Actress: 4 GENA
**Nolo:** 4 PLEA
contendere: 4 PLEA
**No longer:** 3 NOT
here: 4 GONE
hot: 3 OUT
in: 5 DATED PASSE
**Nolte**
Actor: 4 NICK
Cape in a ~: 4 FEAR
**Nomad:** 5 ROVER 6 ROAMER
8 WANDERER
**Nomadic**
Be: 4 ROAM ROVE
tribe: 5 HORDE

**"No man is an island"**
author: 5 DONNE
**"No man ___ island":** 4 ISAN
**No matter what:**
15 COMERAINORSHINE
**Nom de plume:** 5 ALIAS
Lamb's: 4 ELIA
**Nome**
dome home: 5 IGLOO
home: 6 ALASKA
knife: 3 ULU
"___ nome" ("Rigoletto"
highlight): 4 CARO
**Nominate:** 4 NAME
**Nomination**
Kind of: 4 EMMY
**Nominee**
Clio: 5 ADMAN
list: 5 SLATE
**Nomo**
birthplace: 5 OSAKA
Number for: 3 ERA
of baseball: 5 HIDEO
**"No more!":** 5 UNCLE
**Non**
opposite: 3 OUI
**Non ___ (unwelcome):** 5 GRATA
**Nonaffiliated**
(abbr.): 3 IND
**No-name:** 7 GENERIC
**Nonbeliever:** 5 PAGAN
7 ATHEIST
**Nonchalance:** 4 EASE
8 EASINESS
**Nonchalant:** 4 COOL
**Nonchalantly**
Walk: 6 SASHAY
**Nonchooser:** 6 BEGGAR
**Non-clashing**
color: 4 ECRU
**Nonclerical:** 3 LAY 4 LAIC
group: 5 LAITY
**Noncom**
(abbr.): 3 SGT 4 MSGT
Navy: 3 CPO
nickname: 5 SARGE
**Noncombat**
gp.: 4 WAAC
**Noncommercial**
~ TV network: 3 PBS
**Noncommittal**
answer: 5 MAYBE
words: 4 IMAY
**Noncompromiser:** 6 PURIST
**Nonconformist:** 5 FLAKE
6 MISFIT 7 HERETIC
**Nondairy**
spread: 4 OLEO
**None**
of the above: 5 OTHER
**Non-earthling:** 5 ALIEN
**"No need to explain":** 6 IGETIT
**Nonetheless:** 3 YET 6 ANYWAY
EVENSO
~, for short: 3 THO
**Nonexistent:** 3 NIL 4 NULL

**Nonfat**
milk: 4 SKIM
**Nonflowering**
plant: 4 FERN
___ non grata: 7 PERSONA
**Non-Jew:** 7 GENTILE
**Nonkosher**
sandwich: 3 BLT
**Nonnational:** 5 ALIEN
**Nonnative:** 5 ALIEN
Subj. for a: 3 ESL
~ Hawaiian: 5 HAOLE
**No-no:** 4 DONT 5 TABOO
(var.): 4 TABU
**"No ___, no gain":** 4 PAIN
**"No, No, Nanette"**
lyricist Harbach: 4 OTTO
tune: 9 TEAFORTWO
**"No No Song, The"**
singer: 5 STARR
**Non-oyster**
Like ~ months: 5 RLESS
**Nonpastoral:** 4 LAIC
**Nonpayment**
result: 4 REPO
**Non-P.C.**
suffix: 3 ESS 4 ENNE ETTE
**Nonplussed:** 5 ATSEA
**Non-Polynesian:** 5 HAOLE
**Nonpro**
sports gp.: 3 AAU
**Non-pro:** 4 ANTI
**Nonprofessional:** 3 LAY
**Nonprofit**
website suffix: 3 ORG
**Nonreactive:** 5 INERT
**Nonrecurring:** 7 ONESHOT
**Nonresident**
doctor: 6 EXTERN
Place for ~ patients: 6 CLINIC
**Nonreturnable**
It's: 3 ACE
**Non-Rx:** 3 OTC
**Nonsense:** 3 PAP ROT 4 BOSH
HOKE TOSH 5 BILGE
HOOEY TRIPE
6 BUSHWA DRIVEL
7 HOGWASH TWADDLE
10 BALDERDASH
Kind of: 5 UTTER
singing: 4 SCAT
Talk: 4 JIVE
~, to a Brit: 4 TOSH
**"Nonsense!":** 3 BAH 4 BUNK
PISH TOSH 5 NERTS
PSHAW
**Nonsensical:** 5 INANE SILLY
7 ASININE IDIOTIC
**Non-sharer:** 3 HOG
**Nonsmoking ___:** 4 AREA
**Nonstick**
spray: 3 PAM
surface: 6 TEFLON
**Nonstop:** 5 NOEND 7 ENDLESS
ETERNAL 9 CEASELESS
Talk: 5 RUNON

**Non-studio:** 5 INDIE
**Nonsurfer:** 5 HODAD
**Nonverbal**
agreement: 3 NOD
**Nonviolent**
demonstration: 5 SITIN
**Nonwinner:** 7 ALSORAN
**Nonwoody**
plant: 4 HERB
**Nonwritten**
test: 4 ORAL
**Noodge:** 3 NAG 4 PEST
Be a: 6 PESTER
**Noodle:** 4 BEAN
concoction: 4 IDEA
dish: 5 RAMEN
French: 4 TETE
Like a wet: 4 LIMP
Use one's: 5 THINK 6 REASON
**Noodlehead:** 3 OAF SAP
5 SCHMO 9 BIRDBRAIN
**Noodles:** 5 PASTA
Japanese: 5 RAMEN
**Nook:** 6 ALCOVE
Church: 4 APSE
Kitchen: 7 DINETTE
Shady: 5 ARBOR
Sheltered: 4 COVE
**Noon:** 6 MIDDAY
Nap after: 6 SIESTA
~, in France: 4 MIDI
~, to Nero: 3 XII
**"No Ordinary Love"**
singer: 4 SADE
**Noose**
Decorative: 3 TIE
material: 4 ROPE
**"Nope":** 3 NAH 4 UHUH
rebuttal: 3 YUP
**"No problem!":** 4 EASY SURE
5 CANDO
**"___ no questions ...":** 5 ASKME
**Nor**
partner: 7 NEITHER
**Nor.**
neighbor: 3 SWE
**Nora**
Director: 6 EPHRON
portrayer: 5 MYRNA
**Norah**
Father of: 4 RAVI
**Nord**
opposite: 3 SUD
**Nordic**
alternative: 6 ALPINE
carrier: 3 SAS
**Nordland**
native: 4 LAPP
**Nordstrom**
rival: 4 SAKS
**Nor'easter:** 5 STORM
**"No returns":** 4 ASIS
**Norgay, Tenzing:** 6 SHERPA
**Norm:** 3 PAR
(abbr.): 3 STD
Wife of: 4 VERA

~, in golf: 3 PAR
**Norma**
Constellation near: 3 ARA
**"Norma":** 5 OPERA
composer: 7 BELLINI
highlight: 4 ARIA
**"Norma ___":** 3 RAE
**Normal:** 3 PAR 4 SANE
5 USUAL
(abbr.): 3 STD
Not: 3 ODD
prefix: 4 PARA
They're not: 8 DEVIANTS
**Normally:** 7 ASARULE
**Norman**
Author: 6 MAILER
Golfer: 4 GREG
home (abbr.): 4 OKLA
of cosmetics: 5 MERLE
Playwright: 6 MARSHA
Producer: 4 LEAR
Soprano: 6 JESSYE
**Normand**
of silent films: 5 MABEL
**Normandy**
battle site: 4 STLO
city: 4 CAEN
event: 4 DDAY
town: 4 STLO
**Norman Vincent ___:** 5 PEALE
**"Norma Rae"**
director: 4 PITT
**No ___ roses:** 5 BEDOF
**Norris Dam**
project (abbr.): 3 TVA
**Norris Trophy**
winner: 3 ORR
**Norse**
capital: 4 OSLO
chieftain: 5 ROLLO
epic: 4 EDDA
Evil ~ god: 4 LOKI
explorer: 4 ERIC
god: 4 ODIN
goddess: 3 HEL
goddess of love: 5 FREYA
god of discord: 4 LOKI
god of strife: 3 TYR
god of thunder: 4 THOR
god of war: 3 TYR 4 ODIN
Home of the ~ gods: 6 ASGARD
name: 4 OLAF
pantheon: 5 AESIR
Race of ~ gods: 5 AESIR
saint: 4 OLAV
**Norte**
90 degrees from ~: 4 ESTE
opposite: 3 SUR
**North:** 3 SEA
Actress: 6 SHEREE
end: 3 ERN
of Irangate: 5 OLLIE
of Virginia: 5 OLLIE
suffix: 3 ERN
**North Africa**
Much of: 6 SAHARA

**North African**
  capital: 5 RABAT TUNIS
  desert: 6 SAHARA
  tribesman: 6 BERBER
  viper: 3 ASP
**"North and South"**
  novelist: 5 JAKES
**North Atlantic**
  fish: 3 COD
  menace: 4 BERG
**"North by Northwest"**
  costar: 3 EVA
**North Carolina**
  cape: 4 FEAR 8 HATTERAS
  capital: 7 RALEIGH
  college: 4 ELON
  county: 4 ASHE
  fort: 5 BRAGG
  motto beginning: 4 ESSE
  resident: 7 TARHEEL
  senator: 5 HELMS
  university: 4 ELON
**North Dakota**
  city: 5 FARGO MINOT
**Northeast**
  college town: 5 ORONO
**Northeast Corridor**
  train: 5 ACELA
**Northeast India**
  State in: 5 ASSAM
**Northern:** 6 BOREAL
  Bright ~ star: 6 ALTAIR
  capital: 4 OSLO
  constellation: 5 DRACO
  diving bird: 3 AUK
  forest: 5 TAIGA
  highway: 5 ALCAN
**Northern ___ (apple):** 3 SPY
**"Northern Exposure"**
  setting: 6 ALASKA
**Northern Manhattan**
  dweller: 8 UPTOWNER
**Northern Spy:** 5 APPLE
**North Pole**
  explorer: 5 PEARY
  exports: 4 TOYS
  resident: 5 SANTA
  worker: 3 ELF
**Northrop**
  Literary critic: 4 FRYE
**North Sea**
  diver: 3 AUK
  feeder: 3 DEE EMS 4 ELBE
    TYNE YSER 5 MEUSE
  port: 8 ABERDEEN
  structure: 6 OILRIG
  tributary: 5 MEUSE
**Northumberland**
  river: 4 TYNE
**Northwest**
  (abbr.): 4 TERR
  Sound of the: 5 PUGET
**Northwest Rebellion**
  tribe: 4 CREE
**Northwest Territories**
  capital: 11 YELLOWKNIFE

**North Yorkshire**
  river: 3 URE
**Norton**
  and others: 3 EDS
  Boxer: 3 KEN
**Norton, Ed**
  wear: 4 VEST
  workplace: 5 SEWER
  ~, to Ralph Kramden: 3 PAL
**Norton Sound**
  city: 4 NOME
**Norway**
  capital: 4 OSLO
  patron saint: 4 OLAF OLAV
**Norwegian**
  capital: 4 OSLO
  coin: 3 ORE
  composer: 5 GRIEG
  inlet: 5 FJORD
  king: 4 OLAF OLAV
  Northern: 4 LAPP
  playwright: 5 IBSEN
  saint: 4 OLAF OLAV
**"Norwegian Wood"**
  instrument: 5 SITAR
**Nor'wester:** 5 STORM
**Nose**
  around: 3 PRY 5 SNOOP
  Beat by a: 3 NIP 4 EDGE
  Canary's: 4 CERE
  Kind of: 5 ROMAN
  nipper: 9 JACKFROST
  notifier: 5 AROMA
  Offend the: 4 REEK
  On the: 5 EXACT
  (out): 4 EDGE
  prefix: 4 NASI RHIN
  Turn up one's ~ at: 4 SNUB
  What the ~ knows: 4 ODOR
    5 AROMA
  Words before: 3 BYA
  wrinkler: 4 ODOR
  ~, slangily: 5 SNOOT
**"No seats left":** 3 SRO
**Nosebag**
  filler: 4 OATS
**Nosebleed**
  seats: 6 TOPROW
**Nosedive:** 4 FALL 6 TUMBLE
**No-see-um:** 4 GNAT
**Nosegay:** 4 POSY
**Nose-in-the-air**
  type: 4 SNOB
**Nosh:** 3 EAT 4 BITE 5 SNACK
  Nag's: 3 OAT
  on: 3 EAT
**No-show:** 4 AWOL
    8 ABSENTEE
  Literary: 5 GODOT
  Military: 4 AWOL
  Score for a: 4 ZERO
**Nostalgia**
  Bit of: 5 OLDIE
**Nostalgic**
  Be ~ for: 4 MISS
  fashion: 5 RETRO

  location: 10 MEMORYLANE
  pop: 4 NEHI
  song: 5 OLDIE
  style: 5 RETRO
  times: 7 OLDDAYS
  tune: 5 OLDIE
**___ Nostra:** 4 COSA
**Nostradamus:** 4 SEER
  Sign for: 4 OMEN
**Nostrils:** 5 NARES
**"No Strings Attached"**
  pop group: 5 NSYNC
**Nostromo**
  Film set on the spaceship:
    5 ALIEN
**Nostrum:** 6 REMEDY
**"___ No Sunshine":** 4 AINT
**"No sweat!":** 4 EASY
**Nosy**
  Be: 3 PRY
  Get: 3 PRY 5 SNOOP
  sort: 5 SNOOP
**Nosy Parker:** 5 PRIER SNOOP
    YENTA 7 SNOOPER
  Be a: 3 PRY
**Not:** 4 NARY
  And: 3 NOR
  any: 4 NARY NONE
  ~, to a Scot: 3 NAE
**Not ___ (mediocre):** 5 SOHOT
**"Not ___!":** 4 THAT 5 AGAIN
**Nota ___:** 4 BENE
**Notable**
  period: 3 ERA 5 EPOCH
  time: 3 ERA 5 EPOCH
**"Not a chance!":** 5 MYEYE
    NOWAY
**"Not again!":** 4 OHNO
**"No talking!":** 3 SHH
**Notary**
  need: 4 SEAL
**Not at all:** 5 NOHOW 6 HARDLY
    NOWISE 7 INNOWAY
**Notation**
  Editor's: 4 STET
  Env.: 4 ATTN
  ER: 3 DOA
  Invitation: 4 RSVP
  Margin: 4 STET
  Memo: 4 ASAP INRE
  Proofreader's: 4 STET
  Quotation: 4 ANON
  Sale: 4 ASIS
  Staff: 4 CLEF
**"Not ___ bet!":** 3 ONA
**Notch:** 3 VEE 4 NICK
**___ notch:** 3 UPA
**Notched:** 5 JAGGY 7 CRENATE
    SERRATE
  Irregularly: 5 EROSE
**Note:** 3 IOU SOL 4 MEMO
    7 JOTDOWN
  above C: 5 DFLAT
  above G: 5 AFLAT
  after fa: 3 SOL
  High ~ of old: 3 ELA

in the A-major scale: 6 GSHARP
Office: 4 MEMO
Promissory: 3 IOU
Sour: 7 CLINKER
Staff: 3 SOL 4 MEMO
Sticky: 6 POSTIT
Take ~ of: 4 HEED
taker: 5 STENO
**Notebook:** 6 LAPTOP
divider: 3 TAB
Like ~ paper: 5 LINED RULED
maker: 3 IBM
**Noted:** 6 FAMOUS 7 EMINENT
**Notes**
after do: 3 RES 4 REMI
Closing: 4 CODA
End: 4 CODA
Musical: 3 FAS LAS MIS RES
TIS
Pound: 6 ARFARF
Scale: 3 FAS LAS MIS RES
TIS
**"___ note to follow ...":** 3 LAA
**Noteworthy**
period: 3 ERA 5 EPOCH
time: 3 ERA 5 EPOCH
**Not ___ eye in the house:**
4 ADRY
**"Not from where ___":** 4 ISIT
**"Not guilty":** 4 PLEA
**Nothin':** 4 NADA
**"Nothin' ___!":** 4 DOIN
**"Nothin' doin'!":** 4 UHUH
**Nothing:** 3 NIL ZIP 4 NADA
ZERO
at all: 3 NIL
but: 3 ALL 4 MERE ONLY
Did: 3 SAT 5 SATBY
Do: 4 IDLE LAZE LOAF
Doing: 4 IDLE
Have ~ to do with: 4 SHUN
If ~ changes: 6 ASITIS
It beats: 4 PAIR
It means: 3 NIL
It means ~ in tennis: 4 LOVE
It's ~ new: 5 RERUN
7 ROUTINE
It's next to: 3 ONE
more than: 4 MERE ONLY
One with ~ to do: 5 IDLER
special: 4 SOSO
Sweet: 10 ENDEARMENT
Take ~ in: 4 FAST
to write home about: 4 SOSO
~, in French: 4 RIEN
~, in Italian: 6 NIENTE
~, in Spanish: 4 NADA
~, to Nero: 5 NIHIL
**Nothing ___:** 4 LESS
**"Nothing ___!":** 5 DOING
**___ nothing:** 5 ALLOR
**"Nothing new":** 7 SAMEOLD
**"Nothing runs like a ___":**
5 DEERE
**Notice:** 3 SEE 4 ESPY SPOT
6 DETECT

Final: 4 OBIT
Give: 4 QUIT
Give ~ to: 5 ALERT
Passing: 4 OBIT
Put on: 4 WARN
Take: 5 SITUP
**Noticed:** 3 SAW 4 SEEN
6 ESPIED
**Notify:** 5 ALERT 6 ADVISE
INFORM
**Not in:** 4 AWAY 5 PASSE
**Not ___ in the world:** 5 ACARE
**Not in use:** 4 IDLE
**Not in yet:** 7 ONORDER
**Notion:** 4 IDEA
Capricious: 4 WHIM
Nice: 4 IDEE
~, in French: 4 IDEE
**Notions**
case: 4 ETUI
**Not know from ___:** 4 ADAM
**"Not likely!":** 4 IBET
**Not ___ many words:** 4 INSO
**Not miss ___:** 5 ABEAT
**Not much:** 4 ABIT ATAD
**Not now:** 4 THEN 5 LATER
7 LATERON
**"Not on ___!":** 4 ABET
**Notoriety:** 4 FAME 6 REPUTE
7 RECLAME
**"Notorious"**
actor Grant: 4 CARY
**Not quite:** 6 ALMOST
**"No ___ traffic":** 4 THRU
**Notre ___:** 4 DAME
**Notre Dame**
area: 4 APSE
bench: 3 PEW
city: 5 PARIS
coach Parseghian: 3 ARA
coach Rockne: 5 KNUTE
river: 5 SEINE
team: 5 IRISH
**"Not so fast!":** 6 HOLDIT
**Not so many:** 5 FEWER
**Not so much:** 4 LESS
**Nottingham**
John of: 3 LOO
river: 5 TRENT
**"Not to worry!":** 5 ITSOK
**"Not true!":** 7 ITSALIE
9 THATSALIE
**"___ Not Unusual":** 3 ITS
**Not up to much:** 4 IDLE
**Notwithstanding:** 7 DESPITE
~, briefly: 3 THO 5 ALTHO
**Not worth ___:** 4 AFIG ASOU
**Not worth a ___:** 3 FIG SOU
**"Not you ___!":** 5 AGAIN
**Noun**
gender (abbr.): 3 FEM 4 MASC
NEUT
suffix: 4 NESS SION TION
**Noun-forming**
suffix: 3 ION 4 ENCE
**Nourish:** 4 FEED

**Nourished:** 3 FED
**Nourishing**
~, in Latin: 4 ALMA
**Nourishment:** 4 FOOD
**___ nous:** 5 ENTRE
**Nouveau ___:** 5 RICHE
**Nouvelle-Calédonie:** 3 ILE
**Nova:** 3 LOX 4 STAR
follower: 6 SCOTIA
**"Nova"**
network: 3 PBS
subj.: 3 SCI
**Nova ___:** 6 SCOTIA
**___ nova:** 3 ARS 5 BOSSA
**Novak**
Actress: 3 KIM
Onetime partner of:
5 EVANS
**Novarro**
Actor: 5 RAMON
**Novel:** 3 NEW 5 FRESH
ending: 3 IST 4 ETTE
6 EPILOG
idea: 4 PLOT
~ ID: 4 ISBN
**Novell**
city: 4 OREM
state: 4 UTAH
**Novello**
Actor: 4 IVOR
**November**
birthstone: 5 TOPAZ
choice: 4 VOTE
honoree: 3 VET
veggie: 3 YAM
winner: 7 ELECTEE
winners: 3 INS
**Novgorod**
No, in: 4 NYET
**Novice:** 4 TIRO TYRO
6 ROOKIE
10 TENDERFOOT
Internet: 6 NEWBIE
**Novi Sad**
native: 4 SERB
**___ Novo:** 5 PORTO
**Novocain**
Shoot up with: 4 NUMB
6 DEADEN
target: 5 NERVE
**Novotna**
of tennis: 4 JANA
**Novus ___ seclorum:** 4 ORDO
**Now:** 5 TODAY 6 ATONCE
and again: 5 TWICE
7 ATTIMES
10 ONOCCASION
and then: 7 ATTIMES
10 ONOCCASION
From ~ on: 5 HENCE
Not: 4 ANON THEN 5 LATER
7 LATERON
or in the future: 4 EVER
partner: 4 THEN
Until: 3 YET 5 ASYET SOFAR
6 TODATE

Up to: 3 YET 5 ASYET SOFAR
　　6 TODATE
~, in Spanish: 5 AHORA
**"Now!":** 4 ASAP STAT
　　6 ATONCE PRONTO
**Nowadays:** 7 ANYMORE
**"No way!":** 3 NAH 4 ASIF
　　UHUH 5 ICANT MYEYE
　　PSHAW 6 CANTBE
　　10 NOTACHANCE
**"No way, ___!":** 4 JOSE
**"Now hear ___!":** 4 THIS
**Nowhere**
　Going: 6 INARUT
　Went: 5 IDLED
**Nowheresville:** 6 PODUNK
**"Now I get it!":** 3 AHA
**"Now I ___ me down to ...":**
　　3 LAY
**No-win**
　situation: 3 TIE 4 DRAW
**"Now I see!":** 3 AHA 4 AHSO
**"Now ___ it!":** 4 IGET
**"Now it makes sense":** 4 ISEE
**"Now it's clear":** 4 ISEE
**"Now I've ___ everything!":**
　　4 SEEN
**"Now ___ me down ...":** 4 ILAY
**"___ now or never":** 3 ITS
**"Now ___ seen everything!":**
　　3 IVE
**"Now ___ theater near you!":**
　　3 ATA
**"Now, Voyager"**
　actress Chase: 4 ILKA
**"Now We Are Six"**
　author: 5 MILNE
**"Now, where ___?":** 4 WASI
**"Now, where ___ I?":** 3 WAS
**"Now you ___ ...":** 5 SEEIT
**"Now ___ you ...":** 4 IASK
**Noxious**
　emanation: 6 MIASMA
**Noyes**
　Poet: 6 ALFRED
**Nozzle:** 3 JET 6 GASJET
**NPR**
　host Glass: 3 IRA
　host Hansen: 5 LIANE
　puzzlemaster: 6 SHORTZ
　reporter Totenberg: 4 NINA
**NRA:** 4 ASSN
　supporter: 3 FDR
**NRC**
　predecessor: 3 AEC
**NT**
　book: 3 EPH
**Nth**
　(abbr.): 3 ULT
　degree: 3 MAX
**Nuance:** 4 TONE 7 SHADING
**Nuanced:** 6 SUBTLE
**Nubian Desert**
　site: 5 SUDAN
**Nuclear**
　accident site (abbr.): 3 TMI

experiment: 5 ATEST
fission discoverer: 4 HAHN
Former ~ agcy.: 3 AEC
missile acronym: 4 MIRV
physicist Niels: 4 BOHR
physics suffix: 4 TRON
trial: 5 ATEST
weapon: 5 ABOMB HBOMB
**Nuclei:** 5 CORES
**Nucleotide**
　prefix: 3 TRI
**Nucleus:** 4 CORE 5 CADRE
　Part of a cell: 3 RNA
**Nude:** 4 BARE 5 MODEL
　Not: 4 CLAD
**Nudge:** 3 JOG 4 POKE PROD
　　5 ELBOW
　forward: 4 PROD
　rudely: 5 ELBOW
　~, as memory: 3 JOG
**Nudist:** 7 ADAMITE
**Nudnik:** 4 PAIN PEST
　Be a: 6 PESTER
**"___ nuff!":** 3 SHO
**Nugent**
　Guitarist: 3 TED
**Nugget**
　Barbecue: 4 COAL
**___ Nui (Easter Island):** 4 RAPA
**Nuisance:** 4 PAIN PEST
　E-mail: 4 SPAM
　Garden: 4 WEED
**"___ nuit!":** 5 BONNE
**Nuke:** 3 ZAP 6 REHEAT
　　REWARM
　prefix: 4 ANTI
**Nullify:** 4 UNDO VOID
　　6 NEGATE
**Num.**
　follower: 4 DEUT
**Numb:** 6 DEADEN
　~, as a foot: 6 ASLEEP
**Number:** 3 ACT 4 SONG TUNE
　Allowed: 5 QUOTA
　Best-selling: 3 ONE
　Chosen: 3 FEW
　Clock: 3 III VII XII 4 IIII VIII
　Cloud: 4 NINE
　Did a: 4 SANG
　Diva's: 4 ARIA
　Do a: 4 SING
　for Nomo: 3 ERA
　for one: 4 ARIA
　for two: 4 DUET
　Gas pump: 6 OCTANE
　Great: 4 RAFT
　Hole: 3 PAR
　Holiday: 4 NOEL
　in black: 5 ASSET
　Kind of: 6 ATOMIC
　　7 ORDINAL
　Large: 4 HERD HOST SLEW
　Like a certain ~ system:
　　5 OCTAL
　Limited: 3 FEW
　Lonely: 3 ONE

Met: 4 ARIA
next to a plus sign:
　　6 ADDEND
Old: 5 ETHER
Opera: 4 ARIA
Page: 5 FOLIO
Perfect: 3 TEN
Pump: 6 OCTANE
Round: 4 ZERO
Small: 3 FEW
Sundial: 3 III VII XII 4 IIII VIII
Tango: 3 TWO
Three-digit: 8 AREACODE
two: 4 VICE
Unspecified: 3 ANY
Whole: 3 INTEGER
Work with a: 4 OPUS
**Number-calling**
　game: 5 BEANO
**Number cruncher:** 3 CPA
**Numbered**
　club: 4 IRON
　composition: 4 OPUS
　hwy.: 3 RTE
　rd.: 3 RTE
　work: 4 OPUS
**___ number on:** 3 DOA
**"Number One Son"**
　Father of: 4 CHAN
**Numbers**
　after "1": 8 AREACODE
　Bookie's: 4 ODDS
　Box score: 5 STATS
　game: 4 KENO 5 BEANO
　　BINGO LOTTO
　holder: 5 TORAH
　on horses: 4 ODDS
　person: 8 OPERATOR
　Recital: 4 SOLI
　Set of: 6 MEDLEY
　to crunch: 4 DATA
　Track: 4 ODDS
**Numbskull:** 3 ASS OAF 4 BOZO
　　DODO DOPE 5 IDIOT
**Numeral:** 5 DIGIT
　Clock: 3 III VII XII 4 IIII VIII
**Numerals**
　Like our: 6 ARABIC
　Like some: 5 ROMAN
**"Numerals, The"**
　painter: 4 ERTE
**Numerical**
　ending: 3 ETH 4 TEEN
　prefix: 3 TRI 4 DECA HEPT
　　HEXA MONO OCTA OCTO
　　5 PENTA TETRA
　suffix: 3 ETH 4 TEEN
**Numero**
　Important: 3 UNO
　uno: 4 BEST
**Numero ___:** 3 UNO
**Numerous:** 4 MANY 6 LEGION
　　UNTOLD
　Less: 5 FEWER
　Most ~ people: 6 ASIANS
　~, slangily: 5 LOTSA

**Numismatist**
item: 4 COIN
**Numskull:** 3 ASS OAF 4 BOZO
    DODO DOPE 5 IDIOT
**Nun:** 6 SISTER
attire: 5 HABIT
headcloth: 6 WIMPLE
**Nuncupative:** 4 ORAL
**Nunn**
Georgia senator: 3 SAM
**Nuptial**
agreement: 3 IDO
lane: 5 AISLE
pronoun: 4 OURS
starter: 3 PRE
Take a ~ flight: 5 ELOPE
**Nuremberg**
Info: German cue
Never, in: 3 NIE
No, in: 4 NEIN
trial figure: 5 SPEER
**Nureyev:** 7 DANSEUR
Ballet dancer: 6 RUDOLF
**Nurmi**
Olympic medalist: 5 PAAVO
**Nürnberg**
Info: German cue
Never, in: 3 NIE
No, in: 4 NEIN
**Nurse:** 3 SIP 4 FEED 6 SUCKLE
Asian: 4 AMAH
Eastern: 4 AMAH
**Nursemaid:** 5 NANNY
Asian: 4 AMAH
Hindu: 4 AYAH
Indian: 4 AMAH
**Nursery**
color: 4 PINK
cry: 4 MAMA
denizen: 7 NEONATE
furniture: 4 CRIB
product: 3 SOD
purchase: 4 CRIB 5 PLANT
supply: 4 LOAM
**Nursery rhyme**
boy: 5 PETER
girl: 6 BOPEEP
name: 5 SPRAT
residence: 4 SHOE
start: 5 PEASE 6 BAABAA
    10 RUBADUBDUB
trio: 4 MICE
**Nursing**
Need: 3 AIL
**Nurture:** 4 GROW REAR TEND
**Nus**
followers: 3 XIS
~, to us: 3 ENS
**Nut:** 4 KOOK LOON 6 MANIAC
    WEIRDO
cake: 3 BUR 5 TORTE
Car: 3 LUG

center: 4 MEAT
Kind of: 3 LUG 4 KOLA
    5 BEECH BETEL 6 LITCHI
    7 LUNATIC 9 MACADAMIA
Oak: 5 ACORN
partner: 4 BOLT
Pie: 5 PECAN
Praline: 5 PECAN
Soft drink: 4 KOLA
source: 4 TREE
Tough: 5 POSER
tree: 5 BEECH
Tropical: 4 KOLA 5 BETEL
with a cap: 5 ACORN
**Nutcase:** 4 KOOK LOON
    5 WACKO
**Nutcracker**
suite: 4 NEST
**"Nutcracker, The"**
girl: 5 CLARA
**Nuthatch**
home: 4 NEST
**"Nuthin' but a 'G' Thang"**
rapper: 5 DRDRE
**Nutmeg:** 4 SEED
covering: 4 ARIL
spice: 4 MACE
**NutRageous**
maker: 6 REESES
**Nutrient**
Important: 4 IRON
stat.: 3 RDA
**Nutrition**
inits.: 3 RDA
units: 5 GRAMS
**Nutritional**
fig.: 3 CAL RDA
std.: 3 RDA
**Nutritive**
mineral: 4 IRON
**Nuts:** 4 BATS GAGA LOCO
    5 CRAZY KOOKY LOONY
and bolts: 4 ABCS
Be ~ over: 5 ADORE
Go: 4 RAGE RAVE
Like many: 6 SALTED
**"Nuts!":** 3 BAH 4 DARN DRAT
    RATS
___ nutshell: 3 INA
**Nutso:** 4 LOCO 5 LOOPY
**Nutty:** 4 DAFT 5 LOOPY
cake: 5 TORTE
confection: 6 NOUGAT
    7 PRALINE
Not as: 5 SANER
**"Nutty Professor, The"**
actor Murphy: 5 EDDIE
**N.Y.**
college: 3 RPI
hrs.: 3 EST
neighbor: 3 ONT QUE
summer hrs.: 3 EDT

team: 4 METS
winter hrs.: 3 EST
**Nyasaland**
~, today: 6 MALAWI
**NYC**
airport: 3 LGA
arena: 3 MSG
art center: 4 MOMA
Artsy ~ area: 4 SOHO
clock setting: 3 EDT EST
commuter line: 4 LIRR
gallery: 4 MOMA
hours: 3 EST
Part of: 4 CITY
radio station: 4 WABC
subway: 3 IND IRT
subway line: 3 IRT
subway org.: 3 MTA
subway overseer: 3 MTA
summer hours: 3 EDT
They're numbered in: 3 STS
Train line to: 4 LIRR
Uptown, in: 3 NNE
**Nyctophobic:**
    15 AFRAIDOFTHEDARK
**Nye, Bill**
subj.: 3 SCI
**Nykvist**
Cinematographer: 4 SVEN
**Nylon:** 7 POLYMER
**NY Mets:** 5 NLERS
division: 6 NLEAST
**Nymph**
Aquatic: 5 NAIAD
chaser: 5 SATYR
Mountain: 5 OREAD
River: 5 NAIAD
Sea: 6 NEREID 7 OCEANID
who fled Apollo: 6 DAPHNE
Wood: 5 DRYAD
**"Nymphéas"**
painter: 5 MONET
**Nymphet:** 6 LOLITA
**NYPD**
alert: 3 APB
figure: 3 DET
rank: 3 DET SGT
title: 3 DET
**"NYPD Blue"**
actor Jimmy: 5 SMITS
actor Morales: 4 ESAI
network: 3 ABC
**Nyro**
Singer: 5 LAURA
**NYSE:** 3 MKT
competitor: 4 AMEX
cousin: 6 NASDAQ
debut: 3 IPO
listings: 3 COS
regulator: 3 SEC
rival: 4 AMEX
unit: 3 SHR

# Oo

**O:** 3 MAG 4 ELEM RING TYPE
8 for ~: 4 ATNO
Center X or: 3 TAC
Greek: 7 OMICRON
in old radio lingo: 4 OBOE
in REO: 4 OLDS
in SRO: 4 ONLY
of O magazine: 5 OPRAH
preceders: 3 LMN

**Oaf:** 3 APE LUG 4 BOZO CLOD
DOLT LOUT 6 GALOOT
7 PALOOKA

**Oafish:** 5 INEPT

**Oahu**
dance: 4 HULA
goose: 4 NENE
greeting: 5 ALOHA
landmark: 11 DIAMONDHEAD
neighbor: 5 KAUAI
souvenir: 3 LEI
wear: 6 MUUMUU
wingding: 4 LUAU

**Oak:** 4 TREE
California: 5 ROBLE
fruit: 5 ACORN
Future: 5 ACORN
Holm: 4 ILEX
Like ~ leaves: 5 EROSE
LOBED
Live: 6 ENCINA
nut: 5 ACORN
Silver ~ leaf wearer (abbr.):
5 LTCOL
White: 5 ROBLE

**Oakes**
Actress: 5 RANDI

**Oakland**
county: 7 ALAMEDA
neighbor: 7 ALAMEDA
player: 6 RAIDER 8 ATHLETIC
transit sys.: 4 BART

**Oakley**
Sharpshooter: 5 ANNIE

**Oakley, Annie:** 4 PASS
7 DEADEYE
Like the aim of: 4 TRUE

**Oak Ridge Boys**
hit: 6 ELVIRA

**Oar:** 6 PADDLE
pin: 5 THOLE

**Oarlock:** 5 THOLE

**Oar-powered**
ship: 7 TRIREME

**OAS**
member: 4 PERU 5 CHILE
Part of: 3 ORG 4 AMER

**Oasis**
animal: 5 CAMEL

Roadside: 3 INN 8 RESTSTOP

**Oast:** 4 OVEN

**Oater:** 10 HORSEOPERA
actor Jack: 4 ELAM
actor Lash: 5 LARUE
affirmative: 3 YEP YUP
challenge: 4 DRAW
Classic: 5 SHANE
climax: 8 SHOOTOUT
Entered, in an: 8 RODEINTO
group: 5 POSSE
locale: 6 SALOON
omen: 5 NOOSE 6 TOMTOM
prop: 5 LASSO RIATA
Scram, in an: 3 GIT
sound effect: 7 GUNFIRE
sound effects: 5 CLOPS
transport: 5 STAGE
wear: 7 BANDANA

**Oates, Joyce Carol**
novel: 4 THEM

**Oath:** 3 VOW
Administer the ~ to:
7 INSTATE SWEARIN
Affirm under: 7 SWEARTO
Break an: 3 LIE
Kind of: 6 SOLEMN
Mild: 4 DRAT EGAD GOSH
HECK
Name in an old: 4 JOVE
Name on which an ancient ~
was taken: 4 STYX
Old: 4 EGAD 5 NERTS
Start of an: 5 SACRE
Take an: 5 SWEAR
Testify under: 6 DEPONE
DEPOSE

**Oatmeal:** 6 CEREAL
alternative: 6 FARINA

**Oats:** 4 FEED 5 GRAIN
holder: 7 FEEDBAG
Like some: 6 ROLLED

**Oaxaca**
Other, in: 4 OTRA
water: 4 AGUA

**OB-___:** 3 GYN

**"O ___ babbino caro"** (Puccini
aria): 3 MIO

**Obadiah**
Book before: 4 AMOS

**Obdurate:** 4 HARD 5 STONY

**Obedience school**
command: 3 SIT 4 HEEL STAY

**Obedient:** 8 AMENABLE
dogs: 7 STAYERS

**Obeisance:** 6 SALAAM
Show: 5 KNEEL

**Obelisk:** 8 MONUMENT

**Oberon**
Actress: 5 MERLE
Wife of: 7 TITANIA

**"O, beware, my lord, of
jealousy!"**
speaker: 4 IAGO

**Obey:** 4 HEED
10 TOETHELINE
the coxswain: 3 ROW
the drill sergeant:
15 SNAPTOATTENTION
the photographer: 5 SMILE
the sentry: 4 HALT

**Obfuscate:** 5 BEFOG

**OB-GYN**
job: 5 AMNIO

**Obi:** 4 SASH

**Obie:** 5 AWARD
cousin: 4 TONY

**Obit**
word: 3 NEE

**Obi-Wan:** 4 JEDI
portrayer: 4 ALEC EWAN

**Obi-Wan ___:** 6 KENOBI

**Object:** 3 AIM 4 MIND 5 ARGUE
DEMUR THING
of devotion: 4 IDOL
of esteem: 4 ICON
of gossip: 4 ITEM
of loathing: 8 ANATHEMA
of worship: 4 IDOL
Three-dimensional: 5 SOLID
Ultimate: 6 ENDALL

**Objection**
Trivial: 5 CAVIL
Vocal: 3 NAY

**Objective:** 3 AIM END 4 GOAL
5 POINT 6 TARGET
Heist: 4 LOOT
Noble: 5 IDEAL

**Objectivism**
advocate Rand: 3 AYN

**"Object of My Affection, The"**
actor: 4 ALDA

**Objet**
d'art: 5 CURIO

**Objeto**
That: 3 ESO

**"Ob-La-Di, Ob-La-Da"**
Last name in: 5 JONES

**Oblast**
on the Oka: 4 OREL

**Obligated:** 6 LIABLE
Be ~ to: 3 OWE

**Obligation:** 4 DEBT DUTY
MUST ONUS
Govt.: 5 TNOTE
Word of: 5 OUGHT

**Obligatory:** 6 MUSTDO
___ **oblige:** 8 NOBLESSE
**Obliged**
  Be ~ to: 3 OWE
**Obliging**
  spirit: 5 GENIE
**Oblique:** 5 BEVEL
**Obliquely:** 6 ASKANT
  ASLANT
  Move: 5 SIDLE
**Obliterate:** 5 ERASE
**Oblivion:** 5 LETHE
  Consign to: 4 DOOM
**Oblivious:** 7 UNAWARE
  Hardly: 5 AWARE
**Oblong**
  yellow fruit: 5 PAPAW
**Obloquy:** 5 ABUSE
**Oboe:** 4 REED
  Sounding like an: 5 REEDY
**Oboist**
  need: 4 REED
**Obote**
  Deposer of: 4 AMIN
**O'Brian, Hugh**
  TV role: 4 EARP
**O'Brien**
  Actor: 6 EDMOND
  Author: 4 EDNA
  Talk show host: 5 CONAN
  thriller: 3 DOA
**Obringa**
  River known anciently as:
    4 AARE
**OBs:** 3 MDS
**Obscene:** 4 LEWD
  material: 4 SMUT
**Obscenity:** 4 SMUT
**Obscure:** 3 DIM 4 BLUR VEIL
    5 BEDIM BEFOG
    6 DARKEN
  stuff: 7 ESOTERY
**Obsequious**
  Be ~ (to): 6 KOWTOW
  one: 6 FAWNER
**Observance:** 4 RITE
  Hanoi: 3 TET
  Ramadan: 4 FAST
**Observant:** 5 AWARE
  one: 5 NOTER
  Very: 9 EAGLEEYED
**Observation:** 6 ESPIAL
**Observatory**
  find: 4 NOVA
**Observe:** 3 EYE SEE 4 HEED
    NOTE OBEY SPOT VIEW
    5 WATCH 6 BEHOLD
    LOOKAT
**Observer:** 4 EYER 5 NOTER
  U.N.: 3 PLO
**Obsessed**
  by: 4 INTO
  captain: 4 AHAB
  with: 4 INTO
**Obsession:** 5 MANIA
    8 IDEEFIXE

**Obsidian**
  source: 4 LAVA
**Obstacle:** 3 RUB 4 SNAG
  Limbo: 3 BAR
  Slalom: 4 GATE
  Underwater: 4 REEF
  ___ obstat: 5 NIHIL
**Obstetrician**
  Of interest to an:
    8 PRENATAL
**Obstinate:** 5 BALKY 6 ORNERY
  one: 3 ASS 4 MULE
**Obstruct:** 3 DAM 5 DAMUP
    JAMUP 6 IMPEDE
**Obstruction:** 3 DAM
  Blood vessel: 4 CLOT
**Obtain:** 3 GET 4 REAP
  by force: 6 EXTORT
**Obtuse:** 3 DIM 4 DULL
    5 DENSE THICK
  It may be ~ (abbr.): 3 ANG
  one: 6 CRETIN
**Obvious:** 5 OVERT 6 PATENT
    7 EVIDENT
  flirt: 5 OGLER
  It is: 6 TRUISM
**"O Canada":** 6 ANTHEM
**Ocasek**
  Rocker: 3 RIC
**O'Casey**
  Playwright: 4 SEAN
**Occasion**
  Asian: 3 TET
  Festive: 4 GALA 5 PARTY
  March: 6 PARADE
  On a single: 4 ONCE
  Present: 4 XMAS 5 NONCE
  Quilting: 3 BEE
  Suitable for the: 3 APT
**Occasionally:** 7 ATTIMES
    11 EVERANDANON
    15 EVERYNOWANDTHEN
**Occident**
  It is no: 6 ORIENT
**Occult:** 6 MYSTIC
  doctrine: 6 CABALA
**Occupant:** 6 TENANT
**Occupation:** 3 JOB 4 LINE
    5 TRADE 6 METIER
  Start an: 6 MOVEIN
**Occupational**
  suffix: 3 EER IER IST 4 STER
**Occupied:** 4 BUSY 5 INUSE
    TAKEN
**Occupy:** 3 USE 4 FILL 5 TIEUP
    6 LIVEAT TAKEUP
  ~, as a table: 5 SITAT
**Occur:** 5 EXIST
  to: 6 DAWNON
**Occurrence:** 3 HAP 5 EVENT
  March 21: 7 EQUINOX
  Spring: 4 THAW
**Ocean:** 3 SEA TON 4 DEEP
    SLEW 5 BRINE
  (abbr.): 3 ATL
  bottom: 6 DEPTHS

  crosser: 5 LINER
  debris: 7 FLOTSAM
  Dot in the: 5 ISLET
  Drop in the: 3 EBB
  flier: 3 ERN 4 ERNE
  Land in the: 4 ISLE
  liner: 4 SAND
  motion: 4 TIDE
  Mongolian: 5 DALAI
  On the: 4 ASEA 5 ATSEA
  predator: 4 ORCA
  Spot in the: 5 ISLET
  vessel: 4 SHIP
**Oceania**
  Much of: 6 ATOLLS
**Oceanic**
  ice: 4 FLOE
**Océano**
  contents: 4 AGUA
  feeder: 3 RIO
**Oceans:** 4 ALOT 5 DEEPS
**"Ocean's Eleven"**
  star: 7 SINATRA
**Ocean State**
  coll.: 3 URI
**Oceanus:** 5 TITAN
  Wife of: 6 TETHYS
**Ochlocracy:** 7 MOBRULE
**Ocho** ___, **Jamaica:** 4 RIOS
**Ochs**
  of folk: 4 PHIL
**O'clock**
  Five ~ shadow: 7 STUBBLE
  Four ~ drink: 3 TEA
  Four ~ fare: 8 TEACAKES
  Six ~ fare: 4 NEWS
**"**___ **o'clock scholar":** 4 ATEN
**"O Come,** ___ **Faithful":**
    5 ALLYE
**"O Come, O Come Emmanuel":**
    5 CAROL
**O'Connor**
  Actress: 3 UNA
  Singer: 6 SINEAD
**O'Connor, Cardinal**
  successor: 4 EGAN
**O'Connor,** ___ **Day**
  Justice: 6 SANDRA
**OCS**
  driller: 3 SGT
  grads: 3 LTS
  relative: 4 ROTC
**Oct.**
  It used to end in: 3 DST
**Octagon**
  Roadside: 8 STOPSIGN
  Word in an: 4 STOP
**Octave**
  follower: 6 SESTET
**Octavio**
  Author: 3 PAZ
**Octet**
  plus one: 5 NONET
**October**
  birthstone: 4 OPAL
  Many ~ babies: 6 LIBRAS

**October 31**
  option: 5 TREAT
**Octopus**
  arm: 8 TENTACLE
  defense: 3 INK
  eater: 3 EEL
  Female: 3 HEN
  octet: 4 ARMS
**Ocular**
  output: 5 TEARS
  woe: 4 STYE
**"Ocupado": 5 INUSE**
**Odalisque**
  quarters: 6 HAREMS
**O'Day**
  Singer: 5 ANITA
**Odd**: 4 RARE 7 STRANGE
    8 ABNORMAL
  couple: 4 DEES
  It may be: 3 JOB LOT
  Not: 4 EVEN
**Oddball**: 4 KOOK NERD
    5 WACKO 6 WEIRDO
  Carnival: 4 GEEK
**"Odd Couple, The"**
  cop: 6 MURRAY
  director: 4 SAKS 8 GENESAKS
  Half of: 5 OSCAR UNGER
  playwright: 5 SIMON
**Oddity: 5 FREAK**
**Oddly**
  amusing: 5 DROLL
**Odd-numbered**
  page: 5 RECTO
**Odds**
  Betting: 4 LINE
  Long: 8 ONEINTEN
  Partner of: 4 ENDS
  Take: 3 BET
**"Odds ___ ...": 3 ARE**
**Odd-toed**
  ungulate: 5 TAPIR
**Ode**: 4 POEM
  fellow: 4 POET
  preposition: 3 ERE
  subject: 3 URN
  title starter: 3 TOA
**Odense**
  citizen: 4 DANE
**"Odense" Symphony**
  Key of Mozart's: 6 AMINOR
**Oder**
  region: 7 SILESIA
**Odessa**
  native: 5 TEXAN
**"Ode to Psyche"**
  poet: 5 KEATS
**"O Deus Ego ___ Te" (hymn):**
    3 AMO
**Odin**
  hall: 8 VALHALLA
  Home of: 6 ASGARD
  Like: 5 NORSE
  race: 5 AESIR
  Son of: 3 TYR 4 THOR
  Wife of: 5 FRIGG

**Odist: 4 POET**
**Odometer**
  reading: 7 MILEAGE
  unit: 4 MILE
**O'Donnell**
  Actor: 5 CHRIS
  Quarterback: 4 NEIL
  TV host: 5 ROSIE
**O'Donnell, Chris**
  role: 5 ROBIN
**Odor**: 5 SMELL 6 REPUTE
  Agreeable: 5 AROMA
  Foul: 6 STENCH
  Oxygen with an: 5 OZONE
  Slight: 5 WHIFF
**Odorizer: 6 SACHET**
**Odorless**
  gas: 5 ARGON 6 ETHANE
**Odysseus**
  Father of: 7 LAERTES
  Guardian for: 6 ATHENA
  Home of: 6 ITHACA
  Wife of: 8 PENELOPE
  ~, to Polyphemus: 5 NOMAN
**Odyssey**
  maker: 5 HONDA
**"Odyssey": 4 EPIC**
  enchantress: 5 CIRCE
**OED**
  offering: 3 DEF SYN
  Part of: 4 DICT
**"Oedipe"**
  composer Georges: 6 ENESCO
**Oedipus**
  follower: 3 REX
**"Oedipus ___": 3 REX**
**Oenologist**
  Dry, to an: 3 SEC
  interest: 4 WINE YEAR
**O'er**
  Not: 5 NEATH
**O'er and o'er: 3 OFT**
**Oerter**
  and others: 3 ALS
  sport: 6 DISCUS
**"Of ___ and Men": 4 MICE**
**O'Faolain**
  Writer: 4 SEAN
  ___ of Avon, The: 4 BARD
  ___ of Capricorn: 6 TROPIC
**"Of course!": 3 YES 4 ISEE**
    5 NATCH
**"___ of Eden": 4 EAST**
**Off**: 3 ICE 4 AWAY AWRY DOIN
    IDLE LESS SENT
    5 AMISS ASKEW ERASE
    NOTON
  and on: 7 ATTIMES
  base: 4 AWOL 7 ONLEAVE
  course: 4 AWRY 6 AFIELD
    ASTRAY ERRANT
  in the distance: 4 AFAR
  one's feed: 3 ILL
  one's rocker: 4 LOCO
  the boat: 6 ASHORE
  the hook: 4 FREE

  the job: 4 IDLE
  the leash: 5 LOOSE
  the mark: 4 WIDE 6 ERRANT
  the track: 6 ASTRAY
  yonder: 4 AFAR
**Off.**
  helper: 4 ASST
  Naval: 3 ADM CDR ENS
  Not: 3 RES
  Three-star: 5 LTGEN
  ___ off: 4 TEED
**Off-Broadway**
  award: 4 OBIE
**Off-center: 5 ASKEW**
**Off-color**: 3 RAW 4 BLUE LEWD
    RACY 5 SALTY
**Off-duty**: 4 IDLE 7 ONLEAVE
**Offed**: 4 SLEW 5 DIDIN
**Offend**: 4 MIFF 6 INSULT
  the nose: 4 REEK
**Offended**: 4 HURT 5 HUFFY
**Offender: 7 CULPRIT**
  ~, to a cop: 4 PERP
**Offense**: 3 SIN 7 UMBRAGE
  Bum's: 8 VAGRANCY
  Cager's: 4 FOUL
  GI's: 4 AWOL
  Loan shark's: 5 USURY
  Meas. of passing: 3 YDS
  Motorist ~, briefly: 3 DWI
  On ~, on a diamond: 5 ATBAT
  Take ~ at: 6 RESENT
**Offensive**: 4 VILE 5 GROSS
    NASTY
  Some are: 4 ENDS
  time: 3 TET 4 DDAY
  Was: 5 STANK
  ___ Offensive: 3 TET
**Offer**: 3 BID 6 HITMAN
    TENDER 8 ASSASSIN
  AAA: 3 RTE
  Escort: 3 ARM
  for dinner: 7 SERVEUP
  Manufacturer's: 6 REBATE
  One with lots to: 7 REALTOR
  Shark's: 4 LOAN
  Treater's: 4 ONME
**Offering**: 4 ALMS 5 TITHE
  to voters: 5 SLATE
**Offhand**: 5 ADLIB 6 CASUAL
**Office**
  aide (abbr.): 4 ASST SECY
  assistant: 4 AIDE
  communication: 3 FAX
  crew: 5 STAFF
  D.C. ~ shape: 4 OVAL
  diversion: 4 POOL
  fastener: 9 PAPERCLIP
  fill-in: 4 TEMP
  Force from: 6 DEPOSE
  furniture: 4 DESK 5 DESKS
  Kind of: 4 HOME
  Like some ~ jobs: 8 CLERICAL
  machine: 5 ADDER 6 COPIER
    8 SHREDDER
  Many an ~ has one: 4 OATH

Modern ~ staple: 3 PCS
note: 4 MEMO
novice: 7 TRAINEE
Period of: 4 TERM
phone nos.: 4 EXTS
Put back in: 7 REELECT
Put in: 5 ELECT
Remove from: 4 OUST
   6 UNSEAT
Seek: 3 RUN
seeker: 3 POL
skills meas.: 3 WPM
solution: 5 TONER
Sought: 3 RAN
stamp: 4 PAID RECD 5 DATER
supply: 5 TONER 6 ERASER
Those holding: 3 INS
worker: 5 CLERK STENO
**Officeholders:** 3 INS
**Officer**
Antidrug: 4 NARC
Church: 5 ELDER 6 DEACON
Merchant vessel: 5 BOSUN
Nav.: 3 ADM ENS
Navy: 6 ENSIGN
order: 6 ATEASE
ornament: 7 EPAULET
Ottoman: 3 AGA
Patrol ~ rounds: 4 BEAT
University: 6 REGENT
**Officers**
Group of: 5 CADRE
Mil.: 3 LTS
Petty: 6 YEOMEN
**Official:** 3 REF
Ballpark: 3 UMP
College: 4 DEAN
decree: 5 EDICT
emblem: 4 SEAL
mark: 5 STAMP
Muslim: 3 AGA 4 EMIR IMAM
proceedings: 4 ACTA
record: 4 ACTA
Roman: 5 EDILE 7 SENATOR
seal: 6 SIGNET
Turkish: 3 AGA 5 PASHA
**Officiate:** 3 REF UMP
**Offing**
Be in the: 4 PEND
In the: 4 NEAR 5 AHEAD
**Off-limits:** 5 TABOO
item: 4 NONO
(var.): 4 TABU
**Off-peak**
call: 5 YODEL
**Off-ramp:** 4 EXIT
**Off-road**
goer, for short: 3 ATV
vehicle: 8 DIRTBIKE
**Off-season**
in the Alps: 3 ETE
**Offshoot:** 3 ARM 4 SPUR
  5 SCION
Religious: 4 SECT
**Offshore:** 4 ASEA 5 ATSEA
sight: 6 OILRIG

**Offspring:** 3 SON 4 KIDS SONS
  5 BROOD ISSUE SCION
  YOUNG
(abbr.): 4 DESC
**Off-target:** 5 AMISS 6 ERRANT
**"Off the Court"**
autobiographer: 4 ASHE
**Off-the-cuff:** 5 ADLIB
**Off-the-wall:** 3 ODD 4 LOCO
  ZANY 5 MANIC WACKO
  WEIRD
play: 5 CAROM
reply: 4 ECHO
**Off-white:** 4 BONE ECRU
  5 BEIGE IVORY
"___ of God": 5 AGNES
"___ of Honey": 6 ATASTE
"Of ___ I Sing": 4 THEE
"___ of Iwo Jima": 5 SANDS
**O'Flaherty**
Novelist: 4 LIAM
___ of Man: 4 ISLE
**"Of Mice and Men"**
actor Bob: 6 STEELE
___ of office: 4 OATH
"___ of One's Own":
  5 AROOM
"___ of Pooh, The": 3 TAO
"___ of robins ...": 5 ANEST
"Of ___ Sing": 5 THEEI
**Oft-broken**
promise: 3 IDO
**Often:** 4 ALOT
**Often-repeated**
abbr.: 3 ETC
___ of the Apostles, The:
  4 ACTS
"Of Thee ___" (Gershwin
  musical): 5 ISING
"___ of the Flies": 4 LORD
"___ of the Mind" (Shepard
  play): 4 ALIE
**Oft-mispunctuated**
pronoun: 3 ITS
**Oft-stubbed**
digit: 3 TOE
**Oft-told**
tales: 4 LORE
"___ of Two Cities": 5 ATALE
___ of vantage: 5 COIGN
**Ogden**
Humorist/poet: 4 NASH
**Ogle:** 3 EYE 4 LEER 5 STARE
  6 LEERAT 7 STAREAT
  10 MAKEEYESAT
**O'Grady**
of song: 5 ROSIE
**Ogre:** 3 ORC 5 BEAST FIEND
  6 MEANIE
**Oh**
Word before and after: 3 MAN
**"Oh!":** 4 ISEE
~, in German: 3 ACH
**"Oh, ___!":** 4 MAMA
**O'Hara**
home: 4 TARA

**O'Hara, Mary**
Horse in a ~ book: 6 FLICKA
**O'Hara, Scarlett:** 5 BELLE
**O'Hare**
abbr.: 3 ARR ETA
airport designation: 3 ORD
Strand at ~, perhaps: 5 ICEIN
**"Oh, bother!":** 4 DRAT
**"Oh boy!":** 5 GOODY
**"Oh, brother!":** 3 MAN
**"Oh dear!":** 4 ALAS
**O. Henry**
group: 4 MAGI
Like an ~ story: 6 IRONIC
specialty: 5 IRONY
**"Oh, fudge!":** 4 DRAT
**"Ohh, that's why!":**
  8 NOWONDER
**Ohio**
city: 5 AKRON XENIA
  6 DAYTON TOLEDO
college: 7 OBERLIN
political name: 4 TAFT
River to the: 5 MIAMI
~ Indians: 5 ERIES
**Ohm**
Physicist: 5 GEORG
symbol: 5 OMEGA
**"Oh my!":** 4 EGAD GOSH
**"Oh my goodness!":**
  5 EGADS
**"Oh no!":** 4 YIPE
**"Oh, nonsense!":** 4 PISH
**"Oh, sure!":** 4 IBET
**"Oh, that's silly!":** 4 POOH
**"Oh, what's the ___?":** 3 USE
**"Oh, woe!":** 4 ALAS
**"Oh yeah?":** 3 GEE
  7 SAYSWHO
**"Oh yeah? ___ who?":** 3 SEZ
**Oil:** 4 FUEL 8 TEXASTEA
  9 BLACKGOLD
additive: 3 STP
Apply ~ to: 6 ANOINT
Big ~ company, informally:
  3 OXY
Big name in: 4 ARCO HESS
  5 AMOCO GETTY MOBIL
  6 CRISCO WESSON
Burning the midnight:
  6 UPLATE
Canadian ~ company: 4 ESSO
cartel: 4 OPEC
Cook in hot: 3 FRY
Fragrant: 5 ATTAR
gp.: 4 OPEC
Hammer in: 6 ARMAND
holder: 3 CAN 4 DRUM TANK
  5 CRUET EASEL
Like some: 7 IRANIAN
Linseed ~ source: 4 FLAX
Motor ~ abbr.: 3 SAE
Orange blossom: 6 NEROLI
Paint: 7 LINSEED
Perfume: 5 ATTAR 6 NEROLI
Rose: 5 ATTAR

source: 3 SOY 4 PALM WELL
  5 OLIVE SHALE 6 CANOLA
  OLIVES PEANUT SESAME
  7 COCONUT LINSEED
  SOYBEAN
**Oil-bearing**
  rock: 5 SHALE
**Oilcan**
  size: 5 QUART
**Oil-measuring**
  device: 8 DIPSTICK
**Oil of ___**: 4 OLAY
**Oil-rich**
  land: 5 QATAR
  peninsula: 6 ARABIA
  7 ARABIAN
**Oils**: 3 ART
**Oil well**
  firefighter: 5 ADAIR
**Oily**: 5 SLICK
**Oink**
  joint: 3 STY
**Ointment**
  Apply: 5 RUBON
  Fly in the: 4 SNAG
  Hair: 6 POMADE
  ingredient: 7 LANOLIN
  Pharmaceutical: 6 OLEATE
  Soothing: 4 BALM 5 SALVE
**"O! it is my love; O! that she
  knew she were"**
  speaker: 5 ROMEO
**O.J.**
  trial judge: 3 ITO 8 LANCEITO
**OK**: 3 NOD 4 FAIR JAKE
  5 ALLOW 6 ASSENT
  10 ACCEPTABLE
  in any outlet: 4 ACDC
  Radio: 5 ROGER
  sign: 3 NOD
**Oka**
  City on the: 4 OREL
**Okay**: 4 SOSO 5 LEGIT LICIT
**"Okay"**: 4 SURE
  à la Opie: 4 YESM
**O.K. Corral**
  brothers: 5 EARPS
  gunfighter: 4 EARP
  occurrence: 8 SHOOTOUT
**Okeechobee**
  loc.: 3 FLA
**O'Keeffe, Georgia**
  locale: 4 TAOS
**Okefenokee**
  possum: 4 POGO
**Okinawa**
  city: 4 NAHA
  port: 4 NAHA
**Okla.**
  neighbor: 3 KAN TEX 4 KANS
  ~, before 1907: 4 TERR
**Oklahoma**
  athlete: 6 SOONER
  city: 3 ADA 4 ENID 5 TULSA
  native: 3 OTO 4 OTOE
  5 OSAGE 6 PAWNEE

**"Oklahoma!"**
  actor Gordon: 6 MACRAE
  aunt: 5 ELLER
  girl: 8 ADOANNIE
**Okra**
  stew: 5 GUMBO
  unit: 3 POD
**Oksana**
  successor: 4 TARA
**Oktoberfest**
  dance: 5 POLKA
  order: 4 BEER
  souvenir: 5 STEIN
  vessel: 5 STEIN
**Olajuwon**
  of basketball: 5 AKEEM
**Oland**
  role: 4 CHAN
**"Ol' Blue Eyes"**: 7 SINATRA
**Old**: 4 AGED 5 DATED PASSE
  enough: 5 OFAGE
  hand: 3 PRO
  hat: 5 DATED PASSE STALE
  TRITE
  salt: 3 TAR
  saw: 5 ADAGE
  Suffix with: 4 STER
  The ~ man: 3 DAD POP
  5 POPPA
  The ~ Sod: 4 EIRE ERIN
  Very ~ (abbr.): 3 ANC
**Old ___**: 3 VIC
**"Old ___"** (1957 Disney film):
  6 YELLER
**"Old ___ Bucket, The"**:
  5 OAKEN
**"___, old chap!"**: 4 ISAY
**Old ___, Connecticut**: 4 LYME
**"___ old cowhand ..."**: 4 IMAN
**"Old Curiosity Shop, The"**
  girl: 4 NELL
**"Olde"**
  establishment: 6 SHOPPE
**Olden**
  In ~ days: 4 ONCE
**Old English**
  letter: 3 EDH ETH
**Older**
  Grow: 3 AGE
**Old Faithful**: 6 GEYSER
**Old-fashioned**: 5 DATED
  6 STODGY
  Fashionably: 5 RETRO
**Old Glory**: 4 FLAG 6 USFLAG
  15 STARSANDSTRIPES
**"Old Guitarist, The"**
  painter: 7 PICASSO
**"Old MacDonald"**
  refrain: 5 EIEIO
  sound: 4 OINK
**"Old Man and the Sea, The"**
  Old man in: 8 SANTIAGO
**Old Nick**: 5 SATAN
  9 BEELZEBUB
**Olds**
  Middle name of: 3 ELI

  model: 5 ALERO
  Old: 3 REO 5 CIERA
**Olds, Ransom ___**: 3 ELI
**Old Scratch**: 5 SATAN
  7 EVILONE
**Oldsmobile**
  model: 5 ALERO
**Old Sod, The**: 4 EIRE ERIN
**Old Testament**
  boat: 3 ARK
  book: 3 JOB 4 AMOS EZRA
  RUTH 5 HOSEA JONAH
  MICAH 6 ESTHER ISAIAH
  PSALMS 8 JEREMIAH
  priest: 3 ELI
  prophet: 4 AMOS 5 HOSEA
  6 ISAIAH
  scroll: 5 TORAH
  verse: 5 PSALM
**Old-timer**: 3 VET 5 ELDER
**"Old Uncle"**
  in a Stephen Foster song:
  3 NED
**Old West**
  outlaw family: 7 DALTONS
**"Old Wives' Tale, The"**
  dramatist: 5 PEELE
**Old World**
  deer: 3 ROE 4 ROES
  language: 4 ERSE
**"Olé ___"** (1976 hit album):
  3 ELO
**"Oleanna"**
  playwright: 5 MAMET
**Oleo**
  holder: 3 TUB
  square: 3 PAT
**Olfactory**
  stimulus: 4 ODOR 5 AROMA
  SMELL
**Olin**
  Actor: 3 KEN
  Actress: 6 LENA
**Olio**: 6 MEDLEY
  Literary: 3 ANA
**Olive**
  Animated: 3 OYL
  genus: 4 OLEA
  kin: 3 ASH
  lover: 6 POPEYE
  product: 3 OIL
**Olive ___**: 3 OYL 4 DRAB
**Oliver**
  Actor: 5 PLATT
  Actress: 4 EDNA
  Director: 5 STONE
**"Oliver!"**
  choreographer White: 4 ONNA
  composer Lionel: 4 BART
  Oliver of: 4 REED
**"Oliver Twist"**
  dish: 5 GRUEL
  request: 4 MORE
  villain: 5 FAGIN SIKES
**Olives**
  Like some: 7 SPEARED

**Olivier**
role: 4 LEAR 6 HAMLET
**Olla:** 3 POT 7 STEWPOT
**Ollie**
Friend of: 4 FRAN 5 KUKLA
Partner of: 4 STAN
**"Olly, Olly, ___ Free":** 4 OXEN
**"Ol' Man River"**
composer: 4 KERN
**Ologies**
(abbr.): 4 SCIS
**Olsen**
Comic: 3 OLE
**"Olympia"**
painter Édouard: 5 MANET
**Olympian:** 7 ATHLETE
1936 ~: 5 OWENS
hawk: 4 ARES
queen: 4 HERA
quest: 4 GOLD 5 MEDAL
ruler: 4 ZEUS
sword: 4 EPEE
**Olympic**
award: 5 MEDAL
contest: 5 EVENT
host city: *see page 709*
judge: 5 RATER
sled: 4 LUGE
weapon: 4 EPEE
**Olympics**
1936 ~ star: 5 OWENS
1952 ~ site: 4 OSLO
1960 ~ site: 4 ROME
1964 ~ site: 5 TOKYO
1972 ~ site: 7 SAPPORO
1984 ~ site: 8 SARAJEVO
1988 ~ site: 5 KOREA SEOUL
1996 ~ host: 3 USA
1998 ~ site: 6 NAGANO
2000 ~ host: 6 AUSSIE
2000 ~ site: 6 SYDNEY
2002 ~ host: 3 USA
2002 ~ site: 4 UTAH
2004 ~ host: 6 ATHENS
Ancient ~ site: 4 ELIS
broadcaster Jim: 5 MCKAY
chant: 3 USA
event: 4 EPEE
host city: *see page 709*
jump: 4 AXEL
no-no: 7 STEROID
prize: 5 MEDAL
**Olympic Stadium**
team: 5 EXPOS
**Olympus**
neighbor: 4 OSSA
Queen of: 4 HERA
resident: 3 GOD
**"Om":** 6 MANTRA
**Omaha**
beach craft (abbr.): 3 LST
river: 6 PLATTE
state (abbr.): 3 NEB
**Oman**
neighbor: 5 YEMEN
**Omani:** 4 ARAB

money: 4 RIAL
title: 4 EMIR
**Omar**
Actor: 4 EPPS
**O'Meara, Mark**
org.: 3 PGA
**Omega:** 3 END
Its symbol is an: 3 OHM
opposite: 5 ALPHA
preceder: 3 PSI
rival: 5 ROLEX SEIKO
**Omelet**
base: 4 EGGS
Western ~ ingredient: 3 HAM
**Omen:** 4 SIGN 7 PORTENT
Be an ~ of: 4 BODE
interpreter: 4 SEER
Shark: 3 FIN
**"Omen, The"**
boy: 6 DAMIEN
**"O, ___ me the lass that ...":**
Burns: 3 GIE
**"Omigosh!":** 4 EGAD 5 YIKES
**Ominous:** 4 DIRE
**"O mio babbino ___"** (Puccini
aria): 4 CARO
**Omission:** 3 SIN
indication: 8 ELLIPSIS
**Omit:** 4 SKIP
in pronunciation: 5 ELIDE
~, in diners: 4 HOLD
**"Omnia vincit ___",** Virgil:
4 AMOR
**Omnibus**
alternative: 4 TRAM
**"Omnibus"**
host: 5 COOKE
**Omnium-gatherum:** 4 OLIO
**On:** 3 LIT 4 ATOP 6 ABOARD
AIRING 7 ASTRIDE
again: 5 RELIT
Off and: 7 ATTIMES
**On ___:** 4 SPEC 5 AROLL
ATEAR ATOOT THEGO
6 THEDOT
**"___ on $45 a Day":** 6 EUROPE
**Onager:** 3 ASS
**"On Aggression"**
author: 6 LORENZ
**On and on:** 5 NOEND
8 ATLENGTH
**On a scale of one ___:**
5 TOTEN
**Onassis**
nickname: 3 ARI
**On bended ___:** 4 KNEE
**Once:** 8 ASSOONAS
again: 4 ANEW
around: 3 LAP 5 ORBIT
a year: 6 ANNUAL
called: 3 NEE
in a while: 7 ATTIMES
more: 4 ANEW 5 AGAIN
Not: 4 NEER
~, formerly: 4 ERST
**___ once:** 5 ALLAT

**"Once and Again"**
actress Ward: 4 SELA
**Once ___ blue moon:** 3 INA
**"Once ___ Honeymoon"** (1942
film): 5 UPONA
**"Once in Love With ___":** 3 AMY
**"Once Is Not Enough"**
author Jacqueline: 6 SUSANN
**"Once ___ Mattress"** (1959
Broadway show):
5 UPONA
**Once-over**
Give the: 3 EYE 4 OGLE SCAN
**"Once upon ___ ...":** 5 ATIME
**Once ___ while:** 3 INA
**Oncle**
Wife of: 5 TANTE
**One:** 6 UNITED
against: 4 ANTI
and one: 4 PAIR
and only: 4 LONE SOLE
and the other: 4 BOTH
As: 6 UNITED
by one: 6 ELEVEN
Even: 3 ANY
Every: 3 ALL
For: 3 PER 4 APOP 6 APIECE
more: 7 ANOTHER
More than: 6 PLURAL
more time: 4 ANEW 5 AGAIN
Not: 4 NARY
Not ~ or the other:
7 NEITHER
Not just: 4 BOTH
of a kind: 4 UNIT
of fifty: 5 STATE
of five: 5 QUINT
of those: 4 THAT
of two: 4 HALF 6 EITHER
or more: 3 ANY
or the other: 6 EITHER
out: 7 PAROLEE
over par: 5 BOGEY
over there: 4 THAT
Partner of: 4 ONLY
prefix: 3 UNI
The ~ that got away: 4 YARN
~, in French: 3 UNE
~, in German: 3 EIN 4 EINE
EINS
~, in Spanish: 3 UNO
**"One"**
has one (abbr.): 3 SYL
in a one-two: 3 JAB
on a one: 4 UNUM
**One-___:** 4 OCAT 6 REELER
**O'Neal**
Actor: 4 RYAN
Actress: 5 TATUM
nickname: 4 SHAQ
**One-armed**
bandit: 4 SLOT
**One-billionth**
prefix: 4 NANO
**One-celled**
animal: 5 AMEBA 6 AMOEBA

One ___ customer: 3 TOA
"One Day at ___": 5 ATIME
"One Day ___ Time": 3 ATA
One-dimensional: 6 LINEAR
    SCALAR
One-eighty: 3 UEY 5 UTURN
    9 ABOUTFACE
"One Flew Over the Cuckoo's
    Nest"
  author: 5 KESEY
    8 KENKESEY
"One for My Baby"
  composer: 5 ARLEN
O'Neill
  daughter: 4 OONA
  offering: 5 DRAMA
  play: 3 ILE
  title character: 4 ANNA
    6 ICEMAN
  title ender: 4 ELMS 6 COMETH
"One I Love, The"
  group: 3 REM
One ___kind: 3 OFA
"One Life to Live"
  Kristen of: 5 ILENE
  Slezak of: 5 ERICA
One-liner: 3 GAG 4 JOKE QUIP
"One Mic"
  rapper: 3 NAS
One-million
  link: 3 INA
One ___ million: 3 INA
"One More Night"
  singer Collins: 4 PHIL
One-name
  actress: 4 CHER
  designer: 4 ERTE
  folk singer: 6 ODETTA
  Irish singer: 4 ENYA
  musician: 5 YANNI
  Nigerian singer: 4 SADE
  singer: 4 CHER 5 CHARO
  sports star: 4 PELE
  supermodel: 4 EMME IMAN
Oneness: 5 UNITY
"One O'Clock Jump"
  composer: 5 BASIE
"One of ___" (Willa Cather
    novel): 4 OURS
"One of ___ days ...": 5 THESE
One-on-one: 4 DUEL
  sport: 4 EPEE
One-piece
  undergarment: 9 UNIONSUIT
Oner: 4 LULU
"One ringy-dingy"
  lady: 9 ERNESTINE
One-seater
  Speedy: 6 GOKART
One-sided: 6 UNEVEN
  win: 4 ROUT
One-spot: 3 ACE
___ one's time: 4 BIDE
One-striper: 3 PFC
One-time
  link: 3 ATA

One ___ time: 3 ATA
"One Touch of Venus"
  composer: 5 WEILL
One-two
  connector: 4 ANDA
  Start of a: 3 JAB
One-up: 4 BEST 8 OUTSMART
One-way
  sign: 5 ARROW
On-field
  greeting: 5 HIMOM
"___ on first?": 4 WHOS
Ongoing
  saga: 9 SOAPOPERA
  story: 6 SERIAL
"On Golden ___": 4 POND
"On Golden Pond"
  bird: 4 LOON
Onion: 4 BULB
  Cocktail with an: 6 GIBSON
  Kind of: 7 BERMUDA
  relative: 4 LEEK 5 CHIVE
Onions
  partner: 5 LIVER
"___ on it!": 4 STEP
"On Language"
  columnist: 6 SAFIRE
Online
  activity: 4 CHAT
  auction site: 4 EBAY
  bookseller: 6 AMAZON
  brokerage: 6 ETRADE
  group: 5 USERS
  help: 3 FAQ
  message: 5 EMAIL
  newsgroup: 6 USENET
  novice: 6 NEWBIE
  publication: 4 EMAG 5 EZINE
  response to a joke: 3 LOL
  ~ VIP: 5 SYSOP
Only: 3 ONE 4 LONE MERE
    SOLE
  fair: 4 SOSO
"___ Only Just Begun": 4 WEVE
"Only the Lonely"
  Milo of: 5 OSHEA
"Only Time"
  singer: 4 ENYA
"Only When I ___" (1968 British
    comedy): 4 LARF
"On ___ Majesty's Secret
    Service": 3 HER
Ono
  Singer: 4 YOKO
On ___ of: 6 BEHALF
On one's ___: 3 OWN 4 TOES
"___ on parle français": 3 ICI
On-ramp
  sign: 5 MERGE
Onsager
  Nobel chemist: 4 LARS
Onstage
  Go: 5 ENTER
  Overplay: 5 EMOTE
Ont.
  neighbor: 3 QUE

Ontario
  capital: 7 TORONTO
  native: 4 CREE 6 OTTAWA
  neighbor: 4 ERIE
On the ___: 3 LAM SLY 4 OUTS
    5 FRITZ
"On the Beach"
  actress Gardner: 3 AVA
  author: 5 SHUTE
  costar of Gregory: 3 AVA
"On the double!": 3 NOW
    4 ASAP
"On the ___ hand ...":
    5 OTHER
On the qui ___: 4 VIVE
On the qui vive: 5 ALERT
"___ on the Range": 4 HOME
"On the Road Again"
  singer: 6 NELSON
"On the Street Where You
    Live"
  composer: 5 LOEWE
"On the Town"
  actor: 7 SINATRA
On the ___ vive: 3 QUI
"On the Waterfront"
  director: 9 ELIAKAZAN
  director Kazan: 4 ELIA
___ onto: 4 GLOM
Ontologist
  concern: 5 BEING
On ___ with: 4 APAR
"___ on your life!": 3 NOT
Onyx: 3 GEM
Oocytes
  ~, eventually: 3 OVA
Oodles: 4 ALOT GOBS LOTS
    TONS 5 SCADS
    6 OCEANS
Ooh and ___: 3 AAH
"Ooky"
  ~ Addams Family cousin:
    3 ITT
Oologist
  studies: 3 OVA
Oolong: 3 TEA
Oompah
  instrument: 4 TUBA
Oomph: 3 PEP 4 ELAN
  Lose: 3 SAG
"Oops!": 4 OHNO UHOH
Ooze: 4 SEEP 5 EXUDE
Oozing: 5 SEEPY
Op ___: 3 ART
Op. ___: 3 CIT
Opal: 3 GEM 6 SILICA
  Fire: 7 GIRASOL
  suffix: 4 ESCE
"O patria mia"
  singer: 4 AIDA
OPEC: 6 CARTEL
  concern: 3 OIL
  figure: 4 EMIR
  Many ~ delegates: 5 ARABS
  member: 4 IRAN
  unit: 3 BBL 6 BARREL

**Open:** 4 AIRY 5 OVERT UNBAR
   UNCAP 6 UNBOLT
   UNSEAL 7 SINCERE
   8 UNFASTEN
   a bottle: 5 UNCAP
   a gate: 5 UNBAR
   a jacket: 5 UNZIP
   house org.: 3 PTA
   Out in the: 5 OVERT 6 PUBLIC
   Slightly: 4 AJAR
   wide: 4 GAPE YAWN
**"Open ___":** 6 SESAME
**"Open ___ 9":** 3 TIL
**Opener:** 3 KEY 5 INTRO
   7 PASSKEY
   for two tins: 3 RIN
**Open-eyed:** 5 ALERT AWAKE
**Open-handed**
   blow: 4 SLAP
**Opening:** 3 GAP 4 SLOT
   5 INTRO 7 ORIFICE
   at an opening: 6 ACTONE
   bars: 5 INTRO
   day: 4 XMAS
   remarks: 5 INTRO
   run: 4 ABCD
   stake: 4 ANTE
   time: 4 NINE
   word: 6 SESAME
**Openings:** 3 ORA
**Open-mouthed:** 5 AGAPE
   Leave: 5 AMAZE
   stare: 4 GAPE
**Openness:** 6 CANDOR
**Open ___ of worms:** 4 ACAN
**"Open Sesame"**
   sayer: 7 ALIBABA
**Open-textured**
   weave: 4 MESH
**Open-wide**
   word: 3 AAH
**Opera**
   1887 ~ debut: 6 OTELLO
   about an opera singer:
      5 TOSCA
   and others: 4 ARTS
   cast member: 8 BARITONE
   hero, often: 5 TENOR
   NYC ~ house: 3 MET
   opener: 4 ACTI
   Prince of: 4 IGOR
   prop: 5 SPEAR
   set in Egypt: 4 AIDA
   Slave girl of: 4 AIDA
   solo: 4 ARIA
   star: 4 DIVA
   villain, often: 5 BASSO
   villains, often: 5 BASSI
   ___ operandi: 4 MODI 5 MODUS
**Operate:** 3 RUN
   Prepare to: 5 SCRUB
   properly: 4 WORK
**Operated**
   by air: 9 PNEUMATIC
**Operatic**
   Brief ~ solo: 7 ARIETTA

Extended ~ solo: 5 SCENA
   passage: 6 ARIOSO
   prince: 4 IGOR
   slave: 4 AIDA
   solo: 4 ARIA
**Operating:** 5 INUSE
   at a loss: 8 INTHERED
   room pro: 10 SCRUBNURSE
   Start: 9 SETUPSHOP
   system: 4 UNIX
**Operation**
   Kind of: 5 STING
   Sting: 4 TRAP
**Operation Allied Force**
   gp.: 4 NATO
**Operation Overlord**
   time: 4 DDAY
**Operative:** 3 SPY 5 AGENT
   American: 6 CIASPY
   DEA: 4 NARC
   Undercover: 4 MOLE
**Operator**
   Computer: 4 USER
   need: 7 SCALPEL
   Radio: 3 HAM
   wear: 7 HEADSET
**Operetta**
   title character: 6 MIKADO
**Ophelia:** 4 DANE
   Brother of: 7 LAERTES
**Ophthalmologist**
   case: 4 STYE
   study: 3 EYE
**Opie**
   Bee, to ~: 4 AUNT
   Father of: 4 ANDY
   portrayer: 3 RON
**Opinion:** 3 SAY 4 IDEA VIEW
   Ask for an: 4 POLL
   Favorable: 6 ESTEEM
   Form an: 4 DEEM
   Hold the same: 5 AGREE
   Not shy with an: 5 VOCAL
   opener: 8 ASISEEIT
   page, briefly: 4 OPED
   piece: 5 ESSAY
**Opossum**
   gripper: 4 TAIL
**Opp.:** 3 ANT
**Opponent:** 3 FOE 4 ANTI
   5 ENEMY RIVAL
**Opportune:** 4 RIPE 6 TIMELY
**Opportunity:** 4 SHOT
   Equitable: 9 FAIRSHAKE
   Hitting: 5 ATBAT
   Seize an: 7 MAKEHAY
   ~, so to speak: 4 DOOR
**Oppose:** 6 RESIST
   boldly: 5 BEARD
**Opposed:** 4 ANTI 6 AVERSE
   Diametrically: 5 POLAR
   Those: 4 NAYS 5 ANTIS
   to, in the sticks: 4 AGIN
**Opposing:** 4 ANTI
   force: 5 ENEMY
**Opposite:** 5 POLAR

**Opposition**
   member: 4 ANTI
   vote: 3 NAY
**Oppositionist:** 4 ANTI
**"Oppression and Liberty"**
   author Simone: 4 WEIL
**Oppressor:** 6 DESPOT
**Oprah**
   rival, once: 5 ROSIE
**Ops**
   Husband of: 6 SATURN
**Opt:** 5 ELECT 6 CHOOSE
**Optic**
   screens: 7 RETINAE
   ___ optics: 5 FIBER
**Optima**
   automaker: 3 KIA
**Optimally:** 6 ATBEST
**Optimist**
   focus: 6 UPSIDE
   words: 4 ICAN
**Optimistic:** 4 ROSY 6 UPBEAT
   Be: 4 HOPE
   Be unrealistically:
      15 HOPEAGAINSTHOPE
**"Optimist's Daughter, The"**
   author: 5 WELTY
      11 EUDORAWELTY
**Option**
   No longer an: 3 OUT
**Optional**
   Not: 6 NEEDED
   Not ~ (abbr.): 3 REQ
**Options**
   list: 4 MENU
**Optometrist**
   interest: 3 EYE
**Opulence:** 4 LUXE
**Opulent:** 4 LUSH
**Opus ___:** 3 DEI
**OR**
   On the double, in the: 4 STAT
   workers: 3 DRS RNS
**"Or ___!":** 4 ELSE
**Oracle:** 4 SEER
   sire: 6 DELPHI
**Oral:** 4 EXAM
   history: 4 LORE
   poetry: 4 EPOS
   surgeon deg.: 3 DDS
**Orally:** 5 ALOUD
**Orang:** 3 APE
**Orange:** 4 BOWL
   container: 5 CRATE
   cover: 4 PEEL RIND SKIN
   drink: 3 ADE
   feature: 5 NAVEL
   food: 3 YAM
   Inedible: 5 OSAGE
   Kind of: 5 NAVEL OSAGE
      8 MANDARIN
   seed: 3 PIP
**Orange ___:** 5 PEKOE
**___ orange:** 5 OSAGE
**Orange Bowl**
   city: 5 MIAMI

org.: 4 NCAA
**Orange County**
seat: 7 ORLANDO
**"Orange Crush"**
band: 3 REM
**Orangeish:** 5 OCHRE
**___ Orange, New Jersey:**
4 EAST
**Orange-red**
rock: 4 SARD
**Oranges**
and shredded coconut:
8 AMBROSIA
**Orangutan:** 3 APE
**Oranjestad**
island: 5 ARUBA
**Oration:** 6 SPEECH
station: 4 DAIS
**Oratorio**
piece: 4 ARIA
that debuted in 1742:
7 MESSIAH
**Orb:** 6 SPHERE
**Orbison**
hit song: 4 LEAH
Singer: 3 ROY
**Orbit**
bit: 3 ARC
First American in: 5 GLENN
Kind of: 5 LUNAR
Leave: 7 REENTER
period: 4 YEAR
Where electrons: 4 ATOM
**Orbital**
high point: 6 APOGEE
point: 4 NODE 5 APSIS
7 PERIGEE
**Orbs:** 4 EYES
**Orch.**
section: 3 STR
**Orchard**
Banned ~ spray: 4 ALAR
fruit: 4 PEAR
pest: 5 APHID
unit: 4 TREE
**Orchard Field**
~, now: 5 OHARE
**Orchestra**
alternative: 4 LOGE
area: 3 PIT
member: 4 OBOE 5 CELLO
6 OBOIST
output: 5 MUSIC
sec.: 3 STR
section: 5 BRASS REEDS
**Orchestrate:** 4 PLAN
**Orchid**
products: 4 LEIS
starch: 5 SALEP
**Order:** 4 FIAT TELL 5 EDICT
(around): 4 BOSS
In: 4 NEAT 6 ARIGHT
In ~ that: 6 SOASTO
In ~ (to): 4 SOAS
Kind of: 3 GAG
member: 3 NUN

One way to: 4 TOGO
8 ALACARTE
Out of: 5 AMISS
Partner of: 3 LAW
request: 4 ASAP
room service: 5 EATIN
**Ordered:** 4 BADE NEAT
**Orderly:** 4 NEAT TIDY
grouping: 5 ARRAY
**Orders:** 5 DICTA
One who takes: 4 CHEF
Short: 4 BLTS
Take ~ from: 4 OBEY
Take ~, in a way: 4 WAIT
**Ordinal**
ending: 3 ETH
Imprecise: 3 NTH
**Ordinance:** 3 LAW
**Ordinarily:** 7 ASARULE
**Ordinary:** 5 USUAL
7 MUNDANE
Hardly: 3 ODD
language: 5 PROSE
Out of the: 3 ODD 7 STRANGE
**"___ Ordinary Man":** 4 IMAN
**Ordnance**
supplier: 5 ARMER
**Ore**
analysis: 5 ASSAY
carrier: 4 TRAM
deposit: 4 LODE VEIN
ending: 3 ITE
Process: 5 SMELT
**Ore.**
neighbor: 3 CAL IDA NEV
5 CALIF
setting: 3 PST
summer setting: 3 PDT
**Oreck**
product: 3 VAC
**Oregano:** 4 HERB
**Oregon**
capital: 5 SALEM
city: 6 EUGENE 7 ASTORIA
college: 4 REED
motto's first word: 4 ALIS
volcanic peak: 6 MTHOOD
**Oregon Trail**
fort: 5 BOISE
**Ore-Ida**
product: 9 TATERTOTS
**O'Reilly, Radar**
drink: 4 NEHI
rank: 3 CPL
**Orenburg**
river: 4 URAL
**Oreo**
center: 5 CREME
makers: 7 NABISCO
**Org.:** 4 ASSN 5 ASSOC
founded in 1970: 3 EPA
that sticks to its guns: 3 NRA
with a journal: 3 AMA
**Organ**
effect: 7 TREMOLO
Kind of: 4 PIPE REED

knob: 4 STOP
Largest human: 4 SKIN
part: 5 PEDAL
transplant need: 5 DONOR
**Organic**
compound: 4 ENOL 5 AMIDE
ESTER
ending: 3 ENE
fertilizer: 5 GUANO
fuel: 4 PEAT
**Organism**
Plantlike: 4 ALGA
Single-cell: 5 MONAD
6 AMOEBA
**Organisms**
Genetically related: 7 BIOTYPE
**Organization**
(abbr.): 4 ASSN
Worker in a big: 3 COG
**Organized**
crime: 6 THEMOB
It may be: 5 CRIME
**Organizer**
Cry of an: 5 UNITE
**Organs**
Like some: 5 VITAL
**Orient:** 4 EAST
From the: 7 EASTERN
**Oriental:** 7 EASTERN
**Orienteering**
need: 3 MAP
**Orig.**
Not: 4 IMIT
Photo: 3 NEG
**Origami**
bird: 5 CRANE
Do: 4 FOLD
need: 5 PAPER
**Origin:** 4 ROOT SEED
6 SOURCE 7 GENESIS
Find the ~ of: 5 TRACE
suffix: 4 ATOR
**Original:** 5 NOVEL
gardener: 4 ADAM
Highly ~ and influential:
7 SEMINAL
In its ~ form: 5 UNCUT
It may be: 3 SIN
Not the ~ color: 4 DYED
sinner: 3 EVE
**"Original Gangster"**
rapper: 4 ICET
**Originally:** 3 NEE
As ~ placed: 6 INSITU
**Originate:** 4 STEM 5 ARISE
**O-ring:** 6 GASKET
**Orinoco:** 3 RIO
**"Orinoco Flow"**
singer: 4 ENYA
**Oriole:** 4 ALER
home: 3 ELM
**Orion**
has one: 4 BELT
Part of: 4 STAR
Star in: 5 RIGEL
**Ork:** 6 PLANET

**Orlando**
attraction: 5 EPCOT
City NW of: 5 OCALA
**"Orlando"**
author: 5 WOOLF
princess: 5 SASHA
**Orlando-Miami**
dir.: 3 SSE
**Orléans**
Louisiana, in: 4 ETAT
river: 5 LOIRE
**"___ or lose it!":** 5 USEIT
**Orly**
arrival: 5 AVION
plane, once: 3 SST
**Ornament:** 5 ADORN
**Ornamental**
band: 6 ARMLET
case: 4 ETUI
container: 8 CACHEPOT
fabric: 4 LAME
flower: 6 DAHLIA
loop: 5 PICOT
shell: 7 ABALONE
shrub: 6 SPIREA
    8 OLEANDER
stone: 9 TIGERSEYE
style: 6 ROCOCO
trinket: 10 KNICKKNACK
vase: 3 URN
**Ornamentation:** 5 DECOR
**Ornate**
Overly: 6 ROCOCO
**Orne**
City on the: 4 CAEN
**"Oro y ___"** (Montana motto):
    5 PLATA
**Orphan**
Fictional: 4 EYRE
of comics: 5 ANNIE DONDI
Range: 5 DOGIE
**"Orphée"**
painter: 5 COROT
**Orpheus**
instrument: 4 LYRE
poet: 5 RILKE
**Orr**
org.: 3 NHL
teammate, familiarly: 4 ESPO
**Orr, Bobby**
team: 6 BRUINS
**Orsk**
river: 4 URAL
**Orson**
Planet of: 3 ORK
**Orthodontist**
concern: 4 BITE
deg.: 3 DDS
device: 8 RETAINER
org.: 3 ADA
**Orthodox**
prefix: 3 NEO
**Orthopedist**
tool: 4 XRAY
**ORU**
Part of: 4 ORAL

**Orwell, George**
alma mater: 4 ETON
**Orzo:** 5 PASTA
**___ O's** (Post cereal): 4 OREO
**Osage oranges**
Like: 8 INEDIBLE
**Osaka**
City near: 4 KOBE
sash: 3 OBI
**Osbourne**
music: 5 METAL
of rock: 4 OZZY
**Oscar:** *see pages 718–721*
    5 AWARD
1953 ~ winner: 7 SINATRA
1992 ~ winner: 5 TOMEI
Actor/pianist: 6 LEVANT
An ~ is mostly this: 3 TIN
French: 5 CESAR
org.: 5 AMPAS
Three-time ~ winner for
    directing: 5 CAPRA
**Oscar the Grouch**
passion: 5 TRASH
**Oscillated:** 5 SWUNG
**O'Shea**
Actor: 4 MILO
Actress: 6 TESSIE
**"O Ship of State!"**
Words before: 6 SAILON
**Osiris**
Sister/wife of: 4 ISIS
**Oskar**
portrayer: 4 LIAM
**Oslo**
airline: 3 SAS
Word on ~ coins: 5 NORGE
**Osmonds**
birthplace: 5 OGDEN
One of the: 5 DONNY
    MARIE
~, by birth: 7 UTAHANS
**"O Sole ___":** 3 MIO
**Osprey**
asset: 5 TALON
**OSS**
successor: 3 CIA
**Osso ___:** 4 BUCO
**Ostentatious:** 5 SHOWY
    7 SPLASHY
display: 4 POMP RITZ
**Ostracize:** 4 SHUN
**Ostracized**
one: 5 LEPER
**Ostrich:** 6 RATITE
kin: 3 EMU MOA 4 RHEA
**O.T.**
book: 3 EZR GEN ISA LEV
    NEH 4 ECCL ESTH EZEK
    OBAD
**Otalgia:** 7 EARACHE
**"Otello"**
composer: 5 VERDI
offering: 4 ARIA
**"O tempora! O mores!"**
speaker: 6 CICERO

**Oteri**
"SNL" alum: 5 CHERI
**Othello:** 4 MOOR
foe: 4 IAGO
Like: 7 MOORISH
piece: 4 DISC
**"Othello"**
fellow: 4 IAGO
villain: 4 IAGO
**Other:** 4 ELSE
Go to the ~ side: 6 DEFECT
In ~ words: 5 IDEST
Look the ~ way: 6 IGNORE
Not one or the: 7 NEITHER
One and the: 4 BOTH
One behind the: 6 TANDEM
One or the: 6 EITHER
On the ~ hand: 3 BUT YET
side: 3 FOE 5 ENEMY
than that: 4 ELSE
~, in French: 5 AUTRE
~, in Spanish: 4 OTRA OTRO
**Others:** 5 THOSE
And: 6 ETALII
And ~ (abbr.): 4 ETAL
~, in Latin: 4 ALII
**Otherwise:** 4 ELSE 5 IFNOT
**Otherworldly:** 5 EERIE
**Otis**
Inventor: 6 ELISHA
**Otitis:** 7 EARACHE
**Otologist**
study: 3 EAR
**Ott**
of baseball: 3 MEL
**Ottawa**
chief: 7 PONTIAC
prov.: 3 ONT
**Otter**
Friend of: 4 TOAD
**Otto**
1936 Medicine Nobelist ~:
    5 LOEWI
1944 Chemistry Nobelist ~:
    4 HAHN
preceder: 5 SETTE
**Otto I**
Realm of ~ (abbr.): 3 HRE
**Ottoman**
bigwig: 6 SULTAN
governor: 3 BEY
official: 3 AGA 4 AGHA
sultan name: 5 AHMED
title: 5 PASHA
**"Ouch!":** 4 YEOW 5 YOWIE
**Ought**
to have, informally:
    7 SHOULDA
**Oui:** 3 YES
Opposite of: 3 NON
**"___ oui!":** 4 MAIS
**Ouija board**
word: 3 YES
**Ounce**
.035 ~: 4 GRAM
1/8 ~: 4 DRAM

**Ounces**
32,000 ~: 3 TON
Four fluid: 4 GILL
**Our**
genus: 4 HOMO
lang.: 3 ENG
Not: 5 THEIR
~, in French: 5 NOTRE
**Ouray, Chief**
Tribe of: 3 UTE
**"Our Gang"**
actress Hood: 5 DARLA
assent: 4 OTAY
dog: 4 PETE 5 PETEY
girl: 5 DARLA
kid with a cowlick:
    7 ALFALFA
**"___, Our Help in Ages Past":**
    4 OGOD
**"Our Miss Brooks"**
star: 5 ARDEN 8 EVEARDEN
**"Our Town":** 5 DRAMA
character Emily: 4 WEBB
family: 5 WEBBS
heroine: 5 EMILY
**Oust:** 4 BOOT 5 EVICT
    6 DEPOSE UNSEAT
**Out:** 4 AWAY 5 ALIBI NOTIN
    PASSE 6 ASLEEP
    ONLOAN 7 ONADATE
    9 NOTATHOME
for the night: 4 ABED
    6 ASLEEP
in front: 5 AHEAD
in the open: 5 OVERT
Not: 4 SAFE 5 AWAKE
    6 ATHOME
of: 4 FROM
of it: 6 INAFOG
One: 7 PAROLEE
Partner of: 4 OVER
there: 4 AFAR 6 YONDER
**"Out!":** 4 CALL SCAT
Opposite of: 4 SAFE
**___ out**
(cancels): 3 XES
(decline): 3 OPT
(relax): 3 VEG
(scrape by): 3 EKE
**"___ out!":** 3 YER
**"___ out?":** 4 INOR
**___ out a living:** 3 EKE 4 EKED
    EKES 5 EKING
**Out-and-out:** 5 UTTER
**Outback**
bird: 3 EMU
canine: 5 DINGO
hopper: 3 ROO
mineral: 4 OPAL
runner: 3 EMU
**Outbreak:** 4 RIOT 5 ONSET
Unwanted: 4 ACNE
**"Outbreak"**
actress Rene: 5 RUSSO
actress Russo: 4 RENE
**Outbuilding:** 4 SHED

**Outburst:** 3 CRY 5 SPASM
    6 TIRADE
of laughter: 4 GALE
**Outcast:** 5 LEPER 6 MISFIT
    PARIAH
Social: 4 NERD
**"Outcasts of Poker Flat, The"**
author: 5 HARTE
**Outcome:** 3 END 6 RESULT
    UPSHOT
**Outcropping:** 4 CRAG
**Outcry:** 3 HUE 4 ROAR
**Outdo:** 3 TOP 4 BEST 5 ONEUP
    6 SHOWUP
**Outdoor:** 7 OPENAIR
    8 ALFRESCO
party: 4 LUAU
**Outer**
limit: 3 RIM 4 EDGE
prefix: 3 ECT EXO 4 ECTO
**Outerwear**
Arctic: 6 ANORAK
**Outfield**
surface: 3 SOD
**Outfielder**
cry: 4 MINE 6 IGOTIT
**Outfit:** 4 UNIT 5 EQUIP GETUP
    6 ATTIRE
**Outflow**
Opposite of: 6 INTAKE
**Outing**
African: 6 SAFARI
Rural: 7 HAYRIDE
Scout: 4 HIKE
**Outlaw:** 3 BAN
chaser: 5 POSSE
**Outlay:** 4 COST
**Outlet:** 4 VENT 5 STORE
insert: 4 PLUG
option: 4 ACDC
**Outline:** 4 LIMN 6 AGENDA
    SKETCH
Make an ~ of: 5 TRACE
**Outlook:** 4 VIEW 5 VISTA
**Outlying:** 3 FAR
area: 4 BURB 5 EXURB
**Outmoded:** 5 PASSE 6 OLDHAT
**"Out of Africa"**
author Dinesen: 4 ISAK
author Isak: 7 DINESEN
director: 7 POLLACK
star: 6 STREEP
**Out-of-date:** 5 PASSE
    (abbr.): 3 OBS
**Out-of-doors:** 4 OPEN
**"Out of Sight"**
costar of Clooney: 5 LOPEZ
**"Out of sight!":** 3 RAD
**"Out of Time"**
Group with the #1 album:
    3 REM
**Out on ___:** 5 ALIMB
**Outpost:** 4 CAMP FORT
**Outpouring:** 5 SPATE
**Outrage:** 3 IRE 5 ANGER
**Outrageousness:** 8 ENORMITY

**Outs**
partner: 3 INS
**Outscore:** 4 BEAT
**Outshine:** 7 ECLIPSE
**Outside:** 8 EXTERNAL
prefix: 3 EXO
**Outsider:** 5 ALIEN
in Hawaii: 5 HAOLE
**Outstanding:** 4 OWED
    6 UNPAID 7 STELLAR
**"Outta sight!":** 5 NEATO
**Outward**
Growing: 5 ENATE
Turn: 5 EVERT SPLAY
**"Out with it!":** 4 GIVE
**Ouzo**
flavoring: 5 ANISE 7 ANISEED
**Oval:** 7 ELLIPSE
**Oven:** 4 KILN OAST
    7 ROASTER
glove: 4 MITT
output: 4 HEAT
Ready to come out of the:
    4 DONE
setting: 5 BROIL
Use the: 4 BAKE 5 ROAST
**Over:** 4 ANEW ATOP DONE
    PAST UPON 5 ABOVE
    AGAIN ENDED
    6 ACROSS AFRESH
    7 ONTOPOF
again: 4 ANEW 8 ONCEMORE
Do: 7 ITERATE
One: 5 BOGEY
prefix: 3 EPI
there: 3 YON 6 YONDER
there, poetically: 4 YOND
yonder: 5 THERE
~, in French: 3 SUR
~, in German: 4 UBER
~, slangily: 6 FINITO
**"Over ___":** 5 THERE
**___ over:** 4 KEEL TIDE
    5 PORED
**Over-50**
gp.: 4 AARP
**Overabundance:** 4 GLUT
**Overact:** 3 HAM 5 EMOTE
    7 HAMITUP
**Overactor:** 3 HAM
**Overall**
material: 5 DENIM
part: 3 BIB
**Over and over:**
    10 REPEATEDLY
**Overblown:** 5 HYPED
**Overcast:** 4 GRAY
**Overcharge:** 4 SOAK 5 GOUGE
    SCALP STING
**Overcoat:** 6 RAGLAN ULSTER
**Overcome:** 6 DEFEAT
Most: 8 TEARIEST
utterly: 5 WHELM
**Overcook:** 4 CHAR
**Overdone:** 5 BANAL STALE
    TRITE

**Overdue:** 4 LATE
  debt: 6 ARREAR
**Overeater:** 3 PIG
**Overfill:** 4 SATE
**Overflow:** 4 TEEM
  point: 3 RIM
**Overflowing:** 5 AWASH
  Filled to: 5 ABRIM
**Overfond**
  Was: 5 DOTED
**Overgrown**
  ~, in a way: 5 IVIED
**Overhang:** 4 EAVE
**Overhaul:** 4 REDO 5 REFIT
    REHAB 6 REVAMP
**Overhead:** 5 ABOVE ALOFT
  Circle: 4 HALO
  Pack: 4 STOW
  trains: 3 ELS
**"Over here!":** 4 PSST
**Overindulge:** 4 GLUT 5 SPOIL
**Overindulgent:** 4 FOND
  one: 5 DOTER
**Overjoy:** 5 ELATE
**Overlay**
  Map: 4 GRID
  material: 7 ACETATE
**Overload:** 4 CRAM 5 SWAMP
  protection: 4 FUSE
**Overlook:** 4 MISS OMIT
    6 IGNORE 7 NEGLECT
**Overly:** 3 TOO 6 TOOTOO
**Overpermisisve:** 3 LAX
**Overplay:** 5 EMOTE HAMUP
**Overrun:** 6 INFEST
**Overseas:** 6 ABROAD
  carrier: 4 ELAL
**Oversell:** 4 HYPE
**Overshadow:** 7 ECLIPSE
    UPSTAGE
**Overshoe:** 6 GALOSH
  liner: 3 PAC
**Oversight:** 5 LAPSE
**Oversized:** 3 BIG
**Overstuff:** 4 CRAM SATE
**Oversupply:** 4 GLUT 5 SPATE
**"Over the Rainbow"**
  composer Harold: 5 ARLEN

**"Over There"**
  composer: 5 COHAN
**"Over there!":** 4 LOOK
**Overthrow:** 5 ERROR UPEND
**Overthrown**
  leader: 4 SHAH
**Overtime**
  cause: 3 TIE
**Overture**
  follower: 4 ACTI 6 ACTONE
**Overturn:** 3 TIP 5 UPEND
    UPSET 7 CAPSIZE
**Overused:** 5 STALE TRITE
**Overweight:** 5 OBESE
**Overwhelm:** 3 AWE 4 DAZE
    ROUT STUN 5 SWAMP
    8 INUNDATE
**Ovid**
  opus: 6 AMORES
**Ovine**
  utterance: 3 BAA
  whine: 5 BLEAT
**Ovum:** 6 GAMETE
**Owl:** 6 HOOTER
  hangout: 4 BARN
  Like an: 7 TALONED
  question: 3 WHO
  sound: 4 HOOT
**Own:** 4 HAVE
  Come into one's: 7 BLOSSOM
  On one's: 4 SOLO 5 ALONE
  (Scottish): 3 HAE
  Take as one's: 5 ADOPT
  up to: 4 AVOW 5 ADMIT
  (up to): 4 FESS
**Owner:** 6 HOLDER
  certificate: 4 DEED 5 TITLE
**"Owner of a Lonely Heart"**
  band: 3 YES
**Ownership:** 5 TITLE
  Proof of: 4 DEED 5 TITLE
**Owns:** 3 HAS
**Ox:** 5 BOVID
  Indian: 4 ZEBU
  Tibetan: 3 YAK
**Oxen**
  holder: 4 YOKE
  Pair of: 4 SPAN TEAM

**Oxeye**
  Like an ~ window: 4 OVAL
**Oxford:** 4 SHOE
  bigwig: 3 DON
  choice: 3 EEE
  Miss in: 3 OLE
  tie: 4 LACE
  university: 7 OLEMISS
  ___ oxide: 7 NITROUS
**Oxidize:** 4 RUST
**Oxlike**
  antelope: 3 GNU 5 ELAND
**Oxy**
  target: 3 ZIT
**Oxygen**
  container: 4 TENT
  Creature dependent on:
    6 AEROBE
  Fill with: 6 AERATE
  Form of: 5 OZONE
**"Oy ___!":** 3 VEY
**"Oye Como Va"**
  band: 7 SANTANA
  composer Puente: 4 TITO
**Oyster**
  home: 3 BED
  prize: 5 PEARL
**"Oysters ___ season":** 3 RIN
**Oz**
  Author: 4 AMOS
  creator: 4 BAUM
  denizen: 4 LION
  Dog in: 4 TOTO
  Transport to: 7 TORNADO
**"Oz"**
  network: 3 HBO
**Oz.**
  1/6 fl. ~: 3 TSP
  1/2 fl. ~: 4 TBSP
  and others: 3 WTS
  Many: 3 LBS
  Sixteen: 5 ONELB
**Ozone**
  alert prompter: 4 HAZE
**Ozzy**
  Wife of: 6 SHARON

# Pp

**P:** 3 RHO 5 PENCE
  followers: 3 QRS
  Greek: 3 RHO
  of mpg: 3 PER
  of rpm: 3 PER
**PA**
  and others: 3 STS
  announcement: 3 ETA
  neighbor: 3 DEL
  nuclear accident site: 3 TMI
  summer hrs.: 3 EDT
**PABA**
  Part of: 5 AMINO
**Pablo**
  Former drug kingpin:
    7 ESCOBAR
  Poet: 6 NERUDA
**PAC**
  man, often: 6 FATCAT
  Powerful: 3 NRA
**Pac.**
  borderer: 3 CAL
  counterpart: 3 ATL
**Pac-10**
  sch.: 3 ASU ORE USC 4 UCLA
  team: 4 UCLA
**Pace:** 4 CLIP STEP 5 TEMPO
    6 STRIDE
  Easy: 4 LOPE TROT 5 AMBLE
  Fast: 4 CLIP
  Gentle: 7 DOGTROT
  Horse: 4 GAIT TROT
**Pacer:** 5 EDSEL
  maker: 3 AMC
  place: 6 STABLE
**Paces**
  Musical: 5 TEMPI
**Pacesetter:** 6 LEADER
**Pachyderm**
  of fiction: 5 BABAR
  with a horn: 5 RHINO
**Pacific:** 5 OCEAN 6 SERENE
  battle site: 7 OKINAWA
  capital: 4 APIA
  coast land: 4 PERU
  goose: 4 NENE
  greeting: 5 ALOHA
  Half a ~ island city: 4 PAGO
  Half a ~ isle: 4 BORA
  island: 4 OAHU
  islander: 6 SAMOAN
  island nation: 4 FIJI 5 NAURU
  kingdom: 5 TONGA
  party: 4 LUAU
  paste: 3 POI
  phenomenon: 6 ELNINO
  ring: 3 LEI
  sighter: 6 BALBOA

  tuber: 4 TARO
  U.S. ~ island: 4 GUAM
**Pacific ___:** 3 RIM
**Pacific Fur Company**
  founder: 5 ASTOR
**Pacifier:** 3 SOP
**Pacifist:** 4 DOVE
**Pacify:** 5 QUIET 7 APPEASE
    PLACATE
**Pacino**
  and others: 3 ALS
  film: 15 DOGDAYAFTERNOON
  role: 7 SERPICO
**___ Pacis (Rome):** 3 ARA
**Pack:** 4 LADE STOW
  again: 5 REBAG
  Ahead of the: 5 FIRST
  animal: 3 ASS RAT 4 MULE
    5 BURRO LLAMA
  away: 3 EAT 4 STOW
  down: 4 TAMP
  in tightly: 4 CRAM
  it in: 4 QUIT
  Kind of: 3 ICE
  Leader of the: 5 AKELA PACER
  member: 4 BRAT
  of pennies: 4 ROLL
  rat: 5 SAVER
  Trail the: 3 LAG
  up: 6 ENCASE
  Word before or after: 3 RAT
**Pack ___:** 4 ITIN
**Package:** 6 ENCASE PARCEL
  Benefit ~ gp.: 3 HMO
  info: 4 NTWT
  Kind of: 4 CARE
  letters: 3 COD
  string: 5 TWINE
  Wired: 4 BALE
**Packages:** 4 MAIL
  Care: 3 AID
**Packaging**
  abbr.: 5 NETWT
  amt.: 3 GRO
  material: 5 SARAN
  need: 4 TAPE
**Packard:** 4 AUTO
**Packed:** 5 DENSE
  away: 3 ATE
  How tuna is: 5 INOIL
  in: 3 ATE
  Tightly: 5 DENSE
**Packers**
  org.: 3 NFL
**Packing:** 5 ARMED
  a punch: 6 POTENT
  cord: 5 TWINE
  heat: 5 ARMED

  Send: 3 AXE CAN 4 OUST
**Packinghouse**
  stamp: 4 USDA
**Pact:** 6 TREATY
  1990s U.S./Can./Mex.: 5 NAFTA
  city: 6 WARSAW
  Defunct def.: 5 SEATO
  Western: 4 NATO
**Pad:** 4 DIGS 6 TABLET
  Brake: 4 SHOE
  Gym: 3 MAT
  Kind of: 4 KNEE LILY
    5 STENO 7 HEATING
  Mouse: 3 MAT
  Paper for a: 5 LEASE
  Parson: 5 MANSE
  Pig: 3 STY
  Place for a: 4 KNEE
  prefix: 4 HELI
  Rice: 4 DORM
  user: 5 STENO
**Pad ___:** 4 THAI
**Padded**
  covering: 4 COZY
**Paddle:** 3 OAR TAN 5 SPANK
  boat: 5 CANOE
  Do the dog: 4 SWIM
**Paddock**
  female: 4 MARE
  newcomer: 4 FOAL
  parent: 4 SIRE
**Paddy**
  product: 4 RICE
**Padlock**
  piece: 4 HASP
**Padre:** 4 NLER
  brother: 3 TIO
**Padres**
  Former owner of the: 4 KROC
**Pads**
  Lizard with clingy toe:
    5 GECKO
  Things on: 4 MICE
**Padua**
  City near: 4 ESTE
**Paean**
  Poetic: 3 ODE
**Paella**
  accompaniment: 7 SANGRIA
  base: 4 RICE
  pot: 4 OLLA
**Paesano**
  land: 6 ITALIA
**___ Paese cheese:** 3 BEL
**Paganini**
  birthplace: 5 GENOA
**Page:** 4 BEEP LEAF
  Atlas: 3 MAP

Book: 4 LEAF
Essay: 4 OPED
Kind of: 4 OPED
Left-hand: 5 VERSO
Newspaper: 4 OPED
number: 5 FOLIO
Odd-numbered: 5 RECTO
of columns: 4 OPED
of music: 5 PATTI
On this: 4 HERE
Right-hand: 5 RECTO
Singer: 5 PATTI
Society ~ word: 3 NEE
Stock ~ abbr.: 3 OTC 4 AMEX
Title: 4 DEED

**Pageant**
accessory: 4 SASH
crown: 5 TIARA
Like a ~ winner: 7 TIARAED
Parks at a: 4 BERT
prize: 5 TIARA
rating subject: 5 POISE
venue: 12 ATLANTICCITY

**Page-bottom**
abbr.: 4 IBID

**Pageboy:** 6 HAIRDO

**Pager**
letters: 3 MCI
sound: 4 BEEP

**"Pagliacci":** 5 OPERA
clown: 5 TONIO
soprano: 5 NEDDA

**"___, Pagliacci" (aria):** 4 RIDI

**Pagoda**
roofing: 5 TILES
sight: 4 IDOL
sound: 4 GONG

**Pago Pago**
native: 6 SAMOAN
site: 5 SAMOA

**Pah**
lead-in: 3 OOM

**Pahlavi:** 4 SHAH
Shah: 4 REZA

**Pahoehoe:** 4 LAVA

**Paid**
admission: 4 GATE
Debt to be: 3 IOU
holiday: 13 FRINGEBENEFIT
out: 5 SPENT
player: 3 PRO
Price: 4 COST
spots: 3 ADS
(up): 5 ANTED 6 PONIED

**Paige**
of baseball: 7 SATCHEL

**Pail**
Be clumsy with a: 5 SLOSH

**Pain:** 4 ACHE HURT 6 HASSLE
Be a: 5 ANNOY 6 PESTER
Cries of: 3 OWS
Cry of: 4 OUCH YELP YIPE
    YOWL
Dull: 4 ACHE
Feeling no: 4 NUMB
In: 4 HURT 6 ACHING

Intense: 5 AGONY
in the neck: 4 ACHE KINK
    PEST 5 CRICK 6 HASSLE
Lessen a: 4 EASE
Little: 3 IMP
React to: 5 WINCE
Royal: 4 PEST
soother: 4 BALM 6 BENGAY
Spasm of: 5 THROE
Sudden: 6 TWINGE

**Pained**
expression: 4 MOUE

**Painful:** 4 SORE
state: 5 THROE

**Painkiller:** 5 OPIUM
    7 ANODYNE
Popular: 5 ALEVE

**Pain reliever:** 6 OPIATE
    7 ANODYNE
brand: 5 ALEVE BAYER

**Pains:** 4 CARE ILLS
Partner of: 5 ACHES

**Paint:** 4 LIMN
Apply more ~ to: 6 RECOAT
base: 5 LATEX
basecoat: 6 PRIMER SEALER
can direction: 4 STIR
crudely: 4 DAUB
Eggy: 7 TEMPERA
Glossy: 6 ENAMEL
ingredient: 5 LATEX
    7 ACETONE
Kind of: 5 LATEX 6 ENAMEL
    7 ACRYLIC
layer: 4 COAT
like Pollock: 7 SPATTER
oil: 7 LINSEED
pigment: 5 OCHRE
Place to: 7 ATELIER
Poster: 7 TEMPERA
Prepare: 4 STIR
Prepare to: 6 SCRAPE
Remove: 5 STRIP
Smear: 4 DAUB
the town red: 7 CAROUSE
Uneven, as a ~ job:
    7 STREAKY

**Painted**
Freshly: 3 WET
horse: 5 PINTO
It may be: 3 TOE 4 NAIL
tinware: 4 TOLE
vessel: 4 EWER

**Painted Desert**
feature: 4 MESA
site (abbr.): 4 ARIZ

**Painter**
Belgian ~ James: 5 ENSOR
calculation: 4 AREA
choice: 3 HUE
cover-up: 5 SMOCK
Dutch: 4 HALS 5 STEEN
English ~ John: 4 OPIE
French: 5 COROT LEGER
    MANET MONET
    7 MATISSE UTRILLO

Like a: 4 ARTY
Limp watch: 4 DALI
Maja: 4 GOYA
of ballerinas: 5 DEGAS
pigment: 8 OILCOLOR
plaster: 5 GESSO
Pointillist: 6 SEURAT
Spanish: 4 GOYA MIRO SERT
stand: 5 EASEL
Surrealist: 4 DALI 5 ERNST
Swiss: 4 KLEE
~ Ashan: 5 SLOAN
~ Fernand: 5 LEGER
~ Frans: 4 HALS
~ Henri: 7 MATISSE
~ Hieronymus: 5 BOSCH
~ Jan: 5 STEEN
~ Jan Van ___: 4 EYCK
~ Joan: 4 MIRO
~ Mary: 7 CASSATT
~ Maurice: 7 UTRILLO
~ Max: 5 ERNST WEBER
~ Rembrandt: 5 PEALE
~ Richard: 5 ESTES
~ Salvador: 4 DALI

**Painting**
Do finger: 5 SMEAR
genre: 9 LANDSCAPE
guide: 7 STENCIL
(Italian): 4 ARTE
Kind of: 3 OIL
on plaster: 6 FRESCO
Prepare for: 5 PRIME
Put up a: 4 HANG
School of: 6 ASHCAN
surface: 5 GESSO
Wall: 5 MURAL

**Paintings:** 3 ART
Illusory: 5 OPART
Some: 4 OILS

**Pair:** 3 DUO TWO 4 DUAD
    DYAD ITEM 5 BRACE
    6 COUPLE 7 TWOSOME
of nines: 3 ENS
of socks: 6 ONETWO
One of a matched: 3 HIS
    4 HERS
picker: 4 NOAH
The: 4 BOTH
The best: 5 ACES
up: 4 MATE
with drums: 4 EARS
Wrestling: 7 TAGTEAM
Yoked: 4 OXEN

**Pairing:** 5 UNION

**Paisley**
Irish leader: 3 IAN

**"Pajama Party"**
actress: 8 DORISDAY

**Pajamas**
Cat's: 3 FUR
Exec in: 3 HEF

**Pak**
LPGA star: 4 SERI

**Pak, Se Ri**
org.: 4 LPGA

**Pakistan**
city: 6 LAHORE
language: 4 URDU
money: 5 RUPEE
neighbor: 4 IRAN 5 INDIA
river: 5 INDUS
**Pakistani:** 5 ASIAN
president of the 80s: 3 ZIA
**Pal:** 3 BRO BUD 4 CHUM
5 AMIGO BUDDY
French: 3 AMI 4 AMIE
Spanish: 5 AMIGO
Western: 4 PARD
___ pal (girlfriend): 3 GAL
**Palace**
dweller: 5 ROYAL
Like many a: 6 ORNATE
Moorish: 7 ALCAZAR
8 ALHAMBRA
Muslim ~ area: 5 HAREM
Paris: 6 ELYSEE
Pinball: 6 ARCADE
protector: 4 MOAT
resident: 4 EMIR TSAR
Sports: 5 ARENA
**Palais**
resident: 3 ROI
**Palatable:** 5 TASTY
Make: 9 SUGARCOAT
**Palate**
dangler: 5 UVULA
pleasing: 5 TASTY
**Palatine Hill**
site: 4 ROME
**Pale:** 3 WAN 4 ASHY 5 ASHEN
as a ghost: 4 ASHY
color: 4 TINT
drink: 3 ALE
More: 6 ASHIER
Paler than: 4 ASHY
purple: 5 LILAC MAUVE
Turn: 6 BLANCH
Very: 4 ASHY
yellow: 5 MAIZE
**Pale ___:** 3 ALE
**Paleo-**
Opposite of: 3 NEO
**Paleontological**
estimate: 3 AGE
find: 6 FOSSIL
period: 3 ERA
**Paleozoic:** 3 ERA
**Palermo**
Prior ~ pelf: 4 LIRE
**Palestine**
Ancient city of: 6 BETHEL
Ancient neighbor of: 4 EDOM
Northernmost city of ancient:
3 DAN
~, long ago: 6 CANAAN
**Palestinian:** 4 ARAB
Ancient: 6 ESSENE
ascetic: 6 ESSENE
Former ~ leader: 6 ARAFAT
**Palestrina**
piece: 5 MOTET

**Palillo**
Actor: 3 RON
**Palindrome**
center: 3 ERE
Island in a: 4 ELBA
part: 4 EREI
Poetic: 3 ERE
start: 4 AMAN
**Palindromic**
address: 4 MAAM 5 MADAM
animal: 3 EWE
cheer: 3 YAY
comics dog: 4 OTTO
cry: 3 AHA OHO
diarist: 3 NIN
exiled dictator: 6 LONNOL
magazine: 4 ELLE
name: 3 ASA EVE 4 OTTO
nickname: 3 NAN
parent: 3 DAD MOM
plea: 3 SOS
pop group: 4 ABBA
preposition: 3 ERE
principle: 5 TENET
songbird: 3 TIT
spinner: 5 ROTOR
suffix: 4 ETTE
tennis pro: 5 SELES
time: 4 NOON
title: 4 MAAM 5 MADAM
**Palladium:** 5 METAL
**Palliate:** 4 EASE
**Pallid:** 3 WAN 4 ASHY 5 ASHEN
WAXEN
**Palm:** 4 TREE
Asian: 5 ARECA BETEL
Basketry: 4 NIPA
Betel: 5 ARECA
fruit: 4 DATE
Kind of: 4 SAGO 5 BETEL
leaf: 5 FROND
reader: 4 SEER
spring: 5 OASIS
starch: 4 SAGO
Wicker: 6 RATTAN
___ Palmas: 3 LAS
**Palme**
of Sweden: 4 OLOF
**Palme ___ (Cannes award):**
3 DOR
**Palmer**
Actress: 5 LILLI
Golfer: 5 ARNIE
peg: 3 TEE
with an "army": 5 ARNIE
**Palmer, Jim:** 6 ORIOLE
**Palminteri**
Actor: 5 CHAZZ
**Palmist:** 4 SEER
concern: 4 LINE
**Palm Pilot:** 3 PDA
**Palo Alto**
City near: 8 SANMATEO
**Palo ___, California:** 4 ALTO
**Paloma**
Pop of: 5 PABLO

**Palomino**
TV: 4 MRED
**Palooka:** 3 APE OAF 4 LOUT
**Palpable:** 7 EVIDENT
**Paltrow, Gwyneth**
title role: 4 EMMA
**Paltry:** 4 MERE 6 MEASLY
amount: 3 SOU
**Pam**
Actress: 5 GRIER
**Pampas**
bird: 4 RHEA
cowpoke: 6 GAUCHO
**Pamper:** 4 BABY 5 SPOIL
6 CODDLE COSSET
11 MOLLYCODDLE
One to: 3 TOT
Place to ~ oneself: 3 SPA
**Pampering:** 3 TLC
place: 3 SPA
**Pamphlet:** 5 TRACT
suffix: 3 EER
**Pamphleteer**
of 1776: 5 PAINE
**Pamplona**
Info: Spanish cue
pal: 5 AMIGO
runner: 4 TORO
shout: 3 OLE
Stick at: 4 GORE
**Pan:** 4 SLAM
Baking: 3 TIN
creator: 6 BARRIE
Flying: 5 PETER
Frying: 7 SKILLET
handler: 4 CHEF
Opposite of: 4 RAVE
Oven: 7 ROASTER
Played like: 5 PIPED
Stir-fry: 3 WOK
**Panacea:** 7 CUREALL
**Panache:** 4 ELAN 5 STYLE
**Pan Am**
Old ~ rival: 3 TWA 5 USAIR
**Panama:** 3 HAT 7 ISTHMUS
currency: 6 BALBOA
**Panasonic**
rival: 3 RCA 4 AIWA 5 SANYO
**Panatella:** 5 CIGAR
**Pancake**
Fancy: 5 CREPE
French: 5 CREPE
Light: 4 BLIN
Like a: 4 FLAT
palace: 4 IHOP
Russian: 4 BLIN
Russian (plural): 5 BLINI
serving: 5 STACK
Thin: 5 CREPE
topper: 4 OLEO 5 SYRUP
Turn over a: 4 FLIP
**Panchen ___:** 4 LAMA
**Pancho**
Mexican revolutionary:
5 VILLA
pal: 5 AMIGO CISCO

poncho: 6 SERAPE
**Pancreas:** 5 GLAND
**Panda**
Toon: 4 ANDY
**Pandemonium:** 5 CHAOS
    HAVOC
**P&L**
column heading: 3 YTD
preparer: 3 CPA
**Pandora**
released them: 4 ILLS 5 EVILS
**Pandora's box:**
    10 CANOFWORMS
remnant: 4 HOPE
**Pandowdy:** 3 PIE
**Pane**
frame: 4 SASH
**Panel**
Court: 4 JURY
Dress: 5 INSET
Kind of: 5 SOLAR
suffix: 3 IST
**Paneling**
material: 8 MASONITE
**Panelist:** 5 JUROR
**Panels**
Car with removable roof:
    4 TTOP
**Panetta**
Political: 4 LEON
**Pan-fry:** 5 SAUTE
**Pang:** 4 ACHE 5 THROE
    6 TWINGE
Emotional: 6 TWINGE
**Panhandle:** 3 BEG
loc.: 4 OKLA
site: 6 ALASKA
State with a: 5 IDAHO
**Panic**
In a: 6 SCARED
PC ~ button: 3 ESC
Study in a: 4 CRAM
___ **Panisse (restaurant):**
    4 CHEZ
**Panorama:** 4 VIEW 5 VISTA
**Pans**
Partners of: 4 POTS
Some: 7 TINWARE
**Pant:** 4 GASP
**Pantheon**
member: 3 GOD
Norse: 5 AESIR
**Panther:** 5 NHLER
Cartoon ~ color: 4 PINK
**Panthers**
of the Big East: 4 PITT
**Panties**
Short: 7 STEPINS
**Pantomime:** 6 ACTOUT
character: 7 PIERROT
Song title spelled in: 4 YMCA
**Pantomimist**
Jacques: 4 TATI
**Pantry:** 6 LARDER
    9 STOREROOM
items: 4 TINS

pest: 3 ANT
**Pants:** 5 GASPS 6 SLACKS
alternative: 5 SKIRT
Alternative to hot: 4 MINI
Casual: 5 JEANS
feature: 6 CREASE
holder: 6 HANGER
maker Strauss: 4 LEVI
material: 5 CHINO
measure: 6 INSEAM LENGTH
One with ~ on fire: 4 LIAR
part: 3 LEG 4 KNEE SEAT
problem: 3 RIP
Short: 4 TROU
style: 5 CAPRI
___ **pants:** 5 CAPRI
**Pantyhose**
Brand of: 5 LEGGS
shade: 4 ECRU
woe: 4 SNAG
**Pantywaist:** 5 SISSY
**Panza, ___:** 6 SANCHO
**Panza, Sancho**
mount: 3 ASS
**Papa:** 3 DAD
Mama of: 4 NANA
Partner of: 4 MAMA
Stable: 4 SIRE
**"Papa Bear"**
of football: 5 HALAS
**"Papa, Can You Hear Me?"**
Film with the song: 5 YENTL
**Papa Doc**
ruled it: 5 HAITI
**Papa Hemingway:** 6 ERNEST
**Papal**
ambassador: 6 NUNCIO
bull: 5 EDICT
cape: 5 FANON
court: 5 CURIA
headgear: 5 TIARA
name: 4 PIUS
representative: 6 LEGATE
vestment: 5 ORALE
**Papandreou**
Former Greek P.M.:
    7 ANDREAS
**Paparazzi**
target: 4 STAR 5 CELEB
**Paparazzo**
need: 6 CAMERA
prize: 3 PIC
target: 4 STAR 5 CELEB
**Papas**
Actress: 5 IRENE
Singing partner of: 5 MAMAS
**Papeete**
island: 6 TAHITI
**Paper**
24 sheets of: 5 QUIRE
art: 7 ORIGAMI
Baltimore: 3 SUN
Chi-town: 4 TRIB
container: 3 BAG
craft: 7 ORIGAMI
Do ~ work: 4 EDIT

Enjoy the: 4 READ
fastener: 6 STAPLE
Flat: 5 LEASE
flier: 4 KITE
holder: 3 PAD
Holds the ~ to: 4 OWNS
Homeowner: 4 DEED
Kind of: 3 FAX 4 RICE TERM
    5 CREPE GRAPH TRADE
Like India: 4 THIN
Like notebook: 5 LINED
    RULED
money: 4 NOTE
name, briefly: 4 TRIB
Not on: 4 ORAL
Old ~ money: 5 SCRIP
Old ~ part: 4 ROTO
Party: 5 CREPE
Piece of: 4 SLIP 5 SCRAP
    SHEET
Pitch on: 7 PRINTAD
Pulitzer: 5 WORLD
pusher: 7 NEWSBOY
Put on: 5 WRITE
quantity: 4 REAM 5 QUIRE
Renter: 5 LEASE
Scrap: 5 SHRED
section: 6 SPORTS
size: 5 LEGAL
Sleazy: 3 RAG
Term ~ abbr.: 4 IBID
Term ~ citation: 6 IBIDEM
towel: 4 WIPE
Translucent: 9 ONIONSKIN
Travel: 4 VISA
unit: 5 SHEET
Washington: 4 POST
worker: 6 EDITOR
Yellow: 6 MANILA
**Paperback:** 4 BOOK
Big inits. in: 3 NAL
publisher: 4 AVON DELL
    6 SIGNET
**Paperboy**
path: 5 ROUTE
**"Paper Chase, The"**
topic: 3 LAW
**Paper Mate:** 3 PEN
rival: 3 BIC
**"Paper Moon"**
actor or actress: 5 ONEAL
**"Paper Roses"**
singer Marie: 6 OSMOND
**Papers:** 5 MEDIA
(abbr.): 3 MSS
Bundle of: 5 SHEAF
Give walking ~ to: 3 AXE
Research: 6 THESES
Walking: 5 THEAX
**Paperwork:** 5 FORMS
    7 REDTAPE
**Papier-___:** 5 MACHE
**Paprika**
Stew with: 7 GOULASH
**Papua**
city: 3 LAE

**Papyrus:** 5 SEDGE
**Paquin**
  Oscar winner: 4 ANNA
**Par:** 4 NORM
  On a: 4 EVEN
  On a ~, in French: 4 EGAL
  On a ~ with: 7 EQUALTO
  One over: 5 BOGEY
  One under: 6 BIRDIE
  Two under: 5 EAGLE
**Par ___ (airmail label):** 5 AVION
**Parable**
  message: 5 MORAL
**Parabola**
  part: 3 ARC
**Parabolic**
  path: 3 ARC
**Parachute**
  Deliver by: 7 AIRDROP
  Kind of: 6 GOLDEN
  material: 5 NYLON
  part: 4 CORD 6 CANOPY
  Small: 6 DROGUE
**"Parachutes and Kisses"**
  author Erica: 4 JONG
**Parade:** 5 STRUT
  group: 4 VETS
  honoree: 4 HERO 5 STPAT
  NY ~ sponsor: 5 MACYS
  sight: 5 FLOAT
  spinner: 5 BATON
  spoiler: 4 RAIN
  time: 6 EASTER
  Word before: 3 HIT
**"Parade"**
  actor: 4 TATI
**Paradigm:** 5 IDEAL
**Paradise:** 4 EDEN
  evictee: 4 ADAM
  Like: 6 EDENIC
  lost: 4 EDEN
  of Gauguin: 6 TAHITI
  of King Arthur: 6 AVALON
**"Paradise Lost":** 4 EPIC
  character: 4 ADAM
  figure: 5 SATAN
  poet: 6 MILTON
  setting: 4 EDEN
**Paradisiacal:** 6 EDENIC
**"Paradiso"**
  writer: 5 DANTE
**Paradoxical**
  question, in Zen: 4 KOAN
  ~ Greek: 4 ZENO
**Paraffin**
  Like: 4 WAXY
**Paragon:** 5 IDEAL
  8 NONESUCH
**Paragraph**
  Playbill: 3 BIO
  Start a: 6 INDENT
**Parakeet:** 3 PET
  home: 4 CAGE
**Parallel:** 4 AKIN 6 ANALOG
  7 ALIGNED
  Capital on the 60th: 4 OSLO

It's ~ to the radius: 4 ULNA
**Parallelograms**
  Some: 6 RHOMBI
**Paramecium**
  propellers: 5 CILIA
**Paramedic**
  (abbr.): 3 EMT
**Paramount:** 4 MAIN
**Paramour**
  French: 4 AMIE
**Paranoiac**
  worry: 4 PLOT
**Paranormal**
  power: 3 ESP
**Paranormalist**
  ~ Geller: 3 URI
**Paraphernalia:** 4 GEAR
**Paraphrase:** 7 RESTATE
**Parapsychology**
  subj.: 3 ESP
**Parasailing**
  Go: 4 SOAR
**Parasite:** 5 LEECH
  home: 4 HOST
  Plant: 5 APHID
  prefix: 4 ECTO
  Tiny: 4 MITE
  Young: 3 NIT
**Parasites**
  Some: 4 LICE
  Their parents are: 4 NITS
**Parasol:** 8 SUNSHADE
  offering: 5 SHADE
**Paratrooper**
  cry: 8 GERONIMO
  need: 5 CHUTE
**Parboil:** 5 SCALD
**Parcel:** 4 DOLE METE
  Land: 4 ACRE 5 TRACT
  out: 5 ALLOT
  Partner of: 4 PART
  Realty: 3 LOT
**Parched:** 4 ARID SERE
  feeling: 6 THIRST
**Pardon**
  General: 7 AMNESTY
  ~, with "off": 3 LET
**Pardoned**
  president: 5 NIXON
**"Pardon me":** 4 AHEM 5 SORRY
  7 SOSORRY
  abroad: 5 SCUSI
**Pare:** 4 PEEL
  pounds: 4 SLIM
**Parent:** 4 REAR 6 RAISER
  REARER
  New: 5 NAMER
  order: 3 NOW
  Palindromic: 3 DAD MOM POP
  Parisian: 4 MERE PERE
  Piglet: 3 SOW
  Reason from a: 6 ISAYSO
  Show biz: 8 STAGEMOM
  Stable: 4 SIRE
  warning: 4 DONT
**Parenthesis:** 3 ARC

**Parenthetical**
  amount: 4 LOSS
  remark: 5 ASIDE
**Parenthood**
  Plant ~ setting:
    10 GREENHOUSE
**"Parenthood"**
  actress Dianne: 5 WIEST
**Parenting**
  challenges: 5 TEENS
  Do: 4 REAR
**Paretsky**
  Mystery writer: 4 SARA
**Pariah:** 5 LEPER
  Union: 4 SCAB
**Parimutuel:** 4 TOTE
  Use a: 3 BET
**Paris**
  Info: French cue
  abductee: 5 HELEN
  airport: 4 ORLY
  American in: 5 ANGLO
  bank: 4 RIVE
  based org.: 6 UNESCO
  City of: 4 TROY
  divider: 5 SEINE
  evening: 4 SOIR
  Father of: 5 PRIAM
  First bishop of: 7 STDENIS
  foe: 5 ROMEO
  girl: 4 ELLE
  Hot time in: 3 ETE
  museum: 6 LOUVRE
  newspaper, with "Le":
    5 MONDE
  pal: 3 AMI
  palace: 6 ELYSEE
  papa: 4 PERE
  path: 5 ALLEE
  Plaster of: 5 GESSO
  playground: 4 PARC
  possessive: 3 MON SES 4 AMOI
  pronoun: 3 TOI
  river: 5 SEINE
  River near: 4 OISE
  school: 5 ECOLE LYCEE
  springtime: 3 MAI
  star: 6 ETOILE
  Suburb of: 4 ORLY
  subway: 5 METRO
  summer: 3 ETE
  Washington in: 4 ETAT
  Wife of: 6 OENONE
  yes: 3 OUI
  ~ Ltd.: 3 CIE
**"___ Paris" (Cole Porter):**
  5 ILOVE
**Parish**
  leader: 6 RECTOR
  priest: 5 VICAR 6 CURATE
**Parishes**
  Long in the: 4 HUEY
**Parishioners:** 5 LAITY
  donation: 5 TITHE
**Parisian**
  Info: French cue

article: 3 UNE
coin: 5 FRANC
diner: 4 CAFE
goodbye: 5 ADIEU
pal: 3 AMI
palace: 6 ELYSEE
parent: 4 MERE PERE
passion: 5 AMOUR
possessive: 3 SES 4 AMOI
preposition: 4 AVEC
pronoun: 3 ILS
pupil: 5 ELEVE
season: 3 ETE
street: 3 RUE
**Park: 6 AVENUE**
Alberta: 5 BANFF
Animal: 3 ZOO
Big Apple: 4 SHEA
concern (abbr.): 4 ECOL
Copenhagen: 6 TIVOLI
in NYC: 3 AVE
it: 3 SIT
Kind of: 5 THEME 7 TRAILER
London: 4 HYDE
Out of the: 4 GONE
person: 6 RANGER
place: 3 LOT 4 CURB
    6 GARAGE
shelter: 6 GAZEBO
**___ Park**
(California): 5 BUENA MENLO
(Colorado): 5 ESTES
(Illinois): 3 OAK
(New Jersey): 5 MENLO
(New York): 4 REGO
(Pirates' field): 3 PNC
**Parka: 6 ANORAK**
part: 4 HOOD
**Park Avenue: 3 CAR**
**Parkay**
product: 4 OLEO
**Parked**
it: 3 SAT
**Parker: 3 PEN**
Actor: 4 FESS
Actress: 5 POSEY
Car: 5 VALET
Illegal ~ worry: 5 TOWER
Nosy: 5 SNOOP YENTA
**Parker, Charlie**
genre: 5 BEBOP
instrument: 7 ALTOSAX
nickname: 4 BIRD
**Parker, Dorothy**
quality: 3 WIT
**Parker, ___ Jessica: 5 SARAH**
**Parker House: 4 ROLL**
**Parking**
Airport ~ area: 5 APRON
attendant: 5 VALET
lot device: 5 METER
meter opening: 4 SLOT
place: 3 LOT 4 CURB SPOT
    6 GARAGE
**Parkinsonism**
treatment: 5 LDOPA

**Parks**
at a pageant: 4 BERT
Civil rights activist: 4 ROSA
on a bus: 4 ROSA
**Parks, Rosa: 8 ALABAMAN**
**Parliament**
First woman in: 5 ASTOR
Head of: 3 LOO
Israeli: 7 KNESSET
Japanese: 4 DIET
John in: 3 LOO
member: 4 LORD
Russian: 4 DUMA
**Parliamentary**
govt. leaders: 3 PMS
proposal: 6 MOTION
response: 3 AYE
**Parlor**
Beauty: 5 SALON
game: 4 POOL
Ice cream ~ order: 6 FRAPPE
    SUNDAE
letters: 3 OTB
piece: 4 SOFA 5 DIVAN
    6 SETTEE
Spider's ~ invitee: 3 FLY
Stick in a: 3 CUE
~, in Spanish: 4 SALA
**Parmenides**
home: 4 ELEA
**Parmesan**
Prepare: 5 GRATE
**Parody: 3 APE 5 SPOOF**
    6 SENDUP 7 LAMPOON
Yankovic: 5 EATIT
**Paroxysm: 5 THROE**
**Parquet**
Like a ~ floor: 6 INLAID
**Parrot: 3 APE 4 APER ECHO**
    6 REPEAT 7 IMITATE
Colorful: 5 MACAW
cry: 3 AWK
Disney: 4 IAGO
Large: 3 KEA 5 MACAW
Showy: 8 COCKATOO
**Parry: 5 AVERT**
follower: 7 RIPOSTE
Item to ~ with: 4 EPEE
**Parseghian**
Coach: 3 ARA
of football: 3 ARA
**Parsifal**
quest: 5 GRAIL
**Parsing**
choice: 4 NOUN
**Parsley: 4 HERB**
piece: 5 SPRIG
relative: 4 DILL 5 ANISE
    6 FENNEL 8 ANGELICA
With: 5 GARNI
**Parson**
place: 5 MANSE
**Parsonage: 5 MANSE**
    7 RECTORY
**Parsons**
Actress: 7 ESTELLE

Musician: 4 ALAN
**Part: 4 AREA ROLE 6 DIVIDE**
    7 ELEMENT
    8 SEPARATE
Bit: 5 CAMEO
Discrete: 4 UNIT
Do one's: 3 ACT
Essential: 4 PITH
Film: 4 ROLE
of: 4 INON
Worst: 5 DREGS
**Partake**
of: 3 EAT USE 4 HAVE
**Parted**
It ~ in Exodus: 6 REDSEA
**Parthenon**
goddess: 6 ATHENA
**Partial: 6 BIASED**
    8 ONESIDED
**Partiality: 4 BIAS**
**Partially: 4 SOME**
**Participate: 5 ENTER OPTIN**
    SHARE SITIN
Decide to: 5 OPTIN
Hope to: 6 WANTIN
Not ~ in: 6 SITOUT
**Particle: 4 ATOM**
Charged: 3 ION 5 ANION
Cyclotron: 3 ION
Dust: 4 MOTE
Electrolysis: 5 ANION
Elementary: 4 ATOM 5 MESON
    8 NEUTRINO
Hypothetical: 5 AXION
    QUARK
Kind of: 3 PSI 5 ALPHA
    6 LAMBDA
Negative: 5 ANION
Positive: 6 PROTON
prefix: 4 ANTI
Quantum physics: 5 MESON
Small: 4 MOTE
Soot: 4 SMUT
Stable: 3 OAT
Subatomic: 4 MUON PION
    5 MESON 6 PROTON
Tiny: 4 ATOM
Unstable: 4 MUON
**___ particle: 3 PSI TAU**
**Particle accelerator**
particle: 3 ION 4 ATOM
**Particles**
Abrasive: 4 GRIT
Create charged: 6 IONIZE
Remove ~ from: 4 SIFT
Sandy: 4 GRIT
**Particular: 4 ITEM 5 FUSSY**
    6 DETAIL
Agenda: 4 ITEM
Drive nowhere in: 4 SPIN
In ~ (abbr.): 3 ESP
Nobody in: 6 ANYONE
period: 3 ERA
**Parties: 3 DOS**
Like some: 4 STAG
War: 6 ARMIES

**Parting**
Pacific: 5 ALOHA
word: 4 CIAO 5 ADIEU ADIOS
    ALOHA LATER
    7 GOODBYE 8 SAYONARA
words: 4 BYES OBIT TATA
    5 IQUIT OBITS 6 ADIEUS
    8 AUREVOIR
**"Parting is ___ sweet sorrow":**
    4 SUCH
**Partisan**
prefix: 3 NON
**Partisanship:** 4 SIDE
**Partition:** 5 SEVER 6 DIVIDE
Ping-Pong: 3 NET
Safety: 8 FIREWALL
~, with "off": 4 ROPE
**Partitions**
Nasal: 5 SEPTA
**Partly**
coincide: 7 OVERLAP
open: 4 AJAR
**Partner:** 4 ALLY MATE 5 UNITE
Talk show: 6 COHOST
**Partnership:** 7 CAHOOTS
**Partnership for Peace**
gp.: 4 NATO
**Partook**
of: 3 ATE
**Partridge**
boy: 5 DANNY
Eldest: 5 KEITH
perch in song: 8 PEARTREE
Slang expert: 4 ERIC
**Partridge, Laurie**
portrayer: 3 DEY
**"Partridge Family, The"**
actor Bonaduce: 5 DANNY
actress Susan: 3 DEY
**"___ partridge in ...":** 4 ANDA
**"... partridge in ___ tree":**
    5 APEAR
**Parts**
of qts.: 3 PTS
**Part-time**
player: 7 SEMIPRO
worker: 4 TEMP
**Party:** 4 FETE 5 REVEL
1990s ~: 4 RAVE
A ~ to: 4 INON
activist: 3 POL
Afternoon: 3 TEA
All-night: 4 RAVE
animal: 4 STAG 6 DONKEY
attendee: 5 GUEST
big shot: 4 WHIP
Block party: 9 HOMEOWNER
bowlful: 3 DIP
brewer: 3 URN
Bridal: 4 WIFE
cheese: 4 BRIE EDAM
Coming-out: 3 DEB
decoration: 8 STREAMER
Fancy: 4 GALA
follower: 4 GOER
Frat ~ staple: 3 KEG

Frat ~ wear: 4 TOGA
Furnish ~ food: 5 CATER
game pin-on: 4 TAIL
Garden: 3 EVE 4 ADAM
gift: 5 FAVOR
Give a ~ for: 4 FETE
giver: 4 HOST 7 HOSTESS
handout: 5 FAVOR
hearty: 5 REVEL
    8 LIVEITUP
Held by a third: 8 INESCROW
Hostile: 5 ENEMY
invitee: 5 GUEST
Israeli political: 5 LIKUD
Kind of: 3 HEN TEA 4 POOL
    STAG TOGA 6 PAJAMA
Lavish: 4 FETE
Lawn ~ site: 4 YARD
leader: 4 HOST 5 EMCEE
    7 HOSTESS
Life of the:
    15 GOODTIMECHARLIE
Like a dull: 4 DEAD
line: 5 CONGA
    8 WHATSNEW
Lively: 4 BASH
member: 3 HEN
member, briefly: 3 DEM
munchies: 7 CANAPES
Not the ~ sort (abbr.): 3 IND
offering: 5 SLATE
paper: 5 CREPE
Pool: 5 STENO
pooper: 4 BORE DRAG DRIP
    10 WETBLANKET
popper: 4 CORK
purchase: 3 ICE
Quilting: 3 BEE
Quite a: 4 BASH
Search: 5 POSSE
snacks: 4 NUTS
spread: 4 PATE
Stag: 4 DEER
Tea ~ crasher: 5 ALICE
Tea ~ member: 8 DORMOUSE
thrower: 4 HOST
time: 3 EVE
to: 4 INON
Uncrashable: 9 OPENHOUSE
Wild: 4 ORGY
Work: 4 CREW
**Party-giver:** 4 HOST
~ Mesta: 5 PERLE
~ Perle: 5 MESTA
**Parvenu:** 7 UPSTART
**Pas**
Partners of: 3 MAS
**Pas ___:** 4 ALLE SEUL
**"___ pasa?":** 3 QUE
**Pasadena**
parade flowers: 5 ROSES
**Pascal**
Philosopher: 6 BLAISE
thought: 6 PENSEE
**___ Pascal (computer language):**
    5 TURBO

**Pas de ___:** 4 DEUX
**Pas de deux**
part: 6 ADAGIO
**Pass:** 4 GOBY 5 BADGE ENACT
    6 ELAPSE 8 OVERTAKE
again: 5 RELAP
Allow to: 5 LETBY
along: 5 RELAY 6 RELATE
and then some: 3 ACE
by: 6 ELAPSE
catcher: 3 END
Come to: 5 ENSUE OCCUR
    6 BETIDE HAPPEN
Didn't ~ the bar: 5 DRANK
Didn't just: 4 ACED
Don't: 3 BID
Forward: 6 AERIAL
Give a free: 4 COMP
into law: 5 ENACT
Kind of: 7 LATERAL
Long: 4 BOMB
Make a ~ at: 5 HITON
    8 COMEONTO
Mountain: 3 COL GAP
on: 4 SKIP 5 REFER RELAY
out: 4 ZONK 5 ALLOT SWOON
out cards: 4 DEAL
over: 4 OMIT SKIP 5 ELIDE
prefix: 3 SUR
Press: 5 IDTAG
quickly: 4 FLIT
slowly: 4 DRAG 6 WEARON
the time: 4 LAZE
They're hard to: 8 ROADHOGS
through a wall: 4 GATE
Tourney: 3 BYE
~, as time: 5 SPEND
    6 ELAPSE
**"Pass ___!":** 4 ITON
**Passable:** 4 SOSO
**Passage:** 4 PATH
Anatomical: 4 ITER
Brain: 4 ITER
Chimney: 4 FLUE
Closing: 4 CODA
Diary: 5 ENTRY
Melodic: 6 ARIOSO
Mine: 4 ADIT 5 SHAFT
Narrow: 4 LANE 5 ALLEY
    INLET
Narrow water ~ (abbr.): 3 STR
Operatic: 6 ARIOSO
Right of: 8 EASEMENT
Sermon: 4 TEXT
Symbol of safe: 3 ARK
~, in Latin: 4 ITER
**Passages**
Nasal: 5 NARES
**"Passage to India, A"**
author: 9 EMFORSTER
doctor: 4 AZIZ
heroine: 5 ADELA
**Passageway**
Body: 4 ITER
Covered: 6 ARCADE
Vine-covered: 7 PERGOLA

**Passbook**
abbr.: 3 DEP INT
amt.: 3 DEP
**Passé:** 3 OLD OUT 5 DATED
STALE 6 DEMODE
OLDHAT
preposition: 4 UNTO
**Passed:** 3 OKD 6 GONEBY
It may be: 3 ACT HAT
out cards: 5 DEALT
the puck to: 3 FED
**Passel:** 4 SLEW
**Passenger:** 5 RIDER
Ark: 3 HAM
Cheap ~ place: 8 STEERAGE
info: 3 ETA
Limo: 3 VIP
Paying: 4 FARE
Was a: 4 RODE
**Passeport**
info: 3 NOM
**Passer**
Buck: 3 ATM
Charge the: 5 BLITZ
Leading NFL ~ of 1980: 4 SIPE
**"___ Passes" (Rumer Godden
novel):** 5 PIPPA
**"___ Pass Go ...":** 5 DONOT
**Passing**
assistance: 3 YEA
Barely ~ grade: 3 DEE
fancy: 3 FAD 4 WHIM
grade: 3 CEE
mention: 4 OBIT
notice: 4 OBIT
Sounds of time: 5 TICKS
stats (abbr.): 3 YDS
**Passing ___:** 4 LANE
**Passion:** 4 FIRE HEAT LOVE
ZEAL 5 ARDOR
6 FERVOR
Hate with a: 6 DETEST
Parisian: 5 AMOUR
personified: 4 EROS
Uncontrolled: 4 LUST
**Passionate:** 4 AVID 5 AFIRE
6 ARDENT TORRID
7 INTENSE
about: 4 INTO
desire: 4 LUST
**"Passions":** 4 SOAP
**Passive**
Be: 5 SITBY
protest: 5 SITIN
**Passive-aggressive**
response:
15 SILENTTREATMENT
**___ Passos, John:** 3 DOS
**Passover**
meal: 5 SEDER
month: 5 NISAN
staple: 5 MATZO
**Passport**
maker: 5 HONDA
stamp: 4 VISA
**Passports:** 3 IDS

**___ passu (equably):** 4 PARI
**Password**
Fictional ~ user: 7 ALIBABA
Person with a: 4 USER
preceder: 6 USERID
requester: 4 USER
Type a: 5 LOGIN
Verify a: 7 REENTER
What a ~ allows: 5 ENTRY
**Past:** 3 AGO 7 ONETIME
Are in the: 4 WERE
Blast from the: 5 ATEST
NTEST OLDIE
due: 4 LATE
Ending for: 3 URE
Evoking the: 5 RETRO
Fifty minutes: 5 TENTO
Get: 5 ELUDE
Go: 4 OMIT SKIP
In days: 3 AGO
In the: 3 AGO 4 ONCE
In the ~, in the past: 4 ERST
In the recent: 6 LATELY
OFLATE
Is in the: 3 WAS
Long: 6 OFYORE
Not long: 6 RECENT
Of time: 5 OLDEN
one's prime: 4 AGED
or present: 5 TENSE
Piece of the: 3 ERA 5 RELIC
Put one: 3 ACE
Slip: 5 ELUDE
Song from the: 5 OLDIE
The ~, in the past: 3 ELD
the deadline: 4 LATE
Thing of the: 5 RELIC
Time: 4 THEN YORE
Times: 4 ERAS YORE
Went: 8 OVERSHOT
**Pasta**
choice: 4 ZITI 5 PENNE
Corkscrew: 6 ROTINI
dish: 7 LASAGNA
Firm: 7 ALDENTE
Green ~ sauce: 5 PESTO
ingredient: 8 SEMOLINA
in product names: 4 RONI
order: 7 ALDENTE
Popular ~, for short: 3 MAC
Ricelike: 4 ORZO
sauce maker: 4 RAGU
shape: 5 ELBOW SHELL
6 BOWTIE
Soup: 4 ORZO
suffix: 3 INI
topper: 5 PESTO SAUCE
Tubular: 4 ZITI 5 PENNE
8 RIGATONI
With ~, in product names:
5 ARONI
with pockets: 7 RAVIOLI
~, to an athlete: 4 CARB
**Paste:** 4 SOCK 6 WALLOP
Cut and: 4 EDIT
ingredient: 6 TOMATO

Polynesian: 3 POI
Sesame: 6 TAHINI
Soybean: 4 MISO
**Pasted**
in the ring: 3 KOD
**Pastel**
Hardly: 4 NEON
shade: 4 AQUA 5 LILAC
**Pastels:** 3 ART
**Pasternak**
heroine: 4 LARA
**Pasteur**
Chemist: 5 LOUIS
portrayer: 4 MUNI
**Pastiche:** 4 OLIO
**Pastime**
for Prince Charles: 4 POLO
Pub: 5 DARTS
**Pastis**
flavor: 5 ANISE
**Pastoral:** 5 IDYLL RURAL
6 SERENE
deity: 4 FAUN
pipe: 4 REED
place: 3 LEA
poem: 4 IDYL 5 IDYLL
7 ECLOGUE
sound: 3 BAA
**"Pastoral" Symphony**
Like Beethoven's: 3 INF
**Pastrami**
Like good: 4 LEAN
purveyor: 4 DELI
**Pastry**
Breakfast: 6 DANISH
Cream-filled: 6 ECLAIR
finisher: 4 ICER
Flaky: 4 FILO
French: 7 RISSOLE
Fruit: 4 TART 7 STRUDEL
Indian: 6 SAMOSA
Rich: 5 TORTE
shell: 4 PUFF
thickener: 4 AGAR
**Pasture:** 3 LEA 5 FIELD
mom: 3 EWE
sound: 3 BAA MAA MOO
**Pastureland:** 3 LEA
**Pasty:** 3 WAN 5 ASHEN
**Pat:** 3 DAB
Actor: 6 MORITA
Alternative nickname for:
5 TRISH
Didn't stand: 4 DREW
down: 4 TAMP
Former Knicks coach: 5 RILEY
gently: 3 DAB 5 DABAT
Had down: 4 KNEW
Host: 5 SAJAK
of fat: 4 OLEO
on the back: 4 BURP 6 PRAISE
on the buns: 4 OLEO
Vanna, to: 6 COHOST
**Pataki**
Gov. ~ place: 3 NYS
predecessor: 5 CUOMO

**Patch:** 6 REPAIR
  Attach a: 5 SEWON 6 IRONON
  Kind of: 3 PEA 6 IRONON
  More than ~ up: 4 REDO
  Needing a: 4 WORN
  place: 3 EYE 4 KNEE
  Place for a: 3 RIP 4 TEAR
  up: 3 SEW 4 DARN HEAL
    MEND 6 REPAIR
**Patchwork**
  Make a: 3 SEW
  Some: 6 QUILTS
**Patchy:** 4 PIED
**Pat-down:** 5 FRISK
**Paté**
  meat: 5 LIVER
**Paté de foie ___:** 4 GRAS
**Paté de ___ gras:** 4 FOIE
**Patella:** 7 KNEECAP
  place: 4 KNEE
**Patented**
  product names (abbr.): 3 TMS
**Patents**
  Holder of 1,093: 6 EDISON
**Pater ___ (Lord's Prayer):**
    6 NOSTER
**Paternal**
  relative: 6 AGNATE
**Paternity test**
  material: 3 DNA
  site: 6 DNALAB
**Path:** 4 LANE 5 AISLE ROUTE
    TRAIL
  Bridal: 5 AISLE
  Curved: 3 ESS
  Data: 6 UPLINK
  finder: 5 HIKER
  Kind of: 4 BASE
  Like a planetary: 7 ORBITAL
  Mowing: 5 SWATH
  Off the: 6 ASTRAY
  Orbital: 7 ELLIPSE
  Paperboy: 5 ROUTE
  Pendulum: 3 ARC
  Planetary: 5 ORBIT
  Racer's: 4 OVAL
  Runner's: 8 BASELINE
  Slalom ~ part: 3 ESS
  Spiritual: 3 TAO ZEN
  Sprinter: 4 LANE
  Wagon-wheel: 3 RUT
  Winding: 3 ESS
**Pathet ___ (Asian Party):** 3 LAO
**Pathetic:** 3 SAD 4 LAME
  person: 7 SADSACK
**"Pathétique":** 6 SONATA
**Pathfinder**
  challenge: 4 MAZE
  launcher: 4 NASA
  target: 4 MARS
**Pathogen**
  Rod-shaped: 5 ECOLI
**Pathological**
  One might be: 4 LIAR
**Paths**
  Puzzle with: 4 MAZE

**Patience:** 6 VIRTUE
  Her ~ is legendary: 4 ENID
  Paragon of: 3 JOB
  Tax one's: 3 TRY
**Patient**
  Be: 4 WAIT
  gp.: 3 HMO
  people: 7 ABIDERS
  remark: 3 AHH
  responses: 3 AHS
  state: 4 COMA
  wear: 4 GOWN
**Patient-care**
  gp.: 3 HMO
**Patients**
  A number of dental: 3 GAS
  Place for nonresident:
    6 CLINIC
**Patina:** 4 COAT 5 SHEEN
**Patio**
  grill: 7 HIBACHI
**Patisserie**
  product: 6 ECLAIR
  worker: 4 ICER
**Patois:** 5 ARGOT
**Paton**
  Author: 4 ALAN
  ___ patriae (patriotism):
    4 AMOR
**Patriarch:** 5 ELDER
    6 NESTOR
  Biblical: 4 ENOS 5 ABRAM
    ISAAC
  Genesis: 4 ADAM
  ~ Clampett: 3 JED
**Patricia**
  Actress: 4 NEAL
**Patrick:** 5 SAINT
  Mame, to: 6 AUNTIE
  of basketball: 5 EWING
  Tony-winner: 5 MAGEE
**Patriot:** 3 SAM
  Cuban: 5 MARTI
  Hungarian ~ Nagy: 4 IMRE
  Irish: 5 EMMET
  Yugoslav: 4 TITO
  ~ Nathan: 4 HALE
  ~ Silas: 5 DEANE
**"Patriot Games"**
  gp.: 3 IRA
**Patriotic**
  chant: 3 USA 6 USAUSA
  org.: 3 DAR SAR
  symbol: 4 FLAG
  women's org.: 3 DAR
**Patriots**
  gp.: 3 AFC
  org.: 3 NFL
**Patriots' Day**
  month: 5 APRIL
**Patrol**
  Border ~ concern: 6 ALIENS
  car alert (abbr.): 3 APB
  Cop: 4 BEAT
  Vietnam ~ boat:
    8 RIVERRAT

**Patroller**
  Highway: 7 TROOPER
**Patron:** 4 USER 6 CLIENT
  Airlines: 5 FLIER
  Bank: 5 SAVER
  Goya: 4 ALBA
  Library: 4 USER
  Pol: 6 FATCAT
  Renaissance: 4 ESTE
  Restaurant: 5 EATER
  Sailor: 6 STELMO
**Patronage:** 5 AEGIS
**Patronize:** 5 BUYAT 6 SHOPAT
  a motel: 6 STAYAT
  a restaurant: 5 EATAT
    6 DINEAT
**Patronizing**
  person: 4 SNOB
**Patrons**
  Starts to receive: 5 OPENS
**Patron saint**
  of France: 5 DENIS
  of Norway: 4 OLAF OLAV
  of sailors: 4 ELMO
**Patsy:** 3 SAP 4 DUPE FOIL
    5 CHUMP 8 EASYMARK
  Make a ~ of: 3 USE
  Pal of: 5 EDINA
  Singer: 5 CLINE
**Patter**
  Pigeon: 3 COO
**Pattern**
  Behavior: 5 HABIT
  Dance: 4 STEP
  Follow a: 3 SEW
  Graph: 4 GRID
  Ice cream: 5 SWIRL
  Intricate: 3 WEB
  Kilt: 6 TARTAN
  of diamonds: 6 ARGYLE
  Predictable: 8 SYNDROME
  Quatrain: 4 ABBA
  Radial: 5 TREAD
  Ripply: 5 MOIRE
  Sock: 6 ARGYLE
  Tartan: 5 PLAID 6 ARGYLE
  Tire: 5 TREAD
  Wavy: 5 MOIRE
  Wood: 5 GRAIN
**Patterned**
  Delicately: 4 LACY
  fabric: 5 TOILE 6 DAMASK
**Patterns**
  Criminal: 3 MOS
  Paintings with geometric:
    5 OPART
**Patti**
  Singer: 4 PAGE 6 LUPONE
    7 ADELINA LABELLE
**Patton**
  protrayer: 5 SCOTT
**Patty**
  place: 3 BUN
  Rock singer: 5 SMYTH
**Paucity**
  of pep: 6 ANEMIA

**Paul:** 3 MRS 4 POPE TSAR
    5 SAINT 6 BEATLE
    7 APOSTLE
1933 Nobelist ~: 5 DIRAC
1943 Oscar winner ~: 5 LUKAS
1992 presidential hopeful ~:
    7 TSONGAS
Acting daughter of: 4 MIRA
Comedian: 5 LYNDE
Director: 9 VERHOEVEN
Guitarist: 3 LES
Longest letter of: 6 ROMANS
of Peter, Paul, and Mary:
    7 STOOKEY
or Carly: 5 SIMON
Peter and ~ (abbr.): 3 STS
role: 3 ARI
Singer: 4 ANKA
status: 8 SAINTDOM
suffix: 3 INE
Swiss painter: 4 KLEE
**Paula**
Actress: 8 PRENTISS
Newscaster: 4 ZAHN
Singer: 5 ABDUL
**Pauley Pavilion**
team: 4 UCLA
**Pauline**
Film critic: 4 KAEL
problem: 5 PERIL
___ Paulo: 3 SAO
**Paulsen**
Skater: 4 AXEL
**Paul V**
predecessor: 5 LEOXI
**Paunch:** 3 POT
**Pause:** 4 REST 5 LETUP
Cause for: 5 COMMA
    9 SEMICOLON
in the action: 4 LULL
Poet: 7 CAESURA
sign: 5 COMMA
**Pauses**
Speaker: 3 ERS
**Pavarotti:** 5 TENOR
birthplace: 6 MODENA
piece: 4 ARIA
Tenor: 7 LUCIANO
**Pave**
over: 5 RETAR
**Pavement:** 7 MACADAM
caution: 3 SLO
material: 3 TAR
**Paves**
It ~ the way: 3 TAR
    7 ASPHALT
**Pavilion:** 6 GAZEBO
**Pavin**
Golfer: 5 COREY
**Paving**
In need of: 5 RUTTY
material: 3 TAR 7 MACADAM
pieces: 6 STONES
stone: 4 SETT
**Pavlov**
dog output: 6 SALIVA

Nobelist: 4 IVAN
Physiologist: 4 IVAN
**Pavlova**
attire: 4 TUTU
Ballerina: 4 ANNA
portrayal: 4 SWAN
**Paw:** 4 MITT
Cat's: 3 TOM
Pal with a: 3 PET
part: 3 PAD
Partner of: 3 MAW
**Pawn:** 4 DUPE HOCK 5 AGENT
**"Pawnbroker, The"**
actor Rod: 7 STEIGER
**Pawned:** 6 INHOCK
**Pawns:** 5 OCTET
**Pawnshop**
Leave at a: 4 HOCK
**Pax ___:** 6 ROMANA
**Pay:** 5 REMIT WAGES
    6 ANTEUP PONYUP
    SALARY
attention: 6 LISTEN
    9 LENDANEAR
attention to: 4 HEED OBEY
back: 3 OLA 6 AVENGE
Bills to: 5 DEBTS
dirt: 3 ORE
ending: 3 OLA
for: 4 FOOT
for a hand: 4 ANTE
for dinner: 5 TREAT
Have to ~ back: 3 OWE
heed: 4 OBEY
Hourly: 4 WAGE
Kind of: 4 BASE
Need to: 3 OWE
no attention to: 6 IGNORE
    7 NEGLECT
One way to: 4 CASH
    6 CHARGE INCASH
out: 5 SPEND
period: 4 WEEK
phone feature: 4 SLOT
Promise to: 3 IOU
Small price to: 4 CENT
stub: 3 OLA
stub abbr.: 3 YTD
stub fig.: 4 FICA
suffix: 3 OLA
Take-home: 3 NET
They play for: 4 PROS
to play: 4 ANTE
tribute to: 5 HONOR
    6 SALUTE
up: 5 REMIT SPEND
    6 SETTLE
(up): 4 PONY
What you: 4 COST
with plastic: 6 CHARGE
**Payable:** 3 DUE
Become: 7 FALLDUE
It may be ~ (abbr.): 4 ACCT
**Payback**
Get ~ for: 6 AVENGE
Manufacturer: 6 REBATE

**"Payback"**
actor Kristofferson: 4 KRIS
**Paycheck**
abbr.: 4 FICA
booster: 8 OVERTIME
deduction: 8 STATETAX
**Pay dirt:** 3 ORE
**Payee:** 6 BEARER
Apr.: 3 IRS
**Payer**
Dues ~ (abbr.): 3 MEM
Full-price: 5 ADULT
Rent: 6 LESSEE TENANT
**Paying**
attention: 5 ALERT
passenger: 4 FARE
**Payment:** 8 REMITTAL
Car: 4 TOLL
Demand: 3 DUN
Lawyer: 3 FEE
Monthly: 4 RENT
option: 4 CASH
Pester for: 3 DUN
Poker: 4 ANTE
Press for: 3 DUN
Send: 5 REMIT
Simple ~ form: 4 CASH
Tenant: 4 RENT
Tiny: 4 CENT
Under-the-table: 5 BRIBE
Upfront: 4 ANTE
**"Pay ___ mind":** 4 ITNO
**Payne**
Golfer: 7 STEWART
Singer: 5 FREDA
**Payoff:** 3 SOP 6 REWARD
Ransom: 4 DROP
**Payola:** 5 GRAFT
**Payout**
Commuter: 4 TOLL
**Payroll**
Add to the: 4 HIRE
category: 4 RATE
On the: 8 SALARIED
Put on the: 4 HIRE
Put on the ~ again: 6 REHIRE
~ ID: 3 SSN
**Pay-___-view:** 3 PER
**Pb:** 4 LEAD
**PBS**
Charlie of: 4 ROSE
funder: 3 NEA
newsman: 6 LEHRER
NYC ~ flagship: 4 WNET
"science guy": 3 NYE
science show: 4 NOVA
supporter: 3 NEA
**PC**
alternative: 3 MAC 4 IMAC
bailout: 3 ESC
brain: 3 CPU
component: 3 CPU CRT
core: 3 CPU
environment: 5 MSDOS
expert: 4 TECH
format: 5 MSDOS

hookup: 3 CRT LAN
insert: 5 CDROM
key: 3 ALT ESC 5 ENTER
  6 DELETE
Kind of ~ monitor: 3 LCD
letters: 5 EMAIL
linkup: 3 LAN
listing: 4 MENU
maker: 3 IBM
monitor: 3 CRT
owner: 4 USER
panic button: 3 ESC
part: 3 CRT
perch: 3 LAP
person: 4 USER
pic: 4 ICON
platform: 3 DOS
Popular ~ game: 4 DOOM
Portable: 6 LAPTOP
program: 3 APP
screen: 3 CRT
shortcut: 5 MACRO
software: 5 MSDOS
storage medium: 5 CDROM
support staff: 5 TECHS
troubleshooter: 4 TECH

**PCBs**
Org. concerned about: 3 EPA
**P.D.**
alert: 3 APB
employee: 4 INSP
rank: 3 DET 4 INSP
**PDA**
entry: 4 APPT
no.: 4 NSEC
**P. Diddy**
First name of: 4 SEAN
**PDQ:** 4 ASAP
in the ER: 4 STAT
**P/E:** 5 RATIO
**Pea:** 6 LEGUME
holder: 3 CAN POD
jacket: 3 POD
**Pea-___ (dense fog):**
  6 SOUPER
**___' Pea:** 4 SWEE
**Peace**
agreement: 4 PACT
and quiet: 4 CALM
At: 6 SERENE
bird: 4 DOVE
goddess: 5 IRENE
Gp. in ~ accords: 3 IRA
In: 8 SERENELY
Kind of: 5 INNER
maker: 7 ENTENTE
Norse god of: 4 FREY
offering: 6 AMENDS
of mind: 4 EASE REST
  6 REPOSE
personified: 5 IRENE
Promoting: 6 IRENIC
Russian: 3 MIR
suffix: 3 NIK
symbol: 3 VEE 4 DOVE
treaty: 4 PACT

~ Nobelist: *see pages 734–735*
**Peace Corps**
cousin: 5 VISTA
**Peaceful:** 6 IRENIC SERENE
greeting: 6 SALAAM
place: 7 ARCADIA
protest: 5 SITIN
**Peace Garden State**
(abbr.): 4 NDAK
**Peacekeeping**
gp.: 4 NATO
skill: 4 TACT
**Peacenik:** 4 DOVE
slogan: 7 NONUKES
**Peace Nobelist**
1912 ~: 4 ROOT
1962 ~: 12 LINUSPAULING
1969 ~ gp.: 3 ILO
1971 ~: 6 BRANDT
1974 ~: 4 SATO
1978 ~: 5 SADAT
1983 ~: 6 WALESA
1984 ~: 4 TUTU
1987 ~: 5 ARIAS
1989 ~: 9 DALAILAMA
1993 ~: 7 MANDELA
1994 ~: 5 PERES RABIN
  6 ARAFAT
South African: 4 TUTU
~ Cassin: 4 RENE
~ Ducommun: 4 ELIE
~ Eisaku: 4 SATO
~ John Boyd ___: 3 ORR
~ Ralph: 6 BUNCHE
~ Root: 5 ELIHU
~ Sakharov: 6 ANDREI
~ Wiesel: 4 ELIE
**Peace Prize**
city: 4 OSLO
~ Nobelist: *see pages 734–735*
**Peach:** 3 HUE 4 TREE
  5 COLOR
pulpy portion: 5 FLESH
seed: 3 PIT
**Peach ___:** 5 MELBA
**Peachy**
follower: 4 KEEN
Just: 3 AOK 5 SWELL
**"Peachy!":** 4 NEAT 5 NEATO
  NIFTY SWELL
**Peachy-keen:** 4 NEAT 5 NEATO
  NIFTY SWELL
**Peacock**
Act like a: 5 PREEN
constellation: 4 PAVO
feather: 5 PLUME
feather feature: 6 OCELLI
  7 EYESPOT
Like a: 5 PROUD
NBC: 4 LOGO
network: 3 NBC
pride: 4 TAIL 7 PLUMAGE
Strut like a: 6 PARADE
Walk like a: 5 STRUT
**Peacock Throne**
occupant: 4 SHAH

**Peak:** 4 ACME APEX 5 CREST
  MOUNT 6 APOGEE
  8 PINNACLE
At the: 5 ONTOP
Biblical: 5 HOREB
California: 6 SHASTA
Craggy: 3 TOR
Cretan: 3 IDA
French: 4 ALPE
Greek: 4 OSSA
High: 3 ALP
in myth: 4 OSSA
in W. Turkey: 5 MTIDA
Japanese: 4 FUJI
no.: 4 ELEV
On the ~ of: 4 ATOP
Ore.: 6 MTHOOD
peak: 9 MTEVEREST
performance: 5 YODEL
Reach a: 5 CREST
Rocky: 3 TOR
Sicilian: 4 ETNA
Swiss: 3 ALP
Thessaly: 4 OSSA
Turkish: 6 ARARAT
**Peaked**
A bit: 6 PALISH
**Peaks**
(abbr.): 3 MTS 4 MTNS
Austrian: 4 ALPS
Peruvian: 5 ANDES
**Peal:** 4 TOLL
Mournful: 5 KNELL
**Pealed:** 4 RANG
**Peanut:** 6 GOOBER LEGUME
product: 3 OIL
**Peanut butter:** 6 SPREAD
brand: 3 JIF
choice: 6 SMOOTH
container: 3 JAR
cup maker: 6 REESES
**___ Peanut Butter Cups:**
  6 REESES
**Peanut Butter Lovers Mo.:**
  3 NOV
**Peanuts**
Like many: 6 SALTED
**"Peanuts"**
boy: 5 LINUS
Dirty ~ character:
  6 PIGPEN
expletive: 4 RATS
girl: 4 LUCY
One never seen in: 5 ADULT
**Pear:** 4 POME TREE
Alligator: 7 AVOCADO
Prickly: 6 CACTUS
Type of: 6 SECKEL
variety: 4 BOSC 5 ANJOU
**Pearl:** 5 ONION
Fake: 6 OLIVET
Milton: 3 ODE
Perlman who played: 4 RHEA
producer: 6 OYSTER
**Pearl City**
locale: 4 OAHU

**Pearl Harbor**
  attack plane: 4 ZERO
  island: 4 OAHU
  ship: 4 UTAH 6 NEVADA
      7 ARIZONA
**"Pearl Harbor"**
  Baldwin of: 4 ALEC
**Pearl Mosque**
  city: 4 AGRA
**Pearly**
  Show one's ~ whites: 5 SMILE
  whites: 5 TEETH
**Pearly Gates**
  keeper: 7 STPETER
**Pear-shaped**
  fruit: 3 FIG
  instrument: 4 LUTE 5 SITAR
**Pearson**
  Canadian statesman: 6 LESTER
**Peary**
  Of interest to: 5 POLAR
**Peas**
  Resembling two ~ in a pod:
      5 ALIKE
  ~, to a prankster: 4 AMMO
**Peasant:** 4 SERF
  costume part: 6 BODICE
  dress: 6 DIRNDL
  skirt: 6 DIRNDL
**Peat:** 4 MOSS
  source: 3 BOG
**Peau de ___ (silk cloth):** 4 SOIE
**Pebble Beach**
  hazard: 4 TRAP
  pastime: 4 GOLF
  peg: 3 TEE
**Pebbles**
  Fred, to: 3 DAD
  hair accessory: 4 BONE
  Mother of: 5 WILMA
  pet: 4 DINO
**Pec**
  neighbor: 3 LAT
**Pecan:** 3 NUT PIE 4 TREE
  confection: 7 PRALINE
**Peccadillo:** 3 SIN
**Peck:** 4 TYPE
  and Remick film: 7 THEOMEN
  Partner of: 4 HUNT
  pic topic: 4 OMEN
  role: 4 AHAB
**Pecker**
  Woodpecker: 4 BEAK
**Peckinpah**
  Director: 3 SAM
**Pecksniff**
  Dickens's: 4 SETH
**Pecs**
  display case: 3 BOD
  kin: 3 ABS
**Pectin**
  React to: 3 GEL
**Peculiar:** 3 ODD 5 WEIRD
  expression: 5 IDIOM
  It's: 7 ANOMALY
  prefix: 4 IDIO

**Peculiarity:** 5 TRAIT
  Language: 5 IDIOM
**PED ___:** 4 XING
**Pedagogic**
  org.: 3 NEA
**Pedal:** 4 BIKE
  digit: 3 TOE
  pusher: 4 FOOT 5 BIKER
  pushers: 4 FEET
  Put the ~ to the metal: 4 SPED
**Peddle:** 4 HAWK SELL VEND
  Peddlers ~ them: 5 WARES
**Peddler**
  aim: 4 SALE
**Pedestal:** 4 BASE
  figure: 4 IDOL
  part: 4 BASE DADO
  Piece on a: 3 URN
  Put on a: 5 ADORE DEIFY
      EXULT 6 ADORED
      ESTEEM 7 ADULATE
      ELEVATE 8 IDEALIZE
      VENERATE
  topper: 4 IDOL
**Pedestrian**
  Law-breaking: 9 JAYWALKER
  Like an unlucky winter:
      7 SLUSHED
  path: 4 WALK
**Pediatrician**
  Noted: 7 DRSPOCK
**Pedicurist**
  target: 7 TOENAIL
  workplace: 4 TOES 5 SALON
**Pedigree**
  org.: 3 AKC
  part: 4 SIRE
  rival: 4 ALPO
**Pedometer**
  New ~ reading: 3 OOO
**Pedro**
  Info: Spanish cue
  Intro to: 3 SAN SAO
  pal: 5 AMIGO
  parlor: 4 SALA
**Pedro, Dom**
  Wife of: 4 INES
**Peek:** 4 LOOK 6 GLANCE
  follower: 4 ABOO
  in (on): 3 SPY
  Sneak ~ (var.): 6 PREVUE
**Peek-___:** 4 ABOO
**Peekaboo**
  follower: 7 ISEEYOU
  words: 4 ISEE
**Peel:** 4 PARE RIND SKIN
      5 STRIP
  Fruit: 4 RIND
  Fruit with a: 6 BANANA
  in a drink: 5 TWIST
  Lemon: 4 RIND ZEST
**Peel, Mrs.:** 7 AVENGER
  Partner of: 5 STEED
  portrayer: 4 RIGG
**Peeler:** 5 PARER
**"Peel ___ grape":** 3 MEA

**Peeling**
  potatoes, perhaps: 4 ONKP
**Peep**
  Sheep: 3 BAA
**"Peep at Polynesian Life, A"**
  Novel subtitled: 5 TYPEE
**Peeper:** 3 EYE 5 CHICK SNOOP
  place: 7 KEYHOLE
  problem: 4 STYE
  protector: 6 EYELID
**Peepers:** 4 ORBS
  Use one's: 3 SEE
**Peeping Tom:** 4 EYER 5 SPIER
  Play the: 6 PEERIN
**Peeples**
  Actress: 3 NIA
**Peer:** 5 EQUAL
  at a page: 4 READ
  British: 4 EARL LORD
      5 BARON
  group: 4 EYES JURY
  Without: 5 ALONE
**"Peer ___":** 4 GYNT
**Peerage**
  member: 4 EARL
**"Peer Gynt"**
  character: 3 ASE
  composer: 5 GRIEG
  dancer: 6 ANITRA
  playwright: 5 IBSEN
**Peerless:** 4 AONE 5 ALONE
**Peeve:** 3 IRK 4 RILE
  Pet: 4 FLEA
  PETA: 3 FUR
**Peeved:** 4 SORE 5 ANGRY
      CROSS 6 INAPET
      7 INASNIT
  In a ~ mood: 5 TESTY
  mood: 4 SNIT
  More: 5 IRATE
**Peevish:** 4 SOUR 5 TESTY
  complaint: 4 CARP
  state: 4 SNIT
  temper: 4 BILE
**Peevishness:** 4 BILE
**Peewee:** 4 MINI RUNT TINY
      6 TEENSY
**Pee Wee**
  of baseball: 5 REESE
  Teammate of: 3 GIL
**Peg**
  Golf: 3 TEE
  Small: 3 TEE
  Square ~ in a round hole:
      6 MISFIT
  Take down a: 5 ABASE
  Wooden: 5 DOWEL
**Peggy**
  Panelist: 4 CASS
  Singer: 3 LEE
  Speechwriter: 6 NOONAN
**"Peg Woffington"**
  author: 5 READE
**PEI**
  setting: 3 AST
**Pei, Ieoh ___:** 4 MING

**Pei, I.M.**
alma mater: 3 MIT
The "I" of: 4 IEOH
**Pei, ___ Ming:** 4 IEOH
**Peke**
perch: 3 LAP
squeak: 3 YIP
**Peking**
suffix: 3 ESE
**Pekoe:** 3 TEA
holder: 6 TEABAG
server: 6 TEAPOT
unit: 7 TEALEAF
**Pelé**
given name: 5 EDSON
org.: 4 NASL
**Pelée**
spew: 4 LAVA
**Pelion**
neighbor: 4 OSSA
**Pell-___:** 4 MELL
**Pellagra**
preventer: 6 NIACIN
**Pellet:** 7 GRANULE
propeller: 8 AIRRIFLE
shooter: 3 PEA
**Pellets**
Air-gun: 3 BBS
Falling: 4 HAIL
**Peloponnesian**
P: 3 RHO
**Peloponnesian War**
victor: 6 SPARTA
**Pelota**
catcher: 5 CESTA
**Pelt:** 3 FUR 4 HIDE SKIN
5 STONE 6 PEPPER
**Pelvic:** 5 ILIAC
bone: 5 ILIUM
bones: 4 ILIA 5 SACRA
parts: 4 ILIA
**Pelvis**
part: 6 SACRUM 7 HIPBONE
**Pelvis-knee**
connector: 5 FEMUR
**Pemmican**
Language that gives us: 4 CREE
**Pen:** 3 STY 4 SWAN 5 WRITE
6 CORRAL FEMALE
7 ENCLOSE
African cattle: 5 KRAAL
British: 4 GAOL
Bull ~ sound: 5 SNORT
Bull ~ stat: 3 ERA
fare: 4 SLOP
Farm: 3 STY
feature: 7 FELTTIP
filler: 3 INK
Hen's: 4 COOP
holder: 5 STATE
Kind of: 5 STATE
mother: 3 SOW
pal: 3 CON PIG SOW 5 SWINE
6 INMATE OINKER
part: 4 CELL
partner: 3 PAD

point: 3 NIB
resident: 3 CON
sound: 4 OINK
stroke: 5 SERIF
**Penalized:** 5 FINED
**Penalty:** 4 FINE
caller: 3 REF
for not paying on time:
7 LATEFEE
Paid the: 6 ATONED
Subject to a: 7 PASTDUE
**Penance**
Do: 5 ATONE
**Penchant:** 4 BIAS
**Pencil**
end: 6 ERASER
game entries: 7 XSANDOS
holder: 3 EAR
Much-used: 3 NUB 4 STUB
pusher: 5 CLERK 6 WRITER
puzzle: 4 MAZE
Styptic ~ stuff: 4 ALUM
topper: 6 ERASER
Use a ~ end: 5 ERASE
Use a blue: 4 EDIT
**Pencil-and-paper**
game: 4 DOTS MAZE
**Pencil box**
item: 5 RULER
**Penciled**
It may be ~ in: 7 EYEBROW
**"Pencils down":** 7 TIMESUP
**Pendant**
Fashionable: 7 EARDROP
gem shape: 8 TEARDROP
Polynesian: 4 TIKI
**Pending**
item: 6 PATENT
**Pendleton**
Actor: 3 NAT
**Pendulum**
direction: 3 FRO
Like a ~ motion:
8 TOANDFRO
partner: 3 PIT
path: 3 ARC
**Penetrate:** 5 ENTER
Hard to: 5 DENSE
slowly: 4 SEEP
**Penetrating:** 4 KEEN 5 ACUTE
6 ASTUTE COGENT
quality: 4 EDGE
reed: 4 OBOE
**Penguin**
Antarctic: 6 ADELIE
Comics page: 4 OPUS
**Penguins**
1955 ~ hit: 10 EARTHANGEL
org.: 3 NHL
**___ Penh, Cambodia:** 4 PNOM
5 PHNOM
**Penicillin:** 4 DRUG
source: 4 MOLD
target: 5 STREP
**Peninsula**
Adriatic: 6 ISTRIA

Asian: 5 KOREA MALAY
6 ARABIA MALAYA
Black Sea: 6 CRIMEA
European: 6 IBERIA
It is mostly a ~ (abbr.):
3 FLA
Mexican: 4 BAJA
Mideast: 5 SINAI 6 ARABIA
Portugal: 6 IBERIA
Québec: 5 GASPE
Red Sea: 5 SINAI
World's largest: 6 ARABIA
**___ Peninsula:** 6 ARABIA
BALKAN 7 IBERIAN
**Penitence**
Period of: 4 LENT
Show: 5 ATONE
**Penitent:** 6 ATONER
person: 4 RUER 6 ATONER
**Penlight**
battery: 3 AAA
**Penman:** 6 SCRIBE
**Penn:** 4 SEAN 5 ACTOR
(abbr.): 3 STA
Actor: 4 SEAN
Like: 3 IVY
name: 4 SEAN
pal: 6 TELLER
specialty: 5 MAGIC
**Penna**
neighbor: 3 DEL
**Pen name:** 3 BIC 5 ALIAS
FLAIR
Literary: 3 BOZ 4 ELIA SAKI
5 TWAIN
**Pennant:** 4 FLAG
Took the: 3 WON
**Penne:** 5 PASTA
kin: 4 ZITI
**Penned:** 5 WROTE
**Pennies:** 5 ANTES
(abbr.): 3 CTS
Pack of: 4 ROLL
Pinch: 5 SKIMP STINT
**Penniless:** 5 BROKE
person: 4 HOBO
**Penn Sta.**
traffic: 3 RRS
**Penn State**
city: 4 ERIE
coach: 7 PATERNO
**Penn Station**
inits.: 4 LIRR
**Pennsylvania:** 6 AVENUE
(abbr.): 3 AVE
city: 4 ERIE 6 EASTON
7 ALTOONA
county: 4 ERIE
port: 4 ERIE
resort area: 7 POCONOS
sect: 5 AMISH
university: 6 LEHIGH
**Pennsylvania Dutch**
Some: 5 AMISH
**Penny:** 4 CENT
component: 4 ZINC

pincher: 5 MISER PIKER
  6 CHEAPO
portrayal: 7 LAVERNE
Prez on a: 3 ABE
Word on a: 3 GOD ONE
  4 UNUM
**Penny ___:** 4 ANTE
**"... ___ penny earned":** 3 ISA
**Penny-pinching:** 4 MEAN
**Penobscot**
  City on the: 6 BANGOR
    11 BANGORMAINE
**Penobscot River**
  city: 5 ORONO
**Penpoint:** 3 NIB
**"Penrod"**
  pal: 3 SAM
**Pens:** 5 STYLI
**Pension**
  agcy.: 3 SSA
  alternative: 3 IRA
  Become owned, as a: 4 VEST
  On a ~ (abbr.): 3 RET 4 RETD
  plan law: 5 ERISA
  supplement: 3 IRA
**Pensioner:** 7 RETIREE
**Pensive**
  sounds: 3 HMS
**Pent**
  ending: 3 ANE
  up: 5 CAGED
**Penta**
  minus one: 5 TETRA
**Pentacles**
  Deck with: 5 TAROT
**Pentad**
  Common: 6 SENSES
**Pentagon**
  bigwigs: 5 BRASS
**Pentagram:** 4 STAR
**Pentameter**
  parts: 5 IAMBS
**Pentateuch:** 5 TORAH
**Pentathlete**
  weapon: 4 EPEE
**Pentathlon**
  event: 4 EPEE
**Penthouse**
  Escorts to a: 6 SEESUP
  Invite to a: 5 ASKUP
  plus: 4 VIEW
**Pentium**
  maker: 5 INTEL
**Penultimate**
  fairy tale word: 4 EVER
  Greek letter: 3 PSI
  letter: 3 WYE
**Penury:** 4 NEED
**Penzance**
  prison: 4 GAOL
**Peony**
  part: 5 PETAL 6 PISTIL
**People**
  Dear: 4 SIRS
  Home to most: 4 ASIA
  Laid-back ~ category: 5 TYPEB

Med.: 3 DRS
Meet: 6 RACERS
of action: 5 DOERS
Party: 5 HOSTS
people (abbr.): 3 EDS
person: 5 CELEB
PR: 4 AGTS
prefix: 5 ETHNO
Prized: 5 DEARS
Self-employed: 3 EDS
Short ~ write them: 4 IOUS
Some ~ can't take one: 4 HINT
Spirit of a: 5 ETHOS
Those: 4 THEY
to hang with: 4 PALS
Where ~ rush: 4 FRAT
who knead people:
  8 MASSEURS
with pistols: 8 STARTERS
Work with: 4 EDIT
**"People's Court, The"**
  former judge: 4 KOCH
**Pep:** 3 VIM 4 BRIO ELAN ZEST
  5 VIGOR 6 ENERGY
  Full of: 4 PERT SPRY 5 ALIVE
  Give a ~ talk to: 6 EXHORT
  rally cry: 3 RAH
  up: 7 ANIMATE
**Pepe**
  Cartoon skunk: 5 LEPEW
**Pepe Le ___ (Boyer role):**
  4 MOKO
**Pepe Le Pew**
  defense: 4 ODOR
**Peppard, George**
  1980s ~ costar: 3 MRT
  TV series, with "The":
    5 ATEAM
**Pepper**
  (abbr.): 3 SGT
  and others: 3 DRS 4 SGTS
  from above: 6 STRAFE
  Hot: 7 CAYENNE
    8 JALAPENO
  Kind of: 4 BELL 5 BETEL
    7 CAYENNE 8 JALAPENO
  Partner of: 4 SALT
  Pickled ~ measure: 4 PECK
  plant: 5 BETEL
  reaction: 6 SNEEZE
**___ Pepper:** 3 SGT
**Pepperidge Farm**
  cookie brand: 6 MILANO
**Peppermint**
  candy: 6 PATTIE
**Peppermint Patty**
  ~, to Marcie: 3 SIR
**"Peppermint Twist"**
  singer: 7 JOEYDEE
  singer Joey: 3 DEE
**Peppery:** 3 HOT 7 PUNGENT
**Peppy:** 4 SPRY 8 SPIRITED
**Pepsi:** 4 COLA SODA
  bottle size: 5 LITER
  Coke vs. ~ event: 9 TASTETEST
  rival: 4 COKE 6 RCCOLA

**Pepsin:** 6 ENZYME
**Pepsi-owned**
  juice drink: 4 SOBE
**Peptic**
  problem: 5 ULCER
**Pepys:** 7 DIARIST
  kept one: 5 DIARY
**Pequod**
  captain: 4 AHAB
  hand: 7 ISHMAEL
**Per:** 4 APOP EACH 6 APIECE
**Per ___:** 4 DIEM 5 ANNUM
  6 CAPITA
**Pera**
  Author: 3 PIA
**Perambulate:** 4 WALK
**___ Percé:** 3 NEZ
**Perceive:** 4 ESPY FEEL 5 SENSE
  6 DESCRY 7 DISCERN
**Perceived:** 4 KNEW SEEN
  to be: 6 SEENAS
**Percent**
  100 ~: 3 ALL 4 PURE
  Fifty: 4 HALF
  Increase by 200: 6 TREBLE
  suffix: 3 ILE
**Percentage:** 4 PART 5 SHARE
  for the IRS: 7 TAXRATE
**Percenter**
  Ten ~ (abbr.): 3 AGT
**Perception:** 3 EYE 7 INSIGHT
  General: 5 IMAGE
  Of: 7 SENSATE
  Sound: 3 EAR
**Perceptive:** 4 KEEN 5 ACUTE
  SHARP 6 ASTUTE
**Perch:** 3 SIT 5 ROOST
  Bird: 4 WIRE 5 LEDGE ROOST
    7 TREETOP
  Came to: 4 ALIT
  Church: 3 PEW
  Couch potato: 4 SOFA
  Dummy's: 4 KNEE
  Lofty: 7 TREETOP
  Mountain cat: 5 ARETE
  Mountain goat: 4 CRAG
  Muezzin: 7 MINARET
  Pet: 3 LAP
  Pie: 4 SILL
  Pigskin: 3 TEE
  Pub: 5 STOOL
  Toddler: 4 KNEE
  Yodeler: 3 ALP
**Perched:** 3 SAT
  on: 4 ATOP
**Percolate:** 4 OOZE SEEP
  5 LEACH
**Percussion**
  cap: 9 DETONATOR
  Chinese: 4 GONG
  Impromptu: 7 SPOONS
  instrument: 4 DRUM GONG
    5 GOURD 6 BONGOS
    TOMTOM 7 MARIMBA
    9 SNAREDRUM
    10 KETTLEDRUM

set: 7 TYMPANI
**Percussionist**
~ Puente: 4 TITO
**Père**
sibling: 5 ONCLE
**Père ___**: 6 GORIOT
**"Perelandra"**
author: 7 CSLEWIS
**Perennial**
campaign issue: 4 JOBS
defender: 4 EAST
Garden: 7 BEGONIA
Showy: 6 DAHLIA
**Perennials**
Showy: 5 CROCI
**Peres**
of Israel: 6 SHIMON
predecessor: 5 RABIN
**___ Peres, Missouri**: 3 DES
**Peretti**
Designer: 4 ELSA
**Perez**
Actress: 5 ROSIE
**Pérez de Cuéllar**
home: 4 PERU
**Pérez Esquivel, ___**
1980 Peace Nobelist ~:
6 ADOLFO
**Perfboard**
insert: 3 PEG
Repair a: 5 REPEG
**Perfect**: 3 AOK 4 HONE MINT
5 IDEAL 9 ERRORLESS
accord: 6 UNISON
for NASA: 3 AOK
game catcher: 9 YOGIBERRA
In ~ condition: 4 MINT
It may be: 5 TENSE
Like a ~ game: 5 NOHIT
Like a ~ plan: 9 FOOLPROOF
model: 5 IDEAL
Not: 6 FLAWED
number: 3 TEN
or present: 5 TENSE
place: 4 EDEN 6 UTOPIA
prose: 4 EDIT
rating: 3 TEN
score: 3 TEN
serve: 3 ACE
world: 6 UTOPIA
**"Perfect!"**: 3 AOK
**"Perfect Fool, The"**: 6 EDWYNN
**Perfection**
First name in Olympic:
5 NADIA
Gymnastic: 3 TEN
Standard of: 5 IDEAL
**Perfectionist**: 8 STICKLER
aim: 5 IDEAL
**Perfectly**: 3 PAT 4 TOAT
6 TOATEE
clear: 5 LUCID
Do: 4 NAIL
draftable: 4 ONEA
Execute: 4 NAIL
matched: 8 ONETOONE

Not ~ round: 5 OVOID
Served: 4 ACED
timed: 5 ONCUE
vertical: 5 PLUMB
**Perfecto**: 5 CIGAR
**"Perfect Peace, A"**
author: 6 AMOSOZ
**Perfect Sleeper**
maker: 5 SERTA
**"Perfect Spy, A"**
author: 7 LECARRE
**"... ___ perfect union ..."**:
5 AMORE
**Perform**: 3 ACT 6 RENDER
a canticle: 6 INTONE
again: 4 REDO
better than: 5 OUTDO
penance: 5 ATONE
**Performance**: 3 GIG
Diva: 4 ARIA
hall: 5 ODEUM
Individual: 4 SOLO
Jazz: 3 JAM
Kind of: 4 GALA
Like a super: 5 BOFFO
Met: 5 OPERA
Peak: 5 YODEL
Price: 5 OPERA
Repeat: 4 ECHO 6 ENCORE
**Performed**: 3 DID
in Shakespeare: 5 DIDST
Poorly: 4 LAME
satisfactorily: 5 DIDOK
**Performer**: 4 DOER 7 ARTISTE
Aquarium: 4 SEAL
Camel: 6 SKATER
Circus: 4 FLEA SEAL
9 LIONTAMER
15 HUMANCANNONBALL
CPR: 3 EMT
Nightclub: 5 COMIC
Public: 7 ARTISTE
Rodeo: 5 ROPER
Street: 4 MIME
thrill: 15 STANDINGOVATION
"Wave": 3 FAN
with lions: 5 TAMER
**Performing**: 7 ONSTAGE
**Performing ___**: 4 ARTS
**Performs**: 4 DOES
**Perfume**: 5 AROMA ATTAR
CENSE SCENT
7 ESSENCE
Apply: 5 SPRAY
bottle name: 5 ESTEE
brand: 4 TABU
compound: 5 ESTER
holder: 4 VIAL
ingredient: 4 MUSK 5 ATTAR
6 ACETAL
oil: 5 ATTAR 6 NEROLI
Petal: 5 ATTAR
resin: 5 ELEMI
root: 5 ORRIS
**Pergola**: 5 ARBOR
**Perhaps**: 5 MAYBE

**Peri**
Actress: 6 GILPIN
role: 3 ROZ
**Pericles**
Opponent of: 5 CLEON
**___ Perignon**: 3 DOM
**Peril**: 6 DANGER HAZARD
MENACE
Sailor: 4 REEF
**Perimeter**: 3 RIM 4 EDGE
contents: 4 AREA
Green: 5 APRON
**Per ___ income**: 6 CAPITA
**Period**: 3 AGE DOT END ERA
4 TERM 5 EPOCH STAGE
6 TENURE
Calendar: 4 WEEK YEAR
Cong.: 4 SESS
Crisis: 8 REDALERT
Geologic: 3 EON 5 EPOCH
Grace: 4 AMEN
Historical: 3 AGE ERA
5 EPOCH
Interim: 8 MEANTIME
Legal hunting:
10 OPENSEASON
Long: 3 EON 5 EPOCH
Notable: 3 ERA 5 EPOCH
of decline: 7 EBBTIDE
of devotions: 6 NOVENA
of duty: 4 TOUR
of greatest success: 6 HEYDAY
of note: 3 ERA
of office: 4 TERM
of penitence: 4 LENT
of power: 5 REIGN
of time: 4 SPAN 5 SPELL
STINT
on the throne: 5 REIGN
Pay: 4 WEEK
piece: 3 ERA 5 EPOCH
Pique: 4 SNIT
place: 3 END
Postwar: 9 PEACETIME
Preceding: 3 EVE
Prosperous: 4 BOOM
Quiet: 4 LULL
School: 4 TERM
Significant: 3 ERA
"Spring fwd.": 3 DST
Subscription: 4 YEAR
Telegram: 4 STOP
Time: 3 ERA 4 SPAN 5 SPELL
Tiny time ~ (abbr.): 4 NSEC
**Periodical**
Fan ~, for short: 4 ZINE
for short: 3 MAG
Online: 4 EMAG 5 EZINE
piece: 7 ARTICLE
**Periodically**: 7 ATTIMES
**Periodic Table**
abbr.: 4 ATNO ATWT
entry: 7 ELEMENT
stat.: 4 ATNO
**"Periodic Table, The"**
author: 4 LEVI 9 PRIMOLEVI

**Periodontist**
deg.: 3 DDS
gp.: 3 ADA
**Periods**
Good: 3 UPS
Group of: 3 ERA
Morning: 3 AMS
Tie-breaking ~ (abbr.): 3 OTS
**Peripheral:** 5 ADDON
**Periphery:** 3 RIM 4 EDGE
6 FRINGE
**Periscope**
part: 4 LENS 5 PRISM
6 MIRROR
**Perjure**
oneself: 3 LIE
**Perjurer:** 4 LIAR
**Perjury**
Commit: 3 LIE
**Perk:** 6 REWARD
Executive: 11 STOCKOPTION
up: 4 WHET 5 LIVEN
7 ANIMATE
**Perking**
place: 3 URN
**Perkins**
role: 5 BATES
Songwriter: 4 CARL
**Perky:** 4 SPRY
**Perle**
Hostess: 5 MESTA
**Perlman**
Actress: 4 RHEA
instrument: 6 VIOLIN
Violinist: 6 ITZHAK
**Permafrost**
region: 6 TUNDRA
**Permanent**
feature: 4 WAVE
location: 5 SALON
Make: 4 ETCH
mark: 4 SCAR
One sans ~ address:
5 NOMAD
pen pal: 5 LIFER
**Permanently:** 5 ININK
7 FORGOOD
Dwell: 6 RESIDE
Mark: 4 ETCH
~, in poetry: 3 EER
**Permeate:** 4 SEEP 5 IMBUE
**Permed**
Like ~ hair: 4 WAVY
**Permissible:** 5 LICIT
**Permission:** 5 LEAVE
Give ~ to: 3 LET 5 ALLOW
Legal: 7 RELEASE
Refuse to give: 5 SAYNO
to go: 5 LEAVE
**Permissive:** 3 LAX 7 LENIENT
**Permit:** 3 LET 5 ALLOW
6 ENABLE 7 LICENSE
Passport: 4 VISA
**"Permit Me Voyage"**
author: 4 AGEE
**Permitted:** 5 LEGAL LICIT

**Pernod**
flavoring: 5 ANISE
**Peron**
Ms.: 3 EVA
Musical about: 5 EVITA
**Perot:** 7 ALSORAN
Businessman/candidate:
4 ROSS 5 HROSS
Co. founded by: 3 EDS
party (abbr.): 3 IND
Treaty opposed by: 5 NAFTA
**Perp**
alert: 3 APB
Help a: 4 ABET
Pinch a: 3 NAB
prosecutors: 3 DAS
story: 5 ALIBI
**Perpendicular**
to long.: 3 LAT
to radial: 5 AXIAL
to the keel: 5 ABEAM
**Perpetrator:** 4 DOER 5 FELON
7 CULPRIT
Genesis: 4 CAIN
Rue Morgue: 3 APE
**"___ perpetua" (Idaho's motto):**
4 ESTO
**Perpetual:** 7 AGELESS
ENDLESS ETERNAL
~, in poetry: 6 ETERNE
**Perplex:** 5 STUMP 6 BEMUSE
**Perplexed:** 4 ASEA LOST
5 ATSEA 7 ATALOSS
~, after "at": 5 ALOSS
**Perplexing**
path: 4 MAZE
**Perrier**
rival: 5 EVIAN
**Perrins**
Partner of: 3 LEA
**Perry**
creator: 4 ERLE
Designer: 5 ELLIS
secretary: 5 DELLA
Singer: 4 COMO
victory site: 4 ERIE
**Persecute:** 6 HARASS
**Persephone**
Husband of: 5 HADES
Mother of: 7 DEMETER
**Persepolis**
Home of ancient: 4 IRAN
**Perseus**
Monster slain by: 6 MEDUSA
Mother of: 5 DANAE
Person ~ petrified: 5 ATLAS
star: 5 ALGOL
**Persevere:** 4 COPE 6 HANGIN
KEEPAT 7 PRESSON
**Pershing**
nickname: 9 BLACKJACK
~ WWI gp.: 3 AEF
**Persia**
Faith that arose in: 5 BAHAI
Queen of ~, in the Bible:
6 ESTHER

today: 4 IRAN
**Persian:** 3 CAT RUG 5 FARSI
Ancient: 4 MEDE
despot: 6 SATRAP
emperor: 5 CYRUS
fairy: 4 PERI
for "king": 4 SHAH
Former ~ ruler: 4 SHAH
for "rose water": 5 JULEP
Modern: 5 FARSI IRANI
Person in ~ folklore: 7 ALIBABA
plaint: 3 MEW
pleasure: 6 CATNIP
poet: 4 OMAR
religion: 5 BAHAI
royal name: 6 DARIUS
XERXES
ruler: 4 SHAH
Speak: 4 MEOW
**Persian Gulf**
capital: 6 TEHRAN
8 ABUDHABI
emirate: 5 DUBAI QATAR
8 ABUDHABI
fed.: 3 UAE
nation: 4 IRAN 5 QATAR
port: 5 BASRA DUBAI
ruler: 4 EMIR
ship: 5 OILER
**Persiflage:** 6 BANTER
**Persist:** 4 LAST 5 RECUR
6 KEEPAT LINGER
suffix: 3 ENT 4 ENCE
**Persisted:** 6 HUNGON KEPTAT
**"Persistence of Memory, The"**
painter: 4 DALI
**Persistent**
desire: 7 CRAVING
**Persistently**
Bother: 3 NAG 5 EATAT
NAGAT 6 HARASS
PESTER
Follow: 3 DOG
**Person:** 3 ONE 4 NOUN
Accommodating: 5 SPORT
Active: 4 DOER
Adored: 4 IDOL
Any: 3 ONE
August: 3 LEO
Chair: 5 TAMER
Cruel: 4 OGRE
Delivery ~ path: 5 ROUTE
Displaced: 6 EMIGRE
First: 4 ADAM
First ~ in Berlin: 3 ICH
Fourth: 4 ABEL
Funny: 5 CUTUP
Gifted: 5 DONEE
Hilarious: 4 RIOT
Hill ~ (abbr.): 3 SEN
Holy: 6 TERROR
Impertinent: 4 SNIP
In: 4 LIVE
in a mask: 3 UMP
in a pool: 5 STENO
in the left lane: 6 PASSER

of action: 4 DOER
of great interest: 6 USURER
of the Year: *see pages 725–726*
on a soapbox: 6 ORATOR
Patronizing: 4 SNOB
PC: 4 USER
People: 5 CELEB
Per: 4 APOP EACH
Personnel: 5 HIRER
Pompous: 3 ASS
Powerful: 5 NABOB
PR: 5 AGENT
Promising: 5 COMER
Remarkable: 4 LULU
Right-hand: 4 AIDE
Second: 3 EVE YOU
Singular: 4 ONER
Support: 5 AIDER
Time magazine's ~ of the Year:
   *see pages 725–726*
Twisted: 5 SICKO
Unique: 4 ONER
Which: 3 WHO
Wise: 4 SAGE
with a mike: 5 EMCEE
with hives: 8 APIARIST
~, informally: 3 EGG
**Persona:** 4 ROLE 5 IMAGE
Chaplin: 5 TRAMP
Fields: 3 SOT
non grata: 5 LEPER
Public: 5 IMAGE
Skelton: 4 HOBO
**Persona ___ grata:** 3 NON
**Personal:** 3 OWN
account: 6 MEMOIR
ad abbr.: 3 SWF SWM
appearance: 4 MIEN
bugbear: 8 PETPEEVE
creed: 5 ETHIC
history: 4 PAST
instructor: 5 TUTOR
magnetism: 8 CHARISMA
prefix: 4 IDIO
quirk: 3 TIC
Some are: 3 ADS
taste: 8 CUPOFTEA
**Personalities:** 4 EGOS
Split: 4 EXES
**Personality**
aspect: 5 TRAIT
Assertive: 5 ARIES TYPEA
Duel: 4 BURR 6 SECOND
Kind of: 5 ONAIR TYPEA
part: 3 EGO 5 ANIMA
**Personalize:** 7 ENGRAVE
**Personals:** 3 ADS
**Persona non ___:** 5 GRATA
**Personification:** 6 AVATAR
Luck: 4 LADY
Moon: 4 LUNA
of wind: 4 AURA
**Personified:** 9 INCARNATE
Darkness: 6 EREBUS
Love: 4 AMOR EROS
   5 VENUS

Moon: 4 LUNA
Passion: 4 EROS
Peace: 5 IRENE
Sun: 3 SOL
**Personify:** 6 EMBODY
**Personnel:** 5 STAFF
Ambulance: 4 EMTS
director: 5 HIRER
ER: 3 DRS RNS
group: 5 CADRE
listing: 6 ROSTER
Mil.: 4 NCOS
OR: 3 RNS
person: 5 HIRER
**Person of the Year**
Time magazine's ~: *see pages*
   *725–726*
**Person-to-person:**
   8 ONEONONE
**"Person to Person"**
host: 6 MURROW
**Perspective:** 4 VIEW 5 ANGLE
   SLANT
**Perspicacity:** 6 ACUMEN
**Perspiration:** 5 SWEAT
point: 4 PORE
**Persson**
Actress: 4 ESSY
**Persuade:** 4 COAX SELL SWAY
   6 CAJOLE ENTICE
   INDUCE 7 WINOVER
Try to: 4 COAX URGE
**Persuaded:** 4 SOLD
   7 WONOVER
**Pert:** 5 SASSY
blurt: 4 SASS
**Pertain:** 6 RELATE
**Pertaining**
to a manuscript: 7 TEXTUAL
to bees: 5 APIAN
to birds: 5 AVIAN
to life: 6 BIOTIC
to most students: 4 ELHI
to planes: 4 AERO
to plants: 7 BOTANIC
to punishment: 5 PENAL
to spring: 6 VERNAL
**Perth**
pal: 4 MATE
river: 3 TAY
**Perth ___, New Jersey:**
   5 AMBOY
**Pertinent:** 3 APT 7 APROPOS
~, in Latin: 5 ADREM
**Perturb:** 4 FAZE 7 AGITATE
**Perturbed:** 8 INASTATE
state: 4 SNIT
**Peru**
Capital of: 4 LIMA
From early: 5 INCAN
native: 4 INCA
Neighbor of: 7 ECUADOR
range: 5 ANDES
Sumac of: 3 YMA
**Perugia**
Town near: 6 ASSISI

**Peruse:** 4 READ
again: 6 REREAD
**Peruvian**
Ancient: 4 INCA 5 INCAN
beast: 5 LLAMA 6 ALPACA
capital: 4 LIMA
coin: 3 SOL
singer: 8 YMASUMAC
singer Sumac: 3 YMA
~ Peter: 5 PEDRO
**Pervasive**
quality: 4 AURA
**Pervert:** 5 SICKO
**Pesci, Joe**
title role: 5 VINNY
**Peseta**
replacer: 4 EURO
**Pesky**
e-mail: 4 SPAM
flier: 4 GNAT
insect: 4 GNAT 5 MIDGE
   6 TSETSE 7 SKEETER
kid: 4 BRAT PAIN
**Peso**
fraction: 7 CENTAVO
Spanish: 4 DURO
**Pessimist:** 4 BEAR 8 NAYSAYER
reply: 5 ICANT
word: 4 CANT
**Pessimistic:** 4 DOUR
pal of Pooh: 6 EEYORE
sort: 4 BEAR
**Pest:** 4 GNAT TWIT 5 TWERP
   6 NOODGE NUDNIK
African: 6 TSETSE
Closet: 4 MOTH
control brand: 4 DCON
control device:
   10 FLYSWATTER
Cornfield: 4 CROW
Dog: 4 FLEA
Garden: 4 SLUG 5 APHID
Household: 5 ROACH
   6 REDANT
Little: 3 IMP
Pantry: 3 ANT
Picnic: 3 ANT 4 GNAT
Plant: 5 APHID BORER
Subterranean: 4 MOLE
Summer: 4 GNAT
Summer ~, informally:
   7 SKEETER
Tiny: 4 GNAT MITE
Wharf: 3 RAT
**Pester:** 3 BUG NAG 5 ANNOY
   NAGAT TEASE
   6 HARASS HASSLE
   NEEDLE NOODGE
for payment: 3 DUN
like a pup: 5 NIPAT
**Pesticide**
Apple: 4 ALAR
Banned: 3 DDT
mineral: 4 TALC
**Pestle**
Partner of: 6 MORTAR

**Pesto:** 5 SAUCE
  herb: 5 BASIL
  ingredient: 7 PINENUT
**Pet:** 4 SNIT 6 CARESS
  adoption org.: 4 SPCA
  Caged: 8 PARAKEET
  carrier feature: 7 AIRHOLE
  checker: 5 LEASH
  Cuddly: 6 LAPDOG
  Flintstone: 4 DINO
  Green: 4 CHIA
  House: 3 CAT
  Is in a: 5 SULKS
  Kind of: 4 CHIA
  lovers' org.: 4 SPCA
  master: 5 OWNER
  name: 3 HON 4 DEAR FIDO
  Nestlé ~ food brand: 4 ALPO
  peeve: 4 FLEA
  Popular: 3 CAT DOG
  Potted: 4 CHIA
  Primer: 4 SPOT
  protection org.: 4 SPCA
    5 ASPCA
  restraint: 6 TETHER
  rocks, once: 3 FAD
  Screen: 4 ASTA
  store purchase: 4 CAGE
    5 LEASH
  Treat as a: 6 COSSET
**Pet ___:** 5 PEEVE
**___ Pet:** 4 CHIA
**PETA**
  Kin of: 4 SPCA
  peeve: 3 FUR
**Petal**
  perfume: 5 ATTAR
  plucker word: 3 NOT SHE
  pusher: 3 BEE
**Pete**
  Folk singer: 6 SEEGER
**Peter:** 4 TSAR
  Actor: 5 LORRE 6 OTOOLE
  and Annette: 7 OTOOLES
  and Franco: 5 NEROS
  and Paul (abbr.): 3 STS
  Author: 4 MAAS
  Cartoonist: 4 ARNO
  Director: 4 WEIR 5 YATES
  Newsman: 6 ARNETT
  of Herman's Hermits:
    5 NOONE
  of Peter and Gorden: 5 ASHER
  of Peter, Paul, and Mary:
    6 YARROW
  or Paul: 4 TSAR 5 SAINT
    7 APOSTLE
  out: 3 DIE EBB 4 WANE
  Pianist: 4 NERO
  Playwright: 5 WEISS
  Reggae singer: 4 TOSH
  Synonymist: 5 ROGET
  the Great: 4 CZAR TSAR
  ~, Paul, and Mary: 3 STS
    4 TRIO
  ~, Paul, or Mary: 5 SAINT

**"Peter ___":** 4 GUNN
**"Peter and the Wolf"**
  bird: 5 FLUTE SASHA
  duck: 4 OBOE 5 SONIA
**"Peter Grimes":** 5 OPERA
**Peter Pan**
  foe: 4 HOOK
    11 CAPTAINHOOK
  rival: 3 JIF
**"Peter Pan"**
  critter: 4 CROC
  pirate: 4 HOOK SMEE
  playwright: 6 BARRIE
  pooch: 4 NANA
**"Peter, Peter, Pumpkin ___":**
  5 EATER
**Peters**
  Soprano: 7 ROBERTA
**Petersburg, Virginia**
  Base near: 5 FTLEE
**Peterson, Cassandra**
  alter ego: 6 ELVIRA
**Petite:** 4 SIZE
  dessert: 4 TART
  pasta: 4 ORZO
**Petit four:** 4 CAKE
  finisher: 4 ICER
**Petition:** 3 BEG SUE 4 PLEA
  PRAY 5 PLEAD
  7 ENTREAT
  8 ENTREATY
  Devout: 6 ORISON
**Petrarch**
  Beloved of: 5 LAURA
  work: 6 SONNET
**Petri**
  Director: 4 ELIO
**Petri dish**
  gelatin: 4 AGAR
**Petrie, Laura**
  plaint: 5 OHROB
**"Petrified Forest, The"**
  Bogart role in: 6 MANTEE
**Petrifying**
  Her looks were: 6 MEDUSA
**Petrocelli**
  of baseball: 4 RICO
**Petrol**
  brand: 4 ESSO
  measure: 5 LITRE
  unit: 5 LITRE
**Petroleum**
  distillate: 7 NAPHTHA
  gp.: 4 OPEC
  jelly: 8 VASELINE
  name: 4 ARCO 5 AMOCO
  product: 8 KEROSENE
**Petruchio**
  activity: 6 TAMING
**Pet Shop Boys**
  record label: 3 EMI
**Petticoat:** 4 SLIP
  junction: 4 SEAM
**Petting**
  place: 3 ZOO
  zoo animal: 5 LLAMA

**Petty:** 5 SMALL
  Actress: 4 LORI
  clash: 4 SPAT
  officer: 4 BOSN 5 BOSUN
    6 YEOMAN
  or Singer: 4 LORI
  quarrel: 4 SPAT TIFF
  tyrant: 6 SATRAP
**Petty, Richard**
  Son of: 4 KYLE
  sponsor: 3 STP
**Petula**
  Singer: 5 CLARK
**Petunia**
  Boyfriend of: 5 PORKY
  part: 5 PETAL SEPAL
**Peut-___ (maybe, in French):**
  4 ETRE
**Pew**
  adjunct: 7 KNEELER
  area: 4 NAVE
  divider: 5 AISLE
**Pewter:** 5 ALLOY
  component: 3 TIN 4 LEAD
  Kind of: 3 LEY
**Peyote**
  cactus: 6 MESCAL
  Sacramental user of: 3 UTE
**"Peyton Place"**
  actor: 5 ONEAL
  actress Hope: 5 LANGE
  actress Turner: 4 LANA
**PFC**
  superior: 3 CPL
**PG**
  Gave a: 5 RATED
**Pg.**
  Turn to the next: 4 CONT
**PG-13:** 6 RATING
**PGA**
  1965 ~ champ Dave: 4 MARR
  1998 ~ champ: 5 SINGH
  Annual ~ event: 6 USOPEN
  nickname: 4 SEVE 5 ARNIE
  Part of: 4 ASSN
  player: 3 PRO
  Three-time ~ champ:
    5 SNEAD
  Winner of 81 ~ tournaments:
    5 SNEAD
**pH**
  It has a low: 4 ACID
**Phair**
  Singer: 3 LIZ
**Phantom:** 8 SPECTRAL
  portrayer Chaney: 3 LON
**"Phantom Lady"**
  1944 ~ star: 6 RAINES
**"Phantom Menace, The"**
  actor McGregor: 4 EWAN
  boy: 3 ANI
**"Phantom of the Opera, The"**
  1962 ~ star: 3 LOM
  name: 4 ERIK
**Pharaoh**
  cross: 4 ANKH

land: 5 EGYPT
of Genesis: 7 RAMESES
river: 4 NILE
symbol: 3 ASP
**Pharm.**
watchdog: 3 FDA
**Pharmaceutical**
giant: 5 MERCK ROCHE
8 ELILILLY
Lilly of ~ fame: 3 ELI
ointment: 6 OLEATE
watchdog gp.: 3 FDA
**Pharmacist**
compound: 3 SAL
concern: 4 DOSE
item: 4 DRUG
thrice: 3 TER
**Phase:** 4 STEP 5 STAGE
6 ASPECT
out: 3 END
Sea: 4 TIDE
Sleep: 3 REM
Washer: 5 CYCLE
**Phased-out**
flier: 3 SST
toxin: 3 PCB
**Phaser**
Hit with a: 3 ZAP
setting: 4 STUN
**Phat:** 3 RAD
**Ph.D.:** 3 DEG
hurdle: 5 ORALS
**Pheasant**
female: 3 HEN 6 PEAHEN
stew: 5 SALMI
**"Phèdre"**
playwright: 6 RACINE
**Phenom:** 3 ACE
Golf ~ Michelle: 3 WIE
**Phenomena**
Astronomical: 5 NOVAE
Kind of: 3 PSI
**Phenomenon**
Cave: 4 ECHO
Eclipse: 6 CORONA
Foreboding: 4 OMEN
Ocean: 4 TIDE
8 NEAPTIDE
Pacific weather: 6 ELNINO
Sleep: 3 REM 5 APNEA
Solar: 5 FLARE
Spring: 4 THAW
Winter: 8 COLDSNAP
**"Phew!"**
inducer: 4 ODOR
**Phi**
follower: 3 CHI
**Phi Beta Kappa**
concern (abbr.): 3 GPA
**Phidias**
subject: 6 ATHENA
**Phi ___ Kappa:** 4 BETA
**Phil**
Don or ~ of pop: 6 EVERLY
Folk singer: 4 OCHS
of hockey, familiarly: 4 ESPO

Quarterback: 5 SIMMS
Skier: 5 MAHRE
Texas senator: 5 GRAMM
Wife of: 5 MARLO
**Phil.**
Book before: 3 EPH
**Phila.**
clock setting: 3 EST
transit: 5 SEPTA
**Philadelphia**
former mayor: 5 GOODE
founder: 4 PENN
suburb: 5 ASTON PAOLI
university: 6 TEMPLE
7 LASALLE
**"Philadelphia"**
director: 5 DEMME
**Philanderer:** 3 CAD 4 ROUE
of filmdom: 5 ALFIE
**Philanthropic**
Was: 4 GAVE
**Philanthropist:** 5 DONOR
No: 5 MISER
~ Barton: 5 CLARA
~ Cornell: 4 EZRA
~ Yale: 5 ELIHU
**Philatelist**
book: 5 ALBUM
purchase: 4 PANE 5 STAMP
**Philbin**
cohort: 4 RIPA
TV host: 5 REGIS
**Phileas**
Verne hero: 4 FOGG
**Philemon:** 7 EPISTLE
Book before: 5 TITUS
**Philharmonic**
gp.: 4 ORCH
**Philip**
Author: 4 ROTH 5 WYLIE
**Philip II**
fleet: 6 ARMADA
**Philippe:** 3 ROI
**Philippic:** 4 RANT 6 TIRADE
**Philippine**
capital: 6 MANILA
city: 6 ILOILO
Former ~ leader: 5 RAMOS
6 MARCOS
island: 4 CEBU 5 LEYTE
LUZON SAMAR
peak: 3 APO
sea: 4 SULU
~ Muslim: 4 MORO
**Philippines**
1990s ~ president:
5 RAMOS
Capital of the: 6 MANILA
island: 5 LEYTE
Marcos of the: 6 IMELDA
**Philips**
Comic: 3 EMO
product: 5 TVSET
**Philistines**
Where Samson slew the:
4 LEHI

**Phillies**
star Del: 5 ENNIS
**Phillippe**
Actor: 4 RYAN
**Phillips**
and Elliot: 5 MAMAS
head: 5 SCREW
Newsman: 5 STONE
**Phillips Academy**
city: 7 ANDOVER
**Phillips ___ Academy:**
6 EXETER
**Phillips University**
city: 4 ENID
**Phillpotts**
Author: 4 EDEN
**Philly**
player: 5 EAGLE SIXER
**Philo**
S.S. Van Dine sleuth: 5 VANCE
**Philosopher:** 4 SAGE
Chinese: 6 LAOTSE
English: 5 LOCKE
French: 6 PASCAL
German: 4 KANT
Greek: 5 PLATO
Roman: 4 CATO 6 SENECA
**Philosophical:** 4 DEEP
ending: 3 ISM
ideal: 3 TAO
**Philosophy:** 5 CREDO
Chinese: 3 TAO
giant: 4 KANT 5 PLATO
**"Philosophy of Right, The"**
author: 5 HEGEL
**Phinehas**
Father of: 3 ELI
**Phlebotomy**
target: 4 VEIN
**Phnom ___ :** 4 PENH
**Phobia:** 4 FEAR
prefix: 4 ACRO XENO
5 AGORA
**Phobos:** 4 MOON
Father of: 4 ARES
orbits it: 4 MARS
**Phoebe**
Actress: 5 CATES
portrayer: 4 LISA
Sister of: 6 URSULA
**Phoenician:** 6 SEMITE
deity: 4 BAAL
love goddess: 7 ASTARTE
port: 4 TYRE 5 SIDON
**Phoenix**
cager: 3 SUN
City near: 4 MESA 5 TEMPE
setting (abbr.): 3 MST
source: 5 ASHES
team: 4 SUNS
**Phone:** 4 CALL HORN
abbr.: 4 OPER
answerer word: 5 HELLO
attachment: 3 EAR 5 SOUSA
bk. listings: 3 NOS
Bug a: 7 WIRETAP

Bulk-rate ~ line (abbr.):
 4 WATS
Business ~ button: 4 HOLD
button: 4 OPER STAR
 6 REDIAL
Bygone pay ~ amount: 4 DIME
Cell ~ button: 4 SEND
Cell ~ kin: 5 PAGER
Cell ~ maker: 5 NOKIA
cord shape: 4 COIL
crew: 7 LINEMEN
Emergency: 7 HOTLINE
enclosure: 5 BOOTH
In ~ limbo: 6 ONHOLD
Kind of: 4 CELL
Letterless ~ button: 3 ONE
Like most ~ numbers:
 6 LISTED
Like some ~ nos.: 3 RES
Long-distance ~ number part:
 8 AREACODE
menu imperative: 5 PRESS
Modern ~ feature: 6 REDIAL
no. add-on: 3 EXT
Office ~ nos.: 4 EXTS
Old ~ company nickname:
 6 MABELL
Old ~ lack: 4 STAR
Old ~ user: 6 DIALER
part: 7 HANDSET
Pay ~ feature: 4 SLOT
Pioneer cell ~ co.: 3 GTE
prefix: 4 MEGA TELE
Report by: 6 CALLIN
Retro ~ feature: 4 DIAL
Run up a ~ bill: 3 GAB
Send via: 3 FAX
six: 3 MNO
Tie up the: 3 YAK
trio: 3 ABC DEF GHI JKL
 MNO PRS TUV WXY
~ 0: 4 OPER
~ 2: 3 ABC
~ 3: 3 DEF
~ 4: 3 GHI
~ 5: 3 JKL
~ 6: 3 MNO
~ 7: 3 PRS
~ 8: 3 TUV
~ 9: 3 WXY
~, slangily: 4 HORN
**Phone ___:** 3 TAG
**Phoned:** 4 RANG
**Phones**
Like some: 6 ROTARY
**Phonograph**
needles: 5 STYLI
part: 3 ARM
record: 4 DISC
**Phony:** 4 SHAM 5 BOGUS
 FAKER POSER 6 POSEUR
**"Phooey!":** 3 BAH FIE PAH
 4 CRUD DANG DARN
 DRAT NUTS RATS
 5 NERTS 6 DANGIT
 DARNIT

**Phosphate:** 5 ESTER
**Photo:** 3 PIC 4 SNAP
Advertising ~ label: 5 AFTER
book: 5 ALBUM
Brown-tinted: 5 SEPIA
Enlarge a: 6 BLOWUP
finish: 4 STAT 5 GENIC
 MATTE
Frame a ~ again: 5 REMAT
holder: 5 ALBUM
lab svc.: 3 ENL
Locker: 5 PINUP
Magazine: 4 STAT
Old: 5 SEPIA 7 TINTYPE
prefix: 4 TELE
session: 5 SHOOT
Sit for a: 4 POSE
Take a: 4 SNAP 5 SHOOT
tint: 5 SEPIA
Took a: 4 SHOT
**Photo ___:** 3 OPS
**Photocopier**
part: 6 SORTER
problem: 3 JAM
**Photocopy:** 4 STAT 5 REPRO
precursor: 5 DITTO
**Photoelectric cell**
element: 6 CESIUM
**Photoengraving**
innovator Frederic: 4 IVES
**Photog**
choice: 3 SLR
image: 3 NEG
request: 5 SMILE
**Photog.**
service: 3 ENL
**Photograph:** 5 SHOOT
Trim a: 4 CROP
**Photographed:** 4 SHOT
**Photographer**
Civil War: 5 BRADY
request: 5 SMILE
setting: 5 FSTOP
Word to the: 6 CHEESE
Yosemite: 10 ANSELADAMS
~ Adams: 5 ANSEL
~ Arbus: 5 DIANE
~ Cartier-Bresson: 5 HENRI
~ Goldin: 3 NAN
~ Leibovitz: 5 ANNIE
~ Richard: 6 AVEDON
**Photography**
brand: 5 KODAK
First name in: 5 ANSEL
lens: 5 MACRO
light: 6 STROBE
**Photomuralist**
~ Adams: 5 ANSEL
**Photos:** 3 PIX
Some have: 3 IDS
**Phrase**
after break or shake: 4 ALEG
before phrase: 5 COINA
in disco names: 5 AGOGO
Musical: 5 TRALA
of inclusion: 6 ETALII

of understanding: 4 ISEE
Ratio: 4 ISTO
Speller: 4 ASIN
tacked on for emphasis:
 6 NOLESS
Twist of: 7 ANAGRAM
**Phrygia**
King of: 5 MIDAS
**Phx.**
Sch. near: 3 ASU
**Phylicia**
Cosby costar: 6 RASHAD
**Phyllis**
Comic: 6 DILLER
TV husband of: 4 LARS
**Phylum**
subdivision: 5 CLASS
**Phys.:** 3 SCI
**Physical:** 4 EXAM
condition: 5 SHAPE
Having ~ presence:
 15 BRICKSANDMORTAR
likeness: 5 IMAGE
prefix: 4 META
sounds: 3 AHS
**Physician:** 6 HEALER
Ancient: 5 GALEN
Canadian: 5 OSLER
English ~ and scholar:
 5 ROGET
Greek: 5 GALEN
Hypnotism: 6 MESMER
org.: 3 AMA
~, briefly: 3 DOC
**Physicist**
Austrian: 4 MACH 5 PAULI
Danish: 4 BOHR
French: 6 AMPERE
German: 3 OHM
particle: 3 ION
study: 4 ATOM 6 ENERGY
unit: 3 RAD
~ Alessandro: 5 VOLTA
~ Enrico: 5 FERMI
~ Fermi: 6 ENRICO
~ Georg: 3 OHM
~ Mach: 5 ERNST
~ Niels: 4 BOHR
~ Nikola: 5 TESLA
~ Ohm: 5 GEORG
~ Sakharov: 6 ANDREI
**Physics**
Branch of: 6 OPTICS
 7 STATICS
calculation: 4 MASS
concept: 4 MASS
particle: 5 BOSON MESON
prefix: 4 META 5 ASTRO
Suffix in nuclear: 4 TRON
unit: 3 ERG RAD 4 DYNE
**Physics Nobelist:** *see pages*
 *728–730*
1918 ~: 6 PLANCK
1922 ~: 4 BOHR
1933 ~: 5 DIRAC
1938 ~: 5 FERMI

1957 ~ Tsung-___ Lee: 3 DAO
**Physique:** 3 BOD 4 BODY
 5 FRAME SHAPE
 Having a good: 5 BUILT
**Pi:** 5 RATIO
 follower: 3 RHO
**PI:** 3 TEC
**Pia**
 Actress: 6 ZADORA
**Piaf**
 Singer: 5 EDITH
**Pianist**
 Chilean: 5 ARRAU
 Comic: 5 BORGE
 Flamboyant: 8 LIBERACE
 Jazz: 10 COUNTBASIE
 Jazz ~ Allison: 4 MOSE
 Jazz ~ Art: 5 TATUM
 Jazz ~ with eight Grammys:
  5 COREA
 New Age: 5 YANNI
 purchase: 10 SHEETMUSIC
 span: 6 OCTAVE
 ~ André: 5 WATTS
 ~ Chick: 5 COREA
 ~ Claudio: 5 ARRAU
 ~ John: 4 TESH
 ~ Myra: 4 HESS
 ~ Peter: 4 NERO
 ~ Rudolf: 6 SERKIN
**Piano:** 4 SOFT
 Dame of the: 4 HESS
 dedicatee: 5 ELISE
 exercise: 5 ETUDE
 Fix a: 4 TUNE 6 RETUNE
 fixer: 5 TUNER
 Four-hand ~ piece: 4 DUET
 key material: 5 EBONY IVORY
 keys: 7 IVORIES
 Kind of: 6 SPINET
  9 BABYGRAND
 lesson: 5 ETUDE
 Like some ~ keys: 4 EBON
 part: 5 PEDAL
 piece: 3 LEG RAG 5 ETUDE
  6 DAMPER
 pieces: 4 KEYS
 reference point: 7 MIDDLEC
 Sharp and flat ~ keys:
  7 EBONIES
 Small: 6 SPINET
 technician: 5 TUNER
 ~ 88: 4 KEYS
**"Piano, The"**
 actor Harvey: 6 KEITEL
 actor Sam: 5 NEILL
 extra: 5 MAORI
 Heroine in: 3 ADA
 Oscar winner:
  11 HOLLYHUNTER
**"Piano Lesson, The"**
 painter: 7 MATISSE
**"Piano Man"**
 songwriter: 4 JOEL
**Piao**
 of China: 3 LIN

**Piaster**
 place: 5 SYRIA
**Piazza**
 with a fountain: 5 TREVI
**Piazza, Mike:** 3 MET
**Piazza del Campo**
 site: 5 SIENA
**Pic:** 4 FOTO SNAP
 PC: 4 ICON
 Quick: 4 SNAP
 source: 3 NEG
**Pica**
 alternative: 5 ELITE
**Picador**
 cheer: 3 OLE
 target: 4 TORO
**Picante:** 5 ZESTY
**Picard**
 Counselor to: 4 TROI
**Picard, Jean-___**
 Captain: 3 LUC
**Picasso:** 6 CUBIST
 contemporary: 4 DALI MIRO
 Designer: 6 PALOMA
 home: 5 SPAIN
 Painter: 5 PABLO
 phase: 10 BLUEPERIOD
 style: 6 CUBISM
**Picasso, Pablo ___ y:** 4 RUIZ
**Picayune:** 5 PETTY
**Piccadilly Circus**
 Area north of: 4 SOHO
 statue: 4 EROS
**Piccata**
 meat: 4 VEAL
**___ Picchu:** 5 MACHU
**Piccolo**
 player: 4 CAAN
 relative: 4 FIFE 5 FLUTE
**Pick:** 3 OPT TAP 4 CULL
  5 ELECT 6 CHOICE
  SELECT
 a target: 3 AIM
 Bone to: 4 BEEF 5 GRIPE
 Critic: 3 NIT
 Do with a: 4 AFRO
 Draft: 3 ALE
 from the menu: 5 ORDER
 Ice ~, essentially: 3 AWL
 Lousy: 3 NIT
 Menu: 6 ENTREE
 on: 3 NAG 5 TEASE
 out: 4 SPOT 5 ELECT
  6 CHOOSE
 Place for a: 4 AFRO
 preceder: 3 ICE
 prefix: 3 NIT
 Ready to: 4 RIPE
 Something to: 3 NIT 4 BONE
 Take your: 3 OPT 6 CHOOSE
 Top: 4 FAVE
 Try to ~ up: 5 HITON
 up: 3 GET NAB 4 GAIN HEAR
  LIFT TAKE 5 LEARN
  SENSE 6 ARREST
 up, as cubes: 4 TONG

 up on: 5 SENSE
 up the tab: 5 TREAT
 Worker with a: 5 MINER
 ~, with "for": 3 OPT
**Pickable:** 4 RIPE
**Picked:** 5 CHOSE 6 CHOSEN
 from a lineup: 4 IDED
 It can be ~ out: 3 ORE
 It gets ~ in Hawaii: 3 UKE
 It may be: 4 LOCK
 It's ~ up at a pizza place:
  5 AROMA
 Something that's: 3 NIT
 up: 3 GOT 4 ROSE TOOK
 up item: 3 TAB
**Pickens**
 Actor: 4 SLIM
**Picker**
 A ~ may pick one: 5 BANJO
 Apple: 3 EVE
 prefix: 3 NIT
**Picker-upper:** 4 MAID TAXI
  5 TALON
 Ice: 5 TONGS
 Quicker: 3 CAB
**Picket**
 line: 5 FENCE
 line crosser: 4 SCAB
**Picketer**
 foe: 4 SCAB
**Pickle:** 3 FIX JAM 4 BIND CURE
  MESS SPOT 5 SOUSE
 brand: 6 VLASIC
 flavoring: 4 DILL
 holder: 3 JAR
 juice: 5 BRINE
 pick: 4 DILL
 producer: 5 HEINZ
 purveyor: 4 DELI
 ___ pickle: 3 INA 4 DILL
**Pickled:** 6 STINKO
 bud: 5 CAPER
 cheese: 4 FETA
 delicacy: 3 EEL
 Somewhat: 5 TIPSY
 veggie: 4 BEET
**Pickler:** 5 BRINE
**Pick-me-up:** 4 LIFT 5 TONIC
  6 BRACER ELIXIR
 Morning: 5 LATTE
**Pickup**
 Airport: 4 LIMO 6 RENTAL
 Bowling: 5 SPARE
 capacity: 3 TON 6 ONETON
 Curbside: 5 TRASH
 line: 5 HELLO HOPIN
  13 WHATSYOURSIGN
  15 HAVEWEMETBEFORE
 shtick: 4 LINE
 Tow truck: 4 REPO
 Yardage: 4 GAIN
**Pick-up-sticks**
 game: 3 NIM
**Picky**
 Be: 4 CARP
 It is picked by the: 3 NIT

**Picnic**
beverage: 4 COLA
carry-all: 6 BASKET
container: 6 COOLER
event: 8 SACKRACE
hamperer: 3 ANT 4 RAIN
lunch: 10 SANDWICHES
Paris ~ place: 4 PARC
pest: 3 ANT 4 GNAT
side dish: 4 SLAW
    8 COLESLAW
    10 PASTASALAD
Spoil, as a: 6 RAINON
spoiler: 4 ANTS RAIN
take-along: 8 ICECHEST
**"Picnic"**
playwright: 4 INGE
**Picone**
of fashion: 4 EVAN
**Pictograph:** 4 ICON
**Picture:** 3 SEE 4 CINE 5 IMAGE
    7 IMAGINE
Big: 4 EPIC 5 MURAL
Big ~ (abbr.): 3 ENL
book: 5 ALBUM
card: 5 TAROT
Computer: 4 ICON
Enter the: 6 APPEAR
frame shape: 4 OVAL
Get the: 3 SEE
Got the: 3 SAW
holder: 5 ALBUM
Hosp.: 3 MRI
in a picture: 5 INSET
Iron-on: 5 DECAL
Match sound to: 5 SYNCH
Medical: 4 XRAY
Motion: 4 CINE
Move a: 6 REHANG
of health: 4 XRAY
prize: 5 OSCAR
Put up a: 4 HANG
puzzle: 5 REBUS
receivers: 7 RETINAE
Revealing: 4 XRAY
Sacred: 4 ICON
Take a: 5 SHOOT
taker, briefly: 3 CAM
Transfer: 5 DECAL
~, informally: 4 FOTO
**"Picture of Dorian Gray, The"**
writer: 5 WILDE
**"Picture of ___ Gray, The":**
    6 DORIAN
**Pictures**
Dizzying: 5 OPART
Mental: 7 IMAGERY
Pair of: 7 DIPTYCH
**"___ Pictures" (Wyeth):**
    5 HELGA
**Picturesque:** 6 SCENIC
**Piddling:** 6 MEAGER
**Pie:** 4 TART
chart lines: 5 RADII
choice: 5 PECAN
cooling place: 4 SILL

crust ingredient: 4 LARD
cuts, essentially: 5 RADII
fight sound: 5 SPLAT
filling: 3 MUD
French: 5 TARTE
fruit: 5 APPLE
ingredient: 3 MUD 5 MINCE
    PECAN
in the sky: 3 UFO
Italian: 5 PIZZA
Kind of: 3 MUD 5 MINCE
    6 ESKIMO
    11 BANANACREAM
    BOSTONCREAM
Like: 4 EASY
Like many a: 8 HOMEMADE
maker: 3 MOM
Meat: 5 PASTY
nut: 5 PECAN
part: 5 CRUST
perch: 4 SILL
Piece of the: 5 SHARE
portion: 5 SLICE
preference: 7 ALAMODE
    8 DEEPDISH
slice: 5 WEDGE
Small: 4 TART
Tangy ~ flavor: 5 LEMON
**___ Pie:** 5 CUTIE 6 ESKIMO
    TWEETY
**Piece:** 3 BIT 4 ITEM
activists: 3 NRA
Big: 5 CHUNK
Broken: 5 SHARD
End: 4 CODA
goods: 5 CLOTH
In one: 5 WHOLE 6 ENTIRE
It's a ~ of cake: 5 SLICE
maker: 5 REESE
Numbered: 5 OPUS
of advice: 3 TIP
of cake: 4 SNAP TIER 5 CINCH
    WEDGE 6 BREEZE PICNIC
of china: 5 PLATE
of cookware: 7 STEWPAN
of dinnerware: 5 PLATE
of eight piece: 4 REAL
of farmland: 4 ACRE
of history: 3 ERA 5 RELIC
of land: 5 TRACT
of mail (abbr.): 3 LTR
of music: 5 SHEET
of news: 4 ITEM
of paper: 4 SLIP 5 SHEET
of the action: 3 CUT
of the past: 3 ERA 5 RELIC
of the pie: 5 SHARE
of turf: 3 SOD
of work: 3 ERG JOB 4 TASK
on a pedestal: 3 URN
Packing a: 5 ARMED
Parlor: 5 SOFA 5 DIVAN
    6 SETTEE
Period: 5 EPOCH
Practice: 5 ETUDE
Recital: 4 SOLO

Rotating: 3 CAM
Set: 4 PROP
Short opera: 7 ARIETTA
Show: 3 ACT 7 EPISODE
Signature: 3 PEN
Single: 4 UNIT
Thick: 4 SLAB
Top: 3 BRA
Wooden: 4 SLAT
**___ piece (alike):** 3 OFA
**Pieced**
together: 4 SEWN
**Piecemeal:** 8 ALACARTE
**"Piece of cake!":** 4 EASY
    5 CANDO 6 NOPROB
    7 NOSWEAT
**Pieces:** 3 MEN
Go to: 5 PANIC 7 SHATTER
In: 5 APART
Love to: 5 ADORE
Small: 4 NUBS
Tear to: 4 REND 5 RIPUP
    SHRED
Thrill to: 5 ELATE
To: 5 APART
**___ Pieces:** 6 REESES
**Pied-___:** 6 ATERRE
**Pied-à-___:** 5 TERRE
**Piedmont**
capital: 5 TURIN
Carrier that bought: 5 USAIR
province: 4 ASTI
wine center: 4 ASTI
**Pied Piper**
Emulate the: 5 DERAT
follower: 3 RAT
understatement:
    10 ISMELLARAT
**Pie-eyed:** 5 OILED 6 STEWED
    STINKO
Makes: 6 BESOTS
**Pielet:** 4 TART
**Pie ___ mode:** 3 ALA
**Pie-mode**
connection: 3 ALA
**Pier:** 5 WHARF
Architectural: 4 ANTA
gp.: 3 ILA
Landing: 4 DOCK
**Pierce:** 4 STAB 5 LANCE
Author: 4 EGAN
portrayer: 4 ALDA
**Pierce, Hawkeye**
portrayer: 8 ALANALDA
**Pierce Arrow**
rival: 3 REO
**Pierced**
item: 3 EAR
places: 5 LOBES
    8 EARLOBES
**Pierced-lip**
people: 6 UBANGI
**Piercer:** 3 AWL
**Piercing:** 4 KEEN
site: 3 EAR 4 LOBE
tool: 3 ADZ AWL 4 ADZE

**Pierre**
Impressionist: 6 RENOIR
Novelist: 4 LOTI
pal: 3 AMI
South Dakota, to: 4 ETAT
state (abbr.): 4 SDAK
**Pietà**
figure: 4 MARY
**Pietermaritzburg**
province: 5 NATAL
**Pig:** 4 SLOB
Big: 3 HOG 4 BOAR
Comparable to a: 5 ASFAT
Dig like a: 4 ROOT
digs: 3 STY
feed: 4 SLOP
feeder: 6 TROUGH
Kind of: 6 GUINEA
Male: 4 BOAR
nose: 5 SNOUT
of film: 4 BABE
out: 3 EAT 5 BINGE GORGE
7 OVEREAT
place: 3 PEN STY 4 POKE
tail: 3 LET
Wild: 4 BOAR
Word after: 4 IRON
**Pig ___:** 5 LATIN
**Pigeon:** 3 SAP 4 DUPE
Clay: 6 TARGET
Clay ~ sport: 5 SKEET
coop: 4 COTE
follower: 4 TOED
perch: 5 LEDGE
shelter: 4 COTE
sound: 3 COO
Stool: 3 RAT
variety: 7 FANTAIL
Young: 5 SQUAB
**Pigeon-___:** 4 TOED
**Pigeon English:** 3 COO
**Pigeonhole:** 4 SLOT SORT
5 LABEL 6 ASSORT
place: 4 DESK
**Pigged**
out: 3 ATE 7 OVERATE
**Piggery:** 3 STY
**Piggies**
Little: 4 TOES
protector: 6 BOOTEE
**Piggy:** 3 TOE
bank opening: 4 SLOT
Little: 3 TOE
Little ~ cry: 3 WEE
What the fourth little ~ had:
4 NONE
**Piggy bank**
opening: 4 SLOT
**Pig in ___:** 5 APOKE
**Piglet:** 5 SHOAT
Creator of: 5 MILNE
Mom of: 3 SOW
Pal of: 3 ROO 4 POOH
parent: 3 SOW
**Piglike:** 5 MESSY
animal: 5 TAPIR

**Pigment**
Blood: 4 HEME
Brown: 5 SEPIA
deficient: 6 ALBINO
Earthy: 5 OCHER OCHRE
UMBER 6 SIENNA
Paint: 5 OCHER
Red: 4 LAKE
Skin: 7 MELANIN
Yellowish: 5 OCHER
**Pigmented**
eye part: 4 UVEA
**Pigpen:** 3 STY
**Pig-poke**
connector: 3 INA
**Pig ___ poke:** 3 INA
**Pigs:** 5 SWINE
**"___ pig's eye!":** 3 INA
**Pigskin**
Give up the: 4 PUNT
prop: 3 TEE
**Pigsty:** 3 PEN 4 MESS SLUM
**Pigtail:** 5 BRAID PLAIT TRESS
**Pigtails**
Like: 6 TWINED
**Pigweed:** 7 REDROOT
**Pika**
kin: 4 HARE
**Pikake**
Wreath of ~ flowers: 3 LEI
**Pike:** 4 ROAD
**Pikes Peak**
locale (abbr.): 4 COLO
**Pilaf**
staple: 4 RICE
**Pilaster:** 4 ANTA
**Pilate**
Behold, to: 4 ECCE
Word from: 4 ECCE
**Pilates**
alternative: 4 YOGA
**Pile:** 4 HEAP 5 STACK
Atomic: 7 REACTOR
by a pitchfork: 3 HAY
Combustible: 4 PYRE
Ed.'s: 3 MSS
Make a: 5 AMASS STACK
maker: 4 RAKE
Rite: 4 PYRE
up: 5 AMASS 6 RAKEIN
**Piled**
deeply: 5 PLUSH
up: 7 INAHEAP
**Piles:** 4 ALOT
Place on: 4 PIER
Put into: 4 SORT
**Pileup**
Messy: 6 LOGJAM
**Pilfer:** 3 NIP 4 GLOM 5 FILCH
STEAL SWIPE
**Pilfered:** 5 STOLE
**Pilgrim**
Chaucer: 5 REEVE
destination: 5 MECCA
6 SHRINE
Plymouth: 5 ALDEN

to Mecca: 5 HADJI HAJJI
6 MOSLEM
~ John: 5 ALDEN
**Pilgrimage**
destination: 5 MECCA
Muslim: 4 HADJ HAJJ
to Mecca: 4 HADJ HAJJ
**Pill:** 6 TABLET
form: 6 CAPLET
Kind of: 3 PEP
Open a ~ bottle: 5 UNCAP
Sugar: 7 PLACEBO
Take a chill: 6 COOLIT
**Pillage:** 4 LOOT 6 MARAUD
**Pillager:** 3 HUN
**Pillar**
His wife was a: 3 LOT
Inscribed: 5 STELA STELE
Of a stone: 6 STELAR
Stair: 5 NEWEL
Stone: 5 STELA
**Pillars**
It has five: 5 ISLAM
One of the ~ of Islam: 4 HADJ
HAJJ
**Pillbox:** 3 HAT
**Pill-gobbling**
video icon: 6 PACMAN
**Pillow**
cover: 4 CASE SHAM
filler: 4 FOAM 5 EIDER
**Pillowcase**
and others: 5 LINEN
8 BEDLINEN
**"Pillow Talk"**
actress: 3 DAY
actress Day: 5 DORIS
**Pillowy:** 4 SOFT
**Pills**
~, briefly: 4 MEDS
**___ Pills:** 5 DOANS
**Pillsbury**
competitor: 7 SARALEE
**Pillsbury Bake-Off**
fixture: 4 OVEN
**Pilot:** 5 STEER 6 AVIATE
Did a ~ job: 5 RELIT
fig.: 3 ALT
guidepost: 5 PYLON
heading (abbr.): 3 ENE NNE
SSE
Hotshot: 3 ACE
Kind of: 4 TEST
Legendary test: 6 YEAGER
Military ~ post: 7 AIRBASE
place: 5 STOVE 8 GASRANGE
prediction (abbr.): 3 ETA
prefix: 4 AUTO
problem: 3 YAW
Sky: 5 PADRE
UFO: 5 ALIEN
wind problem: 5 SHEAR
worry: 4 FLAK
~, slangily: 6 FLYBOY
**Pilothouse**
abbr.: 3 ENE

**Pilotless**
  plane: 5 DRONE
**Pilots**
  Signal to: 8 AIRALERT
  UFO: 3 ETS
**Pilsener:** 5 LAGER
  holder: 5 STEIN
  kin: 3 ALE
**Piltdown Man:** 4 HOAX
**Pimiento**
  holder: 5 OLIVE
**Pimples:** 4 ACNE
**Pin:** 5 RIVET 6 BROOCH
  Accessory: 6 TIETAC
  Bowling ~ wood: 5 MAPLE
  British bowling: 7 SKITTLE
  Carpentry: 5 DOWEL
  Comparable to a: 6 ASNEAT
  cushion: 3 MAT
  Fastening: 5 RIVET
  Gunwale: 5 THOLE
  Hard to ~ down: 4 EELY
    5 DODGY VAGUE
  Holding: 6 COTTER
  Oar: 5 THOLE
  Place for a: 3 MAT TIE
    5 LAPEL
  Poke with a: 5 PRICK
  Stick with a: 5 BURST
  up: 6 SECURE
  Wooden: 5 DOWEL
**PIN**
  requester: 3 ATM
**Pin ___ :** 3 OAK
**Piña colada**
  ingredient: 3 RUM
**"___ Pinafore"**: 3 HMS
**Pinatubo**
  product: 3 ASH
**Pinball**
  infraction: 4 TILT
  palace: 6 ARCADE
  path: 3 ARC
  problem: 4 TILT
**Pince-___ :** 3 NEZ
**Pincer:** 4 CLAW
**Pincers**
  Insect with: 6 EARWIG
**Pinch:** 3 NAB NIP 5 CRIMP
    STEAL SWIPE 6 ARREST
  One to watch in a: 6 KLEPTO
  pennies: 5 STINT 6 SCRIMP
  Playful: 5 TWEAK
**___ pinch:** 3 INA
**Pincher**
  Penny: 5 MISER PIKER
**Pinch-hit:** 7 STANDIN
**"___ pinch of salt ...":** 4 ADDA
**Pincushion**
  alternative: 4 ETUI
**Pindar:** 5 ODIST
  work: 3 ODE
**Pindaric**
  poem: 3 ODE
**Pine:** 4 ACHE LONG 5 SCENT
    YEARN

  aloud: 4 SIGH
  cone, essentially: 4 SEED
  exudate: 5 RESIN
  family tree: 3 FIR
  (for): 4 ACHE
  leaf: 6 NEEDLE
  Like ~ scent: 6 WOODSY
  product: 3 TAR 5 RESIN
  Sauce with ~ nuts: 5 PESTO
**Pine-___ (cleaning brand):**
  3 SOL
**Pineapple:** 7 GRENADE
  Big name in: 4 DOLE
  island: 5 LANAI
**Pine Tree**
  state: 5 MAINE
**Pine Valley**
  resident: 5 ERICA
**Ping:** 5 NOISE
**Ping-___ :** 4 PONG
**Ping-Pong**
  partition: 3 NET
**Pinhead:** 3 ASS 4 BOOB DODO
    TWIT 5 IDIOT
**Piniella**
  of baseball: 3 LOU
**Pink:** 4 RARE ROSE ROSY
  Deep: 4 ROSE 5 MELON
  Give a ~ slip to: 3 AXE CAN
    9 TERMINATE
  In the: 4 HALE RARE ROSY
    WELL
  lady ingredient: 3 GIN
  Not in the: 3 ILL
  Reddish: 4 RARE
  slip: 13 WALKINGPAPERS
  Tickle: 5 AMUSE ELATE
    6 PLEASE
  Tickled: 4 GLAD
  wine: 4 ROSE
  Yellowish: 7 TEAROSE
**Pinker**
  inside: 5 RARER
**Pinkerton**
  Detective: 5 ALLAN
**Pinkett Smith**
  Actress: 4 JADA
**Pink Floyd**
  album, with "The": 4 WALL
  guitarist Barrett: 3 SYD
**Pinkish:** 4 RARE
  yellow: 5 CORAL
**Pink-legged**
  bird: 5 STILT
**"Pink Panther, The"**
  actor David: 5 NIVEN
  actor Herbert: 3 LOM
**Pink-slip:** 3 AXE CAN 4 BOOT
    FIRE SACK
**Pinky**
  Key hit with a: 5 ENTER
  or Peggy: 3 LEE
**Pinnacle:** 3 TOP TOR 4 ACME
    APEX PEAK 5 SPIRE
  Rocky: 3 TOR
**Pinocchio:** 4 LIAR

  Emulate: 3 LIE
  goldfish: 4 CLEO
  lie detector: 4 NOSE
**Pinochle**
  combo: 4 MELD
  king beater: 3 TEN
  low card: 4 NINE
  play: 4 MELD
**Pin-on**
  Conference: 5 IDTAG
  Party: 4 TAIL
**Pinot ___ (wine):** 4 NOIR
**"___ pin, pick ...":** 4 SEEA
**Pinpoint:** 6 LOCATE
**Pins**
  On ~ and needles: 4 EDGY
    5 ANTSY TENSE
**Pinsk**
  Peace, in: 3 MIR
**Pinstripes**
  Manager in ~, once: 5 TORRE
  wearer: 4 YANK 6 YANKEE
**Pint**
  fraction: 4 GILL
  Half: 3 CUP
  Hearty: 5 STOUT
  Place for a: 3 PUB
  Pub: 3 ALE
**Pinta**
  partner: 4 NINA
**Pintail**
  duck: 4 SMEE
**Pinter**
  Playwright: 6 HAROLD
**Pinto:** 4 BEAN
**Pint-size:** 4 MINI
**Pint-sized:** 4 PUNY TINY
    5 SHORT TEENY
**Pinup**
  '40s ~ Betty: 6 GRABLE
  feature: 3 GAM
  legs: 4 GAMS
  Like a: 4 SEXY
**Pinza**
  and others: 5 BASSI
  Basso: 4 EZIO
  Singer: 4 EZIO
**Pinzón**
  Ship commanded by: 5 PINTA
**Pion**
  Home to a: 4 ATOM
**Pioneer:** 7 SETTLER
    11 TRAILBLAZER
  automaker: 4 OLDS
  cell phone co.: 3 GTE
  computer: 5 ENIAC
  heading: 4 WEST
  in Surrealism: 5 ERNST
  product: 6 STEREO
  vehicle: 5 WAGON
**Pioneer Day**
  Where ~ is celebrated:
    4 UTAH
**Pioneering**
  video game: 4 PONG
  video game system: 5 ATARI

**Pious:** 5 GODLY 6 DEVOUT
   8 REVERENT
**Pip:** 4 LULU ONER SEED
   5 BEAUT PEACH
  Beloved of: 7 ESTELLA
  Card with a single: 3 ACE
**Pipe**
  bend: 3 ELL 5 ELBOW
  cleaner: 5 DRANO
   6 REAMER
  Collar on a: 6 FLANGE
  elbows: 4 ELLS
  joint: 3 ELL TEE
  Kind of: 5 BRIAR
  Large: 4 MAIN
  material: 3 COB 5 BRIAR
   BRIER
  part: 3 ELL 4 BOWL STEM
  Pastoral: 4 REED
  problem: 4 CLOG DRIP LEAK
   RUST
  residue: 6 DOTTLE
  section: 4 TRAP
  type: 3 ELL 5 BRIAR BRIER
   7 CORNCOB
  up: 5 SPEAK 7 CHIMEIN
  Vertical: 5 RISER
  Water: 4 MAIN 6 HOOKAH
**"Pipe down!":** 3 SHH 4 HUSH
  5 SHUSH
**Pipeline**
  Fuel: 7 GASMAIN
**Piper**
  Actress: 6 LAURIE
  Greek: 3 PAN
  Legendary: 3 PAN
  Like the: 4 PIED
  Son of the: 3 TOM
  wear: 4 KILT
  ___ Piper: 4 PIED
**Pipes**
  Some bagpipe: 6 DRONES
**Pipeye**
  Popeye, to: 5 UNCLE
**Piping:** 5 REEDY
**Pippig**
  Marathoner: 3 UTA
**"Pippi Longstocking"**
  author Lindgren: 6 ASTRID
**"Pippin"**
  actress Ryan: 5 IRENE
  director: 5 FOSSE
**Pipsqueak:** 4 RUNT 5 TWERP
  6 SHRIMP
**Piquancy:** 3 NIP 4 TANG ZEST
  5 SPICE
**Piquant:** 4 RACY TART 5 SALTY
  TANGY ZESTY
**Pique:** 3 IRE IRK PET 4 RILE
  SNIT 6 AROUSE
  condition: 3 IRE
  experience: 3 IRE 4 SNIT
  Fit of: 4 HUFF SNIT
  period: 4 SNIT
**Piqued**
  state: 4 HUFF SNIT

**Pirandello**
  Author: 5 LUIGI
**Pirate:** 6 SEADOG 7 CORSAIR
  8 SEAROVER
  captain: 4 KIDD
  feature: 6 PEGLEG
  Fictional: 4 SMEE
  interjections: 3 ARS
  knife: 4 SNEE
  of note:
   15 ROBERTOCLEMENTE
  place: 7 OPENSEA
  plunder: 4 LOOT 5 BOOTY
  potable: 3 RUM 4 GROG
  punishment: 4 LASH
  rival: 5 ASTRO
  ship: 7 CORSAIR 8 SEAROVER
  Start of a ~ chant: 4 YOHO
**"Pirates of the Caribbean"**
  star: 4 DEPP
**Pirelli**
  product: 4 TIRE
**Pirouette:** 5 TWIRL
  follower: 4 PLIE
**Pisa**
  dough, formerly: 4 LIRA
  Emulate the ~ tower: 4 LEAN
  Like the ~ tower: 5 ATILT
  place: 5 ITALY
  river: 4 ARNO
**Pisan**
  payments, formerly: 4 LIRE
**Pisces**
  Sign after: 5 ARIES
**Pistachio:** 3 NUT
**Piste**
  Sport played on a: 4 EPEE
**Pistil**
  partner: 6 STAMEN
**Pistol:** 3 GUN ROD 7 FIREARM
  SIDEARM
  Fully automatic: 7 BURPGUN
  German: 5 LUGER
  kickback: 6 RECOIL
  Kind of: 3 CAP
  Point a: 3 AIM
  pointer: 5 AIMER
  Toy: 6 CAPGUN POPGUN
  Toy ~ ammo: 4 CAPS
  ~, slangily: 3 GAT ROD
   4 IRON
**Pistol-packing:** 5 ARMED
**Piston**
  chamber: 8 CYLINDER
  Press: 3 RAM
**Pit:** 4 SEED
  Bottomless: 5 ABYSM ABYSS
  bull sound: 3 GRR
  Caravan ~ stop: 5 OASIS
  contents: 3 TAR
  Deep: 5 ABYSS CHASM
  Do a ~ job: 6 REFUEL
  Fruit: 5 STONE
  Gaping: 5 ABYSS
  Reed in a: 4 OBOE
  stuff: 3 TAR

  Water: 4 SUMP
  Wind in a: 4 OBOE
**Pit-___ (heart sound):** 3 PAT
**Pita**
  sandwich: 4 GYRO
**"Pit and the Pendulum, The"**
  author: 3 POE
**Pitapat**
  Go: 5 THROB
**Pitch:** 3 TAR 4 HURL SELL
  TONE TOSS 5 ERECT
  RESIN SLANT SLOPE
  SPIEL THROW
  Black as: 4 INKY
  catcher: 4 MITT
  Certain: 8 HARDSELL
  Dangerous: 8 BEANBALL
  High: 3 LOB 4 BALL
  Hit with a: 4 BEAN
  in: 3 AID 4 HELP
  In: 5 TUNED
  indicator: 4 CLEF NOTE
  It may follow a: 4 SALE
  Low: 4 BASS
  Lowest: 8 SOFTSELL
  Musical: 4 TONE
  Of: 5 TONAL
  One way to: 7 OVERARM
  on paper: 7 PRINTAD
  Pitcher's: 6 SLIDER
  preceder: 3 SLO
  Sales: 3 PIE 5 SPIEL
  Slow: 3 LOB
  Softball: 3 ARC
  Successful: 4 SALE
  symbol: 4 CLEF
  tents: 6 ENCAMP
  Tricky: 8 CHANGEUP
  Vocal: 4 TONE
**Pitch-black:** 4 INKY
**Pitchblende:** 3 ORE
**Pitched:** 5 THREW
  It might be: 3 WOO 4 ROOF
  TENT 7 ROOFTOP
  Perfectly: 5 NOHIT
  Properly: 5 ONKEY
  roof: 4 TENT
  too low: 4 FLAT
**Pitcher:** 4 EWER 5 ADMAN
  8 SALESMAN
  1950s ~: 5 LOPAT 6 MAGLIE
  asset: 3 ARM
  Decorative: 4 EWER
  dream: 8 NOHITTER
  Face the: 3 BAT
  Facing the: 5 ATBAT
  handle: 3 EAR
  nicknamed "Tornado":
   4 NOMO
  of milk: 5 ELSIE
  part: 3 EAR LIP
  Perfect game: 6 LARSEN
  place: 5 MOUND
  plant catch: 6 INSECT
  Porcelain: 4 EWER
  pride: 3 ARM

prize: 4 CLIO
Relief: 5 SAVER 7 FIREMAN
Relief ~ goal: 4 SAVE
Star: 3 ACE
stat: 3 ERA
target: 4 MITT
Top: 3 ACE
Water: 4 EWER
with a big mouth: 4 EWER
with a record 5,714 strikeouts:
    4 RYAN
~ Early: 4 WYNN
~ Hideki: 5 IRABU
~ Hideo: 4 NOMO
~ Nolan: 4 RYAN
~ Robb: 3 NEN
~ Ryan: 5 NOLAN
~ Satchel: 5 PAIGE
~ Shawn: 5 ESTES
~ Warren: 5 SPAHN
**Pitcherful**
~, maybe: 3 ALE
**Pitches**
between innings: 3 ADS
Like some: 7 OUTSIDE
    SIDEARM
**Pitchfork**
part: 4 TINE 5 PRONG
Pile by a: 3 HAY
wielder: 5 DEVIL
**Pitchfork-shaped**
letter: 3 PSI
**Pitch ___-hitter:** 3 ANO
**Pitching**
choice: 3 TAR
Game with: 4 GOLF
star: 3 ACE
stat: 3 ERA 4 WINS 5 SAVES
style: 7 SIDEARM
**Pitchman:** 6 BARKER
**___-pitch softball:** 3 SLO
**Pitfall:** 4 TRAP 5 SNARE
**Pith:** 4 MEAT 7 ESSENCE
helmet: 4 TOPI 5 TOPEE
**Pithy:** 5 TERSE
**Pitiful:** 5 SORRY
**Pits:** 5 NADIR
Took ~ from: 6 STONED
**Pit stop**
can: 3 STP
maker: 7 RACECAR
**Pitt**
1995 ~ flick: 5 SEVEN
Actor: 4 BRAD
Penn or: 5 ACTOR
**Pittance:** 3 SOU 4 MITE
preceder: 4 MERE
~, slangily: 3 HAY
**Pitter-patter**
maker: 4 RAIN
**Pitts**
Actress: 4 ZASU
**Pittsburgh**
co.: 7 USSTEEL
German: 5 ESSEN
pro: 7 STEELER

river: 4 OHIO
team: 7 PIRATES 8 STEELERS
**Pituitary:** 5 GLAND
hormone: 4 ACTH
**Pity**
Feeling of: 6 PATHOS
**"Pity!":** 4 ALAS
**Pius**
and others: 5 POPES
**Pivot:** 4 SLUE 6 ROTATE
    SWIVEL
around: 4 SLUE
**Pivotal:** 3 KEY
point: 4 CRUX 5 HINGE
**Pix**
Pose for: 3 SIT
**Pixar**
character: 4 NEMO
**Pixel:** 3 DOT
Alter ~ by pixel: 5 MORPH
**Pixie:** 3 ELF IMP 6 SPRITE
**Pizarro**
City founded by: 4 LIMA
conquest: 4 PERU
gold: 3 ORO
victim: 4 INCA
**Pizazz:** 3 ZIP 4 BRIO ELAN
    ZEST ZING 5 FLAIR
    OOMPH SPICE STYLE
    VERVE
Lacking: 8 LIFELESS
Without: 5 DRYLY
**Piz Bernina:** 3 ALP
**Pizza:** 3 PIE
brand: 7 CELESTE
feature: 5 CRUST
Had a ~ delivered: 5 ATEIN
herb: 7 OREGANO
It's picked up at a ~ parlor:
    5 AROMA
order: 3 PIE 4 TOGO
perimeter: 5 CRUST
piece: 5 SLICE
place: 4 OVEN
portion: 8 ONESLICE
slice, often: 6 EIGHTH
topping: 5 BACON ONION
    6 OLIVES SALAMI
    7 OREGANO SAUSAGE
**Pizza Quick**
sauce maker: 4 RAGU
**Pizzeria**
fixture: 4 OVEN
lure: 5 AROMA
order: 3 PIE 5 SLICE
patron: 5 EATER
**Pizzeria ___ (fast food chain):**
    3 UNO
**Pizzicato**
Not: 4 ARCO
Play: 5 PLUCK
**Pkg.**
Cigarette: 3 CTN
deliverer: 3 UPS
How a ~ may arrive: 3 COD
**Placard:** 6 POSTER

**Placate:** 7 APPEASE
**Place:** 3 LAY PUT SET 4 LIEU
    SITE SPOT 5 LOCUS
    STEAD WHERE
    6 LOCALE 7 SITUATE
All over the: 4 RIFE
At the original: 6 INSITU
At this: 4 HERE
First: 4 EDEN
for an X: 3 MAP
for losers: 3 SPA
for memories: 4 LANE
for portraits: 4 HALL
for sweaters: 3 SPA
for the night: 3 INN
From that: 6 THENCE
From what: 6 WHENCE
In: 3 SET 4 NEAT
In ~ of: 3 FOR
In first: 5 ONTOP
In that: 5 THERE
In the first: 5 AHEAD
in the Old West: 4 ETTA
In this: 4 HERE
of bliss: 4 EDEN
of honor: 4 DAIS
of refuge: 3 ARK 5 HAVEN
on piles: 4 PIER
on the schedule: 4 SLOT
Person, ~, or thing: 4 NOUN
place: 6 SECOND
Put in: 5 SITED
Run in: 4 IDLE
Show: 5 STAGE THIRD
side by side: 6 APPOSE
Take: 5 OCCUR 6 HAPPEN
Taking-off: 3 SPA
Taking the ~ (of): 6 INLIEU
Third: 4 SHOW
to be taken: 9 CLIPJOINT
to build: 4 SITE
to crash: 3 PAD
to do one's bidding: 4 EBAY
to fish: 6 STREAM
to gambol: 3 LEA
to graze: 3 LEA
to kick something: 5 REHAB
to lay over: 3 INN
to live: 5 ABODE
to moor: 5 INLET
Took: 3 WAS
to park: 3 LOT
to play: 5 ARENA 7 RECROOM
to play b-ball: 4 YMCA
to relax: 3 DEN SPA
to roll: 5 AISLE
to sign: 10 DOTTEDLINE
to sit: 5 CHAIR
to stand a round: 3 BAR
to start a hole: 3 TEE
to stay: 3 INN
to step: 5 ASIDE
to surf: 3 NET
to trade: 4 MART
to unwind: 3 SPA
to work: 4 DESK

**"___ Place":** 7 MELROSE
**Placed:** 4 LAID
**Placekicker:** 3 TOE
  prop: 3 TEE
**Place-name**
  Asian ~ ender: 4 STAN
**Places:** 4 LOCI
  To distant: 4 AFAR
**Placid:** 4 LAKE 6 SERENE
**Plácido**
  Tenor: 7 DOMINGO
**Plagiarize:** 4 COPY CRIB LIFT
    5 STEAL
**Plague:** 3 AIL POX VEX 4 PEST
    5 BESET 6 HARASS
    7 BEDEVIL
  Avoid like the: 4 SHUN
  Biblical: 7 LOCUSTS
  ~, to Camus: 5 PESTE
**"Plague, The"**
  setting: 4 ORAN 7 ALGERIA
**Plaid:** 6 TARTAN
  Kind of: 4 GLEN
**Plain:** 3 DRY 4 BARE
    7 GENERIC
  Arctic: 6 TUNDRA
  Argentine: 5 PAMPA
  as day: 8 CLEARCUT
  Author: 5 BELVA
  Grassy: 5 LLANO 7 SAVANNA
  homes: 6 TEPEES
  Just ~ bad: 5 AWFUL
  Lunar: 4 MARE
  Russian: 6 STEPPE
  Southwestern: 5 LLANO
  to see: 5 OVERT
  Treeless: 5 LLANO 6 STEPPE
  Tropical: 7 SAVANNA
  writing: 5 PROSE
  ~ Jane: 4 EYRE
**Plain ___:** 5 TOSEE
**___ Plaines, Illinois:** 3 DES
**Plain-living**
  sect: 5 AMISH
**Plains**
  drifters: 5 BISON
  shelter: 5 TEPEE
  tribe: 3 OTO 4 OTOE OTOS
    5 KIOWA OSAGE
    6 PAWNEE 7 ARAPAHO
**Plains Indian:** 3 OTO 4 OTOE
    5 KIOWA OSAGE
    6 PAWNEE 7 ARAPAHO
**"Plains of Passage, The"**
  author: 4 AUEL
**Plaint**
  Kennel: 4 YELP
  Persian: 3 MEW
  Pooped person's: 6 IMBEAT
  Porker: 4 OINK
**Plaintext**
  Translate from: 6 ENCODE
**Plaintiff:** 4 SUER 7 ACCUSER
  Certain ~, at law: 4 USEE
**Plaintive**
  cry: 3 MEW 4 MEOW

  poem: 5 ELEGY
**"___ plaisir!":** 4 AVEC
**Plait:** 5 BRAID
**Plan:** 4 IDEA 6 AGENDA
    DESIGN INTEND
    SCHEMA SCHEME
  Anti-ICBM: 3 SDI
  Food: 4 DIET
  for later yrs.: 3 IRA
  Game: 8 SCENARIO
    STRATEGY
  General: 7 ROADMAP
  Like a perfect: 9 FOOLPROOF
  Med.: 3 HMO
  Meeting: 6 AGENDA
  Nefarious: 6 SCHEME
  on it: 8 INTENDTO
  part: 4 STEP
  Part of a: 4 STEP
  Retirement ~ name: 5 KEOGH
  Roth: 3 IRA
  Spending: 6 BUDGET
  to lose: 4 DIET
  Vacation: 4 TRIP
  Word with: 4 GAME
**Planchette**
  Board with a: 5 OUIJA
**Plane:** 4 TOOL 6 EVENER
  Attack by: 6 STRAFE
  detector: 5 RADAR
  Famous ~ name part: 5 ENOLA
  Fast: 3 JET
  Fast ~, for short: 3 SST
  flier: 5 PILOT
  Kind of: 6 ASTRAL
  measure: 4 AREA
  Old ~ handle: 5 USAIR
  part: 4 NOSE 7 AILERON
  Pilotless: 5 DRONE
  place: 3 SKY
  prefix: 4 AERO AQUA
  reservation: 4 SEAT
  seating choice: 5 AISLE
  Shuttle: 6 AIRBUS
  site: 6 HANGAR
  Small: 9 ONESEATER
  surface: 6 TARMAC
  WWI: 4 SPAD
  WWII: 4 ZERO
**Plane-regulating**
  gp.: 3 FAA
**Plane-related:** 4 AERO
**Planes**
  Big name in small: 6 CESSNA
  Group of: 5 FLEET
  Large fleet of: 6 ARMADA
  Unidentified: 6 BOGIES
**Planet:** 3 ORB 5 GLOBE
    6 SPHERE
  Fourth: 4 MARS
  of Mork: 3 ORK
  Outer: 6 URANUS
  Poet's: 3 ORB
  Red: 4 MARS
  Ringed: 6 SATURN
  Seventh: 6 URANUS

  Sitcom: 3 ORK
  suffix: 3 OID
  Third: 5 EARTH
  TV: 3 ORK
**Planetarium**
  display: 5 STARS
**Planetary**
  path: 5 ORBIT
  revolution: 4 YEAR
  shadow: 5 UMBRA
**"Planet of the ___":** 4 APES
**"Planet of the Apes"**
  planet: 5 EARTH
**"Planets, The"**
  composer: 5 HOLST
**Plank**
  Playground: 6 SEESAW
**Plankton**
  component: 5 ALGAE
**Planned**
  Intelligently ~ progress:
    7 TELESIS
**Planning**
  Bit of financial: 3 IRA
  Federal financial ~ gp.: 3 OMB
  time: 3 EVE
**Plans:** 8 SCHEMATA
**Plant:** 3 SOW SPY 5 EMBED
  again: 5 RESOW
  anchor: 4 ROOT
  anew: 5 RESOW
  Aquatic: 4 ALGA
  bristle: 3 AWN
  Climbing: 3 IVY 4 VINE
  Dye: 4 ANIL
  firmly: 5 EMBED
  fungus: 5 ERGOT
  life: 5 FLORA
  louse: 5 APHID
  malady: 5 EDEMA
  more seed: 5 RESOW
  Move, as a: 5 REPOT
  Nonflowering: 4 FERN
  Nonwoody: 4 HERB
  of the future: 4 SEED
  one on: 4 KISS
  parasite: 5 APHID
  parenthood setting:
    10 GREENHOUSE
  part: 4 ROOT STEM
  pest: 4 MITE 5 APHID BORER
  Pet: 4 CHIA
  place: 7 NURSERY
  Pond: 4 ALGA
  pores: 7 STOMATA
  pouch: 3 SAC
  Prepare to: 3 HOE
  Prickly: 5 BRIER 6 TEASEL
  Prickly-leafed: 6 TEASEL
  Related to ~ life: 7 BOTANIC
  reproductive part: 5 SPORE
  root: 5 RADIX
  Seedless: 4 FERN
  stem: 5 STALK
  Succulent: 4 ALOE
  suffix: 4 WORT

swelling: 5 EDEMA
Terrarium: 4 FERN
tissue: 5 XYLEM
with a bitter root: 7 DOGBANE
with arrow-shaped leaves:
   5 CALLA
~, so to speak: 5 INTER
**Plantain**
lily: 5 HOSTA
**Plantation**
of fiction: 4 TARA
**Planted:** 4 SOWN
How corn is: 6 INROWS
**Planter**
Large: 3 URN
purchase: 4 SEED
**Planting**
Fall: 4 BULB
Fit for: 6 ARABLE
Prepare for: 4 PLOW
**Plants:** 5 FLORA
Desert: 5 CACTI
**Plant-to-be:** 4 SEED
**Plaque**
place: 4 WALL
**Plasm**
prefix: 4 ECTO ENDO
**Plaster:** 5 BESOT
Apply, as: 4 DAUB
backing: 4 LATH
Harden, as: 3 SET
Painter's: 5 GESSO
Painting on: 6 FRESCO
support: 4 LATII
Wall: 6 STUCCO
**Plastered:** 3 LIT
**Plaster of ___ :** 5 PARIS
**Plasterwork**
Some: 6 STUCCO
**Plastic:** 6 CREDIT
alternative: 4 CASH 5 PAPER
item: 3 BAG
Name in: 4 VISA
Pay with: 6 CHARGE
prefix: 5 OSTEO
Switch from ~ to paper:
   5 REBAG
Transparent: 6 LUCITE
wrap: 5 SARAN
**Plastic ___ Band:** 3 ONO
**Plata**
Partner of: 3 ORO
**Plate**
appearance: 5 ATBAT
cleaner: 3 UMP 7 DISHRAG
Diamond: 4 HOME
Do better at the: 6 OUTHIT
Eucharist: 6 PLATEN
License: 3 TAG
No longer on the: 5 EATEN
scrap: 3 ORT
Step to the: 3 BAT
Still on the: 7 UNEATEN
**Plateau**
boundary: 7 RIMROCK
Western: 4 MESA

**___ Plateau (Missouri region):**
   5 OZARK
**Platform**
Choir: 5 RISER
Golf ball: 3 TEE
Old PC: 3 DOS
over the water: 4 PIER
part: 5 PLANK
Place for a ~ (abbr.): 3 STA
Portable: 4 SKID
Speaker: 4 DAIS
**Platforms:** 5 PODIA 6 ROSTRA
**Plath, Sylvia**
book: 5 ARIEL
novel, with "The":
   7 BELLJAR
**Plating**
material: 3 TIN 4 ZINC
**Platinum:** 5 METAL
Went: 4 DYED
**Platitude:** 6 CLICHE TRUISM
**Plato**
Home of: 6 ATHENS
school: 7 ACADEMY
Teacher of: 8 SOCRATES
**Platoon:** 4 UNIT
**"Platoon"**
actor: 5 DEFOE SHEEN
setting: 3 NAM
**Platte**
People of the: 3 OTO 4 OTOS
**Platter:** 4 DISC
1950s ~: 5 OLDIE
Kind of: 4 PUPU
part: 5 SIDEB
player: 4 HIFI 5 PHONO
Top of a: 5 SIDEA
**___ platter:** 4 PUPU
**Platters**
Groovy: 3 LPS
**Plaudits:** 4 OLES
**Plausible**
Less: 5 LAMER
**Play:** 8 RECREATE
again: 7 REPRISE
an ace: 6 AVIATE
area: 4 YARD 5 ARENA
   7 RECROOM
a role: 3 ACT
(around): 5 HORSE
a round: 4 GOLF
backer: 5 ANGEL
ball: 9 COOPERATE
break: 8 ENTRACTE
Bring into: 3 USE 6 ENTAIL
by oneself: 4 SOLO
Chance to: 4 TURN
Child's: 3 TAG
Did not: 3 SAT
Does not: 5 RESTS
first: 4 STAR
footsie: 5 FLIRT
for a sap: 3 USE
for reading only:
   11 CLOSETDRAMA
for time: 5 STALL

French ~ part: 4 ACTE
ground: 5 ARENA
group: 4 CAST
hard to get: 5 EVADE
How some: 8 FORKEEPS
In: 4 LIVE
in a puddle: 5 SLOSH
in the pool: 6 SPLASH
Lacking: 4 TAUT
lightly: 5 STRUM
Like a short: 6 ONEACT
matchmaker for: 5 FIXUP
mates: 4 CAST
merrily: 6 CAVORT
Off-the-wall: 5 CAROM
One way to: 5 BYEAR
on words: 3 PUN
opener: 4 ACTI
part: 3 ACT 4 ROLE 5 ACTII
   SCENE
Part to: 4 ROLE
Pay to: 4 ANTE
place: 5 ARENA
Put on a: 5 STAGE
Roulette: 3 RED
Serious: 5 DRAMA
start: 4 ACTI
Start of a: 4 ACTI 6 ACTONE
Still in: 4 LIVE 5 ALIVE
Students ~ it: 5 HOOKY
the flute: 6 TOOTLE
the lead: 4 STAR
the part: 3 ACT
the part of: 5 ENACT
the role of: 5 ACTAS
They ~ for pay: 3 PRO
thing: 4 PROP ROLE
time: 6 RECESS
to the balcony: 5 EMOTE
tricks: 4 JAPE
Unable to: 4 HURT
unit: 5 SCENE
up: 6 STRESS
Urban ~ area: 7 SANDLOT
What some ~ for: 5 KEEPS
(with): 3 TOY
with masks: 3 NOH
with matches: 6 TENNIS
with robots: 3 RUR
**Play-___:** 3 DOH
**Playback**
magazine org.: 5 ASCAP
**Playbill**
feature: 3 BIO
listing: 4 CAST ROLE
paragraph: 3 BIO
**Playboy:** 4 ROUE
bunny: 4 LOGO
Featured in: 4 BARE
founder, familiarly: 3 HEF
Like ~ cartoons: 6 RIBALD
Like ~ models: 4 SEXY
publisher: 6 HEFNER
**"Playboy of the Western World,
   The"**
author: 5 SYNGE

**Played**
  again: 5 RERAN
  first: 3 LED
  out: 5 STALE
  over: 5 RERAN
**Player:** 5 GAMER
  Bit: 5 EXTRA
  Bygone: 4 HIFI
  Card ~ cry: 3 GIN
  Contest: 7 ENTRANT
  Golfer: 4 GARY
  in a dome: 5 ASTRO
  J.V.: 4 SOPH
  Key: 7 PIANIST
  Lead: 4 STAR
  Minor: 3 COG
  Money: 3 PRO
  Music: 4 JUKE
  Paid: 3 PRO
  Part: 5 ACTOR
  Part-time: 7 SEMIPRO
  Poker: 6 RAISER
    8 GAMESTER
  Top: 4 STAR
  turn: 4 MOVE
**Players:** 4 CAST
  CD: 3 DJS
  Top: 5 ATEAM
**Playful**
  animal: 5 OTTER
  mammal: 5 OTTER
  one: 3 IMP
  pinch: 5 TWEAK
  prank: 5 ANTIC
  sort: 5 PIXIE
  swimmer: 5 OTTER
**Playfully:** 5 INFUN
  roguish: 4 ARCH
  Run: 4 ROMP
**Playground**
  comeback: 6 CANTOO
  cry: 4 WHEE
  equipment: 5 SWING
    6 SEESAW SLIDES
  game: 3 TAG
  item: 5 SLIDE
  marble: 5 AGATE
  plank: 6 SEESAW
  retort: 4 AMSO 5 AMNOT
    ARESO CANSO ISNOT
    ISTOO
  sight: 5 SLIDE
**Playhouse**
  Parma: 6 TEATRO
**Play ___ in (influence):** 5 AROLE
**Playing**
  field: 5 ARENA
  hard to get: 3 COY
  hooky: 4 AWOL 6 ABSENT
  marble: 3 TAW 5 AGATE
    AGGIE 7 STEELIE
  Not: 4 IDLE
    11 OUTOFACTION
  solitaire: 5 ALONE
  with a full deck: 4 SANE
**Playing card:** 4 TREY

  spot: 3 PIP
**Playing field**
  Level the: 3 MOW
  Like a fair: 5 LEVEL
**"___ Playing Our Song":**
    6 THEYRE
**"Play it, Sam"**
  speaker: 4 ILSA
**"Play It ___, Sam":** 5 AGAIN
**Playlet:** 4 SKIT
**Playoff**
  game: 4 SEMI
**Playpen**
  item: 3 TOY
**Plays**
  6-pt. ~: 3 TDS
  Tic-tac-toe: 7 XSANDOS
**Playskool**
  parent company: 6 HASBRO
**PlayStation**
  maker: 4 SONY
**Playtex**
  parent company: 7 SARALEE
  product: 3 BRA
**Plaything:** 3 TOY
  Beach: 4 PAIL
  Kitten: 4 YARN
**Playthings**
  Construction: 10 TINKERTOYS
**Play to ___ (draw):** 4 ATIE
**Play ___ with (damage):** 3 HOB
**Playwright**
  1953 Pulitzer: 4 INGE
  dream: 4 OBIE
  Kansas: 4 INGE
  turned president: 5 HAVEL
  ~ Clifford: 5 ODETS
  ~ David: 5 MAMET
  ~ Henrik: 5 IBSEN
  ~ Jean: 5 GENET
  ~ Zoe: 5 AKINS
**Plaza:** 4 MALL 6 SQUARE
  of Plato: 5 AGORA
**___ Plaza:** 4 ESSO
**Plaza Hotel**
  imp: 6 ELOISE
**Plea**
  Court ~, for short: 4 NOLO
  Kid's: 4 ICAN
  Sea: 3 SOS
**Plead:** 3 ASK BEG 7 ENTREAT
  a case: 5 ARGUE
  innocent to: 4 DENY
**Pleasant:** 4 NICE 6 POLITE
  and mild: 5 BALMY
  smell: 5 AROMA
  to look at: 6 SCENIC
  way to walk: 5 ONAIR
**Please**
  Hard to: 5 FUSSY PICKY
    6 CHOOSY
  More than: 5 ELATE
  ~, in German: 5 BITTE
  ~, in Siamese: 4 MEOW
**___ please (do one's best):**
    5 AIMTO

**Pleased:** 4 GLAD 5 HAPPY
**"Please stay!":** 6 DONTGO
**"___ please the court ...":** 4 IFIT
**Pleasing:** 4 NICE
  scent: 5 AROMA
**Pleasure**
  boat: 5 SLOOP YACHT
  dome site: 6 XANADU
  Expressed: 5 AAHED OOHED
  Great: 4 GLEE
  seeker: 8 HEDONIST
  Sounds of: 4 AAHS
  Take ~ in: 5 EATUP REVEL
    6 RELISH
  trip: 5 JAUNT
  Unexpected: 5 TREAT
**Pleasure ___ (hedonists):**
    7 SEEKERS
**Pleasure-seeking:** 7 HEDONIC
**Pleat:** 4 FOLD
**Plebe**
  place: 7 ACADEMY
  West Point: 5 CADET
**Pledge:** 3 VOW 4 OATH
    6 COMMIT SURETY
  Courtroom: 4 OATH
  drive reward: 4 TOTE
    7 TOTEBAG
  of fidelity: 5 TROTH
**Pledged:** 5 SWORE
**Pledge of Allegiance**
  ender: 3 ALL
**Pledges**
  Harass the: 4 HAZE
**Pleiades**
  Father of the: 5 ATLAS
  number: 5 SEVEN
  One of the: 4 MAIA
  pursuer: 5 ORION
**Pleistocene:** 5 EPOCH
  beast: 7 MAMMOTH
  epoch: 6 ICEAGE
**Plentiful:** 4 RIFE 5 AMPLE
  Be: 6 ABOUND
**Plenty:** 4 ALOT ATON GOBS
    LOTS TONS 6 OODLES
    8 OPULENCE
  angry: 4 SORE
  Biblical place of: 6 GOSHEN
  Goddess of: 3 OPS
  loud: 5 AROAR
  mad: 4 IRED
  of: 5 AMPLE
  of yore: 4 ENOW
  ~, slangily: 4 ENUF
**"___ Plenty o' Nuttin'"**
    **(Gershwin song):** 4 IGOT
**Plexiglas:** 7 POLYMER
**Plexus**
  Word before: 5 SOLAR
**Pliable:** 5 WAXEN
  leather: 3 ELK
**Plied**
  with port: 5 WINED
**Pliers**
  Kind of: 10 NEEDLENOSE

**Plies**
  a needle: 4 SEWS
**Plight:** 4 MESS
**Plimpton, George**
  1982 ~ bestseller: 4 EDIE
**Pliny the ___:** 5 ELDER
**PLO**
  Arafat of the: 5 YASIR
    6 YASSER
  Former ~ leader: 6 ARAFAT
**Plod**
  along: 4 SLOG 6 TRUDGE
**Plop**
  down: 3 SIT
  prefix: 3 KER
**Plot:** 4 PLAN 5 CABAL TRACT
    6 SCHEME
  Devise, as a: 5 HATCH
  in the suburbs: 4 LAWN
  of land: 4 ACRE 5 TRACT
  outline: 8 SCENARIO
  over: 5 REMAP
  part: 4 ACRE 5 TWIST
  Perfect: 4 EDEN
  Shady: 5 ARBOR
  unit: 4 ACRE
**Plotter**
  Globe: 4 IAGO
**Plotters:** 5 CABAL
**Plotting:** 4 UPTO
  group: 5 CABAL
**"Plough and the Stars, The"**
  playwright: 6 OCASEY
**Plow:** 4 TILL
  Hitch to a: 4 YOKE
  into: 3 RAM
  maker: 5 DEERE
  pioneer: 5 DEERE
  Pull a: 4 TILL
  pullers: 4 OXEN TEAM
  Reason to: 4 SNOW
**Plowshares**
  Beat swords into: 5 UNARM
**Ploy:** 4 RUSE TRAP 6 GAMBIT
    TACTIC
  Marketing: 4 TEST 5 TIEIN
  Poker: 5 BLUFF RAISE
**Pluck:** 4 GRIT 5 MOXIE SPUNK
    6 METTLE SPIRIT
  out: 6 TWEEZE
  Ready to: 4 RIPE
**Plucked**
  instrument: 3 UKE 4 HARP
    LYRE
**Plucky:** 4 GAME 5 BRAVE
**Plug:** 4 TOUT 5 DAMUP
    PROMO
  away: 4 SLOG TOIL
  of tobacco: 4 CHAW
  part: 5 PRONG
  Pull the ~ on: 3 END 4 STOP
  suffix: 3 OLA
  up: 4 FILL
**Plugging**
  away: 4 ATIT
**Plugs:** 3 ADS

**Plum:** 3 HUE 4 TREE 5 COLOR
  center: 3 PIT
  Dried: 5 PRUNE
  Exec: 4 PERK
  finder of rhyme: 6 HORNER
  pudding ingredient: 4 SUET
  relative: 7 MAGENTA
  Tart: 4 SLOE
  variety: 4 GAGE SLOE
    6 DAMSON
  wild: 4 SLOE
**Plumb**
  Actress: 3 EVE
  crazy: 4 LOCO
**Plumb ___:** 4 LOCO
**Plumber**
  Good name for a: 3 FLO
  Job for a: 4 DRIP LEAK
  joint: 3 ELL TEE
  tool: 5 SNAKE
**Plumbing**
  convenience:
    12 RUNNINGWATER
  joint: 3 ELL
  Kind of: 6 INDOOR
  problem: 4 CLOG DRIP LEAK
**Plume**
  owner: 5 TANTE
  source: 5 EGRET
  ___ plume: 5 NOMDE
**Plumed**
  hat: 5 SHAKO
  heron: 5 EGRET
  wader: 5 EGRET
**Plumlike**
  fruit: 4 SLOE
**Plummer**
  Actress: 6 AMANDA
**Plummet:** 4 DIVE DROP FALL
    8 NOSEDIVE
**Plump**
  and then some: 5 OBESE
**Plunder:** 3 ROB 4 LOOT SACK
    SWAG 5 BOOTY RIFLE
    6 MARAUD RAVAGE
  ~, old-style: 5 REAVE
**Plundered**
  ~, old-style: 4 REFT
**Plunderer**
  take: 4 SWAG
**Plunge:** 4 DIVE DROP
  Take the: 3 WED
  Took the: 4 DOVE 5 LEAPT
**Plunk**
  (down): 3 PUT
  preceder: 3 KER
**Pluperfect:** 5 TENSE
**Plural**
  suffix: 3 IES 4 EERS
**Pluralized**
  ~ Y: 3 IES
**Pluralizing**
  letter: 3 ESS
**Plus:** 3 AND 4 ALSO 5 ASSET
  item: 5 ASSET
  others (abbr.): 4 ETAL

**Pluses and minuses**
  It has: 4 MATH
  They have their: 4 IONS
**Plus-size**
  model: 4 EMME
**Plutarch**
  subject: 4 CATO
**Pluto**
  and others: 4 GODS
  ender: 4 CRAT
  realm: 5 HADES
**Plutocrat**
  backer: 6 FATCAT
**Pluvial:** 3 WET 5 RAINY
**Ply:** 3 USE 5 LAYER
  the seas: 4 SAIL
  with a feast: 6 REGALE
**Plymouth**
  1970s ~: 6 DUSTER
  pilgrim: 5 ALDEN
    8 STANDISH
  Standish of: 5 MILES MYLES
**Plymouth Reliant:** 4 KCAR
**Plywood**
  feature: 6 VENEER
  section: 5 PANEL
**P.M.**
  4 ~: 7 TEATIME
  11 ~, to some: 7 BEDTIME
  British ~ Douglas-Home:
    4 ALEC
  British ~ educator: 4 ETON
  British ~ Tony: 5 BLAIR
  Early: 3 AFT
  First Burmese: 3 UNU
  First Indian: 5 NEHRU
  Former British: 4 EDEN PITT
    8 DISRAELI
  Former Greek ~ Papandreou:
    7 ANDREAS
  Former Irish ~ Cosgrave:
    4 LIAM
  Former Israeli: 4 MEIR
  Former Italian: 4 MORO
  Former Japanese: 4 SATO
  Former Swedish ~ Palme:
    4 OLOF
  times: 4 AFTS
**Pmt.**
  Bank: 3 INT
  Homeowner: 4 MTGE
  Loan: 3 INT
  Proof of: 4 RCPT
  Security: 3 DEP
**Pneumo**
  What ~ means: 4 LUNG
**Po**
  City on the: 5 TURIN
  land: 5 ITALY
**P.O.**
  assignment: 3 RTE
  piece: 3 LTR
**Poached**
  edibles: 4 EGGS
**Poacher**
  meal: 4 EGGS

nemesis: **10** GAMEWARDEN
**Pocahontas**
  Husband of: **5** ROLFE
**Pocatello**
  state: **5** IDAHO
**Pocket: 5** STEAL
  bread: **4** PITA
  change sound: **6** JINGLE
  Edible: **4** PITA
  money: **4** CASH
  problem: **4** HOLE
  residue: **4** LINT
  Watch: **3** FOB
**Pocket Books**
  logo: **8** KANGAROO
**Pocketful**
  Golfer: **4** TEES
  Nursery rhyme: **3** RYE
**"Pocketful of Miracles"**
  director: **5** CAPRA
**Pocket protector**
  item: **3** PEN
  wearer: **4** NERD
**Pockets**
  Like rich: **4** DEEP
  Pasta with: **7** RAVIOLI
  They're found in: **4** ORES
**Pod**
  Cotton: **4** BOLL
  Edible: **5** CAROB
  member: **5** WHALE
  prefix: **3** TRI
  veggie: **3** PEA **4** OKRA
    **8** SNAPBEAN
**Podiatrist**
  case: **5** CORNS
**Podium**
  Take the: **5** ORATE
  ___ podrida: **4** OLLA
**Poe**
  family: **5** USHER
  Like ~ works: **5** EERIE
  maiden: **6** LENORE
    **7** ANNABEL
  middle name: **5** ALLAN
  poem: **6** LENORE **7** ULALUME
    **8** THEBELLS THERAVEN
    **9** TAMERLANE
  story setting: **3** PIT
  visitor: **5** RAVEN
**Poe, ___ Allan: 5** EDGAR
**Poe, Edgar ___: 5** ALLAN
**Poem: 5** VERSE
  14-line ~: **6** RONDEL
    SONNET
  Classic: **5** EPODE
  final stanza: **5** ENVOI
  Holiday ~ opener: **4** TWAS
  Inspired: **3** ODE
  Kind of: **3** ODE
  Long: **4** EPIC
  Love ~ of 1849:
    **10** ANNABELLEE
  Lyric: **3** ODE **5** EPODE
  Mournful: **5** ELEGY
  Mystical: **4** RUNE

of 24 books: **5** ILIAD
of homage: **3** ODE
of lament: **5** ELEGY
Old Testament: **5** PSALM
part: **5** CANTO VERSE
  **6** STANZA
Pastoral: **4** IDYL **5** IDYLL
Plaintive: **5** ELEGY
Praiseful: **3** ODE
Sacred: **5** PSALM
Short: **6** RONDEL
Six-line: **6** SESTET
Symphonic ~ creator: **5** LISZT
with 17 syllables: **5** HAIKU
with a punch line: **8** LIMERICK
**"... poem lovely as ___":**
    **5** ATREE
**Poet: 4** BARD
  1948 Pulitzer Prize: **5** AUDEN
  Chilean: **6** NERUDA
  Chinese: **4** LIPO
  Classical lyric: **6** SAPPHO
    **8** ANACREON
  concern: **5** METER
  contraction: **3** EEN TIL TIS
  English: **4** TATE **5** KEATS
  eye: **3** ORB
  foot: **4** IAMB
  Indian: **6** TAGORE
  Irish: **5** YEATS
  Italian: **5** TASSO
  laureate: *see page 725*
  laureate Nicholas: **4** ROWE
  laureate of 1692: **4** TATE
  Lyric: **4** BARD **5** ODIST
  Metaphysical: **5** DONEN
  monogram: **3** TSE
  muse: **5** ERATO
  pause: **7** CAESURA
  Persian: **4** OMAR
  preposition: **3** ERE OER
    **5** ANEAR
  Roman: **4** OVID
  suffix: **4** ICAL
  ~ Crane: **4** HART
  ~ Federico García: **5** LORCA
  ~ Heinrich: **5** HEINE
  ~ Mark Van: **5** DOREN
  ~ Nahum: **4** TATE
  ~ Ogden: **4** NASH
  ~ Stephen Vincent: **5** BENET
  ~ T.S.: **5** ELIOT
  ~ W.H.: **5** AUDEN
**Poetic**
  adverb: **3** EEN EER OFT
    **4** ANON NEER
  conjunction: **3** ERE
  contraction: **3** EEN EER OER
    TIS **4** NEER
  Exaltedly: **4** ODIC
  foot: **4** IAMB
  form: **3** ODE
  It may be: **7** LICENSE
  preposition: **3** ERE OER
  pugilist: **3** ALI
  time: **3** EEN **4** MORN

tribute: **3** ODE
verb: **3** OPE
  ~ Muse: **5** ERATO
**"___ Poetica" (Horace poem):**
    **3** ARS
**Poet laureate:** *see page 725*
  ~ Hughes: **3** TED
  ~ Nahum: **4** TATE
  ~ Nicholas: **4** ROWE
**Poetry: 5** VERSE
  fight: **4** SLAM
  Icelandic: **4** EDDA
  Land of: **4** ERIN
  Muse of: **5** ERATO
  Norse ~ collection: **4** EDDA
  Oral: **4** EPOS
**"___ Poets Society": 4** DEAD
**Pogo: 6** POSSUM **7** OPOSSUM
  cartoonist Kelly: **4** WALT
**Pogs: 3** FAD
**Poi**
  party: **4** LUAU
  source: **4** TARO
**Point: 3** AIM DOT NIB USE
    **4** CRUX GIST ITEM
    NODE TINE
  a finger at: **5** BLAME
    **6** ACCUSE
  after deuce: **4** ADIN
  At any: **4** EVER
  At that: **4** THEN
  at the dinner table: **4** TINE
  At this: **4** HERE
  Ball: **3** TEE
  Break: **5** ADOUT
  Central: **4** CRUX GIST NODE
    **5** MIDST NAVEL
  Come to a: **5** TAPER
  Connecting: **4** NODE
  Crisis: **4** HEAD
  Decimal: **3** DOT
  Drop-off: **4** EDGE
  Fine: **6** DETAIL NICETY
  Focal: **3** HUB **4** NODE
    **9** EPICENTER
  Get the: **3** SEE
  Get to the: **5** TAPER
  Good: **5** ASSET
  Highest: **3** TOP **4** ACME APEX
    **5** CREST **6** APOGEE
    ZENITH **7** EVEREST
  in the right direction:
    **6** ORIENT
  It ends in a: **5** FABLE
  Junction: **4** NODE
  Kind of: **5** FOCAL
  Lookout: **5** AERIE
  Lowest: **5** NADIR
  Made a: **6** SCORED
  Main: **4** CRUX GIST
  Make a: **5** TAPER
  More to the: **6** TERSER
  Needle: **3** ENE ESE **4** EAST
    **5** NORTH
  of decline: **3** EBB
  of no return: **3** ACE

of view: **5** ANGLE SLANT
   STAND
Orbital: **4** NODE **5** APSIS
   **6** APOGEE **7** PERIGEE
Orbital high: **6** APOGEE
out: **7** MENTION
   **15** CALLATTENTIONTO
Overflow: **3** RIM
Perspiration: **4** PORE
Pivotal: **4** CRUX
Regarding this: **6** HERETO
Selling: **5** ASSET KIOSK
   STORE
Starting: **4** GERM **6** ORIGIN
Sticking: **4** CRAW TINE
Strong: **5** ASSET FORTE
Talking: **3** JAW **5** TOPIC
To the: **3** APT **5** PITHY
   TERSE
To this: **3** YET **5** ASYET
   SOFAR
Turning: **4** AXIS AXLE EDDY
   **5** HINGE PIVOT **6** CRISIS
Up to this: **3** YET **5** ASYET
**___ point**
   (never): **4** ATNO
   (somewhat): **5** UPTOA
   (stitch): **4** GROS
**"___ Pointe Blank" (John**
   **Cusack film): 6** GROSSE
**Pointed: 5** SHARP **6** ACUATE
   arch: **4** OGEE **5** OGIVE
   beard: **6** GOATEE
   end: **3** NIB
   remark: **4** BARB
   tool: **3** AWL
**Pointer: 3** TIP **5** ARROW
   **11** INDEXFINGER
   Finger: **7** ACCUSER
   West: **5** CADET
   word: **4** THAT
**Pointer Sisters**
   hit: **6** DAREME **8** HESSOSHY
   One of the: **5** ANITA
**Pointillist**
   painter Georges: **6** SEURAT
   point: **3** DOT
**Pointless: 5** INANE NOUSE
   **6** FUTILE OTIOSE
   event: **4** EPEE
**Point ___ return: 4** OFNO
**Points: 4** FOCI
   High: **6** APICES
**Pointy**
   beard: **6** GOATEE
   shoe wearer: **3** ELF
**Poirot**
   Hercule: **6** SLEUTH
   job: **4** CASE
   portrayer: **7** USTINOV
**Poise: 6** APLOMB
**Poison: 4** BANE **5** TOXIN
   Arrow: **4** INEE **6** CURARE
   checker: **6** TASTER
   conduit: **4** FANG
   Snake: **5** VENOM

**Poison ___: 3** OAK **5** SUMAC
**Poisoner**
   of Britannicus: **4** NERO
**Poison ivy**
   relative: **5** SUMAC
   symptom: **4** ITCH RASH
**Poison Ivy**
   portrayer: **3** UMA
**Poisonous: 5** TOXIC
   plant: **5** SUMAC **7** HENBANE
   **8** OLEANDER
   snake: **3** ASP **5** VIPER
**Poitier**
   Actor: **6** SIDNEY
   film: **15** ARAISININTHESUN
   role: **3** SIR **5** TIBBS
**Poitiers**
   pal: **3** AMI
**Poivre**
   Partner of: **3** SEL
**Poke: 3** JAB **4** GOAD PROD
   **5** NUDGE
   around: **5** SNOOP
   fun at: **3** KID RIB **4** MOCK
   TWIT **5** TEASE **6** NEEDLE
   holes in: **4** STAB
   Sharp: **3** JAB
   with a pin: **5** PRICK
**Pokémon: 3** FAD
**Poker**
   action: **3** BET **4** CALL
   buy-in: **4** ANTE
   card: **3** ACE **4** TREY **5** DEUCE
   declaration: **4** IMIN **5** ICALL
   IFOLD **6** IRAISE
   dream: **10** ROYALFLUSH
   fee: **4** ANTE
   holding: **4** PAIR
   Match in: **3** SEE
   Maximum ~ bet: **5** ALLIN
   payment: **4** ANTE
   phrase: **4** IMIN **5** ICALL
   **6** IRAISE
   player: **6** RAISER
   **8** GAMESTER
   prize: **3** POT
   stake: **4** ANTE
   starter: **4** ANTE
   strategy: **5** BLUFF RAISE
   Stud: **4** SPUR
   token: **4** CHIP
   variety: **4** DRAW STUD
   winnings: **4** POTS
**Poker Flat**
   creator: **5** HARTE
**Poky: 3** CAN JUG **4** SLOW
   STIR
**Pol**
   backer: **6** FATCAT
   Certain: **3** DEM
   concern: **5** IMAGE
   D.C.: **3** SEN
   Minor: **6** HEELER
**Pol.**
   neighbor: **3** GER **4** LITH
   Old ~ division: **3** SSR

**Pola**
   of the silents: **5** NEGRI
**Poland**
   capital: **6** WARSAW
   Gp. joined by: **4** NATO
   Lech of: **6** WALESA
   river: **4** ODER
   Walesa of: **4** LECH
**Poland Spring**
   rival: **5** EVIAN
**Polanski**
   Director: **5** ROMAN
   film: **4** TESS
**Polar: 6** ARCTIC
   buildup: **6** ICECAP
   crew: **5** ELVES
   explorer: **4** BYRD
   feature: **6** ICECAP
   formation: **6** ICECAP
   **8** ICESHEET
   jacket: **6** ANORAK
   worker: **3** ELF
**Polaris: 4** STAR
   place: **9** URSAMINOR
**Polaroid: 4** SNAP
**Pole: 4** SLAV **8** EUROPEAN
   Carved: **5** TOTEM
   Climb a: **4** SHIN
   Fishing: **3** ROD
   Fowl: **5** ROOST
   image: **5** TOTEM
   Indian: **5** TOTEM
   Kind of: **5** TOTEM
   length: **7** TENFEET
   Nautical: **4** MAST SPAR
   **5** SPRIT
   Positive: **5** ANODE
   seeker of 1909: **5** PEARY
   star: **5** CLAUS SANTA
   tossed by Scots: **5** CABER
   Toward Santa's: **5** NORTH
   Used a firehouse: **4** SLID
   vault: **5** EVENT
   vault unit: **5** ZLOTY
   worker: **3** ELF
**___ Pole: 5** TOTEM
**Polecat**
   defense: **4** ODOR
   kin: **6** FERRET
**Pole Position**
   company: **5** ATARI
**Poles**
   Chair on: **5** SEDAN
   Flattened at the: **6** OBLATE
   with footrests: **6** STILTS
**Pole-to-pole**
   line: **4** AXIS
**Poli ___: 3** SCI
**Police: 4** COPS
   1980s TV ~ comedy: **4** ENOS
   action: **4** RAID **6** ARREST
   **8** STAKEOUT
   alert (abbr.): **3** APB
   area: **8** PRECINCT
   blotter entry: **3** AKA **5** ALIAS
   car warning: **5** SIREN

cry: 4 RAID 6 OPENUP
dept. employee: 3 DET
Former East German secret:
    5 STASI
Half a TV ~ duo: 5 LACEY
informer: 7 STOOLIE
    11 STOOLPIGEON
line: 6 CORDON
round: 6 PATROL
search: 7 DRAGNET
team: 4 SWAT
The ~, e.g.: 4 TRIO
WWII USSR secret: 4 NKGB
~, with "the": 3 LAW
**Policeman:** 3 COP
British: 5 BOBBY
insignia: 5 BADGE
patrol: 4 BEAT
**"Police Woman"**
Dickinson of: 5 ANGIE
**Policy**
1970s Nixon ~: 7 DETENTE
Get a: 6 INSURE
gurus: 5 WONKS
opposer: 4 ANTI
position: 5 STAND
reversal: 5 UTURN
    8 FLIPFLOP
Words before: 3 ASA
**Polio**
vaccine developer: 4 SALK
    5 SABIN
**Polish:** 4 BUFF EDIT 5 SHINE
Former ~ capital: 6 KRAKOW
Furniture ~ scent: 5 LEMON
language: 4 EDIT
locale: 4 NAIL
Nail: 6 ENAMEL
Nail ~ brand: 5 CUTEX
off: 3 EAT
Partner of: 4 SPIT
prose: 4 EDIT
remover: 7 ACETONE
river: 4 ODER
sausage: 8 KIELBASA
seaport: 6 GDANSK
Shoe ~ brand: 4 KIWI
    7 SHINOLA
**Polished:** 5 ADEPT SLEEK
    SUAVE 6 SMOOTH
    URBANE 7 ELEGANT
It may be: 4 RICE
off: 3 ATE 5 EATEN
**Polishing**
agent: 5 EMERY
**"Polish Wedding"**
star: 4 OLIN
**Polit.**
label: 3 IND
Old ~ cause: 3 ERA
**Polite:** 5 CIVIL
address: 3 SIR 4 MAAM
    5 MADAM
Far from: 4 RUDE
interruption: 4 AHEM
refusal: 5 NOSIR 6 NOMAAM

response: 7 YESMAAM
Start of a ~ offer:
    9 IFYOUWISH
**Politely**
Ax: 7 EASEOUT
Tip: 4 DOFF
**Political**
1958–71 ~ inits.: 3 UAR
buff channel: 5 CSPAN
cartoonist Thomas: 4 NAST
faction: 4 BLOC
Former ~ divs.: 4 SSRS
funny business: 5 GRAFT
group: 4 CAMP 5 BLOCK
    PARTY
housecleaning: 5 PURGE
influence: 5 CLOUT
intrigue: 5 CABAL
Israeli ~ party: 5 LIKUD
mascot creator: 4 NAST
Occasional suffix on ~ titles:
    5 ELECT
Ohio ~ name: 4 TAFT
pamphlet: 5 TRACT
power structure: 7 APPARAT
prefix: 3 GEO
refugee: 6 EMIGRE
satirist Mort: 4 SAHL
scandal: 6 ABSCAM
slant: 4 SPIN
suffix: 3 IST 4 CRAT
ticket: 5 SLATE
Type of ~ campaign: 5 SMEAR
Wealthy ~ patron: 6 FATCAT
~ VIP: 4 BOSS
**Politically**
incorrect suffix: 4 ETTE
moderate:
    15 MIDDLEOFTHEROAD
neutral sort: 7 MUGWUMP
**"Politically Incorrect"**
host Bill: 5 MAHER
**Politician**
concern: 5 IMAGE
~ Alexander: 5 LAMAR
~ Bob: 4 DOLE
**Politico**
Elected (plural): 3 INS
Nasty: 7 SMEARER
~ Alexander: 5 LAMAR
~ Morris or Stewart:
    5 UDALL
**Politics**
Big name in Chicago: 5 DALEY
First name in Mideast:
    5 YASIR
Long in: 4 HUEY
prefix: 3 GEO
Root of: 5 ELIHU
**Politique**
Division: 4 ETAT
**Polk**
1844 loser to: 4 CLAY
middle name: 4 KNOX
President after: 6 TAYLOR
President before: 5 TYLER

**Poll**
amt.: 3 PCT
category: 5 OTHER
    9 UNDECIDED
finding: 5 TREND
Kind of: 4 EXIT 5 STRAW
suffix: 4 STER
**Pollack**
Director: 3 SYD
kin: 3 COD
**Pollen**
gatherer: 3 BEE
producer: 6 STAMEN
React to: 6 SNEEZE
**Pollen-bearing**
part: 6 ANTHER STAMEN
**Pollinator**
Fig: 4 WASP
**Polliwog**
Adult: 4 TOAD
place: 4 POND
**Pollock**
cousin: 3 COD
Paint like: 7 SPATTER
**"Pollock"**
actress Amy: 7 MADIGAN
**Pollock, Jackson**
player: 8 EDHARRIS
___ polloi: 3 HOI
**Polls**
Big name in: 5 ROPER
Gain in the: 5 SURGE
**Pollster**
discovery: 5 TREND
~ Roper: 4 ELMO
**Pollutant:** 3 ASH
Banned: 3 PCB
Chem.: 3 PCB
**Pollute:** 5 TAINT 6 DEFILE
**Pollution**
Air: 4 SMOG 5 SMAZE
Kind of: 5 NOISE
monitoring org.: 3 EPA
problem: 4 SMOG
**Pollux**
Mother of: 4 LEDA
Twin of: 6 CASTOR
**Polly:** 4 AUNT
Nephew of Aunt ~: 3 TOM
~, to Tom Sawyer: 4 AUNT
**"Pollyanna"**
author Porter: 7 ELEANOR
**Polo:** 5 SHIRT
Actress: 4 TERI
animal: 4 PONY
competitor: 4 IZOD
Explorer: 5 MARCO
grounds: 4 ASIA
homeland: 5 ITALY
in China: 5 MARCO
period: 7 CHUKKER
**Polo, Marco**
crossed it: 4 ASIA
**Polo Grounds**
legend: 3 OTT
team: 6 GIANTS

**Polonaise**
composer: 6 CHOPIN
**Polonius**
Daughter of: 7 OPHELIA
Hiding place for: 5 ARRAS
Son of: 7 LAERTES
**Poltergeist:** 6 SPIRIT
**Poly**
finish: 5 ESTER
kin: 5 MULTI
**Poly ___ (college major):** 3 SCI
**___ Poly (West Coast school):**
3 CAL
**Polyester**
brand: 6 DACRON
film brand: 5 MYLAR
**Polygon**
measurement: 4 AREA
**Polygonal**
recess: 4 APSE
**Polygraph**
test failer: 4 LIAR
wave, maybe: 3 LIE
**Polyhymnia:** 4 MUSE
Sister of: 5 ERATO
**Polynesian**
drink: 4 KAVA
First man, in ~ myth. 4 TIKI
food: 4 TARO
idol: 4 TIKI
kingdom: 5 TONGA
language: 5 MAORI
paste: 3 POI
pendant: 4 TIKI
porch: 5 LANAI
treat: 11 PUPUPLATTER
**Polyp**
Flowerlike: 7 ANEMONE
10 SEAANEMONE
**Polyphemus**
Odysseus, to: 5 NOMAN
**Polyphonic**
piece: 5 MOTET
**___ Polytechnique:** 5 ECOLE
**Polytheist:** 5 PAGAN
**Pom**
alternative: 4 PEKE
**Pomade**
relative: 3 GEL
**Pomegranate**
Like a: 5 SEEDY
**Pomeranian:** 6 LAPDOG
variety: 5 SPITZ
**Pomme de ___ (potato):**
5 TERRE
**Pomp:** 5 ECLAT
Proclaim with: 5 ORATE
**"Pomp and Circumstance"**
composer: 5 ELGAR
**Pompano**
relative: 4 SCAD
**Pompeii**
attraction: 5 RUINS
burier: 3 ASH 4 LAVA
City near: 6 NAPLES

heroine: 4 IONE
**Pompey the Great**
Supporter of: 6 CICERO
**Pompom**
Hat with a: 3 TAM
**Pompous**
people: 5 ASSES
sort: 3 ASS
walk: 5 STRUT
**Pompously**
Speak: 5 ORATE
**Ponce ___:** 6 DELEON
**Ponce de ___:** 4 LEON
**Ponch**
Erik who played ~ on TV:
7 ESTRADA
**Poncho**
relative: 6 SERAPE
**Pond**
denizen: 3 EFT 4 NEWT TOAD
Down at the: 5 EIDER
duck: 4 TEAL
film: 4 SCUM
fish: 4 CARP
floater: 4 ALGA
greenery: 5 ALGAE
High: 4 TARN
Like some ~ life: 5 ALGAL
plant: 4 ALGA
Poetic: 4 MERE
scum: 5 ALGAE
sound: 5 CROAK
swimmer: 4 TEAL
youngster: 3 EFT
**Ponder:** 4 MULL MUSE
5 BROOD WEIGH
8 COGITATE
**Ponderosa:** 6 SPREAD
son: 4 HOSS
**Pong**
maker: 5 ATARI
**Pongid**
Certain: 5 ORANG
**Ponied**
up: 6 AHORSE
**Ponies**
Place to play the ~ (abbr.):
3 OTB
Play the: 3 BET
**Pons**
delivery: 4 ARIA
**Ponselle**
Soprano: 4 ROSA
**Ponta Delgada**
locale: 6 AZORES
**Pont ___ Arts:** 3 DES
**Ponte Vecchio**
river: 4 ARNO
Water under the: 4 ARNO
**Ponti**
Director: 5 CARLO
Wife of: 5 LOREN
**Pontiac**
model: 3 GTO 5 FIERO
7 GRANDAM
Old ~ model: 3 GTO

place (abbr.): 4 MICH
tribe: 6 OTTAWA
**Pontifical:** 5 PAPAL
**Pontificate:** 5 ORATE
**Ponty, Jean-___**
Violinist: 3 LUC
**Pony**
American Indian: 6 CAYUSE
pace: 4 GAIT TROT
player's loc.: 3 OTB
prodder: 4 SPUR
up: 3 PAY
**Pony Express**
employee: 5 RIDER
stop: 4 ELKO
**Ponzi**
scheme: 4 SCAM
**Pooch:** 3 DOG 6 DOGGIE
Big: 3 LAB
Comics: 4 ODIE
Generic: 4 FIDO
Inge: 5 SHEBA
Movie: 4 ASTA
Nickelodeon: 3 REN
Oz: 4 TOTO
Primer: 4 SPOT
Silky-coated: 7 SPANIEL
Snorkel: 4 OTTO
Toon: 3 REN
White House: 4 FALA
**Poodle:** 3 DOG PET
Kind of: 3 TOY
name: 4 FIFI
**Pooh:** 3 BAH 4 BEAR
creator: 5 MILNE
7 AAMILNE
Greeting from: 5 HALLO
pal: 3 ROO 5 KANGA
6 EEYORE PIGLET
TIGGER
**Pooh-bah**
Mideast: 4 AGHA EMIR
Persian: 4 SHAH
**Pooh-pooh:** 5 DECRY SCOFF
6 DERIDE 7 SCOFFAT
SNEERAT
**Pool**
accessory: 3 CUE 4 RACK
5 CHALK
color: 4 AQUA
contents: 5 GENES
distance: 3 LAP
division: 4 LANE
Fix a ~ cue: 5 RETIP
Get in a: 3 BET
Gone across a: 4 SWUM
Kind of: 4 GENE 5 STENO
life: 4 ALGA
Like one end of the: 4 DEEP
member: 5 STENO
Mountain: 4 TARN
Part of a: 4 GENE
party: 5 STENO
Play in the: 6 SPLASH
problem: 5 ALGAE
shot: 5 CAROM MASSE

site: 4 YMCA
stick: 3 CUE
stroke: 5 MASSE
tester: 3 TOE
Toddler in a: 5 WADER
tool: 3 CUE
Type of: 7 SNOOKER
worker: 5 STENO
**Poolroom**
cube: 5 CHALK
ploy: 5 MASSE
stick: 3 CUE
triangle: 4 RACK
**Pools**
Like some: 6 HEATED
   INDOOR
They're in: 5 GENES
**Poolside**
enclosure: 6 CABANA
**Pool table**
feature: 8 SLATEBED
material: 4 FELT
rim: 4 RAIL
**Poona**
place: 5 INDIA
**Poop:** 4 INFO
out: 4 TIRE
**Pooped:** 4 BEAT 5 ALLIN
   WEARY
person's cry: 6 IMBEAT
___ pooped to pop: 3 TOO
**Poor:** 5 NEEDY 6 INNEED
blokes: 4 SODS
dog's portion: 4 NONE
grade: 3 DEE
Like ~ losers: 4 SORE
Like a ~ excuse: 4 LAME
mark: 3 DEE
Money for the: 4 ALMS
movie rating: 7 ONESTAR
woodcutter of folklore:
   7 ALIBABA
**Poor box**
filler: 4 ALMS
___ poor example: 4 SETA
**Poorhouse**
In the: 5 NEEDY
**"Poor Little Fool"**
singer: 11 RICKYNELSON
**Poorly:** 3 ILL
behaved: 3 BAD
Do: 3 AIL
Feel: 3 AIL
Feeling: 3 ILL
kept: 5 SEEDY
lit: 3 DIM
performed: 4 LAME
Treat: 5 ABUSE
**"Poor me!":** 4 ALAS
**"Poor Poor Pitiful Me"**
singer Clark: 5 TERRI
**Poor Richard:** 3 BEN
book: 7 ALMANAC
**"Poor Richard's Almanack"**
tidbit: 5 ADAGE
"___, poor Yorick!": 4 ALAS

**Pop:** 3 DAD 4 SODA 5 DADDY
   6 PARENT
A: 3 PER 4 EACH
Bro of: 3 UNC
Classic: 4 NEHI
Fasten with a: 6 SNAPON
flavor: 4 COLA
follower: 3 ART
hero: 4 IDOL
Jamaican: 3 SKA
John of: 5 ELTON
King of: 6 CAROLE
maker: 6 WEASEL
Mama of: 4 CASS
measure: 5 LITER
Open with a: 6 UNSNAP
Partner of: 3 MOM
Popular: 4 COLA
quiz: 4 TEST
Radar's: 4 NEHI
Singer: 4 IGGY
Sir of: 5 ELTON
star: 4 IDOL
stars, often: 9 TEENIDOLS
the question: 3 ASK
They may ~ up: 3 ADS
up: 5 ARISE 6 APPEAR
Word with: 3 ART
**Popcorn**
additive: 4 SALT
How some ~ is popped:
   5 INAIR
**Pope:** *see pages 726–728*
5th-century: 4 LEOI 5 STLEO
7th-century ~: 5 LEOII
10th-century ~: 5 LEOVI
after Marcellus II: 6 PAULIV
cape: 5 ORALE
from 440 to 461: 4 LEOI
nicknamed "the Great": 4 LEOI
of 1605: 5 LEOXI
output: 4 POEM 5 ESSAY
who persuaded Attila not to
   attack Rome: 4 LEOI
   5 STLEO
**Pope, Alexander**
piece: 5 ESSAY
**Popeil**
of infomercials: 3 RON
**Pope John Paul II**
first name: 5 KAROL
**Pope John XXIII**
first name: 6 ANGELO
**Popes**
First of 13: 4 LEOI
Name of 6: 6 ADRIAN
Name of 8: 5 URBAN
Name of 12: 4 PIUS
Name of 13: 3 LEO
**Popeye:** 6 SAILOR
creator Elzie: 5 SEGAR
Olive of: 3 OYL
phrase: 4 IYAM
power source: 7 SPINACH
rival: 5 BLUTO
Son of: 7 SWEEPEA

sweetie: 5 OLIVE 8 OLIVEOYL
tattoo: 6 ANCHOR
tooter: 4 PIPE
verb: 3 YAM
~, to Pipeye: 5 UNCLE
**Popeyed:** 4 AGOG
**Popinjay:** 3 FOP
**Poplar:** 5 ASPEN
Southwestern: 5 ALAMO
White: 5 ABELE
**Poppaea**
Husband of: 4 NERO
**Popped:** 5 BURST
up: 5 AROSE 6 ARISEN
**Popper**
of song: 6 WEASEL
Party: 4 CORK
**Poppy**
derivative: 6 OPIATE
product: 5 OPIUM
**Poppycock:** 3 ROT 5 BILGE
   HOOEY
**"Poppycock!":** 3 BAH 4 BOSH
**Poppycockish:** 5 INANE
**Pops:** 3 PAS
(abbr.): 3 SRS
**Popsicle**
flavor: 6 ORANGE
**Pop singer**
~ Leo: 5 SAYER
~ Taylor: 5 DAYNE
~ Tori: 4 AMOS
**Popular:** 3 BIG HOT 5 LOVED
Extremely: 3 HOT 4 HUGE
   6 REDHOT
No longer: 3 OUT
Not a ~ type: 4 NERD
resort: 3 RIO
sauce: 4 RAGU
side: 4 SLAW
toast: 3 RYE
___ populi: 3 VOX
**Populous**
area: 3 URB
**Pop-up**
breakfast brand: 4 EGGO
nuisances: 3 ADS
Word after: 4 MENU
**Pop-ups:** 3 ADS
**Porcelain**
Fine: 9 BONECHINA
Japanese: 5 IMARI
making dynasty: 4 MING
pitcher: 4 EWER
Some English: 5 SPODE
**Porch:** 7 VERANDA
Ancient: 4 STOA
Polynesian: 5 LANAI
**Porches**
Glassed-in: 7 SOLARIA
**Porcine**
pad: 3 STY
reply: 4 OINK
title role: 4 BABE
**Porcupine:** 6 RODENT
barb: 5 QUILL SPINE

**Pore**
Leaf: 5 STOMA
over: 4 READ
**Pores**
Plant: 7 STOMATA
**Porfirio**
Mexican dictator: 4 DIAZ
**Porgy:** 4 FISH
Love of: 4 BESS
variety: 4 SCUP
**"Porgy and Bess":** 5 OPERA
**Pork:** 4 MEAT
cut: 4 CHOP LOIN
place: 3 STY
Preserve: 4 SALT
**Pork-barreler:** 3 POL
**Porker**
in pictures: 4 BABE
Mother: 3 SOW
place: 3 STY
plaint: 4 OINK
**Porkpie:** 3 HAT
feature: 4 BRIM
**Porky:** 3 PIG 4 TOON
Love of: 7 PETUNIA
Voice of: 3 MEL
**Porn:** 4 SMUT
**Porous:** 5 LEAKY
**Porridge**
Bear with cold: 4 MAMA
Buckwheat: 5 KASHA
ingredient: 3 OAT
Like some ~, to Goldilocks:
6 TOOHOT
Thin: 5 GRUEL
___ porridge: 5 PEASE
"___ Porridge Hot": 5 PEASE
**Porsche**
Old ~ model: 6 SPYDER
**Port**
alternative: 7 MADEIRA
Any ~ in a storm: 5 HAVEN
Israel: 5 EILAT
Leave: 4 SAIL 7 SETSAIL
of Algeria: 4 ORAN
of Brazil: 5 BELEM
of Crete: 5 CANEA
of Iraq: 5 BASRA
of Okinawa: 4 NAHA
of Phoenicia: 5 SIDON
of Yemen: 4 ADEN
Old Rome: 5 OSTIA
on the Loire: 6 NANTES
on the Seine: 5 ROUEN
opening: 4 HELI
Out of: 4 ASEA 5 TOSEA
prefix: 4 HELI TELE
vessel: 3 VAT 6 CARAFE
**Port-___ (cheese):** 5 SALUT
**Portable**
bed: 3 COT
computer: 6 LAPTOP
cutter: 8 SABERSAW
home: 5 TEPEE
platform: 4 SKID
~ PC: 6 LAPTOP

**Portal:** 4 DOOR GATE
Popular: 5 YAHOO
**Port-au-Prince**
land: 5 HAITI
**Port du ___ (cheese):** 5 SALUT
**Port ___, Egypt:** 4 SAID
**Portend:** 4 BODE
**Portent:** 4 OMEN
**Porter:** 3 ALE 6 BEARER
Baggage: 6 REDCAP
burden: 4 BAGS
or Younger: 4 COLE
Popular: 6 SHERPA
Pullman: 6 REDCAP
Regretful Miss of: 4 OTIS
**Porter, Cole**
1929 ~ song: 5 PAREE
birthplace: 4 PERU
title city: 5 PAREE
tune: 7 ROSALIE
~, schoolwise: 3 ELI
**Porterhouse:** 5 STEAK
alternative: 5 TBONE
request: 4 RARE
**Porters**
Where to find: 3 PUB
**Portfolio**
component: 5 STOCK
item: 5 ASSET
part: 3 IRA 4 FUND
**Porthos**
Friend of: 5 ATHOS
6 ARAMIS
~, to Athos: 3 AMI
**Portico**
Greek: 4 STOA
**Portion:** 4 DOSE METE PART
5 PIECE SHARE
(abbr.): 3 SEG
Butter: 3 PAT
Corn: 3 EAR
Game: 4 HALF
(out): 4 METE
Sound: 5 AUDIO
**Portland**
college: 4 REED
st.: 4 OREG
**Portly:** 5 STOUT 6 ROTUND
plus: 5 OBESE
**Portman**
Actress: 7 NATALIE
**Portnoy**
creator: 4 ROTH
**"Portnoy's Complaint"**
author: 4 ROTH
**Pôrto ___, Brazil:** 6 ALEGRE
**Portoferraio**
island: 4 ELBA
**Portrait:** 5 IMAGE
8 LIKENESS
medium: 4 OILS
Penny: 3 ABE
place: 4 HALL
Sit for a: 4 POSE
Stand for a: 5 EASEL
subject: 4 SELF

**Portraitist**
American Revolutionary:
5 PEALE
Dutch ~ Frans: 4 HALS
Edwardian: 7 SARGENT
medium: 4 OILS
**Portray:** 4 LIMN 5 ENACT
6 DEPICT
again: 7 REENACT
**Portrayer:** 5 ACTOR
**Port St. ___, Florida:** 5 LUCIE
**Portugal**
Euro's predecessor in:
6 ESCUDO
Islands off: 6 AZORES
Lady of: 4 DONA
place: 6 IBERIA
Spain and: 6 IBERIA
**Portuguese**
city: 6 OPORTO
Former ~ colony: 5 MACAO
Former ~ colony in India:
3 GOA
islands: 6 AZORES
king: 3 REI
king, 1861–89: 4 LUIZ
Old ~ money: 6 ESCUDO
speaking land: 6 ANGOLA
title: 4 DONA
wine: 7 MADEIRA
**Pos.**
Opposite of: 3 NEG
**Posada:** 3 INN
**Pose:** 3 SIT
again: 7 REFRAME
**Posed:** 3 PUT SAT
**Poseidon:** 6 SEAGOD
7 NEPTUNE
Mother of: 4 RHEA
realm: 3 SEA
Son of: 5 ORION 6 TRITON
spear: 7 TRIDENT
**Poser:** 5 MODEL 6 ENIGMA
7 TOUGHIE
Present a: 3 ASK
**Posh:** 5 RITZY 7 ELEGANT
Far from: 5 SEEDY
property: 6 ESTATE
**Posit**
prefix: 3 OVI
**Position:** 3 JOB PUT SET
4 RANK ROLE SITE
5 STAND STEAD TENET
6 STANCE
at sea: 4 ALEE
Central: 5 MIDST
In a tough: 5 TREED
It may put you in a difficult:
4 YOGA
Kind of: 4 POLE 5 FETAL
LOTUS
of authority: 5 CHAIR
of control: 4 HELM
Precarious: 7 THINICE
Put in: 3 SET
Put in a: 4 HIRE

Rough: 3 LIE
to fill: 4 ROLE SLOT
Top: 3 ONE
Uncomfortable: 7 HOTSEAT
**Positioned**
Is: 4 LIES
Properly: 7 INPLACE
**Positive:** 4 SURE
aspect: 6 UPSIDE
feedback: 5 YESES
It may be: 3 ION
pole: 5 ANODE
principle: 4 YANG
response: 3 YES
thinker: 5 PEALE
vote: 3 AYE YEA
Was: 4 KNEW
**Positively**
State: 4 AVER 6 ASSERT
**Positron**
place: 4 ATOM
**Posse:** 4 GANG
Picture with a: 5 OATER
**Possess:** 3 OWN 4 HAVE
Does not: 5 HASNT
~, to Burns: 3 HAE
**Possessed:** 3 HAD
**Possesses:** 3 HAS
~, old-style: 4 HATH
**Possession**
Keep ~ of: 6 RETAIN
**"Possession of fools"**
~, to Herodotus: 5 PRIDE
**Possessions**
Worldly: 6 ESTATE
**Possessive**
Biblical: 5 THINE
Dogpatch: 4 HISN
French: 3 SES TES 4 AMOI
   ATOI
Italian: 3 MIO
pronoun: 3 ITS
**Possibilities:** 3 IFS
**Possibility**
Word of: 3 MAY
**Possible**
All: 5 EVERY
Best: 5 IDEAL
Least: 7 MINIMAL
Make: 6 ENABLE
**Possibly:** 5 MAYBE
**Possum**
Comics: 4 POGO
**Post:** 4 MAIL SEND 7 AVIATOR
Aviator: 5 WILEY
delivery (abbr.): 3 ENV
ending: 3 URE
Go from pillar to: 4 ROVE
Hitching: 5 ALTAR
in a flight: 5 NEWEL
Not pre or: 3 MID
of etiquette: 5 EMILY
Opposite of: 3 PRE
position: 6 EDITOR
production: 4 NEWS 6 CEREAL
Read but not: 4 LURK

Ready to: 7 STAMPED
Skipper's: 4 HELM
Stairway: 5 NEWEL
**Post-___:** 6 MORTEM
**Post, Wilbur**
horse: 4 MRED
**Post-accident**
statement: 4 IMOK
**Postage**
item: 5 STAMP
meter unit: 5 OUNCE
sheet: 4 PANE
**Postal**
abbr.: 3 RFD
creed word: 3 NOR
delivery: 4 MAIL
Go: 4 SNAP 6 LOSEIT
**Post-Baroque:** 6 ROCOCO
**Post-blizzard**
stuff: 5 SLUSH
**Postcards**
Like early: 7 ONECENT
**Posted:** 4 SENT
It's: 4 BAIL
**Poster**
1960s ~ genre: 5 OPART
boy: 6 ADONIS
heading: 6 REWARD WANTED
letters: 3 AKA
person: 4 IDOL
**Post-ER**
place: 3 ICU
**Posterior:** 4 HIND
**Postgame**
summary: 5 RECAP
**Postgrad**
deg.: 3 MBA
degrees: 3 MAS
**Postgraduate**
hurdle: 4 ORAL
study: 3 LAW
**Post-It:** 4 NOTE
**"Postman Always Rings Twice,
   The"**
wife: 4 CORA
**Postman's Creed**
word: 3 NOR
**Post-mark**
currency: 4 EURO
**Postmortem**
bio: 4 OBIT
**Post office**
activity: 4 KISS
gizmo: 5 DATER
machine: 6 SORTER
motto word: 3 NOR
**Post-op**
time: 5 REHAB
**Postpaid**
enc.: 4 SASE
**Postpone:** 5 DEFER TABLE
**Postponement:** 4 STAY
cause: 4 RAIN
**Postprandial**
handout: 5 MINTS
libation: 4 PORT

**Postscript**
Literary: 6 EPILOG
Musical: 4 CODA
**PostScript**
creator: 5 ADOBE
**Postscripts:** 7 ADDENDA
**Posture**
Having poor: 7 UNERECT
problem: 5 STOOP
Yoga: 5 ASANA
**Posturepedic**
maker: 5 SEALY
**Postwar**
period: 9 PEACETIME
**Post-workout**
woe: 4 ACHE
**Post-WWII**
alliance: 4 NATO
**Pot:** 6 KETTLE
contents: 4 BETS
Earthen cooking: 4 OLLA
grower: 4 ANTE
Hot: 4 STEW
In debt to the: 3 SHY
It might go into a: 4 CHIT
Meal in a: 4 STEW
Pouring: 5 CRUSE
Spanish: 4 OLLA
starter: 4 ANTE
Sweeten the: 5 RAISE
top: 3 LID
**Potable**
Make: 6 DESALT
Potent: 3 ALE RUM RYE
Pub: 3 ALE 5 STOUT
**Potala Palace**
setting: 5 LHASA TIBET
**Potash**
Caustic: 3 LYE
**Potassium ___ (food
   preservative):** 7 SORBATE
**Potassium hydroxide:** 3 LYE
**Potation**
Pirate: 4 GROG
Pub: 3 ALE
**Potato:** 4 SPUD 5 TUBER
alternative: 4 RICE 5 PASTA
   PILAF
choice: 6 MASHED
covering: 4 SKIN
feature: 3 EYE
holder: 4 SACK
pancake: 5 LATKE
Quality: 5 IDAHO
state: 5 IDAHO
Sweet: 3 YAM 7 OCARINA
tool: 5 RICER
**Potato chip**
accompanier: 8 ONIONDIP
brand: 4 LAYS
feature: 5 RIDGE
flavor: 3 BBQ 5 CHIVE
Like a: 5 SALTY
Like a ~, perhaps: 6 RIDGED
Wise ~ symbol: 3 OWL
~, to a Brit: 5 CRISP

**Potatoes: 5** CARBS
  Meat and: **4** FOOD
  Partner of: **4** MEAT
  Peeling ~, perhaps: **4** ONKP
  Prepare: **4** MASH RICE
  Word before: **5** SMALL
**Potatoes au ___: 6** GRATIN
**Potato sack**
  material: **6** BURLAP
  wt.: **5** TENLB
**Potbelly: 5** STOVE
**Potemkin**
  setting: **6** ODESSA
**Potent**
  mixture: **11** WITCHESBREW
  potable: **3** ALE RYE
  prefix: **4** OMNI
**Potentate: 6** DYNAST
  Mideast: **4** EMIR
  Persian: **4** SHAH
  Turkish: **4** AGHA
**Potential: 6** LATENT
    **7** PROMISE
**Potentially**
  explosive situation:
    **9** POWDERKEG
**"Potent Potables for 200, ___":**
    **4** ALEX
**Pother: 3** ADO **4** STIR
**Pothook**
  shape: **3** ESS
**Potion: 6** ELIXIR
**Potions**
  Potter's ~ professor: **5** SNAPE
**Potluck**
  choice: **4** DISH
  dish: **9** CASSEROLE
    **15** NOODLECASSEROLE
**Potok**
  Author: **5** CHAIM
**Potomac**
  Army of the ~ leader:
    **5** MEADE
**Potpie**
  veggie: **3** PEA
**Potpourri: 4** OLIO
  bag: **6** SACHET
  bit: **5** PETAL
  container: **3** JAR
  ingredient: **9** ROSEPETAL
  Like: **8** AROMATIC
  output: **5** SCENT
**Pots: 7** TINWARE **8** IRONWARE
  Fish caught in: **4** EELS
**Potsdam**
  please: **5** BITTE
**Potshots**
  Take: **5** SNIPE
**Pot-shy**
  Plays: **4** OWES
**Potsie**
  portrayer: **5** ANSON
**Potslicker**
  cooker: **3** WOK
**Potted: 3** LIT
  plant place: **4** SILL **5** LEDGE

**Potter: 8** CERAMIST
  English ~ Josiah: **5** SPODE
  material: **4** CLAY
  need: **4** CLAY SOIL
  oven: **4** KILN
  rank (abbr.): **3** COL
**Potter, Harry: 4** TEEN
  Hedwig belonging to: **3** OWL
  lightning bolt: **4** SCAR
  potions professor: **5** SNAPE
  prop: **4** WAND
  study: **5** MAGIC
**Pottery: 4** WARE
  Blue and white: **5** DELFT
  Dutch: **5** DELFT
  finish: **5** GLAZE
  fragment: **5** SHARD
  oven: **4** KILN
  worker: **8** ENAMELER
**Potting**
  need: **4** SOIL
  soil: **4** LOAM
**POTUS**
  part (abbr.): **4** PRES
  Title akin to: **4** CINC
**Potvin**
  of hockey: **5** DENIS
**Pou ___ (vantage point): 3** STO
**Pouch: 3** SAC
  Anatomical: **3** SAC
  Animal in a: **3** ROO
  Animal with a: **7** OPOSSUM
  Highlander: **7** SPORRAN
**Poughkeepsie**
  college: **6** MARIST VASSAR
**Poultry**
  chicken: **7** ROASTER
  choice: **5** CAPON
  giant: **5** TYSON
  product: **3** EGG
**Pounce**
  (upon): **4** LEAP
**Pound: 4** MASH **5** SMITE
    THROB
  and others: **5** POETS
  and Stone: **5** EZRAS
  (down): **4** TAMP
  Foot in a: **3** PAW
  notes: **6** ARFARF
  of flesh, e.g.: **4** DEBT
  One ~ and one shilling, once:
    **6** GUINEA
  part: **5** OUNCE PENCE
  poem part: **5** CANTO
  Poet: **4** EZRA
  resident: **4** MUTT **5** STRAY
    **8** STRAYDOG
  sound: **3** ARF GRR YAP YIP
    **4** THUD WOOF YELP
  sterling: **4** QUID
  unrelentingly: **4** PELT
**Pound, Ezra: 4** POET
    **7** IDAHOAN
**Pounder**
  Actress: **3** CCH
  Door ~ demand: **6** OPENUP

  Gavel ~ word: **5** ORDER
**Pounding**
  tool: **6** PESTLE
**Pounds**
  2.2 ~: **4** KILO
  14 ~, in Britain: **5** STONE
  100 ~ (abbr.): **3** CWT
  100 ~ of nails: **3** KEG
  140 ~, in Britain:
    **8** TENSTONE
  2,000 ~: **3** TON
  Put on: **4** GAIN
**Pour: 4** RAIN
  down: **4** RAIN
  Here's one ~ vous: **3** UNE
  out: **5** EMPTY **6** DECANT
  Pub: **3** ALE
  Ready to: **5** ONTAP
  ~, as wine: **6** DECANT
**Pour ___: 4** ITON
**Pourer: 4** EWER
  pot: **5** CRUSE
  request: **7** SAYWHEN
**Pout: 4** MOUE SULK
**Poverty: 4** NEED WANT
  ~, symbolically: **4** RAGS
**Poverty-stricken: 5** NEEDY
**POW**
  Sitcom: **5** HOGAN
**"Pow!": 3** BAM **4** WHAM
**Powder: 4** SNOW TALC
  Bath: **4** TALC
  Chilly: **4** SNOW
  Cleansing: **5** BORAX
  holder: **4** HORN
  Printer: **5** TONER
  room: **7** ARSENAL
  Soothing: **4** TALC
  Take a: **3** LAM **5** SCRAM
  Took a: **4** FLED LEFT
**Powdery: 4** FINE
**Powell**
  area: **15** STATEDEPARTMENT
  Frequent ~ costar: **3** LOY
  General: **5** COLIN
  Like Gen. ~: **3** RET
  of baseball: **4** BOOG
  Secretary: **5** COLIN
  Tap dancer: **7** ELEANOR
**Power: 3** GAS **5** JUICE MIGHT
    SINEW **6** ENERGY
  Actor: **6** TYRONE
  Center of: **5** LOCUS
  Centers of: **4** LOCI
  choice: **4** ACDC
  co. product: **4** ELEC
  Exercise: **5** WIELD
  Give ~ to: **4** VEST **6** ENABLE
  Government in: **6** REGIME
  Has ~ over: **4** OWNS
  Have staying: **4** LAST
  High: **3** NTH
  holders: **3** INS
  Increase in: **5** SURGE
  jolt: **5** SURGE
  Kind of: **3** NTH **5** SOLAR

Lost: 4 DIED
Muscle: 5 SINEW
network: 4 GRID
Not at full: 5 ONLOW
period: 5 REIGN
problem: 5 SURGE 6 OUTAGE
Put in: 8 ENTHRONE
Raise to the third: 4 CUBE
Reflective: 6 ALBEDO
Remove from: 8 DETHRONE
source: 5 MOTOR STEAM
Southern ~ inits.: 3 TVA
stats: 3 RBI
Staying: 4 LEGS 7 INERTIA
    STAMINA
Super: 3 ESP
symbol: 3 ORB
Those in: 3 INS
Topple from: 4 OUST
unit: 4 WATT
**"Power"**
star: 4 GERE
**Power ___: 4 LOOM**
**"Power and the Glory, The"**
author: 6 GREENE
**"Power Broker, The"**
author Robert: 4 CARO
**Powerful**
blow: 4 SWAT
person: 5 NABOB
stream: 3 JET
stuff: 3 TNT
**Powerless: 5 ATBAY 6 UNABLE**
to move: 5 INERT
**"Power Lunch"**
network: 4 CNBC
**"Power of Positive Thinking,**
**The"**
author: 5 PEALE
**Powers**
Actress: 4 MALA
Judicial ~ part: 10 ARTICLEIII
or Smart: 5 AGENT
player: 5 MYERS
that be: 3 INS
**Powwow: 4 CHAT TALK**
    7 PALAVER
**Pox: 5 CURSE**
**PR**
concern: 5 IMAGE
output: 4 HYPE
person: 3 AGT 5 AGENT
**Practical: 5 OFUSE UTILE**
It may be: 4 JOKE
joke: 3 GAG 4 JAPE 5 PRANK
    7 LEGPULL
literary genre: 5 HOWTO
Not: 8 ACADEMIC
**Practice: 3 PLY 4 WONT**
    5 DRILL USAGE
a part: 8 REHEARSE
Ballet: 4 LEAP
Customary: 4 RITE 5 USAGE
elocution: 5 ORATE
for a rodeo: 5 LASSO
in the outfield: 4 SHAG

Marching: 5 DRILL
Out of: 5 RUSTY
piece: 5 ETUDE
punching: 4 SPAR
**"Practice, The"**
actress Boyle: 4 LARA
event: 5 TRIAL
**Practicing**
Prevent from: 6 DISBAR
**Practitioner**
Divination: 4 SEER
Yoga: 5 HINDU
**Prado**
Some ~ works: 5 GOYAS
works: 4 ARTE
**Pragmatic**
one: 7 REALIST
**Prague**
native: 5 CZECH
premiere of 1921: 3 RUR
**Prairie**
Argentine: 5 PAMPA
building: 4 SILO
home material: 3 SOD
wolf: 6 COYOTE
**Prairie State**
hub: 5 OHARE
**Praise: 4 LAUD 5 EXALT**
    EXTOL KUDOS
    7 APPLAUD COMMEND
Overdo the: 4 GUSH
Poem of: 3 ODE
Shout of: 7 HOSANNA
Song of: 4 HYMN 5 PAEAN
    8 CANTICLE
to the skies: 5 EXALT EXTOL
Work of: 3 ODE
**"Praise of Folly, The"**
author: 7 ERASMUS
**Praiser**
Poetic: 5 ODIST
**"Praise the Lord!": 8 ALLELUIA**
**Praiseworthy: 8 LAUDABLE**
    11 MERITORIOUS
**Praline**
nut: 5 PECAN
**Prance**
about: 6 CAVORT
**Prancer**
Forest: 4 DEER
**Prank: 3 GAG 4 DIDO 5 ANTIC**
    CAPER TRICK
Major: 4 HOAX
Merry: 4 JEST
Start of a: 4 DARE
suffix: 4 STER
**Prankster: 3 IMP**
projectile: 3 EGG PEA
**Prattle: 3 GAB YAK**
**Pravda**
provider: 4 TASS
**Prawn**
Large: 6 SCAMPI
**Pray: 7 ENTREAT**
One way to: 5 ALOUD
Prepare to: 5 KNEEL

~, in Latin: 3 ORA
**"___ pray": 5 LETUS**
**Prayer: 6 ORISON**
beads: 6 ROSARY
book: 6 MISSAL 7 PSALTER
ending: 4 AMEN
leader: 4 IMAM
period: 6 NOVENA
pronoun: 4 THEE
response: 4 AMEN
Rosary: 8 AVEMARIA
She fought school: 5 OHAIR
Start of a: 4 NOWI 5 OLORD
Use a ~ rug: 5 KNEEL
wheel user: 4 LAMA
**___ prayer: 4 SAYA**
**"Prayer for ___ Meany, A":**
    4 OWEN
**Prayers**
Object of many: 5 ALLAH
**Praying**
figure: 5 ORANT
insect: 6 MANTIS
**Praying ___: 6 MANTIS**
**Preach: 5 ORATE**
**Preacher**
post: 5 ALTAR
subject: 3 SIN
**"Preach on, brother!": 4 AMEN**
**Preakness: 4 RACE**
1942 ~ winner: 5 ALSAB
**Preamble: 5 INTRO PROEM**
**Prebirth**
berth: 4 WOMB
**Precalc**
part: 4 TRIG
**Precambrian: 3 ERA**
**Precarious: 5 SHAKY**
perch: 4 LIMB
position: 7 THINICE
**Precaution**
As a: 6 INCASE
**___ precaution: 3 ASA**
**Precede: 6 FOREGO**
    7 FORERUN
    8 ANTEDATE
    LEADUPTO
**Precedent**
setter: 8 TESTCASE
**___ precedent: 4 SETA**
**Preceding**
period: 3 EVE
**Precept: 4 RULE 5 TENET**
Moral: 5 ETHIC
**Precinct: 4 AREA WARD ZONE**
    6 SECTOR
**Precious: 4 CUTE DEAR**
    6 CUTESY
Act: 7 GETCUTE
instrument: 5 STRAD
metal: 4 GOLD
stone: 3 GEM 5 JEWEL
**Precipice: 4 EDGE**
**Precipitate: 4 RAIN RASH**
    5 HASTY 6 HASTEN
**Precipitation: 4 RAIN**

Icy: 4 HAIL 5 SLEET
Winter: 4 SNOW 5 SLEET
**Precipitous:** 5 STEEP
Make more: 7 STEEPEN
**Precise:** 5 EXACT 6 DEADON
Aim at the ~ center: 6 ZEROIN
**Precisely:** 4 TOAT 6 TOATEE
    11 TOTHELETTER
**Precision**
group: 9 DRILLTEAM
**Preclude:** 5 DEBAR
**Precollege:** 4 ELHI
**Preconditions:** 3 IFS
**Precook:** 7 PARBOIL
**Predator:** 5 SHARK
Black-and-white: 4 ORCA
Ocean: 4 ORCA
    10 NURSESHARK
seabird: 4 ERNE SKUA
Veldt: 4 LION
WWII: 5 UBOAT
Young: 5 OWLET
**Predatory**
bird: 6 RAPTOR
dolphin: 4 ORCA
group: 4 PACK
**Predestine:** 6 ORDAIN
**Predicament:** 3 JAM 4 BIND
    MESS SPOT 6 SCRAPE
Golfer: 6 BADLIE
In a: 8 UPACREEK
**Predictable**
pattern: 8 SYNDROME
**Predicted:** 7 FORESAW
**Prediction**
Capt.'s: 3 ETA
maker: 4 SEER
tool: 5 TAROT
**Predilection:** 4 BENT 5 TASTE
**Predisposed:** 5 PRONE
**Predisposition:** 4 BIAS
**Preface:** 5 INTRO PROEM
**Prefecture**
Honshu: 5 OSAKA
**Prefer:** 5 FAVOR
charges: 3 SUE
**Preference:** 5 TASTE
In ~ to: 4 OVER
Pie: 7 ALAMODE
**Preferred:** 6 BETTER
invitees: 5 ALIST
Most: 3 PET
strategy: 5 PLANA
**Pregame**
ritual: 4 TOSS 6 ANTHEM
**Pregnancy**
Kind of: 5 TUBAL
**Prego**
rival: 4 RAGU
**Prehistoric:** 3 OLD
threat: 4 TREX
time: 8 STONEAGE
**Prejudice:** 4 BIAS
**Prelate**
honorific (abbr.): 4 MSGR
**Prelim:** 5 INTRO

**Preliminary**
races: 4 HEAT
text: 5 DRAFT
Was ~ (to): 5 LEDUP
**Prelude:** 5 INTRO
to a deal: 4 ANTE
to a duel: 4 SLAP
**"Prelude to a Kiss"**
actor Baldwin: 4 ALEC
**Prematurely:** 7 TOOSOON
**Premed**
subj.: 4 ANAT
**Premiere:** 5 DEBUT
sight: 4 LIMO
**Preminger**
1944 ~ suspense classic:
    5 LAURA
Director: 4 OTTO
**Premises**
Remove from the: 5 EVICT
**Premium**
At a: 4 RARE
channel: 3 HBO
Exchange: 4 AGIO
___ **premium (scarce):** 3 ATA
**Premonition:** 5 HUNCH
    6 BODING
Have a: 5 SENSE
**Prenatal**
prefix: 5 UTERO
test, for short: 5 AMNIO
**Preoccupy:** 6 OBSESS
**Preoperative**
delivery of old: 5 ETHER
**Preordain:** 7 DESTINE
**Preowned:** 4 USED
**Prep**
for a marathon, with "up":
    4 CARB
sch.: 4 ACAD
**Prepaid**
Not: 3 COD
**Preparation:** 5 SETUP
Party: 3 DIP
**Preparations**
Make: 4 PLAN
Make final: 4 CRAM
**Prepare:** 3 SET 5 GROOM
    READY TRAIN 6 GETSET
    8 GETREADY
~, as a hook: 4 BAIT
~, as leftovers: 6 REHEAT
~, as mushroom: 5 SAUTE
~, as new students: 6 ORIENT
~, as salad: 4 TOSS
~, as tea: 5 STEEP
**Prepared:** 3 SET 5 READY
    9 MADEREADY
**Preparer**
Food: 4 CHEF COOK
Salad: 6 TOSSER
Tax: 3 CPA
**Preparers**
MS. ~: 3 EDS
**Preposterous:** 5 INANE
    6 INSANE

**Preppy**
brand: 4 IZOD
jacket: 4 ETON
**Preprandial**
drink: 8 APERITIF
**Prep school**
British: 4 ETON
New Hampshire: 6 EXETER
**Prerecorded**
Not: 4 LIVE
**Prerequisite:** 4 NEED
Deal: 4 ANTE
Two-run homer: 5 ONEON
**Prerogative**
Director: 6 RETAKE
Presidential: 4 VETO
**Pres.**
33rd ~: 3 HST
appointee: 4 SECY
Four-term: 3 FDR
New Deal: 3 FDR
title: 3 CIC 4 CINC
**Presbyter:** 5 ELDER
**Preschool**
attendee: 3 TOT
**Preschooler:** 3 TOT
**Preschoolers:** 3 ROE
**Prescient**
one: 4 SEER
**Prescribed:** 3 SET
amount: 4 DOSE
doctrine: 5 DOGMA
**Prescribers**
(abbr.): 3 MDS
**Prescription**
Available without a ~ (abbr.):
    3 OTC
Four times a day, in a: 3 QID
info: 4 DOSE
overseer in D.C.: 3 FDA
phrase: 8 ASNEEDED
Three times a day, in a: 3 TID
Three times, in a: 3 TER
**Presence:** 8 CHARISMA
Having physical:
    15 BRICKSANDMORTAR
Stage: 5 ACTOR
**Present:** 4 GIFT GIVE HERE
    5 NONCE TENSE
    6 ONHAND ONSITE
    9 INTRODUCE
and past: 6 TENSES
a poser: 3 ASK
a problem: 4 POSE
but hidden: 6 LATENT
from birth: 6 INNATE
mo.: 3 DEC
occasion: 5 NONCE
opener: 4 OMNI
prefix: 4 OMNI
Prepare a: 4 WRAP
time: 4 NOEL XMAS
    9 CHRISTMAS
Was: 4 CAME
**Presentation**
Kind of: 4 ORAL

staple: 5 CHART
**Presenter:** 5 EMCEE
**Presently:** 4 ANON SOON
**Preservative**
Common: 3 BHT
**Preserve:** 3 CAN 4 SALT SAVE
for burial: 6 EMBALM
~, as hay: 6 ENSILE
~, as meat: 4 CURE
**Preserved:** 4 KEPT 5 ONICE
**Preserver**
Fossil: 5 AMBER
Life: 4 OBIT
of a sort: 6 SALTER
Secret identity: 4 MASK
The ~, in Hinduism: 6 VISHNU
**Preserves:** 3 JAM
preserver: 3 JAR
**Preside**
at tea: 4 POUR
over: 4 RULE 5 CHAIR
**President:** *see page 723*
2nd: 5 ADAMS
6th: 5 ADAMS
11th ~: 4 POLK
27th ~: 4 TAFT
44th ~: 5 OBAMA
1950s French: 4 COTY
Bolivia: 5 SUCRE
Czech: 5 HAVEL
Disney: 4 IGER
Fair Deal: 6 TRUMAN
First ~ to marry while in office:
   5 TYLER
First AFL-CIO: 5 MEANY
Former Nicaraguan: 6 ORTEGA
Former SAG: 5 ASNER
French ~ residence: 6 ELYSEE
Kenyan: 3 MOI
Last mustachioed: 4 TAFT
Like the U.S. ~ office: 4 OVAL
Mexican War: 4 POLK
Pakistani ~ of the 1980s: 3 ZIA
Philippines: 5 RAMOS
South Korean: 4 RHEE
Syrian: 5 ASSAD
Unlikely class: 4 NERD
Where le ~ presides: 5 SENAT
**President ___ (acting head):**
   6 PROTEM
**___ President:** 5 MADAM
**Presidential**
1992 ~ candidate: 7 TSONGAS
1996 ~ candidate: 5 PEROT
1996 ~ candidate Alexander:
   5 LAMAR
2000 ~ candidate: 4 BUSH
   5 NADER 6 ALGORE
advisory gp.: 3 NSC
Frequent ~ aspirant Harold:
   7 STASSEN
middle name: 4 ALAN
   6 DELANO
monogram: 3 DDE HST
nickname: 3 ABE CAL IKE
   5 TEDDY

office shape: 4 OVAL
time: 4 TERM
turndown: 4 VETO
**President pro ___:** 3 TEM
**Presidents**
Birthplace of seven: 4 OHIO
Name of three: 6 GEORGE
Name of two: 5 ADAMS
**Presidents' Day**
event: 4 SALE
mo.: 3 FEB
**Presley, Elvis**
1958 hit: 4 DONT
hit: 13 JAILHOUSEROCK
middle name: 4 ARON
**Presley, Elvis ___:** 4 ARON
**Presque Isle**
locale: 4 ERIE
**Press:** 4 IRON URGE 5 MEDIA
agent: 4 IRON
conference activity: 5 QANDA
coverage: 3 INK
down: 4 TAMP
for: 4 URGE
for payment: 3 DUN
Hot off the: 3 NEW
into service: 3 USE
Kind of: 5 CIDER DRILL
need: 3 INK
on: 4 URGE 5 IMPEL
pass: 5 IDTAG
Ready the: 3 INK
release: 4 WINE 5 CIDER
suffix: 3 URE
Word with: 3 KIT
~, slangily: 3 INK
**Pressed**
for time: 7 INARUSH
It is ~ for cash: 3 ATM
**Presser**
Bench ~ pride: 4 PECS
Clothes: 4 IRON
**Pressing:** 5 ACUTE
   6 URGENT
need: 4 IRON
One with ~ duties: 6 IRONER
**Press Secretary**
Ford: 6 NESSEN
Former ~ Myers: 6 DEEDEE
George W's: 3 ARI
**Pressure:** 4 HEAT 6 LEANON
   STRESS
Apply: 5 EXERT
Collapse under: 4 GIVE
   5 CHOKE
Give in to: 3 SAG
Grace under: 5 POISE
Its walls withstand a lot of:
   5 AORTA
Kind of: 4 PEER
meas.: 3 PSI
Operated by air:
   9 PNEUMATIC
Position of: 7 HOTSEAT
prefix: 3 ACU
source: 4 PEER

Under: 7 ONADARE
   8 STRESSED
unit: 4 TORR 7 KILOBAR
   8 MILLIBAR
unit (abbr.): 3 PSI
**Prestige:** 6 CACHET
**Prestigious**
boys' school: 4 ETON
institutions: 5 IVIES
prize: 5 NOBEL
sch.: 3 MIT
**Presto:** 5 TEMPO
**"Presto!":** 4 TADA
**Preston:** 3 SGT
**Preston, Robert**
1966 ~ musical: 6 IDOIDO
**Preston, Sgt.**
home: 5 YUKON
org.: 4 RCMP
**Presumed**
facts: 6 GIVENS
**"Presumed Innocent"**
actress Scacchi: 5 GRETA
author: 5 TUROW
   10 SCOTTTUROW
**Presumptive:** 7 APRIORI
**Presupposed:** 7 APRIORI
**Pretend:** 5 FEIGN LETON
   7 PLAYACT
to be: 3 ACT
to sing: 7 LIPSYNC
**Pretended:** 4 SHAM
**Pretense:** 3 ACT 4 AIRS POSE
   SHAM VEIL 5 GUISE
   PUTON 6 FACADE
   7 CHARADE
**Pretentious:** 4 ARTY 5 ARTSY
   6 LADIDA
attitude: 4 AIRS
display: 4 RITZ
**Preternatural:** 5 EERIE
**Prettify:** 5 ADORN PREEN
   PRIMP
**Pretty:** 4 CUTE 5 QUITE
It's not: 7 EYESORE
Make: 5 ADORN
Not a ~ fruit: 4 UGLI
**"___ Pretty":** 5 IFEEL
**"Pretty nice!":** 6 NOTBAD
**"Pretty please?":** 4 CANI
**"Pretty Poison"**
star: 11 TUESDAYWELD
**"Pretty Woman"**
actor Richard: 4 GERE
pretty woman: 7 ROBERTS
**Pretzel**
bag resealer: 4 CLIP
shape: 4 KNOT
topping: 4 SALT
**Pretzels**
Like most: 5 SALTY
**Prevail:** 6 WINOUT
Begin to: 5 SETIN
**Prevailed:** 3 WON
**Prevailing**
conditions: 7 CLIMATE

tendency: 5 TREND
**Préval**
  of Haiti: 4 RENE
**Prevalent:** 4 RIFE
  Become: 5 SETIN
**Prevaricate:** 3 LIE 8 TELLALIE
**Prevaricator:** 4 LIAR
**Prevent:** 3 BAR 5 AVERT
      DEBAR DETER
  from practicing: 6 DISBAR
  legally: 5 ESTOP
**Preventer**
  Slip: 3 MAT
  Whiplash: 8 HEADREST
**Prevention**
  unit: 5 OUNCE
**Preview:** 9 SNEAKPEEK
  Kind of: 5 SNEAK
  TV: 6 TEASER
**Previewer**
  Movie: 5 RATER
**Previn**
  Conductor: 5 ANDRE
**Previous:** 4 PAST
  Not based on ~ study:
      7 APRIORI
  to, old-style: 5 AFORE
**Previously:** 3 NEE 4 ONCE
      5 AFORE 7 ALREADY
      9 ATONETIME
  As ~ mentioned: 4 IDEM
  owned: 4 USED
**Prévost**
  Novelist: 4 ABBE
**Prexy**
  partner: 4 VEEP
**Prey:** 6 VICTIM
  Bird of: 6 RAPTOR
  gripper: 5 TALON
  on the mind: 5 EATAT
  Search for: 5 PROWL
**Prez:** 4 EXEC
  34th ~: 3 IKE
  backup: 4 VEEP
  on a penny: 3 ABE
**Priam**
  home: 4 TROY
  Son of: 5 PARIS 6 HECTOR
      7 TROILUS
  Wife of: 6 HECUBA
**Price:** 4 COST
  abbr.: 3 CTS
  At a reduced: 6 ONSALE
  Change the: 5 RETAG
  For the stock issue: 5 ATPAR
  indicator: 3 TAG
  Kind of: 4 LIST UNIT
      6 ASKING RESALE
  List: 6 RETAIL
  Market: 5 VALUE
  of a ride: 4 FARE
  of a visit: 3 FEE
  offering: 4 ARIA
  or Callas: 4 DIVA
  paid: 4 COST
  performance: 5 OPERA

place: 3 TAG
Put a ~ on freedom:
    7 SETBAIL
Resell at an inflated: 5 SCALP
Retail: 4 COST
Set a: 3 ASK
Small ~ to pay: 4 CENT
Stock: 5 QUOTE
tag: 4 COST
tag qualifier: 4 ASIS
word: 3 PER
___ price: 3 ATA
**Price, T. ___ :** 4 ROWE
**Priced**
  Be ~ at: 7 SELLFOR
  to move: 6 ONSALE
**Price/earnings:** 5 RATIO
**Price-fixing**
  group: 6 CARTEL
**Priceless:** 4 FREE
**Prices**
  Compare: 4 SHOP
  Cut, as: 5 SLASH
  Like some: 3 NET
**Pricey:** 4 DEAR 5 STEEP
  cracker spread: 3 ROE
  fur: 5 SABLE
  gown: 4 DIOR
  import: 3 BMW
  watch: 5 ROLEX
**Pricing**
  Kind of: 4 UNIT
  word: 3 PER 6 APIECE
**Prickle:** 5 THORN
**Prickly**
  heat: 4 RASH
  plant: 5 BRIER 6 CACTUS
      TEASEL
  plants: 5 CACTI
  seed case: 3 BUR
  sensation: 6 TINGLE
**Prickly ___ :** 4 PEAR
**Pride:** 3 EGO SIN
  Burst with: 5 KVELL
  Excessive: 6 HUBRIS
  member: 4 LION
  of Joy: 4 ELSA
  Pitcher's: 3 ARM ERA
  She has her: 7 LIONESS
  sound: 4 ROAR
  Sultan: 5 HAREM
  Swallowed one's: 7 ATEDIRT
**"Pride and Prejudice"**
  author: 6 AUSTEN
**"Pride's Crossing"**
  playwright Howe: 4 TINA
**Prie-___ (prayer bench):** 4 DIEU
**Prie-dieu**
  Use a: 5 KNEEL
**Priest**
  Ancient Celtic: 5 DRUID
  and minister cohort: 5 RABBI
  at a mosque: 4 IMAM
  High ~, in Exodus: 5 AARON
  of I Samuel: 3 ELI
  of the East: 4 LAMA

Old Testament: 3 ELI
Parish: 5 VICAR 6 CURATE
sch.: 3 SEM
Tibetan: 4 LAMA
vestment: 3 ALB
**Priestess**
  at Delphi: 6 ORACLE
  Bizet opera: 5 LEILA
**Priestley**
  Actor: 5 JASON
**Priestly**
  attire: 5 ORALE
  vestment: 3 ALB
**Prig:** 8 BLUENOSE
**Prima**
  ballerina: 6 ETOILE
**Prima donna:** 4 DIVA
  problem: 3 EGO
**Prima ___ evidence:** 5 FACIE
**Primal**
  impulse: 4 URGE
  Visit through ~ therapy:
      6 RELIVE
**"Primal Fear"**
  actor Richard: 4 GERE
**Primary:** 4 MAIN
  color: 3 RED 4 BLUE
  color of printing: 4 CYAN
  strategy: 5 PLANA
**"Primary Colors"**
  author: 5 KLEIN
**Primate:** 3 APE
  Big-eyed: 5 LORIS
  Hypothetical: 6 APEMAN
  Nocturnal: 5 LEMUR
**Primatologist**
  study: 4 APES
  ~ Fossey: 4 DIAN
**Primavera**
  It's sometimes served: 5 PASTA
**Prime:** 4 AONE
  draft status: 4 ONEA
  Even ~ number: 3 TWO
  Past one's: 4 AGED
  purchases: 6 STEAKS
  the pot: 4 ANTE
  time: 4 NINE
  time hour: 6 NINEPM
**Primed:** 3 SET 5 READY
**Prime Minister**
  1950s British ~: 4 EDEN
      6 ATTLEE
  1960s Japanese ~: 4 SATO
  British ~ Benjamin:
      8 DISRAELI
  British ~ William: 4 PITT
  First Burmese: 3 UNU
  First Indian: 5 NEHRU
  Former Israeli ~ Golda:
      4 MEIR
  Former Israeli ~ Shimon:
      5 PERES
  from 1947 to 1964: 5 NEHRU
  Postwar: 6 ATTLEE
**Primer:** 5 PAINT
  pooch: 4 SPOT

subject: 4 ABCS
**Prime rib au ___:** 3 JUS
**Primero**
mes: 5 ENERO
**Primitive:** 5 EARLY
counters: 5 ABACI
creature: 5 AMEBA
home: 3 HUT 5 TEPEE
percussion instrument:
5 GOURD
time: 8 STONEAGE
weapon: 5 SPEAR
**Primo:** 4 AONE
Italian writer: 4 LEVI
**Primogeniture**
beneficiary: 3 SON
**Primordial**
stuff: 4 OOZE
**Primp:** 5 PREEN
**Primrose**
variety: 5 OXLIP
**Prince:** 3 SON 4 HEIR
Arabian: 4 EMIR
Indian: 4 RAJA 5 RAJAH
in Ezekiel: 3 GOG
Mideast: 4 EMIR
of Broadway: 3 HAL
of Darkness: 5 SATAN
of India: 4 RAJA 5 RAJAH
of opera: 4 IGOR
school: 4 ETON
Shakespearean: 3 HAL
**Prince Charles**
Sister of: 4 ANNE
**Prince ___ Coast:** 4 OLAV
**Princedom**
of Charles: 5 WALES
**Prince ___ Khan:** 3 ALY
**Princely**
monogram: 3 HRH
~ Italian surname: 4 ESTE
**"Prince of Tides, The"**
actor Nick: 5 NOLTE
**Princess**
Emerald City: 4 OZMA
Gilbert and Sullivan: 3 IDA
Indian: 4 RANI 5 RANEE
Movie: 4 LEIA
Punjab: 4 RANI 5 RANEE
Sci-fi: 4 LEIA
Spanish: 5 ELENA
topper: 5 TIARA
tormentor: 3 PEA
TV warrior: 4 XENA
vessels: 6 LINERS
**"Princess Bride, The"**
actor Cary: 5 ELWES
director: 6 REINER
**Princess Leia ___:** 6 ORGANA
**Princess of Wales**
Late: 5 DIANA
**Princess Royal:** 4 ANNE
**Princeton**
and others: 5 IVIES
mascot: 5 TIGER
team: 6 TIGERS

**Prince Valiant**
Son of: 3 ARN
Wife of: 5 ALETA
**"Prince Valiant"**
cartoonist Foster: 3 HAL
**Prince William:** 7 ETONIAN
school: 4 ETON
**Principal:** 4 ARCH HEAD MAIN
STAR 5 CHIEF
part: 4 BODY
**Principality**
British: 5 WALES
**Principal McGee**
portrayer: 5 ARDEN
8 EVEARDEN
**Principle:** 5 TENET
Accounting: 4 LIFO
Chinese: 3 TAO
Female: 3 YIN
Guiding: 5 CREDO TENET
Jungian: 5 ANIMA
Kwanzaa: 5 UNITY
Man of: 5 PETER
of economy:
15 WASTENOTWANTNOT
Positive: 4 YANG
Underlying: 5 BASIS
Universal: 5 AXIOM
**Principles**
Basic: 4 ABCS
Lacking: 6 AMORAL
Set of: 5 ETHIC
**Print**
Kind of: 5 LITHO
Like some: 4 FINE
made using stone: 5 LITHO
Malign in: 5 LIBEL
measures: 3 EMS ENS
Ready for: 4 EDIT
See: 3 RUN
tint: 5 SEPIA
Words in: 4 TEXT
**Printed**
matter: 4 TEXT
mistake: 4 TYPO
Was: 3 RAN
**Printemps**
follower: 3 ETE
month: 3 MAI 5 AVRIL
**Printer**
!, to a: 4 BANG
ad abbr.: 3 PPM
company: 5 EPSON
measure: 4 PICA
powder: 5 TONER
primary color: 4 CYAN
problem: 3 JAM
proof: 5 REPRO
spec.: 3 DPI
supplies: 4 INKS
type: 5 LASER 6 INKJET
unit: 4 REAM
widths: 3 EMS ENS
**Printing**
Book: 7 EDITION
flourish: 5 SERIF

measures: 3 EMS ENS
method: 6 OFFSET
mistakes: 6 ERRATA
Prepare for: 4 EDIT
7 TYPESET
press part: 5 INKER
process, for short: 4 ROTO
5 LITHO
woe: 4 BLOT
**Printout**
Hosp.: 3 ECG
**Prints**
and such: 3 ART
Blue: 7 EROTICA
Look for: 4 DUST
**Prior**
From a ~ era: 3 OLD
superior: 5 ABBOT
to: 3 ERE 5 UNTIL
to, old-style: 5 AFORE
**Prioritizing**
Medical: 6 TRIAGE
**Priscilla**
John who courted: 5 ALDEN
**Prison:** 3 PEN
area: 4 WARD YARD
camp: 6 STALAG
guard: 5 SCREW
in a Cash tune: 6 FOLSOM
Like ~ windows: 6 BARRED
Notorious London:
7 NEWGATE
One way out of: 6 PAROLE
sentence: 4 TERM
uprising: 4 RIOT
weapon: 4 SHIV
Women's ~ figure: 6 MATRON
**Prisoner:** 3 CON
for good: 5 LIFER
It's entered by a: 4 PLEA
of Jabba the Hutt: 4 LEIA
Take: 7 CAPTURE
term: 7 STRETCH
**"Prisoner of ___, The":** 5 ZENDA
**Prison-related:** 5 PENAL
**Pristine:** 4 MINT PURE
**Private:** 5 INNER 8 ONEONONE
address: 3 APO
bed: 3 COT
chat: 9 TETEATETE
club: 3 USO
dinner: 4 MESS
filmmaker: 5 INDIE
instructor: 4 TUTOR
language: 4 CANT
lines: 5 ASIDE
response: 5 NOSIR 6 YESSIR
sch.: 4 ACAD
student: 5 TUTEE
~, at times: 7 SALUTER
**"Private Dancer"**
singer Turner: 4 TINA
**Private eye:** 3 TEC 5 SNOOP
6 SHAMUS
Attire popular with a:
10 TRENCHCOAT

Do a ~ job: 6 DETECT
Like Britain's ~ magazine:
    9 SATIRICAL
**Privately:** 8 INCAMERA
**Privileged**
    group: 5 ELITE
    The: 5 HAVES
**Privy:** 3 LOO
    Made ~ to: 7 LETINON
    to: 4 INON
**Prix ___:** 4 FIXE
**Prix fixe**
    offering: 4 MEAL
**Prize:** 5 AWARD VALUE
    6 ESTEEM
    Acting: 5 OSCAR
    Boxing: 4 BELT
    Derby: 5 PURSE ROSES
    Drama: 4 OBIE
    Film: 5 OSCAR
    money: 5 PURSE
    name: 5 NOBEL
    Olympic: 5 MEDAL
    since 1949: 4 EMMY
    Taking the booby: 4 LAST
    Top: 7 JACKPOT
    TV: 4 EMMY
    ___ prize: 5 BOOBY
**"Prize, The"**
    actress Sommer: 4 ELKE
**Prized:** 3 PET
    name: 5 NOBEL
    people: 5 DEARS
    person: 3 GEM
    salmon: 4 TYEE
    violin: 5 AMATI
**Prizm**
    maker: 3 GEO
**"Prizzi's Honor"**
    heroine: 5 IRENE
**PRNDL**
    Part of: 4 PARK
    pick: 4 GEAR
**Pro:** 3 ACE FOR 4 WHIZ
    9 INFAVOROF
    Balancing: 3 CPA
    choice: 4 IRON 7 ONEIRON
    CPR: 3 EMT
    follower: 3 TEM 4 RATA
    5 FORMA
    Kitchen: 4 CHEF
    Not: 4 ANTI
    Numbers: 3 CPA
    opponent: 4 ANTI
    opposite: 3 CON
    or con: 4 SIDE
    shop item: 3 TEE
    Theatrical: 7 ARTISTE
    vote: 3 AYE
**Pro ___:** 3 TEM 4 BONO RATA
    5 FORMA
**Pro-___ (some tourneys):**
    3 AMS
**Probability:** 4 ODDS
    pioneer: 6 PASCAL
**Probable:** 6 LIKELY

___ **probandi (burden of proof):**
    4 ONUS
**Probate**
    subject: 6 ESTATE
**Probe:** 4 FEEL TEST
    Busybody: 4 NOSE
    Surgical: 6 STYLET
    ~, with "into": 5 DELVE
**Problem:** 3 ILL 4 SNAG
    conclusion: 4 ATIC
    for Pauline: 5 PERIL
    of the middle ages: 3 SAG
    Present a: 4 POSE
    Tending to the: 4 ONIT
    Thorny: 7 DILEMMA
**Problematic:** 4 IFFY
**Pro bono:** 6 UNPAID
    ~ TV spot: 3 PSA
**Pro Bowl**
    letters: 3 AFC NFC
**Procedure:** 6 SYSTEM
    (abbr.): 4 SYST
    Backup: 5 PLANB
    part: 4 STEP
**Proceed:** 4 GOON WEND
    tediously: 4 PLOD
**Proceeded:** 4 WENT
    confidently: 6 STRODE
**Proceedings:** 4 ACTA
    Like some legal: 5 INREM
**Proceeds:** 3 SUM 4 GATE GOES
    TAKE
    ~, biblically: 5 GOETH
**Process**
    Part of a: 4 STEP
    Repetitive: 4 ROTE
    ~, as ore: 5 SMELT
**Procession:** 7 CORTEGE
    Public: 6 PARADE
**Proclaim:** 4 AVOW 6 ASSERT
    7 TRUMPET
    noisily: 5 BLARE
    with pomp: 5 ORATE
**Proclamation:** 5 EDICT
    Wedding: 5 BANNS
**Proclivity:** 4 BENT
**Procol ___:** 5 HARUM
**Procrastinator**
    promise: 4 SOON
    word: 5 LATER 6 MANANA
    8 TOMORROW
**Procter & Gamble**
    detergent: 3 ERA 4 TIDE
    shampoo: 4 PERT 5 PRELL
    soap: 3 DUZ 4 LAVA 5 IVORY
**Proctor**
    call: 4 TIME 7 TIMESUP
    handout: 4 TEST
**Procyon**
    constellation:
        10 CANISMINOR
**Prod:** 3 EGG 4 GOAD URGE
    5 EGGON
    gently: 4 COAX 5 NUDGE
**Prodder:** 4 SPUR
**Prodigal:** 7 SPENDER

**Prodigal Son**
    Where the ~ saw the light:
        3 STY
**Prodigy**
    alternative: 3 AOL
**Produce:** 4 SIRE 5 BREED
    SPAWN STAGE YIELD
    8 GENERATE
    hurriedly, with "out":
        5 CHURN
**Producer:** 5 MAKER
    Commercial: 7 SPONSOR
    Oil: 6 ARTIST
    Private film: 5 INDIE
    Wool: 5 LLAMA
**"Producers, The"**
    award: 4 TONY
    director Mel: 6 BROOKS
    Max's partner in: 3 LEO
**Produce-scale**
    word: 4 TARE
**Product**
    End: 6 RESULT
    makers (abbr.): 4 MFRS
    of erosion: 6 RAVINE
    package abbr.: 4 NTWT
        5 NETWT
    rollout: 6 LAUNCH
    testing org.: 3 FDA
**Production:** 6 OUTPUT
    Big: 4 EPIC
    Iron: 5 STEAM
    Met: 5 OPERA
    Post: 4 NEWS 6 CEREAL
**Productive**
    activity: 4 WORK
    one: 4 DOER
**Prof**
    degree: 3 PHD
    helpers: 3 TAS
    Kind of: 4 ASST
    Law ~ degree: 3 LLD
    protection: 6 TENURE
    ___ prof.: 4 ASST
**Profane**
    Least: 7 HOLIEST
**Profanity**
    Bit of: 4 OATH
**Profess:** 4 AVER AVOW
    6 ALLEGE
**Profession:** 5 TRADE 6 CAREER
    METIER
    ~, in slang: 3 BIZ
**Professional**
    org.: 3 AMA 4 ASSN
    payment: 3 FEE
    pitcher: 5 ADMAN
    prefix: 3 NON
    runner: 3 POL
    suffix: 3 IST
**Professor:** 8 EDUCATOR
    Do a ~ job: 5 TEACH
    Hogwarts: 5 SNAPE
    Retired: 8 EMERITUS
    ~ Brainard: 3 NED
    ~ Corey: 5 IRWIN

~ Higgins, to Eliza: 4 ENRY
~ Hill: 5 ANITA
~ Jones: 4 INDY
~ Plum game: 4 CLUE
**"Professor and the Madman, The"**
subj.: 3 OED
**Professors**
Some: 7 EMERITI
**Proficiency:** 4 EASE 5 SKILL
H.S. ~ test: 3 GED
**Proficient:** 4 ABLE 5 ADEPT
in: 6 GOODAT
Not ~ in: 5 BADAT
**Profile**
Distinctive: 4 OGEE
Short: 3 BIO
**Profit:** 3 NET 4 GAIN 5 AVAIL
LUCRE 7 NETGAIN
ending: 3 EER
For no: 6 ATCOST
Net ~ or loss:
10 BOTTOMLINE
Opposite of: 4 LOSS
prefix: 3 NON
Resell for a: 5 SCALP
unfairly:
15 LINEONESPOCKETS
___ profit (make money):
5 TURNA
**Profitable**
~ Internet business: 4 PORN
**Profiteer**
Ticket: 7 SCALPER
**Profits:** 4 TAKE
Deplete, as: 7 EATINTO
**Profligate:** 4 ROUE
**Profound:** 4 DEEP
**Profundity:** 5 DEPTH
___ profundo: 5 BASSO
**Prog.**
New Deal: 3 CCC NRA REA
TVA WPA
Reagan: 3 SDI
Web ~ code: 4 HTML
**Progenitor:** 4 SIRE
**Progeny:** 4 SEED 5 ISSUE
SCION
Some: 4 SONS
**Prognosis**
Unfavorable: 5 WORSE
**Prognosticator:** 4 SEER
**Program:** 4 SHOW
airing: 8 TELECAST
Coll. military: 4 ROTC
Community: 8 OUTREACH
Computer ~ input:
8 DATABASE
Fed. monetary aid: 3 SSI
file extension: 3 EXE
Fix a computer: 5 DEBUG
interruption:
10 NEWSREPORT
interruptions: 3 ADS
listing: 4 CAST
Mail ~ command: 4 SEND

Mil. training: 3 OCS
Moonshot: 6 APOLLO
offerer: 5 USHER
PC: 3 APP
Post-op: 5 REHAB
Reagan R&D: 3 SDI
Small: 6 APPLET
Software: 3 APP
trial: 8 BETATEST
**Programmer:** 5 CODER
output: 4 CODE
solution: 3 APP
**Programming**
language: 4 JAVA 5 COBOL
**Progress:** 5 GAINS 7 HEADWAY
INROADS STRIDES
Delay: 6 RETARD
impeder: 4 SNAG
In: 5 AFOOT
Initial: 7 TOEHOLD
Intelligently planned:
7 TELESIS
Making no: 6 INARUT
Slight: 4 DENT
slowly: 4 INCH
**Progresso**
product: 4 SOUP
**Prohibit:** 3 BAN BAR NIX
5 DEBAR 6 ENJOIN
**Prohibited:** 5 TABOO
7 FORBADE ILLEGAL
ILLICIT
act: 4 NONO
**Prohibition:** 3 BAN 4 NONO
5 TABOO
Apartment: 6 NOPETS
opener: 5 DONOT
promoter: 3 DRY
supporters: 4 DRYS
**Prohibition ___:** 3 ERA
**Prohibitionists:** 4 DRYS
**Project:** 3 JUT 7 RADIATE
conclusion: 3 ILE
Dives into a: 7 HASATIT
FDR: 3 TVA
step: 5 PHASE
TVA: 3 DAM
**Projectile**
path: 3 ARC
Prankster: 3 PEA
Pub: 4 DART
Quitter: 5 TOWEL
**Projecting**
part: 5 PRONG 6 FLANGE
7 SALIENT
window: 5 ORIEL
**Projection:** 4 EAVE 5 LEDGE
Church: 4 APSE
Hook: 4 BARB
Kind of: 6 ASTRAL
Rocky: 4 CRAG
Roof: 4 EAVE
room spool: 4 REEL
Soft palate: 5 UVULA
Warship: 3 RAM
Window: 5 LEDGE

**Prokofiev**
character: 5 PETER
Composer: 6 SERGEI
~ Piano Concerto #1 key:
5 DFLAT
**Prolific**
author: 4 ANON
Be: 4 TEEM
**Prolix:** 5 WORDY 7 VERBOSE
Hardly: 5 TERSE
**Prologue:** 5 INTRO
follower: 4 ACTI 6 ACTONE
**Prolonged**
attack: 5 SIEGE
**Prolonger**
Life ~, supposedly: 6 ELIXIR
**Prom:** 5 DANCE
attendee: 4 TEEN 6 SENIOR
attendees (abbr.): 3 SRS
At the: 7 ONADATE
date: 6 ESCORT
dress fabric: 5 TULLE
night safety gp.: 4 SADD
night woe: 4 ACNE
partner: 4 DATE
pursuit: 4 DATE
queen prop: 5 TIARA
rental: 4 LIMO
ride: 4 LIMO
Unlikely ~ king: 4 NERD
wear: 3 TUX 4 GOWN
6 ORCHID TUXEDO
**Promenade:** 7 SAUNTER
Greek: 4 STOA
Public: 5 PASEO
Tree-lined: 7 ALAMEDA
**Prometheus**
Brother of: 5 ATLAS
Gift from: 4 FIRE
**Prominence:** 3 TOR 4 CRAG
NAME
**Prominent:** 4 STAR 5 NOTED
It has a ~ bridge:
9 ROMANNOSE
time: 3 ERA
~ U.S. mayor: 5 DALEY
**Promise:** 3 VOW 4 OATH OLEO
WORD 6 ASSURE
Bud: 5 BLOOM
Campaign: 6 TAXCUT
Go back on a: 6 RENEGE
Oft-broken: 3 IDO
product: 4 OLEO
Solemn: 3 VOW 4 OATH
to pay: 3 IOU
Words of: 3 IDO
**Promised Land:** 6 CANAAN
UTOPIA
promisee: 7 ABRAHAM
**"Promised Land"**
author: 4 EBAN
**Promises**
Like some: 5 EMPTY
**Promising:** 4 ROSY
letters: 3 IOU
Not: 5 BLEAK

person: 5 COMER
rocks: 3 ORE
words: 3 IDO 4 IDOS OATH
**Promissory**
 Govt. ~ note: 5 TBILL
 note: 3 IOU
**Promo:** 6 TEASER
 Movie: 7 TRAILER
 pro: 5 ADMAN
 tape: 4 DEMO
**Promontory:** 4 NESS
**Promos**
 Some: 3 ADS
**Promote:** 4 ABET SELL TOUT
  5 BOOST EXALT
  6 FOSTER
 Heavily: 4 HYPE
**Promoted**
 Is: 7 MOVESUP
**Promoter**
 H.S.: 3 PTA
 Product: 5 ADMAN
**Promotion**
 basis: 5 MERIT
 recipient: 4 PAWN
**Promotional**
 link: 5 TIEIN
**Prompt:** 3 CUE 4 GOAD SPUR
  URGE 6 ONTIME
  REMIND SPEEDY
  7 INSPIRE
**PrompTer**
 prefix: 4 TELE
**Prompting**
 Urgent: 6 BEHEST
**Promptly:** 4 ASAP SOON
  5 APACE
**Promulgate:** 3 SOW
**Prone:** 3 APT
 Get: 3 LIE
 to fidgeting: 5 ANTSY
 to imitation: 5 APISH
 to pry: 4 NOSY
**Prong:** 4 TINE
**Pronghorn:** 8 ANTELOPE
**"___ pro nobis":** 3 ORA
**Pronoun**
 Biblical: 3 THY 4 THEE THOU
  5 THINE
 Dixie: 4 YALL
 French: 3 CES ILS LUI MOI
  MON SES TES TOI
 German: 3 ICH SIE
 Italian: 3 MIA
 Latin: 3 MEA 4 ILLE
 Nuptial: 4 OURS
 Oft-mispunctuated: 3 ITS
 Pointer: 4 THAT
 Quaker: 3 THY 4 THEE THOU
  5 THINE
 Seagoing: 3 HER SHE
 Spanish: 3 ESA 4 ESAS ESTA
  ESTO 5 ELLAS
**Pronounce:** 3 SAY 5 UTTER
 Fail to: 5 ELIDE
 indistinctly: 4 SLUR

**"___ pronounce ...":** 4 INOW
**Pronouncement:** 5 EDICT
**Pronouncements:** 5 DICTA
 One making: 5 SAYER
**Pronto:** 4 ASAP 6 ATONCE
**Pronunciation**
 mark: 5 BREVE SCHWA
 Omit in: 5 ELIDE
**Proof**
 Burden of: 4 ONUS
 Claim without: 6 ALLEGE
 finale: 3 QED
 Fire: 3 ASH
 letters: 3 QED
 of ownership: 4 DEED 5 TITLE
 of purchase (abbr.): 4 RCPT
 Printer's: 5 REPRO
 Show ~ of: 6 EVINCE
 They have the burden of: 3 TAS
 word: 4 ERAT ERGO STET
**Proofer**
 find: 4 TYPO
 mark: 4 DELE STET
**Proofreader**
 find: 4 TYPO 5 ERROR
 "leave it": 4 STET
 mark: 4 DELE STET
 oversights: 6 ERRATA
**Proofreading**
 mark: 4 STET
 symbol: 5 CARET
**Proofs**
 Go over: 4 EDIT
 of age: 3 IDS
**Prop**
 place: 3 SET
 prefix: 5 TURBO
 suffix: 3 ANE
 up: 5 BRACE SHORE
**Propagate:** 3 SOW
**Propel:** 5 PEDAL
 a boat: 3 OAR ROW
 a gondola: 4 POLE
**Propeller:** 3 OAR 5 SCREW
 holder: 6 BEANIE
 part: 5 BLADE
 Pellet: 8 AIRRIFLE
 sound: 4 WHIR
**Propensity:** 4 BENT
**Proper:** 5 STAID
 As is: 5 APTLY
 Deem: 6 SEEFIT
 In a ~ manner: 4 DULY
 It may be: 4 NOUN
 Like ~ children: 4 SEEN
 Overly ~ person: 5 PRUDE
 Partner of: 4 PRIM
**Properly:** 6 ARIGHT
 Act: 6 BEHAVE
 Operate: 4 WORK
 pitched: 5 ONKEY
 positioned: 7 INPLACE
**Property:** 5 TRAIT 6 ESTATE
  REALTY
 claim: 4 LIEN
 Govt. ~ overseer: 3 GSA

Landed: 6 ESTATE
 recipient: 7 ALIENEE
 right: 4 LIEN
 seller: 7 ALIENOR
 title: 4 DEED
 Turn over a: 6 RESELL
**Prophecies**
 Book of: 4 AMOS 5 HOSEA
  6 ISAIAH
**Prophet:** 4 SEER
 at Delphi: 6 ORACLE
 Minor: 4 AMOS 5 JONAH
  MICAH
 Old Testament: 4 AMOS
  5 HOSEA 6 ISAIAH
**Prophetess:** 5 SIBYL
 of Greek myth: 9 CASSANDRA
**Prophetic:** 8 ORACULAR
 sign: 4 OMEN
**Propitiate:** 7 APPEASE
**Propitiatory**
 present: 3 SOP
**Proportion:** 5 RATIO
**Proportional:** 7 INSCALE
 share: 5 QUOTA
**Proportionately:** 7 TOSCALE
**Proportions**
 Of great: 4 EPIC
**Proposal:** 4 IDEA 5 OFFER
  6 THESIS
 defeated in 1982: 3 ERA
 Freelancer's: 5 QUERY
 Makes a:
  15 POPSTHEQUESTION
 Parliamentary: 6 MOTION
**Propose:** 5 OFFER POSIT
  8 PUTFORTH
 at a meeting: 4 MOVE
 Prepare to: 5 KNEEL
**Proposer**
 prop: 4 KNEE
**Proposition**
 Auxiliary: 5 LEMMA
 Losing: 4 DIET
 Money-losing: 4 SCAM
 Provable: 7 THEOREM
**Proprietor:** 5 OWNER
**Proprietresses**
 Pub: 8 ALEWIVES
**Propyl**
 finish: 3 ENE
 prefix: 3 ISO
**Pros and ___:** 4 CONS
**Prosciutto:** 3 HAM
**Proscribed:** 5 TABOO
  7 FORBADE
**Proscription:** 3 BAN 4 NONO
**Prose**
 piece: 5 ESSAY
 Polish: 4 EDIT
**Prosecute:** 3 TRY
 They ~ perps: 3 DAS
**Prosecutors**
 Perp: 3 DAS
 Subordinate ~ (abbr.): 4 ADAS
**___ prosequi:** 5 NOLLE

**Prosodic**
foot: 4 IAMB
**Prospect**
Derby: 4 COLT
Impractical:
11 PIEINTHESKY
**Prospecting**
tool: 3 PAN
**Prospector**
beast: 4 MULE
find: 3 ORE
property: 5 CLAIM
strike: 4 LODE
**Prosper:** 6 DOWELL THRIVE
French writer: 7 MERIMEE
**Prosperity:** 4 BOOM EASE
6 WEALTH
**Prospero**
Daughter of: 7 MIRANDA
servant: 5 ARIEL
**Prosperous**
Not: 4 LEAN
time: 4 BOOM
times: 3 UPS
**Prost**
of racing: 5 ALAIN
**Prot.:** 3 REL
Certain: 4 EPIS METH
**Protagonist**
Unlikely: 7 NONHERO
8 ANTIHERO
**Protect:** 5 GUARD 6 DEFEND
from floods: 6 EMBANK
~, as freshness: 6 SEALIN
~, in a way: 6 ENCASE
INSURE PATENT
8 LAMINATE
9 INOCULATE
**Protected:** 4 SAFE 6 IMMUNE
area: 7 WETLAND
bird: 5 EGRET
from the elements: 6 INDOOR
from the wind: 4 ALEE
**Protection:** 4 CARE EGIS
5 AEGIS ARMOR
**Protective**
charm: 6 AMULET
container: 3 POD
embankment: 6 ESCARP
garment: 5 SMOCK
plastic: 7 ACETATE
**Protectively**
Hold: 6 CRADLE
**Protectorate**
Former British: 4 ADEN OMAN
6 UGANDA
Former French: 4 LAOS
**Protegé**
maker: 5 MAZDA
**Protein**
acid: 5 AMINO
component: 9 AMINOACID
Muscle: 5 ACTIN
production aid: 3 RNA
source: 3 NUT 4 TOFU
7 SOYBEAN

**Protest:** 4 BEEF 5 DEMUR
SITIN 6 OPPOSE
1960s ~ org.: 3 SDS
French ~ phrase: 4 ABAS
tactic: 5 SITIN
**Protestant**
Certain: 8 LUTHERAN
denom.: 3 BAP 4 EPIS
French: 8 HUGUENOT
**Protester:** 4 ANTI
ploy: 5 SITIN
prop: 8 BULLHORN
**Proteus**
and others: 8 VERONESE
**Proto**
suffix: 5 PLASM
**Protocol:** 6 RUBRIC
**Proton**
holder: 4 ATOM
part: 5 QUARK
prefix: 4 ANTI
**Protopopov**
Skater: 4 OLEG
**Prototype:** 5 MODEL
**Protozoan:** 5 AMEBA 6 AMEBIC
AMOEBA
propellers: 5 CILIA
**Protracted:** 4 LONG
**Protractor**
measure: 5 ANGLE
**Protrude:** 3 JUT 5 BULGE
**Protuberance:** 4 NODE
Small: 3 NUB
Tree: 4 KNAR
**Proudly**
Presents ~, with "out":
5 TROTS
Walk: 5 STRUT
**Proud ___ peacock:** 3 ASA
**Proust**
protagonist: 5 SWANN
Writer: 6 MARCEL
**Prov.**
Book after: 4 ECCL
Canadian: 3 ONT PEI QUE
4 ALTA
**Prove**
false: 5 BELIE
successful: 6 PANOUT
to be human: 3 ERR
useful: 5 AVAIL
**"Proved!"**
letters: 3 QED
**"Prove it!":** 6 SHOWME
**Proven:** 4 SURE 6 TESTED
**Provençal**
pal: 4 AMIE
___ provençale: 3 ALA
**Provence**
city: 5 ARLES
**Proverb:** 3 SAW 5 ADAGE
MAXIM
ending: 3 IAL
**Proverbial**
amount of bricks: 3 TON
backbreaker: 5 STRAW

battlers: 5 SEXES
heirs: 4 MEEK
In the ~ cellar: 4 LAST
More, in a ~ sense: 4 LESS
sword beater: 3 PEN
**Proverbs**
Bk. after: 4 ECCL
**Provide:** 5 ENDUE 6 RENDER
an address: 5 ORATE
an upper surface for: 4 CEIL
food for: 5 CATER
(for): 4 FEND
guidance: 6 MENTOR
new equipment for: 5 REFIT
temporarily: 4 LEND
with funds: 5 ENDOW
with gear: 5 EQUIP
with workers: 5 STAFF
**Provide ___ (save face):**
5 ANOUT
**Provided**
that: 8 ASLONGAS
**Providence**
sch.: 3 URI
**"Providence"**
Lead role in: 3 SYD
**Province:** 4 AREA 5 REALM
Austrian: 5 TYROL
Canadian: 7 ALBERTA
ONTARIO
Chinese: 5 HONAN HUNAN
Italian: 4 ASTI 5 SIENA
UDINE 7 SALERNO
South African: 5 NATAL
Spanish: 4 LEON 5 AVILA
6 ARAGON
**Provinces**
Like some: 8 MARITIME
**Provincetown**
catch: 3 COD
**Provincial:** 4 HICK
one: 5 YOKEL
**Provision**
Contract: 6 CLAUSE
15 ESCALATORCLAUSE
**Proviso**
Auction: 4 ASIS
**Provo**
coll.: 3 BYU
neighbor: 4 LEHI OREM
resident: 5 UTAHN 6 UTAHAN
state: 4 UTAH
**Provocative**
look: 4 LEER
Most: 7 EDGIEST
**Provoke:** 3 IRE IRK VEX
4 DARE GOAD RILE ROIL
SPUR STIR 5 ANGER
TEASE TEMPT
6 AROUSE INCITE
NETTLE STIRUP
**Provoked**
Easily: 5 SHORT
**Prowler**
Night: 6 TOMCAT
8 ALLEYCAT

Proximate: 4 NEAR 7 NEAREST
Proximity: 8 NEARNESS
Prude: 8 BLUENOSE
Prudent: 4 SAGE WARY WISE
Prudential
  rival: 5 AETNA
Prudhomme
  Cajun cookbook author:
    5 ENOLA
Prufrock
  creator: 5 ELIOT 7 TSELIOT
  creator monogram: 3 TSE
Prufrock, J. Alfred
  poet: 3 TSE 7 TSELIOT
Prune: 3 LOP 4 EDIT PARE
  TRIM
  Like a: 5 DRIED
  Prepare a: 4 STEW
  ~, formerly: 4 PLUM
Prurient
  look: 4 LEER
Pruritus: 4 ITCH
Prussian
  Palindromic: 4 OTTO
  pronoun: 3 SIE
Pry: 5 SNOOP
  Apt to: 4 NOSY
  bar: 5 LEVER
Prying: 4 NOSY
Pryor, Richard
  1982 ~ movie: 6 THETOY
Psalm
  word: 5 SELAH
Psalms
  interjection: 5 SELAH
  preceder: 3 JOB
PSAT
  takers: 3 JRS
Pseudo: 4 MOCK
Pseudocultural: 4 ARTY
Pseudodocumentary
  1983 ~: 5 ZELIG
Pseudologue: 4 LIAR
Pseudonym: 5 ALIAS
  Anne Brontë: 5 ACTON
  Lamb: 4 ELIA
  Munro: 4 SAKI
  Romain de Tirtoff: 4 ERTE
Pseudopod
  former: 5 AMEBA 6 AMOEBA
Pseudosophisticated: 4 ARTY
Psi
  follower: 5 OMEGA
  preceder: 3 CHI
"Psst!": 3 HEY 8 OVERHERE
  follower: 6 INHERE
  relative: 4 AHEM
PST
  Part of: 3 STD
Psych
  suffix: 4 OSIS OTIC
Psych.
  research subject: 3 ESP
Psyche
  Damage, as the: 4 SCAR
  Lover of: 4 EROS

part: 3 EGO
parts: 3 IDS
Psyched: 5 EAGER
  about: 5 UPFOR
  up: 4 AGOG
Psychedelic
  drug: 3 LSD
Psychiatrist
  response: 4 ISEE
  ~ Alfred: 5 ADLER
  ~ Carl: 4 JUNG
Psychic: 4 SEER
  A ~ may see it: 4 AURA
  power: 3 ESP
  reading material: 4 AURA
  ~ Edgar: 5 CAYCE
  ~ Geller: 3 URI
  ~ "Miss": 4 CLEO
"Psycho"
  actor Bates: 6 NORMAN
  actress Anne: 5 HECHE
  actress Miles: 4 VERA
  motel: 5 BATES
  setting: 5 MOTEL
Psychoanalysis
  subject: 3 EGO
Psychoanalyst
  term: 12 FREUDIANSLIP
  ~ Fromm: 5 ERICH
Psychological
  shock: 6 TRAUMA
  ~ Burton-Firth film: 5 EQUUS
Psychologist
  Giant of a: 4 JUNG
  study: 6 AUTISM
  Swiss: 6 PIAGET
  ~ Bettelheim: 5 BRUNO
  ~ Jean: 6 PIAGET
  ~ Jung: 4 CARL
  ~ May: 5 ROLLO
Pt.
  or qt.: 3 AMT
P.T.
  boat officer: 3 ENS
  boats are in it: 3 USN
  program: 5 REHAB
PTA
  concern (abbr.): 4 EDUC
  meeting place (abbr.): 3 SCH
  member: 6 PARENT
  part: 4 ASSN
Pterodactyl
  Screen: 5 RODAN
Pts.
  8 ~: 3 GAL
  parts: 3 OZS
  They're worth 6: 3 TDS
Pub
  fixture: 3 TAP
  game: 5 DARTS 7 SNOOKER
  Go from ~ to pub: 6 BARHOP
  order: 3 ALE 4 PINT 5 LAGER
    STEIN STOUT 6 PORTER
    7 PALEALE
  projectile: 4 DART
  proprietresses: 8 ALEWIVES

purchase: 4 PINT
stock: 4 ALES
Public: 5 OVERT
  announcers: 6 CRIERS
  English ~ school: 4 ETON
  hanging: 3 ART
  hangings: 7 ARTSHOW
  house: 3 INN
  image, for short: 3 REP
  In the ~ eye: 4 SEEN
  Make: 3 AIR 4 BARE
    7 RELEASE 8 ANNOUNCE
  opinion: 6 VOXPOP
  outburst: 5 SCENE
  performer: 7 ARTISTE
  persona: 5 IMAGE
  procession: 6 PARADE
  reader: 6 LECTOR
  relations concern: 4 SPIN
    5 IMAGE
  role: 7 PERSONA
  row: 5 SCENE
  sentiment: 5 ETHOS
  Sought ~ office: 3 RAN
  speaker: 6 ORATOR
  speech: 7 ORATION
  square: 5 PLAZA
  square of old: 5 AGORA
  to-do: 5 SCENE
  transport: 3 BUS
  ___ public: 6 NOTARY
  ___ publica: 3 RES
Publican
  potable: 3 ALE
Publication
  Fan: 4 ZINE
  Humor: 11 MADMAGAZINE
  Online: 5 EZINE
  Prepare for: 4 EDIT
Public Citizen
  founder: 5 NADER
Publicist
  concern: 5 IMAGE
Publicity: 3 INK
  Exaggerated: 4 HYPE
  Major: 6 HOOPLA
  person: 5 AGENT
  piece: 7 RELEASE
  seeker act: 5 STUNT
Publicize: 3 AIR
Publish: 5 ISSUE
Published: 3 RAN 7 INPRINT
Publisher: 6 ISSUER
  Available from the: 7 INPRINT
  Big paperback: 3 TOR 4 AVON
  Famous jour.: 3 AMA
  Playboy: 6 HEFNER
  pursuit: 12 SERIALRIGHTS
  ~ Adolph: 4 OCHS
  ~ Ballantine: 3 IAN
  ~ Chandler: 4 OTIS
  ~ Henry: 4 LUCE
Publishers
  Like some textbook: 4 ELHI
Publishing
  Big inits. in paperback: 3 NAL

Big name in book: 5 KNOPF
Big name in newspaper:
　4 OCHS
　employee: 6 EDITOR READER
**Pubmates:** 4 LADS
**Pucci**
　Designer: 6 EMILIO
**Puccini**
　heroine: 5 TOSCA
　opera: 5 EDGAR TOSCA
　　8 LABOHEME
　piece: 4 ARIA 5 OPERA
　work: 5 TOSCA
**Puck:** 3 IMP
　Pass the ~ to: 4 FEED
　stopper: 6 GOALIE
　The ~ stops here: 3 NET
**Pucker:** 5 PURSE
　producing: 4 TART
**Puckered**
　fabric: 6 PLISSE
**Puckish:** 5 ELFIN
**Pudding:** 7 DESSERT
　flavor: 7 TAPIOCA
　ingredient: 3 EGG FIG 4 SAGO
　　SUET
　Kind of: 4 RICE 5 HASTY
　starch: 4 SAGO
**Puddle**
　Play in a: 5 SLOSH 6 SPLOSH
**Puddle-jumper:** 7 AIRTAXI
**Pudgy**
　Beyond: 5 OBESE
**Pueblo**
　chamber: 4 KIVA
　home: 5 ADOBE
　material: 5 ADOBE
　New Mexico: 4 TAOS
　pot: 4 OLLA
**Pueblo Indian:** 4 HOPI ZUNI
**Puente**
　Bandleader: 4 TITO
　music: 5 SALSA
　specialty: 5 MAMBO
**Puerto ___:** 4 RICO 5 RICAN
**Puerto Rican**
　city: 7 ARECIBO
　port: 5 PONCE
**___ Puf (softener brand):** 3 STA
**Puff:** 4 GASP TOKE WISP
　　6 DRAGON
　Cream: 4 WIMP 6 ECLAIR
　Huff and: 4 BLOW PANT
　Move on a ~ of air: 4 WAFT
　of smoke: 4 WISP
　up: 4 RISE 5 BLOAT ELATE
**Puff ___:** 5 ADDER
**Puff Daddy**
　music: 3 RAP
**Puffed:** 4 BLEW
　up: 4 SMUG VAIN 7 SWOLLEN
**Puffin**
　relative: 3 AUK
**Puffy**
　Ex of: 3 JLO
　white hat person: 4 CHEF

**Pug:** 3 DOG
　Practice with a: 4 SPAR
　workplace: 5 ARENA
**Puget Sound**
　city: 6 TACOMA 7 SEATTLE
**Pugilism**
　Practice: 4 SPAR
**Pugilist**
　gp.: 3 IBF WBA
　Poetic: 3 ALI
　punch: 3 JAB
　"Rope-a-dope": 3 ALI
　weapon: 4 FIST
　~ Laila: 3 ALI
**"Puh-leeze!":** 7 SPAREME
**Pulitzer:** *see pages 716–717*
　1934 ~ writer: 4 AGAR
　1953 ~ playwright: 4 INGE
　1958 ~ author: 4 AGEE
　1975 ~ critic: 5 EBERT
　1977 ~ winner: 5 HALEY
　　9 ALEXHALEY
　1999 ~ play: 3 WIT
　category: 5 DRAMA
　critic Richard: 4 EDER
　novelist Glasgow: 5 ELLEN
　paper: 5 WORLD
　playwright Akins: 3 ZOE
　poet Van Duyn: 4 MONA
　Posthumous ~ winner: 4 AGEE
　winner James: 4 AGEE
　winner Pyle: 5 ERNIE
　winner Welty: 6 EUDORA
　winning biographer Leon:
　　4 EDEL
　winning biographer Nevins:
　　5 ALLAN
　winning columnist Mike:
　　5 ROYKO
　winning humorist Barry:
　　4 DAVE
　winning novel of 1925: 5 SOBIG
**Pulka**
　rider: 4 LAPP
**Pull:** 3 TOW TUG 5 CLOUT
　a boner: 3 ERR 4 GOOF
　along: 3 TOW 4 HAUL
　an all-nighter: 4 CRAM
　apart: 4 REND TEAR
　　8 SEPARATE
　a plow: 4 TILL
　a sulky: 4 TROT
　back: 6 REININ
　down: 4 EARN
　Gp. with: 3 ADA
　in: 6 ARRIVE
　(in): 4 REIN
　on: 5 TUGAT
　out: 6 SECEDE
　out all the stops: 6 LETRIP
　Quick: 4 JERK
　the plug on: 3 END 4 STOP
　They have: 4 OXEN
　up stakes: 4 MOVE 6 DECAMP
　up to a bar: 4 CHIN
　with effort: 3 LUG

**Pull-down**
　Word after: 4 MENU
**Pulled:** 4 DREW
　apart: 4 TORE
　It's ~ on a farm: 5 UDDER
　off: 3 DID
**Puller**
　Nail: 4 CLAW
　Plow: 4 TEAM
**Pullers**
　Plow: 4 OXEN TEAM
**Pullet**
　Former: 3 HEN
**Pulley:** 7 MACHINE
**Pulling**
　One ~ strings: 5 TUNER
**Pullman:** 3 CAR
　place: 5 BERTH
　porter: 6 REDCAP
**Pull-off:** 8 RESTAREA
　　RESTSTOP
**Pull ___ one:** 5 AFAST
**Pullover:** 4 POLO
　African: 7 DASHIKI
　Colorful: 7 DASHIKI
**Pulls:** 3 INS
　It ~ a bit: 4 REIN
**Pull-up**
　Do a: 4 CHIN
**Pulp**
　Beat to a: 4 MASH
**"Pulp Fiction"**
　actress Plummer: 6 AMANDA
　actress Thurman: 3 UMA
　costar of John: 3 UMA
　She played Mia in: 3 UMA
　Uma role in: 3 MIA
**Pulpit**
　Early: 4 AMBO
**Pulpits:** 6 ROSTRA
**Pulsate:** 5 THROB
**Pulse**
　alternative: 4 TONE
**Pulver**
　rank (abbr.): 3 ENS
**Pulverize:** 4 MASH 5 CRUSH
　　SMASH
**Puma:** 3 CAT
　rival: 6 ADIDAS
**Pumice**
　feature: 4 PORE
　source: 4 LAVA
**Pummel:** 4 MAUL 6 BEATON
**Pump:** 3 ASK 4 SHOE
　Bodybuilders ~ it: 4 IRON
　Fix a: 6 REHEEL RESOLE
　Gas ~ choice (abbr.): 3 REG
　levy: 6 GASTAX
　number: 6 OCTANE
　Old ~ name: 4 ESSO
　part: 4 HEEL SOLE 6 INSOLE
　Prepare the: 5 PRIME
　preserver: 8 SHOETREE
　rating: 6 OCTANE
　Vital: 5 HEART
**Pumped:** 4 SHOD

It may be: 4 IRON
**Pumper**
  Iron ~ pride: 3 ABS 4 PECS
**Pumpernickel**
  alternative: 3 RYE
**"Pumping ___":** 4 IRON
**Pumpkin**
  and pecan: 4 PIES
  color: 6 ORANGE
  kin: 5 GOURD
  Noted ~ eater: 5 PETER
  seed: 6 PEPITA
**Pumps**
  In: 4 SHOD
  Letters on some: 3 EEE
**Pun:** 7 GROANER
  conclusion: 4 STER
  React to a bad: 4 MOAN OUCH
    5 GROAN WINCE
  response: 4 HAHA 5 GROAN
**Punch:** 3 JAB 4 SOCK TANG
  bowl item: 5 LADLE
  card remnant: 4 CHAD
  in: 5 ENTER
  ingredient: 4 FIST
  It may give ~ punch: 3 RUM
  Juice with: 9 HARDCIDER
  Kind of: 6 ONETWO
  Packing a: 6 POTENT
  Partner of: 4 JUDY
  Pleased as: 4 GLAD 6 ELATED
  Poem with a ~ line:
    8 LIMERICK
  Prepared to: 9 HAULEDOFF
  Quick: 3 JAB
  Reaction to a stomach: 3 OOF
  server: 5 LADLE
  Small: 3 AWL
  sound: 3 POW
  Spike the: 4 LACE
  with punch: 7 SANGRIA
**Puncher**
  Hole: 3 AWL 8 STILETTO
**Punches**
  Roll with the: 5 ADAPT
  Some: 4 AWLS 5 LEFTS
  Trade: 4 SPAR
**Punching**
  Practice: 4 SPAR
  tool: 3 AWL
**Punctual:** 6 ONTIME
**Punctually:** 8 ONTHEDOT
**Punctuation**
  Bit of: 6 EMDASH
  mark: 4 DASH 5 COLON
    COMMA
  Telegram: 4 STOP
**Puncture:** 4 STAB 5 PRICK
  prefix: 3 ACU
  sound: 3 SSS 4 SISS
**Pundit:** 4 SAGE 5 SWAMI
    6 SAVANT
  TV ~ Rooney: 4 ANDY
  ~ Gary: 5 BAUER
**Pungent:** 5 ACRID TANGY
    6 STRONG

bulb: 5 ONION
cheese: 6 ASIAGO
green: 5 CRESS
pepper: 8 JALAPENO
veggie: 5 ONION
**Punic Wars**
  side: 8 CARTHAGE
**Punish:** 7 CHASTEN
  by fine: 6 AMERCE
  Serving to: 5 PENAL
  ~, in a way: 4 CANE FINE
    5 SPANK
**Punishment**
  Civil: 4 FINE
  Kid's: 4 NOTV
  Light: 4 SLAP
  Makeshift ~ tool: 5 RULER
  Partner of: 5 CRIME
  Subject to: 5 PENAL
  symbol: 3 ROD
  unit: 4 LASH
**Punjab**
  Capital of ~ province:
    6 LAHORE
  Early invader of the: 5 ARYAN
  princess: 4 RANI
  sect member: 4 SIKH
**Punjabi**
  believer: 4 SIKH
  princess: 4 RANI
**Punk**
  Feels: 4 AILS
  genre: 3 EMO
  icon Joey: 6 RAMONE
  Pop of: 4 IGGY
  rock outgrowth: 7 NEWWAVE
**"Punk'd"**
  network: 3 MTV
**Punkie:** 4 GNAT
**Punster:** 3 WIT
**Punt:** 4 BOAT
  path: 3 ARC
**Punta ___, Chile:** 6 ARENAS
**Punta del ___, Uruguay:**
    4 ESTE
**Punter:** 7 BOATMAN
**Punxsutawney**
  groundhog: 4 PHIL
**Puny**
  pest: 4 GNAT
**Pup**
  Bite like a: 3 NIP
  cry: 3 YIP 4 YELP
  Primer: 4 SPOT
  Smallest: 4 RUNT
**Pup ___:** 4 TENT
**Pupa**
  graduate: 5 IMAGO
  preceder: 5 LARVA
  protection: 6 COCOON
**Pupil:** 5 TUTEE
  Act like a: 9 TAKENOTES
  Constriction of the: 6 MIOSIS
  controller: 4 IRIS
  French: 5 ELEVE
  of Jane Eyre: 5 ADELE

place: 3 EYE 4 IRIS
protector: 3 LID 6 CORNEA
surrounder: 4 IRIS 6 AREOLA
Where a ~ sits: 4 IRIS
**Puppet**
  dragon: 5 OLLIE
  Kukla's ~ pal: 5 OLLIE
  Shari Lewis: 8 LAMBCHOP
**Puppeteer**
  ~ Baird: 3 BIL
  ~ Bil: 5 BAIRD
  ~ Lewis: 5 SHARI
  ~ Tony: 4 SARG
**Puppies**
  Have: 5 WHELP
  Like: 4 CUTE
**Puppy**
  bite: 3 NIP
  Go after, like a: 5 NIPAT
  love: 5 CRUSH
  sound: 3 YAP YIP 4 YELP
**"Puppy Love"**
  singer: 4 ANKA 6 OSMOND
**Pups**
  Praises for: 4 PATS
  Some: 5 SEALS
**Pupu platter**
  party: 4 LUAU
**___ pura:** 4 AQUA
**Purchase:** 3 BUY
  incentive: 6 REBATE
  Prime: 5 STEAK
  Proof of ~ (abbr.): 4 RCPT
  Risky: 10 PIGINAPOKE
**Purchased**
  How some stocks are: 5 ATPAR
**Purchasing**
  Govt. ~ org.: 3 GSA
**Purdue Univ.**
  major: 3 AGR
**Pure:** 6 CHASTE
  and simple: 4 MERE
  Make: 6 REFINE
**"Pure ___"** (1994 jazz album):
    4 ELLA
**Purebred**
  Not: 4 MUTT
**Purée**
  Red: 10 TOMATOSOUP
**Puréed**
  peas eater: 4 BABY
**Purely**
  academic: 4 MOOT
**"Pure Woman"**
  Hardy's: 4 TESS
**"Purgatorio"**
  poet: 5 DANTE
**Purge:** 3 RID 7 CLEANSE
**Purged:** 3 RID
**Purify:** 6 REFINE 7 CLEANSE
**Purim**
  honoree: 6 ESTHER
  month: 4 ADAR
**Purina**
  rival: 4 ALPO
**Puritan:** 4 PRIG

**Puritanical**
  one: 5 PRISS 8 BLUENOSE
**Purity**
  Mythical symbol of:
    7 UNICORN
  symbol: 4 LILY
  unit: 5 KARAT
**Purlieu:** 4 AREA
**Purloin:** 5 STEAL
**Purloined:** 5 STOLE
**"Purloined Letter, The"**
  detective: 5 DUPIN
  writer: 3 POE
**Purple**
  bloom: 5 LILAC
  Bluish: 5 MAUVE
  Dark: 4 PUCE
  fruit: 4 PLUM SLOE
  Pale reddish: 5 LILAC
  Shade of: 4 PUCE 5 GRAPE
    LILAC MAUVE
**Purple Heart:** 5 MEDAL
**"Purple People Eater, The"**
  singer Wooley: 4 SHEB
**Purplish**
  hue: 5 LILAC
  red: 7 MAGENTA
  shade: 5 MAUVE
  Tree with ~ flowers: 5 PAPAW
**Purport:** 5 CLAIM TENOR
**Purpose:** 3 AIM END USE
    4 SAKE 5 SENSE
    6 INTENT
  For a specific: 5 ADHOC
  Lose on: 5 THROW
  Sans: 4 IDLY
  Serve the: 5 AVAIL
  Serving a: 5 UTILE
  Ultimate: 6 ENDALL ENDUSE
  Walked with: 6 STRODE
  Without: 4 IDLY
**Purposeful:** 7 EARNEST
**Purring**
  animal: 3 CAT
**Purse:** 3 BAG
  alternative: 7 SATCHEL
  holder: 5 STRAP
**Pursue:** 4 HUNT SEEK SHAG
    5 CHASE STALK TRAIL
  as a trade: 3 PLY
  relentlessly: 3 DOG 5 HOUND
**Pursuer**
  of the Pleiades: 5 ORION
  Pusher: 4 NARC
**Pursuing:** 5 AFTER
**Pursuit:** 4 HUNT 5 CHASE
    QUEST
  In ~ of: 5 AFTER
  Vein: 3 ORE
**Purviance**
  Actress: 4 EDNA
**Purview:** 5 SCOPE 6 SPHERE
**Pusan**
  native: 6 KOREAN
**Push:** 4 PROD SELL URGE
    5 SHOVE

(around): 4 BOSS
  forward: 4 URGE 5 IMPEL
  Give a little: 5 NUDGE
  out of bed: 5 ROUST
  roughly: 5 SHOVE
  ~, so to speak: 6 PEDDLE
**Push-button**
  Not: 4 DIAL
**Pushed**
  It may get ~ around: 4 CART
  the doorbell: 4 RANG
**Pusher**
  customer: 4 USER
  Harbor: 3 TUG
  Pedal: 4 FOOT
  Pencil: 6 WRITER
  Petal: 3 BEE
  pursuer: 4 NARC
**Pushkin**
  hero: 5 BORIS 6 ONEGIN
**Pushover:** 5 PATSY 6 SOFTIE
**Pushrod**
  pusher: 3 CAM
**Push-up**
  Kind of: 6 ONEARM
  muscle: 3 PEC
**Pushy**
  Get: 5 PRESS
**Pusillanimous:** 5 TIMID
**Puss:** 3 MUG
  Wear a: 4 POUT
**Pussy**
  foot: 3 PAW
**Pussycat**
  shipmate: 3 OWL
**Pussycats**
  Leader of the: 5 JOSIE
**Pussyfoot:** 5 SNEAK
**Put:** 3 LAY 7 SITUATE
  a cap on: 5 LIMIT
  a match to: 3 LIT 6 IGNITE
  an early end to:
    11 NIPINTHEBUD
  an edge on: 4 HONE WHET
    5 HONED
  an end to: 4 STOP 5 CEASE
  another way: 7 REWRITE
  aside: 5 ALLOT 6 SHELVE
  a strain on: 3 TAX 5 TAXED
  at risk: 7 IMPERIL
    8 ENDANGER
  a value on: 6 ASSESS
  away: 3 ATE EAT ICE 4 ICED
    SAVE STOW 5 EATEN
    SAVED STASH STORE
    6 ENTOMB STORED
    STOWED 7 SHEATHE
    8 STOREDUP
  back: 4 STET 5 RESET
    7 RESTORE
  down: 3 DIS LAY SET 4 LAID
    5 ABASE QUELL WROTE
    6 ABASED BERATE
    DEMEAN DISSED STIFLE
    7 ASPERSE DERIDED
  down in writing: 5 LIBEL

down roots: 6 SETTLE
  forth: 3 ASK 5 EXERT POSIT
  forward: 5 OFFER POSED
    POSIT 6 ASSERT
  in: 3 ADD
  in a kiln: 3 DRY
  in cipher: 6 ENCODE
  in office: 5 ELECT
  in order: 4 SORT 7 ARRANGE
  in place: 5 SITED
  in power: 8 ENTHRONE
  in rollers: 3 SET
  in stitches: 3 SEW 4 DARN
    SEWN SLAY 5 SEWED
  in the bank: 5 SAVED
  in the cup: 5 HOLED
  in the hold: 4 LADE STOW
  in the mail: 4 SEND SENT
  in the pot: 4 ANTE
  into action: 3 USE 5 EXERT
  into law: 5 ENACT
  into motion: 7 ACTUATE
  into piles: 4 SORT
  into service: 3 USE
  into words: 3 SAY 5 UTTER
    7 UTTERED
  it to: 3 ASK
  next to: 6 APPOSE
  Not stay: 4 ROAM
  off: 5 DEFER DELAY DETER
    REPEL TABLE
    8 ALIENATE POSTPONE
  on: 3 ADD DON 4 GAIN WEAR
    5 AIRED APPLY LADED
    STAGE 6 STAGED
  on again: 7 RESTAGE
  on a happy face: 5 SMILE
  on a pedestal: 5 ADORE EXALT
    6 ADORED ESTEEM
    7 ADULATE
  on a scale: 4 RATE
  on a spare tire: 4 GAIN
  on board: 4 LADE STOW
  on cargo: 4 LADE
  on cloud nine: 5 ELATE
  on cuffs: 5 ALTER
  one over on: 6 SNOWED
  one past: 3 ACE 4 ACED
  one's finger on: 7 PINDOWN
  one's foot down: 4 STEP TROD
    5 STOMP
  one's two cents in: 4 ANTE
    5 OPINE
  on ice: 5 CHILL TABLE
  on notice: 4 WARN
  on the books: 5 ENACT
  on the line: 4 RISK
  on the market: 4 SELL
  on the payroll: 4 HIRE
    5 HIRED
  on the rack: 7 TORTURE
  on TV: 3 AIR 5 AIRED
  out: 3 IRK TAG 4 EMIT IRED
    SORE 5 DOUSE EVICT
    IRATE ISSUE 6 DOUSED
    ISSUED

out (effort): 5 EXERT
out of commission: 7 DISABLE
out of sight: 4 HIDE
right: 5 AMEND 6 INDENT
spin on: 4 SKEW
Stay: 6 REMAIN
the collar on: 3 NAB 6 ARREST
the kibosh on: 3 END NIX
    4 VETO 5 ENDED NIXED
the pedal to the metal: 4 SPED
the squeeze on: 5 PRESS
the whammy on: 5 HEXED
They're ~ on: 4 AIRS
through a sieve: 5 RICED
together: 4 MADE 5 AMASS
    RIGUP UNITE
to rest: 5 ALLAY
to shame: 5 ABASH
to sleep: 4 BORE LULL
to the grindstone: 5 HONED
to the test: 3 USE 5 ASSAY
    7 ESSAYED
to use: 5 EXERT
to work: 3 USE 4 USED
    6 EMPLOY
two and two together: 3 ADD
under: 6 SEDATE
up: 4 POST 5 BUILD BUILT
    ERECT HOUSE STORE
    6 HOUSED 7 ERECTED
up a fight: 6 RESIST
up a fuss: 6 BEEFED
up for sale: 5 OFFER
up on the wall: 4 HANG
up with: 5 ABIDE STAND
    STOOD 6 ABIDED
Well: 3 APT
your hands together: 4 CLAP
Put ___ (ask a hard question):
    4 ITTO
"Put a lid ___!": 4 ONIT
"Put a lid on it!": 3 SHH
Put an ___ (stop): 5 ENDTO
"Put a sock ___!": 4 INIT
"Put a sock in it!": 3 SHH
"Put a tiger in your tank"
  company: 4 ESSO
Put-down: 4 SLAP SLUR
Put ___ good word for: 3 INA
"Put ___ Happy Face": 3 ONA

**Putin**
  denial: 4 NYET
  Former ~ org.: 3 KGB
**Putin, Vladimir**
  former org.: 3 KGB
Put in ___ for: 4 ABID
"... ___ put it another way ...":
    4 ORTO
"Put ___ my bill": 4 ITON
"Put ___ my tab": 4 ITON
**Putnam**
  Revolutionary War patriot:
    5 RUFUS
**Put-on:** 3 ACT 4 HOAX SHAM
**Put one's ___ (meddle):**
    5 OARIN
"Put ___ on it!": 4 ALID
**Putt**
  First to ~, usually: 4 AWAY
  Make a: 4 SINK
  Sank, as a: 5 HOLED
  Short: 5 TAPIN
  Sink a: 7 HOLEOUT
  Very short ~, say: 5 GIMME
**Putter**
  Shot: 7 SYRINGE
  target: 3 CUP 4 HOLE
**Putterer:** 7 AMATEUR
"Put the gun down!": 6 DROPIT
"Puttin' On the ___": 4 RITZ
Put ___ to: 5 ANEND ASTOP
Put to ___ (outdo): 5 SHAME
"Put ___ writing": 4 ITIN
"Put Your Head on My
    Shoulder"
  singer: 4 ANKA
**Puzo**
  Author: 5 MARIO
  novel: 6 OMERTA
  subject: 5 MAFIA
**Puzzle:** 5 POSER 6 BEMUSE
    ENIGMA
  pattern: 4 GRID
  Pencil: 4 MAZE
  Picture: 5 REBUS
  Seven-piece: 7 TANGRAM
  solver's shout: 3 AHA
  suffix: 4 MENT
  Tough: 5 POSER
  unit: 5 PIECE

**Puzzled:** 5 ATSEA 7 ATALOSS
  comments: 3 EHS
**Puzzlement:** 6 ENIGMA
**Puzzles:** 8 ENIGMATA
  First word in: 6 ACROSS
**Pvt.**
  Like a ~ washing dishes:
    4 ONKP
  superior: 3 CPL SGT
**PX**
  patrons: 3 GIS 4 NCOS
**Pygmalion**
  Love of: 7 GALATEA
**"Pygmalion"**
  heroine: 5 ELIZA
  monogram: 3 GBS
  playwright: 4 SHAW
**Pygmy**
  antelope: 5 ORIBI
**Pyle**
  Journalist: 5 ERNIE
  of Mayberry: 5 GOMER
  player: 6 NABORS
**Pyle, Gomer:** 6 MARINE
  org.: 4 USMC
**Pym**
  Creator of Miss: 3 TEY
**Pymt.**
  Homeowner: 4 MTGE
**Pyramid:** 4 TOMB
  Bill with a: 3 ONE
  builders: 5 MAYAS 6 MAYANS
  Food ~ org.: 4 USDA
  scheme: 4 SCAM
**Pyramide du Louvre**
  designer: 5 IMPEI
**Pyramus**
  Lover of: 6 THISBE
**Pyrenees**
  **Info:** Spanish cue
  realm: 7 ANDORRA
**Pysanky**
  need: 3 EGG
**Pythagorean**
  proposition: 7 THEOREM
  ~ P: 3 RHO
**Pythias**
  Pal of: 5 DAMON
**Python:** 5 SNAKE
  Kipling: 3 KAA

**Q**
Queue after: 3 RST 4 RSTU
Queue before: 3 NOP 4 MNOP
**Q45**
maker: 8 INFINITI
**Qabus bin Said:** 5 OMANI
country: 4 OMAN
**Qaddafi:** 6 LIBYAN
country: 5 LIBYA
**Q&A**
Part of: 3 ANS
**Qantas**
symbol: 5 KOALA
**Qatar**
capital: 4 DOHA
leader: 4 EMIR
place: 6 ARABIA
resident: 4 ARAB
**Qatari:** 4 ARAB
leader: 4 EMIR
**QB:** 6 PASSER
mistake: 3 INT
stat: 3 TDS YDS
**"QB ___":** 3 VII
**"QB VII"**
author: 4 URIS
**QED**
Part of: 4 ERAT QUOD
**Qintars**
100 ~: 3 LEK
**Qom**
country: 4 IRAN
money: 4 RIAL
resident: 5 IRANI
**"Q ___ queen":** 4 ASIN
**Qt.:** 3 AMT
couple: 3 PTS
**Q-Tip:** 4 SWAB
target: 3 EAR 6 EARWAX
**Qtr.**
starter: 3 OCT
**Qtrs.**
Fifth: 3 OTS
Transient: 3 SRO
**Qts.:** 4 AMTS
Four: 3 GAL
Parts of: 3 PTS
**Qty.:** 3 AMT
Egg: 3 DOZ
**Q-U**
connection: 3 RST
**Quaalude**
Give a ~ to: 6 SEDATE
**Quad**
building: 4 DORM
~ VIP: 4 BMOC
**Quadrennial**
candidate Harold: 7 STASSEN

games org.: 3 IOC
pol. event: 4 CONV
**Quadri-**
Cousin of: 3 TRI UNI 4 HEXA
OCTA 5 TETRA
preceder: 3 TRI
**Quaff**
Green: 7 LIMEADE
Herbal: 3 TEA 7 MINTTEA
Holiday: 3 NOG 6 EGGNOG
Japanese: 4 SAKE
Middle Ages: 4 MEAD
Minty: 5 JULEP
Pub: 3 ALE 4 BEER
Radar's: 4 NEHI
Sailor's: 4 GROG
Summer: 3 ADE
**Quagmire:** 3 BOG FEN
5 MARSH SWAMP
6 MORASS
**Quahog:** 4 CLAM
**Quaid, Dennis**
film: 3 DOA
**Quai d'Orsay**
river: 5 SEINE
**Quail:** 5 COWER
group: 4 BEVY 5 COVEY
**Quaint:** 3 ODD
contraction: 5 TWERE
establishment: 6 SHOPPE
expletive: 4 EGAD
lodging: 3 INN
road: 4 LANE
sigh: 4 AHME
**Quake:** 5 SEISM 6 TREMOR
**Quaker:** 5 ASPEN 6 FRIEND
cereal: 3 OHS
colonist: 4 PENN
in the woods: 5 ASPEN
pronoun: 3 THY 4 THEE
THOU 5 THINE
**Quaker ___:** 4 OATS
**Quakers:** 4 SECT
**Quaker State**
port: 4 ERIE
**Quaking:** 8 ATREMBLE
in one's boots: 6 SCARED
tree: 5 ASPEN
**Qualcomm Stadium**
player: 5 PADRE
**Qualification**
Without: 6 FLATLY
**Qualified:** 3 APT 4 ABLE
8 ELIGIBLE
Most ~ to serve: 4 ONEA
to work: 7 HIRABLE
**Qualifiers:** 3 IFS
**Qualify:** 7 ENTITLE

**Qualifying**
race: 4 HEAT
**Quality:** 4 GOOD ODOR TONE
5 TRAIT
Attractive: 6 APPEAL
Carpet: 4 PILE
Cool: 7 HIPNESS
Gung-ho: 4 ZEAL ZEST
Laid-back: 4 EASE
Muscle: 4 TONE
Pervasive: 4 AURA
Sound: 4 TONE 6 TIMBRE
Valuable: 5 ASSET
Winter air: 3 NIP
**Qualm:** 4 PANG
**___ quam videri (North
Carolina motto):**
4 ESSE
**Quandary:** 3 FIX 7 DILEMMA
In a: 5 ATSEA
**___ quandary:** 3 INA
**___ qua non:** 4 SINE
**Quant, Mary**
design: 4 MINI 9 MINISKIRT
look: 3 MOD
**Quantity:** 6 AMOUNT
(abbr.): 3 AMT
Cookie: 5 BATCH
Fixed: 4 UNIT
Large: 3 SEA 4 HEAP MUCH
RAFT SCAD SLEW
5 OCEAN 6 OODLES
Medicinal: 4 DOSE
Paper: 4 REAM
Small: 4 IOTA
Unspecified: 3 ANY 4 SOME
Yarn: 5 SKEIN
**Quantum:** 6 AMOUNT
event: 4 LEAP
physics particle: 5 MESON
**Quarantine:** 6 ENISLE
7 ISOLATE
**"Quare Fellow, The"**
author: 5 BEHAN
**Quark**
A ~ and an antiquark:
5 MESON
place: 4 ATOM
**Quarrel:** 3 ROW 4 SPAT TIFF
5 ARGUE RUNIN SCRAP
SETTO 6 BICKER
DUSTUP
settler: 4 DUEL
**Quarry:** 3 PIT 4 MINE PREY
Cop's: 4 PERP
Hunter's: 3 ELK
MP's: 4 AWOL
Sniggler's: 3 EEL

**Quart**
British: 5 LITRE
fractions (abbr.): 3 PTS
Metric: 5 LITER
quartet: 4 CUPS
**Quarter:** 4 AREA COIN
        6 LOCALE 7 TWOBITS
Algerian: 6 CASBAH
back: 5 EAGLE
millennium: 3 CCL
of four: 3 ONE
Word on a: 4 UNUM
**Quarterback:** 6 PASSER
        7 OVERSEE
option: 4 PASS 5 SNEAK
setback: 4 LOSS
target: 3 END
**Quarterfinal**
group: 5 OCTET
**Quarter note**
line: 4 STEM
**Quarters:** 5 ABODE AREAS
Camper's: 4 TENT
Campus: 4 DORM
Clergyman's: 5 MANSE
Conical: 5 TEPEE
Cruise: 5 CABIN
Four: 3 ONE 4 YEAR
Frozen: 5 IGLOO
Skier's: 5 LODGE
Two: 4 HALF
**Quartet**
Alphabet: 4 ABCD BCDE
        CDEF *etc.*
Country: 7 ALABAMA
Deck: 4 ACES
Half of a pop: 5 MAMAS PAPAS
member: 4 ALTO BASS
        5 CELLO VIOLA
minus one: 4 TRIO
Swedish: 4 ABBA
"___ Quartet, The": 3 RAJ
**Quartz**
Golden-brown ~ stone:
        9 TIGERSEYE
material: 6 SILICA
variety: 4 ONYX OPAL
        5 AGATE TOPAZ
        6 JASPER
**Quash:** 3 END 4 STOP VETO
**Quasimodo**
creator: 4 HUGO
portrayer: 3 LON
**Quaternary**
division: 6 ICEAGE
**Quatrain:** 6 STANZA
rhyme scheme: 4 ABAA ABAB
        ABBA
**Quatro**
Singer: 4 SUZI
**Quattro**
maker: 4 AUDI
preceder: 3 TRE
Tre plus: 5 SETTE
**Quaver:** 4 NOTE
**Quay:** 4 PIER 5 WHARF

**Quayle**
successor: 4 GORE
Vice president: 3 DAN
**Que**
follower, in song: 4 SERA
**Que.**
neighbor: 3 ONT
"Qué ___ ?": 4 PASA
**Queasiness:** 6 NAUSEA
**Queasy:** 3 ILL
Feel: 3 AIL
feeling: 6 NAUSEA
**Québec**
campus: 5 LAVAL
connections: 3 ETS
friend: 3 AMI
Hot time in: 3 ETE 4 AOUT
Part of many ~ place names:
        3 STE
peninsula: 5 GASPE
school: 5 ECOLE
vote: 3 NON
**Quechua**
speaker: 4 INCA
Where ~ is spoken: 4 PERU
        7 BOLIVIA
**Queeg**
creator: 4 WOUK
ship: 5 CAINE
**Queen:** 4 CARD
Babar's: 7 CELESTE
county: 5 SHIRE
Fairy: 3 MAB
Fit for a: 5 REGAL ROYAL
French: 5 REINE
Hindu: 4 RANI 5 RANEE
Jordanian: 4 NOOR
Land of a biblical: 5 SHEBA
Nile: 4 CLEO
Norse underworld: 3 HEL
of Carthage: 4 DIDO
of fiction: 6 ELLERY
of Persia, in the Bible:
        6 ESTHER
of rap: 7 LATIFAH
of Thebes: 5 NIOBE
        7 JOCASTA
Olympus: 4 HERA
Scat: 4 ELLA
Spanish: 3 ENA
Spartan: 4 LEDA
subject: 3 ANT
topper: 5 TIARA
**Queen ___ :** 3 MUM
**Queendom**
Biblical: 5 SHEBA
Cleopatra's: 5 EGYPT
"___ Queene, The": 6 FAERIE
**Queen Elizabeth II:** 5 LINER
Daughter of: 4 ANNE
Letters that precede: 3 HRH
**Queen ___ lace:** 5 ANNES
**Queenly**
crown: 5 TIARA
**Queen Margarethe**
land: 7 DENMARK

subjects: 5 DANES
**Queen of Country**
singer McEntire: 4 REBA
**Queen of Hearts**
dessert: 5 TARTS
tart thief: 5 KNAVE
**"Queen of Mean"**
~ Helmsley: 5 LEONA
**Queen of Soul**
~ Franklin: 6 ARETHA
**Queens**
section: 7 ASTORIA
stadium: 4 ASHE SHEA
team: 4 METS
**Queenside**
castle, in chess notation: 3 OOO
**Queen Victoria**
granddaughter: 3 ENA
house: 7 HANOVER
prince: 6 ALBERT
**Queequeg:** 6 WHALER
captain: 4 AHAB
**"Queer Eye for the Straight
        Guy"**
channel: 5 BRAVO
**Quemoy**
neighbor: 5 MATSU
**Quench:** 5 SLAKE
**Quencher**
Citrus: 3 ADE 7 LIMEADE
Pub: 3 ALE 4 BEER
Summer: 8 LEMONADE
**___ Quentin:** 3 SAN
**Query:** 3 ASK
Biblical: 5 ISITI
Cabbie's: 7 WHERETO
Comic's: 5 GETIT
Reporter's: 3 HOW WHO WHY
        4 WHAT WHEN 4 WHERE
sounds: 3 EHS
Tot's: 3 WHY
**Ques.**
response: 3 ANS
**Quest**
One on a: 6 SEEKER
**___ Quested:** 5 ADELA
**Question:** 3 ASK 5 DOUBT
        POSIT 9 CHALLENGE
A ~ of identity: 3 WHO
A ~ of motive: 3 WHY
A ~ of timing: 4 WHEN
Biblical: 5 ISITI
Cabbie's: 7 WHERETO
Call into: 6 OPPUGN
Comic's: 5 GETIT
Gift recipient's: 5 FORME
Kind of: 5 YESNO
Long-answer: 5 ESSAY
Optimist's: 6 WHYNOT
Pop the: 7 PROPOSE
Put forth a: 4 POSE
Reporter's: HOW WHO WHY
        4 WHAT WHEN 4 WHERE
Throw in, as a: 9 INTERPOSE
to Mom or Dad: 4 CANI
Tough: 5 POSER

Zen master's: 4 KOAN
**Questionable:** 4 IFFY 5 FISHY
    7 SUSPECT
**Questionnaire**
  choice: 3 YES 4 MALE NONE
    5 OTHER
  datum: 3 AGE SEX
  Kind of: 6 MAILIN
**Quetzalcoatl**
  worshipper: 5 AZTEC MAYAN
    6 TOLTEC
**Queue:** 4 LINE 5 BRAID
    7 PIGTAIL
  after A: 3 BCD
  after Q: 3 RST 4 RSTU
  after R: 3 STU 4 STUV
  before Q: 3 NOP 4 MNOP
    5 LMNOP
  before U: 3 RST
  call: 4 NEXT
  Form a: 6 LINEUP
**Queued up:** 6 INAROW INLINE
    7 INALINE
**Quibble:** 4 CARP 5 CAVIL
    7 NITPICK
**Quiche:** 3 PIE
  ingredient: 3 EGG HAM
    4 EGGS 7 SPINACH
**Quiche Lorraine**
  ingredient: 5 BACON
**Quick:** 3 APT 4 SPRY 5 AGILE
    SHARP WITTY 6 ASTUTE
    SPEEDY
  bread: 5 SCONE
  gait: 4 TROT 6 GALLOP
  look: 4 PEEK 6 GLANCE
  Not very: 5 DENSE
  pull: 4 JERK
  to the helm: 3 YAR
  trip: 4 SPIN
**Quickly:** 4 ASAP FAST SOON
    5 APACE 6 ATONCE
    PRESTO 8 CHOPCHOP
  Very: 8 INAFLASH INATRICE
    INNOTIME
**Quick on the ___:** 6 UPTAKE
**Quick-witted:** 3 APT 4 KEEN
    5 AGILE SHARP SMART
    6 ADROIT
**Quid:** 4 CHAW
**Quiddity:** 7 ESSENCE
**Quid pro ___:** 3 QUO
**Quid pro quo:** 4 SWAP
    9 TITFORTAT
**"Quién ___?":** 4 SABE
**Quiescent:** 6 ATREST
    7 DORMANT
**Quiet:** 3 MUM 4 CALM HUSH
    MUTE 5 MUTED STILL
    6 HUSHED 8 RETICENT
  Be: 4 REST
  Be ~, musically: 5 TACET
  companion: 5 PEACE
  period: 4 LULL
  protest: 5 SITIN
**"Quiet!":** 3 SHH 4 HUSH SHHH

**Quietly**
  Move: 5 STEAL 6 TIPTOE
**"Quiet on the ___!":** 3 SET
**Quill:** 3 NIB 5 SPINE
**Quilled**
  critter: 9 PORCUPINE
**"Quills"**
  subject: 4 SADE
**Quilt**
  Crazy: 4 OLIO
  filler: 5 EIDER
  part: 5 PATCH
  Work on a: 3 SEW
**Quilting**
  party: 3 BEE
**Quince:** 4 POME
**Quincy**
  actor: 3 ITO
  of music: 5 JONES
**Quincy, Dr.**
  and colleagues: 3 MES
**Quindlen**
  Writer: 4 ANNA
**Quinine**
  target: 7 MALARIA
  water: 5 TONIC
**Quinn**
  Actor: 5 AIDAN
  Annie portrayer: 6 AILEEN
**Quinn, Anthony**
  role: 5 ZORBA
**Quint**
  family name: 6 DIONNE
**Quintessence:** 7 EPITOME
**Quintet**
  Alphabet: 5 AEIOU
  Ark: 5 TORAH
  Corporeal: 6 SENSES
  HOMES: 5 LAKES
  member: 4 ALTO
  Vowel: 5 AEIOU
  Wind ~ member: 4 OBOE
    6 OBOIST
**Quintuplet**
  1934 ~: 6 DIONNE
**Quip:** 3 MOT 4 JAPE JEST
  suffix: 4 STER
**Quipster:** 3 WAG WIT
**Quipu**
  maker: 4 INCA
**Quire**
  member: 5 SHEET
**Quirk:** 3 TIC 6 FOIBLE ODDITY
  Language: 5 IDIOM
  Personal: 3 TIC
**Quirky:** 3 ODD
  habit: 3 TIC
**Quisling:** 7 TRAITOR
  City of: 4 OSLO
**Quit:** 4 EXIT FOLD STOP
    5 CEASE 6 RESIGN
**"___ quit!":** 3 ORI
**Quite:** 4 VERY
  a bit: 4 LOTS MANY TONS
    5 OFTEN
  a way: 4 AFAR

  a while: 3 EON 4 AGES
    5 YEARS
  Not: 6 ALMOST HARDLY
    NEARLY
**"Quite contrary"**
  girl: 4 MARY
**Quito**
  Capital south of: 4 LIMA
  coin: 5 SUCRE
  country: 7 ECUADOR
  country (abbr.): 4 ECUA
  quencher: 4 AGUA
**Quitter**
  comment: 5 ICANT
  cry: 5 UNCLE
  throw-in: 5 TOWEL
  word: 4 CANT
**"Quit that!":** 6 STOPIT
**Quitting time:** 4 FIVE
**Quiver:** 5 SHAKE 7 VIBRATE
  carrier: 6 ARCHER
  item: 5 ARROW
**Quivering:** 7 TREMBLY
  tree: 5 ASPEN
**Quiz:** 3 ASK 4 EXAM TEST
  answer: 4 TRUE 5 FALSE
**Quiz show**
  group: 5 PANEL
  host Trebek: 4 ALEX
  Old radio: 4 DRIQ
  sound: 4 DING
**"Quiz Show"**
  actor: 7 FIENNES
**Qum**
  coin: 4 RIAL
  country: 4 IRAN
  native: 5 IRANI
**Qumran**
  dweller: 6 ESSENE
**"Quo ___?":** 5 VADIS
**Quod ___ demonstrandum:**
    4 ERAT
**Quod ___ faciendum:** 4 ERAT
**Quoits**
  Good shot in: 6 RINGER
  target: 3 HOB
**Quorum**
  Company: 3 TWO
  Football: 6 ELEVEN
  Solitaire: 3 ONE
  Tango: 3 TWO
  Teetertotter: 3 TWO
**Quotable**
  catcher: 4 YOGI 5 BERRA
**Quotation**
  notation: 3 SIC 4 ANON
**Quote:** 4 CITE
  Probability: 4 ODDS
**___ quote ...:** 4 ANDI
**"___ quote you?":** 4 CANI
**Quotidian:** 5 DAILY
**"Quo Vadis"**
  role: 4 NERO
**QWERTY**
  alternative: 6 DVORAK
**QxQ:** 4 MOVE

**R**
  Geometry: 6 RADIUS
  Give an ~ to: 4 RATE
  Greek: 3 RHO
  Queue after: 3 STU 4 STUV
  Reason for an ~ rating: 3 SEX
    4 GORE
**R ___:** 4 ANDR
**R2-D2:** 5 DROID
**Ra:** 3 GOD
**Rabanne**
  Fashion designer: 4 PACO
**Rabaud**
  role: 3 ALI
**"Rabbi Ben ___":** 4 EZRA
**Rabbinical**
  text: 6 TALMUD
**Rabbit:** 4 CONY 6 ANGORA
  Cereal promoted by a: 4 TRIX
  chaser: 5 ALICE
  ears: 6 DIPOLE 7 ANTENNA
  Female: 3 DOE
  food: 5 SALAD
  foot: 3 PAW
  fur: 4 CONY 5 LAPIN
    6 ANGORA
  home: 5 HUTCH 6 WARREN
  hunter Fudd: 5 ELMER
  Kind of: 10 COTTONTAIL
  relative: 4 HARE
  Rock: 4 PIKA
  Rodent like a: 6 AGOUTI
  Run like a: 7 SCAMPER
  season: 6 EASTER
  Storied: 5 MOPSY
  tail: 4 SCUT
  title: 4 BRER
  Toon: 5 ROGER
**Rabbit ___:** 4 EARS
**"Rabbit ___":** 5 REDUX
**___ Rabbit:** 4 BRER
**"Rabbit, Run"**
  author: 6 UPDIKE
**Rabble-rouse:** 7 AGITATE
**Rabelaisian**
  giant: 9 GARGANTUA
**Rabi**
  Nobel physicist: 6 ISIDOR
**Rabin:** 7 ISRAELI
  Mrs.: 4 LEAH
  predecessor: 4 MEIR
  successor: 5 PERES
**Raccoon**
  relative: 5 COATI PANDA
**Race:** 3 REV 4 TEAR 5 SPEED
  Alaskan sled dog: 8 IDITAROD
  Annual: 5 DERBY
  Baton-passing: 5 RELAY

  British ~ site: 5 ASCOT
  climax: 7 LASTLAP
  distance: 4 MILE TENK
  Drag: 6 HOTROD
  Early political: 7 PRIMARY
  End of a: 8 ELECTION
  Enter the: 3 RUN
  Fabled ~ loser: 4 HARE
  Fabled ~ winner: 8 TORTOISE
  finish: 4 TAPE WIRE
  French auto: 6 LEMANS
  Harness: 4 TROT
  Harness ~ horse: 5 PACER
  Kind of: 3 RAT 4 ARMS DRAG
    5 ALIEN HUMAN RELAY
  Memorial Day: 4 INDY
  of Norse gods: 5 AESIR
  pace: 4 TROT
  place: 4 INDY OVAL 5 ASCOT
    TRACK 7 DAYTONA
  Qualifying: 4 HEAT
  Sailing: 7 REGATTA
  Short: 4 DASH
  Ski: 6 SLALOM
  starter: 3 EVE 4 ADAM
  unit: 3 LAP LEG
**Racecar**
  feature: 7 ROLLBAR
  gauge: 4 TACH
**Racehorse**
  classification: 3 AGE
  Like a former: 6 ATSTUD
**Racer**
  Downhill: 4 LUGE SLED
    5 LUGER SKIER
  Edge for a: 9 HEADSTART
  Harness: 5 PACER
  Iditarod: 4 SLED
  Kiddie: 6 GOKART
  Miniature: 4 KART 7 SLOTCAR
  Tortoise: 4 HARE
  Toy: 7 SLOTCAR
**"Racer's Edge, The":** 3 STP
**Racetrack:** 4 OVAL
  boundary: 4 RAIL
  figure: 4 TOUT
  info: 4 ODDS
  NYC: 4 BIGA
**Rachel**
  Brother-in-law of: 4 ESAU
  Father of: 5 LABAN
  Husband of: 5 JACOB
  Sister of: 4 LEAH
**Rachmaninoff**
  Composer: 6 SERGEI
  piece: 5 ETUDE
**Racine**
  play part: 4 ACTE

  tragedy: 6 ESTHER PHEDRE
**Racing**
  Big name in: 5 UNSER
  boat: 5 SCULL
  circuit: 3 LAP
  form site, briefly: 3 OTB
  initials: 3 STP
  org.: 6 NASCAR
  sled: 4 LUGE
  vehicle: 4 AUTO 6 GOCART
    GOKART 8 DRAGSTER
**Rack:** 7 ANTLERS
  Discount ~ abbr.: 3 IRR
    5 IRREG
  item: 3 BAT HAT TIE 4 COAT
    5 SPICE
  Kind of: 3 HAT
  Partner of: 4 RUIN 6 PINION
  Put on the: 7 TORTURE
  site: 4 OVEN
**Racket:** 3 ADO DIN 4 SCAM
    5 NOISE 6 CLAMOR
    7 CLATTER
  game: 6 SQUASH
  It makes a: 6 CATGUT
  Suffix with: 3 EER
**Raconteur**
  offering: 4 TALE 8 ANECDOTE
**Racy**
  Hardly: 4 TAME
**"Rad!":** 4 COOL NEAT
    5 NEATO 7 AWESOME
**Radames**
  Love of: 4 AIDA
**Radar**
  anomaly: 3 UFO
  detector: 10 FUZZBUSTER
  Favorite drink of: 4 NEHI
  Home of: 4 IOWA
  Last name of: 7 OREILLY
  principle: 4 ECHO
  screen: 4 GRID
  signal: 4 BLIP
**Radarange**
  maker: 5 AMANA
**Radar gun**
  meas.: 3 MPH
  pointer: 3 COP 7 TROOPER
**Radcliffe**
  grads: 7 ALUMNAE
  Novelist: 3 ANN
**Radial:** 4 TIRE
  British: 4 TYRE
  pattern: 5 TREAD
  Perpendicular to: 5 AXIAL
**Radiance:** 4 AURA GLOW
    5 SHEEN
  Social: 5 ECLAT

**Radians**
Angle measured in: 7 ARCSINE
**Radiant:** 5 AGLOW 6 AGLEAM
glow: 4 AURA
smile: 4 BEAM
**Radiate:** 4 EMIT OOZE
5 EXUDE SHINE
**Radiation**
unit: 3 REM
**Radiator**
adjunct: 7 FANBELT
front: 6 GRILLE
output: 4 HEAT
part: 3 FIN 4 COIL
sound: 3 SSS 4 HISS SSSS
**Radical**
1960s ~ gp.: 3 SDS
1970s ~ gp.: 3 SLA
Sixties: 6 YIPPIE
Vinegar: 6 ACETYL
**Radii**
neighbors: 5 ULNAE
**Radio:** 4 SEND 5 MEDIA
amateur: 3 HAM
Car ~ button: 6 PRESET
Celestial ~ source: 6 PULSAR
component: 6 PREAMP
feature: 4 DIAL KNOB
5 TUNER
format: 4 ROCK TALK
6 OLDIES
Get a program on the:
6 TUNEIN
good buddy: 4 CBER
host Hansen: 5 LIANE
Kind of: 3 HAM 4 AMFM
9 SHORTWAVE
O in old ~ lingo: 4 OBOE
okay: 5 ROGER
Old ~ quiz show: 4 DRIQ
partner of Abner: 3 LUM
partner of Andy: 4 AMOS
personality: 7 DONIMUS
11 HOWARDSTERN
Police ~ alert, briefly: 3 APB
settings: 3 AMS FMS
Sitcom ~ station: 4 WKRP
spots: 3 ADS
talk show participant:
6 CALLER
tube gas: 5 ARGON XENON
**Radioactive**
gas: 5 RADON
isotope: 6 IONIUM
**Radioactivity**
unit: 5 CURIE
**Radio City**
Like: 4 DECO 7 ARTDECO
**Radio Flyer**
bar: 4 AXLE
**Radiola**
maker: 3 RCA
**Radish:** 4 ROOT
**Radium**
discoverer: 5 CURIE
**Radius:** 7 ARMBONE

neighbor: 4 ULNA
**Radner**
Comedienne: 5 GILDA
role: 8 BABAWAWA
**Radon:** 3 GAS
lacks it: 4 ODOR
Like: 5 INERT
___ Rae: 5 NORMA
**Reasonable:** 4 SANE
Sound: 5 ADDUP
**RAF**
award: 3 DSO
flyer: 4 BRIT
~, to Churchill: 5 SOFEW
___ Rafael: 3 SAN
**Raffle**
ticket: 6 CHANCE
**Raft:** 3 TON 4 BEVY HEAP
SLEW
Move a: 4 POLE
operator: 5 POLER
wood: 5 BALSA
**Rafter:** 4 BEAM
connector: 7 TIEBEAM
**Rag:** 3 KID 5 TAUNT TEASE
WIPER 6 TATTER
Chew the: 3 YAK 4 CHAT
**Raga**
First name in: 4 RAVI
instrument: 5 SITAR
rhythm-maker: 5 TABLA
**Ragamuffin:** 4 WAIF 6 URCHIN
**Rage:** 3 FAD IRE 4 FURY
5 ANGER FUROR MANIA
STORM STYLE 6 LATEST
All the: 3 HOT MOD 4 CHIC
6 REDHOT TRENDY
7 INSTYLE POPULAR
**Ragged:** 6 UNEVEN
Make: 4 FRAY
**"Ragged Dick"**
author: 5 ALGER
**Raggedy**
doll: 3 ANN 4 ANDY
**Raggedy Ann:** 4 DOLL
**Raging:** 5 ANGRY 7 ONATEAR
**"Raging Bull"**
subject: 7 LAMOTTA
**"Rag Mop"**
brothers: 4 AMES
**Ragout:** 4 STEW
Game: 5 SALMI
**Rags-to-riches**
author: 5 ALGER
**Ragtime**
Blake of: 5 EUBIE
dance: 7 ONESTEP
**"Ragtime"**
actress Steenburgen: 4 MARY
author: 10 ELDOCTOROW
**Ragú**
rival: 5 PREGO
**Rah**
Ring: 3 OLE
**Rah-rah:** 4 AVID 6 ARDENT
**Raid:** 6 INROAD SORTIE

1976 ~ site: 7 ENTEBBE
Cause of a Boston Harbor:
6 TEAACT
Drug: 4 BUST
Quick: 5 FORAY
rival: 4 DCON
target: 4 PEST 5 ROACH
6 INSECT
the fridge: 4 NOSH
**Raider**
Cornfield: 4 CROW
Corporate ~ Carl: 5 ICAHN
of the 10th century:
8 NORSEMAN
Pantry: 3 ANT
Picnic: 3 ANT
**Raiders**
gp.: 3 DEA FBI
Home of the: 7 OAKLAND
Treasury Dept.: 3 ATF
**"Raiders of the Lost ___":** 3 ARK
**"Raiders of the Lost Ark"**
danger: 4 ASPS
setting: 5 NEPAL
**"Raid on Entebbe"**
airline: 4 ELAL
**Rail**
Ballet: 5 BARRE
Like a: 4 THIN
rider: 4 HOBO
runner: 4 TRAM 5 TRAIN
Short-billed: 4 SORA
support: 3 TIE
Windy City ~ system (abbr.):
3 CTA
**Raillery:** 3 WIT
**Railroad**
area: 4 YARD
bridge: 7 TRESTLE
car: 5 DINER
Certain model ~ *(plural):*
3 HOS
measure: 5 GAUGE
siding: 4 SPUR
station: 5 DEPOT
stop (abbr.): 3 STA
support: 3 TIE
switch: 5 SHUNT
Trans-Siberian ~ city: 4 OMSK
unit: 3 CAR
worker: 6 REDCAP STOKER
**Railway**
car problem: 6 HOTBOX
D.C.: 5 METRO
**Railways**
Raised: 3 ELS
**Raiment:** 4 GARB 6 ATTIRE
Raipur: 4 SARI
Roman: 4 TOGA
**Rain**
alternative: 5 SHINE
Bit of: 4 DROP
check: 4 STUB
clouds: 5 NIMBI
delay protection: 4 TARP
Frozen: 5 SLEET

gear: 7 OILSKIN SLICKER
Hard: 4 HAIL
heavily: 4 POUR TEEM
It may be called on account of:
   3 CAB
Kind of: 4 ACID
The ~ in Spain: 4 AGUA
___ rain: 4 ACID
**Rainbow:** 3 ARC 4 IRIS
color: 6 INDIGO
End of a: 6 VIOLET
goddess: 4 IRIS
Like a: 5 ARCED
maker: 5 PRISM
Part of a: 3 HUE
shape: 3 ARC 4 ARCH
**Rainbow ___:** 5 TROUT
**Rainbow Bridge**
locale: 4 UTAH
**Raincoat**
British: 3 MAC
**Raindrop**
sound: 4 PLOP
**"Raindrops Keep Fallin' ___**
   **Head":** 4 ONMY
**Rainer**
Actress: 5 LUISE
Oscar role for: 4 OLAN
**Raines**
Actress: 4 ELLA
**Rainfall**
measure: 4 INCH
**Rain forest**
feature: 4 MIST
Like a: 4 LUSH 5 DENSE
ruminant: 5 OKAPI
vine: 5 LIANA
**Raingear**
brand: 5 TOTES
**Rainier**
and others (abbr.): 3 MTS
locale: 6 MONACO
**Rainless:** 4 ARID SERE
**Rains**
Actor: 6 CLAUDE
**Rainy:** 3 WET
**Rainy day**
fund: 7 NESTEGG
Prepare for a: 4 SAVE
**Raipur**
wrap: 4 SARI
**Raise:** 3 BET 4 HIKE LIFT
   REAR 5 ERECT EXALT
   HOIST 6 UPREAR
   7 ELEVATE
(abbr.): 4 INCR
a glass to: 5 TOAST
an outcry: 6 CLAMOR
a stink: 4 REEK 5 GRIPE
canines: 6 TEETHE
in relief: 6 EMBOSS
It helps ~ dough: 5 YEAST
Kind of: 5 MERIT
Match a: 3 SEE
Refuse to: 4 CALL
Something to: 4 CAIN HELL

spirits: 5 ELATE
the cost of: 5 BIDUP
the hackles of: 4 RILE
the hem: 5 ALTER
your voice: 4 YELL
~ Cain: 4 RAGE
**Raise ___:** 4 CAIN
**Raised:** 4 BRED 5 ERECT
   UPPED
eyebrow remarks: 3 OHS
He ~ Cain: 4 ADAM
It is ~ on a farm: 4 BARN SILO
platform: 4 DAIS 5 ALTAR
platforms: 6 ROSTRA
railways: 3 ELS
ridge: 4 WELT
seam: 4 WELT
She ~ Cain: 3 EVE
**Raiser:** 6 PARENT
Cain: 3 EVE 4 ADAM
Curtain: 4 ACTI
Dough: 5 YEAST
Hair: 3 GEL
Ham: 4 NOAH
Reindeer: 4 LAPP
Spirit: 6 SEANCE
Tarzan: 3 APE
**Raises:** 3 UPS
**Raisin**
California ~ center: 6 FRESNO
Like a: 5 DRIED
rum cake: 4 BABA
Seedless: 7 SULTANA
~, originally: 5 GRAPE
**Raising**
heck: 5 ROWDY 7 ONATEAR
**"Raisin in the Sun, A"**
heroine: 4 LENA
**Raison ___:** 5 DETRE
**Rajah**
land: 5 INDIA
Wife of: 4 RANI 5 RANEE
**Rajiv**
Mother of: 6 INDIRA
Wife of: 5 SONIA
**Rake:** 3 CAD 4 ROUE
   6 LECHER 8 LOTHARIO
home: 4 SHED
in: 4 EARN
over the coals: 5 ROAST
part: 4 TINE
**Rakehell:** 4 ROUE
**Raleigh**
state (abbr.): 4 NCAR
title: 3 SIR
to Philly heading (abbr.):
   3 NNE
**Rall**
Political cartoonist: 3 TED
**Rally:** 5 ROUSE 7 RECOVER
cry: 3 RAH 6 GOTEAM
Kind of: 3 PEP
They may: 5 CRIES
**Ralph**
1950s slugger ~: 5 KINER
Consumerist: 5 NADER

Designer: 6 LAUREN
Ed, to: 3 PAL
Wife of: 5 ALICE
**Ram:** 4 BUTT MALE
   7 REAREND
Astrological: 5 ARIES
mate: 3 EWE
remark: 3 BAA MAA 5 BLEAT
**RAM**
Part of: 6 ACCESS RANDOM
unit: 3 MEG 4 ONEK
**Rama**
~, to Vishnu: 6 AVATAR
**Ramadan:** 5 MONTH
observance: 4 FAST
**Ramble:** 3 GAD 4 ROAM ROVE
   6 WANDER 7 MEANDER
on: 3 YAK
**Rambler**
maker: 3 AMC 4 NASH
**"Rambling Rose"**
actress Laura: 4 DERN
**"___ ramblin' wreck":** 3 IMA
**"Ramblin' Wreck From**
   **Georgia ___":** 4 TECH
**Rambo:** 5 HEMAN
   10 ONEMANARMY
Like: 5 MACHO
**Rambunctious:** 5 ROWDY
**Ramee**
pen name: 5 OUIDA
**Ramirez**
of tennis: 4 RAUL
**Ramis**
Actor: 6 HAROLD
**Ramone**
Late rocker: 6 DEEDEE
**Ramones, The:**
   11 PUNKROCKERS
music: 4 PUNK
**Ramp**
Off: 4 EXIT
**Rampage:** 4 TEAR
**___ rampage:** 3 ONA
**Rampager**
Ring: 4 TORO
**Rampaging:** 7 ONATEAR
**Rampal**
instrument: 5 FLUTE
**Rampant:** 4 RIFE
**Rampart:** 4 WALL
part: 7 PARAPET
**Rams**
home: 3 STL
Like: 5 OVINE
The ~ sch.: 3 URI
**Ramses I**
Son of: 4 SETI
**Ramses II**
Father of: 4 SETI
Site of ~ temples:
   9 ABUSIMBEL
**"___ Ramsey" (1970s TV**
   **western):** 3 HEC
**Ramshackle**
structure: 7 RATTRAP

**Ran:** 3 LED 4 BLED FLED
    TORE 5 LOPED RACED
  a tab: 4 OWED
  away: 4 FLED
  easily: 5 LOPED
  first: 3 LED
  in: 8 ARRESTED
  in neutral: 5 IDLED
  in the wash: 4 BLED
  into: 3 MET
  like heck: 4 TORE
  off: 6 ELOPED
  on: 6 PRATED
  out: 6 LAPSED
**Ranch**
  alternative: 7 ITALIAN
    RUSSIAN
  brush: 4 SAGE
  bunch: 4 HERD
  Kind of: 4 DUDE
  Large: 8 HACIENDA
  Like a ~ house: 8 ONESTORY
  moniker: 3 TEX
  Pres. with a: 3 LBJ
  rope: 5 RIATA 6 LARIAT
  suffix: 3 ERO
  unit: 4 ACRE HEAD
  visitor: 4 DUDE
  wear: 6 DENIMS
  worker: 4 HAND
    7 COWPOKE
    9 HIREDHAND
**Rancher:** 9 CATTLEMAN
  enemy: 6 COYOTE
  mark: 5 BRAND
**Rancidity**
  retardant: 3 BHT
**Rancor:** 5 SPITE
**Rand**
  Author: 3 AYN
  Shrugger of: 5 ATLAS
**Rand, Ayn**
  book: 6 ANTHEM
    13 ATLASSHRUGGED
**Randall**
  1964 ~ title role: 5 DRLAO
  Actor: 4 TONY
  Dr. played by: 3 LAO
  ~ TV role: 5 UNGER
**R&B**
  1970s ~ member: 4 OJAY
  singer Braxton: 4 TONI
  singer Bryson: 5 PEABO
  singer Hill: 3 DRU
  singer James: 4 ETTA
  singer Redding: 4 OTIS
**R&D**
  Part of: 3 DEV RES
  Reagan ~ program: 3 SDI
**Rand McNally**
  book: 5 ATLAS
**Random:** 5 STRAY
  criticism: 7 POTSHOT
  number generator: 3 DIE
  scrap: 6 TAGEND
  Select at: 4 DRAW

**Random House**
  founder: 4 CERF
**Randomizer:** 3 DIE
**R&R**
  Part of: 4 REST
  place: 3 SPA 6 RESORT
**Randy**
  Country singer: 6 TRAVIS
**Ranee**
  wrap: 5 SAREE
**Rang:** 6 PEALED TOLLED
  out: 6 PEALED 7 SOUNDED
**"___ rang?":** 3 YOU
**Range:** 4 ROAM ROVE
    5 GAMUT SCOPE STOVE
    STRAY SWEEP
  animal: 4 DEER 8 ANTELOPE
  Asian: 5 URALS
  Audible: 7 EARSHOT
  Chilean: 5 ANDES
  Complete: 4 ATOZ 5 GAMUT
  Curriculum ~, briefly: 4 ELHI
  Driving ~ item: 3 TEE
  Entire: 4 ATOZ 5 GAMUT
  Gp. on the: 3 NRA
  Home on the: 5 TEPEE
  influence: 6 SPHERE
  It is within your: 4 OVEN
  Light on the: 5 PILOT
  Low: 4 BASS 5 BASSO
  maker: 5 AMANA
  Minnesota: 6 MESABI
  Name on the: 3 TEX 5 AMANA
  newcomer: 4 CALF
  of view: 5 SCOPE
  of vision: 3 KEN 7 EYESHOT
  orphan: 5 DOGIE
  Peruvian: 5 ANDES
  Rating: 8 ONETOTEN
  rover: 4 HERD 5 STEER
  Rugged: 6 SIERRA
  Russian: 5 URALS
  Sax: 4 ALTO 5 TENOR
  stray: 5 DOGIE
  units (abbr.): 3 MTS 4 MTNS
  Voice: 4 ALTO BASS 5 TENOR
    7 SOPRANO
  Wyoming: 6 TETONS
  Yodeler: 8 FALSETTO
**Ranger:** 5 EDSEL
  sidekick: 5 TONTO
  slugger, once: 4 AROD
**___ Ranger (trendy Londoner):**
    6 SLOANE
**"___ Ranger, The":** 4 LONE
**Rangers**
  gp.: 3 NHL
**Rani**
  wrap: 4 SARI
**Rank:** 4 RATE TIER 5 FETID
    GRADE PLACE
    6 ROTTEN
  GI: 3 PFC
  Mil.: 3 COL MAJ PFC SGT
    5 LTCOL
  Nav.: 3 CPO ENS

  NCO: 4 MSGT SSGT
  Partner of: 4 NAME
  P.D.: 3 DET 4 INSP
  Reduce in: 5 ABASE
    6 DEMOTE
  Scout: 5 EAGLE
  Sign of: 6 STRIPE
  Social: 5 CLASS
  Tournament: 4 SEED
**Ranked:** 4 AROW
**Ranking:** 5 CLASS
  player: 4 SEED
**Rankle:** 3 IRK VEX 5 ANNOY
    6 FESTER 8 EMBITTER
**Ransack:** 4 LOOT RAID 5 RIFLE
**Ransom**
  Automaker: 4 OLDS
  Hold for: 6 KIDNAP
  payoff: 4 DROP
**"Ransom"**
  actress Russo: 4 RENE
  actress Taylor: 4 LILI
**Rant:** 6 TIRADE
  Partner of: 4 RAVE
**"___ Ran the Circus":** 3 IFI
**"___ Ran the Zoo":** 3 IFI
**Raoul**
  Director: 5 WALSH
**Rap:** 3 GAB 4 CHAT 5 BLAME
    14 CRIMINALCHARGE
  artist: 4 ICET 6 COOLIO
  fans: 5 BBOYS
  Give a: 4 CARE
  session: 6 SEANCE
  sheet data: 3 AKA 5 ALIAS
    PRIOR 6 THEFTS
    7 ARRESTS
  variety: 7 GANGSTA
  ~ Dr.: 3 DRE
**Rapa ___ (Easter Island):** 3 NUI
**Rapid:** 6 SPEEDY
  transit: 3 SST
**Rapid-fire**
  weapon: 3 UZI
**Rapidly:** 4 FAST 5 APACE
**Rapids**
  transit: 4 RAFT 5 CANOE
    KAYAK
**Rapier**
  Fencing: 4 EPEE
**Rapper**
  Cool: 4 ICET
  sound: 7 RATATAT
  ~ Dr.: 3 DRE
  ~ Lil': 3 KIM
  ~ Queen: 7 LATIFAH
  ~ Snoop: 4 DOGG
  ~ Tone: 3 LOC
**Rapscallion:** 3 IMP 5 ROGUE
    SCAMP
**Raptor**
  claw: 5 TALON
  Coastal: 3 ERN 4 ERNE
  Young: 6 EAGLET
**Raptors**
  city: 7 TORONTO

**Rapture:** 3 JOY 5 BLISS
**Rapunzel**
  feature: 4 HAIR 5 TRESS
  hair color: 6 FLAXEN
  Like: 6 TRESSY
  prison: 5 TOWER
**Raquel**
  Actress: 5 WELCH
**Rara ___:** 4 AVIS
**Rara avis:** 4 ONER
**Rare:** 4 PINK 6 EXOTIC
    SCARCE
  bill: 3 TWO
  bird: 4 ONER
  blood: 6 TYPEAB
  golf shot: 3 ACE
  It may be: 5 STEAK
  Like a ~ game: 5 NOHIT
  Not even: 3 RAW
  Rarer than: 3 RAW 7 TARTARE
  trick taker: 4 TREY
**"Rare and radiant maiden"**
  of Poe: 6 LENORE
**Rarefied:** 4 THIN
**Rarely:** 6 SELDOM
    15 ONCEINABLUEMOON
**Raring**
  to go: 4 AVID 5 AFIRE EAGER
    6 ALLSET
  ___ rasa: 6 TABULA
**Rascal:** 3 CAD IMP 5 KNAVE
    ROGUE SCAMP
    6 VARLET 8 SCALAWAG
**Rash:** 5 HASTY SPATE
    6 MADCAP SUDDEN
  feature: 7 REDNESS
  reaction: 4 ITCH
  treatment: 4 TALC
**Rashad**
  Sportscaster: 5 AHMAD
**Rasp:** 4 FILE
**Raspberry:** 4 JEER
    10 BRONXCHEER
**Raspy:** 6 HOARSE
**Rasta**
  messiah: 8 SELASSIE
  music: 6 REGGAE
**Rat:** 4 SING TELL 6 TATTLE
    7 STOOLIE TRAITOR
  challenge: 4 MAZE
  Dirty: 5 LOUSE 7 SOANDSO
  Film: 3 BEN
  (on): 4 TELL
  out: 6 TELLON
  Pack: 5 SAVER
  Rug: 3 TOT 4 TYKE
  tail: 4 ATAT
  White: 6 ALBINO
**Rat-___:** 4 ATAT
**Rat-a-___:** 3 TAT
**Ratatouille:** 4 STEW
  ingredient: 8 ZUCCHINI
**Ratched, Nurse**
  creator: 5 KESEY
**Ratchet**
  engager: 4 PAWL

**Rate:** 4 CLIP PACE 5 MERIT
    7 DESERVE
  Data transfer: 4 BAUD
  Flat: 4 RENT
  of return: 5 YIELD
  The going: 4 FARE TOLL
    5 SPEED
  Tpk.: 3 MPH
**Rate ___ (be perfect):** 4 ATEN
**Rated**
  Highly: 3 AAA 4 ACES AONE
**Rater**
  Meat ~ (abbr.): 4 USDA
  Motel: 3 AAA
  MPG: 3 EPA
**Ratfink:** 7 STOOLIE
**Rathbone**
  Actor: 5 BASIL
  role: 6 HOLMES
**Rather:** 4 ABIT 5 QUITE
    6 SORTOF 7 INSTEAD
    8 PREFERTO
  Newsman: 3 DAN
  report: 4 NEWS
  ~, informally: 5 KINDA SORTA
**Rather, Dan:** 7 NEWSMAN
  network: 3 CBS
**Rathskeller:** 8 BEERHALL
  item: 5 STEIN
  quaff: 3 ALE
**Ratify:** 4 PASS
**Rating**
  a 10: 5 IDEAL
  Bond: 3 AAA BBB CCC
  Draft: 4 ONEA
  Excellent: 4 AONE
  Film ~ gp.: 4 MPAA
  Gas: 6 OCTANE
  Kind of: 3 EPA 7 NIELSEN
  Mileage ~ gp.: 3 EPA
  Movie ~ (plural): 3 PGS
  Perfect: 3 TEN
  Poor: 7 ONESTAR
  range: 8 ONETOTEN
  unit: 4 STAR
**Ratio**
  Betting: 4 ODDS
  indicator: 5 COLON
  Math: 4 SINE
  phrase: 4 ISTO
  Speed: 4 MACH
  Trig: 3 COS TAN 4 SINE
    5 COSEC 6 COSINE
    SECANT
**Ration:** 4 DOLE METE
    5 ALLOT
**Rational:** 4 SANE
  religion: 5 DEISM
**Rationality:** 5 SENSE
    8 SANENESS
**Ratios**
  Circle: 3 PIS
**Rat Island**
  resident: 5 ALEUT
**Ratite**
  bird: 3 EMU

**Ratlike**
  rodent: 4 VOLE
**___ Raton:** 4 BOCA
**Rat Pack**
  leader: 7 SINATRA
  name: 4 DINO 5 SAMMY
    10 JOEYBISHOP
**"Rats!":** 4 DARN 6 DARNIT
    PHOOEY
**Ratso**
  portrayer: 6 DUSTIN
**Ratted:** 4 SANG TOLD
**Rattle:** 3 JAR 4 FAZE 6 MARACA
    7 UNHINGE UNNERVE
  in a whistle: 3 PEA
  on: 3 YAK
  sabers: 6 MENACE
  Something to: 4 CAGE
    5 SABER
**Rattletrap:** 5 CRATE
**Rattrap:** 3 STY
**Ratty**
  place: 5 SEWER
**Raucous:** 4 LOUD 5 NOISY
  diver: 4 LOON
  noise: 5 BLARE
**Rave**
  music: 6 TECHNO
  Partner of: 4 RANT
  ~ VIPs: 3 DJS
**Ravel**
  classic: 6 BOLERO
  Composer: 7 MAURICE
**Raveled**
  fuzz: 4 LINT
**Raven**
  call: 3 CAW 5 CROAK
  haven: 4 NEST
  maven: 3 POE
**"Raven, The"**
  actor: 5 LORRE
  author: 3 POE 5 EAPOE
    13 EDGARALLANPOE
  maiden: 6 LENORE
  monogram: 3 EAP
  opener: 4 ONCE
**Ravens**
  God attended by two: 4 ODIN
  gp.: 3 NFL
**Ravi**
  Sitarist: 7 SHANKAR
**Ravioli:** 5 PASTA
**Raw:** 7 TARTARE
  facts: 4 DATA
  fish dish: 5 SUSHI
  In the: 4 BARE NUDE
  It may be: 4 DEAL
  linen color: 4 ECRU
  material: 3 ORE
  Run in the: 6 STREAK
  silk color: 4 ECRU
  ~, as diamonds: 5 UNCUT
**Rawboned:** 5 LANKY
    7 ANGULAR
**Rawhide**
  Cure: 3 TAN

**"Rawhide"**
Eastwood role in: 5 YATES
singer: 5 LAINE
**Rawlings**
Writer: 8 MARJORIE
**Rawls**
Singer: 3 LOU
**Ray**
Actor: 4 ALDO 6 LIOTTA
Big Band singer: 6 EBERLE
Kind of: 4 HEAT 5 GAMMA
   MANTA SKATE
McDonald's founder: 4 KROC
of light: 4 BEAM 7 SUNBEAM
of the Kinks: 6 DAVIES
Shoot a: 4 LASE
Use a ~ gun: 3 ZAP
**Ray, Johnnie**
song: 3 CRY
**Ray, Man**
genre: 4 DADA
**Rayburn**
Game show host: 4 GENE
Politico: 3 SAM
**Raymond**
Actor: 4 BURR 6 MASSEY
Mystery writer: 8 CHANDLER
on TV: 6 ROMANO
Songwriter: 4 EGAN
**Rays**
Catch some: 3 SUN TAN
   4 BASK 6 SUNTAN
   8 SUNBATHE
Give off: 4 EMIT
**Raze:** 5 LEVEL
**Razor**
brand: 3 BIC 4 ATRA
   6 SENSOR 7 NORELCO
brand ___ II: 4 TRAC
feature: 4 EDGE
He had a: 5 OCCAM
Sharpen a: 4 HONE
sharpener: 5 STROP
Use a: 5 SHAVE
**Razor-billed**
bird: 3 AUK
**Razorfish:** 6 WRASSE
**"Razor's ___, The":** 4 EDGE
**Razz:** 4 GIBE JEER 5 TAUNT
   TEASE 6 NEEDLE
**Razzle-dazzle:** 5 ECLAT GLITZ
**RB**
gains: 3 YDS
**RBI:** 4 STAT
Part of: 3 RUN 4 RUNS
recordholder: 5 AARON
**RC:** 4 COLA
rival: 4 COKE 5 PEPSI
**RCA:** 5 LABEL
Nipper of: 3 DOG
products: 3 TVS
rival: 3 EMI
**RCA Dome**
team: 5 COLTS
**Rd.**
Major: 3 HWY

Numbered: 3 RTE
Toll: 3 TPK 4 TPKE
**Re:** 4 ASTO NOTE 5 ANENT
**Reach:** 3 GET 5 GETAT GETTO
   6 ATTAIN 7 CONTACT
across: 4 SPAN
a peak: 5 CREST
for: 6 GRABAT
in amount: 5 RUNTO
the beach: 4 LAND
Within: 4 NEAR 5 HANDY
   6 ATHAND
___ reach: 6 WITHIN
**Reachable:** 7 INRANGE
**Reaches:** 8 GETSUPTO
**React**
Not quick to: 5 INERT
to a blow: 4 REEL 8 SEESTARS
to a pun: 5 WINCE
to snuff: 6 SNEEZE
**Reaction**
Allergic: 4 ITCH RASH
   5 ACHOO 6 ASTHMA
   SNEEZE
Angry: 4 RISE
Bad news: 5 GROAN
Cold: 3 BRR
Gut: 3 OOF
Hostile: 4 FLAK
Kind of: 3 GUT 8 ALLERGIC
   KNEEJERK
Mouse: 3 EEK
Rash: 4 ITCH
Shocked: 4 GASP
source: 3 GUT
**Reactor:** 10 ATOMICPILE
part: 3 ROD 4 CORE
unit: 3 RAD
**Read:** 7 PERUSED
a bar code: 4 SCAN
Make hard to: 6 ENCODE
One way to: 5 ALOUD
quickly: 4 SCAN SKIM
Something to: 4 PALM
   5 METER 7 RIOTACT
**Read ___ (study):** 4 UPON
**"Read 'em and ___!":** 4 WEEP
**Reader**
Manual: 4 USER
Meter: 6 GASMAN
Mind ~ claim: 3 ESP
Palm: 4 SEER
Public: 6 LECTOR
Speed: 5 RADAR
Tarot: 4 SEER
**"___ Reader, The":** 4 UTNE
**"Reader's ___":** 6 DIGEST
**"Reader's Digest"**
Wallace of: 4 LILA
**Readily**
available: 5 ONTAP 6 ONCALL
   ONHAND
**Readiness**
In: 5 ONICE
**Reading:** 4 GAOL
Bar Mitzvah: 5 TORAH

Heavy: 4 TOME
light: 4 LAMP
material: 9 TEALEAVES
Meter: 4 FARE
Odometer: 5 MILES
Restaurant: 4 MENU
room: 3 DEN 5 STUDY
Sunday: 6 COMICS
   8 MASSBOOK
Sundial: 3 III VII XII
Tach: 3 RPM 4 REVS
**"Reading Rainbow"**
host Burton: 5 LEVAR
**Readout**
Digital ~, for short: 3 LCD
Hosp.: 3 ECG EEG EKG
**Read the ___ act:** 4 RIOT
**Ready:** 3 SET 4 PREP RIPE
   5 ALERT ONTAP
   6 ALLSET PRIMED
and willing partner: 4 ABLE
Be ~ for: 5 AWAIT
follower: 3 AIM
for: 4 UPTO 6 OPENTO
for battle: 5 ARMED
   15 ARMEDTOTHETEETH
for drawing: 5 ONTAP
Get: 4 PREP 5 TEEUP
   6 GEARUP 7 PREPARE
to fire: 5 ARMED 6 COCKED
   PRIMED
to go: 3 SET 5 EAGER
   6 ALLSET
to hit: 5 ATBAT
to pluck: 4 RIPE
to roll: 6 INGEAR
to serve: 4 DONE
**"Ready ...":** 5 ORNOT
**Ready for the World**
hit: 8 OHSHEILA
**"Ready or not, ___ ...":** 5 HEREI
**"Ready or not, here ___!":**
   5 ICOME
**"Ready to Wear"**
actor Stephen: 3 REA
**Reagan**
aide Nofziger: 3 LYN
Attorney General under:
   5 MEESE 7 EDMEESE
costar in 1951: 5 BONZO
court appointee: 6 SCALIA
Daughter of: 5 PATTI
era prog.: 3 SDI
First wife of: 5 WYMAN
Interior Secretary under:
   4 WATT
President: 6 RONALD
Secretary of State under:
   4 HAIG
Son of: 3 RON
speechwriter: 6 NOONAN
Surgeon General under:
   4 KOOP
**Real:** 4 TRUE 6 ACTUAL
   INESSE 7 SINCERE
Be: 5 EXIST

For: 5 LEGIT
Not: 4 SHAM 5 BOGUS
"___ real!": 3 GET
**Real estate**
  abbr.: 3 RMS 4 APTS BDRM
    BSMT
  company: 3 ERA
  document: 4 DEED
  info: 5 RENTS
  map: 4 PLAT
  Move, in ~ lingo: 4 RELO
  parcel: 3 LOT
  sign: 4 SOLD
  unit: 4 ACRE
**Realism**
  prefix: 3 NEO
**Reality**: 4 FACT
  In: 7 ATHEART DEFACTO
**Realize**: 3 GET NET SEE
    4 GAIN REAP 6 ATTAIN
    7 ACHIEVE
**Really**: 6 INFACT
"**Really!**": 3 GEE 5 NOLIE
    6 DOTELL
"**Really?**": 4 ITIS 8 ISTHATSO
"___ Really Going Out With
    Him?": 5 ISSHE
"**Really lookin' fine**"
  car in a '64 song: 3 GTO
**Realm**: 4 AREA 6 SPHERE
"___ real nowhere man ...":
    4 HESA
**Realtor**
  database (abbr.): 3 MLS
  Move, in ~ lingo: 4 RELO
  sign: 4 SOLD
  tactic: 9 OPENHOUSE
  unit: 3 LOT 4 ACRE
**Realty**
  unit: 3 LOT 4 ACRE
**Ream**
  fraction: 5 QUIRE
  unit: 5 SHEET
**Reaper**
  tool: 6 SCYTHE
**Rear**: 4 DUFF HIND 5 RAISE
    STERN 6 BREECH
    PARENT 7 TAILEND
  Bringing up the: 4 LAST
  Bring up the: 3 LAG 4 MOON
    5 TRAIL 6 BELAST
  end: 3 RAM 4 PRAT RUMP
    TUSH 5 FANNY
    6 HEINIE
  To the: 3 AFT 5 ABAFT
    6 ASTERN
**Rear-___**: 5 ENDER
**Reason**: 3 WHY 5 CAUSE
    LOGIC 6 DEDUCE
    MOTIVE SANITY
  For any: 5 ATALL
  For this: 5 HENCE
  Partner of: 5 RHYME
  Within: 4 SANE
  ___ reason: 6 WITHIN
**Reasoning**: 5 LOGIC

**Reassurance**
  Words of: 4 IMOK
**Reassuring**
  phrase: 4 IMOK 5 ITSOK
**Reb**
  Foe of: 4 YANK
  outfit: 3 CSA
**Rebate**
  Kind of: 6 MAILIN
**Rebbe**
  locale: 4 SHUL
**Rebecca**
  Author: 4 WEST
  of the WNBA: 4 LOBO
"**Rebecca**"
  1997 Emmy winner for ~:
    4 RIGG
**Rebecca ___ (née Pocahontas)**:
    5 ROLFE
**Rebekah**
  Husband of: 5 ISAAC
  Son of: 4 ESAU
**Rebel**
  ~ Turner: 3 NAT
**Rebel ___**: 4 YELL
"___ Rebel" (Crystals hit):
    4 HESA
**___ Rebellion**
  of 1786: 5 SHAYS
  of 1857–59: 5 SEPOY
**Rebellious**
  time: 5 TEENS
  ~ Turner: 3 NAT
**Rebels**: 5 RIOTS 6 ARISES
    7 UPRISES
**Rebels, The**: 7 OLEMISS
"**Rebel Without a Cause**"
  actor: 8 SALMINEO
    9 JAMESDEAN
  actor Mineo: 3 SAL
  actor Sal: 5 MINEO
"**Rebel Yell**"
  rocker Billy: 4 IDOL
**Rebound**: 5 CAROM
  basket: 5 TAPIN
  Sound: 4 ECHO
**Rebounds**: 4 STAT
**Rebozo**
  Nixon pal: 4 BEBE
**Rebuff**: 4 SLAP SNUB
**Rebuffs**: 3 NOS
**Rebuke**
  Ides: 4 ETTU
  Recital: 3 SHH
  Sharp: 4 SLAP
  Verbal: 6 EARFUL
  Word of: 3 TUT
**Rebukes**
  How some ~ are made:
    7 CROSSLY
  sharply: 7 SNAPSAT
**Rec**
  center: 4 YMCA
  room: 3 DEN
**Recall**
  1982 ~ subject: 7 TYLENOL

  beginning: 9 IREMEMBER
"___ recall ...": 3 ASI
**Recant**: 6 ABJURE
**Recap**: 5 SUMUP
**Recede**: 3 EBB
**Receipt**: 9 SALESSLIP
  Abbr. on a: 3 CHG
  stamp: 4 PAID
**Receipts**: 4 GATE TAKE
**Receive**: 3 GET 5 GREET
    6 ACCEPT
  enthusiastically: 5 LAPUP
**Receiver**: 5 RADIO
  Audio: 3 EAR
  Gift: 5 DONEE
  Image: 6 RETINA
  Pass: 3 END
  Property: 7 ALIENEE
  Signal: 4 DISH 7 ANTENNA
    13 SATELLITEDISH
**Recent**: 3 NEW 4 LATE
  arrival: 6 NEWKID
    7 NEONATE
    8 NEWCOMER
  In ~ times: 6 LATELY OFLATE
  prefix: 3 NEO 4 CENO
  ~, in German: 3 NEU
**Recently**: 5 NEWLY 6 OFLATE
  As ~ as: 4 ONLY
  discovered: 8 NEWFOUND
**Receptacle**
  Barbecue: 6 ASHPIT
  Garbage: 6 ASHCAN
  Holy water: 4 FONT
  Recycling: 3 BIN
**Reception**
  Afternoon: 3 TEA
  aid: 6 AERIAL 7 ANTENNA
  Bad: 4 HISS 6 STATIC
  Handle a: 5 CATER
  Line before a: 3 IDO
  medium: 5 CABLE
  staple: 5 TOAST
  Wedding ~ centerpiece: 4 CAKE
**Receptionist**
  cry: 4 NEXT
**Receptive**: 4 OPEN 7 TUNEDIN
**Recess**: 4 NOOK REST 5 BREAK
    NICHE 6 ALCOVE
  Carpentry: 7 MORTISE
  Church: 4 APSE
  Shoreline: 4 COVE 5 INLET
  Wall: 5 NICHE
**Recession**: 5 SLUMP
    7 DECLINE
**Rechargeable**
  battery: 5 NICAD
**Recharging**
  In need of: 4 DEAD
**Recherché**: 4 RARE 6 ARCANE
**Recipe**
  amt.: 3 TBS TSP 4 TBSP
  direction: 4 BOIL SEAR STIR
    5 SAUTE STEAM
    6 FOLDIN STIRIN
  guesstimate: 4 DASH 5 ADASH

info (abbr.): **3** AMT
phrase: **7** TOTASTE
title words: **3** ALA
**Recipient**
  Award: **7** HONOREE
  Bond: **7** OBLIGEE
  Charity: **5** DONEE
  Check: **5** PAYEE
  Gift: **5** DONEE
  Gold watch: **7** RETIREE
  Legacy: **4** HEIR
  Medal: **4** HERO
  Property: **7** ALIENEE
**Reciprocal**
  Cosecant: **4** SINE
  Sine: **5** COSEC
**Reciprocity**
  Law of quadratic ~ formulator:
    **5** EULER
**Recital**
  hall: **5** ODEUM
  piece: **4** SOLO **5** ETUDE
    **6** SONATA
  pieces: **4** SOLI
  Rosary: **8** AVEMARIA
**Recitation**
  Kindergarten: **4** ABCS
  Religious: **6** ROSARY
    **8** AVEMARIA
  Scout: **4** OATH
**Recite: 3** SAY **6** INTONE
  Easily: **7** REELOFF
**Reckless: 4** RASH **6** MADCAP
  sort: **9** DAREDEVIL
**Recklessly**
  Dance: **4** MOSH
  Drive: **6** CAREEN
**Recklessness**
  Goddess of: **3** ATE
**Reckon: 5** GUESS OPINE
    **6** FIGURE
**Recline: 3** LIE **4** LOLL
**Reclined: 3** LAY **4** LAIN
**Recliner: 5** CHAIR
  part: **7** ARMREST LEGREST
  Room with a: **3** DEN
**Recluse: 5** LONER **6** HERMIT
    SHUTIN **7** EREMITE
**Recognition: 4** FAME **6** CREDIT
  response: **3** AHA
  Words to elicit: **5** ITSME
**Recognize: 3** SEE **4** KNOW
    **7** DISCERN
**Recoil: 3** SHY **4** KICK
**Recolor: 3** DYE
**Recombinant**
  stuff: **3** DNA
**Recommend: 4** URGE
    **6** ADVISE
**Recompense: 5** WAGES
    **6** AMENDS
**Recon**
  unit: **6** PATROL
**Reconcile: 7** IRONOUT
    MEDIATE
**Reconditioned: 4** USED

**Reconnoiter: 5** SCOUT
    **6** PATROL
**Reconsideration**
  Mark of: **4** STET
**Record: 3** LOG **4** DISC TAPE
    **5** ALBUM ENTER
    **6** ANNALS **8** RAPSHEET
  Ancestry: **4** TREE
  book entry: **4** STAT
  Checkbook: **4** STUB
  collection: **8** DATABASE
  company: **5** LABEL
  company receipt: **8** DEMOTAPE
  cutter: **6** STYLUS
  flaw: **4** SKIP
  Half a: **7** SIDEONE
  holder: **4** FILE **6** JACKET
    SLEEVE **7** DOSSIER
    SPINDLE
  label: **3** BMI EMI MCA **4** ATCO
    KTEL **5** ASCAP DECCA
    **6** ARISTA
  material: **5** VINYL
  of one year: **5** ANNAL
  One with a: **3** CON
  output: **5** AUDIO
  Phonograph: **4** DISC
  player: **4** HIFI **5** PHONO
    **6** DEEJAY STEREO
  problem: **4** SKIP
  store purchases: **3** CDS
  store section: **3** RAP
  World: **5** ATLAS
  ___ record: **4** SETA
**Recorded: 5** TAPED
    **6** ONTAPE
  Not: **4** LIVE
  proceedings: **4** ACTA
**Recorder**
  Modern: **4** TIVO
**Recording**
  Early: **4** MONO
  medium: **3** DAT **4** TAPE
  studio effect: **4** ECHO
  Trial: **4** DEMO
**Records**
  Computer: **7** DATASET
  Court: **4** ACTA
  Diamond of: **4** NEIL
  Vinyl: **3** LPS
**Recount: 4** TELL
**Recourse**
  Lender: **4** LIEN
**Recover: 4** HEAL **5** RALLY
  from: **7** GETOVER
**Recovered**
  car: **4** REPO
**Recovery**
  clinic: **5** REHAB
**Recreation: 4** PLAY **5** SPORT
**Recreational**
  four-wheeler: **3** ATV
  vehicle: **10** MOBILEHOME
**Recruit**
  Like a new: **3** RAW
  response: **5** NOSIR **6** YESSIR

**Recruiter**
  Corporate: **10** HEADHUNTER
  Lafayette ~ Silas: **5** DEANE
  Univ.: **4** ROTC
**Recruitment**
  Campus: **4** RUSH
**Rectangle: 6** OBLONG
  (abbr.): **3** OBL
**Rectangular**
  pier: **4** ANTA
**Rector**
  income: **5** TITHE
**Recumbent: 5** LYING
**Recuperate: 4** HEAL MEND
  Place to: **3** SPA
**Recur: 5** ACTUP
**Recurring**
  melody: **5** THEMA
  period: **5** CYCLE
  theme: **5** MOTIF
**Recyclable: 4** USED
  item: **3** CAN **5** EMPTY
    **7** SODACAN **8** ALUMINUM
    **11** ALUMINUMCAN
**Recycling**
  receptacle: **3** BIN
**Red: 3** SEA **4** NLER **5** ROUGE
  algae: **7** SEAMOSS
  bearded god: **4** THOR
  Be in the: **3** OWE
  Big: **3** MAO **5** LENIN **6** STALIN
  buoy: **3** NUN
  cap: **3** FEZ
  carpet recipient: **7** HONOREE
  Cause to see: **6** ENRAGE
  Cheese in: **4** EDAM
  coat: **4** RUST
  coin: **4** CENT
  Comedian: **7** SKELTON
  Cool ~ giant: **5** SSTAR
  Dark: **4** LAKE PUCE RUBY
    WINE **6** CERISE MAROON
  dye: **5** EOSIN HENNA
  Firefighter: **5** ADAIR
  fish: **7** SNAPPER
  flag: **5** ALERT
  Former ~ Rose: **4** PETE
  giant: **7** ANTARES
  head: **3** MAO **5** LENIN
    **6** STALIN
  herring: **4** PLOY
  In the: **4** ASEA **5** OWING
  in the middle: **4** RARE
  It might be: **4** CENT
    **5** ALERT
  letters: **4** USSR
  One in the: **4** OWER
  pigment: **4** LAKE
  planet: **4** MARS
  prefix: **5** INFRA
  Purplish: **4** PUCE WINE
    **5** GRAPE **6** CERISE
    **7** CARMINE MAGENTA
  See: **3** OWE **4** FUME RAGE
    STOP **5** STEAM **6** GETMAD
    SEETHE

Seeing: 3 MAD 4 IRED SORE
   5 IRATE RILED
Shade of: 4 BEET 6 CERISE
sky: 4 OMEN
state: 4 DEBT 5 ALERT
   ANGER
tag event: 4 SALE
team: 3 SOX
Turn: 3 DYE 5 BLUSH FLUSH
   RIPEN SHAME
vegetable: 4 BEET
Vivid: 7 PIMENTO
wine: 4 PORT 5 MEDOC
   PINOT 6 CLARET
   MERLOT 9 PINOTNOIR
~ Muppet: 4 ELMO
**Red ___**: 3 ANT SEA TAI 4 CENT
   HOTS 5 ALERT APPLE
   BARON 7 SNAPPER
**___ red**: 4 BEET
**___ Red**
   (apple variety): 3 IDA
**"Red, The"**
   Explorer called: 4 ERIC
**Red Army**
   founder: 7 TROTSKY
   leader: 3 MAO
   member: 3 ANT
**Red as ___**: 5 ABEET
**"Red Badge of Courage, The"**
   author: 5 CRANE
**Red Baron**: 3 ACE 7 AVIATOR
   foe: 6 SNOOPY
**Red-blooded**: 5 LUSTY
   6 ROBUST
**Redbone**
   Folk singer: 4 LEON
**Redbreast**: 5 ROBIN
**Redcap**
   burden: 4 BAGS
   workplace: 5 DEPOT
**Red carpet**
   recipient: 7 HONOREE
   Roll out the: 5 GREET
**Red Cloud**: 5 SIOUX
**Red Cross**
   course: 3 CPR
   Former ~ head: 4 DOLE
   founder: 6 BARTON
   founder Barton: 5 CLARA
   supply: 4 SERA 5 BLOOD
   6 PLASMA
**Redding**
   Peak north of: 8 MTSHASTA
   Singer: 4 OTIS
**Reddish**: 4 RARE
   purple: 5 LILAC
   yellow: 5 OCHER
**Reddish brown**: 4 RUST
   5 HENNA 6 RUSSET
   SIENNA SORREL TITIAN
   WALNUT 8 MAHOGANY
   gem: 4 SARD
   horse: 3 BAY 4 ROAN
   6 SORREL
**Red-dog**: 5 BLITZ

**Reddy**
   Singer: 5 HELEN
**Reddy, Helen**
   hit: 9 DELTADAWN
**Redecorate**: 6 DOOVER
**Redeem**: 4 CASH SAVE
   6 CASHIN
**Red-eye**
   gravy base: 3 HAM
**Red-faced**: 7 ABASHED
   ASHAMED
**Redford**: 5 BLOND
   1969 ~ role:
     11 SUNDANCEKID
   1975 ~ role:
     11 WALDOPEPPER
   1984 ~ film: 10 THENATURAL
   1984 ~ role: 5 HOBBS
   1992 ~ film: 8 SNEAKERS
   1994 ~ film: 8 QUIZSHOW
**Redgrave**
   1968 ~ film: 7 ISADORA
   Actress: 4 LYNN 7 VANESSA
   title role: 5 JULIA 6 AGATHA
**Red Guard**
   leader: 3 MAO
   member: 6 MAOIST
**Red-handed**
   Catch: 3 NAB 4 NAIL
**Redhead**
   dye: 5 HENNA
   Mayberry: 4 OPIE
   Raggedy: 3 ANN
   Riverdale: 6 ARCHIE
   ~, slangily. 9 CARROTTOP
**Red-hot**: 6 WIENER
   one: 4 MAMA
**"Red House Mystery, The"**
   author: 5 MILNE 7 AAMILNE
**Red-hunting**
   gp.: 4 HUAC
**Red ink**: 4 DEBT
   amount: 4 LOSS
**Redness**
   Symbol of: 4 BEET
**Redo**: 4 EDIT
**Redolence**: 4 ODOR 5 AROMA
   7 PERFUME
**Redress**
   Seek: 3 SUE
**Red Riding Hood**
   accessory: 6 BASKET
   burden: 6 BASKET
**Red River**
   capital: 5 HANOI
**"Red River"**: 5 OATER
   actress Joanne: 3 DRU
**Reds**: 4 TEAM 5 NLERS
   7 SOVIETS
**Red Sea**
   gulf: 5 AQABA
   nation: 5 SUDAN YEMEN
   7 ERITREA
   peninsula: 5 SINAI
   port: 4 ADEN SUEZ
   vessel: 4 DHOW

**"Red Shoes, The"**
   actress Shearer: 5 MOIRA
**Red Skelton**
   catchphrase: 7 IDOODIT
   character: 4 CLEM
**Red Sox**
   Garciaparra of the: 5 NOMAR
**Red-spotted**
   creature: 3 EFT 4 NEWT
**Red Square**
   figure: 5 LENIN
**Reduce**: 4 DIET EASE PARE
   5 ABATE LOWER PRUNE
   6 LESSEN
   to mush: 5 PUREE
**Reduced**: 6 ONSALE
   by: 4 LESS
   fare: 4 DIET
**Reduction**: 3 CUT 4 DROP
   8 CUTPRICE
**Redwood City**
   county: 8 SANMATEO
**Reebok**: 7 SNEAKER
   rival: 4 AVIA FILA NIKE
   PUMA 6 ADIDAS
**Reed**
   Film critic: 3 REX
   home: 5 MARSH
   instrument: 3 SAX 4 OBOE
   Musical: 3 LOU
   of TV: 5 DONNA
   player: 6 OBOIST
   Weaver: 4 SLEY
**Reedlike**: 7 SLENDER
**Reef**
   dweller: 3 EEL 5 MORAY
   material: 5 CORAL
   Ring-shaped: 5 ATOLL
**Reek**: 5 FETOR STINK
**Reel**: 5 DANCE 7 STAGGER
   8 SEESTARS
   Fishing ~ winder: 5 SPOOL
   in: 4 LAND
   off: 6 RECITE
   Partner of: 3 ROD
   person: 5 ACTOR
**Reese**
   Actress: 5 DELLA
   of the Dodgers: 6 PEEWEE
   Singer: 5 DELLA
**Reese, ___ Wee**: 3 PEE
**Reeve**
   role: 4 KENT 8 SUPERMAN
**Reeves**
   Actor: 5 KEANU
   Bodybuilder: 5 STEVE
   Country singer: 3 DEL
   film: 5 SPEED 9 THEMATRIX
   role: 3 NEO
**Ref**
   call: 3 TKO 4 TIME
   counterpart: 3 UMP
**Ref.**
   book: 4 DICT
   Large ~ work: 3 ENC OED
   5 ENCYC

**Refer: 6** ALLUDE
  to: **4** CITE
**Referee: 7** MEDIATE
  ~, slangily: **5** ZEBRA
**Reference: 8** ALLUSION
  20-vol. ~ work: **3** OED
  Annual ~ book: **7** ALMANAC
  Astronomy: **7** STARMAP
  Chef's: **8** COOKBOOK
  Credit as a: **4** CITE
  Geographical: **5** ATLAS
  Make: **6** ALLUDE
  Many ~ works: **5** TOMES
  Microsoft: **7** ENCARTA
  Paper: **8** FOOTNOTE
  Pianist ~ material:
    **10** SHEETMUSIC
  words: **4** INRE
  Writing: **5** ROGET
**Referendum**
  choice: **3** YES
**Refill**
  Needing a: **3** LOW
**Refinable**
  rock: **3** ORE
**Refine: 4** HONE **5** SMELT
**Refined: 6** POLITE **7** ELEGANT
  iron: **5** STEEL
  Not: **3** RAW **4** BASE **5** CRUDE
    **6** COARSE
**Refinement: 5** TASTE **6** NICETY
  **8** ELEGANCE
  Place of: **7** SMELTER
  They lack: **4** ORES
**Refinery**
  refuse: **4** SLAG
**Reflect: 4** MUSE
  Something to ~ on: **6** MIRROR
**Reflection: 5** IMAGE
  ___ reflection: **4** UPON
**"Reflections on Ice-Breaking"**
  poet Ogden: **4** NASH
**Reflex**
  Conditioned ~ researcher:
    **6** PAVLOV
  Gag: **4** HAHA
  test site: **4** KNEE
**Reflux: 3** EBB
**Reform**
  targets: **4** ILLS
**Reformer**
  ~ Bloomer: **6** AMELIA
  ~ Dorothea: **3** DIX
  ~ Jacob: **4** RIIS
  ~ Julia Ward ___: **4** HOWE
  ~ Wells: **3** IDA
**Reformist**
  Aggressive: **9** YOUNGTURK
**Reform Party**
  founder: **5** PEROT
  member: **5** TRUMP
**Refractor**
  Light: **5** PRISM
**Refrain**
  Common: **5** TRALA
    **7** TRALALA

from taking action: **6** SITPAT
  King of Siam: **8** ETCETERA
  "Old MacDonald": **5** EIEIO
  Part of a Beatles: **4** YEAH
  Part of a pirate: **6** YOHOHO
  syllable: **3** SHA TRA **4** LALA
  Tyrolean: **5** YODEL
**Refresh: 6** AERATE
**Refresher**
  Daytime: **3** NAP
  Summer: **3** ADE
**Refreshing**
  place: **3** SPA **5** OASIS
**Refreshment**
  Boardwalk: **3** ICE
  site: **5** OASIS
  Summer: **3** ADE
**Refrigerant: 5** FREON
  Cryogenic: **4** NEON
**Refrigerate: 4** COOL **5** CHILL
**Refrigerator**
  decoration: **6** MAGNET
  name: **5** AMANA
  part: **7** CRISPER
  precursor: **6** ICEBOX
**Refuel: 5** GASUP
**Refueling**
  area: **3** PIT
  opportunity: **7** PITSTOP
**Refuge**
  Place of: **3** ARK **4** LAIR NEST
    **5** HAVEN
  Take: **6** HOLEUP
**Refugee**
  Dust Bowl: **4** OKIE
  Political: **6** EMIGRE
**Refuges: 5** ASYLA
**Refund**
  check issuer (abbr.): **3** IRS
  Due a: **12** OVERWITHHELD
  How a ~ may be made:
    **7** PRORATA
**Refusal**
  Emphatic: **5** NEVER
    NOHOW **6** NOMAAM
    **7** NOSIREE
  French: **3** NON
  German: **4** NEIN
  Polite: **5** NOSIR **6** NOMAAM
  Russian: **4** NYET
  Scottish: **3** NAE
  Slangy: **3** NAH **4** NOPE
  Terse: **5** IWONT
**Refusals: 3** NOS **4** NOES
**Refuse: 3** ASH **4** DENY LEES
    SCUM **5** CHAFF DROSS
    OFFAL SAYNO TRASH
    WASTE **6** LITTER
    **7** GARBAGE
  aid: **8** TRASHCAN
  Kitchen: **4** SLOP
  Metal: **4** SLAG
  to talk: **6** CLAMUP
  to yield: **6** INSIST
  transport: **4** SCOW
  visitor: **3** RAT

**Refuses**
  to: **4** WONT
**Refute: 4** DENY **5** BELIE
  **8** DISPROVE
**Reg.: 3** STD
  City: **3** ORD
**Regal: 7** STATELY
  address: **4** SIRE
  fur: **6** ERMINE
  headwear: **5** TIARA
  letters: **3** HRH
  material: **4** SILK
  residence: **6** PALACE
  symbol: **3** ORB
**Regale: 4** FETE
**Regalia**
  item: **3** ORB
**Regan**
  Father of: **4** LEAR
**Regard: 3** EYE SEE **4** CARE
  DEEM VIEW **6** ESTEEM
  highly: **6** ADMIRE ESTEEM
  In ~ to: **5** ANENT ASFOR
  with awe: **8** VENERATE
**Regarding: 4** ASTO INRE
  **5** ABOUT ANENT
  this point: **6** HERETO
**Regardless: 6** ANYWAY
  **7** ANYWAYS
**Regatta: 4** RACE **8** BOATRACE
  implement: **3** OAR
  racer: **5** SCULL SLOOP
    YACHT
  site: **6** HENLEY
  team: **4** CREW
**Reggae**
  fan: **5** RASTA
  Gregory of: **6** ISAACS
  Kamoze of: **3** INI
  Peter of: **4** TOSH
  relative: **3** SKA
  ___ régime: **6** ANCIEN
**Regimen: 4** DIET **7** PROGRAM
  Pool: **4** LAPS
  Post-op: **5** REHAB
  vitamin: **7** ONEADAY
**Reginald**
  Actor: **4** OWEN
**"Reginald"**
  author: **4** SAKI
**Region: 4** AREA ZONE
  (abbr.): **4** TERR
  Upper ~ of space: **3** SKY
    **5** ETHER
**Regional: 7** ENDEMIC
  dialect: **5** IDIOM **6** PATOIS
  foliage: **5** FLORA
  life: **5** BIOTA
  wildlife: **5** FAUNA
**Regis**
  cohost Kelly: **4** RIPA
**Register: 5** ENROL ENTER
    LOGIN **6** ENLIST
    ENROLL SIGNIN
    SIGNUP SINKIN
  key: **6** NOSALE

output: 7 RECEIPT
signer: 5 GUEST
transaction: 4 SALE
**Registered**
It may be: 9 TRADENAME
**Registration**
datum: 5 OWNER
Mil. ~ group: 3 SSS
**Regret:** 3 RUE 6 LAMENT
7 REMORSE
Express: 4 MOAN SIGH
Word of: 4 ALAS
**Regretful**
feeling: 4 PANG
one: 4 RUER
~ Miss of song: 4 OTIS
**Regrets**
Send ~, maybe: 4 RSVP
**Regrettable:** 3 SAD
**Regular:** 5 USUAL 6 PATRON
7 HABITUE
(abbr.): 3 STD
guy: 3 JOE 4 BEAU
hangout: 5 HAUNT
7 PURLIEU
order: 5 USUAL
**Regulation:** 3 LAW 4 RULE
7 STATUTE
Judge's: 10 COURTORDER
**Regulator**
Current: 8 RHEOSTAT
Former RR: 3 ICC
JFK: 3 FAA
Light: 4 IRIS
NYSE: 3 SEC
TV: 3 FCC
Workplace: 4 OSHA
**Regulatory**
Fed. ~ gp.: 3 AEC FDA
**Rehab**
candidate: 4 USER
process: 5 DETOX
**Rehan**
Actress: 3 ADA
**Rehearsal**
Kind of: 5 DRESS
request: 4 LINE
**Rehearse**
in the ring: 4 SPAR
**Rehem:** 5 ALTER
**Reid**
Actor: 3 TIM
Actress: 4 TARA
**Reign:** 4 RULE
**Rein**
in: 4 CURB
**Reindeer**
herder: 4 LAPP
kin: 3 ELK 7 CARIBOU
name: 5 COMET CUPID
VIXEN 6 DANCER
DASHER DONNER
7 BLITZEN PRANCER
Santa's: 5 OCTAD OCTET
**Reiner**
Director: 3 ROB 4 CARL

**Reinforcement**
Blue jeans: 5 RIVET
Concrete: 5 REBAR
Tire: 3 PLY
**Reinking**
Dancer: 3 ANN
**Reins**
Take the: 4 LEAD 5 STEER
**Reiterate:** 4 ECHO
**Reitman**
Director: 4 IVAN
**Reject:** 3 NIX 4 DENY JILT
VETO 5 SPURN
**Rejection:** 6 REBUFF
Russian: 4 NYET
**Rejections:** 3 NOS 4 NOES
**Rejoice:** 5 EXULT
**Relate:** 4 TELL 5 TIETO
6 BEARON
**Related:** 3 KIN 4 AKIN TOLD
7 SIMILAR
Maternally: 5 ENATE
(to): 4 AKIN TIED
**Relation**
In ~ to: 7 VISAVIS
**Relations:** 7 KINFOLK
Break in: 4 RIFT
Good: 5 AMITY
**Relationship:** 5 RATIO
Kind of: 6 CASUAL
8 ONETOONE
**Relationships**
Like some: 7 SAMESEX
SPATIAL 8 PLATONIC
**Relative:** 3 SIB 5 FLESH
7 KINSMAN
by marriage: 5 INLAW
of mine: 4 OURS
**Relax:** 4 EASE LAZE LOLL
REST 5 CHILL LETUP
6 COOLIT EASEUP
GOEASY LOOSEN
UNWIND 7 TAKETEN
8 CHILLOUT TAKEFIVE
Place to: 3 DEN SPA
6 RESORT
~, as rules: 4 BEND
~, with "out": 3 VEG
**"Relax!":** 6 ATEASE
8 LOOSENUP
**Relaxation:** 4 EASE
**Relaxed:** 4 CALM 5 EASED
LOOSE 6 ATEASE
**Relaxing:** 6 ATEASE
place: 3 SPA
**"Relax, soldier!":** 6 ATEASE
**Relay:** 6 PASSON SENDON
part: 3 LEG
stick: 5 BATON
**Release:** 4 EMIT FREE
5 LETGO UNTIE
6 SPRING 7 SETFREE
8 LETLOOSE
Conditional: 6 PAROLE
Early: 6 PAROLE
money: 4 BAIL

Press: 4 WINE
**Released:** 8 ONPAROLE
Be: 6 GOFREE
**Relent:** 6 EASEUP GIVEIN
**Relevance:** 7 APTNESS
**Relevant:** 3 APT 5 ADREM
7 GERMANE
Be: 5 TIEIN 7 PERTAIN
Be ~ to: 6 BEARON
**Reliable:** 4 SAFE TRUE
5 LOYAL SOLID
6 TRUSTY
**Reliant**
Plymouth: 4 KCAR
**Relief:** 3 AID SUB 4 DOLE
6 SOLACE 7 RESPITE
Carve in: 6 EMBOSS
carving: 5 CAMEO
Cries of: 3 AHS
Cry of: 3 AAH 4 PHEW SIGH
TGIF WHEW 6 ATLAST
Disaster ~ org.: 4 FEMA
It is a: 7 ASPIRIN
Kind of: 3 BAS 5 COMIC
Source of: 4 BALM
spot: 5 OASIS
___ relief: 3 BAS
**Relief pitcher:** 5 SAVER
7 FIREMAN
goal: 4 SAVE
**Relieve:** 3 RID 4 EASE 5 ALLAY
SALVE SLAKE
**Reliever:** 5 EASER
Pain: 6 ICEBAG OPIATE
7 ANODYNE
Pain ~ brand: 5 ALEVE
BAYER
stat: 3 ERA 5 SAVES
**Religion:** 5 FAITH
Japanese: 6 SHINTO
Mideast: 5 ISLAM
Persian: 5 BAHAI
**Religious:** 5 PIOUS
artifact: 4 ICON
belief: 6 THEISM
Bygone ~ group: 7 SHAKERS
ceremony: 4 RITE
council: 5 SYNOD
dissenter: 7 HERETIC
Extremist ~ group: 4 CULT
group: 4 SECT
Iowa ~ sect: 5 AMANA
offshoot: 4 SECT
principle: 5 TENET
recitation: 6 ROSARY
recluse: 4 MONK 7 EREMITE
retreat: 5 ABBEY 6 ASHRAM
sch.: 3 SEM
scroll: 5 TORAH
sculpture: 5 PIETA
symbol: 4 ICON
war: 7 CRUSADE
**Relinquish:** 4 CEDE QUIT
5 DEMIT WAIVE
**Relish:** 4 TANG ZEST 5 EATUP
ENJOY GUSTO SAVOR

**Relocate:** 4 MOVE
**Reluctant:** 3 COY 5 LOATH
    6 AVERSE
**Rely:** 6 DEPEND
  on: 5 TRUST 6 LOOKTO
    7 SWEARBY TRUSTIN
**REM**
  Part of: 3 EYE 5 RAPID
  venue: 3 MTV
  ~ singer Michael: 5 STIPE
**Remain:** 3 ARE 4 BIDE STAY
    6 STAYON
  at home: 6 STAYIN
  How some shall: 8 NAMELESS
  undecided: 4 PEND
**Remainder:** 4 REST
  ~, in French: 5 RESTE
**Remained:** 3 SAT 6 ABIDED
**Remaining:** 4 LEFT 5 OTHER
**Remains:** 4 LEES 5 ASHES
    DREGS 6 DEBRIS
  Smoldering: 6 EMBERS
  to be seen: 5 RUINS
**Remark**
  Barbed: 4 GIBE
  Cutting: 4 BARB
  Defiant: 7 SOTHERE
  Parenthetical: 5 ASIDE
  Sheepish: 3 BAA
  Sotto voce: 5 ASIDE
  Witty: 3 MOT 4 JEST QUIP
**Remarkable:** 6 OFNOTE
    7 AMAZING UNCANNY
    10 NOTEWORTHY
  person: 4 LULU
  thing: 5 DILLY 8 CATSMEOW
**Remarks**
  Like some: 5 SNIDE 6 SEXIST
    7 POINTED
  Opening: 5 INTRO
**Remarque**
  Author: 5 ERICH
**Re/Max**
  rival: 3 ERA
**Rembrandt**
  Artist: 5 PEALE
  Artist ~ van ___: 3 RYN
  Emulate: 4 ETCH
  medium: 4 OILS
**Remedy:** 4 CURE HEAL
    7 REDRESS 8 ANTIDOTE
  Burn: 4 ALOE
  Sunburn ~, originally:
    7 NOXZEMA
**Remember**
  Mission to: 5 ALAMO
  Ship to: 5 MAINE
  Time to: 3 ERA 5 EPOCH
  You must ~ this: 5 ALAMO
**"___ Remember":** 5 TRYTO
**"Remember the ___!":** 5 ALAMO
    MAINE
**Remembrance Day**
  mo.: 3 NOV
**Remind:** 5 NUDGE
  too much: 3 NAG

**Reminder:** 4 NOTE
  Office: 4 MEMO
  product: 6 POSTIT
  Stage: 3 CUE
  Surgery: 4 SCAR
  to Santa: 4 LIST
**Remington**
  rival: 7 NORELCO
  TV detective: 6 STEELE
**"Remington ___":** 6 STEELE
**Remini**
  Actress: 4 LEAH
**Remit:** 3 PAY 4 SEND
**Remnant:** 3 END 4 DREG
    5 SCRAP SHRED TRACE
    6 TAGEND 7 RESIDUE
    VESTIGE
  Fire: 3 ASH 5 EMBER
**___ Remo, Italy:** 3 SAN
**Remora**
  ride: 5 SHARK
**Remorse:** 7 SADNESS
  Feel ~ for: 3 RUE 6 REPENT
**Remorseful**
  one: 4 RUER
**Remote:** 3 FAR 7 FARAWAY
    8 ISOLATED
  ancestor: 4 DIAL
  button: 3 REC 4 MENU MUTE
    6 VOLUME
  location: 4 SOFA
  room: 3 DEN
  target: 3 VCR 5 TVSET
  targets: 3 TVS
**Removable**
  car roof: 4 TTOP
**Remove:** 3 AXE 4 DELE DOFF
    SHED 5 ERASE EVICT
  a splinter: 6 TWEEZE
  branches: 5 PRUNE
  from office: 4 OUST
    6 UNSEAT
  rind: 4 PARE
  the fat from: 4 TRIM
**Removed**
  Commonly ~ tissue: 6 TONSIL
    8 ADENOIDS
**Remover**
  Hair: 5 RAZOR
  Hair ~ brand: 4 NEET
  Mistake: 6 ERASER
  Polish: 7 ACETONE
  Stubble: 5 RAZOR
  Wrinkle: 4 IRON
**Remsen**
  Chemist: 3 IRA
**Remus:** 4 TWIN 5 UNCLE
**Remus, Uncle:** 4 TALE
  address: 4 BRER
**Ren:** 4 TOON
**Renaissance**
  family: 4 ESTE
  fiddle: 5 REBEC
  instrument: 4 LUTE
  patron: 4 ESTE
**Renaissance ___:** 5 FAIRE

**Renata**
  Soprano: 6 SCOTTO
**Renault**
  Old: 5 LECAR
**Rend:** 4 TEAR
**Render**
  harmless: 5 UNARM
    6 DEFUSE DISARM
  speechless: 3 AWE GAG
    4 STUN
  unnecessary: 7 OBVIATE
**"Render therefore ___**
    Caesar ...":** 4 UNTO
**Rendezvous:** 4 MEET 5 TRYST
    6 MEETUP
**Rene**
  Actress: 5 RUSSO
**René**
  1950s French president ~:
    4 COTY
  of tennis: 7 LACOSTE
**Renée**
  Actress: 6 ADOREE
**Renege:** 6 COPOUT
**Renewable**
  energy type: 5 SOLAR
**Renewal**
  Kind of: 5 URBAN
  target: 4 SLUM
**Renfrew**
  org., in old radio: 4 RCMP
**Reno**
  formerly in Washington:
    5 JANET
  predecessor: 4 BARR
  resident: 7 NEVADAN
  roller: 3 DIE
  state: 6 NEVADA
**Renoir**
  subject: 4 NUDE
**Renounce:** 6 DISOWN
**Renown:** 4 FAME 5 ECLAT
    GLORY
**Rent:** 3 LET RIP 4 HIRE TEAR
    TORE TORN 5 LEASE
  again: 5 RELET
  alternative: 3 OWN
  For: 5 TOLET
  payer: 6 LESSEE TENANT
**"Rent"**
  Basis for: 8 LABOHEME
**Rent-___:** 4 ACAR ACOP
**"Rent-___" (1988 film):** 4 ACOP
**Renta, Oscar ___:** 4 DELA
**Rental**
  ad abbr.: 3 RMS
  agent: 6 LEASER
  agreement: 5 LEASE
  Common: 4 TAPE 5 VIDEO
  Lake: 5 CANOE
  Links: 4 CART
  Moving: 5 UHAUL
  Prom: 3 TUX 4 LIMO
**Renter:** 6 LESSEE TENANT
  paper: 5 LEASE
  Room: 3 INN

**Reo:** 3 CAR
 maker: 4 OLDS
 Part of: 3 ELI 4 OLDS
  6 RANSOM
 rival: 5 ESSEX
**Rep:** 5 AGENT
 presentation: 4 DEMO
**Rep.:** 3 AGT
 City council: 3 ALD
 counterpart: 3 SEN
 Legal: 3 ATT 4 ATTY
 Not ~ or Dem.: 3 IND
 rival: 3 DEM
**Repair:** 3 FIX 4 MEND
 cost: 5 LABOR PARTS
 shop substitute: 6 LOANER
 Wreck beyond: 5 TOTAL
**Repairman:** 5 FIXER
 Brand with a lonely:
  6 MAYTAG
**Reparation:** 6 AMENDS
 Make: 5 ATONE
**Repartee:** 3 WIT
 Bit of: 3 MOT
 Part of a: 3 TAT
**Repast:** 4 MEAL
**Repay:** 6 AVENGE
**Repeat:** 4 ECHO 6 PARROT
  7 ITERATE
 performance: 6 ENCORE
 verbatim: 4 ECHO 5 QUOTE
**Repeatedly:** 3 OFT 5 OFTEN
 Say: 7 ITERATE
**Repeating:** 7 ITERANT
  9 ITERATIVE
**Repellent**
 Evil: 6 AMULET
 Insect: 4 DEET
 Moth: 5 CEDAR
 Mugger: 4 MACE
 Vampire: 5 CROSS 6 GARLIC
**Repent:** 5 ATONE
 of: 3 RUE
**Repentant**
 one: 4 RUER
**Repetition**
 Musical ~ mark: 5 SEGNO
 Unthinking: 4 ROTE
**Repetitious:** 7 ITERANT
**Repetitive**
 card game: 3 WAR
 process: 4 ROTE
**Rephrase:** 4 EDIT 5 AMEND
**Replace:** 9 SUPERSEDE
**Replay**
 feature: 5 SLOMO
**Replayed**
 shot: 3 LET
**Replete**
 Render: 4 SATE
**Replica:** 4 COPY 5 MODEL
**Replicate:** 5 CLONE
**Reply:** 4 RSVP
 (abbr.): 3 ANS
 Defiant: 5 NEVER
 Off-the-wall: 4 ECHO

 Private: 5 NOSIR
 Respectful: 4 YESM
 Roll call: 4 HERE
 Sheepish: 3 BAA
 to "Am not!": 4 AMSO 5 ARESO
 to "Am too!": 6 ARENOT
 to "That so?": 4 ITIS
 to the captain: 3 AYE
  6 AYEAYE
 to "You are not!": 5 IAMSO
**Repo**
 man: 6 SEIZER
**Report:** 4 BANG 7 WRITEUP
 1977 ~ author: 4 HITE
 1998 ~ author: 5 STARR
 by phone: 6 CALLIN
 card stat: 3 GPA
 of an insured: 4 LOSS
 of a report:
  15 HEARSAYEVIDENCE
 of a shooting: 4 BANG
 Police ~ letters: 3 AKA
 Rather: 4 NEWS
 Short: 3 POP
**Reporter**
 angle: 5 SLANT
 bailiwick: 4 BEAT
 CNN: 11 WOLFBLITZER
 Comics: 5 STARR
 contact: 6 SOURCE
 coup: 5 SCOOP
 Court: 5 STENO
 Daily Planet· 4 KENT LANE
  LOIS 5 OLSEN
  8 LOISLANE
 need: 7 NOTEPAD
 place: 4 DESK
 query: 3 HOW WHO WHY
  4 WHAT WHEN 5 WHERE
 source: 4 LEAK
 ~ Donaldson: 3 SAM
 ~ Roberts: 5 COKIE
**Reporters:** 5 PRESS
 Like some: 6 ROVING
**Reporting**
 Credit ~ co.: 3 TRW
 to: 5 BELOW UNDER
**Repose:** 4 EASE REST 5 SLEEP
**Reposed:** 4 LAIN
**Repository**
 Corneal: 7 EYEBANK
 Tool: 4 SHED
 Wine: 6 CELLAR
**Reprehensible:** 4 BASE VILE
 Morally: 6 SORDID
**Represent:** 5 ACTAS 6 DENOTE
  8 SPEAKFOR
 What candles sometimes:
  3 AGE
**Representation:** 5 IMAGE
**Representative:** 5 AGENT
  ENVOY TOKEN 6 ICONIC
**Repress:** 5 QUASH 6 HOLDIN
  KEEPIN
**Reprieve:** 4 STAY
  15 STAYOFEXECUTION

**Reprimand:** 5 CHIDE SCOLD
  6 BERATE REBUKE
  7 CENSURE
  15 CALLONTHECARPET
 for Rover: 3 BAD
 ~, with "out": 4 CHEW REAM
**Reprints**
 Magazine of: 4 UTNE
  10 UTNEREADER
**Reproach**
 Famed: 4 ETTU
 Sound of: 3 TSK TUT
  6 TSKTSK
 Word of: 5 SHAME
**Reproduce:** 4 COPY 5 BREED
  SPAWN
**Reproduction**
 Exact: 5 CLONE
 needs: 3 OVA
**Reproductive**
 body: 5 SPORE
 cell: 5 OVULE 6 GAMETE
 cells: 3 OVA
 gland: 5 OVARY
**Reproof**
 Sound of: 3 TUT
**Reps**
 Company whose ~ have a
  calling: 4 AVON
 Several ~, in the gym: 3 SET
**Reptile:** 5 SNAKE 6 LIZARD
 Company with a ~ logo: 4 IZOD
 Long ~, in short: 4 CROC
 Nile: 3 ASP
 prefix: 4 SAUR
**Republic**
 Asian: 4 IRAN LAOS
 Baltic: 7 ESTONIA
 Black Sea: 7 GEORGIA
  ROMANIA
 Caribbean: 5 HAITI
 Irish: 4 EIRE
 Islamic: 4 IRAN
 Landlocked African: 4 MALI
 South Pacific: 4 FIJI
 West African: 4 MALI TOGO
  5 BENIN GABON
  7 NIGERIA
**"Republic, The"**
 author: 5 PLATO
**Republican:** 3 GOP
 elephant creator: 4 NAST
**Repudiate:** 4 DENY 6 DISOWN
**Repugnant:** 6 ODIOUS
 Find: 5 ABHOR
**Repulsive:** 4 ICKY VILE
 Find: 5 ABHOR
**Reputation:** 4 NAME ODOR
 tarnisher: 4 BLOT
 threat: 5 SMEAR
 Worse than a bad: 6 INFAMY
**Repute:** 4 FAME ODOR
**Req.**
 Not: 3 OPT
**Request:** 3 ASK 4 PLEA SEEK
  6 ASKFOR

before a shot: 5 SMILE
sweetener: 6 PLEASE
**Requested**
Do as: 6 OBLIGE
**Requiem**
word: 4 IRAE
**"Requiem for ___" (Faulkner book):** 4 ANUN
**Require:** 4 NEED 6 COMPEL ENTAIL OBLIGE
**Requirement:** 4 MUST NEED
**Requiring**
help: 6 INNEED
**Requisite:** 4 NEED 6 NEEDED
**Requisition:** 6 ASKFOR
**Requital:** 7 PAYMENT
**Requite:** 6 AVENGE
**Rescue:** 3 AID 4 HELP SAVE 7 BAILOUT
squad VIP: 3 EMT
**Rescuer:** 4 HERO 6 SAVIOR
**Research:** 5 DELVE
facil.: 4 INST
institute: 9 THINKTANK
Medical ~ agcy.: 3 NIH
money: 5 GRANT
paper: 6 THESIS
site: 3 LAB
___ **Research Center:** 4 AMES
**Researcher**
quest: 5 GRANT
**Resell**
illegally: 5 SCALP
**Resemble:** 6 BELIKE
Closely: 5 MIMIC
~, with "after": 4 TAKE
**Resembling:** 3 ALA 4 LIKE 5 QUASI
**Resentful:** 4 SORE 6 BITTER
**Resentment:** 3 IRE 5 PIQUE 7 UMBRAGE
Cause: 6 RANKLE
**Reservation:** 3 BUT 5 QUALM
Course: 7 TEETIME
Make a: 4 BOOK
Plane: 4 SEAT
**Reserve:** 4 HOLD SAVE 5 CACHE STORE 7 ICINESS 8 BOTTLEUP SETASIDE 9 RETICENCE
In: 5 APART ASIDE ONICE
**Reserved:** 3 SHY 4 KEPT 5 ALOOF ONICE STAID TAKEN 6 DEMURE SEDATE 8 SETASIDE
**Reserves:** 7 MILITIA
**Reservoir**
filler: 4 RAIN
**Reset**
setting: 3 OOO 4 OOOO
**Reside:** 5 DWELL
**Resided:** 5 DWELT LIVED
**Residence**
(abbr.): 3 HSE
Bird: 4 NEST
Cockney: 3 OME

First family: 4 EDEN
French president: 6 ELYSEE
Northern: 5 IGLOO
Regal: 6 PALACE
Take up: 6 MOVEIN
**Resident:** 6 INTERN
suffix: 3 ESE ITE
**Residents**
(abbr.): 3 DRS MDS
**Residue:** 3 ASH
Chimney: 4 SOOT
Dryer: 4 LINT
Pipe: 6 DOTTLE
Smelting: 4 SLAG
**Resign:** 4 QUIT 5 DEMIT
**Resignation**
Phrase of: 5 IQUIT
**Resignee**
1973 ~: 5 AGNEW
1974 ~: 3 RMN 5 NIXON
**Resilient:** 7 ELASTIC
wood: 3 ASH
**Resin:** 3 LAC
Adhesive: 5 EPOXY
Fossil: 5 AMBER
Fragrant: 5 ELEMI
Varnish: 5 COPAL ELEMI 6 MASTIC
**Resist:** 4 DEFY 6 OPPOSE
change: 8 STANDPAT
Not: 4 OBEY
**Resistance**
Air: 4 DRAG
figure: 6 OHMAGE
Symbol of: 5 OMEGA
to change: 7 INERTIA
unit: 3 OHM
**Resistant:** 6 AVERSE
**Resister:** 5 REBEL
Roman invasion: 5 DRUID
**Res ___ loquitur:** 4 IPSA
**Resnais**
Director: 5 ALAIN
**Resolution**
Accept a: 5 ADOPT
Fill with: 5 STEEL
Printer (abbr.): 3 DPI
Typical New Year: 4 DIET
**Resolve:** 3 VOW 6 SETTLE 7 IRONOUT
Tough to: 5 MESSY
**Resolved:** 7 DEADSET
Not yet: 4 OPEN
**Resonance**
Magnetic ~ device: 6 IMAGER
**Resonant**
Not: 5 TINNY
**Resort**
Belgian: 3 SPA
Brazilian: 3 RIO
California: 5 TAHOE 11 PALMSPRINGS
Caribbean: 5 ARUBA
Colorado: 4 VAIL 5 ASPEN
German: 3 EMS
Health: 3 SPA

Italian: 4 LIDO
Italian ~ lake: 4 COMO
Maine: 9 BARHARBOR
Mediterranean: 7 RIVIERA
near Venezuela: 5 ARUBA
Nevada: 5 TAHOE
New Mexico: 4 TAOS
Pennsylvanian: 7 POCONOS
Riviera: 4 NICE 7 SANREMO
Sicilian: 4 ENNA
Sierra Madres: 4 OJAI
site: 5 SHORE
Utah: 4 ALTA
Vermont: 5 STOWE
**Resound:** 4 ECHO PEAL
**Resource:** 5 ASSET
Natural: 3 ORE
**Resourcefulness:** 4 WITS
**Resp.:** 3 ANS
**Respect:** 6 ADMIRE ESTEEM
In any: 5 ATALL
Indian title of: 3 SRI 5 SAHIB
Japanese title of: 3 SAN
Show: 3 BOW 4 RISE 5 KNEEL
Term of: 4 MAAM 5 MADAM
Treat with: 5 HONOR
With ~ to: 4 INRE 5 ASFOR
**Respected**
one: 5 DOYEN ELDER
**"Respect for Acting"**
author: 8 UTAHAGEN
author Hagen: 3 UTA
**Respectful**
gesture: 6 SALUTE
**Respecting:** 4 ASTO
**Respiration:** 6 BREATH
**Respire:** 7 BREATHE
**Respond:** 6 ANSWER
angrily: 15 BITEONESHEADOFF
suffix: 3 ENT
(to): 5 REACT
to a bore: 4 YAWN
to a sneeze: 5 BLESS
to reveille: 4 RISE 5 ARISE
**Respondent**
911 ~: 3 EMT
**Response**
Glib: 9 PATANSWER
Military: 5 NOSIR 6 YESSIR
Polite: 7 YESMAAM
Positive: 3 YES
Prayer: 4 AMEN
to a compliment: 4 ITRY
to a ques.: 3 ANS
**Responsibilities**
Face: 4 COPE
~, figuratively: 4 HATS
**Responsibility:** 4 DUTY ONUS 5 BLAME
Avoid: 11 PASSTHEBUCK
Falls on, as a: 8 LIESWITH
**Responsible:** 8 INCHARGE
Be ~ for: 5 SEETO
Hold: 5 BLAME
Legally: 5 OFAGE 6 LIABLE

**Rest:** 3 LIE NAP SIT 4 EASE
    6 REPOSE 7 LIEDOWN
against: 6 LEANON
And the ~ (abbr.): 3 ETC
    4 ETAL
area: 3 BED SPA 5 OASIS
area sight: 4 SEMI
At: 4 IDLE
atop: 5 LIEON
Came to: 4 ALIT
Come to: 5 ENDUP
Day of: 7 SABBATH
Lay to: 5 INTER 6 ENTOMB
of the afternoon: 6 SIESTA
Put to: 5 ALLAY
room sign: 3 MEN 5 GENTS
    INUSE 6 LADIES
stop: 3 BED 5 OASIS
**Restaurant**
Avoid the: 5 EATIN
chain: 4 IHOP
employee: 4 CHEF
fish: 7 SEABASS
freebie: 4 MINT ROLL
    5 WATER 8 ICEWATER
Go to a: 5 EATAT 6 EATOUT
Like some ~ orders: 4 TOGO
list: 4 MENU
of "Alice": 4 MELS
offering: 4 MEAL
owner of song: 5 ALICE
review symbol: 4 STAR
Surf, in a: 7 SEAFOOD
Toots in a: 4 SHOR
Word in French ~ names:
    4 CHEZ
___ **Restaurant:** 6 ALICES
**Restaurateur**
New York: 4 SHOR 5 SARDI
**Rested:** 3 SAT 4 LAIN 5 LEANT
**Resting:** 4 ABED 6 ATEASE
on: 4 ATOP
place: 3 BED DEN INN 4 BASE
    LAIR MOOR SOFA TOMB
    5 OASIS ROOST
**Restless:** 4 EDGY 5 ANTSY
    6 UNEASY
desire: 4 ITCH
Have a ~ night: 4 TOSS
on a score: 7 AGITATO
**Restlessness:** 4 ITCH 6 UNEASE
    15 ANTSINONESPANTS
**Restorative:** 5 SALVE TONIC
**Restore**
confidence to: 8 REASSURE
to health: 4 CURE
**Restrain:** 4 BATE CURB REIN
    STEM 6 HOLDIN REININ
    TETHER
**Restraint:** 4 CURB REIN
    5 LEASH 7 LIMITER
Dungeon: 5 IRONS
Free from: 5 UNTIE
Pet: 5 LEASH 6 TETHER
**Restrict:** 5 CRAMP HEMIN
    LIMIT

**Restricted ___:** 4 AREA
**Restriction:** 5 LIMIT
**Restroom:** 3 LAV
**Result:** 3 END 5 ENDUP
    ENSUE 6 UPSHOT
As a: 4 ERGO THUS
As a ~ of: 5 DUETO
End: 6 UPSHOT
Get as a: 4 REAP
in: 6 LEADTO
of a crack: 4 HAHA
Ring: 3 TKO 4 DRAW
Unexpected: 5 UPSET
**Results**
They get: 5 DOERS
**Résumé**
relative: 3 BIO
~, for short: 4 VITA
**Resurrection**
Egyptian symbol of: 6 SCARAB
**"Resurrection"**
composer Gustav: 6 MAHLER
**Ret.**
plan: 3 IRA
**Retail**
area: 5 STRIP
center: 4 MALL
outlet: 4 MART 5 STORE
outlets: 7 EMPORIA
price: 4 COST
revenue: 5 SALES
store opening: 3 WAL
**Retailer:** 6 DEALER SELLER
Swedish: 4 IKEA
**Retain:** 4 HOLD KEEP
**Retainer:** 3 FEE 4 DIKE
**Retaliate:** 7 GETEVEN
**Retardant**
Apple growth: 4 ALAR
Rancidity: 3 BHT
**Retina**
cell: 3 ROD
feature: 4 CONE
layers: 6 TAPETA
**Retin-A**
treats it: 4 ACNE
**Retinue:** 5 TRAIN
**Retire**
Place to: 3 BED
When to: 7 BEDTIME
**Retired:** 4 ABED 8 EMERITA
as a prof.: 4 EMER
flier: 3 SST
His #4 was: 3 OTT 6 MELOTT
His #7 was: 6 MANTLE
His #12 was: 6 NAMATH
professors: 7 EMERITI
quarterback: 7 ESIASON
U.S. brand ~ in 1972: 4 ESSO
**Retiree**
asset: 3 IRA
of 1979: 3 ALI
title: 7 EMERITA
**Retirees**
Agcy. for: 3 SSA
Titled: 7 EMERITI

**Retirement**
agcy.: 3 SSA
benefit: 7 PENSION
home: 3 BED
mecca: 6 STPETE
plan: 5 KEOGH
Put off: 6 STAYUP
savings: 4 IRAS
**Retiring:** 3 SHY 5 TIMID
**Retort**
Cynic's: 4 IBET
Unconcerned: 6 SOWHAT
**Retract:** 5 UNSAY 8 TAKEBACK
**Retraction**
Make a: 7 EATCROW
**Retreat:** 3 DEN SPA 4 EXIT
    LAIR 5 OASIS
    9 BACKPEDAL
Hindu: 6 ASHRAM
Luxurious: 5 VILLA
Mountain: 5 CABIN
Russian: 5 DACHA
Shady: 5 ARBOR
**Retribution:** 9 TITFORTAT
Agent of: 7 NEMESIS
**Retrieve:** 3 GET 6 REELIN
**Retriever**
Type of: 8 LABRADOR
~, for short: 3 LAB
**Retro**
car: 6 BEETLE
hairdo: 4 AFRO
phone feature: 4 DIAL
sign word: 4 OLDE
style: 4 DECO
**Retroactive**
Make: 8 BACKDATE
**Retrovirus**
material: 3 RNA
**Retsyn**
Mint with: 4 CERT
**Return:** 6 PROFIT
addressee: 3 IRS
call: 4 ECHO
Get in: 4 REAP
High: 3 LOB
mail courtesy (abbr.): 4 SASE
Rate of: 5 YIELD
requirement: 7 RECEIPT
    9 SALESSLIP
to base: 5 TAGUP
to office: 7 REELECT
~ ID: 3 SSN
**Returnee**
cry: 6 IMHOME
Lucas: 4 JEDI
**Returnees**
Homecoming: 6 ALUMNI
**Returner**
Hardy: 6 NATIVE
**"Return of the Jedi"**
creature: 4 EWOK
**Returns**
No: 4 ASIS
org.: 3 IRS
**"Return to ___":** 6 SENDER

**Reuben**
bread: 3 RYE
Brother of: 4 LEVI
ingredient: 5 KRAUT SWISS
Mother of: 4 LEAH
**"Reuben, Reuben"**
actor Tom: 5 CONTI
**Reunifier**
German: 4 KOHL
**Reunion**
attendee: 3 SIS 4 ALUM AUNT
GRAD 5 FRERE NIECE
UNCLE
attendee (abbr.): 3 REL
group: 3 KIN 4 CLAN
5 CLASS
**Reuss River**
origin: 3 URI
**Reuters**
rival: 3 UPI
**Reuther, Walter**
org.: 3 UAW
**Rev:** 3 GUN
**Rev.**
address: 3 SER
initials: 3 MLK
~ Jackson: 5 JESSE
~ Roberts: 4 ORAL
**Reveal:** 4 BARE 5 LETON
6 IMPART UNVEIL
7 LAYBARE
by accident: 7 LETSLIP
~, in poetry: 3 OPE
**Revealed:** 3 OUT 4 TOLD
**Revealing:** 8 TELLTALE
10 TATTLETALE
attire: 4 MINI
cry from above: 6 UPHERE
pictures: 5 XRAYS
swimwear: 5 THONG
**Reveille**
horn: 5 BUGLE
Opposite of: 4 TAPS
Respond to: 4 RISE 5 ARISE
**"___ Reveille" (Kyser hit):** 3 TIL
**Revel**
in: 5 EATUP
noisily: 7 ROISTER
**Revelation:** 6 EXPOSE
9 EYEOPENER
Divine: 6 ORACLE
response: 3 AHA
**Revelations**
nation: 5 MAGOG
**Reveler**
Greek ~ utterance: 4 EVOE
Mythical: 5 SATYR
**Revelry**
Wild: 4 ORGY
**Revenge**
Have ~ on: 3 GET
Take: 7 GETEVEN
**Revenue**
sources: 3 ADS
State ~ generator: 5 LOTTO
~, in French: 5 RENTE

**Revenuer:** 4 TMAN
**Reverberate:** 4 ECHO
**Reverberation:** 4 ECHO
**Revere:** 5 ADORE HONOR
6 ESTEEM
When ~ rode: 5 APRIL
**Revered:** 6 SACRED
leader: 9 STATESMAN
one: 4 GURU IDOL
**Reverence:** 3 AWE
9 PIOUSNESS
**Reverend Jim**
Sitcom with: 4 TAXI
**Reverent:** 5 PIOUS
**Reverie:** 5 DREAM
Lost in: 5 MOONY
**Reversal:** 3 UEY 5 UTURN
7 SETBACK
**"Reversal of Fortune"**
star Jeremy: 5 IRONS
**Reverse:** 4 GEAR UNDO
7 COUNTER
a dele: 4 STET
Coin: 5 TAILS
Game with ~ cards: 3 UNO
side: 4 BACK
stitch: 4 PURL
**Reversible**
fabric: 6 DAMASK
**Reversion:** 7 ATAVISM
**Revert:** 5 RESET
**Review:** 6 ASSESS GOOVER
7 BRUSHUP RUNOVER
WRITEUP 8 CRITIQUE
HASHOVER
Bad: 3 PAN
Four-star: 4 RAVE
IRS: 3 AUD
Kind of: 4 RAVE 5 MIXED
**Reviewer**
Book: 3 CPA
~ Reed: 3 REX
~ Roger: 5 EBERT
**Revise:** 4 EDIT 5 AMEND
EMEND
**Revision:** 4 EDIT
**Revival**
shelter: 4 TENT
shout: 4 AMEN
technique: 3 CPR
**Revivalist:** 3 NEO
chic: 5 RETRO
**Revlon**
rival: 4 AVON
**Revolt:** 5 REBEL 6 APPALL
RISEUP UPRISE
8 NAUSEATE
**Revolting:** 4 VILE 5 LURID
one: 5 REBEL
**Revolution:** 5 TWIRL
period: 4 YEAR
**Revolutionary**
French: 5 MARAT
loyalist: 4 TORY
mercenary: 7 HESSIAN
Mexican: 5 VILLA 6 ZAPATA

Old-style: 6 ANARCH
Russian: 5 LENIN
~ Luxemburg: 4 ROSA
**"Revolutionary"**
of Chopin: 5 ETUDE
**Revolve:** 4 SPIN TURN 5 TWIRL
**Revolver:** 3 GUN 4 DOOR
feature: 8 SNUBNOSE
inventor: 4 COLT
Small: 4 EDDY
Space: 6 PLANET
**Revolving**
firework: 8 PINWHEEL
part: 5 ROTOR
**Revue**
1978 Broadway ~: 5 EUBIE
1998 Broadway ~: 5 FOSSE
bit: 4 SKIT
Weekend ~: 3 SNL
**Reward**
Employee: 5 BONUS RAISE
for a dog: 4 BONE 5 TREAT
for a hero: 5 MEDAL
for waiting: 3 TIP
**Rework:** 4 EDIT 5 ADAPT
AMEND
**Rewrite:** 4 EDIT
**Rex**
Contemporary of: 4 ERLE
Critic: 4 REED
Sleuth created by: 4 NERO
**Rey, Lester ___ (sci-fi author):**
3 DEL
**Reykjavik**
nation: 7 ICELAND
**Reynolds**
Actor: 4 BURT
competitor: 5 ALCOA
Pitcher: 5 ALLIE
**Reynolds, Burt**
1976 ~ film: 5 GATOR
1978 ~ film: 6 HOOPER
THEEND
1988 ~ film: 8 RENTACOP
**Reynolds, Debbie**
1973 ~ Broadway revival:
5 IRENE
**Reynolds, R.J.**
brand: 5 DORAL SALEM
**Reza Khan:** 4 SHAH
**RFD**
Part of: 5 RURAL
**RFK:** 4 ATTY
**Rhapsodic**
Make: 5 ELATE
rhyme: 3 ODE
**Rhea**
Daughter of: 4 HERA
relative: 3 EMU
role: 5 CARLA
Roman equivalent of: 3 OPS
**Rhein**
blocker: 3 EIS
city: 4 KOLN
feeder: 3 AAR
**"___ Rheingold":** 3 DAS

**Rheinland**
 route: 4 BAHN
**Rhetoric:** 6 HOTAIR
 Recite: 5 ORATE
**Rhett**
 Last word of: 4 DAMN
 Last words of: 5 ADAMN
**Rhine**
 Catcher in the: 5 SEINE
 City on the: 4 BONN
  5 BASEL
 feeder: 3 AAR 4 AARE RUHR
 Region along the: 6 ALSACE
 siren: 7 LORELEI
 whine: 3 ACH
**Rhine, Dr.**
 Field of: 3 ESP
**Rhineland**
 refusal: 4 NEIN
 region: 4 SAAR
**Rhino**
 feature: 4 HORN
 relative: 5 TAPIR
**Rhinoplasty:** 7 NOSEJOB
**Rho**
 follower: 5 SIGMA
**Rhoda**
 Mom of: 3 IDA
**"Rhoda"**
 David of: 4 GROH
 mom: 3 IDA
 production co.: 3 MTM
 star Harper: 7 VALERIE
**Rhode Island**
 Former ~ senator: 4 PELL
 motto: 4 HOPE
 nickname: 10 OCEANSTATE
 state tree: 8 REDMAPLE
**Rhodes**
 Actor: 4 HARI
 of Rhodesia: 5 CECIL
**Rhododendron**
 kin: 6 AZALEA
**Rhody:** 4 AUNT
 Little: 10 OCEANSTATE
**Rhone**
 capital: 4 LYON 5 LYONS
 City on the: 4 LYON 5 ARLES
 feeder: 5 ISERE SAONE
**Rhubarb:** 3 ADO ROW 5 SCRAP
  SETTO 6 FRACAS
**Rhyme:** 4 POEM
 Dieter of: 5 SPRAT
 Gardener of: 4 MARY
 Nightgown wearer of:
  15 WEEWILLIEWINKIE
 Old king of: 4 COLE
 Rhapsodic: 3 ODE
 Runaway of: 5 SPOON
 scheme: 4 ABAB ABBA
 Seesaw sitter of: 4 ESAU
 Shepherdess of: 6 BOPEEP
 Simpleton of: 5 SIMON
 Start of a counting: 4 EENY
 time: 3 EEN
 Tumbler of: 4 JILL

Without ~ or reason:
 8 ATRANDOM
writer: 11 MOTHERGOOSE
**"Rhyme Pays"**
 rapper: 4 ICET
**Rhymer:** 4 POET
 Wry Rye: 4 NASH
**Rhymes**
 Busta Rhymes: 8 RAPSONGS
 of rap: 5 BUSTA
**Rhys, Jean**
 Sea in a ~ title: 8 SARGASSO
**Rhythm:** 4 BEAT 5 TEMPO
 Dramatic: 6 PACING
 instrument: 4 DRUM
  6 MARACA
 Jaunty: 4 LILT
 keeper: 3 TOE
 Rio: 5 SAMBA
**"___ Rhythm":** 4 IGOT
**Rhythmic:** 6 CADENT
  7 METERED
  8 CADENCED
 cadence: 4 LILT
 dance: 5 SAMBA
 feet: 5 IAMBS
 speech: 4 LILT
**Rial**
 spender: 5 IRANI OMANI
**Rib:** 4 BONE JOSH 5 COSTA
  TEASE 6 NEEDLE
 connection: 7 STERNUM
 Corduroy: 4 WALE
 donor: 4 ADAM
 order: 4 RACK
**Ribald:** 4 LEWD RACY
**Ribbed**
 fabric: 5 TWILL 6 FAILLE
**Ribbon**
 Get a blue: 3 WIN
 ornament: 7 ROSETTE
 Yellow ~ site: 7 OAKTREE
**Ribosomal ___:** 3 RNA
**___ Rica:** 5 COSTA
**Ricardo**
 landlord: 5 MERTZ
 ~, to Mertz: 6 TENANT
**Riccardo**
 Conductor: 4 MUTI
**Ricci**
 Designer: 4 NINA
**Rice**
 athlete: 3 OWL
 Author: 4 ANNE
 Brown or: 3 JIM
 dish: 5 PILAF PILAU
  6 PAELLA 7 RISOTTO
 field: 5 PADDY
 Lyricist: 3 TIM
 pad: 4 DORM
 Playwright: 5 ELMER
 White ~ lack: 4 BRAN
 wine: 4 SAKE
**Rice ___:** 5 PADDY PILAF
**Rice-___:** 5 ARONI
**Rice-A-___:** 4 RONI

**Rice/John**
 musical: 4 AIDA
**Rice-shaped**
 pasta: 4 ORZO
**Rice/Webber**
 musical: 5 EVITA
**Rich:** 6 LOADED
 Actress: 5 IRENE
 deposit: 4 LODE
 dessert: 5 TORTE 6 ECLAIR
 dude: 6 FATCAT
 fertilizer: 5 GUANO
 Kind of: 6 FILTHY
 Like ~ soil: 5 LOAMY
 Poet: 8 ADRIENNE
 soil: 4 LOAM
 tapestry: 5 ARRAS
 voiced: 7 OROTUND
**"Rich and Famous"**
 reporter: 5 LEACH
**Richard**
 1987 Pulitzer critic ~: 4 EDER
 Actor: 4 EGAN GERE
 Anonymous: 3 ROE
 Antarctic explorer: 4 BYRD
 Architect: 5 MEIER
 Author: 5 ADAMS 6 SCARRY
 Comedian: 5 PRYOR
 First VP under: 5 SPIRO
 Virgin tycoon: 7 BRANSON
 who played Jaws: 4 KIEL
**Richard ___:** 3 III
**Richard ___, Sir**
 English essayist: 6 STEELE
**Richard III**
 request: 6 AHORSE
**Richards**
 Former Texas governor: 3 ANN
 of tennis: 5 RENEE
 Rock musician: 5 KEITH
**Richards, Mary**
 Neighbor of: 5 RHODA
**Richardson**
 Nixon attorney general:
  6 ELLIOT
**___ riche:** 7 NOUVEAU
**Richert**
 Actor: 4 NATE
**Richie**
 Dad of ~, to the Fonz: 3 MRC
 Mom of ~, to the Fonz: 4 MRSC
**Richie, Lionel**
 1983 ~ hit: 6 YOUARE
 1984 ~ hit: 5 HELLO
**Richly**
 decorated: 6 ORNATE
 embellish: 4 GILD
**"Rich Man, Poor Man"**
 actor Nick: 5 NOLTE
 actress Kay: 4 LENZ
 author: 4 SHAW
 novelist Shaw: 5 IRWIN
 The rich man in: 4 RUDY
**Richmond**
 Actor: 4 DEON
**Richness:** 4 LUXE

**Richter**
concern: 5 SCALE 6 TREMOR
**Richthofen:** 3 ACE 5 BARON
**Rick**
Disc jockey: 4 DEES
Indy champ: 5 MEARS
Love of: 4 ILSA
Where Ilsa met: 5 PARIS
**Rickenbacker:** 3 ACE 6 AIRACE
Aviator: 5 EDDIE
**Rickety:** 10 RAMSHACKLE
auto: 10 RATTLETRAP
**Rickey**
ingredient: 3 GIN 4 LIME
**Ricki**
rival, once: 5 OPRAH
Talk show host: 4 LAKE
**Rickles**
Comic: 3 DON
riposte: 6 INSULT
**Rickman**
Actor: 4 ALAN
**Rick's**
pianist: 3 SAM
**Ricky**
Bluegrass musician: 6 SKAGGS
Landlady of: 5 ETHEL
Landlord of: 4 FRED
portrayer: 4 DESI
**Rico**
Where ~ shot Tony: 4 COPA
___ **Rico:** 6 PUERTO
**Ricochet:** 5 CAROM
Sonic: 4 ECHO
**"Ricochet"**
rapper: 4 ICET
**Rid:** 6 DIVEST
Get ~ of: 3 AXE 4 LOSE SHED
5 DITCH ERASE SCRAP
6 DELETE 7 ABOLISH
DEEPSIX DISPOSE
of vermin: 5 DERAT
**Riddance**
Good: 6 NOLOSS
**Riddick**
Boxer: 4 BOWE
**Riddle:** 5 POSER 6 ENIGMA
Pose a: 3 ASK
Zen: 4 KOAN
**Riddle-me-___:** 3 REE
**Riddler**
nemesis: 6 BATMAN
**Ride:** 5 TAUNT TEASE
6 HARASS
for E.T.: 3 UFO
Guide the: 5 STEER
in space: 5 SALLY
Long: 4 LIMO
Metered: 3 CAB 4 TAXI
Prepare for a rough:
7 STRAPIN
price: 4 FARE
Short: 4 SPIN
the banister: 5 SLIDE
Toddler's: 5 TRIKE
up the slope: 6 SKITOW

Winter: 4 SLED
**Rider:** 5 ADDON
Broom: 3 HAG
Champion: 5 AUTRY
command: 4 WHOA
Cry of a: 4 WHEE
grip: 4 REIN
Like the ~ of Silver: 4 LONE
Rail: 4 HOBO
Revolutionary: 6 REVERE
Rosinante: 7 QUIXOTE
10 DONQUIXOTE
Scout: 5 TONTO
seat: 6 SADDLE
Sleipnir: 4 ODIN
**"Riders of the Purple Sage"**
author Grey: 4 ZANE
**"Riders to the Sea"**
playwright: 5 SYNGE
**Ridge**
Coin-edge: 5 KNURL
Coral: 4 REEF
Corduroy: 4 WALE
Fingerboard: 4 FRET
Fingerprint: 5 WHORL
Glacial: 5 ARETE ESKER
SERAC
in Washington: 3 TOM
Mountain: 5 ARETE
Rocky: 3 TOR
___ **Ridge (racehorse):** 4 RIVA
**Ridicule:** 4 JEER MOCK TWIT
5 TAUNT 6 DERIDE
7 SNEERAT
**Ridiculous:** 6 INANE NUTTY
SILLY 6 INSANE
7 ASININE
**"Ridiculous!":** 5 PSHAW
**Riding:** 4 ATOP
the waves: 4 ASEA 6 AFLOAT
whip: 4 CROP
**Riefenstahl**
Director: 4 LENI
**Rife:** 5 AWASH 7 TEEMING
Be ~ (with): 4 TEEM
**Riffraff:** 4 SCUM 5 TRASH
6 RABBLE
**Rifle:** 4 LOOT 7 RANSACK
Air: 5 BBGUN
Air ~ ammo: 3 BBS 6 BBSHOT
attachment: 5 SCOPE
7 BAYONET
M-1 ~ inventor: 6 GARAND
part: 4 BUTT 6 BREECH
support: 5 BIPOD
**Rift:** 3 GAP
**Rig**
Big: 4 SEMI
Rod on a: 4 AXLE
**Riga**
resident: 4 LETT 7 LATVIAN
**Rigatoni:** 5 PASTA
kin: 4 ZITI 5 PENNE
**Rigby**
of song: 7 ELEANOR
**Rigel:** 4 STAR

constellation: 5 ORION
**Rigg**
Actress: 5 DIANA
**Rigg, Diana**
role: 7 MRSPEEL
**Rigged:** 5 ARMED
It is: 4 MAST
**Rigging**
support: 4 MAST SPAR
**Right:** 6 PROPER
9 STARBOARD
Ain't: 4 ISNT 5 ARENT
angle: 3 ELL
At ~ angles to the keel:
5 ABEAM
At the ~ time: 5 ONCUE
away: 3 NOW 4 STAT
6 ATONCE PRONTO
away (abbr.): 4 ASAP
Exactly: 6 DEADON SPOTON
Game with a ~ bower:
6 EUCHRE
Go: 3 GEE 4 TURN
Indifferent to ~ and wrong:
6 AMORAL
Is the ~ size: 4 FITS
Just: 4 TOAT 5 IDEAL
6 TOATEE
Leaning to the: 6 ITALIC
Not: 3 ODD OFF 4 LEFT
5 AMISS
Not ~ now: 4 ANON 5 LATER
of decision: 5 SAYSO
of passage: 8 EASEMENT
on the map: 4 EAST
Point in the ~ direction:
6 ORIENT
Set: 4 HEAL MEND TRUE
5 ALIGN AMEND
6 REMEDY 7 REDRESS
8 FINETUNE
**"Right!":** 3 YES
**"___, right!":** 4 YEAH
**Right, Mr.**
Hardly: 3 CAD 5 CREEP
**"Right away!":** 4 ASAP
6 INASEC
**Righteous:** 4 JUST
**Rightful:** 3 DUE 4 JUST
8 DESERVED
**Right Guard**
rival: 5 ARRID
**Right-hand**
man: 4 AIDE
man (abbr.): 4 ASST
page: 5 RECTO
**Rightist**
~, briefly: 6 NEOCON
**"Right on!":** 4 AMEN
**Rights**
Animal ~ org.: 4 PETA SPCA
5 ASPCA
Gun ~ org.: 3 NRA
Human ~ agcy.: 3 ILO
org.: 4 ACLU CORE 5 ASCAP
Transfer: 6 ASSIGN

Workers ~ org.: 4 NLRB
**"Rights of Man"**
  writer: 5 PAINE
**"Right Stuff, The"**
  role: 5 GLENN 6 YEAGER
**Rigid:** 3 SET 5 TENSE
  7 ADAMANT
  bracelet: 6 BANGLE
**"Rigoletto"**
  Beloved, in: 4 CARO
  composer: 5 VERDI
  trio: 4 ACTS
**Rigor:** 8 ASPERITY SEVERITY
**Rigorous:** 5 STERN 6 SEVERE
  exams: 5 ORALS
  ___ rigueur (literally): 3 ALA
**Riis**
  concern: 5 SLUMS
**"Rikki-Tikki-___":** 4 TAVI
**Rile:** 4 STIR 5 GRATE
  up: 5 ANGER 6 ENRAGE
**Riled**
  All ~ up: 5 IRATE 7 INASTIR
  up: 3 HET 4 SORE 6 INAPET
**Riley**
  Former Knicks coach: 3 PAT
  Life of: 4 EASE
    10 EASYSTREET
  pal Digger: 5 ODELL
**Riley, Bridget**
  genre: 5 OPART
**Rill**
  setting: 4 VALE
**Rim:** 4 EDGE 5 VERGE
  Basketball: 4 HOOP
  Projecting metal: 6 FLANGE
  Watch: 5 BEZEL
**Rime:** 4 HOAR
**Rimes**
  Singer: 5 LEANN
**Rind:** 4 PEEL
  Cheese with a: 4 BRIE
  Lemon: 4 ZEST
  Remove: 4 PARE
**Ring:** 4 BAND ECHO HALO
    PEAL TOLL 5 ARENA
    CHIME KNELL PHONE
    8 RESONATE
  activity: 4 BOUT
  Anatomical: 6 AREOLA
  Angelic: 4 HALO
  around the castle: 4 MOAT
  Baby: 7 TEETHER
  bearer: 3 EAR 4 TREE WIFE
    5 FRODO 6 SATURN
  boss: 3 REF
  cheer: 3 OLE
  combo: 6 ONETWO
  count: 3 TEN
  dance: 4 HORA
  decision: 3 TKO
  Floral: 3 LEI
  foe: 4 TORO
  Give a: 5 PHONE
  great: 3 ALI
  Harness: 6 TERRET

Island: 3 LEI
Item thrown in a: 3 HAT
Kind of: 4 MOOD 7 DECODER
leader: 5 CHAMP 6 TORERO
legend: 3 ALI
Light: 4 HALO
master: 7 JEWELER
of color: 6 AREOLA AREOLE
org.: 3 WBA
out: 4 PEAL
Practice in the: 4 SPAR
Reef: 5 ATOLL
Response to a: 5 HELLO
Rubber: 6 GASKET
site: 3 EAR 4 LOBE NOSE
  TREE 5 NAVEL PINKY
  7 BATHTUB EARLOBE
source: 5 ONION
sport: 4 SUMO
Swing in the: 3 BOX
up: 4 CALL DIAL HALO
  5 PHONE
wear: 6 GLOVES
**Ringed**
  planet: 6 SATURN
**Ringer:** 4 BELL 5 CHIME
  Bell: 4 AVON 6 SEXTON
    8 AVONLADY
  Near: 6 LEANER
**Ringing**
  site: 3 EAR
  sound: 4 PEAL TING
**Ringlet:** 4 CURL LOCK
**Ringling Brothers**
  One of the: 4 OTTO
**Ringmaster:** 5 EMCEE
**Ringo:** 6 BEATLE
  Drummer: 5 STARR
  John, to: 3 LOO
  Part of a ~ kit: 5 SNARE
**Rings:** 6 ANNULI
  Car with four linked: 4 AUDI
  Math: 4 TORI
  Things on: 4 KEYS
  What tree ~ indicate: 3 AGE
**Ring-shaped:** 5 TORIC
    7 ANNULAR
  reef: 5 ATOLL
**Ringside**
  shout: 3 OLE
**Ring-tailed**
  critter: 4 COON 5 COATI
**Rink**
  confrontation: 7 FACEOFF
  Enjoy the: 5 SKATE
  fakeout: 4 DEKE
  jump: 4 AXEL LUTZ
  legend: 3 ORR
  shape: 4 OVAL
  surface: 3 ICE
**Rinse**
  Hair: 5 HENNA
  Red: 5 HENNA
  with a solvent: 5 ELUTE
**Rio**
  Airline to: 5 VARIG

automaker: 3 KIA
beach: 7 IPANEMA
  10 COPACABANA
contents: 4 AGUA
peak: 9 SUGARLOAF
rhythm: 5 SAMBA
**Rio ___:** 5 NEGRO 6 GRANDE
**"Rio ___"** (John Wayne film):
  4 LOBO
**Rio de la ___:** 5 PLATA
**Rio Grande**
  city: 6 ELPASO LAREDO
**Rio Grande do ___** (Brazilian
  state): 5 NORTE
**"Rio Lobo"**
  actor Jack: 4 ELAM
  ___ Rios, Jamaica: 4 OCHO
**Riot:** 4 HOOT 5 REBEL
    6 SCREAM
  1886 ~ site , with "Square":
    9 HAYMARKET
  1971 prison ~ site: 6 ATTICA
  follower: 3 ACT
  participant: 6 LOOTER
  Put down a: 5 QUELL
  remedy: 7 TEARGAS
  spray: 4 MACE
  squad item: 7 GASMASK
**Rioter:** 6 STONER
  take: 4 LOOT
  ___ Rio, Texas: 3 DEL
**Riotous**
  crowd: 3 MOB
**Rio Treaty**
  implementer (abbr.): 3 OAS
**Rip:** 4 TEAR 6 SCATHE
  apart: 4 REND
  into: 5 SETAT 6 TEARAT
  off: 3 CON ROB 4 GLOM
    ROOK SCAM 5 STEAL
    SWIPE 6 FLEECE
  up: 4 REND 5 SHRED
**Ripe**
  for planting: 6 ARABLE
  Way past: 6 ROTTEN
**Ripen:** 3 AGE 6 MATURE
**Ripening**
  agent: 4 AGER
**Ripken**
  broke his record: 6 GEHRIG
  of baseball: 3 CAL
  was one: 6 ORIOLE
**Ripley**
  End of a claim by: 3 NOT
    5 ORNOT
  Ready for: 3 ODD
**Ripley, Mr.**
  of film: 5 DAMON
**"Ripley's Believe ___ Not":**
  4 ITOR
**Ripoff:** 4 SCAM 5 THEFT
**Ripped:** 4 RENT TORE TORN
    6 TOREUP
  off: 5 STOLE 6 STOLEN
**Ripple:** 7 WAVELET
  maker: 3 OAR

They ~ on bodybuilders:
4 PECS
tippler: 4 WINO
**Ripsnorter:** 4 LULU
**Rise:** 4 GOUP HIKE HILL
5 CLIMB GETUP STAND
6 ASCEND
(abbr.): 4 INCR
and shine: 6 AWAKEN
Dow: 4 GAIN
Flat-topped: 4 MESA
Get a ~ out of: 6 LEAVEN
Give ~ to: 4 SIRE 5 BREED
SPAWN 8 ENGENDER
high: 4 SOAR
It will get a: 5 YEAST
quickly: 4 SOAR
up: 4 REAR 5 REBEL
**"Rise, Glory, Rise"**
composer: 4 ARNE
**Riser**
Early: 3 SUN
plus tread: 5 STAIR
**Rising**
locale: 4 OVEN
star: 5 COMER
**Rising Sun**
Land of the: 5 JAPAN
**Risk:** 5 PERIL WAGER
6 HAZARD 7 IMPERIL
8 ENDANGER
a fine: 6 LITTER
At: 6 LIABLE 7 INPERIL
8 INDANGER
a ticket: 5 SPEED
Free of: 4 SAFE
Take a: 4 DARE
taker: 5 DARER 9 DAREDEVIL
Transfer the: 8 REINSURE
Worrier: 5 ULCER
**"Risk"**
adversaries: 6 ARMIES
**Risked:** 7 ATSTAKE
**Risk takers**
self-question: 7 DOIDARE
**Risky:** 6 UNSAFE
business: 4 SPEC
purchase: 10 PIGINAPOKE
undertaking: 7 VENTURE
way to run: 7 ONEMPTY
**Risqué:** 4 BLUE RACY 5 SALTY
A bit: 5 SPICY
More than: 4 LEWD
**Ristorante**
beverage: 4 VINO
course: 5 PASTA
courses: 9 ANTIPASTI
dessert: 6 GELATI GELATO
7 TORTONI
dish: 8 CALAMARI
herb: 7 OREGANO
request: 7 ALDENTE
**Rita**
An ex of: 3 ALY 5 ORSON
**Ritchard**
Actor: 5 CYRIL

**Ritchie**
Singer: 6 VALENS
**Rite:** 8 CEREMONY
answer: 3 IDO
Early: 7 BAPTISM
robe: 3 ALB
site: 4 PYRE 5 ALTAR
**Rites**
Waive one's: 5 ELOPE
**Ritter**
Actor: 3 TEX
Singer: 3 TEX
**Ritter, John**
Father of: 3 TEX
**Ritual:** 7 LITURGY
bread: 5 WAFER
greeting: 6 SALAAM
Inauguration: 4 OATH
Nine-day: 6 NOVENA
Poker: 4 ANTE
Pregame: 4 TOSS 6 ANTHEM
Religious: 4 MASS
Tot: 3 NAP
Wedding: 5 TOAST
Yom Kippur: 4 FAST
**Ritz**
owner: 8 HOTELIER
rival: 4 HIHO
**Ritzy:** 4 POSH 5 PLUSH SWANK
7 OPULENT
spread: 6 CAVIAR ESTATE
**Rival:** 3 FOE 4 VIER
**River**
African: 4 NILE 5 NIGER
6 UBANGI
Alpine: 3 AAR 4 AARE 5 ISERE
blocker: 3 DAM
Blue or White: 4 NILE
crosser: 5 FERRY 6 BRIDGE
dam: 4 WEIR
deposit: 4 SILT
embankment: 5 LEVEE
English: 4 AVON TYNE
5 TRENT 6 THAMES
Eurasian: 4 URAL
European: 4 ELBE ODER
5 VOLGA
feature: 3 BED 4 BEND FORK
5 DELTA FALLS MOUTH
feeder: 6 STREAM
French: 4 OISE ORNE 5 ISERE
LOIRE MARNE RHONE
SAONE
German: 3 EMS 4 EDER ELBE
ODER RUHR SAAR
5 RHINE
horse: 5 HIPPO
in a 1957 film: 4 KWAI
inlet: 3 RIA
island: 3 AIT
Longest: 4 NILE
mammal: 5 OTTER
mouth: 5 DELTA
of Hades: 4 STYX 5 LETHE
Sell up the: 6 BETRAY
skipper: 5 STONE

source: 4 HEAD
transport: 4 RAFT 5 BARGE
CANOE
~, in Spanish: 3 RIO
___ River: 4 EAST 5 OLMAN
**Rivera**
Actress: 5 CHITA
Artist: 5 DIEGO
Muralist: 5 DIEGO
**Rivera, Diego**
work: 5 MURAL
**Riverbank**
romper: 5 OTTER
**Riverbed**
Dry: 4 WADI
**Riverboat**
hazard: 4 SNAG 5 SHOAL
**Riverdale**
redhead: 6 ARCHIE
**Rivers**
of comedy: 4 JOAN
**Riveter**
of song: 5 ROSIE
**Riviera**
resort: 4 NICE 7 SANREMO
season: 3 ETE
view: 3 MER
___ Rivoli (of Paris): 5 RUEDE
**Riyadh**
resident: 4 ARAB 5 SAUDI
**Rizzuto**
contemporary: 5 REESE
Ex-Yankee: 4 PHIL
nickname: 7 SCOOTER
**R.L.**
"Goosebumps" author: 5 STINE
**Rm.**
coolers: 3 ACS
**RMN**
Loser to: 3 HHH
**R.N.**
forte: 3 TLC
workplaces: 3 ERS ORS 4 ICUS
**RNA**
component: 6 URACIL
sugar: 6 RIBOSE
**Roach**
Film producer: 3 HAL
killing brand: 4 RAID
**Road**
Bump in the: 4 SNAG
caution: 3 SLO 4 BUMP
closing: 4 STER
Country: 4 LANE
cover: 3 TAR
curve: 3 ESS 4 BEND
Do ~ work: 3 TAR 4 PAVE
Down the: 5 AHEAD LATER
6 INTIME
Fix a: 5 RETAR
groove: 3 RUT
guide: 3 MAP
hazard: 3 ICE 5 SLEET
Hit the: 4 LEFT MOVE RIDE
TOUR WENT 5 LEAVE
SCRAM 6 DEPART

hugger: **10** RADIALTIRE
King of the: **4** HOBO
Mountain ~ sign:
   **10** STEEPGRADE
offense: **3** DWI
One for the: **3** CAR **4** AUTO
On the: **4** AWAY
Prepare for a ~ trip: **5** GASUP
Rig on the: **4** SEMI
Roman: **4** ITER
runner: **3** CAR **4** AUTO
Secluded: **5** BYWAY
shoulder: **4** BERM
sign word: **4** THRU
Toll: **4** PIKE **8** TURNPIKE
Word after: **4** TEST
**"Road"**
destination: **3** RIO **4** BALI
**"___ Road" (Binchy book):**
   **4** TARA
**Roadblock: 4** SNAG **7** IMPASSE
requests: **3** IDS
**Roadhouse: 3** INN
sign: **4** EATS
**Roadie**
load: **3** AMP
ride: **7** TOURBUS
**Road map**
abbr.: **3** RTE
feature: **5** INSET
**Road Runner**
foe: **6** COYOTE
sound: **4** BEEP
**Roads**
(abbr.): **3** STS
Like some: **3** ICY **5** RUTTY
   **7** ONELANE
**Roadside**
distress signal: **5** FLARE
eatery: **5** DINER
grazer: **4** DEER
lodging: **3** INN **5** MOTEL
sign: **3** GAS
stop: **3** INN **5** MOTEL
**Roadster: 8** RUNABOUT
feature: **10** RUMBLESEAT
**"Road to ___": 4** BALI
**Roadwork**
Do: **4** PAVE **5** RETAR
**Roald**
Author: **4** DAHL
**Roam: 5** RANGE
about: **3** GAD **6** WANDER
**Roar: 4** YELL **5** BLARE
in a ring: **3** OLE
**Roarer: 3** LEO **4** LION
**Roaring**
Its films have a ~ start:
   **3** MGM
start: **3** RIP
**Roaring Camp**
creator: **5** HARTE
**Roaring Fork River**
City on the: **5** ASPEN
**Roaring Twenties: 3** ERA
   **6** DECADE

**Roast**
Center for a: **7** HONOREE
French: **4** ROTI
host: **5** EMCEE
hosts: **3** MCS
How a ~ may be served:
   **5** AUJUS
Moisten a: **5** BASTE
spot: **4** DAIS
**Roast beef**
au ___: **3** JUS
order: **4** RARE
**Roaster: 4** OVEN
spot: **4** DAIS
**Roasting**
rod: **4** SPIT
**Rob: 5** RIFLE **6** BURGLE
Actor: **4** LOWE
Director: **6** REINER
**Robb**
Pitcher: **3** NEN
**Robbe-Grillet**
Author: **5** ALAIN
**Robber: 5** THIEF **7** BRIGAND
chaser: **3** COP
Grave: **5** GHOUL
**Robbery: 5** HEIST THEFT
Check out before a: **4** CASE
**Robbie**
Daredevil dad of: **4** EVEL
**Robbins**
Actor: **3** TIM
Author: **6** HAROLD
Choreographer: **6** JEROME
**Robe**
African: **7** DASHIKI
fabric: **5** TERRY
Lounging: **6** CAFTAN
Priest: **3** ALB
Roman: **4** TOGA
**Robert**
Actor: **4** ALDA HAYS RYAN
   **5** DONAT URICH
   **6** DENIRO
Arctic explorer: **5** PEARY
Author: **4** CARO **6** LUDLUM
Baritone: **7** MERRILL
Comedian: **5** KLEIN
Director: **6** ALTMAN
Disney president: **4** IGER
Irish patriot: **5** EMMET
Screenwriter: **5** TOWNE
Synthesizer creator: **4** MOOG
**Robert ___**
Gen.: **4** ELEE
**Roberto**
Boxer: **5** DURAN
of baseball: **6** ALOMAR
   **8** CLEMENTE
**Roberts**
Actor: **4** ERIC
Actress: **5** DORIS JULIA
   TANYA
Evangelist: **4** ORAL
Journalist: **5** COKIE
Writer: **4** NORA

**Roberts, Julia**
Brother of: **4** ERIC
Ex of: **4** LYLE
**Robertson**
Writer: **6** DAVIES
**Robert the ___: 5** BRUCE
**Robes**
Roman: **5** TOGAE
**Robeson**
role: **7** OTHELLO
**Robin**
and Batman: **3** DUO
   **10** DYNAMICDUO
Celeb watcher: **5** LEACH
mentor: **6** BATMAN
residence: **4** NEST
sweetheart: **10** MAIDMARIAN
Ward who played: **4** BURT
**Robin, Christopher**
bear: **4** POOH
**Robin Goodfellow: 3** IMP
**Robin Hood: 6** ARCHER
portrayer: **5** ERROL
   **8** ALANHALE
**"Robin Hood: Men in Tights"**
Roger of: **4** REES
**Robinson**
and Thomas:
   **14** BALLPARKFRANKS
Brooks: **6** ORIOLE
Game show host: **4** ANNE
of song: **3** MRS
Poet: **5** EDWIN
role: **4** RICO
**"___ Robinson": 3** MRS
**Robinson, Mrs.**
Daughter of: **6** ELAINE
portrayer: **8** BANCROFT
**Robot**
banker: **3** ATM
coiner: **5** CAPEK
drama: **3** RUR
of Jewish lore: **5** GOLEM
**Robotic**
rock group: **4** DEVO
**Rob Roy: 4** GAEL SCOT
refusal: **3** NAE
**"Rob Roy"**
actor Neeson: **4** LIAM
star: **6** NEESON
**Robt. ___: 4** ELEE
**Robust: 3** FIT **4** HALE **5** HUSKY
   LUSTY **6** HEARTY
**"Robusto!"**
Maker of ~ sauces: **4** RAGU
**Roc**
Like a: **5** AVIAN
**Rochester**
river: **7** GENESEE
Wife of: **4** EYRE
**Rock: 5** GENRE STONE
   **6** TEETER
1960s ~ musical: **4** HAIR
1986 ~ autobiography: **5** ITINA
Banded: **6** GNEISS
Black: **6** BASALT

blaster: 3 AMP TNT
bottom: 5 LEAST NADIR
Comedian: 5 CHRIS
Crystalline: 6 SCHIST
Crystal-lined: 5 GEODE
Easily split: 5 SLATE
First name in: 4 JIMI 5 ELTON
Fissile: 5 SHALE
Flaky: 4 MICA
forerunner: 5 RANDB
garden herb: 5 SEDUM
group: 4 LODE ORES
growth: 4 MOSS 6 LICHEN
Hollow: 5 GEODE
Igneous: 6 BASALT
Kind of: 4 ACID FOLK PUNK
layers: 6 STRATA
ledge: 5 SHELF
Like a: 4 HARD 5 SOLID
Loose ~ debris: 5 SCREE
Made-up ~ group: 4 KISS
Metallic: 3 ORE
Metamorphic: 5 SLATE
  6 GNEISS SCHIST
Modern ~ genre: 3 EMO
Molten: 4 LAVA 5 MAGMA
Monument: 7 GRANITE
music genre: 5 METAL
Oil-bearing: 5 SHALE
Partner of: 4 ROLL
Pop of: 4 IGGY
rabbit: 4 PIKA
Rugged: 4 CRAG
salt: 6 HALITE
singer: 5 SIREN 7 LORELEI
Soft: 4 TALC
Stone of: 3 SLY
Third ~ from the sun:
  5 EARTH
trailer: 4 ETTE
venue: 5 ARENA
video awards: 4 AVAS
___ Rock: 5 AYERS
"___ Rock": 4 IAMA
"Rock-a-Bye Baby"
  setting: 7 TREETOP
Rock and Roll Hall of Fame
  architect: 3 PEI 5 IMPEI
  singer James: 4 ETTA
  View from the: 4 ERIE
"Rock and Roll, Hoochie ___"
  ('74 song): 3 KOO
Rock-bottom: 5 LEAST
Rock climbing
  grip: 4 CRAG
  need: 7 TOEHOLD
Rock-clinger
  Marine: 7 ABALONE
Rockefeller
  asset: 8 OLDMONEY
  dish: 7 OYSTERS
  Former VP: 6 NELSON
  money source: 3 OIL
  ___ Rockefeller: 7 OYSTERS
Rockefeller Center
  muralist: 4 SERT

Rocker
  Country ~ Steve: 5 EARLE
  Folk ~ DiFranco: 3 ANI
  gear: 3 AMP
  Is not off one's: 4 SITS
  Off one's: 3 MAD 4 BATS DAFT
    LOCO
  On one's: 4 SANE
  site: 5 PORCH
  ~ Billy: 4 IDOL 5 OCEAN
  ~ Bob: 5 SEGER
  ~ Bonnie: 5 RAITT
  ~ Brian: 3 ENO
  ~ Chris: 3 REA
  ~ Elvis: 8 COSTELLO
  ~ Frank: 5 ZAPPA
  ~ Glenn: 4 FREY
  ~ Joan: 4 JETT
  ~ Julian: 6 LENNON
  ~ Marvin: 4 GAYE
  ~ Patty: 5 SMYTH
Rocket: 4 SOAR
  1950s U.S. ~: 4 THOR
  1960s U.S. ~: 8 REDSTONE
  add-on: 3 EER
  Booster: 5 ATLAS
  European: 6 ARIANE
  French: 6 ARIANE
  fuel: 3 LOX
  fuel component: 5 NITRO
  gasket: 5 ORING
  Inits. on a: 3 USA 4 CCCP
  interceptor: 3 ABM
  launcher: 4 NASA 7 BAZOOKA
  launch site: 3 PAD
  Moon: 6 APOLLO
  path: 3 ARC
  pioneer: 7 GODDARD
  section: 5 STAGE
    8 NOSECONE
  stage: 5 AGENA
Rockies: 3 MTS
  Home of the: 8 COLORADO
  Range of the: 5 TETON
  resort: 4 VAIL 5 ASPEN
  summer setting (abbr.): 3 MDT
  wind: 7 CHINOOK
Rockne
  Coach: 5 KNUTE
"Rock 'n' Roll Is King"
  band: 3 ELO
"Rock of ___": 4 AGES
Rocks: 3 ICE
  Hot: 4 LAVA
  Not on the: 4 NEAT
  On the: 4 ICED
  Pet: 3 FAD
  Throw ~ at: 4 PELT 5 STONE
Rock Wren
  habitat: 4 MESA
Rocky
  cliff: 4 SCAR
  debris: 5 SCREE
  Foe of: 6 APOLLO
  peak: 3 TOR
  projection: 4 CRAG

  ridge: 5 ARETE
  ~, for Stallone: 4 ROLE
"Rocky"
  actress Shire: 5 TALIA
  actress Talia: 5 SHIRE
  composer Bill: 5 CONTI
"Rocky II"
  He was dethroned in:
    6 APOLLO
"Rocky III"
  actor: 3 MRT
"Rocky IV"
  actor Lundgren: 5 DOLPH
Rocky Mountain
  Indian: 3 UTE
  state: 4 UTAH
  tree: 5 ASPEN
Rococo: 5 STYLE 6 ORNATE
Rod: 3 GAT 6 HEATER PISTOL
    ROSCOE
  Actor: 7 STEIGER
  attachment: 4 REEL
  Barbecue: 4 SPIT
  Baseball Hall of Famer:
    5 CAREW
  Conducting: 5 BATON
  divs.: 3 YDS
  Ex of: 5 ALANA
  of tennis: 5 LAVER
  Partner of: 4 REEL
  Roasting: 4 SPIT
  Schoolmaster: 6 FERULE
  squad (abbr.): 3 NRA
  Surveyor: 9 RANGEPOLE
  Use a divining: 5 DOWSE
  Wheel: 4 AXLE 5 SPOKE
  Wooden: 5 DOWEL
  ___ Rod: 6 AARONS
Roddick
  of tennis: 4 ANDY
Rodent
  Bushy-tailed: 6 MARMOT
  Rabbitlike: 6 AGOUTI
  Ratlike: 4 VOLE
  Reaction to a: 3 EEK
  South American: 4 PACA
    5 COYPU 6 AGOUTI
  Tailless: 4 PACA
Rodeo
  bucker: 5 BRONC
  bull: 6 BRAHMA
  Compete in a: 4 ROPE
  holler: 5 WAHOO
  Immobilize, at a: 6 HOGTIE
  performer: 5 ROPER
  producer: 5 ISUZU
  rope: 5 LASSO REATA RIATA
    6 LARIAT
  sight: 5 CLOWN 6 BARREL
Rodgers
  and Hart song: 8 BLUEMOON
  Musical partner of: 4 HART
Rodham
  Word before: 3 NEE
Rodin
  Emulate: 6 SCULPT

sculpture: 4 ADAM
**Rodney**
  Quarterback: 5 PEETE
**Rodnina**
  Figure skater: 5 IRINA
**Rodolfo**
  Love of: 4 MIMI
**Rodomontade:** 4 RANT
**Rodriguez**
  Catcher: 4 IVAN
  Golfer: 6 CHICHI
  Shortstop: 4 ALEX
**Rods**
  160 square ~: 4 ACRE
  It has: 6 RETINA
**Rod-shaped**
  germ: 5 ECOLI 7 BACILLI
**Roe:** 4 EGGS
  source: 4 SHAD
**Roebuck:** 4 DEER
  Partner of: 5 SEARS
**Roeper**
  Partner of: 5 EBERT
**Rogaine**
  promise: 4 HAIR
**Roger**
  1960s slugger ~: 5 MARIS
  Actor: 5 MOORE
  Critic: 5 EBERT
  Fictional: 6 RABBIT
  follower: 5 WILCO
  Media exec: 5 AILES
  Newsman: 4 MUDD 5 ONEIL
  Sportswriter: 4 KAHN
**"Roger, ___ and out!":**
  4 OVER
**Rogers**
  Actor: 5 WAYNE
  Actress: 4 MIMI
  Cowboy: 3 ROY
  partner: 7 ASTAIRE
  Sci-fi hero: 4 BUCK
  Singer: 5 KENNY
**Rogers, Buck**
  ladylove: 5 WILMA
**Rogers, Ginger**
  role: 5 FOYLE
    10 KITTYFOYLE
    11 IRENECASTLE
**Rogers, Kenny**
  hit: 4 LADY
**Rogers, Mister:** 4 FRED
**Rogers, Roy**
  movie type: 5 OATER
  Real last name of: 4 SLYE
  Wife of: 4 DALE 5 EVANS
**Rogers, Will**
  prop: 5 LASSO
**Roget**
  wd.: 3 SYN
**Rogue:** 3 CAD 5 SCAMP
  6 PICARO RASCAL
**Roguish:** 3 SLY 4 ARCH
**Rohmer**
  Director: 4 ERIC
  Writer: 3 SAX

**Roker**
  and others: 3 ALS
  show: 5 TODAY
**Rolaids**
  rival: 4 TUMS
**Role:** 4 PART 7 PERSONA
  Has the lead: 5 STARS
  It has a supporting: 3 BRA
  model: 4 HERO IDOL 5 IDEAL
  Play a: 3 ACT
  player: 5 ACTOR
  Play the ~ of: 5 ACTAS
  Primary: 4 LEAD
  Public: 7 PERSONA
  Put in an expected:
    8 TYPECAST
  Small: 5 CAMEO
**Rolex**
  rival: 5 ELGIN OMEGA
**Roll:** 3 WAD 4 LIST
  back: 5 RESET
  Big: 3 WAD 6 ELEVEN
  Common: 5 SEVEN
  Dice: 5 THROW
  Holey: 5 BAGEL
  It may be on a: 4 OLEO
  Kind of: 3 EGG 5 HONOR
    PIANO 6 KAISER
    8 CRESCENT
  of coins: 7 ROULEAU
  of fabric: 4 BOLT
  of stamps: 4 COIL
  On a: 3 HOT
  Onion: 5 BIALY
  out: 6 UNFURL
  partner: 4 ROCK
  Place to: 5 AISLE
  player: 5 PIANO
  up: 4 FURL 5 AMASS
  with the punches: 5 ADAPT
  **___ roll:** 3 BED EGG LOG ONA
    5 HONOR 6 KAISER
    7 TOOTSIE
**Rollaway**
  kin: 3 COT
**Roll-call**
  no-show: 4 AWOL
  response: 3 NAY YEA 4 HERE
**Rolle**
  Actress: 6 ESTHER
**Rolled**
  It can be ~ over: 3 IRA
  items: 4 DICE EGGS EYES
    OATS
  model: 5 PINUP
**Roller:** 5 WHEEL 6 CASTER
  High: 4 SEMI 7 SPENDER
  High ~ roll: 3 WAD
  Mine: 4 TRAM
  on the road: 4 TIRE
  Reno: 3 DIE
  Typewriter: 6 PLATEN
**Rollerblade:** 5 SKATE
  protection: 6 HELMET
    7 KNEEPAD
**Roller coaster:** 4 RIDE

  cry: 4 WHEE
  feature: 4 DROP LOOP
  unit: 3 CAR
**Roller derby**
  item: 3 PAD 5 SKATE
**Rollers**
  High: 3 ELS
  Put in: 3 SET 6 CURLED
  Vegas: 4 DICE
**Rolling**
  Get the ball: 4 OPEN 5 START
  Have ~ in the aisles: 4 SLAY
  in dough: 4 RICH
  lands: 5 HILLS
  musician: 5 STONE
  rock: 4 LAVA
  stone lack: 4 MOSS
  veggie: 3 PEA
**Rolling ___:** 4 INIT 6 STONES
**Rolling Stone**
  founder Jann: 6 WENNER
**Rolling Stones**
  1965 ~ hit:
    15 GETOFFOFMYCLOUD
  1966 ~ hit: 12 PAINTITBLACK
  1967 ~ hit: 11 RUBYTUESDAY
  1968 ~ hit:
    15 JUMPINJACKFLASH
  1973 ~ hit: 5 ANGIE
  1980 ~ hit:
    15 EMOTIONALRESCUE
  Former ~ member Bill:
    5 WYMAN
  label: 3 EMI
  One of the: 5 WATTS
  Richards of the: 5 KEITH
  Wood of the: 3 RON
**Roll-on**
  brand: 3 BAN 5 ARRID
  target: 4 ODOR
**Rollout**
  Ballpark: 4 TARP
  Product: 6 LAUNCH
**Rollover**
  target: 3 IRA
**Rolls**
  filler: 6 PETROL
  Partner of: 5 ROYCE
  radial: 4 TYRE
**Rolls-___:** 5 ROYCE
**Rolodex**
  abbr.: 3 TEL
**Roly-___:** 4 POLY
**Roly-poly:** 5 PLUMP PUDGY
**ROM**
  Part of: 4 ONLY READ
    6 MEMORY
  storage units: 3 CDS
**Rom.**
  Not: 4 ITAL
**Roma**
  Bishop of: 4 PAPA
  currency: 4 LIRE
  Love, in: 5 AMORE
  Seaport southeast of: 6 NAPOLI
  Where ~ is: 6 ITALIA

**Romain de Tirtoff:** 4 ERTE
**Romaine**
lettuce: 3 COS
**Roman**
censor: 4 CATO
commoner: 4 PLEB
date: 4 IDES
dictator: 5 SULLA
emperor: 4 NERO OTHO
6 CAESAR TRAJAN
fountain: 5 TREVI
Four Holy ~ emperors:
5 OTTOS
goddess of agriculture:
5 CERES
goddess of plenty: 3 OPS
goddess of the moon: 4 LUNA
5 DIANA
god of love: 4 AMOR
hearth goddess: 5 VESTA
historian: 4 LIVY
holiday: 5 FESTA
Holy ~ emperor: 4 OTTO
5 OTTOI 7 LOTHAIR
household god: 3 LAR
invasion resister: 5 DRUID
law: 3 LEX
magistrate: 5 EDILE
meeting place: 5 FORUM
naturalist: 5 PLINY
official: 7 SENATOR
orator: 4 CATO 6 CICERO
philosopher: 6 SENECA
poet: 4 OVID
road: 4 ITER
robe: 4 TOGA 5 STOLA
sandal: 5 SOLEA
suffix: 5 ESQUE
sun god: 3 SOL
temple: 8 PANTHEON
trio: 3 TRE
well: 4 BENE
~ Zeus: 4 JOVE
**Roman ___:** 4 NOSE
7 NUMERAL
**___-Roman**
wrestling: 5 GRECO
**___ Romana:** 3 PAX
**Romance:** 3 WOO 4 TALE
5 GENRE GESTE
Big name in ~ fiction: 4 AVON
9 HARLEQUIN
Call off the: 5 ENDIT
French: 5 AMOUR
Hero of medieval:
6 ROLAND
lang.: 4 ITAL
Melville: 4 OMOO
writer award: 4 RITA
**"___ Romance" (Kern tune):**
5 AFINE
**Roman Empire**
invader: 4 GOTH
**Roman-fleuve:** 4 SAGA
**Romanian**
coin: 3 LEU

Former ~ president: 7 ILIESCU
Former ~ president Iliescu:
3 ION
~ Wiesel: 4 ELIE
**"Romanian Rhapsodies"**
composer: 6 ENESCO
**Romano**
cheese source: 3 EWE
TV star: 3 RAY
**Romanov**
ruler: TSAR
**Romans:** 7 EPISTLE
Book before: 4 ACTS
**Romantic:** 5 LOVER
interlude: 4 IDYL 5 IDYLL
lead-in: 3 NEO
Like ~ evenings: 7 MOONLIT
rendezvous: 5 TRYST
situation:
15 ETERNALTRIANGLE
song: 6 BALLAD
writing: 10 LOVELETTER
**Romantically**
Murmur: 3 COO
**Rombauer**
Cookbook author: 4 IRMA
**Rome**
Ancient invader of: 4 GOTH
Behold, in old: 4 ECCE
Bishop of: 4 POPE
Capital of: 4 LIRE
First bishop of: 7 STPETER
It was in old: 4 ERAT
Land in old: 5 TERRA
neighbor: 5 UTICA
7 ATLANTA
Nothing in old: 5 NIHIL
Port of old: 5 OSTIA
River of: 5 TIBER
Road to old: 4 ITER
To be, in old: 4 ESSE
Year in: 4 ANNO
Years in old: 4 ANNI
**Romeo**
Emulate: 5 ELOPE
Juliet, to: 3 SUN
Last words of: 4 IDIE
Rival of: 5 PARIS
**___ Romeo:** 4 ALFA
**"Romeo and Juliet"**
Churchyard tree in: 3 YEW
Like: 6 TRAGIC
setting: 6 VERONA
**"Romeo Is Bleeding"**
actress Lena: 4 OLIN
**Romero**
Actor: 5 CESAR
**Rommel**
Field marshal: 5 ERWIN
milieu: 6 DESERT
nickname: 9 DESERTFOX
Where ~ was routed:
9 ELALAMEIN
**Romp:** 4 LARK SAIL 6 FROLIC
**Romper**
River: 5 OTTER

**"Romper Room"**
role model: 5 DOBEE
**Romulus:** 4 TWIN 6 EPONYM
Twin of: 5 REMUS
**Ron**
Actor: 3 ELY 5 ONEAL
of baseball: 3 CEY
TV Tarzan: 3 ELY
**Rona**
Author: 5 JAFFE
**Ronnie**
Football Hall of Famer: 4 LOTT
Singer: 6 MILSAP
**Ronny**
Role for: 4 OPIE
**Ronny & the Daytonas**
1964 ~ hit: 3 GTO
**Ronstadt**
Singer: 5 LINDA
**Roo**
Mom of: 5 KANGA
Pal of: 6 EEYORE
**Roods**
Four: 4 ACRE
**Roof**
Car ~ variety: 4 TTOP
covering: 3 TAR
edge: 4 EAVE
Hit the: 6 SEERED
Like a bad: 5 LEAKY
of the mouth: 6 PALATE
On the ~ of: 4 ATOP
ornament: 3 EPI
overhang: 4 EAVE
piece: 7 SHINGLE
Restaurant with an orange:
4 HOJO
support: 6 RAFTER
type: 5 SLATE 6 LEANTO
7 MANSARD
**Roofer:** 6 NAILER
**Roofing**
material: 3 TAR 4 TILE
5 SLATE 6 THATCH
8 TARPAPER
specialist: 6 SLATER
**Rooftop**
device: 4 VANE
fixture: 4 DISH
**Rook:** 3 GYP 4 BILK 6 CASTLE
call: 3 CAW
home: 4 NEST
**Rookie:** 4 TIRO TYRO
6 NOVICE
9 GREENHORN
socialite: 3 DEB
**Rookie of the Year**
1951 N.L. ~: 4 MAYS
1964 A.L. ~: 5 OLIVA
1966 A.L. ~: 4 AGEE
1967 NHL ~: 3 ORR
1968 N.L. ~: 5 BENCH
1975 A.L. ~: 4 LYNN
1982 N.L. ~: 8 STEVESAX
1988 N.L. ~: 4 SABO
1993 AFC ~: 5 MIRER

1993 NBA ~: 5 ONEAL
1995 N.L. ~: 4 NOMO
1996 A.L. ~: 5 JETER
1997 N.L. ~: 5 ROLEN
**Room:** 5 SPACE 6 LEEWAY
at the top: 4 LOFT 5 ATTIC
Baby: 7 NURSERY
Chat ~ chuckle: 3 LOL
Clue: 5 STUDY
Cozy: 3 DEN
décor: 9 WALLPAPER
divider: 4 WALL
Drawing: 5 SALON
Family: 3 DEN
Growing: 4 ACRE
Hacienda: 4 SALA
Harem: 3 ODA
Kind of: 3 REC 4 MENS
    5 ELBOW 6 ROMPER
meas.: 4 SQFT
on board: 5 CABIN
Powder: 7 ARSENAL
Provide a ~ for: 6 RENTTO
Reading: 3 DEN
renter: 3 INN
Sitting: 6 LOUNGE PARLOR
Spa: 5 SAUNA
Style of a: 5 DECOR
TV: 3 DEN
Vaulted: 4 APSE
Waiting ~ call: 4 NEXT
Wash: 7 LAUNDRY
Wiggle: 6 LEEWAY
With ~ to spare: 5 AMPLY
~, in French: 5 SALLE
~, in Spanish: 4 SALA
___ room: 3 REC
**Roommate**
of Bert: 5 ERNIE
of Felix: 5 OSCAR
of Madison: 5 UNGER
**"Room of One's Own, A"**
author: 5 WOOLF
**Rooms**
Skylit: 5 ATRIA
**Room to swing ___:** 4 ACAT
**"Room With ___, A":** 5 AVIEW
**Roomy**
bag: 8 CARRYALL
dress: 4 TENT 5 ALINE
vehicle: 3 VAN 5 SEDAN
**Roone**
TV exec: 7 ARLEDGE
**Rooney**
Commentator: 4 ANDY
**Roosevelt:** 4 SARA 5 TEDDY
    7 ELEANOR
**Roosevelt, Teddy**
group: 11 ROUGHRIDERS
Home of: 12 SAGAMOREHILL
**Roost:** 5 PERCH
Lofty: 5 AERIE
**Rooster:** 4 COCK MALE
mate: 3 HEN
Roof: 4 VANE
topper: 4 COMB

**Root:** 5 CAUSE 6 ORIGIN
Agave: 5 AMOLE
Edible: 3 YAM 4 TARO
for: 6 URGEON 7 CHEERON
Fragrant: 5 ORRIS
Nobelist: 5 ELIHU
Plant: 5 RADIX
Poi: 4 TARO
Take: 5 SETIN
Taro: 4 EDDO
vegetable: 7 PARSNIP
word: 3 OLE RAH
**Root beer**
brand: 4 DADS NEHI
    5 AANDW BARQS HIRES
root: 9 SASSAFRAS
**Rooter:** 3 FAN
**Rootlessness:** 6 ANOMIE
**Roots**
Put down: 7 SETTLED
Work on: 3 DYE
**"Roots":** 4 EPIC SAGA
actor Burton: 5 LEVAR
author Alex: 5 HALEY
author Haley: 4 ALEX
Captain Davies on: 7 EDASNER
hero ___ Kinte: 5 KUNTA
role: 5 KINTE
~ Emmy winner: 5 ASNER
    7 EDASNER
**Rope**
Attach with a: 5 TIEON
Bind with: 4 LASH
Cowboy: 5 LASSO REATA
    RIATA
fiber: 4 BAST HEMP JUTE
    5 SISAL
Gaucho: 5 REATA RIATA
Horse-training: 5 LONGE
in: 5 LASSO 7 ENSNARE
Looped: 5 NOOSE
Mooring: 6 HAWSER
Separate ~ strands: 5 UNLAY
Unravel a: 4 FRAY
**"Rope-a-dope"**
boxer: 3 ALI
**Roper**
Pollster: 4 ELMO
report: 4 POLL
**Roper, Mrs.**
portrayer Lindley: 5 AUDRA
**Ropes:** 4 GEAR
One learning the: 7 TRAINEE
Show the ~ to: 5 TEACH
    TRAIN 6 ORIENT
    7 EDUCATE
**Roping**
venue: 5 RODEO
**Roquefort**
hue: 4 BLEU
**Rorem**
Composer: 3 NED
**Rorschach**
image: 4 BLOT 7 INKBLOT
**Rosa**
of civil rights fame: 5 PARKS

**Rosalynn**
Daughter of: 3 AMY
successor: 5 NANCY
**"Rosanna"**
band: 4 TOTO
**Rosary**
prayer: 8 AVEMARIA
Say the: 4 PRAY
unit: 4 BEAD
**Roscoe:** 3 GAT ROD 6 HEATER
**Rose:** 4 GREW 5 STOOD
    7 CLIMBED
home: 3 BED
Love of: 4 ABIE
oil: 5 ATTAR
part: 3 HIP 4 STEM 5 PETAL
protector: 5 THORN
Red: 4 PETE
Rock singer: 3 AXL
shrub family: 4 SLOE
    6 SPIREA
___ Rose: 5 TOKYO
"___ Rose": 4 LIDA
**Roseanne**
1989 ~ film: 8 SHEDEVIL
Comic: 4 BARR
TV daughter of: 7 DARLENE
**"Roseanne"**
actress Gilbert: 4 SARA
Darlene player on: 4 SARA
star: 4 BARR
**Rose Bowl**
20-time ~ winner: 3 USC
city: 8 PASADENA
team: 3 MSU OSU 4 UCLA
**Rosebud:** 4 SLED
owner: 4 KANE
**"Rose is a rose is a rose"**
speaker: 5 STEIN
**Rosemary:** 4 HERB
portrayer: 3 MIA
**"Rosemary's Baby"**
author Ira: 5 LEVIN
author Levin: 3 IRA
**Rosencrantz:** 4 DANE
    8 COURTIER
"___ Rosenkavalier": 3 DER
**"Rose of ___, The":** 6 TRALEE
**"Rose ___ rose ...":** 3 ISA
**Roses**
Goddess with a crown of:
    5 ERATO
Oil of: 5 ATTAR
**"Roses ___ red ...":** 3 ARE
**Rosetta**
river: 4 NILE
**Rosetta Stone**
stuff: 6 BASALT
**Rosewall**
of tennis: 3 KEN
**Rosie**
Actress: 5 PEREZ
Fastener for: 5 RIVET
Muppet friend of: 4 ELMO
of tennis: 6 CASALS
Runner: 4 RUIZ

**Rosie the ___**: 7 RIVETER
**Rosinante**
 rider: 10 DONQUIXOTE
**"Rosmersholm"**
 playwright: 5 IBSEN
**Ross**
 Flagmaker: 5 BETSY
 Singer: 5 DIANA
**Ross, Betsy**
 Emulate: 3 SEW
**Ross, Diana**
 1975 ~ film: 8 MAHOGANY
 1980 ~ hit: 9 ITSMYTURN
 musical: 6 THEWIZ
**Ross, Katharine**
 1969 ~ role: 9 ETTAPLACE
**Rossellini**
 Director: 7 ROBERTO
**Rossi**
 of soccer: 5 PAOLO
**Rossini**
 creation: 5 OPERA
 song: 4 ARIA
 subject: 4 TELL
**Ross Sea**
 sight: 4 FLOE
**Rostand**
 hero: 6 CYRANO
**Rosten**
 Author: 3 LEO
**Roster**: 4 ROLL ROTA
 abbr.: 4 ETAL
 Playbill: 4 CAST
 Society: 5 ALIST
**Rostropovich**
 instrument: 5 CELLO
**Roswell**
 sighting: 3 UFO
 visitor: 5 ALIEN
**Rosy**
 Hardly: 4 GRIM 5 ASHEN
**Rot**: 4 TOSH 5 DECAY GOBAD
       HOOEY 7 TWADDLE
**Rota**
 Composer: 4 NINO
**Rotary**
 current: 4 EDDY
 Use a ~ phone: 4 DIAL
**Rotate**: 4 SPIN TURN 5 TWIRL
**Rotating**
 disc: 3 CAM
**Rotation**
 About the line of: 5 AXIAL
 Center of: 4 AXIS
 Force of: 6 TORQUE
 Star of the: 3 ACE
**ROTC**
 relative: 3 OCS
**Rote**
 exercise: 5 DRILL
**Roth**
 plan: 3 IRA
 Writer: 6 PHILIP
**Rotini**: 5 PASTA
**Rotisserie**: 4 OVEN
 part: 3 ROD 4 SPIT

**Rotten**: 3 BAD 5 AWFUL LOUSY
       6 NOGOOD
 Dirty ~ scoundrel: 5 CREEP
       SWINE
**Rotter**: 3 CAD CUR
**Rotterdam**
 Revered name in: 7 ERASMUS
**Rotunda**
 feature: 4 DOME
**Rouen**
 refusal: 3 NON
 river: 5 SEINE
 room: 5 SALLE
**"Rouen Cathedral"**
 painter: 5 MONET
**Rouge**
 In need of: 4 PALE
 It may be: 3 VIN
**Rough**: 4 RUDE 6 COARSE
       SEVERE 7 CRAGGED
       8 UNGENTLE
 cliff: 4 CRAG
 file: 4 RASP
 guess: 4 STAB
 house: 6 LEANTO
 it: 4 CAMP
 Prepare for a ~ ride:
       7 STRAPIN
 stuff: 3 ORE 5 EMERY GRASS
 up: 4 MAUL 5 ABUSE
 waters: 4 CHOP
**Roughage**: 5 FIBER
**Roughly**: 4 ORSO 5 ABOUT
       CIRCA 6 AROUND
       10 MOREORLESS
 Handle: 4 MAUL 5 PAWAT
 Tear: 8 LACERATE
**Roulette**
 bet: 3 ODD RED 4 EVEN
       NOIR 5 ROUGE
 try: 4 SPIN
**Round**
 Bar: 4 ALES
 building: 4 SILO
 cheese: 4 EDAM
 dance: 4 HORA
 Early: 6 PRELIM
 ender: 4 BELL
 figure: 5 BOXER
 Go a: 4 SPAR
 Kind of: 5 OVATE
 Not quite: 4 OVAL 5 OVOID
 number: 4 ZERO 8 ESTIMATE
 of applause: 4 HAND
 of four: 5 SEMIS
 Pub: 4 ALES
 roof: 4 DOME
 sandwich: 4 OREO
 trip: 5 ORBIT
 window: 5 OXEYE
**Roundabout**
 path: 6 DETOUR
**"Roundabout"**
 band: 3 YES
**"Round and Round"**
 rock group: 4 RATT

 singer Perry: 4 COMO
**Rounded**
 hammer part: 4 PEEN
 lump: 4 GLOB
 up: 6 HERDED
**Roundish**: 4 OVAL 5 OVATE
       OVOID
**Rounds**: 4 AMMO
**Round Table**
 address: 3 SIR
 knight: 3 KAY 4 BORS
       6 GARETH 8 LANCELOT
 ruler: 6 ARTHUR
**Roundup**
 rope: 5 LASSO RIATA
 sound: 3 MOO
**Roundworm**: 8 NEMATODE
**Rouse**: 4 WAKE 6 AWAKEN
**Rouser**: 5 ALARM
**Roush**
 of baseball: 3 EDD
**Rousseau**
 Artist: 5 HENRI
 novel: 5 EMILE
**Roustabout**
 raising: 4 TENT
**Route**: 3 WAY 4 LINE PATH
       6 COURSE
 Bus: 4 LINE
 Cop: 4 BEAT
 Direct: 7 BEELINE
 Main: 7 SEALANE
 Rheinland: 4 BAHN
 Rural: 4 LANE
 Shipping: 7 SEALANE
 Wheelchair: 4 RAMP
**"Route 66"**
 actor George: 7 MAHARIS
 When ~ was on (abbr.):
       3 FRI
**Routes**
 Like some: 6 SCENIC
**Routine**: 4 ROTE 5 DRILL
       HOHUM USUAL
       6 OLDHAT
 Comedy: 3 BIT 6 SHTICK
 Dull: 3 RUT 4 ROTE
 Frenzied: 7 RATRACE
 Healthful: 7 REGIMEN
 Laborious: 5 GRIND
 task: 5 CHORE
**Routing**
 word: 3 VIA
**Rover**: 5 NOMAD
 Command to: 3 SIT 4 HEEL
       STAY 5 FETCH SPEAK
 Friend of: 3 REX 4 FIDO
 Ordeal for: 4 BATH
 Range: 5 STEER
 reprimand: 3 BAD
 restraint: 5 CHAIN LEASH
 reward: 4 BONE
 Scrap for: 3 ORT
 warning: 3 GRR 5 SNARL
**Roving**
 adventurously: 6 ERRANT

**Row:** 3 OAR 4 FRAY RANK
    SPAT TIER 5 MELEE
    SCULL SETTO 6 FRACAS
    STROKE
  Cannery: 4 TINS
  Classroom: 5 DESKS
  of bushes: 5 HEDGE
  One in a: 3 OAR
  Play to the back: 5 EMOTE
  producer: 3 HOE
  Public: 5 SCENE
  Stadium: 4 TIER
  Tough ~ to hoe: 6 ORDEAL
**Rowan**
  Designer: 4 RENA
**Rowboat**
  blade: 3 OAR
  pair: 4 OARS
  Small: 5 SKIFF
**Rowdy ___ ("Rawhide" role):**
  5 YATES
**Rower:** 3 OAR
**Rowing**
  need: 3 OAR
  team: 4 CREW
**Rowland**
  Actress: 4 GENA
  Columnist: 4 EVANS
**Rowling, J.K.**
  creation: 6 POTTER
  Honour given to: 3 OBE
**"Row, Row, Row Your Boat":**
  5 ROUND
  Life, in: 5 DREAM
**"Roxanne"**
  Martin of: 5 STEVE
**Roxette**
  style: 7 EUROPOP
**Roxy Music**
  cofounder: 3 ENO
**Roy**
  Cartoonist: 4 DOTY
  Country singer: 5 ACUFF
  Former Colorado governor:
    5 ROMER
  Lawyer: 4 COHN
  of CORE: 5 INNIS
  Wife of: 4 DALE
**Royal**
  address: 4 SIRE 6 MYLORD
  ball: 3 ORB
  British: 4 ANNE
  decree: 5 EDICT
  domain: 5 REALM
  Eastern: 4 RAJA RANI
  educator: 4 ETON
  elephant: 5 BABAR
  flush card: 3 ACE TEN
  fur: 5 SABLE 6 ERMINE
  headgear: 5 CROWN TIARA
    6 DIADEM
  home: 6 CASTLE PALACE
  Indian: 4 RAJA RANI
  irritant: 3 PEA
  issue: 6 PRINCE
  jelly maker: 3 BEE

  messenger: 6 HERALD
  Mideast ~ name: 4 SAUD
  Norwegian ~ name: 4 OLAF
    OLAV
  pain: 4 PEST
  princess: 4 ANNE
  rule: 5 REIGN
  Russian: 4 TSAR
  Saudi ~ name: 4 FAHD
    6 FAISAL
  seat: 6 THRONE
  symbol: 3 ORB
  wish: 3 SON
**Royal Botanical Gardens**
  locale: 3 KEW
**Royal Crown:** 4 COLA
  brand: 4 NEHI
**Royale**
  automaker: 3 REO
  ___ Royale: 4 ISLE
  "___ Royale": 6 CASINO
**Royalty**
  Indian: 4 RANI 5 RANIS
  receiver: 6 AUTHOR
  Spanish: 5 REYES 6 REINAS
  "Star Wars": 4 LEIA
**ROY G. ___:** 3 BIV
**ROY G. BIV**
  Part of: 3 RED 6 INDIGO
    VIOLET
**Roz**
  portrayer on "Frasier": 4 PERI
  Role for: 4 MAME
**Rozelle**
  Football exec: 4 PETE
**RPI**
  grad: 4 ENGR
  grads: 3 EES
  Part of: 4 INST
**RPM**
  indicator: 4 TACH
  The P in: 3 PER
**RR**
  employee: 4 ENGR
  Former ~ regulator: 3 ICC
  stop: 3 STA STN
**RR ___:** 4 XING
**R-rated**
  ~, maybe: 4 GORY RACY
    5 ADULT 6 EROTIC
    STEAMY
**RSVP**
  enclosure: 4 SASE
  Part of: 3 SIL 4 VOUS
    5 PLAIT
**Rte.:** 3 HWY RDS (plural) TPK
  Backwoods: 3 RFD
  City: 3 AVE
  East Coast: 5 USONE
  recommenders: 3 AAA
**Ruark**
  novel: 5 UHURU
**Rub:** 4 WIPE 6 ABRADE
  and rub: 5 SCOUR
  it in: 5 GLOAT
  off: 6 ABRADE

  on: 6 ANOINT
  out: 3 OFF 4 DOIN KILL SLAY
    5 ERASE
  the right way: 3 PET
  the wrong way: 3 IRK 4 RILE
    5 CHAFE 6 NETTLE
  together: 5 GNASH
  Violinist's: 5 ROSIN
  You might ~ one out: 5 GENIE
**Rub-___:** 4 ADUB
**"Rubáiyát"**
  poet: 4 OMAR
**Rubber:** 5 TIRES 6 ERASER
    7 MASSEUR
    8 MASSEUSE
  Burn: 5 SPEED
  center: 5 AKRON
  ducky spot: 4 BATH
  gasket: 5 ORING
  Hard: 7 EBONITE
  Kind of: 4 FOAM 5 INDIA
  Leave: 5 ERASE
  Letters on a ~ check: 3 NSF
  Pitcher: 4 SLAB
  Prepare to burn: 3 REV
  ring: 6 GASKET
  source: 5 LATEX
  Synthetic ~ componet:
    7 STYRENE
**Rubber ___:** 6 CEMENT
**"Rubber Duckie"**
  singer: 5 ERNIE
**Rubbermaid**
  Home of: 4 OHIO
**Rubberneck:** 3 EYE 4 GAPE
    GAWK OGLE 5 CRANE
    STARE
**Rubber-stamp:** 4 OKAY
**Rubbish:** 3 ROT 4 CRUD
    5 DROSS OFFAL TRIPE
    6 DEBRIS
**Rubble**
  maker: 3 TNT
  Rocky: 5 SCREE
**Rubdown**
  target: 4 ACHE
**Rube:** 4 HICK 5 RURAL YOKEL
    7 HAYSEED
  of Red: 4 CLEM
**Rubella**
  symptom: 4 RASH
**Rubenesque:** 6 ZAFTIG
**Rubicon**
  crosser: 6 CAESAR
**Rubicund:** 3 RED
**Rubik**
  creation: 4 CUBE
**Rubik's Cube**
  inventor Rubik: 4 ERNO
**Rubinstein**
  Pianist: 5 ANTON ARTUR
**Ruble**
  part: 5 KOPEK 6 KOPECK
**Ruby:** 3 GEM 7 CARMINE
    DEEPRED
  Actress: 3 DEE

**Ruby-like**
gem: 6 SPINEL
**Ruckus:** 3 ADO DIN 4 FLAP
STIR TODO 5 HOOHA
MELEE NOISE SCENE
**Rudder**
control: 6 TILLER
locale: 5 STERN
support: 4 SKEG
Take the: 5 STEER
Toward the: 3 AFT 6 ASTERN
**Ruddy**
Hardly: 3 WAN 4 ASHY PALE
5 PASTY
**Rude:** 5 SURLY 8 INSOLENT
Be ~ in line: 5 SHOVE
Less: 5 NICER
look: 4 LEER 5 STARE
one: 3 CAD 4 BOOR 5 CHURL
**Rudely**
Awaken: 5 ROUST
brief: 4 CURT
ignore: 4 SNUB
Nudge: 5 ELBOW
sarcastic: 5 SNIDE
Stare: 4 OGLE
Take: 4 GRAB
Treat: 5 SHOVE
**Rudge**
Fictional: 7 BARNABY
**Rudimentary:** 5 BASIC CRUDE
seed: 5 OVULE
**Rudiments:** 4 ABCS
**Rudner**
Comic: 4 RITA
**Rudolf**
Infamous: 4 HESS
Pianist: 6 SERKIN
**Rudolph**
Runner: 5 WILMA
trademark: 7 REDNOSE
**Rue:** 6 REGRET
Costar of: 3 BEA
the run: 4 ACHE
**Rueful:** 5 SORRY
**"Rue Morgue"**
author: 3 POE
culprit: 3 APE
**Ruff**
stuff: 4 LACE
**Ruffian:** 4 GOON THUG
5 BRUTE 6 MAULER
**Ruffle:** 3 IRK 4 STIR
feathers: 4 RILE
**Rug:** 6 TOUPEE
cleaner, for short: 3 VAC
Cut a: 5 DANCE
fiber: 5 SISAL
Fix a: 7 REWEAVE
Kind of: 3 RYA 4 AREA 5 SISAL
6 NAVAJO
Like a bug in a: 4 SNUG
rat: 3 TOT 4 TYKE 6 MOPPET
Scandinavian: 3 RYA
Shag ~ feature: 4 PILE
Small: 3 MAT

Sweep under the: 4 HIDE
Use a prayer: 5 KNEEL
**Rugby**
formation: 5 SCRUM
**Rugged**
range: 6 SIERRA
ridge: 5 ARETE
rock: 4 CRAG
**Rugrat:** 3 TOT 4 TYKE
6 MOPPET
**"Rugrats"**
dad: 3 STU
Tommy's kid brother on: 3 DIL
**Ruhr**
city: 5 ESSEN
refusal: 4 NEIN
**Ruin:** 3 MAR 4 BANE DOIN
DOOM HARM UNDO
5 WRACK WRECK
Bring ~ on: 6 RAVAGE
Cause of: 4 BANE
Partner of: 4 RACK 5 WRACK
Rack and: 5 HAVOC
~, old-style: 5 STROY
**Ruination:** 4 BANE DOOM
**Ruined:** 4 SHOT 5 KAPUT
6 SPOILT
**Rukeyser**
Host: 5 LOUIS
**Rule:** 5 REIGN 6 GOVERN
Actress: 6 JANICE
As a: 9 INGENERAL
Brief: 3 REG
British ~ in India: 3 RAJ
Corporate: 5 BYLAW
Golden ~ word: 4 UNTO
Kind of: 3 MOB 4 HOME
Last word of the golden:
3 YOU
out: 3 BAN BAR NIX
6 NEGATE
Standard: 5 BYLAW
to live by: 5 TENET
___ rule: 3 ASA
**"Rule, Britannia"**
composer: 4 ARNE
**Ruled:** 3 RAN 4 LINY
**"___ Ruled the World" (1965**
hit): 3 IFI
**Ruler**
at Karnak: 6 RAMSES
Bygone: 3 DEY 4 CZAR SHAH
TSAR
Hereditary: 6 DYNAST
in Borneo: 5 RAJAH
length: 4 FOOT 7 ONEFOOT
Mesopotamian: 6 SARGON
Mideast: 4 EMIR SHAH
5 AMEER EMEER
Olympian: 4 ZEUS
Petty: 6 SATRAP
Terrible: 4 IVAN
Turkish: 5 PASHA
unit: 4 INCH
**Rules**
Follow the: 4 OBEY

maven: 5 HOYLE
of conduct: 6 ETHICS
One who ~ the roast:
5 EMCEE
Org. with eligibility: 4 NCAA
Relax, as: 4 BEND
System of: 4 CODE
**Ruling**
body: 6 REGIME
Court: 3 LET
group: 5 JUNTA
Ref: 3 TKO
**"Ruling Class, The"**
star: 6 OTOOLE
**Rulings:** 5 DICTA
**Rum**
cake: 4 BABA
Cuban: 3 RON
drink: 4 GROG 6 COLADA
MAITAI
~, to some: 5 DEMON
**Rumba:** 5 DANCE
relative: 5 MAMBO
**Rum-based**
liqueur: 8 TIAMARIA
**Rumble:** 4 ROAR 5 MELEE
Car with a ~ seat:
8 ROADSTER
**"Rumble in the Jungle"**
site: 5 ZAIRE
**Rumbler**
Sicilian: 4 ETNA
**Rumblers**
Chicago: 3 ELS
**Ruminant**
chew: 3 CUD
Rain forest: 5 OKAPI
Third stomach of a:
6 OMASUM
**Ruminate:** 4 CHEW MUSE
**Rummikub**
piece: 4 TILE
**Rummy:** 3 SOT 5 SOUSE
game: 3 GIN 4 TONK
variety: 3 GIN 7 CANASTA
**Rumor:** 4 TALE 6 GOSSIP
REPORT
generator: 4 MILL
Nasty: 6 CANARD
starter: 5 IHEAR
**Rumormonger:** 5 YENTA
**Rumors**
Like some: 4 IDLE
**Rump**
neighbor: 7 SIRLOIN
**Rumpelstiltskin**
Imitated: 4 SPUN
**Rumple:** 4 MUSS
**Rumpled:** 5 MESSY
**Rumpus:** 3 ADO 4 TODO
6 SHINDY
**Rumsfeld**
org.: 3 DOD
predecessor: 5 COHEN
**Rum ___ Tugger ("Cats"**
character): 3 TUM

**Run:** 3 HIE LAM 4 COST FLEE LOPE 5 BLEED SCOOT SPATE 6 DIRECT MANAGE SERIES 7 OPERATE
after: 5 CHASE
Alphabet: 3 ABC BCD CDE *etc.*
amok: 4 RIOT
a tab: 3 OWE
away: 4 FLEE
Bond on the: 5 ELOPE
Bull: 3 LEA
Dry: 4 TEST 5 TRIAL
easily: 4 LOPE TROT
Good: 6 STREAK
in: 3 NAB 6 ARREST
in neutral: 4 IDLE
in the raw: 6 STREAK
in the wash: 5 BLEED
into: 3 RAM 4 MEET 7 REAREND
like heck: 4 TEAR
off: 4 BOLT FLEE 5 PRINT REPEL
One on the: 5 FLEER 7 ESCAPEE
One way to: 3 JOG 4 AMOK WILD 6 SCARED
Opening: 4 ABCD
out: 3 END 5 LAPSE 6 ELAPSE EXPIRE
out of: 5 USEUP
out of gas: 4 DIE 4 TIRE
out of steam: 3 DIE 4 TIRE
out on: 6 DESERT 7 ABANDON
playfully: 4 ROMP
Prepare to: 4 EDIT
Risky way to: 7 ONEMPTY
Short: 4 DASH
Ski: 5 PISTE SLOPE
smoothly: 3 HUM 4 FLOW PURR
the show: 4 RULE 5 EMCEE REIGN
They ~ errands: 6 GOFERS
They ~ in the kitchen: 4 TAPS
They ~ when broken: 4 EGGS
through: 4 GORE STAB 5 USEUP 6 IMPALE PIERCE SKEWER 8 REHEARSE
Trial: 4 PREP
up: 5 AMASS INCUR
Wrong way to: 7 AGROUND
**Run ___:** 4 AMOK ATAB
**Run-___ (of hip-hop):** 3 DMC
**"Runaround Sue"**
singer: 4 DION
**Runaway:** 4 ROMP 7 RAMPANT
of rhyme: 5 SPOON
**"Runaway"**
singer Shannon: 3 DEL
**"Runaway Bride"**
Richard of: 4 GERE

**Rundgren**
Singer: 4 TODD
**Rundown:** 5 RECAP
**Run-down:** 5 SEAMY SEEDY 6 SORDID
area: 4 SLUM 6 GHETTO
building: 8 TENEMENT
**Rung:** 4 STEP
Rope ~ on a ship: 7 RATLINE
**Run-in:** 3 ROW 4 SPAT
**Runner:** 5 GOFER 7 ATHLETE
Australian: 3 EMU
Distance: 5 MILER
Easy: 5 LOPER
Errand: 5 GOFER
Fast: 4 HARE
Forest: 3 SAP
goal: 4 TAPE
Graceful: 7 ARABIAN
Maze: 3 RAT 6 LABRAT
Nov.: 3 POL
Pamplona: 4 TORO
path: 8 BASELINE
Road: 3 CAR 4 AUTO
Senate: 4 PAGE
Winter: 4 SLED
**Runners:** 4 LEGS
carry it: 4 SLED
**Runner-up:** 5 LOSER
Fabled: 4 HARE
to Ike: 5 ADLAI
**Running:** 8 ONTHELAM
behind: 4 LATE 5 TARDY
game: 3 TAG
mates: 3 VPS 5 VEEPS
Stop: 3 DIE
things: 8 INCHARGE
Those ~ the place (abbr.): 4 MGMT
total: 5 TALLY
track: 4 OVAL
wild: 4 AMOK 5 ARIOT 7 ONATEAR
**Running mate**
1968 ~ of Wallace: 5 LEMAY
Adlai's: 5 ESTES
Dole's: 4 KEMP
Mondale's: 7 FERRARO
Nixon's: 5 AGNEW
**"Running on Empty"**
singer: 13 JACKSONBROWNE
**"Runnin' Rebels, The":** 4 UNLV
**Run ___ of:** 5 AFOUL
**Runoff**
spot: 6 RAVINE
Typographical: 5 WIDOW
**Run ___ of the law:** 5 AFOUL
**Run-of-the-mill:** 4 SOSO 5 USUAL 6 COMMON 7 AVERAGE
(abbr.): 3 ORD
**"Run ___ Run" (1998 film):** 4 LOLA
**Runs:** 4 GOES
It ~ from stem to stern: 4 KEEL
**Runt:** 8 LITTLEST

Like a: 7 WEAKEST
**Runway:** 6 TARMAC
Banks on the: 4 TYRA
Hit the: 4 LAND 6 ALIGHT
model: 5 PLANE
Move down the: 6 SASHAY
Roll on a: 4 TAXI
walker: 5 MODEL
**Runyon**
Writer: 5 DAMON
**Rupees**
Where ~ are spent: 5 INDIA NEPAL
**Rupert**
Actor: 7 EVERETT
**Rupture:** 4 REND TEAR
**"R.U.R."**
playwright: 5 CAPEK
**Rural:** 6 RUSTIC
carriage: 4 SHAY
expanse: 3 LEA
fight: 6 RASSLE
get-together: 3 BEE
hotel: 3 INN
Like many ~ roads: 7 ONELANE
Not: 5 URBAN
outing: 7 HAYRIDE 9 STATEFAIR
route: 4 LANE
storehouse: 4 SILO
structure: 4 BARN
**Ruse:** 3 CON 4 PLOY WILE
**Rush:** 3 HIE 4 RACE REED ZOOM 5 HASTE HURRY RUNAT SPURT STORM SURGE 6 HASTEN SCURRY 8 STEPONIT
letters: 4 ASAP
People ~ to get in here: 4 FRAT
site: 5 MARSH
Sudden: 5 SPATE
**"Rush!":** 4 ASAP
**Rush, Geoffrey**
Oscar-winning film starring: 5 SHINE
**Rushdie**
Author: 6 SALMAN
Like the Verses of: 7 SATANIC
**Rushed:** 5 HADAT RANAT
**Rush hour:** 3 SIX
subway rarity: 4 SEAT
traffic facilitator: 7 HOVLANE
**"Rush Hour"**
star Jackie: 4 CHAN
**Rushing**
place: 4 FRAT
sound: 6 SWOOSH
**Rushlike**
plant: 5 SEDGE
**"Rushmore"**
director Anderson: 3 WES
___ Rushmore: 5 MOUNT
**"Rush, Rush"**
singer Abdul: 5 PAULA
singer Paula: 5 ABDUL

**Russ**
  Director: 5 MEYER
**Russell**
  Actor: 4 KURT
  Actress: 7 THERESA
  "Felicity" star: 4 KERI
  Oscar winner: 5 CROWE
  Rocker: 4 LEON
**Russell, Rosalind**
  1948 ~ film, with "The":
    11 VELVETTOUCH
  1958 ~ comedy:
    10 AUNTIEMAME
  role: 4 MAME
**Russell Cave Natl. Mon.**
  locale: 3 ALA
**Russert**
  Moderator: 3 TIM
**Russert, Tim**
  venue: 4 CNBC
**Russia**
  Popular game from:
    6 TETRIS
  Trotsky of: 4 LEON
**"___ Russia $1200" (Bob Hope**
    **book):** 4 IOWE
**Russian**
  alternative: 5 RANCH
  auto make: 4 LADA
  ballet company: 5 KIROV
  blue: 3 CAT
  capital: 6 MOSCOW
  carriage: 6 TROIKA
  city: 4 OMSK OREL
  coin: 5 RUBLE
  comrade: 8 TOVARICH
  cooperative: 5 ARTEL
  country home: 5 DACHA
  czar known as "The Great":
    6 PETERI
  dish: 5 BLINI
  empress: 7 TSARINA
  fighter: 3 MIG
  Former ~ council: 6 SOVIET
  Former ~ space station: 3 MIR
  grassland: 6 STEPPE
  John, in: 4 IVAN
  legislature: 4 DUMA
  mountains: 5 URALS
  name meaning holy: 4 OLGA
  news agency: 4 TASS
  novelist: 5 GOGOL GORKI
  Old ~ ruler: 4 CZAR TSAR
  pancakes: 5 BLINI

  peace: 3 MIR
  plain: 6 STEPPE
  range: 5 URALS
  refusal: 4 NYET
  retreat: 5 DACHA
  revolutionary: 5 LENIN
  river: 3 OKA 4 LENA NEVA
    URAL
  urn: 7 SAMOVAR
  wolfhound: 6 BORZOI
**Russian America**
  Capital of: 5 SITKA
**Russian-born**
  artist: 4 ERTE
**Russian Orthodox**
  First ~ saint: 4 OLGA
**Russians**
  Some: 6 ASIANS TATARS
**Russo**
  Actress: 4 RENE
**Rust:** 5 OXIDE 7 OXIDATE
**Rustic:** 4 HICK RUBE 5 YOKEL
  digs: 5 CABIN
  locale: 3 LEA
  pipe: 4 REED
**Rustle:** 5 SWISH
**Rustler**
  chaser: 5 POSSE
  target: 4 HERD
**Rustling**
  sound: 6 SWOOSH
**Rusty**
  of baseball: 5 STAUB
**Rut**
  In a: 5 STUCK
  Words before: 3 INA
**Rutabaga:** 5 SWEDE 6 TURNIP
**Rutger**
  Actor: 5 HAUER
**Rutgers**
  river: 7 RARITAN
  team color: 7 SCARLET
**Ruth**
  Colleague of: 4 ARTE
  Husband of: 4 BOAZ
  Mother-in-law of: 5 NAOMI
  nickname: 4 BABE 7 BAMBINO
    THEBABE
  Retired number of: 5 THREE
  successor: 5 AARON
  sultanate: 4 SWAT
**Ruthless:** 9 CUTTHROAT
    DOGEATDOG
  boss: 4 AXER

**RV**
  connection: 3 STU
  stop: 3 KOA
**R-V**
  hookup: 3 STU
  link: 3 STU
**Rwanda**
  native: 4 HUTU
**RWE**
  Part of: 5 WALDO
**Rwy.**
  stop: 3 STA
**Rx**
  amount: 4 DOSE
  amt.: 3 TSP
  dispenser (abbr.): 4 PHAR
  Four times a day, in an: 3 QID
  Needing no: 3 OTC
  Three times, in an: 3 TER
  watchdog: 3 FDA
  writers: 3 DRS MDS
**Ryan**
  (abbr.): 3 PVT
  Actor: 5 ONEAL
  Actress: 3 MEG 4 JERI
    5 IRENE
  Daughter of: 5 TATUM
  Hall of Fame pitcher:
    5 NOLAN
  Like seven ~ games: 5 NOHIT
  portrayer: 5 DAMON
**Ryan, Meg**
  1989 ~ film: 3 DOA
**Ryan, Nolan**
  ~, once: 5 ASTRO
**Ryan, Robert**
  1949 ~ film: 8 THESETUP
**"Ryan Express, The":**
    5 NOLAN
**"Ryan's Hope"**
  actress Kristen: 5 ILENE
**Ryder**
  Actress: 6 WINONA
  rival: 5 UHAUL
**___-Ryder Open:** 5 DORAL
**Rye:** 5 BREAD
  alternative: 10 WHITEBREAD
    WHOLEWHEAT
  buy: 4 LOAF
  Deli meat on: 8 PASTRAMI
  fungus: 5 ERGOT
  Wry ~ rhymer: 4 NASH
**Ryun, Jim**
  distance: 4 MILE

**S:** 3 DIR 4 SIZE
    15 SYMBOLFORSULFUR
Code word for: 6 SIERRA
in RSVP: 3 SIL
in WASP: 5 SAXON
Not quite: 3 SSE
of CBS: 3 SYS
shape: 4 OGEE

**Saab**
Fashion designer: 4 ELIE
model: 4 AERO

**Saarinen**
Architect: 4 EERO
The elder: 5 ELIEL

**Saatchi & Saatchi**
award: 4 CLIO
employees: 5 ADMEN

**Sábado:** 3 DIA

**Sabbath**
Observe the. 4 REST
talk (abbr.): 3 SER
___ Sabe: 4 KEMO

**Saber**
relative: 4 EPEE

**Saberhagen**
of baseball: 4 BRET

**Saber-rattling:** 6 THREAT

**Sabin**
Like the ~ vaccine: 4 ORAL
rival: 4 SALK

**Sabina, Poppaea**
Husband of: 4 NERO

**Sable:** 3 FUR
kin: 6 MARTEN
maker, for short: 4 MERC

**Sabres**
gp.: 3 NHL

**Sac**
Anatomical: 4 CYST 5 BURSA
Form into a: 6 ENCYST
Of the embryo: 8 AMNIOTIC
prefix: 3 OVI

**SAC**
letters: 4 USAF

**Sacajawea:** 5 GUIDE
craft: 5 CANOE
denomination: 3 ONE

**Saccharin**
discoverer Remsen: 3 IRA

**Saccharine:** 5 SWEET
    6 SUGARY

**Sacco**
of Sacco and Vanzetti:
    6 NICOLA

**Sacher**
dessert: 5 TORTE

**Sachet**
emanation: 5 AROMA SCENT

scent: 5 LILAC

**Sachs**
Poet: 5 NELLY

**Sack:** 3 AXE BAG BED CAN
    ROB 4 BOOT LOOT
    6 RAVAGE 7 PILLAGE
Camp: 3 COT
Give the: 4 FIRE
In the: 4 ABED
Leave the: 5 ARISE
out: 5 SLEEP
Out of the: 5 ASTIR RISEN
Ready for the: 4 BEAT
Simple: 3 COT
sound: 5 SNORE
weight: 5 TENLB

**Sackcloth**
Don: 6 REPENT
partner: 5 ASHES

**Sacked:** 5 INBED
out: 5 INBED SLEPT

**"Sack Look"**
designer Christian: 4 DIOR

**Sacramento**
arena: 4 ARCO
City near: 4 LODI

**"Sacre ___!":** 4 BLEU

**Sacred:** 4 HOLY
beetle: 6 SCARAB
bird: 4 IBIS
bull: 4 APIS
chest: 3 ARK
cow: 4 IDOL
hymn: 5 PSALM
image: 4 ICON IKON
Make: 6 ANOINT
place: 5 ALTAR
poem: 5 PSALM
prefix: 5 HIERO
river: 4 ALPH
scroll: 5 TORAH
song: 5 MOTET PSALM
syllables: 3 OMS
text: 5 KORAN TORAH

**"Sacred Wood, The"**
writer: 5 ELIOT

**Sacrifice**
Certain: 4 BUNT
fly stat: 3 RBI
site: 5 ALTAR

**Sacro**
suffix: 5 ILIAC

**Sacs:** 6 BURSAE
Spore: 4 ASCI

**Sad:** 3 LOW 4 BLUE DOWN
    GLUM 5 TEARY
notice: 4 OBIT
piece: 5 ELEGY

song: 5 DIRGE
sound: 3 SOB
to say: 4 ALAS
___ Sad: 4 NOVI

**Sadat**
of Egypt: 5 ANWAR
predecessor: 6 NASSER

**Saddam:** 5 IRAQI

**Sadden:** 7 DEPRESS

**Saddle**
In the: 7 ASTRIDE
part: 4 HORN

**Saddler**
tool: 3 AWL

**Sad-faced**
comedian: 7 BENBLUE

**"___ Sadie" (Beatles song):**
    4 SEXY

**"Sadly ...":** 4 ALAS

**Sadness:** 3 WOE 5 TEARS
    6 SORROW
Sign of: 4 TEAR
Sound of: 4 MOAN

**"Sad to say ...":** 4 ALAS

**Safari:** 4 TREK
gateway: 7 NAIROBI
leader: 5 BWANA
lodging: 4 TENT
park: 3 ZOO
sight: 3 GNU 4 LION 5 RHINO

**Safe**
deposit box item: 4 DEED
harbor: 4 COVE
havens: 5 ASYLA
Make: 6 SECURE
on board: 4 ALEE
On the ~ side: 4 ALEE
or out: 4 CALL
Person with a ~ job: 4 YEGG
place: 4 BANK 5 HAVEN
    VAULT 6 REFUGE
spot: 4 WALL 5 HAVEN
Symbol of ~ passage: 3 ARK
to consume: 6 EDIBLE

**Safecracker:** 4 YEGG

**Safeguard:** 4 KEEP 6 ENSURE
    INSURE

**Safekeeper**
Sailor's: 6 STELMO

**Safekeeping:** 4 CARE

**Safer**
coworker: 5 STAHL
    8 REASONER
network: 3 CBS
Newsman: 6 MORLEY
On the ~ side: 4 ALEE

**Safety:** 4 BACK
Air ~ gp.: 3 FAA

Auto ~ device: 6 AIRBAG
  7 ROLLBAR
device: 3 NET
gp.: 4 MADD SADD
org.: 4 OSHA
signal: 8 ALLCLEAR
Staircase ~ feature: 4 RAIL
Workplace ~ org.: 4 OSHA
**Saffron**
  Dish made with: 6 PAELLA
**Safin**
  2000 U.S. Open winner ~:
    5 MARAT
**Safire**
  subject: 5 USAGE
**Sag:** 5 DROOP
**SAG**
  Former ~ president: 5 ASNER
  member: 5 ACTOR
**Saga:** 4 EPIC TALE
  Icelandic: 4 EDDA
**Sagacious:** 4 WISE
**Sagacity:** 6 ACUMEN
**Sagal**
  Actress: 5 KATEY
**Sagan**
  Astronomer: 4 CARL
  book and series: 6 COSMOS
  subj.: 4 ASTR
**Sage:** 4 HERB WISE 5 SOLON
  6 SAVANT
  Hindu: 5 RISHI SWAMI
  Sci-fi: 4 YODA
**Sagebrush State:** 6 NEVADA
  native: 7 NEVADAN
**Sage of Concord, The:**
  7 EMERSON
**Sager, ___ Bayer**
  Songwriter: 6 CAROLE
**Saginaw Bay**
  lake: 5 HURON
**Sagittarius:** 6 ARCHER
**Saguaro**
  and others: 5 CACTI
**Sahara:** 6 DESERT
  beast: 5 CAMEL
  Like the: 4 ARID SERE
  rarity: 4 RAIN
  sight: 4 DUNE
  stop: 5 OASIS
  stops: 5 OASES
**Saharan:** 4 ARID
  nation: 4 MALI 5 LIBYA
  sight: 4 DUNE
  wind: 7 SIROCCO
**Sahib**
  in Swahili: 5 BWANA
**Sahl**
  Humorist: 4 MORT
**Said:** 6 STATED 7 UTTERED
  "#@$%!": 5 SWORE
  with a sneer: 5 SNIDE
  ~, old-style: 5 SPAKE
"___ said ...": 3 ASI
**Saigon**
  former enemy: 5 HANOI

site, for short: 3 NAM
~ New Year: 3 TET
**"Saigon"**
  star Alan: 4 LADD
**Sail**
  extender: 5 SPRIT
  Forward: 3 JIB
  holder: 4 MAST
  Ready, as a: 5 ATRIP
  Set: 3 RIG 6 EMBARK
    8 PUTTOSEA
  spar: 5 SPRIT
  support: 4 MAST 7 YARDARM
  through: 3 ACE
  Triangular: 3 JIB 6 LATEEN
    9 GOOSEWING
  Under: 4 ASEA 5 ATSEA
**Sailboat**
  Arab: 4 DHOW
  feature: 4 MAST
  pole: 5 SPRIT
**Sailcloth**
  fiber: 4 HEMP
**Sailed:** 6 BOATED
**Sailer**
  of 1492: 4 NINA
**Sailing:** 4 ASEA 5 ATSEA
    8 OUTTOSEA
  hailing: 4 AHOY
  hazard: 4 REEF 5 SHOAL
  maneuver: 4 TACK
  race: 7 REGATTA
  Small ~ vessel: 4 YAWL
  Smooth: 4 EASE
**Sailor:** 3 GOB TAR 4 SALT
  6 SEAMAN 8 SEAFARER
  command: 5 AVAST
  direction: 4 ALEE
  drink: 4 GROG
  expertise: 5 KNOTS
  greeting: 4 AHOY
  Indian: 6 LASCAR
  jail: 4 BRIG
  left: 4 PORT
  of myth: 6 SINBAD
  or boater: 3 HAT
  patron: 4 ELMO 6 STELMO
  punishment: 4 LASH
  saint: 4 ELMO
  speed: 5 KNOTS
  stop: 5 AVAST
  tale: 4 YARN
  temptress: 7 LORELEI
  Veteran: 6 SEADOG
  yes: 3 AYE
**Sailors:** 4 CREW
**"Sailor's Song"**
  Words repeated in: 5 TOSEA
**Sailplane:** 4 SOAR
**"Sail ___ Ship of State!":** 3 ONO
**Saint**
  Actress: 8 EVAMARIE
  Canterbury: 6 ANSELM
  Fiery: 4 ELMO
  Home of a: 6 ASSISI
  Norwegian: 4 OLAF OLAV

Patron ~ of France: 5 DENIS
picture: 4 ICON
Russian Orthodox: 4 OLGA
Sailor: 4 ELMO
"Venerable": 4 BEDE
**Saint, ___ Marie**
  Actress: 3 EVA
**Saint-___**
  (French resort): 6 TROPEZ
  (Loire's capital): 7 ETIENNE
**Saint-___, Camille**
  Composer: 5 SAENS
**"Saint, The"**
  actor Kilmer: 3 VAL
  actress Elisabeth: 4 SHUE
**Saint Catherine**
  home: 5 SIENA
**Saint Clare**
  home: 6 ASSISI
**Sainted**
  king: 4 OLAV
  ~ 5th-century pope: 4 LEOI
  ~ 7th-century pope: 5 LEOII
**Sainte-___, Quebec:** 3 FOY
**Saint-Exupéry**
  classic:
    15 THELITTLEPRINCE
  Writer ___ de ~: 7 ANTOINE
**Saint Francis**
  home: 6 ASSISI
**Sainthood**
  Fit for: 4 HOLY
**"Saint Joan"**
  monogram: 3 GBS
  playwright: 4 SHAW
  star Jean: 6 SEBERG
**Saintly:** 4 GOOD 7 ANGELIC
  glow: 4 AURA HALO
  symbol: 4 HALO
**Saint Patrick**
  land: 4 EIRE
**Saint Philip ___:** 4 NERI
**Saints**
  gp.: 3 NFC NFL
  Some: 7 MARTYRS
**Saint-___, Switzerland:**
  6 MORITZ
**Saint Teresa**
  Home of: 5 AVILA
**Saint-Tropez**
  locale: 7 RIVIERA
**Saison**
  Une: 3 ETE
**"___ Saison en Enfer":** 3 UNE
**Sajak:** 5 EMCEE
  Request to: 3 ANE
  show: 5 WHEEL
**Sake**
  Dish seasoned with:
    8 TERIYAKI
  For safety's: 6 INCASE
  Source of: 4 RICE
**Sakharov**
  Nobelist: 6 ANDREI
**Saki:** 7 PENNAME
  real name: 5 MUNRO

title: 4 ESME

**Sal**
Actor: 5 MINEO
canal: 4 ERIE
of song: 3 GAL

**Salaam:** 3 BOW 9 OBEISANCE

**Salacious:** 4 LEWD
look: 4 LEER

**Salad**
Bitter ~ item: 6 ENDIVE
　9 DANDELION
Cabbage: 4 SLAW
Caesar ~ ingredient: 3 OVA
cheese: 4 FETA
choice: 6 CAESAR
Cobb ~ ingredient: 5 BACON
Crunchy ~ bit: 4 BACO
dressing choice: 5 RANCH
dressing ingredient: 3 OIL
fish: 4 TUNA
follower: 6 ENTREE
fruit: 4 KIWI 7 AVOCADO
garnish: 5 CRESS
green: 5 CRESS 6 ENDIVE
　8 ESCAROLE
ingredient: 4 CUKE 5 FRUIT
　OLIVE ONION 6 ENDIVE
　TOMATO 7 ARUGULA
　LETTUCE ROMAINE
　8 CHICKPEA
　10 BELLPEPPER
In one's ~ days: 5 YOUNG
Kind of: 4 TACO TUNA
　5 CHEFS PASTA 6 CAESAR
　POTATO
leaf: 6 ENDIVE
Like much: 6 TOSSED
Like some ~ dressings:
　6 ONIONY
oil holder: 5 CRUET
Prepare a: 4 TOSS
preparer: 6 TOSSER
servers: 5 TONGS
slice: 6 RADISH
sort: 5 CHEFS
topping: 3 OIL 8 CROUTONS
veggie: 4 CUKE 5 CRESS
　6 ENDIVE
Waldorf ~ ingredient:
　6 CELERY

**Salad bowl**
wood: 4 TEAK

**Salad dressing**
ingredient: 3 OIL

**Salade Niçoise**
ingredient: 4 TUNA

**Salamander:** 3 EFT 4 NEWT
Two-legged: 6 MUDEEL

**Salami**
choice: 5 GENOA
hangout: 4 DELI

**Salary:** 3 PAY 4 WAGE 5 WAGES
increase: 5 RAISE
limit: 3 CAP

**Salchow**
relative: 4 AXEL

**Sale**
abbr.: 3 IRR
condition: 4 ASIS
Fabrics for: 8 DRYGOODS
item, often: 4 DEMO
Kind of: 6 ESTATE REDTAG
Like some ~ items: 4 USED
Put up for: 5 OFFER
Records a: 7 RINGSUP
sign: 4 ASIS
site: 4 YARD
word: 4 ONLY

**Salem**
City between Boston and:
　4 LYNN
state: 6 OREGON

**Salerno**
**Info:** Italian cue
send-off: 4 CIAO
She, in: 4 ESSA

**Sales**
agents: 4 REPS
booth: 5 KIOSK
dept. worker: 3 AGT
force: 4 REPS
goal: 5 QUOTA
incentive: 6 REBATE
meeting aid: 5 GRAPH
online: 5 ETAIL
pitch: 3 PIE 5 SPIEL
rep.: 3 AGT
slip (abbr.): 3 RCT 4 RCPT
Ticket: 4 GATE

**Salesman:** 3 REP
Fictional: 5 LOMAN
goal: 5 ORDER
Miller: 5 LOMAN
pitch: 5 SPIEL
place: 4 ROAD
stock: 4 LINE

**Salesperson:** 3 REP 5 CLERK

**Salieri**
Slow, to: 5 LENTO

**Saline**
drop: 4 TEAR

**Salinger**
character: 4 ESME 6 HOLDEN
dedicatee: 4 ESME
girl: 4 ESME
hero: 15 HOLDENCAULFIELD
or Trudeau: 6 PIERRE
title character: 4 ESME
　5 ZOOEY

**Salisbury**
Capital once known as:
　6 HARARE

**Salisbury Plain**
monument: 10 STONEHENGE

**Saliva:** 7 SPITTLE

**Salivate:** 5 DROOL

**Salk**
and Pepper (abbr.): 3 DRS
conquest: 5 POLIO
contemporary: 5 SABIN
Dr.: 5 JONAS

**Sallie ___ :** 3 MAE

**Sally**
and Ayn: 5 RANDS
Astronaut: 4 RIDE
~, to Charlie Brown: 6 SISTER

**Sally Ann**
Actress: 5 HOWES

**Sally ___ cake:** 4 LUNN

**Salma**
Actress: 5 HAYEK

**Salmon:** 7 SPAWNER
Brine-cured: 3 LOX
do it: 5 SPAWN
Prized: 4 TYEE
Reproduce like: 5 SPAWN
Smoked: 3 LOX
variety: 4 COHO
Where the ~ flows: 5 IDAHO
Young: 4 PARR 5 SMOLT

**"Salome"**
prop: 4 VEIL
solo: 4 ARIA

**Salon**
activity: 7 STYLING
appliance: 5 DRYER
application: 3 DYE GEL
coloring: 5 HENNA
creation: 4 COIF
cut: 4 SHAG
dye: 5 HENNA
employee: 4 DYER 6 TINTER
　7 STYLIST
goo: 3 GEL
job: 3 CUT SET 4 PERM TINT
　5 RINSE
locks: 4 HAIR
or Slate: 4 EMAG
sound: 4 SNIP
styles: 3 DOS
supplies: 4 DYES GELS
　5 COMBS TINTS
　7 ROLLERS
sweepings: 4 HAIR
Touch up at a: 7 RECOLOR
treatment: 4 PERM
　6 FACIAL

**Salonen, ___-Pekka**
Conductor: 3 ESA

**Salonga**
Actress: 3 LEA

**Salons**
Like some: 6 UNISEX

**Saloon:** 3 BAR 7 CANTINA
bill: 6 BARTAB
Old ~ sight: 5 PIANO
order: 3 ALE RYE
request: 7 ANOTHER
seat: 5 STOOL
sign: 5 ONTAP
worker: 5 BGIRL

**Salsa**
dipper: 5 NACHO
Like some: 4 MILD 5 ZESTY
quality: 4 TANG
singer Blades: 5 RUBEN
singer Cruz: 5 CELIA
topped entrée: 4 TACO

**Salt:** 3 GOB TAR 4 NACL
    6 DEICER SAILOR
    SEADOG
  Add ~ to: 6 SEASON
  amount: 4 DASH
  assent: 3 AYE
  away: 5 STASH STORE
  Call for the: 4 AHOY
  Chemical: 6 IODIDE
  Chemical ~ in ink:
    7 TANNATE
  direction: 4 ALEE
  Element 53: 6 IODATE IODIDE
  Halt, to a: 5 AVAST
  holder: 4 BOAT 6 CELLAR
  lick visitor: 4 DEER
  Old: 3 TAR
  Olive with a little: 3 OYL
  Organic: 5 ESTER
  Rock: 6 HALITE
  Sea: 3 TAR
  shaker: 7 TSUNAMI
  source: 3 SEA
  Soviet ~ lake: 4 ARAL
  Spilled: 4 OMEN
  Table: 4 NACL
  Treat as table: 6 IODIZE
  ~, in French: 3 SEL
  ~, symbolically: 4 NACL
**SALT**
  Part of: 4 ARMS
  signer: 4 USSR
  subject: 4 ICBM 5 NTEST
**Salt-___:** 5 NPEPA
**Salten**
  deer: 5 BAMBI
**Saltimbocca**
  ingredient: 4 VEAL
**Saltine**
  brand: 5 ZESTA
**Salting**
  In need of: 3 ICY
**Salt Lake City**
  athlete: 3 UTE
  City near: 4 OREM 5 OGDEN
  native: 5 UTAHN
  state: 4 UTAH
**Salt-N-___:** 4 PEPA
**Salt-N-Pepa:** 4 TRIO
  Emulate: 3 RAP
**Salton ___:** 3 SEA
**Saltpeter:** 5 NITER
  British: 5 NITRE
**Saltpetre:** 5 NITRE
**Salts**
  Kind of: 5 EPSOM
  Need smelling: 5 SWOON
  ___ salts: 5 EPSOM
**Saltwater**
  catch: 7 SEABASS
  Like ~ taffy: 5 CHEWY
**Salty:** 5 BRINY 6 SALINE
  assents: 4 AYES
  drop: 4 TEAR
  lake: 4 ARAL
  Man with a ~ wife: 3 LOT

  sauce: 3 SOY
  shout: 4 AHOY
**Salutation**
  Islamic: 6 SALAAM
  Island: 5 ALOHA
  Latin: 3 AVE
  Sailor's: 4 AHOY
  Sideline: 5 HIMOM
  Sydney: 4 GDAY
**Salute:** 4 HAIL
  Answer with a: 3 SIR 6 YESSIR
  Gun: 5 SALVO
  Raised glass: 5 TOAST
**Salvador**
  Artist: 4 DALI
  Surrealist: 4 DALI
  ___ Salvador: 3 SAN
**Salvage**
  gear: 5 SONAR
**Salvation**
  Person in need of:
    8 LOSTSOUL
**Salvation Army**
  collection: 4 ALMS
**Salve**
  ingredient: 4 ALOE
**Salyut 7**
  cosmonaut Atkov: 4 OLEG
  Successor to: 3 MIR
**Salzburg**
  vista: 4 ALPS
**Sam:** 5 UNCLE
  Actor: 5 NEILL
  Detective: 5 SPADE
  Director: 5 RAIMI
  Former senator: 4 NUNN
  Golfer: 5 SNEAD
  of Watergate fame: 5 ERVIN
  played for her: 4 ILSA
  Singer: 5 COOKE
**Sam-___ (Seuss character):**
  3 IAM
**"___ Sam" (Sean Penn film):**
  3 IAM
**Samantha**
  Actress: 5 EGGAR
  Sister of: 6 SERENA
**Samara**
  bearer: 3 ELM
**Samaritan**
  Be a good ~ to: 3 AID
**Samba**
  place: 3 RIO
  relative: 7 CARIOCA
**Sambuca**
  flavoring: 5 ANISE
**Same:** 5 ALIKE
  Be of the ~ mind: 5 AGREE
  Do the ~ as: 3 APE
  Feel the ~: 5 AGREE
  In the ~ place: 6 IBIDEM
  In the ~ place (abbr.): 4 IBID
  More of the: 7 WHATNOT
  Much the: 5 ALIKE
  Not the: 7 ALTERED
  Of the ~ cloth: 4 AKIN

  prefix: 3 ISO 4 EQUI
  Regard as the: 6 EQUATE
  The ~ as: 7 EQUALTO
  The ~ as before: 4 IDEM
  Treat the: 6 EQUATE
  ~, in French: 4 EGAL
**"Same here!":** 5 ASAMI DITTO
  METOO SODOI
**Same old, same old:** 3 RUT
  5 USUAL 10 DAILYGRIND
**"Same Time, Next Year"**
  actor: 4 ALDA
**Sam Goody**
  purchases: 3 CDS
**Sami**
  speaker: 4 LAPP
**Samisen**
  player: 6 GEISHA
**Samms**
  Actress: 4 EMMA
**Sammy**
  Composer: 4 FAIN
  Lyricist: 4 CAHN
  of baseball: 4 SOSA
  Slammin': 4 SOSA 5 SNEAD
  Slugger: 4 SOSA
**Samoa**
  Capital of: 4 APIA
  coin: 4 TALA
  staple: 3 POI
  studier: 4 MEAD
**Samos**
  Site of ancient: 5 IONIA
**Samothrace**
  figure: 4 NIKE
**Samovar:** 3 URN
**Sampan**
  paddle: 3 OAR
**Sample:** 3 SIP TRY 4 BITE
  DEMO POLL TEST
  5 TASTE
  Band: 4 DEMO
  check word: 4 VOID
  Cloth: 6 SWATCH
  tray sign: 6 TRYONE
**Sampler:** 6 TESTER
  Music: 4 DEMO
**Sampras**
  asset: 5 SERVE
  feat: 3 ACE
  foe: 6 AGASSI
  of tennis: 4 PETE
  ~, at times: 4 ACER
**Samson**
  Like the weakened: 5 SHORN
  suffix: 3 ITE
  Where ~ defeated the
    Philistines: 4 LEHI
  Where ~ died: 4 GAZA
**"Samson and Delilah"**
  actress Lamarr: 4 HEDY
  Delilah in: 6 LAMARR
**Sam the ___ and the Pharaohs:**
  4 SHAM
**Samuel**
  Diarist: 5 PEPYS

teacher: 3 ELI
with a code: 5 MORSE
**Samurai**
home: 3 EDO
sash: 3 OBI
**"Samurai, The"**
novelist Shusaku: 4 ENDO
**San ___**
(Argentina): 6 ISIDRO
(California): 4 JOSE 5 DIEGO
　　MATEO RAMON
(Italy): 4 REMO
(Puerto Rico): 4 JUAN
(Riviera resort): 4 REMO
(Theological Seminary site):
　7 ANSELMO
(Texas, familiarly): 6 ANTONE
**San'a**
land: 5 YEMEN
native: 6 YEMENI
**San Antonio**
arena: 9 ALAMODOME
cagers: 5 SPURS
landmark: 5 ALAMO
**San Bernardino County**
Part of: 6 MOHAVE MOJAVE
**Sanctified:** 5 BLEST
**Sanctify:** 5 BLESS 6 HALLOW
**Sanction:** 3 LET 4 OKAY
　5 BLESS 6 PERMIT
**"___ Sanction, The";** 5 EIGER
**Sanctioned:** 3 OKD 5 LEGAL
　LEGIT
**Sanctions:** 3 OKS
Subject of U.N.: 4 IRAQ
**Sanctity**
Sign of: 4 HALO
**___ Sanctorum:** 4 ACTA
**Sanctuaries:** 5 ASYLA
**Sanctuary:** 3 ARK 5 HAVEN
　OASIS 6 ASYLUM
　REFUGE
**___ sanctum:** 5 INNER
**"___ Sanctum, The":**
　5 INNER
**Sand:** 4 GRIT
bar: 5 SHOAL
club: 5 WEDGE
hill: 4 DUNE
holder: 4 PAIL TRAP
lover: 6 CHOPIN
~, to Chopin: 4 AMIE
**Sand, George:** 5 ALIAS
　WOMAN
Composer who loved:
　6 CHOPIN
**Sandal**
feature: 5 STRAP THONG
　7 OPENTOE
Japanese: 4 ZORI
Like a: 7 TOELESS
Mexican: 8 HUARACHE
Roman: 5 SOLEA
Sporting a: 4 SHOD
**San ___ Dam, California:**
　4 LUIS

**Sandbank:** 5 SHOAL
**Sandbar:** 5 SHOAL
**Sandberg**
of baseball: 4 RYNE
**Sandbox**
sharer: 8 PLAYMATE
toy: 4 PAIL
**"Sandbox, The"**
playwright: 5 ALBEE
**Sandburg:** 4 POET
Poet: 4 CARL
**Sandcastle**
spot: 5 SHORE
**Sanders**
of football: 5 DEION
rank: 3 COL 7 COLONEL
**Sanders, Colonel**
chain: 3 KFC
feature: 6 GOATEE
**San Diego**
attraction: 3 ZOO
baseballer: 5 PADRE
City near: 6 DELMAR LAMESA
It's south of: 4 BAJA
pro: 5 PADRE
**Sanding**
In need of: 3 ICY
**Sandinista**
leader Daniel: 6 ORTEGA
**S&L**
convenience: 3 ATM
customer: 4 ACCT
offering: 3 IRA
offerings: 3 CDS
payment: 3 INT
**Sandler**
Comic: 4 ADAM
**Sandlot**
game: 7 ONEOCAT
**S&P 500**
stock: 3 AOL
**Sandpaper**
coating: 4 GRIT
Like: 5 ROUGH 6 COARSE
Use: 6 ABRADE
**"Sand Pebbles, The"**
actress Richard: 6 CRENNA
**Sandpiper:** 3 REE
**Sandra**
Actress: 3 DEE
and Ruby: 4 DEES
**Sands**
Singer: 4 EVIE
**"Sands of ___ Jima":** 3 IWO
**Sandstone:**
　15 SEDIMENTARYROCK
**Sandusky**
lake: 4 ERIE
**Sandwich**
Big: 4 HERO
Black and white: 4 OREO
bread: 3 RYE 4 PITA
Cheesy: 4 MELT
cookie: 4 OREO
Crunchy: 3 BLT 4 TACO
Deli: 4 HERO 6 REUBEN

Diner: 3 BLT
filler: 4 TUNA 8 TUNAFISH
fish: 4 TUNA
Greek: 4 GYRO
Grilled: 6 PANINI
Hot: 4 MELT
initials: 3 BLT
Kind of: 4 PITA
Layered: 4 CLUB
Long: 3 SUB
man: 4 EARL
meat: 3 HAM
Mexican: 4 TACO
New Orleans: 5 POBOY
option: 5 WHEAT
　15 WHOLEWHEATBREAD
order: 5 ONRYE
Round: 4 OREO
shop: 4 DELI
spread: 4 MAYO
Submarine: 4 HERO 6 HOAGIE
Sweet: 4 OREO
Trendy: 4 WRAP
with sauerkraut: 6 REUBEN
**Sandy**
color: 4 ECRU 5 BEIGE
expanse: 6 DESERT
Golfer: 4 LYLE
hill: 4 DUNE
of baseball: 6 ALOMAR
owner: 5 ANNIE
particles: 4 GRIT
sound: 3 ARF 6 ARFARF
tract, to a Brit: 4 DENE
**Sane:** 8 ALLTHERE
**San Fernando Valley**
city: 6 ENCINO
**Sanford**
Actress: 6 ISABEL
or son: 7 JUNKMAN
**Sanford, John**
He was born: 8 REDDFOXX
**"Sanford and ___":** 3 SON
**"Sanford and Son"**
actor Foxx: 4 REDD
son: 6 LAMONT
**San Francisco**
and environs: 7 BAYAREA
County north of: 5 MARIN
footballer: 5 NINER
hill: 3 NOB
Late ~ columnist: 4 CAEN
neighbor: 7 OAKLAND
Onetime mayor of: 6 ALIOTO
paper: 8 EXAMINER
sight: 9 CABLECARS
tower: 4 COIT
transport: 8 CABLECAR
**San Francisco Bay**
City on: 7 ALAMEDA
　8 PALOALTO
**Sang:** 6 RATTED
**San Gabriel Valley**
city: 5 AZUSA
**Sang-froid:** 4 CALM COOL
　5 POISE

**San Giacomo**
Actress: 5 LAURA
**San Joaquin Valley**
city: 4 LODI 6 DELANO
FRESNO
**Sank**
a putt: 5 HOLED
into the sofa: 3 SAT
___ San Lucas (Baja resort):
4 CABO
**San Luis ___, California:**
6 OBISPO
**San Marino**
cash: 4 LIRE
surrounder: 5 ITALY
**San ___ Obispo, California:**
4 LUIS
**San Quentin**
room: 4 CELL
**San Rafael**
county: 5 MARIN
**Sans**
company: 5 ALONE
ice: 4 NEAT
Opposite of: 4 AVEC
purpose: 4 IDLY
sense: 5 INANE
**Sans ___ (carefree):** 5 SOUCI
**San Simeon**
builder: 6 HEARST
**Sanskrit**
word for color: 4 RAGA
**Sans-___ type:** 5 SERIF
**Santa**
California: 3 ANA
delivery: 3 TOY
helper: 3 ELF
helpers: 5 ELVES
image creator: 4 NAST
landing spot: 4 ROOF
7 ROOFTOP
Letter to: 8 WISHLIST
Like ~ cheeks: 4 ROSY
Like ~ helpers: 5 ELFIN
mail: 5 LISTS
mo.: 3 DEC
pole: 5 NORTH
reindeer: 5 COMET CUPID
VIXEN 6 DANCER
DASHER DONNER
7 BLITZEN PRANCER
reindeer team: 5 OCTAD
reminder: 4 LIST
sackful: 4 TOYS
season: 4 YULE
Sidewalk: 4 TEMP
soiler: 4 SOOT
sound: 4 HOHO
sounds: 3 HOS
They track: 5 NORAD
transport: 4 SLED
**Santa ___**
(California): 3 ANA 4 CRUZ
ROSA 5 CLARA MARIA
(hot winds): 4 ANAS
(racetrack): 5 ANITA

**Santa Anita**
doings: 5 RACES
**Santa Anita Racetrack**
site: 7 ARCADIA
**Santa Anna**
target: 5 ALAMO
**"Santa Baby"**
singer: 4 KITT
**Santa Barbara**
Resort east of: 4 OJAI
**Santa Claus**
artist: 4 NAST
feature: 5 BEARD
**Santa Fe**
and others: 3 RRS
neighbor: 4 TAOS
**Santa Fe Trail**
town: 4 TAOS
**Santana**
hit: 8 EVILWAYS
9 OYECOMOVA
**"___ santé!":** 6 AVOTRE
**___ Sant'Gria (wine):** 4 YAGO
**Santha Rama ___**
Author: 3 RAU
**Santiago**
backdrop: 5 ANDES
charger: 4 TORO
land: 5 CHILE
**Sanyo**
rival: 3 RCA 4 AIWA SONY
**São ___:** 5 PAULO
**São ___ (Cape Verde island):**
5 TIAGO
**São Miguel**
islands: 6 AZORES
**Saône**
City on the: 4 LYON 5 LYONS
**São Paulo**
Part of: 5 TILDE
**Sap:** 5 CHUMP DRAIN ERODE
6 WEAKEN 8 ENERVATE
Play for a: 3 USE
source: 5 MAPLE
sucker: 5 APHID
**Saperstein**
of basketball: 3 ABE
**___ sapiens:** 4 HOMO
**Sapphire**
Birthstone after: 4 OPAL
mo.: 4 SEPT
**Sappho:** 4 POET
home: 6 LESBOS
Muse of: 5 ERATO
poem: 3 ODE
**Sapporo**
sash: 3 OBI
sport: 4 SUMO
**Sap-sucking**
genus: 5 APHIS
**Sara**
Actress: 3 MIA
in the market: 3 LEE
Poet: 8 TEASDALE
**Saragossa**
river: 4 EBRO

**Sarah**
Son of: 5 ISAAC
**Sarajevo**
locale: 6 BOSNIA
**Saran:** 4 WRAP
**Sarandon**
Actress: 5 SUSAN
**Saratoga Springs:** 3 SPA
**Sarcasm**
Subtle: 5 IRONY
**Sarcastic:** 4 ACID 5 SNIDE
6 IRONIC
response: 4 IBET
syllables: 4 HAHA
**Sarcophagus:** 4 TOMB
**Sardine**
holder: 3 TIN
relative: 7 HERRING
**Sardonic:** 3 WRY
smile: 5 SNEER
**Sarducci, Father ___:** 5 GUIDO
**Sargasso:** 3 SEA
plant: 7 SEAWEED
swimmer: 3 EEL
**Sarge:** 3 NCO 6 NONCOM
pooch: 4 OTTO
superior: 5 LOOIE
**Sargents**
Where ~ hang: 4 TATE
**Sari**
wearer: 4 RANI
**___ Sark:** 5 CUTTY
**Sarnoff**
org.: 3 RCA
**Saroyan**
title character: 4 ARAM
**___ Sarto, Andrea**
Artist: 3 DEL
**Sartre**
Info: French cue
article: 3 LES
being: 4 ETRE
novel: 6 NAUSEA
play: 6 NOEXIT
sea: 3 MER
Soul, to: 3 AME
**SAS**
listing (abbr.): 3 ETA
**SASE:** 3 ENC 4 ENCL
enclosures (abbr.): 3 MSS
Part of: 3 ENV 4 SELF
**Sash**
Kimono: 3 OBI
**Sasha**
Skater: 5 COHEN
**Sashimi**
fare: 3 EEL
Like: 3 RAW
**Sask.**
neighbor: 3 ALB 4 ALTA NDAK
**Saskatchewan**
capital: 6 REGINA
native: 4 CREE
**Sasquatch**
cousin: 4 YETI
**Sass:** 3 LIP 5 CHEEK

Lots of: 5 ESSES
**Sassafras**
Struggle with: 4 LISP
**Sassoon**
Hair maven: 5 VIDAL
**Sassy:** 4 PERT 5 FRESH
one: 4 SNIP
**Sastre**
Supermodel: 4 INES
**Sat:** 5 POSED
around: 5 IDLED
in a cask: 4 AGED
tight: 5 BIDED
**SAT:** 5 BOARD
company: 3 ETS
relative: 3 GRE
section: 4 MATH 6 VERBAL
taker need: 6 PENCIL
takers: 3 SRS
**Satan:** 7 EVILONE
Like: 4 EVIL
work: 4 EVIL
**Satanic:** 4 EVIL
moniker: 7 EVILONE
**"Satanic Verses"**
author: 7 RUSHDIE
**Satchel**
of baseball: 5 PAIGE
**Satchmo**
instrument: 7 TRUMPET
Sound like: 4 RASP
style: 4 JAZZ
**Satellite:** 4 MOON
Communications: 4 ECHO
7 TELSTAR
Data path to a: 6 UPLINK
First man-made: 7 SPUTNIK
French ~ launcher: 6 ARIANE
of Jupiter: 4 LEDA 6 EUROPA
of Saturn: 4 RHEA 5 DIONE
TITAN
path: 5 ORBIT
transmission: 4 FEED
Weather: 4 ESSA 5 TIROS
**Satellite-tracking**
program: 5 NORAD
**Satiate:** 4 CLOY FILL
**Satie**
Composer: 4 ERIK
**Satinlike:** 5 SILKY
**Satire**
magazine: 3 MAD
Voltaire: 7 CANDIDE
**Satirical**
cartoonist: 4 ARNO
essay: 4 SKIT
newspaper, with "The":
5 ONION
**Satirist**
Freberg: 4 STAN
Mort: 4 SAHL
Sahl: 4 MORT
**Satirize:** 7 LAMPOON
**Satisfaction:** 7 REDRESS
Exact ~ for: 6 AVENGE
Focus on: 11 AIMTOPLEASE

Show: 5 GLOAT
Sound of: 3 AAH
Sounds of: 3 AHS 4 AAHS
Ultimate: 9 LASTLAUGH
**Satisfactorily**
Performed: 5 DIDOK
**Satisfactory**
Be: 11 FILLTHEBILL
**Satisfied:** 3 MET
sigh: 3 AAH
sighs: 3 AHS
**Satisfy:** 4 MEET SUIT 5 SLAKE
6 PLEASE
a debt: 5 REPAY
fully: 4 SATE
the munchies: 4 NOSH
**Satori**
Pursuit of: 3 ZEN
**Saturate:** 3 SOP 4 SOAK
5 IMBUE STEEP
**Saturated:** 3 WET
substances: 4 FATS
**"Saturday Night Fever"**
group: 7 BEEGEES
music: 5 DISCO
**"Saturday Night Live"**
announcer: 5 PARDO
piece: 4 SKIT
producer Michaels: 5 LORNE
regular Cheri: 5 OTERI
regular Gasteyer: 3 ANA
**Saturn:** 3 CAR GOD 4 AUTO
5 DEITY
compact: 3 ION
features: 5 RINGS
model: 3 ION VUE
Moon of: 4 RHEA 5 DIONE
TITAN
neighbor: 6 URANUS
vehicle: 3 UFO
Wife of: 3 OPS
**Saturnalia:** 4 ORGY
**Saturnine:** 4 DOUR GLUM
**Satyr:** 4 LECH
Look like a: 4 LEER
stare: 4 LEER
~, in part: 4 GOAT
**Sauce**
Basil: 5 PESTO
Béarnaise ~ herb:
8 TARRAGON
brand: 4 RAGU 5 PREGO
Falafel: 6 TAHINI
Floury: 4 ROUX
Garlicky: 5 AIOLI
Green: 5 PESTO
herb: 5 BASIL
Highly seasoned: 8 RAVIGOTE
Hot: 5 SALSA 7 TABASCO
Italian: 5 PESTO
Kind of: 3 SOY
Off the: 5 SOBER
Pasta ~ maker: 4 RAGU
Salty: 3 SOY
source: 3 SOY
Spicy: 5 SALSA

Steak: 4 AONE
style: 5 BARBQ
Tend the: 4 STIR
thickener: 4 ROUX
with fish: 6 TARTAR
**Saucer**
crew: 3 ETS
Flying: 3 UFO
person: 5 ALIEN
**Sauciness:** 4 SASS
**Saucy:** 4 PERT
sort: 4 SNIP
**Saud**
Brother of: 6 FAISAL
___ Saud: 3 IBN
**Saudi:** 4 ARAB
citizen: 4 ARAB
city: 6 MEDINA
king: 4 FAHD 6 FAISAL
neighbor: 5 OMANI
royal name: 4 FAHD
**Saudi ___:** 6 ARABIA
**Saudi Arabia**
capital: 6 RIYADH
Gulf between ~ and Egypt:
5 AQABA
neighbor: 4 IRAQ OMAN
5 QATAR YEMEN
region: 4 ASIR
**Sauerkraut**
Sandwich with: 6 REUBEN
**Sault ___ Marie:** 3 STE
**Sauna**
attire: 5 TOWEL
Like a: 6 STEAMY
siding: 5 CEDAR
site: 3 SPA
**Saunders**
Jazzman: 4 MERL
**Saunter:** 5 AMBLE MOSEY
**Sausage:** 5 WURST
Deli: 6 SALAMI
Polish: 8 KIELBASA
skin: 6 CASING
Spicy: 6 SALAMI
unit: 4 LINK
**Sausalito**
county: 5 MARIN
**Sauté:** 3 FRY
**Sautéed**
Battered and ~ in butter:
8 MEUNIERE
dish: 4 HASH
shrimp dish: 6 SCAMPI
**Savage:** 5 BEAST BRUTE
CRUEL FERAL
6 FIERCE
on TV: 4 FRED
**Savalas**
Actor: 5 TELLY
**Savalas, Telly**
Like: 4 BALD
role: 5 KOJAK
**Savannah**
summer hrs.: 3 EDT
___ Savant, Marilyn: 3 VOS

**Save:** 3 BUT 6 EXCEPT
RESCUE 8 SALTAWAY
Partner of: 6 SCRIMP
**Saved:** 9 LAIDASIDE
It may be: 4 FACE
on dinner: 5 ATEIN
up: 9 INRESERVE
**"Save Me"**
singer Mann: 5 AIMEE
**"Save me ___"** (movie request):
5 ASEAT
**Saver**
Day: 4 HERO
Life: 4 HERO
option: 3 IRA
Shoe: 4 TREE
**Saves**
on postage: 8 PRESORTS
**"Saving Private ___":** 4 RYAN
**"Saving Private Ryan"**
actor Matt: 5 DAMON
craft: 3 LST
event: 4 DDAY
**Savings:** 7 NESTEGG
acct. earning: 3 INT
bond abbr.: 3 SER
plan: 3 IRA
Some ~ accts.: 3 CDS 4 IRAS
**Savior:** 4 HERO
**Savoie**
Summer in: 3 ETE
**Savoir-faire:** 4 TACT
**Savor:** 5 TASTE
**Savory**
jelly: 5 ASPIC
smell: 5 AROMA
**Savoy ___:** 4 ALPS
**Savvy:** 3 HEP HIP 4 KNOW
5 SMART 6 SMARTS
about: 4 ONTO
**"Savvy?":** 3 SEE 5 GETME
**Saw:** 4 EYED TOOL 5 ADAGE
DATED MAXIM 6 ESPIED
7 NOTICED
10 LAIDEYESON
eye to eye: 6 AGREED
logs: 5 SNORE
red: 4 OWED
suffix: 3 YER
the sights: 6 TOURED
things: 5 TEETH
through: 6 XRAYED
with the grain: 3 RIP
wood: 5 SNORE
**Sawbones:** 3 DOC 6 MEDICO
org.: 3 AMA
**Sawbuck:** 3 TEN 6 TENNER
7 TENSPOT
fraction: 3 ONE
Half a: 3 FIN 4 FIVE
**Sawbucks**
100 ~: 4 ONEG
Bill worth 10: 5 CNOTE
**"... ___ saw Elba":** 4 EREI
**Sawing**
logs: 6 ASLEEP

**Saw-toothed:** 7 SERRATE
formation: 6 SIERRA
**Sawtooth Mountains**
state: 5 IDAHO
**Sawyer**
Journalist: 5 DIANE
pal Huck: 4 FINN
**Sawyer, Tom**
creator: 5 TWAIN
Half brother of: 3 SID
Love of: 5 BECKY
Polly, to: 4 AUNT
**Sax**
How a ~ sounds: 5 REEDY
Kind of: 4 ALTO 5 TENOR
object: 4 REED
player G: 5 KENNY
player Getz: 4 STAN
**Saxon**
prefix: 5 ANGLO
**Saxony**
river: 3 EMS
seaport: 5 EMDEN
**Saxophone:** 4 REED
Kind of: 4 ALTO
part: 4 REED
**Saxophonist**
Popular: 6 KENNYG
~ Getz: 4 STAN
~ Stan: 4 GETZ
~ Zoot: 4 SIMS
**Say:** 5 STATE UTTER
"#@$%!": 4 CUSS 5 SWEAR
again: 4 ECHO 6 REPEAT
9 REITERATE
by heart: 6 RECITE
for sure: 4 AVER
further: 3 ADD
"hey" to: 5 GREET
it isn't so: 4 DENY
it's so: 4 AVER AVOW
Just ~ no: 4 DENY
Never ~ this: 3 DIE
no to: 4 VETO
over: 7 ITERATE
Sad to: 4 ALAS
so: 4 AVER
suddenly: 5 BLURT
yes: 5 AGREE 6 ACCEDE
You can ~ that again!:
6 MANTRA
**"Say ___":** 3 AAH 4 WHEN
**"Say ___?":** 4 WHAT
**Say ___ (deny):** 4 NOTO
**"Say cheese!":** 5 SMILE
**Sayer**
Nae: 4 SCOT
Nay: 4 ANTI
Neigh: 5 HORSE
**Sayers**
detective Lord Peter:
6 WIMSEY
**Say Hey Kid, The:** 4 MAYS
**Saying:** 5 ADAGE
Familiar: 6 OLDSAW
Old: 3 SAW 5 ADAGE

One who sees what you're:
9 LIPREADER
Say without: 5 IMPLY
Trite: 7 BROMIDE
Witty: 3 MOT
**Sayings**
Collected: 3 ANA
**"Say it isn't so!":** 4 OHNO
**"Say it ___ so!":** 4 AINT ISNT
**"___ say more?":** 5 NEEDI
**"Say no more!":** 4 STOP
**"Sayonara"**
~ Oscar-winner Miyoshi:
5 UMEKI
**___ Says (child's game):**
5 SIMON
**Say-so**
On the ~ of: 5 ASPER
**"Say what?":** 3 HUH 5 AGAIN
**"Say You, Say Me"**
singer Lionel: 6 RICHIE
**Scacchi**
Actress: 5 GRETA
**Scads:** 4 ALOT ATON LOTS
SLEW 5 AHEAP
**Scaggs**
Singer: 3 BOZ
**Scalawag:** 5 ROGUE 6 RASCAL
**Scale:** 4 GOUP 5 CLIMB
6 ASCEND
amts.: 3 LBS WTS
button: 4 TARE
divs.: 3 LBS
down: 4 PARE
Fifth on the: 3 SOL
It uses a higher: 5 INSET
Kind of: 4 MOHS 6 POSTAL
model: 6 MOCKUP
notes: 3 FAS LAS MIS RES
TIS
On a grand: 4 EPIC
pair: 4 DORE REMI MIFA
FASO SOLA LATI TIDO
Postal ~ unit: 5 OUNCE
Put on a: 4 RATE
start: 4 DORE 6 DOREMI
Steps on a: 5 TONES
Temperature: 7 CELSIUS
Top of a: 3 TEN
**___ scale:** 4 MOHS
**Scaleless**
fish: 3 EEL
**Scales**
Celestial: 5 LIBRA
They have: 4 MAPS
up: 5 LIBRA
**Scalia**
Justice: 7 ANTONIN
**Scallion:** 4 LEEK
**Scallop:** 8 SEASHELL
Kind of: 3 BAY
**Scaloppine**
Make: 5 SAUTE
~, usually: 4 VEAL
**Scalp**
tickets: 6 RESELL

**Scaly**
squeezer: 3 BOA
**Scam:** 3 CON 4 TAKE
Three-card: 5 MONTE
victims: 4 SAPS
**Scammed:** 3 HAD 4 TOOK
**Scamp:** 5 ROGUE 6 RASCAL
URCHIN
**Scampered:** 3 RAN
**Scampi**
ingredient: 5 PRAWN
6 GARLIC SHRIMP
**Scan:** 4 READ
Brain: 3 EEG
Hosp.: 3 MRI
**Scand.**
land: 3 NOR 4 NORW SWED
**Scandal**
1920s ~: 10 TEAPOTDOME
1950s recording: 6 PAYOLA
1980s ~: 8 IRANGATE
2002 ~: 5 ENRON
fodder: 4 DIRT
sheet: 3 RAG
suffix: 3 OLA 4 GATE
**Scandalous**
gossip: 4 DIRT
~ 1980s initials: 3 PTL
**Scandinavia**
From: 6 NORDIC
native: 4 LAPP
**Scandinavian:** 4 DANE
5 NORSE
capital: 4 OSLO
Certain: 4 LAPP
coin word: 5 NORGE
epic: 4 EDDA
god: 4 ODIN
king: 4 OLAV
native: 4 SAMI
royal name: 4 OLAF
rug: 3 RYA
saint: 4 OLAF
toast: 5 SKOAL
**Scanned**
Something: 3 UPC 7 BARCODE
**Scanner**
Cat: 3 VET
Diagnostic: 3 MRI
Kind of: 7 OPTICAL
Text: 3 OCR
**Scant:** 4 MERE 6 MEAGER
**Scanty:** 4 SLIM 6 SPARSE
~, to a Brit: 6 MEAGRE
**Scar**
Car: 4 DENT
**Scarab:** 6 BEETLE
**Scarce:** 4 RARE
Hardly: 4 RIFE
**Scarcely:** 3 ILL
scruffy: 5 KEMPT
**Scarcity:** 6 DEARTH
**Scare**
It may ~ you: 3 BOO
off: 5 DETER SPOOK
word: 3 BOO

**Scarecrow**
lack: 5 BRAIN
stuffing: 5 STRAW
**Scared**
Visibly: 5 ASHEN
**Scarf:** 3 BOA
Broad: 5 ASCOT
down: 3 EAT 6 INHALE
Feathery: 3 BOA
Furry: 5 STOLE
Spanish: 8 MANTILLA
Wide: 5 STOLE
**Scarface**
portrayer: 6 PACINO
~ Al: 6 CAPONE
**Scarfed**
down: 3 ATE 5 EATEN
**Scarlatti**
Typical ~ work:
10 OPERASERIA
**Scarlet:** 3 RED
bird: 7 TANAGER
It may be: 7 TANAGER
letter: 6 STIGMA
The ~ letter: 4 REDA
**"Scarlet Letter, The"**
woman: 6 HESTER PRYNNE
**Scarlett**
admirer: 5 RHETT
Daughter of: 4 ELLA
First love of: 6 ASHLEY
home: 4 TARA
love: 5 RHETT
11 RHETTBUTLER
of Tara: 5 OHARA
**Scarpia**
killer: 5 TOSCA
**Scary:** 5 EERIE
snake: 3 ASP
street: 3 ELM
**"Scary Movie"**
actress Cheri: 5 OTERI
actress Faris: 4 ANNA
**Scat**
First name in: 4 ELLA
**"Scat, cat!":** 4 SHOO
**Scatter:** 5 STREW
seed: 3 SOW
~ Anita: 4 ODAY
~ Fitzgerald: 4 ELLA
**Scatterbrain:** 4 DITZ
**Scatterbrained:** 5 DITSY
**Scattered:** 6 SPARSE STREWN
~, as seed: 4 SOWN
**Scavenger**
Beach: 4 GULL
Laughing: 5 HYENA
Serengeti: 5 HYENA
**Scene:** 4 VIEW 5 VENUE
At the: 6 ONSITE
Chaotic: 3 ZOO
Chase ~ noise: 5 SIREN
Completed: 4 WRAP
Crime ~ find: 5 PRINT
Crowd ~ actor: 5 EXTRA
Made a: 5 ACTED

Made the: 4 CAME
Mob: 4 RIOT
Nativity: 6 CRECHE
One who makes a: 6 ARTIST
On the: 7 PRESENT
Stable: 6 CRECHE
Temptation: 4 EDEN
**Scene-ending**
cry: 3 CUT
**Scenery**
chewer: 3 HAM 6 EMOTER
Chew the: 5 EMOTE
Part of the: 8 SETPIECE
Stage: 3 SET
**Scenes**
Behind the: 8 OFFSTAGE
**Scenic**
view: 5 VISTA
**Scent:** 4 ODOR 5 AROMA
SMELL
Animal: 4 MUSK
Cleanser: 4 PINE
finder: 4 NOSE
Polish: 5 LEMON
Sachet: 5 LILAC
**Scented**
bag: 6 SACHET
**"Scent of a Woman"**
~ Oscar winner: 6 PACINO
**Scepter:** 3 ROD
Crown and: 7 REGALIA
mate: 3 ORB
**Sch.**
Grade: 4 ELEM
group: 3 PTA
High ~ exam: 4 PSAT
Kind of: 4 ELEM
Prep: 4 ACAD
subject: 3 ENG SCI
supporter: 3 PTA
Technical: 4 INST
Theological: 3 SEM
**Scharnhorst**
admiral: 4 SPEE
**Sched.**
Business: 3 HRS
entry: 3 ETA ETD 4 APPT
Not yet on the: 3 TBA
**Schedule:** 5 SLATE
abbr.: 3 ARR ETA ETD TBA
again: 7 RESLATE
Behind: 4 LATE
contingency: 8 RAINDATE
Meeting: 6 AGENDA
On the: 6 SLATED 7 SLOTTED
opening: 4 SLOT
Part of a flexible:
8 OPENDATE
Space on the: 4 SLOT
TV ~ abbr.: 3 TBA
Was behind: 7 RANLATE
**Schedule A**
Use: 7 ITEMIZE
**Schedule C**
figure: 7 NETLOSS
**Scheduled:** 3 DUE

**Schedules**
  Org. with many: 3 IRS
  They work with: 4 CPAS
**Scheherazade**
  offering: 4 TALE
**Scheme:** 4 PLAN PLOT
    5 CAPER SETUP
  Get-rich-quick: 5 HEIST
  Pyramid: 4 SCAM
  Rhyme: 4 ABAB ABBA
  Sneaky: 4 RUSE
  Support a: 4 ABET
**Schemer**
  "Othello": 4 IAGO
**Schemers:** 5 CABAL
**Scheming**
  bunch: 5 CABAL
**Schenectady**
  river: 6 MOHAWK
**Schiaparelli**
  Designer: 4 ELSA
**Schiele**
  Painter: 4 EGON
**Schifrin**
  Composer: 4 LALO
**Schiller**
  poem used by Beethoven:
    8 ODETOJOY
**Schindler**
  Herr: 5 OSKAR
  portrayer: 6 NEESON
**"Schindler's List"**
  Oskar portrayer in: 4 LIAM
  Schindler of: 5 OSKAR
  star: 6 NEESON
**Schipa**
  Tenor: 4 TITO
**Schiphol Airport**
  Carrier to: 3 KLM
**Schisgal, Murray**
  1964 ~ play: 3 LUV
**Schism:** 4 RIFT SECT
**Schlemiel:** 3 SAP 4 JERK
    5 LOSER
**Schlep:** 3 LUG 4 DRAG HAUL
    TOTE
**Schlepper:** 5 TOTER
**Schlesinger**
  1995 ~ film:
    15 COLDCOMFORTFARM
**Schlessinger, Dr.**
  of radio: 5 LAURA
**Schlimazel:** 5 LOSER
**Schmaltz:** 3 GOO
**Schmear**
  The whole: 3 ALL
**Schmidt**
  of Novell: 4 ERIC
  successor: 4 KOHL
**Schmooze:** 3 GAB
**Schnabel**
  Pianist: 5 ARTUR
**Schnauzer**
  of whodunits: 4 ASTA
**Schneider**
  Actress: 4 ROMY

**Schnoz:** 4 BEAK NOSE
    5 SNOUT 7 SMELLER
**Schnozz**
  suffix: 3 OLA
**Schnozzola:** 4 BEAK NOSE
    5 SNOOT SNOUT
  of vaudeville: 7 DURANTE
**Schoenberg**
  Like ~ music: 6 ATONAL
**Scholar:** 6 SAVANT
  goal: 3 PHD
  Jewish: 5 RABBI
  Legal: 6 JURIST
  Legal ~ deg.: 3 LLD
  Old Jewish: 4 ABBA
  sphere: 8 ACADEMIA
  Venerable: 4 BEDE
  volume: 4 TOME
**Scholarly**
  In a ~ fashion: 9 ERUDITELY
**Scholarship**
  criterion: 4 NEED
  founder: 6 RHODES
  Rhodes with a: 5 CECIL
**Scholastic**
  stereotype: 4 NERD
**Scholasticism**
  founder: 6 ANSELM
**Scholl, Dr.**
  product: 6 INSOLE
**Schon**
  Guitarist: 4 NEAL
**School:** 5 TEACH 7 EDUCATE
  007 ~: 4 ETON
  adviser: 4 DEAN
  assignment: 5 ESSAY
    6 REPORT
  Avoid summer: 4 PASS
  basics: 3 RRR
  book: 4 TEXT
  break: 6 RECESS
  British secondary ~ exam:
    6 ALEVEL OLEVEL
  cheer: 4 YELL 6 GOTEAM
  course part: 4 UNIT
  dance: 3 HOP
  division: 5 GRADE
  Eli: 4 YALE
  furniture: 5 DESKS
  Future: 4 ROE
  gp.: 3 PTA
  grad: 4 ALUM
  Grammar ~ trio: 3 RRR
  group: 4 FISH
  house: 4 FRAT
  Kick out of: 5 EXPEL
  Kind of: 3 MED 4 ELEM PREP
  Martial arts: 4 DOJO
  Med. ~ subj.: 4 ANAT
  Mil.: 4 ACAD
  Military: 7 ACADEMY
  mo.: 3 OCT 4 SEPT
  Night ~ subj.: 3 ESL
  of Buddhism: 3 ZEN
  of the future: 3 ROE
  of thought: 3 ISM

  of whales: 3 GAM POD
  Old ~ figure: 4 MARM
  org.: 3 NEA PTA 4 ROTC
  period: 4 TERM
  prayer fighter: 5 OHAIR
  Preppy: 4 ETON
  Reason to cancel: 4 SNOW
  session: 4 TERM
  setting: 3 SEA
  since 1440: 4 ETON
  Southern: 4 BAMA
  sports org.: 4 NCAA
  Start for: 3 PRE
  Stick in: 5 RULER
  subj.: 3 ENG SCI 4 HIST
    MATH
  tie: 3 PTA
  tool: 5 RULER
  transport: 3 BUS
  website ender: 3 EDU
  zone sign: 3 SLO 4 SLOW
  ~, in French: 5 ECOLE LYCEE
  ___ School: 6 ASHCAN
**Schoolbook:** 4 TEXT
**Schoolboy:** 3 LAD
  collar: 4 ETON
**"Schoolboy"**
  of baseball: 4 ROWE
**Schooling**
  Get: 5 LEARN
**Schoolmarm**
  do: 3 BUN
  Like a: 4 PRIM
  rod: 6 FERULE
**Schoolmaster**
  rod: 6 FERULE
**Schoolroom**
  fixture: 4 DESK
**Schoolteacher**
  Old-time: 4 MARM
**Schoolwork**
  Do: 5 TEACH
  Some: 4 ROTE
**Schoolyard**
  challenge: 4 DARE
    6 MAKEME
  game: 3 TAG
  retort: 4 AMSO
**Schooner**
  filler: 3 ALE 4 BEER
  part: 4 MAST
**Schott**
  Former baseball owner:
    5 MARGE
**Schroeder**
  Former Rep.: 8 PATRICIA
  toy: 5 PIANO
**Schubert**
  chamber work:
    15 THETROUTQUINTET
  song: 4 LIED 8 AVEMARIA
**Schuss:** 3 SKI
**Schusser**
  lift: 4 TBAR
  locale: 5 SLOPE
  ___ Schwarz (toy store): 3 FAO

**Schwarzenegger**
1988 ~ film: 7 REDHEAT
1996 ~ film: 6 ERASER
Gov.: 6 ARNOLD
middle name: 5 ALOIS
role: 5 CONAN
**Schwarzkopf, Gen.**
Like: 3 RET 4 RETD
**Sci.**
Biological: 4 ANAT
course: 4 ANAT
Earth: 4 ECOL GEOL
Environmental: 4 ECOL
of the body: 4 ANAT
of the stars: 4 ASTR
Social: 4 ECON
Structural: 4 ANAT
___ sci (coll. course): 4 POLI
**Science**
Bygone ~ magazine: 4 OMNI
class: 3 LAB
Occult: 6 CABALA
of light: 6 OPTICS
PBS ~ series: 4 NOVA
prefix: 4 OMNI
show: 4 NOVA
Winemaking: 8 OENOLOGY
~, informally: 5 OLOGY
**Science fiction**
award: 4 HUGO
magazine: 6 ANALOG
**"Science Guy"**
~ Bill: 3 NYE
**Sciences**
Partner of: 4 ARTS
**Scientific**
org.: 4 INST
**Scientist**
employer: 4 NASA
hangout: 3 LAB
**Scientology**
founder Hubbard: 4 LRON
**Sci-fi:** 5 GENRE
1956 ~ film:
15 FORBIDDENPLANET
1958 ~ menace: 4 BLOB
1960s ~ series:
11 LOSTINSPACE
1966 ~ film:
15 FANTASTICVOYAGE
1979 ~ film: 5 ALIEN
1982 ~ film: 4 TRON
1986 ~ film: 6 ALIENS
Asimov of: 5 ISAAC
author Ellison: 6 HARLAN
author Frederik: 4 POHL
author Isaac: 6 ASIMOV
author Lester ___ Rey: 3 DEL
author ___ Scott Card:
5 ORSON
Change, in ~ films: 5 MORPH
creatures: 3 ETS
Disney ~ film: 4 TRON
Doctor of: 3 WHO
drug: 3 TEK
Earth, in: 5 TERRA

Earthling, in: 6 TERRAN
escape vehicle: 3 POD
figure: 5 DROID ROBOT
film extra: 5 ALIEN
film extras: 3 ETS
Flying monster of: 5 RODAN
Furry ~ critter: 4 EWOK
Herbert ~ opus: 4 DUNE
killer: 3 RAY
mag of old: 4 OMNI
Miniature ~ vehicle: 3 POD
play: 3 RUR
princess: 4 LEIA
sage: 4 YODA
Serling of: 3 ROD
Shatner ~ novel: 6 TEKWAR
sighting: 3 UFO
Solo of: 3 HAN
subjects: 3 ETS
vehicle: 3 UFO
visitor: 5 ALIEN
visitors: 3 ETS
weapon: 3 RAY 5 LASER
6 PHASER RAYGUN
**Scimitar:** 5 SABER
**Scintilla:** 4 ATOM IOTA
5 SHRED TRACE
**Scion:** 4 HEIR
Woody: 4 ARLO
**Scissor**
sound: 4 SNIP
**Scissorhands**
portrayer: 4 DEPP
**Scissors**
Cut with: 4 SNIP
Place for: 4 ETUI
sound: 4 SNIP
**Scoff:** 4 JEER 5 SNEER
at: 4 GIBE 6 DERIDE
Skeptic's: 4 IBET
**Scoffer**
cry: 3 HAH
**Scold:** 3 NAG 4 LASH RATE
5 CHIDE 6 BERATE
SNAPAT YELLAT
7 BAWLOUT CHEWOUT
REAMOUT
severely: 4 FLAY
**Scolder**
sound: 3 TSK
**Scolding:** 6 EARFUL
8 HARANGUE
sound: 3 TSK
syllable: 3 TUT
word: 3 BAD
**Sconce**
spot: 4 WALL
**Scooby-___ (cartoon dog):**
3 DOO
**Scooby-Doo**
Pal of: 5 VELMA
**Scoop:** 4 DOPE INFO
holder: 4 CONE
Inside: 4 DIRT DOPE
Soup: 5 LADLE
**Scoot:** 3 HIE RUN 4 TEAR

**Scooter:** 5 MOPED
**Scope:** 3 KEN 4 AREA ROOM
5 AMBIT RANGE
Grand in: 4 EPIC
prefix: 4 ENDO PERI TELE
6 STETHO
Use a: 3 AIM
**Scopes**
advocate: 6 DARROW
The ~ ___: 5 TRIAL
**Scopes Trial**
org.: 4 ACLU
**Scorch:** 4 BURN CHAR SEAR
5 SCALD SINGE
**Score:** 6 TWENTY
after deuce: 4 ADIN 5 ADOUT
Arc on a: 4 SLUR
before 15: 4 LOVE
Best golf: 6 FEWEST
Court: 4 ADIN
direction: 8 STACCATO
Early game: 6 ONEONE
Even: 3 TIE
Free throw: 3 ONE
Got a perfect ~ on: 4 ACED
Great: 3 TEN
Half: 3 TEN
Hockey: 4 GOAL
in horseshoes: 6 LEANER
Like a 4-4: 4 TIED
Line ~ letters: 3 RHE
mark: 3 TIE 4 REST SLUR
Miner: 3 ORE
Ore: 4 VEIN
Part of a: 4 ARIA
Settle the: 7 GETEVEN
Slowly, on a: 5 LENTO
Soccer: 4 GOAL
Standard: 3 PAR
Tennis: 4 ADIN 5 ADOUT
Together, on a: 4 ADUE
unit: 4 NOTE
Worst: 4 ZERO
**Scoreboard**
info: 3 PTS 4 DOWN OUTS
RUNS
initials: 3 RHE
**Scorecard**
bunt: 3 SAC
line: 3 PAR
**Score-producing**
stat: 3 RBI
**Scorer**
of 1,281 career goals: 4 PELE
**Scores:** 4 ALOT LOTS MANY
5 DEBTS
Apiece, in: 3 ALL
Lively, in: 7 ANIMATO
NFL: 3 TDS
Smooth, in: 6 LEGATO
**Scorn:** 7 DISDAIN SNEERAT
Show: 5 SNEER
**Scornful**
cry: 3 BAH
look: 5 SNEER
**Scorpio:** 4 SIGN

star: 7 ANTARES
**Scorpion:** 8 ARACHNID
attack: 5 STING
product: 5 VENOM
**Scorpius**
Neighbor of: 3 ARA
Star in: 7 ANTARES
**Scot:** 4 GAEL
Ancient: 4 PICT
Certain: 10 ABERDONIAN
group: 4 CLAN
Not, to a: 3 NAE
topper: 3 TAM
**Scotch**
and Drambuie drink:
9 RUSTYNAIL
concoction: 6 ROBROY
datum: 3 AGE
ingredient: 4 MALT
partner: 4 SODA
servings: 5 SHOTS
**Scotch ___:** 4 PINE TAPE
**___ Scotia:** 4 NOVA
**Scotland**
Island of: 4 IONA
John of: 3 IAN
Longest river of: 3 TAY
Since, in: 4 SYNE
Tiny, in: 3 SMA
**Scotland yard:** 5 METRE
**Scotland Yard**
div.: 3 CID
title (abbr.): 4 INSP
**Scots**
toss it: 5 CABER
trill: 4 BURR
~ Gaelic: 4 ERSE
**"Scots Wha ___" (Burns poem):**
3 HAE
**Scott**
Author: 5 ODELL TUROW
Cartoonist: 5 ADAMS
Historic: 4 DRED
in 1857 news: 4 DRED
Newbery-winning: 5 ODELL
novel: 6 ROBROY 7 IVANHOE
of TV: 4 BAIO
role: 6 PATTON
**Scott, Dred**
~ Chief Justice: 5 TANEY
**Scott, Paul**
series: 13 THERAJQUARTET
**___ Scott Decision:** 4 DRED
**Scott-Heron**
Novelist: 3 GIL
**Scottie:** 7 TERRIER
White House: 4 FALA
**Scottish**
bay: 4 LOCH
cap: 3 TAM
cattle breed: 5 ANGUS
child: 5 BAIRN
county: 6 ARGYLL
dagger: 4 DIRK
dish: 6 HAGGIS
explorer John: 3 RAE

family: 4 CLAN
girl: 4 LASS
highlander: 4 GAEL
hillside: 4 BRAE
inlet: 4 LOCH 5 FIRTH
inventor James: 4 WATT
isle: 4 IONA
lake: 4 LOCH NESS
landholder: 5 LAIRD
loch: 4 NESS
monster: 6 NESSIE
no: 3 NAE
Old ~ landholder: 5 THANE
philosopher David: 4 HUME
quickbread: 5 SCONE
refusal: 3 NAE
river: 3 TAY
topper: 3 TAM
uncle: 3 EME
~ Gaelic: 4 ERSE
~ "Gee!": 3 OCH
~ John: 3 IAN
**Scotto:** 4 DIVA
solo: 4 ARIA
Soprano: 6 RENATA
**Scoundrel:** 3 CAD CUR RAT
4 HEEL 5 KNAVE ROGUE
6 RASCAL 8 DIRTYDOG
SCALAWAG
Dirty rotten: 5 CREEP
Stevenson: 4 HYDE
**Scour:** 4 COMB
**Scourge:** 4 BANE
African: 5 EBOLA 6 TSETSE
**"Scourge of God, The":**
6 ATTILA
**Scout**
creation: 4 KNOT
discovery: 6 TALENT
doing: 4 DEED
group: 3 DEN 5 TROOP
High: 5 EAGLE
job: 5 RECON
Kind of: 6 TALENT
leader: 5 TONTO
master: 5 TONTO
Memorable: 9 KITCARSON
Novice: 10 TENDERFOOT
outing: 4 HIKE 5 RECON
rank: 5 EAGLE
recitation: 4 OATH
skill: 8 EAGLEEYE
Tonto, to: 5 RIDER
Top: 5 EAGLE
unit: 3 DEN 5 TROOP
~, at times: 5 HIKER
**Scow:** 4 BOAT
**Scowcroft**
Bush adviser: 5 BRENT
**Scowl:** 5 GLARE
**Scrabble**
Low-count ~ quintet: 5 AEIOU
piece: 4 TILE
Valuable ~ tile: 3 ESS
~ 3-pointers: 3 EMS
~ 10-pointer: 3 ZEE 5 ZTILE

**Scram**
suffix: 3 OLA
**"Scram!":** 3 GIT 4 SHOO
5 LEAVE 6 BEATIT
GETOUT 7 GETLOST
**Scrambled**
It may be: 3 EGG
**Scrammed:** 3 RAN
**Scrap:** 3 ORT RAG ROW 4 SPAT
5 SETTO 6 TAGEND
7 REMNANT
Food: 3 ORT
paper: 5 SHRED
Random: 6 TAGEND
Stable: 3 OAT
Table: 3 ORT
**Scrapbook**
Affix in a: 5 PASTE
pastings: 3 ANA
**Scrape:** 3 ROW 4 BIND MESS
RASP SKIN 6 ABRADE
8 ABRASION
aftermath: 4 SCAB
Bow and: 4 FAWN
More than: 4 GASH
(out): 3 EKE
site: 4 KNEE
together: 5 RAISE 6 EKEOUT
**Scratch:** 3 MAR 4 CLAW
5 MOOLA 6 MOOLAH
a dele: 4 STET
From: 4 ANEW 6 AFRESH
Needing to: 5 ITCHY
Old: 5 SATAN 7 EVILONE
(out): 3 EKE
Start from: 4 REDO
target: 4 ITCH
the surface: 3 MAR
up: 3 MAR
**Scratcher**
Cat: 4 CLAW
**Scrawny:** 4 BONY THIN
5 GAUNT WEEDY
one: 5 SCRAG
**Scream:** 4 RIOT 6 SHRIEK
Comics: 3 EEK
Type of: 6 PRIMAL
**"Scream"**
actress Campbell: 4 NEVE
director Craven: 3 WES
**"Scream 2"**
actor Omar: 4 EPPS
**Screamers:**
15 BANNERHEADLINES
Some: 4 FANS
**Screecher:** 3 OWL
**Screen:** 4 HIDE SIFT VEIL
award: 5 OSCAR
Big ~ name: 4 IMAX
dot: 5 PIXEL
image: 4 ICON
Kind of: 4 LINT 5 RADAR
letters: 5 EMAIL
Letters on a: 5 EMAIL
material: 4 MESH
PC: 3 CRT

pet: 4 ASTA
Put on the small: 3 AIR
Radar: 4 GRID
Radar ~ image: 4 BLIP
symbol: 4 ICON
TV ~ grid: 6 RASTER
**Screened:** 3 HID
**Screening**
device: 5 VCHIP
**Screenwriter**
1972 Oscar-winning ~: 4 PUZO
creation: 8 SCENARIO
~ Ephron: 4 NORA 5 DELIA
~ James: 4 AGEE
~ Robert: 5 TOWNE
**Screw**
Bar with two ~ threads:
    5 UBOLT
up: 3 ERR
**Screwball:** 3 NUT 4 LOON
    5 WACKO WACKY
    7 NUTCASE
**Screwdriver:** 4 TOOL
hue: 6 ORANGE
Part of a: 5 VODKA
place: 3 BAR
**"Screwtape Letters, The"**
writer: 7 CSLEWIS
**Scribble:** 3 JOT 4 NOTE
    6 DOODLE
**Scribe:** 6 PENMAN
Dead Sea Scrolls: 6 ESSENE
**Scrimp**
partner: 4 SAVE
**Scrimshaw**
medium: 5 IVORY
**Script**
Ignore the: 5 ADLIB
suffix: 3 URE
When the ~ demands:
    5 ONCUE
**Scriptural**
interpretation: 8 EXEGESIS
**Scripture**
Jewish: 5 TORAH
Of Hindu: 5 VEDIC
volume: 5 CODEX
**Scroll**
holder: 3 ARK
Holy: 5 TORAH
Scriptures: 5 CODEX
Synagogue: 4 TORA 5 TORAH
**Scrolls**
site: 7 DEADSEA
**Scrollwork**
shape: 3 ESS
**Scrooge:** 5 MISER
cry: 3 BAH
look: 5 SNEER
portrayer: 3 SIM
~, for short: 4 EBEN
**Scrounge**
(for): 4 GRUB
**Scrub:** 4 WASH 5 ABORT
    SCOUR 6 CANCEL
NASA: 4 NOGO 5 ABORT

nurse sites (abbr.): 3 ORS
**Scrubbed:** 4 NOGO
**Scruff:** 4 NAPE
**Scruffy**
Scarcely: 5 KEMPT
**Scruggs**
Banjoist: 4 EARL
instrument: 5 BANJO
partner: 5 FLATT
**Scrum**
game: 5 RUGBY
**Scrumptious:** 5 YUMMY
**Scruples**
Without: 6 AMORAL
**Scrutinize:** 3 EYE
~, with "over": 4 PORE
**Scrutiny:** 7 PERUSAL
**Scuba**
gear: 4 TANK 7 WETSUIT
**Scud**
downer (abbr.): 3 ABM
**Scuff:** 3 MAR
up: 3 MAR
**Scuffle:** 4 FRAY
More than a: 5 MELEE
**Scull:** 3 OAR
propeller: 3 OAR
Use your: 3 ROW
**Sculler**
need: 3 OAR
**Scully:** 5 AGENT
abbr.: 3 AGT
Agent: 4 DANA
Case for: 5 XFILE
employer: 3 FBI
Sportscaster: 3 VIN
**Sculpt:** 5 SHAPE 6 CHISEL
**Sculpted**
form: 5 TORSO
**Sculpting**
medium: 3 ICE 4 CLAY
**Sculptor**
Dadaist: 3 ARP
French: 5 RODIN
medium: 3 ICE
subject: 4 BUST 5 TORSO
~ Henry: 5 MOORE
~ Hesse: 3 EVA
~ Jean: 3 ARP
~ Nadelman: 4 ELIE
**Sculptors**
Family of: 7 PISANOS
**Sculpture**
alloy: 6 BRONZE
forms: 5 TORSI
Religious: 5 PIETA
subject: 5 TORSO
Type of: 7 RELIEVO
with fixed parts: 7 STABILE
**Scum**
Pond: 4 ALGA 5 ALGAE
**Scummy**
place: 4 POND
**Scurrier**
Little: 3 ANT
Slum: 3 RAT

**Scurrilous:** 6 RIBALD
**Scurry:** 3 HIE RUN
**Scut**
Critter with a: 4 HARE
**Scuttle:** 4 SINK
Coal: 3 HOD
filler: 4 COAL
**Scuttlebutt:** 4 DIRT INFO POOP
    5 RUMOR 7 HEARSAY
**Scuttler**
Ocean: 8 SANDCRAB
**Scythe**
handle: 5 SNATH
Use a: 4 REAP
**S. Dak.**
neighbor: 3 NEB
**SDS**
antithesis: 4 ROTC
target: 3 SSS
**Sea:** 5 BRINY OCEAN
Antarctic: 4 ROSS
Arm of the: 5 INLET
Back at: 3 AFT 6 ASTERN
bird: 3 ERN 4 ERNE GULL
cow: 7 MANATEE
creature: 5 OTTER
    7 ANEMONE
dog: 3 GOB TAR 4 SALT
duck: 5 EIDER
eagle: 3 ERN 4 ERNE
flier: 4 ERNE
god: 7 NEPTUNE
Go out to: 3 EBB
Go to: 4 SAIL
Greek: 6 AEGEAN
growth: 5 ALGAE
Inland: 4 ARAL
Killer at: 4 ORCA
Left at: 4 PORT 5 APORT
letters: 3 HMS USS
life: 5 ALGAE
Like a ~ lion: 5 EARED
monster: 3 ORC
nymph: 6 NEREID 7 OCEANID
Pair at: 4 OARS
palm: 4 KELP
phase: 4 TIDE
plea: 3 SOS
predator: 4 ORCA
Room at: 5 CABIN
salt: 3 TAR
She at: 4 SHIP
shell seller: 3 SHE
spots: 5 ISLES 6 ISLETS
suffix: 5 SCAPE
Support at: 4 MAST
swallow: 4 TERN
urchin food: 4 KELP
Where river meets: 7 ESTUARY
~, in French: 3 MER
~, in Spanish: 3 MAR
**Sea ___:** 5 OTTER
**___ Sea:** 4 ARAL
**Sea-___ Airport:** 3 TAC
**Seabees**
mil. branch: 6 USNAVY

motto: 5 CANDO
**Seabird:** 3 ERN 4 ERNE TERN
  Diving: 3 AUK 6 PETREL
  Predatory: 4 SKUA
  Tube-nosed: 6 PETREL
**Seaboard:** 5 COAST
**Sea-ear:** 7 ABALONE
**Seafarer:** 3 TAR 7 OLDSALT
**Seafood**
  choice: 4 CRAB SOLE
    7 LOBSTER
  delicacy: 3 ROE
  dish: 6 SCAMPI
  entrée: 4 SOLE 5 SCROD
    6 SALMON 8 SCALLOPS
    10 REDSNAPPER
    11 FILETOFSOLE
  lover: 3 ERN
**Seagal, Steven**
  1997 ~ movie:
    13 FIREDOWNBELOW
**Seagoing**
  (abbr.): 4 NAUT
  letters: 3 USS
  pronoun: 3 HER SHE
  sort: 3 TAR
**Seahawks**
  home: 7 SEATTLE
**Seal:** 4 SHUT 6 CACHET
  Baby: 3 PUP
  Eared: 5 OTARY
  hunter: 4 ORCA
  in the juices: 4 SEAR
  Kind of: 5 EARED 6 EASTER
  meal: 3 EEL
  Official: 6 SIGNET
  ring: 6 SIGNET
  Solomon's: 4 STAR
  Young: 3 PUP
**Sealant:** 3 TAR
**Sealed:** 4 SHUT 6 UNOPEN
  They may be: 4 LIPS
**Sealer**
  Carton: 4 TAPE
  Street: 3 TAR
  wax ingredient: 3 LAC
  Windowpane: 5 PUTTY
**Seals**
  Herd of: 3 POD
  Like: 7 AQUATIC
  Like some: 5 EARED
    7 EARLESS
  Male ~ have them:
    6 HAREMS
  singing partner: 6 CROFTS
**Sealskin**
  wearer: 5 ALEUT
**Sealy**
  rival: 5 SERTA
**Seam**
  content: 3 ORE
  Fix a: 3 SEW
  Garment: 4 DART
  Raised: 4 WELT
**Seaman:** 3 TAR 4 SALT
  assent: 3 AYE

**Seams**
  Burst at the: 4 TEEM
  Come apart at the: 4 FRAY
  They come out at the: 4 ORES
**Seamstress**
  fastener: 3 PIN
  ~ Betsy: 4 ROSS
**Seamy**
  stuff: 3 ORE
**Sean**
  Actor: 4 PENN 5 ASTIN
**Séance**
  board: 5 OUIJA
  phenomenon: 6 TRANCE
  sound: 3 RAP
**Sea of ___ (Black Sea arm):**
    4 AZOV
**"Sea of Love"**
  star: 6 PACINO
**Seaplane**
  part: 5 FLOAT
**Seaport**
  Adriatic: 4 BARI
  Alaskan: 4 NOME
  Algerian: 4 ORAN
  Brazilian: 5 BELEM NATAL
  Danish: 6 ODENSE
  French: 5 BREST
  German: 5 EMDEN
  Hawaiian: 4 HILO
  Indian: 6 MADRAS
  Irish: 6 TRALEE
  Israeli: 4 ACRE 5 HAIFA
  Italia: 6 NAPOLI
  Italian: 4 BARI 5 GENOA
    7 SALERNO
  Japanese: 4 KOBE
  Mediterranean: 4 GAZA
  New Jersey: 10 PERTHAMBOY
  Polish: 6 GDANSK
  Saxony: 5 EMDEN
  southeast of Roma: 6 NAPOLI
  south of Milan: 5 GENOA
  Ukrainian: 6 ODESSA
  Vietnamese: 6 DANANG
  Yemen: 4 ADEN
**Seaquake**
  aftermath: 7 TSUNAMI
**Search:** 5 QUEST
  a perp: 5 FRISK
  blindly: 5 GROPE
  engine result: 3 HIT
  for: 4 SEEK
  for food: 6 FORAGE
  for gold: 3 PAN
  for prey: 5 PROWL
  for the unknown:
    7 ALGEBRA
  for water: 5 DOWSE
  high and low: 5 SCOUR
  In ~ of: 5 AFTER
  (into): 5 DELVE
  party: 5 POSSE
  thoroughly: 4 COMB 5 SCOUR
**Searcher**
  need: 7 WARRANT

**Searle**
  Artist: 6 RONALD
**Sears**
  rival: 5 KMART
**Seascape**
  color: 4 AQUA
**"Seascape"**
  playwright: 5 ALBEE
**Seashell**
  Colorful: 6 TRITON
  seller: 3 SHE
**Seashore:** 5 COAST
**Season:** 3 AGE
  Allergy ~ sound: 5 ACHOO
  Christmas: 4 NOEL YULE
  French: 3 ETE
  Like monsoon: 5 RAINY
  opener: 3 MID PRE
  Rabbit: 6 EASTER
**Seasonal**
  air: 4 NOEL
  drink: 3 NOG
  employee: 3 ELF
  schedule abbr.: 3 EDT
  song: 4 NOEL 5 CAROL
  song end: 4 SYNE
  visitor: 5 SANTA
**Seasoned:** 4 AGED
  Highly ~ stew: 6 BURGOO
  one: 3 VET
  pro: 3 ACE
  sailor: 4 SALT
  stew: 6 RAGOUT
  vet: 6 OLDPRO
**Seasoning:** 5 SPICE
  Add: 4 SALT
  Chef: 4 HERB
  French: 3 SEL
  Get some: 3 AGE
  Goulash: 7 PAPRIKA
  Meat: 4 SAGE
  Soup: 5 THYME
  Spaghetti: 7 OREGANO
  Stuffing: 4 SAGE
**Seasons**
  Four: 4 YEAR
  Goddesses of the: 5 HORAE
**"Seasons, The":** 8 ORATORIO
**Seat:** 3 USH
  Airline ~ feature:
    7 ARMREST
  a jury: 7 IMPANEL
  Baby: 3 LAP
  Back ~ driver: 3 NAG
  Bar: 5 STOOL
  Bridge: 4 EAST WEST
    5 NORTH SOUTH
  Catbird: 4 NEST
  Child: 3 LAP
  choice: 5 AISLE
  Church: 3 PEW
  Cowboy: 6 SADDLE
  Deluxe: 3 BOX
  Elephant: 6 HOWDAH
  for two or more: 6 SETTEE
  Give a ~ to: 5 ELECT

Greet and: 5 SEEIN
holders: 3 INS
Judge: 4 BANC
Kind of: 3 BOX 5 AISLE
    6 SENATE
Left one's: 5 AROSE
Occupied, as a: 5 TAKEN
of Allen County: 4 IOLA
of County Kerry: 6 TRALEE
of Garfield County: 4 ENID
of Greene County: 5 XENIA
of Hawaii County: 4 HILO
of Jackson County: 4 EDNA
of Marion County: 5 OCALA
of Silver Bow County: 5 BUTTE
of Ward County: 5 MINOT
of Washoe County: 4 RENO
of White Pine County: 3 ELY
Provide a ~ for: 5 ELECT
Return to one's: 7 REELECT
Saloon: 5 STOOL
seeker: 3 POL
Simple: 5 STOOL
Soft: 4 SOFA 6 SETTEE
Sought a: 3 RAN
Sunday: 3 PEW
Tried to keep one's:
    5 RERAN
**Seater:** 5 USHER
**Seating**
Mass: 3 PEW
request: 5 AISLE
sect.: 4 ORCH
section: 4 TIER
Soft: 4 SOFA
Stadium: 10 GRANDSTAND
**SEATO**
Part of: 4 ASIA EAST
**Seattle**
ballplayer: 7 MARINER
City east of: 8 BELLEVUE
forecast: 4 RAIN
Gp. protested in: 3 WTO
hoopster: 5 SONIC
sound: 5 PUGET
team: 6 SONICS
**Seawater:** 5 BRINE
Like: 6 SALINE
part: 4 NACL
Treat, as: 6 DESALT
**Seaweed:** 4 ALGA KELP
    5 ALGAE
extract: 4 AGAR
product: 4 AGAR
**Seaweed-wrapped**
fare: 5 SUSHI
**SeaWorld**
attraction: 4 ORCA 5 SHAMU
performer: 4 SEAL
**Sebastian**
Explorer: 5 CABOT
Runner: 3 COE
**Sec:** 4 JIFF 5 TRICE
**SEC**
eleven: 4 BAMA
**Secant:** 5 RATIO

**Seceder**
of 1967: 6 BIAFRA
**Secessionist**
of '67: 7 BIAFRAN
**Secessionists**
~, initially: 3 CSA
**Sechs**
Half of: 4 DREI
**Seckel:** 4 PEAR
kin: 4 BOSC
**Secluded**
corner: 4 NOOK
road: 5 BYWAY
spot: 4 GLEN
valley: 4 DELL GLEN
**Second:** 4 ECHO
(abbr.): 4 ASST
afterthought: 3 PPS
Begin a ~ hitch: 4 REUP
busiest U.S. airport:
    5 OHARE
chance:
    15 ANEWLEASEONLIFE
chance for a student:
    6 RETEST
Come in: 4 LOSE 5 PLACE
coming: 6 ENCORE
degree: 3 MBA
Do a ~ draft: 6 RETYPE
Dove into: 4 SLID
Fairy tale ~ word: 4 UPON
family of the 1990s: 5 GORES
Finish: 5 PLACE
First and: 5 GEARS
    8 ORDINALS
Got to ~ base: 5 STOLE
half of an album: 5 SIDEB
Have ~ thoughts: 3 RUE
    8 REASSESS
in a series: 4 BETA
in command: 4 VEEP
man on the moon: 6 ALDRIN
name in inventions: 4 ALVA
name in rock: 4 ARON
of Adam: 4 ABEL
of all: 3 EVE
of Eric: 4 LEIF
of Eve: 4 ABEL
of Frank: 3 AVA
of Henry VIII: 4 ANNE
of Jackie: 3 ARI
of two: 6 LATTER
person: 3 EVE YOU
prefix: 4 NANO
president: 5 ADAMS
section: 5 PARTB
sequel tag: 3 III
shot: 6 RETAKE
showing: 5 RERUN
sight: 3 ESP
sinner: 4 ADAM
son: 4 ABEL
start: 4 NANO
Take: 5 STEAL
Take a ~ look at: 6 REREAD
to none: 4 BEST

**Second ___ (tops):** 6 TONONE
**Second Amendment**
org.: 3 NRA
word: 4 ARMS
**Secondary:** 5 MINOR
British ~ school exam:
    6 OLEVEL
**Second-century**
anatomist: 5 GALEN
**"Second Coming, The"**
poet: 5 YEATS
**Second-generation**
Japanese: 5 NISEI
**Second-guessing:**
    9 HINDSIGHT
**Secondhand:** 4 USED
deal: 6 RESALE
**Second-in-command:**
    6 DEPUTY
**Second-rate:** 6 LESSER
**Seconds:** 4 MORE
Factory ~ (abbr.): 4 IRRS
**Second-stringer:** 3 SUB
    5 SCRUB
**Second-year**
student: 4 SOPH
**Secrecy**
Breach of: 4 LEAK
Sign of: 4 VEIL
**Secret:** 5 CODED INNER
    6 ARCANE CLOSET
agent: 3 SPY
author: 11 GHOSTWRITER
Blonde's: 3 DYE
Chef's: 4 HERB
Chinese ~ society: 4 TONG
competitor: 3 BAN 5 ARRID
doctrine: 6 CABALA
East German ~ police: 5 STASI
ending: 3 IVE
exit: 8 TRAPDOOR
gp.: 3 NSA
language: 4 CODE
Make: 6 ENCODE
meeting: 5 TRYST
Member of a ~ order:
    5 MASON
motive: 5 ANGLE
No longer: 4 SEEN
offering: 6 ROLLON
Redhead's: 5 HENNA
rendezvous: 5 TRYST
retreat: 4 LAIR
society: 5 MAFIA
society secret: 6 RITUAL
Soviet ~ police: 3 KGB
Spill a: 4 BLAB
store: 5 CACHE STASH
stuff: 6 ARCANA
supply: 5 CACHE STASH
target: 4 ODOR
Well-kept ~, to some: 3 AGE
writing: 4 CODE
**Secretarial**
position: 4 DESK
**Secretary:** 4 DESK 5 FILER

Oscar Madison's: 5 MYRNA
Perry's: 5 DELLA
~ Powell: 5 COLIN
**Secretary-General**
First U.N.: 3 LIE
**Secretary of Defense**
Nixon: 5 LAIRD
**Secretary of State**
1960s ~: 4 RUSK
1980s ~: 4 HAIG
Carter's: 5 VANCE
Clinton's: 5 COHEN
Eisenhower's: 6 DULLES
FDR's: 4 HULL
Kennedy's: 4 RUSK
Lincoln's: 6 SEWARD
Reagan's: 4 HAIG
Truman's: 7 ACHESON
~ Vance: 5 CYRUS
**Secretary of the Interior**
Kennedy's: 5 UDALL
**Secretary of War**
First: 4 KNOX
WWII: 7 STIMSON
**Secreted:** 3 HID
**Secreter**
Musk: 5 OTTER
**Secretion**
Resinous: 3 LAC
Squid: 3 INK
**Secretly:** 7 ONTHEQT
tie the knot: 5 ELOPE
watch: 5 SPYON
**"Secret of ___, The":** 4 NIMH
**Secrets:** 6 ARCANA
**Secs.**
60 ~: 3 MIN
**Sect**
Buddhist: 3 ZEN
Iowa religious: 5 AMANA
Lancaster-area: 5 AMISH
leader: 3 TRI
Meditative: 3 ZEN
Mennonite: 5 AMISH
Muslim: 5 SUNNI
Plain-living: 5 AMISH
Punjab ~ member: 4 SIKH
Religious: 4 CULT
suffix: 5 ARIAN
**Sect.**
Bookstore: 4 BIOG
Seating: 4 ORCH
Yearbook: 3 SRS
**Sectarian**
Jamaican: 5 RASTA
**Section:** 4 AREA PART UNIT
ZONE 5 PIECE
Big ~ in a dictionary: 3 ESS
Grass: 3 SOD
of Queens: 7 ASTORIA
Seating: 4 TIER
section: 4 ACRE
Semi: 3 CAB
**Sector:** 4 AREA ZONE
boundary: 3 ARC
**Secular:** 4 LAIC 6 LAICAL

**Secure:** 3 GET ICE TIE 4 MOOR
SAFE SHUT 5 CLAMP
6 ANCHOR ATTACH
ATTAIN FASTEN
OBTAIN
a ship: 4 MOOR
a victory: 3 ICE
tightly: 5 TRUSS
with lines: 4 MOOR
**Secured:**
15 UNDERLOCKANDKEY
**Securities**
Like some: 3 OTC
trader, for short: 3 ARB
**Security**
agreement: 4 LIEN
breach: 4 LEAK
Company with famous: 4 ELAL
concern: 4 LEAK
Form of: 4 LIEN
Govt.: 5 TBILL TNOTE
holder: 6 BAILEE
Loan: 4 LIEN
pmt.: 3 DEP
problem: 4 LEAK
Professor's: 6 TENURE
system part: 6 SENSOR
U.S.: 5 TNOTE
**Security Council**
Former ~ member: 4 USSR
member: 3 USA
vote: 3 NON
**Secy.:** 4 ASST
**Sedaka**
Singer: 4 NEIL
**Sedan:** 3 CAR 4 AUTO
Nissan: 6 ALTIMA
Oldsmobile: 5 ALERO
sweetie: 4 AMIE
**Sedate:** 5 STAID
**Sedation**
Under: 5 DOPED
**Sedative:** 6 OPIATE
**Seder**
serving: 5 MATZO
**Sedgwick**
Actress: 4 KYRA
Warhol pal: 4 EDIE
**Sedgy**
stretch: 5 MARSH
**Sediment:** 4 LEES SILT
5 DREGS
Wine: 4 LEES
**Sedimentary**
rock beds: 6 STRATA
**Sedona**
automaker: 3 KIA
**Seducer**
of Tess: 4 ALEC
**"Seduction of Joe Tynan, The"**
star: 4 ALDA 8 ALANALDA
**"Seduction of the Minotaur"**
author: 3 NIN
**Seductive:** 4 SEXY
**Seductress:** 5 SIREN
**See:** 4 DATE SPOT

Able to ~ through: 4 ONTO
A psychic may ~ it: 4 AURA
As much as one cares to:
6 EYEFUL
Cause to ~ red: 6 ENRAGE
Does more than: 6 RAISES
eye to eye: 4 JIBE 5 AGREE
Fail to: 4 MISS
For all to: 5 OVERT 6 OPENLY
It helps you ~ plays: 5 SLOMO
It may make you ~ things:
3 LSD
Just like you ~ it: 4 ASIS
One way to: 8 EYETOEYE
Plain to: 5 OVERT
red: 3 OWE 4 FUME RAGE
STOP 5 STEAM 6 GETMAD
socially: 4 DATE
stars: 4 GAZE
the old gang: 5 REUNE
the sights: 4 TOUR
to: 4 TEND
You can ~ right through them:
6 LENSES
**See-___:** 4 THRU
**"See?":** 5 GETIT
**"See!":** 10 ITOLDYOUSO
**"See ___" (news program):**
5 ITNOW
**"___ see!":** 3 SOI
**"___ See Clearly Now":** 4 ICAN
**Seed:** 5 SPORE
Caffeinated: 4 KOLA
case: 4 ARIL
Citrus: 3 PIP
coat: 4 ARIL 5 TESTA
covering: 4 ARIL
Feed: 3 OAT
Go to: 3 ROT
Plant more: 5 RESOW
Prickly ~ cover: 3 BUR
Pumpkin: 6 PEPITA
Rudimentary: 5 OVULE
Scatter: 3 SOW
shell: 4 HULL
source: 6 SESAME
Spread: 3 SOW
**Seed-bearing**
organ: 6 PISTIL
**Seeded**
It may be: 3 RYE
**Seedless**
plant: 4 FERN
raisin: 7 SULTANA
**Seeds:** 3 OVA
Apple ~ site: 4 CORE
**Seed-to-be:** 5 OVULE
**Seedy**
joint: 4 DIVE
**Seeger**
Folk singer: 4 PETE
**"See if ___!":** 5 ICARE
**Seeing**
Not ~ eye to eye: 6 ATODDS
red: 3 MAD 4 SORE 5 IRATE
6 INDEBT

Respond to ~ red: 4 STOP
things: 4 EYES
"___ seeing you": 5 ILLBE
"___ see it ...": 3 ASI
Seek
answers: 3 ASK
approval from: 6 PLAYTO
change: 3 BEG
damages: 3 SUE
Didn't go: 3 HID
help from: 6 PRAYTO
TURNTO
info: 3 ASK
the hand of: 3 WOO
What some scouts: 6 TALENT
Seeker
Asylum: 6 EMIGRE
Evaded the: 3 HID
Food: 7 FORAGER
Office: 3 POL
Pleasure: 8 HEDONIST
Pole: 5 PEARY
Solitude: 5 LONER
Vein: 5 MINER
Seeking: 5 AFTER
Seeming: 5 QUASI
Seemingly
boundless: 4 VAST
forever: 3 EON 4 AEON AGES
EONS
limitless: 4 VAST
"___ seems": 4 SOIT
Seen
enough: 5 HADIT
Hardly: 4 RARE
Remains to be: 5 RUINS
Seldom: 4 RARE
"See no ___ ...": 4 EVIL
Seep: 4 OOZE
Seepage
at sea: 5 BILGE
Seer: 6 ORACLE
card: 5 TAROT
deck: 5 TAROT
reading matter: 9 TEALEAVES
sign: 4 OMEN
Spanish: 3 OJO
suffix: 3 ESS
Sees
One who ~ what you mean:
9 LIPREADER
Seesaw: 6 TEETER
requirement: 3 TWO
sitter of rhyme: 4 ESAU
"See Spot run"
book: 6 READER
Seethe: 4 BOIL
Seething: 5 ABOIL
See-through: 5 CLEAR SHEER
item: 5 LENS PANE
wrap: 5 SARAN
"See ya!": 3 BYE 4 CIAO TATA
5 ADIEU ADIOS IMOFF
LATER
Sega
rival: 3 NES

user: 5 GAMER
Segal
Author: 5 ERICH
Segment: 4 PART 5 PIECE
___ segno: 3 DAL
Sego lily
state: 4 UTAH
Segovia
Guitarist: 6 ANDRES
Segue: 6 LEADIN
Communiqué: 4 ASTO
Sei
halved: 3 TRE
Seiji
Conductor: 5 OZAWA
Seine
City on the: 5 PARIS ROUEN
contents: 3 EAU
feeder: 4 OISE 5 MARNE
port: 5 ROUEN
sight: 3 ILE
Summer on the: 3 ETE
tributary: 4 OISE 5 MARNE
"Seinfeld"
A Costanza on: 7 ESTELLE
Any ~ episode, now: 5 RERUN
character Elaine: 5 BENES
character Kramer: 5 COSMO
postal worker: 6 NEWMAN
role: 6 ELAINE GEORGE
KRAMER
uncle: 3 LEO
Seinfeldesque: 3 WRY
Seis
halved: 4 TRES
Seismic
event: 5 QUAKE 6 TREMOR
Seize: 3 NAB 4 GRAB TAKE
5 USURP WREST
6 SNATCH
firmly: 4 GRIP
~, à la Caesar: 5 CARPE
Seized
the opportunity: 7 MADEHAY
vehicle: 4 REPO
Seko, Mobutu ___: 4 SESE
Selassie
of Ethiopia: 5 HAILE
Selassie, Haile
follower: 5 RASTA
~, originally: 9 RASTAFARI
Seldom: 6 RARELY
seen: 4 RARE
Select: 3 OPT TAP 4 CULL PICK
5 ELITE 6 CHOOSE
at random: 4 DRAW
for jury duty: 7 EMPANEL
group: 5 ALIST ELITE
~, with "for": 3 OPT
Selected: 5 CHOSE 6 CHOSEN
Selection
Auto: 5 SEDAN
Brunch: 5 CREPE 6 OMELET
Caucus: 8 DELEGATE
Dairy: 4 OLEO
Golf: 4 IRON

Make a: 3 OPT
Pub: 3 ALE
Selective: 6 CHOOSY
Selena
Music style of: 6 TEJANO
Selene
realm: 4 MOON
Sister of: 3 EOS
Selenic: 5 LUNAR
Seles
of tennis: 6 MONICA
rival: 4 GRAF
Self: 3 EGO
expression: 3 IAM
Inner: 5 ANIMA
prefix: 3 AUT
starter: 3 ESS HER 4 AUTO
Self-___: 7 RELIANT
Self-assurance
Spirited: 4 ELAN
Self-assured: 6 POISED
Self-centered
sort: 6 EGOIST
Self-conceit: 3 EGO
Self-confidence: 5 POISE
6 APLOMB
Destroy the ~ of: 5 ABASH
Self-congratulatory: 4 SMUG
Self-conscious
giggle: 6 TITTER
Self-contradictory
thing: 7 PARADOX
Self-defense: 4 PLEA
method: 4 JUDO 6 KARATE
Self-employed
people: 3 EDS
professional: 9 FREELANCE
Self-esteem: 3 EGO
Self-evident
It's: 6 TRUISM
truth: 5 AXIOM
Self-government
Local: 8 HOMERULE
Self-guided
tour: 7 EGOTRIP
Self-identifying
response: 5 ITSME
Self-image: 3 EGO
Self-importance: 3 EGO
Self-important
pace: 5 STRUT
Self-indulgent
act: 7 EGOTRIP
Selfish
Harbor ~ motives:
15 HAVEANAXTOGRIND
sort: 5 TAKER
14 DOGINTHEMANGER
Selfishness: 6 EGOISM
Self-mover
rental: 5 UHAUL
Self-proclaimed
"greatest": 3 ALI
Self-produced
CD: 4 DEMO
Self-question: 7 DOIDARE

**Self-regard:** 3 EGO
**Self-righteous**
  sort: 4 PRIG
**Self-satisfied:** 4 SMUG
  15 PROUDASAPEACOCK
**Self-server:** 6 EGOIST
**Self-styled**
  superior: 4 SNOB
**Self-titled**
  1982 ~ album: 6 ARETHA
**Sell:** 4 VEND 6 MARKET
  RETAIL
  at an inflated price: 5 SCALP
  Buy and: 5 TRADE 6 DEALIN
  for: 4 COST 5 FETCH
  (for): 3 REP
  off: 6 DIVEST
  out: 5 RATON 6 BETRAY
**Sellecca**
  Actress: 6 CONNIE
  Spouse of: 4 TESH
**Selleck**
  Actor: 3 TOM
  film of 1992: 10 MRBASEBALL
  ~ TV role: 6 MAGNUM
**Seller**
  Birthright: 4 ESAU
  caveat: 4 ASIS
  Insurance: 5 AGENT
  Property: 7 ALIENOR
  Seashell: 3 SHE
  Ticket: 5 AGENT
**Sellers**
  Actor: 5 PETER
  role: 6 ORIENT
  Tip: 5 TOUTS
**Selling**
  liquor: 3 WET
  point: 5 ASSET KIOSK STORE
  well: 3 HOT
**Sellout:** 3 HIT 5 SMASH
  sign: 3 SRO
**"___ sells":** 3 SEX
**"___ sells seashells ...":** 3 SHE
**Selma**
  ~, to Bart: 4 AUNT
**Seltzer**
  starter: 4 ALKA
**Selves:** 4 EGOS
**Sem.**
  study: 3 REL
**Semana**
  part: 3 DIA
**Semaphore**
  equipment: 4 FLAG
**Semblance:** 5 GHOST
**Semester:** 4 TERM
  ender: 4 EXAM
**Semesters**
  Two: 4 YEAR
**Semi:** 3 RIG
  compartment: 3 CAB
  conductor: 4 CBER
  engine: 6 DIESEL
  part: 3 CAB
  support: 4 AXLE

**Semiaquatic**
  salamander: 3 EFT 4 NEWT
**Semicircle:** 3 ARC
**Semicircular**
  molding: 4 TORI
  recess: 4 APSE
**Semi-colon:** 3 DOT
**Semiconductor:** 5 DIODE
**Semidiurnal**
  occurrence: 4 TIDE
**Semiformal**
  outfit: 3 TUX
**Semimonthly**
  tide: 4 NEAP
**Seminary**
  deg.: 3 STB
  subj.: 3 REL
**Seminole**
  leader: 7 OSCEOLA
**Seminoles**
  sch.: 3 FSU
**Semiprecious**
  stone: 5 AGATE
**Semiquaver:** 4 NOTE
**"Semiramide"**
  composer: 7 ROSSINI
**Semiramis**
  realm: 7 ASSYRIA
**Semirural:** 7 EXURBAN
**Semisolid:** 3 GEL
**Semisweet**
  wine: 8 SAUTERNE
**Semite**
  Ancient: 6 ESSENE
**Semitic**
  deity: 4 BAAL
  Demon of ~ lore: 6 LILITH
**"Semi-Tough"**
  actress Lotte: 5 LENYA
**"Semper fidelis":** 5 MOTTO
**"Semper Fidelis"**
  composer: 5 SOUSA
**"___ semper tyrannis":** 3 SIC
**Sen**
  division: 3 RIN
**Senate**
  accusation: 4 ETTU
  attire: 4 TOGA
  declaration: 3 YEA
  employee: 4 PAGE
  event: 6 DEBATE
  Former ~ leader: 4 LOTT
  gofer: 4 PAGE
  Hatch in the: 5 ORRIN
  Lott of the: 5 TRENT
  position: 4 SEAT
  shower: 5 CSPAN
  Speak in the: 5 ORATE
  spot: 4 SEAT
  Words heard in the: 4 ETTU
**Senator**
  California:
    12 BARBARABOXER
  Connecticut: 4 DODD
  Delaware: 4 ROTH 5 BIDEN
  Former ~ Sam: 4 NUNN

  Former Georgia: 4 NUNN
  Former Indiana: 4 BAYH
  Former New York: 6 DAMATO
  Former Rhode Island: 4 PELL
  Former Tennessee: 5 ESTES
  Former Virginia: 4 ROBB
  Hawaiian: 6 INOUYE
  Indiana: 5 LUGAR
  in space: 4 GARN 5 GLENN
  Massachusetts: 5 KERRY
  Mississippi: 4 LOTT
    9 TRENTLOTT
  Nevada: 4 REID
  Six years, to a: 4 TERM
  Vermont: 5 LEAHY
  Watergate: 5 ERVIN
  ~ Bayh: 4 EVAN
  ~ Feinstein: 6 DIANNE
  ~ Hatch: 5 ORRIN
  ~ Kefauver: 5 ESTES
  ~ Kennedy: 3 TED
  ~ Lott: 5 TRENT
  ~ Sam: 5 ERVIN
  ~ Specter: 5 ARLEN
  ~ Thurmond: 5 STROM
  ~ Trent: 4 LOTT
**Senators**
  home: 6 OTTAWA
  org.: 3 NHL
**Send:** 4 SHIP WIRE 5 ELATE
  RADIO REMIT
  again: 6 REPOST RESHIP
  another way: 7 REROUTE
  a telegram: 4 WIRE 6 TAPOUT
  back: 4 ECHO 6 REMAND
  by FedEx: 4 RUSH
  elsewhere: 5 REFER
  forth: 4 EMIT
  headlong: 4 TRIP
  in: 5 REMIT
  off: 4 EMIT SHIP
  on: 5 REFER
  on an impulse: 5 EMAIL
  out: 4 EMIT
  packing: 3 AXE CAN 4 FIRE
  OUST
  payment: 5 REMIT
  sprawling: 4 TRIP
  (to): 5 REFER
  to a mainframe: 6 UPLOAD
  via phone: 3 FAX
**"Send help!":** 3 SOS
**"Send in the Clowns"**
  First word of: 4 ISNT
**Seneca**
  Student of: 4 NERO
**Senegal**
  Capital of: 5 DAKAR
  suffix: 3 ESE
**Senescence:** 6 OLDAGE
**Senile**
  one: 6 DOTARD
**Senior:** 4 YEAR 5 ELDER
  7 OLDSTER
  Coll. ~ test: 3 GRE
  event: 4 PROM

Former: 4 ALUM
in French names: 4 PERE
Junior, to: 8 NAMESAKE
Knievel: 4 EVEL
member: 4 DEAN 5 DOYEN
moment: 4 PROM
org.: 4 AARP
Organization for ~ travelers:
   11 ELDERHOSTEL
**Seniors:** 5 CLASS
exam: 3 SAT
gp.: 4 AARP
**Sennett**
character: 3 KOP
**Señor**
Answer to a: 4 SISI
feature: 5 TILDE
of old TV: 6 WENCES
suffix: 3 ITA
**Señora**
That: 3 ESA
**Señorita:** 6 LATINA
need: 5 TILDE
**Sensation:** 4 VIBE 5 ECLAT
Excited: 6 TINGLE
It's a: 4 ITCH
Lingering: 10 AFTERTASTE
Sudden: 4 STAB
**Sensational:** 5 LURID
Something: 7 SCANDAL
   SHOCKER
**Sense:** 4 FEEL 6 DETECT
6th ~: 3 ESP
Common: 5 SIGHT SMELL
   TASTE 6 SMARTS
Kind of: 5 HORSE
Make: 5 ADDUP
Making no: 5 INANE
Musical: 3 EAR
of completeness: 7 CLOSURE
of humor: 3 WIT
of manliness: 8 MACHISMO
of self: 3 EGO
of taste: 6 PALATE
Sixth: 3 ESP
Uncommon: 3 ESP
___ sense: 3 INA
**"Sense and Sensibility"**
actress Thompson: 4 EMMA
heroine: 6 ELINOR
**Sensed:** 4 FELT
**Senseless:** 5 INANE
Knock: 4 STUN
**Senses**
The human: 6 PENTAD
**Sensible:** 4 SANE
More: 5 SANER WISER
**Sensitive**
spot: 4 SORE
subject: 3 AGE
topic: 8 SORESPOT
Very: 4 KEEN
**Sensitivity:** 3 EAR 4 TACT
**Sensor**
forerunner: 4 ATRA
Oral: 8 TASTEBUD

**Sensory**
stimulus: 4 ODOR
___-sen, Sun: 3 YAT
**Sent**
back (abbr.): 4 RETD
to the mat: 3 KOD
with a click: 7 EMAILED
**Sentence:** 4 DOOM
Analyze a: 5 PARSE
Complete a: 9 SERVETIME
ending abbr.: 3 ETC
Kind of: 5 RUNON
Long: 4 LIFE
modifier: 7 REMORSE
One with a shortened:
   7 PAROLEE
part (abbr.): 4 PRED
Reduce a: 4 EDIT
Serve a: 6 DOTIME
shortener: 6 PAROLE
subject: 4 NOUN
Word preceding a: 6 GUILTY
**Sentences**
Life: 4 OBIT
**Sentient:** 5 AWARE
**Sentiment**
Public: 5 ETHOS
Sampler:
   13 HOMESWEETHOME
Valentine: 4 LOVE
**Sentimental:** 8 DEWYEYED
drivel: 3 GOO
Get: 4 GUSH
one: 6 MOONER SOFTIE
Overly: 4 ICKY 5 SAPPY
song: 6 BALLAD
**Sentimentality**
Contrived: 7 TREACLE
Excessive: 8 SCHMALTZ
**Sentinel**
site: 10 WATCHTOWER
**Sentry**
cry: 4 HALT
Dangerous answer to a: 3 FOE
duty: 5 WATCH
Obey the: 4 HALT
**Seoul**
Citizen of: 6 KOREAN
soldier: 3 ROK
Where ~ is: 5 KOREA
**SEP:** 3 IRA
**Separate:** 5 ALONE SPLIT
   6 DETACH UNGLUE
   7 SPLITUP
flour: 4 SIFT
Go ~ ways: 4 PART
**Separated:** 5 APART
**Separately**
Not: 5 ASONE
When sold: 4 EACH
**"Separate Tables"**
star: 5 NIVEN
**Separation**
Adjective relating to the ~ of
   church and state:
   9 TAXEXEMPT

**Sephia**
maker: 3 KIA
**Sept.**
follower: 3 OCT
**September**
birthstone: 8 SAPPHIRE
bloom: 5 ASTER
Many a ~ birth: 5 VIRGO
The first of: 3 ESS
Third of: 3 PEE
**"September ___" (Neil Diamond**
   **hit):** 4 MORN
**Septembre**
It ends in: 3 ETE
**Septennial**
problem: 4 ITCH
**Septet**
One of a fairy tale: 3 DOC
Salty: 4 SEAS
**Sepulcher:** 4 TOMB 6 ENTOMB
**Sequel**
of 1847: 4 OMOO
Sci-fi: 6 ALIENS
tag: 3 III
Words used in a: 5 SONOF
**Sequence:** 6 SERIES
Alphabet: 3 ABC BCD CDE *etc.*
Boxer: 6 ONETWO
End of a: 3 ZEE
of amino acids:
   11 GENETICCODE
Position in a: 4 SLOT
Scale: 4 DORE REMI MIFA
   FASO SOLA LATI TIDO
that may end in "y": 5 AEIOU
**Sequential**
evidence: 10 PAPERTRAIL
**Sequentially:** 6 INTURN
**Sequester:** 7 ISOLATE
**Sequins:** 8 SPANGLES
**Seraglio:** 5 HAREM
chamber: 3 ODA
**Seraph**
circle: 4 HALO
French: 4 ANGE
**"___ Sera, Sera":** 3 QUE
**Serb:** 4 SLAV
neighbor: 5 CROAT
**Serbian**
city: 3 NIS
**Sere:** 4 ARID
**Serenade:** 6 SINGTO
the moon: 4 HOWL
**Serenaded:** 6 SANGTO
**Serendip**
Land once known as:
   8 SRILANKA
**"Serendipities"**
author: 3 ECO
**Serene:** 4 CALM
**Serengeti**
family: 5 PRIDE
grazer: 3 GNU 5 ELAND
   6 IMPALA
scavenger: 5 HYENA
sound: 4 ROAR

trek: 6 SAFARI
**Serenity:** 4 EASE 5 PEACE
    QUIET
**Serf:** 4 ESNE 5 HELOT
**Sergeant:** 3 NCO
  command: 6 ATEASE FALLIN
  in a 1941 film: 4 YORK
  Obey the drill:
    15 SNAPTOATTENTION
  TV: 5 BILKO
  What to call a: 3 SIR
**Sergeant Friday**
  request: 5 FACTS
**Sergeant Preston**
  horse: 3 REX
**Sergeant York:** 5 ALVIN
**"Sergeant York"**
  star: 6 COOPER
**Sergio**
  Director: 5 LEONE
**Se Ri**
  of the LPGA: 3 PAK
**Serial**
  for lunch: 4 SOAP
  Partner of ~ number and rank:
    4 NAME
  segment: 7 EPISODE
**Serials**
  Spaceman of:
    11 FLASHGORDON
**Series**
  1969 ~ winners: 4 METS
  2000 ~ losers: 4 METS
  CBS hit: 3 CSI
  ender: 3 ETC ZEE 4 ETAL
    5 OMEGA
  End of a: 3 ZED ZEE 5 OMEGA
  First in a: 5 ALPHA
  Fourth in a: 3 DEE
  Last in a: 3 NTH ZEE
    5 OMEGA
  Like one in a: 3 NTH
  of engagements: 4 TOUR
  opener: 3 ESS 5 ALPHA
  prototype: 5 PILOT
  Repeated: 5 CYCLE
  Second in a: 4 BETA
  separator: 5 COMMA
  starter: 6 OPENER
  Start of a German: 4 EINS
  ___ serif: 4 SANS
**Serious:** 4 DIRE 5 ACUTE
    GRAVE SOBER
    6 SOLEMN
    10 NONONSENSE
  about: 4 INTO
  Get: 5 SOBER
    11 KNUCKLEDOWN
  hang-ups: 3 ART
  Isn't: 4 KIDS 5 JESTS
  Not: 6 JOKING
  play: 5 DRAMA
  sign: 4 OMEN
  trouble: 3 WOE 8 HOTWATER
**Seriously**
  Not: 5 INFUN

Take: 4 HEED
**Serkin**
  Pianist: 6 RUDOLF
**Serling**
  Host: 3 ROD
  Like ~ tales: 5 EERIE
  Like ~ tales (var.): 4 EERY
  series:
    15 THETWILIGHTZONE
**Sermon**
  basis: 4 TEXT
  Deliver a: 6 PREACH
  ender: 4 AMEN ETTE
  subject: 3 SIN 4 EVIL
    11 ORIGINALSIN
**Sermonize:** 6 PREACH
**Serpent**
  African: 3 ASP
  Beany's ~ buddy: 5 CECIL
  home: 4 EDEN
  Nine-headed: 5 HYDRA
  sound: 3 SSS 4 HISS
  suffix: 3 INE
  tail: 3 INE
**Serpentine:** 5 SNAKY
  curve: 3 ESS
  shape: 3 ESS
  swimmer: 3 EEL
**"Serpico"**
  author Peter: 4 MAAS
  director Sidney: 5 LUMET
  producer De Laurentiis:
    4 DINO
**Serta**
  rival: 5 SEALY
**Serum**
  holder: 4 VIAL
**Serval:** 3 CAT
**Servant**
  Eastern: 4 AMAH
  Future: 5 ROBOT
  Prospero's: 5 ARIEL
**Servants:** 4 HELP
**Serve:** 5 AVAIL DOFOR LADLE
    6 DOTIME
  a sentence: 6 DOTIME
  at parties: 5 CATER
  drinks: 4 POUR
  Fit to: 4 ONEA
  Great: 3 ACE
  How to ~ Welsh rabbit:
    7 ONTOAST
  in the capacity of: 5 ACTAS
  Net-touching: 3 LET
  Ready to: 4 DONE ONEA
    5 ONTAP
  Score on a: 3 ACE
  soup: 5 LADLE
  Super: 3 ACE
  the purpose: 5 AVAIL
  to be replayed: 3 LET
**Server:** 6 WAITER
  Caesar: 9 SALADBOWL
  Coffee: 3 URN
  Drive-in: 6 CARHOP
  edge: 4 ADIN

Frank: 4 DELI
item: 4 FILE
reward: 3 TIP
Salad: 5 TONGS
Situation for a: 4 ADIN
Soup: 5 LADLE 6 LADLER
Water: 4 EWER
Wheeled: 7 TEACART
**Service**
  Afternoon: 6 TEASET
  Auto: 4 LUBE
  Be of ~ to: 5 AVAIL
  call: 3 LET
  charge: 3 FEE
  Church: 4 MASS
  club: 7 KIWANIS
  expert: 4 ACER
  Fit for: 4 ONEA
  Great: 3 ACE
  group: 6 TEASET
  holder: 5 PADRE
  Join the: 6 ENLIST
  Kind of: 3 CAR LIP TEA
    4 ROOM TAXI WIRE
  Length of: 6 TENURE
  Of: 5 UTILE 6 USABLE
  One in the: 3 HUP
  Out of ~ (abbr.): 3 RET
  Press into: 3 USE
  Put back into: 5 REUSE
  Put into: 3 USE
  Social: 3 TEA
  status: 4 ONEA
  Sunday: 4 MASS
  volunteer: 8 ENLISTEE
  Wire: 3 UPI
  Wonderland: 6 TEASET
**Serviceable:** 4 ONEA 5 OFUSE
    UTILE
**Service station:** 6 CHAPEL
    TEMPLE
  container: 6 OILCAN
  service: 4 LUBE
**Servicewoman**
  British: 4 WREN
**Servile**
  Act: 6 GROVEL
**Servilely:** 7 ADULATE
**Serving:** 9 WAITINGON
  a purpose: 5 UTILE
  bowl: 6 TUREEN
  of butter: 3 PAT
  perfectly: 5 ACING
  Wee: 4 DRAM
**Servitude:** 7 PEONAGE
**Sesame:** 7 OILSEED
  paste: 6 TAHINI
  plant: 3 TIL
  treat (var.): 5 HALVA
  Word before: 4 OPEN
**"Sesame Street"**
  channel: 3 PBS
  character: 4 BERT ELMO
    5 ERNIE 8 THECOUNT
  grouch: 5 OSCAR
  lesson: 4 ABCS

puppeteer: 7 FRANKOZ
Spanish speaker on: 6 ROSITA
**Sess.:** 3 MTG
**Session**
Be in: 3 SIT
Held ~ again: 5 REMET
Kind of: 5 QANDA
Rap: 6 SEANCE
Returned to: 5 RESAT
School: 4 TERM
Training: 7 SEMINAR
Was in: 3 SAT
with an M.D.: 4 APPT
**Sessions**
org. (1987–93): 3 FBI
successor: 5 FREEH
**Set:** 3 GEL 8 ARRANGED
afire: 3 LIT 6 IGNITE
(against): 3 PIT
All: 5 READY
apart: 5 ALLOT 7 ISOLATE
a price: 3 ASK
aside: 4 SAVE 5 ALLOT
   8 RESERVED
back: 7 SCENERY
do-overs: 7 RETAKES
down: 3 LAY PUT 4 ALIT LAID
   5 WROTE
Empty math: 4 NULL
fire to: 5 TORCH
firmly: 5 EMBED
foot in: 5 ENTER
foot (on): 4 TROD
free: 5 UNTIE 7 UNLOOSE
Gym: 4 REPS
Head: 4 EARS EYES
Kind of: 7 DINETTE
   ERECTOR
loose: 5 UNTIE
Mind: 5 IDEAS 6 IMAGES
of beliefs: 5 CREDO
off: 3 IRK 5 APART 6 IGNITE
   8 DETONATE
of moral principles: 5 ETHIC
of plates: 5 ARMOR
of sheets: 4 REAM
of supplies: 3 KIT
of values: 5 ETHIC
(on): 3 SIC
One of a matched: 3 HIS
   4 HERS
one's sights: 3 AIM 5 AIMED
out: 5 ARRAY 6 EMBARK
piece: 4 PROP
right: 4 MEND 5 AMEND
   7 REDRESS
sail: 3 RIG 6 EMBARK
   8 PUTTOSEA
shout: 3 CUT
Smart: 5 MENSA
Sock: 4 PAIR
straight: 4 TRUE 5 ALIGN
   6 ORIENT
Super: 4 KEYS
the pace: 3 LED
to go: 5 READY

to rest: 5 ALLAY
up: 3 RIG 5 ERECT FRAME
   6 RIGGED 7 ARRANGE
   PREPARE
~, in French: 4 FIXE
**Set-___:** 3 TOS
**___ Set:** 7 ERECTOR
**Setback:** 4 LOSS 7 RELAPSE
Minor: 4 SNAG
**Set ___ by:** 5 STORE
**Seth**
Brother of: 4 ABEL
Father of: 4 ADAM
Son of: 4 ENOS
**Seton**
Author: 4 ANYA
**Sets:** 3 TVS 5 JELLS
upon: 5 HASAT
**Sette**
successor: 4 OTTO
**Settee:** 4 SOFA
**Setter**
Precedent: 8 TESTCASE
Trap: 6 SNARER
**Setting:** 5 ARENA PLACE
35mm ~: 5 FSTOP
**Settle:** 3 PAY SAG 4 SINK
   5 REPAY 6 LOCATE
   7 RESOLVE
down: 5 ROOST
in: 4 NEST
once and for all: 8 NAILDOWN
One who won't ~ down:
   5 NOMAD
snugly: 8 ENSCONCE
Tough to: 5 MESSY
up: 5 REPAY
**Settled:** 3 LIT 4 ALIT PAID
down: 4 ALIT
Got: 8 HADASEAT
in: 6 NESTED
**Settlement**
Frontier: 7 OUTPOST
**Settler**
Andes: 4 INCA
building material: 3 SOD
Quarrel: 4 DUEL
Transvaal: 4 BOER
**Set-to:** 3 ROW
**Set-top**
box: 4 TIVO
**Setup**
Circus: 4 TENT
Sound: 6 STEREO
**___ seul (dance solo):** 3 PAS
**Seuss**
character: 5 LORAX 6 SAMIAM
turtle: 6 YERTLE
**Sevareid**
Newsman: 4 ERIC
**Sevastopol**
locale: 6 CRIMEA
**Seven**
Best of: 6 SERIES
City of ~ hills: 4 ROME
Explore the ~ seas: 4 SAIL

Group of: 6 HEPTAD
Largest of: 4 ASIA
One of: 3 SEA 4 ASIA
One of Salome's: 4 VEIL
There are ~ in a semana:
   4 DIAS
Three before: 8 AREACODE
Winner of ~ Emmys: 5 ASNER
~, in Spanish: 5 SIETE
**"Seven Brides for Seven
   Brothers"**
actor Howard: 4 KEEL
**Seven deadly sins**
One of the: 4 ENVY LUST
   5 ANGER PRIDE SLOTH
**Seven Dwarfs**
One of the: 3 DOC 5 DOPEY
   HAPPY 6 GRUMPY
   SLEEPY SNEEZY
   7 BASHFUL
**Seven Little ___:** 4 FOYS
**"Seven-Per-Cent Solution, The"**
actor Williamson: 5 NICOL
author Nicholas: 5 MEYER
**Seven-piece**
puzzle: 7 TANGRAM
**Sevens**
Card game also called:
   6 FANTAN
It uses ~ through aces: 4 SKAT
**Seventh**
grader: 7 PRETEEN
letter: 3 ETA
planet: 6 URANUS
sign: 5 LIBRA
**Seventh-century**
date: 3 DCI DCL
**Seventh heaven:** 5 BLISS
   7 ECSTASY 8 EUPHORIA
   9 CLOUDNINE
In: 6 ELATED
Put in: 5 ELATE
**Seven-time**
batting champ Rod: 5 CAREW
home run champ: 5 KINER
~ Best Actor nominee:
   11 PETEROTOOLE
~ Emmy winner: 5 ASNER
   7 EDASNER
~ Wimbledon champ: 4 GRAF
   7 SAMPRAS
**"Seven Year Itch, The"**
actor Tom: 5 EWELL
**"Seven Years in Tibet"**
star: 4 PITT
**Sever:** 3 CUT HEW LOP
   4 REND
**Several**
czars: 5 IVANS
periods: 4 ERAS
reps: 3 SET
Sondheim's: 5 TONYS
**Severe:** 5 ACUTE HARSH
   STERN
Became less: 8 RELENTED
blow: 4 GALE

Less: 5 LAXER
pang: 5 THROE
test: 6 ORDEAL
**Severinsen**
Bandleader: 3 DOC
**Severity:** 5 RIGOR
**Severn**
feeder: 4 AVON
**Seville:** 3 CAR 4 AUTO
Info: Spanish cue
Lady of: 4 DONA
sir: 5 SENOR
six: 4 SEIS
snack: 4 TAPA
some: 4 UNOS
**Sèvres**
Info: French cue
**Sew**
loosely: 5 BASTE
up: 3 ICE 4 DARN MEND
**Seward**
Folly of: 6 ALASKA
**Seward Peninsula**
city: 4 NOME
**Sewell**
Author: 4 ANNA
**Sewer**
line: 3 HEM 4 SEAM
6 THREAD
of note: 4 ROSS
protector: 7 THIMBLE
~ Howe: 5 ELIAS
**Sewing**
case: 4 ETUI
connection: 4 SEAM
kit item: 3 PIN 5 SPOOL
10 PINCUSHION
requirement: 6 NEEDLE
tool: 3 AWL
**Sewing machine**
attachments: 7 HEMMERS
inventor: 4 HOWE
9 ELIASHOWE
inventor Howe: 5 ELIAS
**Sewn**
edge: 3 HEM
It may be ~ in: 5 IDTAG
**Sex**
An end to: 3 ISM
appeal: 5 OOMPH
determinant:
11 XCHROMOSOME
Intro to: 3 UNI
prefix: 3 UNI
researcher Hite: 5 SHERE
suffix: 3 ISM
**Sex ___:** 6 APPEAL
**"Sex and the City"**
heroine: 6 CARRIE
network: 3 HBO
**Sex-changing**
suffix: 3 INE
**Sexennial**
affair: 10 SENATERACE
**Sexes**
For both: 7 EPICENE

**"sex, lies, and videotape"**
actress MacDowell: 5 ANDIE
**Sexologist**
~ Shere: 4 HITE
**Sextet**
halves: 4 TRIO
Inning: 4 OUTS
**Sexton:** 4 POET
**Sexual**
prefix: 4 AMBI
**Sexy:** 3 HOT
skirt: 4 MINI
skirt feature: 4 SLIT
~ Beatles girl: 5 SADIE
**"___ sez ...":** 3 SOI
**S.F.**
hours: 3 PST
summer setting: 3 PDT
**S.F. Giant:** 4 NLER
**SFO**
posting: 3 ARR ETA ETD
**Sgt.:** 3 NCO
charges: 4 PFCS
**"Sgt. Pepper"**
album song:
15 WHENIMSIXTYFOUR
**Shabbily**
Treat: 3 USE
**Shabby:** 5 RATTY SEEDY
6 RAGTAG
10 DOWNATHEEL
**Shack:** 3 HUT 5 HOVEL
6 LEANTO
Caddy: 6 GARAGE
**Shackle:** 6 FETTER 7 ENSLAVE
LEGIRON
**Shackles:** 5 IRONS
**Shackleton**
Antarctic explorer: 6 ERNEST
**Shad**
delicacy: 3 ROE
Had: 3 ATE
**Shade:** 3 HUE 4 TINT TONE
5 TINGE 6 NUANCE
Beach: 3 TAN
Eye: 5 HAZEL
Fall: 4 RUST
giver: 3 ELM 4 TREE
maker: 3 ELM
Marine: 4 AQUA
Neutral: 3 ASH 4 ECRU
5 BEIGE
of black: 3 JET 4 COAL EBON
5 RAVEN
of blond: 3 ASH
of blue: 3 SKY 4 ANIL AQUA
CYAN NAVY NILE OPAL
TEAL 5 AZURE ROYAL
6 COBALT
of brown: 4 ECRU RUST
5 BEIGE COCOA SEPIA
UMBER
of green: 3 PEA 4 JADE LIME
MOSS NILE 5 BERYL
KELLY OLIVE 7 AVOCADO
of meaning: 6 NUANCE

of purple: 4 PUCE 5 LILAC
MAUVE
of red: 4 BEET 6 CERISE
Pastel: 4 AQUA 5 LILAC
provider: 3 ELM 4 TREE
6 AWNING 7 ELMTREE
Sky: 5 AZURE
Soft: 4 AQUA 6 PASTEL
tree: 3 ELM 5 BEECH
**Shading:** 4 TINT TONE
**Shadow:** 4 TAIL 5 UMBRA
Eclipse: 5 UMBRA
Five o'clock: 7 STUBBLE
Five o'clock ~ remover:
5 RAZOR
Get rid of a: 5 SHAVE
**"Shadow, The"**
actor Baldwin: 4 ALEC
character Cranston:
6 LAMONT
**Shadowbox:** 4 SPAR
**Shadows**
When ~ are shortest: 4 NOON
**Shadowy:** 6 UMBRAL
**Shady**
group: 4 ELMS
It may be: 4 PAST
spot: 5 ARBOR BOWER
**Shaffer**
play: 5 EQUUS
**Shaft**
Auto: 4 AXLE
find: 3 ORE
of light: 3 RAY
They get the: 6 MINERS
Wheel: 4 AXLE
**Shag**
rug feature: 4 PILE
**Shaggy:** 7 HIRSUTE
ape: 5 ORANG
bovine: 5 BISON
ox: 3 YAK
**Shah**
homeland, once: 4 IRAN
subject, once: 5 IRANI
**Shah ___ (Taj Mahal builder):**
5 JAHAN
**Shaheen**
Pol. designation for Gov.
Jeanne: 3 DNH
**Shahn**
Painter: 3 BEN
**___ Shah Pahlavi:** 4 REZA
**Shake:** 3 JAR 4 LOSE 5 ELUDE
6 WAGGLE
a leg: 3 HIE
alternative: 6 MALTED
hands with: 4 MEET
it or break it: 4 ALEG
off: 4 LOSE 5 ELUDE EVADE
slightly: 3 JOG
Something to: 4 HAND
up: 3 JAR MAR 4 FAZE JOLT
ROIL 5 ROUSE SCARE
7 AGITATE STARTLE
**"Shake ___!":** 4 ALEG

**Shake like ___:** 5 ALEAF
**Shaken**
It may be: 4 SALT
**Shaker**
Abbr. after: 3 HTS
contents: 4 SALT
leader: 6 ANNLEE
Mover and: 4 DOER 5 NABOB
Salt: 7 TSUNAMI
shaker: 6 SALTER
**Shaker ___, OH:** 3 HTS
**Shakers**
and others: 5 SECTS
founder Lee: 3 ANN
leader: 6 ANNLEE
partners: 6 MOVERS
**Shakes**
No great: 4 SOSO
Two: 3 SEC
~, for short: 3 DTS
**Shakespeare:** 4 BARD
character Andronicus:
5 TITUS
character Katharina: 5 SHREW
foot: 4 IAMB
king: 4 LEAR
Like a ~ sonnet: 6 IAMBIC
Mrs.: 4 ANNE
Performed, per: 5 DIDST
river: 4 AVON
suffix: 3 ANA
teen: 5 ROMEO
theatre: 5 GLOBE
title starter: 4 ALLS
Trouble, per: 3 ADO
villain: 4 IAGO
Witch, to: 3 HAG
Word repeated in a ~ title:
7 MEASURE
work: 4 PLAY
**Shakespearean**
actor Edmund: 4 KEAN
bad guy: 4 IAGO
contraction: 5 TWERE
ensign: 4 IAGO
exclamation: 3 FIE
forest: 5 ARDEN
king: 4 LEAR 6 OBERON
prince: 3 HAL
setting: 6 VERONA
sprite: 5 ARIEL
suffix: 3 EST ETH
title start: 4 ALLS 5 ASYOU
tragedy: 7 OTHELLO
verb: 4 DOTH HATH
villain: 4 IAGO
~ Moor: 7 OTHELLO
**Shakespeare Festival**
New York ~ founder: 4 PAPP
**"Shakespeare in Love"**
prop: 4 EPEE
~ Oscar winner: 5 DENCH
**Shaking**
spell: 4 AGUE
**Shakur**
Rapper: 5 TUPAC

**Shalala**
Former HHS Secretary:
5 DONNA
**Shale**
extract: 3 OIL
features: 6 STRATA
**Shalhoub, Tony**
~ TV role: 4 MONK
**Shalit**
Critic: 4 GENE
**"... ___ shall die":** 3 ORI
**Shallow**
Bake in a ~ dish: 5 SHIRR
container: 4 TRAY 5 PLATE
Get into ~ water: 4 WADE
Not: 4 DEEP
**"Shallow ___" (Paltrow film):**
3 HAL
**"Shall we?"**
Answer to: 4 LETS
**"Shalom!":** 5 PEACE
**Sham:** 4 FAKE HOAX 5 BOGUS
FALSE 6 ERSATZ
PSEUDO 7 PRETEND
**Shaman:** 6 HEALER
**Shambles:** 4 MESS RUIN
Make a ~ of: 5 TRASH
**Shame**
Crying: 4 PITY
Put to: 5 ABASH
Show: 6 REDDEN
**"Shame ___!":** 5 ONYOU
**Shamefaced:** 7 HANGDOG
**Shameless:** 6 BRAZEN
joy: 4 GLEE
promotion: 4 PLUG
**"Shame on you!":** 3 TSK
**Shampoo**
bottle word: 4 OILY
brand: 5 PRELL
ingredient: 4 ALOE
step: 5 RINSE
**"Shampoo"**
screenwriter Robert: 5 TOWNE
~ Oscar winner:
8 LEEGRANT
**Shamrock**
land: 4 EIRE ERIN
**Shamu:** 4 ORCA
**Shamus:** 3 TEC
**Shandy**
creator: 6 STERNE
ingredient: 3 ALE
8 LEMONADE
**"Shane"**
actor Jack: 7 PALANCE
star: 4 LADD 8 ALANLADD
**Shanghai:** 6 ABDUCT
**"Shanghai Express"**
actress Anna May: 4 WONG
**"Shanghai Noon"**
actor Jackie: 4 CHAN
actor Wilson: 4 OWEN
actress Lucy: 3 LIU
**Shangri-La:** 4 EDEN
Man of: 4 LAMA

**Shankar**
instrument: 5 SITAR
Sitarist: 4 RAVI
tune: 4 RAGA
**Shannon**
Singer: 3 DEL
Where the ~ flows: 4 EIRE
**Shanty:** 3 HUT 5 HOVEL
6 LEANTO
**Shape:** 4 MOLD
Angular: 3 ELL
Bent out of: 5 IRATE
6 WARPED
Get in: 5 TRAIN 6 TONEUP
In fighting: 4 TRIM
In good: 3 FIT 4 HALE TRIM
5 SOUND TONED
In sorry: 5 SEEDY
Out of: 4 BENT SOFT
Take: 4 JELL
Twist out of: 4 WARP 5 GNARL
up: 6 SNAPTO
**Shapeless**
mass: 4 GLOB
**Shapely**
leg: 3 GAM
**Shaper**
Gelatin: 4 MOLD
Shoe: 4 TREE
Shop: 5 LATHE
Tool: 3 DIE
Wood: 3 ADZ
**Shaping**
tool: 4 RASP 5 LATHE
**Shapiro**
Jazzman: 5 ARTIE
**Shaq**
alma mater: 3 LSU
Former teammate of: 4 KOBE
Former team of: 4 HEAT
5 MAGIC 6 LAKERS
of basketball: 5 ONEAL
org.: 3 NBA
**Shar-___ (dog):** 3 PEI
**Share:** 3 CUT 4 DOLE
6 RATION 7 PARTAKE
PORTION
a border with: 4 ABUT
a role: 10 SPLITAPART
Don't: 3 HOG
equally: 5 HALVE SPLIT
Even: 4 HALF
Lion's: 4 MOST
Pay one's ~, with "up":
4 ANTE
Proportional: 5 QUOTA
**Shared:** 6 MUTUAL
between us: 4 OURS
computer sys.: 3 LAN
with: 6 TOLDTO
**Sharer**
Apartment: 6 ROOMIE
Bedroom: 3 SIB
Lead: 6 COSTAR
Legacy: 6 COHEIR
word: 3 OUR 4 OURS

**Shares**
  Corp.: 3 STK
  Fewer than 100: 6 ODDLOT
  How some ~ are bought/sold:
    5 ATPAR
  Like some: 7 PRORATA
**Shari**
  Puppeteer: 5 LEWIS
**Sharif**
  Actor: 4 OMAR
  homeland: 5 EGYPT
  title role: 3 CHE
**Sharing**
  word: 6 APIECE
**Sharjah:** 7 EMIRATE
**Shark:** 8 MANEATER
  clinger: 6 REMORA
  hangout: 8 POOLHALL
  home: 3 SEA 5 OCEAN
  Kind of: 4 LOAN MAKO
  Loan: 6 USURER
  Loan ~ offense: 5 USURY
  movie: 4 JAWS
  offer: 4 LOAN
  omen: 3 FIN
  Small: 7 DOGFISH
  Thresher: 6 SEAFOX
**Sharkey**
  ~ TV rank: 3 CPO
**Sharks**
  or Jets: 4 GANG
**Sharon:** 7 ISRAELI
  Actress: 5 GLESS
  Land of: 6 ISRAEL
  of Israel: 5 ARIEL
**Sharp:** 3 SLY 4 ACID KEEN
    TART 5 ACERB ACRID
    ACUTE ALERT
    6 ASTUTE CLEVER
    POINTY
  bark: 3 YIP 4 YELP
  blow: 4 SLAP
  C: 5 DFLAT
  change in direction: 3 ZIG
  cheese: 6 ROMANO
  competitor: 3 RCA 4 SONY
  curve: 3 ESS
  D: 5 EFLAT
  F: 5 GFLAT
  feller: 3 AXE
  fight: 5 SETTO
  flavor: 4 TANG
  Having one: 3 ING
  Key with one: 6 EMINOR
  knock: 3 RAP
  left or right: 3 JAB
  Like ~ cheese: 4 AGED
  Make a ~ turn: 4 VEER
  Neither ~ nor flat: 5 ONKEY
  part: 4 EDGE
  punch: 3 AWL JAB
  rebuke: 4 SLAP
  ridge: 5 ARETE
  taste: 4 TANG
  turn: 3 ZAG ZIG
  Very: 5 ACUTE

  weapon: 5 SPEAR
**Sharp as ___:** 5 ATACK
**"Sharp Dressed Man"**
  band: 5 ZZTOP
**Sharpen:** 4 EDGE HONE WHET
    5 STROP
  again: 6 REHONE
**Sharpener:** 5 HONER
    8 OILSTONE
  Razor: 5 STROP
**Sharper:** 5 CHEAT
**Sharp-eyed**
  hunter: 5 EAGLE
**Sharply**
  dressed: 5 NATTY
  stinging: 5 ACRID
  Turn: 3 ZIG 4 SLEW VEER
  Whack: 4 SWAT
**Sharpness:** 3 WIT 4 BITE EDGE
    TANG 6 ACUITY
    ACUMEN
**Sharp-pointed**
  instrument: 6 STYLET
**Sharps**
  Having five: 3 INB
  Having four: 3 INE
  Key with four: 6 EMAJOR
  Key with no ~ or flats:
    6 AMINOR
  Key with three ~ (abbr.):
    4 AMAJ
**Sharpshooter:** 7 DEADEYE
  asset: 3 AIM
  ~ Oakley: 5 ANNIE
**Sharp-smelling:** 5 ACRID
**Sharp-tasting:** 4 TART 5 ACRID
    6 ACIDIC
**Sharpton**
  and others: 3 ALS
**Sharp-tongued:** 5 ACERB
**Sharp-toothed**
  fish: 5 MORAY
**Sharp-witted:** 6 ASTUTE
**Shatner**
  sci-fi series: 6 TEKWAR
  Word in ~ titles: 3 TEK
**Shatt-al-Arab**
  port: 5 BASRA
**Shave**
  Close: 5 SCARE
  Prepare to: 6 LATHER
**"Shave ___ haircut":** 4 ANDA
**Shaver**
  brand: 4 ATRA
  Little: 3 LAD TOT 4 TYKE
  need: 5 RAZOR
**Shavers**
  Women with: 3 MAS
**Shavetails**
  (abbr.): 3 LTS
**Shaving**
  accessory: 5 STROP
  brand: 4 ATRA
  mishap: 4 NICK
  stuff: 4 FOAM
  tool: 5 RAZOR

**Shaving cream**
  feature: 4 FOAM
  ingredient: 4 ALOE
**Shaw**
  Author: 5 IRWIN
  Bandleader: 5 ARTIE
  Clarinetist: 5 ARTIE
  Doolittle created by: 5 ELIZA
  play: 7 CANDIDA
  title starter: 4 ARMS
**Shawl:** 4 WRAP
  Fur: 5 STOLE
  Mexican: 6 SERAPE
**Shawm**
  descendant: 4 OBOE
**Shawn**
  Dancer: 3 TED
  of the NBA: 4 KEMP
  Pitcher: 5 ESTES
**Shawnee**
  Honorary: 5 BOONE
**"Shawshank Redemption, The"**
  extra: 6 INMATE
**Shays's Rebellion**
  Shays of: 6 DANIEL
**She**
  gets what she wants: 4 LOLA
  had a little lamb: 3 EWE
  has a ball: 3 DEB
  He and: 4 THEY
  sheep: 3 EWE 4 EWES
  ~, in French: 4 ELLE
  ~, in Italian: 4 ESSA
**Shea**
  and others: 6 STADIA
  player: 3 MET 5 NYMET
  Stadium near: 4 ASHE
**Shearer**
  Actress: 5 MOIRA NORMA
  Ballerina: 5 MOIRA
**Shearing**
  candidate: 3 EWE
  protest: 3 BAA
**Shears**
  Use: 4 SNIP
**Shearson**
  Ex-partner of: 6 LEHMAN
**Sheathe:** 6 ENCASE
**Sheaves**
  Bring in the: 4 REAP
**Sheba**
  creator: 4 INGE
  today: 5 YEMEN
**Shebang**
  The whole: 3 ALL 4 ATOZ
**Shebat**
  follower: 4 ADAR
**She-bear**
  ~, in Latin: 4 URSA
  ~, in Spanish: 3 OSA
**"She Believes ___":** 4 INME
**"___ she blows!":** 4 THAR
**Shed:** 3 HUT 4 CAST EMIT
    LOSE MOLT 6 HANGAR
    LEANTO
  feathers: 4 MOLT

item: 3 HOE 4 RAKE TEAR
tears: 4 WEEP WEPT
**Shed ___**: 5 ATEAR
**"She Done ___ Wrong":**
 3 HIM
**Sheedy**
 Actress: 4 ALLY
**Sheehan**
 Pulitzer writer: 4 NEIL
**Sheehy**
 Author: 4 GAIL
**Sheen**: 6 LUSTER
**Sheena**
 Singer: 6 EASTON
**Sheep**
 Bear young, as: 4 YEAN
 Clip: 5 SHEAR
 coat: 4 WOOL 6 FLEECE
 Dolly the: 5 CLONE
 Female: 3 EWE
 Like: 5 OVINE
 Like clipped: 5 SHORN
 Male: 3 RAM
 place: 3 LEA
 She: 3 EWE 4 EWES
 shelter: 4 COTE
 sound: 3 BAA 5 BLEAT
 Stop counting: 5 SLEEP
 type: 6 MERINO
 Words to a black: 6 BAABAA
 Young: 4 LAMB
**Sheepdog**: 6 HERDER
 British: 7 SHELTIE
 Hungarian: 4 PULI
**Sheepish**: 5 OVINE
 remark: 3 BAA MAA
 6 BAABAA
 Sound: 5 BLEAT
**Sheep-related**: 5 OVINE
**Sheepshank**: 4 KNOT
 Make another: 5 RETIE
**Sheepskin**
 bearer: 4 GRAD
 leather: 4 ROAN
**Sheer**: 5 UTTER
 fabric: 5 NINON TOILE
 VOILE
**Sheet**
 Animation: 3 CEL
 Balance ~ item: 5 ASSET
 Cheat: 4 TROT
 Four-page: 5 FOLIO
 Kind of: 4 SPEC
 material: 5 SATIN 6 MUSLIN
 7 PERCALE
 of glass: 4 PANE
 of ice: 4 FLOE
 of stamps: 4 PANE
 Scandal: 3 RAG
 White as a: 4 PALE 5 ASHEN
**Sheetful**
 of cookies: 5 BATCH
**Sheet music**
 abbr.: 3 ARR
 symbol: 4 CLEF REST
 5 SEGNO

**Sheets**: 5 LINEN 6 STRATA
 24 ~: 5 QUIRE
 500 ~: 4 REAM
 Material in: 4 MICA
 Set of: 4 REAM
 Three ~ to the wind: 3 LIT
 6 BLOTTO
**Sheffield**
 Info: British cue
**She-goat**: 3 DOE
**Sheik**: 4 ARAB
 bevy: 5 HAREM
 of Ray Stevens:
 11 AHABTHEARAB
 peer: 4 EMIR
**Sheikdom**
 Gulf: 7 BAHRAIN
 of song: 5 ARABY
**"Sheik of ___, The"**: 5 ARABY
**Shelby**
 Historian: 5 FOOTE
 Writer: 6 STEELE
**Shelf**: 5 LEDGE
 bracket: 3 ELL
 Fireplace: 3 HOB 6 MANTEL
 Take off the: 3 USE
**Shell**
 alternative: 4 HESS 5 AMOCO
 EXXON GETTY MOBIL
 6 SUNOCO
 Deep-fried: 7 TIMBALE
 figure: 6 OCTANE
 food: 4 TACO
 Food in a: 4 TACO
 game: 4 SCAM
 game need: 3 PEA
 Kind of: 4 TACO
 lining: 5 NACRE
 mover: 3 OAR
 Ornamental: 7 ABALONE
 out: 5 SPEND
 Propel a: 3 OAR
 Racing: 5 SCULL
 Seafood in a: 6 OYSTER
 Seed: 4 HULL
 Spiral: 5 CONCH
 Stick a ~ in: 4 LOAD
 team: 4 CREW
**Shellac**: 4 DRUB 5 TROMP
**Shellacking**: 4 BATH
**Sheller**
 Sea: 6 ARMADA
**Shelley**: 5 ODIST
 Actress: 4 LONG
 alma mater: 4 ETON
 Keats, to: 7 ADONAIS
 Novelist: 4 MARY
 poem: 3 ODE
 queen: 3 MAB
 role: 5 DIANE
 Shortly, to: 4 ANON
 Sundown, to: 3 EEN
**Shellfish**: 7 ABALONE
 bane: 7 REDTIDE
**Shells**: 4 AMMO 5 PASTA
**"___ She Lovely"**: 4 ISNT

**"She loves me"**
 flower: 5 DAISY
**Shelter**: 3 LEE 5 HAVEN
 6 HARBOR HOSTEL
 and food: 5 NEEDS
 Animal: 3 ARK 4 LAIR
 Beach: 6 CABANA
 Camp: 4 TENT
 Crude: 3 HUT
 Dugout: 4 ABRI
 Gave ~ to: 6 HOUSED
 gp.: 4 SPCA
 Leafy: 5 ARBOR BOWER
 Open: 6 RAMADA
 Plains: 5 TEPEE
 Sheep: 4 COTE
 Toward: 4 ALEE
**Sheltered**: 4 ALEE
 inlet: 4 COVE
 side: 3 LEE
 spot: 4 COVE 5 HAVEN
**Shelters**: 5 ASYLA
 Some tax: 8 ROTHIRAS
**"Shelters of Stone, The"**
 author: 4 AUEL
**Shelve**: 5 DEFER TABLE
**Shelved**
 for now: 6 ONHOLD
**Shelves**
 Set of display: 7 ETAGERE
**Shem**
 Father of: 4 NOAH
**Shemp**: 6 STOOGE
 Brother of: 3 MOE
**Shenanigan**: 5 ANTIC PRANK
 Assist in a: 4 ABET
**Shepard**
 Astronaut: 4 ALAN
 Playwright: 3 SAM
**Shepard, Sam**
 genre: 5 DRAMA
**Shepherd**
 boy of opera: 5 AMAHL
 Cry to a: 3 BAA
 Genesis: 4 ABEL
 locale: 3 LEA
**Shepherd, Jean**
 book: 15 ACHRISTMASSTORY
**Shepherdess**
 of rhyme: 6 BOPEEP
**Sheraton**
 Food critic: 4 MIMI
**Sheraton Hotels**
 owner: 3 ITT
**Sherbet**
 choice: 6 ORANGE
 kin: 3 ICE
**Shere**
 Sexologist: 4 HITE
**Sheridan**
 Actress: 3 ANN
**Sheriff**
 aide: 6 DEPUTY
 asst.: 3 DEP
 badge: 4 STAR 7 TINSTAR
 band: 5 POSSE

Mayberry: 4 ANDY
star: 5 BADGE
TV: 4 LOBO
**Sheriff Lobo**
portrayer: 5 AKINS
**Sheriff Taylor**
boy: 4 OPIE
**Sherilyn**
Actress: 4 FENN
**Sherlock**
Going on, to: 5 AFOOT
lead: 4 CLUE
portrayer: 5 BASIL
"The Woman," to: 5 IRENE
**Sherman**
Comic: 5 ALLAN
took it: 7 ATLANTA
War, to: 4 HELL
was his veep: 4 TAFT
**Sherman ___, California:**
4 OAKS
**Sherman Oaks**
City near: 6 ENCINO
**Sherpa**
land: 5 NEPAL
sighting: 4 YETI
**Sherry**
casks: 6 SOLERA
Drank: 5 WINED
Semisweet: 7 OLOROSO
Spanish: 7 AMOROSO
**Sherwood:** 6 FOREST
**"She's a Lady"**
songwriter: 4 ANKA
**"She's ___ Have It":** 5 GOTTA
**"She's So High"**
singer Bachman: 3 TAL
**"___ She Sweet?":** 4 AINT
**Shetland:** 4 PONY
**Shevat**
follower: 4 ADAR
**Shield:** 5 BADGE
border: 4 ORLE
Driver: 5 VISOR
Heat ~ locale: 8 NOSECONE
of Athena: 5 AEGIS
of Zeus: 5 AEGIS
Sun: 7 PARASOL
**"Shield, The"**
actress Pounder: 3 CCH
**Shields**
Lyricist: 3 REN
on stage: 6 BROOKE
**Shields, Brooke**
TV role for: 5 SUSAN
**Shift:** 5 DRESS 7 CHEMISE
Late: 8 DOGWATCH
neighbor: 5 ENTER
start: 4 NINE
Work: 4 DAYS
**Shifted**
They may be: 5 GEARS
9 TENSPEEDS
**Shiftless:** 4 LAZY
**Shifty**
one: 5 SNEAK

**Shih ___:** 3 TZU
**Shih Tzu:** 3 TOY 6 LAPDOG
origin: 5 TIBET
**Shiite**
deity: 5 ALLAH
leader: 4 IMAM
**Shiites:** 4 SECT
**Shill**
Audience: 5 PLANT
for: 4 ABET
**Shilling**
A pound and a: 6 GUINEA
Fifth of a: 5 PENCE
**Shillong**
state: 5 ASSAM
**Shilly-shally:** 5 WAVER
**Shiloh**
commander: 5 GRANT
general: 5 BUELL
priest: 3 ELI
**Shimmering**
stone: 4 OPAL
**"Shimmy, Shimmy, ___-Bop":**
4 KOKO
**Shimon**
of Israel: 5 PERES
**Shinbone:** 5 TIBIA
**Shindig:** 4 BASH GALA 5 PARTY
Island: 4 LUAU
**Shindigs:** 3 DOS
**Shine:** 5 EXCEL GLEAM
7 RADIATE
in ads: 3 GLO
Partner of: 4 RISE
Rise and: 6 AWAKEN
Take a ~ to: 3 WAX 4 LIKE
**"Shine a Little Love"**
rock gp.: 3 ELO
**"Shine On, Harvest Moon"**
co-composer Bayes: 4 NORA
**Shiner:** 4 STAR
Big: 3 SUN
**Shingle**
abbr.: 3 ESQ
letters: 3 DDS
material: 5 CEDAR
words: 5 ATLAW
**Shingles**
Get new: 6 REROOF
**Shining:** 5 AGLOW
brightly: 6 AGLARE
example: 3 SUN
faintly: 8 AGLIMMER
**"Shining, The"**
actor Crothers: 7 SCATMAN
author: 4 KING
**Shinny:** 5 CLIMB
**Shinto**
temple gateway: 5 TORII
**Shiny**
fabric: 4 LAME 6 SATEEN
mineral: 4 MICA
on top: 4 BALD
**"Shiny Happy People"**
band: 3 REM
**Ship:** 4 SEND

1492 ~: 4 NINA 5 PINTA
50-oared ~: 4 ARGO
Any: 3 SHE
backbone: 4 KEEL
Behind, on a: 3 AFT
Big: 5 LINER
board: 5 PLANK
class: 8 STEERAGE
Clumsy: 3 TUB
company: 4 CREW
Crosswise, on a: 5 ABEAM
Cruise: 5 LINER
deck: 5 ORLOP
Easily handled, as a: 4 YARE
Fasten a ~ rope: 5 BELAY
frame: 4 HULL
front: 5 PROW
Gulf: 5 OILER
heading: 3 ENE ESE NNE
SSE
Historic: 4 NINA
in news of 1898: 5 MAINE
landing: 4 PORT
Legendary: 4 ARGO
load: 5 CARGO
Lowest ~ deck: 5 ORLOP
mast: 4 SPAR
Memorable: 5 MAINE
Merchant: 6 ARGOSY
money-handler: 6 PURSER
Mutinied: 7 AMISTAD
of fuels: 5 OILER
of myth: 4 ARGO
part: 4 KEEL
Part of a ~ bow: 5 HAWSE
pole: 4 MAST
pronoun: 3 SHE
Ready to: 6 CRATED
rear: 5 STERN
rope: 3 TYE
Rope rung on a: 7 RATLINE
Secure a: 4 MOOR
shape: 4 HULL
Sinking ~ signal: 3 SOS
stabilizer: 4 KEEL
staff: 4 CREW
Steer a: 4 CONN
steering wheel: 4 HELM
Swerve, as a: 3 YAW
That: 3 HER SHE
To the back, on a: 6 ASTERN
To the left, on a: 5 APORT
wood: 4 TEAK
**Shipboard**
direction: 6 ASTERN
**Shipbuilder**
Biblical: 4 NOAH
**Shipbuilding**
wood: 4 TEAK
**Shipman**
prefix: 3 MID
**Shipped:** 4 SENT
**Shipping**
container: 5 CRATE
deduction: 4 TARE
dept. stamp: 4 RECD

hazard: 4 BERG FLOE
   7 ICEBERG
inquiry: 6 TRACER
line: 6 HAWSER
nickname: 3 ARI
Remove from a ~ box:
   7 UNCRATE
route: 7 SEALANE
unit: 3 TON
weight: 4 TARE

**Ships**
Group of: 5 FLEET
   6 ARGOSY

**Shipshape:** 4 NEAT TIDY TRIM

**Ship-to-ship**
call: 4 AHOY

**Shipworm:** 5 BORER

**Shipwreck**
site: 4 REEF

**Shiraz**
locale: 4 IRAN
native: 5 IRANI
resident: 7 IRANIAN

**Shire**
Actress: 5 TALIA

**Shirelles**
hit: 10 SOLDIERBOY

**Shirk:** 5 EVADE
   15 LIEDOWNONTHEJOB
Shirkers ~ it: 4 DUTY

**Shirley**
1963 role for ~: 4 IRMA
1994 role for ~: 4 TESS
Roommate of: 7 LAVERNE

**Shirt:** 3 TOP
brand: 4 IZOD
Casual: 3 TEE
Kind of: 3 TEE 4 POLO
opponent: 4 SKIN
part: 3 ARM 6 SLEEVE
shape: 3 TEE
size: 5 LARGE
size (abbr.): 3 LGE MED
spoiler: 5 STAIN
Striped ~ wearer: 3 REF
Stuffed: 4 PRIG SNOB
   5 SNOOT
with a slogan: 3 TEE
with a reptilian logo: 4 IZOD
___ shirt: 5 ALOHA

**Shirts**
and skins: 5 TEAMS
Like Hawaiian: 4 LOUD

**Shish ___:** 6 KEBABS

**Shish kebab**
Like: 8 SKEWERED
pin: 6 SKEWER

**Shiva**
Wife of: 4 KALI

**Shiver**
producing: 5 EERIE

**Shivering**
fit: 4 AGUE
sound: 3 BRR

**Shmoo**
creator Al: 4 CAPP

**SHO**
alternative: 3 AMC HBO TMC
   TNT

**Shoal:** 4 REEF
Long: 4 SPIT

**Shoat**
place: 3 STY

**Shock:** 3 JAR ZAP 4 JOLT STUN
   5 AMAZE APPAL
   6 APPALL TRAUMA
Cry of: 4 EGAD
Emotional: 6 TRAUMA
Express: 4 GASP
In: 6 AGHAST
Partner of: 3 AWE
React to a: 4 REEL
Show: 4 GASP

**Shocked:** 5 AGASP 6 AGHAST
reaction: 4 GASP
Visibly: 5 AGAPE ASHEN
"___ shocked!": 3 IAM

**Shocker**
Sea: 3 EEL
Sports: 5 UPSET

**Shocking:** 5 LURID
It can be: 3 EEL 5 TASER
sound: 3 ZAP
swimmer: 3 EEL

**Shock jock**
Don: 4 IMUS
Howard: 5 STERN

**Shoddy:** 4 POOR 5 CHEAP
   6 SLEAZY

**Shoe**
accessory: 6 INSOLE
Big: 3 EEE 4 EEEE
blemish: 5 SCUFF
bottom: 4 SOLE
box letters: 3 AAA EEE
Clunky: 5 SABOT
Comfy: 3 MOC
cover: 4 SPAT
Dancing ~ attachment: 3 TAP
Danish ~ brand: 4 ECCO
designation: 3 EEE
Do a ~ repair: 6 RESOLE
feature: 6 EYELET
forms: 5 LASTS
Golf ~ feature: 5 CLEAT
Heelless: 4 FLAT
holder: 4 TREE
hue: 3 TAN
insert: 4 TREE
lift: 7 HEELTAP
Low-heeled: 6 BROGUE
material: 5 SUEDE
name: 4 MCAN
part: 3 TOE 4 ARCH HEEL
   SOLE WELT 5 UPPER
   6 INSOLE INSTEP
Pointy ~ wearer: 3 ELF
polish brand: 4 KIWI
saver: 4 TREE
seller Thom: 4 MCAN
shaper: 4 TREE
Soft: 3 MOC

style: 7 OPENTOE
Thick-soled: 4 CLOG
tie: 4 LACE
touting dog: 4 TIGE
Wide: 3 EEE
Woman's: 6 TSTRAP WEDGIE
Wooden: 4 CLOG 5 SABOT

**Shoebox**
letters: 3 EEE

**"___ shoe fits ...":** 5 IFTHE

**Shoelace:** 3 TIE
alternative: 6 VELCRO
hole: 6 EYELET
problem: 4 KNOT
tip: 5 AGLET

**Shoeless**
cobbler: 3 PIE

**"Shoeless Joe"**
portrayer: 6 LIOTTA

**Shoemaker**
form: 4 LAST
helper: 3 ELF
McAn: 4 THOM
strip: 4 WELT
Thom: 4 MCAN
tool: 3 AWL

**Shoes**
Big name in: 4 ECCO MCAN
   6 DEXTER
Feature of some: 6 TSTRAP
First name in: 6 IMELDA
Fix: 6 REHEEL RESOLE
Like some: 7 OPENTOE
   TWOTONE
Some: 5 NIKES
Thom of: 4 MCAN
Tied, as: 5 LACED

**"Shoes of the Fisherman, The"**
author: 4 WEST

**Shoestring:** 4 LACE
___ shoestring: 3 ONA

**Shofar**
source: 3 RAM

**Shogun**
capital: 3 EDO
sash: 3 OBI

**Sholem**
Author: 4 ASCH

**Sholom**
Author: 8 ALEICHEM

**"Shoo!":** 3 GIT 4 AWAY SCAT

**Shoo-___:** 3 INS

**"Shooby-doo"**
Sing: 4 SCAT

**Shook**
hands with: 7 GREETED
up: 6 JARRED 8 STARTLED

**"Shoop Shoop Song"**
syllables: 6 NANANA

**Shoot:** 4 DART FILM SPEW
   TWIG 5 SPRIG
a ray: 4 LASE
at: 5 PLINK
down: 3 NIX
End of a: 4 WRAP
for: 5 AIMAT 6 ASPIRE

Get set to: 5 AIMAT
Grafting: 5 SCION
off: 4 EMIT
One about to: 5 AIMER
Prepared to: 4 DREW
Prepare to: 3 AIM
Something to ~ for: 3 PAR
   5 IDEAL SKEET
the breeze: 3 FAN GAB JAW
   RAP YAK 4 CHAT
up: 4 SOAR 5 SPIKE
"Shoot!": 3 ASK 4 DANG DARN
   DRAT 5 ASKME
   6 DARNIT
**Shoot-'em-up:** 5 OATER
**Shooter:** 3 TAW 4 GUNN
  ammo: 3 PEA
  Arrow: 4 EROS
  filler: 4 AMMO
  Glass: 3 TAW
  gp.: 3 NRA
  Hood's: 3 GAT
  order: 9 SAYCHEESE
  pellet: 3 PEA
  setting: 5 FSTOP
  Shot: 4 HYPO
  Showy: 3 TAW
**Shootin'**
  The whole ~ match: 3 ALL
**Shooting**
  End of a: 4 WRAP
  game: 5 SKEET
  Kind of: 5 SKEET
  marble: 5 AGATE IMMIE
  org.: 3 NRA
  Report of a: 4 BANG
  site: 3 SET
  sport: 5 SKEET
  star: 6 METEOR
  Start: 8 OPENFIRE
  The whole ~ match: 3 ALL
**"Shooting of Dan ___, The":**
  6 MCGREW
**Shootout**
  shout: 4 DRAW
  site: 8 OKCORRAL
  time: 4 NOON
**Shop:** 4 MART 5 STORE
  C's in: 6 CLAMPS
  Food: 4 DELI
  holder: 4 VISE 5 CLAMP
    6 CCLAMP
  item: 4 TOOL
  piercer: 3 AWL
  Reason to close: 6 SIESTA
  shaper: 5 LATHE
  Specialty: 5 SALON
  Sweat: 3 SPA
  talk: 5 LINGO
  without buying: 6 BROWSE
**Shopaholic**
  binge: 5 SPREE
  delight: 4 SALE
  heaven: 4 MALL
  ___ Shop Boys: 3 PET
**Shopkeeper:** 6 SELLER

on TV: 3 APU
**Shoplift:** 5 BOOST STEAL
**Shoplifter**
  giveaway: 5 BULGE
**Shoppe**
  sign word: 4 OLDE
**Shopper**
  aid: 4 CART LIST
  bag: 4 TOTE
  binge: 5 SPREE
  burden: 4 BAGS
  Car ~ option: 5 LEASE
  concern: 5 PRICE
  notes: 4 LIST
  stopper: 4 SALE
**Shopping**
  aid: 4 CART LIST
  binge: 5 SPREE
  center: 4 MALL MART
    5 PLAZA
  channel: 3 QVC
  Like some: 7 ONESTOP
  London ~ district: 4 SOHO
  Popular ~ spot: 6 THEWEB
  Tokyo ~ district: 5 GINZA
**Shoptalk:** 5 ARGOT LINGO
**Shopworn:** 5 TRITE
**"Shop ___ you drop":** 3 TIL
**Shore**
  bird: 3 ERN 4 ERNE GULL
    TERN 5 HERON
  dinner entrée: 4 CLAM CRAB
  Far from: 4 ASEA
  Off: 4 ASEA
  Singer: 5 DINAH
  Stay near the: 4 WADE
  thing: 4 DUNE SAND
**Shore, Pauly**
  1992 ~ film: 9 ENCINOMAN
**Shorebird:** 4 GULL TERN
    6 AVOCET PLOVER
**Shoreline**
  feature: 4 COVE 5 INLET
  problem: 7 EROSION
  shelter: 4 COVE
**Shorelines**
  Like some: 6 ERODED
**Short:** 3 SHY 4 CURT 5 BRIEF
  Info: Abbr. cue
  and sweet: 5 TERSE
  Are: 4 LACK
  Be: 3 OWE
  Be ~ with: 6 SNAPAT
  bio: 4 OBIT VITA
  blast: 4 TOOT
  branch track: 4 SPUR
  breath: 4 GASP
  change: 3 CTS
  Come up: 3 OWE 4 FAIL FALL
    LOSE
  coming: 3 ARR
  Cut: 3 BOB END 4 CLIP CROP
    5 ABORT
  cuts: 4 BOBS 5 SNIPS
  distance: 4 STEP
    11 STONESTHROW

dog: 3 POM 4 PEKE
drama: 7 PLAYLET
drink: 4 DRAM
drive: 4 SPIN
end: 4 STUB
end of the stick: 7 BUMDEAL
  RAWDEAL
Fall: 4 FAIL
flight: 3 HOP
form: 4 ABBR
Get ~ with: 6 SNAPAT
haircut: 3 BOB
holiday: 4 XMAS
In ~ supply: 5 SCANT
In a ~ time: 4 ANON
Is: 4 OWES
It may be ~ or long: 3 TON
jacket: 4 ETON
joke: 8 ONELINER
letter: 4 NOTE
life: 3 BIO
meeting: 4 SESS
news bit: 5 SQUIB
No ~ story: 4 EPIC SAGA
note: 4 MEMO
of shut: 4 AJAR
opera piece: 7 ARIETTA
order: 3 BLT
pan: 3 UGH
pants: 4 TROU
Partner of: 5 SWEET
people might write them:
  4 IOUS
period: 3 SEC
poem: 6 RONDEL
punch: 3 JAB
putt: 5 TAPIN
race: 4 DASH 6 SPRINT
relative: 3 SIS
report: 3 POP
ride: 4 SPIN
run: 4 DASH
shot: 3 PIC
skirt: 4 MINI
sleep: 3 NAP
smoke: 3 CIG
snooze: 3 NAP 6 CATNAP
snort: 3 NIP 4 SHOT
sock: 6 ANKLET
solo: 7 ARIETTA
solos: 7 ARIOSOS
stop: 3 STA
stories: 3 LIT
story: 7 NOVELLA
street: 4 LANE
stroke: 4 PUTT
summary: 5 RECAP
swim: 3 DIP
tail: 4 SCUT
Take a ~ cut: 4 SNIP
time: 3 BIT MIN SEC 5 SPELL
  TRICE 6 MOMENT
time out: 4 DOZE
trader: 3 ARB
trip: 3 HOP
wave: 4 PERM

way to go: 3 RTE

**Shortage:** 4 LACK NEED
6 DEARTH
Extreme: 6 FAMINE

**Short-billed**
rail: 4 SORA

**Shortcut:** 10 SIDESTREET
Chore: 9 TIMESAVER
Computer: 5 MACRO

**Shorten:** 3 MOW 4 EDIT
7 ABRIDGE
again: 5 RECUT REHEM
RESAW

**Shortener**
Fight: 3 TKO
List: 3 ETC 4 ETAL
Sentence: 6 PAROLE

**Shortening:** 4 LARD

**Short-fused:** 5 TESTY

**Shorthand**
inventor: 5 GREGG
pro: 5 STENO

**Short-legged**
dog: 6 BASSET

**Short-lived**
fashion: 3 FAD
particle: 4 MUON
success: 13 FLASHINTHEPAN
-- Ford: 5 EDSEL

**Shortly:** 4 ANON SOON
6 INABIT INASEC
before: 3 ERE

**Short-range**
plane: 6 AIRBUS

**Short-sheeting:** 5 PRANK

**Shortsighted**
one: 5 MYOPE

**Shortsightedness:** 6 MYOPIA

**Short-spoken:** 5 TERSE

**Shortstop**
Famous: 5 REESE
Like a: 5 AGILE
nickname: 4 AROD
~ Aparicio: 4 LUIS
~ Derek: 5 JETER
~ Garciaparra: 5 NOMAR
~ Jeter: 5 DEREK
~ Rodriguez: 4 ALEX
~ Vizquel: 4 OMAR

**Short-straw**
drawer: 5 LOSER

**Short-tailed**
wildcat: 4 LYNX

**Short-tempered:** 5 TESTY

**Short-term**
hire: 4 TEMP

**Short-winded:** 5 TERSE

**Shoshone**
speaker: 3 UTE

**Shostakovich**
Composer: 6 DMITRI

**Shot:** 3 BBS TRY 4 AMMO STAB
5 GUESS KAPUT PHOTO
SNORT
A: 3 PER
amount: 4 DOSE

Arcing: 3 LOB
Being: 8 ONCAMERA
Big: 3 VIP 4 CZAR 5 CELEB
MOGUL NABOB 6 FATCAT
7 CLOSEUP
Billiards: 5 CAROM MASSE
Camera: 3 PAN
contents: 4 SERA
Drop: 4 DINK
Easy: 5 TAPIN
from a tee: 5 DRIVE
Give it a: 3 TRY
Good: 4 GOAL
Had a: 5 DRANK
Hot: 3 ACE
Inside: 4 XRAY
in the arm: 4 HYPO 5 BOOST
in the dark: 4 STAB 5 GUESS
Kind of: 3 FLU MUG 4 CHIP
Last: 4 PUTT
Long: 8 ONEINTEN
Movie: 4 TAKE
Not-so-big: 3 BBS
of booze: 4 BELT SLUG
5 SNORT
orderer: 3 DOC
Overhead: 5 SMASH
Prepare to be: 4 POSE
put: 5 EVENT
putter: 7 SYRINGE
Replayed: 3 LET
Second: 6 RETAKE
shooter: 4 HYPO
Small: 3 BBS 6 PELLET
spot: 3 ARM
Sweeping: 3 PAN
Take a ~ at: 3 TRY
Take another: 5 RETRY
Tennis: 3 LOB
Took a: 5 TRIED
Tricky: 5 MASSE
up: 4 GREW
Voided: 3 LET

**Shotgun**
shot: 6 PELLET

**Shots**
Call the: 4 LEAD 6 DIRECT
Some: 8 VACCINES

**Should**
that be the case: 4 IFSO
~, with "to": 5 OUGHT

**Shoulder**
blade: 7 SCAPULA
Cold: 4 SNUB
extension: 6 SLEEVE
Give the cold: 4 SHUN SNUB
5 SPURN 6 IGNORE
muscle: 7 DELTOID ROTATOR
muscle, briefly: 4 DELT
ornament: 7 EPAULET
Road: 4 BERM
Touch on the: 3 TAP
wrap: 5 SHAWL STOLE

**Shouldered:** 5 BORNE

**Shoulders**
It has: 4 ROAD

**Shout:** 3 CRY 4 YELL
from the stands: 3 RAH
in church: 4 AMEN
of adoration: 7 HOSANNA
of disapproval: 3 BOO
of encouragement: 5 CHEER
of praise: 7 HOSANNA
of support: 3 OLE
of surprise: 3 OHO
of triumph: 4 TADA
to an unruly group:
10 ONEATATIME

**Shove:** 4 PUSH
off: 4 SAIL 5 LEAVE 6 DEPART
7 SETSAIL
Upward: 5 BOOST

**Shovel**
Use a: 3 DIG

**Shoving**
match: 4 SUMO

**Show:** 3 AIR 4 BARE 6 EVINCE
7 PRESENT
Afternoon: 7 MATINEE
again: 5 REAIR
appreciation: 4 CLAP
5 THANK
assent: 3 NOD
backer: 5 ANGEL
Big: 4 EXPO
Boffo: 5 SMASH
clearly: 6 EVINCE
concern for: 8 ASKAFTER
contempt: 5 SNEER
curiosity: 3 ASK
Daytime: 4 SOAP
disapproval: 3 BOO
disdain: 5 SCORN SNEER
fear: 4 PALE 5 COWER START
7 TREMBLE
flexibility: 4 BEND 5 ADAPT
gratitude: 5 THANK
Hit ~ sign: 3 SRO
horse: 4 ARAB 5 THIRD
host: 5 EMCEE
how: 5 TEACH
interest in: 8 ASKABOUT
Kick off the: 4 OPEN
Kind of: 4 STAG TENT
5 RAREE 6 ONEMAN
7 PREGAME
Light: 6 AURORA
Like ~ horses: 4 SHOD
mercy to: 5 SPARE
need (abbr.): 3 TKT
off: 5 SPORT 6 FLAUNT
off muscles: 4 FLEX
of hands: 4 VOTE
on TV: 3 AIR
opener: 4 ACTI 5 EMCEE
partner: 4 TELL
piece: 3 ACT 7 EPISODE
place: 5 STAGE THIRD
Postgame: 5 RECAP
presenter: 3 USO
proof of: 6 EVINCE
respect: 4 RISE 5 KNEEL

Run the: 4 RULE 5 EMCEE
   6 DIRECT
Science: 4 NOVA
scorn: 5 SNEER
shame: 6 REDDEN
shock: 4 GASP
showers: 3 TVS
signs of life: 4 STIR
souvenir: 4 STUB
starter: 4 ACTI
stoppers: 3 ADS
Street: 5 RAREE
surprise: 4 GASP
Take the ~ on the road:
   4 TOUR
team spirit: 4 ROOT
the ropes to: 5 TEACH TRAIN
   6 ORIENT
They'll ~ you the world:
   7 ATLASES
to a seat: 3 USH
to be false: 5 BELIE
to be true: 5 PROVE
Trade: 4 EXPO
uncertainty: 6 SEESAW
up: 4 COME 6 APPEAR
   ARRIVE
up again: 5 RECUR
up for: 6 ATTEND
Variety: 5 REVUE
When the ~ must go on:
   7 AIRTIME
with skits: 3 SNL
**Show ___ : 3 BIZ**
**___ show (carnival): 5 RAREE**
**Show biz**
   org.: 5 ASCAP
   parent: 8 STAGEMOM
   prize: 5 OSCAR
**"Show Boat"**
   author Ferber: 4 EDNA
   cap'n: 4 ANDY
   composer Jerome: 4 KERN
   song: 10 OLMANRIVER
**Showdown: 4 DUEL**
**Showed**
   again: 5 RERAN
   interest: 5 SATUP
   up: 4 CAME 6 BLEWIN
**Shower: 4 PELT RAIN 5 BATHE**
   affection: 4 DOTE
   alternative: 4 BATH
   Bridal: 4 RICE
   Cold: 5 SLEET
   gel additive: 4 ALOE
   Get ready to: 6 UNROBE
   House: 5 CSPAN
   Kind of: 6 BRIDAL
   Like a cold: 6 SLEETY
   Local flick: 4 NABE
   part: 6 METEOR
   powder: 4 TALC
   shower: 5 RADAR
   sponge: 5 LOOFA
   square: 4 TILE
   time: 5 APRIL

**Showers**
   Show: 3 TVS
**Showery**
   month: 5 APRIL
**"Show Girl"**
   tune: 4 LIZA
**Showing**
   a fancy for: 4 INTO
   awe: 5 AGAPE
   distress: 6 PAINED
   fatigue: 3 WAN
   off: 10 HOTDOGGING
   Second: 5 RERUN
   wonder: 5 AGAPE
**Showman**
   ~ Ziegfeld: 3 FLO
**"Show Me the Way"**
   band: 4 STYX
**Show-off: 3 HAM**
   Educated: 6 PEDANT
**Showplaces**
   Tree: 8 ARBORETA
**Showroom**
   model: 4 DEMO
**Shows**
   It ~ the way: 5 ARROW
**Showtime**
   rival: 3 HBO
**"___ show time!": 3 ITS**
**Showy: 4 ARTY GALA**
   6 FLORID ORNATE
   bloom: 4 IRIS 5 ASTER
   Culturally: 4 ARTY
   display: 5 ECLAT
   feather: 5 PLUME
   Female with a ~ mate:
     6 PEAHEN
   flower: 4 GLAD IRIS LILY
     ROSE 5 ASTER CALLA
     PEONY 6 AZALEA DAHLIA
     8 HIBISCUS
   flowers: 5 CROCI
     8 GLADIOLI
   lily: 4 SEGO
   moths: 3 IOS
   parrot: 8 COCKATOO
   shooter: 3 TAW
   shrub: 6 AZALEA
   trinket: 4 GAUD
**Shred: 3 RIP 4 ATOM IOTA**
   REND TEAR WHIT
   5 RIPUP 6 TATTER
   TEARUP
**Shredded: 4 TORE TORN**
   9 INTATTERS
**Shredder**
   in the news: 5 ENRON
**Shrek: 4 OGRE**
   Like: 6 RATEDG
**Shrew: 3 HAG NAG 6 VIRAGO**
**Shrewd: 3 SLY 4 CAGY CUTE**
   5 CAGEY CANNY SHARP
   SMART 6 ASTUTE
**Shrewdness: 6 ACUMEN**
**Shriek**
   Comics: 3 EEK 4 YEOW

**Shrill**
   cry: 4 YELP
   insect: 6 CICADA
**Shrimp: 4 RUNT 7 SHORTIE**
   dish: 6 SCAMPI
   kin: 5 PRAWN
**Shrimper**
   needs: 4 NETS
   net: 5 TRAWL
**Shrine**
   Buddhist: 5 STUPA
   Cavelike: 6 GROTTO
   Delphic: 6 ORACLE
   Eastern: 6 PAGODA
   Israeli: 6 MASADA
   San Antonio: 5 ALAMO
   Texas: 5 ALAMO
**Shrine Game**
   side: 4 EAST WEST
**Shriner**
   cap: 3 FEZ
   Humorist: 3 WIL
**Shrink: 3 SHY 7 ANALYST**
   15 PSYCHOTHERAPIST
   in fear: 6 CRINGE
   org.: 3 APA
   reply: 4 ISEE
**Shrinking**
   Like a ~ violet: 3 SHY
   sea: 4 ARAL
**Shrivel: 4 WILT 5 WIZEN**
   6 WITHER
**Shriver**
   Newswoman: 5 MARIA
   of tennis: 3 PAM
   Philanthropist: 6 EUNICE
**Shriver, Maria**
   Mother of: 6 EUNICE
**Shropshire**
   she: 3 EWE
**Shroud**
   site: 5 TURIN
**Shrovetide**
   serving: 5 BLINI
**Shrove Tuesday**
   follower: 4 LENT
**Shrub**
   Asian: 5 HENNA
   Cashew family: 5 SUMAC
   Flowering: 6 AZALEA SPIREA
   Fragrant: 5 LILAC
   Garden: 6 AZALEA
   Indigo: 4 ANIL
   Medicinal: 5 SENNA 6 CASSIA
   Ornamental: 6 SPIREA
   8 OLEANDER
   Poison: 5 SUMAC
   Rose family: 4 SLOE 6 SPIREA
   Showy: 6 AZALEA
**Shrubby**
   wasteland: 5 HEATH
**Shrug**
   Eliciting a ~, maybe: 4 SOSO
   off: 6 IGNORE
**Shtick: 3 ACT BIT**
   Pick up: 4 LINE

**Shucker**
unit: 3 EAR
**"Shucks!":** 4 DANG DARN
  DRAT HECK RATS
  5 AWGEE OHGEE
  6 DARNIT
**Shuffleboard**
locale: 4 DECK
___ shui: 4 FENG
**Shul**
scroll: 5 TORAH
**Shula**
Coach: 3 DON
**Shun:** 5 AVOID 6 ESCHEW
**Shuriken**
thrower: 5 NINJA
**"Shush!":** 5 QUIET
**Shut:** 5 CLOSE
in: 4 PENT
loudly: 4 SLAM
Not quite: 4 AJAR
up: 4 SEAL 5 CLOSE
(up): 4 CLAM PENT
**Shutdown**
End a: 6 REOPEN
**Shute**
Author: 5 NEVIL
**Shuteye:** 5 SLEEP
Get some extra: 7 SLEEPIN
Got some: 5 SLEPT
**Shutout**
line score: 4 OOOO
score: 3 NIL
spoilers: 4 RUNS
**Shutter**
strip: 4 SLAT
**Shutterbug**
request: 5 SMILE
setting: 5 FSTOP
**Shuttle**
org.: 4 NASA
piece: 4 TILE
plane: 6 AIRBUS
seal: 5 ORING
site: 4 LOOM
Use a: 3 TAT 5 WEAVE
**Shuttlecock:** 4 BIRD
**"Shut up!":** 5 CANIT 6 STOWIT
  7 SILENCE
**Shy:** 3 COY 5 SHORT
  6 DEMURE
Be: 3 OWE
creature: 4 DEER
Not: 5 VOCAL
person:
  15 SHRINKINGVIOLET
**Shylock**
doing: 5 USURY
offering: 4 LOAN
Play: 4 LEND
**Sí:** 3 YES
**Sl:** 3 MAG
**Siam**
King of ~ phrase:
  8 ETCETERA
suffix: 3 ESE

Visitor to: 4 ANNA
**Siamang:** 9 LESSERAPE
**Siamese:** 3 CAT 4 THAI
sound: 4 MEOW PURR
Tutor of ~ royalty: 4 ANNA
twin name: 3 ENG
**Sib:** 3 BRO SIS
**Sibelius**
Composer: 4 JEAN
**Siberia**
City in: 4 OMSK
locale: 4 ASIA
People of: 5 YAKUT
Send to: 5 EXILE
**Siberian**
Like ~ winters: 5 HARSH
plain: 6 STEPPE
relative: 5 ALEUT
river: 4 URAL
**Sibilant**
letters: 5 ESSES
Suffer with a: 4 LISP
summons: 4 PSST
**Sibling**
Biblical: 4 ABEL CAIN
Bro: 3 SIS
offspring: 5 NIECE
of Jo, Meg, and Amy: 4 BETH
Sis: 3 BRO
Spouse's: 5 INLAW
**Siblings**
Having no: 4 ONLY
Kid with no: 9 ONLYCHILD
**Sibyl:** 4 SEER 7 SEERESS
**"Sic 'em!":** 6 ATTACK
**Sicilia:** 5 ISOLA
**Sicilian**
city: 4 ENNA 7 PALERMO
peak: 4 ETNA
resort: 4 ENNA
volcano: 4 ETNA
wine: 7 MARSALA
**Sicily**
Capital of: 7 PALERMO
Island near: 5 MALTA
volcano: 4 ETNA 6 MTETNA
**Sick:** 3 ILL
and tired: 5 FEDUP
Feel: 3 AIL
Partner of: 5 TIRED
~, in French: 6 MALADE
**Sick as ___:** 4 ADOG
**Sickle:** 4 TOOL
Use a: 4 REAP
**Sickly**
looking: 6 SALLOW
**"Sic semper tyrannis!"**
crier: 5 BOOTH
**Sid**
TV costar of: 7 IMOGENE
**"Siddhartha"**
author: 5 HESSE
**Side:** 6 ASPECT
Calm: 3 LEE
Chopped: 4 SLAW
Coin: 7 OBVERSE

Cutting: 4 EDGE
Debate: 3 CON PRO 4 ANTI
Diamond: 5 FACET
Favor one: 4 LIMP
Flip: 5 HEADS
Go to the other: 6 DEFECT
It has a broad: 4 BARN
Lean to one: 4 LIST
Lee: 3 CSA 4 GRAY
Move to the: 5 SHUNT
One on your: 4 ALLY
On the other: 3 FOE
On the safe: 4 ALEE
On the small: 3 WEE
Other: 3 FOE 5 ENEMY
South: 3 ERN
squared: 4 AREA
The bright: 4 YANG
The dark: 3 YIN
Tip to one: 6 CAREEN
To one: 5 APART ASKEW
Toward the sheltered: 4 ALEE
track: 4 SPUR
Window: 4 JAMB
with: 4 ABUT
Word on either ~ of "-à-": 3 VIS
**Sidearm**
Cavalry: 5 SABER
**Sideboard:** 8 CREDENZA
**Side by side:** 4 AREA
  7 ABREAST
Live: 7 COEXIST
Place: 6 APPOSE
**Side dish:** 4 SLAW 5 BEANS
  FRIES 8 COLESLAW
  9 RICEARONI
  11 IDAHOPOTATO
**Sidekick:** 3 PAL 4 AIDE
  5 CRONY
Batman's: 5 ROBIN
Boris's: 7 NATASHA
Captain Hook's: 4 SMEE
Garfield's: 4 ODIE
Green Hornet's: 4 KATO
Lone Ranger's: 5 TONTO
Ollie's: 4 STAN
Stimpy's: 3 REN
with a headband: 5 TONTO
**Sideless**
cart: 4 DRAY
**Sidelines**
brand: 8 GATORADE
greeting: 5 HIMOM
shout: 3 RAH
**Sidelong**
glance: 4 LEER
**Sidepiece:** 4 JAMB
**Sides**
Attack from all: 5 BESET
Cricket: 3 ONS
in some wars: 5 GANGS
It has six: 4 UTAH
On both ~ of: 7 ASTRIDE
**Sideshow**
performer: 4 GEEK
setting: 4 TENT

site: 6 MIDWAY
Side-splitter: 4 RIOT
Sidestep: 5 AVERT AVOID
    DODGE ELUDE EVADE
    SKIRT
Sidestroke
    feature: 12 SCISSORSKICK
Side to side
    From: 7 ATHWART
    Move from: 4 SWAY
    Move rapidly from: 6 WAGGLE
Sidewalk
    eatery: 4 CAFE
    edge: 4 CURB
    Install a: 4 PAVE
    stand drink: 3 ADE
    ~ Santa: 4 TEMP
Sideways
    look: 4 LEER
    Move: 4 CRAB
Sidewinder: 5 SNAKE
    React to a: 8 SEESTARS
    trail: 3 ESS
    warning: 6 RATTLE
Siding
    Railroad: 4 SPUR
    wood: 5 CEDAR
Sidle: 4 EDGE
Sidler
    Beach: 4 CRAB
Sidney
    Charlie Chan portrayer:
        5 TOLER
    Director: 5 LUMET
Sieben
    follower: 4 ACHT
Siege
    1836 ~ site: 5 ALAMO
    defense: 4 MOAT
    Under: 5 BESET
Siegfried
    Partner of: 3 ROY
Siegmeister
    Composer: 4 ELIE
Siemens
    Electrical units now called:
        4 MHOS
Sierra ___: 5 LEONE MADRE
    6 NEVADA
Sierra Club
    cofounder: 4 MUIR
    concern (abbr.): 4 ECOL
Sierra Madre
    treasure: 3 ORO
Sierra Madres
    resort: 4 OJAI
Sierra Nevada
    City at the foot of the: 4 RENO
    lake: 5 TAHOE
    resort: 5 TAHOE
Siesta: 3 NAP 4 REST
    5 SLEEP
    covering: 6 SERAPE
    Take a: 4 DOZE REST
    takers: 7 NAPPERS
    time (abbr.): 3 AFT

Siete
    follower: 4 OCHO
    minus seis: 3 UNO
Sieve
    bottom: 4 MESH
    Put through a: 4 RICE
    Use a: 6 STRAIN
Sift
    through: 6 WINNOW
Sigh
    of relief: 4 PHEW
    Quaint: 4 AHME
    Satisfied: 3 AAH
Sighed
    aside: 4 AHME
    line: 4 AHME
Sigher
    word: 4 ALAS
Sighs
    of distress: 3 OHS
Sight: 5 SENSE
    Catch ~ of: 4 ESPY SPOT
        6 DESCRY
    Out of: 4 GONE 6 HIDDEN
    Put out of: 4 HIDE
    Second: 3 ESP
    Stay out of: 4 HIDE 6 HOLEUP
        LIELOW
"___ sight!": 4 OUTA 5 OUTTA
Sighting: 6 ESPIAL
Sights
    See the: 4 TOUR
    Set one's: 3 AIM
    Set one's ~ on: 5 AIMAT
Sightseeing
    trip: 4 TOUR
Sigma
    follower: 3 TAU
    preceder: 3 RHO
Sigma ___: 3 CHI
Sigma Chi
    Sweetheart of: 4 COED
Sigmoid
    shape: 3 ESS
Sigmund: 5 FREUD
    Daughter of: 4 ANNA
Sign: 3 INK 4 OMEN
    an agreement: 9 ENTERINTO
    a new lease: 5 RELET
    Apartment: 5 TOLET
    away: 4 CEDE
    Be a ~ of: 4 BODE
    Broadcast: 5 ONAIR
    Business: 4 ESTD 5 ESTAB
    B'way: 3 SRO
    Danger: 7 REDFLAG
    Diner: 4 EATS 7 EATHERE
    Door: 3 MEN 4 EXIT 5 ENTER
    Fall: 5 LIBRA 7 SCORPIO
    First: 5 ARIES
    Flat: 5 TOLET
    for another hitch: 4 REUP
    Foreboding: 4 OMEN
        7 PORTENT
    for short: 7 INITIAL
    from above: 4 OMEN

gas: 4 NEON
Good: 4 HALO
Healing: 4 SCAB
Hit: 3 SRO
How to: 5 ININK
in the dark: 4 EXIT
Kind of: 4 NEON
Lighted: 4 EXIT
Musical: 4 CLEF
Octagonal: 4 STOP
of a mistake: 7 ERASURE
of approval: 3 NOD
of a winner: 3 VEE
of boredom: 4 YAWN
of disuse: 4 RUST
off: 3 END
off on: 4 OKAY
of life: 5 PULSE
of spring: 4 THAW 5 ARIES
    6 GEMINI
of success: 3 SRO
of summer: 3 LEO 5 VIRGO
    7 THECRAB
of things to come: 4 OMEN
on: 4 HIRE 5 ENROL LOGIN
    6 ENLIST
on again: 4 REUP
over: 4 CEDE
Pause: 5 COMMA
Peace: 4 DOVE
Place to: 10 DOTTEDLINE
Retro ~ word: 4 OLDE
Sale: 4 ASIS
Store: 4 OPEN SALE
Studio: 5 ONAIR
up: 4 JOIN 5 ENROL
    6 ENLIST ENROLL
    HIREON 7 RECRUIT
Signal: 3 CUE 5 NODTO
    a cab: 4 HAIL
    approval: 3 NOD
    for help: 3 SOS
    light: 5 FLARE
    receivers:
        15 SATELLITEDISHES
    Sortie: 8 AIRALERT
    to enter: 3 CUE
    TV ~ carrier: 5 CABLE
    Two-palms-down: 4 SAFE
    Warning: 5 SIREN
Signature
    piece: 3 PEN
Signatures
    Simple: 3 XES
Signe
    Actress: 5 HASSO
Signed: 3 XED
    note: 3 IOU
    off on: 3 OKD
Signer
    ~, at times: 3 XER
Signet: 4 SEAL
Significance: 6 IMPORT
Significant: 3 KEY 5 MAJOR
    6 OFNOTE
    event: 9 MILESTONE

Least: 6 MEREST
period: 3 ERA
They may be: 6 OTHERS
**Significant ___**: 5 OTHER
**Signify:** 4 BODE MEAN
        6 DENOTE 7 ADDUPTO
**Sikorsky**
Inventor: 4 IGOR
**Silas**
Diplomat: 5 DEANE
**"Silas Marner"**
author: 5 ELIOT
girl: 5 EPPIE
**Sildenafil ___ (Viagra):**
        7 CITRATE
**Silence:** 3 GAG 4 HUSH MUTE
        5 SITON STILL
Code of: 6 OMERTA
Musical: 4 REST
**Silenced:** 5 SATON
**"Silence of the Lambs, The"**
director: 5 DEMME
org.: 3 FBI
**Silencer:** 3 SHH
Commercial: 4 MUTE
Squeak: 3 OIL
**Silent:** 3 MUM 4 MUTE 5 TACIT
assent: 3 NOD
Be ~, in music: 5 TACET
communication syst.: 3 ASL
film star: 5 HARPO
greeting: 4 WAVE
one: 4 CLAM
performer: 4 MIME
president: 3 CAL
**"Silent Movie"**
costar: 6 PETERS
**"Silent Running"**
star Bruce: 4 DERN
**Silent-screen**
siren: 4 VAMP
**"Silent Spring"**
killer: 3 DDT
**Silesia**
River of: 4 ODER
**Silica**
gem: 4 OPAL
**Silicate**
Soft: 4 TALC
**Silicon**
gem: 4 OPAL
**Silicone**
valley: 8 CLEAVAGE
**Silicon Valley**
city: 8 PALOALTO
giant: 5 INTEL
**Silk**
fabric: 5 TULLE 6 PONGEE
French ~ center: 4 LYON
        5 LYONS
Indian ~ center: 5 ASSAM
pattern: 5 MOIRE
Raw ~ color: 4 ECRU
tie: 3 OBI
topper: 8 OPERAHAT
wrap: 4 SARI

~, in French: 4 SOIE
**"Silk Stockings"**
actress Charisse: 3 CYD
actress Cyd: 8 CHARISSE
star: 7 ASTAIRE
**"Silkwood"**
character Silkwood: 5 KAREN
star: 6 STREEP
**Silkworm:** 3 ERI
**Silky**
coated cat/rabbit: 6 ANGORA
coated dog: 7 SPANIEL
        11 AFGHANHOUND
synthetic: 5 RAYON
**Sill:** 5 LEDGE
**Silliness**
Symbols of: 5 GEESE
**Sillitoe**
Author: 4 ALAN
**Sills:** 4 DIVA
solo: 4 ARIA
**Silly:** 4 DAFT 5 INANE
        7 ASININE
goose: 3 ASS 5 NINNY
It might be: 4 GRIN
Knock: 4 DAZE
ones: 5 GEESE
Really: 5 APISH
stuff: 5 PUTTY
trick: 5 APERY
**Silly Putty**
holder: 3 EGG
**"___ silly question ...":** 4 ASKA
**Silo**
missile: 5 TITAN
neighbor: 4 BARN
occupant: 4 ICBM
**Silt**
deposit: 5 LOESS
**Silver:** 5 METAL 6 ARGENT
Actor: 3 RON
eagle wearer: 7 COLONEL
Fine: 8 STERLING
lead: 4 REIN
leaf wearer (abbr.): 5 LTCOL
rider: 10 LONERANGER
salmon: 4 COHO
Shout to: 4 HIYO
source: 3 ORE 4 LODE MINE
Take the: 5 PLACE
type (abbr.): 4 STER
~, in Spanish: 5 PLATA
**Silver ___ (cloud seed):**
        6 IODIDE
**"___ Silver, away!":** 4 HIYO
**Silver Bow County**
seat: 5 BUTTE
**Silverdome**
team: 5 LIONS
**Silverheels, Jay**
role: 5 TONTO
**Silvers**
Comedian: 4 PHIL
role: 5 BILKO
**Silversmith**
Colonial: 6 REVERE

**Silver Springs**
neighbor: 5 OCALA
**Silver State (abbr.):** 3 NEV
**Silverstein**
Author: 4 SHEL
**Silverstone**
Actress: 6 ALICIA
**Silver-tongued:** 4 GLIB
speaker: 6 ORATOR
**Silverwork**
Mexican ~ center: 5 TAXCO
**Silvery:** 6 ARGENT
fish: 5 SMELT
gray: 3 ASH
white: 6 ARGENT
**Sim**
Actor: 8 ALASTAIR
**Simba:** 4 LION
cry: 4 ROAR
Mate of: 4 NALA
Uncle of: 4 SCAR
**___ Simbel:** 3 ABU
**Simferopol**
Its capital is: 6 CRIMEA
**Simian:** 3 APE 7 APELIKE
Sumatran: 5 ORANG
**Similar:** 4 AKIN 5 ALIKE
in sound: 8 ASSONANT
prefix: 5 HOMEO
to: 4 LIKE
version: 8 ANALOGUE
**Similarity**
symbol: 5 TILDE
**Similarly:** 5 ALIKE
**Simile**
center: 3 ASA
words: 3 ASA 4 ASAN
**Simmer:** 4 STEW 6 BRAISE
eggs: 5 POACH
More than: 4 BOIL
**Simmering:** 5 ONLOW
**Simmons**
of Kiss: 4 GENE
rival: 5 SEALY SERTA
rock band: 4 KISS
**Simoleon:** 4 BUCK CLAM
Spanish: 6 PESETA
**Simoleons:** 5 MOOLA
**Simon**
Apostle: 5 PETER
Baritone: 5 ESTES
Playwright: 4 NEIL
TV detective: 7 TEMPLAR
Villainous: 6 LEGREE
**Simon ___:** 4 SAYS
**Simon, Carly**
hit: 11 YOURESOVAIN
**Simon, Neil**
play: 10 CHAPTERTWO
        15 CALIFORNIASUITE
**Simon, Paul**
musical: 7 CAPEMAN
song: 7 AMERICA
**Simon & Garfunkel:** 3 DUO
1966 ~ hit: 8 IAMAROCK
hit: 7 CECILIA

**Simone**
Info: French cue
Author: 4 WEIL
Sea, to: 3 MER
Singer: 4 NINA
**Simpatico:** 7 LIKABLE
reply: 8 IHEARYOU
**Simple:** 4 EASY MERE
fellow: 5 SIMON
Pure and: 4 MERE
Something: 4 SNAP
stuff: 4 ABCS
**Simpler**
Make: 4 EASE
**Simpleton:** 3 ASS OAF 4 BOOB
CLOD DODO DOLT DOPE
LOON 5 GOOSE NINNY
NODDY
**Simplicity:** 4 EASE
Epitome of: 3 ABC
**Simplify:** 4 EASE
10 STREAMLINE
**Simpson**
Blue-haired: 5 MARGE
boy: 4 BART
Designer: 5 ADELE
Former Senator: 4 ALAN
Grandpa: 3 ABE
Novelist: 4 MONA
sister: 4 LISA
trial judge: 3 ITO
**Simpson, Homer**
bartender: 3 MOE
Dad of: 3 ABE
favorite bar: 4 MOES
neighbor: 3 NED
outburst: 3 DOH
Son of: 4 BART
**Simpson, Marge**
voice: 6 KAVNER
**"Simpsons, The"**
bartender: 3 MOE
bus driver: 4 OTTO
character Disco ___: 3 STU
character Nahasapeemapetilon:
3 APU
creator Groening: 4 MATT
neighbor Flanders: 3 NED
storekeeper: 3 APU
tavern: 4 MOES
teacher Krabappel: 4 EDNA
**Sims**
of jazz: 4 ZOOT
**Simulate**
~, in a way: 7 REENACT
**Simultaneously:** 7 ATATIME
**Sin:** 3 ERR 5 STRAY
7 MISDEED
A deadly: 4 ENVY LUST
5 ANGER GREED SLOTH
city: 5 SODOM
**Sinai**
and others (abbr.): 3 MTS
climber: 5 MOSES
Desert near: 5 NEGEV
**Sinatra:** 4 TINA 8 BARITONE

1961 ~ album:
13 RINGADINGDING
1993 ~ album: 5 DUETS
circle: 7 RATPACK
employer: 6 DORSEY
Former Mrs.: 3 AVA MIA
hometown: 7 HOBOKEN
standard: 5 MYWAY
9 HIGHHOPES
**Sinbad**
bird: 3 ROC
realm: 3 SEA
transport: 3 ROC
**Since:** 4 ASOF 6 INTHAT
~, in Scotland: 4 SYNE
**Sincere:** 4 REAL TRUE
**"Since ___ You Baby":** 4 IMET
**Sinclair**
Author: 5 UPTON
rival: 4 ESSO
**Sine:** 5 RATIO
language: 4 TRIG
**Sine ___ non:** 3 QUA
**Sine qua non:** 4 NEED
**Sinew:** 6 TENDON
**Sinewy:** 4 WIRY
**Sinful:** 4 EVIL
**Sing:** 3 RAT 4 BLAB 5 TROLL
along: 6 JOININ
cheerfully: 4 LILT
in the Alps: 5 YODEL
in the snow: 5 CAROL
like Bing: 5 CROON
like Ella: 4 SCAT
like the birds: 5 TRILL TWEET
Not really: 7 LIPSYNC
softly: 5 CROON
Something to: 4 TUNE
the blues: 4 WAIL
the praises of: 4 LAUD
5 EXTOL
without words: 3 HUM
Word after: 5 ALONG
**Sing.**
Opposite of: 3 PLU
**Sing-along**
Bar: 7 KARAOKE
syllable: 3 TRA
**"___ Sing America":** 4 ITOO
**Singapore**
Island near: 7 SUMATRA
setting: 4 ASIA
**"Singapore"**
actress Gardner: 3 AVA
**Singaraja**
setting: 4 BALI
**Singe:** 4 CHAR
**Singer:** 3 RAT 4 FINK
7 STOOLIE
Actress: 4 LORI
at Woodstock: 4 BAEZ
Author: 5 ISAAC
One-named: 4 CHER ENYA
SADE 5 CHARO 6 ODETTA
syllable: 3 TRA
syllables: 3 LAS 4 LALA

Synagogue: 6 CANTOR
Use a: 3 SEW
~ Amos: 4 TORI
~ Anita: 4 ODAY
~ Anthony: 4 MARC
~ Arnold: 4 EDDY
~ Billy: 4 JOEL
~ Bonnie: 5 RAITT
~ Bryant: 5 ANITA
~ Burl: 4 IVES
~ Celine: 4 DION
~ Cleo: 5 LAINE
~ Della: 5 REESE
~ Diana: 4 ROSS
~ Dinah: 5 SHORE
~ Ed: 4 AMES
~ Edith: 4 PIAF
~ Frankie: 5 LAINE
~ Irene: 4 CARA
~ Jackson: 6 BROWNE
~ Jacques: 4 BREL
~ Janis: 3 IAN
~ Jennifer: 5 LOPEZ
~ Jerry: 4 VALE
~ Joan: 4 JETT
~ Johnny: 6 MATHIS
~ k.d.: 4 LANG
~ Kiki: 3 DEE
~ K.T.: 5 OSLIN
~ LeAnn: 5 RIMES
~ Lena: 5 HORNE
~ Leon: 7 REDBONE
~ Lou: 5 RAWLS
~ Mariah: 5 CAREY
~ Marvin: 4 GAYE
~ Mel: 5 TORME
~ Nelson: 4 EDDY
~ Patsy: 5 CLINE
~ Patti: 7 LABELLE
~ Paul: 4 ANKA
~ Paula: 5 ABDUL
~ Peggy: 3 LEE
~ Perry: 4 COMO
~ Phil: 4 OCHS
~ Sheena: 6 EASTON
~ Tori: 4 AMOS
~ Travis: 5 TRITT
~ Vikki: 4 CARR
~ Yma: 5 SUMAC
~ Yoko: 3 ONO
**Singers**
Church: 5 CHOIR
Some: 5 ALTOS BASSI
**"Sing, goddess, the wrath of ..."**
It begins: 5 ILIAD
**Singing**
brothers: 4 AMES
cowboy: 5 AUTRY
First name in: 4 ELLA
group: 5 CHOIR
Half a ~ group: 5 MAMAS
PAPAS
One of a ~ quartet: 6 EDAMES
Refrain from: 3 TRA
7 TRALALA
soldier: 6 SADLER

style: 4 SCAT
syllable: 3 TRA
syllables: 4 LALA 5 TRALA
the blues: 3 SAD
voice: 4 ALTO
Wordless: 4 SCAT
**Single:** 3 ONE 4 LONE ONLY
    SOLE 5 UNWED
    7 BASEHIT
A ~ time: 4 ONCE
Card with a ~ pip: 3 ACE
entity: 5 MONAD
Not a ~ person: 5 NOONE
On a ~ occasion: 4 ONCE
out: 6 SELECT
piece: 4 UNIT
With a ~ voice: 5 ASONE
**Single-celled**
organism: 5 AMEBA MONAD
    6 AMOEBA
**Single-channel:** 4 MONO
**Single-handed:** 4 SOLO
    5 ALONE
**Single-handedly:** 5 ALONE
**Single-masted**
vessel: 5 SLOOP
**Single-named**
    4 CHER ENYA SADE
    5 CHARO 6 ODETTA
supermodel: 4 IMAN
**Singles**
players: 3 DJS
Some: 4 EXES
**Single-sailed**
vessel: 7 CATBOAT
**Single-strand**
molecule: 3 RNA
**Singleton:** 3 ONE
**Singly:** 3 PER 4 APOP EACH
    ONCE 5 ALONE
    10 ONEATATIME
**Sing Sing:** 6 PRISON
inhabitant: 3 CON
room: 4 CELL
**Singsong**
syllable: 3 TRA
**Singular:** 3 ODD 4 RARE
person: 4 ONER
**Sinister:** 4 EVIL
look: 4 LEER
**Sink:** 3 EBB SAG SET 4 FALL
    5 BASIN 7 SCUTTLE
    TORPEDO
clutter: 6 DISHES
feature: 5 DRAIN
hole: 5 DRAIN
in the middle: 3 SAG
jam: 4 CLOG
Kitchen ~ item:
    10 LIQUIDSOAP
opposite: 4 SWIM
or swim: 4 VERB
trap shape: 3 ESS
unclogging brand: 5 DRANO
**Sinker**
Lusitania: 5 UBOAT

material: 4 LEAD
Sub: 6 ASHCAN
Titanic: 4 BERG 7 ICEBERG
**Sinking**
It may be: 4 FUND
Not: 6 AFLOAT
signal: 3 SOS
**Sinn ___:** 4 FEIN
**Sinner**
Original: 3 EVE
Second: 4 ADAM
What a ~ does: 7 PENANCE
**Sinn Fein**
land: 4 EIRE
org.: 3 IRA
**Sins**
Deadly ~ number: 5 SEVEN
**Sinuous**
curve: 3 ESS
shocker: 3 EEL
squeezer: 3 BOA
swimmer: 3 EEL
**Sinus:** 4 ITER
specialist, briefly: 3 ENT
suffix: 4 ITIS
**Siouan**
Largest ~ tribe: 6 DAKOTA
speaker: 3 OTO 4 IOWA OTOE
    5 OMAHA OSAGE
**Sioux**
foe: 6 PAWNEE
speaker: 3 OTO 4 OTOE
trophy: 5 SCALP
**Sioux City**
site: 4 IOWA
**Sip:** 5 NURSE TASTE
More than: 4 SWIG
**Sipowicz**
employer: 4 NYPD
**Sipping**
aid: 5 STRAW
**Sir:** 5 TITLE
counterpart: 4 MAAM
    5 MADAM
Deer: 4 STAG
in India: 5 SAHIB
~, in Spanish: 5 SENOR
**Sire:** 5 BEGET
**Sired:** 5 BEGAT BEGOT
**Siren:** 4 VAMP 5 ALARM ALERT
    7 ALLURER LORELEI
    9 SEXKITTEN
on the Rhine: 7 LORELEI
Play the: 4 LURE 5 TEMPT
Sound like a: 4 WAIL
**"Sirens"**
actress Macpherson: 4 ELLE
**Sirius:** 5 ASTAR
**Sirloin:** 5 STEAK
part: 3 TIP
**Sis:** 3 REL SIB
sibling: 3 BRO
**Sisal:** 5 AGAVE
**Siskel**
One-time partner of:
    5 EBERT

**Sissy**
Actress: 6 SPACEK
No: 5 HEMAN
role: 6 CARRIE 7 LORETTA
**Sister**
and brother: 3 KIN
attire: 5 HABIT
Dad's: 4 AUNT
Daughter of: 5 NIECE
Holy: 3 NUN
Mom's: 4 AUNT
Sorority: 4 COED
Word with: 3 SOB
**"Sister Act"**
extra: 3 NUN
**Sisterhood**
member: 3 NUN
**Sisterly:** 7 SORORAL
**"Sisters"**
actress Ward: 4 SELA
sister: 4 ALEX
**Sistine Chapel**
figure: 4 ADAM
**Sit:** 4 POSE REST
around: 4 LOAF
Don't just ~ there: 3 ACT
(down): 4 PLOP
for: 4 POSE
in on: 5 AUDIT 6 ATTEND
in the sun: 4 BASK
in traffic: 4 IDLE
Just ~, like food: 7 GETCOLD
on: 5 QUASH 6 STIFLE
One way to: 4 IDLY
Place to: 5 CHAIR
through again: 5 RESEE
Unable to ~ still: 5 ANTSY
Words after: 4 ONIT
**Sitar**
accompaniment: 5 TABLA
player Shankar: 4 RAVI
**Sitarist**
Ravi: 7 SHANKAR
Shankar: 4 RAVI
**Sitcom**
1950s ~: 9 MRPEEPERS
1950s ~ family: 6 NELSON
1950s ~ mom: 4 REED
1950s ~ name: 4 DESI
1970s ~: 5 ARNIE RHODA
1980s ~: 4 AMEN
1990s ~: 5 ELLEN 7 FRIENDS
alien: 3 ALF
aunt: 3 BEE
British: 5 ABFAB
diner: 4 MELS
Former ABC: 5 ELLEN
Furry: 3 ALF
Groundbreaking: 5 ELLEN
Half a ~ duo: 7 LAVERNE
in a garage: 4 TAXI
landlord: 5 MERTZ
newsman Baxter: 3 TED
Part of a ~ sign-off: 4 NANU
planet: 3 ORK
segment: 7 EPISODE

Self-titled: 4 REBA
set in Korea: 4 MASH
Starring in a: 4 ONTV
station: 4 WKRP
WB: 4 REBA
Young:
    15 FATHERKNOWSBEST
**Site:** 6 LOCALE
of a fall: 4 EDEN
of many firings: 4 KILN
of some famous hangings:
    5 PRADO
**Sites:** 4 LOCI
**Sit-in**
Old ~ org.: 3 SDS
participant: 9 PROTESTER
**Sitka**
of Stooge shorts: 4 EMIL
**Sitter**
charge: 3 TOT
creation: 3 LAP
handful: 3 IMP
on the farm: 3 HEN
**Sitting:** 7 SESSION
around: 4 IDLE
duck: 5 DECOY
muscles: 6 GLUTEI
Not ~ well: 5 ANTSY
on: 4 ATOP
on one's hands: 4 IDLE
room: 6 PARLOR
spot: 5 STOOP
Stand for a: 5 EASEL
**Sitting Bull:** 5 SIOUX 6 DAKOTA
**Situate:** 6 ORIENT
**Situated**
Be ~ above: 7 OVERLIE
Is: 4 LIES
**Situation:** 8 BALLGAME
Embarrassing: 7 HOTSEAT
Handle the: 4 COPE
Kind of: 5 NOWIN
Messy: 5 SNAFU
No-win: 3 TIE 4 DRAW
Potentially explosive:
    9 POWDERKEG
Romantic:
    15 ETERNALTRIANGLE
Tennis: 4 ADIN
Tough: 4 SPOT
Unpleasant: 4 MESS
**Situations**
Like some: 5 NOWIN
**Sit-up**
targets: 3 ABS
**Sitwell**
Poet: 5 EDITH
**Siva**
sounds: 3 OMS
**Six**
It has ~ sides: 4 CUBE UTAH
Last ~ lines of a sonnet:
    6 SESTET
make a fl. oz.: 4 TSPS
o'clock fare: 4 NEWS
on a phone: 3 MNO

years, for a senator: 4 TERM
~, in Italian: 3 SEI
~, in Spanish: 4 SEIS
"Six ___ ...": 5 OFONE
**"Six Characters in Search of an
    Author"**
dramatist:
    15 LUIGIPIRANDELLO
**"Six Days, Seven Nights"**
actress: 5 HECHE
**Six-Day War**
hero: 5 DAYAN
side: 6 ISRAEL
**"Six Feet Under"**
network: 3 HBO
son: 4 NATE
**Six Flags**
attraction: 4 RIDE
**Six-foot**
~ Australian: 3 EMU
**Six-footer:** 3 ANT
**Six-legged**
soldier: 7 ARMYANT
**Six-line**
poem: 6 SESTET
**Six-pack**
component: 3 CAN
makeup: 3 ABS
**Six-packs**
Four: 4 CASE
**Six-pointers:** 3 TDS
**Six-shooter:** 3 GUN
**Six-sided**
state: 4 UTAH
**Six-stringed**
instrument: 4 VIOL
**Sixteen**
Kasparov's: 3 MEN
oz.: 5 ONELB
**Sixth**
Henry VIII's: 4 PARR
president: 5 ADAMS
sense: 3 ESP
~ Greek letter: 4 ZETA
**Sixth-century**
date: 3 DII DLI DXI 4 DIII
storyteller: 5 AESOP
**Sixth-day**
creation: 3 MAN
**"Sixth Sense, The"**
actress Collette: 4 TONI
**Six-time**
homer champ: 3 OTT
~ Rose Bowl champs: 3 OSU
~ Super Bowl coach:
    5 SHULA
~ U.S. Open champ: 5 EVERT
**Sixty**
Of ~ minutes: 5 HORAL
**Six-winged**
angel: 6 SERAPH
**Six-yr.**
term holder: 3 SEN
**Size**
abbr.: 3 LGE MED REG
Battery: 3 AAA

Bed: 4 TWIN
Big: 3 EEE
Book: 6 OCTAVO
Bottle: 5 LITER
Broad: 3 EEE
Clothing: 6 PETITE
Coffee: 4 TALL 5 VENTI
Egg: 5 LARGE
Is the right: 4 FITS
Paper: 5 LEGAL
Type: 4 PICA 5 AGATE ELITE
up: 4 CASE RATE 6 ASSESS
**Sizes**
Ascending ~ (abbr.): 3 SML
Big: 3 XLS
**Sizing**
up: 5 EYING
**Sizzler**
Breakfast: 5 BACON
**Sizzling:** 3 HOT
**Skate:** 3 RAY
kin: 5 MANTA
Loosen, as a: 5 UNTIE
Prepare to: 6 LACEUP
**Skater:** 5 LACER
jump: 4 AXEL LUTZ
surface: 3 ICE
~ Apolo Anton: 4 OHNO
~ Brian: 5 ORSER
~ Katarina: 4 WITT
~ Michelle: 4 KWAN
~ Sonja: 5 HENIE
**Skates**
Kind of: 6 INLINE
**Skating**
event: 5 PAIRS
jump: 4 AXEL 7 SALCHOW
legend: 3 ORR
rink: 4 OVAL
spin: 5 CAMEL
venue: 7 ICERINK
**Skavar:** 4 IVAN
**Sked**
guess: 3 ETA
TV ~ abbr.: 3 TBA
**Skedaddle:** 3 GIT HIE LAM
    4 FLEE SCAT 5 SCOOT
    SCRAM 7 VAMOOSE
**"Skedaddle!":** 3 GIT 4 SHOO
**Skedaddled:** 3 RAN 4 FLED
    TORE
**Skee-Ball**
site: 6 ARCADE
**Skeet**
device: 4 TRAP
target: 10 CLAYPIGEON
**Skeeter**
Smack a: 4 SWAT
**Skein**
formers: 5 GEESE
sound: 4 HONK
**Skeleton**
Kind of: 5 AXIAL
part: 4 BONE ULNA
place: 6 CLOSET
prefix: 3 EXO 4 ENDO

**Skelton**
  catchphrase: 7 IDOODIT
  character: 4 CLEM
  Comic: 3 RED
  persona: 4 HOBO
**Skeptic:** 7 DOUBTER
  grain: 4 SALT
  scoff: 4 IBET
**Skeptical:** 5 LEERY
  Be: 5 DOUBT
  response: 4 IBET
  sort: 5 CYNIC
**Skeptically:** 7 ASKANCE
**Sketch:** 4 DRAW LIMN SKIT
  again: 6 REDRAW
  Brief: 8 VIGNETTE
  Funny: 4 SKIT
  out: 4 PLAN
  TV ~ show: 3 SNL
**Sketched:** 4 DREW 5 DRAWN
**"Sketches by ___":** 3 BOZ
**Skewed:** 4 AWRY 5 ATILT
  view: 4 BIAS
**Skewer:** 4 SPIT STAB
**Skewered**
  meal: 5 KABOB KEBAB
**Ski**
  event: 6 SLALOM
  house style: 6 AFRAME
  lift: 3 TOW 4 TBAR
  lodge fare: 5 COCOA
  run: 5 SLOPE
  trail: 5 PISTE
**Ski-___ (snowmobile):** 3 DOO
**Skidded:** 4 SLID
**Skid row**
  denizen: 4 WINO
  woe: 3 DTS
**Skier**
  aid: 4 JBAR TBAR
  quarters: 5 LODGE
  run: 5 SLOPE
  transport: 4 TBAR
  ~ Hermann: 5 MAIER
  ~ Phil: 5 MAHRE
  ~ Tommy: 3 MOE
**Skies**
  Praise to the: 5 EXALT EXTOL
**Skiff:** 4 BOAT
  mover: 3 OAR
  stabilizer: 4 KEEL
  That: 3 SHE
**Skiing**
  category: 6 ALPINE
  event: 6 SLALOM
  Kind of: 6 NORDIC
  mecca: 4 ALPS 5 ASPEN
  spot: 5 SLOPE
**Skill:** 3 ART 5 CRAFT KNACK
    6 TALENT
  EMT: 3 CPR
  Having: 4 ABLE
  Improve a: 4 HONE
  Lacking: 5 INEPT
  Mediator's: 4 TACT
  Medium's: 3 ESP

  R.N.'s: 3 TLC
  Special: 5 KNACK
  With: 4 ABLY 7 ADEPTLY
    8 ADROITLY
**Skilled:** 4 ABLE DEFT 5 ADEPT
  in: 6 GOODAT
  Not ~ in: 6 POORAT
  stalker: 4 LION
**Skillet:** 3 PAN
  lubricant: 4 OLEO
  material: 4 IRON
**Skillful:** 4 ABLE DEFT 5 ADEPT
    6 ADROIT HABILE
**Skills**
  Basic: 4 ABCS
  Office ~ meas.: 3 WPM
**Skim**
  along: 4 FLIT
  ~, as milk: 5 DEFAT
**Skimmer:** 3 HAT
**Skim milk**
  lack: 3 FAT
  Like: 6 NONFAT
  Produce: 5 DEFAT
**Skimpy**
  skirt: 4 MINI
**Skin:** 4 FLAY HIDE PARE PEEL
    5 FLESH 6 SCRAPE
  Animal: 4 HIDE PELT
  art: 6 TATTOO
  blemish: 4 MOLE WART
  care name: 4 OLAY 5 ESTEE
    NIVEA
  cream ingredient: 4 ALOE
  Get under one's: 3 IRK
  layer: 5 DERMA
  Like a lizard's: 5 SCALY
  Of the: 6 DERMAL
  opening: 4 PORE
  pigment: 7 MELANIN
  prefix: 4 DERM 5 DERMO
  problem: 4 ACNE 5 TINEA
  Shed one's: 4 MOLT
  Soak to the: 6 DRENCH
  soother: 4 ALOE 5 CREAM
    6 LOTION
  Tough: 4 HIDE
**"Skin Deep"**
  actor John: 6 RITTER
**Skinflint:** 5 MISER PIKER
**Skinflinty:** 5 CHEAP
**Skinnay**
  Bandleader: 5 ENNIS
**Skinner**
  Actor: 4 OTIS
**Skinny:** 4 BONY DIRT DOPE
    INFO LEAN POOP SLIM
    THIN 6 LATEST
  dipper: 3 EEL
  one: 5 SCRAG
**Skinny-dipper**
  Like a: 4 BARE NUDE
**Skins**
  Shirts and: 5 TEAMS
**Skin-So-Soft**
  maker: 4 AVON

**Skip:** 4 MISS OMIT 5 ELIDE
    6 PASSUP SITOUT
  along the water: 3 DAP
  a turn: 4 PASS
  Game with ~ cards: 3 UNO
  it: 4 ROPE
  off: 5 ELOPE
  over: 4 OMIT 5 ELIDE
  the commercials: 3 ZAP
  You can ~ it: 4 ROPE
**Skip ___:** 5 ABEAT
**Skipjack:** 4 TUNA
**Skipped:** 6 SATOUT
    8 BYPASSED
**Skipper:** 10 SEACAPTAIN
  Genesis: 4 NOAH
  Nautilus: 4 NEMO
  Pequod: 4 AHAB
  portrayer: 8 ALANHALE
  post: 4 HELM
  River: 5 STONE
  syllable: 3 TRA
  Yankee: 5 TORRE
**"Skip to My ___":** 3 LOU
**Ski resort**
  Alberta: 5 BANFF
  Colorado: 4 VAIL 5 ASPEN
  Utah: 4 ALTA
  Vermont: 4 PICO 5 STOWE
**Skirmish:** 4 FRAY 5 MELEE
    6 TUSSLE
  Marital: 4 SPAT
**Skirt:** 5 AVOID EVADE
    8 SIDESTEP
  Ankle-length: 4 MAXI
  Ballerina: 4 TUTU
  Calf-length: 4 MIDI
  edge: 3 HEM
  feature: 4 SLIT 5 PLEAT
  fold: 5 PLEAT
  Full: 6 DIRNDL
  Hula ~ material: 5 GRASS
  insert: 4 GORE
  Kind of: 4 HULA MAXI MINI
    SLIT 5 ALINE 6 POODLE
  Layered: 4 TUTU
  length: 4 MAXI MIDI MINI
  line: 3 HEM
  Long: 4 MAXI
  panel: 4 GORE
  shape: 4 HOOP
  Short: 4 MINI
**Skit**
  NBC ~ show: 3 SNL
**Skits**
  Show with: 3 SNL 5 REVUE
**Skittish:** 4 WARY 5 TIMID
  Acts: 5 SHIES
  move: 5 START
**Skittle:** 7 NINEPIN
**"Skittle Players"**
  artist: 5 STEEN
**___ Ski Valley:** 4 TAOS
**Skivvies:** 4 BVDS
**Skosh:** 3 TAD
**Skulk:** 4 LURK 5 SNEAK

**Skull:** 7 CRANIUM
**Skull and Bones**
  member: 3 ELI
**Skullcap:** 8 YARMULKE
**Skull Island**
  find: 4 KONG
**Skunk:** 7 POLECAT
  Cartoon: 4 PEPE 5 LEPEW
  City on the: 4 AMES
  defense: 4 ODOR 5 SCENT
  feature: 6 STRIPE
**Sky:** 5 LIMIT
  Altar in the: 3 ARA
  bear: 4 URSA
  blue: 5 AZURE
  box: 4 KITE
  Clear: 5 ETHER
  color: 5 AZURE
  Drops from the: 4 RAIN
  High in the: 5 ALOFT
  light: 3 UFO 4 STAR
    6 AURORA
  Pie in the: 3 UFO
  pilot: 5 PADRE
  Red ~ at morning: 4 OMEN
  shade: 5 AZURE
  Take to the: 6 AVIATE
  ~, in French: 4 CIEL
**Skybox**
  locale: 5 ARENA
**Skydiving**
  need: 5 CHUTE
**SkyDome**
  setting: 7 TORONTO
  song: 7 OCANADA
**Skye**
  Actress: 4 IONE
  cap: 3 TAM
  guy: 4 SCOT
  talk: 4 ERSE
**Sky-high**
  Go: 4 SOAR
**"___ Skylark":** 3 TOA
**Skylighted**
  courts: 5 ATRIA
**Skyline**
  European ~ sight: 3 ALP
  feature: 5 SPIRE 7 STEEPLE
  obscurer: 4 HAZE SMOG
  Rural ~ sight: 4 SILO
**Skylines**
  Like some: 8 STEEPLED
**Skylit**
  courts: 5 ATRIA
**SkyMiles**
  offerer: 5 DELTA
**Skyrocket:** 4 RISE SOAR ZOOM
**Skyscraper**
  Boston ~, with "the": 3 PRU
  He made the ~ possible:
    4 OTIS
  Rural: 4 SILO
  support: 5 IBEAM
**Skywalker:** 4 JEDI
  foe: 5 VADER
  mentor: 4 YODA

**Skywalker, Anakin**
  Son of: 4 LUKE
**Skyward:** 5 ALOFT
  Directed: 6 UPCAST
**SLA**
  Hearst ~ name: 5 TANIA
**Slab**
  Stone: 5 STELE
**Slack:** 6 UNTAUT
  Give some: 6 LOOSEN
  Lacking: 4 TAUT 5 TENSE
    TIGHT
  off: 4 EASE 5 ABATE
**Slacken:** 4 EASE 5 ABATE
**Slacker**
  bane: 3 JOB
**Slack-jawed:** 4 AGOG 5 AGAPE
  feeling: 3 AWE
  Leave: 4 STUN
  look: 4 GAPE
**Slacks**
  material: 5 CHINO
  measure: 6 INSEAM
**Slake:** 4 SATE 6 QUENCH
**Slalom:** 3 SKI
  contestant: 5 SKIER
  curve: 3 ESS
  obstacle: 4 GATE
**Slam:** 4 SHUT
  preventer: 8 DOORSTOP
**Slam-dance:** 4 MOSH
**Slammed:** 7 LITINTO
**Slammer:** 3 PEN 4 COOP JAIL
    STIR 5 CLINK POKEY
    6 PRISON 8 HOOSEGOW
  Ship: 4 BRIG
**"Slammin' Sammy":** 4 SOSA
    5 SNEAD
**Slander:** 3 TAR 5 SMEAR
    7 ASPERSE TRADUCE
  Like: 4 ORAL
**Slang**
  expert Partridge: 4 ERIC
  Shop: 5 LINGO
**Slangy**
  assent: 3 YEH YEP 4 YEAH
  greeting: 4 HIHO
  hat: 3 LID
  intensifier: 3 OLA
  money: 4 KALE
  no: 5 IXNAY
  refusal: 3 NAH NAW 4 NOPE
  suffix: 3 OLA 4 AROO EROO
**Slant:** 4 BIAS CANT LEAN
    SKEW TILT 5 ANGLE
    BEVEL
  Political: 4 SPIN
**Slanted:** 5 ATILT 6 ITALIC
  type: 6 ITALIC
  type (abbr.): 4 ITAL
**Slanting:** 6 ASLOPE
**Slap**
  cuffs on: 3 NAB
  Deserving a: 4 RUDE 5 FRESH
  It may follow a: 4 DUEL
  target: 5 WRIST

**Slapper**
  in shorts: 3 MOE
**Slapstick**
  comedy: 5 FARCE
  missile: 3 PIE
  trio member: 3 MOE
    6 STOOGE
**Slash**
  Bandmate of: 3 AXL
  mark: 4 SCAR
  Words separated by a:
    5 ANDOR
**Slasher**
  of films: 5 ZORRO
**Slat:** 4 LATH
**Slate:** 6 AGENDA ROSTER
  Clean: 10 TABULARASA
  Clear the: 5 ERASE
  name: 7 NOMINEE
  Was on a: 3 RAN
  ~, for one: 4 EMAG
  ~, for short: 4 SKED
**Slaughter:** 4 ROUT
  of baseball: 4 ENOS
**Slaughterhouse:** 8 ABATTOIR
**Slav**
  Certain: 4 SERB
**Slave:** 4 PEON SERF 5 HELOT
    6 THRALL
    11 BONDSERVANT
  away: 4 TOIL
  girl of opera: 4 AIDA
  name: 4 TOBY
  response: 5 GROAN
  ~ Turner: 3 NAT
**Slavery**
  Amendment abolishing: 4 XIII
**Slaves**
  Country founded by:
    7 LIBERIA
**"Slaves of New York"**
  author Janowitz: 4 TAMA
**Slaving**
  away: 4 ATIT
**"Slavonic Dances"**
  composer: 6 DVORAK
**Slaw:** 4 SIDE
**___ slaw:** 4 COLE
**Slay:** 3 OFF 4 DOIN KILL
**Slayer**
  Vampire: 5 STAKE
**"___ slayeth the silly one":**
    4 ENVY
**Slayton**
  Astronaut: 4 DEKE
**Sleaze:** 5 CREEP
**Sleazy:** 6 SORDID
  paper: 3 RAG
**Sled**
  Olympic: 4 LUGE
  Travel by: 4 MUSH
**Sledding**
  spot: 4 HILL
**Sleek**
  fabric: 5 SATIN
  jet: 3 SST

looking: **11** STREAMLINED
swimmer: **5** OTTER
~, in lingo: **4** AERO
**Sleekly**
designed: **4** AERO
**Sleep**
acronym: **3** REM
Bit of: **3** ZEE
Deep: **4** COMA **5** SOPOR
disorder: **5** APNEA
Forego: **6** STAYUP
Get some: **6** RESTUP
He may put you to:
   **7** SANDMAN
inducer: **6** OPIATE
Like ~, ideally: **7** RESTFUL
Lose ~ over: **4** STEW
Put to: **4** BORE LULL
research tool: **3** EEG
restlessly: **4** TOSS
Short: **3** NAP
sound: **5** SNORE
soundly: **5** SNORE
spoiler: **5** ALARM
stage: **3** REM
unit: **3** ZEE
You'll ~ through it: **5** DREAM
**Sleep ___**: **4** ONIT
**Sleeper**: **3** CAR
film of 1978: **4** COMA
Noisy: **6** SNORER
Restless: **6** TOSSER
Sound: **6** SNORER
Storied: **3** RIP
Upside-down: **5** SLOTH
woe: **5** APNEA
**Sleepers**: **7** PAJAMAS
**"___ Sleep, for Every Favor"**:
   **4** EREI
**Sleeping**: **3** OUT **4** ABED
   **5** NOTUP **6** ATREST
disorder: **5** APNEA
Like a ~ bag: **5** LINED
sickness carrier: **6** TSETSE
Stopped: **4** WOKE
**"Sleepless in Seattle"**
director Ephron: **4** NORA
director Nora: **6** EPHRON
**Sleepover**
wear: **3** PJS
**Sleepy**: **5** DWARF
Get: **4** FADE
pal: **3** DOC
**Sleepy Hollow**
character: **4** BROM
**"Sleepy Hollow"**
star: **4** DEPP
**"Sleepy Time ___"**: **3** GAL
**"Sleepy Time Gal"**
songwriter: **4** EGAN
**Sleet**
covered: **3** ICY
Slide in: **4** SKID
**Sleeve**
card: **3** ACE
filler: **3** ARM

**Sleeveless**
cloak: **6** MANTLE
garment: **4** CAPE VEST
**Sleeves**
Discs with: **3** LPS
**Sleigh**
Russian: **6** TROIKA
**Sleighmate**
of Cupid: **5** COMET
**Sleipnir**
rider: **4** ODIN
**Slender**: **4** LANK SLIM THIN
   **5** REEDY
blade: **4** EPEE
candle: **5** TAPER
cigar: **8** PANATELA
dagger: **6** STYLET
   **8** STILETTO
girl: **5** SYLPH
Gracefully: **6** SVELTE
gull: **4** TERN
instrument: **4** OBOE
nail: **4** BRAD
reed: **4** OBOE
stinger: **4** WASP
sword: **6** RAPIER
**Slender-waisted**
insect: **4** WASP
**Sleuth**: **3** TEC
Bogart's: **5** SPADE
dog: **4** ASTA
Film: **4** CHAN
find: **4** CLUE
Hammett's: **5** SPADE
Marquand's: **4** MOTO
Rex's: **4** NERO
~ Charlie: **4** CHAN
~ Lupin: **6** ARSENE
~ Wolfe: **4** NERO
**"Sleuth"**
star: **5** CAINE
**Slew**: **3** TON **4** RAFT **5** DIDIN
   OCEAN SMOTE
Whole ~ of: **7** ZILLION
**Slezak**
Actress: **5** ERIKA
**Slice**: **3** CUT
and dice: **4** HASH
(off): **3** LOP
of history: **3** ERA
Salad: **6** RADISH
Thick: **4** SLAB
Thin: **7** SCALLOP
**Slicer**
site: **4** DELI
**Slick**: **3** ICY WET **4** OILY WILY
   **5** SUAVE
stuff: **3** OIL
**Slicker**: **3** MAC **5** ICIER
   **7** OILSKIN
place: **4** CITY
**Slid**
It may be ~ on: **8** BANISTER
**Slide**
Lab ~ critter: **5** AMEBA
   **6** AMOEBA

Lab ~ subjects: **6** AMEBAE
   **7** AMOEBAE
on ice: **4** SKID **5** SKATE
Spot for a: **4** BASE
Water: **5** CHUTE
Word with: **4** RULE
**Sliding**
machine part: **6** TAPPET
Vehicle with ~ doors: **3** VAN
**Slight**: **4** MERE SNUB
   **6** IGNORE **7** SLENDER
advantage: **4** EDGE
color: **4** TINT **5** TINGE
decrease: **3** DIP
fight: **4** SPAT
odor: **5** WHIFF
progress: **4** DENT
Social: **4** SNUB
variation: **5** SHADE
**Slightest**: **5** LEAST
In the: **5** ATALL
sound: **4** PEEP
The ~ bit: **4** ATAD
**Slightly**: **4** ABIT ATAD
   **7** ALITTLE ATRIFLE
~, in music: **4** POCO
**Slim**
and muscular: **4** WIRY
and trim: **6** SVELTE
swimmer: **3** EEL
Very ~ margin: **4** HAIR
**Slime**: **3** GOO **4** GOOK GOOP
   GUCK GUNK MUCK
   OOZE
**"Slim Shady"**: **6** EMINEM
**Slimy**
stuff: **4** OOZE
**Sling**: **4** HURL
ammo: **5** STONE
mud at: **4** SLUR **5** SMEAR
   **7** ASPERSE
What some slingers: **4** HASH
**Slingshot**
ammo: **5** STONE
Like a: **7** YSHAPED
**Slink**: **4** LURK
**Slinky**: **3** TOY
shape: **4** COIL
**Slip**: **3** ERR **5** ERROR LAPSE
   **7** FAUXPAS
a cog: **3** ERR
away: **5** ELOPE **6** ELAPSE
back: **7** RELAPSE
behind: **3** LAG
by: **5** ELUDE **6** ELAPSE
cover: **5** DRESS
Give a pink ~ to: **3** AXE CAN
Give the ~ to: **4** LOSE
   **5** ELUDE EVADE
into: **3** DON **7** THROWON
(into): **4** EASE
Let: **4** TELL
of the tongue: **5** ERROR
on: **3** DON
Pink: **13** WALKINGPAPERS
preventer: **3** MAT

sort: 3 FOX
stratagem: 4 RUSE
trick: 4 WILE
**Slyly**
Eye: 4 OGLE
suggest: 9 INSINUATE
**Smack:** 3 HIT RAM 4 BUSS
KISS SLAP SWAT
5 PASTE TASTE
6 SMOOCH
dab in the middle:
10 DEADCENTER
in the face: 4 KISS
suffix: 4 EROO
**Smacker:** 3 LIP 4 CLAM
**Smackers:** 4 ONES
100 ~: 5 CNOTE
**Smacking**
sound: 4 WHAP
**Small:** 3 LIL 4 PUNY SIZE
5 DINKY PETTY
6 PETITE
amount: 3 BIT DAB SOU TAD
4 DRAM DRIB IOTA MITE
WHIT 5 TRACE
and mischievous: 5 ELFIN
and weak: 4 PUNY
band: 4 TRIO 5 COMBO
Extremely: 5 MICRO
It carries a ~ charge: 3 ION
Like a ~ garage: 6 ONECAR
suffix: 3 ULE
Very: 3 WEE 4 ITSY TINY
5 TEENY 6 MINUTE
~, in French: 5 PETIT
**Small-business**
mag: 3 INC
**Smaller**
amount: 4 LESS
Get: 6 SHRINK
than small: 6 TEENSY
**Smallest:** 5 LEAST
**Small-minded:** 5 PETTY
**Smallmouth:** 4 BASS
**Small-plane**
maker: 6 CESSNA
**Smallpox**
vaccine discoverer: 6 JENNER
**Small-screen**
heartthrob: 6 TVIDOL
**Small-time:** 5 DINKY 6 TWOBIT
7 TINHORN
9 PENNYANTE
**"Smallville"**
character Lang: 4 LANA
family: 5 KENTS
friend: 5 CHLOE
**"___ small world":** 4 ITSA
**Smarmy:** 4 OILY
**Smart:** 4 ACHE CHIC HURT
NEAT 5 NATTY SASSY
STING
dresser: 3 FOP
employer: 7 CONTROL
Get: 4 SASS 5 LEARN
6 WISEUP

group: 5 MENSA
guy: 4 ALEC 5 ALECK
BRAIN
Not: 3 DIM
or Bond: 5 AGENT
player: 5 ADAMS
set: 5 MENSA
talk: 4 SASS
Unusually: 3 APT
**Smart ___:** 4 ALEC 5 ALECK
**Smart, Maxwell:** 5 AGENT
**Smart-alecky:** 4 FLIP PERT
WISE
**Smarten**
up: 7 GETWISE
**Smartly**
Dress: 5 PREEN
**Smart-mouthed:** 4 PERT
5 SASSY
**Smarts:** 4 WITS 5 SENSE
10 HORSESENSE
Having more: 5 SORER
**Smart ___ whip:** 3 ASA
**Smash:** 3 HIT
Box office: 4 BOFF
into: 3 RAM
Sign of a: 3 SRO
suffix: 4 EROO
up: 4 RUIN 5 TOTAL
**Smashed:** 3 LIT 6 BLOTTO
It may get: 4 ATOM
**Smasheroo:** 3 HIT
**Smashing**
serve: 3 ACE
**Smattering**
A ~ of: 4 SOME
**Smear:** 3 TAR 4 BLUR DAUB
5 LIBEL 6 BEDAUB
STREAK
Ink: 4 BLOT
**Smell:** 4 ODOR REEK 5 SCENT
SENSE STINK WHIFF
Awful: 5 FETOR
bad: 4 REEK
like: 6 REEKOF
Pleasant: 5 AROMA
What the suspicious: 4 ARAT
**Smell ___:** 4 ARAT
**Smeller:** 4 NOSE
**Smelling ___:** 5 SALTS
**Smells**
It: 4 NOSE
**Smelly**
smoke: 6 STOGIE
**Smelter**
input: 3 ORE
waste: 4 SLAG
**Smeltery**
fodder: 7 IRONORE
input: 3 ORE
waste: 4 SLAG 5 DROSS
**Smidge:** 3 DAB TAD
**Smidgen:** 3 BIT DAB JOT TAD
4 ATOM DRIB IOTA
WHIT 5 PINCH SKOSH
SPECK TRACE

**Smile:** 4 BEAM GRIN
Bring a ~ to: 5 AMUSE
Scornful: 5 SNEER
shape: 3 ARC
Word that brings a:
6 CHEESE
**"Smile!":** 9 SAYCHEESE
**"___ Smile":** 4 SARA
**"___ Smile Be Your Umbrella":**
4 LETA
**Smiles**
All: 5 HAPPY
Like some: 6 TOOTHY
**Smiley:** 5 AGENT
creator: 7 LECARRE
**Smiley, Jane**
novel: 3 MOO
**Smiling:** 5 AGRIN RIANT
6 AMUSED
**Smirk:** 4 LEER
**Smirnoff**
Comedian: 5 YAKOV
rival: 5 STOLI
**Smith:** 5 SHOER
and Gore: 3 ALS
and Jones, often: 7 ALIASES
Blues singer: 6 BESSIE
Columnist: 3 LIZ
Did a ~ job: 4 SHOD
5 SHOED
Do a ~ job: 6 RESHOE
Economist: 4 ADAM
Gossipy: 3 LIZ
Granny: 5 APPLE
iron: 5 ANVIL
Jockey: 5 ROBYN
NFL rusher: 6 EMMITT
of tennis: 4 STAN
Partner of: 6 WESSON
Rock singer: 5 PATTI
role: 3 ALI
Singer: 4 KATE
**___ Smith:** 6 GRANNY
**Smith, Buffalo Bob**
puppet: 10 HOWDYDOODY
**Smith, Hannibal**
group: 5 ATEAM
**Smith, John**
~, perhaps: 5 ALIAS
**Smith, Jos.**
follower: 3 LDS
**Smith, Mrs.**
product: 3 PIE
**Smith, ___ Pinkett**
Actress: 4 JADA
**Smith, Snuffy:** 6 RUSTIC
Inquired, to: 3 AST
Son of: 5 TATER
**Smith, Will**
1997 ~ film, briefly: 3 MIB
2001 ~ role: 3 ALI
Mrs.: 4 JADA
songs: 4 RAPS
**Smithereens:** 4 BITS
6 PIECES
Break to: 5 SMASH TOTAL

maker: 3 TNT
**Smithfield**
product: 3 HAM
**Smithsonian**
(abbr.): 4 INST
stuff: 9 AMERICANA
**Smithsonite:** 3 ORE
**Smithy:** 5 FORGE SHOER
Did a ~ job: 5 SHOED
sight: 5 ANVIL
**Smits**
former show: 5 LALAW
of basketball: 3 RIK
**Smitten:** 4 GAGA 6 INLOVE
8 ENAMORED
**Smog:** 4 HAZE
component: 4 SOOT
watchdog (abbr.): 3 EPA
**Smoke:** 3 CIG 4 CURE
Bit of: 4 PUFF WISP
Celebratory: 5 CIGAR
Cheap: 6 STOGIE
conduit: 4 FLUE
detector: 4 NOSE
Good: 6 HAVANA
Mild: 5 CLARO
out: 6 EXPOSE
site: 7 ASHTRAY
Small: 6 CIGARILLO
solids: 3 TAR
___ smoke: 4 UPIN
**Smoked**
delicacy: 3 EEL
meat: 3 HAM
salmon: 3 LOX
**Smoke-filled**
room folks: 4 POLS
**"Smoke Gets In Your Eyes"**
composer: 4 KERN
lyricist Harbach: 4 OTTO
**Smokehouse**
item: 3 HAM
**Smokejumper**
need: 5 CHUTE
**Smoker:** 3 CAR 4 STAG
concern: 3 TAR
purchase: 4 PACK
request: 5 LIGHT
Sicilian: 4 ETNA
**Smokey:** 4 BEAR
spotter: 4 CBER
**Smoking**
alternative: 3 NON
and nonsmoking: 5 AREAS
gun: 5 PROOF
Quit: 12 KICKTHEHABIT
Started: 5 LITUP
**"Smoking or ___?":** 3 NON
**Smoky**
stone: 4 OPAL
**"Smoky Mountain Rain"**
singer Ronnie: 6 MILSAP
**Smoldering**
remains: 5 EMBER
**Smooch:** 4 BUSS KISS
Willing to: 5 KISSY

**Smooth:** 4 EASE EVEN FILE
GLIB IRON SAND
5 SILKY SUAVE
6 FLUENT SATINY
SHAVEN 7 UNLINED
and lustrous: 5 SLEEK
and soft: 6 SILKEN
Make: 4 EASE SAND
Make a ~ transition: 5 SEGUE
musically: 6 LEGATO
out: 4 EVEN
Overly: 4 GLIB
sailing: 4 EASE
the way: 4 EASE
transition: 5 SEGUE
**Smoother:** 4 RASP
Make even: 6 RESAND
**Smoothing**
tool: 6 PLANER
**Smoothly**
Go: 4 FLOW
Mix: 5 BLEND
Move: 5 GLIDE
Run: 3 HUM 4 PURR
Switch: 5 SEGUE
**"Smooth Operator"**
singer: 4 SADE
**Smooth-talking:** 4 GLIB
**Smooth-tongued:** 4 GLIB
**Smothers Brothers:** 3 DUO
One of the: 3 TOM
**Smudge:** 4 BLOT SOIL SPOT
5 SMEAR
Solver's: 7 ERASURE
**Smug**
Be: 5 GLOAT
smile: 5 SMIRK
**Smurf**
Bearded: 4 PAPA
Like a: 4 BLUE
**Smut:** 4 PORN
**Smythe**
Cartoonist: 3 REG
**Sn**
Its symbol is: 3 TIN
**Snack:** 3 EAT 4 BITE NOSH
After-school: 4 OREO
bar: 7 GRANOLA
cake: 5 SUZYQ
Cheesy: 5 NACHO
chip: 5 NACHO
chips: 6 FRITOS
Coffee break: 5 DONUT
Creme-filled: 4 OREO
Have a: 3 EAT 4 NOSH
Hiker's: 4 GORP
Hostess: 5 HOHOS
in a shell: 4 TACO
in a stack: 4 OREO
Marshmallow: 5 SMORE
7 MOONPIE
Mexican: 4 TACO
since 1912: 4 OREO
Snail's: 5 ALGAE
Squirrel: 5 ACORN
Stadium: 6 NACHOS

Tex-Mex: 4 TACO 6 TAMALE
~, in Spanish: 4 TAPA
**Snafu:** 4 MESS 5 MIXUP
6 MESSUP
**Snag:** 3 NET 5 HITCH LASSO
**Snail:** 8 SLOWPOKE
Edible: 8 ESCARGOT
Like a: 4 SLOW
mail attachment: 5 STAMP
Marine: 5 WHELK
snack: 5 ALGAE
trail: 5 SLIME
**Snaillike:** 4 POKY SLOW
___ snail's pace: 3 ATA
**Snake:** 4 APOD
African: 3 ASP 5 MAMBA
charmee: 3 EVE
Charmer's: 5 COBRA
dancers: 4 HOPI
Deadly: 5 COBRA KRAIT
VIPER
eye: 7 ONESPOT
eyes: 3 TWO 4 ONES
Hooded: 3 ASP 5 COBRA
Kind of: 5 ADDER
Longest venomous:
10 BUSHMASTER
Many a: 6 HISSER
Milk: 5 ADDER
Place for a: 5 DRAIN
poison: 5 VENOM
shape: 3 ESS
sound: 3 SSS 4 HISS
Squeezing: 3 BOA
venom: 5 TOXIN
Venomous: 3 ASP 5 ADDER
COBRA KRAIT MAMBA
10 COPPERHEAD
Venomous, as a: 6 ASPISH
Word with: 3 SEA
~, to Medusa: 5 TRESS
**Snake-haired**
woman of myth: 6 MEDUSA
**Snakelike**
fish: 3 EEL
**Snake River**
locale: 5 IDAHO
**Snaky**
curve: 3 ESS
fish: 3 EEL
shape: 3 ESS 4 COIL
sound: 3 SSS
**Snap:** 3 PIC 4 ELAN ZING
5 CINCH CLICK GOAPE
PHOTO 6 LOSEIT
course: 5 EASYA
It's a: 3 PIC 4 HIKE
5 PHOTO
It's heard at a: 3 HUT
Liable to: 5 CROSS
Sit for a: 4 POSE
**Snapper:** 6 TURTLE
competitor: 4 TORO
Swamp: 4 CROC 5 GATOR
trapper: 3 NET
**Snappish:** 4 CURT 5 TESTY

**Snapple**
   rival: 6 NESTEA
   specialty: 3 TEA
**Snappy**
   comeback: 6 RETORT
**Snaps:** 3 PIX 10 BLOWSAFUSE
      15 LOSESONESTEMPER
**Snapshot:** 3 PIC 5 PHOTO
**Snare:** 3 NET 4 DRUM TRAP
      5 NOOSE 6 ENTRAP
   Sniggler: 6 EELPOT
**Snarl:** 4 GNAR 6 TANGLE
   Traffic: 3 JAM
**Snarler**
   Traffic: 5 CRASH
**Snatch:** 4 GRAB
**Snead**
   of golf: 3 SAM
**Sneak**
   a look: 4 PEEK
   attack: 6 AMBUSH
   peek (var.): 6 PREVUE
**Sneak ___:** 5 APEEK
**Sneaker:** 4 SHOE 7 GYMSHOE
   bottoms: 6 TREADS
   brand: 4 KEDS 5 NIKES
   feature: 4 LACE 6 EYELET
   Former ~ brand: 4 AVIA
   problem: 4 ODOR
**Sneakily**
   Criticize: 5 SNIPE
   Injured: 5 KNEED
**Sneaking**
   suspicion: 4 IDEA
**Sneaky:** 3 SLY
   guy: 4 PETE
   laugh: 3 IIEII
   scheme: 4 RUSE
**Sneaky ___:** 4 PETE
**Sneer**
   Said with a: 5 SNIDE
**Sneetches**
   creator: 5 SEUSS
**Sneeze**
   inducer: 7 ALLERGY
   Respond to a: 5 BLESS
   sound: 5 ACHOO
**Sneezy**
   friend: 3 DOC
   Sound from: 5 ACHOO
**Snicker:** 5 TEHEE
   Like a: 5 SNIDE
   sound: 3 HEE
**Snicker-___:** 4 SNEE
**Snickers**
   maker: 4 MARS
**Snick-or-___:** 4 SNEE
**Snidely**
   Look from: 5 SNEER
**Snider**
   teammate: 5 REESE
**Sniff:** 6 INHALE
   out: 6 DETECT
**Sniffer:** 4 NOSE
**Sniffles**
   Get the: 9 CATCHCOLD

Have the: 3 AIL
**Sniggler:** 5 EELER
   quarry: 3 EEL
   snare: 6 EELPOT
**Snip:** 3 CUT
**Snipes**
   Actor: 6 WESLEY
**Snippet**
   Cinema: 4 CLIP
   Dramatic: 5 SCENE
**Snippy:** 4 TART
   Get ~ with: 4 SASS
**Snit**
   fit: 5 ANGER
**Snitch:** 3 RAT
   Act the: 6 TATTLE
   Be a: 4 TELL 5 RATON
**Snitched:** 4 TOLD
**Snitches**
   spill them: 5 BEANS
**Snivel:** 5 WHINE
**"SNL"**
   bit: 4 SKIT
   Early ~ comic: 7 PISCOPO
   Early ~ name: 5 GILDA
   Kevin on: 6 NEALON
   Part of: 4 LIVE
   player Cheri: 5 OTERI
   player Dunn: 4 NORA
   player Kevin: 6 NEALON
   producer Michaels: 5 LORNE
   segment: 4 SKIT
   When ~ ends: 5 ONEAM
**Snob:** 7 ELITIST
**Snobbery:** 7 ELITISM
**Snobbish:** 6 UPPITY
      7 HIGHHAT
   behavior: 4 AIRS
**Snobs**
   put them on: 4 AIRS
**Snockered:** 3 LIT
**Snood:** 7 HAIRNET
**Snooker**
   shot: 5 MASSE
**Snookums:** 3 HON 6 DEARIE
      7 PETNAME
**Snoop:** 3 PRY SPY 5 PRIER
   Act the: 3 PRY
   (around): 4 NOSE
   gp.: 3 CIA
   Like a: 4 NOSY
   Rapper: 4 DOGG
**Snooping:** 4 NOSY
**Snoopy:** 4 NOSY 6 BEAGLE
   foe: 8 REDBARON
**Snoot:** 4 NOSE
**Snootiness:** 4 AIRS
**Snooty**
   one: 4 SNOB
**Snooze:** 3 NAP
   Short: 3 NAP 6 CATNAP
   Sonora: 6 SIESTA
**Snore**
   letter: 3 ZEE
**Snorer**
   disorder: 5 APNEA

**Snorkel:** 5 SARGE
   (abbr.): 3 SGT
   dog: 4 OTTO
**Snorkeler**
   locale: 4 REEF
   sight: 5 CORAL
**Snorkeling**
   accessory: 3 FIN
   milieu: 5 CORAL
   site: 4 REEF
**Snort:** 3 NIP 4 BELT
   Cynic's: 4 IBET
   Short: 3 NIP 4 SHOT
**Snorter**
   Corrida: 4 TORO
   starter: 3 RIP
**Snout**
   Animal with a: 5 TAPIR
**Snow**
   boot: 3 PAC
   Clear: 4 PLOW
   coaster: 4 SLED
   cover: 5 IGLOO
   Glide on: 3 SKI
   Lift in the: 4 TBAR
   Like the driven: 4 PURE
   Loose: 6 POWDER
   pea holder: 3 POD
   prowler: 4 YETI
   remover: 6 SHOVEL
   structure: 4 FORT
   toy: 4 SLED
   unit: 5 FLAKE
   vehicle: 4 SLED
**Snowball:** 8 ESCALATE
**Snowballs:** 4 AMMO
   Attack with: 4 PELT
**Snowbird**
   Resort near: 4 ALTA
**"Snowbird"**
   singer Murray: 4 ANNE
**Snowe, Sen.**
   state: 5 MAINE
**Snowed**
   Not ~ by: 4 ONTO
**Snowfall**
   measure: 4 INCH
**Snowman**
   Abominable: 4 YETI
   carrot: 4 NOSE
   of song: 6 FROSTY
   prop: 4 PIPE
**Snowmass**
   Enjoy: 3 SKI
**Snowmobile**
   part: 3 SKI
**Snow White**
   and the dwarfs: 5 OCTET
   dwarfs: 6 SEPTET
**Snowy**
   bird: 5 EGRET
   Enjoy a ~ slope: 3 SKI
      4 SLED
**Snub:** 4 SHUN 6 IGNORE
      7 HIGHHAT
      12 COLDSHOULDER

**Snub-nosed**
dog: 3 PUG 4 PEKE
**Snuff**
Isn't up to: 4 AILS
Not up to: 3 BAD OFF 4 POOR
6 SUBPAR
React to: 6 SNEEZE
Up to: 4 ABLE
___ snuff: 4 UPTO
**Snuffleupagus**
street: 6 SESAME
**Snug:** 4 COZY 5 COMFY
bug locale: 3 RUG
retreat: 4 NEST
**"Snug as ___ ...":** 4 ABUG
**Snuggle:** 6 NESTLE
up: 6 NESTLE
**Snugly**
Fit: 4 NEST
Settle: 6 NESTLE
8 ENSCONCE
**So:** 4 ERGO NOTE THUS
TRUE
And ~ on: 3 ETC 8 ETCETERA
and so: 5 NOTES
be it: 4 AMEN
Even: 3 YET 5 STILL
far: 3 YET YTD 5 ASYET
6 TODATE 7 UPTONOW
Just: 4 TOAT 6 TOATEE
Like: 4 THUS
Say it ain't: 4 DENY
Say it's: 4 AVER AVOW
to speak: 8 ASITWERE
**"So?":** 15 WHATSTHEBIGDEAL
**"So!":** 3 AHA
**"So ___":** 4 BEIT
**Soak:** 3 SOP SOT 6 DRENCH
flax: 3 RET
in the tub: 5 BATHE
Place for a: 3 SPA
starter: 3 PRE
tea: 5 STEEP
up: 4 BLOT 6 ABSORB
(up): 3 SOP
up again: 6 RESORB
up some sun: 4 BASK
**Soaked:** 3 WET 5 AWASH
SOGGY 6 SODDEN
**Soaking**
Make ~ wet: 3 SOP
spot: 3 TUB 4 BATH
**Soap:** 5 DRAMA 6 SERIAL
acid: 5 OLEIC
Bar of: 4 CAKE
box: 6 TEEVEE
brand: 3 LUX 4 LAVA 5 CAMAY
follower: 5 OPERA
ingredient: 3 LYE 6 OLEATE
POTASH
Like ~ operas: 8 EPISODIC
neighbor: 7 SHAMPOO
opera: 5 DRAMA
plant: 5 AMOLE
Popular: 4 DAYS
segment: 7 EPISODE

substitute: 5 AMOLE
unit: 3 BAR 4 CAKE
Wash off: 5 RINSE
**"Soap"**
family: 5 TATES
family name: 4 TATE
spin-off: 6 BENSON
**Soapbox**
person: 6 ORATOR
Use a: 5 ORATE
**Soap Box Derby**
city: 5 AKRON
entrant: 5 RACER
**Soap-making**
need: 3 LYE
**Soapstone:** 4 TALC
**Soar:** 4 RISE
**Soaring**
hairdo: 7 UPSWEEP
Send spirits: 5 ELATE
**Soave:** 4 WINE
**Sob:** 4 BAWL WAIL WEEP
syllable: 3 HOO
**Sobbed:** 4 WEPT
**Sobbing:** 7 INTEARS
**"So be it":** 4 AMEN
**Sober:** 5 STAID
**Sober-minded:** 5 STAID
**Sobieski**
Actress: 6 LEELEE
**"So Big"**
author Ferber: 4 EDNA
**Sobriquet**
Cowboy's: 3 TEX
Hemingway's: 4 PAPA
Springsteen's: 4 BOSS
Stallone's: 3 SLY
**Soc.**
Patriotic: 3 DAR
**Soccer**
announcer's cry: 4 GOAL
Common ~ score: 6 ONENIL
ONEONE
First name in: 3 MIA
great: 4 PELE
great Rossi: 5 PAOLO
Mia of: 4 HAMM
period: 4 HALF
score: 4 GOAL
shot: 6 HEADER
star: 4 PELE 7 MIAHAMM
**Social:** 3 BEE TEA 5 DANCE
MIXER 8 TEAPARTY
A ~ sci.: 4 ECON
Afternoon: 3 TEA
asset: 4 TACT 5 POISE
blunder: 5 GAFFE
brew: 3 TEA
butterfly: 8 GADABOUT
class: 5 CASTE
climber's goal: 6 STATUS
connections: 3 INS
customs: 5 MORES
division: 5 CASTE
dud: 4 NERD 6 MISFIT
ending: 3 ITE

equal: 4 PEER
finale: 3 ITE
gathering: 3 BEE
group: 5 CASTE
Hindu ~ division: 5 CASTE
insect: 3 ANT
instability: 6 ANOMIE
introduction: 4 ANTI
Lodge: 8 APRESSKI
misfit: 4 GEEK NERD
note: 4 ITEM
outcast: 6 PARIAH
outing: 4 DATE
radiance: 5 ECLAT
rank: 5 CLASS
rebuff: 4 SNUB
reformer Bloomer: 6 AMELIA
reformer Jacob: 4 RIIS
service: 3 TEA
skill: 4 TACT
slight: 4 SNUB
standing: 6 STATUS
stratum: 5 CASTE
suffix: 3 ITE
welfare org.: 6 UNICEF
worker: 3 ANT
worker load: 5 CASES
**"Social Contract, The"**
author: 8 ROUSSEAU
**Socialist**
~ Eugene: 4 DEBS
**Socialite**
~ Maxwell: 4 ELSA
~ Mesta: 5 PERLE
~ Young: 3 DEB
**Socialites**
Certain: 6 JETSET
**Socially**
challenged one: 4 DRIP GEEK
NERD
chosen: 5 ALIST
dominant: 5 ALPHA
inept: 5 NERDY
See: 4 DATE
**Social Register**
word: 3 NEE
**Societal**
breakdown: 5 ANOMY
6 ANOMIE
no-no: 5 TABOO
oddball: 4 GEEK
woes: 4 ILLS
**Society**
Born, in the ~ page: 3 NEE
Chinese secret: 4 TONG
Cream of: 5 ELITE
girl: 3 DEB
High: 4 JETS SOTS 5 ELITE
Levels of: 6 STRATA
newcomer: 3 DEB
page word: 3 NEE
roster: 5 ALIST
Secret: 5 MAFIA
stalwart: 6 PILLAR
**Society Islands**
Largest of the: 6 TAHITI

**"Society's Child"**
singer Janis: 3 IAN
**Sociologist**
~ Durkheim: 5 EMILE
~ Max: 5 WEBER
**Sock**
away: 4 SAVE 5 STASH
clinger: 3 BUR
Fix a: 4 DARN
front: 3 TOE
hard: 5 PASTE
hop: 5 DANCE
hop number: 5 OLDIE
Kind of: 4 TUBE
part: 3 TOE
pattern: 6 ARGYLE
Short: 6 ANKLET
suffix: 4 EROO
**Socket**
filler: 7 EYEBALL
Golf club: 5 HOSEL
Word with: 3 EYE
**Sock-in-the-gut**
sound: 3 OOF
**"Sock it ___!":** 4 TOME
**"Sock ___ me!":** 4 ITTO
**Socks:** 4 HOSE 7 HOSIERY
Darn, as: 4 MEND
Kind of: 4 KNEE
Knock the ~ off: 3 AWE WOW
5 AMAZE 6 DAZZLE
Like matched: 6 PAIRED
Like some: 3 ODD
Pair of: 6 ONETWO
set: 4 PAIR
**"Socrate"**
composer Erik: 5 SATIE
**Socrates**
end: 5 OMEGA
Student of: 5 PLATO
**Soc. Sec.**
On: 3 RET 4 RETD
supplement: 3 IRA
**Soda**
bottle size: 5 LITER
can feature: 3 TAB
choice: 5 PEPSI
Classic ~ brand: 4 NEHI
Club: 7 SELTZER
container: 3 CAN
11 ALUMINUMCAN
flavor: 4 COLA 5 GRAPE
Fruit ~ brand: 5 FANTA
Kind of: 3 SAL 6 BAKING
Per bottle of: 4 APOP
server: 4 JERK
___ soda: 3 SAL
**Soda fountain**
choice: 4 COKE MALT
freebie: 5 STRAW
New England: 3 SPA
**Sodium**
chloride: 4 SALT
hydroxide: 3 LYE 4 NAOH
**Sodom**
escapee: 3 LOT

**"___ So Easy":** 3 ITS
**Soeur**
sibling: 5 FRERE
**Sofa:** 4 SEAT 5 DIVAN
6 SETTEE
Backless: 5 DIVAN
Convertible: 3 BED
feature: 3 ARM
How to move a: 7 ENDWISE
Relax on the: 4 LOLL
Sank into the: 3 SAT
**Sofer**
Soap actress: 4 RENA
**"So few"**
of WWII: 3 RAF
**Sofia:** 5 REINA
portrayer: 5 OPRAH
**"___ So Fine":** 3 HES
**Soft:** 5 DOWNY PIANO
7 LENIENT
and smooth: 6 SILKEN
and wet: 7 SQUISHY
ball: 4 NERF
cheese: 4 BRIE
diet: 3 PAP
ending: 4 WARE
fabric: 5 TERRY 6 SATEEN
felt hat: 6 FEDORA
food: 3 PAP
Go: 4 MELT
kid: 5 SUEDE
leather: 5 SUEDE
metal: 3 TIN
mineral: 4 TALC
Not too: 7 ALDENTE
rock: 4 TALC
seat: 4 SOFA 6 SETTEE
shade: 6 PASTEL
shoe: 3 MOC
shot: 3 LOB
spread: 4 OLEO
suffix: 4 WARE
throw: 3 LOB
tissue: 7 KLEENEX
touch: 3 DAB PAT
**Soft & ___:** 3 DRI
**Softball**
team: 3 TEN
**Soft drink:** 4 COLA SODA
7 SODAPOP
brand: 4 NEHI 6 RCCOLA
SHASTA
Classic: 4 NEHI
nut: 4 KOLA
Popular: 4 COKE COLA
size: 5 LITER
**Soften:** 4 EASE MELT 5 ALLAY
6 EASEUP RELENT
up: 4 THAW
~, with "down": 4 TONE
**Softener**
Skin: 4 ALOE 5 CREAM
**Softest**
mineral: 4 TALC
**Soft-focus**
effect: 4 HAZE

**Softhead:** 3 SAP
**Softly:** 5 PIANO
Sing: 5 CROON
Very, very ~, in music: 3 PPP
Walk: 3 PAD 6 TIPTOE
**Soft-money**
source: 3 PAC
**Soft palate:** 5 VELUM
Of the: 5 VELAR
projection: 5 UVULA
**Soft-shell**
clam: 7 STEAMER
**Software**
All-in-one: 5 SUITE
Big name in: 5 ADOBE LOTUS
box encl.: 5 CDROM
buyer: 4 USER
Newer: 7 UPGRADE
Old PC: 5 MSDOS
Prerelease ~ version: 4 BETA
program: 3 APP
security fix: 5 PATCH
selection: 4 MENU
test version: 4 BETA
**Soggy:** 3 WET
ground: 4 MIRE
**Soglow**
Cartoonist: 4 OTTO
**"So help me!":** 6 HONEST
**Soho**
digs: 4 LOFT
Like some ~ shops: 4 ARTY
social: 3 TEA
So long, in: 4 TATA
**Soil:** 4 DIRT 5 EARTH
Clayey: 4 MARL 5 ADOBE
component: 5 HUMUS
embankment: 4 BERM
Fertile: 4 LOAM 5 LOESS
Like ~ near trees: 5 ROOTY
Like good: 5 LOAMY
Loamy: 5 LOESS
prefix: 4 AGRO
Rich: 4 LOAM
sweetener: 4 LIME
Windblown: 5 LOESS
Work the: 3 HOE 4 TILL
**Soiled:** 5 DIRTY
**Soissons**
summer: 3 ETE
**"___ soit qui mal y pense":**
4 HONI
**"So it's you!":** 3 AHA
**Sojourn:** 4 STAY
**Sojourner**
Cell: 3 CON
**Sokolova**
Skater: 5 ELENA
**Sol:** 4 NOTE
Impresario: 5 HUROK
prefix: 4 AERO
Where el ~ rises: 4 ESTE
**Sol.:** 3 ANS
**Solar**
deity: 4 ATEN
event: 7 ECLIPSE

phenomenon: 5 FLARE
  6 CORONA 7 SUNSPOT
product: 3 RAY
system model: 6 ORRERY
**Solar ___: 6 SYSTEM**
**"Solaris"**
  author Stanislaw: 3 LEM
**Sold**
  Bought and: 5 DEALT
  It's ~ in bags: 3 ICE
  It's ~ in bars: 4 OLEO SOAP
  It's ~ in sticks: 4 OLEO
  out: 4 GONE
  When ~ separately: 4 EACH
**Solder**
  element: 3 TIN
**Soldier**
  assignment: 4 DUTY
  Career: 5 LIFER
  Cavalry: 6 LANCER
  Confederate: 3 REB
  cops: 3 MPS
  CSA: 3 REB
  Down Under: 5 ANZAC
  French: 5 POILU
  helmet: 6 TINHAT
  Inept: 7 SADSACK
  in gray: 3 REB 5 REBEL
  knapsack: 6 KITBAG
  Korean: 3 ROK
  material: 3 TIN
  of fortune: 4 MERC
  Small: 3 ANT
  Seoul: 3 ROK
  topper: 6 TINHAT
  Toy: 5 GIJOE
  utensils: 7 MESSKIT
**Soldiers: 3 GIS**
**Sold-out**
  sign: 3 SRO
**Sole: 3 ONE 4 LONE ONLY**
  attachment: 5 CLEAT
  Kind of: 5 CREPE
  pattern: 5 TREAD
  point: 5 CLEAT
**Soleil Moon ___: 4 FRYE**
**Solely: 3 ALL**
**Solemn: 5 GRAVE**
  ceremony: 4 RITE
  promise: 3 VOW 4 OATH
  response: 4 AMEN
  song: 5 DIRGE
  stretch: 4 LENT
  vow: 4 OATH
**"___ Solemnis": 5 MISSA**
**Solemnly**
  affirm: 7 SWEARTO
  state: 4 AVOW
**Solicit: 3 BEG 6 ASKFOR**
  from: 5 ASKOF HITUP
**Solicitous**
  reply: 4 ISEE
**Solid**
  alcohol: 6 STEROL
  Become: 3 GEL
  Biochemical: 6 STEROL

Freeze: 5 ICEUP
ground: 10 TERRAFIRMA
Not: 4 IFFY
On ~ ground: 6 ASHORE
suffix: 3 ITY
**Solidarity**
  city: 6 GDANSK
  First name in: 4 LECH
  name: 6 WALESA
**Solidify: 3 GEL SET 4 CAKE**
  CLOT JELL
**Solidity**
  Symbol of: 3 OAK
**Solids**
  Geometric: 4 TORI
**Soliloquy**
  start: 4 TOBE
**Solitaire: 3 GEM**
  Playing: 5 ALONE
  stone: 4 OPAL
**Solitary: 3 ONE 4 LONE**
  5 ALONE
  one: 5 LONER 7 EREMITE
**Solitude**
  seeker: 5 LONER
**Solo: 4 ARIA LONE STAG**
  5 ALONE 6 ONEMAN
  7 UNAIDED
  8 ALLALONE
  9 GOITALONE
  in space: 3 HAN
  org.: 5 UNCLE
  performance: 4 ARIA
  Short vocal: 6 ARIOSO
**Solo, Han**
  love: 4 LEIA
**Soloist: 5 LONER**
**Solomon: 4 SAGE**
  asset: 6 WISDOM
  Like: 4 SAGE WISE
  seal: 4 STAR
**"Solomon and Sheba"**
  costar: 4 GINA
**"So long!": 4 CIAO TATA**
  5 ADIOS SEEYA
**"___ So Long": 4 BEEN**
**Solti**
  Conductor: 5 GEORG
  Slowly, to: 5 LENTO
  Smoothly, to: 6 LEGATO
  Softly, to: 5 PIANO
  Speeds, to: 5 TEMPI
**Solution**
  (abbr.): 3 ANS
  Bleaching: 3 LYE
  Caustic: 3 LYE
  Hospital: 6 SALINE
  Office: 5 TONER
  Pickling: 5 BRINE
  product: 3 ION
  Programmer's: 3 APP
  strength: 5 TITER
  Strong-smelling: 7 AMMONIA
  Temporary: 7 STOPGAP
**Solve: 5 CRACK 7 UNRAVEL**
  a cryptogram: 6 DECODE

Confident way to: 5 ININK
  INPEN
**Solvent: 6 AFLOAT**
  Alcohol-based: 6 ACETAL
  Common: 5 ETHER
  7 ACETONE
  Financially: 6 AFLOAT
  Hydrocarbon: 6 HEXANE
  Paint: 6 ACETAL
  7 ACETONE
  Rinse, as with: 5 ELUTE
  Volatile: 5 ETHER
**Solver**
  Confident ~ tool: 3 PEN
  cry: 3 AHA
  need: 6 ERASER
  smudge: 7 ERASURE
**Solzhenitsyn**
  punishment: 5 EXILE
  topic: 5 GULAG
**Somalia**
  Gulf near: 4 ADEN
**Somalian**
  model: 4 IMAN
**Somber: 4 GRIM 5 GRAVE**
  In a ~ way: 5 SADLY
**Sombrero: 3 HAT**
**Some: 3 ANY 4 ABIT AFEW**
  ATAD 6 ABITOF
  7 ALITTLE
  ~, in Spanish: 4 UNOS
**"So ___ me!": 3 SUE**
**Somebody: 4 NAME**
**Somebody ___ (not mine):**
  5 ELSES
**Somehow: 8 INASENSE**
  15 ONEWAYORANOTHER
**"Some ___ meat and canna**
  **eat": 3 HAE**
**Somersault: 4 FLIP ROLL**
**Something**
  Certain: 4 AURA
  Come up with: 6 IDEATE
  Do: 3 ACT
  Do ~ with: 3 USE
  Have: 3 AIL EAT 4 DINE
  Have ~ at home: 5 EATIN
  It may follow: 4 ELSE
**"___ something I said?": 4 ISIT**
**"Something's ___ Give":**
  5 GOTTA
**"Something to Talk About"**
  singer Bonnie: 5 RAITT
**Sometime: 6 ONEDAY**
**"Sometimes a Great Notion"**
  author: 5 KESEY
**"Sometimes you feel like ___":**
  4 ANUT
**Somewhat: 4 ABIT ATAD**
  5 SORTA 6 KINDOF
  RATHER SORTOF
  8 INASENSE
  suffix: 3 ISH
  ~, in music: 4 POCO
**"Somewhere in Time"**
  actor: 5 REEVE

**Somme**
Info: French cue
city: 6 AMIENS
Set, in: 4 FIXE
state: 4 ETAT
summer: 3 ETE
**Sommelier**
Do a ~ job: 6 DECANT
offering: 3 RED 4 WINE
prefix: 4 OENO
**Sommer**
Actress: 4 ELKE
**"Sommersby"**
actor: 4 GERE
**Sommers, Jaime**
Like: 6 BIONIC
**Somnambulist**
Like a: 6 ASLEEP
**"So Much in Love"**
singers: 5 TYMES
**Son:** 8 MANCHILD
Favorite ~, perhaps: 6 ELDEST
of a son: 3 III
~, in French: 4 FILS
**Sonar**
signal: 4 ECHO
sound: 4 PING
spot: 4 BLIP
**Sonata:** 4 OPUS
finale: 4 CODA
movement: 5 RONDO
**Sondheim**
character: 4 TODD
**Song**
Alpine: 5 YODEL
and dance: 4 ARTS
Battle: 4 ARIA
Biblical: 5 PSALM
Cheerful: 4 LILT
Christmas: 4 NOEL 5 CAROL
Church: 4 HYMN
ending: 4 FEST
For a: 5 CHEAP
   9 DIRTCHEAP
Kind of: 4 SWAN 5 SIREN
Like a: 6 ARIOSE ARIOSO
Minstrel: 3 LAY
Nostalgic: 5 OLDIE
of praise: 3 ODE 4 HYMN
   5 PAEAN 8 CANTICLE
Part: 4 GLEE
Sacred: 5 MOTET PSALM
Sad: 5 DIRGE
section: 5 VERSE
Sentimental: 6 BALLAD
Simple: 5 DITTY
syllable: 3 TRA
syllables: 3 LAS 4 LALA
   5 LALAS TRALA
thrush: 5 MAVIS
Words of a: 5 LYRIC 6 LYRICS
___ song (cheaply): 4 FORA
"___ Song" (John Denver hit):
   6 ANNIES
**Song-and-dance**
act: 5 REVUE

**Songbird**
Small: 3 TIT 4 LARK WREN
   5 PIPIT VIREO 6 TOMTIT
   7 SPARROW
"___ Song Go Out of My
   Heart": 5 ILETA
**Songka River**
capital: 5 HANOI
**Songlike:** 6 ARIOSE ARIOSO
**"Song of the Golden Calf":**
   4 ARIA
**"Song of the South"**
syllables: 4 ADEE
title: 4 BRER
**Songs**
Art: 6 LIEDER
for one: 4 SOLI
for two: 5 DUETS
German: 6 LIEDER
Top 40: 4 HITS
**Songsmith**
~ Jacques: 4 BREL
**"Son ___ gun!":** 3 OFA
**Songwriter**
org.: 5 ASCAP
~ Gus: 4 KAHN
~ Jacques: 4 BREL
~ Leonard: 5 COHEN
~ Sammy: 4 CAHN
**Sonia**
Actress: 5 BRAGA
**Sonic**
boom source: 3 SST
bounce: 4 ECHO
unit: 4 MACH
**Sonic the Hedgehog**
maker: 4 SEGA
**Son-in-law**
of LBJ: 4 ROBB
of Muhammad: 3 ALI
**Sonja**
Skater: 5 HENIE
**Sonnet:** 4 POEM
component: 7 COUPLET
ending: 3 EER 6 SESTET
Italian ~ closing: 6 SESTET
starter: 5 OCTET
unit: 4 IAMB
**Sonneteer:** 4 BARD POET
Muse of a: 5 ERATO
**Sonnets**
Like most: 6 IAMBIC
**"Sonnets of Orpheus, The"**
poet: 5 RILKE
**Sonntag**
Never, on: 3 NIE
**Sonny**
Boxer: 6 LISTON
boy: 3 LAD
Ex of: 4 CHER
or Chastity: 4 BONO
sibling: 3 SIS
**"Son of"**
in Arabic: 3 IBN
**"Son of ___!":** 4 AGUN
**"Son of a gun!":** 5 ILLBE

**"Son of Frankenstein"**
role: 4 YGOR
**Sonoma**
neighbor: 4 NAPA
**Sonora**
Info: Spanish cue
shawl: 6 SERAPE
snack: 4 TACO
snooze: 6 SIESTA
"so long": 5 ADIOS
**Sons**
Fathers and: 3 HES
of, in Hebrew: 4 BNAI
Some: 3 JRS
**Sontag**
Writer: 5 SUSAN
**Sony**
cofounder Morita: 4 AKIO
product: 7 WALKMAN
rival: 3 RCA 4 AIWA 5 SANYO
**Soon:** 4 ANON 7 ERELONG
   SHORTLY 9 INAMINUTE
after: 4 UPON
As ~ as: 4 ONCE
None too: 6 ATLAST
Sometime: 6 ONEDAY
Start too: 10 JUMPTHEGUN
Very: 6 INASEC
~, in poems: 4 ANON
**Sooner**
Certain: 6 TULSAN
city: 4 ENID 5 TULSA
migrant: 4 OKIE
state (abbr.): 4 OKLA
**Sooner State**
native: 4 OTOE
**Soot**
particle: 4 SMUT
**Sooth**
Word following: 5 SAYER
**Soothe:** 4 EASE LULL 5 ALLAY
**Soother:** 4 BALM
Burn: 4 ALOE 8 ALOEVERA
Mineral: 4 TALC
Skin: 4 BALM 6 LOTION
Sprain: 6 ICEBAG
   8 LINIMENT
Throat: 7 LOZENGE
**Soothing**
hue: 4 AQUA
medicine: 7 NERVINE
ointment: 4 BALM 5 SALVE
plant: 4 ALOE
powder: 4 TALC
sound: 3 AAH
spot: 3 SPA
**Soothsayer:** 4 SEER 5 SIBYL
clue: 4 OMEN
**Sooty**
spot: 4 FLUE
**Soph.**
and others: 3 YRS
**Sophia**
Actress: 5 LOREN
Carlo, husband of: 5 PONTI
Husband of: 5 CARLO

**Sophie**
  Oscar winner as: 5 MERYL
**"Sophie's Choice"**
  actress: 6 STREEP
  author: 6 STYRON
  Sophie, in: 5 MERYL
**Sophisticated: 5 SUAVE**
      6 URBANE
  Like ~ software: 8 HIGHTECH
**Sophisticates**
  they're not: 5 HICKS RUBES
**Sophocles**
  tragedy: 4 AJAX 7 ELECTRA
      8 ANTIGONE
      10 OEDIPUSREX
**Sophomore: 4 YEAR**
  Former: 6 JUNIOR
**Sophs.**
  in two years: 3 SRS
**Soporific: 6 OPIATE**
  substance: 6 OPIATE
**Soprano**
  nicknamed "Bubbles": 5 SILLS
  Puccini: 5 TOSCA
  Range below: 4 ALTO
  solo: 4 ARIA
  ~ Beverly: 5 SILLS
  ~ Jenny: 4 LIND
  ~ Lily: 4 PONS
  ~ Nellie: 5 MELBA
  ~ Renata: 6 SCOTTO
  ~ Wagner: 3 EVA
**Soprano, A.J.**
  Robert who plays: 4 ILER
**Soprano, Tony**
  Mother of: 5 LIVIA
**"Sopranos, The"**
  actor Robert: 4 ILER
  actress Falco: 4 EDIE
  actress Turturro: 4 AIDA
  award: 4 EMMY
  Carmela portrayer on: 4 EDIE
  James role on: 4 TONY
  network: 3 HBO
**Sorbet: 3 ICE**
**Sorbonne: 5 ECOLE**
  **Info:** French cue
  article: 3 UNE
  Head of the: 4 TETE
  student: 5 ELEVE
  summer: 3 ETE
  To be, at the: 4 ETRE
**Sorcerer: 4 MAGE**
**Sorcerers: 4 MAGI**
**Sorceress**
  of myth: 5 CIRCE MEDEA
**Sorcery: 10 BLACKMAGIC**
  Goddess of: 6 HECATE
  West Indies: 5 OBEAH
**Sordid: 5 SEAMY**
**Sore: 3 MAD 4 ACHY 5 IRATE**
      IRKED ULCER VEXED
      6 ACHING TENDER
  Be: 4 ACHE
  Eye: 4 STYE
  Feel: 4 ACHE

  Feeling: 4 ACHY
  loser attitude:
      10 SOURGRAPES
  More: 6 ACHIER
  spot: 4 ACHE
  throat cause: 5 STREP
**Soreness: 4 ACHE**
**Sorenstam**
  Golfer: 6 ANNIKA
  org.: 4 LPGA
**Sorghum**
  variety: 4 MILO 5 DURRA
**Sor Juana ___**
  Poet: 4 INES
**Sorority**
  letter: 3 CHI ETA PHI PSI
      RHO 4 ZETA 5 DELTA
      OMEGA THETA
  member: 4 COED
**Sorrel**
  Cold ~ dish: 5 SCHAV
  horse: 4 ROAN
  Wood: 3 OCA 6 OXALIS
**Sorrow: 3 RUE WOE 5 DOLOR**
      TEARS
  Expression of: 4 ALAS
      6 LAMENT
  Feel ~ for: 3 RUE
  Sign of: 4 TEAR 8 TEARDROP
  Sound of: 4 SIGH
**Sorrowful**
  poem: 5 ELEGY
  sigh: 4 ALAS
  sound: 3 SOB 6 PLAINT
  words: 4 AHME
**Sorry: 3 SAD 4 LAME**
  Be ~ for: 4 PITY
  Being ~ for: 5 RUING
  Feel ~ about: 3 RUE
      6 LAMENT
  Feel ~ for: 4 PITY 6 REPENT
  In ~ shape: 5 SEEDY
  situations: 4 ILLS
  sort: 4 RUER
  to say: 4 ALAS
**"Sorry!": 4 OOPS**
      8 PARDONME
**"___ sorry!": 4 IMSO**
**"Sorry about that!": 4 OOPS**
**"Sorry to say ...": 4 ALAS**
**Sort: 3 ILK 4 KIND TYPE**
  of: 6 INAWAY RATHER
      8 INASENSE
**Sortie: 4 RAID**
**Sorting**
  device: 5 SIZER
**"Sort of"**
  suffix: 3 ISH OID
**Sorts**
  Out of: 3 ILL 5 ALIBI UPSET
**Sorvino**
  Actress: 4 MIRA
**SOS**
  alternative: 6 BRILLO
  part, supposedly: 3 OUR
  responder: 4 USCG

**"S.O.S."**
  band: 4 ABBA
**Sosa: 3 CUB**
  Stat for: 3 HRS RBI
  stick: 3 BAT
**"So ___ say": 4 THEY**
**So-so: 4 FAIR**
  connection: 3 AND
  grade: 3 CEE
**So ___ so forth: 5 ONAND**
**"So's ___ old man!": 3 YER**
**Sot: 4 LUSH 5 TOPER**
      7 TOSSPOT
  Certain: 4 WINO
  Mayberry: 4 OTIS
  problem: 3 DTS
  sound: 3 HIC
  spot: 3 BAR
  state: 6 STUPOR
  symptoms: 3 DTS
  Walk like a: 4 REEL
**"So that's it!": 3 AHA OHO**
**"So that's your game!": 3 OHO**
**Sotheby's**
  signal: 3 BID NOD
  stock: 3 ART
**"So there!": 3 HAH SEE 4 TADA**
**Sothern**
  Actress: 3 ANN
**Sothern, Ann**
  role: 6 MAISIE
**Sotto ___: 4 VOCE**
**Sotto voce**
  Not: 5 ALOUD
  remark: 5 ASIDE
**Souchong: 3 TEA**
**___ souci: 4 SANS**
**Soufflé**
  Like a: 4 EGGY
  start: 4 EGGS
**Sought: 7 QUESTED**
  an office: 6 RANFOR
  answers: 5 ASKED
  a seat: 5 RAN
  damages: 4 SUED
  office: 3 RAN
**Soul: 5 ANIMA**
  mate: 4 BODY
  Nary a: 5 NOONE 6 NOTONE
  Not a: 5 NOONE
  Queen of: 6 ARETHA
  Solitary: 5 LONER
  Sorry: 4 RUER
  ~, in French: 3 AME
**"Soul Food"**
  actress Long: 3 NIA
**Sound: 4 GOOD HALE OKAY**
      SANE TOLL TONE WELL
      5 AUDIO INLET SOLID
      6 COGENT
  asleep: 5 SNORE
  at the door: 3 RAP
  bite: 5 QUOTE
  booster: 3 AMP
  effect: 4 ECHO
  investment: 3 AMP 6 STEREO

Make: 4 HEAL
Of ~ mind: 4 SANE
Of ~ quality: 5 TONAL
off: 4 RANT 5 OPINE ORATE
Ominous: 5 KNELL
portion: 5 AUDIO
purchase: 6 STEREO
quality: 4 TONE 6 HEALTH
   TIMBRE
reasonable: 5 ADDUP
rebound: 4 ECHO
setup: 6 STEREO
sleeper: 6 SNORER
start: 5 ULTRA
the alarm: 4 WARN
track: 5 AUDIO
unit: 4 SONE
upstairs: 4 SANE
~, as a bell: 4 PEAL
**Sounded:** 4 RANG
**"Sounder"**
  actress Cicely: 5 TYSON
**Soundness**
  of mind: 6 SANITY
**"Sound of Music, The"**
  backdrop: 4 ALPS
  extra: 3 NUN
  figure: 6 ABBESS
  heroine: 5 MARIA
  name: 5 TRAPP
  song: 5 MARIA
**"Sounds good to me!":** 4 IMIN
**Sound system:** 4 HIFI
   6 STEREO
  Old ~ component:
   8 TAPEDECK
**Soundtrack**
  Fix the: 5 REDUB
  Work on a: 3 DUB
**Soup**
  alternative: 5 SALAD
  bean: 4 LIMA 6 LENTIL
  Chilled: 5 SCHAV
  Clear: 8 CONSOMME
  container: 3 CAN
  cracker: 7 SALTINE
  Duck: 4 EASY
  flavoring: 4 DILL
  holder: 3 CAN 6 TUREEN
  Hot and sour ~ ingredient:
   4 TOFU
  ingredient: 6 LENTIL
   OXTAIL
  Italian ~ ingredient: 4 ORZO
   9 SPLITPEAS
  Japanese: 4 MISO 5 RAMEN
  legume: 3 PEA 6 LENTIL
  pasta: 4 ORZO
  pod: 4 OKRA
  scoop: 5 LADLE
  Serve: 5 LADLE
  served cold: 5 SCHAV
  served with sour cream:
   7 BORSCHT
  server: 5 LADLE 6 LADLER
   TUREEN

Simple: 5 BROTH
source: 3 CAN
spheroid: 3 PEA
Thick: 5 PUREE 6 POTAGE
Thin: 5 BROTH
veggie: 3 PEA 4 LEEK OKRA
vessel: 3 POT
with sushi: 4 MISO
**Soupçon:** 3 TAD 4 DASH HINT
   TANG 5 TASTE TINGE
   TRACE
**Soup du ___:** 4 JOUR
**Souped-up**
  car: 6 HOTROD
**Soupy**
  Comic: 5 SALES
**Sour:** 4 TART 5 ACERB ACIDY
   SPOIL 6 ACETIC ACIDIC
   CURDLE MOROSE
  brew: 6 ALEGAR
  fruit: 4 SLOE 5 LEMON
  Go: 4 TURN
  note: 7 CLINKER
  Without a ~ note: 6 INTUNE
**Sour ___:** 4 MASH
**Sourball**
  Like a: 4 TART
**Source:** 4 FONT LODE ROOT
   5 FOUNT 6 ORIGIN
**Sourdough**
  find: 3 ORE
**Sourpuss:** 4 CRAB
**Sour-tasting:** 4 ACID TART
   5 ACERB
**Sousaphone**
  kin: 4 TUBA
**Souse**
  Sitcom: 4 OTIS
**Soused:** 3 LIT
**Souter**
  Justice replaced by:
   7 BRENNAN
**South:** 5 DIXIE
  Commodity in the old:
   10 KINGCOTTON
  end: 3 ERN
  Go ~, maybe: 7 MIGRATE
  side: 3 ERN
  suffix: 3 ERN
  The ~, once: 3 CSA
  ~, in Spanish: 3 SUR
**South Africa**
  area: 5 NATAL
  Country inside: 7 LESOTHO
  Golfer from: 3 ELS
  Mandela of: 6 NELSON
**South African**
  Certain: 4 BOER
  fox: 4 ASSE
  grassland: 4 VELD 5 VELDT
  money: 4 RAND
  playwright Fugard: 5 ATHOL
  pres.: 7 PWBOTHA
  president: 5 BOTHA
  province: 5 NATAL
  ~ Peace Nobelist: 4 TUTU

**South America**
  Flightless bird of: 4 RHEA
  It's spotted in: 6 OCELOT
  Landlocked country of:
   7 BOLIVIA
**South American**
  Ancient: 4 INCA
  beast: 5 LLAMA
  bird: 4 RHEA
  capital: 4 LIMA 5 LAPAZ
   QUITO SUCRE
  dance: 5 SAMBA
  monkey: 4 TITI
  plain: 5 LLANO
  range: 5 ANDES
  rodent: 4 CAVY PACA 5 COYPU
   6 AGOUTI
  tuber: 3 OCA
  ~ Indian: 4 INCA
**South Australia**
  Capital of: 8 ADELAIDE
**South Beach ___:** 4 DIET
**South Bend**
  City near: 7 ELKHART
**South Carolina**
  motto word: 5 SPERO
**South Dakota**
  athlete: 6 COYOTE
  capital: 6 PIERRE
  city: 5 HURON 7 YANKTON
  feature: 7 BADLAND
  ~, to Pierre: 4 ETAT
**South Devon**
  river: 3 EXE
**Southeast Asian:** 3 LAO 4 THAI
**Southeastern Conference**
  team, informally: 4 BAMA
**Southend-on-Sea**
  site: 5 ESSEX
**Southern**
  bread: 4 PONE
  breakfast dish: 5 GRITS
  city: 8 SAOPAULO
  constellation: 3 ARA
  gal: 5 BELLE
  legume: 6 COWPEA
  lights: 15 AURORAAUSTRALIS
  power inits.: 3 TVA
  school: 4 BAMA
  sibling: 4 BRER
  side: 4 OKRA
  vacation spot: 3 RIO
**Southernmost**
  of the Marianas: 4 GUAM
  ~ Great Lake: 4 ERIE
  ~ U.S. city: 4 HILO
**Southfork:** 5 RANCH
  matriarch: 5 ELLIE
**South ___, Indiana:** 4 BEND
**South Korea**
  capital: 5 SEOUL
  First president of: 4 RHEE
  Roh ___ Woo of: 3 TAE
  Syngman of: 4 RHEE
**South Korean**
  1950s ~ president: 4 RHEE

auto: 3 KIA
port: 5 PUSAN
**South-of-the-border**
Info: Spanish cue
friend: 5 AMIGO
shout: 3 OLE
uncle: 3 TIO
**South Pacific**
island: 5 SAMOA 6 EASTER
  TAHITI 8 BORABORA
kingdom: 5 TONGA
region: 7 OCEANIA
republic: 4 FIJI
**"South Pacific"**
actor Pinza: 4 EZIO
actress Gaynor: 5 MITZI
director Josh: 5 LOGAN
Emile portrayer in: 4 EZIO
girl: 4 LIAT
hero: 5 EMILE
heroine: 6 NELLIE
song: 7 BALIHAI
**"South Park"**
casualty: 5 KENNY
character Cartman: 4 ERIC
creator Parker: 5 TREY
creator Stone: 4 MATT
kid: 3 IKE 4 KYLE STAN
voice actor Hayes: 5 ISAAC
**Southpaw:** 5 LEFTY
strength: 4 LEFT
Winningest: 5 SPAHN
**South Pole**
explorer Amundsen: 5 ROALD
**South Seas**
attire: 6 SARONG
island: 6 TAHITI
islander: 6 SAMOAN
island group: 4 FIJI 5 SAMOA
kingdom: 5 TONGA
staple: 4 TARO
tale: 4 OMOO
**South Vietnam**
president Ngo Dinh: 4 DIEM
**Southwest**
friend: 5 AMIGO
poplar: 5 ALAMO
sight: 4 MESA
~ Indian: 4 HOPI PIMA
**Southwestern**
art colony: 4 TAOS
brick: 5 ADOBE
gulch: 6 ARROYO
monster: 4 GILA
native: 3 UTE
plateau: 4 MESA
poplar: 5 ALAMO
pot: 4 OLLA
river: 4 GILA
saloon: 7 CANTINA
stewpot: 4 OLLA
~ Indian: 3 UTE 4 HOPI
**Souvenir:** 5 RELIC TOKEN
  7 MEMENTO
item: 3 TEE 6 TSHIRT
  8 TEESHIRT

**Souvlaki**
ingredient: 4 LAMB
" ___ So Vain": 5 YOURE
**Sovereign:** 5 ROYAL RULER
stand-in: 6 REGENT
**Sovereignty:** 6 THRONE
Symbol of: 3 ORB
**Soviet**
co-op: 5 ARTEL
First ~ premier: 5 LENIN
Former ~ First Lady: 5 RAISA
founder: 5 LENIN
labor camp: 5 GULAG
military force: 7 REDARMY
news agency: 4 TASS
Old ~ initials: 4 CCCP
satellite: 7 SPUTNIK
space probe: 4 LUNA
spy agcy.: 3 KGB
**Sow:** 3 SHE 4 SEED 5 PLANT
  6 FEMALE
chow: 4 SLOP
mate: 4 BOAR
pen: 3 STY
sound: 4 OINK
"___ sow ...": 4 ASYE
"So what?!": 7 BIGDEAL
"So what ___ is new?": 4 ELSE
**Sowing**
machine: 6 SEEDER
**Sox**
city: 3 CHI
on scoreboards: 3 BOS
**Soy**
product: 4 TOFU
What ~ can mean: 3 IAM
**Soybean**
product: 4 TOFU
soup: 4 MISO
**Soyuz**
Inits. on a ~ rocket: 4 CCCP
launcher: 4 USSR
**Spa:** 5 BATHS 6 HOTTUB
  RESORT
Day ~ offering: 4 ROBE
English: 4 BATH
feature: 5 SAUNA 6 HOTTUB
French: 5 EVIAN
German: 5 BADEN
  10 BADENBADEN
handout: 5 TOWEL
Lake Geneva: 5 EVIAN
offering: 5 SAUNA
  7 MUDBATH
sounds: 3 AHS 4 AAHS
treatment: 6 FACIAL
**Space:** 3 AIR GAP 4 AREA
  HOLE ROOM VOID
  5 REALM
between: 5 AISLE
between teeth: 8 DIASTEMA
Buzz in: 6 ALDRIN
cadet's place: 8 LALALAND
chimp: 4 ENOS
cloud: 6 NEBULA
Empty: 4 VOID

explorer: 5 PROBE
Fill: 3 ARE
First guy in: 4 YURI
Had ~ for: 6 SEATED
heater: 3 SOL
Intro to: 4 AERO
invaders: 3 ETS
Kind of: 5 OUTER
leader: 4 AERO
Like outer: 4 VAST
Link in: 4 DOCK
occupier: 6 MATTER
on a schedule: 4 SLOT
opening: 4 AERO
org.: 4 NASA
prefix: 4 AERO
revolver: 6 PLANET
Ride in: 5 SALLY
rock: 6 METEOR
Senator in: 4 GARN 5 GLENN
Shepard in: 4 ALAN
shuttle org.: 4 NASA
Solo in: 3 HAN
Soviet ~ program: 6 VOSTOK
spiral: 6 NEBULA
Tight on: 7 CRAMPED
Upper regions of: 5 ETHER
Vaulted: 4 APSE
walk (abbr.): 3 EVA
~, poetically: 5 ETHER
**Space ___:** 5 CADET
**___ space:** 5 OUTER
**Spacecraft**
component: 3 POD
segment: 6 MODULE
**Space Invaders**
maker: 5 ATARI
**Spacek**
Actress: 5 SISSY
role: 4 LYNN
**Spaceman**
of serials: 11 FLASHGORDON
**Space Needle**
city: 7 SEATTLE
**Space-saving**
abbr.: 3 ETC 4 ETAL
**Spaceship**
Mork's: 3 EGG
**Spaceship Earth**
setting: 5 EPCOT
**Space station**
1970s ~: 6 SKYLAB
Former Russian: 3 MIR
**Spacewalk**
initials: 3 EVA
**Spacey**
Actor: 5 KEVIN
**Spacious:** 4 AIRY 5 AMPLE
  ROOMY
**Spackle**
target: 8 NAILHOLE
**Spade:** 6 SLEUTH
Doesn't call a ~ a spade:
  4 ERRS
portrayer: 6 BOGART
the sleuth: 3 SAM

Use a: 3 DIG
~, to Bogart: 4 ROLE
**Spades:** 4 SUIT
Game with 13 ~ laid out:
    4 FARO
**Spaghetti:** 5 PASTA
specification: 7 ALDENTE
strainer: 5 SIEVE
topping: 5 SAUCE
**Spaghetti sauce**
brand: 4 RAGU 5 PREGO
herb: 5 BASIL
**Spaghetti western**
director Sergio: 5 LEONE
topper: 7 STETSON
**Spain**
and Portugal: 6 IBERIA
Capital of: 6 MADRID
City in: 4 LEON 5 AVILA
    LORCA 6 ORENSE
    OVIEDO TOLEDO
is in it (abbr.): 3 EEC
Lady of: 4 DONA 6 SENORA
Money of: 6 PESETA
Onetime queen of: 3 ENA
Province in: 4 LEON 5 AVILA
Region in: 6 ARAGON
River in: 4 EBRO
The rain in: 4 AGUA
**Spam:** 4 MEAT
container: 3 CAN TIN 5 EMAIL
maker: 6 HORMEL
Much: 3 ADS
**Span:** 5 CROSS
Animals in a: 4 OXEN
Calendar: 4 YEAR
Geological: 3 EON
Historical: 3 ERA
Pianist's: 6 OCTAVE
Singer's: 5 RANGE
**Spanakopita**
cheese: 4 FETA
**Spandau**
Last inmate at: 4 HESS
**Spangle:** 6 SEQUIN
**Spaniard**
Legendary: 5 ELCID
**Spaniel**
breed: 8 SPRINGER
Kind of: 6 SUSSEX
**Spanish**
1930s ~ queen: 3 ENA
actress Carmen: 5 MAURA
and pearl: 6 ONIONS
appetizer: 4 TAPA
article: 3 LAS LOS UNA UNO
aunt: 3 TIA
ayes: 3 SIS 4 SISI
babe: 4 NENE
beach: 5 PLAYA
bear: 3 OSO
bread: 6 PESETA
cheer: 3 OLE
Common ~ verb: 4 ESTA
count start: 3 UNO
cowboy: 7 LLANERO

crowd: 4 TRES
custard: 4 FLAN
day: 3 DIA
dessert: 4 FLAN
dessert wine: 6 MALAGA
diminutive: 3 ITA
direction: 3 SUR 4 ESTE
dish: 6 PAELLA
Dry ~ wine: 5 RIOJA
explorer: 6 DESOTO
eye: 3 OJO
girlfriend: 5 AMIGA
gold: 3 ORO
grocery: 6 BODEGA
hand: 4 MANO
hero: 5 ELCID
house: 4 CASA
inn: 6 POSADA
king: 3 REY
lady: 4 DONA 6 SENORA
language drama of 1984:
    7 ELNORTE
liqueur: 4 ANIS
love: 4 AMOR
mark: 5 TILDE
miss (abbr.): 4 SRTA
muralist: 4 SERT
nobleman: 7 GRANDEE
Old ~ coins: 6 REALES
or Denver: 6 OMELET
painter: 4 DALI GOYA MIRO
    SERT
poet: 5 LORCA
port: 5 CADIZ
pot: 4 OLLA
princess: 5 ELENA
pronoun: 3 ESA ESO 4 ELLO
    ESAS ESTA ESTO
    5 ELLAS
queen: 5 REINA
rice: 5 ARROZ
rice dish: 6 PAELLA
river: 3 RIO 4 EBRO
room: 4 SALA
root word: 3 OLE
royalty: 5 REYES 6 REINAS
shawl: 6 SERAPE
sherry: 7 AMOROSO
silver: 5 PLATA
sir: 5 SENOR
snack: 4 TAPA
stew: 4 OLLA
stewpot: 4 OLLA
surrealist: 4 DALI MIRO
tar: 4 BREA
tourist town: 5 AVILA
uncle: 3 TIO
vessel: 4 OLLA
walled city: 5 AVILA
water: 4 AGUA
wave: 3 OLA
~ Mrs.: 3 SRA
~ Muppet: 6 ROSITA
**Spanish ___:** 6 OMELET
**"Spanish Harlem"**
singer: 6 ARETHA

**Spanish Steps**
city: 4 ROME
**"Spanish Tragedy, The"**
dramatist Thomas: 3 KYD
**Spank:** 3 TAN 4 LICK SWAT
**Spanker:** 4 SAIL
**Spanking**
follower: 3 NEW
spot: 4 KNEE REAR
**Spanky**
Pal of: 7 ALFALFA
~, for one: 6 RASCAL
**Spann**
Bluesman: 4 OTIS
**Spar:** 3 BOX 4 MAST POLE
    YARD
Sail: 5 SPRIT
**Spare:** 4 LEAN TIRE
    7 AUSTERE
change: 4 TIRE
hair: 3 WIG
holder: 5 TRUNK
part: 3 PIN RIB
Put on a ~ tire: 4 GAIN
Seek ~ change: 3 BEG
target: 6 TENPIN 7 NINEPIN
With room to: 5 AMPLY
**Spared**
It may be: 6 THEROD
**Spare tire:** 3 FAT 4 FLAB
site: 5 WAIST
**Spark:** 4 ELAN GERM
    6 EXCITE 7 ANIMATE
    8 CATALYST
Creative: 4 IDEA
follower: 4 PLUG
plug feature: 3 GAP
**Sparkle:** 3 PEP 4 ELAN
    5 ECLAT GLINT SHINE
    6 ESPRIT 7 GLISTEN
Add some: 6 AERATE
Wine with a: 4 ASTI
**Sparkled:** 5 SHONE
**Sparkler:** 3 GEM
**Sparkling:** 8 AGLITTER
headwear: 5 TIARA
It might be: 4 WINE
wine: 4 ASTI
**Sparks**
City near: 4 RENO
loc.: 3 NEV
Old film comic: 3 NED
setting: 6 NEVADA
**Sparky**
Cy Young winner: 4 LYLE
**Sparrow:** 5 FINCH
**Sparrow of Paris, The**
Singer known as: 4 PIAF
**Sparse:** 4 THIN 6 SCANTY
**Sparta**
Rival of: 5 ARGOS
Serf of ancient: 5 HELOT
**Spartacus:** 5 SLAVE
**Spartan:** 5 HARSH STARK
    7 AUSTERE
foe: 8 ATHENIAN

queen: 4 LEDA
serf: 5 HELOT
**Spasm:** 3 TIC 4 PANG 5 THROE
Neck: 5 CRICK
**Spasmodic:** 5 JERKY
**Spat:** 3 ROW 4 TIFF TODO
5 SETTO
Public: 5 SCENE
spot: 5 ANKLE
**Spate:** 4 RASH 7 TORRENT
**Spathe**
Flower with a: 5 CALLA
**Spatting:** 4 ATIT
**Spatula**
Toss with a: 4 FLIP
**Spawn:** 3 OVA ROE
**Spawning**
fish: 3 EEL 4 SHAD
**Spay:** 6 NEUTER
**SPCA**
Part of: 3 SOC
**Speak:** 3 SAY 4 TALK 5 ORATE
UTTER
As we: 3 NOW
at all: 6 SAYBOO
at length: 5 ORATE RUNON
derisively: 5 SCOFF
hesitantly: 3 HAW
hoarsely: 4 RASP
in a monotone: 5 DRONE
irritably to: 6 SNAPAT
like a tough guy: 4 RASP
like Sylvester: 4 LISP
lovingly: 3 COO
off the cuff: 5 ADLIB
one's mind: 5 OPINE
pompously: 5 ORATE
slowly: 5 DRAWL
So to: 8 ASITWERE
unclearly: 4 SLUR
with a Jersey accent: 3 MOO
~, old-style: 5 SAYST
___ speak: 4 SOTO
**Speakeasy**
event: 4 RAID
**Speaker**
aid: 5 NOTES
Loud: 6 RANTER 7 STENTOR
of baseball: 4 TRIS
Old ~ name: 4 NEWT
part: 7 TWEETER
pauses: 3 ERS
platform: 4 DAIS
Public: 6 ORATOR
spot: 4 DAIS 7 LECTERN
systems, for short: 3 PAS
**Speaking**
Generally: 7 ASARULE
Manner of: 4 TONE 5 IDIOM
Plain: 5 PROSE
sites: 6 ROSTRA
**Spear**
carrier: 5 EXTRA
carrier venue: 5 OPERA
handle: 5 SHAFT
Poseidon's: 7 TRIDENT

**Spearhead:** 4 LEAD
**Spears, Britney**
fan: 4 TEEN
hit: 15 OOPSIDIDITAGAIN
Product hawked by: 5 PEPSI
**Spec.**
Not: 3 GEN
Shoe: 3 EEE
**Special:** 3 PET 6 ENTREE
attention, for short: 3 TLC
case: 4 ETUI
connections: 3 INS
edition: 5 EXTRA
group: 5 ELITE
Kind of: 5 KMART
Nothing: 4 SOSO
skill: 4 GIFT 5 KNACK
suffix: 3 IST
They may be: 9 INTERESTS
time: 3 ERA
vocabulary: 5 ARGOT
**Special Forces**
cap: 5 BERET
unit: 5 ATEAM
weapon: 3 UZI
**Special-interest**
gp.: 3 ORG 4 ASSN
**Specialist:** 3 PRO 5 MAVEN
**Specialized**
angler: 5 EELER
idiom: 5 ARGOT
sch.: 4 ACAD
slang: 5 LINGO
**Specialty:** 4 AREA 5 FIELD
FORTE NICHE
6 METIER
**Specific**
For a ~ purpose: 5 ADHOC
Get: 9 NAMENAMES
**Specifically:** 5 TOWIT
**Specification:** 6 DETAIL
**Specifics:** 7 DETAILS
**Specified:** 3 SET
**Specify:** 4 NAME
**Specimen**
Assay: 3 ORE
collector: 4 SWAB
holder: 4 VIAL
New: 7 NEOTYPE
**Specious**
debater: 7 SOPHIST
**Speck:** 3 DOT TAD 4 ATOM
IOTA MOTE
in the ocean: 4 ISLE 5 ISLET
**Speckled**
fish: 5 TROUT
horse: 4 ROAN
**Spectacle:** 5 SCENE
**Spectacles**
Spot for: 4 NOSE
**Spectacular:** 4 EPIC
7 AWESOME
star: 4 NOVA
**Spectator**
No mere: 4 DOER
Unhappy: 5 BOOER

**Spectator, The**
essayist: 6 STEELE
**Specter:** 5 BOGIE GHOST
6 WRAITH
Senator: 5 ARLEN
**Spectra**
maker: 3 KIA
**Spectrum**
band: 3 HUE
Beyond the visible:
8 ULTRARED
11 ULTRAVIOLET
component: 3 RED 4 BLUE
6 INDIGO
One end of the: 3 RED
producer: 5 PRISM
The whole: 4 ATOZ
**Speculative:** 5 RISKY
Least: 6 SAFEST
**Sped:** 3 RAN ZIP 4 FLEW
TORE
**Speech:** 7 ADDRESS ORATION
Acceptance ~ word: 5 THANK
Body of a: 4 TEXT
characteristic: 6 ACCENT
difficulty: 4 LISP
enlivener: 8 ANECDOTE
Figure of: 5 IDIOM TROPE
6 ORATOR
Formal: 7 ORATION
Free ~ obstacle: 3 GAG
Give a: 5 ORATE
Imperfect: 4 LISP
Informal: 5 SLANG
Long ~, often: 4 BORE
Make a: 5 ORATE
Omit, in: 5 ELIDE
Part of: 4 NOUN 8 SENTENCE
problem: 4 LISP
Pt. of: 3 ADV 4 PRON
Public: 7 ORATION
Some ~ sounds: 6 NASALS
study: 9 PHONETICS
stumbles: 3 UHS
Sun.: 3 SER
**Speechify:** 5 ORATE
**Speechless:** 3 MUM 4 MUTE
6 AGHAST SILENT
Leave: 3 AWE 4 STUN
one: 5 MIMER
**Speechwriter**
~ Peggy: 6 NOONAN
**Speed:** 3 HIE 5 HASTE
6 GOFAST
At full: 5 AMAIN
Built for: 5 SLEEK
Burst of: 6 SPRINT
Check: 4 TIME
contest: 4 RACE
demon: 5 RACER
Demonstrate raw: 6 STREAK
Hi-tech ~ rate: 4 BAUD
limit letters: 3 MPH
Musical: 5 TEMPO
prefix: 3 VEL
ratio: 4 MACH

reader: 5 RADAR
   8 RADARGUN
Tape ~ (abbr.): 3 IPS
Undue: 5 HASTE
unit: 4 KNOT MACH
up: 3 REV
Up to: 4 ABLE
Walking: 4 PACE
With: 5 APACE
Word with: 4 TRAP
**"Speed"**
   actor: 6 REEVES
   actor Reeves: 5 KEANU
   actress Bullock: 6 SANDRA
   setting: 3 BUS
**"Speed ___": 5 RACER**
**Speeder**
   A ~ makes it: 5 HASTE
   A ~ steps on it: 3 GAS
   penalty: 4 FINE
   spotter: 5 RADAR
   stopper: 3 COP
**Speedily: 5 APACE**
**Speed-of-sound**
   exceeder: 3 SST
   number: 4 MACH
**Speedometer**
   letters: 3 MPH
**Speeds**
   Musical: 5 TEMPI
**Speedster**
   Retired: 3 SST
**Speed Stick**
   maker: 6 MENNEN
**___ Speedwagon: 3 REO**
**Speedway**
   Florida: 7 DAYTONA
**Speedy: 4 FAST 5 FLEET**
   RAPID
   flier: 3 SST
   one-seater: 6 GOKART
   steed: 4 ARAB
**Speleologist: 5 CAVER**
**Spell: 3 HEX 4 BOUT 5 STINT**
   7 RELIEVE
   Bad: 3 HEX
   Cold: 6 ICEAGE
   For a: 6 AWHILE
   of excess: 5 SPREE
   Sit a: 4 REST
   Under Cupid's: 6 INLOVE
   Under the ~ (of):
     8 ENAMORED
   Voodoo: 4 MOJO
   Where one stands for a: 3 BEE
**Spellbinding**
   sort: 6 ORATOR
**Spellbound: 4 AGOG AWED**
   RAPT
**Spelled**
   Not ~ out: 5 TACIT
   Song title ~ out: 4 YMCA
**Speller**
   phrase: 4 ASIN
**Spelling**
   Actress: 4 TORI

Alt.: 3 VAR
and Amos: 5 TORIS
contest: 3 BEE
game: 5 GHOST
TV producer: 5 AARON
**Spell-off: 3 BEE**
**Spelunker: 5 CAVER**
**Spelunking**
   site: 4 CAVE 6 GROTTO
**Spend: 5 USEUP**
   the night: 4 STAY
**Spender**
   Big: 10 HIGHROLLER
**Spending**
   binge: 5 SPREE
   limit: 3 CAP
**Spendthrift: 7 WASTREL**
   Not a: 5 MISER SAVER
**Spenser**
   portrayer: 5 URICH
**"Spenser: For Hire"**
   actor Robert: 5 URICH
**Spenserian**
   work: 6 SONNET
**Spent: 4 WORN 5 ALLIN TIRED**
   WEARY 6 POOPED
   USEDUP 7 ALLGONE
   Money: 5 OUTGO
**Spew: 4 EMIT**
   fire and brimstone: 4 RANT
   forth: 4 GUSH 5 ERUPT
   SPOUT SPUME
   Volcanic: 3 ASH
**Spewer**
   Sicilian: 4 ETNA
**Sphagnous: 5 MOSSY**
**Sphagnum: 4 MOSS**
   moss: 4 PEAT
**Sphere: 3 ORB 4 AREA**
   5 ARENA GLOBE REALM
   6 REGION
   prefix: 3 ECO 4 ATMO HEMI
   IONO 5 TROPO 6 STRATO
**Spherical: 5 ORBIC ROUND**
   veggies: 4 PEAS
**Spheroid: 3 ORB**
   Edible: 3 PEA
   hairdo: 4 AFRO
**Sphinx**
   site: 4 GIZA
   ~, in part: 4 LION
**Spice: 4 ZEST**
   Add ~ to: 6 SEASON
   amt.: 3 TSP
   Cookie: 6 GINGER
   Eggnog: 6 NUTMEG
   holder: 4 RACK
   Nutmeg: 4 MACE
   rack spice: 9 ONIONSALT
**Spiced**
   It may be: 3 TEA
   stew: 4 OLLA
   tea: 4 CHAI
**Spice Girls**
   genre: 7 EUROPOP
   singer Halliwell: 4 GERI

**Spick-and-span: 4 NEAT**
**Spicy: 3 HOT 5 ZESTY**
   7 PEPPERY
   candies: 7 REDHOTS
   cuisine: 4 THAI 5 CAJUN
   HUNAN 6 CREOLE
   TEXMEX 7 MEXICAN
   dip: 5 SALSA
   ingredient: 5 CHILI
   Not: 4 MILD 5 BLAND
   sauce: 5 SALSA
   sausage: 6 SALAMI
   stew: 4 OLLA SAMI
   6 RAGOUT
   Very: 6 REDHOT
**Spider**
   creation: 3 WEB 6 COBWEB
   maker: 4 FIAT
   prey: 3 FLY
   She was changed into a:
     7 ARACHNE
   web: 4 TRAP
**Spiderlike**
   bug: 13 DADDYLONGLEGS
**Spider-Man**
   creator: 7 STANLEE
   creator Lee: 4 STAN
   creator Stan: 3 LEE
**"Spider-Man"**
   actress Kirsten: 5 DUNST
   director: 5 RAIMI 8 SAMRAIMI
**___ Spiegel: 3 DER**
**Spiegelman, Art**
   critter: 4 MAUS
**Spiel: 4 LINE 5 ORATE**
   6 PATTER
   Emcee: 5 INTRO
   Sales: 5 PITCH
**Spielberg**
   Director: 6 STEVEN
   film: 4 JAWS 7 AMISTAD
**Spiff**
   (up): 6 SPRUCE
**Spiffy: 4 NEAT POSH 6 RAKISH**
   Make: 4 DOUP
**Spigot: 3 TAP**
   Container with a: 3 URN
**Spike: 4 LACE**
   Climbing: 5 PITON
   Corn: 3 EAR
   Director: 3 LEE
   Golden ~ state: 4 UTAH
   greeting: 3 GRR
   Shoe: 5 CLEAT
   Volleyball: 8 KILLSHOT
**Spiked**
   club: 4 MACE
**Spikes**
   They might end in: 3 TDS
**Spike TV**
   former name: 3 TNN
**Spiky**
   Doll with ~ hair: 5 TROLL
**Spill: 4 TRIP 5 WASTE**
   6 HEADER TUMBLE
   Clean, as a: 5 MOPUP

(over): 4 SLOP
Snitches ~ them: 5 BEANS
the beans: 3 RAT 4 BLAB
   SING TALK TELL
   5 BLURT LETON
   6 TATTLE

**Spilt**
Cry over ~ milk: 5 WHINE

**Spin:** 4 REEL TURN 5 TWIRL
   6 ROTATE 7 REVOLVE
Apply: 4 SKEW
Go for a: 4 REEL
Put a ~ on: 5 SLANT
Rink: 5 CAMEL
What DJs: 3 LPS
You might go for a ~ in it:
   4 TUTU

**Spinach**
Like: 5 LEAFY

**Spinach-like**
plant: 5 ORACH

**Spinal**
column feature: 4 DISC

**Spinal cord**
Brain and ~ (abbr.): 3 CNS
Of the: 6 NEURAL

**"Spin City"**
star: 5 SHEEN

**Spindle:** 3 MAR 4 AXLE
Grinding wheel:
   7 MANDREL

**Spin doctor:** 5 PRMAN
concern: 5 IMAGE

**Spine**
line: 5 TITLE

**Spine-chilling:** 5 EERIE

**Spiner**
Actor: 5 BRENT
role: 4 DATA

**Spine-tingling:** 5 EERIE

**Spingarn Medal**
awarder: 5 NAACP

**Spinks**
Boxer: 4 LEON
defeater: 3 ALI

**Spin like ___:** 4 ATOP

**Spinnaker:** 4 SAIL
site: 5 YACHT

**Spinner:** 3 TOP 4 GYRO
   5 PRMAN
of lore:
   15 RUMPELSTILTSKIN
Plane: 4 PROP
Record: 6 DEEJAY
Yarn: 5 LIAR

**Spinners:** 3 DJS

**Spinning:** 5 AREEL
   6 AWHIRL
part: 5 ROTOR
toy: 3 TOP
wheels, perhaps: 5 MIRED

**Spin-off**
Religious: 4 SECT

**Spiny**
anteater: 7 ECHIDNA
cactus: 6 CHOLLA

houseplant: 4 ALOE
plant: 6 CACTUS
plants: 5 CACTI

**Spiny-rayed**
fish: 7 CICHLID

**Spiral:** 4 LOOP 5 HELIX
   6 GYRATE
shell: 5 CONCH 6 TRITON
Space: 6 NEBULA

**Spiral-horned**
antelope: 4 KUDU 5 ELAND

**Spiral-shelled**
mollusk: 5 SNAIL WHELK
   6 TRITON

**Spirit:** 3 PEP VIM 4 AURA BRIO
   ELAN LIFE SOUL
   5 ARDOR GENIE GHOST
   HEART SPUNK
   6 MORALE WRAITH
Blithe: 4 ELAN
Bottled: 5 GENIE
Break the ~ of: 5 UNMAN
Community: 5 ETHOS
Evil: 5 DEMON
Full of school: 6 RAHRAH
Group: 6 MORALE
Household: 3 LAR
Indomitable: 4 GRIT
Irish: 7 BANSHEE
Islamic: 5 DJINN
Kind of: 4 TEAM
Obliging: 5 GENIE
of a people: 5 ETHOS
of the time: 9 ZEITGEIST
raiser: 6 SEANCE
Shakespearean: 5 ARIEL
Show team: 4 ROOT
Word before: 4 TEAM

**Spirited**
attack: 5 SALVO
horse: 4 ARAB 5 STEED
self-assurance: 4 ELAN
session: 6 SEANCE

**Spiritedness:** 4 ELAN

**Spirits:** 7 ALCOHOL
Bottled: 5 GENII
Evil: 6 INCUBI
Guardian: 5 GENII
High: 3 PEP 4 GLEE 5 CHEER
   7 ELATION
home: 3 BAR
In low: 3 SAD
Island: 4 RUMS
Japanese: 5 SAKES SAKIS
Lift the ~ of: 5 ELATE
Roman household: 5 LARES

**Spiritual:** 4 SONG 5 INNER
adviser: 4 GURU
Endow with ~ awareness:
   6 ENSOUL
guide: 4 GURU
Islamic ~ leader: 6 CALIPH
leader: 5 REBBE
path: 3 TAO ZEN

**Spiritualist**
session: 6 SEANCE

**Spiritually**
Uplift: 5 EDIFY

**Spiro**
predecessor: 6 HUBERT
Vice President: 5 AGNEW

**Spit**
Frog: 4 ALGA
out: 4 SPEW
Ready to: 5 IRATE

**Spitchcock:** 3 EEL

**Spite:** 5 VENOM 6 MALICE
In ~ of: 3 THO 5 ALTHO

**Spiteful:** 4 MEAN 5 CATTY
   NASTY

**Spitfire**
fliers: 3 RAF

**Spitter**
sound: 4 PTUI
South American: 5 LLAMA

**Spitting**
sound: 4 PTUI
thing: 5 IMAGE

**Splash:** 4 ELAN SLOP
Big: 5 ECLAT
Cause of a big:
   9 BELLYFLOP
Make a: 4 PLOP

**Splasher**
Playful: 5 OTTER

**Splashy**
resort: 3 SPA

**Splatter**
protector: 3 BIB

**Spleen:** 3 IRE 4 BILE

**Splendid:** 5 GRAND REGAL
   SUPER
array: 7 PANOPLY

**"Splendid Splinter, The"**
~ Williams: 3 TED

**Splendor:** 4 POMP

**"Splendor in the Grass"**
screenwriter: 4 INGE

**Splice:** 4 EDIT

**Spliced**
Get: 3 WED
item: 4 GENE

**Splicer**
need: 3 DNA
target: 4 GENE

**Splint**
site: 4 SHIN

**Splinter**
group: 4 SECT
Remove a: 6 TWEEZE

**"Splish Splash"**
singer Bobby: 5 DARIN

**Split:** 3 RAN 4 BOLT CHAP
   GAPE GULF PART REND
   RENT RIFT RIVE TEAR
   TORE 5 CLEFT HALVE
   INTWO LEAVE RIVED
   RIVEN 6 BISECT
   CLEAVE CLOVEN
   DIVIDE
apart: 4 REND
bit: 4 ATOM

country: 5 KOREA
decision: 7 DIVORCE
Easily ~ rock: 4 MICA 5 SLATE
evenly: 6 BISECT
Family: 6 ESTATE
for church: 5 TITHE
hairs: 7 NITPICK
in two: 6 CLEAVE
It might be: 3 PEA 4 ATOM
land: 5 KOREA
open: 3 RIP
personalities: 4 EXES
Some are: 4 ENDS
They've: 4 EXES
to unite: 5 ELOPE
up: 7 DIVORCE
**Split-off**
group: 4 SECT
**Split ___ soup:** 3 PEA
**Splitsville:** 4 RENO
parties: 4 EXES
**Splitter**
Beam: 5 PRISM
Wood: 3 AXE
**Splitting**
headache:
13 CUSTODYBATTLE
**Splotch:** 4 BLOB
**Spock**
(abbr.): 3 CDR
forte: 5 LOGIC
Like: 7 LOGICAL
portrayer: 5 NIMOY
**Spode**
offering: 6 TEASET
**Spoil:** 3 MAR ROT 4 RUIN
TURN 5 GOBAD GUMUP
TAINT
a picnic: 6 RAINON
Didn't: 4 KEPT
~, with "on": 4 DOTE
**Spoiled:** 3 BAD 6 BRATTY
8 INEDIBLE
kid: 4 BRAT
**Spoiler:** 4 BANE 6 RUINER
~, of a sort: 5 DOTER
**Spoils:** 4 LOOT SWAG 5 BOOTY
7 DOTESON
taker: 6 VICTOR
**Spoilsport:** 9 SORELOSER
**Spoke:** 4 SAID
(up): 5 PIPED
**Spoken:** 4 ORAL SAID
5 ALOUD 6 STATED
for: 5 TAKEN
Not: 5 TACIT
**Spokes:** 5 RADII
center: 3 HUB
Umbrella: 4 RIBS
**Spokescow:** 5 ELSIE
**Spokes-elf:** 5 ERNIE
**Spokeslizard:** 5 GECKO
**Spokesman**
for Moses: 5 AARON
Keebler: 3 ELF
~ Fleischer: 3 ARI

**Sponge:** 3 BUM DAB SOT
4 GRUB 5 CADGE DIPSO
LEECH MOOCH
6 CADGER 7 MOISTEN
8 FREELOAD
Bath: 5 LOOFA 6 LOOFAH
feature: 4 PORE
gently: 5 DABAT
target: 4 SLOP
**Spongy**
cake: 5 BABKA
earth: 4 MIRE
ground: 3 BOG
toy ball: 4 NERF
**Sponsor**
GI show: 3 USO
Jack Benny: 5 JELLO
Racecar: 3 STP
spots: 3 ADS
Words from the: 3 ADS
**Sponsored**
One ~ at baptism: 6 GODSON
**Sponsorship:** 4 EGIS 5 AEGIS
**Spontaneous**
response: 5 ADLIB
**Spoof:** 5 PUTON
1966 spy ~:
11 OURMANFLINT
1974 Sutherland/Gould ~:
4 SPYS
**Spook:** 3 SPY 5 SCARE
gp.: 3 CIA
**Spooky:** 4 EERY 5 EERIE
SCARY WEIRD
In a ~ way: 6 EERILY
sight: 3 UFO
**Spool**
Film: 4 REEL
**Spoon:** 7 UTENSIL
Greasy: 5 DINER
Greasy ~ sign: 4 EATS
Use a: 4 STIR
___ spoon (diner): 6 GREASY
**Spoon-bender**
~ Geller: 3 URI
**Spoonbill**
cousin: 4 IBIS
**Spoonful:** 4 DOSE 5 TASTE
6 DOLLOP
**Spoon-playing**
site: 4 KNEE
**Spoons**
Like some: 7 SLOTTED
**Spoony**
Make: 6 ENAMOR
**Sporadic:**
15 ONAGAINOFFAGAIN
**Spore**
prefix: 4 ENDO
producer: 4 FERN
sacs: 4 ASCI
**Spork**
part: 4 TINE
**Sport:** 4 JEST
blade: 4 EPEE
Clay pigeon: 5 SKEET

Court: 7 JAIALAI
Cowboy: 5 RODEO
for heavyweights: 4 SUMO
full of traps: 5 SKEET
Japanese: 4 SUMO
NCAA: 8 LACROSSE
Royal: 4 POLO
Self-defense: 4 JUDO
Shooting: 5 SKEET
Sword: 4 EPEE
Winter: 4 LUGE
with horses: 4 POLO
World Cup: 6 SOCCER
**Sport ___:** 3 UTE 4 TRAC
**Sportage**
maker: 3 KIA
**Sported:** 4 WORE 5 HADON
**Sporting**
blade: 4 EPEE
sandals: 4 SHOD
**Sports:** 5 HASON WEARS
2001 ~ biopic: 3 ALI
Amateur ~ org.: 4 NCAA
Annual ~ event: 6 USOPEN
arenas: 6 STADIA
award: 4 ESPY
basket: 5 CESTA
Big name in ~ cards: 5 FLEER
Cable ~ award: 4 ESPY
center: 5 ARENA
College ~ org.: 4 NCAA
column: 4 LOSS WINS
complex: 5 ARENA
data: 5 STATS
drink suffix: 3 ADE
elite: 6 ALLPRO
event: 4 MEET
facilities: 6 STADIA
facility: 5 ARENA
figure: 4 STAT
Former ~ org.: 3 AFL
gp.: 3 AAU
HBO ~ agent: 6 ARLISS
Like many ~ telecasts: 4 LIVE
Like no-holds-barred:
7 EXTREME
mag: 4 ESPN
Nonpro ~ org.: 3 AAU
NYC ~ venue: 3 MSG
org.: 4 NCAA
page number: 4 STAT
palace: 5 ARENA
replay tool: 5 SLOMO
shocker: 5 UPSET
show tool: 5 SLOMO
squad: 4 TEAM
stadium: 5 ARENA
surprise: 5 UPSET
team: 5 SQUAD
trivia: 5 STATS
Univ. ~ gp.: 4 NCAA
venue: 5 ARENA
**Sports car:** 3 JAG 4 ALFA
Classic: 5 TBIRD
engine: 5 TURBO
English: 3 JAG

Italian: 4 ALFA
**Sports cars**
British: 3 MGS
Some: 3 GTS
**Sportscast**
feature: 5 RECAP SLOMO
insight: 5 COLOR
**Sportscaster**
device: 5 SLOMO 6 REPLAY
offering: 5 COLOR
~ Dick: 6 ENBERG
~ Howard: 6 COSELL
~ Mel: 5 ALLEN
~ Merlin: 5 OLSEN
**"SportsCenter"**
network: 4 ESPN
**Sportsman**
Sports Illustrated's 1974 ~ of
the Year: 3 ALI
Sports Illustrated's ~ of the
Century: 3 ALI
**Sportster**
Chevy: 5 VETTE
**Sportswear**
brand: 4 IZOD
**Sporty**
auto: 3 GTO 6 CAMARO
car roof: 4 TTOP
scarf: 5 ASCOT
truck: 3 UTE
~ Chevy: 5 VETTE 6 CAMARO
~ Ford: 5 TBIRD
~ Italian car: 4 ALFA
~ Mazda: 5 MIATA
~ Pontiac: 3 GTO
~ Studebaker: 6 AVANTI
~ Volkswagen: 3 GTI
**Spot:** 3 DAB EYE SEE SPY
4 AREA ESPY LOAN
SITE TVAD 5 PLACE
STAIN 6 DAPPLE
LOCALE LOCATE
broadcast: 5 PROMO
checker: 5 ASPCA LEASH
markers: 4 EXES
of land: 4 ISLE
of relief: 5 OASIS
of wine: 4 ASTI
on radar: 4 BLIP
**Spotless:**
15 CLEANASAWHISTLE
**Spots:** 3 ADS 4 LOCI
Central: 4 LOCI
Paid: 3 ADS
TV: 3 ADS
**Spotted:** 3 SAW 4 LENT SEEN
6 CALICO
beetle: 7 LADYBUG
butterfly: 6 SATYR
cat: 6 OCELOT
cavy: 4 PACA
predator: 5 HYENA
~, to Tweety: 3 TAW
**Spotter**
Smokey: 4 CBER
Speeder: 5 RADAR

**Spouse:** 4 MATE 7 PARTNER
8 HELPMATE
denial: 6 NODEAR
kin: 5 INLAW
sibling: 5 INLAW
Take a: 3 WED
**Spouses**
Former: 4 EXES
of a sultan: 5 HAREM
**Spout:** 5 ORATE
off: 5 ORATE
**Spouter**
Sicilian: 4 ETNA
**Sprain**
soother: 6 ICEBAG
8 LINIMENT
spot: 5 ANKLE
Treat a: 3 ICE
**Sprang:** 5 AROSE LEAPT
up: 5 AROSE
**Sprat:** 5 EATER
regimen: 5 NOFAT
**Sprat, Jack**
bane: 3 FAT
choice: 4 LEAN
diet: 4 LEAN
**Sprawl:** 3 LIE
Kind of: 5 URBAN
**Sprawling**
Send: 4 TRIP
**Spray:** 3 WET 4 MIST
7 AEROSOL
alternative: 6 ROLLON
Anti-attacker: 4 MACE
Asthma: 8 INHALANT
Banned: 4 ALAR
can: 7 AEROSOL
Cooking: 3 PAM
Fine: 4 MIST
Kind of: 5 NASAL
Nasal: 5 SINEX
target: 4 ODOR
**Spread:** 3 SOW 4 FARM MEAL
5 FEAST SPLAY STREW
WIDEN
apart: 5 SPLAY
around: 5 STREW
BLT: 4 MAYO
Bread: 3 JAM 4 MAYO OLEO
Deli: 4 MAYO
Expensive: 3 ROE 6 CAVIAR
Fancy: 4 PATE
Garlicky: 5 AIOLI
Had a: 5 DINED
Hors d'oeuvre: 4 PATE
in a tub: 4 OLEO
joy: 5 ELATE
Nondairy: 4 OLEO
out: 3 FAN 4 SOWN 5 ARRAY
SPLAY 6 SPARSE
Part of a: 4 ACRE
Party: 4 BRIE PATE
seed: 5 SOWED
Significant: 6 ESTATE
Sweet: 5 ICING
thickly: 7 SLATHER

Thinly: 6 SPARSE
unchecked: 4 RAGE
Vegetable: 4 OLEO
**Spreadable**
cheese: 4 BRIE
stick: 4 OLEO
**Spreading**
tree: 3 ELM
**Spreadsheet**
entry: 5 DATUM
filler: 4 DATA
Like a: 7 TABULAR
line: 3 ROW
pros: 4 CPAS
**"Sprechen ___ Deutsch?":**
3 SIE
**Spree:** 3 JAG 4 LARK ORGY
TEAR TOOT 5 BINGE
6 BENDER
Go on a: 5 SPEND
site: 4 MALL
**Spreeing:** 7 ONATEAR
**Sprightly:** 4 PERT 5 AGILE
ELFIN
**Spring:** 3 HOP SPA 4 COIL
LEAP 5 ARISE BOUND
LETGO 6 SEASON
7 EMANATE
ahead, perhaps: 5 RESET
bloom: 4 IRIS 5 LILAC PEONY
6 AZALEA CROCUS
cleaning event: 7 TAGSALE
collection org.: 3 IRS
Do a ~ chore: 5 CLEAN
event: 4 THAW
11 APRILSHOWER
feast: 5 SEDER
feature: 4 COIL
festival: 6 EASTER
formal: 4 PROM
harbinger: 5 ROBIN
Like many ~ days: 4 MILD
locale: 3 SPA 5 OASIS
Mineral: 3 SPA
mo.: 3 APR MAR
month: 3 MAY
Opposite of: 4 NEAP
Pertaining to: 6 VERNAL
purchase: 4 SEED
Showy ~ flower: 5 PEONY
Sign of: 4 THAW 5 ARIES
ROBIN 6 GEMINI
sound: 5 BOING
summer: 3 CPA
thing: 4 COIL
time: 3 MAY 4 LENT 5 APRIL
7 EQUINOX
Toy on a: 9 POGOSTICK
up: 5 ARISE
**Spring ___ (start dripping):**
5 ALEAK
**"Spring ahead"**
hrs.: 3 DST
**Springlike:** 6 VERNAL
**Springs**
It ~ eternal: 4 HOPE

___ Springs, Florida:
   9 ALTAMONTE
**Springsteen**
  birthplace: 3 USA
  nickname: 7 THEBOSS
  tune: 8 IMONFIRE
**Springtime**
  dance site: 7 MAYPOLE
  hunter's find: 9 EASTEREGG
**Springy:** 6 VERNAL 7 ELASTIC
**Sprinkle**
  around: 5 STREW
  Post-shower: 4 TALC
  Scientist's: 4 NACL
  with oil: 6 ANOINT
  ~, as powdered sugar: 4 SIFT
**Sprinkler**
  attachment: 4 HOSE
**Sprint:** 3 RUN 4 DASH RACE
  rival: 3 MCI
**Sprinted:** 3 RAN
**Sprinter**
  assignment: 4 LANE
  goal: 4 TAPE
  path: 4 LANE
**Sprite:** 3 ELF IMP 4 PERI PIXY
    5 PIXIE
  Mischievous: 5 PIXIE
  rival: 6 FRESCA
  Shakespearean: 5 ARIEL
  Water: 5 NIXIE
**Spritely:** 5 ELFIN 6 ELFISH
**Sprocket:** 3 COG
**Sprout:** 3 LAD TOT 4 GROW
  Bean: 3 EAR 4 IDEA
  up: 4 GROW
**Spruce:** 4 NEAT TIDY TRIM
    5 NATTY 6 DAPPER
  relative: 3 FIR
  up, in a way: 6 REFACE
**Spruced**
  All ~ up: 4 NEAT
  up: 8 NEATENED
**Sprung:** 6 ARISEN
**Spry:** 5 AGILE
**Spud:** 5 TATER
  bud: 3 EYE
  source: 5 IDAHO
**Spuds**
  Prepare: 4 MASH
**Spumante**
  source: 4 ASTI
  ___ spumante: 4 ASTI
**Spun:** 7 ROTATED
  It may be: 4 TALE YARN
  tales: 6 YARNED
  Yarn that is: 4 TALE
**Spunk:** 4 GRIT 5 MOXIE
    6 METTLE SPIRIT
  Full of: 6 FEISTY
**Spur:** 4 GOAD PROD URGE
    5 EGGON IMPEL ROUSE
    6 INCITE
  part: 5 ROWEL
  Silver: 4 HIYO
**Spurt:** 5 SPASM

Had a growth: 6 SHOTUP
  of activity: 5 SPASM
**Sputnik**
  coverer: 4 TASS
  letters: 4 CCCP
  Month when ~ was launched:
    7 OCTOBER
**Sputter**
  and stall: 3 DIE
**Spy:** 4 MOLE 5 AGENT PLANT
  alias: 8 CODENAME
  Biblical: 5 CALEB
  disguise: 5 COVER
  exchanged for Powers: 4 ABEL
  Fictional ~ Helm: 4 MATT
  Former ~ org.: 3 KGB
  Northern: 5 APPLE
  Old ~ org.: 3 OSS
  org.: 3 CIA
  Seductive: 8 MATAHARI
  writing: 4 CODE
  WWII ~ org.: 3 OSS
  ~ Aldrich: 4 AMES
**Spydom**
  First name in: 4 MATA
  Last name in: 4 HARI
**Spyglass**
  Use a: 4 PEER
**"Spy in the House of Love, A"**
  novelist: 3 NIN 8 ANAISNIN
**Spymaster**
  worry: 4 MOLE
**Spyri, Johanna**
  classic novel: 5 HEIDI
**S*P*Y*S**
  org.: 3 CIA
**"Spy vs. Spy"**
  magazine: 3 MAD
**"Spy Who Came In From the
    Cold, The"**
  spy: 4 ALEC
**Squabble:** 3 ADO 4 FEUD RIFT
    SPAT TIFF 5 ARGUE
    RUNIN SCRAP 6 BICKER
    HASSLE 7 RHUBARB
**Squabbling:** 4 ATIT
**Squad:** 4 TEAM
  car: 7 CRUISER
  Crack: 8 ATEAM
  Firing: 3 NRA
  Football: 6 ELEVEN
  Military: 4 UNIT
  Rescue ~ VIP: 3 EMT
  Riot ~ item: 7 GASMASK
**"___ Squad, The":** 3 MOD
**Squads**
  GI: 3 KPS
**Squalid:** 5 DIRTY SEAMY
    SEEDY 6 SORDID
  digs: 4 SLUM
**Squander:** 4 BLOW BURN
    LOSE 5 WASTE
**Squandered:** 4 BLEW
**Square:** 4 BOXY EVEN KNOT
    NERD 5 ALIGN NERDY
    UNHIP 6 HONEST

¹/₆₄₀ of a ~ mile: 4 ACRE
100 ~ meters: 3 ARE
160 ~ rods: 4 ACRE
4,840 ~ yards: 4 ACRE
    7 ONEACRE
6,272,640 ~ inches: 4 ACRE
Butter: 3 PAT
Calendar: 3 DAY
Ceramic: 4 TILE
Floor: 4 TILE
footage: 4 AREA SIZE
Glass: 4 PANE
Grass: 3 SOD
Greek: 5 AGORA
Half the ~ dancers: 4 GALS
It can be measured in ~ feet:
    4 AREA
It may be: 4 MEAL
matrix, in math: 7 ADJOINT
measure: 4 AREA
mileage: 4 AREA
Monopoly: 4 JAIL 6 CHANCE
Not: 3 HEP
one: 5 GETGO START
On the: 7 ETHICAL
peg in a round hole: 6 MISFIT
Public: 5 AGORA PLAZA
They may be: 5 DEALS
things: 5 AMEND ATONE
Town: 5 PLAZA
(with): 5 AGREE
**Square dance**
  call: 6 DOSIDO
  group: 5 OCTET
  neckwear: 4 BOLO
  partner: 3 GAL
  site: 4 BARN
**Square-ended**
  boat: 4 SCOW
**Squarely:** 8 SMACKDAB
  Met: 5 FACED
**Square-mile**
  fraction: 4 ACRE
**Square one**
  From: 4 ANEW 5 AGAIN
    6 AFRESH
  Go back to: 9 STARTANEW
  Take from: 4 REDO
**Squaretail:** 5 TROUT
**Squarish:** 4 BOXY
**Squash:** 9 VEGETABLE
  Kind of: 5 ACORN
**Squashed**
  circle: 4 OVAL
**Squat:** 3 NIL
  (down): 6 HUNKER
  One ~, say: 3 REP
**Squawk:** 4 YAWP
  box: 8 INTERCOM
**Squawker**
  Colorful: 5 MACAW
**Squeak**
  Fix a: 3 OIL
  (out): 3 EKE
  Peke: 3 YIP
  silencer: 3 OIL

**Squeakers:** 4 MICE
**Squeaky:** 7 UNOILED
  clean: 6 CHASTE
  wheel need: 3 OIL
**Squeal:** 3 RAT 4 SING TELL
    6 TATTLE
  Cartoon: 3 EEK
**Squealed:** 4 SANG
**Squeegee:** 4 WIPE 5 WIPER
**Squeeze:** 3 HUG 4 BEAU CRAM
    5 PRESS
  (from): 5 EXACT
  It may put the ~ on you: 3 BOA
    8 ANACONDA
  (out): 3 EKE
  play start: 4 BUNT
  Suicide ~ stat: 3 RBI
**Squeezer:** 3 BOA 4 VISE
**Squelch:** 5 SITON 6 STIFLE
**Squelched:** 5 SATON
**Squib:** 4 ITEM 5 BLURB
**Squid**
  on a plate: 8 CALAMARI
  relatives: 6 OCTOPI
  squirt: 3 INK
  squirter: 6 INKSAC
**Squiggle**
  Sheet music: 4 CLEF
  Type: 5 TILDE
**Squiggles**
  Make: 6 DOODLE
**Squiggly**
  mark: 5 TILDE
**Squint:** 4 PEER
**Squinting**
  eye: 4 SLIT
**Squirm:** 6 WIGGLE WRITHE
**Squirrel:** 6 RODENT STORER
  away: 4 SAVE 5 HOARD
    STASH STORE
  food: 3 NUT 5 ACORN
  Go like a flying: 5 GLIDE
  hangout: 3 OAK
  home: 4 TREE
**Squirt:** 3 TOT 4 TYKE 6 SPRITZ
**Squirter:** 6 INKSAC OILCAN
**Sr.**
  and jr.: 3 YRS
  test: 3 GRE SAT 4 LSAT
**Sra.**
  French: 3 MME
**Sri ___ :** 5 LANKA
**Sri Lanka**
  capital: 7 COLOMBO
  export: 3 TEA 5 PEKOE
    8 PEKOETEA
  language: 5 TAMIL
  money: 5 RUPEE
  native: 5 TAMIL
  ~, formerly: 6 CEYLON
**SRO**
  affair: 7 SELLOUT
  Part of: 4 ONLY
  show: 3 HIT
**Srta.**
  French: 4 MLLE

**SSE:** 3 DIR
  Opposite of: 3 NNW
**S-shaped**
  molding: 4 OGEE
**SSS**
  category: 4 ONEA
  Eligible, to the: 4 ONEA
  Pt. of: 3 SYS 4 SYST
**SST**
  It's crossed by an: 3 ATL
  Part of: 5 SONIC
**SSW**
  Opposite of: 3 NNE
**St.**
  Broad: 3 AVE
  crosser: 3 AVE
**St. ___ :** 5 CROIX LUCIA MARYS
    6 MORITZ
**Stab:** 3 TRY 5 GUESS SPEAR
    7 ATTEMPT BAYONET
  Take a ~ (at): 5 LUNGE
  Take another ~ at: 5 RETRY
**Stabber:** 4 TINE
**Stability**
  Symbol of: 8 EVENKEEL
**Stabilize:** 6 STEADY
**Stabilizer**
  Cello: 4 KNEE
  Food: 4 AGAR
  Kite: 4 TAIL
  Ship: 4 KEEL 7 BALLAST
**Stable**
  area: 5 STALL
  babe: 4 FOAL
  bit: 3 OAT
  British: 4 MEWS
  diet: 3 HAY 4 OATS
  employee: 6 OSTLER
  Gave birth in a: 6 FOALED
  locks: 4 MANE
  mate: 4 MARE
  More: 5 SANER
  parent: 4 SIRE
  scene: 6 CRECHE
  sound: 4 BRAY CLOP 5 NEIGH
    SNORT
  staple: 3 HAY OAT 4 OATS
  talker: 4 MRED
**Staccato**
  Not: 6 LEGATO
  symbol: 3 DOT
**Stack:** 4 PILE
  Cafeteria: 5 TRAYS
  DJ's: 3 CDS
  In a: 5 PILED
  Monopoly: 5 DEEDS
  role: 4 NESS
  Snack in a: 4 OREO
  Teller's: 4 ONES
**Stackable**
  snack: 4 OREO
**Stacked:** 7 INAPILE
**Stacks**
  Chain with: 4 IHOP
  It's found in: 4 SOOT
  Lighted: 5 PYRES

**Stadia:** 6 ARENAS
**Stadium:** 4 OVAL PARK
    5 ARENA
  area: 4 TIER
  Big Apple: 4 ASHE SHEA
  cheer: 3 RAH
  cover: 4 DOME
  D.C.: 3 RFK
  feature: 4 TIER
  hoverer: 5 BLIMP
  level: 4 LOGE TIER
  Like a ~ crowd: 5 AROAR
  receipts: 4 GATE
  shot: 3 RAH
  snack: 6 NACHOS
  sound: 3 RAH 4 ROAR
  stat: 3 RBI 5 SEATS
  walkway: 4 RAMP
  worker: 5 USHER
**Stadiumgoer:** 3 FAN
**Staff:** 3 MAN ROD 4 CANE
    5 AIDES
  Add: 4 HIRE
  anew: 5 REMAN
  associate: 3 ROD
  Captain's: 4 CREW
  Ceremonial: 4 MACE
  Cut from the: 3 AXE
  Executive's: 5 AIDES
  leader: 4 CLEF 5 CCLEF
    GCLEF
  Lines on a: 5 EGBDF
  Mag: 3 EDS
  member: 4 NOTE REST
  Music ~ symbol: 4 CLEF
    5 CCLEF
  note: 3 SOL 4 MEMO
  of Life: 3 EDS
  Part of a univ.: 3 FAC
  PC support: 5 TECHS
  Sails: 4 MAST
  sgt.: 3 NCO
  Silence of the: 4 REST
  Supply: 3 MAN
  Support: 4 CANE
  symbol: 4 CLEF REST
    5 GCLEF
**Staffer:** 4 AIDE
  Hosp.: 3 LPN
  Hospital: 4 AIDE
  Tabloid: 6 EDITOR
**Staffers**
  Hosp.: 3 DRS MDS RNS
**Stafford**
  Singer ~, et al.: 3 JOS
**Staffordshire**
  river: 5 TRENT
**Stag:** 4 DEER HART MALE
    SOLO 5 ALONE
  attendees: 3 MEN
  partner: 3 DOE
  party: 4 DEER
**Stage:** 3 LEG 4 STEP 5 PHASE
  accessory: 4 PROP
  All the world is his: 5 ACTOR
  area: 5 APRON

assistant: 4 CUER
award: 4 OBIE
Bean on: 5 ORSON
Chase on: 4 ILKA
comment: 5 ASIDE
construction: 3 SET
curtain: 5 SCRIM
direction: 4 EXIT 5 ENTER
Do ~ work: 3 ACT
Early: 5 ONSET
Final: 7 ENDGAME
front: 5 APRON
Go on: 5 ENTER
Got ~ fright: 5 FROZE
Has the: 4 ISON
hog: 3 HAM
Insect: 4 PUPA 5 IMAGO
      LARVA
item: 4 PROP
Leave the: 4 EXIT
Moon: 5 PHASE
of a race: 3 LEG
of development: 5 PHASE
opening: 4 ACTI
org.: 4 ANTA
Overdo on the: 5 EMOTE
part: 4 ROLE
Perform on: 3 ACT
piece: 4 PROP
presence: 5 ACTOR
prompt: 3 CUE
remark: 5 ASIDE
Rocket: 5 AGENA
scenery: 3 SET
signal: 3 CUE
Sleep: 3 REM
success sgn: 3 SRO
Terrible age: 4 TWO3
whisper: 5 ASIDE
**Stagecoach**
controls: 5 REINS
**Stagehand:** 4 GRIP
**Stagg, ___ Alonzo:** 4 AMOS
**Stagg, Amos ___:** 6 ALONZO
**Stagger:** 4 REEL 5 LURCH
      SHOCK 6 CAREEN
**Staggering:** 5 AREEL
**Stagnant**
water problem: 4 ALGA
**Stagnation:** 3 RUT
**St. Agnes's ___:** 3 EVE
**Stain:** 3 DYE MAR 4 BLOT
      SLUR SOIL 5 SULLY
      TAINT 6 BLOTCH
      IMBRUE 7 SPLOTCH
Biological: 5 EOSIN
Collar: 4 RING
Garage: 3 OIL
Ink: 4 BLOT
**Stained-glass**
site: 4 APSE
**Stainless:** 6 CHASTE
What ~ steel is resistant to:
      4 RUST
**Stair**
part: 4 STEP 5 RISER TREAD

post: 5 NEWEL
**Staircase**
safety feature: 4 RAIL
shape: 6 SPIRAL
support: 5 NEWEL
**Stake:** 3 BET 5 WAGER
driver: 4 MAUL 6 SLEDGE
Initial: 4 ANTE
Thing to have a ~ in: 4 TENT
**Staked**
Something: 5 CLAIM
**"Stakeout"**
Richard's costar in: 6 EMILIO
**Stakes**
Pull up: 4 MOVE 6 DECAMP
Put down: 4 ANTE
race stakes: 5 PURSE
**Stalactite**
former: 4 DRIP
site: 4 CAVE 6 CAVERN
**"Stalag 17"**
star: 6 HOLDEN
**Stale:** 3 OLD 5 DATED TIRED
      TRITE
**Stalemate:** 3 TIE 7 IMPASSE
**Stalin**
challenger: 4 TITO
domain: 4 USSR
predecessor: 5 LENIN
State under: 3 SSR
**Stalk:** 4 HUNT STEM
      6 PREYON
Marsh: 4 REED
Salad: 6 CELERY
**Stalker**
Skilled: 4 LION
**Stall**
bedding: 5 STRAW
call: 5 SNORT
Mall: 5 KIOSK
Sputter and: 3 DIE
**Stalling**
Stop: 3 ACT
**Stallion**
mate: 4 MARE
Young: 4 COLT
**Stallone**
nickname: 3 SLY
role: 5 DREDD RAMBO
      ROCKY
**Stalls**
Place with:
      10 FLEAMARKET
**Stalwart**
Society: 6 PILLAR
**Stamen**
counterpart: 6 PISTIL
**Stamina:** 4 WIND
Have: 4 LAST
Lose: 4 FADE
**Stammerer**
sounds: 3 ERS
words: 5 IMEAN
**Stamp:** 4 SEAL
Actor: 7 TERENCE
Bill: 3 DUE 4 PAID

Christmas ~ subject:
      7 MADONNA
Food: 4 USDA
Invoice: 4 PAID
mill input: 3 ORE
of approval: 4 USDA
Office: 4 RECD 5 DATER
Passport: 4 VISA
purchase: 4 COIL
sheet: 4 PANE
**Stampeders:** 4 HERD
**Stamper**
need: 3 PAD
**Stamps:** 7 POSTAGE
Letters without: 5 EMAIL
Roll of: 4 COIL
Sheet of: 4 PANE
**Stan**
Funny: 6 LAUREL
Jazzman: 4 GETZ
of hockey: 6 MIKITA
Partner of: 6 OLLIE
Spider-Man creator: 3 LEE
**Stance:** 4 POSE
**Stand:** 4 BEAR DAIS RISE
      5 ABIDE ARISE EASEL
      GETUP GROVE
      7 STOMACH
      8 TOLERATE
against: 6 OPPOSE
Artist's: 5 EASEL
at a wake: 4 BIER
at home: 3 BAT
Bric-a-brac: 7 ETAGERE
buy: 3 ADE
by: 5 AWAIT
Can't: 4 HATE 5 ABHOR
      HATES 6 DETEST
      LOATHE 7 DETESTS
Didn't ~ pat: 4 DREW
Don't just ~ there: 5 REACT
Famous last: 5 ALAMO
firm: 6 INSIST
for: 4 MEAN 5 ABIDE
      6 DENOTE
Hat: 4 HEAD
in: 3 SUB
in line: 4 WAIT
Kind of: 4 TAXI
Let: 4 STET
Mall: 5 KIOSK
One way to: 3 PAT 4 TALL
      5 ALONE INAWE ONEND
      6 UNITED
One way to ~ by: 4 IDLY
out: 5 EXCEL SHINE
Place to ~ a round: 3 BAR
Sidewalk ~ buy: 3 ADE
Something to ~ on: 3 LEG
Take the: 7 TESTIFY
The way things ~ now:
      6 ASITIS
up: 4 RISE 5 ARISE
up and speak: 5 ORATE
up for: 6 DEFEND
up to: 4 DEFY FACE 6 RESIST

You ~ to lose it: 3 LAP
**"Stand"**
band: 3 REM
**"___ stand" (Martin Luther):**
    5 HEREI
**"Stand and Deliver"**
star Edward James: 5 OLMOS
**Standard:** 3 PAR 4 NORM
    5 STOCK 6 NORMAL
axes: 5 XANDY
Clock ~ (abbr.): 3 GMT
deviation symbol: 5 SIGMA
Double: 3 TWO
Gold: 5 KARAT
High: 5 IDEAL
Links: 3 PAR
Moral: 5 ETHIC
Naval: 6 ENSIGN
of excellence: 5 IDEAL
partner: 5 POORS
product: 3 OIL
score: 3 PAR
stuff: 3 OIL 4 GOLD
**Standard & ___ :** 5 POORS
**Standard Oil**
acronym: 4 ESSO
**Standards:** 8 CRITERIA
**"Stand by Me"**
actor Wheaton: 3 WIL
singer King: 4 BENE
**Standee**
support: 5 STRAP
**Stand-in:** 3 SUB
Rest-of-the-team: 4 ETAL
**Standing:** 4 RANK 5 ERECT
    ONEND PLACE
    6 REPUTE
by: 5 ONICE
Of long: 3 OLD
on: 4 ATOP
rule: 5 BYLAW
Run while: 4 IDLE
Social: 5 CASTE 6 ESTATE
    STATUS
straight: 5 ERECT
**Stand in good ___ :** 5 STEAD
**Standings**
column: 4 WINS 6 LOSSES
**Standish**
Pilgrim: 5 MYLES
**Standoff:** 3 TIE 7 IMPASSE
**Standoffish:** 3 ICY 5 ALOOF
**Standout:** 4 STAR
**Standstill:** 4 HALT
**___ standstill:** 3 ATA
**Stand-up**
guy: 5 COMIC
offering: 3 BIT
staple: 4 JOKE
**Stanford-Binet**
figs.: 3 IQS
**Stanford-___ test:** 5 BINET
**Stanislaw**
Author: 3 LEM
**Stanley**
Director: 5 DONEN 6 KRAMER

Jazzman: 6 CLARKE
Mystery writer: 5 ELLIN
offering: 4 TOOL
**Stanley Cup**
org.: 3 NHL
winners of 1999: 5 STARS
**Stanley Falls**
river: 8 THECONGO
**Stannary**
stock: 3 TIN
**Stannous**
element: 3 TIN
**Stansfield**
Pop singer: 4 LISA
**St. Anthony's cross:** 3 TAU
**Stanton, Elizabeth ___**
Suffragist: 4 CADY
**Stanza**
Final: 5 ENVOI
Six-line: 6 SESTET
**Staple**
Bar: 3 RYE
Breakfast: 3 EGG 4 EGGS
Brunch: 6 OMELET
Cajun: 4 OKRA
Daytime TV: 5 OPRAH
Dorm room: 6 STEREO
Drawing board: 7 TSQUARE
Frat party: 3 KEG
Italian: 5 PASTA
Luau: 3 POI
Passover: 5 MATZO
Presentation: 5 CHART
South Seas: 4 TARO
Stable: 3 HAY OAT 4 OATS
Sushi bar: 8 SOYSAUCE
Table: 4 SALT
Vegan: 4 TOFU
Wedding: 4 BAND
**Staples**
purchase: 4 REAM
Sci-fi: 3 ETS
**Staples Center:** 5 ARENA
Former ~ center: 4 SHAQ
    5 ONEAL
player: 5 LAKER
**Staple Singers**
#1 hit:
    15 ILLTAKEYOUTHERE
**Stapleton**
Actress: 4 JEAN
**Star:** 4 HERO 5 CELEB
    6 ETOILE
bit: 5 CAMEO
Bright: 4 BETA NOVA
Dog: 4 ASTA 5 BENJI
    6 LASSIE
Exploding: 4 NOVA
Faded: 7 HASBEEN
Falling: 6 METEOR
followers: 4 MAGI
go-between: 5 AGENT
It can move a: 4 LIMO
Kind of: 5 NATAL
Little: 5 CELEB
material: 3 TIN

Matinee: 4 IDOL
Night: 4 LENO
One-named: 8 ROSEANNE
Our: 3 SOL SUN
Pitching: 3 ACE
Pop: 4 IDOL 8 TEENIDOL
prefix: 4 MEGA
quality: 4 AURA
rep: 5 AGENT
Rising: 5 COMER
Shooting: 6 METEOR
Spectacular: 4 NOVA
vehicle: 4 LIMO
witnesses: 4 MAGI
~, in French: 6 ETOILE
**"Star ___":** 4 TREK WARS
**Starboard**
Opposite of: 4 PORT
**Starbuck**
boss: 4 AHAB
Skater: 4 JOJO
**Starbucks**
asset: 5 AROMA
container: 3 URN
flavor: 5 MOCHA
order: 5 DECAF LATTE
    MOCHA 6 GRANDE
    8 ESPRESSO
size: 5 VENTI 6 GRANDE
**Starch**
Palm: 4 SAGO
source: 4 TARO
~, for short: 4 CARB
**Starched**
collar: 4 ETON
**Starchy**
pudding stuff: 4 SAGO
tuber: 3 YAM
**Star-crossed**
lover: 5 ROMEO
**Stare:** 4 GAPE GAWK GAZE
at: 4 OGLE
Impertinent: 4 OGLE
Like an unfriendly: 3 ICY
open-mouthed: 4 GAPE
Satyr's: 4 LEER
stupidly: 4 GAWK
**Stares**
Like some: 3 ICY 6 VACANT
**Starfire:** 4 OLDS
**Starfleet Academy**
grad.: 3 ENS
**Staring:** 5 AGAZE
angrily: 6 AGLARE
**Stark**
raving sort: 6 MANIAC
**Starker**
Cellist: 5 JANOS
**Starless**
Like a ~ night: 4 INKY
**Starlet**
dream: 4 FAME
persona: 7 INGENUE
**Starlike:** 6 ASTRAL
**Starling**
org.: 3 FBI

relative: 4 MYNA
**Starliters, The**
Joey of: 3 DEE
**"Starpeace"**
musician: 3 ONO
**Starr**
of song: 3 KAY
of the Beatles: 5 RINGO
of the Wild West: 5 BELLE
Quarterback: 4 BART
**Starring**
in a sitcom: 4 ONTV
role: 4 LEAD
**Starry:** 6 ASTRAL
bear: 4 URSA
**Stars**
Give ~ to: 4 RATE
Give more ~ to: 6 RERATE
Give no: 3 PAN
Movie that rates 0: 7 STINKER
Of the: 6 ASTRAL
Wearer of three ~ (abbr.):
    5 LTGEN
~, in Latin: 5 ASTRA
**"Stars above!":** 6 DEARME
**Stars and Bars**
org.: 3 CSA
**Stars and Stripes**
land: 3 USA
**"Stars and Stripes Forever"**
composer: 5 SOUSA
**Star-shaped:** 6 ASTRAL
    8 STELLATE
flower: 5 ASTER
**Starship**
1986 ~ hit: 4 SARA
**Starsky**
Partner of: 5 HUTCH
**"Star-Spangled Banner"**
lyricist: 3 KEY
word: 3 OER
**Start:** 5 GETGO ONSET SCARE
    WINCE 6 ADVENT
    LAUNCH OPENER
    OUTSET SETOUT
**Info:** Prefix cue
again: 6 REOPEN
a hand: 4 ANTE DEAL
a hole: 5 TEEUP
all over: 4 REDO
an occupation: 6 MOVEIN
another hitch: 4 REUP
a pot: 4 ANTE
eating: 5 DIGIN
fishing: 4 CAST
from scratch: 4 REDO
From the: 4 ANEW
Head: 4 EDGE
of a polite offer:
    9 IFYOUWISH
over: 4 REDO
up: 4 BOOT 8 INITIATE
**Starter**
**Info:** Prefix cue
need: 3 GUN
**Starters:** 5 ATEAM

**"Star Time"**
star Michael: 8 STGERARD
**Starting:** 4 ASOF
from: 4 ASOF
gait: 4 TROT
gate: 4 POST
lineup: 4 ABCD
on: 4 ASOF
place: 4 EDEN
point: 4 GERM SEED WOMB
    5 GITGO 6 ORIGIN
points: 7 GENESES
stake: 4 ANTE
to develop: 7 NASCENT
with: 4 ASOF
**Startled**
cries: 3 OHS
**Star-to-be:** 5 COMER
**Start-over**
button: 5 RESET
**"Star Trek"**
actor Burton: 5 LEVAR
actor George: 5 TAKEI
actor Spiner: 5 BRENT
address: 6 MRSULU
android: 4 DATA
bad guy: 7 ROMULAN
communications officer:
    5 UHURA
counselor Deanna: 4 TROI
doctor: 5 MCCOY
engineer: 6 SCOTTY
extra: 5 ALIEN
genre: 5 SCIFI
helmsman: 5 SULU
lieutenant: 5 UHURA
navigator: 4 SULU
phaser setting: 4 STUN
rank (abbr.): 3 ENS
speed: 4 WARP
star: 5 NIMOY
weapon: 6 PHASER
**"Star Trek: Deep Space Nine"**
character: 3 ODO
**"Star Trek II"**
villain: 4 KHAN
**"Star Trek: The Next
    Generation"**
actor Burton: 5 LEVAR
counselor Deanna: 4 TROI
role: 4 TROI
**"Star Trek: Voyager"**
actress Kate: 7 MULGREW
actress Ryan: 4 JERI
**Starts**
Partner of: 4 FITS
**Star-___ tuna:** 4 KIST
**Starve:** 8 EMACIATE
**Star Wars**
inits.: 3 SDI
**"Star Wars"**
actor Guinness: 4 ALEC
character: 11 JARJARBINKS
character Han: 4 SOLO
creature: 4 EWOK
director George: 5 LUCAS

droid: 5 ARTOO
gangster: 5 JABBA
knight: 4 JEDI
mentor: 4 YODA
name: 3 HAN 5 VADER
princess: 4 LEIA
prog.: 3 SDI
role for Ford: 4 SOLO
sage: 4 YODA
star: 12 ALECGUINNESS
villain: 5 VADER
    10 DARTHVADER
warrior: 4 JEDI
**Starwood**
acquisition: 3 ITT
**Starwort:** 5 ASTER
**Stash:** 4 HIDE STOW
away: 4 SAVE STOW 5 HOARD
finder: 4 NARC
Secret: 5 CACHE
**Stashed:** 3 HID
**Stat:** 3 PDQ 4 ASAP 6 ATONCE
    PRONTO
prefix: 4 RHEO
**"Stat!":** 3 NOW 4 ASAP
    6 PRONTO
**State:** 4 AVER AVOW 5 VOICE
    6 ASSERT 7 DECLARE
as fact: 4 AVER 5 SAYSO
bird: *see page 723*
confidently: 4 AVER 6 ASSERT
    ASSURE
firmly: 4 AVER
flower: *see page 724*
further: 3 ADD
of mind: 4 MOOD
one's view: 5 OPINE
positively: 4 AVER 6 ASSERT
since 1948: 6 ISRAEL
solemnly: 4 AVOW
tree: *see page 724*
treasury: 4 FISC
~, in French: 4 ETAT
**Stated:** 3 PUT 4 SAID
one's case: 4 PLED
**"State Fair"**
setting: 4 IOWA
**State Farm**
rival: 5 AETNA
**Statehouse**
~ VIP: 3 GOV
**Stately:** 5 NOBLE REGAL
dance: 6 MINUET PAVANE
home: 5 MANOR MANSE
shade-giver: 3 ELM
    7 ELMTREE
**Statement**
Court: 4 PLEA
Definitive: 8 LASTWORD
of belief: 5 CREDO CREED
Sworn: 4 OATH
**Staten Island**
boat: 5 FERRY
**State-of-the-art:** 6 NEWEST
**State-run**
game: 5 LOTTO

**Statesman**
Israeli: 4 EBAN
Roman: 4 CATO
**Statesmen**
Like some: 5 ELDER
**Static:** 5 NOISE
**Static ___:** 5 CLING
**Station:** 4 DESK STOP 5 DEPOT
Bus: 5 DEPOT
High: 3 MIR
Kind of: 3 GAS WAY 5 RELAY
     6 AMTRAK
Military: 4 POST
Old ~ name: 4 ESSO
sign: 5 ONAIR
Sub: 4 DELI
suffix: 3 ARY ERY
Took to the ~ house: 5 RANIN
Train: 4 STOP 5 DEPOT
Union: 5 ALTAR
wagon abroad: 9 ESTATECAR
Work: 4 DESK
___ Station: 4 PENN
**Stationary:** 5 STILL 6 ATREST
Be ~, nautically: 5 LIETO
**Stationed:** 3 PUT 5 BASED
**Stationer**
supply: 4 PADS PENS
**Stationery**
brand: 5 EATON
imprint: 10 LETTERHEAD
quantity: 4 REAM
store stock (abbr.): 4 ENVS
**Station wagon**
abroad: 9 ESTATECAR
**Statistic**
Court: 6 ASSIST
Econ.: 3 GNP
Gazetteer: 4 AREA
Vital: 3 AGE
**Statistical**
boundary: 8 QUARTILE
info: 4 DATA
measure: 4 MEAN MODE
     5 RANGE
**Statistician:** 11 BEANCOUNTER
**Statistics:** 4 DATA
Like some: 5 VITAL
**Stats:** 4 DATA INFO RECS
**Statuary**
Bit of: 5 TORSO
**Statue**
base: 6 PLINTH
Gold: 5 OSCAR
inscription: 8 EPIGRAPH
Made like a: 5 FROZE
Michelangelo: 5 PIETA
place: 5 NICHE
**Statue of Liberty**
ship: 5 ISERE
skin: 6 COPPER
**Statues**
Giant: 7 COLOSSI
**Statuesque:** 4 TALL
**Statuette**
Cinema: 5 OSCAR

Winged: 4 EMMY
**Status**
Attain: 4 RISE
Current: 4 ACDC
Draft: 4 ONEA 5 ONTAP
follower: 3 QUO
Have: 4 RATE
Service: 4 ONEA
**Status ___:** 3 QUO
**Statute:** 3 ACT LAW
Make a: 5 ENACT
**Staunch:** 4 TRUE 8 TRUEBLUE
**Stave**
off: 5 AVERT REPEL
**Stay:** 4 BIDE 5 ABIDE VISIT
     6 REMAIN
away from: 4 SHUN 5 AVOID
     NOTDO
behind: 6 REMAIN
dry: 8 TEETOTAL
fresh: 4 KEEP
glued to: 7 STAREAT
home for dinner: 5 EATIN
How long one might:
     6 AWHILE
idle: 3 SIT
in the cooler: 6 DOTIME
Not ~ put: 4 ROAM
out of sight: 4 HIDE
     6 HOLEUP LIELOW
Place to: 3 INN
put: 6 REMAIN
Some ~ at home: 4 DADS
still, at sea: 5 LIETO
to the finish: 4 LAST
**"Stay!":** 6 DONTGO
**"Stay (I Missed You)"**
singer Lisa: 4 LOEB
singer Loeb: 4 LISA
**Staying**
Have ~ power: 4 LAST
power: 4 LEGS 6 TENURE
     7 INERTIA STAMINA
**St. Bernard**
bark: 4 WOOF
**St. Catherine**
Home of: 5 SIENA
**St. Clare**
Home of: 6 ASSISI
**Std.**
Not: 3 IRR
**Stead:** 4 LIEU
**Steadfast:** 4 TRUE 5 LOYAL
     6 STABLE
**Steadily**
Keep at: 7 STANDTO
Pursued: 5 PLIED
**Steady:** 4 BEAU SURE
     5 BRACE
devotion: 9 ADHERENCE
flow: 6 STREAM
Go ~ with: 4 DATE
Jacques': 4 AMIE
**"Steady Eddie"**
of baseball: 5 LOPAT
**"Steady ___ goes":** 5 ASSHE

**Steadying**
rope: 3 GUY
**Steak:** 4 MEAT
Blacken, as: 4 CHAR
Char a: 4 SEAR
Club: 9 DELMONICO
Cook, as: 5 BROIL
cut: 5 FLANK TBONE
Hearty: 5 TBONE
Kind of: 4 TUNA 5 STRIP
     SWISS
Like ~ tartare: 3 RAW
Like a good: 6 TENDER
Loin: 5 TBONE
order: 4 RARE WELL
     5 TBONE
Pink, as a: 4 RARE
sauce brand: 4 AONE
style: 5 DIANE 7 TARTARE
type: 5 TBONE
**Steak ___:** 5 DIANE 7 TARTARE
**Steakhouse**
offering: 5 TBONE 6 RIBEYE
order: 4 RARE 5 TBONE
sound: 6 SIZZLE
**Steak tartare**
ingredient: 6 RAWEGG
**Steal:** 3 ROB 4 GLOM TAKE
     5 POACH SWIPE
     6 PILFER THIEVE
attention from: 7 UPSTAGE
away: 5 ELOPE
cattle: 6 RUSTLE
from: 3 ROB
It's a: 5 THEFT
steers: 6 RUSTLE
**Stealth**
Move with: 6 TIPTOE
What ~ may avoid: 5 RADAR
**Stealthily**
Approach: 7 CREEPUP
Enter: 6 EDGEIN
Move: 5 SKULK SLINK
     SNEAK
Moved: 5 CREPT
Pick up: 4 PALM
**"Steal This Book"**
author Hoffman: 5 ABBIE
**Stealthy:** 7 CATLIKE
sort: 5 NINJA SNEAK
**Steam:** 5 VAPOR
bath: 5 SAUNA
Blow off: 4 HISS RANT VENT
Burn with: 5 SCALD
It blows off: 6 GEYSER
Lose: 4 TIRE
room: 5 SAUNA
Run out of: 3 DIE 4 TIRE
up: 3 IRE 4 RILE 5 ANGER
**Steamed:** 3 MAD 4 IRED SORE
     5 ANGRY IRATE LIVID
     RILED 6 FUMING
     INAPET 7 INARAGE
     INASNIT
dish: 6 TAMALE
Get: 4 BOIL 6 SEERED

Get ~ up: 4 FUME
up: 4 IRED
**Steam engine**
developer: 4 WATT
**Steamer**
creator: 7 STANLEY
trunk feature: 4 HASP
**Steaming:** 5 IRATE
**Steamroll:** 7 RUNOVER
**Steamy:** 3 HOT 4 DAMP
6 EROTIC RRATED
TORRID
spot: 5 SAUNA
~ 1998 Broadway revue:
5 FOSSE
**Steed:** 5 HORSE
Speckled: 4 ROAN
Spirited: 4 ARAB 7 ARABIAN
steerer: 4 REIN
Swift: 4 ARAB
**Steel**
component: 4 IRON
factory input: 7 IRONORE
German ~ city: 5 ESSEN
girder: 5 IBEAM
industry pioneer:
8 BESSEMER
Man of: 5 ROBOT
8 CARNEGIE
Man of ~ portrayer: 5 REEVE
mill refuse: 4 SLAG
plow maker: 5 DEERE
source: 4 IRON 7 PIGIRON
toughener: 8 TITANIUM
Use ~ wool: 5 SCOUR
**Steele**
Partner of: 7 ADDISON
**Steeler**
Former ~ coach Chuck:
4 NOLL
**Steelhead:** 5 TROUT
**Steelie**
alternative: 5 AGATE
**Steelworkers**
Former ~ head: 4 ABEL
**Steely Dan**
album: 3 AJA
**Steen**
Painter: 3 JAN
Stand for: 5 EASEL
**Steenburgen**
Actress: 4 MARY
**Steep:** 4 BREW DEAR SOAK
5 CLIFF
cliff: 4 CRAG
slope: 4 DROP 5 SCARP
6 ESCARP
**Steeple:** 5 SPIRE
**Steep-roofed**
house: 6 AFRAME
**Steep-sided**
valley: 6 RAVINE
**Steer:** 3 TIP 5 PILOT
clear of: 4 SHUN 5 AVOID
ELUDE EVADE
**Steerer:** 6 DROVER

**Steering**
adjustment: 5 TOEIN
aid: 6 RUDDER
station: 4 CONN HELM
strap: 4 REIN
system link: 6 TIEROD
wheel: 4 HELM
**Stefani**
Singer: 4 GWEN
**Steffi**
of tennis: 4 GRAF
**Stein**
and Stiller: 4 BENS
filler: 3 ALE 4 BEER 5 LAGER
Part of a ~ line: 3 ISA
5 AROSE
relative: 7 TANKARD
**Stein, Jean**
bestseller: 4 EDIE
**Steinbeck**
birthplace: 7 SALINAS
character: 4 OKIE
family: 5 JOADS
migrant: 4 OKIE
name: 4 JOAD
novel: 10 CANNERYROW
title varmints: 4 MICE
**Steinful:** 3 ALE 5 LAGER
**Steinway**
product: 5 PIANO
**Ste. Jeanne ___:** 4 DARC
**Stellar:** 6 ASTRAL
altar: 3 ARA
bear: 4 URSA
spectacular: 4 NOVA
**"St. Elmo's Fire"**
actor: 4 LOWE
**Stem:** 4 PROW 6 ARREST
Base of a plant: 4 CORM
joint: 4 NODE
Mushroom: 5 STIPE
Opposite of: 5 STERN
Plant: 5 STALK 6 STOLON
to stern runner: 4 KEEL
Twining: 4 BINE
___ Ste. Marie: 5 SAULT
**Stemmed**
It may be: 4 TIDE
**Stemware:** 7 GLASSES
**Sten**
or Magnani: 4 ANNA
**Stench:** 4 ODOR REEK 5 FETOR
7 MALODOR
**Stengel**
1960s ~ crew: 4 METS
of baseball: 5 CASEY
**Steno**
need: 3 PAD 7 NOTEPAD
**Stenographer**
group: 4 POOL
**Step:** 3 PAS 4 PACE 5 STAIR
TREAD
Ballet: 3 PAS
Big: 6 STRIDE
Bouncy: 4 LILT
Dance: 3 CHA PAS

down: 8 ABDICATE
Gliding dance: 6 CHASSE
in: 5 ENTER
into character: 3 ACT
Ladder: 4 RUNG
Laundering: 5 RINSE
Miss a: 6 FALTER
on a scale: 4 TONE
One: 5 STAIR
on it: 3 GAS HIE 4 PATH SOLE
5 PEDAL SCALE 6 INSOLE
8 GASPEDAL
on the scale: 3 SOL
part: 5 RISER
Place to: 5 ASIDE
Project: 5 PHASE
**"Step ___!" ("Hurry!"):** 4 ONIT
**"Step by Step"**
actress Keanan: 5 STACI
**"Stepford Wives, The"**
author: 8 IRALEVIN
author Levin: 3 IRA
___ step further: 3 GOA
**Stephanie**
Father of: 5 EFREM
**Stephen**
Actor: 3 REA 4 BOYD
Brother of ~ and Billy: 4 ALEC
~, in French: 7 ETIENNE
**Stephen Vincent ___**
Poet: 5 BENET
**"Step on it!":** 5 HURRY
**Stepped:** 4 TROD
down: 4 ALIT
on: 4 TROD
on it: 4 SPED
**"Steppenwolf"**
author: 5 HESSE
**Steppes**
settler: 5 TATAR
**Steps**
alternative: 4 RAMP
Castle with many: 5 IRENE
over a fence: 5 STILE
Porch: 5 STOOP
Take: 3 ACT
Take baby: 6 TODDLE
Took: 6 STRODE
**"Steps in Time"**
autobiographer: 7 ASTAIRE
**Stepsisters**
Like Cinderella's: 4 UGLY
**Stereo**
component: 3 AMP 5 TUNER
forerunner: 4 MONO
Not: 4 MONO
system: 4 HIFI
**Stereotype**
Studious: 4 NERD
**Sterile**
hybrid: 4 MULE
**Sterling**
Pound: 4 QUID
**Stern:** 4 REAR
Article in: 3 EIN
Opposite of: 4 STEM

rival: 4 IMUS
Toward the: 3 AFT
Violinist: 5 ISAAC
with a bow: 5 ISAAC
___ Stern (German newspaper):
  3 DER
**Sternutation:** 6 SNEEZE
**Sternward:** 3 AFT 5 ABAFT
**Steroid**
  Kind of: 8 ANABOLIC
**Stertorous**
  Be: 5 SNORE
**Stet:** 7 LEAVEIN
  Opposite of: 4 DELE
**Stethoscope**
  sound: 5 THUMP
  user: 3 DOC
**St.-Étienne**
  capital: 5 LOIRE
**Stetson:** 3 HAT
  Like a: 7 BRIMMED
**Steve**
  Host: 5 ALLEN
  Muscleman: 6 REEVES
  Quarterback: 6 MCNAIR
  Runner: 5 OVETT
  Singer: 5 EARLE
  Singing partner of: 5 EYDIE
  Skier: 5 MAHRE
**"Steve Allen Show, The"**
  regular: 3 NYE
**Stevedore:** 4 LADE 5 LADER
  6 LOADER
  concern: 5 CARGO
  org.: 3 ILA
**Steven**
  Actor: 6 SEAGAL
**Stevens**
  Actress: 5 INGER 6 STELLA
  Senator: 3 TED
**Stevenson**
  fiend: 4 HYDE
  Politician: 5 ADLAI
  retirement home: 5 SAMOA
  scoundrel: 6 MRHYDE
**Stevie**
  Singer: 5 NICKS
**Stew:** 4 FRET OLIO SNIT
  SULK 6 RAGOUT
  SEETHE SIMMER
  bean: 4 LIMA
  cooker: 3 POT
  First name in: 5 DINTY
  Get into a: 3 EAT
  Highly seasoned: 6 BURGOO
  ingredient: 3 PEA 4 LEEK
    OKRA
  It may be in a: 5 LADLE
  Kind of: 5 IRISH 6 HOTPOT
  Okra: 5 GUMBO
  Spicy: 4 OLLA 5 SALMI
    6 RAGOUT
**Steward**
  offer: 4 WINE
**Stewart**
  film: 6 DESTRY

Golfer: 5 PAYNE
Journalist: 5 ALSOP
Politico: 5 UDALL
role: 4 DOWD
Singer: 3 ROD
Style expert: 6 MARTHA
successor on the bench:
  7 OCONNOR
**Stewart, Jimmy**
  Speak like: 5 DRAWL
  syllables: 3 AWS
**Stewbum:** 3 SOT
**Stewed:** 3 LIT 5 OILED TIPSY
  6 BLOTTO WASTED
  dude: 3 SOT
**Stewpot:** 4 OLLA
**"St. ___ Fire":** 5 ELMOS
**St. Francis**
  Home of: 6 ASSISI
**St.-Germain**
  river: 5 SEINE
**St. Helens**
  and others: 3 MTS
**Stick:** 4 CANE POKE STAB
  5 CLING PASTE
  6 ADHERE CLEAVE
  COHERE
  around: 4 STAY WAIT
  a shell in: 4 LOAD
  Beat with a: 4 FLOG
  Candy on a: 5 LOLLY
  Dangerous: 3 TNT
  Fiddle: 3 BOW
  Game: 6 CROSSE
  Get the short end of the:
    7 LOSEOUT
  Grocery: 4 OLEO
  in a paint can: 7 STIRRER
  in school: 5 RULER
  in the fridge: 4 OLEO
  in the mud: 4 MIRE 5 EMBED
  in the water: 3 OAR
  it in your ear: 4 QTIP
  it out: 4 STAY
  it to: 5 SHAFT
  Kind of: 4 JOSS POGO
  Knight: 5 LANCE
  like glue: 6 ADHERE
  Magic: 4 WAND
  Night: 5 ROOST
  on: 3 ADD 5 AFFIX 6 ATTACH
    GLUETO
  on a stick: 6 IMPALE
  or split: 6 CLEAVE
  out: 3 JUT 4 SHOW 5 BULGE
    6 ENDURE 8 PROTRUDE
  (out): 3 JUT
  Place to ~ a pick: 4 AFRO
  Pool: 3 CUE
  Short end of the: 7 BUMDEAL
    RAWDEAL
  Swizzle: 7 STIRRER
  (to): 6 ADHERE CLEAVE
  together: 4 BIND GLUE
    5 CLUMP PASTE
    6 COHERE

up: 3 ROB
Walking: 4 CANE
Where something may: 4 CRAW
with: 6 HOLDTO
  8 ADHERETO
with a kick: 3 TNT
with a pin: 5 BURST
Yellow: 4 OLEO
**Stick ___ (maltreat):** 4 ITTO
**___ stick**
  (clarinet): 8 LICORICE
  (toy): 4 POGO
**Stickball**
  venue: 6 STREET
**"Stick 'em up!":** 5 REACH
**Sticker:** 3 BUR PIN 4 GLUE
  HYPO TACK 5 DECAL
  EPOXY THORN
  6 CACTUS NEEDLE
  7 IMPALER 8 PRICETAG
  Direct-mail: 3 YES
  Food: 4 TINE
  Game: 5 SPEAR
  Leather: 3 AWL
  Price: 3 TAG
  response: 4 HONK
  stat: 3 MPG
  Window: 5 DECAL
**Sticking**
  point: 3 RUT 4 CRAW SNAG
  TINE 5 THORN
**Stick in one's ___:** 4 CRAW
**Stick-in-the-mud:** 4 FOGY
**Stickler:** 6 PURIST
**Stick-on:** 5 DECAL
**Sticks**
  Gp. that ~ to its guns: 3 NRA
  It comes in: 3 GUM
  partners: 6 STONES
**Stick-to-it-___:** 3 IVE
**Stick-to-itiveness:** 4 GRIT
**Stickum:** 4 GLUE 5 PASTE
**Sticky:** 5 GOOEY HUMID
  6 VISCID
  roll: 4 TAPE
  strip: 4 TAPE
  stuff: 3 GOO TAR 4 GLUE
  GOOK GOOP TAPE
  5 EPOXY PASTE
**Sticky-tongued**
  critter: 4 TOAD
**Stiff:** 4 TAUT 6 FRIGID
  WOODEN
  and sore: 4 ACHY
  collar: 4 ETON
  drink: 6 BRACER
  hair: 4 SETA
  hairs: 5 SETAE
  Not: 4 LIMP
  wind: 4 GALE
  Working: 4 PEON 5 PROLE
**Stiff ___ board:** 3 ASA
**Stiffen:** 3 SET 5 STEEL TENSE
**Stiffener**
  Collar: 4 STAY
  Laundry: 6 STARCH

**Salon:** 3 GEL
**Stiffly**
  formal: 4 PRIM 7 STILTED
  Walk: 5 STALK
**Stiffness:** 4 KINK
**Stiff-upper-lip**
  sort: 5 STOIC
**Still:** 3 YET 4 CALM EVEN IDLE
    MUTE 5 INERT
    6 ATREST EVENSO
    SILENT 8 STAGNANT
  and all: 3 YET
  Be ~, at sea: 5 LIETO
  for rent: 5 UNLET
  fresh: 7 UNJADED
  going: 5 ALIVE
  not there: 4 LATE
  on the plate: 7 UNEATEN
  Stood: 5 FROZE
  stuff: 7 ALCOHOL
  Unable to sit: 5 ANTSY
  with us: 5 ALIVE
  ~, in poetry: 3 EEN
**"Still ___" (1999 rap song):**
    3 DRE
**"Still Crazy"**
  star Stephen: 3 REA
**"Stille ___":** 5 NACHT
**Stiller**
  Comedian: 3 BEN
  Partner of: 5 MEARA
**Stiller, Ben**
  ~, to Meara: 3 SON
**Still-life**
  item: 4 PEAR
  subject: 3 URN 4 EWER VASE
    5 FRUIT
**Stills**
  bandmate: 4 NASH
  Crosby, ~, and Nash: 4 TRIO
**Stillwater**
  City near: 4 ENID
**Stilt**
  relative: 6 AVOCET
  spot: 4 NEST
**Stimpy:** 3 CAT 4 TOON
  pal: 3 REN
**Stimulant:** 5 UPPER
  yielder: 4 COCA
**Stimulate:** 4 FUEL PROD SPUR
    URGE WHET 5 PIQUE
    6 AROUSE EXCITE
**Stimulating**
  drink: 6 BRACER
  nut: 4 KOLA
**Stimulus:** 4 GOAD PROD
    SPUR
  Olfactory: 4 ODOR 5 AROMA
    SMELL
  Respond to a: 5 REACT
  Taste: 4 ODOR
**Sting:** 3 CON 4 BILK SCAM
    TRAP 5 SMART
  It has no: 5 DRONE
  operation: 4 TRAP
  Ring king with a: 3 ALI

**"Sting, The"**
  character Henry: 8 GONDORFF
  Oscar winner: 4 HEAD
**Stinger:** 3 BEE 4 WASP
    6 HORNET 8 SCORPION
  Big: 9 BUMBLEBEE
**Stinging:** 4 ACID 5 ACRID
  insect: 4 WASP 6 HORNET
  remark: 4 BARB
  shot: 3 BBS
**Stingless**
  bee: 5 DRONE
**"... sting like ___":** 4 ABEE
**"Sting like a bee"**
  boxer: 3 ALI
**Stingy:** 4 MEAN NEAR 5 CHEAP
    CLOSE 11 TIGHTFISTED
  one: 5 MISER PIKER
**Stink:** 3 ADO 4 ODOR REEK
    5 SMELL
  Make a: 3 ROT 4 REEK
  suffix: 4 AROO EROO
  to high heaven: 4 REEK
**Stinker:** 3 RAT 5 LOUSE
    SKUNK 6 MEANIE
  Real: 7 SOANDSO
  Warner Bros.: 4 PEPE
**Stinkeroo**
  Cinematic: 4 BOMB
**Stinkpot:** 6 MEANIE
**Stint**
  Do another: 4 REUP
**Stipe, Michael**
  band: 3 REM
**Stipend:** 3 FEE PAY 4 WAGE
**Stipulation:** 5 GIVEN
  Added: 3 AND
  Auction: 4 ASIS
**Stipulations:** 3 IFS
**Stir:** 3 ADO MIX 4 RILE ROIL
    TODO WAKE 5 BUDGE
    HOOHA ROUSE
    6 AROUSE HOOPLA
    INCITE THECAN
  in: 3 ADD
  It can cause a: 5 SPOON
  to action: 4 PROD URGE
    6 AROUSE
  up: 3 FAN 4 RILE ROIL
    5 ROUSE STOKE WAKEN
    6 AROUSE EXCITE
    FOMENT INCITE
    7 AGITATE
**"Stir Crazy"**
  actor Richard: 5 PRYOR
**Stir-fry**
  pan: 3 WOK
  tidbit: 7 SNOWPEA
**Stirred:** 4 WOKE
**Stirrer:** 5 SPOON
  Cauldron: 3 HAG
**Stirrup**
  site: 3 EAR
**Stitch:** 3 SEW
  caretaker: 4 LILO
  Knitting: 4 PURL

  loosely: 5 BASTE
  over: 5 RESEW
  Pal of: 4 LILO
  up: 3 SEW
  Without a: 5 NAKED
**Stitched:** 4 SEWN
  fold: 5 PLEAT
**Stitches**
  In: 4 SEWN
  It may need: 4 GASH
  Line of: 4 SEAM
  Put in: 3 SEW 4 DARN KNIT
    SEWN SLAY 5 BASTE
  Remove ~ from: 5 UNSEW
**Stitching**
  Towel: 3 HIS 4 HERS
**St. Ives**
  riddle start: 3 ASI
**St.-John's-___:** 4 WORT
**St. Johns, ___ Rogers**
  Author: 5 ADELA
**St. Kitts**
  partner: 5 NEVIS
**St. Louis**
  bridge designer: 4 EADS
  footballer: 3 RAM
  hrs.: 3 CST
  landmark: 4 ARCH
  summer setting: 3 CDT
**St. Louis Browns**
  successor: 6 ORIOLE
**St. Moritz**
  backdrop: 4 ALPS
**Stock:** 5 BROTH GOODS
    HOARD
  (abbr.): 4 MDSE
  buyer's objective: 6 GROWTH
  collection: 4 HERD
  European ~ exchange:
    6 BOURSE
  figure: 3 PAR 5 RATIO
  For the ~ issue price: 5 ATPAR
  holder: 3 PEN 4 BARN SAFE
    5 LADLE LASSO STORE
  In: 6 ONHAND UNSOLD
  Kind of: 5 NOPAR
  Lock, ~, and barrel: 3 ALL
  market abbr.: 3 IPO OTC
  Not in ~ yet: 7 ONORDER
  option: 3 PUT 5 TRADE
  or bond: 5 ASSET
  page abbr.: 3 OTC 4 AMEX
  phrase: 5 ATPAR NOPAR
  response: 3 MOO
  Risky ~ tradng: 4 SPEC
  S&P 500: 3 AOL
  Secret: 5 STASH
  suffix: 3 ADE
  Take: 5 LASSO 6 RUSTLE
  Take ~ of: 6 ASSESS
  Tech: 3 IBM
  Tech-heavy ~ exchange:
    6 NASDAQ
  ticker inventor: 6 EDISON
  unit: 3 COW 4 HEAD 5 SHARE
    STEER

unit (abbr.): 3 SHR
Unload: 4 SELL
up: 5 HOARD
up on: 5 AMASS
up on again: 7 REORDER
word: 3 PAR
**Stockbroker**
freebie: 3 TIP
**Stockdale**
was his running mate:
 5 PEROT
**Stock exchange:** 3 MOO
area: 3 PIT
membership: 4 SEAT
worker: 6 TRADER
**Stockholder**
vote: 5 PROXY
**Stockholm**
Airline to: 3 SAS
Capital west of: 4 OSLO
coin: 5 KRONA
native: 5 SWEDE
sedan: 4 SAAB
**Stocking**
flaws: 4 RUNS
lines: 5 SEAMS
material: 5 LISLE NYLON
merchandise: 4 TOYS
No longer: 5 OUTOF
problem: 4 SNAG
shade: 4 ECRU NUDE
 5 BEIGE
stuffer: 3 TOE TOY 5 SANTA
stuffer for a brat: 4 COAL
**Stockings:** 4 HOSE
Like some: 6 SEAMED
 8 SEAMLESS
**Stockpile:** 5 AMASS CACHE
 HOARD 6 GATHER
 SAVEUP
**Stogie:** 5 CIGAR
**Stoic**
Original: 4 ZENO
**Stoicism**
Founder of: 4 ZENO
**Stoker**
Author: 4 BRAM
**Stole:** 3 FUR 4 WRAP 5 CREPT
 6 LIFTED SWIPED
Feathered: 3 BOA
material: 4 MINK
**Stolen**
goods: 4 LOOT
It can be: 4 BASE 5 SCENE
Like ~ goods: 3 HOT
**Stoltz**
Actor: 4 ERIC
**Stomach:** 3 GUT MAW 5 ABIDE
 BROOK STAND
 6 ENDURE 8 TOLERATE
Animal: 4 CRAW
Can't: 4 HATE 5 ABHOR
 6 LOATHE
muscles: 3 ABS
settler: 5 BROMO 6 BICARB
 7 ANTACID

Sound of a ~ punch: 3 OOF
woe: 4 KNOT 5 ULCER
**Stomachache**
cause: 5 ECOLI
**Stomachs**
Like some: 8 CASTIRON
**Stomp:** 5 DANCE 7 TRAMPLE
**"Stompin' at the ___":** 5 SAVOY
**Stone**
Actress: 6 SHARON
and Pound: 5 EZRAS
and Stallone: 4 SLYS
Banded: 5 AGATE
Blue: 5 LAPIS
Cameo: 4 ONYX
Cherry: 3 PIT
Crystal-lined: 5 GEODE
for a Libra: 4 OPAL
foundation: 6 RIPRAP
Glittery: 5 GEODE
Green: 4 JADE
Hollow: 5 GEODE
Inscribed: 5 STELA STELE
Iridescent: 4 OPAL
Letters carved in: 3 RIP
Marbled: 5 AGATE
marker: 5 STELA STELE
memorial: 5 CAIRN
Milky: 4 OPAL
mound: 5 CAIRN
name: 7 ROSETTA
of rock: 3 SLY
Ornamental: 9 TIGERSEYE
pillar: 5 STELA
Precious: 3 GEM 5 JEWEL
Print made using: 5 LITHO
Rolling ~ lack: 4 MOSS
Smoky: 4 OPAL
Striped: 5 AGATE
Unlike a rolling: 5 MOSSY
Weight of a: 5 CARAT
Words in: 7 EPITAPH
___ Stone: 7 ROSETTA
**Stone, Oliver**
film: 3 JFK 5 NIXON
**Stone Age**
implement: 7 NEOLITH
tool: 6 EOLITH
**"Stoned Soul Picnic"**
songwriter Laura: 4 NYRO
**Stone-faced:** 6 STOLID
**Stonehenge**
worker: 4 CELT
worshipper: 5 DRUID
**Stones:** 4 BAND
Board game with: 5 PENTE
Spa rooms with heated:
 6 SAUNAS
**Stoneworker:** 5 MASON
**"Stoney End"**
composer Laura: 4 NYRO
**Stood:** 4 ROSE 5 AROSE
 BORNE GOTUP
firm: 4 HELD
for: 5 MEANT
on a soapbox: 6 ORATED

still: 5 FROZE
up: 5 AROSE
up to: 5 FACED
**Stooge:** 3 MOE 5 CURLY LARRY
 SHEMP
Head: 3 MOE
with bangs: 3 MOE
**Stooges:** 4 TRIO
**Stool:** 4 SEAT 5 PERCH
**Stoolie:** 3 RAT
Play the: 4 BLAB
~, to a Brit: 4 NARK
**Stool pigeon:** 3 RAT
Be a: 4 SING
**"___ Stoops to Conquer":** 3 SHE
**Stop:** 3 DIE END 4 CORK HALT
 QUIT 5 CEASE DEPOT
 DETER EMBAR LETUP
 6 DESIST
 11 CALLITQUITS
by: 5 ENDAT POPIN VISIT
 6 DROPIN
Didn't: 4 WENT 5 RANON
Don't: 6 KEEPAT
fasting: 3 EAT
Kind of: 3 BUS 4 REST
on a line: 3 STA 5 DEPOT
One way to: 7 ONADIME
on the way: 8 RESTAREA
order: 4 DONT
Put a ~ to: 3 END 5 CEASE
running: 3 DIE
signal: 3 RED
start: 3 NON
talking: 6 CLAMUP
Train ~ (abbr.): 3 STA
Travel: 3 INN 5 MOTEL
Truck: 5 DINER
Truckee: 4 RENO
up: 3 DAM 4 CLOG CORK
 PLUG
Wayside: 3 INN
working: 6 RETIRE
~, in French: 5 ARRET
**"Stop!":** 4 DONT HALT WHOA
 5 AVAST 6 ENOUGH
 NOMORE
**"Stop already!":** 6 ENOUGH
**"Stop behaving like a child!":**
 10 ACTYOURAGE
**Stop ___ dime:** 3 ONA
**Stoplight**
color: 3 RED
**Stop on ___:** 5 ADIME
**Stopover:** 3 INN 5 MOTEL
Cruise: 4 ISLE
Desert: 5 OASIS
in la mar: 3 ILE
**Stoppage**
Blood flow: 4 CLOT
Flow: 6 STASIS
WBA: 3 TKO
**Stopped**
fasting: 3 ATE
lying: 5 AROSE
sleeping: 4 WOKE

**Stopper:** 4 CORK PLUG
    5 BRAKE
  Bottle: 4 CORK
  Debate: 7 GAGRULE
  Fight: 3 TKO
  Flow: 4 CLOG
  Keg: 4 BUNG
  Parade: 4 RAIN
  Shopper: 4 SALE
  Speeder: 3 COP
**Stoppers**
  Show: 3 ADS
**Stopping**
  place: 3 INN
  Without: 7 ATACLIP
**"Stop right there!":** 4 HALT
    WHOA 6 HOLDIT
**Stops**
  It ~ often: 5 LOCAL
  Pull out all the: 6 LETRIP
  Rest: 5 OASES
  Where the buck: 3 DOE
    4 HERE
**"Stop that!":** 4 DONT
**"Stop the clock!":** 4 TIME
**Stopwatch**
  button: 5 RESET
  Use a: 4 TIME
**Storage**
  area: 5 ATTIC 6 GARAGE
  battery type: 5 NICAD
  box: 3 BIN
  building: 4 SHED
  Coal: 3 BIN
  Computer ~ acronym: 5 ASCII
  container: 3 BIN
  cylinder: 4 SILO
  Farm ~ area: 4 SILO
  Food ~ material: 5 SARAN
  Hay ~ space: 4 LOFT
  PC ~ medium: 5 CDROM
  place: 3 BIN 6 CLOSET
  room: 5 ATTIC
  space: 3 BIN 5 ATTIC
    6 CLOSET
  unit: 4 BYTE
**Store:** 4 FILE MART STOW
    5 CACHE
  Be in ~ for: 5 AWAIT
  event: 4 SALE
  goods (abbr.): 4 MDSE
  Kind of: 4 DIME
  of ore: 4 LODE
  on a farm: 6 ENSILE
  posting (abbr.): 3 HRS
  prefix: 4 MEGA
  Retail: 4 MART
  Retail ~ opening: 3 WAL
  Secret: 5 CACHE STASH
  selection: 5 SIZES
  sign: 4 OPEN SALE
  up: 8 PUTASIDE
  wine: 6 CELLAR
  ~, as fodder: 6 ENSILE
**Stored:** 6 LAIDUP
  in barrels: 4 AGED

  on board: 5 LADED
**Storefront**
  cover: 6 AWNING
  sign: 4 OPEN
**Storehouse**
  Rural: 4 SILO
**Stores:** 7 EMPORIA
  Mil.: 3 PXS
**Stories:** 4 LORE
  Body of legendary: 6 MYTHOS
  Like ghost: 5 EERIE
**Stork**
  kin: 4 IBIS 5 CRANE
**Storm:** 4 RAGE 6 ASSAIL
    ATTACK
  Away from a: 4 ALEE
  center: 3 EYE
  Let up, as a: 5 ABATE
  maker: 3 GEO
  preceder: 4 CALM
  tracker: 5 RADAR
**Stormy**
  bird: 6 PETREL
**"Stormy Weather"**
  composer: 5 ARLEN
  singer: 5 HORNE
  singer Horne: 4 LENA
**Stornoway**
  It's spoken in: 4 ERSE
**Storrs**
  coll.: 5 UCONN
**Storting**
  Where the ~ meets: 4 OSLO
**Story:** 4 MYTH TALE
    7 ACCOUNT
  approach: 5 ANGLE
  Bear of: 4 PAPA
  Bedtime: 5 DREAM
  Big: 4 EPIC
  connector: 5 STAIR
  Continuing: 6 SERIAL
  Cover: 5 ALIBI
  Creative: 3 LIE
  dance: 4 HULA
  Epic: 4 SAGA
  Fairy: 4 TALE
  Final: 4 OBIT
  Fish: 3 LIE 4 TALE YARN
  Fish ~ suffix: 3 EST
  Folk: 4 TALE
  Heroic: 4 EPIC
  It's a long: 4 EPIC SAGA
  It's an old: 5 FABLE
  Kind of: 3 SAD SOB
  Legendary: 4 MYTH
  Life: 3 BIO
  Like a hard-to-believe: 4 TALL
  line: 4 PLOT 5 ANGLE
  Long: 4 SAGA
  Make a long ~ short: 4 EDIT
    5 RECAP
  Never-ending: 4 SOAP
    9 SOAPOPERA
  of Jesus: 7 PARABLE
  Old war: 5 ILIAD
  Ongoing: 6 SERIAL

  setting: 5 SCENE
  Shorter: 7 NOVELLA
  starter: 4 ONCE
  Suspect's: 5 ALIBI
  Sweeping: 4 EPIC
  Tall: 4 TALE YARN
  Tell a: 7 NARRATE
  teller: 4 LIAR
  that may hold secrets: 5 ATTIC
  Troy: 5 ILIAD
  Trumped-up: 3 LIE
  Unlikely: 4 TALE
  War: 5 ILIAD
  with a moral: 7 PARABLE
  ~, in French: 5 ETAGE
**Storybook**
  elephant: 5 BABAR
  ending: 5 MORAL
  How a ~ is read: 5 ALOUD
  monster: 4 OGRE
  start: 4 ONCE
**"Story of Civilization, The"**
  author: 6 DURANT
**"Story of ___ H., The":** 5 ADELE
**Storyteller:** 4 LIAR 6 FIBBER
    7 RELATER
  Noted: 5 AESOP
**Storytelling**
  ~ Uncle: 5 REMUS
**Stout:** 3 ALE 5 BEEFY LUSTY
    6 PORTLY ROTUND
  Half ale, half:
    11 BLACKANDTAN
  Make: 4 BREW 6 FATTEN
  Mystery writer: 3 REX
  relative: 3 ALE
  sleuth: 4 NERO
**Stove**
  Bubbling on the: 5 ABOIL
  light: 5 PILOT
  option: 3 GAS
  section: 4 OVEN
  workspace: 7 COOKTOP
**Stovepipe:** 3 HAT
**Stoves**
  Like some: 5 SETIN
**Stovetop**
  sights: 4 PANS POTS
  whistler: 6 KETTLE
**Stow**
  cargo: 4 LADE
**Stowe**
  1856 ~ novel: 4 DRED
  character: 3 EVA 5 TOPSY
  Enjoy: 3 SKI
  gear: 4 SKIS
  tow: 4 TBAR
  villain: 6 LEGREE
**St. Patrick**
  Home of: 4 EIRE ERIN
**St. Paul:** 8 TWINCITY
  architect: 4 WREN
**St. Pete**
  Home of: 3 FLA
**St. Peter**
  was the first: 4 POPE

**St. Petersburg**
neighbor: 5 TAMPA
river: 4 NEVA
st.: 3 FLA
**St. Philip ___: 4 NERI**
**St. Pierre: 3 ILE**
and others: 4 ILES
**Strabismus: 8 CROSSEYE**
**Straddle: 4 SPAN**
**Straddling: 4 ATOP 6 ACROSS**
7 ASTRIDE
**Stradivari**
Teacher of: 5 AMATI
**Strads**
Some: 5 CELLI
**Straggle: 3 LAG**
**Straight: 3 DUE 4 NEAT TRUE**
6 HETERO HONEST
LINEAR UNBENT
and tall: 5 ERECT
Didn't go: 5 ARCED
Don't go: 4 VEER
Get: 5 ALIGN
Get ~ A's: 5 EXCEL
Isn't: 5 LEANS
Isn't ~ with: 6 LIESTO
line through a circle:
6 SECANT
Make: 6 NEATEN
man: 4 FOIL 6 STOOGE
Not: 3 GAY WRY 4 ALOP
AWRY BENT WAVY
5 ATILT CURLY 6 ANGLED
Not walk: 4 REEL
path: 7 BEELINE
prefix: 5 ORTHO
Set: 4 TRUE 5 ALIGN
6 ORIENT
Standing: 5 ERECT
up: 4 NEAT 5 ERECT
Wasn't: 4 LIED
**Straight ___ arrow: 4 ASAN**
**Straight as ___: 4 ADIE**
**Straightaway: 3 NOW**
**Straight-billed**
game bird: 5 SNIPE
**Straight-bladed**
dagger: 4 DIRK
**Straighten: 5 ALIGN**
6 UNBEND UNCURL
8 UNTANGLE
up: 6 NEATEN
**Straightened: 4 NEAT**
**Straightforward**
Less: 5 SLIER
**Straight-grained**
wood: 3 ASH
**Straightness**
Epitome of: 5 ARROW
**"Straight Up"**
singer: 5 ABDUL
**Strain: 3 TAX 4 ONUS 5 BREED**
EXERT 6 MELODY
STRESS 9 OVEREXERT
Dangerous: 5 EBOLA ECOLI
One with "I": 6 EGOIST

Put a ~ on: 3 TAX 5 TAXED
**Strain at a ___: 4 GNAT**
**Strained**
Became: 6 TENSED
**Strainer: 5 SIEVE**
8 COLANDER
**Strains: 5 TRIES**
**Strait**
European: 7 OTRANTO
___ Strait: 6 BERING
**Strait-laced: 4 PRIM 5 STAID**
9 VICTORIAN
one: 5 PRISS
**Strait of ___ (Malaysia):**
7 MALACCA
**Strait of Dover**
county: 4 KENT
French city on the: 6 CALAIS
**Strait of Hormuz**
land: 4 IRAN OMAN
**Strait of Messina**
monster: 6 SCYLLA
**Straits**
In dire: 5 NEEDY
Like some: 4 DIRE
___ Straits: 4 DIRE
**Strand: 5 BEACH LEAVE**
SHORE 6 DESERT
ENISLE MAROON
Curly: 7 TENDRIL
in winter: 5 ICEIN
Thin: 4 WISP
**Stranded**
It's: 3 DNA RNA
motorist's need: 3 TOW
5 FLARE
**Strands**
Separate rope: 5 UNLAY
**Strange: 3 ODD 5 ALIEN EERIE**
OUTRE
Frightfully: 5 EERIE
In a ~ way: 5 ODDLY
6 EERILY
sighting: 3 UFO
sounding city: 4 ERIE
to say: 5 ODDLY
Very: 5 WEIRD
**Strangelove**
and No: 3 DRS
**"Strange Magic"**
band: 3 ELO
**"Stranger, The"**
author Albert: 5 CAMUS
**"Strangers and Brothers"**
novelist: 6 CPSNOW
**Strap**
Bridle: 4 REIN
Jockey: 4 REIN
Kind of: 3 BRA
Sandal: 5 THONG
**Straphanger: 7 STANDEE**
buy: 5 TOKEN
lack: 4 SEAT
**Strapped: 5 BROKE NEEDY**
for cash: 5 SHORT
**Strapping: 6 ROBUST**

**Strasbourg**
Info: French cue
school: 5 ECOLE
summer: 3 ETE
**Strata: 6 LAYERS**
Social: 6 CASTES
**Stratagem: 4 PLAN PLOY RUSE**
6 TACTIC
Sly: 4 RUSE
Tennis: 3 LOB
**Strategically**
Arrange: 6 DEPLOY
**Stratego**
piece: 3 SPY 4 FLAG
**Strategy: 8 GAMEPLAN**
Backup: 5 PLANB
Desperate: 10 LASTRESORT
Fallback: 5 PLANB
First: 5 PLANA
Poker: 5 RAISE
Wall St.: 3 LBO
**Stratford**
river: 4 AVON
**Stratford-___-Avon: 4 UPON**
**Stratosphere**
Head for the: 4 SOAR
**Stratum: 5 LAYER**
Coal: 4 SEAM
Social: 5 CASTE CLASS ELITE
Thin: 4 SEAM
**Strauss**
Composer: 6 JOHANN
Jeans maker: 4 LEVI
opera: 6 DAPHNE SALOME
waltz river: 6 DANUBE
**Stravinsky**
ballet: 4 AGON
Composer: 4 IGOR
**Straw**
Bundled, as: 5 BALED
Drink with a: 5 FLOAT
hat: 6 BOATER
in the wind: 4 OMEN
It contains: 5 ADOBE
Japanese ~ mat: 6 TATAMI
Last: 5 LIMIT
Like the unlucky: 5 SHORT
Small bundle of: 4 WISP
Use a: 4 SUCK
**Strawberry: 5 EXMET**
was one: 3 MET
**Strawberry ___: 4 ROAN**
**Stray: 3 ERR SIN 4 ROAM**
WAIF 6 ERRANT
8 ALLEYCAT
animal: 4 WAIF
calf: 5 DOGIE
Cowboy's: 5 DOGIE
from the script: 5 ADLIB
gp.: 5 ASPCA
Take in a: 5 ADOPT
**Straying: 6 ERRANT**
**Streak**
Go on a winning: 6 GETHOT
On a lucky: 3 HOT
Ready to: 5 NAKED

Talk a blue: 3 GAB YAK
    4 CUSS 5 RUNON SWEAR
Winning: 3 RUN
**Streaked:** 4 LINY SPED TORE
    7 STRIATE
**Streaker**
  Celestial: 5 COMET 6 METEOR
  European: 3 SST
  Sleek: 3 SST
**Stream:** 5 CREEK
  Block, as a: 5 DAMUP
  Burns: 5 AFTON
  Cross a: 4 WADE
  Electron: 7 BETARAY
  Shakespeare: 4 AVON
  Small: 4 RILL 5 BROOK
  spot: 4 VALE
  Swiss: 3 AAR 4 AARE
  Word before: 3 AIR
**Streambed**
  African: 4 WADI
**"Streamers"**
  playwright David: 4 RABE
**Streamlet:** 3 RIA 4 RILL
**Streamlined:** 5 SLEEK
**Streep**
  Actress: 5 MERYL
  film: 8 SHEDEVIL
  Title role for: 6 SOPHIE
  ~ Oscar role: 6 KRAMER
**Street:** 4 ROAD
  34th ~ happening:
    7 MIRACLE
  Back: 5 ALLEY
  border: 4 CURB
  boss: 5 MASON
  caution: 3 SLO
  Central: 4 MAIN
  Common ~ name: 3 ELM
    4 MAIN
  Complete a: 3 TAR
  crosser: 6 AVENUE
  Dead-end: 8 CULDESAC
  fixture: 4 LAMP
  fleet: 4 CABS
  Freddy's: 3 ELM
  Horror film: 3 ELM
  Is not on the: 4 AINT
  Memphis: 5 BEALE
  Narrow: 4 LANE
  Nightmare: 3 ELM
  of fiction: 5 DELLA
  of Olympics fame: 6 PICABO
  Parisian: 3 RUE
  performer: 4 MIME
  Reason for a ~ closing:
    10 BLOCKPARTY
  Scary: 3 ELM
  shader: 3 ELM
  Short: 4 LANE
  show: 5 RAREE
  sign: 5 YIELD 6 ONEWAY
  urchin: 5 GAMIN
    10 RAGAMUFFIN
    11 GUTTERSNIPE
  vendor: 7 PEDDLER

**Street ___ (believability):**
  4 CRED
**Streetcar:** 4 TRAM 7 TROLLEY
**"Streetcar Named Desire, A"**
  role: 6 STELLA
**Street corner**
  box: 6 USMAIL
  sign: 4 STOP
**Streets**
  Like some: 4 THRU
  Protest in the: 4 RIOT
**Street-smart:** 5 CANNY
**Streisand**
  Film directed by: 5 YENTL
  title role: 5 YENTL
  ~, familiarly: 4 BABS
**Strength:** 5 FORTE MIGHT
    POWER SINEW
    7 POTENCE
  Brute: 8 RAWPOWER
  Current: 8 AMPERAGE
  Drain: 3 SAP
  Gather one's: 6 RESTUP
  Kind of: 5 INNER 7 TENSILE
  Lose: 3 EBB 4 FADE FLAG
    TIRE WANE
  Muscular: 5 SINEW
  Solution: 5 TITER
  Source of: 5 ASSET UNITY
    6 SINEWS
  Symbol of: 3 OAK 5 STEEL
  With all one's: 5 AMAIN
  ~, in Latin: 3 VIS
**Strengthen:** 4 GIRD TONE
    6 ANNEAL BEEFUP
    TONEUP
**Strengthener**
  Ab: 5 SITUP
**Stress:** 4 AGER 7 ITERATE
  Sign of: 6 ACCENT 7 ITALICS
**Stressed:** 4 BOLD 5 TENSE
  type (abbr.): 4 ITAL
**Stressful**
  spot: 7 HOTSEAT
**Stress-reducing**
  discipline: 4 YOGA
**Stretch:** 4 AREA 5 CRANE
    STINT TRACT
    8 ELONGATE
  across: 4 SPAN
  in a stretch: 8 LIMORIDE
  Intervening: 8 MEANTIME
  It can be a: 4 LIMO
  Long: 3 EON
  More than a: 3 LIE
  of land: 5 TRACT
  out: 3 LIE 8 ELONGATE
  (out): 3 EKE
  Sedgy: 5 MARSH
  Significant: 3 ERA
  Solemn: 4 LENT
  the truth: 3 LIE
  time: 7 SEVENTH
**Stretchable:** 7 ELASTIC
**Stretched**
  out: 4 LAIN

  Tightly: 4 TAUT
**Stretcher**
  Pay: 3 OLA
  Shoe: 4 TREE
**Stretching**
  muscle: 6 TENSOR
**Stretchy:** 7 ELASTIC
**Strict**
  Hardly: 3 LAX
  Less: 5 LAXER 6 EASIER
  Morally: 7 PURITAN
  Not: 7 LENIENT
  suffix: 3 URE
**Strictly**
  precise: 5 EXACT
**Strictness:** 5 RIGOR
**Stride:** 4 PACE STEP
  Easy: 4 LOPE
  Steed: 4 GAIT
**Strident:** 5 HARSH
  sound: 5 BLARE
**Stridex**
  target: 4 ACNE
**Strife**
  Free from: 7 ATPEACE
  Norse god of: 3 TYR
**Strike:** 3 HIT NIX 4 DELE XOUT
    5 CLOUT SMITE
    6 ATTACK DELETE
    SEEMTO
  back: 5 REACT
  caller: 3 UMP 5 UNION
    6 UMPIRE
  Didst: 5 SMOTE
  down: 5 SMITE
  from a list: 4 XOUT
  lightly: 3 TAP
  Lucky: 3 OIL ORE 5 TROVE
  Not quite a: 5 SPARE
  out: 3 FAN 4 DELE FAIL
    OMIT 5 ERASE 6 DELETE
  participant: 3 PIN
  Prepare to: 4 COIL
  setting: 4 LANE
  site: 5 ALLEY
  Try to: 5 HITAT
  Wildcat: 3 OIL
  zone: 4 LANE
  zone boundary: 5 KNEES
**Strike ___:** 5 ADEAL APOSE
**Strike ___ blow:** 4 ALOW
**Strikebreaker:** 4 SCAB
**Strikeout**
  king Nolan: 4 RYAN
  king Ryan: 5 NOLAN
**Striker**
  anathema: 4 SCAB
  cry: 5 UNITE
**Strikers**
  demand: 5 RAISE
  org.: 3 PBA
**"Strike up the band!":** 5 HITIT
**Strike while the iron ___:**
  5 ISHOT
**Striking**
  end: 4 PEEN

**String**
Drum: 5 SNARE
group: 5 OCTET
Item attached to a: 6 TEABAG
of flowers: 3 LEI
Package: 5 TWINE
sound: 5 TWANG
Strong: 5 TWINE
tie: 4 BOLO
Toy on a: 4 KITE YOYO
Word after: 5 ALONG
**String bean**
opposite: 5 FATSO
**Stringed**
instrument: 4 HARP LYRE
VIOL 5 CELLO 6 ZITHER
toy: 4 YOYO
**String quartet**
member: 5 CELLO VIOLA
**Strings**
Hawaiian: 3 UKE 7 UKELELE
UKULELE
Heavenly: 4 HARP
Old: 5 LYRES
One pulling: 5 TUNER
Precious: 5 STRAD
Pull: 5 STRUM
Some: 5 CELLI
**Stringy:** 4 ROPY
**Strip:** 4 PARE PEEL SLAT
5 SWATH 6 UNROBE
7 DISROBE
a ship: 5 UNRIG
Backing: 4 LATH
Barrel: 5 STAVE
Blind: 4 SLAT
blubber: 6 FLENSE
Decorative ~ of fabric:
6 RIBAND
Mideast: 4 GAZA
Musical based on a: 5 ANNIE
Narrow: 4 SLAT 7 ISTHMUS
Shoe: 4 WELT
Stem-to-stern: 4 KEEL
Sticky: 4 TAPE
Wood: 4 LATH SLAT
6 SPLINE
___ Strip: 4 GAZA 6 MOBIUS
**Stripe:** 3 ILK 4 KIND
Lowest: 4 NINE
Tear a ~ off: 6 DEMOTE
**Striped**
animal: 5 OKAPI TIGER
cat: 5 TABBY
chalcedony: 5 AGATE
equine: 5 ZEBRA
fish: 4 BASS
shirt wearer: 3 REF
stone: 5 AGATE
**Stripling:** 3 LAD
**Stripped**
They're sometimes: 5 GEARS
**Stripper**
garb: 7 GSTRING
**Strips**
of land: 6 ISTHMI

**Stritch**
Tony winner: 6 ELAINE
**Strive:** 3 TRY VIE 5 ASSAY
6 ASPIRE
**Stroheim, Erich ___ :** 3 VON
**Stroke:** 3 PET RUB 6 CARESS
Back: 3 PAT
Billiards: 5 MASSE
Finishing: 4 COUP
Gentle: 6 CARESS
gently: 3 PAT PET
Golf: 4 PUTT SHOT
of luck: 5 BREAK FLUKE
of the pen: 5 SERIF
Short: 4 PUTT
Something to: 3 EGO
Swimming: 5 CRAWL
Tennis: 3 LOB 4 CHOP
Violin: 5 UPBOW
**Strokes**
Like some swimming:
7 OVERARM
**Stroll:** 4 ROAM WALK 5 AMBLE
MOSEY 6 RAMBLE
Easy: 5 PASEO
Leisurely: 5 PASEO
**Stroller**
London: 4 PRAM
**Strolling**
area: 4 PIER
**Stromboli**
output: 4 LAVA
**Strong:** 5 HARDY 6 POTENT
7 INTENSE
acid: 3 HCL 6 NITRIC
adhesive: 5 EPOXY
alkali: 3 LYE
and sharp: 5 ACRID
cleaner: 3 LYE
cord: 4 ROPE
cotton: 4 PIMA
craving: 4 LUST
criticism: 4 FLAK
desire: 3 YEN
fiber: 5 RAMIE
glue: 5 EPOXY
Going: 4 ATIT
impulse: 4 URGE
insect: 3 ANT
It may be: 4 SUIT
Lean and: 4 WIRY
point: 5 ASSET FORTE
preference: 4 BIAS
string: 5 TWINE
suit: 5 ARMOR FORTE
wind: 4 GALE
**Strong-arm:** 6 COERCE
**Strong as ___ :** 4 ANOX
**Strongbox:** 4 SAFE 5 CHEST
6 COFFER
**"Strong Enough to Bend"**
singer Tucker: 5 TANYA
**Stronghold:** 4 FORT 7 BASTION
CITADEL
Military: 4 FORT
Mormon: 4 UTAH

**Strongman**
Biblical: 6 SAMSON
Mythical: 5 ATLAS
Onetime African: 4 AMIN
**Strong ___ ox:** 4 ASAN
**"Strong Poison"**
author: 6 SAYERS
**Strong-scented**
herb: 3 RUE
**Strong-willed:** 4 IRON
**Strop:** 4 HONE
user: 5 HONER
**Stroud, Robert**
nickname: 7 BIRDMAN
**Strove:** 4 VIED
**Struck:** 7 EXEDOUT
by Cupid: 7 SMITTEN
down: 5 SMOTE
hard: 5 SMOTE
It may be: 3 OIL 4 POSE
out: 4 EXED 5 DELED
prefix: 4 DUMB
~, old-style: 4 SMIT
**Structural**
beam: 4 IBAR
member: 5 IBEAM
sci.: 4 ANAT
support: 6 PILING
**Structure**
Baglike: 3 SAC
Circus: 4 TENT
Cylindrical: 4 SILO
Farm: 4 BARN SILO
Multiroofed: 6 PAGODA
Offshore: 3 RIG
prefix: 5 INFRA
Ramshackle: 7 RATTRAP
Snow: 4 FORT
Storage: 4 SHED
**Struggle:** 3 VIE WAR 6 TUSSLE
Class: 4 TEST
for air: 4 GASP
(through): 4 SLOG
Violent: 5 THROE
with struggle: 4 LISP
**Struggling:** 7 INAHOLE
**Strummed**
instrument: 3 UKE
**Strung**
along: 5 LEDON
tightly: 4 TAUT
**Strut:** 6 SASHAY 7 SWAGGER
like a peacock: 6 PARADE
**Sts.:** 3 RDS
**St. Teresa**
Home of: 5 AVILA
**St. Thomas:** 4 ISLE
who was murdered:
6 BECKET
**Stu**
Actor: 5 IRWIN
**Stuart**
CSA general: 3 JEB
Last ~ monarch: 4 ANNE
**Stuart, J.E.B.**
country: 3 CSA

**Stuarti**
Singer: 4 ENZO
**"Stuart Little"**
actress Davis: 5 GEENA
**Stub ___:** 4 ATOE
**Stubbed**
item: 3 TOE
**Stubble**
remover: 5 RAZOR
**Stubborn:** 6 MULISH
animal: 4 MULE
dirt: 5 GRIME
one: 3 ASS 4 MULE
things of Twain: 5 FACTS
**Stubborn as ___:** 5 AMULE
**Stubbornness**
Symbol of: 4 MULE
**Stubbs**
of the Four Tops: 4 LEVI
**Stubby:** 4 KAYE
**Stuck:** 5 GLUED MIRED TREED
6 INAFIX INAJAM
INARUT LODGED
7 ADHERED INABIND
INASPOT UPATREE
around: 6 STAYED
by a thorn: 7 PRICKED
Get: 5 LODGE
on oneself: 4 VAIN
Place to get: 4 MIRE
**Stuck in ___:** 4 ARUT
**Stuck-up**
sort: 4 SNOB 7 EGOTIST
**Stud:** 5 HEMAN POKER
7 EARRING
Emulate a: 4 SIRE
Farm: 8 STALLION
fee: 4 ANTE
Pay a ~ fee: 6 ANTEUP
poker: 4 SPUR
remark: 4 IMIN
site: 3 EAR 4 LOBE
7 EARLOBE
**Studdard**
"American Idol" winner:
5 RUBEN
**Studebaker**
Sporty: 6 AVANTI
**Student:** 5 PUPIL TUTEE
7 LEARNER
Academy: 5 CADET
book: 4 TEXT
concern: 4 EXAM
driver, usually: 4 TEEN
First-year law: 4 ONEL
Flight ~ test: 4 SOLO
focused org.: 3 PTA
jottings: 5 NOTES
Kind of: 3 MED
Mil. ~ body: 4 ROTC
Military: 5 CADET
New Haven: 3 ELI 5 YALIE
of Seneca: 4 NERO
of Socrates: 5 PLATO
of Zeno: 5 STOIC
overseer: 4 DEAN

Private: 5 TUTEE
purchase: 4 TEXT
res.: 4 DORM
second chance: 6 RETEST
Second-yr.: 4 SOPH
stat: 3 GPA
surprise: 7 POPQUIZ
West Point: 5 CADET
Yale: 3 ELI
Yeshiva: 3 JEW
~, in French: 5 ELEVE
**Students**
Fourth-yr.: 3 SRS
Group of: 5 CLASS
Like Anna's: 7 SIAMESE
Pertaining to most: 4 ELHI
play it: 5 HOOKY
Prepare new: 6 ORIENT
Some college: 5 COEDS
**Studied**
~, with "over": 5 PORED
**Studio:** 7 ATELIER
alert: 5 ONAIR
Artist's: 7 ATELIER
Ball's: 6 DESILU
Dance ~ feature: 5 BARRE
Film: 3 LOT
output: 7 RELEASE
sight: 3 SET
sign: 5 ONAIR
stand: 5 EASEL 6 TRIPOD
stock: 4 REEL
structure: 3 SET
with a lion: 3 MGM
with a troubled history:
5 ORION
worker: 6 ARTIST
**Study:** 3 DEN 4 READ ROOM
6 BONEUP PERUSE
7 EXAMINE LIBRARY
8 POREOVER
Advanced ~ group: 7 SEMINAR
at the last minute: 4 CRAM
Field of: 4 AREA
hard: 4 CRAM
Not based on previous:
7 APRIORI
**Stuff:** 3 RAM 4 CRAM FILL
GEAR GLUT SATE
5 ITEMS 7 SATIATE
and nonsense: 3 ROT
in a cell: 3 RNA
in a closet: 5 LINEN
one's face: 6 PIGOUT
to the gills: 4 SATE 5 GORGE
Unimportant: 6 TRIVIA
Unusual: 6 CURIOS
**Stuffed:** 7 OVERFED REPLETE
animal of the '80s:
8 CAREBEAR
Get: 7 OVEREAT
It might be: 9 BALLOTBOX
shirt: 4 PRIG SNOB 5 SNOOT
~ Italian pockets: 7 RAVIOLI
**Stuffer**
Bagel: 3 LOX 4 NOVA

Stocking: 3 TOE TOY 4 COAL
FOOT 5 SANTA
**Stuffers**
Wallet: 4 ONES
**Stuffing**
Cotton: 4 BATT
herb: 4 SAGE
Pillow: 5 EIDER KAPOK
Scarecrow: 5 STRAW
**Stuffy:** 4 PRIM
sounding: 5 NASAL
**Stumble:** 3 ERR 4 TRIP
6 FALTER
**Stumblebum:** 3 OAF 4 CLOD
LOUT 5 KLUTZ
**Stumbles**
Verbal: 3 ERS UHS UMS
**Stumbling**
block: 4 SNAG
**Stump**
man: 6 ORATOR
Take the: 5 ORATE
**Stumped:** 5 ATSEA 7 ATALOSS
UPATREE
Help for the: 4 HINT
**Stumper:** 3 POL 6 ENIGMA
ORATOR
**Stun:** 3 AWE JAR WOW ZAP
4 DAZE 5 AMAZE
FLOOR
gun: 5 TASER
**Stung**
He ~ like a bee: 3 ALI
**Stunned:** 5 AGAPE AGASP
INAWE 7 INADAZE
state: 4 DAZE
**Stunning**
It's: 6 PHASER
success: 4 COUP
swimmer: 3 EEL
**Stunt:** 4 FEAT 5 CAPER
double: 7 STANDIN
Plane: 4 LOOP
**Stunted:** 5 RUNTY
**Stuntman**
Knievel: 4 EVEL
**"Stunt Man, The"**
star: 6 OTOOLE
**Stunts**
First name in: 4 EVEL
**Stupefy:** 3 AWE 4 DAZE STUN
5 AMAZE BESOT
6 BEMUSE BOGGLE
with drink: 5 BESOT
**Stupid:** 5 DENSE DOPEY
INANE 7 ASININE
jerk: 3 ASS 4 BOZO 5 SCHMO
**Stupidly**
Stare: 4 GAPE GAWK
**"Stupid me!":** 3 DOH 4 OOPS
**Stupor:** 4 DAZE
**Sturdiness**
Symbol of: 3 OAK
**Sturdy:** 5 OAKEN
cart: 4 DRAY
wood: 3 ASH OAK

**Sturgeon**
output: 3 ROE
**Sturluson**
Icelandic poet: 6 SNORRI
work: 4 EDDA
**Sturm ___ Drang:** 3 UND
**Sturm und ___:** 5 DRANG
**Stuttered**
Name ~ in a song: 4 KATY
**Stuttgart**
title: 4 HERR
**Stutz**
auto: 7 BEARCAT
contemporary: 3 REO
**Stutz Bearcat**
contemporary: 3 REO
**Sty**
cry: 4 OINK
dweller: 3 HOG SOW
fare: 4 SLOP 5 SWILL
guy: 4 BOAR
offspring: 5 STOAT
resident: 3 PIG
sound: 4 OINK 5 GRUNT
       SNORT
**Style:** 4 ELAN MODE VEIN
       5 DECOR GENRE TASTE
       TREND 6 MANNER
       7 PANACHE
1920s ~: 7 ARTDECO
1960s ~: 3 MOD 5 OPART
In the ~ of: 3 ALA
No longer in: 5 PASSE
Nostalgic: 5 RETRO
of a room: 5 DECOR
of dress: 5 ALINE
Ornate: 6 ROCOCO
Out of: 5 DATED PASSE
Suffix of: 5 ESQUE
Type: 5 ELITE
~, in French: 3 TON
**Styling**
goo: 3 GEL
**Stylish:** 3 MOD 4 CHIC TONY
       5 DASHY SHARP
       6 CLASSY
dresser: 3 FOP
Elegantly: 6 CLASSY
More: 6 TONIER 7 SMARTER
Overly: 6 CHICHI
suit: 6 ARMANI
**Stylishly**
old: 5 RETRO
smooth: 5 SLEEK
**Stylist**
spot: 5 SALON
**Stylistically**
bold: 5 AVANT
**Stylus**
channel: 6 GROOVE
**Styne**
Tony winner: 4 JULE
**Styptic**
stuff: 4 ALUM
**Styron**
heroine: 6 SOPHIE

~ Turner: 3 NAT
**Styx**
ferryman: 6 CHARON
setting: 5 HADES
**Suave:** 6 URBANE
competitor: 5 PRELL
Overly: 4 OILY
**"___ Suave":** 4 RICO
**Sub:** 4 HERO TEMP 5 UBOAT
       6 HOAGIE 7 STANDIN
Attack a: 3 EAT
contractor: 4 DELI
detector: 5 SONAR
Downed a: 3 ATE
German: 5 UBOAT
Ill-fated: 5 KURSK
in a tub: 4 OLEO
launching: 7 TORPEDO
New Orleans: 7 POORBOY
sinker: 4 MINE 6 ASHCAN
station: 4 DELI
system: 5 SONAR
viewer: 5 SCOPE
WWII: 5 UBOAT
**Sub ___ (in secret):** 4 ROSA
**Subarctic**
forest: 5 TAIGA
**Subatomic**
particle: 4 MUON PION
       5 MESON QUARK
       6 PROTON
**Subbed:** 5 SATIN
**Subcompact:** 4 MINI
**Subcontinental**
prefix: 4 INDO
**Subdivision**
Family: 5 GENUS
Military: 4 UNIT
of a legion: 7 MANIPLE
Phylum: 5 CLASS
subdivision: 3 LOT 4 ACRE
**Subdivisions**
Taxonomic: 5 PHYLA
**Subdue:** 4 TAME
**Subdued:** 4 TAME
color: 6 PASTEL
**Subject:** 4 NOUN 5 THEME
       TOPIC 6 MATTER
preceder: 5 INRE
word: 4 NOUN
**Subjective**
atmosphere: 4 AURA
**Subjoin:** 3 ADD 6 APPEND
**Sublease:** 5 RELET
**Sublime:** 8 ETHEREAL
**Submachine gun**
British: 4 STEN
Clip-fed: 4 BREN
Israeli: 3 UZI
**Submarine:** 4 HERO
       12 HEROSANDWICH
base: 4 DELI
class: 4 ALFA
detector: 5 SONAR
First atomic: 8 NAUTILUS
German: 5 UBOAT

on sonar: 4 BLIP
sandwich: 4 HERO 6 HOAGIE
Work on a: 3 EAT
WWII: 5 UBOAT
**Submariner**
Fictional: 4 NEMO
**Submerged:** 4 SANK SUNK
Partially ~ part: 4 HULL
**Submission**
Aspiring singer's: 4 DEMO
Contest: 5 ENTRY
enc.: 4 SASE
**Submissions**
to eds.: 3 MSS
**Submissive:** 4 MEEK TAME
       6 DOCILE
group: 5 SHEEP
**Submit:** 3 BOW 5 ENTER
       OFFER YIELD 6 ACCEDE
       HANDIN SENDIN
       TENDER
**Submitted:** 6 SENTIN
**Subordinate**
Brig. Gen.: 3 COL
Claus's: 3 ELF
deity: 6 DAEMON
Looie: 5 SARGE
ruler: 6 SATRAP
Santa's: 3 ELF
title (abbr.): 4 ASST
**Subordinates**
Capt.: 3 LTS
**Subpoena:** 4 WRIT
**Subscriber:** 4 USER
option: 7 RENEWAL
**Subscription**
End, as a: 5 LAPSE
Extend a: 5 RENEW
period: 4 YEAR
**Subsection**
Document: 7 ARTICLE
**Subsequently:** 4 THEN 5 AFTER
       HENCE LATER SINCE
**Subservience**
Show: 5 KNEEL
**Subside:** 3 EBB 4 WANE
       5 ABATE 6 LESSEN
**Subsidiary:** 4 UNIT
ExxonMobil: 4 ESSO
GE: 3 NBC
Maytag: 5 AMANA
theorem: 5 LEMMA
**Subsidy:** 3 AID
**Subsist:** 3 ARE 4 LIVE
**Subspecies**
Adaptable: 7 ECOTYPE
**Substance:** 4 GIST MEAT
Lacking: 4 AIRY 5 INANE
Slick: 3 OIL
Soothing: 5 SALVE
**Substantial:** 5 AMPLE HEFTY
       LARGE MEATY
**Substantive:** 5 MEATY
**Substitute:** 5 PROXY SCRUB
       6 FILLIN 8 ALTEREGO
As a: 7 INSTEAD

Butter: 4 OLEO
Chocolate: 5 CAROB
Fat: 5 OLEAN 7 OLESTRA
for: 5 ACTAS
Gelatin: 4 AGAR
Meat: 4 TOFU
Money: 5 SCRIP
place: 5 STEAD
Repair shop: 6 LOANER
ruler: 6 REGENT
Soap: 5 AMOLE
spread: 4 OLEO
Sugar: 4 DEAR
**Substituted:** 7 STOODIN
**Substitution**
    word: 4 LIEU
**Subterfuge:** 4 RUSE TRAP
    5 TRICK
**Subterranean**
    dwarf: 5 GNOME
    pest: 4 MOLE
    soldier: 3 ANT
**Subtle:** 4 FINE
    atmosphere: 4 AURA
    difference: 6 NUANCE
    emanation: 4 AURA
    tone: 3 HUE
**Subtlety:** 6 NUANCE
    Lacking: 5 CORNY
**Subtraction**
    Account: 5 DEBIT
    amt.: 3 DIF
    subject: 4 MATH
    word: 4 LESS
**Suburb:** 4 AREA
**Suburban**
    expanse: 4 LAWN
    hangout: 4 MALL
    plot: 4 ACRE
    suffix: 3 ITE
**Suburbanite**
    concern: 4 LAWN
**Suburbia**
    sight: 4 LAWN
**Subway:** 5 METRO
    alternative: 3 BUS CAB 4 TAXI
    alternatives: 3 ELS
    barrier: 5 STILE
    coin: 5 TOKEN
    entrance: 5 STILE
    fare: 4 HERO
    handhold: 5 STRAP
    map point: 4 STOP
    NYC: 3 BMT IND IRT MTA
    NYC ~ stop, for short: 3 LEX
    of song: 6 ATRAIN
    Paris: 5 METRO
    S.F. ~ system: 4 BART
    stop (abbr.): 3 STA
    track: 4 RAIL
    wish: 4 SEAT
    ~, to a Brit: 4 TUBE
**"Subway Series"**
    manager: 5 TORRE
    stop: 4 SHEA
    team: 4 METS

**Succeed:** 5 ENSUE GOFAR
    6 FOLLOW MAKEIT
    PANOUT 7 PROSPER
    REPLACE 8 GETAHEAD
    GOPLACES
    Might: 8 HASASHOT
**Success:** 3 HIT
    Achieve: 6 ARRIVE
    Big: 3 HIT 5 ECLAT SMASH
    Brilliant: 5 ECLAT
    Letters of: 3 SRO
    Short-lived:
        13 FLASHINTHEPAN
    Sign of: 3 SRO
**Successful:** 5 ONTOP
    Become: 6 GETHOT
    Very: 5 BOFFO SOCKO
    Where the ~ go: 3 FAR
**Succession**
    Arranged in: 7 SERIATE
**Successively:** 5 ONEND
    6 INTURN
**Successor:** 4 HEIR
**Succinct:** 5 BRIEF PITHY
    TERSE
**Succor:** 3 AID
**Succotash**
    bean: 4 LIMA
    morsel: 8 LIMABEAN
**Succulent**
    Soothing: 4 ALOE
    They're: 5 CACTI
**Suck**
    in: 4 LURE 6 ENTICE
    up: 6 ABSORB
**Sucker:** 3 SAP 5 PATSY
    7 ENSNARE LIVEONE
    8 LOLLIPOP
    British: 5 LOLLY
    It's for a: 5 STRAW
    Play for a: 3 USE
    Sap: 5 APHID
**Sucking**
    fish: 6 REMORA
**Suckling**
    spot: 4 TEAT
**Sucks**
    It: 6 VACUUM
**Sucres**
    Where to spend: 7 ECUADOR
**Sucrose**
    source: 4 BEET
**Suction**
    device: 6 SIPHON
    9 ASPIRATOR
    prefix: 4 LIPO
**Sud**
    Opposite of: 4 NORD
**Sudan**
    neighbor: 4 CHAD
    river: 4 NILE
    suffix: 3 ESE
**Sudden:** 6 ABRUPT
    attack: 4 RAID
    burst: 4 GUST 5 SPASM
        SPURT

enlightenment: 6 SATORI
fancy: 4 WHIM
fright: 5 PANIC START
impulse: 4 URGE
move: 4 DART
outpouring: 5 SPATE
pain: 6 TWINGE
rush: 5 SPATE SURGE
sensation: 4 STAB
thought: 4 IDEA
transition: 4 LEAP
wind: 4 GUST
**Suddenly**
    Appear: 5 POPUP
    Awaken: 5 ROUST
    Become ~ aware: 6 SNAPTO
    Erupt: 5 FLARE
    Intensify: 7 FLAREUP
    Move: 4 DART
    Open: 3 POP
    Pull: 4 JERK
    Say: 5 BLURT
    Seize: 4 GRAB 6 SNATCH
    Turn: 6 SWERVE
    Veer: 3 ZAG
**"Suddenly"**
    singer: 10 BILLYOCEAN
**Suds:** 4 BEER BREW FOAM
    Bath: 3 ALE
    Get the ~ off: 5 RINSE
    holder: 3 KEG
    Make: 4 BREW
    Pub: 3 ALE
    source: 3 PUB TAP
**Suez ___:** 5 CANAL
**Suez Canal**
    land: 5 EGYPT
    sight: 5 OILER
    terminus: 6 REDSEA
**Suffer:** 3 AIL 7 AGONIZE
    a "brain cramp": 3 ERR
    defeat, slangily: 5 EATIT
    from: 4 HAVE
    humiliation: 7 EATCROW
    in summer: 7 SWELTER
    suffix: 4 ANCE
**Sufferer**
    Allergy: 7 SNEEZER
    Cold ~ sound: 7 SNIFFLE
**Suffering:** 3 ILL WOE
    Intense: 5 AGONY
    partner: 4 PAIN
**"... ___ suffer the slings ...":**
    4 ORTO
**Suffice:** 11 FILLTHEBILL
    More than: 4 SATE
**"Suffice ___ say ...":** 4 ITTO
**Sufficient:** 5 AMPLE 6 ENOUGH
    Barely: 5 SCANT 6 SKIMPY
    Fully: 5 AMPLE
    Marginally: 4 MERE
    ~, informally: 4 ENUF
    ~, poetically: 4 ENOW
**Suffragist**
    ~ Carrie: 4 CATT
**Suffuse:** 5 BATHE IMBUE

Sugar: 3 HON 4 CARB DOLL
Add ~ to: 7 SWEETEN
amt.: 3 TSP
bowl marchers: 4 ANTS
coat: 5 GLAZE ICING
Corn: 8 DEXTROSE
cube: 4 LUMP
in some fruits: 7 GLUCOSE
Like table: 8 GRANULAR
Milk: 7 LACTOSE
pill: 7 PLACEBO
Potatoes high in: 4 YAMS
source: 4 BEET CANE
   5 MAPLE
Sprinkle: 4 SIFT
substitute: 4 DEAR
suffix: 3 OSE
unit: 4 CUBE LUMP
Sugar ___: 3 PIE 4 BEET
   5 MAPLE
**Sugar Bowl**
1993 ~ champs: 4 BAMA
Eight-time ~ champs: 4 BAMA
**Sugarcoat:** 5 GLAZE
**Sugarcoated:** 5 GLACE
**Sugar-free:** 5 NOCAL
**"Sugar Lips"**
trumpeter: 4 HIRT
**Sugarloaf**
1970 ~ hit:
   13 GREENEYEDLADY
**Sugarloaf Mountain**
city: 3 RIO
**Sugary:** 5 SWEET
drink: 3 ADE
Sort of: 8 SWEETISH
suffix: 3 OSE
**Suggest:** 4 MEAN 5 GETAT
   IMPLY INFER OPINE
   POSIT 6 HINTAT
   7 CONNOTE PROPOSE
More than: 4 URGE
**Suggested**
amt.: 3 RDA
**Suggestion:** 4 HINT IDEA
   5 SCENT
**Suggestions:** 5 INPUT
**Suggestive:** 4 RACY 6 RISQUE
look: 4 LEER
**Suicidal:** 8 KAMIKAZE
**"Suicide Blonde"**
rock group: 4 INXS
**Suicide squeeze**
stat: 3 RBI
**Suit:** 4 CASE EXEC 5 BEFIT
accessory: 3 TIE
Big: 3 CEO
Birthday: 4 SKIN
Change to: 5 ADAPT
Dark: 6 SPADES
fabric: 4 WOOL 5 SERGE
   TWEED TWILL
Fail to follow: 6 RENEGE
in a suit: 6 LAWYER
Kind of: 4 ZOOT 5 CIVIL
   LIBEL UNION

Knight: 5 ARMOR
Like a leisure ~, now:
   5 RETRO
Long: 5 ASSET FORTE
Man in a: 5 SANTA
One in a: 3 ACE
One in a black: 5 SPADE
part: 4 VEST 5 PANTS
Press a: 3 WOO
Reason for a: 4 TORT
Revealing: 6 BIKINI
spec: 4 LONG
Strong: 5 ARMOR FORTE
Stylish: 6 ARMANI
Tarot: 4 CUPS
Three-piece ~ part: 4 VEST
top: 3 ACE BRA
___ suit: 4 ZOOT
**Suitability:** 7 APTNESS
**Suitable:** 3 APT
for all audiences: 6 RATEDG
for evening wear: 6 DRESSY
for farming: 6 ARABLE
for service: 4 ONEA
In a ~ manner: 5 FITLY
Not: 5 INAPT UNFIT
place: 5 NICHE
**Suitcase:** 3 BAG 4 GRIP
   6 VALISE
**Suite:** 7 RETINUE
amenity: 6 WETBAR
section: 4 ROOM
spot: 5 HOTEL
**Suited**
Best: 6 APTEST
Not: 5 UNFIT
___ suiter: 4 ZOOT
**Suitor:** 4 BEAU 5 SWAIN
It's pitched by a: 3 WOO
**Suits**
It ~ you: 6 ATTIRE
**"Suits me!":** 7 IMHAPPY
**Suit to ___:** 4 ATEE
**Sukiyaki**
ingredient: 4 TOFU
**Sulawesi**
Former name of: 7 CELEBES
**Sulf-**
suffix: 3 IDE
**Sulk:** 4 MOPE POUT SNIT
**Sulky:** 6 INAPET MOROSE
gait: 4 TROT
horse: 7 TROTTER
leader: 5 PACER
Pull a: 4 TROT
state: 3 PET
**Sullen:** 4 DOUR GLUM
   5 POUTY 6 MOROSE
Look: 4 POUT
**Sullivan**
and others: 3 EDS
had a really big one: 4 SHEW
**Sully:** 3 MAR TAR 4 SOIL
   5 STAIN TAINT
   6 DEFILE SMIRCH
   7 BESMEAR

**Sultan**
Spouses of a: 5 HAREM
**Sultana**
chamber: 3 ODA
**"Sultan after Sultan with his
   Pomp"**
poet: 4 OMAR
**Sultanate**
Arabian: 4 OMAN
Diamond: 4 SWAT
Pacific: 6 BRUNEI
**"Sultan of Sulu, The"**
writer: 3 ADE
**Sultans**
One of three Ottoman:
   5 AHMED
**Sulu**
portrayer: 5 TAKEI
shipmate: 5 UHURA
**Sum:** 5 TOTAL
Considerable:
   11 PRETTYPENNY
In: 7 ALLTOLD
part: 6 ADDEND
thing: 6 ADDEND
Tidy: 4 PILE
Tiny: 4 MITE
total: 6 AMOUNT
total (abbr.): 3 AMT
up: 3 ADD 5 RECAP
**Sumac**
Singer: 3 YMA
**Sumatra**
neighbor: 4 JAVA
simian: 5 ORANG
Three-toed ~ beast: 5 TAPIR
**Summa cum ___:** 5 LAUDE
**Summa ___ laude:** 3 CUM
**Summarize:** 5 RECAP
**Summary:** 5 RECAP 6 APERCU
   PRECIS
holder: 8 NUTSHELL
**Summation:** 5 RECAP
**Summer:** 6 SEASON
A ~ place: 4 CAMP
attire: 6 SHORTS
Avoid ~ school: 4 PASS
clock setting (abbr.): 3 DST
   EDT
cooler: 3 ADE FAN 4 POOL
   6 ICETEA 7 ICEDTEA
coolers: 3 ACS 4 ICES
cottage: 6 RENTAL
D.C. ~ hrs.: 3 EDT
Denver ~ hrs.: 3 MDT
drink: 3 ADE
ermine: 5 STOAT
fare: 7 REPEATS
footwear: 6 SANDAL
   7 SANDALS
getaway: 4 CAMP
hire: 4 TEMP
hrs.: 3 DST EDT MDT
KS ~ hrs.: 3 CDT
L.A. ~ hrs.: 3 PDT
Like ~ drinks: 4 ICED

Middle of: 3 EMS
mo.: 3 AUG JUL
music: 5 DISCO
music festival site: 5 ASPEN
Part of a ~ forecast: 4 HAZE
pest: 4 GNAT 7 SKEETER
quaff: 3 ADE
shade: 3 TAN
shirt: 3 TEE
shoe: 6 SANDAL
Showed during the: 5 RERAN
Sign of: 3 LEO 5 VIRGO
    7 THECRAB
Singer: 5 DONNA
Spring: 3 CPA
Sticky in: 5 HUMID
Sultry part of: 7 DOGDAYS
top: 3 TEE 6 HALTER
wear: 3 TEE
~, in French: 3 ETE
~ TV fare: 5 RERUN
**Summer, Donna**
song: 10 ONTHERADIO
**"Summer and Smoke"**
heroine: 4 ALMA
**Summer Games**
event: 4 EPEE
org.: 3 IOC
**Summerhouse:** 6 GAZEBO
**Summerlike:** 7 ESTIVAL
**"Summer Nights"**
Musical with the song:
    6 GREASE
**"Summer of ___":** 3 SAM
**"Summer of Sam"**
director Spike: 3 LEE
**"Summer Place, A"**
actor Richard: 4 EGAN
actress Sandra: 3 DEE
**Summers**
in the East: 5 ABACI
**"Summertime":** 4 ARIA
**"Summertime, Summertime"**
group: 6 JAMIES
**Summery:** 7 ESTIVAL
**Summing**
up: 5 INALL
**Summit:** 3 TIP TOP 4 ACME
    APEX 6 VERTEX
1945 ~ site: 5 YALTA
At the ~ of: 4 ATOP 5 ONTOP
Gangland ~ figure: 3 DON
offering: 5 VISTA
**Summon:** 4 CALL PAGE
    7 SENDFOR
up: 5 EVOKE 6 MUSTER
with a beeper: 4 PAGE
~, in a way: 4 BEEP
**Summoned:** 4 BADE RANG
    7 SENTFOR
**Summoner:** 5 PAGER
Genie: 7 ALADDIN
**Summons:** 4 BEEP CALL
(abbr.): 3 CIT
Answered a: 4 CAME
Brief: 5 SEEME

Court: 8 SUBPOENA
from the boss: 5 SEEME
Furtive: 4 PSST
Gave a ~ to: 5 CITED
Sibilant: 4 PSST
Teacher's: 5 SEEME
**Sumner, Gordon**
stage name: 5 STING
**Sumo**
land: 5 JAPAN
Like ~ wrestlers: 5 OBESE
**Sumptuous:** 4 POSH RICH
    7 OPULENT
meal: 5 FEAST
**Sumptuously**
Eat: 5 FEAST
**Sumptuousness:** 4 LUXE
**Sumter:** 4 FORT
and others (abbr.): 3 FTS
**Sun:** 3 ORB SOL
Bit of: 3 RAY
block: 5 CLOUD 7 ECLIPSE
    PARASOL
dancer: 4 HOPI 7 ARAPAHO
Egyptian: 4 ATEN
emanations: 4 RAYS
Enjoy the: 4 BASK
follower: 3 MON 6 MOONIE
Get some: 3 TAN
He flew too near to the:
    6 ICARUS
Indian with a ~ dance: 3 UTE
Lie in the: 4 BAKE BASK
Look into the: 6 SQUINT
offering: 4 JAVA
Of the: 5 SOLAR
Once around the: 4 YEAR
orbiter: 6 PLANET
or moon: 3 ORB
Our: 3 SOL
prefix: 5 HELIO
Roman ~ god: 3 SOL
Sag in the: 4 WILT
screen: 5 VISOR
Setting of the: 3 SKY
shade: 3 TAN
Shade from the: 3 TAN
shield: 5 VISOR 6 AWNING
    7 PARASOL
Soak up some: 4 BASK
The ~ is one: 5 GSTAR
Third rock from the:
    5 EARTH
Where the ~ comes up: 4 EAST
~, in French: 6 SOLEIL
~, in Spanish: 3 SOL
**Sun.**
delivery: 3 SER
follower: 3 MON
speech: 3 SER
talk: 3 SER
**Sunbather**
goal: 3 TAN
Riverside: 4 CROC
**Sunbathers**
catch them: 4 RAYS

**Sunbeam:** 3 RAY
**Sunblock:** 6 LOTION
letters: 3 SPF
**Sunbow**
producer: 4 MIST
**Sun Bowl**
city: 6 ELPASO
**Sunburn**
Get a: 3 FRY
Lose a: 4 PEEL
Product once sold as a ~
    remedy: 7 NOXZEMA
soother: 4 ALOE
**Sunburned:** 3 RED
**Sun-cracked:** 4 SERE
**Sundance Kid:** 5 ALIAS
girlfriend: 4 ETTA
partner: 5 BUTCH
**Sunday**
address (abbr.): 3 SER
celebration: 4 MASS
clothes: 6 FINERY
delivery: 6 SERMON
dinner: 5 ROAST 8 POTROAST
drive: 4 SPIN
Put on one's ~ best:
    7 DRESSUP
reading: 6 COMICS
    8 MASSBOOK
seat: 3 PEW
service: 4 MASS
supplement: 6 INSERT
talk topic: 3 SIN
wrap-up: 4 AMEN
**Sundays**
A month of: 3 EON 4 AGES
**Sun Devils**
sch.: 3 ASU
**Sundial**
numeral: 3 III VII XII 4 IIII
    VIII
**Sundown**
~, poetically: 3 EEN
**Sun-dried**
brick: 5 ADOBE
**Sundry:** 7 DIVERSE
**Sunfish:** 5 BREAM
**Sunflower:** 5 OXEYE
or daisy: 5 ASTER
product: 3 OIL
seed: 6 ACHENE
start: 4 SEED
**"Sunflowers"**
setting: 5 ARLES
**Sunflower St.:** 3 KAN
**Sunflower State:** 6 KANSAS
**Sung**
syllable: 3 TRA
**Sunken**
cooking site: 7 FIREPIT
**Sun King**
number: 3 XIV
**Sunni:** 4 SECT
faith: 5 ISLAM
**Sunny:** 5 SOLAR
opening: 5 HELIO

**"Sunny"**
singer Bobby: 4 HEBB
**Sunnyside up**
It may be served: 3 EGG
The sun in: 4 YOLK
**Sunrise:** 4 DAWN
direction: 4 EAST
Sonora: 4 ESTE
to sunset to sunrise: 5 CYCLE
**"Sun ___ Rises, The":** 4 ALSO
**Sunrooms:** 7 SOLARIA
**Suns:** 4 TEAM
Exploding: 5 NOVAE
spot: 7 PHOENIX
**Sunscreen:** 6 AWNING
abbr.: 3 SPF
ingredient: 4 ALOE PABA
**Sunset**
direction: 4 WEST
Like a: 3 RED
On ~ Blvd., perhaps: 4 INLA
shade: 4 ROSE
time, in verse: 3 EEN
**"Sunset Boulevard"**
actress Nancy: 5 OLSON
heroine Desmond: 5 NORMA
**Sunshade:** 7 PARASOL
**Sunshine**
Bit of: 3 RAY
cracker: 4 HIHO
~, in French: 6 SOLEIL
**Sunshine St.:** 3 FLA
**Sunshine State**
city: 5 MIAMI OCALA
**Sun-Times**
rival: 4 TRIB
**Sunup**
direction: 4 EAST
**Sun Valley**
setting: 5 IDAHO
**"Sun Valley Serenade"**
star: 5 HENIE
**Sup:** 3 EAT 4 DINE
**Super:** 4 AONE PHAT 5 GREAT
    ULTRA
apartment: 4 AONE
bargain: 5 STEAL
duper: 5 FRAUD
mark: 5 APLUS
power: 3 ESP
serve: 3 ACE
server: 4 ACER
set: 4 KEYS
star: 4 NOVA
time (abbr.): 3 TUE
**"Super!":** 5 NEATO
**Super ___:** 3 NES
**Superabundance:** 4 GLUT
**Superaggressive**
one: 5 RAMBO
**Superb:** 4 AONE
**Superbly**
Did: 5 SHONE
Serve: 3 ACE
**Super Bowl**
1984 ~ champs: 7 RAIDERS

1999 ~ MVP: 5 ELWAY
2000 ~ champs: 4 RAMS
2002 ~ champs: 4 PATS
First ~ MVP: 5 STARR
Five-time ~ champs:
    8 STEELERS
Four-time ~ winning coach:
    4 NOLL
Namath: 3 III
sight: 5 BLIMP
Six-time ~ coach: 5 SHULA
stat: 3 TDS
Three-time ~ MVP:
    10 JOEMONTANA
~ MVP: *see page 709*
~ MVP Brett: 5 FAVRE
**Super Bowl I**
winner: 8 GREENBAY
**Super Bowl III**
winners: 4 JETS
~ MVP: 6 NAMATH
**Super Bowl VII**
winner: 5 MIAMI
**Super Bowl VIII**
~ MVP Larry: 6 CSONKA
**Super Bowl X**
~ MVP Swann: 4 LYNN
**Super Bowl XIV**
losers: 4 RAMS
winners: 8 STEELERS
**Super Bowl XX**
winning coach: 5 DITKA
**Super Bowl XXI**
~ MVP: 5 SIMMS
**Super Bowl XXIX**
winners: 6 NINERS
**Super Bowl XXXIII**
~ MVP: 5 ELWAY
**Super Bowl XXXIV**
champs: 4 RAMS
**Super Bowl XXXV**
champs: 6 RAVENS
**Superboy**
girlfriend Lana: 4 LANG
girlfriend Lang: 4 LANA
**Supercharger:** 5 TURBO
**Supercilious**
sort: 4 SNOB
**Superciliousness:** 4 AIRS
**Supercomputer**
name: 4 CRAY
**Superdome**
team: 6 SAINTS
**Super-duper:** 4 ACES AONE
    TOPS 5 GREAT NEATO
**Superfecta:** 3 BET
**Superficial:** 5 SLICK
    7 SHALLOW
**Superfluous:** 5 EXTRA
**Superfund**
org.: 3 EPA
**Supergarb:** 4 CAPE
**Supergiant**
in Scorpius: 7 ANTARES
**Supergirl**
alias Linda: 3 LEE

Krypton name of: 4 KARA
**Supergroup**
Comics: 4 XMEN
**Superhero**
accessory: 4 CAPE MASK
Diminutive DC Comics:
    4 ATOM
garment: 4 CAPE
group: 4 XMEN
Marvel Comics: 4 THOR
    7 IRONMAN
**Superimpose:** 7 OVERLAY
**Superimposed:** 4 ATOP
**Superior:** 4 AONE BEST LAKE
    5 ELECT 6 CHOICE
    8 HIGHERUP
Be: 5 EXCEL
Be ~ to: 8 OUTCLASS
city: 6 DULUTH
group: 5 ELITE
inferior: 4 ERIE
skill: 3 ART
to: 4 ATOP OVER 5 ABOVE
**Superlative**
ending: 3 EST
suffix: 3 EST 4 IEST
**Superman**
accessory: 4 CAPE
alias: 4 KENT
birth name: 5 KALEL
co-creator: 6 SIEGEL
Father of: 5 JOREL
insignia: 3 ESS
Like: 6 HEROIC
Mother of: 4 LARA
portrayer: 4 CAIN 5 REEVE
skill: 10 XRAYVISION
symbol: 3 ESS
~, to Reeve or Reeves: 4 ROLE
**"Superman"**
actor Christopher: 5 REEVE
Margot's ~ role: 4 LOIS
star: 5 REEVE
villainess: 4 URSA
villain Luthor: 3 LEX
**"Super, man!":** 3 RAD
**Supermarket**
area: 5 AISLE
chain: 5 AANDP
checkout item: 7 SCANNER
division: 5 AISLE
Do a ~ job: 3 BAG
employee: 6 PRICER
It's bagged at the: 3 TEA
lines: 8 BARCODES
section: 4 DELI 5 AISLE
    DAIRY MEATS
**Supermodel**
One-named: 4 EMME IMAN
    5 FABIO
~ Carol: 3 ALT
~ Heidi: 4 KLUM
**Super Monkey Ball**
producer: 4 SEGA
**Supernatural:** 5 EERIE
    6 OCCULT

**Superpower**
Former: 4 USSR
**Supersecret**
org.: 3 NSA
**Super-secure**
carrier: 4 ELAL
**Super-sharp**
knife: 5 GINSU
**Supersized:** 5 LARGE
**Supersonic**
reading: 4 MACH
**Superstar**
Temporary: 4 NOVA
**Superstation**
Cable: 3 TBS
**Supervise:** 7 OVERSEE
**Supervised:** 7 OVERSAW
**Supervision:** 4 CARE
**Supervisor:** 4 BOSS
8 OVERSEER
Casino: 7 PITBOSS
**Supervisors**
Dorm: 3 RAS
**Superwide:** 3 EEE
**Supped:** 3 ATE
**Supper:** 6 DINNER REPAST
IIas: 5 DINES
in a sty: 4 SLOP 5 SWILL
It's set for: 5 TABLE
Saved on ~, perhaps: 5 ATEIN
scrap: 3 ORT
Serve ~ to: 4 FEED
**Suppertime**
~, for some: 3 SIX
**Supple:** 5 LITHE 7 LISSOME
**Supplement:** 3 ADD 5 ADDIN
ADDON ADDTO
7 ADDONTO
Article: 7 SIDEBAR
Pension: 3 IRA
Sunday: 6 INSERT
Vitamin: 4 IRON
Will: 7 CODICIL
~, with "out": 3 EKE
**Supplements:** 7 ADDENDA
**Supplicate:** 4 PRAY
**Supplied:** 3 FED
**Supply:** 4 FUND 5 EQUIP
6 SELLTO
Hidden: 5 CACHE STASH
In short: 5 SCANT 6 SCARCE
SPARSE
more weapons to: 5 REARM
of arms: 7 ARSENAL
Partner of: 6 DEMAND
the food: 5 CATER SERVE
with weapons: 3 ARM
**Supply-and-demand**
subj.: 4 ECON
**Support:** 3 AID 4 ABET BACK
HELP PROP 5 AEGIS
BRACE CHEER
6 PROPUP UPHOLD
7 BOLSTER 8 UNDERPIN
a foundation: 6 DONATE
a scheme: 4 ABET

at sea: 4 MAST
beam: 4 IBAR
Give ~ to: 4 BACK
group: 4 BRAS 6 ALANON
In ~ of: 3 FOR
Insincere: 10 LIPSERVICE
Kind of: 4 TECH 7 SPOUSAL
Letter-shaped: 5 IBEAM
Limited: 5 RAILS
person: 5 AIDER
piece: 4 SLAT
provider: 3 BRA
Sound of: 3 RAH
system: 3 BRA 7 SHORING
Use for: 6 LEANON RELYON
Vote of: 3 YEA
Without: 5 ALONE
Words of: 5 ICARE
~, with "up": 4 PROP
~, with "with": 4 SIDE
___ support: 4 TECH
**Supporter:** 3 LEG PRO 4 ALLY
CANE 6 PATRON
of arms: 3 NRA
of the arts: 5 DONOR EASEL
**Supporting:** 3 FOR PRO
Not: 4 ANTI
vote: 3 YEA
**Supportive**
of: 3 FOR
**Suppose:** 4 DEEM 5 GUESS
OPINE
**"Suppose ...":** 6 WHATIF
**Suppositions:** 3 IFS
**Suppress:** 5 QUASH QUELL
SITON 6 STIFLE
**Suppressed:** 5 SATON
6 PENTUP
**"___ supra" (as above):** 3 UBI
**Supreme**
being: 3 GOD
leader: 4 ROSS
ruler: 7 EMPEROR
~ Diana: 4 ROSS
~ Greek deity: 4 ZEUS
~ Norse deity: 4 ODIN
~ Supreme: 4 ROSS 5 DIANA
~ Theban deity: 6 AMENRA
**Supreme Court**
1973 ~ case: 3 ROE
count: 4 NINE
David of the: 6 SOUTER
justices, e.g.: 6 ENNEAD
justice since 1975: 7 STEVENS
middle name: 5 BADER
Reagan ~ nominee: 4 BORK
6 SCALIA
Scott of an 1857 ~ case:
4 DRED
**Supremes, The:** 4 TRIO
**___ supuesto (of course, in
Spanish):** 3 POR
**Sur**
Opposite of: 5 NORTE
**Suras**
It has 114: 5 KORAN

**Sure**
Be ~ of: 4 KNOW
competitor: 3 BAN 5 ARRID
Isn't: 6 DOUBTS
Make: 7 SEETOIT
Make ~ of: 3 ICE 5 SEETO
Say for: 4 AVER
shooter: 7 DEADEYE
target: 4 ODOR
thing: 4 FACT 5 CINCH
6 SHOOIN
to succeed: 5 ONICE
Was ~ of: 4 KNEW
**"Sure!":** 3 YEP YES 5 NATCH
6 YOUBET
**Surefire:** 6 NORISK
winner: 6 SHOOIN
**Sure-footed**
animal: 3 ASS
goat: 4 IBEX
**"Surely you ___!":** 4 JEST
**"Surely you jest":** 4 UHUH
**"Sure thing!":** 3 YES 4 OKAY
6 RIGHTO YOUBET
**Sure-to-succeed:** 6 NOLOSE
**"Sure, why not?":** 4 LETS
OKAY
**Surf**
feature: 5 SPRAY
in restaurants: 7 SEAFOOD
Loud, as the: 5 AROAR
Place to: 3 NET
Prepare to: 5 LOGIN
LOGON
Slog through the: 4 WADE
sound: 4 ROAR
Tho "turf" in ~ and turf:
5 STEAK
Wade through the: 4 SLOG
**Surface:** 4 PAVE 5 ARISE
6 EMERGE
Condense on the: 6 ADSORB
Downy: 3 NAP
Flat: 5 PLANE
Near the: 4 RISE
On the: 6 INAREA
**Surfaced:** 5 AROSE
**Surfboard**
coat: 3 WAX
flaw: 4 DING
**Surfeit:** 4 CLOY SATE
7 SATIATE SATIETY
**Surfer:** 4 USER
enabler: 5 MODEM
entry: 3 URL
mart: 4 EBAY
Net: 4 USER
spot: 3 WEB
surface: 4 WAVE
wannabe: 5 HODAD
**Surfing:** 6 ONLINE
equipment: 5 MODEM
mecca: 4 OAHU
site: 3 NET WEB 6 THENET
the Net: 6 ONLINE
wannabe: 5 HODAD

**Surg.**
locales: 3 ORS
specialty: 4 ORTH
**Surge:** 6 ONRUSH
**Surgeon:** 6 DOCTOR
Army ~ Walter: 4 REED
assistant: 5 NURSE
Immediately, to a: 4 STAT
insertion: 5 STENT
Kind of: 4 ORAL
Noted heart: 7 DEBAKEY
Oral ~ deg.: 3 DDS
outfit: 6 SCRUBS
prefix: 5 NEURO
tool: 6 LANCET
Unwelcome word from a:
4 OOPS
**Surgeon General**
Former: 4 KOOP 6 ELDERS
Former ~ C. Everett: 4 KOOP
under Reagan: 4 KOOP
**Surgery**
Before: 5 PREOP
Do eye: 4 LASE
Eye ~ procedure: 5 LASIK
Fat-removing: 4 LIPO
Get ready for: 4 PREP
It may require: 4 TREE
Kind of: 4 ORAL 5 LASER
9 OPENHEART
reminder: 4 SCAR
sites: 3 ORS
souvenir: 4 SCAR
**Surgical**
beam: 5 LASER
dressing: 5 GAUZE
glove material: 5 LATEX
instrument: 6 LANCET
Modern ~ tool: 5 LASER
opening: 5 NEURO
probe: 6 STYLET
tube: 5 STENT
Use a ~ beam: 4 LASE
**Suribachi**
~, et al.: 3 MTS
**Suriname**
neighbor: 6 GUYANA
region: 6 GUIANA
**Surly:** 5 GRUFF 6 ORNERY
sort: 3 CUR 5 CHURL
**Surmise:** 5 INFER
**Surmounting:** 4 ATOP
**Surname**
Common: 5 SMITH
Fictional ~ of 1847: 4 EYRE
French ~ start: 3 DES
Italian noble: 4 ESTE
Marionette: 5 DOODY
Number One Son's: 4 CHAN
O.K. Corral: 4 EARP
Singing brothers': 4 AMES
Steinbeck: 4 JOAD
Tara: 5 OHARA
**Surnames**
Abbr. before multiple:
6 MESSRS

**Surpass:** 3 TOP 5 EXCEL
ONEUP OUTDO
UPEND 7 ECLIPSE
OVERTOP
**Surplus:** 4 GLUT
**Surprise**
attack: 4 RAID
By: 5 ABACK 8 UNAWARES
Cry of: 3 AHA GEE HEY OHO
4 YIPE 5 WOWIE
from a lamp: 5 GENIE
greatly: 4 STUN
Grunt of: 3 HUH
hit: 7 SLEEPER
Show: 4 GASP 5 REACT
Sounds of: 3 EHS OHS
5 GASPS
Sports: 5 UPSET
Student: 4 QUIZ
**Surprised**
Cry of ~ disgust: 3 ACK
Obviously: 5 AGAPE
**"Surprised by Joy"**
autobiographer: 7 CSLEWIS
**Surprisingly:** 6 NOLESS
**Surreal**
suffix: 3 ISM
**Surrealism**
pioneer: 5 ERNST
**Surrealist**
German: 5 ERNST
Mustachioed: 4 DALI
Some ~ works: 5 DALIS
MIROS
Spanish: 4 MIRO
~ Jean: 3 ARP
~ Joan: 4 MIRO
~ Max: 5 ERNST
~ Salvador: 4 DALI
**Surrender:** 4 CEDE
Cry of: 5 IQUIT UNCLE
Formally: 4 CEDE
Word of: 5 UNCLE
**Surreptitious:** 3 SLY
look: 4 PEEK
summons: 4 PSST
**Surrey**
town: 5 EPSOM
**Surrogate**
Child in a 1980s ~ case:
5 BABYM
**Surround:** 4 GIRD 5 BATHE
HEMIN 6 ENFOLD
ENWRAP 7 BESIEGE
ENCLOSE
snugly: 5 EMBED
with an aura: 6 ENHALO
**Surrounded:** 4 GIRT 5 BESET
by: 4 AMID 5 AMONG
6 AMIDST 7 AMONGST
~, poetically: 6 ENGIRT
**Surrounder**
Lagoon: 5 ATOLL
Pupil: 4 IRIS 6 AREOLA
San Marino: 5 ITALY
Shower: 4 TILE

**Surrounding**
Completely: 7 AMBIENT
glow: 4 AURA
light: 4 HALO
**Surroundings:** 6 MILIEU
**Surveil:** 5 SPYON
**Survey:** 4 POLL
choice: 3 YES 4 MALE
5 OTHER 6 FEMALE
no.: 3 PCT
Unscientific: 8 SPOTTEST
~, for short: 5 RECON
**Surveyor**
assistant: 6 RODMAN
calculation: 4 AREA
map: 4 PLAT
support: 6 TRIPOD
unit: 4 ACRE
**Survive:** 4 LAST 5 GETBY
7 OUTLIVE
**Surviving**
trace: 5 RELIC
**Survivor**
concern:
11 ESTATETAXES
Flood: 4 NOAH
Lions' den: 6 DANIEL
Sodom: 3 LOT
**"Survivor"**
group: 5 TRIBE
network: 3 CBS
**Susan**
Actress: 3 DEY 5 ANTON
Author: 6 ISAACS
Emmy role for: 5 ERICA
Essayist: 6 SONTAG
Lazy: 4 TRAY
of soaps: 5 LUCCI
**Susceptible**
Not: 6 IMMUNE
**Sushi**
bar staple: 8 SOYSAUCE
condiment: 6 WASABI
Drink with: 4 SAKE
fish: 3 EEL TAI 4 TUNA
7 ABALONE
ingredient: 4 KELP RICE
item: 3 UNI
land: 5 JAPAN
Like: 3 RAW
Soup with: 4 MISO
supplier: 5 EELER
Tuna belly: 4 TORO
wrap: 7 SEAWEED
**Suspect:** 5 SENSE
dishonesty: 9 SMELLARAT
story: 5 ALIBI
**Suspected**
More than: 4 KNEW
"___ suspected!": 3 ASI
**Suspects**
Like some: 5 USUAL
**Suspend:** 4 HALT HANG
5 PAUSE
**Suspended**
ride: 4 TRAM

**Suspender**
Curtain: 3 ROD
**Suspends**
One who ~ an action:
6 ABATOR
**Suspenseful**
ending: 11 CLIFFHANGER
**Suspicion:** 5 DOUBT
Sneaking: 4 IDEA
**"Suspicion"**
studio: 3 RKO
**Suspicious:** 4 WARY 5 FISHY
LEERY
Be: 9 SMELLARAT
More than ~ of: 4 ONTO
of: 4 ONTO
What ~ folks smell: 4 ARAT
~, as in Hamlet's Denmark:
6 ROTTEN
**Susquehanna**
City on the: 7 ONEONTA
**Sussex**
**Info:** British cue
school exam: 6 ALEVEL
stoolie: 4 NARK
streetcar: 4 TRAM
sword: 5 SABRE
**Sustain:** 4 FEED 5 INCUR
**Sustenance:** 4 FOOD FUEL
7 ALIMENT
**Sutcliffe**
Early Beatle: 3 STU
**Sutherland:** 4 DIVA
1971 ~ title role: 5 KLUTE
1974 ~ film: 4 SPYS
Actor: 6 DONALD KIEFER
oong: 4 ARIA
**"___ Sutra":** 4 KAMA
**Sutton**
Golfer: 3 HAL
**SUV:** 3 UTE
Chevy: 5 TAHOE 6 BLAZER
**Suva**
land: 4 FIJI
**Suvari**
Actress: 4 MENA
**Suzanne**
Actress: 6 SOMERS
Singer: 4 VEGA
**"Suzanne"**
songwriter Leonard:
5 COHEN
**Svelte:** 4 SLIM THIN TRIM
**Sven**
Cousin of: 4 LARS
**Svgs.**
fund: 3 IRA
**Swab:** 3 MOP TAR 5 MATEY
6 WETMOP
again: 5 REMOP
Cotton: 4 QTIP
**Swabber:** 3 MOP
org.: 3 USN
**Swabbie:** 3 GOB TAR
**Swaddle:** 4 WRAP
**Swag:** 4 LOOT 5 BOOTY

**Swagger:** 4 BRAG 5 STRUT
SWASH 7 BRAVADO
**Swahili:** 5 BANTU
for "boss": 5 BWANA
for "freedom": 5 UHURA
**Swain:** 4 BEAU 5 ROMEO
WOOER 6 SUITOR
**SWAK**
Part of: 4 KISS 6 SEALED
**Swallow:** 4 DOWN GULP SWIG
6 ACCEPT INGEST
flat: 4 NEST
It may be hard to: 4 PILL
Prepare to: 4 CHEW
Sea: 4 TERN
up: 6 ENGULF
**Swallowed:** 3 ATE
one's pride: 7 ATEDIRT
**Swallower**
Jonah's: 5 WHALE
**Swallow-tailed**
bird: 4 KITE
**Swami:** 4 GURU SAGE SEER
5 HINDU
**Swamp:** 3 BOG FEN 4 MIRE
5 DROWN MARSH
6 ENGULF MORASS
critter: 4 CROC 5 GATOR
goo: 4 OOZE
plant: 4 REED 5 SEDGE
Stalk in the: 4 REED
thing: 4 CROC PEAT REED
5 GATOR
**Swampland**
swindle: 5 BUNCO
**Swamplike:** 4 MIRY
**"Swamp Thing"**
director Craven: 3 WES
**Swampy**
ground: 3 BOG 4 MIRE
stretch: 5 SWALE
**Swan**
City on the: 5 PERTH
lady: 4 LEDA
Male: 3 COB
song: 3 END
Star in the ~ constellation:
5 DENEB
Young: 6 CYGNET
**Swank:** 4 CHIC 5 RITZY
6 CLASSY 7 ELEGANT
Husband of: 4 LOWE
**Swanky:** 4 POSH
**"Swan Lake"**
heroine: 6 ODETTE
role: 5 ODILE
skirt: 4 TUTU
swan: 5 ODILE
**Swann**
of football: 4 LYNN
**"Swann's Way"**
author: 6 PROUST
**Swansea**
locale: 5 WALES
**Swanson**
film: 15 SUNSETBOULEVARD

**Swap:** 5 TRADE 6 BARTER
**Swarm:** 3 MOB 4 HOST TEEM
5 HORDE
**Swarming:** 5 ALIVE
**Swarms**
Like some: 5 APIAN
**Swarthy:** 4 DARK
**Swashbuckler**
Flynn: 5 ERROL
weapon: 5 SABER SWORD
**Swath**
producer: 6 SCYTHE
**SWAT team**
member: 6 SNIPER
**Sway:** 4 REEL ROLL TILT
6 CAREEN TOTTER
7 IMPRESS
Hold: 4 RULE 5 REIGN
**Swayback**
woe: 3 SAG
**Swayze**
1987 ~ film:
12 DIRTYDANCING
1990 ~ film: 5 GHOST
**Swe.**
neighbor: 3 NOR
**Swear:** 4 AVER AVOW
6 ATTEST
by, with "on": 4 RELY
word: 4 OATH
words: 3 IDO
**Swearing-in:** 4 OATH
words: 3 IDO 4 OATH
**Swear ___ stack of Bibles:**
3 ONA
**Sweat**
Bit of: 4 BEAD
bullets: 4 FRET STEW
Don't ~ it: 8 RESTEASY
drop: 4 BEAD
it: 4 FRET
It might make you: 3 SPA
it out: 6 ENDURE
No: 4 EASY
Place to ~ it out: 5 SAUNA
shop: 3 SPA
spot: 4 PORE 5 SAUNA
**Sweatband**
spot: 5 WRIST
**Sweater:** 3 TOP 4 KNIT PORE
eater: 4 MOTH
Hole in a: 4 PORE
Kind of: 5 VNECK 6 PULLON
RAGLAN 8 PULLOVER
10 TURTLENECK
letter: 3 ETA RHO VEE 4 ZETA
5 THETA
Make a: 4 KNIT
material: 6 ANGORA MOHAIR
problem: 4 SNAG
size: 5 LARGE
style: 5 VNECK
synthetic: 5 ORLON
Work up a: 4 KNIT
**"Sweater Girl"**
~ Turner: 4 LANA

**Sweaters**
Pair of ~ worn together:
7 TWINSET
**Sweatshirt**
part: 4 HOOD
**Swed.**
neighbor: 3 NOR 4 NORW
**Sweden**
Airline to: 3 SAS
capital: 3 ESS
Coin of: 5 KRONA
Furniture store from: 4 IKEA
Import from: 4 SAAB
**Swedish**
auto: 4 SAAB
chain: 4 IKEA
city: 7 UPPSALA
diva Jenny: 4 LIND
flier: 3 SAS
Flower named for a ~ botanist:
6 DAHLIA
Former ~ P.M. Palme:
4 OLOF
import: 4 SAAB 5 VOLVO
money: 5 KRONA
quartet: 4 ABBA
**"Swedish Nightingale, The":**
4 LIND
**"Sweeney ___":** 4 TODD
**Sweeney, Julia**
film: 6 ITSPAT
**"Sweeney Todd"**
actor Cariou: 3 LEN
prop: 5 RAZOR
**Sweep:** 3 OAR 5 CLEAN
GAMUT 7 EXPANSE
Like a chimney: 5 SOOTY
target: 4 SOOT
under the rug: 4 HIDE
**Sweeper:** 5 BROOM
accessory: 7 DUSTPAN
**Sweeping:** 3 BIG 4 EPIC VAST
5 BROAD 7 OVERALL
cut: 5 SLASH
shot: 3 PAN
story: 4 EPIC
**Sweepings**
Salon: 4 HAIR
**Sweepstakes**
hopeful: 7 ENTRANT
Mailed, as a ~ entry:
6 SENTIN
**Sweet:** 4 DEAR KIND
Be ~ on: 5 ADORE
cherry: 4 BING
drink: 4 COLA MEAD 5 JULEP
6 NECTAR
ending: 3 OSE
flower: 5 AFTON
It may be: 5 TOOTH
Least: 6 DRIEST
liqueur: 5 CREME
8 ANISETTE
Not: 3 DRY SEC
nothing: 10 ENDEARMENT
potato: 3 YAM 7 OCARINA

prefix: 4 SEMI
sandwich: 4 OREO
Short and: 5 TERSE
spread: 5 ICING
stuff: 5 SUGAR 6 NECTAR
7 TREACLE
suffix: 3 OSE
They can be: 4 PEAS
treat: 3 ICE 4 FLAN 5 FUDGE
7 DESSERT
Whisper ~ nothings: 3 COO
Whisper ~ nothings to: 3 WOO
wine: 4 PORT 6 MALAGA
7 MARSALA 8 MUSCATEL
**"Sweet"**
girl of song: 7 ADELINE
herb: 5 BASIL
stream of poetry: 5 AFTON
**"Sweet!":** 3 RAD 5 NEATO
**Sweet 16**
org.: 4 NCAA
**"Sweet and Lowdown"**
actress Thurman: 3 UMA
**"Sweet as apple cider"**
girl: 3 IDA
**Sweetbrier:** 8 WILDROSE
**"Sweet Dreams"**
Singer profiled in: 5 CLINE
**Sweeten:** 5 SUGAR
the pot: 5 RAISE
**Sweetener**
brand: 5 EQUAL
Request: 6 PLEASE
Soil: 4 LIME
**"Sweetest Taboo, The"**
singer: 4 SADE
**Sweetheart:** 4 BABY BEAU
DEAR LASS LOVE
5 DEARY FLAME HONEY
6 DEARIE 8 TRUELOVE
**"Sweetheart of Sigma ___,
The":** 3 CHI
**"Sweet Home ___":**
7 ALABAMA
**"Sweet Home Alabama"**
actress Witherspoon: 5 REESE
**Sweetie:** 3 HON 4 DEAR DOLL
LAMB 5 ANGEL FLAME
SUGAR TOOTS
8 SUGARPIE
pie: 3 HON 4 DEAR DOLL
LOVE 5 CUTEY CUTIE
HONEY TOOTS
**"Sweet Liberty"**
director/star: 4 ALDA
**"Sweet Love"**
singer Anita: 5 BAKER
**Sweetly**
(Italian): 5 DOLCE
**Sweetness:** 5 SAPOR
Overwhelm with: 4 CLOY
**Sweet 'N Low**
rival: 5 EQUAL
**Sweet-sounding:** 6 DULCET
**Sweet-talk:** 4 COAX
**Sweetums:** 3 HON 5 TOOTS

**Swell:** 3 FOP 4 NICE RISE
WAVE 5 BLOAT NEATO
SUPER 7 BREAKER
ENLARGE
Cause to: 5 BLOAT
place: 3 SEA 5 OCEAN
**"Swell!":** 5 NEATO
**Swelled**
head: 3 EGO
**Swellhead:** 7 EGOTIST
indulgence: 7 EGOTRIP
problem: 3 EGO
**Swelling**
Eyelid: 4 STYE
Plant: 5 EDEMA
reducer: 3 ICE 6 ICEBAG
Where ~ occurs: 3 SEA
**Swelter:** 3 FRY 4 BOIL 5 BROIL
ROAST
**Sweltering:** 3 HOT
**Swenson**
Actress: 4 INGA
**Swerve:** 4 VEER
off course: 3 YAW
**Swift:** 4 FAST 5 RAPID
6 SPEEDY 8 SATIRIST
bird: 3 EMU
boat: 4 PROA
forte: 5 IRONY
horse: 4 ARAB
9 HOUYHNHNM
Not too: 5 DENSE 7 SLOWISH
piece: 6 SATIRE
vehicle: 6 SATIRE
watercraft: 9 HYDROFOIL
work: 5 ESSAY 6 SATIRE
**Swift, Jonathan:** 8 SATIRIST
1729 ~ pamphlet:
15 AMODESTPROPOSAL
piece: 6 SATIRE
**Swiftly:** 5 APACE
Move: 4 DART DASH TEAR
**Swiftness:** 5 HASTE
**Swifty**
Hollywood agent: 5 LAZAR
**Swig**
Big: 4 BELT CHUG
**Swill:** 4 SLOP
**Swim**
alternative: 4 SINK
competition: 4 MEET
Quick: 3 DIP
Sink or: 4 VERB
**Swimmer**
1920s Olympics ~: 6 EDERLE
Aquarium: 5 TETRA
assignment: 4 LANE
Channel ~ Gertrude:
6 EDERLE
concern: 5 CRAMP
count: 3 LAP
Electric: 3 EEL
Furry: 5 OTTER
Lab: 5 AMEBA
Long-jawed: 3 GAR
Long-nosed: 4 PIKE

Park: 4 SWAN
Playful: 5 OTTER
Pond: 4 TEAL
regimen: 4 LAPS
Slippery: 3 EEL
~ Janet: 5 EVANS
~ Kristin: 4 OTTO
~ Mark: 5 SPITZ
~ Matt: 6 BIONDI
~ Thorpe: 3 IAN
**Swimmers**
Leggy: 6 OCTOPI
One-celled: 7 AMOEBAE
**Swimming:** 6 NATANT
competition: 4 MEET
Like some ~ strokes:
7 OVERARM
site: 4 HOLE LAKE POND
POOL
**Swimming pool**
shade: 4 AQUA
site: 4 YMCA 5 MOTEL
sound: 6 SPLASH
tester: 3 TOE
**Swimsuit**
brand: 6 SPEEDO
part: 3 BRA
Revealing: 5 THONG
**Swimwear**
Big name in: 6 SPEEDO
Minimal: 5 THONG
**Swindle:** 3 CON GYP RIP ROB
4 BILK BURN CLIP DOIN
HOSE ROOK SCAM
5 BUNKO CHEAT COZEN
GOUGE GRIFT MULCT
6 CHISEL CONJOB
EUCHRE FLEECE
RIPOFF 7 CONGAME
9 SHELLGAME
**Swindled:** 5 STUNG
**Swindler:** 5 CHEAT CROOK
SHARP THIEF
6 CONMAN
~, slangily: 5 GANEF
**Swine:** 4 BOAR
food: 4 SLOP
She turned men into: 5 CIRCE
spot: 3 STY
**Swing:** 3 BAT
and others: 4 ERAS
around: 4 SLUE
a sickle: 4 REAP
Couples may ~ here: 3 TEE
First name in: 5 ARTIE
in a ring: 3 BOX
Kind of: 4 MOOD
Makeshift: 4 TIRE
music: 4 JIVE
One way to: 3 FRO
One who knows how to:
7 GOLFPRO
Ready to: 5 ATBAT
site: 3 TEE
wildly: 5 FLAIL
**Swinger:** 6 HEPCAT

club: 3 BAT
joint: 5 HINGE
Jungle: 3 APE
Sumatra: 5 ORANG
**Swingers**
org.: 3 PGA
**Swinging:** 3 HIP
Word after: 4 DOOR
**"Swing Time"**
star: 7 ASTAIRE
**Swipe:** 3 COP 4 GLOM 5 STEAL
**Swiped:** 4 TOOK 5 STOLE
TAKEN 6 STOLEN
**Swirl:** 4 EDDY
**Swiss**
A ~ army knife has many:
4 USES
abstractionist Paul: 4 KLEE
canton: 3 URI 4 BERN
6 GENEVA
capital: 4 BERN 5 BERNE
FRANC
chard: 4 BEET
city: 5 BASEL BERNE
cottage: 6 CHALET
hero: 4 TELL
It has ~ banks: 4 AARE
mathematician: 5 EULER
miss: 5 HEIDI
Of ~ peaks: 6 ALPINE
painter Paul: 4 KLEE
peak: 3 ALP
river: 3 AAR 4 AARE
skyline: 3 ALP
state: 6 CANTON
stream: 3 AAR
tourist center: 7 LUCERNE
vendor: 4 DELI
watch: 5 OMEGA
**Swiss cheese:** 7 GRUYERE
feature: 4 HOLE
hole: 3 EYE
Like: 5 HOLEY
**"Swiss Family Robinson"**
author Johann: 4 WYSS
**Swit**
Actress: 7 LORETTA
costar: 4 ALDA
**Switch:** 4 SWAP 9 TRANSPOSE
Bait and: 6 TACTIC
ending: 4 EROO
handles: 6 RENAME
Kind of: 5 ONOFF 6 DIMMER
material: 5 BIRCH
partner: 4 BAIT
position: 3 OFF
positions: 3 ONS 4 OFFS
Radio: 4 AMFM
Railroad: 5 SHUNT
suffix: 4 EROO
words: 5 ONOFF
**Switchback**
curve: 3 ESS
**Switchblade:** 4 SHIV
**Switz.**
neighbor: 3 AUS

Where ~ is: 3 EUR
**Switzerland**
canton: 3 URI
Capital of: 3 ESS 4 BERN
It has banks in: 4 AARE
loc.: 3 EUR
river: 4 AARE
**Swiveling**
joint: 3 HIP
**Swizzle:** 4 STIR
stick: 7 STIRRER
Use a ~ stick: 4 STIR
**Swoboda**
of baseball: 3 RON
**Swoon:** 5 FAINT
cause: 4 IDOL
**Swoop:** 6 POUNCE
**Swoopes**
gp.: 4 WNBA
**Swoosh**
company: 4 NIKE
Nike's: 4 LOGO
**Swoosie**
Tony winner: 5 KURTZ
**Sword**
beater: 3 PEN
Blunted: 4 EPEE
Cavalry: 5 SABER
Curved: 5 SABER 8 SCIMITAR
Fencing: 4 EPEE 5 SABER
6 RAPIER
fight: 4 DUEL
handle: 4 HAFT HILT
of Damocles: 5 PERIL
Olympic: 4 EPEE
Put a ~ away: 7 SHEATHE
Slender: 6 RAPIER
with a guarded tip: 4 EPEE
**Swordfight**
reminder: 4 SCAR
**Swordplay**
Japanese: 5 KENDO
**Swords**
Beat ~ into plowshares:
5 UNARM
Crossing: 6 ATWAR
Like: 5 EDGED
**Sword-shaped**
Plant with ~ leaves: 4 IXIA
5 YUCCA 8 GLADIOLA
**Swordsman:** 5 BLADE
Dumas: 5 ATHOS
Masked: 5 ZORRO
ploy: 5 LUNGE
**Swore:** 6 CUSSED
by: 8 RELIEDON
**Sworn:** 6 AVOWED
statement: 3 VOW 4 OATH
They may be: 7 ENEMIES
**Sycophant:** 5 TOADY 6 LACKEY
YESMAN
response: 3 YES
**Sydney**
Astrologer: 5 OMARR
band: 4 ACDC
salutation: 4 GDAY

st.: 3 NSW
**Sylphlike:** 6 SVELTE
**Sylvan:** 5 WOODY
deity: 5 SATYR
**Sylvania**
unit: 4 WATT
**Sylvester**
costar: 5 TALIA
problem letters: 5 ESSES
Speak like: 4 LISP
~, to Tweety: 3 TAT
**Sylvia**
Singer: 4 SYMS
**Sylvius**
Aqueduct of: 4 ITER
**Symbol:** 4 ICON 5 TOKEN
　　6 EMBLEM
of Americanism:
　　8 APPLEPIE
of authority: 6 MANTLE
of craziness: 4 LOON
of easiness: 3 ABC PIE
of elusiveness: 3 EEL
of freshness: 5 DAISY
of goodness: 4 HALO
of grace: 4 SWAN
of happiness: 4 CLAM
of holiness: 4 HALO
of industry: 3 ANT
of life: 4 ANKH
of love: 7 REDROSE
of meanness:
　　11 JUNKYARDDOG
of might: 3 OAK
of redness: 4 BEET
of resistance: 5 OMEGA
of royalty: 3 ORB
of slowness: 5 SNAIL
of stability: 8 EVENKEEL
of strength: 3 OAK 5 STEEL
of stubbornness: 4 MULE
**Symmetry**
Kind of: 5 AXIAL 6 RADIAL
**Sympathetic:** 4 KIND 5 HUMAN
　　6 CARING
attention: 3 EAR
Make: 6 ENDEAR
sounds: 3 AWS
**Sympathy**
Feel ~ (for): 4 ACHE

partner: 3 TEA
Words of: 5 ICARE
**Symphonic**
poem creator: 5 LISZT
**"Symphonie espagnole"**
composer Édouard: 4 LALO
**"Symphonie fantastique"**
composer: 7 BERLIOZ
**Symphony:** 4 OPUS
member: 4 OBOE
nickname: 6 EROICA
performers (abbr.): 4 ORCH
**"Symphony ___" (Bizet):** 3 INC
**"Symphony of a Thousand"**
composer: 6 MAHLER
**"Symposium"**
author: 5 PLATO
**Symptom:** 4 SIGN
suffix: 4 ATIC
**Synagogue:** 4 SHUL
chest: 3 ARK
leader: 5 RABBI
scroll: 4 TORA 5 TORAH
singer: 6 CANTOR
**Sync**
Get in ~ again: 6 RETUNE
In: 5 ASONE
**Synchronous:** 7 INPHASE
**Syncopated**
music: 3 RAG
**Syndicate:** 3 MOB 6 CARTEL
boss: 4 CAPO
head: 3 DON
**Syndicated**
astrologer: 5 OMARR
deejay: 4 IMUS
**Synfuel**
source: 5 SHALE
**Syngman**
of Korea: 4 RHEE
**Synonym**
man: 5 ROGET
**Synonymist**
~ Peter: 5 ROGET
**Syntax**
Analyze the ~ of: 5 PARSE
**Synthesizer**
inventor: 4 MOOG
Speech: 7 VOCODER
**___ synthesizer:** 4 MOOG

**Synthetic:** 4 FAUX MADE
　　6 ERSATZ 7 MANMADE
　　8 TESTTUBE
fabric: 5 ORLON
fiber: 5 ARNEL NYLON
　　ORLON RAYON
　　7 ACETATE
rubber component: 7 STYRENE
Silky: 5 RAYON
**Syr.**
and Eg., once: 3 UAR
neighbor: 3 ISR LEB
**Syracuse**
athletes: 9 ORANGEMEN
City near: 5 UTICA
College in: 7 LEMOYNE
Lake near: 6 ONEIDA
**Syria**
and Egypt, once: 3 UAR
Bashar of: 5 ASSAD
Capital of ancient: 7 ANTIOCH
Great Mosque site of:
　　6 ALEPPO
**Syrian:** 4 ARAB
city: 4 HAMA 6 ALEPPO
Early: 7 HITTITE
leader: 5 ASSAD
**Syringe:** 4 HYPO
amt.: 3 CCS
**Syrup**
brand: 4 KARO
flavor: 5 MAPLE
Item with: 5 CREPE
Medicinal: 6 IPECAC
source: 3 SAP 4 CORN
　　5 MAPLE
**System:** 6 METHOD
Belief: 3 ISM
Exercise: 4 YOGA 5 TAEBO
Kind of: 5 CASTE MERIT
　　SOLAR
Learning: 4 ROTE
Operating: 4 UNIX 5 MSDOS
Power: 4 GRID
prefix: 3 ECO
Sound: 4 HIFI 6 STEREO
Sub: 5 SONAR
Support: 3 BRA 7 SHORING
Value: 5 ETHIC
**Systematize:** 4 SORT 6 CODIFY

# Tt
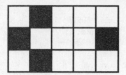

**T:** 5 SHIRT
  Greek: 3 TAU
  Morse: 4 DASH
  or F: 3 ANS
**T. ___:** 3 REX
**___ T:** 3 TOA
**Tab:** 4 BILL COLA 8 DIETCOLA
    DIETSODA
  Accumulate a: 5 RUNUP
  competitor: 8 DIETCOKE
  Have a: 3 OWE
  Opening for a: 4 SLOT
  Pick up the: 3 PAY 5 TREAT
  Run a: 3 OWE
  Settle a: 5 PAYUP
**Tabasco**
  **Info:** Spanish cue
  quality: 4 ZEST
**Tabby:** 3 CAT
  cry: 4 MEOW
  mate: 3 TOM
  tempter: 6 CATNIP
  treater: 3 VET
  Word to a: 4 SCAT
**Table:** 5 DEFER
  Bar on the: 4 OLEO
  Buffet ~ item: 3 URN
      6 STERNO
  Chip on the: 4 ANTE
  Clear the: 3 BUS
  Coffee ~ item: 7 ARTBOOK
  Dinner: 4 MENU
  extender: 4 LEAF
  Find another ~ for: 6 RESEAT
  Have a ~ for one:
      8 EATALONE
  insert: 4 LEAF
  It's found in a: 7 ELEMENT
  It's shaken at the: 4 SALT
  Like ~ sugar: 8 GRANULAR
  linen: 6 NAPERY
  linen fabric: 6 DAMASK
  No longer at the: 5 EATEN
  Occupy a: 5 SITAT
  part: 3 LEG
  Point at the: 4 TINE
  protector: 6 TRIVET
      8 PLACEMAT
  salt: 4 NACL 8 CHLORIDE
  scrap: 3 ORT
  spread: 4 OLEO
  staple: 4 SALT
  support: 3 LEG
  tennis need: 6 PADDLE
  Three-legged ornamental:
      6 TEAPOY
  Under the: 3 LIT
  wine: 4 ROSE

**Tablecloth**
  material: 4 LACE 5 LINEN
**Tablecloths**
  and such: 6 NAPERY
**Table d'___:** 4 HOTE
**Table-hop:** 3 MIX
**Tableland:** 4 MESA 7 PLATEAU
**Tables**
  Clear: 3 BUS
  How times ~ are learned:
      6 BYROTE
  Like some: 6 NESTED
  Workplaces with: 3 ORS
**Tablet:** 3 PAD 4 DOSE PILL
  holder: 3 ARK
  Writing: 3 PAD
**Tabletop**
  farm animals: 4 ANTS
**Tablets:** 4 MEDS
  He took two: 5 MOSES
  Holder of two: 3 ARK
  Two: 4 DOSE
**Tabloid:** 3 RAG
  abductor: 5 ALIEN
  couple: 4 ITEM
  fliers: 3 ETS
  fodder: 4 DIRT
  Like ~ stories: 5 LURID
  monster: 6 NESSIE
  staffer: 6 EDITOR
  subject: 3 UFO
  talk: 4 DIRT
  target: 5 CELEB
  tidbit: 4 ITEM
  topic: 3 UFO
  twosome: 4 ITEM
**Taboo:** 3 BAN 4 NONO
      8 VERBOTEN
**Taboos:** 5 DONTS
**Tabouli**
  bread: 4 PITA
**Tabriz**
  country: 4 IRAN
  resident: 5 IRANI
**Tabula ___:** 4 RASA
**"___ Tac Dough":** 3 TIC
**Tach**
  reading: 3 RPM 4 REVS
**Tachometer**
  abbr.: 3 RPM
**Tacit:** 6 UNSAID
      8 UNSPOKEN
  approval: 3 NOD
**Taciturn:** 11 TIGHTLIPPED
**Tack**
  Like a: 5 SHARP
  Sharp as a: 4 KEEN 5 ACUTE
      SMART 6 ASTUTE

**Tacked**
  on: 5 ADDED
**Tackle:** 3 TRY 4 GEAR
      7 ATTEMPT
  box item: 4 LURE 5 SNELL
      6 SCALER
  Get up after a: 6 UNPILE
  hard: 4 NAIL
  teammate: 3 END
**Tacks**
  Spots for: 4 TIES
**Tacky:** 5 SHARP
**Taco**
  alternative: 7 TOSTADA
  topper: 5 SALSA
**Taconite:** 7 IRONORE
**Tact**
  suffix: 3 ILE
**Tactful**
  one: 8 DIPLOMAT
**Tactfully**
  Remove: 7 EASEOUT
**Tactic:** 4 PLOY RUSE
  Basketball: 5 PRESS
      9 FASTBREAK
  Campaign: 5 SMEAR
  Deceptive: 4 RUSE
  Economic warfare:
      7 EMBARGO
  Evasive: 6 ENDRUN
  Ring: 3 JAB
  Tennis: 3 LOB
  Wheedler: 5 GUILE
**Tactical**
  station: 3 OPS
**Tactile**
  Like ~ hair: 7 SENSORY
**Tactless:** 5 BLUNT
      10 INDELICATE
**Tad:** 3 KID TOT 4 IOTA
      MITE
**"Ta-da!":** 5 THERE VOILA
**Tadpole**
  home: 4 POND
**Tadzhik**
  ~, once (abbr.): 3 SSR
**TAE**
  Part of: 4 ALVA
**Tae ___ do:** 4 KWON
**___ Tafari (Haile Selassie):**
      3 RAS
**Taffy**
  Like: 5 CHEWY
**Taft**
  alma mater: 4 YALE
  birth state: 4 OHIO
**Tag:** 5 LABEL
  abbr.: 3 LGE

along: 4 COME
disclaimer: 4 ASIS
Dog ~ datum: 5 OWNER
Gift ~ word: 4 FROM
info: 4 SIZE
line: 4 ASIS 5 NOTIT PRICE
Price: 4 COST
pursuers: 3 ITS
Red ~ event: 4 SALE
Sale: 4 ASIS
Sale ~ (abbr.): 3 IRR
Second sequel: 3 III
___ tag: 5 PHONE
"___ Tag!": 5 GUTEN
**Tagalong**
 cry: 5 METOO
**Tagging**
 along: 5 INTOW
**Tags:** 3 IDS
 Switch: 6 RENAME
**Tagus**
 City on the: 6 LISBON
**Tahini**
 base: 6 SESAME
**Tahiti:** 3 ILE
 Island near: 8 BORABORA
**Tahitian**
 Language akin to: 5 MAORI
 port: 7 PAPEETE
**Tahoe:** 4 LAKE
 City near: 4 RENO
 topper: 6 SKICAP
 ___ tai: 3 MAI
**Tail:** 3 DOG 5 TRAIL
 6 SHADOW
 **Info:** Suffix cue
 Buck: 4 AROO
 Chick: 4 ADEE
 Dino: 4 SAUR
 Dog with a curled: 3 PUG
 5 AKITA
 end: 4 REAR
 Gator: 3 ADE
 Hippo: 5 DROME
 Human: 3 OID
 Meteor: 3 ITE
 Move one's: 3 WAG
 off: 5 ABATE
 Ox: 3 IDE
 Pig: 3 LET
 prefix: 3 URO
 Rabbit: 4 SCUT
 Rat: 4 ATAT
 Rocket: 3 EER
 Serpent: 3 INE
 Toward the: 3 AFT
 Toy with a: 4 KITE
 Turn: 3 RUN 4 FLEE
**Tailbone:** 6 COCCYX
**Tailless**
 amphibian: 4 TOAD
 cat: 4 MANX
 primate: 3 APE
 rodent: 4 PACA
 simian: 3 APE
**Taillike:** 6 CAUDAL

**Tailor:** 3 SEW 5 ADAPT
 6 MENDER SEAMER
 7 ALTERER
 concern: 3 FIT HEM
 Do a ~ job: 3 HEM SEW
 line: 4 SEAM
 measurement: 6 INSEAM
 of yore: 6 SARTOR
 tool: 6 SHEARS
 11 TAPEMEASURE
**Tails**
 It goes with: 6 TOPHAT
**Tailward:** 3 AFT
**Taina**
 Dancer: 3 ELG
**Taint:** 3 MAR 7 CORRUPT
**Tainted**
 Least: 6 PUREST
**Taipei**
 Where ~ is: 6 TAIWAN
**Taiwan**
 capital: 6 TAIPEI
 is in it: 8 CHINASEA
 ~, formerly: 7 FORMOSA
**Taiwanese:** 5 ASIAN
**Taj ___ :** 5 MAHAL
**Taj Mahal**
 city: 4 AGRA
 site: 4 AGRA
**Take:** 3 NAB 4 GATE GRAB
 5 CHEAT
 after: 7 EMULATE
 apart: 4 UNDO
 as a given: 5 POSIT
 as one's own: 5 ADOPT
 away: 4 LESS 6 DEDUCT
 REMOVE 7 DETRACT
 back: 4 UNDO 5 UNSAY
 6 RECANT
 by force: 5 SEIZE USURP
 WREST
 Can't: 5 ABHOR
 care of: 4 TEND 5 SEETO
 6 HANDLE TENDTO
 8 SEEAFTER
 cover: 4 HIDE
 credit: 3 OWE
 Did a double: 6 RESHOT
 Didn't ~ part, with "out":
 5 OPTED
 Do a double: 5 REACT
 effect: 5 INURE SETIN
 exception: 5 DEMUR
 five: 4 REST 5 RELAX
 Get ready to ~ off: 4 TAXI
 Give and: 4 SWAP 5 TRADE
 Give or: 4 ORSO 5 ABOUT
 home: 3 NET
 in: 3 EAT SEE 4 EARN
 5 ADOPT ALTER
 It doesn't ~ much: 4 TREY
 it easy: 4 LOLL REST
 most of: 3 HOG
 Not ~ off: 4 STAY
 off: 3 LAM 4 SHED SOAR
 6 DEPART

 on: 4 HIRE 5 ADOPT
 out: 4 DATE DELE
 over: 5 USURP
 Put in or ~ out: 4 EDIT
 Some people can't ~ them:
 5 HINTS
 steps: 3 ACT 4 PACE
 turns: 6 ROTATE
 ~, as advice: 5 ACTON
**Take-___ :** 5 ALONG
**"Take ___"**
 (host's request): 5 ASEAT
 (Madonna song): 4 ABOW
**"Take ___!":** 4 THAT
**"Take a Chance on Me"**
 group: 4 ABBA
**Take a crack ___ :** 4 ATIT
**"Take a hike!":** 5 SCRAM
**"Take a load off!":** 3 SIT
**"... ___ take arms against ...":**
 4 ORTO
**Take-away**
 game: 3 NIM
**Takeback**
 Bank: 4 REPO
**"Take care of that!":** 7 SEETOIT
**Take down ___ :** 4 APEG
**Take ___ down memory lane:**
 5 ATRIP
**Take ___ for the worse:**
 5 ATURN
**"Take ___ from me":** 4 ATIP
**Take-home:** 3 NET 6 NETPAY
**Takei, George**
 role: 4 SULU
**"Take it easy!":** 5 RELAX
 6 NOWNOW
**"Take it or leave it":** 4 ASIS
**"Take ___ leave it!":** 4 ITOR
**"Take my wife, please!"**
 speaker Youngman: 5 HENNY
**Taken:** 3 HAD 5 INUSE
 alone: 5 PERSE
 by force, once: 4 REFT
 How some are: 5 ABACK
 in: 3 HAD 4 SEEN
 Not ~ in by: 4 ONTO
 One ~ in: 7 ADOPTEE
**Taken ___ :** 5 ABACK
**Takeoff:** 5 SPOOF 6 PARODY
 SATIRE
 approx.: 3 ETD
 Clear for: 5 DEICE
 Do a ~ on: 3 APE
 Prepare for: 4 TAXI
**"Take one!":** 4 HERE
**Takeout**
 Chinese ~ freebie: 4 RICE
 choice: 7 CHINESE
 For: 4 TOGO
 Get: 5 EATIN
 order: 4 DELE
**Takeover**
 Corp.: 3 LBO
 Sudden: 4 COUP
**"___ takers?":** 3 ANY

driver: 4 ALEX
Judd on: 4 ALEX
Marilu on: 6 ELAINE
mechanic: 5 LATKA
**Taxidermy**
Perform: 5 STUFF
**Taxing**
Do ~ work: 6 ASSESS
Less: 6 EASIER
mo.: 3 APR
org.: 3 IRS
trip: 4 TREK
**Taxonomic**
subdivisions: 5 PHYLA
suffix: 3 OTA
**Taxpayer:** 5 FILER
dread: 5 AUDIT 8 IRSAUDIT
~ ID: 3 SSN
**Tay:** 4 LOCH
Tiny, on the: 3 SMA
**Taylor**
1963 ~ role: 4 CLEO
A ~ husband: 4 TODD
Actress: 4 LILI 5 RENEE
Blues singer: 4 KOKO
boy: 4 OPIE
Entertainer: 3 RIP
nickname: 3 LIZ
Pop singer: 5 DAYNE
predecessor: 4 POLK
~, for one: 4 WHIG
**Taylor, Claudia ___:** 4 ALTA
**Tazer**
Use a ~ on: 4 STUN
**T-bar:** 3 TOW
**T-Bird**
Old ~ features: 4 FINS
**T-bone:** 5 STEAK
**Tbsp.:** 3 AMT
fractions: 4 TSPS
**Tchaikovsky**
ballet: 8 SWANLAKE
ballet role: 4 SWAN
middle name: 5 ILICH
**Tchotchke:** 7 TRINKET
holder: 7 ETAGERE
**TDK**
rival: 7 MEMOREX
**Te-___ (cigar brand):** 3 AMO
**Tea:** 6 SOCIAL
biscuit: 5 SCONE
Black: 5 PEKOE
brand: 6 LIPTON SALADA
6 TETLEY
Brit's bit of: 4 SPOT
Chinese: 3 CHA
Grade of: 5 PEKOE
growing state: 5 ASSAM
holder: 3 BAG TIN
Iced ~ garnish: 5 LEMON
Interpret ~ leaves: 4 READ
leaf reader: 4 SEER
Like some: 4 ICED 6 HERBAL
party member: 5 ALICE
8 DORMOUSE
Prepare: 4 BREW 5 STEEP

quantity: 4 SPOT
server: 3 URN
Spiced: 4 CHAI
Texas: 3 OIL
time: 4 FOUR
type: 5 PEKOE 6 HERBAL
OOLONG
**Téa**
Actress: 5 LEONI
**Teach:** 5 TRAIN 7 EDUCATE
**Teacher:** 4 PROF
Bauhaus: 4 KLEE
charges: 5 CLASS
favorite: 3 PET
goal: 6 TENURE
Hindu: 4 GURU 5 SWAMI
Jewish: 5 REBBE
joy: 8 ASTUDENT
Martial arts: 6 SENSEI
of Bart: 4 EDNA
of Heifetz: 4 AUER
of Luke: 4 YODA
of Samuel: 3 ELI
of Stradivari: 5 AMATI
org.: 3 NEA
request: 5 SEEME
TV: 4 GABE
Wise: 6 MENTOR
Word a ~ likes to hear: 3 AHA
~, sometimes: 6 TESTER
**Teaching**
deg.: 3 EDB EDD MED 4 BSED
Do a ~ job: 5 GRADE
Elders: 4 LORE
**"Teach not thy lip such ___":**
5 SCORN
**Teacup**
handle: 3 EAR
**"Tea for Two"**
musical: 11 NONONANETTE
**Teal**
Color similar to: 4 AQUA
hangout: 4 POND
**Team:** 4 SIDE 5 SQUAD
6 TANDEM
Competing: 4 SIDE
Crew: 4 OARS
Farm: 4 OXEN SPAN
Football: 6 ELEVEN
Greet the opposing: 3 BOO
Hockey: 6 SEXTET
It keeps the ~ together:
4 YOKE
Kind of: 3 TAG 4 AWAY FARM
SWAT
Lacrosse: 3 TEN
leader: 7 CAPTAIN
lineup: 6 ROSTER
members: 4 OXEN
morale: 6 SPIRIT
Mule: 4 ARMY
Police: 4 SWAT
Show ~ spirit: 4 ROOT
Small: 3 DUO
Sports: 5 SQUAD
The other: 4 THEM

Word to a: 4 MUSH
**Teamsters**
notable: 5 HOFFA
rig: 4 SEMI
**Teamwork**
deterrent: 3 EGO
**Teapot**
cover: 4 COZY
feature: 5 SPOUT
Tempest in a: 3 ADO 4 FUSS
**Teapot Dome**
figure: 10 ALBERTFALL
**Tear:** 3 RIP 4 RACE REND
RENT 5 SPREE
8 LACERATE
apart: 3 RIP 4 REND RIVE
carrier: 4 DUCT
Doesn't just ~ up: 4 SOBS
down: 4 RAZE
down (British): 4 RASE
Fix a: 4 DARN
in little pieces: 5 SHRED
into: 6 ASSAIL ATTACK
It brings a ~ to the eye:
4 DUCT
jerker: 5 ONION
More than ~ up: 4 BAWL
WEEP
open: 5 UNRIP
Partner of: 4 WEAR
roughly: 8 LACERATE
Shed a: 4 WEPT
to pieces: 4 REND 5 RIPUP
up: 3 CRY RIP 4 MIST REND
WEEP
Wear and: 3 USE
Words before: 3 ONA
**Tearful:** 3 SAD 5 WEEPY
**Tearjerker:** 5 ONION
necessity: 6 TISSUE
React to a: 3 CRY
**Tearoom:** 4 CAFE
**Tears**
Blur with: 5 BLEAR
into: 5 HASAT
Like: 5 SALTY 6 SALINE
Shed: 4 WEEP WEPT
**Teasdale**
Poet: 4 SARA
**Tease:** 3 KID RAG RIB 4 BAIT
JOSH RAZZ RIDE TWIT
5 RAGON 6 LEADON
NEEDLE
**Teased:** 4 RODE
**Teaser**
Kitty: 6 CATNIP
TV: 5 PROMO
**Teasing**
result: 7 BIGHAIR
**Teaspoon:** 4 DOSE
**Teatime**
treat: 5 SCONE
**Teatro alla ___:** 5 SCALA
**Teatro Costanzi**
debut of 1900: 5 TOSCA
**Teatro ___ Scala:** 4 ALLA

**Takes**
Having what it: 4 ABLE
It ~ two: 4 TREY
off: 4 GOES
too much: 3 ODS
**"Take ___, She's Mine":** 3 HER
**Take ___ stride:** 4 ITIN
**"Take that!":** 7 SOTHERE
**"Take this!":** 4 HERE
**"Take ___ Train":** 4 THEA
**"Take ___ your leader":**
4 METO
**"Take your pick":** 3 ANY
8 EITHEROR
**"Take your time!":** 6 NORUSH
**Taking**
after: 3 ALA
For the: 4 FREE
liberty: 6 ASHORE
One ~ off: 4 APER
**Taking-off**
place: 3 SPA
**"Takin' ___ the Streets":** 4 ITTO
**Talbot**
Actress: 4 NITA
**Talcum**
and walcum rhymer: 4 NASH
target: 4 RASH
**Tale:** 4 YARN 5 STORY
Epic: 4 SAGA
Grand-scale: 4 EPIC
Heroic: 4 EPIC SAGA
Moralistic: 5 FABLE
of adventure: 4 GEST 5 GESTE
of woe: 8 SOBSTORY
Old wives': 4 MYTH
starter: 4 ONCE
Tall: 4 YARN
teller: 3 POE 4 BARD LIAR
Told, as a: 4 SPUN
**Talent:** 4 BENT GIFT 5 KNACK
SKILL 8 APTITUDE
Furnish with: 5 ENDOW
Look for: 5 SCOUT
Medium's: 3 ESP
Musical: 3 EAR
Natural: 4 GIFT 5 FLAIR
Special: 5 KNACK
**Talented:** 3 APT 4 ABLE
5 ADEPT
**"Talented Mr. Ripley, The"**
actor Jude: 3 LAW
actor Matt: 5 DAMON
**"Tale of ___ Saltan, The":**
4 TSAR
**Tales**
Folk ~ and such: 4 LORE
Like some: 4 TALL
Tell: 3 LIE 7 NARRATE
**"Tales From the Vienna Woods"**
composer: 7 STRAUSS
**Tales of ___:** 3 WOE
**"... tale told by an ___":**
5 IDIOT
**Talia**
Actress: 5 SHIRE

Cousin of: 7 NICOLAS
**Taliban**
mullah: 4 OMAR
**Talisman:** 4 MOJO 5 CHARM
6 AMULET FETISH
Egyptian: 6 SCARAB
**Talk:** 3 GAB 4 CHAT
a blue streak: 4 CUSS
5 RUNON SWEAR
about: 7 SPEAKOF
amorously: 3 COO
and talk: 3 YAK
Baby: 6 GOOGOO
Back: 3 LIP 4 ECHO GUFF
SASS 6 STATIC
big: 4 BRAG CROW 5 BOAST
Casual: 4 CHAT
Colorful: 5 SLANG
effusively: 4 GUSH
Empty: 3 GAS 4 WIND
6 HOTAIR
First name in: 4 MERV
5 CONAN ELLEN LEEZA
OPRAH REGIS RICKI
ROSIE 6 MONTEL
7 ARSENIO
Fresh: 4 SASS
incessantly: 3 YAP
Insincere: 4 CANT
It's mostly: 7 AMRADIO
Jazzy: 4 JIVE
Kind of: 3 PEP
King of: 5 LARRY
like crazy: 4 RANT
Like some: 5 SMALL
Loose: 5 SLANG
(over): 4 HASH
Playful: 6 BANTER
Small: 4 CHAT 8 CHITCHAT
Something to ~ about: 5 TOPIC
Sun.: 3 SER
too much: 4 BLAB 6 YAMMER
Trade: 5 ARGOT
up: 4 HYPE PRAY TOUT
wildly: 4 RANT
with one's hands: 4 SIGN
**Talk ___:** 4 SHOP
**"___ talk?":** 5 CANWE
**Talkathon:** 7 GABFEST
**Talkative:** 4 GLIB 6 CHATTY
bird: 4 MYNA
**Talked**
a blue streak: 5 SWORE
monotonously: 8 DRONEDON
**Talker**
Caged: 4 MYNA
Morning: 4 IMUS
**Talking**
bird: 4 MYNA
bird of poetry: 5 RAVEN
heads: 5 PANEL
horse of TV: 4 MRED
Not: 3 MUM
point: 3 JAW 5 TOPIC
She's not: 4 MIME
Stop: 6 CLAMUP

trees: 4 ENTS
**Talking-___ (lectures):** 3 TOS
**"Talking in Your Sleep"**
singer: 5 GAYLE
**"Talking Straight"**
author: 7 IACOCCA
**"Talk Radio"**
actor Baldwin: 4 ALEC
director Oliver: 5 STONE
**Talks**
It: 5 MONEY
**Talk show**
group: 5 PANEL
host Jay: 4 LENO
host Joe: 4 PYNE
host Tom: 6 SNYDER
lineup: 6 GUESTS
partner: 6 COHOST
pioneer: 4 PAAR
Radio ~ participant:
6 CALLER
Try to reach a: 6 DIALIN
**Tall**
and trim: 4 LANK
bird: 3 EMU
hat wearer: 4 CHEF
It may be: 4 TALE
stalk: 4 REED
story: 4 TALE YARN
Straight and: 5 ERECT
tale: 4 YARN
**Tallchief, Maria**
tribe: 5 OSAGE
**Taller**
Get: 4 GROW
**Tallies**
NBA: 3 PTS
**Tallinn**
native: 4 ESTH
resident: 8 ESTONIAN
**Tallow**
ingredient: 4 SUET
**Tally:** 3 ADD
mark: 5 NOTCH
**Talmadge**
Actress: 5 NORMA
**Talmud**
expert: 5 RABBI
language: 6 HEBREW
**Talmudic**
Noted ~ sage: 6 HILLEL
**Talon:** 4 CLAW
**Talus**
area: 5 ANKLE
**Tam:** 3 CAP
wearer's tongue: 4 ERSE
**Tamale**
topping: 5 SALSA
**Tamblyn**
Actor: 4 RUSS
**"Tamburlaine the Great"**
playwright: 7 MARLOWE
**Tamed**
Easily ~ bird: 3 EMU
**"Tamerlane"**
dramatist Nicholas: 4 ROWE

**"Taming of the Shrew, The"**
  setting: 5 PADUA
  shrew: 4 KATE
**Tamiroff**
  Actor: 4 AKIM
**Tammany Hall**
  caricaturist: 4 NAST
  leader: 5 TWEED
**Tammy**
  Actress: 6 GRIMES
  Jim and ~ gp.: 3 PTL
  Singer: 7 WYNETTE
**"Tammy"**
  singer Debbie: 8 REYNOLDS
**Tammy Faye**
  former org.: 3 PTL
**Tampa**
  City south of: 8 SARASOTA
  neighbor: 6 STPETE
  paper, for short: 4 TRIB
**Tampa Bay**
  player, for short: 3 BUC
**Tamper**
  with: 3 RIG
**Tamper-resistant:** 6 SEALED
**Tan:** 3 SUN 4 ECRU
  Author: 3 AMY
  Black and ~ ingredient: 3 ALE
  Light: 4 ECRU
  too long: 4 BAKE
**Tandem**
  Go by: 5 PEDAL
**Tandoor:** 4 OVEN
  baked bread: 3 NAN
**Tang:** 3 NIP 4 ZEST
**T'ang dynasty**
  poet: 4 LIPO
**Tangelo**
  variety: 4 UGLI
**Tangent:** 5 RATIO
  Go off on a: 7 DIGRESS
**Tangible:** 4 REAL 8 CONCRETE
**Tangier**
  Port east of: 4 ORAN
**Tangle:** 3 MAT WEB 5 MELEE
     RAVEL SKEIN SNARL
     6 ENMESH 7 ENSNARL
  Bureaucratic: 7 REDTAPE
  Traffic: 5 SNARL
  up: 6 ENMESH 7 ENSNARL
**Tangled:** 5 MESSY
**Tanglewood**
  town: 5 LENOX
**Tango:** 5 DANCE
  move: 3 DIP
  number: 3 TWO
**Tanguy**
  Painter: 4 YVES
**Tangy**
  drink: 7 LIMEADE
  Most: 7 TARTEST
  pie flavor: 5 LEMON
**Tank:** 3 VAT
  Brewery: 3 VAT
  filler: 3 GAS
  Fill the: 5 GASUP

fish: 5 TETRA
Kind of: 6 SEPTIC 7 SHERMAN
Rainwater: 7 CISTERN
suffix: 3 ARD
top: 6 GASCAP TURRET
**Tankard**
  filler: 3 ALE
**Tanker:** 4 SHIP 5 OILER
  mishap: 5 SPILL
**Tankful:** 3 GAS
**"Tank Girl"**
  actress Petty: 4 LORI
  rapper: 4 ICET
**Tanks:** 7 AQUARIA
  and such: 5 ARMOR
**Tanned**
  Hardly: 4 PALE
**Tanner:** 3 SUN
  tub: 3 VAT
  wares: 5 HIDES
**Tanners**
  catch them: 4 RAYS
**Tannery**
  tool: 3 AWL
**Tanning**
  abbr.: 3 UVA
  lotion letters: 3 SPF
**Tannish:** 4 ECRU
**Tantalize:** 5 TEMPT
**Tantalus**
  Daughter of: 5 NIOBE
**Tantara:** 5 BLARE
**Tantrum:** 3 FIT 4 RAGE
**Tanzanian**
  neighbor: 7 RWANDAN
  park: 9 SERENGETI
  tongue: 7 SWAHILI
**Tao**
  founder: 6 LAOTSE
  ~, literally: 6 THEWAY
**Taoism**
  emerging dynasty: 4 CHOU
  founder: 6 LAOTSE
**Taormina**
  Peak near: 4 ETNA
**Taos**
  material: 5 ADOBE
**Tap:** 6 DRAWON SPIGOT
  Back: 3 PAT
  choice: 3 ALE
  Green: 4 PUTT
  label: 3 HOT
  Morse: 3 DIT
  output: 3 ALE
  problem: 4 DRIP
  Type of: 6 SPINAL
**"Tap"**
  Gregory of: 5 HINES
**Tape**
  Audition: 4 DEMO
  Beat to the: 6 OUTRAN
    7 OUTRACE
  Break the: 3 WIN
  Clear the: 5 ERASE
  deck button: 3 REC 5 EJECT
    ERASE

holder: 8 CASSETTE
Kind of: 4 BETA DEMO DUCT
  5 VIDEO
Linen: 5 INKLE
Not on: 4 LIVE
Obsolete: 10 EIGHTTRACK
over: 5 ERASE
rec. jack: 3 MIC
Ticker: 3 EKG
Trimming: 5 INKLE
**Taper:** 3 VCR
  off: 4 WANE 5 ABATE
**Tapered**
  Cylindrical and: 6 TERETE
  end: 5 POINT
  feature: 7 STEEPLE
  tuck: 4 DART
**Tapestry:** 5 ARRAS
  beast: 7 UNICORN
**Tapioca**
  source: 7 CASSAVA
**Tapir**
  feature: 5 SNOUT
**Tappan ___ Bridge:** 3 ZEE
**Tapped**
  It's: 3 KEG
**Taproom**
  site: 3 INN
**"Taps"**
  instrument: 5 BUGLE
  time: 3 TEN
**Taqueria**
  order: 7 TOSTADA
**Tar:** 3 GOB 4 SALT SWAB
    6 SEADOG SEAMAN
  British: 5 LIMEY
  tale: 4 YARN
  ~, in Spanish: 4 BREA
**Tara**
  Butler at: 5 RHETT
  family: 6 OHARAS
  Scarlett of: 5 OHARA
**Taradiddle:** 3 FIB
**Tarantino**
  Director: 7 QUENTIN
  Like most ~ films: 6 RATEDR
**Tarantula:** 6 SPIDER
**"Taras Bulba"**
  author: 5 GOGOL
  extra: 7 COSSACK
**Tarbell**
  Author: 3 IDA
**Tarboosh**
  feature: 6 TASSEL
  kin: 3 FEZ
**Tardiness**
  excuse: 8 LATEPASS
**Tardy:** 4 LATE
  Somewhat: 6 LATISH
**Target:** 3 AIM 4 PREY
    5 AIMAT
  1969 ~: 4 MOON
  competitor: 5 KMART SEARS
  On: 3 APT
  Pick a: 3 AIM
  Tell tale: 5 APPLE

---

**Tar Heel State**
  (abbr.): 4 NCAR
  campus: 4 ELON
  sch.: 3 UNC
**Tariff:** 3 FEE
  1930 ~ cosponsor: 5 SMOOT
  eliminating pact: 5 NAFTA
**Tariq**
  Former Iraqi diplomat: 4 AZIZ
**Tarkenton**
  of football: 4 FRAN
**Tarkington**
  novel: 6 PENROD
**Tarmac**
  Hit the: 4 LAND
  Touched the: 4 ALIT
**"Tarnation!":** 4 EGAD
**Tarnish:** 3 MAR 4 SOIL 5 STAIN
    TAINT
**Tarnisher**
  Reputation: 4 BLOT
**Taro**
  dish: 3 POI
  root: 4 EDDO
**Tarot**
  reader: 4 SEER
  suit: 4 CUPS
**Tarpon:** 4 FISH
**Tarragon:** 4 HERB
**Tarry:** 4 BIDE
**Tarsal**
  prefix: 4 META
**Tart:** 4 ACID 5 ACERB ACRID
    6 ACIDIC
  fruit: 4 SLOE
  taste: 4 TANG
  thief: 5 KNAVE
  Very: 5 ACERB
**Tartan**
  cap: 3 TAM
  garb: 4 KILT
  pattern: 5 PLAID
  sporters: 4 CLAN
**"Tartuffe"**
  author: 7 MOLIERE
**Tarzan:** 6 APEMAN
  actor Ely: 3 RON
  actor Ron: 3 ELY
  companion: 3 APE
  kid: 3 BOY
  mate: 4 JANE
  transportation: 4 VINE
**Task:** 3 JOB 5 CHORE STINT
  Equal to the: 4 ABLE
  Is up to the: 3 CAN
  Not up to the: 5 INEPT
  Routine: 5 CHORE
  Tough: 4 ONUS
  Up to the: 4 ABLE
**Tasman**
  Explorer: 4 ABEL
**Tasmania**
  capital: 6 HOBART
  Peak in: 4 OSSA
**Tass**
  country: 4 USSR

**Tasseled**
  topper: 3 FEZ TAM
**Taste:** 3 BIT SIP TRY 5 SENSE
    6 LIKING SAMPLE
  Enjoy the: 5 SAVOR
  Personal: 8 CUPOFTEA
  Sense of: 6 PALATE
  Sharp: 4 TANG
  Small: 3 SIP
  stimulus: 4 ODOR
  test label: 6 BRANDX
  Zingy: 4 TANG
**Tasteless:** 4 BLAH 5 BLAND
    CRASS GAUDY TACKY
**Tastelessly**
  affected: 6 TOOTOO
**"Taste of Honey, A"**
  playwright: 7 DELANEY
**Taster**
  Wine ~ concern: 4 YEAR
**"Tastes awful!":** 3 UGH
**Tastiness:** 5 SAPOR
**Tasting**
  Bitter: 5 ACERB
  like Tokay: 4 WINY
  of wood: 4 OAKY
  Wine: 3 SIP
**Tasty:** 4 GOOD 5 SAPID
  dish: 5 VIAND
  mushroom: 5 MOREL
  tuber: 3 YAM
**"Tasty!":** 3 MMM YUM
    4 MMMM
**Tat**
  equivalent: 3 TIT
**"Ta-ta!":** 4 CIAO 5 ADIEU
    SEEYA 7 CHEERIO
**Tatar**
  ruler: 4 KHAN
**Tate**
  British poet: 5 NAHUM
  collection: 3 ART
**Tater:** 4 SPUD
  state: 5 IDAHO
**Taters**
  Some: 7 IDAHOES
**Tater Tots**
  maker: 6 OREIDA
**Tati**
  character: 5 HULOT
**"Tatler, The"**
  founder: 6 STEELE
**Tatter:** 3 RAG
  product: 4 LACE
**Tattered:** 4 TORN WORN
    5 RATTY 6 INRAGS
  attire: 4 RAGS
**"Tattered Tom"**
  author: 5 ALGER
**Tatting**
  material: 4 LACE
**Tattle:** 3 RAT 4 BLAB TELL
    6 TELLON
**Tattled:** 4 TOLD
**Tattletale:** 3 RAT 6 SNITCH
    7 BLABBER

**Tattoo**
  fluid: 3 INK
  for kids: 5 DECAL
  Popeye: 6 ANCHOR
  site: 3 ARM
  word: 3 MOM
**"Tattooed lady"**
  of song: 5 LYDIA
**Tatum**
  Father of: 4 RYAN
  Jazzman: 3 ART
  Oscar winner: 5 ONEAL
**Tatyana**
  Singer: 3 ALI
**Taught:** 8 SCHOOLED
**Taunt:** 4 GIBE GOAD JEST
    TWIT 5 RAGON TEASE
**Taunting**
  cry: 3 OHO
  remark: 4 GIBE
**Tauromachian**
  cheer: 3 OLE
**Taurus:** 3 CAR 4 AUTO
  Constellation next to: 5 ORION
  Sign after: 6 GEMINI
  Sign before: 5 ARIES
  Star in: 9 ALDEBARAN
**Taut:** 12 TIGHTASADRUM
**Tautness**
  Lose: 3 SAG 5 DROOP
**Tauto-**
  What ~ means: 4 SAME
**Tavern:** 3 BAR INN PUB
  inventory: 4 KEGS
  offering: 4 BEER
  order: 3 ALE RYE
  sign abbr.: 4 ESTD 5 ESTAB
  temptress: 5 BGIRL
**Tax:** 3 TRY 4 DUTY LEVY
  agcy.: 3 IRS
  British: 4 CESS
  cheat catchers: 4 TMEN
  cheat's risk: 5 AUDIT
  form ID: 3 SSN
  form info (abbr.): 3 IRA
  Imposed a: 6 LEVIED
  Kind of: 3 SIN USE 6 EXCISE
  mo.: 3 APR
  pro: 3 CPA 8 ASSESSOR
  Protectionist: 6 TARIFF
  Some ~ shelters: 8 ROTHIRAS
  time: 5 APRIL
**Tax-___:** 6 EXEMPT
**Tax-deferred**
  acct.: 3 IRA 7 ROTHIRA
**Taxes**
  Earn after: 3 NET
  Impose: 4 LEVY
  Take home, after: 5 CLEAR
**Taxi:** 3 CAB 4 HACK
  feature: 4 HORN 5 METER
  fee: 4 FARE
  Like a: 7 METERED
  Typical: 5 SEDAN
**"Taxi"**
  Danny on: 5 LOUIE

**Tebaldi**
Soprano: 6 RENATA
**Tech**
sch. grad.: 4 ENGR
stock: 3 IBM
___ Tech: 3 CAL
**Techie**
client: 4 USER
Kind of:
14 SYSTEMSANALYST
~, maybe: 4 NERD
"___ Te Ching": 3 TAO
**Technical**
data: 5 SPECS
sch.: 4 INST
**Technicality**
Kind of: 4 MERE
**Technician**
Piano: 5 TUNER
spot: 3 LAB
**Technique**: 3 ART 4 MODE
Film editing: 4 WIPE
Jazz: 4 SCAT
Memorization: 4 ROTE
Mosaic: 5 INLAY
Mountain climbing: 6 RAPPEL
Replay: 5 SLOMO
**Techno**
Popular ~ musician: 4 MOBY
suffix: 4 CRAT
**Technological**
advance of the 50's:
7 COLORTV
marvel of 1951: 6 UNIVAC
**Technologically**
advanced:
13 STATEOFTHEART
**Technology**
prefix: 4 NANO
**Techs**
It has many: 6 NASDAQ
**Tecs**: 3 PIS
**Tecumseh**: 7 SHAWNEE
**Ted**
Rocker: 6 NUGENT
**Teddies**: 8 LINGERIE
**Teddy**
Eleanor, to: 5 NIECE
**Tedious**: 5 PROSY
8 TIRESOME
situation: 4 DRAG
task: 4 ONUS 5 CHORE
**Tediously**
Proceed: 4 PLOD
**Tedium**: 5 ENNUI
**Tee**
follower: 3 HEE
Hit from a: 5 DRIVE
off: 3 IRE IRK 4 RILE
5 ANGER DRIVE
preceder: 3 ESS
To a: 3 PAT
user: 6 GOLFER
___ tee: 3 TOA
**Teed**
off: 4 SORE 5 IRATE

**Tee-hee**
More than a: 4 HAHA
**Teem**: 6 ABOUND
**Teeming**: 4 RIFE 6 ASWARM
**Teen**: 7 MALLRAT
affliction: 4 ACNE
fave: 4 IDOL 7 POPSTAR
hangout: 4 MALL
Much ~ talk: 5 SLANG
of comics: 6 ARCHIE
outcast: 4 NERD
party: 9 SLEEPOVER
spots: 4 ACNE
suffix: 4 AGER
wall décor: 6 POSTER
woe: 3 ZIT 4 ACNE
**Teen** ___: 4 IDOL
**Teena**
Singer: 5 MARIE
**Teenage**
hooligan, to a Brit: 3 YOB
Like some ~ turtles:
6 MUTANT
**Teenage Mutant** ___ **Turtles:**
5 NINJA
**Teenager**
Many a ~ room: 4 MESS
woe: 4 ACNE
"___ Teen-age Werewolf":
5 IWASA
**Teens**
Great, to: 3 RAD
Not for most: 6 RATEDR
Rock star, to: 4 IDOL
**Teensy**: 3 WEE
bit: 4 ATOM IOTA
**Teeny**: 3 WEE 4 ITSY 5 BITSY
6 PETITE 9 ITSYBITSY
parasites: 5 MITES
**Teeter-totter**: 6 SEESAW
**Teeth**: 4 COGS
Deg. with: 3 DDS
Gear: 4 COGS
Grind, as: 5 GNASH
Grinding: 6 MOLARS
Like hen's: 4 RARE
One with sharp: 3 SAW
Sink one's ~ into: 4 BITE
Space between: 8 DIASTEMA
Tool with: 3 SAW 4 RAKE
**Teetotaler**: 3 DRY 7 NONUSER
order: 4 SODA
**Teflon**
maker: 6 DUPONT
"**Teflon Don, The**": 5 GOTTI
**Teheran**
City SW of: 3 QOM
coin: 4 RIAL
country: 4 IRAN
Former ~ ruler: 4 SHAH
native: 5 IRANI
tongue: 5 FARSI
**Tehrani**
tongue: 5 FARSI
**Tejano**
singer: 6 SELENA

**Te Kanawa**
Soprano: 4 KIRI
**Tel.**
book listings: 3 NOS
line: 3 EXT
**Tel** ___: 4 AVIV
**Tel Aviv**
Airline to: 4 ELAL
Airport near: 3 LOD
native: 5 SABRA 7 ISRAELI
server: 4 ELAL
**Telecast**
component: 5 AUDIO
over: 5 RERUN
**Telecom**
Former ~ giant: 3 GTE ITT
giant: 3 ATT
**Telecommunications**
Old ~ name: 5 NYNEX
speed unit: 4 BAUD
**Telecommuter**
Where a ~ works: 6 ATHOME
**Telegram**: 4 WIRE
period: 4 STOP
Send, as a: 6 TAPOUT
**Telegrams**
Like some: 4 SUNG
**Telegraph**
click: 3 DIT
inventor: 5 MORSE
key: 6 TAPPER
**Telepathy**: 3 ESP PSI
**Telephone**: 4 CALL
6 on a ~: 3 MNO
abbr.: 4 OPER
button: 4 STAR
button with no letters: 3 ONE
greeting: 5 HELLO
location: 5 BOOTH
part: 4 CORD 6 CRADLE
7 HANDSET
trio: 3 ABC DEF GHI JKL
MNO PRS TUV WXY
user: 5 PARTY
~, in slang: 4 HORN
**Telephoned**: 4 RANG
"**Telephone Line**"
gp.: 3 ELO
**TelePrompter**
filler: 4 TEXT
input: 6 SCRIPT
**Telescope**
Hale ~ site: 7 PALOMAR
part: 4 LENS
pioneer: 7 GALILEO
sights: 5 STARS
Small: 8 SPYGLASS
**Telescopium**
Constellation next to: 3 ARA
**Telesthesia**: 3 ESP
**TeleTax**
org.: 3 IRS
**Televise**: 3 AIR
**Television**: 5 MEDIA
announcer Don: 5 PARDO
award: 4 EMMY

cabinet: 7 CONSOLE
Show on: 3 AIR
**Tell:** 6 INFORM RELATE
    7 NARRATE
a good one: 3 LIE
all: 4 BLAB SING
a thing or two: 5 SCOLD
a whopper: 3 LIE
Could: 6 SENSED
Didn't mean to: 7 LETSLIP
forte: 7 ARCHERY
it like it isn't: 3 LIE
It's hard to: 4 SAGA
projectile: 5 ARROW
tales: 3 LIE 7 NARRATE
**Tell-___ (some biographies):**
    4 ALLS
**Tell, William:** 6 ARCHER
canton: 3 URI
**Teller:** 3 RAT
Bygone tale: 4 BARD
call: 4 NEXT
Fortune: 4 SEER 5 TAROT
    6 ORACLE
Partner of: 4 PENN
post: 4 CAGE
stack: 4 ONES TENS
Tale: 3 POE 4 LIAR
**Telling:** 6 COGENT
trial: 8 ACIDTEST
**"Tell It to My Heart"**
singer Taylor: 5 DAYNE
**"Tell ___ lies":** 4 MENO
**"Tell Mama"**
singer James: 4 ETTA
**"Tell ___ story":** 3 MEA
**Telltale**
sign: 4 ODOR OMEN
**"Tell-Tale Heart, The"**
author: 3 POE
**"Tell ___ the judge!":** 4 ITTO
**"Tell ___ the Marines!":** 4 ITTO
**Telly**
network: 3 BBC
on the telly: 7 SAVALAS
**Temp**
Year-end: 5 SANTA
**Tempe**
sch.: 3 ASU
**Temper:** 3 IRE 4 HUFF MOOD
    5 IRISH 6 ANNEAL
Ill: 3 IRE 4 BILE
Lose one's:
    13 HITTHECEILING
**Tempera**
painting surface: 5 GESSO
**Temperament:** 4 MOOD
    6 NATURE
**Temperamental:** 5 MOODY
star: 4 DIVA
tizzy: 4 SNIT
**Temperate:** 4 MILD
**Temperature:** 4 HEAT
Body ~, etc.: 6 VITALS
scale: 7 CELSIUS
taker: 5 NURSE

___ temperature: 4 RANA
**Temperatures**
Freezing: 5 TEENS
**Tempest:** 5 STORM
in a teapot: 3 ADO 4 FUSS
**"Tempest, The"**
fairy: 5 ARIEL
king: 6 ALONSO
magician: 8 PROSPERO
Sci-fi version of:
    15 FORBIDDENPLANET
slave: 7 CALIBAN
**Tempest ___ teapot:** 3 INA
**Temple**
athlete: 3 OWL
Chinese: 6 PAGODA
Common ~ name: 7 EMANUEL
Greek: 4 NAOS
image: 4 IDOL
leader: 5 RABBI
Object near a: 3 EAR
player: 3 OWL
Roman: 8 PANTHEON
Shinto ~ gateway: 5 TORII
text: 5 TORAH
**Temple, Shirley**
role: 5 HEIDI
**Temple of ___:** 4 ARES ZEUS
**Temple of Apollo**
site: 6 DELPHI
**Temple of Zeus**
site: 5 NEMEA
**Temples**
Site of two: 9 ABUSIMBEL
They're found beside:
    7 GLASSES
**Templeton**
Pianist: 4 ALEC
**Tempo:** 4 PACE RATE
    5 SPEED
Fast: 6 PRESTO
Slow: 5 LARGO LENTO
**Temporarily:** 6 FORNOW
    8 FORATIME
be: 5 ACTAS
Give: 4 LEND LOAN
Joined: 5 SATIN
put aside: 5 ONICE
**Temporary:** 5 ADHOC 6 ACTING
    7 INTERIM
fashion: 3 FAD
fix: 7 STOPGAP
gift: 4 LOAN
money: 5 SCRIP
wheels: 6 LOANER
**Tempt:** 4 BAIT LURE 6 ENTICE
    SEDUCE
fate: 4 DARE
**Temptation**
Dieter's: 5 AROMA
location: 4 EDEN
**"Temptation of St. Anthony,**
    **The"**
artist: 5 BOSCH ERNST
**Temptations**
1965 ~ hit: 6 MYGIRL

**Tempted**
It may be: 4 FATE
**Tempter:** 5 SATAN SIREN
    WOOER
Eve: 7 SERPENT
Fish: 4 LURE
**Temptress:** 5 SIREN
Joe Hardy: 4 LOLA
Play the: 6 SEDUCE
Rhine: 7 LORELEI
Tavern: 5 BGIRL
**Ten**
Hang: 4 SURF
or higher: 5 HONOR
percenter (abbr.): 3 AGT
prefix: 4 DECA
sawbucks: 5 CNOTE
Take: 4 REST
Top ~, for one: 4 LIST
Top ~ item: 3 HIT
Worth a: 5 IDEAL
**Tenacious:** 6 DOGGED
**Tenant:** 6 LESSEE RENTER
    ROOMER
Feudal: 6 VASSAL
Find a new ~ for: 5 RELET
Joint: 3 CON 5 FELON
Mall: 4 SHOP 5 STORE
payment: 4 RENT
protest: 10 RENTSTRIKE
Tent: 6 CAMPER
Throw out a: 5 EVICT
**Ten Commandments**
mount: 5 SINAI
word: 5 SHALT
~, for the most part: 5 NONOS
**"Ten Commandments, The":**
    4 EPIC
actress Debra: 5 PAGET
director: 7 DEMILLE
Ramses portrayer, in: 3 YUL
**Tend:** 5 SEETO
**Tended:** 5 SAWTO
**Tendency:** 4 BENT 5 TREND
Had a: 5 LEANT
toward chaos: 7 ENTROPY
**Tender:** 4 SORE
Bar: 9 BEERMONEY
ender: 4 LOIN
Some legal: 6 TNOTES
spot: 3 BAR 4 SORE
Tijuana: 4 PESO
touch: 6 CARESS
**"Tender ___":** 7 MERCIES
**Tenderfoot:** 4 TYRO
org.: 3 BSA
**Tender-hearted:** 4 SOFT
**Tenderized**
cut: 9 CUBESTEAK
**Tendon:** 5 SINEW
connector: 5 BURSA
**Tendril:** 4 WISP
**Tenement**
locale: 4 SLUM
___ tenens (substitute):
    5 LOCUM

Tenerife: 4 ISLA
Tenet: 5 CREDO DOGMA
**Tenet, George**
  org.: 3 CIA
**"Ten-hut!"**
  opposite: 6 ATEASE
**Tenn.**
  athlete: 3 VOL
  hours: 3 CST
  neighbor: 3 ALA 4 NCAR
**Tennessee**
  aluminum town: 5 ALCOA
  athlete: 3 VOL
  footballer: 3 VOL 5 TITAN
  Former ~ senator Kefauver:
    5 ESTES
  singer Ford: 5 ERNIE
  state flower: 4 IRIS
  Veep from: 6 ALGORE
**Tennille**
  Singer: 4 TONI
**Tennis:** 5 SPORT
  1965 NCAA ~ champ:
    4 ASHE
  1970s ~ star: 4 ASHE BORG
  call: 3 LET
  Czech ~ player: 5 LENDL
  deuce: 3 TIE
  divider: 3 NET
  do-over: 3 LET
  drop shot: 4 DINK
  First name in 1970s: 4 ILIE
  game point: 4 ADIN
  Great ~ server: 4 ACER
  instructor: 3 PRO
  miscue: 5 FAULT
  New York ~ stadium: 4 ASHE
  Palindromic ~ star: 5 SELES
  ploy: 3 LOB
  Quick round of: 6 ONESET
  ranking: 4 SEED
  score: 4 ADIN 5 ADOUT
  score after deuce: 4 ADIN
  shot: 3 LOB
  Start a ~ game: 5 SERVE
  whiz: 4 ACER
  zero: 4 LOVE
**"Tennis, ___?":** 6 ANYONE
**Tennis player**
  ~ Andre: 6 AGASSI
  ~ Arthur: 4 ASHE
  ~ Becker: 5 BORIS
  ~ Borg: 5 BJORN
  ~ Edberg: 6 STEFAN
  ~ Emerson: 3 ROY
  ~ Fraser: 5 NEALE
  ~ Gibson: 6 ALTHEA
  ~ Hingis: 7 MARTINA
  ~ Hoad: 3 LEW
  ~ Huber: 4 ANKE
  ~ Ilie: 7 NASTASE
  ~ Kournikova: 4 ANNA
  ~ Lacoste: 4 RENE
  ~ Lendl: 4 IVAN
  ~ Makarova: 5 ELENA
  ~ Mandlikova: 4 HANA

  ~ Martina: 6 HINGIS
  ~ Michael: 5 CHANG
  ~ Monica: 5 SELES
  ~ Nastase: 4 ILIE
  ~ René: 7 LACOSTE
  ~ Richards: 5 RENEE
  ~ Rod: 5 LAVER
  ~ Sampras: 4 PETE
  ~ Shriver: 3 PAM
  ~ Smith: 4 STAN
  ~ Steffi: 4 GRAF
  ~ Tanner: 6 ROSCOE
  ~ Williams: 5 VENUS
    6 SERENA
**"Ten North Frederick"**
  writer: 5 OHARA
**Tennyson**
  Arden of: 5 ENOCH
  lady: 4 ENID
  maid: 6 ELAINE
  poem: 5 IDYLL
**Tenochtitlán**
  resident: 5 AZTEC
**Tenor**
  top note: 5 HIGHC
  tune: 4 ARIA
  Voice above: 4 ALTO
  warhorse: 8 OSOLEMIO
**Tenpenny:** 4 NAIL
**Ten-percenter:** 5 AGENT
**Tense:** 4 EDGY TAUT
    6 ONEDGE
  Get less: 4 THAW
  Kind of: 4 PAST
  Make less: 6 DEFUSE
  ~, with "up": 5 KEYED
**Ten-sided**
  figure: 7 DECAGON
**Tension:** 6 STRESS
**Ten-speed:** 4 BIKE
**Tent**
  caterpillar: 5 EGGER
  Conical: 5 TEPEE
  event: 4 SALE
  furnishing: 3 COT
  holder: 3 PEG 5 STAKE
  Mongol: 4 YURT
  Pitch a: 4 CAMP 6 ENCAMP
  tenant: 6 CAMPER
**Tentacle:** 3 ARM
**Tentacled**
  animal: 5 POLYP SQUID
    7 ANEMONE
    10 SEAANEMONE
**Tentative**
  taste: 3 SIP
**Tenterhooks**
  On: 4 EDGY 5 TENSE
**Tenth**
  anniversary gift: 3 TIN
  Break the ~ Commandment:
    5 COVET
  part: 5 TITHE
  prefix: 4 DECI
**Tenth-grader:** 4 SOPH
    9 SOPHOMORE

**Tentmaker**
  Literary: 4 OMAR
**Tenuous:** 8 ETHEREAL
**Tenure:** 5 STINT
  Military: 4 TOUR
  of office: 4 TERM
**Tenzing**
  Sherpa guide: 6 NORGAY
**Teo**
  of racing: 4 FABI
**Tepee**
  makeup: 4 HIDE
  shape: 4 CONE
  shaped: 5 CONIC
**Tequila**
  serving: 4 SHOT
  source: 5 AGAVE
**Teresa, Mother:** 3 NUN
  ~, by birth: 8 ALBANIAN
**Teresa, Saint**
  birthplace: 5 AVILA
**Terfel**
  Opera singer: 4 BRYN
**Terhune**
  classic: 7 LADADOG
  dog: 3 LAD
**Teri**
  Actress: 4 GARR
  Role for: 4 LOIS
**Teriyaki**
  seasoning: 6 GINGER
**Terkel**
  Author: 5 STUDS
**Term:** 5 STINT 7 SESSION
  Academic: 8 SEMESTER
  of affection: 5 CUTIE
  of endearment: 3 HON PET
    4 BABE 5 HONEY
    TOOTS
    10 HONEYBUNCH
  of respect: 3 SIR 4 MAAM
  paper abbr.: 4 IBID
  paper citation: 6 IBIDEM
  Prison: 7 STRETCH
**Termagant:** 5 SHREW
    8 SHREWISH
**Term-ending**
  test: 5 FINAL
**Terminal:** 3 END 5 DEPOT
    FATAL
  abbr.: 3 POS
  Battery: 5 ANODE
  Battery ~ (abbr.): 3 NEG POS
  Cell: 7 CATHODE
  Chicago: 5 OHARE
  info: 3 ETA
  JFK: 3 TWA
  Like a battery: 6 ANODAL
  list (abbr.): 4 ARRS
  Network: 4 NODE
  posting: 3 ETA
  R.R.: 3 STA
**"Terminal Bliss"**
  actress Chandler: 5 ESTEE
**Terminate:** 3 AXE CAN END
    4 FIRE 5 CEASE

**Terminator**
Pasta: 3 INI
**"Terminator, The"**
heroine: 5 SARAH
**Termini:** 4 ENDS
Modem: 3 EMS
**Terminus:** 3 END
Chisholm Trail: 7 ABILENE
I-79: 4 ERIE
Iditarod: 4 NOME
Race: 4 TAPE
Suez Canal: 6 REDSEA
**Termitarium:** 4 NEST
**Termite:** 4 PEST
hunter: 8 ANTEATER
relative: 3 ANT
**Terms**
Come to: 5 AGREE
**Tern:** 7 SEABIRD
**Terpsichore**
Sister of: 5 ERATO
**Terr.**
Former U.S.: 3 DAK
**Terra ___:** 5 COTTA FIRMA
**Terra firma:** 4 LAND SOIL
5 EARTH
On: 6 ASHORE
**Terrapin:** 6 TURTLE
**Terrarium**
growth: 4 MOSS
plant: 4 FERN
youngster: 3 EFT
**Terre**
Opposite of: 3 MER
**Terre ___:** 5 HAUTE
**Terre Haute**
river: 6 WABASH
sch.: 3 ISU
**Terrestrial**
newt: 3 EFT
**Terrible**
He was: 4 IVAN
More: 5 DIRER
time: 4 TWOS
twos: 5 PHASE
type: 6 ENFANT
**"Terrible"**
tsar: 4 IVAN 6 IVANIV
**___ terrible (brat):** 6 ENFANT
**"... ___ terrible thing to waste":**
3 ISA
**Terribly**
Bother: 5 EATAT
**Terrier**
cry: 3 ARF
Kind of: 4 SKYE 5 CAIRN
8 AIREDALE WIREHAIR
Largest: 8 AIREDALE
Movie: 4 ASTA TOTO
type: 7 SCOTTIE
Welsh: 8 SEALYHAM
White: 6 WESTIE
**"Terrif!":** 3 FAB
**Terrific:** 5 GREAT SUPER SWELL
time: 5 BLAST
~, in slang: 4 PHAT

**Terrified:** 5 ASHEN
Was ~ by: 7 DREADED
**Terrify:** 5 SCARE
**Terrifying:** 5 SCARY
**Territory:** 4 AREA LAND ZONE
6 DOMAIN
Canadian: 5 YUKON
east of Manila: 4 GUAM
Former U.S.: 6 DAKOTA
Fowl: 4 COOP 5 ROOST
Gang: 4 TURF
Give up: 4 CEDE
Gold rush: 5 YUKON
Indian: 5 DELHI
Kind of: 5 ENEMY
**Terror**
Cry of: 5 OHGOD
Prehistoric: 4 TREX
Squeals of: 4 EEKS
**Terrorism**
prefix: 3 ECO
**Terrorist**
Kenyan: 6 MAUMAU
of renown: 5 CARLO
weapon: 3 UZI
**Terrorize:** 6 MENACE
**Terry**
Clockmaker: 3 ELI
garment: 4 ROBE
Teammate of Hubbell and:
3 OTT
**Terse:** 4 CURT 5 PITHY SHORT
denial: 5 NOTME
review: 3 UGH
summons: 5 SEEME
warning: 4 DONT
**Tertiary Period**
epoch: 6 EOCENE
**Terza ___:** 4 RIMA
**Tesla**
Inventor: 6 NICOLA
**Tessie**
Actress: 5 OSHEA
**"Tess of the D'Urbervilles"**
seducer: 4 ALEC
**Test:** 3 TRY 4 EXAM 5 TRIAL
8 TRIALRUN
answer: 4 TRUE 5 FALSE
area: 3 LAB
Big: 5 FINAL
Brain: 3 EEG
Breeze through a: 3 ACE
choice: 4 TRUE
Diagnostic: 4 SCAN
Difficult: 6 ORDEAL
ER: 3 ECG EKG
F on a: 5 FALSE
for a sr.: 3 GRE
for fit: 5 TRYON
Geometry ~ answer: 4 AREA
Hosp.: 3 ECG EKG
H.S. junior: 4 PSAT
H.S. proficiency: 3 GED
IQ ~ name: 5 BINET
Kind of: 3 DNA 4 ACID BETA
ORAL 5 ESSAY TASTE

M.A. entry: 3 GRE
material: 3 DNA
Nonwritten: 4 ORAL
Prenatal: 5 AMNIO
Preop: 3 ECG EKG
Prepare for a: 5 STUDY
proctor call: 4 TIME
Put to the: 3 TRY USE
5 ASSAY ESSAY
site: 3 LAB
Some ~ answers: 5 TRUES
Tough: 4 ORAL
**Testarossa**
and others: 8 FERRARIS
**Test-driven**
car: 4 DEMO
**Tester**
Air ~ (abbr.): 3 EPA
Beta: 4 USER
IQ: 5 BINET
Water: 3 TOE
**Testify:** 4 AVOW 5 SWEAR
6 DEPONE DEPOSE
**Testimonial**
dinner: 5 HONOR 7 TRIBUTE
**Testimony**
Like court: 5 SWORN
Like some: 4 ORAL
starter: 4 OATH
Take ~ from: 4 HEAR
**Testing**
site: 3 LAB
**Test-marketing**
city: 6 PEORIA
**Testy:** 5 SHORT
Get ~ with: 6 SNAPAT
state: 4 SNIT
**Tet**
observer: 5 ASIAN
**Tête**
thought: 4 IDEE
topper: 5 BERET
**Tête-à-tête:** 4 CHAT TALK
Have a ~ with:
8 SEEALONE
**Tether:** 5 LEASH
**Tethys**
Daughter of: 7 OCEANID
**Tetley**
alternative: 6 NESTEA
SALADA
product: 3 TEA
**Tet Offensive**
city: 6 SAIGON
**Tetra-**
~, twice: 4 OCTA OCTO
**Tetrazzini**
Soprano: 5 LUISA
**Teutonic:** 8 GERMANIC
cry: 3 ACH
lang.: 3 GER
name part: 3 VON
three: 4 DREI
turndown: 4 NEIN
**Tevere**
city: 4 ROMA

**Takes**
Having what it: 4 ABLE
It ~ two: 4 TREY
off: 4 GOES
too much: 3 ODS
**"Take ___, She's Mine":** 3 HER
**Take ___ stride:** 4 ITIN
**"Take that!":** 7 SOTHERE
**"Take this!":** 4 HERE
**"Take ___ Train":** 4 THEA
**"Take ___ your leader":**
4 METO
**"Take your pick":** 3 ANY
8 EITHEROR
**"Take your time!":** 6 NORUSH
**Taking**
after: 3 ALA
For the: 4 FREE
liberty: 6 ASHORE
One ~ off: 4 APER
**Taking-off**
place: 3 SPA
**"Takin' ___ the Streets":** 4 ITTO
**Talbot**
Actress: 4 NITA
**Talcum**
and walcum rhymer: 4 NASH
target: 4 RASH
**Tale:** 4 YARN 5 STORY
Epic: 4 SAGA
Grand-scale: 4 EPIC
Heroic: 4 EPIC SAGA
Moralistic: 5 FABLE
of adventure: 4 GEST 5 GESTE
of woe: 8 SOBSTORY
Old wives': 4 MYTH
starter: 4 ONCE
Tall: 4 YARN
teller: 3 POE 4 BARD LIAR
Told, as a: 4 SPUN
**Talent:** 4 BENT GIFT 5 KNACK
SKILL 8 APTITUDE
Furnish with: 5 ENDOW
Look for: 5 SCOUT
Medium's: 3 ESP
Musical: 3 EAR
Natural: 4 GIFT 5 FLAIR
Special: 5 KNACK
**Talented:** 3 APT 4 ABLE
5 ADEPT
**"Talented Mr. Ripley, The"**
actor Jude: 3 LAW
actor Matt: 5 DAMON
**"Tale of ___ Saltan, The":**
4 TSAR
**Tales**
Folk ~ and such: 4 LORE
Like some: 4 TALL
Tell: 3 LIE 7 NARRATE
**"Tales From the Vienna Woods"**
composer: 7 STRAUSS
**Tales of ___:** 3 WOE
**"... tale told by an ___":**
5 IDIOT
**Talia**
Actress: 5 SHIRE

Cousin of: 7 NICOLAS
**Taliban**
mullah: 4 OMAR
**Talisman:** 4 MOJO 5 CHARM
6 AMULET FETISH
Egyptian: 6 SCARAB
**Talk:** 3 GAB 4 CHAT
a blue streak: 4 CUSS
5 RUNON SWEAR
about: 7 SPEAKOF
amorously: 3 COO
and talk: 3 YAK
Baby: 6 GOOGOO
Back: 3 LIP 4 ECHO GUFF
SASS 6 STATIC
big: 4 BRAG CROW 5 BOAST
Casual: 4 CHAT
Colorful: 5 SLANG
effusively: 4 GUSH
Empty: 3 GAS 4 WIND
6 HOTAIR
First name in: 4 MERV
5 CONAN ELLEN LEEZA
OPRAH REGIS RICKI
ROSIE 6 MONTEL
7 ARSENIO
Fresh: 4 SASS
incessantly: 3 YAP
Insincere: 4 CANT
It's mostly: 7 AMRADIO
Jazzy: 4 JIVE
Kind of: 3 PEP
King of: 5 LARRY
like crazy: 4 RANT
Like some: 5 SMALL
Loose: 5 SLANG
(over): 4 HASH
Playful: 6 BANTER
Small: 4 CHAT 8 CHITCHAT
Something to ~ about: 5 TOPIC
Sun.: 3 SER
too much: 4 BLAB 6 YAMMER
Trade: 5 ARGOT
up: 4 HYPE PRAY TOUT
wildly: 4 RANT
with one's hands: 4 SIGN
**Talk ___:** 4 SHOP
**"___ talk?":** 5 CANWE
**Talkathon:** 7 GABFEST
**Talkative:** 4 GLIB 6 CHATTY
bird: 4 MYNA
**Talked**
a blue streak: 5 SWORE
monotonously: 8 DRONEDON
**Talker**
Caged: 4 MYNA
Morning: 4 IMUS
**Talking**
bird: 4 MYNA
bird of poetry: 5 RAVEN
heads: 5 PANEL
horse of TV: 4 MRED
Not: 3 MUM
point: 3 JAW 5 TOPIC
She's not: 4 MIME
Stop: 6 CLAMUP

trees: 4 ENTS
**Talking-___ (lectures):** 3 TOS
**"Talking in Your Sleep"**
singer: 5 GAYLE
**"Talking Straight"**
author: 7 IACOCCA
**"Talk Radio"**
actor Baldwin: 4 ALEC
director Oliver: 5 STONE
**Talks**
It: 5 MONEY
**Talk show**
group: 5 PANEL
host Jay: 4 LENO
host Joe: 4 PYNE
host Tom: 6 SNYDER
lineup: 6 GUESTS
partner: 6 COHOST
pioneer: 4 PAAR
Radio ~ participant:
6 CALLER
Try to reach a: 6 DIALIN
**Tall**
and trim: 4 LANK
bird: 3 EMU
hat wearer: 4 CHEF
It may be: 4 TALE
stalk: 4 REED
story: 4 TALE YARN
Straight and: 5 ERECT
tale: 4 YARN
**Tallchief, Maria**
tribe: 5 OSAGE
**Taller**
Get: 4 GROW
**Tallies**
NBA: 3 PTS
**Tallinn**
native: 4 ESTH
resident: 8 ESTONIAN
**Tallow**
ingredient: 4 SUET
**Tally:** 3 ADD
mark: 5 NOTCH
**Talmadge**
Actress: 5 NORMA
**Talmud**
expert: 5 RABBI
language: 6 HEBREW
**Talmudic**
Noted ~ sage: 6 HILLEL
**Talon:** 4 CLAW
**Talus**
area: 5 ANKLE
**Tam:** 3 CAP
wearer's tongue: 4 ERSE
**Tamale**
topping: 5 SALSA
**Tamblyn**
Actor: 4 RUSS
**"Tamburlaine the Great"**
playwright: 7 MARLOWE
**Tamed**
Easily ~ bird: 3 EMU
**"Tamerlane"**
dramatist Nicholas: 4 ROWE

**"Taming of the Shrew, The"**
setting: 5 PADUA
shrew: 4 KATE
**Tamiroff**
Actor: 4 AKIM
**Tammany Hall**
caricaturist: 4 NAST
leader: 5 TWEED
**Tammy**
Actress: 6 GRIMES
Jim and ~ gp.: 3 PTL
Singer: 7 WYNETTE
**"Tammy"**
singer Debbie: 8 REYNOLDS
**Tammy Faye**
former org.: 3 PTL
**Tampa**
City south of: 8 SARASOTA
neighbor: 6 STPETE
paper, for short: 4 TRIB
**Tampa Bay**
player, for short: 3 BUC
**Tamper**
with: 3 RIG
**Tamper-resistant:** 6 SEALED
**Tan:** 3 SUN 4 ECRU
Author: 3 AMY
Black and ~ ingredient: 3 ALE
Light: 4 ECRU
too long: 4 BAKE
**Tandem**
Go by: 5 PEDAL
**Tandoor:** 4 OVEN
baked bread: 3 NAN
**Tang:** 3 NIP 4 ZEST
**T'ang dynasty**
poet: 4 LIPO
**Tangelo**
variety: 4 UGLI
**Tangent:** 5 RATIO
Go off on a: 7 DIGRESS
**Tangible:** 4 REAL 8 CONCRETE
**Tangier**
Port east of: 4 ORAN
**Tangle:** 3 MAT WEB 5 MELEE
RAVEL SKEIN SNARL
6 ENMESH 7 ENSNARL
Bureaucratic: 7 REDTAPE
Traffic: 5 SNARL
up: 6 ENMESH 7 ENSNARL
**Tangled:** 5 MESSY
**Tanglewood**
town: 5 LENOX
**Tango:** 5 DANCE
move: 3 DIP
number: 3 TWO
**Tanguy**
Painter: 4 YVES
**Tangy**
drink: 7 LIMEADE
Most: 7 TARTEST
pie flavor: 5 LEMON
**Tank:** 3 VAT
Brewery: 3 VAT
filler: 3 GAS
Fill the: 5 GASUP

fish: 5 TETRA
Kind of: 6 SEPTIC 7 SHERMAN
Rainwater: 7 CISTERN
suffix: 3 ARD
top: 6 GASCAP TURRET
**Tankard**
filler: 3 ALE
**Tanker:** 4 SHIP 5 OILER
mishap: 5 SPILL
**Tankful:** 3 GAS
**"Tank Girl"**
actress Petty: 4 LORI
rapper: 4 ICET
**Tanks:** 7 AQUARIA
and such: 5 ARMOR
**Tanned**
Hardly: 4 PALE
**Tanner:** 3 SUN
tub: 3 VAT
wares: 5 HIDES
**Tanners**
catch them: 4 RAYS
**Tannery**
tool: 3 AWL
**Tanning**
abbr.: 3 UVA
lotion letters: 3 SPF
**Tannish:** 4 ECRU
**Tantalize:** 5 TEMPT
**Tantalus**
Daughter of: 5 NIOBE
**Tantara:** 5 BLARE
**Tantrum:** 3 FIT 4 RAGE
**Tanzanian**
neighbor: 7 RWANDAN
park: 9 SERENGETI
tongue: 7 SWAHILI
**Tao**
founder: 6 LAOTSE
~, literally: 6 THEWAY
**Taoism**
emerging dynasty: 4 CHOU
founder: 6 LAOTSE
**Taormina**
Peak near: 4 ETNA
**Taos**
material: 5 ADOBE
**Tap:** 6 DRAWON SPIGOT
Back: 3 PAT
choice: 3 ALE
Green: 4 PUTT
label: 3 HOT
Morse: 3 DIT
output: 3 ALE
problem: 4 DRIP
Type of: 6 SPINAL
**"Tap"**
Gregory of: 5 HINES
**Tape**
Audition: 4 DEMO
Beat to the: 6 OUTRAN
7 OUTRACE
Break the: 3 WIN
Clear the: 5 ERASE
deck button: 3 REC 5 EJECT
ERASE

holder: 8 CASSETTE
Kind of: 4 BETA DEMO DUCT
5 VIDEO
Linen: 5 INKLE
Not on: 4 LIVE
Obsolete: 10 EIGHTTRACK
over: 5 ERASE
rec. jack: 3 MIC
Ticker: 3 EKG
Trimming: 5 INKLE
**Taper:** 3 VCR
off: 4 WANE 5 ABATE
**Tapered**
Cylindrical and: 6 TERETE
end: 5 POINT
feature: 7 STEEPLE
tuck: 4 DART
**Tapestry:** 5 ARRAS
beast: 7 UNICORN
**Tapioca**
source: 7 CASSAVA
**Tapir**
feature: 5 SNOUT
**Tappan ___ Bridge:** 3 ZEE
**Tapped**
It's: 3 KEG
**Taproom**
site: 3 INN
**"Taps"**
instrument: 5 BUGLE
time: 3 TEN
**Taqueria**
order: 7 TOSTADA
**Tar:** 3 GOB 4 SALT SWAB
6 SEADOG SEAMAN
British: 5 LIMEY
tale: 4 YARN
~, in Spanish: 4 BREA
**Tara**
Butler at: 5 RHETT
family: 6 OHARAS
Scarlett of: 5 OHARA
**Taradiddle:** 3 FIB
**Tarantino**
Director: 7 QUENTIN
Like most ~ films: 6 RATEDR
**Tarantula:** 6 SPIDER
**"Taras Bulba"**
author: 5 GOGOL
extra: 7 COSSACK
**Tarbell**
Author: 3 IDA
**Tarboosh**
feature: 6 TASSEL
kin: 3 FEZ
**Tardiness**
excuse: 8 LATEPASS
**Tardy:** 4 LATE
Somewhat: 6 LATISH
**Target:** 3 AIM 4 PREY
5 AIMAT
1969 ~: 4 MOON
competitor: 5 KMART SEARS
On: 3 APT
Pick a: 3 AIM
Tell tale: 5 APPLE

**Tar Heel State**
(abbr.): 4 NCAR
campus: 4 ELON
sch.: 3 UNC
**Tariff:** 3 FEE
1930 ~ cosponsor: 5 SMOOT
eliminating pact: 5 NAFTA
**Tariq**
Former Iraqi diplomat: 4 AZIZ
**Tarkenton**
of football: 4 FRAN
**Tarkington**
novel: 6 PENROD
**Tarmac**
Hit the: 4 LAND
Touched the: 4 ALIT
**"Tarnation!":** 4 EGAD
**Tarnish:** 3 MAR 4 SOIL 5 STAIN
TAINT
**Tarnisher**
Reputation: 4 BLOT
**Taro**
dish: 3 POI
root: 4 EDDO
**Tarot**
reader: 4 SEER
suit: 4 CUPS
**Tarpon:** 4 FISH
**Tarragon:** 4 HERB
**Tarry:** 4 BIDE
**Tarsal**
prefix: 4 META
**Tart:** 4 ACID 5 ACERB ACRID
6 ACIDIC
fruit: 4 SLOE
taste: 4 TANG
thief: 5 KNAVE
Very: 5 ACERB
**Tartan**
cap: 3 TAM
garb: 4 KILT
pattern: 5 PLAID
sporters: 4 CLAN
**"Tartuffe"**
author: 7 MOLIERE
**Tarzan:** 6 APEMAN
actor Ely: 3 RON
actor Ron: 3 ELY
companion: 3 APE
kid: 3 BOY
mate: 4 JANE
transportation: 4 VINE
**Task:** 3 JOB 5 CHORE STINT
Equal to the: 4 ABLE
Is up to the: 3 CAN
Not up to the: 5 INEPT
Routine: 5 CHORE
Tough: 4 ONUS
Up to the: 4 ABLE
**Tasman**
Explorer: 4 ABEL
**Tasmania**
capital: 6 HOBART
Peak in: 4 OSSA
**Tass**
country: 4 USSR

**Tasseled**
topper: 3 FEZ TAM
**Taste:** 3 BIT SIP TRY 5 SENSE
6 LIKING SAMPLE
Enjoy the: 5 SAVOR
Personal: 8 CUPOFTEA
Sense of: 6 PALATE
Sharp: 4 TANG
Small: 3 SIP
stimulus: 4 ODOR
test label: 6 BRANDX
Zingy: 4 TANG
**Tasteless:** 4 BLAH 5 BLAND
CRASS GAUDY TACKY
**Tastelessly**
affected: 6 TOOTOO
**"Taste of Honey, A"**
playwright: 7 DELANEY
**Taster**
Wine ~ concern: 4 YEAR
**"Tastes awful!":** 3 UGH
**Tastiness:** 5 SAPOR
**Tasting**
Bitter: 5 ACERB
like Tokay: 4 WINY
of wood: 4 OAKY
Wine: 3 SIP
**Tasty:** 4 GOOD 5 SAPID
dish: 5 VIAND
mushroom: 5 MOREL
tuber: 3 YAM
**"Tasty!":** 3 MMM YUM
4 MMMM
**Tat**
equivalent: 3 TIT
**"Ta-ta!":** 4 CIAO 5 ADIEU
SEEYA 7 CHEERIO
**Tatar**
ruler: 4 KHAN
**Tate**
British poet: 5 NAHUM
collection: 3 ART
**Tater:** 4 SPUD
state: 5 IDAHO
**Taters**
Some: 7 IDAHOES
**Tater Tots**
maker: 6 OREIDA
**Tati**
character: 5 HULOT
**"Tatler, The"**
founder: 6 STEELE
**Tatter:** 3 RAG
product: 4 LACE
**Tattered:** 4 TORN WORN
5 RATTY 6 INRAGS
attire: 4 RAGS
**"Tattered Tom"**
author: 5 ALGER
**Tatting**
material: 4 LACE
**Tattle:** 3 RAT 4 BLAB TELL
6 TELLON
**Tattled:** 4 TOLD
**Tattletale:** 3 RAT 6 SNITCH
7 BLABBER

**Tattoo**
fluid: 3 INK
for kids: 5 DECAL
Popeye: 6 ANCHOR
site: 3 ARM
word: 3 MOM
**"Tattooed lady"**
of song: 5 LYDIA
**Tatum**
Father of: 4 RYAN
Jazzman: 3 ART
Oscar winner: 5 ONEAL
**Tatyana**
Singer: 3 ALI
**Taught:** 8 SCHOOLED
**Taunt:** 4 GIBE GOAD JEST
TWIT 5 RAGON TEASE
**Taunting**
cry: 3 OHO
remark: 4 GIBE
**Tauromachian**
cheer: 3 OLE
**Taurus:** 3 CAR 4 AUTO
Constellation next to: 5 ORION
Sign after: 6 GEMINI
Sign before: 5 ARIES
Star in: 9 ALDEBARAN
**Taut:** 12 TIGHTASADRUM
**Tautness**
Lose: 3 SAG 5 DROOP
**Tauto-**
What ~ means: 4 SAME
**Tavern:** 3 BAR INN PUB
inventory: 4 KEGS
offering: 4 BEER
order: 3 ALE RYE
sign abbr.: 4 ESTD 5 ESTAB
temptress: 5 BGIRL
**Tax:** 3 TRY 4 DUTY LEVY
agcy.: 3 IRS
British: 4 CESS
cheat catchers: 4 TMEN
cheat's risk: 5 AUDIT
form ID: 3 SSN
form info (abbr.): 3 IRA
Imposed a: 6 LEVIED
Kind of: 3 SIN USE 6 EXCISE
mo.: 3 APR
pro: 3 CPA 8 ASSESSOR
Protectionist: 6 TARIFF
Some ~ shelters: 8 ROTHIRAS
time: 5 APRIL
**Tax-___:** 6 EXEMPT
**Tax-deferred**
acct.: 3 IRA 7 ROTHIRA
**Taxes**
Earn after: 3 NET
Impose: 4 LEVY
Take home, after: 5 CLEAR
**Taxi:** 3 CAB 4 HACK
feature: 4 HORN 5 METER
fee: 4 FARE
Like a: 7 METERED
Typical: 5 SEDAN
**"Taxi"**
Danny on: 5 LOUIE

driver: 4 ALEX
Judd on: 4 ALEX
Marilu on: 6 ELAINE
mechanic: 5 LATKA
**Taxidermy**
Perform: 5 STUFF
**Taxing**
Do ~ work: 6 ASSESS
Less: 6 EASIER
mo.: 3 APR
org.: 3 IRS
trip: 4 TREK
**Taxonomic**
subdivisions: 5 PHYLA
suffix: 3 OTA
**Taxpayer:** 5 FILER
dread: 5 AUDIT 8 IRSAUDIT
~ ID: 3 SSN
**Tay:** 4 LOCH
Tiny, on the: 3 SMA
**Taylor**
1963 ~ role: 4 CLEO
A ~ husband: 4 TODD
Actress: 4 LILI 5 RENEE
Blues singer: 4 KOKO
boy: 4 OPIE
Entertainer: 3 RIP
nickname: 3 LIZ
Pop singer: 5 DAYNE
predecessor: 4 POLK
~, for one: 4 WHIG
**Taylor, Claudia ___:** 4 ALTA
**Tazer**
Use a ~ on: 4 STUN
**T-bar:** 3 TOW
**T-Bird**
Old ~ features: 4 FINS
**T-bone:** 5 STEAK
**Tbsp.:** 3 AMT
fractions: 4 TSPS
**Tchaikovsky**
ballet: 8 SWANLAKE
ballet role: 4 SWAN
middle name: 5 ILICH
**Tchotchke:** 7 TRINKET
holder: 7 ETAGERE
**TDK**
rival: 7 MEMOREX
**Te-___ (cigar brand):** 3 AMO
**Tea:** 6 SOCIAL
biscuit: 5 SCONE
Black: 5 PEKOE
brand: 6 LIPTON SALADA
    6 TETLEY
Brit's bit of: 4 SPOT
Chinese: 3 CHA
Grade of: 5 PEKOE
growing state: 5 ASSAM
holder: 3 BAG TIN
Iced ~ garnish: 5 LEMON
Interpret ~ leaves: 4 READ
leaf reader: 4 SEER
Like some: 4 ICED 6 HERBAL
party member: 5 ALICE
    8 DORMOUSE
Prepare: 4 BREW 5 STEEP

quantity: 4 SPOT
server: 3 URN
Spiced: 4 CHAI
Texas: 3 OIL
time: 4 FOUR
type: 5 PEKOE 6 HERBAL
    OOLONG
**Téa**
Actress: 5 LEONI
**Teach:** 5 TRAIN 7 EDUCATE
**Teacher:** 4 PROF
Bauhaus: 4 KLEE
charges: 5 CLASS
favorite: 3 PET
goal: 6 TENURE
Hindu: 4 GURU 5 SWAMI
Jewish: 5 REBBE
joy: 8 ASTUDENT
Martial arts: 6 SENSEI
of Bart: 4 EDNA
of Heifetz: 4 AUER
of Luke: 4 YODA
of Samuel: 3 ELI
of Stradivari: 5 AMATI
org.: 3 NEA
request: 5 SEEME
TV: 4 GABE
Wise: 6 MENTOR
Word a ~ likes to hear: 3 AHA
~, sometimes: 6 TESTER
**Teaching**
deg.: 3 EDB EDD MED 4 BSED
Do a ~ job: 5 GRADE
Elders: 4 LORE
**"Teach not thy lip such ___":**
    5 SCORN
**Teacup**
handle: 3 EAR
**"Tea for Two"**
musical: 11 NONONANETTE
**Teal**
Color similar to: 4 AQUA
hangout: 4 POND
**Team:** 4 SIDE 5 SQUAD
    6 TANDEM
Competing: 4 SIDE
Crew: 4 OARS
Farm: 4 OXEN SPAN
Football: 6 ELEVEN
Greet the opposing: 3 BOO
Hockey: 6 SEXTET
It keeps the ~ together:
    4 YOKE
Kind of: 3 TAG 4 AWAY FARM
    SWAT
Lacrosse: 3 TEN
leader: 4 CAPTAIN
lineup: 6 ROSTER
members: 4 OXEN
morale: 6 SPIRIT
Mule: 4 ARMY
Police: 4 SWAT
Show ~ spirit: 4 ROOT
Small: 3 DUO
Sports: 5 SQUAD
The other: 4 THEM

Word to a: 4 MUSH
**Teamsters**
notable: 5 HOFFA
rig: 4 SEMI
**Teamwork**
deterrent: 3 EGO
**Teapot**
cover: 4 COZY
feature: 5 SPOUT
Tempest in a: 3 ADO 4 FUSS
**Teapot Dome**
figure: 10 ALBERTFALL
**Tear:** 3 RIP 4 RACE REND
    RENT 5 SPREE
    8 LACERATE
apart: 3 RIP 4 REND RIVE
carrier: 4 DUCT
Doesn't just ~ up: 4 SOBS
down: 4 RAZE
down (British): 4 RASE
Fix a: 4 DARN
in little pieces: 5 SHRED
into: 6 ASSAIL ATTACK
It brings a ~ to the eye:
    4 DUCT
jerker: 5 ONION
More than ~ up: 4 BAWL
    WEEP
open: 5 UNRIP
Partner of: 4 WEAR
roughly: 8 LACERATE
Shed a: 4 WEPT
to pieces: 4 REND 5 RIPUP
up: 3 CRY RIP 4 MIST REND
    WEEP
Wear and: 3 USE
Words before: 3 ONA
**Tearful:** 3 SAD 5 WEEPY
**Tearjerker:** 5 ONION
necessity: 6 TISSUE
React to a: 3 CRY
**Tearoom:** 4 CAFE
**Tears**
Blur with: 5 BLEAR
into: 5 HASAT
Like: 5 SALTY 6 SALINE
Shed: 4 WEEP WEPT
**Teasdale**
Poet: 4 SARA
**Tease:** 3 KID RAG RIB 4 BAIT
    JOSH RAZZ RIDE TWIT
    5 RAGON 6 LEADON
    NEEDLE
**Teased:** 4 RODE
**Teaser**
Kitty: 6 CATNIP
TV: 5 PROMO
**Teasing**
result: 7 BIGHAIR
**Teaspoon:** 4 DOSE
**Teatime**
treat: 5 SCONE
**Teatro alla ___:** 5 SCALA
**Teatro Costanzi**
debut of 1900: 5 TOSCA
**Teatro ___ Scala:** 4 ALLA

**Tebaldi**
Soprano: 6 RENATA
**Tech**
sch. grad: 4 ENGR
stock: 3 IBM
___ Tech: 3 CAL
**Techie**
client: 4 USER
Kind of:
14 SYSTEMSANALYST
~, maybe: 4 NERD
**"___ Te Ching":** 3 TAO
**Technical**
data: 5 SPECS
sch.: 4 INST
**Technicality**
Kind of: 4 MERE
**Technician**
Piano: 5 TUNER
spot: 3 LAB
**Technique:** 3 ART 4 MODE
Film editing: 4 WIPE
Jazz: 4 SCAT
Memorization: 4 ROTE
Mosaic: 5 INLAY
Mountain climbing: 6 RAPPEL
Replay: 5 SLOMO
**Techno**
Popular ~ musician: 4 MOBY
suffix: 4 CRAT
**Technological**
advance of the 50's:
7 COLORTV
marvel of 1951: 6 UNIVAC
**Technologically**
advanced:
13 STATEOFTHEART
**Technology**
prefix: 4 NANO
**Techs**
It has many: 6 NASDAQ
**Tecs:** 3 PIS
**Tecumseh:** 7 SHAWNEE
**Ted**
Rocker: 6 NUGENT
**Teddies:** 8 LINGERIE
**Teddy**
Eleanor, to: 5 NIECE
**Tedious:** 5 PROSY
8 TIRESOME
situation: 4 DRAG
task: 4 ONUS 5 CHORE
**Tediously**
Proceed: 4 PLOD
**Tedium:** 5 ENNUI
**Tee**
follower: 3 HEE
Hit from a: 5 DRIVE
off: 3 IRE IRK 4 RILE
5 ANGER DRIVE
preceder: 3 ESS
To a: 3 PAT
user: 6 GOLFER
___ tee: 3 TOA
**Teed**
off: 4 SORE 5 IRATE

**Tee-hee**
More than a: 4 HAHA
**Teem:** 6 ABOUND
**Teeming:** 4 RIFE 6 ASWARM
**Teen:** 7 MALLRAT
affliction: 4 ACNE
fave: 4 IDOL 7 POPSTAR
hangout: 4 MALL
Much ~ talk: 5 SLANG
of comics: 6 ARCHIE
outcast: 4 NERD
party: 9 SLEEPOVER
spots: 4 ACNE
suffix: 4 AGER
wall décor: 6 POSTER
woe: 3 ZIT 4 ACNE
**Teen ___:** 4 IDOL
**Teena**
Singer: 5 MARIE
**Teenage**
hooligan, to a Brit: 3 YOB
Like some ~ turtles:
6 MUTANT
**Teenage Mutant ___ Turtles:**
5 NINJA
**Teenager**
Many a ~ room: 4 MESS
woe: 4 ACNE
**"___ Teen-age Werewolf":**
5 IWASA
**Teens**
Great, to: 3 RAD
Not for most: 6 RATEDR
Rock star, to: 4 IDOL
**Teensy:** 3 WEE
bit: 4 ATOM IOTA
**Teeny:** 3 WEE 4 ITSY 5 BITSY
6 PETITE 9 ITSYBITSY
parasites: 5 MITES
**Teeter-totter:** 6 SEESAW
**Teeth:** 4 COGS
Deg. with: 3 DDS
Gear: 4 COGS
Grind, as: 5 GNASH
Grinding: 6 MOLARS
Like hen's: 4 RARE
One with sharp: 3 SAW
Sink one's ~ into: 4 BITE
Space between: 8 DIASTEMA
Tool with: 3 SAW 4 RAKE
**Teetotaler:** 3 DRY 7 NONUSER
order: 4 SODA
**Teflon**
maker: 6 DUPONT
**"Teflon Don, The":** 5 GOTTI
**Teheran**
City SW of: 3 QOM
coin: 4 RIAL
country: 5 IRAN
Former ~ ruler: 4 SHAH
native: 5 IRANI
tongue: 5 FARSI
**Tehrani**
tongue: 5 FARSI
**Tejano**
singer: 6 SELENA

**Te Kanawa**
Soprano: 4 KIRI
**Tel.**
book listings: 3 NOS
line: 3 EXT
**Tel ___:** 4 AVIV
**Tel Aviv**
Airline to: 4 ELAL
Airport near: 3 LOD
native: 5 SABRA 7 ISRAELI
server: 4 ELAL
**Telecast**
component: 5 AUDIO
over: 5 RERUN
**Telecom**
Former ~ giant: 3 GTE ITT
giant: 3 ATT
**Telecommunications**
Old ~ name: 5 NYNEX
speed unit: 4 BAUD
**Telecommuter**
Where a ~ works: 6 ATHOME
**Telegram:** 4 WIRE
period: 4 STOP
Send, as a: 6 TAPOUT
**Telegrams**
Like some: 4 SUNG
**Telegraph**
click: 3 DIT
inventor: 5 MORSE
key: 6 TAPPER
**Telepathy:** 3 ESP PSI
**Telephone:** 4 CALL
6 on a ~: 3 MNO
abbr.: 4 OPER
button: 4 STAR
button with no letters: 3 ONE
greeting: 5 HELLO
location: 5 BOOTH
part: 4 CORD 6 CRADLE
7 HANDSET
trio: 3 ABC DEF GHI JKL
MNO PRS TUV WXY
user: 5 PARTY
~, in slang: 4 HORN
**Telephoned:** 4 RANG
**"Telephone Line"**
gp.: 3 ELO
**TelePrompter**
filler: 4 TEXT
input: 6 SCRIPT
**Telescope**
Hale ~ site: 7 PALOMAR
part: 4 LENS
pioneer: 7 GALILEO
sights: 5 STARS
Small: 8 SPYGLASS
**Telescopium**
Constellation next to: 3 ARA
**Telesthesia:** 3 ESP
**TeleTax**
org.: 3 IRS
**Televise:** 3 AIR
**Television:** 5 MEDIA
announcer Don: 5 PARDO
award: 4 EMMY

cabinet: 7 CONSOLE
Show on: 3 AIR
**Tell:** 6 INFORM RELATE
    7 NARRATE
a good one: 3 LIE
all: 4 BLAB SING
a thing or two: 5 SCOLD
a whopper: 3 LIE
Could: 6 SENSED
Didn't mean to: 7 LETSLIP
forte: 7 ARCHERY
it like it isn't: 3 LIE
It's hard to: 4 SAGA
projectile: 5 ARROW
tales: 3 LIE 7 NARRATE
**Tell-___ (some biographies):**
    4 ALLS
**Tell, William:** 6 ARCHER
canton: 3 URI
**Teller:** 3 RAT
Bygone tale: 4 BARD
call: 4 NEXT
Fortune: 4 SEER 5 TAROT
    6 ORACLE
Partner of: 4 PENN
post: 4 CAGE
stack: 4 ONES TENS
Tale: 3 POE 4 LIAR
**Telling:** 6 COGENT
trial: 8 ACIDTEST
**"Tell It to My Heart"**
singer Taylor: 5 DAYNE
**"Tell ___ lies":** 4 MENO
**"Tell Mama"**
singer James: 4 ETTA
**"Tell ___ story":** 3 MEA
**Telltale**
sign: 4 ODOR OMEN
**"Tell-Tale Heart, The"**
author: 3 POE
**"Tell ___ the judge!":** 4 ITTO
**"Tell ___ the Marines!":** 4 ITTO
**Telly**
network: 3 BBC
on the telly: 7 SAVALAS
**Temp**
Year-end: 5 SANTA
**Tempe**
sch.: 3 ASU
**Temper:** 3 IRE 4 HUFF MOOD
    5 IRISH 6 ANNEAL
Ill: 3 IRE 4 BILE
Lose one's:
    13 HITTHECEILING
**Tempera**
painting surface: 5 GESSO
**Temperament:** 4 MOOD
    6 NATURE
**Temperamental:** 5 MOODY
star: 4 DIVA
tizzy: 4 SNIT
**Temperate:** 4 MILD
**Temperature:** 4 HEAT
Body ~, etc.: 6 VITALS
scale: 7 CELSIUS
taker: 5 NURSE

___ temperature: 4 RANA
**Temperatures**
Freezing: 5 TEENS
**Tempest:** 5 STORM
in a teapot: 3 ADO 4 FUSS
**"Tempest, The"**
fairy: 5 ARIEL
king: 6 ALONSO
magician: 8 PROSPERO
Sci-fi version of:
    15 FORBIDDENPLANET
slave: 7 CALIBAN
**Tempest ___ teapot:** 3 INA
**Temple**
athlete: 3 OWL
Chinese: 6 PAGODA
Common ~ name: 7 EMANUEL
Greek: 4 NAOS
image: 4 IDOL
leader: 5 RABBI
Object near a: 3 EAR
player: 3 OWL
Roman: 8 PANTHEON
Shinto ~ gateway: 5 TORII
text: 5 TORAH
**Temple, Shirley**
role: 5 HEIDI
**Temple of ___:** 4 ARES ZEUS
**Temple of Apollo**
site: 6 DELPHI
**Temple of Zeus**
site: 5 NEMEA
**Temples**
Site of two: 9 ABUSIMBEL
They're found beside:
    7 GLASSES
**Templeton**
Pianist: 4 ALEC
**Tempo:** 4 PACE RATE
    5 SPEED
Fast: 6 PRESTO
Slow: 5 LARGO LENTO
**Temporarily:** 6 FORNOW
    8 FORATIME
be: 5 ACTAS
Give: 4 LEND LOAN
Joined: 5 SATIN
put aside: 5 ONICE
**Temporary:** 5 ADHOC 6 ACTING
    7 INTERIM
fashion: 3 FAD
fix: 7 STOPGAP
gift: 4 LOAN
money: 5 SCRIP
wheels: 6 LOANER
**Tempt:** 4 BAIT LURE 6 ENTICE
    SEDUCE
fate: 4 DARE
**Temptation**
Dieter's: 5 AROMA
location: 4 EDEN
**"Temptation of St. Anthony,**
**The"**
artist: 5 BOSCH ERNST
**Temptations**
1965 ~ hit: 6 MYGIRL

**Tempted**
It may be: 4 FATE
**Tempter:** 5 SATAN SIREN
    WOOER
Eve: 7 SERPENT
Fish: 4 LURE
**Temptress:** 5 SIREN
Joe Hardy: 4 LOLA
Play the: 6 SEDUCE
Rhine: 7 LORELEI
Tavern: 5 BGIRL
**Ten**
Hang: 4 SURF
or higher: 5 HONOR
percenter (abbr.): 3 AGT
prefix: 4 DECA
sawbucks: 5 CNOTE
Take: 4 REST
Top ~, for one: 4 LIST
Top ~ item: 3 HIT
Worth a: 5 IDEAL
**Tenacious:** 6 DOGGED
**Tenant:** 6 LESSEE RENTER
    ROOMER
Feudal: 6 VASSAL
Find a new ~ for: 5 RELET
Joint: 3 CON 5 FELON
Mall: 4 SHOP 5 STORE
payment: 4 RENT
protest: 10 RENTSTRIKE
Tent: 6 CAMPER
Throw out a: 5 EVICT
**Ten Commandments**
mount: 5 SINAI
word: 5 SHALT
~, for the most part: 5 NONOS
**"Ten Commandments, The":**
    4 EPIC
actress Debra: 5 PAGET
director: 7 DEMILLE
Ramses portrayer, in: 3 YUL
**Tend:** 5 SEETO
**Tended:** 5 SAWTO
**Tendency:** 4 BENT 5 TREND
Had a: 5 LEANT
toward chaos: 7 ENTROPY
**Tender:** 4 SORE
Bar: 9 BEERMONEY
ender: 4 LOIN
Some legal: 6 TNOTES
spot: 3 BAR 4 SORE
Tijuana: 4 PESO
touch: 6 CARESS
**"Tender ___":** 7 MERCIES
**Tenderfoot:** 4 TYRO
org.: 3 BSA
**Tender-hearted:** 4 SOFT
**Tenderized**
cut: 9 CUBESTEAK
**Tendon:** 5 SINEW
connector: 5 BURSA
**Tendril:** 4 WISP
**Tenement**
locale: 4 SLUM
**___ tenens (substitute):**
    5 LOCUM

**Tenerife:** 4 ISLA
**Tenet:** 5 CREDO DOGMA
**Tenet, George**
  org.: 3 CIA
**"Ten-hut!"**
  opposite: 6 ATEASE
**Tenn.**
  athlete: 3 VOL
  hours: 3 CST
  neighbor: 3 ALA 4 NCAR
**Tennessee**
  aluminum town: 5 ALCOA
  athlete: 3 VOL
  footballer: 3 VOL 5 TITAN
  Former ~ senator Kefauver:
    5 ESTES
  singer Ford: 5 ERNIE
  state flower: 4 IRIS
  Veep from: 6 ALGORE
**Tennille**
  Singer: 4 TONI
**Tennis:** 5 SPORT
  1965 NCAA ~ champ:
    4 ASHE
  1970s ~ star: 4 ASHE BORG
  call: 3 LET
  Czech ~ player: 5 LENDL
  deuce: 3 TIE
  divider: 3 NET
  do-over: 3 LET
  drop shot: 4 DINK
  First name in 1970s: 4 ILIE
  game point: 4 ADIN
  Great ~ server: 4 ACER
  instructor: 3 PRO
  miscue: 5 FAULT
  New York ~ stadium: 4 ASHE
  Palindromic ~ star: 5 SELES
  ploy: 3 LOB
  Quick round of: 6 ONESET
  ranking: 4 SEED
  score: 4 ADIN 5 ADOUT
  score after deuce: 4 ADIN
  shot: 3 LOB
  Start a ~ game: 5 SERVE
  whiz: 4 ACER
  zero: 4 LOVE
**"Tennis, ___?":** 6 ANYONE
**Tennis player**
  ~ Andre: 6 AGASSI
  ~ Arthur: 4 ASHE
  ~ Becker: 5 BORIS
  ~ Borg: 5 BJORN
  ~ Edberg: 6 STEFAN
  ~ Emerson: 3 ROY
  ~ Fraser: 5 NEALE
  ~ Gibson: 6 ALTHEA
  ~ Hingis: 7 MARTINA
  ~ Hoad: 3 LEW
  ~ Huber: 4 ANKE
  ~ Ilie: 7 NASTASE
  ~ Kournikova: 4 ANNA
  ~ Lacoste: 4 RENE
  ~ Lendl: 4 IVAN
  ~ Makarova: 5 ELENA
  ~ Mandlikova: 4 HANA

  ~ Martina: 6 HINGIS
  ~ Michael: 5 CHANG
  ~ Monica: 5 SELES
  ~ Nastase: 4 ILIE
  ~ René: 7 LACOSTE
  ~ Richards: 5 RENEE
  ~ Rod: 5 LAVER
  ~ Sampras: 4 PETE
  ~ Shriver: 3 PAM
  ~ Smith: 4 STAN
  ~ Steffi: 4 GRAF
  ~ Tanner: 6 ROSCOE
  ~ Williams: 5 VENUS
    6 SERENA
**"Ten North Frederick"**
  writer: 5 OHARA
**Tennyson**
  Arden of: 5 ENOCH
  lady: 4 ENID
  maid: 6 ELAINE
  poem: 5 IDYLL
**Tenochtitlán**
  resident: 5 AZTEC
**Tenor**
  top note: 5 HIGHC
  tune: 4 ARIA
  Voice above: 4 ALTO
  warhorse: 8 OSOLEMIO
**Tenpenny:** 4 NAIL
**Ten-percenter:** 5 AGENT
**Tense:** 4 EDGY TAUT
    6 ONEDGE
  Get less: 4 THAW
  Kind of: 4 PAST
  Make less: 6 DEFUSE
  ~, with "up": 5 KEYED
**Ten-sided**
  figure: 7 DECAGON
**Tension:** 6 STRESS
**Ten-speed:** 4 BIKE
**Tent**
  caterpillar: 5 EGGER
  Conical: 5 TEPEE
  event: 4 SALE
  furnishing: 3 COT
  holder: 3 PEG 5 STAKE
  Mongol: 4 YURT
  Pitch a: 4 CAMP 6 ENCAMP
  tenant: 6 CAMPER
**Tentacle:** 3 ARM
**Tentacled**
  animal: 5 POLYP SQUID
    7 ANEMONE
    10 SEAANEMONE
**Tentative**
  taste: 3 SIP
**Tenterhooks**
  On: 4 EDGY 5 TENSE
**Tenth**
  anniversary gift: 3 TIN
  Break the ~ Commandment:
    5 COVET
  part: 5 TITHE
  prefix: 4 DECI
**Tenth-grader:** 4 SOPH
    9 SOPHOMORE

**Tentmaker**
  Literary: 4 OMAR
**Tenuous:** 8 ETHEREAL
**Tenure:** 5 STINT
  Military: 4 TOUR
  of office: 4 TERM
**Tenzing**
  Sherpa guide: 6 NORGAY
**Teo**
  of racing: 4 FABI
**Tepee**
  makeup: 4 HIDE
  shape: 4 CONE
  shaped: 5 CONIC
**Tequila**
  serving: 4 SHOT
  source: 5 AGAVE
**Teresa, Mother:** 3 NUN
  ~, by birth: 8 ALBANIAN
**Teresa, Saint**
  birthplace: 5 AVILA
**Terfel**
  Opera singer: 4 BRYN
**Terhune**
  classic: 7 LADADOG
  dog: 3 LAD
**Teri**
  Actress: 4 GARR
  Role for: 4 LOIS
**Teriyaki**
  seasoning: 6 GINGER
**Terkel**
  Author: 5 STUDS
**Term:** 5 STINT 7 SESSION
  Academic: 8 SEMESTER
  of affection: 5 CUTIE
  of endearment: 3 HON PET
    4 BABE 5 HONEY
    TOOTE
    10 HONEYBUNCH
  of respect: 3 SIR 4 MAAM
  paper abbr.: 4 IBID
  paper citation: 6 IBIDEM
  Prison: 7 STRETCH
**Termagant:** 5 SHREW
    8 SHREWISH
**Term-ending**
  test: 5 FINAL
**Terminal:** 3 END 5 DEPOT
    FATAL
  abbr.: 3 POS
  Battery: 5 ANODE
  Battery ~ (abbr.): 3 NEG POS
  Cell: 7 CATHODE
  Chicago: 5 OHARE
  info: 3 ETA
  JFK: 3 TWA
  Like a battery: 6 ANODAL
  list (abbr.): 4 ARRS
  Network: 4 NODE
  posting: 3 ETA
  R.R.: 3 STA
**"Terminal Bliss"**
  actress Chandler: 5 ESTEE
**Terminate:** 3 AXE CAN END
    4 FIRE 5 CEASE

**Terminator**
Pasta: 3 INI
**"Terminator, The"**
heroine: 5 SARAH
**Termini:** 4 ENDS
Modem: 3 EMS
**Terminus:** 3 END
Chisholm Trail: 7 ABILENE
I-79: 4 ERIE
Iditarod: 4 NOME
Race: 4 TAPE
Suez Canal: 6 REDSEA
**Termitarium:** 4 NEST
**Termite:** 4 PEST
hunter: 8 ANTEATER
relative: 3 ANT
**Terms**
Come to: 5 AGREE
**Tern:** 7 SEABIRD
**Terpsichore**
Sister of: 5 ERATO
**Terr.**
Former U.S.: 3 DAK
**Terra ___:** 5 COTTA FIRMA
**Terra firma:** 4 LAND SOIL
5 EARTH
On: 6 ASHORE
**Terrapin:** 6 TURTLE
**Terrarium**
growth: 4 MOSS
plant: 4 FERN
youngster: 3 EFT
**Terre**
Opposite of: 3 MER
**Terre ___:** 5 HAUTE
**Terre Haute**
river: 6 WABASH
sch.: 3 ISU
**Terrestrial**
newt: 3 EFT
**Terrible**
He was: 4 IVAN
More: 5 DIRER
time: 4 TWOS
twos: 5 PHASE
type: 6 ENFANT
**"Terrible"**
tsar: 4 IVAN 6 IVANIV
**___ terrible (brat):** 6 ENFANT
**"... ___ terrible thing to waste":**
3 ISA
**Terribly**
Bother: 5 EATAT
**Terrier**
cry: 3 ARF
Kind of: 4 SKYE 5 CAIRN
8 AIREDALE WIREHAIR
Largest: 8 AIREDALE
Movie: 4 ASTA TOTO
type: 7 SCOTTIE
Welsh: 8 SEALYHAM
White: 6 WESTIE
**"Terrif!":** 3 FAB
**Terrific:** 5 GREAT SUPER SWELL
time: 5 BLAST
~, in slang: 4 PHAT

**Terrified:** 5 ASHEN
Was ~ by: 7 DREADED
**Terrify:** 5 SCARE
**Terrifying:** 5 SCARY
**Territory:** 4 AREA LAND ZONE
6 DOMAIN
Canadian: 5 YUKON
east of Manila: 4 GUAM
Former U.S.: 6 DAKOTA
Fowl: 4 COOP 5 ROOST
Gang: 4 TURF
Give up: 4 CEDE
Gold rush: 5 YUKON
Indian: 5 DELHI
Kind of: 5 ENEMY
**Terror**
Cry of: 5 OHGOD
Prehistoric: 4 TREX
Squeals of: 4 EEKS
**Terrorism**
prefix: 3 ECO
**Terrorist**
Kenyan: 6 MAUMAU
of renown: 5 CARLO
weapon: 3 UZI
**Terrorize:** 6 MENACE
**Terry**
Clockmaker: 3 ELI
garment: 4 ROBE
Teammate of Hubbell and:
3 OTT
**Terse:** 4 CURT 5 PITHY SHORT
denial: 5 NOTME
review: 3 UGH
summons: 5 SEEME
warning: 4 DONT
**Tertiary Period**
epoch: 6 EOCENE
**Terza ___:** 4 RIMA
**Tesla**
Inventor: 6 NICOLA
**Tessie**
Actress: 5 OSHEA
**"Tess of the D'Urbervilles"**
seducer: 4 ALEC
**Test:** 3 TRY 4 EXAM 5 TRIAL
8 TRIALRUN
answer: 4 TRUE 5 FALSE
area: 3 LAB
Big: 5 FINAL
Brain: 3 EEG
Breeze through a: 3 ACE
choice: 4 TRUE
Diagnostic: 4 SCAN
Difficult: 6 ORDEAL
ER: 3 ECG EKG
F on a: 5 FALSE
for a sr.: 3 GRE
for fit: 5 TRYON
Geometry ~ answer: 4 AREA
Hosp.: 3 ECG EKG
H.S. junior: 4 PSAT
H.S. proficiency: 3 GED
IQ ~ name: 5 BINET
Kind of: 3 DNA 4 ACID BETA
ORAL 5 ESSAY TASTE

M.A. entry: 3 GRE
material: 3 DNA
Nonwritten: 4 ORAL
Prenatal: 5 AMNIO
Preop: 3 ECG EKG
Prepare for a: 5 STUDY
proctor call: 4 TIME
Put to the: 3 TRY USE
5 ASSAY ESSAY
site: 3 LAB
Some ~ answers: 5 TRUES
Tough: 4 ORAL
**Testarossa**
and others: 8 FERRARIS
**Test-driven**
car: 4 DEMO
**Tester**
Air ~ (abbr.): 3 EPA
Beta: 4 USER
IQ: 5 BINET
Water: 3 TOE
**Testify:** 4 AVOW 5 SWEAR
6 DEPONE DEPOSE
**Testimonial**
dinner: 5 HONOR 7 TRIBUTE
**Testimony**
Like court: 5 SWORN
Like some: 4 ORAL
starter: 4 OATH
Take ~ from: 4 HEAR
**Testing**
site: 3 LAB
**Test-marketing**
city: 6 PEORIA
**Testy:** 5 SHORT
Get ~ with: 6 SNAPAT
state: 4 SNIT
**Tet**
observer: 5 ASIAN
**Tête**
thought: 4 IDEE
topper: 5 BERET
**Tête-à-tête:** 4 CHAT TALK
Have a ~ with:
8 SEEALONE
**Tether:** 5 LEASH
**Tethys**
Daughter of: 7 OCEANID
**Tetley**
alternative: 6 NESTEA
SALADA
product: 3 TEA
**Tet Offensive**
city: 6 SAIGON
**Tetra-**
~, twice: 4 OCTA OCTO
**Tetrazzini**
Soprano: 5 LUISA
**Teutonic:** 8 GERMANIC
cry: 3 ACH
lang.: 3 GER
name part: 3 VON
three: 4 DREI
turndown: 4 NEIN
**Tevere**
city: 4 ROMA

**Tevye**
portrayer: 5 TOPOL
**Tex**
Animator: 5 AVERY
Singer: 6 RITTER
**Tex.**
neighbor: 4 OKLA
or Mex.: 4 ABBR
**Tex-___ :** 3 MEX
**Texaco**
symbol: 4 STAR
**"Texaco Star Theater"**
star: 5 BERLE
**Texan**
Many a: 5 OILER
tie: 4 BOLO
**"Texan, The"**
actor Calhoun: 4 RORY
**Texas**
border city: 6 DELRIO ELPASO
    LAREDO
border river: 6 SABINE
city: 4 WACO 6 DALLAS
    ELPASO LAREDO ODESSA
city on the Brazos: 4 WACO
city on the Rio Grande:
    6 LAREDO
cook-off dish: 5 CHILI
county: 5 LAMAR
flag symbol: 4 STAR
Houston of: 3 SAM
Hutchinson of: 3 KAY
landmark: 5 ALAMO
leaguer: 5 ASTRO
mission: 5 ALAMO
oil city: 6 ODESSA
player: 5 ASTRO
Richards of: 3 ANN
sch.: 3 SMU
shortstop, once: 4 AROD
shrine: 5 ALAMO
state flower: 10 BLUEBONNET
state tree: 5 PECAN
tea: 3 OIL
town: 4 WACO 5 ENNIS
    PLANO
university: 5 LAMAR
**Texas ___ :** 3 TEA
**Texas A&M**
player: 5 AGGIE
**Texas Mustangs (abbr.):** 3 SMU
**Tex-Mex**
condiment: 5 SALSA
sauce: 5 SALSA
snack: 4 TACO 6 TAMALE
treat: 6 FAJITA TAMALE
**Text**
Authoritative: 5 BIBLE
Change: 4 EDIT
Computer: 5 ASCII
Correct: 5 EMEND
ending: 3 URE
Fix: 4 EDIT 5 EMEND
Islamic: 5 KORAN
Rabbinical: 6 TALMUD
Remove from: 4 DELE

Sacred: 5 KORAN TORAH
Tilted ~ (abbr.): 4 ITAL
**Textbook**
division: 4 UNIT
Like some ~ publishing:
    4 ELHI
**Textile**
colorer: 3 DYE
French ~ city: 5 LILLE
trademark: 5 ARNEL
Trousers: 5 CHINO
worker: 4 DYER
**Texts**
Orig.: 3 MSS
**TGIF**
Part of: 3 FRI ITS
**Thai:** 5 ASIAN
currency: 4 BAHT
language: 3 LAO
neighbor: 3 LAO
Some: 3 LAO
**Thailand**
neighbor: 4 LAOS
~, once: 4 SIAM
**Thais:** 6 ASIANS
**Thalia**
Sister of: 4 CLIO 5 ERATO
**Thames**
College on the: 4 ETON
Land in the: 3 AIT
town: 4 ETON
**"Thank God ___ Country Boy":**
    3 IMA
**"Thank goodness!":** 4 PHEW
**"Thank Heaven for Little Girls"**
musical: 4 GIGI
**Thankless**
one: 7 INGRATE
**Thanks**
Island: 6 MAHALO
~, in French: 5 MERCI
~, in German: 5 DANKE
**"Thanks ___!":** 4 ALOT
**"Thanks a ___!":** 3 MIL
**Thanksgiving**
Alice's ~ guest: 4 ARLO
celebration: 5 FEAST
day (abbr.): 5 THURS
dish: 4 YAMS
Do the ~ honors: 5 CARVE
Hymn of: 5 PAEAN
mo.: 3 NOV
veggie: 3 YAM
**Thanksgiving Day**
event: 6 PARADE
**"Thanks, I already ___":** 3 ATE
**"Thank U"**
singer Morissette: 6 ALANIS
**Thank you**
(Japanese): 7 ARIGATO
partner: 6 PLEASE
**"Thank You"**
singer: 4 DIDO
**Thank-you-___ :** 4 MAAM
**Thank-yous**
Brits': 3 TAS

**"Thar ___ blows!":** 3 SHE
**Tharp**
Choreographer: 5 TWYLA
**That**
and that: 5 THOSE
being the case: 4 IFSO
guy's: 3 HIS
is: 5 IDEST
objeto: 3 ESO
This and: 4 BOTH OLIO
    5 THESE
~, in French: 3 CET
~, in Spanish: 3 ESA ESO
~, once: 3 YON
**"___ That a Shame":** 4 AINT
**Thataway:** 6 YONDER
**Thatch**
Bit of: 4 REED
**Thatcher, Margaret:** 4 TORY
**Thatching**
palm: 4 NIPA
**"That ___ excuse!":** 4 ISNO
**"That feels good!":** 3 AAH OOH
**"That Girl"**
actress Thomas: 5 MARLO
girl: 3 ANN
**"That hurts!":** 3 YOW 4 OUCH
**"That is" (to Caesar):** 5 IDEST
**"That is ___ ...":** 5 TOSAY
**"That is a riot!":** 4 HAHA
    7 GOODONE
**"That is my understanding":**
    10 IBELIEVESO
**"That is right!":** 4 TRUE
**"That is so funny!":** 4 HAHA
**"That is to say ...":** 5 IMEAN
**"That'll be the day!":** 4 IBET
**"That'll show you!":** 3 HAH
**"That makes me mad!":** 3 GRR
**"That makes sense!":** 4 ISEE
**"That means ___!":** 3 YOU
**"That's ___!":** 4 ALIE
**"That's ___ ...":** 3 ODD
**"That's ___" (Dean Martin hit):**
    5 AMORE
**"That's a go":** 3 YES
**"That's a laugh!":** 3 HAH
**"That's a lie!":** 5 NOTSO
    6 UNTRUE
**"That's all, folks!"**
speaker: 8 PORKYPIG
voice: 5 BLANC
**"That's all there ___ it!":** 4 ISTO
**"That's all ___ wrote!":** 3 SHE
**"That's a relief!":** 4 WHEW
**"That's a riot!":** 4 HAHA
**"That's ___ ask!":** 4 ALLI
**"That's awful!":** 3 UGH
**"That's ___ blow!":** 4 ALOW
**"That's cheating!":** 6 NOFAIR
**"That's clear":** 4 ISEE
**"That's disgusting!":** 3 ICK
    UGH 4 YECH 5 YECCH
**"That's enough!":** 4 STOP
    6 NOMORE STOPIT
    11 PUTALIDONIT

"That's gotta hurt!": 3 OOH
"That's gross!": 3 UGH
"That's ___ haven't heard":
    4 ONEI
"That's it!": 3 AHA 5 BINGO
"That's nice!": 3 AAH
"That's not ___!": 4 ATOY
"That sounds good!": 3 OOH
"___ that special!": 4 ISNT
"That's really something!":
    3 MAN
"That's right!": 4 TRUE
"That's show ___!": 3 BIZ
"That's so-o-o-o nice!": 3 AAH
"That's so true": 6 IAGREE
"That's ___ subject": 5 ASORE
"That's terrible!": 4 OHNO
"That's the way ___": 4 ITIS
"that thing you do!"
    setting: 4 ERIE
"That was close!": 4 PHEW
    WHEW
"That wasn't nice!": 3 TSK
"That Was the Week That Was"
    host: 10 DAVIDFROST
"That ___ you!": 4 ISSO
Thaw: 4 MELT 5 DEICE
    7 DETENTE
The ___ (Netherlands city):
    5 HAGUE
Theater: 4 CINE
    abbr.: 3 SRO
    Ancient Greek: 5 ODEON
    and other things: 4 ARTS
    area: 4 LOGE 6 RIALTO
    award: 4 OBIE TONY
    backdrop: 5 SCRIM
    Best of: 4 EDNA
    Big-screen: 4 IMAX
    box: 4 LOGE
    Classic ~ name: 4 ROXY
        6 RIALTO
    company, briefly: 3 REP
    district: 6 RIALTO
    divider: 5 AISLE
    employee: 5 USHER
    for some vets: 3 NAM
    guide: 5 USHER
    Harlem: 6 APOLLO
    Holds, as a: 5 SEATS
    level: 4 LOGE TIER
    light: 4 SPOT
    litter: 5 STUBS
    Local ~, in slang: 4 NABE
    London: 6 OLDVIC
    Movie: 4 CINE 6 CINEMA
    section: 4 LOGE
    Shakespeare: 5 GLOBE
    sign: 3 SRO 4 EXIT
    Some: 7 CABARET
    sound: 3 SHH
    souvenir: 4 STUB
    space: 8 ENTRACTE
    ticket word: 3 ROW
    walkway: 5 AISLE
    warning: 3 SHH

Worth of the: 5 IRENE
Theater of the Absurd
    pioneer: 7 IONESCO
Theaters
    Ancient: 4 ODEA
    Big name in: 5 LOEWS
    Bygone: 4 RKOS
    They are shared in:
        8 ARMRESTS
Théâtre
    division: 4 ACTE
Theatrical: 5 SHOWY
    award: 4 OBIE
    backdrop: 5 SCRIM
    Be: 5 EMOTE
    Extravagantly: 4 CAMP
    Overly: 5 STAGY
    pro: 7 ARTISTE
    Wax: 5 EMOTE
Theban
    deity: 4 AMON
    Supreme ~ deity: 6 AMENRA
Thebes
    Opera set in: 4 AIDA
    Queen of: 5 NIOBE
"The best ___ to come":
    5 ISYET
___ the chase: 5 CUTTO
Theda
    Actress: 4 BARA
    Vamp: 4 BARA
"The Day the Earth Stood Still"
    robot: 4 GORT
"The doctor ___": 4 ISIN
"The heck with you!": 5 NERTS
"The jig ___!": 4 ISUP
"The joke is ___!": 4 ONME
    5 ONYOU
The ___ knees: 4 BEES
"The lady ___ protest ...":
    4 DOTH
"The law is a ___": Mr. Bumble:
    3 ASS
"The light dawns!": 3 AHA
    4 ISEE
Thelma
    Actress: 4 TODD
    Movie partner of: 6 LOUISE
"Thelma & Louise"
    actress Davis: 5 GEENA
    star: 10 GEENADAVIS
    Thelma in: 5 GEENA
"The loneliest number": 3 ONE
Thelonious
    Jazzman: 4 MONK
Them: 5 ENEMY 6 OTHERS
    ~, to us: 4 FOES 5 ENEMY
"Them": 3 FOE 5 ENEMY
    author: 5 OATES
    or "us": 4 SIDE
"Them!"
    creatures: 4 ANTS
"The magic word": 6 PLEASE
Theme: 4 IDEA 5 ESSAY MOTIF
    TOPIC
    Main: 5 MOTIF

Recurring: 5 MOTIF
"___ Theme": 5 LARAS
Theme park
    acronym: 5 EPCOT
    attraction: 4 RIDE
Then
    Now and: 7 ATTIMES
    ~, in French: 5 ALORS
"Then what?": 3 AND
Theobald
    Flute innovator: 5 BOEHM
    ___ the occasion: 6 RISETO
Theocracy
    Mideast: 4 IRAN
Theocritus
    work: 4 IDYL
Theodore
    Eleanor, to: 5 NIECE
    of Broadway: 5 BIKEL
    ~, to Wally: 4 BEAV
Theodore Roosevelt Award
    org.: 4 NCAA
Theologian
    Kierkegaard: 5 SOREN
    sch.: 3 SEM
    subj.: 3 REL
    who opposed Martin Luther:
        3 ECK
Theological
    no-no: 3 SIN
    sch.: 3 SEM
"The one that got away":
    4 YARN
Theophilus
    New Haven founder: 5 EATON
Theorem
    Auxiliary: 5 LEMMA
    ender: 3 QED
    name: 6 FERMAT
Theoretically: 7 ONPAPER
Theory: 3 ISM
    In: 7 IDEALLY
    Put forth a: 5 POSIT
    suffix: 3 ISM
"The other white meat":
    4 PORK
___ the rainbow: 4 OVER
"___ the ramparts ...": 3 OER
Therapeutic
    bath: 4 SITZ
    Employ a ~ technique:
        8 ROLEPLAY
    plant: 4 ALOE
    scent: 5 AROMA
Therapist
    Animated: 4 KATZ
    response: 4 ISEE
    Speech ~ concern: 4 LISP
Therapy
    Kind of: 4 GENE
    Primal ~ sound: 6 SCREAM
    prog.: 5 REHAB
    Visit through primal: 6 RELIVE
There
    All: 4 SANE 6 INTACT
    Be: 6 ATTEND

Get: 6 ARRIVE MAKEIT
Go here and: 4 ROAM ROVE
Here and: 5 ABOUT APART
  6 PASSIM
Here, ~, and everywhere:
  7 ALLOVER
is, in French: 4 ILYA
It's up: 3 SKY
Neither here nor: 7 ENROUTE
  INLIMBO
Not all: 5 DOTTY
Out: 4 AFAR 6 YONDER
Over: 3 YON 6 YONDER
Still not: 4 LATE
The one over: 4 THAT
Way out: 4 AFAR
"There!": 4 LOOK TADA
  5 VOILA
"___ there?": 4 WHOS
Thereabout: 4 ORSO
"There ___ atheists ...":
  5 ARENO
"There but for the grace of
  God ___": 3 GOI
"Thereby hangs ___": 5 ATALE
"___ there, done that": 4 BEEN
Therefore: 4 ERGO THUS
  5 ANDSO HENCE
"There Is Nothin' Like ___":
  5 ADAME
"There it is!": 3 AHA
"There'll be ___ time ...":
  4 AHOT
"There oughta be ___!":
  4 ALAW
Theresa
  St. ~ home: 5 AVILA
"There's a Wocket in My
  Pocket!"
  writer: 5 SEUSS
Thérèse: 3 STE
___ Thérèse, Quebec: 3 STE
"Thérèse Raquin"
  novelist: 4 ZOLA
"There's ___ every crowd!":
  5 ONEIN
"There's many ___ ...":
  5 ASLIP
"There's more ...": 3 AND
"The rest ___ to you": 4 ISUP
"The results ___!": 5 AREIN
"There, there": 5 ITSOK
"There ___ tide ...": 3 ISA
"There was ___ woman ...":
  5 ANOLD
Therewithal: 4 ALSO
"___ there yet?": 5 AREWE
"There you are!": 3 AHA
Therm
  prefix: 3 ISO
Thermal
  prefix: 3 GEO ISO
Thermodynamics
  Second law of: 7 ENTROPY
Thermometer
  Kind of: 4 ORAL

Thermonuclear
  explosive: 5 HBOMB
Thermopylae
  victor: 6 XERXES
Thermos
  inventer James: 5 DEWAR
Thermostat: 6 SENSOR
Thesaurus
  author: 5 ROGET
  entry (abbr.): 3 SYN
These
  Not: 5 THOSE 6 OTHERS
  ~, in French: 3 CES
  ~, in Spanish: 5 ESTAS ESTOS
Theseus
  land: 6 ATTICA
  She helped ~ escape:
    7 ARIADNE
"The sign of extra service"
  sloganeer: 4 ESSO
Thesis
  defense: 4 ORAL
  prefix: 3 SYN
Thespian: 5 ACTOR
  part: 4 ROLE
Thessaly
  peak: 4 OSSA
"The sweetest gift of heaven":
  Virgil: 5 SLEEP
Theta
  Letter after: 4 IOTA
  Letter before: 3 ETA
"The ___ Tale" (Chaucer
  segment): 6 REEVES
"The ___ the limit!": 4 SKYS
"The thief of bad gags":
  5 BERLE
"___ the Top" (Porter tune):
  5 YOURE
"The Twilight ___": 4 ZONE
"The very ___!": 4 IDEA
"___ the Walrus" (Beatles tune):
  3 IAM
___ the way: 4 PAVE
"The wolf ___ the door": 4 ISAT
The writing ___ the wall: 4 ISON
They
  ~, in French: 3 ILS 5 ELLES
  ~, in Italian: 4 ESSE
"They Died With Their Boots
  On": 5 OATER
"They're ___!": 3 OFF
"They're ___ again!": 4 ATIT
"___ they run": 6 SEEHOW
Thiamine
  deficiency: 8 BERIBERI
Thick: 3 FAT 5 DENSE MIDST
  as a brick: 5 DENSE
  carpet: 4 SHAG
  cornmeal mush: 7 POLENTA
  cut: 4 SLAB
  fog: 7 PEASOUP
  hair: 3 MOP 4 MANE
  In the ~ of: 3 MID 4 AMID
    5 AMONG 6 AMIDST
  Lay on: 7 SLATHER

liqueur: 5 CREME
  piece: 4 SLAB
  slice: 4 SLAB
  soup: 5 PUREE 6 POTAGE
    7 CHOWDER
Thick ___ brick: 3 ASA
Thicke
  Actor: 4 ALAN
Thicken: 4 CLOT
Thickener
  Food: 4 AGAR
  Sauce: 4 ROUX
  Soup: 4 OKRA
Thickening: 4 CLOT
  agent: 4 AGAR
Thicket: 5 COPSE
Thickheaded: 5 DENSE
  6 OBTUSE
Thickly
  packed: 5 DENSE
  Spread: 7 SLATHER
Thickness: 3 PLY
  measure: 3 MIL
  measurer: 7 CALIPER
Thick ___ plank: 3 ASA
Thick-skinned
  creature: 5 RHINO
Thick-soled
  shoe: 4 CLOG
Thick-trunked
  tree: 6 BAOBAB
Thief
  Give relief to a: 4 ABET
  "savings": 5 STASH
  Seagoing: 6 PIRATE
  Tart: 5 KNAVE
"Thief"
  actor James: 4 CAAN
"Thief of Bagdad, The"
  star: 4 SABU
Thieves
  hangout: 3 DEN
  take: 4 HAUL
Thigh
  muscles: 5 QUADS
Thighbone: 5 FEMUR
Thimbleful: 3 SIP
Thimblerig
  item: 3 PEA
"Thimble Theater"
  name: 3 OYL
Thimbleweed: 7 ANEMONE
Thin: 4 LANK LEAN RARE
    SLIM 6 SPARSE WATERY
  and nasal: 5 REEDY
  and slippery: 7 EELLIKE
  board: 4 SLAT
  coat: 4 FILM
  coin: 4 DIME
  fastener: 4 BRAD
  fog: 4 MIST
  layer: 6 LAMINA VENEER
  layers: 7 LAMINAE
  mattress: 5 FUTON
  model: 4 WAIF
  nail: 4 BRAD

opening: 4 SLIT
out: 9 ATTENUATE
pancake: 5 CREPE
paper: 9 ONIONSKIN
porridge: 5 GRUEL
puff: 4 WISP
slice: 7 SCALLOP
soup: 5 BROTH
strand: 4 WISP
stratum: 4 SEAM
strip: 4 SLAT
tie: 4 BOLO
Very: 4 LANK
wedge: 4 SHIM
**Thin ___**: 7 ASARAIL
**Thin as ___**: 5 ARAIL AREED
**Thing**: 4 ITEM 6 ENTITY
Directed against a: 5 INREM
Good: 4 PLUS 5 ASSET
Had a ~ for: 5 LIKED
In: 5 STYLE
Latest: 4 RAGE
Legal: 3 RES
Living: 5 BEING
Not a: 3 NIL
of the past: 5 RELIC
of value: 5 ASSET
One ~ after another: 6 SERIES
Play: 4 PROP ROLE
Tell a ~ or two: 5 SCOLD
to avoid: 4 NONO
Wonderful:
   12 THEBEESKNEES
**"Thing, The"**
He played the Thing in:
   6 ARNESS
**Thingamabob**: 6 DOODAD
**Thingamajig**: 5 GIZMO
   6 DOODAD 7 WHATSIT
**Thingie**: 6 DOODAD GADGET
**Things**: 5 STUFF
Fine: 4 ARTS
lacking: 5 NEEDS
One of those: 4 THAT
Saw: 5 TEETH
The way ~ are going: 5 TREND
The way ~ stand: 6 ASITIS
to do: 5 TASKS 6 AGENDA
   7 ERRANDS
to mind: 7 PSANDQS
What little ~ mean: 4 ALOT
**Thingy**: 4 ITEM 6 DOODAD
**"Thin Ice"**
skater Sonja: 5 HENIE
**Think**: 5 OPINE 6 IDEATE
ahead: 4 PLAN
alike: 5 AGREE
fit: 5 DEIGN
hard: 8 COGITATE
highly of: 6 ADMIRE ESTEEM
logically: 6 REASON
of it: 4 IDEA
One way to: 5 ALOUD
out loud: 5 OPINE
(over): 4 MULL
piece: 4 IDEA 5 ESSAY

Something to ~ about: 4 IDEA
the world of: 5 ADORE
   6 ADMIRE
Things to ~ about: 5 IDEAS
through: 6 REASON
up: 6 DEVISE IDEATE
**Thinker**: 4 SAGE
French: 4 TETE
Positive: 5 PEALE
**"Thinker, The"**
creator: 5 RODIN
**Thinking**
Kind of: 9 NONLINEAR
Positive ~ proponent: 5 PEALE
Say without: 5 BLURT
Way of: 7 MINDSET
Wishful: 5 IHOPE
Without: 6 RASHLY
**"Think nothing ___!"**: 4 OFIT
**ThinkPad**
maker: 3 IBM
**Think tank**
member: 7 IDEAMAN
output: 4 IDEA
**"... think, therefore ___"**: 3 IAM
**Thinly**
spread: 6 SPARSE
**"Thin Man, The"**
actress Loy: 5 MYRNA
actress Myrna: 3 LOY
dog: 4 ASTA
wife: 4 NORA
**Thinner**
component: 7 ACETONE
**Thinness**
Epitome of: 4 RAIL REED
   5 RAZOR
**Thinnest**
coin: 4 DIME
**"Thin Red Line, The"**
actor Sean: 4 PENN
**Thin-waisted**
flier: 4 WASP
**Third**
Adam's: 4 SETH
Beethoven's: 6 EROICA
century date: 3 CCI
Come in: 4 SHOW
degree: 3 PHD
Finish: 4 SHOW
Frank's: 3 MIA
from center: 3 END
Give the ~ degree: 5 GRILL
Held by a ~ party:
   8 INESCROW
man: 4 ABEL
man in the ring: 3 REF
of eight: 5 EARTH
of September: 3 PEE
party holding: 6 ESCROW
place: 4 SHOW
Raise to the ~ power: 4 CUBE
rock from the sun: 5 EARTH
Scarlett's: 5 RHETT
smallest of eight: 4 MARS
Taylor's: 4 TODD

~ Greek letter: 5 GAMMA
**"Third Man, The"**
actress Valli: 5 ALIDA
setting: 6 VIENNA
star: 6 WELLES
**"Third of May"**
painter: 4 GOYA
**Thirds**
Cut in: 7 TRISECT
**Third-stringer**: 5 SCRUB
**Thirst**: 3 YEN
Quench, as: 5 SLAKE
quencher: 3 ADE
**Thirsty**: 3 DRY
**Thirteen**
popes: 4 LEOS
**"Thirty days ___ ..."**: 4 HATH
**"thirtysomething"**
actor Ken: 4 OLIN
actress Harris: 3 MEL
**This**
and that: 4 BOTH OLIO
   5 THESE
Apart from: 4 ELSE
At ~ point: 4 HERE
Exactly like: 6 JUSTSO
Give ~ for that: 5 TRADE
In ~ manner: 6 LIKESO
In ~ way: 4 THUS 6 LIKESO
instant: 3 NOW
is one: 4 CLUE
Never say: 3 DIE
Not: 4 THAT
one and that: 4 BOTH
Other than: 4 ELSE
way, or that: 3 FRO
What ~ isn't: 4 THAT
~, in French: 3 CET
~, in Spanish: 4 ESTA ESTE
   ESTO
**"This ___"** (1979 Loggins hit):
   4 ISIT
**"This ___"** (carton label):
   5 ENDUP
**This-and-that**
dish: 4 STEW
**"This can't be!"**: 4 OHNO
**"This comes ___ surprise"**:
   4 ASNO
**___ this earth**: 5 NOTOF
**"This Gun for Hire"**
star: 4 LADD
**"This guy walks into ___ ..."**:
   4 ABAR
**"This instant!"**: 6 ATONCE
**"This is ___"**: 5 ATEST
**"This is fun!"**: 4 WHEE
**"This is just ___"**: 5 ATEST
**"This is no joke!"**: 7 IMEANIT
**"This is only ___"**: 5 ATEST
**"This is serious!"**: 7 IMEANIT
**"This looks bad"**: 4 UHOH
**"This means ___!"**: 3 WAR
**"This must weigh ___!"**: 4 ATON
**"This Old House"**
network: 3 PBS

"This one's ___!": 4 ONME
"This ___ outrage!": 4 ISAN
"This ___ recording": 3 ISA
"This round is ___!": 4 ONME
"This ___ stickup!": 3 ISA
"This ___ sudden!": 4 ISSO
"This ___ test": 3 ISA
"This won't hurt ___!": 4 ABIT
**Thom**
  Shoemaker: 4 MCAN
**Thomas**
  Actress: 5 MARLO
  Author: 5 WOLFE
  Cartoonist: 4 NAST
  Clockmaker: 4 SETH
  Colleague of Kennedy and:
    6 SCALIA
  Columnist: 3 CAL
  Composer: 4 ARNE
  Doubting: 5 CYNIC
  Dramatist: 3 KYD
  of basketball: 5 ISIAH
  Pamphleteer: 5 PAINE
  Poet: 5 DYLAN
  Revolutionary War general:
    4 GAGE
  Skater: 4 DEBI
  Soul singer: 4 IRMA
**"Thomas Crown Affair, The"**
  actress: 9 RENERUSSO
**Thomas Stearns ___ : 5 ELIOT**
**Thompson**
  Actress: 3 LEA 4 EMMA SADA
  Oscar winner: 4 EMMA
**Thompson, Kay**
  character: 6 ELOISE
**Thong: 5 STRAP**
**"Thong Song"**
  rapper: 5 SISQO
**Thor**
  and others: 5 AESIR
  Father of: 4 ODIN
  Like: 5 NORSE
**Thoracic**
  muscle: 3 PEC
**Thorn**
  relative: 3 EDH
  Stuck by a: 7 PRICKED
**"Thorn Birds, The"**
  novelist McCullough:
    7 COLLEEN
**Thornburgh**
  predecessor: 5 MEESE
    7 EDMEESE
**Thornfield Hall**
  governess: 4 EYRE
**Thorny: 6 BRIERY**
  bloom: 4 ROSE
  subject: 5 BRIAR
    8 ROSEBUSH
**Thorough: 10 EXHAUSTIVE**
**Thoroughfare: 4 ROAD**
    6 AVENUE STREET
  German: 7 STRASSE
**Thoroughfares**
  (abbr.): 3 STS

**Thoroughly: 4 ATOZ 5 NOEND**
    15 FROMSTEMTOSTERN
  enjoyed: 5 ATEUP
  investigate: 3 VET
**Thorpe**
  Swimmer: 3 IAN
**Those**
  against: 5 ANTIS
  for: 4 YEAS
  Not: 5 THESE
  One of: 4 THAT
  over there: 4 THEM
  people: 4 THEY
  ~, in Spanish: 4 ESAS ESOS
**"Those ___ the Days": 4 WERE**
**Thoth**
  had the head of one: 4 IBIS
**Thou: 3 GEE 4 ONEG 5 GRAND**
  A thousand: 3 MIL
  squared: 3 MIL
  Verb with: 4 DOST HAST
**Though: 6 ALBEIT**
  Even: 6 ALBEIT
**Thought: 4 IDEA 5 MUSED**
    6 OPINED 7 IDEATED
  Lines of: 4 EEGS
  Lost in: 7 PENSIVE
  prefix: 4 IDEO
  School of: 3 ISM
  the world of: 6 ADORED
  waves: 3 ESP
  Without: 4 IDLY
**Thought-provoking: 4 DEEP**
**Thoughts**
  Have second: 3 RUE
  Have second ~ about:
    8 REASSESS
  Offer: 5 OPINE
**"Thou ___ not ...": 5 SHALT**
**"___ Thou Now O Soul"**
  (Whitman poem):
    6 DAREST
**Thousand**
  thou: 3 MIL
  ~, in French: 5 MILLE
**Thousand ___, California:**
    4 OAKS
**Thousandth**
  of a yen: 3 RIN
  One: 5 MILLI
**"... ___ thousand times ...":**
    3 NOA
**Thou-shall-not: 4 NONO**
**"Thpeak like thith": 4 LISP**
**Thrash: 3 LAM TAN 4 FLOG**
    5 BASTE FLAIL WHALE
    6 LARRUP
**Thread**
  and other things:
    7 NOTIONS
  Cotton: 5 LISLE
  Fine: 5 LISLE
  holder: 5 SPOOL
  Twisted: 5 LISLE
  Unit of wound: 5 SKEIN
  Use needle and: 3 SEW

**Threadbare: 4 WORN 5 RATTY**
    6 SHABBY
**Threaded**
  fastener: 4 TNUT 5 SCREW
**Threads: 6 ATTIRE**
**Threat: 5 PERIL 6 MENACE**
  ender: 4 ELSE 6 ORELSE
**Threaten: 4 WARN 6 IMPEND**
    MENACE
  like a dog: 7 SNARLAT
**Threatening**
  word: 4 ELSE
  words: 6 ORELSE
**Threats**
  Like some: 4 IDLE
**Three: 4 TREY**
  About ~ grains: 5 CARAT
  are a match: 4 SETS
  before seven: 8 AREACODE
  Consisting of: 6 TRIUNE
  dots: 3 ESS
  Group of: 5 TRIAD
  in one: 6 TRIUNE
  (Italian): 3 TRE
  months abroad: 3 ETE
  on a clock: 3 III
  One of ~ squares: 4 MEAL
  or four: 4 AFEW
  sheets to the wind: 3 LIT
    6 BLOTTO
  times, in an Rx: 3 TER
  wood: 5 SPOON
  ~, at times: 5 CROWD
  ~, in French: 5 TROIS
  ~, in German: 4 DREI
**Three Bears**
  One of the: 4 MAMA PAPA
**Three B's**
  One of the: 4 BACH
**Three-card**
  game: 5 MONTE
  monte: 4 SCAM
**"Three Coins in the Fountain"**
  fountain: 5 TREVI
  lyricist: 4 CAHN
**Three-digit**
  number: 8 AREACODE
**Three-dimensional: 5 CUBIC**
    SOLID 7 SPATIAL
**Three-faced**
  woman: 3 EVE
**"Three Faces ___, The":**
    5 OFEVE
**Three-handed**
  card game: 4 SKAT
**Three-horse**
  carriage: 6 TROIKA
**Three-layer**
  snack: 4 OREO
**Three-legged**
  endeavor: 4 RACE
  table: 6 TEAPOY
**Three-letter**
  sequence: 7 TRIGRAM
**Three-line**
  verse: 5 HAIKU

**Three Little Kittens**
reward: 3 PIE
"___ Three Lives": 4 ILED
**Three-match**
link: 3 ONA
**Three ___ match:** 3 ONA
**"Three men in ___":** 4 ATUB
**Three-mile**
Area beyond the ~ limit:
7 OPENSEA
**Three Musketeers**
One of the: 5 ATHOS
6 ARAMIS
unit: 3 BAR
**Three-note**
chord: 5 TRIAD
**Three-panel**
picture: 8 TRIPTYCH
**"Threepenny Opera"**
composer: 5 WEILL
**Three-piece**
apparel: 4 SUIT
suit piece: 4 VEST
**Threepio**
pal: 5 ARTOO
**Three-pronged**
weapon: 7 TRIDENT
**Three-reeler:** 5 MOVIE
**"Three's Company"**
actor John: 6 RITTER
actress Suzanne: 6 SOMERS
**Threescore:** 5 SIXTY
**Three-seater:** 4 SOFA
**Three-sided**
sword: 4 EPEE
**"Three Sisters"**
sister: 4 OLGA 5 IRINA
MASHA
**Threesome:** 4 TRIO
Easy: 3 ABC
TV: 4 SONS
**Three-spot:** 4 TREY
**Three-star**
off.: 5 LTGEN
**Three Stooges**
One of the: 3 MOE 5 SHEMP
**Three-strikes**
result: 3 OUT
**Three-striper**
(abbr.): 3 NCO SGT
**"Three Tall Women"**
playwright: 5 ALBEE
**Three-time**
heavyweight champ: 3 ALI
~ 60-homer man: 4 SOSA
~ A.L. batting champ:
5 BRETT OLIVA
~ A.L. MVP: 5 BERRA
~ Best Director: 5 CAPRA
~ Burmese leader: 3 UNU
~ Cy Young Award winner:
6 SEAVER
~ French Open champ:
5 SELES
~ Hart Trophy winner:
3 ORR

~ Masters champ: 5 FALDO
SNEAD 8 SAMSNEAD
~ PGA champ: 5 SNEAD
~ Super Bowl MVP:
10 JOEMONTANA
~ U.S. Open champ: 5 LENDL
9 IVANLENDL
~ Wimbledon champ: 5 EVERT
6 TILDEN 7 MCENROE
**Three-toed**
animal: 5 TAPIR
bird: 4 RHEA
**Three-way**
joint: 3 TEE
**Threnody:** 5 ELEGY 6 LAMENT
**Thresh:** 5 FLAIL
**Thresher**
shark: 6 SEAFOX
**Threshing**
tool: 5 FLAIL
**Threshold:** 3 EVE 4 DOOR
EDGE SILL 5 BRINK
Cross the: 5 ENTER 6 STEPIN
**Thrice**
daily, in prescriptions: 3 TID
~, in prescriptions: 3 TER
**Thrift shop**
condition: 4 USED
stipulation: 4 ASIS
What a ~ does: 7 RESELLS
**Thrifty**
competitor: 4 AVIS
one: 5 SAVER
Too: 6 SKIMPY
**Thrill:** 3 WOW 4 KICK RUSH
SEND 5 ELATE
**"Thrilla in Manila"**
boxer: 3 ALI
**Thrilled:** 4 GLAD SENT
**"Thriller"**
singer nickname: 5 JACKO
**Thrilling:** 5 HEADY
8 ELECTRIC
**"Thrill Is Gone, The"**
singer: 6 BBKING
**Thrill-seeker**
cord: 6 BUNGEE
**Throat**
ailment: 5 STREP
clearer: 4 AHEM
dangler: 5 UVULA
feature: 6 TONSIL
problem: 4 FROG
___ throat: 5 STREP
___ Throat (of Watergate):
4 DEEP
**Throat-clearing**
sound: 4 AHEM
**Throat-culture**
finding: 5 STREP
**Throaty:** 6 HOARSE
**Throb:** 4 ACHE PANG 5 POUND
PULSE
**Throne**
eyer: 4 HEIR
Hold the: 5 REIGN

Occupy the: 3 SIT 4 RULE
On the: 7 REGNANT
Place for a: 4 DAIS
**Throneberry**
of baseball: 4 MARV
~, once: 3 MET
**Throng:** 3 MOB 4 HOST SLEW
5 CROWD HORDE
**"___ Thro' the Rye":** 5 COMIN
**Throttle:** 3 GAS
At full: 5 AMAIN
**Through:** 3 PER VIA 4 DONE
OVER 5 ENDED
Get ~ to: 5 REACH
Go: 4 SIFT 5 SPEND
Run: 4 GORE STAB 6 PIERCE
8 REHEARSE
**Throw:** 3 PEG 4 CAST FAZE
HURL TOSS 5 AMAZE
HEAVE
A: 4 EACH
dice: 4 CAST ROLL
down the gauntlet: 4 DARE
Easy: 3 LOB 4 TOSS
in: 3 ADD 9 INTERPOSE
in the towel: 4 QUIT
off: 4 EMIT SHED
out: 3 CAN 4 CAST TOSS
5 EJECT EVICT EXPEL
SCRAP
rocks at: 4 PELT
Slow: 3 LOB
water on: 5 DOUSE
with effort: 5 HEAVE
**Throw ___:** 4 AFIT
**Throwaway**
Apple: 4 CORE
Cookout: 3 COB
Fruit: 4 RIND SEED
**Throwback:** 7 ATAVISM
**Thrower**
Party: 4 HOST
**Throwing**
in the towel result: 3 TKO
**Thrown**
disk: 7 FRISBEE
Item ~ in a ring: 3 HAT
**Thrown for ___:** 5 ALOOP
ALOSS
**Thrush:** 5 VEERY
Song: 5 MAVIS
**Thrust:** 4 STAB 5 LUNGE
**Thrusting**
sword: 6 RAPIER
**Thu.**
follower: 3 FRI
**Thud**
Loud: 3 BAM
**Thug:** 3 APE 4 GOON HOOD
5 BRUTE 7 GORILLA
knife: 4 SHIV
**Thumb:** 5 HITCH
owner: 5 EBERT
(through): 4 LEAF
**Thumb-and-forefinger**
sign: 4 OKAY

**Thumb-raising**
critic: 5 EBERT
**Thumbs**
All: 5 INEPT 6 CLUMSY
7 AWKWARD
down: 3 NAY
down reactions: 4 NOES
Give a ~ down: 3 NIX PAN
ups: 3 YES
**Thumbscrew**
ridge: 5 KNURL
**Thumbs-up:** 3 YES 4 OKAY
6 ASSENT
Gave the ~ to: 3 OKD
response: 3 AOK
vote: 3 YEA YES
write-up: 4 RAVE
**Thumb-twiddling:** 4 IDLE
**Thump:** 3 RAP
**Thumper**
pal: 5 BAMBI
**Thunder:** 4 ROAR
God of: 4 THOR
sound: 4 CLAP PEAL
**Thunder Bay**
prov.: 3 ONT
**Thundering:** 5 AROAR
group: 4 HERD
**Thunderstorm**
product: 5 OZONE
**Thunderstruck:** 4 AWED
5 AGAPE INAWE
**Thurber**
dreamer: 5 MITTY
**Thurible**
Use a: 5 CENSE
**Thüringen**
Info: German cue
trio: 4 DREI
**Thurman**
Actress: 3 UMA
role: 4 PEEL
**Thurmond**
of basketball: 4 NATE
Senator: 5 STROM
**Thurs.**
follower: 3 FRI
___ Thursday: 6 MAUNDY
**Thus:** 3 SIC 4 ERGO
far: 3 YET 5 ASYET TONOW
6 TODATE
**Thusly:** 6 LIKESO
**Thwack:** 3 RAP
**Thwart:** 4 FOIL 5 AVERT CROSS
DETER 6 STYMIE
7 PREVENT
**"Thy hair ___ a flock of goats":**
4 ISAS
**Thyme:** 4 HERB 7 POTHERB
**"Thy Neighbor's Wife"**
author: 6 TALESE
**Thyroid:** 5 GLAND
treatment: 6 IODINE
**Tia**
Actress: 7 CARRERE
___ Tiago: 3 SAO

**Tiant**
of baseball: 4 LUIS
**Tiara**
inlays: 4 GEMS
wearer: 4 POPE
**Tibbets, Colonel**
Mother of: 5 ENOLA
**Tiber**
City on the: 4 ROME
River connected to the: 4 ARNO
**Tiberius**
Mother of: 5 LIVIA
That is, to: 5 IDEST
To be, to: 4 ESSE
**Tibet**
capital: 5 LHASA
From: 5 ASIAN
neighbor: 5 NEPAL
setting: 4 ASIA
**Tibetan**
legend: 4 YETI
monk: 4 LAMA
ox: 3 YAK
prefix: 4 SINO
**Tibia:** 4 BONE SHIN
connectors: 5 TARSI
**Tic:** 5 SPASM
follower: 3 TAC
**Tic ___ :** 3 TAC
**"Tic ___ Dough":** 3 TAC
**Tick**
away: 6 ELAPSE
off: 3 IRE IRK 4 GALL LIST
MIFF RILE 5 ANGER
ANNOY COUNT PEEVE
6 ENRAGE 7 INCENSE
**Ticked:** 3 MAD 4 SORE 5 IRATE
Get ~ off: 5 STEAM 6 SEERED
off: 3 MAD 4 SORE 5 ANGRY
IRATE 7 INASNIT
(off): 4 TEED
**Ticker**
locale (abbr.): 4 NYSE
tape (abbr.): 3 ECG EKG
Taxi: 5 METER
**Ticket:** 4 CITE 5 DUCAT SLATE
buyer alert: 3 SRO
category: 5 ADULT
end: 4 STUB
Free: 4 COMP PASS
Give a ~ to: 4 CITE
High-priced ~ area: 4 LOGE
info: 3 ROW 4 GATE SEAT
TIER
issuer: 3 COP
Kind of: 4 MEAL 5 LOTTO
SPLIT 6 SEASON
leftover: 4 STUB
Overcharge for a: 5 SCALP
Political: 5 SLATE
profiteer: 7 SCALPER
Risk a: 5 SPEED
sales: 4 GATE
seller: 5 AGENT 9 BOXOFFICE
word: 3 ROW 5 ADMIT
**Tickle:** 5 AMUSE ELATE

pink: 5 ELATE 6 PLEASE
the ivories: 4 PLAY
**Tickled:** 4 GLAD
He's: 4 ELMO
pink: 4 GLAD
**Tickled-pink**
feeling: 4 GLEE
**"Tickle Me"**
doll: 4 ELMO
**Ticklish**
doll: 4 ELMO
**Tic-tac-toe**
loser: 3 OOX OXO XOO XXO
plays: 7 XSANDOS
win: 3 OOO
**Tic-___-toe:** 3 TAC
**Tidal**
reflux: 3 EBB
wave: 7 TSUNAMI
**Tidbit:** 4 ITEM 6 MORSEL
Try a: 5 TASTE
**Tiddlywink:** 4 DISC
**Tide**
Kind of: 3 EBB 4 NEAP YULE
Receding: 3 EBB
rival: 3 ALL ERA FAB
Semimonthly: 4 NEAP
target: 4 DIRT 5 STAIN
**Tidy:** 4 NEAT TRIM
9 SHIPSHAPE
sum: 4 PILE
up: 6 NEATEN
**Tie:** 4 DRAW KNOT YOKE
5 NEXUS TRUSS UNITE
6 CRAVAT 8 DEADHEAT
Broad: 5 ASCOT
Eastern: 3 OBI
fabric: 3 REP
Fancy: 5 ASCOT
holder: 3 TAC
indicator: 3 ALL
Parts to: 4 ENDS
School: 3 PTA
Shoe: 4 LACE
String: 4 BOLO
the knot: 3 WED
type: 4 BOLO 5 ASCOT
up: 4 BIND DOCK LACE LASH
5 TRUSS 6 TETHER
up at the dock: 4 MOOR
up the line: 3 YAK
**Tie ___ :** 3 TAC
**Tiebreaker:** 7 PLAYOFF
**Tiebreakers:** 3 OTS
**Tied:** 4 EVEN 10 EVENSTEVEN
All ~ up: 4 EVEN
bundle: 4 BALE
Fit to be: 3 MAD 5 IRATE
LOOSE RILED 7 INARAGE
STEAMED
It's ~ at the back: 3 OBI
It's fit to be: 7 SNEAKER
up: 4 EVEN 5 BOUND
6 MOORED
**Tie-dye**
alternative: 5 BATIK

**Tier:** 5 LAYER
**Tierney**
Actress: 5 MAURA
**Tierney, Gene**
role: 5 LAURA
**Tierra del ___:** 5 FUEGO
**Tierra del Fuego**
sight: 5 ANDES
**Tierra ___ Fuego:** 3 DEL
**Ties:** 8 NECKWEAR
Like some: 6 CLIPON
**Tie-twiddling**
comedian: 5 OLLIE
**Tie-up:** 5 SNARL
Traffic: 3 JAM 5 SNARL
10 BOTTLENECK
**Tiff:** 3 ROW 4 SNIT SPAT
5 RUNIN
**Tiffin**
Take: 3 EAT
**Tiger:** 3 CAT 8 MANEATER
Cereal box: 4 TONY
Comic strip: 6 HOBBES
cry: 4 FORE
feet: 4 PAWS
game: 4 GOLF
Like a: 6 FIERCE
org.: 3 PGA
pocketful: 4 TEES
position: 3 LIE
Start of a rhyme about a:
4 EENY
support: 3 TEE
target: 4 HOLE
tooth: 4 FANG
with a club: 5 WOODS
**Tiger Beat**
reader: 4 TEEN
**Tiger-in-your-tank**
brand: 4 ESSO
**Tigers:** 4 TEAM
of South Carolina: 7 CLEMSON
sch.: 3 LSU
**"Tiger Walks, A"**
star: 4 SABU
**Tigger**
Friend of: 3 ROO 4 POOH
**Tiggywinkle:** 3 MRS
**Tight:** 4 SNUG TAUT 5 TENSE
6 STINGY
Close: 6 SEALUP
Got: 6 TENSED
He may be: 3 END
hold: 4 GRIP
Make: 4 SEAL
Not: 5 LOOSE SOBER
Not quite: 4 SNUG
Not shut: 4 AJAR
Sit: 4 BIDE STAY
spot: 4 BIND
~, budgetwise: 7 AUSTERE
**Tight as ___:** 5 ADRUM
**Tighten:** 5 RETIE
up: 5 TENSE
**Tightener**
Tummy: 5 SITUP 6 CORSET

**Tight-fisted:** 5 CHEAP
**Tightfitting:** 4 SNUG
**Tight-knit**
group: 5 CADRE
**Tight-lipped:** 3 MUM
**Tightly**
packed: 5 DENSE
stretched: 4 TAUT
**Tightwad:** 5 MISER PIKER
**Tiglon:** 6 HYBRID
**Tigris**
land: 4 IRAQ
**Tijuana**
Info: Spanish cue
gold: 3 ORO
region: 4 BAJA
tender: 4 PESO
That, in: 3 ESA ESO
This, in: 4 ESTO
title: 5 SENOR
toast: 5 SALUD
Today, in: 3 HOY
Tomorrow, in: 6 MANANA
treat: 4 TACO
two: 3 DOS
**Tijuana Brass**
leader: 6 ALPERT
**Tiki**
carver: 5 MAORI
**Tikkanen**
of hockey: 3 ESA
**Tilde**
PC ~ topper: 3 ESC
wearers: 3 ENS
**Tilden**
topper: 5 HAYES
**Tile**
Clean a ~ floor, maybe:
7 DAMPMOP
protector: 7 BATHMAT
**Tiler**
need: 5 GROUT
**Tiles**
Game with: 8 SCRABBLE
**Till:** 3 HOE 4 PLOW UPTO
6 DRAWER
bill: 3 ONE
compartment: 4 ONES TENS
fill: 4 CASH ONES
now: 3 YET
stack: 4 ONES TENS
**Tiller**
locale: 4 HELM
prefix: 4 ROTO
Take the: 5 STEER
**Tillie**
Novelist: 5 OLSEN
**Tilling**
tool: 3 HOE
**Tillis**
Singer: 3 MEL PAM
**Tilly**
Actress: 3 MEG
**Tilt:** 3 TIP 4 CANT LEAN LIST
5 TIPUP
Going full: 4 ATIT

**Tilt-a-Whirl:** 4 RIDE
**Tilted:** 5 LEANT 6 ASLANT
ASLOPE
type, for short: 4 ITAL
**Tilter**
mount: 5 STEED
weapon: 5 LANCE
**Tilting**
tower town: 4 PISA
weapon: 5 LANCE
**Tim**
Actor: 4 REID
collaborator: 5 ELTON
of comedy: 5 ALLEN
of the Yankees: 6 RAINES
**Timber**
problem: 6 DRYROT
Stem-to-stern: 4 KEEL
tab: 5 TENON
tool: 3 ADZ 4 ADZE
tree: 3 ASH
Western: 6 REDFIR
wolf: 4 LOBO
**Timbering**
tool: 3 AXE
**Timberlake, Justin**
band: 5 NSYNC
**Timberwolves**
org.: 3 NBA
**Timbuktu**
land: 4 MALI
**Time:** 3 ERA 4 AGER HOUR
5 CLOCK
15 FOURTHDIMENSION
after time: 5 OFTEN
Ahead of: 5 EARLY
All the: 4 ALOT 5 OFTEN
and again: 3 OFT 5 OFTEN
and time again: 4 EONS ERAS
Another: 5 AGAIN
Any: 5 ISSUE
Any ~ now: 4 SOON
At another: 4 ANON
At any: 4 EVER
At no: 4 NEER 5 NEVER
At that: 4 THEN
At the ~ of: 4 UPON
At the right: 5 ONCUE
At what: 4 WHEN
Back in: 3 AGO
Bad: 4 IDES
before: 3 EVE
Before this: 6 ERENOW
Behind: 4 LATE
being: 5 NONCE
Big: 3 AGE ERA 4 ALOT
Cold: 6 ICEAGE
critic: 4 AGEE
Dark: 5 NIGHT
Decisive: 4 DDAY
delay: 3 LAG
div.: 3 MIN
division: 4 ZONE
During the ~ that: 5 WHILE
Fast: 4 LENT 7 RAMADAN
Festive: 4 YULE

follower: 4 SPAN
for a revolution: 4 YEAR
for one doing time: 7 STRETCH
For the ~ being: 6 PROTEM
For the second: 4 ANEW
frame: 3 ERA
Gay: 8 NINETIES
Get to work on: 4 EDIT
Give a hard ~ to: 6 HASSLE
gone by: 4 PAST
Great: 3 ERA GAS 4 BALL
    5 BLAST
High: 4 BOOM NOON
Hit the big: 6 ARRIVE
    MAKEIT
Holiday: 4 YULE
Important: 3 ERA
In a short: 4 ANON
In due: 4 ANON
in history: 3 AGE EON ERA
In no: 4 SOON
Keep: 3 TAP 5 RENEW
keeper: 6 EDITOR
Kill: 4 IDLE
Kind of: 3 NAP TEE 4 REAL
Knight: 4 YORE
Length of: 5 SPELL
Life: 3 AGE
line segment: 3 ERA
Long: 3 AGE CEN EON
    4 AEON AGES 5 EPOCH
    YEARS 7 DOGSAGE
long past: 4 YORE
Make-or-break: 4 DDAY
Many a: 3 OFT 5 OFTEN
March: 4 IDES
Mark: 4 IDLE TICK
Memorable: 3 ERA 5 EPOCH
Notable: 3 ERA
Not in: 4 LATE 5 TARDY
    7 TOOLATE
Of all: 4 EVER
of anticipation: 3 EVE
of decision: 4 DDAY
off: 4 REST 5 LEAVE RANDR
    7 HOLIDAY LEISURE
of note: 3 ERA
of one's life: 3 AGE
of the year: 6 SEASON
One: 5 ISSUE
One more: 4 ANEW 5 AGAIN
on end: 3 EON
on the job: 5 STINT
Opening: 4 NINE
out: 3 NAP 4 COMA REST
    6 RECESS
Palindromic: 4 NOON
Partner of: 5 AGAIN
Pass, as: 5 SPEND 6 ELAPSE
Past: 4 YORE
period: 3 ERA 4 SPAN
    5 SPELL
piece: 3 ERA MIN 6 OCLOCK
pieces: 3 HRS
Play for: 5 STALL
Poetic: 3 EEN 4 MORN

Present: 4 NOEL XMAS
Pressed for: 7 INARUSH
Primitive: 8 STONEAGE
Quiet: 4 LULL
Short: 3 BIT MIN SEC
    5 TRICE 6 MOMENT
Single: 4 ONCE
Some: 6 AWHILE
Some ~ ago: 4 ONCE
Some ~ back: 9 AWHILEAGO
Some other: 5 LATER
Spring: 3 MAY 4 LENT
    7 EQUINOX
Stretch: 7 SEVENTH
Take more: 5 RENEW
Terrible: 4 TWOS
Terrific: 5 BLAST
Tiny ~ div.: 4 MSEC NSEC
to act: 4 DDAY
to beware: 4 IDES
to celebrate: 3 EVE
to crow: 4 DAWN
to dye: 6 EASTER
to give up: 4 LENT
to remember: 3 ERA
Trying: 6 ORDEAL
Up to the ~ that: 5 UNTIL
Very long: 3 EON 4 AEON
    8 BLUEMOON
Waste: 4 IDLE KILL
    6 DAWDLE
when both hands are up:
    4 NOON
While away the: 4 LAZE
Whistle: 4 NOON
Wild: 5 SPREE
without end: 4 AEON
~ Magazine's Person of the
    Year: see pages 725–726
~, so to speak: 5 SANDS
"Time ___" (old sci-fi series):
    4 TRAX
___ time: 4 ATNO INNO
"___ time": 3 ITS
"___ Time" (1970s musical):
    5 ONEMO
Time and ___: 5 AHALF
"Time ___ a premium": 4 ISAT
Timecard
    (abbr.): 3 HRS
Time-consuming: 4 LONG
"Timecop"
    actress Mia: 4 SARA
Timed
    Perfectly: 5 ONCUE
    ___ time flat: 4 INNO
Time ___ half: 4 ANDA
Time-honored
    practice: 4 RITE
    saying: 5 ADAGE
"Time in a Bottle"
    singer Jim: 5 CROCE
"Time is money": 5 ADAGE
    AXIOM
Timeless: 7 ETERNAL
    ~, to a poet: 6 ETERNE

Timeline
    division: 3 ERA
Timely
    benefit: 4 BOON
    In a ~ way: 5 ONCUE
"Time Machine, The"
    people: 4 ELOI
Time Magazine
    ~ Person of the Year: see pages
      725–726
"Time ___ My Side": 4 ISON
Time-out: 3 NAP
Timepiece: 5 WATCH
    Novelty: 11 CUCKOOCLOCK
    Pricey: 5 ROLEX
Timer
    Lot: 5 METER
    place: 4 OVEN
Times
    At all: 4 EVER
    Change with the: 5 ADAPT
    Good: 3 UPS
    High: 3 UPS
    Old: 4 YORE
    P.M.: 3 NTS 4 AFTS
Timesaver
    PC: 5 MACRO
"Time's a-wastin'!": 4 CMON
Time-share: 6 RENTAL
"Times of Your Life"
    singer: 4 ANKA
Timetable: 4 SKED
    abbr.: 3 ARR ETD
"Time ___ the essence": 4 ISOF
"... ___ time to do't": Lady
    Macbeth: 3 TIS
Time Warner
    buyer: 3 AOL
Timeworn: 3 OLD
Timex
    rival: 5 CASIO SEIKO
Timid: 3 SHY 5 MOUSY
    creature: 4 DEER
    one: 5 MOUSE
Timing
    A question of: 4 WHEN
Timmy
    Dog of: 6 LASSIE
Timothy
    1960s tripper: 5 LEARY
    Actor: 4 DALY
Timothy Q. Mouse
    Friend of: 5 DUMBO
Timpani: 4 DRUM
Tin
    alloy: 6 PEWTER
    Award that is mostly: 5 OSCAR
    Fish in a: 7 SARDINE
    foil: 4 WRAP
Tina
    Ex of: 3 IKE
    "SNL" writer: 3 FEY
Tin ___ Alley: 3 PAN
"Tin Cup"
    actress Rene: 5 RUSSO
    costar of Kevin: 4 RENE

**"Tin Drum, The"**
  author Gunter: 5 GRASS
**Tine:** 5 PRONG
**Tined**
  tool: 4 FORK
**Tinged:** 4 HUED
**Tiniest**
  bit: 4 ATOM DROP IOTA
    5 LEAST SHRED
  The ~ bit: 7 ONEIOTA
**Tinker:** 3 CUB
  target: 5 EVERS
  with: 4 EDIT
**Tinkerbell:** 5 PIXIE
  prop: 4 WAND
**"Tinker to ___ to Chance":**
  5 EVERS
**Tin Lizzie:** 6 MODELT
**Tin Man**
  Dorothy, to the: 5 OILER
  necessity: 6 OILCAN
  need: 3 OIL
  portrayer: 5 HALEY
**Tinny:** 7 STANNIC
**Tin Pan Alley**
  Ardor, in: 4 PASH
  org.: 5 ASCAP
  product: 4 SONG
**Tinsel:** 7 ADORNER
**Tint:** 3 DYE HUE 5 COLOR
    SHADE
  Photo: 5 SEPIA
**Tintern:** 5 ABBEY
  ___ Tin Tin: 3 RIN
**Tintinnabulation:** 4 PEAL
**Tintype**
  tint: 5 SEPIA
**Tinware**
  Painted: 4 TOLE
**Tiny:** 3 WEE 4 ITSY 5 ELFIN
    MICRO 6 MINUTE
  amount: 3 SOU TAD 4 ATOM
    DRIB IOTA MITE WHIT
    5 AMITE GRAIN TRACE
  buzzer: 4 GNAT
  (Scottish): 3 SMA
**"Tiny"**
  guy: 3 TIM
**"Tiny ___":** 5 ALICE
**"Tiny Alice"**
  playwright: 5 ALBEE
**"Tiny Bubbles"**
  singer: 5 DONHO
**Tiny-capped**
  mushroom: 5 ENOKI
**Tiny Tim**
  Father of: 3 BOB
  flower: 5 TULIP
  instrument: 3 UKE
    7 UKELELE UKULELE
  ~, to Bob Cratchit: 3 SON
**Tiomkin**
  Film composer: 6 DMITRI
**Tip:** 3 END 4 ACME DOFF HINT
    LEAN 5 STEER UPEND
  **Info:** Suffix cue

a hat: 4 DOFF
Follow a: 5 ACTON
for a dealer: 4 TOKE
Leave no: 5 STIFF
of a wing tip: 3 TOE
off: 4 CLUE TELL WARN
    5 ALERT 6 CLUEIN
    8 FOREWARN
of the House: 6 ONEILL
politely: 4 DOFF
seller: 4 TOUT
suffix: 4 STER
to one side: 6 CAREEN
Tout: 5 HORSE
**Tippecanoe**
  mate: 5 TYLER
**Tipped**
  It may be: 3 HAT
**Tipper**
  Mate of: 6 ALGORE
  or Al: 4 GORE
**Tipperary**
  County west of: 5 CLARE
**Tippi**
  Actress: 6 HEDREN
  Daughter of: 7 MELANIE
**Tippled:** 7 HADANIP
**Tippler:** 3 SOT
  Big: 4 WINO
  Mayberry: 4 OTIS
**Tippy**
  craft: 5 CANOE
**Tips:** 6 INCOME
**Tipsy:** 4 HIGH
  Beyond: 3 LIT 6 STEWED
**Tiptoe:** 5 SNEAK STEAL
**Tiptop:** 4 ACME AONE APEX
    PEAK
**Tirade:** 4 RANT
  One on a: 6 RANTER
**Tiranë**
  land: 7 ALBANIA
  land (abbr.): 3 ALB
**Tire**
  abbr.: 3 PSI
  channel: 3 RUT
  filler: 3 AIR
  in the trunk: 5 SPARE
  Leaky ~ sound: 4 SSSS
  meas.: 3 PSI
  Ohio ~ city: 5 AKRON
  (out): 4 POOP
  part: 5 TREAD
  pattern: 5 TREAD
  Put on a spare: 4 GAIN
  reinforcement: 3 PLY
  Spare: 3 FAT 4 FLAB
  Spare ~ site: 5 WAIST
  Type of: 5 RECAP 6 RADIAL
    7 RETREAD
  ~, in French: 4 PNEU
**Tired:** 5 ALLIN STALE TRITE
    WEARY
  Sick and: 3 ILL 5 FEDUP
**Tireless**
  It's: 4 SLED

**Tires**
  Feature of some: 9 STEELBELT
  Like most: 7 TREADED
  Like old: 4 BALD
  Work on: 5 ALIGN
**Tiresias:** 4 SEER
**Tiresome:** 3 OLD
  Become: 4 PALL WEAR
  grind: 3 RUT
  one: 4 BORE
**Tirtoff**
  alias: 4 ERTE
**Tishri**
  Month before: 4 ELUL
**Tissue**
  additive: 4 ALOE
  Connective: 6 TENDON
  Fatty: 4 SUET
  Kind of: 4 SCAR
  layer: 3 PLY
  Mass of: 4 NODE
  Plant: 5 XYLEM
  Relating to: 5 TELAR
  Soft: 7 KLEENEX
  suffix: 5 PLASM
  Throat: 6 TONSIL
**Tit**
  for tat: 4 TYPO 5 TRADE
**Titan**
  Memorable: 5 ATLAS
  place: 4 SILO
**Titania:** 4 MOON
  Husband of: 6 OBERON
**Titanic:** 5 LINER
  casualty: 5 ASTOR
  It was left on the: 4 PORT
  message: 3 SOS
  sinker: 4 BERG 7 ICEBERG
  totaler: 4 BERG
**"Titanic"**
  actor Billy: 4 ZANE
  actress Winslet: 4 KATE
  director: 7 CAMERON
  heroine: 4 ROSE
  sight: 4 BERG
  soundtrack singer: 4 DION
**Titan II:** 4 ICBM
**Titans**
  Father of the: 6 URANUS
  Mother of the: 4 GAEA
  One of the: 5 ATLAS
    7 OCEANUS
  org.: 3 NFL
  quarterback Steve: 6 MCNAIR
**Tit for ___:** 3 TAT
**Tithe**
  amount: 5 TENTH
**Tither**
  amount: 8 ONETENTH
**Titian Venus:** 4 NUDE
**Titicaca:** 4 LAGO
**Titillating:** 4 RACY SEXY
    6 EROTIC
**Titillation:** 5 AROMA
**Title:** 4 DEED NAME
  bandit of opera: 6 ERNANI

British: 4 DAME EARL
car of song: 3 GTO
cloud: 4 LIEN
Common ~ word: 3 THE
document: 4 DEED
Eastern: 3 AGA
Esteemed: 3 SIR
Have ~ to: 3 OWN
Hindu: 3 SRI
holder: 5 CHAMP OWNER
Islamic: 4 EMIR
Knight: 3 SIR
Lady: 3 MRS 5 MADAM
Muslim: 4 IMAM
of respect: 3 SIR SRI 5 SAHIB
page: 4 DEED
Palindromic: 3 AGA 4 MAAM
   5 MADAM
Property: 4 DEED
Retiree: 7 EMERITA
Take the: 3 WIN
Turkish: 3 AGA 4 AGHA
   5 PASHA
~, in French: 3 MME 4 MLLE
~, in Spanish: 3 SRA 4 SRTA
**Titled:** 5 NOBLE
lady: 4 DAME
nobleman: 4 LORD
**Titleist**
holder: 3 TEE
**Titmouse**
Kind of: 6 TUFTED
**Tito**
Bandleader: 6 PUENTE
predecessor: 7 PETERII
Real first name of: 5 JOSIP
Real name of: 4 BROZ
**Titter:** 5 TEHEE
**Tittle:** 4 IOTA
**TiVo**
alternative: 3 VCR
**Tivoli**
family name: 4 ESTE
Three, in: 3 TRE
**Tix:** 6 DUCATS
Free: 5 COMPS
**Tizzy:** 4 SNIT 5 HOOHA
   6 LATHER
In a: 4 AGOG 5 MANIC
   UPSET
**TKO**
caller: 3 REF
**Tlaloc**
~, to the Aztecs: 7 RAINGOD
**TLC**
dispensers: 3 RNS
Part of: 4 CARE
provider: 5 NURSE
~, for one: 4 TRIO
**T-man:** 3 FED
**T-men:** 4 FEDS
**TNT**
alternative: 3 AMC HBO SHO
   USA
ending: 3 ENE
inventor: 5 NOBEL

Part of: 3 TRI 5 NITRO
   7 TOLUENE
Use: 5 BLAST
**To**
any extent: 5 ATALL
a tee: 3 PAT
be *(plural)*: 3 ARE
be, in French: 4 ETRE
be, in Latin: 4 ESSE
be, in Spanish: 3 SER 5 ESTAR
boot: 3 TOO 4 ALSO
   6 NOLESS
date: 3 YET 4 AFAR 5 ASYET
   SOFAR
have, in French: 5 AVOIR
love (Italian): 5 AMARE
me, in French: 4 AMOI
Partner of: 3 FRO
pieces: 5 APART
wit: 6 NAMELY
**To ___:** 4 AMAN ATEE
**"To a …"**
poem: 3 ODE
**Toad**
feature: 4 WART
**"Toad of Toad Hall"**
playwright: 7 AAMILNE
**Toadstool**
Unlike a: 6 EDIBLE
**Toady:** 6 YESMAN
   13 APPLEPOLISHER
Acted the: 5 YESED
response: 3 YES
**To and ___:** 3 FRO
**Toast:** 4 CHAR 5 SKOAL
   6 SALUTE 7 DRINKTO
choice: 3 RYE 5 WHEAT
Cockney ~ start: 4 ERES
Danish: 5 SKOAL
Dish served on: 7 RAREBIT
French: 5 SALUT
French ~ portion: 5 SANTE
German: 6 PROSIT
Kind of: 5 MELBA
On ~, at a diner: 4 DOWN
opener: 5 HERES
   7 HERESTO
Spanish: 5 SALUD
topper: 3 JAM 4 OLEO
   5 JELLY
Yuletide: 7 WASSAIL
~, to a GI: 7 SHINGLE
**___ toast:** 5 MELBA
**Toasted**
brand: 4 EGGO
sandwich, for short: 3 BLT
**Toaster**
oven setting: 5 BROIL
sound: 5 CLINK
treat: 7 POPTART
type: 5 POPUP
waffle brand: 4 EGGO
word: 5 SKOAL
**Toastmaster:** 5 EMCEE
**"Toastmaster General":**
   6 JESSEL

**"Toast of the Town"**
host: 10 EDSULLIVAN
**Toasty:** 4 WARM
**"To Autumn":** 3 ODE
**Tobacco:** 4 ROAD
Coarse: 4 SHAG
holder: 3 TIN
kiln: 4 OAST
Kind of: 9 SMOKELESS
mouthful: 4 CHAW
Pack down: 4 TAMP
pipe part: 4 STEM
Plug of: 4 CHAW
~, et al. (abbr.): 3 RDS
**Tobacconist**
offering: 5 BLEND
**"To be, or not to be"**
speaker: 6 HAMLET
**Tobias**
Author: 5 WOLFF
**Toboggan:** 4 SLED
site: 4 HILL
**Toby ___, Sir:** 5 BELCH
**Today**
~, in Italian: 4 OGGI
~, in Spanish: 3 HOY
**"Today"**
cohost Lauer: 4 MATT
cohost Matt: 5 LAUER
forecaster Al: 5 ROKER
Former ~ cohost Couric:
   5 KATIE
weatherman: 7 ALROKER
**___ Today:** 3 USA
**Todd**
of baseball: 5 ZEILE
Oldtime actress: 6 THELMA
**Todd, Mary**
Hubby of: 3 ABE
**Todd, Sweeney**
weapon: 5 RAZOR
**Toddler:** 3 TOT 4 TYKE
   6 RUGRAT
break: 3 NAP
glassful: 4 WAWA
perch: 3 LAP 4 KNEE
place: 4 CRIB
query: 3 WHY
taboo: 4 NONO
**To-do:** 3 ROW 4 FLAP FUSS
   SPAT STIR 6 FRACAS
   HOOPLA
list: 6 AGENDA
list item: 4 TASK 5 CHORE
Public: 5 SCENE
**Toe:** 5 DIGIT PIGGY 6 DACTYL
cover: 4 NAIL
Hurt a: 4 STUB
in the water: 4 TEST
More than dip a: 4 WADE
the line: 4 OBEY
woe: 4 CORN GOUT
**Toes**
On one's: 4 ATIP 5 ALERT
   AWAKE READY
She's on her: 9 BALLERINA

"... to fetch ___ of water":
   5 APAIL
**Tofu**
  base: 3 SOY 7 SOYBEAN
  source: 4 SOYA
**Tog**
  up: 6 ENROBE
**Toga**
  party site: 4 FRAT
  sporter: 5 ROMAN
**Together:** 3 ONE WED 4 SANE
    5 ASONE INALL
    6 INSYNC 7 ATATIME
    ENMASSE 8 INTANDEM
  All: 5 ASONE 6 INTOTO
    7 ENMASSE
  Band: 5 UNITE 6 TEAMUP
  Bring: 5 UNITE
  Come: 3 GEL 4 JELL KNIT
    MASS MESH 5 AMASS
    MERGE UNITE
    8 COALESCE
  Do: 5 COACT
  Fit: 4 MESH NEST
  Gather: 5 AMASS
  Get: 4 MEET 5 AMASS UNITE
  Get ~ again: 5 REUNE
  Got: 3 MET
  Grind: 5 GNASH
  Grow: 7 ACCRETE
  Hold: 6 COHERE
  Join: 4 YOKE 5 UNITE
  Melt: 4 FUSE
  Mix: 4 STIR 5 BLEND
  Most: 6 SANEST
  musically: 4 ADUE
  Not: 5 APART
  Pieced: 4 SEWN
  Put: 4 MADE 5 AMASS RIGUP
    UNITE
  Rub: 5 GNASH
  Scrape: 5 RAISE 6 EKEOUT
  Stick: 4 GLUE JOIN 5 PASTE
    6 COHERE
  They're no longer: 4 EXES
  When both hands are: 4 NOON
  (with): 5 ALONG
  Working: 6 INSYNC
    8 INLEAGUE
**Togetherness:** 5 UNITY
    6 UNISON
**Toggery:** 5 DRESS
**Tognazzi**
  Actor: 3 UGO
**Togo**
  capital: 4 LOME
  neighbor: 5 BENIN GHANA
  ___ Toguri (Tokyo Rose): 3 IVA
"To ___ his own": 4 EACH
"To ___ human ...": 5 ERRIS
**Toil:** 5 LABOR SLAVE
  and trouble: 3 ADO
  wearily: 4 SLOG
  with a crew: 3 OAR
**Toiler:** 4 PEON SERF
  Autumn: 5 RAKER

Tiny: 3 ANT
**Toiletries**
  case: 4 ETUI
**Toiling**
  away: 4 ATIT
"To ___ is human ...": 3 ERR
**Token:** 4 SIGN 7 MEMENTO
    8 KEEPSAKE
  Counterfeit: 4 SLUG
  Engagement: 4 RING
  Monopoly: 3 HAT 4 IRON
    SHOE
  of welcome: 3 LEI
  Poker: 4 CHIP
  taker: 4 SLOT 5 STILE
"To Kill a Mockingbird"
  actor Gregory: 4 PECK
  author: 9 HARPERLEE
  author Harper: 3 LEE
  author Lee: 6 HARPER
**Toklas**
  partner: 5 STEIN
**Tokyo**
  Airline to: 3 ANA
  airport: 6 NARITA
  carrier: 3 JAL
  district: 5 GINZA
  Former name of: 3 EDO
  island: 6 HONSHU
  Singer born in: 3 ONO
  tie-on: 3 OBI
  trasher: 5 RODAN
**Told**
  all: 4 SANG
  a tale: 4 SPUN
  a whopper: 4 LIED
  Do as: 4 OBEY
  on: 6 RATTED
"___ Told Every Little Star":
    3 IVE
"Told you!": 3 HAH SEE
    7 IKNEWIT SOTHERE
**Toledo**
  Info: Spanish cue
  lake: 4 ERIE
  river: 6 MAUMEE
  title: 5 SENOR
  viewer: 7 ELGRECO
  View from: 8 LAKEERIE
**Tolerable:** 4 SOSO
**Tolerate:** 4 BEAR TAKE
    5 ABIDE BROOK STAND
    6 ENDURE 7 STOMACH
    8 STANDFOR
"To Live and Die ___": 4 INLA
**Tolkien**
  beast: 3 ORC
  creature: 3 ENT 6 HOBBIT
  protagonist: 5 FRODO
  tree creature: 3 ENT
  wrote one: 7 TRILOGY
**Toll:** 3 FEE 5 KNELL
    7 USERFEE
  rd.: 3 TPK 4 TPKE
  road: 4 PIKE
  Take a: 3 TAX 4 PEAL

  unit: 4 AXLE
**Tollbooth**
  area: 5 PLAZA
**Tolled:** 4 RANG
**Toll-free**
  Part of a ~ number: 3 ATT
**Tolls**
  For whom the bell: 4 THEE
**Tolstoy**
  Author: 3 LEO
  heroine: 4 ANNA 8 KARENINA
  novel: 11 WARANDPEACE
**Tom:** 3 CAT
  Actor: 5 EWELL WOPAT
  Author: 5 WOLFE
  cry: 4 MEOW
  Father of: 5 PIPER
  Golfer: 4 KITE 6 WATSON
  Lyricist: 5 ADAIR
  mate: 3 HEN
  Oscar role for: 7 FORREST
  Peeping: 4 EYER 5 SPIER
  Polly, to: 4 AUNT
  Talk host: 6 SNYDER
  ~, Dick, and Harry: 4 TRIO
    5 MALES
  ~, Dick, or Harry: 4 NAME
    6 ANYONE 8 FORENAME
**Tomahawk:** 3 AXE
**Tomás**
  Info: Spanish cue
**Tomato:** 9 LOVEAPPLE
  blight: 5 EDEMA
  jelly: 5 ASPIC
  Tossed ~ sound: 5 SPLAT
  variety: 4 PLUM ROMA
**Tomb**
  His ~ was found in 1922:
    3 TUT
**Tomboy:** 6 HOYDEN
"Tomb Raider"
  character Croft: 4 LARA
  character Lara: 5 CROFT
**Tombstone**
  inscription: 3 RIP
  lawman: 4 EARP
  locale: 7 ARIZONA
  newspaper: 7 EPITAPH
"Tombstone"
  actor Kilmer: 3 VAL
  role: 4 EARP
**Tomcat:** 3 GIB
**Tome:** 4 BOOK
  Brit. ref.: 3 OED
  filling tales: 5 SAGAS
  ___ Tomé: 3 SAO
**Tomei**
  Oscar winner: 6 MARISA
**Tomlin, Lily**
  character: 8 EDITHANN
  character Ernestine:
    8 OPERATOR
**Tommie**
  of baseball: 4 AGEE
**Tommy**
  gun: 4 STEN

of Broadway: 4 TUNE
Rocker: 3 LEE
Singer: 3 ROE
Skier: 3 MOE
**"Tommy":** 5 OPERA
band: 6 THEWHO
**Tommy Lee ___:** 5 JONES
**Tomorrow**
Here today, gone:
9 EPHEMERAL
School of: 3 ROE
~, in Spanish: 6 MANANA
**"Tomorrow"**
musical: 5 ANNIE
**"___ Tomorrow" (Sammy Kaye
tune):** 5 UNTIL
**Tomorrow's**
woman: 4 GIRL
**Tomoyuki**
Godzilla creator: 6 TANAKA
**"Tom Sawyer"**
author: 5 TWAIN
**"Tom's Diner"**
singer Suzanne: 4 VEGA
**"Tom Thumb"**
composer: 4 ARNE
star Tamblyn: 4 RUSS
**Tom-tom:** 4 DRUM
**Ton:** 4 LOTS 5 LOADS PILES
SCADS
fractions (abbr.): 3 LBS
portion (abbr.): 3 CWT
Type of: 6 METRIC
**Tone**
arm item: 6 NEEDLE
Complexion: 5 OLIVE
down: 4 EASE MUTE
6 SOFTEN SUBDUE
Earth: 4 ECRU 5 OCHER
OCHRE
Nasal: 5 TWANG
Neutral: 4 ECRU
Photo: 5 SEPIA
Subtle: 3 HUE
Triangle: 4 TING
Word after: 4 DEAF
**Toner:** 6 DRYINK
**Tongue**
Asian: 4 THAI
Boot ~ (abbr.): 4 ITAL
Caesar's: 5 LATIN
Celtic: 4 ERSE
Dog with a blue-black: 4 CHOW
Gaelic: 4 ERSE
Indian: 3 UTE 4 ZUNI 5 TAMIL
of Jesus: 7 ARAMAIC
Pakistani: 4 URDU
Siouan: 5 OMAHA OSAGE
Speak with forked: 3 LIE
Tehran: 5 FARSI
tip: 3 ESE
Turkic: 5 TATAR
**Tongue-clucking**
sound: 3 TSK
**Tongue-lash:** 5 SCOLD
6 BERATE

**Tongue-lashing:** 6 TIRADE
**Tongues**
do it: 3 WAG
Like gossiping: 4 AWAG
**Tongue-tied**
one: 4 SHOE
**Toni**
Pop singer: 7 BRAXTON
**Tonic**
partner: 3 GIN
prefix: 3 ISO
**Tonics**
and tablets, briefly: 4 MEDS
**"Tonight Show, The"**
first host: 5 ALLEN
former announcer Hall: 3 EDD
host: 4 LENO
host before Carson: 4 PAAR
**Tonkin**
delta city: 5 HANOI
**To no ___:** 5 AVAIL
**"To ___ not to ...":** 4 BEOR
**Tons:** 4 LOTS MANY 5 AHEAP
ALOAD HEAPS SCADS
SLEWS 6 OCEANS
OODLES
**Tonsil**
neighbor: 5 UVULA
suffix: 4 ITIS
**Tonsillitis**
cause: 5 STREP
**Tonsorial**
offering: 5 SHAVE
touch up: 4 TRIM
**Tony:** *see pages 722–723* 4 CHIC
5 AWARD
1964 ~ winner: 4 LAHR
1980 ~ winner: 5 EVITA
1982 ~ winner: 4 NINE
1996 ~ winner: 4 RENT
1998 ~ winner: 3 ART
Actor: 5 DANZA
Batting champ: 5 OLIVA
British P.M.: 5 BLAIR
candidate: 4 PLAY
kin: 4 OBIE
Middleweight champ: 4 ZALE
of baseball: 4 PENA 5 OLIVA
PEREZ
of golf: 4 LEMA
Puppeteer: 4 SARG
winner: 10 HELENHAYES
winner Caldwell: 3 ZOE
winner Hagen: 3 UTA
winner Judith: 4 IVEY
winner Neuwirth: 4 BEBE
winner Rivera: 5 CHITA
winner Styne: 4 JULE
winner Swoosie: 5 KURTZ
winner Uta: 5 HAGEN
winner Worth: 5 IRENE
winning role for Morse: 3 TRU
**Too:** 4 ALSO 6 ASWELL OVERLY
big: 5 OBESE
hasty: 4 RASH
inquisitive: 4 NOSY

much, musically: 6 TROPPO
quickly: 7 INHASTE
snug: 5 TIGHT
**"Too bad!":** 4 ALAS PITY
5 TOUGH
**"Toodle-oo!":** 4 TATA
Toulouse: 5 ADIEU
**"Toodles!":** 3 BYE 4 TATA
5 IMOFF 6 SOLONG
**Took:** 5 STOLE 7 FLEECED
care of: 5 SAWTO
charge: 3 LED
cover: 3 HID
first: 3 WON
five: 6 RESTED
from the top: 5 REDID
home: 6 NETTED
in: 3 ATE
measures: 5 ACTED
notice: 5 SATUP
off: 3 RAN 4 FLED FLEW
LEFT WENT
off on: 4 APED
on: 5 HIRED
out: 5 DELED
place: 3 WAS
steps: 5 ACTED 6 STRODE
the cake: 3 ATE WON
the wrong way: 5 STOLE
too much: 4 ODED
up: 7 GOTINTO
**Tool:** 4 PAWN 7 CATSPAW
Abrasive: 7 SCRAPER
arm: 6 SCYTHE
Axelike: 4 ADZE
Boring: 5 AUGER 6 REAMER
Branding: 4 IRON
building: 4 SHED
Carpentry: 3 ADZ SAW 4 RASP
VISE 5 DRILL LEVEL
PLANE 6 RIPSAW
Climbing: 5 PITON
Cutting: 3 ADZ AXE BUR
4 ADZE
Digging: 5 SPADE 6 SHOVEL
Duel: 4 EPEE
Fall: 4 RAKE
Garden: 3 HOE 4 RAKE
5 EDGER SPADE
6 WEEDER
Grinding: 6 PESTLE
Kitchen: 6 PEELER
Metalworker: 8 BALLPEEN
Piercing: 3 AWL
shaper: 3 DIE
Shaping: 4 RASP
sharpener: 8 OILSTONE
Surgical: 5 LASER
Threshing: 5 FLAIL
Trimming: 3 ADZ 5 EDGER
Turning: 5 LATHE
with a belt: 6 SANDER
with teeth: 3 SAW 4 RAKE
Woodworking: 3 ADZ 4 ADZE
5 LATHE 6 CHISEL
SHAPER

**"Too many cooks ...": 5** ADAGE
**Toon**
Blue: 5 SMURF
chihuahua: 3 REN
dog: 3 REN
Early ~ clown: 4 KOKO
fowl: 9 DAFFYDUCK
frame: 3 CEL
Futuristic ~ family:
7 JETSONS
MTV: 3 REN
panda: 4 ANDY
pooch: 3 REN
rabbit: 5 ROGER
skunk: 9 PEPELEPEW
Twister-like: 3 TAZ
unit: 3 CEL
~ Betty: 4 BOOP
___ to one's ears: 4 INUP
"___ Too Proud to Beg": 4 AINT
**"Too-Ra-Loo-Ra-Loo-___":**
3 RAL
**Toot:** 3 JAG 4 BEEP BLOW
TEAR 5 BINGE SPREE
6 BENDER
one's own horn: 4 CROW
5 BOAST
**Tooter**
Popeye's: 4 PIPE
**Tooth:** 3 COG
Artificial: 7 DENTURE
Back: 5 MOLAR
covering: 6 ENAMEL
Gear: 3 COG
Long: 4 FANG
Long in the: 3 OLD 4 AGED
Machine: 3 COG
org.: 3 ADA
part: 4 ROOT 6 ENAMEL
Partner of: 4 NAIL
prefix: 5 DENTI 6 ODONTO
trouble: 4 ACHE 5 DECAY
Wheel: 3 COG
Wisdom: 5 MOLAR
**Toothbrush**
brand: 5 ORALB
**Toothed:** 7 DENTATE
tool: 3 SAW 4 RAKE
**Toothless:** 8 EDENTATE
**Toothpaste**
box abbr.: 3 ADA
brand: 5 CREST
Classic: 5 IPANA
holder: 4 TUBE
type: 3 GEL
**Toothpick**
item: 5 OLIVE
**Toothsome:** 5 TASTY
**Toothy**
fish: 3 GAR
menace: 4 CROC
tool: 3 SAW
**Toots:** 3 HON 5 HONEY
Restaurateur: 4 SHOR
**"Tootsie"**
actress Garr: 4 TERI

actress Jessica: 5 LANGE
~ Oscar nominee: 8 TERIGARR
**Tootsies**
Tabby: 4 PAWS
**Top:** 3 BRA CAP LID TOY
4 ACME APEX BEST
PEAK 5 OUTDO
6 BLOUSE
athlete: 7 ALLSTAR
banana: 4 STAR
Big: 4 TENT
Bikini: 3 BRA
Blow one's: 5 ERUPT
Box: 3 LID
card: 3 ACE
Casual: 3 TEE 6 TSHIRT
choices: 5 ALIST
Come out on: 3 WIN
contractor: 6 ROOFER
dog: 5 CHAMP MRBIG
9 NUMEROUNO
draft level: 4 ONEA
floor: 5 ATTIC
From the: 4 ANEW 5 AGAIN
From the ~, in music:
6 DACAPO
grade: 5 APLUS
gun: 3 ACE
kick: 6 NONCOM
Kind of: 4 TANK 6 HALTER
of some scales: 3 TEN
of the head: 4 PATE
of the morning: 5 ONEAM
of the world: 4 POLE
On: 5 AHEAD
On ~ of: 4 OVER UPON
5 ABOVE
position: 3 ONE
prize: 7 JACKPOT
rating: 3 TEN 4 AONE
scout: 5 EAGLE
spot: 4 ACME APEX
Take from the: 4 REDO SKIM
Take off the: 4 SKIM
Tank: 6 GASCAP TURRET
Tatar: 4 KHAN
Tube: 3 CAP
Very: 4 ACME
Wave: 5 CREST
Way to get to the: 6 SKITOW
**Top 40**
song list: 9 HITPARADE
songs: 4 HITS
**Topaz:** 3 GEM
**"Topaz"**
author Leon: 4 URIS
**Top-drawer:** 4 AONE 5 ELITE
**Topeka**
state (abbr.): 4 KANS
**Toper:** 3 SOT 4 SOAK
Mayberry: 4 OTIS
**Top-flight:** 4 AONE
**"Top Hat"**
star: 7 ASTAIRE
**Topiary**
Like: 6 SHAPED

**Topic:** 5 THEME
list: 6 AGENDA
of gossip: 4 ITEM
**"Top ___ morning!":** 4 OTHE
**Top-notch:** 3 ACE 4 ACES
AONE 5 APLUS
**Top-of-the-line:** 4 AONE BEST
**Topology**
shapes: 4 TORI
**Topper:** 3 CAP HAT LID TAM
**Topple:** 5 UPEND UPSET
6 UNSEAT
from power: 4 OUST
(over): 4 KEEL
**Topps**
rival: 5 FLEER
**Top-rated:** 4 AONE
**Tops:** 4 AONE BEST 6 ATMOST
ONEUPS
~, in sports:
11 ALLAMERICAN
**Top-shelf:** 4 AONE
**Topsoil**
Added ~ to: 6 LOAMED
Lose: 5 ERODE
**Topsy**
playmate: 3 EVA
**Topsy-turvy:** 7 INAMESS
Turn: 5 UPEND UPSET
**Toque:** 3 HAT
**Torah**
holder: 3 ARK
teacher: 5 RABBI
**Torch**
1996 Olympic ~ lighter: 3 ALI
carrier: 6 SCONCE
Carry a ~ (for): 4 PINE
crime: 5 ARSON
job: 5 ARSON
Kind of: 4 TIKI
user: 6 WELDER
**Torched:** 3 LIT
**Torch Red**
Car available in: 5 TBIRD
**Tore:** 3 RAN 4 SPED
down: 5 RAZED
**Toreador**
Cheer for a: 3 OLE
**"To recap ...":** 5 INSUM
**"To reiterate ...":** 7 ASISAID
**Torero**
encouragement: 3 OLE
**Tori**
Singer: 4 AMOS
**Torino**
Info: Italian cue
locale: 6 ITALIA
Three, in: 3 TRE
**Tormé**
forte: 4 SCAT
nickname, with "The":
9 VELVETFOG
Singer: 3 MEL
**Torment:** 3 VEX 4 BAIT RIDE
5 AGONY EATAT NAGAT
TEASE

**Tormentor**
of Curly: 3 MOE
of Margaret: 6 DENNIS
Princess: 3 PEA
Tiny: 4 GNAT
**Torn:** 4 RENT
Actor: 3 RIP
and tattered: 5 RATTY
**Tornado:** 8 ACTOFGOD
siren: 5 ALERT
**"Tornado"**
Pitcher nicknamed: 4 NOMO
**Toro**
competitor: 5 DEERE
opponent: 7 MATADOR
___ Toro, Benicio: 3 DEL
**Toronto**
media inits.: 3 CBC
team: 4 JAYS 5 LEAFS
   10 MAPLELEAFS
~ Argonauts' org.: 3 CFL
**Toronto Maple ___:** 5 LEAFS
**Torpedo:** 3 SUB 4 RUIN SINK
vessel: 5 EBOAT UBOAT
**Torpor:** 7 INERTIA
**Torquato**
Italian poet: 5 TASSO
**Torre**
team member: 6 YANKEE
**Torrent:** 4 RAIN RASH 5 SPATE
   6 DELUGE ONRUSH
**Torrijos**
of Panama: 4 OMAR
**Torso:** 4 BODY 6 MIDDLE
**Torte**
Top a: 3 ICE
topper: 4 ICER
**Tortelli, Carla**
portrayer: 11 RHEAPERLMAN
**Tortilla**
chip dip: 5 SALSA
Filled: 4 TACO
sandwich: 4 WRAP
snack: 5 NACHO
**"Tortilla Soup"**
actress Elizabeth: 4 PENA
**Tortoise**
and hare event: 4 RACE
racer: 4 HARE
**"Tortoise and the Hare, The":**
   5 FABLE
writer: 5 AESOP
**Tortosa**
river: 4 EBRO
**Torts**
prof.'s degree: 3 LLD
**Tortuga**
neighbor: 5 HAITI
**Torture**
device: 4 RACK
**Torturer:** 6 SADIST
**Tory**
rival: 4 WHIG
**"Tosca":** 5 OPERA
composer: 7 PUCCINI
tune: 4 ARIA

**Toscanini:** 7 MAESTRO
Conductor: 6 ARTURO
Together, to: 4 ADUE
~, et al.: 7 MAESTRI
**Tosh, Peter:** 5 RASTA
**Toshiba**
competitor: 3 NEC RCA
   4 SONY 5 SANYO
**"To Sir With Love"**
singer: 4 LULU
**Toss:** 3 LOB 4 FLIP HURL
   5 THROW
about: 5 STREW
High: 3 LOB
option: 5 TAILS
out: 4 BOOT EMIT 5 EJECT
   EVICT SCRAP 6 DEPOSE
Scots ~ it: 5 CABER
**Tossed**
dish: 5 SALAD
It may be: 5 SALAD
**Tosser**
Caber: 4 SCOT
Mortarboard: 4 GRAD
**Tosspot:** 3 SOT
**"To summarize ...":** 7 INSHORT
**Tot:** 3 ADD 4 DRAM 5 CHILD
break: 3 NAP
piggies: 4 TOES
Reminder to a: 9 SAYPLEASE
ritual: 3 NAP
Seat for a: 4 KNEE
song start: 4 ABCD
spot: 4 CRIB
tender: 5 NANNY
toter: 4 PRAM
trailer: 5 WAGON
wheels: 5 TRIKE
Words to a: 7 ISEEYOU
**Tot.:** 3 AMT
**Total:** 3 ADD SUM 4 FULL RUIN
   5 ADDUP INALL RUNTO
   UTTER 6 ALLOUT
   AMOUNT COMETO
   ENTIRE 7 ADDUPTO
   8 DEMOLISH
(abbr.): 3 AMT
again: 5 READD
confusion: 5 CHAOS
failure: 6 FIASCO
reversal: 5 UTURN
Running: 5 TALLY
Sum: 6 AMOUNT
**"Total ___" (1990 film):**
   6 RECALL
**Totaled:** 5 RANTO
**Totality:** 3 ALL
**Totally:** 3 ALL 5 INALL
**"Totally rad":** 7 AWESOME
**"Total Recall"**
setting: 4 MARS
**"Total Request Live"**
network: 3 MTV
**Tote:** 3 LUG 5 CARRY 6 SCHLEP
   8 CARRYALL
figures: 4 ODDS

Roadie: 3 AMP
**Totenberg**
of NPR: 4 NINA
**Toter**
Blanket: 5 LINUS
**To the ___:** 3 MAX 4 HILT
**To the ___ degree:** 3 NTH
**"To ___ their golden eyes"**
   ("Cymbeline"): 3 OPE
**"To the max"**
indicator: 3 EST
**"To thine own ___ be true":**
   4 SELF
**Toto**
hit song: 7 ROSANNA
**Tottenham**
Info: British cue
**Totter:** 4 REEL
**Toucan**
feature: 4 BEAK
**Touch:** 3 BIT TAD TAG 4 ABUT
   HINT 5 SENSE
base: 5 TAGUP
down: 4 LAND
Encouraging: 3 PAT
Gentle: 6 CARESS
Get in: 7 CONTACT
Kind of: 5 MIDAS
Light: 3 PAT
lovingly: 6 FONDLE
Nice: 6 CARESS
of color: 5 TINCT
off: 4 TRIP 5 SPARK START
of frost: 3 NIP
on: 4 ABUT
on the shoulder: 3 TAP
Perceive by: 4 FEEL
Special: 3 TLC
up: 4 EDIT 5 AMEND EMEND
   6 REVISE 7 ENHANCE
up, at the salon: 7 RECOLOR
upon: 4 ABUT
**Touchdown:** 7 ARRIVAL
Chicago: 5 OHARE
datum: 3 ETA
Made a: 4 ALIT
spot: 7 AIRPORT
time (abbr.): 3 ETA
**Touched:** 5 DOTTY
down: 4 ALIT
**"Touched by an Angel"**
actress Downey: 4 ROMA
actress Reese: 5 DELLA
costar: 5 REESE
role: 4 TESS
**Touching:** 7 TANGENT
**"Touch of Evil"**
director Orson: 6 WELLES
**"Touch the Wind"**
Hit subtitled: 6 ERESTU
**Touch-up:** 4 TRIM
**Touchy:** 7 TACTILE
subject: 3 AGE 8 SORESPOT
**Touchy-___:** 5 FEELY
**Tough:** 4 GOON HARD HOOD
   THUG 9 HARDNOSED

boss: **10** TASKMASTER
companion: **4** MOLL
curve: **3** ESS
exam: **4** ORAL
exterior: **4** HIDE
guy: **7** IRONMAN **8** HARDNOSE
In a ~ spot: **5** TREED
journey: **4** TREK
look: **5** SNEER
Make: **5** STEEL
Mob: **8** ENFORCER
Not so: **8** TENDERER
nut: **5** POSER
nut to crack: **6** ENIGMA
question: **5** POSER
row to hoe: **6** ORDEAL
situation: **4** SPOT
spot: **3** JAM **4** BIND HOLE
    KNOT MESS **5** PINCH
    **6** PLIGHT SCRAPE
    **8** KNOTHOLE
task: **4** ONUS
test: **4** ORAL
to climb: **5** STEEP
to grasp: **4** DEEP
to settle: **5** MESSY
trip: **4** TREK
watchdog: **5** AKITA
wood: **3** ASH **5** LARCH
**Toughen: 5** ENURE INURE
up: **5** INURE STEEL
    **6** ANNEAL
**Toughener**
Steel: **8** TITANIUM
**Tough-guy**
actor Ray: **4** ALDO
**Toughie: 5** POSER
**"Tough-Minded Optimist, The"**
author: **5** PEALE
**Toughness**
symbol: **5** NAILS
**Toujours ___: 3** GAI
**Toulon**
**Info:** French cue
To be, in: **4** ETRE
View from: **3** MER
**Toulouse**
**Info:** French cue
Thanks, in: **5** MERCI
time: **3** ETE
To be, in: **4** ETRE
"Toodle-oo" in: **5** ADIEU
**Toulouse-___: 7** LAUTREC
**Toulouse-Lautrec**
album of women: **5** ELLES
Artist: **5** HENRI
**Toupee: 3** RUG WIG
**Tour**
gp.: **3** PGA **4** LPGA
guide listings: **4** INNS
helper: **6** ROADIE
leader: **5** GUIDE
of duty: **5** STINT
Take a: **8** SIGHTSEE
**Tour de France**
entrant: **6** CYCLER

**Touring**
car: **5** SEDAN
company: **8** ROADSHOW
Early ~ car: **3** REO
prefix: **3** ECO
troupe: **8** ROADSHOW
**Tourist**
aid: **3** MAP **5** GUIDE
draw: **5** MECCA
tote: **6** CAMERA
transport: **3** CAB
**Tourist spot**
Arizona: **6** SEDONA
Indian: **4** AGRA
Mediterranean: **5** IBIZA
New Mexico: **4** TAOS
San Diego: **3** ZOO
Spanish: **5** AVILA
Swiss: **7** LUCERNE
**Tournament**
Big: **4** OPEN
Early ~ match: **6** PRELIM
exemption: **3** BYE
favorite: **4** SEED
Hoops: **3** NIT **4** NCAA
Kind of: **4** OPEN **5** PROAM
Like many ~ events: **5** TIMED
match: **4** SEMI
pass: **3** BYE
ranking: **4** SEED
round: **5** SEMIS
type: **4** OPEN
**Tourney**
Hoops: **3** NIT
March: **4** NCAA
pass: **3** BYE
rank: **4** SEED
round: **5** SEMIS
type: **4** OPEN **5** PROAM
**Tours**
**Info:** French cue
river: **5** LOIRE
season: **3** ETE
Ta-ta, in: **5** ADIEU
thanks: **5** MERCI
toast: **5** SALUT
To be, in: **4** ETRE
turndown: **3** NON
with: **4** AVEC
Yours, in: **4** ATOI
**Tousle: 4** MUSS
**Tout: 4** LAUD
figures: **4** ODDS
hangout (abbr.): **3** OTB
spot: **4** RAIL
tidbit: **6** HOTTIP
tip: **5** HORSE
**Toves**
Like Carroll's: **6** SLITHY
**Tow: 4** HAUL
Horse: **4** SHAY
job: **4** REPO
Ski: **4** TBAR
Tug: **5** BARGE
**Toward**
Head: **7** MAKEFOR

Lean: **5** FAVOR **6** PREFER
Move: **4** NEAR
Point: **5** AIMAT
shelter: **4** ALEE
sunrise: **4** EAST
sunset: **4** WEST
the back: **5** AREAR
the dawn: **4** EAST
the mouth: **4** ORAD
the rear: **3** AFT **4** ASTERN
the rudder: **3** AFT **6** ASTERN
the stern: **3** AFT
Turn: **4** FACE
**Towel**
feature: **3** NAP
holder: **3** ROD
inscription: **3** HIS **4** HERS
material: **5** TERRY
Needing a: **3** WET
off: **3** DRY
Result of throwing in the:
    **3** TKO
Throw in the: **4** QUIT
word: **3** HIS **4** HERS
**Tower: 4** LOOM SOAR
Bell ~ emanation: **4** PEAL
Biblical: **5** BABEL
Bridge: **5** PYLON
Control ~ image: **4** BLIP
Farm: **4** SILO
in the water: **3** TUG
Leaning ~ home: **4** PISA
Mosque: **7** MINARET
over: **5** DWARF
Rural: **4** SILO
site: **4** PISA **5** BABEL
    **6** LONDON
topper: **5** SPIRE
town: **4** PISA
**___ Tower**
(Chicago): **5** SEARS
(Honolulu): **5** ALOHA
(San Francisco): **4** COIT
**"Tower, The"**
poet: **5** YEATS
**Towering: 4** TALL **5** LOFTY
**"Towering Inferno, The"**
~ Oscar nominee: **7** ASTAIRE
**Tower of London**
treasure: **11** CROWNJEWELS
**"To what do I ___ ...?": 3** OWE
**"To whom ___ concern ...":**
    **5** ITMAY
**"To ___ With Love": 3** SIR
**Town: 4** BURG
Bean: **4** LIMA
destroyed during WWI:
    **5** YPRES
destroyed in 1944: **4** STLO
employee: **5** CRIER
German: **5** STADT
In: **5** LOCAL
in a novel: **5** ADANO
in County Kerry: **6** TRALEE
Italian: **6** ASSISI
Italian wine: **4** ASTI

Like a tiny: 8 ONEHORSE
Market: 5 BOURG
meeting: 5 FORUM
near Bangor: 5 ORONO
near Caen: 4 STLO
near Padua: 4 ESTE
Noted cathedral: 3 ELY
official: 5 CRIER
on the Thames: 4 ETON
on the Vire: 4 STLO
Outlying: 5 EXURB
Out of: 4 AWAY
outside Harrisburg: 5 ENOLA
Paint the ~ red: 7 CAROUSE
Skip: 4 FLEE 5 ELOPE
Small: 4 BURG
Spanish wine: 5 JEREZ
square: 5 PLAZA
~ NNE of Santa Fe: 4 TAOS
Town ___: 5 CRIER
"___ Town" (Wilder play):
    3 OUR
Townhouse
    type: 5 CONDO
Townie: 5 LOCAL
Town-line
    sign (abbr.): 4 ESTD
Townshend
    of the Who: 4 PETE
    Rocker: 4 PETE
"To Wong ___, Thanks for
    Everything, Julie
    Newmar: 3 FOO
"___ to worry!": 3 NOT
Tow truck
    abbr.: 3 AAA
    pickup, at times: 4 REPO
Toxic
    compound (abbr.): 3 PCB
    shrub: 5 SUMAC
Toxin
    fighters: 4 SERA
Toy
    ball: 4 NERF
    Beach: 4 PAIL
    block: 4 LEGO
    boat spot: 4 POND
    Boy: 3 KEN
    Building: 4 LEGO
    Child's: 10 JACKINABOX
    Christmas: 4 SLED
    Crib: 6 RATTLE
    disk: 7 FRISBEE
    dog: 4 PEKE
    for windy days: 4 KITE
    gun ammo: 4 CAPS
    Musical: 5 KAZOO
    on a string: 4 KITE YOYO
    Paper: 4 KITE
    racer: 7 SLOTCAR
    Sandbox: 4 PAIL
    since 1902: 9 TEDDYBEAR
    Snow: 4 SLED
    soldier: 5 GIJOE
    Spinning: 3 TOP
    Spring: 6 SLINKY

that does tricks: 4 YOYO
Ticklish: 4 ELMO
train maker: 6 LIONEL
truck: 5 TONKA
Wind-up: 4 KITE
Winter: 4 SLED
with a tail: 4 KITE
Toyland
    visitors: 5 BABES
Toymaker: 3 ELF
Toyota
    model: 5 CAMRY PASEO
        SUPRA 6 AVALON CELICA
        TERCEL 7 COROLLA
"To your health!": 5 SALUD
        SKOAL 6 PROSIT
Tpk.: 3 RTE
    rate: 3 MPH
Tra ___: 4 LALA
Trace: 4 CLUE HINT IOTA
        WISP 7 SOUPCON
        VESTIGE 9 SCINTILLA
    Memory: 6 ENGRAM
    of color: 5 TINGE
    of dishonor: 5 TAINT
    of smoke: 4 WISP
Tracey
    Comedienne: 6 ULLMAN
Trac II
    alternative: 4 ATRA
Track: 3 DOG 4 OVAL RAIL
        SONG
    action: 3 BET
    Animal: 5 SPOOR
    athlete: 5 MILER
    Auxiliary: 4 SPUR
    Back at the: 5 BETON
    down: 6 LOCATE
    event: 4 DASH HEAT MEET
        RACE TROT 5 RELAY
        6 SPRINT
        11 HAMMERTHROW
    figure: 4 TOUT
    figures: 4 ODDS
    Go off the: 6 DERAIL
    has-been: 3 NAG
    Laugh ~ sound: 4 HAHA
    Like some ~ meets: 4 DUAL
    Lose: 6 DERAIL
    numbers: 4 ODDS
    official: 5 TIMER
    Off the: 6 ASTRAY
    Once around the: 3 LAP
    Pass again on the: 5 RELAP
    Race: 4 OVAL
    Railroad ~ part: 8 CROSSTIE
    regular: 6 BETTOR
    shape: 4 OVAL
    Slalom: 3 ESS
    specialist: 5 MILER
    support: 7 TRESTLE
    tipster: 4 TOUT
    transaction: 3 BET
    trial: 4 HEAT
    Trodden: 4 PATH
    Wheel: 3 RUT

Track-and-field
    org.: 3 AAU
Trackball
    alternatives: 4 MICE
Tracker: 3 GEO
    Airplane: 5 RADAR
    Storm: 5 RADAR
    UV index: 3 EPA
Tracking
    device: 5 RADAR
Tracks
    (down): 5 HUNTS
    Made: 3 RAN 4 FLED SPED
        TORE
    Make: 3 HIE LAM SKI 4 FLEE
        RACE 6 HASTEN
Tract: 3 LOT 4 AREA PLOT
    Low: 4 VALE
    Open: 3 LEA 5 LLANO
    Overgrown: 5 HEATH
    Peaty: 4 MOOR
    Uncultivated: 5 HEATH
    Wet: 4 MIRE
Traction
    aid: 5 CLEAT
    Lose: 4 SKID
    Lost: 4 SLID
Tractor
    blade: 4 PLOW
    handle: 5 DEERE
    maker: 5 DEERE
    name: 5 DEERE
Tractor-trailer: 3 RIG 4 SEMI
Tracy
    of the comics: 4 DICK
Tracy, Dick
    Mrs.: 4 TESS
Tracy, Spencer
    film of 1958:
        13 THELASTHURRAH
Tracy/Hepburn
    1949 ~ film: 8 ADAMSRIB
    1957 ~ film: 7 DESKSET
Trade: 3 BIZ 4 LINE SWAP
        5 SKILL 6 BARTER
        CAREER METIER
        8 EXCHANGE
    Carry on: 3 PLY
    center: 4 MART
    International ~ spot:
        8 OPENPORT
    jabs: 4 SPAR
    Make a: 4 SWAP
    Place to: 4 MART
    punches: 4 SPAR
    show: 4 EXPO
    talk: 5 ARGOT
    Where some stks.: 3 OTC
    ___ trade: 3 RAG
Trade-in
    item: 7 USEDCAR
    reason: 5 DENTS
Trademark: 4 LOGO 5 BRAND
        LABEL
    Chevalier: 8 STRAWHAT
    Churchill: 5 VSIGN

Elvis: 5 SNEER
Indiana Jones: 6 FEDORA
Tangelo: 4 UGLI
Textile: 5 ARNEL
**Trader**
Bond ~ phrase: 5 ATPAR
Kind of: 3 DAY FUR
place: 3 PIT
Wall St.: 3 ARB
**Trader ___:** 4 VICS
**Trading**
abbr.: 3 OTC
area: 3 PIT
card name: 5 FLEER
center: 4 MART
Early ~ town: 7 ASTORIA
letters: 4 NYSE
Nonstandard ~ unit:
   6 ODDLOT
Risky stock: 4 SPEC
U.S. ~ partner: 3 EEC
**"Trading Spaces":** 6 TVSHOW
Emulate ~ folk: 4 REDO
**Tradition**
Kind of: 4 ORAL
Local: 4 LORE
**Traditional**
knowledge: 4 LORE
saying: 5 ADAGE
**Trafalgar Square**
honoree: 6 NELSON
**Traffic:** 5 TRADE
Air ~ control device: 5 RADAR
Air ~ screen sight: 4 BLIP
Blend with: 5 MERGE
caution: 3 SLO
circle: 6 ROTARY
cone: 5 PYLON
controller: 5 LIGHT
cop, at times: 5 CITER
director: 4 CONE 5 ARROW
jam: 5 SNARL TIEUP
Kind of: 4 THRU
light color: 5 AMBER
marker: 4 CONE
problem: 5 SNARL
   8 GRIDLOCK
Rush-hour ~ facilitator:
   7 HOVLANE
Sit in: 4 IDLE
slower: 9 SPEEDBUMP
snarl: 3 JAM
sound: 5 BLARE
tie-up: 3 JAM 5 SNARL
   10 BOTTLENECK
**"Traffic"**
cop: 4 NARC
org.: 3 DEA
**Traffic ___:** 4 CONE
**Traffic-stopping**
org.: 3 DEA
**Tragedy**
Euripides: 5 MEDEA
   7 ORESTES
King of: 4 LEAR
Racine: 6 ESTHER PHEDRE

Shakespearean: 7 OTHELLO
Sophocles: 4 AJAX 7 ELECTRA
   8 ANTIGONE
   10 OEDIPUSREX
**"Tragedy of ___, The":** 3 NAN
**Tragic**
It may be: 4 FLAW
**Trail:** 3 LAG 4 PATH 5 SCENT
Animal: 5 SPOOR
Blazed a: 3 LED
Follow a: 4 HIKE
Hound: 5 SCENT
Hunter: 5 SPOOR
On the ~ of: 5 AFTER
shelter: 6 LEANTO
Ski: 5 PISTE SLOPE
Snail: 5 SLIME
the pack: 3 LAG
**___ Trail:** 7 TAMIAMI
**Trailblazer:** 7 PIONEER
**Trailer:** 5 PROMO
**Info:** Suffix cue
Boat: 4 WAKE
hauler: 7 TRACTOR
Motor: 4 CADE
Movie: 4 GOER
Rock: 4 ETTE
Tot: 5 WAGON
unit: 5 SCENE
**Trailing:** 5 INTOW
**Trail mix:** 4 GORP
fruit: 6 RAISIN
**Train:** 5 COACH TEACH TUTOR
Amtrak's bullet: 5 ACELA
bridge: 7 TRESTLE
cos.: 3 RRS
Drive ~ part: 4 AXLE
for a match: 4 SPAR
Freight ~ part: 6 BOXCAR
Half a: 4 CHOO
Last ~ car: 7 CABOOSE
line to NYC: 4 LIRR
name: 6 LIONEL
On the: 6 ABOARD
part: 3 CAR
Place on a: 5 BERTH
schedule abbr.: 3 ETD
schedule listing: 4 STOP
Slow: 5 LOCAL
Speedy: 5 ACELA
station: 4 STOP 5 DEPOT
stop (abbr.): 3 STA
Took the: 4 RODE
Toy ~ maker: 6 LIONEL
track: 4 RAIL
unit: 3 CAR
Wagon ~ direction: 4 WEST
with gloves: 4 SPAR
**Trained**
Better: 5 ABLER
**Trainee:** 5 CADET 6 INTERN
education: 5 ROPES
**Trainer**
Ali: 6 ANGELO
Lt.: 3 OTC
place: 3 GYM

**Training**
group: 5 CADRE
Kind of: 5 BASIC
Like some: 6 ONSITE
Mil. ~ acad.: 3 OCS
Military ~ group: 5 CADRE
Military ~ site: 8 BOOTCAMP
Pugilist in:
   11 SHADOWBOXER
session: 7 SEMINAR
**Trains**
Big name in: 4 TYCO
   6 AMTRAK LIONEL
Chicago: 3 ELS
Overhead: 3 ELS
**"Trainspotting"**
actor McGregor: 4 EWAN
**Trait**
carrier: 4 GENE
Desirable: 5 ASSET
transmitter: 4 GENE
**Traitor:** 5 JUDAS REBEL
Noted: 6 ARNOLD
**Traits**
Like some: 7 GENETIC
**Trajan**
Year ~ conquered Dacia: 3 CVI
Year ~ was born: 4 LIII
Year in the reign of ~: 3 CII
**Trajectory:** 3 ARC
**Tralee**
county: 5 KERRY
**Tram**
load: 3 ORE
**Tramp:** 4 HOBO 7 TRAIPSE
Love of: 4 LADY
**Tramped:** 4 TROD
**Trample:** 6 STEPON
   7 TREADON
**Trampled:** 4 TROD
**Tranquil:** 4 CALM 6 SERENE
   7 ATPEACE
discipline: 4 YOGA
**Tranquilize:** 6 SEDATE
**Tranquilizer:** 6 OPIATE
transport: 7 DARTGUN
**Tranquillity:** 4 EASE 6 REPOSE
**Transaction:** 4 DEAL
Bank: 4 LOAN
Business: 4 DEAL
Flea market: 6 RESALE
Team: 5 TRADE
Track: 3 BET
Used car: 6 RESALE
Video store: 6 RENTAL
**Transactional analysis**
phrase: 4 IMOK
**Transatlantic**
flyer: 3 SST
**Transcriber**
~, for short: 5 STENO
**Transcript**
fig.: 3 GPA
letter: 5 GRADE
**Transcriptionist:** 5 STENO
**Transfer:** 5 DECAL

Data ~ speed rate: 4 BAUD
port: 6 DECANT
property: 6 ASSIGN
title: 4 DEED
**Transfer ___**: 3 RNA
**Transferee**
concern (abbr.): 4 RELO
**Transfix**: 5 RIVET 6 IMPALE
**Transform**: 5 MORPH
**Transfusion**
fluids: 4 SERA
**Transgress**: 3 ERR 7 VIOLATE
**Transgression**: 3 SIN
    7 OFFENSE
**Transient**
qtrs.: 3 SRO
**Transistor**
electrode: 7 EMITTER
forerunner: 6 TRIODE
**Transit**
Boston ~ syst.: 3 MTA
Capital: 5 METRO
Like some: 5 RAPID
Mass ~ carrier: 3 BUS
Rapid: 3 SST
Rapids: 5 CANOE KAYAK
    RAFTS
Some ~ lines: 6 METROS
**Transition**: 5 SEGUE
Abrupt: 4 LEAP
Astrological ~ point: 4 CUSP
Logician: 4 ERGO
Make a slow: 6 EASEIN
Smooth: 5 SEGUE
**Transitional**
being: 6 APEMAN
**Transitory**: 10 FLYBYNIGHT
**Translate**: 6 DECODE
from plaintext: 6 ENCODE
**Translation**
Bible ~ (abbr.): 3 VER
**Translator**: 8 LINGUIST
obstacle: 5 IDIOM
**Translucent**
computer: 4 IMAC
gem: 4 OPAL
mineral: 4 MICA 5 TOPAZ
paper: 9 ONIONSKIN
**Transmission**
part: 4 GEAR
Satellite: 4 FEED
Sound: 5 AUDIO
**Transmit**: 3 FAX 4 SEND
**Transmitted**: 4 SENT
**Transmitter**: 6 SENDER
Impulse: 4 AXON
Neural: 4 AXON
prefix: 5 NEURO
Trait: 4 GENE
**Transmitting**: 5 ONAIR
**Transmutation**
Process of: 7 ALCHEMY
**Transparency**: 7 ACETATE
**Transparent**: 5 SHEER
    7 SEETHRU
It's: 4 PANE

linen: 5 TOILE
Not: 6 OPAQUE
plastic: 6 LUCITE
wrap: 5 SARAN
**Transpire**: 5 OCCUR 6 HAPPEN
**Transplant**: 5 REPOT 6 REROOT
Kind of: 5 ORGAN
Prepare to: 5 UNPOT
taker: 5 DONEE
**Transplanting**
need: 4 SOIL
**Transport**
Bermuda: 5 MOPED
D-Day: 3 LST
E.T.: 3 UFO
Final: 6 HEARSE
Golfer's: 4 CART
Huck: 4 RAFT
Kiddie: 7 SCOOTER
Off-road: 3 ATV
on treads: 6 SNOCAT
School: 3 BUS
sci-fi style: 6 BEAMUP
Skier's: 4 TBAR
Tippy: 5 CANOE
to Oz: 7 TORNADO
Tot's: 5 TRIKE
Tourist: 3 CAB
Urban: 3 BUS CAB
Western: 5 STAGE
Winter: 4 SLED
**Transportation**
Urban: 3 ELS
**Transported**: 5 BORNE
    6 ENRAPT
**Trans ___ range**: 4 ALAI
**Trans-Siberian Railroad**
city: 4 OMSK
**Transvaal**
settler: 4 BOER
**Transversely**: 6 ACROSS
**Trans World Dome**
player: 3 RAM
**Transylvania**
locale: 7 ROMANIA
**Trap**: 3 NAB YAP 5 ICEIN
    SNARE 7 ENSNARE
Booby: 5 SNARE
Dryer ~ content: 4 LINT
Fly: 3 WEB
It's a: 5 SNARE
Like a dryer: 5 LINTY
Lint: 5 INNIE
setter: 6 SNARER
Simple: 5 SNARE
trigger: 8 TRIPWIRE
Type of: 5 STEEL
**Trapeze**
expert: 9 AERIALIST
**Trapped**: 5 ATBAY 6 INAJAM
    7 INABIND INASPOT
    UPATREE 8 ENSNARED
**Trapped like ___**: 4 ARAT
**Trapper**
Bug: 5 RESIN
device: 5 SNARE

prize: 4 PELT
Snapper: 3 NET
**Trapper John**
Last name of: 8 MCINTYRE
**Trappist**
Head: 5 ABBOT
**Trapshooting**: 5 SKEET
**Trash**: 3 DIS 4 JUNK 5 WASTE
    6 GRUNGE REFUSE
bag accessory: 3 TIE
collector: 3 BIN 8 WASTEBIN
Desktop ~ can: 4 ICON
place: 4 DUMP
prefix: 4 EURO
Talk ~ to: 4 SASS
**Trask**
One of the ~ brothers:
    4 ARON
**Trattoria**
bottle: 4 VINO
course: 5 PASTA
dessert: 7 TORTONI
order: 7 LASAGNA RISOTTO
quaff: 4 VINO
sauce: 5 PESTO
topping: 5 PESTO
treat: 6 GELATO
treats: 6 GELATI
tubes: 4 ZITI
**Trauma**
ctrs.: 3 ERS
evidence: 4 SCAR
Teen: 4 ACNE
**Travel**
agent suggestion: 7 AIRLINE
aimlessly: 3 GAD
Air ~ expediter: 7 ETICKET
around: 4 TOUR
before takeoff: 4 TAXI
by air: 4 WAFT
Fast way to: 5 BYAIR
method: 3 AIR
need: 4 VISA
on snow: 3 SKI
option: 4 RAIL
org.: 3 AAA
papers: 5 VISAS
Ready to: 6 ABOARD
stop: 3 INN
When ~ is restricted:
    7 WARTIME
**Traveler**: 4 GOER 5 FARER
aid: 3 MAP 5 ATLAS
bag: 6 VALISE
digs: 5 HOTEL
info: 3 ETA
need: 4 VISA
reference: 5 ATLAS
stop: 3 INN 5 MOTEL
Time ~ stop: 4 PAST
**Travelers**
Horse-and-buggy: 5 AMISH
to Bethlehem: 4 MAGI
**Travel guide**: 3 MAP
list: 4 INNS
name: 5 FODOR

**Traveling:** 4 AWAY 6 AFIELD
    9 ONTHEROAD
  carriage: 4 SHAY
  trio: 4 MAGI
**Traveling Wilburys**
  Bob of the: 5 DYLAN
**"Travelin' Man"**
  Opening words of: 3 IMA
**Travels**
  Fabric that ~ well: 5 ORLON
**Travesty:** 5 FARCE
**Travis**
  Country singer: 5 MERLE
    RANDY TRITT
  Fictional sleuth: 5 MCGEE
  Last stand for: 5 ALAMO
**Travolta**
  1980 ~ film:
    11 URBANCOWBOY
  musical: 6 GREASE
**Trawl**
  Use a: 4 DRAG
**Trawled:** 6 SEINED
**Trawler**
  gear: 3 NET
**Tray**
  cheese: 4 EDAM
  deposit: 3 ASH
  Sign on a ~ of samples:
    6 TRYONE
**Tre**
  ~ + quattro: 5 SETTE
  ~ + tre: 3 SEI
**Treacherous:** 5 FALSE
  one: 5 VIPER
  sort: 15 SNAKEINTHEGRASS
  type: 7 SERPENT
**Tread:** 4 STEP
  mate: 5 RISER
  plus riser: 5 STAIR
  tediously: 4 PLOD
  the boards: 3 ACT
**Tread-bare:** 4 BALD
**Treading**
  the boards: 7 ONSTAGE
**Treadless:** 4 BALD
**Treadmill**
  ordeal: 10 STRESSTEST
  unit: 4 MILE
**Treasure:** 3 GEM 5 ADORE
    TROVE 6 ESTEEM
    7 CHERISH
  Buried: 3 ORE
  cache: 5 TROVE
  guardian: 5 GNOME
  Hidden: 5 TROVE
  holder: 5 CHEST
  hunter aid: 3 MAP
  Legendary ~ city: 8 ELDORADO
  map measure: 4 PACE
  Spanish: 3 ORO
**Treasure-___:** 5 TROVE
**Treasured**
  violin: 5 AMATI
**"Treasure Island"**
  character: 4 GUNN

  monogram: 3 RLS
**Treasurer**
  Corp.: 3 CPA
**Treasure State**
  capital: 6 HELENA
**Treasure-trove:** 4 LODE
**Treasury**
  bill: 3 TEN
  State: 4 FISC
**Treasury Dept.**
  branch: 3 ATF IRS
**Treasury secretary**
  Former: 5 RUBIN
  of Bush: 6 ONEILL
**Treat:** 3 PAY 6 PAYFOR
    11 FOOTTHEBILL
  as a celebrity: 7 LIONIZE
  badly: 5 ABUSE
  Black-and-white: 4 OREO
  Breakfast: 5 CREPE
    12 CINNAMONROLL
  Campfire: 5 SMORE
  Carnival: 7 SNOCONE
  Cool: 7 SHERBET SNOCONE
  Custard: 4 FLAN
  Dog: 4 BONE
  Dutch: 4 EDAM 5 GOUDA
  Fountain: 4 MALT 6 MALTED
    11 BANANASPLIT
  harshly: 5 ABUSE
  like a dog: 3 PET
  like dirt: 5 ABUSE
  Luau: 3 POI 4 HULA
  Lunchbox: 4 OREO
  maliciously: 5 SPITE
  meat: 4 CORN CURE
  Meat-filled: 4 TACO
  poorly: 5 ABUSE
  Rich: 5 TORTE
  salt: 6 IODIZE
  Sesame ~ (var.): 5 HALVA
  shabbily: 3 USE
  Teatime: 5 SCONE
  Tex-Mex: 4 TACO 6 FAJITA
    TAMALE
  Toaster: 7 POPTART
  Tubular: 7 CANNOLI
  Twisted: 7 PRETZEL
  with contempt: 5 SPURN
    6 DERIDE
  with gas: 6 AERATE
  with milk: 4 OREO
  with tea: 5 SCONE
**Treater**
  phrase: 4 ONME 7 ITSONME
  pickup: 3 TAB
**"Treatise of Human Nature, A"**
  author: 4 HUME
**Treatment**
  Bad: 5 ABUSE
  Emergency: 8 FIRSTAID
  Harsh: 4 GAFF
  Ill: 5 ABUSE
  Kind of: 3 VIP 5 ROYAL
  Rash: 4 TALC
  R.N.: 3 TLC

  Salon: 4 PERM 6 FACIAL
  Window: 5 DRAPE 7 DRAPERY
**Treaty:** 4 PACT
  1814 ~ city: 5 GHENT
  1993 ~: 5 NAFTA
  Defunct ~ org.: 5 SEATO
  gp. since 1948: 3 OAS
  Joined by: 6 ALLIED
  signer: 4 ALLY
  subject: 4 ARMS 7 TESTBAN
  Western ~ gp.: 3 OAS
**Trebek**
  Emcee: 4 ALEX
**Trebek, Alex:** 5 EMCEE
    8 CANADIAN
**Treble:** 4 CLEF
  clef lines: 5 EGBDF
  clef reader: 4 ALTO
**Tree**
  African: 4 KOLA 5 MAMBA
  Bark up the wrong: 3 ERR
  branch: 4 LIMB
  Chinese: 6 LITCHI
  chopper: 3 AXE
  Christmas: 3 FIR
  Cone-bearing: 3 FIR
    7 CYPRESS
  Cottonwood: 5 ALAMO
  creature: 3 ENT
  Cut down a: 4 FELL
  Dwarf: 6 BONSAI
  European: 4 SORB
  Evergreen: 4 YEW
  exudate: 3 SAP
  Fam. ~ member: 4 DESC
  Fam. ~ word: 3 NEE
  feller: 3 AXE
  fluid: 3 SAP
  Fluttering: 5 ASPEN
  Fruit: 4 PEAR
  Hardwood: 3 ASH 5 MAPLE
  Hawaiian: 3 KOA
  house: 4 NEST
  in Miami: 4 PALM
  juice: 3 SAP
  knot: 4 BURL KNAR 5 GNARL
  Liberty: 3 ELM
  Like soil around a: 5 ROOTY
  Like some ~ trunks: 5 MOSSY
  Mighty: 3 OAK
  Mountain: 3 ASH
  Nut: 5 BEECH
  of life locale: 4 EDEN
  Quaking: 5 ASPEN
  ring: 7 ANNULUS
  rings indication: 3 AGE
  Shade: 3 ELM
  Slippery: 3 ELM
  Small: 6 ACACIA
  Spreading: 3 ELM
  State: *see page 724*
  Sturdy: 3 OAK
  surgeon: 6 PRUNER
  that spreads: 6 BANYAN
  Thick-trunked: 6 BAOBAB
  Trembling: 5 ASPEN

Trim a: 3 LOP
Tropical: 4 PALM 5 CACAO
trunk: 4 BOLE
type: 3 ASH
  with catkins: 5 ALDER
  with cones: 4 PINE
  with triangular nuts:
    5 BEECH
  with yellow ribbons: 3 OAK
  ___ tree: 3 UPA 5 TULIP
Treebeard: 3 ENT
Tree-dwelling: 8 ARBOREAL
  primate: 5 LEMUR
"___ tree falls ...": 3 IFA
"Tree Grows in Brooklyn, A"
  family: 5 NOLAN
Treeless
  expanse: 5 PAMPA
  plain: 5 LLANO 6 STEPPE
Tree-lined
  Like a ~ area: 5 SHADY
  promenade: 7 ALAMEDA
  walk: 5 ALLEE
Tree-man: 3 ENT
Tree of Knowledge
  site: 4 EDEN
Tree-planting
  org.: 3 CCC
"Trees"
  poet Kilmer: 5 JOYCE
Treetop
  ornament: 5 ANGEL
Trek
  Great ~ participant: 4 BOER
  to Mecca: 4 HADJ
Trekker
  Transvaal: 4 BOER
Trekkers
  Star: 4 MAGI
Trellis: 8 ESPALIER
  climber: 3 IVY
Tremble: 5 QUAKE 6 DODDER
    QUAVER QUIVER
Trembled: 5 SHOOK
Trembling: 6 ASHAKE
  tree: 5 ASPEN
Tremendous: 4 EPIC HUGE
Tremendously: 4 ALOT
Tremor: 5 QUAKE SEISM
Trench
  Lunar: 4 RILL 5 RILLE
  suffix: 4 COAT
  Watery: 4 MOAT
Trencherman: 5 EATER
Trend
  determiner: 4 POLL
  Hot: 3 FAD
Trendy: 3 HIP HOT NOW
    4 CHIC 6 LATEST
    WITHIT
  cuisine: 4 THAI
  protein source: 4 TOFU
  sandwich: 4 WRAP
Trent
  Senator: 4 LOTT
Trepidation: 5 DREAD

Tres
  menos dos: 3 UNO
  y cinco: 4 OCHO
  y tres: 4 SEIS
"Très ___!": 4 BIEN
Trespass: 3 SIN
Tresses: 4 HAIR 5 LOCKS
  Long: 5 MANES
Trevanian
  novel peak: 5 EIGER
Trevi Fountain
  coin: 4 LIRA
  coins: 4 LIRE
  locale: 4 ROME
Trevino
  Golfer: 3 LEE
Trevor
  Director: 4 NUNN
Trey: 4 CARD
  Loser to a: 5 DEUCE
  topper: 4 FOUR
Tri
  plus two: 5 PENTA
Triage
  ctrs.: 3 ERS
  team member: 5 MEDIC
Trial: 3 WOE 4 TEST 6 ORDEAL
    7 TESTRUN
  Avoid a: 6 SETTLE
  balloon: 4 TEST 6 FEELER
  Bikini: 5 ATEST
  Conclusive: 8 ACIDTEST
  evidence: 3 DNA
  Explosive: 5 NTEST
  figure: 5 STENO
  Military: 5 NTEST
  partner: 5 ERROR
  Program: 8 BETATEST
  run: 4 PREP TEST
  setting: 5 VENUE
  Telling: 8 ACIDTEST
  town: 5 SALEM
  Track: 4 HEAT
"Trial, The"
  author: 5 KAFKA
Triangle
  Kind of: 7 SCALENE
  part: 3 LEG
  part (abbr.): 3 HYP
  Pool: 4 RACK
  ratio: 4 SINE
  River: 5 DELTA
  tone: 4 TING
Triangular
  deposit: 5 DELTA
  formation: 5 DELTA
  house: 6 AFRAME
  road sign: 5 YIELD
  sail: 3 JIB 6 LATEEN
    9 GOOSEWING
Triangular-bladed
  weapon: 4 EPEE
Triathlete: 7 IRONMAN
  quality: 7 STAMINA
Triathlon
  leg: 3 RUN 4 SWIM

  need: 4 BIKE
Tribal
  chief: 4 KHAN 6 SACHEM
  doctor: 6 SHAMAN
  figure: 5 TOTEM
  history: 4 LORE
  leader: 5 ELDER
  magician: 6 SHAMAN
  symbol: 5 TOTEM
  tales: 4 LORE
  warrior: 5 BRAVE
Tribe
  called the Cat Nation: 4 ERIE
  defeated by the Iroquois:
    4 ERIE
  Eastern: 4 ERIE
  for whom a sea is named:
    5 CARIB
  Indian: 6 NATION
  Lake: 4 ERIE
  Largest U.S.: 6 NAVAJO
  Midwest: 4 OTOE
  Plains: 4 OTOE 5 KIOWA
    6 PAWNEE
  Respected ~ member: 5 ELDER
  Western: 3 UTE 4 UTES
TriBeCa
  neighbor: 4 SOHO
Tribes
  One of the 12: 3 DAN 4 LEVI
    5 ASHER
Tribesman
  North African: 6 BERBER
  Plains: 3 OTO
  Western: 3 UTE
Tribulation: 3 WOE 6 ORDEAL
Tribunal
  Vatican: 4 ROTA
Tributary: 6 FEEDER
Tribute: 4 KUDO 6 HOMAGE
  Comic: 5 ROAST
  Flowery: 3 ODE
  Pay ~ to: 5 HONOR 6 SALUTE
  Poetic: 3 ODE
  Spoken: 6 EULOGY
Triceratops
  feature: 4 HORN
Trick: 3 CON FOX 4 DUPE
    RUSE SCAM WILE
    5 CATCH 6 DELUDE
    ENTRAP LEADON
    TAKEIN 7 MISLEAD
    SLEIGHT
  Beguiling: 4 WILE
  Does a dog: 4 BEGS
  Do the: 5 AVAIL
  joint: 4 KNEE
  Part of a hat: 4 GOAL
  Playful: 5 ANTIC
  Rare ~ taker: 4 TREY
  Silly: 5 APERY
  Sly: 4 WILE
  suffix: 3 ERY 4 STER
  taker: 3 ACE
Tricked
  Not ~ by: 4 ONTO 6 WISETO

**Trickery:** 3 ART 5 WILES
   6 DECEIT
**Trickle:** 4 DRIP OOZE SEEP
**"Trick or ___":** 5 TREAT
**Trick-or-treater:** 5 GHOST
**Tricks**
  Play: 4 JAPE
**Trickster:** 3 IMP
  of myth: 4 LOKI
**"Tricksy spirit":** 5 ARIEL
**Trick-taking**
  game: 5 WHIST 6 ECARTE
    EUCHRE
**Tricky:** 3 SLY 4 WILY
  curve: 3 ESS
  maneuver: 4 PLOY
  shot: 5 MASSE
**Trident**
  feature: 4 TINE
  Like a: 5 TINED
  shaped letter: 3 PSI
**Tried:** 6 TESTED
  and true: 5 SOLID
    6 TESTED
  Fit to be: 4 SANE
  hard: 6 STROVE
  Partner of: 4 TRUE
  ~, with "at": 6 HADAGO
**Trieste**
  **Info:** Italian cue
  They, in: 4 ESSE
**Trifecta:** 3 BET
**Trifle:** 3 SOU TOY
**Trifling:** 4 MERE 5 PETTY
    7 NOMINAL
  amount: 3 FIG SOU 4 IOTA
    MITE
  fruit: 3 FIG
  Most: 5 LEAST
**Trig:** 4 MATH
  abbr.: 3 COS TAN
  function: 4 SINE 5 COSEC
    COTAN 6 COSINE SECANT
    7 ARCSINE
  ratio: 4 SINE 5 COSEC
**Trigger:** 8 PALOMINO
  puller: 4 REIN
  rider: 3 ROY
  tidbit: 3 OAT
  Trap: 8 TRIPWIRE
**Triglyceride:** 5 ESTER
**Trigonometric**
  function: 4 SINE
**Trigonometry**
  abbr.: 3 COS
  ratio: 4 SINE 6 SECANT
**Trigram**
  Cinema: 3 MGM
  Phone: 3 ABC DEF GHI JKL
    MNO PRS TUV WXY
**Trike**
  power: 5 PEDAL
**Trilby:** 3 HAT
**Trill**
  Insect: 5 CHIRR
  Sheep: 3 BAA

**Trillion**
  About 5.88 ~ mi.: 4 LTYR
  prefix: 4 TERA
**Trillions**
  No. in ~ of dollars: 3 GNP
**Trilogy**
  Aeschylus: 8 ORESTEIA
  Dos Passos: 3 USA
**Trim:** 3 LOP MOW 4 CROP
    LEAN NEAT PARE SNIP
    5 ADORN PRUNE SHAVE
    6 EDGING
  and graceful: 5 SLEEK
  Auto: 6 CHROME
  Decorative: 4 LACE
  Not just: 5 SLASH
  Robe: 6 ERMINE
  Slim and: 6 SVELTE
  to fit: 4 EDIT
**Trimmer**
  Lawn: 5 EDGER
  Wood: 4 ADZE
**Trimming**
  Ready for ~, as a sail: 5 ATRIP
  tape: 5 INKLE
  tool: 3 ADZ 5 EDGER
**Trinidad**
  partner: 6 TOBAGO
**Trinity**
  Hindu ~ member: 4 SIVA
    5 SHIVA
  member: 3 SON
**"Trinity"**
  author: 4 URIS
**Trinity College Library**
  architect: 4 WREN
**Trinket:** 5 CHARM 6 BAUBLE
    10 KNICKKNACK
  Exquisite: 5 BIJOU
  Showy: 4 GAUD
**Trio**
  Alphabetic: 3 ABC BCD CDE
    *etc.*
  Basic ed: 3 RRR
  Biblical: 4 MAGI
  Female rap: 3 TLC
  German: 4 DREI
  Italian: 3 TRE
  Mythological: 5 FATES HORAE
  One of a 1492: 4 NINA
    5 PINTA
  One of a daily: 4 MEAL
  One of a Latin: 3 AMO 4 AMAS
    AMAT VENI
  One of a slapstick: 3 MOE
  Phone: 3 ABC DEF GHI JKL
    MNO PRS TUV WXY
  Pop: 3 AHA
  Rock: 5 ZZTOP
  times two: 6 SESTET
  Traveling: 4 MAGI
  trebled: 5 NONET
  Trident: 5 TINES
  Triple: 5 NONET
  Upscale: 6 DOREMI
  Yule: 4 MAGI

**___ Triomphe:** 5 ARCDE
**Trip:** 3 ERR 5 JAUNT 6 VOYAGE
  choice (abbr.): 3 RTE
  Guided: 4 TOUR
  Hard: 4 TREK
  inducer: 3 LSD
  Kind of: 3 EGO LSD
  Newlywed: 9 HONEYMOON
  odometer button: 5 RESET
  Oversea: 6 SAFARI
  part: 3 LEG
  Prepare for a: 5 GASUP
  Quick: 4 SPIN
  Round: 5 ORBIT
  segment: 3 LEG
  Sightseeing: 4 TOUR
  starter: 3 LEG
  taker: 3 EGO
  Took a: 4 FELL
  to the plate: 5 ATBAT
  Tough: 4 TREK
  up: 6 ASCENT
  Wee-hours: 6 REDEYE
**Triple**
  in a triple play: 4 OUTS
  trio: 5 NONET
**Triple ___:** 3 SEC
**Triple Crown**
  1930 ~ jockey: 5 SANDE
  1930 ~ winner:
    10 GALLANTFOX
  1935 ~ winner: 5 OMAHA
  1937 ~ winner:
    10 WARADMIRAL
  1978 ~ winner: 8 AFFIRMED
  stat: 3 RBI
  Two-time ~ jockey: 6 ARCARO
**Triple-decker**
  lunch: 12 CLUBSANDWICH
  treat: 4 OREO
**Triple sec**
  flavoring: 6 ORANGE
**Triplets:** 6 THREES
**Tripmeter**
  button: 5 RESET
**Tripod**
  feature: 3 LEG
**Tripoli**
  land: 5 LIBYA
  resident: 6 LIBYAN
**Tripper**
  turn-on: 3 LSD
**Tripping**
  air: 4 LILT
**Triptik**
  abbr.: 3 RTE
  org.: 3 AAA
**Trireme**
  gear: 4 OARS
**Tristan**
  Love of: 6 ISOLDE
**"___ Triste":** 5 VALSE
**"Tristia"**
  poet: 4 OVID
**Tristram**
  Beloved of: 6 ISEULT ISOLDE

"Tristram ___": 6 SHANDY
"Tristram Shandy"
  author: 6 STERNE
Trite: 3 PAT 5 BANAL CORNY
    DATED STALE
  saying: 3 SAW 7 BROMIDE
  writer: 4 HACK
Tritt
  Country singer: 6 TRAVIS
Triumph: 3 WIN 7 PREVAIL
    SUCCESS
  Cry of: 3 AHA HAH
  Reliever: 4 SAVE
  Shout of: 4 TADA
  Song of: 5 PAEAN
Triumphant
  cry: 3 AHA 4 IWON TADA
  shout: 3 YES
Triumphed: 3 WON
"Triumph of the Will"
  director Riefenstahl: 4 LENI
Triumvirate: 6 TROIKA
Trivia
  Bit of: 4 FACT 7 FACTOID
  category: 6 SPORTS
  collection: 3 ANA
  Sports: 5 STATS
Trivial: 5 MINOR 6 PALTRY
    13 NICKELANDDIME
  detail: 3 NIT
  objection: 5 CAVIL
Trivial Pursuit
  edition: 5 GENUS
  piece: 3 PIE
Trixie
  Pal of: 5 ALICE
Trodden
  track: 4 PATH
Troglodyte
  home: 4 CAVE
Troilus
  Lover of: 8 CRESSIDA
Trois
  less deux: 3 UNE
Trojan
  hero: 6 AENEAS
  horse: 4 RUSE
  rival: 5 BRUIN UCLAN
Trojans, The: 3 USC 5 SOCAL
Trojan War
  adviser: 6 NESTOR
  beauty: 5 HELEN
  epic: 5 ILIAD
  hero: 4 AJAX 6 AENEAS
    HECTOR
  king: 5 PRIAM
Troll: 5 GNOME
Trolley: 4 TRAM
  Off one's: 4 DAFT 5 NUTSY
    NUTTY
  shelter: 7 CARBARN
  sound: 5 CLANG
Trollhättan
  Car from: 4 SAAB
Trollop: 6 HARLOT
Trombone: 5 BRASS

attachment: 4 MUTE
  feature: 5 SLIDE
Trombonist
  ~ "Kid": 3 ORY
  ~ Winding: 3 KAI
Trompe l'___: 4 OEIL
Trône
  occupant: 3 ROI
Troon
  Info: Scottish cue
  Tiny, in: 3 SMA
Troop
  carrier (abbr.): 3 LST
  encampment: 5 ETAPE
  entertainment spon.: 3 USO
  gp.: 3 BSA 4 REGT
  group: 4 ARMY UNIT
    7 BRIGADE
  movement: 6 SORTIE
  truant: 4 AWOL
Trooper
  maker: 5 ISUZU
  Tempt a: 5 SPEED
Troops
  Have more ~ than:
    6 OUTMAN
  Move: 6 DEPLOY
  WWI: 3 AEF
Trophy: 3 CUP 5 AWARD PRIZE
  Branch in a ~ room:
    6 ANTLER
  Frontier: 5 SCALP
  locale: 3 DEN
  NHL: 4 HART
  shelf: 6 MANTEL
  Took the: 3 WON
  Trapper: 4 PELT
  TV: 4 EMMY
Tropical
  animal: 5 TAPIR
  bird: 3 ANI 5 MACAW
    6 TOUCAN
  climber: 5 LIANA
  cocktail: 6 MAITAI
  cooler: 9 TRADEWIND
  cuckoo: 3 ANI
  evergreen: 5 CACAO
  fish: 4 SCAD 5 TETRA
  fruit: 4 DATE 5 DATES GUAVA
    MANGO 6 BANANA
    PAPAYA
  jelly source: 5 GUAVA
  lizard: 6 IGUANA
  nut: 4 KOLA 5 BETEL
    6 CASHEW
  palm: 5 ARECA
  parrot: 5 MACAW
  plain: 7 SAVANNA
  ray: 5 MANTA
  root: 4 TARO
  spot: 4 ISLE
  tree: 4 PALM 5 CACAO
    6 BAOBAB
  tuber: 4 TARO
  vine: 5 LIANA LIANE
  wader: 4 IBIS

Tropicana
  rival: 10 MINUTEMAID
Tropicana Field
  locale: 6 STPETE
Trot: 4 GAIT
  Hot to: 4 AGOG AVID KEEN
    5 EAGER
  More than a: 4 LOPE
Trotsky
  Revolutionary: 4 LEON
Trotter
  rhythm: 4 PACE
Troubadour
  instrument: 4 LUTE
  song: 3 LAI
Trouble: 3 ADO AIL ILL IRK
    VEX WOE 4 CARE FLAP
    5 BESET EATAT
    6 HARASS 7 DISTURB
    8 HOTWATER
  Athlete ~ spot: 4 KNEE
  Big: 8 HOTWATER
  Cause:
    15 CREATEANUISANCE
  Eye: 4 STYE
  Get out of: 6 RESCUE
  Have ~ deciding: 6 SEESAW
  Having: 7 INASPOT
  Hose: 4 SNAG
  "I": 6 EGOISM
  In: 8 UPACREEK
  Partner of: 4 TOIL
  Ready for: 7 ONALERT
  Serious: 8 HOTWATER
  Sleep: 5 APNEA
  spots: 4 ACNE
  Tap: 4 DRIP LEAK
  Teen: 4 ACNE
  Throat: 4 FROG 5 STREP
  Timber: 6 DRYROT
  Tooth: 5 DECAY
  Tummy: 4 ACHE 5 ULCER
  with esses: 4 LISP
"T-R-O-U-B-L-E"
  singer Travis: 5 TRITT
Troubled: 5 ATEAT
  Not: 6 ATEASE
  state: 6 UNREST
Troublemaker: 3 IMP 4 BRAT
    6 BADLOT 7 GREMLIN
    HELLION
Troubleshooter
  PC: 4 TECH
Trough
  filler: 4 SLOP
  Mason: 3 HOD
  site: 3 STY 4 EAVE
Trounce: 4 ROUT 5 WHOMP
Troupe
  gp.: 3 USO
  group: 6 ACTORS
  Touring: 8 ROADSHOW
Trouser
  cuffs: 7 TURNUPS
  fold: 6 CREASE
  part: 3 LEG

**Trousers:** 5 PANTS 6 SLACKS
  Old-fashioned: 9 KNEEPANTS
  textile: 5 CHINO
**Trout**
  fisherman's wear: 6 WADERS
  tempter: 4 LURE
  Way to prepare:
    8 AMANDINE
**Troutlike**
  fish: 5 SMELT
**Troy**
  Ancient: 5 ILIUM
  coll.: 3 RPI
  Counselor at: 6 NESTOR
  It's headquartered in:
    5 KMART
  King of: 5 PRIAM
  lady: 5 HELEN
  Mount near: 3 IDA
  sch.: 3 RPI
  story: 5 ILIAD
  Tactics at: 5 SIEGE
  Tale of: 5 ILIAD
  Warrior at: 4 AJAX
**Troyanos**
  Opera singer: 7 TATIANA
**TRS-80**
  computer maker: 5 TANDY
**Truant**
  Mil.: 4 AWOL
**Truce**
  talk: 6 PARLEY
**Trucial**
  potentate: 4 EMIR
**Truck**
  All-purpose: 3 UTE
  British: 5 LORRY
  Chevy: 5 TAHOE
  compartment: 3 CAB
  Dump ~ filler: 6 LOADER
  Fire ~ item: 3 AXE
  garage: 4 BARN
  GMC: 6 SIERRA
  Large: 4 SEMI
  Like a money: 7 ARMORED
  name: 4 MACK
  part: 3 CAB
  Rental ~ company: 5 RYDER
  Shallow: 7 FLATBED
  Sporty: 3 UTE
  Versatile: 3 UTE
  weight: 4 TARE 6 ONETON
**Truckee**
  Source of the ~ River:
    5 TAHOE
  stop: 4 RENO
**Trucker**
  competition: 6 ROADEO
  expense: 5 TOLLS
  in a union: 8 TEAMSTER
  rig: 4 SEMI
  watchdog (abbr.): 3 ICC
  with a handle: 4 CBER
**Trucking**
  rig: 4 SEMI
**Truckload:** 3 TON 4 ALOT

**Trucks**
  Big name in: 5 TONKA
  Co. with brown: 3 UPS
  Gas company known for toy:
    4 HESS
  initials: 3 GMC
  Some toy: 6 TONKAS
**Truck stop:** 5 DINER
  fare: 4 HASH
  sight: 3 RIG 4 SEMI
  sign: 4 EATS
**Trudeau**
  Canadian P.M.: 6 PIERRE
  Cartoonist: 5 GARRY
**Trudge:** 4 PLOD SLOG TREK
**True:** 4 REAL 5 ALIGN LEVEL
    LOYAL
  blue: 5 LOYAL
  It's: 4 FACT
  It's not: 4 MYTH
  Make: 5 ALIGN
  partner: 5 TRIED
  Regard as: 6 ACCEPT
  Show to be: 5 PROVE
  Tried and: 6 TESTED
  up: 5 ALIGN ALINE
**"True ___" (Wayne film):** 4 GRIT
**"___ true!":** 3 ITS
**"True Colors"**
  singer Lauper: 5 CYNDI
**"True Grit"**
  ~ Oscar winner: 5 WAYNE
**Trueheart**
  beau: 5 TRACY
  of the comics: 4 TESS
**True-to-life:** 4 REAL
**Truffaut**
  character: 5 ADELE
**Truffle**
  and others: 5 FUNGI
  coating: 5 COCOA
**Truism:** 4 FACT 5 ADAGE
    AXIOM
**Truly:** 3 YEA 5 QUITE
    6 INDEED 7 FORREAL
**Truman**
  adviser: 7 ACHESON
  birthplace: 5 LAMAR
  Mrs.: 4 BESS
  nuclear agcy.: 3 AEC
  program: 8 FAIRDEAL
  veep Barkley: 5 ALBEN
**"Truman"**
  portrayer: 6 SINISE
**Trump:** 4 BEST
  Former Mrs.: 5 IVANA MARLA
  Game with ~ cards: 4 SKAT
  ~, at times: 5 CLUBS
    6 HEARTS SPADES
    8 DIAMONDS
**Trumped-up**
  story: 3 LIE
**Trumpet:** 4 HORN
  accessory: 4 MUTE
  blast: 7 TANTARA
  feature: 5 VALVE

  Half a ~ sound: 3 WAH
  muffler: 4 MUTE
  sound: 4 WAWA 5 BLARE
    7 CLARION
**Trumpeter:** 4 SWAN
  accessory: 4 MUTE
  Jazz: 6 ALHIRT
**Trumpeting:** 6 ABLARE
**Trumpets:** 5 BRASS
**Truncation**
  abbreviation: 3 ETC
**Trunk:** 4 BOLE 5 AORTA
    TORSO
  fastener: 4 HASP
  growth: 4 MOSS
  Human: 5 TORSO
  item: 4 JACK TIRE 5 FLARE
    SPARE 8 TIREIRON
    9 SPARETIRE
  It has a: 4 TREE
  line: 5 AORTA
  Main: 5 AORTA
  One year in a: 4 RING
  site: 4 TREE
  Tree: 4 BOLE
  with a chest: 5 TORSO
**Trunkmate**
  of McCarthy: 5 SNERD
**Trunks:** 5 TORSI 6 TORSOS
**Trust:** 6 BANKON RELYON
    8 RELIANCE
  Have: 4 RELY
  Hold in: 6 ESCROW
  Kind of: 5 BLIND
  prefix: 4 ANTI
  ~, with "on": 4 BANK RELY
**Trusted**
  friend: 8 ALTEREGO
**Trustful:** 7 RELIANT
**Trusting**
  act: 11 LEAPOFFAITH
  Less: 6 WARIER
**Trustworthy:** 4 SURE
    8 RELIABLE
  sort: 7 GOODEGG
**Trusty**
  mount: 5 STEED
**Truth**
  Absolute: 6 GOSPEL
  Assumed: 5 AXIOM
  Central: 3 TAO
  It's the: 4 FACT
  Kind of: 5 NAKED
  Not facing the: 8 INDENIAL
  Old-style: 5 SOOTH
  Self-evident: 5 AXIOM
  Stretch the: 3 FIB LIE
  twister: 4 LIAR
**Truth ___:** 5 SERUM
**Truthful:** 6 HONEST
**Try:** 3 TAX VIE 4 SHOT STAB
    TEST 5 TASTE 6 SAMPLE
    7 HAVEAGO
  again: 6 REHEAR
  Eager to: 6 KEENON
  Give a: 5 ESSAY

hard: **6** STRIVE
Hardly: **5** COAST
out: **4** TEST
They ~ harder: **4** AVIS
Willing to: **6** OPENTO
~, as a case: **4** HEAR
**Trying**
experience: **6** ORDEAL
one: **7** ESSAYER
**"Try ___ might ...": 3** ASI
**Tryon, Thomas**
novel, with "The": **5** OTHER
**Tryout: 4** TEST **7** TESTRUN
Bikini: **5** ATEST
of a sort: **10** SCREENTEST
**Trypanosome**
transmitter: **6** TSETSE
**Trypsin: 6** ENZYME
**Tryptophan: 9** AMINOACID
**"Try ___ see": 5** ITAND
**Tryst**
spot: **5** MOTEL
**"Try this!": 4** HERE **5** TASTE
**T.S. ___ (poet): 5** ELIOT
**Tsar**
"Terrible": **4** IVAN **6** IVANIV
**Tse-___, Mao: 4** TUNG
**Tse-tung, ___: 3** MAO
**T-shirt**
Old ~, perhaps: **3** RAG
size: **5** LARGE
size (abbr.): **3** LGE
**"Tsk!": 3** TUT **4** PITY
**Tsp.: 3** AMT
**Tswana**
pest: **6** TSETSE
**T ___ Tom: 4** ASIN
**"___ Tu" (1974 hit): 4** ERES
**"___ tu" (Verdi aria): 3** ERI
**Tu-144: 3** SST
**Tub: 4** BATH SCOW
contents: **4** OLEO
**9** MARGARINE
Hot: **3** SPA
Industrial: **3** VAT
Linger in the: **4** SOAK
Soak in the: **5** BATHE
Spread in a: **4** OLEO
Sub in a: **4** OLEO
**Tuba: 8** BASSHORN
role: **8** BASSPART
sound: **3** PAH **6** OOMPAH
**Tubb**
Country singer: **6** ERNEST
**Tubby: 3** FAT
More than: **5** OBESE
**Tube: 5** TVSET **6** TEEVEE
Air on the: **8** TELECAST
Boob: **5** TVSET
Electron: **5** DIODE **6** TRIODE
Exhaust: **8** TAILPIPE
Kind of: **4** BOOB **5** INNER
Lab: **5** PIPET **7** PIPETTE
Old: **6** TRIODE
Radio ~ gas: **5** ARGON
XENON

Surgical: **5** STENT
Toothpaste ~ abbr.: **3** ADA
top: **3** CAP
traveler: **4** OVUM
travelers: **3** OVA
**___ tube: 5** INNER
**Tube-nosed**
seabird: **6** PETREL
**Tuber**
Edible: **3** OCA YAM **4** TARO
**Tubes**
Boob: **3** TVS
Inner ~, e.g.: **4** TORI
Pasta: **4** ZITI **5** PENNE
**8** RIGATONI
**9** MANICOTTI
**Tubing**
Insulating: **9** SPAGHETTI
**Tubman: 7** HARRIET
**Tub-thump: 4** RANT
**Tubular**
fare: **4** ZITI **5** PENNE
**8** RIGATONI
treat: **7** CANNOLI
**Tuck**
away: **3** EAT **4** STOW
partner: **3** NIP
Tapered: **4** DART
title: **5** FRIAR
**Tucked**
away: **3** ATE
in: **4** ABED SNUG
**Tucker**
Country singer: **5** TANYA
Entertainer: **6** SOPHIE
out: **4** TIRE
partner: **3** BIB
**Tuckered**
out: **4** BEAT **5** ALLIN SPENT
**Tucson**
plants: **5** CACTI
**Tudor**
queen: **4** MARY
**Tues.**
preceder: **3** MON
**Tuesday**
at the movies: **4** WELD
~, in French: **5** MARDI
**___ Tuesday: 5** SUPER
**6** SHROVE
(Mardi Gras): **3** FAT
**___ Tuesday (1980s pop group):**
**3** TIL
**Tuffet**
Use a: **3** SIT
**Tuft**
Ornamental: **6** POMPOM
Thin: **4** WISP
**Tufts**
Cat with ear: **4** LYNX
**Tug: 4** YANK
task: **3** TOW
tow: **4** SCOW **5** BARGE
**Tugboat**
line: **7** TOWROPE
sound: **4** TOOT

**Tuition**
Kind of: **7** INSTATE
**Tulip**
Future: **4** BULB
**Tulips**
Traverse the: **6** TIPTOE
**"Tulips and Chimneys"**
poet: **10** EECUMMINGS
**Tully**
Philanthropist: **5** ALICE
**Tulsa**
City south of: **3** ADA
City west of: **4** ENID
sch.: **3** ORU
state (abbr.): **4** OKLA
**Tumble: 4** FALL
**Tumbler: 5** GLASS **7** ACROBAT
of rhyme: **4** JILL
**"Tumbleweeds"**
cartoonist: **6** TKRYAN
cartoonist Tom: **4** RYAN
**Tumbling**
need: **3** MAT
**Tummy**
muscles: **3** ABS
tightener: **6** CORSET
trouble: **4** ACHE **5** ULCER
upsetter: **4** ACID
**Tums**
alternative: **7** ROLAIDS
**Tumult: 3** ADO **4** ROAR STIR
**6** CLAMOR
**Tumultuous: 6** STORMY
**Tuna: 4** FISH
at a sushi bar: **4** TORO
container: **3** TIN
Hawaiian: **3** AHI
How some ~ is ordered:
**7** ONTOAST
How some ~ is packed:
**5** INOIL
type: **8** ALBACORE
**Tuna ___: 4** MELT
**"Tuna Fishing"**
artist: **4** DALI
**___ Tunas: 3** LAS
**Tundra**
Like the: **8** TREELESS
wanderer: **3** ELK
**Tune: 3** AIR **4** SONG **6** MELODY
1950s ~: **5** OLDIE
Cheery: **4** LILT
for two: **4** DUET
Holiday: **4** NOEL **5** CAROL
Light: **4** LILT
Nostalgic: **5** OLDIE
Operatic: **4** ARIA
out: **6** IGNORE
**Tuned**
in: **5** AWARE
**Tuneful: 7** MELODIC
transition: **5** SEGUE
**Tuner: 4** DIAL
choices: **4** AMFM
**___ Tunes (cartoon series):**
**6** LOONEY

**Tunesmith**
  org.: 5 ASCAP
**Tune-up**
  item: 9 SPARKPLUG
**Tunic**
  Knight's: 6 TABARD
  Roman: 5 STOLA
**Tuning fork**
  Orchestral: 4 OBOE
**Tunis**
  gp.: 3 PLO
**Tunisian**
  Old ~ title: 3 BEY CEY
  port: 4 SFAX
**Tunnel**
  maker: 3 ANT 4 MOLE
  ___ tunnel syndrome: 6 CARPAL
**Tunney**
  Boxer: 4 GENE
**Tupolev**
  creation: 3 SST
**Tupperware**
  Mr. Tupper of: 4 EARL
  sound: 4 BURP
**"Turandot"**
  slave girl: 3 LIU
**Turban**
  wearer: 4 SIKH 5 SWAMI
**Turbid**
  Make: 3 MUD
**Turbine**
  part: 5 ROTOR
  pivot: 6 STATOR
**Turbo**
  maker: 4 SAAB
**Turbulent**
  water: 3 RIP
**Turcotte**
  Jockey: 3 RON
**Tureen**
  spoon: 5 LADLE
**Turf: 3 SOD 4 AREA 5 SWARD**
  Cover with: 3 SOD
  grabber: 5 CLEAT
  group: 4 GANG
  Homeboy: 4 HOOD
  in "surf and turf": 5 STEAK
**Turgenev**
  Author: 4 IVAN
  birthplace: 4 OREL
  heroine: 5 ELENA
**Turin**
  Info: Italian cue
  City near: 4 ASTI
  Cloth of: 6 SHROUD
  goodbye: 4 CIAO
  Three, in: 3 TRE
  Today, in: 4 OGGI
**Turing**
  Mathematician: 4 ALAN
**Turk**
  neighbor: 3 SYR 5 IRANI
    IRAQI
  title: 3 AGA
**Turkey: 3 DUD 4 FLOP NERD
  5 LEMON**

Capital of: 6 ANKARA
follower: 4 TROT
Fruit from: 6 CASABA
Go cold: 4 QUIT
helping: 3 LEG
herb: 4 SAGE
Highest point in: 6 ARARAT
Male: 3 TOM
Moisten a: 5 BASTE
neighbor: 4 IRAN IRAQ
  5 SYRIA
part: 3 LEG 9 ASIAMINOR
Peak in: 5 MTIDA
roaster: 4 OVEN
Tend to a: 5 BASTE
topper: 5 GRAVY
Young: 5 POULT
**Turkic**
  speaker: 5 TATAR
**Turkish**
  bigwig: 3 AGA 4 AGHA
    5 PASHA
  city: 5 ADANA
  coin: 4 LIRA
  fruit: 3 FIG
  honorific: 3 AGA 4 AGHA
  inn: 5 SERAI 6 IMARET
  money: 4 LIRA
  mount: 6 ARARAT
  native: 4 KURD
  title: 3 AGA 4 AGHA 5 PASHA
**Turkish Empire**
  founder: 5 OSMAN
**Turkmenistan**
  neighbor: 4 IRAN
**Turks**
  Home to most: 4 ASIA
  Like most: 5 ASIAN
**Turmoil: 4 STIR 5 MELEE
  6 UNREST**
  Inner: 5 ANGST
**Turn: 4 MOVE SOUR VEER
  5 SPOIL**
  180-degree ~: 3 UEY
  about: 4 SLUE 6 ROTATE
  abruptly: 6 SWERVE
  aside: 4 SNUB 5 AVERT
    PARRY SHUNT 6 DIVERT
  away: 5 AVERT REPEL
    SPURN
  back: 5 REPEL 6 REVERT
  blue: 3 DYE 6 SADDEN
  color: 5 RIPEN
  down: 3 DIM 4 DENY VETO
    5 LOWER SPURN
    6 PASSUP REFUSE
    REJECT
  in: 6 RETIRE
  Indicate a: 6 SIGNAL
  informer: 3 RAT
  inside out: 5 EVERT
  Kind of: 7 HAIRPIN
  left: 3 HAW
  loose: 7 RELEASE
  Make a sharp: 4 VEER
  off: 8 ALIENATE

off course: 4 VEER
on: 5 START 6 AROUSE
on an axis: 4 SLUE 6 ROTATE
out: 5 ENDUP
out to be: 5 ENDUP
outward: 5 EVERT SPLAY
over: 4 CEDE GIVE 5 UPEND
  6 HANDIN INVERT
pale: 6 BLANCH
Partner of: 4 TOSS
Player's: 4 MOVE ROLL
Ready to ~ in: 6 SLEEPY
red: 3 DYE 5 BLUSH RIPEN
right: 3 GEE
Sharp: 3 ZAG ZIG
sharply: 3 ZIG 4 VEER
  5 ANGLE
Skip a: 4 PASS
suddenly: 6 SWERVE
tail: 3 RUN WAG 4 FLEE
Takes a: 4 GOES
Took a: 4 WENT
toward: 4 FACE
Tricky: 3 ESS
up one's nose at: 4 SNUB
___-turn: 3 NOU
**Turnaround: 3 UIE**
**Turncoat: 8 DESERTER
  RENEGADE**
**Turndown**
  Emphatic: 5 NOSIR
  Polite: 5 NOSIR 6 NOMAAM
  Presidential: 4 VETO
  Slangy: 3 NAH NAW 4 NOPE
  Teutonic: 4 NEIN
  Tours: 3 NON
  Vocal: 3 NAY
  words: 3 NOS
**Turndowns: 3 NOS 4 NOES**
**Turned: 5 SWUNG**
  into: 6 BECAME
  on: 3 LIT
  on by: 4 INTO
**Turner**
  Actress: 4 LANA
  autobiography: 5 ITINA
  Cable kingpin: 3 TED
  creation: 3 CNN
  Head: 4 HUNK
  Insurrectionist: 3 NAT
  of records: 3 IKE
  Rebellious: 3 NAT
  Singer: 4 TINA
  Tycoon: 3 TED
  Wheel: 4 AXLE
**Turner Field**
  site: 7 ATLANTA
  team, on scoreboards: 3 ATL
**Turning**
  meas.: 3 RPM RPS
  part: 5 ROTOR
  point: 3 ELL HUB 4 AXIS
    AXLE DDAY EDDY
    5 HINGE PIVOT 6 CRISIS
  tool: 5 LATHE
  WWII ~ point: 4 DDAY

**Turnip: 4 ROOT**
  variety: 8 RUTABAGA
**Turnoff: 4 EXIT**
  Turnpike: 4 RAMP
    8 RESTAREA
**Turn-on**
  Certain: 3 LSD
**"Turn on, tune in, drop out"**
  adviser: 5 LEARY
**Turnover: 5 KNISH**
  Small: 6 SAMOSA
**Turnovers**
  Small Russian: 8 PIROSHKI
**Turnpike: 4 ROAD**
  charge: 4 TOLL
  no-no: 5 UTURN
  turnoff: 4 EXIT RAMP
    8 RESTSTOP
**Turn ___ profit: 4 ANET**
**Turns**
  It ~ in its work: 5 LATHE
  Some: 5 LEFTS
  Take: 6 ROTATE
**Turnstile**
  coin: 5 TOKEN
**Turntable**
  speed (abbr.): 3 RPM
  topper: 5 ALBUM
  turners: 3 LPS
**"Turn to Stone"**
  gp.: 3 ELO
**"Turn! Turn! Turn!"**
  group: 5 BYRDS
  songwriter: 6 SEEGER
**Turow, Scott**
  book: 4 ONEL
**Turpentine**
  source: 4 PINE
**Turpitude: 4 EVIL**
**Turquoise: 4 AQUA**
    8 GEMSTONE
  relative: 4 AQUA 8 NILEBLUE
**Turret**
  site: 4 TANK
**Turtle**
  shell: 8 CARAPACE
**"Turtle, The"**
  poet: 4 NASH
**Turtledove: 4 DEAR**
**Turtles**
  Like some teenage: 5 NINJA
    6 MUTANT
**Turtles, The**
  1968 hit song by ~:
    7 ELENORE
**Turturro**
  Actress: 4 AIDA
**Tuscaloosa**
  univ.: 4 BAMA
**Tuscan**
  city: 5 SIENA
  island: 4 ELBA
  marble city: 5 MASSA
  river: 4 ARNO
**Tuscany**
  city: 4 PISA 5 SIENA

island: 4 ELBA
Old name for: 7 ETRURIA
river: 4 ARNO
Talk of ~ (abbr.): 4 ITAL
wine: 7 CHIANTI
**Tush: 4 REAR**
**"Tush!": 4 POOH**
**Tushingham**
  Actress: 4 RITA
**Tusk**
  material: 5 IVORY
**Tusked**
  animal: 4 BOAR 6 WALRUS
**Tussaud**
  establishment:
    9 WAXMUSEUM
  first name: 5 MARIE
  medium: 3 WAX
  Title for: 3 MME 6 MADAME
**Tussle: 5 SCRAP**
  Brief: 5 SETTO
**Tut**
  country: 5 EGYPT
  relative: 3 TSK
**Tutee**
  Henry's: 5 ELIZA
**Tutor**
  Fictional: 4 ANNA
  session: 6 LESSON
**Tutu: 5 SKIRT**
  material: 5 TULLE
**Tutuila**
  harbor: 8 PAGOPAGO
**Tuxedo**
  button: 4 STUD
  Like many a: 6 RENTED
  Put on a: 7 DRESSUP
**TV**
  adjunct: 3 VCR
  adjustment: 3 HOR
  alien: 3 ALF 4 MORK
  angel portrayer: 5 REESE
  antenna: 6 AERIAL
    10 RABBITEARS
  appearance: 6 AIRING
  award: 4 EMMY
  band: 3 UHF VHF
  cabinet: 7 CONSOLE
  cartoon dog: 3 REN 5 ASTRO
  chef: 4 KERR
  choice: 3 RCA
  clown: 4 BOZO
  collie: 6 LASSIE
  commercial: 4 SPOT
  component: 3 CRT
  control: 3 VOL 4 DIAL TINT
  diner: 4 MELS
  doctor: 4 PHIL 5 ULENE
  dog: 3 REN 6 LASSIE
  et al.: 5 MEDIA
  from D.C.: 5 CSPAN
  genie: 4 EDEN
  guide: 6 RATING
  handyman: 4 VILA
  hookup: 3 VCR
  horse: 4 MRED

host: 5 EMCEE
hosts: 3 MCS
inits.: 3 RCA
inits. since 1975: 3 SNL
interference: 4 SNOW
interruptions: 3 ADS
judge: 3 AMY
knob: 4 TINT
lawyer: 4 ALLY
listing: 4 SKED 7 AIRTIME
maker: 3 RCA 4 SONY
monitor: 3 FCC 5 VCHIP
music vendor: 4 KTEL
news source: 3 CNN
palomino: 4 MRED
part: 3 CRT 4 TELE
planet: 3 ORK
preview: 6 TEASER
receiver: 4 DISH
remote button: 3 SEL
room: 3 DEN
screen grid: 6 RASTER
series precursor: 5 PILOT
sheriff: 4 LOBO
sked letters: 3 TBA
spots: 3 ADS
studio sign: 5 ONAIR
teaser: 5 PROMO
trophy: 4 EMMY
Unpaid ~ ad: 3 PSA
warrior: 4 XENA
Was on: 5 AIRED
watchdog: 3 FCC
Weekend ~ show: 3 SNL
Words mouthed to a ~ camera:
  5 HIMOM
workers' union: 5 AFTRA
~ E.T.: 3 ALF
~ Marine: 4 PYLE
**TVA**
  output: 4 ELEC
  project: 3 DAM
  proponent: 3 FDR
**TV Guide**
  abbr.: 3 TBS
  notation: 3 TBA
  span: 4 WEEK
**TWA**
  exec Carl: 5 ICAHN
  Former ~ rival: 5 PANAM
**Twaddle: 3 PAP ROT 4 BOSH**
    5 PRATE 6 DRIVEL
**Twain**
  character: 4 FINN HUCK
    6 SAWYER
  contemporary: 5 HARTE
  Country singer: 6 SHANIA
  frog: 4 DANL
  Onetime ~ home: 6 ELMIRA
  resting place: 6 ELMIRA
**Twain, Mark: 7 PENNAME**
**Twain/Harte**
  play: 5 AHSIN
**Twangy: 5 NASAL**
**TWA Terminal**
  designer Saarinen: 4 EERO

Tweak: 3 NIP 8 FINETUNE
**Tweed**
Boss ~ caricaturist: 4 NAST
___ Tweed (fabric): 6 HARRIS
**Tweeter**
output: 6 TREBLE
**Tweety**
home: 4 CAGE
Sylvester, to: 3 TAT
**"Twelfth Night"**
Belch of: 4 TOBY
countess: 6 OLIVIA
duke: 6 ORSINO
role: 5 VIOLA
Sir Toby of: 5 BELCH
**Twelve:** 4 NOON
A cube has: 5 EDGES
doz.: 3 GRO
**Twelve ___:** 4 OAKS
**"Twelve Days of Christmas, The"**
musician: 5 PIPER
**Twelve Oaks**
neighbor: 4 TARA
**Twelve-year-old:** 7 PRETEEN
Last year's: 4 TEEN
**Twenties**
dispenser: 3 ATM
Roaring: 3 ERA
**Twenty**
Change for a: 4 TENS
fins: 5 CNOTE
**"Twenty-One"**
host: 5 BARRY
**Twenty Questions**
answer: 3 YES
category: 6 ANIMAL
**Twice:** 3 BIS 5 AGAIN
chewed food: 3 CUD
Pass: 5 RELAP
Price: 5 RETAG
tetra: 4 OCTA OCTO
tre: 4 SEIS
**Twiddled**
one's thumbs: 5 IDLED
**Twiddling**
one's thumbs: 4 IDLE
**Twig**
Basketry: 5 OSIER
broom: 5 BESOM
Willow: 5 OSIER
**Twiggy**
abode: 4 NEST
**Twigs**
Digs of: 4 NEST 5 NESTS
**Twilight**
times: 4 EVES
~, old-style: 5 GLOAM
~, to a poet: 3 EEN
**"Twilight Zone, The"**
host: 10 RODSERLING
host Serling: 3 ROD
Like: 5 EERIE
**Twill**
Khaki: 5 CHINO

**Twilled**
fabric: 5 SERGE
**Twin:** 4 DUAL
Biblical: 4 ESAU
in chemistry: 6 ISOMER
Minnesota: 6 STPAUL
of Abby: 3 ANN
of Apollo: 7 ARTEMIS
of Artemis: 6 APOLLO
of Bert: 3 NAN
of Chang: 3 ENG
of Esau: 5 JACOB
of Jacob: 4 ESAU
of myth: 5 REMUS
of Pollux: 6 CASTOR
of Romulus: 5 REMUS
**Twin Cities**
suburb: 5 EDINA
**Twine:** 4 CORD 6 ENLACE
fiber: 5 SISAL
**Twin Falls**
Capital NW of: 5 BOISE
**Twinge:** 4 ACHE PANG
**Twining**
stem: 4 BINE
**Twinings**
product: 3 TEA
**Twinkie**
alternatives: 5 HOHOS
filler: 5 CREME
maker: 7 HOSTESS
**Twinkler:** 4 STAR
**Twinkle-toed:** 4 SPRY 5 AGILE
**Twinkling:** 5 TRICE
**"Twin Peaks"**
actress Piper: 6 LAURIE
**Twins**
Father of: 5 ISAAC
Minnesota: 3 ENS
**"Twins"**
twin: 6 DEVITO
**Twirl:** 4 SPIN
**Twirler**
stick: 5 BATON
**Twist:** 4 SKEW WARP 5 DANCE
GNARL SCREW
7 CONTORT
about: 7 ENTWINE
creator: 7 DICKENS
derivative: 4 FRUG
Double: 3 ESS
Fruit for a: 4 LIME
Humor with a: 5 IRONY
It might have a: 4 PLOT
Novel: 6 OLIVER
of phrase: 7 ANAGRAM
out of shape: 4 WARP 5 GNARL
together: 6 ENLACE
Wry: 5 IRONY
**Twistable**
cookie: 4 OREO
**Twisted:** 3 WRY 4 AWRY BENT
SICK 5 WOUND
Antelope with ~ horns: 5 ELAND
Mentally: 4 SICK

person: 5 SICKO
They can be: 6 ANKLES
thread: 5 LISLE
treat: 7 PRETZEL
**Twister**
Truth: 4 LIAR
Wrist: 4 ULNA
~ Joey: 3 DEE
**Twister-like**
toon: 3 TAZ
**Twisting:** 5 SNAKY
Act of: 7 TORSION
the truth: 5 LYING
turns: 5 ESSES
**Twit:** 5 TAUNT
**Twitch:** 3 TIC 5 SPASM
**Twitter:** 4 PEEP
**"Twittering Machine"**
artist: 4 KLEE
**Twix**
maker: 4 MARS
**Two:** 4 BOTH PAIR
Any one of: 6 EITHER
bells: 3 ONE 5 ONEPM
Bicycle for: 6 TANDEM
bits: 7 QUARTER
Break in: 5 HALVE
Brew for: 3 TEA
caplets: 4 DOSE
cents worth: 3 SAY 7 OPINION
Contest for: 4 DUEL
cups: 3 BRA
Dance for: 5 TANGO
Divisible by: 4 EVEN
fins: 3 TEN 7 TENSPOT
Game with ~ bases: 7 ONEACAT
Give ~ thumbs down to: 3 PAN
Group of: 4 DYAD
hearts: 3 BID
He put ~ and two together: 4 NOAH
He took ~ tablets: 5 MOSES
How ~ hearts may beat: 5 ASONE
In ~ parts: 4 DUAL
It has ~ doors: 5 COUPE
It takes: 4 TREY
Music for: 4 DUET
Number: 4 VEEP VICE
of a kind: 4 PAIR
of fifty: 4 EFFS
of nine: 3 ENS
One of: 6 EITHER
or three: 4 AFEW
out of two: 4 BOTH
points: 5 COLON
Put ~ and two together: 3 ADD
6 TOTEUP
Put in ~ cents' worth: 4 ANTE
5 OPINE
quarters: 4 HALF
Seat for ~ or more: 6 SETTEE
Second of: 6 LATTER
shakes: 3 SEC
Song for: 4 DUET

Split in: 6 CLEAVE
together: 4 BOTH
trios: 6 SEXTET
under par: 5 EAGLE
~, in Spanish: 3 DOS
Two-\_\_\_: 6 SEATER
Two-bagger
(abbr.): 3 DBL
Two-band
radio: 4 AMFM
Two-by-four: 5 BOARD
Trim a: 3 SAW
Two-by-two
vessel: 3 ARK
"Two by Two"
focus: 8 NOAHSARK
role: 4 NOAH
Two-dimensional: 5 PLANE
6 PLANAR
measure: 4 AREA
Two-door: 5 COUPE
Two-faced: 5 FALSE
deity: 5 JANUS
Two-finger
sign: 3 VEE
Two fives for \_\_\_: 4 ATEN
Twofold: 4 DUAL
Two-footed
animal: 5 BIPED
"Two Laundresses"
painter: 5 DEGAS
Two-legged
salamander: 6 MUDEEL
Two-masted
vessel: 4 BRIG YAWL
5 KETCH
"Two Mules for Sister \_\_\_":
4 SARA
Two-palms-down
signal: 4 SAFE
Two-part: 4 DUAL
Two-piece: 6 BIKINI
piece: 3 BRA
Two-player
hoops game: 8 ONEONONE
Two-pointer: 6 SAFETY
Easy: 4 DUNK 5 TIPIN
Two-run
homer prerequisite: 5 ONEON
Two-seaters
Classic: 3 MGS
Two-\_\_\_ sloth: 4 TOED
Twosome: 3 DUO 4 DYAD ITEM
PAIR
Tabloid: 4 ITEM
Two-stage
missile: 5 TITAN
Two-star: 4 SOSO
Two-syllable
foot: 4 IAMB

Two-tiered
galley: 6 BIREME
Two-ton
beast: 5 RHINO
Two-tone
treat: 4 OREO
"Two Treatises of Government"
author: 5 LOCKE
"Two Virgins"
musician: 3 ONO
Two-way
preposition: 3 ERE
Two-wheeled
carriage: 4 SHAY
Two-wheeler: 4 BIKE 5 MOPED
7 SCOOTER
Old: 7 CHARIOT
"Two Women"
~ Oscar winner: 5 LOREN
Two-year-old: 3 TOT
stride: 6 TODDLE
"Two Years Before the \_\_\_":
4 MAST
"Two Years Before the Mast"
author: 4 DANA
Twyla
Choreographer: 5 THARP
Ty
of baseball: 4 COBB
Tycho
Astronomer: 5 BRAHE
Tycoon: 5 BARON
Fur: 5 ASTOR
nickname: 3 ARI
Virgin: 7 BRANSON
"Tyger! Tyger!"
poet: 5 BLAKE
Tyke: 3 TAD TOT
"Blondie": 4 ELMO
Mayberry: 4 OPIE
Unruly: 4 BRAT
Tylenol
alternative: 5 ADVIL ALEVE
6 ANACIN
target: 4 ACHE PAIN
Tyler
Actress: 3 LIV
Author: 4 ANNE
successor: 4 POLK
~, politically: 4 WHIG
Tympanic
membrane: 7 EARDRUM
Tynan, Joe
portrayer: 4 ALDA
Tyne
Actress: 4 DALY
Type: 3 ILK 4 KIND SORT
choice: 4 FONT
detail: 5 SERIF
in again: 5 REKEY 7 REENTER

measures: 3 EMS ENS
redundantly: 7 ENTERIN
Slanted ~ (abbr.): 4 ITAL
Stressed ~ (abbr.): 4 ITAL
Type A
ailment: 5 ULCER
"Typee"
sequel: 4 OMOO
Typeface: 4 FONT
detail: 5 SERIF
extension: 4 KERN
PC: 5 ARIAL
Typesetter
option: 4 FONT
unit: 4 PICA
Typesetting
unit: 4 PICA
units: 3 ENS
Typewriter
feature: 6 TABSET
key: 3 TAB 5 SHIFT
6 RETURN SPACER
part: 6 PLATEN
settings: 4 TABS
type: 4 PICA
Typical: 5 USUAL
Least: 6 ODDEST
prefix: 5 PROTO
Typically: 9 ONAVERAGE
Typing
Blood ~ system: 3 ABO
Typist
purchase: 4 REAM
stat: 3 WPM
Typo: 5 ERROR
Typographic
unit: 4 PICA
Typographical
runover: 5 WIDOW
Typos: 6 ERRATA
Check for: 4 EDIT
Tyrannical: 8 DESPOTIC
sort: 4 OGRE
Tyrannosaurus \_\_\_: 3 REX
Tyranny
First name in: 3 IDI
Tyrant: 4 OGRE 6 DESPOT
Petty: 6 SATRAP
Tyre
King of: 5 HIRAM
Tyro: 6 NEWBIE ROOKIE
Tyrolean
garb: 6 DIRNDL
refrain: 5 YODEL
Tyrrhenian Sea
island: 4 ELBA
Tyson
Actress: 6 CICELY
moniker: 8 IRONMIKE
\_\_\_ Tzu: 4 SHIH

**U**
Drainpipe: 4 TRAP
follower: 4 HAUL
of the United Nations:
  5 THANT
Queue before: 3 RST 4 QRST
senior test: 3 GRE
**U2**
lead singer: 4 BONO
**UAE**
Part of: 4 ARAB
**UAR**
Half the ~, once: 3 SYR
  5 SYRIA
Part of: 4 ARAB
**Ubangi**
River to the: 4 UELE
**Ucayali**
Where the ~ flows: 4 PERU
**UCLA**
Part of: 3 CAL LOS 4 UNIV
  5 CALIF
rival: 3 USC
team: 6 BRUINS
**Udder**
part: 4 TEAT
**Udon**
Order with: 5 SUSHI
**Uffizi**
display: 3 ART 4 ARTE
**UFO**
crew: 3 ETS 6 ALIENS
shape: 4 DISK
**Uganda**
Amin of: 3 IDI
city: 7 ENTEBBE
Deposed ~ leader: 5 OBOTE
despot: 4 AMIN 7 IDIAMIN
neighbor: 5 KENYA SUDAN
  6 RWANDA
**"Ugh!":** 3 ICK 4 YECH
  8 ITSAMESS
**Ugly**
Make: 3 MAR
weather: 5 SLEET
**Ugly Duckling**
~, eventually: 4 SWAN
**U-Haul**
rival: 5 RYDER
unit: 3 VAN
Use: 4 RENT
**UHF**
Part of: 5 ULTRA
**"Uh-huh":** 3 YEP 4 ISEE YEAH
**"Uh-oh!":** 4 OOPS
**"Uh-uh!":** 3 NAH 4 NOPE
  5 NOWAY 6 NODICE
  NOSOAP

**Uintah Reservation**
~ Indian: 3 UTE
**U.K.**
award: 3 MBE OBE
Fast way to the: 3 SST
fliers: 3 RAF
honour: 3 MBE OBE
Inc., in the: 3 LTD
lexicon: 3 OED
locale: 3 EUR
native: 4 BRIT
network: 3 BBC
Part of the: 3 ENG IRE
record label: 3 EMI
**Ukr.**
neighbor: 3 RUS
~, once: 3 SSR
**Ukraine**
capital: 4 KIEV
citizen: 7 ODESSAN
city: 4 LVOV 5 YALTA
  6 ODESSA
port: 6 ODESSA
~, once (abbr.): 3 SSR
**Ukulele**
Play a: 5 STRUM
**"Ulalume"**
poet: 3 POE
**Ulan ___:** 5 BATOR
**Ullman**
Comedienne: 6 TRACEY
**Ullmann**
Actress: 3 LIV
**Ulna:** 4 BONE
neighbor: 6 RADIUS
**Ulrich**
Metallica drummer: 4 LARS
**Ulster:** 4 COAT
**Ultimate:** 3 END NTH 4 LAST
  5 FINAL 6 ENDALL
  8 EVENTUAL
purpose: 6 ENDALL ENDUSE
**Ultimatum:** 6 THREAT
ender: 4 ELSE 6 ORELSE
**Ultrasecret**
org.: 3 NSA
**Ultraviolet**
blocker: 5 OZONE
**Ulvaeus**
group: 4 ABBA
**"Ulysses"**
author: 5 JOYCE
Last word of: 3 YES
**Uma**
1998 ~ role: 4 EMMA
role: 3 MIA
**Umberto**
Author: 3 ECO

**Umbrage:** 3 IRE
Take ~ at: 4 MIND
  6 RESENT
**Umbrella:** 5 AEGIS
Lightweight: 7 PARASOL
part: 3 RIB
**Umbrian**
city: 6 ASSISI
**Umlaut**
Half an: 3 DOT
Rotated: 5 COLON
**Ump**
call: 3 OUT 4 SAFE TIME
  6 STRIKE
Kin of: 3 REF
**"Um, pardon me":** 4 AHEM
**Umpire**
call: 3 LET OUT 4 SAFE
  TIME
**Umpteen:** 4 MANY 5 SCADS
**U.N.**
ambassador under JFK: 3 AES
  15 ADLAIESTEVENSON
Annan of the: 4 KOFI
delegate (abbr.): 3 AMB
First ~ head: 3 LIE
First Israeli ~ ambassador:
  4 EBAN 8 ABBAEBAN
Former ~ member: 4 USSR
  6 TAIWAN
Hammarskjöld of the: 3 DAG
head of the 1960s: 6 UTHANT
headquarters site: 3 NYC
intervention site: 7 SOMALIA
Kofi of the: 5 ANNAN
member since 1949: 3 ISR
  6 ISRAEL
member since 1960: 4 TOGO
observer group: 3 PLO
worker agency: 3 ILO
~ Security Council member:
  3 USA
**Unable**
Is ~ to: 4 CANT
to decide: 4 TORN
to escape: 5 TREED
to flee: 5 ATBAY
to play: 4 HURT
to sit still: 5 ANTSY
**Unabridged:** 6 ENTIRE
dictionary: 4 TOME
**Unacceptable:** 6 NOGOOD
Is: 6 WONTDO
**Unaccompanied:** 4 LONE SOLE
  SOLO STAG 5 ALONE
part song: 4 GLEE
**"Unaccustomed ___ am ...":**
  3 ASI

**Unacquainted**
Be ~ with:
    15 NOTKNOWFROMADAM
**Unadorned:** 4 BARE 5 NAKED
    PLAIN
**Unadulterated:** 4 PURE
**Unaffected:** 4 REAL 5 NAIVE
    manner: 4 EASE
**Unaffiliated**
    (abbr.): 3 IND
    ~, slangily: 5 INDIE
**Unagi:** 3 EEL
**Unaided:** 5 ALONE
    sight: 8 NAKEDEYE
**Unalaska**
    resident: 5 ALEUT
**Unanimously:** 5 ASONE
    6 TOAMAN
**"Unanswered Question, The"**
    composer: 4 IVES
**Unappealing:** 4 BLAH UGLY
    15 NOTONESCUPOFTEA
**Unappetizing:** 7 INSIPID
    food: 4 GLOP MUSH SLOP
    5 GRUEL
**Unarmed:** 5 CLEAN
**Unassuming:** 3 SHY 4 MEEK
    6 MODEST
**Unattached:** 6 SINGLE
**Unattended:** 4 LONE
    8 SOLITARY
**Unattractive**
    feature: 4 WART
    fruit: 4 UGLI
**Unbalanced:** 4 ALOP
**"Un Ballo in Maschera"**
    aria: 5 ERITU
**Unbar**
    ~, to Byron: 3 OPE
**"Unbearable Bassington, The"**
    author: 4 SAKI 5 MUNRO
**"Unbearable Lightness of**
    **Being, The"**
    author Kundera: 5 MILAN
**Unbegotten:** 7 ETERNAL
**Unbelievable:** 4 TALL
**"Unbelievable"**
    rock band: 3 EMF
**Unbending:** 4 TAUT 5 RIGID
    6 STEELY
**Unbleached**
    hue: 4 ECRU
**Unbound:** 5 LOOSE
**Unbreakable:** 8 IRONCLAD
**Unbroken:** 3 ONE 4 WILD
    5 SOLID 6 ENTIRE
**Unburden:** 3 RID
**Uncalled**
    for: 8 NEEDLESS
**Uncanny:** 5 EERIE WEIRD
    ability: 3 ESP
**Uncap:** 4 OPEN
**Unceasingly:** 4 EVER
**Uncertain:** 4 IFFY 5 ATSEA
    ROCKY 7 NOTSURE
    things: 3 IFS 6 DOUBTS

___ **uncertain terms:** 4 INNO
**Uncertainty**
    Schedule ~ (abbr.): 3 TBA
    Show: 6 SEESAW
**Unchanged:** 4 ASIS SAME
**Unchanging:** 6 STABLE STATIC
**Unchecked:** 7 RAMPANT
    Spread: 4 RAGE
**Unchic:** 5 PASSE
**Uncivil:** 4 RUDE
**Uncle:** 3 MAN
    (abbr.): 3 REL
    American: 3 SAM
    Chekov: 5 VANYA
    Fictional: 5 REMUS
    of a donkey: 3 ASS
    of a monkey: 3 APE
    of Antigone: 5 CREON
    of Simba: 4 SCAR
    Scottish: 3 EME
    Seinfeld: 3 LEO
    She may cry: 5 NIECE
    ~, in Spanish: 3 TIO
**"Uncle!":** 5 IGIVE
**Uncle ___:** 3 SAM 4 BENS
**"Uncle ___" (Chekov):** 5 VANYA
**Unclear:** 4 HAZY 6 OPAQUE
**Unclearly**
    Speak: 4 SLUR
**Uncle Ben**
    speciality: 4 RICE
**"Uncle Miltie":** 5 BERLE
**Uncle Remus**
    character: 7 BRERFOX
    8 BRERBEAR
    offering: 4 TALE
    title: 4 BRER
**"Uncle Tom's Cabin"**
    author: 5 STOWE
    Friend of Topsy in: 3 EVA
    girl: 3 EVA
**"Uncle Vanya"**
    role: 5 ELENA
**Unclose:** 3 OPE
**Uncluttered:** 4 NEAT
**Uncomfortable:** 9 ILLATEASE
    position: 7 HOTSEAT
    weather measure (abbr.):
    3 THI
**Uncommon:** 4 RARE
    bill: 3 TWO
    major: 5 CFLAT
    sense: 3 ESP
    ~, in Latin: 4 RARA
**Uncomplaining:** 5 STOIC
**Uncomplicate:** 4 EASE
**Uncompromising:** 5 RIGID
    STERN
    offer: 9 ALLORNONE
**Unconcealed:** 5 OVERT
**Unconcerned:** 5 ALOOF
    retort: 6 SOWHAT
    with right and wrong:
    6 AMORAL
**Unconfined:** 5 LOOSE
**Unconscious:** 3 OUT

    state: 4 COMA
**Uncontaminated:** 4 PURE
**Uncontrolled:** 4 AMOK
    cry: 3 SOB
**Unconventional:** 5 OUTRE
    7 OFFBEAT
**Unconvincing:** 4 LAME
**Uncooked:** 3 RAW 7 TARTARE
**Uncool**
    sort: 4 NERD 5 DWEEB
**Uncountable**
    years: 3 EON
**Uncouth:** 4 RUDE 5 CRASS
    CRUDE
    one: 3 APE
**Uncover:** 4 OPEN 5 DIGUP
    6 DETECT REVEAL
**Uncovered:** 4 BARE
**Uncrashable**
    party: 9 OPENHOUSE
**Uncreative**
    response: 4 ROTE
**Uncredited**
    actor: 5 EXTRA
**Unctuous:** 4 OILY 6 SMARMY
    flattery: 5 SMARM
**Uncultivated:** 6 FALLOW
    tract: 5 HEATH
**Uncut:** 6 ENTIRE
**U.N. Day**
    month: 3 OCT
___ **und Drang:** 5 STURM
**Undecided:** 4 OPEN TORN
    10 ONTHEFENCE
    Be: 4 HANG 5 WAVER
    Remain: 4 PEND
    seat: 5 FENCE
**Undecorated:** 4 BARE
**Undeliverable**
    letter: 5 NIXIE
**Undemanding:** 4 EASY
    5 CUSHY
**Undeniable:** 4 TRUE
**Under:** 5 BELOW 6 NETHER
    7 SEDATED
    any circumstances: 5 ATALL
    control: 4 TAME 6 INHAND
    INLINE
    debate: 7 ATISSUE
    Go: 4 SINK
    Not: 7 ATLEAST
    pressure: 8 STRESSED
    Put: 6 SEDATE
    sail: 4 ASEA 5 ATSEA
    siege: 5 BESET
    the covers: 4 ABED 5 INBED
    the deck: 5 BELOW
    the spell (of): 8 ENAMORED
    the table: 3 LIT
    the weather: 3 ILL 4 SICK
    way: 5 AFOOT BEGUN
    7 STARTED
    wraps: 6 SECRET
    ~, in verse: 5 NEATH
**Underage**
    temptation: 8 JAILBAIT

**"Under a Glass Bell"**
author: 3 NIN
**Underbodice:** 8 CAMISOLE
**Undercoat:** 6 PRIMER SEALER
**Undercover**
agent: 3 SPY 4 NARC
Like some ~ cops: 5 WIRED
operation: 5 STING
Went: 5 SPIED
**Undercut:** 6 ERODED
**Underdog**
win: 5 UPSET
**Underestimate:** 9 SELLSHORT
**Underfoot**
It may be: 3 RUG 6 INSOLE
**Undergarment:** 3 BRA 4 SLIP
5 PANTY TEDDY
6 PANTIE
One-piece: 9 UNIONSUIT
**Undergoes:** 3 HAS
**Undergrad:** 4 SOPH
degs.: 3 BAS
Some ~ studies: 6 PRELAW
**Underground**
chamber: 4 CAVE 5 CRYPT
8 CATACOMB
conduit: 5 SEWER
deposit: 3 ORE
figure: 4 MOLE
Go: 4 HIDE
org.: 3 UMW
Paris: 5 METRO
**Underground Railroad**
leader: 6 TUBMAN
**Underhanded:** 3 SLY 5 CHEAP
one: 5 SNEAK 6 WEASEL
**Underline:** 6 STRESS
**Underling:** 4 AIDE 6 MENIAL
MINION STOOGE
(abbr.): 4 ASST
Hook: 4 SMEE
**Underlining**
equiv.: 4 ITAL
**Underlying:** 5 BASIC
cause: 4 ROOT
principle: 5 BASIS
**Undermine:** 3 SAP 5 ERODE
6 WEAKEN
**Underscore:** 6 STRESS
**Underside:** 4 SOLE
**"Under Siege"**
star Steven: 6 SEAGAL
**Understand:** 3 DIG GET SEE
4 READ 5 GRASP
Hard to: 6 OPAQUE
~, à la Heinlein: 4 GROK
**"Understand?":** 5 GETME
**Understanding:** 3 KEN 4 GRIP
ONTO 5 GRASP
7 ENTENTE
Phrase of: 4 AHSO ISEE
6 IGETIT
Political: 7 ENTENTE
Sounds of: 3 AHS
**Understated:** 6 LOWKEY
SUBTLE

**Understood:** 3 DUG GOT
4 KNEW 5 CLEAR
KNOWN TACIT
**"Understood!":** 4 ISEE
Slangy: 4 IDIG 5 IMHIP
**Undertake:** 4 GOAT WAGE
5 START
**Undertaking:** 3 ACT 4 TASK
**Under-the-table**
activity: 8 KNEESIES
**Underwater**
asteroid: 7 SEASTAR
device: 5 SONAR
habitat: 6 SEALAB
missile: 7 POLARIS
obstacle: 4 REEF
shelf: 5 LEDGE
shocker: 3 EEL
**Underway:** 5 AFOOT BEGUN
Get: 5 START
**Underwear:** 6 BRIEFS
8 SKIVVIES
brand: 4 BVDS 5 HANES
Kind of: 7 THERMAL
**Underwood**
Pound on an: 4 TYPE
**Underworld**
boss: 4 CAPO
Egyptian ~ god: 6 OSIRIS
Egyptian ~ queen: 4 ISIS
Greek: 5 HADES
Norse ~ queen: 3 HEL
river: 4 STYX 5 LETHE
**Underwrite:** 4 FUND 6 ASSURE
7 SPONSOR
**Undeserved**
charge: 6 BADRAP BUMRAP
**Undesirable**
condition: 6 MALADY
**Undiluted:** 4 NEAT PURE
6 STRONG
**Undissembling:** 7 SINCERE
**Undisturbed:** 6 INSITU
**Undivided:** 3 ONE 4 RAPT
SOLE 5 WHOLE
6 ENTIRE
**Undo:** 4 RUIN 5 ANNUL
6 NEGATE REPEAL
7 REVERSE
a dele: 4 STET
PC ~ key: 3 ESC
**Undocumented**
one: 5 ALIEN
**Undoing:** 4 BANE RUIN
**Undone**
Wish: 3 RUE 6 REGRET
**"Undoubtedly":** 3 YES
**Undress:** 4 PEEL
**Undulate:** 4 ROLL WAVE
**Unduly:** 3 TOO
interested: 4 NOSY
**Undying:** 7 AGELESS
ETERNAL
**Unearned**
run cause: 5 ERROR
**Unearth:** 5 DIGUP

**Unearthly:** 5 ALIEN EERIE
WEIRD
**Uneasy**
feeling: 5 ANGST DREAD
QUALM
**Unedited:** 3 RAW 5 ROUGH
version: 5 DRAFT
**Unemotional:** 3 DRY 5 STOIC
STONY 6 STOLID
**Unemployed:** 4 IDLE
**Unending:** 7 ETERNAL
**Unenthusiastic:** 5 TEPID
**Unequal:** 5 ALONE
on all three sides: 7 SCALENE
**Unescorted:** 4 SOLO 5 ALONE
**Uneven:** 3 ODD 4 ALOP
5 EROSE JERKY
7 STREAKY
hairdo: 4 SHAG
**Unexciting:** 4 BLAH DRAB FLAT
SOSO TAME
grade: 3 CEE
poker hand: 4 PAIR
**Unexpected:** 6 ABRUPT
blow: 4 GUST
development: 5 TWIST
11 TWISTOFFATE
pleasure: 5 TREAT
result: 5 UPSET
**Unexploded:** 4 LIVE
**Unfair:** 6 BIASED 8 ONESIDED
shake: 6 BUMRAP
**Unfairly**
Depict: 4 SKEW
Treat: 5 SHAFT WRONG
**"Unfaithful"**
costar: 4 GERE
**Unfamiliar:** 3 NEW 5 ALIEN
7 STRANGE
with: 5 NEWAT
**Unfavorable:** 7 ADVERSE
prognosis: 5 WORSE
**Unfavorably:** 3 ILL
Review: 3 PAN
**Unfeeling:** 4 COLD NUMB
5 STONY 8 RUTHLESS
**Unfettered:** 4 FREE 5 LOOSE
**Unflappable:** 4 CALM
6 SERENE STOLID
**Unfold:** 4 OPEN 6 EVOLVE
OPENUP
~, in verse: 3 OPE
**"Unforgettable"**
singer: 4 COLE
~ Cole: 3 NAT
**Unforseen**
problem: 4 SNAG
**Unfortunate:** 3 SAD 7 HAPLESS
**"Unfortunately ...":** 4 ALAS
**Unfounded**
~, as gossip: 4 IDLE
**Unfriendly:** 3 ICY 4 COLD
quality: 7 ICINESS
welcome:
15 CHILLYRECEPTION
**Unger, Felix:** 9 NEATFREAK

Daughter of: 4 EDNA
Like: 4 NEAT TIDY
**Ungulate**
Odd-toed: 5 TAPIR
**"Unhand me!": 5 LETGO**
**Unhastily: 9 ATLEISURE**
**Unhealthy**
atmosphere: 6 MIASMA
**Unhearing: 4 DEAF**
**Unheeding: 4 DEAF**
**Unhinged: 3 MAD 4 BATS**
Become: 4 SNAP
**Unhip**
type: 4 NERD
**Unholster: 4 DRAW**
**Unholy: 4 EVIL**
**"Unholy Loves"**
author: 5 OATES
**"Un Homme et une Femme"**
actress: 10 ANOUKAIMEE
**Unhurried: 4 EASY SLOW**
8 LEISURED
**Unicellular**
critter: 5 AMEBA
**Unidentified**
man: 7 JOHNDOE MISTERX
plane: 5 BOGIE
woman: 7 JANEDOE
**Unification Church**
head: 4 MOON
member: 6 MOONIE
**Unified: 3 ONE 5 ASONE**
ATONE
**Uniform: 4 EVEN 5 DRESS**
color: 5 KHAKI OLIVE
9 OLIVEDRAB
fabric: 5 CHINO KHAKI
frill: 7 EPAULET
GI ~ (plural): 3 ODS
Lady in: 3 WAC 4 WAAC
part: 3 CAP
**Uniform Crime Report**
org.: 3 FBI
**Unifying**
idea: 5 THEME
**Unimaginative: 4 ARID**
**Unimportant: 4 MERE 5 MINOR**
**Unimpressed: 5 BLASE**
**Uninteresting: 3 DRY 4 ARID**
BLAH DRAB DULL
5 BLAND HOHUM
**Uninvited**
Enter: 5 CRASH
guest: 11 GATECRASHER
**Uninvolved: 5 ALOOF**
7 NEUTRAL
**Union: 4 BLOC 7 WEDDING**
(abbr.): 3 STA
Actors': 3 SAG
agreement: 3 IDO
branch: 5 LOCAL
concern: 4 JOBS 5 LABOR
dealing agcy.: 4 NLRB
demand: 5 RAISE
Detroit: 3 UAW
foe: 3 REB 4 SCAB

Former ~ member (abbr.):
3 SSR
Largest U.S.: 3 NEA
Leave the: 6 SECEDE
letters: 3 AFL SSR
Media: 5 AFTRA
member: 5 BRIDE STATE
6 YANKEE
of D.C.: 3 STA
site: 5 ALTAR
10 CLOSEDSHOP
Teachers': 3 NEA
TV: 5 AFTRA
Waterfront: 3 ILA
**Unique: 4 ONLY SOLE**
5 ALONE
person: 4 ONER
~, in Latin: 4 RARA
**Uniquely: 4 ONCE**
___ **Unis: 5 ETATS**
**Unison**
In: 5 ASONE 8 ASONEMAN
In ~, musically: 4 ADUE
**Unit**
A/C: 3 BTU
Animation: 3 CEL
Astronomical: 6 PARSEC
Auction: 3 LOT
Bridge toll: 4 AXLE
Burpee: 4 SEED
Butter: 3 PAT
Capacitance: 5 FARAD
Cargo: 3 TON
Cloth: 4 BOLT
Conductance: 3 MHO
Corn: 3 COB EAR
Cotton: 4 BALE
Dance: 4 STEP
Dorm: 4 ROOM
Dosage: 3 RAD 4 PILL
Ecological: 5 BIOME
Electrical: 3 AMP OHM REL
4 VOLT WATT 5 FARAD
TESLA 6 AMPERE
Energy: 3 ERG 4 DYNE
5 JOULE
Exercise: 3 REP 5 SITUP
Farm: 4 ACRE
Film: 4 REEL
Flight: 5 STAIR
Force: 4 DYNE
Frequency: 5 HERTZ
Fuse: 3 AMP 6 AMPERE
Glazier: 4 PANE
Grass: 5 BLADE
Hay: 4 BALE
Heat: 5 THERM
Heredity: 4 GENE
Hospital: 3 BED 4 WARD
Information: 3 BIT 4 BYTE
Jeweler: 5 CARAT KARAT
Kind of: 4 ARMY 6 METRIC
Land: 4 ACRE
Leaf: 4 PAGE
Lettuce: 4 HEAD
Light: 5 LUMEN

Loudness: 3 BEL 4 SONE
7 DECIBEL
Magnetic: 5 GAUSS TESLA
WEBER
Mall: 5 STORE
Marathon: 4 MILE
Metric: 4 GRAM IAMB KILO
5 STERE TONNE
Mil.: 4 REGT
Monogram ~ (abbr.): 4 INIT
NYSE: 3 SHR
Per: 4 APOP 6 APIECE
Petrol: 5 LITRE
Play: 5 SCENE
Power: 4 WATT
Pressure: 4 TORR
Printing: 4 PICA REAM
Punishment: 4 LASH
Race: 3 LAP LEG
Radiation: 3 REM
Rating: 4 STAR
Recon: 6 PATROL
Resistance: 3 OHM
Rosary: 4 BEAD
Soap: 4 CAKE
Sound: 3 BEL 4 PHON SONE
7 DECIBEL
Special forces: 5 ATEAM
Speed: 4 KNOT
Stock: 5 SHARE STEER
Sugar: 4 LUMP
Train: 3 CAR
UPS: 3 CTN
USAF: 3 SAC
Work: 3 ERG 4 CREW WEEK
5 JOULE
Zoning: 4 ACRE
**Unitas**
team: 5 COLTS
**Unite: 3 WED 4 JOIN KNIT**
WELD 5 MERGE
6 SPLICE
Split to: 5 ELOPE
**United: 3 ONE WED 5 ASONE**
7 AIRLINE
Be: 6 COHERE
group: 4 BLOC
rival: 3 TWA 8 AMERICAN
**United Arab Emirates**
capital: 8 ABUDHABI
neighbor: 4 OMAN
**United ___ Emirates: 4 ARAB**
**United Nations**
display: 5 FLAGS
**United Nations Day**
mo.: 3 OCT
**"___: United States Marshal"**
(Wayne film): 6 CAHILL
**Unity: 7 ONENESS**
**"Unity of India, The"**
writer: 5 NEHRU
**Univ.: 3 SCH**
aides: 3 TAS
conference: 3 ACC
dorm supervisors: 3 RAS
hotshot: 4 BMOC

military program: 4 ROTC
sports gp.: 4 NCAA
teacher: 4 PROF
test: 3 GRE
**Universal:** 6 COSMIC
blood recipient: 6 TYPEAB
donor: 5 TYPEO
ideal: 3 TAO
principle: 5 AXIOM
**Universal Studios**
company: 3 MCA
**Universe:** 6 COSMOS
Egyptian god of the:
  6 AMENRA
Protomatter of the: 4 YLEM
**University**
Atlanta: 5 EMORY
Chicago: 6 LOYOLA
Denver: 5 REGIS
English ~ city: 5 LEEDS
founder Cornell: 4 EZRA
head: 5 PREXY
Houston: 4 RICE
life: 8 ACADEMIA
Long Island: 7 ADELPHI
Maine ~ town: 5 ORONO
New Orleans: 6 TULANE
New York: 7 CORNELL
North Carolina: 4 ELON
Oxford: 7 OLEMISS
Philadelphia: 7 LASALLE
Swedish: 7 UPPSALA
~ URL ending: 3 EDU
~ VIP: 4 DEAN 6 REGENT
**University of California**
site: 5 DAVIS
**University of Cincinnati**
player: 7 BEARCAT
**University of Wyoming**
site: 7 LARAMIE
**Unjust**
charge: 6 BUMRAP
**Unkempt:** 5 MESSY SEEDY
  6 RAGGED
one: 4 SLOB
place: 3 STY
**Unkept**
Like ~ yards: 5 WEEDY
**Unkeyed:** 6 ATONAL
**Unkind:** 4 MEAN 5 CATTY
nickname: 5 FATSO
**Unknown**
author (abbr.): 4 ANON
influence: 7 XFACTOR
sched.: 3 TBA
Search for the: 7 ALGEBRA
~ John: 3 DOE
**Unlatch**
~, in poetry: 3 OPE
**Unlawful**
firing: 5 ARSON
removal: 5 THEFT
**Unleaded**
alternative (abbr.): 3 REG
**Unleash:** 3 SIC 4 FREE
  5 WREAK

**Unless**
~, in law: 4 NISI
**Unlikely:** 4 SLIM 6 REMOTE
class president: 4 NERD
donor: 5 MISER
protagonist: 7 NONHERO
  8 ANTIHERO
story: 4 TALE
to bite: 4 TAME
**Unlit:** 4 DARK 5 SOBER
**Unload:** 3 RID 4 DUMP SELL
**Unlock:** 4 OPEN
~, in verse: 3 OPE
**Unlucky:** 7 HAPLESS
**UNLV**
Part of: 3 LAS
**Unmannered:** 5 CRASS
sort: 3 CAD 4 BOOR
**Unmask:** 6 REVEAL
**Unmatched:** 3 ODD 4 AONE
  SOLE
**Unmitigated:** 5 UTTER
  6 ARRANT
**Unmixed:** 4 NEAT PURE
**Unmoved:** 5 STOIC 6 INSITU
**Unmoving:** 5 INERT
**Unnamed**
alternative: 4 ELSE
litigant: 3 ROE
ones: 4 THEM THEY
**Unnatural:** 5 EERIE 6 FORCED
blonde: 4 DYER
**Unnecessary**
Render: 7 OBVIATE
**Unnerve:** 3 COW 4 FAZE
  5 DAUNT 6 DISMAY
**Uno:** 6 NUMERO
and dos: 4 TRES
and due: 3 TRE
and uno: 3 DOS
minus uno: 4 CERO
___ uno: 6 NUMERO
**Unobtainable**
Nearly: 4 RARE
**Unoccupied:** 4 IDLE
**Unoriginal:** 5 APISH STALE
  TRITE
reply: 4 ECHO
**Unpaid**
debt: 6 ARREAR
Have ~ bills: 3 OWE
servant: 5 ROBOT
~ TV ad (abbr.): 3 PSA
**Unpleasant:** 4 GRIM SOUR
  5 MESSY
fuss: 5 STINK
look: 4 LEER
situation: 4 MESS
Very: 4 VILE 5 NASTY
"___ Unplugged": 6 ALANIS
**Unpolished:** 4 RUDE 5 CRASS
leather: 6 RUSSET
**Unpopular**
More than: 5 HATED
one: 4 NERD
spots: 4 ACNE

worker: 4 SCAB
**Unpredictable:** 7 ERRATIC
**Unpretentious:** 5 LOWLY
  6 MODEST
  11 DOWNTOEARTH
**Unprincipled:** 6 AMORAL
person: 6 RASCAL
**Unprocessed:** 3 RAW 5 CRUDE
**Unproductive:** 6 INARUT
  7 STERILE
**Unprotected:** 5 NAKED
**Unproven**
ability: 3 ESP
**Unqualified:** 5 UTTER
**Unravel:** 4 FRAY 5 SOLVE
**Unreactive:** 5 INERT
**Unrealistic**
hope: 9 PIPEDREAM
**Unrealized**
gain: 11 PAPERPROFIT
**Unrefined:** 3 RAW 4 BASE
  5 CRASS CRUDE
  6 COARSE EARTHY
metal: 3 ORE
**Unrehearsed:** 5 ADLIB
**Unreliable**
witness: 4 LIAR
**Unrepaired:** 4 ASIS
**Unresolved**
detail: 8 LOOSEEND
Leave things:
  15 AGREETODISAGREE
**Unrest**
1965 ~ site: 5 WATTS
Urban: 4 RIOT
**Unrestricted:** 4 OPEN 5 LOOSE
**Unreturnable**
serve: 3 ACE
**Unruffled:** 4 CALM COOL
  6 PLACID SEDATE
  SERENE
**Unruly:** 4 WILD 5 ROWDY
bunch: 3 MOB 4 HERD
  5 HORDE 6 RABBLE
locks: 3 MOP
**"Unsafe at Any Speed"**
author: 5 NADER
**Unsaid:** 5 TACIT
Leave: 4 OMIT
**Unsatisfactory:** 4 POOR
grade: 3 DEE
Most: 5 WORST
outcome: 3 TIE
**Unsavory:** 5 SHADY
one: 5 CREEP 6 SLEAZE
**Unscheduled**
(abbr.): 3 TBA
**Unscrupulous:** 6 AMORAL
sort: 6 RASCAL
**Unseal:** 4 OPEN
**Unseat:** 4 OUST 6 DEPOSE
**Unseen**
Hang around: 4 LURK
Present but: 6 LATENT
**Unseld**
of basketball: 3 WES

**Unselfish**
sort: 5 GIVER
**Unsers**
of racing: 3 ALS
**Unsettle:** 3 JAR
**Unsettled:** 4 OPEN 6 QUEASY
10 INQUESTION
Remain: 4 PEND
**Unshackle:** 4 FREE
**Unskilled:** 4 POOR
worker: 4 PEON
writer: 4 HACK
**Unsmiling:** 5 STERN 6 SOLEMN
**Unsociable**
sort: 5 LONER
**Unsophisticated:** 5 NAIVE
6 RUSTIC
sort: 4 RUBE
**Unsound:** 6 FAULTY
**Unspecified**
amount: 3 ANY 4 SOME
degree: 3 NTH
person: 3 ONE
**Unspoiled:** 4 PURE
spot: 4 EDEN
**Unspoken:** 5 TACIT
**Unstable**
Be: 6 TEETER
particle: 4 MUON
**Unstamped**
letters: 5 EMAIL
**Unstated:** 5 TACIT
**Unsteady:** 5 SHAKY TIPSY
Be: 4 REEL
**Unstressed**
vowel: 5 SCHWA
**Unstrict:** 3 LAX
**Unstructured:** 5 LOOSE
**Unsubstantial:** 4 AERY AIRY
**Unsuccessful**
one: 7 ALSORAN
**Unsuitable:** 5 INAPT
**Unsullied:** 4 PURE 6 CHASTE
**Unsurpassed:** 4 BEST
7 ALLTIME
**Untagged:** 5 NOTIT
**Untainted:** 4 PURE 5 CLEAN
**Untamed:** 4 WILD 5 FERAL
6 SAVAGE
**Unter**
Opposite of: 4 UBER
**Unthought-out:** 4 RASH
**Untidy:** 5 MESSY
one: 4 SLOB 6 SLOVEN
**Until:** 4 UPTO
now: 3 YET 5 ASYET SOFAR
6 TODATE
~, in Spanish: 5 HASTA
"___ unto Caesar ...": 6 RENDER
___ unto himself: 4 ALAW
**"Unto the Sons"**
author Gay: 6 TALESE
**Untouchable:** 4 SAFE 6 SACRED
~ Eliot: 4 NESS
~ Ness: 5 ELIOT
**Untouchables:** 4 TMEN 5 CASTE

**"Untouchables, The":** 4 FEDS
TMEN
composer Morricone: 5 ENNIO
leader: 4 NESS 9 ELIOTNESS
role for Costner: 4 NESS
villain: 5 NITTI
~ Oscar winner: 7 CONNERY
**"Unto us ___ is given ...":**
4 ASON
**Untrained:** 3 RAW
**Untroubled:** 7 ATPEACE
PACIFIC
**Untrue:** 5 NOTSO
Declare: 4 DENY
**Untrustworthy**
one: 3 CAD 5 SNEAK
**Untruth:** 3 LIE
**Untruthful**
Be ~ with: 5 LIETO
**Untruths**
Many: 10 PACKOFLIES
**Unused:** 3 NEW 4 IDLE
Remain: 4 IDLE
**Unusual:** 3 ODD 4 RARE
item: 5 CURIO
partner: 5 CRUEL
**Unveiling**
cry: 4 TADA
**Unwakable**
state: 4 COMA
**Unwanted**
buildup: 4 LINT 6 TARTAR
e-mail: 4 SPAM
flora: 4 WEED
look: 4 LEER
**Unwarm**
welcome: 4 HISS
**Unwashed**
Like ~ hair: 4 OILY
The great: 5 PLEBS
**Unwavering:** 5 SOLID
6 STEADY
**Unwelcome**
guest: 4 PEST
look: 5 SNEER
mail: 4 BILL
one: 6 PARIAH
**Unwell:** 3 ILL
Be: 3 AIL
**Unwilling:** 5 LOATH 6 AVERSE
to listen: 4 DEAF
**Unwind:** 4 REST 5 RELAX
Place to: 3 SPA TUB
**Unwise**
undertaking: 5 FOLLY
**Unwitting**
one: 4 DUPE PAWN
**Unworldly:** 5 NAIVE
**Unwrap:** 4 OPEN
in a hurry: 8 TEAROPEN
**Unwritten:** 4 ORAL
**Unyielding:** 4 GRIM IRON
5 RIGID STERN STIFF
STOIC 6 STEELY
7 ADAMANT
8 HARDLINE OBDURATE

**Up:** 5 AHEAD ALOFT ASTIR
ATBAT AWAKE BOOST
RAISE RISEN 6 ARISEN
7 ELEVATE 8 INCREASE
above: 4 ATOP
and about: 5 ASTIR AWAKE
RISEN 6 ACTIVE ARISEN
for grabs: 4 FREE 7 ANYONES
for it: 4 GAME
in arms: 5 IRATE
in the air: 4 IFFY 5 ALOFT
Is ~ to the task: 3 CAN
Not: 3 SAD 4 ABED 5 INBED
Not ~ (to): 6 UNABLE
Not ~ to much: 4 IDLE
One who is: 6 BATTER
Partner of: 5 ABOUT
the ante: 5 RAISE
the creek: 7 INASPOT
9 INTROUBLE
to: 3 TIL 5 UNTIL 6 ATMOST
to it: 4 ABLE
to now: 3 YET 5 ASYET SOFAR
to the task: 4 ABLE
**Up ___:** 5 ATREE
**___ up**
(admit): 4 FESS
(angry): 3 HET
(clinch): 3 SEW
(dress): 3 TOG
(get ready): 4 GEAR
(hide): 4 HOLE
(invigorate): 3 PEP
(prepare to drive): 3 TEE
**"Up and ___!":** 4 ATEM
**Up-and-comer:** 7 STARLET
**Up-and-up**
On the: 5 LEGAL LEGIT LICIT
6 KOSHER RISING
**Upbraid:** 5 SCOLD
**UPC**
Part of: 4 CODE
**Update:** 4 REDO 7 REFRESH
a chart: 5 REMAP
a factory: 6 RETOOL
**"___ up, doc?":** 5 WHATS
**Up-front**
money: 4 ANTE
**Up ___ good:** 4 TONO
**Upgrade:** 4 REDO
**Upheaval:** 5 THROE
**Upholstered**
piece: 4 SOFA
Thickly ~ seat: 9 CLUBCHAIR
**Upholstery**
fabric: 5 FRISE TOILE
flaw: 3 RIP
**Uplift:** 4 BUOY 5 EDIFY RAISE
**Uplifting**
attire: 3 BRA
talk (abbr.): 3 SER
**Upon:** 4 ATOP
**"___ upon a time":** 4 ONCE
**Upper**
body: 5 TORSO
crust: 5 ELITE

hand: 4 EDGE
house: 6 SENATE
left key: 3 ESC
limit: 3 CAP MAX
regions: 5 ETHER SKIES
story: 4 LOFT
**Upper ___ (Burkina Faso):**
     5 VOLTA
**Upperclassmen**
     (abbr.): 3 SRS
**Uppity**
one: 4 SNOB 5 SNOOT
**Up ___ point:** 3 TOA
**Upright:** 4 POST 5 ERECT
     MORAL ONEND PIANO
     PROUD 6 HONEST
     SPINET 7 ETHICAL
     8 GOALPOST
Door frame: 4 JAMB
Not: 5 ALIST ATILT
**Uprising:** 4 RIOT 6 REVOLT
     1976 ~ site: 6 SOWETO
**Uproar:** 3 ADO DIN 4 RIOT
     TODO 5 FUROR HAVOC
     HOOHA 6 OUTCRY
     TUMULT
**___ uproar:** 4 INAN
**Ups:** 5 HIKES
It has its ~ and downs:
     4 YOYO 6 SEESAW
     8 ELEVATOR
Switch: 3 ONS
**UPS**
delivery: 3 CTN PKG
rival: 5 FEDEX
Use: 4 SHIP
**Upscale:** 4 TONY 5 ELITE
More: 5 NICER
trio: 6 DOREMI
wheels: 3 BMW
**Upset:** 3 ADO 4 IRED RILE
     SORE 5 EVERT IRKED
     RILED 6 RATTLE
     7 AGITATE
with: 5 MADAT
**Upshot:** 3 END 6 RESULT
**Upside-down**
"e": 5 SCHWA
sleeper: 5 SLOTH
**Upsilon**
follower: 3 PHI
preceder: 3 TAU
**Upstairs:** 5 ABOVE
Sound: 4 SANE
**___ upswing:** 4 ONAN
**Uptake**
Quick on the: 3 APT 5 ALERT
     SMART 6 ASTUTE
Slow on the: 5 DENSE
**Uptight:** 4 EDGY 5 TENSE
     6 ONEDGE
**Up-to-date:** 3 MOD
Most: 6 LATEST
Not be: 3 LAG
**Upton**
Writer: 8 SINCLAIR

**Uptown**
in NYC: 3 NNE
**"___ up to you":** 3 ITS
**Upturn**
Brief: 4 BLIP
Sudden: 5 SPIKE
**Upturned:** 5 ONEND
slope: 4 RISE 6 ASCENT
**"Up, up and away"**
co.: 3 TWA
**"Up Where We Belong":**
     4 DUET
**Ur**
Locale of ancient: 5 SUMER
**Uracil**
It contains: 3 RNA
**Uraeus**
figure: 3 ASP
**Ural**
City on the: 4 ORSK
**Urals**
East of the: 4 ASIA
West of the: 6 EUROPE
**Urania:** 4 MUSE
Sister of: 5 ERATO
**Uranium**
~ 235 or 238: 7 ISOTOPE
**Uranus**
Moon of: 5 ARIEL 6 OBERON
     7 MIRANDA TITANIA
Wife of: 4 GAEA
**Urban:** 5 CIVIC
air problem: 4 SMOG 5 SMAZE
blight: 4 SLUM
play area: 7 SANDLOT
polluter: 5 NOISE
problem: 6 SPRAWL
suffix: 3 ITE
unrest: 4 RIOT
vehicle: 3 BUS CAB 4 TAXI
vermin: 3 RAT
**Urbane:** 5 SUAVE
**Urchin**
Street: 4 WAIF 5 GAMIN
     SCAMP 11 GUTTERSNIPE
**Urge:** 3 YEN 4 GOAD ITCH
     PROD 5 IMPEL PRESS
     6 EXHORT
(on): 4 SPUR
to attack: 3 SIC
**Urgency:** 5 HASTE
**Urgent:** 4 DIRE STAT 5 ACUTE
call: 3 SOS
letters: 4 ASAP
need: 6 DEMAND
request: 6 BEHEST
**Uriah ___ (Dickens character):**
     4 HEEP
**Urich, Robert**
~ TV series: 5 VEGAS
**Uris**
Author: 4 LEON
hero: 3 ARI
novel: 5 QBVII TOPAZ
     6 THEHAJ
novel, with "The": 3 HAJ

**URL**
ending: 3 COM EDU GOV NET
     ORG
part: 3 DOT
start: 4 HTTP
**Urn:** 4 VASE
Decorative: 7 SAMOVAR
Russian: 7 SAMOVAR
tribute: 3 ODE
**Ursula**
Author: 6 LEGUIN
**Uru.**
neighbor: 3 ARG
**Uruguay:** 3 RIO
**Us**
Not: 4 THEM
Still with: 5 ALIVE
Them, to: 4 FOES
**U.S.**
currency: *see page 724*
First ~ capital: 3 NYC
Former ~ territory:
     6 DAKOTA
From the: 4 AMER
president: *see page 723*
Southernmost ~ city: 4 HILO
The ~, to Mexicans:
     7 ELNORTE
trading partner: 3 EEC
vice president: *see page 723*
**USA**
50 of the ~: 3 STS
alternative: 3 TBS TNT
Part of: 4 AMER
~ ID: 3 SSN
**"U.S.A.":** 7 TRILOGY
**Usable**
Make: 5 ADAPT
**USAF**
bigwig: 3 GEN
unit: 3 SAC
~ NCO: 4 TSGT
**U.S. Airways**
rival: 3 TWA
**U.S. Army**
medal: 3 DSC
**"___ us a son ...":** 4 UNTO
**USC**
athlete: 6 TROJAN
rival: 4 UCLA
**U.S./Canadian**
security acronym: 5 NORAD
**USCG**
call: 3 SOS
rank: 3 CPO ENS
**U.S. Constitution**
article: 3 THE
**USDA**
Part of: 3 AGR 4 DEPT
rating: 6 CHOICE
**Use:** 3 PLY 4 WEAR 5 AVAIL
     6 EMPLOY
Allow to: 4 LEND
Already in: 5 TAKEN
Be of: 5 AVAIL SERVE
Do not: 4 OMIT 5 WASTE

Have no ~ for: 4 HATE
  5 ABHOR 6 DETEST
In widespread: 4 RIFE
Make good ~ of: 3 TAP
  6 DRAWON
Not in: 4 FREE IDLE
Of no: 6 OTIOSE
Put to: 5 APPLY EXERT
Ready to: 5 ONTAP
**Used:** 3 OLD 4 WORN
  Get ~ (to): 5 ADAPT ENURE
    INURE
  Hardly: 7 LIKENEW
  Not: 3 NEW 4 LEFT
  to be: 3 WAS 4 WERE
  to own: 3 HAD
  up: 4 GONE 5 SPENT
**Useful:** 5 HANDY UTILE
  article: 3 THE
  Prove: 5 AVAIL
  thing: 5 ASSET
**Useless:** 6 NOGOOD NOHELP
  7 INUTILE
**User:** 6 ADDICT
  Kind of: 3 END
**U.S./Eur.**
  link: 3 ATL
**U-shaped**
  river bend: 5 OXBOW
**Usher:** 6 ESCORT LEADIN
    SEATER
  beat: 5 AISLE
  creator: 3 POE
  in: 4 SEAT 5 ADMIT
    6 HERALD
  offering: 3 ARM 4 SEAT
**Using:** 3 VIA
**USMA**
  freshman: 4 PLEB
  grads: 3 LTS
  Part of: 4 ACAD
**USMC**
  Highest ~ rank: 3 GEN
  one-striper: 3 PFC
  Part of: 5 CORPS
**USN**
  rank: 3 ADM CDR CPO ENS
    4 CAPT CMDR
**USNA**
  freshman: 5 PLEBE
  grad: 3 ENS
  Part of: 3 NAV 4 ACAD
**USO**
  attendees: 3 GIS
**U.S. Open:** *see page 713*
  1955 ~ winner: 7 TRABERT
  1966 ~ winner: 6 STOLLE
  1968 ~ winner: 4 ASHE

1972 ~ runner-up: 4 ASHE
1972 ~ winner: 7 NASTASE
1977 ~ winner: 5 VILAS
1991–92 ~ winner: 5 SELES
1992 ~ winner: 4 KITE
  7 TOMKITE
1994 ~ winner: 3 ELS
1997 ~ winner: 3 ELS
1999 ~ winner: 6 AGASSI
2000 ~ winner: 5 SAFIN
2000 ~ winner Safin: 5 MARAT
Former ~ site:
  11 FORESTHILLS
Six-time ~ winner: 5 EVERT
stadium: 4 ASHE
Three-time ~ winner: 5 LENDL
  9 IVANLENDL
Two-time ~ winner: 3 ELS
  5 PAYNE SELES 6 AGASSI
  8 ERNIEELS
Two-time ~ winner Fraser:
  5 NEALE
unit: 3 SET
___ **U.S. Pat. Off.:** 3 REG
**U.S. president:** *see page 723*
  11th ~: 4 POLK
  27th ~: 4 TAFT
**USPS**
  alternative: 3 FAX 5 EMAIL
  delivery: 3 LTR
  limbo: 3 DLO
  option: 3 COD
**USSR**
  Part of: 3 SOV
  state (abbr.): 3 RUS
  successor: 3 CIS
**U.S. Steel**
  founder: 8 JPMORGAN
**Ustinov**
  Actor: 5 PETER
**Usual:** 3 PAR 6 NORMAL
  7 ROUTINE
  (abbr.): 3 STD
  routine (abbr.): 3 SOP
**Usually:** 7 ASARULE
**Usurer:** 9 LOANSHARK
  offering: 4 LOAN
**U.S. vice president:** *see page 723*
**Uta**
  Tony winner: 5 HAGEN
**Utah**
  canyon: 4 SEGO 5 BRYCE
  city: 4 OREM 5 OGDEN
    PROVO
  Hatch of: 5 ORRIN
  landmark:
    13 GREATSALTLAKE
  lily: 4 SEGO

mountain range: 5 UINTA
national park: 4 ZION
ski resort: 4 ALTA
Young in ~ history:
  7 BRIGHAM
**Utensil:** 4 TOOL
  Cooking: 3 PAN WOK
  Holey: 5 SIEVE
  Kitchen: 5 CORER PARER
**Utensils:** 8 FLATWARE
  Military ~ set: 7 MESSKIT
**UTEP**
  Part of: 4 PASO
**Utica**
  county: 6 ONEIDA
**Utility**
  (abbr.): 3 TEL 4 ELEC
  bill enc.: 3 SAE
  customer: 4 USER
  pipe: 4 MAIN
**Utilize:** 6 DRAWON
**Utmost:** 3 NTH 7 EXTREME
  9 NTHDEGREE
**Utopia:** 4 EDEN 9 SHANGRILA
  Onetime New York: 6 ONEIDA
**Utopian:** 5 IDEAL 8 IDEALIST
  novel: 7 EREWHON
**Utrecht**
  From: 5 DUTCH
**Utrillo**
  Stand for: 5 EASEL
**Uttar Pradesh**
  city: 4 AGRA
**Utter:** 3 SAY 4 EMIT PURE
  TELL 5 SHEER STATE
  TOTAL 6 ENTIRE
  suffix: 4 ANCE
**Uttered:** 4 ORAL SAID
  6 SPOKEN
  with contempt: 4 SPAT
**U-turn**
  from ENE: 3 WSW
  from ESE: 3 WNW
  from NNE: 3 SSW
  from NNW: 3 SSE
  from SSE: 3 NNW
  from SSW: 3 NNE
  from WNW: 3 ESE
  from WSW: 3 ENE
**UV**
  index tracker: 3 EPA
**Uzbek**
  body of water: 7 ARALSEA
**Uzbekistan**
  sea: 4 ARAL
  ~, once (abbr.): 3 SSR
**Uzi:** 3 GUN
  relative: 4 STEN

**V:** 4 FIVE
  formers: 5 GEESE
  preceders: 3 STU 4 RSTU
  sign: 5 PEACE
**V8**
  ingredient: 6 CELERY
    TOMATO 7 SPINACH
**V-8:** 6 ENGINE
  unit (abbr.): 3 CYL
**Vacances**
  Time for les: 3 ETE
**Vacancy:** 4 VOID
  sign: 5 TOLET
**Vacant:** 5 EMPTY INANE
    UNLET
  look: 5 STARE
**Vacation:** 4 TRIP 7 GETAWAY
    HOLIDAY
  aid: 3 MAP
  home: 5 VILLA 7 COTTAGE
  On: 3 OFF 4 AWAY
  plan: 4 REST TRIP 5 RANDR
  Popular ~ spot: 3 RIO 4 KEYS
    5 ARUBA CRETE
    7 BAHAMAS POCONOS
    RIVIERA
  rental: 3 CAR
  souvenir: 3 LEI TEE
    6 TSHIRT
  spot: 3 SPA 4 CAPE ISLE
    LAKE 5 SHORE 6 RESORT
    7 SEASIDE 8 SEASHORE
  stop: 3 INN
  time in France: 3 ETE
  Wild: 6 SAFARI
**Vacationing:** 3 OFF 4 AWAY
    7 ONATRIP
**Vaccination:** 4 SHOT
  fluids: 4 SERA
**Vaccine**
  developer Salk: 5 JONAS
  Smallpox ~ developer:
    6 JENNER
  Type of: 4 ORAL SALK
**Vaccines:** 5 SERA
**Vacillate:** 4 SWAY YOYO
    5 HEDGE WAVER
    6 SEESAW TEETER
**Vaclav**
  Czech leader: 5 HAVEL
**Vacuous:** 5 INANE
**Vacuum:** 4 VOID 5 CLEAN
  part: 3 BAG 4 HOSE
  target: 4 DIRT 5 CRUMB
**Vacuum tube**
  gas: 5 ARGON
  Type of: 5 DIODE 6 TRIODE
**___ Vader:** 5 DARTH

**Vader, Darth**
  Like: 4 EVIL
**Vaderesque:** 4 EVIL
**"___ Vadis?":** 3 QUO
**Vagabond:** 4 HOBO 5 NOMAD
    ROGUE ROVER
    TRAMP 6 PICARO
    ROAMER
**Vagrant:** 3 BUM 4 HOBO
    5 TRAMP
**Vague:** 4 HAZY
  quality: 4 AURA
**Vail**
  alternative: 5 ASPEN
  Enjoy: 3 SKI
  surface: 4 SNOW
  trail: 6 SKIRUN
  visitor: 5 SKIER
**Vain**
  claim: 5 BOAST
  voyage: 7 EGOTRIP
  walk: 5 STRUT
**"Valachi Papers, The"**
  author Peter: 4 MAAS
**Valais**
  capital: 4 SION
**Val d'___:** 4 ARNO
**Valdai Hills**
  river: 5 VOLGA
**Valdez**
  vessel: 5 OILER
**Vale:** 4 DELL GLEN
**Valedictorian**
  pride (abbr.): 3 GPA
**Valedictory**
  Give a: 5 ORATE
**Valencia**
  Info: Spanish cue
  conqueror: 5 ELCID
  Very, in: 3 MUY
**Valens, Ritchie**
  hit song: 5 DONNA
**Valentine:** 5 HEART SAINT
  Actress: 5 KAREN
  figure: 4 EROS 5 CUPID
  flowers: 5 ROSES
  month (abbr.): 3 FEB
  team: 4 METS
  word: 4 LOVE
  words: 5 ILOVE
**Valentine's Day**
  gift: 4 CARD 5 ROSES
  letters: 3 FTD
**Valentino**
  Lover of: 5 NEGRI
  role: 5 SHEIK
**Valhalla**
  ~ VIP: 4 ODIN

**Valiant:** 5 BRAVE GUTSY
    6 HEROIC
**Valid:** 5 LEGIT SOUND
  Established as: 8 PROBATED
  No longer: 4 NULL VOID
**Valium**
  manufacturer: 5 ROCHE
**Valkyries:** 5 NORSE
  God attended by the: 4 ODIN
  Mother of the: 4 ERDA
**___ Vallarta:** 6 PUERTO
**Valle del Bove**
  site: 4 ETNA
**Valle del Cauca**
  capital: 4 CALI
**Vallee**
  Singer: 4 RUDY
**Vallejo**
  City near: 4 NAPA
**Valletta**
  island: 5 MALTA
**Valley:** 4 DALE DELL GLEN
  California: 4 NAPA SIMI
  French wine: 5 LOIRE
  German: 4 RUHR SAAR
    5 MOSEL RHINE
  Moon: 5 RILLE
  Wine: 4 NAPA
**Valley ___:** 5 FORGE
**___ Valley:** 4 SIMI
**"Valley Girl"**
  singer: 5 ZAPPA
**"Valley of the Dolls"**
  actress: 4 TATE
  author: 6 SUSANN
  character: 5 NEELY
**Valli**
  Actress: 5 ALIDA
**Valor:** 6 METTLE
**Valorous:** 5 BRAVE
**Valova**
  Skater: 5 ELENA
**"Valse ___":** 6 TRISTE
**Valuable:** 4 DEAR 5 OFUSE
    UTILE 6 NEEDED
  collection: 5 TROVE
  deposit: 3 ORE 4 LODE
  item: 5 ASSET
  Least ~ part: 5 DREGS
  quality: 5 ASSET
**Value:** 5 PRIZE WORTH
    6 ASSESS ESTEEM
    8 APPRAISE
  Add ~ to: 6 ENRICH
  Base: 3 PAR
  Of: 5 UTILE 7 AINTHAY
  system: 5 ETHIC ETHOS
  Thing of: 5 ASSET

Without: 4 NULL
Without face: 5 NOPAR
Valued: 4 DEAR
Valve
  Place for a: 5 AORTA
  prefix: 3 UNI
  Type of: 6 AORTIC INTAKE
    MITRAL
"Vamoose!": 3 GIT 4 SCAT
    SHOO 5 SCRAM
    6 GETOUT
Vamp: 5 FLIRT SIREN TEASE
    6 SEDUCE 7 SEDUCER
  accessory: 3 BOA
Vampire
  Anne Rice: 6 LESTAT
  Famous: 7 DRACULA
  feature: 5 FANGS
  Female: 5 LAMIA
  hideaway: 4 TOMB
  killer: 5 STAKE
  repellent: 5 CROSS 6 GARLIC
Van: 7 VEHICLE
  starter: 4 MINI
  Took the: 3 LED
Van ___, Anthony
  Artist: 4 DYCK
Van ___, Charles
  Quiz show contestant:
    5 DOREN
Van ___, Eddie
  Guitarist: 5 HALEN
Van ___, Gus
  Director: 4 SANT
Van ___, Jan
  Artist: 4 EYCK
Van ___, Jean-Claude
  Actor: 5 DAMME
Van ___, Mark
  Poet: 5 DOREN
Van ___, Martin
  President: 5 BUREN
Van ___, Rembrandt
  Artist: 3 RYN
Van ___, Vincent
  Artist: 4 GOGH
Van ___, William
  Architect: 4 ALEN
Van ___, California: 4 NUYS
Vance
  (abbr.): 3 AFB
  Detective: 5 PHILO
Vance AFB
  locale: 4 ENID
Vance Air Force Base
  City near: 4 ENID
Van Cleef
  Actor: 3 LEE
Vandal: 3 HUN 7 RAVAGER
Vandalize: 3 MAR 5 TRASH
    6 DAMAGE DEFACE
Vandenberg: 3 AFB
Van der ___, Jan
  Artist: 4 MEER
Van Der Beek, James
  role: 6 DAWSON

Vanderbilt: 3 AMY 6 GLORIA
    9 CORNELIUS
___ van der Rohe, Ludwig
  Architect: 4 MIES
van der Rohe, Mies
  motto: 10 LESSISMORE
Van Devere
  Actress: 5 TRISH
Van Doren
  Actress: 5 MAMIE
  of quiz show fame: 7 CHARLES
Van Duyn
  Poet: 4 MONA
Vandyke: 5 BEARD
Van Dyke
  Actor: 4 DICK
  role: 6 PETRIE
Vane
  dir.: 3 ENE ESE NNE NNW
    SSE SSW WNW WSW
  direction: 4 EAST WEST
    5 NORTH SOUTH
  turner: 4 WIND
Vanessa
  Role for: 7 ISADORA
Van Gogh, Vincent: 6 ARTIST
    7 PAINTER
  Brother of: 4 THEO
  home: 5 ARLES
  offering: 3 EAR
  painting: 6 IRISES
Vanguard
  Took the: 3 LED
Vanilla: 5 PLAIN
  Rapper: 3 ICE
___ Vanilli: 5 MILLI
Vanish: 4 FADE 9 DISAPPEAR
    EVAPORATE
  Cause to: 6 DISPEL
Vanished: 4 GONE
Vanishing
  sound: 4 POOF
Vanity: 3 EGO 5 PRIDE
  affair: 7 EGOTRIP
  Sign of: 4 AIRS
  Voyage of: 7 EGOTRIP
Vanna
  Boss of: 4 MERV
  Partner of: 3 PAT
  Request to: 3 ANA ANO
  ~, to Pat: 6 COHOST
Vannelli
  Singer: 4 GINO
Vanquish: 4 BEAT BEST
    ROUT 6 DEFEAT
    8 OVERCOME
Van Sant
  Director: 3 GUS
van Susteren
  Analyst: 5 GRETA
Vantage
  point: 4 VIEW 5 ANGLE
    COIGN PERCH
Vanuatu
  neighbor: 4 FIJI
  Part of: 7 OCEANIA

Vanzetti
  partner: 5 SACCO
___ vapeur: 3 ALA
Vapor: 4 MIST 5 STEAM
Vaporize: 8 EVANESCE
Vaquero
  rope: 5 LASSO REATA RIATA
Vardalos
  Actress: 3 NIA
Vargas ___, Mario
  Author: 5 LLOSA
Variable
  star: 4 NOVA
Varicolored: 4 PIED
  horse: 5 PINTO
  Most: 8 MOTLIEST
Varied: 8 ECLECTIC
  mixture: 4 OLIO
Variegated: 4 PIED
Variety: 3 ILK 4 KIND SORT
    TYPE 5 GENRE
  Lacking in: 7 ONENOTE
  show: 5 REVUE
Various: 6 SUNDRY
Varner
  Faulkner character: 4 EULA
Varney, Jim
  character: 6 ERNEST
Varnish: 5 STAIN
  ingredient: 3 LAC 5 RESIN
    7 TUNGOIL
  resin: 5 ELEMI 6 MASTIC
  thinner: 7 ACETONE
Varsity: 5 ATEAM
  award: 6 LETTER
Vasarely
  genre: 5 OPART
Vasco ___
  Explorer: 6 DAGAMA
Vasco da ___
  Explorer: 4 GAMA
Vase: 3 URN 4 EWER
  handle: 4 ANSA
  handles: 5 ANSAE
  Valuable: 4 MING
  Verse on a: 3 ODE
Vassal: 4 SERF 5 LIEGE
Vassar
  Like: 4 COED
Vast: 5 BROAD LARGE
    7 IMMENSE OCEANIC
  amount: 5 OCEAN
  chasm: 5 ABYSS
  expanse: 3 SEA 5 OCEAN
  extents: 5 DEEPS
  ~, old-style: 5 ENORM
Vat: 3 TUN 4 CASK
  Wine ~ waste: 4 LEES
  worker: 4 DYER
Vatican
  court: 4 ROTA
  emissary: 6 NUNCIO
  figure: 4 POPE
  government: 7 HOLYSEE
  locale: 4 ROME
  period: 6 PAPACY

Related to the: 5 PAPAL
  sculpture: 5 PIETA
  vestment: 3 ALB
**Vaudeville**
  bit: 3 ACT 4 SKIT
  brothers: 4 RITZ
  family: 4 FOYS
  prop: 3 BOA 4 CANE
  Sad-faced ~ comedian:
    7 BENBLUE
  show: 5 REVUE
  star: 9 TOPBANANA
**Vaughan**
  Jazz singer: 5 SARAH
  nickname: 5 SASSY
  of baseball: 4 ARKY
**Vaughan, ___ Ray**
  Guitarist: 6 STEVIE
**Vaughn**
  Actor: 5 VINCE
**Vault:** 4 ARCH LEAP SAFE
  Burial: 5 CRYPT
  cracker: 4 YEGG
  locale: 4 APSE BANK
  part: 3 RIB
**Vaulted**
  area: 4 APSE
**Vaulter**
  aid: 4 POLE
**Vaunt:** 4 BRAG 5 BOAST
    9 BRAGABOUT
**"Vaya Con ___":** 4 DIOS
**Vb.**
  form: 3 INF
  target: 3 OBJ
  Type of: 3 AUX IRR 4 INTR
**V-chip**
  target: 4 GORE PORN
**VCR**
  alternative: 4 TIVO
  button: 3 REC REW 4 PLAY
    5 EJECT PAUSE RESET
    6 REWIND
  connections: 3 TVS
  feature: 5 TIMER
  format: 3 VHS 4 BETA
  insert: 4 TAPE
  location: 3 DEN
  maker: 3 RCA 4 SONY
    5 SANYO
  The "V" of: 5 VIDEO
**Veal:** 4 MEAT
  cut: 4 CHOP
  serving: 6 CUTLET
**___ Vecchio:** 5 PONTE
**Veda**
  devotee: 5 HINDU
  language: 8 SANSKRIT
**V-E Day**
  celebrants: 6 ALLIES
  initials: 3 HST
**Vedder**
  Illustrator: 5 ELIHU
**Vedic**
  deity: 5 INDRA
  god of fire: 4 AGNI

**Vee, Bobby**
  hit song: 8 RUNTOHIM
**Veejay**
  employer: 3 MTV
**Veep**
  before Al: 3 DAN
  before Ford: 5 AGNEW
  of Coolidge: 5 DAWES
  of LBJ: 3 HHH
  of Nixon: 5 AGNEW SPIRO
**Veer:** 3 ZAG 4 SKEW 6 CAREEN
    SWERVE
**Vega**
  constellation: 4 LYRA
**Vegan**
  no-no: 4 MEAT 5 STEAK
  staple: 4 TOFU
**Vegas**
  area: 5 STRIP 8 THESTRIP
  attraction: 4 SLOT 6 CASINO
  calculation: 4 ODDS
  casino of old: 5 SANDS
  cubes: 4 DICE
  game: 4 FARO KENO
  Hot, in: 7 ONAROLL
  machine: 4 SLOT
  natural: 5 SEVEN 6 ELEVEN
  opening: 3 LAS
  Run off to: 5 ELOPE
  sign: 4 NEON
  TV show set in: 3 CSI
**"Vega$"**
  actor: 5 URICH
**___ Vegas:** 3 LAS
**Vegetable**
  Borscht: 4 BEET
  Cabbagelike: 4 KALE
  container: 3 POD 6 PEAPOD
  Creole: 4 OKRA
  fat: 4 OLEO
  fuel: 4 PEAT
  Gumbo: 4 OKRA
  Japanese: 3 UDO
  Leafy: 4 KALE 5 CRESS
  Pungent: 5 ONION
  Red: 4 BEET
  Root: 7 PARSNIP
  Salad: 4 CUKE 5 CRESS
    6 ENDIVE
  Soup: 3 PEA 4 LEEK OKRA
  sponge: 4 LOOFA
  spread: 4 OLEO
**Vegetable oil:** 5 ESTER
  part: 5 OLEIN
**Vegetarian**
  no-no: 4 MEAT
  staple: 4 TOFU
**Vegetation:** 4 ALGA 5 FLORA
  Like desert: 6 SPARSE
  Lush with: 7 VERDANT
**Veg out:** 4 LAZE LOAF LOLL
**Vehemence:** 4 HEAT 5 ARDOR
**Vehicle:** 3 CAR 4 AUTO
  All-purpose: 3 UTE
  Apollo: 3 LEM
  Army: 4 JEEP TANK

  Auctioned: 4 REPO
  Autobahn: 4 AUDI
  Celebrity: 4 LIMO
  E.T.: 3 UFO
  Family: 5 SEDAN
  Farm: 7 TRACTOR
  Grocery: 4 CART
  Iditarod: 4 SLED
  Metered: 3 CAB 4 TAXI
  Mine: 4 TRAM
  Moving: 3 VAN
  Musher: 4 SLED
  NASA: 3 LEM 7 SHUTTLE
  Off-road: 8 DIRTBIKE
  Olympics: 5 KAYAK
    7 BOBSLED
  Racing: 4 AUTO 6 GOKART
    7 RACECAR 8 DRAGSTER
    STOCKCAR
  Roomy: 5 SEDAN
  Sci-fi: 3 UFO 8 STARSHIP
  Seized: 4 REPO
  Swift: 6 SATIRE
  Urban: 3 BUS CAB 4 TAXI
  Winter: 4 SLED 6 SNOCAT
**Veil**
  material: 5 TULLE
**Veiled**
  oath: 3 IDO
**Vein:** 4 LODE SEAM 7 DEPOSIT
  contents: 3 ORE
  Leaf: 3 RIB 6 MIDRIB
  Leaf ~ space: 6 AREOLA
  seeker: 5 MINER
  site: 4 MINE
**Velcro**
  alternative: 4 SNAP 5 LACES
    6 ZIPPER
**Veldt**
  grazer: 5 ELAND HIPPO
  predator: 4 LION
  vacation: 6 SAFARI
**Velez**
  Actress: 4 LUPE
**Velocity:** 5 SPEED
  Meas. of: 3 FPS IPS
**Velodrome**
  vehicle: 7 BICYCLE
**___ Velva:** 4 AQUA
**Velveeta**
  maker: 5 KRAFT
**Velvet**
  finish: 3 EEN
  Lustrous: 5 PANNE
**Velvet Fog, The:** 5 TORME
**Velvety**
  growth: 4 MOSS
**Vena ___:** 4 CAVA
**Vena cava**
  neighbor: 5 AORTA
**Venae ___:** 5 CAVAE
**Vend:** 4 SELL 6 PEDDLE
**Vendetta:** 4 FEUD
**Vending machine**
  input: 4 ONES
  purchase: 4 COLA SODA

**Vendor**
stand: 4 CART
Street: 7 PEDDLER
**Veneer:** 4 COAT FACE FILM
5 LAYER 6 FACADE
**Veneman, Ann**
dept.: 3 AGR
**Venerable:** 3 OLD
one: 5 ELDER
ref. set: 3 OED
saint: 4 BEDE
**Venerate:** 5 ADORE HONOR
6 ADMIRE HALLOW
**Venerated**
symbol: 5 TOTEM
tribe member: 5 ELDER
**Veneration:** 3 AWE
**Venetian**
blind part: 4 SLAT
explorer: 4 POLO
magistrate: 4 DOGE
painter: 6 TITIAN
resort: 4 LIDO
taxi: 7 GONDOLA
villain: 4 IAGO
___ **Veneto:** 3 VIA
**Venezuela**
capital: 7 CARACAS
export: 3 OIL
Group that includes ~ (abbr.):
4 OPEC
Island near: 5 ARUBA
neighbor: 6 GUYANA TOBAGO
river: 7 ORINOCO
**Vengeful**
feeling: 5 SPITE
**Veni:** 5 ICAME
**Venice**
City near: 5 UDINE
Coin of old: 5 DUCAT
marketplace: 6 RIALTO
Resort near: 4 LIDO
**Venice-to-Naples**
dir.: 3 SSE
**Venison:** 4 MEAT
Like: 4 GAMY
source: 4 DEER
**"Veni, ___, vici":** 4 VIDI
**"Veni, vidi, ___":** 4 VICI
**Venner**
of fiction: 5 ELSIE
**Venom:** 4 BILE HATE 5 TOXIN
6 MALICE
Snake: 5 TOXIN
source: 3 ASP 5 SNAKE
**Venomous**
snake: 3 ASP 5 ADDER
COBRA KRAIT MAMBA
10 COPPERHEAD
**Venous**
prefix: 5 INTRA
**Vent:** 4 EMIT SLIT 6 AIRWAY
OUTLET
**Ventilate:** 3 AIR 6 AERATE
AIROUT
**Ventilated:** 4 AIRY 5 AIRED

**Ventilation:** 3 AIR
channel: 4 DUCT
source: 7 AIRHOLE
**Ventral**
Fish without ~ fins: 3 EEL
**Ventricle**
Left ~ attachment: 5 AORTA
**Ventriloquist**
Head-in-a-box: 6 WENCES
~ Bergen: 5 EDGAR
~ Lewis: 5 SHARI
**Ventura**
Former governor: 5 JESSE
**Ventura County**
city: 6 OXNARD
valley: 4 SIMI
**Venture:** 3 BET TRY 4 DARE
RISK
**Venue:** 4 SITE 6 LOCALE
Hockey: 4 RINK
Mead: 5 SAMOA
NYC opera: 6 THEMET
NYC sports: 3 MSG
Olympics: 4 OSLO
Roping: 5 RODEO
Skiing: 5 SLOPE
Sports: 5 ARENA
Workout: 3 SPA
**Venus:** 3 ORB 5 DEITY
6 PLANET
home: 4 MILO
neighbor: 5 EARTH
Sister of: 6 SERENA
Son of: 4 AMOR
**"Venus"**
pop group: 10 BANANARAMA
singer: 6 AVALON
**"Venus and ___":** 6 ADONIS
**"Venus and Adonis"**
painter: 6 RUBENS
**Venus de ___:** 4 MILO
**Venus de Milo**
lack: 4 ARMS
**Venus Flytrap**
radio station: 4 WKRP
**Venusian:** 5 ALIEN
(plural): 3 ETS
**"___ Vep" (1996 film):** 4 IRMA
**Vera**
Actress: 5 MILES
Fashion designer: 4 WANG
**Vera ___:** 4 CRUZ
___ **vera:** 4 ALOE
**Veracious:** 4 TRUE
**Veranda:** 5 PORCH
Hawaiian: 5 LANAI
**Verb**
Archaic ~ ending: 3 ETH
Biblical: 4 DOST DOTH HAST
HATH 5 HADST SHALT
Biblical ~ ending: 3 EST ETH
British ~ ending: 3 ISE
ending: 3 OSE
French 101: 4 ETRE
Latin 101: 3 AMO 4 AMAS
AMAT ESSE

preceder: 4 NOUN
Spanish 101: 4 ESTA
suffix: 3 ING
type (abbr.): 3 INT IRR 4 INTR
~, for one: 4 NOUN
**Verbal**
assault: 4 SLAM
gem: 3 MOT
hesitations: 3 ERS UMS
nudge: 4 PSST
white flag: 5 UNCLE
**Verbatim:** 7 LITERAL
Quoted: 3 SIC
Repeat: 4 ECHO 5 QUOTE
**Verbena:** 7 LANTANA
tree: 4 TEAK
**Verbose:** 5 GASSY WORDY
opposite: 5 TERSE
**Verboten:** 5 TABOO 6 BANNED
act: 4 NONO
(var.): 4 TABU
**Verdant:** 4 LUSH 5 GREEN
___ **Verde:** 4 MESA
**Verde Sao ___:** 5 TIAGO
**Verdi**
aria: 5 ERITU
genre: 5 OPERA
heroine: 4 AIDA
opera: 4 AIDA 6 ERNANI
OTELLO 8 FALSTAFF
solo: 4 ARIA
Very, to: 5 ASSAI MOLTO
villain: 4 IAGO
**Verdict**
Hand down, as a: 6 RENDER
Unjust: 6 BUMRAP
**"Verdict, The"**
actor Milo: 5 OSHEA
**Verdigris:** 6 PATINA
**Verdon**
Dancer: 4 GWEN
**Verdon, Gwen**
role: 4 LOLA
**Verdugo**
Actress: 5 ELENA
**Verdun**
Done, in: 4 FINI
river: 5 MEUSE
**Vereen**
Tony winner: 3 BEN
**Vereen, Ben**
musical: 6 PIPPIN
**Verge:** 4 EDGE 5 BRINK
Is on the ~ of: 5 NEARS
on: 4 ABUT
**Vergil:** 4 POET
epic: 6 AENEID
hero: 6 AENEAS
**Verifier**
Balance sheet ~ (abbr.):
3 AUD
**Verily:** 3 YEA 4 AMEN 5 TRULY
6 INDEED
**"___, verily!":** 3 YEA
**Verizon**
predecessor: 3 GTE

**Vermeer**
contemporary: 4 HALS
  5 STEEN
Painter: 3 JAN
**Vermin:** 4 LICE RATS 5 PESTS
Clear of: 5 DERAT
**Vermont**
city: 5 BARRE 7 RUTLAND
harvest: 3 SAP
patriot Allen: 5 ETHAN
product: 5 SYRUP
senator: 5 LEAHY
ski area: 4 PICO
ski resort: 5 STOWE
stop: 3 INN
**Vermouth:** 8 APERITIF
name: 5 ROSSI
**Vern**
Neighbor of: 6 ERNEST
**Vernacular:** 5 ARGOT LINGO
  SLANG
**Verne**
Author: 5 JULES
captain: 4 NEMO
genre: 5 SCIFI
traveler: 4 FOGG
**Vernon**
Dancing partner of: 5 IRENE
**Verona**
A gentleman of: 5 ROMEO
family name: 7 CAPULET
wine: 5 SOAVE
**Veronese**
painter: 5 PAOLO
**Veronica**
Actress: 4 LAKE 5 HAMEL
Supermodel: 4 WEBB
**"Veronica's Closet"**
actress: 5 ALLEY
  12 KIRSTIEALLEY
**Véronique:** 3 STE
___ versa: 4 VICE
**Versace**
Designer: 6 GIANNI
**Versailles**
agreement: 6 TREATY
Eye, in: 4 OEIL
ruler: 3 ROI
verb: 4 ETRE
Very, in: 4 TRES
**Versatile**
bean: 4 SOYA
Electrically: 4 ACDC
opener: 11 SKELETONKEY
transport: 3 ATV
vehicle: 3 UTE 4 JEEP
**Verse:** 4 POEM 6 POETRY
  STANZA
adverb: 3 EEN EER
Analyze: 4 SCAN
Japanese: 5 HAIKU
Narrative: 4 EPOS
on a vase: 3 ODE
prefix: 3 UNI
reciter: 4 BARD
tribute: 3 ODE

writer: 4 POET
**Versed:** 5 ADEPT
in: 4 UPON
**Versifier:** 4 BARD POET
**Version**
Basic ~ (abbr.): 3 STD
Easier ~, in music: 5 OSSIA
New: 6 REMAKE 7 REWRITE
Pop song: 5 REMIX
Similar: 8 ANALOGUE
Small: 4 MINI
Software: 4 BETA
**Verso:** 4 PAGE
counterpart: 5 RECTO
**Vert.**
opposite: 3 HOR
**Vertebra**
locale: 5 SPINE
Type of: 6 LUMBAR
**Vertical:** 5 APEAK
graph line: 5 YAXIS
Not exactly: 5 ATILT
Perfectly: 5 PLUMB
pipe: 5 RISER
stabilizer: 3 FIN 4 KEEL
~, at sea: 5 APEAK
**"Vertigo"**
actress Kim: 5 NOVAK
actress Novak: 3 KIM
**Verve:** 3 PEP 4 BRIO ELAN
  ZEST 6 ESPRIT SPIRIT
  7 PANACHE
**Very:** 4 MOST OHSO SAME
  SUCH 5 QUITE
~, in French: 4 TRES
~, in German: 4 SEHR
~, in music: 5 ASSAI MOLTO
**"Very funny!":** 4 HAHA
**Very much:** 4 ALOT 5 NOEND
  6 SORELY
**"Very well!":** 6 SOBEIT
**Vespasian**
Son of: 5 TITUS
**Vespers**
preceder: 5 NONES
time: 7 EVENING
**Vespucci**
Explorer: 7 AMERIGO
**Vessel:** 4 BOAT SHIP 5 CRAFT
15th-century ~: 4 NINA
  5 PINTA
Ablutionary: 4 EWER
Beer: 5 STEIN
Biblical: 3 ARK
Blood: 5 AORTA 6 ARTERY
Coffee: 3 URN
D-Day: 3 LST
Harbor: 3 TUG 7 TOWBOAT
Indian Ocean: 4 DHOW
Jason's: 4 ARGO
Kitchen: 3 POT
Lake: 5 CANOE
Large: 3 VAT
Ocean: 4 SHIP 5 LINER
Port: 3 VAT
Queeg's: 5 CAINE

Red Sea: 4 DHOW
Sailing: 4 YAWL 5 SLOOP
Spanish: 4 OLLA
That: 3 SHE
Torpedo: 5 EBOAT
Vintner's: 3 TUN VAT
Wine: 3 VAT 6 CARAFE
WWII: 3 LST 5 UBOAT
  6 PTBOAT
**Vest**
lack: 7 SLEEVES
**Vesta:** 8 ASTEROID
**Vestibule:** 5 ENTRY FOYER
  7 HALLWAY
**Vestige:** 4 DREG SIGN 5 RELIC
  SHRED TRACE
**Vestment:** 3 ALB 5 AMICE
Papal: 5 ORALE
**Vesture:** 4 ROBE
**Vesuvio**
City near: 6 NAPOLI
**Vesuvius**
City near: 6 NAPLES
output: 3 ASH 4 LAVA
Vent, like: 5 ERUPT
**Vet:** 3 DOC 4 EXGI 6 OLDPRO
  7 OLDHAND
  8 OLDTIMER
task: 5 SPAY 6 DEFLEA
text: 4 EDIT
theater, maybe: 3 NAM
**Veteran:** 3 PRO 6 OLDPRO
  7 OLDHAND
  8 OLDTIMER SEASONED
sailor: 3 TAR 4 SALT
  6 SEADOG 7 OLDSALT
**Veto:** 3 NIX 4 KILL 6 REJECT
  8 OVERRULE
Opposite of: 6 ASSENT
**Vex:** 3 IRK 4 GALL RILE ROIL
  5 EATAT 6 PESTER
**Vexation:** 3 IRE
___ vez (again, in Spanish):
  4 OTRA
**Vezina Trophy**
org.: 3 NHL
**V-formation**
group: 5 GEESE
  8 SQUADRON
**VFW**
Part of: 4 WARS
**VH1**
rival: 3 MTV
**VHS**
alternative: 4 BETA
**Via:** 3 PER 5 USING
**Via ___ (Rome):** 6 VENETO
**Viacom**
cable channel: 3 TNN
**Via del Corso**
locale: 4 ROMA
**Viagra**
alternative: 6 CIALIS
maker: 6 PFIZER
**Vial:** 6 AMPULE
**Viands:** 7 EDIBLES

**Via Veneto**
car: 4 FIAT
**Vibes:** 4 AURA
Pick up: 5 SENSE
**Vibrant:** 5 ALIVE
Not: 4 DRAB
**Vibrating**
effect: 7 TREMOLO
**Vibration:** 6 TREMOR
**Vibrato:** 7 TREMOLO
**Vic**
Radio wife of: 4 SADE
Singer: 6 DAMONE
**"Vic and ___" (old radio show):**
4 SADE
**Vicar of Christ:** 4 POPE
**Vice ___ :** 5 VERSA
**"___ Vice":** 5 MIAMI
**Vice president:** *see page 723*
First: 5 ADAMS
under Clinton: 4 GORE
6 ALGORE
under Coolidge: 5 DAWES
under Lincoln: 6 HAMLIN
under Madison: 5 GERRY
~ Agnew: 5 SPIRO
**Vichy:** 3 SPA
verb: 4 ETRE
Very, in: 4 TRES
Void, in: 3 NUL
water: 3 EAU
**Vichyssoise**
ingredient: 4 LEEK 6 POTATO
**Vicinity:** 4 AREA 6 LOCALE
REGION
In the: 4 NEAR 5 ABOUT
6 AROUND
**Vicious:** 4 EVIL 5 CRUEL
Punk rocker: 3 SID
**Vicksburg**
fighter: 3 REB
victor: 5 GRANT
**Victim:** 4 GOAT PREY
April 1st: 4 FOOL
Blight: 3 ELM
Corday: 5 MARAT
Genesis: 4 ABEL
of Brutus: 6 CAESAR
of deflation: 3 EGO
Pizarro: 4 INCA
Raid: 4 PEST 5 ROACH
**Victimize:** 6 PREYON
**Victor:** 5 CHAMP
Actor: 5 BUONO
Author: 4 HUGO
by one electoral vote: 5 HAYES
Comedic musician: 5 BORGE
Cry of a: 4 IWIN IWON
Gettysburg: 5 MEADE
initials: 3 RCA
___ Victor: 3 RCA
**Victoria:** 4 LAKE
Novelist: 4 HOLT
**Victoria Island**
explorer: 3 RAE
**Victorian:** 4 PRIM

expletive: 4 EGAD
time period: 3 ERA
type: 5 PRUDE
**Victorian ___ :** 3 ERA
**Victoria's Secret**
item: 3 BRA
**Victories**
Ring: 3 KOS
**Victorious:** 5 ONTOP
**Victory:** 3 WIN
Clinch, as a: 3 ICE 5 SEWUP
Easy: 4 ROMP ROUT
7 RUNAWAY
emblem: 6 LAUREL
goddess: 4 NIKE
Narrow margin of: 4 NOSE
One-sided: 9 LANDSLIDE
sign: 3 VEE
Unexpected: 5 UPSET
~, in German: 4 SIEG
**"Victory ___!":** 5 ATSEA
**"___ victory!":** 4 ONTO
**Victrola**
company: 3 RCA
**Victuals:** 4 EATS
**Vicuna**
home: 5 ANDES
kin: 5 LLAMA
Like the: 6 ANDEAN
**Vidal**
Author: 4 GORE
book: 4 BURR
character Breckenridge:
4 MYRA
**Vidalia:** 5 ONION
**Video**
dot: 5 PIXEL
Make a: 4 TAPE
meaning: 4 ISEE
network: 3 MTV
Old ~ format: 4 BETA
partner: 5 AUDIO
recorder, for short: 3 CAM
**Video game:** 6 PACMAN
TETRIS
adventurer: 5 MARIO
company: 4 SEGA 5 ATARI
Early: 4 PONG
hangout: 6 ARCADE
letters: 3 NES
**Video store**
offering: 3 DVD 6 RENTAL
section: 5 DRAMA SCIFI
6 HORROR
**Vidi**
meaning: 4 ISAW
**Vie:** 7 COMPETE CONTEND
**"___ Vie" (novel):** 3 UNE
**Vienna**
group (abbr.): 4 OPEC
home (abbr.): 3 AUS
**Vientiane**
land: 4 LAOS
native: 3 LAO 7 LAOTIAN
**Vier**
Half of: 4 ZWEI

preceder: 4 DREI
**Viet ___ :** 4 CONG
**Vietnam**
capital: 5 HANOI
coin: 3 HAO
dictator: 4 DIEM
general: 6 ABRAMS
holiday: 3 TET
neighbor: 4 LAOS
patrol boat: 8 RIVERRAT
port: 6 DANANG
suffix: 3 ESE
**Vietnam Veterans Memorial**
designer: 3 LIN 7 MAYALIN
**View:** 3 EYE SEE 5 SCENE
7 EYESHOT OPINION
Come into: 4 LOOM
6 EMERGE
Express a: 5 OPINE
Extensive: 5 VISTA
finder: 3 EYE
Have in: 6 INTEND
In: 4 SEEN
Inside: 4 XRAY
Nice: 3 MER
Open to: 5 OVERT
Panoramic: 5 VISTA
Point of: 5 ANGLE SLANT
quickly: 6 PEEKAT
Scenic: 8 PANORAMA
Skewed: 4 BIAS
**"View, The"**
cohost: 5 BEHAR
**Viewable:** 7 INSIGHT
**Viewer:** 4 EYER
MTV: 4 TEEN
**Viewpoint:** 5 ANGLE SLANT
6 ASPECT
page: 4 OPED
**Vigilant:** 5 ALERT AWARE
7 ONALERT
Wasn't: 5 SLEPT
**Vigilius**
Year of ~ papacy: 3 DLI
**Vigoda**
Actor: 3 ABE
**Vigor:** 3 PEP ZIP 4 BRIO ELAN
Lack of: 6 ANEMIA
Lose: 3 SAG
partner: 3 VIM
**Vigorous:** 4 HALE 5 PEPPY
6 HEARTY ROBUST
dance: 8 FLAMENCO
effort: 11 ELBOWGREASE
spirit: 4 ELAN
**Viking**
destination: 4 MARS
of the comics: 5 HAGAR
**Vikki**
Singer: 4 CARR
**Vile:** 4 BASE EVIL 5 NASTY
SLIMY 6 SORDID
smile: 5 SNEER
**Vilify:** 5 SMEAR 6 DEFAME
**Villa**
Russian: 5 DACHA

**Villa ___:** 5 DESTE
**Villa d'___:** 4 ESTE
**Villa d'Este**
  city: 6 TIVOLI
**Village:** 4 DORP
  African: 4 STAD
  Tiny: 6 HAMLET
**Village People**
  hit song: 4 YMCA
**Village Voice**
  award: 4 OBIE
**Villain:** 6 BADDIE BADMAN
  Biblical: 5 HEROD
  expletive: 6 CURSES
  Fairytale: 4 OGRE
  Greet the: 3 BOO 4 HISS
  Opera ~, often: 5 BASSO
  ~, at times: 7 SNEERER
**Villainous:** 4 EVIL MEAN
  look: 4 LEER 5 SNEER
**Villechaize**
  Actor: 5 HERVE
**Villon**
  offering: 5 POEME
    7 RONDEAU
**Vim:** 3 PEP 4 ELAN ZEST
    5 GUSTO
**Vin**
  choice: 5 BLANC
**Viña ___ Mar:** 3 DEL
**Vince**
  Country singer: 4 GILL
**Vincent**
  Actor: 5 SPANO
  Brother of: 4 THEO
**Vincente**
  Daughter of: 4 LIZA
**___ vincit amor:** 5 OMNIA
**Vindictive**
  goddess: 4 HERA
**Vine**
  Climbing: 3 IVY
  Tropical: 5 LIANA
**Vine-covered**
  area: 5 ARBOR
  passageway: 7 PERGOLA
**Vinegar**
  bottle: 5 CRUET
  Full of: 6 ACETIC
  partner: 3 OIL
  prefix: 5 ACETO
  radical: 6 ACETYL
  type: 8 BALSAMIC
**Vinegary:** 6 ACETIC
  Prefix meaning: 5 ACETO
**Vineyard**
  container: 4 CASK
  French: 3 CRU
  valley: 4 NAPA
**Vingt-___ (blackjack):** 4 ETUN
**Vinland**
  discoverer: 8 ERICSSON
**Vino**
  region: 4 ASTI
**Vintage:** 3 OLD 4 YEAR
  auto: 3 REO 5 ESSEX

~ Ford: 6 MODELA
~ Jag: 3 XKE
**Vintner**
  cache: 7 RESERVE
  dregs: 4 LEES
  Prefix used by a: 3 OEN
    4 OENO
  valley: 4 NAPA
  vessel: 3 TUN VAT
**Vinton**
  Singer: 5 BOBBY
**Vinton, Bobby**
  hit song: 11 ROSESARERED
    14 RAINRAINGOAWAY
**Vinyl**
  records: 3 LPS
**Viol**
  precursor: 5 REBEC
**Viola**
  kin: 5 CELLO
  range: 5 TENOR
  Valuable: 5 AMATI
**Viola da ___:** 5 GAMBA
**Violation:** 7 OFFENSE
  Commandment: 3 SIN
**Violent:** 4 GORY 5 ROUGH
    6 STORMY
  Like a ~ film: 6 RATEDR
  struggles: 6 THROES
  weather: 5 STORM
**Violet:** 5 PANSY
  Kind of: 7 AFRICAN
  Like a shrinking: 3 SHY
  prefix: 5 ULTRA
**Violin**
  holder: 4 CHIN
  Like a ~ bow: 6 ROSINY
  maker Amati: 6 NICOLO
  part: 4 NECK
  precursor: 5 REBEC
  string holder: 3 PEG
  stroke: 5 UPBOW
  Valuable: 5 AMATI STRAD
**Violinist**
  accessory: 5 ROSIN
**Violist**
  clef: 4 ALTO
**VIP:** 4 EXEC 5 MOVER
    6 CHEESE 7 SOMEONE
  Ambulance: 3 EMT
  Business: 3 CEO
  Campus: 4 BMOC DEAN PROF
  Capitol: 3 SEN
  Church: 5 ELDER
  Computer: 5 SYSOP
  Cotillion: 3 DEB
  Court ~, in 1995: 3 ITO
  Mideast: 4 AMIR EMIR
    5 EMEER.6 SULTAN
  Mosque: 4 IMAM
  Political: 4 BOSS
  Valhalla: 4 ODIN
  vehicle: 4 LIMO
**Viper:** 3 ASP 5 ADDER SNAKE
  feature: 4 FANG
  home: 4 NEST

sound: 3 SSS
**VIPs**
  Baseball: 3 GMS
  Courtroom: 3 DAS
  Hospital: 3 DRS MDS RNS
  Magazine: 3 EDS
  Radio: 3 DJS
**Vire**
  Town on the: 4 STLO
**Virgil:** 4 POET
  epic: 6 AENEID
  hero: 6 AENEAS
**Virgin:** 6 UNTROD
  Like a: 6 CHASTE VESTAL
    9 UNTRODDEN
  tycoon: 7 BRANSON
**Virginia**
  Author: 5 WOOLF
  city: 7 ROANOKE
  dance: 4 REEL
  family: 4 LEES
  North of: 5 OLLIE
  player: 3 CAV
  resource: 8 COALMINE
  senator: 4 ROBB
  settler: 5 ROLFE
  willow: 4 ITEA
**Virginia ___:** 4 REEL
**"Virginian, The"**
  actor Doug: 7 MCCLURE
  actor Gulager: 3 CLU
  actor McClure: 4 DOUG
  author Wister: 4 OWEN
**Virgin Islands**
  Smallest of the: 6 STJOHN
  Westernmost of the:
    8 STTHOMAS
  ~, for one (abbr.): 4 TERR
**Virgo**
  Sign after: 5 LIBRA
  Sign before: 3 LEO
  star: 5 SPICA
**Virgule:** 5 SLASH
**Virile:** 5 MACHO MANLY
  person: 5 HEMAN
**Virna**
  Actress: 4 LISI
**Virtue**
  Paragon of: 5 SAINT
  Symbol of: 4 HALO
**Virtuoso:** 3 ACE 4 WHIZ
**Virtuous:** 5 PURE 5 MORAL
    6 CHASTE
**Virus**
  African: 5 EBOLA
  carrier, sometimes: 5 EMAIL
  type: 3 RNA
**Visa**
  rival: 4 AMEX
  statement abbr.: 3 APR
**Visage**
  Villainous: 4 LEER 5 SNEER
**Viscosity**
  symbol: 3 ETA
**Viscount**
  superior: 4 EARL

**Viscous: 5** SLIMY
 substance: **4** GOOP
**Vise**
 part: **5** CLAMP
 Portable: **6** CCLAMP
**Vishnu: 3** GOD
 avatar: **4** RAMA **7** KRISHNA
 Rama, to: **6** AVATAR
 Sounds of: **3** OMS
 worshiper: **5** HINDU
**Visibility**
 problem: **3** FOG **4** HAZE MIST
  SMOG **5** SMAZE
**Visible: 4** SEEN
 Barely: **5** FAINT
 Become: **6** EMERGE
**Visine**
 units: **5** DROPS
**Vision: 4** IDEA **5** DREAM
  SIGHT
 Dull: **5** BLEAR
 Having keen: **9** EAGLEEYED
 Inner: **4** XRAY
 Night: **5** DREAM
 Person of: **4** SEER **6** ORACLE
 prefix: **4** TELE
 Range of: **7** EYESHOT
**Visionary: 4** SEER **6** DREAMY
  **7** DREAMER UTOPIAN
  **8** IDEALIST
 drama: **3** RUR
 words: **4** ISEE
**Visit: 3** SEE **5** GOSEE POPIN
  **6** CALLON DROPIN
  STOPBY STOPIN
  **8** CALLUPON
**Visited: 3** SAW **6** CAMEBY
**"Visit From St. Nicholas, A"**
 opener: **4** TWAS
 poet: **5** MOORE
**Visitor: 5** GUEST **6** DROPIN
 China: **4** POLO
 Christmas: **5** SANTA
 Holiday: **5** INLAW
 Sci-fi: **3** UFO **5** ALIEN
 Siam: **4** ANNA
**Visored**
 cap: **4** KEPI
 helmet: **5** ARMET
**"Vissi d'arte": 4** ARIA
 opera: **5** TOSCA
**Vista: 5** SCAPE SCENE
 Desert: **5** CACTI
**___ Vista**
 (battle site): **5** BUENA
 (San Diego suburb): **5** CHULA
**Vistula River**
 city: **6** WARSAW
**Visual: 5** OPTIC **6** OCULAR
 aid: **5** SPECS
 assent: **3** NOD
 illusions: **5** OPART
 prefix: **5** AUDIO
**Visualize: 3** SEE
**Vital: 3** KEY **5** ALIVE BASIC
  **6** NEEDED

 fluid: **3** SAP
 sign: **5** PULSE
 Some are: **6** ORGANS
 statistic: **3** AGE
 vessel: **5** AORTA
**Vitality: 3** PEP **4** ELAN LIFE
  ZING **5** OOMPH PULSE
  VERVE
 Lacking: **6** ANEMIC
 Lack of: **6** ANEMIA
 Lose: **3** SAG
**Vitamin**
 acid: **5** FOLIC
 bottle abbr.: **3** RDA
 prefix: **5** MULTI
 regimen: **7** ONEADAY
 supplement: **4** IRON
**Vitamin A: 7** RETINOL
 source: **8** CAROTENE
  **12** BETACAROTENE
**Vitamin B: 6** NIACIN
**Vitamin C: 4** ACID
 source: **3** ADE **4** LIME
**Vit. info: 3** RDA
**Vitro**
 In ~ items: **3** OVA
**Vittles: 4** CHOW EATS GRUB
**Vittorio**
 Director: **6** DESICA
**Vituperate: 5** ABUSE
  **7** CURSEAT
**Viva ___: 4** VOCE
**Vivacious**
 wit: **6** ESPRIT
**Vivacity: 4** BRIO DASH ELAN
  LIFE **6** ESPRIT
**___ vivant: 3** BON
**Vivarin**
 rival: **5** NODOZ
**"Viva ___ Vegas": 3** LAS
**Viva voce: 4** ORAL **5** ALOUD
**"Viva Zapata!"**
 star: **6** BRANDO
**"Vive ___!": 5** LEROI
**"Vive le ___!": 3** ROI
**Vivid: 5** LURID **7** GRAPHIC
 display: **4** RIOT
 red: **7** PIMENTO
**Vizquel**
 of baseball: **4** OMAR
**VJ**
 employer: **3** MTV
**V-J Day**
 It ended with: **4** WWII
 pres.: **3** HST
**Vladivostok**
 villa: **5** DACHA
**Vlad the Impaler: 6** DESPOT
**V-mail**
 address: **3** APO
**VMI**
 program: **4** ROTC
 student: **5** CADET
**V-neck: 7** SWEATER
**Vocabulary**
 Specialized: **5** ARGOT

**Vocal: 4** ORAL
 cords: **5** PIPES
 effect: **7** TREMOLO
 group: **5** OCTET
 part: **6** ARIOSO
 quality: **4** TONE
 range: **4** ALTO
 solo: **4** ARIA
**Vocalize: 5** SPEAK UTTER
  **6** INTONE
**Vocalized: 4** SUNG
**Vocally: 5** ALOUD
 expressed: **4** ORAL
**Vocation: 6** CAREER
**Voce**
 Not sotto: **5** ALOUD
 Viva: **4** ORAL **5** ALOUD
**___ voce: 4** VIVA **5** SOTTO
**"___ voce poco va": 3** UNA
**Vociferate: 4** YELL **5** SHOUT
**Vodka**
 (abbr.): **3** ALC
 brand, familiarly: **5** STOLI
 cocktail: **6** GIMLET
**Vogue: 4** RAGE **5** STYLE
  TREND
 competitor: **4** ELLE
 In: **4** CHIC **6** TRENDY
 No longer in: **3** OUT **5** PASSE
 photographer: **6** AVEDON
**Voice**
 above tenor: **4** ALTO
 a view: **5** OPINE
 below soprano: **4** ALTO
 Choir: **4** ALTO
 Give ~ to: **5** UTTER
 Like a whiny: **5** NASAL
 Low: **4** BASS **5** BASSO
 of Bugs: **3** MEL
 of Elmer: **3** MEL
 of Porky: **3** MEL
 quality: **4** TONE
 range: **4** ALTO BASS **5** TENOR
  **7** SOPRANO
 vote: **3** NAY YEA
 With a single: **5** ASONE
**Voiced: 4** ORAL SAID TOLD
  **6** SONANT
**Voice of America**
 gp.: **4** USIA
**"Voice of Israel"**
 author: **4** EBAN
**Voices: 4** ALTI **5** BASSI
**"Voices Carry"**
 pop group: **10** TILTUESDAY
**Void: 3** GAP **5** ANNUL
  **6** CANCEL NEGATE
  **7** INVALID
 Make: **5** ANNUL
 partner: **4** NULL
 ~, in Vichy: **3** NUL
**Voided: 5** UNDID
 tennis play: **3** LET
**Voight**
 Actor: **3** JON
 role: **6** COSELL

"Voilà!": 4 TADA 5 THERE
  6 PRESTO
Voir ___: 4 DIRE
Vojvodina
  resident: 4 SERB
Volatile
  liquid: 5 NITRO
  solvent: 5 ETHER
    7 ACETONE
"___ volat propriis" (Oregon
    motto): 4 ALIS
Volcanic
  crater: 7 CALDERA
  output: 3 ASH 4 LAVA
    5 MAGMA
  peak: 6 MTHOOD SHASTA
  rock: 6 BASALT
Volcano: 6 SPEWER
  Alaskan: 6 KATMAI
  Japanese: 4 FUJI
  Martinique: 5 PELEE
  output: 3 ASH 4 LAVA SLAG
  part: 4 CONE
  Sicilian: 4 ETNA 6 MTETNA
"Volcano Lover, The"
  author: 6 SONTAG
___ volente (God willing):
    3 DEO
Volga
  dweller: 5 TATAR
  outlet: 7 CASPIAN
  River to the: 3 OKA
Volkswagen
  model: 3 GTI 4 GOLF 5 JETTA
    6 PASSAT
  rival: 4 OPEL
Volley: 5 BURST SALVO
    7 BARRAGE
Volleyball
  birthplace: 7 HOLYOKE
  divider: 3 NET
  player: 6 SETTER
  smash: 4 KILL 5 SPIKE
Volt: 4 UNIT
Voltage
  letters: 3 EMF
Voltaire
  satire: 7 CANDIDE
  ~, religiously: 5 DEIST
Volume: 4 BOOK TOME
    5 ATLAS
  Metric: 5 STERE
  supporter: 7 BOOKEND
  Two-dimensional: 4 AREA
  unit: 4 SONE
Volunteer: 5 ENROL OFFER
    6 ENLIST 8 ENLISTEE

phrase: 4 ICAN 5 IWILL
Volunteer State
  (abbr.): 4 TENN
Voluptuous: 4 SEXY
Volvo: 4 AUTO
  competitor: 4 SAAB
von ___, Carl Maria
  Composer: 5 WEBER
von Bismarck
  Chancellor: 4 OTTO
von Bulow: 5 CLAUS
  portrayer: 5 IRONS
von Dohnányi
  Composer: 4 ERNO
von Furstenberg
  Designer: 4 EGON 5 DIANE
Vonnegut
  Author: 4 KURT
von Richtofen
  title: 5 BARON
von Sternberg
  Director: 5 JOSEF
von Stroheim
  Director: 5 ERICH
von Sydow
  Actor: 3 MAX
von Trapp
  family member: 4 KURT
    5 GEORG MARIA MARTA
  title: 5 BARON
von Trier
  Director: 4 LARS
Voodoo
  charm: 4 MOJO
  cousin: 5 OBEAH
Voom
  preceder: 4 VAVA
Vortex: 4 EDDY
"___ Vos Prec" (T.S. Eliot work):
    3 ARA
Vote
  Affirmative: 3 AYE YEA
  Decline to: 7 ABSTAIN
  French: 3 NON OUI
  German: 4 NEIN
  in: 5 ELECT
  Negative: 3 NAY
  out: 6 UNSEAT
  Russian: 4 NYET
  to accept: 5 ADOPT
  Type of: 4 ORAL
Voters: 10 ELECTORATE
  Like-minded: 4 BLOC
  problem: 6 APATHY
  Some: 4 INDS
Voting
  district: 4 WARD

group: 4 BLOC
no: 4 ANTI
place: 4 POLL
Voucher: 4 CHIT
Vous
  Verb with: 4 ETES
"___ vous plait": 3 SIL
Vow: 4 OATH 5 SWEAR
    7 PROMISE
  Altar: 3 IDO
  taker: 3 NUN 4 MONK
Vowel
  Greek: 3 ETA 4 IOTA
  group: 5 AEIOU
  slur: 5 ELIDE
  sound: 5 SCHWA
  Unstressed: 5 SCHWA
Vows
  Exchange: 3 WED
  Like some: 6 SACRED
    7 NUPTIAL
  Wedding: 4 IDOS
Voyage: 4 TREK TRIP
  end: 8 LANDFALL
  for the vain: 7 EGOTRIP
  preceder: 3 BON
  type: 6 MAIDEN
"___ voyage!": 3 BON
Voyager: 7 MINIVAN
Voyageurs Natl. Park
  locale (abbr.): 4 MINN
Voyeur: 6 PEEPER
VP: 4 EXEC
  of LBJ: 3 HHH
"VR.5"
  actress Singer: 4 LORI
V-shaped
  cut: 5 NOTCH
  fortification: 5 REDAN
Vt.
  neighbor: 3 QUE
___ vu: 4 DEJA
Vulcan: 5 ALIEN
  home: 4 ETNA
Vulcanologist
  study: 4 LAVA
Vulgar: 3 RAW 5 CRASS
  person: 6 SLEAZE
Vulgarian: 4 BORE LOUT SLOB
    5 YAHOO 6 SLEAZE
Vulnerable
  area: 10 UNDERBELLY
  hero: 8 ACHILLES
  to shooting: 7 INRANGE
Vulpine: 3 SLY
VW: 4 AUTO 6 BEETLE
  predecessors: 3 STU 4 RSTU

**W:** 8 TUNGSTEN
  Affiliation of: 3 GOP
  Brother of: 3 JEB
**W-2**
  info: 3 SSN 5 WAGES
**Wabbit**
  chaser: 5 ELMER
**Wacko:** 3 MAD NUT 4 DAFT
    LOON NUTS 5 LOONY
**Wacky:** 4 DAFT LOCO NUTS
    ZANY 5 AMISS 6 INSANE
**Wad**
  Tobacco: 4 CHAW
  Wallet: 4 ONES
**Wade**
  across: 4 FORD
  of baseball: 5 BOGGS
  opponent: 3 ROE
  through: 4 SLOG 5 SLOSH
**Wader**
  Everglades: 5 EGRET
  Marsh: 4 IBIS 5 EGRET
    HERON
  Pinkish: 8 FLAMINGO
  White: 4 IBIS 5 EGRET
**Wading**
  bird: 4 IBIS RAIL 5 CRANE
    EGRET HERON SNIPE
    STILT STORK
    8 FLAMINGO
**Wadkins**
  Golfer: 5 LANNY
**Wafer**
  Like a: 4 THIN
  Nabisco: 5 NILLA
**Wafer-and-creme**
  cookie: 4 OREO
**Waffle:** 5 HEDGE 6 SEESAW
  brand: 4 EGGO
  topping: 5 SYRUP
**Waffling**
  Stop: 3 OPT
**Wag:** 4 CARD 5 JOKER
    8 JOKESTER
  words: 4 QUIP
**Wage:** 6 SALARY
  Hourly: 4 RATE
  Minimum: 5 SCALE
**Wage ___:** 6 EARNER
**Wager:** 3 BET PUT 5 PUTUP
    STAKE
  Extra: 7 SIDEBET
  handler (abbr.): 3 OTB
  Place a ~ towards: 5 BETON
  Risked a: 6 STAKED
  type: 6 EXACTA PARLAY
**Wagered:** 4 LAID
  Amount: 5 STAKE

**Wagering**
  locale (abbr.): 3 OTB
**Wages:** 3 PAY 6 INCOME
  Like some: 6 HOURLY
**Wagga Wagga**
  resident: 6 AUSSIE
**Waggish:** 5 DROLL 7 JOCULAR
**Waggle**
  dancer: 3 BEE
**Waggoner**
  Actor: 4 LYLE
**Wagnalls**
  collaborator: 4 FUNK
**Wagner**
  Father-in-law of: 5 LISZT
  hero: 7 TRISTAN
  heroine: 6 ISOLDE
  of baseball: 5 HONUS
  opera: 6 RIENZI 8 PARSIFAL
  soprano: 3 EVA 4 ELSA
  Very, to: 4 SEHR
  work: 5 OPERA
**Wagon:** 4 CART DRAY
    9 CONESTOGA
  On the: 5 SOBER
  part: 4 AXLE
  track: 3 RUT
**Wagons-___:** 3 LIT
**Wagon train**
  direction: 4 WEST
**"Wag the Dog"**
  actress Anne: 5 HECHE
**Wahine**
  dance: 4 HULA
  feast: 4 LUAU
  gift: 3 LEI
  wear: 3 LEI
  welcome: 5 ALOHA
**Wahlberg**
  Singer: 6 DONNIE
**Waif:** 5 GAMIN STRAY
    6 URCHIN
**Waiflike:** 4 THIN
**Waikiki**
  locale: 4 OAHU
  wannabe: 5 HODAD
  wear: 3 LEI
  welcome: 3 LEI 5 ALOHA
  wiggle: 4 HULA
  wingding: 4 LUAU
  woman: 6 WAHINE
  wreath: 3 LEI
**Wail:** 3 CRY SOB 4 BAWL KEEN
    YOWL
  Dramatic: 4 ALAS
  Warning: 5 SIREN
**Wailer**
  Irish: 7 BANSHEE

Warning: 5 SIREN
**Waist**
  circler: 3 OBI 4 BELT
  type: 4 WASP
**Waistband:** 4 SASH
**Waist-length**
  jacket: 4 ETON
**Waistline:** 6 MIDDLE
  It lacks a: 9 TENTDRESS
**Wait:** 3 SIT 4 BIDE 8 SITTIGHT
  After a long: 6 ATLAST
  at the light: 4 IDLE
  impatiently: 4 PACE
  Lie in: 4 LURK 5 SKULK
  Long: 3 EON
  on: 3 SIT 4 TEND 5 SERVE
    6 ATTEND 7 CATERTO
  Some ~ for this: 3 CUE TIP
**"Wait ___!":** 4 ASEC
**___ wait:** 5 LIEIN
**Waite**
  Hall of Fame pitcher: 4 HOYT
**Waiter:** 6 SERVER
  Airport: 3 CAB 4 TAXI
  boss: 7 MAITRED
  burden: 4 TRAY
  French: 6 GARCON
  handout: 4 MENU
  helper: 6 BUSBOY
  on wheels: 6 CARHOP
  parting word: 5 ENJOY
  Place for a: 4 LINE
  request: 5 ORDER
  reward: 3 TIP
  type: 4 DUMB
**"Waiter, there's a fly ___**
    soup!":** 4 INMY
**Waiting:** 4 IDLE 6 INLINE
    ONDECK ONHOLD
    7 INSTORE
  area: 6 LOUNGE
    8 ANTEROOM
    9 GREENROOM
  period: 3 EON
  Reward for: 3 TIP
  room call: 4 NEXT
**"Waiting for ___":** 5 GODOT
**"Waiting for Lefty"**
  playwright: 5 ODETS
**"Waiting for the Robert ___":**
    4 ELEE
**"Waiting to ___" (McMillan**
    novel):** 6 EXHALE
**"Wait just a minute!":**
    4 WHOA
**Waitress**
  at Mel's Diner: 3 FLO 4 VERA
    5 ALICE

**Waits, Tom**
Sing like: 4 RASP
**"Wait ___ the Sun Shines, Nellie":** 3 TIL
**"Wait Until Dark"**
actor: 5 ARKIN
**Waitz**
Marathoner: 5 GRETE
**Waitz, Grete**
birthplace: 4 OSLO
**Waive**
your rites: 5 ELOPE
**Wakayama**
woofer: 5 AKITA
**Wake**
Begin to: 4 STIR
site: 3 AFT 6 ASTERN
up: 5 ARISE ROUSE
6 COMETO
**Wakefield**
cleric: 5 VICAR
**Wake Island:** 5 ATOLL
**Waken:** 5 ROUSE 6 AROUSE
rudely: 5 ROUST
**Waker-upper:** 5 ALARM BUGLE
6 ROUSER
**Wake-up**
call: 5 ALARM 7 AROUSAL
**"Wake Up Little ___":** 5 SUSIE
**Waking:** 5 ASTIR
**"Waking ___ Devine" (1998 film):** 3 NED
**Walden:** 4 POND
**Waldheim**
predecessor: 5 THANT
6 UTHANT
Secretary General: 4 KURT
**Waldorf**
salad ingredient: 4 MAYO
6 CELERY 7 WALNUTS
serving: 5 SALAD
**Wales**
capital: 7 CARDIFF
dog: 5 CORGI
Former Princess of: 5 DIANA
Motto of the Prince of:
7 ICHDIEN
symbol: 4 LEEK
~ John: 4 EVAN
**Walesa**
homeland: 6 POLAND
Polish leader: 4 LECH
**Walk:** 4 GAIT 5 AMBLE LEGIT
TREAD 6 HOOFIT
14 CONSTITUTIONAL
a beat: 6 PATROL
all over: 3 USE
back and forth: 4 PACE
Faster than a: 4 TROT
heavily: 4 PLOD SLOG
5 CLOMP STOMP TRAMP
TROMP
in the woods: 4 HIKE
It is used to ~ the dog: 4 YOYO
leisurely: 5 AMBLE 6 SASHAY
STROLL

like a cat: 5 PROWL
like a child: 6 TODDLE
like a duck: 6 WADDLE
Long: 4 HIKE
One learning to: 3 TOT
out: 4 EXIT QUIT
over: 6 STEPON
proudly: 5 STRUT
Shady: 5 ALLEE 7 ALAMEDA
Sloping: 4 RAMP
slowly: 5 MOSEY
softly: 3 PAD 6 TIPTOE
Space ~ (abbr.): 3 EVA
through water: 4 WADE
5 SLOSH
unsteadily: 4 REEL
Waterfront: 4 PIER
Where the elated: 5 ONAIR
Where to ~ very carefully:
6 ONEGGS
with effort: 4 PLOD SLOG
6 TRUDGE
**Walk-___:** 3 ONS
**"Walk ___" (Warwick hit):**
4 ONBY
**"Walkabout"**
director Nicolas: 4 ROEG
**"Walk Away ___" (1966 hit):**
5 RENEE
**"Walk, Don't Run"**
costar: 5 EGGAR
**Walked:** 4 TROD 6 STRODE
**"___ Walked Into My Life":**
4 IFHE
**Walker**
Author: 5 ALICE
Beat: 3 COP
Cartoonist: 4 MORT
Distiller: 5 HIRAM
New: 3 TOT
of football: 4 DOAK
Runway: 5 MODEL
~, for short: 3 PED
**Walker, Mort**
pooch: 4 OTTO
**Walkie-talkie**
word: 4 OVER 5 ROGER
**Walking:** 5 AFOOT 6 ONFOOT
difficulty: 4 GIMP LIMP
on air: 6 ELATED
papers: 5 THEAX 7 RELEASE
speed: 4 PACE
stick: 4 CANE
Way of: 4 GAIT
**Walking ___:** 5 ONAIR
**"Walking Man"**
of baseball: 4 YOST
**"Walking on Thin Ice"**
singer: 3 ONO
**"Walk Like ___" (Four Seasons hit):** 4 AMAN
**Walkman**
batteries: 3 AAS
maker: 4 SONY
**Walk of Fame**
sight: 4 STAR

**Walk-on**
role: 5 CAMEO
**"Walk on the Wild Side"**
singer: 4 REED
**Walkover:** 4 ROMP
**"___ walks in beauty ...": Byron:**
3 SHE
**Walk-up**
resident: 6 TENANT
**Walkway:** 4 PATH 5 AISLE
Covered: 4 STOA
material: 5 SLATE
Stadium: 4 RAMP
Tree-lined: 7 ALAMEDA
**Wall:** 6 STREET
Bounce off the: 4 ECHO
bracket: 6 SCONCE
British ~ builder: 7 HADRIAN
climber: 3 IVY
covering: 5 PAINT PAPER
décor: 5 MURAL
Defensive: 7 PARAPET
Drive up the: 3 IRK
6 MADDEN
hanging: 3 ART OIL 5 ARRAS
6 POSTER
hanging for an M.D.: 3 DEG
Hole in the: 4 SAFE VENT
6 SOCKET
layer: 4 COAT
Off the: 4 LOCO 5 DAFFY
NUTTY WACKO
Pass through a: 4 GATE
plaster: 5 GROUT 6 STUCCO
Put up on the: 4 HANG
recess: 5 NICHE
tapestry: 5 ARRAS
Word on a: 4 MENE
work: 3 ART OIL 6 POSTER
Writing on the: 4 OMEN
SIGN
**Wallace**
Actor: 5 BEERY
Actress: 3 DEE
Author: 3 LEW
cohort: 5 SAFER
of Reader's Digest: 4 LILA
Running mate of: 5 LEMAY
**Wallace, George**
Home of: 7 ALABAMA
**Wallach**
Actor: 3 ELI
**Wallboard:** 5 PANEL
**Walled**
~ Spanish city: 5 AVILA
**Wallenda**
patriarch: 4 KARL
**Waller**
Jazzman: 4 FATS
**Wallet**
items: 3 IDS 7 IDCARDS
material: 3 EEL 7 EELSKIN
stuffers: 4 CASH ONES
wad: 4 ONES
**Walletful:** 3 WAD
**Walleye:** 8 PICKEREL

**Wallflower**
Like a: 3 SHY 4 MEEK
   5 TIMID
**Wallop:** 3 TAG 4 BANG BELT
   DECK SLUG SOCK
   5 PASTE SMITE
Added a ~ to: 5 LACED
Packing a: 6 POTENT
**Wallow**
Place to: 3 STY 4 MIRE
**Walls**
Bouncing off the: 5 HYPER
Its ~ can withstand a lot of
   pressure: 5 AORTA
Like some college: 5 IVIED
**Wall Street**
Boesky of: 4 IVAN
deal (abbr.): 3 LBO
debut (abbr.): 3 IPO
deg.: 3 MBA
Good news on: 3 UPS 4 RISE
   5 RALLY
gp.: 4 AMEX NASD NYSE
index: 3 DOW
index (abbr.): 5 SANDP
letters: 4 AMEX NASD NYSE
optimist: 4 BULL
org.: 3 ASE
pessimist: 4 BEAR
purchase: 5 STOCK 6 OPTION
regulator (abbr.): 3 SEC
site: 13 STOCKEXCHANGE
transaction: 3 BUY PUT
   4 SELL 5 TRADE
whiz, for short: 3 ARB
worker: 6 BROKER TRADER
   7 ANALYST
worry: 5 PANIC
**Wally**
Bother of: 4 BEAV
Cookie maker: 4 AMOS
**Wal-Mart:** 5 CHAIN
competitor: 5 SEARS
   6 TARGET
founder: 9 SAMWALTON
founder Walton: 3 SAM
**Walnut:** 4 TREE
**Walpole**
title: 4 EARL
**Walrus**
feature: 4 TUSK
**Walsh**
Director: 5 RAOUL
**Walsh, M. ___**
Actor: 5 EMMET
**Walston**
Actor: 3 RAY
**Walter**
Army surgeon: 4 REED
Cartoonist: 5 LANTZ
Conductor: 5 BRUNO
Golfer: 5 HAGEN
Labor leader: 7 REUTHER
Singer: 4 EGAN
Thurber character: 5 MITTY
**Walter ___, Sir:** 5 SCOTT

**Walton**
Author: 5 IZAAK
daughter: 4 ERIN
Grandpa ~ portrayer: 4 GEER
   8 WILLGEER
of Wal-Mart: 3 SAM
**Walton, Izaak**
Pastime of: 7 FISHING
___ Walton League: 5 IZAAK
**"Waltons, The"**
actor Ralph: 5 WAITE
actor Will: 4 GEER
actress Corby: 5 ELLEN
character: 4 ERIN 6 OLIVIA
   7 GRANDPA
**Waltz**
King of: 7 STRAUSS
**Waltzing**
woman: 7 MATILDA
**"Waltzing Matilda"**
First words of: 5 ONCEA
**Waltz King, The:** 7 STRAUSS
**Wampum:** 5 BEADS
**Wan:** 4 ASHY PALE 5 ASHEN
   6 PALLID
Rather: 6 PALISH
**Wanamaker**
Actress: 3 ZOE
**Wand**
Conductor: 5 BATON
Majorette: 5 BATON
**Wander:** 3 ERR GAD 4 ROAM
   ROVE
about: 5 MOSEY
aimlessly: 4 MILL 5 DRIFT
   6 STROLL 7 MEANDER
   TRAIPSE
off: 5 STRAY
**Wanderer:** 4 HOBO 5 GYPSY
   NOMAD ROVER STRAY
   8 WAYFARER
Alley: 8 STRAYDOG
Web: 6 SURFER
**Wandering:** 6 ADRIFT
   ASTRAY ERRANT
   7 NOMADIC
**Wane:** 3 EBB LAG SAG
   5 ABATE
**Wang**
Designer: 4 VERA
**Wangle:** 7 FINAGLE
**Wankle:** 6 ENGINE
engine part: 5 ROTOR
**"Wanna ___?":** 3 BET
**"___ Wanna Do":** 4 ALLI
**"Wanna make ___?":** 4 ABET
**Want:** 4 NEED 5 CRAVE
   6 DEARTH DESIRE
badly: 5 COVET
to avoid: 5 DREAD
to know: 3 ASK
**Want ad**
abbr.: 3 EEO EOE
listing (abbr.): 4 APTS
**Wanted**
Help ~ notice: 3 SOS

**Wanted poster**
letters: 3 AKA
word: 5 ALIAS ARMED
**"___ want for Christmas":**
   4 ALLI
**Wanting:** 5 NEEDY 6 INNEED
company: 8 LONESOME
**"___ want is a room
   somewhere ...":** 4 ALLI
**Wanton**
look: 4 LEER
**Wants**
He ~ you: 8 UNCLESAM
**Wapiti:** 3 ELK
kin: 5 MOOSE
**War**
1899–1902 ~ participant:
   4 BOER
1950s ~ site: 5 KOREA
1960s ~ zone: 3 NAM
1967 ~ site: 5 SINAI
1991 ~ zone: 4 IRAQ
2003 invasion locale: 4 IRAQ
Act of: 3 TUG
correspondent Pyle: 5 ERNIE
Drawn-out ~ tactic: 5 SIEGE
ender: 4 PACT 6 TREATY
film, when tripled: 4 TORA
First Secretary of: 4 KNOX
Friend in: 4 ALLY
game: 8 STRATEGO
god: 4 ARES MARS
goddess: 6 ATHENA
Holy: 5 JIHAD 7 CRUSADE
horse: 5 STEED
party: 4 ARMY
Prepare for: 3 ARM
Pro: 4 HAWK
Religious: 7 CRUSADE
room item: 3 MAP
Side in a 1980s: 4 IRAN
stat.: 3 MIA
story: 5 ILIAD
~, to Sherman: 4 HELL
___ War: 4 MANO
**"War and Peace"**
actor Herbert: 3 LOM
author: 7 TOLSTOY
heroine: 7 NATASHA
**Warble:** 5 CROON TRILL
**Warbled:** 4 SANG SUNG
**Warbucks**
Annie, to: 4 WARD
henchman: 3 ASP 6 THEASP
ward: 5 ANNIE
**Ward:** 5 STAVE
Actress: 4 SELA
healers (abbr.): 3 MDS RNS
heeler: 3 POL
Hosp.: 3 ICU
off: 4 FEND 5 AVERT DETER
   REPEL
Satirist: 3 NED
**Ward-___ (politico):** 6 HEELER
**Ward ___, Julia**
Reformer: 4 HOWE

**Ward County**
seat: 5 MINOT
**Warden**
Kind of: 4 GAME
**Wardrobe:** 7 ARMOIRE
___ ware: 5 IMARI
**Warehouse:** 4 STOW 5 DEPOT
STORE
supply (abbr.): 4 CTNS
**Warfare**
Kind of: 4 GANG GERM
5 CLASS
tactic: 5 SIEGE 7 EMBARGO
**"WarGames"**
org.: 5 NORAD
**Warhead**
toter: 4 ICBM
**Warhol:** 9 POPARTIST
Artist: 4 ANDY
genre: 6 POPART
protegé Sedgwick: 4 EDIE
subject: 3 MAO 7 SOUPCAN
**"War is ___":** 4 HELL
**Warm:** 4 NEAR 6 TOASTY
TROPIC 7 AFFABLE
and comfy: 4 COZY SNUG
5 HOMEY 6 TOASTY
drink: 5 COCOA TODDY
Getting: 4 NEAR 5 CLOSE
Nice ~ time: 3 ETE
Set to keep: 5 ONLOW
the bench: 3 SIT
up: 4 THAW
up again: 6 REHEAT
welcome: 3 HUG 5 ALOHA
When it's ~ in Chile: 5 ENERO
**Warmer**
Egg: 3 HEN
Hand: 4 GLOVE 6 MITTEN
Winter: 4 WOOL 5 COCOA
SCARF STOLE
~, perhaps: 4 HINT
**Warm-hearted:** 4 KIND NICE
**Warmth:** 5 ARDOR
Without: 5 ICILY
**Warm-up:** 4 PREP 7 PRELUDE
**Warn:** 5 ALERT 6 TIPOFF
7 CAUTION
**Warner**
Chan portrayer: 5 OLAND
Revolutionary War hero:
4 SETH
**Warner ___:** 4 BROS
**Warner Bros.**
collectible: 3 CEL
creation: 4 TOON
toon: 4 FUDD
Work for: 7 ANIMATE
**Warning:** 5 ALERT 6 CAVEAT
TIPOFF
Advance: 5 ALERT
Fairway: 4 FORE
Fencer: 7 ENGARDE
Highway: 3 SLO 5 FLARE
Jungle: 4 ROAR
Library: 3 SHH

sign: 4 OMEN
10 DONOTENTER
sound: 3 GRR 4 HISS
5 GROWL SIREN SNARL
Studio ~ sign: 5 ONAIR
Theater: 3 SHH
Word of: 4 DONT
Words of: 5 DONOT 6 ORELSE
7 LOOKOUT
**War of 1812**
battle site: 4 ERIE
treaty site: 5 GHENT
**"War of the ___":** 5 ROSES
**"War of the ___, The":**
6 WORLDS
**"War of the Worlds, The"**
author: 5 WELLS
enemy: 4 MARS 7 MARTIAN
invader: 4 MARS 7 MARTIAN
**War on Poverty**
org.: 3 OEO
**Warp:** 4 SKEW
**Warp-knit**
fabric: 6 TRICOT
**Warplane:** 6 BOMBER
10 DIVEBOMBER
fleet: 6 ARMADA
**Warrant:** 3 LET
officer (abbr.): 4 BOSN
**Warranty**
purchaser: 4 USER
Without: 4 ASIS
**Warren**
Football player: 4 SAPP
Hall of Fame pitcher: 5 SPAHN
Jurist: 4 EARL
resident: 4 HARE 6 RABBIT
Wife of: 7 ANNETTE
**Warren, Robert ___**
Author: 4 PENN
**Warrior**
Female: 6 AMAZON
Fifth-century: 3 HUN
Japanese: 5 NINJA 7 SAMURAI
Olympian: 4 ARES
princess: 4 XENA
Trojan War: 4 AJAX 6 AENEAS
**"Warrior Princess"**
of TV: 4 XENA
**Warriors**
org.: 3 NBA
**"___ Wars":** 4 STAR
**Warsaw**
coin: 5 ZLOTY
native: 4 POLE
resident: 4 POLE
river: 7 VISTULA
**Warsaw ___:** 4 PACT
**Warsaw Pact**
Former ~ member: 4 USSR
**"War Scenes"**
composer: 8 NEDROREM
**Warship:** 7 FRIGATE
9 DESTROYER
danger: 4 MINE
group: 5 FLEET 6 ARMADA

Old: 7 TRIREME
projection: 3 RAM
**Wars of the Roses**
house: 4 YORK
**Wartime**
Detain during: 6 INTERN
sub: 5 UBOAT
**Warts**
and all: 4 ASIS
**Warty**
hopper: 4 TOAD
**Warwick**
hit: 5 ALFIE
Singer: 6 DIONNE
**Warwickshire**
forest: 5 ARDEN
**Wary:** 5 LEERY
**Was**
What: 4 PAST
~, in Latin: 4 ERAT
**"Was ___ blame?":** 3 ITO
**Wash:** 4 LAVE 5 BATHE
7 CLEANSE
against: 5 LAPAT
away: 5 ERODE
Bleed in the: 3 RUN
cycle: 4 SPIN 5 RINSE
Dry: 4 WADI
English river to the: 4 OUSE
out: 4 FADE 5 ERODE RINSE
room: 7 LAUNDRY
Run in the: 5 BLEED
thoroughly: 5 SCRUB
**Wash.**
bigwig: 3 SEN
hours: 3 PST
neighbor: 3 IDA ORE 4 OREG
**Washboard**
muscles: 3 ABS
**Washbowl:** 5 BASIN
**Washday**
brand: 3 ALL DUZ 4 TIDE
unit: 4 LOAD
**Washed-out:** 3 WAN 4 PALE
5 ASHEN FADED
**Washer**
Beach: 4 TIDE
companion: 5 DRYER
cycle: 4 SPIN 5 RINSE
Shore: 4 TIDE
**Washerful:** 4 LOAD
**Washing:** 6 LAVAGE
**Washington:** 4 CITY 5 MOUNT
STATE
(abbr.): 3 GEN
Actor: 6 DENZEL
airport: 6 SEATAC
and others (abbr.): 3 MTS
bill: 3 ONE
Bill in: 5 GATES
biographer: 5 WEEMS
Blues singer: 5 DINAH
city: 6 TACOMA 7 SPOKANE
10 WALLAWALLA
city, when doubled: 5 WALLA
gallery: 5 FREER

insider: 3 POL 8 POLITICO
Lyricist: 3 NED
Mrs.: 6 MARTHA
neighbor: 6 OREGON
paper: 4 POST
Part of a ~ address:
    15 ICANNOTTELLALIE
post: 10 SENATESEAT
Pres.: 3 GEO
product: 5 APPLE
river: 7 POTOMAC
Send to: 5 ELECT
sound: 5 PUGET
stadium: 3 RFK
successor: 5 ADAMS
summit: 7 RAINIER
What ~ could not tell:
    4 ALIE
wheeler-dealer: 3 POL
    8 POLITICO
**Washington, Denzel**
movie: 5 GLORY
role: 8 MALCOLMX
    15 HURRICANECARTER
**Washington Sq.**
School at: 3 NYU
**"Washington Week"**
airer: 3 PBS
**Wash n ___**: 3 DRI
**Washoe**
~ County seat: 4 RENO
**Washout**: 3 DUD 4 FLOP
**Washroom**: 3 LAV
**Washstand**
pitcher: 4 EWER
**"___ was in the beginning"**:
    4 ASIT
**Wasp**
home: 4 NEST
nest site: 4 EAVE
type: 3 MUD
    12 YELLOWJACKET
woe: 5 STING
**WASP**
part: 5 ANGLO SAXON
**Wassailing**
Go: 5 CAROL
quaff: 6 EGGNOG
song: 4 NOEL
**"___ was saying"**: 3 ASI
**Wasser**
Frozen: 3 EIS
**Wasserstein, Wendy**
heroine: 5 HEIDI
**Waste**: 4 LOSE SLAG 5 DROSS
    6 DEBRIS SEWAGE
allowance: 4 TRET
away: 3 ROT 5 ERODE
effort: 14 SPINONESWHEELS
Go to: 3 ROT
Lay ~ to: 4 RUIN
maker: 5 HASTE
not: 3 USE
pipe: 5 SEWER
receptacle: 3 BIN 6 ASHCAN
Smeltery: 4 SLAG 5 DROSS

time: 4 LOAF 6 DAWDLE
    DIDDLE
watchers (abbr.): 3 EPA
Wine: 4 LEES
~, as time: 4 KILL
**Wasted**: 4 ICED 6 STINKO
**Wasteland**: 4 MOOR 5 HEATH
**"Waste Land, The"**
monogram: 3 TSE
poet: 5 ELIOT 7 TSELIOT
**"Waste not, want not"**:
    5 ADAGE
**Waster**
Time: 5 IDLER 7 DAWDLER
**"Was to be"**
~, in Latin: 4 ERAT
**Watch**: 3 EYE 4 TEND 5 GUARD
    VIGIL
Adjust a: 3 SET
again: 5 RESEE
brand: 5 CASIO OMEGA
    SEIKO 6 BULOVA
chain: 3 FOB
closely: 3 EYE
    15 KEEPASHARPEYEON
display, briefly: 3 LCD LED
face: 4 DIAL
for: 5 AWAIT
innards: 5 WORKS
Limp ~ painter: 4 DALI
One to ~ in a pinch: 6 KLEPTO
over: 4 TEND
part: 4 FACE STEM 5 BEZEL
    STRAP
Place for a: 5 WRIST
pocket: 3 FOB
secretly: 5 SPYON
Something to: 4 STEP
sound: 4 TICK
the figures: 4 OGLE
the kids: 3 SIT 7 BABYSIT
type: 6 ANALOG
wide-eyed: 6 GAPEAT
winder: 4 STEM
**Watchband**: 5 STRAP
**Watchdog**
Airline ~ gp.: 3 FAA
breed: 5 AKITA
Ecol.: 3 EPA
Govt. narcotics: 3 DEA
org.: 4 SPCA 5 ASPCA
Rx: 3 FDA
Trucking: 3 ICC
TV: 3 FCC
Wall St.: 3 SEC
warning: 3 GRR
Workplace ~ org.: 4 OSHA
**Watched**: 3 SAW
Just: 5 SATBY
**Watcher**: 4 EYER
Bambino: 5 MAMMA
Junior: 6 SITTER
Kid: 6 SITTER
**Watchful**: 5 ALERT
    8 OPENEYED
one: 4 EYER

**Watching**: 7 ONALERT
Tanks for: 7 AQUARIA
**"Watching ___"** (Julia
    Louis-Dreyfus sitcom):
    5 ELLIE
**"Watch it, buster!"**: 3 HEY
**"Watch out!"**: 4 FORE
**Water**: 4 AQUA 8 IRRIGATE
Add ~ to: 6 DILUTE
balloon sound: 5 SPLAT
barrier: 4 DIKE MOAT
    5 LEVEE
Bath: 4 AVON
Bath ~ unit: 5 LITRE
bird: 4 COOT SWAN
Body of: 3 SEA 4 POND
    5 OCEAN 6 LAGOON
Burn with: 5 SCALD
cannon target: 6 RIOTER
carrier: 4 MAIN PAIL VASE
channel: 6 SLUICE
Clean ~ org.: 3 EPA
color: 4 AQUA
cooler: 3 ICE
edge: 5 SHORE
French ~ source: 5 EVIAN
gate: 3 DAM
Hard: 3 ICE 4 HAIL 5 SLEET
hazard: 4 REEF
High ~ alternative: 4 HELL
holder: 3 DAM JUG 4 PAIL
    VASE WELL 5 BASIN
    GLASS
Holy ~ receptacle: 4 FONT
Italian body of: 4 LAGO
It gets into hot: 5 PASTA
    6 TEABAG
It will not hold: 3 NET 5 SIEVE
Lake name meaning big:
    5 TAHOE
Land in the: 4 ISLE 5 ISLET
Leaves in hot: 3 TEA
Like running: 7 EROSIVE
Muddy the: 4 ROIL
Narrow body of ~ (abbr.):
    3 STR
Narrow passage of: 5 INLET
nymph: 5 NAIAD
park feature: 5 CHUTE SLIDE
pipe: 4 BONG MAIN
pitcher: 4 EWER
plant: 4 ALGA
platform: 4 PIER 5 WHARF
Playful ~ animal: 5 OTTER
prefix: 5 HYDRO
Put in boiling: 5 STEEP
Salt: 5 BRINE
Scottish body of: 4 LOCH
Search for: 5 DOWSE
skiing apparatus: 4 RAMP
Skip on: 3 DAP
slide: 5 CHUTE
source: 3 TAP 4 MAIN WELL
sprite: 5 NIXIE
tester: 3 TOE
Test the: 3 SIP

No: 3 NAH 4 ASIF IBET
UHUH 5 ICANT NEVER
6 CANTBE
10 NOTACHANCE
Not in any: 5 NOHOW
6 NOWISE
off: 3 FAR 4 AFAR RAMP
6 REMOTE
of walking: 4 GAIT
On the: 3 DUE 4 SENT
5 ALONG 7 ENROUTE
out: 4 AFAR DOOR EXIT
5 ALIBI 6 EGRESS ESCAPE
PORTAL
out there: 4 AFAR
Show the: 5 POINT 6 LEADIN
Smooth the: 4 EASE PAVE
The ~ things stand: 6 ASITIS
This ~ or that: 3 FRO
to go: 4 EXIT PATH ROAD
5 ROUTE 6 AVENUE
to go (abbr.): 3 RTE
to stand: 3 PAT
to the altar: 5 AISLE
to walk: 5 ONAIR
Under: 5 AFOOT BEGUN
7 STARTED
up: 4 RAMP STEP 5 STAIR
6 ASCENT
up the slope: 4 TBAR
9 CHAIRLIFT
Wild ~ to go: 3 APE
Wild ~ to run: 4 AMOK
with words: 4 TACT
Wrong ~ to run: 7 AGROUND
___ way: 3 INA
___ Way (Rome): 6 APPIAN
**Wayans**
brother: 5 DAMON 6 KEENEN
**"Way cool!": 3 RAD**
**Wayfarer**
stop: 3 INN
**Waylay**: 6 ACCOST
**Wayne**
Author: 4 DYER
Buddy of: 5 GARTH
**Wayne, Bruce**
butler: 6 ALFRED
cavemate: 3 BAT
home: 5 MANOR
~, to Batman: 8 ALTEREGO
**Wayne, John**
birthplace: 4 IOWA
film: 3 MCQ 5 HONDO
6 DAKOTA HATARI
7 BIGJAKE RIOLOBO
8 ELDORADO RIOBRAVO
THEALAMO TRUEGRIT
10 FORTAPACHE
14 SANDSOFIWOJIMA
15 LEGENDOFTHELOST
REUNIONINFRANCE
TALLINTHESADDLE
film, with "The": 5 ALAMO
genre: 5 OATER
9 SHOOTEMUP

nickname: 4 DUKE
role: 14 ROOSTERCOGBURN
title word: 3 RIO
**"Wayne's World"**
actor Carvey: 4 DANA
actor Mike: 5 MYERS
actress Carrere: 3 TIA
Where ~ began (abbr.): 3 SNL
word: 3 NOT
**"Way of All ___, The": 5 FLESH**
**"Way of the gods": 6 SHINTO**
**Ways**
partner: 5 MEANS
**Wayside**
stop: 3 INN
**"Way to go!": 7 NICEONE**
8 ATTAGIRL
**Wayward**
Like a ~ GI: 4 AWOL
**"Wayward Wind, The"**
singer Grant: 4 GOGI
**"Way We ___, The": 4 WERE**
**WB**
competitor: 3 UPN
network mascot: 4 FROG
sitcom: 4 REBA
**WBA**
official: 3 REF
outcome: 3 TKO
stats: 3 KOS 4 TKOS
**W.C.**
in the U.K.: 3 LOO
**Wd.**
part: 3 LTR SYL
**We**
As ~ speak: 3 NOW
**Weak**: 4 PUNY SOFT THIN
6 ANEMIC FEEBLE
7 FLACCID
brew: 8 NEARBEER
~, as an excuse: 4 LAME
**"___ Weak" (Belinda Carlisle
hit): 4 IGET**
**Weaken**: 3 EBB SAG SAP
4 FADE 5 ABATE ERODE
6 DILUTE 8 ENERVATE
**"Weakest Link, The"**
host Robinson: 4 ANNE
**Weakness**: 6 ANEMIA
9 BLINDSPOT
**"___ we all?": 5 ARENT**
**Wealth**: 3 FAT 5 MEANS
6 ASSETS RICHES
A lot of: 6 ESTATE
Inherited: 8 OLDMONEY
Source of sudden: 7 JACKPOT
**Wealthy**: 10 RAKINGITIN
WELLHEELED
contributor: 6 FATCAT
one: 4 HAVE 5 NABOB
~, in Spanish: 4 RICO
**Weapon**
Animal: 4 CLAW 5 TALON
Antitank: 7 BAZOOKA
Cavalry: 5 LANCE SABER
Caveman: 4 CLUB

David's: 5 SLING
Defense system without a:
4 JUDO
Fencing: 4 EPEE FOIL
5 SABER SWORD
Gangster: 3 GAT 4 SHIV
6 ROSCOE
Gaucho: 4 BOLA
Guided ~, for short: 4 ICBM
handle: 4 HAFT HILT
in Clue: 4 ROPE 8 LEADPIPE
REVOLVER
Jousting: 5 LANCE
Medieval: 4 MACE PIKE
6 POLEAX 7 POLEAXE
8 CROSSBOW
Mob ~: 7 GAROTTE
GARROTE
Nuclear: 5 ABOMB HBOMB
Olympic: 4 EPEE
Sci-fi: 3 RAY 5 LASER
6 PHASER RAYGUN
Sharp: 5 LANCE SABER
SPEAR
Slapstick: 3 PIE
Special Forces: 3 UZI
Sport: 4 EPEE
Take away a: 5 UNARM
Terrorist: 3 UZI
Tilting: 5 LANCE
WWII: 4 STEN
~, in French: 4 ARME
**"___ Weapon": 6 LETHAL**
**Weaponry**: 4 ARMS
**Weapons**: 4 ARMS
Big: 9 ARTILLERY
experiment, for short: 5 NTEST
Search for: 5 FRISK
supply: 6 ARMORY
7 ARSENAL
Supply more ~ to: 5 REARM
**Wear**: 5 ERODE SPORT
6 ATTIRE HAVEON
7 APPAREL
After-bath: 4 ROBE
a long face: 4 MOPE POUT
and tear: 3 USE
at the edges: 4 FRAY
away: 4 FRET 5 ERODE
6 ABRADE
Casual: 3 TEE
down: 4 TIRE 5 ERODE
6 ABRADE 7 TIREOUT
Formal: 3 TUX 5 TAILS
6 TUXEDO
Hard: 5 ARMOR
out: 4 TIRE
out your welcome:
8 OVERSTAY
Partner of: 4 WASH
Summer: 3 TEE
well: 4 LAST
___ wear: 4 MENS
**"___ we are!": 4 HERE**
**Wearily**
Walk: 4 PLOD SLOG

**Weariness:** 5 ENNUI
**Wearing:** 7 EROSIVE
Is: 5 HASON
**Wearisome**
Become: 4 PALL
**Wears:** 5 HASON
**Weary:** 4 BEAT FLAG LIMP
TIRE
Sound: 4 SIGH
**Weasel:** 3 RAT 5 SNEAK
6 FISHER
10 EQUIVOCATE
kin: 4 MINK 5 OTTER SABLE
6 MARTEN 7 POLECAT
out: 6 RENEGE
out of: 5 EVADE
type: 5 STOAT 6 ERMINE
word: 3 POP 5 MAYBE
**Weather:** 5 ERODE 6 ENDURE
8 ELEMENTS
Be under the: 3 AIL
forecasting aid: 5 RADAR
indicator: 4 VANE
Like some winter: 5 SNOWY
6 SLEETY
London: 3 FOG
map area: 3 LOW 4 HIGH
5 FRONT
map line: 6 ISOBAR
Mild, as: 5 BALMY
phenomenon: 6 ELNINO
LANINA
Prevailing: 5 CLIME
satellite: 4 ESSA 5 TIROS
stat: 3 LOW 4 HIGH
system: 3 LOW 4 HIGH
Under the: 3 ILL 4 SICK
Wet: 4 RAIN
**Weathercock:** 4 VANE
**Weatherman**
TV: 7 ALROKER
**Weatherspoon**
of the WNBA: 6 TERESA
**Weave:** 4 MESH
Partner of: 3 BOB
**Weaver**
apparatus: 4 LOOM
Basket ~ material: 5 OSIER
Fictional: 6 MARNER
Former manager: 4 EARL
of myth: 7 ARACHNE
reed: 4 SLEY
**Weaver, Charley**
hometown: Mount ___: 3 IDY
**Weaver, Sigourney**
film: 5 ALIEN
role: 10 DIANFOSSEY
sequel: 6 ALIENS
**Weavers, The**
One of: 6 SEEGER
**Web**
Access the: 5 LOGON
Bit of ~ programming:
10 JAVAAPPLET
conversation: 4 CHAT
letters: 5 EMAIL

Make a: 4 SPIN
master: 6 SPIDER
place: 4 SITE
pop-ups: 3 ADS
surfer: 4 USER 7 NETIZEN
user: 6 SURFER
user's need: 5 MODEM
**Web address**
(abbr.): 3 URL
ending: 3 COM EDU GOV NET
ORG
part: 3 DOT
start: 4 HTTP
**Webb, Karrie**
org.: 4 LPGA
**Webber, Andrew Lloyd:**
6 KNIGHT
musical: 4 CATS 5 EVITA
title: 3 SIR
**Weber**
One ~ per square meter:
5 TESLA
**Web-footed**
mammal: 5 OTTER
swallow: 4 TERN
**Web page**
feature: 4 LINK
Main: 4 HOME
**Web site:** 4 FOOT 5 ATTIC
Auction: 4 EBAY
help: 3 FAQ
language: 4 JAVA
unit: 4 PAGE
visit: 3 HIT
worker: 5 SYSOP
**Webster**
Emulate: 5 ORATE
Wordsmith: 4 NOAH
~, for short: 4 DANL
**Webster, Daniel:** 6 ORATOR
**Webster, Norma ___:** 3 RAE
**Webzine:** 4 EMAG
**Wed:** 3 TIE 5 UNITE
on the run: 5 ELOPE
**Wed.**
follower: 3 THU
preceder: 3 TUE
**"___ We Dance?":** 5 SHALL
**Wedded:** 3 ONE
**Wedding:** 4 RITE 5 UNION
anniversary: *see page 725*
announcement: 5 BANNS
band: 4 RING 5 OCTET
cake feature: 4 TIER
dance: 4 HORA
day sight: 4 LIMO
dessert: 4 CAKE
helper: 5 USHER
keepsake: 5 ALBUM
Like a ~ cake: 6 TIERED
Make ~ plans: 8 SETADATE
Many ~ guests: 3 KIN
page word: 3 NEE
ritual: 5 TOAST
seater: 5 USHER
shower: 4 RICE

site: 5 ALTAR 6 CHAPEL
symbol: 4 BAND
vow: 3 IDO
wear: 3 TUX 4 VEIL
6 TUXEDO
~ VIP: 5 BRIDE 7 BESTMAN
10 RINGBEARER
**"___ Wedding":** 6 BETSYS
**Wedel:** 3 SKI
**"___ we devils?":** 5 ARENT
**Wedge:** 4 SHIM
driver: 4 MAUL
Wheel: 5 CHOCK
**Wedges**
It has: 3 PIE
**Wednesday**
was named for him: 4 ODIN
___ **Wednesday:** 3 ASH
**Wednesday's child**
Fate of: 3 WOE
**"We Do Our Part"**
org.: 3 NRA
**Wee:** 3 LIL SMA 4 PUNY TINY
5 SMALL TEENY
6 MINUTE TEENSY
bit: 3 TAD 4 ATOM IOTA
MITE
hour: 3 ONE TWO 5 ONEAM
THREE TWOAM
6 FOURAM
hour flight: 6 REDEYE
hours: 4 LATE
one: 3 ELF TAD TOT 4 RUNT
TYKE 6 INFANT
worker: 3 ANT
~, in Scotland: 3 SMA
**Wee ___:** 3 UNS
**Weed:** 3 CIG
Biblical: 4 TARE
killer: 3 HOE 4 HOER
whacker: 3 HOE 4 HOER
**Week**
before Easter:
10 PALMSUNDAY
Big ~ in TV: 6 SWEEPS
Day of the ~ (abbr.): 3 FRI
MON SAT SUN THU TUE
WED
ending abbr.: 4 TGIF
~, in Spanish: 6 SEMANA
**Weekend**
getaway site: 3 INN
inits.: 4 TGIF
~ TV show: 3 SNL
**Weena:** 4 ELOI
**Weenie:** 4 NERD 5 TWERP
**Weep:** 3 CRY SOB
**Weeper:** 5 LOSER
of myth: 5 NIOBE
**Weevil**
home: 4 BOLL
___ **weevil:** 4 BOLL
**"We ___ Family":** 3 ARE
**"___ we forget ...":** 4 LEST
**"... we have seen his ___ the
east":** 6 STARIN

**Wendy**
  Dog of: 4 NANA
  Kidnapper of: 4 HOOK
**Wendy's**
  Went to: 6 ATEOUT
**"We ___ Not Alone":** 3 ARE
**Went**
  after: 4 SUED 5 SETAT
    WOOED 6 CHASED
    8 ASSAILED
  ahead: 3 LED
  alone: 6 SOLOED
  around: 7 AVOIDED
  astray: 5 ERRED
  bad: 6 ROTTED SOURED
  ballistic: 5 RAGED 6 LOSTIT
  down: 4 FELL SANK SLID
  fast: 3 RAN 4 FLEW HIED
    SPED TORE 5 RACED
    RANBY 7 SCOOTED
  for: 5 CHOSE LIKED
    7 AIMEDAT
    9 HOMEDINON
  gaga over: 5 LOVED
    6 ADORED
  off: 4 BLEW 5 ERRED
  off course: 5 YAWED
  out: 5 EBBED 6 EXITED
  out of business: 8 FOLDEDUP
  out with: 5 DATED
  over: 7 RANLATE
  too far: 9 OVERDIDIT
  too fast: 4 SPED
  under: 4 DOVE SANK
  undercover: 5 SPIED
  underground: 3 HID
  wild: 5 RAVED 7 RANRIOT
  with: 5 DATED
  wrong: 5 ERRED
**"___ Went Mad": Riley:** 4 EREI
**" ___ went thataway!":** 4 THEY
**"We ___ Overcome":** 5 SHALL
**"We ___ please":** 5 AIMTO
**Wept:** 5 CRIED
  **___ were:** 4 ASIT
**"___ Were a Rich Man":** 3 IFI
**"We're in big trouble!":**
    4 OHOH
**"We're number ___!":** 3 ONE
**"We're Off ___ the Wizard":**
    5 TOSEE
**" ___ Were the Days":** 5 THOSE
**"Werewolves of London"**
  singer: 5 ZEVON
**" ___ were you ...":** 3 IFI
**"Were you born in ___?":**
    5 ABARN
**Werner**
  Actor: 5 OSKAR
**Wertmuller**
  Director: 4 LINA
**Wesley, John**
  denom.: 4 METH
**West**
  Actress: 3 MAE
  Contest in the: 5 RODEO

end: 3 ERN
  Land ~ of Nod: 4 EDEN
  of Batman: 4 ADAM
**West ___:** 6 INDIES
  **___ West:** 3 MAE
**West, Mae**
  Final film of: 8 SEXTETTE
  Move like: 5 SLINK
  play: 10 DIAMONDLIL
  song: 10 MYOLDFLAME
  wraparound: 3 BOA
**West African**
  desert: 5 NAMIB
  republic: 4 MALI 5 BENIN
    GABON 7 NIGERIA
    10 IVORYCOAST
**West Bank**
  gp.: 3 PLO
**West Coast**
  sch.: 4 UCLA
  time: 3 PDT
**Western:** 5 OATER
  airline: 5 ALOHA
  alliance: 3 OAS 4 NATO
  capital: 5 BOISE SALEM
    6 HELENA
  classic of 1953: 5 SHANE
  elevation: 4 MESA
  film: 5 OATER
  friend: 4 PARD
  hat: 7 STETSON
  law group: 5 POSSE
  lily: 4 SEGO
  locale: 4 FORT
  moniker: 3 TEX
  Old ~ fort: 3 ORD
  omelet ingredient: 3 HAM
  plateau: 4 MESA
  resort lake: 5 TAHOE
  show: 5 RODEO
  star Lash: 5 LARUE
  tie: 4 BOLO
  timber: 6 REDFIR
  topper: 7 STETSON
  treaty org.: 3 OAS
  tribe: 3 UTE 4 OTOE UTES
  TV: 6 LAREDO
  wine valley: 4 NAPA
  wolf: 4 LOBO
  writer: 4 GREY 5 HARTE
  writer Grey: 4 ZANE
  writer Wister: 4 OWEN
**Western Athletic Conference**
  sch.: 3 SMU TCU 4 UTEP
**Western Australia**
  capital: 5 PERTH
**Westernmost**
  African capital: 5 DAKAR
  Aleutian: 4 ATTU
**Western Samoa**
  capital: 5 APIA
**Western Union**
  founder Cornell: 4 EZRA
**West Indies:** 5 ISLES
  island: 5 ARUBA 7 ANTIGUA
  language: 5 CARIB

music: 7 CALYPSO
  native: 5 CARIB
  sorcery: 5 OBEAH
**Westminster:** 5 ABBEY
**"Westminster Alice, The"**
  author: 4 SAKI
**West Point**
  alt.: 4 ROTC
  athletes: 4 ARMY
  frosh: 5 PLEBE
  sch.: 4 ACAD USMA
  student: 5 CADET
**"West Side Story"**
  actor Tamblyn: 4 RUSS
  actress Moreno: 4 RITA
  gang: 4 JETS 6 SHARKS
  girl: 5 ANITA MARIA
  Maria's friend in: 5 ANITA
  role: 4 TONY 5 ANITA
  song: 5 MARIA 7 AMERICA
    TONIGHT
  ~ Oscar winner: 6 MORENO
    10 RITAMORENO
**West Virginia**
  resource: 8 COALMINE
**"West Wing, The"**
  actor Rob: 4 LOWE
  award: 4 EMMY
  network: 3 NBC
  star: 5 SHEEN
  worker: 4 AIDE
**"Westworld"**
  actor Brynner: 3 YUL
**Wet:** 4 DAMP DEWY SOAK
    5 RAINY 7 MOISTEN
  bar: 4 SOAP
  behind the ears: 3 RAW
    5 NAIVE
  blanket: 7 KILLJOY
    11 PARTYPOOPER
  course: 4 SOUP
  Get one's feet: 4 WADE
  Like ~ ink: 6 SMEARY
  Like a ~ noodle: 4 LIMP
  nurse: 4 AMAH
  septet: 4 SEAS
  Sound of ~ impact: 5 SPLAT
  weather: 4 RAIN
  wiggler: 3 EEL
  zapper: 3 EEL
**"We ___ the Champions"**
    **(Queen hit):** 3 ARE
**"We, the Living"**
  author: 4 RAND 7 AYNRAND
**" ___ we there yet?":** 3 ARE
**"We ___ the World":** 3 ARE
**Wetland:** 3 BOG FEN
    5 MARSH
**"We try harder"**
  company: 4 AVIS
**"We've got trouble!":** 4 UHOH
**"We want ___!" (ballpark**
    **chant):** 4 AHIT
**Whack:** 3 BAT BOP HIT OFF
    RAP 4 BELT STAB SWAT
    5 SMITE

Out of: 4 AWRY 5 AMISS
    ASKEW 8 COCKEYED
**Whacker**
    Weed: 3 HOE 4 HOER
**Whale**
    Baby: 4 CALF
    Female: 3 COW
    finder: 5 SONAR
    First name of a: 4 MOBY
    group: 3 GAM POD
    Killer: 4 ORCA
    Kind of: 5 SPERM
    movie: 4 ORCA
    One in a: 5 JONAH
    SeaWorld: 5 SHAMU
    White ~ pursuer: 4 AHAB
**Whaler:** 6 SEAMAN
    direction: 4 THAR
    Melville: 4 AHAB
**"Wham!":** 3 POW 5 KAPOW
**Whammy:** 3 HEX
**Wham-O**
    fad item: 8 HULAHOOP
**Wharf:** 4 PIER QUAY
    locale: 4 PORT
    pest: 3 RAT
    worker org.: 3 ILA
**Wharton**
    deg.: 3 MBA
    grad: 3 MBA
    subj.: 4 ECON
    title character: 5 ETHAN
        FROME
    Writer: 5 EDITH
**What**
    a mess: 3 STY
    Give ~ for: 5 SCOLD
        7 TELLOFF
    Having ~ it takes: 4 ABLE
    In ~ way?: 3 HOW 5 HOWSO
    No matter:
        15 COMERAINORSHINE
    Then: 3 AND
    this is not: 4 THAT
    to do: 4 TASK 6 AGENDA
    we have: 4 OURS
    you eat: 4 DIET
    you will: 6 ESTATE
    ~, in French: 4 QUOI
    ~, in Spanish: 3 QUE
**"What?":** 3 HUH
    syllables: 3 EHS
    Words after: 5 ISAID
**"What ___!":** 4 AGAS 5 ADEAL
        AMESS
**"What ___ ...":** 3 THE
**"What ___ ?":** 4 ELSE
**"What, again?!":** 4 OHNO
**"What a Girl Wants"**
    singer Christina: 8 AGUILERA
**"What a good boy ___!":** 3 AMI
**"What am ___?" (auction**
        **query):** 4 IBID
**"What am I supposed to ___?":**
        5 DONOW
**"What a pity!":** 4 ALAS

**"What a rare mood ___":**
        4 IMIN
**"What a relief!":** 3 AAH
        4 PHEW
**"What are the ___?":** 4 ODDS
**"What a ride!":** 4 WHEE
**"What a shame!":** 4 ALAS
        6 TOOBAD
**"What a surprise!":** 3 OHO
**"What a week!":** 4 TGIF
**"What ___ can I say?":** 4 ELSE
**"Whatcha ___?":** 4 DOIN
**"What ___, chopped liver?":**
        3 AMI
**"What'd ___" (Ray Charles hit):**
        4 ISAY
**"What did I tell you?":** 3 SEE
**"What'd I tell ya?":** 3 SEE
**"What'd you say?":** 3 HUH
**"What else?":** 3 AND
**Whatever:** 3 ANY
**"Whatever":** 9 IDONTCARE
**"Whatever ___ Wants" (1955**
        **song):** 4 LOLA
**"What fools these mortals be"**
    writer: 6 SENECA
**"What ___ for Love":** 4 IDID
**"What ___ God wrought?":**
        4 HATH
**"What happened next?":** 3 AND
**"What have we here?!":** 3 OHO
**"What I Am"**
    singer Brickell: 4 EDIE
**"What ___ is new?":** 4 ELSE
**"What Kind of Fool ___?":**
        3 AMI
**"What Kind of Fool Am I?"**
    singer Anthony: 6 NEWLEY
**"What'll ___?":** 4 ITBE
**"What, me ___?":** 5 WORRY
**"What ___ mind reader?":**
        4 AMIA
**"What ___ now?":** 4 ISIT
**What's**
    expected: 4 NORM
    happening: 4 NEWS 5 EVENT
        TREND
    here: 5 THESE
    left: 4 REST 6 ESTATE
    more: 3 AND 4 ALSO
    up: 3 SKY
**"What's ___?":** 3 NEW
**"What ___ say?":** 4 CANI
**"What's ___ for me?":** 4 INIT
**"What's Going On?"**
    singer: 4 GAYE
**"What's gotten ___ you?":**
        4 INTO
**"What's in ___?": Shakespeare:**
        5 ANAME
**"What's more ...":** 3 AND
**"What's My Line?"**
    crew: 5 PANEL
    panelist Bennett: 4 CERF
    panelist Francis: 6 ARLENE
**Whatsoever:** 5 ATALL

**"What's the ___?":** 3 DIF USE
**"What's the big ___?":** 4 IDEA
**"What's this?":** 5 HELLO
**"What's up, ___?":** 3 DOC
**"What's ___ you?":** 4 ITTO
        6 EATING
**"What ___ that?":** 3 WAS
**"What the Butler Saw"**
    playwright: 5 ORTON
**"What ___ the odds?":** 3 ARE
**"What time ___?":** 4 ISIT
**"What've you been ___?":**
        4 UPTO
**"What was ___ do?":** 3 ITO
**"What was that?":** 3 HUH
**"What was ___ think?":** 3 ITO
**"What Women Want"**
    actor Alan: 4 ALDA
    actress Marisa: 5 TOMEI
**"Whazzat?":** 3 HUH
**Wheat:** 4 CROP 5 GRAIN
    Beat the: 6 THRESH
    bundle: 5 SHEAF
    covering: 3 AWN
    holder: 4 SILO
    husk: 4 BRAN
    Pasta: 5 DURUM
    Type of: 5 SPELT
**Wheaties**
    box figure: 7 ATHLETE
**Wheaton**
    Actor: 3 WIL
**Wheedle:** 4 COAX 6 CAJOLE
**Wheedler**
    tactic: 5 GUILE
**Wheel**
    alignment: 5 TOEIN
    Be at the: 5 STEER
    Big: 5 CHIEF NABOB
    Color ~ display: 5 TONES
    connector: 4 AXLE
    cover: 6 HUBCAP
    Engine: 3 CAM
    hub: 4 NAVE
    Kind of: 3 MAG
    man: 5 SAJAK 6 FERRIS
    part: 3 HUB RIM 5 SPOKE
    Pet on a: 7 HAMSTER
    shaft: 4 AXLE
    Ship: 4 HELM
    spokes: 5 RADII
    Spur: 5 ROWEL
    Take the: 5 STEER
    Tend the squeaky: 3 OIL
    tooth: 3 COG
    track: 3 RUT
    turner: 4 AXLE
**Wheelchair**
    access: 4 RAMP
**Wheeler-dealer:** 8 OPERATOR
    D.C.: 3 POL
    Wall St.: 3 ARB
**Wheelhouse**
    direction: 4 ALEE
**Wheeling**
    River of: 4 OHIO

**Wheelless**
vehicle: 6 SLEDGE
**"Wheel of Fortune"**
buy: 3 ANA ANE ANI ANO
5 VOWEL
category: 5 EVENT THING
6 PHRASE
choice: 4 SPIN
creator Griffin: 4 MERV
host: 5 SAJAK
quintet: 5 AEIOU
singer: 5 STARR
**Wheels:** 3 CAR 4 AUTO
10 AUTOMOBILE
Early: 5 TRIKE
Eccentric: 4 CAMS
Fast: 7 PORSCHE
Furniture: 7 CASTERS
Homes on: 3 RVS
Off-road ~, for short: 3 ATV
Teamster: 4 SEMI
Temporary: 6 LOANER
Upscale: 3 BMW
Vintage: 3 REO
VIP: 4 LIMO
**Whelk:** 5 SNAIL
**W. Hemisphere**
gp.: 3 OAS
**When:** 8 ASSOONAS
Back: 3 AGO
**"___ when?":** 5 SINCE
**"When ___ door ...?":** 3 ISA
**"When ___ eat?":** 4 DOWE
**Whenever**
you like: 6 ATWILL
**"Whenever":** 7 ANYTIME
**"When Harry Met Sally"**
actress Ryan: 3 MEG
director Rob: 6 REINER
**"When hell freezes over!":**
5 NEVER
**"When in ___ ...":** 4 ROME
**"When in Rome, ___ the ...":**
4 DOAS
**"When I put out ___"**
Tennyson: 5 TOSEA
**"When it's ___" (old riddle**
answer): 4 AJAR
**"When I was ___ ...":** 4 ALAD
**"When pigs fly!":** 5 NEVER
**"When ___ said and done ...":**
4 ALLS
**"When the frost ___ the**
punkin ...": 4 ISON
**"When the moon hits your eye"**
emotion: 5 AMORE
**"When We Were Kings"**
subject: 3 ALI
**"When Will ___ Loved":** 3 IBE
**"When You Wish Upon ___":**
5 ASTAR
**Where**
From: 6 WHENCE
to get down: 5 EIDER
to get off: 4 EXIT STOP
you live: 5 ABODE

~, in Latin: 3 UBI
**Where ___:** 5 ITSAT
**"Where ___?":** 3 AMI 4 WASI
**Whereabouts:** 4 AREA SITE
**"Where America's Day Begins":**
4 GUAM
**"Where Angels Fear to Tread"**
author: 7 FORSTER
**"Where Eagles Dare"**
actress Mary: 3 URE
gun: 4 STEN
**Wherefores**
Partner of: 4 WHYS
**"Wherefore ___ thou ...":** 3 ART
**"Where pines and maples**
grow"
Words before: 7 OCANADA
**"Where's ___?" (1970 film):**
5 POPPA
**"Where's Daddy?"**
dramatist: 4 INGE
**"Where's Poppa?"**
actor George: 5 SEGAL
**"Where the Boys ___":** 3 ARE
**"Where the heart is":** 4 HOME
**"Where there's ___ ...":**
5 AWILL
**"Where the Wild Things ___":**
3 ARE
**Wherewithal:** 5 MEANS
Lacks the: 6 CANNOT
Provide the: 5 EQUIP
**"Where ___ you?":** 4 WERE
**Wherry:** 4 BOAT
**Whet:** 4 HONE 6 AROUSE
**Whether ___:** 4 ORNO
**"Whether ___ nobler ...":**
Hamlet: 3 TIS
**Whetstone**
Use a: 4 HONE
**"Whew!":** 3 BOY MAN
6 IMBEAT
Reason to say: 8 NEARMISS
**Whey**
companion: 5 CURDS
**Wheyfaced:** 3 WAN 5 ASHEN
**Which**
By ~, in Latin: 3 QUA
person: 3 WHO
**Whichever:** 3 ANY
**"___ which will live in infamy":**
FDR: 5 ADATE
**Whiff:** 3 FAN 4 HINT ODOR
5 SMELL
Get a ~ of: 5 SCENT SMELL
SNIFF
king Ryan: 5 NOLAN
**Whiffenpoof:** 3 ELI
**Whig**
leader: 4 CLAY
orator William: 4 PITT
rival: 4 TORY
**While:** 8 SOLONGAS
A ~ back: 4 ONCE
After a: 4 ANON
away: 4 IDLE LAZE

Give for a: 4 LEND
In a: 4 ANON SOON 5 LATER
lead-in: 4 ERST
Once in a: 7 ATTIMES
Quite a: 3 EON 4 AGES
5 YEARS
**"While ___ it ...":** 4 IMAT
**"While you're ___ ...":** 4 ATIT
**Whillikers**
lead-in: 3 GEE
**___ whim:** 3 ONA
**Whimper:** 3 SOB 4 MEWL
PULE WEEP
**Whimsical:** 3 FEY 5 DROLL
**Whine:** 4 MEWL PULE
6 SNIVEL YAMMER
Rhine: 3 ACH
**Whinny:** 5 NEIGH
**Whip:** 3 TAN 4 BEST LASH
Like a: 5 SMART
mark: 4 WALE WELT
One with a: 5 TAMER
9 LIONTAMER
Riding: 4 CROP
up: 5 CHURN 7 PREPARE
**"Whip It"**
band: 4 DEVO
**Whiplash**
of cartoons: 7 SNIDELY
preventer: 8 HEADREST
**Whiplash, Snidely**
Emulate: 5 SNEER
**Whipped:** 6 BEATEN
cream serving: 4 GLOP
6 DOLLOP
dessert: 6 MOUSSE
up: 4 MADE
**Whippersnapper:** 5 WHELP
**Whipping**
boy: 4 GOAT
**Whirl:** 3 TRY 4 EDDY REEL
SPIN
Give it a: 3 TRY
**Whirling:** 5 AREEL ASPIN
water: 4 EDDY 6 VORTEX
**Whirlpool:** 4 EDDY 6 VORTEX
competitor: 5 AMANA
6 MAYTAG
feature: 3 JET
site: 3 SPA
**Whirlybird**
relative: 4 GIRO
whirler: 5 ROTOR
**Whirring**
sound: 4 BIRR
**Whisker**
Beat by a: 4 EDGE
**Whiskers**
Animal with: 3 CAT 4 SEAL
**Whiskey**
drink: 4 SOUR 6 ROBROY
9 MANHATTAN
follower: 4 SOUR 5 AGOGO
grain: 3 RYE
Kind of: 3 RYE 5 IRISH
Language that gives us: 4 ERSE

Noted name in: 5 DEWAR
Walker of: 5 HIRAM
**Whisper**
Furtive: 4 PSST
Stage: 5 ASIDE
sweet nothings: 3 COO
**Whispering**
No: 3 SHH
**Whistle:** 5 ALERT
blower: 3 COP REF 6 TOOTER
Blow the: 3 RAT 4 TELL TOOT
cord: 7 LANYARD
hour: 4 NOON
Kitchen ~ cause: 5 STEAM
Old ~ tune: 5 DIXIE
part: 3 PEA
sound: 4 TOOT 5 TWEET
**Whistler:** 3 REF 4 WOLF
6 ARTIST KETTLE
TEAPOT 7 REFEREE
9 TEAKETTLE
**Whistles**
partners: 5 BELLS
**Whit:** 3 FIG 4 ATOM IOTA
**Whitcomb**
Poet: 5 RILEY
**White:** 3 SEA WAN 4 ASHY
PALE 5 ANGLO ASHEN
SNOWY
animal: 6 ALBINO
Celtics great: 4 JOJO
cheese: 4 BRIE
chip, often: 4 ANTE
Choreographer: 4 ONNA
cliffs locale: 5 DOVER
Compliment of: 4 YOLK
Creamy: 5 IVORY
dwarf: 3 DOC
flag message: 5 TRUCE
fur: 6 ERMINE
Great ~ ___: 5 HERON
hat wearer: 4 CHEF HERO
5 NURSE
heron: 5 EGRET
house: 5 IGLOO
lie: 3 FIB
Little ~ thing: 3 LIE
Lustrous: 6 PEARLY
Milky ~ gem: 4 OPAL
oak: 5 ROBLE
of the eye: 6 SCLERA
poplar: 5 ABELE
sale item: 5 LINEN SHEET
TOWEL
Silvery: 6 ARGENT
The other ~ meat: 4 PORK
Verbal ~ flag: 5 UNCLE
vestment: 3 ALB 5 AMICE
wader: 4 IBIS 5 EGRET
water: 6 RAPIDS
whale pursuer: 4 AHAB
wine: 5 PINOT RHINE SOAVE
8 SAUTERNE
wine aperitif: 3 KIR
**White ___:** 3 ANT SOX
5 NOISE

**White, Perry:** 5 CHIEF
6 EDITOR
employee: 8 LOISLANE
**White, Snow**
and the dwarfs: 5 OCTET
**Whiteboard**
wiper: 6 ERASER
**"White Christmas"**
Danny of: 4 KAYE
The "white" of: 4 SNOW
**Whiteclaw**
Journalist: 4 REID
**White Cloud**
People of: 4 IOWA
**White-collar**
crook: 5 KITER
worker: 6 CLERIC PRIEST
**"White Fang"**
author: 6 LONDON
**Whitefish:** 4 CHUB 5 CISCO
**White-haired**
fellow: 7 GRANDPA
**Whitehall**
whitewall: 4 TYRE
**Whitehorse**
Chief: 4 OTOE
**White House**
dog: 3 HER HIM 4 FALA
monogram: 3 DDE FDR HST
RMN
nickname: 3 ABE CAL IKE
RON
spokesman Fleischer: 3 ARI
staffer: 4 AIDE
~ Office: 4 OVAL
~ Room: 4 EAST 5 GREEN
~ Spring: 4 FALA
**White Rabbit:** 6 ALBINO
cry: 6 IMLATE
Like the: 4 LATE
**Whites**
Flash the pearly: 5 SMILE
Pearly: 5 TEETH
**Whitetail:** 4 DEER
**White-tailed**
bird: 3 ERN 4 ERNE
**Whitewash:** 4 HIDE LIME
7 COVERUP
**Whitewater**
craft: 4 RAFT 5 CANOE
KAYAK
~ VIP: 5 STARR
**Whitey**
teammate: 4 YOGI
**Whitman**
bloomer: 5 LILAC
Poet: 4 WALT
**Whitman, C. Todd**
org.: 3 EPA
**Whitney**
and others (abbr.): 3 MTS
Author: 4 OTTO
invention: 9 COTTONGIN
Inventor: 3 ELI
Partner of ~ in planes:
5 PRATT

**Whittle:** 4 PARE
away: 5 ERODE
**Whitty, May**
title: 4 DAME
**Whiz:** 3 ACE PRO ZIP 4 GURU
5 MAVEN SPEED
6 EXPERT
Computer: 6 TECHIE
Electronics: 6 TECHIE
Gee: 4 GOSH
opener: 3 GEE
Shorthand: 5 STENO
Tennis: 4 ACER
Wall St.: 3 ARB
**Who**
follower: 3 AMI
**"Who ___?":** 3 DAT 4 ISIT
6 DOESNT
**"___ who?":** 3 SEZ
**Who, The**
Like ~, in the 1960s: 3 MOD
Townshend of: 4 PETE
**"Whoa, ___!":** 6 NELLIE
**"Who am ___ judge?":** 3 ITO
**"Who am ___ say?":** 3 ITO
**"Who cares?":** 6 SOWHAT
**"Who Do You Love?"**
singer: 9 BODIDDLEY
**Whodunit**
plot element: 6 MOTIVE
suspect: 4 HEIR
terrier: 4 ASTA
**"Who goes there?"**
Word before: 4 HALT
**"Who is there?"**
reply: 5 ITSME
**"Who knew?!":**
10 IHADNOIDEA
**Whole:** 3 ONE 6 ENTIRE
INTACT 7 UNITARY
As a: 5 INALL 6 ENBLOC
bunch: 3 TON 4 ALOT LOTS
RAFT SCAD SLEW
6 OCEANS 9 AGGREGATE
Double ~ note: 5 BREVE
lot: 3 TON 4 RAFT SCAD
SLEW 6 OCEANS
9 AGGREGATE
Make: 4 HEAL MEND
number: 7 INTEGER
Opposite of: 6 NONFAT
Part of a: 4 UNIT
slew of: 8 ZILLIONS
The ~ shebang: 3 ALL 4 ATOZ
**"Whole ___ Love" (1970 hit):**
5 LOTTA
**"Whole ___ Shakin' Goin' On":**
5 LOTTA
**"Who Let the Dogs Out"**
band: 7 BAHAMEN
**Wholly:** 3 ALL 6 INTOTO
absorbed: 4 RAPT
**"Who, me?":** 3 MOI
**Whoop:** 4 YELL 5 SHOUT
YAHOO
it up: 5 PARTY REVEL

**Whoop-de-do:** 4 STIR
　5 HOOHA
**Whooped:** 5 SMOTE
**"Whoopee!":** 3 YAY 6 HURRAY
**Whooping**
　bird: 5 CRANE
**"Whoops!":** 4 OHOH UHOH
**Whopper:** 3 LIE 4 LULU TALE
　YARN
　rival: 6 BIGMAC
　teller: 4 LIAR
　topper: 5 ONION 7 KETCHUP
**"Who's Afraid of Virginia
　Woolf?"**
　playwright: 5 ALBEE
**"Whose Life ___ Anyway?"
　(1981 movie):** 4 ISIT
**"Who's on ___?":** 5 FIRST
**"Who's on First?"**
　comic: 6 ABBOTT
**"Who's That Girl?"**
　rapper: 3 EVE
**"Who's the Boss?"**
　costar: 5 DANZA
　role: 4 MONA
**"Who's there?"**
　response: 5 ITISI ITSME
**"Who's Who"**
　entry: 3 BIO
**"Who Wants to Be a
　Millionaire"**
　network: 3 ABC
　option: 8 LIFELINE
**"Who ___ we kidding?":** 3 ARE
**"Who ___ you?":** 3 ARE
**Whup:** 3 TAN 4 BEAT FLOG
　LICK
**Why:** 6 REASON
**"Why don't we ?":** 4 LETS
**"Why not?":** 4 OKAY SURE
**"Why should ___?":** 5 ICARE
**"Why should ___ you?":** 4 ILET
**"Why would ___?":** 4 ILIE
**Wiccan:** 8 PAGANIST
**Wichita**
　winter hrs.: 3 CST
**Wicked:** 4 EVIL VILE
　6 UNHOLY
**"Wicked Game"**
　singer Chris: 5 ISAAK
**Wicker**
　material: 6 RATTAN
　palm: 6 RATTAN
　source: 5 OSIER
　willow: 5 OSIER
**Wicket**
　Cricket: 3 END
**Wickiup:** 3 HUT
**Wide**
　belt: 4 SASH
　body: 3 SEA
　Give a ~ berth: 5 AVOID
　key: 5 ENTER
　of the mark: 3 OFF 6 ERRANT
　Open: 4 GAPE YAWN
　opening: 5 AGAPE 6 GAPING

　Partner of: 3 FAR
　shoe size: 3 EEE
　tie: 5 ASCOT
**Wide-area**
　alert: 3 APB
**Widebody:** 3 JET
**Wide-eyed:** 4 AGOG GAGA
　5 ALERT
**Widen:** 4 REAM 5 FLARE
　6 DILATE
**"Wide Sargasso Sea"**
　author Jean: 4 RHYS
**"___ Wide Shut":** 4 EYES
**Widespread:** 4 RIFE VAST
　5 BROAD 7 GENERAL
　RAMPANT 8 EPIDEMIC
　damage: 5 HAVOC
**"Wide World of Sports"**
　creator Arledge: 5 ROONE
**Width**
　Lacking ~ and depth:
　4 ONED
　Length ×: 4 AREA
　Shoe: 3 EEE
**___ Wiedersehen:** 3 AUF
**Wield:** 3 PLY USE 5 EXERT
　6 EMPLOY
**Wiener**
　holder: 4 ROLL
**Wiener schnitzel**
　meat: 4 VEAL
**Wiesbaden**
　state: 5 HESSE
**Wiesel**
　birthplace: 7 ROMANIA
　Nobelist: 4 ELIE
**Wiest**
　Oscar winner: 6 DIANNE
**Wife:** 3 MRS 4 MATE 5 WOMAN
　6 MISSUS 7 OLDLADY
　Run for your: 5 ELOPE
　~, in legalese: 4 UXOR
**Wiggle**
　room: 4 PLAY 6 LEEWAY
　Wahine: 4 HULA
　Waikiki: 4 HULA
**Wiggy**
　Get all: 9 GOBANANAS
**Wight:** 4 ISLE
**Wigwam:** 4 TENT 5 TEPEE
**Wilcox, ___ Wheeler**
　Poet: 4 ELLA
**Wild:** 4 AMOK ZANY 5 FERAL
　OUTRE 6 MADCAP
　SAVAGE UNTAME
　7 LAWLESS UNTAMED
　about: 4 INTO
　animal home: 4 LAIR
　animal trail: 5 SPOOR
　blue yonder: 3 SKY 5 ETHER
　bugler: 3 ELK
　bunch: 3 MOB 4 PACK
　Call of the: 4 ROAR
　cat: 4 LION PUMA
　dog: 5 DINGO 6 JACKAL
　fancy: 5 DREAM

　Go: 4 RIOT 7 RUNAMOK
　goat: 4 IBEX
　Going: 7 ONATEAR
　guess: 4 SHOT STAB
　Not: 4 SANE TAME 5 STAID
　party: 4 BASH ORGY RAVE
　5 BLAST
　pig: 4 BOAR
　plum: 4 SLOE
　Running: 4 AMOK 5 ARIOT
　They may be: 4 OATS
　6 DEUCES
　thing: 6 SAVAGE
　throw: 5 ERROR
　time: 5 SPREE
　way to go: 3 APE
　way to run: 4 AMOK
**Wildcat**
　Short-tailed: 4 LYNX
　Spotted: 6 OCELOT
　strike: 3 OIL
**Wildcats**
　of the Big 12 Conf.: 3 KSU
　org.: 4 NCAA
**Wildcatter**
　dream: 6 GUSHER
　find: 3 OIL
**"Wild Duck, The"**
　playwright: 5 IBSEN
**Wilde**
　forte: 5 FARCE
　genre: 5 FARCE
　play: 6 SALOME
　quality: 3 WIT
　Writer: 5 OSCAR
**Wildebeest:** 3 GNU
**Wilder**
　Actor: 4 GENE
　Author: 5 LAURA
**Wilderness Road**
　blazer: 5 BOONE
**Wildflower**
　Yellow: 9 BUTTERCUP
**Wildlife**
　marker: 6 EARTAG
　refuge: 4 LAIR
**"Wild Swans at Coole, The"**
　poet: 5 YEATS
**"Wild Thing"**
　rapper: 7 TONELOC
**Wild West:** 3 MAE
　justice: 5 NOOSE
　knot: 5 NOOSE
　showman: 4 CODY
　vehicle: 5 STAGE
　watering hole: 6 SALOON
**Wile E. Coyote**
　Supply company to: 4 ACME
**Wilhelm**
　Hall of Fame pitcher: 4 HOYT
**Wilkes-___, Pennsylvania:**
　5 BARRE
**Will**
　be, in song: 4 SERA
　beneficiary: 4 HEIR
　Having a: 7 TESTATE

Ill: 3 IRE 4 HATE 5 SPITE
  6 ANIMUS ENMITY
  MALICE RANCOR
matter: 6 ESTATE
subject: 6 ESTATE
supplement: 7 CODICIL
What you: 6 ESTATE
**Willa**
Novelist: 6 CATHER
**Willamette**
Capital on the: 5 SALEM
**"Will & Grace"**
actor McCormack: 4 ERIC
actress Messing: 5 DEBRA
actress Mullally: 5 MEGAN
Grace on: 5 ADLER
Maid on: 7 ROSARIO
**Willard**
Boxing champ: 4 JESS
**"Will be"**
What ~ will be: 3 ARE
Word before and after: 4 BOYS
"___ will be done ...": 3 THY
**Willem**
Actor: 5 DEFOE
**Willful:** 10 HEADSTRONG
**Willfully**
Behave: 5 ACTUP
**William:** 6 PRINCE
Actor: 6 DEVANE
Archer: 4 TELL
Bathysphere designer:
  5 BEEBE
Ex-Defense Secretary:
  5 COHEN
Mother of: 5 DIANA
of westerns: 4 BOYD
Playwright: 4 INGE
Quaker: 4 PENN
**William ___, Sir:** 5 OSLER
**William of ___:** 5 OCCAM
**William Randolph**
Publisher: 6 HEARST
**Williams**
Actress: 6 JOBETH
Adventure hero: 4 REMO
of baseball: 3 TED
of tennis: 5 VENUS
  6 SERENA
Singer: 4 ANDY
Talk host: 6 MONTEL
title start: 5 CATON
  6 CATONA
**Williams, Andy**
hit tune: 9 DEARHEART
  10 LIPSOFWINE
**Williams, Billy ___**
Actor: 3 DEE
**Williams, Robin**
film: 4 TOYS 7 ALADDIN
  JUMANJI
  10 PATCHADAMS
film role: 4 GARP 5 GENIE
~ TV role: 4 MORK
**Williams, Ted**
number: 4 NINE

**Williamson**
Actor: 5 NICOL
**William the Conqueror**
Daughter of: 5 ADELA
Son of: 6 HENRYI
**Willie**
Hall of Famer: 4 MAYS
Pool champ: 7 MOSCONI
**Willing:** 4 GAME GLAD
Is ~ to: 5 WOULD
More: 5 GAMER
partner: 4 ABLE
to try: 6 OPENTO
**Willingly:** 4 FAIN LIEF
**Willis, Bruce**
Ex of: 4 DEMI 5 MOORE
film: 7 DIEHARD
**Willow:** 4 TREE 5 OSIER
relative: 6 POPLAR
**Will-___-wisp:** 4 OTHE
**Willy**
Fictional salesman: 5 LOMAN
follower: 5 NILLY
**"Willy Wonka and the
  Chocolate Factory"**
song part: 5 OOMPA
**Wilmington**
state (abbr.): 3 DEL
**Wilson**
Cartoonist: 5 GAHAN
Former Philly mayor: 5 GOODE
Jazz pianist: 5 TEDDY
Pianist-actor: 6 DOOLEY
President before: 4 TAFT
**Wilson, Marie**
role: 4 IRMA
**Wilson, Woodrow**
school: 9 PRINCETON
**Wilt:** 3 SAG
Built like: 4 TALL
**Wily:** 3 SLY
**Wimbledon:** *see page 712*
1955 ~ champ: 7 TRABERT
1956–57 ~ champ Lew:
  4 HOAD
1960 ~ champ Fraser:
  5 NEALE
1972 ~ champ Smith: 4 STAN
1975 ~ champ: 4 ASHE
1976–80 ~ champ: 4 BORG
1988 ~ champ: 4 GRAF
  6 EDBERG
1991 ~ champ: 5 STICH
1992 ~ champ: 6 AGASSI
1998 ~ champ Novotna:
  4 JANA
call: 3 LET
Five-time ~ champ: 4 BORG
  9 BJORNBORG
Four-time ~ champ: 5 LAVER
Seven-time ~ champ: 4 GRAF
Three-time ~ champ: 5 EVERT
  6 TILDEN 7 MCENROE
unit: 3 SET
**Wimp:** 4 WUSS 5 SISSY
  7 MILKSOP NEBBISH

**Wimple**
wearer: 3 NUN
**Wimpy:** 4 MEEK
Hardly: 5 MACHO
They are hardly: 5 HEMEN
**Wimsey**
creator: 6 SAYERS
title: 4 LORD
**Win:** 4 REAP 6 GARNER
  OBTAIN 7 TRIUMPH
back: 6 RECOUP
Boxing: 3 TKO 4 KAYO
Easy: 4 ROMP
every game: 5 SWEEP
Lopsided: 4 ROUT
of an underdog: 5 UPSET
over: 6 ENDEAR SEDUCE
the heart of: 6 ENAMOR
Try to: 3 WOO
Wrestling: 3 PIN
**Winans**
Singer: 4 BEBE CECE
**Win by ___:** 5 ANECK ANOSE
**Wince:** 5 REACT
**Winchester:** 5 RIFLE
Rank of: 3 MAJ
**Wind**
word form: 5 ANEMO
**Windbag**
output: 6 HOTAIR
**Windblown:** 6 EOLIAN
soil: 5 LOESS
**Winder**
Fishing reel: 5 SPOOL
Watch: 4 STEM
**Windex**
target: 4 PANE
**Windfall:** 4 BOON 7 BONANZA
**Windflower:** 7 ANEMONE
**Winding**
path: 3 ESS
Trombonist: 3 KAI
way: 3 ESS
**"Wind in the Willows, The"**
author: 7 GRAHAME
character: 4 TOAD 5 OTTER
**Windless:** 4 CALM 5 STILL
**Windmill**
part: 4 VANE 5 BLADE
**Window**
alternative: 5 AISLE
Bay: 5 ORIEL
blind piece: 4 SLAT
Choose the ~ instead of the
  aisle: 5 ELOPE
dressing: 5 DRAPE 6 FACADE
  7 DRAPERY
frame: 4 SASH
inset: 6 SCREEN
It may have a ~ (abbr.): 3 ENV
ledge: 4 SILL
Look through a: 6 PEERIN
Oval: 5 OXEYE
Oxeye ~ shape: 4 OVAL
part: 4 PANE SASH SILL
Projecting: 5 ORIEL

Round: 5 OXEYE
Ship: 8 PORTHOLE
side: 4 JAMB
sign: 4 OPEN SALE 5 TOLET
sticker: 5 DECAL
treatment: 5 DRAPE 6 FACADE
   7 DRAPERY
Upstairs: 6 DORMER
**"___ Window":** 4 REAR
**Windows**
  boxes: 3 PCS
  Like: 5 PANED
  picture: 4 ICON
  predecessor: 3 DOS 5 MSDOS
  typeface: 5 ARIAL
**Windpipe:** 6 AIRWAY
   7 TRACHEA
**Winds**
  California: 8 SANTAANA
**Windshield**
  cleaner: 5 WIPER
  Clear a: 5 DEFOG DEICE
  option: 4 TINT
  sticker: 5 DECAL
**"Winds of ___, The":** 3 WAR
**Windsor:** 4 KNOT 6 CASTLE
  prov.: 3 ONT
  river: 6 THAMES
  School near: 4 ETON
**Windswept**
  spot: 3 TOR
**Windup:** 3 END 6 FINALE
**Wind-up**
  toy: 4 KITE
**Windward**
  Not: 4 ALEE
**Windy**
  Not: 5 TERSE
**Windy City**
  airport: 5 OHARE
  train initials: 3 CTA
  trains: 3 ELS
  ~, briefly: 3 CHI
**Wine**
  Amber: 7 MADEIRA
  and dine: 3 WOO 4 FETE
    6 REGALE
  Big name in: 5 GALLO
  Bordeaux: 5 MEDOC
    6 CLARET
  bottle datum: 4 YEAR
  bottle word: 3 CRU SEC
  bouquet: 4 NOSE 5 AROMA
  California ~ region: 4 NAPA
    6 SONOMA
  cask: 3 TUN
  choice: 4 ROSE
  container: 3 JUG VAT 4 CASK
    6 BARREL CELLAR
    FLAGON
  Dessert: 4 PORT 8 SAUTERNE
  Dry, as: 3 SEC
  expert: 6 TASTER
  French ~ region: 6 ALSACE
  German: 5 RHINE 7 MOSELLE
  grape: 5 PINOT 8 RIESLING

Hungarian: 5 TOKAY
Italian: 4 VINO 5 SOAVE
  7 MARSALA
Italian ~ area: 4 ASTI
Like fine: 4 AGED
order: 6 CARAFE
Partner of: 4 DINE
Piedmont ~ center: 4 ASTI
Portuguese: 7 MADEIRA
Pour, as: 6 DECANT
prefix: 3 OEN 4 OENO
Red: 5 MEDOC PINOT
  6 CLARET 7 CHIANTI
  9 PINOTNOIR
Rice: 4 SAKE
Seal the ~ bottle again:
  6 RECORK
sediment: 4 LEES
Sicilian: 7 MARSALA
source: 5 GRAPE
Sparkling: 4 ASTI
Sweet: 4 PORT 6 MALAGA
  7 MARSALA 8 MUSCATEL
  SAUTERNE
valley: 4 NAPA 5 LOIRE
  MOSEL RHINE
Very dry, as: 4 BRUT
waste: 4 LEES
White: 5 BLANC SOAVE
  7 CHABLIS
White ~ aperitif: 3 KIR
word form: 4 OENO
**Wineglass**
  part: 4 STEM
**Winemaker**
  ~ Carlo: 5 ROSSI
  ~ Ernest or Julio: 5 GALLO
**Winemaking**
  partner of Martini: 5 ROSSI
  science: 8 OENOLOGY
**Winery**
  fixture: 3 VAT
  process: 5 AGING
**Wineshop:** 6 BODEGA
**Winfield**
  General: 5 SCOTT
**Winfrey**
  Former ~ rival: 7 DONAHUE
  of TV: 5 OPRAH
**Wing:** 3 ELL 4 SIDE 5 ANNEX
  FLANK
  Building: 3 ELL
  Dumbo: 3 EAR
  it: 3 JAM 5 ADLIB
  measurement: 4 SPAN
  New: 5 ANNEX
  prefix: 4 PTER 5 PTERO
  Take: 3 FLY 4 SOAR 6 AVIATE
  Take under one's: 5 ADOPT
  tip: 4 SHOE
  Wright: 3 ELL
**Wingding:** 4 BASH FETE GALA
  5 ROAST
  Waikiki: 4 LUAU
**Winged:** 4 ALAR 5 ALATE
  god: 4 EROS

  youth: 4 EROS
**Winger**
  Actress: 5 DEBRA
**Wingless**
  parasites: 4 LICE
**Winglike:** 4 ALAR 5 ALATE
**Wings**
  ~, in Latin: 4 ALAE
**"Wings"**
  actress: 8 CLARABOW
**Wink**
  Done with a: 3 SLY
**Winks**
  count: 5 FORTY
**Winless**
  horse: 6 MAIDEN
**Winnebago**
  nation member: 4 OTOE
  ~ County seat: 7 OSHKOSH
**Winnebagos:** 3 RVS
**Winner:** 5 CHAMP 6 VICTOR
  Be a bad: 4 CROW 5 GLOAT
  Cry of a game: 3 GIN
  Headpiece of a: 5 TIARA
  Not a: 7 ALSORAN
  November: 7 ELECTEE
  Olympic: 8 MEDALIST
  Sign of a: 3 VEE
  Take of a: 3 ALL POT
  Tic-tac-toe: 3 OOO
**Winners**
  Bred: 5 SIRED
  Clio: 3 ADS
  Election: 3 INS
**Winnie ___:** 3 MAE
**"Winnie ___ Pu":** 4 ILLE
**"Winnie-the-___":** 4 POOH
**"Winnie-the-Pooh"**
  baby: 3 ROO
  creator: 5 MILNE 7 AAMILNE
  friend: 3 OWL 6 EEYORE
**Winning:** 5 AHEAD ONTOP
  Barely: 5 UPONE
  Go on a ~ streak: 6 GETHOT
  margin: 4 EDGE NOSE
  roll at Caesar's: 3 VII
  streak: 3 RUN
**"Winning ___ everything!":**
  4 ISNT
**Winnings:** 3 POT 5 PURSE
**Winnow:** 4 CULL SIFT SORT
**Winona**
  Actress: 5 RYDER
**Winslet**
  Actress: 4 KATE
**Winslow**
  Painter: 5 HOMER
**Winsome:** 7 LIKABLE
**Winsor**
  Cartoonist: 5 MCCAY
**Winston Cup**
  org.: 6 NASCAR
**Winter**
  ailment: 3 FLU 4 COLD
    6 GRIPPE
  air: 4 NOEL 5 CAROL

air quality: 3 NIP
apple: 6 RUSSET
arrival: 6 PISCES
blanket: 4 SNOW
break: 4 THAW 7 SNOWDAY
budget item: 4 HEAT
bug: 3 FLU 4 COLD
coat: 4 HOAR RIME 5 FROST
   6 ANORAK ULSTER
comment: 4 BRRR
drink: 3 NOG 5 COCOA
   TODDY
fall: 4 SNOW 5 SLEET
fish: 4 SHAD
forecast: 4 SNOW 5 SLEET
forecast word: 5 TEENS
fruit: 9 SNOWAPPLE
hat part: 6 EARLAP
   7 EARFLAP
hazard: 3 ICE 5 SLEET
hrs. in Wichita: 3 CST
Like ~ roads: 3 ICY
melon: 6 CASABA
mo.: 3 DEC FEB JAN
pear: 4 BOSC 5 ANJOU
toy: 4 SLED
vehicle: 4 SLED 6 SNOCAT
wear: 4 WOOL 5 PARKA
   SCARF 7 WOOLENS
   8 OVERCOAT
**Wintergreen**
   fruit: 8 TEABERRY
**Winter Olympian:** 5 LUGER
   SKIER
**Winter Olympics**
   1952 ~ site: 4 OSLO
   1984 ~ site: 8 SARAJEVO
   2002 ~ host: 3 USA
   2002 ~ site: 4 UTAH
   event: 4 LUGE 6 SLALOM
   7 SKIJUMP
   10 SKIJUMPING
**Winter Palace**
   resident: 4 CZAR TSAR
**Wintry:** 3 ICY 4 COLD
**Winwood**
   Actress: 7 ESTELLE
**Wipe**
   out: 3 END 5 ERASE PURGE
   6 DELETE EFFACE
   NEGATE 8 MASSACRE
   9 ERADICATE
**Wiped**
   out: 5 SPENT TIRED
**Wipe out:** 5 ERASE
**Wire:** 5 CABLE TELEX
   7 MESSAGE
   8 TELEGRAM
   Live: 4 DOER 6 DYNAMO
   measure: 3 MIL
   nail: 4 BRAD
   point: 4 BARB
   service inits.: 3 UPI
**Wired:** 4 EDGY 5 HYPER
   TENSE 6 ONLINE
**Wirehair:** 7 TERRIER

Fictional: 4 ASTA
**Wiry**
   dog: 8 AIREDALE
**Wisc.**
   neighbor: 4 MICH MINN
**Wisconsin**
   city: 6 BELOIT
   college: 5 RIPON 6 BELOIT
   senator Herb: 4 KOHL
**Wisdom**
   Folk: 4 LORE
   Goddess of: 6 ATHENA
   tooth: 5 MOLAR
   Unit of: 5 PEARL
   Words of: 5 ADAGE 6 ADAGES
**Wise:** 3 HEP 4 SAGE
   about: 4 ONTO
   competitor: 4 LAYS
   guy: 3 OWL 4 GURU SAGE
   5 SWAMI 6 SMARTY
   11 SMARTYPANTS
   men: 4 MAGI
   one: 3 OWL 4 GURU SAGE
   SEER YOGI 5 ELDER
   SOLON SWAMI 6 ORACLE
   PUNDIT SAVANT SMARTY
   saying: 5 ADAGE
   teacher: 6 MENTOR
   to: 4 INON
   trio: 4 MAGI
   Word to the: 3 TIP 6 TIPOFF
**Wisecrack:** 4 GIBE QUIP
**"Wiseguy"**
   writer Nicholas: 7 PILEGGI
**Wiseman, Joseph**
   role: 4 DRNO
**Wisenheimer:** 6 SMARTY
   9 KNOWITALL
   10 SMARTALECK
**Wise ___ owl:** 4 ASAN
**Wiser:** 5 SAGER
   partner: 5 OLDER
**Wish**
   (for): 4 HOPE LONG PINE
   5 YEARN
   granter: 5 GENIE
   Royal: 3 SON
   undone: 3 RUE 6 REGRET
   ~, with "to": 6 ASPIRE
   ___ wish!: 3 YOU
**Wishful**
   words: 5 IHOPE 7 IHOPESO
**"Wish I could help":**
   7 NOCANDO
**"Wishing won't make ___":**
   4 ITSO
**"Wish ___, wish ...":** 4 IMAY
**Wishy-___:** 5 WASHY
**Wishy-washy**
   Be: 6 WAFFLE
**Wisk**
   rival: 3 ALL ERA
**Wister**
   Author: 4 OWEN
**Wistful**
   wishing: 3 YEN

word: 4 ALAS
**Wistfully**
   thoughtful: 7 PENSIVE
**Wit:** 3 WAG 4 CARD SALT
   Biting: 4 ACID
   Bit of: 3 PUN
   Lively: 6 ESPRIT
   To: 6 NAMELY
**Witch:** 3 HAG 5 CRONE
   Biblical ~ place: 5 ENDOR
   blemish: 4 WART
   Comic strip: 10 BROOMHILDA
   concoction: 4 BREW
   craft: 5 BROOM
   trials town: 5 SALEM
   work: 3 HEX 5 CURSE SPELL
**Witchcraft**
   Goddess of: 6 HECATE
   West Indies: 5 OBEAH
**Witches**
   brew ingredient: 4 NEWT
   Group of: 5 COVEN
**"Witches, The"**
   director: 4 ROEG
**Witching**
   hour: 3 XII
**"Witching Hour, The"**
   author: 8 ANNERICE
**With**
   it: 3 HEP HIP NOW 4 CHIC
   5 ALERT AWARE SHARP
   SMART 7 TUNEDIN
   ~, in French: 4 AVEC
   ~, in Spanish: 3 CON
   "___ With a View": 5 AROOM
   "With a wink and ___": 4 ANOD
   "___ With a Z": 4 LIZA
**Withdraw:** 4 QUIT WEAN
   6 BOWOUT RECEDE
   RETIRE SECEDE
**Withdrawal**
   site: 3 ATM
**Withdrawn:** 3 SHY 7 ASOCIAL
**Wither:** 5 DRYUP 7 SHRIVEL
**Withered:** 4 SERE
**Withers, Bill**
   tune: 5 USEME 8 LEANONME
**Witherspoon**
   Actress: 4 CORA 5 REESE
**Withhold:** 4 DENY KEEP
**Within:** 4 AMID
   Fit: 4 NEST
   It is ~ range: 4 OVEN
   prefix: 4 ENDO ENTO
   5 INTRA
   reach: 4 NEAR 5 HANDY
   6 ATHAND
**"With ___ in My Heart":**
   5 ASONG
**Within ___ of:** 5 ANACE
**"___, With Love":** 5 TOSIR
**"___ With Music":** 5 SAYIT
**"With ___ of thousands!":**
   5 ACAST
**"With or Without You"**
   singer: 4 BONO

Without: 4 LESS SANS
    5 MINUS
 a bal.: 3 PPD
 Cannot do: 4 NEED
 ~, in French: 4 SANS
 ~, in Latin: 4 SINE
Without ___: 4 ANET 5 ACARE
    ACENT
"Without further ___ ...": 3 ADO
"With Reagan"
 author: 7 EDMEESE
Withstand: 4 BEAR 5 ABIDE
    6 RESIST
"With the jawbone of ___":
    5 ANASS
Witness: 3 SEE 6 LOOKON
 Bear: 6 ATTEST
 Unreliable: 4 LIAR
 vow: 4 OATH
 words: 3 IDO
"Witness"
 actor Lukas: 4 HAAS
 director Peter: 4 WEIR
 sect: 5 AMISH
Witnesses
 Like some: 7 HOSTILE
 Star: 4 MAGI
"Witness for the Prosecution"
 Tyrone's wife in:
    7 MARLENE
Wits
 Battle of: 5 CHESS
Witt
 Actress: 6 ALICIA
 jump: 4 AXEL
Witticism: 3 MOT 4 JEST JOKE
    QUIP
 Critical: 4 BARB
"Wiz, The"
 Glinda in: 4 LENA 5 HORNE
    9 LENAHORNE
 star: 4 ROSS
 Wiz in: 5 PRYOR
Wizard: 4 GURU SAGE
    8 SORCERER
"Wizard ___, The": 4 OFID
    OFOZ
"Wizard of Menlo Park, The":
    6 EDISON
"Wizard of Oz, The"
 actor: 4 LAHR 5 HALEY
 actor Bert: 4 LAHR
 author: 4 BAUM
 composer: 5 ARLEN
 dog: 4 TOTO
 farmhand: 4 ZEKE
 producer: 5 LEROY
 prop: 6 OILCAN
 revealer: 4 TOTO
 studio: 3 MGM
Wizardry: 5 MAGIC
Wizards: 5 MAGES
 org.: 3 NBA
Wizened: 7 DRIEDUP
WJM
 anchorman: 3 TED

Wk.
 Day of the: 3 FRI MON SAT
    SUN THU TUE WED
"WKRP"
 actress Anderson: 4 LONI
 Nessman of: 3 LES
 news director Les:
    7 NESSMAN
 She was Jennifer on: 4 LONI
 Tim of: 4 REID
WNBA
 Lisa of the: 6 LESLIE
 Rebecca of the: 4 LOBO
WNW
 opposite: 3 ESE
Woe: 3 ILL 6 SORROW
 Word of: 4 ALAS 5 ALACK
 Words of: 4 AHME OHME
    OHNO 5 OYVEY
"Woe ___" (grammar
    bestseller): 3 ISI
"Woe ___!": 4 ISME
Woebegone: 3 SAD
"Woe is me!": 4 ALAS 5 ALACK
Wok: 3 PAN
 Use a: 3 FRY 5 SAUTE
    7 STIRFRY
Wolf: 5 SCARF 6 CANINE
    8 PREDATOR
 down: 3 EAT 6 DEVOUR
    INHALE
 Feminist author: 5 NAOMI
 Gray: 4 LOBO
 in a Kipling tale: 5 AKELA
 Kind of: 4 LONE
 Look like a: 4 LEER OGLE
 pack member: 5 UBOAT
 pack rank: 5 ALPHA
 Prairie: 6 COYOTE
 preceder: 3 SHE 4 WERE
 Timber: 4 LOBO
Wolfe
 Detective: 4 NERO
Wolfgang
 Physicist: 5 PAULI
Wolfhound
 Russian: 6 BORZOI
Wolflike: 6 LUPINE
Woman
 Fr. holy: 3 STE
 in distress: 6 DAMSEL
 Loos: 7 LORELEI
 Low-voiced: 4 ALTO
 name suffix: 4 ETTE
 of distinction: 4 DAME
 of letters: 5 VANNA
 of the haus: 4 FRAU
 of tomorrow: 4 GIRL
 Old: 5 CRONE
 Sp.: 3 SRA
 That: 3 HER SHE
 Waikiki: 6 WAHINE
 Witchy: 5 CRONE
 Young: 4 LASS
"Woman"
 The woman in: 3 ONO

"___ Woman"
 (Beatles tune): 5 SHESA
 (Maria Muldaur tune):
    3 IMA
 (Reddy tune): 3 IAM
"Woman ___, The"
 (1984 Wilder film): 5 INRED
Womanizer: 4 RAKE ROUE
"Woman With a ___"
    (Vermeer): 4 LUTE
Wombs: 5 UTERI
Women: 4 GALS
 Figure in a prison for:
    6 MATRON
 (French abbr.): 4 MMES
 Group of: 5 HAREM
 Magazine for: 4 ELLE SELF
    5 COSMO
 Org. of: 3 DAR 4 LPGA
 Without: 4 STAG
 ~, to poets: 7 FAIRSEX
"Women, The"
 playwright: 4 LUCE
 writer: 4 LOOS
"Women and Love"
 author: 4 HITE
"Women Ironing"
 artist: 5 DEGAS
"Women, Race and Class"
 author Davis: 6 ANGELA
Women's ___: 3 LIB
"Women Who Run With the
    Wolves"
 author: 5 ESTES
Won
 every game: 5 SWEPT
Won ___: 3 TON
Wonder: 3 AWE
 Full of: 5 INAWE
 Kind of: 6 ONEHIT
 of music: 6 STEVIE
 Word of: 3 GEE
Wonder, Stevie
 tune: 5 IWISH
Wonderful: 5 NEATO SUPER
 thing, once:
    12 THEBEESKNEES
 ~, in slang: 3 RAD
"Wonderful!": 3 AAH
"___ Wonderful Life": 4 ITSA
Wonderland
 bird: 4 DODO
 cake phrase: 5 EATME
 character: 4 HARE
 girl: 5 ALICE
 Like the ~ Hatter: 3 MAD
Wonderment: 3 AWE
 Show: 3 AAH OOH
Wonder Woman: 6 AMAZON
 alias: 5 DIANA
Wonder-worker
 Hindu: 5 FAKIR
Wong, ___ May: 4 ANNA
Wonka
 creator: 4 DAHL
"___ won't!": 3 NOI

"___ won't be afraid" ("Stand by Me" lyric): 3 NOI
**Woo:** 7 ROMANCE
**Woo, Roh ___ (of South Korea):** 3 TAE
**Wood**
Actress: 4 LANA 7 NATALIE
alternative: 4 IRON
Archery: 3 YEW
basecoat: 6 SEALER
Bat: 3 ASH
Bowling pin: 5 MAPLE
Cabinet: 5 ALDER
Chest: 5 CEDAR
cutter: 3 ADZ AXE SAW
    4 ADZE 6 RIPSAW
Durable: 3 ASH ELM OAK
    4 TEAK
file: 4 RASP
finish: 5 STAIN
Fragrant: 5 CEDAR
    8 REDCEDAR
Guitarist: 3 RON
Hard: 3 ASH ELM OAK
    4 TEAK 5 EBONY LARCH
Knotty: 4 PINE
Light: 5 BALSA
Model: 5 BALSA
nymph: 5 DRYAD
pattern: 5 GRAIN
problem: 6 DRYROT
Saw: 5 SNORE
Shipbuilding: 4 TEAK
Smooth: 4 SAND
sorrel: 3 OCA 6 OXALIS
strip: 4 LATH SLAT 6 SPLINE
Three: 5 SPOON
trimmer: 3 ADZ AXE SAW
    4 ADZE
Two: 7 BRASSIE
Wickerwork: 5 OSIER
Work on: 7 WHITTLE
**Woodard**
Actress: 5 ALFRE
"... ___ woodchuck": 3 IFA
**Woodcutter**
of fiction: 7 ALIBABA
**Wooded:** 6 SYLVAN
shelter: 5 ARBOR
valley: 4 DELL
**Wooden**
container: 6 BARREL
duck: 5 DECOY
pin: 3 PEG 5 DOWEL
shoe: 5 SABOT
**Wooden, John**
team: 4 UCLA
**Woodhouse**
of fiction: 4 EMMA
**Woodland**
creature: 4 DEER
deity: 4 FAUN 5 SATYR
**Woods**
Actor: 5 JAMES
Babe in the: 4 FAWN NAIF
Golfer: 5 TIGER

Neck of the: 4 AREA
org.: 3 PGA
prop: 3 TEE
Quaker in the: 5 ASPEN
Walk in the: 4 HIKE
Way into the: 4 PATH
**Woodskin:** 5 CANOE
**Woodstock**
do: 4 AFRO
First name at: 4 ARLO JIMI
gear: 4 AMPS
setting: 4 FARM
Singer at: 4 BAEZ
**Woodward**
Actress: 6 JOANNE
Husband of: 6 NEWMAN
**Woodward, Joanne**
role: 3 EVE
**Woodwind:** 4 OBOE REED
**Woodworking**
groove: 4 DADO
tool: 3 ADZ AWL 4 ADZE RASP
    5 LATHE PLANE 6 RIPSAW
    SHAPER
**Woody**
Arlo, to: 3 SON
Colleague of Ted and: 4 RHEA
Ex of: 3 MIA
Filmmaker: 5 ALLEN
Son of: 4 ARLO
vine: 5 LIANA
Wife of: 6 SOONYI
**Woody Woodpecker**
creator: 5 LANTZ
**Wooer:** 4 BEAU 6 SUITOR
of Cleo: 4 MARC
**"Woof!":** 3 ARF
**Woofer**
output: 3 ARF 4 BASS
Wakayama: 5 AKITA
**Wool:** 7 TEXTILE
Coarse ~ cloth: 5 TWEED
fat: 7 LANOLIN
Fine: 6 ANGORA MERINO
Harvest: 5 SHEAR
Kind of: 5 LAMBS STEEL
Low-grade: 5 MUNGO
source: 3 EWE 5 LLAMA
    6 ALPACA ANGORA
**Woolen**
cap: 3 TAM
**Wooley**
Actor and singer: 4 SHEB
**Woolly:** 5 OVINE 6 LANATE
    LANOSE
mama: 3 EWE
yarn: 4 TALE
~ Andean: 5 LLAMA
**Woolworth's**
First ~ store city: 5 UTICA
**Woosnam**
Golfer: 3 IAN
**Word:** 3 VOW 4 NEWS 5 SAYSO
Encouraging: 3 OLE RAH TRY
    YES 4 AMEN CMON
    7 ATTABOY 8 ATTAGIRL

Final: 3 END 4 AMEN OBIT
    5 ADIEU SAYSO
for the wise: 4 SAGE
game: 5 GHOST
Get the: 4 HEAR
Give one's: 5 SWEAR
    6 ASSURE
on either side of -à-: 3 VIS
    4 TETE
on the wall: 4 MENE
origin: 6 ETYMON
part (abbr.): 3 SYL
The magic: 6 PLEASE
to the wise: 3 TIP
You can take his ~ for it:
    5 ROGET
**Word for word:** 3 MOT
    7 LITERAL 8 VERBATIM
**Wordless**
agreement: 3 NOD
singing: 4 SCAT
**Wordplay**
Some: 4 PUNS
**Word processor**
command: 4 REDO SAVE
    SORT UNDO 5 PASTE
function: 6 TABSET
menu: 4 EDIT
**Words**
Have ~ with: 4 SPAR 5 ARGUE
    6 TALKTO
In other: 5 IDEST 6 THATIS
Man of many: 5 ROGET
    7 WEBSTER
to live by: 5 ADAGE AXIOM
    CREDO CREED DOGMA
    MORAL MOTTO TENET
**Wordsmith**
~ Webster: 4 NOAH
**Wordsworth:** 5 ODIST
    8 LAKEPOET
muse: 5 ERATO
work: 3 ODE 4 POEM
**Wordy:** 4 LONG
Not: 5 TERSE
**Wore:** 5 HADON
away: 3 ATE 6 ERODED
He ~ a 4: 3 ORR OTT
    6 MELOTT
**Workhorse**
Harbor: 3 TUG
**Working:** 4 ATIT 6 ONDUTY
class: 5 PROLE
Get by: 4 EARN
In ~ order: 6 USABLE
    8 OPERABLE
No longer ~ (abbr.): 3 RET
    4 RETD
Not: 3 OFF 4 DEAD IDLE
    6 BROKEN 7 ONLEAVE
    RETIRED 8 ONSTRIKE
on a chair: 6 CANING
stiff: 4 PEON 5 PROLE
Stop: 6 RETIRE
together: 6 TEAMED
    8 INLEAGUE

**"Working Girl"**
actress Griffith: 7 MELANIE
girl: 4 TESS
**Working without ___:** 4 ANET
**Workout**
Achy after a: 4 SORE
aftereffect: 4 ACHE
center: 3 GYM SPA 4 YMCA
exercise: 5 SITUP
result: 5 SWEAT
spot: 3 GYM SPA 4 YMCA
system: 5 TAEBO
target: 4 DELT FLAB LATS
   PECS
type: 7 AEROBIC
unit: 3 REP SET
wear: 6 SWEATS
woe: 4 SORE
**Workplace**
safety org.: 4 OSHA
**Workshop:** 7 ATELIER
of Hephaestus: 4 ETNA
tool: 4 RASP VISE 5 CLAMP
   PLANE
**Work ___ sweat:** 3 UPA
**Workweek**
Cry at the end of a: 4 TGIF
**World**
book: 5 ATLAS
College: 7 ACADEME
   8 ACADEMIA
Dead to the: 5 INERT
   6 ASLEEP 7 OUTCOLD
End of the: 4 POLE
financial gp.: 3 IMF
Game of ~ conquest: 4 RISK
Go around the: 5 ORBIT
In the: 7 ONEARTH
It goes around the: 7 ORBITER
It might go around the: 4 YOYO
Lat.: 5 MUNDI
leader: 6 NETHER
leader, 1959–2008: 6 CASTRO
leader, 1961–71: 6 UTHANT
Man of the: 5 ATLAS
Out of this: 5 ALIEN EERIE
record: 5 ATLAS
religion: 5 ISLAM
(Russian): 3 MIR
They'll show you the:
   7 ATLASES
Think the ~ of: 5 ADORE
   6 ADMIRE ESTEEM
~, in French: 5 MONDE
~, in Spanish: 5 MONDO
**World ___:** 6 SERIES
**"___ World":** 6 WAYNES
**"___ World, The" (MTV):** 4 REAL
**"World According to ___, The":**
   4 GARP
**World Bank**
offering: 3 AID
**World Court**
site: 5 HAGUE
**World Cup**
1958 ~ sensation: 4 PELE

1974 ~ site:
   11 WESTGERMANY
1982 ~ site: 5 SPAIN
1994 ~ host: 3 USA
1998 ~ winner: 6 FRANCE
2002 ~ cohost: 5 KOREA
cry: 3 OLE
power (abbr.): 3 ARG 4 ITAL
powerhouse: 5 ITALY
sport: 6 SOCCER
**World Heritage**
gp.: 6 UNESCO
**Worldly:** 5 SUAVE 7 SECULAR
Least: 7 NAIVEST
**"World of Suzie ___, The":**
   4 WONG
**World Series**
1956 ~ perfect game pitcher:
   6 LARSEN
1960 ~ hero, familiarly: 3 MAZ
1969 ~ champs: 4 METS
1972–74 ~ champs: 5 THEAS
1973 ~ site: 4 SHEA
1975–76 ~ champs: 4 REDS
1979 ~ champs: 7 PIRATES
1983 ~ champs: 7 ORIOLES
1984 ~ champs: 6 TIGERS
1986 ~ champs: 4 METS
1986 ~ site: 4 SHEA
1990 ~ champs: 4 REDS
1990 ~ MVP: 4 RIJO
1991 ~ champs: 5 TWINS
1992–93 ~ champs:
   8 BLUEJAYS
1992–93 ~ site: 7 TORONTO
1995 ~ champs (abbr.): 3 ATL
1999 ~ losers: 7 ATLANTA
2000 ~ MVP: 5 JETER
   10 DEREKJETER
2000 ~ site: 4 SHEA
2000 ~ team: 4 METS
2002 ~ champs: 6 ANGELS
College ~ site: 5 OMAHA
Four-game: 5 SWEEP
mo.: 3 OCT
winning manager in '98, '99,
   and '00: 5 TORRE
~ MVP: *see page 710*
**World Series of Golf**
site: 5 AKRON
**World's Fair**
1962 ~ city: 7 SEATTLE
1964 ~ symbol:
   9 UNISPHERE
1970 ~ site: 5 OSAKA
~, for short: 4 EXPO
**"___ World Turns":** 5 ASTHE
**World War I**
battle site: 6 VERDUN
   7 ARGONNE
**World War II**
gun: 4 STEN
**World-weariness:** 5 ENNUI
**World-weary:** 5 BLASE JADED
**Worldwide**
(abbr.): 4 INTL

law enforcement group:
   8 INTERPOL
workers gp.: 3 ILO
**Worm:** 4 BAIT
container: 3 CAN
follower: 5 EATEN
Like the bird that catches the:
   5 EARLY
product: 4 SILK
**Worms**
conclave: 4 DIET
Like: 7 LEGLESS
One in: 3 EIN
**Worn:** 3 OLD 4 USED
   7 ABRADED
away: 5 EATEN 6 ERODED
down: 6 ERODED 7 ABRADED
out: 3 OLD 4 SHOT 5 JADED
   SPENT 6 DONEIN
to a frazzle: 4 SHOT 5 TIRED
Unevenly: 5 EROSE
**Worrier**
risk: 5 ULCER
**Worry:** 3 NAG 4 CARE FRET
   STEW 5 ANGST BROOD
   EATAT SWEAT
   7 SWEATIT
Bank: 3 RUN
excessively: 4 FUSS 6 OBSESS
Freedom from: 4 EASE
Grower's: 6 FREEZE
Illegal parker: 5 TOWER
Not: 8 RESTEASY
Not to: 4 IMOK 5 ITSOK
Old car: 4 RUST
Things to ~ over: 5 BEADS
Winter: 3 ICE
**"___ worry!":** 5 NOTTO
**Worry-free**
locale: 4 EDEN
**Worrywart**
Act the: 4 FRET STEW
woe: 5 ULCER
**Worse**
Could be: 4 SOSO
   8 NOTSOBAD
None the: 6 UNHURT
   9 UNSCARRED
**"___ worse than death":**
   5 AFATE
**Worship:** 5 ADORE 6 REVERE
   9 ADORATION
House of: 4 SHUL 5 ABBEY
   6 CHURCH TEMPLE
Nature: 5 WICCA
Object of: 3 GOD 4 HERO
   5 DEITY IDOLS
Place of: 5 ALTAR 6 CHAPEL
Seat of: 3 PEW
Where some ~ from: 4 AFAR
Worthy of: 4 HOLY 6 SACRED
**Worshiper:** 5 DEIST 6 ADORER
Haile Selassie: 5 RASTA
Hero: 7 LEANDER
Idol: 3 FAN
Islamic: 6 MUSLIM

Machu Picchu: 4 INCA
Quetzalcoatl: 5 AZTEC MAYAN
   6 TOLTEC
Shiva: 5 HINDU
Stonehenge: 5 DRUID
Tree: 5 DRUID
Vishnu: 5 HINDU
**Worst:** 6 DEFEAT
  Absolute: 4 PITS
  In the ~ way: 5 BADLY
   6 SORELY
  score: 4 ZERO
**Worsted**
  cloth: 5 SERGE 6 TRICOT
**Worth:** 5 MERIT VALUE
   8 VALUEDAT
  a C: 4 FAIR SOSO
  Actress: 5 IRENE
  a D: 4 POOR
  having: 5 OFUSE UTILE
  Is ~ it: 4 PAYS
  mentioning: 6 OFNOTE
  Not ~ debating: 4 MOOT
  Two cents': 3 SAY 5 INPUT
   7 OPINION
**Worthless:** 3 BUM TIN 4 NULL
   7 INUTILE
  amount: 3 FIG
  coin: 3 SOU
  talk: 5 BILGE 6 DRIVEL
**Worthwhile:** 5 UTILE
  Is: 4 PAYS
**Worthy:** 3 FIT
  Be ~ of: 4 EARN RATE
   5 MERIT 7 DESERVE
  of worship: 4 HOLY
   6 SACRED
**Wouk**
  ship: 5 CAINE
  work: 5 NOVEL
**"Would I lie?":** 6 HONEST
**"Would ___ to you?":** 4 ILIE
**"Would you look at that?!":**
  5 ILLBE
**Wound:** 4 GASH HURT SORE
   6 COILED INJURE
   LESION
  cover: 4 SCAB
  Item that is: 5 SKEIN
  Old: 4 SCAR
  Piercing: 4 STAB
  Seriously: 4 MAIM
  Shaving: 4 NICK
  Small: 5 PRICK
  up: 5 ENDED TENSE WIRED
   6 ONEDGE
**Wounded Knee**
  locale (abbr.): 4 SDAK
**Woven:** 7 BRAIDED
  fabric: 4 MESH 6 DAMASK
   7 TEXTILE
  rattan: 4 CANE
**Wow:** 3 AWE 4 SLAY STUN
  5 AMAZE
**"Wow!":** 3 GEE MAN OOH
  12 HOLYMACKEREL

**Wozniak**
  Computer pioneer: 5 STEVE
**"Wozzeck":** 5 OPERA
  composer: 4 BERG
**WPM**
  part: 3 MIN PER WDS
**Wraith:** 5 SPOOK 7 SPECTER
**Wrangle:** 4 SPAR 6 HAGGLE
**Wrangler:** 4 JEEP
  alternative: 3 LEE 5 LEVIS
  rope: 6 LARIAT
**Wrap:** 3 BOA FUR OBI 4 COAT
   FOIL PITA SARI 5 SARAN
   SAREE SHAWL STOLE
   6 ENFOLD ENROBE
   MANTLE SARONG
   SERAPE 7 SWADDLE
   TINFOIL 8 ENVELOPE
  around: 4 FURL 5 TWINE
   7 ENTWINE
  artist: 7 CHRISTO
  Delhi: 4 SARI
  Feathery: 3 BOA
  Fur: 5 STOLE
  Indian: 4 SARI
  like a baby: 7 SWADDLE
  Mexican: 6 SERAPE
  Neck: 5 SCARF
  Plastic: 5 SARAN
  Ranee: 5 SAREE
  Roman: 4 TOGA 5 STOLA
  tightly: 4 BIND 6 SWATHE
  up: 3 END ICE 6 ENCASE
   ENFOLD 7 ENVELOP
  (up): 3 SEW
**"___ wrap!":** 4 ITSA
**Wraparound**
  dress: 4 SARI
  Japanese: 3 OBI
  Polynesian: 5 PAREU
   6 SARONG
  Tartan: 4 KILT
**Wrapped**
  up: 4 CLAD DONE OVER
**Wrapper**
  Body: 4 SKIN
  Flapper: 3 BOA
  weight: 4 TARE
**Wrapping**
  material: 5 SARAN
**Wraps**
  Keep under: 4 HIDE 5 SITON
  Under: 6 SECRET 7 CLOAKED
**Wrap-up**
  Musical: 4 CODA
  Play: 6 EPILOG
  Sports: 5 RECAP
**Wrath:** 3 IRE 4 FURY 5 ANGER
  Fit of: 4 RAGE
  Roman: 4 IRAE
**Wray**
  Actress: 3 FAY
**Wreak**
  Bad thing to: 5 HAVOC
**Wreath**
  Hawaiian floral: 3 LEI

  Head: 6 ANADEM
**Wreck:** 3 MAR 4 BUST RAZE
   RUIN 5 TOTAL TRASH
   6 DERAIL
**Wreckage:** 4 RUIN 6 DEBRIS
**Wrecked:** 4 SHOT
**Wrecker**
  Home: 6 VANDAL 7 TERMITE
  Job for a: 3 TOW
**Wrecking ball**
  alternative: 3 TNT
  Use a: 4 RAZE
**"Wreck of the Mary ___, The":**
  5 DEARE
**"Wreck of the Mary Deare,**
  **The"**
  author: 5 INNES
**Wren:** 4 BIRD 6 TOMTIT
  Wing of: 3 ELL
**Wrench:** 4 TOOL TURN
   6 SPRAIN 7 SPANNER
  Monkey: 4 SNAG
  type: 5 ALLEN 6 SOCKET
   7 SPANNER
**Wrestle:** 6 TUSSLE
  (with): 7 GRAPPLE
**Wrestler:** 6 PINNER
  goal: 3 PIN
  Japanese: 4 SUMO
  knowledge: 5 HOLDS
  surface: 3 MAT
  ~ Hogan: 4 HULK
**Wrestling**
  contest: 4 MEET
  event: 4 MEET
  Giant of: 5 ANDRE
  hold: 4 LOCK 6 NELSON
   9 WRISTLOCK
  Hulk of: 5 HOGAN
  Japanese: 4 SUMO
  Kind of: 3 ARM 4 SUMO
   6 INDIAN
  move: 12 SCISSORSHOLD
  official: 3 REF
  pair: 7 TAGTEAM
  round: 4 FALL
  surface: 3 MAT 6 CANVAS
  venue: 3 MUD 5 ARENA
  win: 3 PIN
**Wretched:** 5 LOUSY RATTY
   SEEDY 6 ROTTEN
   SORDID
**Wretchedness:** 3 WOE
**Wriggler:** 3 EEL 4 WORM
**Wriggling:** 4 EELY
**Wriggly**
  fish: 3 EEL
  swimmer: 3 EEL
**Wright:** 4 ISLE 5 MAKER
  Actress: 6 TERESA
  angle: 3 ELL
  Comic: 6 STEVEN
  Do the ~ thing: 6 AVIATE
  wing: 3 ELL
**Wright, Steven**
  quip: 8 ONELINER

**Wright brothers:** 7 OHIOANS
    8 AVIATORS
  home: 4 OHIO
  hometown: 6 DAYTON
**Wrigley**
  field: 3 GUM
**Wrigley Field**
  flora: 3 IVY
  Like ~ walls: 5 IVIED
  slugger: 4 SOSA
  team: 4 CUBS
**Wrinkle:** 4 SEAM 6 CREASE
    RUMPLE
  a brow: 4 KNIT
  cause: 3 AGE
  remover: 4 IRON
**Wrinkled:** 4 LINY 7 CREASED
    9 DEPRESSED
**Wrinkler**
  Nose: 4 ODOR
**Wrinkle-resistant**
  fabric: 5 ORLON 6 DACRON
**Wrinkly**
  canine: 3 PUG 7 SHARPEI
  fruit: 4 UGLI 5 PRUNE
**Wrist**
  action: 5 FLICK
  attachment: 4 ULNA
  bones: 5 CARPI
  Of the: 6 CARPAL
**Writ**
  of a debtor: 6 ELEGIT
**Write:** 3 JOT PEN 6 NOTATE
    9 DROPALINE
  anew: 5 REPEN
  down: 3 LOG
  for another: 5 GHOST
  illegibly: 6 SCRAWL
  Nothing to ~ home about:
    4 SOSO
  on metal: 4 ETCH
    7 ENGRAVE
  quickly: 3 JOT 9 DROPALINE
  software: 4 CODE
  up: 4 CITE
  with a point: 4 ETCH
**Write-off:** 4 LOSS 7 BADDEBT
**Writer:** 3 PEN 6 AUTHOR
    PENMAN SCRIBE
  A ~ may work on it: 4 SPEC
  Bakery: 4 ICER
  Check: 5 PAYER
  deg.: 3 MFA
  Jingle: 5 ADMAN
  Mediocre: 4 HACK
  Praiseful: 5 ODIST
  problem: 5 CRAMP
  reference: 5 ROGET
  rep: 5 AGENT
  Slogan: 5 ADMAN
  submissions (abbr.): 3 MSS
  Unknown ~ (abbr.): 4 ANON
  Verse: 4 POET
  woe: 5 CRAMP
**Writers**
  Rx: 3 DRS MDS

**Write-up**
  Doctor: 9 CASESTUDY
  Preliminary: 5 DRAFT
  Research: 9 LABREPORT
**Writing:** 5 PROSE
  Dull, as: 5 PROSY
  Icelandic: 4 EDDA
  on the wall: 4 OMEN SIGN
  pad: 6 TABLET
  point: 3 NIB
  Portable ~ surface:
    9 CLIPBOARD
  Put down in: 3 PAN 5 LIBEL
  Secret: 4 CODE
  style: 8 LONGHAND
  table: 4 DESK
  tablet: 3 PAD
**Writings**
  Some ancient: 6 PAPYRI
**Writ of ___ corpus:** 6 HABEAS
**Written**
  As: 3 SIC
  assurance: 9 GUARANTEE
  It is: 4 TEXT
  Not: 4 ORAL
  record: 4 MEMO 5 ANNAL
    ENTRY
  Wrong: 3 SIN 4 AWRY TORT
    5 ABUSE AMISS
    7 INERROR
  Civil: 4 TORT
  Completely: 6 ALLWET
  end: 4 DOER
  Go: 3 ERR
  Gone: 4 AWOL
  Isn't: 4 AINT
  Legal: 4 TORT
  move: 5 ERROR
  prefix: 3 MIS
  Prove: 6 NEGATE
  Right, as a: 6 AVENGE
  Rub the ~ way: 3 IRK 4 RILE
    5 CHAFE 6 ABRADE
    NETTLE
  Sense of right and:
    6 MORALS
  start: 3 MIS
  Take the ~ way: 3 ROB
    5 STEAL
  way to run: 7 AGROUND
  Went: 5 ERRED
**"Wrong!":** 5 NOTSO
**Wrongdoing:** 3 SIN 4 EVIL
    5 ERROR
  Assist in: 4 ABET
**Wrongful**
  act: 4 TORT
**Wrote:** 6 PENNED
    7 EMAILED
  for: 7 GHOSTED
**Wrought**
  It may be: 4 IRON
  Richly: 6 ORNATE
**Wry:** 5 DROLL
  Catcher in the: 5 BERRA
  twist: 5 IRONY

**W's**
  One of the five: 3 WHO WHY
    4 WHAT WHEN 5 WHERE
**WSW**
  Opposite of: 3 ENE
**Wt.**
  Sack: 5 TENLB
  system: 5 AVOIR
  units: 3 LBS
**Wts.**
  Heavy: 3 TNS
**Wurst:** 7 SAUSAGE
**Wuss:** 5 PANSY SISSY WEENY
**"Wuthering Heights"**
  actress Oberon: 5 MERLE
  author: 6 BRONTE
  setting: 4 MOOR
**WWI**
  battle site: 5 MARNE SOMME
    YPRES
  line: 6 TRENCH
  plane: 4 SPAD
  river: 4 YSER 5 MARNE
  spy: 8 MATAHARI
  troops: 3 AEF
  victor: 3 AEF
  ~ French soldier: 5 POILU
  ~ German admiral: 4 SPEE
  ~ U.S. soldier: 4 YANK
    8 DOUGHBOY
**WWII**
  ¹/₃ of a ~ film title: 4 TORA
  admiral: 6 HALSEY
  ally: 4 USSR
  anti-subversive gp.: 4 HUAC
  arena: 3 ETO
  battle site: 4 STLO 6 BATAAN
  battle site, for short: 3 IWO
  beach: 5 OMAHA
  beachhead: 5 ANZIO
  buy: 5 EBOND
  captive: 3 POW
  center of French resistance:
    4 LYON
  code machine: 6 ENIGMA
  command: 3 ETO
  conference site: 5 CAIRO
    YALTA
  correspondent: 4 PYLE
    9 ERNIEPYLE
  correspondent Pyle: 5 ERNIE
  covert gp.: 3 OSS
  craft: 3 LST 5 EBOAT UBOAT
    6 PTBOAT
  enlistee: 5 GIJOE 7 DOGFACE
  enlistees: 3 GIS
  entertainers: 3 USO
  female enlistee: 3 WAC 4 SPAR
    WAAC
  general: 11 OMARBRADLEY
  gun: 4 STEN
  hero Murphy: 5 AUDIE
  island: 4 TRUK 5 LEYTE
  journalist: 4 PYLE
    9 ERNIEPYLE
  losers: 4 AXIS

menace: 5 UBOAT
neutral country (abbr.): 3 ARG
nickname: 3 IKE 4 DUCE
  5 MONTY
pinup: 6 GRABLE
plane: 4 ZERO 5 STUKA
  8 ENOLAGAY
power: 4 USSR
pres.: 3 FDR
prison camp: 6 STALAG
rationing agcy.: 3 OPA
rifle: 6 GARAND
riveter: 5 ROSIE
side: 4 AXIS
spy gp.: 3 OSS
sub: 5 UBOAT
tank: 6 PANZER 7 SHERMAN
town: 4 STLO 6 BATAAN
turning point: 4 DDAY
vessel: 3 LST 5 EBOAT
  UBOAT 6 PTBOAT

weapon: 4 STEN 6 GARAND
  7 ENFIELD
winners: 6 ALLIES
~ Brit. flyers: 3 RAF
~ GI: 5 AMVET
~ Japanese general: 4 TOJO
~ Russian leader: 6 STALIN
**WWW**
address: 3 URL
address starter: 4 HTTP
moniker: 6 USERID
One way to the: 3 AOL
Part of: 3 WEB
**Wyatt**
Marshal: 4 EARP
**Wye**
follower: 3 ZED ZEE
**Wyeth**
Artist: 5 JAMIE 6 ANDREW
**Wyeth, Andrew**
subject/model: 5 HELGA

**Wyeth, ___ Convers:** 6 NEWELL
**Wylie**
Poet: 6 ELINOR
**Wynken**
Partner of: 3 NOD
**Wynn**
Actor: 6 KEENAN
and others: 3 EDS
of baseball: 5 EARLY
**Wynn, Ed**
Son of: 6 KEENAN
**Wynonna**
Mother of: 5 NAOMI
**Wyo.**
neighbor: 3 IDA NEB 4 NEBR
  SDAK
**Wyoming**
city: 6 CASPER 7 LARAMIE
neighbor: 4 UTAH
range: 5 TETON 6 TETONS
river: 7 LARAMIE

**X:** 3 CHI TEN 4 KISS 5 TIMES 15 SIMPLESIGNATURE
(abbr.): 3 LTR
Center: 3 TAC
First: 3 TIC
Greek: 3 CHI
on a map: 4 HERE
out: 6 DELETE
rating: 3 TEN
Third: 3 TOE
~, Y, or Z: 4 AXIS
**Xanadu**
resident: 4 KANE
**"Xanadu"**
rock gp.: 3 ELO
**Xanthippe:** 3 NAG
Where ~ shopped: 5 AGORA
**Xavier**
Bandleader: 5 CUGAT
ex: 5 CHARO
Singer with: 4 ABBE
**Xavier, Professor**
Team of: 4 XMEN
**Xbox**
fan: 5 GAMER
**Xena**
foe: 4 ARES
portrayer Lucy: 7 LAWLESS
**"Xena: Warrior Princess"**
actress O'Connor: 5 RENEE

god: 4 ARES
**Xenia**
locale: 4 OHIO
**Xenon:** 3 GAS 7 RAREGAS 8 INERTGAS
Like: 5 INERT
**Xenophobe**
dread: 5 ALIEN
___ Xer: 3 GEN
**Xerox**
competitor: 5 RICOH
insert (abbr.): 4 ORIG
**Xerxes**
land: 6 PERSIA
**"X-Files, The"**
actor Nicholas: 3 LEA
agent: 6 SCULLY
agent Monica: 5 REYES
agent Scully: 4 DANA
extras: 3 ETS 4 GMEN
Like: 5 EERIE
network: 3 FOX
org.: 3 FBI 4 SETI
role for Gillian: 4 DANA
sight: 3 UFO
subject: 3 ETS
worker: 5 AGENT
**X-Games**
network: 4 ESPN
**Xhosa:** 5 BANTU

**Xi**
preceders: 3 NUS
**Xiamen:** 4 AMOY
**Xiaoping**
Chinese leader: 4 DENG
___ Xing: 3 PED 4 DEER
**Xings**
They have: 3 RRS
**XL:** 4 SIZE
**Xmas**
mo.: 3 DEC
poem opener: 4 TWAS
**"X-Men"**
actor McKellen: 3 IAN
**X-rated:** 5 ADULT DIRTY
stuff: 4 SMUT
**X-ray**
alternative: 3 MRI
blocker: 4 LEAD
discoverer: 8 ROENTGEN
dose: 3 RAD
subject: 7 INSIDES
unit: 3 RAD
vision blocker: 4 LEAD
**XXX:** 4 CHIS
counterpart: 3 OOO
**X ___ xylophone:** 4 ASIN
**Xylophone**
need: 6 MALLET
relative: 7 MARIMBA

# Yy

**Y:** 4 AXIS
  (abbr.): 3 LTR
  chromosome carrier: 4 MALE
  Like: 10 NEXTTOLAST
  of YSL: 4 YVES
  room: 3 GYM
  Series that may end in:
    5 AEIOU
  sporter: 3 ELI
  wearer: 3 ELI
  X, ~, or Z: 4 AXIS

**Y2K**
  Language linked to ~ problem:
    5 COBOL

**Y.A.**
  Giants QB: 6 TITTLE

**Yacht**
  maneuver: 4 TACK
  Maneuverable, as a: 4 YARE
  spot: 4 PIER 5 BASIN
    6 MARINA
  yes: 3 AYE
  Yonder: 3 SHE

**Yachting:** 4 ASEA 5 ATSEA
  event: 7 REGATTA 3EARAOE
  Go: 4 SAIL
  hazard: 4 REEF
  woe: 4 CALM

**"Yadda yadda yadda":** 3 ETC
    6 ETCETC 7 ANDSOON
    8 ETCETERA

**Yagudin**
  Skater: 6 ALEXEI

**Yahoo:** 4 BOOR HICK LOUT

**Yahoo!:** 3 ISP 6 PORTAL
  competitor: 3 AOL
  feature: 5 EMAIL

**Yahoo.com:** 4 SITE

**Yahtzee**
  cube: 3 DIE
  equipment: 4 DICE

**Yak:** 3 GAB JAW 4 BLAB
    5 RUNON 6 NATTER
  home: 5 TIBET
  pack: 4 OXEN

**Yakutsk**
  river: 4 LENA

**Yale:** 3 IVY
  alumni: 4 ELIS
  and others: 5 IVIES
  Either Clinton, to: 4 ALUM
  founder: 5 ELIHU
  Half a ~ cheer: 5 BOOLA
  NFL Hall of Famer: 4 LARY
  student: 3 ELI
  students since 1969:
    5 COEDS

**Yalie:** 3 ELI

**"Y'all"**
  Say: 5 ELIDE

**Yalow**
  Nobelist: 7 ROSALYN

**Yalta**
  attendee: 6 STALIN
  monogram: 3 FDR

**Yam**
  sayer: 6 POPEYE

**Yamaguchi**
  Figure skater: 6 KRISTI
  rival: 3 ITO

**Yamaha**
  product: 5 PIANO
  user: 5 BIKER

**Yamuna**
  City on the ~ river: 4 AGRA

**Yang**
  Concept with yin and: 3 TAO
  opposite: 3 YIN

**Yangtze**
  feeder: 3 HAN

**Yank:** 3 TUG 4 ALER PULL
  ally: 4 BRIT
  foe: 3 REB
  out of bed: 5 ROUST

**Yankee:** 4 ALER 6 GRINGO
  admonition: 6 GOHOME
  announcer: 8 MELALLEN
  div.: 6 ALEAST
  epithet: 4 DAMN
  home: 5 BRONX
  manager Joe: 5 TORRE
  manager Stengel: 5 CASEY
  nickname: 4 AROD YOGI
    5 DIMAG
  number 3: 4 RUTH
  pitcher Eddie: 5 LOPAT
  Quotable: 5 BERRA

**Yankee Clipper**
  airline: 5 PANAM

**Yankee Conference**
  town: 5 ORONO

**Yankee Doodle**
  feather: 8 MACARONI

**"Yankee Doodle Dandy"**
  beginning: 3 IMA
  songwriter: 5 COHAN

**"Yank in the ___, A":** 3 RAF

**Yankovic, "___ Al":** 5 WEIRD

**Yankovic, "Weird Al"**
  hit: 5 EATIT

**"Yanks"**
  star: 4 GERE

**Yao**
  of basketball: 4 MING

**Yap:** 4 TRAP 5 MOUTH
    6 KISSER

**Yaphet**
  Actor: 5 KOTTO
  role: 3 IDI

**Yapper:** 7 SCOTTIE
  Little: 4 PEKE

**Yarborough**
  Racer: 4 CALE

**Yard:** 4 LAWN
  Big ~, perhaps: 4 ACRE
  contents: 3 ALE
  Do ~ work: 3 MOW SOD
    4 RAKE
  enclosure: 5 FENCE HEDGE
  follower: 4 SALE
  holder: 4 MAST
  It's served by the: 3 ALE
  part: 4 FOOT
  pest: 4 MOLE
  tool: 4 RAKE 5 EDGER

**Yardage**
  pickup: 4 GAIN

**Yardarm:** 4 SPAR

**Yardbirds**
  tune: 6 IMAMAN

**Yards**
  5.5 ~: 3 ROD
  1,760 ~: 4 MILE
  4,840 square ~: 4 ACRE
    7 ONEACRE
  About 1.3 cubic: 5 STERE
  About 120 square: 3 ARE
  The whole nine: 3 ALL 4 ATOZ

**Yard sale**
  buys: 3 LPS
  caveat: 4 ASIS
  label: 3 TAG
  tag: 4 ASIS

**Yardstick:** 5 GAUGE
  (abbr.): 3 STD
  Econ.: 3 GNP

**Yarn:** 4 TALE
  Ball of: 4 CLEW
  Bit of: 4 HANK
  Embroidery: 6 CREWEL
  Fishy: 4 TALE
  quantity: 5 SKEIN
  spinner: 4 LIAR
  Work with: 4 KNIT

**Yashin**
  of hockey: 6 ALEXEI

**Yashmak:** 4 VEIL

**Yasir**
  Former Palestinian leader:
    6 ARAFAT

**Yasmine**
  Actress: 6 BLEETH

**Yastrzemski**
  of baseball: 4 CARL

Yat-___, Sun: 3 SEN
Yaw: 4 VEER
Yawl: 4 BOAT 5 YACHT
  call: 4 AHOY
  relative: 5 KETCH
Yawn: 4 GAPE
  Cause to: 4 BORE
  inducer: 4 BORE
  sound: 5 HOHUM
Yawner: 4 BORE
Yawn-inducing: 4 BLAH DULL
    5 BANAL HOHUM
Yawning: 4 DEEP 5 AGAPE
  fissure: 5 CHASM
  gulf: 5 ABYSS
"Yay!": 3 OLE RAH 6 HOORAH
"Yay, team!": 3 RAH
Ye
  follower: 4 OLDE
Yea
  opposite: 3 NAY
"Yeah, ___!": 3 YOU
"Yeah, man!": 4 IDIG
"Yeah, right!": 3 HAH 4 ASIF
    IBET 6 ILLBET IMSURE
    OHSURE
"Yeah, sure!": 4 ASIF IBET
Yeanling
  producer: 3 EWE
Year
  Add another: 5 RENEW
  divs.: 3 MOS
  Lunar new: 3 TET
  Once a: 6 ANNUAL
  One ~ in a trunk: 4 RING
  record: 5 ANNAL
  ~, in French: 5 ANNEE
  ~, in Italian: 4 ANNO
  ~, in Spanish: 3 ANO
  ___ year: 4 LEAP
Yearbook: 6 ANNUAL
  sect.: 3 SRS
Year-end
  reward: 5 BONUS
  temp: 5 SANTA
"Yearling, The"
  animal: 4 DEER
Yearly: 6 ANNUAL
  record: 5 ANNAL
Yearn: 4 ACHE LONG PINE
    6 ASPIRE HUNGER
  for: 4 MISS NEED 5 COVET
    CRAVE 6 DESIRE
Yearning: 3 YEN 4 ACHE ITCH
    LUST
Years
  A billion: 3 EON 4 AEON
  Add ~ to: 3 AGE
  ago: 4 ONCE
  Early: 5 YOUTH
  Getting on in: 6 OLDISH
  Golden: 6 OLDAGE
  of note: 3 ERA
  Ten: 6 DECADE
  Uncountable: 3 EON
  Up in: 4 AGED 5 OLDER

~, in Italian: 4 ANNI
Years ___: 3 AGO
"Years Alone, The"
  Biography subtitled:
    7 ELEANOR
Years and years: 3 EON 4 AGES
    EONS 7 DECADES
Yearwood
  Singer: 6 TRISHA
Yeast
  Add ~ to: 6 LEAVEN
  React to: 4 RISE
Yeasty
  brew: 3 ALE
Yeats: 4 POET
  heroine: 7 DEIRDRE
  Home for: 4 EIRE ERIN
    7 IRELAND
"Yea, verily": 6 ITISSO
"Yecch!": 3 UGH
Yegg: 11 SAFECRACKER
  haul: 3 ICE
  target: 4 SAFE
Yell: 3 CRY 5 SHOUT 6 HOLLER
  Bowl: 3 RAH
  Outfielder: 6 IGOTIT
  Sporting: 3 RAH
Yeller
  Old: 5 CRIER
___ Yello (soda brand):
    5 MELLO
Yellow: 3 SEA 5 AMBER MAIZE
    OCHER RIPEN 6 AFRAID
    CRAVEN FLAXEN
  blazer: 3 SUN
  brown: 5 TAWNY
  cheese: 4 EDAM
  flower: 5 TANSY
    9 BUTTERCUP
  fruit: 5 GUAVA PAPAW
    6 BANANA CASABA
    PAPAYA
  Grayish: 4 ECRU
  jacket: 4 WASP
  Pale: 5 MAIZE
  paper: 6 MANILA
  part: 4 YOLK
  Pinkish: 5 CORAL 7 APRICOT
  Reddish: 5 OCHER
  spread: 4 OLEO
  Tree with ~ ribbons: 3 OAK
  wildflower: 9 BUTTERCUP
Yellowbelly: 6 COWARD
Yellow fever
  fighter: 4 REED
  mosquito: 5 AEDES
Yellowfin: 4 TUNA
  tuna: 3 AHI
Yellowish: 5 OCHER 6 SALLOW
  brown: 5 AMBER CAMEL
    OCHER TAWNY 6 SIENNA
    7 CARAMEL
  pigment: 5 OCHER
  pink: 6 SALMON 7 TEAROSE
  red: 5 CORAL SANDY
  white: 8 EGGSHELL

Yellow Pages
  entries: 3 ADS
"___ yellow ribbon ...":
    4 TIEA
Yellowstone: 4 PARK
  animal: 3 ELK 4 BEAR
    5 BISON 6 WAPITI
  City near: 4 CODY
  figure: 6 RANGER
    10 PARKRANGER
  spewer: 6 GEYSER
"Yellow Submarine"
  villain: 6 MEANIE
Yelp
  Mouse-induced: 3 EEK
Yeltsin
  Mr.: 5 BORIS
  Mrs.: 5 NAINA
  successor: 5 PUTIN
  villa: 5 DACHA
Yemana
  portrayer: 3 SOO
Yemen
  capital: 4 ADEN SANA
    5 SANAA
  city: 4 ADEN TAIZ
  gulf: 4 ADEN
  native: 5 ADENI
  neighbor: 4 OMAN
  peninsula: 6 ARABIA
  port: 4 ADEN
  ~, long ago: 5 SHEBA
Yemeni: 4 ARAB
  money: 4 RIAL 5 RIYAL
  neighbor: 5 OMANI
  port: 4 ADEN
Yen: 4 ACHE ITCH URGE
    6 DESIRE
  Have a: 4 ACHE
  Have a ~ for: 4 WANT
    5 CRAVE 6 HANKER
  part: 3 SEN
  thousandth: 3 RIN
Yenta
  Like a: 4 NOSY
Yeoman
  yes: 3 AYE
"Yep"
  on a yacht: 3 AYE
  opposite: 4 NOPE
"Yer darn ___!": 6 TOOTIN
"___ yer old man!": 3 SOS
"Yertle the Turtle"
  author: 5 SEUSS
Yes
  at sea: 3 AYE
  Emphatic: 6 IDOIDO
  Emphatic ~, in Spanish:
    4 SISI
  follower: 5 SIREE
  (Japanese): 3 HAI
  Say: 5 AGREE 6 ASSENT
  Say ~ to: 6 ACCEDE
    ACCEPT
  vote: 3 AYE
  ~, in French: 3 OUI

"Yes!": 4 AMEN
10 ABSOLUTELY
BYALLMEANS
11 BUTOFCOURSE
"Yes ___?": 4 ORNO
"Yes, ___!": 4 MAAM
6 SIRREE
"Yes ___" (Sammy Davis Jr.
bio): 4 ICAN
"Yes ___, Bob!": 6 SIRREE
Yeshiva
graduate: 5 RABBI
teacher: 5 REBBE
Ye ___ Shoppe: 4 OLDE
Yes-man: 5 TOADY 6 NODDER
8 ASSENTER
Yesterday
~, in French: 4 HIER
~, in Italian: 4 IERI
"Yesterday!": 4 ASAP
Yesteryear: 4 YORE
"Yes, there is ___!": 4 AGOD
"Yes! Yes!": 6 IDOIDO
Yet: 5 BYNOW SOFAR
6 TODATE
again: 4 ANEW
As: 5 SOFAR 6 ERENOW
Not in: 7 ONORDER
to come: 5 AHEAD
~, poetically: 3 EEN
Yiddish
gossip: 5 YENTE
plaints: 3 OYS
writer Aleichem: 6 SHOLOM
Yield: 3 BOW PAY 4 BEAR
BEND CAVE CEDE EMIT
GIVE 5 DEFER 6 ASSENT
GIVEIN RELENT
RETURN 7 SUCCUMB
Field: 4 CROP
Maple: 3 SAP
Mine: 3 ORE
Refuse to: 6 INSIST
Yielding: 6 PLIANT
"Yikes!": 3 EEK 4 EGAD OHNO
5 EGADS 7 OMIGOSH
Yin
opposite: 4 YANG
"Yipe!": 4 EGAD
"Yippee!": 5 OHBOY WAHOO
Yitzhak
predecessor: 5 GOLDA
YM: 3 MAG
Yma
Singer: 5 SUMAC
YMCA
class: 3 CPR
part: 4 ASSN MENS
"Yo!": 3 HEY 6 HEYYOU
Subtle: 4 PSST
Yodel
recall: 4 ECHO
Yodeler
perch: 3 ALP
range: 8 FALSETTO
reply: 4 ECHO

Yoga
accessory: 3 MAT
position: 5 ASANA LOTUS
practitioner: 5 HINDU
type: 5 HATHA
___ yoga: 5 HATHA
Yogi: 4 BEAR
Baseball catcher: 5 BERRA
Buddy of: 10 BOOBOOBEAR
Yogi Bear: 4 TOON
co-creator: 5 HANNA
Voice of: 4 DAWS
Yogurt
Like some: 5 NOFAT 6 NONFAT
Yoke: 5 UNITE
mates: 4 OXEN
The ~ is on them: 4 OXEN
Yokel: 4 BOOR CLOD RUBE
Yoko
Singer: 3 ONO
Son of: 4 SEAN
Yokohama
drama: 3 NOH
yes: 3 HAI
Yokozuna
Its champion is called: 4 SUMO
Yokum
boy: 5 ABNER
creator: 4 CAPP 6 ALCAPP
dad: 5 PAPPY
mom: 5 MAMMY
Yokum, Daisy ___: 3 MAE
Yokum, Mammy
First name of: 5 PANSY
Yolk
encloser: 3 SAC
Yom ___: 3 TOV
Yom Kippur
Observe: 5 ATONE
observer: 6 ATONER
ritual: 4 FAST
Yon: 4 AFAR
companion: 6 HITHER
damsel: 3 HER SHE
"Yond Cassius has ___ and
hungry look": 5 ALEAN
Yonder: 4 AFAR THAT 5 THERE
Off: 4 AFAR
Over: 4 THAR 5 THERE
woman: 3 SHE
yacht: 3 SHE
Yoo
follower: 3 HOO
"Yoo-___!": 3 HOO
"Yoo-hoo!": 8 OVERHERE
Yoplait
competitor: 6 DANNON
Yorba ___: 5 LINDA
Yore
Car of: 3 GTO
Days of: 3 ELD 4 PAST
News source of: 5 CRIER
Oath of: 4 EGAD
Of: 3 AGO 4 PAST 5 OLDEN
Ruler of: 4 TSAR 6 SHOGUN
Your of: 3 THY 5 THINE

Yorick
Like: 4 POOR
Word for: 4 ALAS
York: 3 NCO SGT
Actress: 8 SUSANNAH
John of: 3 LOO
river: 4 OUSE
Sergeant: 5 ALVIN
Yorkshire
city: 5 LEEDS
literary name: 6 BRONTE
river: 3 URE 4 AIRE OUSE
Yosemite: 4 PARK
photographer: 5 ADAMS
10 ANSELADAMS
Yossarian
bunkmate: 3 ORR
"Yo te ___": 3 AMO
Yothers
Actress: 4 TINA
You
are here: 5 EARTH
~, formerly: 4 THEE THOU
~, in French: 3 TOI
~, in German: 3 SIE
~, in Spanish: 5 USTED
~, right now: 6 SOLVER
You ___!": 6 BETCHA
"You ___?": 4 RANG
"You ___" (Lionel Richie hit):
3 ARE
"You are ___": 4 HERE
"You are here"
place: 3 MAP
"You Are My Destiny"
singer Paul: 4 ANKA
"You are not!"
reply: 5 IAMSO 6 IAMTOO
"You are, too!"
preceder: 6 IAMNOT
"___ you asked ...": 5 SINCE
"___ You Babe": 4 IGOT
"You ___ Beautiful" (Joe Cocker
hit): 5 ARESO
"You Belong to Me"
singer Glenn: 4 FREY
"You bet!": 3 YEP YES 4 SURE
YEAH 6 ANDHOW
"You betcha!": 3 YEP YES YUP
4 SURE 8 YESSIREE
"You Bet Your Life"
prop: 5 CIGAR
sponsor: 6 DESOTO
"You ___ bother!":
6 NEEDNT
"You Can Call Me Al"
singer Paul: 5 SIMON
"You can count on me!":
7 ILLDOIT
"You can ___ horse ...":
5 LEADA
"You can observe a lot by
watching"
speaker: 5 BERRA
"You can say that again!":
4 AMEN

**"You can't play at my house!":**
  6 GOHOME
**"You Can't Take It With You"**
  director: 5 CAPRA
  playwright: 8 MOSSHART
  star: 10 JEANARTHUR
**"You can't teach ___ dog ...":**
  5 ANOLD
**"You da ___!":** 3 MAN
**"___ you don't!":** 4 OHNO
**"You Don't Bring Me Flowers":**
  4 DUET
**"You don't mean me?!":** 3 MOI
**"You don't say!":** 3 GEE
  6 INDEED
**"You don't think I'd do it, do**
  **you?":** 6 DAREME
**"You ___ for it!":** 5 ASKED
**"___ you for real?":** 3 ARE
**"___ you glad ...":** 5 ARENT
**"___ You Glad You're You?":**
  5 ARENT
**"You go not till ___ you up a**
  **glass":** 4 ISET
**"You gotta be kidding!":**
  4 OHNO
**"You got that right!":** 6 ILLSAY
**"You haven't started yet, have**
  **you?":** 7 AMILATE
**"You have to see this!":**
  6 OHLOOK
**"You ___ here":** 3 ARE
**"You ___ kidding!":** 5 ARENT
**"___ you kidding?":** 3 ARE
**"You know how ___":** 4 ITIS
**"You Light Up My Life"**
  singer Boone: 5 DEBBY
**"You'll regret it otherwise!":**
  6 ORELSE
**"You look like you ___ ghost!":**
  4 SAWA
**"___ you loud and clear!":**
  5 IREAD
**Youmans**
  heroine: 7 NANETTE
  musical: 11 NONONANETTE
**"You missed it":** 7 TOOLATE
**"You ___ mouthful!":** 5 SAIDA
**"You Must Remember This"**
  author: 5 OATES
**"You ___ My Sunshine":** 3 ARE
**Young**
  Actor: 4 ALAN
  Actress: 4 SEAN 7 LORETTA
  bear: 3 CUB
  Bear ~, as sheep: 4 YEAN
  "Blondie" creator: 4 CHIC
  boy: 3 LAD TAD
  codfish: 5 SCROD
  deer: 4 FAWN
  eel: 5 ELVER
  follower: 3 UNS
  Forever: 7 AGELESS
  fowl: 5 POULT
  fox: 3 KIT
  goat: 3 KID

haddock: 5 SCROD
hare: 7 LEVERET
hooter: 5 OWLET
horse: 4 COLT FOAL
hotshot: 6 PHENOM
lady: 4 GIRL LASS MISS
lady of Sp.: 4 SRTA
lion: 5 WHELP
man: 3 BOY LAD
newt: 3 EFT
Not: 4 AGED
of Utah history: 7 BRIGHAM
Org. for ~ men: 3 BSA
Partner of ~ in accounting:
  5 ERNST
pig: 5 SHOAT
pigeon: 5 SQUAB
predator: 5 OWLET
raptor: 6 EAGLET
salmon: 4 PARR 5 SMOLT
seal: 3 PUP
sheep: 4 LAMB
Singer: 4 NEIL
socialite: 3 DEB
suffix: 4 STER
swan: 6 CYGNET
turkey: 5 POULT
wolf: 5 WHELP
woman: 4 LASS
**Young ___:** 3 UNS
**Young, Brigham**
  place: 4 UTAH
**Young, Robert**
  sitcom:
    15 FATHERKNOWSBEST
**"Young and the Restless, The":**
  4 SOAP 9 SOAPOPERA
**Youngest**
  Greek god: 4 EROS
**"Young Frankenstein"**
  Actress Garr: 4 TERI
  assistant: 4 IGOR
  role for Marty: 4 IGOR
  woman: 4 INGA
**Youngman**
  Funnyman: 5 HENNY
  specialty: 8 ONELINER
**Youngster:** 3 KID LAD TAD TOT
  4 TYKE 5 CHILD
  6 SHAVER
**Young 'un:** 3 LAD TAD TOT
  4 TYKE
**"___ you nuts?":** 3 ARE
**"___ you one!":** 4 IOWE
**Your**
  and my: 3 OUR
  highness: 4 SIRE
  of yore: 3 THY
  ~, in French: 3 TES
**"You rang?":** 3 YES
**"___ your disposal":** 4 IMAT
**"You're it!"**
  Word before: 3 TAG
**"You're joshing!":** 5 PSHAW
**"You're ___ mistaken!":**
  5 SADLY

**"You're ___ Need to Get By":**
  4 ALLI
**"You're on!":** 8 ITSADEAL
**"Your Erroneous Zones"**
  author Wayne: 4 DYER
**"You're So ___" (Carly Simon**
  **hit):** 4 VAIN
**"You're ___ talk!":** 5 ONETO
**"You're the ___ Care For":**
  4 ONEI
**"You're ___, ya know that?":**
  Archie Bunker: 4 APIP
**"You ___ right!":** 5 ARESO
**"___ your life!":** 5 NOTON
**"Your majesty":** 4 SIRE
**"___ your pardon!":** 4 IBEG
**"Your point being ...?":** 3 AND
**Yours**
  and mine: 4 OURS
  Not: 4 MINE
  of yore: 5 THINE
  ~, in French: 4 ATOI
**Yours ___:** 5 TRULY
**"___ yourself":** 5 BRACE
**"Your Show of Shows"**
  regular: 4 COCA
**"Yours truly":** 5 CLOSE
**"Your turn":** 4 OVER
**"You said it!":** 3 YES 4 AMEN
  6 ANDHOW 7 RIGHTON
**"___ you serious?":** 3 ARE
**"You sly one, you!":** 3 OHO
**"You stink!":** 3 BOO
**Youth:** 3 LAD 5 MINOR TEENS
  9 SALADDAYS
  Goddess of: 4 HEBE
  Impudent: 5 WHELP
  org.: 3 BSA 4 YMCA YMHA
  Winged: 4 EROS
**"You there!":** 3 HEY
**"You there?":** 5 HELLO
**"You ___ There":** 3 ARE
**Youthful**
  times: 9 SALADDAYS
**"You've got ___":** 5 ADEAL
**"You've Got ___":** 4 MAIL
**"You've got mail"**
  co.: 3 AOL
  One who hears: 5 AOLER
**"You've Got Mail"**
  director Ephron: 4 NORA
  Ryan of: 3 MEG
**"You've Made ___ Very Happy":**
  4 MESO
**"You ___ what you eat":** 3 ARE
**"You will regret it otherwise!":**
  6 ORELSE
**"You win":** 5 ILOSE
**"You wish!":** 4 ASIF
  7 DREAMON
**"You Won't ___" (Beatles tune):**
  5 SEEME
**"You ___ worry":** 6 NEEDNT
**"You wouldn't dare!"**
  response: 5 TRYME
**"Yow!":** 4 OUCH

**Yowler**
Alley: 3 TOM
**Yo-yo:** 3 TOY
maker: 6 DUNCAN
trick: 13 WALKINGTHEDOG
**"___ y Plata"** (Montana's
motto): 3 ORO
**Yr.**
end adviser: 3 CPA
ender: 3 DEC
fourth: 3 QTR
parts: 3 MOS
School ~ part: 3 SEM
**Yrs.**
100 ~: 3 CEN
Golden ~ cache: 3 IRA
**YSL**
part: 4 YVES
**Yttrium:** 9 RAREEARTH
**Yucatán**
Early ~ dweller: 4 MAYA
yay!: 3 OLE
year: 3 ANO
you: 5 USTED

~ Indian: 5 MAYAN
**Yucca**
family: 5 AGAVE
fiber: 5 ISTLE
relative: 4 ALOE
**"Yuck!":** 3 UGH
**Yugo.**
neighbor: 3 ALB
**Yugoslav**
Former ~ leader: 4 TITO
**Yugoslavs**
Many: 5 SERBS
**Yukon:** 4 TERR
country: 6 CANADA
letters: 3 GMC
**"Yuk yuk":** 4 HAHA
**Yule:** 4 NOEL
drink: 3 NOG
garland: 6 WREATH
song: 4 NOEL
trio: 4 MAGI
~, informally: 4 XMAS
**Yuletide:** 4 NOEL
décor: 5 HOLLY

door décor: 6 WREATH
drink: 3 NOG 6 EGGNOG
song: 4 NOEL 5 CAROL
sweet: 4 CANE
trio: 4 MAGI
visitor: 5 SANTA
**"Yum!":** 5 TASTY
**Yuma**
river: 4 GILA
**Yummy:** 4 GOOD
**"Yummy":** 3 MMM
**Yup**
opposite: 4 NOPE
**Yuppie**
auto: 3 BMW
**Yuri**
Love of: 4 LARA
player: 4 OMAR
**Yutang**
Author: 3 LIN
**Yvonne**
Actress: 7 DECARLO
**YWCA**
part: 4 ASSN

# Zz

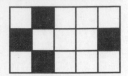

**Z**
- A to: 5 GAMUT
- British: 3 ZED
- Greek: 4 ZETA
- X, Y, or: 4 AXIS

**"Z"**
- actor Montand: 4 YVES
- actress Papas: 5 IRENE
- ___ Z: 3 ATO
- From: 3 ATO

**Z3:** 3 BMW

**Zadora**
- Actress/singer: 3 PIA

**Zag:** 3 YAW 4 VEER

**Zagreb**
- location: 7 CROATIA
- resident: 5 CROAT
  - 8 CROATIAN

**Zahn**
- Newswoman: 5 PAULA

**Zaire**
- dictator Mobuto ___ Seko:
  - 4 SESE
- dictator Mobuto Sese ___:
  - 4 SEKO

**Zaius, Dr.:** 3 APE

**Zambia**
- neighbor: 6 ANGOLA

**Zamboni**
- site: 4 RINK
- surface: 3 ICE

**Zane**
- Author: 4 GREY

**Zany:** 6 MADCAP

**Zap:** 4 LASE NUKE STUN

**Zapata**
- Info: Spanish cue
- Zilch, to: 4 NADA

**"___ Zapata":** 4 VIVA

**Zappa**
- Daughter of Frank:
  - 8 MOONUNIT

**Zappa, Moon ___:** 4 UNIT

**Zapped**
- They might be: 3 ADS

**Zapper:** 3 EEL
- target: 3 ADS BUG

**Zaragoza**
- river: 4 EBRO

**Zasu**
- Comic: 5 PITTS

**Zátopek**
- Olympic runner: 4 EMIL

**Zayak**
- Skater: 6 ELAINE

**Zeal:** 5 ARDOR

**Zealot:** 3 NUT 5 ULTRA
- 6 MANIAC 7 FANATIC

**Zealous:** 4 AVID 5 EAGER
- 6 ABLAZE ARDENT

**Zebra:** 3 REF 6 EQUINE
- feature: 4 MANE
- relative: 3 ASS

**Zebulon**
- Explorer: 4 PIKE

**Zedong, ___:** 3 MAO

**Zee**
- preceder: 3 WYE

**Zeke**
- portrayer: 4 LAHR

**"Zelig"**
- director: 5 ALLEN

**Zelle**
- familiar name: 4 HARI

**Zellweger**
- Actress: 5 RENEE

**Zelnicek, ___:** 5 IVANA

**Zen:** 4 SECT
- Do: 8 MEDITATE
- enlightenment: 6 SATORI

**Zenith:** 3 TOP 4 ACME APEX
- 6 APOGEE
- opposite: 5 NADIR
- product: 3 VCR
- rival: 3 RCA

**Zeno**
- birthplace: 4 ELEA
- follower: 5 STOIC
- platform: 4 STOA

**Zephyr:** 6 BREEZE

**Zephyrous:** 4 AIRY

**___ Zeppelin:** 3 LED

**Zeppo:** 4 MARX
- Brother of: 5 CHICO
  - HARPO

**Zero:** 3 NIL 4 LOVE NADA
- NONE NULL 5 AUGHT
- 6 NAUGHT NOTANY
- NOTONE 7 NOTABIT
- 8 GOOSEEGG
- Actor: 6 MOSTEL
- Less than ~ (abbr.): 3 NEG
- Letters above: 4 OPER
- Put back to: 5 RESET
- With ~ chance: 5 NOHOW

**Zero-star**
- fare: 4 SLOP
- movie: 4 BOMB
- review: 3 PAN

**Zero-wheeled**
- vehicle: 4 SLED

**Zest:** 4 BRIO ELAN RIND
- 5 GUSTO SAVOR
- Fruit: 4 PEEL RIND

**Zesty**
- dip: 5 SALSA

**Zeta**
- follower: 3 ETA

**Zetterling**
- Actress: 3 MAI

**Zeus**
- abductee: 6 EUROPA
- Consort of: 4 HERA
- Daughter of: 4 HEBE 5 HELEN
  - 6 ATHENA
- Mother of: 4 RHEA
- Queen wooed by: 4 LEDA
- Roman: 4 JOVE
- Shield of: 5 AEGIS
- Son of: 4 ARES 6 APOLLO
- temple site: 5 NEMEA
- Wife of: 4 HERA

**Zhivago**
- Love of: 4 LARA
- portrayer: 6 SHARIF

**Zhou**
- Communist leader: 5 ENLAI

**Ziegfeld**
- designer: 4 ERTE
- Producer: 3 FLO
- production: 5 REVUE

**"Ziegfeld Follies"**
- designer: 4 ERTE
- star Naldi: 4 NITA
- Ziegfeld of: 3 FLO

**Ziering**
- Actor: 3 IAN

**Zig:** 3 YAW 4 TURN VEER

**Ziggy**
- Jazz trumpeter: 5 ELMAN

**Zigzag:** 3 SEW 5 WEAVE
- 6 SLALOM

**Zilch:** 3 NIL 4 NADA NONE
- ZERO 6 NAUGHT
- NOTANY

**Zillion:** 3 TON 4 MANY

**Zillions:** 4 ALOT
- of years: 3 EON

**Zimbabwe**
- capital: 3 ZEE 6 HARARE
- Lang. of: 3 ENG
- ~, formerly: 8 RHODESIA

**Zimbalist**
- Actor: 5 EFREM
- Violinist: 5 EFREM

**Zinc**
- sulfide: 6 BLENDE

**Zinc ___:** 5 OXIDE

**Zine**
- Online: 4 EMAG

**Zinfandel**
- Like: 3 DRY

**Zing:** 3 PEP 4 ELAN 5 NOISE
- OOMPH

**Zinger:** 3 MOT 4 BARB
  6 RETORT 7 RIPOSTE
  8 ONELINER
  producer: 3 WIT
**Zingy**
  taste: 4 TANG
**Zinnemann**
  Director: 4 FRED
**Zion National Park**
  home: 4 UTAH
**Zip:** 3 NIL PEP 4 DART ELAN
  NADA NONE NULL
  TEAR ZERO 5 SPEED
  ZILCH 6 ENERGY
  7 NOTAONE
  8 GOOSEEGG
  Bike that can: 5 MOPED
  Full of: 4 PERT
**"Zip-A-Dee-___-Dah":** 3 DOO
**"Zip-A-Dee-Doo-___":** 3 DAH
**"Zip-A-___-Doo-Dah":** 3 DEE
**Zip code**
  10001 ~: 4 NYNY
**"Zip-___-Doo-Dah":** 4 ADEE
**Zipped:** 4 FLEW SPED TORE
  through: 4 ACED
**Zipper**
  alternative: 4 SNAP 6 VELCRO
  cover: 3 FLY
  Name on a: 4 IZOD
**Zippo:** 3 NIL 4 NADA NONE
  part: 4 WICK
**Zippy**
  dip: 5 SALSA
  flavor: 4 TANG
  watercraft: 6 JETSKI
**Zither**
  Japanese: 4 KOTO
**Ziti:** 5 PASTA
  relative: 5 PENNE
**Zodiac**
  animal: 3 RAM 4 BULL CRAB
  GOAT LION 8 SCORPION
  border: 4 CUSP
  sign: 3 LEO 5 ARIES LIBRA
  VIRGO 6 GEMINI PISCES
  symbol: 6 ARCHER SCALES
**Zoe**
  Friend of: 4 ELMO
  Playwright: 5 AKINS

**Zog I**
  domain: 7 ALBANIA
**Zola**
  Author: 5 EMILE
  heroine: 4 NANA
  letter: 7 JACCUSE
  novel: 4 NANA \
  portrayer: 4 MUNI
**Zoltan**
  Director: 5 KORDA
**Zone:** 4 AREA 6 REGION
  SECTOR
  Canal: 3 EAR
  Flying: 8 AIRSPACE
  Narrow: 4 BELT
  School ~ sign: 3 SLO 4 SLOW
  Strike ~ boundary: 5 KNEES
  Time: 3 CST EST PST
  War: 3 NAM 4 IRAQ 5 ARENA
  6 SECTOR
  WWII: 3 ETO
**Zoning**
  unit: 4 ACRE
**Zoo**
  barrier: 4 MOAT
  beast: 3 APE 5 HIPPO KOALA
  LLAMA ORANG OTTER
  PANDA RHINO TIGER
  enclosure: 4 CAGE
  Floating: 3 ARK
  section: 6 AVIARY
  sound: 4 ROAR
  trench: 4 MOAT
**Zoo de Madrid**
  animal: 3 OSO 5 TIGRE
**Zooey**
  Father of: 3 LES
**Zool.:** 3 SCI
**Zoologist**
  study: 5 FAUNA
  ~ Fossey: 4 DIAN
**Zoology:** 7 SCIENCE
  bones: 4 OSSA
  classification: 6 FAMILY
  foot: 3 PES
  mouths: 3 ORA
**Zoom:** 4 LENS SOAR TEAR
  5 NOISE SPEED
  photo: 7 CLOSEUP
**Zoophyte:** 7 ANEMONE

**"Zoo Story, The":** 8 ONEACTER
  playwright: 5 ALBEE
**Zoot**
  Jazzman: 4 SIMS
**"Zorba the Greek"**
  actress Irene: 5 PAPAS
  actress Papas: 5 IRENE
**Zoroastrian:** 5 PARSI
  scriptures: 4 ZEND 6 AVESTA
**Zorro**
  Daughter of: 5 ELENA
  garb: 4 CAPE
  mark: 3 ZEE 4 SCAR
**"Zounds!":** 4 EGAD 5 EGADS
**Zoysia:** 5 GRASS
**Z's**
  Catch some: 3 NAP 4 DOZE
  5 SLEEP 6 SNOOZE
  Catch some extra: 7 SLEEPIN
  ~, in Zaragoza: 6 SIESTA
**Zsa Zsa:** 5 GABOR
  Sister of: 3 EVA 5 MAGDA
  8 EVAGABOR
**Zubin**
  Conductor: 5 MEHTA
**"Zuckerman Unbound"**
  author: 4 ROTH
**Zugspitze:** 3 ALP
**Zuider ___:** 3 ZEE
**Zukor**
  Producer: 6 ADOLPH
**Zulu:** 5 BANTU
**Zumwalt**
  Admiral: 4 ELMO
**Zurich**
  peak: 3 ALP
**Zurich-to-Munich**
  dir.: 3 ENE
**Zuyder ___:** 3 ZEE
**Zwei**
  cubed: 4 ACHT
  doubled: 4 VIER
  follower: 4 DREI
  Half of: 4 EINS
**Zygomatic**
  Flex one's ~ muscles:
  5 SMILE
**Z ___ zebra:** 4 ASIN
**ZZ Top:** 4 TRIO
**Zzz:** 5 SNORE

## Olympic Games Host Cities

1896 Athens
1900 Paris
1904 St. Louis
1908 London
1912 Stockholm
1916 Berlin (canceled)
1920 Antwerp
1924 (S) Paris
     (W) Chamonix
1928 (S) Amsterdam
     (W) St. Moritz
1932 (S) Los Angeles
     (W) Lake Placid
1936 (S) Berlin
     (W) Garmisch-Partenkirchen
1940 (S) Tokyo (canceled)
     (W) Sapporo (canceled)
1944 (S) London (canceled)
     (W) Cortina d'Ampezzo (canceled)
1948 (S) London
     (W) St. Moritz
1952 (S) Helsinki
     (W) Oslo
1956 (S) Melbourne
        (equestrian events in Stockholm)
     (W) Cortina d'Ampezzo
1960 (S) Rome
     (W) Squaw Valley
1964 (S) Tokyo
     (W) Innsbruck
1968 (S) Mexico City
     (W) Grenoble
1972 (S) Munich
     (W) Sapporo
1976 (S) Montreal
     (W) Innsbruck
1980 (S) Moscow
     (W) Lake Placid
1984 (S) Los Angeles
     (W) Sarajevo
1988 (S) Seoul
     (W) Calgary
1992 (S) Barcelona
     (W) Albertville
1994 (W) Lillehammer
1996 (S) Atlanta
1998 (W) Nagano
2000 (S) Sydney
2002 (W) Salt Lake City
2004 (S) Athens
2006 (W) Turin
2008 (S) Beijing
2010 (W) Vancouver
2012 (S) London
2014 (W) Sochi

## Super Bowl MVPs

1967 (I) Bart Starr
1968 (II) Bart Starr
1969 (III) Joe Namath
1970 (IV) Len Dawson
1971 (V) Chuck Howley
1972 (VI) Roger Staubach
1973 (VII) Jake Scott
1974 (VIII) Larry Csonka
1975 (IX) Franco Harris
1976 (X) Lynn Swann
1977 (XI) Fred Biletnikoff
1978 (XII) Randy White
            Harvey Martin
1979 (XIII) Terry Bradshaw
1980 (XIV) Terry Bradshaw
1981 (XV) Jim Plunkett
1982 (XVI) Joe Montana
1983 (XVII) John Riggins
1984 (XVIII) Marcus Allen
1985 (XIX) Joe Montana
1986 (XX) Richard Dent
1987 (XXI) Phil Simms
1988 (XXII) Doug Williams
1989 (XXIII) Jerry Rice
1990 (XXIV) Joe Montana
1991 (XXV) Ottis Anderson
1992 (XXVI) Mark Rypien
1993 (XXVII) Troy Aikman
1994 (XXVIII) Emmitt Smith
1995 (XXIX) Steve Young
1996 (XXX) Larry Brown
1997 (XXXI) Desmond Howard
1998 (XXXII) Terrell Davis
1999 (XXXIII) John Elway
2000 (XXXIV) Kurt Warner
2001 (XXXV) Ray Lewis
2002 (XXXVI) Tom Brady
2003 (XXXVII) Dexter Jackson
2004 (XXXVIII) Tom Brady
2005 (XXXIX) Deion Branch
2006 (XL) Hines Ward
2007 (XLI) Peyton Manning
2008 (XLII) Eli Manning

## NBA MVPs
1956 Bob Pettit
1957 Bob Cousy
1958 Bill Russell
1959 Bob Pettit
1960 Wilt Chamberlain
1961 Bill Russell
1962 Bill Russell
1963 Bill Russell
1964 Oscar Robertson
1965 Bill Russell
1966 Wilt Chamberlain
1967 Wilt Chamberlain
1968 Wilt Chamberlain
1969 Wes Unseld
1970 Willis Reed
1971 Kareem Abdul-Jabbar
       (as Lew Alcindor)
1972 Kareem Abdul-Jabbar
1973 Dave Cowens
1974 Kareem Abdul-Jabbar
1975 Bob McAdoo
1976 Kareem Abdul-Jabbar
1977 Kareem Abdul-Jabbar
1978 Bill Walton
1979 Moses Malone
1980 Kareem Abdul-Jabbar
1981 Julius Erving
1982 Moses Malone
1983 Moses Malone
1984 Larry Bird
1985 Larry Bird
1986 Larry Bird
1987 Magic Johnson
1988 Michael Jordan
1989 Magic Johnson
1990 Magic Johnson
1991 Michael Jordan
1992 Michael Jordan
1993 Charles Barkley
1994 Hakeem Olajuwon
1995 David Robinson
1996 Michael Jordan
1997 Karl Malone
1998 Michael Jordan
1999 Karl Malone
2000 Shaquille O'Neal
2001 Allen Iverson
2002 Tim Duncan
2003 Tim Duncan
2004 Kevin Garnett
2005 Steve Nash
2006 Steve Nash
2007 Dirk Nowitzki
2008 Kobe Bryant

## World Series MVPs
1955 Johnny Podres
1956 Don Larsen
1957 Lew Burdette
1958 Bob Turley
1959 Larry Sherry
1960 Bobby Richardson
1961 Whitey Ford
1962 Ralph Terry
1963 Sandy Koufax
1964 Bob Gibson
1965 Sandy Koufax
1966 Frank Robinson
1967 Bob Gibson
1968 Mickey Lolich
1969 Donn Clendenon
1970 Brooks Robinson
1971 Roberto Clemente
1972 Gene Tenace
1973 Reggie Jackson
1974 Rollie Fingers
1975 Pete Rose
1976 Johnny Bench
1977 Reggie Jackson
1978 Bucky Dent
1979 Willie Stargell
1980 Mike Schmidt
1981 Ron Cey
       Pedro Guerrero
       Steve Yeager
1982 Darrell Porter
1983 Rick Dempsey
1984 Alan Trammell
1985 Bret Saberhagen
1986 Ray Knight
1987 Frank Viola
1988 Orel Hershiser
1989 Dave Stewart
1990 José Rijo
1991 Jack Morris
1992 Pat Borders
1993 Paul Molitor
1994 no World Series
1995 Tom Glavine
1996 John Wetteland
1997 Liván Hernández
1998 Scott Brosius
1999 Mariano Rivera
2000 Derek Jeter
2001 Randy Johnson
       Curt Schilling
2002 Troy Glaus
2003 Josh Beckett
2004 Manny Ramírez
2005 Jermaine Dye
2006 David Eckstein
2007 Mike Lowell
2008 Cole Hamels

## Cy Young Award Winners

1956 Don Newcombe
1957 Warren Spahn
1958 Bob Turley
1959 Early Wynn
1960 Vern Law
1961 Whitey Ford
1962 Don Drysdale
1963 Sandy Koufax
1964 Dean Chance
1965 Sandy Koufax
1966 Sandy Koufax
1967 (AL) Jim Lonborg
     (NL) Mike McCormick
1968 (AL) Denny McLain
     (NL) Bob Gibson
1969 (AL) Mike Cuellar
     Denny McLain
     (NL) Tom Seaver
1970 (AL) Jim Perry
     (NL) Bob Gibson
1971 (AL) Vida Blue
     (NL) Ferguson Jenkins
1972 (AL) Gaylord Perry
     (NL) Steve Carlton
1973 (AL) Jim Palmer
     (NL) Tom Seaver
1974 (AL) Catfish Hunter
     (NL) Mike Marshall
1975 (AL) Jim Palmer
     (NL) Tom Seaver
1976 (AL) Jim Palmer
     (NL) Randy Jones
1977 (AL) Sparky Lyle
     (NL) Steve Carlton
1978 (AL) Ron Guidry
     (NL) Gaylord Perry
1979 (AL) Mike Flanagan
     (NL) Bruce Sutter
1980 (AL) Steve Stone
     (NL) Steve Carlton
1981 (AL) Rollie Fingers
     (NL) Fernando Valenzuela
1982 (AL) Pete Vuckovich
     (NL) Steve Carlton
1983 (AL) LaMarr Hoyt
     (NL) John Denny
1984 (AL) Willie Hernández
     (NL) Rick Sutcliffe

1985 (AL) Bret Saberhagen
     (NL) Dwight Gooden
1986 (AL) Roger Clemens
     (NL) Mike Scott
1987 (AL) Roger Clemens
     (NL) Steve Bedrosian
1988 (AL) Frank Viola
     (NL) Orel Hershiser
1989 (AL) Bret Saberhagen
     (NL) Mark Davis
1990 (AL) Bob Welch
     (NL) Doug Drabek
1991 (AL) Roger Clemens
     (NL) Tom Glavine
1992 (AL) Dennis Eckersley
     (NL) Greg Maddux
1993 (AL) Jack McDowell
     (NL) Greg Maddux
1994 (AL) David Cone
     (NL) Greg Maddux
1995 (AL) Randy Johnson
     (NL) Greg Maddux
1996 (AL) Pat Hentgen
     (NL) John Smoltz
1997 (AL) Roger Clemens
     (NL) Pedro Martínez
1998 (AL) Roger Clemens
     (NL) Tom Glavine
1999 (AL) Pedro Martínez
     (NL) Randy Johnson
2000 (AL) Pedro Martínez
     (NL) Randy Johnson
2001 (AL) Roger Clemens
     (NL) Randy Johnson
2002 (AL) Barry Zito
     (NL) Randy Johnson
2003 (AL) Roy Halladay
     (NL) Eric Gagné
2004 (AL) Johan Santana
     (NL) Roger Clemens
2005 (AL) Bartolo Colón
     (NL) Chris Carpenter
2006 (AL) Johan Santana
     (NL) Brandon Webb
2007 (AL) C.C. Sabathia
     (NL) Jake Peavey
2008 (AL) Cliff Lee
     (NL) Tim Lincecum

## Wimbledon Singles Winners
(since 1922)

| Men | Women | Men | Women |
|---|---|---|---|
| 1922 Gerald Patterson | Suzanne Lenglen | 1969 Rod Laver | Ann Jones |
| 1923 Bill Johnston | Suzanne Lenglen | 1970 John Newcombe | Margaret Smith Court |
| 1924 Jean Borotra | Kitty McKane | 1971 John Newcombe | Evonne Goolagong |
| 1925 René Lacoste | Suzanne Lenglen | 1972 Stan Smith | Billie Jean King |
| 1926 Jean Borotra | Kitty McKane Godfree | 1973 Jan Kodeš | Billie Jean King |
| 1927 Henri Cochet | Helen Wills | 1974 Jimmy Connors | Chris Evert |
| 1928 René Lacoste | Helen Wills Moody | 1975 Arthur Ashe | Billie Jean King |
| 1929 Henri Cochet | Helen Wills Moody | 1976 Björn Borg | Chris Evert |
| 1930 Bill Tilden | Helen Wills Moody | 1977 Björn Borg | Virginia Wade |
| 1931 Sidney Wood | Cilly Aussem | 1978 Björn Borg | Martina Navrátilová |
| 1932 Ellsworth Vines | Helen Wills Moody | 1979 Björn Borg | Martina Navrátilová |
| 1933 Jack Crawford | Helen Wills Moody | 1980 Björn Borg | Evonne Goolagong |
| 1934 Fred Perry | Dorothy Round | | Cawley |
| 1935 Fred Perry | Helen Wills Moody | 1981 John McEnroe | Chris Evert-Lloyd |
| 1936 Fred Perry | Helen Jacobs | 1982 Jimmy Connors | Martina Navrátilová |
| 1937 Don Budge | Dorothy Round | 1983 John McEnroe | Martina Navrátilová |
| 1938 Don Budge | Helen Wills Moody | 1984 John McEnroe | Martina Navrátilová |
| 1939 Bobby Riggs | Alice Marble | 1985 Boris Becker | Martina Navrátilová |
| 1940–1945 (no competition) | | 1986 Boris Becker | Martina Navrátilová |
| 1946 Yvon Petra | Pauline Betz | 1987 Pat Cash | Martina Navrátilová |
| 1947 Jack Kramer | Margaret Osborne | 1988 Stefan Edberg | Steffi Graf |
| 1948 Bob Falkenburg | Louise Brough | 1989 Boris Becker | Steffi Graf |
| 1949 Ted Schroeder | Louise Brough | 1990 Stefan Edberg | Martina Navrátilová |
| 1950 Budge Patty | Louise Brough | 1991 Michael Stich | Steffi Graf |
| 1951 Dick Savitt | Doris Hart | 1992 Andre Agassi | Steffi Graf |
| 1952 Frank Sedgman | Maureen Connolly | 1993 Pete Sampras | Steffi Graf |
| 1953 Vic Seixas | Maureen Connolly | 1994 Pete Sampras | Conchita Martínez |
| 1954 Jaroslav Drobný | Maureen Connolly | 1995 Pete Sampras | Steffi Graf |
| 1955 Tony Trabert | Louise Brough | 1996 Richard Krajicek | Steffi Graf |
| 1956 Lew Hoad | Shirley Fry | 1997 Pete Sampras | Martina Hingis |
| 1957 Lew Hoad | Althea Gibson | 1998 Pete Sampras | Jana Novotná |
| 1958 Ashley Cooper | Althea Gibson | 1999 Pete Sampras | Lindsay Davenport |
| 1959 Alex Olmedo | Maria Bueno | 2000 Pete Sampras | Venus Williams |
| 1960 Neale Fraser | Maria Bueno | 2001 Goran Ivaniševic | Venus Williams |
| 1961 Rod Laver | Angela Mortimer | 2002 Lleyton Hewitt | Serena Williams |
| 1962 Rod Laver | Karen Hantze Susman | 2003 Roger Federer | Serena Williams |
| 1963 Chuck McKinley | Margaret Smith | 2004 Roger Federer | Maria Sharapova |
| 1964 Roy Emerson | Maria Bueno | 2005 Roger Federer | Venus Williams |
| 1965 Roy Emerson | Margaret Smith | 2006 Roger Federer | Amélie Mauresmo |
| 1966 Manolo Santana | Billie Jean King | 2007 Roger Federer | Venus Williams |
| 1967 John Newcombe | Billie Jean King | 2008 Rafael Nadel | Venus Williams |
| 1968 Rod Laver | Billie Jean King | | |

## U.S. Open Tennis Singles Winners
### (since 1968)

| Men | Women |
|---|---|
| 1968 Arthur Ashe | Virginia Wade |
| 1969 Rod Laver | Margaret Court |
| 1970 Ken Rosewall | Margaret Court |
| 1971 Stan Smith | Billie Jean King |
| 1972 Ilie Năstase | Billie Jean King |
| 1973 John Newcombe | Margaret Court |
| 1974 Jimmy Connors | Billie Jean King |
| 1975 Manuel Orantes | Chris Evert |
| 1976 Jimmy Connors | Chris Evert |
| 1977 Guillermo Vilas | Chris Evert |
| 1978 Jimmy Connors | Chris Evert |
| 1979 John McEnroe | Tracy Austin |
| 1980 John McEnroe | Chris Evert |
| 1981 John McEnroe | Tracy Austin |
| 1982 Jimmy Connors | Chris Evert |
| 1983 Jimmy Connors | Martina Navrátilová |
| 1984 John McEnroe | Martina Navrátilová |
| 1985 Ivan Lendl | Hana Mandlíková |
| 1986 Ivan Lendl | Martina Navrátilová |
| 1987 Ivan Lendl | Martina Navrátilová |
| 1988 Mats Wilander | Steffi Graf |
| 1989 Boris Becker | Steffi Graf |
| 1990 Pete Sampras | Gabriela Sabatini |
| 1991 Stefan Edberg | Monica Seles |
| 1992 Stefan Edberg | Monica Seles |
| 1993 Pete Sampras | Steffi Graf |
| 1994 Andre Agassi | Arantxa Sánchez Vicario |
| 1995 Pete Sampras | Steffi Graf |
| 1996 Pete Sampras | Steffi Graf |
| 1997 Patrick Rafter | Martina Hingis |
| 1998 Patrick Rafter | Lindsay Davenport |
| 1999 Andre Agassi | Serena Williams |
| 2000 Marat Safin | Venus Williams |
| 2001 Lleyton Hewitt | Venus Williams |
| 2002 Pete Sampras | Serena Williams |
| 2003 Andy Roddick | Justine Henin |
| 2004 Roger Federer | Svetlana Kuznetsova |
| 2005 Roger Federer | Kim Clijsters |
| 2006 Roger Federer | Maria Sharapova |
| 2007 Roger Federer | Justine Henin |
| 2008 Roger Federer | Serena Williams |

## U.S. Open Golf Winners
### (since World War II)

1946 Lloyd Mangrum
1947 Lew Worsham
1948 Ben Hogan
1949 Cary Middlecoff
1950 Ben Hogan
1951 Ben Hogan
1952 Julius Boros
1953 Ben Hogan
1954 Ed Furgol
1955 Jack Fleck
1956 Cary Middlecoff
1957 Dick Mayer
1958 Tommy Bolt
1959 Billy Casper
1960 Arnold Palmer
1961 Gene Littler
1962 Jack Nicklaus
1963 Julius Boros
1964 Ken Venturi
1965 Gary Player
1966 Billy Casper
1967 Jack Nicklaus
1968 Lee Trevino
1969 Orville Moody
1970 Tony Jacklin
1971 Lee Trevino
1972 Jack Nicklaus
1973 Johnny Miller
1974 Hale Irwin
1975 Lou Graham
1976 Jerry Pate
1977 Hubert Green
1978 Andy North
1979 Hale Irwin
1980 Jack Nicklaus
1981 David Graham
1982 Tom Watson
1983 Larry Nelson
1984 Fuzzy Zoeller
1985 Andy North
1986 Ray Floyd
1987 Scott Simpson
1988 Curtis Strange
1989 Curtis Strange
1990 Hale Irwin
1991 Payne Stewart
1992 Tom Kite
1993 Lee Janzen
1994 Ernie Els
1995 Corey Pavin
1996 Steve Jones
1997 Ernie Els
1998 Lee Janzen
1999 Payne Stewart
2000 Tiger Woods
2001 Retief Goosen
2002 Tiger Woods
2003 Jim Furyk
2004 Retief Goosen
2005 Michael Campbell
2006 Geoff Ogilvy
2007 Ángel Cabrera
2008 Tiger Woods

## British Open Winners
## (since World War II)

1946 Sam Snead
1947 Fred Daly
1948 Henry Cotton
1949 Bobby Locke
1950 Bobby Locke
1951 Max Faulkner
1952 Bobby Locke
1953 Ben Hogan
1954 Peter Thomson
1955 Peter Thomson
1956 Peter Thomson
1957 Bobby Locke
1958 Peter Thomson
1959 Gary Player
1960 Kel Nagle
1961 Arnold Palmer
1962 Arnold Palmer
1963 Bob Charles
1964 Tony Lema
1965 Peter Thomson
1966 Jack Nicklaus
1967 Roberto DeVicenzo
1968 Gary Player
1969 Tony Jacklin
1970 Jack Nicklaus
1971 Lee Trevino
1972 Lee Trevino
1973 Tom Weiskopf
1974 Gary Player
1975 Tom Watson
1976 Johnny Miller
1977 Tom Watson
1978 Jack Nicklaus
1979 Seve Ballesteros
1980 Tom Watson
1981 Bill Rogers
1982 Tom Watson
1983 Tom Watson
1984 Seve Ballesteros
1985 Sandy Lyle
1986 Greg Norman
1987 Nick Faldo
1988 Seve Ballesteros
1989 Mark Calcavecchia
1990 Nick Faldo
1991 Ian Baker-Finch
1992 Nick Faldo
1993 Greg Norman
1994 Nick Price
1995 John Daly
1996 Tom Lehman
1997 Justin Leonard
1998 Mark O'Meara
1999 Paul Lawrie
2000 Tiger Woods
2001 David Duval
2002 Ernie Els
2003 Ben Curtis
2004 Todd Hamilton
2005 Tiger Woods
2006 Tiger Woods
2007 Pádraig Harrington
2008 Pádraig Harrington

## Indianapolis 500 Winners
## (since World War II)

1946 George Robson
1947 Mauri Rose
1948 Mauri Rose
1949 Bill Holland
1950 Johnnie Parsons
1951 Lee Wallard
1952 Troy Ruttman
1953 Bill Vukovich
1954 Bill Vukovich
1955 Bob Sweikert
1956 Pat Flaherty
1957 Sam Hanks
1958 Jimmy Bryan
1959 Rodger Ward
1960 Jim Rathmann
1961 A.J. Foyt
1962 Rodger Ward
1963 Parnelli JOnes
1964 A.J. Foyt
1965 Jim Clark
1966 Graham Hill
1967 A.J. Foyt
1968 Bobby Unser
1969 Mario Andretti
1970 Al Unser
1971 Al Unser
1972 Mark Donohue
1973 Gordon Johncock
1974 Johnny Rutherford
1975 Bobby Unser
1976 Johnny Rutherford
1977 A.J. Foyt
1978 Al Unser
1979 Rick Mears
1980 Johnny Rutherford
1981 Bobby Unser
1982 Gordon Johncock
1983 Tom Sneva
1984 Rick Mears
1985 Danny Sullivan
1986 Bobby Rahal
1987 Al Unser
1988 Rick Mears
1989 Emerson Fittipaldi
1990 Arie Luyendyk
1991 Rick Mears
1992 Al Unser Jr.
1993 Emerson Fittipaldi
1994 Al Unser Jr.
1995 Jacques Villeneuve
1996 Buddy Lazier
1997 Arie Luyendyk
1998 Eddie Cheever Jr.
1999 Kenny Bräck
2000 Juan Pablo Montoya

2001 Hélio Castroneves
2002 Hélio Castroneves
2003 Gil de Ferran
2004 Buddy Rice
2005 Dan Wheldon
2006 Sam Hornish Jr.
2007 Dario Franchitti
2008 Scott Dixon

## Kentucky Derby Winners (since 1917)

1917 Omar Khayyam
1918 Exterminator
1919 Sir Barton
1920 Paul Jones
1921 Behave Yourself
1922 Morvich
1923 Zev
1924 Black Gold
1925 Flying Ebony
1926 Bubbling Over
1927 Whiskery
1928 Reigh Count
1929 Clyde Van Dusen
1930 Gallant Fox
1931 Twenty Grand
1932 Burgoo King
1933 Brokers Tip
1934 Cavalcade
1935 Omaha
1936 Bold Venture
1937 War Admiral
1938 Lawrin
1939 Johnstown
1940 Gallahadion
1941 Whirlaway
1942 Shut Out
1943 Count Fleet
1944 Pensive
1945 Hoop Jr.
1946 Assault
1947 Jet Pilot
1948 Citation
1949 Ponder
1950 Middleground
1951 Count Turf
1952 Hill Gail
1953 Dark Star
1954 Determine
1955 Swaps
1956 Needles
1957 Iron Liege
1958 Tim Tam

1959 Tomy Lee
1960 Venetian Way
1961 Carry Back
1962 Decidedly
1963 Chateaugay
1964 Northern Dancer
1965 Lucky Debonair
1966 Kauai King
1967 Proud Clarion
1968 Forward Pass
      Dancer's Image (disqualified)
1969 Majestic Prince
1970 Dust Commander
1971 Canonero II
1972 Riva Ridge
1973 Secretariat
1974 Cannonade
1975 Foolish Pleasure
1976 Bold Forbes
1977 Seattle Slew
1978 Affirmed
1979 Spectacular Bid
1980 Genuine Risk
1981 Pleasant Colony
1982 Gato Del Sol
1983 Sunny's Halo
1984 Swale
1985 Spend a Buck
1986 Ferdinand
1987 Alysheba
1988 Winning Colors
1989 Sunday Silence
1990 Unbridled
1991 Strike the Gold
1992 Lil E. Tee
1993 Sea Hero
1994 Go for Gin
1995 Thunder Gulch
1996 Grindstone
1997 Silver Charm
1998 Real Quiet
1999 Charismatic
2000 Fusaichi Pegasus
2001 Monarchos
2002 War Emblem
2003 Funny Cide
2004 Smarty Jones
2005 Giacomo
2006 Barbaro
2007 Street Sense
2008 Big Brown

## American Crossword Puzzle Tournament Champions

1978 Nancy Schuster
1979 Miriam Raphael
1980 Daniel Pratt
1981 Philip Cohen
1982 Stanley Newman
1983 David Rosen
1984 John McNeill
1985 David Rosen
1986 David Rosen
1987 David Rosen
1988 Douglas Hoylman
1989 Jon Delfin
1990 Jon Delfin
1991 Jon Delfin
1992 Douglas Hoylman
1993 Trip Payne
1994 Douglas Hoylman
1995 Jon Delfin
1996 Douglas Hoylman
1997 Douglas Hoylman
1998 Trip Payne
1999 Jon Delfin
2000 Douglas Hoylman
2001 Ellen Ripstein
2002 Jon Delfin
2003 Jon Delfin
2004 Trip Payne
2005 Tyler Hinman
2006 Tyler Hinman
2007 Tyler Hinman
2008 Tyler Hinman

## Pulitzer Drama Winners

1918 Jesse Lynch Williams, *Why Marry?*
1919 no award
1920 Eugene O'Neill, *Beyond the Horizon*
1921 Zona Gale, *Miss Lulu Bett*
1922 Eugene O'Neill, *Anna Christie*
1923 Owen Davis, *Icebound*
1924 Hatcher Hughes, *Hell-Bent Fer Heaven*
1925 Sidney Howard, *They Knew What They Wanted*
1926 George Kelly, *Craig's Wife*
1927 Paul Green, *In Abraham's Bosom*
1928 Eugene O'Neill, *Strange Interlude*
1929 Elmer Rice, *Street Scene*
1930 Marc Connelly, *The Green Pastures*
1931 Susan Glaspell, *Alison's House*
1932 George S. Kaufman, Morrie Ryskind, Ira Gershwin, *Of Thee I Sing*
1933 Maxwell Anderson, *Both Your Houses*
1934 Sidney Kingsley, *Men in White*
1935 Zoe Akins, *The Old Maid*
1936 Robert E. Sherwood, *Idiot's Delight*
1937 Moss Hart, George S. Kaufman, *You Can't Take It With You*
1938 Thornton Wilder, *Our Town*
1939 Robert E. Sherwood, *Abe Lincoln in Illinois*
1940 William Saroyan, *The Time of Your Life*

1941 Robert E. Sherwood, *There Shall Be No Night*
1942 no award
1943 Thornton Wilder, *The Skin of Our Teeth*
1944 no award
1945 Mary Coyle Chase, *Harvey*
1946 Russel Crouse, Howard Lindsay, *State of the Union*
1947 no award
1948 Tennessee Williams, *A Streetcar Named Desire*
1949 Arthur Miller, *Death of a Salesman*
1950 Richard Rodgers, Oscar Hammerstein II, Joshua Logan, *South Pacific*
1951 no award
1952 Joseph Kramm, *The Shrike*
1953 William Inge, *Picnic*
1954 John Patrick, *The Teahouse of the August Moon*
1955 Tennessee Williams, *Cat on a Hot Tin Roof*
1956 Albert Hackett and Frances Goodrich, *The Diary of a Young Girl*
1957 Eugene O'Neill, *Long Day's Journey Into Night*
1958 Ketti Frings, *Look Homeward, Angel*
1959 Archibald MacLeish, *J.B.*
1960 Jerome Weidman, George Abbott, Jerry Bock, Sheldon Harnick, *Fiorello!*
1961 Tad Mosel, *All the Way Home*
1962 Frank Loesser, Abe Burrows, *How to Succeed in Business Without Really Trying*
1963 no award
1964 no award
1965 Frank D. Gilroy, *The Subject Was Roses*
1966 no award
1967 Edward Albee, *A Delicate Balance*
1968 no award
1969 Howard Sackler, *The Great White Hope*
1970 Charles Gordone, *No Place to Be Somebody*
1971 Paul Zindel, *The Effect of Gamma Rays on Man-in-the-Moon Marigolds*
1972 no award
1973 Jason Miller, *That Championship Season*
1974 no award
1975 Edward Albee, *Seascape*
1976 Michael Bennett, Nicholas Dante, James Kirkwood, Jr., Marvin Hamlisch, Edward Kleban, *A Chorus Line*
1977 Michael Cristofer, *The Shadow Box*
1978 Donald L. Coburn, *The Gin Game*
1979 Sam Shepard, *Buried Child*
1980 Lanford Wilson, *Talley's Folly*
1981 Beth Henley, *Crimes of the Heart*
1982 Charles Fuller, *A Soldier's Play*
1983 Marsha Norman, *'Night, Mother*

1984 David Mamet, *Glengarry Glen Ross*
1985 James Lapine, Stephen Sondheim, *Sunday in the Park With George*
1986 no award
1987 August Wilson, *Fences*
1988 Alfred Uhry, *Driving Miss Daisy*
1989 Wendy Wasserstein, *The Heidi Chronicles*
1990 August Wilson, *The Piano Lesson*
1991 Neil Simon, *Lost in Yonkers*
1992 Robert Schenkkan, *The Kentucky Cycle*
1993 Tony Kushner, *Angels in America: Millennium Approaches*
1994 Edward Albee, *Three Tall Women*
1995 Horton Foote, *The Young Man From Atlanta*
1996 Jonathan Larson, *Rent*
1997 no award
1998 Paula Vogel, *How I Learned To Drive*
1999 Margaret Edson, *Wit*
2000 Donald Margulies, *Dinner With Friends*
2001 David Auburn, *Proof*
2002 Suzan-Lori Parks, *Topdog/Underdog*
2003 Nilo Cruz, *Anna in the Tropics*
2004 Doug Wright, *I Am My Own Wife*
2005 John Patrick Shanley, *Doubt, a Parable*
2006 no award
2007 David Lindsay-Abaire, *Rabbit Hole*
2008 Tracy Letts, *August: Osage County*

## Pulitzer Fiction Winners

1948 *Tales of the South Pacific* by James A. Michener
1949 *Guard of Honor* by James Gould Cozzens
1950 *The Way West* by A. B. Guthrie, Jr.
1951 *The Town* by Conrad Richter
1952 *The Caine Mutiny* by Herman Wouk
1953 *The Old Man and the Sea* by Ernest Hemingway
1954 no award
1955 *A Fable* by William Faulkner
1956 *Andersonville* by MacKinlay Kantor
1957 no award
1958 *A Death in the Family* by James Agee
1959 *The Travels of Jaimie McPheeters* by Robert Lewis Taylor
1960 *Advise and Consent* by Allen Drury
1961 *To Kill a Mockingbird* by Harper Lee
1962 *The Edge of Sadness* by Edwin O'Connor
1963 *The Reivers* by William Faulkner
1964 no award
1965 *The Keepers of the House* by Shirley Ann Grau
1966 *The Collected Stories of Katherine Anne Porter* by Katherine Anne Porter

1967 *The Fixer* by Bernard Malamud
1968 *The Confessions of Nat Turner* by William Styron
1969 *House Made of Dawn* by N. Scott Momaday
1970 *The Collected Stories of Jean Stafford* by Jean Stafford
1971 no award
1972 *Angle of Repose* by Wallace Stegner
1973 *The Optimist's Daughter* by Eudora Welty
1974 no award
1975 *The Killer Angels* by Michael Shaara
1976 *Humboldt's Gift* by Saul Bellow
1977 no award
1978 *Elbow Room* by James Alan McPherson
1979 *The Stories of John Cheever* by John Cheever
1980 *The Executioner's Song* by Norman Mailer
1981 *A Confederacy of Dunces* by John Kennedy Toole
1982 *Rabbit Is Rich* by John Updike
1983 *The Color Purple* by Alice Walker
1984 *Ironweed* by William Kennedy
1985 *Foreign Affairs* by Alison Lurie
1986 *Lonesome Dove* by Larry McMurtry
1987 *A Summons to Memphis* by Peter Taylor
1988 *Beloved* by Toni Morrison
1989 *Breathing Lessons* by Anne Tyler
1990 *The Mambo Kings Play Songs of Love* by Oscar Hijuelos
1991 *Rabbit at Rest* by John Updike
1992 *A Thousand Acres* by Jane Smiley
1993 *A Good Scent from a Strange Mountain* by Robert Olen Butler
1994 *The Shipping News* by E. Annie Proulx
1995 *The Stone Diaries* by Carol Shields
1996 *Independence Day* by Richard Ford
1997 *Martin Dressler: The Tale of an American Dreamer* by Steven Millhauser
1998 *American Pastoral* by Philip Roth
1999 *The Hours* by Michael Cunningham
2000 *Interpreter of Maladies* by Jhumpa Lahiri
2001 *The Amazing Adventures of Kavalier & Clay* by Michael Chabon
2002 *Empire Falls* by Richard Russo
2003 *Middlesex* by Jeffrey Eugenides
2004 *The Known World* by Edward P. Jones
2005 *Gilead* by Marilynne Robinson
2006 *March* by Geraldine Brooks
2007 *The Road* by Cormac McCarthy
2008 *The Brief Wondrous Life of Oscar Wao* by Junot Diaz

## Best Picture Oscar Winners

1928 *Wings*
1929 *The Broadway Melody*
1930 *All Quiet on the Western Front*
1931 *Cimarron*
1932 *Grand Hotel*
1933 *Cavalcade*
1934 *It Happened One Night*
1935 *Mutiny on the Bounty*
1936 *The Great Ziegfeld*
1937 *The Life of Emile Zola*
1938 *You Can't Take It With You*
1939 *Gone With The Wind*
1940 *Rebecca*
1941 *How Green Was My Valley*
1942 *Mrs. Miniver*
1943 *Casablanca*
1944 *Going My Way*
1945 *The Lost Weekend*
1946 *The Best Years of Our Lives*
1947 *Gentleman's Agreement*
1948 *Hamlet*
1949 *All the King's Men*
1950 *All About Eve*
1951 *An American in Paris*
1952 *The Greatest Show on Earth*
1953 *From Here to Eternity*
1954 *On the Waterfront*
1955 *Marty*
1956 *Around the World in Eighty Days*
1957 *The Bridge on the River Kwai*
1958 *Gigi*
1959 *Ben-Hur*
1960 *The Apartment*
1961 *West Side Story*
1962 *Lawrence of Arabia*
1963 *Tom Jones*
1964 *My Fair Lady*
1965 *The Sound of Music*
1966 *A Man for All Seasons*
1967 *In the Heat of the Night*
1968 *Oliver!*
1969 *Midnight Cowboy*
1970 *Patton*
1971 *The French Connection*
1972 *The Godfather*
1973 *The Sting*
1974 *The Godfather, Part II*
1975 *One Flew Over the Cuckoo's Nest*
1976 *Rocky*
1977 *Annie Hall*
1978 *The Deer Hunter*
1979 *Kramer vs. Kramer*
1980 *Ordinary People*
1981 *Chariots of Fire*
1982 *Gandhi*
1983 *Terms of Endearment*
1984 *Amadeus*
1985 *Out of Africa*
1986 *Platoon*
1987 *The Last Emperor*
1988 *Rain Man*

1989 *Driving Miss Daisy*
1990 *Dances With Wolves*
1991 *The Silence of the Lambs*
1992 *Unforgiven*
1993 *Schindler's List*
1994 *Forrest Gump*
1995 *Braveheart*
1996 *The English Patient*
1997 *Titanic*
1998 *Shakespeare in Love*
1999 *American Beauty*
2000 *Gladiator*
2001 *A Beautiful Mind*
2002 *Chicago*
2003 *The Lord of the Rings: The Return of the King*
2004 *Million Dollar Baby*
2005 *Crash*
2006 *The Departed*
2007 *No Country for Old Men*

## Best Director Oscar Winners (movie is noted when it differs from the Best Picture winner)

1928 Lewis Milestone (comedy), *Two Arabian Nights*
　　 Frank Borzage (drama), *7th Heaven*
　　 Charles Chaplin (special award), *The Circus*
1929 Frank Lloyd, *The Divine Lady*
1930 Lewis Milestone
1931 Norman Taurog, *Skippy*
1932 Frank Borzage, *Bad Girl*
1933 Frank Lloyd
1934 Frank Capra
1935 John Ford, *The Informer*
1936 Frank Capra, *Mr. Deeds Goes to Town*
1937 Leo McCarey, *The Awful Truth*
1938 Frank Capra
1939 Victor Fleming
1940 John Ford, *The Grapes of Wrath*
1941 John Ford
1942 William Wyler
1943 Michael Curtiz
1944 Leo McCarey
1945 Billy Wilder
1946 William Wyler
1947 Elia Kazan
1948 John Huston, *The Treasure of the Sierra Madre*
1949 Joseph L. Mankiewicz, *A Letter to Three Wives*
1950 Joseph L. Mankiewicz
1951 George Stevens, *A Place in the Sun*
1952 John Ford, *The Quiet Man*
1953 Fred Zinnemann
1954 Elia Kazan
1955 Delbert Mann
1956 George Stevens, *Giant*
1957 David Lean
1958 Vincente Minnelli

1959 William Wyler
1960 Billy Wilder
1961 Robert Wise, Jerome Robbins
1962 David Lean
1963 Tony Richardson
1964 George Cukor
1965 Robert Wise
1966 Fred Zinnemann
1967 Mike Nichols, *The Graduate*
1968 Carol Reed
1969 John Schlesinger
1970 Franklin J. Schaffner
1971 William Friedkin
1972 Bob Fosse, *Cabaret*
1973 George Roy Hill
1974 Francis Ford Coppola
1975 Milos Forman
1976 John G. Avildsen
1977 Woody Allen
1978 Michael Cimino
1979 Robert Benton
1980 Robert Redford
1981 Warren Beatty, *Reds*
1982 Richard Attenborough
1983 James L. Brooks
1984 Milos Forman
1985 Sydney Pollack
1986 Oliver Stone
1987 Bernardo Bertolucci
1988 Barry Levinson
1989 Oliver Stone, *Born on the Fourth of July*
1990 Kevin Costner
1991 Jonathan Demme
1992 Clint Eastwood
1993 Steven Spielberg
1994 Robert Zemeckis
1995 Mel Gibson
1996 Anthony Minghella
1997 James Cameron
1998 Steven Spielberg, *Saving Private Ryan*
1999 Sam Mendes
2000 Steven Soderbergh, *Traffic*
2001 Ron Howard
2002 Roman Polanski, *The Pianist*
2003 Peter Jackson
2004 Clint Eastwood
2005 Ang Lee, *Brokeback Mountain*
2006 Martin Scorsese
2007 Joel Coen, Ethan Coen

## Best Actor Oscar Winners
1928 Emil Jannings
1929 Warner Baxter
1930 George Arliss
1931 Lionel Barrymore
1932 Fredric March
    Wallace Beery
1933 Charles Laughton
1934 Clark Gable
1935 Victor McLaglen

1936 Paul Muni
1937 Spencer Tracy
1938 Spencer Tracy
1939 Robert Donat
1940 James Stewart
1941 Gary Cooper
1942 James Cagney
1943 Paul Lukas
1944 Bing Crosby
1945 Ray Milland
1946 Fredric March
1947 Ronald Colman
1948 Laurence Olivier
1949 Broderick Crawford
1950 José Ferrer
1951 Humphrey Bogart
1952 Gary Cooper
1953 William Holden
1954 Marlon Brando
1955 Ernest Borgnine
1956 Yul Brynner
1957 Alec Guinness
1958 David Niven
1959 Charlton Heston
1960 Burt Lancaster
1961 Maximilian Schell
1962 Gregory Peck
1963 Sidney Poitier
1964 Rex Harrison
1965 Lee Marvin
1966 Paul Scofield
1967 Rod Steiger
1968 Cliff Robertson
1969 John Wayne
1970 George C. Scott
1971 Gene Hackman
1972 Marlon Brando
1973 Jack Lemmon
1974 Art Carney
1975 Jack Nicholson
1976 Peter Finch
1977 Richard Dreyfuss
1978 Jon Voight
1979 Dustin Hoffman
1980 Robert De Niro
1981 Henry Fonda
1982 Ben Kingsley
1983 Robert Duvall
1984 F. Murray Abraham
1985 William Hurt
1986 Paul Newman
1987 Michael Douglas
1988 Dustin Hoffman
1989 Daniel Day-Lewis
1990 Jeremy Irons
1991 Anthony Hopkins
1992 Al Pacino
1993 Tom Hanks
1994 Tom Hanks
1995 Nicolas Cage
1996 Geoffrey Rush

1997 Jack Nicholson
1998 Roberto Benigni
1999 Kevin Spacey
2000 Russell Crowe
2001 Denzel Washington
2002 Adrien Brody
2003 Sean Penn
2004 Jamie Foxx
2005 Philip Seymour Hoffman
2006 Forest Whitaker
2007 Daniel Day-Lewis

## Best Supporting Actor Oscar Winners
1936 Walter Brennan
1937 Joseph Schildkraut
1938 Walter Brennan
1939 Thomas Mitchell
1940 Walter Brennan
1941 Donald Crisp
1942 Van Heflin
1943 Charles Coburn
1944 Barry Fitzgerald
1945 James Dunn
1946 Harold Russell
1947 Edmund Gwenn
1948 Walter Huston
1949 Dean Jagger
1950 George Sanders
1951 Karl Malden
1952 Anthony Quinn
1953 Frank Sinatra
1954 Edmond O'Brien
1955 Jack Lemmon
1956 Anthony Quinn
1957 Red Buttons
1958 Burl Ives
1959 Hugh Griffith
1960 Peter Ustinov
1961 George Chakiris
1962 Ed Begley
1963 Melvyn Douglas
1964 Peter Ustinov
1965 Martin Balsam
1966 Walter Matthau
1967 George Kennedy
1968 Jack Albertson
1969 Gig Young
1970 John Mills
1971 Ben Johnson
1972 Joel Grey
1973 John Houseman
1974 Robert De Niro
1975 George Burns
1976 Jason Robards
1977 Jason Robards
1978 Christopher Walken
1979 Melvyn Douglas
1980 Timothy Hutton
1981 John Gielgud
1982 Louis Gossett Jr.
1983 Jack Nicholson

1984 Haing S. Ngor
1985 Don Ameche
1986 Michael Caine
1987 Sean Connery
1988 Kevin Kline
1989 Denzel Washington
1990 Joe Pesci
1991 Jack Palance
1992 Gene Hackman
1993 Tommy Lee Jones
1994 Martin Landau
1995 Kevin Spacey
1996 Cuba Gooding Jr.
1997 Robin Williams
1998 James Coburn
1999 Michael Caine
2000 Benicio del Toro
2001 Jim Broadbent
2002 Chris Cooper
2003 Tim Robbins
2004 Morgan Freeman
2005 George Clooney
2006 Alan Arkin
2007 Javier Bardem

## Best Actress Oscar Winners
1928 Janet Gaynor
1929 Mary Pickford
1930 Norma Shearer
1931 Marie Dressler
1932 Helen Hayes
1933 Katharine Hepburn
1934 Claudette Colbert
1935 Bette Davis
1936 Luise Rainer
1937 Luise Rainer
1938 Bette Davis
1939 Vivien Leigh
1940 Ginger Rogers
1941 Joan Fontaine
1942 Greer Garson
1943 Jennifer Jones
1944 Ingrid Bergman
1945 Joan Crawford
1946 Olivia de Havilland
1947 Loretta Young
1948 Jane Wyman
1949 Olivia de Havilland
1950 Judy Holliday
1951 Vivien Leigh
1952 Shirley Booth
1953 Audrey Hepburn
1954 Grace Kelly
1955 Anna Magnani
1956 Ingrid Bergman
1957 Joanne Woodward
1958 Susan Hayward
1959 Simone Signoret
1960 Elizabeth Taylor
1961 Sophia Loren
1962 Anne Bancroft

1963 Patricia Neal
1964 Julie Andrews
1965 Julie Christie
1966 Elizabeth Taylor
1967 Katharine Hepburn
1968 Katharine Hepburn
     Barbra Streisand
1969 Maggie Smith
1970 Glenda Jackson
1971 Jane Fonda
1972 Liza Minnelli
1973 Glenda Jackson
1974 Ellen Burstyn
1975 Louise Fletcher
1976 Faye Dunaway
1977 Diane Keaton
1978 Jane Fonda
1979 Sally Field
1980 Sissy Spacek
1981 Katharine Hepburn
1982 Meryl Streep
1983 Shirley MacLaine
1984 Sally Field
1985 Geraldine Page
1986 Marlee Matlin
1987 Cher
1988 Jodie Foster
1989 Jessica Tandy
1990 Kathy Bates
1991 Jodie Foster
1992 Emma Thompson
1993 Holly Hunter
1994 Jessica Lange
1995 Susan Sarandon
1996 Frances McDormand
1997 Helen Hunt
1998 Gwyneth Paltrow
1999 Hilary Swank
2000 Julia Roberts
2001 Halle Berry
2002 Nicole Kidman
2003 Charlize Theron
2004 Hilary Swank
2005 Reese Witherspoon
2006 Helen Mirren
2007 Marion Cotillard

## Best Supporting Actress Oscar Winners
1936 Gale Sondergaard
1937 Alice Brady
1938 Fay Bainter
1939 Hattie McDaniel
1940 Jane Darwell
1941 Mary Astor
1942 Teresa Wright
1943 Katina Paxinou
1944 Ethel Barrymore
1945 Anne Revere
1946 Anne Baxter
1947 Celeste Holm

1948 Claire Trevor
1949 Mercedes McCambridge
1950 Josephine Hull
1951 Kim Hunter
1952 Gloria Grahame
1953 Donna Reed
1954 Eva Marie Saint
1955 Jo Van Fleet
1956 Dorothy Malone
1957 Miyoshi Umeki
1958 Wendy Hiller
1959 Shelley Winters
1960 Shirley Jones
1961 Rita Moreno
1962 Patty Duke
1963 Margaret Rutherford
1964 Lila Kedrova
1965 Shelley Winters
1966 Sandy Dennis
1967 Estelle Parsons
1968 Ruth Gordon
1969 Goldie Hawn
1970 Helen Hayes
1971 Cloris Leachman
1972 Eileen Heckart
1973 Tatum O'Neal
1974 Ingrid Bergman
1975 Lee Grant
1976 Beatrice Straight
1977 Vanessa Redgrave
1978 Maggie Smith
1979 Meryl Streep
1980 Mary Steenburgen
1981 Maureen Stapleton
1982 Jessica Lange
1983 Linda Hunt
1984 Peggy Ashcroft
1985 Angelica Huston
1986 Dianne Wiest
1987 Olympia Dukakis
1988 Geena Davis
1989 Brenda Fricker
1990 Whoopi Goldberg
1991 Mercedes Ruehl
1992 Marisa Tomei
1993 Anna Paquin
1994 Dianne Wiest
1995 Mira Sorvino
1996 Juliette Binoche
1997 Kim Basinger
1998 Judi Dench
1999 Angelina Jolie
2000 Marcia Gay Harden
2001 Jennifer Connelly
2002 Catherine Zeta-Jones
2003 Renée Zellweger
2004 Cate Blanchett
2005 Rachel Weisz
2006 Jennifer Hudson
2007 Tilda Swinton

## Best Play Tony Winners

1948 *Mister Roberts*
1949 *Death of a Salesman*
1950 *The Cocktail Party*
1951 *The Rose Tattoo*
1952 *The Fourposter*
1953 *The Crucible*
1954 *The Teahouse of the August Moon*
1955 *The Desperate Hours*
1956 *The Diary of Anne Frank*
1957 *Long Day's Journey Into Night*
1958 *Sunrise at Campobello*
1959 *J.B.*
1960 *The Miracle Worker*
1961 *Becket*
1962 *A Man for All Seasons*
1963 *Who's Afraid of Virginia Woolf?*
1964 *Luther*
1965 *The Subject Was Roses*
1966 *Marat/Sade*
1967 *The Homecoming*
1968 *Rosencrantz & Guildenstern Are Dead*
1969 *The Great White Hope*
1970 *Borstal Boy*
1971 *Sleuth*
1972 *Sticks and Bones*
1973 *That Championship Season*
1974 *The River Niger*
1975 *Equus*
1976 *Travesties*
1977 *The Shadow Box*
1978 *Da*
1979 *The Elephant Man*
1980 *Children of a Lesser God*
1981 *Amadeus*
1982 *The Life and Adventures of Nicholas Nickleby*
1983 *Torch Song Trilogy*
1984 *The Real Thing*
1985 *Biloxi Blues*
1986 *I'm Not Rappaport*
1987 *Fences*
1988 *M. Butterfly*
1989 *The Heidi Chronicles*
1990 *The Grapes of Wrath*
1991 *Lost in Yonkers*
1992 *Dancing at Lughnasa*
1993 *Angels in America: Millennium Approaches*
1994 *Angels in America: Perestroika*
1995 *Love! Valour! Compassion!*
1996 *Master Class*
1997 *The Last Night of Ballyhoo*
1998 *'Art'*
1999 *Side Man*
2000 *Copenhagen*
2001 *Proof*
2002 *The Goat, or, Who is Sylvia?*
2003 *Take Me Out*
2004 *I Am My Own Wife*
2005 *Doubt, a Parable*
2006 *The History Boys*
2007 *The Coast of Utopia*
2008 *August: Osage County*

## Best Musical Tony Winners

1949 *Kiss Me, Kate*
1950 *South Pacific*
1951 *Guys and Dolls*
1952 *The King and I*
1953 *Wonderful Town*
1954 *Kismet*
1955 *The Pajama Game*
1956 *Damn Yankees*
1957 *My Fair Lady*
1958 *The Music Man*
1959 *Redhead*
1960 *The Sound of Music*
     *Fiorello!*
1961 *Bye Bye Birdie*
1962 *How to Succeed in Business Without Really Trying*
1963 *A Funny Thing Happened on the Way to the Forum*
1964 *Hello, Dolly!*
1965 *Fiddler on the Roof*
1966 *Man of La Mancha*
1967 *Cabaret*
1968 *Hallelujah, Baby!*
1969 *1776*
1970 *Applause*
1971 *Company*
1972 *Two Gentlemen of Verona*
1973 *A Little Night Music*
1974 *Raisin*
1975 *The Wiz*
1976 *A Chorus Line*
1977 *Annie*
1978 *Ain't Misbehavin'*
1979 *Sweeney Todd*
1980 *Evita*
1981 *42nd Street*
1982 *Nine*
1983 *Cats*
1984 *La Cage aux Folles*
1985 *Big River*
1986 *The Mystery of Edwin Drood*
1987 *Les Misérables*
1988 *The Phantom of the Opera*
1989 *Jerome Robbins' Broadway*
1990 *City of Angels*
1991 *The Will Rogers Follies*
1992 *Crazy for You*
1993 *Kiss of the Spider Woman*
1994 *Passion*
1995 *Sunset Boulevard*
1996 *Rent*
1997 *Titanic*
1998 *The Lion King*
1999 *Fosse*
2000 *Contact*
2001 *The Producers*
2002 *Thoroughly Modern Millie*

2003 *Hairspray*
2004 *Avenue Q*
2005 *Monty Python's Spamalot*
2006 *Jersey Boys*
2007 *Spring Awakening*
2008 *In the Heights*

## U.S. Presidents and Vice Presidents

| # | President | Vice President |
|---|-----------|----------------|
| 1 | George Washington | John Adams |
| 2 | John Adams | Thomas Jefferson |
| 3 | Thomas Jefferson | Aaron Burr |
|   |  | George Clinton |
| 4 | James Madison | George Clinton |
|   |  | Elbridge Gerry |
| 5 | James Monroe | Daniel Tompkins |
| 6 | John Quincy Adams | John Calhoun |
| 7 | Andrew Jackson | John Calhoun |
|   |  | Martin Van Buren |
| 8 | Martin Van Buren | Richard Johnson |
| 9 | William H. Harrison | John Tyler |
| 10 | John Tyler | vacant |
| 11 | James K. Polk | George Dallas |
| 12 | Zachary Taylor | Millard Fillmore |
| 13 | Millard Fillmore | vacant |
| 14 | Franklin Pierce | William King |
| 15 | James Buchanan | John Breckinridge |
| 16 | Abraham Lincoln | Hannibal Hamlin |
|   |  | Andrew Johnson |
| 17 | Andrew Johnson | vacant |
| 18 | Ulysses S. Grant | Schuyler Colfax |
|   |  | Henry Wilson |
| 19 | Rutherford B. Hayes | William Wheeler |
| 20 | James Garfield | Chester A. Arthur |
| 21 | Chester A. Arthur | vacant |
| 22 | Grover Cleveland | Thomas Hendricks |
| 23 | Benjamin Harrison | Levi P. Morton |
| 24 | Grover Cleveland | Adlai E. Stevenson |
| 25 | William McKinley | Garret Hobart |
|   |  | Theodore Roosevelt |
| 26 | Theodore Roosevelt | Charles Fairbanks |
| 27 | William H. Taft | James Sherman |
| 28 | Woodrow Wilson | Thomas Marshall |
| 29 | Warren G. Harding | Calvin Coolidge |
| 30 | Calvin Coolidge | Charles Dawes |
| 31 | Herbert Hoover | Charles Curtis |
| 32 | Franklin D. Roosevelt | John Nance Garner |
|   |  | Henry Wallace |
|   |  | Harry S Truman |
| 33 | Harry S Truman | Alben Barkley |
| 34 | Dwight D. Eisenhower | Richard Nixon |
| 35 | John F. Kennedy | Lyndon Johnson |
| 36 | Lyndon Johnson | Hubert Humphrey |
| 37 | Richard Nixon | Spiro Agnew |
|   |  | Gerald Ford |
| 38 | Gerald Ford | Nelson Rockefeller |
| 39 | Jimmy Carter | Walter Mondale |
| 40 | Ronald Reagan | George H.W. Bush |
| 41 | George H.W. Bush | Dan Quayle |
| 42 | Bill Clinton | Al Gore |
| 43 | George W. Bush | Dick Cheney |
| 44 | Barack Obama | Joe Biden |

## State Birds

| State | Bird |
|-------|------|
| Alabama | Yellowhammer |
|  | Wild turkey (game bird) |
| Alaska | Willow ptarmigan |
| Arizona | Cactus wren |
| Arkansas | Mockingbird |
| California | California quail |
| Colorado | Lark bunting |
| Connecticut | American robin |
| Delaware | Blue hen chicken |
| D.C. | Wood thrush |
| Florida | Mockingbird |
| Georgia | Brown thrasher |
|  | Bobwhite quail (game bird) |
| Hawaii | Hawaiian goose (nene) |
| Idaho | Mountain bluebird |
| Illinois | Cardinal |
| Indiana | Cardinal |
| Iowa | Eastern goldfinch |
| Kansas | Western meadowlark |
| Kentucky | Cardinal |
| Louisiana | Eastern brown pelican |
| Maine | Black-capped chickadee |
| Maryland | Baltimore oriole |
| Massachusetts | Black-capped chickadee |
|  | Wild turkey (game bird) |
| Michigan | American robin |
| Minnesota | Common loon |
| Mississippi | Mockingbird |
|  | Wood duck (waterfowl) |
| Missouri | Eastern bluebird |
| Montana | Western meadowlark |
| Nebraska | Western meadowlark |
| Nevada | Mountain bluebird |
| New Hampshire | Purple finch |
| New Jersey | Eastern goldfinch |
| New Mexico | Roadrunner |
| New York | Eastern bluebird |
| North Carolina | Cardinal |
| North Dakota | Western meadowlark |
| Ohio | Cardinal |
| Oklahoma | Scissor-tailed flycatcher |
| Oregon | Western meadowlark |
| Pennsylvania | Ruffed grouse |
| Rhode Island | Rhode Island Red chicken |
| South Carolina | Mockingbird (former) |
|  | Carolina wren |
|  | Wild turkey (game bird) |
| South Dakota | Ring-necked pheasant |
| Tennessee | Mockingbird |
|  | Bobwhite quail (game bird) |
| Texas | Mockingbird |
| Utah | California gull |
| Vermont | Hermit thrush |
| Virginia | Cardinal |
| Washington | Willow goldfinch |
| West Virginia | Cardinal |
| Wisconsin | American robin |
| Wyoming | Western meadowlark |

## State Trees

| | | | |
|---|---|---|---|
| Alabama | Longleaf pine | Delaware | Peach blossom |
| Alaska | Sitka spruce | Florida | Orange blossom |
| Arizona | Palo verde | Georgia | Cherokee rose |
| Arkansas | Pine | Hawaii | Hibiscus (former) |
| California | California redwood | | Yellow hibiscus |
| Colorado | Colorado blue spruce | Idaho | Syringa (mock orange) |
| Connecticut | White oak | Illinois | Violet |
| D.C. | Scarlet oak | Indiana | Carnation, zinnia, dogwood |
| Delaware | American holly | | blossom (former) |
| Florida | Sabal palmetto palm | | Peony |
| Georgia | Live oak | Iowa | Wild rose |
| Hawaii | Candlenut (kukui) | Kansas | Sunflower |
| Idaho | White pine | Kentucky | Goldenrod |
| Illinois | White oak | Louisiana | Magnolia |
| Indiana | Tulip tree | Maine | White pine cone and tassel |
| Iowa | Oak | Maryland | Black-eyed susan |
| Kansas | Cottonwood | Massachusetts | Mayflower |
| Kentucky | Tulip poplar | Michigan | Apple blossom |
| Louisiana | Bald cypress | Minnesota | Showy lady's-slipper |
| Maine | Eastern white pine | Mississippi | Magnolia |
| Maryland | White oak | Missouri | Hawthorn |
| Massachusetts | American elm | Montana | Bitterroot |
| Michigan | White pine | Nebraska | Goldenrod |
| Minnesota | Red pine | Nevada | Sagebrush |
| Mississippi | Magnolia | New Hampshire | Purple lilac |
| Missouri | Flowering dogwood | New Jersey | Purple violet |
| Montana | Ponderosa pine | New Mexico | Yucca |
| Nebraska | Cottonwood | New York | Rose |
| Nevada | Single-leaf piñon | North Carolina | Dogwood |
| New Hampshire | White birch | North Dakota | Wild prairie rose |
| New Jersey | Red oak | Ohio | Scarlet carnation |
| New Mexico | Piñon | Oklahoma | Mistletoe (former) |
| New York | Sugar maple | | Oklahoma rose |
| North Carolina | Pine | Oregon | Oregon grape |
| North Dakota | American elm | Pennsylvania | Mountain laurel |
| Ohio | Buckeye | Rhode Island | Violet |
| Oklahoma | Redbud | South Carolina | Yellow jessamine |
| Oregon | Douglas fir | South Dakota | Pasqueflower |
| Pennsylvania | Hemlock | Tennessee | Iris |
| Rhode Island | Red maple | Texas | Bluebonnet |
| South Carolina | Palmetto | Utah | Sego lily |
| South Dakota | Black Hills spruce | Vermont | Red clover |
| Tennessee | Tulip poplar | Virginia | Dogwood |
| Texas | Pecan | Washington | Coast rhodendron |
| Utah | Blue spruce | West Virginia | Rhododendron |
| Vermont | Sugar maple | Wisconsin | Wood violet |
| Virginia | Dogwood | Wyoming | Indian paintbrush |
| Washington | Western hemlock | | |
| West Virginia | Sugar maple | | |

## U.S. Currency

| Wisconsin | Sugar maple | $1 | George Washington |
|---|---|---|---|
| Wyoming | Cottonwood | $2 | Thomas Jefferson |
| | | $5 | Abraham Lincoln |

## State Flowers

| | | $10 | Alexander Hamilton |
|---|---|---|---|
| Alabama | Goldenrod (former) | $20 | Andrew Jackson |
| | Camellia | $50 | Ulysses S. Grant |
| Alaska | Forget-me-not | $100 | Benjamin Franklin |
| Arizona | Saguaro cactus blossom | $500 | William McKinley |
| Arkansas | Apple blossom | $1,000 | Grover Cleveland |
| California | Golden poppy | $5,000 | James Madison |
| Colorado | Rocky Mountain columbine | $10,000 | Salmon P. Chase |
| Connecticut | Mountain laurel | $100,000 | Woodrow Wilson |

## Wedding Anniversary (Traditional and Modern)

| | | |
|---|---|---|
| 1st | Paper | Clocks |
| 2nd | Cotton | China |
| 3rd | Leather | Crystal/Glass |
| 4th | Fruit/Flowers | Appliances |
| 5th | Wood | Silverware |
| 6th | Candy/Iron | Wood |
| 7th | Wool/Copper | Desk sets |
| 8th | Bronze/Pottery | Linens/Lace |
| 9th | Pottery | Leather |
| 10th | Tin/Aluminum | Diamond jewelry |
| 11th | Steel | Fashion jewelry |
| 12th | Silk/Linen | Pearls |
| 13th | Lace | Textiles/Furs |
| 14th | Ivory | Gold jewelry |
| 15th | Crystal | Watches |
| 16th | | Silver hollowware |
| 17th | | Furniture |
| 18th | | Porcelain |
| 19th | | Bronze |
| 20th | China | Platinum |
| 25th | Silver | Sterling silver |
| 30th | Pearl | Diamond |
| 35th | Coral/Jade | Jade |
| 40th | Ruby | Ruby |
| 45th | Sapphire | Sapphire |
| 50th | Gold | Gold |
| 55th | Emerald | Emerald |
| 60th | Diamond | Diamond |
| 65th | Star sapphire | Star sapphire |
| 70th | Platinum | Platinum |
| 75th | Diamond | Diamond |

## Birthstones

| | |
|---|---|
| January | Garnet |
| February | Amethyst |
| March | Aquamarine, bloodstone |
| April | Diamond |
| May | Emerald, agate |
| June | Pearl, moonstone |
| July | Ruby, onyx |
| August | Peridot, carnelian |
| September | Sapphire, chrysolite |
| October | Opal, beryl, tourmaline |
| November | Topaz |
| December | Turquoise, zircon |

## Poets Laureate of England
(year appointed)
1591 Edmund Spenser (unofficial)
1599 Samuel Daniel (unofficial)
1619 Ben Jonson (unofficial)
1638 William Davenant (unofficial)
1668 John Dryden
1689 Thomas Shadwell
1692 Nahum Tate
1715 Nicholas Rowe
1718 Laurence Eusden
1730 Colley Cibber
1757 William Whitehead
1785 Thomas Warton
1790 Henry James Pye
1813 Robert Southey
1843 William Wordsworth
1850 Alfred, Lord Tennyson
1896 Alfred Austin
1913 Robert Bridges
1930 John Masefield
1967 Cecil Day-Lewis
1972 Sir John Betjeman
1984 Ted Hughes
1999 Andrew Motion

## U.S. Poets Laureate
(year appointed)
1986 Robert Penn Warren
1987 Richard Wilbur
1988 Howard Nemerov
1990 Mark Strand
1991 Joseph Brodsksy
1992 Mona Van Duyn
1993 Rita Dove
1995 Robert Haas
1997 Robert Pinsky
2000 Stanley Kunitz
2001 Billy Collins
2003 Louise Glück
2004 Ted Kooser
2006 Donald Hall
2007 Charles Simic
2008 Kay Ryan

## Time Magazine's Person of the Year
1927 Charles Lindbergh
1928 Walter Chrysler
1929 Owen D. Young
1930 Mahatma Gandhi
1931 Pierre Laval
1932 Franklin D. Roosevelt
1933 Hugh Samuel Johnson
1934 Franklin D. Roosevelt
1935 Haile Selassie I
1936 Wallis Simpson
1937 Chiang Kai-shek
      Soong May-ling
1938 Adolf Hitler
1939 Joseph Stalin
1940 Winston Churchill
1941 Franklin D. Roosevelt
1942 Joseph Stalin
1943 George Marshall
1944 Dwight D. Eisenhower
1945 Harry S. Truman
1946 James F. Byrnes
1947 George Marshall
1948 Harry S. Truman
1949 Winston Churchill
1950 The American Fighting Man
1951 Mohammed Mossadegh
1952 Elizabeth II
1953 Konrad Adenauer
1954 John Foster Dulles

| | |
|---|---|
| 1955 Harlow Curtice | **Popes** |
| 1956 Hungarian Freedom Fighter | 32–67 St. Peter |
| 1957 Nikita Khrushchev | 67–76 St. Linus |
| 1958 Charles de Gaulle | 76–88 St. Anacletus (Cletus) |
| 1959 Dwight D. Eisenhower | 88–97 St. Clement I |
| 1960 U.S. Scientists | 97–105 St. Evaristus |
| 1961 John F. Kennedy | 105–115 St. Alexander I |
| 1962 Pope John XXIII | 115–125 St. Sixtus I |
| 1963 Martin Luther King Jr. | 125–136 St. Telesphorus |
| 1964 Lyndon B. Johnson | 136–140 St. Hyginus |
| 1965 William Westmoreland | 140–155 St. Pius I |
| 1966 The Generation Twenty-Five and Under | 155–166 St. Anicetus |
| 1967 Lyndon B. Johnson | 166–175 St. Soter |
| 1968 The Apollo 8 astronauts (Frank Borman, | 175–189 St. Eleutherius |

Popes

1955 Harlow Curtice
1956 Hungarian Freedom Fighter
1957 Nikita Khrushchev
1958 Charles de Gaulle
1959 Dwight D. Eisenhower
1960 U.S. Scientists
1961 John F. Kennedy
1962 Pope John XXIII
1963 Martin Luther King Jr.
1964 Lyndon B. Johnson
1965 William Westmoreland
1966 The Generation Twenty-Five and Under
1967 Lyndon B. Johnson
1968 The Apollo 8 astronauts (Frank Borman,
    Jim Lovell, and William Anders)
1969 The Middle Americans
1970 Willy Brandt
1971 Richard Nixon
1972 Richard Nixon
    Henry Kissinger
1973 John Sirica
1974 King Faisal
1975 American women
1976 Jimmy Carter
1977 Anwar Sadat
1978 Deng Xiaoping
1979 Ayatollah Khomeini
1980 Ronald Reagan
1981 Lech Walesa
1982 The Computer
1983 Ronald Reagan
    Yuri Andropov
1984 Peter Ueberroth
1985 Deng Xiaoping
1986 Corazon C. Aquino
1987 Mikhail Gorbachev
1988 The Endangered Earth
1989 Mikhail Gorbachev
1990 George H.W. Bush
1991 Ted Turner
1992 Bill Clinton
1993 The Peacemakers (Nelson Mandela, F.W.
    de Klerk, Yasser Arafat, Yitzhak Rabin)
1994 Pope John Paul II
1995 Newt Gingrich
1996 David Ho
1997 Andy Grove
1998 Bill Clinton
    Kenneth Starr
1999 Jeffrey P. Bezos
2000 George W. Bush
2001 Rudolph Giuliani
2002 The Whistleblowers (Cynthia Cooper,
    Sherron Watkins, Coleen Rowley)
2003 The American Soldier
2004 George W. Bush
2005 The Good Samaritans (Bono, Bill Gates,
    Melinda Gates)
2006 You
2007 Vladimir Putin
2008 Barack Obama

32–67 St. Peter
67–76 St. Linus
76–88 St. Anacletus (Cletus)
88–97 St. Clement I
97–105 St. Evaristus
105–115 St. Alexander I
115–125 St. Sixtus I
125–136 St. Telesphorus
136–140 St. Hyginus
140–155 St. Pius I
155–166 St. Anicetus
166–175 St. Soter
175–189 St. Eleutherius
189–199 St. Victor I
199–217 St. Zephyrinus
217–222 St. Callistus I
222–230 St. Urban I
230–235 St. Pontain
235–236 St. Anterus
236–250 St. Fabian
251–253 St. Cornelius
253–254 St. Lucius I
254–257 St. Stephen I
257–258 St. Sixtus II
260–268 St. Dionysius
269–274 St. Felix I
275–283 St. Eutychian
283–296 St. Caius
296–304 St. Marcellinus
308–309 St. Marcellus I
309–310 St. Eusebius
311–314 St. Miltiades
314–335 St. Sylvester I
    336 St. Marcus
337–352 St. Julius I
352–366 Liberius
366–383 St. Damasus I
384–399 St. Siricius
399–401 St. Anastasius I
401–417 St. Innocent I
417–418 St. Zosimus
418–422 St. Boniface I
422–432 St. Celestine I
432–440 St. Sixtus III
440–461 St. Leo I (the Great)
461–468 St. Hilarius
468–483 St. Simplicius
483–492 St. Felix III (numbering skips
           Pope Felix II, now considered
           an antipope)
492–496 St. Gelasius I
496–498 Anastasius II
498–514 St. Symmachus
514–523 St. Hormisdas
523–526 St. John I
526–530 St. Felix IV
530–532 Boniface II
533–535 John II
535–536 St. Agapetus I
536–537 St. Silverius
537–555 Vigilius

556–561 Pelagius I
561–574 John III
575–579 Benedict I
579–590 Pelagius II
590–604 St. Gregory I (the Great)
604–606 Sabinian
607 Boniface III
608–615 St. Boniface IV
615–618 St. Deusdedit (Adeodatus I)
619–625 Boniface V
625–638 Honorius I
640 Severinus
640–642 John IV
642–649 Theodore I
649–655 St. Martin I
655–657 St. Eugene I
657–672 St. Vitalian
672–676 Adeodatus (II)
676–678 Donus
678–681 St. Agatho
682–683 St. Leo II
684–685 St. Benedict II
685–686 John V
686–687 Conon
687–701 St. Sergius I
701–705 John VI
705–707 John VII
708 Sisinnius
708–715 Constantine
715–731 St. Gregory II
731–741 St. Gregory III
741–752 St. Zachary
752 Stephen II (died before being consecrated)
752–757 Stephen III
757–767 St. Paul I
767–772 Stephen IV
772–795 Adrian I
795–816 St. Leo III
816–817 Stephen V
817–824 St. Paschal I
824–827 Eugene II
827 Valentine
827–844 Gregory IV
844–847 Sergius II
847–855 St. Leo IV
855–858 Benedict III
858–867 St. Nicholas I (the Great)
867–872 Adrian II
872–882 John VIII
882–884 Marinus I
884–885 St. Adrian III
885–891 Stephen VI
891–896 Formosus
896 Boniface VI
896–897 Stephen VII
897 Romanus
897 Theodore II
898–900 John IX
900–903 Benedict IV
903 Leo V

904–911 Sergius III
911–913 Anastasius III
913–914 Lando
914–928 John X
928 Leo VI
929–931 Stephen VIII
931–935 John XI
936–939 Leo VII
939–942 Stephen IX
942–946 Marinus II
946–955 Agapetus II
955–963 John XII
963–964 Leo VIII
964 Benedict V
965–972 John XIII
973–974 Benedict VI
974–983 Benedict VII
983–984 John XIV
985–996 John XV
996–999 Gregory V
999–1003 Sylvester II
1003 John XVII
1003–1009 John XVIII
1009–1012 Sergius IV
1012–1024 Benedict VIII
1024–1032 John XIX
1032–1045 Benedict IX*
1045 Sylvester III
1045 Benedict IX*
1045–1046 Gregory VI
1046–1047 Clement II
1047–1048 Benedict IX*
1048 Damasus II
1049–1054 St. Leo IX
1055–1057 Victor II
1057–1058 Stephen X
1058–1061 Nicholas II
1061–1073 Alexander II
1073–1085 St. Gregory VII
1086–1087 Blessed Victor III
1088–1099 Blessed Urban II
1099–1118 Paschal II
1118–1119 Gelasius II
1119–1124 Callistus II
1124–1130 Honorius II
1130–1143 Innocent II
1143–1144 Celestine II
1144–1145 Lucius II
1145–1153 Blessed Eugene III
1153–1154 Anastasius IV
1154–1159 Adrian IV
1159–1181 Alexander III
1181–1185 Lucius III
1185–1187 Urban III
1187 Gregory VIII
1187–1191 Clement III
1191–1198 Celestine III
1198–1216 Innocent III
1216–1227 Honorius III
1227–1241 Gregory IX
1241 Celestine IV

1243–1254 Innocent IV
1254–1261 Alexander IV
1261–1264 Urban IV
1265–1268 Clement IV
1271–1276 Blessed Gregory X
1276 Blessed Innocent V
1276 Adrian V
1276–1277 John XXI
1277–1280 Nicholas III
1281–1285 Martin IV
1285–1287 Honorius IV
1288–1292 Nicholas IV
1294 St. Celestine V
1294–1303 Boniface VIII
1303–1304 Blessed Benedict XI
1305–1314 Clement V
1316–1334 John XXII
1334–1342 Benedict XII
1342–1352 Clement VI
1352–1362 Innocent VI
1362–1370 Blessed Urban V
1370–1378 Gregory XI
1378–1389 Urban VI
1389–1404 Boniface IX
1404–1406 Innocent VII
1406–1415 Gregory XII
1417–1431 Martin V
1431–1447 Eugene IV
1447–1455 Nicholas V
1455–1458 Callistus III
1458–1464 Pius II
1464–1471 Paul II
1471–1484 Sixtus IV
1484–1492 Innocent VIII
1492–1503 Alexander VI
1503 Pius III
1503–1513 Julius II
1513–1521 Leo X
1522–1523 Adrian VI
1523–1534 Clement VII
1534–1549 Paul III
1550–1555 Julius III
1555 Marcellus II
1555–1559 Paul IV
1559–1565 Pius IV
1566–1572 St. Pius V
1572–1585 Gregory XIII
1585–1590 Sixtus V
1590 Urban VII
1590–1591 Gregory XIV
1591 Innocent IX
1592–1605 Clement VIII
1605 Leo XI
1605–1621 Paul V
1621–1623 Gregory XV
1623–1644 Urban VIII
1644–1655 Innocent X
1655–1667 Alexander VII
1667–1669 Clement IX
1670–1676 Clement X
1676–1689 Blessed Innocent XI
1689–1691 Alexander VIII

1691–1700 Innocent XII
1700–1721 Clement XI
1721–1724 Innocent XIII
1724–1730 Benedict XIII
1730–1740 Clement XII
1740–1758 Benedict XIV
1758–1769 Clement XIII
1769–1774 Clement XIV
1775–1799 Pius VI
1800–1823 Pius VII
1823–1829 Leo XII
1829–1830 Pius VIII
1831–1846 Gregory XVI
1846–1878 Blessed Pius IX
1878–1903 Leo XIII
1903–1914 St. Pius X
1914–1922 Benedict XV
1922–1939 Pius XI
1939–1958 Pius XII
1958–1963 Blessed John XXIII
1963–1978 Paul VI
1978 John Paul I
1978–2005 John Paul II
2005– Benedict XVI
* twice removed and restored

## Physics Nobelists
1901 Wilhelm Conrad Röntgen
1902 Hendrik A. Lorentz
Pieter Zeeman
1903 Henri Becquerel
Pierre Curie
Marie Curie
1904 Lord Rayleigh
1905 Philipp Lenard
1906 J.J. Thomson
1907 Albert A. Michelson
1908 Gabriel Lippmann
1909 Ferdinand Braun
Guglielmo Marconi
1910 Johannes Diderik van der Waals
1911 Wilhelm Wien
1912 Gustaf Dalén
1913 Heike Kamerlingh Onnes
1914 Max von Laue
1915 William Bragg
Lawrence Bragg
1916 no award
1917 Charles Glover Barkla
1918 Max Planck
1919 Johannes Stark
1920 Charles Edouard Guillaume
1921 Albert Einstein
1922 Niels Bohr
1923 Robert A. Millikan
1924 Manne Siegbahn
1925 James Franck
Gustav Hertz
1926 Jean Baptiste Perrin
1927 Arthur H. Compton
C.T.R. Wilson
1928 Owen Willans Richardson

1929 Louis de Broglie
1930 Sir Venkata Raman
1931 no award
1932 Werner Heisenberg
1933 Paul A.M. Dirac
    Erwin Schrödinger
1934 no award
1935 James Chadwick
1936 Carl D. Anderson
    Victor F. Hess
1937 Clinton Davisson
    George Paget Thomson
1938 Enrico Fermi
1939 Ernest Lawrence
1940–42 no award
1943 Otto Stern
1944 Isidor Isaac Rabi
1945 Wolfgang Pauli
1946 Percy W. Bridgman
1947 Edward V. Appleton
1948 Patrick M.S. Blackett
1949 Hideki Yukawa
1950 Cecil Powell
1951 John Cockcroft
    Ernest T.S. Walton
1952 Felix Bloch
    E.M. Purcell
1953 Frits Zernike
1954 Max Born
    Walther Bothe
1955 Polykarp Kusch
    Willis E. Lamb
1956 John Bardeen
    Walter H. Brattain
    William B. Shockley
1957 Tsung-Dao Lee
    Chen Ning Yang
1958 Pavel A. Cherenkov
    Il´ja M. Frank
    Igor Y. Tamm
1959 Owen Chamberlain
    Emilio Segrè
1960 Donald A. Glaser
1961 Robert Hofstadter
    Rudolf Mössbauer
1962 Lev Landau
1963 Maria Goeppert-Mayer
    J. Hans D. Jensen
    Eugene Wigner
1964 Nicolay G. Basov
    Aleksandr M. Prokhorov
    Charles H. Townes
1965 Richard P. Feynman
    Julian Schwinger
    Sin-Itiro Tomonaga
1966 Alfred Kastler
1967 Hans Bethe
1968 Luis Alvarez
1969 Murray Gell-Mann
1970 Hannes Alfvén
    Louis Néel
1971 Dennis Gabor

1972 John Bardeen
    Leon N. Cooper
    Robert Schrieffer
1973 Leo Esaki
    Ivar Giaever
    Brian D. Josephson
1974 Antony Hewish
    Martin Ryle
1975 Aage N. Bohr
    Ben R. Mottelson
    James Rainwater
1976 Burton Richter
    Samuel C.C. Ting
1977 Philip W. Anderson
    Sir Nevill F. Mott
    John H. van Vleck
1978 Pyotr Kapitsa
    Arno Penzias
    Robert Woodrow Wilson
1979 Sheldon Glashow
    Abdus Salam
    Steven Weinberg
1980 James Cronin
    Val Fitch
1981 Nicolaas Bloembergen
    Arthur L. Schawlow
    Kai M. Siegbahn
1982 Kenneth G. Wilson
1983 Subramanyan
    Chandrasekhar
    William A. Fowler
1984 Carlo Rubbia
    Simon van der Meer
1985 Klaus von Klitzing
1986 Gerd Binnig
    Heinrich Rohrer
    Ernst Ruska
1987 J. Georg Bednorz
    K. Alex Müller
1988 Leon M. Lederman
    Melvin Schwartz
    Jack Steinberger
1989 Hans G. Dehmelt
    Wolfgang Paul
    Norman F. Ramsey
1990 Jerome I. Friedman
    Henry W. Kendall
    Richard E. Taylor
1991 Pierre-Gilles de Gennes
1992 Georges Charpak
1993 Russell A. Hulse
    Joseph H. Taylor Jr.
1994 Bertram N. Brockhouse
    Clifford G. Shull
1995 Martin L. Perl
    Frederick Reines
1996 David M. Lee
    Douglas D. Osheroff
    Robert C. Richardson
1997 Steven Chu
    Claude Cohen-Tannoudji
    William D. Phillips

1998 Robert B. Laughlin
  Horst L. Störmer
  Daniel C. Tsui
1999 Gerardus 't Hooft
  Martinus J.G. Veltman
2000 Zhores I. Alferov
  Jack S. Kilby
  Herbert Kroemer
2001 Eric A. Cornell
  Wolfgang Ketterle
  Carl E. Wieman
2002 Raymond Davis Jr.
  Riccardo Giacconi
  Masatoshi Koshiba
2003 Alexei A. Abrikosov
  Vitaly L. Ginzburg
  Anthony J. Leggett
2004 David J. Gross
  H. David Politzer
  Frank Wilczek
2005 Roy J. Glauber
  John L. Hall
  Theodor W. Hänsch
2006 John C. Mather
  George F. Smoot
2007 Albert Fert
  Peter Grünberg
2008 Makoto Kobayashi
  Toshihide Maskawa
  Yoichiro Nambu

## Chemistry Nobelists
1901 Jacobus H. van 't Hoff
1902 Emil Fischer
1903 Svante Arrhenius
1904 Sir William Ramsay
1905 Adolf von Baeyer
1906 Henri Moissan
1907 Eduard Buchner
1908 Ernest Rutherford
1909 Wilhelm Ostwald
1910 Otto Wallach
1911 Marie Curie
1912 Victor Grignard
  Paul Sabatier
1913 Alfred Werner
1914 Theodore W. Richards
1915 Richard Willstätter
1916–17 no award
1918 Fritz Haber
1919 no award
1920 Walther Nernst
1921 Frederick Soddy
1922 Francis W. Aston
1923 Fritz Pregl
1924 no award
1925 Richard Zsigmondy
1926 The Svedberg
1927 Heinrich Wieland
1928 Adolf Windaus
1929 Arthur Harden
  Hans von Euler-Chelpin

1930 Hans Fischer
1931 Friedrich Bergius
  Carl Bosch
1932 Irving Langmuir
1933 no award
1934 Harold C. Urey
1935 Frédéric Joliot
  Irène Joliot-Curie
1936 Peter Debye
1937 Norman Haworth
  Paul Karrer
1938 Richard Kuhn
1939 Adolf Butenandt
  Leopold Ruzicka
1940–42 no award
1943 George de Hevesy
1944 Otto Hahn
1945 Artturi Virtanen
1946 John H. Northrop
  Wendell M. Stanley
  James B. Sumner
1947 Sir Robert Robinson
1948 Arne Tiselius
1949 William F. Giauque
1950 Kurt Alder
  Otto Diels
1951 Edwin M. McMillan
  Glenn T. Seaborg
1952 Archer J.P. Martin
  Richard L.M. Synge
1953 Hermann Staudinger
1954 Linus Pauling
1955 Vincent du Vigneaud
1956 Sir Cyril Hinshelwood
  Nikolay Semenov
1957 Lord Todd
1958 Frederick Sanger
1959 Jaroslav Heyrovsky
1960 Willard F. Libby
1961 Melvin Calvin
1962 John C. Kendrew
  Max F. Perutz
1963 Giulio Natta
  Karl Ziegler
1964 Dorothy Crowfoot
  Hodgkin
1965 Robert B. Woodward
1966 Robert S. Mulliken
1967 Manfred Eigen
  Ronald G.W. Norrish
  George Porter
1968 Lars Onsager
1969 Derek Barton
  Odd Hassel
1970 Luis Leloir
1971 Gerhard Herzberg
1972 Christian Anfinsen
  Stanford Moore
  William H. Stein
1973 Ernst Otto Fischer
  Geoffrey Wilkinson
1974 Paul J. Flory

1975 John Cornforth
Vladimir Prelog
1976 William Lipscomb
1977 Ilya Prigogine
1978 Peter Mitchell
1979 Herbert C. Brown
Georg Wittig
1980 Paul Berg
Walter Gilbert
Frederick Sanger
1981 Kenichi Fukui
Roald Hoffmann
1982 Aaron Klug
1983 Henry Taube
1984 Bruce Merrifield
1985 Herbert A. Hauptman
Jerome Karle
1986 Dudley R. Herschbach
Yuan T. Lee
John C. Polanyi
1987 Donald J. Cram
Jean-Marie Lehn
Charles J. Pedersen
1988 Johann Deisenhofer
Robert Huber
Hartmut Michel
1989 Sidney Altman
Thomas R. Cech
1990 Elias James Corey
1991 Richard R. Ernst
1992 Rudolph A. Marcus
1993 Kary B. Mullis
Michael Smith
1994 George A. Olah

1995 Paul J. Crutzen
Mario J. Molina
F. Sherwood Rowland
1996 Robert F. Curl Jr.
Sir Harold Kroto
Richard E. Smalley
1997 Paul D. Boyer
Jens C. Skou
John E. Walker
1998 Walter Kohn
John Pople
1999 Ahmed Zewail
2000 Alan Heeger
Alan G. MacDiarmid
Hideki Shirakawa
2001 William S. Knowles
Ryoji Noyori
K. Barry Sharpless
2002 John B. Fenn
Koichi Tanaka
Kurt Wüthrich
2003 Peter Agre
Roderick MacKinnon
2004 Aaron Ciechanover
Avram Hershko
Irwin Rose
2005 Yves Chauvin
Robert H. Grubbs
Richard R. Schrock
2006 Roger D. Kornberg
2007 Gerhard Ertl
2008 Martin Chalfie
Osamu Shimomura
Roger Y. Tsien

## Medicine Nobelists

1901 Emil von Behring
1902 Ronald Ross
1903 Niels Ryberg Finsen
1904 Ivan Pavlov
1905 Robert Koch
1906 Camillo Golgi
    Santiago Ramón y Cajal
1907 Alphonse Laveran
1908 Paul Ehrlich
    Ilya Mechnikov
1909 Theodor Kocher
1910 Albrecht Kossel
1911 Allvar Gullstrand
1912 Alexis Carrel
1913 Charles Richet
1914 Robert Bárány
1915–18 no award
1919 Jules Bordet
1920 August Krogh
1921 no award
1922 Archibald V. Hill
    Otto Meyerhof
1923 Frederick G. Banting
    John Macleod
1924 Willem Einthoven
1925 no award
1926 Johannes Fibiger
1927 Julius Wagner-Jauregg
1928 Charles Nicolle
1929 Christiaan Eijkman
    Sir Frederick Hopkins
1930 Karl Landsteiner
1931 Otto Warburg
1932 Edgar Adrian
    Sir Charles Sherrington
1933 Thomas H. Morgan
1934 George R. Minot
    William P. Murphy
    George H. Whipple
1935 Hans Spemann
1936 Sir Henry Dale
    Otto Loewi
1937 Albert Szent-Györgyi
1938 Corneille Heymans
1939 Gerhard Domagk
1940–42 no award
1943 Henrik Dam
    Edward A. Doisy
1944 Joseph Erlanger
    Herbert S. Gasser
1945 Ernst B. Chain
    Sir Alexander Fleming
    Sir Howard Florey
1946 Hermann J. Muller
1947 Carl Cori
    Gerty Cori
    Bernardo Houssay
1948 Paul Müller
1949 Walter Hess
    Egas Moniz
1950 Philip S. Hench
    Edward C. Kendall

    Tadeus Reichstein
1951 Max Theiler
1952 Selman A. Waksman
1953 Hans Krebs
    Fritz Lipmann
1954 John F. Enders
    Frederick C. Robbins
    Thomas H. Weller
1955 Hugo Theorell
1956 André F. Cournand
    Werner Forssmann
    Dickinson W. Richards
1957 Daniel Bovet
1958 George Beadle
    Joshua Lederberg
    Edward Tatum
1959 Arthur Kornberg
    Severo Ochoa
1960 Sir Frank Macfarlane Burnet
    Peter Medawar
1961 Georg von Békésy
1962 Francis Crick
    James Watson
    Maurice Wilkins
1963 Sir John Eccles
    Alan L. Hodgkin
    Andrew F. Huxley
1964 Konrad Bloch
    Feodor Lynen
1965 François Jacob
    André Lwoff
    Jacques Monod
1966 Charles B. Huggins
    Peyton Rous
1967 Ragnar Granit
    Haldan K. Hartline
    George Wald
1968 Robert W. Holley
    H. Gobind Khorana
    Marshall W. Nirenberg
1969 Max Delbrück
    Alfred D. Hershey
    Salvador E. Luria
1970 Julius Axelrod
    Sir Bernard Katz
    Ulf von Euler
1971 Earl W. Sutherland Jr.
1972 Gerald M. Edelman
    Rodney R. Porter
1973 Konrad Lorenz
    Nikolaas Tinbergen
    Karl von Frisch
1974 Albert Claude
    Christian de Duve
    George E. Palade
1975 David Baltimore
    Renato Dulbecco
    Howard M. Temin
1976 Baruch S. Blumberg
    D. Carleton Gajdusek
1977 Roger Guillemin
    Andrew V. Schally

Rosalyn Yalow
1978 Werner Arber
Daniel Nathans
Hamilton O. Smith
1979 Allan M. Cormack
Godfrey N. Hounsfield
1980 Baruj Benacerraf
Jean Dausset
George D. Snell
1981 David H. Hubel
Roger W. Sperry
Torsten N. Wiesel
1982 Sune K. Bergström
Bengt I. Samuelsson
John R. Vane
1983 Barbara McClintock
1984 Niels K. Jerne
Georges J.F. Köhler
César Milstein
1985 Michael S. Brown
Joseph L. Goldstein
1986 Stanley Cohen
Rita Levi-Montalcini
1987 Susumu Tonegawa
1988 Sir James W. Black
Gertrude B. Elion
George H. Hitchings
1989 J. Michael Bishop
Harold E. Varmus
1990 Joseph E. Murray
E. Donnall Thomas
1991 Erwin Neher
Bert Sakmann
1992 Edmond H. Fischer
Edwin G. Krebs
1993 Richard J. Roberts
Phillip A. Sharp
1994 Alfred G. Gilman
Martin Rodbell
1995 Edward B. Lewis
Christiane Nüsslein-Volhard
Eric F. Wieschaus
1996 Peter C. Doherty
Rolf M. Zinkernagel
1997 Stanley B. Prusiner
1998 Robert F. Furchgott
Louis J. Ignarro
Ferid Murad
1999 Günter Blobel
2000 Arvid Carlsson
Paul Greengard
Eric R. Kandel
2001 Leland H. Hartwell
Tim Hunt
Sir Paul Nurse
2002 Sydney Brenner
H. Robert Horvitz
John E. Sulston
2003 Paul C. Lauterbur
Sir Peter Mansfield
2004 Richard Axel
Linda B. Buck

2005 Barry J. Marshall
J. Robin Warren
2006 Andrew Z. Fire
Craig C. Mello
2007 Mario R. Capecchi
Sir Martin J. Evans
Oliver Smithies
2008 Françoise Barré-Sinoussi
Luc Montagnier
Harald zur Hausen

**Literature Nobelists**
1901 Sully Prudhomme
1902 Theodor Mommsen
1903 Bjørnstjerne Martinus Bjørnson
1904 José Echegaray
Frédéric Mistral
1905 Henryk Sienkiewicz
1906 Giosuè Carducci
1907 Rudyard Kipling
1908 Rudolf Eucken
1909 Selma Lagerlöf
1910 Paul Heyse
1911 Maurice Maeterlinck
1912 Gerhart Hauptmann
1913 Rabindranath Tagore
1914 no award
1915 Romain Rolland
1916 Verner von Heidenstam
1917 Karl Gjellerup
Henrik Pontoppidan
1918 no award
1919 Carl Spitteler
1920 Knut Hamsun
1921 Anatole France
1922 Jacinto Benavente
1923 William Butler Yeats
1924 Wladyslaw Reymont
1925 George Bernard Shaw
1926 Grazia Deledda
1927 Henri Bergson
1928 Sigrid Undset
1929 Thomas Mann
1930 Sinclair Lewis
1931 Erik Axel Karlfeldt
1932 John Galsworthy
1933 Ivan Bunin
1934 Luigi Pirandello
1935 no award
1936 Eugene O'Neill
1937 Roger Martin du Gard
1938 Pearl Buck
1939 Frans Eemil Sillanpää
1940–43 no award
1944 Johannes V. Jensen
1945 Gabriela Mistral
1946 Hermann Hesse
1947 André Gide
1948 T.S. Eliot
1949 William Faulkner
1950 Bertrand Russell
1951 Pär Lagerkvist

| | |
|---|---|
| 1952 François Mauriac | **Peace Nobelists** |
| 1953 Winston Churchill | 1901 Henry Dunant |
| 1954 Ernest Hemingway | Frédéric Passy |
| 1955 Halldór Laxness | 1902 Élie Ducommun |
| 1956 Juan Ramón Jiménez | Albert Gobat |
| 1957 Albert Camus | 1903 Randal Cremer |
| 1958 Boris Pasternak | 1904 Institute of International Law |
| 1959 Salvatore Quasimodo | 1905 Bertha von Suttner |
| 1960 Saint-John Perse | 1906 Theodore Roosevelt |
| 1961 Ivo Andric | 1907 Ernesto Teodoro Moneta |
| 1962 John Steinbeck | Louis Renault |
| 1963 Giorgos Seferis | 1908 Klas Pontus Arnoldson |
| 1964 Jean-Paul Sartre | Fredrik Bajer |
| 1965 Mikhail Sholokhov | 1909 Auguste Beernaert |
| 1966 Shmuel Agnon | Paul Henri d'Estournelles de Constant |
| Nelly Sachs | 1910 Permanent International Peace |
| 1967 Miguel Angel Asturias | Bureau |
| 1968 Yasunari Kawabata | 1911 Tobias Asser |
| 1969 Samuel Beckett | Alfred Fried |
| 1970 Alexandr Solzhenitsyn | 1912 Elihu Root |
| 1971 Pablo Neruda | 1913 Henri La Fontaine |
| 1972 Heinrich Böll | 1914–16 no award |
| 1973 Patrick White | 1917 International Committee of the Red |
| 1974 Eyvind Johnson | Cross |
| Harry Martinson | 1918 no award |
| 1975 Eugenio Montale | 1919 Woodrow Wilson |
| 1976 Saul Bellow | 1920 Léon Bourgeois |
| 1977 Vicente Aleixandre | 1921 Hjalmar Branting |
| 1978 Isaac Bashevis Singer | Christian Lange |
| 1979 Odysseus Elytis | 1922 Fridtjof Nansen |
| 1980 Czeslaw Milosz | 1923–24 no award |
| 1981 Elias Canetti | 1925 Sir Austen Chamberlain |
| 1982 Gabriel García Márquez | Charles G. Dawes |
| 1983 William Golding | 1926 Aristide Briand |
| 1984 Jaroslav Seifert | Gustav Stresemann |
| 1985 Claude Simon | 1927 Ferdinand Buisson |
| 1986 Wole Soyinka | Ludwig Quidde |
| 1987 Joseph Brodsky | 1928 no award |
| 1988 Naguib Mahfouz | 1929 Frank B. Kellogg |
| 1989 Camilo José Cela | 1930 Nathan Söderblom |
| 1990 Octavio Paz | 1931 Jane Addams |
| 1991 Nadine Gordimer | Nicholas Murray Butler |
| 1992 Derek Walcott | 1932 no award |
| 1993 Toni Morrison | 1933 Sir Norman Angell |
| 1994 Kenzaburo Oe | 1934 Arthur Henderson |
| 1995 Seamus Heaney | 1935 Carl von Ossietzky |
| 1996 Wislawa Szymborska | 1936 Carlos Saavedra Lamas |
| 1997 Dario Fo | 1937 Robert Cecil |
| 1998 José Saramago | 1938 Nansen International Office for |
| 1999 Günter Grass | Refugees |
| 2000 Gao Xingjian | 1939–43 no award |
| 2001 V.S. Naipaul | 1944 International Committee of the Red |
| 2002 Imre Kertész | Cross |
| 2003 J.M. Coetzee | 1945 Cordell Hull |
| 2004 Elfriede Jelinek | 1946 Emily Greene Balch |
| 2005 Harold Pinter | John R. Mott |
| 2006 Orhan Pamuk | 1947 Friends Service Council |
| 2007 Doris Lessing | American Friends Service Committee |
| 2008 Jean-Marie Gustave Le Clézio | 1948 no award |
| | 1949 Lord Boyd Orr |
| | 1950 Ralph Bunche |
| | 1951 Léon Jouhaux |
| | 1952 Albert Schweitzer |

1953 George C. Marshall
1954 Office of the United Nations High
    Commissioner for Refugees
1955–56 no award
1957 Lester Bowles Pearson
1958 Georges Pire
1959 Philip Noel-Baker
1960 Albert Lutuli
1961 Dag Hammarskjöld
1962 Linus Pauling
1963 International Committee of the Red
    Cross
    League of Red Cross Societies
1964 Martin Luther King Jr.
1965 United Nations Children's Fund
1966–67 no award
1968 René Cassin
1969 International Labour Organization
1970 Norman Borlaug
1971 Willy Brandt
1972 no award
1973 Le Duc Tho
    Henry Kissinger
1974 Seán MacBride
    Eisaku Sato
1975 Andrei Sakharov
1976 Betty Williams
    Mairead Corrigan
1977 Amnesty International
1978 Anwar al-Sadat
    Menachem Begin
1979 Mother Teresa
1980 Adolfo Pérez Esquivel
1981 Office of the United Nations High
    Commissioner for Refugees
1982 Alfonso García Robles
    Alva Myrdal
1983 Lech Walesa
1984 Desmond Tutu

1985 International Physicians for the
    Prevention of Nuclear War
1986 Elie Wiesel
1987 Oscar Arias Sánchez
1988 United Nations Peacekeeping Forces
1989 The 14th Dalai Lama
1990 Mikhail Gorbachev
1991 Aung San Suu Kyi
1992 Rigoberta Menchú Tum
1993 F.W. de Klerk
    Nelson Mandela
1994 Yasser Arafat
    Shimon Peres
    Yitzhak Rabin
1995 Pugwash Conferences on Science and
    World Affairs
    Joseph Rotblat
1996 Carlos Filipe Ximenes Belo
    José Ramos-Horta
1997 International Campaign to Ban
    Landmines
    Jody Williams
1998 John Hume
    David Trimble
1999 Médecins Sans Frontières
2000 Kim Dae-jung
2001 United Nations
    Kofi Annan
2002 Jimmy Carter
2003 Shirin Ebadi
2004 Wangari Maathai
2005 International Atomic Energy Agency
    Mohamed ElBaradei
2006 Grameen Bank
    Muhammad Yunus
2007 Intergovernmental Panel on Climate
    Change
    Al Gore
2008 Martti Ahtisaari

## Economics Nobelists

1969 Ragnar Frisch
     Jan Tinbergen
1970 Paul A. Samuelson
1971 Simon Kuznets
1972 Kenneth J. Arrow
     John R. Hicks
1973 Wassily Leontief
1974 Gunnar Myrdal
     Friedrich August von Hayek
1975 Leonid Vitaliyevich Kantorovich
     Tjalling C. Koopmans
1976 Milton Friedman
1977 James E. Meade
     Bertil Ohlin
1978 Herbert A. Simon
1979 Sir Arthur Lewis
     Theodore W. Schultz
1980 Lawrence R. Klein
1981 James Tobin
1982 George J. Stigler
1983 Gerard Debreu
1984 Richard Stone
1985 Franco Modigliani
1986 James M. Buchanan Jr.
1987 Robert M. Solow
1988 Maurice Allais
1989 Trygve Haavelmo
1990 Harry M. Markowitz
     Merton H. Miller
     William F. Sharpe
1991 Ronald H. Coase

1992 Gary S. Becker
1993 Robert W. Fogel
     Douglass C. North
1994 John C. Harsanyi
     John F. Nash Jr.
     Reinhard Selten
1995 Robert E. Lucas Jr.
1996 James A. Mirrlees
     William Vickrey
1997 Robert C. Merton
     Myron S. Scholes
1998 Amartya Sen
1999 Robert A. Mundell
2000 James J. Heckman
     Daniel L. McFadden
2001 George A. Akerlof
     A. Michael Spence
     Joseph E. Stiglitz
2002 Daniel Kahneman
     Vernon L. Smith
2003 Robert F. Engle III
     Clive W.J. Granger
2004 Finn E. Kydland
     Edward C. Prescott
2005 Robert J. Aumann
     Thomas C. Schelling
2006 Edmund S. Phelps
2007 Leonid Hurwicz
     Eric S. Maskin
     Roger B. Myerson
2008 Paul Krugman

## Themes in Crosswords

In the early days of crosswords, puzzles consisted of nothing but unrelated intersecting words. Over the years, constructors began using unifying gimmicks, or *themes*, in order to make their puzzles more interesting and enjoyable. Not only does a theme break the monotony of straight clues and answers, it provides an "Aha!" moment for the solver when it is finally revealed.

Thematic answers are almost always the longest ones in a puzzle grid and are placed in symmetrically matching positions. These long answers are related in some way, and the earlier you can figure it out, the more help it will be with solving the other theme entries as well as the rest of the puzzle. A simple theme might include answers like these:

RED RIDING HOOD
WHITE ELEPHANT
BLUE IN THE FACE

The first word in each answer represents one of the colors of the U.S. flag (red, white, and blue). This is a rather basic theme and represents only one type. There are many other theme types, some more challenging than others. Theme types are sometimes combined to create new varieties. The following outline describes many of the theme types found in mainstream crossword puzzles today.

## Theme Types

**Addition:** Theme entries are created by adding a letter, letters, or word to a word or phrase.
Examples:
1. E added at end of phrases: CHECKERED PASTE, CRITICAL MASSE, PATERNITY SUITE
2. ET added to end of a word in phrases: CABINET FEVER, WALLET PAPER, ROCKET BOTTOM
3. BOY added to phrases: HOMEBOY TEAM, PAPERBOY WORK, BELLBOY RINGER, CASH COWBOY

**Alliteration:** Theme entries are two-word (or longer) phrases that have a common first letter or letter combination.
Example:
HAPPY HOUR, HEAD HONCHO, HO-HUM, HIRED HAND, HIGH HAT, HOBBIT HOLE

**Anagram:** All or a portion of each theme entry is anagrammed.
Examples:
1. Anagrammed last word (in this case, the entries also have a movie theme): LORD OF THE FILES (flies), PLANET OF THE PEAS (apes), DAY OF THE CLOUTS (locust)
2. Anagram pairs: STRANGE GARNETS, REMOTE METEOR, CLARET CARTEL, STORIED EDITORS
3. Entire entry anagrammed (usually for this sort of theme, all entries will be derived from the same set of letters, like "mixed METAPHORS"): RASH TEMPO, HART POEMS, MOT SHAPER, MOP HATERS, MATH POSER

**Antonyms:** Theme entries have opposite meanings or contain words that have opposite meanings.
Examples:
1. Pairs of entries have opposite meanings: NOT AT ALL / THUMBS UP, NO WAY JOSE / OKEY-DOKEY
2. Each entry contains opposing words: SWEET AND SOUR PORK, UP AND DOWN MARKET, BLACK AND WHITE TV, LIFE AND DEATH SITUATION, ON AND OFF ROMANCE

**Bookends:** Starting and ending letters form a word or phrase in each theme entry.
Examples:
1. LO at start and VE at end: LOOK ALIVE, LOST ONE'S NERVE, LOCAL DIVE, LOCOMOTIVE
2. First and last words form well-known names: TIGER IN THE WOODS, SALLY NEEDS A RIDE, JOHNNY OUT OF CASH

**Category:** Entries or words within entries are members of a specific category.
Examples:
1. Entire entry (dances): GRIZZLY BEAR, TURKEY TROT, BLACK BOTTOM, CHARLESTON
2. First word of phrase (fingers): THUMB DRIVE, INDEX CARDS, MIDDLE AGES, RING BINDER, PINKY SWEAR

**Chain:** Theme entries are words linked together in end-to-end fashion forming a long chain, with each word connected to the adjacent word(s).

Example:
> BREAD/BASKET/BALL/PLAYER, PIANO/BENCH/PRESS/KIT/BAG, LADY/BIRD/FOOD/TRUCK/FARM, FRESH/AIR/TANK/TOP/BANANA (BANANA links back to BREAD at the start)

**Circles in squares:** Circled squares contain letters that spell out a hidden theme word or phrase.

**Compound:** Words used in theme entries that can come before or after a target word, usually included as a short entry in the puzzle.

Examples:
1. Ending words can precede ROOM: LUCILLE BALL, TAKE A POWDER, IT'S A LIVING, MEAT LOCKER
2. Starting words can follow FLAG: FOOTBALL PADS, POLE POSITION, STAFF OF LIFE, DAY-GLO PAINT

**Container:** Theme entries contain a "hidden" word or letter sequence.

Examples:
1. Same hidden word throughout (GPA): WRITING PAPER, GROWING PAINS, LANDING PARTY, DANGLING PARTICIPLES, STANDING PAT, BOARDING PASS
2. Different hidden words, but all belong to same category (in this case, fish): DIRECT ROUTE, TURNPIKE EXIT, CIGARILLO, KAREN CARPENTER, MAUSOLEUM, U.S. AMBASSADOR, DISCO DIVA, BANTU NATIVE

**Definition:** Theme entries are in the form of a definition, while the clues are usually related and carry the theme.

Examples:
1. Four clues for "Buck": ONE SMACKER, NOVELIST PEARL, KIND OF PRIVATE, MALE RABBIT
2. Clues for related words: MONTHS OF SPRING (clue for MAYS), LAYER OF THE EARTH (clue for MANTLE), MORE DEROGATORY (clue for SNIDER)

**Deletion:** Theme entries created by deleting a letter, letters, or word from a word or phrase.

Examples:
1. T deleted from front of phrases: APE MEASURE, RUST BUSTER, RAILBLAZER, AX ASSESSOR
2. BR deleted from front end: EAST PLATE, ANDY ALEXANDER, INK OF DISASTER, ACE AND BIT
3. IT deleted from end of phrases: ONE-ARMED BAND, DOUBLE DIG, LEARNERS PERM

**Direction change:** Entries change direction as they are entered in the grid.

Example:
> MICHAEL DELL, NORMAN FELL, WILLIAM TELL, JOSHUA BELL (each entry turns to make a right angle in the grid at the "ELL")

**Double/Triple letters:** Words or phrases containing double or triple letters are featured.

Examples:
1. Single per entry: OOM-PAH-PAHS, OOH AND AHH, OONA O'NEILL, OOLONG TEA
2. Multiple per entry ARTOO-DETOO, BAMBOO SHOOT, WHOOP-DE-DOOS, POOH-POOHED

**Featured letter(s):** Entries feature or highlight a given letter or group of letters.

Examples:
1. The only vowel used in the entire puzzle is A.
2. A rare letter, such as Q or X or Z, is used in abundance.
3. All entries contain letters found only on the left-hand side of the keyboard.

**Grid design:** The arrangement of black and white squares plays into the theme.

Example:
> Black squares form a large S in the center of the grid, and all clues start with an S.

**Holidays and special occasions:** Theme is related to the day on which it appears in the newspaper.

Example:
> MARTIN, LUTHER, I HAVE A DREAM, NOBEL PEACE PRIZE, KING JR, CIVIL RIGHTS (appearing on Martin Luther King Jr. Day)

**Homophones:** Theme entries have words that sound like other words.
Examples:
1. Same-sounding words throughout: CIVIL RIGHT, PLEASE WRITE, STRIDE RITE, WHEELWRIGHT
2. Different homophones with a common theme: BEAR ESSENTIALS, BEE CAREFUL, GNU ARRIVAL, GORILLA WARFARE

**Joke/Riddle:** A joke or riddle is related by the theme entries.
Examples:
1. Joke: KNOCK KNOCK / WHO'S THERE / THE HANDY MAN YOUR / DOORBELL'S / ON THE BLINK
2. Riddle: WHAT CAN YOU USE / TO FIX A BROKEN / JACK O'LANTERN / A PUMPKIN PATCH

**Language/Accent:** Theme entries use another language, accent, or manner of speech
Example (Pig Latin):
OKAY COLLEGE, ASHTRAY COMPACTOR, QUILTING EBAY, ELWAY SUITED, OLAY PROFILE, WOMEN'S AIRWAY, LOOT AND UNDERPLAY

**Mini-theme:** Two related entries in an otherwise themeless puzzle
Example:
ORANGE ROUGHY, LIME SMOOTHIE

**Pairs/Triplets/N-tuplets:** Theme entries consist of two or more words/phrases from the same category.
Examples:
1. Rock group pairings: POISON AIR SUPPLY, MEATLOAF PLATTERS, HEART ASSOCIATION
2. Triplets: SONY RCA MAGNAVOX (clued as "TV series"), MARS SATURN VENUS (clued as "World series"), LITTLE TINY SHORT (clued as "Mini series")
3. Magazine n-tuplets: STAR WIRED PARENTS MONEY, MAD CONSUMER REPORTS SPY, JET THE ATLANTIC MONTHLY

**Palindromes:** Theme entries read the same forward and backward.
Example (religiously themed):
MA IS A NUN AS I AM, DO GEESE SEE GOD, WE PANIC IN A PEW

**Positional:** Theme entries are positioned in specific grid locations or are positioned relative to each other.
Examples:
1. Positioned by direction: WESTCHESTER, NORTH DAKOTA, EAST HAMPTON, SOUTH AFRICA
2. By relative position: ON TOP OF positioned above THE WORLD, BENEATH positioned under CONTEMPT

**Proper names:** Theme involves a shared characteristic of (or wordplay with) proper names.
Example:
F. LEE BAILEY, G. GORDON LIDDY, C. EVERETT KOOP, L. FRANK BAUM (well-known names with first initials)

**Punch lines:** Theme entries are punch lines led into by the clues.
Example (puzzle titled "I wanted to be a ..."):
(clue)... sumo wrestler, but I ...
(entry) QUIT WHEN PUSH CAME TO SHOVE
(clue)... mime, but I ...
(entry) TALKED MYSELF OUT OF IT

**Puns:** Theme relies on the usually humorous use of a word in such a way as to suggest two or more of its meanings or the meaning of another word similar in sound.
Examples:
1. Words used with multiple meanings (same spelling): I'LL DRAW TWO CARDS (clue: Artist's comment at the poker game), I HOPE I WIN THIS POT (clue: Chef's comment at the poker game)
2. Similar-sounding words with different meanings and spellings: CHANGES ATTIRE, TURNS ON THE VIPER, ADJUSTS THE MIR

**Quips/Quotes:** Theme entries reveal a quip (generally written specifically to fit a puzzle grid) or quote (for which the constructor must find one that can be broken into symmetric segments).
Examples:
1. Quip: DIETING IS FOR / THOSE WHO / ARE THICK / AND TIRED OF IT
2. Quote (by Will Rogers): I DON'T / MAKE JOKES / I JUST WATCH THE / GOVERNMENT AND / REPORT THE / FACTS

**Rebus:** Theme entries contain a segment
that consists of a picture or string of letters
to be entered in a single square.
  Examples:
  1. Single rebus: ♥THROBS, ♥BEATS,
     PURPLE ♥, SWEET♥, ♥ OF GOLD,
     BROKEN ♥
  2. Multiple rebuses of tree varieties:
     S[TEAK] SAUCE, [TEA K]ETTLE,
     LUC[Y EW]ING, E[YEW]ASH, TRASH
     [FIR]ES, SEMI[FIR]M, CR[OAK],
     S[OAK] IN, AL[PINE], S[PINE]LESS

**Redivision:** Theme entries are regular
phrases clued as if the division between
words were different than usual.
  Example:
     BALAAM SASS, THE LORD
     SPRAYER, WOMEN SWEAR DAILY,
     MRS. O'LEARY SCOW

**Repetition:** Theme entries contain
repeated words or sounds.
  Examples:
  1. Same word appears in each entry:
     QUILTING BEE, OKEECHOBEE,
     BEEHIVE OVEN, FRISBEE
  2. Same sound appears multiple times
     in each entry: IMPALA À LA OCALA,
     KOALA À LA MARSALA, FALA À LA
     SCALA
  3. Doubled words: BORA BORA,
     BADEN-BADEN, PAGO PAGO,
     WALLA WALLA

**Reversal:** Part or all of the theme entries
are in reverse.
  Examples:
  1. Full entry: KCAB ELBUOD, SRAEG
     ESREVER, YTHGIE-ENO A OD,
     DNUORA NRUT
  2. Last word: GO WITH THE WOLF,
     MINIATURE FLOG, TREASURE
     SPAM, SHOOTING RATS

**Rhymes:** Theme entries rhyme or contain
rhyming portions.
  Examples:
  1. Full entry: DING-DONG, KING
     KONG, PING-PONG, SINGSONG
  2. Front-end rhyme: GOBBLEDYGOOK,
     BOBBLEHEAD DOLL,
     COBBLESTONES

**Sequence:** Series of words or phrases that
produce a sequence from theme entry to
theme entry.
  Examples:
  1. Numbers: FIRST AID STATION,
     SECONDHAND SMOKE, THIRD
     BASE UMPIRE, FOURTH-CLASS
     MAIL
  2. Phrase (in first words): FAITH
     HEALER, HOPE AGAINST HOPE,
     CHARITY BALL
  3. Clued sequence: ONCE IN A WHILE,
     EVERY NOW AND THEN, ON A
     REGULAR BASIS
  4. Word ladder (series of words that
     change one letter to move from one
     word to the next—an invention of
     Lewis Carroll): **HEAT** WAVE, **BEAT**
     THE CLOCK, **BOAT** WHISTLE,
     **BOLT** CUTTERS, **COLT** REVOLVER,
     **COLD** SNAP
  5. Vowel sequence (set of words that
     differ only by one vowel): THE LAST
     MILE, LEST WE FORGET, THE
     LIST, THE LOST WORLD, LUST
     FOR LIFE

**Shared centers:** Two words or phrases
that share an intervening word or segment.
  Example:
     PIN**BALL**PARK, OLD**MAID**MARIAN,
     BLACK**JACK**RABBIT,
     BACCA**RAT**TRAP

**Shared initials:** Theme entries are phrases
that share the same initial letters, excluding
alliterations.
  Example:
     IAN MCKELLEN, IMPORT MODEL,
     IMPOSSIBLE MISSION, INBOARD
     MOTOR

**Shift:** Theme entries consistently shift a
letter or letters from one position to another.
  Example:
     Shift IN from front end to a later
     position: DIANA IN HOOSIERS,
     FIELD IN HITS, TRAM IN URALS,
     COME IN STATEMENT

**Spoonerisms:** Phrases or words with
swapped sounds. The name Spoonerism
comes from the Reverend William Archibald
Spooner who is reputed to have been
particularly prone to making this type of
verbal slip.
  Example:
     COURT OF PAUL (port of call),
     CLUTCH OF TASS (touch of class),
     MENTOR OF SASS (center of mass),
     WALL OF BACKS (ball of wax)

**Stacked 15's:** Fifteen-letter entries stacked on each other in a themeless puzzle.

**String:** Theme entries formed of words strung together in end-to-end fashion forming a long string. The individual words are usually related to a selected word.
Example:
All words can follow ROAD: RUNNER/TAR/MAP/WAY, BIKE/WORK/BED/SIGN, GRADER/AGENT/TRIP, SHOW/HOG/SIDE/TEST, HOUSE/ROLLER/RAGE

**Substitutions:** One letter, group of letters, sound, or word(s) is (are) substituted for another in the theme entries.
Examples:
1. U substituted for ME: SEIZE THE MOUNT, CORPORATE URGERS, FRAU OF REFERENCE
2. "Tee" sound substituted for "two" sound: POWER TEAL, TIER DE FRANCE, KING TUT'S TEAM
3. Element abbr. substitution: PT BLONDE, AG TONGUED, SN LIZZIE, AU DIGGER, FE CURTAIN
4. Double substitution (ALL for ONE and ONE for ALL): TALL OF VOICE, SOUP BALLS, NOSE CALLS, STALL MASONS, SHOWER STONE, CONES HOME, BEAN BONES, WALKING TONE
5. Thematic:
   a. Times advanced: LUNCH AT TIFFANY'S, SUNDAY NIGHT LIVE, SEVEN DAYS IN JUNE
   b. Names subbed for initials: JIM PALMER MORGAN, ANNE JACKSON FOYT, ANSEL ADAMS MILNE

**Switch:** Letters or words within theme entry phrases switch positions.
Examples:
1. Letters: BALL OF FIRE, BILL OF FARE, CONVERSATION, CONSERVATION, LIMESTONE, MILESTONE
2. Words: CONTENTS OF TABLE, RECORD OF CLIENTS, CLOTHES OF CHANGE

**Synonyms:** Theme entries or words within theme entries that have like meanings.
Examples:
1. Full entry: ASK ME IF I CARE, WHAT'S THE BIG DEAL, WHO GIVES A FIG
2. First word: DOUBLE FEATURE, TWIN SISTERS, PAIR OF PANTS, TWO CENTS' WORTH

**Tribute:** Theme entries create a puzzle tribute to a person or place.
Example:
BOB KEESHAN, CAPTAIN KANGAROO, CLOWN HALL OF FAME, HOWDY DOODY

**Verse:** Theme entries combine to create a verse, poem, limerick, or other similar form. Similar to a quip puzzle, except it rhymes.
Example:
I MEET SANTA MORE AND MORE / MANY STORES ENTHRONE HIM / SOMEONE MUST BE JOKING OR / THEY'VE BEGUN TO CLONE HIM

Any of the above theme types may be combined to create even trickier themes. Sometimes you'll come across an innovative puzzle that does something new and unclassifiable, but most crossword theme types can be found somewhere on this list.

Top 3-Letter Answers
(by rank)

| | | | | | | |
|---|---|---|---|---|---|---|
| 1. ERA | 62. RTE | 123. EDS | 184. OTT | 248. TDS | 312. DIE | 376. ARS |
| 2. ERE | 63. ETE | 124. ETC | 185. OWE | 249. LED | 313. YEA | 377. TAT |
| 3. ORE | 64. SSE | 125. URN | 186. LEN | 250. NAT | 314. PIE | 378. SUE |
| 4. ELI | 65. EER | 126. PTA | 187. OBI | 251. MET | 315. WAR | 379. REM |
| 5. ONE | 66. AXE | 127. ETS | 188. ATA | 252. BAA | 316. OAK | 380. LAM |
| 6. ALE | 67. EON | 128. INN | 189. ABA | 253. OPT | 317. LAP | 381. AGA |
| 7. ALI | 68. LIE | 129. NEA | 190. ERN | 254. EMS | 318. REP | 382. HOE |
| 8. ARE | 69. LEA | 130. TRA | 191. DOE | 255. ALS | 319. HAT | 383. ATL |
| 9. ETA | 70. AGO | 131. NIL | 192. EEE | 256. AMP | 320. ROD | 384. SOD |
| 10. ATE | 71. STE | 132. LET | 193. ERG | 257. SCI | 321. SIN | 385. ONT |
| 11. OLE | 72. ROE | 133. USA | 194. INA | 258. YEN | 322. DOT | 386. STP |
| 12. ENE | 73. OAR | 134. RAH | 195. AWE | 259. TOT | 323. ROO | 387. AFT |
| 13. ERR | 74. ADS | 135. ASP | 196. TRI | 260. ALT | 324. THE | 388. CAT |
| 14. ESS | 75. ELL | 136. TAN | 197. MAE | 261. ENG | 325. ARK | 389. AWL |
| 15. ALA | 76. TNT | 137. OER | 198. ITO | 262. RID | 326. SKI | 390. NCO |
| 16. SPA | 77. ORR | 138. APT | 199. AIL | 263. SIS | 327. RAW | 391. ISM |
| 17. ASH | 78. ARC | 139. ELO | 200. DES | 264. ASI | 328. NOD | 392. IOU |
| 18. IRE | 79. ANN | 140. RAT | 201. AAA | 265. ITE | 329. TAP | 393. CRO |
| 19. IRA | 80. ECO | 141. ION | 202. LAS | 266. SOL | 330. TAB | 394. EIN |
| 20. NEE | 81. AIR | 142. AVE | 203. BRA | 267. YET | 331. NOS | 395. SOT |
| 21. ADO | 82. NOR | 143. AND | 204. RYE | 268. TIS | 332. OHO | 396. INT |
| 22. ESE | 83. RED | 144. NTH | 205. STA | 269. DEL | 333. POE | 397. EDT |
| 23. EAR | 84. EWE | 145. SOS | 206. SRA | 270. SAG | 334. ENT | 398. RIM |
| 24. ODE | 85. AMI | 146. REO | 207. TIN | 271. HAS | 335. AMO | 399. UPS |
| 25. END | 86. RIO | 147. ILL | 208. ODD | 272. AER | 336. NEW | 400. ATT |
| 26. ARI | 87. IDO | 148. ELM | 209. ROT | 273. RAP | 337. ITA | 401. LSD |
| 27. SEE | 88. RNA | 149. ENO | 210. TAI | 274. LOU | 338. SIT | 402. ESC |
| 28. ACE | 89. RAE | 150. SRI | 211. ORA | 275. INK | 339. BAH | 403. MIR |
| 29. ANT | 90. AMA | 151. ARA | 212. EEN | 276. SAO | 340. RIP | 404. AHS |
| 30. EGO | 91. ADE | 152. ERS | 213. TOO | 277. ALP | 341. TAO | 405. EEK |
| 31. APE | 92. EMU | 153. SAL | 214. SEN | 278. CEE | 342. MAT | 406. LOS |
| 32. EEL | 93. PER | 154. RCA | 215. MAR | 279. ORB | 343. SAS | 407. UNE |
| 33. AGE | 94. IDA | 155. DNA | 216. TET | 280. REC | 344. UNI | 408. COO |
| 34. TEE | 95. RAN | 156. REA | 217. SSR | 281. ARR | 345. CAN | 409. OOH |
| 35. EVE | 96. EPA | 157. AVA | 218. EBB | 282. INS | 346. MOE | 410. SAC |
| 36. EAT | 97. LES | 158. IRS | 219. SRS | 283. PSI | 347. DER | 411. BAT |
| 37. SEA | 98. ACT | 159. ARM | 220. SLO | 284. SAM | 348. ITT | 412. OUT |
| 38. ART | 99. DEN | 160. ELK | 221. SEC | 285. PAT | 349. NBA | 413. TOM |
| 39. ASS | 100. RES | 161. TON | 222. STS | 286. KEN | 350. ISH | 414. TOR |
| 40. EST | 101. TIE | 162. ANY | 223. AIM | 287. PET | 351. PEN | 415. CHE |
| 41. TEA | 102. SRO | 163. SSS | 224. NAP | 288. TRY | 352. LOT | 416. SSN |
| 42. AHA | 103. NEO | 164. EKE | 225. ANI | 289. OLA | 353. TLC | 417. TRE |
| 43. ANA | 104. LEI | 165. OLD | 226. BEE | 290. CIA | 354. NIP | 418. DDE |
| 44. NET | 105. EYE | 166. ADD | 227. AOL | 291. ABS | 355. WEE | 419. SGT |
| 45. TAR | 106. ILE | 167. SAD | 228. CPA | 292. LIL | 356. GEL | 420. DAS |
| 46. SHE | 107. SIR | 168. DEE | 229. HAL | 293. MEL | 357. ARF | 421. OAF |
| 47. ONO | 108. TED | 169. CAR | 230. OCT | 294. PRE | 358. NOT | 422. SPY |
| 48. ICE | 109. ASA | 170. OVA | 231. IVE | 295. AID | 359. OWN | 423. RNS |
| 49. SST | 110. OAT | 171. RUE | 232. REF | 296. EOS | 360. RBI | 424. FEE |
| 50. TEN | 111. NRA | 172. HER | 233. EGG | 297. IDS | 361. TAG | 425. NIN |
| 51. ELS | 112. SAT | 173. LEO | 234. EAU | 298. INE | 362. RHO | 426. EMT |
| 52. SET | 113. UTE | 174. SLY | 235. ELF | 299. OUR | 363. AAH | 427. MAO |
| 53. TSE | 114. EVA | 175. PEA | 236. MER | 300. RAM | 364. ANE | 428. TWO |
| 54. USE | 115. TOE | 176. GAS | 237. ETO | 301. URI | 365. RAY | 429. MAD |
| 55. YES | 116. ORO | 177. PRO | 238. SAN | 302. TAD | 366. BOA | 430. IMP |
| 56. ENS | 117. NNE | 178. ONA | 239. SAP | 303. MIA | 367. TAU | 431. REB |
| 57. STY | 118. NED | 179. REN | 240. ASK | 304. STU | 368. CSA | 432. ISA |
| 58. LEE | 119. IAN | 180. ATM | 241. SNO | 305. LAD | 369. IKE | 433. WET |
| 59. ABE | 120. OIL | 181. SON | 242. PAL | 306. APR | 370. REL | 434. TIC |
| 60. ESP | 121. ITS | 182. TEL | 243. HEN | 307. BAR | 371. LYE | 435. NAY |
| 61. ALL | 122. ADA | 183. GEE | 244. PAR | 308. RDA | 372. CBS | 436. CON |
| | | | 245. RON | 309. AKA | 373. REV | 437. RAD |
| | | | 246. UMA | 310. SEW | 374. CAL | 438. CEL |
| | | | 247. UNO | 311. LIT | 375. DYE | 439. GAL |

440. AYE
441. LOA
442. ORS
443. NAN
444. IST
445. IDI
446. DRE
447. ISR
448. DOS
449. PLO
450. RET
451. IMA
452. CDS
453. CEO
454. DAD
455. MAS
456. LOO
457. ANO
458. SHA
459. MOO
460. TIA
461. CHI
462. DAN
463. SNL
464. OSE
465. RAG
466. NIT
467. LAW
468. BRO
469. LIP
470. PAS

471. NON
472. YRS
473. NAB
474. PAN
475. UAR
476. TKO
477. SAW
478. INC
479. VEE
480. VIA
481. MAC
482. YDS
483. HOT
484. TAE
485. NIA
486. HEE
487. ARP
488. NSA
489. NAE
490. ROB
491. OOP
492. DAM
493. ALF
494. OPE
495. ETH
496. HEM
497. ACH
498. III
499. TSK
500. ZEN

## Top 3-Letter Answers (alphabetical)

| | | | | |
|---|---|---|---|---|
| AAA (201) | ASH (17) | EBB (218) | HEE (486) | LSD (401) |
| AAH (363) | ASI (264) | ECO (80) | HEM (496) | LYE (371) |
| ABA (189) | ASK (240) | EDS (123) | HEN (243) | MAC (481) |
| ABE (59) | ASP (135) | EDT (397) | HER (172) | MAD (429) |
| ABS (291) | ASS (39) | EEE (192) | HOE (382) | MAE (197) |
| ACE (28) | ATA (188) | EEK (405) | HOT (483) | MAO (427) |
| ACH (497) | ATE (10) | EEL (32) | IAN (119) | MAR (215) |
| ACT (98) | ATL (383) | EEN (212) | ICE (48) | MAS (455) |
| ADA (122) | ATM (180) | EER (65) | IDA (94) | MAT (342) |
| ADD (166) | ATT (400) | EGG (233) | IDI (445) | MEL (293) |
| ADE (91) | AVA (157) | EGO (30) | IDO (87) | MER (236) |
| ADO (21) | AVE (142) | EIN (394) | IDS (297) | MET (251) |
| ADS (74) | AWE (195) | EKE (164) | III (498) | MIA (303) |
| AER (272) | AWL (389) | ELF (235) | IKE (369) | MIR (403) |
| AFT (387) | AXE (66) | ELI (4) | ILE (106) | MOE (346) |
| AGA (381) | AYE (440) | ELK (160) | ILL (147) | MOO (459) |
| AGE (33) | BAA (252) | ELL (75) | IMA (451) | NAB (473) |
| AGO (70) | BAH (339) | ELM (148) | IMP (430) | NAE (489) |
| AHA (42) | BAR (307) | ELO (139) | INA (194) | NAN (443) |
| AHS (404) | BAT (411) | ELS (51) | INC (478) | NAP (224) |
| AID (295) | BEE (226) | EMS (254) | INE (298) | NAT (250) |
| AIL (199) | BOA (366) | EMT (426) | INK (275) | NAY (435) |
| AIM (223) | BRA (203) | EMU (92) | INN (128) | NBA (349) |
| AIR (81) | BRO (468) | END (25) | INS (282) | NCO (390) |
| AKA (309) | CAL (374) | ENE (12) | INT (396) | NEA (129) |
| ALA (15) | CAN (345) | ENG (261) | ION (141) | NED (118) |
| ALE (6) | CAR (169) | ENO (149) | IOU (392) | NEE (20) |
| ALF (493) | CAT (388) | ENS (56) | IRA (19) | NEO (103) |
| ALI (7) | CBS (372) | ENT (334) | IRE (18) | NET (44) |
| ALL (61) | CDS (452) | EON (67) | IRS (158) | NEW (336) |
| ALP (277) | CEE (278) | EOS (296) | ISA (432) | NIA (485) |
| ALS (255) | CEL (438) | EPA (96) | ISH (350) | NIL (131) |
| ALT (260) | CEO (453) | ERA (1) | ISM (391) | NIN (425) |
| AMA (90) | CHE (415) | ERE (2) | ISR (447) | NIP (354) |
| AMI (85) | CHI (461) | ERG (193) | IST (444) | NIT (466) |
| AMO (335) | CIA (290) | ERN (190) | ITA (337) | NNE (117) |
| AMP (256) | CON (436) | ERR (13) | ITE (265) | NOD (328) |
| ANA (43) | COO (408) | ERS (152) | ITO (198) | NON (471) |
| AND (143) | CPA (228) | ESC (402) | ITS (121) | NOR (82) |
| ANE (364) | CRO (393) | ESE (22) | ITT (348) | NOS (331) |
| ANI (225) | CSA (368) | ESP (60) | IVE (231) | NOT (358) |
| ANN (79) | DAD (454) | ESS (14) | KEN (286) | NRA (111) |
| ANO (457) | DAM (492) | EST (40) | LAD (305) | NSA (488) |
| ANT (29) | DAN (462) | ETA (9) | LAM (380) | NTH (144) |
| ANY (162) | DAS (420) | ETC (124) | LAP (317) | OAF (421) |
| AOL (227) | DDE (418) | ETE (63) | LAS (202) | OAK (316) |
| APE (31) | DEE (168) | ETH (495) | LAW (467) | OAR (73) |
| APR (306) | DEL (269) | ETO (237) | LEA (69) | OAT (110) |
| APT (138) | DEN (99) | ETS (127) | LED (249) | OBI (187) |
| ARA (151) | DER (347) | EVA (114) | LEE (58) | OCT (230) |
| ARC (78) | DES (200) | EVE (35) | LEI (104) | ODD (208) |
| ARE (8) | DIE (312) | EWE (84) | LEN (186) | ODE (24) |
| ARF (357) | DNA (155) | EYE (105) | LEO (173) | OER (137) |
| ARI (26) | DOE (191) | FEE (424) | LES (97) | OHO (332) |
| ARK (325) | DOS (448) | GAL (439) | LET (132) | OIL (120) |
| ARM (159) | DOT (322) | GAS (176) | LIE (68) | OLA (289) |
| ARP (487) | DRE (446) | GEE (183) | LIL (292) | OLD (165) |
| ARR (281) | DYE (375) | GEL (356) | LIP (469) | OLE (11) |
| ARS (376) | EAR (23) | HAL (229) | LIT (311) | ONA (178) |
| ART (38) | EAT (36) | HAS (271) | LOA (441) | ONE (5) |
| ASA (109) | EAU (234) | HAT (319) | LOO (456) | ONO (47) |
| | | | LOS (406) | ONT (385) |
| | | | LOT (352) | OOH (409) |
| | | | LOU (274) | OOP (491) |

OPE (494)
OPT (253)
ORA (211)
ORB (279)
ORE (3)
ORO (116)
ORR (77)
ORS (442)
OSE (464)
OTT (184)
OUR (299)
OUT (412)
OVA (170)
OWE (185)
OWN (359)
PAL (242)
PAN (474)
PAR (244)
PAS (470)
PAT (285)
PEA (175)
PEN (351)
PER (93)
PET (287)
PIE (314)
PLO (449)
POE (333)
PRE (294)
PRO (177)
PSI (283)
PTA (126)
RAD (437)
RAE (89)
RAG (465)
RAH (134)
RAM (300)
RAN (95)
RAP (273)
RAT (140)
RAW (327)
RAY (365)
RBI (360)
RCA (154)
RDA (308)
REA (156)
REB (431)
REC (280)
RED (83)
REF (232)
REL (370)
REM (379)
REN (179)
REO (146)
REP (318)
RES (100)
RET (450)
REV (373)
RHO (362)
RID (262)
RIM (398)
RIO (86)
RIP (340)
RNA (88)

RNS (423)
ROB (490)
ROD (320)
ROE (72)
RON (245)
ROO (323)
ROT (209)
RTE (62)
RUE (171)
RYE (204)
SAC (410)
SAD (167)
SAG (270)
SAL (153)
SAM (284)
SAN (238)
SAO (276)
SAP (239)
SAS (343)
SAT (112)
SAW (477)
SCI (257)
SEA (37)
SEC (221)
SEE (27)
SEN (214)
SET (52)
SEW (310)
SGT (419)
SHA (458)
SHE (46)
SIN (321)
SIR (107)
SIS (263)
SIT (338)
SKI (326)
SLO (220)
SLY (174)
SNL (463)
SNO (241)
SOD (384)
SOL (266)
SON (181)
SOS (145)
SOT (395)
SPA (16)
SPY (422)
SRA (206)
SRI (150)
SRO (102)
SRS (219)
SSE (64)
SSN (416)
SSR (217)
SSS (163)
SST (49)
STA (205)
STE (71)
STP (386)
STS (222)
STU (304)
STY (57)
SUE (378)

TAB (330)
TAD (302)
TAE (484)
TAG (361)
TAI (210)
TAN (136)
TAO (341)
TAP (329)
TAR (45)
TAT (377)
TAU (367)
TDS (248)
TEA (41)
TED (108)
TEE (34)
TEL (182)
TEN (50)
TET (216)
THE (324)
TIA (460)
TIC (434)
TIE (101)
TIN (207)
TIS (268)
TKO (476)
TLC (353)
TNT (76)
TOE (115)
TOM (413)
TON (161)
TOO (213)
TOR (414)
TOT (259)
TRA (130)
TRE (417)
TRI (196)
TRY (288)
TSE (53)
TSK (499)
TWO (428)
UAR (475)
UMA (246)
UNE (407)
UNI (344)
UNO (247)
UPS (399)
URI (301)
URN (125)
USA (133)
USE (54)
UTE (113)
VEE (479)
VIA (480)
WAR (315)
WEE (355)
WET (433)
YDS (482)
YEA (313)
YEN (258)
YES (55)
YET (267)
YRS (472)
ZEN (500)

## Top 4-Letter Answers (by rank)

1. AREA
2. ERIE
3. EDEN
4. ANTE
5. ALOE
6. ARIA
7. IDEA
8. OREO
9. ELSE
10. OLEO
11. ASEA
12. ORAL
13. ACRE
14. STAR
15. ODOR
16. ASIA
17. ALAS
18. ERAS
19. ENOS
20. EROS
21. ETNA
22. EASE
23. EPEE
24. TREE
25. ECHO
26. ANTI
27. ERIC
28. ANON
29. IRON
30. ALAN
31. ELLA
32. ONES
33. ETAL
34. ASHE
35. ALEC
36. TSAR
37. ANNE
38. EDIT
39. ETON
40. ARAB
41. ISEE
42. ELIA
43. ONCE
44. STIR
45. REST
46. IDOL
47. OGRE
48. OMAR
49. AMEN
50. EDGE
51. ACHE
52. ENDS
53. OBOE
54. ALEE
55. ERLE
56. OTTO
57. RENE
58. ORES
59. IRAN
60. ELAN
61. ERIN
62. ISLE
63. ENID
64. EMIT
65. OPAL
66. EAST
67. ADAM
68. ALTO
69. AERO
70. ETTE
71. ITEM
72. ARLO
73. ARES
74. ERRS
75. RARE
76. EIRE
77. OSLO
78. USER
79. EVIL
80. ATOM
81. STET
82. ELAL
83. UTAH
84. NERO
85. RENO
86. ALOT
87. ESAU
88. ABET
89. ESSO
90. INTO
91. INRE
92. ASAP
93. EVER
94. ELLE
95. ALES
96. EPIC
97. ONTO
98. IDLE
99. OGLE
100. SLED
101. AFAR
102. ANNA
103. OTIS
104. ALAI
105. ELSA
106. ARID
107. URGE
108. NESS
109. ALIT
110. ABLE
111. NEST
112. UNIT
113. EDIE
114. ANTS
115. IGOR
116. EMIR
117. ETTA
118. ANEW
119. NEAT
120. SSTS
121. APSE
122. EDNA
123. IOTA
124. ATOP
125. KNEE
126. AURA
127. AVER
128. EGAD
129. OVER
130. STEP
131. ALSO
132. NEAR
133. AONE
134. NEED
135. ASTI
136. OMIT
137. ERTE
138. EVEN
139. STAT
140. ODES
141. ETRE
142. ASTA
143. AJAR
144. ABEL
145. OMEN
146. PSST
147. ESTE
148. STAN
149. REAR
150. URAL
151. AGEE
152. ECRU
153. OVAL
154. NEON
155. TERI
156. EARL
157. IRIS
158. INCA
159. AGRA
160. ACES
161. ESSE
162. ARTE
163. SCAR
164. SNAP
165. ICON
166. OPEN
167. TALE
168. ARTS
169. EDAM
170. LEER
171. URSA
172. REED
173. ARNO
174. EELS
175. NERD
176. SENT
177. ADEN
178. OLIO
179. EWER
180. SERA
181. ASST
182. TARA
183. AMOS

| | | | | | |
|---|---|---|---|---|---|
| 184. STOP | 237. SEMI | 290. PERU | 343. UCLA | 396. SERE | 449. SETH |
| 185. ALOU | 238. SLOE | 291. ILIE | 344. MESA | 397. OLES | 450. OLLA |
| 186. ALDA | 239. EMMA | 292. SPAS | 345. OBIE | 398. SECT | 451. RAIN |
| 187. ONEA | 240. SANE | 293. REAL | 346. AWOL | 399. EZRA | 452. LIEN |
| 188. STEM | 241. AIDE | 294. ATIT | 347. AUTO | 400. REBA | 453. STOW |
| 189. ODIE | 242. ETCH | 295. AQUA | 348. SLAT | 401. SODA | 454. ERNE |
| 190. ASTO | 243. NOEL | 296. EXIT | 349. STAY | 402. SALE | 455. SAGA |
| 191. ARAL | 244. TEAR | 297. RISE | 350. AMID | 403. GNAT | 456. ANNO |
| 192. ASIS | 245. AHAB | 298. DELI | 351. APER | 404. NASA | 457. OLEG |
| 193. TRIO | 246. SETS | 299. STAG | 352. ACED | 405. CEDE | 458. RHEA |
| 194. SARI | 247. HALO | 300. SPED | 353. TROT | 406. OLGA | 459. SOHO |
| 195. ACME | 248. SOSO | 301. REDS | 354. IRMA | 407. ESAI | 460. SLOT |
| 196. SPAR | 249. TEEN | 302. PETE | 355. SALT | 408. HARE | 461. LORE |
| 197. ERSE | 250. DEER | 303. SIRE | 356. UNDO | 409. SOAR | 462. OBIT |
| 198. SARA | 251. OVEN | 304. SEEN | 357. TRUE | 410. ATTA | 463. ABCS |
| 199. AMES | 252. AMOR | 305. SCAT | 358. NINA | 411. MESS | 464. SHOE |
| 200. SEER | 253. OHIO | 306. ABUT | 359. OHNO | 412. TONI | 465. SILO |
| 201. ASPS | 254. IVAN | 307. TALC | 360. AXLE | 413. SEES | 466. SCOT |
| 202. SNIT | 255. LENO | 308. TATA | 361. LAIR | 414. TETE | 467. YENS |
| 203. ABBA | 256. AGES | 309. IDES | 362. SHEA | 415. OLIN | 468. EWES |
| 204. NILE | 257. NATO | 310. NOAH | 363. NCAA | 416. UPON | 469. RIDE |
| 205. STEW | 258. LESS | 311. NEMO | 364. NINE | 417. ARCH | 470. SEEP |
| 206. TIER | 259. INON | 312. ETTU | 365. URIS | 418. SCAN | 471. NOTE |
| 207. TESS | 260. ONUS | 313. EYES | 366. EXES | 419. ASSN | 472. ADES |
| 208. AFRO | 261. ERAT | 314. TIRE | 367. TACO | 420. IVES | 473. ASKS |
| 209. ACTS | 262. HERO | 315. ODIN | 368. AHEM | 421. DESI | 474. TEES |
| 210. TEST | 263. ESTA | 316. EMIL | 369. SEAL | 422. TINA | 475. YSER |
| 211. EARN | 264. TRAP | 317. ATRA | 370. RITA | 423. LARA | 476. RAIL |
| 212. EURO | 265. RIOT | 318. EERO | 371. REAP | 424. IRAE | 477. SPAN |
| 213. ELIE | 266. GENE | 319. ERMA | 372. ALMA | 425. NARC | 478. ELEE |
| 214. RENT | 267. OPIE | 320. AGED | 373. ADOS | 426. OPEC | 479. COLA |
| 215. LIAR | 268. EARS | 321. EAVE | 374. SEED | 427. STEN | 480. ATTN |
| 216. NORA | 269. AGAR | 322. USSR | 375. RANT | 428. DRAT | 481. HAHA |
| 217. REDO | 270. IAGO | 323. MERE | 376. ENYA | 429. AKIN | 482. AINT |
| 218. ERGO | 271. EONS | 324. USED | 377. YALE | 430. OARS | 483. RAGE |
| 219. STAB | 272. ROAR | 325. SEND | 378. NEER | 431. OREL | 484. LOSE |
| 220. ROLE | 273. EATS | 326. SNAG | 379. RTES | 432. AGER | 485. AVID |
| 221. ULNA | 274. LAVA | 327. TAXI | 380. SPAT | 433. ORSO | 486. NONE |
| 222. ELMO | 275. INGE | 328. ANKA | 381. ERST | 434. DATA | 487. ROSA |
| 223. NETS | 276. LENA | 329. ARGO | 382. ACNE | 435. LOLA | 488. ARNE |
| 224. EGOS | 277. LIRA | 330. OTOE | 383. NANA | 436. SATE | 489. PEER |
| 225. AIDA | 278. APES | 331. SPOT | 384. INNS | 437. OSHA | 490. SOLO |
| 226. EDDY | 279. REEL | 332. AGOG | 385. ALEX | 438. IOWA | 491. ICED |
| 227. RATE | 280. TENT | 333. PESO | 386. OAHU | 439. ATEE | 492. NADA |
| 228. SASS | 281. OMNI | 334. ROSE | 387. SOLE | 440. RILE | 493. RATS |
| 229. AVON | 282. OKRA | 335. ANAT | 388. HALE | 441. ILSA | 494. EASY |
| 230. ETAT | 283. ALAR | 336. NOSE | 389. ACID | 442. SEAT | 495. UTES |
| 231. OMAN | 284. YEAR | 337. OXEN | 390. LEAR | 443. RACE | 496. OMOO |
| 232. SORE | 285. ELIS | 338. IRAS | 391. OOZE | 444. ALPO | 497. ALPS |
| 233. ETAS | 286. HERE | 339. SMEE | 392. REIN | 445. READ | 498. EBAN |
| 234. MENU | 287. ODDS | 340. OATH | 393. TBAR | 446. RASP | 499. SNIP |
| 235. USES | 288. UNTO | 341. SCAM | 394. TONE | 447. PLEA | 500. AMMO |
| 236. ORCA | 289. ADDS | 342. LANE | 395. RAVE | 448. NONO | |

| | | | | |
|---|---|---|---|---|
| ABBA (203) | ANEW (118) | EARN (211) | ETAL (33) | LENA (276) | OMAR (48) |
| ABCS (463) | ANKA (328) | EARS (268) | ETAS (233) | LENO (255) | OMEN (145) |
| ABEL (144) | ANNA (102) | EASE (22) | ETAT (230) | LESS (258) | OMIT (136) |
| ABET (88) | ANNE (37) | EAST (66) | ETCH (242) | LIAR (215) | OMNI (281) |
| ABLE (110) | ANNO (456) | EASY (494) | ETNA (21) | LIEN (452) | OMOO (496) |
| ABUT (306) | ANON (28) | EATS (273) | ETON (39) | LIRA (277) | ONCE (43) |
| ACED (352) | ANTE (4) | EAVE (321) | ETRE (141) | LOLA (435) | ONEA (187) |
| ACES (160) | ANTI (26) | EBAN (498) | ETTA (117) | LORE (461) | ONES (32) |
| ACHE (51) | ANTS (114) | ECHO (25) | ETTE (70) | LOSE (484) | ONTO (97) |
| ACID (389) | AONE (133) | ECRU (152) | ETTU (312) | MENU (234) | ONUS (260) |
| ACME (195) | APER (351) | EDAM (169) | EURO (212) | MERE (323) | OOZE (391) |
| ACNE (382) | APES (278) | EDDY (226) | EVEN (138) | MESA (344) | OPAL (65) |
| ACRE (13) | APSE (121) | EDEN (3) | EVER (93) | MESS (411) | OPEC (426) |
| ACTS (209) | AQUA (295) | EDGE (50) | EVIL (79) | NADA (492) | OPEN (166) |
| ADAM (67) | ARAB (40) | EDIE (113) | EWER (179) | NANA (383) | OPIE (267) |
| ADDS (289) | ARAL (191) | EDIT (38) | EWES (468) | NARC (425) | ORAL (12) |
| ADEN (177) | ARCH (417) | EDNA (122) | EXES (366) | NASA (404) | ORCA (236) |
| ADES (472) | AREA (1) | EELS (174) | EXIT (296) | NATO (257) | OREL (431) |
| ADOS (373) | ARES (73) | EERO (318) | EYES (313) | NCAA (363) | OREO (8) |
| AERO (69) | ARGO (329) | EGAD (128) | EZRA (399) | NEAR (132) | ORES (58) |
| AFAR (101) | ARIA (6) | EGOS (224) | GENE (266) | NEAT (119) | ORSO (433) |
| AFRO (208) | ARID (106) | EIRE (76) | GNAT (403) | NEED (134) | OSHA (437) |
| AGAR (269) | ARLO (72) | ELAL (82) | HAHA (481) | NEER (378) | OSLO (77) |
| AGED (320) | ARNE (488) | ELAN (60) | HALE (388) | NEMO (311) | OTIS (103) |
| AGEE (151) | ARNO (173) | ELEE (478) | HALO (247) | NEON (154) | OTOE (330) |
| AGER (432) | ARTE (162) | ELIA (42) | HARE (408) | NERD (175) | OTTO (56) |
| AGES (256) | ARTS (168) | ELIE (213) | HERE (286) | NERO (84) | OVAL (153) |
| AGOG (332) | ASAP (92) | ELIS (285) | HERO (262) | NESS (108) | OVEN (251) |
| AGRA (159) | ASEA (11) | ELLA (31) | IAGO (270) | NEST (111) | OVER (129) |
| AHAB (245) | ASHE (34) | ELLE (94) | ICED (491) | NETS (223) | OXEN (337) |
| AHEM (368) | ASIA (16) | ELMO (222) | ICON (165) | NILE (204) | PEER (489) |
| AIDA (225) | ASIS (192) | ELSA (105) | IDEA (7) | NINA (358) | PERU (290) |
| AIDE (241) | ASKS (473) | ELSE (9) | IDES (309) | NINE (364) | PESO (333) |
| AINT (482) | ASPS (201) | EMIL (316) | IDLE (98) | NOAH (310) | PETE (302) |
| AJAR (143) | ASSN (419) | EMIR (116) | IDOL (46) | NOEL (243) | PLEA (447) |
| AKIN (429) | ASST (181) | EMIT (64) | IGOR (115) | NONE (486) | PSST (146) |
| ALAI (104) | ASTA (142) | EMMA (239) | ILIE (291) | NONO (448) | RACE (443) |
| ALAN (30) | ASTI (135) | ENDS (52) | ILSA (441) | NORA (216) | RAGE (483) |
| ALAR (283) | ASTO (190) | ENID (63) | INCA (158) | NOSE (336) | RAIL (476) |
| ALAS (17) | ATEE (439) | ENOS (19) | INGE (275) | NOTE (471) | RAIN (451) |
| ALDA (186) | ATIT (294) | ENYA (376) | INNS (384) | OAHU (386) | RANT (375) |
| ALEC (35) | ATOM (80) | EONS (271) | INON (259) | OARS (430) | RARE (75) |
| ALEE (54) | ATOP (124) | EPEE (23) | INRE (91) | OATH (340) | RASP (446) |
| ALES (95) | ATRA (317) | EPIC (96) | INTO (90) | OBIE (345) | RATE (227) |
| ALEX (385) | ATTA (410) | ERAS (18) | IOTA (123) | OBIT (462) | RATS (493) |
| ALIT (109) | ATTN (480) | ERAT (261) | IOWA (438) | OBOE (53) | RAVE (395) |
| ALMA (372) | AURA (126) | ERGO (218) | IRAE (424) | ODDS (287) | READ (445) |
| ALOE (5) | AUTO (347) | ERIC (27) | IRAN (59) | ODES (140) | REAL (293) |
| ALOT (86) | AVER (127) | ERIE (2) | IRAS (338) | ODIE (189) | REAP (371) |
| ALOU (185) | AVID (485) | ERIN (61) | IRIS (157) | ODIN (315) | REAR (149) |
| ALPO (444) | AVON (229) | ERLE (55) | IRMA (354) | ODOR (15) | REBA (400) |
| ALPS (497) | AWOL (346) | ERMA (319) | IRON (29) | OGLE (99) | REDO (217) |
| ALSO (131) | AXLE (360) | ERNE (454) | ISEE (41) | OGRE (47) | REDS (301) |
| ALTO (68) | CEDE (405) | EROS (20) | ISLE (62) | OHIO (253) | REED (172) |
| AMEN (49) | COLA (479) | ERRS (74) | ITEM (71) | OHNO (359) | REEL (279) |
| AMES (199) | DATA (434) | ERSE (197) | IVAN (254) | OKRA (282) | REIN (392) |
| AMID (350) | DEER (250) | ERST (381) | IVES (420) | OLEG (457) | RENE (57) |
| AMMO (500) | DELI (298) | ERTE (137) | KNEE (125) | OLEO (10) | RENO (85) |
| AMOR (252) | DESI (421) | ESAI (407) | LAIR (361) | OLES (397) | RENT (214) |
| AMOS (183) | DRAT (428) | ESAU (87) | LANE (342) | OLGA (406) | REST (45) |
| ANAT (335) | EARL (156) | ESSE (161) | LARA (423) | OLIN (415) | RHEA (458) |
| | | ESSO (89) | LAVA (274) | OLIO (178) | RIDE (469) |
| | | ESTA (263) | LEAR (390) | OLLA (450) | RILE (440) |
| | | ESTE (147) | LEER (170) | OMAN (231) | RIOT (265) |

| | | | | |
|---|---|---|---|---|
| RISE (297) | SSTS (120) | **Top 5-Letter Answers** | 123. GEESE | 187. ATTIC |
| RITA (370) | STAB (219) | **(by rank)** | 124. ASHEN | 188. AMATI |
| ROAR (272) | STAG (299) | | 125. EATEN | 189. STATE |
| ROLE (220) | STAN (148) | 1. ARENA | 62. TEASE | 126. SENOR | 190. STORE |
| ROSA (487) | STAR (14) | 2. ERASE | 63. DEERE | 127. ALTAR | 191. AMINO |
| ROSE (334) | STAT (139) | 3. EERIE | 64. EVADE | 128. EVENT | 192. TAROT |
| RTES (379) | STAY (349) | 4. OPERA | 65. ARIEL | 129. ABATE | 193. SLEET |
| SAGA (455) | STEM (188) | 5. ALONE | 66. ERECT | 130. ORION | 194. ASTOR |
| SALE (402) | STEN (427) | 6. IRENE | 67. INERT | 131. AVAIL | 195. SALEM |
| SALT (355) | STEP (130) | 7. ADORE | 68. ENOLA | 132. ALIBI | 196. EDENS |
| SANE (240) | STET (81) | 8. ELATE | 69. ASIDE | 133. SALSA | 197. TESTS |
| SARA (198) | STEW (205) | 9. ENTER | 70. ERICA | 134. AMORE | 198. OILER |
| SARI (194) | STIR (44) | 10. ATONE | 71. EMILE | 135. ENSUE | 199. IDEAS |
| SASS (228) | STOP (184) | 11. ELITE | 72. ARIES | 136. TRESS | 200. AGAPE |
| SATE (436) | STOW (453) | 12. ORATE | 73. ANISE | 137. AGAIN | 201. TEENS |
| SCAM (341) | TACO (367) | 13. ASSET | 74. STEER | 138. AWARE | 202. INSET |
| SCAN (418) | TALC (307) | 14. IRATE | 75. ONSET | 139. RADAR | 203. ARSON |
| SCAR (163) | TALE (167) | 15. ERATO | 76. ESSAY | 140. OMEGA | 204. SANTA |
| SCAT (305) | TARA (182) | 16. ESTEE | 77. AGILE | 141. REHAB | 205. ALICE |
| SCOT (466) | TATA (308) | 17. AROMA | 78. ADELE | 142. ELDER | 206. ATBAT |
| SEAL (369) | TAXI (327) | 18. ERODE | 79. ETHER | 143. SALAD | 207. ANNIE |
| SEAT (442) | TBAR (393) | 19. SENSE | 80. ASTRO | 144. PASTA | 208. NIECE |
| SECT (398) | TEAR (244) | 20. INANE | 81. EDSEL | 145. IRANI | 209. EVITA |
| SEED (374) | TEEN (249) | 21. ALIEN | 82. OBESE | 146. AGORA | 210. TEPEE |
| SEEN (304) | TEES (474) | 22. ATSEA | 83. ASTER | 147. DENSE | 211. SASSY |
| SEEP (470) | TENT (280) | 23. ELIOT | 84. AARON | 148. ARNIE | 212. EAGER |
| SEER (200) | TERI (155) | 24. REESE | 85. TESLA | 149. ELTON | 213. ULTRA |
| SEES (413) | TESS (207) | 25. OTTER | 86. EGRET | 150. TAHOE | 214. SEINE |
| SEMI (237) | TEST (210) | 26. ATLAS | 87. ATRIA | 151. ELMER | 215. OPINE |
| SEND (325) | TETE (414) | 27. ATARI | 88. TENET | 152. IMAGE | 216. SNORE |
| SENT (176) | TIER (206) | 28. ERNIE | 89. AMANA | 153. RETRO | 217. USERS |
| SERA (180) | TINA (422) | 29. ALOHA | 90. OHARA | 154. SNARE | 218. LASSO |
| SERE (396) | TIRE (314) | 30. ALERT | 91. ADIEU | 155. ILIAD | 219. NOLTE |
| SETH (449) | TONE (394) | 31. ALAMO | 92. ECLAT | 156. ATEAM | 220. OCTET |
| SETS (246) | TONI (412) | 32. ESSEN | 93. OLIVE | 157. ONION | 221. ATOLL |
| SHEA (362) | TRAP (264) | 33. ANITA | 94. ERRED | 158. LEASE | 222. PASTE |
| SHOE (464) | TREE (24) | 34. ELENA | 95. TASTE | 159. EAGLE | 223. ALTER |
| SILO (465) | TRIO (193) | 35. AREAS | 96. RESET | 160. CANOE | 224. TSARS |
| SIRE (303) | TROT (353) | 36. ESTES | 97. ALIAS | 161. RODEO | 225. STEAM |
| SLAT (348) | TRUE (357) | 37. AORTA | 98. ETHAN | 162. SELES | 226. MIAMI |
| SLED (100) | TSAR (36) | 38. AROSE | 99. EMCEE | 163. ASIAN | 227. LEAVE |
| SLOE (238) | UCLA (343) | 39. STENO | 100. ESTER | 164. NEEDS | 228. ONTAP |
| SLOT (460) | ULNA (221) | 40. OMAHA | 101. ASONE | 165. TRADE | 229. INLET |
| SMEE (339) | UNDO (356) | 41. OCEAN | 102. STERN | 166. STEAL | 230. STOLE |
| SNAG (326) | UNIT (112) | 42. EMAIL | 103. ADOBE | 167. SCENE | 231. OPART |
| SNAP (164) | UNTO (288) | 43. ONEAL | 104. RAISE | 168. TREAT | 232. AHEAD |
| SNIP (499) | UPON (416) | 44. TIARA | 105. NOONE | 169. ORONO | 233. ABASE |
| SNIT (202) | URAL (150) | 45. AGREE | 106. UNITE | 170. ASSES | 234. ALGAE |
| SOAR (409) | URGE (107) | 46. ELOPE | 107. AESOP | 171. ERROL | 235. ENDED |
| SODA (401) | URIS (365) | 47. AISLE | 108. TENOR | 172. ACTOR | 236. EASES |
| SOHO (459) | URSA (171) | 48. SNEER | 109. TERSE | 173. STARE | 237. ASCOT |
| SOLE (387) | USED (324) | 49. EMOTE | 110. NEATO | 174. OTHER | 238. OMANI |
| SOLO (490) | USER (78) | 50. IDEAL | 111. UBOAT | 175. OCALA | 239. ANAIS |
| SORE (232) | USES (235) | 51. ARISE | 112. ETUDE | 176. ORDER | 240. STONE |
| SOSO (248) | USSR (322) | 52. AMASS | 113. ADAGE | 177. IDEST | 241. START |
| SPAN (477) | UTAH (83) | 53. ISAAC | 114. ELECT | 178. ARTIE | 242. AGATE |
| SPAR (196) | UTES (495) | 54. OSCAR | 115. ONAIR | 179. ALIVE | 243. TITLE |
| SPAS (292) | YALE (377) | 55. ESSES | 116. IDAHO | 180. RINSE | 244. LILAC |
| SPAT (380) | YEAR (284) | 56. EASEL | 117. EPEES | 181. ASTIR | 245. INNER |
| SPED (300) | YENS (467) | 57. AERIE | 118. LLAMA | 182. ARUBA | 246. ECOLE |
| SPOT (331) | YSER (475) | 58. ENERO | 119. NESTS | 183. OHARE | 247. ASNER |
| | | 59. TENSE | 120. ELLEN | 184. ASPEN | 248. NEEDY |
| | | 60. AGENT | 121. ASHES | 185. HANOI | 249. SEDER |
| | | 61. ERROR | 122. RENEE | 186. OLLIE | 250. ALARM |

| | | | | | |
|---|---|---|---|---|---|
| 251. ENTRE | 293. RELIC | 335. PASSE | 377. SEEDY | 419. NAIVE | 461. AVILA |
| 252. ANDES | 294. ALLOT | 336. SANER | 378. SIREN | 420. ISSUE | 462. CARAT |
| 253. ITEMS | 295. TETRA | 337. ROTOR | 379. OREOS | 421. SADAT | 463. TESTY |
| 254. IRISH | 296. ODORS | 338. ICIER | 380. NASAL | 422. STAND | 464. AMAZE |
| 255. EDDIE | 297. INTRO | 339. ANGST | 381. ACUTE | 423. ELAND | 465. LINEN |
| 256. ABETS | 298. EDITS | 340. ETHOS | 382. UNION | 424. ASCAP | 466. LOOSE |
| 257. ENACT | 299. HESSE | 341. SOLAR | 383. ARMOR | 425. IDIOM | 467. TRAIT |
| 258. OSAGE | 300. SKATE | 342. ELUDE | 384. ENLAI | 426. SAMOA | 468. RASTA |
| 259. STEED | 301. ISLET | 343. EVERT | 385. DRESS | 427. ALLEN | 469. ATILT |
| 260. ACHES | 302. EGADS | 344. NEARS | 386. ATALL | 428. APRIL | 470. AMOUR |
| 261. STYLE | 303. SLATE | 345. ETHEL | 387. STAGE | 429. SNERD | 471. ASYET |
| 262. IONIA | 304. UNTIE | 346. AROAR | 388. DANTE | 430. TREND | 472. SODAS |
| 263. ALOES | 305. LEAST | 347. ELLIS | 389. AMEND | 431. MATTE | 473. ELIHU |
| 264. NEPAL | 306. ADIOS | 348. SPREE | 390. KOREA | 432. EXTRA | 474. ATEIN |
| 265. TERRA | 307. EDGES | 349. ADMIT | 391. REEVE | 433. DIANE | 475. SPASM |
| 266. EATAT | 308. ERNST | 350. ALIST | 392. SETTO | 434. EPSOM | 476. ELCID |
| 267. NEHRU | 309. TBONE | 351. INTER | 393. LASER | 435. ADORN | 477. SPEAR |
| 268. ARENT | 310. ADEPT | 352. PANEL | 394. ISLES | 436. STRAP | 478. ALEUT |
| 269. INDIA | 311. SEDAN | 353. LAINE | 395. ADLIB | 437. ABODE | 479. GESTE |
| 270. ADLAI | 312. TOSCA | 354. OASIS | 396. ASKED | 438. STEVE | 480. AWAIT |
| 271. UTTER | 313. ENEMY | 355. IBSEN | 397. HORSE | 439. ANDRE | 481. OATER |
| 272. STARR | 314. AFIRE | 356. ELIAS | 398. ROMEO | 440. ARIAS | 482. NOLAN |
| 273. TORSO | 315. ISLAM | 357. ALINE | 399. SINAI | 441. YEAST | 483. LEONE |
| 274. SLEDS | 316. AMISS | 358. TOTAL | 400. AETNA | 442. ARETE | 484. BALSA |
| 275. ETHIC | 317. DELTA | 359. RIATA | 401. THERE | 443. ALLAH | 485. EWERS |
| 276. ODETS | 318. ALOUD | 360. IDIOT | 402. APSES | 444. RARER | 486. TOAST |
| 277. ONICE | 319. STALE | 361. OSAKA | 403. EASED | 445. ACTED | 487. STEPS |
| 278. PIANO | 320. CEASE | 362. OLDIE | 404. PARIS | 446. NAOMI | 488. LEVEE |
| 279. APART | 321. EBERT | 363. ONEND | 405. APACE | 447. PETER | 489. STRAW |
| 280. ANTES | 322. LAURA | 364. SARAH | 406. OZONE | 448. SMART | 490. SATIN |
| 281. ARLEN | 323. AMUSE | 365. ATTAR | 407. UNCLE | 449. SATAN | 491. ITALY |
| 282. ANODE | 324. ANTIC | 366. OMENS | 408. ROAST | 450. EXILE | 492. STEEP |
| 283. MELEE | 325. USUAL | 367. POSSE | 409. EMEND | 451. EARTH | 493. STAIR |
| 284. EIDER | 326. ANEAR | 368. USHER | 410. EMERY | 452. PERIL | 494. RERAN |
| 285. ELSIE | 327. SEETO | 369. REELS | 411. ARABS | 453. ENROL | 495. INUSE |
| 286. SONAR | 328. RESTS | 370. AVERT | 412. YESES | 454. MENSA | 496. ENTRY |
| 287. AIMEE | 329. ELIDE | 371. MAINE | 413. REACT | 455. IRONY | 497. SCRAP |
| 288. RECAP | 330. AFTER | 372. DEEDS | 414. EIEIO | 456. UTILE | 498. SCRAM |
| 289. STEEL | 331. ESSEX | 373. OASES | 415. ARLES | 457. SNEAK | 499. TONER |
| 290. IRONS | 332. ADAPT | 374. RENEW | 416. NOOSE | 458. LEERS | 500. TAMPA |
| 291. ACRES | 333. ABOUT | 375. SCENT | 417. ANGER | 459. AGNES | |
| 292. NOISE | 334. ACORN | 376. SCALE | 418. PSALM | 460. ACHOO | |

## Top 5-Letter Answers (alphabetical)

AARON (84)
ABASE (233)
ABATE (129)
ABETS (256)
ABODE (437)
ABOUT (333)
ACHES (260)
ACHOO (460)
ACORN (334)
ACRES (291)
ACTED (445)
ACTOR (172)
ACUTE (381)
ADAGE (113)
ADAPT (332)
ADELE (78)
ADEPT (310)
ADIEU (91)
ADIOS (306)
ADLAI (270)
ADLIB (395)
ADMIT (349)
ADOBE (103)
ADORE (7)
ADORN (435)
AERIE (57)
AESOP (107)
AETNA (400)
AFIRE (314)
AFTER (330)
AGAIN (137)
AGAPE (200)
AGATE (242)
AGENT (60)
AGILE (77)
AGNES (459)
AGORA (146)
AGREE (45)
AHEAD (232)
AIMEE (287)
AISLE (47)
ALAMO (31)
ALARM (250)
ALERT (30)
ALEUT (478)
ALGAE (234)
ALIAS (97)
ALIBI (132)
ALICE (205)
ALIEN (21)
ALINE (357)
ALIST (350)
ALIVE (179)
ALLAH (443)
ALLEN (427)
ALLOT (294)
ALOES (263)
ALOHA (29)
ALONE (5)
ALOUD (318)
ALTAR (127)

ALTER (223)
AMANA (89)
AMASS (52)
AMATI (188)
AMAZE (464)
AMEND (389)
AMINO (191)
AMISS (316)
AMORE (134)
AMOUR (470)
AMUSE (323)
ANAIS (239)
ANDES (252)
ANDRE (439)
ANEAR (326)
ANGER (417)
ANGST (339)
ANISE (73)
ANITA (33)
ANNIE (207)
ANODE (282)
ANTES (280)
ANTIC (324)
AORTA (37)
APACE (405)
APART (279)
APRIL (428)
APSES (402)
ARABE (411)
AREAS (35)
ARENA (1)
ARENT (268)
ARETE (442)
ARIAS (440)
ARIEL (65)
ARIES (72)
ARISE (51)
ARLEN (281)
ARLES (415)
ARMOR (383)
ARNIE (148)
AROAR (346)
AROMA (17)
AROSE (38)
ARSON (203)
ARTIE (178)
ARUBA (182)
ASCAP (424)
ASCOT (237)
ASHEN (124)
ASHES (121)
ASIAN (163)
ASIDE (69)
ASKED (396)
ASNER (247)
ASONE (101)
ASPEN (184)
ASSES (170)
ASSET (13)
ASTER (83)
ASTIR (181)

ASTOR (194)
ASTRO (80)
ASYET (471)
ATALL (386)
ATARI (27)
ATBAT (206)
ATEAM (156)
ATEIN (474)
ATILT (469)
ATLAS (26)
ATOLL (221)
ATONE (10)
ATRIA (87)
ATSEA (22)
ATTAR (365)
ATTIC (187)
AVAIL (131)
AVERT (370)
AVILA (461)
AWAIT (480)
AWARE (138)
BALSA (484)
CANOE (160)
CARAT (462)
CEASE (320)
DANTE (388)
DEEDS (372)
DEERE (63)
DELTA (317)
DENSE (147)
DIANE (433)
DRESS (385)
EAGER (212)
EAGLE (159)
EARTH (451)
EASED (403)
EASEL (56)
EASES (236)
EATAT (266)
EATEN (125)
EBERT (321)
ECLAT (92)
ECOLE (246)
EDDIE (255)
EDENS (196)
EDGES (307)
EDITS (298)
EDSEL (81)
EERIE (3)
EGADS (302)
EGRET (86)
EIDER (284)
EIEIO (414)
ELAND (423)
ELATE (8)
ELCID (476)
ELDER (142)
ELECT (114)
ELENA (34)
ELIAS (356)
ELIDE (329)
ELIHU (473)
ELIOT (23)
ELITE (11)

ELLEN (120)
ELLIS (347)
ELMER (151)
ELOPE (46)
ELSIE (285)
ELTON (149)
ELUDE (342)
EMAIL (42)
EMCEE (99)
EMEND (409)
EMERY (410)
EMILE (71)
EMOTE (49)
ENACT (257)
ENDED (235)
ENEMY (313)
ENERO (58)
ENLAI (384)
ENOLA (68)
ENROL (453)
ENSUE (135)
ENTER (9)
ENTRE (251)
ENTRY (496)
EPEES (117)
EPSOM (434)
ERASE (2)
ERATO (15)
ERECT (66)
ERICA (70)
ERNIE (28)
ERODE (18)
ERRED (94)
ERROL (171)
ERROR (61)
ESSAY (76)
ESSEN (32)
ESSES (55)
ESSEX (331)
ESTEE (16)
ESTER (100)
ESTES (36)
ETHAN (98)
ETHEL (345)
ETHER (79)
ETHIC (275)
ETHOS (340)
ETUDE (112)
EVADE (64)
EVENT (128)
EVERT (343)
EVITA (209)
EWERS (485)
EXILE (450)
EXTRA (432)
GEESE (123)
GESTE (479)
HANOI (185)
HESSE (299)
HORSE (397)
IBSEN (355)
ICIER (338)
IDAHO (116)

IDEAL (50)
IDEAS (199)
IDEST (177)
IDIOM (425)
IDIOT (360)
ILIAD (155)
IMAGE (152)
INANE (20)
INDIA (269)
INERT (67)
INLET (229)
INNER (245)
INSET (202)
INTER (351)
INTRO (297)
INUSE (495)
IONIA (262)
IRANI (145)
IRATE (14)
IRENE (6)
IRISH (254)
IRONS (290)
IRONY (455)
ISAAC (53)
ISLAM (315)
ISLES (394)
ISLET (301)
ISSUE (420)
ITALY (491)
ITEMS (253)
KOREA (390)
LAINE (353)
LASER (393)
LASSO (218)
LAURA (322)
LEASE (158)
LEAST (305)
LEAVE (227)
LEERS (458)
LEONE (483)
LEVEE (488)
LILAC (244)
LINEN (465)
LLAMA (118)
LOOSE (466)
MAINE (371)
MATTE (431)
MELEE (283)
MENSA (454)
MIAMI (226)
NAIVE (419)
NAOMI (446)
NASAL (380)
NEARS (344)
NEATO (110)
NEEDS (164)
NEEDY (248)
NEHRU (267)
NEPAL (264)
NESTS (119)
NIECE (208)
NOISE (292)
NOLAN (482)
NOLTE (219)

| | | | | |
|---|---|---|---|---|
| NOONE (105) | OSCAR (54) | SALAD (143) | SONAR (286) | TEPEE (210) |
| NOOSE (416) | OTHER (174) | SALEM (195) | SPASM (475) | TERRA (265) |
| OASES (373) | OTTER (25) | SALSA (133) | SPEAR (477) | TERSE (109) |
| OASIS (354) | OZONE (406) | SAMOA (426) | SPREE (348) | TESLA (85) |
| OATER (481) | PANEL (352) | SANER (336) | STAGE (387) | TESTS (197) |
| OBESE (82) | PARIS (404) | SANTA (204) | STAIR (493) | TESTY (463) |
| OCALA (175) | PASSE (335) | SARAH (364) | STALE (319) | TETRA (295) |
| OCEAN (41) | PASTA (144) | SASSY (211) | STAND (422) | THERE (401) |
| OCTET (220) | PASTE (222) | SATAN (449) | STARE (173) | TIARA (44) |
| ODETS (276) | PERIL (452) | SATIN (490) | STARR (272) | TITLE (243) |
| ODORS (296) | PETER (447) | SCALE (376) | START (241) | TOAST (486) |
| OHARA (90) | PIANO (278) | SCENE (167) | STATE (189) | TONER (499) |
| OHARE (183) | POSSE (367) | SCENT (375) | STEAL (166) | TORSO (273) |
| OILER (198) | PSALM (418) | SCRAM (498) | STEAM (225) | TOSCA (312) |
| OLDIE (362) | RADAR (139) | SCRAP (497) | STEED (259) | TOTAL (358) |
| OLIVE (93) | RAISE (104) | SEDAN (311) | STEEL (289) | TRADE (165) |
| OLLIE (186) | RARER (444) | SEDER (249) | STEEP (492) | TRAIT (467) |
| OMAHA (40) | RASTA (468) | SEEDY (377) | STEER (74) | TREAT (168) |
| OMANI (238) | REACT (413) | SEETO (327) | STENO (39) | TREND (430) |
| OMEGA (140) | RECAP (288) | SEINE (214) | STEPS (487) | TRESS (136) |
| OMENS (366) | REELS (369) | SELES (162) | STERN (102) | TSARS (224) |
| ONAIR (115) | REESE (24) | SENOR (126) | STEVE (438) | UBOAT (111) |
| ONEAL (43) | REEVE (391) | SENSE (19) | STOLE (230) | ULTRA (213) |
| ONEND (363) | REHAB (141) | SETTO (392) | STONE (240) | UNCLE (407) |
| ONICE (277) | RELIC (293) | SINAI (399) | STORE (190) | UNION (382) |
| ONION (157) | RENEE (122) | SIREN (378) | STRAP (436) | UNITE (106) |
| ONSET (75) | RENEW (374) | SKATE (300) | STRAW (489) | UNTIE (304) |
| ONTAP (228) | RERAN (494) | SLATE (303) | STYLE (261) | USERS (217) |
| OPART (231) | RESET (96) | SLEDS (274) | TAHOE (150) | USHER (368) |
| OPERA (4) | RESTS (328) | SLEET (193) | TAMPA (500) | USUAL (325) |
| OPINE (215) | RETRO (153) | SMART (448) | TAROT (192) | UTILE (456) |
| ORATE (12) | RIATA (359) | SNARE (154) | TASTE (95) | UTTER (271) |
| ORDER (176) | RINSE (180) | SNEAK (457) | TBONE (309) | YEAST (441) |
| OREOS (379) | ROAST (408) | SNEER (48) | TEASE (62) | YESES (412) |
| ORION (130) | RODEO (161) | SNERD (429) | TEENS (201) | |
| ORONO (169) | ROMEO (398) | SNORE (216) | TENET (88) | |
| OSAGE (258) | ROTOR (337) | SODAS (472) | TENOR (108) | |
| OSAKA (361) | SADAT (421) | SOLAR (341) | TENSE (59) | |

Top 6-Letter Answers
(by rank)

| | | | |
|---|---|---|---|
| 1. ATEASE | 50. ARREST | 99. ASSERT | 151. OSIRIS | 203. OCTANE |
| 2. ESTATE | 51. AMOEBA | 100. ONEILL | 152. SENECA | 204. ORNERY |
| 3. TSETSE | 52. AZALEA | 101. IRISES | 153. STENOS | 205. ENTAIL |
| 4. ELAINE | 53. AROUSE | 102. RAREST | 154. DELETE | 206. ENAMOR |
| 5. ORIOLE | 54. ATLAST | 103. ARIOSO | 155. ACTONE | 207. PAROLE |
| 6. ODESSA | 55. ENDEAR | 104. ELECTS | 156. HONEST | 208. ANOINT |
| 7. STEREO | 56. ISRAEL | 105. ESCAPE | 157. ESSENE | 209. UNEASE |
| 8. ARENAS | 57. APOLLO | 106. ATTILA | 158. ATTEST | 210. ATREST |
| 9. ARARAT | 58. ADESTE | 107. SHASTA | 159. NEGATE | 211. OSCARS |
| 10. ORELSE | 59. SIESTA | 108. SETTEE | 160. AMULET | 212. AVENUE |
| 11. ERASER | 60. AGASSI | 109. SECEDE | 161. IGUANA | 213. ARMADA |
| 12. ORANGE | 61. ATONCE | 110. ALGORE | 162. SIERRA | 214. IGNORE |
| 13. ORIENT | 62. ALASKA | 111. RENEGE | 163. SPARTA | 215. ADORED |
| 14. OTOOLE | 63. SEESAW | 112. ASLEEP | 164. ALLEGE | 216. REBATE |
| 15. ELAPSE | 64. ELATED | 113. AMPERE | 165. STREAM | 217. ACROSS |
| 16. EMERGE | 65. NEEDLE | 114. SOIREE | 166. OREGON | 218. SEERED |
| 17. ENTREE | 66. ELPASO | 115. INTOTO | 167. ICEAGE | 219. TATTOO |
| 18. ERRATA | 67. SENATE | 116. ERODES | 168. ASPIRE | 220. STOLEN |
| 19. SESAME | 68. EROICA | 117. ASTUTE | 169. OVERDO | 221. RESALE |
| 20. SERENE | 69. SALAMI | 118. ORATES | 170. OTTAWA | 222. TEASET |
| 21. ESTEEM | 70. ONEIDA | 119. ARETHA | 171. ISLAND | 223. ARISEN |
| 22. ERNEST | 71. PRESTO | 120. ADONIS | 172. ARABIA | 224. ARRIVE |
| 23. STEELE | 72. ELEVEN | 121. HASSLE | 173. OPERAS | 225. IRONIC |
| 24. AMORAL | 73. SPARSE | 122. SEETHE | 174. ASSAIL | 226. INHALE |
| 25. SNEERS | 74. IBERIA | 123. ENIGMA | 175. LAREDO | 227. ONIONS |
| 26. ORACLE | 75. OPIATE | 124. SAFARI | 176. TAHITI | 228. ANKARA |
| 27. ONSALE | 76. ESSAYS | 125. ENTERS | 177. AVATAR | 229. ELDEST |
| 28. ORNATE | 77. ELOISE | 126. EDISON | 178. REDSEA | 230. ARISTA |
| 29. ENAMEL | 78. ASTERN | 127. AMELIA | 179. INNATE | 231. TASSEL |
| 30. EDITOR | 79. SENORA | 128. ESTHER | 180. TENURE | 232. EASELS |
| 31. ORATOR | 80. ATHOME | 129. STREET | 181. NESTLE | 233. HARASS |
| 32. TERESA | 81. ETERNE | 130. STRATA | 182. ASPENS | 234. ELICIT |
| 33. ENTIRE | 82. OPENER | 131. OBERON | 183. ALERTS | 235. ISOLDE |
| 34. ERASES | 83. ASSENT | 132. ETHANE | 184. HELENA | 236. DETEST |
| 35. ELNINO | 84. SEDATE | 133. ELATES | 185. ANEMIA | 237. ONLINE |
| 36. AVIATE | 85. EASTER | 134. ENLIST | 186. ASSURE | 238. PARADE |
| 37. AERATE | 86. STRESS | 135. SATIRE | 187. ARCANE | 239. ERODED |
| 38. ASSESS | 87. STOOGE | 136. OCEANS | 188. TALENT | 240. ERRORS |
| 39. ATHENA | 88. AURORA | 137. ONEDGE | 189. ARISES | 241. STALAG |
| 40. SAHARA | 89. SPHERE | 138. UTOPIA | 190. REESES | 242. TOMATO |
| 41. OMELET | 90. SLEEVE | 139. SCENES | 191. ENRAGE | 243. AGATHA |
| 42. APIECE | 91. EDSELS | 140. ATTIRE | 192. INTERN | 244. TEETER |
| 43. AGENDA | 92. ANIMAL | 141. INSTEP | 193. LARIAT | 245. ASTRAL |
| 44. ASSISI | 93. ERECTS | 142. SENSES | 194. STEEDS | 246. TOATEE |
| 45. OCELOT | 94. ERRANT | 143. ATONES | 195. ARLENE | 247. OATERS |
| 46. ADHERE | 95. ASHORE | 144. ENCORE | 196. ARDENT | 248. EGRESS |
| 47. AVERSE | 96. EMIGRE | 145. AGHAST | 197. SETTER | 249. EDERLE |
| 48. ALIENS | 97. AROMAS | 146. SANEST | 198. OPENED | 250. AGENTS |
| 49. ASSETS | 98. CAESAR | 147. RELATE | 199. ERMINE | |
| | | 148. SEESTO | 200. OTELLO | |
| | | 149. PESETA | 201. LENORE | |
| | | 150. IDEATE | 202. ATTEND | |

## Top 6-Letter Answers (alphabetical)

| | | | |
|---|---|---|---|
| ACROSS (217) | ASSENT (83) | ENAMEL (29) | NEEDLE (65) | SCENES (139) |
| ACTONE (155) | ASSERT (99) | ENAMOR (206) | NEGATE (159) | SECEDE (109) |
| ADESTE (58) | ASSESS (38) | ENCORE (144) | NESTLE (181) | SEDATE (84) |
| ADHERE (46) | ASSETS (49) | ENDEAR (55) | OATERS (247) | SEERED (218) |
| ADONIS (120) | ASSISI (44) | ENIGMA (123) | OBERON (131) | SEESAW (63) |
| ADORED (215) | ASSURE (186) | ENLIST (134) | OCEANS (136) | SEESTO (148) |
| AERATE (37) | ASTERN (78) | ENRAGE (191) | OCELOT (45) | SEETHE (122) |
| AGASSI (60) | ASTRAL (245) | ENTAIL (205) | OCTANE (203) | SENATE (67) |
| AGATHA (243) | ASTUTE (117) | ENTERS (125) | ODESSA (6) | SENECA (152) |
| AGENDA (43) | ATEASE (1) | ENTIRE (33) | OMELET (41) | SENORA (79) |
| AGENTS (250) | ATHENA (39) | ENTREE (17) | ONEDGE (137) | SENSES (142) |
| AGHAST (145) | ATHOME (80) | ERASER (11) | ONEIDA (70) | SERENE (20) |
| ALASKA (62) | ATLAST (54) | ERASES (34) | ONEILL (100) | SESAME (19) |
| ALERTS (183) | ATONCE (61) | ERECTS (93) | ONIONS (227) | SETTEE (108) |
| ALGORE (110) | ATONES (143) | ERMINE (199) | ONLINE (237) | SETTER (197) |
| ALIENS (48) | ATREST (210) | ERNEST (22) | ONSALE (27) | SHASTA (107) |
| ALLEGE (164) | ATTEND (202) | ERODED (239) | OPENED (198) | SIERRA (162) |
| AMELIA (127) | ATTEST (158) | ERODES (116) | OPENER (82) | SIESTA (59) |
| AMOEBA (51) | ATTILA (106) | EROICA (68) | OPERAS (173) | SLEEVE (90) |
| AMORAL (24) | ATTIRE (140) | ERRANT (94) | OPIATE (75) | SNEERS (25) |
| AMPERE (113) | AURORA (88) | ERRATA (18) | ORACLE (26) | SOIREE (114) |
| AMULET (160) | AVATAR (177) | ERRORS (240) | ORANGE (12) | SPARSE (73) |
| ANEMIA (185) | AVENUE (212) | ESCAPE (105) | ORATES (118) | SPARTA (163) |
| ANIMAL (92) | AVERSE (47) | ESSAYS (76) | ORATOR (31) | SPHERE (89) |
| ANKARA (228) | AVIATE (36) | ESSENE (157) | OREGON (166) | STALAG (241) |
| ANOINT (208) | AZALEA (52) | ESTATE (2) | ORELSE (10) | STEEDS (194) |
| APIECE (42) | CAESAR (98) | ESTEEM (21) | ORIENT (13) | STEELE (23) |
| APOLLO (57) | DELETE (154) | ESTHER (128) | ORIOLE (5) | STENOS (153) |
| ARABIA (172) | DETEST (236) | ETERNE (81) | ORNATE (28) | STEREO (7) |
| ARARAT (9) | EASELS (232) | ETHANE (132) | ORNERY (204) | STOLEN (220) |
| ARCANE (187) | EASTER (85) | HARASS (233) | OSCARS (211) | STOOGE (87) |
| ARDENT (196) | EDERLE (249) | HASSLE (121) | OSIRIS (151) | STRATA (130) |
| ARENAS (8) | EDISON (126) | HELENA (184) | OTELLO (200) | STREAM (165) |
| ARETHA (119) | EDITOR (30) | HONEST (156) | OTOOLE (14) | STREET (129) |
| ARIOSO (103) | EDSELS (91) | IBERIA (74) | OTTAWA (170) | STRESS (86) |
| ARISEN (223) | EGRESS (248) | ICEAGE (167) | OVERDO (169) | TAHITI (176) |
| ARISES (189) | ELAINE (4) | IDEATE (150) | PARADE (238) | TALENT (188) |
| ARISTA (230) | ELAPSE (15) | IGNORE (214) | PAROLE (207) | TASSEL (231) |
| ARLENE (195) | ELATED (64) | IGUANA (161) | PESETA (149) | TATTOO (219) |
| ARMADA (213) | ELATES (133) | INHALE (226) | PRESTO (71) | TEASET (222) |
| AROMAS (97) | ELDEST (229) | INNATE (179) | RAREST (102) | TEETER (244) |
| AROUSE (53) | ELECTS (104) | INSTEP (141) | REBATE (216) | TENURE (180) |
| ARREST (50) | ELEVEN (72) | INTERN (192) | REDSEA (178) | TERESA (32) |
| ARRIVE (224) | ELICIT (234) | INTOTO (115) | REESES (190) | TOATEE (246) |
| ASHORE (95) | ELNINO (35) | IRISES (101) | RELATE (147) | TOMATO (242) |
| ASLEEP (112) | ELOISE (77) | IRONIC (225) | RENEGE (111) | TSETSE (3) |
| ASPENS (182) | ELPASO (66) | ISLAND (171) | RESALE (221) | UNEASE (209) |
| ASPIRE (168) | EMERGE (16) | ISOLDE (235) | SAFARI (124) | UTOPIA (138) |
| ASSAIL (174) | EMIGRE (96) | ISRAEL (56) | SAHARA (40) | |
| | | LAREDO (175) | SALAMI (69) | |
| | | LARIAT (193) | SANEST (146) | |
| | | LENORE (201) | SATIRE (135) | |

**Top 7-Letter Answers
(by rank)**

1. ELEANOR
2. IRONORE
3. ASTAIRE
4. ETERNAL
5. ERASURE
6. INERTIA
7. ASARULE
8. ERASERS
9. ESTATES
10. ESSENCE
11. OTHELLO
12. ATLANTA
13. ESTELLE
14. ISRAELI
15. EVEREST
16. ALABAMA
17. ALSORAN
18. ONTARIO
19. ABALONE
20. RELEASE
21. ENTENTE
22. ITERATE
23. ALAMODE
24. ENMASSE
25. ANTENNA
26. ALDENTE
27. ALIBABA
28. ESTONIA
29. ATLARGE
30. AAMILNE
31. ENHANCE
32. ENSNARE
33. SARALEE
34. EYESORE
35. ASININE
36. OCANADA
37. ENROUTE
38. ONATEAR
39. ENTERED
40. EDASNER
41. OPERATE
42. ATHLETE
43. ANAGRAM
44. ATLEAST
45. SIAMESE
46. ELASTIC
47. IRELAND
48. ELEMENT
49. ACETATE

50. EPISODE
51. ADAMANT
52. ASTORIA
53. DESERTS
54. ORIGAMI
55. ONLEAVE
56. STEEPLE
57. SEESRED
58. ALIENEE
59. ESTEEMS
60. SENATOR
61. CELESTE
62. STPETER
63. ENEMIES
64. ATTESTS
65. ARTDECO
66. EGOTRIP
67. ERNESTO
68. ARSENAL
69. ETAGERE
70. ELEVATE
71. ANIMATE
72. SATIATE
73. ENLARGE
74. ORIOLES
75. AMERICA
76. TRESTLE
77. LORELEI
78. ATALOSS
79. ELEGANT
80. ENDORSE
81. RESENTS
82. ONELANE
83. INERROR
84. RATRACE
85. SOANDSO
86. SINATRA
87. ABILENE
88. EARLOBE
89. ALTOONA
90. DETENTE
91. EMANATE
92. OREGANO
93. RESTORE
94. SEERESS
95. ISOLATE
96. ADDENDA
97. STALEST
98. REMORSE

99. ANATOLE
100. TSELIOT
101. DESSERT
102. TABASCO
103. ARALSEA
104. OCEANIA
105. ARRESTS
106. OPENSEA
107. SATIRES
108. CANASTA
109. STOPGAP
110. PESETAS
111. APOSTLE
112. ALIASES
113. APPEASE
114. ACETONE
115. INTENSE
116. AGITATE
117. ANEMONE
118. INAHOLE
119. STERILE
120. RATATAT
121. REDTAPE
122. ENTREAT
123. ONAROLL
124. ELLIPSE
125. ERASMUS
126. TSETSES
127. UTENSIL
128. ANALYST
129. APRIORI
130. ESCAPEE
131. ERITREA
132. OTTOMAN
133. AVARICE
134. NEMESIS
135. ANOTHER
136. ELECTRA
137. ANTARES
138. STRANGE
139. STREETS
140. SEATTLE
141. NATALIE
142. ATLASES
143. ANNETTE
144. EROTICA
145. STENCIL
146. ORESTES
147. AMNESIA
148. IRANIAN
149. ATELIER
150. LARAMIE

151. TREETOP
152. EMINENT
153. ENTITLE
154. ALAMEDA
155. STAMINA
156. AVIATOR
157. EMERSON
158. ARAPAHO
159. AMASSED
160. ARTICLE
161. UNEATEN
162. ERECTED
163. ONESTEP
164. SEESAWS
165. ATSTAKE
166. UPATREE
167. ATTIMES
168. RELAPSE
169. MASCARA
170. ASPECTS
171. STEELIE
172. ONADARE
173. ORLANDO
174. ESTRADA
175. ATTACHE
176. TRAINEE
177. MINARET
178. ONADATE
179. AVERAGE
180. ORIENTS
181. EVILEYE
182. SNEERAT
183. TREMOLO
184. TRIESTE
185. IMEANIT
186. ONETIME
187. ECLIPSE
188. SENSATE
189. YESORNO
190. POSSESS
191. ARRANGE
192. ONESTAR
193. ORACLES
194. NESTEGG
195. TANTARA
196. EMERALD
197. ADELINE
198. ACROBAT
199. STEAMER
200. NEMESES
201. ATEDIRT
202. INITIAL

203. ARABIAN
204. NIAGARA
205. ONSTAGE
206. REENTER
207. ALADDIN
208. NATASHA
209. IRONAGE
210. ROSETTA
211. ASTRIDE
212. ATPEACE
213. ALERTED
214. ENTRANT
215. OCARINA
216. SEASIDE
217. SAHARAN
218. MAEWEST
219. ROSSSEA
220. ONENOTE
221. EPAULET
222. ROASTER
223. REASONS
224. USELESS
225. ACTRESS
226. ALCOHOL
227. NARRATE
228. ECUADOR
229. LATERAL
230. TORONTO
231. AVOCADO
232. ARIADNE
233. LASAGNA
234. REFEREE
235. ELECTED
236. ACADEME
237. OPENTOE
238. ASSENTS
239. AERATOR
240. REAREND
241. ISADORA
242. REGATTA
243. SEDATES
244. STOOLIE
245. IVANHOE
246. CABARET
247. SCOTTIE
248. IMITATE
249. EMULATE
250. BEELINE

Top 7-Letter Answers
(alphabetical)

AAMILNE (30)
ABALONE (19)
ABILENE (87)
ACADEME (236)
ACETATE (49)
ACETONE (114)
ACROBAT (198)
ACTRESS (225)
ADAMANT (51)
ADDENDA (96)
ADELINE (197)
AERATOR (239)
AGITATE (116)
ALABAMA (16)
ALADDIN (207)
ALAMEDA (154)
ALAMODE (23)
ALCOHOL (226)
ALDENTE (26)
ALERTED (213)
ALIASES (112)
ALIBABA (27)
ALIENEE (58)
ALSORAN (17)
ALTOONA (89)
AMASSED (159)
AMERICA (75)
AMNESIA (147)
ANAGRAM (43)
ANALYST (128)
ANATOLE (99)
ANEMONE (117)
ANIMATE (71)
ANNETTE (143)
ANOTHER (135)
ANTARES (137)
ANTENNA (25)
APOSTLE (111)
APPEASE (113)
APRIORI (129)
ARABIAN (203)
ARALSEA (103)
ARAPAHO (158)
ARIADNE (232)
ARRANGE (191)
ARRESTS (105)
ARSENAL (68)
ARTDECO (65)
ARTICLE (160)
ASARULE (7)
ASININE (35)
ASPECTS (170)
ASSENTS (238)
ASTAIRE (3)
ASTORIA (52)
ASTRIDE (211)
ATALOSS (78)
ATEDIRT (201)
ATELIER (149)
ATHLETE (42)
ATLANTA (12)

ATLARGE (29)
ATLASES (142)
ATLEAST (44)
ATPEACE (212)
ATSTAKE (165)
ATTACHE (175)
ATTESTS (64)
ATTIMES (167)
AVARICE (133)
AVERAGE (179)
AVIATOR (156)
AVOCADO (231)
BEELINE (250)
CABARET (246)
CANASTA (108)
CELESTE (61)
DESERTS (53)
DESSERT (101)
DETENTE (90)
EARLOBE (88)
ECLIPSE (187)
ECUADOR (228)
EDASNER (40)
EGOTRIP (66)
ELASTIC (46)
ELEANOR (1)
ELECTEE (235)
ELECTRA (136)
ELEGANT (79)
ELEMENT (48)
ELEVATE (70)
ELLIPSE (124)
EMANATE (91)
EMERALD (196)
EMERSON (157)
EMINENT (152)
EMULATE (249)
ENDORSE (80)
ENEMIES (63)
ENHANCE (31)
ENLARGE (73)
ENMASSE (24)
ENROUTE (37)
ENSNARE (32)
ENTENTE (21)
ENTERED (39)
ENTITLE (153)
ENTRANT (214)
ENTREAT (122)
EPAULET (221)
EPISODE (50)
ERASERS (8)
ERASMUS (125)
ERASURE (5)
ERECTED (162)
ERITREA (131)
ERNESTO (67)
EROTICA (144)
ESCAPEE (130)
ESSENCE (10)
ESTATES (9)

ESTEEMS (59)
ESTELLE (13)
ESTONIA (28)
ESTRADA (174)
ETAGERE (69)
ETERNAL (4)
EVEREST (15)
EVILEYE (181)
EYESORE (34)
IMEANIT (185)
IMITATE (248)
INAHOLE (118)
INERROR (83)
INERTIA (6)
INITIAL (202)
INTENSE (115)
IRANIAN (148)
IRELAND (47)
IRONAGE (209)
IRONORE (2)
ISADORA (241)
ISOLATE (95)
ISRAELI (14)
ITERATE (22)
IVANHOE (245)
LARAMIE (150)
LASAGNA (233)
LATERAL (229)
LORELEI (77)
MAEWEST (218)
MASCARA (169)
MINARET (177)
NARRATE (227)
NATALIE (141)
NATASHA (208)
NEMESES (200)
NEMESIS (134)
NESTEGG (194)
NIAGARA (204)
OCANADA (36)
OCARINA (215)
OCEANIA (104)
ONADARE (172)
ONADATE (178)
ONAROLL (123)
ONATEAR (38)
ONELANE (82)
ONENOTE (220)
ONESTAR (192)
ONESTEP (163)
ONETIME (186)
ONLEAVE (55)
ONSTAGE (205)
ONTARIO (18)
OPENSEA (106)
OPENTOE (237)
OPERATE (41)
ORACLES (193)
OREGANO (92)
ORESTES (146)
ORIENTS (180)
ORIGAMI (54)
ORIOLES (74)
ORLANDO (173)

OTHELLO (11)
OTTOMAN (132)
PESETAS (110)
POSSESS (190)
RATATAT (120)
RATRACE (84)
REAREND (240)
REASONS (223)
REDTAPE (121)
REENTER (206)
REFEREE (234)
REGATTA (242)
RELAPSE (168)
RELEASE (20)
REMORSE (98)
RESENTS (81)
RESTORE (93)
ROASTER (222)
ROSETTA (210)
ROSSSEA (219)
SAHARAN (217)
SARALEE (33)
SATIATE (72)
SATIRES (107)
SCOTTIE (247)
SEASIDE (216)
SEATTLE (140)
SEDATES (243)
SEERESS (94)
SEESAWS (164)
SEESRED (57)
SENATOR (60)
SENSATE (188)
SIAMESE (45)
SINATRA (86)
SNEERAT (182)
SOANDSO (85)
STALEST (97)
STAMINA (155)
STEAMER (199)
STEELIE (171)
STEEPLE (56)
STENCIL (145)
STERILE (119)
STOOLIE (244)
STOPGAP (109)
STPETER (62)
STRANGE (138)
STREETS (139)
TABASCO (102)
TANTARA (195)
TORONTO (230)
TRAINEE (176)
TREETOP (151)
TREMOLO (183)
TRESTLE (76)
TRIESTE (184)
TSELIOT (100)
TSETSES (126)
UNEATEN (161)
UPATREE (166)
USELESS (224)
UTENSIL (127)
YESORNO (189)

AAA | Motorists' org. | Battery size | Battery type | Rte. recommenders | Bond rating

AAH | "That feels good!" | Satisfied sound | Sound of relief | Word to a doctor | Sigh of contentment

ABA | Lawyers' org. | Attorneys' org. | Legal org. | "The ___ Daba Honeymoon" | Litigator's org.

ABE | Presidential nickname | Justice Fortas | Actor Vigoda | Playwright Burrows | Tad's dad

ABS | Tummy muscles | Stomach muscles, for short | Bodybuilder's pride | Exercise target | They're below pecs

ACE | Expert | Whiz | King topper | Crackerjack | High card

ACH | Rhine whine | Essen exclamation | "___ du Lieber!" | German cry | Cologne cry

ACT | Take steps | Do something | Pretense | Play part | Tread the boards

ADA | Nabokov novel | Oklahoma city | Boise's county | Toothpaste tube abbr. | Nabokov title heroine

ADD | Say further | Tack on | Put in | Contribute | Sum up

ADE | Summer drink | Summer cooler | Citrus drink | Fruity drink | Lime drink

ADO | Fuss | Hubbub | Commotion | Bustle | Flap

ADS | Spots | Pitches | Commercials | Some are classified | Show stoppers?

AER | ___ Lingus | Atmospheric prefix | Fizzy prefix

AFT | Toward the stern | Sternward | Toward the rudder | Toward the rear | Back at sea

AGA | Turkish title | ___ Khan | Turkish bigwig | Turkish leader | Turkish honorific

AGE | Ripen | Mature | Epoch | Long time | Historical period

AGO | In the past | Gone by | Past | Before now | Back

AHA | "So that's it!" | "Eureka!" | "Gotcha!" | "Bingo!" | Cry of discovery

AHS | Sounds of relief | Sounds of contentment | Satisfied sighs | Sounds of delight | Checkup sounds

AID | Lend a hand | Help | Assistance | Pitch in | Succor

AIL | Feel poorly | Be under the weather | Have a bug | Feel off | Have the blahs

AIM | Objective | Intention | Goal | Draw a bead | Crest competitor

AIR | Broadcast | Televise | Make public | Ventilate | Balloon filler

AKA | Rap sheet letters | Alias letters | Alias | Wanted poster letters

ALA | In the style of | Pie ___ mode | Like | According to | Chicken ___ king

ALE | Pub order | Pub pint | Ginger ___ | Tankard filler | Draft choice

ALF | Politico Landon | TV alien | Franklin's 1936 opponent | TV extraterrestrial

ALI | ___ Baba | Actress MacGraw | Poetic pugilist | Clay, today | Boxer Laila

ALL | The whole shebang | 100% | The works | Completely | The lot

ALP | Swiss peak | Mont Blanc, for one | High mountain | Matterhorn, for one | Climber's challenge

ALS | Capp and Capone | Gore and more | The Unsers of Indy | Pacino et al.

ALT | PC key | Cockpit abbr. | Model Carol | Hgt. | Elev.

AMA | Doctors' org. | Doc bloc | Physicians' org. | Anti-smoking org. | Professional org. since 1847

AMI | French friend | "___ dreaming?" | "What ___, chopped liver?" | "What Kind of Fool ___?" | "___ Blue?"

AMO | Latin 101 word | I love: Latin | Latin lover's word

AMP | Roadie's load | Fuse unit | Band aid | Rock blaster | Gig gear

ANA | Santa ___ winds | Santa ___, California | Literary collection | Actress ___ Alicia

AND | Plus | In addition | What's more | Furthermore | Clause connector

ANE | Hydrocarbon suffix | Chemical suffix | Actress Sue ___ Langdon | Suffix with meth- | "Wheel of Fortune" purchase

ANI | Singer DiFranco | Black cuckoo | "Wheel of Fortune" purchase | Game show request

ANN | Raggedy doll | Massachusetts cape | Abby's twin | Actress Sothern | Author Beattie

ANO | Pitch ___-hitter | "It's ___-win situation!" | "Wheel of Fortune" purchase | Year, in Yucatán | "Is that ___?"

ANT | Hill dweller | Picnic pest | Colony member | Industrious insect | Aardvark morsel

ANY | Whichever | Whatever | One or more | "___ takers?" | "___ luck?"

AOL | "You've got mail" co. | Popular ISP | Part of many e-mail addresses | Earthlink competitor | Big name on the Internet

APE | Mimic | Copy | Galoot | Imitate | Make like

APR | Spring mo. | Financing abbr. | Earth Day mo. | Tax mo. | Car ad abbr.

APT | Fitting | Likely | Appropriate | Inclined | Well-put

ARA | Coach Parseghian | Altar constellation | Southern constellation | Neighbor of Scorpius

ARC | Circle segment | Rainbow shape | Pendulum's path | Bow | ___ de Triomphe

ARE | Exist | Live and breathe | "You ___ here" | "Chances ___" | "We ___ the World"

ARF | Pound sound | Canine comment | Comics bark | Sandy's sound | Declaration of puppy love?

ARI | Jackie's second | "Exodus" hero | Bush spokesman Fleischer | Uris hero | Actress Meyers

ARK | Biblical boat | Two-by-two vessel | Sacred chest | Place of refuge | Torah holder

ARM | Hand holder | Shirt part | Escort's offer | Pitcher's asset | Branch

ARP | Dadaist Jean | Dada pioneer | Duchamp contemporary

ARR | JFK posting | Sheet music abbr. | LAX posting | Airport monitor abbr. | Timetable abbr.

ARS | "___ Poetica" | Start of MGM's motto | "___ gratia artis" | "___ longa, vita brevis"

ART | College major | Skill | Knack | Gallery display | Actor Carney

ASA | Simile center | Botanist Gray | Flat ___ pancake | Congressman Hutchinson | ___ rule

ASH | Bat wood | Blonde shade | Volcanic output | Grate stuff | Louisville Slugger wood

ASI | "___ was saying ..." | "Just ___ suspected!" | Do-say link | "___ live and breathe!" | Faulkner's "___ Lay Dying"

ASK | "Shoot!" | Inquire | "Don't ___!" | Request | Pop the question

ASP | Nile reptile | Egyptian cobra | Cleopatra's undoing | Horned viper

ASS | Beast of burden | Nincompoop | Fool | Ninny | Pompous sort

ATA | ___ glance | One ___ time | ___ standstill | One-time link | Loss leader?

ATE | Chowed down | Consumed | Put away | Broke bread | Downed

ATL | Part of NATO (abbr.) | The Braves, on scoreboards | It borders Fla. | Pac.'s counterpart | Iceland's ocean (abbr.)

ATM | PIN requester | Cash dispenser, for short | S&L convenience | 24-hr. bank feature

ATT | ABA member | Court fig. | Lawyer (abbr.) | Part of an 800 collect call number | J.D. holder (abbr.)

AVA | Actress Gardner | Clark's "Mogambo" costar | An ex of Frank

AVE | "___ Maria" | Forum greeting | St. crosser | Hail, to Caesar | Blvd.

AWE | Wonderment | Blow away | Reverence | Amazement | Bowl over

AWL | Hole maker | Leatherworker's tool | Piercing tool | Punching tool | Leather sticker

AXE | Fire | Pink-slip | Chopper | Bunyan's tool | Can

AYE | Sailor's assent | Word of assent | Yeoman's "Yes!" | Vote of confidence | Affirmative on board

BAA | Ram's remark | Ewe said it | Ovine utterance | Sheep sound | Kid's cry

BAH | "Phooey!" | Ebenezer's exclamation | Scrooge's cry | "___, humbug!" | "Nuts!"

BAR | Tavern | Prohibit | Watering hole | Sot's spot | Keep out

BAT | Cave dweller | Take one's cuts | Diamond club | Flying mammal | Louisville Slugger

BEE | Spelling contest | Spell-off | Buzzer | Quilting party | Comb maker

BOA | Feathery wrap | Fluffy scarf | ___ constrictor | Fancy wrap | Flapper wrapper

BRA | Bikini top | Lingerie item | Swimsuit part | Two-piece piece | Victoria's Secret purchase

BRO | Sis's sib | Buddy | Dude | "My man!" | Friend in the 'hood

CAL | Iron man Ripken | Presidential nickname | "Silent" prez | White House nickname

CAN | Fire | Corn holder | Soup container | Soda container | Preserve, in a way

CAR | Saturn or Mercury | Train unit | Jam ingredient? | One for the road? | Railroad unit

CAT | Hipster | House pet | Jazzman | Friskies eater | Dude

CBS | "60 Minutes" network | "Survivor" network | Letterman's network | "CSI" network | "JAG" network

CDS | LP successors | DJ's assortment | Audiophile's collection | Bank offerings | Record store purchases

CEE | Average grade | Mediocre mark | Clamp shape | Middling mark | Bee follower

CEL | Animation frame | Cartoon collectible | "Fantasia" frame | Disney frame

CEO | Corporate VIP | Corp. bigwig | Biz biggie | Business VIP

CHE | "Evita" role | Friend of Fidel | Revolutionary Guevara | "Evita" narrator

CHI | Greek X | Frat letter | X | Phi follower | Psi preceder

CIA | Spy org. | "The Company" | KGB counterpart | Cloak-and-dagger org. | OSS successor

CON | Hoodwink | Bamboozle | Jailbird | Take in | Swindle

COO | Bill's partner | Whisper sweet nothings | Dove's sound | Pigeon sound | Murmur

CPA | Busy one in Apr. | Tax pro | IRS employee | H&R Block employee | Book reviewer, for short

CRO | ___-Magnon man | Early man prefix | Vel attachment?

CSA | Civil War letters | Jefferson Davis's org. | Union foe (abbr.)

DAD | June honoree | Pop | Family member | Father | Mom's mate

DAM | Hoover, for one | It holds water | Hydroelectric project | Block up | Beaver's work

DAN | Newsman Rather | Dapper dude? | Blocker of "Bonanza" | Veep before Al | Actor Aykroyd

DAS | "___ Kapital" | German article | Prosecutors (abbr.) | Court figs. | They prosecute perps

DDE | HST's successor | JFK predecessor | ETO commander | Ike's monogram | Presidential inits.

DEE | Poor grade | Ruby or Sandra | Billy ___ Williams | Wallace of "E.T."

DEL | Singer Shannon | Costa ___ Sol | Dover's state (abbr.) | Pa. neighbor | Tierra ___ Fuego

DEN | Family room | Lair | Reading room | Cub Scout group | Study

DER | German article | "___ Rosenkavalier" | Austrian article | "___ Spiegel" | ___ Stern (German newspaper)

DES | ___ Moines, Iowa | ___ Plaines, Illinois

DIE | Conk out | Casino cube | Go kaput | Yahtzee cube | Tool's partner

DNA | Genetic letters | Kind of test | Kind of fingerprint | Chromosome component | Evidence type

DOE | Forest female | Anonymous John | Buck's mate | John ___ | Female rabbit

DOS | John ___ Passos | Hairstyles | Windows precursor | ___ and don'ts | Parties

DOT | Part of an e-mail address | Point | Semi-colon? | Speck | Ellipsis part

DRE | Rap's Dr. ___ | "Still ___" (1999 rap song)

DYE | Hair coloring | Batiking need | Salon supply | Turn blue? | Tint

EAR | Attention | Corn unit | Musical ability | Canal site | Listening device

EAT | Chow down | Consume | Polish off | Dig in | Put away

EAU | Vichy water | ___ de Cologne | Mer contents | ___ de toilette | French water

EBB | Recede | Fall back | Decline | Go out | Subside

ECO | Author Umberto | "Foucault's Pendulum" author | Prefix with system | Prefix with friendly | Prefix with sphere

EDS | Magazine VIPs | Ames and Asner | Both Begleys | Mag. staffers | Ms. reviewers

EDT | NYC summer clock setting | D.C. summer clock setting

EEE | Shoebox letters | Wide shoe width | Big foot? | Shoe specification

EEK | "A mouse!" | Comics cry | Cartoon squeal | It's a scream

EEL | Slippery swimmer | Snakelike fish | Snaky swimmer | Moray | Sushi fish

EEN | Velvet finish? | Dusk, to Donne | Poetic contraction | Bard's nightfall

EER | Poetic adverb | Alway | Always, poetically | Auction ending | Occupational suffix

EGG | Silly Putty holder | Deviled item | Heckler's missile | Poultry product | Cackleberry

EGO | Swelled head | Conceit | Self-image | Self | Freudian topic

EIN | German article | "Ich bin ___ Berliner" | Article in Der Spiegel | Article of Cologne | A as in Austria

EKE | Squeeze (out) | ___ out a living | Barely make, with "out" | Supplement, with "out" | Scratch (out)

ELF | Pixie | Brownie | Sprite | Arctic assistant | North Pole worker

ELI | Inventor Whitney | Actor Wallach | Yale student | Yalie | Ivy Leaguer

ELK | Lodge member | Wapiti | Antlered animal | Caribou kin | Fraternal fellow

ELL | Building wing | Wing | Pipe joint | Annex | Right-angle shape

ELM | Shade tree | Common street name | Shade provider | Freddy Krueger's street | Nightmare street of film

ELO | "Hold On Tight" gp. | "Xanadu" gp. | "Do Ya" rock gp. | "Rock 'n' Roll Is King" gp.

ELS | Golfer Ernie | Overhead trains | High rollers? | Loop loopers | 1997 U.S. Open winner

EMS | Printer's measures | Dash lengths | German spa | German river | Els' followers

EMT | CPR expert | 911 respondent | Ambulance VIP

EMU | Big bird | Flightless bird | Outback runner | Cassowary cousin | Australian bird

END | Wrap up | Conclusion | Finish | Finale | Wind up

ENE | Chemical suffix | Hydrocarbon suffix | Opposite of WSW | Wind dir. | Compass dir.

ENG | Chang's twin | High school subj. | H.S. requirement | Part of the U.K. | Coll. major

ENO | Rock producer Brian | Brian of Roxy Music | Musician Brian

ENS | USNA grad | Nav. rank | Printer's measures | Pulver's rank (abbr.) | Naval off.

ENT | Med. specialty | Tolkien creature | Adjective suffix | Suffix with differ | Suffix with absorb

EON | Long, long time | Ages and ages | Time on end | One billion years

EOS | Dawn goddess | Canon camera | Aurora's counterpart | Daughter of Hyperion

EPA | Ecol. watchdog | Clean air org. | MPG rater | Pollution monitoring org. | Ecology org.

ERA | Pitcher's stat | Historical period | Big time | Important time | Epoch

ERE | Poetic preposition | Before | Afore | Prior to | Palindromic preposition

ERG | Work unit | Bit of work | Fraction of a joule | Unit of energy | Physics unit

ERN | Directional suffix | Sea eagle | West ender? | East ender?

ERR | Blow it | Slip up | Drop the ball | Mess up | Go astray

ERS | Hosp. areas | Sounds of hesitation | Trauma ctrs. | Triage ctrs.

ESC | PC key | Computer key | Upper-left key | Key abbr. | Bailout key

ESE | Language suffix | Compass reading | Legal conclusion?

ESP | Sixth sense | Mentalist's claim | Psychic's claim | Uncommon sense | Clairvoyance

ESS | Slalom curve | Double curve | Pothook shape | Road curve | Curvy letter

EST | Superlative suffix | Superlative ending | Guess (abbr.) | Ballpark fig. | Guinness suffix | Cornerstone abbr. | Guinness Book suffix

ETA | Greek vowel | Hellenic H | LAX posting | Zeta follower | Fraternity letter

ETC | Catchall abbr. | List-ending abbr. | Space-saving abbr. | And so on (abbr.)

ETE | Somme summer | Printemps follower | Summer on the Seine | Summer, in Lyon | When the French fry

ETH | Ordinal ending | Biblical verb ending | Numerical suffix | Shakespearean suffix

ETO | DDE's command | WWII arena | WWII command | Ike's command (abbr.)

ETS | UFO pilots | French connections | Aliens, briefly | Sci-fi visitors | "The X-Files" extras

EVA | Zsa Zsa's sister | One of the Gabors | "Uncle Tom's Cabin" girl | Stowe character

EVE | Night before | First lady | Time before | First mate? | She raised Cain

EWE | Farm female | She sheep | Ram's mate | Fleecy female | Meadow mother

EYE | Storm center | CBS logo | Check out | Needle hole | Looker

FEE | Charge | Service charge | Lawyer's charge | Honorarium

GAL | Guy's date | Square dance partner | Eight pts. | Lass | "My ___ Sal"

GAS | Tank filler | Auto fuel | Beetle juice? | Krypton, for one | Blast

GEE | Thou | "Golly!" | "That's amazing!" | "How about that!" | "Fancy that!"

GEL | Toothpaste type | Hair goo | Come together | Set | Solidify

HAL | Shakespearean prince | "2001" computer | Actor Linden | Actor Holbrook | Prince of Broadway

HAS | Owns | Possesses | Suffers from | Is down with | Holds

HAT | Monopoly token | Topper | Beanie or beret | Head cover | Bowler or boater

HEE | "___ Haw" | Laugh syllable | Half a laugh | Tee follower | Bray beginning

HEM | Haw's partner | Clothes line | Bottom line? | Skirt edge | Hesitate

HEN | Biddy | Female lobster | Farm female | Layer | Egg warmer

HER | That girl | That woman | Self starter? | Part of HRH | That lady

HOE | Ground breaker | Weed whacker | Clod chopper | Garden tool | Tilling tool

HOT | On a roll | In | Very popular | Like stolen goods

IAN | Author Fleming | Singer Janis | Actor McKellen | Golfer Woosnam

ICE | Rink surface | Rocks | Hard water | Swelling reducer | Hotel freebie

IDA | Actress Lupino | Wyo. neighbor | Author Tarbell | Gilbert and Sullivan princess | Rhoda's mom

IDI | Dictator Amin | First name in tyranny | First name in despotism

IDO | Swear words? | Altar words | Promising words | Wedding words | Bachelor's last words

IDS | Psyche sections | Fingers | Bouncers' requests | Freudian topics | Some have photos

III | Sundial reading | Son of a son | Junior's junior | "Richard ___" | George ___

IKE | Tina's ex | Presidential nickname | Mamie's man | 1950s campaign nickname | Clanton gang leader

ILE | ___ de France | Seine sight | ___ du Diable | French spot of land | Martinique, par exemple

ILL | Under the weather | Out of sorts | Laid up | Indisposed | Poorly

IMA | "___ little teapot ..." | The Monkees' "___ Believer" | "___ Yankee Doodle Dandy" | "Hallelujah, ___ Bum"

IMP | Little devil | Little rascal | Mischief-maker | Troublemaker | Little pest

INA | Actress Balin | One ___ million | "___ pig's eye!" | Once ___ while | Actress Claire

INC | Business abbr. | Business mag | Business letters | Co. name ender | Ltd., in the U.S.

INE | Suffix with serpent | Chemical suffix | Like Bruckner's Symphony No. 7 | Suffix with elephant | Having four sharps

INK | Publicity | Sign | Pen filler | Squid's squirt | Bic filler

INN | Bed-and-breakfast | Roadhouse | B and B | Hostelry | Rural hotel

INS | Connections | Officeholders | Electees | Social connections | Election winners

INT | Acct. addition | CD earnings | Bankbook abbr. | Bank acct. entry | QB's mistake

ION | Charged particle | Charged atom | It's charged | Saturn model | Cyclotron bit

IOU | Debtor's letters | Marker | Chit | Promise to pay | Promissory note

IRA | Lyricist Gershwin | Author Levin | 401(k) alternative | George's brother

IRE | Wrath | Anger | High dudgeon | Spleen | Dander

IRS | Apr. addressee | Returns org. | Form letters? | 1040EZ issuer | Collection agcy.

ISA | "This ___ bust!" | "This ___ test" | "This ___ stickup!" | "This ___ surprise!" | "The Lady ___ Tramp"

ISH | "Sort of" suffix | Relative of -esque | Language suffix | It's like -like | Suffix with bull or bear

ISM | Doctrine | Belief | School of thought | Belief system | Theory

ISR | Neighbor of Leb. | Syr. neighbor | Medit. country | Mideast land (abbr.) | 1949 U.N. entrant

IST | Adherent's suffix | Professional suffix | Follower's suffix | Doer's suffix | Occupational suffix

ITA | Call ___ day | "Give ___ rest!" | Señor suffix | Give ___ go | Give ___ whirl

ITE | Mineral suffix | Suffix with Israel | Follower's suffix | Native's suffix | Ore suffix

ITO | Skater Midori | Simpson trial judge | "How was ___ know?" | Judge Lance

ITS | Part of TGIF | "___ up to you" | "___ De-Lovely" | "___ a deal!"

ITT | Addams Family cousin | Telecom giant, once

IVE | "___ Got a Secret" | "___ had it!" | "___ been had!" | "Now ___ seen everything!" | "___ got it!"

KEN | Barbie's beau | Understanding | He's a doll | Boy toy | Author Kesey

LAD | Young fellow | Boy | Youngster | Stripling | Little shaver

LAM | Hasty escape | On the ___ (fleeing) | Flight | Flee

LAP | Once around the track | Racing circuit | Luxurious place? | Napkin's place

LAS | ___ Cruces, New Mexico | Vegas opening | ___ Vegas | Spanish article | Scale notes

LAW | Statute | Jurisprudence | Ordinance | Bailey's bailiwick | Order's partner

LEA | Meadow | Pasture | Grazing ground | Actress Thompson | Grassland

LED | Was ahead | Conducted | Went first | Blazed a trail | Headed up

LEE | Director Spike | Golfer Trevino | Jeans brand | "Malcolm X" director | "Crooklyn" director

LEI | Hula hoop? | Island chain? | Oahu souvenir | Hawaiian garland | Kauai keepsake

LEN | Author Deighton | Sportscaster Berman | Actor Cariou | Football Hall of Famer Ford | Quarterback Dawson

LEO | Sign of summer | Name of 13 popes | Zodiac sign | Feline sign

LES | Guitarist Paul | Bandleader Brown | "___ Misérables" | French article | "___ Miz"

LET | Allow | Permit | Court call | Tennis call | Rent

LIE | Whopper | Prevaricate | Tell it like it isn't | Tell a whopper | Golfer's concern

LIL | "___ Abner" | Diamond ___ | Dogpatch adjective

LIP | Back talk | Sass | Mouth piece | Edge | It may be glossed over

LIT | Ignited | Put a match to | Plastered | English ___ | Blotto

LOA | Mauna ___ | End of a Hawaiian volcano | "Long," in Hawaiian

LOO | Card game | Elton's john | John, to Ringo | Canterbury can | London lavatory

LOS | ___ Alamos, New Mexico | Part of UCLA | Spanish article | The "L" of L.A. | ___ Angeles

LOT | Parking place | Fate | Auction offering | Destiny | Kit and caboodle

LOU | Singer Rawls | Bud's bud | Comic Costello | Baseball great Gehrig | Reed of rock

LSD | Acid | It was dropped in the '60s | Acid letters | Timothy Leary's turn-on | Kind of trip

LYE | Soap ingredient | Caustic stuff | Strong cleaner | Strong alkali | Bleaching agent

MAC | Bub | Buddy | PC alternative | Brit's raincoat | Singer Davis

MAD | "Spy vs. Spy" magazine | Steamed | Satire magazine | Boiling | Irate

MAE | West of Hollywood | Fannie ___ | Ginnie ___ | Daisy ___ | Actress West

MAO | Long March leader | Chinese Chairman | ___ Tse-tung | Warhol subject | Kind of jacket

MAR | Spoil | Deface | Damage | Disfigure | Scratch

MAS | Bell and Barker | Pas' partners | More, in México | Barker and Kettle | Some advanced degs.

MAT | Wrestling surface | Slip preventer | Framer's need | Gym pad | "Welcome" site

MEL | Actor Gibson | Blanc or Brooks | Singer Tormé | Sportscaster Allen | Actress Harris

MER | Mal de ___ | French sea | Debussy subject | Sea, to Marie | View from Marseille

MET | Encountered | Bumped into | Ran into | Satisfied | Came across

MIA | Actress Farrow | Soccer star Hamm | "Mamma ___!" | War stat. | Woody's ex

MIR | Russian space station | Earth orbiter

MOE | A Stooge | One of the Three Stooges | "The Simpsons" bartender | Broadway's "Five Guys Named ___" | Skier Tommy

MOO | Low | Herd word | Bossy remark? | Speak with a Jersey accent? | Pasture sound

NAB | Collar | Arrest | Pinch | Catch in the act | Slap the cuffs on

NAE | Dundee denial | Scot's negative | Angus's refusal | Scottish refusal | Burns not?

NAN | Bert Bobbsey's twin | Photographer Goldin | Indian bread

NAP | Siesta | Forty winks | Short snooze | Day break? | Fuzz

NAT | Rebellious Turner | ___ King Cole | Writer Hentoff | Singer Cole | Insurrectionist Turner

NAY | Dissenting vote | No vote | Vote against | Thumbs-down | Voice vote

NBA | Hoops gp. | Warriors' gp. | Magic org. | Lakers' org. | Jazz gp.

NCO | Sgt., e.g. | Sgt. or cpl. | Cpl., e.g.

NEA | Teachers' org. | PBS benefactor | Pedagogic org. | AFT rival

NED | Actor Beatty | Composer Rorem | Nancy Drew's beau | Homer's neighbor | Writer Buntline

NEE | Society page word | Born | Maiden name preceder | Wedding page word | Once called

NEO | Opposite of paleo- | Prefix with natal | Prefix with classical | New beginning?

NET | Bottom line | Court divider | Take home | Clear | Profit

NEW | Just out | Fresh | Unfamiliar | Unused | Novel

NIA | Actress Peeples | Actress Long | Actress Vardalos

NIL | Zilch | Zip | Zero | Nothing | Nada

NIN | Diarist Anaïs | "Delta of Venus" author | "Seduction of the Minotaur" author | Palindromic diarist | French diarist

NIP | Tuck's partner | Pinch | Short snort | Chill | Small bite

NIT | Something to pick | Prefix for picker | NCAA rival | Coll. hoops competition | Louse-to-be

NNE | U-turn from SSW | Vane dir. | Compass reading | Wind dir.

NOD | Affirmative action | Silent assent | Doze | Auction action

NON | Oui's opposite | "Smoking or ___?" | Rouen refusal | Tours turndown | Alternative to smoking

NOR | Neither's partner | And not | Hide-hair link | Postal creed word | Negative conjunction

NOS | Turndowns | Refusals | Figs. | Discouraging words | Negative votes

NOT | "As if!" | "Kidding!" | "Wayne's World" word | "She loves me ___" | "___ to worry"

NRA | Big D.C. lobby | Heston's org. | FDR program | New Deal agcy. | Blue Eagle org.

NSA | Hush-hush org. | Code-cracking org. | CIA relative

NTH | Utmost | Ultimate degree | High degree | To the ___ degree | Ultimate

OAF | Klutz | Lummox | Stumblebum | Clod | Blockhead

OAK | Symbol of strength | Symbol of might | Furniture wood | Acorn source | Hard wood

OAR | Paddle | Scull | Boat propeller | Crew member | Galley tool

OAT | Bran source | Cereal grain | Feedbag morsel | Meal starter | Cereal grass

OBI | Kimono sash | Japanese sash | Kimono accessory | Geisha's sash | ___-Wan Kenobi

OCT | World Series mo. | Halloween mo. | Fall mo. | Columbus Day mo. | U.N. Day month

ODD | Unmatched | Roulette bet | Uneven? | Strange | Peculiar

ODE | Praiseful poem | Lyric poem | Keats creation | Horatian creation | Poetic tribute

OER | Not 'neath | Anthem contraction | Poetic preposition | "___ the ramparts ..." | Above, poetically

OHO | Sound of surprise | Surprised cry | "Gotcha!" | "So that's your game!" | Cry of discovery

OIL | Peanut product | Black gold | Texas tea | Fix a squeak | Lubricate

OLA | Pay stub? | Suffix with pay | Slangy suffix | Pay back? | Suffix with schnozz

OLD | Ancient | Vintage | Done to death | Antique | Getting on

OLE | Grand ___ Opry | Corrida cry | Bullring cheer | ___ Miss | Chihuahua cheer

ONA | Three ___ match | ___ roll | Stop ___ dime | Out ___ limb | "___ Clear Day ..."

ONE | Single | United | Unified | Indivisible | Small bill

ONO | Yoko ___ | Lennon's lady | Plastic ___ Band | Lennon's love | Singer Yoko

ONT | Toronto's prov. | Mich. neighbor | N.Y. neighbor | Ottawa's prov. | Canadian prov.

OOH | "I'm impressed!" | Sound of awe | "Wow!" | La-la lead-in | Aah's partner

OOP | Alley ___ | Alley follower | "Alley ___" | Alley in a cave | Caveman Alley

OPE | Unlock, poetically | Unlock, in verse | Reveal, in poetry | Expose, in verse | Unfold, in verse

OPT | Make a choice | Choose | Go (for) | Select, with "for" | Make a selection

ORA | Man-mouse link | ___ pro nobis | Mouths | Man-mouse connection | "Are you a man ___ mouse?"

ORB | Sphere | Globe | Sun or moon | Eyeball | Heavenly body

ORE | Mine find | Pay dirt | Lode load | You can dig it | Tram filler

ORO | Spanish gold | Acapulco gold | Guadalajara gold | Pizarro's quest | ___ y plata (Montana's motto)

ORR | Hockey great Bobby | Bobby of hockey | Bruins legend | Three-time Hart Trophy winner | Eight-time Norris Trophy winner

ORS | Hosp. areas | Surgery sites, briefly | IV sites | Alternatives | Places for M.D.'s

OSE | Sugar suffix | Verb ending | Sweet suffix

OTT | Baseball great Mel | Slugger Mel | Polo Grounds legend | Giant Mel | Giant of old

OUR | "___ Town" | "___ Gang" | Lord's Prayer start | Sharer's word | Your and my

OUT | Ump's call | In the open | Loophole | No longer hot | Escape clause

OVA | Eggs | Reproductive cells | Egg cells | In vitro items | Lab eggs

OWE | See red? | Be in the red | Be indebted to | Have debts | Have a tab

OWN | Have | Possess | Have title to | Part of BYOB | Personal

PAL | Buddy | Chum | Bud | Sidekick | Amigo

PAN | Bad review | Go for the gold? | Sweeping shot | Skillet | Criticize

PAR | Golfer's goal | Average | Hole goal | Something to shoot for | Standard

PAS | Ballet step | Faux ___ | Dance step | ___ de deux | Audio systems, for short

PAT | One way to stand | Butter portion | Back stroke? | Frisk, with "down" | Butter unit

PEA | Soup veggie | Shooter ammo | Green shade | Potpie spheroid | Shooter pellet

PEN | Farm enclosure | Corral | Write | Compose | Proverbial sword beater

PER | According to | A pop | For each | ___ capita | Apiece

PET | Favorite | Cat or canary | Teacher's favorite | Stroke | Four-footed friend

PIE | Chart shape | Kind of chart | Dessert choice | Pizza | Epitome of easiness

PLO | Arafat's org. | Mideast gp. | Arafat's gp. | West Bank gp.

POE | Usher's creator | "The Gold Bug" author | "Ulalume" poet | "The Bells" poet | "Annabel Lee" writer

PRE | Opposite of post- | Season opener? | Grand ___ ("Evangeline" setting) | Relative of ante- | Historic leader?

PRO | Paid player | Old hand | In favor of | Debate side | Expert

PSI | Greek letter | Pressure meas. | Inflation meas. | Telepathy, e.g. | Trident-shaped letter

PTA | School org. | School gp. | Mom-and-pop org. | "Harper Valley ___" | Bake sale org.

RAD | "Awesome!" | "Far out!" | "Cool!" | "Way cool!" | Physicist's unit

RAE | "Norma ___" | Actress Charlotte | Actress ___ Dawn Chong | Arctic explorer John | Comic Charlotte

RAG | Tease | Scott Joplin piece | Dustcloth | Sleazy paper | Scandal sheet

RAH | "Yay, team!" | Stadium cheer | "Go, team!" | Bowl yell | Cheering word

RAM | Ewe's mate | Hit head-on | Smash into | Zodiac animal | Hit hard

RAN | Managed | Sought office | Sought a seat | Took off | Operated

RAP | Séance sound | Grammy category | Blame | Criminal charge | Record store section

RAT | Scoundrel | Squealer | Squeal | Snitch | No-goodnik

RAW | Uncooked | Wet behind the ears | Rarer than rare | Green | Like steak tartare

RAY | Bit of sunshine | Beam | Sunbeam | Bit of hope | Light line

RBI | Baseball stat | Diamond stat | Stat for Sosa | Hitter's stat | Slugger's stat

RCA | Color TV pioneer | Victor's initials? | Magnavox competitor | NBC's former owner | ___ Victor

RDA | Nutritional abbr. | Nutritional std. | Vitamin bottle abbr. | Cereal box initials | Cereal box abbr.

REA | Actor Stephen | Stephen of "The Crying Game" | New Deal agcy. | "Citizen X" actor | "Bad Behaviour" star Stephen

REB | Yank's foe | Johnny ___ | Confederate soldier | Graycoat | One of Lee's soldiers

REC | VCR button | Kind of room | ___ room | ___ center | Tape deck button

RED | Blushing | Flushed | Scarlet | Roulette bet | Checkers color

REF | Boxing official | Whistle blower | TKO caller | Third man in the ring | Striped-shirt wearer

REL | Fam. member | Fam. reunion attendee | Seminary subj. | Electrical unit | Kin (abbr.)

REM | Sleep acronym | "Losing My Religion" band | Sleep phenomenon | Dreamer's acronym | Radiation unit

REN | Stimpy's pal | Cartoon Chihuahua | Cartoon dog | Stimpy's sidekick | Cartoon canine

REO | Classic car | ___ Speedwagon | Antique auto | Classic auto | Stutz contemporary

REP | Agent | Agt. | Iron-pumper's unit | Good name, briefly | House mem.

RES | Scale notes | Legal thing | In medias ___ | Legal matter | Hi-___ monitor

RET | Emeritus (abbr.) | No longer working (abbr.) | On Soc. Sec. | Like Gen. Powell | On a pension (abbr.)

REV | Gun | Gun the engine | Prepare to drag | Increase, with "up" | Ministerial nickname

RHO | Pi follower | Greek letter | Frat letter | Letter before sigma | Campus letter

RID | Disencumber | Free (of) | Purge | Clear (of) | Unburden

RIM | Canyon edge | Edge | Crater feature | Lip | Wheel part

RIO | Carnival city | ___ Grande | Brazilian resort | Copacabana site | Hope-Crosby destination

RIP | Tear | Letters carved in stone | Upholstery flaw | Roaring start? | Stretch of turbulent water

RNA | Genetic letters | Genetic material | Genetic stuff | Messenger ___ | Genetic initials

RNS | Hosp. workers | Hosp. employees | ER workers | OR personnel | TLC givers

ROB | Hold up | Stick up | Knock over | Rip off | Steal from

ROD | Curtain holder | Gat | Staff | Towel holder | Fishing pole

ROE | Fish eggs | Caviar | Future fish | Lobster eggs | Shad delicacy

RON | Director Howard | Jockey Turcotte | Wood of the Rolling Stones | Darling of the diamond | Actor Silver

ROO | Kanga's kid | Milne marsupial | Pooh pal | Pal of Piglet | Aussie hopper

ROT | Go bad | Balderdash | Poppycock | Nonsense | Baloney

RTE | Hwy. | Map abbr. | AAA suggestion | Numbered hwy. | Way to go (abbr.)

RUE | Regret | Wish undone | Feel bad about | Bemoan | Wish one hadn't

RYE | Deli bread | Reuben bread | White alternative | Bar order | Manhattan ingredient

SAC | Cul-de-___ | Pouch | Anatomical pouch | Bag | Fluid container

SAD | Blue | Down | Down in the dumps | Bummed out | Melancholy

SAG | Droop | Mattress problem | Give in to gravity | Decline | Give in to pressure

SAL | Actor Mineo | Mule of song | Gal of song | Erie Canal mule | "My Gal ___"

SAM | America's Uncle | Houston of Texas | Uncle ___ | "Casablanca" pianist | Muppet eagle

SAN | Japanese honorific | ___ Quentin | ___ Clemente | ___ Diego, California | ___ Marino

SAO | ___ Paulo | ___ Paulo, Brazil | ___ Tomé | ___ Tomé and Príncipe

SAP | Easy mark | Patsy | Dupe | Maple output | Syrup source

SAS | Carrier to Copenhagen | Airline to Stockholm | KLM rival | Airline to Sweden | European airline

SAT | Posed | Took a load off | Made a lap | Rode the bench | Took a chair

SAW | Adage | Toothed tool | Spotted | Noticed | Observed

SCI | Chem. or biol. | Poli ___ | School subj. | Bill Nye subj. | H.S. subject

SEA | Poseidon's realm | Where the buoys are | Ocean | Swell place? | Mermaid's habitat

SEC | Jiffy | Dry, as wine | Instant | Blink of an eye | Wall St. regulator

SEE | "Get it?" | Get the picture | Go out with | "I told you so!" | Notice

SEN | D.C. VIP | Rep.'s counterpart | Sun Yat-___ | One of a D.C. 100

SET | Complete collection | Harden | Ready to go | Match part | Gel

SEW | Put in stitches | Wrap (up) | Darn | Stitch up | Use a needle

SGT | Cpl.'s superior | Certain NCO | Bilko's rank (abbr.) | Pepper, for one (abbr.) | York, for one (abbr.)

SHA | ___ Na Na | Doo-wop syllable | Al Green's "___ La La" | Refrain syllable | Manfred Mann's "___ La La"

SHE | That girl | Cow or sow | Seashell seller | That woman | "Thar ___ blows!"

SIN | Fall from grace | Transgression | Sloth, for one | It may be original | Go astray

SIR | Knight's title | Round Table title | Military address | Polite address | Peppermint Patty, to Marcie

SIS | Family nickname | Bro's sib | Marie, to Donny | Boom-bah preceder | Bro's counterpart

SIT | Take a load off | Obedience school command | Command to Fido | Canine command | Be in session

SKI | Hit the slopes | Tackle moguls | Kind of mask | Slalom | Schuss

SLO | ___-mo replay | Pavement caution | Traffic caution | ___-pitch softball | Highway warning

SLY | Foxy | Cunning | Underhanded | Arch | Guileful

SNL | Debut of Oct. 11, 1975 | Where "Wayne's World" began (abbr.) | NBC show since '75 | Inits. in comedy | NBC weekend comedy

SNO | ___-Cat (winter vehicle) | ___-cone (summer treat) | Cone or Cat preceder | Hostess ___ Balls

SOD | Turf | Ground cover | Lay down the lawn | Grass section | Instant lawn

SOL | The sun | Costa del ___ | Impresario Hurok | Our sun | Fa follower

SON | Mama's boy | Heir, often | Trinity member | Junior | Michael Douglas, to Kirk

SOS | Brillo rival | Call for help | Distress signal | Sea plea | "Help!"

SOT | Lush | Barfly | Foster Brooks persona | W.C. Fields persona | Rummy

SPA | Health resort | Fitness center | Hot tub | Sauna site | Health haven

SPY | Le Carré character | Bond, for one | Mata Hari, for one | Undercover agent | Snoop

SRA | Madrid Mrs. | Mexican Mrs. | Lady of Sp. | Sp. title | Mme., across the Pyrenees

SRI | ___ Lanka | Hindu honorific | Hindu title | Indian honorific | Hindu title of respect

SRO | Sellout sign | Hit sign | Sign of success | B.O. sign | B'way hit sign

SRS | SAT takers | Grads-to-be (abbr.) | Yearbook sect. | AARP members | Gown renters (abbr.)

SSE | Wind dir. | U-turn from NNW | Compass dir. | Dallas-to-Houston dir. | Vane dir.

SSN | Nine-digit ID | Payroll ID | W-2 ID | Taxpayer's ID | Tax return ID

SSR | Ukr., once | Georgia, once (abbr.) | Lith., once | Latvia, once (abbr.) | Outdated atlas abbr.

SSS | Draft org. | Former draft org. | Conscription org. | Puncture sound | Serpent's sound

SST | Atl. crosser | Fast flier | Concorde, e.g. | JFK arrival | Mach 1 breaker

STA | RR stop | Depot (abbr.) | B&O stop | Railroad stop (abbr.) | Amtrak stop (abbr.)

STE | Sault ___ Marie | Fr. holy woman | Jeanne d'Arc, e.g. (abbr.) | Part of many Québec place names | ___-Foy, Quebec

STP | "The Racer's Edge" | Indy 500 letters | Oil additive | Nascar sponsor | Fuel additive brand

STS | Ave. crossers | Peter, Paul, and Mary (abbr.) | Blvds. | Ave. intersectors | Holy men (abbr.)

STU | Actor Erwin | Early Beatle Sutcliffe | R-V link | "Rugrats" dad | Apt name for a cook?

STY | Pig's digs | Mudhole | Porker's pad | Messy place | Hog heaven?

SUE | Take to court | Petition | "So ___ me!" | Good name for a lawyer? | Girl or boy of song

TAB | Bar bill | Bill | Typewriter key | Can opener | Check

TAD | Smidgen | Wee bit | Bit | Small amount | Lincoln son

TAE | ___ kwon do | Menlo Park monogram | Inventor's monogram | ___-Bo (exercise system) | South Korea's Roh ___ Woo

TAG | Playground game | It's game | Kids' game | Phone ___ | Price place

TAI | Mai ___ | ___ chi | Skater Babilonia | ___ chi ch'uan | Half a drink

TAN | Sunbather's goal | Whip but good | Whup | Catch some rays | Beachgoer's goal

TAO | Eastern way | Lao-Tzu's "way" | Confucian path | Eastern ideal | Universal ideal

TAP | Spigot | Faucet | Select | Water source | Keep time

TAR | Old salt | Sea dog | Sailor | Besmirch | Pitch

TAT | Make lace | Tit for ___ | Use a shuttle | Sylvester, to Tweety | End of a retaliatory phrase

TAU | Sigma follower | Greek cross | Greek letter | Frat letter | Letter before upsilon

TDS | NFL scores | NFL stats | NFL 6-pointers | QB stats

TEA | Afternoon social | Oolong or pekoe | Tetley product | Mad hatter's drink | Sri Lanka export

TED | Actor Danson | Poet Hughes | Newsman Koppel | Slugger Williams

TEE | Pipe joint | Golf gadget | Driving aid | Shirt with a slogan | Kicker's aid

TEL | ___ Aviv | Business card abbr. | Rolodex no.

TEN | Half a score | Sawbuck | Gymnast's goal | Hamilton's bill | Perfect rating

TET | Asian holiday | Hanoi holiday | Vietnamese New Year | Asian occasion | ___ Offensive

THE | Common article | Not just any | French beverage | Café alternative | Common title word

TIA | Spanish aunt | ___ Maria | Actress Carrere | Acapulco aunt | Argentine aunt

TIC | Quirk | Spasm | Twitch | Personal quirk | Eccentricity

TIE | Dead heat | Draw | No-win situation | Deadlock | Overtime cause

TIN | Pewter component | Sardine holder | Badge material | Soft metal | Can material

TIS | "___ the season ..." | Carol contraction | Poetic contraction | Scale notes | "___ the season to be jolly"

TKO | Ref's decision | Ring decision | Fight stopper, briefly | Ring letters | Bout decision

TLC | RN's specialty | Special attention, for short | Pampering, briefly | Gentle handling, initially | Mom's offering

TNT | Explosive letters | Blaster's need | Cable channel | Big bang producer | It's a blast

TOE | Water tester | Low digit | Sock part | Little piggy | Hose part

TOM | Male turkey | Mr. Turkey | Barnyard male | Alley prowler | Cartoon cat

TON | Heavy weight | Freight weight | Won ___ soup | Great deal | Whole lot

TOO | As well | Overly | Also | In addition | Unduly

TOR | Rocky peak | Rocky pinnacle | Craggy hill | Craggy peak | Anderson's "High ___"

TOT | Little one | Rug rat | Preschooler | Wee one | Tyke

TRA | Singing syllable | La-la lead-in | Refrain syllable | ___ la la | Song syllable

TRE | Three, in Napoli | Due follower | Uno + due | It's past due | Half of sei

TRI | Numerical prefix | Part of TNT | Prefix with athlete | Cycle starter | Prefix with state

TRY | Have a go at | Attempt | Stab | Sample | Give it a whirl

TSE | Mao ___-tung | Literary monogram | Lao-___ | Literary inits. | "The Waste Land" poet's monogram

TSK | Condescending cluck | "For shame!" | Sound of disapproval | Tut's cousin | Tongue-clucking sound

TWO | Pair | Couple | Snake eyes | Double standard? | Teetertotter quorum

UAR | Former Mideast org. | Old Mideast inits. | Nasser's org. | Egypt and Syria, once (abbr.)

UMA | Actress Thurman | She was June in "Henry & June" | Ethan's ex-wife | John's "Pulp Fiction" costar

UNE | French article | Article in Le Monde | Arles article | French one | Half of deux

UNI | Prefix with cycle | Prefix with sex | Bi- halved | Mono- relative | Prefix with color

UNO | Numero ___ | Popular card game | Family card game | Important numero | Game with 108 cards

UPS | FedEx rival | Good times | Raises | Increases | Hikes

URI | Swiss canton | Mentalist Geller | William Tell's canton | Spoon-bender Geller | Altdorf's canton

URN | Samovar | Coffee server | Coffee maker | Java holder | Keats subject

USA | Olympics chant | Mex. neighbor | Made in the ___ | NATO member | 2002 Winter Olympics host

USE | Take advantage of | Employ | Put to work | Purpose | Bring into play

UTE | Western Indian | 4×4 | All-purpose truck | Colorado native | Beehive State athlete

VEE | Neckline shape | Churchillian sign | Neckline type | Flight formation | Victory sign

VIA | By way of | Itinerary word | Through | Routing word | Using

WAR | Armed conflict | Kids' card game | "This means ___!" | Wouk's "The Winds of ___" | Combat

WEE | Tiny | Itty-bitty | Minute | Minuscule | Very early

WET | Drenched | Dripping | Soaked | Freshly painted | Allowing alcohol

YDS | NFL gains | Gridiron gains (abbr.) | QB's gains | Football gains (abbr.) | NFL stats

YEA | Thumbs-up vote | Pro vote | Affirmative vote | Indeed | Word of support

YEN | Itch | Hankering | Longing | Craving | Kobe currency

YES | "You bet!" | "Absolutely!" | Thumbs-up vote | "You rang?" | "May I help you?"

YET | Still | So far | Nevertheless | To date | Up to now

YRS | Mos. and mos. | Decade divs. | Jr. and sr. | Soph. and jr. | Century divs.

ZEN | Buddhist sect | Meditative sect | Buddhist discipline | "___ and the Art of Motorcycle Maintenance" | Meditative discipline

ABBA | "Dancing Queen" group | Palindromic pop group | Eban of Israel | "Waterloo" group | "Fernando" singers

ABCS | Basics | Fundamentals | Rudiments | Kindergarten basics | Kid stuff

ABEL | Genesis victim | Explorer Tasman | Cain's brother | Cain's victim | Third man

ABET | Help in a heist | Aid in crime | Aid's partner | Help in crime | Help a hood

ABLE | Competent | Up to the task | Qualified | Fit | Skilled

ABUT | Border on | Touch on | Neighbor | Lie next to | Be adjacent to

ACED | Got 100 on | Scored 100 on | Didn't just pass | Breezed through | Served perfectly

ACES | High cards | Deck quartet | Super-duper | Breezes through | Experts

ACHE | Yearn | Tylenol target | Tummy trouble | Feel sore | Sore spot

ACID | Etcher's need | Corrosive chemical | Kind of rock | Litmus reddener | Kind of rain

ACME | High point | Pinnacle | Zenith | Ne plus ultra | Peak

ACNE | Clearasil target | Teen's woe | Teen spots? | Teen trouble | Prom night woe

ACRE | Farm unit | Land unit | 43,560 square feet | Part of a plot | Zoning unit

ACTS | Play parts | New Testament book | Does something | Circus lineup | Deeds

ADAM | Economist Smith | First of all | He raised Cain | Fall guy? | First person

ADDS | Tacks on | Throws in | Puts two and two together | Says further | Contributes

ADEN | Yemeni port | Mideast's Gulf of ___ | Gulf port | Yemeni city | Arabian gulf

ADES | Citrus drinks | Fruity drinks | Summer drinks | Summer coolers | Summer quaffs

ADOS | Fusses | Commotions | Hubbubs | Brouhahas | Hullabaloos

AERO | Prefix with dynamic | Dynamic start | Flying start? | Dynamic leader? | Dynamic opening?

AFAR | At a distance | Way off | Yonder | Way out there | Off in the distance

AFRO | Bushy hairdo | Big do | Spheroid hairdo | Curly coif | '60s do

AGAR | Food thickener | Culture medium | Ice cream thickener | Lab gel | Thickening agent

AGED | Like fine wine | Long in the tooth | Matured | Elderly | Like sharp cheese

AGEE | "A Death in the Family" author | Pulitzer winner James | "The Night of the Hunter" screenwriter | "The Morning Watch" author | "The African Queen" screenwriter

AGER | Maturing agent | Ripening agent | Antiquing agent | Teen follower? | "Ain't She Sweet?" composer

AGES | A long time | Matures | Quite a while | Mellows | Ripens

AGOG | Wide-eyed | Bug-eyed | Enthralled | Awestruck | Eagerly excited

AGRA | Taj Mahal site | Taj Mahal city | Uttar Pradesh city | Indian tourist city | Pearl Mosque site

AHAB | Jezebel's husband | Pequod captain | "Moby Dick" captain | Ishmael's captain | Starbuck's captain

AHEM | Throat-clearing sound | "Excuse me ..." | Attention-getter | "Pardon me!"

AIDA | Verdi heroine | Verdi opera | Opera set in Egypt | "O patria mia" singer | Turturro of "The Sopranos"

AIDE | Helper | Assistant | White House staffer | Gofer | Man Friday

AINT | "___ Misbehavin'" | Isn't wrong? | "It ___ Necessarily So" | "Is so!" rebuttal | "___ it the truth!"

AJAR | Slightly open | Not quite shut | Close to closed | Open a crack | Cracked

AKIN | Related | Similar | Analogous | Comparable | Similar in nature

ALAI | Jai ___ | Kyrgyzstan range | Half court game? | Merry, in Basque | Game ending?

ALAN | Astronaut Shepard | King of comedy | Greenspan of the Fed | Actor Rickman | Actor Arkin

ALAR | Winglike | Winged | Banned apple spray | Having wings | Controversial orchard spray

ALAS | Word of regret | "Woe is me!" | "Ah, me!" | Word of woe | "Too bad!"

ALDA | "M*A*S*H" star | Hawkeye Pierce portrayer | Actor Alan | "Sweet Liberty" director | Swit's costar

ALEC | Actor Baldwin | Actor Guinness | Novelist Waugh | One of the Baldwins | He played Obi-Wan

ALEE | Away from the wind | Toward shelter | Nautical adverb | Sheltered | Downwind

ALES | Pub orders | Porters | Pub potables | Pub quaffs | Saloon selections

ALEX | "Roots" author Haley | "Jeopardy!" host Trebek | Emcee Trebek | Quizmaster Trebek | Haley or Trebek

ALIT | Touched down | Landed | Dismounted | Came down to earth | Got down

ALMA | ___ mater | Soprano Gluck | Michigan college | Diva Gluck | ___-Ata, Kazakhstan

ALOE | Lotion ingredient | Sunburn soother | Spiny houseplant | Skin soother | ___ vera

ALOT | Oodles | Heaps | Scads | Loads | Very much

ALOU | Baseball family name | Moises of baseball | Felipe of baseball | Diamond family name | 1966 N.L. batting champ Matty

ALPO | Kal-Kan competitor | Brand for Bowser | Purina competitor | Food for Fido | Chow chow chow

ALPS | Heidi's home | Swiss peaks | Skiing mecca | Hannibal's hurdle | "The Sound of Music" backdrop

ALSO | To boot | What's more | As well | Besides | In addition

ALTO | Choir voice | Chorus member | Violist's clef | Sax type | Countertenor

AMEN | "You said it!" | "You can say that again!" | Grace period? | Word of agreement | "Right on!"

AMES | Iowa city | Iowa college town | Singing brothers | Skunk River city | Iowa State site

AMID | In the thick of | Surrounded by | In the center of | During | Betwixt and between

AMMO | Bullets | Magazine contents | Shells, e.g. | Cartridges | Shots, for short

AMOR | Love personified | Cupid | Love god | Latin love | Archer of myth

AMOS | Singer Tori | Book after Joel | Biblical prophet | Author Oz | "Famous" cookie maker

ANAT | Med school subj. | Gray's subj. | Sci. course | Structural sci. | Biol. subject

ANEW | From the top | From square one | Over | From scratch | Once more

ANKA | "Diana" singer | Singer Paul | "Lonely Boy" singer | "My Way" songwriter | "Puppy Love" singer

ANNA | Visitor to Siam | Ballerina Pavlova | Soprano Moffo | Sigmund's daughter | "The King and I" role

ANNE | Green Gables girl | Diarist Frank | Author Rice | Actress Heche | Elizabeth I's mother

ANNO | Part of A.D. | ___ Domini | Cornerstone word | The "A" in A.D.

ANON | Shortly | Soon | By and by | In a bit | In a while

ANTE | Pay to play | Poker stake | Poker payment | Start a pot | Chip in

ANTI | Opposed to | Con | Nay sayer | Against | Not pro

ANTS | Picnic pests | Hill dwellers | Hill builders | Tiny colonists | Some carpenters

AONE | Top-notch | Tops | First-rate | Excellent | Top-drawer

APER | Mimic | Copycat | Impressionist | Imitator | Parrot

APES | Mimics | Simians | "Planet of the ___" | Tarzan's neighbors | Goons

APSE | Church recess | Church area | Church section | Cathedral area | Nave neighbor

AQUA | Water color | Blue hue | Greenish blue | Blue shade

ARAB | Kaffiyeh wearer | Part of UAR | Saudi, for one | Riyadh resident | Burnoose wearer

ARAL | Asia's ___ Sea | Asian inland sea | Shrinking sea | Sea east of the Caspian | Uzbekistan's ___ Sea

ARCH | St. Louis landmark | Foot part | Roguish | Eyebrow shape | Flatfoot's lack

AREA | Vicinity | Neighborhood | Neck of the woods | Region | Zone

ARES | Greek war god | Bellicose god | Son of Zeus | God of war | Lover of Aphrodite

ARGO | Jason's ship | Golden Fleece ship | Jason's craft | Ship that sailed to Colchis | Medea rode on it

ARIA | Opera solo | La Scala highlight | Diva's delivery | Sills solo | Opera highlight

ARID | Saharan | Parched | Desertlike | Bone-dry | Like the Gobi

ARLO | Singer Guthrie | Woody's son | He sang about Alice | Woody's boy | Alice's chronicler

ARNE | "Rule, Britannia" composer | "Alfred" composer | "Judith" composer | "Artaxerxes" composer

ARNO | Florence's river | Cartoonist Peter | Pisa's river | River under the Ponte Vecchio | River to the Ligurian Sea

ARTE | Commedia dell'___ | Johnson of "Laugh-In" | Comic Johnson | Museo offering | Jocular Johnson

ARTS | Part of A&E | Sciences' partner | Fine things? | Crafts' companion | Liberal ___

ASAP | PDQ | Pronto | Quickly, quickly | Letters of urgency | PDQ relative

ASEA | On the briny | Out of port | Cruising | Sailing | On the ocean

ASHE | Arthur of tennis | 1975 Wimbledon champ | Queens stadium | Tennis great

ASIA | China setting | Largest continent | Part of SEATO | The East | Largest of seven

ASIS | Warts and all | Sale condition | Closeout caveat | Sale sign | Without warranties

ASKS | Inquires | Questions | Sets a price | Invites | Quizzes

ASPS | Nile reptiles | Egyptian cobras | Poisonous snakes | Horned vipers | African snakes

ASSN | Org. | Pt. of AARP | Organization (abbr.) | Pt. of NAACP | Pt. of NCAA

ASST | Helper (abbr.) | Aide (abbr.) | Mgr.'s helper | Kind of prof. | Kind of D.A.

ASTA | Hammett hound | "The Thin Man" dog | Movie terrier | Nick and Nora's dog | Film terrier

ASTI | Italian wine region | ___ spumante | Piedmont province | Piedmont wine center | Piedmont city

ASTO | Concerning | Regarding | About | In the matter of | Memo words

ATEE | Suit to ___ | To ___ (perfectly) | To ___ (exactly) | Fit to ___ | To ___

ATIT | Working hard | Plugging away | Busy | Fighting | Arguing

ATOM | Molecule part | Tiny particle | Energy source | Quark's place | Scintilla

ATOP | On | Resting on | Surmounting | At the summit of | Perched on

ATRA | Razor brand | Gillette product | Razor name | Blade brand | Razor handle?

ATTA | "___ girl!" | "___ boy!" | Kofi ___ Annan | Boy or girl preceder | "___ baby!"

ATTN | Envelope abbr. | Memo abbr. | Business letter abbr. | Env. notation | Envelope letters

AURA | Mystique | Atmosphere | Ambience | Distinctive air | Pervasive quality

AUTO | Garage occupant | Car | Mercury or Saturn | Self starter? | Road runner?

AVER | Declare | Maintain | State | Profess | Allege as fact

AVID | Gung-ho | Enthusiastic | Zealous | Rah-rah | Eager

AVON | Bard's river | Stratford's river | Mary Kay competitor | Calling company? | Shakespeare's river

AWOL | MP's quarry | Illegally off base | GI offense | Mil. truant | Off base, in a way

AXLE | Car bar | Wheel shaft | Wheel connector | Rod between wheels | Wagon part

CEDE | Give up | Yield | Relinquish | Hand over | Turn over

COLA | Soft drink | Cuba libre ingredient | Fizzy drink | Pepsi, for one | Popular pop

DATA | Facts and figures | Information | Facts | Figures | Info

DEER | Bucks and does | A few bucks? | Bambi and kin | Venison source | Timid creature

DELI | Sandwich shop | Supermarket section | Food shop | Where heroes are made | Frank server

DESI | He loved Lucy | Lucie's dad | Lucy's partner | Ricky's portrayer | First name in '50s TV

DRAT | "Phooey!" | Mild oath | "Doggone it!" | "Shucks!" | "Fiddlesticks!"

EARL | Viscount's superior | British noble | Countess's spouse | Banjoist Scruggs | James ___ Carter

EARN | Merit | Pull down | Take home | Make | Bring in

EARS | Corn units | Listening devices | Dumbo's wings | Rabbit ___ | Jug handles

EASE | Facility | Comfort | Relaxation | Simplicity | Naturalness

EAST | Bridge seat | Sunrise direction | Orient | Right on the map | Down ___ (Maine)

EASY | Simple | "Piece of cake!" | Effortless | "Duck soup!" | Like falling off a log

EATS | Grub | Diner sign | Chow | Vittles | Breaks bread

EAVE | Roof overhang | Icicle site | Roof edge | Roof projection | Gutter site

EBAN | Israel's Abba | "Voice of Israel" author | Israeli diplomat Abba | Israeli statesman | "My Country" author

ECHO | Reverberate | Bounce back | Canyon comeback | Parrot | Repeat

ECRU | Light brown | Stocking shade | Hosiery shade | Neutral hue | Beige

EDAM | Dutch cheese | Dutch export | Ball-shaped cheese | Red-wrapped cheese | Wax-coated cheese

EDDY | Whirlpool | Whirling water | Swirl | Countercurrent | Vortex

EDEN | Genesis garden | Paradise | Perfect place | First place | Utopia

EDGE | Advantage | Upper hand | Leg up | Nose (out) | Brink

EDIE | Singer Adams | Falco of "The Sopranos" | Singer Brickell | Actress McClurg | Peter Gunn's girlfriend

EDIT | Blue-pencil | Cut and paste | Prepare for publication | Check copy | Correct copy

EDNA | Author Ferber | Novelist Ferber | Poet ___ St. Vincent Millay | Best or Ferber | Dame ___ Everage

EELS | Sushi fish | Snakelike fish | Congers | Slippery swimmers | Wriggly swimmers

EERO | Architect Saarinen | First name in architecture | Eliel's son | A Saarinen | Gateway Arch designer Saarinen

EGAD | "Zounds!" | "Yikes!" | Mild oath | Old-time oath | "Omigosh!"

EGOS | Swelled heads | Self-images | Freudian subjects | They may be inflated | Psyche parts

EIRE | Green land | The Emerald Isle | De Valera's land | Land of the leprechauns | Hibernia

ELAL | Israeli airline | Airline to Tel Aviv | Mideast carrier | Carrier to Ben-Gurion | Airline since 1948

ELAN | Verve | Panache | Pizazz | Dash | Enthusiasm

ELEE | Gen. Robert ___ | Robt. ___ | "Waiting for the Robert ___" | Part of a CSA signature | Robert ___

ELIA | Director Kazan | Lamb's pen name | Essayist's alias | "Essays of ___" | Lamb's pseudonym

ELIE | Nobelist Wiesel | Author Wiesel | "Night" author Wiesel | Sculptor Nadelman | Peace Nobelist Ducommun

ELIS | Yalies | Yale students | New Haven collegians | Crimson rivals | Some Ivy Leaguers

ELLA | Singer Fitzgerald | First name in scat | Actress Raines | First name in jazz | Poet ___ Wheeler Wilcox

ELLE | Model Macpherson | Fashion magazine | Vogue rival | Vogue competitor

ELMO | Sailor's saint | Ticklish doll | Pollster Roper | Red Muppet | Admiral Zumwalt

ELSA | "Born Free" lioness | Actress Lanchester | Designer Schiaparelli | Lohengrin's love | Film feline

ELSE | Otherwise | Choice word | In addition | If not | Alternatively | Different | Besides

EMIL | Actor Jannings | Pianist Gilels | Runner Zátopek | Disney's "___ and the Detectives" | Biographer Ludwig

EMIR | Kuwaiti ruler | Kuwaiti bigwig | Islamic leader | Mideast bigwig | Arab ruler

EMIT | Give off | Send out | Radiate | Discharge | Give out

EMMA | Jane Austen novel | Austen heroine | Actress Thompson | Madame Bovary | Poet Lazarus

ENDS | Winds up | Wraps up | Finishes | Pulls the plug on | Means justifiers

ENID | Oklahoma city | City west of Tulsa | Author Bagnold | Writer Bagnold | Geraint's wife

ENOS | Son of Seth | Grandson of Adam | Slaughter of baseball | Genesis name

ENYA | "Orinoco Flow" singer | "Only Time" singer | New Age singer | One-named Irish singer | Irish folk singer

EONS | Ages and ages | Seemingly forever | Years and years | Ages on end | Almost forever

EPEE | Fencing sword | Blunted blade | Fencing blade | One-on-one sport | Sporting blade

EPIC | Larger-than-life | Monumental | Sweeping | On a grand scale | It's a long story

ERAS | Historical periods | Historic times | Important times | Times to remember | Notable periods

ERAT | Part of QED | Quod ___ demonstrandum | The "E" in QED | Proof word

ERGO | Therefore | Hence | Thus | Consequently | So

ERIC | Guitarist Clapton | Newsman Sevareid | Skater Heiden | Leif's father | Author Ambler

ERIE | Pennsylvania port | Toledo's lake | Buffalo's lake | Cleveland's lake | Part of HOMES

ERIN | Leprechaun land | Hibernia | Oscar role for Julia | The Emerald Isle | Ireland

ERLE | Perry's creator | ___ Stanley Gardner | Della's creator | First name in mysteries

ERMA | Humorist Bombeck | First name in humor | Writer Bombeck | Columnist Bombeck

ERNE | Sea eagle | River to Donegal Bay | Fish-eating eagle | Shore bird | Sea bird

EROS | Love god | Son of Aphrodite | Cupid, to the Greeks | Piccadilly Circus statue | Winged god

ERRS | Goofs | Blows it | Makes a mistake | Messes up | Slips

ERSE | Gaelic | Gaelic tongue | Scots Gaelic | Highland tongue | Irish Gaelic

ERST | Once, once | Formerly, formerly | Prefix for while | Once, once upon a time | At one time, at one time

ERTE | Art Deco designer | Art Deco artist | Harper's Bazaar illustrator | One-named designer

ESAI | Actor Morales | Morales of "La Bamba" | Morales of "Bad Boys" | Morales of "NYPD Blue"

ESAU | Jacob's twin | Biblical twin | Birthright seller | Genesis twin | Son of Isaac

ESSE | Latin being | Start of North Carolina's motto | In ___ (actually) | Latin 101 verb | To be, to Tiberius

ESSO | Sinclair rival | Exxon, formerly | Old gas brand | "Happy Motoring" company | Exxon, in Canada

ESTA | "¿Cómo ___ usted?" | Spanish 101 verb | This, in Toledo | Are, in Aragón

ESTE | Villa d'___ | Ferrara family name | Italian noble surname | Punta del ___, Uruguay | Renaissance family

ETAL | List-ending abbr. | And others (abbr.) | Bibliography abbr. | List shortener | Catchall abbr.

ETAS | Greek vowels | LAX postings | JFK postings | Hellenic H's | H lookalikes

ETAT | Coup d'___ | French state | Coup target | South Dakota, to Pierre | State of France

ETCH | Work with acid | Delineate | Cut glass | Impress deeply | Outline clearly

ETNA | Sicilian spouter | Sicilian spewer | Sicilian volcano | European erupter | Erupter of 2002

ETON | Harrow rival | British prep school | School on the Thames | School founded by Henry VI | Prince William's school

ETRE | Raison d'___ | French 101 verb | To be, in Toulouse

ETTA | Singer James | James of jazz | Kett of the comics | Sundance's girlfriend | Singer James or Jones

ETTE | Diminutive suffix | Suffix with cigar | Luncheon ending | Suffix with disk | Novel ending

ETTU | "___, Brute?" | Words to Brutus | Ides rebuke | Caesar's accusation | Words to a traitor

EURO | Continental currency | New money | Continental prefix | New currency | Mark's replacement

EVEN | Neck and neck | Tied | Roulette bet | Level | Flush

EVER | At any time | Always | In any way | Continuously | At any point

EVIL | Wicked | Bad to the bone | Diabolical | Nefarious | Devil's doings

EWER | Water pitcher | Pitcher | Decorative pitcher | Still life subject | Basin accessory

EWES | Farm females | Flock members | She sheep | Meadow mamas | Rams' mates

EXES | Former spouses | Split personalities? | They've split | Old flames | Divorcées

EXIT | Way out | Leave the stage | Leave | Where to get off | Theater sign

EYES | Peepers | Potato features | Baby blues | Ogles | Seeing things

EZRA | Poet Pound | Book before Nehemiah | University founder Cornell | Old Testament book | Book after II Chronicles

GENE | Trait carrier | Kind of pool | Kind of therapy | Actor Wilder | Chromosome part

GNAT | Pesky flier | Pesky insect | No-see-um | Punkie | Bitty biter

HAHA | "Very funny!" | Gag reflex? | Result of a crack? | "LOL," vocalized | "That's a riot"

HALE | Robust | Hearty partner | Patriot Nathan | Vigorous | Sound

HALO | Nimbus | Light ring | Angel topper | Good sign? | Head light?

HARE | Fabled also-ran | Aesop's also-ran | Fabled runner-up | Long-eared hopper | Rabbit relative

HERE | Roll call response | "Take this!" | In this place | At this point | Present

HERO | Long lunch? | Man of the hour | Submarine | Leander's love | Medal recipient

IAGO | "Othello" villain | Verdi villain | Othello's betrayer | Cassio's rival | Shakespearean villain

ICED | On the rocks | Frosted | Bumped off | Sewed up | Like some tea

ICON | Computer image | Screen symbol | Computer symbol | Religious image | Something to click on

IDEA | Brainstorm | Notion | Concept | Brainchild | Inkling

IDES | March time | Midmonth day | Bad day for Caesar | Fateful March day | Time to beware

IDLE | Not working | Run in neutral | Doing nothing | Inactive | Goofing off

IDOL | Hero | Pedestal topper | Role model | Admired one | Adored one

IGOR | Composer Stravinsky | Operatic prince | Inventor Sikorsky | Borodin's prince | Frankenstein's assistant

ILIE | Nastase of tennis | Netman Nastase | "Would ___ to you?" | Rival of Björn | "Would ___?"

ILSA | Rick's love | Ingrid's "Casablanca" role | "Casablanca" heroine | Rick's old flame | Mrs. Victor Laszlo

INCA | Ancient Peruvian | Machu Picchu resident | Quechua speaker | Ancient Andean | Early Peruvian

INGE | "Picnic" playwright | "Bus Stop" playwright | "Come Back, Little Sheba" playwright | "A Loss of Roses" playwright | "Splendor in the Grass" screenwriter

INNS | Lodges | Rural stopovers | Hostelries | Bed-and-breakfasts | Roadside stops

INON | Privy to | A party to | Aware of | Get ___ the ground floor | Involved with

INRE | Concerning | About | Memo starter | As to | Regarding

INTO | Division word | Absorbed by | Fascinated by | A fan of | Gung-ho about

IOTA | Smidgen | Tiny bit | Bit | Tiny amount | Scintilla

IOWA | Corn Belt state | Hawkeye State | "The Music Man" setting | Corn country | "Field of Dreams" locale

IRAE | "Dies ___" | Requiem Mass word | Wrath, to Romulus

IRAN | Persia, today | Where Farsi is spoken | Shah's land, once | OPEC member | Turkmenistan neighbor

IRAS | Some nest eggs | Gershwin and Levin | 401(k) cousins | Nest eggs, briefly | Bank offerings

IRIS | Eye part | Pupil's place | Rainbow goddess | Spring bloom | Fleur-de-lis

IRMA | "___ la Douce" | Cookbook author Rombauer | "My Friend ___" | Cookery's Rombauer | Role for Shirley

IRON | Press | Wrinkle remover | Dumbbell material | Monopoly token | Pressing need

ISEE | "Gotcha" | Words of understanding | "Aha!" | "Got it!" | "Uh-huh"

ISLE | Man, for one | Capri, for one | Key | Castaway's home | Spot of land

ITEM | Particular | News bit | Bit of gossip | Tabloid twosome | Part of a list

IVAN | Lendl of tennis | Novelist Turgenev | Nobelist Pavlov | "Terrible" czar

IVES | Currier's partner | Singer Burl | Composer Charles | "A Little Bitty Tear" singer, 1962 | "Concord Sonata" composer

KNEE | Leg joint | Patella's place | Proposer's prop | Pants part | Dummy's perch

LAIR | Den | Hideout | Hideaway | Retreat | Animal house

LANE | Pool division | Swimmer's assignment | Lois of the Daily Planet | Country road | Highway division

LARA | Zhivago's love | Superman's mother | Actress ___ Flynn Boyle | Pasternak heroine | "Doctor Zhivago" heroine

LAVA | Molten rock | Hot stuff | Volcanic flow | Pumice source | Hot issue

LEAR | Shakespearean king | Regan's father | Cordelia's father | Goneril's father | TV producer Norman

LEER | Impolite look | Sly look | Lascivious look | Lecherous look | Ogle

LENA | Singer Horne | Actress Olin | Musical Horne | Olin or Horne | Olin of "Chocolat"

LENO | Letterman rival | Carson's successor | Late-night name | He follows the news | Lantern-jawed celeb

LESS | Minus | Not as much | Discounted by | Reduced by | More or ___

LIAR | Perjurer | Makeup artist? | Storyteller | Tall tale teller | Prevaricator

LIEN | Legal claim | Property claim | Bank claim | Mortgage, e.g. | Bank holding

LIRA | Italian money | Turkish money | Capri cash | Money in Milan | 100 kurus

LOLA | "Damn Yankees" vamp | 1970 Kinks hit | She gets what she wants

LORE | Traditional knowledge | Folk history | Folk wisdom | Anecdotal knowledge | Tribal tales

LOSE | Misplace | Come in second | Shake | Give the slip to | Take it on the chin

MENU | Waiter's handout | List of choices | Bill of fare | Diner's card | Beanery handout

MERE | Insignificant | Nothing more than | Simple | Paltry | Only

MESA | City near Phoenix | Arizona city | Tableland | Flat-topped hill | Big butte

MESS | Military meal | Clutter | Disorder | Predicament | Hodgepodge

NADA | Zilch | Zip | Zippo | Nothin' | Big zero

NANA | "Peter Pan" pooch | Zola heroine | Granny | Zola novel | Grandma

NARC | DEA agent | Buster? | Bust maker | Antidrug cop | Drug agent

NASA | Space shuttle gp. | Rocket launcher | Space org. | Astronaut's org. | Launching org.

NATO | Defense org. since 1949 | Defense gp. | Alliance acronym | Brussels-based alliance

NCAA | March Madness org. | Final Four org. | Sweet 16 org. | School sports org.

NEAR | Approach | At hand | Close by | Close | Within earshot

NEAT | In apple-pie order | Tidy | Shipshape | Without ice | Spiffy

NEED | Require | Requirement | Have to have | Exigency | Cry out for

NEER | Not e'en once | Poetic adverb | Opposite of alway | Literary adverb | Beginning to do-well?

NEMO | Verne captain | Nautilus captain | Nautilus skipper

NEON | Light gas | Element #10 | Sign gas | It's a gas | Inert gas

NERD | Dweeb | Geek | Social misfit | Uncool one | Square

NERO | Pianist Peter | Rex's sleuth | Infamous emperor | Detective Wolfe | Fiddling emperor

NESS | Legendary loch | Capone's nemesis | Stack role | 1987 Costner role | Monster's loch

NEST | Tree house | Egg holder | Robin's residence | Hotbed | Catbird seat?

NETS | Takes home | New Jersey five | Clears | Fishing gear | Earns after taxes

NILE | World's longest river | Khartoum's river | Cairo's river | Shade of green | Christie's "Death on the ___"

NINA | Ship of 1492 | Historic caravel | Actress Foch | One of Columbus's ships | One of a 1492 trio

NINE | Muse count | Mudville complement | Opening time, maybe | Low card in pinochle | Prime-time hour

NOAH | Ark builder | Flood survivor | Wordsmith Webster | Biblical boat builder | Ham's father

NOEL | Christmas carol | Carol | Playwright Coward | Winter air | Yuletide

NONE | Zero | Zilch | Not any | Zip | Poor dog's portion

NONO | Taboo | Forbidden thing | Taboo thing | Something to avoid | It's frowned upon

NORA | Director Ephron | "A Doll's House" heroine | Writer Ephron | Asta's mistress | Mrs. Nick Charles

NOSE | It smells | Narrow margin of victory | Wine's bouquet | Bridge site | Scents organ

NOTE | Memo | E or G, e.g. | Staff member? | Post-It, e.g. | Musical symbol

OAHU | Honolulu's island | Diamond Head locale | Hawaiian island | Pearl Harbor locale | Waikiki locale

OARS | Boat propellers | Boathouse inventory | Galley propellers | Sculls | Rowing needs

OATH | Vow | Solemn promise | Swear words | Inauguration highlight | It may be minced

OBIE | Theater award | Tony's cousin | Village Voice bestowal | Off-Broadway award | Big Apple award

OBIT | Newspaper notice | Passing notice | Final notice | Last words? | Life lines?

OBOE | Woodwind | Double-reed instrument | Woodwind instrument | Mitch Miller's instrument | Clarinet cousin

ODDS | Chances | Track numbers | Bookie's concern | Vegas line | Probabilities

ODES | Poems of praise | Lyric poems | Poetic tributes | Keats creations | Lofty poems

ODIE | Garfield's foil | Garfield's pal | Comics canine | "Garfield" dog | Jon Arbuckle's dog

ODIN | Norse god | Valhalla VIP | Norse war god | Thor's father | Frigg's husband

ODOR | Aroma | Smell | Scent | Fragrance | Bouquet

OGLE | Stare at | Gawk at | Eye amorously | Eyeball | Make eyes at

OGRE | Shrek, for one | Folklore fiend | Meanie | Monster | Brute

OHIO | The Buckeye State | Home to Columbus | Louisville's river | Buckeye's home

OHNO | "Yikes!" | "This can't be!" | "Horrors!" | "Say it ain't so!" | Cry of dismay

OKRA | Gumbo ingredient | Gumbo vegetable | Gumbo pod | Pod vegetable | Creole veggie

OLEG | Designer Cassini | Cassini of fashion | First name in fashion | Designer for Jackie | Couturier Cassini

OLEO | Bread spread | Butter substitute | Toast topper | Margarine | Muffin topper

OLES | Corrida cries | Bullring cheers | Corrida cheers | Cries at the bullfight | Encouraging words

OLGA | Gymnast Korbut | One of Chekhov's "Three Sisters" | "Three Sisters" sister | First name in gymnastics | "Eugene Onegin" mezzo-soprano

OLIN | Actress Lena | Lena of "Chocolat" | Lena of "Havana" | Actor Ken | Ken of "thirtysomething"

OLIO | Hodgepodge | Mishmash | Miscellany | Mixed bag | Potpourri

OLLA | Stewpot | Earthen pot | ___ podrida | Spicy stew | It's a crock

OMAN | Arabian sultanate | Yemen neighbor | Neighbor of Saudi Arabia | Muscat's land | Arab League member

OMAR | General Bradley | Actor Sharif | Actor Epps | Poet Khayyám | Baseball's Vizquel

OMEN | Portent | Sign | Handwriting on the wall | Augury | Harbinger

OMIT | Leave out | Skip | Drop | Pass over | Fail to mention

OMNI | Old Dodge | Former Atlanta arena | Present opener? | Word form for "all" | Science magazine

OMOO | Melville novel | Melville work | Melville tale | "Typee" sequel

ONCE | Formerly | In the past | As soon as | A single time | Story starter

ONEA | Draft status | Draftable | ___-Day vitamins | Fit to serve | Suitable for service

ONES | Change for a five | Small bills | Singles | Individuals | Addition column

ONTO | Aware of | Not fooled by | Not tricked by | Cognizant of | In the know about

ONUS | Burden | Responsibility | Blame | Load | Weight

OOZE | Seep | Move like molasses | Slime | Exude | Flow slowly

OPAL | October birthstone | Fall birthstone | Milky gem | Iridescent gem | Australian gem

OPEC | Oil cartel | Cartel letters | Oil gp. | Fuel org. since 1960

OPEN | Ready for business | Store sign | Frank | Dentist's request | Unlock

OPIE | Mayberry moppet | Mayberry kid | Ronny Howard role | '60s TV boy

ORAL | Spoken | Like some vaccines | Kind of exam | Vocal | Voiced

ORCA | Killer whale | Shamu, for one | Willy or Shamu | "Jaws" boat | Largest dolphin

OREL | Pitcher Hershiser | Hurler Hershiser | City south of Moscow | City on the Oka | Turgenev's birthplace

OREO | Sandwich cookie | Nabisco cookie | Sweet sandwich | Black-and-white treat | Creme-filled cookie

ORES | Mine finds | Tram loads | Metallic rocks | Vein pursuits | They lack refinement

ORSO | Roughly | Approximately | About | Estimator's words | Thereabouts

OSHA | Dept. of Labor agency | Workers' protection org. | Worker welfare org. | Job-safety org.

OSLO | Capital on a fjord | Norway's capital | 1952 Winter Olympics site | European capital | Kon-Tiki Museum site

OTIS | Singer Redding | Elevator man | Elevator inventor | Mayberry tippler | Porter's regretful Miss

OTOE | Siouan speaker | Oklahoma native | Western Indian | Plains Indian | Nebraska City's county

OTTO | Director Preminger | Conductor Klemperer | "Beetle Bailey" dog | One of the Ringling Brothers | Grid great Graham

OVAL | Track shape | Elliptical | Cameo shape | Roundish | Track

OVEN | Hot spot | Bakery fixture | Pizzeria fixture | Kitchen appliance | Dutch ___

OVER | Finished | [see other side] | Walkie-talkie word | Finito | More than

OXEN | The yoke's on them | Farm team | Plow pullers | Yoked beasts | Draft animals

PEER | Equal | Jury member | Social equal | Look closely | Kind of pressure

PERU | Lima's land | Llama land | Chile neighbor | Cuzco's land | OAS member

PESO | Cancún coin | Mexican money | 100 centavos | Cuban coin | Mexican moolah

PETE | Townshend of the Who | Folk singer Seeger | Sneaky guy? | Fountain of jazz | Red Rose

PLEA | Entreaty | Court statement | Answer to a charge | Appeal | Nolo contendere, e.g.

PSST | "Hey, you!" | "Hey, over here!" | "Hey!" | Attention-getting sound | Attention-getter

RACE | Track event | Marathon, e.g. | Derby | Dash | Battle the clock

RAGE | Fury | Go ballistic | Latest thing | Storm | Foam at the mouth

RAIL | Racetrack fence | Commuter line | Marsh bird | Epitome of thinness | Banister

RAIN | April forecast | Drops from the sky | Picnic spoiler | Parade spoiler | Shower

RANT | Carry on | Talk wildly | Deliver a tirade | Go on and on | Harangue

RARE | Steak order | Seldom seen | Hard to find | Like hen's teeth | Exceptional

RASP | Coarse file | Grate | Wood file | Grating sound | Irritate

RATE | Assess | Clip | Appraise | Size up | Have status

RATS | "Phooey!" | Charlie Brown expletive | "Darn!" | "Peanuts" expletive | Hamelin pests

RAVE | Four-star review | Carry on | Glowing review | Pan's opposite | All-night bash

READ | Interpret | Peruse | Try for a part | Enjoy a novel | Crack the books

REAL | Genuine | Honest-to-goodness | Concrete | Bona fide | Authentic

REAP | Harvest | Bring in | Gather grain | Bring in the sheaves | Use a sickle

REAR | Bring up | Stern | Back | Derrière | Caboose

REBA | Singer McEntire | First name in country | McEntire of country | "Fancy" singer McEntire | Musical McEntire

REDO | Make over | Fix up | Overhaul | Decorate anew | Change the décor

REDS | Cincinnati team | 1990 World Series champs | Half the checkers | Beatty Oscar film | Some wines

REED | Marsh plant | Cattail, e.g. | Critic Rex | Bassoon, e.g. | Oboist's need

REEL | Film holder | Stagger | Lively dance | It holds the line | Rod's partner

REIN | Check | Bit attachment | Bridle strap | Pull (in) | Jockey strap

RENE | Actress Russo | Philosopher Descartes | Painter Magritte | Lacoste of tennis | Russo of "Ransom"

RENO | Nevada city | Casino city | Ashcroft's predecessor | Betting setting | Clinton's attorney general

RENT | Tenant's payment | Let | Monthly payment | Torn | Flat fee

REST | Take five | Take a break | What's left | Break | Take a breather

RHEA | Perlman of "Cheers" | Mother of Zeus | Moon of Saturn | Three-toed bird | Ostrich relative

RIDE | Roller coaster, e.g. | Fair attraction | Harass | Hitchhike | Astronaut Sally

RILE | Tick off | Stir up | Irritate | Nettle | Vex

RIOT | Knee-slapper | Barrel of laughs | Scream | Laughfest | Sidesplitter

RISE | Get up | Go up | Greet the day | Ascend | Respond to reveille

RITA | Comic Rudner | Singer Coolidge | Meter maid of song | Actress Moreno | Actress Hayworth

ROAR | Crowd sound | Surf sound | Laugh loudly | Bellow | Din

ROLE | Part to play | Part | Function | Stage part | Auditioner's goal

ROSA | Civil rights activist Parks | Santa ___ | Parks on a bus | Painter Bonheur | Soprano Ponselle

ROSE | Wine choice | Kennedy matriarch | Got up | "Titanic" heroine | American Beauty, e.g.

RTES | Hwys. | AAA suggestions | Numbered rds. | 66 and others (abbr.) | U.S. 1 and others

SAGA | Long story | Heroic tale | Long tale | Epic tale | Major account

SALE | Garage event | Shopper stopper | Mall event | Store sign | Red tag event

SALT | Shaker contents | Tar | Pretzel topper | Pepper partner | Preserve, in a way

SANE | All there | Compos mentis | Sensible | Lucid | Of sound mind

SARA | Poet Teasdale | Gilbert of "Roseanne" | FDR's mom | Franklin D.'s mother | 1986 #1 hit for Starship

SARI | Delhi wrap | Delhi dress | Rani's wrap | Hindu garment | Calcutta coverup

SASS | Back talk | Lip | Impudence | Talk back to | Cheek

SATE | Stuff | Fill up | Fill to the gills | Glut | Gorge

SCAM | Con game | Swindle | Sting | Ripoff | Fleece

SCAN | Read a bar code | Give the once-over | Glance over | CAT ___ | Capture electronically

SCAR | Lasting impression | "The Lion King" villain | Mark for life | Surgery souvenir | Kind of tissue

SCAT | "Shoo!" | "Out!" | "Beat it!" | Fitzgerald forte | "Vamoose!"

SCOT | Highlander | Dundee denizen | Nae sayer | Sean Connery, for one | Edinburgh native

SEAL | Navy commando | Circus barker | Aquatic mammal | Shut up | Close up

SEAT | Pants part | Spot in the Senate | Exchange membership | Chair | Usher's offering

SECT | Splinter group | Faction | Religious group | Religious offshoot | Denomination

SEED | Progeny | Germ | Tournament ranking | Ranking player | Plant-to-be

SEEN | Spotted | Caught in the act | Witnessed | Observed | Taken in

SEEP | Ooze | Trickle | Flow slowly | Percolate | Dribble

SEER | Visionary | Clairvoyant | Prophet | Fortuneteller | Merlin, e.g.

SEES | Goes out with | Dates | Notices | Gets the picture | Bishoprics

SEMI | Big rig | Highway hauler | 18-wheeler | Rig | Final Four game

SEND | Transmit | E-mail command | Thrill | Dispatch | Fax, say

SENT | E-mailed | Dispatched | Mailed | On its way | Shipped

SERA | Antitoxins | Vaccines | Hospital supplies | Blood fluids | Flu fighters

SERE | Withered | Parched | Dried out | Dry | Arid

SETH | Clockmaker Thomas | Genesis son | Adam's third | Brother of Cain and Abel | Father of Enos

SETS | Hardens | Tennis units | Complete collections | Match parts | Solidifies

SHEA | Queens stadium, once | Mets' home, once | Mets' stadium, once | Big Apple ballpark, once | Flushing stadium, once

SHOE | Brake part | It's about a foot | Loafer, for one | Oxford, e.g. | Monopoly token

SILO | Missile housing | Farm structure | Fodder holder | Cylindrical structure | Rural storage site

SIRE | Beget | Father | Stable parent | Kingly address | Royal address

SLAT | Blind part | Bed support | Mattress support | Louver part | Crate component

SLED | Winter toy | Musher's vehicle | Coaster | Downhill racer | Snow vehicle

SLOE | Gin flavoring | Blackthorn fruit | ___ gin fizz | Wild plum | Plumlike fruit

SLOT | Job opening | Pigeonhole | One-armed bandit | Token taker | Vegas machine

SMEE | Barrie baddie | "Peter Pan" pirate | Hook's mate | Captain Hook's cohort

SNAG | Hitch | Catch | Fly in the ointment | Unforeseen obstacle | Glitch

SNAP | Lose it | Ginger cookie | Piece of cake | Breeze | Rice Krispies sound

**SNIP** | Barbershop sound | Salon sound | Scissors sound | Impertinent one | Quick cut

**SNIT** | Huff | Tizzy | Agitated state | Fit of pique | Peeved mood

**SOAR** | Fly high | Skyrocket | Fly like an eagle | Take off | Get really high

**SODA** | Pop | Carbonated drink | Soft drink | Scotch partner | Fizzy drink

**SOHO** | London district | TriBeCa neighbor | Big Apple neighborhood | Manhattan neighborhood | Slice of the Big Apple

**SOLE** | Exclusive | Unique | Only | Shoe bottom | Pump part

**SOLO** | Go it alone | Recital piece | Unaccompanied | Han of "Star Wars" | Fly alone

**SORE** | Ticked off | Achy | Like some losers | Miffed | Teed off

**SOSO** | Mediocre | Fair | Middling | Average | Passable

**SPAN** | Bridge | Reach across | Time period | Go over | Stretch across

**SPAR** | Practice boxing | Practice in the ring | Practice pugilism | Rigging support | Go a few rounds

**SPAS** | Health resorts | Restful resorts | Watering holes | Pampering places | Mineral springs

**SPAT** | Tiff | Petty quarrel | Squabble | Falling-out | Minor argument

**SPED** | Risked a ticket | Hightailed it | Tore | Made tracks | Exceeded the limit

**SPOT** | Notice | Predicament | Dick and Jane's dog | Catch sight of | Smudge

**SSTS** | Concordes | Fast fliers | Sleek jets | Barrier breakers | Fast fleet

**STAB** | Wild guess | Attempt | Run through | Try | Pierce

**STAG** | Dateless | For men only | Male deer | Party animal? | Doe's mate

**STAN** | Getz of jazz | Kenton of jazz | Cartoonist Drake | Ollie's partner | Spider-Man creator Lee

**STAR** | Headliner | Lead | Top banana | Rating unit | Asterisk

**STAT** | RBI, e.g. | Sports figure | ER order | "Now!" | Ballpark figure

**STAY** | Command to Fido | Collar insert | Hang around | Remain | Corset part

**STEM** | Check | Goblet part | Hold back | Wineglass part | Plant part

**STEN** | British gun | Anna of "Nana" | British submachine gun | British weapon | WWII gun

**STEP** | Put one's foot down | Part of a process | Plan part | Short distance | Rung

**STET** | Editor's mark | Proofreader's mark | [ignore this deletion] | Manuscript marking | Leave in, to an editor

**STEW** | Fret | Worry | Bouillabaisse, e.g. | Do a slow burn | Hobo fare

**STIR** | Swizzle | Hoosegow | Commotion | Recipe direction | To-do

**STOP** | Station | Organ knob | Where to get off | Knock off | Cease

**STOW** | Put away | Pack away | Put in the hold | Stash away | Put belowdecks

**TACO** | Snack in a shell | Sonora snack | Crunchy munchie | ___ Bell | Meal in a shell

**TALC** | Soft mineral | Bath powder | Baby powder | After-bath application | Soft rock

**TALE** | Story | Narrative | Yarn | Account | Whopper

**TARA** | Skater Lipinski | Scarlett's home | Mitchell mansion | "Gone With the Wind" plantation | The O'Hara place

**TATA** | "Cheerio!" | "Later" | "Toodle-oo" | "So long!" | "Ciao"

**TAXI** | Curbside call | Hack | Metered vehicle | Prepare to take off | Kind of stand

**TBAR** | Ski lift | Skier's lift | Skier's transport | Lift up a mountain | Skier's aid

TEAR | Eye drop | Rip | Spree | Shed item | Salty drop

TEEN | Adolescent | High schooler | Prom attendee | Many a new driver | Adult-to-be

TEES | Driving aids | Golf gadgets | Place-kickers' props | Golf props | Golf pegs

TENT | Mobile home | Bivouac shelter | Caterpillar construction | Jamboree sight | Camper's shelter

TERI | Actress Garr | Actress Hatcher | Garr of "Mr. Mom" | Hatcher of "Lois & Clark" | Garr of "Tootsie"

TESS | Hardy heroine | Mrs. Dick Tracy | Actress Harper | Tracy's Trueheart | "___ of the D'Urbervilles"

TEST | Try out | Dry run | Exam | Examination | Midterm, e.g.

TETE | Head: Fr. | Henri's head | Nantes noggin | French bean | French noodle?

TIER | Level | Stadium level | Wedding cake feature | Bleacher feature | Layer

TINA | Singer Turner | Ike's ex | Rocker Turner | One of the Sinatras | She played Ginger on "Gilligan's Island"

TIRE | Poop out | Flag | Lose energy | Grow weary | Trunk item

TONE | Muscle quality | Sound quality | Pitch | Vocal quality | Muscular fitness

TONI | Singer Braxton | Singer Tennille | Author Morrison | Nobelist Morrison

TRAP | Golf hazard | Mouth, slangily | Snare | Pitfall | Lint collector

TREE | Leaves home? | Corner | Sloth's home | Genealogy chart | Elder or alder

TRIO | Small combo | Threesome | Peter, Paul, and Mary, e.g. | The Supremes, e.g. | The Andrews Sisters, e.g.

TROT | Jog | Bring (out) | Race pace | Horse's gait | Harness race

TRUE | Factual | Loyal | In alignment | So | Faithful

TSAR | Autocrat | Onetime Russian ruler | Despot | Winter Palace resident | Romanov ruler

UCLA | Bruins' sch. | Pac-10 team | Bruins' home | Arthur Ashe's alma mater | The Bruins

ULNA | Forearm bone | Arm bone | Radius neighbor | Humerus neighbor | Radius partner

UNDO | Reverse | Take apart | Bring to ruin | Nullify | Word processing command

UNIT | Troop group | Condo division | Part of BTU | Hand or foot | Military group

UNTO | Golden rule word | Biblical preposition | Golden rule preposition | "Do ___ others ..." | Passé preposition

UPON | Atop | Abreast of | Familiar with | "___ my word!" | Versed in

URAL | Russian river | Russia's ___ Mountains | River to the Caspian | Caspian Sea feeder | Orsk's river

URGE | Impulse | Press | Hankering | Egg on | Push

URIS | "Exodus" author | "Topaz" author | "Mila 18" author | "Trinity" author | "QB VII" author

URSA | ___ Major | Celestial bear | ___ Minor | Sky bear | Bear in the air

USED | Secondhand | Not new | Took advantage of | Not mint | Previously owned

USER | Mouse manipulator | Software buyer | Computer owner | Consumer | Manipulative one

USES | Applications | Takes advantage of | Puts to work | Employs | Exploits

USSR | Former U.N. member | Red letters? | Cold war inits. | Former geopolitical initials | Soyuz launcher

UTAH | Four Corners state | The Beehive State | Six-sided state | Bryce Canyon locale | Jazz home

UTES | Western Indians | Beehive State natives | Western tribe | Colorado natives | Versatile vehicles

YALE | New Haven school | Harvard rival | Brown rival | Bush's alma mater | Ivy League school

YEAR | Once around the sun | Four quarters | Four seasons | Wine bottle datum | Fiscal period

YENS | Hankerings | Desires | Cravings | Itches | Longings

YSER | North Sea feeder | River of Flanders | Belgian river | River to the North Sea | River through Belgium

AARON | Composer Copland | Brother of Moses | Hammerin' Hank | Biblical brother | High priest in Exodus

ABASE | Humiliate | Humble | Belittle | Put down | Degrade

ABATE | Lessen | Let up | Die down | Diminish | Taper off

ABETS | Encourages | Helps a hood | Helps in wrongdoing | Supports, in a way | Helps a felon

ABODE | Dwelling | Where you live | Home | Domicile | Quarters

ABOUT | More or less | Circa | Give or take | Approximately | Close to

ACHES | Flu symptoms | Partner of pains | Feels sore | Sore spots | Throbs

ACHOO | Blessing preceder | Allergy season sound | Allergic reaction | Cold response?

ACORN | Kind of squash | Squirrel snack | Oak fruit | Something squirreled away

ACRES | Lots of lots | Farm units | Field units | Land measures | "Green ___"

ACTED | Took steps | Performed | Played a role | Didn't just sit there | Made a scene?

ACTOR | Cast member | Thespian | Stage presence? | Role player | Penn or Pitt

ACUTE | Sharp | Like some French accents | Less than 90 degrees | Penetrating | Critical

ADAGE | Saw | Proverb | Old saying | Words of wisdom | Maxim

ADAPT | Go with the flow | Modify | Show flexibility | Get used (to) | Customize

ADELE | Designer Simpson | Fred Astaire's sister | "Die Fledermaus" maid | One of the Astaires

ADEPT | Skilled | Expert | Masterful | Proficient | Crack

ADIEU | Parting word | French farewell | Gallic goodbye | It may be bid | Toulouse toodle-oo

ADIOS | Parting word | "Later!" | "So long" | "See ya" | Felipe's farewell

ADLAI | Two-time loser to Dwight | Statesman Stevenson | Ike's two-time opponent

ADLIB | Wing it | Improvise | Off-the-cuff | Stray from the script | Unrehearsed

ADMIT | Let in | Fess up | Word on a ticket | Acknowledge | Confess

ADOBE | Sun-dried brick | Pueblo material | Hacienda brick | Building block | Pueblo home

ADORE | Worship | Idolize | Like a lot | Think the world of | Love to pieces

ADORN | Decorate | Gussy up | Deck out | Festoon | Embellish

AERIE | Eagle's nest | High home | Lofty nest | Cliff hanger? | Mountain home

AESOP | Man of morals | Greek fabulist | "Belling the Cat" author | Fabulous fellow?

AETNA | Prudential rival | MetLife competitor | Big name in insurance | Allstate rival | State Farm rival

AFIRE | Blazing | In flames | Burning | Flaming | Lit

AFTER | Following | In pursuit of | Subsequently | Gunning for | In search of

AGAIN | Once more | Over | From the top | Another time | "Not ___!"

AGAPE | Slack-jawed | Wide open | Open-mouthed | In awe | Yawning

AGATE | Playing marble | Steelie alternative | Small type | Striped chalcedony | Quartz variety

AGENT | Representative | Ten-percenter | Operative | 007, for one | Cut taker

AGILE | Nimble | Like a gymnast | Light on one's feet | Quick | Spry

AGNES | Moorehead of "Bewitched" | Choreographer de Mille | Infamous 1972 hurricane | "___ of God"

AGORA | Greek marketplace | Ancient marketplace | Prefix with phobia | Plato's plaza

AGREE | See eye to eye | Concur | Come to terms | Match | Jibe

AHEAD | Leading | In front | In the lead | Winning | In the offing

AIMEE | Actress Anouk | Evangelist McPherson | Pop singer Mann | Name meaning "beloved"

AISLE | Bridal path | Usher's beat | Window alternative | Supermarket section | Place to roll?

ALAMO | Crockett's last stand | San Antonio shrine | Memorable mission | Bowie's last stand | Battle site of 1836

ALARM | Frighten | Burglar deterrent | Sleep spoiler | Auto option | Waker-upper

ALERT | On the ball | On one's toes | Argus-eyed | Vigilant | On the qui vive

ALEUT | Native Alaskan | Certain Alaskan | Alaskan islander | Attu resident | Sealskin wearer, maybe

ALGAE | Seaweed | Aquarium problem | Aquatic organisms | Pool problem | Plankton components

ALIAS | Assumed name | Pseudonym | Rap sheet info | Nom de plume | Jennifer Garner TV series

ALIBI | Suspect's story | Out | Cover story? | Excuse | It may be airtight

ALICE | Dennis the Menace's mother | Mrs. Kramden | Wonderland girl | "The Color Purple" author Walker | "The Brady Bunch" housekeeper

ALIEN | Little green man | Out of this world | Strange | Extraterrestrial | Foreigner

ALINE | Dress style | Skirt style | Roomy dress | Dress with a flare | Drop ___ (write)

ALIST | Select group | Elite group | Most-wanted invitees | Society roster | Desirable guests

ALIVE | Still in the game | Still in contention | Full of energy | Breathing | Kicking partner

ALLAH | God of the Koran | God of Islam | Koran Creator | Shiite's deity | Muslim's Almighty

ALLEN | Kind of wrench | ___ wrench | "Annie Hall" director | Sportscaster Mel | "Home Improvement" star

ALLOT | Distribute | Parcel out | Dole out | Apportion | Set apart

ALOES | Healing plants | Medicinal plants | Fugard's "A Lesson From ___" | Soothing plants | Lily plants

ALOHA | Hilo hello | Island greeting | Wahine's welcome | Waikiki welcome | Hawaiian hello

ALONE | Unaccompanied | Solo | Without company | Stag | Single-handedly

ALOUD | Vocally | For all to hear | One way to read | Audibly | Not sotto voce

ALTAR | Rite site | Hitching post? | Wedding site | Union station? | It may have a cross to bear

ALTER | Change | Take in or let out | Modify | Make fit | Rehem, perhaps

AMANA | Appliance maker | Microwave maker | Range maker | Maytag rival | Whirlpool competitor

AMASS | Pile up | Accumulate | Stockpile | Gather together | Collect

AMATI | Valuable violin | Stradivari's teacher | Fine fiddle | Cremona craftsman

AMAZE | Dumbfound | Astound | Floor | Bowl over | Flabbergast

AMEND | Make changes to | Make better | Put right | Change for the better | Modify

AMINO | Kind of acid | ___ acid | Essential acid | Acid in proteins

AMISS | Out of whack | Not quite right | Wrong | Faulty | Out of kilter

AMORE | Love, Italian-style | Love, to Luigi | Dean Martin's "That's ___" | Love, in Lombardy | Dean Martin song subject

AMOUR | Love affair | Love, in Lille | Love, in Lourdes | Affaire de coeur | Parisian passion

AMUSE | Entertain | Tickle | Divert | Beguile | Cause to laugh

ANAIS | Diarist Nin | Novelist Nin | First name in diaries | "Henry & June" character

ANDES | Much of Chile | Aconcagua's range | Lake Titicaca locale | Peruvian peaks | Chilean range

ANDRE | Conductor Previn | Pianist Watts | Netman Agassi | Brooke's ex

ANEAR | Keep ___ to the ground | Lend ___ (listen) | Close by, once | Words after bend or lend

ANGER | Steam up | Tee off | Rile up | A deadly sin | Inflame

ANGST | Feeling of dread | Uneasy feeling | Apprehension | Existential woe | Dread

ANISE | Ouzo flavoring | Liqueur flavoring | Licorice flavoring | Pernod flavoring | Cordial flavoring

ANITA | Singer Baker | Actress Ekberg | Writer Loos | Santa ___ | Singer O'Day

ANNIE | Sandy's owner | Photographer Leibovitz | "Tomorrow" musical | Sharpshooter Oakley | Daddy Warbucks's kid

ANODE | Battery terminal | Positive pole | Battery post | Cathode's counterpart | + end

ANTES | Starts the pot | Pays to play | Stud stakes | Pot starters | Chips in

ANTIC | Caper | Ludicrous | Shenanigan | Prank | Bit of high jinks

AORTA | Main artery | Blood line | It comes from the heart | Main line | Major artery

APACE | Swiftly | Quickly | Lickety-split | Without delay | On the double

APART | In pieces | Separated | To pieces | Here and there? | In reserve

APRIL | Patriots' Day month | Shower time | 30-day month | March follower | Earth Day month

APSES | Church areas | Church recesses | Basilica parts | Vaulted recesses

ARABS | Spirited horses | Burnoose wearers | Most Jordanians | Some OPEC ministers | Iraqis and Qataris

AREAS | Regions | Zones | Fields | Neighborhoods | Vicinities

ARENA | Where the action is | Fight site | Sports venue | Sports stadium | Sports center

ARENT | Don't exist | "___ we all?" | Ain't right? | "You ___ serious?" | "You ___ kidding!"

ARETE | Mountain ridge | Rugged ridge | Glacial ridge | Sharp ridge | Craggy ridge

ARIAS | Puccini pieces | La Scala solos | Met highlights | Opera solos | Opera songs

ARIEL | The Little Mermaid | Sharon of Israel | Shakespearean sprite | Disney mermaid | Historian Durant

ARIES | Sign of spring | Old Dodge | First sign | Zodiac sign | Astrological ram

ARISE | Get up | Greet the day | Come up | Crop up | Respond to reveille

ARLEN | Senator Specter | "Over the Rainbow" composer Harold | "Stormy Weather" composer | "I Love a Parade" composer | "One for My Baby" composer

ARLES | City on the Rhone | Van Gogh locale | Where Van Gogh painted "Sunflowers" | "Sunflowers" setting | Burgundy by another name

ARMOR | Tanks and such | Strong suit | Knight wear | Knight's protection | Hard wear?

ARNIE | "L.A. Law" lawyer | Golfer with an "army" | Golfer Palmer, informally | 1970s sitcom | PGA nickname

AROAR | Bellowing | Clamorous | Loud, as a crowd | Cheering | Plenty loud

AROMA | Bouquet | Scent | Fragrance | Bakery enticement | Coffee allure

AROSE | Came up | Got up | Cropped up | Stood | Originated

ARSON | Fiery crime | Burning desire? | Fiery felony | Bad lighting? | Torch job

ARTIE | Bandleader Shaw | Clarinetist Shaw | Shaw of swing | Ex of Ava and Lana | First name in swing

ARUBA | Island off Venezuela | Curaçao neighbor | Island near Curaçao | Caribbean resort island | Its capital is Oranjestad

ASCAP | Songwriters' org. | Tin Pan Alley org. | BMI rival | Music creators' org. | Record label abbr.

ASCOT | Fancy tie | Broad necktie | Wide tie | Broad tie | Knotted scarf

ASHEN | Pale | Wan | Gray | Whitish | Ghostly

ASHES | Fireplace residue | Grate stuff | "Angela's ___" | Hibachi residue | Fire proof

ASIAN | Kind of flu | ___ flu | Like most Turks | One of 3.5 billion | Thai, for one

ASIDE | In reserve | Out of the way | Stage whisper | Comment to the audience | Parenthetical comment

ASKED | Invited | Popped the question | Inquired | Made a request | Set, as a price

ASNER | Grant portrayer | "Lou Grant" star | Seven-time Emmy winner | Moore's TV boss | "Roots" Emmy winner

ASONE | In unison | Together | In concert | United | Unanimously

ASPEN | Colorado resort | Rockies resort | Forest quaker | City on the Roaring Fork River | Quaking tree

ASSES | Beasts of burden | Fools | Dolts | Ninnies | Jerks

ASSET | Plus | Good thing | It's a good thing | Selling point | Valuable quality

ASTER | Fall flower | Fall bloomer | Autumn bloomer | Michaelmas daisy | Late bloomer

ASTIR | Up and about | Moving | Moving about | On the move | Out of bed

ASTOR | Fur tycoon | Furrier John Jacob | Mary of "The Maltese Falcon" | New York's ___ Place | Pacific Fur Company founder

ASTRO | Elroy Jetson's dog | Houston player | Houston pro | George Jetson's dog | Houston ballplayer

ASYET | So far | To date | Thus far | Up to now | To this point

ATALL | In any way | To any extent | Whatsoever | In the least | To any degree

ATARI | Video game pioneer | Video game name | Pong maker | Pong producer | Arcade name

ATBAT | Up | Facing the pitcher | In the box | Ready to swing | Trip to the plate

ATEAM | First-stringers | Special forces unit | Elite group | Mr. T's group | Varsity starters

ATEIN | Had a home-cooked meal | Dined at home | Enjoyed home cooking | Had a TV dinner | Had dinner at home

ATILT | Listing | Leaning | Lopsided | Like the Tower of Pisa | Not quite erect

ATLAS | World book | Book of maps | Country album? | Book with legends | Bodybuilder Charles

ATOLL | Bikini, for one | Coral island | Ring-shaped reef | Lagoon surrounder | Wake Island, e.g.

ATONE | Make amends | Make up (for) | Do penance | Observe Yom Kippur | Expiate

ATRIA | Skylit lobbies | Heart chambers | Skylit courts | Open courtyards | Places in the heart

ATSEA | Perplexed | Befuddled | Bewildered | Confused | Lost

ATTAR | Fragrant oil | Rose oil | Essence of roses | Petal product | Rose extract

ATTIC | Room at the top | Web site? | Storage area | Loft | Cobwebby area

AVAIL | Be of use | Profit | Benefit | To no ___ (useless) | Help

AVERT | Ward off | Turn away | Turn aside | Prevent | Head off

AVILA | St. Teresa's birthplace | Walled city near Madrid | St. Teresa's town | City near Madrid

AWAIT | Expect | Anticipate | Look forward to | Look for | Hang around for

AWARE | In the know | Cognizant | Conscious | Mindful | Informed

BALSA | Model wood | Light wood | Model material | Raft material | Model airplane wood

CANOE | Lake craft | Birchbark | Indian craft | Tippy transport | Lake rental

CARAT | Jeweler's unit | Jeweler's weight | Gem weight | 200 milligrams | Diamond weight

CEASE | Discontinue | Stop | Cut out | Put a stop to | Come to a halt

DANTE | "The Divine Comedy" poet | "La vita nuova" poet | "The Inferno" author

DEEDS | Monopoly stack | Exploits | Owners' papers | 1936 Cooper role | Title documents

DEERE | Plow pioneer | Tractor maker | Tractor name | Caterpillar competitor | Big name in farm equipment

DELTA | "Animal House" house | Continental competitor | Atlanta-based airline | Mouth of the Mississippi | Triangular formation

DENSE | Thickheaded | Tightly packed | Thick | Slow-witted | Slow on the uptake

DIANE | Steak ___ | Photographer Arbus | Sawyer of TV news | Newswoman Sawyer | "Cheers" role

DRESS | Attire | Code subject | Slip cover? | Getup | Toggery

EAGER | Raring to go | Gung-ho | Champing at the bit | Avid | Hot to trot

EAGLE | Colonel's insignia | Birdie beater | Top scout | Scout rank | Quarter back?

EARTH | Soil | Third rock from the sun | Third of eight | Our planet | You're on it

EASED | Let up | Alleviated | Slackened | Made bearable | Lightened

EASEL | Studio stand | Stand for a sitting | Art supporter | Stand for a portrait | Artist's stand

EASES | Alleviates | Lets up | Simplifies | Relieves | Lightens

EATAT | Annoy | Bother | Worry | Really bother | Bother terribly

EATEN | Consumed | Gobbled up | Put away | Downed | Worn away

EBERT | "I Hated, Hated, Hated This Movie" author | Critic Roger | Reviewer Roger | Movie critic Roger | Thumb-raising critic

ECLAT | Brilliance | Showy display | Razzle-dazzle | Acclaim | Brilliant success

ECOLE | French school | Élève's place | Sorbonne, e.g. | Jules's school | Where to study mathématiques

EDDIE | "Frasier" dog | Jockey Arcaro | Actor Albert | Wally Cleaver's pal | Murphy of "The Nutty Professor"

EDENS | Paradises | Perfect places | Idyllic spots | Utopias | Shangri-las

EDGES | Borders | Boundaries | Noses (out) | Outer limits | Rims

EDITS | Blue-pencils | Prepares for publication | Checks for typos | Rewrites | Cuts and pastes

EDSEL | '50s Ford | Car bomb? | Henry Ford's son | Ford flop | Detroit dud

EERIE | Spooky | Spine-tingling | Weird | Creepy | Chilling

EGADS | "Zounds!" | "Holy cow!" | Old oath | "Yikes!" | "Good grief!"

EGRET | White wader | Wading bird | Everglades wader | Marsh bird | Plume source

EIDER | Down source | Duck down | Where to get down | Downy duck | Sea duck

EIEIO | Children's song refrain | "Old MacDonald" refrain | Kids' song refrain | Refrain from farming? | Letters for Old MacDonald

ELAND | African antelope | Spiral-horned antelope | Twisty-horned antelope | Serengeti grazer | Cousin of a gazelle

ELATE | Tickle pink | Make jubilant | Make happy | Fill with joy | Overjoy

ELCID | Spanish hero | 1961 Heston role | Castilian hero | Legendary Spaniard

ELDER | Church official | Church leader | Senior | Like some statesmen | Born first

ELECT | Vote in | Choose | Put in office | Vote into office | Chosen ones

ELENA | Actress Verdugo | Skater Valova | "Maria ___" (1940s song) | Daughter of Juan Carlos I | "Uncle Vanya" role

ELIAS | Inventor Howe | Walt Disney's middle name | Sewing machine inventor Howe | 1846 patentee Howe | 1981 Literature Nobelist Canetti

ELIDE | Omit in pronunciation | Slur over | Skip over | Skip | Say "nothin'," say

ELIHU | Philanthropist Yale | Nobelist Root | Statesman Root | Mr. Yale | Friend of Job

ELIOT | Prufrock's creator | "Middlemarch" author | "The Waste Land" poet | "Silas Marner" author | Untouchable Ness

ELITE | Upper crust | Cream of the crop | Crème de la crème | Top-drawer | Best of the best

ELLEN | Actress Burstyn | Comic DeGeneres | Actress Barkin | Barkin or Burstyn | Columnist Goodman

ELLIS | Designer Perry | New York island | ___ Island (immigrants' spot) | Island in New York Bay | Jazz pianist Marsalis

ELMER | Playwright Rice | Bugs bugs him | Toon Fudd | Borden bull | "___ Gantry"

ELOPE | Take the honey and run | Split to unite | Avoid a big wedding | Bypass the altar | Bond on the run

ELSIE | Beast of Borden | Pitcher of milk? | Borden bovine | Borden's cow | Corporate cow | Milk pitcher?

ELTON | Rocker John | Singer John | John of song | Pop's John | John of England

ELUDE | Give the slip to | Get away from | Duck | Shake off | Dodge

EMAIL | Cyberspace letters | AOL delivery | PC-to-PC communication | PC messages | AOL offering

EMCEE | Roast host | Host | Mike holder | TV host | Banquet host

EMEND | Edit | Correct | Make corrections to | Touch up | Fix, as text

EMERY | Manicurist's board | Board material | Nail file material | Filer | Abrasive stuff

EMILE | Author Zola | Novelist Zola | Rousseau novel | "South Pacific" hero | Boxer Griffith

EMOTE | Ham it up | Chew the scenery | Overact | Play to the balcony | Get melodramatic

ENACT | Make into law | Pass | Put on the books | Put into law | Establish as law

ENDED | Over | Wound up | Broke off | Wrapped up | Finished

ENEMY | Foe | Adversary | Other side | "Them" | Opposing force

ENERO | Año starter | Diciembre follower | January, in Juárez | Calendario opener | Juan's January

ENLAI | Zhou ___ | China's Zhou ___ | Chou ___ | China's Chou | Big name in Chinese history

ENOLA | ___ Gay | "___ Gay" (WWII plane) | Name on a bomber

ENROL | Sign up | Register | Join | Matriculate | Join up

ENSUE | Follow | Come after | Come next | Result | Succeed

ENTER | Go in | Stage direction | Computer key | Maze word | Shift neighbor

ENTRE | ___ nous | ___ nous (confidentially) | Between: Fr. | ___ nous (between ourselves)

ENTRY | Door | Contest submission | Diary passage, e.g. | Access | Log item

EPEES | Fencing swords | Sporting blades | Olympic weapons | Blunted blades | Foil relatives

EPSOM | ___ salts | English Derby site | Derby town | Derby site

ERASE | Obliterate | Rub out | Wipe clean | Wipe out | Clear the board

ERATO | Poetry Muse | Poetic Muse | Sister of Clio | Poet's Muse | Sister of Calliope

ERECT | Put up | Build | Upright | Construct | At attention

ERICA | Author Jong | Writer Jong | "Fear of Flying" author Jong | Susan's "All My Children" role | Susan Lucci role

ERNIE | Bert's buddy | Banks of Chicago | Journalist Pyle | Comic Kovacs | Els with tees

ERNST | Dadaist Max | Surrealist Max | Director Lubitsch | Artist Max | Physicist Mach

ERODE | Wear away | Eat away at | Chip away at | Wear down | Eat into

ERRED | Blew it | Goofed | Messed up | Miscalculated | Made a boo-boo

ERROL | Swashbuckler Flynn | Swashbuckling Flynn | Flynn of film | Actor Flynn | Flamboyant Flynn

ERROR | Miscue | Diamond flaw? | Overthrow, e.g. | Flub | Baseball blunder

ESSAY | Test type | School assignment | Lamb product | Attempt | Opinion piece

ESSEN | Ruhr Valley city | Ruhr city | German industrial city | Krupp works city | German steel city

ESSES | Double curves | Snaky shapes | Twisty turns | Tricky curves | Pluralizers

ESSEX | English county | Colchester's county | Devereux's earldom | Vintage auto | Elizabeth's favorite

ESTEE | Cosmetician Lauder | First name in cosmetics | Lauder of cosmetics | Helena rival | Makeup name

ESTER | Fragrant compound | Aromatic compound | Banana oil, for one | Organic compound | Fruity-smelling compound

ESTES | ___ Park, Colorado | Senator Kefauver | Adlai's running mate

ETHAN | Actor Hawke | Fictional Frome | Patriot Allen | Revolutionary Allen | Frome of fiction

ETHEL | Lucy's landlady | Lucy's pal | One of the Barrymores | Singer Merman | A Barrymore

ETHER | Old anesthetic | Old number? | It'll knock you out | Heavens | Clear sky

ETHIC | Code of conduct | Moral principle | Body of values | Set of principles | Work ___

ETHOS | Community spirit | Cultural values | Spirit of a people | Group character | Cultural character

ETUDE | Practice piece | Chopin piece | Piano piece | Chopin composition | Liszt piece

EVADE | Duck | Dodge | Get around | Sidestep | Give the slip to

EVENT | Happening | Occurrence | Episode | It happens | It may be blessed

EVERT | Navratilova rival | Turn outward | Three-time Wimbledon champ | Six-time U.S. Open champ | Goolagong rival

EVITA | Madonna role | Lloyd Webber musical | 1980 Tony winner | Musical set in Argentina | "Don't Cry for Me, Argentina" musical

EWERS | Water pitchers | Pitchers | Washstand accessories | Still-life subjects | Wide-spouted pitchers

EXILE | Banish | Cast out | Napoleon, notably | Send to Siberia | Force to leave

EXTRA | Special edition | Newsboy's cry | Crowd-scene character | Bonus | Cavalryman in an oater, e.g.

GEESE | V-formation fliers | Honkers | Gaggle members | Ninnies | Skein formers

GESTE | Beau ___ | Exploit | Tale of derring-do | Romance in verse

HANOI | Vietnam's capital | Asian capital | Capital on the Red River | Capital west of Haiphong | Le Duc Tho's capital

HESSE | "Steppenwolf" author | "Siddhartha" author | 1946 Literature Nobelist | Wiesbaden's state | Novelist Hermann

HORSE | Mount | Fool (around) | Centaur, in part | Neigh sayer | Chestnut, e.g.

IBSEN | "The Wild Duck" playwright | "Ghosts" playwright | "Peer Gynt" playwright | "A Doll's House" playwright

ICIER | More slippery | More aloof | Less friendly | More frosty | More frigid

IDAHO | Boise's state | The Gem State | Sun Valley setting | Spud source

IDEAL | Perfect | Utopian | Paragon | Just right | Model

IDEAS | Brainstorms | Inspirations | Think tank output | Bean sprouts? | "Don't get any funny ___!"

IDEST | That is: Latin | That is | In other words | Latin clarifier

IDIOM | Figure of speech | Dialect | Manner of speaking | Distinct style | Language peculiarity

IDIOT | Dunderhead | Dimwit | Bonehead | Doofus | Blockhead

ILIAD | Troy story | Homeric epic | Trojan War epic | Old war story | War story

IMAGE | Spin doctor's concern | Publicist's concern | Public persona | Candidate's concern | Reflection

INANE | Silly | Pointless | Cockamamie | Nonsensical | Senseless

INDIA | Kind of ink | "Gunga Din" setting | "Kim" setting | Where the Ganges flows | Land of a billion

INERT | Not moving | Like krypton | Lifeless | Motionless | Like some gases

INLET | Cove | Small bay | Estuary | Place to moor | Arm of the sea

INNER | Private | Secret | Word with city or circle | Kind of circle | Kind of tube

INSET | Map within a map | Atlas feature | Map closeup | Map feature

INTER | Bury | Lay to rest | Part of ICBM | Prefix with face or faith | ___ alia

INTRO | Opening | Emcee's task | Opening bars | Emcee's opening | Prelim

INUSE | Occupied | Not available | Busy | Currently employed | Taken

IONIA | Ancient Greek colony | Ancient Greek region | Asia Minor region | Aegean region

IRANI | Farsi speaker | Teheran native | Shiraz native | Tabriz resident | Qom resident

IRATE | Fit to be tied | Furious | Steamed | Hopping mad | Ticked off

IRENE | Actress Dunne | Goodnight girl of song | Singer Cara | Castle of dance | Goddess of peace

IRISH | March marchers | Dander | Kind of coffee | Corkers? | From Killarney

IRONS | Shackles | Presses | Wrinkle removers | "Reversal of Fortune" star | Decreases?

IRONY | O. Henry specialty | Literary device | Wry twist | Swift forte

ISAAC | Stern with a bow | Violinist Stern | Designer Mizrahi | Writer Asimov | Son of Sarah

ISLAM | Koran religion | Mideast belief | Its emblem is the crescent | Mideast religion | Muhammad's faith

ISLES | Cruise stopovers | British ___ | Lands in water | Wight and Man | Vacation spots

ISLET | Key | Spot in the ocean | Dot in the ocean | Cay | ___ of Langerhans

ISSUE | Magazine copy | Any Time | Offspring | Progeny | Debate topic

ITALY | Europe's "boot" | Pisa place | San Marino surrounder | Boot-shaped country | New York's Little ___

ITEMS | List components | Agenda entries | Particulars | News bits

KOREA | Divided land | Asian peninsula | Divided country | "M*A*S*H" setting | Where Seoul is

LAINE | Singer Frankie | "Mule Train" singer | Frankie or Cleo | Singer Cleo

LASER | Kind of printer | Kind of surgery | Modern surgical tool | CD player part | Light in a light show

LASSO | Rodeo rope | Dogie catcher | Will Rogers prop | Cow catcher | Cowboy's rope

LAURA | Designer Ashley | Mrs. Bush | Hillary's successor | Actress San Giacomo | Actress Dern

LEASE | Rental agreement | Buy alternative | Charter | Paper for a pad | Rent

LEAST | Minimal | Minimum | Smallest | Most trifling | Slightest

LEAVE | Bequeath | Split | Permission | Exit | Go away

LEERS | Sly looks | Glances from Groucho | Sly glances | Dirty looks | Lascivious looks

LEONE | Sierra ___ | Spaghetti western director Sergio | Freetown currency unit

LEVEE | River embankment | Dike | Flood barrier | Embankment | It may get high marks

LILAC | Pale purple | Purple shade | Whitman's dooryard bloomer | Sachet scent | Light purple

LINEN | Flaxen fabric | Tablecloth material | Flax fabric | Sheets | Flax product

LLAMA | Wool source | Andean animal | Beast of burden | Guanaco relative

LOOSE | On the lam | Off the leash | Not tight | Baggy | Relaxed

MAINE | Down East | Pine Tree State | Acadia National Park locale | Ship to remember

MATTE | Photo finish | Dull finish | Finish option | Not glossy | Lusterless finish

MELEE | Free-for-all | Donnybrook | Fracas | Confused conflict | Rumble

MENSA | Smart set | Bright bunch | Brainy bunch | Collection of brains | High-IQ group

MIAMI | Dolphins' home | Orange Bowl site | Biscayne Bay city | Home of the Heat | Hurricane home

NAIVE | Unsophisticated | Gullible | Easily duped | Green | Unworldly

NAOMI | Supermodel Campbell | One of the Judds | Wynonna's mom | Ruth's mother-in-law | Ashley Judd's mom

NASAL | Twangy | Like Fran Drescher's voice | Kind of spray | Like Willie Nelson's voice | Stuffy-sounding

NEARS | Approaches | Closes in on | Comes close | Gets closer to | Draws nigh

NEATO | "Cool!" | "Peachy keen!" | "Keen!" | "Peachy!" | "Rad!"

NEEDS | Has to have | Requirements | Cries out for | Can't do without | Requires

NEEDY | Destitute | Hard up | Indigent | Strapped | Impoverished

NEHRU | India's first prime minister | India's first P.M. | Kind of jacket | Indira Gandhi's father | '60s jacket style

NEPAL | Himalayan kingdom | High land | Sherpa's home | Katmandu's land | Tibet neighbor

NESTS | Bird houses | Settles in | Egg holders | Snug retreats | Tree houses

NIECE | Dorothy, to Em | Reunion attendee | Bridget Fonda, to Jane | Family girl | Eleanor, to Teddy

NOISE | Din | Racket | Library no-no | Static | Hubbub

NOLAN | Pitcher Ryan | Fireballer Ryan | Hall of Famer Ryan | Hurler Ryan | Actor Lloyd

NOLTE | "Cape Fear" actor | Nick of "Cape Fear" | "Lorenzo's Oil" star | Actor Nick | Nick of "The Prince of Tides"

NOONE | Nary a soul | Not a soul | Peter of Herman's Hermits | Who might be to blame | Everybody's opposite

NOOSE | Lasso loop | Choker | Hangman's knot | Gallows loop | Wild West justice

OASES | Refuges | Caravan stops | Desert havens | Wet spots | Desert refuges

OASIS | Desert stopover | Haven | Watering hole | Where to get a date? | Spot of relief

OATER | Horse opera | Western | Western film | Many a John Wayne flick | Mix movie

OBESE | More than plump | Like Santa Claus | Too big | Like Humpty Dumpty | Corpulent

OCALA | Florida city | City west of Daytona Beach | City south of Gainesville | Florida citrus center

OCEAN | Indian, for one | Continental divide? | Indian ___ | Sea | Where the buoys are

OCTET | Group of eight | Largish combo | Chamber group | Square dance group | Good-sized combo

ODETS | "Waiting for Lefty" playwright | "Golden Boy" playwright | Playwright Clifford | "Awake and Sing!" playwright

ODORS | Smells | Aromas | Scents | Kitchen emanations | Household spray targets

OHARA | "BUtterfield 8" author | Scarlett of Tara | Butler's love | "My Friend Flicka" author | "Pal Joey" author

OHARE | Chicago airport | Midway alternative | Midwest hub | Chicago hub | Windy City airport

OILER | Crude carrier | Ship of fuels | Edmonton skater | Persian Gulf ship | Edmonton hockey player

OLDIE | Blast from the past | It may be golden | Nostalgic tune | '50s tune | Any Platters platter

OLIVE | Martini garnish | Oil source | Antipasto morsel | Green shade | Popeye's gal

OLLIE | North of Virginia | Stan's pal | Stan's partner | Kukla's pal | Kukla's colleague

OMAHA | Nebraska city | D-Day beach | College World Series site | Cornhusker city | 1935 Triple Crown winner

OMANI | Muscat native | Muscat resident | Muscat citizen | Muscateer? | Yemeni's neighbor

OMEGA | Alpha's opposite | Last of a series | Greek letter | The end | Psi follower

OMENS | Portents | Harbingers | Signs | Straws in the wind | Signs to heed

ONAIR | Studio sign | Broadcasting | TV studio sign | Studio warning sign | Walking ___ (elated)

ONEAL | Ryan or Tatum | Center of Phoenix | Hoopster Shaq | Shaq of the NBA

ONEND | Upright | Continuously | Without letup | Without interruption | Ceaselessly

ONICE | In reserve | Chilling | Chilled | Standing by | In abeyance

ONION | Gibson garnish | Burger topper | Pizza topping | Hamburger topping | Pungent bulb

ONSET | Beginning | Start | Get-go | Commencement | Kickoff

ONTAP | Available | Ready to pour | Ready to draw | Ready | Ready to serve

OPART | Dizzying designs | Eyeball benders | Bridget Riley's genre | Victor Vasarely's genre | '60s poster genre

OPERA | Wagner work | Met offering | La Scala offering | "Carmen," for one | Wagnerian work

OPINE | State one's views | Suppose | Sound off | Think out loud | Suggest

ORATE | Speechify | Hold forth | Make a speech | Give a speech | Emulate Demosthenes

ORDER | Command | Law partner? | Direct | "Law & ___" | Mandate

OREOS | Sandwich cookies | Lunchbox treats | Two-tone treats | After-lunch sandwiches | Sweet sandwiches

ORION | Heavenly hunter | Hunter in the heavens | Betelgeuse's constellation | Rigel's constellation | Pursuer of the Pleiades

ORONO | Maine college town | Home of the Black Bears | Town near Bangor | Maine university town | University of Maine city

OSAGE | Missouri feeder | Missouri river | Inedible orange | River to the Missouri | Oklahoma tribe

OSAKA | Honshu port | Japanese city | Honshu city | Japanese port | 1970 World's Fair site

OSCAR | Film award | Felix's roommate | Grouchy Muppet | Academy Award | "The Odd Couple" role

OTHER | None of the above | Different | Additional | Survey choice | Not listed above

OTTER | Aquatic mammal | Furry swimmer | Playful swimmer | Playful animal | Riverbank romper

OZONE | Endangered layer | Atmospheric layer | Form of oxygen | Damaged layer | 22-mile-high layer

PANEL | Discussion group | Expert group | Committee | Plywood section | Cartoon part

PARIS | Helen's abductor | Where Ilsa met Rick | Louvre locale | Romeo's rival | City of Light

PASSE | Old hat | Out | Out of style | Outmoded | Out of fashion

PASTA | Noodles | Ziti, e.g. | Italian staple | Elbows, but not knees | Macaroni, e.g.

PASTE | Wallop | Cheap jewelry | Cut's partner | Stickum | Fake jewelry

PERIL | Danger | Jeopardy | Problem for Pauline | Risk | Hazard

PETER | Flying Pan | Jane's brother | A Fonda | Man of Principle | Prokofiev character

PIANO | Basie's instrument | Kind of bar | Softly | Eighty-eight | Schroeder's toy

POSSE | Sheriff's band | Oater group | Search party | Deputized group | Chasers

PSALM | Sacred song | Biblical song | Sacred poem | Davidic song | Old Testament poem

RADAR | Tracking device | "M*A*S*H" clerk | Kind of screen | Speeder spotter | Nehi drinker on TV

RAISE | Bring up | Bluffer's ploy | Union demand | Salary increase | Strikers' demand

RARER | Harder to find | Less common | Less cooked | Not as common | Closer to extinction

RASTA | Jamaican sectarian | Haile Selassie worshiper | Dreadlocked one | Dreadlocks wearer | Haile Selassie disciple

REACT | Flinch, say | Do a double take | Strike back | Respond (to) | Respond to a stimulus

RECAP | Summary | Sum up | News summary | Rundown | Postgame summary

REELS | Staggers | Film units | Lively dances | Reacts to a haymaker | Movie spools

REESE | Actress Witherspoon | Witherspoon of "Legally Blonde" | Della of "Touched by an Angel" | Singer Della | Piece maker

REEVE | Christopher of "Superman" | Actor Christopher | Chaucer pilgrim | "Rear Window" star, 1998 | "The Canterbury Tales" pilgrim

REHAB | Post-op program | Post-op time | Back-to-health process | Recovery clinic | "Get clean" program

RELIC | Memento | Museum piece | Thing of the past | Dig find | Keepsake

RENEE | Actress Zellweger | Taylor of "The Nanny" | Actress Taylor | Actress Adorée | Soprano Fleming

RENEW | Extend a subscription | Take up again | Extend, in a way | Continue a subscription | Extend, as a lease

RERAN | Showed again | Aired again | Played over | Showed over | Tried to keep one's seat

RESET | Bowling alley button | VCR button | Bowling lane button | Bowler's button | Furnace button

RESTS | Takes five | Breaks | Takes a breather | Takes it easy | Takes ten

RETRO | Fashionably old-fashioned | Back in | Nostalgic style | So out it's in | Fashionably nostalgic

RIATA | Lasso | Gaucho's rope | Dogie catcher | Rodeo rope | Calf catcher

RINSE | Washer cycle | Dentist's request | Dentist's directive | Salon service | Dishwasher cycle

ROAST | Friars Club event | Cook one's goose | Rake over the coals | Cook in the oven | Swelter

RODEO | Cowboy contest | Drive in Beverly Hills | Copland ballet | Wild West show | Where the big bucks are?

ROMEO | Ladies' man | Juliet's beloved | Lover | Loverboy | Mercutio's friend

ROTOR | Chopper blade | Turbine part | Chopper topper | Helicopter part | Turning part

SADAT | Anwar of Egypt | 1978 co-Nobelist | Time's 1977 Man of the Year | 1978 Peace Nobelist | Nobelist Anwar

SALAD | Bar fare | Light lunch | Course with greens | Dinner course | Leaves for lunch?

SALEM | "The Crucible" setting | Oregon's capital | Capital on the Willamette | Western capital | Beaver State capital

SALSA | Chip dip | Taco topper | Zesty dip | Latin music | Hot stuff

SAMOA | Pago Pago's place | Mead subject | Margaret Mead topic | Pacific island group | Island group near Fiji

SANER | More rational | More sensible | More lucid | More balanced | Less loco

SANTA | Year-end temp | Stocking stuffer | Nick name? | December temp | ___ Clara, California

SARAH | Fergie, formally | Skater Hughes | Abraham's wife | Vaughan of jazz | Miles of film

SASSY | Fresh | Impudent | Impertinent | Fresh-mouthed | Pert

SATAN | Old Nick | Beelzebub | Old Scratch | Prince of Darkness | "Paradise Lost" figure

SATIN | Gown material | Fine fabric | Sheet material | Lustrous fabric | Subbed with the band

SCALE | Climb | Map feature | Actor's minimum wage | Weighing device | Bathroom item

SCENE | Part of an act | Embarrassing display | Public to-do | Public spat | Play unit

SCENT | Bloodhound's trail | Hound's hint | Pine, e.g. | Bouquet | Aroma

SCRAM | "Get lost!" | "Beat it!" | Take a powder | "Git!"

SCRAP | Deep-six | Toss out | Throw out | Quarrel | Fragment

SEDAN | Family car | Family auto | Auto style | Alternative to a convertible | Roomy vehicle

SEDER | Passover meal | Passover feast | Exodus commemoration | Passover dinner | Meal with matzoh

SEEDY | Run-down | Disreputable | Poorly kept | Down at the heels | In sorry shape

SEETO | Take care of | Handle | Look after | Mind | Make sure of

SEINE | Paris divider | Left Bank river | Rouen's river | Fishing net | River of Paris

SELES | Tennis star Monica | Graf rival | Two-time U.S. Open winner | Hingis rival

SENOR | Mexican mister | Man of La Mancha | Madrid mister | Toledo title | Málaga mister

SENSE | Intuit | Have a feeling | Have a hunch | Pick up on | Touch or taste

SETTO | Brief brawl | Brief fight | Fistfight | Brawl | Fracas

SINAI | Mideast peninsula | Red Sea peninsula | Egyptian peninsula | Ten Commandments mount | Moses's mount

SIREN | Femme fatale | Temptress | Ambulance attachment | Seductress | Warning wailer

SKATE | Emulate Sarah Hughes | Play in the NHL | Do figure eights | Sarah Hughes footwear | Blade site

SLATE | List of candidates | Roofing material | Schedule | Walkway material | Ticket

SLEDS | Coasters | Mushers' vehicles | Iditarod vehicles | Winter transports | Flexible Flyers

SLEET | Winter fall | Winter hazard | Driving hazard | Wintry forecast | Icy rain

SMART | Sting | Quick-witted | Like some bombs | Brainy | Whiplike?

SNARE | Trap | Entrap | Catch | Capture | Entangle

SNEAK | Dishonest sort | Move furtively | Kind of preview | Move stealthily | Underhanded type

SNEER | Villain's look | Villainous look | Contemptuous look | Scornful look | Curl one's lip

SNERD | Bergen dummy | Dummy Mortimer | McCarthy's trunkmate | Bergen spoke for him

SNORE | Sound asleep? | Sleep soundly? | Night noise | Saw wood | Zzz

SODAS | Pops | Fast-food drinks | Fountain treats | Fountain drinks | Ice cream drinks

SOLAR | Kind of energy | Kind of battery | Kind of panel | Clean kind of energy | Kind of system

SONAR | Sub detector | Submarine detector | Sub system | Destroyer detector | Fish finder

SPASM | Tic | Muscle contraction | Jerk | Muscle twitch | Muscle problem

SPEAR | Primitive weapon | Asparagus unit | Javelin | Opera prop | Bit of broccoli

SPREE | Binge | Toot | Mall binge | Wild time | Shopaholic's binge

STAGE | Put on | Phase | Carry out | Rocket section | Show place

STAIR | Flight part | Flight segment | Way up | Step | Way up or down

STALE | Old hat | No longer fresh | Hackneyed | Like week-old bread | Played out

STAND | Get up | Position | Put up with | Rise | Cope with

STARE | Blank look | It may be blank | Rubberneck | Gawk | Impolite look

STARR | Brenda of the comics | One of the Fab Four | Football legend Bart | Harrison associate | First Super Bowl MVP

START | Begin | Get going | Maze word | Skittish move | Turn on

STATE | Condition | Express | Washington, for one | Alaska or Hawaii | Union member

STEAL | Great bargain | Real bargain | Swipe | Take the wrong way? | Lift

STEAM | Fulton's power | Iron output | Geyser output | Cook clams | Water vapor

STEED | Mount | Charger | War horse | Spirited horse | Trusty mount

STEEL | Symbol of strength | Pittsburgh product | Mill output | Refined iron | Mill product

STEEP | Pricey | Brew | Exorbitant | Precipitous | Expensive

STEER | Beef on the hoof | Direct | Take the wheel | Take the helm | Take the tiller

STENO | Dictation taker | Shorthand pro | Pool member | Pad user | Pool party?

STEPS | Stair parts | Action | Way up | Phases | Measures

STERN | Uncompromising | Violinist Isaac | Back of a boat | Back | Forbidding

STEVE | Martin or McQueen | Canyon of the comics | Allen or Martin | Actor McQueen | Funnyman Martin

STOLE | Wrap | Ripped off | Took the wrong way? | Lifted | Filched

STONE | Boulder | Brit's weight | "JFK" director Oliver | Sling ammo | Backgammon piece

STORE | Mall unit | Squirrel away | Put away | Boutique | Outlet

STRAP | Thong | Subway handhold | Sandal feature | Watchband | Watch part

STRAW | Scarecrow stuffing | Proverbial backbreaker | Barn bedding | Sipper's aid | Soda shop freebie

STYLE | Panache | Fashion | Flair | Elegance | Pizazz

TAMPA | Buccaneers' home | Busch Gardens locale | St. Petersburg neighbor | Florida city | The Bucs stop here

TAHOE | Sierra Nevada lake | Lake near Carson City | Western lake | Chevy SUV | Western resort lake

TAROT | Diviner's deck | Seer's deck | Fortuneteller's card | Seer's card | 22-card deck

TASTE | Sample | Discrimination | One of the senses | Refinement | It may be acquired

TBONE | Steakhouse offering | Beef cut | Steak cut | Delmonico alternative

TEASE | Needle | Make fun of | Poke fun at | Rib | Kid

TEENS | Adolescents | High schoolers | Music store frequenters | Most high schoolers | MTV fans

TENET | Belief | Doctrine | Principle | Basic belief | Article of faith

TENOR | Drift | Pavarotti, e.g. | Pavarotti or Domingo | Domingo, for one | Purport

TENSE | Uptight | Wound up | Keyed up | On edge | High-strung

TEPEE | Home on the range | Crow's home | Conical quarters | Home with a flap door | Ute hostel?

TERRA | ___ firma | Land | Earth, in sci-fi | ___ incognita | ___ cotta

TERSE | To the point | Clipped | Short and sweet | Concise | Pithy

TESLA | Inventor Nikola | Induction motor inventor | Edison contemporary | Physicist Nikola | Electrical pioneer Nikola

TESTS | Lab work | Tries out | Exams | Trial runs | Examinations

TESTY | Snappish | Irritable | Irascible | Peevish | Short-tempered

TETRA | Aquarium fish | Aquarium favorite | Di- doubled | Fish in a tank | Penta- minus one

THERE | Yonder | "Ta-da!" | "Voila!" | "Over ___" | Over yonder

TIARA | Princess's headgear | Pageant crown | Jeweled crown | Pageant prize | Small crown

TITLE | Championship | Name | Sir or madam | Challenger's quest | Ownership

TOAST | A goner | Raise a glass to | Wedding ritual | Brown bread | Part of a wedding reception

TONER | Copier additive | Copier chemical | Copier need | Copier powder | Printer powder

TORSO | Trunk | Upper body | Bit of statuary | Human trunk | Common sculpture

TOSCA | Puccini opera | Puccini heroine | Puccini classic | Opera about an opera singer | Teatro Costanzi premiere of 1900

TOTAL | Absolute | Wreck | All-out | General Mills brand | Bottom line

TRADE | Barter | Swap | Traffic | Living | Profession

TRAIT | Characteristic | Attribute | Mannerism | Feature | Genetic attribute

TREAT | Grab the tab | Pick up the tab | Halloween option | Unexpected pleasure | Doctor

TREND | Vogue | Pollster's discovery | The way things are going | Current fashion | Tendency

TRESS | Lock | Lock of hair | Long lock | Head lock | Hair piece

TSARS | Winter Palace residents | Ivan and Nicholas | Peter and Paul | Autocrats | Peter and Paul, but not Mary

UBOAT | German sub | WWII sub | Lusitania sinker | Wolf pack member | WWII threat

ULTRA | Extremist | Extreme | Part of UHF | Excessive | Fanatic

UNCLE | "I give up!" | Quitter's cry | "I give!" | Cry of defeat | Verbal white flag

UNION | Strike caller | Workers' group | Civil War side | "Local" group | Marriage

UNITE | Bring together | Come together | Join forces | Get together | Band together

UNTIE | Loosen | Free | Set free | Release | Set loose

USERS | Employers | Software buyers | Computer operators | Addicts | Mouse manipulators

USHER | Theater guide | Theater employee | Wedding worker | Program offerer | Theater worker

USUAL | Customary | Bar order, with "the" | Run-of-the-mill | Ordinary | Commonplace

UTILE | Of service | Serviceable | Handy | Of value | Functional

UTTER | Out-and-out | Absolute | Complete | Say | Total

YEAST | Brewer's need | Baker's need | Leavening agent | Brewery supply | Dough raiser

YESES | Approvals | Thumbs-up votes | Okays | Votes in favor | Affirmatives

ACROSS | Unlike this answer | Down's opposite | Over | Like this clue | Clue column heading

ACTONE | Play opener | Moss Hart autobiography | Broadway opening? | Overture follower | Start of a play

ADESTE | Carol starter | "___ Fideles" | Carol opener | Start of a Christmas carol

ADHERE | Stick | Cling | Stick (to) | Hold fast | Stick like glue

ADONIS | Hunk | Handsome guy | Beloved of Aphrodite | Handsome hunk | "Venus and ___" (Shakespeare poem)

ADORED | Put on a pedestal | Like an idol | Worshiped | Doted on | Cherished

AERATE | Make bubbly | Make fizzy | Add fizz to | Freshen | Refresh, as a room | Treat with gas

AGASSI | 1992 Wimbledon winner | Two-time U.S. Open champ | 1999 U.S. Open champ | 1992 Wimbledon champ | Sampras foe

AGATHA | Hercule's creator | First name in mysteries | Contemporary of Erle | 1979 Vanessa Redgrave title role | Christie of mystery

AGENDA | Ax to grind | Meeting plan | "To do" list | Things to do | Meeting schedule

AGENTS | Operatives | FBI employees

AGHAST | Shocked | Horrified | Horror-struck | In shock | Speechless

ALASKA | The 49th state | Panhandle site | "Seward's Folly" | $7.2 million purchase of 1867 | Baked ___

ALERTS | Tips off | Warns | Warnings | Flashing lights, say | Advisories

ALGORE | "Earth in the Balance" author | Dick Cheney's predecessor | Tipper's mate | Big Tipper fan | Candidate of 2000

ALIENS | 1986 sci-fi sequel | Foreigners | Little green men | UFO crew | Men from Mars and women from Venus

ALLEGE | Claim | Assert without proof | Maintain | Bring charges | Profess

AMELIA | Aviator Earhart | First name in aviation | Social reformer Bloomer | Flier Earhart | First name in flight

AMOEBA | It multiplies by dividing | One-celled organism | One-celled animal | Protozoan | Microscopic critter

AMORAL | Unprincipled | Ethically neutral | Ethically indifferent | Lacking principles | Without scruples

AMPERE | Current unit | Fuse unit | French physicist | Current measure | One coulomb per second

AMULET | Charm | Lucky charm | Magic charm | Talisman | Gris-gris or juju

ANEMIA | Lack of vigor | Lack of vitality | Paucity of pep | Iron target | Weakness

ANIMAL | Brute | 20 Questions category | Beast | Skink or skunk | "___ Crackers"

ANKARA | Turkish capital | Capital of Turkey | Ataturk mausoleum city | Capital since 1923 | NATO country capital

ANOINT | Consecrate | Sprinkle with oil | Make sacred | Apply holy oil to | Rub on

APIECE | Each | Per | Individually | For one | Pricing word

APOLLO | Historic Harlem theater | Handsome god | Storied Harlem theater | Artemis's twin | NASA project

ARABIA | Kuwait's peninsula | World's largest peninsula | Lawrence's land | Yemen's peninsula | Asian peninsula

ARARAT | Turkish mount | Biblical landfall | Genesis locale | Noah's landfall | Biblical landing place

ARCANE | Esoteric | Mysterious | Secret | Known by few | Like Federal tax laws

ARDENT | Passionate | Impassioned | Gung-ho | Devoted | Fervid

ARENAS | Sports venues | Stadiums | Fight sites | Sports centers | Gladiatorial sites

ARETHA | First name in soul | Franklin of soul | Singer Franklin | Soul singer Franklin | "Spanish Harlem" singer

ARIOSO | Melodic | Melodic passage |
Melodic piece | Operatic passage |
Songlike

ARISEN | Up | Up and about | Gotten out
of bed | Up and at 'em | Popped up

ARISES | Crops up | Comes up | Comes to
mind | Gets up | Rebels

ARISTA | Grain bristle | Grain appendage |
Popular record label | Whitney Houston's
record label | The Grateful Dead label

ARLENE | Actress Dahl | Francis of
"What's My Line?" | Francis or Dahl |
Garfield's girlfriend | Actress Francis

ARMADA | Fleet | Fighting force | Big fleet
| Fleet of warships | Philip II's fleet

AROMAS | Bouquets | Oven emanations |
Coffee shop emanations | Bakery
emanations | Nasal appraisals

AROUSE | Stir up | Stir to action | Excite |
Stir | Work up

ARREST | Run in | Collar | Check | Take
into custody | Nab

ARRIVE | Make it | Achieve success | Get in
| Come | Hit the big time

ASHORE | On land | Off the boat | On dry
land | Taking liberty | On the beach

ASLEEP | Numb, as a foot | Out | Out for
the night | Dead to the world | Like a
somnambulist

ASPENS | Trembling trees | Quaking trees
| Fluttering trees | Quakers | Poplars

ASPIRE | Aim | Have high hopes | Shoot
for, with "to" | Hope | Wish, with "to"

ASSAIL | Attack vigorously | Go after |
Tear into | Lash out at | Light into

ASSENT | Agreement | Agree | Thumbs-up
| Concurrence | Nod

ASSERT | Maintain | Declare | State
positively | State with conviction | Put
forward

ASSESS | Size up | Evaluate | Take stock of
| Weigh | Judge

ASSETS | Ledger column | Resources |
They may be fixed | Desirable qualities |
Holdings

ASSISI | Birthplace of St. Francis | Umbrian
town | St. Francis's home | Whence St.
Clare

ASSURE | Guarantee | Give confidence to |
Make certain | Promise | Give a
guarantee

ASTERN | To the rear | Back at sea | Away
from the bow | Backward | Toward the
rudder

ASTRAL | Stellar | Star-shaped | Starlike |
Of the stars | Kind of projection

ASTUTE | Shrewd | Sharp as a tack | Sharp
| Quick | Keen

ATEASE | Relaxed | Military command |
"Relax, soldier!" | Comfortable | "Relax,
and that's an order!"

ATHENA | Greek goddess of wisdom |
Phidias subject | Parthenon goddess |
Parthenon figure

ATHOME | In | Not out | Where
telecommuters work | Comfortable |
Not away

ATLAST | "Finally!" | "It's about time!" |
After a long wait | Cry of relief

ATONCE | Stat | Immediately | Pronto |
"This instant!" | Without delay

ATONES | Makes amends | Observes Yom
Kippur | Does penance | Makes up (for) |
Expiates

ATREST | Not moving | Still | Motionless |
Stationary | Quiescent

ATTEND | Go to | Be there | Come to | Sit
in on | Show up for

ATTEST | Bear witness | Certify | Swear |
Swear (to) | Bear witness (to)

ATTILA | Number one Hun | Fifth-century
scourge | Head Hun | Hun-armed bandit?
| King of the Huns

ATTIRE | Duds | Garb | Habit | Outfit | It
suits you

AURORA | Dawn goddess | Light show |
Goddess of the dawn | ___ borealis |
Natural light show

AVATAR | Hindu incarnation | Embodiment
| Personification | Rama, to Vishnu |
Incarnation

AVENUE | Means | Means of access | Pennsylvania, for one | Street crosser | Park, for one

AVERSE | Disinclined | Loath | Reluctant | Opposed | Unwilling

AVIATE | Fly | Pilot | Emulate Earhart | Take to the air | Do the Wright thing

AZALEA | Showy shrub | Flowering shrub | Spring bloomer | Rhododendron relative

CAESAR | Salad type | Rubicon crosser | Kind of salad | Victim of Brutus | Salad choice

DELETE | Erase | Computer key | Strike | PC key | X out

DETEST | Abominate | Can't stand | Loathe | More than dislike | Hate

EASELS | Stands for sittings | Stands in a studio | Supporters of the arts? | Stands for things

EASTER | Rabbit season? | Lent ender | Spring festival | Kind of seal | A time to dye?

EDERLE | Channel swimmer Gertrude | Swimmer in 1926 news | Channel crosser of 1926 | 1924 gold medal swimmer

EDISON | Holder of 1,093 patents | The Wizard of Menlo Park | Inventor of the stock ticker | Kinetoscope inventor | Eponymic New Jersey city

EDITOR | Perry White, e.g. | Time keeper? | Paper worker | Money manager? | Post position?

EDSELS | Ford flops | Detroit duds | Corsair and Citation, for two | '50s autos | The Ranger and the Corsair

EGRESS | Way out | Exit | Go out | Way out, to Barnum | Way to go

ELAINE | "Seinfeld" role | May or Stritch | "Seinfeld" character | Jerry's friend | Director May

ELAPSE | Go by | Pass, as time | Pass by | Slip by | Run out

ELATED | On cloud nine | Pleased as punch | Walking on air | Very happy | In seventh heaven

ELATES | Thrills | Puts on cloud nine | Makes rhapsodic | Tickles pink | Makes very happy

ELDEST | Firstborn | Favorite son, maybe | Most senior | Child with responsibilities, traditionally | Meg, among the "little women"

ELECTS | Chooses | Puts into office | Picks | Picks out | Votes in

ELEVEN | Football team | Big roll | Craps natural | Gridiron complement | Football squad

ELICIT | Draw out | Bring out | Draw forth | Bring to the surface | Extract

ELNINO | Meteorological menace | Pacific phenomenon | Cause of chaotic weather | Climatologist's concern | Weather-changing current

ELOISE | Plaza Hotel imp | Fictional Plaza Hotel brat | Kay Thompson character | Plaza Hotel heroine | Ava's role in "Mogambo"

ELPASO | Rio Grande city | Sun Bowl site | Sun Bowl city | Texas city | Fort Bliss location

EMERGE | Come out | Come forth | Come into view | Surface | Exit one's cocoon

EMIGRE | Political refugee | Political asylum seeker | Asylum seeker | New citizen, perhaps | Political escapee

ENAMEL | Crown covering | Canine's coat | Glossy paint | Nail polish | Tooth covering

ENAMOR | Charm | Captivate | Fill with love | Win the heart of | Bewitch

ENCORE | "More!" | Concert bonus | Repeat performance | Concert hall cry | Shout when the band leaves the stage

ENDEAR | Make beloved | Win over | Make lovable | Ingratiate | Charm

ENIGMA | Puzzle | Riddle | Stumper | Mystery | Poser

ENLIST | Sign up | Join up | Join the service | Beat the draft? | Join the military

ENRAGE | Infuriate | Really rile | Incense | Tick off | Make angry

ENTAIL | Involve | Necessitate | Call for | Bring into play | Require

ENTERS | Goes in | Records | Walks onstage | Punches in | Puts in

ENTIRE | Complete | Unbroken | Whole | Unabridged | Missing nothing

ENTREE | Main course | Access | Main dish | Menu selection | Way in

ERASER | Pencil topper | One end of a #2 | Boo-boo remover | Rubber | It gets the lead out

ERASES | Rubs out | Obliterates | Deletes | Wipes away | Leaves rubber?

ERECTS | Puts up | Builds | Sets up | Raises | Pitches, in a way

ERMINE | Regal fur | Royal fur | White fur | Furrier's offering | Politically incorrect coat

ERNEST | Writer Hemingway | Actor Borgnine | English poet Dowson | Country singer Tubb | Jim Varney character

ERODED | Wore away | Worn away | Worn down | Like many shorelines | Ate into

ERODES | Wears away | Destroys slowly | Eats away at | Washes away | Wears down

EROICA | Beethoven's Third | Beethoven's Symphony No. 3 | Beethoven symphony | Symphony Beethoven originally dedicated to Napoleon | Symphony that includes a funeral march

ERRANT | Wandering | Off-course | Straying | Off the mark | Wide of the mark

ERRATA | Book boo-boos | Slips | Printing mistakes | Printing goofs | Slips on a slip?

ERRORS | Boo-boos | Blunders | Faults | Goofs | Baseball misplays

ESCAPE | Get away | Break out | Get away from | Way out | Turn tail

ESSAYS | Op-Ed pieces | Attempts | Lamb pieces | Opinion pieces | Literary pieces

ESSENE | Ancient ascetic | Ancient Palestinian | Ancient Palestinian ascetic | Dead Sea Scrolls scribe

ESTATE | What you will | Landed property | A lot of wealth? | What's left | House and grounds

ESTEEM | Regard highly | Prize | Treasure | Regard | High regard

ESTHER | Old Testament book | Job preceder | Book before Job | Queen of Persia, in the Bible | Purim honoree

ETERNE | Everlasting, old-style | Perpetual, in poesy | E'erlasting | Timeless, to a poet

ETHANE | Natural gas component | Flammable gas | Simple hydrocarbon | Fuel gas | Odorless gas

HARASS | Badger | Plague | Bother continually | Dog | Persecute

HASSLE | Inconvenience | Headache | Bother | Annoyance | Pain in the neck

HELENA | Treasure State capital | Montana's capital | Western capital | Montana city built around Last Chance Gulch

HONEST | "I swear!" | Truthful | "So help me!" | "Would I lie?" | Straight

IBERIA | Spain and Portugal | European peninsula | Portugal's place | Albeniz piano work | Airline to Madrid

ICEAGE | Cold time | Ancient epoch | Cold era | When mammoths lived | Glacial epoch

IDEATE | Conceive | Brainstorm | Conceptualize | Think up | Imagine

IGNORE | Tune out | Pay no attention to | Shrug off | Disregard | Slight, in a way

IGUANA | Large lizard | Galapagos critter | Galápagos creature | Arboreal lizard | Galápagos Islands critter

INHALE | Get some air | "... but I didn't ___" | Scarf down | Fill the lungs | Sniff

INNATE | Hereditary | Deep-seated | Present from birth | Natural | Congenital

INSTEP | Shoe part | Foot part | Part of the foot | Marching together | Like a marching band

INTERN | Trainee | Apprentice | Trainee or detainee | Hospital worker | Medical resident

INTOTO | Completely | Entirely | Altogether | Counting everything | All together

IRISES | Van Gogh masterpiece | Light regulators | Bearded bloomers | Places for pupils | Camera parts

IRONIC | Double-edged | Like "The Gift of the Magi" | Unexpected, in a way | Sarcastic | Arch

ISLAND | Manhattan, for one | Montreal, for one | Nantucket, for one | Archipelago component | Hawaii component

ISOLDE | Tristan's love | Wagner heroine | King Mark's bride | Tristram's love | Heroine of Arthurian romance

ISRAEL | Sharon's land | State since 1948 | Jerusalem's country | Acre land | Its flag is blue and white

LAREDO | Texas city | Rio Grande city | City on the Rio Grande | Texas border city

LARIAT | Cow catcher | Rodeo rope | Wrangler's rope | It may be thrown from a horse

LENORE | "The Raven" maiden | 1831 Poe poem | "The Raven" name

NEEDLE | Tease | Razz | Poke fun at | Haystack hider | Rib

NEGATE | Nullify | Cancel out | Cancel | Undo | Make invalid

NESTLE | Get cozy | Big name in chocolate | Get comfy | Snuggle up | Cozy up

OATERS | Horse operas | Westerns | Wayne vehicles | B westerns | Mix movies, e.g.

OBERON | King of the fairies | Moon of Uranus | Fairy king | "A Midsummer Night's Dream" king | Actress Merle

OCEANS | A whole lot | Lots and lots | Vast amounts | Indian and others | Oodles

OCELOT | Spotted cat | Spotted wildcat | Endangered cat | Leopardlike cat | Spotted feline

OCTANE | Gas rating | Pump number | Engine-knock reducer | Gas pump number | It's often in the 90s

ODESSA | Black Sea port | Texas oil city | Ukrainian seaport | West Texas city

OMELET | Egg dish | Brunch entrée | Brunch selection | Breakfast dish | Frittata

ONEDGE | Tense | Jittery | Jumpy | Uptight | Nervous

ONEIDA | New York lake | Iroquois tribe | Iroquoian language | Lake near Syracuse | Onetime New York utopia

ONEILL | "The Iceman Cometh" playwright | Tip of Massachusetts | "Mourning Becomes Electra" playwright | Treasury Secretary Paul

ONIONS | Whopper toppers | Pearl and Spanish | Burger topping | They may smother a dish | Kitchen tearjerkers

ONLINE | Connected to the Internet | Surfing, perhaps | Surfing the Net | Connected to the Web | Having a chat, maybe

ONSALE | Marked down | Reduced | Discounted | Clearance sign | Priced to move

OPENED | Bid first | Began playing on Broadway | Kicked off the show | Kicked off | Broke the seal on

OPENER | First game | First game of a doubleheader | Start of a series | Intro | Church key

OPERAS | Musical dramas | La Scala offerings | "Aida" and "The Magic Flute" | Met productions | "Carmen" and "Norma"

OPIATE | Sleep inducer | Narcotic | Sedative | Calmer | Soporific

ORACLE | Delphic medium | Prophet at Delphi | Delphic shrine | Divine revelation | Larry Ellison's company

ORANGE | Halloween hue | Fall color | Popsicle flavor | Triple sec flavoring | Screwdriver hue

ORATES | Gives a speech | Addresses the crowd | Bloviates | Proclaims with pomp | Holds forth

ORATOR | Daniel Webster, for one | Silver-tongued speaker | Figure of speech? | Public speaker | Person on a soapbox

OREGON | The Beaver State | Salem's state | Coos Bay's state | Where to find Eugene | Crater Lake locale

ORELSE | Ultimatum words | Threat ender | Threatening words | Words of warning | Ultimatum ender

ORIENT | Familiarize | Point in the right direction | East | "Murder on the ___ Express" | Prepare, as new students

ORIOLE | Camden Yards player | Baltimore athlete | Firebird | Brightly colored bird | Baltimore bird

ORNATE | Richly decorated | Baroque | Flowery | Rococo | Busy

ORNERY | Cantankerous | Obstinate | Ill-tempered | Mean | Crabbed

OSCARS | Movie awards | Annual TV event, with "the" | Hepburn's quartet | Academy Awards | Film awards

OSIRIS | Egyptian god of the underworld | Egyptian king of the dead | Brother of Isis | Egyptian pantheon bigwig | God of fertility

OTELLO | Verdi opera | Opera set in Cyprus | Verdi opera based on a Shakespeare play | 1887 La Scala premiere

OTOOLE | "Becket" star | "My Favorite Year" star | Lawrence portrayer | "The Stunt Man" star | Peter of "Lawrence of Arabia"

OTTAWA | Canadian capital | Canada's capital | Chrétien's capital | Pontiac, e.g. | River to the St. Lawrence

OVERDO | Exaggerate | Take too far | Go to extremes | Go too far | Work too hard

PARADE | Easter event | Flaunt | Thanksgiving Day event | Columbus Day event | Strut like a peacock

PAROLE | Sentence shortener | Conditional release | Early release | Inmate's hope | One way out of prison

PESETA | 100 centimos | Euro preceder | Madrid monetary unit | Barcelona buck | Spanish simoleon

PRESTO | Magic word | Magician's word | Quickly | Magician's exclamation | Wand waver's word

RAREST | Most uncommon | Least cooked | Most unusual | Least common | Most difficult to find

REBATE | Sales incentive | Purchase incentive | Discount | Money back | Car buyer's incentive

REDSEA | It had a part in the Bible | Exodus crossing | Suez Canal terminus | Obstacle for Moses | Biblical locale

REESES | ___ Pieces | Candy brand | ___ Peanut Butter Cups | ___ NutRageous candy bar | Mason and Della

RELATE | Tell | Empathize | Give an account of | Have a connection | Pertain

RENEGE | Weasel out | Go back | Go back on one's word | Bridge blunder | Go back on a promise

RESALE | Used car transaction | Kind of price | Used car deal | Antique shop deal | Secondhand shop deal

SAFARI | African adventure | Hunting expedition | African outing | Bush jacket wearer's undertaking | Game expedition

SAHARA | African desert | 1943 Bogart film | African hot spot | African expanse | "The English Patient" setting

SALAMI | Deli meat | Deli dangler | Deli sausage | Spicy sausage | Antipasto ingredient

SANEST | Most rational | Most together | Most lucid | Most sensible | Most balanced

SATIRE | Lampoon | Swift vehicle | Mad's genre | Paddy Chayefsky's forte | Fun-making skit

SCENES | Dramatic snippets | Trailer units | Public flaps | Vistas | Play parts

SECEDE | Withdraw | Pull out | Leave the country? | Leave the union | Break away

SEDATE | Put under | Unruffled | Composed | Calm | Calm down

SEERED | Fume | Get angry | Hit the roof | Get mad | Go ballistic

SEESAW | It has its ups and downs | Vacillate | Have trouble deciding | Playground plank | Show uncertainty

SEESTO | Takes care of | Looks after | Handles | Is responsible for | Takes charge of

SEETHE | Do a slow burn | Boil | Stew | Get all worked up | Be livid

SENATE | Upper house | 100-member group | Boxer's group | "Julius Caesar" setting | Kind of seat

SENECA | Nero's tutor | "What fools these mortals be" writer | Roman philosopher | Cayuga relative | Member of the Iroquois Confederacy

SENORA | Lady of Spain | Lady of la casa | Spanish lady's title | Married madrileña | Andalusian title

SENSES | Feels | Sight, smell, taste, touch, and hearing | Corporeal quintet | Sight and hearing | Has a feeling

SERENE | Tranquil | Unruffled | Calm | At peace | Composed

SESAME | Opening word? | Seed source | Oil source | Snuffleupagus's street | Bagel flavoring

SETTEE | Parlor piece | Small sofa | Living room piece | Soft seat | Seat for two or more

SETTER | Hunting dog | Irish ___ | Volleyball player | Canine hunter

SHASTA | California peak | Cascades peak | Cascade Range peak | Kind of daisy | Soft drink brand

SIERRA | ___ Leone | ___ Club | Rugged range | Word before Nevada or Leone | Code word for "S"

SIESTA | Rest of the afternoon | Sonora snooze | Break of day? | Nap | Reason to close up shop

SLEEVE | Record holder | Record protector | Ace place? | Shoulder extension | Magician's hiding place

SNEERS | Contemptuous looks | Shows contempt | Exhibits scorn | Bad looks | Villainous visages

SOIREE | Evening do | Evening party | Evening affair | Evening get-together | Formal bash

SPARSE | Few and far between | Thin | Thinly spread | Spread out | Meager

SPARTA | Peloponnesian War victor | Athens rival | Greek city-state | Rival of Athens | Ancient Greek city

SPHERE | Globe | Bailiwick | Orb | Realm | Ball

STALAG | "Hogan's Heroes" setting | German prison camp | WWII camp | Certain camp | Place of confinement

STEEDS | Mounts | Spirited horses | War horses | Mighty mounts | Spirited mounts

STEELE | Brosnan TV role | Addison's publishing partner | "Remington ___" | Writer Shelby | The Spectator essayist

STENOS | Shorthand pros | Dictation takers | They serve dictators | Pool parties? | Dictator's aides

STEREO | Sound system | Sound investment? | Record player | Home music system | Audiophile's setup

STOLEN | Hot | Ripped off | Like some kisses and bases | In a chop shop, say | Like second, sometimes

STOOGE | Straight man | Fall guy | Curly or Moe | Underling | Flunky

STRATA | Layers | Levels of society | Rock layers | Cloud layers | Levels

STREAM | Flow | Steady flow | Place to fish | Small river | Mill site

STREET | Thoroughfare | Avenue crosser | Easy ___ | Bourbon, for one | Certain fair site

STRESS | Pressure | Underline | Underscore | Cause of burnout | High anxiety

TAHITI | Gauguin's island home | Destination of the Bounty | Papeete's island | Largest of the Society Islands

TALENT | Ability | Kind of scout | Scout's quest | Concern of some agencies | Pageant element

TASSEL | Mortarboard attachment | Loafer attachment | Corn feature | Dangler | String decoration

TATTOO | Arm art | Body work? | Body image? | Ring around the biceps, perhaps | Popeye's anchor, e.g.

TEASET | Afternoon service | China shop purchase | Wonderland service | It might include a sugar bowl | Wonderland dishes

TEETER | Move unsteadily | Wobble | Rock | Rock on the edge | Seesaw

TENURE | Professor's goal | Teacher's goal | Professor's prize | Academic fire insurance? | Prof's goal

TERESA | Mother ___ | Singer Brewer | Mother of Calcutta | Mezzo Berganza | Mother of mercy

TOATEE | Perfectly | Precisely | Just so | Exactly | Just right

TOMATO | Salad ingredient | Gazpacho ingredient | Love apple | BLT part | Killer in a cult classic

TSETSE | African fly | Dangerous fly | African scourge | Sleeping sickness carrier

UNEASE | Discomfort | Disquiet | Nervousness | Anxiety | Creepy feeling

UTOPIA | More work | Heaven on earth | Dreamland | Ideal place | Perfect world

AAMILNE | "It's Too Late Now" autobiographer | Pooh's creator | "Toad of Toad Hall" playwright | "The Red House Mystery" author | Winnie-the-Pooh's creator

ABALONE | Mother-of-pearl source | Ornamental shell | Seaweed eater | Edible mollusk | Marine rock-clinger

ABILENE | Chisholm Trail terminus | Eisenhower Center city | Ike's hometown | Eisenhower's boyhood home | Home to Dyess AFB

ACADEME | College life | It's far removed from the real world | Scholar | Campus community | Dean's milieu

ACETATE | Overlay material | Transparency | Film material | Synthetic fiber | Film maker?

ACETONE | Polish remover | Paint solvent | Common solvent | Paint ingredient | Organic solvent

ACROBAT | Flipper? | Tumbler | Circus star | Showy gymnast | Aerial artist

ACTRESS | Cast member | Starlet, e.g. | Lucci or Leoni | Julia Roberts, but not Raul Julia | Close, for example

ADAMANT | Unyielding | Inflexible | Not budging | Far from easygoing | Rigid

ADDENDA | Supplements | Book supplements | Book ends? | Postscripts | Extras

ADELINE | "The flower of my heart" | "Sweet" girl of song | "The flower of my heart," in old song | "Sweet ___" (quartet tune) | Barbershop girl

AERATOR | Aquarium device | Aquarium bubbler | Faucet attachment | Machine that adds carbonation | Greenskeeper's gizmo

AGITATE | Stir up | Shake up | Perturb | Whip into a lather | Stir

ALABAMA | Mobile home? | Country quartet | "Take Me Down" band | Home of Horseshoe Bend National Military Park | Crimson Tide

ALADDIN | Genie summoner | Disney hit of '92 | Robin Williams had a voice in it | Rubber of myth | Genie's boss

ALAMEDA | Oakland's county | City on San Francisco Bay | Oakland neighbor | Tree-lined promenade

ALAMODE | Like some desserts | Apple-pie order | With ice cream | Pie order | Chic

ALCOHOL | Whiskey component | Hooch | Breathalyzer find | Fermentation product

ALDENTE | Just firm enough | Spaghetti specification | Not overboiled | Firm, as pasta | Not too soft

ALERTED | Warned | Tipped off | Gave a heads-up to | On one's toes | Notified of danger

ALIASES | Smith and Jones, often | Rap sheet list | Dossier list | Wanted poster info | Made-up monikers

ALIBABA | He said "Open sesame!" | "Arabian Nights" hero | Poor woodcutter of folklore | Kasim's brother, in Persian folklore | Fictional password user

ALIENEE | Property receiver | Property recipient | Heir, at law

ALSORAN | Loser | Election loser | Late finisher | One who's back in the pack | Unsuccessful contender

ALTOONA | Pennsylvania city | Keystone State city | City near Horseshoe Curve | Penn State campus site

AMASSED | Gathered | Piled up | Stockpiled | Built up | Accumulated

AMERICA | "West Side Story" song | Paul Simon song | Bernstein song | Song that starts "My country, 'tis of thee" | Statue of Liberty's home

AMNESIA | Loss of memory | Condition sometimes treated by hypnosis | Result of a conk on the head, perhaps | "Regarding Henry" malady | Blackout

ANAGRAM | Twist of phrase, perhaps | Make cats scat | Get Meg Ryan out of Germany?

ANALYST | Shrink | Wall Street worker | CIA job | Market watcher | Person who breaks down

ANATOLE | Author France | France of France | France, for one | Novelist France | Director Litvak

ANEMONE | Windflower | Buttercup family member | Sea creature | Buttercup relative | Flowerlike sea creature

ANIMATE | Bring to life | Spark | Energize | Pep up | Work for Warner Bros., maybe

ANNETTE | Warren's wife | One of the original Mouseketeers | Actress Bening | Bening or Funicello | 1950s Mouseketeer

ANOTHER | One more | Saloon request | Baldwin's "___ Country" | Something different | Seconds

ANTARES | Brightest star in Scorpio | Star in Scorpius | Red giant in Scorpius | Binary star in Scorpio

ANTENNA | Feeler | Reception helper | Aerial | Wave catcher | Ham's need

APOSTLE | Peter or Paul, but not Mary | Peter or Paul | Early Christian | Title role for Robert Duvall | Last Supper guest

APPEASE | Pacify | Propitiate | Emulate Chamberlain | Mollify | Quiet

APRIORI | Not based on previous study | Presumptive | Deductive | Kind of assumption | Based on hypothesis

ARABIAN | Graceful horse | The Black Stallion, e.g. | High-spirited horse | Graceful runner | Fine horse

ARALSEA | About 25,000 square miles of Asia | Body of water south of Orsk | Kazakhstan border water | Fourth-largest lake | Uzbek lake

ARAPAHO | Fox relative | Plains Indian | Algonquian language | Cheyenne ally of old | Oklahoma tribe member

ARIADNE | Daughter of King Minos | Dionysus' bride, in myth | Without her, Theseus didn't have a clue | Half sister of the Minotaur

ARRANGE | Put in order | Set up | Handle | Work with music | Systematize

ARRESTS | Takes into custody | Collars | Picks up | Rap sheet data | Pinches

ARSENAL | Magazine | Weapons supply | Powder room? | Supply of arms | Gun stock

ARTDECO | Like Radio City Music Hall | Erté's style | Like the Chrysler Building | Style of the '20s and '30s | Empire State Building décor

ARTICLE | Document subsection | People feature | Periodical staple | Constitution clause | A, for example

ASARULE | By and large | Ordinarily | Generally | In the main | Usually

ASININE | Silly | Ill-considered | Cockamamie | Featherbrained | Knuckleheaded

ASPECTS | Phases | Views | Facets | Sides | Looks

ASSENTS | Gives in | Yeses | Agreements | Goes along with | Acceptances

ASTAIRE | "Top Hat" star | "Steps in Time" autobiographer | Dancing man in "Dancing Lady" | "Swing Time" star | Rogers partner

ASTORIA | Oregon city | Early Northwest trading town | Section of Queens | Columbia River city | Waldorf-___

ASTRIDE | On both sides of | With a leg on each side of | In the saddle of | Straddling | Bridging

ATALOSS | Puzzled | Baffled | Bewildered | Clueless | Perplexed

ATEDIRT | Was humbled | Was humiliated | Swallowed one's pride | Humbled oneself | Acted humble

ATELIER | Artist's studio | Place to paint | Studio | Workshop | Where pictures may be made

ATHLETE | Jock | Olympian, e.g. | Hurler or curler | Jim Thorpe, for one | Tinactin user, presumably

ATLANTA | Home of the Braves | Martin Luther King Jr.'s birthplace | Carter Library site | Morehouse College locale | Setting for Tom Wolfe's "A Man in Full"

ATLARGE | On the loose | Loose | Free | Wanted by the police, maybe | Like some representatives in Washington

ATLASES | Motorists' references | They'll show you the world | Map collections | World books | World records?

ATLEAST | Minimally | In any case | No less than | Not under | No fewer than

ATPEACE | Free from strife | Untroubled | Tranquil | Content | Free from friction

ATSTAKE | On the line | Hanging in the balance | In danger of being lost | Risked | Being risked

ATTACHE | Case for a lawyer | Kind of case | Newspaper carrier, at times | Embassy worker | Executive's burden

ATTESTS | Certifies | Bears witness | Swears | Swears (to) | Affirms

ATTIMES | Now and then | Occasionally | Once in a while | Off and on | Periodically

AVARICE | Greed | Cupidity | Midas's downfall | Insatiable greed | One of a sinful septet | Sin of the beady-eyed | Itching palm

AVERAGE | Fair | Garden-variety | Middling | Not at all extraordinary | Just okay

AVIATOR | Joystick expert | One who may raise a flap | Howard Hughes was one | Red Baron, e.g. | Fly guy

AVOCADO | Green shade | Guacamole ingredient | Alligator pear | Salad fruit | Popular salad ingredient

BEELINE | Direct route | Direct path

CABARET | Some theater | Club with a floor show | Singer's locale | Tony winner of 1967 and 1998 | Fosse musical

CANASTA | Rummy variation | Rummy variety | Card-melding game | Game with four jokers | Melder's game

CELESTE | Babar's wife | Name that means "heavenly" | Actress Holm | Holm of "All About Eve"

DESERTS | They may be just | Gobi and Kalahari | Strands | Comeuppance | Takes off wrongly

DESSERT | Feast finale | Calorie-crammed course | Last course | Napoleon, for one | Banquet finale

DETENTE | Thaw | Nixon policy | Diplomat's quest | Cold War lull | Peace negotiator's goal

EARLOBE | Ring site | Stud site | Place for a ring | Place for a hanging? | Stud holder

ECLIPSE | Overshadow | Sun block | Outshine | Cover-up at the highest levels? | Lunar event

ECUADOR | Where to spend sucres | Galápagos owner | Peru neighbor | Country on the equator | Big banana exporter

EDASNER | Lou Grant portrayer | He played Captain Davies on "Roots" | Seven-time Emmy winner | Mary Tyler Moore's "boss" | "Roots" Emmy winner, 1977

EGOTRIP | Vanity case? | Vanity affair | Conceit | I movement? | Self-motivated journey?

ELASTIC | Flexible | Springy | Adaptable | Stretchy | Stretchable

ELEANOR | "The Lion in Winter" queen | Queen of Henry II | Tap dancer Powell | Bess's predecessor | Rigby or Roosevelt

ELECTEE | In | November winner | Successful candidate | Winner of a race | Ballot choice

ELECTRA | Sister of Orestes | Sophocles tragedy | Clytemnestra's daughter | Plane in which Amelia Earhart disappeared | Sophocles subject

ELEGANT | Chic | Posh | White-tie, say | Classy | Polished

ELEMENT | Natural habitat | Part | Comfortable space | Home environment | Gold or silver

ELEVATE | Up | Lift up | Raise | Uplift | Boost up

ELLIPSE | Oval | Orbital path | Orbital shape | Closed curve | Squashed circle

EMANATE | Flow out | Spring | Flow forth | Issue | Flow (from)

EMERALD | May birthstone | 55th anniversary gift | Deep green | Clear, deep green | Tiny type size

EMERSON | The Sage of Concord | "Nature" essayist | "Shot heard round the world" writer | Transcendentalist Ralph Waldo | Boston college

EMINENT | Celebrated | Noted | Distinguished | Illustrious | August

EMULATE | Act like | Try to equal | Be like | Take after | Copy

ENDORSE | Back | Get behind | Give backing to | Stand behind | Support publicly

ENEMIES | Foes | They may be bitter | "Wise men learn much from ___": Aristophanes | Hostile parties | Those opposed

ENHANCE | Intensify | Better | Improve | Magnify | Heighten

ENLARGE | Blow up | Swell | Broaden | Expand | Turn into something big

ENMASSE | All together | As a group | Together | Not singly | As a body

ENROUTE | On the way | Coming or going | Along the way | Coming | Neither here nor there

ENSNARE | Catch | Trap | Capture | Rope in | Sucker

ENTENTE | International agreement | International accord | Understanding | Political understanding | Alliance

ENTERED | Came in | Typed in | Penetrated | Signed up for | Went in

ENTITLE | Authorize | Qualify | Give a name to | Make a baron, say | Put a name to

ENTRANT | Competitor | Contest hopeful | Contest player | Contest contestant | Sweepstakes hopeful

ENTREAT | Beseech | Plead | Beg | Implore | Importune

EPAULET | Officer's ornament | Shoulder ornament | Uniform frill | Shoulder adornment | Military decoration

EPISODE | Serial segment | Show piece? | Incident | Happening | Sitcom segment

ERASERS | Office supplies | Board clearers | Classroom needs | Pink Pearls, e.g. | They get the graphite out

ERASMUS | Dutch humanist | "The Praise of Folly" author | Catholic Reformation writer | Name revered in Rotterdam | "Colloquia" author

ERASURE | Sign of a mistake | Sign of a slip | Start of a correction | Sign of imperfection | Strike-out

ERECTED | Built | Put up | Put together | Made | Set up

ERITREA | Asmara is its capital | Land on the Red Sea | Red Sea nation | Neighbor of Djibouti | United Nations member since 1993

ERNESTO | Carmaker Maserati | Auto designer Maserati | Che Guevara's real first name | "Don Pasquale" role | Mexican president Zedillo

EROTICA | Blue books? | Blue prints | Literary genre | Anaïs Nin output | A nice word for dirt?

ESCAPEE | Fugitive | Coop flier | One on the run | Tim Robbins, in "The Shawshank Redemption" | Object of a manhunt

ESSENCE | Perfume | Gist | Core | Quiddity | Heart

ESTATES | Posh properties | Big spreads | Will subjects | They may be taxed | Ritzy homes

ESTEEMS | Regards highly | Values highly | Prizes | Holds in high regard | Prizes highly

ESTELLE | Actress Parsons | Getty or Parsons | One of the Costanzas, on "Seinfeld" | Actress Getty | 1967 Oscar winner Parsons

ESTONIA | Baltic republic | It regained independence in 1991 | Land on the Gulf of Finland | Country with a blue, black, and white flag | Ill-fated ferry of 1994

ESTRADA | "CHiPs" star Erik | Spanish highway

ETAGERE | Tchotchke holder | Bric-a-brac stand | Bust site | Display unit | Stand for trinkets

ETERNAL | Timeless | Enduring | Undying | Everlasting | God, with "the"

EVEREST | Hillary's conquest | High point | Challenge for Hillary | Chomolungma alias | News locale of 5/28/53

EVILEYE | Look bringing bad luck, supposedly | Hex of a sort | "Bad luck" look | Curse, of sorts | Nasty look?

EYESORE | It doesn't look good | Dump | Blot on the landscape | Urban blight | Stye, for one

IMEANIT | "This is no joke!" | "No kidding!" | "This is serious!" | "Don't test me!" | "Seriously!"

IMITATE | Ape | Copy | Parrot | Flatter, in a way | Mirror

INAHOLE | Behind the eight ball | Financially compromised | Struggling | Way behind, in Vegas | Financially strapped

INERROR | Mistakenly | By mistake | Off base | Wrong | Not perfect

INERTIA | Resistance to change | It'll keep you going | Subject of the first law of motion | Sluggishness | Inactivity

INITIAL | OK, in a way | First | Monogram character | Approve, in a way | Part of JFK?

INTENSE | Strong | Deep | Deeply felt | Fervid | Passionate

IRANIAN | Like some oil | Shiraz resident | Middle Easterner | Isfahan inhabitant | Qom native

IRELAND | Cork's place | Cork setting | Where the Boyne flows | Eire | Yeats's home

IRONAGE | When forging began | Period in human development | It began around 1100 B.C. in Europe | When coins came into general use | Primitive period

IRONORE | Mined find | Smeltery fodder | Blast furnace input | Raw material for smelting | Mesabi Range output

ISADORA | Dancer Duncan | First name in dance | 1960 dance biography | 1968 Vanessa Redgrave movie

ISOLATE | Cut off | Quarantine | Set apart | Keep apart | Maroon

ISRAELI | Begin, e.g. | Tel Aviv native | Begin or Rabin | Nazareth native | Sharon, e.g.

ITERATE | Repeat | Echo | Do over | Go over again | Say repeatedly

IVANHOE | Fictional knight | Rowena's lover | Athelstane's romantic rival | Cedric the Saxon's son | Novel that includes Robin Hood

LARAMIE | Wyoming city | University of Wyoming site | Colorado-Wyoming river | Cheyenne's county | Fort on the Oregon Trail

LASAGNA | Layered entrée | Layered pasta dish | Garfield's favorite food | Ristorante order | Italian entrée

LATERAL | Certain pass | Football throw | Sidelong pass | Pass in some bowls | Sidewise

LORELEI | Loos woman | Siren on the Rhine | Siren luring sailors to shipwreck | Many a sailor's downfall | Temptress of sailors

MAEWEST | Lifeboat vest named for an actress | Life saver | "Sextette" was her last film | WWII life jacket

MASCARA | Lash cosmetic | The eyes have it | It runs in the rain | War paint, so to speak

MINARET | Mosque tower | Muezzin's perch | Source of many calls | Cairo skyline feature | Prayer tower

NARRATE | Tell tales | Tell | Do the commentary | Chronicle | Spin a story

NATALIE | Merchant of music | Wood in Hollywood | Actress Portman | Wood on a screen | Wood or Cole

NATASHA | "War and Peace" heroine | Boris's sidekick | Boris Badenov's partner | Bullwinkle foe | "Rocky and Bullwinkle" baddie

NEMESES | Banes | Agents of retribution | Batman and Robin, to Catwoman | Baddies | Mortal enemies

NEMESIS | Archenemy | Unbeatable foe | Moby Dick, to Ahab | Moriarty, to Holmes | Formidable opponent

NESTEGG | Savings | Mutual fund holdings, often | IRA, e.g. | Savings for a rainy day | You may use it after retiring

NIAGARA | Falls on the border | Falls for a lover? | Honeymoon haven | Falls for the Maid of the Mist | Horseshoe locale

OCANADA | Words before "Where pines and maples grow" | National anthem up north | Face-off preceder, often | Song played before some hockey games | It's heard at some ball games

OCARINA | Egg-shaped instrument | Simple wind instrument | Sweet potato | Crude instrument | Harmonica-like instrument

OCEANIA | South Seas islands | "1984" setting | Pacific group | Solomons locale | Polynesia's place

ONADARE | Due to being challenged | When challenged | Impetuously, maybe | Under pressure, perhaps

ONADATE | At the movies, perhaps | Out for the evening, maybe | Out, maybe | Out (with) | Courting, perhaps

ONAROLL | Hot | Hot, in Vegas | Doing great | Winning steadily, as in gambling | Batting a thousand

ONATEAR | Rampaging | Carousing | Going wild | Out of control | Raging

ONELANE | Like some rural bridges | Narrow, in a way | Narrow, as a bridge | Like most covered bridges | Not suitable for passing

ONENOTE | Monotonous | Lacking in variety | Johnny's last name? | Not varied at all | Rodgers and Hart's "Johnny ___"

ONESTAR | Poor movie rating | Like a brigadier general | Poor, to a film critic | Poor rating | Low-quality

ONESTEP | Ragtime dance | Ballroom dance | Round dance | Very simple, as a process | Lively ballroom dance

ONETIME | Former | Past | Previous

ONLEAVE | Off base, perhaps | Taking a break | Furloughed | Away, in a way | Off-duty

ONSTAGE | Performing | Treading the boards | In a cast | Making a scene? | Behind the proscenium

ONTARIO | Smallest Great Lake | Where London is | London locale | Canadian province

OPENSEA | International waters | Bounding main | Where clippers go at a clip | View from a porthole | Pirates' place

OPENTOE | Shoe style | Sandal feature | Like some shoes | Like some sandals | Digital window?

OPERATE | Run | Act the cutup? | Handle, as machinery | Perform surgery | Be in charge of

ORACLES | Medium settings? | Wise counsels | Future presenters, in the past | Answer sources | Divine revelations

OREGANO | Mint family member | Pizza herb | Ristorante herb | Italian herb | Pizza topper

ORESTES | Electra's brother | Son of Agamemnon | Euripides tragedy | Clytemnestra's slayer

ORIENTS | Positions | Sets straight | Adjusts | Gives bearings | Finds one's bearings

ORIGAMI | Paper craft | Paper art | Its business is folding | Traditional Japanese art form | Work for a folder

ORIOLES | 1983 World Series champs | Browns, now | Camden Yards team | Maryland songbirds | Baltimore birds

ORLANDO | Home of Disney World | Magic city | Home of the NBA's Magic | Seat of Orange County | Florida tourist mecca

OTHELLO | He "lov'd not wisely but too well" | Role for Robeson | Shakespearean Moor | Shakespearean tragedy | Play set mostly in Cyprus

OTTOMAN | Backless divan | Empire builder | ___ Empire | Place to put the feet up | Relaxation aid

PESETAS | Spanish bread, once | Bygone money | Euros replaced them | Spanish money, once | Barcelona bread, once

POSSESS | Boast | Have | Own | Haunt | Take over

RATATAT | Knocking sound | Machine gun sound | Drumming syllables | Rapper's beat | Machine gun noise

RATRACE | Daily grind | Grind | Frenzied routine | Corporate routine | Hustle and bustle

REAREND | Hit from behind | Ram | Collide with, in a way | Run into | Bump from behind

REASONS | Justifications | Bases | Explanations | Thinks logically | Whys

REDTAPE | Bureaucratic tangle | Bureaucratic stuff | Bureaucratic form-filling | Procedural complication | Barrier to progress

REENTER | Type in again | Key in again | One might do it after being stamped | What astronauts do to the atmosphere | Leave orbit

REFEREE | Court arbiter | Time caller | One may use hand signals | "Foul!" caller | Maker of many calls

REGATTA | Sailing race | Annual Henley-on-Thames event | Breezy competition | Occasion for flags | Boat race

RELAPSE | Backslide | Fall back | Slip back | Backslide, medically | Health setback

RELEASE | Free | Publicity piece | Liberate from the can | Film event | Loose

REMORSE | Compunction | Contrition | Guilt | Sackcloth and ashes | Regret

RESENTS | Takes umbrage at | Minds | Takes exception to | Is insulted by | Harbors ill feelings towards

RESTORE | Bring back | Put back | Make good as new | Give back | Make like new

ROASTER | Oven pan | Cooker | Fowl variety | Bigger than a frier | Poultry chicken

ROSETTA | Stone name | Hieroglyphic stone locale | Nile delta town | Tablet-discovery site | City of northern Egypt

ROSSSEA | Arm of the Antarctic Ocean | Antarctic waters | It borders Marie Byrd Land | Arm of the Pacific Ocean | Bay of Whales locale

SAHARAN | Dry | Dry as a desert | Desertlike | Hot and dry | Far from wet

SARALEE | Pillsbury competitor | Big name in cakes | Corporate baker | Cake maker | Name on a cake

SATIATE | Fill beyond full | Glut | Gorge | Stuff | Fill to excess

SATIRES | Swift works | Eveyln Waugh works | Swift pieces | Sendups | Biting pieces

SCOTTIE | Terrier type | Wire-haired yapper | Pippen of the court | Fox hunter, familiarly | George W.'s Barney, for one

SEASIDE | Vacation spot | Place for a boardwalk | Like many a resort | Fun-in-the-sun spot | Oceanfront

SEATTLE | Puget Sound city | Seahawks' home | 1962 World's Fair city | Home to the Museum of Flight | Bill Gates locale

SEDATES | Calms | Knocks out | Calms down | Puts under | Tranquilizes

SEERESS | Sibyl | Certain prophesier | Prophetic figure | She knows what's happening | Prophesying woman

SEESAWS | Vacillates | Goes up and down | Waffles | Has one's ups and downs | Playground items

SEESRED | Fumes | Goes ballistic | Bristles | Steams | Hits the roof

SENATOR | Roman official | Kennedy or Clinton | Gramm or Grams | Hill worker | Six-year-term politician

SENSATE | Feeling | Having feeling | Able to feel | Of perception | Having perceptions

SIAMESE | Cat breed | "Lady and the Tramp" breed | Like Anna's students | Closely connected | Elegant cat

SINATRA | Bishop cohort | "The Voice" | 1953 Oscar winner | Founder of Reprise Records | Rat Pack member

SNEERAT | Pooh-pooh | Make fun of | Make a mockery of | Dismiss casually | Show disrespect for

SOANDSO | Dirty rat | Stinker | No-goodnik | Some #@%*& individual | What's-his-name

STALEST | Least fresh | Least original | Showing the least originality | Superlatively trite | Most familiar

STAMINA | Staying power | Endurance | Marathoner's need | Inner strength | Lasting quality

STEAMER | Soft-shell clam | Clambake delicacy | Type of clam or trunk | Trunk or vessel | Carpet cleaner

STEELIE | Metal marble | Playing marble | Shooting marble | Shooter banned from tournaments | Rainbow trout

STEEPLE | Church topper | Bell site | Jack's workplace? | Peak in the skyline | Tower

STENCIL | Lettering device | Designer's device | Letter-writing device | Trace element? | Graphic designer's tool

STERILE | Germ-free | Unproductive | Like a mule | Germless | Ultraclean, as a lab

STOOLIE | Informer | Rat | One who sings | Cop's contact | Squealer

STOPGAP | Makeshift | Temporary fix | Improvised | Band-aid | It'll do for now

STPETER | Brother of the Apostle Andrew | Gatekeeper | First bishop of Rome | Final admissions supervisor? | Guard of the highest gate

STRANGE | Out of the ordinary | Odd | Golfer Curtis | Idiosyncratic | Off-center

STREETS | Thoroughfares | D and C, in D.C. | Map features | Some are mean | Where some jams are made

TABASCO | Hot sauce | Hot stuff | Cajun condiment | Sauce with a bite | Fiery sauce

TANTARA | Trumpet blast | Clarion blast | Fanfare | Brass production | Horn sound

TORONTO | CN Tower city | City on Lake Ontario | Where the Raptors play | Home of the Blue Jays | Ontario capital

TRAINEE | New hire | Apprentice | One learning the ropes | One new to a line | Cadet

TREETOP | "Rock-a-Bye, Baby" setting | Nursery song locale | Aerie area | Baby's spot in song

TREMOLO | Organ device | Vibrating effect | Organ effect | Vocal effect | Cheap trill

TRESTLE | Bridge support | Track support | Railroad bridge | Gorge crosser | Train bridge

TRIESTE | Adriatic port | Italian port | Miramare Castle locale | Italian province | Onetime rival of Venice

TSELIOT | J. Alfred Prufrock's creator | 1948 literature Nobelist | "The Waste Land" poet | "Murder in the Cathedral" playwright | "Gerontion" poet

TSETSES | Flies over the equator? | Dangerous flies | African carriers | Flies over the Nile | African bloodsuckers

UNEATEN | Like leftovers | Left over | Still on the plate | Like orts

UPATREE | Stuck | Trapped | Stumped | In a difficult situation | Cornered

USELESS | Futile | Good-for-nothing | To no avail | Like a fifth wheel | Of no value

UTENSIL | Kitchen item | Fork or spoon | Fork, e.g. | Funnel or stirrer | Kitchen help

YESORNO | "Don't evade the question!" | Kind of question | Simple answer choice | "Give me your answer" | Response request

# About the Authors

KEVIN MCCANN is an Internet technologies specialist and creator of cruciverb.com, a website for crossword constructors. In his spare time Kevin enjoys guitar, billiards, golf, the music of Leon Redbone, and, of course, crossword puzzles. He dedicates this book to his wife, Paula, to their two Chihuahuas, Archie and Mindy, and to the rest of his family, who have been very patient during the creation of this book.

MARK DIEHL has been a full-time dentist for over 30 years with the Veterans Affairs Hospital in Palo Alto, California. When time allows, he constructs crosswords for *The New York Times*, the *Los Angeles Times*, and other puzzle venues. He dedicates this book to his wife, Lee Ann; daughters, Erin, Brynn, and Megan; son-in-law, Tim; and granddaughters, Reagan and Lorelai—without whom he would be at a loss for words.

# Index to Lists